Merchandising Transactions, 168–175
Mortgages Payable, 562–563
Natural Resources Transactions, 408–409
Net Purchases, 170
Noninfluential and Noncontrolling Investments, Ap-65–Ap-67
Notes Payable, 436–437
Notes Receivable Transactions, 323–325
Operating Activities—Analysis of Transactions, 1104–1111
Owner's Investment, 17, 56
Owner's Withdrawals, 20, 60
Partnership—Distribution of Income and Losses, Ap-39–Ap-45
Partners' Investments, Ap-38–Ap-39
Patent, 410–411
Payment of a Liability, 18, 58
Payment of Expenses in Advance, 57
Payroll, 447
Payroll Register, 447
Payroll Taxes, 449
Payroll Transactions, 445–449
Pensions, 567–568
Percentage of Net Sales Method, 312–313
Periodic Versus Perpetual Inventory System, 364–366
Perpetual Inventory System, 364–366
Plant Asset Exchange—Gain Not Recognized, 407–408
Plant Asset Exchange—Gain Recognized, 407
Plant Asset Exchange—Loss Not Recognized, 406–407
Plant Asset Exchange—Loss Recognized, 406
Plant Assets Sold for Cash, 404–405
Prepaid Expenses, 95–97
Prior Period Adjustments, 501
Process, 411
Process Cost System Transactions:
  Average Method, 730–733
  FIFO Method, 715–725
Product Warranty Liability, 440–441
Property Taxes Payable, 440
Purchase of Assets by Incurring a Liability, 17, 58
Purchase of Assets with Cash, 17, 57
Purchase of Assets with Partial Payment, 57
Purchase of Bonds between Interest Rates, Ap-52
Purchase of Interest from Partner, Ap-46–Ap-47
Purchase of Treasury Stock, 506–507
Purchases, 170
Purchases Discounts—Gross Method, 172–173
Purchases Discounts—Net Method, 174–175
Purchases Journal, 259–261
Purchases Returns and Allowances, 171–172
Raw-in-Process Inventory, 1007–1009
Realized Exchange Gain or Loss, Ap-59
Receipt of Notes Receivable, 323
Recording a Dishonored Note, 323
Recovery of Accounts Receivable Written Off, 316–317
Retained Earnings Transactions, 501–509
Retirement of Treasury Stock, 508
Revenue Expenditures, 401–402
Revenue Received in Advance, 59
Revenues, 18, 59, 60
Revenues from Sales, 168–170
Reversing Entries, 140–144
Revision of Depreciation Rates, 398–399
Sale of Treasury Stock, 507–508
Sales, 168–170
Sales and Excise Taxes Payable, 438
Sales Discounts, 169–170
Sales Journal Transactions, 256–259
Sales of Bonds between Interest Dates, 557–559
Sales Returns and Allowances, 169
Sales Taxes, 259
Service Company Transactions, 16–20, 56–62
Short-Term Investments, 307–309
Special-Purpose Journals, 256–268
Standard Costing, Initial Recording, 842–843
Standard Costing Variance Transactions, 854–856
Stock Dividends, 502–504
Stock Issuance Transactions, 477–482
Stock Splits, 504–505
Stock Subscriptions, 481–482
Subsidiary Ledger, 256–258
Trademark, 411
Treasury Stock Transactions, 505–508
Uncollectible Accounts Expense, 309–315
Uncollectible Account Written Off, 315–317
Unearned or Deferred Revenues, 439
Unrealized Exchange Gain or Loss, Ap-59
Unrecorded or Accrued Revenues, 100
Vacation Pay Liability, 441–442
Withdrawal of Partner by Removing Assets, Ap-50–Ap-51
Withdrawal of Partner by Selling Interest, Ap-49–Ap-50

Financial & Managerial Accounting

Note to Students:

For business majors, this may be the **only** accounting textbook you purchase during your college career.

The author and the publisher want you to be aware that your copy of ***Financial & Managerial Accounting,* Third Edition**, is a valuable investment toward your success in this **and** other business courses. Principles of accounting is the foundation of the business curriculum; you will find that other business courses require you to use information learned from this text. You will enhance your success as a business major if, after completing this course, you retain this textbook as a reference. The following list, while not exhaustive, indicates those courses for which this book will be an asset:

Economics: ***Financial & Managerial Accounting*** is useful in understanding microeconomic topics such as costs of doing business, marginal cost analysis, profitability analysis, profit maximization, and foreign exchange rates; and macroeconomic topics such as money and banking, national income accounting, and foreign exchange transactions.

Finance: ***Financial & Managerial Accounting*** is useful in understanding the topics of financial statement analysis; cash flow analysis; capital budgeting; the time value of money; credit and banking transactions; working capital management (including cash, investments, receivables, and inventories); short- and long-term financing using notes, bonds, leases, and capital stocks; and mergers and acquisitions.

Information Systems: ***Financial & Managerial Accounting*** is useful in understanding accounting and computer systems, system documentation, internal control, and purchasing and payroll systems.

Management: ***Financial & Managerial Accounting*** is useful in understanding forms of business organizations, characteristics of corporations, performance measurement, and managers' internal use of accounting information.

Marketing: ***Financial & Managerial Accounting*** is useful in understanding pricing policies, the relationship of sales to profitability, and incentive plans.

We are very proud of ***Financial & Managerial Accounting,* Third Edition.** We encourage you to keep it and to refer to it often throughout your college and professional career.

Belverd E. Needles, Jr.
Professor of Accounting
DePaul University
Chicago, IL

Henry R. Anderson
Professor of Accounting
University of Central Florida
Orlando, FL

James C. Caldwell
Partner, Change
Management Services
Andersen Consulting
Dallas/Fort Worth

Financial & Managerial Accounting

Third Edition

Belverd E. Needles, Jr.

Ph.D., C.P.A., C.M.A.
Arthur Andersen & Co. Alumni
Distinguished Professor of Accounting
DePaul University

Henry R. Anderson

Ph.D., C.P.A., C.M.A.
Professor of Accounting
Director, School of Accounting
University of Central Florida

James C. Caldwell

Ph.D., C.P.A.
Partner, Change Management Services
Andersen Consulting
Dallas/Fort Worth

Houghton Mifflin Company **Boston** **Toronto**

Geneva, Illinois Palo Alto Princeton, New Jersey

To: **Professor Reginald R. Rushing**
Texas Tech University

Professor S. James Galley
Augustana College (Illinois)

Professor W. Baker Flowers
University of Alabama

For motivating and guiding us through our undergraduate accounting programs and inspiring us to become accounting educators.

Senior Sponsoring Editor: *Donald Golini*
Associate Sponsoring Editor: *Margaret E. Monahan*
Senior Project Editor: *Paula Kmetz*
Production/Design Coordinator: *Sarah L. Ambrose*
Senior Manufacturing Coordinator: *Marie Barnes*
Marketing Manager: *Karen Natale*

Cover design: Ron Kosciak, Dragonfly Design.
Cover photograph: Ralph Mercer Photography.

Printed in the U.S.A.

Library of Congress Catalog Card Number: 93-78706

Student Book ISBN: 0-395-67693-2

Exam Copy ISBN: 0-395-68548-6

123456789-VH-97 96 95 94 93

To the Student:

How to Study Accounting Successfully

Success in your accounting class depends first on your desire to learn and your willingness to work hard. But it also depends on your understanding of how the text complements the way your instructor teaches and the way you learn. An understanding of how this text is structured will help you to study more efficiently, make better use of classroom time, and improve your performance on exams.

The Teaching/Learning Cycle™

Both teaching and learning have natural, parallel, and mutually compatible cycles. This teaching/learning cycle, as shown in Figure 1 on page vi, interacts with the basic structure of learning objectives in this text.

The Teaching Cycle. Refer to the inner circle in Figure 1, which shows the steps an instructor takes in teaching a chapter. Your teacher *assigns* material, *presents* the subject in lecture, *explains* by going over assignments and answering questions, *reviews* the subject prior to an exam, and *tests* your knowledge and understanding on the exam.

The Learning Cycle. Now refer in Figure 1 to the next circle, which shows the steps you should take in studying a chapter. You should *preview* the material, *read* the chapter, *apply* your understanding by working the assignments, *review* the chapter prior to the examination, and *recall* and *demonstrate* your knowledge and understanding of the material on the exam. Your textbook supports these cycles through the use of integrated learning objectives. **Learning objectives** are simply statements of what you should be able to do after you have completed a chapter.

Integrated Learning Objectives. In Figure 1, the outside circle shows how learning objectives are integrated into your text and other study aids and how they interact with the teaching/learning cycle.

1. Learning objectives appear at the beginning of the chapter, as an aid to your teacher in making assignments and as a preview of the chapter for you.
2. Each learning objective is repeated in the text at the point where that subject is covered to assist your teacher in presenting the material and to help you in reading the material.

Figure 1. Teaching/Learning Cycles with Learning Objectives

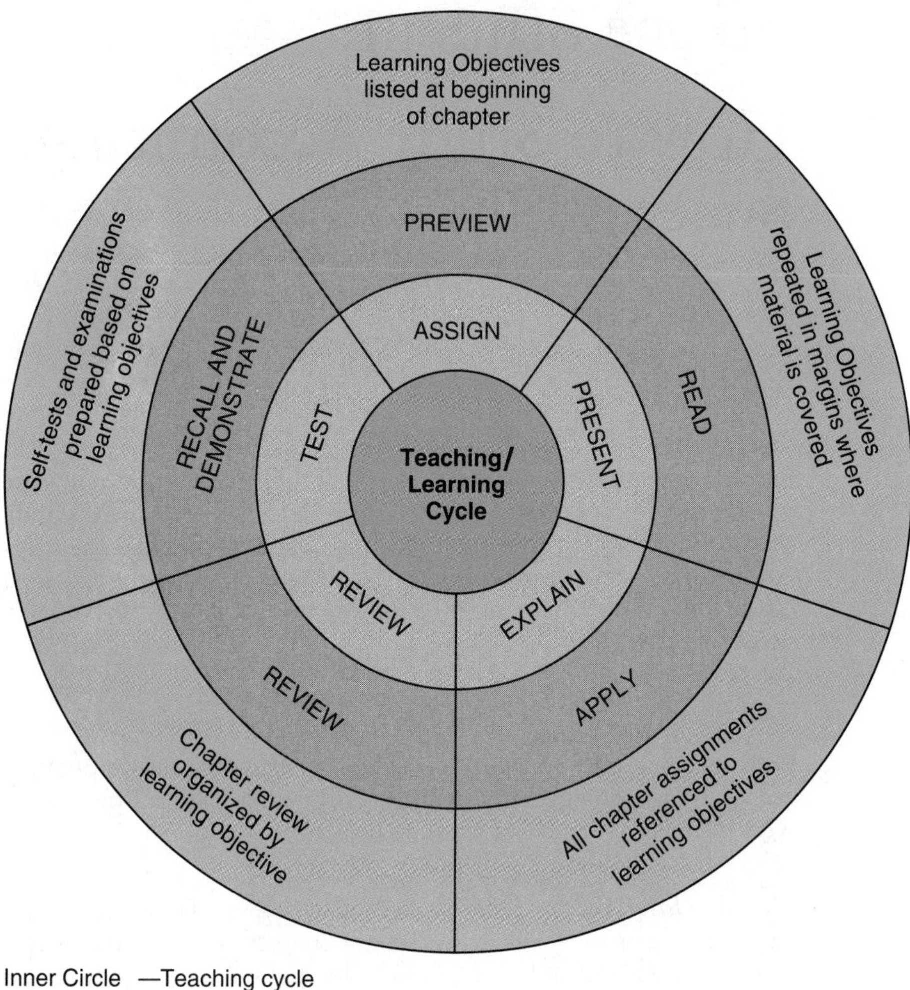

Inner Circle —Teaching cycle
Middle Circle—Learning cycle
Outer Circle —Learning objectives structure

3. Every exercise, problem, and case in the chapter assignments shows the applicable learning objective(s) so that you can refer to the text if you need help.
4. A summary of the key points for each learning objective, a list of new concepts and terms referenced by learning objectives, and a review problem covering key learning objectives assist you in reviewing each chapter. Your Study Guide, also organized by learning objectives, provides for additional review.
5. Finally, a self-test in each chapter review helps you prepare for the examination that your teacher will give based on the learning objectives assigned and covered in class. The questions, exercises, and problems in the Study Guide also help you prepare for examinations.

Why Students Succeed. Students succeed in their accounting course when their personal learning cycle is in phase with their instructor's cycle. Students who do a good job of previewing their assignments, reading the chapters before the instructor is ready to present them, preparing homework assignments before they are to be gone over in class, and reviewing carefully will ultimately achieve their potential on exams. Those who get out of phase with their instructor, for whatever reason, will do poorly or fail. To ensure that you are in phase with your instructor, check your study habits against these suggestions.

Previewing the Chapter

1. Read the learning objectives at the beginning of the chapter. These learning objectives are specific action statements of what you should be able to do after completing the chapter.
2. Study your syllabus. Know where you are in the course and where you are going. Know the rules of the course.
3. Studying accounting is not like studying history or political science. Each assignment builds on previous ones. If you do poorly in Chapter 1, you may have difficulty in Chapter 2 and be lost in Chapter 3.

Reading the Chapter

1. As you read each chapter, be aware of the learning objectives in the margins. They will tell you why the material is relevant.
2. Allow yourself plenty of time to read the text. Accounting is a technical subject. Accounting books are condensed and almost every sentence is important.
3. Strive to be able to say "I understand why they do that." Accounting is logical and requires reasoning. If you understand why something is done in accounting, there is little need to memorize.
4. Relate each new topic to its learning objective and be able to explain it in your own words.
5. Be aware of colors as you read. They are designed to help you understand the text.

Teal green All learning objectives and references to them are in teal green, as well as all key terms. Make sure you know their meanings. Remember, they are listed with definitions in the chapter reviews. All accounting forms and working papers are shown in teal green as well.

Gray All financial statements, the final product of the accounting process, are shown in gray.

6. If there is something you do not understand, prepare specific questions for your instructor. Pinpoint the topic or concept that confuses you. Some students keep a notebook of points with which they have difficulty.

Applying the Chapter

1. In addition to understanding "why they do that," you must also be able to do it yourself by working exercises, problems, and cases. Accounting is a "do-it-yourself" course.
2. Read assignments and the instructions carefully. The wording is precise, and a clear understanding of it will save time and improve your performance.
3. Try to work exercises, problems, and cases without flipping back to the chapter. If you cannot work the assignment without looking in the chapter, you will not be able to work a similar problem on an exam. After you have tried on your own, refer to the chapter (based on the learning objective reference) and check your answer. Try to understand any mistakes you may have made.
4. Be neat and orderly. Sloppy calculations, messy papers, and general carelessness cause most errors on accounting assignments.
5. Allow plenty of time to work the chapter assignments. Assignments are harder to work and more errors occur when prepared under time pressure.

6. Keep up with your class. Check your problem against the solution presented in class. Find your mistakes. Be sure you understand the correct solution.
7. Note the part of an exercise, problem, or case with which you have difficulty so that you can ask for help.
8. Attend class. Most instructors design classes to help you and to answer your questions. Absence from even one class can have a negative effect on your performance.

Reviewing the Chapter

1. Read the summary of learning objectives in the chapter review. Be sure you know all the words in the review of concepts and terminology.
2. Take the chapter self-test and review the learning objective for any question you answered incorrectly.
3. Review all assigned exercises, problems, and cases. Know them "cold!" Be sure you can work these assignments without the aid of the book.
4. Determine the learning objectives for which most of the problems were assigned. These are the topics that your instructor is most likely to emphasize on an exam. Scan the text for these learning objectives and pay particular attention to the examples and illustrations.
5. Look for and scan other similar assignments that cover the same learning objectives. These may be helpful on an exam.
6. Review quizzes. These questions are often similar to longer exams.
7. Attend any labs or visit any tutors your school provides, or see your instructor during office hours to get assistance. Be sure to have specific questions ready.

Taking the Exam

1. Arrive at class early so you can get the feel of the room and make a last minute review of your notes.
2. Have plenty of sharp pencils and your calculator (if allowed) ready.
3. Review the exam quickly when it is handed out to get an overview of your task. Start with a part you know. It will give you confidence and save time.
4. Allocate your time to the various parts of the exam, and stick to your schedule. Every exam has an element of speed. You need to move ahead and make sure you attempt all parts of the exam.
5. Read the questions carefully. Some may not be exactly like a homework assignment. They may approach the material from a slightly different angle to test your understanding and ability to reason, rather than your ability to memorize.
6. Be neat, use good form, and show calculations. These techniques prevent errors.
7. Relax. If you have followed the above guidelines, your effort will be rewarded.

Contents in Brief

I. The Basic Accounting Model

1. Accounting as an Information System 2
2. Measuring and Recording Business Transactions 46
3. Business Income and Accrual Accounting 89
4. Completing the Accounting Cycle 129

COMPREHENSIVE PROBLEM: *Joan Miller Advertising Agency* 161

II. Extensions of the Basic Accounting Model

5. Accounting for Merchandising Operations 166
6. Accounting Concepts and Classified Financial Statements 208
7. Accounting Systems and Internal Control 249

COMPREHENSIVE PROBLEM: *Fenwick Fashions Company* 300

III. Measuring and Reporting Assets and Current Liabilities

8. Short-Term Liquid Assets 306
9. Inventories 353
10. Long-Term Assets: Acquisition, Depreciation, and Disposal 386
11. Current Liabilities 433

IV. Accounting for Corporations

12. Contributed Capital 466
13. Retained Earnings and Corporate Income Statements 500

COMPREHENSIVE PROBLEM: *Sundial Corporation* 542

14. Long-Term Liabilities 544

V. Basic Concepts of Management Accounting

15. Introduction to Management Accounting 588
16. Cost Behavior and Cost-Volume-Profit Analysis 630
17. Cost Allocation and the Job Order Costing System 667

COMPREHENSIVE PROBLEM: *Silvoso Computer Systems, Inc.* 710

18. The Process Cost System 712

VI. Management Planning and Control

19. Responsibility Accounting and Performance Evaluation 754
20. The Budgeting Process 798
21. Standard Costing and Variance Analysis 838

VII. Accounting for Management Decision Making

22. Pricing Decisions, Including Transfer Pricing 882
23. Short-Run Decision Analysis 919
24. Capital Expenditure Decisions 954

VIII. Management Accounting Changes Caused by Global Competition

25. The Just-in-Time Operating Environment and Automation 992
26. Cost Management Systems, Including Activity-Based Costing and Measures of Quality 1044

IX. Special Reports and Analyses of Accounting Information

27. The Statement of Cash Flows 1098
28. Financial Statement Analaysis 1150

Appendix A. The Annotated Annual Report of Toys "R" Us, Inc. Ap-1
Appendix B. The Time Value of Money Ap-14
Appendix C. Future Value and Present Value Tables Ap-29
Appendix D. Accounting for Partnerships Ap-36
Appendix E. International Accounting Ap-55
Appendix F. Intercompany Investments Ap-64
Appendix G. Overview of Governmental and Not-for-Profit Accounting Ap-81
Appendix H. Overview of Income Taxes for Individuals Ap-97

Contents

Notes: *The topic of income tax is integrated throughout the book. It is covered at those points where it is relevant to the discussion.*

Each chapter concludes with a Chapter Review consisting of Review of Learning Objectives, Review of Concepts and Terminology, and Review Problem with Answer. Each set of Chapter Assignments includes Discussion Questions, Communication Skills Exercises, Classroom Exercises, Interpretation Cases from Business, 'A' and 'B' Problem Sets, and one or more Financial Decision Cases.

Preface xxvii

Part One
The Basic Accounting Model

1. Accounting as an Information System 2

Decision Point: Gerber Products Company 2
Accounting Defined 2
Accounting Information and Decision Making 4
Decision Makers: The Users of Accounting Information 5
Financial and Management Accounting 9
Accounting Measurement 12
Forms of Business Organization 13
Financial Position and the Accounting Equation 15
Communication Through Financial Statements 20
Professional Ethics and the Accounting Profession 25
Chapter Review 29
Chapter Assignments 34
Communications Skills Exercises
Foote, Cone & Belding 36
Ethics Exercise: Professional Ethics 36
Interpretation Case from Business
Merrill Lynch & Co., Inc. 40
Financial Decision Case
Henderson Lawn Care Company 44

2. Measuring and Recording Business Transactions 46

Decision Point: UAL Corporation and The Boeing Company 46
Measurement Issues 47
Accounts 48
The Double-Entry System: The Basic Method of Accounting 53
Recording Transactions 62
The Trial Balance 66
Some Notes on Presentation 68
Chapter Review 68
Chapter Assignments 74
Communication Skills Exercises
The Foxboro Company 75
Ethics Exercise: Penn Office Supplies Corporation 75
Interpretation Case from Business
First Chicago Corporation 80
Financial Decision Case
Obi Repairs Company 87

The following computer-assisted practice sets may be used after Chapter 2:
Parks Computer Company, Second Edition Matthew Sports Company, Second Edition Cooks Solar Energy Systems, Second Edition Sounds Abound, Second Edition

3. Business Income and Accrual Accounting 89

Decision Point: Never Flake Company 89
The Measurement of Business Income 90
Accrual Accounting 93
The Adjustment Process 95
Decision Point: Joan Miller Advertising Agency 101
Correcting Errors 103
A Note About Journal Entries 105
Summary of the Accounting System 105
Chapter Review 106
Chapter Assignments 113
Communication Skills Exercises
Takashimaya Company, Limited 113
Ethics Exercise: Central Appliance Service Co., Inc. 113
The Lyric Opera of Chicago 114
Interpretation Case from Business
City of Chicago 118
Financial Decision Case
Alvarez Systems Company 127

4. Completing the Accounting Cycle 129

Decision Point: Maintenance Management Company 129
The Work Sheet: A Tool of Accountants 130

Steps in Preparing the Work Sheet 130
Using the Work Sheet 132
Required Closing Entries 136
The Post-Closing Trial Balance 140
Reversing Entries: The Optional First Step in the Next Accounting Period 140
Chapter Review 144
Chapter Assignments 147
Communication Skills Exercises
Ethics Exercise: Ethics and Time Pressure 148
Way Heaters Company 148
Interpretation Case from Business
H&R Block 151
Financial Decision Case
Adele's Secretarial Service 159

COMPREHENSIVE PROBLEM: *Joan Miller Advertising Agency* 161

Part Two
Extensions of the Basic Accounting Model

5. Accounting for Merchandising Operations 166
Decision Point: Target Stores 166
The Income Statement for a Merchandising Concern 166
Revenues from Sales 168
The Cost of Goods Sold 170
Operating Expenses 177
Handling the Merchandise Inventory Account at the End of the Accounting Period 178
Work Sheet for a Merchandising Concern 180
Income Statement Illustrated 188
Chapter Review 188
Chapter Assignments 194
Communication Skills Exercises
Ethics Exercise: Files, Folders, & Clips 196
The Book Nook 196
Interpretation Case from Business
Wal-Mart versus Kmart 199
Financial Decision Case
Diamond Apparel Company 206

6. Accounting Concepts and Classified Financial Statements 208
Decision Point: The Gap, Inc. 208
Objectives of Financial Information 209
Qualitative Characteristics of Accounting Information 210
Conventions That Help in the Interpretation of Financial Information 211
Financial Accounting Concepts and Ethical Reporting 214
Classified Balance Sheet 216

Forms of the Income Statement 221
Other Financial Statements 224
Using Classified Financial Statements 225
Chapter Review 231
Chapter Assignments 237
Communication Skills Exercises
Mason Parking 237
Ethics Exercise: Salem Software 238
Ethics Exercise: Treon Microsystems, Inc. 238
Interpretation Case from Business
Albertson's, Inc., A&P, and American Stores Co. 242
Financial Decision Case
Cruz Tapestries Company 247

Additional Ethics Exercises
Accounting Concepts and Conventions (Exercise 6-1) 238
Accounting Conventions (Problem 6A-1) 242
Accounting Conventions (Problem 6B-1) 245

7. Accounting Systems and Internal Control 249

Decision Point: Fine Arts Gallery and Framing 249
Principles of Accounting Systems Design 250
Computerized Data Processing 251
Manual Data Processing: Journals and Procedures 255
Internal Control Structure: Basic Elements and Procedures 268
Internal Control over Merchandising Transactions 271
Chapter Review 278
Chapter Assignments 285
Communication Skills Exercises
Ethics Exercise: Ethics and Commissions on Sales 286
Kroch's & Brentano's 286
Interpretation Case from Business
B. Dalton Bookseller and Waldenbooks 291
Financial Decision Case
RW Finer Foods Company 298

COMPREHENSIVE PROBLEM: *Fenwick Fashions Company* 300

The following computer-assisted practice sets may be used after Chapter 7:
Micro-Tec, Third Edition
Collegiate Ts: Three-in-One Financial Practice Set

Part Three
Measuring and Reporting Assets and Current Liabilities

8. Short-Term Liquid Assets 306

Decision Point: Bell Atlantic Corporation 306
Accounting for Cash and Short-Term Investments 307
Accounting for Accounts Receivable 309
Decision Point: Fleetwood Enterprises, Inc. 317
Accounting for Notes Receivable 319
Decision Point: Marriott Corporation 323

Banking Transactions 326
Decision Point: National Realty 331
Petty Cash Procedures 332
Chapter Review 333
Chapter Assignments 339
Communication Skills Exercises
Ethics Exercise: Fitzsimmons Designs 340
Mitsubishi Corporation 341
Siegel Appliances, Inc. 341
Interpretation Case from Business
AmeriBank 345
Financial Decision Case
Bates Christmas Tree Company 352

9. Inventories 353

Decision Point: Amoco Corporation 353
Inventories and Income Determination 354
Inventory Measurement 357
Pricing the Inventory at Cost 358
Application of the Perpetual Inventory System 364
Valuing the Inventory at the Lower of Cost or Market (LCM) 367
Valuing Inventory by Estimating 368
Chapter Review 370
Chapter Assignments 375
Communication Skills Exercises
Ethics Exercise: Flare, Inc. 376
The Foot Joint, Inc. 376
Interpretation Case from Business
Hershey Foods Corporation 380
Financial Decision Case
BRT Company 385

10. Long-Term Assets: Acquisition, Depreciation, and Disposal 386

Decision Point: H. J. Heinz Company 386
Long-Term Assets 386
Acquisition Cost of Property, Plant, and Equipment 389
Accounting for Depreciation 390
Methods of Computing Depreciation 392
Decision Point: Choice of Depreciation Methods and Income Taxes: 600 Large Companies 395
Special Problems of Depreciating Plant Assets 397
Decision Point: Amre, Inc. 400
Capital Expenditures and Revenue Expenditures 401
Disposal of Depreciable Assets 403
Accounting for Natural Resources 408

Accounting for Intangible Assets 409
Chapter Review 413
Chapter Assignments 418
Communication Skills Exercises
Ethics Exercise: Signal Corporation 420
General Motors Corp. 420
The Quaker Oats Company 420
Grand Metropolitan 420
Interpretation Case from Business
Century Steelworks Company 424
Financial Decision Case
Kho Computer Company 432

11. Current Liabilities 433

Decision Point: USAir Group Inc. 433
Nature and Measurement of Liabilities 434
Common Categories of Current Liabilities 435
Contingent Liabilities 442
Introduction to Payroll Accounting 443
Chapter Review 449
Chapter Assignments 454
Communication Skills Exercise
Ethics Exercise: Tower Restaurant 455
Interpretation Cases from Business
Trans World Airlines, Inc. (TWA) 457
Texaco, Inc. 458
Financial Decision Case
Lafayette Television Repair 463

The following computer-assisted practice set may be used after Chapter 11:
College Words and Sounds Store, Fourth Edition

Part Four
Accounting for Corporations

12. Contributed Capital 466

Decision Point: Time Warner, Inc. 466
The Corporation 467
Organization Costs 471
The Components of Stockholders' Equity 471
Accounting for Stock Issuance 477
Exercising Stock Options 482
Chapter Review 483
Chapter Assignments 489
Communication Skills Exercises
Ethics Exercise: The Corporate Form of Business and Ethical Considerations for the Accounting Profession 490
Tucson Electric Company 490
Interpretation Case from Business
United Airlines 493
Financial Decision Case
Infinite Systems Corporation 498

13. Retained Earnings and Corporate Income Statements 500

Decision Point: International Business Machines Corporation (IBM) 500
Retained Earnings Transactions 501
Restrictions on Retained Earnings 508
The Statement of Stockholders' Equity 509
Stock Values 511
Decision Point: Eastman Kodak Company 512
The Corporate Income Statement 513
Chapter Review 521
Chapter Assignments 529
- Communication Skills Exercises
  - *Ethics Exercise: Bass Products Corporation* 529
  - Atlantic Richfield Company 529
- Interpretation Case from Business
  - Ford Motor Company 534
- Financial Decision Case
  - Borders Steel Corporation 540

COMPREHENSIVE PROBLEM: *Sundial Corporation* 542

14. Long-Term Liabilities 544

Decision Point: RJR Nabisco 544
The Nature of Bonds 545
Accounting for Bonds Payable 546
Amortizing a Bond Discount 550
Amortizing a Bond Premium 555
Other Bonds Payable Issues 557
Other Long-Term Liabilities 562
Chapter Review 569
Chapter Assignments 574
- Communication Skills Exercises
  - *Ethics Exercise: Xetol Corporation* 575
  - RJR Nabisco 575
  - Sumitomo Corporation 576
- Interpretation Case from Business
  - The Times Mirror Company 579
- Financial Decision Case
  - Coniglio Chemical Corporation 584

Part Five
Basic Concepts of Management Accounting

15. Introduction to Management Accounting 588

Decision Point: Caterpillar, Inc. 588
What Is Management Accounting? 589
Management Accounting versus Financial Accounting 590
The Information Needs of Management 593

Analysis of Nonfinancial Data 595
Merchandising versus Manufacturing Companies 598
Manufacturing Cost Elements 600
Manufacturing Inventory Accounts 603
Manufacturing and Reporting 607
Standards of Ethical Conduct for Management Accountants 611
Chapter Review 612
Chapter Assignments 618
Communication Skills Exercises
Ethics Exercise: Comparing Management Accounting and Financial Accounting 618
Barnett Banks, Inc. 618
Interpretation Case from Business
Cresep Enterprises 623
Management Decision Case
St. Peter Municipal Hospital 629
The following computer-assisted practice set may be used after Chapter 15:
The Windham Company, Second Edition

16. Cost Behavior and Cost-Volume-Profit Analysis 630

Decision Point: Carey Construction Company 630
Cost Behavior Patterns 631
Cost Behavior in a Service-Oriented Business 640
Cost-Volume-Profit Analysis 642
Breakeven Analysis 644
Decision Point: Mobay Chemical Corp. 644
Contribution Margin 645
Profit Planning 647
Cost-Volume-Profit Applications 648
Chapter Review 651
Chapter Assignments 656
Communication Skills Exercises
Carolina Keys Shrimp Company 656
Orlando Medical Center (OMC) and Infante Lawn Maintenance Company 656
Ethics Exercise: Breaking Even and Ethics 657
Interpretation Case from Business
Trevor Corporation 660
Management Decision Case
Homan-Rodrigue, Ltd. 665

17. Cost Allocation and the Job Order Costing System 667

Decision Point: Southwestern Bell Telephone Co. 667
Cost Allocation 668
Assigning the Costs of Supporting Service Functions 671

The Concept of Absorption Costing 675
Predetermined Overhead Rates 676
Product Costing Systems—Job Order Costing 680
Chapter Review 691
Chapter Assignments 697
Communication Skills Exercises
Roland County Community Hospital 698
Sally Industries, Inc.
Ethics Exercise: Ethical Job Order Costs 699
Interpretation Case from Business
Jones Company and Proctor Corporation 702
Management Decision Case
Pearson Manufacturing Company 708

COMPREHENSIVE PROBLEM: *Silvoso Computer Systems, Inc.* **710**

The following computer-assisted practice set may be used after Chapter 17:
The Windham Company, Second Edition

18. The Process Cost System 712

Decision Point: Banyon Industries 712
The Process Cost Accounting System 713
The Concept of Equivalent Production 717
Cost Analysis Schedules 721
Journal Entry Analysis 725
Illustrative Problem: Two Production Departments 727
Accounting for Joint Production Costs 733
Chapter Review 735
Chapter Assignments 741
Communication Skills Exercises
Euro-Continental, Inc. 741
Hi-Tec Semiconductor Corp. 741
Ethics Exercise: Ethics and JIT Implementation 742
Interpretation Case from Business
Tucker Tire Corporation 745
Management Decision Case
Murvin Cola, Inc. 751

The following computer-assisted practice sets may be used after Chapter 18:
Aspen Food Products Company: Three-in-One Managerial Practice Case

Part Six
Management Planning and Control

19. Responsibility Accounting and Performance Evaluation 754

Decision Point: Martin Industries, Inc. 754
Responsibility Accounting 755
Performance Evaluation 761
Implementing a Performance Reporting System 763

Chapter Review 773

Chapter Assignments 778

Communication Skills Exercises
Weyerhaeuser Company 778
Ethics Exercise: Watts Insurance Agency 778
Ethics Exercise: Grant Boutique 779
Interpretation Case from Business
Wisconsin Produce Company 784
Management Decision Case
Kroovand Petroleum Company 795

20. The Budgeting Process 798

Decision Point: Lord Corporation 798

The Budgeting Process 799

The Master Budget 805

Decision Point: Cardinal Industries, Inc. 815

Cash Budgeting 815

Chapter Review 819

Chapter Assignments 824

Communication Skills Exercises
University of Southern California 824
SubRunners 825
Ethics Exercise: Ethical Considerations in the Budgeting Process 825
Interpretation Case from Business
Hugo Corporation 829
Management Decision Case
Hayes Enterprises 836

The following computer-assisted practice set may be used after Chapter 20:

McHenry Hotels, Inc., Second Edition

21. Standard Costing and Variance Analysis 838

Decision Point: Hewlett-Packard 838

Standard Cost Accounting 839

Cost Control Through Variance Analysis 843

Performance Evaluation 856

Three-Variance Approach to Factory Overhead Variance Analysis 857

Chapter Review 860

Chapter Assignments 867

Communication Skills Exercises
United States Air Force 867
Hernden Company 867
Ethics Exercise: An Ethical Question Involving Standard Costs 868
Interpretation Case from Business
Gordon Realtors, Inc. 871
Management Decision Case
Annuity Life Insurance Company 878

Part Seven

Accounting for Management Decision Making

22. Pricing Decisions, Including Transfer Pricing 882

Decision Point: American Transtech, Inc. 882
The Pricing Decision 883
Cost-Based Pricing Methods 889
Pricing Using Target Costing 894
Transfer Pricing 895
Measuring Performance by Using Transfer Prices 899
Final Note on Transfer Prices 900
Chapter Review 900
Chapter Assignments 906
Communication Skills Exercises
The National Association of Printers and Lithographers 906
Maytag Corporation 906
Ethics Exercise: Norris Company 907
Interpretation Case from Business
Prescott Industries, Inc. 910
Management Decision Case
Heitz Company 917

23. Short-Run Decision Analysis 919

Decision Point: Fireman's Fund Insurance Company 919
The Decision-Making Process 920
Accounting Tools and Reports for Decision Analysis 922
Operating Decisions of Management 927
Chapter Review 936
Chapter Assignments 941
Communication Skills Exercises
Norfield Manufacturing Co. 942
Adolf Coors Brewing Company 942
Ethics Exercise: Bannister Corp. 942
Interpretation Case from Business
Hess Can Opener Company 947
Management Decision Case
Tyndall Company 952

24. Capital Expenditure Decisions 954

Decision Point: United Architects, Inc. 954
The Capital Expenditure Decision Process 955
Capital Expenditure Evaluation Methods 963
Income Taxes and Business Decisions 969
Ranking Capital Expenditure Proposals 971
Capital Expenditure Decisions in a Globally Competitive Business Environment 972
Chapter Review 973
Chapter Assignments 979
Communication Skills Exercises
The Upjohn Company 980

Hurco, Inc. 980
Ethics Exercise: Belstar Corporation 981
Interpretation Case from Business
Santa Cruz Federal Bank 984
Management Decision Case
Mesa Grande Photo, Inc. 989

Part Eight
Management Accounting Changes Caused by Global Competition

25. The Just-in-Time Operating Environment and Automation 992

Decision Point: Grand Rapids Spring & Wire Company 992
The New Manufacturing Environment: Automation and JIT Operations 993
Implementing a JIT Operating Environment 994
Traditional versus Just-in-Time Production 997
Accounting for Product Costs in the New Manufacturing Environment 1002
The Raw in Process Inventory Account 1007
JIT and Automation Are Changing Management Accounting 1009
Automation: Product Costing Issues 1010
Chapter Review 1017
Chapter Assignments 1024
Communication Skills Exercises
J. I. Case Company 1025
General Motors Company 1025
Ethics Exercise: Barineau Company 1026
Interpretation Case from Business
Hamby Woodworks, Inc. 1030
Management Decision Case
Kingsley Iron Works 1041

26. Cost Management Systems, Including Activity-Based Costing and Measures of Quality 1044

Decision Point: Sola Optical Company 1044
Cost Management Systems 1045
Accounting for Product and Service Quality 1051
Performance Measures for JIT/FMS Operating Control 1059
Full Cost Profit Margin 1063
JIT/FMS Management Reporting Guidelines 1067
Chapter Review 1069
Chapter Assignments 1075
Communication Skills Exercises
IBM Corporation 1076
Elgin Sweeper Company 1076
Ethics Exercise: Townsend Enterprises 1076
Interpretation Case from Business
Nease Corporation 1081
Management Decision Case
Cooplan Saddle Company 1094

The following computer-assisted practice set may be used after Chapter 26:
Callson Industries

Part Nine
Special Reports and Analyses of Accounting Information

27. The Statement of Cash Flows 1098

Decision Point: Marriott Corporation 1098
Purposes, Uses, and Components of the Statement of Cash Flows 1099
Preparing the Statement of Cash Flows 1103
Decision Point: Survey of Large Companies 1106
Interpretation of the Statement of Cash Flows 1116
Preparing the Work Sheet 1119
Chapter Review 1124
Chapter Assignments 1131
Communication Skills Exercises
Ethics Exercise: Chemical Waste Treatment, Inc. 1132
Tandy Corporation 1132
Interpretation Case from Business
Airborne Freight Corporation 1138
Financial Decision Case
Hashimi Print Gallery, Inc. 1148

The following computer-assisted practice sets may be used after Chapter 27:
Heartland Airways, Inc., Third Edition Richland Home Centers, Inc., Third Edition

28. Financial Statement Analysis 1150

Decision Point: Moody's Investors Service 1150
Objectives of Financial Statement Analysis 1151
Standards for Financial Statement Analysis 1152
Decision Point: Eastman Kodak Company 1153
Sources of Information 1154
Evaluating a Company's Quality of Earnings 1156
Tools and Techniques of Financial Analysis 1159
Survey of Commonly Used Ratios 1166
Chapter Review 1174
Chapter Assignments 1182
Communication Skills Exercises
Helene Curtis 1183
International Business Machines Corporation (IBM) 1183
Interpretation Cases from Business
Ford Motor Company 1188
PepsiCo, Inc. 1189
Financial Decision Case
Uribe Corporation 1198

Ethics Exercise
Effect of Internal Accounting Methods (Exercise 28-1) 1184

The following computer-assisted practice sets may be used after Chapter 28:

Heartland Airways, Inc., Third Edition   Richland Home Centers, Inc., Third Edition

Appendix A The Annotated Annual Report of Toys "R" Us, Inc. Ap-1

Letter to the Stockholders Ap-1
Financial Highlights (Figure 1) Ap-1
Consolidated Statements of Earnings (Figure 2) Ap-3
Consolidated Balance Sheets (Figure 3) Ap-3
The Consolidated Statements of Stockholders' Equity Ap-6
The Consolidated Statements of Cash Flows (Figure 4) Ap-6
Notes to Consolidated Financial Statements Ap-8
Report of Management's Responsibilities Ap-9
Management's Discussion and Analysis Ap-10
Report of Certified Public Accountants (Figure 5) Ap-10
Questions Ap-12
Classroom Exercises Ap-12
Problem Ap-13

Appendix B The Time Value of Money Ap-14

Simple Interest and Compound Interest Ap-14
Present Value Ap-17
Time Periods Ap-20
Applications of Present Value to Accounting Ap-21
Questions Ap-25
Classroom Exercises Ap-25
Problems Ap-27

Appendix C Future Value and Present Value Tables Ap-29

Appendix D Accounting for Partnerships Ap-36

Partnership Characteristics Ap-36
Accounting for Partners' Equity Ap-38
Distribution of Partnership Income and Losses Ap-39
Dissolution of a Partnership Ap-45
Liquidation of a Partnership Ap-51
Questions Ap-51
Classroom Exercises Ap-52
Problems Ap-53

Appendix E International Accounting Ap-55

International Accounting Ap-55
Questions Ap-62
Classroom Exercises Ap-62
Problems Ap-62

Appendix F Intercompany Investments Ap-64

Intercompany Investments Ap-64
Consolidated Financial Statements Ap-69
Questions Ap-76
Classroom Exercises Ap-77
Problems Ap-78

Appendix G Overview of Governmental and Not-for-Profit Accounting Ap-81

Governmental, Not-for-Profit, and Business Accounting Ap-81
Not-for-Profit Organizations Ap-85
Summary of Funds Ap-87
Budgeting in Not-for-Profit Organizations Ap-87
Expenditure Control—Governmental and Not-for-Profit Organizations Ap-92
Questions Ap-93
Classroom Exercises Ap-94
Problems Ap-95

Appendix H Overview of Income Taxes for Individuals Ap-97

Some Basic Concepts Related to Federal Income Taxes Ap-97
Income Tax for Individuals Ap-99
Questions Ap-103
Classroom Exercise Ap-103

Index of Company Names I-1
Subject Index I-3

Preface

FINANCIAL & MANAGERIAL ACCOUNTING, Third Edition, is a comprehensive first course in accounting for students with no previous training in accounting or business. Designed for both business and accounting majors, it is intended for use in two-semester, two-quarter, or three-quarter sequences in which there is an equal emphasis on financial and managerial accounting. The textbook is part of a well-integrated package of materials for students and instructors, including both manual and computer ancillaries.

Objectives of This Textbook

Our discussions with college and university instructors throughout the country lead us to believe that in today's environment there is a desire on the part of many of our colleagues for a new organization to the principles of accounting course, one that devotes approximately the same amount of time to managerial accounting as it does to financial accounting while maintaining the same pedagogical method that has been used successfully in the principles course for many years. The success of the first two editions of FINANCIAL & MANAGERIAL ACCOUNTING confirmed this belief. Specifically, our objectives for the Third Edition remain the same as those for the prior editions:

1. To provide equal coverage of financial accounting and managerial accounting;
2. To provide more coverage of managerial accounting than is found in the typical principles of accounting textbook; and
3. To cover both topics at a level suitable for freshman and sophomore students.

Equal Coverage of Financial and Managerial Accounting

This text contains twenty-eight chapters. Chapters 1–14 cover financial accounting topics, and Chapters 15–28 cover managerial accounting topics. Sometimes considered to be financial accounting topics, the statement of cash flows and financial statement analysis, Chapters 27 and 28, respectively, may be inserted immediately after 14, if desired.

Comprehensive Coverage of Managerial Accounting

With twelve chapters devoted to managerial accounting, our text provides the most complete coverage of managerial accounting of any principles textbook. This coverage is equivalent to that found in single-volume managerial accounting books and means that students are introduced to the field of management accounting in a patient, pedagogically sound way. The managerial topics are covered thoroughly enough to give students an understanding of management accounting that they can use throughout their future business and accounting careers.

Coverage at the Principles Level

Using the time-tested approach to the principles course, this text presents the accounting cycle and merchandising accounting (Chapters 1–5) based on the sole proprietorship. The approach used in Chapter 6 and following chapters is the same type as that used in single-volume accounting texts based on the corporate approach. Thus, freshmen and sophomore students are introduced to accounting in a way they can understand. At the same time, they are introduced to all the topics necessary to understand at this level the financial reporting of modern corporations. We have judiciously chosen the topics to be covered so that they can be presented with the same readability, pacing of topics, clarity of presentation, and balance of concepts and practices that appear in an optimally organized principles textbook. To provide maximum flexibility, we have also provided a series of eight appendices of optional topics, each presented in a mini-chapter format with exercises and problems.

Features of This Textbook

In writing FINANCIAL & MANAGERIAL ACCOUNTING, we have included the same features that have made our previous textbooks among the most widely-used textbooks in accounting education. These features include:

1. Readability and clarity of presentation
2. Integrated learning objectives throughout the package
3. Authoritative, practical, and contemporary content
4. Decision-making emphasis
5. Strict system of quality control
6. Most complete and flexible package

Readability and Clarity of Presentation

The text's intended audience, the freshman or sophomore student, has influenced the organization of the book in several ways. first, we have carefully planned the timing of new concepts and techniques to facilitate learning. The pace enables the student to grasp and retain the material. Second, we have taken special care, particularly in the early part of the book, to limit the number of difficult concepts or practices in each chapter. Third, clarity of presentation, consistent reading level, and uniform terminology have been rigorously applied throughout the text, including the chapter assignment material Fourth, we focus throughout on understanding, rather than mere memorization. We believe that concepts take on meaning when applied, and practices are most easily understood if related to a conceptual foundation. Fifth, we emphasize concepts and practices that will be useful to students throughout their careers.

Learning by Objectives

We take a definite pedagogical approach to writing FINANCIAL & MANAGERIAL ACCOUNTING. We have made extensive use of integrated learning objectives and learning theory. Learning objectives are integrated throughout the package, from the preview and presentation of the chapters to the assignment material, chapter reviews, study aids, and the testing and evaluation materials.

Authoritative, Practical, and Contemporary

This book presents accounting as it is practiced, but the concepts underlying each accounting practice are also carefully explained. Accounting terms and concepts are defined according to current pronouncements of the AICPA, APB, and FASB. The Statements of Financial Accounting Concepts of the FASB's Conceptual Framework Study form the theoretical underpinning of the book and are used to assess various accounting situations and controversies. In addition, we have taken steps to assure that, to the extent possible within the framework of introductory accounting, the practical material is realistic in terms of how accounting is practiced today.

Decision-Making Emphasis

Another objective has been to present the contemporary business world and the real-life complexities of accounting in a clear, concise, easy-to-understand manner. Accounting is treated as an information system that helps management, investors, and creditors make economic decisions.

Quality Control

Together with our publisher, we developed a system of quality control for all parts of the package to ensure the most technically and conceptually accurate program possible. This system, which utilizes an innovative computer database technology, involves many steps, including thorough reviews by users, visits to and discussions with users by the authors, extensive in-house editorial review, accuracy checking by over forty introductory accounting teachers, and finally, class testing.

Complete and Flexible Learning System

We believe that FINANCIAL & MANAGERIAL ACCOUNTING, Third Edition, represents the most complete and flexible package available for a first course in accounting. All parts of the package fit within the exclusive pedagogical system of integrated learning by objectives established by the authors. This system fits within the framework of the Teaching/Learning Cycle, which is described in detail in the To the Student section at the beginning of this text and in the following sections.

Objectives of the Third Edition

In addition to the objectives encompassed by the fundamental approach described above, the Third Edition was written with the following objectives in mind: (1) to enhance the clarity of presentation and ease of use whenever possible, (2) to improve the coverage of managerial accounting; (3) to increase the real-world emphasis of the text and chapter assignments; (4) to provide an abundant variety and depth of chapter assignment materials; (5) to provide multimedia enhancements for students and teachers; (6) to introduce more coverage, examples, and opportunities for discussion of international business, ethical considerations, and governmental and not-for-profit organizations; and (7) to introduce the development of communication and critical thinking skills into the beginning accounting course. These objectives reflect needs expressed by reviewers, information gathered by us through campus travel and interviews, and editorial input; they make the book fully responsive to the goals of the Accounting Education Change Commission for the first course in accounting.

To Enhance the Clarity of Presentation and Ease of Use Whenever Possible

Thorough Editing for Writing Clarity. Authors and editors worked together to make this text the easiest from which to teach and learn. Special attention was paid to parts One and Two, which include the basic accounting model and its extensions, as well as to parts Five, Six, Seven, Eight, and Nine, which encompass the managerial accounting chapters.

Revision of Chapter Assignments. More than 90 percent of the exercises and problems have been revised in three significant ways. First, we selected new names for individuals and companies, in an effort to reflect the richly diversified multicultural world in which we live. Second, we recast the numbers so that the chapter assignments contain fresh, realistic figures. And third, to avoid confusion on the part of students, we paid particular attention to the wording of transactions and of "Required" statements.

Revised Learning Objectives. Learning objectives organize text, reviews, and assignments, providing an unsurpassed internal reference system for instructors and students alike. Close attention was paid to their use in this edition. We carefully reviewed and revised all learning objectives for clarity as necessary. These action-oriented objectives located at the beginning of each chapter indicate in precise terms what students should be able to do when they complete the chapter. Then, each objective is restated in the margin beside pertinent text. All end-of-chapter components—Review of Learning Objectives, Review of Concepts and Terminology, Self-Test, and Review Problem—are clearly referenced to learning objectives and end-of-chapter assignments are keyed to specific objectives as well.

Key Terms. Throughout the book, key accounting terms are emphasized in bold, teal green type and are clearly defined in context the first time they are used. All of these terms are listed alphabetically with definitions and learning objective references in each Chapter Review.

Transaction Index. The unique index of transactions, which appears inside the front cover of the text, allows students to look up any transaction and find the page number on which it is discussed and illustrated. The transaction index is especially helpful to students when solving homework assignments.

Guide to Accounting Formats and Financial Statements. Inside the back cover of the text, we provide a guide to accounting formats and financial statements. This guide illustrates the proper formats for financial statements and references pages on which common accounting forms and financial statements can be found.

Index of Company Names. A separate index listing the over 150 real-world companies used in examples and cases is provided as a new reference tool that is useful for finding citations used in the book.

Chapter Review. An important feature of each chapter is the review section designed to promote effective learning. The Review of Learning Objectives summarizes the chapter's main points in relation to the learning objectives. The Review of Concepts and Terminology presents all key terms from the chapter with definitions and learning objective references. The Review Problem, with a complete solution, demonstrates the chapter's major procedures before students work the exercises and problems. The Self-Test reviews the basic concepts taught in the chapter and all Self-Test questions are referenced to learning objectives. The Answers to Self-Test section provides immediate feedback to students and is located at the end of each chapter.

To Improve the Coverage of Managerial Accounting

We have accomplished a comprehensive revision of the managerial accounting chapters. First, based on reviewer comments, we reorganized chapters to emphasize decision making. The chapter on cost behavior and cost-volume-profit analysis now follows the introductory chapter, to ensure students have a firm understanding of cost concepts before studying the more procedural product costing chapters. Second, the new operating environment, including just-in-time methods, activity-based costing, and measures of quality, constitutes two chapters (Chapter 25 and 26). Third, the entire text of the managerial chapters has been thoroughly reorganized, rewritten, and edited, to improve the clarity of presentation. We paid particular attention to the correlation of the assignment material to the text, and we simplified many of the exercises and problems, based on customer suggestions.

To Increase the Real-World Emphasis of the Text and Chapter Assignments

Decision Points. A new feature of the Third Edition is Decision Points. Decision Points are short vignettes based on real companies that show how accounting is used in decision making by managers, investors, and creditors. A Decision Point introduces each chapter, showing the relevance of the material in the chapter to decision makers. In addition, many chapters present a second Decision Point later in the chapter to illustrate key concepts.

Citations of Real Companies. Information from annual reports of real companies and articles about them in business journals such as *Business Week, Forbes,* and the *Wall Street Journal* is included to enhance students' appreciation of the usefulness and relevance of accounting information. In total, more than one hundred publicly held companies appear in the text as examples or in the chapter assignments. In addition, Chapter 28 demonstrates financial statement analysis using the financial statements of Eastman Kodak Company, and Appendix A contains the annotated financial statements of Toys "R" Us, Inc.

Real-World Graphic Illustrations. Graphs or tables illustrating how actual business practices relate to chapter topics are presented in several chapters. Many of these illustrations are based on data from studies of 600 annual reports published in *Accounting Trends & Techniques.* Chapter 6 features new graphics that show ratios for selected industries based on Dun & Bradstreet data. Most Interpretation Cases from Business are based on the published financial reports of real companies.

Business Practice Interviews. Periodically, the authors conduct interviews of businesspeople to ascertain current business practices. For example, Chapter 8, *Short-Term Liquid Assets,* and Chapter 11, *Current Liabilities,* have been revised based on interviews with officials in the banking industry.

Real Companies in Chapter Assignments. Almost one hundred Communication Skills Exercises and Interpretation Cases from Business, based on real companies, appear in the chapter assignments.

Moody's Company Data Software. Both an academic and student edition are available for use with the text. The student edition provides the annual report and comprehensive data for twenty well-known companies, in each of ten industries, so that students can perform comparative financial analyses. The academic edition, available to instructors, contains a database of more than eighty companies' financial histories for five years. This data may be manipulated and displayed in a number of ways, including search functions and spreadsheet options. In addition to the software, we provide a booklet of assignments, tied directly to the textbook, which are designed to familiarize students with manipulating Moody's Company Data Software.

To Provide an Abundant Variety and Depth of Chapter Assignment Materials

Questions. Review questions at the end of each chapter focus on major concepts and terms and provide thought-provoking topics for discussion.

Communication Skills Exercises. These exercises, identified by icon, are designed to help students develop their abilities to understand and communicate accounting information successfully. A new feature of this edition, Communication Skills Exercises address real accounting issues and concepts based on real companies and situations. They are designed so that a written solution is appropriate, but most may be used to develop other kinds of communication modes: they may form the basis of class discussion, small group activities, or student presentations. At least one Communications Skills Exercise addresses ethical issues faced in business and accounting. The final Communication Skills Exercise in each chapter focuses on basic research skills. These exercises are intended to acquaint students with business periodicals, use of annual reports and business references, and use of the library. Some are designed to improve interviewing and observation skills through field activities at actual businesses.

Classroom Exercises. Classroom Exercises provide practice in applying concepts and procedures taught in the chapter and are effective in illustrating lecture points. Each exercise is keyed to one or more learning objective. In addition, solutions transparencies are available for all exercise solutions.

Interpretation Cases from Business. These cases require students to interpret published financial information based on excerpts from actual reports and published articles about well-known corporations and organizations such as K Mart, Wal-Mart, Toys "R" Us, Inc., and UAL (United Airlines). Each case requires students to analyze published information by extracting data and making computations and interpretations.

A and B Problems. The text offers two sets of problems to provide maximum flexibility in homework assignments. Generally, the problems are arranged in order of difficulty, with problems A-1 and B-1 for each chapter being the simplest. A and B problems have been matched by topic, thus A-1 and B-1 are equivalent in content and level of difficulty. In addition, all problems are keyed to the learning objectives in the chapter. For each problem, ratings of difficulty, time estimates, and solutions are available to the instructor, as are transparencies of all solutions.

Financial/Management Decision Cases. Each chapter contains a case that emphasizes the usefulness of accounting information in decision making. The business background and financial information for each case are presented in the context of the decision. In the role of a manager, an investor, an analyst, or a creditor, the student is asked to extract relevant data from the case, make computations as necessary, and arrive at a decision.

Comprehensive Problems. Comprehensive Problems covering several chapters give students the opportunity to apply accounting procedures to help them understand an entire process. Following Chapter 4, the first Comprehensive Problem covers the second month of operations for Joan Miller Advertising Agency, the service company which introduces the accounting cycle in Chapters 2 through 4. After Chapter 7, the second Comprehensive Problem covers the accounting cycle for a merchandising concern, Fenwick Fashions, using special-purpose journals. Fenwick Fashions is the same company that introduces merchandising in Chapter 5. Following Chapter 13, comprehensive stockholders' equity transactions for Sundial Corporation are recorded and a statement of stockholders' equity is prepared. After Chapter 17, a new Comprehensive Problem focuses on the procedural aspects of a job order cost system at Silvoso Computer Systems, Inc. This Comprehensive Problem covers journal entry preparation, job order cost sheet maintenance, T account posting, and the computation of final inventory amounts.

To Provide Multimedia Enhancements for Students and Teachers

The advent of the 'information age' is changing the way in which students learn about business today. Increasingly, graduates of business, accounting and other disciplines are required to have microcomputer and other technology-based skills to secure the positions upon which they will build successful careers. For this reason, working with our publisher, we have developed a number of high-quality technology-related assignment options that will enhance the teaching and learning process in a more integrated fashion than is otherwise available:

- Specific problems, identified with the icon, have been set up to be solved either with pencil and paper or by using the commercial-quality general ledger package developed by the publisher.
- Lotus Templates for Accounting: A Working Papers Approach, second edition. Using this worktext and accompanying software templates, students are able to solve almost any of the chapter assignments using the LOTUS 1-2-3 spreadsheet, in effect producing electronic working papers.
- Moody's Company Data, Student Edition, adds additional depth to many of the Interpretation Cases from Business and Financial/Management Decision Cases by providing vast new information resources about American companies for student analysis and understanding.
- Exercises and Problems that are integrated with the Student Resource Videos are identified with the icon.

In addition to the above, using Houghton Mifflin's unique A.S.S.E.T. Preparation and Presentation software and Moody's Company Data, Academic Edition, instructors are able to reinforce the information technology component of accounting procedures: A.S.S.E.T.'s assignment-based spreadsheet files, lecture outlines, and graphics, as well as Moody's annual reports, financial statements, and analyses may be manipulated and displayed in class. Using any of these materials improves the realism and the effectiveness of the instructor's presentations.

To Introduce More Coverage, Examples, and Opportunities for Discussion of Ethical Considerations, International Accounting, and Governmental and Not-for-Profit Organizations

Ethical Considerations. Because accounting and business students must be exposed to ethical considerations in all their courses, we introduce ethical situations in the text. Every chapter has at least one assignment, identified by icon, that addresses ethical issues.

International Accounting. In recognition of the global economy in which all businesses operate today, international accounting and examples are introduced in Chapter 1 and integrated as appropriate throughout the text.

Governmental and Not-for-Profit Organizations. Because of the importance of governmental and not-for-profit organizations in our society, discussion and examples citing such organizations as the City of Chicago and the Lyric Opera are used at appropriate points. Appendix G provides an introduction to accounting for governmental and not-for-profit organizations and now includes a discussion of the managerial accounting issues facing these organizations.

To Introduce the Development of Communication and Critical Thinking Skills into the Beginning Accounting Course

To help students sharpen writing and speaking skills, we provide over two hundred opportunities for students to practice communication skills. All sections of the end-of-chapter material now contain writing assignments, many of which are suitable for small group assignments and oral presentations. In particular, the new Communication Skills Exercises, Interpretation Cases from Business, and Financial/Management Decision Cases are excellent vehicles for this kind of experience.

Critical thinking involves the ability to use analytical skills and to deal with unstructured problems that have more than one desirable solution. To achieve this objective, we have added to each chapter Decision Points involving the use of accounting information in key decision-making situations. In addition, we provide many unstructured assignments including Communication Skills Exercises, Interpretation Cases from Business, and Financial/Management Decision Cases. Further, the Moody's Company Data provides ample resources for cases, unstructured problems, and financial analysis.

Summary of Changes in the Third Edition

The process of revising a textbook offers authors the opportunity to improve their text by responding to the evolving need of instructors and students. The previous sections of this Preface describe our responses to concerns regarding managerial coverage, real-world applications, decision making, communication and critical thinking skills, and clarity of text presentation and assignments. Specific changes in chapter content, resulting from reviewer and customer comments, follow:

Chapter 1: Accounting as an Information System. We added sections on the relationship of GAAP to the independent CPA's report and on the applicability of accounting to governmental and not-for-profit organizations.

Chapter 4: Completing the Accounting Cycle. The presentation of the worksheet for a service organization, Joan Miller Advertising Agency, is presented on transparent mylar pages to help students better visualize the five steps used in preparing a worksheet.

Chapter 5: Accounting for Merchandising Operations. An illustration and discussion of bar coding and the Universal Product Code (UPC) is new, as well as an illustration depicting the effects of inventory adjustments and closing entries on the income summary accounts.

Chapter 6: Accounting Concepts and Classified Financial Statements. We deleted discussions of accounting systems installation and data processing perspectives to make the chapter more concise. Sections on the basic elements of computer systems, special-purpose journals, and controlling accounts and subsidiary ledgers can now be found in Chapter 7. The section on accounting concepts, an appendix in the previous edition, now appears in this chapter, as well as classified financial statements (from Chapter 7 in the previous edition). To add realism, we present charts that show ratios for selected industries from data published by Dun & Bradstreet. Included are examples from service, merchandising, and manufacturing industries. The ratios of Shafer Auto Parts, the example company in the chapter, are compared with the auto and home supply industry figures.

Chapter 7: Accounting Systems and Internal Control. We shifted discussions of classified financial statements from this chapter in the previous edition to Chapter 6, and in their place we added coverage of basic computer systems, special-purpose journals, and controlling accounts and subsidiary ledgers. We relocated bank reconciliations to Chapter 8.

Chapter 8: Short-Term Liquid Assets. We now define and discuss the term *cash equivalents,* and introduce a section on financing accounts receivable. We added the more common practice of selling notes receivable to the presentation of discounting notes receivable. The discussion of bank reconciliations, previously located in Chapter 7, now appears in this chapter.

Chapter 9: Inventories. A more understandable table illustrating the effects of errors in inventory on net income is included in this chapter.

Chapter 11: Current Liabilities. We extensively revised this chapter to include a new introduction to short- and long-term liabilities. The section on disclosure of liabilities now contains discussions of disclosure of financial instruments and off-balance-sheet liabilities. We added a new section on bank loans and commercial paper. We changed the procedure for accounting for notes payable with interest in the face amount to use the Discount on Notes Payable account. And finally, we updated payroll tax categories and rates.

Chapter 12: Contributed Capital. A new illustration in this chapter shows U.S. common stock, preferred stock, and bond issues over a recent five-year period.

Chapter 13: Retained Earnings and Corporate Income Statements. We now regard reissuance of treasury stock as a sale of treasury stock.

Chapter 14: Long-Term Liabilities. We added new sections on installment notes receivable and other post-retirement benefits.

Chapter 15: Introduction to Management Accounting. We streamlined the coverage of the original content of this chapter and added material on terms, classification, and reporting of operating costs from Chapter 16 in the second edition. We also revised the coverage of ethical standards of management accountants

Chapter 16: Cost Behavior and Cost-Volume-Profit Analysis. This newly structured chapter has been repositioned to introduce the concepts of cost behavior and C-V-P analysis before the student studies the product costing systems chapters. We expanded the coverage of cost-volume-profit analysis and linked it with cost behavior. We also introduce cost variability for a service-oriented business.

Chapter 17: Cost Allocation and the Job Order Costing System. We introduce and illustrate cost allocation before we discuss the computation of the predetermined overhead rate. In response to user preference, we discontinued the use of a separate factory overhead applied account and now use only the Factory Overhead Control account for recording both the incurrence and application of factory overhead costs.

Chapter 18: The Process Cost System. Because recent studies have shown that the FIFO method of process costing is the dominant method used in practice, the FIFO method is now the featured approach to process costing. The average costing approach is covered as an Alternative Method. Accounting for joint costs concludes this chapter.

Chapter 19: Responsibility Accounting and Performance Evaluation. This chapter precedes the budgeting chapter so students can understand that budgets are built along responsibility lines.

Chapter 20: The Budgeting Process. We restructured and expanded this chapter so that all examples of the master budget are from a single company. The chapter also has an extra decision point dealing with cash budgeting.

Chapter 22: Pricing Decisions, Including Transfer Pricing. We tightened this chapter by eliminating one of the cost-based approaches. In addition, we introduce and explain target costing, a method used currently by the Japanese to establish competitive prices that also ensure profitability.

Chapter 24: Capital Expenditure Decisions. We expanded this chapter to include a discussion of qualitative considerations required for decisions affected by the new globally competitive economic structure.

Chapter 25: The Just-in-Time Operating Environment and Automation. We restructured the just-in-time chapter to emphasize the impact of automation on management accounting techniques. We removed the section on activity-based costing in favor of expanded coverage of the subject in a new chapter.

Chapter 26: Cost Management Systems, Including Activity-Based Costing and Measures of Quality. With the focus on cost management systems, this new chapter first looks at the concept and application of activity-based costing. Then we introduce the total quality management operating philosophy, along with the various ways that management accountants measure quality. We conclude the chapter with a look at new performance measurement and reporting guidelines in the globally-competitive operating environment.

Chapter 28: Financial Statement Analysis. We added an example from *Moody's Handbook of Dividend Achievers* to the section on sources of information; an Interpretation Case from Business relates to this illustration. We updated the illustrated analysis of Eastman Kodak Company.

Appendix A: The Annotated Annual Report of Toys "R" Us, Inc. We made this popular feature of prior editions an appendix to improve flexibility of use during the course.

Appendix B: The Time Value of Money. We expanded this appendix significantly to include more applications of present and future concepts to accounting. We added appropriate assignment materials where necessary.

Appendix F: Intercompany Investments. This is an entirely new appendix.

Appendix G: Overview of Governmental and Not-for-Profit Accounting. We expanded this appendix to include managerial accounting issues for these types of entities and we added appropriate assignment materials.

Appendix H: Overview of Income Taxes for Individuals. We have updated tax rates in this appendix.

Supplementary Learning Ancillaries

The supplementary learning ancillaries provide a variety of useful items for students and instructors. A complete description is contained in the Instructor's Handbook. Briefly, they consist of the following:

Study Guide
Working Papers, two sets
Traditional Practice Sets, including
- Micro-Tec, Third Edition
  - A Merchandising Sole Proprietorship Practice Set, in narrative and working-papers formats

- College Words and Sounds Store, Fourth Edition
  - A Sole Proprietorship Merchandising Business with Payroll Practice Set
- The Windham Company, Second Edition
  - A Managerial Accounting Practice Set
- Collegiate Ts: Three-in-One Retail Merchandising Practice Set for Financial & Managerial Accounting

Practice Analysis Cases, including

- Richland Home Centers, Inc. Annual Report, Third Edition
  - A Practice Case in Financial Analysis
- Heartland Airways, Inc. Annual Report, Third Edition
  - A Practice Case in Financial Analysis
- McHenry Hotels, Inc., Third Edition
  - A Practice Case in Managerial Accounting
- General Mills, Inc. Practice Case, Second Edition
- Callson Industries, Inc.
  - A Practice Case in Managerial Accounting
- Aspen Food Products Company: Three-in-One Process Costing Practice Case for Financial & Managerial Accounting

Computer-Assisted Practice Sets

- Parks Computer Company, Second Edition
- Matthew Sports Company, Second Edition
- Cooks Solar Energy Systems, Second Edition
- Sounds Abound, Second Edition
- Polyform, Inc.
  - A Computerized Decision Case in Cost and Managerial Accounting

Other Computerized Study Materials

- Lotus® Templates for Accounting: A Working Papers Approach, Second Edition
- General Ledger Software for Selected Problems
- The Accounting Transaction Tutor, Chapters 1–4

Check List of Key Figures

Student Resource Videos, Third Edition

Moody's Company Data™ Student Edition

Moody's Company Data Student Assignments and Cases

- Moody's Handbook of Dividend Achievers—1993 Houghton Mifflin Educational Edition

Business Readings in Financial and Managerial Accounting

Instructor's Ancillaries

Print-Based Materials

- Instructor's Handbook
- Instructor's Solutions Manual, Volume 1: Chapters 1–14
- Instructor's Solutions Manual, Volume 2: Chapters 15–28 and Appendices
- Test Bank with Achievement Tests with Answers, Volume 1: Chapters 1–14
- Test Bank with Achievement Tests with Answers, Volume 2: Chapters 15–28 and Appendices
- Teaching Transparencies
- Solutions Transparencies

Guide to Student Resource Videos
Videodisc Guide
Moody's Company Data Student Assignments and Cases Instructor's Solutions Manual

Microcomputer-Based Materials

Computerized Test Bank
Presentation Software: A.S.S.E.T.: Accounting Software System for Electronic Transparencies
Moody's Company Data™ Academic Edition
Videodisc

Acknowledgments

Developing the Third Edition of Financial & Managerial Accounting was a long and demanding project that could not succeed without the help of one's colleagues.

We are also grateful to a large number of professors and other professional colleagues as well as students for constructive comments that have led to improvements in the text. Unfortunately, space does not permit us to mention all those who have contributed to this volume.

We would like to thank the following individuals for their contributions to the textbook and the ancillary program. Many have been supportive and have had an impact on the text and ancillaries as reviewers. Others have contributed greatly by reviewing and checking the end-of-chapter assignment materials.

Professor Charles D. Adkins
Casper College

Professor Marilyn L. Allan
Central Michigan University

Professor Gerald Ashley
Grossmont College

Professor Sue Atkinson
Tarleton State University

Professor Dale Bandy
University of Central Florida

Professor Abdul K. Baten
Northern Virginia Community College—Manassas Campus

Professor Robert H. Bauman
Alan Hancock College

Professor Cindi S. Bearden
University of North Alabama

Professor Lon Behmer
Northeast Community College

Professor Frank R. Beigbeder
Rancho Santiago Community College

Professor Teri Bernstein
Santa Monica College

Kristi S. Bianco

Professor Ronald W. Bolenz
Kellogg Community College

Professor Marvin L. Bouillon
Iowa State University

Professor Richard Bowden
Oakland Community College—Auburn Hills Campus

Professor Gary R. Bower
Community College of Rhode Island

Professor Russell L. Breslauer
Chabot College

Professor Sarah Brown
University of North Alabama

Professor Roy Broxterman
Hutchinson Community College

Professor Lois D. Bryan
Robert Morris College

Professor JoAnn Buchmann
Rockland Community College

Professor Edward F. Callanan
DeKalb College—North Campus

Professor Eric Carlsen
Kean College of New Jersey

Professor John A. Caspari
Grand Valley State University

Professor Donna M. Chadwick
Sinclair Community College

Professor B. Lynette Chapman
Southwest Texas State University

Professor William C. Chapman
East Central University

Professor Stanley Chu
Borough of Manhattan Community College

Adam J. Collins

Professor Judith Cook
Grossmont College

Ann Cosby

Professor Sharon A. Cotton
Schoolcraft College

Professor Mickey W. Cowan
East Central University

Gregory A. Crook

Professor Billie M. Cunningham
Collin County Community College

Professor Robert L. Dan
San Antonio College

Professor Elizabeth Davis
Baylor University

Professor Jo Ann DeVries
University of Central Oklahoma

Professor Walter A. Doehring
Genesee Community College

Professor Margaret Douglas
University of Arkansas

Professor John Elfrink
Ferris State University

Professor Richard F. Emery
Linfield College

Margaret Eshoo

Professor Estelle Faier
Metropolitan Community College (Fort)

Professor Robert E. Fellowes
Christopher Newport College

Professor Albert Fisher
Community College of Southern Nevada

Professor Ronald E. Fisher
Camden County College

Professor E. A. Fornstrom
University of Wyoming

Professor Jeanne C. Franco
Paradise Valley Community College

Professor Victoria A. Fratto
Robert Morris College

Professor Mark L. Frigo
DePaul University

Professor Ralph B. Fritzsch
Midwestern State University

Professor Diane Glowacki
Tarrant County Junior College—Northeast Campus

Professor Larry Goode
Missouri Southern State College

Professor Debra Goorbin
Westchester Community College

Professor Parker Granger
Jacksonville State University

Professor Dennis Greer
Utah Valley Community College

Professor Barbara Saar-Gregorio
Nassau Community College

Professor Robert B. Gronstal
Metropolitan Community College

Professor William Grollman
Fordham University

Professor Beverly J. Grunder
Cowley County Community College

Professor Lawrence Gulley
Norfolk State University

Professor Rama R. Guttikonda
Auburn University at Montgomery

Professor Dennis A. Gutting
Orange County Community College

Tal Hagigi

Professor Carolyn B. Harris
University of Texas at San Antonio

Professor Darrell D. Haywood
North Harris County College

Professor Paula E. Hegner
Heald College

Professor Alene G. Helling
Stark Technical Community College

Professor Linda Hemmingway
Athens State College

Ira M. Hirsch

Professor Paul E. Holt
Texas A&I University

Professor Anita Hope
Tarrant County Junior College—Northeast Campus

Professor Charles W. Hope
Tarrant County Junior College—Northwest Campus

Professor Bambi A. Hora
University of Central Oklahoma

Professor Kendra Huff
Texas A&I University

Professor Samuel J. Hughson
New York City Technical College

Professor Sid N. Hyder
Indiana University of Pennsylvania

Professor Anthony W. Jackson
Central State University

Professor Gloria M. Jackson
San Antonio College

Professor Sharon S. Jackson
Auburn University at Montgomery

Professor John S. Jeter
Cameron University

Professor David M. Johnson
Pepperdine University

Professor Herbert J. Johnson
Blinn College

Professor David T. Jones
California University of Pennsylvania

Professor Richard W. Jones
Lamar University

Professor Rita C. Jones
Georgia College

Professor Peter B. Kenyon
Humboldt State University

Professor Vicky Arnold King
University of Arkansas at Little Rock

Professor Roberta L. Klein
SUNY, Brockport

Professor Jack L. Kockentiet
Columbus State Community College

Professor Cynthia Kreisner
Austin Community College

Professor Linda Kropp
Modesto Junior College

Professor Cathy Xanthaky Larson
Middlesex Community College

Professor William C. Lathen
Boise State University

Professor Paul J. Lisowski
Edinboro University of Pennsylvania

Professor Leonard T. Long
Fisher College

Professor Katherine A. Longbotham
Richland College

Professor George Loughron
Tomball College

Professor Nancy Pennoyer Lynch
West Virginia University

Professor L. Kevin McNelis
Eastern New Mexico University

Professor Donald L. Madden
University of Kentucky

Professor Lois Mahoney
University of Central Florida

Professor James P. Makofske
Fresno City College

Professor Gary L. Merz
Clarion University of Pennsylvania

Michael F. Monahan

Professor Doug Morrison
Clark College

Jenine Moscove

Professor Susan Murphy
Monroe Community College

Professor C. Lynn Murray
Florida Community College at Jacksonville

Professor Leila Newkirk
Garland County Community College

Professor Terry J. Nunley
University of North Carolina at Charlotte

Professor Harris M. O'Brien
North Harris County College

Professor Marilyn Okleshen
Mankato State University

Professor Anne M. Oppegard
Augustana College

Professor Lynn Mazzola Paluska
Nassau Community College

Professor Rukshad Patel
College of DuPage

Professor Ralph L. Peck
Utah State University

Professor Paul E. Pettit
Snead State Junior College

Professor Wayne E. Pfingsten
Belleville Area College

Professor Orrel E. Picklesimer
University of Texas at San Antonio

Professor Elden Price
Bee County College

Robert J. Pytell

Holly Qian

Professor LaVonda Ramey
Schoolcraft College

Professor Robert Randall
Moorpark College

Mark T. Rasimas

Professor Edward R. Rayfield
Suffolk County Community College—Western Campus

Professor David A. Reese
Southern Utah University

Professor Sara Reese
Virginia Union University

Professor Cheri Reither
Midwestern State University

Harold F. Ripley
Orange County Community College

Professor Jep Robertson
New Mexico State University

Professor Margo Rock
Hillsborough Community College

Professor Yasuo Saito
Los Angeles Trade Technical College

Professor Marilyn Salter
University of Central Florida

Martha H. Sandler

Professor Dennis Schirf
Quincy College

Professor Donal R. Schmidt, Jr.
Tarleton State University

Professor James Seivwright
Hillsborough Community College—Dale Mabry Campus

Professor Gary C. Sell
Madison Area Technical College

Professor Robbie Sheffy
Tarrant County Junior College—South Campus

Professor Margaret L. Shelton
University of Houston—Downtown Campus

Professor Arthur Silva
Community College of Rhode Island

Professor S. Murray Simons
Northeastern University

Professor Jill M. Smith
Idaho State University

Professor Ron Stunda
Samford University

Professor Ellen L. Sweatt
DeKalb College—North Campus

Professor Marion Taube
University of Pittsburgh

Professor Beverly B. Terry
Central Piedmont Community College

Professor Kathryn Verrenult
University of Massachusetts—Lowell

Professor Mike Watters
New Mexico State University

Professor Robert R. Wennagel
College of the Mainland

Professor Kathleen A. Wessman
Montgomery College—Rockville

Professor Dale Westfall
Midland College

Professor Kenneth Winter
University of Wisconsin—La Crosse

Professor Stanley J. Yerep
Indiana University of Pennsylvania

Professor Marilyn J. Young
Tulsa Junior College

Professor Thomas E. Zaher
Bucks County Community College

We wish to express our deep appreciation to our colleagues at DePaul University and the University of Central Florida, who have been extremely supportive and encouraging.

The thoughtful and meticulous work of Edward Julius (California Lutheran University) is reflected not only in the Study Guide and Instructor's Handbook, but in many other ways. Kim Lazar also has contributed significantly to the quality of the Study Guide. We also wish to thank David D. Byrd and Sandra D. Byrd (Southwest Missouri State University) for their assistance in preparing the Test Bank.

We wish to express our appreciation to William P. Stevens of DePaul University for his assistance in the preparation of Appendix G, *Overview of Governmental and Not-for-Profit Accounting.*

Very important to the quality of this book is the supportive collaboration of our sponsoring editor, Don Golini. We further benefitted from the ideas and guidance of our associate sponsoring editor, Peggy Monahan, as well as the efficiency and patience of our project editor, Paula Kmetz. Also very helpful were Fred Shafer and Tari Szatkowski for their assistance with the preparation of the manuscript.

Without the help of these and others, this book would not have been possible.
B.E.N. H.R.A. J.C.C.

Financial & Managerial Accounting

FINANCIAL & MANAGERIAL ACCOUNTING

FINANCIAL ACCOUNTING

PART ONE
The Basic Accounting Model

Chapter 1
Accounting as an Information System
Chapter 2
Measuring and Recording Business Transactions
Chapter 3
Business Income and Accrual Accounting
Chapter 4
Completing the Accounting Cycle

PART TWO
Extensions of the Basic Accounting Model

PART THREE
Measuring and Reporting Assets and Current Liabilities

PART FOUR
Accounting for Corporations

MANAGERIAL ACCOUNTING

PART FIVE
Basic Concepts of Management Accounting

PART SIX
Management Planning and Control

PART SEVEN
Accounting for Management Decision Making

PART EIGHT
Management Accounting Changes Caused by Global Competition

PART NINE
Special Reports and Analyses of Accounting Information

Accounting is an information system for measuring, processing, and communicating information that is useful in making economic decisions. Part One presents the fundamental concepts and techniques of the basic accounting system, including accounting for a complete cycle of business activities for a service enterprise.

PART ONE

The Basic Accounting Model

Chapter 1 explores the nature and environment of accounting, with special emphasis on the users of accounting information, the roles of accountants in society, and the organizations that influence accounting practice. It introduces the four basic financial statements, the concept of accounting measurement, and the effects of business transactions on financial position. Chapter 1 concludes with a discussion of the ethical responsibilities in the accounting profession.

Chapter 2 continues with accounting measurement by focusing on the issues of recognition, valuation, and classification and how they are solved in the recording of business transactions.

Chapter 3 defines the accounting concept of business income, discusses the role of adjusting entries in its measurement, and demonstrates the preparation of financial statements.

Chapter 4 completes the accounting system with a presentation of the work sheet and closing entries.

LEARNING OBJECTIVES

1. *Define* accounting *and describe its role in making informed decisions.*
2. *Identify the many users of accounting information in society.*
3. *Distinguish between financial and management accounting, define* generally accepted accounting principles (GAAP), *and identify the organizations that influence GAAP.*
4. *Explain the importance of business transactions, money measure, and separate entity to accounting measurement.*
5. *Identify the three basic forms of business organization.*
6. *Define* financial position, *state the accounting equation, and show how they are affected by simple transactions.*
7. *Identify the four basic financial statements.*
8. *Describe accounting as a profession with ethical responsibilities and a wide career choice.*

CHAPTER 1

Accounting as an Information System

Your first accounting course starts with a general view of the accounting discipline and profession. In this chapter, you begin the study of accounting measurement of business transactions and communication through financial statements. You also learn about the important roles that accountants play in society and about the organizations where accountants work. After studying this chapter, you should be able to meet the learning objectives listed on the left.

DECISION POINT
Gerber Products Company

■ Top management of Gerber Products Company, a leader in baby and toddler food products, children's clothes, and other markets, set the following financial goals in its 1989 annual report to the company's stockholders:

1. Seek real earnings growth of 6 to 8 percent annually.
2. Sustain a return on equity of at least 22 percent.
3. Maintain cash flow from operations (earnings before interest, taxes, and depreciation) at a minimum of 15 percent of revenues.
4. Increase dividends commensurate with earnings growth.

Management views these goals as essential to building the long-term wealth of the company's owners. What financial knowledge do the company's managers need in order to achieve these goals?

Each of these goals is stated in terms of financial results. Gerber's managers must have a thorough knowledge of accounting in order to understand how the operations for which they are responsible contribute to the firm's overall financial health as reflected by these goals. This requires a knowledge of the terminology and concepts that underlie accounting, of the way in which financial information is generated, and of the way in which that information is interpreted and analyzed. The purpose of this textbook is to provide that knowledge. ■

Accounting Defined

Early definitions of accounting generally focused on the traditional recordkeeping functions of the accountant. In 1941 the American Institute of Certified Public Accountants (AICPA) defined accounting as "the art of recording, classifying, and summarizing in a significant manner and in terms of money, transactions and events which are, in part at least, of a financial character, and interpreting the results thereof."[1]

OBJECTIVE 1
Define accounting and describe its role in making informed decisions

The modern definition of accounting is much broader. In 1970 the AICPA stated that the function of accounting is "to provide quantitative information, primarily financial in nature, about economic entities that is intended to be useful in making economic decisions."[2] (An economic entity is a unit—a business, for example—that exists independently.)

The modern accountant is concerned not only with recordkeeping but also with a whole range of activities that involve planning and problem solving; control and attention directing; and evaluation, review, and auditing. Today's accountant focuses on the ultimate needs of those who use accounting information, whether the users are inside or outside the business. **Accounting** "is not an end in itself."[3] It is **an information system that measures, processes, and communicates financial information about an identifiable economic entity**. This information allows users to make "reasoned choices among alternative uses of scarce resources in the conduct of business and economic activities."[4]

According to this definition, accounting is a service activity. As shown in Figure 1-1, accounting is a link between business activities and decision makers. First, accounting measures business activities by recording data about them for future use. Second, the data are stored until needed and then processed to become useful information. Third, the information is communicated, through reports, to decision makers. We might say that data about business activities are the input to the accounting system and that useful information for decision makers is the output.

Figure 1-1. Accounting as an Information System for Business Decisions

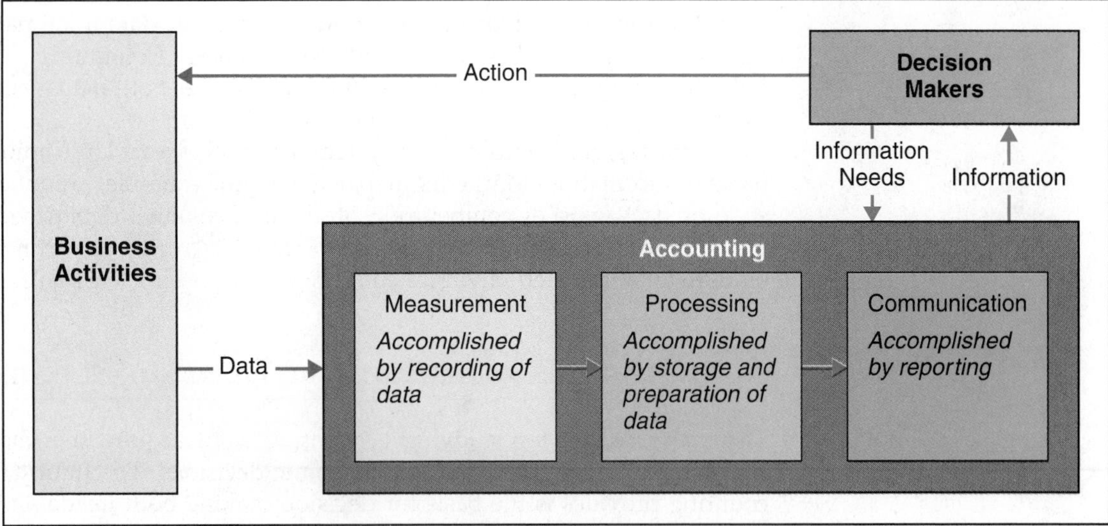

1. Committee on Accounting Terminology, *Accounting Terminology Bulletin No. 1* (New York: American Institute of Certified Public Accountants, 1953), par. 9.
2. *Statement of the Accounting Principles Board No. 4,* "Basic Concepts and Accounting Principles Underlying Financial Statements of Business Enterprises" (New York: American Institute of Certified Public Accountants, 1970), par. 40.
3. *Statement of Financial Accounting Concepts No. 1,* "Objectives of Financial Reporting by Business Enterprises" (Stamford, Conn.: Financial Accounting Standards Board, 1978), par. 9.
4. Ibid.

To avoid misunderstandings about accounting, it is important to clarify its relationship with bookkeeping, the computer, and management information systems.

People often fail to understand the difference between accounting and bookkeeping. **Bookkeeping** is the process of recording financial transactions and keeping financial records. Mechanical and repetitive, bookkeeping is only a small—but important—part of accounting. Accounting, on the other hand, includes the design of an information system that meets the user's needs. The major goals of accounting are the analysis, interpretation, and use of information. Accountants look for important relationships in the information they produce. They are interested in finding trends and studying the effects of different alternatives. Accounting includes systems design, budgeting, cost analysis, auditing, and tax planning and preparation.

The **computer** is an electronic tool that is used to collect, organize, and communicate vast amounts of information with great speed. Accountants were among the earliest and most enthusiastic users of computers, and today they use microcomputers in all aspects of their work. It may appear that the computer is doing the accountant's job; in fact, it is only a tool that is instructed to do routine bookkeeping and to perform complex calculations. It is important that the user of accounting information and the new accountant understand the processes underlying accounting. For this reason, most of the examples in this book describe manual operations. You should remember, however, that most accounting operations are now computerized.

With the widespread use of the computer today, many of these varied information needs are being organized into what is called a **management information system (MIS)**. The management information system consists of the interconnected subsystems that provide the information needed to run a business. The accounting information system is the most important subsystem because it plays the key role of managing the flow of economic data to all parts of a business and to interested parties outside the business. Accounting is the financial hub of the management information system. It gives both management and outsiders a complete view of the business organization.

The management information system also processes a large amount of nonfinancial information. Marketing departments, for example, are interested in the style or packaging of competitors' products. Personnel departments keep employees' health and employment records. Manufacturing departments must operate in an automated environment.

Accounting Information and Decision Making

The major reason for studying accounting is to acquire the knowledge and skills to participate in important economic decisions. The information that accounting provides is the basis for decision making both inside and outside the business enterprise. Accounting information

> is a tool and, like most tools, cannot be of much direct help to those who are unable or unwilling to use it or who misuse it. Its use can be learned, however, and [accounting] should provide information that can be used by all—nonprofessionals as well as professionals—who are willing to use it properly.[5]

The first step in the learning process is to understand how decisions are made and how accountants can contribute to decision making. To make a wise

5. Ibid., par. 36.

decision and carry it out effectively, the decision maker must answer the following questions:

What is the goal? (Step 1)

What different means are available to reach the goal? (Step 2)

Which alternative provides the best way to achieve the goal? (Step 3)

What action should be taken? (Step 4)

Was the goal met? (Step 5)

Figure 1-2 shows the steps in making a decision.

When a decision involves business and economic questions, accounting information is essential to the decision-making process. It provides quantitative information for three functions: planning, control, and evaluation.

Planning is the process of formulating a course of action. It includes setting a goal, finding alternative ways of meeting the goal, and deciding which alternative is the best. In this stage, the accountant should be able to present a clear statement of financial alternatives. Accounting information that deals with projected income and budgets is also an important element of planning.

Control is the process of seeing that plans are carried out. At this point, the accountant might be expected to present information that compares actual costs and revenues with those projected.

Evaluation is the examination of the whole decision process to the end of improving it. It asks the question: Was the original goal satisfactorily met? If the answer is no, it looks for the reason. Was the problem in planning or control? Was the goal the right one? Much of the feedback used to evaluate a decision comes from the financial statements the accountant prepares.

Decision Makers: The Users of Accounting Information

OBJECTIVE 2
Identify the many users of accounting information in society

Accounting and accounting information are used more widely than is commonly realized. The users of accounting information can be divided roughly into three groups: (1) those who manage a business; (2) those outside a business enterprise who have a direct financial interest in the business; and (3) those people, organizations, and agencies that have an indirect financial interest in the business. These groups are shown in Figure 1-3.

Figure 1-2. The Decision-making Process

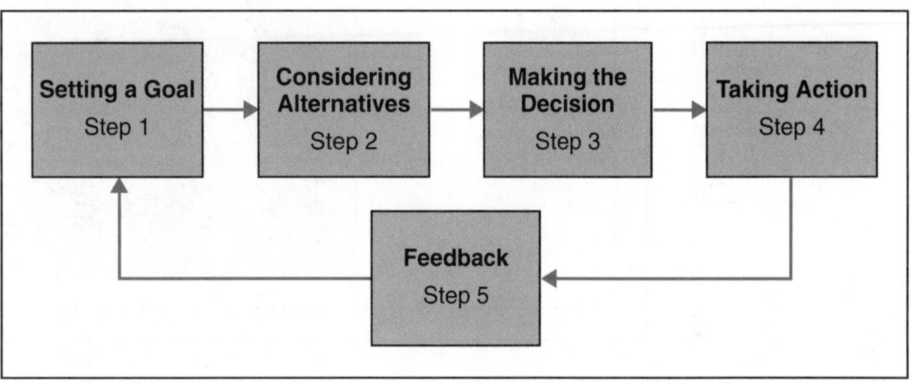

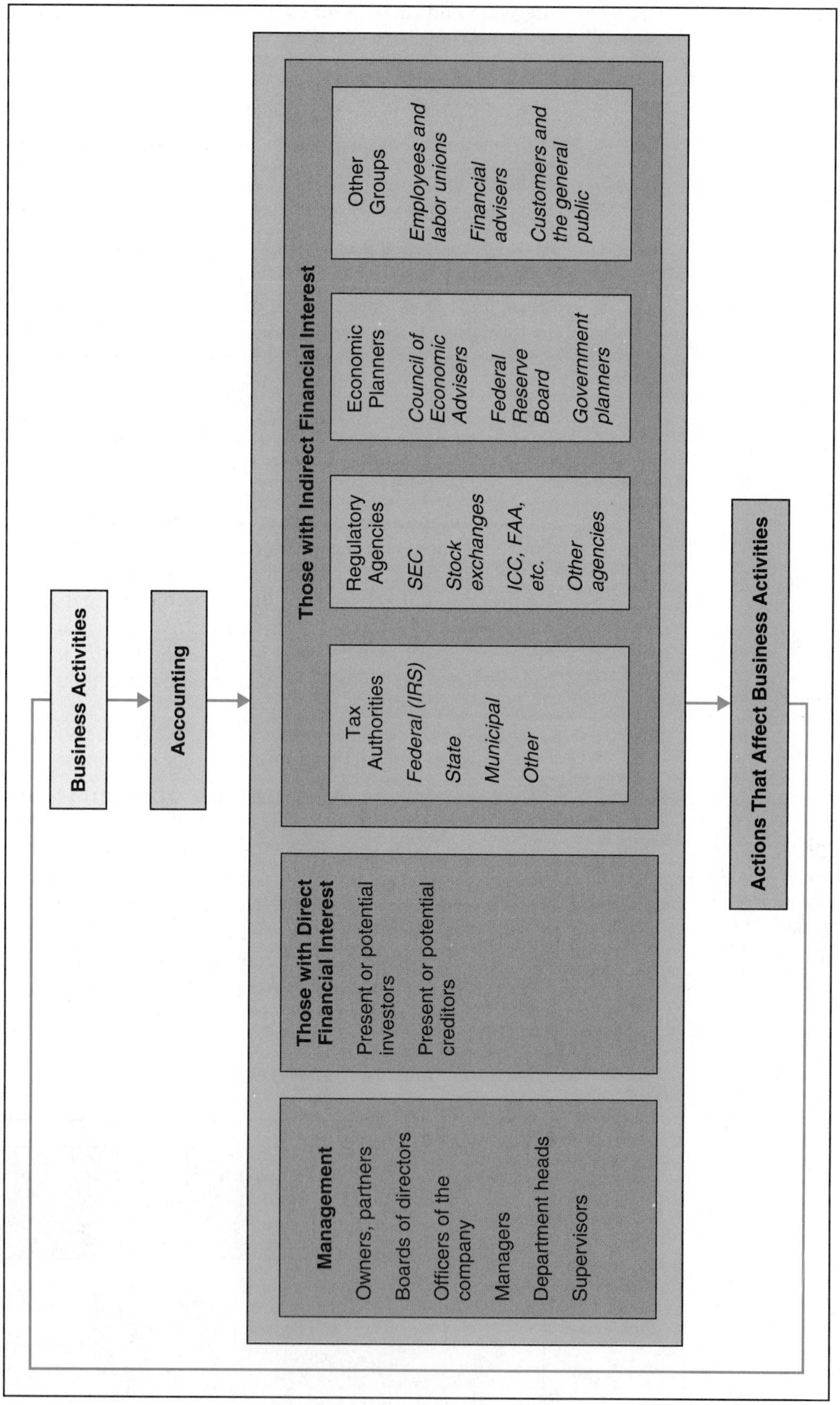

Figure 1-3. The Users of Accounting Information

Business Activities

Accounting

Management
- Owners, partners
- Boards of directors
- Officers of the company
- Managers
- Department heads
- Supervisors

Those with Direct Financial Interest
- Present or potential investors
- Present or potential creditors

Those with Indirect Financial Interest

Tax Authorities
- *Federal (IRS)*
- *State*
- *Municipal*
- *Other*

Regulatory Agencies
- *SEC*
- *Stock exchanges*
- *ICC, FAA, etc.*
- *Other agencies*

Economic Planners
- *Council of Economic Advisers*
- *Federal Reserve Board*
- *Government planners*

Other Groups
- *Employees and labor unions*
- *Financial advisers*
- *Customers and the general public*

Actions That Affect Business Activities

Management

Management is the group of people who have overall responsibility for operating a business and for meeting the company's goals. In a small business, management may include the owners. In a large business, management more often consists of people who have been hired. Business enterprises have many varied and often complex objectives. These goals include maintaining an acceptable level of earnings, providing quality goods and services at low cost, creating new and improved products, increasing the number of jobs available, and improving the environment. To accomplish these and other tasks, the company must be successful. Success and survival in a competitive business environment require that management concentrate much of its effort on two important goals: profitability and liquidity. **Profitability** is the ability to earn enough income to attract and hold investment capital. **Liquidity** means having enough funds on hand to pay debts when they fall due.

Managers must decide what to do, how to do it, and whether the results match their original plans. Successful managers consistently make the right decisions on the basis of timely and valid information. What was the company's net income during the past quarter? Is the rate of return to the owners adequate? Does the company have enough cash? Which products are most profitable? What is the cost of manufacturing each product? Many of these decisions are based on an analysis of accounting data. For this reason, management is one of the most important users of accounting information.

Users with a Direct Financial Interest

Another major function of accounting is to measure and report information about how a business has performed. Most businesses periodically publish a set of general-purpose financial statements that report their success in meeting the objectives of profitability and liquidity. These statements show what has happened in the past and are important indicators of what is going to happen in the future. Many people outside the company carefully study these financial reports.

Present or Potential Investors. Those who invest or may invest in a company are interested in the past success of the business and its potential earnings. A thorough study of the company's financial statements helps potential investors judge the prospects for a profitable investment. After investing in a company, investors continually must review their commitment, again by examining the company's financial statements.

Present or Potential Creditors. Most companies borrow money for both long- and short-term operating needs. Creditors, those who lend money or deliver goods and services before being paid, are interested mainly in whether a company is going to have the cash to pay the interest charges and repay the debt at the appropriate time. They study the company's liquidity and cash flow as well as its profitability. Banks, finance companies, mortgage companies, securities firms, insurance firms, suppliers, and others who lend money must analyze a company's financial position before they make a loan to the company.

Users with an Indirect Financial Interest

Society as a whole, through government and public groups, in recent years has become one of the biggest and most important users of accounting information.

Users who need accounting information to make decisions on public issues include (1) tax authorities, (2) regulatory agencies, (3) economic planners, and (4) other groups.

Tax Authorities. Our governments are financed through the collection of taxes. Under federal, state, and local laws, companies and individuals pay many kinds of taxes, including federal, state, and city income taxes, social security and other payroll taxes, excise taxes, and sales taxes. Each tax requires special tax returns and often a complex set of records as well. Proper reporting is generally a matter of law and can be very complicated. The Internal Revenue Code, for instance, contains thousands of rules governing the preparation of the accounting information used in computing federal income taxes.

Regulatory Agencies. Most companies must report to one or more regulatory agencies at the federal, state, and local levels. All public corporations must report periodically to the Securities and Exchange Commission (SEC). This body, which was set up by Congress to protect the public, regulates the issuing, buying, and selling of stocks in the United States. Companies that are listed on a stock exchange also must meet the special reporting requirements of their exchange. The Interstate Commerce Commission (ICC) regulates the trucking industry and railroads, and the Federal Aviation Administration (FAA) regulates airlines. Most public utilities—for example, electric and gas companies—are regulated and must defend their rates with accounting reports. Accounting reports also are required by new and broader regulations, like those of the Environmental Protection Agency (EPA), which is concerned with, among other things, the cost and speed of reducing environmental pollution.

Economic Planners. Since the 1930s the federal government's commitment to a more active role in planning and forecasting economic activity has led to greater use of accounting and accounting information. A system of accounting for the whole economy, called *national income accounting*, deals with the total production, inventories, income, dividends, taxes, and so forth of our economy. Economic planners, among them members of the President's Council of Economic Advisers and the Federal Reserve Board, use this information to set economic policies and evaluate economic programs.

Other Groups. Labor unions study the financial statements of corporations as part of preparing for contract negotiations. A company's income and costs often play an important role in these negotiations. Those who advise investors and creditors—financial analysts and advisers, brokers, underwriters, lawyers, economists, and the financial press—also have an indirect interest in the financial performance and prospects of a business. And consumers' groups, customers, and the general public have become more concerned about the financing and earnings of corporations as well as with the effects that corporations have on inflation, the environment, social problems, and the quality of life.

Government and Not-for-Profit Organizations

More than 30 percent of the U.S. economy is generated by government and not-for-profit organizations (hospitals, universities, professional organizations, and charities). Like the heads of private firms, the managers of these diverse entities need accounting information. They need to raise funds and deploy scarce resources. They need to plan to pay for operations and repay creditors on a timely basis. Moreover, they have an obligation to report their financial performance to legislators, boards, and contributors. Although most of the examples in this text focus on business enterprises, the same basic principles apply to government and not-for-profit organizations. We discuss accounting for these types of organizations in an appendix to the textbook.

Financial and Management Accounting

OBJECTIVE 3
Distinguish between financial and management accounting, define generally accepted accounting principles (GAAP), *and identify the organizations that influence GAAP*

Accounting was defined earlier as an information system that measures, processes, and communicates information that is useful for decision making. A distinction commonly is made between the fields of management accounting and financial accounting. **Management accounting** produces all the accounting information that is measured, processed, and communicated for the internal use of management. **Financial accounting** generates the accounting information that, in addition to being used internally by management, is communicated to those outside the organization. Chapters 1 through 14 of this book focus on financial accounting; Chapters 15 through 26 are concerned primarily with management accounting. Chapters 27 and 28 may be considered either financial accounting or management accounting.

Generally Accepted Accounting Principles

Because it is important that all who receive accounting reports be able to interpret them, a set of practices has developed that provides guidelines for financial accounting, called **generally accepted accounting principles (GAAP)**. Although the term has several meanings in the literature, perhaps this is the best definition: "Generally accepted accounting principles encompass the conventions, rules, and procedures necessary to define accepted accounting practice at a particular time."[6] In other words, GAAP arise from wide agreement on the theory and practice of accounting at a particular time. These "principles" are not like the unchangeable laws of nature found in chemistry. They are developed by accountants and businesses to serve the needs of decision makers, and they can be altered as better methods evolve or as circumstances change.

In this book, we present accounting practice, or GAAP, as it is today. We also try to explain the reasons or theory on which the practice is based. Both theory and practice are part and parcel of the study of accounting. However, you should realize that accounting is a discipline that is always growing, changing, and improving. Just as years of research are necessary before a new surgical method or lifesaving drug can be introduced, it may take years for research and new discoveries in accounting to become common practice. As a result, you may come across practices that seem contradictory. In some cases, we point out new directions in accounting. Your instructor also may mention certain weaknesses in current theory or practice.

GAAP and the Independent CPA's Report

Because financial statements are prepared by the management of the company and could be falsified for personal gain, all companies that sell ownership to the public and many companies that apply for sizable loans have their financial statements audited by an independent certified public accountant. **Certified**

6. *Statement of the Accounting Principles Board No. 4*, par. 138.

public accountants (CPAs) are licensed by all states for the same reason that lawyers and doctors are—to protect the public by ensuring the quality of professional service. One important attribute of CPAs is **independence**: They have no financial or other compromising ties with the companies they audit. This gives the public confidence in their work.

An independent CPA makes an **audit**, an examination of a company's financial statements and the accounting systems, controls, and records that produced them. The purpose of the audit is to ascertain that the financial statements have been prepared in accordance with generally accepted accounting principles. If the independent accountant is satisfied that this standard has been met, his or her report contains the following language:

> In our opinion, the financial statements . . . present fairly, in all material respects . . . in conformity with generally accepted accounting principles.

This wording emphasizes the fact that accounting and auditing are not an exact science. Because the framework of GAAP provides room for interpretation and their application necessitates the making of estimates, the auditor can render an opinion or judgment only that the financial statements *present fairly* or conform *in all material respects* to GAAP. The accountant's report does not preclude minor or immaterial errors in the financial statements. However, it does imply that on the whole, investors and creditors can rely on those statements. Historically, the reputation of auditors for competence and independence has been highly regarded. As a result, banks, investors, and creditors are willing to rely on an auditor's opinion when deciding to invest in a company or to make loans to a firm that has been audited. The independent audit is an important factor in the worldwide growth of financial markets.

Organizations That Influence Current Practice

Many organizations directly or indirectly influence GAAP and so influence much of what is in this book. The most important of these organizations are the Financial Accounting Standards Board, the American Institute of Certified Public Accountants, the Securities and Exchange Commission, the Internal Revenue Service, and the Governmental Accounting Standards Board. There are international and other groups that also influence accounting practices.

Financial Accounting Standards Board. Founded in 1973, the **Financial Accounting Standards Board (FASB)** has the primary responsibility for developing and issuing rules on accounting practice. This independent body issues Statements of Financial Accounting Standards. Departures from these standards must be justified and reported in a company's financial statements. The FASB is governed by the Financial Accounting Foundation.

American Institute of Certified Public Accountants. The **American Institute of Certified Public Accountants (AICPA)** has been concerned with accounting practice longer than most other groups. From 1938 to 1958 the AICPA's Committee on Accounting Procedures issued a series of pronouncements dealing with accounting principles, procedures, and terms. In 1959 the AICPA organized the Accounting Principles Board (APB) to replace the committee. The board published a number of APB Opinions on accounting practice, many of which are still in effect even though the APB was disbanded in 1973, the year when the FASB took over the standard-setting authority. The AICPA still influences accounting practice through the activities of its senior technical committees.

Securities and Exchange Commission. The **Securities and Exchange Commission (SEC)** is a U.S. government agency that has the legal power to set and enforce accounting practices for companies whose securities are offered for sale to the general public. As such, it has enormous influence on accounting practice. Because the APB failed to solve some of the major problems and abuses in accounting practice, the SEC began to play a larger and more aggressive part in formulating the rules of accounting. The FASB represents a major effort on the part of accountants to limit the SEC to its traditional role, allowing the accounting profession to regulate itself. The success or failure of the FASB will be important in determining how much influence the SEC will have on accounting in the future.

Internal Revenue Service. U.S. tax laws govern the assessment and collection of revenue for operating the government. Because a major source of the government's revenue is the income tax, the law specifies the rules for determining taxable income. These rules are interpreted and enforced by the **Internal Revenue Service (IRS)**. In some cases, these rules conflict with good accounting practice, but they still are an important influence on that practice. Businesses use certain accounting practices simply because they are required by the tax laws. Sometimes companies follow an accounting practice specified in the tax laws to take advantage of rules that can help them financially. Cases where the tax laws affect accounting practice are noted throughout this book.

Governmental Accounting Standards Board. The **Governmental Accounting Standards Board (GASB)**, which was established in 1984 under the same governing body as the Financial Accounting Standards Board, is responsible for issuing accounting standards for state and local governments. The GASB has a great influence on financial reporting by these units.

International Organizations. With the growth of financial markets throughout the world, the need for financial statements that can be understood by investors and auditors in different countries has increased. As a result, worldwide cooperation in the development of accounting principles has become a priority. The International Accounting Standards Committee (IASC) has approved more than twenty international standards, which have been translated into six languages. In 1977 the International Federation of Accountants (IFAC), made up of professional accounting bodies from more than sixty countries, was founded to promote international agreement on accounting questions.

Other Organizations. The Institute of Management Accountants (IMA), composed mainly of accountants in business, engages in education and research, with an emphasis on management accounting and accounting for management decisions. The Financial Executives Institute (FEI) is made up of people who hold the highest financial positions in large businesses. It is most interested in standards and research in financial accounting.

The American Accounting Association (AAA) was founded in 1935, succeeding the American Association of University Instructors in Accounting, which was started in 1916. This group has an academic and theoretical focus. Its members have contributed greatly to the development of accounting theory.

Accounting Measurement

OBJECTIVE 4
Explain the importance of business transactions, money measure, and separate entity to accounting measurement

Accounting is an information system that measures, processes, and communicates financial information. In this section, you begin the study of the measurement aspects of accounting. Here you learn what accounting actually measures and study the effects of certain transactions on a company's financial position.

To make an accounting measurement, the accountant must answer four basic questions:

1. What is measured?
2. When should the measurement be made?
3. What value should be placed on what is measured?
4. How should what is measured be classified?

All the questions deal with basic underlying assumptions and generally accepted accounting principles, and their answers establish what accounting is and what it is not. Accountants in industry, professional associations, public accounting, government, and academic circles debate the answers to these questions constantly, and the answers change as new knowledge and practice require. But the basis of today's accounting practice rests on a number of widely accepted concepts and conventions, which are described in this book. Questions **2**, **3**, and **4** are examined in the chapter on measuring and recording business transactions. Here we focus on question **1**, What is measured?

What Is Measured?

The world contains an unlimited number of things to measure and ways to measure them. For example, consider a machine that makes bottle caps. How many measurements of this machine could you make? You might start with size and then go on to location, weight, cost, or one of many other units of measurement. Some of these measurements are relevant to accounting; some are not. Every system must define what it measures, and accounting is no exception. Basically, **financial accounting is concerned with measuring the impact of business transactions on separate business entities in terms of money measures**. The concepts of business transactions, money measure, and separate entity are discussed in the next sections.

Business Transactions as the Object of Measurement

Business transactions are economic events that affect the financial position of a business entity. Business entities can have hundreds or even thousands of transactions every day. These business transactions are the raw material of accounting reports.

A transaction can be an exchange of value (a purchase, sale, payment, collection, or loan) between two or more independent parties. A transaction also can be an economic event that has the same effect as an exchange transaction but does not involve an exchange. Some examples of "nonexchange" transactions are losses from fire, flood, explosion, and theft; physical wear and tear on machinery and equipment; and the day-by-day accumulation of interest.

To be recorded, a transaction must relate directly to a business entity. For example, suppose a customer buys a shovel from Ace Hardware but has to buy a hoe from a competing store because Ace is sold out of hoes. The transaction for selling the shovel is recorded in Ace's records. However, the purchase of the hoe from the competitor is not recorded in Ace's records because even though it indirectly affects Ace economically, it does not involve a direct exchange of value between Ace and the customer.

Money Measure

All business transactions are recorded in terms of money. This concept is called the **money measure**. Of course, information of a nonfinancial nature can be recorded, but it is only through the recording of dollar amounts that the diverse transactions and activities of a business are measured. Money is the only factor common to all business transactions, so it is the only practical unit of measurement that can produce financial data that can be compared.

The monetary unit used by a business depends on the country in which it exists. For example, in the United States, the basic unit of money is the dollar. In Japan, it is the yen; in France, the franc; in Germany, the mark; and in the United Kingdom, the pound. When transactions take place between businesses in two countries, the units must be translated from one currency to another. Our discussion in this book focuses on dollars.

The Concept of Separate Entity

For accounting purposes, a business is a **separate entity**, distinct not only from its creditors and customers but also from its owner or owners. It should have a completely separate set of records and its financial records and reports should refer only to its own financial affairs.

For example, the Jones Florist Company should have a bank account that is separate from the account of Kay Jones, the owner. Kay Jones may own a home, a car, and other property, and she may have personal debts, but these are not the Jones Florist Company's resources or debts. Kay Jones also may own another business, say a stationery shop. If she does, she should have a completely separate set of records for each business.

Forms of Business Organization

OBJECTIVE 5
Identify the three basic forms of business organization

There are three basic forms of business organization: sole proprietorships, partnerships, and corporations. Accountants recognize each form as an economic unit separate from its owners, although legally only the corporation is considered separate from its owners. Other legal differences among the three forms are summarized in Table 1-1 and discussed briefly below. In this book, we begin with accounting for the sole proprietorship because it is the simplest form of accounting. At critical points, however, we call attention to its essential differences from accounting for partnerships and corporations. Later we deal specifically with corporation and partnership accounting.

Sole Proprietorships

A **sole proprietorship** is a business owned by one person. This form of business gives the individual a means of controlling the business apart from his or her personal interests. Legally, however, the proprietorship is the same economic unit as the individual. The individual receives all profits or losses and is liable for all obligations of the business. Proprietorships represent the largest number of businesses in the United States, but typically they are the smallest in size. The life of a sole proprietorship ends when the owner wants it to or at the owner's death or incapacity.

Table 1-1. Comparative Features of the Forms of Business Organization

	Sole Proprietorship	Partnership	Corporation
1. Legal status	Not a separate legal entity	Not a separate legal entity	Separate legal entity
2. Risk of ownership	Owner's personal resources at stake	Partners' personal resources at stake	Limited to investment in corporation
3. Duration or life	Limited by choice or death of owner	Limited by choice or death of any partner	Indefinite, possibly unlimited
4. Transferability of ownership	Sale by owner establishes new company	Changes in any partner's percentage of interest requires new partnership	Transferable by sale of stock
5. Accounting treatment	Separate economic unit	Separate economic unit	Separate economic unit

Partnerships

A **partnership** is like a proprietorship in most ways except that it has more than one owner. A partnership is not a legal entity separate from the owners but an unincorporated association that brings together the talents and resources of two or more people. The partners share the profits and losses of the partnership according to an agreed-on formula. Generally, any partner can bind the partnership to another party, and, if necessary, the personal resources of each partner can be called on to pay the obligations of the partnership. In some cases, one or more partners limit their liability, but at least one partner must have unlimited liability. A partnership must be dissolved when ownership changes—for example, when a partner leaves or dies. For the business to continue as a partnership, a new partnership must be formed.

Corporations

A **corporation** is a business unit that is legally separate from its owners (the stockholders). The owners, whose ownership is represented by shares of stock in the corporation, do not control the operations of the corporation directly. Instead, they elect a board of directors, which appoints managers to run the corporation for the benefit of the stockholders. In exchange for limited involvement in the corporation's actual operations, stockholders enjoy limited liability. That is, their risk of loss is limited to the amount they paid for their shares. If they want, stockholders can sell their shares to other people, without affecting corporate operations. Because of this limited liability, stockholders often are willing to invest in riskier, but potentially more profitable, activities. Also, because ownership can be transferred without dissolving the corporation, the life of the corporation is unlimited; it is not subject to the whims or health of a proprietor or of a partner.

Corporations have several important advantages over proprietorships and partnerships that make them very efficient in amassing capital for the formation and growth of very large companies (see the chapter on contributed capital). Even though corporations are fewer in number than proprietorships and partnerships, they contribute much more to the U.S. economy in monetary terms. For example, in 1992 General Motors generated more revenue than all but fifteen of the world's countries.

Financial Position and the Accounting Equation

OBJECTIVE 6
Define financial position, *state the accounting equation, and show how they are affected by simple transactions*

Financial position refers to the economic resources that belong to a company and the claims against those resources at a point in time. Another term for claims is *equities*. Therefore, a company can be viewed as economic resources and equities:

Economic resources = equities

Every company has two types of equities, creditors' equity and owner's equity. Thus,

Economic resources = creditors' equity + owner's equity

In accounting terminology, economic resources are called *assets* and creditors' equities are called *liabilities*. So the equation can be written like this:

Assets = liabilities + owner's equity

This equation is known as the **accounting equation**. The two sides of the equation always must be equal, or "in balance."

Assets

Assets are "probable future economic benefits obtained or controlled by a particular entity as a result of past transactions or events."[7] In other words, they are economic resources owned by a business that are expected to benefit future operations. Certain kinds of assets—for example, cash and money owed to the company from customers (called *accounts receivable*)—are monetary items. Other assets—inventories (goods held for sale), land, buildings, and equipment—are nonmonetary physical things. Still other assets—the rights granted by patent, trademark, or copyright—are nonphysical.

Liabilities

Liabilities are "probable future sacrifices of economic benefits arising from present obligations of a particular entity to transfer assets or provide services to other entities in the future as a result of past transactions or events."[8] Among these are debts of the business, amounts owed to creditors for goods or services bought on credit (called *accounts payable*), borrowed money (for example, money owed on loans payable to banks), salaries and wages owed to employees, taxes owed to the government, and services to be performed.

As debts, liabilities are claims recognized by law. That is, the law gives creditors the right to force the sale of a company's assets if the company fails to pay its debts. Creditors have rights over owners and must be paid in full before the owners receive anything, even if payment of a debt uses up all the assets of a business.

7. *Statement of Financial Accounting Concepts No. 6*, "Elements of Financial Statements" (Stamford, Conn.: Financial Accounting Standards Board, December 1985), par. 25.
8. Ibid., par. 35.

Owner's Equity

Equity is "the residual interest in the assets of an entity that remains after deducting its liabilities."[9] In a business, equity is called the ownership interest or **owner's equity**. Owner's equity represents the claims by an owner against the assets of a business. Owner's equity also is known as *residual equity* because, theoretically, it is what would be left over if all the liabilities were paid. Transposing the accounting equation, we can define owner's equity this way:

Owner's equity = assets – liabilities

Because it equals the assets after deducting the liabilities, owner's equity sometimes is said to equal **net assets**.

The four types of transactions that affect owner's equity are shown in Figure 1-4. Two of these transactions, **owner's investments** and **owner's withdrawals**, are assets that the owner either puts into the business or takes out of the business. For instance, if the owner of Shannon Realty, John Shannon, takes cash out of his personal bank account and deposits it in the business bank account, he has made an owner's investment. The assets (cash) of the business increase, and John Shannon's equity in those assets also increases. Conversely, if John Shannon takes cash out of the business bank account and deposits it in his personal bank account, he has made a withdrawal from the business. The assets of the business decrease, and John Shannon's equity in the business also decreases.

The other two types of transactions that affect owner's equity are revenues and expenses. Simply stated, **revenues** and **expenses** are the increases and decreases in owner's equity that result from operating a business. For example, the cash a customer pays (or agrees to pay in the future) to Shannon Realty in return for a service provided by the company is a revenue. The assets (cash or accounts receivable) of Shannon Realty increase, and the owner's equity in those assets also increases. On the other hand, the cash Shannon Realty pays out (or agrees to pay in the future) in the process of providing a service is an expense. Now the assets (cash) decrease or the liabilities (accounts payable) increase, and the owner's equity in the assets decreases. Generally speaking, a company is successful if its revenues exceed its expenses. When revenues exceed expenses, the difference is called **net income**; when expenses exceed revenues, the difference is called **net loss**.

Some Sample Transactions

Let us examine the effect of some of the most common business transactions on the accounting equation. Suppose that John Shannon opens a real estate agency

Figure 1-4. Four Types of Transactions That Affect Owner's Equity

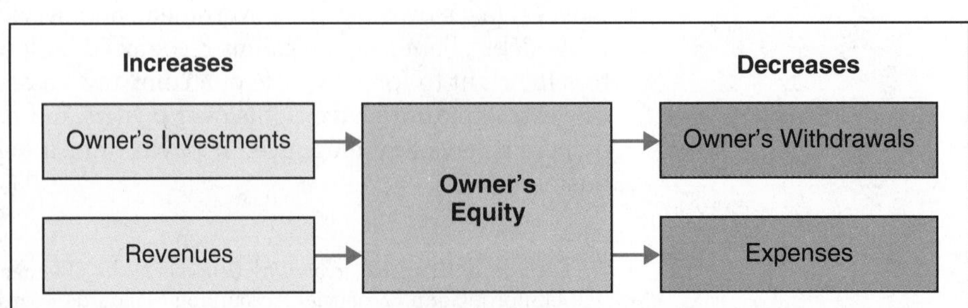

9. Ibid., par. 49.

called Shannon Realty on December 1. During December, his business engages in the transactions described in the following paragraphs.

Owner's Investments. John starts his business by depositing $50,000 in a bank account in the name of Shannon Realty. The transfer of cash from his personal account to the business account is an owner's investment. It increases the assets (Cash) and the owner's equity (John Shannon, Capital):

	Assets	=	Owner's Equity	
	Cash		John Shannon, Capital	Type of OE Transaction
1.	$50,000		$50,000	Owner's Investment

At this point, the company has no liabilities, so its assets equal the owner's equity. The labels *Cash* and *John Shannon, Capital* are called **accounts**. Accounts are used by accountants to accumulate amounts produced from like transactions. Transactions that affect owner's equity are identified by type so that similar types can be grouped together on accounting reports.

Purchase of Assets with Cash. John finds a good location for his business and purchases with cash a lot for $10,000 and a small building on the lot for $25,000. This transaction does not change the total assets, liabilities, or owner's equity of Shannon Realty, but it does change the composition of the assets—decreasing Cash and increasing Land and Building:

	Assets			=	Owner's Equity	
	Cash	Land	Building		John Shannon, Capital	Type of OE Transaction
bal.	$50,000				$50,000	
2.	−35,000	+$10,000	+$25,000			
bal.	$15,000	$10,000	$25,000		$50,000	
	$50,000					

Purchase of Assets by Incurring a Liability. Assets do not always have to be purchased with cash. They also can be purchased on credit, that is, on the basis of an agreement to pay for them later. Suppose John buys office supplies for $500 on credit. This transaction increases both the assets (Supplies) and the liabilities (an account called *Accounts Payable*) of Shannon Realty:

	Assets				=	Liabilities	+	Owner's Equity	
	Cash	Supplies	Land	Building		Accounts Payable		John Shannon, Capital	Type of OE Transaction
bal.	$15,000		$10,000	$25,000				$50,000	
3.		+$500				+$500			
bal.	$15,000	$500	$10,000	$25,000		$500		$50,000	
	$50,500					$50,500			

Notice that this transaction increases both sides of the accounting equation to $50,500.

Payment of a Liability. If John later pays $200 of the $500 owed for the supplies, both assets (Cash) and liabilities (Accounts Payable) decrease, but Supplies is unaffected:

	Assets				=	Liabilities	+	Owner's Equity	
	Cash	Supplies	Land	Building		Accounts Payable		John Shannon, Capital	Type of OE Transaction
bal.	$15,000	$500	$10,000	$25,000		$500		$50,000	
4.	−200					−200			
bal.	$14,800	$500	$10,000	$25,000		$300		$50,000	
	$50,300					$50,300			

Notice that the accounting equation is still equal on both sides, although now at a total of $50,300.

Revenues. Shannon Realty earns revenues in the form of commissions received from selling houses for clients. Sometimes these commissions are paid immediately in cash, and sometimes the client agrees to pay a commission later. In either case, the commission is recorded when it is earned, and Shannon Realty has a right to a current or future receipt of cash.

First, assume that Shannon Realty sells a house and receives a commission in cash of $1,500. This transaction increases assets (Cash) and owner's equity (John Shannon, Capital):

	Assets				=	Liabilities	+	Owner's Equity	
	Cash	Supplies	Land	Building		Accounts Payable		John Shannon, Capital	Type of OE Transaction
bal.	$14,800	$500	$10,000	$25,000		$300		$50,000	
5.	+1,500							+1,500	Commissions Revenue
bal.	$16,300	$500	$10,000	$25,000		$300		$51,500	
	$51,800					$51,800			

Now assume that John sells a house, earning a commission of $2,000, but agrees to wait for payment. Because the commission is earned now, a bill or invoice is sent to the client and the transaction is recorded now. This revenue transaction increases both assets and owner's equity as before, but a new asset account, Accounts Receivable, shows that Shannon Realty is waiting for the receipt of the commission:

	Assets					=	Liabilities	+	Owner's Equity	
	Cash	Accounts Receivable	Supplies	Land	Building		Accounts Payable		John Shannon, Capital	Type of OE Transaction
bal.	$16,300		$500	$10,000	$25,000		$300		$51,500	
6.		+$2,000							+2,000	Commissions Revenue
bal.	$16,300	$2,000	$500	$10,000	$25,000		$300		$53,500	
	$53,800						$53,800			

The use of separate accounts for revenue accounts, like Commissions Revenue, is introduced in the chapter on measuring and recording business transactions.

Collection of Accounts Receivable. Let us assume that a few days later Shannon Realty receives $1,000 from the client in transaction **6**. The asset Cash increases and the asset Accounts Receivable decreases:

	Assets					=	Liabilities	+	Owner's Equity	
	Cash	Accounts Receivable	Supplies	Land	Building		Accounts Payable		John Shannon, Capital	Type of OE Transaction
bal.	$16,300	$2,000	$500	$10,000	$25,000		$300		$53,500	
7.	+1,000	−1,000								
bal.	$17,300	$1,000	$500	$10,000	$25,000		$300		$53,500	
	$53,800						$53,800			

Notice that this transaction does not affect owner's equity because the commission revenue already has been recorded in transaction **6**. Also notice that the balance of Accounts Receivable is $1,000, which means that $1,000 still has to be collected.

Expenses. Just as revenues are recorded when they are earned, expenses are recorded when they are incurred. Expenses can be paid in cash when they occur, or they can be paid later. If payment is going to be made later, a liability—for example, Accounts Payable or Wages Payable—increases. In both cases, owner's equity decreases. Assume that John Shannon pays $1,000 to rent some equipment for the office and $400 in wages to a part-time helper. These transactions reduce assets (Cash) and owner's equity (John Shannon, Capital):

	Assets					=	Liabilities	+	Owner's Equity	
	Cash	Accounts Receivable	Supplies	Land	Building		Accounts Payable		John Shannon, Capital	Type of OE Transaction
bal.	$17,300	$1,000	$500	$10,000	$25,000		$300		$53,500	
8.	−1,000								−1,000	Equip. Rental Expense
9.	−400								−400	Wages Expense
bal.	$15,900	$1,000	$500	$10,000	$25,000		$300		$52,100	
	$52,400						$52,400			

Now assume that John has not paid the $300 bill for utility expenses incurred by Shannon Realty in December. In this case, the effect on owner's equity is the same as when the expense is paid in cash, but instead of a reduction in assets, there is an increase in liabilities (Accounts Payable):

	Assets					=	Liabilities	+	Owner's Equity	
	Cash	Accounts Receiv-able	Supplies	Land	Building		Accounts Payable		John Shannon, Capital	Type of OE Transaction
bal.	$15,900	$1,000	$500	$10,000	$25,000		$300		$52,100	
10.							+300		−300	Utility Expense
bal.	$15,900	$1,000	$500	$10,000	$25,000		$600		$51,800	
			$52,400					$52,400		

The use of separate accounts for expenses is introduced in the chapter on measuring and recording business transactions.

Owner's Withdrawals. John now withdraws $600 in cash from Shannon Realty and deposits it in his personal account. This transaction reduces assets (Cash) and owner's equity (John Shannon, Capital). Although, as can be seen below, withdrawals have the same effect on the accounting equation as expenses (see transactions **8** and **9**), it is important not to confuse them. Withdrawals are not expenses: Withdrawals are personal distributions of assets to the owner; expenses are incurred by the business in its operations.

	Assets					=	Liabilities	+	Owner's Equity	
	Cash	Accounts Receiv-able	Supplies	Land	Building		Accounts Payable		John Shannon, Capital	Type of OE Transaction
bal.	$15,900	$1,000	$500	$10,000	$25,000		$600		$51,800	
11.	−600								−600	Owner's Withdrawal
bal.	$15,300	$1,000	$500	$10,000	$25,000		$600		$51,200	
			$51,800					$51,800		

Summary. A summary of the eleven sample transactions is shown in Exhibit 1-1.

Communication Through Financial Statements

OBJECTIVE 7
Identify the four basic financial statements

Financial statements are a central feature of accounting because they are the primary means of communicating important accounting information to users. It is helpful to think of these statements as models of the business enterprise because they show the business in financial terms. As is true of all models, however, financial statements are not perfect pictures of the real thing but rather the accountant's best effort to represent what is real.

Four major financial statements are used to communicate accounting information about a business. One is the *income statement,* which reports the firm's income-generating activities or earnings over a period of time (the accounting period). A second statement, called the *statement of owner's equity,* shows the changes in the owner's interest in the business over the same period of time. These statements are prepared from the four types of transactions that affect owner's equity. This is why in the examples above and in Exhibit 1-1, these transactions are identified by type.

Exhibit 1-1. Summary of Effects of Sample Transactions on the Accounting Equation

	Assets					= Liabilities +	Owner's Equity	
	Cash	Accounts Receivable	Supplies	Land	Building	Accounts Payable	John Shannon, Capital	Type of OE Transaction
1.	$50,000						$50,000	Owner's Investment
2.	−35,000			+$10,000	+$25,000			
bal.	$15,000			$10,000	$25,000		$50,000	
3.			+$500			+$500		
bal.	$15,000		$500	$10,000	$25,000	$500	$50,000	
4.	−200					−200		
bal.	$14,800		$500	$10,000	$25,000	$300	$50,000	
5.	+1,500						+1,500	Commissions Revenue
bal.	$16,300		$500	$10,000	$25,000	$300	$51,500	
6.		+$2,000					+2,000	Commissions Revenue
bal.	$16,300	$2,000	$500	$10,000	$25,000	$300	$53,500	
7.	+1,000	−1,000						
bal.	$17,300	$1,000	$500	$10,000	$25,000	$300	$53,500	
8.	−1,000						−1,000	Equip. Rental Expense
9.	−400						−400	Wages Expense
bal.	$15,900	$1,000	$500	$10,000	$25,000	$300	$52,100	
10.						+300	−300	Utility Expense
bal.	$15,900	$1,000	$500	$10,000	$25,000	$600	$51,800	
11.	−600						−600	Owner's Withdrawal
bal.	$15,300	$1,000	$500	$10,000	$25,000	$600	$51,200	
			$51,800				$51,800	

A third financial statement is the *balance sheet*. The balance sheet shows the financial position of the business at a particular date, the end of the accounting period, for example. A fourth statement, called the *statement of cash flows*, summarizes all the changes in cash that result from operating activities, investing activities, and financing activities.

Exhibit 1-2 illustrates the relationship among the first three statements by showing how they would appear for Shannon Realty after the eleven sample transactions shown in Exhibit 1-1. It is assumed that the time period covered is the month of December 19xx. Notice that each statement is headed in a similar way. Each heading identifies the company and the kind of statement. The income statement and the statement of owner's equity give the time period to which they apply; the balance sheet gives the specific date to which it applies. These statements are typical for proprietorships. Statements for corporations and partnerships, which are similar to those for a proprietorship, are discussed in the chapters on accounting for corporations and the appendix on accounting for partnerships.

The Income Statement

The **income statement** is a financial statement that summarizes the amount of revenues earned and expenses incurred by a business over a period of time. Many people consider it the most important financial report because it shows whether or not a business achieved its primary objective, earning an acceptable income. In Exhibit 1-2, Shannon Realty had revenues in commissions earned of $3,500. From this amount, total expenses of $1,700 were deducted (equipment rental expense of $1,000, wages expense of $400, and utility expense of $300), to arrive at a net income of $1,800. To show that it applies to a period of time, the statement is dated "For the Month Ended December 31, 19xx."

The Statement of Owner's Equity

The **statement of owner's equity** shows the changes in the owner's capital account over a period of time. In Exhibit 1-2, the beginning capital is zero because the company was started in this accounting period. During the month, John Shannon made an investment in the business of $50,000, and the company earned income (as shown on the income statement) of $1,800, for a total increase of $51,800. Deducted from this amount are the withdrawals for the month of $600, leaving an ending balance of $51,200 in the Capital account.

The Balance Sheet

The purpose of a **balance sheet** is to show the financial position of a business on a certain date. For this reason, it often is called the *statement of financial position* and is dated as of a certain date. The balance sheet presents a view of the business as the holder of resources or assets that are equal to the claims against or sources of those assets. The claims or sources consist of the company's liabilities and the owner's equity in the company. In Exhibit 1-2, Shannon Realty has several categories of assets, which total $51,800. These assets equal the total liabilities of $600 (Accounts Payable) plus the ending balance of owner's equity of $51,200 (John Shannon, Capital). Notice that the Capital account on the balance sheet comes from the ending balance on the statement of owner's equity.

The Statement of Cash Flows

Over the last three decades, it has become clear that the income statement has a serious deficiency: It shows only the changes in financial position caused by

Exhibit 1-2. Income Statement, Statement of Owner's Equity, and Balance Sheet for Shannon Realty

Shannon Realty
Income Statement
For the Month Ended December 31, 19xx

Revenues		
Commissions Revenue		$3,500
Expenses		
Equipment Rental Expense	$1,000	
Wages Expense	400	
Utility Expense	300	
Total Expenses		1,700
Net Income		**$1,800**

Shannon Realty
Statement of Owner's Equity
For the Month Ended December 31, 19xx

John Shannon, Capital, December 1, 19xx		$ 0
Add: Investments by John Shannon	$50,000	
Net Income for the Month	**1,800**	51,800
Subtotal		$51,800
Less Withdrawals by John Shannon		600
John Shannon, Capital, December 31, 19xx		**$51,200**

Shannon Realty
Balance Sheet
December 31, 19xx

Assets		**Liabilities**	
Cash	$15,300	Accounts Payable	$ 600
Accounts Receivable	1,000		
Supplies	500	**Owner's Equity**	
Land	10,000		
Building	25,000	**John Shannon, Capital**	**51,200**
Total Assets	$51,800	Total Liabilities and Owner's Equity	$51,800

those operations that produce a net income or loss. Many important events, especially those relating to investing and financing activities, can take place during an accounting period and not appear on the income statement. For example, the owner may put more money into the business or take it out. Buildings, equipment, or other assets may be bought or sold. New liabilities may be incurred or old ones paid off. Today, the **statement of cash flows** is widely used to show the cash produced by operating a business as well as important investing and financing transactions that take place over an accounting period.

Exhibit 1-3 shows the statement of cash flows for Shannon Realty. Notice that the name of the company, the title of the statement, and the period covered by the statement are identified. Also notice that the statement explains how the

Exhibit 1-3. Statement of Cash Flows for Shannon Realty

Shannon Realty Statement of Cash Flows For the Month Ended December 31, 19xx		
Cash Flows from Operating Activities		
Net Income		$ 1,800
Noncash Expenses and Revenues Included in Income		
Increase in Accounts Receivable	$ (1,000)*	
Increase in Supplies	(500)	
Increase in Accounts Payable	600	(900)
Net Cash Flows from Operating Activities		$ 900
Cash Flows from Investing Activities		
Purchase of Land	$(10,000)	
Purchase of Building	(25,000)	
Net Cash Flows from Investing Activities		(35,000)
Cash Flows from Financing Activities		
Investments by John Shannon	$ 50,000	
Withdrawals by John Shannon	(600)	
Net Cash Flows from Financing Activities		49,400
Net Increase (Decrease) in Cash		**$15,300**
Cash at Beginning of Month		0
Cash at End of Month		$15,300

* Parentheses refer to a negative amount.

Cash account changed during the period. Cash increased by $15,300. Operating activities produced net cash flows of $900, and financing activities produced net cash flows of $49,400. Investment activities used cash flows of $35,000.

This statement is related directly to the other three statements. Notice that net income comes from the income statement and that investments and withdrawals by John Shannon come from the statement of owner's equity. The other items in the statement represent changes in the balance sheet accounts: Accounts Receivable, Supplies, Accounts Payable, Land, and Building. You should focus here on the importance and overall structure of the statement. Its construction and use are discussed in detail in the chapter on the statement of cash flows.

Relationships Among the Four Statements

At this stage, you are not expected to understand all the fine points and terminology of these four statements. They are presented to show that accounting tries to sum up in a meaningful and useful way the financial history of a business, no matter how large and complex, in four relatively simple financial statements—an amazing feat. Two of the statements—the income statement and the statement of cash flows—deal with the activities of the business over time. One—the balance sheet—shows the financial position of the business at a particular point in time. Another—the statement of owner's equity—ties the income statement and balance sheet together over a period of time. Much of this book deals with how to develop, use, and interpret these four statements.

Professional Ethics and the Accounting Profession

OBJECTIVE 8
Describe accounting as a profession with ethical responsibilities and a wide career choice

Ethics is a code of conduct that applies to everyday life. It addresses the question of whether actions are right or wrong. Ethical actions are the product of individual decisions. You are faced with many ethical situations every day. Some may be potentially illegal—the temptation to take office supplies from your employer to use when you do homework, for example. Others are not illegal but are equally unethical—for example, deciding not to tell a fellow student who missed class that a test has been announced for the next class period. When an organization is said to act ethically or unethically, it means that individuals within the organization have made a decision to act ethically or unethically. When a company uses false advertising, cheats a customer, pollutes the environment, treats employees poorly, or misleads investors by presenting false financial statements, members of management and other employees of the company consciously have made a decision to act unethically. In the same way, ethical behavior within a company is a direct result of the actions and decisions of the company's employees.

Professional ethics is a code of conduct that applies to the practice of a profession. Like the ethical conduct of a company, the ethical actions of a profession are a collection of individual actions. As members of a profession, accountants have a responsibility, not only to their employers and clients but to society as a whole, to uphold the highest ethical standards. A recent survey of over one thousand prominent people in business, education, and government ranked the accounting profession second only to the clergy as having the highest ethical standards.[10]

The accounting function is as old as the need to exchange things of value and keep track of wealth. The commercial and trading revolution of the Renaissance increased the need for accounting, as did the Industrial Revolution. The enormous growth of industry and government in the twentieth century has expanded the need for accountants even further. Today, the accounting profession offers interesting, challenging, well-paying, and satisfying careers. It is the responsibility of every person who becomes an accountant to uphold the high standards of the profession regardless of the field of accounting the individual enters.

The profession can be divided into four broad fields: (1) management accounting, (2) public accounting, (3) government and not-for-profit accounting, and (4) accounting education.

Management Accounting

An accountant who is employed by a business is said to be in **management accounting**. A small business may have only one person doing this work; a medium-sized or large company may have hundreds of accountants working under a chief accounting officer called a *controller, treasurer,* or *financial vice president*. Other positions that can be held by accountants at lower managerial levels are assistant controller, chief accountant, accounting manager, internal auditor, plant accountant, systems analyst, financial accountant, and cost accountant.

Because of their familiarity with all aspects of a company's operations, management accountants often have an important effect on the firm's decision making. Many top-level business executives have backgrounds in accounting and finance. Just a few of the well-known companies whose presidents or chairmen

10. Touche Ross & Co., "Ethics in American Business" (New York: Touche Ross & Co., 1988), p. 7.

of the board are (or have been) accountants are American Airlines (AMR Corporation), General Foods, International Business Machines, Caterpillar, General Motors, Kennecott Copper, Ford, General Electric, Consolidated Edison, International Telephone and Telegraph, and Minnesota Mining and Manufacturing.

The main task of management accountants is to give management the information it needs to make wise decisions. Management accountants also set up systems of internal control to increase efficiency and prevent fraud. They help plan, budget, and control costs. It is their responsibility to see that a company has good records, prepares proper financial reports, and complies with tax laws and government regulations. Management accountants also need to keep up with the latest developments in the uses of computers and in computer systems design.

Management accountants can certify their professional competence and training by qualifying for the status of **certified management accountant (CMA)**, which is awarded to qualified accountants by the Institute of Certified Management Accountants of the Institute of Management Accountants. Under the CMA program, candidates must pass an examination consisting of several parts and meet educational and professional standards.

The Institute of Management Accountants (formerly the National Association of Accountants) has adopted the Code of Professional Conduct for Management Accountants. This ethical code emphasizes that management accountants have a responsibility to be competent at their jobs, to keep information confidential except when authorized or legally required to disclose it, to maintain integrity and avoid conflicts of interest, and to communicate information objectively and without bias.[11]

Public Accounting

The field of **public accounting**, which is practiced by certified public accountants, offers auditing, tax, and management consulting services to the public for a fee. Since about 1900, public accounting in this country has gained a stature similar to that of the older professions of law and medicine.

Requirements. To become a CPA, an applicant must meet rigorous requirements. These requirements vary from state to state but have certain characteristics in common. An applicant must be a person of integrity and have at least a high school education. Most states require four years of college (a few require five years now and many are changing to a five-year requirement) with a major in accounting, and the AICPA has voted to make 150 college-level semester hours of education (that is, five years) a requirement for membership after the year 2000. Also, the applicant must pass a difficult, comprehensive two-and-one-half-day examination in accounting practice, accounting theory, auditing, and business law. Although the examination is uniform in all states, some states also require an examination in such areas as economics and professional ethics. The examination is prepared by the AICPA and is given twice a year. Most states also require one to five years' experience in the office of a certified public accountant or acceptable equivalent experience. In some cases, additional education can be substituted for one or more years of accounting experience.

Professional Ethics. To ensure that its members understand the responsibilities of being professional accountants, the AICPA and each state have adopted codes of professional conduct. Fundamental to these codes is responsibility to

11. *Statement Number 1C*, "Standards of Ethical Conduct for Management Accountants" (Montvale, N.J.: Institute of Management Accountants, June 1, 1983).

the public, including clients, creditors, investors, and anyone else who relies on the work of the public accountant. In resolving conflicts among these groups, the accountant must act with integrity even to the sacrifice of personal benefit. **Integrity** means that the accountant is honest and candid and subordinates personal gain to service and the public trust. The accountant also must be objective. **Objectivity** means that he or she is impartial and intellectually honest. Furthermore, the accountant must be independent. **Independence** means avoiding all relationships that impair or even appear to impair the accountant's objectivity. One way in which an auditor of a company maintains independence is by having no direct financial interest in the company and not being an employee of the company. The accountant must exercise **due care** in all activities, carrying out professional responsibilities with competence and diligence. For example, an accountant must not accept a job for which he or she is not qualified, even at the risk of losing a client to another firm; and careless work is not acceptable. These broad principles are supported by more specific rules that public accountants must follow (for instance, with certain exceptions, client information must be kept confidential). Accountants who violate the rules can be disciplined or suspended from practice.

Accounting Firms. Certified public accountants offer their services to the public for a fee, just as doctors and lawyers do. Accounting firms are made up of partners, who must be CPAs, and staff accountants, many of whom are CPAs and hope to become partners someday. Accounting firms vary in size from large international firms with hundreds of partners and thousands of employees to small one- or two-person firms. The firms listed in Table 1-2 employ about 25 percent of all CPAs.

The work of the public accountant is varied, complex, and interesting. Most accounting firms organize themselves into several principal areas of specialization, among them (1) auditing, (2) tax services, (3) management advisory services, and (4) small business services.

Auditing. The most important and distinctive function of a certified public accountant is **auditing** (also called the **attest function**), the examination and testing of financial statements for the purpose of rendering an opinion on the preparation of the statements in accordance with GAAP. Society relies heavily on the auditing function to vouch for the credibility of financial reports. All public corporations and many companies that apply for sizable loans must have their financial statements and records audited by an independent certified public accountant.

Table 1-2. Large International Certified Public Accounting Firms

Firm	Home Office	Some Major Clients
Arthur Andersen & Co.	Chicago	ITT, Texaco, United Airlines
Coopers & Lybrand	New York	AT&T, Ford
Deloitte & Touche	New York	General Motors, Procter & Gamble, Sears
Ernst & Young	New York	Coca-Cola, McDonald's, Mobil
KPMG Peat Marwick	New York	General Electric, Xerox
Price Waterhouse	New York	Du Pont, Exxon, IBM
Grant Thornton	Chicago	Fretter, Grainger, Home Shopping Network

Tax Services. In the area of **tax services**, public accountants help businesses and individuals prepare tax returns and comply with tax laws. They also help plan business decisions to reduce taxes in the future. Tax accounting work calls for specific knowledge and skill regardless of the size of a business. Most business decisions have some effect on taxes.

Management Advisory Services. An increasingly important part of most public accounting firms' practice is **management advisory services**, or consulting. With their intimate knowledge of a business's operations, auditors can and usually do make important suggestions for improvements. In the past, these recommendations dealt mainly with accounting records, budgeting, and cost accounting. But in the last few years they have expanded into marketing, organizational planning, personnel and recruiting, production, and many other business areas. The wide use of computers has led to services in systems design and control and to the use of mathematical and statistical decision models. All of these different services combined make up management advisory services.

Small Business Services. Many small business owners look to their CPAs for advice on operating their businesses and keeping their accounting records. Although small CPA firms have traditionally performed these functions, large firms also are establishing small business practice units. Among the types of services a CPA might provide are setting up or revising an accounting system, compiling monthly financial statements, preparing a budget of cash needs over the coming year, and helping the client obtain a bank loan.

Government and Other Not-for-Profit Accounting

Agencies and departments at all levels of government hire accountants to prepare reports so that officials can carry out their duties responsibly. Millions of income, payroll, and sales tax returns must be checked and audited. The Federal Bureau of Investigation and the Internal Revenue Service use thousands of accountants. The General Accounting Office audits government activities for Congress, using auditors and other accounting specialists all over the world. Federal agencies—among them the Securities and Exchange Commission, the Interstate Commerce Commission, and the Federal Communications Commission—hire accountants. State agencies such as those that regulate public utilities or collect taxes also use the services of accountants.

Many other not-for-profit enterprises employ accountants. Hospitals, colleges, universities, and foundations, like the government, are interested in complying with the law and using public resources efficiently. They account for over 25 percent of the gross output of our economy. Clearly, the role of accountants in helping these organizations use their resources wisely is important to our society.

Accounting Education

Training new accountants is a challenging and rewarding career, and instructors of accounting are in great demand today. Accounting instructors at the secondary level must have a college degree with a major in accounting and must meet state teacher certification requirements. One entry-level requirement for teaching at the smaller and two-year colleges is a master's degree. Faculty members at most larger universities must have a Ph.D. and do research. In many schools, holding a CPA, CMA, or **CIA (certified internal auditor)** certificate can help an instructor to advance professionally.

Chapter Review

Review of Learning Objectives

1. **Define *accounting* and describe its role in making informed decisions.**
Accounting is an information system that measures, processes, and communicates information, primarily financial in nature, about an identifiable entity for the purpose of making economic decisions. It is not an end in itself but a tool that provides the information that is necessary to make reasoned choices among alternative uses of scarce resources in the conduct of business and economic activities.

2. **Identify the many users of accounting information in society.**
Accounting plays a significant role in society by providing information to managers of all institutions and to individuals with direct financial interest in those institutions, including present or potential investors or creditors. Accounting information is also important to those with an indirect financial interest in the business—for example, tax authorities, regulatory agencies, and economic planners.

3. **Distinguish between financial and management accounting, define *generally accepted accounting principles (GAAP)*, and identify the organizations that influence GAAP.**
Management accounting refers to the preparation of information primarily for internal use by management. Financial accounting refers to the development and use of accounting reports that are communicated to those external to the business organization as well as to management. Acceptable accounting practice consists of those conventions, rules, and procedures that make up generally accepted accounting principles at a particular time. GAAP are essential to the preparation and interpretation of financial accounting reports. Among the organizations that influence the formulation of GAAP are the Financial Accounting Standards Board, the American Institute of Certified Public Accountants, the Securities and Exchange Commission, and the Internal Revenue Service. Other organizations with an interest in accounting are the Institute of Management Accountants, the Financial Executives Institute, and the American Accounting Association.

4. **Explain the importance of business transactions, money measure, and separate entity to accounting measurement.**
To make an accounting measurement, the accountant must determine what is measured, when the measurement should be made, what value should be placed on what is measured, and how what is measured should be classified. Generally accepted accounting principles define the objects of accounting measurement as business transactions, money measures, and separate entities. Relating these three concepts, financial accounting measures the impact of business transactions on separate entities in terms of money measures.

5. **Identify the three basic forms of business organization.**
The three basic forms of business organization are sole proprietorships, partnerships, and corporations. Sole proprietorships, which are formed by one individual, and partnerships, which are formed by more than one individual, are not separate economic units from a legal standpoint. In accounting, however, they are treated separately. Corporations, whose ownership is represented by shares of stock, are separate entities for both legal and accounting purposes.

6. **Define *financial position*, state the accounting equation, and show how they are affected by simple transactions.**
Financial position is the economic resources that belong to a company and the claims against those resources at a point in time. The accounting equation shows financial position in equation form (Assets = liabilities + owner's equity). Business transactions affect financial position by decreasing or increasing assets, liabilities, or owner's equity in such a way that the accounting equation is always in balance.

7. **Identify the four basic financial statements.**
   Financial statements are the means by which accountants communicate the financial condition and activities of a business to those who have an interest in the business. The four basic financial statements are the income statement, the statement of owner's equity, the balance sheet, and the statement of cash flows.
8. **Describe accounting as a profession with ethical responsibilities and a wide career choice.**
   All accountants are required to follow a code of professional ethics, the foundation of which is responsibility to the public. Accountants must act with integrity, objectivity, and independence, and they must exercise due care in all their activities.
   The people who provide accounting information to users make up the accounting profession. They can work in management accounting, public accounting, or government or other not-for-profit accounting. Another career choice open to accountants is accounting education. Each type of accounting is an important specialization and represents a challenging career.

Review of Concepts and Terminology

The following concepts and terms were introduced in this chapter:

(L.O. 1) **Accounting:** An information system that measures, processes, and communicates financial information about an identifiable economic entity.

(L.O. 6) **Accounting equation:** Assets = liabilities + owner's equity, or Owner's equity = assets − liabilities.

(L.O. 6) **Accounts:** The labels used by accountants to accumulate the amounts produced from similar transactions.

(L.O. 3) **American Institute of Certified Public Accountants (AICPA):** The professional association of certified public accountants.

(L.O. 6) **Assets:** Probable future economic benefits obtained or controlled by a particular entity as a result of past transactions or events.

(L.O. 8) **Attest function:** The examination and testing of financial statements by a certified public accountant.

(L.O. 3, 8) **Audit:** An examination of the financial statements of a company in order to render an independent professional opinion that they have been presented fairly and prepared in conformity with generally accepted accounting principles. Also called the *attest function*.

(L.O. 7) **Balance sheet:** The financial statement that shows the assets, liabilities, and owner's equity of a business at a point in time. Also called a *statement of financial position*.

(L.O. 1) **Bookkeeping:** The process of recording financial transactions and keeping financial records.

(L.O. 4) **Business transactions:** Economic events that affect the financial position of a business entity.

(L.O. 8) **Certified internal auditor (CIA):** The professional certification for auditors who carry out their work within a company.

(L.O. 8) **Certified management accountant (CMA):** The status awarded to qualified accountants by the Institute of Certified Management Accountants.

(L.O. 3, 8) **Certified public accountants (CPA):** Public accountants who have met the stringent licensing requirements set by the individual states.

(L.O. 1) **Computer:** An electronic tool for the rapid collection, organization, and communication of large amounts of information.

(L.O. 1) **Control**: The process of seeing that plans are carried out.

(L.O. 5) **Corporation**: A business unit that is legally separate from its owners.

(L.O. 8) **Due care**: The act of carrying out professional responsibilities competently and diligently.

(L.O. 6) **Equity**: The residual interest in the assets of a business entity that remains after deducting its liabilities.

(L.O. 8) **Ethics**: A code of conduct that addresses whether everyday actions are right or wrong.

(L.O. 1) **Evaluation**: The examination of the entire decision-making process with a view to improving it.

(L.O. 6) **Expenses**: Decreases in owner's equity that result from operating a business.

(L.O. 3) **Financial accounting**: The process of generating accounting information that, in addition to being used internally by management, is communicated in the form of financial statements to those outside the organization.

(L.O. 3) **Financial Accounting Standards Board (FASB)**: The body that has primary responsibility for developing and issuing Statements of Financial Accounting Standards, rules on accounting practice.

(L.O. 6) **Financial position**: The economic resources that belong to a company and the claims against those resources at a point in time.

(L.O. 7) **Financial statements**: The primary means of communicating important accounting information to users.

(L.O. 3) **Generally accepted accounting principles (GAAP)**: The conventions, rules, and procedures that define accepted accounting practice at a particular time.

(L.O. 3) **Governmental Accounting Standards Board (GASB)**: The board responsible for issuing accounting standards for state and local governments.

(L.O. 7) **Income statement**: The financial statement that summarizes the amount of revenues earned and expenses incurred by a business over a period of time.

(L.O. 3, 8) **Independence**: The avoidance of all relationships that impair or appear to impair an accountant's objectivity.

(L.O. 8) **Integrity**: Honesty, candidness, and the subordination of personal gain to service and the public trust.

(L.O. 3) **Internal Revenue Service (IRS)**: The federal agency that interprets and enforces the tax laws governing the assessment and collection of revenue for operating the national government.

(L.O. 6) **Liabilities**: Probable future sacrifices of economic benefits arising from present obligations of a particular entity to transfer assets or provide services to other entities in the future as a result of past transactions or events.

(L.O. 2) **Liquidity**: Having enough funds on hand to pay debts when they are due.

(L.O. 2) **Management**: The group of people who have overall responsibility for operating a business and for meeting its goals.

(L.O. 3, 8) **Management accounting**: The process of producing accounting information for the internal use of a company's management.

(L.O. 8) **Management advisory services**: One of the consulting services offered by public accountants.

(L.O. 1) **Management information system (MIS)**: The interconnected subsystems that provide the information necessary to operate a business.

(L.O. 4) **Money measure**: The recording of all business transactions in terms of money.

(L.O. 6) **Net assets**: Owner's equity, or assets minus liabilities.

(L.O. 6) **Net income**: The difference between revenues and expenses when revenues exceed expenses.

(L.O. 6) **Net loss:** The difference between expenses and revenues when expenses exceed revenues.

(L.O. 8) **Objectivity:** Impartiality and intellectual honesty.

(L.O. 6) **Owner's equity:** The claims by an owner against the assets of a business. Also called *residual equity*.

(L.O. 6) **Owner's investments:** The assets that the owner puts into a business.

(L.O. 6) **Owner's withdrawals:** The assets that the owner takes out of a business.

(L.O. 5) **Partnership:** A business owned by two or more people.

(L.O. 1) **Planning:** The process of formulating a course of action.

(L.O. 8) **Professional ethics:** A code of conduct that applies to the practice of a profession.

(L.O. 2) **Profitability:** The ability to earn enough income to attract and hold investment capital.

(L.O. 8) **Public accounting:** The field of accounting that offers auditing, tax, and management consultant services to the public for a fee.

(L.O. 6) **Revenues:** Increases in owner's equity that result from operating a business.

(L.O. 3) **Securities and Exchange Commission (SEC):** An agency of the federal government that has the legal power to set and enforce accounting practices for firms whose securities are sold to the general public.

(L.O. 4) **Separate entity:** A business that is treated as distinct from its creditors, customers, and owners.

(L.O. 5) **Sole proprietorship:** A business owned by one person.

(L.O. 7) **Statement of cash flows:** The financial statement that shows the inflows and outflows of cash from operating activities, investing activities, and financing activities over a period of time.

(L.O. 7) **Statement of owner's equity:** The financial statement that shows the changes in the owner's capital account over a period of time.

(L.O. 8) **Tax services:** The services offered by public accountants in tax planning, compliance, and reporting.

Self-Test

Test your knowledge of the chapter by choosing the best answer for each of the following items.

(L.O. 1) 1. Which of the following is an important reason for studying accounting?
   a. Accounting information is useful in making economic decisions.
   b. Accounting plays an important role in society.
   c. The study of accounting can lead to a challenging career.
   d. All of the above are important reasons for studying accounting.

(L.O. 2) 2. Which of the following groups uses accounting information for planning a company's profitability and liquidity?
   a. Management
   b. Investors
   c. Creditors
   d. Economic planners

(L.O. 3) 3. Generally accepted accounting principles
   a. define accounting practice at a point in time.
   b. are similar in nature to the principles of chemistry or physics.
   c. rarely change.
   d. are not affected by changes in the ways businesses operate.

(L.O. 4) 4. Economic events that affect the financial position of a business are called
   a. separate entities.
   b. business transactions.
   c. money measures.
   d. financial actions.

(L.O. 5) 5. Which of the following forms of organization is not treated as a separate economic unit in accounting?
   a. Sole proprietorship
   b. Committee
   c. Partnership
   d. Corporation

(L.O. 6) 6. If a company has liabilities of $19,000 and owner's equity of $57,000, its assets are
   a. $38,000.
   b. $76,000.
   c. $57,000.
   d. $19,000.

(L.O. 6) 7. The payment of a liability
   a. increases both assets and liabilities.
   b. increases assets and decreases liabilities.
   c. decreases assets and increases liabilities.
   d. decreases both assets and liabilities.

(L.O. 7) 8. The balance sheet is related to the income statement in the same way that a
   a. point in time is related to a period of time.
   b. period of time is related to a point in time.
   c. point in time is related to another point in time.
   d. period of time is related to another period of time.

(L.O. 7) 9. Expenses and withdrawals appear, respectively, on the
   a. balance sheet and income statement.
   b. income statement and balance sheet.
   c. statement of owner's equity and balance sheet.
   d. income statement and statement of owner's equity.

(L.O. 8) 10. Auditing, tax services, and management consulting are services provided by
   a. government accountants.
   b. certified management accountants.
   c. certified public accountants.
   d. accounting educators.

Answers to the Self-Test are at the end of this chapter.

Review Problem
The Effect of Transactions on the Accounting Equation

(L.O. 6) Charlene Rudek finished law school in June and immediately set up her own law practice. During the first month of operation, she completed the following transactions:

a. Began the law practice by placing $2,000 in a bank account established for the business.
b. Purchased a law library for $900 cash.
c. Purchased office supplies for $400 on credit.
d. Accepted $500 in cash for completing a contract.
e. Billed clients $1,950 for services rendered during the month.
f. Paid $200 of the amount owed for office supplies.
g. Received $1,250 in cash from one client who had been billed previously for services rendered.
h. Paid rent expense for the month in the amount of $1,200.
i. Withdrew $400 from the practice for personal use.

Required

Show the effect of each of these transactions on the accounting equation by completing a table similar to Exhibit 1-1. Identify each owner's equity transaction.

Answer to Review Problem

	Assets				=	Liabilities	+	Owner's Equity	
	Cash	Accounts Receivable	Office Supplies	Law Library		Accounts Payable		C. Rudek, Capital	Type of OE Transaction
a.	$2,000							$2,000	Owner's Investment
b.	−900			+$900					
bal.	$1,100			$900				$2,000	
c.			+$400			+$400			
bal.	$1,100		$400	$900		$400		$2,000	
d.	+500							+500	Service Revenue
bal.	$1,600		$400	$900		$400		$2,500	
e.		+$1,950						+1,950	Service Revenue
bal.	$1,600	$1,950	$400	$900		$400		$4,450	
f.	−200					−200			
bal.	$1,400	$1,950	$400	$900		$200		$4,450	
g.	+1,250	−1,250							
bal.	$2,650	$ 700	$400	$900		$200		$4,450	
h.	−1,200							−1,200	Rent Expense
bal.	$1,450	$ 700	$400	$900		$200		$3,250	
i.	−400							−400	Owner's Withdrawal
bal.	$1,050	$ 700	$400	$900		$200		$2,850	
		$3,050					$3,050		

Chapter Assignments

Questions

1. Why is accounting considered an information system?
2. Distinguish among these terms: *accounting, bookkeeping,* and *management information systems.*
3. How are decisions made? What is the role of accounting in the decision-making process?
4. What decision makers use accounting information?
5. What broad management objectives are facilitated through the use of accounting information?
6. Why are investors and creditors interested in reviewing the financial statements of a company?
7. Why is it that society as a whole has become one of the largest users of accounting information?
8. Among those who use accounting information are the people and organizations with an indirect interest in the business entity. Briefly describe these people and organizations.
9. Distinguish between management accounting and financial accounting.
10. What are GAAP? Why are they important to the readers of financial statements?
11. What do auditors mean by the phrase "in all material respects" when they state that financial statements "present fairly, in all material respects . . . in conformity with generally accepted accounting principles"?

12. What organization has the most influence on GAAP?
13. Use the terms *business transaction, money measure,* and *separate entity* in a single sentence that demonstrates their relevance to financial accounting.
14. How do sole proprietorships, partnerships, and corporations differ?
15. Define assets, liabilities, and owner's equity.
16. What four elements affect owner's equity? How?
17. Arnold Smith's company has assets of $22,000 and liabilities of $10,000. What is the amount of his owner's equity?
18. Give examples of the types of transactions that (a) increase assets and (b) increase liabilities.
19. Why is the balance sheet sometimes called the statement of financial position?
20. Contrast the objectives of the balance sheet with those of the income statement.
21. How does the income statement differ from the statement of cash flows?
22. What is the function of the statement of owner's equity?
23. A statement for an accounting period that ends in June can be headed "June 30, 19xx" or "For the Year Ended June 30, 19xx." Which heading is appropriate in (a) a balance sheet and (b) an income statement?
24. Discuss the importance of professional ethics in the accounting profession.
25. What are some of the fields encompassed by the accounting profession?
26. List several activities performed by management accountants.
27. How is a public accountant different from a management accountant?
28. Describe in general terms (a) the requirements that an individual must meet to become a CPA and (b) the four major activities of CPAs.
29. Accounting can be viewed as (a) an intellectual discipline, (b) a profession, or (c) a social force. In what sense is it each of these?
30. Compare and contrast the professional ethics of public accountants and management accountants as reflected by their respective codes of professional conduct.

Communication Skills Exercises

Communication Skills Exercises are real accounting problems that allow you to improve your communication skills as future managers and accountants. Most of these exercises can be completed as written assignments, but your instructor also may want to use them as discussion cases, group exercises, or presentation assignments.

Communication 1-1. Users of Accounting Information *(L.O. 2)*

Public companies report annually on their success or failure in making a net income. Suppose that the following item appeared in the newspaper:

New York. Commonwealth Power Company, a major electric utility, reported yesterday that its net income for the year just ended represented a 50 percent increase over last year. . . .

Explain why each of the following individuals or groups might be interested in seeing the accounting reports that support this statement.

1. The management of Commonwealth Power
2. The stockholders of Commonwealth Power
3. The creditors of Commonwealth Power
4. Potential stockholders of Commonwealth Power
5. The Internal Revenue Service
6. The Securities and Exchange Commission
7. The electrical workers' union
8. A consumers' group called Public Cause
9. An economic adviser to the president

Communication 1-2.
Concept of an Asset
(L.O. 6)

Foote, Cone & Belding is one of the largest and most successful advertising agencies in the world. Its 1989 annual report carried the following statement: "Our principal asset is our people. Our success depends in large part on our ability to attract and retain personnel who are competent in the various aspects of our business." Are personnel considered assets in financial statements? In what sense does Foote, Cone & Belding consider its employees its principal asset?

Communication 1-3.
Professional Ethics
(L.O. 8)

Discuss the ethical choices in the situations below. In each case, determine the alternative courses of action, describe the ethical dilemma, and tell what you would do.

1. You are the payroll accountant for a small business. A friend asks you how much another employee is paid per hour.
2. As an accountant for the branch office of a wholesale supplier, you become aware that several of the receipts the branch manager has submitted for reimbursement as selling expense actually represented "nights out" with his spouse.
3. You are an accountant in the purchasing department of a construction company. When you arrive home from work on December 22, you find a large ham in a box marked "Happy Holidays—It's a pleasure to work with you." The gift is from a supplier who has bid on a contract your employer plans to award next week.
4. As an auditor with one year's experience at a local CPA firm, you are expected to complete a certain part of an audit in twenty hours. Because of your lack of experience, you know you cannot finish the job within that time. Rather than admit this, you are thinking about working late to finish the job and not telling anyone.
5. You are a tax accountant at a local CPA firm. You help your neighbor fill out her tax return, and she pays you $200 in cash. Because there is no record of this transaction, you are considering not reporting it on your tax return.
6. The accounting firm for which you work as a CPA has just won a new client, a firm in which you own 200 shares of stock that you received as an inheritance from your grandmother. Because it is only a small number of shares and you think the company will be very successful, you are thinking about not disclosing the investment.

Communication 1-4.
Basic Research Skills
(L.O. 1, 2)

Clip an article about a company from the business section of your local paper or a nearby metropolitan daily. List all the financial and accounting terms used in the article. Bring the article to class and be prepared to discuss how a knowledge of accounting would help a reader understand the content of the article.

Classroom Exercises

Exercise 1-1.
The Nature of Accounting
(L.O. 1, 2, 3)

Match the terms on the left with the descriptions on the right.

____	1. Bookkeeping	a. Function of accounting
____	2. Creditors	b. Often confused with accounting
____	3. Measurement	c. User(s) of accounting information
____	4. Financial Accounting Standards Board (FASB)	d. Organization that influences current practice
____	5. Tax authorities	e. Tool that facilitates the practice of accounting
____	6. Computer	
____	7. Communication	
____	8. Securities and Exchange Commission (SEC)	
____	9. Investors	
____	10. Processing	
____	11. Management	
____	12. Management information system	

Exercise 1-2.
Separate Entity
(L.O. 4)

Theresa owns and operates a minimart. State which of the transactions below are related to the business. Explain why the others are not regarded as transactions.

1. Theresa buys a loaf of bread and a gallon of milk from a grocery store for use at home over the weekend.
2. Theresa pays a high school student cash for cleaning up the driveway behind the market.
3. Theresa fills her son's car with gasoline in payment for restocking the vending machines and the snack food shelves.
4. Theresa pays interest to herself on a loan she made three years ago to the business.

Exercise 1-3.
Accounting Concepts
(L.O. 4, 5)

Financial accounting is concerned with measuring the impact of business transactions on separate business entities in terms of money measures. For each of the following words or phrases, tell whether it relates most closely to (a) a business transaction, (b) a separate entity, or (c) a money measure.

1. Corporation
2. French franc
3. Sale of products
4. Receipt of cash
5. Sole proprietorship
6. U.S. dollar
7. Partnership
8. Owner's investments
9. Japanese yen
10. Purchase of supplies

Exercise 1-4.
The Accounting Equation
(L.O. 6)

Use the accounting equation to answer each question below. Show any calculations you make.

1. The assets of Newport Company are $650,000, and the owner's equity is $360,000. What is the amount of the liabilities?
2. The liabilities and owner's equity of Fitzgerald Company are $95,000 and $32,000 respectively. What is the amount of the assets?
3. The liabilities of Emerald Co. equal one-third of the total assets, and owner's equity is $120,000. What is the amount of the liabilities?
4. At the beginning of the year, Sherman Company's assets were $220,000 and its owner's equity was $100,000. During the year, assets increased $60,000 and liabilities decreased $10,000. What was the owner's equity at the end of the year?

Exercise 1-5.
Owner's Equity Transactions
(L.O. 6)

Identify the following transactions by marking each an owner's investment (I), owner's withdrawal (W), revenue (R), expense (E), or not an owner's equity transaction (NOE).

a. Received cash for providing a service.
b. Took assets out of the business for personal use.
c. Received cash from a customer previously billed for a service.
d. Transferred assets to the business from a personal account.
e. Paid a service station for gasoline for business vehicle.
f. Performed a service and received a promise of payment.
g. Paid cash to purchase equipment.
h. Paid cash to an employee for services performed.

Exercise 1-6.
Effect of Transactions on the Accounting Equation
(L.O. 6)

During the month of April, Andres Company had the following transactions:

a. Paid salaries for April, $5,400.
b. Purchased equipment on credit, $9,000.
c. Purchased supplies with cash, $300.
d. Additional investment by owner, $12,000.
e. Received payment for services performed, $1,800.
f. Made partial payment on equipment purchased in transaction **b**, $3,000.
g. Billed customers for services performed, $4,800.
h. Cash withdrawal by owner, $4,500.
i. Received payment from customers billed in transaction **g**, $900.
j. Received utility bill, $210.

On a sheet of paper, list the letters **a** through **j**, with columns labeled Assets, Liabilities, and Owner's Equity. In the columns, indicate whether each transaction caused an increase (+), a decrease (–), or no change (NC) in assets, liabilities, and owner's equity.

Exercise 1-7.
Examples of Transactions
(L.O. 6)

For each of the following categories, describe a transaction that would have the required effect on the elements of the accounting equation.

1. Increase one asset and decrease another asset.
2. Decrease an asset and decrease a liability.
3. Increase an asset and increase a liability.
4. Increase an asset and increase owner's equity.
5. Decrease an asset and decrease owner's equity.

Exercise 1-8.
Effect of Transactions on the Accounting Equation
(L.O. 6)

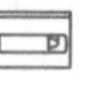

The total assets and liabilities at the beginning and end of the year for Pizarro Company are listed below.

	Assets	Liabilities
Beginning of the year	$110,000	$ 45,000
End of the year	200,000	120,000

Determine Pizarro Company's net income for the year under each of the following alternatives:

1. The owner made no investments in or withdrawals from the business during the year.
2. The owner made no investments in the business, but the owner withdrew $22,000 during the year.
3. The owner made an investment of $13,000 but made no withdrawals during the year.
4. The owner made an investment of $10,000 in the business and withdrew $22,000 during the year.

Exercise 1-9.
Identification of Accounts
(L.O. 6, 7)

1. Indicate below whether each of the following accounts is an asset (A), a liability (L), or a part of owner's equity (OE):

_____ a. Cash
_____ b. Salaries Payable
_____ c. Accounts Receivable
_____ d. T. Booth, Capital
_____ e. Land
_____ f. Accounts Payable
_____ g. Supplies

2. Indicate below whether each account would be shown on the income statement (IS), the statement of owner's equity (OE), or the balance sheet (BS):

_____ a. Repair Revenue
_____ b. Automobile
_____ c. Fuel Expense
_____ d. Cash
_____ e. Rent Expense
_____ f. Accounts Payable
_____ g. T. Booth, Withdrawals

Exercise 1-10.
Preparation of a Balance Sheet
(L.O. 7)

Listed in random order below are the balances for balance sheet items for the Glick Company as of June 30, 19xx.

Accounts Payable	$20,000	Accounts Receivable	$25,000
Building	45,000	Cash	10,000
R. Glick, Capital	85,000	Equipment	20,000
Supplies	5,000		

Sort the balances and prepare a balance sheet similar to the one in Exhibit 1-2.

Exercise 1-11. Completion of Financial Statements
(L.O. 7)

Determine the amounts that correspond to the letters by completing the following independent sets of financial statements. (Assume no new investments by the owners.)

Income Statement	**Set A**	**Set B**	**Set C**
Revenues	$1,100	$ g	$240
Expenses	a	5,200	m
Net Income	$ b	$ h	$ 80
Statement of Owner's Equity			
Beginning Balance	$2,900	$15,400	$200
Net Income	c	1,600	n
Less Withdrawals	(200)	i	o
Ending Balance	$3,000	$ j	$ p
Balance Sheet			
Total Assets	$ d	$21,000	$ q
Liabilities	$1,600	$ 5,000	$ r
Owner's Equity	e	k	280
Total Liabilities and Owner's Equity	$ f	$ l	$480

Exercise 1-12. Preparation of Financial Statements
(L.O. 7)

Strickland Company engaged in the following activities during the year: Service Revenues, $52,800; Rent Expense, $4,800; Wages Expense, $33,080; Advertising Expense, $5,400; Utility Expense, $3,600; and Bill Strickland, Withdrawals, $2,800. In addition, the year-end balances of selected accounts were as follows: Cash, $6,200; Accounts Receivable, $3,000; Supplies, $400; Land, $4,000; Accounts Payable, $1,800; and Bill Strickland, Capital, $8,680.

Using good form, prepare the income statement, statement of owner's equity, and balance sheet for Strickland Company (assume the year ends on June 30, 19x2). **Hint:** The amount given for Bill Strickland, Capital is the beginning balance.

Exercise 1-13. Revenues, Expenses, and Cash Flows
(L.O. 7)

Lorraine, an attorney, bills her clients at a rate of $100 per hour. During July, she worked 150 hours for clients and billed them appropriately. By the end of July, 80 of these hours remained unpaid. At the beginning of the month, clients owed Lorraine $8,000, of which $5,600 was paid during July.

Lorraine has one employee, a secretary who is paid $20 per hour. During July, the secretary worked 170 hours, of which 16 hours were to be paid in August. The rest were paid in July. Also, Lorraine paid the secretary for 8 hours worked in June.

Determine for the month of July: (1) the amount of revenue from clients, (2) wages expense for the secretary, (3) cash received from customers, and (4) cash paid to the secretary.

Exercise 1-14. Statement of Cash Flows
(L.O. 7)

Diamond Company began the year 19x2 with cash of $86,000. In addition to earning a net income of $50,000 and making an owner's withdrawal of $30,000 for his personal use, Diamond borrowed $120,000 from the bank and purchased equipment for $180,000 with cash. Also, Accounts Receivable increased by $12,000 and Accounts Payable increased by $18,000.

Determine the amount of cash on hand at the end of the year (December 31) by preparing a statement of cash flows similar to the one in Exhibit 1-3.

Exercise 1-15.
Accounting Abbreviations
(L.O. 3, 8)

Identify the accounting meaning of each of the following abbreviations: AICPA, SEC, GAAP, FASB, IRS, GASB, IASC, IFAC, IMA, FEI, AAA, CMA, CPA, and CIA.

Interpretation Case from Business

Merrill Lynch & Co., Inc.
(L.O. 6, 7)

Merrill Lynch & Co., Inc. is a U.S.-based global financial services firm. Condensed and adapted balance sheets for 1990 and 1989 from the company's 1990 annual report are presented below. (All numbers are in thousands.) The owner's equity section has been adapted for use in this case.

Merrill Lynch & Co., Inc.
Condensed Balance Sheets
December 31, 1990 and 1989

	1990	1989
Assets		
Cash	$ 1,786,779	$ 2,051,347
Marketable Securities	17,283,836	15,721,216
Accounts Receivable	32,260,458	31,644,718
Property and Equipment	1,646,276	1,669,406
Other Assets	15,152,178	12,855,576
Total Assets	$68,129,527	$63,942,263
Liabilities		
Short-Term Liabilities	$58,562,538	$53,893,811
Long-Term Liabilities	6,341,559	6,897,109
Total Liabilities	$64,904,097	$60,790,920
Owner's Equity		
Merrill Lynch, Capital	3,225,430	3,151,343
Total Liabilities and Owner's Equity	$68,129,527	$63,942,263

Three students who were looking at Merrill Lynch's annual report were overheard to make the following comments:

Student A: What a great year Merrill Lynch had in 1990! The company earned net income of $4,187,264 because its total assets increased by that amount ($68,129,527 – $63,942,263).

Student B: But the change in total assets is not the same as net income! The company had a net loss of $264,568, because cash decreased by that amount ($2,051,347 – $1,786,779).

Student C: I see from the annual report that Merrill Lynch paid cash dividends of $127,637 in 1990. Don't you have to take this fact into consideration when analyzing the company's performance? (*Note:* For a corporation, cash dividends are similar to owner's withdrawals in a sole proprietorship.)

Required

1. Comment on the interpretations of Students A and B, and then answer Student C's question.
2. Calculate Merrill Lynch's net income for 1990.

Problem Set A

Problem 1A-1.
Effect of Transactions on the Accounting Equation
(L.O. 6)

The Creative Frames Shop was started by Rosa Partridge in a small shopping center. In the first weeks of operation, she completed the following transactions:

a. Deposited $21,000 in an account in the name of the company to start the business.
b. Paid the current month's rent, $1,500.
c. Purchased store equipment on credit, $10,800.
d. Purchased framing supplies for cash, $5,100.
e. Received framing revenues, $2,400.
f. Billed customers for services, $2,100.
g. Paid utility expense, $750.
h. Received payment from customers in transaction **f**, $600.
i. Made payment on store equipment purchased in transaction **c**, $5,400.
j. Withdrew cash for personal expenses, $1,200.

Required

1. Arrange the following asset, liability, and owner's equity accounts in an accounting equation similar to Exhibit 1-1: Cash, Accounts Receivable, Framing Supplies, Store Equipment, Accounts Payable, and Rosa Partridge, Capital.
2. Show by addition and subtraction, as in Exhibit 1-1, the effects of the transactions on the accounting equation. Show new balances after each transaction, and identify each owner's equity transaction by type.

Problem 1A-2.
Effect of Transactions on the Accounting Equation
(L.O. 6)

The Quality Courier Company was founded by Johnny Hui on March 1 and engaged in the following transactions:

a. Deposited $18,000 in a bank account established in the name of Quality Courier Company to start the business.
b. Purchased a motor bike on credit, $6,200.
c. Purchased delivery supplies for cash, $400.
d. Billed a customer for a delivery, $200.
e. Received delivery fees in cash, $600.
f. Made a payment on the motor bike, $1,400.
g. Paid expenses, $240.
h. Received payment from customer billed in transaction **d**, $100.
i. Withdrew cash for personal expenses, $300.

Required

1. Arrange the following asset, liability, and owner's equity accounts in an accounting equation similar to Exhibit 1-1: Cash, Accounts Receivable, Delivery Supplies, Motor Bike, Accounts Payable, and Johnny Hui, Capital.
2. Show by addition and subtraction, as in Exhibit 1-1, the effects of the transactions on the accounting equation. Show new balances after each transaction, and identify each owner's equity transaction by type.

Problem 1A-3.
Effect of Transactions on the Accounting Equation
(L.O. 6)

After completing his Ph.D. in management, Tony Rosello set up a consulting practice. At the end of his first month of operation, Dr. Rosello had the following account balances: Cash, $5,860; Accounts Receivable, $2,800; Office Supplies, $540; Office Equipment, $8,400; Accounts Payable, $3,800; and Tony Rosello, Capital, $13,800. Soon thereafter, the following transactions were completed:

a. Paid current month's rent, $800.
b. Made payment toward accounts payable, $900.
c. Billed clients for services performed, $1,600.
d. Received payment from clients billed last month, $2,000.
e. Purchased office supplies for cash, $160.
f. Paid secretary's salary, $1,700.
g. Paid utility expense, $180.
h. Paid telephone expense, $100.
i. Purchased additional office equipment for cash, $800.
j. Received cash from clients for services performed, $2,400.
k. Withdrew cash for personal use, $1,000.

Required

1. Arrange the following asset, liability, and owner's equity accounts in an accounting equation similar to Exhibit 1-1: Cash, Accounts Receivable, Office Supplies, Office Equipment, Accounts Payable, and Tony Rosello, Capital.
2. Enter the beginning balances of the assets, liabilities, and owner's equity.
3. Show by addition and subtraction, as in Exhibit 1-1, the effects of the transactions on the accounting equation. Show new balances after each transaction, and identify each owner's equity transaction by type.

Problem 1A-4. Preparation of Financial Statements *(L.O. 7)*

At the end of its first month of operation, March 19xx, Ellis Plumbing Company had the following account balances:

Cash	$58,600	Tools	$7,600
Accounts Receivable	10,800	Accounts Payable	8,600
Delivery Truck	38,000		

In addition, during the month of March, the following transactions affected owner's equity:

Investment by J. Ellis	$40,000	Repair revenue	$ 5,600
Withdrawal by J. Ellis	4,000	Salaries expense	16,600
Further investment by J. Ellis	60,000	Rent expense	1,400
Contract revenue	23,200	Fuel expense	400

Required

Using Exhibit 1-2 as a model, prepare an income statement, a statement of owner's equity, and a balance sheet for Ellis Plumbing Company. (**Hint**: The final balance of J. Ellis, Capital is $106,400.)

Problem 1A-5. Effect of Transactions on the Accounting Equation and Preparation of Financial Statements *(L.O. 6, 7)*

Arrow Copying Service began operations and engaged in the following transactions during August 19xx:

a. Investment by owner, Myra Lomax, $10,000.
b. Paid current month's rent, $900.
c. Purchased copier for cash, $5,000.
d. Copying job payments received in cash, $1,780.
e. Copying job billed to major customer, $1,360.
f. Paid cash for paper and other copier supplies, $380.
g. Paid wages to part-time employees, $560.
h. Purchased additional copier supplies on credit, $280.
i. Received partial payment from customer in transaction **e**, $600.
j. Paid current month's utility bill, $180.
k. Made partial payment on supplies purchased in transaction **h**, $140.
l. Withdrew cash for personal use, $1,400.

Required

1. Arrange the asset, liability, and owner's equity accounts in an accounting equation similar to Exhibit 1-1, using these account titles: Cash, Accounts Receivable, Supplies, Copier, Accounts Payable, and M. Lomax, Capital.
2. Show by addition and subtraction, as in Exhibit 1-1, the effects of the transactions on the accounting equation. Show new balances after each transaction, and identify each owner's equity transaction by type.
3. Using Exhibit 1-2 as a guide, prepare an income statement, a statement of owner's equity, and a balance sheet for Arrow Copying Service.

Problem Set B

Problem 1B-1. Effect of Transactions on the Accounting Equation *(L.O. 6)*

John Unger, after receiving his degree in computer science, started his own business, Regency Business Services Company. He completed the following transactions soon after starting the business:

a. Deposited $18,000 in the bank to start the business and purchased a systems library with an additional investment of $1,840.
b. Paid current month's rent on an office, $720.
c. Purchased a minicomputer for cash, $14,000.

d. Purchased computer supplies on credit, $1,200.
e. Received revenue from a client, $1,600.
f. Billed a client on completion of a short project, $1,420.
g. Paid wages, $800.
h. Received a partial payment from the client billed in transaction **f**, $160.
i. Withdrew cash for personal expenses, $500.
j. Made a partial payment on the computer supplies purchased in transaction **d**, $400.

Required

1. Arrange the asset, liability, and owner's equity accounts in an accounting equation similar to Exhibit 1-1, using the following account titles: Cash, Accounts Receivable, Supplies, Equipment, Systems Library, Accounts Payable, and John Unger, Capital.
2. Show by addition and subtraction, as in Exhibit 1-1, the effects of the transactions on the accounting equation. Show new balances after each transaction, and identify each owner's equity transaction by type.

Problem 1B-2.
Effect of Transactions on the Accounting Equation
(L.O. 6)

On October 1, Oscar Melendez started a new business, the Melendez Transport Company. During the month of October, the firm completed the following transactions:

a. Deposited $132,000 in a new bank account to establish Melendez Transport Company.
b. Purchased two trucks for cash, $86,000.
c. Purchased equipment on credit, $18,000.
d. Billed a customer for hauling goods, $2,400.
e. Received cash for hauling goods, $4,600.
f. Received cash payment from the customer billed in transaction **d**, $1,200.
g. Made a payment on the equipment purchased in transaction **c**, $10,000.
h. Paid expenses in cash, $3,400.
i. Withdrew cash from the business for personal use, $2,400.

Required

1. Arrange the asset, liability, and owner's equity accounts in an accounting equation similar to Exhibit 1-1, using the following account titles: Cash, Accounts Receivable, Trucks, Equipment, Accounts Payable, and Oscar Melendez, Capital.
2. Show by addition and subtraction, as in Exhibit 1-1, the effects of the transactions on the accounting equation. Show new balances after each transaction, and identify each owner's equity transaction by type.

Problem 1B-3.
Effect of Transactions on the Accounting Equation
(L.O. 6)

Dr. Barbara Getz, a psychologist, moved from her home town to set up an office in St. Louis. After one month, the business had the following assets: Cash, $5,600; Accounts Receivable, $1,360; Office Supplies, $600; and Office Equipment, $15,000. Owner's equity—the capital account—consisted of $17,360. The Accounts Payable were $5,200 for purchases of office equipment on credit. During a short period of time, the following transactions were completed:

a. Paid one month's rent, $700.
b. Billed patient for services rendered, $120.
c. Made payment on accounts owed, $600.
d. Paid for office supplies, $200.
e. Paid the secretary's salary, $600.
f. Received payment for services rendered from patients not previously billed, $1,600.
g. Made payment on accounts owed, $720.
h. Withdrew cash for living expenses, $1,000.
i. Paid telephone bill for current month, $140.
j. Received payment from patients previously billed, $580.
k. Purchased additional office equipment on credit, $600.

Required

1. Arrange the asset, liability, and owner's equity accounts in an accounting equation similar to Exhibit 1-1, using the following account titles: Cash, Accounts Receivable, Office Supplies, Office Equipment, Accounts Payable, and Barbara Getz, Capital.
2. Enter the beginning balances for assets, liabilities, and owner's equity in your equation.

3. Show by addition and subtraction, as in Exhibit 1-1, the effects of the transactions on the accounting equation. Show new balances after each transaction, and identify each owner's equity transaction by type.

Problem 1B-4. Preparation of Financial Statements
(L.O. 7)

At the end of August 19xx, the Sheri Alexander, Capital account had a balance of $74,600. After operating during September, her Moon Valley Riding Club had the following account balances:

Cash	$17,400	Building	$60,000
Accounts Receivable	2,400	Horses	20,000
Supplies	2,000	Accounts Payable	35,600
Land	42,000		

In addition, the following transactions affected owner's equity:

Withdrawal by Sheri Alexander	$ 6,400	Salaries expense	$4,600
Investment by Sheri Alexander	32,000	Feed expense	2,000
Riding lesson revenue	12,400	Utility expense	1,200
Locker rental revenue	3,400		

Required

Using Exhibit 1-2 as a model, prepare an income statement, a statement of owner's equity, and a balance sheet for Moon Valley Riding Club. (**Hint**: The final balance of Sheri Alexander, Capital is $108,200.)

Problem 1B-5. Effect of Transactions on the Accounting Equation and Preparation of Financial Statements
(L.O. 6, 7)

On April 1, 19xx, Dependable Taxi Service began operation and engaged in the following transactions during April:

a. Investment by owner, Madeline Curry, $42,000.
b. Purchase of taxi for cash, $19,000.
c. Purchase of uniforms on credit, $400.
d. Taxi fares received in cash, $3,200.
e. Paid wages to part-time drivers, $500.
f. Purchased gasoline during month for cash, $800.
g. Purchased car washes during month on credit, $120.
h. Further investment by owner, $5,000.
i. Paid part of the amount owed for the uniforms purchased in transaction **c**, $200.
j. Billed major client for fares, $900.
k. Paid for automobile repairs, $250.
l. Withdrew cash from business for personal use, $1,000.

Required

1. Arrange the asset, liability, and owner's equity accounts in an accounting equation similar to Exhibit 1-1, using these account titles: Cash, Accounts Receivable, Uniforms, Taxi, Accounts Payable, and Madeline Curry, Capital.
2. Show by addition and subtraction, as in Exhibit 1-1, the effects of the transactions on the accounting equation. Show new balances after each transaction, and identify each owner's equity transaction by type.
3. Using Exhibit 1-2 as a guide, prepare an income statement, a statement of owner's equity, and a balance sheet for Dependable Taxi Service.

Financial Decision Case

Henderson Lawn Care Company
(L.O. 6, 7)

Instead of hunting for a summer job after finishing her junior year in college, Lucy Henderson organized a lawn service company in her neighborhood. To start her business on June 1, she deposited $1,350 in a new bank account in the name of her company. The $1,350 consisted of a $500 loan from her father and $850 of her own money.

Using the money in this checking account, Lucy rented lawn equipment, purchased supplies, and hired neighborhood high school students to mow and trim the lawns of neighbors who had agreed to pay her for the service. At the end of each month, she mailed bills to her customers.

On August 31, Lucy was ready to dissolve her business and go back to school for the fall quarter. Because she had been so busy, she had not kept any records other than her checkbook and a list of amounts owed to her by customers.

Her checkbook had a balance of $1,760, and the amount owed to her by customers totaled $435. She expected these customers to pay her during October. She planned to return unused supplies to Suburban Landscaping Company for a full refund of $25. When she brought back the rented lawn equipment, Suburban Landscaping also would return a deposit of $100 she had made in June. She owed Suburban Landscaping $260 for equipment rentals and supplies. In addition, she owed the students who had worked for her $50, and she still owed her father $350. Although Lucy feels she did quite well, she is not sure just how successful she was.

Required

1. Prepare a balance sheet dated June 1 and one dated August 31 for Henderson Lawn Care Company.
2. Comment on the performance of Henderson Lawn Care Company by comparing the two balance sheets. Did the company have a profit or a loss? (Assume that Lucy used none of the company's assets for personal purposes.)
3. If Lucy wants to continue her business next summer, what kind of information from her recordkeeping system would help make it easier to tell whether or not she is earning a profit?

Answers to Self-Test

1. d	3. a	5. b	7. d	9. d
2. a	4. b	6. b	8. a	10. c

LEARNING OBJECTIVES

1. *Explain, in simple terms, the generally accepted ways of solving the measurement issues of recognition, valuation, and classification.*
2. *Define and use the terms account and general ledger.*
3. *Recognize commonly used asset, liability, and owner's equity accounts.*
4. *Define double-entry system, and state the rules for debits and credits.*
5. *Apply the procedure for transaction analysis to simple transactions.*
6. *Record transactions in the general journal.*
7. *Post transactions from the journal to the ledger.*
8. *Prepare a trial balance, and describe its value and limitations.*

CHAPTER 2

Measuring and Recording Business Transactions

In the chapter on accounting as an information system, you learned the answer to the question What is measured? This chapter opens with a discussion of three other questions: When should the measurement be made? What value should be placed on what is measured? And how should what is measured be classified? Then, as our focus shifts from accounting concepts to actual practice, you begin working with the double-entry system, applying it to the analysis and recording of business transactions. After studying this chapter, you should be able to meet the learning objectives listed on the left.

DECISION POINT

UAL Corporation and The Boeing Company[1]

■ In October 1990 UAL Corporation, United Airlines' parent company, announced that it had ordered up to 128 Boeing wide-body jets: 68 of the long-awaited 777 models and 60 747-400 models. This order, which was estimated to come to more than $22 billion, was the largest order ever placed for commercial aircraft. The agreement included firm orders for half the aircraft and options to buy the other half. Boeing is manufacturing the aircraft for UAL, and the new planes will be delivered beginning in 1995. How should this important order be recorded, if at all, in the records of UAL and of Boeing? When should the forthcoming purchase and sale be recorded in the companies' records?

The order obviously was an important event, one that carried long-term consequences for both companies. But, as you will see in this chapter, it was not recorded in the accounting records of either company. At the time the order was placed, the aircraft were yet to be manufactured and would not begin to be delivered for five years. For half the aircraft, UAL was given an option that could be accepted or refused. Even for the "firm" orders, Boeing cautioned in its 1989 annual report that "an economic downturn could result in airline equipment requirements less than currently anticipated resulting in requests to negotiate the rescheduling or possible cancellation of firm orders." The aircraft are not assets of UAL, and the company has not incurred a liability. No aircraft have been delivered or even built, so UAL is not obligated to pay at this point. And Boeing cannot record any revenue until the aircraft are manufactured and delivered to UAL, until title to (ownership of) the aircraft shifts from Boeing to UAL.

1. Information from the *Wall Street Journal*, October 16, 1990, p. A3, and excerpts from the 1989 Annual Report of The Boeing Company.

To understand and use financial statements, it is important to know how to analyze events in order to determine the extent of their impact on those statements. ■

Measurement Issues

OBJECTIVE 1
Explain, in simple terms, the generally accepted ways of solving the measurement issues of recognition, valuation, and classification

We have defined business transactions as economic events that affect the financial position of a business entity. To measure a business transaction, the accountant must decide when the transaction occurred (the recognition issue), what value to place on the transaction (the valuation issue), and how the components of the transaction should be categorized (the classification issue).

These three issues—recognition, valuation, and classification—underlie almost every major decision in financial accounting today. They lie at the heart of accounting for pension plans, of mergers of giant companies, and of international transactions; and they allow the accountant to project and plan for the effects of inflation. In discussing the three basic issues, we follow generally accepted accounting principles and use an approach that promotes the understanding of the basic ideas of accounting. Keep in mind, however, that controversy does exist, and some solutions to problems are not as cut-and-dried as they appear.

The Recognition Issue

The **recognition** issue refers to the difficulty of deciding when a business transaction should be recorded. Often the facts of a situation are known, but there is disagreement about *when* the event should be recorded. Suppose, for instance, that a company orders, receives, and pays for an office desk. Which of the following actions constitutes a recordable event?

1. An employee sends a purchase requisition to the purchasing department.
2. The purchasing department sends a purchase order to the supplier.
3. The supplier ships the desk.
4. The company receives the desk.
5. The company receives the bill from the supplier.
6. The company pays the bill.

The answer to this question is important because amounts in the financial statements are affected by the date on which a purchase is recorded. According to accounting tradition, the transaction is recorded when title to the desk passes from the supplier to the purchaser, creating an obligation to pay. Thus, depending on the details of the shipping agreement, the transaction is recognized (recorded) at the time of either action **3** or action **4**. This is the guideline that we generally use in this book. However, in many small businesses that have simple accounting systems, the transaction is not recorded until the bill is received (action **5**) or paid (action **6**) because these are the implied points of title transfer. The predetermined time at which a transaction should be recorded is the **recognition point**.

The recognition problem is not always solved easily. Consider the case of an advertising agency that is asked by a client to prepare a major advertising campaign. People may work on the campaign several hours a day for a number of weeks. Value is added to the plan as the employees develop it. Should this added value be recognized as the campaign is being produced or at the time it is completed? Normally, the increase in value is recorded at the time the plan is finished and the client is billed for it. However, if a plan is going to take a long period to develop, the agency and the client may agree that the client will be billed at key points during its development.

The Valuation Issue

The **valuation** issue is perhaps the most controversial issue in accounting. It focuses on assigning a monetary value to a business transaction. Generally accepted accounting principles state that the appropriate value to assign to all business transactions—and therefore to all assets, liabilities, components of owner's equity, revenues, and expenses acquired by a business—is the original cost (often called *historical cost*). **Cost** is defined here as the exchange price associated with a business transaction at the point of recognition. According to this guideline, the purpose of accounting is not to account for "value," which can change after a transaction occurs, but to account for the cost or value at the time of the transaction. For example, the cost of assets is recorded when they are acquired, and their value is held at that level until they are sold, expire, or are consumed. In this context, *value* means the cost at the time of the transaction. The practice of recording transactions at cost is referred to as the **cost principle**.

Suppose that a person offers a building for sale at $120,000. It may be valued for real estate taxes at $75,000, and it may be insured for $90,000. One prospective buyer may offer $100,000 for the building, and another may offer $105,000. At this point, several different, unverifiable opinions of value have been expressed. Finally, the seller and a buyer may settle on a price and complete the sale for $110,000. All of these figures are values of one kind or another, but only the last is sufficiently reliable to be used in the records. The market value of the building may vary over the years, but it will remain on the new buyer's records at $110,000 until it is sold again. At that point, the accountant will record the new transaction at the new exchange price, and a profit or loss will be recognized.

The cost principle is used because the cost is verifiable. It results from the actions of independent buyers and sellers who come to an agreement on price. An exchange price is an objective price that can be verified by evidence created at the time of the transaction. It is this final price, verified by agreement of the two parties, at which the transaction is recorded.

The Classification Issue

The **classification** issue has to do with assigning all the transactions in which a business engages to appropriate categories, or accounts. For example, a company's ability to borrow money can be affected by the way in which its debts are categorized. Or a company's income can be affected by whether purchases of small items such as tools are considered repair expenses (a component of owner's equity) or equipment (assets). Proper classification depends not only on the correct analysis of the effect of each transaction on the business, but also on maintaining a system of accounts that reflects that effect. The rest of this chapter explains the classification of accounts and the analysis and recording of transactions.

Accounts

OBJECTIVE 2
Define and use the terms account *and* general ledger

In the measurement of business transactions, large amounts of data are gathered. These data require a method of storage. Business people should be able to retrieve transaction data quickly and in usable form. In other words, there should be a filing system to sort out or classify all the transactions that occur in a business. This filing system consists of accounts. An **account** is the basic storage unit for accounting data. An accounting system has separate accounts for each asset, each liability, and each component of owner's equity, including revenues and expenses. Whether a company keeps records by hand or by computer, management must be able to refer to accounts so that it can study the company's financial history and plan for the future. A very small company may need only a few dozen accounts; a multinational corporation may have thousands.

In a manual accounting system, each account is kept on a separate page or card. These pages or cards are placed together in a book or file called the **general ledger**. In the computerized systems that most companies have today, accounts are maintained on magnetic tapes or disks. However, as a matter of convenience, accountants still refer to the group of company accounts as the general ledger, or simply the *ledger*.

To help identify accounts in the ledger and to make them easy to find, the accountant often numbers them. A list of these numbers with the corresponding account names is called a **chart of accounts**. A very simple chart of accounts appears in Exhibit 2-1. Notice that the first digit refers to the major financial

Exhibit 2-1. Chart of Accounts for a Small Business

Assets		**Liabilities**	
Cash	111	Notes Payable	211
Notes Receivable	112	Accounts Payable	212
Accounts Receivable	113	Unearned Art Fees	213
Fees Receivable	114	Wages Payable	214
Art Supplies	115	Mortgage Payable	221
Office Supplies	116		
Prepaid Rent	117	**Owner's Equity**	
Prepaid Insurance	118	Joan Miller, Capital	311
Land	141	Joan Miller, Withdrawals	312
Buildings	142	Income Summary	313
Accumulated Depreciation, Buildings	143		
Art Equipment	144	**Revenues**	
Accumulated Depreciation, Art Equipment	145	Advertising Fees Earned	411
Office Equipment	146	Art Fees Earned	412
Accumulated Depreciation, Office Equipment	147		
		Expenses	
		Office Wages Expense	511
		Utility Expense	512
		Telephone Expense	513
		Rent Expense	514
		Insurance Expense	515
		Art Supplies Expense	516
		Office Supplies Expense	517
		Depreciation Expense, Buildings	518
		Depreciation Expense, Art Equipment	519
		Depreciation Expense, Office Equipment	520
		Interest Expense	521

statement classifications. An account number that begins with the digit 1 is an asset, an account number that begins with a 2 is a liability, and so forth. The second and third digits refer to individual accounts.

You will be introduced to these accounts here and in the next two chapters through the sample case of the Joan Miller Advertising Agency. At this time, notice the gaps among the sequences of numbers. These gaps allow the accountant to expand the number of accounts. Of course, every company develops a chart of accounts for its own needs. Seldom do two companies have exactly the same chart of accounts, and larger companies need more digits to accommodate all of their accounts. But, in keeping its records, each company should follow a consistent framework for its own chart of accounts.

Types of Commonly Used Accounts

OBJECTIVE 3
Recognize commonly used asset, liability, and owner's equity accounts

The specific accounts used by a company depend on the nature of the company's business. A steel company is going to have many equipment and inventory accounts; an advertising agency may have just a few. Each company must design its accounts in a way that reflects the nature of its business and the needs of its management. There are, however, accounts that are common to most businesses. We describe several of them below.

Asset Accounts. A company must keep records of the increases and decreases in each asset that it owns. Some of the more common asset accounts are listed here.

Cash. Cash is the account used to record increases and decreases in cash. Cash consists of money or any medium of exchange that banks accept at face value for deposit. Included are coins, currency, checks, postal and express money orders, and money on deposit in a bank. The Cash account also includes cash on hand, money that is kept in a cash register or a safe.

Notes Receivable. A promissory note is a written promise to pay a definite sum of money at a fixed future date. Amounts due from others in the form of promissory notes are recorded in an account called Notes Receivable.

Accounts Receivable. Companies often sell goods and services on the basis of customers' oral or implied promises to pay in the future (in thirty days or on the first of the month). These sales are called *credit sales,* or *sales on account,* and the promises to pay are recorded in an account called Accounts Receivable. Credit sales increase Accounts Receivable, and collections from customers decrease Accounts Receivable. Of course, it is necessary to keep a record of how much each customer owes the company. We explain how these records are kept in the chapter on special-purpose journals.

Prepaid Expenses. At times, companies pay for goods and services before they receive or use them. Prepaid expenses are considered assets until they are used, or expire, at which time they become expenses. There should be a separate account for each prepaid expense.

An example of a prepaid expense is insurance. Insurance protection against fire, theft, and other hazards usually is paid in advance for a period of one to five years. When the premiums are paid, the Prepaid Insurance (or Unexpired Insurance) account increases. The coverage expires day by day and month by month. Therefore, at intervals (usually at the end of the accounting period), Prepaid Insurance must be reduced by the amount of insurance that has expired. Another common type of prepaid expense is office supplies. Stamps, stationery, pencils, pens, and paper are assets when they are purchased and are recorded as an increase in the Office Supplies account. As the supplies are used, the account is reduced. Other typical prepaid expenses that are assets when they are purchased and become expenses through use or the passage of time are prepaid rent (rent paid for more than one month in advance), store supplies, and prepaid taxes.

Land. Purchases of property that is going to be used in the ordinary operations of the business are recorded in an account called Land.

Buildings. Purchases of structures that are going to be used in the business are recorded in an account called Buildings. Although a building cannot be separated from the land it occupies, it is important to maintain separate accounts for land and buildings. Buildings are subject to wear and tear, but land is not. Later in this book, the subject of depreciation is introduced. Wear and tear is an important aspect of depreciation.

Equipment. A company may own many different types of equipment. Usually, there is a separate account for each type. Transactions involving desks, chairs, office machines, filing cabinets, and typewriters are recorded in an account called Office Equipment. Increases and decreases in cash registers, counters, showcases, shelves, and similar items are recorded in the Store Equipment account. A company that has a factory may own lathes, drill presses, and other equipment; it would record changes in these items in Machinery and Equipment. And some companies use a Trucks and Automobiles account.

Liability Accounts. Another word for *liability* is *debt.* Most companies have fewer liability accounts than asset accounts. But it is just as important to keep records of what the company owes as well as what it owns (assets). There are two types of liabilities: short-term and long-term. The distinction between them is introduced in the chapter on current liabilities. Here, we describe examples of both types.

Short-Term Liabilities. The Notes Payable account is the opposite of Notes Receivable. It is used to record increases and decreases in promissory note amounts owed to creditors within the next year or operating cycle.

Similarly, Accounts Payable is the opposite of Accounts Receivable. It represents amounts owed to creditors on the basis of an oral or implied promise to pay. Accounts payable usually arise as the result of the purchase of merchandise, services, supplies, or equipment on credit. When Company A buys an item from Company B and promises to pay for it at the beginning of the month, the amount of the transaction is an account payable on Company A's books and an account receivable on Company B's books. Like accounts receivable, the amounts owed to individual creditors must be recorded. The chapter on current liabilities describes the process.

Other short-term liability accounts are Wages Payable, Taxes Payable, Rent Payable, and Interest Payable. Also, customers often make deposits on, or pay in advance for, goods and services to be delivered in the future. These deposits are recorded as liabilities too because they represent claims by the customers for those goods or services. These kinds of liability accounts often are called Unearned Fees, Customer Deposits, Advances from Customers, or, more commonly, Unearned Revenues.

Long-Term Liabilities. The most common types of long-term liabilities are notes due in more than one year, bonds, and property mortgages. Because a wide variety of bonds and mortgages have been developed for special financing needs, it is difficult to classify them. They may or may not require the backing of certain of the company's assets for security. For example, a mortgage holder may have the right to force the sale of certain assets if the mortgage debt is not paid when it is due.

Owner's Equity Accounts. In the chapter on accounting as an information system, you saw that several transactions affect owner's equity. The effects of these transactions were shown by the increases or decreases in the single column representing owner's equity (see the exhibit "Summary of Effects of Sample Transactions on the Accounting Equation" in the chapter on accounting as an information system). For legal and managerial reasons, it is important to sort these transactions into separate owner's equity accounts. Among the most important information that management receives for business planning is a detailed breakdown of revenues and expenses. For income tax reporting, financial reporting, and other reasons, the law requires that owner's investments and withdrawals be separated from revenues and expenses. Ownership and equity accounts, especially those for corporations, are covered in detail in the chapters on accounting for corporations. The following accounts, whose relationships are shown in Figure 2-1, are important to the study of sole proprietorships.

Capital Account. When someone invests in his or her own company, the amount of the investment is recorded in a capital account. For instance, in the chapter on accounting as an information system, John Shannon's investment of his personal resources in the firm was recorded in the owner's equity account called John Shannon, Capital. Any additional investments by John Shannon in his firm would be recorded in this account.

Figure 2-1. Relationships of Owner's Equity Accounts

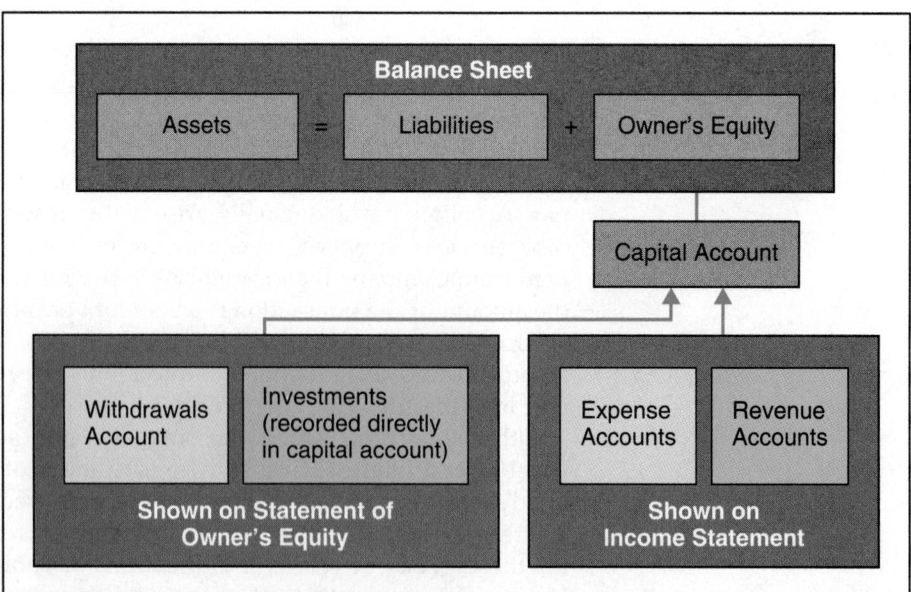

Withdrawals Account. A person who invests in a business usually expects to earn an income, to use at least part of the assets earned from operations to pay personal living expenses. Because a company's income is determined at the end of the accounting period, the owner often finds it necessary to withdraw assets from the business for living expenses long before the firm's income has been determined. We do not describe these withdrawals as salary, although the owner might think of them as such, because there is no change in the ownership of the money withdrawn. We simply say that the owner has withdrawn assets for personal use. As a result, it is common practice to set up a withdrawals account to record these payments, which are made with the expectation of earning an income. For example, an account called John Shannon, Withdrawals would be used to record John Shannon's withdrawals from his firm. In practice, the withdrawals account often goes by several other names, among them Personal and Drawing. Corporations do not use a withdrawals account.

Revenue and Expense Accounts. Revenues increase owner's equity, and expenses decrease owner's equity. The greater the revenues, the more owner's equity increases. The greater the expenses, the more the owner's equity decreases. Of course, when revenues are greater than expenses, the company has earned a profit, or net income. When expenses are more than revenues, the company has suffered a loss, or net loss. Management's primary goal is to earn net income, and an important function of accounting is to give management the information it needs to meet this goal. One way of doing this is to have a ledger account for every revenue and expense item. From these accounts, which are included in the income statement, management can identify exactly the source of all revenues and the nature of all expenses. A particular company's revenue and expense accounts depend on the nature of its business and operations. A few of the revenue accounts used in this book are Commissions Earned, Advertising Fees Earned, and Sales. Some of the expense accounts are Wages Expense, Supplies Expense, Rent Expense, and Advertising Expense.

Account Titles

The names of accounts often confuse beginning accounting students because some of the words are new or have technical meanings. Also, the same asset, liability, or owner's equity account can have different names in different companies. (Actually, this is not so strange. People, too, often are called different names by their friends, families, and associates.) For example, Fixed Assets, Plant and Equipment, Capital Assets, and Long-Lived Assets are all names for long-term assets accounts. Even the most acceptable names change over time, and, by habit, some companies use names that are out of date.

In general, an account title should describe what is recorded in the account. When you come across an account title that you do not recognize, you should examine the context of the name—whether it is classified as asset, liability, owner's equity, revenue, or expense on the financial statements—and look for the kind of transaction that gave rise to the account.

The Double-Entry System: The Basic Method of Accounting

The double-entry system, the backbone of accounting, evolved during the Renaissance. The first systematic description of double-entry bookkeeping

OBJECTIVE 4
Define double-entry system, *and state the rules for debits and credits*

appeared in 1494, two years after Columbus discovered America, in a mathematics book written by Fra Luca Pacioli, a Franciscan monk who was a friend of Leonardo da Vinci. Goethe, the famous German poet and dramatist, referred to double-entry bookkeeping as "one of the finest discoveries of the human intellect." And Werner Sombart, an eminent economist-sociologist, believed that "double-entry bookkeeping is born of the same spirit as the system of Galileo and Newton."

What is the significance of the double-entry system? The system is based on the *principle of duality,* which means that every economic event has two aspects—effort and reward, sacrifice and benefit, source and use—that offset or balance each other. In the **double-entry system**, each transaction must be recorded with at least one debit and one credit, so that the total dollar amount of debits and the total dollar amount of credits equal each other. Because of the way it is designed, the whole system is always in balance. All accounting systems, no matter how sophisticated, are based on the principle of duality.

The T Account

The T account is a good place to begin the study of the double-entry system. In its simplest form, an account has three parts: (1) a title, which describes the asset, the liability, or the owner's equity account; (2) a left side, which is called the **debit** side; and (3) a right side, which is called the **credit** side. This form of the account, called a **T account** because it resembles the letter *T*, is used to analyze transactions. It looks like this:

Title of Account	
Debit (left) side	Credit (right) side

Any entry made on the left side of the account is a debit, or debit entry; and any entry made on the right side of the account is a credit, or credit entry. The terms *debit* (abbreviated Dr., from the Latin *debere*) and *credit* (abbreviated Cr., from the Latin *credere*) are simply the accountant's words for "left" and "right" (not for "increase" or "decrease"). We present a more formal version of the T account later in this chapter, where we examine the ledger account form.

The T Account Illustrated

In the chapter on accounting as an information system, Shannon Realty had several transactions that involved the receipt or payment of cash. (See the exhibit "Summary of Effects of Sample Transactions on the Accounting Equation" in the chapter on accounting as an information system for a summary of the numbered transactions listed below.) These transactions can be summarized in the Cash account by recording receipts on the left (debit) side of the account and payments on the right (credit) side of the account:

Cash			
(1)	50,000	(2)	35,000
(5)	1,500	(4)	200
(7)	1,000	(8)	1,000
		(9)	400
		(11)	600
	52,500		37,200
Bal.	15,300		

The cash receipts on the left total $52,500. (The total is written in small-sized figures so that it cannot be confused with an actual debit entry.) The cash payments on the right side total $37,200. These totals are simply working totals, or **footings**. Footings, which are calculated at the end of each month, are an easy way to determine cash on hand. The difference in dollars between the total debit footing and the total credit footing is called the **balance** or *account balance.* If the balance is a debit, it is written on the left side. If it is a credit, it is written on the right. Notice that Shannon Realty's Cash account has a debit balance of $15,300 ($52,500 – $37,200). This is the amount of cash the business has on hand at the end of the month.

Analysis of Transactions

The rules of double-entry bookkeeping are that every transaction affects at least two accounts and that total debits must equal total credits. In other words, for every transaction, one or more accounts must be debited and one or more accounts must be credited, and the total dollar amount of the debits must equal the total dollar amount of the credits.

Look again at the accounting equation:

Assets = liabilities + owner's equity

You can see that if a debit increases assets, then a credit must be used to increase liabilities or owner's equity because they are on opposite sides of the equal sign. Likewise, if a credit decreases assets, then a debit must be used to decrease liabilities or owner's equity. These rules can be shown as follows:

Assets		=	**Liabilities**		+	**Owner's Equity**	
Debit for increases	Credit for decreases		Debit for decreases	Credit for increases		Debit for decreases	Credit for increases

1. Increases in assets are debited to asset accounts; decreases in assets are credited to asset accounts.
2. Increases in liabilities and owner's equity are credited to liability and owner's equity accounts; decreases in liabilities and owner's equity are debited to liability and owner's equity accounts.

One of the more difficult points to understand is the application of these rules to the owner's equity components of revenues, expenses, and withdrawals. Because revenues increase owner's equity and expenses and withdrawals decrease it, the following relationships hold:

Owner's Equity

Decreases (debits)	Increases (credits)

Expenses

Increases (debits)	Decreases (credits)

Withdrawals

Increases (debits)	Decreases (credits)

Revenues

Decreases (debits)	Increases (credits)

Thus, a transaction that increases revenues by a credit also increases owner's equity by a credit. However, expenses and withdrawals, which are increased by debits, decrease owner's equity. In other words, the more expenses and withdrawals are *increased* by debits, the more these debits *decrease* owner's equity; and the more expenses and withdrawals are *decreased* by credits, the more these credits *increase* owner's equity. Why? Because expenses and withdrawals are components of owner's equity, which is on the right side of the accounting equation.

Now, we can explain how to analyze transactions. Transactions usually are supported by some kind of source document—an invoice, a receipt, a check, or a contract. These documents provide the basis for analyzing each transaction. As an example, suppose that Jones Company borrows $1,000 from its bank on a promissory note. The procedure is as follows:

1. Analyze the effect of the transaction on assets, liabilities, and owner's equity. In this case, both an asset (Cash) and a liability (Notes Payable) increase.
2. Apply the correct double-entry rules. Increases in assets are recorded by debits. Increases in liabilities are recorded by credits.
3. Make the entry. The increase in assets is recorded by a debit to the Cash account; the increase in liabilities is recorded by a credit to the Notes Payable account.

Cash	
1,000	

Notes Payable	
	1,000

The debit to Cash of $1,000 equals the credit to Notes Payable of $1,000.

Later in this chapter, we explain the journal form of this entry:

	Dr.	Cr.
Cash	1,000	
Notes Payable		1,000

Transaction Analysis Illustrated

OBJECTIVE 5
Apply the procedure for transaction analysis to simple transactions

In the next few pages, we describe the transactions for the Joan Miller Advertising Agency during the month of January. We use the transactions to illustrate the principle of duality and to show how they are recorded in the accounts.

January 1: Joan Miller invests $10,000 to start her own advertising agency.

Cash	
Jan. 1 10,000	

Joan Miller, Capital	
	Jan. 1 10,000

Transaction: Owner's investment.
Analysis: Assets increase. Owner's equity increases.
Rules: Increases in assets are recorded by debits. Increases in owner's equity are recorded by credits.
Entry: The increase in assets is recorded by a debit to Cash. The increase in owner's equity is recorded by a credit to Joan Miller, Capital.

	Dr.	Cr.
Cash	10,000	
Joan Miller, Capital		10,000

If Joan Miller had invested assets other than cash in the business, the appropriate asset accounts would be debited.

January 2: Rents an office, paying two months' rent, $800, in advance.

Cash

Jan. 1	10,000	Jan. 2	800

Prepaid Rent

Jan. 2	800		

Transaction: Expense paid in advance.
Analysis: Assets increase. Assets decrease.
Rules: Increases in assets are recorded by debits. Decreases in assets are recorded by credits.
Entry: The increase in assets is recorded by a debit to Prepaid Rent. The decrease in assets is recorded by a credit to Cash.

	Dr.	Cr.
Prepaid Rent	800	
Cash		800

January 3: Orders art supplies, $1,800, and office supplies, $800.

Analysis: No entry is made because no transaction has occurred. According to the recognition issue, there is no liability until the supplies are shipped or received and there is an obligation to pay for them.

January 4: Purchases art equipment, $4,200, with cash.

Cash

Jan. 1	10,000	Jan. 2	800
		4	4,200

Art Equipment

Jan. 4	4,200		

Transaction: Purchase of equipment.
Analysis: Assets increase. Assets decrease.
Rules: Increases in assets are recorded by debits. Decreases in assets are recorded by credits.
Entry: The increase in assets is recorded by a debit to Art Equipment. The decrease in assets is recorded by a credit to Cash.

	Dr.	Cr.
Art Equipment	4,200	
Cash		4,200

January 5: Purchases office equipment, $3,000, from Morgan Equipment; pays $1,500 in cash and agrees to pay the rest next month.

Cash

Jan. 1	10,000	Jan. 2	800
		4	4,200
		5	1,500

Office Equipment

Jan. 5	3,000		

Accounts Payable

		Jan. 5	1,500

Transaction: Purchase of equipment and partial payment.
Analysis: Assets increase. Assets decrease. Liabilities increase.
Rules: Increases in assets are recorded by debits. Decreases in assets are recorded by credits. Increases in liabilities are recorded by credits.
Entry: The increase in assets is recorded by a debit to Office Equipment. The decrease in assets is recorded by a credit to Cash. The increase in liabilities is recorded by a credit to Accounts Payable.

	Dr.	Cr.
Office Equipment	3,000	
Cash		1,500
Accounts Payable		1,500

January 6: Purchases art supplies, $1,800, and office supplies, $800, from Taylor Supply Company, on credit.

Art Supplies

Jan. 6	1,800		

Office Supplies

Jan. 6	800		

Accounts Payable

		Jan. 5	1,500
		6	2,600

Transaction: Purchase of supplies on credit.
Analysis: Assets increase. Liabilities increase.
Rules: Increases in assets are recorded by debits. Increases in liabilities are recorded by credits.
Entry: The increase in assets is recorded by debits to Art Supplies and Office Supplies. The increase in liabilities is recorded by a credit to Accounts Payable.

	Dr.	Cr.
Art Supplies	1,800	
Office Supplies	800	
Accounts Payable		2,600

January 8: Pays for a one-year insurance policy, $480, with coverage effective January 1.

Cash

Jan. 1	10,000	Jan. 2	800
		4	4,200
		5	1,500
		8	480

Prepaid Insurance

Jan. 8	480		

Transaction: Payment in advance for insurance coverage.
Analysis: Assets increase. Assets decrease.
Rules: Increases in assets are recorded by debits. Decreases in assets are recorded by credits.
Entry: The increase in assets is recorded by a debit to Prepaid Insurance. The decrease in assets is recorded by a credit to Cash.

	Dr.	Cr.
Prepaid Insurance	480	
Cash		480

January 9: Pays Taylor Supply Company $1,000 of the amount owed.

Cash

Jan. 1	10,000	Jan. 2	800
		4	4,200
		5	1,500
		8	480
		9	1,000

Accounts Payable

Jan. 9	1,000	Jan. 5	1,500
		6	2,600

Transaction: Partial payment on a liability.
Analysis: Assets decrease. Liabilities decrease.
Rules: Decreases in assets are recorded by credits. Decreases in liabilities are recorded by debits.
Entry: The decrease in liabilities is recorded by a debit to Accounts Payable. The decrease in assets is recorded by a credit to Cash.

	Dr.	Cr.
Accounts Payable	1,000	
Cash		1,000

January 10: Performs a service by placing advertisements for an automobile dealer in the newspaper and collects a fee, $1,400.

Cash

Jan. 1	10,000	Jan. 2	800
10	1,400	4	4,200
		5	1,500
		8	480
		9	1,000

Advertising Fees Earned

		Jan. 10	1,400

Transaction: Revenue earned and cash collected.
Analysis: Assets increase. Owner's equity increases.
Rules: Increases in assets are recorded by debits. Increases in owner's equity are recorded by credits.
Entry: The increase in assets is recorded by a debit to Cash. The increase in owner's equity is recorded by a credit to Advertising Fees Earned.

	Dr.	Cr.
Cash	1,400	
Advertising Fees Earned		1,400

January 12: Pays the secretary two weeks' wages, $600.

Cash

Jan. 1	10,000	Jan. 2	800
10	1,400	4	4,200
		5	1,500
		8	480
		9	1,000
		12	600

Office Wages Expense

Jan. 12	600		

Transaction: Payment of wages expense.
Analysis: Assets decrease. Owner's equity decreases.
Rules: Decreases in assets are recorded by credits. Decreases in owner's equity are recorded by debits.
Entry: The decrease in owner's equity is recorded by a debit to Office Wages Expense. The decrease in assets is recorded by a credit to Cash.

	Dr.	Cr.
Office Wages Expense	600	
Cash		600

January 15: Accepts an advance fee, $1,000, for artwork to be done for another agency.

Cash

Jan. 1	10,000	Jan. 2	800
10	1,400	4	4,200
15	1,000	5	1,500
		8	480
		9	1,000
		12	600

Unearned Art Fees

		Jan. 15	1,000

Transaction: Payment received for future services.
Analysis: Assets increase. Liabilities increase.
Rules: Increases in assets are recorded by debits. Increases in liabilities are recorded by credits.
Entry: The increase in assets is recorded by a debit to Cash. The increase in liabilities is recorded by a credit to Unearned Art Fees.

	Dr.	Cr.
Cash	1,000	
Unearned Art Fees		1,000

January 19: Performs a service by placing several major advertisements for Ward Department Stores. The fee, $2,800, is billed now but will be collected next month.

Accounts Receivable

Jan. 19 2,800	

Advertising Fees Earned

	Jan. 10 1,400
	19 2,800

Transaction: Revenue earned, to be received later.
Analysis: Assets increase. Owner's equity increases.
Rules: Increases in assets are recorded by debits. Increases in owner's equity are recorded by credits.
Entry: The increase in assets is recorded by a debit to Accounts Receivable. The increase in owner's equity is recorded by a credit to Advertising Fees Earned.

	Dr.	Cr.
Accounts Receivable	2,800	
Advertising Fees Earned		2,800

January 25: Joan Miller withdraws $1,400 from the business for personal living expenses.

Cash

Jan. 1	10,000	Jan. 2	800
10	1,400	4	4,200
15	1,000	5	1,500
		8	480
		9	1,000
		12	600
		25	1,400

Joan Miller, Withdrawals

Jan. 25 1,400	

Transaction: Owner's withdrawal for personal use.
Analysis: Assets decrease. Owner's equity decreases.
Rules: Decreases in assets are recorded by credits. Decreases in owner's equity are recorded by debits.
Entry: The decrease in owner's equity is recorded by a debit to Joan Miller, Withdrawals. The decrease in assets is recorded by a credit to Cash.

	Dr.	Cr.
Joan Miller, Withdrawals	1,400	
Cash		1,400

January 26: Pays the secretary two more weeks' wages, $600.

Cash

Jan. 1	10,000	Jan. 2	800
10	1,400	4	4,200
15	1,000	5	1,500
		8	480
		9	1,000
		12	600
		25	1,400
		26	600

Office Wages Expense

Jan. 12 600	
26 600	

Transaction: Payment of wages expense.
Analysis: Assets decrease. Owner's equity decreases.
Rules: Decreases in assets are recorded by credits. Decreases in owner's equity are recorded by debits.
Entry: The decrease in owner's equity is recorded by a debit to Office Wages Expense. The decrease in assets is recorded by a credit to Cash.

	Dr.	Cr.
Office Wages Expense	600	
Cash		600

January 29: Receives and pays the utility bill, $100.

Cash

Jan. 1	10,000	Jan. 2	800
10	1,400	4	4,200
15	1,000	5	1,500
		8	480
		9	1,000
		12	600
		25	1,400
		26	600
		29	100

Utility Expense

Jan. 29	100		

Transaction: Payment of utility expense.
Analysis: Assets decrease. Owner's equity decreases.
Rules: Decreases in assets are recorded by credits. Decreases in owner's equity are recorded by debits.
Entry: The decrease in owner's equity is recorded by a debit to Utility Expense. The decrease in assets is recorded by a credit to Cash.

	Dr.	Cr.
Utility Expense	100	
Cash		100

January 30: Receives (but does not pay) the telephone bill, $70.

Accounts Payable

Jan. 9	1,000	Jan. 5	1,500
		6	2,600
		30	70

Telephone Expense

Jan. 30	70		

Transaction: Expense incurred, to be paid later.
Analysis: Liabilities increase. Owner's equity decreases.
Rules: Increases in liabilities are recorded by credits. Decreases in owner's equity are recorded by debits.
Entry: The decrease in owner's equity is recorded by a debit to Telephone Expense. The increase in liabilities is recorded by a credit to Accounts Payable.

	Dr.	Cr.
Telephone Expense	70	
Accounts Payable		70

Summary of Transactions

If you look closely at the examples above, you can see that there are only a few ways in which transactions can affect the accounting equation:

Effect of Transactions	Example Transactions
1. Increase both assets and liabilities	Jan. 6, 15
2. Increase both assets and owner's equity	Jan. 1, 10, 19
3. Decrease both assets and liabilities	Jan. 9
4. Decrease both assets and owner's equity	Jan. 12, 25, 26, 29
5. Increase one asset and decrease another	Jan. 2, 4, 8
6. Increase one liability or component of owner's equity and decrease another liability or component of owner's equity	Jan. 30
7. No effect	Jan. 3

The January 5 transaction is a slightly more complex transaction: It increases one asset (Office Equipment), decreases another asset (Cash), and increases a liability (Accounts Payable). All of these transactions are shown in Exhibit 2-2 in their correct accounts. Their relation to the accounting equation is also shown.

Exhibit 2-2. Summary of Sample Accounts and Transactions for Joan Miller Advertising Agency

Assets = **Liabilities** + **Owner's Equity**

Assets

Cash			
Jan. 1	10,000	Jan. 2	800
10	1,400	4	4,200
15	1,000	5	1,500
		8	480
		9	1,000
		12	600
		25	1,400
		26	600
		29	100
	12,400		**10,680**
Bal.	**1,720**		

Accounts Receivable			
Jan. 19	2,800		

Art Supplies			
Jan. 6	1,800		

Office Supplies			
Jan. 6	800		

Prepaid Rent			
Jan. 2	800		

Prepaid Insurance			
Jan. 8	480		

Art Equipment			
Jan. 4	4,200		

Office Equipment			
Jan. 5	3,000		

Liabilities

Accounts Payable			
Jan. 9	1,000	Jan. 5	1,500
		6	2,600
		30	70
	1,000		**4,170**
		Bal.	**3,170**

Unearned Art Fees			
		Jan. 15	1,000

Owner's Equity

Joan Miller, Capital			
		Jan. 1	10,000

Joan Miller, Withdrawals			
Jan. 25	1,400		

Advertising Fees Earned			
		Jan. 10	1,400
		19	2,800
		Bal.	**4,200**

Office Wages Expense			
Jan. 12	600		
26	600		
Bal.	**1,200**		

Utility Expense			
Jan. 29	100		

Telephone Expense			
Jan. 30	70		

Recording Transactions

OBJECTIVE 6
Record transactions in the general journal

We have been analyzing transactions by entering them directly into the T accounts. We used this method because it is very simple and effective. Advanced accounting students and professional accountants often use T accounts to analyze very complicated transactions.

The formal process for recording the debits and credits of business transactions, however, involves the following three steps:

1. Analyze the transactions from the source documents.
2. Enter the transactions into the journal (a procedure called *journalizing*).
3. Post the entries to the ledger (a procedure called *posting*).

The General Journal

As you have seen, transactions can be recorded directly into the accounts. But this method makes it very difficult to identify individual transactions or find errors because the debit is recorded in one account and the credit in another. The solution is to record all transactions chronologically in a **journal**. The journal is sometimes called the *book of original entry* because this is where transactions are first recorded. Later, the debit and credit portion of each transaction can be transferred to the appropriate accounts in the ledger.

A separate **journal entry** is used to record each transaction, and the process of recording transactions is called **journalizing**.

Most businesses have more than one kind of journal. The simplest and most flexible type is the **general journal**, the one we focus on in this chapter. Entries in the general journal include the following information about each transaction:

1. The date
2. The names of the accounts debited and the dollar amounts in the debit column on the same lines
3. The names of the accounts credited and the dollar amounts in the credit column on the same lines
4. An explanation of the transaction
5. The account identification numbers, if appropriate

We have recorded two transactions for the Joan Miller Advertising Agency in Exhibit 2-3. As shown in that exhibit, the procedure for recording transactions in the general journal is as follows:

1. Record the date by writing the year in small figures on the first line at the top of the first column, the month on the next line of the first column, and the day in the second column opposite the month. For subsequent entries on the same page for the same month and year, the month and year can be omitted.
2. Write the exact names of the accounts debited and credited under the heading "Description." Write the name of the account debited next to the left margin of

Exhibit 2-3. The General Journal

General Journal					Page 1
Date		Description	Post. Ref.	Debit	Credit
19xx					
Jan.	6	Art Supplies		1,800	
		Office Supplies		800	
		Accounts Payable			2,600
		Purchase of art and office			
		supplies on credit			
	8	Prepaid Insurance		480	
		Cash			480
		Paid one-year insurance			
		premium			

the second line, and indent the name of the account credited. The explanation is placed on the next line and further indented. It should be brief but sufficient to explain and identify the transaction. A transaction can have more than one debit or credit entry; this is called a **compound entry**. In a compound entry, all debit accounts involved are listed before any credit accounts. (The January 6 transaction of Joan Miller Advertising Agency is an example of a compound entry; see Exhibit 2-3.)

3. Write the debit amounts in the appropriate column opposite the accounts to be debited, and write the credit amounts in the appropriate column opposite the accounts to be credited.
4. At the time the transactions are recorded, nothing is placed in the Post. Ref. (posting reference) column. (This column is sometimes called *LP* or *Folio*.) Later, if the company uses account numbers to identify accounts in the ledger, fill in the account numbers to provide a convenient cross-reference from the general journal to the ledger and to indicate that the entry has been posted to the ledger. If the accounts are not numbered, use a checkmark (✓).
5. It is customary to skip a line after each journal entry.

The General Ledger

OBJECTIVE 7
Post transactions from the journal to the ledger

The general journal is used to record the details of each transaction. The **general ledger** is used to update each account.

The Ledger Account Form. The T account is a simple, direct means of recording transactions. In practice, a somewhat more complicated form of the account is needed to record more information. The **ledger account form**, with four columns for dollar amounts, is illustrated in Exhibit 2-4.

The account title and number appear at the top of the account form. The date of the transaction appears in the first two columns as it does in the journal. The Item column is used only rarely to identify transactions because explanations already appear in the journal. The Post. Ref. column is used to note the journal page where the original entry for the transaction can be found. The dollar amount of the entry is entered in the appropriate Debit or Credit column, and a new account balance is computed in the final two columns after each entry. The advantage of this form of account over the T account is that the current balance of the account is readily available.

Posting to the Ledger. After the transactions have been entered in the journal, they must be transferred to the general ledger. The process of transferring

Exhibit 2-4. Accounts Payable in the General Ledger

General Ledger

Accounts Payable — **Account No.** *212*

Date		Item	Post. Ref.	Debit	Credit	Balance	
						Debit	Credit
19xx							
Jan.	5		J1		1,500		1,500
	6		J1		2,600		4,100
	9		J1	1,000			3,100
	30		J2		70		3,170

journal entry information from the journal to the ledger is called **posting**. Posting usually is done after several entries have been made—for example, at the end of each day or less frequently, depending on the number of transactions.

Through posting, each amount in the Debit column of the journal is transferred into the Debit column of the appropriate account in the ledger, and each amount in the Credit column of the journal is transferred into the Credit column of the appropriate account in the ledger (Exhibit 2-5). These are the steps in the posting process:

1. In the ledger, locate the debit account named in the journal entry.
2. Enter the date of the transaction and, in the Post. Ref. column of the ledger, the journal page number from which the entry comes.
3. Enter in the Debit column of the ledger account the amount of the debit as it appears in the journal.
4. Calculate the account balance and enter it in the appropriate balance column.

Exhibit 2-5. Posting from the General Journal to the Ledger

General Journal — (2) Page 2

Date		Description	Post. Ref.	Debit	Credit
19xx	(2)	(1)	(5)	(3)	
Jan.	30	Telephone Expense	513	70	
		Accounts Payable	212		70
		Received bill for telephone expense			

General Ledger

Accounts Payable — Account No. 212

Date		Item	Post. Ref.	Debit	Credit	Balance Debit	Balance Credit
19xx							
Jan.	5		J1		1,500		1,500
	6		J1		2,600		4,100
	9		J1	1,000			3,100
	30		J2		70		3,170

General Ledger

Telephone Expense — Account No. 513

Date		Item	Post. Ref.	Debit	Credit	Balance Debit	Balance Credit
19xx						(4)	
Jan.	30		J2	70		70	

5. Enter in the Post. Ref. column of the journal the account number to which the amount has been posted.
6. Repeat these five steps for the credit side of the journal entry.

Notice that step **5** is the last step in the posting process for each debit and credit. In addition to serving as an easy reference between the journal entry and the ledger account, this entry in the Post. Ref. column of the journal indicates that all of the steps for the item have been completed. This allows accountants who have been called away from their work to easily find where they were before the interruption.

In a computerized accounting system, posting is done automatically by the computer after the transactions have been entered. The computer also carries out the next step in the accounting cycle, preparing a trial balance.

The Trial Balance

OBJECTIVE 8
Prepare a trial balance, and describe its value and limitations

For every amount debited in the ledger, an equal amount must be credited. This means that the total of debits and credits in the ledger must be equal. To test this, the accountant periodically prepares a **trial balance**. Exhibit 2-6 shows a trial balance for the Joan Miller Advertising Agency. It was prepared from the accounts in Exhibit 2-2, on page 62.

The trial balance may be prepared at any time but is usually prepared on the last day of the month. Here are the steps in preparing a trial balance:

1. List each ledger account that has a balance, with debit balances in the left column and credit balances in the right column. Accounts are listed in the order in which they appear in the ledger.
2. Add each column.
3. Compare the totals of each column.

In carrying out steps **1** and **2**, remember that the account form in the ledger has two balance columns, one for debit balances and one for credit balances. In accounts in which increases are recorded by debits, then, the **normal balance** (the usual balance) is a debit balance; where increases are recorded by credits, the normal balance is a credit balance. The following table summarizes the normal account balances of the major account categories. According to the table, the ledger account Accounts Payable (a liability) typically has a credit balance and is copied into the trial balance as a credit balance.

	Increases Recorded by		Normal Balance	
Account Category	**Debit**	**Credit**	**Debit**	**Credit**
Asset	x		x	
Liability		x		x
Owner's Equity:				
Capital		x		x
Withdrawals	x		x	
Revenues		x		x
Expenses	x		x	

Exhibit 2-6. Trial Balance

Joan Miller Advertising Agency Trial Balance January 31, 19xx		
Cash	$ 1,720	
Accounts Receivable	2,800	
Art Supplies	1,800	
Office Supplies	800	
Prepaid Rent	800	
Prepaid Insurance	480	
Art Equipment	4,200	
Office Equipment	3,000	
Accounts Payable		$ 3,170
Unearned Art Fees		1,000
Joan Miller, Capital		10,000
Joan Miller, Withdrawals	1,400	
Advertising Fees Earned		4,200
Office Wages Expense	1,200	
Utility Expense	100	
Telephone Expense	70	
	$18,370	$18,370

Once in a while, a transaction leaves an account with a balance that is not "normal." For example, when a company overdraws its account at the bank, its Cash account (an asset) is going to show a credit balance instead of a debit balance. The "abnormal" balance should be copied into the trial balance columns as it stands, as a debit or credit.

The trial balance proves whether or not the ledger is in balance. *In balance* means that equal debits and credits have been recorded for all transactions so that total debits equal total credits. But the trial balance does not prove that the transactions were analyzed correctly or recorded in the proper accounts. For example, there is no way of determining from the trial balance that a debit should have been made in the Art Equipment account rather than the Office Equipment account. And the trial balance does not detect whether transactions have been omitted because equal debits and credits will have been omitted. Also, if an error of the same amount is made in both a debit and a credit, it will not be discovered by the trial balance. The trial balance proves only that the debits and credits in the accounts are in balance.

If the debit and credit columns of the trial balance do not equal each other, look for one or more of the following errors: (1) A debit was entered in an account as a credit, or vice versa; (2) the balance of an account was computed incorrectly; (3) an error was made in carrying the account balance to the trial balance; or (4) the trial balance was summed incorrectly.

Other than simply adding the columns wrong, the two most common mistakes in preparing a trial balance are (1) recording an account with a debit balance as a credit, or vice versa, and (2) transposing two numbers in an amount when transferring it to the trial balance (for example, entering $23,459 as $23,549). The first of these mistakes causes the trial balance to be out of balance by an amount divisible by 2. The second causes the trial balance to be out of balance by a number divisible by 9. Thus, if a trial balance is out of balance and the addition has been verified, determine the amount by which the trial balance is out of balance and divide it first by 2 and then by 9. If the amount is divisible by 2, look in the trial balance for an amount equal to the quotient. If you find the amount, it is probably in the wrong column. If the amount is divisible by 9, trace each amount to the ledger account balance, checking carefully for a transposition error. If neither of these techniques identifies the error, first recompute the balance of each account in the ledger, and, then, if the error still has not been found, retrace each posting from the journal to the ledger.

Some Notes on Presentation

Ruled lines appear in financial reports before each subtotal or total to indicate that the amounts above are added or subtracted. It is common practice to use a double line under a final total to show that it has been checked, or verified.

Dollars signs ($) are required in all financial statements, including the balance sheet and income statement, and in the trial balance and other schedules. On these statements, a dollar sign should be placed before the first amount in each column and before the first amount in a column following a ruled line. Dollar signs in the same column are aligned. Dollar signs are not used in journals and ledgers.

On unruled paper, commas and decimal points are used in dollar amounts. On paper with ruled columns—like the paper in journals and ledgers—commas and periods are not needed. In this book, because most problems and illustrations are in whole dollar amounts, the cents column usually is omitted. When accountants deal with whole dollars, they often use a dash in the cents column to indicate whole dollars rather than take the time to write zeros.

Chapter Review

Review of Learning Objectives

1. **Explain, in simple terms, the generally accepted ways of solving the measurement issues of recognition, valuation, and classification.**
   To measure a business transaction, the accountant must determine when the transaction occurred (the recognition issue), what value should be placed on the transaction (the valuation issue), and how the components of the transaction should be categorized (the classification issue). In general, recognition occurs when title passes, and a transaction is valued at the exchange price, the cost at the time the transaction is recognized. Classification refers to the categorizing of transactions according to a system of accounts.
2. **Define and use the terms *account* and *general ledger*.**
   An account is a device for storing data from transactions. There is one account for each asset, liability, and component of owner's equity, including revenues and expenses. The general ledger is a book or file consisting of all of a company's accounts arranged according to a chart of accounts.
3. **Recognize commonly used asset, liability, and owner's equity accounts.**
   Commonly used asset accounts are Cash, Notes Receivable, Accounts Receivable, Prepaid Expenses, Land, Buildings, and Equipment. Common liability accounts are Notes Payable, Accounts Payable, Wages Payable, and Mortgages Payable. Common owner's equity accounts are Capital, Withdrawals, and revenue and expense accounts.

4. **Define *double-entry system,* and state the rules for debits and credits.**
   In the double-entry system, each transaction must be recorded with at least one debit and one credit so that the total dollar amount of the debits equals the total dollar amount of the credits. The rules for debit and credit are (1) increases in assets are debited to asset accounts; decreases in assets are credited to asset accounts; and (2) increases in liabilities and owner's equity are credited to those accounts; decreases in liabilities and owner's equity are debited to those accounts.
5. **Apply the procedure for transaction analysis to simple transactions.**
   The procedure for analyzing transactions is (1) analyze the effect of the transaction on assets, liabilities, and owner's equity; (2) apply the appropriate double-entry rule; and (3) make the entry.
6. **Record transactions in the general journal.**
   The general journal is a chronological record of all transactions. That record contains the date of each transaction, the names of the accounts and the dollar amounts debited and credited, an explanation of each entry, and the account numbers to which postings have been made.
7. **Post transactions from the journal to the ledger.**
   After transactions have been entered in the general journal, they are posted to the general ledger. Posting is done by transferring each amount in the Debit column of the general journal to the Debit column of the appropriate account in the general ledger, and transferring each amount in the Credit column of the general journal to the Credit column of the appropriate account in the general ledger. After each entry is posted, a new balance is entered in the appropriate Balance column.
8. **Prepare a trial balance, and describe its value and limitations.**
   A trial balance is used to check that the debit and credit balances in the ledger are equal. It is prepared by listing each account with its balance in the Debit or Credit column. Then, the two columns are added and compared to test their balances. The major limitation of the trial balance is that even if debit and credit balances are equal, this does not necessarily mean that the transactions were analyzed correctly or recorded in the proper accounts.

Review of Concepts and Terminology

The following concepts and terms were introduced in this chapter:

(L.O. 2) **Account:** The basic storage unit of accounting data. There is a separate account for each asset, liability, and component of owner's equity, including revenues and expenses.

(L.O. 4) **Balance:** The difference in total dollars between the total debit footing and the total credit footing of an account. Also called *account balance.*

(L.O. 2) **Chart of accounts:** A scheme that assigns a unique number to each account to facilitate finding the account in the ledger; also, the list of account numbers and titles.

(L.O. 1) **Classification:** The process of assigning transactions to the appropriate accounts.

(L.O. 6) **Compound entry:** A journal entry that has more than one debit or credit entry.

(L.O. 1) **Cost:** The exchange price associated with a business transaction at the point of recognition.

(L.O. 1) **Cost principle:** The practice of recording transactions at cost and maintaining this cost in the records until an asset, liability, or component of owner's equity is sold, expires, is consumed, is satisfied, or otherwise is disposed of.

(L.O. 4) **Credit:** The right side of an account.

(L.O. 4) **Debit:** The left side of an account.

(L.O. 4) **Double-entry system:** The accounting system in which each transaction is recorded with at least one debit and one credit so that the total dollar amount of debits and the total dollar amount of credits equal each other.

(L.O. 4) **Footings:** Working totals of columns of numbers. To *foot* means to total a column of numbers.

(L.O. 6) **General journal:** The simplest and most flexible type of journal.

(L.O. 2, 7) **General ledger:** The book or file that contains all or groups of the company's accounts, arranged in the order of the chart of accounts. Also called *ledger.*

(L.O. 6) **Journal:** A chronological record of all transactions; the place where transactions are first recorded.

(L.O. 6) **Journal entry:** The notations in the journal that are used to record a single transaction.

(L.O. 6) **Journalizing:** The process of recording transactions in a journal.

(L.O. 7) **Ledger account form:** The form of account that has four columns, one for debit entries, one for credit entries, and two columns (debit and credit) for showing the balance of the account.

(L.O. 8) **Normal balance:** The usual balance of an account; also the side (debit or credit) that increases the account.

(L.O. 7) **Posting:** The process of transferring journal entry information from the journal to the ledger.

(L.O. 1) **Recognition:** The determination of when a business transaction should be recorded.

(L.O. 1) **Recognition point:** The predetermined time at which a transaction should be recorded; usually, the point at which title passes to the buyer.

(L.O. 4) **T account:** The simplest form of an account; used to analyze transactions.

(L.O. 8) **Trial balance:** A comparison of the total of debit and credit balances in the ledger, to check that they are equal.

(L.O. 1) **Valuation:** The process of assigning a value to all business transactions.

Self-Test

Test your knowledge of the chapter by choosing the best answer for each of the following items.

(L.O. 1) 1. Deciding whether to record a sale when the order for services is received or when the services are performed is an example of a
   a. recognition issue.
   b. valuation issue.
   c. classification issue.
   d. communication issue.

(L.O. 2) 2. Which of the following statements is true?
   a. The chart of accounts usually is presented in alphabetical order.
   b. The general ledger contains all the accounts found in the chart of accounts.
   c. The general journal contains a list of the chart of accounts.
   d. Most companies use the same chart of accounts.

(L.O. 3) 3. Which of the following is a liability account?
   a. Accounts Receivable
   b. Withdrawals
   c. Rent Expense
   d. Accounts Payable

(L.O. 4) 4. The left side of an account is referred to as
   a. the balance.
   b. a debit.
   c. a credit.
   d. a footing.

(L.O. 4) 5. Although debits increase assets, they also
   a. decrease assets.
   b. increase owner's equity.
   c. increase expenses.
   d. increase liabilities.

(L.O. 5) 6. Payment for a two-year insurance policy is a debit to
   a. Prepaid Insurance.
   b. Insurance Expense.
   c. Cash.
   d. Accounts Payable.

(L.O. 5) 7. An agreement to spend $100 a month on advertising beginning next month requires
   a. a debit to Advertising Expense.
   b. a debit to Prepaid Advertising.
   c. no entry.
   d. a credit to Cash.

(L.O. 6) 8. Transactions initially are recorded in the
a. trial balance.
b. T account.
c. journal.
d. ledger.

(L.O. 7) 9. In posting from the general journal to the general ledger, the page number on which the transaction is recorded appears in the
a. Post. Ref. column of the general ledger.
b. Item column of the general ledger.
c. Post. Ref. column of the general journal.
d. Description column of the general journal.

(L.O. 8) 10. To test that the total of debits and the total of credits are equal, the accountant periodically prepares a
a. trial balance.
b. T account.
c. general journal.
d. ledger.

Answers to the Self-Test are at the end of this chapter.

Review Problem
Transaction Analysis, General Journal, Ledger Accounts, and Trial Balance

(L.O. 5, 6, 7, 8) After graduation from veterinary school, Laura Cox entered private practice. The transactions of the business through May 27 are as follows:

19xx
May 1 Laura Cox deposited $2,000 in her business bank account.
3 Paid $300 for two months' rent in advance for an office.
9 Purchased medical supplies for $200 in cash.
12 Purchased $400 of equipment on credit, making a 25 percent down payment.
15 Delivered a calf for a fee of $35.
18 Made a partial payment of $50 on the equipment purchased May 12.
27 Paid a utility bill of $40.

Required

1. Record these entries in the general journal.
2. Post the entries from the journal to the following accounts in the ledger: Cash (111); Medical Supplies (115); Prepaid Rent (116); Equipment (141); Accounts Payable (211); Laura Cox, Capital (311); Veterinary Fees Earned (411); and Utility Expense (511).
3. Prepare a trial balance.

Answer to Review Problem

1. Record the journal entries.

General Journal **Page 1**

Date		Description	Post. Ref.	Debit	Credit
19xx					
May	1	Cash	111	2,000	
		Laura Cox, Capital	311		2,000
		Deposited $2,000 in the business bank account			

(continued)

General Journal					Page 1
Date		Description	Post. Ref.	Debit	Credit
	3	Prepaid Rent	116	300	
		Cash	111		300
		Paid two months' rent in advance for an office			
	9	Medical Supplies	115	200	
		Cash	111		200
		Purchased medical supplies for cash			
	12	Equipment	141	400	
		Accounts Payable	211		300
		Cash	111		100
		Purchased equipment on credit, paying 25 percent down			
	15	Cash	111	35	
		Veterinary Fees Earned	411		35
		Collected fee for delivery of a calf			
	18	Accounts Payable	211	50	
		Cash	111		50
		Partial payment for equipment purchased May 12			
	27	Utility Expense	511	40	
		Cash	111		40
		Paid utility bill			

2. Post the transactions to the ledger accounts.

General Ledger

Cash — Account No. 111

Date		Item	Post. Ref.	Debit	Credit	Balance Debit	Balance Credit
19xx							
May	1		J1	2,000		2,000	
	3		J1		300	1,700	
	9		J1		200	1,500	
	12		J1		100	1,400	
	15		J1	35		1,435	
	18		J1		50	1,385	
	27		J1		40	1,345	

(continued)

Medical Supplies — Account No. *115*

Date		Item	Post. Ref.	Debit	Credit	Balance Debit	Balance Credit
19xx May	9		J1	200		200	

Prepaid Rent — Account No. *116*

Date		Item	Post. Ref.	Debit	Credit	Balance Debit	Balance Credit
19xx May	3		J1	300		300	

Equipment — Account No. *141*

Date		Item	Post. Ref.	Debit	Credit	Balance Debit	Balance Credit
19xx May	12		J1	400		400	

Accounts Payable — Account No. *211*

Date		Item	Post. Ref.	Debit	Credit	Balance Debit	Balance Credit
19xx May	12		J1		300		300
	18		J1	50			250

Laura Cox, Capital — Account No. *311*

Date		Item	Post. Ref.	Debit	Credit	Balance Debit	Balance Credit
19xx May	1		J1		2,000		2,000

Veterinary Fees Earned — Account No. *411*

Date		Item	Post. Ref.	Debit	Credit	Balance Debit	Balance Credit
19xx May	15		J1		35		35

Utility Expense — Account No. *511*

Date		Item	Post. Ref.	Debit	Credit	Balance Debit	Balance Credit
19xx May	27		J1	40		40	

3. Prepare a trial balance.

Laura Cox, Veterinarian Trial Balance May 31, 19xx		
Cash	$1,345	
Medical Supplies	200	
Prepaid Rent	300	
Equipment	400	
Accounts Payable		$ 250
Laura Cox, Capital		2,000
Veterinary Fees Earned		35
Utility Expense	40	
	$2,285	$2,285

Chapter Assignments

Questions

1. What three issues underlie most accounting measurement decisions?
2. Why is recognition an issue for accountants?
3. A customer asks the owner of a store to save an item for him and says that he will pick it up and pay for it next week. The owner agrees to hold it. Should this event be recorded as a sale? Explain your answer.
4. Why is it practical for accountants to rely on original cost for valuation purposes?
5. Under the cost principle, changes in value after a transaction is recorded are not usually recognized in the accounts. Comment on this possible limitation of using original cost in accounting measurements.
6. What is an account, and how is it related to the ledger?
7. In the preparation of owner's equity accounts, how are owner's investments and withdrawals treated? Explain your answer.
8. Tell whether each of the following accounts is an asset account, a liability account, or an owner's equity account:
   a. Notes Receivable
   b. Land
   c. Withdrawals
   d. Bonds Payable
   e. Prepaid Rent
   f. Insurance Expense
   g. Service Revenue
9. Why is the system of recording entries called the double-entry system? What is so special about this system?
10. "Double-entry accounting refers to entering a transaction in both the journal and the ledger." Comment on this statement.
11. "Debits are bad; credits are good." Comment on this statement.
12. What are the rules of debits and credits for (a) assets, (b) liabilities, and (c) owner's equity?
13. Why are the rules of debits and credits the same for liabilities and owner's equity?
14. Explain why debits, which decrease owner's equity, also increase expenses, which are a component of owner's equity.
15. What is the meaning of the statement, "The Cash account has a debit balance of $500"?
16. What are the three steps in transaction analysis?

17. In recording entries in a journal, which is written first, the debit or the credit? How is indentation used in the general journal?
18. What is the relationship between the journal and the ledger?
19. Describe each of the following:

a. Account	d. Book of original entry	g. Posting
b. Journal	e. Post. Ref. column	h. Footings
c. Ledger	f. Journalizing	i. Compound entry

20. Is it a good idea to forgo the journal and enter a transaction directly into the ledger? Explain your answer.
21. What does a trial balance prove?
22. Can errors be present even though a trial balance balances? Explain your answer.
23. What is the normal balance of Accounts Payable? Under what conditions could Accounts Payable have a debit balance?
24. List the following six items in sequence to illustrate the flow of events through the accounting system:
    a. Analysis of the transaction
    b. Debits and credits posted from the journal to the ledger
    c. Occurrence of the business transaction
    d. Preparation of the financial statements
    e. Entry made in the journal
    f. Preparation of the trial balance

Communication Skills Exercises

Communication 2-1. Valuation Issue
(L.O. 1)

The Foxboro Company manufactures and markets a comprehensive family of products for automating the industrial process. In one of the company's recent annual reports, under Summary of Significant Accounting Policies, the following statement was made: "Property, plant and equipment was stated at cost."[2] Given the fact that the property, plant, and equipment undoubtedly were purchased over several years and that the current value of those assets was likely to be very different from their original cost, what authoritative basis is there for carrying the assets at cost? Does accounting generally recognize changes in value subsequent to the purchase of property, plant, and equipment?

Communication 2-2. Recognition Point and Ethical Considerations
(L.O. 1)

One of ***Penn Office Supplies Corporation***'s sales representatives, Jerry Hasbrow, is compensated on a commission basis and receives a substantial bonus for meeting his annual sales goal. The company's recognition point for sales is the day of shipment. On December 31, Jerry realizes that he needs sales of $2,000 to reach his sales goal and receive the bonus. He calls a purchaser for a local insurance company, whom he knows well, and asks him to buy $2,000 worth of copier paper today. The purchaser says, "But Jerry, that's more than a year's supply for us." Jerry says, "Buy it today. If you decide it's too much, you can return however much you want for full credit next month." The purchaser says, "Okay, ship it." The paper is shipped on December 31 and recorded as a sale. On January 15, the purchaser returns $1,750 worth of paper for full credit (okayed by Jerry) against the bill. Should the shipment on December 31 be recorded as a sale? Discuss the ethics of Jerry's action.

Communication 2-3. Basic Research Skills
(L.O. 5, 6)

Obtain a recent issue of one of the following business journals: *Barrons, Business Week, Forbes, Fortune,* or the *Wall Street Journal.* Find an article on a company you recognize or on a company in a business that interests you. Read the article carefully, noting any references to transactions that the company engages in. These may be normal transactions (sales, purchases) or unusual transactions (a merger, the purchase of another company). Bring a copy of the article to class and be prepared to describe how you would analyze and record the transactions you have noted.

2. Excerpt from the 1989 annual report of The Foxboro Company.

Classroom Exercises

Exercise 2-1. Recognition
(L.O. 1)

Which of the following events would be recognized and recorded in the accounting records of the Sabatini Company on the date indicated?

Feb. 17 Sabatini Company offers to purchase a tract of land for $280,000. There is a high likelihood the offer will be accepted.
Mar. 7 Sabatini Company receives notice that its rent will be increased from $1,000 per month to $1,200 per month effective April 1.
Apr. 28 Sabatini Company receives its utility bill for the month of April. The bill is not due until May 10.
May 19 Sabatini Company places a firm order for new office equipment costing $42,000.
June 27 The office equipment ordered on May 19 arrives. Payment is not due until September 1.

Exercise 2-2. Application of Recognition Point
(L.O. 1)

Infelice's Body Shop uses a large amount of supplies in its business. The following table summarizes selected transaction data for orders of supplies purchased:

Order	Date Shipped	Date Received	Amount
a	April 28	May 7	$300
b	May 8	13	750
c	10	16	400
d	15	21	600
e	25	June 1	750
f	June 3	9	500

Determine the total purchases of supplies for May alone under each of the following assumptions:

1. Infelice's Body Shop recognizes purchases when orders are shipped.
2. Infelice's Body Shop recognizes purchases when orders are received.

Exercise 2-3. Classification of Accounts
(L.O. 3, 8)

Listed below are the ledger accounts of the Kedzie Service Company:

a. Cash
b. Accounts Receivable
c. Sandra Kedzie, Capital
d. Sandra Kedzie, Withdrawals
e. Service Revenue
f. Prepaid Rent
g. Accounts Payable
h. Investments in Stocks and Bonds
i. Bonds Payable
j. Land
k. Supplies Expense
l. Prepaid Insurance
m. Utility Expense
n. Fees Earned
o. Unearned Revenue
p. Office Equipment
q. Rent Payable
r. Notes Receivable
s. Interest Expense
t. Notes Payable
u. Supplies
v. Interest Receivable

Complete the following table, indicating with two Xs for each account its classification and its normal balance (whether a debit or credit increases the account):

	Type of Account						Normal Balance (increases balance)	
			Owner's Equity					
Item	Asset	Liability	Owner's Capital	Owner's Withdrawals	Revenue	Expense	Debit	Credit
a.	x						x	

Exercise 2-4.
Transaction Analysis
(L.O. 5)

Analyze each of the following transactions, using the form shown in the example below the list.

a. Benny James established Benny's Barber Shop by placing $2,400 in a bank account.
b. Paid two months' rent in advance, $840.
c. Purchased supplies on credit, $120.
d. Received cash for barbering services, $100.
e. Paid for supplies purchased in **c**.
f. Paid utility bill, $72.
g. Took cash out of the business for personal expenses, $100.

Example

a. The asset Cash was increased. Increases in assets are recorded by debits. Debit Cash $2,400. A component of owner's equity, Benny James, Capital, was increased. Increases in owner's equity are recorded by credits. Credit Benny James, Capital $2,400.

Exercise 2-5.
Recording Transactions in T Accounts
(L.O. 5)

Open the following T accounts: Cash; Repair Supplies; Repair Equipment; Accounts Payable; Michelle Donato, Capital; Michelle Donato, Withdrawals; Repair Fees Earned; Salaries Expense; and Rent Expense. Record the following transactions for the month of June directly in the T accounts; use the letters to identify the transactions in your T accounts. Determine the balance in each account.

a. Michelle Donato opened the Eastmoor Repair Service by investing $4,300 in cash and $1,600 in repair equipment.
b. Paid $400 for current month's rent.
c. Purchased repair supplies on credit, $500.
d. Purchased additional repair equipment for cash, $300.
e. Paid salary to a helper, $450.
f. Paid $200 of amount purchased on credit in **c**.
g. Withdrew $600 from business for living expenses.
h. Accepted cash for repairs completed, $860.

Exercise 2-6.
Trial Balance
(L.O. 8)

After recording the transactions in Exercise 2-5, prepare a trial balance in proper sequence for Eastmoor Repair Service, June 30, 19xx.

Exercise 2-7.
Analysis of Transactions
(L.O. 5)

Explain each transaction (a through h) entered below.

Cash

	Debit		Credit
a.	60,000	b.	15,000
g.	1,500	e.	3,000
h.	900	f.	4,500

Accounts Receivable

	Debit		Credit
c.	6,000	g.	1,500

Equipment

	Debit		Credit
b.	15,000	h.	900
d.	9,000		

Accounts Payable

	Debit		Credit
f.	4,500	d.	9,000

Seymour, Capital

	Debit		Credit
		a.	60,000

Service Revenue

	Debit		Credit
		c.	6,000

Wages Expense

	Debit		Credit
e.	3,000		

Exercise 2-8.
Analysis of Transactions
(L.O. 5)

Dover Cleanup Company provided monthly waste removal services for Permamove Company, which resulted in the following transactions in Dover's records:

Cash

Debit		Credit	
Sept. 27	1,000		

Accounts Receivable

Debit		Credit	
Aug. 31	1,500	Sept. 27	1,000

Waste Removal Service Revenue

Debit		Credit	
		Aug. 31	1,500

Using T accounts, prepare the corresponding entries in Permamove's records.

Exercise 2-9.
Analysis of Unfamiliar Transactions
(L.O. 5)

Managers and accountants often encounter transactions with which they are unfamiliar. Use your analytical skills to analyze and record in general journal form the transactions below, which have not yet been discussed in the text.

a. Purchased merchandise inventory on account, $1,600.
b. Purchased marketable securities for cash, $4,800.
c. Returned part of merchandise inventory purchased in **a** for full credit, $500.
d. Sold merchandise inventory on account, $1,600 (record sale only).
e. Purchased land and a building for $600,000. Payment is $120,000 cash and a thirty-year mortgage for the remainder. The purchase price is allocated $200,000 to the land and $400,000 to the building.
f. Received an order for $24,000 in services to be provided. With the order was a deposit of $8,000.

Exercise 2-10.
Recording Transactions in the General Journal and Posting to the Ledger Accounts
(L.O. 6, 7)

Open a general journal form like the one in Exhibit 2-3, and label it Page 10. After completing the form, record the following transactions in the journal.

Dec. 14 Purchased an item of equipment for $6,000, paying $2,000 as a cash down payment.
28 Paid $3,000 of the amount owed on the equipment.

Prepare three ledger account forms like those shown in Exhibit 2-4. Use the following account numbers: Cash, 111; Equipment, 143; and Accounts Payable, 212. Then post the two transactions from the general journal to the ledger accounts, at the same time making proper posting references.

Assume that the Cash account has a debit balance of $8,000 on the day prior to these transactions.

Exercise 2-11.
Preparation of a Ledger Account
(L.O. 7)

Below is a T account showing cash transactions for the month of July.

Cash

Debit		Credit	
July 1	18,800	July 3	1,800
9	2,400	7	400
16	8,000	13	3,400
23	400	15	10,000
29	12,800	27	1,200

Prepare the account in ledger form for Cash (Account 111). (See Exhibit 2-4 for an example.)

Exercise 2-12.
Preparing a Trial Balance
(L.O. 8)

The following accounts of the Barnes Service Company as of October 31, 19xx, are listed in alphabetical order. The amount of Accounts Payable is omitted.

Accounts Payable	?	Equipment	$24,000
Accounts Receivable	$ 6,000	Land	10,400
Alvin Barnes, Capital	62,900	Notes Payable	40,000
Building	68,000	Prepaid Insurance	2,200
Cash	18,000		

Prepare a trial balance with the proper heading (see Exhibit 2-6) and with the accounts listed in the chart of accounts sequence (see Exhibit 2-1). Compute the balance of Accounts Payable.

Exercise 2-13.
Effect of Errors on Trial Balance
(L.O. 8)

Which of the following errors would cause a trial balance to have unequal totals? Explain your answers.

a. A payment to a creditor was recorded as a debit to Accounts Payable for $172 and a credit to Cash for $127.
b. A payment of $200 to a creditor for an account payable was debited to Accounts Receivable and credited to Cash.
c. A purchase of office supplies of $560 was recorded as a debit to Office Supplies for $56 and a credit to Cash for $56.
d. A purchase of equipment for $600 was recorded as a debit to Supplies for $600 and a credit to Cash for $600.

Exercise 2-14.
Correcting Errors in a Trial Balance
(L.O. 8)

This was the trial balance for Gilliam Services at the end of September:

Gilliam Services
Trial Balance
September 30, 19xx

Cash	$ 3,840	
Accounts Receivable	5,660	
Supplies	120	
Prepaid Insurance	180	
Equipment	8,400	
Accounts Payable		$ 4,540
R. Gilliam, Capital		11,560
R. Gilliam, Withdrawals		700
Revenues		5,920
Salaries Expense	2,600	
Rent Expense	600	
Advertising Expense	340	
Utility Expense	26	
	$21,766	$22,720

The trial balance does not balance because of a number of errors. Gilliam's accountant compared the amounts in the trial balance with the ledger, recomputed the account balances, and compared the postings. He found the following errors:

a. The balance of Cash was understated by $400.
b. A cash payment of $420 was credited to Cash for $240.
c. A debit of $120 to Accounts Receivable was not posted.
d. Supplies purchased for $60 were posted as a credit to Supplies.
e. A debit of $180 to Prepaid Insurance was not posted.

f. The Accounts Payable account had debits of $5,320 and credits of $9,180.
g. The Notes Payable account, with a credit balance of $2,400, was not included in the trial balance.
h. The debit balance of R. Gilliam, Withdrawals was listed in the trial balance as a credit.
i. A $200 debit to R. Gilliam, Withdrawals was posted as a credit.
j. The actual balance of Utility Expense, $260, was listed as $26 in the trial balance.

Prepare a correct trial balance.

Exercise 2-15. Preparing a Trial Balance *(L.O. 8)*

The Ferraro Construction Company builds foundations for buildings and parking lots. The following alphabetical list shows the account balances as of November 30, 19xx.

Accounts Payable	$ 11,700	Notes Payable	$60,000
Accounts Receivable	30,360	Office Trailer	6,600
Cash	?	Prepaid Insurance	13,800
Construction Supplies	5,700	Revenue Earned	52,200
Equipment	73,500	Supplies Expense	21,600
Fred Ferraro, Capital	120,000	Utility Expense	1,260
Fred Ferraro, Withdrawals	23,400	Wages Expense	26,400

Prepare a trial balance for the company with the proper heading and with the accounts in chart of accounts sequence. Determine the correct balance for the Cash account on November 30, 19xx.

Interpretation Case from Business

First Chicago Corporation *(L.O. 3, 5)*

First Chicago Corporation is the largest bank holding company in Illinois. Selected accounts from the company's 1990 annual report are as follows (in millions):

Cash and Due from Banks	$ 3,571
Loans to Customers	27,706
Investment Securities	1,810
Deposits by Customers	32,543

Required

1. Indicate whether each of the accounts listed above is an asset, a liability, or a component of owner's equity on First Chicago's balance sheet.
2. Assume that you are in a position to do business with First Chicago. Prepare the general journal entry (in First Chicago's records) to record each of the following transactions:

   a. You sell securities in the amount of $2,000 to the bank.
   b. You deposit the $2,000 received in step **a** in the bank.
   c. You borrow $5,000 from the bank.

Problem Set A

Problem 2A-1. Transaction Analysis, T Accounts, and Trial Balance *(L.O. 5, 8)*

Elena Garcia established a small business, Garcia Training Center, to teach individuals how to use spreadsheet analysis, word processing, and other techniques on microcomputers.

a. Garcia began by transferring the following assets to the business:

Cash	$18,400
Furniture	6,200
Microcomputers	14,600

b. Paid the first month's rent on a small storefront, $560.
c. Purchased computer software on credit, $1,500.

d. Paid for an advertisement in the local newspaper, $200.
e. Received enrollment applications from five students for a five-day course to start next week. Each student will pay $400 if he or she actually begins the course.
f. Paid wages to a part-time helper, $300.
g. Received cash payments from three of the students enrolled in **e**, $1,200.
h. Billed the two other students in **e**, who attended but did not pay in cash, $800.
i. Paid the utility bill for the current month, $220.
j. Made a payment on the software purchased in **c**, $500.
k. Received payment from one student billed in **h**, $400.
l. Purchased a second microcomputer for cash, $9,400.
m. Transferred cash to a personal checking account, $600.

Required

1. Set up the following T accounts: Cash; Accounts Receivable; Software; Furniture; Microcomputers; Accounts Payable; Elena Garcia, Capital; Elena Garcia, Withdrawals; Tuition Revenue; Wages Expense; Utility Expense; Rent Expense; and Advertising Expense.
2. Record the transactions listed above by entering debits and credits directly in the T accounts, using the transaction letter to identify each debit and credit.
3. Prepare a trial balance using the current date.

Problem 2A-2. Transaction Analysis, T Accounts, General Journal, and Trial Balance *(L.O. 5, 6, 8)*

Bob Reeves won a concession to rent bicycles in the local park during the summer. In the month of May, Reeves completed the following transactions for his bicycle rental business:

May 3 Began business by placing $14,400 in a business checking account.
4 Purchased ten bicycles for $5,000, paying $2,400 down and agreeing to pay the rest in thirty days.
5 Purchased a small shed to hold the bicycles and to use for other operations for $5,800 in cash.
6 Paid $800 in cash for shipping and installation costs (considered an addition to the cost of the shed) to place the shed at the park entrance.
7 Purchased supplies on account for $300.
8 Received $940 in cash for rentals during the first week of operation.
14 Received $1,000 in cash for rentals during the second week of operation.
15 Hired a part-time assistant to help out on weekends at $8 per hour.
16 Paid a maintenance person $150 to clean the grounds.
18 Paid the assistant $160 for a weekend's work.
19 Paid $300 for the supplies purchased on May 7.
20 Paid a $110 repair bill on bicycles.
21 Received $1,100 in cash for rentals during the third week of operation.
23 Paid the assistant $160 for a weekend's work.
24 Billed a company $220 for bicycle rentals for an employees' outing.
26 Paid the $200 fee for May to the Park District for the right to the bicycle concession.
28 Received $820 in cash for rentals during the week.
30 Paid the assistant $160 for a weekend's work.
31 Transferred $1,000 to a personal checking account.

Required

1. Prepare journal entries to record these transactions in the general journal.
2. Set up the following T accounts and post all the journal entries: Cash; Accounts Receivable; Supplies; Shed; Bicycles; Accounts Payable; Bob Reeves, Capital; Bob Reeves, Withdrawals; Rental Revenue; Wages Expense; Maintenance Expense; Repair Expense; and Concession Fee Expense.
3. Prepare a trial balance for Reeves Rentals as of May 31, 19xx.
4. Compare how recognition applies to the transactions of May 24 and 28 and how classification applies to the transactions of May 7 and 16.

Problem 2A-3. Transaction Analysis, General Journal, Ledger Accounts, and Trial Balance
(L.O. 5, 6, 7, 8)

Cindy Liang opened a photography and portrait studio on July 1. The studio completed the following transactions during the month:

July 1 Opened the business checking account, $51,000.
3 Paid two months' rent in advance for a studio, $2,700.
5 Transferred to the business personal photography equipment valued at $12,900.
7 Ordered additional photography equipment, $7,500.
8 Purchased office equipment for cash, $5,400.
10 Received and paid for the photography equipment ordered on July 7, $7,500.
12 Purchased photography supplies on credit, $2,100.
13 Received cash for portraits, $1,140.
17 Billed customers for portraits, $2,250.
19 Paid for half the supplies purchased on July 12, $1,050.
25 Paid the utility bill for July, $360.
26 Paid the telephone bill for July, $210.
28 Received payments from the customers billed on July 17, $750.
29 Paid wages to assistant, $1,200.
31 Withdrew cash for personal expenses, $3,600.

Required

1. Prepare journal entries to record these transactions in the general journal (Pages 1 and 2).
2. Set up the following ledger accounts and post the journal entries: Cash (111); Accounts Receivable (113); Photography Supplies (115); Prepaid Rent (116); Photography Equipment (141); Office Equipment (143); Accounts Payable (211); Cindy Liang, Capital (311); Cindy Liang, Withdrawals (312); Portrait Revenue (411); Wages Expense (511); Utility Expense (512); and Telephone Expense (513).
3. Prepare a trial balance for Liang Portrait Studio as of July 31, 19xx.

Problem 2A-4. Transaction Analysis, General Journal, Ledger Accounts, and Trial Balance
(L.O. 5, 6, 7, 8)

Fulton Security Service provides ushers and security personnel for athletic events and other functions. Here is Fulton's trial balance at the end of October:

Fulton Security Service
Trial Balance
October 31, 19xx

Cash (111)	$ 26,600	
Accounts Receivable (113)	18,800	
Supplies (115)	1,120	
Prepaid Insurance (116)	1,200	
Equipment (141)	15,600	
Accounts Payable (211)		$ 10,600
LeRoy Fulton, Capital (311)		42,320
LeRoy Fulton, Withdrawals (312)	4,000	
Security Services Revenue (411)		56,000
Wages Expense (512)	32,000	
Rent Expense (513)	6,400	
Utility Expense (514)	3,200	
	$108,920	$108,920

During November, Fulton engaged in the following transactions:

Nov. 1 Received cash from customers billed last month, $8,400.
3 Made a payment on accounts payable, $6,200.

Nov. 5 Purchased a new one-year insurance policy in advance, $7,200.
7 Purchased supplies on credit, $860.
8 Billed a client for security services, $4,400.
10 Made a rent payment for November, $1,600.
11 Received cash from customers for security services, $3,200.
12 Paid wages to the security staff, $2,800.
14 Ordered equipment, $1,600.
15 Paid the current month's utility bill, $800.
17 Received and paid for the equipment ordered on November 14, $1,600.
19 Returned for full credit some of the supplies purchased on November 7 because they were defective, $240.
20 Withdrew cash for personal expenses, $2,000.
21 Paid for the supplies purchased on November 7, less the return on November 19, $620.
23 Billed a customer for security services performed, $3,600.
30 Paid wages to the security staff, $2,100.

Required

1. Prepare journal entries to record these transactions in the general journal (Pages 26 and 27).
2. Open ledger accounts for the accounts shown in the trial balance. Enter the October 31 trial balance amounts in the ledger.
3. Post the journal entries to the ledger.
4. Prepare a trial balance as of November 30, 19xx.

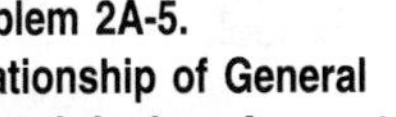

Problem 2A-5. Relationship of General Journal, Ledger Accounts, and Trial Balance
(L.O. 5, 6, 7, 8)

Boulevard Communications Company is a public relations firm. On April 30, 19xx, the company's trial balance looked like this:

Boulevard Communications Company
Trial Balance
April 30, 19xx

Cash (111)	$20,400	
Accounts Receivable (113)	11,000	
Supplies (115)	1,220	
Office Equipment (141)	8,400	
Accounts Payable (211)		$ 5,200
Ramesh Mehta, Capital (311)		35,820
	$41,020	$41,020

During the month of May, the company completed the following transactions:

May 3 Paid rent for May, $1,300.
5 Received cash from customers on account, $4,600.
6 Ordered supplies, $760.
8 Billed customers for services provided, $5,600.
10 Made a payment on accounts payable, $2,200.
13 Received the supplies ordered on May 6 and agreed to pay for them in thirty days, $760.
15 Paid salaries for the first half of May, $3,800.
16 Discovered some of the supplies were not as ordered and returned them for a full credit, $160.
18 Received cash from a customer for services provided, $9,600.

May 22 Paid the utility bill for May, $320.
23 Paid the telephone bill for May, $240.
27 Received a bill, to be paid in June, for advertisements placed during the month of May in the local newspaper to promote Boulevard Communications, $1,400.
28 Billed a customer for services provided, $5,400.
30 Paid salaries for the last half of May, $3,800.
31 Withdrew cash for personal use, $2,400.

Required

1. Enter these transactions in the general journal (Pages 22 and 23).
2. Open accounts in the ledger for the accounts in the trial balance and the following accounts: Ramesh Mehta, Withdrawals (312); Public Relations Fees (411); Salaries Expense (511); Rent Expense (512); Utility Expense (513); Telephone Expense (514); and Advertising Expense (515).
3. Enter the April 30 account balances from the trial balance in the appropriate ledger account.
4. Post the entries to the ledger accounts. Be sure to make the appropriate posting references in the journal and ledger as you post.
5. Prepare a trial balance as of May 31, 19xx.

Problem Set B

Problem 2B-1. Transaction Analysis, T Accounts, and Trial Balance
(L.O. 5, 8)

Donna Polonsky opened a secretarial school called Village Business School.

a. She contributed the following assets to the business:

Cash	$11,400
Word processors	8,600
Office equipment	7,200

b. Found a location for the business and paid the first month's rent, $520.
c. Paid for an advertisement announcing the opening of the school, $380.
d. Received applications from three students for a four-week secretarial program and two students for a ten-day keyboarding course. The students will be billed a total of $2,600.
e. Purchased supplies on credit, $660.
f. Billed the enrolled students, $2,600.
g. Paid an assistant one week's salary, $440.
h. Purchased a word processor, $960, and office equipment, $760, on credit.
i. Paid for the supplies purchased on credit in **e**, $660.
j. Repaired a broken word processor, paid cash, $80.
k. Billed new students who enrolled late in the course, $880.
l. Transferred cash to a personal checking account, $600.
m. Received partial payment from students previously billed, $2,160.
n. Paid the utility bill for the current month, $180.
o. Paid an assistant one week's salary, $440.
p. Received cash revenue from another new student, $500.

Required

1. Set up the following T accounts: Cash; Accounts Receivable; Supplies; Word Processors; Office Equipment; Accounts Payable; Donna Polonsky, Capital; Donna Polonsky, Withdrawals; Tuition Revenue; Salaries Expense; Utility Expense; Rent Expense; Repair Expense; and Advertising Expense.
2. Record the transactions by entering debits and credits directly in the T accounts, using the transaction letter to identify each debit and credit.
3. Prepare a trial balance using today's date.

Problem 2B-2. Transaction Analysis, T Accounts, General Journal, and Trial Balance
(L.O. 5, 6, 8)

Jerry Green is a house painter. During the month of June, he completed the following transactions:

June 3 Began his business with equipment valued at $2,460 and placed $14,200 in a business checking account.
5 Purchased a used truck costing $3,800. Paid $1,000 in cash and signed a note for the balance.
7 Purchased supplies on account for $640.
8 Completed a painting job and billed the customer $960.
10 Received $300 in cash for painting two rooms.
11 Hired an assistant to work with him at $12 per hour.
12 Purchased supplies for $320 in cash.
13 Received a $960 check from the customer billed on May 8.
14 Paid $800 for an insurance policy for eighteen months' coverage.
16 Billed a customer $1,240 for a painting job.
18 Paid the assistant $300 for twenty-five hours' work.
19 Paid $80 for a tune-up for the truck.
20 Paid for the supplies purchased on June 7.
21 Purchased a new ladder (equipment) for $120 and supplies for $580, on account.
23 Received a telephone bill for $120, due next month.
24 Received $660 in cash from the customer billed on May 16.
25 Transferred $600 to a personal checking account.
26 Received $720 in cash for painting a five-room apartment.
28 Paid $400 on the note signed for the truck.
29 Paid the assistant $360 for thirty hours' work.

Required

1. Prepare journal entries to record these transactions in the general journal. Use the accounts listed below.
2. Set up the following T accounts and post all the journal entries: Cash; Accounts Receivable; Supplies; Prepaid Insurance; Equipment; Truck; Notes Payable; Accounts Payable; Jerry Green, Capital; Jerry Green, Withdrawals; Painting Fees Earned; Wages Expense; Telephone Expense; and Truck Expense.
3. Prepare a trial balance for Green Painting Service as of June 30, 19xx.
4. Compare how recognition applies to the transactions of June 8 and 10 and how classification applies to the transactions of June 14 and 18.

Problem 2B-3. Transaction Analysis, General Journal, Ledger Accounts, and Trial Balance
(L.O. 5, 6, 7, 8)

Kwan Lee began a rug cleaning business on October 1 and engaged in the following transactions during the month:

Oct. 1 Began business by transferring $6,000 from his personal bank account to the business bank account.
2 Ordered cleaning supplies, $500.
3 Purchased cleaning equipment for cash, $1,400.
4 Leased a van by making two months' lease payment in advance, $600.
7 Received the cleaning supplies ordered on October 2 and agreed to pay half the amount in ten days and the rest in thirty days.
9 Paid for repairs on the van with cash, $40.
12 Received cash for cleaning carpets, $480.
17 Paid half of the amount owed on supplies purchased on October 7, $250.
21 Billed customers for cleaning carpets, $670.
24 Paid for additional repairs on the van with cash, $40.
27 Received $300 from the customers billed on October 21.
31 Withdrew $350 from the business for personal use.

Required

1. Prepare journal entries to record the above transactions in the general journal (Pages 1 and 2). Use the accounts listed below.
2. Set up the following ledger accounts and post the journal entries: Cash (111); Accounts Receivable (113); Cleaning Supplies (115); Prepaid Lease (116); Cleaning

Equipment (141); Accounts Payable (211); Kwan Lee, Capital (311); Kwan Lee, Withdrawals (312); Cleaning Revenues (411); Repair Expense (511).

3. Prepare a trial balance for Lee Carpet Cleaning Service as of October 31, 19xx.

Problem 2B-4. Transaction Analysis, General Journal, Ledger Accounts, and Trial Balance
(L.O. 5, 6, 7, 8)

The account balances for Ramirez Lawn Service at the end of February are presented in the trial balance below.

Ramirez Lawn Service
Trial Balance
February 28, 19xx

Cash (111)	$ 6,200	
Accounts Receivable (113)	440	
Supplies (115)	920	
Prepaid Insurance (116)	800	
Equipment (141)	8,800	
Notes Payable (211)		$ 6,000
Accounts Payable (212)		1,400
Oscar Ramirez, Capital (311)		8,400
Oscar Ramirez, Withdrawals (312)	840	
Service Revenue (411)		2,980
Lease Expense (512)	580	
Pickup Expense (513)	200	
	$18,780	$18,780

During March, Oscar Ramirez completed the following transactions:

Mar. 3 Paid for supplies purchased on credit last month, $280.
5 Billed customers for services, $820.
6 Paid the lease on a pickup truck, $580.
7 Purchased supplies on credit, $300.
8 Received cash from customers not previously billed, $580.
9 Purchased new equipment from Carson Manufacturing Company on account, $2,600.
11 Received a bill for an oil change on the truck, $80.
13 Returned a portion of the equipment that was purchased on March 9 for a credit, $640.
14 Received payments from customers previously billed, $380.
16 Paid the bill received on March 11.
18 Took cash from the business for personal use, $220.
20 Paid for the supplies purchased on March 7.
21 Billed customers for services, $540.
22 Purchased equipment from a friend who is retiring, $560. Payment was made from Oscar's personal checking account, but the equipment will be used in the business. (**Hint:** Treat this as an owner's investment.)
24 Received payments from customers previously billed, $780.
28 Purchased gasoline for the truck with cash, $60.
30 Made a payment to reduce the principal of the note payable, $1,200.

Required

1. Prepare journal entries to record the March transactions in the general journal (Pages 11, 12, and 13).
2. Open ledger accounts for the accounts shown in the trial balance. Enter the February 28 trial balance amounts in the ledger accounts.
3. Post the entries to the ledger accounts.
4. Prepare a trial balance as of March 31, 19xx.

Problem 2B-5.
Relationship of General Journal, Ledger Accounts, and Trial Balance
(L.O. 5, 6, 7, 8)

The Progressive Child Care Company provides babysitting and child-care programs. On August 31, 19xx, this was the company's trial balance:

Progressive Child Care Company
Trial Balance
August 31, 19xx

Cash (111)	$ 3,740	
Accounts Receivable (113)	3,400	
Equipment (141)	2,080	
Buses (143)	34,800	
Notes Payable (211)		$30,000
Accounts Payable (212)		3,280
Sharon Bromberg, Capital (311)		10,740
	$44,020	$44,020

During the month of September, the company completed the following transactions:

Sept. 3 Paid this month's rent, $540.
5 Received fees for this month's services, $1,300.
7 Purchased supplies on account, $170.
8 Reimbursed the bus driver for gas expenses, $80.
9 Ordered playground equipment, $2,000.
10 Paid part-time assistants for two weeks' services, $460.
12 Made a payment on account, $340.
13 Received payments from customers on account, $2,400.
15 Billed customers who had not yet paid for this month's services, $1,400.
16 Paid for the supplies purchased on September 7.
18 Purchased playground equipment for cash, $2,000.
19 Withdrew cash for personal expenses, $220.
20 Contributed equipment to the business, $580.
21 Paid this month's utility bill, $290.
23 Paid part-time assistants for two weeks' services, $460.
25 Received payment for one month's services from customers previously billed, $1,000.
26 Purchased gas and oil for the bus on account, $70.
29 Paid for a one-year insurance policy, $580.

Required

1. Enter these transactions in the general journal (Pages 17, 18, and 19).
2. Open accounts in the ledger for the accounts in the trial balance and the following accounts: Supplies (115); Prepaid Insurance (116); Sharon Bromberg, Withdrawals (312); Service Revenue (411); Rent Expense (511); Bus Expense (512); Wages Expense (513); and Utility Expense (514).
3. Enter the August 31, 19xx, account balances from the trial balance.
4. Post the entries to the ledger accounts. Be sure to make the appropriate posting references in the journal and ledger as you post.
5. Prepare a trial balance as of September 30, 19xx.

Financial Decision Case

Obi Repairs Company
(L.O. 5, 6, 7, 8)

Benjamin Obi hired an attorney to help him start Obi Repairs Company. On June 1, Mr. Obi invested $23,000 in cash in the business. When he paid the attorney's bill of $1,400, the attorney advised him to hire an accountant to keep his records. However, Mr. Obi was so busy that it was June 30 before he asked you to straighten out his records. Your first task is to develop a trial balance based on the June transactions.

After the investment and payment to the attorney, Mr. Obi borrowed $10,000 from the bank. He later paid $520, which included interest of $120, on this loan. He also purchased a pickup truck in the company's name, paying $5,000 down and financing $14,800. The first payment on the truck is due July 15. Mr. Obi then rented an office and paid three months' rent, $1,800, in advance. Credit purchases of office equipment for $1,400 and repair tools for $1,000 must be paid by July 13.

In June, Obi Repairs completed repairs of $2,600—$800 were cash transactions. Of the credit transactions, $600 was collected during June, and $1,200 remained to be collected at the end of June. Wages of $800 were paid to employees. On June 30, the company received a $150 bill for June utility expense and a $100 check from a customer for work to be completed in July.

Required

1. Record the June transactions in the general journal.
2. Set up and determine the balance of each T account by posting the general journal entries to T accounts and determining the balance of each account.
3. Prepare a June 30 trial balance for Obi Repairs Company.
4. Benjamin Obi is unsure how to evaluate the trial balance. His Cash account balance is $24,980, which exceeds his original investment of $23,000 by $1,980. Did he make a profit of $1,980? Explain why the Cash account is not an indicator of business earnings. Cite specific examples to show why it is difficult to determine net income by looking solely at figures in the trial balance.

Answers to Self-Test

1. a	3. d	5. c	7. c	9. a
2. b	4. b	6. a	8. c	10. a

LEARNING OBJECTIVES

1. *Define* net income *and its two major components,* revenues *and* expenses.
2. *Explain the difficulties of income measurement caused by (a) the accounting period issue, (b) the continuity issue, and (c) the matching issue.*
3. *Define* accrual accounting *and explain two broad ways of accomplishing it.*
4. *State the four principal situations that require adjusting entries.*
5. *Prepare typical adjusting entries.*
6. *Prepare financial statements from an adjusted trial balance.*
7. *Prepare correcting entries.*
8. *State all the steps in the accounting cycle.*

CHAPTER 3

Business Income and Accrual Accounting

In this chapter, you will learn how accountants define business income and the problems of assigning income to specific time periods. Then, working with realistic examples, you will come to understand the adjustment process necessary for measuring periodic business income. Finally, you will prepare financial statements from the adjusted trial balance. After studying this chapter, you should be able to meet the learning objectives listed on the left.

For a business to succeed or even to survive, it must earn a profit. A major function of accounting is to measure and report the success or failure of a company in achieving this goal.

Profit has many meanings. One is the increase in owner's equity that results from business operations. However, even this definition can be interpreted differently by economists, lawyers, business people, and the public. Because the word *profit* has more than one meaning, accountants prefer to use the term *net income*, a term that can be defined precisely from an accounting point of view. To the accountant, net income equals revenues minus expenses, provided revenues exceed expenses.

DECISION POINT

Never Flake Company

■ Never Flake Company, which operated in the northeastern part of the United States, provided a rust prevention coating for the underside of new automobiles. The company advertised widely and offered its services through new car dealers. When a dealer sold a new car, the dealer attempted to sell the rust prevention coating as an option. The protective coating was supposed to make cars last longer in the severe northeastern winters. A key selling point was Never Flake's warranty, which stated that it would repair any damage due to rust at no charge as long as the buyer owned the car.

During the 1970s and most of the 1980s, Never Flake was very successful in generating enough cash to continue operations. But in 1988 the company suddenly declared bankruptcy. Company officials said that the firm had only $5.5 million in assets against liabilities of $32.9 million. Most of the liabilities represented potential claims under the company's lifetime warranty. It seemed that owners were keeping their cars longer in the 1980s than they had in the 1970s. Therefore, more damage was being attributed to rust. What accounting decisions could have helped Never Flake to survive under these circumstances?

According to the concepts of accrual accounting and the matching rule, which you will learn about in this chapter, the accountant must estimate and record (accrue) the expenses associated with a sale even though cash may not be paid out until future years. This procedure enables management to tell whether a company is earning an income and to make informed decisions. In other words, whenever Never Flake sold a rust prevention job, there was a warranty expense associated with the job that the company could expect to pay in future years. If warranty expenses had been estimated and recorded correctly in the years sales were made, Never Flake's management would have realized that it was either charging too little for the rust prevention service or being too generous in the period covered by the warranty. The failure to follow good accrual accounting practices in the measurement of business income undoubtedly led to poor management decisions, and, eventually, to the company's bankruptcy. ■

The Measurement of Business Income

Businesses are in the business of earning income. Their activities do not necessarily coincide with standard periods of time, but the business environment requires that firms report income or loss regularly. For example, owners must receive income reports every year, and the government requires corporations to pay taxes on annual income. Within the business, management uses financial statements—prepared every month or more often—to monitor performance.

Because of these demands, a primary objective of accounting is measuring net income in accordance with generally accepted accounting principles. Readers of financial reports who are familiar with these principles understand how the accountant defines net income and are aware of its strengths and weaknesses as a measurement of company performance.

Net Income

OBJECTIVE 1
Define net income *and its two major components,* revenues *and* expenses

Net income is the net increase in owner's equity that results from the operations of a company. Net income, in its simplest form, is measured by the difference between revenues and expenses when revenues exceed expenses:

$$\text{Net income} = \text{revenues} - \text{expenses}$$

When expenses exceed revenues, a **net loss** occurs.

Revenues. **Revenues** "are inflows or other enhancements of assets of an entity or settlement of its liabilities (or a combination of both) from delivering or producing goods, rendering services, or other activities that constitute the entity's ongoing major or central operations."[1] In the simplest case, revenues equal the price of goods sold and services rendered over a specific period of time. When a business delivers a product or provides a service to a customer, it usually receives either cash or a promise to pay cash in the near future. The promise to pay is recorded in either Accounts Receivable or Notes Receivable. The revenue for a given period equals the total of cash and receivables generated from goods and services provided to customers during that period.

As shown in the chapter on accounting as an information system, revenues increase owner's equity. Liabilities generally are not affected by revenues, and some transactions that increase cash and other assets are not revenues. For example, a bank loan increases liabilities and cash but does not produce revenue. The collection of accounts receivable, which increases cash and decreases ac-

1. *Statement of Financial Accounting Concepts No. 6*, "Elements of Financial Statements" (Stamford, Conn.: Financial Accounting Standards Board, December 1985), par. 78.

counts receivable, does not produce revenue either. Remember that when a sale on credit takes place, the asset account Accounts Receivable increases; at the same time, an owner's equity revenue account increases. So counting the collection of the receivable as revenue later would be counting the same sale twice.

Not all increases in owner's equity arise from revenues. An owner's investment increases owner's equity but is not revenue.

Expenses. **Expenses** are "outflows or other using up of assets or incurrences of liabilities (or a combination of both) from delivering or producing goods, rendering services, or carrying out other activities that constitute the entity's ongoing major or central operations."[2] In other words, expenses are the costs of the goods and services used up in the course of earning revenues. Often called the *cost of doing business,* expenses include the costs of goods sold, the costs of activities necessary to carry on a business, and the costs of attracting and serving customers. Examples are salaries, rent, advertising, telephone service, and depreciation (allocation of cost) of a building or office equipment.

Expenses are the opposite of revenues: They decrease owner's equity. They also produce a decrease in assets or an increase in liabilities. Just as not all cash receipts are revenues, not all cash payments are expenses. A cash payment to reduce a liability does not result in an expense. The liability, however, may have come from incurring a previous expense, such as advertising, that is to be paid later. There also may be two steps before an expenditure of cash becomes an expense. For example, prepaid expenses or plant assets (such as machinery and equipment) are recorded as assets when they are acquired. Later, as their usefulness expires in the operation of the business, their cost is allocated to expenses. In fact, expenses sometimes are called *expired costs.*

Not all decreases in owner's equity arise from expenses. Withdrawals from the company by the owner decrease owner's equity, but they are not expenses.

Temporary and Permanent Accounts. Revenues and expenses can be recorded directly in owner's equity as increases and decreases. In practice, however, management and others want to know the details of the increases and decreases in owner's equity produced by revenues and expenses. For this reason, separate accounts for each revenue and expense are needed to accumulate the amounts. Because the balances of these income statement accounts apply only to the current accounting period, they are called **temporary accounts**. Temporary accounts, or *nominal accounts,* show the accumulation of revenues and expenses over the accounting period. At the end of the accounting period, their balances are transferred to owner's equity. Thus, nominal accounts start each accounting period with zero balances and then accumulate the specific revenues and expenses of that period. On the other hand, the balance sheet accounts—assets, liabilities, and the owner's Capital account—are called **permanent accounts**, or *real accounts,* because their balances extend beyond the end of an accounting period. The process of transferring totals from the temporary revenue and expense accounts to the permanent owner's equity accounts is described in the chapter on completing the accounting cycle.

The Accounting Period Issue

The **accounting period issue** addresses the difficulty of assigning revenues and expenses to a short period of time, such as a month or a year. Not all transactions can be assigned easily to specific time periods. Purchases of buildings and

2. Ibid., par. 80.

OBJECTIVE 2a
Explain the difficulties of income measurement caused by the accounting period issue

equipment, for example, have an effect that extends over many years. Accountants solve this problem by estimating the number of years the buildings or equipment will be in use and the cost that should be assigned to each year. In the process, they make an assumption about **periodicity**: that the net income for any period of time less than the life of the business although tentative is still a useful estimate of the net income for the period.

Generally, the time periods are of equal length to make comparisons easier. And the time period should be noted in the financial statements. Financial statements may be prepared for any time period. Accounting periods of less than one year—for example, monthly or quarterly—are called *interim periods.* The twelve-month accounting period used by a company is called its **fiscal year**. Many companies use the calendar year, January 1 to December 31, for their fiscal year. Others find it convenient to choose a fiscal year that ends during a slack season rather than a peak season. In this case, the fiscal year corresponds to the company's yearly cycle of business activity. The list below shows the diverse fiscal years used by some well-known companies.

Company	Last Month of Fiscal Year
American Greetings Corp.	February
Caesars World, Inc.	July
The Walt Disney Company	September
Eastman Kodak Company	December
Fleetwood Enterprises, Inc.	April
Lorimar	March
Mattel, Inc.	December
MGM/UA Communications Co.	August
Polaroid Corp.	December

Many government and educational units use fiscal years that end June 30 or September 30.

The Continuity Issue

OBJECTIVE 2b
Explain the difficulties of income measurement caused by the continuity issue

The process of measuring business income requires that certain expense and revenue transactions be allocated over several accounting periods. The number of accounting periods raises the **continuity issue**: How long will the business entity last? Many businesses last less than five years, and, in any given year, thousands go bankrupt. To prepare financial statements for an accounting period, the accountant must make an assumption about the ability of the business to survive. Specifically, unless there is evidence to the contrary, the accountant assumes that the business will continue to operate indefinitely, that the business is a **going concern**. Justification for all the techniques of income measurement rests on the assumption of continuity. For example, this assumption allows the cost of certain assets to be held on the balance sheet to a future year when it will become an expense on the income statement.

Another example has to do with the value of assets on the balance sheet. In the chapter on measuring and recording business transactions, we pointed out that the accountant records assets at cost and does not record subsequent changes in their value. But the value of assets to a going concern is much higher than the value of assets to a firm facing bankruptcy. Here, the accountant may be asked to set aside the assumption of continuity and to prepare financial statements based on the assumption that the firm will go out of business and sell all of its assets at liquidation value—that is, for what they will bring in cash.

The Matching Issue

OBJECTIVE 2c
Explain the difficulties of income measurement caused by the matching issue

Revenues and expenses can be accounted for on a cash received and cash paid basis. This practice is known as the **cash basis of accounting**. In certain cases, an individual or business may use the cash basis of accounting for income tax purposes. Under this method, revenues are reported in the period in which cash is received, and expenses are reported in the period in which cash is paid. Taxable income, therefore, is calculated as the difference between cash receipts from revenues and cash payments for expenses.

Although the cash basis of accounting works well for some small businesses and many individuals, it does not meet the needs of most businesses. As explained above, revenues can be earned in a period other than when cash is received, and expenses can be incurred in a period other than when cash is paid. To measure net income adequately, revenues and expenses must be assigned to the appropriate accounting period. The accountant solves this problem by applying the **matching rule**:

> **Revenues must be assigned to the accounting period in which the goods are sold or the services performed, and expenses must be assigned to the accounting period in which they are used to produce revenue.**

Direct cause-and-effect relationships seldom can be demonstrated for certain, but many costs appear to be related to particular revenues. The accountant recognizes these expenses and the related revenues in the same accounting period. Examples are the costs of goods sold and sales commissions. When there is no direct means of connecting expenses and revenues, the accountant tries to allocate costs in a systematic way among the accounting periods that benefit from the costs. For example, a building is converted from an asset to an expense by allocating its cost over the years that benefit from its use.

Accrual Accounting

OBJECTIVE 3
Define accrual accounting and explain two broad ways of accomplishing it

To apply the matching rule, accountants have developed accrual accounting. **Accrual accounting** "attempts to record the financial effects on an enterprise of transactions and other events and circumstances . . . in the periods in which those transactions, events, and circumstances occur rather than only in the periods in which cash is received or paid by the enterprise."[3] That is, accrual accounting consists of all the techniques developed by accountants to apply the matching rule. It is done in two general ways: (1) by recording revenues when earned and expenses when incurred and (2) by adjusting the accounts.

Recognizing Revenues When Earned and Expenses When Incurred

We illustrated the first method of accrual accounting several times in the chapter on measuring and recording business transactions. For example, when the Joan Miller Advertising Agency made a sale on credit by placing advertisements for a client (in the January 19 transaction), revenue was recorded at the time of the sale by debiting Accounts Receivable and crediting Advertising Fees Earned. This is how the accountant recognizes the revenue from a credit sale before the cash is collected. Accounts Receivable serves as a holding account

3. *Statement of Financial Accounting Concepts No. 1*, "Objectives of Financial Reporting by Business Enterprises" (Stamford, Conn.: Financial Accounting Standards Board, 1978), par. 44.

until payment is received. The process of determining when a sale takes place is called **revenue recognition.**

When the Joan Miller Advertising Agency received the telephone bill on January 30, the expense was recognized both as having been incurred and as helping to produce revenue in the current month. The transaction was recorded by debiting Telephone Expense and crediting Accounts Payable. Until the bill is paid, Accounts Payable serves as a holding account. Notice that recognition of the expense does not depend on the payment of cash.

Adjusting the Accounts

An accounting period, by definition, ends on a particular day. The balance sheet must list all assets and liabilities as of the end of that day, and the income statement must contain all revenues and expenses applicable to the period ending on that day. Although operating a business is a continuous process, there must be a cutoff point for the periodic reports. Some transactions invariably span the cutoff point; as a result, some accounts need adjustment.

For example, some of the accounts in the end-of-the-period trial balance for the Joan Miller Advertising Agency (Exhibit 3-1) do not show the correct balances for preparing the financial statements. The January 31 trial balance lists prepaid rent of $800. At $400 per month, this represents rent for the months of January and February. So on January 31, one-half of the $800, or $400, represents rent expense for January; the remaining $400 represents an asset that is going to be used in February. An adjustment is needed to reflect the $400 balance in the Prepaid Rent account on the balance sheet and the $400 rent expense on the income statement. As you will see on the following pages, several other accounts in the Joan Miller Advertising Agency trial balance do not reflect their correct balances. Like the Prepaid Rent account, they need to be adjusted.

Exhibit 3-1. Trial Balance for the Joan Miller Advertising Agency

Joan Miller Advertising Agency
Trial Balance
January 31, 19xx

Cash	$ 1,720	
Accounts Receivable	2,800	
Art Supplies	1,800	
Office Supplies	800	
Prepaid Rent	800	
Prepaid Insurance	480	
Art Equipment	4,200	
Office Equipment	3,000	
Accounts Payable		$ 3,170
Unearned Art Fees		1,000
Joan Miller, Capital		10,000
Joan Miller, Withdrawals	1,400	
Advertising Fees Earned		4,200
Office Wages Expense	1,200	
Utility Expense	100	
Telephone Expense	70	
	$18,370	$18,370

The Adjustment Process

OBJECTIVE 4
State the four principal situations that require adjusting entries

Accountants use **adjusting entries** to apply accrual accounting to transactions that span more than one accounting period. Adjusting entries have at least one balance sheet (or permanent) account entry and at least one income statement (or temporary) account entry. Adjusting entries never involve the Cash account. They are needed when deferrals or accruals exist. A **deferral** is the postponement of the recognition of an expense already paid or incurred or of a revenue already received. Deferrals are used in two instances:

1. Costs have been recorded that must be apportioned between two or more accounting periods. Examples are the costs of a building, prepaid insurance, and supplies. The adjusting entry in this case involves an asset account and an expense account.
2. Revenues have been recorded that must be apportioned between two or more accounting periods. An example is payments collected for services yet to be rendered. The adjusting entry involves a liability account and a revenue account.

An **accrual** is the recognition of a revenue or expense that has arisen but has not yet been recorded. Accruals are required in these two cases:

1. There are unrecorded revenues. An example is fees earned but not yet collected or billed to customers. The adjusting entry involves an asset account and a revenue account.
2. There are unrecorded expenses. Examples are the wages earned by employees in the current accounting period but after the last pay period. The adjusting entry involves an expense account and a liability account.

Once again, we use the Joan Miller Advertising Agency to illustrate the kinds of adjusting entries that most businesses must make.

Apportioning Recorded Expenses Between Two or More Accounting Periods (Deferral Expenses)

OBJECTIVE 5
Prepare typical adjusting entries

Companies often make expenditures that benefit more than one period. These expenditures generally are debited to an asset account. At the end of the accounting period, the amount that has been used is transferred from the asset account to an expense account. Two of the more important kinds of adjustments are for prepaid expenses and the depreciation of plant and equipment.

Prepaid Expenses. Some expenses customarily are paid in advance. These expenditures are called **prepaid expenses**. Among them are rent, insurance, and supplies. At the end of an accounting period, a portion (or all) of these goods or services will have been used up or will have expired. The part of the expenditure that has benefited current operations is treated as an expense of the period. The part that has not been consumed or has not expired is treated as an asset applicable to the company's future operations. If adjusting entries for prepaid expenses are not made at the end of the period, both the balance sheet and the income statement will reflect information that is incorrect: The assets of the company will be overstated, and the expenses of the company will be understated. This means that owner's equity on the balance sheet and net income on the income statement will be overstated.

At the beginning of the month, the Joan Miller Advertising Agency paid two months' rent in advance. This expenditure resulted in an asset consisting of the right to occupy the office for two months. As each day in the month passed, part of the asset's cost expired and became an expense. By January 31, one-half had expired and should be treated as an expense. Here is the analysis of this economic event:

Prepaid Rent (Adjustment a)

Prepaid Rent			
Jan. 2	800	Jan. 31	400

Rent Expense			
Jan. 31	400		

Transaction: Expiration of one month's rent.
Analysis: Assets decrease. Owner's equity decreases.
Rules: Decreases in assets are recorded by credits. Decreases in owner's equity are recorded by debits.
Entries: The decrease in owner's equity is recorded by a debit to Rent Expense. The decrease in assets is recorded by a credit to Prepaid Rent.

	Dr.	Cr.
Rent Expense	400	
Prepaid Rent		400

The Prepaid Rent account now has a balance of $400, which represents one month's rent paid in advance. The Rent Expense account reflects the $400 expense for the month of January.

Besides rent, the Joan Miller Advertising Agency prepaid expenses for insurance, art supplies, and office supplies, all of which call for adjusting entries.

On January 8, the agency purchased a one-year insurance policy, paying for it in advance. Like prepaid rent, prepaid insurance offers benefits (in this case, protection) that expire day by day. By the end of the month, one-twelfth of the protection had expired. The adjustment is analyzed and recorded like this:

Prepaid Insurance (Adjustment b)

Prepaid Insurance			
Jan. 8	480	Jan. 31	40

Insurance Expense			
Jan. 31	40		

Transaction: Expiration of one month's insurance.
Analysis: Assets decrease. Owner's equity decreases.
Rules: Decreases in assets are recorded by credits. Decreases in owner's equity are recorded by debits.
Entries: The decrease in owner's equity is recorded by a debit to Insurance Expense. The decrease in assets is recorded by a credit to Prepaid Insurance.

	Dr.	Cr.
Insurance Expense	40	
Prepaid Insurance		40

The Prepaid Insurance account now shows the correct balance, $440, and Insurance Expense reflects the expired cost, $40, for the month.

Early in the month, the Joan Miller Advertising Agency purchased art supplies and office supplies. As Joan Miller did artwork for various clients during the month, art supplies were consumed. And her secretary used office supplies.

There is no need to account for these supplies every day because the financial statements are not prepared until the end of the month and the recordkeeping would involve too much work. Instead, Joan Miller makes a careful inventory of the art and office supplies at the end of the month. This inventory records the number and cost of those supplies that are still assets of the company—that are yet to be consumed.

Suppose the inventory shows that art supplies costing $1,300 and office supplies costing $600 are still on hand. This means that of the $1,800 of art supplies originally purchased, $500 worth were used up (became an expense) in January. Of the original $800 of office supplies, $200 worth were consumed. These transactions are analyzed and recorded as follows:

Art Supplies and Office Supplies (Adjustments c and d)

Art Supplies

Jan. 6	1,800	Jan. 31	500

Art Supplies Expense

Jan. 31	500		

Office Supplies

Jan. 6	800	Jan. 31	200

Office Supplies Expense

Jan. 31	200		

Transaction: Consumption of supplies.
Analysis: Assets decrease. Owner's equity decreases.
Rules: Decreases in assets are recorded by credits. Decreases in owner's equity are recorded by debits.
Entries: The decreases in owner's equity are recorded by debits to Art Supplies Expense and Office Supplies Expense. The decreases in assets are recorded by credits to Art Supplies and Office Supplies.

	Dr.	Cr.
Art Supplies Expense	500	
Art Supplies		500
Office Supplies Expense	200	
Office Supplies		200

The asset accounts Art Supplies and Office Supplies now reflect the correct balances, $1,300 and $600 respectively, of supplies that are yet to be consumed. In addition, the amount of art supplies used up during the accounting period is reflected as $500 and the amount of office supplies used up is reflected as $200.

Depreciation of Plant and Equipment. When a company buys a long-lived asset—a building, equipment, trucks, automobiles, a computer, store fixtures, or office furniture—it basically is prepaying for the usefulness of that asset for as long as it benefits the company. In other words, the asset is a deferral of an expense. So the accountant must allocate the cost of the asset over its estimated useful life. The amount allocated to any one accounting period is called **depreciation**, or *depreciation expense*. Depreciation, like other expenses, is incurred during an accounting period to obtain revenue.

It is often impossible to tell how long an asset will last or how much of the asset is used in any one period. For this reason, depreciation must be estimated. Accountants have developed a number of methods for estimating depreciation and for dealing with the other complex problems concerning depreciation. Here we look at the simplest case.

Suppose that the Joan Miller Advertising Agency estimates that its art equipment and office equipment will last five years (60 months) and will be worthless at the end of that time. The depreciation for the month of art equipment and office equipment is $70 ($4,200 ÷ 60 months) and $50 ($3,000 ÷ 60 months) respectively. These amounts represent the costs allocated to the month, and they are the amounts by which the asset accounts must be reduced and the expense accounts increased (reducing owner's equity).

Art Equipment and Office Equipment (Adjustments e and f)

Art Equipment

Jan. 4 4,200	

Accumulated Depreciation, Art Equipment

	Jan. 31 70

Office Equipment

Jan. 5 3,000	

Accumulated Depreciation, Office Equipment

	Jan. 31 50

Depreciation Expense, Art Equipment

Jan. 31 70	

Depreciation Expense, Office Equipment

Jan. 31 50	

Transaction: Recording the depreciation expenses.
Analysis: Assets decrease. Owner's equity decreases.
Rules: Decreases in assets are recorded by credits. Decreases in owner's equity are recorded by debits.
Entries: The owner's equity is decreased by debits to Depreciation Expense, Art Equipment and Depreciation Expense, Office Equipment. The assets are decreased by credits to Accumulated Depreciation, Art Equipment and Accumulated Depreciation, Office Equipment.

	Dr.	Cr.
Depreciation Expense, Art Equipment	70	
Accumulated Depreciation, Art Equipment		70
Depreciation Expense, Office Equipment	50	
Accumulated Depreciation, Office Equipment		50

Accumulated Depreciation—A Contra Account. Notice that in the analysis above, the asset accounts are not credited directly. Instead, new accounts—Accumulated Depreciation, Art Equipment and Accumulated Depreciation, Office Equipment—are credited. These **accumulated depreciation** accounts are contra-asset accounts used to total the past depreciation expense on a specific long-lived asset. A **contra account** is a separate account that is paired with a related asset account. The balance of the contra account is shown on the financial statement as a deduction from the related asset account. There are several types of contra accounts. In this case, the balance of Accumulated Depreciation, Art Equipment is shown on the balance sheet as a deduction from the associated account Art Equipment. Likewise, Accumulated Depreciation, Office Equipment is a deduction from Office Equipment. Exhibit 3-2 shows the plant and equipment section of the balance sheet for the Joan Miller Advertising Agency after these adjusting entries have been made.

The contra account is used for two very good reasons. First, it recognizes that depreciation is an estimate. Second, the contra account preserves the original cost of the asset: In combination with the asset account, it shows how much of the asset has been allocated as an expense as well as the balance left to be depreciated. As the months pass, the amount of the accumulated depreciation grows, and the net amount shown as an asset declines. In six months, Accumulated Depreciation, Art Equipment will show a balance of $420; when this

Exhibit 3-2. Plant and Equipment Section of the Balance Sheet

Joan Miller Advertising Agency
Partial Balance Sheet
January 31, 19xx

Plant and Equipment		
Art Equipment	$4,200	
Less Accumulated Depreciation	70	$4,130
Office Equipment	$3,000	
Less Accumulated Depreciation	50	2,950
Total Plant and Equipment		$7,080

amount is subtracted from Art Equipment, a net amount of $3,780 will remain. This net amount is referred to as the carrying value, or *book value*, of the asset.

Other names also are used for accumulated depreciation, among them *allowance for depreciation*. But *accumulated depreciation* is the newer, better term.

Apportioning Recorded Revenues Between Two or More Accounting Periods (Deferral Revenues)

Just as expenses can be paid before they are used, revenues can be received before they are earned. When revenues are received in advance, the company has an obligation to deliver goods or perform services. Therefore, unearned revenues are shown in a liability account. For example, publishing companies usually receive payment in advance for magazine subscriptions. These receipts are recorded in a liability account. If the company fails to deliver the magazines, subscribers are entitled to their money back. As the company delivers each issue of the magazine, it earns a part of the advance payments. This earned portion must be transferred from the Unearned Subscription account to the Subscription Revenue account.

During the month of January, the Joan Miller Advertising Agency received $1,000 as an advance payment for artwork to be done for another agency. Assume that by the end of the month, $400 of the artwork was done and accepted by the other agency. Here is the transaction analysis:

Unearned Art Fees (Adjustment g)

Unearned Art Fees

Jan. 31	400	Jan. 15	1,000

Art Fees Earned

		Jan. 31	400

Transaction: Performance of services paid for in advance.
Analysis: Liabilities decrease. Owner's equity increases.
Rules: Decreases in liabilities are recorded by debits. Increases in owner's equity are recorded by credits.
Entries: The decrease in liabilities is recorded by a debit to Unearned Art Fees. The increase in owner's equity is recorded by a credit to Art Fees Earned.

	Dr.	Cr.
Unearned Art Fees	400	
Art Fees Earned		400

The liability account Unearned Art Fees now reflects the amount of work still to be performed, $600. The revenue account Art Fees Earned reflects the services performed and the revenue earned for those services during the month, $400.

Recognizing Unrecorded Revenues (Accrued Revenues)

Accrued revenues are revenues for which a service has been performed or goods delivered but for which no entry has been recorded. Any revenues that have been earned but not recorded during the accounting period call for an adjusting entry that debits an asset account and credits a revenue account. For example, the interest on a note receivable is earned day by day but may not be received until another accounting period. Interest Receivable should be debited and Interest Income should be credited for the interest accrued at the end of the current period.

Suppose that the Joan Miller Advertising Agency has agreed to place a series of advertisements for Marsh Tire Company and that the first appears on January 31, the last day of the month. The fee of $200 for this advertisement, which has been earned but not recorded, should be recorded this way:

Accrued Advertising Fees (Adjustment h)

Fees Receivable

Debit		Credit	
Jan. 31	200		

Advertising Fees Earned

Debit		Credit	
		Jan. 10	1,400
		19	2,800
		31	200

Transaction: Accrual of unrecorded revenue.
Analysis: Assets increase. Owner's equity increases.
Rules: Increases in assets are recorded by debits. Increases in owner's equity are recorded by credits.
Entries: The increase in assets is recorded by a debit to Fees Receivable. The increase in owner's equity is recorded by a credit to Advertising Fees Earned.

	Dr.	Cr.
Fees Receivable	200	
Advertising Fees Earned		200

Now both the asset and the revenue accounts show the correct balance: The $200 in Fees Receivable is owed to the company, and the $4,400 in Advertising Fees has been earned by the company during the month. Marsh will be billed for the series of advertisements when they are completed. At that time, Accounts Receivable will be debited and Fees Receivable will be credited.

Recognizing Unrecorded Expenses (Accrued Expenses)

At the end of an accounting period, there are usually expenses that have been incurred but not recorded in the accounts. These expenses require adjusting entries. One such case is interest on borrowed money. Each day, interest accumulates on the debt. An adjusting entry at the end of each accounting period records this accumulated interest, which is an expense of the period, and the corresponding liability to pay the interest. Other unrecorded expenses are taxes, wages, and salaries. As the expense and the corresponding liability accumulate, they are said to *accrue*—hence the term **accrued expenses**.

Suppose the calendar for January looks like this:

January

Su	M	T	W	Th	F	Sa
	1	2	3	4	5	6
7	8	9	10	11	12	13
14	15	16	17	18	19	20
21	22	23	24	25	26	27
28	29	30	31			

By the end of business on January 31, the Joan Miller Advertising Agency's secretary will have worked three days (Monday, Tuesday, and Wednesday) beyond the last biweekly pay period, which ended on January 26. The employee has earned the wages for these days, but they are not due to be paid until the regular payday in February. The wages for these three days are rightfully an expense for January, and the liabilities should reflect the fact that the company owes the secretary for those days. Because the secretary's wage rate is $600 every two weeks or $60 per day ($600 ÷ 10 working days), the expense is $180 ($60 × 3 days).

Accrued Wages (Adjustment i)

Wages Payable

		Jan. 31	180

Office Wages Expense

Jan. 12	600		
26	600		
31	180		

Transaction: Accrual of unrecorded expense.
Analysis: Liabilities increase. Owner's equity decreases.
Rules: Increases in liabilities are recorded by credits. Decreases in owner's equity are recorded by debits.
Entries: The decrease in owner's equity is recorded by a debit to Office Wages Expense. The increase in liabilities is recorded by a credit to Wages Payable.

	Dr.	Cr.
Office Wages Expense	180	
Wages Payable		180

The liability of $180 is now reflected correctly in the Wages Payable account. The actual expense incurred for office wages during the month, $1,380, is also correct.

DECISION POINT
Joan Miller Advertising Agency

■ In one example used in this chapter, an accrual is made on January 31 for wages payable in the amount of $180. Joan Miller might ask, "Why go to the trouble of making this adjustment? Why worry about it? Doesn't everything come out in the end, when the secretary is paid in February? Because wages expense in total is the same for the two months, isn't the net income in total unchanged?" Give three reasons why adjusting entries can help Joan Miller assess the performance of her business.

Adjusting entries are important because they help accountants compile information that is useful to management and owners. First, adjusting entries are necessary to measure income and financial position in a relevant and useful way. Joan Miller should know how much the agency has earned each month and what its liabilities and assets are on the last day of the month. For instance, if the three days' accrued wages for the secretary are not recorded, the income of the agency will be overstated by $180, or 9 percent ($180 ÷ $1,990). Second, adjusting entries allow financial statements to be compared from one accounting period to the next. Joan Miller can see whether the company is making progress toward earning a profit or if the company has improved its financial position. To return to our example, if the adjustment for accrued wages is not recorded, not only will the net income for January be overstated by $180, but the net income for February (the month when payment will be made) will be understated by $180. This error will make February's earnings, whatever they may be, appear worse than they actually are. Third, even though one adjusting entry may seem insignificant, the cumulative effect of all adjusting entries can be great. Look back over all the adjustments made by the Joan Miller Advertising Agency for prepaid rent and insurance, art and office supplies, depreciation of art and office equipment, unearned art fees, accrued advertising fees, and accrued wages. These are normal adjustments. Their effect on net income in January is to increase expenses by $1,440 and revenues by $600, for a net effect of minus $840, or 42 percent ($840 ÷ $1,990) of net income. If adjusting entries had not been made, Joan Miller would have had a false impression of her company's performance. ■

Using the Adjusted Trial Balance to Prepare Financial Statements

OBJECTIVE 6
Prepare financial statements from an adjusted trial balance

In the chapter on measuring and recording business transactions, a trial balance was prepared before any adjusting entries were recorded. Here, we prepare an **adjusted trial balance**, a list of the accounts and balances after the adjusting entries have been recorded and posted. The adjusted trial balance for the Joan Miller Advertising Agency is shown on the left side of Exhibit 3-3. Notice that some accounts, such as Cash and Accounts Receivable, have the same balances they have in the trial balance (see Exhibit 3-1 on page 94) because no adjusting entries affected them. Other accounts, such as Art Supplies, Office Supplies, Prepaid Rent, and Prepaid Insurance, have different balances from those in the trial balance because adjusting entries did affect them. If the adjusting entries have been posted correctly to the accounts, the adjusted trial balance should have equal debit and credit totals.

From the adjusted trial balance, the financial statements can be prepared easily. The income statement is prepared from the revenue and expense accounts, as shown in Exhibit 3-3. Then, as shown in Exhibit 3-4, the statement of owner's equity and the balance sheet are prepared. Notice that the net income from the income statement is combined with investments and withdrawals on the statement of owner's equity to give the net change in Joan Miller's Capital account. The resulting balance of Joan Miller, Capital at January 31 is used on the balance sheet, as are the asset and liability accounts. In more complex situations, accountants use a work sheet to prepare financial statements. The preparation of a work sheet is covered in the chapter on completing the accounting cycle.

Exhibit 3-3. Relationship of the Adjusted Trial Balance to the Income Statement

Joan Miller Advertising Agency
Adjusted Trial Balance
January 31, 19xx

Cash	$ 1,720	
Accounts Receivable	2,800	
Art Supplies	1,300	
Office Supplies	600	
Prepaid Rent	400	
Prepaid Insurance	440	
Art Equipment	4,200	
Accumulated Depreciation, Art Equipment		$ 70
Office Equipment	3,000	
Accumulated Depreciation, Office Equipment		50
Accounts Payable		3,170
Unearned Art Fees		600
Joan Miller, Capital		10,000
Joan Miller, Withdrawals	1,400	
Advertising Fees Earned		4,400
Office Wages Expense	1,380	
Utility Expense	100	
Telephone Expense	70	
Rent Expense	400	
Insurance Expense	40	
Art Supplies Expense	500	
Office Supplies Expense	200	
Depreciation Expense, Art Equipment	70	
Depreciation Expense, Office Equipment	50	
Art Fees Earned		400
Fees Receivable	200	
Wages Payable		180
	$18,870	$18,870

Joan Miller Advertising Agency
Income Statement
For the Month Ended January 31, 19xx

Revenues		
Advertising Fees Earned	**$4,400**	
Art Fees Earned	**400**	
Total Revenues		$4,800
Expenses		
Office Wages Expense	**$1,380**	
Utility Expense	**100**	
Telephone Expense	**70**	
Rent Expense	**400**	
Insurance Expense	**40**	
Art Supplies Expense	**500**	
Office Supplies Expense	**200**	
Depreciation Expense, Art Equipment	**70**	
Depreciation Expense, Office Equipment	**50**	
Total Expenses		2,810
Net Income		$1,990

Correcting Errors

OBJECTIVE 7
Prepare correcting entries

When an error is discovered in either the journal or the ledger, it must be corrected. The method of correction depends on the kind of error. However, the error must *never* be erased because this action would seem to indicate an effort to hide something. If an error is discovered in a journal entry before it is posted to the ledger, a line drawn through the incorrect item and the correct item written above suffices. Similarly, when a posting error involves entering an incorrect amount in the ledger, it is acceptable to draw a line through the wrong amount and write in the correct amount.

Exhibit 3-4. Relationship of the Adjusted Trial Balance to the Balance Sheet and the Statement of Owner's Equity

Joan Miller Advertising Agency
Adjusted Trial Balance
January 31, 19xx

Cash	$ 1,720	
Accounts Receivable	2,800	
Art Supplies	1,300	
Office Supplies	600	
Prepaid Rent	400	
Prepaid Insurance	440	
Art Equipment	4,200	
Accumulated Depreciation, Art Equipment		$ 70
Office Equipment	3,000	
Accumulated Depreciation, Office Equipment		50
Accounts Payable		3,170
Unearned Art Fees		600
Joan Miller, Capital		10,000
Joan Miller, Withdrawals	1,400	
Advertising Fees Earned		4,400
Office Wages Expense	1,380	
Utility Expense	100	
Telephone Expense	70	
Rent Expense	400	
Insurance Expense	40	
Art Supplies Expense	500	
Office Supplies Expense	200	
Depreciation Expense, Art Equipment	70	
Depreciation Expense, Office Equipment	50	
Art Fees Earned		400
Fees Receivable	200	
Wages Payable		180
	$18,870	$18,870

Joan Miller Advertising Agency
Balance Sheet
January 31, 19xx

Assets		
Cash		$ 1,720
Accounts Receivable		2,800
Fees Receivable		200
Art Supplies		1,300
Office Supplies		600
Prepaid Rent		400
Prepaid Insurance		440
Art Equipment	$4,200	
Less Accumulated Depreciation	70	4,130
Office Equipment	$3,000	
Less Accumulated Depreciation	50	2,950
Total Assets		$14,540
Liabilities		
Accounts Payable	$3,170	
Unearned Art Fees	600	
Wages Payable	180	
Total Liabilities		$ 3,950
Owner's Equity		
Joan Miller, Capital		10,590
Total Liabilities and Owner's Equity		$14,540

Joan Miller Advertising Agency
Statement of Owner's Equity
For the Month Ended January 31, 19xx

Joan Miller, Capital, January 1, 19xx		—
Add: **Investment by Joan Miller**	$10,000	
Net Income	1,990	$11,990
Subtotal		$11,990
Less **Withdrawals**		1,400
Joan Miller, Capital, January 31, 19xx		$10,590

From Income Statement in Exhibit 3-3.

If a journal entry has been posted to the wrong account in the ledger, however, it is necessary to prepare another journal entry to correct the error. For example, suppose that a purchase of art equipment was recorded like this:

Feb. 20	Art Supplies	100	
	Cash		100
	To record the purchase of art equipment		

It is clear that the debit should be to Art Equipment, not to Art Supplies. Therefore, the following entry is needed to correct the error:

Feb. 24	Art Equipment	100	
	Art Supplies		100
	To correct error of Feb. 20, when Art Supplies was debited for the purchase of art equipment		

The explanation provides a record for those who later might question the entry. The Cash account is not involved in the correction because it was correct originally. The effect of the correction is to reduce Art Supplies by $100 and increase Art Equipment by $100.

A Note About Journal Entries

Throughout this chapter and the chapter on measuring and recording business transactions, we have presented journal entries with a full analysis of each transaction. The analyses showed you the thought process behind each entry. By now, you should be fully aware of the effects of transactions on the accounting equation and the rules of debit and credit. For this reason, journal entries are presented in the rest of the book without a full analysis.

Summary of the Accounting System

OBJECTIVE 8
State all the steps in the accounting cycle

The **accounting system** encompasses the sequence of steps followed in the accounting process. This chapter and the chapter on measuring and recording business transactions have presented the steps in this system, from analyzing transactions to preparing financial statements. This system is sometimes called the **accounting cycle**. The purpose of the system, as illustrated in Figure 3-1 on page 106, is to treat the business transactions as raw material and develop the finished product of accounting—the financial statements—in a systematic way. The steps in this system may be summarized as follows:

1. The transactions are *analyzed* from the *source documents.*
2. The transactions are *recorded* in the *journal.*
3. The entries are *posted* to the *ledger.*
4. The *accounts* are *adjusted* at the end of the period to achieve the *adjusted trial balance.*
5. *Financial statements* are *prepared* from the adjusted trial balance.
6. The *accounts* are *closed* to conclude the current accounting period and prepare for the beginning of the new accounting period.

Step 6 of the accounting system, closing the accounts, is the only step that has not been presented thus far. Since the closing process is covered in detail in the chapter on completing the accounting cycle, it is necessary here to understand only the nature and function of closing entries. *Closing entries* are journal entries prepared by accountants on the last day of the accounting period for the purpose of transferring the balances of the temporary accounts and the With-

Figure 3-1. An Overview of the Accounting System

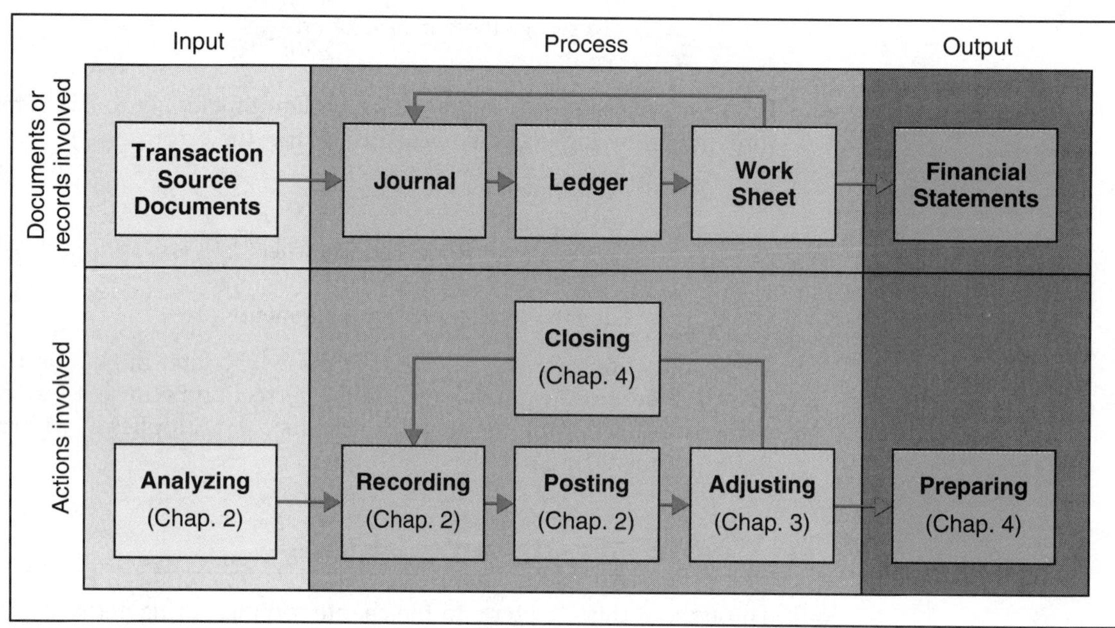

drawals account to the owner's Capital account. As a result of this process, the Capital account will reflect the owner's equity in the business as of the last day of the accounting period. In addition, all the revenue and expense accounts are set equal to zero so that they may be used again in the next accounting period.

Chapter Review

Review of Learning Objectives

1. **Define *net income* and its two major components, *revenues* and *expenses*.**
   Net income is the net increase in owner's equity that results from the operations of a company. Net income equals revenues minus expenses, unless expenses exceed revenues, in which case a net loss results. Revenues equal the price of goods sold and services rendered during a specific period. Expenses are the costs of goods and services used up in the process of earning revenues.

2. **Explain the difficulties of income measurement caused by (a) the accounting period issue, (b) the continuity issue, and (c) the matching issue.**
   The accounting period issue recognizes that net income measurements for short periods of time are necessarily tentative. The continuity issue recognizes that even though businesses face an uncertain future, without evidence to the contrary, accountants must assume that a business will continue indefinitely. The matching issue has to do with the difficulty of assigning revenues and expenses to a period of time. It is solved by applying the matching rule: Revenues must be assigned to the accounting period in which the goods are sold or the services performed, and expenses must be assigned to the accounting period in which they are used to produce revenue.

3. **Define *accrual accounting* and explain two broad ways of accomplishing it.**
   Accrual accounting consists of all the techniques developed by accountants to apply the matching rule. The two general ways of accomplishing accrual accounting are (1) by recognizing revenues when earned and expenses when incurred and (2) by adjusting the accounts.

4. **State the four principal situations that require adjusting entries.**
   Adjusting entries are required (1) when recorded expenses have to be apportioned between two or more accounting periods, (2) when recorded revenues must be apportioned between two or more accounting periods, (3) when unrecorded revenues exist, and (4) when unrecorded expenses exist.
5. **Prepare typical adjusting entries.**
   The preparation of adjusting entries is summarized in the following table:

Type of Adjusting Entry	Type of Account Debited	Type of Account Credited	Examples
Deferrals			
1. Apportioning recorded expenses (recorded, not expensed)	Expense	Asset (or contra asset)	Prepaid Rent Prepaid Insurance Supplies Buildings Equipment
2. Apportioning recorded revenues (recorded, not earned)	Liability	Revenue	Commissions Received in Advance
Accruals			
1. Accrued revenues (earned, not received)	Asset	Revenue	Commissions Receivable Interest Receivable
2. Accrued expenses (incurred, not paid)	Expense	Liability	Wages Payable Interest Payable

6. **Prepare financial statements from an adjusted trial balance.**
   An adjusted trial balance is prepared after adjusting entries have been posted to the ledger accounts. Its purpose is to test the balance of the ledger after the adjusting entries are made and before the financial statements are prepared. The income statement is prepared from the revenue and expense accounts. The balance sheet is prepared from the asset and liability accounts in the adjusted trial balance and from the statement of owner's equity.
7. **Prepare correcting entries.**
   Correcting entries are made to adjust the appropriate accounts to the correct balances. A full explanation should accompany each correcting entry.
8. **State all the steps in the accounting cycle.**
   The steps in the accounting cycle are to (1) analyze the transactions from the source documents, (2) record the transactions in the journal, (3) post the entries to the ledger, (4) adjust the accounts at the end of the period, (5) prepare the financial statements, and (6) close the accounts.

Review of Concepts and Terminology

The following concepts and terms were introduced in this chapter:

(L.O. 2) **Accounting period issue:** The difficulty of assigning revenues and expenses to a short period of time.

(L.O. 8) **Accounting system:** The sequence of steps followed in the accounting process. Also called *accounting cycle.*

(L.O. 4) **Accrual:** The recognition of an expense that has been incurred or a revenue that has been earned but that has not yet been recorded.

(L.O. 3) **Accrual accounting:** The attempt to record the financial effects on an enterprise of transactions and other events in the periods in which those transactions or events occur rather than only in the periods in which cash is received or paid by the enterprise; all the techniques developed by accountants to apply the matching rule.

(L.O. 5) **Accrued expenses:** Expenses that have been incurred but are not recognized in the accounts; unrecorded expenses.

(L.O. 5) **Accrued revenues:** Revenues for which a service has been performed or goods have been delivered but for which no entry has been made; unrecorded revenues.

(L.O. 5) **Accumulated depreciation account:** A contra-asset account used to accumulate the depreciation expense of a specific long-lived asset.

(L.O. 6) **Adjusted trial balance:** A trial balance prepared after all adjusting entries have been posted to the accounts.

(L.O. 4) **Adjusting entries:** Entries made to apply accrual accounting to transactions that span more than one accounting period.

(L.O. 5) **Carrying value:** The unexpired portion of the cost of an asset. Also called *book value.*

(L.O. 2) **Cash basis of accounting:** Accounting for revenues and expenses on a cash received and cash paid basis.

(L.O. 2) **Continuity issue:** The difficulty associated with not knowing how long a business entity will survive.

(L.O. 5) **Contra account:** An account whose balance is subtracted from an associated account in the financial statements.

(L.O. 4) **Deferral:** The postponement of the recognition of an expense that already has been paid or incurred or of a revenue that already has been received.

(L.O. 5) **Depreciation:** The periodic allocation of the cost of a tangible long-lived asset over its estimated useful life. Also called *depreciation expense.*

(L.O. 1) **Expenses:** The cost of goods and services used up in the course of earning revenues.

(L.O. 2) **Fiscal year:** Any twelve-month accounting period used by an economic entity.

(L.O. 2) **Going concern:** The assumption, unless there is evidence to the contrary, that the business entity will continue to operate indefinitely.

(L.O. 2) **Matching rule:** Revenues must be assigned to the accounting period in which the goods are sold or the services performed, and expenses must be assigned to the accounting period in which they are used to produce revenue.

(L.O. 1) **Net income:** The net increase in owner's equity that results from business operations; revenues less expenses when revenues exceed expenses.

(L.O. 1) **Net loss:** The net decrease in owner's equity that results when expenses exceed revenues.

(L.O. 2) **Periodicity:** The recognition that net income for any period less than the life of the business, although tentative, is still a useful estimate of net income for that period.

(L.O. 1) **Permanent accounts:** Balance sheet accounts; accounts whose balances can extend past the end of an accounting period. Also called *real accounts.*

(L.O. 5) **Prepaid expenses:** Expenses paid in advance that do not expire during the current accounting period; an asset account.

(L.O. 1) **Profit:** The increase in owner's equity that results from business operations.

(L.O. 3) **Revenue recognition:** In accrual accounting, the process of determining when a sale takes place.

(L.O. 1) **Revenues:** The price of goods sold and services rendered over a specific period of time.

(L.O. 1) **Temporary accounts:** Accounts that show the accumulation of revenues and expenses over one accounting period; at the end of the accounting period, these account balances are transferred to owner's equity. Also called *nominal accounts.*

(L.O. 5) **Unearned revenues:** Revenues received in advance for which the goods will not be delivered or the services performed during the current accounting period; a liability account.

Self-Test

Test your knowledge of the chapter by choosing the best answer for each of the following items.

(L.O. 1) 1. The net increase in owner's equity that results from business operations is called
   a. net income.
   b. revenue.
   c. an expense.
   d. an asset.

(L.O. 1) 2. In general, the accounts in the income statement are
   a. permanent accounts.
   b. temporary accounts.
   c. unearned revenue accounts.
   d. contra-asset accounts.

(L.O. 2) 3. A business can choose a fiscal year that corresponds to
   a. the calendar year.
   b. the natural business year.
   c. any twelve-month period.
   d. any of the above.

(L.O. 2) 4. Assigning revenues to the accounting period in which goods are delivered or services performed and expenses to the accounting period in which they are used to produce revenues is called the
   a. accounting period.
   b. continuity assumption.
   c. matching rule.
   d. recognition rule.

(L.O. 3) 5. Accrual accounting involves all of the following except
   a. recording all revenues when cash was received.
   b. applying the matching rule.
   c. recognizing expenses when incurred.
   d. adjusting the accounts.

(L.O. 4) 6. Which of the following is an example of a deferral?
   a. Apportioning costs between two or more periods
   b. Recognizing an accrued expense
   c. Recognizing an unrecorded revenue
   d. Recognizing an accrued revenue

(L.O. 5) 7. Prepaid Insurance shows an ending balance of $2,300. During the period, insurance in the amount of $1,200 expired. The adjusting entry would debit
   a. Prepaid Insurance for $1,200.
   b. Insurance Expense for $1,200.
   c. Unexpired Insurance for $1,100.
   d. Insurance Expense for $1,100.

(L.O. 6) 8. The adjusted trial balance is a list of accounts and their balances at
   a. the beginning of the accounting period.
   b. the end of the accounting period.
   c. the end of the accounting period immediately after adjusting entries have been posted.
   d. any point during the accounting period.

(L.O. 7) 9. A purchase of office supplies that was recorded in the Office Equipment account would require a correcting entry that
   a. credits Office Supplies.
   b. credits Cash.
   c. debits Office Equipment.
   d. credits Office Equipment.

(L.O. 8) 10. Which of the following sequences of actions describes the proper sequence of the accounting cycle?
   a. Post, record, analyze, prepare, close, adjust
   b. Analyze, record, post, adjust, prepare, close
   c. Prepare, record, post, adjust, analyze, close
   d. Enter, record, close, prepare, adjust, analyze

Answers to the Self-Test are at the end of this chapter.

Review Problem
Adjusting Entries, T Accounts, and Adjusted Trial Balance

(L.O. 5, 6) This was the unadjusted trial balance for Certified Answering Service on December 31, 19x2:

Certified Answering Service
Trial Balance
December 31, 19x2

Cash	$2,160	
Accounts Receivable	1,250	
Office Supplies	180	
Prepaid Insurance	240	
Office Equipment	3,400	
Accumulated Depreciation, Office Equipment		$ 600
Accounts Payable		700
Unearned Revenue		460
James Neal, Capital		4,870
James Neal, Withdrawals	400	
Answering Service Revenue		2,900
Wages Expense	1,500	
Rent Expense	400	
	$9,530	$9,530

The following information is also available:

a. Insurance that expired during December amounted to $40.
b. Office supplies on hand at the end of December totaled $75.
c. Depreciation for the month of December totaled $100.
d. Accrued wages at the end of December totaled $120.
e. Revenues earned for services performed but not yet billed on December 31 totaled $300.
f. Revenues earned for services performed that were paid in advance totaled $160.

Required

1. Prepare T accounts for the accounts in the trial balance and enter the balances.
2. Determine the required adjusting entries and record them directly in the T accounts. Open new T accounts as needed.
3. Prepare an adjusted trial balance.
4. Prepare an income statement, statement of owner's equity, and a balance sheet for the month ended December 31, 19x2. Assume that James Neal made no new investments during the month.

Answer to Review Problem

1. Set up the T accounts and enter the amounts from the trial balance.
2. Record the adjusting entries.

Cash

Bal.	2,160		

Accounts Receivable

Bal.	1,250		

Service Revenue Receivable

(e)	300		

Office Supplies

Bal.	180	(b)	105
Bal.	**75**		

Prepaid Insurance

Bal.	240	(a)	40
Bal.	**200**		

Office Equipment

Bal.	3,400		

Accumulated Depreciation, Office Equipment

		Bal.	600
		(c)	100
		Bal.	**700**

Accounts Payable

		Bal.	700

Unearned Revenue

(f)	160	Bal.	460
		Bal.	**300**

Wages Payable

		(d)	120

James Neal, Capital

		Bal.	4,870

James Neal, Withdrawals

Bal.	400		

Answering Service Revenue

		Bal.	2,900
		(e)	300
		(f)	160
		Bal.	**3,360**

Wages Expense

Bal.	1,500		
(d)	120		
Bal.	**1,620**		

Rent Expense

Bal.	400		

Insurance Expense

(a)	40		

Office Supplies Expense

(b)	105		

Depreciation Expense, Office Equipment

(c)	100		

3. Prepare an adjusted trial balance.

Certified Answering Service
Adjusted Trial Balance
December 31, 19x2

Cash	$ 2,160	
Accounts Receivable	1,250	
Service Revenue Receivable	300	
Office Supplies	75	
Prepaid Insurance	200	
Office Equipment	3,400	
Accumulated Depreciation, Office Equipment		$ 700
Accounts Payable		700
Unearned Revenue		300
Wages Payable		120
James Neal, Capital		4,870
James Neal, Withdrawals	400	
Answering Service Revenue		3,360
Wages Expense	1,620	
Rent Expense	400	
Insurance Expense	40	
Office Supplies Expense	105	
Depreciation Expense, Office Equipment	100	
	$10,050	$10,050

4. Prepare the financial statements.

Certified Answering Service
Income Statement
For the Month Ended December 31, 19x2

Revenues		
Answering Service Revenue		$3,360
Expenses		
Wages Expense	$1,620	
Rent Expense	400	
Insurance Expense	40	
Office Supplies Expense	105	
Depreciation Expense, Office Equipment	100	
Total Expenses		2,265
Net Income		$1,095

Certified Answering Service
Statement of Owner's Equity
For the Month Ended December 31, 19x2

James Neal, Capital, November 30, 19x2	$4,870
Net Income	1,095
Subtotal	$5,965
Less Withdrawals	400
James Neal, Capital, December 31, 19x2	$5,565

Certified Answering Service
Balance Sheet
December 31, 19x2

Assets		
Cash		$2,160
Accounts Receivable		1,250
Service Revenue Receivable		300
Office Supplies		75
Prepaid Insurance		200
Office Equipment	$3,400	
Less Accumulated Depreciation	700	2,700
Total Assets		$6,685
Liabilities		
Accounts Payable		$ 700
Unearned Revenue		300
Wages Payable		120
Total Liabilities		$1,120
Owner's Equity		
James Neal, Capital		5,565
Total Liabilities and Owner's Equity		$6,685

Chapter Assignments

Questions

1. Why does the accountant use the term *net income* instead of *profit*?
2. Define the terms *revenues* and *expenses*.
3. Why are income statement accounts called *temporary accounts*?
4. Why does the need for an accounting period cause problems?
5. What is the significance of the continuity assumption?
6. "The matching rule is the most significant concept in accounting." Do you agree with this statement? Explain your answer.
7. What is the difference between the cash basis and the accrual basis of accounting?
8. In what two ways is accrual accounting accomplished?
9. Why do adjusting entries have to be made?
10. What are the four situations that require adjusting entries? Give an example of each.
11. "Some assets are expenses that have not expired." Explain this statement.
12. What do plant and equipment, office supplies, and prepaid insurance have in common?
13. What is the difference between accumulated depreciation and depreciation expense?
14. What is a contra account? Give an example.
15. Why are contra accounts used to record depreciation?
16. How does unearned revenue arise? Give an example.
17. Where does unearned revenue appear on the balance sheet?
18. What accounting problem does a magazine publisher who sells three-year subscriptions have?
19. Under what circumstances does a company have accrued revenues? Give an example. What asset arises when the adjustment is made?
20. What is an accrued expense? Give three examples.
21. "Why worry about adjustments? Doesn't it all come out in the wash?" Discuss these questions.
22. Why is the income statement usually the first statement prepared from the adjusted trial balance?
23. What is the difference between an adjusting entry and a correcting entry?
24. Arrange the following activities in proper order by placing the numbers 1 through 6 in the blanks:
    ______ a. The transactions are entered in the journal.
    ______ b. Financial statements are prepared.
    ______ c. The transactions are analyzed from the source documents.
    ______ d. A trial balance and adjusted trial balance are prepared.
    ______ e. Closing entries are prepared.
    ______ f. The transactions are posted to the ledger.

Communication Skills Exercises

Communication 3-1. Account Identification *(L.O. 2, 3, 4)*

Takashimaya Company, Limited is Japan's largest department store chain. On Takashimaya's balance sheet is an account called Gift Certificates, which contains ¥26,156 million ($176 million). Is this account an asset or a liability? What transaction gives rise to the account? How is this account an example of the application of accrual accounting? Explain the conceptual issues that must be resolved in order for an adjusting entry to be valid.

Communication 3-2. Importance of Adjustments *(L.O. 2, 3, 4)*

Central Appliance Service Co., Inc. has achieved fast growth in the St. Louis area by selling service contracts on large appliances, such as washers, dryers, and refrigerators. For a fee, Central Appliance agrees to provide all parts and labor on an appliance after the regular warranty runs out. For example, by paying a fee of $200, a person who buys a dishwasher can add two years (Years 2 and 3) to the regular one-year (Year 1) warranty on the appliance. In 1991, the company sold service contracts in the amount of $1.8 million, all of which applied to future years. Management wanted all the sales recorded as revenues in 1991, contending that the amount of the contracts could be determined and the cash had been received. Do you agree with this logic? How would you record these cash receipts? What assumptions do you think should be made? Would you consider it unethical to follow management's recommendation?

Communication 3-3. Application of Accrual Accounting
(L.O. 3, 4)

The Lyric Opera of Chicago is one of the largest and best-managed opera companies in the United States. Managing opera productions requires advance planning, including the development of scenery, costumes, and stage properties; the sale of tickets; and the collection of contributions. To measure how well the company is operating in any given year, accrual accounting must be applied to these and other transactions. At year's end, February 28, 1990, Lyric Opera of Chicago's balance sheet showed Deferred Production and Other Costs of $412,858, Deferred Revenue from Sales of Tickets of $3,127,237, and Deferred Revenue from Contributions of $2,314,626. What accounting policies and adjusting entries are applicable to these accounts? Why are they important to Lyric Opera's management?

Communication 3-4. Basic Research Skills
(L.O. 4)

Go to the Yellow Pages of your local telephone directory. Find the names of five different kinds of service businesses. List the types of adjusting entries you think each business regularly makes. List any adjustments you think may be unique to each business.

Classroom Exercises

Exercise 3-1. Applications of Accounting Concepts Related to Accrual Accounting
(L.O. 2, 3)

The accountant for Marina Company makes the following assumptions or performs the following activities:

a. In estimating the life of a building, assumes that the business will last indefinitely.
b. Records a sale at the point in time when the customer is billed.
c. Postpones the recognition as an expense of a one-year insurance policy by initially recording the expenditure as an asset.
d. Recognizes the usefulness of financial statements prepared on a monthly basis even though they are based on estimates.
e. Recognizes, by making an adjusting entry, wages expense that has been incurred but not yet recorded.
f. Prepares an income statement that shows the revenues earned and the expenses incurred during the accounting period.

Tell which of the following concepts of accrual accounting most directly relates to each of the assumptions and actions above: (1) periodicity, (2) going concern, (3) matching rule, (4) revenue recognition, (5) deferral, and (6) accrual.

Exercise 3-2. Revenue Recognition
(L.O. 5)

Lifestyle Company of Toledo, Ohio publishes a monthly magazine featuring local restaurant reviews and upcoming social, cultural, and sporting events. Subscribers pay for subscriptions either one year or two years in advance. Cash received from subscribers is credited to an account called Magazine Subscriptions Received in Advance. On December 31, 19x3, the end of the company's fiscal year, the balance of this account was $1,000,000. Expiration of subscriptions was as follows:

During 19x3	$200,000
During 19x4	500,000
During 19x5	300,000

Prepare the adjusting journal entry for December 31, 19x3.

Exercise 3-3. Adjusting Entries for Prepaid Insurance
(L.O. 5)

An examination of the Prepaid Insurance account shows a balance of $4,112 at the end of an accounting period before adjustment. Prepare journal entries to record the insurance expense for the period under each of the following independent assumptions:

1. An examination of the insurance policies shows unexpired insurance that cost $1,974 at the end of the period.
2. An examination of the insurance policies shows insurance that cost $694 has expired during the period.

Exercise 3-4.
Supplies Account: Missing Data
(L.O. 5)

Each column below represents a supplies account:

	a	b	c	d
Supplies on hand October 1	$396	$ 651	$294	$?
Supplies purchased during the month	78	?	261	2,892
Supplies consumed during the month	291	1,458	?	2,448
Supplies on hand October 31	?	654	84	1,782

1. Determine the amounts indicated by the question marks in the columns.
2. Make the adjusting entry for Column **a**, assuming supplies purchased are debited to an asset account.

Exercise 3-5.
Adjusting Entry for Accrued Salaries
(L.O. 5)

Tru Vent has a five-day workweek and pays salaries of $70,000 each Friday.

1. Make the adjusting entry required on July 31, assuming that August 1 falls on a Wednesday.
2. Make the entry to pay the salaries on August 3.

Exercise 3-6.
Revenue and Expense Recognition
(L.O. 5)

Orlando Company produces computer software that is sold by Bond Systems Company. Orlando receives a royalty of 15 percent of sales. Royalties are paid by Bond Systems and received by Orlando semiannually on May 1 for sales made July through December of the previous year and on November 1 for sales made January through June of the current year. Royalty expense for Bond Systems and royalty income for Orlando in the amount of $12,000 were accrued on December 31, 19x2. Cash in the amounts of $12,000 and $20,000 was paid and received on May 1 and November 1, 19x3, respectively. Software sales during the July to December, 19x3, period totaled $300,000.

1. Calculate the amount of royalty expense for Bond Systems and royalty income for Orlando during 19x3.
2. Record the appropriate adjusting entries made by each of the companies on December 31, 19x3.

Exercise 3-7.
Adjusting Entries
(L.O. 5)

Prepare year-end adjusting entries for each of the following:

1. Office Supplies had a balance of $168 on January 1. Purchases debited to Office Supplies during the year amount to $830. A year-end inventory reveals supplies of $570 on hand.
2. Depreciation of office equipment is estimated to be $4,260 for the year.
3. Property taxes for six months, estimated at $1,750, have accrued but have not been recorded.
4. Unrecorded interest receivable on U.S. government bonds is $1,700.
5. Unearned Revenue has a balance of $1,800. Services for $600 received in advance have now been performed.
6. Services totaling $400 have been performed; the customer has not yet been billed.

Exercise 3-8.
Relationship of Cash to Expenses Paid
(L.O. 5)

After adjusting entries had been made, the 19x3 and 19x4 balance sheets of Hampton Company showed the following asset and liability amounts at the end of each year:

	19x3	19x4
Prepaid Insurance	$1,450	$1,200
Wages Payable	1,100	600
Unearned Fees	950	2,100

From the accounting records, the following amounts of cash disbursements and cash receipts for 19x4 were determined:

Cash disbursed to pay insurance premiums	$1,900
Cash disbursed to pay wages	9,750
Cash received for fees	4,450

Calculate the amount of insurance expense, wages expense, and fees earned that should be reported on the 19x4 income statement.

Exercise 3-9. Relationship of Expenses to Cash Paid *(L.O. 5)*

The income statement for Jarvis Company included the following expenses for 19xx:

Rent Expense	$ 5,200
Interest Expense	7,800
Salaries Expense	83,000

Listed below are the related balance sheet account balances at year end for last year and this year:

	Last Year	This Year
Prepaid Rent	—	$ 900
Interest Payable	$1,200	—
Salaries Payable	5,000	9,600

1. Compute the cash paid for rent during the year.
2. Compute the cash paid for interest during the year.
3. Compute the cash paid for salaries during the year.

Exercise 3-10. Accounting for Revenue Received in Advance *(L.O. 5, 6)*

Antonia Soria, a lawyer, was paid $72,000 on April 1 to represent a client in certain real estate negotiations over the next twelve months.

1. Record the entries required in Soria's records on April 1 and at the end of the year, December 31.
2. How would this transaction be reflected in the income statement and balance sheet on December 31?

Exercise 3-11. Identification of Accruals *(L.O. 5)*

Northwest Refrigeration Company has the following liabilities at year end:

Notes Payable	$30,000
Accounts Payable	20,000
Contract Revenue Received in Advance	18,000
Wages Payable	4,900
Interest Payable	1,400
Income Taxes Payable	2,500

1. Which of these accounts probably was created at the end of the fiscal year as a result of an accrual? Which probably was adjusted at year end?
2. Which adjustments probably reduced net income? Which probably increased net income?

Exercise 3-12. Analysis of Deferrals and Accruals *(L.O. 5)*

The following amounts are taken from the balance sheets of Green Bay Company:

	December 31	
	19x1	19x2
Prepaid Expenses	$ 45,000	$56,000
Accrued Liabilities	103,000	88,000

During 19x2, $114,000 was expended in cash and charged to Prepaid Expenses, and $212,000 was expended in cash for amounts related to the accrued liabilities. Determine the amount of expense related to Prepaid Expenses and to Accrued Liabilities for 19x2.

Exercise 3-13. Determining Cash Flows
(L.O. 5)

Horowitz Newspaper Agency delivers morning, evening, and Sunday city newspapers to subscribers who live in the suburbs. Customers can pay a yearly subscription fee in advance (at a savings) or pay monthly after delivery of their newspapers. The following data are available for the Subscriptions Receivable and Unearned Subscriptions accounts at the beginning and end of October 19xx:

	October 1	October 31
Subscriptions Receivable	$ 7,600	$ 9,200
Unearned Subscriptions	22,800	19,600

The income statement shows subscriptions revenue for October of $44,800. Determine the amount of cash received from customers for subscriptions during October.

Exercise 3-14. Preparation of Financial Statements
(L.O. 6)

Prepare the monthly income statement, statement of owner's equity, and balance sheet for Rogers Custodial Services from the data provided in this adjusted trial balance. Assume that no new investment was made by Chuck Rogers.

Rogers Custodial Services
Adjusted Trial Balance
August 31, 19xx

Cash	$ 4,590	
Accounts Receivable	2,592	
Prepaid Insurance	380	
Prepaid Rent	200	
Cleaning Supplies	152	
Cleaning Equipment	3,200	
Accumulated Depreciation, Cleaning Equipment		$ 320
Truck	7,200	
Accumulated Depreciation, Truck		720
Accounts Payable		420
Wages Payable		80
Unearned Janitorial Revenue		920
Chuck Rogers, Capital		15,034
Chuck Rogers, Withdrawals	2,000	
Janitorial Revenue		14,620
Wages Expense	5,680	
Rent Expense	1,200	
Gas, Oil, and Other Truck Expense	580	
Insurance Expense	380	
Supplies Expense	2,920	
Depreciation Expense, Cleaning Equipment	320	
Depreciation Expense, Truck	720	
	$32,114	$32,114

Exercise 3-15. Correction of Errors
(L.O. 7)

A number of errors in journalizing and posting transactions are described below. Prepare the journal entries to correct the errors.

1. The rent payment of $900 for the current month was recorded as a debit to Prepaid Rent and a credit to Cash.
2. A payment of $890 to a creditor was recorded in the amount of $980 as a debit to Accounts Payable and a credit to Cash.
3. A $760 cash payment for equipment repair expense was recorded as a debit to Equipment.
4. Payment of the gas and oil bill of $180 for the owner's personal car was recorded as a debit to Delivery Truck Expense and a credit to Cash.
5. A cash receipt of $300 for services yet to be performed was debited to Cash and credited to Service Revenue.

Interpretation Case from Business

City of Chicago
(L.O. 2, 3)

In 1979, Jane Byrne won the mayoral election in the city of Chicago partly on the basis of her charge that Michael Bilandic, the former mayor, was responsible for the budget deficit. Taking office in 1980, she hired a major international accounting firm, Peat, Marwick, Mitchell & Co. (now known as KPMG Peat Marwick), to straighten things out. This excerpt appeared in an article from a leading Chicago business publication:

> [A riddle]
> Q: When is a budget deficit not a deficit?
> A: When it is a surplus, of course.

> Chicago Mayor Jane Byrne was once again caught with egg on her face last week as she and her financial advisers tried to defend that riddle. On one hand, Comptroller Daniel J. Grim [a Byrne appointee], explaining $75 million in assets the mayor [Byrne] hopes to hold in reserve in the 1981 Chicago city budget, testified in hearings that the city had actually ended 1979 with a $6 million surplus, not the much-reported deficit. He said further that the modest surplus grew to $54 million as a result of tax-enrichment supplements to the 1979 balance sheet.
>
> On the other hand, the mayor stuck by the same guns she used last year on her predecessor. The city had ended 1979, under the Michael Bilandic Administration, not merely without a surplus, but with a deficit. The apparent discrepancy can be explained.[4]

Like most U.S. cities, Chicago operates under a modified accrual accounting basis. This is a combination of the straight cash basis and the accrual basis. The modified accrual basis differs from the accrual method in that an account receivable is recorded only when it is collected in the next accounting period. The collection of Chicago's parking tax, which is assessed on all city parking lots and garages, is an example:

> The tax is assessed and collected on a quarterly basis but the city doesn't collect the amount due for the last quarter of 1980 until the first quarter of 1981. Under ideal accrual methods, the parking revenues should be recorded in the 1980 financial statement. Under a cash approach, the revenues would be recorded in the 1981 budget. What the city did before was to record the money whenever it was advantageous politically. That, combined with the infamous revolving funds, allowed the city to hide the fact it was running large deficits under [former] Mayor Bilandic. That also means that no one really knew where the city stood.[5]

The auditors are now reallocating the parking revenues to the 1981 budget but are accruing other revenues by shifting the period of collection from a year in the past. Overall, more revenues were moved into earlier fiscal years than into later years, inflating those budgets. Thus, the 1979 deficit is a surplus. The article concluded:

> The upshot is that both Mayor Byrne and Mr. Grim [the comptroller] were correct. There was a deficit in the 1979 corporate or checkbook fund, but because of corrections taking place now, a surplus exists.[6]

Required

1. Do you agree with the way the auditors handled parking revenues? Support your answer by explaining which method of accounting you think a city should use.
2. "Systematically applied accounting principles will allow all to know exactly where the city stands." Comment on this statement made in another part of the article quoted above.

Problem Set A

Problem 3A-1. Preparation of Adjusting Entries
(L.O. 5)

On May 31, the end of the current fiscal year, the information on page 119 was available to help Costa Company's accountants make adjusting entries:

4. Reprinted with permission from the December 8, 1980 issue of *Crain's Chicago Business.* Copyright 1980 by Crain Communications Inc.
5. Ibid.
6. Ibid.

a. The Supplies account showed a beginning balance of $4,348. Purchases during the year were $9,052. The end-of-year inventory revealed supplies on hand that cost $2,794.
b. The Prepaid Insurance account showed the following on May 31:

Beginning Balance	$ 7,160
February 1	8,400
April 1	14,544

The beginning balance represents the portion of a one-year policy that remained unexpired at the beginning of the current fiscal year. The February 1 entry represents a new one-year policy, and the April 1 entry represents additional coverage in the form of a three-year policy.
c. The table below contains the cost and annual depreciation for buildings and equipment, all of which were purchased before the current year.

Account	Cost	Annual Depreciation
Buildings	$572,000	$29,000
Equipment	748,000	70,800

d. On March 1, the company completed negotiations with a client and accepted payment of $33,600, which represented one year's services paid in advance. The $33,600 was credited to Unearned Services Revenue.
e. The company calculated that as of May 31, it had earned $8,000 on a $22,000 contract that would be completed and billed in September.
f. Among the liabilities of the company is a note payable in the amount of $600,000. On May 31, the accrued interest on this note amounted to $30,000.
g. On Saturday, June 2, the company, which is on a six-day workweek, will pay its regular salaried employees $24,600.
h. On May 29, the company completed negotiations and signed a contract to provide services to a new client at an annual rate of $35,000.

Required

Prepare adjusting entries for each item listed above.

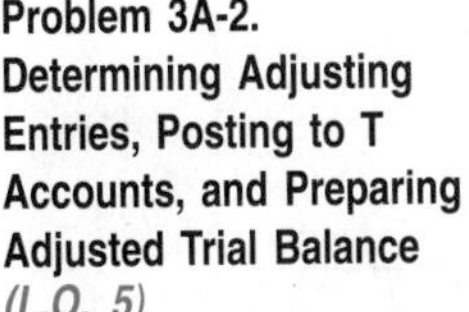

Problem 3A-2. Determining Adjusting Entries, Posting to T Accounts, and Preparing Adjusted Trial Balance *(L.O. 5)*

Here is the trial balance for Crown Advisory Services on July 31:

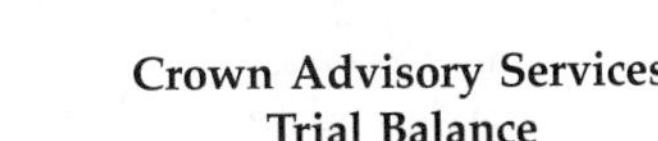

Crown Advisory Services
Trial Balance
July 31, 19xx

Cash	$ 8,250	
Accounts Receivable	4,125	
Office Supplies	1,331	
Prepaid Rent	660	
Office Equipment	4,620	
Accumulated Depreciation, Office Equipment		$ 770
Accounts Payable		2,970
Notes Payable		5,500
Unearned Fees		1,485
Molly Sklar, Capital		12,001
Molly Sklar, Withdrawals	11,000	
Fees Revenue		36,300
Salaries Expense	24,700	
Rent Expense	2,200	
Utility Expense	2,140	
	$59,026	$59,026

The following information is also available:

a. Ending inventory of office supplies, $132.
b. Prepaid rent expired, $220.
c. Depreciation of office equipment for the period, $330.
d. Accrued interest expense at the end of the period, $275.
e. Accrued salaries at the end of the month, $165.
f. Fees still unearned at the end of the period, $583.
g. Fees earned but unrecorded, $1,100.

Required

1. Open T accounts for the accounts in the trial balance plus the following: Fees Receivable; Interest Payable; Salaries Payable; Office Supplies Expense; Depreciation Expense, Office Equipment; and Interest Expense. Enter the balances.
2. Determine the adjusting entries and post them directly to the T accounts.
3. Prepare an adjusted trial balance.

Problem 3A-3. Determining Adjusting Entries and Tracing Their Effects to Financial Statements *(L.O. 5, 6)*

The Foremost Janitorial Service is owned by Ron Hudson. After six months of operation, the September 30, 19xx trial balance for the company was prepared.

Foremost Janitorial Service
Trial Balance
September 30, 19xx

Cash	$ 1,524	
Accounts Receivable	1,828	
Prepaid Insurance	760	
Prepaid Rent	1,400	
Cleaning Supplies	2,792	
Cleaning Equipment	3,480	
Truck	7,200	
Accounts Payable		$ 340
Unearned Janitorial Fees		960
Ron Hudson, Capital		14,190
Ron Hudson, Withdrawals	6,000	
Janitorial Fees		14,974
Wages Expense	4,800	
Gas, Oil, and Other Truck Expenses	680	
	$30,464	$30,464

The balance of the Capital account reflects investments made by Ron Hudson. The following information is also available:

a. Cleaning supplies of $234 are on hand.
b. Prepaid Insurance represents the cost of a one-year policy purchased on April 1.
c. Prepaid Rent represents a $200 payment made on April 1 toward the last month's rent of a three-year lease plus $200 rent per month for each of the past six months.
d. The cleaning equipment and trucks are depreciated at the rate of 20 percent per year (10 percent for each six-month period).
e. The unearned revenue represents a six-month payment in advance made by a customer on August 1.
f. During the last week of September, Ron completed the first stage of work on a contract that will not be billed until the contract is completed. The price of this stage is $800.
g. On Saturday, October 3, Ron will owe his employees $1,080 for one week's work (six-day workweek).

Required

1. Open T accounts for the accounts in the trial balance plus the following: Fees Receivable; Accumulated Depreciation, Cleaning Equipment; Accumulated Depreciation, Truck; Wages Payable; Rent Expense; Insurance Expense; Cleaning Supplies Expense; Depreciation Expense, Cleaning Equipment; and Depreciation Expense, Truck.
2. Determine the adjusting entries and post them directly to the T accounts.
3. Prepare an adjusted trial balance, an income statement, a statement of owner's equity, and a balance sheet.

Problem 3A-4. Determining Adjusting Entries and Tracing Their Effects to Financial Statements
(L.O. 5, 6)

At the end of the first three months of operations, this was the trial balance of the A-1 Answering Service:

A-1 Answering Service
Trial Balance
October 31, 19x4

Cash (111)	$ 5,524	
Accounts Receivable (112)	8,472	
Office Supplies (115)	1,806	
Prepaid Rent (116)	1,600	
Prepaid Insurance (117)	1,440	
Office Equipment (141)	4,600	
Communications Equipment (143)	4,800	
Accounts Payable (211)		$ 5,346
Unearned Answering Service Revenue (213)		1,776
Terry Mei, Capital (311)		11,866
Terry Mei, Withdrawals (312)	4,260	
Answering Service Revenue (411)		18,004
Wages Expense (511)	3,800	
Office Cleaning Expense (513)	690	
	$36,992	$36,992

Terry Mei, the owner of the answering service company, hired an ccountant to prepare financial statements in order to determine how well the company was doing after three months. On examining the accounting records, the accountant found the following items of interest:

a. An inventory of office supplies reveals supplies on hand of $266.
b. The Prepaid Rent account includes the rent for the first three months plus a deposit for the last month's rent.
c. Prepaid Insurance reflects a one-year policy purchased on August 4.
d. Depreciation is estimated at $204 on the office equipment and $212 on the communications equipment for the first three months.
e. The balance of the Unearned Answering Service Revenue account represents a twelve-month service contract paid in advance on September 1.
f. On October 31, accrued wages totaled $160.

The balance of the Capital account represents investments by Terry Mei.

Required

1. Record the adjusting entries in the general journal (Pages 12 and 13).
2. Open ledger accounts for the accounts in the trial balance plus the following: Accumulated Depreciation, Office Equipment (142); Accumulated Depreciation, Communications Equipment (144); Wages Payable (212); Rent Expense (512); Insurance Expense (514); Office Supplies Expense (515); Depreciation Expense, Office Equipment (516); and Depreciation Expense, Communications Equipment (517). Record the balances shown in the trial balance.

3. Post the adjusting entries from the general journal to the ledger accounts, showing the correct references.
4. Prepare an adjusted trial balance.
5. Prepare an income statement, a statement of owner's equity, and a balance sheet.
6. Give examples to show how the techniques of accrual accounting affect A-1's income statement.

Problem 3A-5. Determining Adjusting Entries and Tracing Their Effects to Financial Statements
(L.O. 5, 6)

Here is the trial balance for Century Dance School at the end of its current fiscal year:

Century Dance School
Trial Balance
July 31, 19x4

Cash (111)	$ 3,084	
Accounts Receivable (112)	1,551	
Supplies (115)	510	
Prepaid Rent (116)	1,200	
Prepaid Insurance (117)	1,080	
Equipment (141)	12,300	
Accumulated Depreciation, Equipment (142)		$ 1,200
Accounts Payable (211)		1,140
Unearned Dance Fees (213)		2,700
Loretta Harper, Capital (311)		7,500
Loretta Harper, Withdrawals (312)	36,000	
Dance Fees (411)		62,985
Wages Expense (511)	9,600	
Rent Expense (512)	6,600	
Utility Expense (515)	3,600	
	$75,525	$75,525

Loretta Harper, the owner, made no investments in the business during the year. The following information is available to help in the preparation of adjusting entries:

a. An inventory of supplies reveals $276 still on hand.
b. Prepaid Rent reflects the rent for July plus the rent for the last month of the lease.
c. Prepaid Insurance consists of a two-year policy purchased on February 1, 19x4.
d. Depreciation on equipment is estimated at $2,400.
e. Accrued wages are $195 on July 31.
f. Two-thirds of the unearned dance fees had been earned by July 31.

Required

1. Record the adjusting entries in the general journal (Page 53).
2. Open ledger accounts for the accounts in the trial balance plus the following: Wages Payable (212); Supplies Expense (513); Insurance Expense (514); and Depreciation Expense, Equipment (516). Record the balances shown in the trial balance.
3. Post the adjusting entries from the general journal to the ledger accounts, showing the correct references.
4. Prepare an adjusted trial balance, an income statement, a statement of owner's equity, and a balance sheet.

Problem Set B

Problem 3B-1. Preparation of Adjusting Entries
(L.O. 5)

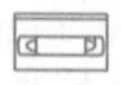

On June 30, the end of the current fiscal year, the following information was available to aid the Sterling Company accountants in making adjusting entries:

a. Among the liabilities of the company is a mortgage payable in the amount of $240,000. On June 30, the accrued interest on this mortgage amounted to $12,000.

b. On Friday, July 2, the company, which is on a five-day workweek and pays employees weekly, will pay its regular salaried employees $19,200.
c. On June 29, the company completed negotiations and signed a contract to provide services to a new client at an annual rate of $3,600.
d. The Supplies account showed a beginning balance of $1,615 and purchases during the year of $3,766. The end-of-year inventory revealed supplies on hand that cost $1,186.
e. The Prepaid Insurance account showed the following entries on June 30:

Beginning Balance	$1,530
January 1	2,900
May 1	3,366

The beginning balance represents the portion of a one-year policy that remained unexpired at the beginning of the current fiscal year. The January 1 entry represents a new one-year policy, and the May 1 entry represents additional coverage in the form of a three-year policy.
f. The table below contains the cost and annual depreciation for buildings and equipment, all of which were purchased before the current year:

Account	Cost	Annual Depreciation
Buildings	$185,000	$ 7,300
Equipment	218,000	21,800

g. On June 1, the company completed negotiations with another client and accepted a payment of $21,000, representing one year's services paid in advance. The $21,000 was credited to Services Collected in Advance.
h. The company calculated that as of June 30 it had earned $3,500 on a $7,500 contract that would be completed and billed in August.

Required

Prepare adjusting entries for each item listed above.

Problem 3B-2. Determining Adjusting Entries, Posting to T Accounts, and Preparing Adjusted Trial Balance *(L.O. 5)*

This is the trial balance for the Executive Advisory Company on March 31, 19x3:

Executive Advisory Company
Trial Balance
March 31, 19x3

Cash	$ 25,572	
Accounts Receivable	49,680	
Office Supplies	1,982	
Prepaid Rent	2,800	
Office Equipment	13,400	
Accumulated Depreciation, Office Equipment		$ 3,200
Accounts Payable		3,640
Notes Payable		20,000
Unearned Fees		5,720
Barbara Podolski, Capital		58,774
Barbara Podolski, Withdrawals	30,000	
Fees Revenue		117,000
Salaries Expense	66,000	
Utility Expense	3,500	
Rent Expense	15,400	
	$208,334	$208,334

The following information is also available:

a. Ending inventory of office supplies, $172.
b. Prepaid rent expired, $1,400.
c. Depreciation of office equipment for the period, $1,200.
d. Interest accrued on the note payable, $1,200.
e. Salaries accrued at the end of the period, $400.
f. Fees still unearned at the end of the period, $2,820.
g. Fees earned but not billed, $1,200.

Required

1. Open T accounts for the accounts in the trial balance plus the following: Fees Receivable; Interest Payable; Salaries Payable; Office Supplies Expense; Depreciation Expense, Office Equipment; and Interest Expense. Enter the balances.
2. Determine the adjusting entries and post them directly to the T accounts.
3. Prepare an adjusted trial balance.

Problem 3B-3. Determining Adjusting Entries and Tracing Their Effects to Financial Statements
(L.O. 5, 6)

Having graduated from college with a degree in accounting, Joyce Ozaki opened a small tax preparation service. At the end of its second year of operation, the Ozaki Tax Service has the following trial balance:

Ozaki Tax Service
Trial Balance
December 31, 19xx

Cash	$ 2,268	
Accounts Receivable	1,031	
Prepaid Insurance	240	
Office Supplies	782	
Office Equipment	4,100	
Accumulated Depreciation, Office Equipment		$ 410
Copier	3,000	
Accumulated Depreciation, Copier		360
Accounts Payable		635
Unearned Tax Fees		219
Joyce Ozaki, Capital		5,439
Joyce Ozaki, Withdrawals	6,000	
Fees Revenue		21,926
Office Salaries Expense	8,300	
Advertising Expense	650	
Rent Expense	2,400	
Telephone Expense	218	
	$28,989	$28,989

Joyce Ozaki made no investments in her business during the year. The following information was also available:

a. Supplies on hand, December 31, 19xx, were $227.
b. Insurance still unexpired amounted to $120.
c. Estimated depreciation of office equipment was $410.
d. Estimated depreciation of the copier was $360.
e. The telephone expense for December was $19. This bill has been received but not recorded.
f. The services for all unearned tax fees had been performed by the end of the year.

Required

1. Open T accounts for the accounts in the trial balance plus the following: Insurance Expense; Office Supplies Expense; Depreciation Expense, Office Equipment; Depreciation Expense, Copier. Record the balances as shown in the trial balance.

2. Determine the adjusting entries and post them directly to the T accounts.
3. Prepare an adjusted trial balance, an income statement, a statement of owner's equity, and a balance sheet.

Problem 3B-4. Determining Adjusting Entries and Tracing Their Effects to Financial Statements
(L.O. 5, 6)

At the end of its fiscal year, the trial balance for North Star Dry Cleaners appears as shown below. Jason Graves, the owner, made no investments during the year.

North Star Dry Cleaners
Trial Balance
June 30, 19x3

Cash (111)	$ 17,682	
Accounts Receivable (112)	39,741	
Prepaid Insurance (115)	5,100	
Cleaning Supplies (116)	11,061	
Land (141)	27,000	
Building (142)	243,000	
Accumulated Depreciation, Building (143)		$ 60,600
Delivery Trucks (144)	34,500	
Accumulated Depreciation, Delivery Trucks (145)		7,800
Accounts Payable (212)		30,600
Unearned Dry Cleaning Revenue (215)		2,400
Mortgage Payable (221)		180,000
Jason Graves, Capital (311)		84,840
Jason Graves, Withdrawals (312)	30,000	
Dry Cleaning Revenue (411)		180,501
Laundry Revenue (412)		55,950
Plant Wages Expense (511)	97,680	
Sales and Delivery Wages Expense (512)	54,315	
Cleaning Equipment Rent Expense (513)	9,000	
Delivery Trucks Expense (514)	6,561	
Interest Expense (519)	16,500	
Other Expenses (520)	10,551	
	$602,691	$602,691

The following information is also available:

a. A study of insurance policies shows that $1,020 is unexpired at the end of the year.
b. An inventory of cleaning supplies shows $1,866 on hand.
c. Estimated depreciation for the year is $12,900 on the building and $6,300 on the delivery trucks.
d. Accrued interest on the mortgage payable amounts to $1,500.
e. On May 1, the company signed a contract effective immediately with Kane County Hospital to dry-clean, for a fixed monthly charge of $600, the uniforms used by doctors in surgery. The hospital paid for four months' service in advance.
f. Unrecorded plant wages total $2,946.
g. Sales and delivery wages are paid on Saturday. The weekly payroll is $1,440. June 30 falls on a Thursday, and the company has a six-day workweek.

Required

1. Determine adjusting entries and enter them in the general journal (Pages 42 and 43).
2. Open ledger accounts for each account in the trial balance plus the following: Plant Wages Payable (213); Interest Payable (214); Insurance Expense (515); Cleaning Supplies Expense (516); Depreciation Expense, Building (517); and Depreciation Expense, Delivery Trucks (518). Record the balances shown in the trial balance.
3. Post the adjusting entries to the ledger accounts, showing the correct references.

4. Prepare an adjusted trial balance.
5. Prepare an income statement, a statement of owner's equity, and a balance sheet for the year ended June 30, 19x3.
6. Give examples of how the techniques of accrual accounting affect the income statement.

Problem 3B-5. Determining Adjusting Entries and Tracing Their Effects to Financial Statements
(L.O. 5, 6)

The Westland Limo Service was organized on January 1, 19x2 to provide limousine service between the airport and various suburban locations. It has just completed its second year of business. Its trial balance appears below. John Cummings, the owner, made no investments during the year.

Westland Limo Service
Trial Balance
December 31, 19x3

Cash (111)	$ 19,624	
Accounts Receivable (112)	28,454	
Prepaid Rent (117)	24,000	
Prepaid Insurance (118)	9,800	
Prepaid Maintenance (119)	24,000	
Spare Parts (141)	22,620	
Limousines (142)	400,000	
Accumulated Depreciation, Limousines (143)		$ 50,000
Notes Payable (211)		90,000
Unearned Passenger Service Revenue (212)		60,000
John Cummings, Capital (311)		156,422
John Cummings, Withdrawals (312)	40,000	
Passenger Service Revenue (411)		856,996
Gas and Oil Expense (511)	178,600	
Salaries Expense (512)	412,720	
Advertising Expense (513)	53,600	
	$1,213,418	$1,213,418

The following information is also available:

a. To obtain space at the airport, Westland paid two years' rent in advance when it began business.
b. An examination of the firm's insurance policies reveals that $5,600 expired during the year.
c. To provide regular maintenance for the vehicles, a deposit of $24,000 was made with a local garage. An examination of maintenance invoices reveals that there are $21,888 in charges against the deposit.
d. An inventory of spare parts shows $3,804 on hand.
e. All of the Westland Limo Service's limousines are depreciated at the rate of 12.5 percent a year. No limousines were purchased during the year.
f. A payment of $21,000 for one year's interest on notes payable is now due.
g. Unearned Passenger Service Revenue on December 31 includes $35,630 in tickets that were purchased by employers for use by their executives and that have not been redeemed.

Required

1. Record the adjusting entries in the general journal (Pages 14 and 15).
2. Open ledger accounts for the accounts in the trial balance plus the following: Interest Payable (213); Rent Expense (514); Insurance Expense (515); Spare Parts Expense (516); Depreciation Expense, Limousines (517); Maintenance Expense (518); and Interest Expense (519). Record the balances shown in the trial balance.

3. Post the adjusting entries from the general journal to the ledger accounts, showing the correct references.
4. Prepare an adjusted trial balance, an income statement, a statement of owner's equity, and a balance sheet.

Financial Decision Case

Alvarez Systems Company
(L.O. 5, 6)

Juan Alvarez began his new business, called Alvarez Systems Company, on January 1, 19xx. The company writes computer programs with special applications for businesses that own small computers. During the first six months of operation, the business was so successful that Alvarez had to hire new employees on several occasions. Yet, he continually had to put off creditors because he lacked the funds to pay them. He wants to apply for a bank loan, but after preparing a statement showing the totals of receipts of cash and payments of cash, he wonders whether a bank will make a loan to him on the basis of what seem to be poor results. Deciding that he needs some accounting help, Alvarez asks you to review the statement and the company's operating results.

Alvarez Systems Company
Statement of Cash Receipts and Payments
For the Six Months Ended June 30, 19xx

Receipts from		
Investment by Juan Alvarez		$ 45,000
Customers for Programming Services Provided		75,600
Total Cash Receipts		$120,600
Payments for		
Wages	$29,340	
Insurance	7,200	
Rent	12,600	
Supplies	5,940	
Office Equipment	18,600	
Computer Rental	24,000	
Maintenance	2,700	
Service Van	15,000	
Oil and Gas Reimbursements	2,070	
Utility	1,620	
Telephone	900	
Total Cash Payments		119,970
Bank Balance		$ 630

After verifying the information in Alvarez's statement, you assemble these additional facts about Alvarez Systems Company:

a. In addition to the amount received from customers, programming services totaling $29,100 have been performed but are not yet paid for.
b. Employees have been paid all the wages owed to them except for $1,050 earned since the last payday. The next regular payday is July 3.
c. The insurance account represents a two-year policy purchased on January 3.
d. The Rent account represents rent of $1,800 per month, including the rent for July.
e. In examining the expenditures for supplies, you find invoices for $1,950 that have not been paid, and an inventory reveals $2,625 of unused supplies on hand.
f. The office equipment is fully paid for. You estimate it will last five years and be worthless at the end of that time.

g. The computer rental agreement provides for a security deposit of $6,000 plus monthly payments of $3,000.
h. The maintenance account represents a one-year maintenance agreement, paid in advance on January 2.
i. The Service Van account represents the down payment on a van purchased on June 29 for $45,000. Before this purchase, the company had reimbursed employees for oil and gas when they used their own cars for business. A study of the documents shows that $360 in employee oil and gas receipts still must be reimbursed.
j. The utility and telephone expenses are paid through the end of June.

Required

1. From the information given, open T accounts and record the transactions and any adjustments. Use letters to identify transactions.
2. Prepare an adjusted trial balance, an income statement, and a balance sheet for Alvarez Systems Company.
3. What is your assessment of the company's performance? If you were a bank loan officer, would you approve a loan application from Alvarez Systems Company?

Answers to Self-Test

1. a	3. d	5. a	7. b	9. d
2. b	4. c	6. a	8. c	10. b

CHAPTER 4

Completing the Accounting Cycle

LEARNING OBJECTIVES

1. *Prepare a work sheet.*
2. *Identify the three principal uses of a work sheet.*
3. *Prepare financial statements from a work sheet.*
4. *Record the adjusting entries from a work sheet.*
5. *Explain the purposes of closing entries.*
6. *Prepare the required closing entries.*
7. *Prepare the post-closing trial balance.*
8. *Prepare reversing entries as appropriate.*

In this chapter, you complete the accounting cycle. First, you study the uses and preparation of the work sheet, an important tool for accountants. Then, in the final step in the accounting cycle, you learn how to prepare closing entries.

In previous chapters, the main focus was on measurement. In this chapter, the emphasis is on the sequence of steps used by the accountant to complete the accounting cycle. An important part of the accounting system involves the preparation of a work sheet, so we present, in detail, each step in its preparation. We also explain how the work sheet is used to carry out the end-of-period procedures: to record the adjusting entries, to prepare the financial statements, and to close the accounts. The optional first step of the next accounting period, the preparation of reversing entries, also is discussed. This chapter may be omitted in courses that take a less procedural approach to accounting. After studying this chapter, you should be able to meet the learning objectives listed on the left.

DECISION POINT

Maintenance Management Company

■ Shortly after the end of Maintenance Management Company's fiscal year, December 31, 1991, the company's accountants submitted the financial statements for the year. The management of the company, which provides janitorial services to major office buildings in the San Francisco area, was surprised to see a fairly substantial loss for the year, and, as a result, determined to pay closer attention to operating results during 1992. The accountants suggested that the company begin preparing *interim statements,* that is, financial statements that are prepared quarterly or monthly, so that management can see operating results more often than once a year. Management agreed that this sounded like a good idea, but wondered how much it would cost in time and money to prepare financial statements more frequently.

The preparation of interim financial statements requires more effort than simply preparing one set of financial statements for the year, which means that Maintenance Management Company would have to hire more accounting staff. Each time the financial statements are prepared, adjusting entries must be determined, prepared, and recorded. In addition, the ledger accounts have to be prepared for beginning the next accounting period. The advantages of preparing interim financial statements usually outweigh the costs, however, because these statements give management timely information that help it make the decisions that are necessary to improve a company's operations. This chapter explains the procedures that are carried out to prepare financial statements at the end of an accounting period, whether that period is a month, a quarter, or a year. ■

The Work Sheet: A Tool of Accountants

OBJECTIVE 1
Prepare a work sheet

As seen earlier, the flow of information that affects a business does not stop arbitrarily at the end of an accounting period. In order to prepare financial reports, accountants must collect relevant data to determine what should be included. For example, they have to examine insurance policies to see how much prepaid insurance has expired, examine plant and equipment records to determine depreciation, take an inventory of supplies on hand, and calculate the amount of accrued wages. These calculations, together with other computations, analyses, and preliminary drafts of statements, make up the accountants' **working papers**. Working papers are important for two reasons. First, they help accountants organize their work so that they do not omit important data or steps that affect the accounting statements. Second, they provide evidence of what has been done so that accountants or auditors can retrace their steps and support the information in the financial statements.

A special kind of working paper is the **work sheet**. The work sheet often is used as a preliminary step in the preparation of financial statements. Using a work sheet lessens the possibility of leaving out an adjustment, helps the accountant check the arithmetical accuracy of the accounts, and facilitates the preparation of financial statements. The work sheet is never published and is rarely seen by management: It is a tool for the accountant.

Because preparing a work sheet is a very mechanical process, many accountants use a microcomputer. In some cases, accountants use a spreadsheet program to prepare the work sheet. In other cases, general ledger software is used to prepare financial statements from the adjusted trial balance.

Steps in Preparing the Work Sheet

In the chapter on business income and accrual accounting, the adjustments were entered directly in the journal and posted to the ledger, and the financial statements were prepared from the adjusted trial balance. The process was relatively simple because the Joan Miller Advertising Agency is a small company. For larger companies, which may require many adjusting entries, a work sheet is essential. To illustrate the preparation of the work sheet, we continue with the Joan Miller Advertising Agency case.

A common form of work sheet has one column for account names and/or numbers and ten more columns with the headings shown in Exhibit 4-1. Notice that the work sheet is identified by a heading that consists of (1) the name of the company, (2) the title "Work Sheet," and (3) the period of time covered (as on the income statement).

There are five steps in the preparation of a work sheet:

1. Enter and total the account balances in the Trial Balance columns.
2. Enter and total the adjustments in the Adjustments columns.
3. Enter and total the account balances as adjusted in the Adjusted Trial Balance columns.
4. Extend the account balances from the Adjusted Trial Balance columns to the Income Statement columns or the Balance Sheet columns.

5. Total the Income Statement columns and the Balance Sheet columns. Enter the net income or net loss in both pairs of columns as a balancing figure, and recompute the column totals.

1. Enter and total the account balances in the Trial Balance columns. The titles and balances of the accounts as of January 31 are copied directly from the ledger into the Trial Balance columns, as shown in Exhibit 4-1. This trial balance is the same one illustrated in the chapter on business income and accrual accounting. When a work sheet is used, the accountant does not have to prepare a separate trial balance.

2. Enter and total the adjustments in the Adjustments columns. The required adjustments for the Joan Miller Advertising Agency were explained in the chapter on business income and accrual accounting. If you place the acetate page displaying Exhibit 4-2 over Exhibit 4-1, you can see that the same adjustments are entered in the Adjustments columns of the work sheet. As each adjustment is entered, a letter is used to identify the debit and credit parts of the same entry. The first adjustment, identified by the letter *a,* is to recognize rent expense, which results in a debit to Rent Expense and a credit to Prepaid Rent. In practice, this letter can be used to reference the supporting computations or documentation underlying the adjusting entry and can simplify the recording of adjusting entries in the general journal.

If the adjustment calls for an account that has not been used in the trial balance, the new account is added below the accounts listed in the trial balance. The trial balance includes only those accounts that have balances. For example, Rent Expense has been added in Exhibit 4-2. The only exception to this rule is the accumulated depreciation accounts, which have a zero balance only in the initial period of operation. Accumulated depreciation accounts are listed immediately after their associated asset accounts.

When all the adjustments have been made, the two Adjustments columns must be totaled. This step proves that the debits and credits of the adjustments are equal and generally reduces errors in the preparation of the work sheet.

3. Enter and total the account balances as adjusted in the Adjusted Trial Balance columns. By placing the acetate containing Exhibit 4-3 over Exhibit 4-2, you can see the adjusted trial balance. It is prepared by combining the amount of each account in the original Trial Balance columns with the corresponding amounts in the Adjustments columns and entering the combined amounts on a line-by-line basis in the Adjusted Trial Balance columns.

Some examples from Exhibit 4-3 illustrate **crossfooting**, or adding and subtracting a group of numbers horizontally. The first line shows Cash with a debit balance of $1,720. Because there are no adjustments to the Cash account, $1,720 is entered in the debit column of the Adjusted Trial Balance columns. The second line is Accounts Receivable, which shows a debit of $2,800 in the Trial Balance columns. Because there are no adjustments to Accounts Receivable, the $2,800 balance is carried over to the debit column of the Adjusted Trial Balance columns. The next line is Art Supplies, which shows a debit of $1,800 in the Trial Balance columns and a credit of $500 from adjustment **c** in the Adjustments columns. Subtracting $500 from $1,800 leaves a $1,300 debit balance in the Adjusted Trial Balance columns. This process is repeated for all the accounts, including those added below the trial balance. The Adjusted Trial Balance columns are then footed (totaled) to check the accuracy of the crossfooting.

4. Extend the account balances from the Adjusted Trial Balance columns to the Income Statement columns or the Balance Sheet columns. Every account in the adjusted trial balance is either a balance sheet account or an income statement account. Each account is extended to its correct place as a debit or credit in either the Income Statement columns or the Balance Sheet columns. The result of extending the accounts is apparent when you place the acetate showing Exhibit 4-4 over Exhibit 4-3. Revenue and expense accounts are extended (copied) to the Income Statement columns. Assets, liabilities, and the Capital and Withdrawals accounts are extended to the Balance Sheet columns. To avoid overlooking an account, extend the accounts line by line, beginning with the first line (Cash) and being sure not to leave out any subsequent lines. For instance, the Cash debit balance ($1,720) is extended to the debit column of the Balance Sheet columns, the Accounts Receivable debit balance ($2,800) is extended to the same debit column, and so forth. Each amount is carried forward to only one column.

5. Total the Income Statement columns and the Balance Sheet columns. Enter the net income or net loss in both pairs of columns as a balancing figure, and recompute the column totals. This last step, which you can see when you place the acetate depicting Exhibit 4-5 over Exhibit 4-4, is necessary to compute net income or net loss and to prove the arithmetical accuracy of the work sheet.

Net income (or net loss) equals the difference between the debit and credit columns of the income statement. It also equals the difference between the debit and credit columns of the balance sheet.

Revenues (Income Statement credit column total)	$4,800
Expenses (Income Statement debit column total)	(2,810)
Net Income	$1,990

In this case, revenues (the credit column) exceeds expenses (the debit column). Consequently, the company has a net income of $1,990. The same difference is shown between the debits and credits of the Balance Sheet columns.

The $1,990 is entered on the debit side of the Income Statement columns and on the credit side of the Balance Sheet columns, to balance the columns. Remember that excess revenue—net income—increases owner's equity, and that increases in owner's equity are recorded by credits.

When a net loss occurs, the opposite rule applies. The excess of expenses—net loss—is placed on the credit side of the Income Statement columns as a balancing figure. It then is extended to the debit side of the Balance Sheet columns because a net loss decreases owner's equity, and decreases in owner's equity are recorded by debits.

As a final check, the four columns are totaled again. If the Income Statement columns and the Balance Sheet columns do not balance, an account may have been extended or sorted to the wrong column, or an error may have been made in adding the columns. Of course, equal totals in the two pairs of columns are not absolute proof of accuracy. If an asset has been carried to the debit Income Statement column and if a similar error involving revenues or liabilities has been made, the work sheet still balances, but the net income figure is wrong.

Using the Work Sheet

OBJECTIVE 2
Identify the three principal uses of a work sheet

The completed work sheet helps the accountant in three principal ways: (1) preparing the financial statements, (2) recording the adjusting entries, and (3) recording the closing entries in the general journal in order to prepare the records for the beginning of the next period.

Preparing the Financial Statements

OBJECTIVE 3
Prepare financial statements from a work sheet

After completing the work sheet, it is simple to prepare the financial statements because the account balances have been sorted into Income Statement and Balance Sheet columns. The income statement shown in Exhibit 4-6 was prepared from the accounts in the Income Statement columns of Exhibit 4-5.

The statement of owner's equity and the balance sheet of the Joan Miller Advertising Agency are shown in Exhibits 4-7 and 4-8. The account balances for these statements are drawn from the Balance Sheet columns of the work sheet shown in Exhibit 4-5. Notice that the totals of the assets and of the liabilities and owner's equity in the balance sheet do not agree with the totals in the Balance Sheet columns in the work sheet. The Accumulated Depreciation and Withdrawals accounts have different normal balances than their associated accounts on the balance sheet. In addition, the Capital account on the balance sheet is the amount determined on the statement of owner's equity. At this point, the financial statements have been prepared from the work sheet, not from the ledger accounts. For the ledger accounts to show the correct balances, the adjusting entries have to be journalized and posted to the ledger.

Recording the Adjusting Entries

OBJECTIVE 4
Record the adjusting entries from a work sheet

For the Joan Miller Advertising Agency, the adjustments were determined during completion of the work sheet because they are essential to the preparation of the financial statements. The adjusting entries could have been recorded in the general journal at that point. However, it is usually convenient to delay recording them until after the work sheet and the financial statements have been prepared because this task can be done at the same time the closing entries are

Exhibit 4-6. Income Statement for the Joan Miller Advertising Agency

Joan Miller Advertising Agency
Income Statement
For the Month Ended January 31, 19xx

Revenues		
Advertising Fees Earned	$4,400	
Art Fees Earned	400	
Total Revenues		$4,800
Expenses		
Office Wages Expense	$1,380	
Utility Expense	100	
Telephone Expense	70	
Rent Expense	400	
Insurance Expense	40	
Art Supplies Expense	500	
Office Supplies Expense	200	
Depreciation Expense, Art Equipment	70	
Depreciation Expense, Office Equipment	50	
Total Expenses		2,810
Net Income		$1,990

Exhibit 4-7. Statement of Owner's Equity for the Joan Miller Advertising Agency

Joan Miller Advertising Agency Statement of Owner's Equity For the Month Ended January 31, 19xx		
Joan Miller, Capital, January 1, 19xx		—
Add: Investment by Joan Miller	$10,000	
Net Income	1,990	$11,990
Subtotal		$11,990
Less Withdrawals		1,400
Joan Miller, Capital, January 31, 19xx		$10,590

recorded, a process described in the next section. Recording the adjusting entries with appropriate explanations in the general journal, as shown in Exhibit 4-9, is an easy step. The information can simply be copied from the work sheet. Adjusting entries are then posted to the general ledger.

Exhibit 4-8. Balance Sheet for the Joan Miller Advertising Agency

Joan Miller Advertising Agency Balance Sheet January 31, 19xx		
Assets		
Cash		$ 1,720
Accounts Receivable		2,800
Fees Receivable		200
Art Supplies		1,300
Office Supplies		600
Prepaid Rent		400
Prepaid Insurance		440
Art Equipment	$4,200	
Less Accumulated Depreciation	70	4,130
Office Equipment	$3,000	
Less Accumulated Depreciation	50	2,950
Total Assets		$14,540
Liabilities		
Accounts Payable	$3,170	
Unearned Art Fees	600	
Wages Payable	180	
Total Liabilities		$ 3,950
Owner's Equity		
Joan Miller, Capital		10,590
Total Liabilities and Owner's Equity		$14,540

Exhibit 4-9. Adjustments on the Work Sheet Entered in the General Journal

General Journal					Page 3
Date		Description	Post. Ref.	Debit	Credit
19xx Jan.	31	Rent Expense	514	400	
		Prepaid Rent	117		400
		To recognize the expiration of one month's rent			
	31	Insurance Expense	515	40	
		Prepaid Insurance	118		40
		To recognize the expiration of one month's life insurance			
	31	Art Supplies Expense	516	500	
		Art Supplies	115		500
		To recognize art supplies used during the month			
	31	Office Supplies Expense	517	200	
		Office Supplies	116		200
		To recognize office supplies used during the month			
	31	Depreciation Expense, Art Equipment	519	70	
		Accumulated Depreciation, Art Equipment	145		70
		To record depreciation of art equipment for one month			
	31	Depreciation Expense, Office Equipment	520	50	
		Accumulated Depreciation, Office Equipment	147		50
		To record depreciation of office equipment for one month			
	31	Unearned Art Fees	213	400	
		Art Fees Earned	412		400
		To recognize the performance of services paid for in advance			
	31	Fees Receivable	114	200	
		Advertising Fees Earned	411		200
		To accrue unrecorded revenue			
	31	Office Wages Expense	511	180	
		Wages Payable	214		180
		To accrue unrecorded wages			

Recording the Closing Entries

OBJECTIVE 5
Explain the purposes of closing entries

Closing entries are journal entries made at the end of an accounting period. They accomplish two purposes. First, closing entries set the stage for the next accounting period by clearing revenue and expense accounts of their balances.

Remember that the income statement reports net income (or loss) for a single accounting period and shows revenues and expenses only for that period. For this reason, the revenue and expense accounts must be closed (cleared of their balances) at the end of the period so that the next period begins with a zero balance in those same accounts. The Withdrawals account is closed similarly.

Second, closing entries summarize a period's revenues and expenses. This is done by transferring the balances of revenues and expenses to the Income Summary account to record the net profit or loss in that account. **Income Summary**, a new temporary account, appears in the chart of accounts between the Withdrawals account and the first revenue account. This account provides a place to summarize all revenues and expenses in a single net figure before transferring the result to the Capital account. It is used only in the closing process and never appears in the financial statements.

The balance of Income Summary equals the net income or loss reported on the income statement. The net income or loss then is transferred to the owner's Capital account. Why? Because even though revenues and expenses are recorded in revenue and expense accounts, they actually represent increases and decreases in owner's equity. Closing entries transfer the net effect of increases (revenues) and decreases (expenses) to the owner's Capital account.

As stated in the chapter on business income and accrual accounting, revenue and expense accounts are temporary, or nominal, accounts. Temporary accounts begin each period with a zero balance, accumulate a balance during the period, and then are cleared by means of closing entries. The accountant uses these accounts to keep track of the increases and decreases in owner's equity in a way that is helpful to management and others interested in the success or progress of the company. Temporary accounts are different from balance sheet accounts. Balance sheet accounts are permanent: They carry the end-of-period balance into the next accounting period.

Required Closing Entries

OBJECTIVE 6
Prepare the required closing entries

There are four important steps in the preparation of closing entries:

1. Transferring the credit balances from income statement accounts to the Income Summary account
2. Transferring the debit balances from income statement accounts to the Income Summary account
3. Transferring the Income Summary account balance to the Capital account
4. Transferring the Withdrawals account balance to the Capital account

With the exception of the Withdrawals account balance, all the data needed to perform these closing steps are found in the Income Statement columns of the work sheet.

Closing the Credit Balances from Income Statement Accounts to the Income Summary Account

In the credit side of the Income Statement columns of the work sheet in Exhibit 4-5, two revenue accounts show balances: Advertising Fees Earned and Art Fees Earned. An entry debiting each of these accounts in the amount of its balance is needed to close the accounts. The Income Summary account is credited for the total (which can be found in the credit side of the Income Statement columns of the work sheet). The compound entry that closes the two revenue accounts for the Joan Miller Advertising Agency is as follows:

Jan. 31	Advertising Fees Earned	411	4,400	
	Art Fees Earned	412	400	
	Income Summary	313		4,800
	To close the revenue accounts			

The effect of posting the entry is shown in Exhibit 4-10. Notice that the entry (1) sets the balances of the revenue accounts to zero, and (2) transfers the total revenues to the credit side of the Income Summary account. If a work sheet is not used, this data can be found in the appropriate general ledger accounts after the adjusting entries have been posted.

Closing the Debit Balances from Income Statement Accounts to the Income Summary Account

On the debit side of the Income Statement columns of the work sheet in Exhibit 4-5, several expense accounts show balances. A compound entry is needed to credit each of these expense accounts for its balance and to debit the Income Summary account for the total (which can be found in the debit side of the Income Statement columns):

Jan. 31	Income Summary	313	2,810	
	Office Wages Expense	511		1,380
	Utility Expense	512		100
	Telephone Expense	513		70
	Rent Expense	514		400
	Insurance Expense	515		40
	Art Supplies Expense	516		500
	Office Supplies Expense	517		200
	Depreciation Expense, Art Equipment	519		70
	Depreciation Expense, Office Equipment	520		50
	To close the expense accounts			

Exhibit 4-10. Posting the Closing Entry of the Credit Balances from the Income Statement Accounts to the Income Summary Account

Advertising Fees Earned — Account No. 411

Date	Item	Post. Ref.	Debit	Credit	Balance Debit	Balance Credit
Jan. 10		J2		1,400		1,400
19		J2		2,800		4,200
31	Adj. (h)	J3		200		4,400
31	Closing	J4	4,400			—

Income Summary — Account No. 313

Date	Item	Post. Ref.	Debit	Credit	Balance Debit	Balance Credit
Jan. 31	Closing	J4		4,800		4,800

4,400
400
4,800

Art Fees Earned — Account No. 412

Date	Item	Post. Ref.	Debit	Credit	Balance Debit	Balance Credit
Jan. 31	Adj. (g)	J3		400		400
31	Closing	J4	400			—

The effect of posting the closing entries to the ledger accounts is shown in Exhibit 4-11. Notice again how the closing entries (1) reduce the expense account balances to zero and (2) transfer the total of the account balances to the debit side of the Income Summary account.

Closing the Income Summary Account to the Capital Account

After the entries closing the revenue and expense accounts have been posted, the balance of the Income Summary account equals the net income or loss for the period. A net income is indicated by a credit balance; a net loss, by a debit

Exhibit 4-11. Posting the Closing Entry of the Debit Balances from the Income Statement Accounts to the Income Summary Account

Office Wages Expense — Account No. 511

Date	Item	Post. Ref.	Debit	Credit	Balance Debit	Balance Credit
Jan. 12		J2	600		600	
26		J2	600		1,200	
31	Adj. (i)	J3	180		1,380	
31	Closing	J4		1,380	—	

Utility Expense — Account No. 512

Date	Item	Post. Ref.	Debit	Credit	Balance Debit	Balance Credit
Jan. 29		J2	100		100	
31	Closing	J4		100	—	

Telephone Expense — Account No. 513

Date	Item	Post. Ref.	Debit	Credit	Balance Debit	Balance Credit
Jan. 30		J2	70		70	
31	Closing	J4		70	—	

Rent Expense — Account No. 514

Date	Item	Post. Ref.	Debit	Credit	Balance Debit	Balance Credit
Jan. 31	Adj. (a)	J3	400		400	
31	Closing	J4		400	—	

Insurance Expense — Account No. 515

Date	Item	Post. Ref.	Debit	Credit	Balance Debit	Balance Credit
Jan. 31	Adj. (b)	J3	40		40	
31	Closing	J4		40	—	

Art Supplies Expense — Account No. 516

Date	Item	Post. Ref.	Debit	Credit	Balance Debit	Balance Credit
Jan. 31	Adj. (c)	J3	500		500	
31	Closing	J4		500	—	

1,380
100
70
400
40
500
50
70
200
2,810

Income Summary — Account No. 313

Date	Item	Post. Ref.	Debit	Credit	Balance Debit	Balance Credit
Jan. 31	Closing	J4		4,800		4,800
31	Closing	J4	2,810			1,990

Office Supplies Expense — Account No. 517

Date	Item	Post. Ref.	Debit	Credit	Balance Debit	Balance Credit
Jan. 31	Adj. (d)	J3	200		200	
31	Closing	J4		200	—	

Depreciation Expense, Art Equipment — Account No. 519

Date	Item	Post. Ref.	Debit	Credit	Balance Debit	Balance Credit
Jan. 31	Adj. (e)	J3	70		70	
31	Closing	J4		70	—	

Depreciation Expense, Office Equipment — Account No. 520

Date	Item	Post. Ref.	Debit	Credit	Balance Debit	Balance Credit
Jan. 31	Adj. (f)	J3	50		50	
31	Closing	J4		50	—	

Exhibit 4-12. Posting the Closing Entry of the Income Summary Account to the Capital Account

Income Summary					Account No. 313	
					Balance	
Date	Item	Post. Ref.	Debit	Credit	Debit	Credit
Jan. 31	Closing	J4		4,800		4,800
31	Closing	J4	2,810			1,990
31	Closing	J4	1,990			—

Joan Miller, Capital					Account No. 311	
					Balance	
Date	Item	Post. Ref.	Debit	Credit	Debit	Credit
Jan. 1		J1		10,000		10,000
31	Closing	J4		1,990		11,990

balance. At this point, the Income Summary balance, whether debit or credit, must be closed to the Capital account. For the Joan Miller Advertising Agency, the entry is as follows:

Jan. 31 Income Summary	313	1,990	
Joan Miller, Capital	311		1,990
To close the Income Summary account			

The effect of posting the closing entry is shown in Exhibit 4-12. Notice the dual effect of (1) closing the Income Summary account and (2) transferring the balance, net income in this case, to Joan Miller's Capital account.

Closing the Withdrawals Account to the Capital Account

The Withdrawals account shows the amount by which capital is reduced during the period by withdrawals of cash or other assets from the business for the owner's personal use. The debit balance of the Withdrawals account is closed to the Capital account, as shown below.

Jan. 31 Joan Miller, Capital	311	1,400	
Joan Miller, Withdrawals	312		1,400
To close the Withdrawals account			

This closing entry, as shown in Exhibit 4-13, (1) closes the Withdrawals account and (2) transfers the balance to the Capital account.

The Accounts After Closing

After all the steps in the closing process have been completed and all of the adjusting and closing entries have been posted to the accounts, the stage is set

Exhibit 4-13. Posting the Closing Entry of the Withdrawals Account to the Capital Account

Joan Miller, Withdrawals					Account No. 312	
					Balance	
Date	Item	Post. Ref.	Debit	Credit	Debit	Credit
Jan. 25		J2	1,400		1,400	
31	Closing	J4		1,400	—	

Joan Miller, Capital					Account No. 311	
					Balance	
Date	Item	Post. Ref.	Debit	Credit	Debit	Credit
Jan. 1		J1		10,000		10,000
31	Closing	J4		1,990		11,990
31	Closing	J4	1,400			10,590

for the next accounting period. The ledger accounts of the Joan Miller Advertising Agency as they appear at this point are shown in Exhibit 4-14. The revenue, expense, and Withdrawals accounts (temporary accounts) have zero balances. The Capital account has been increased to reflect the agency's net income and the owner's withdrawals. The balance sheet accounts (permanent accounts) show the correct balances, which are carried forward to the next period.

The Post-Closing Trial Balance

OBJECTIVE 7
Prepare the post-closing trial balance

Because it is possible to make an error in posting the adjustments and closing entries to the ledger accounts, it is necessary to determine that all temporary (nominal) accounts have zero balances and to check again that total debits equal total credits by preparing a new trial balance. This final trial balance, called the **post-closing trial balance**, is shown in Exhibit 4-15 for the Joan Miller Advertising Agency. Notice that only the balance sheet (permanent) accounts show balances because the income statement accounts and the Withdrawals account have all been closed.

Reversing Entries: The Optional First Step in the Next Accounting Period

OBJECTIVE 8
Prepare reversing entries as appropriate

At the end of each accounting period, adjusting entries are made to bring revenues and expenses into conformity with the matching rule. A **reversing entry** is a general journal entry made on the first day of the new accounting period that is the exact reverse of an adjusting entry made at the end of the previous period. Reversing entries are optional. They simplify the bookkeeping process for transactions involving certain types of adjustments. Not all adjusting entries can be reversed. For the system of recording used in this book, only adjustments for accruals (accrued revenues and accrued expenses) can be reversed. Deferrals cannot be reversed because reversing adjustments for deferrals would not simplify the bookkeeping process in future accounting periods.

To show how reversing entries can be helpful, consider the adjusting entry made in the records of the Joan Miller Advertising Agency to accrue office wages expense:

Jan. 31	Office Wages Expense	180	
	Wages Payable		180
	To accrue unrecorded wages		

When the secretary is paid on the next regular payday, the accountant would make this entry:

Feb. 9	Wages Payable	180	
	Office Wages Expense	420	
	Cash		600
	Payment of two weeks' wages to secretary, $180 of which accrued in the previous period		

Notice that when the payment is made, if there is not a reversing entry, the accountant must look in the records to find out how much of the $600 applies to

Exhibit 4-14. The Accounts After Closing Entries Are Posted

Cash — Account No. 111

Date	Item	Post. Ref.	Debit	Credit	Balance Debit	Balance Credit
Jan. 1		J1	10,000		10,000	
2		J1		800	9,200	
4		J1		4,200	5,000	
5		J1		1,500	3,500	
8		J1		480	3,020	
9		J1		1,000	2,020	
10		J2	1,400		3,420	
12		J2		600	2,820	
15		J2	1,000		3,820	
25		J2		1,400	2,420	
26		J2		600	1,820	
29		J2		100	1,720	

Accounts Receivable — Account No. 113

Date	Item	Post. Ref.	Debit	Credit	Balance Debit	Balance Credit
Jan. 19		J2	2,800		2,800	

Fees Receivable — Account No. 114

Date	Item	Post. Ref.	Debit	Credit	Balance Debit	Balance Credit
Jan. 31	Adj. (h)	J3	200		200	

Art Supplies — Account No. 115

Date	Item	Post. Ref.	Debit	Credit	Balance Debit	Balance Credit
Jan. 6		J1	1,800		1,800	
31	Adj. (c)	J3		500	1,300	

Office Supplies — Account No. 116

Date	Item	Post. Ref.	Debit	Credit	Balance Debit	Balance Credit
Jan. 6		J1	800		800	
31	Adj. (d)	J3		200	600	

Prepaid Rent — Account No. 117

Date	Item	Post. Ref.	Debit	Credit	Balance Debit	Balance Credit
Jan. 2		J1	800		800	
31	Adj. (a)	J3		400	400	

Prepaid Insurance — Account No. 118

Date	Item	Post. Ref.	Debit	Credit	Balance Debit	Balance Credit
Jan. 8		J1	480		480	
31	Adj. (b)	J3		40	440	

Art Equipment — Account No. 144

Date	Item	Post. Ref.	Debit	Credit	Balance Debit	Balance Credit
Jan. 4		J1	4,200		4,200	

Accumulated Depreciation, Art Equipment — Account No. 145

Date	Item	Post. Ref.	Debit	Credit	Balance Debit	Balance Credit
Jan. 31	Adj. (e)	J3		70		70

Office Equipment — Account No. 146

Date	Item	Post. Ref.	Debit	Credit	Balance Debit	Balance Credit
Jan. 5		J1	3,000		3,000	

Accumulated Depreciation, Office Equipment — Account No. 147

Date	Item	Post. Ref.	Debit	Credit	Balance Debit	Balance Credit
Jan. 31	Adj. (f)	J3		50		50

Accounts Payable — Account No. 212

Date	Item	Post. Ref.	Debit	Credit	Balance Debit	Balance Credit
Jan. 5		J1		1,500		1,500
6		J1		2,600		4,100
9		J1	1,000			3,100
30		J2		70		3,170

Unearned Art Fees — Account No. 213

Date	Item	Post. Ref.	Debit	Credit	Balance Debit	Balance Credit
Jan. 15		J2		1,000		1,000
31	Adj. (g)	J3	400			600

Wages Payable — Account No. 214

Date	Item	Post. Ref.	Debit	Credit	Balance Debit	Balance Credit
Jan. 31	Adj. (i)	J3		180		180

(continued)

Exhibit 4-14. *(continued)*

Joan Miller, Capital — Account No. 311

Date	Item	Post. Ref.	Debit	Credit	Balance Debit	Balance Credit
Jan. 1		J1		10,000		10,000
31	Closing	J4		1,990		11,990
31	Closing	J4	1,400			10,590

Joan Miller, Withdrawals — Account No. 312

Date	Item	Post. Ref.	Debit	Credit	Balance Debit	Balance Credit
Jan. 25		J2	1,400		1,400	
31	Closing	J4		1,400	—	

Income Summary — Account No. 313

Date	Item	Post. Ref.	Debit	Credit	Balance Debit	Balance Credit
Jan. 31	Closing	J4		4,800		4,800
31	Closing	J4	2,810			1,990
31	Closing	J4	1,990			—

Advertising Fees Earned — Account No. 411

Date	Item	Post. Ref.	Debit	Credit	Balance Debit	Balance Credit
Jan. 10		J2		1,400		1,400
19		J2		2,800		4,200
31	Adj. (h)	J3		200		4,400
31	Closing	J4	4,400			—

Art Fees Earned — Account No. 412

Date	Item	Post. Ref.	Debit	Credit	Balance Debit	Balance Credit
Jan. 31	Adj. (g)	J3		400		400
31	Closing	J4	400			—

Office Wages Expense — Account No. 511

Date	Item	Post. Ref.	Debit	Credit	Balance Debit	Balance Credit
Jan. 12		J2	600		600	
26		J2	600		1,200	
31	Adj. (i)	J3	180		1,380	
31	Closing	J4		1,380	—	

Utility Expense — Account No. 512

Date	Item	Post. Ref.	Debit	Credit	Balance Debit	Balance Credit
Jan. 29		J2	100		100	
31	Closing	J4		100	—	

Telephone Expense — Account No. 513

Date	Item	Post. Ref.	Debit	Credit	Balance Debit	Balance Credit
Jan. 30		J2	70		70	
31	Closing	J4		70	—	

Rent Expense — Account No. 514

Date	Item	Post. Ref.	Debit	Credit	Balance Debit	Balance Credit
Jan. 31	Adj. (a)	J3	400		400	
31	Closing	J4		400	—	

Insurance Expense — Account No. 515

Date	Item	Post. Ref.	Debit	Credit	Balance Debit	Balance Credit
Jan. 31	Adj. (b)	J3	40		40	
31	Closing	J4		40	—	

Art Supplies Expense — Account No. 516

Date	Item	Post. Ref.	Debit	Credit	Balance Debit	Balance Credit
Jan. 31	Adj. (c)	J3	500		500	
31	Closing	J4		500	—	

Office Supplies Expense — Account No. 517

Date	Item	Post. Ref.	Debit	Credit	Balance Debit	Balance Credit
Jan. 31	Adj. (d)	J3	200		200	
31	Closing	J4		200	—	

Depreciation Expense, Art Equipment — Account No. 519

Date	Item	Post. Ref.	Debit	Credit	Balance Debit	Balance Credit
Jan. 31	Adj. (e)	J3	70		70	
31	Closing	J4		70	—	

Depreciation Expense, Office Equipment — Account No. 520

Date	Item	Post. Ref.	Debit	Credit	Balance Debit	Balance Credit
Jan. 31	Adj. (f)	J3	50		50	
31	Closing	J4		50	—	

Exhibit 4-15. Post-Closing Trial Balance

Joan Miller Advertising Agency Post-Closing Trial Balance January 31, 19xx		
Cash	$ 1,720	
Accounts Receivable	2,800	
Fees Receivable	200	
Art Supplies	1,300	
Office Supplies	600	
Prepaid Rent	400	
Prepaid Insurance	440	
Art Equipment	4,200	
Accumulated Depreciation, Art Equipment		$ 70
Office Equipment	3,000	
Accumulated Depreciation, Office Equipment		50
Accounts Payable		3,170
Unearned Art Fees		600
Wages Payable		180
Joan Miller, Capital		10,590
	$14,660	$14,660

the current accounting period and how much is applicable to the previous period. This may seem easy in our examples, but think of how difficult and time consuming it would be if a company has hundreds of employees, especially if some of them are paid on different schedules. A reversing entry is an accounting procedure that helps solve the problem of applying revenues and expenses to the correct accounting period. A reversing entry is exactly what its name implies: a reversal of the adjusting entry made by debiting the credits and crediting the debits of the adjusting entry.

For example, notice the following sequence of entries and their effects on the ledger account Office Wages Expense:

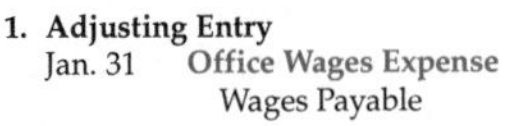

1. **Adjusting Entry**
   Jan. 31 Office Wages Expense 180
   Wages Payable 180
2. **Closing Entry**
   Jan. 31 Income Summary 1,380
   Office Wages Expense 1,380
3. **Reversing Entry**
   Feb. 1 Wages Payable 180
   Office Wages Expense 180
4. **Payment Entry**
   Feb. 9 Office Wages Expense 600
   Cash 600

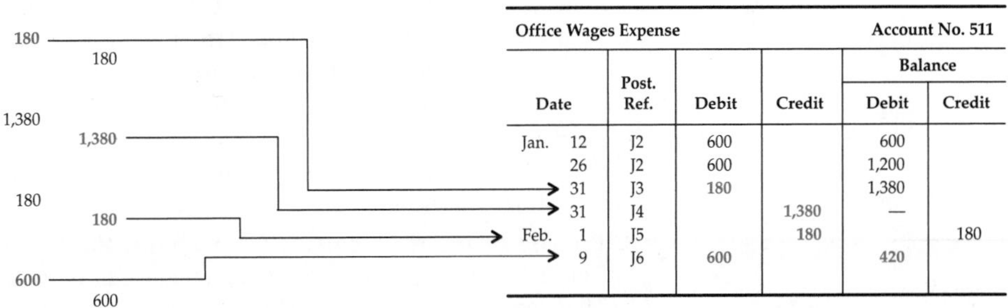

Office Wages Expense — Account No. 511

Date		Post. Ref.	Debit	Credit	Balance Debit	Balance Credit
Jan.	12	J2	600		600	
	26	J2	600		1,200	
	31	J3	180		1,380	
	31	J4		1,380	—	
Feb.	1	J5		180		180
	9	J6	600		420	

Entry 1 adjusted Office Wages Expense to accrue $180 in the January accounting period.

Entry 2 closed the $1,380 in Office Wages Expense for January to Income Summary, leaving a zero balance.

Entry 3, the reversing entry, set up a credit balance of $180 on February 1 in Office Wages Expense equal to the expense recognized through the adjusting entry in January (and also reduced the liability account Wages Payable to a zero balance).

Notice that the reversing entry always sets up a non-normal balance in the income statement account and produces a zero balance in the balance sheet account.

Entry 4 recorded the $600 payment of two weeks' wages as a debit to Office Wages Expense, automatically leaving a balance of $420, which represents the correct wages expense to date in February.

The reversing entry simplified the process of making the payment entry on February 9.

Reversing entries apply to any accrued expenses or revenues. In the case of the Joan Miller Advertising Agency, office wages expense was the only accrued expense. However, the asset account Fees Receivable was created as a result of the adjusting entry made to accrue fees earned but not yet billed. The adjusting entry for this accrued revenue requires a reversing entry like this:

Feb.	1	Advertising Fees Earned	200	
		Fees Receivable		200
		To reverse the adjusting entry for accrued fees receivable		

When the series of advertisements is finished, the accountant can credit the entire proceeds to Advertising Fees Earned without worry about the amount accrued in the previous period. The credit automatically will be reduced to the amount earned during February by the $200 debit in the account.

As noted above, under the system of recording used in this book, reversing entries apply only to accruals. For this reason, reversing entries do not apply to deferrals, such as those that involve supplies, prepaid rent, prepaid insurance, depreciation, and unearned art fees.

Chapter Review

Review of Learning Objectives

1. **Prepare a work sheet.**
   There are five steps in the preparation of a work sheet: (1) Enter and total the account balances in the Trial Balance columns; (2) enter and total the adjustments in the Adjustments columns; (3) enter and total the adjusted account balances in the Adjusted Trial Balance columns; (4) extend the account balances in the Adjusted Trial Balance columns to the Income Statement or Balance Sheet columns; and (5) total the Income Statement and Balance Sheet columns, enter the net income or net loss in both pairs of columns, and then total the columns to be sure they balance.
2. **Identify the three principal uses of a work sheet.**
   A work sheet is useful in (1) preparing the financial statements, (2) recording the adjusting entries, and (3) recording the closing entries.
3. **Prepare financial statements from a work sheet.**
   The balance sheet and income statement can be prepared directly from the Balance Sheet and Income Statement columns of the completed work sheet. The statement of owner's equity is prepared using withdrawals, net income, additional investments, and the beginning balance of the owner's Capital account. Notice that the ending balance of owner's equity does not appear on the work sheet but is a result of it.
4. **Record the adjusting entries from a work sheet.**
   Adjusting entries can be recorded in the general journal directly from the Adjustments columns of the work sheet.
5. **Explain the purposes of closing entries.**
   Closing entries have two objectives. First, they clear the balances of all temporary accounts (revenue and expense accounts, and withdrawals) so that they have zero

balances at the beginning of the next accounting period. Second, they summarize a period's revenues and expenses in the Income Summary account so that the net income or loss for the period can be transferred as a total to owner's equity.

6. **Prepare the required closing entries.**
   Closing entries are prepared by first transferring the revenue and expense account balances (credit and debit entries in the Income Statement columns of the work sheet) to the Income Summary account. Then the balance of the Income Summary account is transferred to the Capital account. And, finally, the balance of the Withdrawals account is transferred to the Capital account.
7. **Prepare the post-closing trial balance.**
   As a final check on the balance of the ledger and to ensure that all temporary (nominal) accounts have been closed, a post-closing trial balance is prepared after the closing entries are posted to the ledger accounts.
8. **Prepare reversing entries as appropriate.**
   Reversing entries are optional entries made on the first day of a new accounting period to simplify routine bookkeeping procedures. They reverse certain adjusting entries made in the previous period. Under the system used in this text, they apply only to accruals.

Review of Concepts and Terminology

The following concepts and terms were introduced in this chapter:

(L.O. 5) **Closing entries:** Journal entries made at the end of an accounting period that set the stage for the next accounting period by clearing the temporary accounts of their balances and that summarize a period's revenues and expenses.

(L.O. 1) **Crossfooting:** Adding and subtracting numbers across a row.

(L.O. 5) **Income Summary:** A temporary account used during the closing process that holds a summary of all revenues and expenses before the net income or loss is transferred to the Capital account.

(L.O. 7) **Post-closing trial balance:** A trial balance prepared at the end of the accounting period after all adjusting and closing entries have been posted; a final check on the balance of the ledger.

(L.O. 8) **Reversing entry:** An entry made on the first day of a new accounting period that is used to reverse certain adjusting entries and designed to simplify the bookkeeping process for the next accounting period.

(L.O. 1) **Working papers:** Documents prepared and used by accountants to help them organize their work and to support the information in the financial statements.

(L.O. 1) **Work sheet:** A type of working paper that is used as a preliminary step and tool in the preparation of financial statements.

Self-Test

Test your knowledge of the chapter by choosing the best answer for each of the following items.

(L.O. 1) 1. The work sheet is a type of
   a. ledger.
   b. journal.
   c. working paper.
   d. financial statement.

(L.O. 1) 2. Which of the following is shown directly on the work sheet?
   a. Ending owner's capital
   b. Total assets
   c. Net income
   d. Total liabilities

(L.O. 2) 3. The work sheet can be used
   a. to prepare financial statements.
   b. to record adjusting entries.
   c. to record closing entries.
   d. for all of the above.

(L.O. 3) 4. Which of the following statements may be prepared from the work sheet but does not have a set of columns denoted to it?
a. Balance sheet
b. Income statement
c. Statement of owner's equity
d. Statement of cash flows

(L.O. 5) 5. One important purpose of closing entries is to
a. adjust the accounts in the ledger.
b. set balance sheet accounts to zero in order to begin the next accounting period.
c. set income statement accounts to zero to begin the next accounting period.
d. summarize assets and liabilities.

(L.O. 6) 6. In preparing closing entries, it is helpful to refer first to the
a. Adjustments columns of the work sheet.
b. Adjusted Trial Balance columns of the work sheet.
c. Income Statement columns of the work sheet.
d. general journal.

(L.O. 6) 7. After all the closing entries have been posted, the balance of the Income Summary account should be
a. a debit if a net income has been earned.
b. a debit if a net loss has been incurred.
c. a credit if a net loss has been incurred.
d. zero.

(L.O. 6) 8. After the closing entries have been posted, all of the following accounts have a zero balance *except*
a. Service Revenue Earned.
b. Depreciation Expense.
c. Unearned Service Revenue.
d. Service Wages Expense.

(L.O. 7) 9. The post-closing trial balance
a. lists income statement accounts only.
b. lists balance sheet accounts only.
c. lists both income statement and balance sheet accounts.
d. is prepared before closing entries are posted to the ledger.

(L.O. 8) 10. For which of the following adjustments would a reversing entry facilitate bookkeeping procedures?
a. An adjustment for depreciation expense
b. An adjustment to allocate prepaid insurance to the current period
c. An adjustment made as a result of an inventory of supplies
d. An adjustment for wages earned but not yet paid to employees

Answers to the Self-Test are at the end of this chapter.

Review Problem
Preparation of a Work Sheet, Financial Statements, Adjusting Entries, and Closing Entries

(L.O. 1, 3, 4, 6, 7) This chapter contains an extended example of the preparation of a work sheet and the last two steps of the accounting cycle for the Joan Miller Advertising Agency. Instead of studying a review problem, carefully review and retrace the steps through the illustrations in the chapter.

Required

1. In Exhibit 4-5, the figures in the Trial Balance columns come from the balances of the accounts in the general ledger after all transactions during the accounting period have been recorded and posted.
2. Trace the amounts in the Income Statement and Balance Sheet columns of Exhibit 4-5 to the income statement in Exhibit 4-6, the statement of owner's equity in Exhibit 4-7, and the balance sheet in Exhibit 4-8.
3. Trace the entries in the Adjustments columns of Exhibit 4-5 to the journal entries in Exhibit 4-9.

4. Trace the amounts in the Income Statement columns and the Withdrawals account balance in Exhibit 4-5 to the closing entries on pages 137–139.
5. Trace the journal entries in Exhibit 4-9 to the ledger accounts in Exhibit 4-14.
6. Trace the closing entries on pages 137–139 to the ledger accounts in Exhibit 4-14.
7. Trace the balances of the ledger accounts in Exhibit 4-14 to the post-closing trial balance in Exhibit 4-15.

Chapter Assignments

Questions

1. Why are working papers important to the accountant?
2. Why are work sheets never published and rarely seen by management?
3. How might accountants use computer software to accomplish the objectives of the work sheet?
4. Can the work sheet be used as a substitute for the financial statements? Explain your answer.
5. At the end of the accounting period, does the posting of adjusting entries to the ledger precede or follow the preparation of the work sheet?
6. What is the normal balance (debit or credit) of the following accounts?
   a. Cash
   b. Accounts Payable
   c. Prepaid Rent
   d. Sam Jones, Capital
   e. Commission Revenue
   f. Sam Jones, Withdrawals
   g. Rent Expense
   h. Accumulated Depreciation, Office Equipment
   i. Office Equipment
7. What is the probable cause of a credit balance in the Cash account?
8. Should the Adjusted Trial Balance columns of the work sheet be totaled before or after the adjusted amounts are carried to the Income Statement and Balance Sheet columns? Discuss your answer.
9. What sequence should be followed in extending the Adjusted Trial Balance columns to the Income Statement and Balance Sheet columns? Discuss your answer.
10. Do the Income Statement columns and Balance Sheet columns of the work sheet balance after the amounts from the Adjusted Trial Balance columns are extended?
11. Do the totals of the Balance Sheet columns of the work sheet agree with the totals on the balance sheet? Explain your answer.
12. What is the purpose of the Income Summary account?
13. Should adjusting entries be posted to the ledger accounts before or after the closing entries? Explain your answer.
14. What is the difference between adjusting and closing entries?
15. What are the four basic tasks of closing entries?
16. Which of the following accounts do not show a balance after the closing entries are prepared and posted?
    a. Insurance Expense
    b. Accounts Receivable
    c. Commission Revenue
    d. Prepaid Insurance
    e. Supplies
    f. The owner's Withdrawals account
    g. Supplies Expense
    h. The owner's Capital account
17. What is the significance of the post-closing trial balance?
18. Which of the following accounts would you expect to find on the post-closing trial balance?
    a. Accounts Receivable
    b. Insurance Expense
    c. Commission Revenue
    d. Prepaid Insurance
    e. The owner's Withdrawals account
    f. Supplies
    g. Supplies Expense
    h. The owner's Capital account
19. How do reversing entries simplify the bookkeeping process?
20. To what types of adjustments do reversing entries apply? To what types do they not apply?

Communication Skills Exercises

Communication 4-1. Ethics and Time Pressure
(L.O. 1, 3)

Jay Wheeler, the assistant accountant for WB, Inc., has made adjusting entries and is preparing the adjusted trial balance for the first six months of the year. Financial statements must be delivered to the bank by 5 o'clock to support a critical loan agreement. By noon, Jay cannot balance the adjusted trial balance. The figures are off by $1,320, so he increases the balance of the capital account by $1,320. He prepares the statements and sends them to the bank on time. Jay hopes that no one will notice the problem and believes he can find the error and correct it by the end of next month. Are Jay's actions ethical? Why or why not? Did Jay have other alternatives?

Communication 4-2. Accounting Efficiency
(L.O. 4, 8)

Way Heaters Company is a small, successful manufacturer of industrial heaters, which it sells to some of its customers on credit with generous terms. The terms usually specify payment six months after purchase and an interest rate based on current bank rates. Because the interest on these loans accrues a little bit every day but is not paid until the due date of the note, it is necessary to make an adjusting entry at the end of each accounting period to debit Interest Receivable and credit Interest Income for the amount of the interest accrued but not paid to date. The company prepares financial statements every month. Keeping track of what has been accrued in the past is time consuming because the notes carry different dates and interest rates. How can this process be simplified?

Communication 4-3. Basic Research Skills
(L.O. 1, 2, 3, 4, 6, 7, 8)

Interview the owner, manager, or accountant of a local service or retail business for an hour to learn about its accounting cycle. Ask this person to show you his or her accounting records and to explain how such transactions as sales, purchases, payments, and payroll are handled. Look at any journals, ledgers, or work sheets that he or she uses. Does the business use a computer? Does it use its own accounting system, or does it use an outside or centralized service? Does it use the cash or accrual basis of accounting? When does it prepare adjusting entries? When does it prepare closing entries? How often does it prepare financial statements? Does it prepare reversing entries? How do its procedures differ from those described in the text? After the interview, organize your findings and be prepared to present them in class.

Classroom Exercises

Exercise 4-1. Preparation of a Trial Balance
(L.O. 1)

The following alphabetical list represents the accounts and balances for Natraj Realty on June 30, 19x3. All the accounts have normal balances.

Accounts Payable	$15,420	Natraj, Withdrawals	$27,000
Accounts Receivable	7,650	Office Equipment	15,510
Accumulated Depreciation,		Prepaid Insurance	1,680
Office Equipment	1,350	Rent Expense	7,200
Advertising Expense	1,800	Revenue from Commissions	57,900
Cash	7,635	Supplies	825
Natraj, Capital	30,630	Wages Expense	36,000

Prepare a trial balance by listing the accounts in the correct order, with the balances in the appropriate debit or credit column.

Exercise 4-2. Completion of a Work Sheet
(L.O. 1)

The following is a list of alphabetically arranged accounts and balances, in highly simplified form. This information is for the month ended October 31, 19xx.

Trial Balance Accounts and Balances

Accounts Payable	$4	Rita Wilkins, Capital	$12
Accounts Receivable	7	Rita Wilkins, Withdrawals	6
Accumulated Depreciation,		Service Revenue	23
Office Equipment	1	Supplies	4
Cash	4	Unearned Revenue	3
Office Equipment	8	Utility Expense	2
Prepaid Insurance	2	Wages Expense	10

1. Prepare a work sheet, entering the trial balance accounts in the order in which they would normally appear, and arranging the balances in the correct debit or credit column.
2. Complete the work sheet using the following information:
   a. Expired insurance, $1.
   b. Of the unearned revenue balance, $2 has been earned by the end of the month.
   c. Estimated depreciation on office equipment, $1.
   d. Accrued wages, $1.
   e. Unused supplies on hand, $1.

Exercise 4-3. Preparation of a Statement of Owner's Equity
(L.O. 3)

The Capital, Withdrawals, and Income Summary accounts for Wendell's Barber Shop are shown in T account form below. The closing entries have been recorded for the year ended December 31, 19xx.

Wendell Ross, Capital

12/31	4,500	Beg. bal.	13,000
		12/31	9,500
		Bal.	**18,000**

Wendell Ross, Withdrawals

4/1	1,500	12/31	4,500
7/1	1,500		
10/1	1,500		
Bal.	—		

Income Summary

12/31	21,500	12/31	31,000
12/31	9,500		
Bal.	—		

Prepare a statement of owner's equity for Wendell's Barber Shop.

Exercise 4-4. Derivation of Adjusting Entries from Trial Balance and Income Statement Columns
(L.O. 3, 4)

Below is a partial work sheet in which the Trial Balance and Income Statement columns have been completed. All amounts shown are in dollars.

Account Name	Trial Balance Debit	Trial Balance Credit	Income Statement Debit	Income Statement Credit
Cash	14			
Accounts Receivable	24			
Supplies	22			
Prepaid Insurance	16			
Building	50			
Accumulated Depreciation, Building		16		
Accounts Payable		8		
Unearned Revenue		4		
T. L., Capital		64		
Revenue		88		92
Wages Expense	54		60	
	180	180		
Insurance Expense			8	
Supplies Expense			16	
Depreciation Expense, Building			4	
			88	92
Net Income			4	
			92	92

1. Determine the adjustments that have been made. (Assume that no adjustments have been made to Accounts Receivable or Accounts Payable.)
2. Prepare a balance sheet.

Exercise 4-5.
Preparation of Adjusting and Reversing Entries from Work Sheet Columns
(L.O. 4, 8)

The items below are from the Adjustments columns of a work sheet dated June 30.

Account Name	Adjustments			
	Debit		Credit	
Prepaid Insurance			(a)	240
Office Supplies			(b)	630
Accumulated Depreciation, Office Equipment			(c)	1,400
Accumulated Depreciation, Store Equipment			(d)	2,200
Office Salaries Expense	(e)	240		
Store Salaries Expense	(e)	480		
Insurance Expense	(a)	240		
Office Supplies Expense	(b)	630		
Depreciation Expense, Office Equipment	(c)	1,400		
Depreciation Expense, Store Equipment	(d)	2,200		
Salaries Payable			(e)	720
		5,190		5,190

1. Prepare the adjusting entries.
2. Where required, prepare appropriate reversing entries.

Exercise 4-6.
Preparation of Closing Entries from the Work Sheet
(L.O. 6)

The items below are from the Income Statement columns of the work sheet of the DiPietro Repair Shop for the year ended December 31, 19xx.

Account Name	Income Statement	
	Debit	Credit
Repair Revenue		25,620
Wages Expense	8,110	
Rent Expense	1,200	
Supplies Expense	4,260	
Insurance Expense	915	
Depreciation Expense, Repair Equipment	1,345	
	15,830	25,620
Net Income	9,790	
	25,620	25,620

Prepare entries to close the revenue, expense, Income Summary, and Withdrawals accounts. Mr. DiPietro withdrew $5,000 during the year.

Exercise 4-7.
Reversing Entries
(L.O. 8)

Selected June T accounts for Holmes Company are presented at the top of page 151.

Supplies

6/1 Bal.	860	6/30 Adjust.	1,280
June purchases	940		
Bal.	**520**		

Supplies Expense

6/30 Adjust.	1,280	6/30 Closing	1,280
Bal.	—		

Wages Payable

		6/30 Adjust.	640
		Bal.	**640**

Wages Expense

June wages	3,940	6/30 Closing	4,580
6/30 Adjust.	640		
Bal.	—		

1. In which of these accounts would a reversing entry be helpful? Why?
2. Prepare the appropriate reversing entry.
3. Prepare the entry to record payments on July 3 for wages totaling $3,140. How much of this amount represents wages expense for July?

Interpretation Case from Business

H&R Block, Inc.
(L.O. 5, 6)

H&R Block, Inc. is the world's largest tax preparation service firm. In its 1990 annual report, the statement of earnings (in thousands, without earnings per share information) for the year ended April 30, 1990 looked like this:

Revenues	
Service Revenues	$ 937,796
Royalties	89,800
Investment Income	15,852
Other Revenues	9,248
Total Revenues	$1,052,696
Expenses	
Employee Compensation and Benefits	$ 492,840
Occupancy and Equipment Expense	152,370
Marketing and Advertising	69,367
Supplies, Freight, and Postage	43,516
Other Operating Expenses	94,069
Total Expenses	$ 852,162
Earnings Before Income Taxes	$ 200,534
Income Taxes	77,005
Net Earnings	$ 123,529

Elsewhere in H&R Block's financial statements, the company reported distributing cash in the amount of $69,539,000 to the owners in 1990.

Required

1. Prepare, in general journal form, the closing entries that would have been made by H&R Block on April 30, 1990. Treat cash distributions as a withdrawal.
2. On the basis of the way you handled expenses and cash distributions in **1** and their ultimate effect on the owner's capital, what theoretical reason can you give for not including expenses and cash distributions in the same closing entry?

Problem Set A

Problem 4A-1. Preparation of Financial Statements and End-of-Period Entries
(L.O. 3, 6, 8)

Benzinger Trailer Rental owns thirty small trailers that are rented by the day for local moving jobs. The adjusted trial balance for Benzinger Trailer Rental for the year ended December 31, 19x4, the end of the current fiscal year, is shown at the top of page 152.

Benzinger Trailer Rental
Adjusted Trial Balance
For the Year Ended December 31, 19x4

Cash	$ 1,384	
Accounts Receivable	1,944	
Supplies	238	
Prepaid Insurance	720	
Trailers	24,000	
Accumulated Depreciation, Trailers		$ 14,400
Accounts Payable		542
Wages Payable		400
Frank Benzinger, Capital		11,388
Frank Benzinger, Withdrawals	14,400	
Trailer Rentals		91,092
Wages Expense	46,800	
Insurance Expense	1,440	
Supplies Expense	532	
Depreciation Expense, Trailers	4,800	
Other Expenses	21,564	
	$117,822	$117,822

Required

1. Prepare an income statement, a statement of owner's equity, and a balance sheet. Assume no additional investments by Frank Benzinger.
2. From the information given, record the closing entries.
3. Assuming Wages Payable represents wages accrued at the end of the period, record the required reversing entry on January 1.

Problem 4A-2. Preparation of a Work Sheet and Financial Statements
(L.O. 1, 3)

The trial balance below was taken from the ledger of Holiday Bowling Lanes at the end of the company's fiscal year.

Holiday Bowling Lanes
Trial Balance
June 30, 19x4

Cash	$ 32,428	
Accounts Receivable	14,776	
Supplies	2,608	
Prepaid Insurance	3,600	
Prepaid Advertising	1,800	
Land	10,000	
Building	200,000	
Accumulated Depreciation, Building		$ 44,800
Equipment	250,000	
Accumulated Depreciation, Equipment		44,000
Accounts Payable		30,088
Notes Payable		140,000
Unearned Revenues		4,600
Marty Kern, Capital		121,626
Marty Kern, Withdrawals	48,000	
Revenues		1,232,526
Wages Expense	754,228	
Advertising Expense	28,600	
Utility Expense	84,400	
Maintenance Expense	168,200	
Miscellanous Expense	19,000	
	$1,617,640	$1,617,640

Required

1. Enter the trial balance amounts in the Trial Balance columns of a work sheet, and complete the work sheet using the following information:
   a. Inventory of unused office supplies, $312.
   b. Expired insurance, $3,000.
   c. Expired advertising, $1,800.
   d. Estimated depreciation on building, $9,600.
   e. Estimated depreciation on equipment, $22,000.
   f. Previously unearned revenues now earned, $4,000.
   g. Accrued but unpaid wages, $7,924.
   h. Accrued but unpaid property taxes, $20,000.
2. Prepare an income statement, a statement of owner's equity, and a balance sheet. Assume no additional investments by Marty Kern.

Problem 4A-3. Preparation of a Work Sheet; Financial Statements; and Adjusting, Closing, and Reversing Entries
(L.O. 1, 3, 4, 6, 8)

Donald Leung began his consulting practice immediately after graduating with his M.B.A. To help him get started, several clients paid him retainers (payment in advance) for future services. Other clients paid when service was provided. After one year, this was the firm's trial balance:

Donald Leung, Consultant
Trial Balance
June 30, 19x5

Cash	$ 9,750	
Accounts Receivable	8,127	
Office Supplies	1,146	
Office Equipment	11,265	
Accounts Payable		$ 3,888
Unearned Retainers		15,000
Donald Leung, Capital		12,000
Donald Leung, Withdrawals	18,000	
Consulting Fees		54,525
Rent Expense	5,400	
Utility Expense	2,151	
Wages Expense	29,574	
	$85,413	$85,413

Required

1. Enter the trial balance amounts in the Trial Balance columns of a work sheet. Remember that accumulated depreciation is listed with its asset account. Complete the work sheet using the following information:
   a. Inventory of unused supplies, $174.
   b. Estimated depreciation on equipment, $1,800.
   c. Services rendered during the month but not yet billed, $2,175.
   d. Services rendered to clients who paid in advance that should be applied against unearned retainers, $9,450.
   e. Wages earned by employees but not yet paid, $360.
2. Prepare an income statement, statement of owner's equity, and balance sheet. Assume no additional investments by Donald Leung.
3. Prepare adjusting, closing, and, if required, reversing entries.
4. How would you evaluate Mr. Leung's first year in practice?

Problem 4A-4. Preparation of a Work Sheet; Financial Statements; and Adjusting, Closing, and Reversing Entries
(L.O. 1, 3, 4, 6, 8)

At the end of the current fiscal year, this was the trial balance of the Drexel Theater:

Drexel Theater
Trial Balance
June 30, 19x5

Cash	$ 31,800	
Accounts Receivable	18,544	
Prepaid Insurance	19,600	
Office Supplies	780	
Cleaning Supplies	3,590	
Land	20,000	
Building	400,000	
Accumulated Depreciation, Building		$ 39,400
Theater Furnishings	370,000	
Accumulated Depreciation, Theater Furnishings		65,000
Office Equipment	31,600	
Accumulated Depreciation, Office Equipment		15,560
Accounts Payable		45,506
Gift Books Liability		41,900
Mortgage Payable		300,000
Ruth Otero, Capital		312,648
Ruth Otero, Withdrawals	60,000	
Ticket Sales Revenue		411,400
Theater Rental Revenue		45,200
Usher Wages Expense	157,000	
Office Wages Expense	24,000	
Utility Expense	112,700	
Interest Expense	27,000	
	$1,276,614	$1,276,614

Required

1. Enter the trial balance amounts in the Trial Balance columns of a work sheet, and complete the work sheet using the following information:
   a. Expired insurance, $17,400.
   b. Inventory of unused office supplies, $244.
   c. Inventory of unused cleaning supplies, $468.
   d. Estimated depreciation on the building, $14,000.
   e. Estimated depreciation on the theater furnishings, $36,000.
   f. Estimated depreciation on the office equipment, $3,160.
   g. The company credits all gift books sold during the year to the Gift Books Liability account. Gift books are booklets of ticket coupons that are purchased in advance as a gift. The recipient redeems the coupons at some point in the future. On June 30 it was estimated that $37,800 worth of the gift books had been redeemed.
   h. Accrued but unpaid usher wages at the end of the accounting period, $860.
2. Prepare an income statement, a statement of owner's equity, and a balance sheet. Assume no additional investments by Ruth Otero.
3. Prepare adjusting, closing, and, if required, reversing entries.

Problem 4A-5. The Complete Accounting Cycle: Two Months
(L.O. 1, 3, 4, 6, 7)

During its first two months of operation, the Rawls Repair Store completed the following transactions:

Oct.	1	Began business by making a deposit in a company bank account, $12,000.
	1	Paid the premium on a one-year insurance policy, $1,200.
	1	Paid the current month's rent, $1,040.

Oct. 3 Purchased repair equipment from Conklin Company, $4,400. The terms were $600 down and $200 per month for nineteen months. The first payment is due November 1.
8 Purchased repair supplies from McKenna Company on credit, $390.
12 Paid utility bill for October, $154.
16 Cash bicycle repair revenue for the first half of October, $1,362.
19 Made payment to McKenna Company, $200.
27 Owner's withdrawal for personal living expenses, $800.
31 Cash bicycle repair revenue for the last half of October, $1,310.

Nov. 1 Paid the monthly rent, $1,040.
1 Made the monthly payment to Conklin Company, $200.
7 Purchased repair supplies on credit from McKenna Company, $894.
12 Cash bicycle repair revenue for the first half of November, $1,050.
16 Paid the utility bill for November, $166.
17 Paid McKenna Company on account, $400.
25 Owner's withdrawal for personal living expenses, $800.
30 Cash bicycle repair revenue for the last half of November, $1,374.

Required

1. Prepare journal entries to record the October transactions.
2. Open the following accounts: Cash (111); Prepaid Insurance (117); Repair Supplies (119); Repair Equipment (144); Accumulated Depreciation, Repair Equipment (145); Accounts Payable (212); Andre Rawls, Capital (311); Andre Rawls, Withdrawals (312); Income Summary (313); Bicycle Repair Revenue (411); Store Rent Expense (511); Utility Expense (512); Insurance Expense (513); Repair Supplies Expense (514); and Depreciation Expense, Repair Equipment (515). Post the October journal entries to the ledger accounts.
3. Prepare a trial balance in the Trial Balance columns of a work sheet, and complete the work sheet using the following information:
   a. One month's insurance has expired.
   b. The remaining inventory of repair supplies is $194.
   c. The estimated depreciation on repair equipment is $70.
4. From the work sheet, prepare an income statement, a statement of owner's equity, and a balance sheet for October.
5. From the work sheet, prepare and post adjusting and closing entries for October.
6. Prepare a post-closing trial balance.
7. Prepare and post the journal entries to record the November transactions.
8. Prepare a trial balance for November in the Trial Balance columns of a work sheet, and complete the work sheet based on the following information:
   a. One month's insurance has expired.
   b. The inventory of repair supplies is $418.
   c. The estimated depreciation on repair equipment is $70.
9. From the work sheet, prepare an income statement, a statement of owner's equity, and a balance sheet for November.
10. From the work sheet, prepare and post adjusting and closing entries for November.
11. Prepare a post-closing trial balance.

Problem Set B

Problem 4B-1. Preparation of Financial Statements and End-of-Period Entries
(L.O. 3, 6, 8)

Lancaster Recreational Park, owned by Betty Schultz, rents campsites in a wooded park. The adjusted trial balance for Lancaster Recreational Park on June 30, 19x3, the end of the current fiscal year, is shown at the top of page 156.

Required

1. From the information given, prepare an income statement, a statement of owner's equity, and a balance sheet. Assume no additional investments by the owner.
2. Record the closing entries in the general journal.
3. Assuming that Wages Payable represents wages accrued at the end of the accounting period, record the reversing entry required on July 1.

Lancaster Recreational Park
Adjusted Trial Balance
June 30, 19x3

Cash	$ 4,080	
Accounts Receivable	7,320	
Supplies	228	
Prepaid Insurance	1,188	
Land	30,000	
Building	91,800	
Accumulated Depreciation, Building		$ 21,000
Accounts Payable		3,450
Wages Payable		1,650
Betty Schultz, Capital		93,070
Betty Schultz, Withdrawals	36,000	
Campsite Rentals		88,200
Wages Expense	23,850	
Insurance Expense	3,784	
Utility Expense	1,800	
Supplies Expense	1,320	
Depreciation Expense, Building	6,000	
	$207,370	$207,370

Problem 4B-2. Preparation of a Work Sheet and Financial Statements
(L.O. 1, 3)

The following trial balance was taken from the ledger of County Line Tennis Club at the end of the company's fiscal year.

County Line Tennis Club
Trial Balance
June 30, 19x5

Cash	$ 26,200	
Prepaid Advertising	14,100	
Supplies	7,200	
Land	745,200	
Equipment	156,000	
Accumulated Depreciation, Equipment		$ 38,400
Accounts Payable		303,000
Unearned Revenue, Locker Fees		12,600
Mary Ong, Capital		471,150
Mary Ong, Withdrawals	54,000	
Revenue from Court Fees		678,100
Wages Expense	342,000	
Maintenance Expense	51,600	
Advertising Expense	35,250	
Water and Utility Expense	64,800	
Miscellaneous Expense	6,900	
	$1,503,250	$1,503,250

Required

1. Enter the trial balance amounts in the Trial Balance columns of a work sheet, and complete the work sheet using the following information:
   a. Expired advertising, $4,500.
   b. Inventory of unused supplies, $1,200.
   c. Estimated depreciation on equipment, $12,000.
   d. Previously unearned locker fee revenues now earned, $9,600.
   e. Accrued but unpaid property taxes, $22,500.
   f. Accrued but unpaid wages, $9,000.
2. Prepare an income statement, a statement of owner's equity, and a balance sheet. Assume no additional investments by Mary Ong.

Problem 4B-3. Preparation of a Work Sheet; Financial Statements; and Adjusting, Closing, and Reversing Entries
(L.O. 1, 3, 4, 6, 8)

Jose Vargas opened his executive search service on July 1, 19x1. Some customers paid for his services after they were rendered, and others paid in advance for one year of service. After six months of operation, Jose wanted to know how his business stood. The trial balance on December 31 appears below:

Vargas Executive Search Service
Trial Balance
December 31, 19x1

Cash	$ 1,713	
Prepaid Rent	1,800	
Office Supplies	413	
Office Equipment	3,750	
Accounts Payable		$ 3,173
Unearned Revenue		1,823
Jose Vargas, Capital		10,000
Jose Vargas, Withdrawals	7,200	
Search Revenue		10,140
Telephone and Utility Expense	1,260	
Wages Expense	9,000	
	$25,136	$25,136

Required

1. Enter the trial balance amounts in the Trial Balance columns of the work sheet. Remember that accumulated depreciation is listed with its asset account. Complete the work sheet using the following information:
   a. One year's rent had been paid in advance when Jose began business.
   b. Inventory of unused office supplies, $75.
   c. One-half year's depreciation on office equipment, $300.
   d. Services rendered that had been paid for in advance, $863.
   e. Executive search services rendered during the month of December but not yet billed, $270.
   f. Wages earned by employees but not yet paid, $188.
2. From the work sheet, prepare an income statement, a statement of owner's equity, and a balance sheet.
3. From the work sheet, prepare adjusting and closing entries and, if required, reversing entries.
4. What is your evaluation of Jose's first six months in business?

Problem 4B-4. Preparation of a Work Sheet; Financial Statements; and Adjusting, Closing, and Reversing Entries
(L.O. 1, 3, 4, 6, 8)

The trial balance below was taken from the ledger of Robinson Delivery Service on December 31, 19x4, the end of the company's fiscal year.

Robinson Delivery Service
Trial Balance
December 31, 19x4

Cash	$ 10,072	
Accounts Receivable	29,314	
Prepaid Insurance	5,340	
Delivery Supplies	14,700	
Office Supplies	2,460	
Land	15,000	
Building	196,000	
Accumulated Depreciation, Building		$ 53,400
Trucks	103,800	
Accumulated Depreciation, Trucks		30,900
Office Equipment	15,900	
Accumulated Depreciation, Office Equipment		10,800
Accounts Payable		9,396
Unearned Lockbox Fees		8,340
Mortgage Payable		72,000
Pearl Robinson, Capital		128,730
Pearl Robinson, Withdrawals	30,000	
Delivery Services Revenue		283,470
Lockbox Fees Earned		28,800
Truck Drivers' Wages Expense	120,600	
Office Salaries Expense	44,400	
Gas, Oil, and Truck Repairs Expense	31,050	
Interest Expense	7,200	
	$625,836	$625,836

Required

1. Enter the trial balance amounts in the Trial Balance columns of a work sheet, and complete the work sheet using the following information:
   a. Expired insurance, $3,060.
   b. Inventory of unused delivery supplies, $1,430.
   c. Inventory of unused office supplies, $186.
   d. Estimated depreciation, building, $14,400.
   e. Estimated depreciation, trucks, $15,450.
   f. Estimated depreciation, office equipment, $2,700.
   g. The company credits the lockbox fees of customers who pay in advance to the Unearned Lockbox Fees account. Of the amount credited to this account during the year, $5,630 had been earned by December 31.
   h. Lockbox fees earned but unrecorded and uncollected at the end of the accounting period, $816.
   i. Accrued but unpaid truck drivers' wages at the end of the year, $1,920.
2. Prepare an income statement, a statement of owner's equity, and a balance sheet. Assume no additional investments by Pearl Robinson.
3. Prepare adjusting, closing, and, if required, reversing entries from the work sheet.

Problem 4B-5. The Complete Accounting Cycle: Two Months
(L.O. 1, 3, 4, 6, 7)

On August 1, 19xx, Carl Luzinski opened Luzinski Appliance Service. During the month, he completed the following transactions for the company:

Aug. 1 Deposited $10,000 of his savings in a bank account for the company.
1 Paid the rent for a store for one month, $850.

Aug.	1	Paid the premium on a one-year insurance policy, $960.
	5	Purchased repair equipment from Jensen Company for $8,400 on the basis of a $1,200 down payment and $600 per month for one year. The first payment is due September 1.
	9	Purchased repair supplies from Marco Company on credit, $936.
	12	Purchased for cash an advertisement in a local newspaper, $120.
	16	Received cash repair revenue for the first half of the month, $800.
	25	Made a payment to Marco Company, $450.
	27	Withdrew cash from the company bank account to pay living expenses, $900.
	31	Received cash repair revenue for the second half of August, $1,950.

Required for August

1. Prepare journal entries to record the August transactions.
2. Open the following accounts: Cash (111); Prepaid Insurance (117); Repair Supplies (119); Repair Equipment (144); Accumulated Depreciation, Repair Equipment (145); Accounts Payable (212); Carl Luzinski, Capital (311); Carl Luzinski, Withdrawals (312); Income Summary (313); Repair Revenue (411); Store Rent Expense (511); Advertising Expense (512); Insurance Expense (513); Repair Supplies Expense (514); and Depreciation Expense, Repair Equipment (515). Post the August journal entries to the ledger accounts.
3. Prepare a trial balance in the Trial Balance columns of a work sheet, and complete the work sheet using the following information:
   a. One month's insurance has expired.
   b. The remaining inventory of repair supplies is $338.
   c. The estimated depreciation on repair equipment is $140.
4. From the work sheet, prepare an income statement, a statement of owner's equity, and a balance sheet for August.
5. From the work sheet, prepare and post the adjusting and closing entries.
6. Prepare a post-closing trial balance.

During September, Carl Luzinski completed the following transactions for Luzinski Appliance Service:

Sept.	1	Paid the monthly rent, $850.
	1	Made monthly payment to Jensen Company, $600.
	7	Purchased additional repair supplies on credit from Marco Company, $1,726.
	15	Received cash repair revenue for the first half of the month, $1,828.
	18	Purchased for cash an additional advertisement in the local newspaper, $120.
	20	Paid the Marco Company on account, $1,200.
	25	Withdrew cash from the company for living expenses, $900.
	30	Received cash repair revenue for the last half of the month, $1,634.

Required for September

7. Prepare and post journal entries to record the September transactions.
8. Prepare a trial balance in the Trial Balance columns of a work sheet, and complete the work sheet based on the following information:
   a. One month's insurance has expired.
   b. The inventory of unused repair supplies is $826.
   c. The estimated depreciation on repair equipment is $140.
9. From the work sheet, prepare the September income statement, statement of owner's equity, and balance sheet.
10. From the work sheet, prepare and post the adjusting and closing entries.
11. Prepare a post-closing trial balance.

Financial Decision Case

Adele's Secretarial Service
(L.O. 3)

Adele's Secretarial Service is a very simple business. Adele provides typing services for students at the local university. Her accountant prepared the income statement that appears at the top of page 160 for the year ended June 30, 19x4.

Adele's Secretarial Service
Income Statement
For the Year Ended June 30, 19x4

Revenues		
Typing Services		$20,980
Expenses		
Rent Expense	$2,400	
Depreciation Expense, Office Equipment	2,200	
Supplies Expense	960	
Other Expenses	1,240	
Total Expenses		6,800
Net Income		$14,180

In reviewing this statement, Adele is puzzled. She knows she withdrew $15,600 in cash for personal expenses, yet the cash balance in the company's bank account increased from $460 to $3,100 from last June 30 to this June 30. She wants to know how her net income could be less than the cash she took out of the business if there is an increase in the cash balance.

Her accountant shows her the balance sheet for June 30, 19x4 and compares it to the one for June 30, 19x3. She explains that besides the change in the cash balance, accounts receivable from customers decreased by $1,480 and accounts payable increased by $380 (supplies are the only items Adele buys on credit). The only other asset or liability account that changed during the year was Accumulated Depreciation, Office Equipment, which increased by $2,200.

Required

1. Explain to Adele why the accountant is answering her question by pointing out year-to-year changes in the balance sheet.
2. Verify the cash balance increase by preparing a statement that lists the receipts of cash and the expenditures of cash during the year.
3. How did you treat depreciation expense? Why?

Answers to Self-Test

1. c
2. c
3. d
4. c
5. c
6. c
7. d
8. c
9. b
10. d

Comprehensive Problem: Joan Miller Advertising Agency

This problem continues with the Joan Miller Advertising Agency, the company we used to illustrate the accounting cycle in the chapters on measuring and recording business transactions, business income and accrual accounting, and completing the accounting cycle. It is necessary in some instances to refer to these chapters in completing this problem.

The January 31, 19xx post-closing trial balance for the Joan Miller Advertising Agency is as follows:

Cash	$ 1,720	
Accounts Receivable	2,800	
Fees Receivable	200	
Art Supplies	1,300	
Office Supplies	600	
Prepaid Rent	400	
Prepaid Insurance	440	
Art Equipment	4,200	
Accumulated Depreciation, Art Equipment		$ 70
Office Equipment	3,000	
Accumulated Depreciation, Office Equipment		50
Accounts Payable		3,170
Unearned Art Fees		600
Wages Payable		180
Joan Miller, Capital		10,590
	$14,660	$14,660

During February, the agency engaged in the following transactions:

Feb. 1 Received an additional investment of cash from Joan Miller, $6,000.

2 Purchased additional office equipment with cash, $800.

5 Received art equipment transferred to the business from Joan Miller, $1,400.

6 Purchased additional office supplies with cash, $80.

7 Purchased additional art supplies on credit from Taylor Supply Company, $500.

8 Completed the series of advertisements for Marsh Tire Company that began on January 31 and billed Marsh Tire Company for the total services performed, including the accrued revenues (fees receivable) that had been recognized in an adjusting entry in January, $800.

9 Paid the secretary for two weeks' wages, $600.

12 Paid the amount due to Morgan Equipment for the office equipment purchased last month, $1,500 (see page 57).

13 Accepted an advance fee in cash for artwork to be done for another agency, $1,800.

14 Purchased a copier (office equipment) from Morgan Equipment for $2,100, paying $350 in cash and agreeing to pay the rest in equal payments over the next five months.

15 Performed advertising services and accepted a cash fee, $1,050.

16 Received payment on account from Ward Department Stores for services performed last month, $2,800 (see page 60).

19 Paid amount due for the telephone bill that was received and recorded at the end of January, $70 (see page 61).

20 Performed advertising services for Ward Department Stores and agreed to accept payment next month, $3,200.

Feb. 21 Performed art services for a cash fee, $580.
22 Received and paid the utility bill for February, $110.
23 Paid the secretary for two weeks' wages, $600.
26 Paid the rent for March in advance, $400.
27 Received the telephone bill for February, which is to be paid next month, $80.
28 Paid out cash to Joan Miller as a withdrawal for personal living expenses, $1,400.

Required

1. Record in the general journal and post to the general ledger the reversing entries necessary on February 1 for Wages Payable and Fees Receivable (see pages 100–101). (Begin the general journal on Page 5.)
2. Record the transactions for February in the general journal.

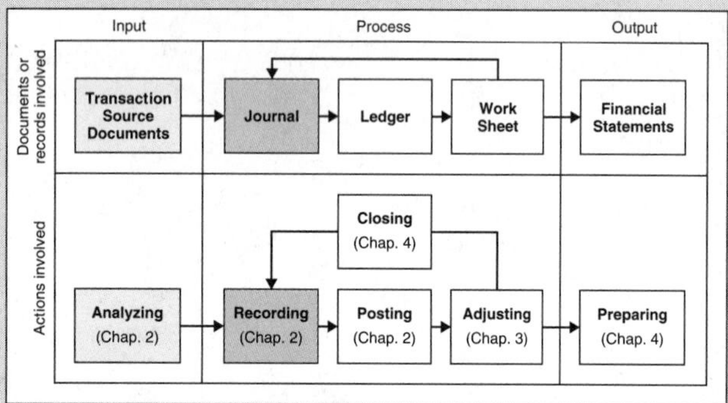

3. Post the February transactions to the general ledger accounts.

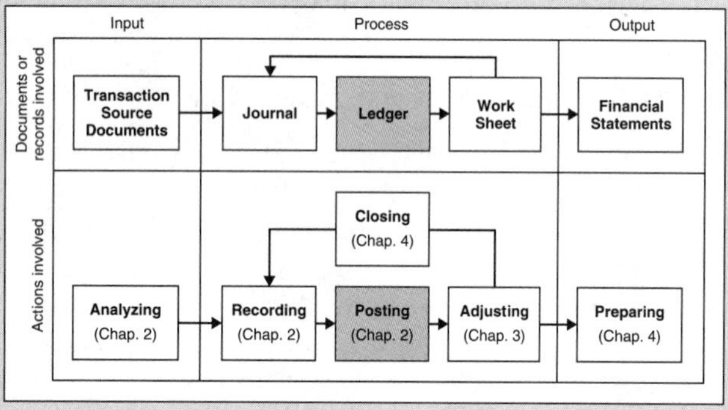

4. Prepare a trial balance in the Trial Balance columns of a work sheet.
5. Prepare adjusting entries and complete the work sheet using the following information:
   a. One month's prepaid rent has expired, $400.
   b. One month's prepaid insurance has expired, $40.
   c. An inventory of art supplies reveals $720 still on hand on February 28.
   d. An inventory of office supplies reveals $380 still on hand on February 28.
   e. Depreciation on Art Equipment for February is calculated to be $90.
   f. Depreciation on Office Equipment for February is calculated to be $100.
   g. Art services performed for which payment has been received in advance total $1,400.

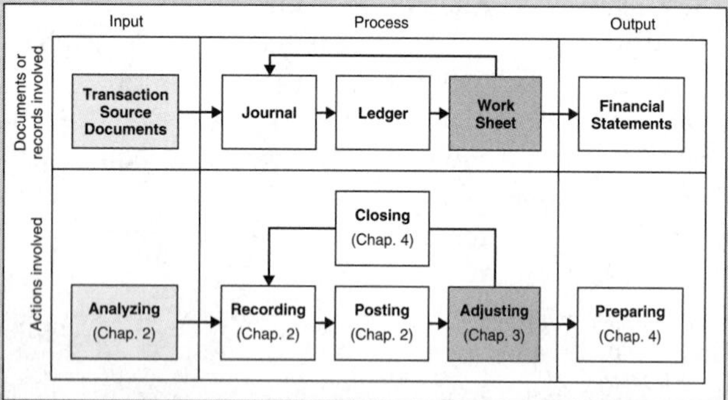

h. Advertising services performed that will not be billed until March total $340.
i. Three days' worth of secretarial wages had accrued by the end of February.

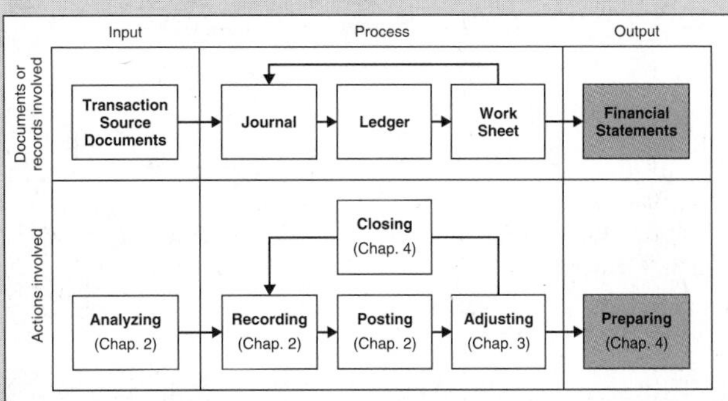

6. From the work sheet prepare an income statement, a statement of owner's equity, and a balance sheet.

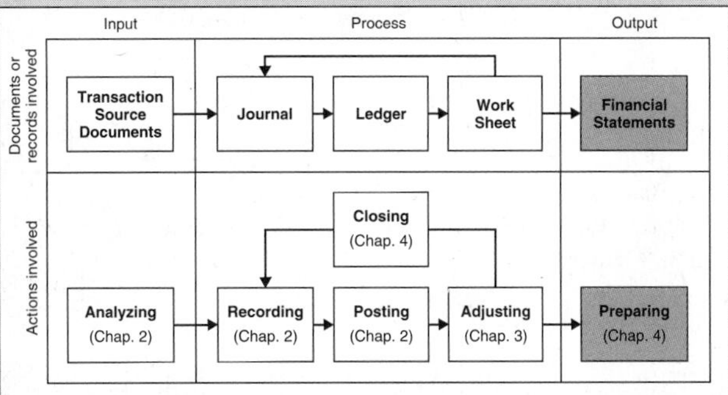

7. Record the adjusting entries in the general journal, and post them to the general ledger.
8. Record the closing entries in the general journal, and post them to the general ledger.
9. Prepare a post-closing trial balance.

This Comprehensive Problem covers all of the Learning Objectives in the chapters on measuring and recording business transactions, business income and accrual accounting, and completing the accounting cycle.

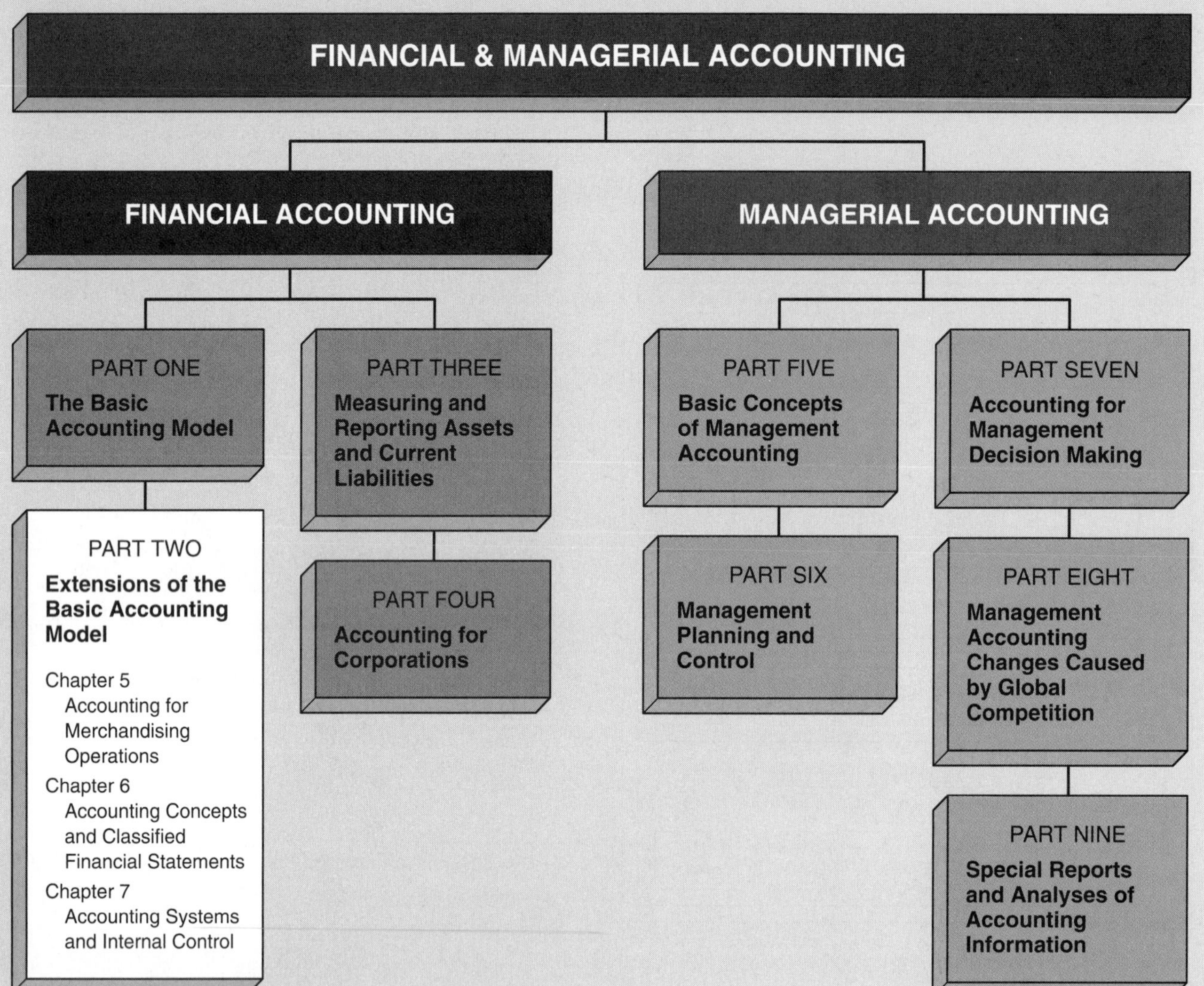

Accounting, as you have seen, is an information system that measures, processes, and communicates information, primarily financial in nature, for decision making. Part One presented the principles and practices of the basic accounting system. In Part Two, the basic accounting system is extended to more complex applications.

PART TWO

Extensions of the Basic Accounting Model

Chapter 5 deals with accounting for merchandising companies, which are companies that sell products, as opposed to the companies you studied earlier, which sell services.

Chapter 6 addresses the goals of organizing accounting systems in order to process a large number of transactions in an efficient and time-saving way.

Chapter 7 first introduces classified financial statements and then describes the basic principles of internal control.

CHAPTER 5

Accounting for Merchandising Operations

LEARNING OBJECTIVES

1. Compare the income statements for service and merchandising concerns.
2. Record transactions involving revenues for merchandising concerns.
3. Calculate the cost of goods sold.
4. Record transactions involving purchases of merchandise.
5. Distinguish between the perpetual inventory system and the periodic inventory system.
6. Explain the objectives of handling merchandise inventory at the end of the accounting period and two approaches to achieving them.
7. Prepare a work sheet for a merchandising concern under one of two alternative methods.
8. Prepare adjusting and closing entries for a merchandising concern.
9. Prepare an income statement for a merchandising concern.

Up to this point, you have studied accounting records and reports for the simplest type of business—the service company. In this chapter, you will study a more complex form of business—the merchandising company. We focus on the merchandising company's special buying and selling transactions and their effects on the income statement. After studying this chapter, you should be able to meet the learning objectives listed on the left. (Objectives 7 and 8 may be omitted if Chapter 4 was not covered.)

DECISION POINT
Target Stores

■ The management of merchandising companies has two key decisions to make: the price at which merchandise is sold and the level of service the company provides. For instance, a department store can set the price of its merchandise at a relatively high level and provide a great deal of service. A discount store, on the other hand, may price its merchandise at a relatively low level and provide limited service.

When Target Stores, a division of Dayton-Hudson Corporation, became a discount merchandiser of brand-name apparel and other products, it had to make these decisions. By emphasizing brand-name merchandise at low prices, the company chose to differentiate itself from department and specialty stores that sell at full price and from other discount chains that sell low-priced but less well known merchandise. Target Stores decided to operate in very large stores that could be controlled by a minimum number of employees. The company planned to earn income by selling a large volume of merchandise. By 1990, Target Stores was one of the most successful merchandising companies in the United States. It operated over four hundred stores and earned income (before interest and income taxes) of $466 million on sales of $8.2 billion.[1] ■

The Income Statement for a Merchandising Concern

OBJECTIVE 1
Compare the income statements for service and merchandising concerns

Service companies such as advertising agencies and law firms perform a service for a fee or commission. To determine their net income, a simple income statement is often all that is needed. As shown in Figure 5-1, these companies measure net income as the difference between revenues and expenses.

1. Bill Saporito, "Is Wal-Mart Unstoppable?" *Fortune,* May 6, 1991, p. 52.

Figure 5-1. The Components of Income Statements for Service and Merchandising Companies

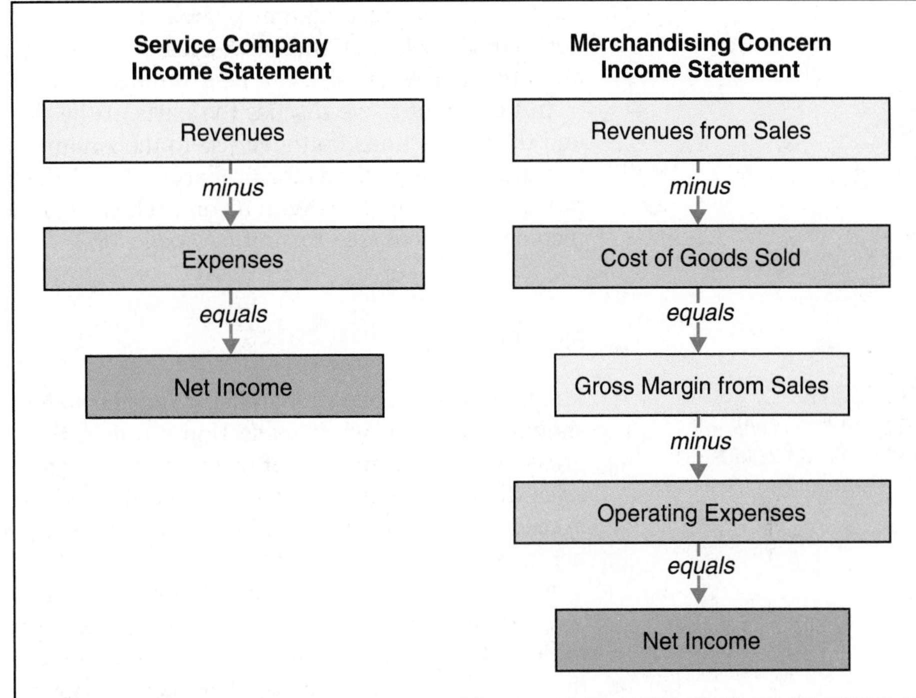

Merchandising companies earn income by buying and selling products or merchandise. These companies, whether wholesale or retail, use the same basic accounting methods as do service companies, but the buying and selling of merchandise adds several steps to the process and produces a more complicated income statement than that needed by a service business.

As shown in Figure 5-1, the income statement for a merchandising concern has three major parts: (1) revenues from sales, (2) the cost of goods sold, and (3) operating expenses. Such an income statement differs from the income statement for a service firm in that gross margin from sales must be computed before operating expenses are deducted in order to arrive at net income.

Revenues from sales arise from sales of goods by the merchandising company, and the **cost of goods sold** tells how much the merchant paid for the goods that were sold. The difference between revenues from sales and the cost of goods sold is called **gross margin from sales**, or simply *gross margin* (or *gross profit*). To be successful, the merchant must sell the goods for an amount greater than cost—that is, gross margin from sales must be large enough to pay operating expenses and provide an adequate income. **Operating expenses** are those expenses, other than the cost of goods sold, that are incurred in running a business. Operating expenses in a merchandising company are similar to the expenses in a service company. **Net income** for merchandising companies is what is left after deducting operating expenses from gross margin.

All of the parts of the merchandising income statement are important to a company's management. Management is interested both in the percentage of gross margin from sales and in the amount of gross margin. This information is helpful in planning business operations. For instance, management may try to increase total sales dollars by reducing the selling price. This strategy reduces the percentage of gross margin. It works if the total items sold increase enough to raise gross margin (which raises income from operations). On the other hand, management may increase operating expenses (such as advertising expense) in an effort to increase sales dollars and the amount of gross margin. If the increase in gross margin is greater than the increase in advertising outlay, net income goes up. Other strategies, such as reducing the cost of goods sold or operating expenses, also can be examined.

In this chapter, we discuss the parts of the merchandising income statement and the transactions that give rise to the amounts in each part. Then we present two alternative methods for preparing the work sheet for a merchandising company. The chapter ends with a comprehensive illustration of the merchandising income statement (see Exhibit 5-7, page 187).

Revenues from Sales

OBJECTIVE 2
Record transactions involving revenues for merchandising concerns

The first part of the merchandising income statement is revenues from sales, as shown in Exhibit 5-1. This section requires the computation of **net sales**, the gross proceeds from sales of merchandise less sales returns and allowances and sales discounts. For a business to survive, net sales must be great enough to exceed the cost of goods sold and operating expenses and to provide sufficient net income.

Management, investors, and others use the amount and trend of sales as indicators of a firm's progress. Increasing sales suggest growth; decreasing sales indicate the possibility of decreased earnings and other financial problems in the future. To detect trends, then, comparisons frequently are made between the net sales of different periods.

Gross Sales

Under accrual accounting, revenues from the sale of merchandise are earned in the accounting period in which title for the goods passes from seller to buyer. **Gross sales** consist of total sales for cash and total sales on credit during a given accounting period. Even though the cash for the sale may not be collected until the following period, under the revenue recognition rule, the revenue is recognized as being earned at the time of the sale.

The Sales account is used to record sales of merchandise, whether a sale is made for cash or on credit. The journal entry to record a sale of merchandise for cash looks like this:

Sept. 16	Cash	1,286	
	Sales		1,286
	Sale of merchandise for cash		

Exhibit 5-1. Partial Income Statement: Revenues from Sales

Fenwick Fashions Company Partial Income Statement For the Year Ended December 31, 19xx		
Revenues from Sales		
Gross Sales		$246,350
Less: Sales Returns and Allowances	$2,750	
Sales Discounts	4,275	7,025
Net Sales		$239,325

This entry records the sale of merchandise on credit:

Sept. 16	Accounts Receivable	746	
	Sales		746
	Sale of merchandise on credit		

Trade Discounts

In order to avoid reprinting wholesale and retail catalogues and price lists every time there is a price change, some manufacturers and wholesalers quote prices of merchandise at a discount (usually 30 percent or more) off the list or catalogue price. These discounts are called **trade discounts**. For example, the seller of an article listed at $1,000 with a trade discount of 40 percent, or $400, would record the sale at $600; and the buyer would record the transaction as a purchase of $600. If the seller wants to change the selling price, this can be done by increasing or decreasing the trade discount. The list price and related trade discounts are used only to arrive at the agreed on price; they do not appear in the accounting records.

Sales Returns and Allowances

If a customer receives a defective or otherwise unsatisfactory product, the seller may allow the buyer to return the item for a cash refund or credit on account, or the seller may give the buyer an allowance off the sales price. A good accounting system provides management with the information it needs to determine the reason for sales returns and allowances because these transactions may reveal unsatisfactory products and dissatisfied customers.

Each return or allowance is recorded as a debit to an account called **Sales Returns and Allowances**. Here is an example:

Sept. 17	Sales Returns and Allowances	76	
	Accounts Receivable (or Cash)		76
	Return or allowance on unsatisfactory merchandise		

If the accountant debited Sales instead of Sales Returns and Allowances, management would not know the extent of customer dissatisfaction. Sales Returns and Allowances is a contra-revenue account with a normal debit balance. This means it is deducted from gross sales in the income statement (see Exhibit 5-1).

Sales Discounts

When goods are sold on credit, both parties should understand the amount and timing of payment. The terms usually are printed on the sales invoice and constitute part of the sales agreement. Customary terms differ from industry to industry. In some industries payment is expected in a short period of time, such as ten days or thirty days. In these cases, the invoice is marked "n/10" or "n/30" (read as "net ten" or "net thirty"), meaning that the amount of the invoice is due ten days or thirty days, respectively, after the invoice date. If the invoice is due ten days after the end of the month, it is marked "n/10 eom."

Some industries give **sales discounts**, discounts for early payment. This practice increases the seller's liquidity by reducing the amount of money tied up in accounts receivable. Examples of these invoice terms are "2/10, n/30" or "2/10, n/60." Terms of 2/10, n/30 mean the buyer can take a 2 percent discount if the invoice is paid within ten days of the invoice date. Otherwise, the buyer can wait thirty days and then pay the full amount of the invoice.

Because it usually is not possible to know at the time of the sale whether the customer will take advantage of the discount by paying within the discount period, sales discounts are recorded only at the time the customer pays. For example, assume that Fenwick Fashions Company sells merchandise to a customer on September 20 for $300, on terms of 2/10, n/60. This is the entry at the time of the sale:

Sept. 20	Accounts Receivable	300	
	Sales		300
	Sale of merchandise on credit, terms 2/10, n/60		

The customer can take advantage of the sales discount any time on or before September 30, ten days after the date of the invoice. If he or she pays on September 29, the entry in Fenwick's records would look like this:

Sept. 29	Cash	294	
	Sales Discounts	6	
	Accounts Receivable		300
	Payment for Sept. 20 sale; discount taken		

If the customer does not take advantage of the sales discount but waits until November 19 to pay for the merchandise, the entry would be as follows:

Nov. 19	Cash	300	
	Accounts Receivable		300
	Payment for Sept. 20 sale; no discount taken		

At the end of the accounting period, the Sales Discounts account has accumulated all the sales discounts taken during the period. Because sales discounts reduce revenues from sales, Sales Discounts is a contra-revenue account with a normal debit balance, which is deducted from gross sales in the income statement (see Exhibit 5-1).

The Cost of Goods Sold

OBJECTIVE 3
Calculate the cost of goods sold

Every merchandising business has goods on hand that it holds for sale to customers. The amount of goods on hand at any one time is known as **merchandise inventory**. The cost of **goods available for sale** during the year is the sum of two factors—merchandise inventory at the beginning of the year plus net purchases during the year.

If a company sold all the goods available for sale during a given accounting period or year, the cost of goods sold would equal the goods that were available for sale. In most cases, however, a business has goods still unsold and on hand at the end of the year. To find out how much the merchant paid for the goods that actually were sold (the cost of goods sold), the merchandise inventory at the end of the year must be subtracted from the goods available for sale.

The partial income statement in Exhibit 5-2 shows the cost of goods sold section of the Fenwick Fashions Company income statement. In this case, goods costing $179,660 were available and could have been sold; Fenwick Fashions started with $52,800 in merchandise inventory at the beginning of the year and purchased a net of $126,860 in goods during the year. At the end of the year, $48,300 in goods were left unsold. This amount appears as merchandise inventory on the balance sheet. When this unsold merchandise inventory is sub-

Exhibit 5-2. Partial Income Statement: Cost of Goods Sold

Fenwick Fashions Company
Partial Income Statement
For the Year Ended December 31, 19xx

Cost of Goods Sold				
Merchandise Inventory, January 1, 19xx			$ 52,800	
Purchases		$126,400		
Less: Purchases Returns and Allowances	$5,640			
Purchases Discounts	2,136	7,776		
		$118,624		
Freight In		8,236		
Net Purchases			126,860	
Goods Available for Sale			$179,660	
Less Merchandise Inventory, December 31, 19xx			48,300	
Cost of Goods Sold				$131,360

tracted from the total available goods that could have been sold, the resulting cost of goods sold is $131,360, which appears on the income statement.

To understand the concept of the cost of goods sold, it is necessary to examine net purchases and merchandise inventory.

Net Purchases

OBJECTIVE 4
Record transactions involving purchases of merchandise

Net purchases consist of gross purchases less purchases returns and allowances and purchases discounts plus any freight charges on the purchases.

Purchases. Merchandise bought for resale is debited to the Purchases account at the gross purchase price:

Nov. 12	Purchases	1,500	
	Accounts Payable		1,500
	Purchases of merchandise, terms 2/10, n/30		

This system of recording purchases initially at the gross purchase price is called the **gross method**. The **Purchases** account, a temporary account, is used only for merchandise purchased for resale. Its sole purpose is to accumulate the total cost of merchandise purchased during an accounting period. (Purchases of other assets, such as equipment, should be recorded in the appropriate asset account, not the Purchases account.) An examination of the Purchases account alone does not indicate whether merchandise has been sold or is still on hand.

Purchases Returns and Allowances. For various reasons, a company may have to return merchandise acquired for resale. The firm may not have been able to sell the merchandise. Or the merchandise may be defective or damaged in some way. The supplier can offer a full credit on the goods or an allowance as an alternative to returning the goods for full credit. These transactions are recorded in the **Purchases Returns and Allowances** account. The journal entry looks like this:

Nov. 14	Accounts Payable	200	
	Purchases Returns and Allowances		200
	Return of damaged merchandise purchased November 12		

Here, the purchaser receives "credit" (in the seller's accounts receivable) for the returned merchandise. The Purchases Returns and Allowances account is used only for returns and allowances of merchandise purchased for resale. Other returns, such as office supplies or equipment, are credited directly to the related asset account.

Purchases Returns and Allowances is a contra-purchases account with a normal credit balance; its balance is deducted from purchases in the income statement (see Exhibit 5-2). It is important that a separate account be used to record purchases returns and allowances because management needs the information to make decisions. It can be very costly to return merchandise for credit, and many costs (ordering costs, accounting costs, sometimes freight costs, interest on the money invested in the goods) cannot be recovered. And there are the costs of lost sales resulting from poor ordering or unusable goods. Excessive returns can indicate a need for new purchasing procedures or new suppliers.

Purchases Discounts. Merchandise purchases usually are made on credit and commonly involve **purchases discounts** for early payment. It is almost always worthwhile for a company to take a discount if offered. For example, the terms 2/10, n/30 offer a 2 percent discount for paying only twenty days early (before the period including the eleventh and the thirtieth days). This is an effective interest rate of 36 percent on a yearly basis,[2] and most companies can borrow money for much less than this rate. The amount of discounts taken forms a separate account. When payment is made, the journal entry looks like this:

Nov. 22	Accounts Payable		1,300	
	Purchases Discounts			26
	Cash			1,274
	Paid the invoice of Nov. 12			
	Purchase Nov. 12	$1,500		
	Less return Nov. 14	200		
	Net purchase	$1,300		
	Discount: 2%	26		
	Cash paid	$1,274		

If the purchase is not paid for within the discount period, this is the entry:

Dec. 12	Accounts Payable	1,300	
	Cash		1,300
	Paid the invoice of Nov. 12 on due date; no discount taken		

Like Purchases Returns and Allowances, Purchases Discounts is a contra-purchases account with a normal credit balance that is deducted from Purchases on the income statement (see Exhibit 5-2). If a company makes only a partial payment on an invoice, most creditors allow the company to take the

2. 360 days ÷ 20 days × 2% = 36%.

discount applicable to the partial payment. The discount usually does not apply to freight, postage, taxes, or other charges that might appear on the invoice.

Good management of cash resources normally calls for both taking discounts and waiting as long as possible to pay. To accomplish these two objectives, some companies file invoices according to their due dates as they get them. Each day, the invoices due on that day are pulled from the file and paid. In this way, the company uses cash as long as possible and also takes advantage of the discounts. Another method commonly used to control purchases discounts—the net method—is illustrated on pages 174–175.

Freight In. In some industries, it is customary for the supplier (seller) to pay transportation costs (and to charge a price that includes those costs). In other industries, it is customary for the purchaser to pay transportation charges on merchandise. These charges, called **freight in** or *transportation in*, logically are included in the cost of purchases, but, like purchases discounts, they should be accumulated in the Freight In account so that management can monitor them. The entry for the purchaser is as follows:

Nov. 12	Freight In	134	
	Cash (or Accounts Payable)		134
	Incurred freight charges on merchandise purchased		

Special terms designate whether the supplier or the purchaser pays the freight charges. **FOB shipping point** means that the supplier places the merchandise "free on board" at the point of origin, and the buyer bears the shipping costs from that point. In addition, the title to the merchandise passes to the buyer at that point. When you buy a car, you know that if the sales agreement says "FOB Detroit," you must pay the freight from Detroit to wherever you are.

On the other hand, **FOB destination** means that the supplier bears the transportation costs to the destination. In this case, title remains with the supplier until the merchandise reaches its destination. The supplier normally prepays the amount, in which case the buyer makes no entry for freight. In rare cases, the buyer may pay the charges and then deduct them from the invoice.

The effects of these special shipping terms are summarized below:

Shipping Term	Where Title Passes	Who Bears the Cost of Transportation
FOB shipping point	At origin	Buyer
FOB destination	At destination	Seller

In some cases, the supplier pays the freight charges but bills the buyer, including the charges as a separate item on the sales invoice. Here, the buyer still should record the purchase and the freight in in separate accounts. For example, assume that an invoice for a purchase of merchandise totaling $1,890 included the cost of merchandise of $1,600, freight charges of $290, and terms of 2/10, n/30. The entry to record this transaction looks like this:

Nov. 25	Purchases	1,600	
	Freight In	290	
	Accounts Payable		1,890
	Purchased merchandise for $1,600; included in the invoice are freight charges of $290 and terms of 2/10, n/30		

If the invoice is paid within ten days, the discount is $32 (.02 × $1,600): The discount does not apply to freight charges.

It is important not to confuse freight-in costs with freight-out or delivery costs. If you, the seller, agree to pay transportation charges on goods you have sold, the expense is a cost of *selling* merchandise, not a cost of *purchasing* merchandise. Freight Out Expense appears as an operating expense on the income statement.

Controlling Purchases Discounts Using the Net Method

Alternative Method

As noted earlier, it is usually worthwhile to pay invoices promptly to qualify for purchases discounts. Generally, it is bad management not to take advantage of these discounts. The gross method, however, has the disadvantage of telling management only about discounts that were taken. It records no information about discounts that were not taken, or, in other words, those discounts that were "lost."

A procedure called the **net method** of recording purchases identifies the discounts that are lost by requiring that purchases be recorded initially at their net price. Then, if a discount is not taken, a special account is debited for the amount of the lost discount.

For example, suppose that a company purchases goods on November 12 for $1,500, with terms of 2/10, n/30, and that it returns $200 worth of merchandise on November 14. If payment is not made until December 12, the company is not eligible for the 2 percent discount. The entries to record these three transactions are as follows:

			Debit	Credit
Nov. 12	Purchases		1,470	
	Accounts Payable			1,470
	Purchases of merchandise at net price, terms 2/10, n/30			
	$1,500 – (.02 × $1,500) = $1,470			
Nov. 14	Accounts Payable		196	
	Purchases Returns and Allowances			196
	Return of damaged merchandise purchased on November 12 and recorded at net price			
	$200 – (.02 × $200) = $196			
Dec. 12	Accounts Payable		1,274	
	Purchases Discounts Lost		26	
	Cash			1,300
	Paid invoice of Nov. 12; no discount taken			
	Purchase Nov. 12	$1,500		
	Less return Nov. 14	200		
	Net purchase	$1,300		
	Discount lost: .02 × $1,300 = $26			

Notice that, if a company makes a payment after the discount period, the lost discount is debited to the Purchases Discounts Lost account. The balance in Purchases Discounts Lost is shown as an operating expense on the income statement. And it allows management to see at a glance the total of discounts lost.

If the company pays the invoice by November 22 and uses the net method of recording purchases, it makes a payment of $1,274. Because the invoice is paid in time to secure the discount, the Purchases Discounts Lost account is not necessary. The entry would be recorded as follows:

Nov. 22	Accounts Payable	1,274	
	Cash		1,274
	Payment of Nov. 12 invoice; discount taken		

Merchandise Inventory

OBJECTIVE 5
Distinguish between the perpetual inventory system and the periodic inventory system

The inventory of a merchandising concern consists of the goods on hand and available for sale to customers. For a grocery store, inventory would be the meats, vegetables, canned goods, and other items for sale. For a service station, it would be gasoline, oil, and automobile parts. Merchandising concerns purchase their inventories from wholesalers, manufacturers, and other suppliers.

The merchandise inventory on hand at the beginning of the accounting period is called the **beginning inventory**; the merchandise inventory on hand at the end of the accounting period is called the **ending inventory**. As we have seen, beginning and ending inventories are used to calculate the cost of goods sold on the income statement. Ending Inventory also appears on the balance sheet as an asset. It becomes a part of the cost of goods sold in a later period, when it is sold. This period's beginning inventory was last period's ending inventory.

Measuring Merchandise Inventory. Merchandise inventory is a key factor in determining the cost of goods sold. Because merchandise inventory represents goods available for sale that are still unsold, there must be a method for determining both the quantity and the cost of the goods on hand. The two basic systems of accounting for the number of items in the merchandise inventory are the periodic inventory system and the perpetual inventory system.

Under the **periodic inventory system**, the inventory on hand is counted periodically, usually at the end of an accounting period: No detailed records of the actual inventory on hand are maintained during the period. Under the **perpetual inventory system**, records are kept of the quantity and, usually, the cost of individual items of inventory as they are bought and sold.

The cost of goods sold under the periodic inventory system is determined at the end of the accounting period in much the same way that supplies expenses are calculated. In the simplest case, the cost of inventory purchased is accumulated in a Purchases account. Then, at the end of the accounting period, the actual count of the physical inventory is deducted from the total of purchases plus beginning merchandise inventory to determine the cost of goods sold.

Under the perpetual inventory system, the cost of each item is debited to the Merchandise Inventory account as it is purchased. As items are sold, the Merchandise Inventory account is credited and the Cost of Goods Sold account is debited for the cost of the items sold. In this way, the balance of Merchandise Inventory always equals the cost of goods on hand at a point in time, and Cost of Goods Sold equals the total cost associated with items sold to that point in time. The Purchases account is not used in a perpetual inventory system.

Traditionally, the periodic inventory system has been used by companies that sell items of low value at high volume because of the difficulty and expense of accounting for the purchase and sale of each item. Examples of such companies are drugstores, automobile parts stores, department stores, discount stores, and grain companies. In contrast, companies that sell items of high unit value, such as appliances or automobiles, tended to use the perpetual inventory system. This distinction between high and low unit value for inventory systems has blurred considerably in recent years because of the widespread use of the computer. Although the periodic inventory system still is widely used, the use of the perpetual inventory system has increased greatly. For example, many grocery stores, which traditionally used the periodic inventory system, now employ bar coding. Electronic markings on each product, called bar codes or universal product codes (UPC), are used to update the physical inventory as items are sold by linking their cash registers to a computer (see Figure 5-2). Bar coding has become common in all types of retail companies, as well as in manufacturing firms and hospitals. It has become common for some retail businesses to use the perpetual system for keeping track of the physical flow of inventory and the periodic system for preparing the financial statements.

The periodic inventory system for determining the cost of goods sold is described in this chapter. The perpetual inventory system is discussed further in the chapter on inventories and the chapter on cost allocation and the job order costing system.

The Periodic Inventory System. Most companies rely on an actual count of goods on hand at the end of an accounting period to determine ending inventory and, indirectly, the cost of goods sold. The procedure for determining the merchandise inventory under the periodic inventory system involves three steps:

1. Make a physical count of the merchandise on hand at the end of the accounting period.
2. Multiply the quantity of each type of merchandise by its unit cost.
3. Add the resulting costs of each type of merchandise to obtain a total. This amount is the ending merchandise inventory.

The cost of the ending merchandise inventory is deducted from goods available for sale to determine the cost of goods sold. The ending inventory of one period is the beginning inventory of the next. Entries are made at the end of the accounting period to remove the beginning inventory (the last period's ending inventory) and to enter the ending inventory of the current period. These entries are the only ones made to the Merchandise Inventory account during the period. Consequently, only on the balance sheet date and after the adjusting or closing entries does the account reflect the actual inventory on hand. As soon as

Figure 5-2. Example of Universal Product Code (UPC)

purchases or sales are made, the figure becomes a historical amount and remains so until the new inventory is entered at the end of the accounting period.

Physical Inventory. Making a physical count of all merchandise on hand is called taking a **physical inventory**. This can be a difficult task because it is easy to leave items out or to count them twice. A physical inventory must be taken under both the periodic and perpetual inventory systems.

Merchandise inventory includes all salable goods owned by the concern regardless of where they are located—on shelves, in storerooms, in warehouses, in trucks en route between warehouses and stores. It includes goods in transit from suppliers if title to the goods has passed to the merchant. Ending inventory does not include merchandise sold to customers but not delivered or goods that cannot be sold because they are damaged or obsolete. If the damaged or obsolete goods can be sold at a reduced price, however, they should be included in ending inventory at their reduced value.

The actual count usually is taken after the close of business on the last day of the fiscal year. Many companies end their fiscal year in a slow season to facilitate taking the physical inventory when inventories are at relatively low levels. Retail department stores often end their fiscal year in January or February, for example. After hours, at night or on the weekend, employees count and record all items on numbered inventory tickets or sheets, following procedures to make sure that no items are missed. Sometimes a store closes for all or part of a day for inventory taking. The use of bar coding has greatly facilitated the taking of a physical inventory in many companies.

Inventory Losses

Many companies have substantial losses in merchandise inventory from spoilage, shoplifting, and employee pilferage. Management, of course, wants to take steps to prevent these losses from occurring. But if they do occur, the periodic inventory system provides no means of tracking them because their costs automatically are included in the cost of goods sold. For example, assume that a company lost $1,250 during an accounting period in merchandise that was stolen or spoiled. When the physical inventory is taken, the missing items are not in stock, so they cannot be counted. Because the ending inventory does not contain these items, the amount subtracted from goods available for sale is less than it would be if the goods were in stock. The cost of goods sold, then, is overstated by $1,250. In a sense, the cost of goods sold is inflated by the amount of merchandise that has been lost. If the perpetual inventory system is used, it is easier to identify these types of losses. Because the merchandise inventory account continuously is updated for sales, purchases, and returns, the loss shows up as the difference between the inventory records and the physical inventory taken at the end of the accounting period.

Operating Expenses

Operating expenses are another major part of the income statement for a merchandising concern. These are the expenses, other than the cost of goods sold, that are necessary to run the business. It is customary to group operating expenses into categories. Selling expenses and general and administrative expenses are two common categories. Selling expenses include the costs of storing and preparing goods for sale; displaying, advertising, and otherwise promoting sales; making the sales; and delivering the goods to the buyer if the seller bears the cost of delivery. Among the general and administrative expenses are general office expenses, those for accounting, personnel, and credit and collections, and any other expenses that apply to the overall operation of the company. Although general occupancy expenses, such as rent expense and utility expenses, often are classified as general and administrative expenses, they can be allocated between the selling and the general and administrative categories on a basis determined by management.

Handling the Merchandise Inventory Account at the End of the Accounting Period

OBJECTIVE 6
Explain the objectives of handling merchandise inventory at the end of the accounting period and two approaches to achieving them

Remember that under the periodic inventory system, purchases of merchandise are accumulated in the Purchases account. During the accounting period, no entries are made to the Merchandise Inventory account. Its balance at the end of the period, before adjusting and closing entries, is the same as it was at the beginning of the period. Thus, its balance at this point represents beginning merchandise inventory. Remember also that the cost of goods sold is determined by adding beginning merchandise inventory to net purchases and then subtracting ending merchandise inventory. The objectives of handling merchandise inventory at the end of the period are to (1) remove the beginning balance from the Merchandise Inventory account, (2) enter the ending balance into the Merchandise Inventory account, and (3) enter the beginning inventory as a debit and the ending inventory as a credit to the Income Summary account to calculate net income. Using the figures for Fenwick Fashions, the T accounts below show how these objectives can be met:

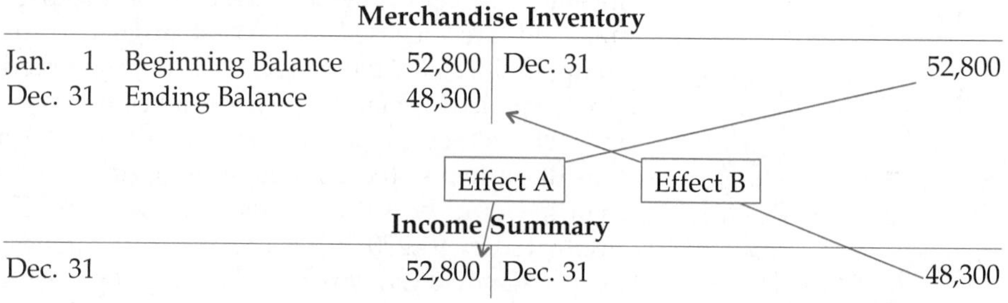

Merchandise Inventory

Jan. 1	Beginning Balance	52,800	Dec. 31	52,800
Dec. 31	Ending Balance	48,300		

Effect A — Effect B

Income Summary

Dec. 31	52,800	Dec. 31	48,300

In this example, merchandise inventory was $52,800 at the beginning of the year and $48,300 at the end of the year. Effect A removes the $52,800 from Merchandise Inventory, leaving a zero balance, and transfers it to Income Summary. In Income Summary, the $52,800 is in effect added to net purchases because, like expenses, the balance of the Purchases account is debited to Income Summary in a closing entry. Effect B establishes the ending balance of Merchandise Inventory, $48,300, and enters it as a credit in the Income Summary account. The credit entry in Income Summary has the effect of deducting the ending inventory from goods available for sale because both purchases and beginning inventory are entered on the debit side. In other words, beginning merchandise inventory and purchases are debits to Income Summary, and ending merchandise inventory is a credit to Income Summary.

So, the three objectives stated above are accomplished if Effects A and B both occur. The question now is how to achieve the effects. Two acceptable methods are available: the adjusting entry method and the closing entry method. Each produces exactly the same result, so only one of them would be used by a company. However, because practice varies in different regions of the country, both are described here. Each method is simply a bookkeeping technique designed to deal with the Merchandise Inventory account under the periodic inventory system.

Using the *adjusting entry method,* the two entries indicated by Effects A and B are prepared at the same time the other adjusting entries are made:

Adjusting Entries

Dec. 31	Income Summary	52,800	
	Merchandise Inventory		52,800
	To remove the beginning balance of the Merchandise Inventory account and transfer it to the Income Summary account		
31	**Merchandise Inventory**	48,300	
	Income Summary		48,300
	To establish the ending balance of the Merchandise Inventory account and deduct it from goods available for sale in the Income Summary account		

The *closing entry method* makes the debit and the credit to Merchandise Inventory by including them among the closing entries:

Closing Entries

Dec. 31	Income Summary	Total of credits	
	Merchandise Inventory		52,800
	Expenses and Other Income Statement Accounts with Debit Balances		Various amounts
	To close temporary expense and revenue accounts with debit balances and to remove the beginning inventory		
31	**Merchandise Inventory**	48,300	
	Revenues and Other Income Statement Accounts with Credit Balances	Various amounts	
	Income Summary		Total of debits
	To close temporary expense and revenue accounts with credit balances and to establish the ending inventory		

Notice that under both methods, Merchandise Inventory is credited for the beginning balance and debited for the ending balance and that the opposite entries are made to the Income Summary account.

Work Sheet for a Merchandising Concern

OBJECTIVE 7
Prepare a work sheet for a merchandising concern under one of two alternative methods (This objective may be omitted if the chapter on completing the accounting cycle was not covered.)

In the chapter on completing the accounting cycle, the work sheet was presented as a useful tool in preparing financial statements and adjusting and closing entries. The work sheet of a merchandising business is basically the same as that of a service business, except that it has to deal with the new accounts that are needed to handle merchandising transactions. These accounts include Sales, Sales Returns and Allowances, Sales Discounts, Purchases, Purchases Returns and Allowances, Purchases Discounts, Freight In, and Merchandise Inventory. Except for Merchandise Inventory, these accounts are treated much as revenue and expense accounts are for a service company. They are transferred to the Income Summary account in the closing process. On the work sheet, they are extended to the Income Statement columns.

The way in which Merchandise Inventory is handled, however, depends on whether the adjusting entry method or the closing entry method is used. You need to learn only one of these methods because they are both acceptable and they accomplish the same objectives. You should ask your instructor which method is going to be used in your course.

The Adjusting Entry Method

The work sheet for Fenwick Fashions Company using the adjusting entry method is shown in Exhibit 5-3. Each pair of columns in the work sheet and the adjusting and closing entries are discussed below.

Trial Balance Columns. The first step in the preparation of the work sheet is to enter the balances from the ledger accounts into the Trial Balance columns. You already are familiar with this procedure. Total the Trial Balance columns to prove that the total of debits and the total of credits are equal.

Adjustments Columns. Under the adjusting entry method of handling merchandise inventory, the first two adjusting entries entered in the work sheet were explained in the previous section. The first entry transfers beginning merchandise inventory to the Income Summary account by debiting Income Summary and crediting Merchandise Inventory for $52,800 (adjustment **a**). The second entry establishes the ending merchandise inventory by debiting Merchandise Inventory and crediting Income Summary for $48,300 (adjustment **b**). Notice that the Income Summary account is listed immediately below the trial balance totals. The remaining adjustments for Fenwick Fashions are familiar to you. They involve insurance expired during the period (adjustment **c**), store and office supplies used (adjustments **d** and **e**), and depreciation of building and office equipment (adjustments **f** and **g**). After the adjusting entries are entered on the work sheet, the Adjustments columns are totaled to prove that total debits equal total credits.

Omission of Adjusted Trial Balance Columns. These two columns, which appeared in the work sheet for a service company, can be omitted. These columns are optional; they should be used only when there are many adjusting entries to record. When only a few adjusting entries are required, as is the case for Fenwick Fashions Company, the columns can be left out to save time.

Income Statement and Balance Sheet Columns. After the Trial Balance columns have been totaled, the adjustments entered, and the equality of the

Exhibit 5-3. Work Sheet for Fenwick Fashions Company: Adjusting Entry Method

Fenwick Fashions Company
Work Sheet
For the Year Ended December 31, 19xx

	Trial Balance		Adjustments		Income Statement		Balance Sheet	
Account Name	**Debit**	**Credit**	**Debit**	**Credit**	**Debit**	**Credit**	**Debit**	**Credit**
Cash	29,410						29,410	
Accounts Receivable	42,400						42,400	
Merchandise Inventory	52,800		(b) 48,300	(a) 52,800			48,300	
Prepaid Insurance	17,400			(c) 5,800			11,600	
Store Supplies	2,600			(d) 1,540			1,060	
Office Supplies	1,840			(e) 1,204			636	
Land	4,500						4,500	
Building	20,260						20,260	
Accumulated Depreciation, Building		5,650		(f) 2,600				8,250
Office Equipment	8,600						8,600	
Accumulated Depreciation, Office Equipment		2,800		(g) 2,200				5,000
Accounts Payable		25,683						25,683
Gloria Fenwick, Capital		118,352						118,352
Gloria Fenwick, Withdrawals	20,000						20,000	
Sales		246,350				246,350		
Sales Returns and Allowances	2,750				2,750			
Sales Discounts	4,275				4,275			
Purchases	126,400				126,400			
Purchases Returns and Allowances		5,640				5,640		
Purchases Discounts		2,136				2,136		
Freight In	8,236				8,236			
Sales Salaries Expense	22,500				22,500			
Freight Out Expense	5,740				5,740			
Advertising Expense	10,000				10,000			
Office Salaries Expense	26,900				26,900			
	406,611	406,611						
Income Summary			(a) 52,800	(b) 48,300	52,800	48,300		
Insurance Expense, Selling			(c) 1,600		1,600			
Insurance Expense, General			(c) 4,200		4,200			
Store Supplies Expense			(d) 1,540		1,540			
Office Supplies Expense			(e) 1,204		1,204			
Depreciation Expense, Building			(f) 2,600		2,600			
Depreciation Expense, Office Equipment			(g) 2,200		2,200			
			114,444	114,444	272,945	302,426	186,766	157,285
Net Income					29,481			29,481
					302,426	302,426	186,766	186,766

columns proved, the balances are extended to the Income Statement and Balance Sheet columns. Again, begin with the Cash account at the top of the work sheet and move sequentially down the work sheet one account at a time. Each account balance is entered in the proper column of the Income Statement or Balance Sheet columns. The only exception to this rule is that both the debit (beginning merchandise inventory of $52,800) and the credit (ending merchandise inventory of $48,300) to Income Summary are extended to the corresponding Income Statement columns. The reason for this is that both the beginning and ending inventory figures are needed to prepare the cost of goods sold section of the income statement.

After all the items have been extended to the correct columns, the four columns are totaled. The net income or net loss is the difference in the debit and credit columns of the Income Statement columns. In this case, Fenwick Fashions Company has earned a net income of $29,481, which is extended to the credit side of the Balance Sheet columns. The four columns then are added to prove that total debits equal total credits.

OBJECTIVE 8
Prepare adjusting and closing entries for a merchandising concern (This objective may be omitted if the chapter on completing the accounting cycle was not covered.)

Adjusting Entries. Now, the adjusting entries are entered into the general journal from the work sheet and posted to the ledger, as they would be in a service company. The only difference is that under the adjusting entry method, the two adjustments involving Merchandise Inventory and Income Summary, already illustrated on page 179, appear among the adjusting entries.

Closing Entries. The closing entries for Fenwick Fashions Company under the adjusting entry method are shown in Exhibit 5-4. These closing entries are very similar to those for a service company except that the new accounts for merchandising companies also must be closed to Income Summary. All income statement accounts with debit balances, including Sales Returns and Allowances, Sales Discounts, Purchases, and Freight In, are credited in the first entry. All income statement accounts with credit balances, including Sales, Purchases Returns and Allowances, and Purchases Discounts, are debited in the second entry. When copying the accounts and their balances from the Income Statement columns of the work sheet, do not include the debit and credit merchandise inventory amounts already in the Income Summary account. The third entry closes the Income Summary account, transferring net income to the Capital account. The fourth entry closes the Withdrawals account to the Capital account. After adjusting and closing entries are posted, the Income Summary account may be summarized in T account form as follows:

Income Summary

Dec. 31	Removal of beginning inventory	52,800	Dec. 31	Establishment of ending inventory	48,300
Dec. 31	Closing of expense and revenue accounts with debit balances	220,145	Dec. 31	Closing of expense and revenue accounts with credit balances	254,126
Dec. 31	Closing of Income Summary account	29,481			
Bal.		0			

Exhibit 5-4. Closing Entries for a Merchandising Concern: Adjusting Entry Method

General Journal					Page 10
Date		Description	Post. Ref.	Debit	Credit
19xx		*Closing entries:*			
Dec.	31	Income Summary		220,145	
		Sales Returns and Allowances			2,750
		Sales Discounts			4,275
		Purchases			126,400
		Freight In			8,236
		Sales Salaries Expense			22,500
		Freight Out Expense			5,740
		Advertising Expense			10,000
		Office Salaries Expense			26,900
		Insurance Expense, Selling			1,600
		Insurance Expense, General			4,200
		Store Supplies Expense			1,540
		Office Supplies Expense			1,204
		Depreciation Expense, Building			2,600
		Depreciation Expense, Office Equipment			2,200
		To close temporary expense and revenue accounts with debit balances			
	31	Sales		246,350	
		Purchases Returns and Allowances		5,640	
		Purchases Discounts		2,136	
		Income Summary			254,126
		To close temporary expense and revenue accounts with credit balances			
	31	Income Summary		29,481	
		Gloria Fenwick, Capital			29,481
		To close the Income Summary account			
	31	Gloria Fenwick, Capital		20,000	
		Gloria Fenwick, Withdrawals			20,000
		To close the Withdrawals account			

The Closing Entry Method

Alternative Method

The work sheet for Fenwick Fashions Company using the closing entry method is shown in Exhibit 5-5. Each pair of columns in the work sheet and the adjusting and closing entries are discussed below.

Trial Balance Columns. The first step in the preparation of the work sheet is to enter the balances from the ledger accounts into the Trial Balance columns. You already are familiar with this procedure.

Exhibit 5-5. Work Sheet for Fenwick Fashions Company: Closing Entry Method

Fenwick Fashions Company
Work Sheet
For the Year Ended December 31, 19xx

Account Name	Trial Balance		Adjustments		Income Statement		Balance Sheet	
	Debit	Credit	Debit	Credit	Debit	Credit	Debit	Credit
Cash	29,410						29,410	
Accounts Receivable	42,400						42,400	
Merchandise Inventory	52,800				52,800	48,300	48,300	
Prepaid Insurance	17,400			(a) 5,800			11,600	
Store Supplies	2,600			(b) 1,540			1,060	
Office Supplies	1,840			(c) 1,204			636	
Land	4,500						4,500	
Building	20,260						20,260	
Accumulated Depreciation, Building		5,650		(d) 2,600				8,250
Office Equipment	8,600						8,600	
Accumulated Depreciation, Office Equipment		2,800		(e) 2,200				5,000
Accounts Payable		25,683						25,683
Gloria Fenwick, Capital		118,352						118,352
Gloria Fenwick, Withdrawals	20,000						20,000	
Sales		246,350				246,350		
Sales Returns and Allowances	2,750				2,750			
Sales Discounts	4,275				4,275			
Purchases	126,400				126,400			
Purchases Returns and Allowances		5,640				5,640		
Purchases Discounts		2,136				2,136		
Freight In	8,236				8,236			
Sales Salaries Expense	22,500				22,500			
Freight Out Expense	5,740				5,740			
Advertising Expense	10,000				10,000			
Office Salaries Expense	26,900				26,900			
	406,611	406,611						
Insurance Expense, Selling			(a) 1,600		1,600			
Insurance Expense, General			(a) 4,200		4,200			
Store Supplies Expense			(b) 1,540		1,540			
Office Supplies Expense			(c) 1,204		1,204			
Depreciation Expense, Building			(d) 2,600		2,600			
Depreciation Expense, Office Equipment			(e) 2,200		2,200			
			13,344	13,344	272,945	302,426	186,766	157,285
Net Income					29,481			29,481
					302,426	302,426	186,766	186,766

Adjustments Columns. Under the closing entry method of handling merchandise inventory, the adjusting entries for Fenwick Fashions Company are entered in the Adjustments columns in the same way that they were for service companies. They involve insurance expired during the period (adjustment **a**), store and office supplies used during the period (adjustments **b** and **c**), and the depreciation of building and office equipment (adjustments **d** and **e**). No adjusting entry is made for merchandise inventory. After the adjusting entries are entered on the work sheet, the columns are totaled to prove that total debits equal total credits.

Omission of Adjusted Trial Balance Columns. These two columns, which appeared in the work sheet for a service company, can be omitted. See the discussion under the adjusting entry method on page 180.

Income Statement and Balance Sheet Columns. After the Trial Balance columns have been totaled, the adjustments entered, and the equality of the columns proved, the balances are extended to the Income Statement and Balance Sheet columns. Again, begin with the Cash account at the top of the work sheet and move sequentially down the work sheet, one account at a time, entering each account balance in the correct Income Statement or Balance Sheet column.

The "problem" extension here is in the Merchandise Inventory row. The beginning inventory balance of $52,800 (which is already in the trial balance) is extended to the debit column of the Income Statement column, as shown in Exhibit 5-5. This procedure has the effect of adding beginning inventory to net purchases because the Purchases account is also in the debit column of the Income Statement columns. The ending inventory balance of $48,300 (which is determined by the physical inventory and is not in the trial balance) then is inserted in the credit column of the Income Statement columns. This procedure has the effect of subtracting the ending inventory from goods available for sale in order to calculate the cost of goods sold. Finally, the ending merchandise inventory ($48,300) is inserted in the debit side of the Balance Sheet columns because it will appear on the balance sheet.

After all the items have been extended into the correct columns, the four columns are totaled. The net income or net loss is the difference between the debit and credit Income Statement columns. In this case, Fenwick Fashions Company has earned a net income of $29,481, which is extended to the credit side of the Balance Sheet columns. The four columns then are added to prove that total debits equal total credits.

Adjusting Entries. The adjusting entries now are entered from the work sheet into the general journal and posted to the ledger, as they would be in a service company. Under the closing entry method, there is no difference in this procedure between a service company and a merchandising company.

Closing Entries. The closing entries for Fenwick Fashions Company under the closing entry method appear in Exhibit 5-6. Notice that Merchandise Inventory is credited in the first entry for the amount of beginning inventory ($52,800) and debited in the second entry for the amount of the ending inventory ($48,300), as shown on page 179. Otherwise, these closing entries are very similar to those for a service company except that the new merchandising accounts introduced in this chapter also must be closed to Income Summary. All

Exhibit 5-6. Closing Entries for a Merchandising Concern: Closing Entry Method

General Journal — **Page 10**

Date		Description	Post. Ref.	Debit	Credit
19xx		*Closing entries:*			
Dec.	31	Income Summary		272,945	
		Merchandise Inventory			52,800
		Sales Returns and Allowances			2,750
		Sales Discounts			4,275
		Purchases			126,400
		Freight In			8,236
		Sales Salaries Expense			22,500
		Freight Out Expense			5,740
		Advertising Expense			10,000
		Office Salaries Expense			26,900
		Insurance Expense, Selling			1,600
		Insurance Expense, General			4,200
		Store Supplies Expense			1,540
		Office Supplies Expense			1,204
		Depreciation Expense, Building			2,600
		Depreciation Expense, Office Equipment			2,200
		To close temporary expense and revenue accounts with debit balances and to remove the beginning inventory			
	31	Merchandise Inventory		48,300	
		Sales		246,350	
		Purchases Returns and Allowances		5,640	
		Purchases Discounts		2,136	
		Income Summary			302,426
		To close temporary expense and revenue accounts with credit balances and to establish the ending inventory			
	31	Income Summary		29,481	
		Gloria Fenwick, Capital			29,481
		To close the Income Summary account			
	31	Gloria Fenwick, Capital		20,000	
		Gloria Fenwick, Withdrawals			20,000
		To close the Withdrawals account			

income statement accounts with debit balances—Sales Returns and Allowances, Sales Discounts, Purchases, and Freight In—are credited in the first entry. The total of these accounts ($272,945) equals the total of the debit column in the Income Statement columns of the work sheet. All income statement ac-

Exhibit 5-7. Income Statement for Fenwick Fashions Company

Fenwick Fashions Company
Income Statement
For the Year Ended December 31, 19xx

Revenues from Sales				
Gross Sales				$246,350
Less: Sales Returns and Allowances			$ 2,750	
Sales Discounts			4,275	7,025
Net Sales				$239,325
Cost of Goods Sold				
Merchandise Inventory, January 1, 19xx			$ 52,800	
Purchases		$126,400		
Less: Purchases Returns and Allowances	$5,640			
Purchases Discounts	2,136	7,776		
		$118,624		
Freight In		8,236		
Net Purchases			126,860	
Goods Available for Sale			$179,660	
Less Merchandise Inventory, December 31, 19xx			48,300	
Cost of Goods Sold				131,360
Gross Margin from Sales				$107,965
Operating Expenses				
Selling Expenses				
Sales Salaries Expense		$ 22,500		
Freight Out Expense		5,740		
Advertising Expense		10,000		
Insurance Expense, Selling		1,600		
Store Supplies Expense		1,540		
Total Selling Expenses			$ 41,380	
General and Administrative Expenses				
Office Salaries Expense		$ 26,900		
Insurance Expense, General		4,200		
Office Supplies Expense		1,204		
Depreciation Expense, Building		2,600		
Depreciation Expense, Office Equipment		2,200		
Total General and Administrative Expenses			37,104	
Total Operating Expenses				78,484
Net Income				$ 29,481

counts with credit balances—Sales, Purchases Returns and Allowances, and Purchases Discounts—are debited in the second entry. The total of these accounts ($302,426) equals the total of the Income Statement credit column in the work sheet. The third and fourth entries are used to close the Income Summary account and transfer net income to the Capital account, and to close the Withdrawals account to the Capital account. After closing entries are posted, the Income Summary account may be summarized in T account form as follows:

Income Summary

Dec. 31	Closing of expense and revenue accounts with debit balances	272,945	Dec. 31	Closing of expense and revenue accounts with credit balances	302,426
Dec. 31	Closing of Income Summary account	29,481			
Bal.		0			

Income Statement Illustrated

OBJECTIVE 9 *Prepare an income statement for a merchandising concern*

In this chapter, we've presented the parts of the income statement for a merchandising concern and discussed the transactions pertaining to each part. Exhibit 5-7 pulls the parts together in the complete income statement for Fenwick Fashions Company. The statement can be prepared by referring to the accounts in the ledger that pertain to the income statement, or by taking the account balances from the Income Statement columns of the work sheet. In practice, the statement of owner's equity and balance sheet also would be prepared. They are not presented here because they are like those of service companies, with the exception of Merchandise Inventory, which is listed among the assets on the balance sheet.

Chapter Review

Review of Learning Objectives

1. **Compare the income statements for service and merchandising concerns.** The merchandising company differs from the service company in that it earns income by buying and selling merchandise rather than by offering services. In the simplest case, the income statement for a service company consists only of revenues and expenses. The income statement for a merchandising company has three major parts: (1) revenues from sales, (2) the cost of goods sold, and (3) operating expenses. Gross margin from sales is the difference between revenues from sales and the cost of goods sold. Net income is the difference between gross margin from sales and operating expenses. Merchandisers must sell their merchandise for more than cost to pay operating expenses and earn an adequate profit.
2. **Record transactions involving revenues for merchandising concerns.** Revenues from sales consist of gross sales less sales returns and allowances and sales discounts. The amount of a sales discount is determined from the terms of the sale. Revenue transactions for merchandising firms can be summarized as follows:

Transaction	Related Accounting Entries: Debit	Related Accounting Entries: Credit
Sell merchandise to customer	Cash (or Accounts Receivable)	Sales
Allow customers to return merchandise or grant a reduction on original price	Sales Returns and Allowances	Accounts Receivable (or Cash)
Receive payment for merchandise sold on credit	Cash (and Sales Discounts, if applicable)	Accounts Receivable

The Sales account is used only to record sales of merchandise to customers.

3. **Calculate the cost of goods sold.**
To compute the cost of goods sold, add net purchases to the beginning merchandise inventory to determine the goods available for sale:

$$\text{Beginning merchandise inventory} + \text{net purchases} = \text{goods available for sale}$$

Then, subtract ending merchandise inventory from the goods available for sale:

$$\text{Goods available for sale} - \text{ending merchandise inventory} = \text{cost of goods sold}$$

Net purchases are calculated by subtracting the purchases returns and allowances and the purchases discounts from gross purchases, and then adding any freight-in charges on the purchases:

$$\text{Gross purchases} - \text{purchases returns and allowances} - \text{purchases discounts} + \text{freight in} = \text{net purchases}$$

4. **Record transactions involving purchases of merchandise.**
The transactions involving purchases of merchandise can be summarized as follows:

Transaction	Related Accounting Entries: Debit	Related Accounting Entries: Credit
Purchase merchandise for resale	Purchases	Cash (or Accounts Payable)
Incur transportation charges on merchandise purchased for resale	Freight In	Cash (or Accounts Payable)
Return unsatisfactory merchandise to supplier, or obtain a reduction from original price	Accounts Payable (or Cash)	Purchases Returns and Allowances
Pay for merchandise purchased on credit	Accounts Payable	Cash (and Purchases Discounts, if applicable)

The Purchases account is debited only for merchandise purchased for resale. Its sole purpose is to accumulate the total cost of merchandise purchased during an accounting period.

5. **Distinguish between the perpetual inventory system and the periodic inventory system.**

Merchandise inventory includes all salable goods owned, regardless of where they are located. Merchandise inventory can be determined by one of two systems. Under the *periodic inventory system,* the company usually waits until the end of an accounting period to take a physical inventory; it does not maintain detailed records of physical inventory on hand during the period. The cost of goods sold is computed after a physical inventory is taken. Under the *perpetual inventory system,* records are kept of the quantity and usually the cost of individual items of inventory throughout the year, as items are bought and sold. The cost of goods sold is recorded as goods are transferred to customers, and the inventory balance is kept current throughout the year, as items are bought and sold.

6. **Explain the objectives of handling merchandise inventory at the end of the accounting period and two approaches to achieving them.**

At the end of the accounting period under a periodic inventory system, it is necessary to (1) remove the beginning balance from the Merchandise Inventory account, (2) enter the ending balance in the Merchandise Inventory account, and (3) enter these two amounts in the Income Summary account to calculate net income. These objectives are accomplished by debiting Income Summary and crediting Merchandise Inventory for the beginning balance, and debiting Merchandise Inventory and crediting Income Summary for the ending balance.

Inventory Procedures at End of Period	Related Accounting Entries	
	Debit	**Credit**
Transfer the balance of the beginning inventory to the Income Summary account	Income Summary	Merchandise Inventory
Take a physical inventory of the goods on hand at the end of the period, and establish the balance of the ending inventory	Merchandise Inventory	Income Summary

There are two ways of accomplishing these effects. Under the adjusting entry method, the entries are included among the adjusting entries. Under the closing entry method, the entries are included among the closing entries.

7. **Prepare a work sheet for a merchandising concern under one of two alternative methods.**

The major difference between preparing a work sheet for a merchandising concern and preparing one for a service company is in the accounts relating to merchandising transactions. The accounts necessary to compute the cost of goods sold appear in the Income Statement columns. The Merchandise Inventory account is treated differently under each of the following two methods:

Adjusting entry method: Under this method, the beginning inventory is debited to Income Summary and credited to Merchandise Inventory in the Adjustments columns—clearing the beginning inventory from the Merchandise Inventory account. Then, the ending inventory is debited to Merchandise Inventory and credited to Income Summary. Both the debit and credit to Income Summary are entered in the appropriate Income Statement columns; and the debit to Merchandise Inventory is entered in the Balance Sheet debit column.

Closing entry method: Under this method, the beginning inventory from the trial balance is extended to the debit column of the Income Statement columns, and the ending balance of Merchandise Inventory is inserted in both the credit column of the Income Statement columns and the debit column of the Balance Sheet columns.

8. **Prepare adjusting and closing entries for a merchandising concern.**
The adjusting and closing entries for a merchandising concern are similar to those for a service business. The major difference is in handling merchandise inventory, which is summarized in this table:

Method	Adjusting Entries	Closing Entries
Adjusting entry method	Dr. Income Summary Cr. Merchandise Inventory for amount of beginning inventory Dr. Merchandise Inventory Cr. Income Summary for the amount of ending inventory	Follow procedures for service companies
Closing entry method	Follow procedures for service companies	Include among closing entries the following: Dr. Income Summary Cr. Merchandise Inventory for amount of beginning inventory Dr. Merchandise Inventory and Cr. Income Summary for amount of ending inventory

9. **Prepare an income statement for a merchandising concern.**
The income statement of a merchandising company is made up of several major sections. The revenues from sales section shows gross sales, with contra-revenue accounts deducted to arrive at net sales. The cost of goods sold section shows the accounts that make up goods available for sale. Net sales less the cost of goods sold equal the gross margin from sales. The operating expenses section divides the expenses into categories, such as selling expenses and general and administrative expenses. Net income equals revenues from sales less the cost of goods sold (the gross margin from sales) less operating expenses.

Review of Concepts and Terminology

The following concepts and terms were introduced in this chapter:

(L.O. 5) **Beginning inventory:** Merchandise (for sale to customers) on hand at the beginning of an accounting period.

(L.O. 1) **Cost of goods sold:** The amount paid for the goods sold during an accounting period.

(L.O. 5) **Ending inventory:** Merchandise (for sale to customers) on hand at the end of an accounting period.

(L.O. 4) **FOB destination:** A term related to transportation charges that means that the seller bears transportation costs to the destination.

(L.O. 4) **FOB shipping point:** A term related to transportation charges that means that the buyer bears transportation costs from the point of origin.

(L.O. 4) **Freight in:** Transportation charges on merchandise purchased for resale. Also called *transportation in.*

(L.O. 3) **Goods available for sale:** The total goods available for sale to customers during the year; beginning merchandise inventory plus net purchases.

(L.O. 1) **Gross margin from sales:** The revenues from sales remaining after deducting the cost of goods sold. Also called *gross margin* or *gross profit.*

(L.O. 4) **Gross method:** The system of recording purchases initially at the gross purchase price.

(L.O. 2) **Gross sales:** Total sales for cash and on credit during an accounting period.

(L.O. 3) **Merchandise inventory:** The goods on hand at any one time that are available for sale to customers.

(L.O. 1) **Net income:** For merchandising companies, what is left after deducting operating expenses from the gross margin from sales.

(L.O. 4) **Net method:** A method of recording purchases that identifies discounts that are lost by requiring that purchases be recorded initially at their net price.

(L.O. 4) **Net purchases:** Gross purchases less purchases returns and allowances and purchases discounts plus any freight charges on the purchases.

(L.O. 2) **Net sales:** The gross proceeds from sales of merchandise less sales returns and allowances and sales discounts.

(L.O. 1) **Operating expenses:** Those expenses, other than the cost of goods sold, that are incurred in running a business.

(L.O. 5) **Periodic inventory system:** A system for determining the cost of goods sold by deducting the ending inventory (based on a physical count of the inventory) from the beginning inventory plus total purchases over the period.

(L.O. 5) **Perpetual inventory system:** A system for determining the cost of goods sold by keeping continuous records of the physical inventory as goods are bought and sold.

(L.O. 5) **Physical inventory:** An actual count of all merchandise on hand at the end of an accounting period.

(L.O. 4) **Purchases:** A temporary account used to accumulate the total cost of all merchandise purchased for resale during an accounting period.

(L.O. 4) **Purchases discounts:** Allowances made for prompt payment for merchandise purchased for resale; the Purchases Discounts account is a contra-purchases account.

(L.O. 4) **Purchases Returns and Allowances:** The account used to accumulate cash refunds and other allowances made by suppliers on merchandise originally purchased for resale; a contra-purchases account.

(L.O. 1) **Revenues from sales:** The amount received for the goods sold during an accounting period.

(L.O. 2) **Sales discounts:** Discounts given to customers for early payment for sales made on credit; the Sales Discounts account is a contra-revenue account.

(L.O. 2) **Sales Returns and Allowances:** The account used to accumulate cash refunds and other allowances related to prior sales; a contra-revenue account.

(L.O. 2) **Trade discounts:** Deductions (usually 30 percent or more) off list or catalogue price.

Self-Test

Test your knowledge of the chapter by choosing the best answer for each of the following items.

(L.O. 1) 1. A net income always results when
   a. the cost of goods sold exceeds operating expenses.
   b. revenues exceed the cost of goods sold.
   c. revenues exceed operating expenses.
   d. the gross margin from sales exceeds operating expenses.

(L.O. 2) 2. A sale is made on June 1 for $200, terms 2/10, n/30, on which a sales return of $50 is granted on June 7. The dollar amount received for payment in full on June 9 is
a. $200.
b. $150.
c. $147.
d. $196.

(L.O. 3) 3. If beginning and ending merchandise inventories are $400 and $700, respectively, and the cost of goods sold is $3,400, net purchases
a. are $3,700.
b. are $3,400.
c. are $3,100.
d. cannot be determined.

(L.O. 4) 4. The entry to record the payment within the discount period for a purchase of $1,000 under terms of 2/10, n/30 on which a purchase return of $300 was made would include a credit to Cash for
a. $980.
b. $700.
c. $686.
d. $680.

(L.O. 4) 5. A purchase of merchandise for $750 including freight of $50 under terms of 2/10, n/30, FOB shipping point would include a
a. debit to Freight In of $50.
b. debit to Purchases of $750.
c. credit to Accounts Payable of $700.
d. credit to Freight Payable of $50.

(L.O. 4) 6. Which of the following accounts is used only under the net method of recording purchases?
a. Purchases Returns and Allowances
b. Purchases Discounts Lost
c. Purchases
d. Purchases Discounts

(L.O. 5) 7. Under which of the following inventory systems would a wholesaler most likely know the exact quantity in inventory of a particular item on hand in the middle of a month?
a. Periodic inventory system
b. Perpetual inventory system
c. Either the periodic or the perpetual inventory system
d. Neither the periodic nor the perpetual inventory system

(L.O. 6) 8. Samuel's Company shows a beginning merchandise inventory of $12,000 and an ending merchandise inventory of $14,000. Under the periodic inventory system, what is the balance of the Merchandise Inventory account at the end of the accounting period before and after the adjusting and closing entries?
a. $12,000 and $14,000
b. $14,000 and $12,000
c. $14,000 and $14,000
d. $12,000 and $12,000

(L.O. 8) 9. The closing entries for a merchandising concern would contain a debit to
a. Sales Discounts.
b. Purchases.
c. Freight In.
d. Purchases Discounts.

(L.O. 9) 10. Which of the following appears as an operating expense on the income statement of a merchandising concern?
a. Freight In
b. Freight Out
c. Sales Returns and Allowances
d. Purchases Returns and Allowances

Answers to the Self-Test are at the end of this chapter.

Review Problem
Methods of Recording Purchases and Sales Contrasted

(L.O. 2, 4) Newcomb Discount Warehouse Corporation purchased $80,000 of merchandise, terms 2/10, n/30, from Videotex Corporation on September 14.

Required

1. Give the entries in Newcomb's records to record the purchase and payment under each of the following situations.
   a. Purchases are recorded at the gross amount, and payment is made on September 24.
   b. Purchases are recorded at the gross amount, and payment is made on October 14.
   c. Purchases are recorded at the net amount, and payment is made on September 24.
   d. Purchases are recorded at the net amount, and payment is made on October 14.

2. Give the entries on Videotex's records to record the sale and its collection under each of the four situations above. Assume all sales are recorded at their gross amounts.

Answer to Review Problem

Situation	Date	1. Newcomb's Records			2. Videotex's Records		
a.	Sept. 14	Purchases	80,000		Accounts Receivable	80,000	
		Accounts Payable		80,000	Sales		80,000
		To record purchase—gross method			To record sale		
	Sept. 24	Accounts Payable	80,000		Cash	78,400	
		Purchases Discount		1,600	Sales Discounts	1,600	
		Cash		78,400	Accounts Receivable		80,000
		To record payment—gross method			To record collection		
b.	Sept. 14	Purchases	80,000		Accounts Receivable	80,000	
		Accounts Payable		80,000	Sales		80,000
		To record purchase—gross method			To record sale		
	Oct. 14	Accounts Payable	80,000		Cash	80,000	
		Cash		80,000	Accounts Receivable		80,000
		To record payment—gross method			To record collection		
c.	Sept. 14	Purchases	78,400		Accounts Receivable	80,000	
		Accounts Payable		78,400	Sales		80,000
		To record purchase—net method			To record sale		
	Sept. 24	Accounts Payable	78,400		Cash	78,400	
		Cash		78,400	Sales Discounts	1,600	
		To record payment—net method			Accounts Receivable		80,000
					To record collection		
d.	Sept. 14	Purchases	78,400		Accounts Receivable	80,000	
		Accounts Payable		78,400	Sales		80,000
		To record purchase—net method			To record sale		
	Oct. 14	Accounts Payable	78,400		Cash	80,000	
		Purchases Discounts Lost	1,600		Accounts Receivable		80,000
		Cash		80,000	To record collection		
		To record payment—net method					

Chapter Assignments

Questions

1. What is the primary difference between the operations of a merchandising concern and those of a service concern, and how is it reflected on the income statement?
2. What is the source of revenues for a merchandising concern?
3. Define *gross margin from sales.* Why is it important?

4. Kumler Nursery had a cost of goods sold during its first year in operation of $64,000 and a gross margin from sales equal to 40 percent of sales. What was the dollar amount of the company's sales?
5. Could Kumler Nursery (in question **4**) have a net loss for the year? Explain your answer.
6. Why is it advisable to maintain an account for Sales Returns and Allowances when the same result could be obtained by debiting each return or allowance to the Sales account?
7. What is a sales discount? If the terms are 2/10, n/30, what is the length of the credit period? What is the length of the discount period?
8. What two related transactions are reflected in the T accounts below?

Cash

	Debit		Credit
(b)	980		

Accounts Receivable

	Debit		Credit
(a)	1,000	(b)	1,000

Sales

	Debit		Credit
		(a)	1,000

Sales Discounts

	Debit		Credit
(b)	20		

9. What is the normal balance of the Sales Discounts account? Is it an asset, liability, expense, or contra-revenue account?
10. In taking a physical inventory, a clerk counts a $200 item twice. What effect does this error have on the income statement and the balance sheet?
11. Hornberger Hardware purchased the following items: (a) a delivery truck, (b) two dozen hammers, (c) supplies for its office workers, and (d) a broom for the janitor. Which item(s) should be debited to the Purchases account?
12. What three related transactions are reflected in the T accounts below?

Cash

	Debit		Credit
		(c)	441

Accounts Payable

	Debit		Credit
(b)	50	(a)	500
(c)	450		

Purchases

	Debit		Credit
(a)	500		

Purchases Returns and Allowances

	Debit		Credit
		(b)	50

Purchases Discounts

	Debit		Credit
		(c)	9

13. How would the transactions in question **12** differ if you used the net method of recording purchases?
14. Is freight in an operating expense? Explain your answer.
15. These prices and terms on 50 units of product are quoted by two companies:

	Price	Terms
Supplier A	$20 per unit	FOB shipping point
Supplier B	$21 per unit	FOB destination

Which supplier is quoting the better deal? Explain your answer.

16. Which inventory figure—beginning or ending inventory—appears in the year-end unadjusted trial balance prepared by a company that uses the periodic inventory system?
17. Under the periodic inventory system, how is the amount of inventory at the end of the year determined?
18. "The perpetual inventory system is the best system because management always needs to know how much inventory it has." Discuss this statement.

19. Why is the handling of merchandise inventory at the end of the accounting period of special importance in determining net income? How should the Merchandise Inventory account be handled in the accounting records?
20. What are the principal differences between the work sheet for a merchandising company and that for a service company? Discuss in terms of both the adjusting or closing entry methods, according to your instructor's wishes.

Communication Skills Exercises

Communication 5-1. Ethics and Timely Payments
(L.O. 4)

Files, Folders, & Clips, with five branch stores, is the area's largest office supply chain. Francesca Gonzales, a new accountant in charge of accounts payable, is told by her supervisor that many of the company's suppliers allow a 2 percent discount if payment for a purchase is made within ten days. She is instructed to write all checks for the net amount taking into account the amount of the discount, and then date them ten days following the invoice date. The checks are not to be mailed until there is enough money in the bank to pay them. The supervisor says that, although most checks must be held a week or more after the discount date, suppliers usually allow the discount anyway because they do not want to lose business. He tells Gonzales: "This is business as usual and just good cash management. Last year we got discounts of $30,000." Gonzales wonders if this is true and, more importantly, whether or not the practice is ethical. Is this practice ethical? Would anyone be harmed by it? What other courses of action are available to Gonzales?

Communication 5-2. Periodic versus Perpetual Inventory Systems
(L.O. 5)

The Book Nook is a well-established chain of twenty book stores in eastern Michigan. In recent years the company has grown rapidly, adding five new stores in regional malls. Management has relied on the manager of each store to place orders keyed to the market in his or her neighborhood, selected from a master list of available titles provided by the central office. Every six months, a physical inventory is taken and financial statements are prepared using the periodic inventory system. At that time, books that have not sold well are placed on sale or, whenever possible, returned to the publisher. As a result of the company's fast growth, management has found that the newer store managers do not have the same ability to judge the market as managers of the older, established stores. Thus, management is considering a recommendation to implement a perpetual inventory system and carefully monitor sales from the central office. Do you think The Book Nook should switch to the perpetual inventory system or stay with the periodic inventory system? What are the advantages and disadvantages of each?

Communication 5-3. Basic Research Skills
(L.O. 5)

Identify three retail businesses in your local shopping area or a local shopping mall. Choose three different types of retail concerns—a book store, a clothing shop, a gift shop, a grocery, a hardware store, a car dealership. In each business, ask to speak to someone who is knowledgeable about the store's inventory methods. Find out the answers to the following questions: How is each item of inventory identified? Does the business have a computerized or a manual inventory system? Which inventory system, periodic or perpetual, is used? How often do employees take a physical inventory? What procedures are followed in taking a physical inventory? What kinds of inventory reports are prepared or received? Prepare a table that summarizes your findings. In the table, use columns to represent the types of businesses and rows to represent the questions. Be prepared to discuss your findings in class.

Classroom Exercises

Exercise 5-1. Computation of Net Sales
(L.O. 2)

During 19xx, the Facets Corporation had total credit sales of $110,000. Of this amount, $90,000 was collected during the year. In addition, the corporation had cash sales of $60,000, customers returned merchandise for credit of $4,000, and cash discounts of $2,000 were allowed. How much were 19xx net sales for the Facets Corporation?

Exercise 5-2.
Sales Transactions
(L.O. 2)

On June 15, the Jackson Company sold merchandise for $2,600 on terms of 2/10, n/30 to Clement Company. Give the entries to record (1) the sale, (2) a return of merchandise of $600, June 20, (3) receipt of the balance from Clement Company assuming payment on June 25, (4) receipt of balance from Clement Company assuming receipt of a check on July 15.

Exercise 5-3.
Parts of the Income Statement: Missing Data
(L.O. 3, 9)

Compute the dollar amount of each item indicated by a letter in the table below. Treat each horizontal row of numbers as a separate problem.

Sales	Beginning Inventory	Net Purchases	Ending Inventory	Cost of Goods Sold	Gross Margin	Operating Expenses	Income (Loss)
$250,000	$ a	$ 70,000	$ 20,000	$ b	$ 80,000	$ c	$24,000
d	24,000	e	36,000	216,000	120,000	80,000	40,000
460,000	44,000	334,000	f	g	100,000	h	(2,000)
780,000	80,000	i	120,000	j	k	240,000	80,000

Exercise 5-4.
Gross Margin from Sales Computation: Missing Data
(L.O. 3)

Determine the amount of gross purchases by preparing a partial income statement showing the calculation of gross margin from sales from the following data: purchases discounts, $3,500; freight in, $13,000; cost of goods sold, $185,000; sales, $275,000; beginning inventory, $25,000; purchases returns and allowances, $4,000; ending inventory, $12,000.

Exercise 5-5.
Purchases and Sales Involving Discounts
(L.O. 2, 4)

The Fellini Company purchased $9,200 of merchandise, terms 2/10, n/30, from the Vance Company and paid for the merchandise within the discount period. Give the entries (1) by the Fellini Company to record the purchase and payment, assuming purchases are recorded at the gross purchase price, and (2) by the Vance Company to record the sale and receipt of payment.

Exercise 5-6.
Gross and Net Methods of Recording Purchases Contrasted
(L.O. 4)

Westland Corporation purchased $9,400 of merchandise, terms 2/10, n/30, on June 10. Give the entries to record purchase and payment under each of the four assumptions below.

1. Purchases are recorded at gross amount, and payment is made June 20.
2. Purchases are recorded at gross amount, and payment is made July 10.
3. Purchases are recorded at net amount, and payment is made June 20.
4. Purchases are recorded at net amount, and payment is made July 10.

Exercise 5-7.
Recording Purchases: Gross and Net Methods
(L.O. 4)

Give the entries to record each of the following transactions, (1) using the gross method and (2) using the net method:

a. Purchased merchandise on credit, terms 2/10, n/30, FOB shipping point, $7,500.
b. Paid freight on the shipment in transaction **a**, $405.
c. Purchased merchandise on credit, terms 2/10, n/30, FOB destination, $4,200.
d. Purchased merchandise on credit, terms 2/10, n/30, FOB shipping point, $7,800, which includes freight paid by the supplier of $600.
e. Returned part of the merchandise purchased in transaction **c**, $1,500.
f. Paid the amount owed on the purchases in transactions **a** and **d**, respectively, within the discount periods. (Record as two transactions.)
g. Paid the amount owed on the purchase in transaction **c** less the return, but not within the discount period.

Exercise 5-8.
Preparation of a Work Sheet
(L.O. 7)

Here, in alphabetical order, are simplified trial balance accounts and their balances at year-end December 31, 19xx: Accounts Payable, $6; Accounts Receivable, $50; Accumulated Depreciation, Store Equipment, $12; Angela Beard, Capital, $134; Angela Beard, Withdrawals, $24; Cash, $24; Freight In, $4; General Expenses, $30; Merchandise Inventory (beginning), $16; Prepaid Insurance, $4; Purchases, $70; Purchases Returns and

Allowances, $4; Sales, $194; Sales Discounts, $6; Selling Expenses, $44; Store Equipment, $60; and Store Supplies, $18.

Copy the trial balance accounts and amounts onto a work sheet in general ledger order. Complete the work sheet, using either the adjusting entry method or the closing entry method and the following information: estimated depreciation on store equipment, $6; ending inventory of store supplies, $4; expired insurance, $2; ending merchandise inventory, $14.

Exercise 5-9. Preparation of the Income Statement from a Work Sheet
(L.O. 9)

Here are selected items from the Income Statement columns of the December 31, 19xx work sheet of the Mill Pond General Store for the year ended December 31, 19xx.

Account Name	Income Statement	
	Debit	Credit
Sales		297,000
Sales Returns and Allowances	11,000	
Sales Discounts	4,200	
Purchases	114,800	
Purchases Returns and Allowances		1,800
Purchases Discounts		2,200
Freight In	5,600	
Selling Expenses	48,500	
General and Administrative Expenses	37,200	

Beginning merchandise inventory was $26,000; ending merchandise inventory is $22,000. From the information given, prepare a 19xx income statement for the company.

Exercise 5-10. Preparation of Closing Entries
(L.O. 8)

Using either the adjusting entry method or the closing entry method, prepare closing entries from the information given in Exercise 5-9, assuming that Mill Pond General Store is owned by Ed Pioutek and that he made withdrawals of $34,000 during the year.

Exercise 5-11. Merchandising Income Statement: Missing Data, Multiple Years
(L.O. 9)

Determine the missing data for each letter in the three income statements below for Lopata Office Supplies Company (in thousands). (**Hint:** Data from one year may be needed to solve subsequent years.)

	19x5	19x4	19x3
Gross Sales	$ p	$ h	$572
Sales Returns and Allowances	38	24	28
Sales Discounts	10	14	a
Net Sales	q	634	b
Merchandise Inventory, Jan. 1	r	i	76
Purchases	384	338	c
Purchases Returns and Allowances	46	j	26
Purchases Discounts	16	10	8
Freight In	s	58	44
Net Purchases	378	k	d
Goods Available for Sale	444	424	364
Merchandise Inventory, Dec. 31	78	l	84
Cost of Goods Sold	t	358	e
Gross Margin from Sales	284	m	252
Selling Expenses	u	156	f
General and Administrative Expenses	78	n	66
Total Operating Expenses	260	256	g
Net Income	v	o	54

Interpretation Case from Business

Wal-Mart versus Kmart
(L.O. 1)

Wal-Mart Stores, Inc. and Kmart Corp., two of the largest and most successful retailers in the United States, have different approaches to retailing. You can see the difference by analyzing their respective income statements and merchandise inventories. Selected information from their annual reports for the year ended January 31, 1990, is presented below. (All amounts are in millions.)

Wal-Mart: Net Sales, $25,810; Cost of Goods Sold, $20,070; Operating Expenses, $4,069; Ending Inventory, $4,428

Kmart: Net Sales, $29,793; Cost of Goods Sold, $21,745; Operating Expenses, $7,282; Ending Inventory, $6,933

Required

1. Prepare a schedule computing the gross margin from sales and net income (ignore income taxes) for both companies as dollar amounts and as percentages of net sales. Also, compute inventory as a percentage of the cost of goods sold. (Round to one decimal place.)
2. From what you know about the different retailing approaches of these two companies, do the gross margin and net income computations you computed in item **1** seem compatible with these approaches? What is it about the nature of Wal-Mart's operations that produces lower gross margin from sales and lower operating expenses in percentages than Kmart? Which company's approach was more successful in 1990? Explain your answer.
3. Both companies have chosen a fiscal year that ends on January 31. Why do you suppose they made this choice? How realistic do you think the inventory figures are as indicators of inventory levels during the rest of the year?

Problem Set A

Problem 5A-1. Merchandising Transactions
(L.O. 2, 4)

Heritage Company, which uses the periodic inventory system, engaged in the following transactions in October:

Oct. 1 Purchased merchandise on credit from Dascenzo Company, terms 2/10, n/30, FOB shipping point, $3,900.
2 Paid Kendall Company for shipping charges on merchandise received, $218.
7 Sold merchandise on credit to Larry Hill, terms 2/10, n/60, $3,000.
9 Purchased merchandise on credit from Tower Company, terms 1/10, n/30, FOB shipping point, $6,000.
10 Purchased merchandise on credit from Center Company, terms 2/10, n/30, FOB shipping point, $9,600, including $600 freight costs paid by Center.
10 Paid Kendall Company for shipping charges on merchandise received, $254.
11 Paid Dascenzo Company for purchase of October 1.
13 Purchased office supplies on credit from Phelan Company, terms n/15, $2,400.
14 Sold merchandise on credit to Mary Walton, terms 2/10, n/30, $2,400.
14 Returned damaged merchandise received from Tower Company on October 9 for credit, $600.
17 Received check from Larry Hill for his purchase of October 7.
18 Returned a portion of the office supplies received on October 13 for credit because the wrong items were sent, $400.
19 Sold merchandise for cash, $1,800.
20 Paid Center Company for purchase of October 10.
21 Paid Tower Company the balance from transactions of October 9 and October 14.
24 Received payment in full from Mary Walton for sale of merchandise on October 14.

Oct. 28 Paid Phelan Company for purchase of October 13 less the return for credit on October 18.

31 Sold merchandise for cash, $1,500.

Required

1. Prepare general journal entries to record the transactions, assuming purchases are recorded initially at their gross purchase price.
2. Which entries would be different if the purchases were recorded initially at their net purchase price and purchases discounts lost were recognized? What advantages does the net method have over the gross method?

Problem 5A-2. Income Statement for a Merchandising Concern *(L.O. 9)*

At the end of the fiscal year, March 31, 19x4, selected accounts from the adjusted trial balance for Helen's New Styles Shop looked like this:

Helen's New Styles Shop
Partial Adjusted Trial Balance
March 31, 19x4

Sales		330,000
Sales Returns and Allowances	4,000	
Purchases	140,400	
Purchases Returns and Allowances		2,800
Purchases Discounts		2,400
Freight In	4,600	
Store Salaries Expense	65,250	
Office Salaries Expense	25,750	
Advertising Expense	48,600	
Rent Expense	4,800	
Insurance Expense	2,400	
Utility Expense	3,120	
Store Supplies Expense	5,760	
Office Supplies Expense	2,350	
Depreciation Expense, Store Equipment	2,100	
Depreciation Expense, Office Equipment	1,600	

The merchandise inventory for Helen's New Styles Shop was $76,400 at the beginning of the year and $58,800 at the end of the year.

Required

1. Using the information given, prepare an income statement for Helen's New Styles Shop. Store Salaries Expense; Advertising Expense; Store Supplies Expense; and Depreciation Expense, Store Equipment are selling expenses. The other expenses are general and administrative expenses.
2. Based on your knowledge at this point in the course, how would you use the income statement for Helen's New Styles Shop to evaluate the company's profitability?

Problem 5A-3. Work Sheet, Financial Statements, and Closing Entries for a Merchandising Company *(L.O. 7, 8, 9)*

The year-end trial balance at the top of page 201 was taken from the ledger of Mendez Party Supplies Company at the end of its annual accounting period, on September 30, 19x4.

Mendez Party Supplies Company
Trial Balance
September 30, 19x4

Cash	$ 21,150	
Accounts Receivable	74,490	
Merchandise Inventory	214,200	
Store Supplies	11,400	
Prepaid Insurance	14,400	
Store Equipment	153,900	
Accumulated Depreciation, Store Equipment		$ 76,500
Accounts Payable		116,850
Flora Mendez, Capital		484,050
Flora Mendez, Withdrawals	72,000	
Sales		1,125,750
Sales Returns and Allowances	14,070	
Sales Discounts	11,370	
Purchases	754,800	
Purchases Returns and Allowances		9,450
Purchases Discounts		8,700
Freight In	31,200	
Sales Salaries Expense	193,800	
Rent Expense	144,000	
Other Selling Expenses	98,730	
Utility Expense	11,790	
	$1,821,300	$1,821,300

Required

1. Enter the trial balance on a work sheet, and complete the work sheet using the following information: ending merchandise inventory, $266,700; ending store supplies inventory, $1,650; expired insurance, $7,200; estimated depreciation on store equipment, $15,000; sales salaries payable, $1,950; and accrued utility expense, $300. Use the adjusting entry method or the closing entry method.
2. Prepare an income statement, a statement of owner's equity, and a balance sheet. Sales Salaries Expense; Other Selling Expenses; Store Supplies Expense; and Depreciation Expense, Store Equipment are selling expenses.
3. From the work sheet, prepare the closing entries.

Problem 5A-4. Journalizing the Transactions of a Merchandising Company *(L.O. 2, 4)*

Here is a list of transactions for the month of March 19xx:

Mar.	1	Sold merchandise on credit to M. Gaberman, terms 2/10, n/60, FOB shipping point, $2,200.
	3	Purchased merchandise on credit from King Company, terms 2/10, n/30, FOB shipping point, $12,800.
	4	Received freight bill for shipment received on March 3, $900.
	6	Sold merchandise for cash, $1,100.
	7	Sold merchandise on credit to B. Gomez, terms 2/10, n/60, $2,400.
	9	Purchased merchandise from Armstrong Company, terms 1/10, n/30, FOB shipping point, $6,180, including freight charges of $400.
	10	Sold merchandise on credit to G. Horn, terms 2/10, n/20, $4,400.
	10	Received check from M. Gaberman for payment in full for sale of March 1.
	11	Purchased merchandise from King Company, terms 2/10, n/30, FOB shipping point, $16,400.
	12	Received freight bill for shipment of March 11, $1,460.

Mar. 13 Paid King Company for purchase of March 3.
14 Returned merchandise from the March 9 shipment that was the wrong size and color, for credit, $580.
16 G. Horn returned some of the merchandise sold to him on March 10 for credit, $400.
17 Received payment from B. Gomez for half of his purchase on March 7. A discount is allowed on partial payment.
18 Paid Armstrong Company balance due on account from transactions on March 9 and 14.
20 In checking the purchase of March 11 from King Company, the accounting department found an overcharge of $800. King agreed to issue a credit.
21 Paid freight company for freight charges of March 4 and 12.
23 Purchased cleaning supplies on credit from Moon Company, terms n/5, $500.
24 Discovered that some of the cleaning supplies purchased on March 23 had not been ordered. Returned them to Moon Company for credit, $100.
25 Sold merchandise for cash, $1,600.
27 Paid Moon Company for the March 23 purchase less the March 24 return.
28 Received payment in full from G. Horn for transactions on March 10 and 16.
29 Paid King Company for purchase of March 11 less allowance of March 20.
31 Received payment for balance of amount owed from B. Gomez from transactions of March 7 and 17.

Required

1. Prepare general journal entries to record the transactions, assuming that the periodic inventory system is used and that purchases are recorded initially at their gross purchase price.
2. Tell how the entries would differ if the net method of recording purchases was used.

Problem 5A-5. Work Sheet, Income Statement, and Closing Entries for a Merchandising Concern
(L.O. 7, 8, 9)

This is the year-end trial balance for Griffin Sporting Goods Store:

Griffin Sporting Goods Store
Trial Balance
January 31, 19x4

Cash	$ 16,500	
Accounts Receivable	12,644	
Merchandise Inventory	187,500	
Store Supplies	14,340	
Prepaid Insurance	10,800	
Store Equipment	303,600	
Accumulated Depreciation, Store Equipment		$ 84,400
Accounts Payable		107,340
Albert Griffin, Capital		252,674
Albert Griffin, Withdrawals	54,000	
Sales		1,971,420
Sales Returns and Allowances	16,200	
Purchases	1,406,950	
Purchases Returns and Allowances		24,750
Purchases Discounts		23,700
Freight In	9,600	
Rent Expense	74,400	
Store Salaries Expense	226,500	
Advertising Expense	113,310	
Utility Expense	17,940	
	$2,464,284	$2,464,284

Required

1. Copy the trial balance amounts into the Trial Balance columns of a work sheet, and complete the work sheet using the following information: ending merchandise inventory, $172,480; ending store supplies inventory, $1,740; insurance unexpired at end of period, $5,400; estimated depreciation, store equipment, $31,800; and accrued store salaries, $750. Use either the adjusting entry method or the closing entry method.
2. Prepare an income statement for the store. Store Salaries Expense; Advertising Expense; Store Supplies Expense; and Depreciation Expense, Store Equipment are selling expenses. The other expenses are general and administrative expenses.
3. From the work sheet, prepare the closing entries.

Problem Set B

Problem 5B-1. Merchandising Transactions
(L.O. 2, 4)

Nakayama Company, which uses the periodic inventory system, engaged in the following transactions in July:

July 1 Sold merchandise to Bernice Wilson on credit, terms 2/10, n/30, $2,100.
3 Purchased merchandise on credit from Simic Company, terms 2/10, n/30, FOB shipping point, $3,800.
5 Paid Banner Freight for freight charges on merchandise received, $290.
6 Purchased store supplies on credit from Hayes Supply Company, terms n/20, $636.
7 Purchased merchandise on credit from Kroll Company, terms 2/10, n/30, FOB shipping point, $2,400.
7 Paid Banner Freight for freight charges on merchandise received, $194.
8 Purchased merchandise on credit from Salinas Company, terms 2/10, n/30, FOB shipping point, $3,600, including $200 freight costs paid by Salinas Company.
9 Received full payment from Bernice Wilson for her July 1 purchase.
10 Paid Simic Company for purchase of July 3.
12 Returned some of the merchandise received on July 7 for credit, $600.
15 Sold merchandise on credit to Marc Singer, terms 2/10, n/30, $1,200.
16 Returned some of the store supplies purchased on July 6 for credit, $200.
17 Sold merchandise for cash, $1,000.
18 Paid Salinas Company for purchase of July 8.
24 Paid Kroll Company for purchase of July 7 less return of July 12.
25 Received full payment from Marc Singer for his July 15 purchase.
27 Paid Hayes Supply Company for purchase of July 6 less return on July 16.
31 Sold merchandise for cash, $1,350.

Required

1. Prepare general journal entries to record the transactions, assuming purchases are recorded initially at the gross purchase price.
2. Which entries would differ if the purchases were recorded initially at the net purchase price and discounts lost were recognized? What advantages does this method have over the gross method?

Problem 5B-2. Income Statement for a Merchandising Concern
(L.O. 9)

The data at the top of page 204 come from Dubinsky Lighting Shop's adjusted trial balance as of the fiscal year ended September 30, 19x5.

The company's beginning inventory was $162,444; ending merchandise inventory is $153,328.

Dubinsky Lighting Shop Partial Adjusted Trial Balance September 30, 19x5		
Sales		867,824
Sales Returns and Allowances	22,500	
Purchases	442,370	
Purchases Returns and Allowances		52,900
Purchases Discounts		7,576
Freight In	20,156	
Store Salaries Expense	215,100	
Office Salaries Expense	53,000	
Advertising Expense	36,400	
Rent Expense	28,800	
Insurance Expense	5,600	
Utility Expense	37,520	
Store Supplies Expense	928	
Office Supplies Expense	1,628	
Depreciation Expense, Store Equipment	3,600	
Depreciation Expense, Office Equipment	3,700	

Required

1. Prepare an income statement for Dubinsky Lighting Shop. Store Salaries Expense; Advertising Expense; Store Supplies Expense; and Depreciation Expense, Store Equipment are selling expenses. The other expenses are general and administrative expenses.
2. Based on your knowledge at this point in the course, how would you use Dubinsky's income statement to evaluate the company's profitability?

Problem 5B-3. Work Sheet, Financial Statements, and Closing Entries for a Merchandising Company
(L.O. 7, 8, 9)

The following trial balance was taken from the ledger of Metzler Music Store at the end of its annual accounting period:

Metzler Music Store Trial Balance November 30, 19x4		
Cash	$ 18,075	
Accounts Receivable	27,840	
Merchandise Inventory	88,350	
Store Supplies	5,733	
Prepaid Insurance	4,800	
Store Equipment	111,600	
Accumulated Depreciation, Store Equipment		$ 46,800
Accounts Payable		36,900
Susan Metzler, Capital		125,982
Susan Metzler, Withdrawals	36,000	
Sales		306,750
Sales Returns and Allowances	2,961	
Purchases	189,600	
Purchases Returns and Allowances		58,965
Purchases Discounts		4,068
Freight In	6,783	
Sales Salaries Expense	64,050	
Rent Expense	10,800	
Other Selling Expenses	7,842	
Utility Expense	5,031	
	$579,465	$579,465

Required

1. Enter the trial balance on a work sheet, and complete the work sheet using the following information: ending merchandise inventory, $99,681; ending store supplies inventory, $912; unexpired prepaid insurance, $600; estimated depreciation on store equipment, $12,900; sales salaries payable, $240; and accrued utility expense, $450. Use the adjusting entry method or the closing entry method.
2. Prepare an income statement, a statement of owner's equity, and a balance sheet. Sales Salaries Expense; Other Selling Expenses; Store Supplies Expense; and Depreciation Expense, Store Equipment are all selling expenses.
3. From the work sheet, prepare the closing entries.

Problem 5B-4. Journalizing the Transactions of a Merchandising Company *(L.O. 2, 4)*

Below is a list of transactions for the month of December 19xx:

Dec. 1 Purchased merchandise on credit from Bickford Company, terms 2/10, n/30, FOB destination, $14,800.
2 Sold merchandise on credit to D. Loo, terms 1/10, n/30, FOB shipping point, $2,000.
3 Sold merchandise for cash, $1,400.
5 Purchased and received merchandise on credit from Parillo Company, terms 2/10, n/30, FOB shipping point, $8,400.
6 Received freight bill from Runyon Freight for shipment received on December 5, $1,140.
8 Sold merchandise on credit to T. Mitchell, terms 1/10, n/30, FOB destination, $7,600.
9 Purchased merchandise from Bickford Company, terms 2/10, n/30, FOB shipping point, $5,300, including freight costs of $300.
10 Received freight bill from Runyon Freight for sale to T. Mitchell on December 8, $582.
11 Paid Bickford Company for purchase of December 1.
12 Received payment in full for D. Loo's purchase on December 2.
15 Paid Parillo Company half the amount owed on the December 5 purchase.
16 Returned faulty merchandise worth $600 to Bickford Company for credit against purchase of December 9.
17 Purchased office supplies from Zucker Company, terms n/10, $956.
18 Received payment from T. Mitchell for half of the purchase on December 8.
19 Paid Bickford Company in full for the amount owed on the purchase of December 9 less the return on December 16.
19 Sold merchandise to R. Godfrey on credit, terms 2/10, n/30, FOB shipping point, $1,560.
20 Returned for credit several items of office supplies purchased on December 17, $256.
23 Issued a credit to R. Godfrey for returned merchandise, $360.
24 Paid for purchase of December 17 less return on December 20.
27 Paid freight company for freight charges for December 6 and 10.
28 Received payment of amount owed by R. Godfrey from purchase of December 19 less credit of December 23.
29 Paid Parillo Company for balance of December 5 purchase.
31 Sold merchandise for cash, $1,946.

Required

1. Prepare general journal entries to record the transactions, assuming that the periodic inventory system is used and that purchases are recorded initially at their gross purchase price.
2. Tell how the entries would differ under the net method of recording purchases.

Problem 5B-5. Work Sheet, Income Statement, and Closing Entries for a Merchandising Concern
(L.O. 7, 8, 9)

The year-end trial balance for Dodge Luggage Store appears below:

Dodge Luggage Store
Trial Balance
April 30, 19x4

Cash	$ 10,430	
Accounts Receivable	38,614	
Merchandise Inventory	53,000	
Store Supplies	1,902	
Prepaid Insurance	5,200	
Store Equipment	64,000	
Accumulated Depreciation, Store Equipment		$ 36,800
Accounts Payable		44,732
Roy Dodge, Capital		127,202
Roy Dodge, Withdrawals	30,000	
Sales		211,080
Sales Returns and Allowances	4,300	
Purchases	120,030	
Purchases Returns and Allowances		34,620
Purchases Discounts		2,600
Freight In	4,288	
Rent Expense	9,600	
Store Salaries Expense	83,200	
Advertising Expense	28,112	
Utility Expense	4,358	
	$457,034	$457,034

Required

1. Copy the trial balance amounts into the Trial Balance columns of a work sheet, and complete the work sheet using the following information: ending merchandise inventory, $61,280; ending store supplies inventory, $576; expired insurance, $4,800; estimated depreciation, store equipment, $17,600; advertising expenses include $2,940 for May clearance sale advertisements, which will begin appearing on May 1; and accrued store salaries, $640. Use either the adjusting entry method or the closing entry method.
2. Prepare an income statement for the store. Store Salaries Expense; Advertising Expense; Store Supplies Expense; and Depreciation Expense, Store Equipment are selling expenses. The other expenses are general and administrative expenses.
3. From the work sheet you prepared for Dodge Luggage Store in **1** above, derive the closing entries.

Financial Decision Case

Diamond Apparel Company
(L.O. 3)

In 19x3 Paul Diamond opened a small retail store in a suburban mall. Called Diamond Apparel Company, the shop sold designer jeans. Paul worked fourteen hours a day and controlled all aspects of the operation. All sales were for cash or bank credit card. The business was such a success that in 19x4 Paul decided to open a second store in another mall. Because the new shop needed his attention, he hired a manager to work in the original store with two sales clerks. During 19x4 the new store was successful, but the operations of the original store did not match the first year's performance.

Concerned about this turn of events, Paul compared the two years' results for the original store. The figures are as follows:

	19x4	19x3
Net Sales	$650,000	$700,000
Cost of Goods Sold	450,000	450,000
Gross Margin from Sales	$200,000	$250,000
Operating Expenses	150,000	100,000
Net Income	$ 50,000	$150,000

In addition, Paul's analysis revealed that the cost and selling price of jeans were about the same in both years and that the level of operating expenses was roughly the same in both years except for the new manager's $50,000 salary. Sales returns and allowances were insignificant amounts in both years.

Studying the situation further, Paul discovered the following facts about the cost of goods sold:

	19x4	19x3
Gross purchases	$400,000	$542,000
Total purchases allowances and discounts	30,000	40,000
Freight in	38,000	54,000
Physical inventory, end of year	64,000	106,000

Still not satisfied, Paul went through all the individual sales and purchase records for the year. Both sales and purchases were verified. However, the 19x4 ending inventory should have been $114,000 given the unit purchases and sales during the year. After puzzling over all this information, Paul comes to you for accounting help.

Required

1. Using Paul's new information, recompute the cost of goods sold for 19x3 and 19x4, and account for the difference in net income between 19x3 and 19x4.
2. Suggest at least two reasons for the difference. (Assume that the new manager's salary is correct.) How might Paul improve the management of the original store?

Answers to Self-Test

1. d	3. a	5. a	7. b	9. d
2. c	4. c	6. b	8. a	10. b

LEARNING OBJECTIVES

1. *State the objectives of financial reporting.*
2. *State the qualitative characteristics of accounting information and describe their interrelationships.*
3. *Define and describe the use of the conventions of* comparability *and* consistency, materiality, conservatism, full disclosure, *and* cost-benefit.
4. *Summarize the concepts that underlie financial accounting and their relationship to ethical financial reporting.*
5. *Identify and describe the basic components of a classified balance sheet.*
6. *Prepare multistep and single-step classified income statements.*
7. *Use classified financial statements for the simple evaluation of liquidity and profitability.*

CHAPTER 6

Accounting Concepts and Classified Financial Statements

Financial statements are the most important means of communicating accounting information to decision makers. For decision makers outside the business, the financial statements, which usually are audited by independent accountants, often are the only information available directly from the company. It is essential, then, that all business students have a thorough knowledge of the objectives and concepts that underlie financial reporting, as well as the forms and methods of evaluating financial statements. This knowledge provides the foundation for the further study of accounting. After studying this chapter, you should be able to meet the learning objectives listed on the left.

DECISION POINT
The Gap, Inc.

■ Corporations issue annual reports in order to distribute their financial statements and communicate other relevant information to stockholders and others outside the business. Because these users have no direct access to the accounting records, they must depend on the information contained in the report. Beyond the financial statements and accompanying notes and text, management must devise its own methods to help the reader understand the data in the statements.

The management of The Gap, Inc., one of the most successful U.S. specialty retailers of casual and active wear for men, women, and children, helped readers of its 1989 annual report by presenting on the first page a series of statistics called "Financial Highlights." Most of the statistics in the series were based on figures from the financial statements for the preceding three years. Along with such important information as net sales, net earnings, and total assets, a number of ratios appeared, including working capital, current ratio, debt to equity, net earnings as a percentage of net sales, and return on average stockholders' equity. Of course, these ratios are meaningless unless the individual understands both their components and their implications. Because learning how to read and interpret financial statements is so important, this chapter describes the categories and classifications used in balance sheets and income statements and explains some of the most important financial statement analysis ratios. The chapter begins by describing the objectives, characteristics, and conventions that underlie the preparation of financial statements. The annotated financial statements of Toys "R" Us, Inc., a major U.S. corporation, can be found in an appendix to this text. ■

Objectives of Financial Information[1]

OBJECTIVE 1
State the objectives of financial reporting

The United States has a highly developed exchange economy. In this kind of economy, most goods and services are exchanged for money or claims to money instead of being used or bartered by their producers. Much business is done by sole proprietorships and partnerships. But as noted earlier (in the chapter on accounting as an information system), most business is carried on through investor-owned companies that are called corporations. Among them are many large corporations that buy, sell, and obtain financing in U.S. and world markets.

By issuing stocks and bonds that are traded in the financial market, businesses can raise capital for production and marketing activities. Investors are interested mainly in returns from dividends and in an increase in the market price of their investments, rather than in managing the company. Creditors want to know if the business can repay a loan (plus interest) according to its terms. Thus, investors and creditors both need to know if a company can generate favorable cash flows. Financial statements are important to both groups in making this judgment. They offer valuable information that helps investors and creditors judge a company's ability to pay dividends and repay debts with interest. In this way, the market puts scarce resources to work in companies that can use them most efficiently.

The needs of users and the general business environment described above are the basis for the Financial Accounting Standards Board's three objectives of financial reporting:[2]

1. *To furnish the information useful in making investment and credit decisions* Financial reporting should offer information that can help present and potential investors (owners) and creditors make rational investment and credit decisions. The reports should be in a form that makes sense to those who have some understanding of business and are willing to study the information carefully.
2. *To provide information useful in assessing cash flow prospects* Financial reporting should supply information to help present and potential investors (owners) and creditors judge the amounts, timing, and risk of expected cash receipts from dividends or interest and the proceeds from the sale, redemption, or maturity of stocks or loans.
3. *To provide information about business resources, claims to those resources, and changes in them* Financial reporting should give information about the company's assets, liabilities, and owner's equity, and the effects of transactions on its assets, liabilities, and owner's equity.

General-purpose external financial statements are the most important way of periodically presenting to parties outside the business the information that has been gathered and processed in the accounting system. For this reason, these statements—the balance sheet, the income statement, the statement of owner's equity, and the statement of cash flows—are the most important output of the accounting system. These financial statements are "general purpose" because of their wide audience. They are "external" because the users are outside the business. Because of a potential conflict of interest between managers, who must prepare the statements, and the investors or creditors, who invest in or lend money to the business, these statements often are audited by outside accountants to increase confidence in their reliability.

1. This discussion is based on "Objectives of Financial Reporting by Business Enterprises," *Statement of Financial Accounting Concepts No. 1* (Stamford, Conn.: Financial Accounting Standards Board, 1978), pars. 6–16 and 28–40.
2. Ibid., pars. 32–54.

Qualitative Characteristics of Accounting Information[3]

OBJECTIVE 2
State the qualitative characteristics of accounting information and describe their interrelationships

It is easy for students in their first accounting course to get the idea that accounting is 100 percent accurate. This idea is reinforced by the fact that all the problems in this and other introductory books can be solved. The numbers all add up; what is supposed to equal something else does. Accounting seems very much like mathematics in its precision. In this course, the basics of accounting are presented in a simple form at first, to help you understand them. In practice, however, accounting information is neither simple nor precise, and it rarely satisfies all criteria. The FASB emphasizes this fact in the following statement:

> The information provided by financial reporting often results from approximate, rather than exact, measures. The measures commonly involve numerous estimates, classifications, summarizations, judgments and allocations. The outcome of economic activity in a dynamic economy is uncertain and results from combinations of many factors. Thus, despite the aura of precision that may seem to surround financial reporting in general and financial statements in particular, with few exceptions the measures are approximations, which may be based on rules and conventions, rather than exact amounts.[4]

The goal of accounting information—to provide the basic data that different users need to make informed decisions—is an ideal. The gap between the ideal and the actual provides much of the interest and controversy in accounting. To facilitate the process of interpretation of accounting information, the FASB has described the **qualitative characteristics** of accounting information, which are standards for judging that information. In addition, there are generally accepted conventions for recording and reporting that simplify interpretation. The relationships among these concepts are shown in Figure 6-1.

The most important qualitative characteristics are understandability and usefulness. **Understandability** depends on both the accountant and the decision maker. The accountant prepares the financial statements in accordance with accepted practices, generating important information that is believed to be understandable. But the decision maker must interpret the information and use it in making decisions. The decision maker must judge what information to use, how to use it, and what it means.

For accounting information to meet the standard of **usefulness**, it must have two major qualitative characteristics: relevance and reliability. **Relevance** means that the information can make a difference in the outcome of a decision. In other words, another decision would have been made if the relevant information was not available. To be relevant, information must provide feedback, help predict future conditions, and be timely. For example, the income statement provides information about how a company did over the past year (feedback), and it helps in planning for the next year (prediction). To be useful, however, it also must be communicated soon enough after the end of the financial period to enable the reader to make a decision (timeliness).

In addition to being relevant, accounting information must have **reliability**. In other words, the user must be able to depend on the information. It must represent what it is meant to represent. It must be credible and verifiable by independent parties using the same methods of measuring. It also must be neu-

3. The discussion in this section is based on "Qualitative Characteristics of Accounting Information," *Statement of Financial Accounting Concepts No. 2* (Stamford, Conn.: Financial Accounting Standards Board, 1980).
4. *Statement of Financial Accounting Concepts No. 1*, par. 20.

Figure 6-1. Qualitative Characteristics and the Conventions of Accounting Information

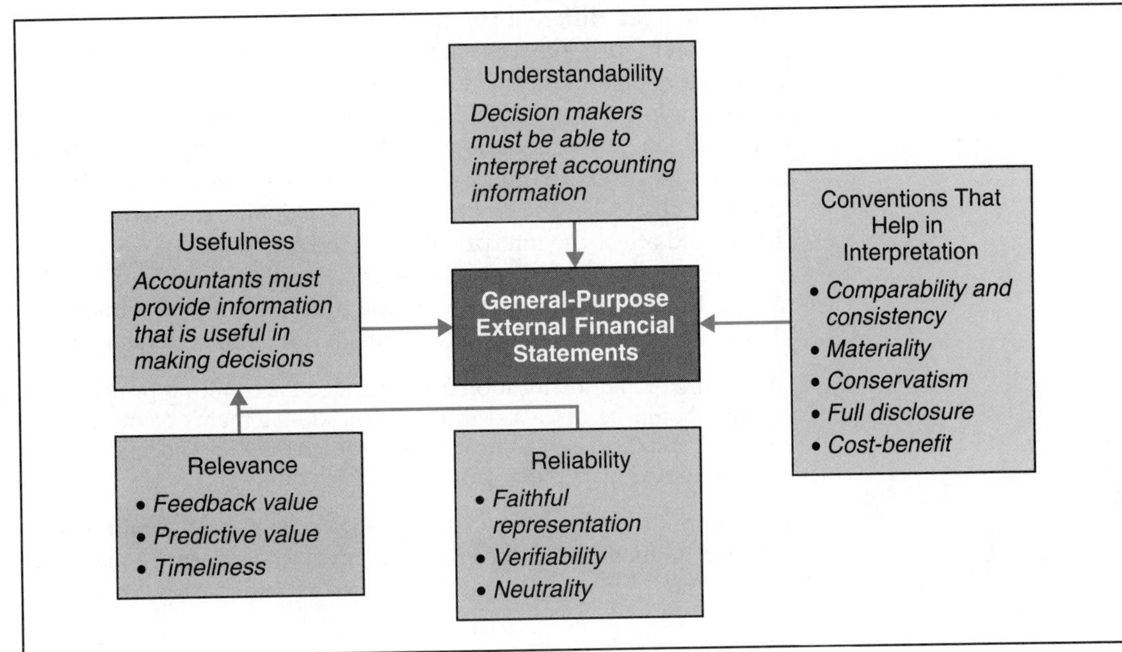

tral. Accounting should convey business activity as faithfully as possible without coloring the picture being presented in order to influence anyone in a certain direction. For example, the balance sheet should represent the economic resources, obligations, and owner's equity of a business as faithfully as possible in accordance with generally accepted accounting principles, and this balance sheet should be verifiable by an auditor.

Conventions That Help in the Interpretation of Financial Information

OBJECTIVE 3
Define and describe the use of the conventions of comparability *and* consistency, materiality, conservatism, full disclosure, *and* cost-benefit

To a large extent, financial statements are based on estimates and arbitrary accounting rules of recognition and allocation. In this book, we point out a number of difficulties with financial statements. One is failing to recognize the changing value of the dollar due to inflation. Another is treating intangibles, like research and development costs, as assets if they are purchased outside the company and as expenses if they are developed within the company. These problems do not mean that financial statements are useless; they are essential. However, users must know how to interpret them. To help in this interpretation, accountants depend on five **conventions**, or rules of thumb, in recording transactions and preparing financial statements: (1) comparability and consistency, (2) materiality, (3) conservatism, (4) full disclosure, and (5) cost-benefit.

Comparability and Consistency

A characteristic that increases the usefulness of accounting information is comparability. Information about a company is more useful if it can be compared with similar facts about the same company over several time periods or with another company for the same time period. The convention of **comparability** means that the information is presented in such a way that the decision maker can recognize similarities, differences, and trends between different time periods or between different companies.

Consistent use of accounting measures and procedures is important in achieving comparability. The **consistency** convention requires that a particular accounting procedure, once adopted by a company, remain in use from one period to the next unless users are informed of a change. Thus, without a note to the contrary, users of financial statements can assume that there has been no arbitrary change in the treatment of a particular transaction, account, or item that would affect the interpretation of the statements.

If management decides that a certain procedure is not appropriate and should be changed, generally accepted accounting principles require that the change and its dollar effect be described in the notes to the financial statements:

> The nature of and justification for a change in accounting principle and its effect on income should be disclosed in the financial statements of the period in which the change is made. The justification for the change should explain clearly why the newly adopted accounting principle is preferable.[5]

For example, during the current year, a company might report that it has changed its method of accounting for inventories because management feels the new method reflects actual cost flows more realistically.

Materiality

The term **materiality** refers to the relative importance of an item or event. If an item or event is material, it probably is relevant to the user of financial statements. In other words, an item is material if the user would have done something differently if he or she had not known about the item. The accountant often is faced with decisions about small items or events that make little difference to users no matter how they are handled. For example, in the chapter on the acquisition, depreciation, and disposal of long-term assets, we suggest that it is more practical to charge small tools as expenses than to depreciate them. Also, small capital expenditures, less than $500, usually are charged as an expense rather than recorded as long-term assets and depreciated.

In general, an item is material if there is a reasonable expectation that knowing about it would influence the decisions of users of financial statements. The materiality of an item normally is determined by relating its dollar value to parts of the financial statements, such as net income or total assets. Some accountants feel that when an item is 5 percent or more of net income, it is material. However, materiality also depends on the nature of the item as well as its value. For example, in a multimillion-dollar company, a mistake in recording an item of $5,000 may not be important, but the discovery of a $5,000 bribe or theft can be very important. Also, a great many small errors combined can result in a material amount. Accountants judge the materiality of many things, and the users of financial statements depend on their judgment being fair and accurate.

Conservatism

Accountants try to base their decisions on logic and evidence that lead to the fairest report of what happened. In judging and estimating, however, accountants often are faced with uncertainties. In these cases, they look to the convention of **conservatism**. This convention means that when accountants face major

5. Accounting Principles Board, "Accounting Changes," *Opinion No. 20* (New York: American Institute of Certified Public Accountants, 1971), par. 17.

uncertainties about which accounting procedure to use, they generally choose the one that is least likely to overstate assets and income.

One of the most common applications of the conservatism convention is the use of the lower-of-cost-or-market method in accounting for short-term investments (see the chapter on short-term liquid assets) and for inventories (see the chapter on inventories). Under this method, if the market value is greater than cost, the more conservative cost figure is used. If the market value is less than cost, the more conservative market value is used.

Conservatism can be a useful tool in doubtful cases, but the abuse of this convention leads to incorrect and misleading financial statements. Suppose that someone incorrectly applies the conservatism convention by expensing a long-term asset in the period of purchase. In this case, there is no uncertainty. Income and assets for the current period would be understated, and income in future periods would be overstated. For this reason, accountants depend on the conservatism convention only when there is uncertainty about which accounting procedure to use.

Full Disclosure

The convention of **full disclosure** requires that financial statements and their footnotes present all information relevant to the user's understanding of the statements. In other words, accounting information should offer any explanation that is needed to keep it from being misleading. Explanatory notes are considered an integral part of the financial statements. For instance, as noted earlier, a change from one accounting procedure to another should be reported. In general, the form of the financial statements can affect their usefulness in making certain decisions. Also, certain items, such as the amount of depreciation expense on the income statement and the accumulated depreciation on the balance sheet, are essential to the readers of financial statements.

Other examples of disclosures required by the Financial Accounting Standards Board and other official bodies are the accounting procedures used in preparing the statements, important terms of the company's debt, commitments and contingencies, and important events taking place after the date of the statements. However, there is a point where the statements become so cluttered that notes impede rather than help understanding. Beyond required disclosures, the application of the full-disclosure convention is based on the judgment of management and of the accountants who prepare the financial statements.

In recent years, the principle of full disclosure also has been influenced by users of accounting information. Independent auditors, the stock exchanges, and the SEC have made more demands for disclosure by publicly owned companies to protect investors and creditors. The SEC has been pushing especially hard for the enforcement of full disclosure. So today, more and better information about corporations is available to the public than ever before.

Cost-Benefit

The **cost-benefit** convention underlies all the qualitative characteristics and conventions. It holds that the benefits to be gained from providing new accounting information should be greater than the costs of providing it. Of course, certain minimum levels of relevance and reliability must be reached for accounting information to be useful. Beyond these minimum levels, however, it is up to the FASB and the SEC, which require the information, and the accountant, who provides the information, to judge the costs and benefits in each case. Most of the costs of providing information fall at first on the preparers; the benefits are reaped by both preparers and users. Finally, both the costs and the benefits are passed on to society in the form of prices and social benefits from more efficient allocation of resources.

The costs and benefits of a particular requirement for an accounting disclosure are both direct and indirect, immediate and deferred. For example, it is hard to judge the final costs and benefits of a far-reaching and costly regulation. The FASB, for instance, allows certain large companies to make a supplemental disclosure in their financial statements of the effects of changes on current costs (we talk about this in the appendices on international accounting and intercompany investments). Most companies choose not to present this information because they believe the costs of producing and providing it exceed the benefits to the readers of their financial statements. Cost-benefit is a question faced by all regulators, including the FASB and the SEC. Even though there are no definitive ways of measuring costs and benefits, much of an accountant's work deals with these concepts.

Financial Accounting Concepts and Ethical Reporting

OBJECTIVE 4
Summarize the concepts that underlie financial accounting and their relationship to ethical financial reporting

We have emphasized the relationships of financial accounting concepts to accounting techniques and procedures, as well as the judgment that underlies their application. Here, we summarize the financial accounting concepts presented to this point and make clear that the use of judgment in their application places an ethical responsibility on the preparer.

Summary of Financial Accounting Concepts

The first figure in this textbook introduced accounting as an information system that helps management make business decisions. That information system is expanded in Figure 6-2 to include the financial accounting concepts introduced thus far. In overview, Figure 6-2 shows the information system as a circular, continuous process. People make decisions and take actions; these decisions and actions affect economic activities, which in turn are measured, processed, and communicated back to the decision makers in the form of financial statements that meet their information needs or objectives.

The decision makers consist of internal users (management) and direct and indirect external users of accounting information. Present and potential investors and creditors are direct users; tax authorities, regulatory agencies, citizens and citizens' groups, and economic planners are indirect users. Accountants measure some but not all economic activities for various economic entities (businesses, government units, not-for-profit organizations, and individuals). In the case of specific business entities, accountants measure business transactions in terms of money.

The measurement, processing, and communication of accounting information is governed by generally accepted accounting principles that encompass all the rules, procedures, and conventions necessary to define accounting practices at a given point in time. The most important source of GAAP is the Financial Accounting Standards Board, but other sources include other authoritative bodies, such as the American Institute of CPAs, as well as traditional practices.

In measuring a business transaction, three characteristics must be identified. First, recognition focuses on when a transaction took place. Second, valuation focuses on what value to place on the transaction. The usual value assigned to a transaction is cost (the value exchanged at the time the transaction is recog-

Figure 6-2. Summary of Financial Accounting Concepts

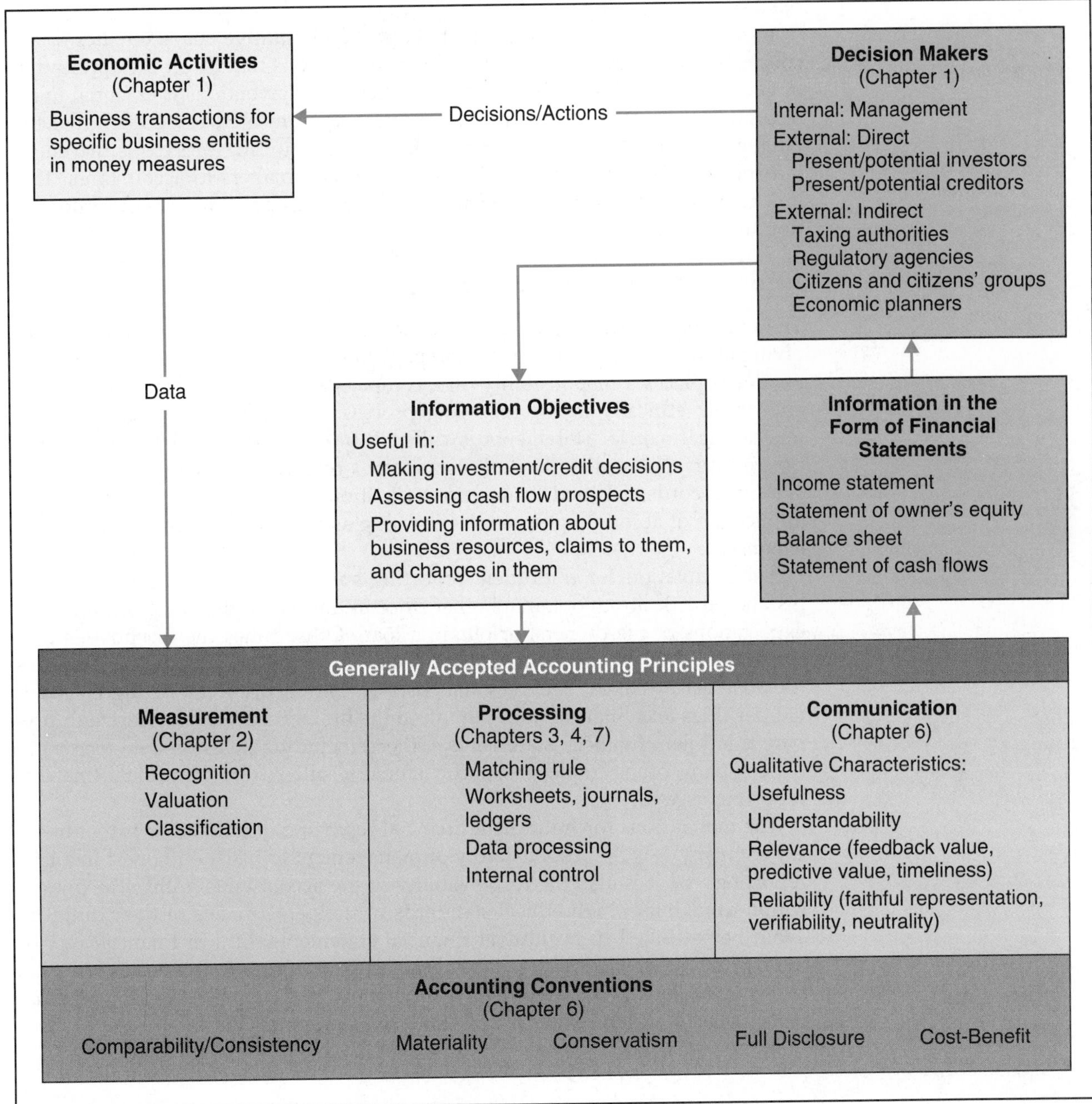

nized). Third, classification requires the identification of the specific accounts in which the transaction should be recorded. When these three determinations are made in accordance with GAAP, the transaction can be recorded in the accounting records.

The processing of accounting data is facilitated if the data are stored in a manner that permits quick and easy retrieval for preparing reports and financial statements. Manual or computerized accounting, using worksheets, journals, and ledgers, assists this effort. Furthermore, it is important to establish internal accounting controls over the processing of accounting data so that assets are safeguarded and accurate records are maintained. Lastly, the matching rule is applied through accrual accounting so that the income earned by the business is reported properly.

In this chapter, you have learned about the qualitative characteristics of accounting information and the accounting conventions that direct the application of GAAP. Knowledge of these characteristics and conventions is essential to interpreting the financial statements that are communicated to decision makers. Finally, it is important to understand that the accounting process is driven by information objectives communicated by decision makers to accountants. This link reinforces the primary function of accounting: providing useful information to decision makers.

Ethics and Financial Reporting

The users of financial statements depend on the judgment of preparers in applying accounting concepts to the preparation of financial statements. This dependence places a responsibility on a company's management and its accountants to act ethically in the reporting process. The intentional preparation of misleading financial statements is called **fraudulent financial reporting**[6] and can result from the distortion of a company's records—the manipulation of inventory records, falsified transactions (fictitious sales or orders)—or the misapplication of accounting principles (treating as an asset an item that should be expensed).

The motivation for fraudulent reporting springs from various sources—for instance, the desire to obtain a higher price in the sale of the company, meet the expectations of the owners, or obtain a loan. Other times the incentive is personal gain, such as additional compensation, promotion, or avoiding penalties for poor performance. The personal costs of these actions can be high—criminal penalties and financial loss can fall to the individuals who authorize or prepare fraudulent financial statements. Others, including investors and lenders to the company, other employees, and customers, suffer from fraudulent financial reporting as well.

The motivations for fraudulent financial reporting exist to some extent in every company. It is the responsibility of management to insist on honest financial reporting, but it is also the responsibility of the accountants within the organization to maintain high ethical standards in the performance of their duties to avoid being linked to fraudulent financial statements. Ethical financial reporting demands that accountants apply financial accounting concepts in a way that presents a fair view of the company's operations and financial position and that does not mislead the readers of the financial statements.

Classified Balance Sheet

OBJECTIVE 5
Identify and describe the basic components of a classified balance sheet

The balance sheets you have seen to this point in the book list the accounts in categories of assets, liabilities, and owner's equity. Because even a fairly small company can have hundreds of accounts, simply listing accounts by these broad categories is not particularly helpful to a statement user. Setting up subcategories within the major categories often makes the financial statements much more useful. Investors and creditors study and evaluate the relationships among the subcategories. General-purpose external financial statements that are divided into useful subcategories are called **classified financial statements**.

6. National Commission on Fraudulent Financial Reporting, *Report of the National Commission on Fraudulent Financial Reporting* (Washington, D.C., 1987), p. 2.

The balance sheet presents the financial position of a company at a particular time. The subdivisions of the classified balance sheet shown in Exhibit 6-1 are typical of most companies in the United States. The subdivisions under owner's equity, of course, depend on the form of business.

Assets

The assets of a company often are divided into four categories: (1) current assets; (2) investments; (3) property, plant, and equipment; and (4) intangible assets. Some companies use a fifth category, "other assets," for miscellaneous assets that do not fall into any of the other groups. These categories are listed in the order of their presumed liquidity (the ease with which an asset can be converted into cash). For example, current assets are considered more liquid than property, plant, and equipment.

Current Assets. **Current assets** are cash or other assets that are reasonably expected to be realized in cash, sold, or consumed over the next year or normal operating cycle of a business, whichever is longer. The normal operating cycle of a company is the average time needed to go from cash to cash. As illustrated in Figure 6-3, cash is used to buy merchandise inventory, which is sold for cash or for a promise of cash (a receivable) if the sale is made on account (for credit). If a sale is made on account, the resulting receivable must be collected before the cycle is completed.

The normal operating cycle for most companies is less than one year, but there are exceptions. Tobacco companies, for example, must cure the tobacco for two or three years before their inventory can be sold. The tobacco inventory still is considered a current asset because it will be sold within the normal operating cycle. Another example is a company that sells on the installment basis. The collection payments for a television set or stove can be extended over twenty-four or thirty-six months, but these receivables still are considered current assets.

Cash is obviously a current asset. Temporary investments, notes and accounts receivable, and inventory are also current assets because they are expected to be converted to cash within the next year or during the normal operating cycle of most firms. On the balance sheet, they are listed in the order of the ease of their conversion into cash. Accounting for these short-term assets is presented in the chapter on short-term liquid assets.

Prepaid expenses, such as rent and insurance paid for in advance, and inventories of various supplies bought for use rather than for sale also should be classified as current assets. These kinds of assets are current in the sense that if they had not been bought earlier, a current outlay of cash would be needed to obtain them.[7]

In deciding whether or not an asset is current or noncurrent, the idea of "reasonable expectation" is important. For example, Short-Term Investments is an account used for temporary investments of idle cash or cash not immediately required for operating purposes. Management can reasonably expect to sell these securities as cash needs arise over the next year or operating cycle. Investments in securities that management does not expect to sell within the next year and that do not involve the temporary use of idle cash should be shown in the investments category of a classified balance sheet.

7. *Accounting Research and Terminology Bulletin,* final ed. (New York: American Institute of Certified Public Accountants, 1961), p. 20.

Exhibit 6-1. Classified Balance Sheet for Shafer Auto Parts Company

Shafer Auto Parts Company Balance Sheet December 31, 19xx			
Assets			
Current Assets			
Cash		$10,360	
Short-Term Investments		2,000	
Notes Receivable		8,000	
Accounts Receivable		35,300	
Merchandise Inventory		60,400	
Prepaid Insurance		6,600	
Store Supplies		1,060	
Office Supplies		636	
Total Current Assets			$124,356
Investments			
Land Held for Future Use			5,000
Property, Plant, and Equipment			
Land		$ 4,500	
Building	$20,650		
Less Accumulated Depreciation	8,640	12,010	
Delivery Equipment	$18,400		
Less Accumulated Depreciation	9,450	8,950	
Office Equipment	$ 8,600		
Less Accumulated Depreciation	5,000	3,600	
Total Property, Plant, and Equipment			29,060
Intangible Assets			
Trademark			500
Total Assets			$158,916
Liabilities			
Current Liabilities			
Notes Payable		$15,000	
Accounts Payable		25,683	
Salaries Payable		2,000	
Total Current Liabilities			$ 42,683
Long-Term Liabilities			
Mortgage Payable			17,800
Total Liabilities			$ 60,483
Owner's Equity			
Fred Shafer, Capital			98,433
Total Liabilities and Owner's Equity			$158,916

Figure 6-3. The Operating Cycle

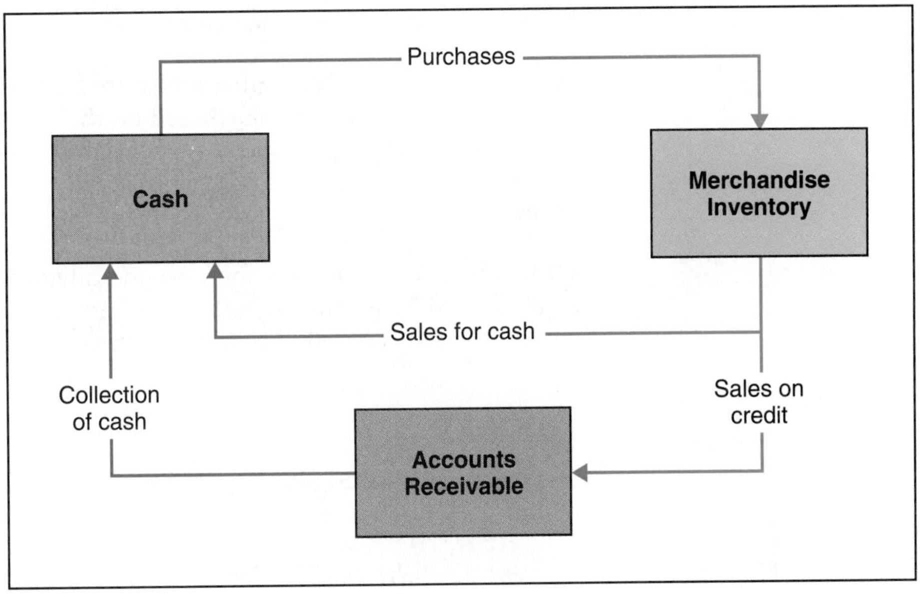

Purchases
Cash
Merchandise Inventory
Sales for cash
Collection of cash
Sales on credit
Accounts Receivable

Investments. The **investments** category includes assets, generally of a long-term nature, that are not used in the normal operation of a business and that management does not plan to convert to cash within the next year. Items in this category are securities held for long-term investment, long-term notes receivable, land held for future use, plant or equipment not used in the business, and special funds established to pay off a debt or buy a building. Also in this category are large permanent investments in another company for the purpose of controlling that company. These topics are covered in the appendix on intercompany investments.

Property, Plant, and Equipment. The **property, plant, and equipment** category includes long-term assets that are used in the continuing operation of the business. They represent a place to operate (land and buildings) and equipment to produce, sell, deliver, and service the company's goods. For this reason, these assets are called *operating assets* or, sometimes, *fixed assets, tangible assets*, or *long-lived assets*. You know that through depreciation, the cost of these assets (except land) is spread over the periods they benefit. Past depreciation is recorded in the Accumulated Depreciation accounts. The exact order in which property, plant, and equipment are listed on the balance sheet is not the same everywhere; in practice, various accounts often are combined to make the financial statement less cluttered. For example:

Property, Plant, and Equipment

Land		$ 4,500
Buildings and Equipment	$47,650	
Less Accumulated Depreciation	23,090	24,560
Total Property, Plant, and Equipment		$29,060

Property, plant, and equipment also includes natural resources owned by the company, such as forest lands, oil and gas properties, and coal mines. Assets that are not used in the regular course of business should be listed in the investments category, as noted above. The chapter on long-term assets is devoted largely to property, plant, and equipment.

Intangible Assets. **Intangible assets** are long-term assets that have no physical substance but have a value based on the rights or privileges that belong to the owner. Examples are patents, copyrights, goodwill, franchises, and trademarks. These assets are recorded at cost, which is spread over the expected life of the right or privilege.

Other Assets. Some companies use the category **other assets** to group all the assets owned by a company other than current assets and property, plant, and equipment. Other assets can include investments and intangible assets.

Liabilities

Liabilities are divided into two categories: current liabilities and long-term liabilities.

Current Liabilities. The category **current liabilities** consists of obligations due within a year or within the normal operating cycle of the business, whichever is longer. These liabilities generally are paid from current assets or by incurring new short-term liabilities. Under this heading are notes payable, accounts payable, the current portion of long-term debt, salaries and wages payable, taxes payable, and customer advances (unearned revenues). Current liabilities are discussed in more detail in the chapter on current liabilities.

Long-Term Liabilities. The debts of a business that fall due more than one year ahead or beyond the normal operating cycle, or that are to be paid out of noncurrent assets, are **long-term liabilities**. Mortgages payable, long-term notes, bonds payable, employee pension obligations, and long-term lease liabilities generally fall in this category. Long-term liabilities are described in a later chapter.

Owner's Equity

The terms *owner's equity, proprietorship, capital,* and *net worth* are used interchangeably. They all stand for the owner's interest in the company. The first three terms are better usage than *net worth* because most assets are recorded at original cost, not at current value. For this reason, ownership does not represent "worth." It is really a claim against the assets of the company.

The accounting treatment of assets and liabilities generally is not affected by the form of business organization. However, the owner's equity section of the balance sheet is different depending on whether the business is a sole proprietorship, a partnership, or a corporation.

Sole Proprietorship. You already are familiar with the owner's equity section of a sole proprietorship, like the one shown in the balance sheet for Shafer Auto Parts Company (see Exhibit 6-1):

Owner's Equity	
Fred Shafer, Capital	$98,433

Partnership. The owners' equity section of the balance sheet for a partnership is called partners' equity and is much like that of the sole proprietorship. It might appear as follows:

Partners' Equity

A. J. Martin, Capital	$21,666	
R. C. Moore, Capital	35,724	
Total Partners' Equity		$57,390

Corporation. Corporations are by law legal entities that are separate from their owners. The owners are the stockholders. The owners' equity section of a balance sheet for a corporation is called stockholders' equity and has two parts: contributed or paid-in capital and retained earnings or earned capital. It might appear like this:

Stockholders' Equity

Contributed Capital		
Common Stock—$10 par value, 5,000 shares authorized, issued, and outstanding	$50,000	
Paid-in Capital in Excess of Par Value	10,000	
Total Contributed Capital		$60,000
Retained Earnings		37,500
Total Stockholders' Equity		$97,500

Remember that owner's equity accounts show the sources of and claims on assets. Of course, these claims are not on any particular asset but on the assets as a whole. It follows, then, that a corporation's Contributed and Earned Capital (retained earnings) accounts measure its stockholders' claims on assets and also indicate the sources of the assets. The **contributed capital** accounts reflect the amounts of assets invested by stockholders themselves. Generally, contributed capital is shown on corporate balance sheets by two amounts: (1) the face or par value of issued stock and (2) the amounts paid in or contributed in excess of the face or par value per share. In the illustration above, stockholders invested amounts equal to par value of the outstanding stock (5,000 × $10) plus $10,000 more.

The **Retained Earnings** account is sometimes called Earned Capital because it represents the stockholders' claim to the assets earned from operations and plowed back into, or reinvested in, corporate operations. Distributions of assets to shareholders, called *dividends,* reduce the Retained Earnings account balance just as withdrawals of assets by the owner of a business lower the Capital account balance in a sole proprietorship. Thus, the Retained Earnings account balance, in its simplest form, represents the earnings of the corporation less dividends paid to stockholders over the life of the business.

Forms of the Income Statement

OBJECTIVE 6
Prepare multistep and single-step classified income statements

For internal management, a detailed income statement similar to the one you learned about in the chapter on accounting for merchandising operations and the one for Shafer Auto Parts Company in Exhibit 6-2 is helpful in analyzing the company's performance. In the Shafer statement, gross margin from sales less operating expenses is called **income from operations,** and a new section,

Exhibit 6-2. Income Statement for Shafer Auto Parts Company

Shafer Auto Parts Company Income Statement For the Year Ended December 31, 19xx			
Revenues from Sales			
Gross Sales			$299,156
Less: Sales Returns and Allowances	$ 6,300		
Sales Discounts	3,200		9,500
Net Sales			$289,656
Cost of Goods Sold			
Merchandise Inventory, January 1, 19xx		$ 64,800	
Purchases	$168,624		
Freight In	8,236	176,860	
Goods Available for Sale		$241,660	
Merchandise Inventory, December 31, 19xx		60,400	
Cost of Goods Sold			181,260
Gross Margin from Sales			$108,396
Operating Expenses			
Selling Expenses			
Sales Salaries Expense	$ 22,500		
Rent Expense, Store Fixtures	5,600		
Freight Out Expense	5,740		
Advertising Expense	10,000		
Insurance Expense, Selling	1,600		
Store Supplies Expense	1,540		
Depreciation Expense, Building	2,600		
Depreciation Expense, Delivery Equipment	5,200		
Total Selling Expenses		$ 54,780	
General and Administrative Expenses			
Office Salaries Expense	$ 26,900		
Insurance Expense, General	4,200		
Office Supplies Expense	1,204		
Depreciation Expense, Office Equipment	2,200		
Total General and Administrative Expenses		34,504	
Total Operating Expenses			89,284
Income from Operations			$ 19,112
Other Revenues and Expenses			
Interest Income		$ 1,400	
Less Interest Expense		2,631	
Excess of Other Expenses over Other Revenues			1,231
Net Income			$ 17,881

other revenues and expenses, has been added to include nonoperating revenues and expenses. The latter section includes revenues from investments (such as dividends and interest from stocks and bonds and savings accounts) and interest earned on credit or notes extended to customers. It also includes interest expense and other expenses that result from borrowing money or from credit being extended to the company. If the company has other revenues and expenses that are not related to normal business operations, they too are classified in this part of the income statement. Thus, an analyst wanting to compare two companies independent of their financing methods—that is, before considering other revenues and expenses—would focus on income from operations. Income taxes expense and earnings per share information do not appear on the income statement for Shafer Auto Parts Company because they apply to accounting for corporations.

For external reporting purposes, the income statement usually is presented in condensed form. **Condensed financial statements** present only the major categories of the financial statement. There are two common forms of the condensed income statement, the multistep form and the single-step form. The **multistep form**, illustrated in Exhibit 6-3, derives net income in the same step-by-step fashion as the detailed income statement for Shafer Auto Parts Company in Exhibit 6-2 except that only the totals of significant categories are given. Usually, some breakdown is shown for operating expenses, such as the totals for selling expenses and for general and administrative expenses. Other revenues and expenses also usually are broken down. The **single-step form**, illustrated in Exhibit 6-4, derives net income in a single step by putting the major categories of revenues in the first part of the statement and the major categories of costs and expenses in the second part. Each of these forms has its advantages. The multistep form shows the components used in deriving net income; the single-step form has the advantage of simplicity. About an equal number of large U.S. companies use each form in their public reports.

Exhibit 6-3. Condensed Multistep Income Statement for Shafer Auto Parts Company

Shafer Auto Parts Company
Income Statement
For the Year Ended December 31, 19xx

Revenues from Sales		$289,656
Cost of Goods Sold		181,260
Gross Margin from Sales		$108,396
Operating Expenses		
Selling Expenses	$54,780	
General and Administrative Expenses	34,504	
Total Operating Expenses		89,284
Income from Operations		$ 19,112
Other Revenues and Expenses		
Interest Income	$ 1,400	
Less Interest Expense	2,631	
Excess of Other Expenses over Other Revenues		1,231
Net Income		$ 17,881

Exhibit 6-4. Condensed Single-Step Income Statement for Shafer Auto Parts Company

Shafer Auto Parts Company Income Statement For the Year Ended December 31, 19xx		
Revenues		
Net Sales		$289,656
Interest Income		1,400
Total Revenues		$291,056
Costs and Expenses		
Cost of Goods Sold	$181,260	
Selling Expenses	54,780	
General and Administrative Expenses	34,504	
Interest Expense	2,631	
Total Costs and Expenses		273,175
Net Income		$ 17,881

Other Financial Statements

Two other statements that are necessary to an understanding of a company's financial operations are the statement of owner's equity and the statement of cash flows.

The statement of owner's equity for Shafer Auto Parts Company is shown in Exhibit 6-5. The statement of retained earnings for a corporation is very similar. In place of the beginning and ending balances of capital are the beginning and ending balances of retained earnings. Instead of withdrawals, there are dividends paid to stockholders. Net income is added in a similar way in the statement of retained earnings. The chapters on contributed capital and retained earnings and corporate income statements deal with the special problems of the equity section of the balance sheet for corporations.

A simple form of the statement of cash flows was shown in the chapter on accounting as an information system. This important statement is explained in detail in the chapter on the statement of cash flows.

Exhibit 6-5. Statement of Owner's Equity for Shafer Auto Parts Company

Shafer Auto Parts Company Statement of Owner's Equity For the Year Ended December 31, 19xx	
Fred Shafer, Capital, January 1, 19xx	$100,552
Net Income for the Year	17,881
	$118,433
Less Withdrawals	20,000
Fred Shafer, Capital, December 31, 19xx	$ 98,433

Using Classified Financial Statements

OBJECTIVE 7
Use classified financial statements for the simple evaluation of liquidity and profitability

Earlier in this chapter, you learned that the objectives of financial reporting, according to the Financial Accounting Standards Board, are to provide information that is useful in making investment and credit decisions, in judging cash flow prospects, and in understanding business resources, claims to those resources, and changes in them. These objectives are related to two of the more important goals of management—maintaining adequate liquidity and achieving satisfactory profitability—because the decisions made by investors and creditors are based largely on their assessment of a company's potential liquidity and profitability. The following analysis focuses on these two important goals.

In this section a series of charts shows average ratios for six industries based on data obtained from *Industry Norms and Ratios,* a publication of Dun and Bradstreet. There are two examples from service industries, accounting and bookkeeping services and interstate trucking; two from merchandising industries, auto and home supply and grocery stores; and two from manufacturing, pharmaceuticals and household appliances. Shafer Auto Parts Company, the example used in this chapter, falls into the auto and home supply industry.

Evaluation of Liquidity

Liquidity means having enough money on hand to pay a company's bills when they are due and to take care of unexpected needs for cash. Two measures of liquidity are working capital and the current ratio.

Working Capital. The first measure, **working capital**, is the amount by which total current assets exceed total current liabilities. This is an important measure of liquidity because current liabilities are debts that must be paid within one year and current assets are assets that are going to be realized in cash or used up within one year or one operating cycle, whichever is longer. By definition, current liabilities are paid out of current assets. So the excess of current assets over current liabilities is the net current assets on hand to continue business operations. It is the working capital that can be used to buy inventory, obtain credit, and finance expanded sales. Lack of working capital can lead to the failure of a company.

For Shafer Auto Parts Company, working capital is computed as follows:

Current assets	$124,356
Less current liabilities	42,683
Working capital	$ 81,673

Current Ratio. The second measure of liquidity, the current ratio, is closely related to working capital and is believed by many bankers and other creditors to be a good indicator of a company's ability to pay its bills and to repay outstanding loans. The **current ratio** is the ratio of current assets to current liabilities. For Shafer Auto Parts Company, it would be computed like this:

$$\text{Current ratio} = \frac{\text{current assets}}{\text{current liabilities}} = \frac{\$124{,}356}{\$42{,}683} = 2.9$$

Based on the current ratio, Shafer has $2.90 of current assets for each $1.00 of current liabilities. Is this rate good or bad? The answer involves comparing this year's ratio with those of earlier years and with similar measures of successful companies in the same industry. The average current ratio varies widely from industry to industry, as shown in Figure 6-4. For interstate trucking companies,

Figure 6-4. Average Current Ratio in Selected Industries

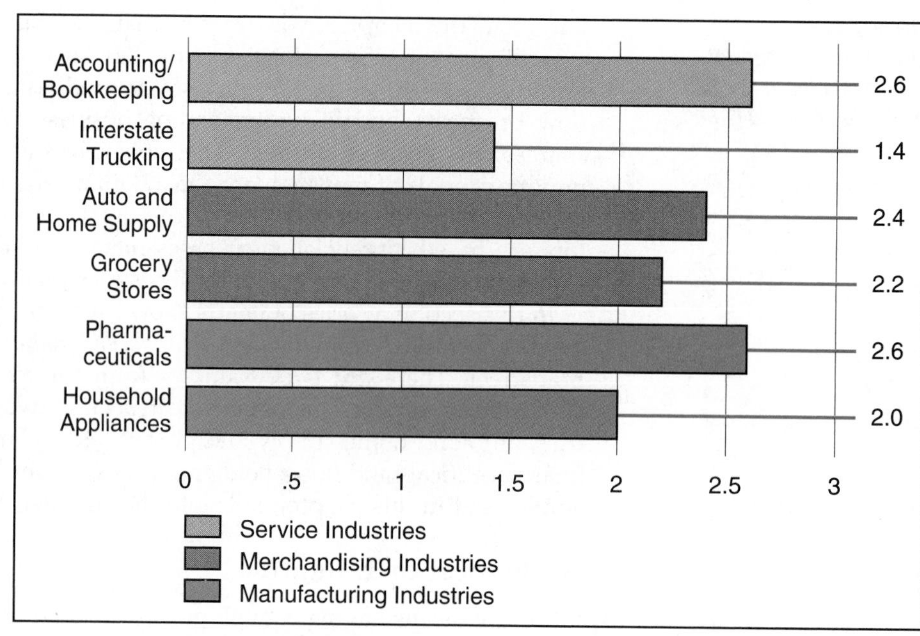

Source: Data from Dun and Bradstreet, *Industry Norms and Ratios*, 1990–91.

which have no merchandise inventory, the current ratio is 1.4. In contrast, accounting and bookkeeping and pharmaceuticals have current ratios of 2.6. Shafer Auto Parts Company, with a ratio of 2.9, exceeds the auto and home supply industry average of 2.4. A very low current ratio, of course, can be unfavorable, but so can a very high one. The latter may indicate that the company is not using its assets effectively.

Evaluation of Profitability

Equally important as paying bills on time is **profitability**—the ability to earn a satisfactory income. As a goal, profitability competes with liquidity for managerial attention because liquid assets, although important, are not the best profit-producing resources. Cash, for example, means purchasing power, but a satisfactory profit can be made only if purchasing power is used to buy profit-producing (and less liquid) assets, such as inventory and long-term assets.

Among the common measures that have to do with a company's ability to earn income are (1) profit margin, (2) asset turnover, (3) return on assets, (4) debt to equity, and (5) return on equity. To evaluate a company meaningfully, one must relate a company's profit performance to its past performance and prospects for the future as well as to the norms (averages) of other companies competing in the same industry.

Profit Margin. The **profit margin** shows the percentage of each sales dollar that produces net income. It is figured by dividing net income by net sales. It should not be confused with gross margin, which is not a ratio but rather the amount by which revenues exceed the cost of goods sold.

Shafer Auto Parts Company has a profit margin of 6.2 percent:

$$\text{Profit margin} = \frac{\text{net income}}{\text{net sales}} = \frac{\$17{,}881}{\$289{,}656} = .062\ (6.2\%)$$

On each dollar of net sales, Shafer Auto Parts Company made 6.2 cents. A difference of 1 or 2 percent in a company's profit margin can mean the difference between a fair year and a very profitable one.

Asset Turnover. **Asset turnover** measures how efficiently assets are used to produce sales. It is computed by dividing net sales by average total assets and shows how many dollars of sales were generated by each dollar of assets. A company with a higher asset turnover uses its assets more productively than one with a lower asset turnover. Average total assets is computed by adding total assets at the beginning of the year to total assets at the end of the year and dividing by 2.

Assuming that total assets for Shafer Auto Parts Company were $148,620 at the beginning of the year, its asset turnover is computed as follows:

$$\text{Asset turnover} = \frac{\text{net sales}}{\text{average total assets}}$$

$$= \frac{\$289{,}656}{(\$148{,}620 + \$158{,}916)/2}$$

$$= \frac{\$289{,}656}{\$153{,}768} = 1.88 \text{ times}$$

Shafer Auto Parts Company produces $1.88 in sales for each $1.00 in average total assets. This ratio shows a meaningful relationship between an income statement figure and a balance sheet figure.

Return on Assets. Both the profit margin and asset turnover ratios have some limitations. The profit margin ratio does not take into consideration the assets necessary to produce income, and the asset turnover ratio does not take into account the amount of income produced. The **return on assets** ratio overcomes these deficiencies by relating net income to average total assets. It is computed as follows:

$$\text{Return on assets} = \frac{\text{net income}}{\text{average total assets}}$$

$$= \frac{\$17{,}881}{(\$148{,}620 + \$158{,}916)/2}$$

$$= \frac{\$17{,}881}{\$153{,}768} = .116 \text{ (or 11.6\%)}$$

For each dollar invested, Shafer Auto Parts Company's assets generated 11.6 cents of net income. This ratio indicates the income-generating strength (profit margin) of the company's resources and how efficiently the company is using all its assets (asset turnover).

Return on assets, then, combines profit margin and asset turnover:

$$\text{Profit margin} \times \text{asset turnover} = \text{return on assets}$$

$$6.2\% \times 1.88 \text{ times} = 11.6\%$$

Thus, a company's management can improve overall profitability by increasing its profit margin or asset turnover or both. Similarly, in evaluating a company's overall profitability, the financial statement user must consider the interaction of both ratios to produce return on assets.

Careful study of Figures 6-5, 6-6, and 6-7 shows the different ways in which the selected industries combine profit margin and asset turnover to produce

Figure 6-5. Average Profit Margin for Selected Industries

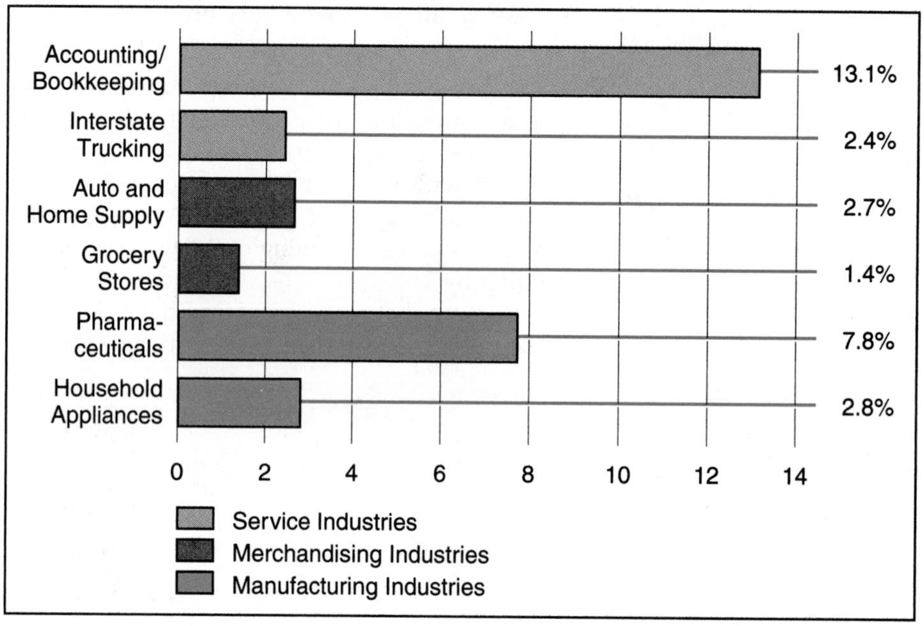

Accounting/ Bookkeeping 13.1%
Interstate Trucking 2.4%
Auto and Home Supply 2.7%
Grocery Stores 1.4%
Pharma-ceuticals 7.8%
Household Appliances 2.8%
0 2 4 6 8 10 12 14
Service Industries
Merchandising Industries
Manufacturing Industries

Source: Data from Dun and Bradstreet, *Industry Norms and Ratios*, 1990–91.

return on assets. For instance, grocery stores and pharmaceutical companies have a similar return on assets, but they achieve it in very different ways. Grocery stores have a very small profit margin, 1.4 percent, which when multiplied by a high asset turnover, 5.6 times, gives a return on assets of 7.8 percent. Pharmaceutical manufacturers, on the other hand, have a high profit margin, 7.8

Figure 6-6. Asset Turnover for Selected Industries

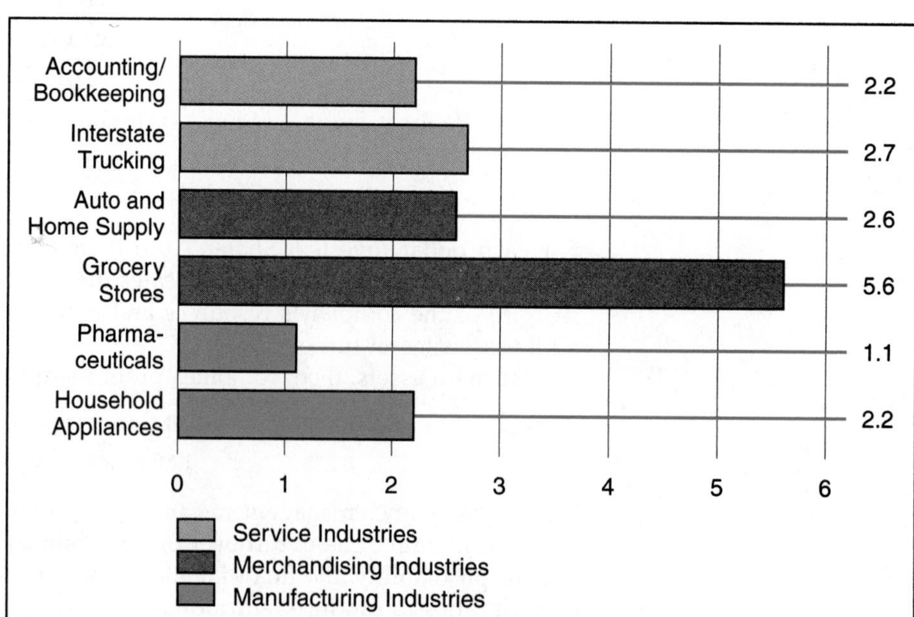

Source: Data from Dun and Bradstreet, *Industry Norms and Ratios*, 1990–91.

Figure 6-7. Return on Assets for Selected Industries

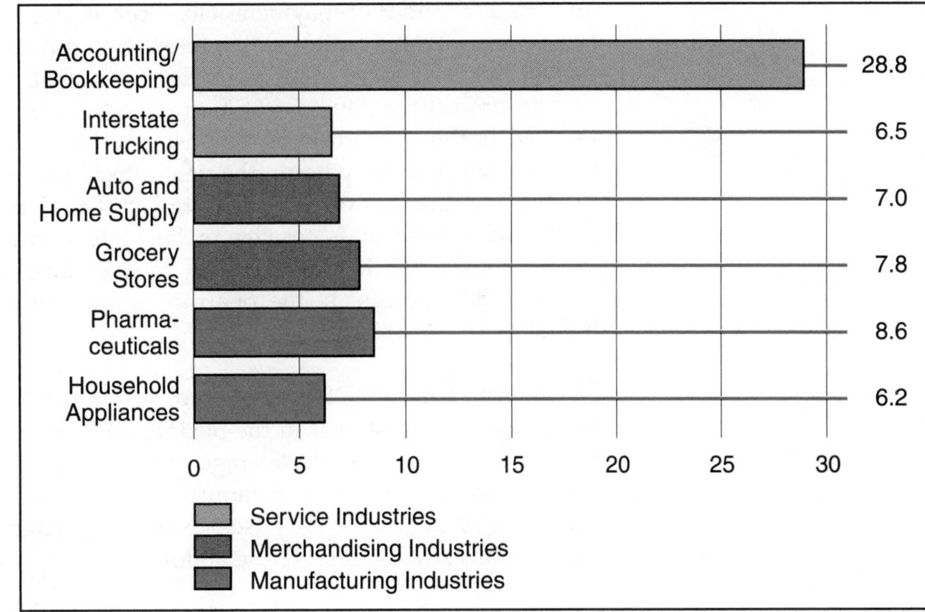

Source: Data from Dun and Bradstreet, *Industry Norms and Ratios*, 1990–91.

percent, and a low asset turnover, 1.1 times, producing a return on assets of 8.6 percent. Accounting and bookkeeping services have the best return on assets, 28.8 percent, because they have a good profit margin, 13.1 percent, combined with a fairly good asset turnover, 2.2 times.

Shafer Auto Parts Company's profit margin of 6.2 percent is more than double the auto and home supply industry average of 2.7 percent, but its turnover of 1.88 times lags behind the industry average of 2.6 times. Shafer is sacrificing asset turnover to achieve a high profit margin. It is clear that this strategy is working, because Shafer's return on assets of 11.6 percent exceeds the industry average of 7.0 percent.

Debt to Equity. Another useful measure is the **debt to equity** ratio, which shows the proportion of the company financed by creditors in comparison to that financed by the owner. This ratio is computed by dividing total liabilities by owner's equity. A debt to equity ratio of 1.0 means that total liabilities equal owner's equity, that half of the company's assets are financed by creditors. A ratio of .5 would mean that one-third of the assets are financed by creditors. A company with a high debt to equity ratio is more vulnerable in poor economic times because it must continue to repay creditors. Owner's investments, on the other hand, do not have to be repaid and withdrawals can be deferred if the company is suffering because of a poor economy.

The Shafer Auto Parts debt to equity ratio is computed as follows:

$$\text{Debt to equity} = \frac{\text{total liabilities}}{\text{owner's equity}} = \frac{\$60{,}483}{\$98{,}433} = .614 \text{ (or 61.4\%)}$$

Because its ratio of debt to equity is 61.4 percent, about 40 percent of Shafer Auto Parts Company is financed by creditors and roughly 60 percent is financed by Fred Shafer.

The debt to equity ratio does not fit neatly into either the liquidity or profitability category. It is clearly very important to liquidity analysis because it relates to debt and its repayment. However, it also is relevant to profitability for two reasons. First, creditors are interested in the proportion of the business that is debt financed because the more debt a company has, the more profit it must earn to protect the payment of interest to the creditors. Second, owners are interested in the proportion of the business that is debt financed. The amount of interest that must be paid on the debt affects the amount of profit that is left to provide a return on owner's investment. The debt to equity ratio also shows how much expansion is possible by borrowing additional long-term funds. Figure 6-8 shows that the debt to equity ratio in our selected industries varies from a low of 52.8 percent in the pharmaceuticals industry to 109.2 percent in the interstate trucking industry.

Return on Equity. Of course, Fred Shafer is interested in how much he has earned on his investment in the business. His **return on equity** is measured by the ratio of net income to average owner's equity. The beginning and ending owner's equity needed to compute average owner's equity are found in the statement of owner's equity (see Exhibit 6-5, page 224). The return on equity for the company is computed as follows:

$$\text{Return on equity} = \frac{\text{net income}}{\text{average owner's equity}}$$

$$= \frac{\$17{,}881}{(\$100{,}552 + \$98{,}433)/2}$$

$$= \frac{\$17{,}881}{\$99{,}492.50} = .180 \text{ (or 18.0\%)}$$

Figure 6-8. Average Debt to Equity for Selected Industries

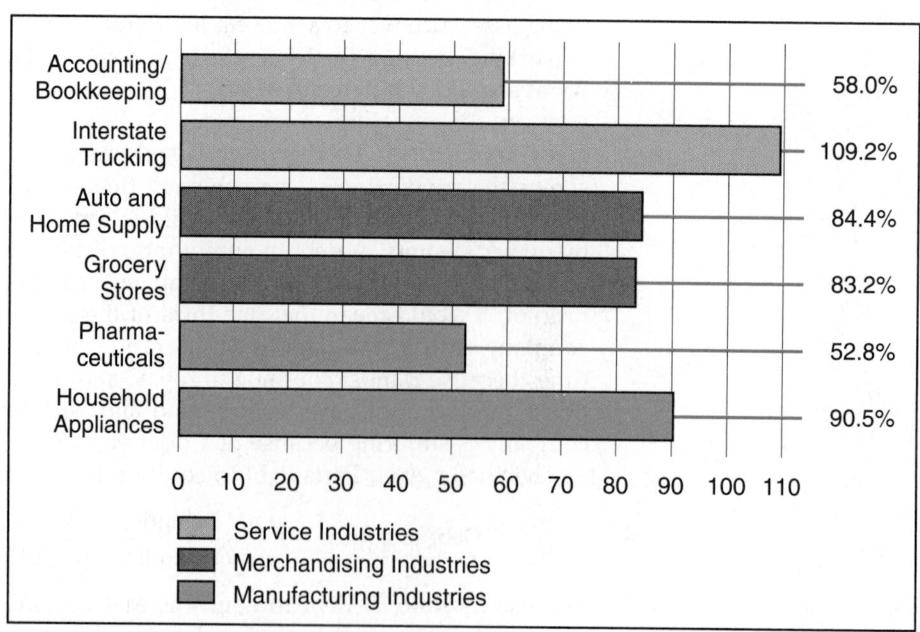

Source: Data from Dun and Bradstreet, *Industry Norms and Ratios*, 1990–91.

Figure 6-9. Average Return on Owner's Equity

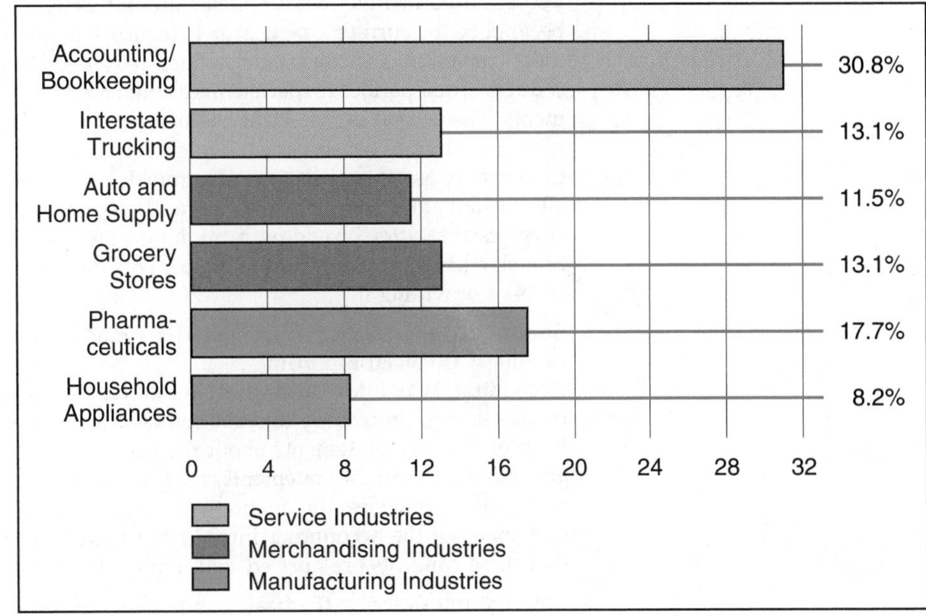

Source: Data from Dun and Bradstreet, *Industry Norms and Ratios*, 1990–91.

In 19xx, Shafer Auto Parts Company earned 18 cents for every dollar invested by the owner, Fred Shafer.

Whether or not this is an acceptable return depends on several factors, such as how much the company earned in prior years and how much other companies in the same industry earned. As measured by return on equity (Figure 6-9), accounting and bookkeeping services are the most profitable of our sample industries, with a return on equity of 30.8 percent. Household appliances are the least profitable, with a return on equity of 8.2 percent. Shafer Auto Parts Company's average return on equity of 18.0 percent exceeds the auto and home supply industry average of 11.5 percent.

Chapter Review

Review of Learning Objectives

1. **State the objectives of financial reporting.**
   The objectives of financial reporting are (1) to furnish the information needed to make investment and credit decisions, (2) to provide information that can be used to assess cash flow prospects, and (3) to provide information about business resources, claims to those resources, and changes in them.
2. **State the qualitative characteristics of accounting information and describe their interrelationships.**
   Understandability depends on the knowledge of the user and the ability of the accountant to provide useful information. Usefulness is a function of two primary characteristics, relevance and reliability. Information is relevant when it affects the outcome of a decision. Information that is relevant has feedback value and predictive value, and is timely. To be reliable, information must represent what it is supposed to represent, must be verifiable, and must be neutral.

3. **Define and describe the use of the conventions of *comparability* and *consistency, materiality, conservatism, full disclosure,* and *cost-benefit.***
Because accountants' measurements are not exact, certain conventions have come to be applied in current practice to help users interpret financial statements. One of these conventions is consistency, which requires the use of the same accounting procedures from period to period and enhances the comparability of financial statements. The second is materiality, which has to do with the relative importance of an item. The third is conservatism, which entails using the procedure that is least likely to overstate assets and income. The fourth is full disclosure, which means including all relevant information in the financial statements. The fifth is cost-benefit, which suggests that after providing a minimum level of information, additional information should be provided only if the benefits derived from the information exceed the costs of providing it.

4. **Summarize the concepts that underlie financial accounting and their relationship to ethical financial reporting.**
Accounting is an information system that facilitates the making of business decisions by measuring, processing, and communicating to decision makers information in the form of financial statements about the transactions of a business entity. To interpret and use the financial statements, it is important to understand generally accepted accounting principles, the qualitative characteristics, and the accounting conventions that underlie the accounting information system. Ethical financial reporting means that these concepts are applied with the intent to enlighten, not to mislead.

5. **Identify and describe the basic components of a classified balance sheet.**
The classified balance sheet is subdivided as follows:

Assets	**Liabilities**
Current Assets	Current Liabilities
Investments	Long-Term Liabilities
Property, Plant, and Equipment	
Intangible Assets	**Owner's Equity**
(Other Assets)	(Category depends on the form of business)

A current asset is an asset that can reasonably be expected to be realized in cash during the next year or normal operating cycle, whichever is longer. Investments are long-term assets that generally are not used in the normal operation of a business. Property, plant, and equipment are long-term assets that are used in day-to-day operations. Intangible assets are long-term assets whose value stems from the rights or privileges they extend to the owner. A current liability is a liability that can reasonably be expected to be paid during the next year or normal operating cycle, whichever is longer. Long-term liabilities are debts that fall due more than one year ahead or beyond the normal operating cycle. The owners' (stockholders') equity section for a corporation differs from that of a proprietorship in that it has subdivisions of contributed capital (the assets invested by stockholders) and retained earnings (stockholders' claim to assets earned from operations and reinvested in operations).

6. **Prepare multistep and single-step classified income statements.**
Condensed income statements for external reporting can be in multistep or single-step form. The multistep form arrives at net income through a series of steps; the single-step form arrives at net income in a single step. There is usually a separate section in the multistep form for other revenues and expenses.

7. **Use classified financial statements for the simple evaluation of liquidity and profitability.**
One major use of classified financial statements is to evaluate a company's liquidity and profitability. Two simple measures of liquidity are working capital and the current ratio. Five simple measures of profitability are profit margin, asset turnover, return on assets, debt to equity, and return on equity.

Review of Concepts and Terminology

The following concepts and terms were introduced in this chapter:

(L.O. 7) **Asset turnover:** A ratio that measures how efficiently assets are used to produce sales; net sales divided by average total assets.

(L.O. 5) **Classified financial statements:** General-purpose external financial statements that are divided into subcategories.

(L.O. 3) **Comparability:** The convention of presenting information in such a way that decision makers can recognize similarities, differences, and trends in different time periods or companies.

(L.O. 6) **Condensed financial statements:** Financial statements for external reporting purposes that present only the major categories of information.

(L.O. 3) **Conservatism:** The convention that mandates that, when faced with two equally acceptable alternatives, the accountant must choose the one less likely to overstate assets and income.

(L.O. 3) **Consistency:** The convention that an accounting procedure, once adopted, is not changed from one period to another unless users are informed of the change.

(L.O. 5) **Contributed capital:** The accounts that reflect the stockholders' investment in a corporation. Also called *Paid-in Capital.*

(L.O. 3) **Convention:** Rule of thumb or customary way of recording transactions or preparing financial statements.

(L.O. 3) **Cost-benefit:** The convention that benefits gained from providing accounting information should be greater than the costs of providing that information.

(L.O. 5) **Current assets:** Cash or other assets that are reasonably expected to be realized in cash, sold, or consumed within one year or within a normal operating cycle, whichever is longer.

(L.O. 5) **Current liabilities:** Obligations due within one year or within the normal operating cycle, whichever is longer.

(L.O. 7) **Current ratio:** A measure of liquidity; current assets divided by current liabilities.

(L.O. 7) **Debt to equity:** A ratio that measures the relationship of assets provided by creditors to those provided by owners; total liabilities divided by owner's equity.

(L.O. 4) **Fraudulent financial reporting:** The intentional preparation of misleading financial statements.

(L.O. 3) **Full disclosure:** The convention that requires that financial statements and the notes to them present all information relevant to the users' understanding of the company's financial condition.

(L.O. 1) **General-purpose external financial statements:** The medium through which information gathered and processed in the accounting system periodically is communicated to investors, creditors, and other interested parties outside the business.

(L.O. 6) **Income from operations:** Gross margin from sales less operating expenses.

(L.O. 5) **Intangible assets:** Long-term assets that have no physical substance but have a value based on rights or privileges that accrue to the owner.

(L.O. 5) **Investments:** Assets, generally of a long-term nature, that are not used in the normal operation of a business and that management does not intend to convert to cash within the next year.

(L.O. 7) **Liquidity:** Having enough money on hand to pay a company's bills when they are due and to take care of unexpected needs for cash.

(L.O. 5) **Long-term liabilities:** Debts of a business that fall due more than one year ahead or beyond the normal operating cycle; debts to be paid out of noncurrent assets.

(L.O. 3) **Materiality:** The convention that requires that an item or event in a financial statement be important to the users of financial statements.

(L.O. 6) **Multistep form:** A form of income statement that arrives at net income in steps.

(L.O. 5) **Other assets:** All of the assets owned by a company other than current assets and property, plant, and equipment.

(L.O. 6) **Other revenues and expenses:** The section of a classified income statement that includes nonoperating revenues and expenses.

(L.O. 7) **Profitability:** The ability of a business to earn a satisfactory income.

(L.O. 7) **Profit margin:** A measure of profitability; the percentage of each sales dollar that results in net income; net income divided by net sales.

(L.O. 5) **Property, plant, and equipment:** Tangible assets of a long-term nature that are used in the continuing operation of a business. Also called *operating assets, fixed assets, tangible assets,* or *long-lived assets.*

(L.O. 2) **Qualitative characteristics:** Standards for judging the information that accountants give to decision makers.

(L.O. 2) **Relevance:** Bearing directly on the outcome of a decision; a qualitative characteristic of accounting information.

(L.O. 2) **Reliability:** Having the traits of representational faithfulness, verifiability, and neutrality; a qualitative characteristic of accounting information.

(L.O. 5) **Retained Earnings:** The account that reflects the stockholders' claim to the assets earned from operations and reinvested in corporate operations. Also called *Earned Capital.*

(L.O. 7) **Return on assets:** A measure of profitability that shows how efficiently a company is using its assets; net income divided by average total assets.

(L.O. 7) **Return on equity:** A measure of profitability related to the amount earned by a business in relation to the owner's investment in the business; net income divided by average owner's equity.

(L.O. 6) **Single-step form:** A form of income statement that arrives at net income in a single step.

(L.O. 2) **Understandability:** Carrying intended meaning; a qualitative characteristic of accounting information.

(L.O. 2) **Usefulness:** Having the traits of relevance and reliability; a qualitative characteristic of accounting information.

(L.O. 7) **Working capital:** A measure of liquidity; the amount by which total current assets exceed total current liabilities.

Self-Test

Test your knowledge of the chapter by choosing the best answer for each of the following items.

(L.O. 1) 1. Financial reporting provides information that is useful in each of the following situations *except*
   a. making investment and credit decisions.
   b. assessing cash flow prospects.
   c. making employment decisions.
   d. assessing business resources, claims to those resources, and changes in them.

(L.O. 2) 2. Accounting information is said to be useful if it is
   a. timely and biased.
   b. relevant and reliable.
   c. relevant and uncertain.
   d. accurate and faithful.

(L.O. 3) 3. To ignore an amount because it is small in relation to the financial statements taken as a whole is an application of
   a. materiality.
   b. conservatism.
   c. full disclosure.
   d. comparability.

(L.O. 4) 4. Accounting is concerned with providing information to decision makers. The overall framework of rules within which accountants work to provide this information is best described as
a. business transactions.
b. data processing.
c. generally accepted accounting principles.
d. income tax laws.

(L.O. 5) 5. A note receivable due in two years normally would be classified as
a. a current asset.
b. an investment.
c. property, plant, and equipment.
d. an intangible asset.

(L.O. 5) 6. The current portion of long-term debt is normally classified as
a. a current asset.
b. a current liability.
c. a long-term liability.
d. owner's equity.

(L.O. 6) 7. A disadvantage of the single-step income statement is that
a. gross margin from sales is not disclosed separately.
b. other revenues and expenses are separated from operating items.
c. interest expense is not disclosed.
d. the cost of goods sold cannot be determined.

(L.O. 7) 8. Which of the following ratios is a measure of liquidity?
a. Return on equity
b. Return on assets
c. Profit margin
d. Current ratio

(L.O. 7) 9. Net income is a component in determining each of the following ratios *except*
a. profit margin.
b. return on assets.
c. debt to equity.
d. return on equity.

(L.O. 7) 10. If a company has a profit margin of 4.0 percent and an asset turnover of 3.0 times, its return on assets is approximately
a. 1.3 percent.
b. 3.0 percent.
c. 4.0 percent.
d. 12.0 percent.

Answers to the Self-Test are at the end of this chapter.

Review Problem
Analyzing Liquidity and Profitability Using Ratios

(L.O. 7) Flavin Shirt Company has faced increased competition from imported shirts in recent years. Presented below is summary information for the last two years:

	19x2	19x1
Current Assets	$ 200,000	$ 170,000
Total Assets	880,000	710,000
Current Liabilities	90,000	50,000
Long-Term Liabilities	150,000	50,000
Owner's Equity	640,000	610,000
Sales	1,200,000	1,050,000
Net Income	60,000	80,000

Total assets and owner's equity at the beginning of 19x1 were $690,000 and $590,000, respectively.

Required

Use (1) liquidity analysis and (2) profitability analysis to document the declining financial position of Flavin Shirt Company.

Answer to Review Problem

1. Liquidity analysis

	Current Assets	Current Liabilities	Working Capital	Current Ratio
19x1	$170,000	$50,000	$120,000	3.40
19x2	200,000	90,000	110,000	2.22
Increase (decrease) in working capital			$ (10,000)	
Decrease in current ratio				1.18

Both working capital and the current ratio declined because, although current assets increased by $30,000 ($200,000 − $170,000), current liabilities increased by a greater amount, $40,000 ($90,000 − $50,000), from 19x1 to 19x2.

2. Profitability analysis

		Sales		Average Total Assets			Average Owner's Equity	
	Net Income	Sales	Profit Margin	Amount	Asset Turnover	Return on Assets	Amount	Return on Equity
19x1	$ 80,000	$1,050,000	7.6%	$700,000[1]	1.50	11.4%	$600,000[3]	13.3%
19x2	60,000	1,200,000	5.0%	795,000[2]	1.51	7.5%	625,000[4]	9.6%
Increase (decrease)	$(20,000)	$ 150,000	(2.6)%	$ 95,000	0.01	(3.9)%	$ 25,000	(3.7)%

[1] ($690,000 + $710,000) ÷ 2
[2] ($710,000 + $880,000) ÷ 2
[3] ($590,000 + $610,000) ÷ 2
[4] ($610,000 + $640,000) ÷ 2

Net income decreased by $20,000 in spite of an increase in sales of $150,000 and an increase in average total assets of $95,000. The results were decreases in profit margin from 7.6 percent to 5.0 percent and in return on assets from 11.4 percent to 7.5 percent. Asset turnover showed almost no change, and so did not contribute to the decline in profitability. The decrease in return on equity from 13.3 percent to 9.6 percent was not as much as the decrease in return on assets because the growth in total assets was financed by debt instead of owner's equity, as shown by the capital structure analysis below.

	Total Liabilities	Owner's Equity	Debt to Equity Ratio
19x1	$100,000	$610,000	16.4%
19x2	240,000	640,000	37.5%
Increase	$140,000	$ 30,000	21.1%

Total liabilities increased by $140,000, while owner's equity increased by $30,000. As a result, the amount of the business financed by debt in relation to the amount of business financed by owner's equity increased from 16.4 percent to 37.5 percent.

Chapter Assignments

Questions

1. What are the three objectives of financial reporting?
2. What are the qualitative characteristics of accounting information, and what is their significance?
3. What are the accounting conventions? How does each help in the interpretation of financial information?
4. What is the relationship among objectives of financial information, financial statements, decision makers, economic activities, and ethical financial reporting?
5. What is the purpose of classified financial statements?
6. What are four common categories of assets?
7. What criteria must an asset meet to be classified as current? Under what condition is an asset considered current even though it is not going to be realized as cash within a year? What are two examples of assets that fall into this category?
8. In what order should current assets be listed?
9. What is the difference between a short-term investment in the current assets section and a security in the investments section of the balance sheet?
10. What is an intangible asset? Give at least three examples.
11. Name the two major categories of liabilities.
12. What are the primary differences between the owner's equity section for a sole proprietorship or partnership and the corresponding section for a corporation?
13. Explain the difference between contributed capital and retained earnings.
14. Explain how the multistep form of the income statement differs from the single-step form. What are the relative merits of each?
15. Why are other revenues and expenses separated from operating revenues and expenses in the multistep income statement?
16. Define *liquidity* and name two measures of liquidity.
17. How is the current ratio computed and why is it important?
18. Which is the more important goal—liquidity or profitability? Explain your answer.
19. Name five measures of profitability.
20. "Return on assets is a better measure of profitability than profit margin." Evaluate this statement.

Communication Skills Exercises

Communication 6-1. Accounting Conventions *(L.O. 3)*

Mason Parking, which operates a seven-story parking building in downtown Chicago, has a calendar year end. It serves daily and hourly parkers, as well as monthly parkers who pay a fixed monthly rate in advance. The company traditionally has recorded all cash receipts as revenues when received. Most monthly parkers pay in full during the month prior to that in which they have the right to park. The company's auditors have said that beginning in 1991, the company should consider recording the cash receipts from monthly parking on an accrual basis, crediting Unearned Parking Fees. Total cash receipts for 1991 were $2,500,000, and the cash receipts received in 1991 and applicable to January 1992 were $125,000. Discuss the relevance of the accounting conventions of consistency, materiality, and full disclosure to the decision to record the monthly parking revenues on an accrual basis.

Communication 6-2. Ethics and Financial Reporting
(L.O. 4)

Salem Software, located outside Boston, develops computer software and licenses it to financial institutions. The firm uses an aggressive accounting method that records revenues from the systems it has sold on a percentage of completion basis. This means that revenue for partially completed projects is recognized based on the proportion of the project that is completed. If a project is 50 percent completed, then 50 percent of the contracted revenue is recognized. In 1992, preliminary estimates for a $5 million project are that the project is 75 percent complete. Because the estimate of completion is a matter of judgment, management asks for a new report showing the project to be 90 percent complete. This change will enable management to meet its financial goals for the year and thus receive substantial year-end bonuses. Do you think management's action is ethical? If you were the company controller and were asked to prepare the new report, would you do it? What action would you take?

Communication 6-3. Ethics and Financial Reporting
(L.O. 4)

Treon Microsystems, Inc., a Silicon Valley manufacturer of microchips for personal computers, has just completed its year-end physical inventory in advance of preparing financial statements. To celebrate, the entire accounting department goes out for a New Year's Eve party at a local establishment. As senior accountant, you join the fun. At the party, you fall into conversation with an employee of one of your main competitors. After a while, the employee reveals that the competitor plans to introduce a new product in sixty days that will make Treon's principal product obsolete.

On Monday morning, you go to the financial vice president with this information, stating that the inventory may have to be written down and net income reduced. To your surprise, the financial vice president says that you were right to come to him, but urges you to say nothing about the problem. He says, "It is probably a rumor, and even if it is true, there will be plenty of time to write down the inventory in sixty days." You wonder if this is the appropriate thing to do. You feel confident that your source knew what he was talking about. You know that the salaries of all top managers, including the financial vice president, are tied to net income. What is fraudulent financial reporting? Is this an example of fraudulent financial reporting? What action would you take?

Communication 6-4. Basic Research Skills
(L.O. 7)

Most college and public libraries have on file the annual reports of major public corporations. In some libraries, these annual reports are on microfiche. Go to the library and obtain the annual report for a company that you recognize. In the annual report, identify the four basic financial statements and the notes to the financial statements. Perform a liquidity analysis, including the calculation of working capital and the current ratio. Perform a profitability analysis, calculating profit margin, asset turnover, return on assets, debt to equity, and return on equity.

Classroom Exercises

Exercise 6-1. Accounting Concepts and Conventions
(L.O. 3)

Each of the statements below violates a convention in accounting. State which of the following concepts or conventions is violated: comparability and consistency, materiality, conservatism, full disclosure, or cost-benefit.

1. A series of reports that are time consuming and expensive to prepare is presented to the board of directors each month even though the reports are never used.
2. A company changes its method of accounting for depreciation.
3. The company in **2** does not indicate in the financial statements that the method of depreciation was changed, nor does it specify the effect of the change on net income.
4. A new office building next to the factory is debited to the Factory account because it represents a fairly small dollar amount in relation to the factory.
5. The asset account for a pickup truck still used in the business is written down to salvage value even though the carrying value under conventional depreciation methods is higher.

Exercise 6-2.
Financial Accounting Concepts
(L.O. 1, 2, 3, 4)

The lettered items below represent a classification scheme for the concepts of financial accounting. Match each term with the letter indicating the category in which it belongs.

a. Decision makers (users of accounting information)
b. Business activities or entities relevant to accounting measurement
c. Objectives of accounting information
d. Accounting measurement considerations
e. Accounting processing considerations
f. Qualitative characteristics
g. Accounting conventions
h. Financial statements

_____ 1. Conservatism
_____ 2. Verifiability
_____ 3. Statement of cash flows
_____ 4. Materiality
_____ 5. Reliability
_____ 6. Recognition
_____ 7. Cost-benefit
_____ 8. Understandability
_____ 9. Business transactions
_____ 10. Consistency
_____ 11. Full disclosure
_____ 12. Furnishing information that is useful to investors and creditors
_____ 13. Specific business entities
_____ 14. Classification
_____ 15. Management
_____ 16. Neutrality
_____ 17. Internal accounting control
_____ 18. Valuation
_____ 19. Investors
_____ 20. Timeliness
_____ 21. Relevance
_____ 22. Furnishing information that is useful in assessing cash flow prospects

Exercise 6-3.
Classification of Accounts: Balance Sheet
(L.O. 5)

The lettered items below represent a classification scheme for a balance sheet, and the numbered items are account titles. Match each account with the letter indicating in which category it belongs.

a. Current assets
b. Investments
c. Property, plant, and equipment
d. Intangible assets
e. Current liabilities
f. Long-term liabilities
g. Owner's equity
h. Not on balance sheet

_____ 1. Patent
_____ 2. Building Held for Sale
_____ 3. Prepaid Rent
_____ 4. Wages Payable
_____ 5. Note Payable in Five Years
_____ 6. Building Used in Operations
_____ 7. Fund Held to Pay Off Long-Term Debt
_____ 8. Inventory
_____ 9. Prepaid Insurance
_____ 10. Depreciation Expense
_____ 11. Accounts Receivable
_____ 12. Interest Expense
_____ 13. Revenue Received in Advance
_____ 14. Short-Term Investments
_____ 15. Accumulated Depreciation
_____ 16. M. Cepeda, Capital

Exercise 6-4.
Classified Balance Sheet Preparation
(L.O. 5)

The following data pertain to a corporation: Cash, $31,200; Investment in Six-Month Government Securities, $16,400; Accounts Receivable, $38,000; Inventory, $40,000; Prepaid Rent, $1,200; Investment in Corporate Securities (long-term), $20,000; Land, $8,000; Building, $70,000; Accumulated Depreciation, Building, $14,000; Equipment, $152,000; Accumulated Depreciation, Equipment, $17,000; Copyright, $6,200; Accounts Payable, $51,000; Revenue Received in Advance, $2,800; Bonds Payable, $60,000; Common Stock—$10 par, 10,000 shares authorized, issued, and outstanding, $100,000; Paid-in Capital in Excess of Par Value, $50,000; and Retained Earnings, $88,200.

Prepare a classified balance sheet; omit the heading.

Exercise 6-5.
Classification of Accounts: Income Statement
(L.O. 6)

Using the classification scheme below for a multistep income statement, match each account with the category in which it belongs.

a. Revenues from sales
b. Cost of goods sold
c. Selling expenses
d. General and administrative expenses
e. Other revenues and expenses
f. Not on income statement

_____ 1. Purchases
_____ 2. Sales Discounts
_____ 3. Beginning Merchandise Inventory
_____ 4. Dividend Income
_____ 5. Advertising Expense
_____ 6. Office Salaries Expense
_____ 7. Freight Out Expense
_____ 8. Prepaid Insurance
_____ 9. Utility Expense
_____ 10. Sales Salaries Expense
_____ 11. Rent Expense
_____ 12. Purchases Returns and Allowances
_____ 13. Freight In
_____ 14. Depreciation Expense, Delivery Equipment
_____ 15. Taxes Payable
_____ 16. Interest Expense

Exercise 6-6.
Preparation of Income Statements
(L.O. 6)

The following data pertain to a sole proprietorship: Sales, $405,000; Cost of Goods Sold, $220,000; Selling Expenses, $90,000; General and Administrative Expenses, $60,000; Interest Expense, $4,000; and Interest Income, $3,000.

1. Prepare a condensed single-step income statement.
2. Prepare a condensed multistep income statement.

Exercise 6-7.
Condensed Multistep Income Statement
(L.O. 6)

A condensed single-step income statement appears below. Present this information in a condensed multistep income statement, and tell what insights can be obtained from the multistep form as opposed to the single-step form.

Narajan Furniture Company
Income Statement
For the Year Ended June 30, 19xx

Revenues		
Net Sales	$1,197,132	
Interest Income	5,720	
Total Revenues		$1,202,852
Costs and Expenses		
Cost of Goods Sold	$ 777,080	
Selling Expenses	203,740	
General and Adminstrative Expenses	100,688	
Interest Expense	13,560	
Total Costs and Expenses		1,095,068
Net Income		$ 107,784

Exercise 6-8.
Liquidity Ratios
(L.O. 7)

The following accounts and balances are taken from the general ledger of Mount Cedar Company:

Accounts Payable	$ 49,800
Accounts Receivable	30,600
Cash	4,500
Current Portion of Long-Term Debt	30,000
Long-Term Investments	31,200
Marketable Securities	37,800
Merchandise Inventory	76,200
Notes Payable, 90 days	45,000
Notes Payable, 2 years	60,000
Notes Receivable, 90 days	78,000
Notes Receivable, 2 years	30,000
Prepaid Insurance	1,200
Property, Plant, and Equipment	180,000
Retained Earnings	84,900
Salaries Payable	2,550
Supplies	1,050
Property Taxes Payable	3,750
Unearned Revenue	2,250

Compute (1) working capital and (2) current ratio.

Exercise 6-9.
Profitability Ratios
(L.O. 7)

The following end-of-year amounts are taken from the financial statements of Overton Company: Total Assets, $852,000; Total Liabilities, $344,000; Owner's Equity, $508,000; Net Sales, $1,564,000; Cost of Goods Sold, $972,000; Operating Expenses, $404,000; and Withdrawals, $80,000. During the past year, total assets increased by $150,000. Total owner's equity was affected only by net income and withdrawals.

Compute (1) profit margin, (2) asset turnover, (3) return on assets, (4) debt to equity, and (5) return on equity.

Exercise 6-10.
Computation of Ratios
(L.O. 7)

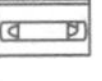

The simplified balance sheet and income statement for a sole proprietorship appear as follows:

Balance Sheet
December 31, 19xx

Assets		**Liabilities**	
Current Assets	$100,000	Current Liabilities	$ 40,000
Investments	20,000	Long-Term Liabilities	60,000
Property, Plant, and Equipment	293,000	Total Liabilities	$100,000
Intangible Assets	27,000	**Owner's Equity**	
Total Assets	$440,000	S. Carroll, Capital	340,000
		Total Liabilities and Owner's Equity	$440,000

Income Statement
For the Year Ended December 31, 19xx

Revenue from Sales (net)	$820,000
Cost of Goods Sold	500,000
Gross Margin from Sales	$320,000
Operating Expenses	270,000
Net Income	$ 50,000

Total assets and owner's equity at the beginning of 19xx were $360,000 and $280,000, respectively.

1. Compute the following liquidity measures: (a) working capital and (b) current ratio.
2. Compute the following profitability measures: (a) profit margin, (b) asset turnover, (c) return on assets, (d) debt to equity, and (e) return on equity.

Interpretation Case from Business

Albertson's, Inc., A&P, and American Stores Co.[8]
(L.O. 7)

Three of the largest chains of grocery/drug stores in the United States are Albertson's, Inc.; The Great Atlantic & Pacific Tea Company, Inc. (A&P); and American Stores Co. (Jewel, Alpha Beta, Osco, Skaggs, and others). In the fiscal years ending in 1990, Albertson's, A&P, and American had net income of $196.6 million, $146.7 million, and $118.1 million, respectively. It is difficult to judge which company is the most profitable from these figures alone because they do not take into account the relative sales, sizes, and investments of the companies. Data (in millions) are presented here to complete a financial analysis of the three companies.

	Albertson's	A&P	American Stores
1990 net sales	$7,422.7	$11,148.0	$22,004.1
1990 total assets	1,591.0	2,831.6	7,398.0
1989 total assets	1,862.7	2,640.4	7,010.4
1990 total liabilities	933.2	1,739.4	6,196.2
1989 total liabilities	790.5	1,669.5	5,892.0
1990 stockholders' equity	929.5	1,092.2	1,201.8
1989 stockholders' equity	800.5	970.8	1,118.4

Required

1. Determine which company was most profitable in 1990 by computing profit margin, asset turnover, return on assets, debt to equity, and return on equity for the three companies. Comment on the relative profitability of the three companies.
2. What do the ratios tell you about the factors that go into achieving an adequate return on assets in the grocery industry?
3. How would you characterize the use of debt financing in the grocery industry and the use of debt by the three companies?

Problem Set A

Problem 6A-1. Accounting Conventions
(L.O. 3)

In each case below, accounting conventions may have been violated.

1. After careful study, Gerson Company, which has offices in forty states, has determined that in the future its method of depreciating office furniture should be changed. The new method is adopted for the current year, and the change is noted in the financial statements.

8. Information excerpted from the 1990 annual reports of Albertson's, Inc.; The Great Atlantic & Pacific Tea Company, Inc.; and American Stores Co.

2. Jafari Corporation in the past has recorded operating expenses in general accounts for each classification (for example, Salaries Expense, Depreciation Expense, and Utility Expense). Management has determined that in spite of the additional record-keeping costs, the company's income statement should break down each operating expense into its selling expense and administrative expense components.
3. Corey, the auditor of Addison Corporation, discovered that an official of the company may have authorized the payment of a $3,000 bribe to a local official. Management argued that because the item was so small in relation to the size of the company ($3,000,000 in sales), the illegal payment should not be disclosed.
4. Farrell Book Store built a small addition to the main building to house a new computer games division. Because of uncertainty about whether the computer games division would succeed, the accountant took a conservative approach, recording the addition as an expense.
5. Since its origin ten years ago, Vazquez Company has used the same generally accepted inventory method. Because there has been no change in the inventory method, the company does not declare in its financial statements what inventory method it uses.

Required

In each case, state the convention that is applicable, explain briefly whether or not the treatment is in accord with the convention and with generally accepted accounting principles, and explain why.

Problem 6A-2. Forms of the Income Statement
(L.O. 6)

The July 31, 19x3 year-end income statement accounts that follow are for Kissell Hardware Company. Beginning merchandise inventory was $172,800 and ending merchandise inventory is $145,000. The Kissell Hardware Company is a sole proprietorship.

Account Name	Debit	Credit
Sales		922,200
Sales Returns and Allowances	42,400	
Sales Discounts	11,400	
Purchases	449,000	
Purchases Returns and Allowances		16,240
Purchases Discounts		7,600
Freight In	34,800	
Sales Salaries Expense	124,320	
Sales Supplies Expense	3,280	
Rent Expense, Selling Space	14,400	
Utility Expense, Selling Space	5,920	
Advertising Expense	33,600	
Depreciation Expense, Delivery Equipment	8,800	
Office Salaries Expense	58,480	
Office Supplies Expense	19,520	
Rent Expense, Office Space	4,800	
Utility Expense, Office Space	2,000	
Postage Expense	4,640	
Insurance Expense	5,360	
Miscellaneous Expense	2,880	
General Management Salaries Expense	84,000	
Interest Expense	11,200	
Interest Income		840

Required

From the information provided, prepare the following:

1. A detailed income statement.
2. A condensed income statement in multistep form.
3. A condensed income statement in single-step form.

Problem 6A-3. Classified Balance Sheet *(L.O. 5)*

Accounts from the July 31, 19x3 post-closing trial balance of Kissell Hardware Company appear below.

Account Name	Debit	Credit
Cash	31,000	
Short-Term Investments	33,000	
Notes Receivable	10,000	
Accounts Receivable	276,000	
Merchandise Inventory	145,000	
Prepaid Rent	1,600	
Prepaid Insurance	4,800	
Sales Supplies	1,280	
Office Supplies	440	
Deposit for Future Advertising	3,680	
Building, Not in Use	49,600	
Land	22,400	
Delivery Equipment	41,200	
Accumulated Depreciation, Delivery Equipment		28,400
Franchise Fee	4,000	
Accounts Payable		114,600
Salaries Payable		5,200
Interest Payable		840
Long-Term Notes Payable		80,000
Warren Kissell, Capital		394,960

Required

From the information provided, prepare a classified balance sheet.

Problem 6A-4. Ratio Analysis: Liquidity and Profitability *(L.O. 7)*

Criss Products Company has been disappointed with its operating results for the past two years. As accountant for the company, you have the following information available to you:

	19x3	19x2
Current Assets	$ 45,000	$ 35,000
Total Assets	145,000	110,000
Current Liabilities	20,000	10,000
Long-Term Liabilities	20,000	—
Owner's Equity	105,000	100,000
Net Sales	262,000	200,000
Net Income	16,000	11,000

Total assets and owner's equity at the beginning of 19x2 were $90,000 and $80,000, respectively.

Required

1. Compute the following measures of liquidity for 19x2 and 19x3: (a) working capital and (b) the current ratio. Comment on the differences between the years.
2. Compute the following measures of profitability for 19x2 and 19x3: (a) profit margin, (b) asset turnover, (c) return on assets, (d) debt to equity, and (e) return on equity. Comment on the change in performance from 19x2 to 19x3.

Problem 6A-5. Classified Financial Statement Preparation and Evaluation
(L.O. 5, 6, 7)

Wu Company sells outdoor sports equipment. At the December 31, 19x4 year end, the following financial information was available from the income statement: Administrative Expenses, $175,600; Cost of Goods Sold, $700,840; Interest Expense, $45,280; Interest Income, $5,600; Net Sales, $1,428,780; and Selling Expenses, $440,400.

The following information was available from the balance sheet (after closing entries were made): Accounts Payable, $65,200; Accounts Receivable, $209,600; Accumulated Depreciation, Delivery Equipment, $34,200; Accumulated Depreciation, Store Fixtures, $84,440; Cash, $56,800; Ming Wu, Capital, $718,600; Delivery Equipment, $177,000; Inventory, $273,080; Investment in Rosenberg Corporation (long term), $112,000; Investment in U.S. Government Securities (short term), $79,200; Long-Term Notes Payable, $200,000; Short-Term Notes Payable, $100,000; Short-Term Prepaid Expenses, $11,520; and Store Fixtures, $283,240.

Total assets on December 31, 19x3 were $1,048,800, and withdrawals during 19x4 were $120,000.

Required

1. From the information above, prepare (a) an income statement in single-step form, (b) a statement of owner's equity, and (c) a classified balance sheet.
2. From the statements you have prepared, compute the following measures: (a) working capital and current ratio (for liquidity); and (b) profit margin, asset turnover, return on assets, debt to equity, and return on equity (for profitability).

Problem Set B

Problem 6B-1. Accounting Conventions
(L.O. 3)

In each case below, accounting conventions may have been violated.

1. Wolin Manufacturing Company uses the cost method for computing the balance sheet amount of inventory unless the market value of the inventory is less than the cost, in which case the market value is used. At the end of the current year, the market value is $221,000 and the cost is $240,000. Wolin uses the $221,000 figure to compute net income because management feels it is the more cautious approach.
2. Mesic Company has annual sales of $15,000,000. It follows a practice of charging any items that cost less than $300 to expenses in the year purchased. During the current year, it purchased several chairs for the executive conference rooms at $291 each, including freight. Although the chairs were expected to last for at least ten years, they were charged as an expense in accordance with company policy.
3. Hayden Company closed its books on July 31, 19x2 before preparing its annual report. On July 30, 19x2, a fire destroyed one of the company's two factories. Although the company had fire insurance and would not suffer a loss on the building, a significant decrease in sales in 19x3 was expected because of the fire. The fire damage was not reported in the 19x2 financial statements because the operations for that year were not affected by the fire.
4. Padron Drug Company spends a substantial portion of its profits on research and development. The company has been reporting its $7,500,000 expenditure for research and development as a lump sum, but management recently decided to begin classifying the expenditures by project even though its recordkeeping costs will increase.
5. During the current year, Schiff Company changed from one generally accepted method of accounting for inventories to another generally accepted method.

Required

In each case, state the convention that is applicable, and explain briefly whether or not (and why) the treatment is in accord with the convention and generally accepted accounting principles.

Problem 6B-2. Forms of the Income Statement
(L.O. 6)

Income statement accounts from the June 30, 19x2 year-end adjusted trial balance of Tasheki Hardware Company appear as follows. Beginning merchandise inventory was $175,200 and ending merchandise inventory is $157,650. Tasheki Hardware Company is a sole proprietorship.

Account Name	Debit	Credit
Sales		541,230
Sales Returns and Allowances	10,228	
Sales Discounts	5,070	
Purchases	212,336	
Purchases Returns and Allowances		4,282
Purchases Discounts		1,877
Freight In	11,221	
Sales Salaries Expense	102,030	
Sales Supplies Expense	1,642	
Rent Expense, Selling Space	18,000	
Utility Expense, Selling Space	11,256	
Advertising Expense	21,986	
Depreciation Expense, Selling Fixtures	6,778	
Office Salaries Expense	47,912	
Office Supplies Expense	782	
Rent Expense, Office Space	4,000	
Depreciation Expense, Office Equipment	3,251	
Utility Expense, Office Space	3,114	
Postage Expense	626	
Insurance Expense	2,700	
Miscellaneous Expense	481	
Interest Expense	3,600	
Interest Income		800

Required

From the information provided, prepare the following:

1. A detailed income statement.
2. A condensed income statement in multistep form.
3. A condensed income statement in single-step form.

Problem 6B-3.
Classified Balance Sheet
(L.O. 5)

Accounts from the June 30, 19x2 post-closing trial balance of Tasheki Hardware Company appear below.

Account Name	Debit	Credit
Cash	24,000	
Short-Term Investments	13,150	
Notes Receivable	45,000	
Accounts Receivable	76,570	
Merchandise Inventory	156,750	
Prepaid Rent	2,000	
Prepaid Insurance	1,200	
Sales Supplies	426	
Office Supplies	97	
Land Held for Future Expansion	11,500	
Selling Fixtures	72,400	
Accumulated Depreciation, Selling Fixtures		22,000
Office Equipment	24,100	
Accumulated Depreciation, Office Equipment		12,050
Trademark	4,000	
Accounts Payable		109,745
Salaries Payable		787
Interest Payable		600
Notes Payable (due in three years)		36,000
Thomas Tasheki, Capital		250,011

Required

From the information provided, prepare a classified balance sheet.

Problem 6B-4.
Ratio Analysis: Liquidity and Profitability
(L.O. 7)

Here is a summary of data taken from the income statements and balance sheets for D'Angelo Construction Supply for the past two years:

	19x4	19x3
Current Assets	$ 366,000	$ 310,000
Total Assets	2,320,000	1,740,000
Current Liabilities	180,000	120,000
Long-Term Liabilities	800,000	580,000
Owner's Equity	1,340,000	1,040,000
Net Sales	4,600,000	3,480,000
Net Income	300,000	204,000

Total assets and owner's equity at the beginning of 19x3 were $1,360,000 and $840,000, respectively.

Required

1. Compute the following liquidity measures for 19x3 and 19x4: (a) working capital and (b) current ratio. Comment on the differences between the years.
2. Compute the following measures of profitability for 19x3 and 19x4: (a) profit margin, (b) asset turnover, (c) return on assets, (d) debt to equity, and (e) return on equity. Comment on the change in performance from 19x3 to 19x4.

Problem 6B-5.
Classified Financial Statement Preparation and Evaluation
(L.O. 5, 6, 7)

The following accounts (in alphabetical order) and amounts were taken or calculated from the June 30, 19x4 year-end adjusted trial balance of Skowron Lawn Equipment Center: Accounts Payable, $72,600; Accounts Receivable, $169,400; Accumulated Depreciation, Building, $52,400; Accumulated Depreciation, Equipment, $34,800; Building, $220,000; Cash, $21,280; Cost of Goods Sold, $492,000; Dividend Income, $2,560; Equipment, $151,200; General and Administrative Expenses, $121,200; Interest Expense, $24,400; Inventory, $112,300; Land (used in operations), $58,000; Land Held for Future Use, $40,000; Mortgage Payable, $180,000; Notes Payable (short-term), $50,000; Notes Receivable (short-term), $24,000; Sales (net) $896,000; Selling Expenses, $202,700; Short-Term Investment (100 shares of General Motors), $13,000; Ann Skowron, Capital, $422,420; Ann Skowron, Withdrawals, $47,800; and Trademark, $13,500. Total assets on June 30, 19x3 were $687,900.

Required

1. From the information above, prepare (a) an income statement in condensed multi-step form, (b) a statement of owner's equity, and (c) a classified balance sheet.
2. Calculate these measures of liquidity: (a) working capital and (b) current ratio.
3. Calculate these measures of profitability: (a) profit margin, (b) asset turnover, (c) return on assets, (d) debt to equity, and (e) return on equity.

Financial Decision Case

Cruz Tapestries Company
(L.O. 7)

Carla Cruz is the principal stockholder and president of Cruz Tapestries Company, which wholesales fine tapestries to retail stores. Because Cruz was not satisfied with the company earnings in 19x3, she raised prices in 19x4, increasing gross margin from sales from 30 percent in 19x3 to 35 percent in 19x4. Cruz is pleased that net income did go up from 19x3 to 19x4, as shown in the following comparative income statements:

	19x4	19x3
Revenues		
Net Sales	$611,300	$693,200
Costs and Expenses		
Cost of Goods Sold	397,345	485,240
Selling and Administrative Expenses	154,199	152,504
Total Costs and Expenses	$551,544	$637,744
Net Income	$ 59,756	$ 55,456

Total assets for Cruz Tapestries Company for 19x2, 19x3, and 19x4 were $623,390, $693,405, and $768,455, respectively.

Required

1. Has Cruz Tapestries' profitability really improved? **Hint:** Compute profit margin and return on assets, and comment.
2. What factors has Cruz overlooked in evaluating the profitability of the company? **Hint:** Compute asset turnover and comment on the role it plays in profitability.

Answers to Self-Test

1. c	3. a	5. b	7. a	9. c
2. b	4. c	6. b	8. d	10. d

LEARNING OBJECTIVES

1. Identify the principles of accounting systems design.
2. Identify the basic elements of computer systems in mainframe and microcomputer contexts.
3. Explain the objectives and uses of special-purpose journals.
4. Construct and use the following types of special-purpose journals: sales journal, purchases journal, cash receipts journal, cash payments journal, and others as needed.
5. Explain the purposes and relationships of controlling accounts and subsidiary ledgers.
6. Define internal control and identify the three elements of the internal control structure, including seven examples of control procedures.
7. Describe the inherent limitations of internal control.
8. Apply control procedures to certain merchandising transactions.

CHAPTER 7

Accounting Systems and Internal Control

Knowledge of accounting systems for processing information is very important today because of the many different systems in use and the rapidly changing needs of businesses. In this chapter, you first study the principles of accounting systems design. You then learn about data processing, with and without a computer. Because the idea behind special-purpose journals is basic to all accounting systems, particular attention is given to the way these journals are used in manual data processing. This chapter also introduces the concept of internal control and its application to certain merchandising transactions, including banking transactions and voucher system transactions. All of the control techniques described in this chapter are applicable to other types of businesses, such as service organizations and manufacturers. The application of these techniques to merchandising transactions is simply a convenient introduction. After studying this chapter, you should be able to meet the learning objectives listed on the left.

DECISION POINT

Fine Arts Gallery and Framing

■ Fine Arts Gallery and Framing, located in South Fork Mall, was established two years ago to provide framing services. At that time, Gary Hoben, the owner, set up a simple manual accounting system—with a general journal and a general ledger—for a service business. Because all sales were for cash or by credit card and because Hoben made a practice of paying all bills by the end of the month, the shop had few receivables or payables. Over the past year, Hoben added an inventory of color prints and posters, which carry a high profit margin. In addition, the various suppliers offer generous terms for payment. As a result, Hoben has been able to allow customers to pay over a period of three months when they buy framed prints or posters. With the increased number and complexity of transactions involving inventory, accounts receivable, and accounts payable, his simple accounting system quickly became a burden for Hoben. What kind of an accounting system could Hoben adopt to handle the increased number and complexity of the store's transactions?

After analyzing the transactions in which his business engages, Hoben divided the transactions into five categories: credit sales, credit purchases, cash receipts, cash payments, and miscellaneous. Because more than 95 percent of the store's transactions fall into the first four categories, he decided to set up a separate journal for each of these types of transactions, and to use the general journal to handle the miscellaneous transactions that do not fall into any of these categories. Next, Hoben investigated small, inexpensive business accounting systems available for use with microcomputers. He was pleasantly surprised to find that several integrated general ledger software packages were organized according to the major types of transactions he had identified. Over the next three months, Hoben purchased and implemented a new accounting system. This chapter discusses the principles to consider in designing or buying an accounting system and describes the basics of both computerized and manual accounting systems. ■

Principles of Accounting Systems Design

OBJECTIVE 1
Identify the principles of accounting systems design

Accounting systems gather data from all parts of a business, put them into useful form, and communicate the results to management. Management uses system output to make all kinds of business decisions. As businesses have grown larger and more complicated, the role of accounting systems also has grown. Today, the need for a total information system with accounting as its base has become more pressing. For this reason, the accountant must understand all phases of the company's operations as well as the latest developments in systems design and technology.

The accountant also may have a voice in choosing the firm's processing system. **Data processing** is the means by which the accounting system gathers data, organizes them into useful form, and issues the resulting information to users. The two extremes of data processing systems are computerized systems and manual systems, both of which do the same job. In this chapter, we examine the main features of computer systems and their use in data processing, as well as the basic ways of handling a large amount of data using manual data processing. First, however, we discuss the four general principles of accounting systems design: (1) the cost-benefit principle, (2) the control principle, (3) the compatibility principle, and (4) the flexibility principle.

Cost-Benefit Principle

The most important systems principle, the **cost-benefit principle**, holds that the benefits derived from an accounting system and the information it generates must be equal to or greater than its cost. Beyond certain routine tasks—preparing payroll and tax reports and financial statements, and maintaining internal control—management may want or need other information. That information must be reliable, timely, and useful. The benefits of additional information must be weighed against both the tangible and intangible costs of gathering it. Among the tangible costs are those for personnel, forms, and equipment. One of the intangible costs is the cost of wrong decisions that stem from the lack of good information. For instance, wrong decisions can lead to loss of sales, production losses, or inventory losses. Some companies have spent thousands of dollars on computer systems that do not offer enough benefits. On the other hand, some managers have failed to realize important benefits that could be gained from investing in more advanced systems. It is the job of the accountant, as systems analyst, to weigh the costs and benefits.

Control Principle

The **control principle** requires that an accounting system provide all the features of internal control needed to protect the firm's assets and to be sure data are reliable. For example, expenditures should be approved by a responsible member of management before they are made.

Compatibility Principle

The **compatibility principle** holds that the design of a system must be in harmony with the organizational and human factors of a business. The organizational factors have to do with the enterprise's kind of business and how the different units of the business are formally related in meeting its objectives. For example, a company can organize its marketing efforts by region or by product. If a company is organized by region, major reports should present revenues and expenses by region. A company organized by product, on the other hand, should have a system that reports revenues and expenses first by product and then by region.

The human factors of business have to do with the people within the organization and their abilities, behaviors, and personalities. The interest, support, and competence of these people are very important to the success or failure of systems design. In changing systems or installing new ones, the accountant must deal with the people presently carrying out or supervising existing procedures. These people must understand, accept, and, in many cases, be trained in the new procedures. The new system cannot succeed unless the system and the people in the organization are compatible.

Flexibility Principle

The **flexibility principle** calls for an accounting system that has enough flexibility to allow the volume of transactions to grow and organizational changes to be made. Businesses do not stay the same. They grow, offer new products, add new branch offices, sell existing divisions, or make other changes that require adjustments in the accounting system. A carefully designed system allows a business to grow and change without it being necessary to make major alterations. For example, the chart of accounts should be designed to allow the addition of new asset, liability, owner's equity, revenue, and expense accounts.

Computerized Data Processing

Most data processing in business today is done by computer. Computers are able to process large volumes of data very quickly. The development of mainframe computer systems has allowed the largest companies to centralize their accounting operations and eliminate much of the work that used to be done by hand. And the development of minicomputers and microcomputers has made it possible for even the smallest company to keep its accounting records on a computer.

The Elements of a Computer System

OBJECTIVE 2
Identify the basic elements of computer systems in mainframe and microcomputer contexts

Regardless of the size of a computerized data processing system, it consists of three basic elements: hardware, software, and personnel.

Hardware. **Hardware** is all the equipment needed to operate a computerized data processing system. Figure 7-1 shows the hardware in a typical mainframe computer system; Figure 7-2 shows the hardware in a typical microcomputer system. In both, there are devices that help input data to the system, process and store data, and output information. In a mainframe system, for example, data related to a purchase transaction might be input through a remote data entry device (a terminal) to the central processor, where it is recorded for future processing on a magnetic tape using a magnetic disk drive or on a disk using a

Figure 7-1. Mainframe Computer System

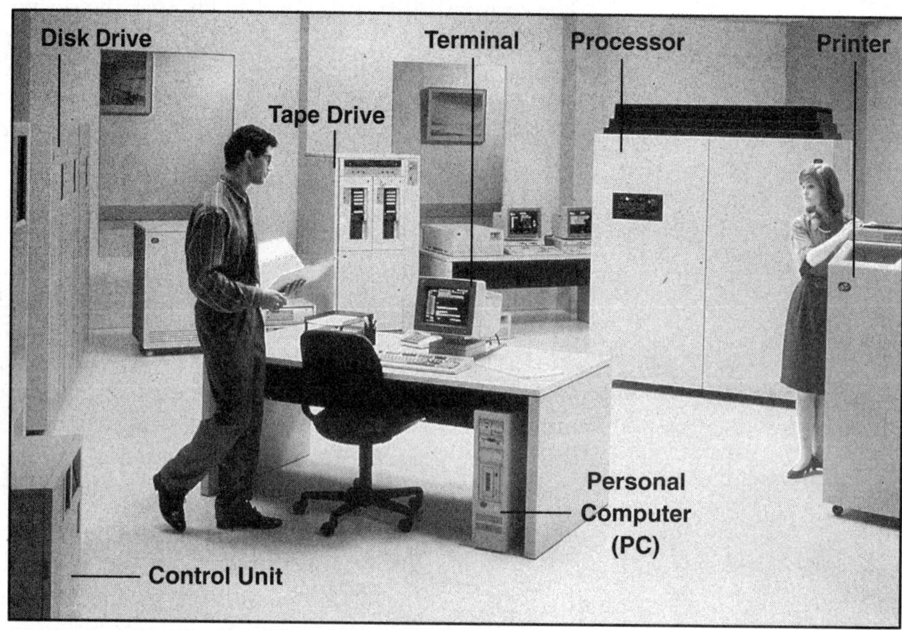

Source: Courtesy of IBM.

disk drive. After processing the data, accounting reports can be prepared on an output device, such as a printer. In a microcomputer system, the day's transactions can be input through the keyboard and monitor onto a floppy disk or a hard disk. A daily transaction report then can be printed.

Figure 7-2. Microcomputer System

Source: Courtesy of IBM.

Software. In a manual system, someone actually records transactions in a journal, posts to a ledger, and then prepares a trial balance and financial statements. The computer performs these steps internally, following a set of instructions called a **program**. Programs are known collectively as **software**. Several programs are needed to instruct the computer to record and post transactions and to prepare financial statements. On a mainframe computer, these programs are written in languages the computer understands, such as COBOL, PL/1, or FORTRAN. Programs for microcomputers often are written in BASIC or PASCAL. In addition, many programs are available commercially to do specialized accounting tasks, such as LOTUS® 1-2-3 for financial analysis and spreadsheet applications; dBASE IV for organizing, storing, and retrieving large quantities of data; and general accounting systems for keeping records and preparing financial statements.

Personnel. The important personnel in a computer system are the systems analyst, the programmer, and the computer operator. The **systems analyst** designs the system on the basis of information needs, the **programmer** writes instructions for the computer, and the **computer operator** runs the computer. In large organizations, the accountant works closely with the systems analyst to make sure that the accounting data processing system is designed in accordance with the informational needs of the company. In smaller organizations that use a microcomputer system and that do not have computer experts for all these positions, the company's owners or management often work with a certified public accountant to purchase and install commercial software that meets the company's needs.

Mainframe Accounting Systems

The parts of a computerized data processing system can be put together in many different ways, and companies use their computers for many purposes besides accounting. The company's overall goal is to meet all its computing needs at the lowest cost. For the accounting system, it is important to coordinate all tasks in order to provide management with the reports and statements it needs on a timely basis.

Most mainframe computer systems take two approaches in processing business transactions and preparing financial reports. The first is called **batch processing**, in which processing tasks are scheduled in logical order. For example, transactions for a day or a week are processed together (as a batch). Later, a separate program is run to update the ledger and prepare the trial balance and financial statements. The processing of employees' time cards, preparation of the company's payroll, and printing of paychecks on a specific day each week or month are examples of batch processing.

Most mainframe systems also allow **on-line processing**, in which remote terminals are linked to the central processor, and files are updated virtually as soon as transactions occur. For example, at the time it takes place, a credit sale can be entered into a remote terminal that records and posts the transaction in the appropriate accounts and updates the trial balance.

Microcomputer Accounting Systems

Most small businesses purchase commercial accounting systems that already are programmed to perform accounting functions. Most of these systems rely on a variation of batch processing, in which a part of the software performs each major task of the accounting system. Although the configuration of such systems, often called **general ledger software**, differs from system to system, a

Figure 7-3. Microcomputer Accounting System

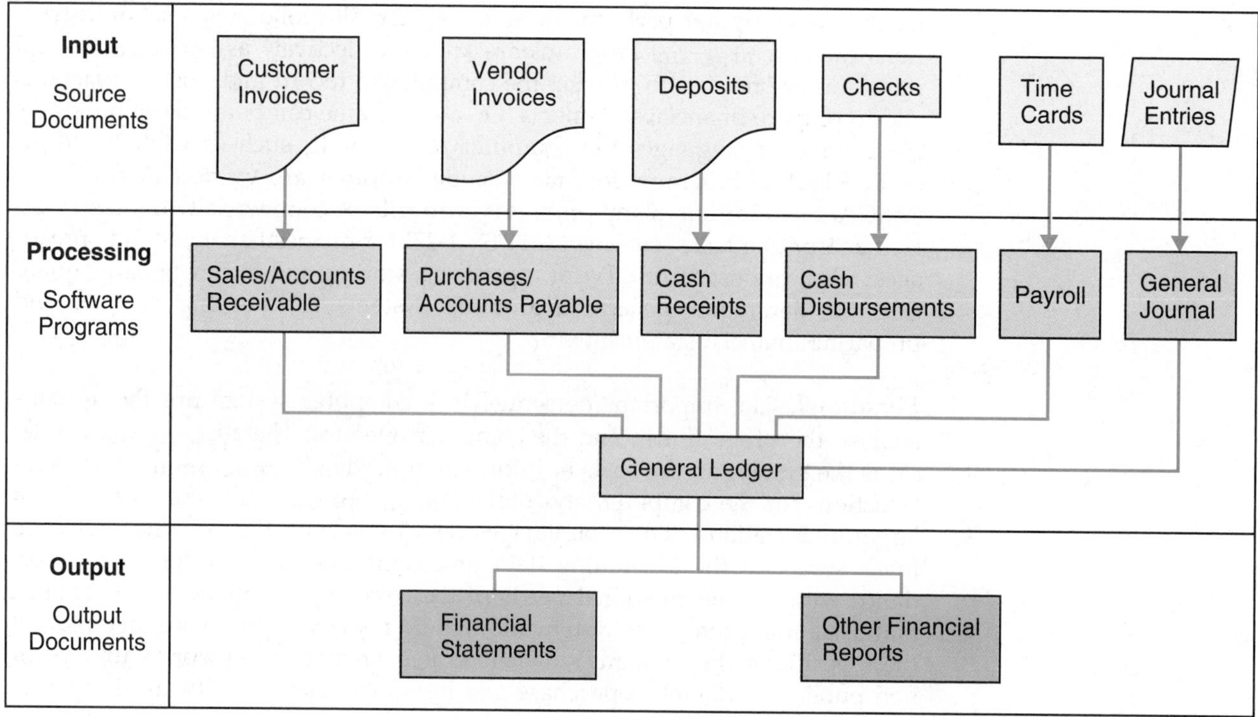

typical configuration appears in Figure 7-3. Notice that there is a software program for each of the major accounting functions—sales/accounts receivable, purchases/accounts payable, cash receipts, cash disbursements, payroll, and general journal. If these software packages interact with one another, they are called *integrated programs.*

The transactions for these functions are based on **source documents**, the written evidence that supports each transaction. Source documents verify the fact that a transaction occurred and provide the details of the transaction. For example, a customer's invoice should support each sale on account, and a vendor's invoice should support each purchase. Even though the transactions are recorded by the computer in a file (on floppy disks or hard disks), the documents should be kept so that they can be examined at a later date if a question arises about the accuracy of the accounting records. The source documents for each function are gathered together in a batch and processed in order with the appropriate program. The scheduling of these programs depends on the function. For example, cash transactions and sales usually are processed daily; payroll may be processed only once every week or two.

After the transactions are processed, a procedure is followed to post to and update the ledgers and to prepare the trial balance. Finally, the financial statements and other accounting reports are prepared.

The batch processing systems used in microcomputer accounting systems very closely resemble the manual accounting systems using special-purpose journals that have been in existence for decades. In fact, their basic goal is to computerize existing accounting systems to make them less time consuming and more accurate and dependable. However, it is important for you to understand, in principle, just what the computer is accomplishing. Knowledge of the underlying accounting process helps ensure that the accounting records are accurate, helps protect the assets of the business, and helps analyze the company's financial statements.

Manual Data Processing: Journals and Procedures

OBJECTIVE 3
Explain the objectives and uses of special-purpose journals

The system of accounting described so far in this book, and presented in Figure 7-4, is a form of **manual data processing**. It has been a useful way to present basic accounting theory and practice in small businesses. Data input is done manually, by entering each transaction from a source document to the general journal (input device in a computer system). Then, each debit and credit is posted to the correct ledger account (processor and memory device). A work sheet (output device) is used as a tool in preparing the financial statements (output devices) that are distributed to users. This system, although useful for explaining the basic concepts of accounting, is limited in practice to only the smallest of companies.

Companies that are faced with larger numbers of transactions, perhaps hundreds or thousands every week or every day, must have a more efficient and economical way of recording transactions in the journal and posting entries to the ledger. The easiest approach is to group the company's typical transactions into common categories and use an input device, called a **special-purpose journal**, for each category. The objectives of special-purpose journals are efficiency, economy, and control. In addition, although manual special-purpose journals are used by companies that have not yet computerized their systems, the concepts underlying special-purpose journals also underlie the programs that drive computerized accounting systems.

Most business transactions—90 to 95 percent—fall into one of four categories. Each kind of transaction can be recorded in a special-purpose journal:

Transaction	Special-Purpose Journal	Posting Abbreviation
Sale of merchandise on credit	Sales journal	S
Purchase of merchandise on credit	Purchases journal	P
Receipt of cash	Cash receipts journal	CR
Disbursement of cash	Cash payments journal	CP

Notice that these special-purpose journals correspond to the accounting functions shown in the microcomputer system in Figure 7-3, except for payroll, which we discuss in the chapter on current liabilities.

Figure 7-4. Steps and Devices in a Manual Accounting System

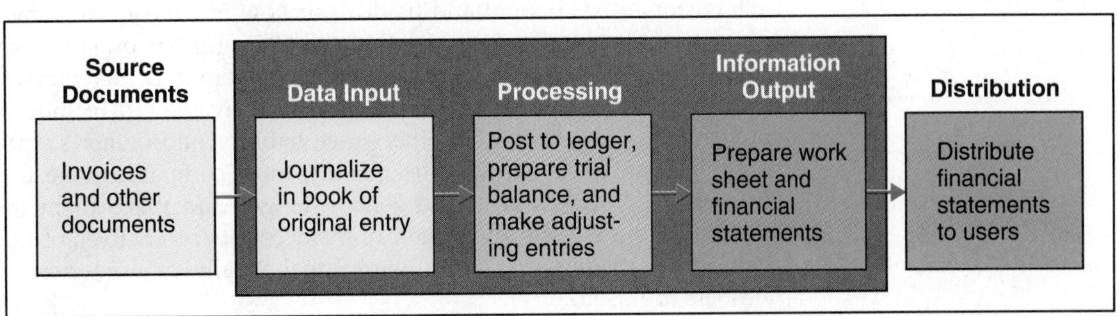

The general journal is used to record transactions that do not fall into any of the special categories. For example, purchase returns, sales returns, and adjusting and closing entries are recorded in the general journal. (When transactions are posted from the general journal to the ledger accounts, the posting abbreviation used is **J**.)

Using special-purpose journals greatly reduces the work involved in entering and posting transactions. For example, instead of posting every debit and credit for each transaction, in most cases only column totals—the sum of many transactions—are posted. In addition, labor can be divided, each journal assigned to a different employee. This division of labor is important in establishing good internal control.

Sales Journal

OBJECTIVE 4
Construct and use the following types of special-purpose journals: sales journal, purchases journal, cash receipts journal, cash payments journal, and others as needed

Special-purpose journals are designed to record particular kinds of transactions. All transactions in a special-purpose journal result in debits and credits to the same accounts. The **sales journal**, for example, is designed to handle all credit sales, and only credit sales. Cash sales are recorded in the cash receipts journal.

Exhibit 7-1 illustrates a page from a typical sales journal. Six sales transactions involving five customers are recorded in this sales journal. As each sale takes place, several copies of the sales invoice are made. The seller's accounting department uses one copy to make the entry in the sales journal. The date, the customer's name, the invoice number, the amount of the sale, and sometimes the credit terms are copied from the invoice. These data correspond to the columns of the sales journal.

Notice how the sales journal saves time:

1. Only one line is needed to record each transaction. Each entry consists of a debit to each customer in Accounts Receivable. The corresponding credit to Sales is understood.
2. The account names do not have to be written out because each entry automatically is debited to Accounts Receivable and credited to Sales.
3. No explanations are necessary because the function of the special-purpose journal is to record just one type of transaction. Only credit sales are recorded in the sales journal. Sales for cash are recorded in the cash receipts journal.
4. Only one amount—the total credit sales for the month—has to be posted. It is posted twice: once as a debit to Accounts Receivable and once as a credit to Sales. You can see the time this saves in Exhibit 7-1, with just six transactions. Imagine the time saved when there are hundreds of sales transactions.

OBJECTIVE 5
Explain the purposes and relationships of controlling accounts and subsidiary ledgers

Controlling Accounts and Subsidiary Ledgers. Every entry in the sales journal represents a debit to a customer's account in Accounts Receivable. In previous chapters, we've posted all of these transactions to Accounts Receivable. However, a single entry in Accounts Receivable does not tell how much each customer has bought and paid for or how much each customer still owes. In practice, almost all companies that sell to customers on credit keep an individual accounts receivable record for each customer. If the company has 6,000 credit customers, there are 6,000 accounts receivable. To include all these accounts in the ledger with the other asset, liability, and owner's equity accounts would make it very bulky. Consequently, most companies take the individual customers' accounts out of the general ledger and place them in a separate ledger, called a **subsidiary ledger**. In the accounts receivable subsidiary ledger, customers' accounts are filed either alphabetically or numerically (if account numbers are used).

Exhibit 7-1. Sales Journal and Related Ledger Accounts

Sales Journal Page 1

Date		Account Debited	Invoice Number	Post. Ref.	Amount (Debit / Credit Accounts Receivable / Sales)
July	1	Peter Clark	721	✓	750
	5	Georgetta Jones	722	✓	500
	8	Eugene Cumberland	723	✓	335
	12	Maxwell Gertz	724	✓	1,165
	18	Peter Clark	725	✓	1,225
	25	Michael Powers	726	✓	975
					4,950
					(114/411)

Post total at **end of month.**

Accounts Receivable 114

Date		Post. Ref.	Debit	Credit	Balance Debit	Balance Credit
July	31	S1	4,950		4,950	

Sales 411

Date		Post. Ref.	Debit	Credit	Balance Debit	Balance Credit
July	31	S1		4,950		4,950

When a company puts its individual customers' accounts in an accounts receivable subsidiary ledger, it still must maintain an Accounts Receivable account in the general ledger. The Accounts Receivable account "controls" the subsidiary ledger and is called a **controlling account**, or *control account*. It controls in the sense that the total of the individual account balances in the subsidiary ledger must equal the balance in the controlling account. The balance of this account on the balance sheet date appears as Accounts Receivable. In transactions that involve accounts receivable, such as credit sales, entries must be posted to the individual customers' accounts every day. Postings to the controlling account in the general ledger are made at least once a month. If a wrong amount has been posted, the sum of all the customers' account balances in the subsidiary accounts receivable ledger will not equal the balance of the Accounts Receivable controlling account in the general ledger. When these amounts do not match, the accountant knows there is an error to find and correct.

Exhibit 7-2 shows how controlling accounts work. The single controlling account in the general ledger summarizes all the individual accounts in the subsidiary ledger. Because the individual accounts are recorded daily and the controlling account is posted monthly, the total of the individual accounts in the accounts receivable ledger equals the controlling account only after the monthly posting. The monthly trial balance is prepared using only the general ledger accounts.

Most companies use an accounts payable subsidiary ledger as well. It is also possible to use a subsidiary ledger for almost any account in the general ledger

Exhibit 7-2. Relationship of Sales Journal, General Ledger, and Accounts Receivable Subsidiary Ledger and the Posting Procedure

Sales Journal — Page 1

Date		Account Debited	Invoice Number	Post. Ref.	Amount (Debit / Credit Accounts Receivable / Sales)
July	1	Peter Clark	721	✓	750
	5	Georgetta Jones	722	✓	500
	8	Eugene Cumberland	723	✓	335
	12	Maxwell Gertz	724	✓	1,165
	18	Peter Clark	725	✓	1,225
	25	Michael Powers	726	✓	975
					4,950
					(114/411)

Post individual amounts **daily** to subsidiary ledger accounts.

Post total at **end of month** to general ledger accounts.

Accounts Receivable Subs. Ledger

Peter Clark

Date		Post. Ref.	Debit	Credit	Balance
July	1	S1	750		750
	18	S1	1,225		1,975

Eugene Cumberland

Date		Post. Ref.	Debit	Credit	Balance
July	8	S1	335		335

Continue posting to Maxwell Gertz, Georgetta Jones, and Michael Powers.

General Ledger

Accounts Receivable — 114

Date		Post. Ref.	Debit	Credit	Balance Debit	Balance Credit
July	31	S1	4,950		4,950	

Sales — 411

Date		Post. Ref.	Debit	Credit	Balance Debit	Balance Credit
July	31	S1		4,950		4,950

for which management wants a specific account for individual items, such as Merchandise Inventory; Notes Receivable; Temporary Investments; Property, Plant, and Equipment; and Notes Payable.

Summary of the Sales Journal Procedure. Exhibit 7-2 illustrates the procedure for using a sales journal:

1. Enter each sales invoice in the sales journal on a single line. Record the date, the customer's name, the invoice number, and the amount. No column is needed for the terms if the terms on all sales are the same.

2. At the end of each day, post each individual sale to the customer's account in the accounts receivable ledger. As each sale is posted, place a checkmark (or customer account number, if used) in the Post. Ref. (posting reference) column of the sales journal to indicate that it has been posted. In the Post. Ref. column of each customer's account, place an **S** and the sales journal page number (**S1** means Sales Journal—Page 1) to indicate the source of the entry.
3. At the end of the month, sum the Amount column in the sales journal to determine the total credit sales, and post the total to the general ledger accounts (debit Accounts Receivable and credit Sales). Place the numbers of the accounts debited and credited beneath the total in the sales journal to indicate that this step has been completed. In the general ledger, indicate the source of the entry in the Post. Ref. column of each account.
4. Verify the accuracy of the posting by adding the account balances of the accounts receivable ledger and by matching the total with the Accounts Receivable controlling account balance in the general ledger. You can do this by listing the accounts in a schedule of accounts receivable, like the one shown in Exhibit 7-3 in the order the accounts are maintained. This step is performed after collections on account in the cash receipts journal and sales returns and allowances from the general journal have been posted.

Sales Taxes. Other columns, such as a column for credit terms, can be added to the sales journal. The nature of the company's business determines whether they are needed.

Many cities and states require retailers to collect a sales tax from their customers and periodically remit the total collected to the city or state. In this case, an additional column is needed in the sales journal to record the credit to Sales Taxes Payable on credit sales. The form of the entry is shown in Exhibit 7-4. The procedure for posting to the ledger is exactly the same as described above except that the total of the Sales Taxes Payable column must be posted as a credit to the Sales Taxes Payable account at the end of the month.

Most companies also make cash sales. Cash sales usually are recorded in a column of the cash receipts journal, as discussed later in the chapter.

Purchases Journal

The **purchases journal** is used to record purchases on credit. It can take the form of either a single-column journal or a multicolumn journal. In the single-column journal, shown in Exhibit 7-5, only credit purchases of merchandise for resale to customers are recorded. This kind of transaction is recorded with a debit to Purchases and a credit to Accounts Payable. When the single-column

Exhibit 7-3. Schedule of Accounts Receivable

Mitchell's Used Car Sales Schedule of Accounts Receivable July 31, 19xx	
Peter Clark	$ 625
Eugene Cumberland	335
Maxwell Gertz	1,130
Georgetta Jones	—
Michael Powers	975
Total Accounts Receivable	$3,065

Exhibit 7-4. Section of a Sales Journal with a Column for Sales Taxes

Sales Journal							Page 7
					Debit	Credits	
Date		Account Debited	Invoice Number	Post. Ref.	Accounts Receivable	Sales Taxes Payable	Sales
Sept.	1	Ralph P. Hake	727	✓	206	6	200

purchases journal is used, credit purchases of things other than merchandise are recorded in the general journal. Cash purchases are never recorded in the purchases journal; they are recorded in the cash payments journal, which we explain later.

Like Accounts Receivable, the Accounts Payable account in the general ledger is used by most companies as a controlling account. So that the company knows how much it owes each supplier, it keeps a separate account for each supplier in an accounts payable subsidiary ledger. The process described above for using the accounts receivable subsidiary ledger and general ledger control account applies also to the accounts payable subsidiary ledger and general ledger control account. Thus, the total of the separate accounts in the accounts payable subsidiary ledger should equal the balance of the Accounts Payable controlling account in the general ledger. Here, too, the monthly total of the credit purchases posted to the individual accounts each day must equal the total credit purchases posted to the controlling account each month.

The procedure for using the purchases journal is much like that for using the sales journal:

1. Enter each purchase invoice in the purchases journal on a single line. Record the date, the supplier's name, the invoice date, the terms (if given), and the amount. It is not necessary to record the shipping terms in the terms column because they do not affect the payment date.
2. At the end of each day, post each individual purchase to the supplier's account in the accounts payable subsidiary ledger. As each purchase is posted, place a checkmark in the Post. Ref. column of the purchases journal to show that it has been posted. Also place a **P** and the page number in the purchases journal (**P1** stands for Purchases Journal—Page 1) in the Post. Ref. column of each supplier's account to show the source of the entry.
3. At the end of the month, sum the Amount column, and post the total to the general ledger accounts (a debit to Purchases and a credit to Accounts Payable). Place the numbers of the accounts debited and credited beneath the totals in the purchases journal to show that this step has been carried out.
4. Check the accuracy of the posting by adding the balances of the accounts payable subsidiary ledger accounts and matching the total with the balance of the Accounts Payable controlling account in the general ledger. This step can be carried out by preparing a schedule of accounts payable, similar to the schedule of accounts receivable.

The single-column purchases journal can be expanded to record credit purchases of things other than merchandise by adding a separate debit column for other accounts that are used often. For example, the multicolumn purchases journal in Exhibit 7-6 has columns for Freight In, Store Supplies, Office Supplies, and Other Accounts. Here, the total credits to Accounts Payable ($9,637)

Exhibit 7-5. Relationship of Single-Column Purchases Journal to the General Ledger and the Accounts Payable Subsidiary Ledger

Purchases Journal Page 1

Date		Account Credited	Date of Invoice	Terms	Post. Ref.	Amount (Debit / Credit Purchases / Accounts Payable)
July	1	Jones Chevrolet	7/1	2/10, n/30	✓	2,500
	2	Marshall Ford	7/2	2/15, n/30	✓	300
	3	Dealer Sales	7/3	n/30	✓	700
	12	Thomas Auto	7/11	n/30	✓	1,400
	17	Dealer Sales	7/17	2/10, n/30	✓	3,200
	19	Thomas Auto	7/17	n/30	✓	1,100
						9,200
						(511/212)

Post individual amounts **daily.**

Post total at **end of month.**

Accounts Payable Subs. Ledger

Dealer Sales

Date		Post. Ref.	Debit	Credit	Balance
July	3	P1		700	700
	17	P1		3,200	3,900

Jones Chevrolet

Date		Post. Ref.	Debit	Credit	Balance
July	1	P1		2,500	2,500

Continue posting to Marshall Ford and Thomas Auto.

General Ledger

Accounts Payable 212

Date		Post. Ref.	Debit	Credit	Balance Debit	Balance Credit
July	31	P1		9,200		9,200

Purchases 511

Date		Post. Ref.	Debit	Credit	Balance Debit	Balance Credit
July	31	P1	9,200		9,200	

equal the total debits to Purchases, Freight In, Store Supplies, Office Supplies, and Parts ($9,200 + $50 + $145 + $42 + $200). Again, the individual transactions in the Accounts Payable column are posted regularly to the accounts payable subsidiary ledger, and the totals of each column (except Other Accounts) in the journal are posted monthly to the correct general ledger accounts.

Cash Receipts Journal

All transactions involving receipts of cash are recorded in the **cash receipts journal**. Examples of these transactions are cash from cash sales, cash from

Exhibit 7-6. A Multicolumn Purchases Journal

Purchases Journal													Page 1
					Credit	Debits							
										Other Accounts			
Date		Account Credited	Date of Invoice	Terms	Post. Ref.	Accounts Payable	Purchases	Freight In	Store Supplies	Office Supplies	Account	Post. Ref.	Amount
July	2	Jones Chevrolet	7/1	2/10, n/30	✓	2,500	2,500						
	2	Marshall Ford	7/2	2/15, n/30	✓	300	300						
	2	Shelby Car Delivery	7/2	n/30	✓	50		50					
	3	Dealer Sales	7/3	n/30	✓	700	700						
	12	Thomas Auto	7/11	n/30	✓	1,400	1,400						
	17	Dealer Sales	7/17	2/10, n/30	✓	3,200	3,200						
	19	Thomas Auto	7/17	n/30	✓	1,100	1,100						
	25	Osborne Supply	7/21	n/10	✓	187			145	42			
	28	Auto Supply	7/28	n/10	✓	200					Parts	120	200
						9,637	9,200	50	145	42			200
						(212)	(511)	(514)	(132)	(133)			(✓)

credit customers in payment of their accounts, and cash from other sources. The cash receipts journal must have several columns because, although all cash receipts are alike in that they require a debit to Cash, they are different in that they require a variety of credit entries. You should be alert, then, to several important differences between the cash receipts journal and the other journals we have described. Among these differences are an Other Accounts column, the use of account numbers in the Post. Ref. column, and the daily posting of the credits to other accounts.

The cash receipts journal illustrated in Exhibit 7-7 is based on the following selected transactions for July:

July 1 Henry Mitchell invested $20,000 in a used-car business.
5 Sold a used car for $1,200 cash.
8 Collected $500 less a 2 percent sales discount from Georgetta Jones.
13 Sold a used car for $1,400 cash.
16 Collected $750 from Peter Clark.
19 Sold a used car for $1,000 cash.
20 Sold some equipment no longer used in the business for $500 cash. The carrying value of the equipment was $500.
24 Signed a note at the bank for a loan of $5,000.
26 Sold a used car for $1,600 cash.
28 Collected partial payment of $600 less a 2 percent sales discount from Peter Clark.

The cash receipts journal shown in Exhibit 7-7 has three debit columns and three credit columns. The three debit columns are as follows:

1. *Cash* Each entry must have an amount in this column because each transaction must be a receipt of cash.
2. *Sales Discounts* This company allows a 2 percent discount for prompt payment. Therefore, it is useful to have a column for sales discounts. Notice that in the transactions of July 8 and 28, the debits to Cash and Sales Discounts equal the credits to Accounts Receivable.
3. *Other Accounts* The Other Accounts column (sometimes called *Sundry Accounts*) is used for transactions that involve both a debit to Cash and a debit to some other account besides Sales Discounts.

Exhibit 7-7. Relationship of the Cash Receipts Journal to the General Ledger and the Accounts Receivable Subsidiary Ledger

Cash Receipts Journal — Page 1

Date		Account Debited / Credited	Post. Ref.	Debits: Cash	Debits: Sales Discounts	Debits: Other Accounts	Credits: Accounts Receivable	Credits: Sales	Credits: Other Accounts
July	1	Henry Mitchell, Capital	311	20,000					20,000
	5	Sales		1,200				1,200	
	8	Georgetta Jones	✓	490	10		500		
	13	Sales		1,400				1,400	
	16	Peter Clark	✓	750			750		
	19	Sales		1,000				1,000	
	20	Equipment	151	500					500
	24	Notes Payable	213	5,000					5,000
	26	Sales		1,600				1,600	
	28	Peter Clark	✓	588	12		600		
				32,528	22		1,850	5,200	25,500
				(111)	(412)		(114)	(411)	(✓)

Post individual amounts in Accounts Receivable Ledger columns **daily**.

Post totals at **end of month**.

Total not posted.

Post individual amounts in Other Accounts column **daily**.

General Ledger

Cash — 111

Date		Post. Ref.	Debit	Credit	Balance: Debit	Balance: Credit
July	31	CR1	32,528		32,528	

Accounts Receivable — 114

Date		Post. Ref.	Debit	Credit	Balance: Debit	Balance: Credit
July	31	S1	4,950		4,950	
	31	CR1		1,850	3,100	

Equipment — 151

Date		Post. Ref.	Debit	Credit	Balance: Debit	Balance: Credit
Bal.					500	
July	20	CR1		500	—	

Accounts Receivable Subsidiary Ledger

Peter Clark

Date		Post. Ref.	Debit	Credit	Balance
July	1	S1	750		750
	16	CR1		750	—
	18	S1	1,225		1,225
	28	CR1		600	625

Georgetta Jones

Date		Post. Ref.	Debit	Credit	Balance
July	5	S1	500		500
	8	CR1		500	—

Continue posting to Notes Payable and Henry Mitchell, Capital.

Continue posting to Sales and Sales Discounts.

These are the credit columns:

1. *Accounts Receivable* This column is used to record collections on account from customers. The customer's name is written in the Account Debited/Credited column so that the payment can be entered in the corresponding account in the accounts receivable subsidiary ledger. Postings to the individual accounts receivable accounts usually are done daily so that each customer's account balance is up to date.
2. *Sales* This column is used to record all cash sales during the month. Retail firms that use cash registers would make an entry at the end of each day for the total sales from each cash register for that day. The debit, of course, is in the Cash debit column.
3. *Other Accounts* This column is used for the credit portion of any entry that is neither a cash collection from accounts receivable nor a cash sale. The name of the account to be credited is indicated in the Account Debited/Credited column. For example, the transactions of July 1, 20, and 24 involve credits to accounts other than Accounts Receivable or Sales. These individual postings should be done daily (or weekly if there are just a few of them). If a company finds that it consistently is crediting a certain account in the Other Accounts column, it can add another credit column to the cash receipts journal for that particular account.

The procedure for posting the cash receipts journal, shown in Exhibit 7-7, is as follows:

1. Post the Accounts Receivable column daily to each individual account in the accounts receivable subsidiary ledger. The amount credited to the customer's account is the same as that credited to Accounts Receivable. A checkmark in the Post. Ref. column of the cash receipts journal indicates that the amount has been posted, and a **CR1** (Cash Receipts Journal—Page 1) in the Post. Ref. column of each ledger account indicates the source of the entry.
2. Post the debits/credits in the Other Accounts columns daily, or at convenient short intervals during the month, to the general ledger accounts. Write the account number in the Post. Ref. column of the cash receipts journal as the individual items are posted to indicate that the posting has been done, and write **CR1** in the Post. Ref. column of each ledger account to indicate the source of the entry.
3. At the end of the month, total the columns in the cash receipts journal. The sum of the Debits column totals must equal the sum of the Credits column totals:

Debits Column Totals		**Credits Column Totals**	
Cash	$32,528	Accounts Receivable	$ 1,850
Sales Discounts	22	Sales	5,200
Other Accounts	0	Other Accounts	25,500
Total Debits	$32,550	Total Credits	$32,550

This step is called *crossfooting*—a procedure we encountered earlier.
4. Post the Debits column totals as follows:
   a. *Cash* Posted as a debit to the Cash account.
   b. *Sales Discounts* Posted as a debit to the Sales Discounts account.
5. Post the Credits column totals as follows:
   a. *Accounts Receivable* Posted as a credit to the Accounts Receivable controlling account.
   b. *Sales* Posted as a credit to the Sales account.

6. Write the account numbers below each column in the cash receipts journal as they are posted to indicate that this step has been completed. A **CR1** is written in the Post. Ref. column of each account to indicate the source of the entry.
7. Notice that the Other Accounts column totals are not posted by total because each entry is posted separately when the transaction occurs. The individual accounts are posted in step **2**. Place a checkmark at the bottom of each column to show that postings in that column have been made and that the total is not posted.

Cash Payments Journal

All transactions involving payments of cash are recorded in the **cash payments journal** (also called the *cash disbursements journal*). Examples of these transactions are cash purchases and payments of obligations resulting from earlier purchases on credit. The form of the cash payments journal is much like that of the cash receipts journal.

The cash payments journal illustrated in Exhibit 7-8 is based on the following selected transactions of Mitchell's Used Car Sales in July:

July 2 Issued check no. 101 for merchandise (a used car) from Sondra Tidmore, $400.
6 Issued check no. 102 for newspaper advertising in the *Daily Journal*, $200.
8 Issued check no. 103 for one month's land and building rent to Siviglia Agency, $250.
11 Issued check no. 104 to Jones Chevrolet for July 1 invoice (recorded in the purchases journal in Exhibit 7-5), $2,500 less 2 percent purchases discount.
16 Issued check no. 105 to Charles Kuntz, a salesperson, for his salary, $600.
17 Issued check no. 106 to Marshall Ford for July 2 invoice (recorded in the purchases journal in Exhibit 7-5), $300 less 2 percent purchases discount.
24 Issued check no. 107 to Grabow & Company for two-year insurance policy, $480.
27 Issued check no. 108 to Dealer Sales for July 17 invoice (recorded in the purchases journal in Exhibit 7-5), $3,200 less 2 percent purchases discount.
30 Purchased office equipment for $400 and service equipment for $500 from A&B Equipment Company. Issued check no. 109 for the total amount.
31 Purchased land for $15,000 from Burns Real Estate. Issued check no. 110 for $5,000 and note payable for $10,000.

The cash payments journal shown in Exhibit 7-8 has three credit columns and two debit columns. The credit columns are as follows:

1. *Cash* Each entry must have an amount in this column because each transaction must involve a payment of cash.
2. *Purchases Discounts* When purchases discounts are taken, they are recorded in this column.
3. *Other Accounts* This column is used to record credits to accounts other than Cash or Purchases Discounts. Notice that the July 31 transaction shows a purchase of Land for $15,000, with a check for $5,000 and a note payable for $10,000.

The debit columns for the cash payments journal are as follows:

1. *Accounts Payable* This column is used to record payments to suppliers that have extended credit to the company. Each supplier's name is written in the Payee

Exhibit 7-8. Relationship of the Cash Payments Journal to the General Ledger and the Accounts Payable Subsidiary Ledger

Cash Payments Journal

Page 1

Date		Ck. No.	Payee	Account Credited / Debited	Post. Ref.	Credits: Cash	Credits: Purchases Discounts	Credits: Other Accounts	Debits: Accounts Payable	Debits: Other Accounts
July	2	101	Sondra Tidmore	Purchases	511	400				400
	6	102	Daily Journal	Advertising Expense	612	200				200
	8	103	Siviglia Agency	Rent Expense	631	250				250
	11	104	Jones Chevrolet		✓	2,450	50		2,500	
	16	105	Charles Kuntz	Salary Expense	611	600				600
	17	106	Marshall Ford		✓	294	6		300	
	24	107	Grabow & Company	Prepaid Insurance	119	480				480
	27	108	Dealer Sales		✓	3,136	64		3,200	
	30	109	A&B Equipment Company	Office Equipment	144	900				400
				Service Equipment	146					500
	31	110	Burns Real Estate	Notes Payable	213	5,000		10,000		
				Land	141					15,000
						13,710	120	10,000	6,000	17,830
						(111)	(512)	(✓)	(212)	(✓)

Post individual amounts in Other Accounts column **daily.**

Post individual amounts in Accounts Payable column **daily.**

Post totals at **end of month.**

Totals not posted.

General Ledger

Cash 111

Date		Post. Ref.	Debit	Credit	Balance Debit	Balance Credit
July	31	CR1	32,528		32,528	
	31	CP1		13,710	18,818	

Prepaid Insurance 119

Date		Post. Ref.	Debit	Credit	Balance Debit	Balance Credit
July	24	CP1	480		480	

Continue posting to Land, Office Equipment, Service Equipment, Notes Payable, Purchases, Salary Expense, Advertising Expense, and Rent Expense.

Continue posting to Purchases Discounts and Accounts Payable.

Accounts Payable Subsidiary Ledger

Jones Chevrolet

Date		Post. Ref.	Debit	Credit	Balance
July	1	P1		2,500	2,500
	11	CP1	2,500		—

Marshall Ford

Date		Post. Ref.	Debit	Credit	Balance
July	2	P1		300	300
	17	CP1	300		—

Dealer Sales

Date		Post. Ref.	Debit	Credit	Balance
July	3	P1		700	700
	17	P1		3,200	3,900
	27	CP1	3,200		700

column so that the payment can be entered in its account in the accounts payable subsidiary ledger.

2. *Other Accounts* Cash can be expended for many reasons. Thus, an Other Accounts or Sundry Accounts column is needed in the cash payments journal. The title of the account to be debited is written in the Account Credited/Debited column, and the amount is entered in the Other Accounts debit column. If a company finds that a particular account appears often in the Other Accounts column, it can add another debit column to the cash payments journal.

The procedure for posting the cash payments journal, shown in Exhibit 7-8, is as follows:

1. Post the Accounts Payable column daily to each individual account in the accounts payable subsidiary ledger. Place a checkmark in the Post. Ref. column of the cash payments journal to indicate that the posting has been made.
2. Post the debits/credits in the Other Accounts debit/credit columns to the general ledger daily or at convenient short intervals during the month. Write the account number in the Post. Ref. column of the cash payments journal as the individual items are posted to indicate that the posting has been completed and **CP1** (Cash Payments Journal—Page 1) in the Post. Ref. column of each ledger account.
3. At the end of the month, the columns are footed and crossfooted. That is, the sum of the Credits column totals must equal the sum of the Debits column totals, as follows:

Credits Column Totals		**Debits Column Totals**	
Cash	$13,710	Accounts Payable	$ 6,000
Purchases Discounts	120	Other Accounts	17,830
Other Accounts	10,000	Total Debits	$23,830
Total Credits	$23,830		

4. Post the column totals for Cash, Purchases Discounts, and Accounts Payable at the end of the month to their respective accounts in the general ledger. Write the account number below each column in the cash payments journal as it is posted to indicate that this step has been completed and a CP1 in the Post. Ref. column of each ledger account. Place a checkmark under the total of each Other Accounts column in the cash payments journal to indicate that the postings in the column have been made and that the total is not posted.

General Journal

Transactions that do not involve sales, purchases, cash receipts, or cash payments should be recorded in the general journal. Usually, there are only a few of these transactions. The two examples that follow require entries that do not fit in a special-purpose journal: a return of merchandise and an allowance from a supplier for credit. Adjusting and closing entries also are recorded in the general journal.

July 25 Returned one of the two used cars purchased on credit from Thomas Auto on July 12, $700 credit.

26 Agreed to give Maxwell Gertz a $35 allowance on his account because a tire blew out on the car he purchased.

These entries are shown in Exhibit 7-9. Notice that the entries include a debit or a credit to a controlling account (Accounts Payable or Accounts Receivable).

Exhibit 7-9. Transactions Recorded in the General Journal

General Journal					Page 1
Date		Description	Post. Ref.	Debit	Credit
July	25	Accounts Payable, Thomas Auto	212/✓	700	
		Purchases Returns and Allowances	513		700
		Returned used car for credit; invoice date: 7/12			
	26	Sales Returns and Allowances	413	35	
		Accounts Receivable, Maxwell Gertz	114/✓		35
		Allowance for faulty tire			

The name of the customer or supplier also is given here. When this kind of debit or credit is made to a controlling account in the general journal, the entry must be posted twice: once in the controlling account and once in the individual account in the subsidiary ledger. This procedure keeps the subsidiary ledger equal to the controlling account. Notice that the July 26 transaction is posted by a debit to Sales Returns and Allowances in the general ledger (shown by the account number 413), by a credit to the Accounts Receivable controlling account in the general ledger (account number 114), and by a credit to the Maxwell Gertz account in the accounts receivable subsidiary ledger (checkmark).

The Flexibility of Special-Purpose Journals

Special-purpose journals reduce and simplify the work in accounting and allow for the division of labor. These journals should be designed to fit the business in which they are used. As noted earlier, if certain accounts show up often in the Other Accounts column of a journal, it is a good idea to add a column for those accounts when a new page of a special-purpose journal is prepared.

Also, if certain transactions appear repeatedly in the general journal, it is a good idea to set up a new special-purpose journal. For example, if Mitchell's Used Car Sales finds that it often gives allowances to customers, it may want to set up a sales returns and allowances journal specifically for these transactions. Sometimes, a purchases returns and allowances journal is in order. In short, special-purpose journals should be designed to take care of the kinds of transactions a company commonly encounters.

Internal Control Structure: Basic Elements and Procedures

Accounting for merchandising companies focuses on buying and selling. These transactions involve asset accounts—Cash, Accounts Receivable, and Merchandise Inventory—that are vulnerable to theft and embezzlement. There are two reasons for this vulnerability. One is that cash and inventory are fairly easy to steal. The other is that these assets involve a large number of transactions—cash sales, receipts on account, payments for purchases, receipts and shipments of inventory, and so on. A merchandising company can have high losses of cash and inventory if it does not take steps to protect its assets. The best way to do this is to set up and maintain a good internal control structure.

Internal Control Defined

OBJECTIVE 6
Define internal control *and identify the three elements of the internal control structure, including seven examples of control procedures*

Internal control traditionally has been defined as all the policies and procedures management uses to protect the firm's assets and to ensure the accuracy and reliability of the accounting records. It also includes controls that deal with operating efficiency and adherence to management's policies. In other words, management wants not only to safeguard assets and have reliable records, but also to maintain an efficient operation that follows its policies. To this end, it establishes an **internal control structure** that consists of three elements: the control environment, the accounting system, and control procedures.[1]

The **control environment** reflects the overall attitude, awareness, and actions of the owners and management of the business. It includes management's philosophy and operating style, the company's organizational structure, methods of assigning authority and responsibility, and personnel policies and practices. Personnel should be qualified to handle responsibilities, which means that employees must be trained and informed. For example, the manager of a retail store should train employees to follow prescribed procedures for handling cash sales, credit card sales, and returns and refunds. It is clear that an accounting system, no matter how well designed, is only as good as the people who run it. The control environment also includes regular reviews for compliance with procedures. For example, large companies often have a staff of internal auditors who review the company's system of internal control to see that it is working properly and that procedures are being followed. In smaller businesses, owners and managers should conduct these reviews.

The **accounting system** consists of the methods and records established by management to identify, assemble, analyze, classify, record, and report a company's transactions, and to provide assurance that the objectives of internal control are being met.

Finally, management has many **control procedures** in its toolbox to safeguard the company's assets and to ensure the reliability of the accounting records:

1. **Authorization** All transactions and activities should be properly authorized by management. In a retail store, for example, some transactions, such as normal cash sales, are authorized routinely; others, such as issuing a refund, may require the manager's approval.
2. **Recording transactions** All transactions should be recorded to facilitate preparation of financial statements and to establish accountability for assets. In a retail store, for example, the cash register records sales, refunds, and other transactions internally on a paper tape or computer disk so that the cashier can be held responsible for the cash that has been received and the merchandise that has been removed during his or her shift.
3. **Documents and records** The design and use of adequate documents help ensure the proper recording of transactions. For example, to ensure that all transactions are recorded, invoices and other documents should be prenumbered and all numbers should be accounted for.

1. *Professional Standards* (New York: American Institute of Certified Public Accountants, June 1, 1989), Vol. 1, Sec. AU 319.06–.11.

4. **Limited access** Access to assets should be permitted only with management's authorization. For example, retail stores should use cash registers, and only the cashier responsible for the cash in the register should have access to it. Other employees should not be able to open the cash drawer if the cashier is not present. Likewise, warehouses and storerooms should be accessible only to authorized personnel. Access to accounting records, including company computers, also should be controlled.
5. **Periodic independent verification** The records should be checked against the assets by someone other than the persons responsible for the records and the assets. For example, at the end of each shift or day, the owner or store manager should count the cash in the cash drawer and compare the amount to the amounts recorded in the cash register on the tape or computer disk. Other examples of independent verification are the monthly bank reconciliation and periodic counts of physical inventory.
6. **Separation of duties** The organizational plan should separate functional responsibilities. Authorizing transactions, operating a department, handling assets, and keeping the records of assets for the department should not be the responsibility of one person. For example, in an appliance or stereo store, each employee should oversee only a single part of a transaction. A sales employee takes the order and writes out an invoice. Another employee receives the customer's money or credit card. Once the customer has a paid receipt, and only then, a third employee obtains the item from the warehouse and gives it to the customer. A person in the accounting department subsequently records the sales from the tape in the cash register, comparing them with the sales invoices and updating the inventory in the records. The separation of duties means that a mistake, honest or not, cannot be made without being seen by at least one other person.
7. **Sound personnel procedures** Sound practices should be followed in managing the people who carry out the duties and functions of each department. Among these practices are supervision, rotation of key people among different jobs, insistence that employees take vacations, and bonding of personnel who handle cash or inventories. **Bonding** means carefully checking an employee's background and insuring the company against any theft by that person. Bonding does not guarantee the prevention of theft, but it does prevent or reduce economic loss if theft occurs. These personnel procedures help ensure that employees know their jobs, are honest, and will find it difficult to carry out and conceal embezzlement over time.

Limitations of Internal Control

OBJECTIVE 7
Describe the inherent limitations of internal control

No system of internal control is without certain weaknesses. As long as people must carry out control procedures, the internal control system is vulnerable to human error. Errors may arise because of a misunderstanding, mistakes in judgment, carelessness, distraction, or fatigue. Separation of duties can be defeated through collusion—employees secretly agreeing to deceive the company. Also, procedures designed by management may be ineffective against employees' errors or dishonesty. Or, controls that may have been effective at first may later become ineffective because of changing conditions.[2] In some cases, the costs of establishing and maintaining elaborate systems may exceed the benefits. In a small business, for example, active involvement by the owner can be a practical substitute for certain separation of duties.

2. Ibid., Sec. AU 320.35.

Internal Control over Merchandising Transactions

OBJECTIVE 8
Apply control procedures to certain merchandising transactions

Sound internal control procedures are needed in all aspects of a business, but particularly when assets are involved. Assets are especially vulnerable when they enter or leave the business. When sales are made, for example, cash or other assets enter the business, and goods or services leave the business. Procedures must be set up to prevent theft during these transactions. Likewise, purchases of assets and payments of liabilities must be controlled. The majority of these transactions can be safeguarded by adequate purchasing and payroll systems. In addition, assets on hand, such as cash, investments, inventory, plant, and equipment, must be protected.

In this section, we apply internal control procedures to such merchandising transactions as cash sales, receipts, purchases, and cash payments. Internal control for other kinds of transactions is covered later in the book. As mentioned previously, similar procedures are applicable to service and manufacturing businesses.

When a system of internal control is applied effectively to merchandising transactions, it can achieve important goals for accounting as well as for general management. For example, here are two goals for accounting:

1. To prevent losses of cash or inventory from theft or fraud
2. To provide accurate records of merchandising transactions and account balances

And here are three broader goals for management:

1. To keep enough inventory on hand to sell to customers without overstocking
2. To keep enough cash on hand to pay for purchases in time to receive purchases discounts
3. To keep credit losses as low as possible by restricting credit sales to those customers who are likely to pay on time

One control to meet broad management goals is the cash budget, which projects future cash receipts and disbursements. By maintaining adequate cash balances, the company is able to take advantage of discounts on purchases, prepare to borrow money when necessary, and avoid the damaging effects of not being able to pay bills when they are due. On the other hand, if the company has excess cash at a particular time, it can be invested, earning interest until it is needed.

A more specific accounting control is the separation of duties involving the handling of cash. This separation means that theft without detection is extremely unlikely except through the collusion of two or more employees. The subdivision of duties is easier in large businesses than in small ones, where one person may have to carry out several duties. The effectiveness of internal control over cash varies, depending on the size and nature of the company. Most firms, however, should use the following procedures:

1. Separate the functions of authorization, recordkeeping, and the custodianship of cash.
2. Limit the number of people who have access to cash.
3. Specifically designate the people who are responsible for handling cash.
4. Use banking facilities as much as possible, and keep the amount of cash on hand to a minimum.
5. Bond all employees who have access to cash.

6. Physically protect cash on hand by using cash registers, cashiers' cages, and safes.
7. Have a person who does not handle or record cash make surprise audits of the cash on hand.
8. Record all cash receipts promptly.
9. Deposit all cash receipts promptly.
10. Make payments by check rather than by currency.
11. Have a person who does not authorize, handle, or record cash transactions reconcile the Cash account.

Notice that each of these procedures helps safeguard cash by making it more difficult for any one person to have access to cash and to steal or misuse it undetected.

Control of Cash Sales Receipts

Cash receipts for sales of goods and services can be received by mail or over the counter in the form of checks or currency. Whatever the source, cash should be recorded immediately on receipt. This generally is done by making an entry in a cash receipts journal. As shown earlier in the chapter, this step establishes a written record of cash receipts and should prevent errors and make theft more difficult.

Control of Cash Received Through the Mail. Cash receipts received through the mail are vulnerable to being stolen by the employees who receive them. This way of doing business is increasing, however, because of the expansion of mail order sales. To control these receipts, customers should be urged to pay with a check instead of currency.

Also, cash that comes in through the mail should be handled by two or more employees. The employee who opens the mail should make a list in triplicate of the money received. The list should contain each payer's name, the purpose for which the money was sent, and the amount. One copy goes with the cash to the cashier, who deposits the money. The second copy goes to the accounting department to be recorded in the cash receipts journal. The person who opens the mail keeps the third copy of the list. Errors can be caught easily because the amount deposited by the cashier must agree with the amount received and the amount recorded in the cash receipts journal.

Control of Cash Received over the Counter. Two common means of controlling cash sales receipts are through the use of cash registers and prenumbered sales tickets. The amount of a cash sale should be rung up on a cash register at the time of the sale. The cash register should be placed so that the customer can see the amount recorded. Each cash register should have a locked-in tape on which it prints the day's transactions. At the end of the day, the cashier counts the cash in the cash register and turns it in to the cashier's office. Another employee takes the tape out of the cash register and records the cash receipts for the day in the cash receipts journal. The amount of cash turned in and the amount recorded on the tape should agree; if not, any differences must be accounted for. Large retail chains commonly perform this function by having each cash register tied directly into a computer. In this way, each transaction is recorded as it occurs. This method separates the responsibility for cash receipts, cash deposits, and recordkeeping, ensuring good internal control.

In some stores, internal control is strengthened further by the use of prenumbered sales tickets and a central cash register or cashier's office, where all sales are rung up and collected by a person who does not participate in the sale. Under this procedure, the salesperson completes a prenumbered sales ticket at the time of sale, giving one copy to the customer and keeping a copy. At the end of the day, all sales tickets must be accounted for, and the sales total computed from the sales tickets should equal the total sales recorded on the cash register.

Cash Short or Over. When there are numerous transactions involving cash receipts, small mistakes are bound to happen. For example, cash registers in grocery and retail stores often have a cash shortage or overage at the end of the day. When the shortages are consistent or large for a particular cash register or cashier, they should be investigated.

The **Cash Short or Over** account is debited for shortages and credited for overages. If, at the end of a day, a cash register shows recorded cash sales of $675 but contains only $670 in cash, the following entry would record the sales:

Cash	670	
Cash Short or Over	5	
Sales		675
To record cash sales; a cash shortage of $5 was discovered		

The use of a separate account to record cash short or over calls management's attention to irregular activity. At the end of an accounting period, a debit balance in Cash Short or Over is reported as a general operating expense on the income statement; a credit balance is reported as other revenue.

Control of Purchases and Cash Disbursements

Cash disbursements are particularly vulnerable to fraud and embezzlement. In one recent case, the treasurer of one of the nation's largest jewelry retailers was charged with having stolen over $500,000 by systematically overpaying federal income taxes and pocketing the refund checks as they came back to the company.

To avoid this kind of theft, cash should be paid only on the basis of specific authorization that is supported by documents that establish the validity and amount of the claim. In addition, maximum possible use should be made of the principle of separation of duties in the purchase of goods and services and the payment for them. The amount of separation of duties varies, depending on the size of the business. Figure 7-5 shows how this kind of control can be achieved in companies large enough for maximum separation of duties. In this example, five internal units (the requesting department, the purchasing department, the accounting department, the receiving department, and the treasurer) and two external contacts (the supplier and the banking system) all play a role in the internal control plan. Notice that business documents also play an important role in the plan. The plan is summarized in Table 7-1. Under this plan, every action is documented and subject to verification by at least one other person. For instance, the requesting department cannot work out a kickback scheme with the supplier because the receiving department independently records receipts and the accounting department verifies prices. The receiving department cannot steal goods because the receiving report must equal the invoices. For the same reason, the supplier cannot bill for more goods than it ships. The accounting department's work is verified by the treasurer, and the treasurer ultimately is checked by the accounting department.

Figure 7-5. Internal Control for Purchasing and Paying for Goods and Services

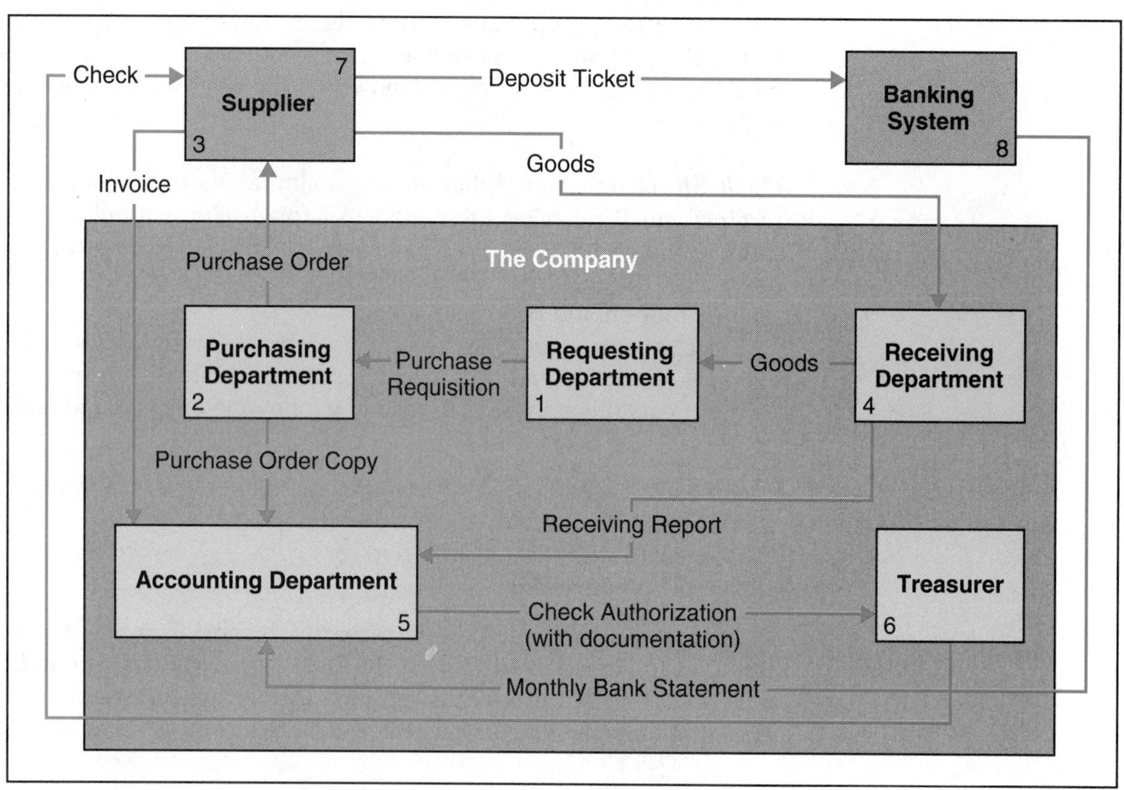

Figures 7-6 through 7-10, which show typical documents used in this internal control plan, follow the purchase of twenty boxes of FAX paper rolls. To begin, the credit office (requesting department) of Martin Maintenance Company fills out a **purchase requisition** for twenty boxes of FAX paper rolls (Figure 7-6). The department head approves it and forwards it to the purchasing department. The people in the purchasing department prepare a **purchase order**, as shown in Figure 7-7. The purchase order is addressed to the vendor (seller) and contains a description of the items ordered; the expected price, terms, and shipping date; and other shipping instructions. Martin Maintenance Company does not pay any bill that is not accompanied by a purchase order number.

After receiving the purchase order, the vendor, Henderson Supply Company, ships the goods (in this case delivers them) and sends an **invoice**, or bill (Figure 7-8, page 277) to Martin Maintenance Company. The invoice gives the quantity and a description of the goods delivered and the terms of payment. If all goods cannot be shipped immediately, the estimated date for shipment of the remainder is indicated.

When the goods reach the receiving department of Martin Maintenance Company, an employee in the department writes the description, quantity, and condition of the goods on the **receiving report**. The receiving department does not receive a copy of the purchase order or invoice, so the people in it do not know what should be received. Thus, they are not tempted to steal any excess that may be delivered.

The receiving report is sent to the accounting department, where it is compared with the purchase order and the invoice. If all is correct, the accounting

Table 7-1. Internal Control Plan for Purchases and Cash Disbursements

Business Document	Prepared by	Sent to	Verification and Related Procedures
1. Purchase requisition	Requesting department	Purchasing department	Purchasing verifies authorization.
2. Purchase order	Purchasing department	Supplier	Supplier sends goods or services in accordance with purchase order.
3. Invoice	Supplier	Accounting department	Accounting receives invoice from supplier.
4. Receiving report	Receiving department	Accounting department	Accounting compares invoice, purchase order, and receiving report. Accounting verifies prices.
5. Check authorization (or voucher)	Accounting department	Treasurer	Accounting attaches check authorization to invoice, purchase order, and receiving report.
6. Check	Treasurer	Supplier	Treasurer verifies all documents before preparing check.
7. Deposit ticket	Supplier	Supplier's bank	Supplier compares check with invoice. Bank deducts check from buyer's account.
8. Bank statement	Buyer's bank	Accounting department	Accounting compares amount and payee's name on returned check with check authorization.

department completes a **check authorization** and attaches it to the three supporting documents. The check authorization form shown in Figure 7-9 has a space for each item to be checked off as it is examined. Notice that the accounting department has all the documentary evidence for the transaction but does not have access to the assets purchased. Nor does it write the checks for payment. This means that the people performing the accounting function cannot gain by falsifying documents in an effort to conceal fraud.

Finally, the treasurer examines all the documents and issues a **check** (Figure 7-10) for the amount of the invoice less any appropriate discount. In some systems, the accounting department fills out the check so that all the treasurer has to do is inspect and sign it. The check then is sent to the supplier, with a remittance advice, which shows what the check is paying. A supplier who is not paid

Figure 7-6. Purchase Requisition

PURCHASE REQUISITION No. 7077

Martin Maintenance Company

From: Credit Office Date: September 6, 19xx

To: Purchasing Department Suggested Vendor: Henderson Supply Company

Please purchase the following items:

Quantity	Number	Description
20 boxes	X 144	FAX paper rolls

Reason for Request	To be filled in by Purchasing Department
Six months' supply for office	Date ordered 9/8/xx P.O. No. J 102
Approved B.M.	

Figure 7-7. Purchase Order

PURCHASE ORDER No. J 102

Martin Maintenance Company
8428 Rocky Island Avenue
Chicago, Illinois 60643

To: Henderson Supply Company
2525 25th Street
Mesa, Illinois 61611

Date September 8, 19xx

FOB Destination

Ship by September 12, 19xx

Ship to: Martin Maintenance Company
Above Address

Terms 2/10, n/30

Please ship the following:

Quantity	✓	Number	Description	Price	Per	Amount
20 boxes		X 144	FAX paper rolls	12.00	box	$240.00

Purchase order number must appear on all shipments and invoices.

Ordered by Marsha Owen

Figure 7-8. Invoice

INVOICE No. 0468

Henderson Supply Company
2525 25th Street
Mesa, Illinois 61611

Date September 12, 19xx

Your Order No. J 102

Sold to:

Martin Maintenance Company
8428 Rocky Island Avenue
Chicago, Illinois 60643

Ship to:

Same

Sales Representative: Joe Jacobs

Quantity		Description	Price	Per	Amount
Ordered	Shipped				
20	20	X 144 FAX paper rolls	12.00	box	$240.00

FOB Destination	Terms: 2/10, n/30	Date Shipped: 9/12/xx	Via: Self

the proper amount will complain, of course, thus providing a form of outside control over the payment. The supplier deposits the check in the bank, which returns the canceled check with Martin Maintenance Company's next bank statement. If the treasurer has made the check out for the wrong amount (or altered a prefilled-in check), the problem shows up at this point in the bank reconciliation.

Figure 7-9. Check Authorization

CHECK AUTHORIZATION

	NO.	CHECK
Requisition	7077	✓
Purchase Order	J 102	✓
Receiving Report	JR 065	✓
INVOICE	0468	
Price		✓
Calculations		✓
Terms		✓

Approved for Payment J. Joseph

Figure 7-10. Check with Attached Remittance Advice

NO. 1787

9/21 19 xx

PAY TO
THE ORDER OF Henderson Supply Company $ 235.20

Two hundred thirty-five and 20/100 ———————————— Dollars

THE LAKE PARK NATIONAL BANK
Chicago, Illinois

Martin Maintenance Company

by Arthur Martin

⑆031130153⑆ ⑈8030 647 4⑈

Remittance Advice

Date	P.O. No.	DESCRIPTION	AMOUNT
9/21/xx	J 102	20 X 144 FAX paper rolls Supplied Inv. No. 0468 Less 2% discount Net Martin Maintenance Company	 $240.00 4.80 $235.20

There are many variations of the system just described. This example is offered as a simple system that provides adequate internal control.

Chapter Review

Review of Learning Objectives

1. **Identify the principles of accounting systems design.**
   In designing an accounting system, the system designer must keep in mind the four principles of systems design: the cost-benefit principle, the control principle, the compatibility principle, and the flexibility principle.
2. **Identify the basic elements of computer systems in mainframe and microcomputer contexts.**
   Computerized data processing systems are the most advanced type of data processing systems, in which recording, posting, and other bookkeeping tasks are done with the help of a computer. The typical computer system consists of hardware, software, and personnel. The internal processing is specified in the form of programs, which can be designed to allow batch processing (grouping of similar transactions to be done at a specified time) or on-line processing (recording transactions as they occur). Commercial accounting packages for microcomputer systems typically use a batch processing approach.
3. **Explain the objectives and uses of special-purpose journals.**
   The typical manual data processing system consists of several special-purpose journals, each of which is designed to record one kind of transaction. Recording only transactions of one kind in each journal reduces and simplifies the bookkeeper's task and allows for the division of labor. This division of labor is important for internal control purposes.

4. **Construct and use the following types of special-purpose journals: sales journal, purchases journal, cash receipts journal, cash payments journal, and others as needed.**
A special-purpose journal is constructed by devoting a single column to a particular account (for example, debits to Cash in the cash receipts journal and credits to Cash in the cash payments journal). Other columns in the journal depend on the kinds of transactions in which the company normally engages. Special-purpose journals also have columns for transaction dates and explanations or subsidiary account names, and reference columns.

5. **Explain the purposes and relationships of controlling accounts and subsidiary ledgers.**
Subsidiary ledgers contain individual accounts of a certain kind, such as customers' accounts (accounts receivable) or suppliers' accounts (accounts payable). The individual account records are kept separately in a subsidiary ledger to avoid making the general ledger too bulky. The total of the balances of the subsidiary accounts should equal the balance of the controlling account in the general ledger because the individual items are posted daily to the subsidiary accounts and the column totals are posted to the general ledger account monthly from the special-purpose journal.

6. **Define *internal control* and identify the three elements of the internal control structure, including seven examples of control procedures.**
Internal controls are the policies and procedures management uses to protect the organization's assets and to ensure the accuracy and reliability of accounting records. They also work to maintain efficient operations and compliance with management's policies. The internal control structure consists of three elements: the control environment, the accounting system, and control procedures. Examples of control procedures are proper authorization of transactions; recording transactions to facilitate preparation of financial statements and to establish accountability for assets; use of well-designed documents and records; limited access to assets; periodic independent comparison of records and assets; separation of duties into the functions of authorization, operations, custody of assets, and recordkeeping; and use of sound personnel procedures.

7. **Describe the inherent limitations of internal control.**
A system of internal control relies on the people who implement it. Thus, the effectiveness of internal control is limited by the people involved. Human error, collusion, the interference of management, and the failure to recognize changed conditions all can contribute to a system's failure.

8. **Apply control procedures to certain merchandising transactions.**
Certain procedures strengthen internal control over sales, cash receipts, purchases, and cash disbursements. First, the functions of authorization, recordkeeping, and custody should be kept separate. Second, the accounting system should provide for physical protection of assets (especially cash and merchandise inventory), use of banking services, prompt recording and deposit of cash receipts, and payment by check. Third, the people who have access to cash and merchandise inventory should be specifically designated and their number limited. Fourth, employees who have access to cash or merchandise inventory should be bonded. Fifth, the Cash account should be reconciled each month, and surprise audits of cash on hand should be made by an individual who does not authorize, handle, or record cash transactions.

Review of Concepts and Terminology

The following concepts and terms were introduced in this chapter:

(L.O. 1, 6) **Accounting systems:** The process that gathers data, puts them into useful form, and communicates the results, including analyzing and recording transactions, posting entries, adjusting and closing the accounts, and preparing financial statements.

(L.O. 2) **Batch processing:** The form of data processing in which processing tasks are scheduled in a logical order.

(L.O. 6) **Bonding:** The process of carefully checking an employee's background and insuring the company against theft by that person.

(L.O. 4) **Cash payments journal:** A multicolumn special-purpose journal used to record payments of cash. Also called *cash disbursements journal.*

(L.O. 4) **Cash receipts journal:** A multicolumn special-purpose journal used to record transactions involving the receipt of cash.

(L.O. 8) **Cash Short or Over:** The account debited for cash shortages and credited for overages; used to call management's attention to irregular activity.

(L.O. 8) **Check:** A written order to a bank to pay the amount specified from funds on deposit.

(L.O. 8) **Check authorization:** A form prepared by the accounting department after it has compared the receiving report for goods received with the purchase order and the invoice.

(L.O. 1) **Compatibility principle:** The principle that holds that the design of an accounting system be in harmony with the organizational and human factors of a business.

(L.O. 2) **Computer operator:** The person who runs a computer.

(L.O. 6) **Control environment:** The overall attitude, awareness, and actions of the owners and management of a business, as reflected in philosophy and operating style, organizational structure, methods of assigning authority and responsibility, and personnel policies and practices.

(L.O. 5) **Controlling account:** An account in the general ledger that summarizes the total balance of a group of related accounts in a subsidiary ledger. Also called *control account.*

(L.O. 1) **Control principle:** The principle that holds that an accounting system must provide all the features of internal control needed to protect the firm's assets and to be sure the data are reliable.

(L.O. 6) **Control procedures:** Procedures and policies established by management to ensure that the objectives of internal control are being met.

(L.O. 1) **Cost-benefit principle:** The principle that holds that the benefits derived from an accounting system and the information it generates should equal or exceed its cost.

(L.O. 1) **Data processing:** The means by which an accounting system gathers data, organizes them into useful forms, and issues the resulting information to users.

(L.O. 1) **Flexibility principle:** The principle that holds that the design of an accounting system must have enough flexibility to allow the volume of transactions to grow and organizational changes to be made.

(L.O. 2) **General ledger software:** The computer programs that direct the computer to carry out the major accounting functions.

(L.O. 2) **Hardware:** The equipment needed to operate a computerized data processing system.

(L.O. 6) **Internal control:** All the policies and procedures a company uses to safeguard its assets, check the accuracy and reliability of its accounting data, promote operational efficiency, and encourage adherence to its policies.

(L.O. 6) **Internal control structure:** A structure established to safeguard the assets of a business and provide reliable accounting records; consists of the control environment, the accounting system, and control procedures.

(L.O. 8) **Invoice:** A form sent or delivered to the purchaser by the vendor that describes the quantity and price of the goods or services delivered and the terms of payment.

(L.O. 3) **Manual data processing:** A system of accounting in which each transaction is entered manually from a source document into the general journal (input device) and each debit and credit is posted manually to the correct ledger account (processor and memory device) for the eventual preparation of financial statements (output devices).

(L.O. 2) **On-line processing:** The form of data processing in which remote terminals are linked to a central processor, and files are updated virtually as transactions occur.

(L.O. 2) **Program:** The set of instructions and steps that bring about the wanted results in a computerized data processing system.

(L.O. 2) **Programmer:** The person who writes instructions for a computer.

(L.O. 8) **Purchase order:** A form prepared by a company's purchasing department and sent to a vendor that describes the items ordered; their expected price, terms, and shipping date; and other shipping instructions.

(L.O. 8) **Purchase requisition:** A formal written request for a purchase, prepared by a department in the organization and sent to its purchasing department.

(L.O. 4) **Purchases journal:** A single-column or multicolumn special-purpose journal used to record all purchases on credit.

(L.O. 8) **Receiving report:** A form prepared by the receiving department of a company that describes the quantity and condition of goods received.

(L.O. 4) **Sales journal:** A type of special-purpose journal used to record credit sales.

(L.O. 2) **Software:** The programs in a computerized data processing system.

(L.O. 2) **Source documents:** The written evidence that supports the transactions for each major accounting function.

(L.O. 3) **Special-purpose journal:** An input device in an accounting system that is used to record a single type of transaction.

(L.O. 5) **Subsidiary ledger:** A ledger separate from the general ledger that contains a group of related accounts; the total of the balances in the subsidiary ledger accounts must equal the balance of a controlling account in the general ledger.

(L.O. 2) **Systems analyst:** The person who designs a computerized data processing system on the basis of the organization's information needs.

Self-Test

Test your knowledge of the chapter by choosing the best answer for each of the following items.

(L.O. 1) 1. Designing a system that allows a retailer to expand to multiple locations and products is probably the result of applying the
   a. cost-benefit principle.
   b. control principle.
   c. compatibility principle.
   d. flexibility principle.

(L.O. 2) 2. An example of a hardware output device in a microcomputer system is a
   a. hard disk.
   b. computer program.
   c. central processor.
   d. printer.

(L.O. 3) 3. Special-purpose journals are used primarily because most businesses have many transactions that
   a. are difficult to classify.
   b. are essentially identical.
   c. use only a very few ledger accounts.
   d. are easy to classify.

(L.O. 4) 4. The total of a single-column sales journal is posted as a
   a. debit to Sales and a credit to Accounts Receivable.
   b. debit to Accounts Receivable and a credit to Sales.
   c. debit to Cash and a credit to Sales.
   d. debit to Sales and a credit to Cash.

(L.O. 4) 5. The daily total of sales for cash is recorded in the
a. sales journal.
b. purchases journal.
c. cash payments journal.
d. cash receipts journal.

(L.O. 5) 6. The failure to post the receipt of a customer's payment in the customer's account in the subsidiary ledger most likely would be discovered when
a. the cash receipts journal is footed and crossfooted.
b. the trial balance is prepared.
c. the total of the subsidiary ledger is compared to the balance of the accounts receivable controlling account.
d. assets are compared with the liabilities and owner's equity on the balance sheet.

(L.O. 6) 7. The internal control structure encompasses all of the following except the
a. attitude of management toward controls.
b. accounting records and system.
c. amount of autonomy held by various divisions within a company.
d. specific procedures for controlling transactions.

(L.O. 6) 8. The separation of duties in terms of cash transactions means that separate individuals should be responsible for authorization, custody, and
a. approval.
b. recordkeeping.
c. control.
d. protection.

(L.O. 7) 9. Which of the following is least likely to lead to a breakdown in internal control?
a. Human errors and mistakes
b. Employees carrying out their duties as prescribed
c. Management taking full control of an operation
d. Two employees working together to steal assets

(L.O. 8) 10. Which of the following documents should be presented and agreed on before a check authorization is prepared?
a. Purchase requisition and purchase order
b. Purchase order and receiving report
c. Purchase requisition, purchase order, and invoice
d. Purchase order, invoice, and receiving report

Answers to the Self-Test are at the end of this chapter.

Review Problem
Purchases Journal

(L.O. 1, 3, 4) Caraban Company is a retail seller of hiking and camping gear. The company is installing a manual accounting system, and the accountant is trying to decide whether to use a single-column or a multicolumn purchases journal. Here is a list of several transactions related to purchases in the month of January:

Jan. 5 Received a shipment of merchandise from Simons Corporation, terms 2/10, n/30, FOB shipping point, invoice dated January 4, $2,875.
10 Received a bill from Allied Freight for the freight charges on the January 5 shipment, terms n/30, invoice dated January 4, $416.
15 Returned some of the merchandise received from Simons Corporation because it was not what was ordered, $315.
20 Purchased store supplies of $56 and office supplies of $117 from Mason Company, terms n/30, invoice dated January 20.
25 Received a shipment from Thomas Manufacturing, $1,882, which included supplier-paid freight charges of $175, terms n/30, FOB shipping point, invoice dated January 23.

Required

1. Record the transactions above using a single-column purchases journal and a general journal, and show the posting reference for each journal entry. Use the following accounts: Store Supplies (116), Office Supplies (117), Accounts Payable (211), Purchases (611), Purchases Returns and Allowances (612), and Freight In (613).
2. Record the transactions above using a multicolumn purchases journal and a general journal, total the purchases journal, and show the posting reference for each journal entry.
3. Using the principles of systems design as a basis for your answer, compare the two systems in terms of the number of journal entries and postings.

Answer to Review Problem

1. Record the transactions in a single-column purchases journal and the general journal. Show the posting references.

Purchases Journal — **Page 1**

Date		Account Credited	Date of Invoice	Terms	Post. Ref.	Amount
Jan.	5	Simons Corporation	1/4	2/10, n/30	✓	2,875

General Journal — **Page 1**

Date		Description	Post. Ref.	Debit	Credit
Jan.	10	Freight In	613	416	
		Accounts Payable, Allied Freight	211/✓		416
		Freight charges on Simons Corporation shipment, terms n/30, invoice dated January 4			
	15	Accounts Payable, Simons Corporation	211/✓	315	
		Purchases Returns and Allowances	612		315
		Returned merchandise not ordered			
	20	Store Supplies	116	56	
		Office Supplies	117	117	
		Accounts Payable, Mason Company	211/✓		173
		Purchased supplies, terms n/30, invoice dated January 20			
	25	Purchases	611	1,707	
		Freight In	613	175	
		Accounts Payable, Thomas Manufacturing	211/✓		1,882
		Purchased merchandise, terms n/30; supplier paid shipping, invoice dated January 23			

2. Record the transactions in a multicolumn purchases journal and the general journal. Total the journals and show posting references.

Purchases Journal — Page 1

Date		Account Credited	Date of Invoice	Terms	Post. Ref.	Credit: Accounts Payable	Debits: Purchases	Freight In	Store Supplies	Office Supplies
Jan.	5	Simons Corporation	1/4	2/10, n/30	✓	2,875	2,875			
	10	Allied Freight	1/4	n/30	✓	416		416		
	20	Mason Company	1/20	n/30	✓	173			56	117
	25	Thomas Manufacturing	1/23	n/30	✓	1,882	1,707	175		
						5,346	4,582	591	56	117
						(211)	(611)	(613)	(116)	(117)

Each of these accounts is posted **daily** to the appropriate account in the subsidiary ledger.

Each of these totals is posted **monthly** to the applicable general ledger account.

General Journal — Page 1

Date		Description	Post. Ref.	Debit	Credit
Jan.	15	Accounts Payable, Simons Corporation	211/✓	315	
		Purchases Returns and Allowances	612		315
		To record return of merchandise not ordered			

This amount is posted both to the controlling account and to the subsidiary account.

This amount is posted to the general ledger account.

3. The first system (single-column purchases journal) requires four general journal entries plus one purchases journal entry, or twenty-three separate lines, including explanations. In addition, fifteen postings to the general ledger and the accounts payable subsidiary ledger are necessary. (Also, the total of the purchases journal must be posted twice at the end of the month: once as a credit to Accounts Payable and once as a debit to Purchases). The second system (multicolumn purchases journal) calls for just one general journal entry and four purchases journal entries. Only ten lines need to be written, and only seven postings must be made (in addition, the column totals in the purchases journal must be posted at the end of the month).

In applying the cost-benefit principle, the benefits of the expanded purchases journal in terms of journalizing and posting time saved are clear from the analysis above. In addition, there are fewer chances for error when using the expanded purchases journal. So the control principle is better achieved under the second system. It is not possible to decide which system better meets the compatibility principle because we do not know the relative proportion of transaction types. For instance, if the number of transactions like the one for January 5 exceeds all the others by ten to one, the first system may be more compatible with the needs of the company. On the other hand, if there are great numbers of transactions like those for January 10, 20, and 25, the second system may be more compatible. Finally, in terms of the flexibility principle, the multicolumn purchases journal is obviously more flexible because it can handle more kinds of transactions and can be expanded to include columns for other accounts if necessary.

Chapter Assignments

Questions

1. What is the relationship of accounting systems to data processing?
2. What is the function of data processing?
3. Describe the four principles of accounting systems design.
4. What are the three basic elements of a computerized data processing system?
5. What is the difference between hardware and software?
6. What is the purpose of a computer program?
7. What is the difference between batch processing and on-line processing?
8. Data are the raw material of a computer system. Trace the flow of data through the different parts of a microcomputer accounting system.
9. How do special-purpose journals save time in entering and posting transactions?
10. Long Transit had 1,700 sales on credit during the current month.
    a. If the firm uses a two-column general journal to record sales, how many times will the word *Sales* be written?
    b. How many postings to the Sales account will have to be made?
    c. If the firm uses a sales journal, how many times will the word *Sales* be written?
    d. How many postings to the Sales account will have to be made?
11. What is the purpose of the Accounts Receivable controlling account? What is its relationship to the accounts receivable subsidiary ledger?
12. Why are the cash receipts journal and cash payments journal crossfooted? When is this step performed?
13. A company has the following numbers of accounts with balances: 18 asset accounts, including the Accounts Receivable account but not the individual customers' accounts; 200 customer accounts; 8 liability accounts, including the Accounts Payable account but not the individual creditors' accounts; 100 creditor accounts; and 35 owner's equity accounts, including income statement accounts—a total of 361 accounts. How many accounts in total would appear in the general ledger?
14. Most people think of internal control as a means of making fraud harder to commit and easier to detect. Can you think of some other important purposes of internal control?
15. What are the three elements of the internal control structure?
16. What are some examples of control procedures?
17. Why is the separation of duties necessary to ensure sound internal control?
18. In a small business, it is sometimes impossible to separate duties completely. What are three other practices that a small business can follow to achieve the objectives of internal control over cash?
19. At Thrifty Variety Store, each sales clerk counts the cash in his or her cash drawer at the end of the day and then removes the cash register tape and prepares a daily cash form, noting any discrepancies. This information is checked by an employee in the cashier's office, who counts the cash, compares the total with the form, and then gives the cash to the cashier. What is the weakness in this system of internal control?
20. How does a movie theater control cash receipts?

21. What does a credit balance in the Cash Short or Over account indicate?
22. At the end of the day, the combined count of cash for all cash registers in a store reveals a cash shortage of $17.20. In what account would this cash shortage be recorded? Would the account be debited or credited?
23. One of the basic principles of internal control is separation of duties. What does this principle assume about the relationships of employees in a company and the possibility of two or more of them stealing from the company?

Communication Skills Exercises

Communication 7-1. Ethics and Commissions on Sales *(L.O. 1)*

Herb Sanders, CPA, provides consulting services to Page Engineering Company. After several years of rapid growth, Page has determined that it needs a new computerized accounting system and has asked Sanders to do a systems investigation and make a recommendation for a new system. Sanders has completed the investigation, and has found that two systems meet Page's needs. The supplier of one of the systems, which is priced about 5 percent higher than the other, has offered Sanders a commission of 10 percent if its system is purchased by Page. Both systems are in the $20,000–$25,000 price range that Page had decided was feasible. Because he is especially familiar with the higher-priced system, Sanders would be better able to provide further services to Page if that system were purchased. Thus, Sanders plans to recommend the higher-priced system without mentioning the other one. What are the ethical implications of Sanders's plan? What alternatives might Sanders consider?

Communication 7-2. Switching to a Computer System *(L.O. 1)*

Kroch's & Brentano's, the fourth largest seller of books in the United States, operates full-service bookstores throughout the Chicago area. The firm is well known for excellent service and large inventories of books in a wide number of fields, such as art, history, business, technology, travel, and fiction. The company is willing to order any book in print.

The following paragraphs are from an article describing a change in the firm's data processing system:

> In a Wabash Avenue office brimming with hip-high piles of books, William Rickman agonizes over computerizing Kroch's & Brentano's 200,000-title inventory.
>
> The new technology, he frets, could make customers think Kroch's and its employees have become cold and distant. But Mr. Rickman, the 42-year-old president of Kroch's, doesn't know which books are selling or where—basic information most retailers cherish. Amazingly, the 20-store chain still uses manual inventory and sales systems.
>
> "We know we need the information, so we're doing it, but we want to make every effort to stay friendly and personal," he says.[3]

Do you think Mr. Rickman's fears are justified? What advantages related to merchandise inventory and sales will stem from implementing the new computer system? How can the possible disadvantages of the new system be overcome?

Communication 7-3. Basic Research Skills *(L.O. 2)*

In your school's library, find the back issues for the past year of one of the following magazines: *PC World, MacUser,* or *MacWorld.* Locate an article that surveys or evaluates general ledger accounting packages. Study the article and compare the product to the microcomputer accounting system shown in Figure 7-3 and the manual accounting system using special-purpose journals described in this chapter. What similarities and differences do you find? Do you think the problems in this chapter could be worked on one of these systems? Why or why not? Be prepared to discuss your findings in class.

3. Lisa Collins, "Top-Seller Kroch's Seeks a New Plot," *Crain's Chicago Business,* October 22, 1990.

Classroom Exercises

Exercise 7-1. Matching Transactions to Special-Purpose Journals *(L.O. 3)*

A company uses a single-column sales journal, a single-column purchases journal, a cash receipts journal, a cash payments journal, and a general journal. In which journal would each of the following transactions be recorded?

1. Sold merchandise on credit
2. Sold merchandise for cash
3. Gave a customer credit for merchandise purchased on credit and returned
4. Paid a creditor
5. Paid office salaries
6. Customer paid for merchandise previously purchased on credit
7. Recorded adjusting and closing entries
8. Purchased merchandise on credit
9. Purchased sales department supplies on credit
10. Purchased office equipment for cash
11. Returned merchandise purchased on credit
12. Paid taxes

Exercise 7-2. Characteristics of Special-Purpose Journals *(L.O. 3, 5)*

Kua Corporation uses a single-column sales journal, a single-column purchases journal, a cash receipts journal, a cash payments journal, and a general journal.

1. In which of the journals listed above would you expect to find the fewest transactions recorded?
2. At the end of the accounting period, to which account or accounts should the total of the sales journal be posted as a debit and/or credit?
3. At the end of the accounting period, to which account or accounts should the total of the purchases journal be posted as a debit and/or credit?
4. What two subsidiary ledgers probably would be associated with the journals listed above? From which journals would postings normally be made to each of the two subsidiary ledgers?
5. In which of the journals are adjusting and closing entries made?

Exercise 7-3. Identifying the Content of a Special-Purpose Journal *(L.O. 4)*

Answer the following questions about the page from a special journal, shown below.

1. What kind of journal is this?
2. Explain each of the transactions in the journal entries.
3. Explain the following: (a) the numbers under the bottom lines, (b) the checkmarks in the Post. Ref. column, (c) the numbers 115 and 715 in the Post. Ref. column, and (d) the checkmark below the Other Accounts column.

Date		Account Credited	Post. Ref.	Debits		Credits		
				Cash	Sales Discounts	Accounts Receivable	Sales	Other Accounts
		Balance Forward		79,598	1,574	20,408	8,564	52,200
May	25	Mae Johnson	✓	980	20	1,000		
	26	Notes Receivable	115	2,240				2,000
		Interest Income	715					240
	27	Cash Sale		1,920			1,920	
	31	Virgil Thomas	✓	400		400		
				85,138	1,594	21,808	10,484	54,440
				(111)	(412)	(114)	(411)	(✓)

Exercise 7-4.
Multicolumn Purchases Journal
(L.O. 4)

Gordon Company uses a multicolumn purchases journal similar to the one shown in Exhibit 7-6.

During the month of July, Gordon made the following purchases:

July 1 Purchased merchandise from Lujack Company on account for $5,400, invoice dated July 1, terms 2/10, n/30.
3 Received freight bill dated July 1 from Olinsky Freight for merchandise purchased July 1, $350, terms n/30.
18 Purchased supplies from Hobbs Company for $240; allocated half to the store and half to the office; invoice dated July 16, terms n/30.
23 Purchased merchandise from Pascale Company on account for $1,974; total included freight in of $174; invoice dated July 20, terms n/30, FOB shipping point.
27 Purchased office supplies from Hobbs Company for $96, invoice dated July 27, terms n/30.
31 Purchased a one-year insurance policy from Rathbun Associates, $480, invoice dated July 31, terms n/30.

1. Set up a multicolumn purchases journal similar to the one in Exhibit 7-6.
2. Enter the transactions listed above in the purchases journal. Then foot and crossfoot the columns.

Exercise 7-5.
Finding Errors in Special-Purpose Journals
(L.O. 4, 5)

A company records purchases in a single-column purchases journal and records purchases returns in its general journal. During the past month, an accounting clerk made each of the errors described below. Explain how each error might be discovered.

1. Correctly recorded a $191 purchase in the purchases journal but posted it to the creditor's account as a $119 purchase.
2. Made an additional error in totaling the Amount column of the purchases journal.
3. Posted a purchases return from the general journal to the Purchases Returns and Allowances account and the Accounts Payable account but did not post it to the creditor's account.
4. Made an error in determining the balance of a creditor's account.
5. Posted a purchases return to the Accounts Payable account but did not post it to the Purchases Returns and Allowances account.

Exercise 7-6.
Posting from a Sales Journal
(L.O. 4, 5)

Prokop Corporation began business on June 1. The company maintains a sales journal. At the end of the month, the sales journal looked like this:

Sales Journal **Page 1**

Date		Account Debited	Invoice Number	Post. Ref.	Amount
June	3	Fran Smiley	1001		516
	8	Steve Pearl	1002		951
	12	Byung Koh	1003		642
	18	Fran Smiley	1004		291
	27	Maria Campos	1005		1,299
					3,699

1. Open general ledger accounts for Accounts Receivable (112) and Sales (411) and an accounts receivable subsidiary ledger with an account for each customer. Make the appropriate postings from the sales journal, indicating the posting references that would be made in the sales journal and inserting the posting references in the ledger accounts as you work.
2. Prove the accounts receivable subsidiary ledger by preparing a schedule of accounts receivable.

Exercise 7-7. Identification of Transactions *(L.O. 4, 5)*

Herrera Company uses a manual accounting system with a sales journal, purchases journal, cash receipts journal, cash payments journal, and general journal similar to those illustrated in the text.

On October 31, the Sales account in the general ledger looked like this:

Sales **Account No. 411**

Date		Item	Post. Ref.	Debit	Credit	Balance Debit	Balance Credit
Oct.	31		S11		74,842		74,842
	31		CR7		42,414		117,256
	31		J17	117,256			—

On October 31, the J. Tanner account in the accounts receivable subsidiary ledger looked like this:

J. Tanner **Account No. 10012**

Date		Item	Post. Ref.	Debit	Credit	Balance
Oct.	8		S10	4,216		4,216
	12		J14		564	3,652
	18		CR6		1,000	2,652

1. Write an explanation of each entry in the Sales account, including the journal from which the entry was posted.
2. Write an explanation of each entry in the J. Tanner account receivable, including the journal from which the entry was posted.

Exercise 7-8. Identification of Transactions *(L.O. 4, 5)*

Medina Company uses a sales journal, single-column purchases journal, cash receipts journal, cash payments journal, and general journal similar to those shown in the text. On April 30, the D. Peters account in the accounts receivable subsidiary ledger appeared as follows:

D. Peters

Date		Item	Post. Ref.	Debit	Credit	Balance
Mar.	31		S4	2,448		2,448
Apr.	7		J7		192	2,256
	12		CR5		600	1,656
	17		S6	684		2,340

On April 30, the Yung Company account in the accounts payable subsidiary ledger appeared as follows:

Yung Company

Date		Item	Post. Ref.	Debit	Credit	Balance
Apr.	18		P7		6,078	6,078
	20		J9	636		5,442
	25		CP8	5,442		—

1. Write an explanation of each entry that affected the D. Peters account receivable, including the journal from which the entry was posted.
2. Write an explanation of each entry that affected the Yung Company account payable, including the journal from which the entry was posted.

Exercise 7-9.
Use of Accounting Records in Internal Control
(L.O. 6)

Careful scrutiny of accounting records and financial statements can lead to the discovery of fraud or embezzlement. Each of the following situations may indicate a breakdown in internal control. Indicate what the possible fraud or embezzlement is in each situation.

1. Wages expense for a branch office was 30 percent higher in 19x2 than in 19x1, even though the office was authorized to employ only the same four employees and raises were only 5 percent in 19x2.
2. Sales returns and allowances increased from 5 percent to 20 percent of sales in the first two months of 19x2, after record sales in 19x1 resulted in large bonuses being paid the sales staff.
3. Gross margin decreased from 40 percent of net sales in 19x1 to 30 percent in 19x2, even though there was no change in pricing. Ending inventory was 50 percent less at the end of 19x2 than it was at the beginning of the year. There is no immediate explanation for the decrease in inventory.
4. A review of daily cash register receipts records shows that one cashier consistently accepts more discount coupons for purchases than do the other cashiers.

Exercise 7-10.
Control Procedures
(L.O. 6)

Sean O'Mara, who operates a small grocery store, has established the following policies with regard to the check-out cashiers:

_____ 1. Each cashier has his or her own cash drawer, to which no one else has access.
_____ 2. Each cashier may accept checks for purchases under $50 with proper identification. Checks over $50 must be approved by O'Mara before they are accepted.
_____ 3. Every sale must be rung up on the cash register and a receipt given to the customer. Each sale is recorded on a tape inside the cash register.
_____ 4. At the end of each day O'Mara counts the cash in the drawer and compares it to the amount on the tape inside the cash register.

Identify by letter which of the following conditions for internal control apply to each of the above policies:

a. Transactions are executed in accordance with management's general or specific authorization.
b. Transactions are recorded as necessary to (1) permit preparation of financial statements and (2) maintain accountability for assets.
c. Access to assets is permitted only as allowed by management.
d. The recorded accountability for assets is compared with the existing assets at reasonable intervals.

Exercise 7-11. Internal Control Procedures
(L.O. 6)

Ruth's Video Store maintains the following policies with regard to purchases of new videotapes at each of its branch stores:

_____ 1. Employees are required to take vacations, and duties of employees are rotated periodically.
_____ 2. Once each month a person from the home office visits each branch to examine the receiving records and to compare the inventory of tapes with the accounting records.
_____ 3. Purchases of new tapes must be authorized by purchase order in the home office and paid for by the treasurer in the home office. Receiving reports are prepared in each branch and sent to the home office.
_____ 4. All new personnel receive a one-hour orientation on receiving and cataloging new tapes.
_____ 5. The company maintains a perpetual inventory system that keeps track of all tapes purchased, sold, and on hand.

Indicate by letter which of the following control procedures apply to each of the above policies (some may have several answers):

a. Authorization
b. Recording transactions
c. Documents and records
d. Limited access
e. Periodic independent verification
f. Separation of duties
g. Sound personnel policies

Exercise 7-12. Internal Control Evaluation
(L.O. 6)

Developing a convenient means of providing sales representatives with cash for their incidental expenses, such as entertaining a client at lunch, is a problem many companies face. One company has a plan whereby the sales representatives receive advances in cash from the petty cash fund. Each advance is supported by an authorization from the sales manager. The representative returns the receipt for the expenditure and any unused cash, which is replaced in the petty cash fund. The cashier of the petty cash fund is responsible for seeing that the receipt and the cash returned equal the advance. At the time that the petty cash fund is reimbursed, the amount of the representative's expenditure is debited to Direct Sales Expense.

What is the weak point in this system? What fundamental principle of internal control is being ignored? What improvement in the procedure can you suggest?

Exercise 7-13. Internal Control Evaluation
(L.O. 6, 8)

An accountant and his assistants are responsible for the following procedures: (a) receiving all cash; (b) maintaining the general ledger; (c) maintaining the accounts receivable subsidiary ledger; (d) maintaining the journals for recording sales, purchases, and cash receipts; and (e) preparing monthly statements to be sent to customers. As a service to customers and employees, the company allows the accountant to cash checks of up to $50 with money from the cash receipts. When deposits are made, the checks are included in place of the cash receipts.

What weakness in internal control exists in this system?

Interpretation Case from Business

B. Dalton and Waldenbooks
(L.O. 1, 2)

In the mid-1960s, a new and tempting mass market was emerging. Americans were becoming better educated and more affluent. Also, the increasing number of shopping centers provided the perfect setting for a chain of national bookstores. Taking advantage of this opportunity, Minneapolis-based Dayton-Hudson Corporation launched its B. Dalton Bookseller, and Los Angeles–based Carter Hawley Hale began expanding its Waldenbooks division. By 1982, these two chains were by far the biggest book retailers in the country and were very competitive with each other. Dalton had 575 stores and planned to add 556 more by 1987. Waldenbooks had 750 outlets and planned to add 80 to 90 more each year.

Forbes magazine reported that although Waldenbooks had more outlets, Dalton "looks like the leader in the fight." Each chain had roughly $250 million in sales in 1980, but Dalton sold an estimated $132 worth of books per square foot of store space to

Waldenbooks' $114. *Forbes* stated that "a computerized inventory system installed in 1966 is what gives Dalton its edge—and is a key to why its 10% pretax profits are well above Walden's." In the book business today, "Success depends far more on fast, high efficiency distribution than on any fundamental appreciation of literature. . . . Order a little of everything and remain secure in your capabilities to restock quickly those titles the computer says are selling fast."[4]

Required

1. Describe, in your own words, how you believe Dalton used the four principles of systems design in 1966 to design its computerized inventory system so that it was able to grow rapidly and to become more profitable than Waldenbooks.
2. Describe, in your own words, how the following parts of a computerized inventory system would allow Dalton to restock fast-selling books quickly: source documents, data input, processing, information output, and distribution.

Problem Set A

Problem 7A-1.
Special-Purpose Journals and Subsidiary Ledgers
(L.O. 4, 5)

Manner Company is a small retail business that uses a manual accounting system similar to the one described in this chapter. At the end of April 19xx, the firm's accounts receivable and accounts payable subsidiary ledgers showed the following balances:

Accounts Receivable		Accounts Payable	
A. Barlett	$430	Baylor Company	$1,300
L. Lozowich	330	Gentrol Company	890
Total Accounts Receivable	$760	Total Accounts Payable	$2,190

During May, the company engaged in the following transactions:

May 2 Sold merchandise on credit to R. Wood, a new customer, $570, terms 2/10, n/30, invoice no. 1001.
4 Received payment in full from L. Lozowich, no discount allowed.
5 Paid Baylor Company the full amount owed less a 2 percent discount, check no. 201.
8 Agreed to accept a return of merchandise for credit from R. Wood, $170.
9 Paid Gentrol Company the full amount owed, no discount allowed, check no. 202.
12 Received payment from R. Wood for amount due less discount.
15 Received partial payment from A. Barlett, no discount allowed, $230.
22 Purchased merchandise from Baylor Company, $1,200, terms 2/10, n/30, FOB destination, invoice dated May 22.
23 Sold merchandise on credit to L. Lozowich, $670, terms 2/10, n/30, invoice no. 1002.
26 Purchased merchandise from Gentrol Company, $1,500, terms 2/10, n/30, FOB destination, invoice dated May 23.
31 Returned merchandise to Gentrol Company for full credit, $600.

Required

1. Prepare a single-column sales journal, a single-column purchases journal, a cash receipts journal, a cash payments journal, and a general journal similar to the ones illustrated in the chapter. Manner Company uses the gross method to record purchases. Use Page 1 for all references.
2. Open the following general ledger accounts: Accounts Receivable (112) and Accounts Payable (211).
3. Open the following accounts receivable subsidiary ledger accounts: A. Barlett, L. Lozowich, and R. Wood.
4. Open the following accounts payable subsidiary ledger accounts: Baylor Company and Gentrol Company.

4. Jeff Blyskal, "Dalton, Walden and the Amazing Money Machine," *Forbes*, January 18, 1982, p. 47.

5. Enter the transactions in the journals and post to the appropriate subsidiary ledger and general ledger accounts.
6. Foot and crossfoot the journals, and make the end-of-month postings applicable to Accounts Receivable and Accounts Payable.
7. Prove the control balances of Accounts Receivable and Accounts Payable by preparing schedules of accounts receivable and accounts payable.

Problem 7A-2. Cash Receipts and Cash Payments Journals
(L.O. 4)

Stigman Company is a small retail business that uses a manual data processing system similar to the one described in the chapter. Among its special-purpose journals are multicolumn cash receipts and cash payments journals. These were the cash transactions for Stigman Company during the month of November:

Nov. 1 Paid November rent to R. Carsello, $1,000, with check no. 782.
3 Paid Cronos Wholesale on account, $2,300 less a 2 percent discount, check no. 783.
4 Received payment in full, less 2 percent discount, for $1,000 amount due from J. Wilkes.
5 Cash sales, $2,632.
8 Paid Murray Freight on account, $598, with check no. 784.
9 The owner, Jerry Stigman, invested an additional $10,000 in cash and a truck valued at $14,000 in the business.
11 Paid Escobar Supply on account, $284, with check no. 785.
14 Cash sales, $2,834.
15 Paid Murray Freight $310 for the freight on a shipment of merchandise received today, with check no. 786.
16 Paid Ludlow Company on account, $1,600 less a 2 percent discount, with check no. 787.
17 Received payment on account from P. Sibley, $120.
18 Cash sales, $1,974.
19 Received payment on a note receivable, $1,800 plus $36 interest.
20 Purchased office supplies from Escobar Supply, $108, with check no. 788.
21 Paid a note payable in full to Kenilworth Bank, $4,100 including $100 interest, with check no. 789.
24 Cash sales, $2,964.
25 Paid $500 on account to Cronos Wholesale, with check no. 790. The discount period had passed.
26 Paid Linda Bisby, a sales clerk, $1,100 for her monthly salary, with check no. 791.
27 Purchased equipment from Buffalo Corporation for $16,000, paying $4,000 with check no. 792 and signing a note payable for the difference.
30 Jerry Stigman withdrew $1,200 from the business, using check no. 793.

Required

1. Enter these transactions in the cash receipts and cash payments journals.
2. Foot and crossfoot the journals.

Problem 7A-3. Purchases and General Journals
(L.O. 4, 5)

Mejias Lawn Supply Company uses a multicolumn purchases journal and general journal similar to those illustrated in the text. The company also maintains an accounts payable subsidiary ledger. The items below represent the company's credit transactions for the month of July.

July 2 Purchased merchandise from Noonan Fertilizer Company, $2,640.
3 Purchased office supplies of $166 and store supplies of $208 from Pagone Supply, Inc.
5 Purchased cleaning equipment from Whitlock Company, $1,856.
7 Purchased display equipment from Pagone Supply, Inc., $4,700.
10 Purchased lawn mowers from Toledo Lawn Equipment Company, for resale, $8,400 (which included transportation charges of $350).
14 Purchased merchandise from Noonan Fertilizer Company, $3,444.
18 Purchased a lawn mower from Toledo Lawn Equipment Company to be used in the business, $950.

July 23 Purchased store supplies from Pagone Supply, Inc., $54.
27 Returned a defective lawn mower purchased on July 10 for full credit, $750.

Required

1. Enter these transactions in a multicolumn purchases journal and the general journal. Assume that all terms are n/30 and that invoice dates are the same as the transaction dates.
2. Foot and crossfoot the purchases journal.
3. Open the following general ledger accounts: Store Supplies (116), Office Supplies (117), Lawn Equipment (142), Display Equipment (144), Cleaning Equipment (146), Accounts Payable (211), Purchases (611), Purchases Returns and Allowances (612), and Freight In (613). Open accounts payable subsidiary ledger accounts as needed. Post from the journals to the ledger accounts and the subsidiary ledgers.

Problem 7A-4. Comprehensive Use of Special-Purpose Journals *(L.O. 4, 5)*

Bromberg Book Store opened its doors for business on May 1. During May, the following transactions took place:

May 1 Linda Bromberg started the business by depositing $42,000 in the new company's bank account.
3 Issued check no. C001 to Lomax Rentals for one month's rent, $1,000.
4 Received a shipment of books from Osgood Books, Inc., $15,680, invoice dated May 3, terms 5/10, n/60, FOB shipping point.
5 Received a bill dated May 4 for freight from Linden Shippers for previous day's shipment, $790, terms n/30.
6 Received a shipment from Forrest Books, $11,300, invoice dated May 6, terms 2/10, n/30, FOB shipping point.
7 Issued check no. C002 to Pappas Freight for transportation charges on previous day's shipment, $574.
8 Issued check no. C003 to Yoo Equipment Company for store equipment, $10,400.
9 Sold books to Horizon Center, $1,564, terms 5/10, n/30, invoice no. 1001.
10 Returned books to Osgood Books, Inc., for credit, $760.
11 Issued check no. C004 to WCAM for radio commercials, $470.
12 Issued check no. C005 to Osgood Books, Inc., for balance of amount owed less discount.
13 Cash sales for the first two weeks, $4,018. (To shorten this problem, cash sales are recorded at intervals instead of daily, as they would be in actual practice.)
14 Issued check no. C006 to Forrest Books, $6,000 less discount.
15 Signed a 90-day, 10 percent note for a bank loan and received the $20,000 in cash.
15 Sold books to Yosh Kawano, $260, terms n/30, invoice no. 1002.
16 Issued a credit memorandum to Horizon Center for returned books, $124.
17 Received payment in full from Horizon Center for balance owed less discount.
18 Sold books to Ruth Mayhew, $194, terms n/30, invoice no. 1003.
19 Received a shipment from Patton Publishing Company, $4,604, invoice dated May 18, terms 5/10, n/60.
21 Sold books to Horizon Center, $1,634, terms 5/10, n/30, invoice no. 1004.
23 Received a shipment from Osgood Books, Inc., $2,374, invoice dated May 19, terms 5/10, n/60, FOB shipping point.
24 Issued check no. C007 to Linden Shippers for balance owed on account plus shipping charges of $194 on previous day's shipment.
27 Cash sales for the second two weeks, $7,488.
29 Issued check no. C008 to Payroll Account for sales salaries for first four weeks of the month, $1,400.
31 Cash sales for the last four days of the month, $554.

Required

1. Prepare a sales journal, a multicolumn purchases journal, a cash receipts journal, a cash payments journal, and a general journal. Use Page 1 for all journal references.
2. Open the following general ledger accounts: Cash (111), Accounts Receivable (112), Store Equipment (141), Accounts Payable (211), Notes Payable (212), Linda Bromberg, Capital (311), Sales (411), Sales Discounts (412), Sales Returns and Allowances (413), Purchases (511), Purchases Discounts (512), Purchases Returns and Allowances (513), Freight In (514), Sales Salaries Expense (611), Advertising Expense (612), and Rent Expense (613).
3. Open the following accounts receivable subsidiary ledger accounts: Horizon Center, Yosh Kawano, and Ruth Mayhew.
4. Open the following accounts payable subsidiary ledger accounts: Forrest Books; Linden Shippers; Osgood Books, Inc.; and Patton Publishing Company.
5. Enter the transactions in the journals and post as appropriate.
6. Foot and crossfoot the journals, and make the end-of-month postings.
7. Prepare a trial balance of the general ledger, and prove the control balances of Accounts Receivable and Accounts Payable by preparing schedules of accounts receivable and accounts payable.

Problem 7A-5. Internal Control *(L.O. 6, 7)*

Lyons Company, a large merchandising concern that stocks over 85,000 different items in inventory, has just installed a new computer system for inventory control. The computer's data storage system provides for direct access to up-to-date inventory records and carries all pertinent data relating to individual items of inventory. The system is equipped with fifteen remote computer terminals, distributed at various locations throughout the warehouse and sales areas. Using these terminals, employees can obtain information from the computer system about the status of any inventory item. To make an inquiry, they use a keyboard similar to a typewriter's. The answer is relayed back instantaneously on the screen. As inventory is received, shipped, or transferred, employees update the inventory records in the computer system by means of the remote terminals.

Required

1. What potential weakness in internal control exists in the system?
2. What suggestions do you have for improving the company's internal control?

Problem Set B

Problem 7B-1. Special-Purpose Journals and Subsidiary Ledgers *(L.O. 4, 5)*

Sachs Company, a small retail business, uses a manual accounting system similar to the one illustrated in this chapter. At the end of May 19xx, the accounts in the accounts receivable and accounts payable subsidiary ledgers showed the following balances:

Accounts Receivable		Accounts Payable	
T. Bakof	$ 870	Cellcor Inc.	$2,900
R. Banz	650	Visidyne Company	460
Total Accounts Receivable	$1,520	Total Accounts Payable	$3,360

During June, the company engaged in the following transactions:

June 2 Sold merchandise on credit to R. Banz, $920, terms 2/10, n/30, invoice no. 4001.
4 Received payment in full from R. Banz for the amount due at the beginning of June less a 2 percent discount.
5 Paid Cellcor Inc. full amount owed less a 2 percent discount, check no. 501.
8 Accepted a return of merchandise from R. Banz, $220.
9 Paid Visidyne Company the full amount owed, no discount allowed, check no. 502.
12 Received payment from R. Banz for the amount due less the discount.
15 Received partial payment from T. Bakof, no discount allowed, $300.
22 Purchased merchandise from Visidyne Company, $1,700, terms 2/10, n/30, FOB destination, invoice dated June 21.

June 23 Sold merchandise on credit to F. Younger, \$2,450, terms 2/10, n/30, invoice no. 4002.
26 Purchased merchandise from Cellcor Inc., \$1,500, terms 2/10, n/30, FOB destination, invoice dated June 24.
30 Returned merchandise to Visidyne Company for full credit, \$600.

Required

1. Prepare a sales journal, a single-column purchases journal, a cash receipts journal, a cash payments journal, and a general journal similar to the ones illustrated in the chapter. Sachs Company uses the gross method to record purchases. Use Page 1 for all references.
2. Open the following general ledger accounts: Accounts Receivable (112) and Accounts Payable (211).
3. Open the following accounts receivable subsidiary ledger accounts: T. Bakof, R. Banz, and F. Younger.
4. Open the following accounts payable subsidiary ledger accounts: Cellcor Inc. and Visidyne Company.
5. Enter the transactions in the journals and post to the appropriate subsidiary ledger and general ledger accounts.
6. Foot and crossfoot the journals, and make the end-of-month postings applicable to Accounts Receivable and Accounts Payable.
7. Prove the control balances of Accounts Receivable and Accounts Payable by preparing schedules of accounts receivable and accounts payable.

Problem 7B-2.
Cash Receipts and Cash Payments Journals
(L.O. 4)

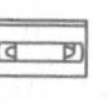

The items below detail all cash transactions by Baylor Company for the month of July. The company uses multicolumn cash receipts and cash payments journals similar to those illustrated in the chapter.

July 1 The owner, Eugene Baylor, invested \$50,000 cash and \$24,000 in equipment in the business.
2 Paid rent to Leonard Agency, \$600, with check no. 75.
3 Cash sales, \$2,200.
6 Purchased store equipment for \$5,000 cash from Gilmore Company, with check no. 76.
7 Purchased merchandise for cash, \$6,500, from Pascual Company, with check no. 77.
8 Paid Audretti Company invoice, \$1,800, less 2 percent discount, with check no. 78 (assume that a payable has already been recorded).
9 Paid advertising bill, \$350, to WOSU, with check no. 79.
10 Cash sales, \$3,910.
12 Received \$800 on account from B. Erring.
13 Purchased used truck for cash, \$3,520, from Pettit Company, with check no. 80.
19 Received \$4,180 from Monroe Company, in settlement of a \$4,000 note plus interest.
20 Received \$1,078 (\$1,100 less \$22 cash discount) from Young Lee.
21 Paid Baylor \$2,000 from business for personal use by issuing check no. 81.
23 Paid Dautley Company invoice, \$2,500, less 2 percent discount, with check no. 82.
26 Paid Haywood Company for freight on merchandise received, \$60, with check no. 83.
27 Cash sales, \$4,800.
28 Paid C. Murphy for monthly salary, \$1,400, with check no. 84.
31 Purchased land from N. Archibald for \$20,000, paying \$5,000 with check no. 85 and signing a note payable for \$15,000.

Required

1. Enter the preceding transactions in the cash receipts and cash payments journals.
2. Foot and crossfoot the journals.

Problem 7B-3. Purchases and General Journals
(L.O. 4, 5)

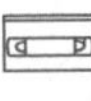

The following items represent the credit transactions for McGarry Company during the month of August. The company uses a multicolumn purchases journal and a general journal similar to those illustrated in the text.

Aug. 2 Purchased merchandise from Alvarez Company, $1,400.
5 Purchased truck to be used in the business from Meriweather Company, $8,000.
8 Purchased office supplies from Daudridge Company, $400.
12 Purchased filing cabinets from Daudridge Company, $550.
14 Purchased merchandise, $1,400, and store supplies, $200, from Petrie Company.
17 Purchased store supplies from Alvarez Company, $100, and office supplies from Hollins Company, $50.
20 Purchased merchandise from Petrie Company, $1,472.
24 Purchased merchandise from Alvarez Company, $2,452; the $2,452 invoice total included shipping charges, $232.
26 Purchased office supplies from Daudridge Company, $150.
30 Purchased merchandise from Petrie Company, $290.
31 Returned defective merchandise purchased from Petrie Company on August 20 for full credit, $432.

Required

1. Enter the preceding transactions in the purchases journal and the general journal. Assume that all terms are n/30 and that invoice dates are the same as the transaction dates. Use Page 1 for all references.
2. Foot and crossfoot the purchases journal.
3. Open the following general ledger accounts: Store Supplies (116), Office Supplies (117), Trucks (142), Office Equipment (144), Accounts Payable (211), Purchases (611), Purchases Returns and Allowances (612), and Freight In (613). Open accounts payable subsidiary ledger accounts as needed. Post from the journals to the ledger accounts.

Problem 7B-4. Comprehensive Use of Special-Purpose Journals
(L.O. 4, 5)

The following transactions were completed by Majid's Men's Wear during the month of May, its first month of operation:

May 1 Farouk Majid deposited $40,000 in the new company's bank account.
2 Issued check no. 101 to O'Neal Realty for one month's rent, $2,400.
3 Received merchandise from Worth Company, $14,000, invoice dated May 2, terms 2/10, n/60, FOB shipping point.
4 Received freight bill on merchandise purchased from Chappell Freight Company, $1,928, terms n/20.
5 Issued check no. 102 to Kwan Company for store equipment, $14,800.
6 Borrowed $16,000 from the bank on a 90-day, 9 percent note.
7 Cash sales for the first week, $3,964. (To shorten this problem, cash sales are recorded weekly instead of daily, as they would be in actual practice.)
8 Sold merchandise to Newfield School, $1,800, terms 2/10, n/30, invoice no. 1001.
9 Sold merchandise to Scott Kravitz, $600, terms n/20, invoice no. 1002.
10 Purchased advertising in the *News-Chronicle*, $300, terms n/15.
11 Issued check no. 103 for purchase of May 3 less discount.
12 Issued a credit memorandum for merchandise returned by Scott Kravitz, $60.
15 Cash sales for the second week, $6,984.
16 Received merchandise from Worth Company, $3,800, invoice dated May 15, terms 2/10, n/60, FOB shipping point.
17 Received freight bill on merchandise purchased from Chappell Freight Company, $524, terms n/20.
18 Received merchandise from Merullo Company, $2,800, invoice dated May 16, terms 1/10, n/60, FOB destination.
18 Received payment in full less discount from Newfield School.

May 20 Received a credit memorandum from Worth Company of $200 for merchandise returned to them from purchase of May 3.
21 Cash sales for the third week, $5,824.
23 Issued check no. 104 for the total amount owed Chappell Freight Company.
24 Sold merchandise to Newfield School, $1,368, terms 2/10, n/30, invoice no. 1003.
25 Issued check no. 105 in payment of the amount owed Worth Company less discount.
26 Sold merchandise to Judy Ming, $744, terms n/20, invoice no. 1004.
27 Issued check no. 106 for the amount owed the *News-Chronicle.*
28 Cash sales for the fourth week, $3,948.
31 Issued check no. 107 to Payroll Account for sales salaries for the month of May, $7,200.

Required

1. Prepare a sales journal, a multicolumn purchases journal, a cash receipts journal, a cash payments journal, and a general journal. Use Page 1 for all journal references.
2. Open the following general ledger accounts: Cash (111), Accounts Receivable (112), Store Equipment (141), Accounts Payable (211), Notes Payable (212), Farouk Majid, Capital (311), Sales (411), Sales Discounts (412), Sales Returns and Allowances (413), Purchases (511), Purchases Discounts (512), Purchases Returns and Allowances (513), Freight In (514), Sales Salaries Expense (611), Advertising Expense (612), and Rent Expense (613).
3. Open the following accounts receivable subsidiary ledger accounts: Scott Kravitz, Judy Ming, and Newfield School.
4. Open the following accounts payable subsidiary ledger accounts: Chappell Freight Company, Merullo Company, the *News-Chronicle,* and Worth Company.
5. Enter the transactions in the journals and post as appropriate.
6. Foot and crossfoot the journals, and make the end-of-month postings.
7. Prepare a trial balance of the general ledger and prove the control balances of Accounts Receivable and Accounts Payable by preparing schedules of accounts receivable and accounts payable.

Problem 7B-5. Internal Control
(L.O. 6, 7)

Ravikumar Company, a small concern, is attempting to organize its accounting department to achieve maximum internal control, subject to the constraint of limited resources. There are three employees (1, 2, and 3) in the accounting department, each of whom has some accounting experience. The accounting department must accomplish the following functions: (a) maintain the general ledger, (b) maintain the accounts payable subsidiary ledger, (c) maintain the accounts receivable subsidiary ledger, (d) prepare checks for signature, (e) maintain the cash payments journal, (f) issue credits on returns and allowances, (g) reconcile the bank account, and (h) handle and deposit cash receipts.

Required

1. Assuming that each employee does only the jobs assigned, assign the functions to the three employees in a way that ensures the highest degree of internal control possible.
2. Identify four possible unsatisfactory combinations of functions.

Financial Decision Case

RW Finer Foods Company
(L.O. 3, 4, 5)

RW Finer Foods Company, owned by Robert Washington, is a local grocery store that accepts cash or checks in payment for food. Known for its informality, the store has been very successful and has grown with the community. Along with that growth, however, has come an increase in the number of bad checks written for purchases by customers. Washington is concerned about the difficulty of accounting for these returned checks, so he asks you to look into the problem.

In addition to a purchases journal and a cash payments journal, the company has a combination single-column sales and cash receipts journal. This combination journal has worked in the past because all sales are for cash (including checks), and almost all cash receipts represent sales transactions. Thus, the single column represents a debit to Cash and a credit to Sales.

The bad checks are recorded individually in the general journal by debiting Accounts Receivable and crediting Cash. When a customer pays off a bad check, another entry is made in the general journal debiting Cash and crediting Accounts Receivable. Washington keeps the returned checks in an envelope. When a customer comes in to pay one off, he gives the check back. No other records of the returned checks are maintained.

In studying the problem, you discover that the company is averaging ten returned checks a day, totaling $1,000. As part of the solution, you recommend to Washington that he issue check-cashing cards to customers whose credit is approved in advance. The card must be presented when a customer offers a check in payment for groceries. You recommend further that a special journal be established for the returned checks, that a subsidiary ledger be maintained, and that the combination sales/cash receipts journal be expanded.

Required

1. Draw and label the columns for the new returned checks journal and the expanded sales/cash receipts journal.
2. Assume that there are 300 returned checks and 280 collections a month and that the records are closed each month. How many written lines can be saved each month in recording returned checks and subsequent collections in the special journals? How many postings can be saved each month? (Ignore the effect of the subsidiary ledger.)
3. Describe the nature and use of the subsidiary ledger. What advantages do you see in having a subsidiary ledger?
4. Assuming that it takes approximately two and a half minutes to make each entry and related postings under the old system of recording bad checks and one minute to make each entry and related postings under the new system, what are the monthly savings if the cost is $20 an hour? What further, and possibly more significant, savings may be realized using the new system?

Answers to Self-Test

1. d	3. b	5. d	7. c	9. b
2. d	4. b	6. c	8. b	10. d

Comprehensive Problem: Fenwick Fashions Company

Fenwick Fashions Company was introduced in the chapter on accounting for merchandising operations. Here, we continue the Fenwick Fashions example by completing the accounting cycle for the month of January 19x2, using special-purpose journals.

The chart of accounts and December 31, 19x1, post-closing trial balance for Fenwick Fashions Company are as follows:

Account Name	Account Number	Debit	Credit
Cash	111	$ 29,410	
Accounts Receivable	112	42,400	
Merchandise Inventory	113	48,300	
Prepaid Insurance	114	11,600	
Store Supplies	115	1,060	
Office Supplies	116	636	
Land	141	4,500	
Building	142	20,260	
Accumulated Depreciation, Building	143		$ 8,250
Office Equipment	144	8,600	
Accumulated Depreciation, Office Equipment	145		5,000
Accounts Payable	211		25,683
Gloria Fenwick, Capital	311		127,833
Gloria Fenwick, Withdrawals	312		
Income Summary	314		
Sales	411		
Sales Returns and Allowances	412		
Sales Discounts	413		
Purchases	511		
Purchases Returns and Allowances	512		
Purchases Discounts	513		
Freight In	514		
Sales Salaries Expense	611		
Freight Out Expense	612		
Advertising Expense	613		
Insurance Expense, Selling	614		
Store Supplies Expense	615		
Office Salaries Expense	621		
Insurance Expense, General	622		
Office Supplies Expense	623		
Telephone Expense	624		
Utility Expense	625		
Depreciation Expense, Building	626		
Depreciation Expense, Office Equipment	627		
Totals		$166,766	$166,766

The company's accounts receivable and accounts payable subsidiary ledgers showed the following accounts and balances on December 31, 19x1:

Schedule of Accounts Receivable

Boris Acton	$ 2,300
Liza Cartwright	1,800
Henry Montin	—
Turnstyle Apparel Centers	38,300
Total Accounts Receivable	$42,400

Schedule of Accounts Payable

Daily Gazette	—
Easton Freight	$ 350
Jason Styles	4,500
Jones Supply House	—
Modern Fashions	8,900
Zalesk Shoes	11,933
Total Accounts Payable	$25,683

During the month of January 19x2, Fenwick Fashions engaged in the following transactions:

Jan. 2 Received payment on account from Turnstyle Apparel Centers, no discount allowed, $12,000.

4 Sold merchandise to Liza Cartwright on credit, terms 2/10, n/30, FOB destination, invoice no. 2330, $1,400.

4 Received a bill for shipping costs on above merchandise from Easton Freight, dated today, terms n/30, $90.

5 Paid amount owed to Jason Styles less 2 percent discount for payment within ten days, check no. 1441.

6 Accepted defective merchandise back from Boris Acton and gave full credit on account, $1,100.

8 Returned merchandise to Zalesk Shoes for full credit, $753.

9 Received payment on account from Liza Cartwright, 2 percent discount allowed, for sale in December.

10 Received a shipment of merchandise from Modern Fashions, invoice dated January 8, terms 2/10, n/30, FOB shipping point, $1,900.

10 Received a bill for shipping costs on above merchandise from Easton Freight, dated today, terms n/30, $180.

11 Paid Easton Freight for amount owed at the beginning of the month, check no. 1442, $350.

12 Made partial payment on account to Zalesk Shoes, no discount allowed, check no. 1443, $8,000.

14 Received payment in full for January 4 sale to Liza Cartwright less 2 percent discount.

15 Sold merchandise to Turnstyle Apparel Centers on account, terms n/30, FOB shipping point, invoice no. 2331, $5,000.

16 Cash sales for the first half of January, $9,110.

16 Paid salaries for the first half of January, check no. 1444, payable to Payroll Account, $2,000. Salaries are allocated $1,100 to sales salaries and $900 to office salaries.

Jan. 17 Paid Modern Fashions in full the amount owed on account on December 31 (no discount allowed) and for the purchase received January 10, invoice dated January 8, less discount, check no. 1445.
19 Sold merchandise to Henry Montin on credit, terms 2/10, n/30, FOB destination, invoice no. 2332, $900.
19 Received a bill for shipping costs on above merchandise from Easton Freight, dated today, terms n/30, $50.
20 Received a bill from the *Daily Gazette* for advertisements, dated January 15, terms n/30, $850.
21 Received a shipment of supplies from Jones Supply House, invoice dated January 18, terms n/30, FOB destination, $360. The supplies are allocated $200 to store supplies and $160 to office supplies.
22 Paid MidBell for January telephone bill, check no. 1446, $120.
23 Received a shipment of merchandise from Jason Styles, invoice dated January 22, terms 2/10, n/30, FOB shipping point, $4,100.
23 Received a bill for shipping costs on above merchandise from Easton Freight, dated today, terms n/30, $220.
25 Sold merchandise to Liza Cartwright on credit, terms 2/10, n/30, FOB destination, invoice no. 2333, $1,400.
25 Received a bill for shipping costs on above merchandise from Easton Freight, dated today, terms n/30, $90.
26 Made a check payable to Gloria Fenwick for her monthly withdrawal, check no. 1447, $1,900.
27 Paid Common Utility for January utilities, check no. 1448, $410.
28 Received payment from Henry Montin for half of the sale on January 19 less the discount.
31 Paid salaries for the last half of January, check no. 1449, payable to Payroll Account, $2,000. Salaries are allocated $1,100 to sales salaries and $900 to office salaries.
31 Cash sales for the last half of January, $6,960.

Fenwick Fashions Company uses a single-column sales journal, a multi-column purchases journal, a cash receipts journal, a cash payments journal, and a general journal. It also has subsidiary ledgers for accounts receivable and accounts payable. General ledger accounts are maintained for each account in the trial balance. Assume all journals begin January on Page 13, except for the general journal, which starts on Page 20.

Required

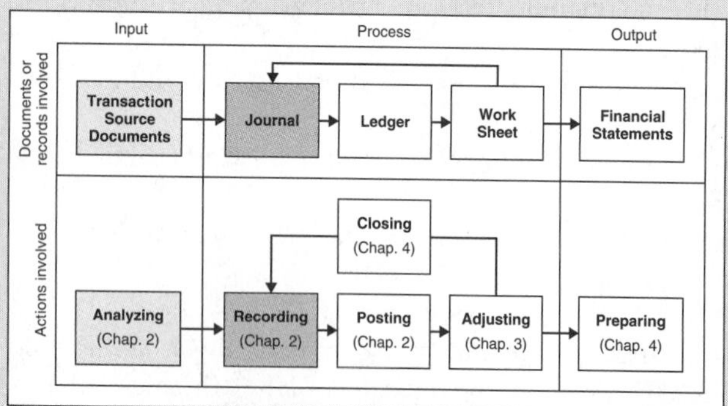

1. Record the January transactions in the journals and make individual postings as appropriate.

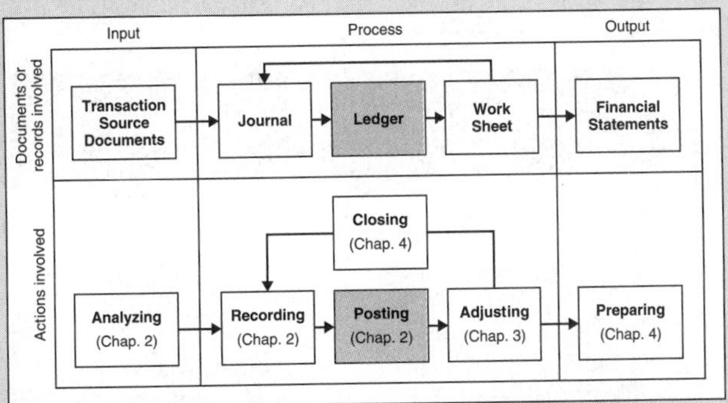

2. Foot and crossfoot the journals and make the end-of-month postings.

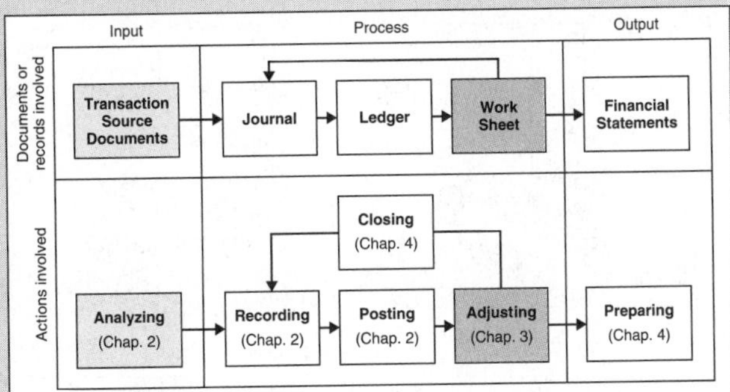

3. Prepare a trial balance in the Trial Balance columns of a work sheet, and complete the work sheet using the following information:
   a. Ending merchandise inventory, $42,300.
   b. Expired insurance (allocated 30 percent to selling and 70 percent to general), $900.
   c. Ending store supplies inventory, $590.
   d. Ending office supplies inventory, $280.
   e. Estimated depreciation on building, $220.
   f. Estimated depreciation on office equipment, $200.

   In preparing the work sheet, use either the adjusting entry or the closing entry method.

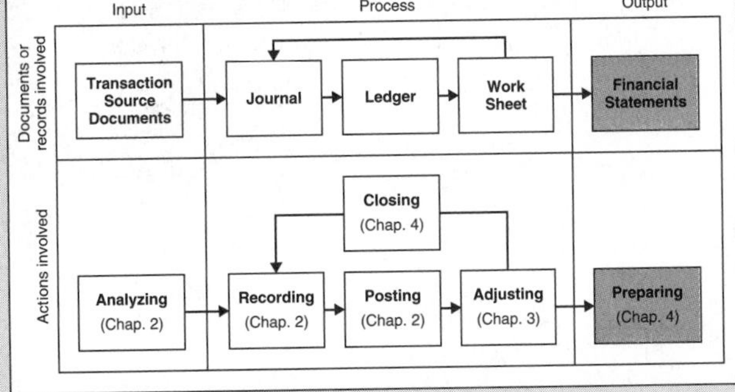

4. From the work sheet, prepare an income statement, statement of owner's equity, and a balance sheet.

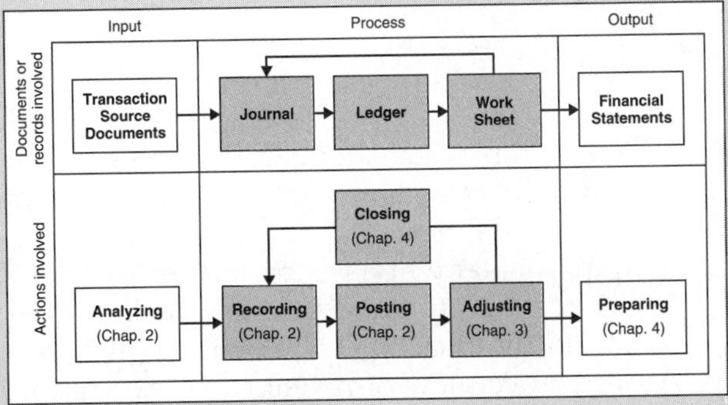

5. Prepare a schedule of accounts receivable and a schedule of accounts payable to prove the balances of the controlling accounts.
6. From the work sheet, record and post the adjusting entries.
7. From the work sheet, record and post the closing entries.
8. Prepare a post-closing trial balance.

This Comprehensive Problem covers all of the Learning Objectives in the chapter on accounting for merchandising operations and Learning Objectives 3 through 5 in the chapter on accounting systems and internal control.

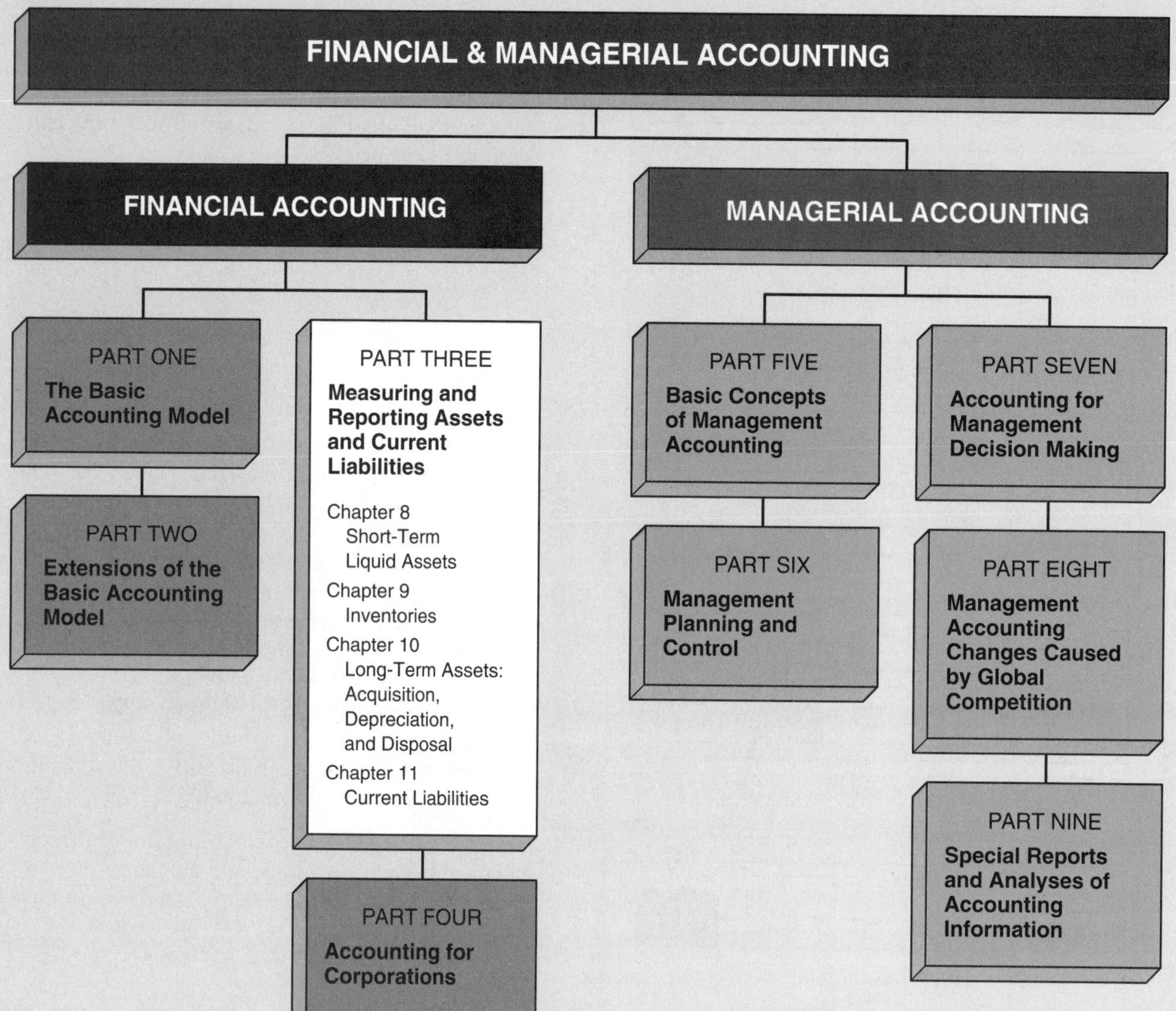

Part Three considers each of the major types of assets as well as the category of current liabilities and payroll accounting, with particular emphasis on the effect of their measurement on net income and their presentation in the financial statements. It also provides an overview of revenue and expense issues and accounting for natural resources and intangible assets.

PART THREE

Measuring and Reporting Assets and Current Liabilities

Chapter 8 focuses on the major types of short-term liquid assets: cash and short-term investments, accounts receivable, and notes receivable.

Chapter 9 presents the accounting concepts and techniques associated with inventories and discusses their importance to income measurement.

Chapter 10 discusses the acquisition of property, plant, and equipment, and the concept and techniques of depreciation. It applies the matching rule to capital and revenue expenditures and to disposal of depreciable assets. In addition, accounting for long-term assets such as natural resources and for intangible assets is covered.

Chapter 11 deals with current liabilities.

LEARNING OBJECTIVES

1. *Account for cash and short-term investments.*
2. *Define accounts receivable, and explain the relationships among credit policies, sales, and uncollectible accounts.*
3. *Apply the allowance method of accounting for uncollectible accounts, including using the percentage of net sales method and the accounts receivable aging method to estimate uncollectible accounts.*
4. *Identify methods of financing accounts receivable and other issues related to accounts receivable.*
5. *Define and describe a promissory note, and make calculations involving promissory notes.*
6. *Journalize entries involving notes receivable.*
7. *Describe a bank account and demonstrate the control of cash by preparing a bank reconciliation.*
8. *Demonstrate the use of a simple imprest system.*

CHAPTER 8

Short-Term Liquid Assets

In the chapters on accounting as an information system and on accounting concepts and classified financial statements, profitability and liquidity were identified as two major concerns of management. In this chapter, you will study the assets that are most closely associated with the liquidity of business. **Short-term liquid assets** are financial assets that arise from cash transactions, the investment of cash, and the extension of credit. They include cash, short-term investments, accounts receivable, and notes receivable. Short-term liquid assets are useful because they are usually quickly available for paying current obligations. Other assets—such as inventories; property, plant, and equipment; natural resources; and intangibles—are less liquid. After studying this chapter, you should be able to meet the learning objectives listed on the left.

DECISION POINT
Bell Atlantic Corporation

■ Management must use a company's assets to maximize income earned while maintaining the company's liquidity. This responsibility applies to the company's short-term liquid assets as well as to productive assets such as property, plant, and equipment. Bell Atlantic Corporation, a leading provider of voice and data communications, mobile telephone services, computer maintenance services, and equipment leasing and financing products, manages almost $3 billion in short-term liquid assets. As reported on the balance sheet in the company's 1990 annual report, these assets were as follows at the end of 1990 (in millions):

Cash and Cash Equivalents	$ 94.7
Short-Term Investments	15.0
Accounts Receivable, Net of Allowances of $123.9	2,080.2
Notes Receivable, Net	605.0
Total Short-Term Liquid Assets	$2,794.9

Although these assets make up only a little more than 10 percent of Bell Atlantic's total assets, they are very important to the company's strategy for meeting its goals. The asset management techniques employed at Bell Atlantic ensure that these assets remain liquid and usable for the company's operations. These techniques also maximize the interest earned on the assets and minimize losses from any decrease in the investments' market value or from the failure of customers to pay their bills. Moreover, the company keeps cash at a minimum by investing the cash that is not currently needed. This chapter emphasizes the accounting for, and management of, these short-term liquid assets. ■

Accounting for Cash and Short-Term Investments

OBJECTIVE 1
Account for cash and short-term investments

The annual report of Bell Atlantic Corporation refers to *cash and cash equivalents.* Of these two terms, *cash* is the easier to understand. It is the most liquid of all assets and the most readily available to pay debts. We discussed the control of cash receipts and cash payments in the chapter on accounting for merchandising operations, but we did not deal with the content of the Cash account on the balance sheet. **Cash** normally consists of coin and currency on hand, checks and money orders from customers, and deposits in bank checking accounts. Cash may also include a **compensating balance**, an amount that is not entirely free to be spent. A compensating balance is a minimum amount that a bank requires a company to keep in its bank account as part of a credit-granting arrangement. Such an arrangement restricts cash and may reduce a company's liquidity. Therefore, the SEC requires companies to disclose the amount of any compensating balance in a note to the financial statements.

The term *cash equivalents* is a little harder to understand. At times a company may find it has more cash on hand than it needs to pay current obligations. This excess cash should not remain idle, especially during periods of high interest rates. Thus, management may periodically invest the idle funds in time deposits or certificates of deposit at banks and other financial institutions, in government securities such as U.S. Treasury notes, or in other securities. These actions are rightfully called investments. However, if these investments have a term of less than ninety days, they are often called **cash equivalents**, because the funds revert to cash so quickly that they are regarded as cash on the balance sheet. Bell Atlantic follows this practice. Its policy is stated as follows: "The Company considers all highly liquid investments with a maturity of 90 days or less when purchased to be cash equivalents. Cash equivalents are stated at cost, which approximates market value." A recent survey of the practices of 600 large U.S. corporations found that 134 of them, or 22 percent, used the term *cash* as the balance sheet caption and 358, or 60 percent, used the phrase *cash and cash equivalents* or *cash and equivalents.* Ninety-three companies, or 16 percent, combined cash with marketable securities.[1] The average amount of cash held can also vary by industry.

When investments have a maturity of more than ninety days but are intended to be held only until cash is needed for current operations, they are called **short-term investments** or **marketable securities.** Bell Atlantic states its policy on short-term investments as follows: "Short-term investments consist of investments that mature in 91 days to 12 months from the date of purchase." Investments that are intended to be held for more than one year are called long-term investments. As discussed in the chapter on accounting concepts and classified financial statements, long-term investments are classified in an investments section of the balance sheet, not in the current assets section. Although these investments may be just as marketable as short-term assets, management intends to hold them for an indefinite period of time.

1. *Accounting Trends & Techniques* (New York: American Institute of CPAs, 1990), p. 88.

Short-term investments are first recorded at cost. Suppose that on March 1, ST Company paid $97,000 for U.S. Treasury bills, which are short-term debt of the U.S. government. The bills will mature in 120 days at $100,000. The following entry would be made by ST Company:

Mar. 1	Short-Term Investments	97,000	
	Cash		97,000
	Purchase of U.S. Treasury bills that mature in 120 days at $100,000		

Income on short-term investments is recorded as received. Dividends and interest on stocks and bonds held as short-term investments would be recorded as Dividend Income or Interest Income when received. For example, ST Company receives interest on the Treasury bills when the bills mature, as shown in the following entry:

June 29	Cash	100,000	
	Interest Income		3,000
	Short-Term Investments		97,000
	Receipt of cash on U.S. Treasury bills and recognition of related income		

When short-term investments are sold, a gain or loss usually results. Suppose that ST Company sells 5,000 shares of an investment in Mobil Corporation on December 5. It bought the shares for $70 per share, including broker's commission. When it sells them at $60 per share net of (after) broker's commissions, the following entry results:

Dec. 5	Cash	300,000	
	Loss on Sale of Investments	50,000	
	Short-Term Investments		350,000
	Sale of 5,000 shares of Mobil Corporation at $60, net of commissions		

In the *Statement of Financial Accounting Standards No. 12,* the Financial Accounting Standards Board requires that investments in debt securities, such as U.S. Treasury bills or corporate debt, be listed at cost, unless there is reason to believe that the value of the security is permanently impaired. However, the board requires that investments in equity securities, such as capital stock, be reported at the lower of the historical cost or the market value on the balance sheet date.[2] For example, assume that at its year end of December 31, ST Company still owns 10,000 shares of Mobil Corporation that it purchased for $70 per share and that are now worth $60 per share. An adjusting entry is made to recognize the loss in value and to reduce the asset amount by means of a contra account, as follows:

Dec. 31	Loss on Decline in Short-Term Investments	100,000	
	Allowance to Reduce Short-Term Investments to Market		100,000
	To recognize decline in market value of short-term investments		

2. *Statement of Financial Accounting Standards No. 12,* "Accounting for Certain Marketable Securities" (Stamford, Conn.: Financial Accounting Standards Board, 1975).

The loss is reported on the income statement. Although it is not usually shown as a separate item, the allowance account is reflected in the value assigned to short-term investments on the balance sheet, as follows:

Current Assets

Short-Term Investments (at lower of cost or market; cost equals $700,000)	$600,000

Subsequent increases in the investment's market value may be recorded, but only to bring it back up to cost. Increases in market value per share above cost are not recorded. When investments that previously have been written down are sold, the gain or loss is measured by the difference between the sale price and the original purchase cost, regardless of any balance in Allowance to Reduce Short-Term Investments to Market. For instance, if ST Company sells 2,000 of the Mobil shares it owned at year end on January 15 for $62 per share, the entry would be:

Jan. 15	Cash	124,000	
	Loss on Sale of Investments	16,000	
	Short-Term Investments		140,000
	Sale of 2,000 shares of Mobil at a loss: 2,000 shares × ($70 − $62) = $16,000		

At the end of the next accounting period, the balance in the allowance account is adjusted up or down to reflect any difference between the total cost and the total market value of any short-term investments held at the end of the accounting period. The credit balance in the allowance account may be reduced to zero (resulting in a gain) if the market value exceeds the cost of the short-term investments. Short-term investments, however, are never increased to a value above cost. If the company has more than one investment, these rules are applied to the total value of the investments at the end of each accounting period.

Accounting for investments is inconsistent with the concept of historical cost. Under historical cost, the cost value would be maintained on the balance sheet until the asset is sold. Accountants justify this inconsistency on the basis of the conservatism convention. That is, they recognize the potential loss immediately but put off recognition of any potential gain until it is actually realized.

Accounting for Accounts Receivable

OBJECTIVE 2
Define accounts receivable, and explain the relationships among credit policies, sales, and uncollectible accounts

The other major types of short-term liquid assets are accounts receivable and notes receivable. Both result from credit sales to customers. Retail companies such as Sears, Roebuck have made credit available to nearly every responsible person in the United States. Every field of retail trade has expanded by allowing customers to make payments a month or more after the date of sale. What is not so apparent is that credit has expanded even more in the wholesale and manufacturing industries than at the retail level. The rest of this chapter discusses accounting for accounts receivable and notes receivable, which play a key role in the credit expansion.

Accounts receivable are short-term liquid assets that arise from sales on credit to customers by wholesalers or retailers. This type of credit is often called **trade credit**.

Credit Policies and Uncollectible Accounts

Companies that sell on credit naturally want customers who will pay. Therefore, most companies develop control procedures to increase the likelihood of selling only to customers who will pay when they are supposed to. As a result of these procedures, a company generally has a credit department. This department's responsibilities include the examination of each person or company that applies for credit and the approval or rejection of a credit sale to that customer. Typically, the credit department will ask for information on the customer's financial resources and debts. In addition, it may check personal references and established credit bureaus, which may provide further information about the customer. On the basis of this information, the credit department will decide whether to extend credit to that customer. It may recommend the payment amount, limit the amount of credit, or request that the customer put up certain assets as security.

Regardless of how thorough and efficient its credit control system is, a company will always have some customers who cannot or will not pay. The accounts owed by such customers are called **uncollectible accounts**, or bad debts, and are a loss or an expense of selling on credit. Why does a company sell on credit if it expects that some of its accounts will not be paid? The answer is that the company expects to sell much more than it would if it did not sell on credit, thereby increasing its earnings.

Matching Losses on Uncollectible Accounts with Sales

Accounting for uncollectible accounts is based on the matching rule. Expenses should be matched against the sales they help to produce. If bad debt losses are incurred in the process of increasing sales revenues, they should be charged against those sales revenues. A company does not know when it makes a credit sale that the debt will not be collected. In fact, it may take a year or more to exhaust every possible means of collection. Even though the loss may not be specifically identified until a later accounting period, it is still an expense of the period in which the sale was made. Therefore, losses from uncollectible accounts must be estimated, and this estimate becomes an expense in the fiscal year when the sales were made. This method of accounting for uncollectible accounts is called the **allowance method**.

For example, let us assume that Cottage Sales Company made most of its sales on credit during its first year of operation. At the end of the year, accounts receivable amounted to $100,000. On this date, management reviewed the collectible status of the accounts receivable. Approximately $6,000 of the $100,000 of accounts receivable were estimated to be uncollectible. Therefore, the uncollectible accounts expense for the first year of operation was estimated to be $6,000. The following adjusting entry would be made on December 31 of that year:

Dec. 31	Uncollectible Accounts Expense	6,000	
	Allowance for Uncollectible Accounts		6,000
	To record the estimated uncollectible accounts expense for the year 19x1		

Uncollectible Accounts Expense appears on the income statement as an operating expense. **Allowance for Uncollectible Accounts** appears on the balance sheet as a contra-asset account that is deducted from Accounts Receivable.[3] It reduces the accounts receivable to the amount that is expected to be realized, or collected in cash, as follows:

Current Assets		
Cash		$ 10,000
Short-Term Investments		15,000
Accounts Receivable	$100,000	
Less Allowance for Uncollectible Accounts	6,000	94,000
Inventory		56,000
Total Current Assets		$175,000

The allowance method of accounting for uncollectible accounts argues that, in accordance with the matching rule, a business should assume that a loss from an uncollectible account occurs at the moment the sale is made to the customer. However, the company will not know until some time after the sale that the customer will not pay. The amount of the loss must be estimated if it is to be matched against the sales or revenue for the period. The estimated uncollectible amount cannot be credited to the account of any particular customer. Nor can it be credited to the Accounts Receivable controlling account because doing so would cause the controlling account to be out of balance with the total customers' accounts in the subsidiary ledger. The estimated uncollectible amount is instead credited to Allowance for Uncollectible Accounts.

The allowance account will often have other titles such as Allowance for Doubtful Accounts or Allowance for Bad Debts. Once in a while, the older phrase Reserve for Bad Debts will be seen, but in modern practice it should not be used. Bad Debts Expense is often used as another title for Uncollectible Accounts Expense.

Estimating Uncollectible Accounts Expense

Because it is impossible to know which accounts will be uncollectible at the time financial statements are prepared, it is necessary to estimate the expense to cover the expected losses for the year. Of course, estimates can vary widely. If management takes an optimistic view and projects a small loss from uncollectible accounts, the resulting net accounts receivable will be larger than if management takes a pessimistic view. The net income will also be larger under the optimistic view because the estimated expense will be smaller. The company's accountant makes an estimate based on past experience and current economic conditions. For example, losses from uncollectible accounts are normally expected to be greater in a recession than during a period of economic growth. The final decision, made by management, of what the expense will be will depend on objective information such as the accountant's analyses and on certain qualitative factors such as how investors, bankers, creditors, and others may view the performance of the company. Regardless of the qualitative considerations, the estimated losses from uncollectible accounts should be realistic.

3. The purpose of the Allowance for Uncollectible Accounts account is to reduce the gross accounts receivable to the amount collectible (estimated value). The purpose of another contra account, the Accumulated Depreciation account, is *not* to reduce the gross plant and equipment accounts to realizable value. Rather, its purpose is to show how much of the cost of the plant and equipment has been allocated as an expense to previous accounting periods.

The accountant has two common methods available for estimating uncollectible accounts expense for an accounting period: the percentage of net sales method and the accounts receivable aging method.

OBJECTIVE 3
Apply the allowance method of accounting for uncollectible accounts, including using the percentage of net sales method and the accounts receivable aging method to estimate uncollectible accounts

Percentage of Net Sales Method. The **percentage of net sales method** asks the question, How much of this year's net sales will not be collected? The answer determines the amount of uncollectible accounts expense for the year.

For example, assume that the following balances represent the ending figures for Hassel Company for the year 19x9:

Sales	
	645,000

Sales Returns and Allowances	
40,000	

Sales Discounts	
5,000	

Allowance for Uncollectible Accounts	
	3,600

Assume also that actual losses from uncollectible accounts for the past three years have been as follows:

Year	Net Sales	Actual Losses from Uncollectible Accounts	Percentage
19x6	$ 520,000	$10,200	1.96
19x7	595,000	13,900	2.34
19x8	585,000	9,900	1.69
Total	$1,700,000	$34,000	2.00

Net sales is understood in many businesses to approximate net credit sales. If there are substantial cash sales, then net credit sales should be used. Management believes that uncollectible accounts will continue to average about 2 percent of net sales. The uncollectible accounts expense for the year 19x9 is therefore estimated to be:

$$.02 \times (\$645{,}000 - \$40{,}000 - \$5{,}000) = .02 \times \$600{,}000 = \$12{,}000$$

The entry to record this estimate is:

Date	Account	Debit	Credit
Dec. 31	Uncollectible Accounts Expense	12,000	
	Allowance for Uncollectible Accounts		12,000
	To record uncollectible accounts expense at 2 percent of $600,000 net sales		

Allowance for Uncollectible Accounts will have a balance of $15,600 after the above entry is posted, as follows:

Allowance for Uncollectible Accounts

Date	Item	Debit	Credit	Balance Debit	Balance Credit
Dec. 31	Balance				3,600
31	Adjustment		12,000		15,600

The balance consists of the $12,000 estimated uncollectible accounts receivable from 19x9 sales and the $3,600 estimated uncollectible accounts receivable from previous years. The latter have not yet been matched with specific uncollectible accounts receivable resulting from sales in those years.

Accounts Receivable Aging Method. The **accounts receivable aging method** asks the question, How much of the year-end balance of Accounts Receivable will not be collected? The answer determines the year-end balance of Allowance for Uncollectible Accounts. The difference between this amount and the actual balance of Allowance for Uncollectible Accounts is the expense for the year. In theory, this method should produce the same result as the percentage of net sales method, but in practice it rarely does.

The **aging of accounts receivable** is the process of listing each accounts receivable customer according to the due date of the account. If the customer's account is past due, there is a possibility that the account will not be paid. And, the further past due an account is, the greater that possibility. The aging of accounts receivable is useful to management in evaluating its credit and collection policies and alerting it to possible problems. The aging of accounts receivable for Myer Company is shown in Exhibit 8-1. Each account receivable is classified as being not yet due or as 1–30 days, 31–60 days, 61–90 days, or over 90 days past due. The percentage uncollectible in each category is also shown.

The accountant uses the aging of accounts receivable method to determine the proper balance of Allowance for Uncollectible Accounts. In Exhibit 8-2, past experience shows that only an estimated 1 percent of the accounts not yet due and 2 percent of the 1–30 days past due accounts will not be collected. Past experience also indicates that of the accounts 31–60 days, 61–90 days, and over 90 days past due, 10 percent, 30 percent, and 50 percent, respectively, will not be collected. In total, it is estimated that $2,459 of the $44,400 accounts receivable will not be collected.

Let us assume that the December 31 credit balance of Allowance for Uncollectible Accounts for Myer Company is $800. Thus, the estimated uncollectible accounts expense for the year is $1,659, which is calculated as shown under Exhibit 8-2 on page 314.

Exhibit 8-1. Analysis of Accounts Receivable by Age

Myer Company
Analysis of Accounts Receivable by Age
December 31, 19xx

Customer	Total	Not Yet Due	1–30 Days Past Due	31–60 Days Past Due	61–90 Days Past Due	Over 90 Days Past Due
A. Arnold	$ 150		$ 150			
M. Benoit	400			$ 400		
J. Connolly	1,000	$ 900	100			
R. DiCarlo	250				$ 250	
Others	42,600	21,000	14,000	3,800	2,200	$1,600
Totals	$44,400	$21,900	$14,250	$4,200	$2,450	$1,600
Percentage Uncollectible		1.0	2.0	10.0	30.0	50.0

Exhibit 8-2. Calculation of Estimated Uncollectible Accounts

Myer Company Estimated Uncollectible Accounts December 31, 19xx			
	Amount	Percentage Considered Uncollectible	Allowance for Uncollectible Accounts
Not yet due	$21,900	1	$ 219
1–30 days	14,250	2	285
31–60 days	4,200	10	420
61–90 days	2,450	30	735
Over 90 days	1,600	50	800
	$44,400		$2,459

Estimated Uncollectible Accounts	$2,459
Less Credit Balance—Allowance for Uncollectible Accounts	800
Uncollectible Accounts Expense	$1,659

The uncollectible accounts expense is recorded as follows:

Dec. 31	Uncollectible Accounts Expense	1,659	
	Allowance for Uncollectible Accounts		1,659
	To record the allowance for uncollectible accounts to the level of estimated losses		

The resulting balance of Allowance for Uncollectible Accounts is $2,459, as follows:

Allowance for Uncollectible Accounts

Date	Item	Debit	Credit	Balance Debit	Balance Credit
Dec. 31	Balance				800
31	Adjustment		1,659		2,459

Since an $800 credit balance in this account was carried over because fewer accounts than estimated at the beginning of the accounting period had been written off thus far, an adjustment of only $1,659 is needed to bring Allowance for Uncollectible Accounts to its estimated level. If, however, Allowance for Uncollectible Accounts has a debit balance of $800, the estimated uncollectible accounts expense for the year will be $3,259, calculated as follows:

Estimated Uncollectible Accounts	$2,459
Plus Debit Balance—Allowance for Uncollectible Accounts	800
Uncollectible Accounts Expense	$3,259

The uncollectible accounts expense will be recorded as shown at the top of the next page.

Dec. 31	Uncollectible Accounts Expense	3,259	
	Allowance for Uncollectible Accounts		3,259
	To record the allowance for uncollectible accounts to the level of estimated losses		

After this entry, Allowance for Uncollectible Accounts has a credit balance of $2,459, as follows:

Allowance for Uncollectible Accounts

Date	Item	Debit	Credit	Balance Debit	Balance Credit
Dec. 31	Balance			800	
31	Adjustment		3,259		2,459

In this case, $800 more in accounts were written off because of uncollectibility than had been provided for in the adjustment for estimated uncollectible accounts in the prior period. In order to bring Allowance for Uncollectible Accounts to the new estimate of $2,459, the uncollectible accounts expense for the period had to be $3,259.

Comparison of the Two Methods. Both methods of estimating try to determine the uncollectible accounts expense for the current period in accordance with the matching rule, but they do so in different ways. The percentage of net sales method represents an income statement viewpoint. It assumes that for each dollar of sales a certain proportion will not be collected, and this proportion is the expense for the year. Because this method matches expenses against revenues, it is in accordance with the matching rule. However, this method ignores the current balance of Allowance for Uncollectible Accounts. The estimated proportion of net sales not expected to be collected is added to the current balance of the allowance account.

The accounts receivable aging method represents a balance sheet viewpoint and is a more direct valuation method. It assumes that for each dollar of accounts receivable outstanding, a certain proportion will not be collected, and this proportion is the balance of the allowance account at the end of the year. This method also agrees with the matching rule because the expense is the difference between what the account is and what it should be. The difference is assumed to be applicable to the current year.

Writing Off an Uncollectible Account

When it becomes clear that a specific account receivable will not be collected, the amount should be written off to Allowance for Uncollectible Accounts. Remember that the uncollectible amount was already accounted for as an expense when the allowance was established. For example, assume that R. Deering, who owes the Myer Company $250, is declared bankrupt by a federal court. The entry to *write off* this account is as follows:

Jan. 15	Allowance for Uncollectible Accounts	250	
	Accounts Receivable, R. Deering		250
	To write off receivable from R. Deering as uncollectible; Deering declared bankrupt on January 15		

Although the write-off removes the uncollectible amount from Accounts Receivable, it does not affect the estimated net value of accounts receivable. The write-off simply reduces R. Deering's account to zero and reduces Allowance for Uncollectible Accounts by a similar amount, as the following table shows:

	Balances Before Write-off	Balances After Write-off
Accounts Receivable	$44,400	$44,150
Less Allowance for Uncollectible Accounts	2,459	2,209
Estimated Net Value of Accounts Receivable	$41,941	$41,941

Why Accounts Written Off Will Differ from Estimates. The total of accounts receivable written off in any given year will rarely equal the estimated uncollectible accounts. The allowance account will show a credit balance when the accounts written off are less than the estimated uncollectible accounts. The allowance account will show a debit balance when the accounts written off are greater than the estimated uncollectible accounts.

The adjusting entry that is made to record the estimated uncollectible accounts expense for the current year will eliminate any debit balance at the end of the accounting period. If the percentage of net sales method is used, the new balance of the allowance account after the adjusting entry will equal the percentage of sales estimated to be uncollectible minus the old debit balance. If the accounts receivable aging method is used, the amount of the adjustment must equal the estimated uncollectible accounts plus the debit balance in Allowance for Uncollectible Accounts. Of course, if the estimates are consistently wrong, the balance of the allowance account will become unusually large, indicating that management should reexamine the company's estimation rates.

Recovery of Accounts Receivable Written Off. Sometimes a customer whose account has been written off as uncollectible will later be able to pay the amount owed in full or in part. When this happens, two journal entries must be made: one to reverse the earlier write-off (which is now incorrect) and another to show the collection of the account.

For example, assume that on September 1, R. Deering, after his bankruptcy on January 15, notified the company that he would be able to pay $100 of his account and sent a check for $50. The entries to record this transaction are as follows:

Sept. 1	Accounts Receivable, R. Deering	100	
	Allowance for Uncollectible Accounts		100
	To reinstate the portion of the account of R. Deering now considered collectible; originally written off January 15		
1	Cash	50	
	Accounts Receivable, R. Deering		50
	Collection from R. Deering		

The collectible portion of R. Deering's account must be restored to his account and credited to Allowance for Uncollectible Accounts for two reasons.

First, it turned out to be wrong to write off the full $250 on January 15 because only $150 was actually uncollectible. Second, the accounts receivable subsidiary account for R. Deering should reflect his ability to pay a portion of the money he owed in spite of his bankruptcy. Documentation of this action will give a clear picture of his credit record for future credit action.

DECISION POINT

Fleetwood Enterprises, Inc.[4]

■ In 1987, Fleetwood Enterprises, Inc., the nation's leading producer of recreational vehicles and manufactured homes, established Fleetwood Credit Corporation to finance sales of its RV products. Fleetwood Credit has grown rapidly; by 1990, it financed over 35 percent of all Fleetwood sales. Since buyers of recreational vehicles and manufactured homes can take several years to pay, what method can Fleetwood use to accelerate the cash flow from these receivables?

Fleetwood's management decided to sell significant amounts of the receivables held by Fleetwood Credit Corporation to provide the company with financial flexibility and to provide funds for future growth. In 1990, $143.3 million of its receivables were sold to investors, and the outstanding balance of sold receivables was $191.8 million. Even though the receivables have been sold, the company can be liable for an amount up to $15.5 million for sold receivables that are not paid. If the receivables are paid as expected, Fleetwood has no further liability. ■

Financing Accounts Receivable

OBJECTIVE 4
Identify methods of financing accounts receivable and other issues related to accounts receivable

Financial flexibility is important to most companies. Companies that have significant amounts of assets tied up in accounts receivable may be unwilling or unable to wait until the receivables are collected to receive the cash they represent. Many companies have set up finance companies to help their customers finance the purchase of their products. For example, Ford Motor Co. has Ford Motor Credit Company (FMCC), General Motors Corp. has General Motors Acceptance Corporation (GMAC), and Sears has Sears Roebuck Acceptance Corporation (SRAC). Some companies borrow funds by pledging their accounts receivable as collateral for the loans. If the company does not pay back the loan, the creditor can take the collateral, in this case the accounts receivable, and convert it to cash to satisfy the loan.

Companies can also raise funds by selling or transferring accounts receivable to another entity, called a **factor**. This sale or transfer of accounts receivable is called **factoring**, and it can be done with or without recourse. *Without recourse* means that the factor who buys the accounts receivable bears any losses from uncollectible accounts. A company's acceptance of credit cards like VISA, MasterCard, or American Express is an example of factoring without recourse because the credit card issuers accept the risk of nonpayment. *With recourse* means that the seller of the receivables is liable to the purchaser if the receivable is not collected. The factor, of course, charges a fee for its service. The fee for sales with recourse is usually about 1 percent of the accounts receivable. The fee is higher for sales without recourse because the factor's risk is greater.

4. Information excerpted from the 1990 annual report of Fleetwood Enterprises, Inc.

Other Issues Related to Receivables

Installment Accounts Receivable. Installment sales make up a significant portion of the accounts receivable of many retail companies. Department stores, appliance stores, and retail chains all sell goods that are paid for in a series of time payments. Companies such as J. C. Penney and Sears have millions of dollars in these **installment accounts receivable**. Although the payment period may be twenty-four months or more, installment accounts receivable are classified as current assets if such credit policies are customary in the industry. There are special accounting rules that apply to installment sales. Because these rules can be very complicated, their study is usually deferred until a more advanced accounting course.

Credit Card Sales. Many retailers allow customers to charge their purchases to a third-party company that the customer will pay later. These transactions are normally handled with credit cards. The five most widely used credit cards are American Express, Carte Blanche, Diners Club, MasterCard, and VISA. The customer establishes credit with the lender (the credit card issuer) and receives a plastic card to use in making charge purchases. If the seller accepts the card, an invoice is prepared and signed by the customer at the time of the sale. The seller then sends the invoice to the lender and receives cash. Because the seller does not have to establish the customer's credit, collect from the customer, or tie money up in accounts receivable, the seller receives an economic benefit that is provided by the lender. For this reason, the lender does not pay 100 percent of the total amount of the invoices. The lender takes a discount of 2 to 6 percent on the credit card sales invoices.

One of two procedures is used in accounting for credit card sales, depending on whether the seller must wait for collection from the lender or may deposit the sales invoices in a checking account immediately. The following example illustrates the first procedure. Assume that, at the end of the day, a restaurant has American Express invoices totaling $1,000 and that the discount charged by American Express is 4 percent. These sales are recorded as follows:

Accounts Receivable, American Express	960	
Credit Card Discount Expense	40	
Sales		1,000
Sales made on American Express cards; discount fee is 4 percent		

The seller sends the American Express invoices to American Express and later receives payment for them at 96 percent of their face value. When cash is received, the entry is as follows:

Cash	960	
Accounts Receivable, American Express		960
Receipt of payment from American Express for invoices at 96 percent of face value		

The second procedure is typical of sales made through bank credit cards such as VISA and MasterCard. Assume that the restaurant made sales of $1,000 on VISA credit cards and that VISA takes a 4 percent discount on the sales. Assume also that the sales invoices are deposited in a special VISA bank account in the name of the company, in much the same way that checks from cash sales are deposited. These sales are recorded as follows:

Cash	960	
Credit Card Discount Expense	40	
Sales		1,000
Sales on VISA cards		

Direct Charge-off Method. Some companies debit an expense account directly when an uncollectible account is written off instead of using Allowance for Uncollectible Accounts. This **direct charge-off method** is not in accordance with good accounting theory because it makes no attempt to match revenues and expenses. Uncollectible accounts are charged to expenses in the accounting period in which they are discovered rather than in the period of the sale. On the balance sheet, the accounts receivable are shown at gross value, not realizable value, because there is no Allowance for Uncollectible Accounts. Only the direct charge-off method, however, can be used to compute taxable income under federal income tax regulations. The allowance method is still used for financial reporting because it is better from the standpoint of accounting theory.

Credit Balances in Accounts Receivable. Sometimes customers overpay their accounts by mistake or in anticipation of future purchases. When customer accounts in the accounts receivable ledger show credit balances, the balance of the Accounts Receivable controlling account should not appear on the balance sheet as the total of all accounts receivable. The total of those customers' accounts with credit balances should be shown as a current liability because the company is liable to those customers for their overpayments.

Other Accounts Receivable. On the balance sheet, the title Accounts Receivable should be reserved for sales made to regular customers in the ordinary course of business. If loans or sales that do not fall in this category are made to employees, officers of the corporation, or owners, they should be shown separately on the balance sheet with an asset title such as Receivables from Employees and Officers.

Accounting for Notes Receivable

OBJECTIVE 5
Define and describe a promissory note and make calculations involving promissory notes

A **promissory note** is an unconditional promise to pay a definite sum of money on demand or at a future date. The person who signs the note and thereby promises to pay is called the *maker* of the note. The person to whom payment is to be made is called the *payee.* The promissory note in Figure 8-1 is dated May 20, 19x1 and is an unconditional promise by the maker, Samuel Mason, to pay a definite sum or principal ($1,000) to the payee, Cook County Bank & Trust Company, at the future date of August 18, 19x1. The promissory note bears an interest rate of 8 percent. The payee regards all promissory notes it holds that are due in less than one year as **notes receivable** in the current assets section of the balance sheet. The makers regard them as **notes payable** in the current liabilities section of the balance sheet.

This portion of the chapter is concerned primarily with notes received from customers. The nature of a business generally determines how frequently promissory notes are received from customers. Firms selling durable goods of high value, such as farm machinery and automobiles, will often accept promissory notes. Among the advantages of promissory notes are that they produce interest income and represent a stronger legal claim against the creditor than do accounts receivable. In addition, selling promissory notes to banks is a common

Figure 8-1. A Promissory Note

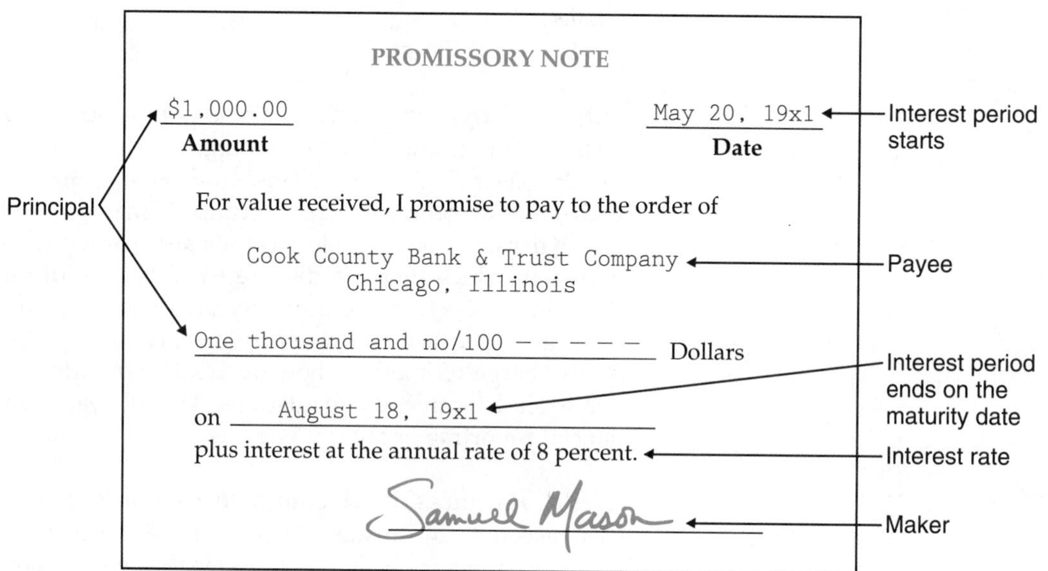
PROMISSORY NOTE

$1,000.00	May 20, 19x1
Amount	Date

For value received, I promise to pay to the order of

Cook County Bank & Trust Company
Chicago, Illinois

One thousand and no/100 ----- Dollars

on August 18, 19x1

plus interest at the annual rate of 8 percent.

Samuel Mason

financing method. Almost all companies will occasionally receive a note, and many companies obtain notes receivable in settlement of past-due accounts.

Computations for Promissory Notes

In accounting for promissory notes, several terms are important to remember. These terms are (1) maturity date, (2) duration of note, (3) interest and interest rate, (4) maturity value, (5) discount, and (6) proceeds from discounting.

Maturity Date. The **maturity date** is the date on which the note must be paid. It must either be stated on the promissory note or be determinable from the facts stated on the note. Among the most common statements of maturity date are the following:

1. A specific date, such as "November 14, 19xx"
2. A specific number of months after the date of the note, for example, "3 months after date"
3. A specific number of days after the date of the note, for example, "60 days after date"

There is no problem in determining the maturity date when it is stated. When the maturity date is a number of months from the date of the note, one simply uses the same day in the appropriate future month. For example, a note dated January 20 that is due in two months would be due on March 20.

When the maturity date is a specific number of days from the date of the note, it must be based on the exact number of days. In computing the maturity date, it is important to exclude the date of the note. For example, a note dated May 20 and due in 90 days would be due on August 18, computed as follows:

Days remaining in May (31 − 20)	11
Days in June	30
Days in July	31
Days in August	18
Total days	90

Duration of Note. Determining the **duration of note**, or its length of time in days, is the opposite problem from determining the maturity date. Knowing the duration of the note is important because interest is calculated for the exact number of days. There is no problem when the maturity date is stated as a specific number of days from the date of the note. However, if the maturity date is a specified date, the exact number of days must be determined. Assume that a note issued on May 10 matures on August 10. The duration of the note is 92 days, determined as follows:

Days remaining in May (31 – 10)	21
Days in June	30
Days in July	31
Days in August	10
Total days	92

Interest and Interest Rate. The **interest** is the cost of borrowing money or the return for lending money, depending on whether one is the borrower or the lender. The amount of interest is based on three factors: the principal (the amount of money borrowed or lent), the rate of interest, and the loan's length of time. The formula used in computing interest is as follows:

Principal × rate of interest × time = interest

Interest rates are usually stated on an annual basis. For example, the interest on a $1,000, one-year, 8 percent note would be $80 ($1,000 × 8/100 × 1 = $80).

If the term, or time period, of the note were three months instead of a year, the interest charge would be $20 ($1,000 × 8/100 × 3/12 = $20).

When the term of a note is expressed in days, the exact number of days must be used in computing the interest. To keep the computation simple, let us compute interest on the basis of 360 days per year.[5] Therefore, if the term of the above note were 45 days, the interest would be $10, computed as follows: $1,000 × 8/100 × 45/360 = $10.

Maturity Value. The **maturity value** of a note is the total proceeds of the note at the maturity date. Maturity value is the face value of the note plus interest. The maturity value of a 90-day, 8 percent, $1,000 note is computed as follows:

Maturity value = principal + interest
= $1,000 + ($1,000 × 8/100 × 90/360)
= $1,000 + $20
= $1,020

There are also so-called non-interest-bearing notes. The maturity value is the face value or principal amount. In this case, the principal includes an implied interest cost.

Discount. To **discount** a note means to take out the interest in advance. The **discount** is the amount of interest deducted. Banks often use this method when lending money on promissory notes. The amount of the discount is computed as follows:

Discount = maturity value × discount rate × time

5. Practice varies in the computation of interest. Many banks use a 360-day year for commercial loans and a 365-day year for consumer loans. Other banks use a 365-day year for all loans. In Europe, use of a 360-day year is common. In this book, we use a 360-day year to keep the computations simple.

For example, assume that a note has a maturity value of \$1,000, is due in 90 days, and is discounted at a 10 percent rate of interest.

$$\text{Discount} = \$1{,}000 \times 10/100 \times 90/360 = \$25$$

Proceeds from Discounting. Normally, when someone borrows money on a note, the amount he or she receives or borrows is the face value or principal. But when a note receivable is discounted, the amount the borrower actually receives, called the **proceeds from discounting**, is computed as follows:

$$\textbf{Proceeds} = \textbf{maturity value} - \textbf{discount}$$

Thus, in the preceding example, the proceeds would be computed as follows:

$$\begin{aligned}\text{Proceeds} &= \$1{,}000 - (\$1{,}000 \times 10/100 \times 90/360)\\ &= \$1{,}000 - \$25\\ &= \$975\end{aligned}$$

This calculation is very simple when the maturity value is given, as illustrated here. However, the calculation is more complicated when the maturity value must be calculated, as when an interest-bearing note from a customer is discounted to the bank. Here, the maturity value must first be computed, using the formula presented earlier. Then the discount is computed on the maturity value. Finally, the proceeds are determined by deducting the discount from the maturity value. For example, the proceeds of a \$2,000, 8 percent, 90-day note, discounted at the bank at 10 percent on the date it is drawn, would be \$1,989:

$$\begin{aligned}\textbf{Maturity value} &= \textbf{principal + interest}\\ &= \$2{,}000 + (\$2{,}000 \times 8/100 \times 90/360)\\ &= \$2{,}000 + \$40\\ &= \$2{,}040\end{aligned}$$

$$\begin{aligned}\textbf{Discount} &= \textbf{maturity value} \times \textbf{discount rate} \times \textbf{time}\\ &= \$2{,}040 \times 10/100 \times 90/360\\ &= \$51\end{aligned}$$

$$\begin{aligned}\textbf{Proceeds} &= \textbf{maturity value} - \textbf{discount}\\ &= \$2{,}040 - \$51\\ &= \$1{,}989\end{aligned}$$

In this example, the note was discounted to the bank on the same day it was written. Usually, time will pass between the date the note is written and the date it is discounted. In such a case, the number of days used in computing the discount should be the days remaining until the maturity date, because that is the length of time for which the bank is lending the money to the company holding the note. For example, assume that for the previous note the company holding it waits 30 days to discount the note to the bank. In other words, at the date of discounting, there are 60 (90 – 30) days remaining until the maturity date. The proceeds are determined as follows:

$$\begin{aligned}\textbf{Maturity value} &= \textbf{principal + interest}\\ &= \$2{,}040 \text{ (from above)}\end{aligned}$$

$$\begin{aligned}\textbf{Discount} &= \textbf{maturity value} \times \textbf{discount rate} \times \textbf{time}\\ &= \$2{,}040 \times 10/100 \times 60/360\\ &= \$34\end{aligned}$$

$$\begin{aligned}\textbf{Proceeds} &= \textbf{maturity value} - \textbf{discount}\\ &= \$2{,}040 - \$34\\ &= \$2{,}006\end{aligned}$$

The difference of $17 ($51 − $34) in the discount between the two cases is equal to the discount on the 30 days that have lapsed between writing and discounting the note ($2,040 × 10/100 × 30/360 = $17).

Illustrative Accounting Entries

OBJECTIVE 6
Journalize entries involving notes receivable

The accounting entries for promissory notes receivable fall into five groups: (1) receipt of a note, (2) collection on a note, (3) recording a dishonored note, (4) discounting a note, and (5) recording adjusting entries.

Receipt of a Note. Assume that on June 1 a 12 percent, 30-day note is received from a customer, J. Halsted, in settlement of an existing account receivable of $4,000. The entry for this transaction is as follows:

June 1	Notes Receivable	4,000	
	Accounts Receivable, J. Halsted		4,000
	Received 12 percent, 30-day note in payment of account		

Collection on a Note. When the note plus interest is collected 30 days later, the entry is as follows:

July 1	Cash	4,040	
	Notes Receivable		4,000
	Interest Income		40
	Collected 12 percent, 30-day note from J. Halsted		

Recording a Dishonored Note. When the maker of a note does not pay the note at maturity, the note is said to be dishonored. The holder or payee of a **dishonored note** should make an entry to transfer the total amount due from Notes Receivable to an account receivable from the debtor. If J. Halsted dishonors his note on July 1, the following entry would be made:

July 1	Accounts Receivable, J. Halsted	4,040	
	Notes Receivable		4,000
	Interest Income		40
	12 percent, 30-day note dishonored by J. Halsted		

The interest earned is recorded because, although J. Halsted did not pay the note, he is still obligated to pay both the principal and the interest.

Two things are accomplished by transferring a dishonored note receivable into an accounts receivable account. First, it leaves the Notes Receivable account with only notes that have not matured and are presumably negotiable and collectible. Second, it establishes a record in the borrower's accounts receivable account that he or she has dishonored a note receivable. This information may be helpful in deciding whether to extend future credit to this customer.

DECISION POINT
Marriott Corporation

■ Marriott Corporation is the world's largest operator of hotels and a leader in food and services management. The company has investments in various affiliated companies that own hotel properties, and it assists in the financing of some of their operations. To provide cash for various purposes, management has sold portions of the notes receivable from affiliates. How can Marriott improve its cash flow for the notes it receives from its affiliated companies?

Many companies raise money for operations by selling unmatured notes receivable to banks or financial companies for cash. In Marriott's 1989 annual report, the notes to the financial statements show that the company sold $61 million of its notes receivable in 1989 and $128 million in 1988. At December 29, 1989, the aggregate unpaid balance of notes receivable sold with recourse was $55 million. As will be explained in the next section, this practice is called discounting, and the $55 million represents a contingent liability. ■

Discounting a Note. Selling notes receivable is usually called discounting because the bank deducts the interest from the maturity value of the note to determine the proceeds. The holder of the note (usually the payee) endorses the note and delivers it to the bank. The bank expects to collect the maturity value of the note (principal plus interest) on the maturity date but also has recourse against the endorser or seller of the note. If the maker fails to pay, the endorser is liable to the bank for payment. In accounting terminology, the endorser is said to be contingently liable. A **contingent liability** is a potential liability that can develop into a real liability if a possible subsequent event occurs. In this case, the subsequent event would be the nonpayment of the note by the maker.

Although sales of notes receivable are made to many different purchasers, we will assume for this example that a $1,000, 12 percent, 90-day note is taken to the bank 60 days before maturity and that the bank discounts it at 15 percent. The cash to be received (proceeds from discounting) is calculated as the maturity value less the discount and is recorded as follows:

Cash	1,004.25	
Notes Receivable		1,000.00
Interest Income		4.25
Discounting of a 12 percent, 90-day note with 60 days left at 15 percent		

Maturity value:		
$1,000 + ($1,000 × 12/100 × 90/360)	=	$1,030.00
Less discount:		
$1,030 × 15/100 × 60/360	=	25.75
Proceeds from discounted note receivable		$1,004.25

Since the interest to be received at maturity of $30.00 exceeds the interest cost or discount, the difference of $4.25 is credited to Interest Income. If the proceeds had been less than the face value of the note receivable, the difference would have been recorded as a debit to Interest Expense. For example, if the proceeds had been $995.75 instead of $1,004.25, the Interest Expense account would have been debited for $4.25, and there would have been no entry to the Interest Income account.

Note that neither the length of the discounting period nor the discount rate is the same as the term or the rate of interest of the note. This situation is typical. Also, notice that the Notes Receivable account is credited. Although this entry removes the note from the records, remember that if the maker cannot or will not pay the bank, the endorser is liable to the bank for the note.

Before the maturity date of the discounted note, the bank will notify the maker that it is holding the note and that payment should be made directly to the bank. If the maker pays the bank as agreed, no entry is required in the records of the endorser. If the maker does not pay the note and interest on the due date, the note is dishonored. To hold the endorser liable for the note, the bank must notify the endorser that the note is dishonored. The bank will normally notify the endorser by protesting the note. The bank does this by preparing and mailing a notice of protest to the endorser. The **notice of protest** is a sworn statement that the note was presented to the maker for payment and the maker refused to pay. The bank typically charges a **protest fee** for protesting the note, which must be paid when the endorser pays the bank the amount due on the dishonored note.

If the note discounted in the previous example is dishonored by the maker on the maturity date, the following entry would be made by the endorser when paying the obligation:

Accounts Receivable, Name of Maker	1,040	
Cash		1,040
Payment of principal and interest on discounted note (maturity value of \$1,030), plus a protest fee of \$10 to bank; the note was dishonored by the maker		

Additional interest accrues on the maturity value plus the protest fee until the note is paid or written off as uncollectible.

Recording Adjusting Entries. A promissory note received in one period might not be due until a following accounting period. Because the interest on the note accrues by a small amount each day of the note's duration, it is necessary, according to the matching rule, to apportion the interest earned to the period in which it belongs. For example, assume that on August 31 a 60-day, 8 percent, \$2,000 note was received and that the company prepares financial statements monthly. The following adjusting entry on September 30 is necessary to show how the interest earned for September has accrued:

Sept. 30	Interest Receivable	13.33	
	Interest Income		13.33
	To accrue 30 days' interest earned on note receivable $\$2,000 \times 8/100 \times 30/360 = \$13.33$		

The account Interest Receivable is a current asset on the balance sheet. Upon receiving payment of the note plus interest on October 30, the following entry is made:[6]

Oct. 30	Cash	2,026.67	
	Notes Receivable		2,000.00
	Interest Receivable		13.33
	Interest Income		13.34
	Receipt of note receivable plus interest		

As seen from these transactions, both September and October receive the benefit of one-half the interest earned.

6. Some firms may follow the practice of reversing the September 30 adjusting entry. Here we assume that a reversing entry is not made.

Banking Transactions

Banking facilities are an important aid to businesses in controlling their short-term liquid assets. Banks are safe depositories for cash, negotiable instruments, and other valuable business documents, such as stocks and bonds. The use of bank checks for cash disbursements improves a company's control by minimizing the amount of currency on hand and by providing a permanent record of all cash payments. Furthermore, banks can serve as agents for a company in a variety of important transactions, such as the collection and payment of certain kinds of debts and the exchange of foreign currencies.

Bank Account

OBJECTIVE 7
Describe a bank account and demonstrate the control of cash by preparing a bank reconciliation

A bank account is an account a business opens with a bank, into which cash is deposited for safekeeping and from which cash is withdrawn by writing checks. The procedure for establishing a bank account varies. In small towns, where bank personnel are familiar with local activities, it can be very easy to open an account. In large metropolitan areas, a bank may require financial information and references.

A verification document that is used for a bank account is a **signature card**. When a business opens an account, this card must be signed by the depositor in exactly the same way that he or she expects to sign the checks. A signature card is required so that a bank teller can authenticate the signature on checks. When a business opens an account, the owners must sign an authorization giving a particular official or officials the right to sign checks. The bank receives a copy of the authorization.

Deposits

When making a deposit, the depositor fills out a **deposit ticket** (usually in duplicate), as shown in Figure 8-2. Space is provided for listing each check and the amounts of coin and currency deposited.

Bank Statement

Once a month, the bank sends a statement to each depositor and returns the canceled checks that it has paid and charged to the depositor's account. The returned checks are called *canceled checks* because the bank stamps, or cancels, them to show that they have been paid. The **bank statement** shows the balance at the beginning of the month, the deposits, the checks paid, other debits and credits during the month, and the balance at the end of the month. A bank statement is illustrated in Figure 8-3.

Preparing a Bank Reconciliation

Rarely does the balance of a company's Cash account exactly equal the cash balance shown on its bank statement. Certain transactions that appear in the company's records may not be recorded by the bank, and certain bank transactions may not appear in the company's records. Therefore, a necessary step in internal control is to prove both the balance on the bank statement and the balance of Cash in the accounting records. **Bank reconciliation** is the process of accounting for the differences between the balance on the bank statement and the balance of Cash according to the company's records. This process involves making additions to and subtractions from the two balances to arrive at the adjusted cash balance.

Figure 8-2. Deposit Ticket

DEPOSIT TICKET
THE LAKE PARK NATIONAL BANK
Chicago, Illinois

Date 10/6/xx

Checking Acct No 8030-647-4

Name Martin Maintenance Company
Address 8428 Rocky Island Avenue
Chicago, Illinois 60643

CASH	CURRENCY	22	00
	COIN	2	50
	CHECKS – LIST SINGLY		
	G. Mason	30	00
	R Enterprises	39	00
	Preston Company	206	50
TOTAL		300	00
Less Cash Received			—
NET DEPOSIT		300	00

The most common examples of transactions shown in the company's records but not entered in the bank's records are the following:

1. **Outstanding checks** These are checks issued and recorded by the company that do not yet appear on the bank statement.
2. **Deposits in transit** These are deposits mailed or taken to the bank but not received in time to be recorded on the bank statement.

Transactions that may appear on the bank statement but that have not been recorded by the company include the following:

1. **Service charges (SC)** Banks cannot profitably handle small accounts without making a service charge. Many banks base their service charge on a number of factors, such as the average balance of the account during the month or the number of checks drawn.
2. **Nonsufficient funds (NSF) checks** An NSF check is a check deposited by a company that is not paid when the company's bank presents it to the maker's bank. The bank charges the company's account and returns the check so that the company can try to collect the amount due. If the bank has deducted the NSF check from the bank statement but the company has not deducted it from its own book balance, an adjustment must be made in the bank reconciliation. The

Figure 8-3. Bank Statement

Statement of Account with
THE LAKE PARK NATIONAL BANK
Chicago, Illinois

Martin Maintenance Company
8428 Rocky Island Avenue
Chicago, Illinois 60643

Checking Acct No
8030-647-4
Period covered
Sept. 30-Oct. 31, 19xx

Previous Balance	Checks/Debits—No.	Deposits/Credits—No.	S.C.	Current Balance
$2,645.78	$4,319.33 --15	$5,157.12 --7	$12.50	$3,471.07

CHECKS/DEBITS			DEPOSITS/CREDITS		DAILY BALANCES	
Posting Date	Check No.	Amount	Posting Date	Amount	Date	Amount
					09/30	2,645.78
10/01	564	100.00	10/01	586.00	10/01	2,881.78
10/01	565	250.00	10/05	1,500.00	10/04	2,825.60
10/04	567	56.18	10/06	300.00	10/05	3,900.46
10/05	566	425.14	10/16	1,845.50	10/06	4,183.34
10/06	568	17.12	10/21	600.00	10/12	2,242.34
10/12	569	1,705.80	10/24	300.00CM	10/16	3,687.84
10/12	570	235.20	10/31	25.62IN	10/17	3,589.09
10/16	571	400.00			10/21	4,189.09
10/17	572	29.75			10/24	3,745.59
10/17	573	69.00			10/25	3,586.09
10/24	574	738.50			10/28	3,457.95
10/24		5.00DM			10/31	3,471.07
10/25	575	7.50				
10/25	577	152.00				
10/28		128.14NSF				
10/31		12.50SC				

Explanation of Symbols:

CM – Credit Memo
DM – Debit Memo
NSF – Nonsufficient Funds

SC – Service Charge
EC – Error Correction
OD – Overdraft
IN – Interest on Average Balance

The last amount in this column is your balance.

Please examine; if no errors are reported within ten (10) days, the account will be considered to be correct.

depositor usually reclassifies the NSF check from Cash to Accounts Receivable because the company now must collect from the person or company that wrote the check.

3. **Interest income (IN)** It is very common for banks to pay interest on a company's average balance. These accounts sometimes are called *NOW* or *money market accounts* but can take other forms. The interest is reported on the bank statement.
4. **Miscellaneous charges and credits** Banks also charge for other services, such as the collection and payment of promissory notes, stopping payment on checks, and printing checks. The bank notifies the depositor of each deduction by including a debit memorandum (DM) with the monthly statement. A bank sometimes serves as an agent in collecting on promissory notes for the depositor. In such a case, a credit memorandum (CM) is included in the statement.

An error by either the bank or the depositor requires immediate correction.

Steps in Reconciling the Bank Balance. The steps in preparing a bank reconciliation are as follows:

1. Compare the deposits listed on the bank statement with the deposits shown in the accounting records. Any deposits in transit should be added to the bank balance. (Immediately investigate any deposits in transit from last month that still are not listed on the bank statement.)
2. Trace returned checks to the bank statement, making sure that all checks have been issued by the company, properly charged to the company's account, and properly signed.
3. Arrange the canceled checks returned with the bank statement in numerical order, and compare them with the record of checks issued. List checks issued but not on the bank statement. (Be sure to include any checks still outstanding from prior months; investigate any checks outstanding for more than a few months.) Deduct outstanding checks from the bank balance.
4. Deduct from the balance per books any debit memoranda issued by the bank (such as NSF checks and service charges) that are not yet recorded on the company's records.
5. Add to the balance per books any interest earned or credit memoranda issued by the bank (collection of a promissory note) that are not yet recorded on the company's books.
6. Make journal entries for any items on the bank statement that have not been recorded in the company's books, as well as any necessary correcting entries for errors made by the company.

Illustration of a Bank Reconciliation. A bank statement can be dated any day of the month. The monthly bank reconciliation is conducted as of whatever day the bank statement is dated. The October bank statement dated October 31 for Martin Maintenance Company (Figure 8-3) indicates a balance of $3,471.07. Let's assume that Martin Maintenance Company has a cash balance in its records on October 31 of $2,405.91. The purpose of a bank reconciliation is to identify the items that make up the difference between these amounts and to determine the correct cash balance. The bank reconciliation for Martin Maintenance Company is shown in Exhibit 8-3. The numbered items in the exhibit refer to the following:

1. A deposit in the amount of $276.00 was mailed to the bank on October 31 and had not been recorded by the bank.
2. Five checks issued in October or prior months have not yet been paid by the bank:

Check No.	Date	Amount
551	Sept. 14	$150.00
576	Oct. 30	40.68
578	Oct. 31	500.00
579	Oct. 31	370.00
580	Oct. 31	130.50

3. The deposit for cash sales of October 6 was recorded incorrectly in the company's records as $330.00. The bank correctly recorded the deposit as $300.00.
4. Among the returned checks was a credit memorandum showing that the bank had collected a promissory note from A. Jacobs in the amount of $280.00, plus

Exhibit 8-3. Bank Reconciliation

Martin Maintenance Company
Bank Reconciliation
October 31, 19xx

Balance per bank, October 31		$3,471.07
① Add deposit of October 31, in transit		276.00
		$3,747.07
② Less outstanding checks:		
No. 551	$150.00	
No. 576	40.68	
No. 578	500.00	
No. 579	370.00	
No. 580	130.50	1,191.18
Adjusted bank balance, October 31		**$2,555.89**
Balance per books, October 31		$2,405.91
Add:		
④ Notes receivable collected by bank, including $20.00 of interest income	$300.00	
⑦ Interest income	25.62	325.62
		$2,731.53
Less:		
③ Overstatement of deposit of October 6	$ 30.00	
④ Collection fee	5.00	
⑤ NSF check of Arthur Clubb	128.14	
⑥ Service charge	12.50	175.64
Adjusted book balance, October 31		**$2,555.89**

Note: The circled numbers refer to the items listed in the text on pages 329–330.

$20.00 in interest on the note. A debit memorandum also was enclosed for the $5.00 collection fee. No entry had been made in Martin Maintenance Company's records.

5. Also returned with the bank statement was an NSF check for $128.14. This check had been received from a customer named Arthur Clubb. The NSF check from Clubb was not reflected in the company's accounting records.
6. A debit memorandum was enclosed for the regular monthly service charge of $12.50. This charge was not yet recorded by Martin Maintenance Company.
7. Interest earned by the company on the average balance was reported as $25.62.

Exhibit 8-3 shows that, starting from their separate balances, the bank and book amounts are adjusted to $2,555.89. This adjusted balance is the amount of cash owned by the company on October 31; it is the amount that should appear on its October 31 balance sheet.

Recording Transactions After Reconciliation. The adjusted balance of cash differs from both the bank statement and the company's records. The bank balance will be corrected when the outstanding checks are presented for payment and when the deposit in transit is received and recorded by the bank. The company must make entries to correct the book balance. All the items reported by the bank but not yet recorded by the company must be recorded in the general journal, as well as the entry correcting the error:

			Debit	Credit
Oct.	31	Cash	300.00	
		Notes Receivable		280.00
		Interest Income		20.00
		Note receivable of $280.00 and interest of $20.00 collected by bank from A. Jacobs		
	31	Cash	25.62	
		Interest Income		25.62
		Interest on average bank account balance		
	31	Sales	30.00	
		Cash		30.00
		Correction of error in recording a $300.00 deposit on October 6 as $330.00		
	31	Accounts Receivable, Arthur Clubb	128.14	
		Cash		128.14
		NSF check from Arthur Clubb returned by bank		
	31	Bank Service Charges Expense	17.50	
		Cash		17.50
		Bank service charge ($12.50) and collection fee ($5.00) for October		

Or, the entries can be recorded in one or two compound entries, to save time and space:

			Debit	Credit
Oct.	31	Cash	149.98	
		Sales	30.00	
		Accounts Receivable, Arthur Clubb	128.14	
		Bank Service Charges Expense	17.50	
		Notes Receivable		280.00
		Interest Income		45.62
		Items from bank reconciliation		

DECISION POINT
National Realty

■ National Realty is a medium-sized real estate agency with offices in fourteen states. The firm specializes in commercial properties and leases. Typically, the firm acts as the leasing agent for large office buildings. To attract important leases, agents often have to make out-of-pocket expenditures for presentations, meals, entertainment, taxis and other transportation, express mail, and additional items. Over a period of a month, individual agents can incur expenditures of several hundred dollars. In the past, the home office reimbursed these expenses after the agent completed an expense report with receipts attached. Agents, however, complained that reimbursement took too long and discouraged them at times from taking needed action. What type of system would allow the agents to be reimbursed sooner and still maintain control over expenditures?

National Realty used an imprest system to establish a petty cash fund, generally in the amount of $500, at each of the firm's offices. The fund is controlled by the assistant manager of each office. Under this system, agents receive immediate reimbursement for an approved expenditure on presentation of a receipt. The funds are subject to audits without notification by the firm's internal audit department. The procedures for creating, using, and replenishing a petty cash fund are described in the next section. ■

Petty Cash Procedures

OBJECTIVE 8
Demonstrate the use of a simple imprest system

Under some circumstances, it is not practical to make all disbursements by check. In most businesses, for example, it is sometimes necessary to make small payments of cash for such things as postage stamps, incoming postage, shipping charges due, or minor purchases of pens, paper, and the like.

For those situations in which it is inconvenient to pay with a check, most companies set up a **petty cash fund**. One of the best methods of maintaining control over the fund is to use the **imprest system.** Under this system, a petty cash fund is established for a fixed amount and periodically is reimbursed for the exact amount necessary to bring it back to the fixed amount.

Establishing the Petty Cash Fund

Some companies have a regular cashier, secretary, or receptionist who administers the petty cash fund. To establish the fund, the company issues a check for an amount that is intended to cover two to four weeks of small expenditures. The check is cashed, and the money is placed in the petty cash box, drawer, or envelope.

The only entry required when the fund is established is to record the check:

Oct. 14	Petty Cash	100.00	
	Cash		100.00
	To establish the petty cash fund		

Making Disbursements from the Petty Cash Fund

The custodian of the petty cash fund should prepare a **petty cash voucher**, or written authorization, for each expenditure, as shown in Figure 8-4. On each petty cash voucher, the custodian enters the date, amount, and purpose of the expenditure. The voucher is signed by the person who receives the payment.

The custodian should be informed that surprise audits of the fund will be made occasionally. The cash in the fund plus the sum of the petty cash vouchers should equal the amount shown in the Petty Cash account at all times.

Reimbursing the Petty Cash Fund

At specified intervals, when the fund becomes low, and at the end of an accounting period, the petty cash fund is replenished by a check issued to the custodian for the exact amount of the expenditures. From time to time, there may be minor discrepancies in the amount of cash left in the fund at the time of

Figure 8-4. Petty Cash Voucher

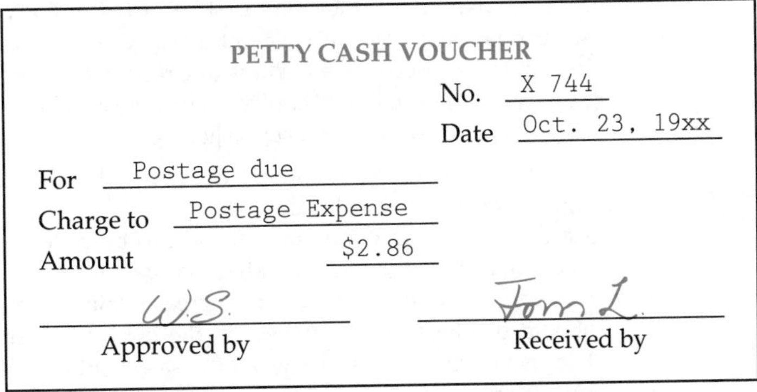

PETTY CASH VOUCHER

No. X 744

Date Oct. 23, 19xx

For Postage due

Charge to Postage Expense

Amount $2.86

W.S. — Approved by

Tom L. — Received by

reimbursement. In these cases, the amount of the discrepancy is recorded in Cash Short or Over, as a debit if short or as a credit if over.

Assume that after two weeks the petty cash fund established earlier has a cash balance of $14.27 and petty cash vouchers as follows: postage, $25.00; supplies, $30.55; and freight in, $30.00. This is the entry to replenish, or restore, the fund:

Oct. 28	Postage Expense	25.00	
	Supplies	30.55	
	Freight In	30.00	
	Cash Short or Over	.18	
	Cash		85.73
	To replenish the petty cash fund		

Notice that the Petty Cash account is debited only when the fund is established. Expense or asset accounts are debited each time the fund is replenished. In most cases, no further entries to the Petty Cash account are needed unless the firm wants to change the fixed amount of the fund.

The petty cash fund should be replenished at the end of an accounting period to bring it up to its fixed amount and ensure that changes in the other accounts involved are reflected in the current period's financial statements. If, through an oversight, the petty cash fund is not replenished at the end of the period, expenditures for the period still must appear on the income statement. They are shown through an adjusting entry debiting the expense accounts and crediting Petty Cash. The result is a reduction in the petty cash fund and the Petty Cash account by the amount of the adjusting entry. On the financial statements, the balance of the Petty Cash account usually is combined with other cash accounts.

Chapter Review

Review of Learning Objectives

1. **Account for cash and short-term investments.**
   Cash consists of coin and currency on hand, checks and money orders received from customers, and deposits in bank accounts. Short-term investments, sometimes called

marketable securities, include time deposits, certificates of deposit, government securities, stocks, and other securities intended to be held for short periods of time (usually less than a year) and are first recorded at cost. Afterwards, investments in debt securities are carried at cost unless there is a permanent drop in the market value. Investments in equity securities are reported at the lower of cost or market. If cost exceeds market value of equity securities, an allowance to reduce short-term investments to market value is established.

2. **Define *accounts receivable*, and explain the relationships among credit policies, sales, and uncollectible accounts.**
Accounts receivable are amounts still to be collected from credit sales to customers. The amounts still owed by individual customers are found in the subsidiary ledger.
Because credit is offered to increase sales, bad debts associated with the sales should be charged as expenses in the period in which the sales are made. However, because of the time lag between the sales and the time the accounts are judged to be uncollectible, the accountant must estimate the amount of bad debts in any given period.

3. **Apply the allowance method of accounting for uncollectible accounts, including using the percentage of net sales method and the accounts receivable aging method to estimate uncollectible accounts.**
Uncollectible accounts expense is estimated by either the percentage of net sales method or the accounts receivable aging method. When the first method is used, bad debts are judged to be a certain percentage of sales during the period. When the second method is used, certain percentages are applied to groups of the accounts receivable that have been arranged by due dates. A third method, the direct charge-off method, is required when filing federal income tax returns but is not used in the accounting records because it does not follow the matching rule.
Allowance for Uncollectible Accounts is a contra-asset account to Accounts Receivable. When the estimate of uncollectible accounts is made, debit Uncollectible Accounts Expense and credit the allowance account. When an individual account is determined to be uncollectible, it is removed from Accounts Receivable by debiting the allowance account and crediting Accounts Receivable. If the written-off account should later be collected, the earlier entry should be reversed and the collection recorded in the normal way.

4. **Identify methods of financing accounts receivable and other issues related to accounts receivable.**
Methods of financing accounts receivable include pledging accounts receivable as collateral for loans and selling or factoring accounts receivable with or without recourse.
Accounts of customers with credit balances should not be classified as negative accounts receivable but as current liabilities on the balance sheet. Installment accounts receivable are classified as current assets if such credit policies are followed in the industry. Receivables from credit card companies should be classified as current assets. Receivables from employees, officers, stockholders, and others made outside the normal course of business should not be listed among accounts receivable. They may be either short- or long-term assets depending on when collection is expected to take place.

5. **Define and describe a *promissory note*, and make calculations involving promissory notes.**
A promissory note is an unconditional promise to pay a definite sum of money on demand or at a future date. Companies selling durable goods of high value such as farm machinery and automobiles often accept promissory notes, which can be sold to banks as a financing method.
In accounting for promissory notes, it is important to know how to calculate the following: maturity date, duration of note, interest and interest rate, maturity value, discount, and proceeds from discounting. Discounting is the act by which the lender takes out the interest in advance when making a loan on a note.

6. **Journalize entries involving notes receivable.**
   The accounting entries for promissory notes receivable fall into five groups: receipt of a note, collection on a note, recording a dishonored note, discounting a note, and recording adjusting entries.
7. **Describe a bank account and demonstrate the control of cash by preparing a bank reconciliation.**
   A bank account is an account a company opens with a bank, into which cash is deposited for safekeeping and from which cash is withdrawn primarily by writing checks. The term *bank reconciliation* means accounting for the difference between the balance that appears on the bank statement and the balance in the company's Cash account. It involves adjusting both balances to arrive at the adjusted cash balance. The bank balance is adjusted for outstanding checks and deposits in transit. The depositor's book balance is adjusted for service charges, NSF checks, interest earned, and miscellaneous debits and credits.
8. **Demonstrate the use of a simple imprest system.**
   An imprest system is a method of controlling small cash expenditures by setting up a fund at a fixed amount. A petty cash fund, one example of the application of an imprest system, is established by a debit to Petty Cash and a credit to Cash. It is replenished by debits to various expense or asset accounts and a credit to Cash. Each expenditure should be supported by a petty cash voucher.

Review of Concepts and Terminology

The following concepts and terms were introduced in this chapter:

(L.O. 2) **Accounts receivable:** Short-term liquid assets that arise from sales on credit at the wholesale or the retail level.

(L.O. 3) **Accounts receivable aging method:** A method of estimating uncollectible accounts based on the assumption that a predictable portion of accounts receivable will not be collected.

(L.O. 3) **Aging of accounts receivable:** The process of listing each customer in accounts receivable according to the due date of the account.

(L.O. 2) **Allowance for Uncollectible Accounts:** A contra-asset account that serves to reduce accounts receivable to the amount that is expected to be collected in cash.

(L.O. 2) **Allowance method:** A method of accounting for uncollectible accounts whereby estimated uncollectible accounts are expenses in the period in which the related sales take place.

(L.O. 7) **Bank reconciliation:** A procedure to account for the difference between the cash balance that appears on the bank statement and the balance of the Cash account in the depositor's records.

(L.O. 7) **Bank statement:** A statement that shows the balance in a bank account at the beginning of the month, the deposits, the checks paid, other debits and credits during the month, and the balance at the end of the month.

(L.O. 1) **Cash:** Coins and currency on hand, checks and money orders from customers, and deposits in bank checking accounts.

(L.O. 1) **Cash equivalents:** Short-term investments that will revert to cash in less than ninety days.

(L.O. 1) **Compensating balance:** A minimum amount that a bank requires be kept in an account as part of a credit-granting arrangement.

(L.O. 6) **Contingent liability:** A potential liability that can develop into a real liability if a possible subsequent event occurs.

(L.O. 7) **Deposit ticket:** A form filled out by a depositor listing the amounts of coin and currency and each check being deposited in the bank.

(L.O. 4) **Direct charge-off method:** A method of accounting for uncollectible accounts by debiting expenses directly when bad debts are discovered instead of using the allowance method; this method violates the matching rule but is required for federal income tax computations.

(L.O. 5) **Discount:** (Verb) To take out interest in advance; (noun) the interest amount deducted in advance.

(L.O. 6) **Dishonored note:** A promissory note that the maker cannot or will not pay at the maturity date.

(L.O. 5) **Duration of note:** Length of time in days between the issue date of a promissory note and its maturity date.

(L.O. 4) **Factor:** An entity that buys accounts receivable.

(L.O. 4) **Factoring:** The selling or transferring of accounts receivable.

(L.O. 8) **Imprest system:** A system for controlling small cash disbursements by establishing a fund at a fixed amount and periodically reimbursing the fund by the amount necessary to bring the fund back to the fixed amount.

(L.O. 4) **Installment accounts receivable:** Accounts receivable that are payable in a series of time payments.

(L.O. 5) **Interest:** The cost of borrowing money or the return for lending money, depending on whether one is the borrower or the lender.

(L.O. 5) **Maturity date:** The due date of a promissory note.

(L.O. 5) **Maturity value:** The total proceeds of a promissory note including principal and interest at the maturity date.

(L.O. 5) **Notes payable:** Collective term for promissory notes owed by the person who promises to pay (maker) to other entities.

(L.O. 5) **Notes receivable:** Collective term for promissory notes held by the entity to whom payment is promised (payee).

(L.O. 6) **Notice of protest:** A sworn statement that a promissory note was presented to the maker for payment and the maker refused to pay.

(L.O. 3) **Percentage of net sales method:** A method of estimating uncollectible accounts based on the assumption that a predictable portion of sales will not be collected.

(L.O. 8) **Petty cash fund:** A fund established by a business for making small payments of cash.

(L.O. 8) **Petty cash voucher:** A form signed by each person who receives a cash payment from a business, listing the date, amount, and purpose of the expenditure.

(L.O. 5) **Proceeds from discounting:** The amount received by the borrower when a promissory note is discounted; proceeds = maturity value – discount.

(L.O. 5) **Promissory note:** An unconditional promise to pay a definite sum of money on demand or at a future date.

(L.O. 6) **Protest fee:** The charge made by a bank for preparing and mailing a notice of protest.

(L.O. 1) **Short-term investments (marketable securities):** Temporary investments of excess cash, intended to be held until needed to pay current obligations.

(L.O. 1) **Short-term liquid assets:** Financial assets that arise from cash transactions, the investment of cash, and the extension of credit.

(L.O. 7) **Signature card:** A card signed by a depositor in exactly the same way he or she expects to sign checks; used to authenticate the signature on the company's checks.

(L.O. 2) **Trade credit:** Credit granted to customers by wholesalers or retailers.

(L.O. 2) **Uncollectible accounts:** Accounts receivable from customers who cannot or will not pay.

Self-Test

Test your knowledge of the chapter by choosing the best answer for each of the following items.

(L.O. 1) 1. A $100,000 U.S. Treasury bill due in ninety days is purchased for $97,000. When cash in the amount of $100,000 is received, the journal entry would contain
   a. a credit to Interest Income for $3,000.
   b. a debit to Gain on Investment for $3,000.
   c. a credit to Investment Loss for $3,000.
   d. a credit to Gain on Investment for $3,000.

(L.O. 2) 2. The matching rule
   a. necessitates the recording of an estimated amount for bad debts.
   b. is violated when the allowance method is employed.
   c. results in the recording of an exact amount for bad debt losses.
   d. requires that bad debt losses be recorded when an individual customer defaults.

(L.O. 3) 3. Using the percentage of net sales method, uncollectible accounts expenses for the year are estimated to be $54,000. If the balance of Allowance for Uncollectible Accounts is a $16,000 credit before adjustment, what is the balance after adjustment?
   a. $16,000
   b. $38,000
   c. $54,000
   d. $70,000

(L.O. 3) 4. Using the accounts receivable aging method, estimated uncollectible accounts are $74,000. If the balance of Allowance for Uncollectible Accounts is an $18,000 credit before adjustment, what is the balance after adjustment?
   a. $18,000
   b. $56,000
   c. $74,000
   d. $92,000

(L.O. 4) 5. A retailer had VISA charge sales totaling $400 and deposited the charge slips in the bank. Assuming a credit card discount expense of 5 percent, what would be the debit to Cash and the credit to Sales for this transaction?
   a. $400 and $400
   b. $380 and $400
   c. $380 and $380
   d. $400 and $380

(L.O. 5) 6. Each of the following is a characteristic of a promissory note, with the exception of
   a. a payee who has an unconditional right to receive a definite amount on a definite date.
   b. an amount to be paid that can be determined on the date the note is signed.
   c. a due date that can be determined on the date the note is signed.
   d. a maker who agrees to pay a definite sum subject to conditions to be determined at a later date.

(L.O. 5) 7. The maturity value of a $6,000, 90-day note at 10 percent is
   a. $600.
   b. $5,850.
   c. $6,600.
   d. $6,150.

(L.O. 6) 8. A $1,000 interest-bearing note is discounted at the bank, generating $1,024 in proceeds. The endorser's (payee's) entry to record this would include a
   a. debit to Cash for $1,024.
   b. debit to Interest Income for $24.
   c. credit to Notes Receivable for $1,024.
   d. debit to Notes Receivable for $1,000.

(L.O. 7) 9. On a bank reconciliation, which of the following would be added to the balance per bank?
   a. Outstanding checks
   b. Deposits in transit
   c. A service charge
   d. Interest on the balance

(L.O. 8) 10. The entry to replenish a $50 petty cash fund that has $20 cash and a receipt for $30 of postage would include a credit to
   a. Cash.
   b. Petty Cash.
   c. Postage Expense.
   d. Prepaid Postage.

Answers to the Self-Test are at the end of this chapter.

Review Problem
Entries for Uncollectible Accounts Expense and Notes Receivable Transactions

(L.O. 3, 5, 6) The Farm Implement Company sells merchandise on credit and also accepts notes for payment, which are discounted to the bank. During the year ended June 30, the company had net sales of $1,200,000 and at the end of the year had Accounts Receivable of $400,000 and a debit balance in Allowance for Uncollectible Accounts of $2,100. In the past, approximately 1.5 percent of net sales have proved uncollectible. Also, an aging analysis of accounts receivable reveals that $17,000 in accounts receivable appears to be uncollectible.

The Farm Implement Company sold a tractor to R. C. Sims. Payment was received in the form of a $15,000, 9 percent, 90-day note dated March 16. On March 31, the note was discounted to the bank at 10 percent. On June 14, the bank notified the company that Sims had dishonored the note. The company paid the bank the maturity value of the note plus a protest fee of $15. On June 29, the company received payment in full from Sims plus additional interest from the date of the dishonored note.

Required

1. Prepare journal entries to record uncollectible accounts expense using (a) the percentage of net sales method and (b) the accounts receivable aging method.
2. Prepare journal entries relating to the note received from R. C. Sims.

Answer to Review Problem

1. Prepare journal entries to record uncollectible accounts expense.

   a. Percentage of net sales method:

June 30	Uncollectible Accounts Expense	18,000	
	Allowance for Uncollectible Accounts		18,000
	To record estimated uncollectible accounts expense at 1.5 percent of $1,200,000		

   b. Accounts receivable aging method:

June 30	Uncollectible Accounts Expense	19,100	
	Allowance for Uncollectible Accounts		19,100
	To record estimated uncollectible accounts expense. The debit balance in the allowance account must be added to the estimated uncollectible accounts: $2,100 + $17,000 = $19,100		

2. Prepare journal entries related to note.

Date		Account / Explanation	Debit	Credit
Mar.	16	Notes Receivable	15,000.00	
		Sales		15,000.00
		Tractor sold to R. C. Sims; terms of note: 9 percent, 90 days		
	31	Cash	15,017.97	
		Notes Receivable		15,000.00
		Interest Income		17.97
		Note discounted at bank at 10 percent		
		Maturity value:		
		$15,000 + ($15,000 × 9/100 × 90/360)	= $15,337.50	
		Less discount:		
		$15,337.50 × 10/100 × 75/360	= 319.53	
		Proceeds from discounted note receivable	$15,017.97	
June	14	Accounts Receivable, R. C. Sims	15,352.50	
		Cash		15,352.50
		Payment of maturity value on discounted note plus a $15 protest fee; the note was dishonored by Sims		
	29	Cash	15,410.07	
		Accounts Receivable, R. C. Sims		15,352.50
		Interest Income		57.57
		Received payment in full from R. C. Sims		
		$15,352.50 + ($15,352.50 × 9/100 × 15/360)		
		$15,352.50 + $57.57 = $15,410.07		

Chapter Assignments

Questions

1. What items are included in the Cash account? What is a compensating balance?
2. Why does a business need short-term liquid assets? Why is it acceptable to account for certain short-term investments by the lower-of-cost-or-market method?
3. Why does a company sell on credit if it expects that some of the accounts will not be paid? What role does a credit department play in selling on credit?
4. According to generally accepted accounting principles, at what point in the cycle of selling and collecting does the bad debt loss occur?
5. If management estimates that $5,000 of the year's sales will not be collected, what entry should be made at year end?
6. After adjusting and closing entries at the end of the year, suppose that Accounts Receivable is $176,000 and Allowance for Uncollectible Accounts is $14,500. (a) What is the realizable collectible value of Accounts Receivable? (b) If the $450 account of a bankrupt customer is written off in the first month of the new year, what will be the resulting collectible value of Accounts Receivable?
7. What is the effect on net income of an optimistic versus a pessimistic view by management of estimated uncollectible accounts?
8. In what ways is Allowance for Uncollectible Accounts similar to Accumulated Depreciation? In what ways is it different?
9. What procedure for estimating uncollectible accounts also gives management a view of the status of collections and the overall quality of accounts receivable?
10. What is the underlying reasoning behind the percentage of net sales method and the accounts receivable aging method of estimating uncollectible accounts?

11. Are the following terms different in any way: allowance for bad debts, allowance for doubtful accounts, allowance for uncollectible accounts?
12. Why should the entry for an account that has been written off as uncollectible be reinstated if the amount owed is subsequently collected?
13. What is a factor, and what do the terms *factoring with recourse* and *factoring without recourse* mean?
14. What accounting rule is violated by the direct charge-off method of recognizing uncollectible accounts? Why?
15. Which of the following lettered items should be in Accounts Receivable? For those that do not belong in Accounts Receivable, tell where on the balance sheet they do belong: (a) installment accounts receivable from regular customers, due monthly for three years; (b) debit balances in customers' accounts; (c) receivables from employees; (d) credit balances in customers' accounts; (e) receivables from officers of the company.
16. What is a promissory note? Who is the maker? Who is the payee?
17. What are the due dates of the following notes: (a) a 3-month note dated August 16, (b) a 90-day note dated August 16, (c) a 60-day note dated March 25?
18. What is the difference between a cash discount and a discount on a note?
19. What is the difference between the interest on a note and the discount on a note?
20. Why is a bank reconciliation prepared?
21. Assume that each of the items below appeared on a bank reconciliation. Which item would be (1) an addition to the balance on the bank statement, (2) a deduction from the balance on the bank statement, (3) an addition to the balance on the books, or (4) a deduction from the balance on the books? Write the correct number next to each item.
    a. Outstanding checks
    b. Deposits in transit
    c. Bank service charge
    d. NSF check returned with statement
    e. Note collected by bank

    Which of the above items require a journal entry?
22. What is the purpose of a petty cash fund? From the standpoint of internal control, what is the significance of the level at which the fund is established?
23. What account or accounts are debited when a petty cash fund is established? What account or accounts are debited when a petty cash fund is replenished?
24. Should a petty cash fund be replenished as of the last day of the accounting period? Explain your answer.

Communication Skills Exercises

Communication 8-1. Ethics, Uncollectible Accounts, and Short-Term Objectives
(L.O. 2, 3)

Fitzsimmons Designs is a successful retail furniture company located in an affluent suburb in which a major insurance company has just announced a restructuring that will lay off 4,000 employees. Fitzsimmons sells quality furniture, usually on credit. Accounts Receivable represents one of the major assets of the company and, although the company's annual uncollectible accounts losses are not out of line, they represent a sizable amount. The company depends on bank loans for its financing. Sales and net income in the past year have declined, and some customers are falling behind in paying their accounts. George Fitzsimmons, owner of the business, has instructed the controller to underestimate the estimated uncollectible accounts this year in order to show a small growth in earnings because he knows that the bank's loan officer likes to see a steady performance. Fitzsimmons believes the short-term action is justified because future successful years will average out the losses, and since the company has a history of success, the adjustments are meaningless accounting measures anyway. Are Fitzsimmons's actions ethical? Would any parties be harmed by his actions? How important is it to try to be accurate in estimating losses from uncollectible accounts?

Communication 8-2. Role of Credit Sales
(L.O. 2)

Mitsubishi Corporation,[7] a broadly diversified Japanese corporation, instituted a credit plan, called Three Diamond, for customers who buy its major electronic products, such as large-screen televisions and videotape recorders, from specified retail dealers. Under this plan, which was introduced in 1990, approved customers who make purchases in November do not have to make any payments until April and pay no interest for the intervening months. Mitsubishi pays the dealer the full amount less a small fee, sends the customer a Mitsubishi credit card, and collects from the customer at the specified time. What is Mitsubishi's motivation for establishing these generous credit terms? What costs are involved? What are the accounting implications?

Communication 8-3. Asset Financing
(L.O. 4, 6)

Siegel Appliances, Inc. is a small manufacturer of washing machines and dryers located in central Michigan. Siegel sells most of its appliances to large, established discount retail companies that market the appliances under their own names. Siegel sells the appliances on trade credit terms of n/60. If a customer wants a longer term, however, Siegel will accept a note with a term of up to nine months for payment. At present, the company is having cash flow troubles. The company needs $5 million immediately. Its cash balance is $200,000, its accounts receivable balance is $2.3 million, and its notes receivable balance is $3.7 million. How might Siegel's management use its accounts receivable and notes receivable to raise the cash it needs? What are the company's prospects for raising the needed cash?

Communication 8-4. Basic Research Skills
(L.O. 1)

Find a recent issue of the *Wall Street Journal* in your school library. Turn to the third or C section, entitled "Money & Investing," and take notes on the stock and treasury investments, as instructed. Find in the index at the top of the page the location of New York Stock Exchange (NYSE) stocks and turn to that page. From the listing of stock, find five companies you have heard of. They may be companies like IBM, Deere, McDonald's, or Ford. Copy down the range of the stock price for the last year and the current closing price. Also, copy down the dividend, if any, per share. How much did the market values of the common stocks you picked vary in the last year? Do these data demonstrate the need to value short-term investments of this type at the lower of cost or market? How does accounting for short-term investments in these common stocks differ from accounting for short-term investments in U.S. Treasury bills? How are dividends received on investments in these common stocks accounted for? Be prepared to hand in your notes and to discuss the results of your investigation in class.

Classroom Exercises

Exercise 8-1. Accounting for Short-Term Investments in Equities
(L.O. 1)

On September 29, 19x3, Chelsea Corporation acquired the following short-term securities:

270 shares of IBM	$15,000
350 shares of General Motors	14,000
Total acquisition cost	$29,000

Chelsea received dividends from IBM of $2.20 per share and from General Motors of $.80 per share on November 30. IBM stock is selling for $60 per share and General Motors for $35 at the end of the year. On January 13, 19x4, Chelsea sells the General Motors shares for $13,000.

1. Prepare the journal entry to record the acquisition.
2. Prepare the journal entry to record receipt of the dividends.
3. Calculate the market value of the portfolio on December 31, 19x3 and prepare the journal entry to record the loss.
4. Prepare the presentation for short-term investments on the December 31, 19x3 balance sheet.
5. Prepare the journal entry for January 13, 19x4 to record the sale.

7. Information based on promotional brochures received from Mitsubishi Corporation.

Exercise 8-2.
Accounting for Short-Term Investments
(L.O. 1)

During certain periods of its fiscal year, Nicks Company invests its excess cash until it is needed. On January 16, the company invested $146,000 in 90-day U.S. Treasury bills that had a maturity value of $150,000. On April 15, Nicks purchased 10,000 shares of Goodrich Paper common stock at $40 per share and 5,000 shares of Keuron Power common stock at $30 per share. The Treasury bills matured on April 16, and the company received $150,000 in cash. On May 15, it received quarterly dividends of 92.25 cents per share from Keuron Power and 60 cents per share from Goodrich Paper. On June 15, the company sold all the shares of Goodrich Paper for $48 per share. On June 30, the value of the Keuron Power stock was $28 per share.

Prepare journal entries to record the transactions on January 16, April 15, April 16, May 15, June 15, and June 30. Also, show the balance sheet presentation of short-term investments on June 30. Round to the nearest whole dollar.

Exercise 8-3.
Adjusting Entries: Accounts Receivable Aging Method
(L.O. 3)

Accounts Receivable of Kinsella Company shows a debit balance of $52,000 at the end of the year. An aging analysis of the individual accounts indicates estimated uncollectible accounts to be $3,350.

Give the general journal entry to record the uncollectible accounts expense under each of the following independent assumptions: (a) Allowance for Uncollectible Accounts has a credit balance of $400 before adjustment and (b) Allowance for Uncollectible Accounts has a debit balance of $400 before adjustment.

Exercise 8-4.
Adjusting Entry: Percentage of Net Sales Method
(L.O. 3)

At the end of the year, Lockport Enterprises estimates the uncollectible accounts expense to be .7 percent of net sales of $30,300,000. The current credit balance of Allowance for Uncollectible Accounts is $51,600. Give the general journal entry to record the uncollectible accounts expense.

Exercise 8-5.
Aging Method and Net Sales Method Contrasted
(L.O. 3)

At the beginning of 19xx, the balances for Accounts Receivable and Allowance for Uncollectible Accounts were $430,000 and $31,400, respectively. During the current year, credit sales were $3,200,000 and collections on account were $2,950,000. In addition, $35,000 in uncollectible accounts were written off. Using T accounts, determine year-end balances of Accounts Receivable and Allowance for Uncollectible Accounts. Then, make the year-end adjusting entry to record the uncollectible accounts expense, and show the year-end balance sheet presentation of Accounts Receivable and Allowance for Uncollectible Accounts under each of the following conditions:

a. Management estimates the percentage of uncollectible credit sales to be 1.2 percent of total credit sales. (Use a separate account from **b.**)
b. Based on an aging of accounts receivable, management estimates the end-of-year uncollectible accounts receivable to be $38,700. (Use a separate account from **a.**)

Post the results of each entry to Allowance for Uncollectible Accounts.

Exercise 8-6.
Entries for Uncollectible Accounts Expense
(L.O. 3)

The Cordero Office Supply Company sells merchandise on credit. During the fiscal year ended July 31, the company had net sales of $4,600,000. At the end of the year, it had Accounts Receivable of $1,200,000 and a debit balance in Allowance for Uncollectible Accounts of $6,800. In the past, approximately 1.4 percent of net sales have proved uncollectible. Also, an aging analysis of accounts receivable reveals that $60,000 of the receivables appear to be uncollectible. Prepare journal entries to record uncollectible accounts expense using: (a) the percentage of net sales method and (b) the accounts receivable aging method.

What is the resulting balance of Allowance for Uncollectible Accounts under each method? How would your answers change if Allowance for Uncollectible Accounts had a credit balance of $6,800 instead of a debit balance?

Exercise 8-7.
Accounts Receivable Transactions
(L.O. 3)

Assuming that the allowance method is being used, prepare journal entries to record the following transactions:

July 12, 19x4 Sold merchandise to Vera Barnes for $1,800, terms n/10.
Oct. 18, 19x4 Received $600 from Vera Barnes on account.

May 8, 19x5 Wrote off as uncollectible the balance of the Vera Barnes account when she was declared bankrupt.
June 22, 19x5 Unexpectedly received a check for $200 from Vera Barnes.

Exercise 8-8. Credit Card Sales Transactions *(L.O. 4)*

Prepare journal entries to record the following transactions for Toni's Novelties Store:

Apr. 8 A tabulation of invoices at the end of the day showed $2,200 in American Express invoices and $1,200 in Diners Club invoices. American Express takes a discount of 4 percent, and Diners Club takes a 5 percent discount.
15 Received payment from American Express at 96 percent of face value and from Diners Club at 95 percent of face value.
19 A tabulation of invoices at the end of the day showed $800 in VISA invoices, which are deposited in a special bank account at full value less 5 percent discount.

Exercise 8-9. Interest Computations *(L.O. 5)*

Determine the interest on the following notes:

a. $22,800 at 10 percent for 90 days
b. $16,000 at 12 percent for 60 days
c. $18,000 at 9 percent for 30 days
d. $30,000 at 15 percent for 120 days
e. $10,800 at 6 percent for 60 days

Exercise 8-10. Discounting Notes *(L.O. 5)*

To raise cash, Perkowski Company discounted two notes at the bank on September 15. The bank charged a discount rate of 15 percent on the maturity value. Compute the proceeds from discounting each of the following notes:

Date of Note	Amount	Interest Rate	Life of Note
a. Aug. 1	$19,000	10	120 days
b. July 20	$36,000	12	90 days

Exercise 8-11. Notes Receivable Transactions *(L.O. 6)*

Prepare general journal entries to record the following transactions:

Jan. 16 Sold merchandise to Brighton Corporation on account for $36,000, terms n/30.
Feb. 15 Accepted a $36,000, 10 percent, 90-day note from Brighton Corporation in lieu of payment on account.
Mar. 17 Discounted Brighton Corporation note at bank at 12 percent.
May 16 Received notice that Brighton Corporation dishonored the note. Paid the bank the maturity value of the note plus a protest fee of $15.
June 15 Received payment in full from Brighton Corporation, including interest at 10 percent from the date the note was dishonored.

Exercise 8-12. Adjusting Entries: Interest Income *(L.O. 6)*

Prepare journal entries (assuming reversing entries were not made) to record the following:

Dec. 1 Received a 90-day, 12 percent note for $10,000 from a customer for a sale of merchandise.
31 Made end-of-year adjustment for interest income.
Mar. 1 Received payment in full for note and interest.

Exercise 8-13. Comprehensive Notes Receivable Transactions *(L.O. 6)*

Prepare general journal entries to record these transactions:

Jan. 5 Accepted a $4,800, 60-day, 10 percent note dated this day in granting a time extension on the past-due account of B. Martinez.
Mar. 6 B. Martinez paid the maturity value of his $4,800 note.
9 Accepted a $3,000, 60-day, 12 percent note dated this day in granting a time extension on the past-due account of L. Waters.

May	8	L. Waters dishonored his note when presented for payment.
	12	Accepted a $3,600, 90-day, 12 percent note in granting a time extension on the past-due account of T. Linker.
	16	Discounted the T. Linker note at the bank at 15 percent.
Aug.	14	Since no notice protesting the T. Linker note has been received, assumed that it had been paid.
	14	Accepted a $2,400, 60-day, 10 percent note dated August 14 in granting a time extension on the past-due account of T. Chao.
Sept.	6	Discounted the T. Chao note at the bank at 15 percent.
Oct.	13	Received notice protesting the T. Chao note. Paid the bank the maturity value of the note plus a $40 protest fee.
	14	Received a $6,000, 60-day, 12 percent note dated this day from F. Mendel in granting a time extension on his past-due account.
Nov.	13	Discounted the F. Mendel note at the bank at 15 percent.
Dec.	14	Received notice protesting the F. Mendel note. Paid the bank the maturity value of the note plus a $40 protest fee.
	27	Received payment from F. Mendel of the maturity value of his dishonored note, the protest fee, and the interest on both for 14 days beyond maturity at 12 percent.
	31	Wrote off the account of L. Waters against the allowance for uncollectible accounts.

Exercise 8-14.
Bank Reconciliation
(L.O. 7)

Prepare a bank reconciliation from the following information:

a. Balance per bank statement as of October 31, $8,454.54.
b. Balance per books as of October 31, $6,138.04.
c. Deposits in transit, $1,134.42.
d. Outstanding checks, $3,455.92.
e. Bank service charge, $5.00.

Exercise 8-15.
Bank Reconciliation: Missing Data
(L.O. 7)

Compute the correct amounts to replace each letter in the following table:

Balance per bank statement	$ a	$26,700	$945	$5,970
Deposits in transit	1,800	b	150	375
Outstanding checks	4,500	3,000	c	225
Balance per books	10,350	28,200	675	d

Exercise 8-16.
Collection of a Note by a Bank
(L.O. 7)

Edmunds Corporation received a notice with its bank statement that the bank had collected a note for $4,000 plus $20 interest from B. Regalado and credited Edmunds Corporation's account for the total less a collection charge of $30.

Explain the effect that these items have on the bank reconciliation. Prepare a general journal entry to record the information on the books.

Exercise 8-17.
Petty Cash Entries
(L.O. 8)

The petty cash fund of Lemke Company appeared as follows on July 31, 19xx (the end of the accounting period):

Cash on hand		$122.46
Petty cash vouchers		
Freight in	$45.72	
Postage	42.38	
Flowers for a sick employee	37.00	
Office supplies	52.44	177.54
Total		$300.00

Because there is cash on hand, is there a need to replenish the petty cash fund on July 31? Explain your answer. Prepare, in general journal form, an entry to replenish the fund.

Exercise 8-18.
Petty Cash Transactions
(L.O. 8)

A small company maintains a petty cash fund for minor expenditures. In September and October, the following transactions took place:

a. The fund was established in the amount of $100.00 on September 1 from the proceeds of check no. 2707.
b. On September 30, the petty cash fund had cash of $15.46 and the following receipts on hand: postage, $40.00; supplies, $24.94; delivery service (for goods sold), $12.40; and rubber stamp, $7.20. Check no. 2778 was drawn to replenish the fund.
c. On October 31, the petty cash fund had cash of $22.06 and the following receipts on hand: postage, $34.20; supplies, $32.84; and delivery service, $6.40. The petty cash custodian could not account for the shortage. Check no. 2847 was drawn to replenish the fund.

Prepare the general journal entries necessary to record each transaction.

Interpretation Case from Business

AmeriBank
(L.O. 2, 3, 5, 6)

AmeriBank is a large banking and financial institution with branches throughout the world. The following data about AmeriBank's loans and lease financing come from its 1990 and 1991 annual reports:

(in millions of dollars)	December 31, 1991	December 31, 1990
Loans and Lease Financing, Net (Notes 2, 3, and 4)		
Consumer (Net of unearned discount of $3,674 in 1991 and $4,154 in 1990)	$ 78,959	$ 68,243
Commercial (Net of unearned discount of $598 in 1991 and $467 in 1990)	55,754	59,439
Lease Financing	3,372	3,222
Loans and Lease Financing, Net of Unearned Discount	$138,085	$130,904
Allowance for Possible Credit Losses	(4,618)	(1,698)
Total Loans and Lease Financing, Net	$133,467	$129,206

The following additional data come from Note 4 of the same report:

4. Changes in the Allowance for Possible Credit Losses

(in millions of dollars)	1991	1990
Balance at Beginning of Year	$1,698	$1,235
Deductions		
Consumer loan and lease losses	$1,271	$1,172
Consumer loan and lease recoveries	(247)	(214)
Net consumer loan and lease losses	$1,024	$ 958
Commercial loan and lease losses	$ 617	$ 489
Commercial loan and lease recoveries	(144)	(76)
Net commercial loan and lease losses	$ 473	$ 413
Additions		
Provision for possible credit losses	$4,410	$1,825
Other (Principally from allowance balances of acquired companies and translation of overseas allowance balances)	7	9
Balance at End of Year	$4,618	$1,698

Required

1. Did AmeriBank experience a higher loss rate for commercial loans or for consumer loans? Did AmeriBank's loss experience improve from 1990 to 1991? **Hint:** Compute the ratio of net consumer loan and lease losses to consumer loans and the ratio of net commerical loan and lease losses to commercial loans for both years. Ignore the effects of lease financing as immaterial.
2. Did AmeriBank's expectation about overall future losses become more optimistic or more pessimistic from 1990 to 1991? **Hint:** Calculate the ratio of the allowance for possible credit losses to loans and lease financing, net of unearned discount, for both years.
3. Prepare the general journal entries for 1991 to record the losses and recoveries for commercial loans and leases and consumer loans and leases and the provision for possible credit losses.
4. Both the consumer and commercial loans are listed as net of unearned discount. What is an unearned discount? Assuming that AmeriBank made a 90-day commercial loan with a maturity value of $1,200 at an annual discount rate of 12 percent, how would the entry be recorded? What entry would be made when the loan is collected in full?

Problem Set A

Problem 8A-1. Percentage of Net Sales Method
(L.O. 3)

On December 31 of last year, the balance sheet of Marzano Company had Accounts Receivable of $298,000 and a credit balance in Allowance for Uncollectible Accounts of $20,300. During the current year, the company's records included the following selected activities: sales on account, $1,195,000; sales returns and allowances, $73,000; collections from customers, $1,150,000; accounts written off as worthless, $16,000; written-off accounts unexpectedly collected, $2,000. In the past, the company had found that 1.6 percent of net credit sales would not be collected.

Required

1. Open ledger accounts for the Accounts Receivable controlling account (112) and Allowance for Uncollectible Accounts (113). Then enter the beginning balances in these accounts.
2. Prepare separate journal entries to record in summary form each of the five activities listed above.
3. Give the general journal entry on December 31 of the current year to record the estimated uncollectible accounts expense for the year.
4. Post the appropriate parts of the transactions in **2** and **3** to the accounts opened in **1**.

Problem 8A-2. Accounts Receivable Aging Method
(L.O. 3, 4)

Pokorny Company uses the accounts receivable aging method to estimate uncollectible accounts. The Accounts Receivable controlling account had a debit balance of $88,430 and Allowance for Uncollectible Accounts had a credit balance of $7,200 at the beginning of the year. During the year, the company had sales on account of $473,000, sales returns and allowances of $4,200, worthless accounts written off of $7,900, and collections from customers of $450,730. At the end of the year (December 31), a junior accountant for the company was preparing an aging analysis of accounts receivable. At the top of page 6 of the report, the following totals appeared:

Customer Account	Total	Not Yet Due	1–30 Days Past Due	31–60 Days Past Due	61–90 Days Past Due	Over 90 Days Past Due
Balance Forward	$89,640	$49,030	$24,110	$9,210	$3,990	$3,300

The following accounts remained to finish the analysis:

Account	Amount	Due Date
K. Foust	$ 930	Jan. 14 (next year)
K. Groth	620	Dec. 24
R. Mejias	1,955	Sept. 28
C. Polk	2,100	Aug. 16
M. Spears	375	Dec. 14
J. Yong	2,685	Jan. 23 (next year)
A. Zorr	295	Nov. 5
	$8,960	

The company has found from past experience that the following rates are realistic to estimate uncollectible accounts:

Time	Percentage Considered Uncollectible
Not yet due	2
1–30 days past due	4
31–60 days past due	20
61–90 days past due	30
Over 90 days past due	50

Required

1. Complete the aging analysis of accounts receivable.
2. Determine the end-of-year balances (before adjustments) of the Accounts Receivable controlling account and Allowance for Uncollectible Accounts.
3. Prepare an analysis computing the estimated uncollectible accounts.
4. Prepare a general journal entry to record the estimated uncollectible accounts expense for the year. (Round adjustment to the nearest dollar.)

Problem 8A-3. Notes Receivable Transactions
(L.O. 5, 6)

Calderon Manufacturing Company engaged in the following transactions involving promissory notes:

Jan. 14 Sold merchandise to Wynton Bell Company for $37,000, terms n/30.
Feb. 13 Received $8,400 in cash from Wynton Bell Company and a 90-day, 8 percent promissory note for the balance of the account.
23 Discounted the Wynton Bell Company note at the bank at 15 percent.
May 14 Because no notice of dishonor was received, it was assumed that Wynton Bell Company paid the bank.
15 Received a 60-day, 12 percent note from Ted Feller Company in payment of a past-due account, $12,000.
30 Discounted the Ted Feller Company note at the bank at 15 percent.
July 14 Received notice that Ted Feller Company dishonored the note. Paid the bank the maturity value of the note plus a protest fee of $40.
20 Received a check from Ted Feller Company for payment of the maturity value of the note, the $40 protest fee, and interest at 12 percent for the six days beyond maturity.
25 Sold merchandise to Marie Luciano Company for $36,000, with payment of $6,000 cash and the remainder on account.
31 Received a $30,000, 45-day, 10 percent promissory note from Marie Luciano Company for the outstanding account receivable.
Aug. 5 Discounted the Marie Luciano Company note at the bank at 15 percent.
Sept. 14 Received notice that Marie Luciano Company dishonored the note. Paid the bank the maturity value of the note plus a protest fee of $40.
25 Wrote off the Marie Luciano Company account as uncollectible following news that the company had been declared bankrupt.

Required

Prepare general journal entries to record these transactions.

Problem 8A-4.
Notes Receivable Transactions
(L.O. 5, 6)

Walter's Auto Store engaged in the following transactions:

Jan. 2 Accepted a $28,200, 90-day, 14 percent note from Tom Carson as an extension on his past-due account.
5 Accepted an $8,700, 90-day, 12 percent note from Judy Leckler in payment of a past-due account receivable.
10 Accepted a $13,500, 90-day, 10 percent note from Sung Ko as an extension of a past-due account.
12 Discounted Tom Carson's note at the bank at 14 percent.
25 Discounted Sung Ko's note at the bank at 14 percent.
30 Accepted a $15,600, 90-day, 12 percent note from Myra Alvarez in lieu of payment of a past-due account.
Apr. 2 Received notice that Tom Carson had dishonored his note. Paid the bank the maturity value plus a protest fee of $75.
5 Judy Leckler dishonored her note.
10 Received no notice of dishonor by Sung Ko and assumed he paid his obligation to the bank.
22 Received payment from Tom Carson for the total amount owed including maturity value, protest fee, and interest at 15 percent for the twenty days past maturity.
25 Wrote off the Judy Leckler account as uncollectible because she could not be located.
30 Myra Alvarez paid her note plus interest in full.

Required

Prepare general journal entries to record these transactions.

Problem 8A-5.
Short-Term Financing by Discounting Customers' Notes
(L.O. 5, 6)

The Beloit Company is faced with a severe cash shortage because of slowing sales and past-due accounts. The financial vice president has studied the situation and has found a number of large past-due accounts. He recommends (a) that the company seek promissory notes from past-due accounts to encourage the customers to pay on time and to earn interest on these accounts, and (b) that the company generate cash by discounting the notes at the bank at the going rate of interest. During the first month of this program, the company was successful, as indicated by the following table:

Company	Amount of Note	Length of Note	Date of Note	Interest Rate	Discount Date	Discount Rate
Rivera Manufacturing Company	$420,000	60 days	Apr. 5	15%	Apr. 7	15%
Jawali Company	340,000	60 days	Apr. 10	12%	Apr. 13	15%
Tisdale Corporation	220,000	60 days	Apr. 15	14%	Apr. 20	15%

Rivera Manufacturing Company and Jawali Company paid their notes on the due dates. Tisdale Corporation dishonored its note on the due date. The latter note was paid by Beloit Company, including a bank protest fee of $100.

Required

1. Prepare appropriate general journal entries for April 5, 7, 10, 13, 15, and 20.
2. What was the total cash generated during April by the vice president's plan?
3. Prepare appropriate general journal entries for June 4, 9, and 14.
4. What is your evaluation of the plan? What offsetting factors occur in later months such as June?

Problem 8A-6.
Bank Reconciliation
(L.O. 7)

The following information is available for Hernandez Company as of November 30, 19xx:

a. Cash on the books as of November 30 amounted to $113,675.28. Cash on the bank statement for the same date was $141,717.08.
b. A deposit of $14,249.84, representing cash receipts of November 30, did not appear on the bank statement.

c. Outstanding checks totaled $7,293.64.
d. A check for $2,420.00 returned with the statement was recorded in the cash payments journal as $2,024.00. The check was for advertising.
e. The bank service charge for November amounted to $26.00.
f. The bank collected $36,400.00 for Hernandez Company on a note. The face value of the note was $36,000.00.
g. An NSF check for $1,140.00 from a customer, Emma Matthews, was returned with the statement.
h. The bank mistakenly deducted a check for $800.00 drawn by Mota Corporation.
i. The bank reported a credit of $960.00 for interest on the average balance.

Required

1. Prepare a bank reconciliation for Hernandez Company as of November 30, 19xx.
2. Prepare the journal entries necessary from the reconciliation.
3. State the amount of cash that should appear on the balance sheet as of November 30.

Problem Set B

Problem 8B-1. Percentage of Net Sales Method
(L.O. 3)

Chappell Company had an Accounts Receivable balance of $320,000 and a credit balance in Allowance for Uncollectible Accounts of $16,700 at January 1, 19xx. During the year, the company recorded the following transactions:

a. Sales on account, $1,052,000.
b. Sales returns and allowances by credit customers, $53,400.
c. Collections from customers, $993,000.
d. Worthless accounts written off, $19,800.
e. Written-off accounts collected, $4,200.

In addition, the company's past history indicates that 2.5 percent of net credit sales will not be collected.

Required

1. Open ledger accounts for the Accounts Receivable controlling account (112) and Allowance for Uncollectible Accounts (113). Then enter the beginning balances in these accounts.
2. Record separate general journal entries for each of the five items listed above, summarizing the year's activity.
3. Record the general journal entry on December 31 for the estimated uncollectible accounts expense for the year.
4. Post the appropriate parts of the transactions in **2** and **3** to Accounts Receivable and Allowance for Uncollectible Accounts.

Problem 8B-2. Accounts Receivable Aging Method
(L.O. 3, 4)

The DiPalma Jewelry Store uses the accounts receivable aging method to estimate uncollectible accounts. The balance of the Accounts Receivable controlling account was a debit of $446,341 and the balance of Allowance for Uncollectible Accounts was a credit of $43,000 at February 1, 19x1. During the year, the store had sales on account of $3,724,000, sales returns and allowances of $63,000, worthless accounts written off of $44,300, and collections from customers of $3,214,000. As part of end-of-year (January 31, 19x2) procedures, an aging analysis of accounts receivable is prepared. The analysis is partially complete. The totals of the analysis follow.

Customer Account	Total	Not Yet Due	1–30 Days Past Due	31–60 Days Past Due	61–90 Days Past Due	Over 90 Days Past Due
Balance Forward	$793,791	$438,933	$149,614	$106,400	$57,442	$41,402

The following accounts remain to be classified in order to finish the analysis:

Account	Amount	Due Date
H. Caldwell	$10,977	January 15
D. Carlson	9,314	February 15 (next fiscal year)
M. Guokas	8,664	December 20
F. Javier	780	October 1
B. Loo	14,810	January 4
S. Qadri	6,316	November 15
A. Rosenthal	4,389	March 1 (next fiscal year)
	$55,250	

From past experience, the company has found that the following rates are realistic to estimate uncollectible accounts:

Time	Percentage Considered Uncollectible
Not yet due	2
1–30 days past due	5
31–60 days past due	15
61–90 days past due	25
Over 90 days past due	50

Required

1. Complete the aging analysis of accounts receivable.
2. Determine the end-of-year balances (before adjustments) of Accounts Receivable and Allowance for Uncollectible Accounts.
3. Prepare an analysis computing the estimated uncollectible accounts.
4. Prepare a general journal entry to record the estimated uncollectible accounts expense for the year (round the adjustment to the nearest whole dollar).

Problem 8B-3. Notes Receivable Transactions
(L.O. 5, 6)

Minarcik Manufacturing Company sells truck beds. To improve its liquidity, Minarcik discounts any promissory notes it receives. The company engaged in the following transactions involving promissory notes:

Jan. 10 Sold beds to Glynn Company for $60,000, terms n/10.
20 Accepted a 90-day, 12 percent promissory note in settlement of the account from Glynn.
31 Discounted the note from Glynn Company at the bank at 14 percent.
Apr. 20 Having received no notice that the note had been dishonored, assumed Glynn Company paid the bank.
May 5 Sold beds to Nanni Company for $40,000, terms n/10.
15 Received $8,000 cash and a 60-day, 13 percent note for $32,000 in settlement of the Nanni Company account.
25 Discounted the note from Nanni to the bank at 14 percent.
July 14 Received notice that Nanni dishonored the note. Paid the bank the maturity value of the note plus a protest fee of $40.
Aug. 2 Wrote off the Nanni Company account as uncollectible after news that the company declared bankruptcy.
5 Received a 90-day, 11 percent note for $30,000 from Sayeed Company in settlement of an account receivable.
15 Discounted the note from Sayeed Company at the bank at 14 percent.
Nov. 3 Received notice that Sayeed Company dishonored the note. Paid the bank the maturity value of the note plus a protest fee of $40.
9 Received payment in full from Sayeed Company, including 15 percent interest for the 6 days since the note was dishonored.

Required

Prepare general journal entries to record these transactions.

Problem 8B-4. Notes Receivable Transactions
(L.O. 5, 6)

The Hazlett Company accepts notes as payment for sales to key customers. The transactions involving notes for August and October follow.

Aug.	6	Accepted a $27,000, 60-day, 10 percent note from Coughlin Company in payment for merchandise.
	8	Accepted a $21,000, 60-day, 11 percent note from Papadakis Electronics in payment for merchandise.
	13	Discounted the Coughlin Company note at the bank at 15 percent.
	23	Discounted the Papadakis Electronics note at the bank at 15 percent.
	28	Accepted a $63,000, 60-day, 9 percent note from Lai Company in payment for purchase of merchandise.
	30	Accepted a $42,000, 60-day, 12 percent note from Bishop Company in payment for merchandise.
Oct.	5	Receiving no notice of dishonor by Coughlin Company, Hazlett Company assumed Coughlin paid its obligation to the bank.
	7	Received notice from the bank that Papadakis Electronics dishonored its note. Paid the bank the maturity value plus a protest fee of $54.
	27	Lai Company paid its note and interest.
	29	Bishop Company dishonored its note.

Required

Prepare general journal entries to record these transactions.

Problem 8B-5. Short-Term Financing by Discounting Customers' Notes
(L.O. 5, 6)

The management of Vogel Lawn Products sells its goods to distributors 120 days before the summer season. Mr. Vogel has worked out a plan with his bank to finance receivables from sales. The plan calls for the company to receive a 120-day, 10 percent note for each sale to a distributor. Each note will be discounted at the bank at the rate of 12 percent. This plan will provide Vogel with adequate cash flow to operate the company.

During January and February, Vogel made the following sales under the plan:

Company	Amount of Note	Date of Note	Discount Date*
Mears Hardware	$ 920,000	Jan. 7	Jan. 9
Fromm Stores	1,640,000	12	15
Shin Markets	580,000	19	Feb. 18

*Assume 28 days in February.

During May, all the distributors paid on their respective due dates except Fromm Stores, which defaulted on its note. The note was paid in full 30 days late, including additional interest at 10 percent on the maturity value and a bank protest fee of $100.

Required

1. Prepare general journal entries to record Vogel Lawn Products's transactions (round calculations to nearest dollar) for January 7, 9, 12, 15, 19 and February 18.
2. What was the total amount of cash generated in January by discounting the notes receivable?
3. Prepare general journal entries to record the transactions on Vogel Lawn Products's records for May 12 and June 11.
4. What is your evaluation of the plan? What risk is management taking?

Problem 8B-6. Bank Reconciliation
(L.O. 7)

This information is available for Jorge Mendoza Company as of October 31, 19xx:

a. Cash on the books as of October 31 amounted to $21,327.08. Cash on the bank statement for the same date was $26,175.73.
b. A deposit of $2,610.47, representing cash receipts of October 31, did not appear on the bank statement.
c. Outstanding checks totaled $1,968.40.
d. A check for $960.00 returned with the statement was recorded incorrectly in the cash payments journal as $690.00. The check was made for a cash purchase of merchandise.
e. Bank service charges for October amounted to $12.50.

f. The bank collected for Jorge Mendoza Company $6,120.00 on a note. The face value of the note was $6,000.00.
g. An NSF check for $91.78 from a client, Beth Franco, came back with the statement.
h. The bank mistakenly charged to the company account a check for $425.00 drawn by another company.
i. The bank reported that it had credited the account for $170.00 in interest on the average balance for October.

Required

1. Prepare a bank reconciliation for Jorge Mendoza Company as of October 31, 19xx.
2. Prepare the journal entries necessary to adjust the accounts.
3. State the amount of cash that should appear on the balance sheet as of October 31.

Financial Decision Case

Bates Christmas Tree Company
(L.O. 1)

The Bates Christmas Tree Company's business is seasonal: the growing and selling of Christmas trees. By January 1, after a successful season, the company has cash on hand that will not be needed for several months. The company has minimal expenses from January to October and heavy expenses during the harvest and shipping months of November and December. The company's management follows the practice of investing the idle cash in marketable securities, which can be sold as the funds are needed for operations. The company's fiscal year ends on June 30. On January 10 of the current year, the company has cash of $408,300 on hand. It keeps $20,000 on hand for operating expenses and invests the rest as follows:

$100,000 3-month Treasury bill	$ 97,800
1,000 shares of Ford Motor Co. ($50 per share)	50,000
2,500 shares of McDonald's ($50 per share)	125,000
2,100 shares of IBM ($55 per share)	115,500
Total short-term investments	$388,300

During the next few months, the company receives two quarterly cash dividends from each company (assume February 10 and May 10): $.40 per share from Ford, $.10 from McDonald's, and $1.04 from IBM. The Treasury bill is redeemed at face value on April 10. On June 1 management sells 500 shares of McDonald's at $55 per share. On June 30 the market values of the investments are as follows:

Ford Motor Co.	$61 per share
McDonald's	$46 per share
IBM	$50 per share

Another quarterly dividend is received from each company (assume August 10). All the remaining shares are sold on November 1 at the following prices:

Ford Motor Co.	$55 per share
McDonald's	$44 per share
IBM	$60 per share

Required

1. Record the investment transactions that occurred on January 10, February 10, April 10, May 10, and June 1. Prepare the required adjusting entry on June 30, and record the investment transactions on August 10 and November 1.
2. How would the short-term investments be shown on the balance sheet on June 30?
3. After November 1, what is the balance of the account called Allowance to Reduce Short-Term Investments to Market, and what will happen to this account next June?
4. What is your assessment of Bates Christmas Tree Company's strategy with regard to idle cash?

Answers to Self-Test

1. a	3. d	5. b	7. d	9. b
2. a	4. c	6. d	8. a	10. a

LEARNING OBJECTIVES

1. *Define* merchandise *inventory, and show how inventory measurement affects income determination.*
2. *Define* inventory cost, *and relate it to goods flow and cost flow.*
3. *Calculate the pricing of inventory, using the cost basis according to the (a) specific identification method; (b) average-cost method; (c) first-in, first-out (FIFO) method; (d) last-in, first-out (LIFO) method.*
4. *State the effects of each method on income determination and income taxes in periods of changing prices.*
5. *Apply the perpetual inventory system to accounting for inventories and cost of goods sold.*
6. *Apply the lower-of-cost-or-market rule to inventory valuation.*
7. *Estimate the cost of ending inventory using the (a) retail inventory method and (b) gross profit method.*

CHAPTER 9

Inventories

The major source of revenues for retail and wholesale businesses is the sale of merchandise. In terms of dollars, the inventory of goods held for sale is one of the largest assets of a merchandising business. The cost of goods sold is the largest deduction from sales because merchandise is continually being bought and sold. In fact, this cost is often larger than the total of other expenses. Inventories are also important to manufacturing companies. These companies have three kinds of inventory: raw materials to be used in making products, partly complete products (often called work in process), and finished goods ready for sale.

Many companies, especially those in manufacturing, are attempting to reduce their inventory assets by changing to a **just-in-time operating environment**. In this environment, rather than stockpiling inventories for later use, the companies work closely with suppliers to coordinate and schedule shipments so that the goods arrive "just in time" to be used. Less money is thereby tied up in inventories, and the costs associated with carrying inventories are reduced. This chapter deals with inventory measurement, emphasizing its importance to income determination and explaining several different ways of determining, valuing, and estimating inventories. Although the examples used in this chapter mostly relate to merchandising businesses, the concepts and techniques are also applicable to manufacturing companies. After studying this chapter, you should be able to meet the learning objectives listed on the left.

Assets may be divided into two categories. Financial assets, such as those studied in the chapter on short-term liquid assets, include cash, short-term investments, accounts receivable, and notes receivable. These assets represent a right to cash or are assets that can be easily converted into cash. The second type of asset represents an unexpired cost that has not yet been matched against revenues. Among these assets are prepaid expenses; inventories; property, plant, and equipment; natural resources; and intangibles.

DECISION POINT

Amoco Corporation[1]

■ The most important accounting issue faced by management in connection with the second type of asset is how to apply the matching rule in order to measure income. In applying the matching rule, two important questions must be answered: (1) How much of the asset has expired or been used up during the current accounting period and should be shown as an expense on the income statement? (2) How much of the asset is still unused or unexpired and should remain on the balance sheet

1. Information excerpted from the 1990 annual report of Amoco Corporation.

as an asset? These questions are particularly important to companies like Amoco Corporation, one of the largest companies in the world. This leading petroleum and chemical company has huge investments in inventories, prepaid expenses, and long-term assets. In 1990, Amoco had more than $24 billion invested in these assets. Variations in applying the matching rule to these assets can have an effect of $1 billion or more in any one year on Amoco's net income, which totaled $1.9 billion in 1990. In this chapter you learn to apply the matching rule to inventories. In later chapters you will learn to apply the matching rule to long-term assets, including property, plant, and equipment; natural resources; and intangibles. ■

Inventories and Income Determination

OBJECTIVE 1
Define merchandise inventory, *and show how* inventory measurement *affects* income determination

Merchandise inventory consists of all goods that are owned and held for sale in the regular course of business, including goods in transit. Because it will normally be converted into cash within a year's time, merchandise inventory is considered a current asset. It appears on the balance sheet just below Accounts Receivable because it is less liquid.

The American Institute of Certified Public Accountants states, "A major objective of accounting for inventories is the proper determination of income through the process of matching appropriate costs against revenues."[2] Note that the objective is to determine the best measure of income, not the most realistic inventory value. As you will see, the two objectives are sometimes incompatible, in which case the objective of income determination takes precedence over a realistic inventory figure for the balance sheet.

Review of Gross Margin and Cost of Goods Sold Computations

A review should show how the cost assigned to inventory affects gross margin and cost of goods sold. The gross margin on sales is computed by deducting cost of goods sold from the net sales of the period. Cost of goods sold is measured by deducting ending inventory from cost of goods available for sale. Because of these relationships, the higher the cost of ending inventory, the lower the cost of goods sold will be and the higher the resulting gross margin. Conversely, the lower the value assigned to ending inventory, the higher the cost of goods sold will be and the lower the gross margin. *In effect, the value assigned to the ending inventory determines what portion of the cost of goods available for sale will be deducted from net sales as cost of goods sold and what portion will be carried to the next period as beginning inventory.* Remember that the cost of goods available for sale includes the beginning inventory (unexpired costs carried over from the last period) plus net purchases during this period. The effects on income of errors in the cost of ending inventory are demonstrated in the next section.

Effects of Errors in Inventory Measurement

The basic problem of separating goods available for sale into two components—goods sold and goods not sold—is that of assigning a cost to the goods not sold, the ending inventory. That portion of the goods available for sale not assigned to the ending inventory is used to determine the cost of goods sold.

2. American Institute of Certified Public Accountants, *Accounting Research Bulletin No. 43* (New York: AICPA, 1953), Ch. 4.

For this reason, an error made in determining the inventory figure at the end of the period will cause an equal error in gross margin and net income in the income statement. The amount of assets and owner's equity on the balance sheet will also be misstated by the same amount. The consequences of overstatement and understatement of inventory are illustrated in the three simplified examples that follow. In each case, beginning inventory, net purchases, and cost of goods available for sale have been stated correctly. In the first example, ending inventory has been stated correctly. In the second example, inventory is overstated by $6,000; in the third example, inventory is understated by $6,000.

Example 1. Ending Inventory Correctly Stated at $10,000

Cost of Goods Sold for the Year	
Beginning Inventory	$12,000
Net Purchases	58,000
Cost of Goods Available for Sale	$70,000
Ending Inventory	10,000
Cost of Goods Sold	$60,000

Income Statement for the Year	
Net Sales	$100,000
Cost of Goods Sold	60,000
Gross Margin from Sales	$ 40,000
Operating Expenses	32,000
Net Income	$ 8,000

Example 2. Ending Inventory Overstated by $6,000

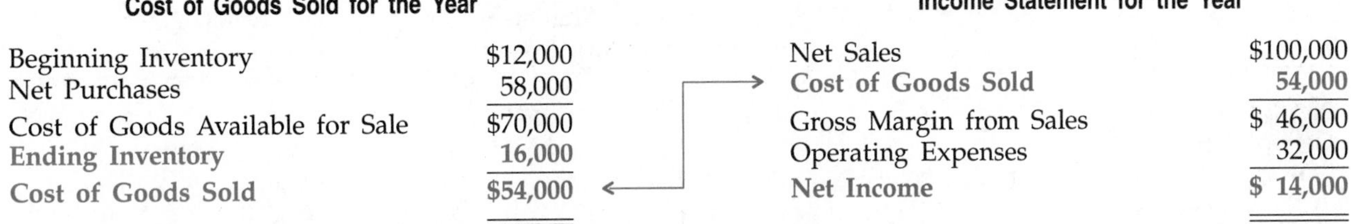

Cost of Goods Sold for the Year	
Beginning Inventory	$12,000
Net Purchases	58,000
Cost of Goods Available for Sale	$70,000
Ending Inventory	16,000
Cost of Goods Sold	$54,000

Income Statement for the Year	
Net Sales	$100,000
Cost of Goods Sold	54,000
Gross Margin from Sales	$ 46,000
Operating Expenses	32,000
Net Income	$ 14,000

Example 3. Ending Inventory Understated by $6,000

Cost of Goods Sold for the Year	
Beginning Inventory	$12,000
Net Purchases	58,000
Cost of Goods Available for Sale	$70,000
Ending Inventory	4,000
Cost of Goods Sold	$66,000

Income Statement for the Year	
Net Sales	$100,000
Cost of Goods Sold	66,000
Gross Margin from Sales	$ 34,000
Operating Expenses	32,000
Net Income	$ 2,000

In all three examples, the total cost of goods available for sale was $70,000. The difference in net income resulted from how this $70,000 was divided between ending inventory and cost of goods sold.

Because the ending inventory in one period becomes the beginning inventory in the following period, it is important to recognize that an error in inventory valuation affects not only the current period but also the following period. Using the same figures in Examples **1** and **2**, the income statements for two successive years in Exhibit 9-1 illustrate this carryover effect.

Note that over a two-year period the errors in net income will offset or counterbalance each other. In Exhibit 9-1, for example, the overstatement of ending inventory in 19x1 caused a $6,000 overstatement of beginning inventory in the following year, resulting in an understatement of income by $6,000 in the second year. This offsetting effect is shown in the table under Exhibit 9-1.

Exhibit 9-1. Effect of Error in Ending Inventory on Current and Succeeding Years

Effect of Error in Inventory on Current Year
Income Statement
For the Year Ended December 31, 19x1

	Correct Statement of Ending Inventory		Overstatement of Ending Inventory	
Net Sales		$100,000		$100,000
Cost of Goods Sold				
Beginning Inventory, Jan. 1, 19x1	$12,000		$12,000	
Net Purchases	58,000		58,000	
Cost of Goods Available for Sale	$70,000		$70,000	
Less Ending Inventory, Dec. 31, 19x1	**10,000**		**16,000**	
Cost of Goods Sold		60,000		54,000
Gross Margin from Sales		$ 40,000		$ 46,000
Operating Expenses		32,000		32,000
Net Income		$ 8,000		$ 14,000

Effect on Succeeding Year
Income Statement
For the Year Ended December 31, 19x2

	Correct Statement of Beginning Inventory		Overstatement of Beginning Inventory	
Net Sales		$130,000		$130,000
Cost of Goods Sold				
Beginning Inventory, Jan. 1, 19x2	**$10,000**		**$16,000**	
Net Purchases	68,000		68,000	
Cost of Goods Available for Sale	$78,000		$84,000	
Less Ending Inventory, Dec. 31, 19x2	13,000		13,000	
Cost of Goods Sold		65,000		71,000
Gross Margin from Sales		$ 65,000		$ 59,000
Operating Expenses		50,000		50,000
Net Income		$ 15,000		$ 9,000

		With Inventory at Dec. 31, 19x1 Overstated	
	With Inventory Correctly Stated	**Reported Net Income Will Be**	**Reported Net Income Will Be Overstated (Understated)**
Net Income for 19x1	$ 8,000	$14,000	$ 6,000
Net Income for 19x2	15,000	9,000	(6,000)
Total Net Income for Two Years	$23,000	$23,000	—

Because the total income for the two years is the same, there may be a tendency to think that one does not need to worry about inventory errors. However, the errors violate the matching rule. In addition, many decisions by management, creditors, and investors are made on an annual basis and depend on the accountant's determination of net income. The accountant has an obligation to make the net income figure for each year as useful as possible.

The effects of errors in inventory on net income are as follows:

Year 1	Year 2
Ending inventory overstated Cost of goods sold understated Net income overstated	**Beginning inventory overstated** Cost of goods sold overstated Net income understated
Ending inventory understated Cost of goods sold overstated Net income understated	**Beginning inventory understated** Cost of goods sold understated Net income overstated

If we assume no income tax effects, a change or error in inventory results in a change or error in net income of the same amount. Thus, the measurement of inventory is important and is the subject of the remainder of this chapter.

Inventory Measurement

The cost assigned to ending inventory depends on two measurements: quantity and price. At least once each year, a business must take an actual physical count of all items of merchandise held for sale. This process is called taking a physical inventory, or simply taking inventory, as described in the chapter on accounting for merchandising operations. Although companies may take inventory at other times during the year, most companies take inventory only at the end of their fiscal year. Taking the inventory consists of: (1) counting, weighing, or measuring the items on hand, (2) pricing each item, and (3) extending (multiplying) to determine the total cost.

Merchandise in Transit

Because merchandise inventory includes all items owned by the company and held for sale, the status of any merchandise in transit, either being sold or purchased by the inventorying company, must be examined to determine if it should be included in the inventory count. As explained in the chapter on accounting for merchandising operations, the terms of the shipping agreement will indicate if title has passed. Outgoing goods shipped FOB destination would be included in merchandise inventory, whereas those shipped FOB shipping point would not. Conversely, incoming goods shipped FOB shipping point would be included in merchandise inventory, but those shipped FOB destination would not.

Merchandise on Hand Not Included in Inventory

At the time a physical inventory is taken, there may be merchandise on hand to which the company does not hold title. One category of such goods includes merchandise sold and awaiting delivery to the buyer. Since the sale has been completed, title of the goods has passed to the buyer, and the merchandise should not be included in the inventory. A second category is goods held on consignment. A **consignment** is the placing of goods by their owner (known as the *consignor*) on the premises of another company (the *consignee*). Title to consigned goods remains with the consignor until the consignee sells the goods.

Thus, consigned goods should not be included in the physical inventory of the consignee because they still belong to the consignor.

Pricing the Inventory at Cost

OBJECTIVE 2
Define inventory cost, and relate it to goods flow and cost flow

The pricing of inventory is one of the most interesting and most widely debated problems in accounting. As demonstrated, the value placed on ending inventory may have a dramatic effect on net income for each of two consecutive years. Federal income taxes are based on income, so the valuation of inventory may also have a considerable effect on the income taxes to be paid. Federal income tax authorities have, therefore, been interested in the effects of various inventory valuation procedures and have specific regulations about the acceptability of different methods. As a result, the accountant is sometimes faced with the problem of balancing the goals of proper income determination with those of minimizing income taxes.

There are a number of acceptable methods of valuing inventories on the financial statements. Most are based either on cost or on the lower of cost or market. Both methods are acceptable for income tax purposes. We will first explain variations of the cost basis of inventory valuation and then turn to the lower-of-cost-or-market method.

Cost Defined

According to the AICPA, "The primary basis of accounting for inventories is cost, which has been defined generally as the price paid or consideration given to acquire an asset."[3] This definition of **inventory cost** has generally been interpreted to include the following costs: (1) invoice price less purchases discounts; (2) freight or transportation in, including insurance in transit; and (3) applicable taxes and tariffs. Other costs—for ordering, receiving, and storing—should in principle also be included in inventory cost. In practice, however, it is so difficult to allocate these costs to specific inventory items that they are usually considered an expense of the accounting period instead of an inventory cost.

Methods of Pricing Inventory at Cost

The prices of most kinds of merchandise vary during the year. Identical lots of merchandise may have been purchased at different prices. Also, when identical items are bought and sold, it is often impossible to tell which have been sold and which are still in inventory. For this reason, it is necessary to make an assumption about the order in which items have been sold. Because the assumed order of sale may or may not be the same as the actual order of sale, the assumption is really an assumption about the *flow of costs* rather than the *flow of physical inventory.*

Thus, the term **goods flow** refers to the actual physical movement of goods in the operations of the company, and the term **cost flow** refers to the association of costs with their *assumed* flow in the operations of the company. The assumed cost flow may or may not be the same as the actual goods flow. This statement may seem strange at first, but several assumed cost flows are available under generally accepted accounting principles. In fact, it is sometimes preferable to use an assumed cost flow that bears no relationship to goods flow because it gives a better estimate of income, which, as stated earlier, is the major goal of inventory valuation.

3. Ibid.

Accountants usually price inventory by using one of the following generally accepted methods, each based on a different assumption of cost flow: (1) specific identification method; (2) average-cost method; (3) first-in, first-out (FIFO) method; and (4) last-in, first-out (LIFO) method. The choice of method depends on the nature of the business, the financial effects of the methods, and the costs of implementing them.

To illustrate the four methods, the following data for the month of June will be used:

Inventory Data, June 30

June 1	Inventory	50 units @ $1.00	$ 50
6	Purchased	50 units @ $1.10	55
13	Purchased	150 units @ $1.20	180
20	Purchased	100 units @ $1.30	130
25	Purchased	150 units @ $1.40	210
Goods Available for Sale		500 units	$625
Sales		280 units	
On hand June 30		220 units	

Notice that there is a total of 500 units available for sale at a total cost of $625. Stated simply, the problem of inventory pricing is to divide the $625 between the 280 units sold and the 220 units on hand.

OBJECTIVE 3a
Calculate the pricing of inventory, using the cost basis according to the specific identification method

Specific Identification Method. If the units in the ending inventory can be identified as coming from specific purchases, the **specific identification method** may be used to price the inventory. For instance, assume that the June 30 inventory consisted of 50 units from the June 1 inventory, 100 units of the purchase of June 13, and 70 units of the purchase of June 25. The cost to be assigned to the inventory under the specific identification method would be $268, determined as follows:

Inventory, June 30—Specific Identification Method

50 units @ $1.00	$ 50	Cost of Goods Available for Sale	$625
100 units @ $1.20	120	→ Less June 30 Inventory	268
70 units @ $1.40	98	Cost of Goods Sold	$357
220 units at cost of	$268 ←		

The specific identification method might be used in the purchase and sale of high-priced articles, such as automobiles, heavy equipment, and works of art. Although this method may appear logical, it is not used by many companies because it has two definite disadvantages. First, in many cases, it is difficult and impractical to keep track of the purchase and sale of individual items. Second, when a company deals in items of an identical nature, deciding which items are sold becomes arbitrary; thus, the company can raise or lower income by choosing to sell the high- or low-cost items.

OBJECTIVE 3b
Calculate the pricing of inventory, using the cost basis according to the average-cost method

Average-Cost Method. Under the **average-cost method**, it is assumed that the cost of inventory is based on the average cost of the goods available for sale during the period. Average cost is computed by dividing the total cost of goods available for sale by the total units available for sale. This gives a weighted-average unit cost that is applied to the units in the ending inventory. In our illustration, the ending inventory would be $275, or $1.25 per unit, determined as follows:

Inventory, June 30—Average-Cost Method

June 1	Inventory	50 @ $1.00	$ 50
6	Purchased	50 @ $1.10	55
13	Purchased	150 @ $1.20	180
20	Purchased	100 @ $1.30	130
25	Purchased	150 @ $1.40	210
Totals		500 units	$625

Average unit cost: $625 ÷ 500 = $1.25
Ending inventory: 220 units @ $1.25 = $275

Cost of Goods Available for Sale	$625
Less June 30 Inventory	275
Cost of Goods Sold	$350

The average-cost method tends to level out the effects of cost increases and decreases because the cost for the ending inventory calculated under this method is influenced by all the prices paid during the year and by the beginning inventory price. Some, however, criticize the average-cost method because they believe that recent costs are more relevant for income measurement and decision making.

OBJECTIVE 3c
Calculate the pricing of inventory, using the cost basis according to the first-in, first-out (FIFO) method

First-In, First-Out (FIFO) Method. The **first-in, first-out (FIFO) method** is based on the assumption that the costs of the first items acquired should be assigned to the first items sold. The costs of the goods on hand at the end of a period are assumed to be from the most recent purchases, and the costs assigned to goods that have been sold are assumed to be from the earliest purchases. The FIFO method of determining inventory cost may be adopted by any business, regardless of the actual physical flow of goods, because the assumption is made regarding the flow of costs and not the flow of goods.

In our illustration, the June 30 inventory would be $301 when the FIFO method is used. It is computed as follows:

Inventory, June 30—First-In, First-Out Method

150 units at $1.40 from purchase of June 25	$210
70 units at $1.30 from purchase of June 20	91
220 units at a cost of	$301
Cost of Goods Available for Sale	$625
Less June 30 Inventory	301
Cost of Goods Sold	$324

The effect of the FIFO method is to value the ending inventory at the most recent costs and include earlier ones in cost of goods sold. During periods of consistently rising prices, the FIFO method yields the highest possible amount of net income, since cost of goods sold will show costs closer to the price level at the time the goods were purchased. Another reason for this result is that businesses tend to increase selling prices as costs rise, regardless of the fact that inventories may have been purchased before the price rise. The reverse effect occurs in periods of price decreases. For these reasons a major criticism of FIFO is that it magnifies the effects of the business cycle on income.

OBJECTIVE 3d
Calculate the pricing of inventory, using the cost basis according to the last-in, first-out (LIFO) method

Last-In, First-Out (LIFO) Method. The **last-in, first-out (LIFO) method** of costing inventories is based on the assumption that the costs of the last items purchased should be assigned to the first items used or sold and that the cost of the ending inventory reflects the cost of merchandise purchased earliest.

Under this method, the June 30 inventory would be $249, computed as follows:

Inventory, June 30—Last-In, First-Out Method

50 units at $1.00 from June 1 inventory	$ 50
50 units at $1.10 from purchase of June 6	55
120 units at $1.20 from purchase of June 13	144
220 units at a cost of	$249
Cost of Goods Available for Sale	$625
Less June 30 Inventory	249
Cost of Goods Sold	$376

The effect of LIFO is to value inventory at earliest prices and to include in cost of goods sold the cost of the most recently purchased goods. This assumption, of course, does not agree with the actual physical movement of goods in most businesses.

However, there is a strong logical argument to support this method, based on the fact that a certain size inventory is necessary in a going concern. When inventory is sold, it must be replaced with more goods. The supporters of LIFO reason that the fairest determination of income occurs if the current costs of merchandise are matched against current sales prices, regardless of which physical units of merchandise are sold. When prices are moving either upward or downward, LIFO will mean that the cost of goods sold will show costs closer to the price level at the time the goods were sold. As a result, the LIFO method tends to show a smaller net income during inflationary times and a larger net income during deflationary times than other methods of inventory valuation. Thus, the peaks and valleys of the business cycle tend to be smoothed out. The important factor here is that in inventory valuation the flow of costs and hence income determination is more important than the physical movement of goods and balance sheet valuation.

An argument may also be made against the LIFO method. Because the inventory valuation on the balance sheet reflects earlier prices, this value is often unrealistic with respect to the current value of the inventory. Thus, such balance sheet measures as working capital and current ratio may be distorted and must be interpreted carefully.

Comparison and Effects of the Alternative Methods of Pricing Inventory

OBJECTIVE 4
State the effects of each method on income determination and income taxes in periods of changing prices

The specific identification, average-cost, FIFO, and LIFO methods of pricing inventory have now been illustrated. The specific identification method is based on actual costs, whereas the other three methods are based on assumptions regarding the flow of costs. Let us now compare the effects of the four methods on net income using the same data as before and assuming sales during June of $500.

	Specific Identification Method	Average-Cost Method	First-In, First-Out Method	Last-In, First-Out Method
Sales	$500	$500	$500	$500
Cost of Goods Sold				
Beginning Inventory	$ 50	$ 50	$ 50	$ 50
Purchases	575	575	575	575
Cost of Goods Available for Sale	$625	$625	$625	$625
Less Ending Inventory	**268**	**275**	**301**	**249**
Costs of Goods Sold	**$357**	**$350**	**$324**	**$376**
Gross Margin from Sales	**$143**	**$150**	**$176**	**$124**

Keeping in mind that June was a period of rising prices, we can see that LIFO, which charges the most recent and in this case the highest prices to cost of goods sold, resulted in the lowest gross margin. Conversely, FIFO, which charges the earliest and in this case the lowest prices to cost of goods sold, produced the highest gross margin. The gross margin under the average-cost method is somewhere between those computed under LIFO and FIFO. Thus, it is clear that this method has a less pronounced effect.

During a period of declining prices, the reverse would occur. The LIFO method would produce a higher gross margin than the FIFO method. It is apparent that the method of inventory valuation has the greatest importance during prolonged periods of price changes in one direction, either up or down.

Effect on the Financial Statements. Each of these four methods of inventory pricing is acceptable for use in published financial statements. The FIFO, LIFO, and average-cost methods are widely used, as can be seen in Figure 9-1, which shows the inventory cost methods used by six hundred large companies. Each has its advantages and disadvantages, and none can be considered best or perfect. The factors that should be considered in choosing an inventory method are the effects of each method on financial statements, income taxes, and management decisions.

A basic problem in determining the best inventory measure for a particular company is that inventory appears on both the balance sheet and the income statement. As we have seen, the LIFO method is best suited for the income statement because it matches revenues and cost of goods sold. But it is not the best measure of the current balance sheet value of inventory, particularly during a prolonged period of price increases or decreases. The FIFO method, on the other hand, is best suited to the balance sheet because the ending inventory is closest to current values and thus gives a more realistic view of the current financial assets of a business. Readers of financial statements must be alert to inventory methods and be able to assess their effects.

Effect on Income Taxes. The Internal Revenue Service has developed several rules for valuing inventories for federal income tax purposes. A company has a wide choice of methods, including specific identification, average cost, FIFO and LIFO, as well as lower of cost or market. But once a method is chosen, it must be used consistently from one year to the next. The IRS must approve any

Figure 9-1. Inventory Costing Methods Used by 600 Large Companies

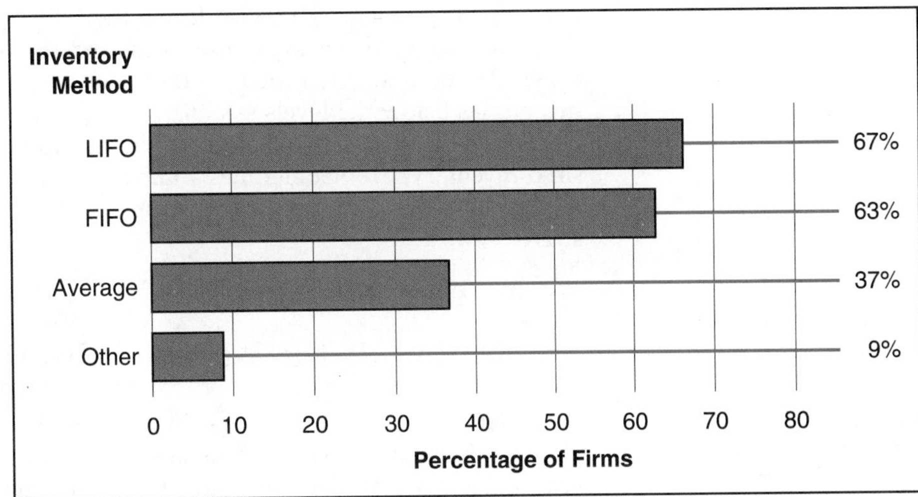

Total percentage exceeds 100 because some companies used different methods for different types of inventory.

Source: American Institute of Certified Public Accountants, *Accounting Trends & Techniques* (New York: AICPA, 1985). Reprinted by permission.

change in the inventory valuation method for income tax purposes.[4] This requirement agrees with the rule of consistency in accounting since changes in inventory method may cause income to fluctuate too much and would make income statements hard to interpret from year to year. A company may change its inventory method if there is a good reason for doing so. The nature and effect of the change must be shown on its financial statements.

Many accountants believe that the use of FIFO or average-cost methods in periods of rising prices causes businesses to report more than their true profit, resulting in the payment of excess income taxes. The profit is overstated because cost of goods sold is understated, relative to current prices. The company must buy replacement inventory at higher prices, but additional funds are also needed to pay income taxes. During the rapid inflation of 1979 to 1982, billions of dollars reported as profits and paid in income taxes were believed to be the result of poor matching of current costs and revenues under the FIFO and average-cost methods. Consequently, many companies have since switched to the LIFO inventory method encouraged by the belief that prices will continue to rise.

If a company uses the LIFO method in reporting income for tax purposes, the IRS requires that the LIFO method also be used in the accounting records. Also, the IRS will not allow the use of the lower-of-cost-or-market rule if LIFO is used to determine inventory cost. In this case, only the LIFO cost can be used. This rule, however, does not preclude a company from using lower of LIFO cost or market for financial reporting purposes. (The use of lower of cost or market is discussed later in this chapter.)

Over a period of rising prices, a business that uses the LIFO basis may find that its inventory is valued for balance sheet purposes at a cost figure far below

4. A single exception to this rule is that taxpayers must notify the IRS of a change to LIFO from another method, but do not need to have advance IRS approval.

what it currently pays for the same items. Management must monitor this situation carefully, because, if it should let the inventory quantity at year end fall below the beginning-of-the-year level, it will find itself paying income taxes on the difference between the current cost and the old LIFO cost in the records. When this occurs, it is called a **LIFO liquidation** because sales have reduced inventories below the levels established in prior years. A LIFO liquidation may be prevented by making enough purchases prior to year end to restore the desired inventory level. Sometimes a LIFO liquidation cannot be avoided because the products are discontinued or supplies are interrupted, as in the case of a strike.

Application of the Perpetual Inventory System

OBJECTIVE 5
Apply the perpetual inventory system to accounting for inventories and cost of goods sold

The inventory system used so far in this book has been the **periodic inventory system**. Under this system no detailed record of inventory is kept during the year and a physical inventory must be taken at the end of the year to establish ending inventory. The cost of goods sold cannot be determined until the physical inventory is completed.

Periodic inventory systems are used in many retail and wholesale businesses because they do not require a large amount of clerical work. The primary disadvantage of periodic inventory systems is the lack of detailed records as to what items of inventory are on hand at a given point in time. Such detailed data would enable management to respond to customers' inquiries concerning product availability, order inventory more effectively to avoid being out of stock, and control the financial costs associated with the money invested in the inventory.

The system that provides this type of data is the **perpetual inventory system**. Under this system, a continuous record of the inventory is maintained by keeping detailed records of the purchases and sales of inventory. As a result, the amount of inventory on hand and the cost of goods sold are known throughout the accounting period. In the past, the high clerical cost of maintaining this type of system meant that it was used primarily for goods of high value and low volume. However, with the advent of the computer and of electronic tags and markings, the perpetual inventory system has become easier and less expensive to operate and, consequently, much more prevalent. For example, the electronic markings of grocery items enable grocery stores to maintain perpetual inventory records; and the tags attached to products sold by clothing, department, and discount stores such as Sears and Kmart enable them to have tight controls over inventory and ordering.

Handling the Perpetual Inventory System in the Accounting Records

The primary difference in accounting between the perpetual and the periodic inventory systems is that under the perpetual inventory system, the Merchandise Inventory account is continuously adjusted by entering purchases, sales, and other inventory transactions as they occur. Under the periodic inventory system, the Merchandise Inventory account stays at the beginning level until the physical inventory is recorded at the end of the period. Under the perpetual system, the Cost of Goods Sold account is used as sales occur to accumulate the cost of goods sold to customers. To illustrate these differences, the transactions of an office supply wholesaler are recorded under both the periodic and perpetual inventory systems as follows:

1. Received 100 cases of floppy disks at a cost of $12,000; terms 2/10, n/30, FOB destination. The net method of recording purchases is used.

Perpetual Inventory System			Periodic Inventory System		
Merchandise Inventory	11,760		Purchases	11,760	
Accounts Payable		11,760	Accounts Payable		11,760
Purchase of merchandise at net purchase price; terms 2/10, n/30, FOB destination			Purchase of merchandise at net purchase price; terms 2/10, n/30, FOB destination		

2. Sold 20 cases of floppy disks to a retailer at a total price of $3,000, terms n/10, FOB shipping point.

Perpetual Inventory System			Periodic Inventory System		
Accounts Receivable	3,000		Accounts Receivable	3,000	
Sales		3,000	Sales		3,000
Sale of 20 cases; terms n/10, FOB shipping point			Sale of 20 cases; terms n/10, FOB shipping point		
Cost of Goods Sold	2,352				
Merchandise Inventory		2,352			
To record cost of goods sold 20 cases × $117.60 = $2,352					

3. Arranged to return 10 cases of the floppy disks to supplier for full credit.

Perpetual Inventory System			Periodic Inventory System		
Accounts Payable	1,176		Accounts Payable	1,176	
Merchandise Inventory		1,176	Purchases Returns and Allowances		1,176
To record purchase return 10 cases × $117.60 = $1,176			To record purchase return		

4. Paid supplier in full within the discount period.

Perpetual Inventory System			Periodic Inventory System		
Accounts Payable	10,584		Accounts Payable	10,584	
Cash		10,584	Cash		10,584
Payment to supplier $11,760 − $1,176 = $10,584			Payment to supplier $11,760 − $1,176 = $10,584		

Note the differences in the first three transactions. In each case, under the perpetual inventory system, the Merchandise Inventory account is updated for the effect on the physical inventory; the Purchases and Purchases Returns and Allowances accounts are not used. Also, in transaction **2**, the Cost of Goods Sold account is updated at the time of a sale.

At the end of the year, neither adjustments to Merchandise Inventory nor corresponding debits or credits to Income Summary are needed under the perpetual inventory system. Because the Merchandise Inventory account has been continually updated during the year, there is no need to establish the ending inventory in the records. The required entry closes Cost of Goods Sold to Income Summary.

Maintaining the Detailed Perpetual Inventory Records

To keep track of the quantities and costs of the individual items stocked in merchandise inventory under the perpetual inventory system, it is necessary to maintain an individual record for each type of inventory. The Merchandise Inventory account is a controlling account for a subsidiary file of individual inventory records. This mechanism is similar to the Accounts Receivable controlling account and its subsidiary ledger. In the Merchandise Inventory subsidiary file, each item has a card (or file in a computer system) on which purchases and sales are entered as they take place. A sample perpetual inventory card of our office supply wholesaler is shown in Exhibit 9-2. At any time, the card will show the number of pencil sharpeners on hand. The total of all the cards is equal to the merchandise inventory.

As shown in Exhibit 9-2, on June 1 there is a balance of 60 pencil sharpeners that cost $5 each. A sale on June 4 reduces the balance by 10 pencil sharpeners. On June 10, 100 pencil sharpeners are purchased at $6 each. Now the inventory consists of 50 pencil sharpeners purchased at $5 each and 100 pencil sharpeners purchased at $6 each. The method of inventory valuation in Exhibit 9-2 is FIFO, as can be determined by looking at the June 20 sale. The entire sale of 30 pencil sharpeners is taken from the 50 sharpeners still left from the beginning inventory. If the LIFO method were used, the sale would be deducted from the latest purchase of 100 pencil sharpeners at $6 each. Under LIFO the resulting balance would be $670 [(50 × $5) + (70 × $6)]. An example showing both the FIFO and LIFO methods appears in this chapter's Review Problem.

Need for Physical Inventories Under the Perpetual Inventory System

The use of the perpetual inventory system does not eliminate the need for a physical inventory at the end of the accounting period. The perpetual inventory records show what should be on hand, not necessarily what is on hand. There

Exhibit 9-2. Perpetual Inventory Record Card, FIFO

Item: Pencil Sharpener, Model D-222

	Purchased			Sold			Balance		
Date	Units	Cost	Total	Units	Cost	Total	Units	Cost	Balance
June 1							60	5.00	300.00
4				10	5.00	50.00	50	5.00	250.00
10	100	6.00	600.00				50 100	5.00 6.00	850.00
20				30	5.00	150.00	20 100	5.00 6.00	700.00

may be losses due to spoilage, employee pilferage, theft, or other causes. If a loss has occurred, it is reflected in the accounts by a debit to Inventory Shortage Expense and a credit to Merchandise Inventory. The individual inventory cards, which may also be the subsidiary ledger, must also be adjusted.

Valuing the Inventory at the Lower of Cost or Market (LCM)

OBJECTIVE 6
Apply the lower-of-cost-or-market rule to inventory valuation

Although cost is usually the most appropriate basis for valuation of inventory, there are times when inventory may properly be shown in the financial statements at less than its cost. If by reason of physical deterioration, obsolescence, or decline in price level the market value of the inventory falls below the cost, a loss has occurred. This loss may be recognized by writing the inventory down to market. The term **market** is used here to mean current replacement cost. For a merchandising company, market is the amount that the company would pay at the present time for the same goods, purchased from the usual suppliers, and in the usual quantities. It may help in applying the **lower-of-cost-or-market (LCM) rule** by thinking of it as the "lower-of-cost-or-replacement-cost" rule.[5]

Methods of Applying LCM

There are three basic methods of valuing inventories at the lower of cost or market: (1) the item-by-item method, (2) the major category method, and (3) the total inventory method. For example, a stereo shop could determine lower of cost or market for each kind of speaker, receiver, and turntable (item by item); for all speakers, all receivers, and all turntables (major categories); or for all speakers, receivers, and turntables together (total inventory).

Item-by-Item Method. When the **item-by-item method** is used, cost and market are compared for each item in the inventory. The individual items are then valued at their lower price.

Lower of Cost or Market with Item-by-Item Method

		Per Unit		
	Quantity	Cost	Market	Lower of Cost or Market
Category I				
Item a	200	**$1.50**	$1.70	$ 300
Item b	100	2.00	**1.80**	180
Item c	100	**2.50**	2.60	250
Category II				
Item d	300	5.00	**4.50**	1,350
Item e	200	**4.00**	4.10	800
Inventory at the lower of cost or market				**$2,880**

5. In some cases, *market value* is determined by the *realizable value* of the inventory—the amount for which the goods can be sold rather than the amount for which the goods can be replaced. The circumstances in which realizable value determines market value are encountered in practice only occasionally, and the valuation procedures are technical enough to be addressed in a more advanced accounting course.

Major Category Method. Under the **major category method**, the total cost and total market for each category of items are compared. Each category is then valued at its lower amount.

Lower of Cost or Market with Major Category Method

		Per Unit		Total		
	Quantity	**Cost**	**Market**	**Cost**	**Market**	**Lower of Cost or Market**
Category I						
Item a	200	$1.50	$1.70	$ 300	$ 340	
Item b	100	2.00	1.80	200	180	
Item c	100	2.50	2.60	250	260	
Totals				**$ 750**	$ 780	**$ 750**
Category II						
Item d	300	5.00	4.50	$1,500	$1,350	
Item e	200	4.00	4.10	800	820	
Totals				$2,300	**$2,170**	**2,170**
Inventory at the lower of cost or market						**$2,920**

Total Inventory Method. Under the **total inventory method**, the entire inventory is valued at both cost and market, and the lower price is used to value inventory. Since this method is not acceptable for federal income tax purposes, it is not illustrated here.

Valuing Inventory by Estimation

It is sometimes necessary or desirable to estimate the value of ending inventory. The methods most commonly used for this purpose are the retail method and the gross profit method.

Retail Method of Inventory Estimation

OBJECTIVE 7a
Estimate the cost of ending inventory using the retail inventory method

The **retail method**, as its name implies, is used in retail merchandising businesses. There are two principal reasons for the use of the retail method. First, management usually requires that financial statements be prepared at least once a month and, as it is time-consuming and expensive to take a physical inventory each month, the retail method is used to estimate the value of inventory on hand. Second, because items in a retail store normally have a price tag or a universal product code, it is a common practice to take the physical inventory at retail from these price tags and codes and reduce the total value to cost through use of the retail method. The term *at retail* means the amount of the inventory at the marked selling prices of the inventory items.

When the retail method is used to estimate an ending inventory, the records must show the beginning inventory at cost and at retail. The records must also show the amount of goods purchased during the period both at cost and at retail. The net sales at retail is, of course, the balance of the Sales account less returns and allowances. A simple example of the retail method follows.

The Retail Method of Inventory Valuation

	Cost	Retail
Beginning Inventory	$ 40,000	$ 55,000
Net Purchases for the Period (excluding Freight In)	107,000	145,000
Freight In	3,000	
Merchandise Available for Sale	**$150,000**	**$200,000**
Ratio of Cost to Retail Price: $\frac{\$150,000}{\$200,000} = 75\%$		
Net Sales During the Period		160,000
Estimated Ending Inventory at Retail		$ 40,000
Ratio of Cost to Retail	75%	
Estimated Cost of Ending Inventory	$ 30,000	

Merchandise available for sale is determined both at cost and at retail by listing beginning inventory and net purchases for the period at cost and at the expected selling price of the goods, adding freight to the cost column, and totaling. The ratio of these two amounts (cost to retail price) provides an estimate of the cost of each dollar of retail sales value. The estimated ending inventory at retail is then determined by deducting sales for the period from the retail price of the goods that were available for sale during the period. The inventory at retail is then converted to cost on the basis of the ratio of cost to retail.

The cost of ending inventory may also be estimated by applying the ratio of cost to retail to the total retail value of the physical count of the ending inventory. Applying the retail method in practice is often more difficult than this simple example because of certain complications, such as changes in the retail price that take place during the year, different markups on different types of merchandise, and varying volumes of sales for different types of merchandise.

Gross Profit Method of Inventory Estimation

OBJECTIVE 7b
Estimate the cost of ending inventory using the gross profit method

The **gross profit method** assumes that the ratio of gross margin for a business remains relatively stable from year to year. It is used in place of the retail method when records of the retail prices of beginning inventory and purchases are not kept. It is considered acceptable for estimating the cost of inventory for interim reports, but is not an acceptable method for valuing inventory in the annual financial statements. It is also useful in estimating the amount of inventory lost or destroyed by theft, fire, or other hazards. Insurance companies often use this method to verify loss claims.

The gross profit method is simple to use. First, figure the cost of goods available for sale in the usual way (add purchases to beginning inventory). Second, estimate the cost of goods sold by deducting the estimated gross margin from sales. Third, deduct the estimated cost of goods sold from the goods available for sale in order to estimate the cost of ending inventory. This method is shown at the top of page 370.

The Gross Profit Method of Inventory Valuation

1. Beginning Inventory at Cost		$ 50,000
Purchases at Cost		290,000
Cost of Goods Available for Sale		$340,000
2. Less Estimated Cost of Goods Sold		
Sales at Selling Price	$400,000	
Less Estimated Gross Margin of 30%	120,000	
Estimated Cost of Goods Sold		280,000
3. Estimated Cost of Ending Inventory		$ 60,000

Chapter Review

Review of Learning Objectives

1. **Define *merchandise inventory*, and show how inventory measurement affects income determination.**
   Merchandise inventory consists of all goods owned and held for sale in the regular course of business. The objective of accounting for inventories is the proper determination of income. If the value of ending inventory is understated or overstated, a corresponding error—dollar for dollar—will be made in net income. Furthermore, because the ending inventory of one period is the beginning inventory of the next, the misstatement affects two accounting periods, although the effects are opposite.

2. **Define *inventory cost*, and relate it to goods flow and cost flow.**
   The cost of inventory includes (1) invoice price less purchases discounts, (2) freight or transportation in, including insurance in transit, and (3) applicable taxes and tariffs. Goods flow relates to the actual physical flow of merchandise, whereas cost flow refers to the assumed flow of costs in the operation of the business.

3. **Calculate the pricing of inventory, using the cost basis according to the (a) specific identification method; (b) average-cost method; (c) first-in, first-out (FIFO) method; (d) last-in, first-out (LIFO) method.**
   The value assigned to the ending inventory is the result of two measurements: quantity and price. Quantity is determined by taking a physical inventory. The pricing of inventory is usually based on the assumed cost flow of the goods as they are bought and sold. One of four assumptions is usually made regarding cost flow. These assumptions are represented by four inventory methods. Inventory pricing could be determined by the specific identification method, which associates the actual cost with each item of inventory but is rarely used. The average-cost method assumes that the cost of inventory is the average cost of goods available for sale during the period. The first-in, first-out (FIFO) method assumes that the costs of the first items acquired should be assigned to the first items sold. The last-in, first-out (LIFO) method assumes that the costs of the last items acquired should be assigned to the first items sold. The inventory method chosen may or may not be equivalent to the actual physical flow of goods.

4. **State the effects of each method on income determination and income taxes in periods of changing prices.**
   During periods of rising prices, the LIFO method will show the lowest net income; FIFO, the highest; and average cost, in between. The opposite effects occur in periods of falling prices. No generalization can be made regarding the specific identification method. The Internal Revenue Service requires that if LIFO is used for tax purposes, it must also be used for book purposes, and that the lower-of-cost-or-market rule cannot be applied to the LIFO method.

5. **Apply the perpetual inventory system to accounting for inventories and cost of goods sold.**
Under the periodic inventory system, inventory is determined by a physical count at the end of the accounting period. Under the perpetual inventory system, the Merchandise Inventory control account is constantly updated as sales and purchases are made during the accounting period. Also, as sales are made, the Cost of Goods Sold account is used to accumulate the costs of those sales.

6. **Apply the lower-of-cost-or-market (LCM) rule to inventory valuation.**
The lower-of-cost-or-market rule can be applied to the above methods of determining inventory at cost. This rule states that if the replacement cost (market) of the inventory is lower than the inventory cost, the lower figure should be used.

7. **Estimate the cost of ending inventory using the (a) retail inventory method and (b) gross profit method.**
Two methods of estimating the value of inventory are the retail inventory method and the gross profit method. Under the retail inventory method, inventory is determined at retail prices and is then reduced to estimated cost by applying a ratio of cost to retail price. Under the gross profit method, cost of goods sold is estimated by reducing sales by estimated gross margin. The estimated cost of goods sold is then deducted from cost of goods available for sale to estimate the inventory.

Review of Concepts and Terminology

The following concepts and terms were introduced in this chapter:

(L.O. 3) **Average-cost method:** An inventory cost method that assumes the cost of inventory is based on the average cost of all goods available for sale.

(L.O. 1) **Consignment:** The placing of goods by the owner of the goods (the consignor) on the premises of another company (the consignee).

(L.O. 2) **Cost flow:** Association of costs with their assumed flow within the operations of the company.

(L.O. 3) **First-in, first-out (FIFO) method:** An inventory cost method based on the assumption that the costs of the first items acquired should be assigned to the first items sold.

(L.O. 2) **Goods flow:** The actual physical movement of goods in the operations of the company.

(L.O. 7) **Gross profit method:** A method of inventory estimation that assumes the ratio of gross margin for a business remains relatively stable from year to year.

(L.O. 2) **Inventory cost:** The price paid or consideration given to acquire an asset; includes invoice price less purchases discounts, plus freight or transportation in, and applicable taxes or tariffs.

(L.O. 6) **Item-by-item method:** A lower-of-cost-or-market method of valuing inventory in which cost and market are compared for each item in the inventory, with each item then valued at its lower price.

(L.O. 1) **Just-in-time operating environment:** An operating environment that seeks to reduce the levels of inventory whereby companies work with suppliers to coordinate and schedule deliveries so that goods arrive just at the time they are needed.

(L.O. 3) **Last-in, first-out (LIFO) method:** An inventory cost method that assumes that the costs of the last items purchased should be assigned to the first items sold.

(L.O. 4) **LIFO liquidation:** The reduction of inventory below previous levels so that income is increased by the amount current prices exceed the historical cost of the inventory under LIFO.

(L.O. 6) **Lower-of-cost-or-market (LCM) rule:** A method of valuing inventory at an amount below cost if the replacement (market) value is less than cost.

(L.O. 6) **Major category method:** A lower-of-cost-or-market method for valuing inventory in which the total cost and total market for each category of items are compared, with each category then valued at its lower amount.

(L.O. 6) **Market:** Current replacement cost of inventory.

(L.O. 1) **Merchandise inventory:** All goods that are owned and held for sale in the regular course of business.

(L.O. 5) **Periodic inventory system:** The method of accounting for the physical quantity of inventory by taking a count at the end of the period and then adjusting the inventory account for the new balance.

(L.O. 5) **Perpetual inventory system:** The method of accounting for the physical quantity and costs of inventory by keeping continuous detailed records of purchases and sales.

(L.O. 7) **Retail method:** A method of inventory estimation used in retail businesses by which inventory at retail value is reduced by the ratio of cost to retail price.

(L.O. 3) **Specific identification method:** A method of determining the cost of inventory by identifying the cost of each item.

(L.O. 6) **Total inventory method:** A lower-of-cost-or-market method of valuing inventory in which the entire inventory is valued at both cost and market, and the lower price is used; not an acceptable method for federal income tax purposes.

Self-Test

Test your knowledge of the chapter by choosing the best answer for each of the following items.

(L.O. 1) 1. An overstatement of ending inventory in one period results in
   a. an overstatement of the ending inventory of the next period.
   b. an understatement of net income of the next period.
   c. an overstatement of net income of the next period.
   d. no effect on net income of the next period.

(L.O. 2) 2. Which of the following costs would *not* be included in the cost of inventory?
   a. Goods held on consignment
   b. Purchased goods in transit, FOB shipping point
   c. Freight In
   d. Invoice price

(L.O. 3) 3. Sept. 1 Inventory 10 @ \$4.00
   8 Purchased 40 @ \$4.40
   17 Purchased 20 @ \$4.20
   25 Purchased 30 @ \$4.80 Sold 70

   Using this information, cost of goods sold under the average-cost method is
   a. \$133.20.
   b. \$444.00.
   c. \$310.80.
   d. \$304.50.

(L.O. 3) 4. Assuming the same facts as in **3**, cost of goods sold under the first-in, first-out (FIFO) method is
   a. \$144.00.
   b. \$300.00.
   c. \$388.50.
   d. \$444.00.

(L.O. 3) 5. Assuming the same facts as in **3**, ending inventory under the last-in, first-out (LIFO) method is
   a. \$316.
   b. \$444.
   c. \$300.
   d. \$128.

(L.O. 4) 6. In a period of rising prices, which of the following inventory methods generally results in the lowest net income figure?
   a. Average-cost method
   b. FIFO method
   c. LIFO method
   d. Cannot tell without more information

(L.O. 5) 7. Under the perpetual inventory method, a purchase of merchandise is recorded as a debit to
a. Income Summary.
b. Cost of Goods Sold.
c. Purchases.
d. Merchandise Inventory.

(L.O. 6) 8. When applying the lower-of-cost-or-market method to inventory, "market" generally means
a. original cost, less physical deterioration.
b. resale value.
c. original cost.
d. replacement cost.

(L.O. 7) 9. Which of the following companies would be most likely to use the retail inventory method?
a. A farm supply company
b. A TV repair company
c. A dealer in heavy machinery
d. A men's clothing shop

(L.O. 7) 10. A retail company has goods available for sale of $1,000,000 at retail and $600,000 at cost and ending inventory of $100,000 at retail. What is the estimated cost of goods sold?
a. $60,000
b. $100,000
c. $900,000
d. $540,000

Answers to the Self-Test are at the end of this chapter.

Review Problem
Periodic and Perpetual Inventory Systems

(L.O. 3, 5) The following table summarizes the beginning inventory, purchases, and sales of Psi Company's single product during January.

	Beginning Inventory			Purchases			
Date	Units	Cost	Total	Units	Cost	Total	Sales Units
Jan. 1	1,400	$19	$26,600				
4							300
8				600	$20	$12,000	
10							1,300
12				900	21	18,900	
15							150
18				500	22	11,000	
24				800	23	18,400	
31							1,350
Totals	1,400		$26,600	2,800		$60,300	3,100

1. Assuming that the company uses the periodic inventory system, compute the cost that should be assigned to ending inventory using (a) a FIFO basis and (b) a LIFO basis.
2. Assuming that the company uses the perpetual inventory system, compute the cost that should be assigned to ending inventory using (a) a FIFO basis and (b) a LIFO basis. (**Hint:** It is helpful to use a form similar to the perpetual inventory card in Exhibit 9-2.)

Answer to Review Problem

	Units	Dollars
Beginning Inventory	1,400	$26,600
Purchases	2,800	60,300
Available for Sale	4,200	$86,900
Sales	3,100	
Ending Inventory	1,100	

1. Periodic inventory system
   a. FIFO basis
      Ending inventory consists of
         January 24 purchases (800 × $23) $18,400
         January 18 purchases (300 × $22) 6,600 $25,000
   b. LIFO basis
      Ending inventory consists of
         Beginning inventory (1,100 × $19) $20,900

2. Perpetual inventory system
   a. FIFO basis

	Purchased			Sold			Balance		
Date	Units	Cost	Total	Units	Cost	Total	Units	Cost	Total
Jan. 1							1,400	$19	$26,600
4				300	$19	$ 5,700	1,100	19	20,900
8	600	$20	$12,000				1,100 600	19 20	32,900
10				1,100 200	19 20	24,900	400	20	8,000
12	900	21	18,900				400 900	20 21	26,900
15				150	20	3,000	250 900	20 21	23,900
18	500	22	11,000				250 900 500	20 21 22	34,900
24	800	23	18,400				250 900 500 800	20 21 22 23	53,300
31				250 900 200	20 21 22	28,300	**300** **800**	**22** **23**	**25,000**

b. LIFO basis

Date	Purchased			Sold			Balance		
	Units	Cost	Total	Units	Cost	Total	Units	Cost	Total
Jan. 1							1,400	$19	$26,600
4				300	$19	$ 5,700	1,100	19	20,900
8	600	$20	$12,000				1,100 600	19 20	32,900
10				600 700	20 19	25,300	400	19	7,600
12	900	21	18,900				400 900	19 21	26,500
15				150	21	3,150	400 750	19 21	23,350
18	500	22	11,000				400 750 500	19 21 22	34,350
24	800	23	18,400				400 750 500 800	19 21 22 23	52,750
31				800 500 50	23 22 21	30,450	**400** **700**	**19** **21**	**22,300**

Chapter Assignments

Questions

1. How does inventory differ from short-term liquid assets, and what measurements of inventory must be taken to make a proper income determination? What is the relationship of inventory to the matching rule?
2. What is merchandise inventory, and what is the primary objective of inventory measurement?
3. If the merchandise inventory is mistakenly overstated at the end of 19x8, what is the effect on (a) 19x8 net income, (b) 19x8 year-end balance sheet value, (c) 19x9 net income, and (d) 19x9 year-end balance sheet value?
4. Fargo Sales Company is very busy at the end of its fiscal year on June 30. There is an order for 130 units of product in the warehouse. Although the shipping department tries, it cannot ship the product by June 30, and title has not yet passed. Should the 130 units be included in the year-end count of inventory? Why or why not?
5. What does the term *taking a physical inventory* mean?
6. What items are included in the cost of inventory?
7. What is the difference between goods flow and cost flow?
8. In periods of steadily rising prices, which of the three inventory methods—average-cost, FIFO, or LIFO—will give the (a) highest inventory cost, (b) lowest inventory cost, (c) highest net income, and (d) lowest net income?
9. May a company change its inventory cost method from year to year? Explain.

10. Do the FIFO and LIFO inventory methods result in different quantities of ending inventory?
11. Under which method of cost flow are (a) the earliest costs assigned to ending inventory, (b) the latest costs assigned to ending inventory, (c) the average costs assigned to inventory?
12. What are the relative advantages and disadvantages of FIFO and LIFO from management's point of view?
13. What effects does inventory valuation have on income taxes?
14. Which is more expensive to maintain: a perpetual inventory system or a periodic inventory system? Why?
15. What differences occur in recording sales, purchases, and closing entries under the perpetual and periodic inventory systems?
16. In the phrase *lower of cost or market*, what is meant by the word *market*?
17. What methods can be used to determine lower of cost or market?
18. What are some reasons management may use the gross profit method of determining inventory?
19. Does using the retail inventory method mean that inventories are measured at retail value on the balance sheet? Explain.
20. Which of the following inventory systems do not require taking a physical inventory: (a) perpetual, (b) periodic, (c) retail, (d) gross profit?

Communication Skills Exercises

Communication 9-1. Inventories, Income Determination, and Ethics *(L.O. 1)*

Flare, Inc., which has a December 31 year end, designs and sells fashions for young professional women. Sandra Mason, president of the company, feared that the forecasted 1992 profitability goals would not be reached. She was pleased when Flare received a large order on December 30 from The Executive Woman, a retail chain of upscale stores for business women. Mason immediately directed the controller to record the sale, which represented 13 percent of Flare's annual sales, but directed the inventory control department not to separate the goods for shipment until after January 1. Separated goods are not included in inventory because they have been sold. On December 31 the company's auditors arrived to observe the year-end taking of the physical inventory under the periodic inventory system. What will be the effect of Mason's action on Flare's 1992 profitability? What will be the effect on 1993 profitability? Is Mason's action ethical?

Communication 9-2. LIFO Inventory Method *(L.O. 4)*

In 1989, 96 percent of paper companies used the LIFO inventory method for the costing of inventories, whereas only 24 percent of electronic equipment companies used LIFO.[6] Describe the LIFO inventory method. What effects does it have on reported income and income taxes during periods of price changes? Can you think of a reason why the paper industry would use LIFO and most of the electronics industry would not?

Communication 9-3. Periodic Versus Perpetual Inventory Systems *(L.O. 5)*

The Foot Joint, Inc. operates four sports shoe stores in Omaha-area malls. The company uses the periodic inventory system and takes a quarterly physical inventory in order to prepare financial statements at the end of each quarter. The company lost money during the last two quarters of 1992 and the first quarter of 1993. Part of the problem, management believes, is that some stores have run out of merchandise while other stores have too much on hand. Top management is certain that if more timely monthly financial statements were prepared, the company could adapt to varying sales patterns during a quarter. Managers have proposed that the company switch to the perpetual inventory system in the second quarter of 1993 and prepare financial statements at the end of each month. Every shoe will be tagged with a machine-readable identification label, which will be scanned as each sale is made. Trends in shoe sales will be monitored so that purchases, shipments, and promotions for each store can be modified on a monthly basis. Monthly physical inventories will be unnecessary under this plan because the amount of the ending merchandise inventory will be available from perpetual inventory

6. American Institute of Certified Public Accountants, *Accounting Trends & Techniques* (New York: AICPA, 1990), p. 106.

records. What changes in the method of recording transactions will be needed in order to adopt the perpetual inventory system? What advantages do you see in the new system? What disadvantages? Will quarterly physical inventories still be necessary?

Communication 9-4. Basic Research Skills *(L.O. 2, 5)*

Visit a local retail business—a grocery, clothing, book, music, or appliance store, for example—and make an appointment to interview the manager for thirty minutes about the company's inventory accounting system. The store may be a branch of a larger company. Find out answers to the following questions, summarize the answers in a paper to be handed in, and be prepared to discuss your results in class.

What is the physical flow of merchandise into the store and what documents are used in connection with this flow?

What documents are prepared when merchandise is sold?

Does the store keep perpetual inventory records? If so, are the records in units only or do they keep track of cost as well? If not, what system does the store use?

How often does the company take a physical inventory?

How are financial statements generated for the store?

What method does the company use to price its inventory for financial statements?

Classroom Exercises

Exercise 9-1. Effects of Inventory Errors *(L.O. 1)*

Condensed income statements for Hamlin Company for two years are shown below.

	19x4	19x3
Sales	$126,000	$105,000
Cost of Goods Sold	75,000	54,000
Gross Margin on Sales	$ 51,000	$ 51,000
Operating Expenses	30,000	30,000
Net Income	$ 21,000	$ 21,000

After the end of 19x4 it was discovered that an error had been made that resulted in a $9,000 understatement of the 19x3 ending inventory.

Compute the corrected net income for 19x3 and 19x4. What effect will the error have on net income and owner's equity for 19x5?

Exercise 9-2. Inventory Costing Methods *(L.O. 3)*

Helen's Farm Store had the purchases and sales of fertilizer during the year that follow:

Jan. 1	Beginning Inventory	250 cases @ $23	$ 5,750
Feb. 25	Purchased	100 cases @ $26	2,600
June 15	Purchased	400 cases @ $28	11,200
Aug. 15	Purchased	100 cases @ $26	2,600
Oct. 15	Purchased	300 cases @ $28	8,400
Dec. 15	Purchased	200 cases @ $30	6,000
Total Goods Available for Sale		1,350	$36,550
Total Sales		1,000 cases	
Dec. 31	Ending Inventory	350 cases	

Assume that all of the June 15 purchase and 200 cases each from the January 1 beginning inventory, the October 15 purchase, and the December 15 purchase were sold.

Determine the costs that should be assigned to ending inventory and cost of goods sold under each of the following assumptions: (1) costs are assigned by the specific identification method; (2) costs are assigned on an average-cost basis; (3) costs are assigned on a FIFO basis; (4) costs are assigned on a LIFO basis. What conclusions can be drawn as to the effect of each method on the income statement and the balance sheet of Helen's Farm Store?

Exercise 9-3.
Inventory Costing Methods
(L.O. 3)

During its first year of operation, Jefferson Company purchased 5,600 units of a product at $21 per unit. During the second year, it purchased 6,000 units of the same product at $24 per unit. During the third year, it purchased 5,000 units at $30 per unit. Jefferson Company managed to have an ending inventory each year of 1,000 units. The company sells goods at a 100 percent markup over cost.

Prepare cost of goods sold statements that compare the value of ending inventory and the cost of goods sold for each of the three years using (1) the FIFO method and (2) the LIFO method. What conclusions can you draw from the resulting data about the relationships between changes in unit price and changes in the value of ending inventory?

Exercise 9-4.
Effects of Inventory Methods on Cash Flows
(L.O. 4)

Ross Products, Inc. sold 120,000 cases of glue at $40 per case during 19x1. Its beginning inventory consisted of 20,000 cases at a cost of $24 per case. During 19x1 it purchased 60,000 cases at $28 per case and later 50,000 cases at $30 per case. Operating expenses were $1,100,000, and the applicable income tax rate is 30 percent.

Using the periodic inventory system, compute net income using the FIFO basis and the LIFO basis for costing inventory. Which alternative produces the larger cash flow? The company is considering a purchase of 10,000 cases at $30 per case just before the year end. What effect on net income and on cash flow will this proposed purchase have under each basis? (**Hint:** What are the income tax consequences?)

Exercise 9-5.
Inventory Costing Method Characteristics
(L.O. 3, 4)

The lettered items in the list below represent inventory costing methods. In the blank next to each numbered statement, write the letter of the method to which the statement is *most* applicable.

a. Specific identification
b. Average cost
c. First-in, first-out (FIFO)
d. Last-in, first-out (LIFO)

____ 1. Matches recent costs with recent revenues
____ 2. Assumes that each item of inventory is identifiable
____ 3. Results in most realistic balance sheet valuation
____ 4. Results in lowest net income in periods of deflation
____ 5. Results in lowest net income in periods of inflation
____ 6. Matches oldest costs with recent revenues
____ 7. Results in highest net income in periods of inflation
____ 8. Results in highest net income in periods of deflation
____ 9. Tends to level out the effects of inflation
____ 10. Is unpredictable as to the effects of inflation

Exercise 9-6.
Periodic Inventory System and Inventory Costing Methods
(L.O. 3, 4)

In chronological order, the inventory, purchases, and sales of a single product for a recent month are as follows:

		Units	Amount per Unit
June 1	Beginning Inventory	300	$10
4	Purchase	800	11
8	Sale	400	20
12	Purchase	1,000	12
16	Sale	700	20
20	Sale	500	22
24	Purchase	1,200	13
28	Sale	600	22
30	Sale	400	22

Using the periodic inventory system, compute the cost of ending inventory, cost of goods sold, and gross margin from sales. Use the FIFO and LIFO inventory costing methods. Explain the difference in gross margin from sales produced by the two methods.

Exercise 9-7.
Inventory Costing Methods: Periodic and Perpetual Systems
(L.O. 3, 5)

During July 19x2, Servex, Inc. sold 250 units of its product Dervex for $2,000 from the following units available:

	Units	Cost
Beginning Inventory	100	$1
Purchase 1	40	2
Purchase 2	60	3
Purchase 3	70	4
Purchase 4	80	5
Purchase 5	90	6

A sale of 100 units was made after purchase 1, and a sale of 150 units was made after purchase 4. Of the units sold, 100 came from beginning inventory and 150 from purchases 3 and 4.

Determine cost of goods available for sale and ending inventory in units. Then determine the costs that should be assigned to cost of goods sold and ending inventory under each of the following assumptions: (1) Costs are assigned under the periodic inventory system using (a) the specific identification method, (b) the average-cost method, (c) the FIFO method, and (d) the LIFO method. (2) Costs are assigned under the perpetual inventory system using (a) the FIFO method and (b) the LIFO method. For each alternative, show the gross margin from sales.

Exercise 9-8.
Perpetual Inventory System and Inventory Costing Methods
(L.O. 3, 5)

Using the data provided in Exercise 9-6 and assuming the perpetual inventory system, compute the cost of ending inventory, cost of goods sold, and gross margin from sales. Use the FIFO and LIFO inventory costing methods. Explain the difference in gross margin from sales produced by the two methods.

Exercise 9-9.
Perpetual and Periodic Inventory Systems
(L.O. 5)

Record general journal entries using the net purchase method to record the following transactions under (1) the perpetual inventory system and (2) the periodic inventory system.

Mar. 11 Received 4,000 cases of chloride tablets at a cost of $200 per case, terms 2/10, n/30, FOB destination.
15 Sold 200 cases of tablets for $300 per case, terms n/10, FOB shipping point.
17 Returned 50 cases of tablets that were damaged to suppliers for full credit.
20 Paid the supplier in full for the amount owed on the purchase of March 11.

Exercise 9-10.
Lower-of-Cost-or-Market Rule
(L.O. 6)

Mercurio Company values its inventory, shown below, at the lower of cost or market. Compute Mercurio's inventory value using (1) the item-by-item method and (2) the major category method.

		Per Unit	
	Quantity	Cost	Market
Category I			
Item aa	200	$ 2.00	$ 1.80
Item bb	240	4.00	4.40
Item cc	400	8.00	7.50
Category II			
Item dd	300	12.00	13.00
Item ee	400	18.00	18.20

Exercise 9-11.
Retail Method
(L.O. 7)

Roseanne's Dress Shop had net retail sales of $500,000 during the current year. The following additional information was obtained from the accounting records:

	At Cost	At Retail
Beginning Inventory	$ 80,000	$120,000
Net Purchases (excluding Freight In)	280,000	440,000
Freight In	20,800	

1. Estimate the company's ending inventory at cost using the retail method.
2. Assume that a physical inventory taken at year end revealed an inventory on hand of $36,000 at retail value. What is the estimated amount of inventory shrinkage (loss due to theft, damage, and so forth) at cost?
3. Prepare the journal entry to record the inventory shrinkage.

Exercise 9-12.
Gross Profit Method
(L.O. 7)

Dale Nolan was at home watching television when he received a call from the fire department. His business was a total loss from fire. The insurance company asked him to prove his inventory loss. For the year, until the date of the fire, Dale's company had sales of $450,000 and purchases of $280,000. Freight in amounted to $13,700, and the beginning inventory was $45,000. It was Dale's custom to price goods in such a way as to have a gross margin of 40 percent on sales.

Compute Dale's estimated inventory loss.

Interpretation Case from Business

Hershey Foods Corporation[7]
(L.O. 2, 4)

A portion of the income statements for 1990 and 1989 for Hershey Foods Corporation, famous for its chocolate and confectionery products, follows (in thousands).

	1990*	1989
Net Sales	$2,715,609	$2,420,988
Cost of Goods Sold	1,588,360	1,455,612
Gross Margin	$1,127,249	$ 965,376
Selling, General, and Administrative Expense	776,668	655,040
Income from Operations	$ 350,581	$ 310,336
Interest Expense	24,603	20,414
Income Before Income Taxes	$ 325,978	$ 289,922
Provision for Income Taxes	145,636	118,868
Net Income (from operations)	$ 180,342	$ 171,054

*1990 excludes net gain on business restructuring of $35,540.

In a note on supplemental balance sheet information, Hershey indicated that most of its inventories are maintained on a last-in, first-out (LIFO) basis. The company also reported that inventories on a LIFO cost basis were $309,837 in 1989 and $379,108 in 1990. In addition, it reported that if valued on a first-in, first-out (FIFO) basis, inventories would have been $371,697 in 1989 and $434,774 in 1990.

Required

1. Prepare a schedule comparing net income for 1990 on a LIFO basis with what it would have been on a FIFO basis. Use a corporate income tax rate of 45 percent (Hershey's average tax rate in 1990).
2. Why do you suppose Hershey's management chooses to use the LIFO inventory method? On what economic conditions, if any, do these reasons depend? Given your calculations in **1** above, do you believe the economic conditions relevant to Hershey were advantageous for using LIFO in 1990? Explain your answer.

7. Information excerpted from the 1990 and 1989 annual reports of Hershey Foods Corporation.

Problem Set A

Problem 9A-1.
Inventory Costing Methods
(L.O. 3)

The Pascual Door Company sold 2,200 doors during 19x2 at $320 per door. Its beginning inventory on January 1 was 130 doors at $112. Purchases made during the year were as follows:

February	225 doors @ $124
April	350 doors @ $130
June	700 doors @ $140
August	300 doors @ $132
October	400 doors @ $136
November	250 doors @ $144

The company's selling and administrative costs for the year were $202,000, and the company uses the periodic inventory system.

Required

1. Prepare a schedule to compute the cost of goods available for sale.
2. Prepare an income statement under each of the following assumptions: (a) costs are assigned to inventory on an average-cost basis; (b) costs are assigned to inventory on a FIFO basis; (c) costs are assigned to inventory on a LIFO basis.

Problem 9A-2.
Lower-of-Cost-or-Market Rule
(L.O. 6)

The employees of Kuberski's Shoes completed their physical inventory as follows:

		Per Unit	
	Pairs of Shoes	Cost	Market
Men			
Black	400	$44	$48
Brown	325	42	42
Blue	100	50	46
Tan	200	38	20
Women			
White	300	52	64
Red	150	46	40
Yellow	100	60	50
Blue	250	50	66
Brown	100	40	60
Black	150	40	50

Required

Determine the value of inventory at lower of cost or market using (1) the item-by-item method and (2) the major category method.

Problem 9A-3.
Periodic Inventory System
(L.O. 3)

The beginning inventory, purchases, and sales of Product LMR for May and June are presented below. The company closes its books at the end of each month. It uses a periodic inventory system.

May	1	Beginning Inventory	60 units @ $147
	9	Sales	20 units
	12	Purchases	100 units @ $156
	25	Sales	70 units
June	5	Purchases	120 units @ $159
	9	Sales	110 units
	14	Purchases	50 units @ $162
	19	Sales	80 units
	24	Purchases	100 units @ $165
	28	Sales	100 units

Required

1. Compute the cost of the ending inventory on May 31 and June 30 on a FIFO basis. In addition, determine cost of goods sold for May and June.
2. Compute the cost of the ending inventory on May 31 and June 30 on a LIFO basis. In addition, determine cost of goods sold for May and June.
3. Prepare a general journal entry to record the sale on June 28 to Panchali Company on credit for $27,300.

Problem 9A-4.
Perpetual Inventory System
(L.O. 3, 5)

Assume the data presented in Problem 9A-3, except the company uses a perpetual inventory system.

Required

1. Assume that the company maintains inventory on a FIFO basis and uses perpetual inventory cards similar to the one illustrated in Exhibit 9-2. Record the transactions on a card using two or more lines as needed. Also, determine cost of goods sold for May and June.
2. Assuming that the company keeps its records on a LIFO basis, record the transactions on a second record card and determine cost of goods sold for both months.
3. Prepare general journal entries to record the credit purchase on June 14 and the credit sale on June 28 for $27,300, assuming the LIFO basis of costing inventory. What is the amount and LIFO cost of the inventory at the end of June?
4. On June 30, the company counted a physical inventory of 22 units. Record any inventory shrinkage necessary, assuming a LIFO basis.

Problem 9A-5.
Retail Inventory Method
(L.O. 7)

Overland Company switched recently to the retail inventory method to estimate the cost of ending inventory. To test this method, the company took a physical inventory one month after its implementation. Cost, retail, and the physical inventory data are as follows:

	At Cost	At Retail
July 1 Beginning Inventory	$472,132	$ 622,800
Purchases	750,000	1,008,400
Purchases Returns and Allowances	(25,200)	(34,800)
Freight In	8,350	
Sales		1,060,000
Sales Returns and Allowances		(28,000)
July 31 Physical Inventory		508,200

Required

1. Prepare a schedule to estimate the dollar amount of Overland's July 31 inventory using the retail method.
2. Use Overland's cost ratio to reduce the retail value of the physical inventory to cost.
3. Calculate the estimated amount of inventory shortage at cost and at retail.

Problem 9A-6.
Gross Profit Method
(L.O. 7)

Brandon Oil Products warehouses its oil field products in a West Texas warehouse. The warehouse and most of its inventory were completely destroyed by a tornado on April 27. The company found some of its records, but it does not keep perpetual inventory records. The warehouse manager must estimate the amount of the loss. He found the following information in the records:

Beginning Inventory, January 1	$1,320,000
Purchases, January 2 to April 27	780,000
Purchases Returns, January 2 to April 27	(30,000)
Freight In since January 2	16,000
Sales, January 2 to April 27	1,840,000
Sales Returns, January 2 to April 27	(40,000)

Inventory costing $420,000 was recovered and could be sold. The manager remembers that the average gross margin on oil field products is 48 percent.

Required

Prepare a schedule to estimate the inventory destroyed by the tornado.

Problem Set B

Problem 9B-1.
Inventory Costing Methods
(L.O. 3)

Lattimer Company merchandises a single product called Rulex. The following data represent beginning inventory and purchases of Rulex during the past year: January 1 inventory, 68,000 units at $22.00; February purchases, 80,000 units at $24.00; March purchases, 160,000 units at $24.80; May purchases, 120,000 units at $25.20; July purchases, 200,000 units at $25.60; September purchases, 160,000 units at $25.20; and November purchases, 60,000 units at $26.00. Sales of Rulex totaled 786,000 units at $40 per unit. Selling and administrative expenses totaled $10,204,000 for the year, and Lattimer Company uses a periodic inventory system.

Required

1. Prepare a schedule to compute the cost of goods available for sale.
2. Prepare an income statement under each of the following assumptions: (a) costs are assigned to inventory on an average-cost basis; (b) costs are assigned to inventory on a FIFO basis; (c) costs are assigned to inventory on a LIFO basis.

Problem 9B-2.
Lower-of-Cost-or-Market Rule
(L.O. 6)

After taking the physical inventory, the accountant for Dorsey Company prepared the inventory schedule that follows:

		Per Unit	
	Quantity	Cost	Market
Product line 1			
Item 11	190	$ 27	$ 30
Item 12	270	12	15
Item 13	210	24	21
Product line 2			
Item 21	160	45	51
Item 22	400	63	60
Item 23	70	54	60
Product line 3			
Item 31	290	78	60
Item 32	310	90	84
Item 33	120	102	117

Required

Determine the value of the inventory at lower of cost or market using (1) the item-by-item method and (2) the major category method.

Problem 9B-3.
Periodic Inventory System
(L.O. 3)

The beginning inventory of Product H and data on purchases and sales for a two-month period follow. The company closes its books at the end of each month. It uses a periodic inventory system.

Sept. 1	Inventory	50 units @ $204
9	Sale	30 units
15	Purchase	100 units @ $220
20	Sale	60 units
Oct. 4	Purchase	100 units @ $216
10	Sale	110 units
16	Purchase	50 units @ $224
20	Sale	40 units
23	Purchase	60 units @ $234
25	Sale	30 units
31	Sale	20 units

Required

1. Compute the value of the ending inventory of Product H on September 30 and October 31 on a FIFO basis. In addition, determine cost of goods sold for September and October.
2. Compute the value of the ending inventory of Product H on September 30 and October 31 on a LIFO basis. In addition, determine cost of goods sold for September and October.
3. Prepare a general journal entry to record the sale on October 31 to Telander Corporation on credit for $8,000.

Problem 9B-4. Perpetual Inventory System
(L.O. 3, 5)

Assume the data presented in Problem 9B-3, except that the company uses a perpetual inventory system.

Required

1. Assume that the company maintains inventory on a FIFO basis and uses perpetual inventory cards similar to the one illustrated in Exhibit 9-2. Record the transactions on a card using two or more lines as needed. Also, determine cost of goods sold for September and October.
2. Assuming that the company keeps its records on a LIFO basis, record the transactions on a second record card and determine cost of goods sold for both months.
3. Assuming that the October 31 sale was made to Telander Corporation on credit for $8,000, prepare a general journal entry to record the sale and cost of goods sold on a LIFO basis.
4. Assuming that the company takes a periodic physical inventory on October 31, that the value of the Product H inventory was $13,800, and that the FIFO basis of evaluating inventory is used, record an inventory shrinkage if necessary.

Problem 9B-5. Retail Inventory Method
(L.O. 7)

Maywood Company operates a large discount store and uses the retail inventory method to estimate the cost of ending inventory. Management suspects that in recent weeks there have been unusually heavy losses from shoplifting or employee pilferage. To estimate the amount of the loss, the company has taken a physical inventory and will compare the results with the estimated cost of inventory. Data from the accounting records of Maywood Company are as follows:

	At Cost	At Retail
March 1 Beginning Inventory	$102,976	$148,600
Purchases	143,466	217,000
Purchases Returns and Allowances	(4,086)	(6,400)
Freight In	1,900	
Sales		218,366
Sales Returns and Allowances		(1,866)
March 31 Physical Inventory		124,900

Required

1. Prepare a schedule to estimate the dollar amount of the store's year-end inventory using the retail method.
2. Use the store's cost ratio to reduce the retail value of the physical inventory to cost.
3. Calculate the estimated amount of inventory shortage at cost and at retail.

Problem 9B-6. Gross Profit Method
(L.O. 7)

Jauss and Sons is a large retail furniture company that operates in two adjacent warehouses. One warehouse is a showroom, and the other is used for storage of merchandise. On the night of May 9, a fire broke out in the storage warehouse and destroyed the merchandise. Fortunately, the fire did not reach the showroom, so all the merchandise on display was saved.

Although the company maintained a perpetual inventory system, its records were rather haphazard, and the last reliable physical inventory was taken on December 31. In addition, there was no control of the flow of the goods between the showroom and the warehouse. Thus, it was impossible to tell what goods should be in either place. As a result, the insurance company required an independent estimate of the amount of loss.

The insurance company examiners were satisfied when they were provided with the following information:

1. Merchandise Inventory on December 31	$1,454,800
2. Purchases, January 1 to May 9	2,412,200
3. Purchases Returns, January 1 to May 9	(10,706)
4. Freight In, January 1 to May 9	53,100
5. Sales, January 1 to May 9	3,959,050
6. Sales Returns, January 1 to May 9	(29,800)
7. Merchandise inventory in showroom on May 9	402,960
8. Average gross profit margin	44 percent

Required

Prepare a schedule that estimates the amount of the inventory lost in the fire.

Financial Decision Case

BRT Company
(L.O. 3, 4)

Bell Refrigerated Trucks Company (BRT Company) buys large refrigerated trucks from the manufacturer and sells them to companies and independent truckers who haul perishable goods for long distances. BRT has been successful in this specialized niche of the industry because it provides a unique product and service. Because of the high cost of these trucks and of financing inventory, BRT tries to maintain as small an inventory as possible. In fact, at the beginning of July the company had no inventory or liabilities, as shown by the following balance sheet:

BRT Company
Balance Sheet
July 1, 19xx

Assets		Owner's Equity	
Cash	$800,000	Larry Bell, Capital	$800,000
Total Assets	$800,000	Total Owner's Equity	$800,000

On July 9, BRT takes delivery of a truck at a price of $300,000. On July 19, after a rise in price, an identical truck is delivered to the company at a price of $320,000. On July 28, the company sells one of the trucks for $390,000. During July expenses totaled $30,000. All transactions were paid in cash.

Required

1. Prepare income statements and balance sheets for BRT on July 31 using (a) the FIFO method of inventory valuation and (b) the LIFO method of inventory valuation. Explain the effects that each method has on the financial statements.
2. Assume that Larry Bell, owner of BRT Company, follows the policy of withdrawing cash each period that is exactly equal to net income. What effects does this action have on each balance sheet prepared in **1**, and how do they compare with the balance sheet at the beginning of the month? Which inventory method, if either, do you feel is more realistic in representing BRT's income?
3. Assume that BRT receives notice of another price increase of $20,000 on refrigerated trucks, to take effect on August 1. How does this information relate to the withdrawal policy of the owner, and how will it affect next month's operations?

Answers to Self-Test

1. b	3. c	5. d	7. d	9. d
2. a	4. b	6. c	8. d	10. d

LEARNING OBJECTIVES

1. *Describe the nature, types, and issues of accounting for long-term assets.*
2. *Account for the cost of property, plant, and equipment.*
3. *Define depreciation, state the factors that affect its computation, and show how to record it.*
4. *Compute periodic depreciation under the (a) straight-line method, (b) production method, and (c) accelerated methods, including (1) sum-of-the-years'-digits method and (2) declining-balance method.*
5. *Apply depreciation methods to problems of partial years, revised rates, items of low unit cost, groups of similar items, and accelerated cost recovery.*
6. *Apply the matching rule to capital expenditures and revenue expenditures.*
7. *Account for disposal of depreciable assets not involving exchanges.*
8. *Account for disposal of depreciable assets involving exchanges.*
9. *Identify natural resource accounting issues and compute depletion.*
10. *Apply the matching rule to intangible asset accounting issues, including research and development costs and goodwill.*

CHAPTER 10

Long-Term Assets: Acquisition, Depreciation, and Disposal

This chapter focuses on the major categories of long-term assets, accounting for their acquisition cost, and disposal. You will also study the allocation of the costs of plant assets over their useful lives through depreciation, as well as other special accounting issues related to long-term assets. After studying this chapter, you should be able to meet the learning objectives listed on the left.

DECISION POINT

H. J. Heinz Company

■ The effects of management's decisions regarding long-term assets are most apparent in the areas of reported total assets and net income. An idea of the extent and importance of these assets can be gained from the following figures taken from the 1990 annual report of the H. J. Heinz Company, one of the world's largest food companies. Of the company's more than $4 billion in assets, about one-third consists of property, plant, and equipment, and another 15 percent is intangible assets. The depreciation and amortization associated with these assets are equal to more than one-third of the company's $504 million in net income. Further, in 1990 the company spent $355 million on new long-term assets. The methods used in accounting for these assets and expenditures can make a difference of millions of dollars in reported net income and income taxes paid. Among the issues management and the company's accountants must consider are how to account for acquisition costs, how to estimate how long the assets will last, what methods to use in allocating the cost, how to handle special capital and revenue expenditures, how to account for gains and losses when these assets are sold or otherwise disposed of, and how to account for intangible assets, such as trademarks. The purpose of this chapter is to provide answers to these questions. ■

Long-Term Assets

Let us take a closer look at long-term assets, which were defined briefly in the chapter on inventories. **Long-term assets** are assets that (1) have a useful life of more than one year, (2) are acquired for use in the operation of the business, and (3) are not intended for resale to customers. For many years, it was common to refer to long-term assets as **fixed assets**, but use of this term is declining because the word *fixed* implies that they last forever.

Although there is no strict minimum length of time for an asset to be classified as long term, the most common criterion is that the asset must be capable of repeated use for a period of at least a year. Included in this category is equipment that is used only in peak or emergency periods, such as a generator.

Assets not used in the normal course of business should not be included in this category. Thus, land held for speculative reasons or buildings that are no longer used in ordinary business operations should not be included in the property, plant, and equipment category. Instead, they should be classified as long-term investments.

Finally, if an item is held for resale to customers, it should be classified as inventory—not plant and equipment—no matter how durable it is. For example, a printing press held for sale by a printing press manufacturer would be considered inventory, whereas the same printing press would be plant and equipment for a printing company that buys the press to use in its operations.

Life of Long-Term Assets

OBJECTIVE 1
Describe the nature, types, and issues of accounting for long-term assets

The primary accounting issue in dealing with short-term assets such as inventory and prepaid assets was to determine how much of the asset benefited the current period and how much should be carried forward as an asset to benefit future periods. The matching rule requires that costs be allocated to the periods that benefit from the use of the asset. The same matching issue applies to long-term assets since they are long-term unexpired costs.

It is helpful to think of a long-term asset as a bundle of services that is to be used in the operation of the business over a period of years. A delivery truck may provide 100,000 miles of service over its life. A piece of equipment may have the potential to produce 500,000 parts. A building may provide shelter for fifty years. As each of these assets is purchased, the company is paying in advance (prepaying) for 100,000 miles, the capacity to produce 500,000 parts, or fifty years of service. In essence, each of these assets is a type of long-term prepaid expense. The accounting problem is to spread the cost of these services over the useful life of the asset. As the services benefit the company over the years, the cost becomes an expense rather than an asset.

Types of Long-Term Assets

Long-term assets are customarily divided into the following categories:

Asset	Expense
Tangible Assets	
Land	None
Plant, buildings, and equipment (plant assets)	Depreciation
Natural resources	Depletion
Intangible Assets	Amortization

Tangible assets have physical substance. Land is a tangible asset, and because it has an unlimited life it is the only tangible asset not subject to depreciation or other expense. Plant, buildings, and equipment (referred to hereafter as plant assets) are subject to depreciation. **Depreciation** is the periodic allocation of the cost of tangible long-lived assets (other than land and natural resources) over their useful lives. The term applies to manufactured assets only. Note that accounting for depreciation is an allocation process, not a valuation process. This point is discussed in more detail later.

Natural resources differ from land in that they are purchased for the substances that can be taken from the land and used up rather than for the value of their location. Among natural resources are ore from mines, oil and gas from oil and gas fields, and lumber from forests. Natural resources are subject to depletion rather than to depreciation. The term **depletion** refers to the exhaustion of a natural resource through mining, cutting, pumping, or otherwise using up the resource, and to the way in which the cost is allocated.

Intangible assets are long-term assets that do not have physical substance and in most cases have to do with legal rights or advantages held. Intangible assets include patents, copyrights, trademarks, franchises, organization costs, leaseholds, leasehold improvements, and goodwill. The allocation of the cost of intangible assets to the periods they benefit is called **amortization**. Although the current assets accounts receivable and prepaid expenses do not have physical substance, they are not intangible assets because they are not long term.

The unexpired part of the cost of an asset is generally called its book value or *carrying value.* The latter term is used in this book when referring to long-term assets. The carrying value of plant assets, for instance, is cost less accumulated depreciation.

Issues of Accounting for Long-Term Assets

As with inventories and prepaid expenses, there are two important accounting problems connected with long-term assets. The first is determining how much of the total cost should be allocated to expense in the current accounting period. The second is figuring how much should remain on the balance sheet as an asset to benefit future periods. To solve these problems, four important questions (shown in Figure 10-1) must be answered:

1. How is the cost of the long-term assets determined?
2. How should the expired portion of the cost of the long-term assets be allocated against revenues over time?
3. How should later expenditures such as repairs, maintenance, and additions be treated?
4. How should disposal of long-term assets be recorded?

Figure 10-1. Issues of Accounting for Long-Term Assets

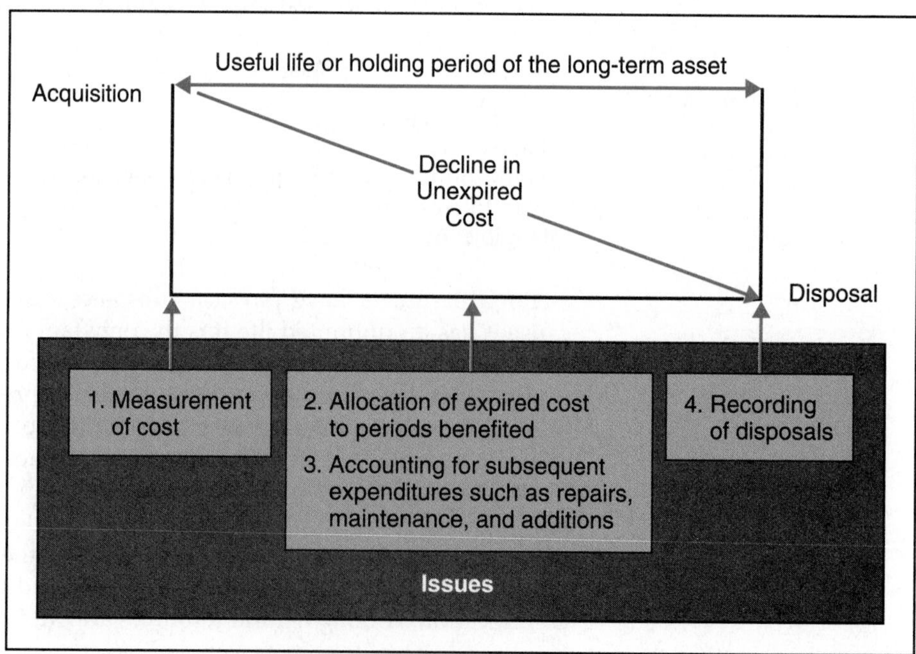

This chapter deals with the answers to these questions. Specific discussion of natural resources and intangibles is also included in this chapter.

Acquisition Cost of Property, Plant, and Equipment

OBJECTIVE 2
Account for the cost of property, plant, and equipment

The acquisition cost of property, plant, and equipment includes all expenditures reasonable and necessary to get them in place and ready for use. For example, the cost of installing and testing a machine is a legitimate cost of the machine. However, if the machine is damaged during installation, the cost of repairing the machine is an operating expense and not an acquisition cost.

Cost is easiest to determine when a transaction is made for cash. In this case, the cost of the asset is equal to the cash paid for the asset plus expenditures for freight, insurance while in transit, installation, and other necessary related costs. If a debt is incurred in the purchase of the asset, the interest charges are not a cost of the asset but a cost of borrowing the money to buy the asset. They are therefore an operating expense. An exception to this principle is that interest costs during the construction of an asset are properly included as a cost of the asset.[1]

Expenditures such as freight, insurance while in transit, and installation are included in the cost of the asset because these expenditures are necessary for the asset to function. Following the matching rule, they are allocated to the useful life of the asset rather than charged as an expense in the current period.

Some of the problems of determining the cost of a long-lived asset are demonstrated in the illustrations for land, buildings, equipment, land improvements, and group purchases presented in the next few sections.

Land

There are often expenditures in addition to the purchase price of the land that should be debited to the Land account. Some examples are commissions to real estate agents; lawyers' fees; accrued taxes paid by the purchaser; cost of preparing the land to build on, such as draining, tearing down old buildings, clearing, and grading; and assessments for local improvements such as streets and sewage systems. The cost of landscaping is usually debited to the Land account because these improvements are relatively permanent. Land is not subject to depreciation because land does not have a limited useful life.

Let us assume that a company buys land for a new retail operation. It pays a net purchase price of $170,000, pays brokerage fees of $6,000 and legal fees of $2,000, pays $10,000 to have an old building on the site torn down, receives $4,000 salvage from the old building, and pays $1,000 to have the site graded. The cost of the land will be $185,000, determined as follows:

Net purchase price		$170,000
Brokerage fees		6,000
Legal fees		2,000
Tearing down old building	$10,000	
Less salvage	4,000	6,000
Grading		1,000
		$185,000

1. "Capitalization of Interest Cost," *Statement of Financial Accounting Standards No. 34* (Stamford, Conn.: Financial Accounting Standards Board, 1979), par. 9–11.

Land Improvements

Improvements to real estate such as driveways, parking lots, and fences have a limited life and thus are subject to depreciation. They should be recorded in an account called Land Improvements rather than in the Land account.

Buildings

When an existing building is purchased, its cost includes the purchase price plus all repairs and other expenses required to put it in usable condition. Buildings are subject to depreciation because they have a limited useful life. When a business constructs its own building, the cost includes all reasonable and necessary expenditures, such as those for materials, labor, part of the overhead and other indirect costs, the architects' fees, insurance during construction, interest on construction loans during the period of construction, lawyers' fees, and building permits. If outside contractors are used in the construction, the net contract price plus other expenditures necessary to put the building in usable condition are included.

Equipment

The cost of equipment includes all expenditures connected with purchasing the equipment and preparing it for use. These expenditures include invoice price less cash discounts; freight or transportation, including insurance; excise taxes and tariffs; buying expenses; installation costs; and test runs to ready the equipment for operation. Equipment is subject to depreciation.

Group Purchases

Sometimes land and other assets are purchased for a lump sum. Because land is a nondepreciable asset and because it has an unlimited life, separate ledger accounts must be kept for land and the other assets. For this reason, the lump-sum purchase price must be apportioned between the land and the other assets. For example, assume that a building and the land on which it is situated are purchased for a lump-sum payment of $85,000. The apportionment can be made by determining the price of each if purchased separately and applying the appropriate percentages to the lump-sum price. Assume that appraisals yield estimates of $10,000 for the land and $90,000 for the building, if purchased separately. In that case, 10 percent, or $8,500, of the lump-sum price would be allocated to the land and 90 percent, or $76,500, would be allocated to the building, as shown below:

	Appraisal	Percentage	Apportionment
Land	$ 10,000	10 ($10,000/$100,000)	$ 8,500 ($85,000 × 10%)
Building	90,000	90 ($90,000/$100,000)	76,500 ($85,000 × 90%)
Totals	$100,000	100	$85,000

Accounting for Depreciation

OBJECTIVE 3
Define depreciation, state the factors that affect its computation, and show how to record it

Depreciation accounting is described by the AICPA as follows:

The cost of a productive facility is one of the costs of the services it renders during its useful economic life. Generally accepted accounting principles require that this cost be spread over the expected useful life of the facility in such a way as to allocate it as equitably as possible to the periods during which services are obtained from the use of the facility. This procedure is known as depreciation accounting, a system of accounting which aims to distribute the cost or other basic value of tangible capital assets, less salvage (if any), over the estimated useful life of the unit . . . in a systematic and rational manner. It is a process of allocation, not of valuation.[2]

This description contains several important points. First, all tangible assets except land have a limited useful life. Because of the limited useful life, the costs of these assets must be distributed as expenses over the years they benefit. Physical deterioration and obsolescence are the major causes of the limited useful life of a depreciable asset. The **physical deterioration** of tangible assets results from use and from exposure to the elements, such as wind and sun. Periodic repairs and a sound maintenance policy may keep buildings and equipment in good operating order and extract the maximum useful life from them, but every machine or building at some point must be discarded. The need for depreciation is not eliminated by repairs. **Obsolescence** is the process of becoming out of date. With fast-changing technology as well as fast-changing demands, machinery and even buildings often become obsolete before they wear out. Accountants do not distinguish between physical deterioration and obsolescence because they are interested in the length of the useful life of the asset regardless of what limits that useful life.

Second, the term *depreciation,* as used in accounting, does not refer to the physical deterioration of an asset or the decrease in market value of an asset over time. Depreciation means the allocation of the cost of a plant asset to the periods that benefit from the services of the asset. The term is used to describe the gradual conversion of the cost of the asset into an expense.

Third, depreciation is not a process of valuation. Accounting records are kept in accordance with the cost principle; they are not indicators of changing price levels. It is possible that, through an advantageous buy and specific market conditions, the market value of a building may rise. Nevertheless, depreciation must continue to be recorded because it is the result of an allocation, not a valuation, process. Eventually the building will wear out or become obsolete regardless of interim fluctuations in market value.

Factors That Affect the Computation of Depreciation

Four factors affect the computation of depreciation. They are: (1) cost, (2) residual value, (3) depreciable cost, and (4) estimated useful life.

Cost. As explained earlier, cost is the net purchase price plus all reasonable and necessary expenditures to get the asset in place and ready for use.

Residual Value. The **residual value** of an asset is its estimated net scrap, salvage, or trade-in value as of the estimated date of disposal. Other terms often used to describe residual value are **salvage value** and **disposal value.**

Depreciable Cost. The **depreciable cost** of an asset is its cost less its residual value. For example, a truck that costs $12,000 and has a residual value of $3,000 would have a depreciable cost of $9,000. Depreciable cost must be allocated over the useful life of the asset.

Estimated Useful Life. The **estimated useful life** of an asset is the total number of service units expected from the asset. Service units may be measured in

2. *Financial Accounting Standards: Original Pronouncements as of July 1, 1977* (Stamford, Conn.: Financial Accounting Standards Board, 1977), ARB No. 43, Ch. 9, Sec. C, par. 5.

terms of years the asset is expected to be used, units expected to be produced, miles expected to be driven, or similar measures. In computing the estimated useful life of an asset, the accountant should consider all relevant information, including (1) past experience with similar assets, (2) the asset's present condition, (3) the company's repair and maintenance policy, (4) current technological and industry trends, and (5) local conditions such as weather.

As introduced in the chapter on business income and accrual accounting, depreciation is recorded at the end of the accounting period by an adjusting entry that takes the following form:

Depreciation Expense, Asset Name	XXX	
Accumulated Depreciation, Asset Name		XXX
To record depreciation for the period		

Methods of Computing Depreciation

OBJECTIVE 4
Compute periodic depreciation under each of four methods

Many methods are used to allocate the cost of plant assets to accounting periods through depreciation. Each of them is proper for certain circumstances. The most common methods are (1) the straight-line method, (2) the production method, and (3) two accelerated methods known as the sum-of-the-years'-digits method and the declining-balance method.

Straight-Line Method

OBJECTIVE 4a
Compute periodic depreciation under the straight-line method

When the **straight-line method** is used to allocate depreciation, the depreciable cost of the asset is spread evenly over the estimated useful life of the asset. The straight-line method is based on the assumption that depreciation depends only on the passage of time. The depreciation expense for each period is computed by dividing the depreciable cost (cost of the depreciating asset less its estimated residual value) by the number of accounting periods in the asset's estimated useful life. The rate of depreciation is the same in each year. Suppose, for example, that a delivery truck costs $10,000 and has an estimated residual value of $1,000 at the end of its estimated useful life of five years. In this case, the annual depreciation would be $1,800 under the straight-line method, calculated as follows:

$$\frac{\text{Cost} - \text{residual value}}{\text{Estimated useful life}} = \frac{\$10,000 - \$1,000}{5} = \$1,800$$

The depreciation for the five years would be as follows:

Depreciation Schedule, Straight-Line Method

	Cost	Yearly Depreciation	Accumulated Depreciation	Carrying Value
Date of purchase	$10,000	—	—	$10,000
End of first year	10,000	$1,800	$1,800	8,200
End of second year	10,000	1,800	3,600	6,400
End of third year	10,000	1,800	5,400	4,600
End of fourth year	10,000	1,800	7,200	2,800
End of fifth year	10,000	1,800	9,000	1,000

There are three important points to note from the schedule for the straight-line depreciation method. First, the depreciation is the same each year. Second, the accumulated depreciation increases uniformly. Third, the carrying value decreases uniformly until it reaches the estimated residual value.

Production Method

OBJECTIVE 4b
Compute periodic depreciation under the production method

The **production method** of depreciation is based on the assumption that depreciation is solely the result of use and that the passage of time plays no role in the depreciation process. If we assume that the delivery truck from the previous example has an estimated useful life of 90,000 miles, the depreciation cost per mile would be determined as follows:

$$\frac{\text{Cost} - \text{residual value}}{\text{Estimated units of useful life}} = \frac{\$10{,}000 - \$1{,}000}{90{,}000 \text{ miles}} = \$.10 \text{ per mile}$$

If we assume that the mileage use of the truck was 20,000 miles for the first year, 30,000 miles for the second, 10,000 miles for the third, 20,000 miles for the fourth, and 10,000 miles for the fifth, the depreciation schedule for the delivery truck would appear as follows:

Depreciation Schedule, Production Method

	Cost	Miles	Yearly Depreciation	Accumulated Depreciation	Carrying Value
Date of purchase	$10,000	—	—	—	$10,000
End of first year	10,000	20,000	$2,000	$2,000	8,000
End of second year	10,000	30,000	3,000	5,000	5,000
End of third year	10,000	10,000	1,000	6,000	4,000
End of fourth year	10,000	20,000	2,000	8,000	2,000
End of fifth year	10,000	10,000	1,000	9,000	1,000

There is a direct relation between the amount of depreciation each year and the units of output or use. Also, the accumulated depreciation increases each year in direct relation to units of output or use. Finally, the carrying value decreases each year in direct relation to units of output or use until it reaches the estimated residual value.

Under the production method, the unit of output or use that is used to measure estimated useful life for each asset should be appropriate for that asset. For example, the number of items produced may be appropriate for one machine, whereas the number of hours of use may be a better indicator of depreciation for another. The production method should be used only when the output of an asset over its useful life can be estimated with reasonable accuracy.

Accelerated Methods

Accelerated methods of depreciation result in relatively large amounts of depreciation in the early years and smaller amounts in later years. These methods, which are based on the passage of time, assume that many kinds of plant assets are most efficient when new, so they provide more and better service in the early years of useful life. It is consistent with the matching rule to allocate more depreciation to the early years than to later years if the benefits or services received in the early years are greater.

The accelerated methods also recognize that changing technologies make some equipment lose service value rapidly. Thus, it is realistic to allocate more to depreciation in the early years than in later years. New inventions and products result in obsolescence of equipment bought earlier, making it necessary to replace equipment sooner than if technology changed more slowly.

Another argument in favor of accelerated methods is that repair expense is likely to be greater in later years than in early years. Thus, the total of repair and depreciation expense remains fairly constant over a period of years. This result naturally assumes that the services received from the asset are roughly equal from year to year.

OBJECTIVE 4c(1)
Compute periodic depreciation under the sum-of-the-years'-digits method

Sum-of-the-Years'-Digits Method. The **sum-of-the-years'-digits method** is an accelerated method of depreciation in which the years in the service life of an asset are added. Their sum becomes the denominator of a series of fractions that are applied against the depreciable cost of the asset in allocating the total depreciation over the estimated useful life. The numerators of the fractions are the individual years in the estimated useful life of the asset in their reverse order.

For the delivery truck used in the illustrations above, the estimated useful life is five years. The sum of the years' digits is as follows:[3]

$$1 + 2 + 3 + 4 + 5 = 15$$

The annual depreciation is then determined by multiplying the depreciable cost of $9,000 ($10,000 – $1,000) by each of the following fractions: 5/15, 4/15, 3/15, 2/15, 1/15. The depreciation schedule for the sum-of-the-years'-digits method is as follows:

Depreciation Schedule, Sum-of-the-Years'-Digits Method

	Cost	Yearly Depreciation		Accumulated Depreciation	Carrying Value
Date of purchase	$10,000		—	—	$10,000
End of first year	10,000	(5/15 × $9,000)	$3,000	$3,000	7,000
End of second year	10,000	(4/15 × $9,000)	2,400	5,400	4,600
End of third year	10,000	(3/15 × $9,000)	1,800	7,200	2,800
End of fourth year	10,000	(2/15 × $9,000)	1,200	8,400	1,600
End of fifth year	10,000	(1/15 × $9,000)	600	9,000	1,000

From the schedule, note that the yearly depreciation is greatest in the first year and declines each year after that. Also, the accumulated depreciation increases by a smaller amount each year. Finally, the carrying value decreases each year by the amount of depreciation until it reaches the residual value.

OBJECTIVE 4c(2)
Compute periodic depreciation under the declining-balance method

Declining-Balance Method. The **declining-balance method** is an accelerated method of depreciation in which depreciation is computed by applying a fixed rate to the carrying value (the declining balance) of a long-lived asset. It is based on the same assumption as the sum-of-the-years'-digits method. Both methods result in higher depreciation charges during the early years of an asset's life. Though any fixed rate might be used under the method, the most common rate is a percentage equal to twice the straight-line percentage. When twice the straight-line rate is used, the method is usually called the **double-declining-balance method**.

3. The denominator used in the sum-of-the-years'-digits method can be computed quickly from the following formula:

$$S = \frac{N(N + 1)}{2}$$

where S equals the sum of the digits and N equals the number of years in the estimated useful life. For example, for an asset with an estimated useful life of ten years, the sum of the digits equals 55, calculated as follows:

$$S = \frac{10(10 + 1)}{2} = \frac{110}{2} = 55$$

In our earlier example, the delivery truck had an estimated useful life of five years. Consequently, under the straight-line method, the percentage depreciation for each year was 20 percent (100 percent ÷ 5 years).

Under the double-declining-balance method, the fixed percentage rate is therefore 40 percent (2 × 20 percent). This fixed rate of 40 percent is applied to the *remaining carrying value* at the end of each year. Estimated residual value is not taken into account in figuring depreciation except in the last year of an asset's useful life, when depreciation is limited to the amount necessary to bring the carrying value down to the estimated residual value. The depreciation schedule for this method is as follows:

Depreciation Schedule, Double-Declining-Balance Method

	Cost	Yearly Depreciation		Accumulated Depreciation	Carrying Value
Date of purchase	$10,000		—	—	$10,000
End of first year	10,000	(40% × $10,000)	$4,000	$4,000	6,000
End of second year	10,000	(40% × $6,000)	2,400	6,400	3,600
End of third year	10,000	(40% × $3,600)	1,440	7,840	2,160
End of fourth year	10,000	(40% × $2,160)	864	8,704	1,296
End of fifth year	10,000		296*	9,000	1,000

*Depreciation limited to amount necessary to reduce carrying value to residual value: $296 = $1,296 (previous carrying value) – $1,000 (residual value).

Note that the fixed rate is always applied to the carrying value at the end of the previous year. Next, the depreciation is greatest in the first year and declines each year after that. Finally, the depreciation in the last year is limited to the amount necessary to reduce carrying value to residual value.

Comparing the Four Methods

A visual comparison may provide a better understanding of the four depreciation methods described above. Figure 10-2 compares yearly depreciation and carrying value under the four methods. In the graph that shows yearly depreciation, straight-line depreciation is uniform over the five-year period at $1,800. However, both accelerated depreciation methods (sum-of-the-years'-digits and declining-balance) begin at amounts greater than straight-line ($3,000 and $4,000, respectively), and decrease each year to amounts less than straight-line ($600 and $296, respectively). The production method does not produce a regular pattern of depreciation because of the random fluctuation of the depreciation from year to year. These yearly depreciation patterns are reflected in the carrying value graph. In the graph, each method starts in the same place (cost of $10,000) and ends at the same place (residual value of $1,000). It is the patterns during the useful life of the asset that differ for each method. For instance, the carrying value for the straight-line method is always greater than that for the accelerated methods, except at the end of useful life.

DECISION POINT

Choice of Depreciation Methods and Income Taxes: 600 Large Companies

■ Most companies choose the straight-line method of depreciation for financial reporting purposes, as indicated in Figure 10-3. This chart,

Figure 10-2. Graphical Comparison of Four Methods of Determining Depreciation

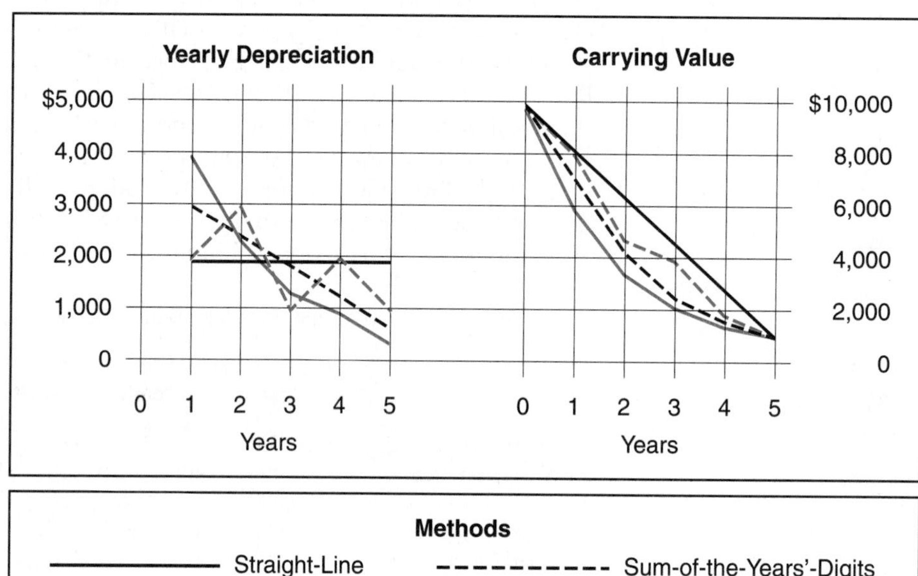

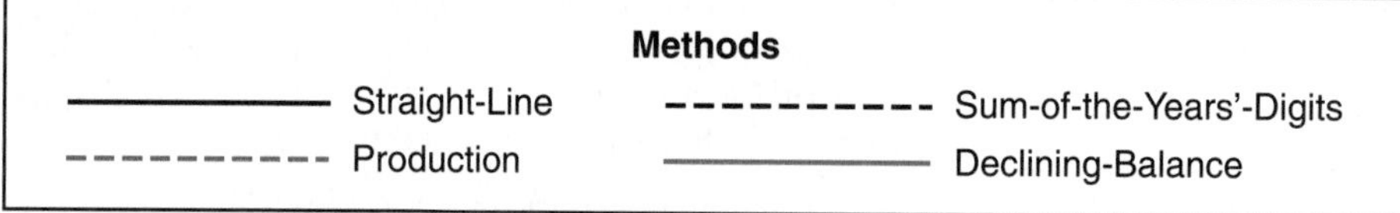

however, tends to be misleading about the importance of accelerated depreciation methods. Federal income tax laws allow either the straight-line method or an accelerated method at one and one-half or two times the straight-line rate. According to *Accounting Trends and Techniques*, 454, or

Figure 10-3. Depreciation Methods Used by 600 Large Companies

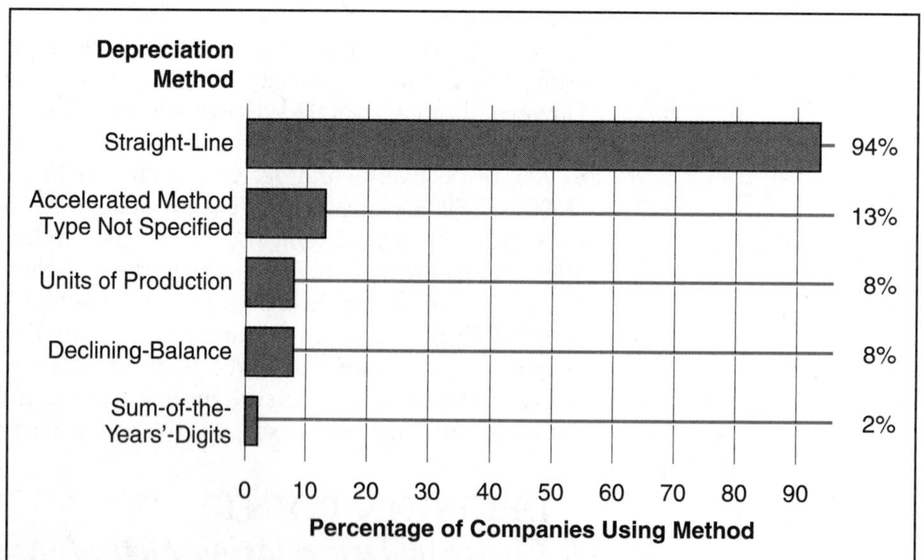

Total percentage exceeds 100 because some companies used different methods for different types of depreciable assets.

Source: American Institute of Certified Public Accountants, *Accounting Trends & Techniques* (New York: AICPA, 1990), p. 261.

about 75 percent, of the 600 large companies studied chose the accelerated method for tax purposes. Although the straight-line method used for financial reporting usually produces the highest net income, the accelerated method results in lower income taxes. ■

Special Problems of Depreciating Plant Assets

The illustrations used so far in this chapter have been simplified to explain the concepts and methods of depreciation. In real business practice, there is often a need to (1) calculate depreciation for partial years, (2) revise depreciation rates on the basis of new estimates of the useful life or residual value, (3) develop more practical ways of depreciating items of low unit cost, (4) group together items that are alike in order to calculate depreciation, and (5) use the accelerated cost recovery method for tax purposes. The next sections discuss these five cases.

Depreciation for Partial Years

OBJECTIVE 5
Apply depreciation methods to problems of partial years, revised rates, items of low unit cost, groups of similar items, and accelerated cost recovery

So far, the illustrations of the depreciation methods have assumed that the plant assets were purchased at the beginning or end of the accounting period. However, business people do not often buy assets exactly at the beginning or end of the accounting period. In most cases, they buy the assets when they are needed and sell or discard them when they are no longer useful or needed. The time of the year is normally not a factor in the decision. Consequently, it is often necessary to calculate depreciation for partial years.

For example, assume that a piece of equipment is purchased for $3,500 and that it has an estimated useful life of six years, with an estimated residual value of $500. Assume also that it is purchased on September 5 and that the yearly accounting period ends on December 31. Depreciation must be recorded for four months, September through December, or four-twelfths of the year. This factor is applied to the calculated depreciation for the entire year. The four months' depreciation under the straight-line method is calculated as follows:

$$\frac{\$3{,}500 - \$500}{6 \text{ years}} \times 4/12 = \$167$$

For the other depreciation methods, most companies will compute the first year's depreciation and then multiply by the partial year factor. For example, if the company used the double-declining-balance method on the above equipment, the depreciation on the asset would be computed as follows:

$$\$3{,}500 \times .33 \times 4/12 = \$385$$

Typically, the depreciation calculation is rounded off to the nearest whole month because a partial month's depreciation is not usually material and the calculation is easier. In this case, depreciation was recorded from the beginning of September even though the purchase was made on September 5. If the equipment had been purchased on September 16 or thereafter, depreciation would be charged beginning October 1, as if the equipment were purchased on that date. Some companies round off all partial years to the nearest one-half year for ease of calculation (half-year convention).

For all methods, the remainder ($^8/_{12}$) of the first year's depreciation is recorded in the next annual accounting period together with $^4/_{12}$ of the second year's depreciation.

When an asset is disposed of, its depreciation must be updated. For example, if the asset is not disposed of at either the beginning or end of the year, depreciation must be recorded for a partial year, reflecting the time to the date of disposal.

Revision of Depreciation Rates

Because depreciation rates are based on an estimate of the useful life of an asset, the periodic depreciation charge is seldom precisely accurate. Sometimes it is very inadequate or excessive. This situation may result from an underestimate or overestimate of the asset's useful life or from a wrong estimate of the residual value. What action should be taken when it is found, after using a piece of equipment for several years, that the equipment will not last as long as—or will last longer than—originally thought? Sometimes it is necessary to revise the estimate of the useful life, so that the periodic depreciation expense increases or decreases. In such a case, the method for correcting depreciation is to spread the remaining depreciable cost of the asset over the years of remaining useful life.

With this technique, the annual depreciation expense is increased or decreased so that the remaining depreciation reduces the asset's carrying value to its residual value at the end of the remaining useful life. To illustrate, assume that a delivery truck was purchased for a price of $7,000, with a residual value of $1,000. At the time of the purchase, it was thought that the truck would last six years, and it was depreciated on the straight-line basis. However, after two years of intensive use, it is determined that the delivery truck will last only two more years and will continue to carry an estimated residual value of $1,000 at the end of the two years. In other words, at the end of the second year, the estimated useful life is reduced from six years to four years. At that time, the asset account and its related accumulated depreciation account would appear as follows:

Delivery Truck

Cost 7,000	

Accumulated Depreciation, Delivery Truck

	Depreciation, year 1	1,000
	Depreciation, year 2	1,000

The remaining depreciable cost is computed as follows:

cost	minus	depreciation already taken	minus	residual value		
$7,000	–	$2,000	–	$1,000	=	$4,000

The new annual periodic depreciation charge is computed by dividing the remaining depreciable cost of $4,000 by the remaining useful life of two years. Therefore, the new periodic depreciation charge is $2,000. The annual adjusting entry for depreciation for the next two years would be as follows:

Dec. 31	Depreciation Expense, Delivery Truck	2,000	
	Accumulated Depreciation, Delivery Truck		2,000
	To record depreciation expense for the year		

This method of revising depreciation is used widely in industry. It is also supported by the Accounting Principles Board of the AICPA in Accounting Principles Board *Opinion No. 9* and *Opinion No. 20*.

Accounting for Assets of Low Unit Cost

Some classes of plant assets are made up of many individual items of low unit cost. Included in this category are small tools such as hammers, wrenches, and drills, as well as dies, molds, patterns, and spare parts. Because of their large numbers, hard usage, breakage, and pilferage, assets such as these are relatively short-lived and require constant replacement. It is impractical to use the ordinary depreciation methods for such assets, and it is often costly to keep records of individual items.

There are two basic methods for accounting for plant assets of low unit cost. The first method is simply to charge the items as expenses when they are purchased. This method assumes that the annual loss on these items from use, depreciation, breakage, and other causes will approximately equal the cost of the items purchased during the year.

The second method used for plant assets of low unit cost is to account for them on an inventory basis. The inventory basis of accounting for items of low unit cost is very similar to the method of accounting for supplies, which you already know. This method is best used when the number of items purchased varies greatly from year to year. Let us assume that a company's asset account for Spare Parts on hand at the beginning of the accounting period is represented by a debit balance. As spare parts are purchased during the accounting period, their cost is debited to this account. At the end of the period, a physical inventory of usable spare parts on hand in the factory is taken. This inventory amount is subtracted from the end-of-period balance in the Spare Parts account to determine the cost of spare parts lost, broken, and used during this period. This cost, assumed in this case to be $700, is then charged to an expense account as a work sheet adjustment with the adjusting entry as follows:

Dec. 31	Spare Parts Expense	700	
	Spare Parts		700
	To record cost of spare parts used or lost during the period		

Group Depreciation

To say that the estimated useful life of an asset, such as a piece of equipment, is six years means that the average piece of equipment of that type is expected to last six years. In reality, some equipment may last only two or three years, and other equipment may last eight or nine years, or longer. For this reason, and for reasons of convenience, large companies will group items of similar assets, such as trucks, power lines, office equipment, or transformers, for purposes of calculating depreciation. This method is called **group depreciation**. Group depreciation is used widely in all fields of industry and business. A recent survey of large businesses indicated that 65 percent used group depreciation for all or part of their plant assets.[4]

4. Edward P. McTague, "Accounting for Trade-Ins of Operational Assets," *The National Public Accountant* (January 1986), p. 39.

Cost Recovery for Federal Tax Purposes

In 1981, Congress dramatically changed the rules for tax depreciation by substituting for depreciation methods similar to those used for financial reporting a new method called **Accelerated Cost Recovery System (ACRS)**. ACRS was a completely new and mandatory cost recovery system that for tax purposes discarded the concepts of estimated useful life and residual value and instead required that a cost recovery allowance be computed (1) on the unadjusted cost of property being recovered, and (2) over a period of years prescribed by the law for all property of similar types. Recovery allowances could be calculated by the straight-line method or by prescribed percentages that approximated 150 percent of the declining-balance method with a half-year convention. ACRS recovery property is generally defined as tangible property subject to depreciation and placed in service after December 31, 1980 and before January 1, 1987. Property purchased before January 1, 1981, is subject to the accounting depreciation methods presented earlier in this chapter.

In 1986, Congress passed the **Tax Reform Act of 1986**, arguably the most sweeping revision of federal tax laws since the original enactment of the Internal Revenue Code in 1913. The new **Modified Accelerated Cost Recovery System (MACRS)** retains the ACRS concepts of prescribed recovery periods for different classes of property, calculation of recovery allowances on the basis of the unadjusted cost of property, and elective use of the straight-line method or an accelerated method of cost recovery. The accelerated method prescribed under MACRS for most property other than real estate is 200 percent declining balance with a half-year convention (only one half-year's depreciation is allowed in the year of purchase and one half-year is taken in the last year). In addition, the period over which the cost may be recovered has been increased. Recovery of the cost of property placed in service after December 31, 1986 is calculated as prescribed in the new law.

The intent of Congress, in both ACRS and MACRS, was to encourage businesses to invest in new plant and equipment by allowing them to write the assets off rapidly. Both ACRS and MACRS accelerate the write-off of these investments in two ways. First, the recovery periods they prescribe are often shorter than the estimated useful lives used for calculating depreciation for the financial statements. Second, the accelerated methods allowed under ACRS and MACRS provide for recovery of most of the cost of the investments early in the recovery period. Recovery will generally be more rapid under MACRS than under ACRS because of the faster accelerated method allowed.

Tax methods of depreciation are not usually acceptable for financial reporting under generally accepted accounting principles because the recovery periods used are shorter than the depreciable assets' estimated useful lives. Accounting for the effects of differences between tax and book depreciation is discussed in the chapter on retained earnings and corporate income statements.

DECISION POINT
Amre, Inc.

■ In 1991, after an investigation by the Securities and Exchange Commission, Amre, Inc., a maker of aluminum siding and kitchen cabinets, announced that it had overstated its profits in 1987 and 1988 and understated its losses in 1989. Results for 1990 were also restated and the company's two top officers resigned. According to reports in the *Wall Street*

Journal, a primary reason for the adjustments was that Amre improperly recorded its marketing costs, such as the cost of purchasing mailing lists, as assets instead of as expenses. Because the costs were treated as assets, they appeared on Amre's balance sheet and the company was able to spread them over time, thereby improving its profits. For example, its 1988 net income should have been $2.9 million, not the reported $7.3 million.[5] What is management's role in determining accounting policy?

Determining when a payment is an expense and when it is an asset is a matter of judgment in which management takes a leading role. Sometimes management has wide latitude in making these decisions. Management decisions about accounting can affect not only a company's net income, income taxes, and stock price, but they also can have severe consequences when the decisions are wrong. In the case of Amre, the SEC is expected to take action against the former management and the company is expected to be involved in litigation by stockholders for an extended period of time. The next section addresses the important issue of when a payment is an asset and when it is an expense. ■

Capital Expenditures and Revenue Expenditures

OBJECTIVE 6
Apply the matching rule to capital expenditures and revenue expenditures

The term **expenditure** refers to a payment or an obligation to make future payment for an asset, such as a truck, or a service received, such as a repair. When the payment or debt is for an asset or a service, it is correctly called an expenditure. A **capital expenditure** is an expenditure for the purchase or expansion of long-term assets and is recorded in the asset accounts. Expenditures for repairs, maintenance, fuel, or other things needed to maintain and operate plant and equipment are called **revenue expenditures** because they are immediately charged as expenses against revenues. They are recorded by debits to expense accounts. Revenue expenditures are charged to expense because the benefits from the expenditures are used up in the current period. For this reason, they are deducted from the revenues of the current period in determining net income. In summary, any expenditure that benefits several accounting periods is considered a capital expenditure. Any expenditure that benefits only the current accounting period is called a revenue expenditure.

It is important to note this careful distinction between capital and revenue expenditures. In accordance with the matching rule, expenditures of any type should be charged to the period that they benefit. For example, if the purchase of an automobile is mistakenly charged as a revenue expenditure, the expense for the current period is overstated on the income statement. As a result, current net income is understated, and in future periods net income will be overstated. If, on the other hand, a revenue expenditure such as the painting of a building were charged to an asset account, the expense of the current period would be understated. Current net income would be overstated by the same amount, and net income of future periods would be understated.

For practical purposes many companies establish policies for what constitutes a revenue or a capital expenditure. For example, small expenditures for items that normally would be treated as capital expenditures may be treated as revenue expenditures because the amounts involved are not material in relation

5. Karen Blumenthal, "Amre Overstated Financial Results for Three Fiscal Years," *Wall Street Journal*, August 7, 1991, p. B8.

to net income. Thus, a wastebasket, which might last for years, would be recorded as a supplies expense rather than as a depreciable asset.

In addition to the acquisition of plant assets, natural resources, and intangible assets, capital expenditures also include additions and betterments. **Additions** are enlargements to the physical layout of a plant asset. If a new wing is added to a building, the benefits from the expenditure will be received over several years, and the amount paid for it should be debited to the asset account. **Betterments** are improvements to plant assets that do not add to the physical layout of the asset. Installation of an air-conditioning system is an example of an expenditure for a betterment that will offer benefits over a period of years and so should be charged to an asset account.

Among the more usual kinds of revenue expenditures for plant equipment are the ordinary repairs, maintenance, lubrication, cleaning, and inspection necessary to keep an asset in good working condition.

Repairs fall into two categories: ordinary repairs and extraordinary repairs. **Ordinary repairs** are expenditures that are necessary to maintain an asset in good operating condition. Trucks must have tune-ups, tires and batteries must be replaced regularly, and other ordinary repairs must be made. Offices and halls must be painted regularly and have broken tiles or woodwork replaced. Such repairs are a current expense.

Extraordinary repairs are repairs of a more significant nature—they affect the estimated residual value or estimated useful life of an asset. For example, a boiler for heating a building may receive a complete overhaul, at a cost of several thousand dollars, that will extend the useful life of the boiler five years.

Typically, extraordinary repairs are recorded by debiting the Accumulated Depreciation account, under the assumption that some of the depreciation previously recorded has now been eliminated. The effect of this reduction in the Accumulated Depreciation account is to increase the book or carrying value of the asset by the cost of the extraordinary repair. Consequently, the new carrying value of the asset should be depreciated over the new estimated useful life. Let us assume that a machine costing $10,000 had no estimated residual value and an original estimated useful life of ten years. After eight years, the accumulated depreciation (straight-line method assumed) would be $8,000, and the carrying value would be $2,000 ($10,000 – $8,000). Assume that, at this point, the machine was given a major overhaul costing $1,500. This expenditure extends the useful life three years beyond the original ten years. The entry for extraordinary repair would be as follows:

Mar. 14	Accumulated Depreciation, Machinery	1,500	
	Cash		1,500
	Extraordinary repair to machinery		

The annual periodic depreciation for each of the five years remaining in the machine's useful life would be calculated as follows:

Carrying value before extraordinary repairs	$2,000
Extraordinary repairs	1,500
Total	$3,500

$$\text{Annual periodic depreciation} = \frac{\$3{,}500}{5 \text{ years}} = \$700$$

If the machine remains in use for the five years expected after the major overhaul, the annual depreciation charges of $700 will exactly write off the new carrying value, including the cost of the extraordinary repair.

Disposal of Depreciable Assets

OBJECTIVE 7
Account for disposal of depreciable assets not involving exchanges

When plant assets are no longer useful in a business because they have become worn out or obsolete, they may be discarded, sold, or traded in on the purchase of new plant and equipment. A comprehensive illustration is presented in the following sections to show how these disposals are recorded in the accounting records.

Assumptions for the Comprehensive Illustration

For accounting purposes, a plant asset may be disposed of in three ways: (1) discarded, (2) sold for cash, or (3) exchanged for another asset. To illustrate how each of these cases is recorded, assume the following facts. MGC Corporation purchased a machine on January 1, 19x0 for $6,500 and depreciated it on a straight-line basis over an estimated useful life of ten years. The residual value at the end of ten years was estimated to be $500. On January 1, 19x7, the balances of the relevant accounts in the plant asset ledger appear as follows:

Machinery		Accumulated Depreciation, Machinery	
6,500			4,200

On September 30, management disposes of the asset. The next few sections illustrate the accounting treatment to record depreciation for the partial year and the disposal under several assumptions.

Depreciation for Partial Year Prior to Disposal

When items of plant assets are discarded or disposed of in some other way, it is first necessary to record depreciation expense for the partial year up to the date of disposal. This step is required because the asset was used until that date and, under the matching rule, the accounting period should receive the proper allocation of depreciation expense.

The depreciation expense for the partial year before disposal is calculated in exactly the same way as it is calculated for the partial year after purchase illustrated earlier in this chapter.

In this comprehensive illustration, MGC Corporation disposes of the machinery on September 30. The entry to record the depreciation for the first nine months of 19x7 is as follows:

Sept. 30	Depreciation Expense, Machinery	450	
	Accumulated Depreciation, Machinery		450
	To record depreciation up to date of disposal		

$$\frac{\$6{,}500 - \$500}{10} \times \frac{9}{12} = \$450$$

The relevant accounts in the plant asset ledger appear as follows after the entry is posted:

Machinery		Accumulated Depreciation, Machinery	
6,500			4,650

Recording Discarded Plant Assets

Even though it is depreciated over its estimated life, a plant asset rarely lasts exactly as long as its estimated life. If it lasts longer than its estimated life, it is not depreciated past the point that its carrying value equals its residual value. The purpose of depreciation is to spread the depreciable cost of the asset over the life of the asset. Thus, the total accumulated depreciation should never exceed the total depreciable cost. If the asset is still used in the business beyond the end of its estimated life, its cost and accumulated depreciation remain in the ledger accounts. Proper records will thus be available for maintaining control over plant assets. If the residual value is zero, the carrying value of a fully depreciated asset is zero until the asset is disposed of. If such an asset is discarded, no gain or loss results.

In the comprehensive illustration, however, the discarded equipment has a carrying value of $1,850 at the time of disposal. The carrying value from the ledger account above is computed as machinery of $6,500 less accumulated depreciation of $4,650. A loss equal to the carrying value should be recorded when the machine is discarded:

Sept. 30	Accumulated Depreciation, Machinery	4,650	
	Loss on Disposal of Machinery	1,850	
	Machinery		6,500
	Discarded machine no longer used in the business		

Gains and losses on disposals of long-term assets are classified as other revenues and expenses on the income statement.

Recording Plant Assets Sold for Cash

The entry to record an asset sold for cash is similar to the one illustrated above except that the receipt of cash should also be recorded. The following entries show how to record the sale of a machine under three assumptions about the selling price. In the first case, the $1,850 cash received is exactly equal to the carrying value of the machine ($1,850), so no gain or loss results.

Sept. 30	Cash	1,850	
	Accumulated Depreciation, Machinery	4,650	
	Machinery		6,500
	Sale of machine for carrying value; no gain or loss		

In the second case, the $1,000 cash received is less than the carrying value of $1,850, so a loss of $850 is recorded.

Sept. 30	Cash	1,000	
	Accumulated Depreciation, Machinery	4,650	
	Loss on Sale of Machinery	850	
	Machinery		6,500
	Sale of machine at less than carrying value; loss of $850 ($1,850 – $1,000) recorded		

In the third case, the $2,000 cash received exceeds the carrying value of $1,850, so a gain of $150 is recorded.

Sept. 30	Cash	2,000	
	Accumulated Depreciation, Machinery	4,650	
	Gain on Sale of Machinery		150
	Machinery		6,500
	Sale of machine at more than the carrying value; gain of $150 ($2,000 – $1,850) recorded		

Recording Exchanges of Plant Assets

OBJECTIVE 8
Account for disposal of depreciable assets involving exchanges

Businesses also dispose of plant assets by trading them in on the purchase of other plant assets. Exchanges may involve similar assets, such as an old machine traded in on a newer model, or dissimilar assets, such as a machine being traded in on a truck. In either case, the purchase price is reduced by the amount of the trade-in allowance given for the asset traded in.

The basic accounting for exchanges of plant assets is similar to accounting for sales of plant assets for cash. If the trade-in allowance received is greater than the carrying value of the asset surrendered, there has been a gain. If the allowance is less, there has been a loss. There are special rules for recognizing these gains and losses depending on the nature of the assets exchanged.

Exchange	Losses Recognized	Gains Recognized
For financial accounting purposes		
Of dissimilar assets	Yes	Yes
Of similar assets	Yes	No
For income tax purposes		
Of dissimilar assets	Yes	Yes
Of similar assets	No	No

Both gains and losses are recognized when a company exchanges dissimilar assets. Assets are dissimilar when they perform different functions; assets are similar when they perform the same function. For financial accounting purposes, gains on exchanges of similar assets are not recognized because the earning lives of the assets surrendered are not considered to be completed. When a company trades in an older machine on a newer machine of the same type, the economic substance of the transaction is the same as a major renovation and upgrading of the older machine. You could think of the trade-in as an extension of the life and usefulness of the original machine. Instead of recognizing a gain at the time of the exchange, the company records the new machine at the sum of the book value of the older machine plus any cash paid.[6]

Accounting for exchanges of similar assets is complicated by the fact that neither gains nor losses are recognized for income tax purposes. This is important because many companies choose to follow this practice in their accounting records, usually for convenience. Thus, in practice, accountants face cases where both gains and losses are recognized (exchanges of dissimilar assets), where losses are recognized and gains are not (exchanges of similar assets), and where neither gains nor losses are recognized (exchanges of similar assets for income tax purposes). Since all these options are used in practice, they are all illustrated in the following paragraphs.

6. Accounting Principles Board, *Opinion No. 29,* "Accounting for Nonmonetary Transactions" (New York: American Institute of Certified Public Accountants, 1973); also see James B. Hobbs and D. R. Bainbridge, "Nonmonetary Exchange Transactions: Clarification of APB Opinion No. 29," *The Accounting Review* (January 1982).

Loss Recognized on the Exchange. A loss is recognized for financial accounting purposes on all exchanges in which a material loss occurs. To illustrate the recognition of a loss, let us assume that the firm in our comprehensive example exchanges the machine for a newer, more modern machine on the following terms:

Price of new machine	$12,000
Trade-in allowance for old machine	(1,000)
Cash payment required	$11,000

In this case the trade-in allowance ($1,000) is less than the carrying value ($1,850) of the old machine. The loss on the exchange is $850 ($1,850 – $1,000). The following journal entry records this transaction under the assumption that the loss is to be recognized:

Sept. 30	Machinery (new)	12,000	
	Accumulated Depreciation, Machinery	4,650	
	Loss on Exchange of Machinery	850	
	Machinery (old)		6,500
	Cash		11,000
	Exchange of machines—cost of old machine and its accumulated depreciation removed from the records; new machine recorded at list price; loss recognized		

Loss Not Recognized on the Exchange. In the previous example in which a loss was recognized, the new asset was recorded at the purchase price of $12,000 and a loss of $850 was recorded. If the transaction is for similar assets and is to be recorded for income tax purposes, the loss should not be recognized. In this case, the cost basis of the new asset will reflect the effect of the unrecorded loss. The cost basis is computed by adding the cash payment to the carrying value of the old asset:

Carrying value of old machine	$ 1,850
Cash paid	11,000
Cost basis of new machine	$12,850

Note that no loss is recognized in the entry to record this transaction:

Sept. 30	Machinery (new)	12,850	
	Accumulated Depreciation, Machinery	4,650	
	Machinery (old)		6,500
	Cash		11,000
	Exchange of machines—cost of old machine and its accumulated depreciation removed from the records; new machine recorded at amount equal to carrying value of old machine plus cash paid; no loss recognized		

Note that the new machinery is reported at the purchase price of $12,000 plus the unrecognized loss of $850. The nonrecognition of the loss on the exchange is, in effect, a postponement of the loss. Since depreciation of the new machine will be computed based on a cost of $12,850 instead of $12,000, the "unrecognized" loss is reflected by more depreciation each year on a new machine than if the loss had been recognized.

Gain Recognized on the Exchange. Gains are recognized for accounting purposes on exchanges when dissimilar assets are exchanged. To illustrate the recognition of a gain, we continue with our example, assuming the following terms for the exchange in which the machines serve different functions:

Price of new machine	$12,000
Trade-in allowance for old machine	(3,000)
Cash payment required	$ 9,000

Here the trade-in allowance ($3,000) exceeds the carrying value ($1,850) of the old machine by $1,150. Thus, there is a gain on the exchange, assuming that the price of the new machine has not been inflated to allow for an excessive trade-in value. In other words, a gain exists if the trade-in allowance represents the fair market value of the old machine. Assuming that this condition is true, the entry to record the transaction is as follows:

Sept. 30	Machinery (new)	12,000	
	Accumulated Depreciation, Machinery	4,650	
	Gain on Exchange of Machinery		1,150
	Machinery (old)		6,500
	Cash		9,000
	Exchange of machines—cost of old machine and its accumulated depreciation removed from the records; new machine recorded at sales price; gain recognized		

Gain Not Recognized on the Exchange. A gain on an exchange should not be recognized in the accounting records if the machines perform similar functions. The cost basis of the new machine must indicate the effect of the unrecorded gain. This cost basis is computed by adding the cash payment to the carrying value of the old asset:

Carrying value of old machine	$ 1,850
Cash paid	9,000
Cost basis of new machine	$10,850

The entry to record the transaction is as follows:

Sept. 30	Machinery (new)	10,850	
	Accumulated Depreciation, Machinery	4,650	
	Machinery (old)		6,500
	Cash		9,000
	Exchange of machines—cost of old machine and its accumulated depreciation removed from the records; new machine recorded at amount equal to carrying value of old machine plus cash paid; no gain recognized		

Similar to the nonrecognition of losses, the nonrecognition of the gain on exchange is, in effect, a postponement of the gain. In the previous illustration, when the new machine is eventually discarded or sold, its cost basis will be $10,850 instead of its original price of $12,000. Since depreciation will be computed on the cost basis of $10,850, the "unrecognized" gain is reflected in less depreciation each year on new equipment than if the gain had been recognized.

Accounting for Natural Resources

OBJECTIVE 9
Identify natural resource accounting issues and compute depletion

Natural resources are also known as **wasting assets**. Examples of natural resources are standing timber, oil and gas fields, and mineral deposits. The distinguishing characteristic of these wasting assets is that they are converted into inventory by cutting, pumping, or mining. For example, an oil field is a reservoir of unpumped oil, and a coal mine is a deposit of unmined coal.

Natural resources are shown on the balance sheet as long-term assets with such descriptive titles as Timber Lands, Oil and Gas Reserves, and Mineral Deposits. When the timber is cut, the oil is pumped, or the coal is mined, it becomes an inventory of the product to be sold. Natural resources are recorded at acquisition cost, which may also include some costs of development. As the resource is converted through the process of cutting, pumping, or mining, the asset account must be proportionally reduced. The carrying value of oil reserves on the balance sheet, for example, is reduced by a small amount for each barrel of oil pumped. As a result, the original cost of the oil reserves is gradually reduced, and depletion is recognized by the amount of the decrease.

Depletion

The term **depletion** is used to describe not only the exhaustion of a natural resource but also the proportional allocation of the cost of a natural resource to the units extracted. The costs are allocated in a way that is much like the production method used to calculate depreciation. When a natural resource is purchased or developed, there must be an estimate of the total units that will be available, such as barrels of oil, tons of coal, or board-feet of lumber. The depletion cost per unit is determined by dividing the cost (less residual value, if any) of the natural resource by the estimated number of units available. The amount of the depletion cost for each accounting period is then computed by multiplying the depletion cost per unit by the number of units pumped, mined, or cut. For example, for a mine having deposits of an estimated 1,500,000 tons of coal, a cost of $1,800,000, and an estimated residual value of $300,000, the depletion charge per ton of coal is $1. Thus, if 115,000 tons of coal are mined and sold during the first year, the depletion charge for the year is $115,000. This charge is recorded as follows:

Dec. 31	Depletion Expense, Coal Deposits	115,000	
	Accumulated Depletion, Coal Mine		115,000
	To record depletion of coal mine: $1 per ton for 115,000 tons mined and sold		

On the balance sheet, the mine would be presented as follows:

Coal Deposits	$1,800,000	
Less Accumulated Depletion	115,000	$1,685,000

A natural resource that is extracted in one year may not be sold until a later year. It is important to note that it would then be recorded as a depletion *expense* in the year it is *sold*. The part not sold is considered inventory.

Depreciation of Closely Related Plant Assets

Natural resources often require special on-site buildings and equipment such as conveyors, roads, tracks, and drilling and pumping devices that are necessary to extract the resource. If the useful life of these assets is longer than the estimated time it will take to deplete the resource, a special problem arises. Because these long-term assets are often abandoned and have no useful purpose beyond the time when the resources are extracted, they should be depreciated on the same basis as the depletion is computed. For example, if machinery with a useful life of ten years is installed on an oil field that is expected to be depleted in eight years, the machinery should be depreciated over the eight-year period using the production method. In other words, each year's depreciation charge should be proportional to the depletion charge. If one-sixth of the oil field's total reserves is pumped in one year, then the depreciation should be one-sixth of the machinery's cost minus the scrap value. If the useful life of a long-term asset is less than the expected life of the depleting asset, the shorter life should be used to compute depreciation. In this case or when an asset is not to be abandoned when the reserves are fully depleted, other depreciation methods such as straight-line or accelerated methods are appropriate.

Accounting for Intangible Assets

OBJECTIVE 10
Apply the matching rule to intangible asset accounting issues, including research and development costs and goodwill

The purchase of an intangible asset is a special kind of capital expenditure. An intangible asset is long term, but it has no physical substance. Its value comes from the long-term rights or advantages that it offers to the owner. Among the most common examples are patents, copyrights, leaseholds, leasehold improvements, trademarks and brand names, franchises, licenses, formulas, processes, and goodwill. Some current assets, such as accounts receivable and certain prepaid expenses, have no physical nature, but they are not classified as intangible assets because they are short term. Intangible assets are both long term and nonphysical.

Intangible assets are accounted for at acquisition cost, that is, the amount paid for them. Some intangible assets such as goodwill or trademarks may have been acquired at little or no cost. Even though they may have great value and are needed for profitable operations, they should not appear on the balance sheet unless they have been purchased from another party at a price established in the marketplace.

The accounting issues connected with intangible assets are the same as those connected with other long-lived assets. The Accounting Principles Board, in its *Opinion No. 17*, lists them as follows:

1. Determining an initial carrying amount
2. Accounting for that amount after acquisition under normal business conditions —that is, through periodic write-off or amortization—in a manner similar to depreciation
3. Accounting for that amount if the value declines substantially and permanently[7]

7. Adapted from Accounting Principles Board, *Opinion No. 17*, "Intangible Assets" (New York: American Institute of Certified Public Accountants, 1970), par. 2.

Besides these three problems, an intangible asset has no physical qualities and so in some cases may be impossible to identify. For these reasons, its value and its useful life may be quite hard to estimate.

The Accounting Principles Board has decided that a company should record as assets the costs of intangible assets acquired from others. However, the company should record as expenses the costs of developing intangible assets. Also, intangible assets that have a determinable life, such as patents, copyrights, and leaseholds, should be written off through periodic amortization over that useful life in much the same way that plant assets are depreciated. Even though some intangible assets, such as goodwill and trademarks, have no measurable limit on their lives, they should also be amortized over a reasonable length of time (not to exceed forty years).

To illustrate these procedures, assume that Soda Bottling Company purchases a patent on a unique bottle cap for $18,000. The entry to record the patent would be as follows:

Patent	18,000	
Cash		18,000
Purchase of bottle cap patent		

Note that if Soda Bottling Company had developed the bottle cap internally instead of purchasing it from a third party, the costs of developing the cap, such as salaries of researchers, supplies used in testing, and costs of equipment, would have been expensed as incurred.

Assume now that Soda's management determines that, although the patent for the bottle cap will last for seventeen years, the product using the cap will be sold only for the next six years. The entry to record the annual amortization would be as follows:

Amortization of Patent	3,000	
Patent		3,000
Annual amortization of patent: $18,000 ÷ 6 years = $3,000		

Note that the Patent account is reduced directly by the amount of the amortization expense. This is in contrast to other long-term asset accounts in which depreciation or depletion is accumulated in a separate contra account.

If the patent becomes worthless before it is fully amortized, the remaining carrying value is written off as a loss. For instance, assume that after the first year Soda's chief competitor offers a bottle with a new type of cap that makes Soda's cap obsolete. The entry to record the loss would be as follows:

Loss on Patent	15,000	
Patent		15,000
Loss resulting from patent's becoming worthless		

Accounting for the different types of intangible assets is outlined in Table 10-1.

Research and Development Costs

Most successful companies carry out activities, possibly within a separate department, involving research and development. Among these activities are development of new products, testing of existing and proposed products, and pure research. In the past, some companies would record as an asset those costs of research and development that could be directly traced to the development

Table 10-1. Accounting for Intangible Assets

Type	Description	Special Accounting Problems
Patent	An exclusive right granted by the federal government for a period of 17 years to make a particular product or use a specific process.	The cost of successfully defending a patent in a patent infringement suit is added to the acquisition cost of the patent. Amortize over the useful life, which may be less than the legal life of 17 years.
Copyright	An exclusive right granted by the federal government to the possessor to publish and sell literary, musical, and other artistic materials for a period of the author's life plus 50 years. Includes computer programs.	Record at acquisition cost and amortize over the useful life, which is often much shorter than the legal life, but not to exceed 40 years. For example, the cost of paperback rights to a popular novel would typically be amortized over a useful life of two to four years.
Leasehold	A right to occupy land or buildings under a long-term rental contract. For example, Company A, which owns but does not want to use a prime retail location, sells Company B the right to use it for 10 years in return for one or more rental payments. Company B has purchased a leasehold.	Debit Leasehold for the amount of the rental payment made, and amortize it over the remaining life of the lease. Payments to the lessor during the life of the lease should be debited to Lease Expense.
Leasehold Improvements	Improvements to leased property that become the property of the lessor (the person who owns the property) at the end of the lease.	Debit Leasehold Improvements for the cost of improvements, and amortize the cost of the improvements over the remaining life of the lease.
Trademark, Brand Name	A registered symbol or name giving the holder the right to use it to identify a product or service.	Debit the trademark or brand name for the acquisition cost, and amortize it over a reasonable life, not to exceed 40 years.
Franchise, License, Formula, Process	A right to an exclusive territory or to exclusive use of a formula, technique, or design.	Debit the franchise, license, formula, or process for the acquisition cost, and amortize it over a reasonable life, not to exceed 40 years.
Goodwill	The excess of the cost of a group of assets (usually a business) over the fair market value of the net assets if purchased individually.	Debit Goodwill for the acquisition cost, and amortize it over a reasonable life, not to exceed 40 years.

of certain patents, formulas, or other rights. Other costs, such as those for testing and pure research, were treated as expenses of the accounting period and deducted from income.

The Financial Accounting Standards Board has stated that all research and development costs should be treated as revenue expenditures and charged to expense in the period when incurred.[8] The board argues that it is too hard to trace specific costs to specific profitable developments. Also, the costs of research and development are continuous and necessary for the success of a business and so should be treated as current expenses. To support this conclusion, the board cites studies showing that 30 to 90 percent of all new products fail and that three-fourths of new product expenses go to unsuccessful products. Thus, their costs do not represent future benefits.

Computer Software Costs

Many companies develop computer programs or software to be sold or leased to individuals and companies. The costs incurred in creating a computer software product are considered research and development costs until the product has been proved to be technologically feasible. As a result, costs incurred to this point in the process should be charged to expense as incurred. A product is deemed to be technologically feasible when a detailed working program has been designed. After the working program is developed, all software production costs are recorded as assets and amortized over the estimated economic life of the product using the straight-line method. If at any time the company cannot expect to realize from the software product the amount of its unamortized costs on the balance sheet, the asset should be written down to the amount expected to be realized.[9]

Goodwill

The term **goodwill** is widely used by business people, lawyers, and the public to mean different things. In most cases goodwill is taken to mean the good reputation of a company. From an accounting standpoint, goodwill exists when a purchaser pays more for a business than the fair market value of the net assets if purchased separately. Because the purchaser has paid more than the fair market value of the physical assets, there must be intangible assets. If the company being purchased does not have patents, copyrights, trademarks, or other identifiable intangible assets of value, the excess payment is assumed to be for goodwill. Goodwill exists because most businesses are worth more as going concerns than as collections of assets. Goodwill reflects all the factors that allow a company to earn a higher-than-market rate of return on its assets, including customer satisfaction, good management, manufacturing efficiency, the advantages of holding a monopoly, good locations, and good employee relations. The payment above and beyond the fair market value of the tangible assets and other specific intangible assets is properly recorded in the Goodwill account.

In *Opinion No. 17*, the Accounting Principles Board states that the benefits arising from purchased goodwill will in time disappear. It is hard for a company to keep having above-average earnings unless new factors of goodwill replace the old ones. For this reason, goodwill should be amortized or written

8. *Statement of Financial Accounting Standards No. 2*, "Accounting for Research and Development Costs" (Stamford, Conn.: Financial Accounting Standards Board, 1974), par. 12.
9. *Statement of Financial Accounting Standards No. 86*, "Accounting for the Costs of Computer Software to Be Sold, Leased, or Otherwise Marketed" (Stamford, Conn.: Financial Accounting Standards Board, 1985).

off by systematic charges to income over a reasonable number of future time periods. The time period should in no case be more than forty years.[10]

Chapter Review

Review of Learning Objectives

1. **Describe the nature, types, and issues of accounting for long-term assets.**
Long-term assets are assets that are used in the operation of the business, are not intended for resale, and have a useful life of more than one year. Long-term assets are either tangible or intangible. In the former category are land, plant assets, and natural resources. In the latter are trademarks, patents, franchises, goodwill, and other rights. The issues associated with accounting for long-term assets are the determination of cost, the allocation of expired cost, and the handling of repairs, maintenance, additions, and disposals.

2. **Account for the cost of property, plant, and equipment.**
The acquisition cost of property, plant, and equipment includes all expenditures that are reasonable and necessary to get the asset in place and ready for use. These expenditures include such payments as purchase price, installation cost, freight charges, and insurance.

3. **Define *depreciation,* state the factors that affect its computation, and show how to record it.**
Depreciation is the periodic allocation of the cost of a plant asset over its estimated useful life. It is recorded by debiting Depreciation Expense and crediting a related contra-asset account called Accumulated Depreciation. Factors that affect the computation of depreciation are cost, residual value, depreciable cost, and estimated useful life.

4. **Compute periodic depreciation under the (a) straight-line method, (b) production method, and (c) accelerated methods, including (1) sum-of-the-years'-digits method and (2) declining-balance method.**
Depreciation is commonly computed by the straight-line method, the production method, or one of the accelerated methods. The two most widely used accelerated methods are the sum-of-the-years'-digits method and the declining-balance method. The straight-line method is related directly to the passage of time, whereas the production method is related directly to use. Accelerated methods, which result in relatively large amounts of depreciation in the early years and reduced amounts in later years, are based on the assumption that plant assets provide greater economic benefit in their early years than in later years.

5. **Apply depreciation methods to problems of partial years, revised rates, items of low unit cost, groups of similar items, and accelerated cost recovery.**
In the application of depreciation methods, it may be necessary to calculate depreciation for partial years and to revise depreciation rates. In addition, it may be practical to apply these methods to groups of similar assets and to apply an inventory method to items of low unit cost. For income tax purposes, rapid write-offs of depreciable assets are allowed through the accelerated cost recovery system.

6. **Apply the matching rule to capital expenditures and revenue expenditures.**
It is important to distinguish between capital expenditures, which are recorded as assets, and revenue expenditures, which are recorded as expenses. The error of classifying one as the other will have an important effect on net income. Expenditures for plant assets, additions, betterments, and intangible assets are capital expenditures. Extraordinary repairs, which increase the residual value or extend the life of an asset, are also treated as capital expenditures, whereas ordinary repairs are revenue expenditures.

10. Accounting Principles Board, *Opinion No. 17*, par. 29.

7. **Account for disposal of depreciable assets not involving exchanges.**
Long-term assets may be disposed of by being discarded, sold, or exchanged. In the disposal of long-term assets, it is necessary to record the depreciation up to the date of disposal and to remove the carrying value from the accounts by removing the cost from the asset account and the depreciation to date from the accumulated depreciation account. If a long-term asset is sold at a price different from carrying value, there is a gain or loss that should be recorded and reported on the income statement.

8. **Account for disposal of depreciable assets involving exchanges.**
In recording exchanges of similar plant assets, a gain or loss may also arise. According to the Accounting Principles Board, losses, but not gains, should be recognized at the time of the exchange (as long as no money is received). When a gain is not recognized, the new asset is recorded at the carrying value of the old asset plus any cash paid. For income tax purposes, neither gains nor losses are recognized in the exchange of similar assets. When dissimilar assets are exchanged, gains and losses are recognized under both accounting and income tax rules.

9. **Identify natural resource accounting issues and compute depletion.**
Natural resources are wasting assets, which are converted to inventory by cutting, pumping, mining, or other forms of extraction. Natural resources are recorded at cost as long-term assets. They are allocated as expenses through depletion charges as the resources are sold. The depletion charge is based on the ratio of the resource extracted to the total estimated resource.

10. **Apply the matching rule to intangible asset accounting issues, including research and development costs and goodwill.**
Purchases of intangible assets should be treated as capital expenditures and recorded at acquisition cost, which in turn should be amortized over the useful life of the assets (but not more than forty years). The FASB requires that research and development costs be treated as revenue expenditures and charged as expense in the period of the expenditure. Software costs are treated as research and development costs and expensed until a feasible working program is developed, after which time the costs may be capitalized and amortized over a reasonable estimated life. Goodwill is the excess of the amount paid over the fair market value of the net assets in the purchase of a business and is usually related to the superior earning potential of the business. It should be recorded only if paid for in connection with the purchase of a business, and it should be amortized over a period not to exceed forty years.

Review of Concepts and Terminology

The following concepts and terms were introduced in this chapter:

(L.O. 5) **Accelerated Cost Recovery System (ACRS):** A mandatory system enacted by Congress in 1981 that requires that a cost recovery allowance be computed (1) on the unadjusted cost of property being recovered, and (2) over a period of years prescribed by the law for all property of similar types.

(L.O. 4) **Accelerated methods:** Methods of depreciation that allocate relatively large amounts of the depreciable cost of the asset to earlier years and reduced amounts to later years.

(L.O. 6) **Additions:** Enlargements to the physical layout of a plant asset.

(L.O. 1) **Amortization:** The periodic allocation of the cost of an intangible asset over its useful life.

(L.O. 6) **Betterments:** Improvements to plant assets that do not add to the physical layout of the asset.

(L.O. 10) **Brand name:** A registered name that gives the holder the right to use it to identify a product or service.

(L.O. 6) **Capital expenditure:** An expenditure for the purchase or expansion of long-term assets, recorded in the asset accounts.

(L.O. 10) **Copyright:** An exclusive right granted by the federal government to the possessor to publish and sell literary, musical, and other artistic materials for a period of the author's life plus fifty years.

(L.O. 4) **Declining-balance method:** An accelerated method of depreciation in which depreciation is computed by applying a fixed rate to the carrying value (the declining balance) of a tangible long-lived asset.

(L.O. 1, 9) **Depletion:** The proportional allocation of the cost of a natural resource to the units removed; the exhaustion of a natural resource through mining, cutting, pumping, or otherwise using up the resource.

(L.O. 3) **Depreciable cost:** The cost of an asset less its residual value.

(L.O. 1) **Depreciation:** The periodic allocation of the cost of tangible long-lived assets (other than land and natural resources) over their estimated useful lives.

(L.O. 4) **Double-declining-balance method:** An accelerated method of depreciation that applies a fixed rate percentage equal to twice the straight-line percentage to the carrying value of a tangible long-term asset.

(L.O. 3) **Estimated useful life:** The total number of service units expected from a long-term asset.

(L.O. 6) **Expenditure:** A payment or an obligation to make future payment for an asset or a service received.

(L.O. 6) **Extraordinary repairs:** Repairs that affect the estimated residual value or estimated useful life of an asset.

(L.O. 1) **Fixed assets:** Another name, no longer widely used, for long-term assets.

(L.O. 10) **Franchise:** The right to an exclusive territory or market.

(L.O. 10) **Goodwill:** The excess of the cost of a group of assets (usually a business) over the market value of the assets individually.

(L.O. 5) **Group depreciation:** The grouping of items of similar plant assets together for purposes of calculating depreciation.

(L.O. 1) **Intangible assets:** Long-term assets that have no physical substance but have a value based on rights or advantages accruing to the owner.

(L.O. 10) **Leasehold:** A right to occupy land or buildings under a long-term rental contract.

(L.O. 10) **Leasehold improvements:** Improvements to leased property that become the property of the lessor at the end of the lease.

(L.O. 10) **License:** Official or legal permission to do or own a specific thing.

(L.O. 1) **Long-term assets:** Assets that (1) have a useful life of more than one year, (2) are acquired for use in the operation of the business, and (3) are not intended for resale to customers.

(L.O. 5) **Modified Accelerated Cost Recovery System (MACRS):** A modification of the accelerated cost recovery system (ACRS) made by the Tax Reform Act of 1986.

(L.O. 1) **Natural resources:** Long-term assets purchased for the physical substances that can be taken from the land and used up rather than for the value of their location.

(L.O. 3) **Obsolescence:** The process of becoming out of date; a contributor, together with physical deterioration, to the limited useful life of tangible assets.

(L.O. 6) **Ordinary repairs:** Expenditures, usually of a recurring nature, that are necessary to maintain an asset in good operating condition.

(L.O. 10) **Patent:** An exclusive right granted by the federal government for a period of seventeen years to make a particular product or use a specific process.

(L.O. 3) **Physical deterioration:** Limitations on the useful life of a depreciable asset resulting from use and from exposure to the elements.

(L.O. 4) **Production method:** A method of depreciation that bases the depreciation charge for a period of time solely on the amount of use of the asset during the period of time.

(L.O. 3) **Residual value (salvage value, disposal value):** The estimated net scrap, salvage, or trade-in value of a tangible asset at the estimated date of disposal.

(L.O. 6) **Revenue expenditures:** Expenditures for repairs, maintenance, or other services needed to maintain or operate plant assets. Recorded by debits to expense accounts.

(L.O. 4) **Straight-line method:** A method of depreciation that assumes that depreciation is dependent on the passage of time and that allocates an equal amount of depreciation to each period of time.

(L.O. 4) **Sum-of-the-years'-digits method:** An accelerated method of depreciation in which the years in the service life of an asset are added; their sum becomes the denominator of a series of fractions that are applied against the depreciable cost of the asset in allocating the total depreciation over the estimated useful life.

(L.O. 1) **Tangible assets:** Long-term assets that have physical substance.

(L.O. 5) **Tax Reform Act of 1986:** The most sweeping revision of federal tax laws since the original enactment of the Internal Revenue Code in 1913.

(L.O. 10) **Trademark:** A registered symbol that gives the holder the right to use it to identify a product or service.

(L.O. 9) **Wasting assets:** Another term for natural resources; long-term assets purchased for the physical substances that can be taken from the land and used up rather than for the value of their location.

Self-Test

Test your knowledge of the chapter by choosing the best answer for each of the following items.

(L.O. 1) 1. Which of the following is *not* a characteristic of all long-term assets?
   a. Used in operation of business
   b. Possess physical substance
   c. Useful life of more than a year
   d. Not for resale

(L.O. 2) 2. Which of the following would *not* be included in the cost of land?
   a. Cost of paving the land for parking
   b. Assessment from local government for sewer
   c. Cost of clearing an unneeded building from the land
   d. Commission to real estate agent

(L.O. 3) 3. Which of the following most appropriately describes depreciation?
   a. Allocation of cost of plant asset
   b. Decline in value of plant asset
   c. Gradual obsolescence of plant asset
   d. Physical deterioration of plant asset

(L.O. 4) 4. If an asset cost $48,000 and has a residual value of $6,000 and a useful life of six years, the depreciation in the second year, using the sum-of-the-years'-digits method, would be
   a. $13,714.
   b. $12,000.
   c. $11,428.
   d. $10,000.

(L.O. 5) 5. Equipment costing $27,000 with a residual value of $3,000 and an estimated life of six years has been depreciated using the straight-line method for two years. Assuming a revised estimated total life of four years and the same estimated residual value, the depreciation expense for the third year will be
   a. $4,000.
   b. $4,750.
   c. $8,000.
   d. $9,500.

(L.O. 6) 6. The primary difference between ordinary and extraordinary repairs is that extraordinary repairs
   a. extend the useful life of the asset.
   b. are an expense of the current period.
   c. are necessary in order to maintain the asset in good operational condition.
   d. are periodic in nature.

(L.O. 7) 7. The sale of equipment costing $16,000 with accumulated depreciation of $13,400 and a sale price of $4,000 would result in a
   a. gain of $4,000.
   b. gain of $1,400.
   c. loss of $1,400.
   d. loss of $12,000.

(L.O. 8) 8. A truck that cost $16,800 and on which $12,600 of accumulated depreciation has been recorded was disposed of on January 1, the first day of the year. Assume the truck was traded for a similar truck having a price of $19,600, that a $2,000 trade-in was allowed, and that the balance was paid in cash. Following APB rules, the amount of the gain or loss recognized on this transaction would be
   a. $2,200 gain.
   b. $2,200 loss.
   c. no gain or loss recognized.
   d. none of the above.

(L.O. 9) 9. A specialized piece of equipment closely associated with a mine is most likely to be depreciated over a shorter-than-normal useful life because
   a. management wants to increase expenses.
   b. the equipment contains certain defects.
   c. the mine is expected to be fully depleted in the shorter length of time.
   d. the equipment will be fully utilized.

(L.O. 10) 10. According to generally accepted accounting principles, the proper accounting treatment for the cost of a trademark that management feels will retain its value indefinitely is to
   a. amortize the cost over a period not to exceed forty years.
   b. amortize the cost over five years.
   c. carry the cost of the asset indefinitely.
   d. write the cost off immediately.

Answers to the Self-Test are at the end of this chapter.

Review Problem
Depreciation Methods and Partial Years

(L.O. 3, 4, 5) Norton Construction Company purchased a cement mixer for $14,500. The mixer is expected to have a useful life of five years and a residual value of $1,000. The company engineers estimate the mixer will have a useful life of 7,500 hours, of which 2,625 hours were used in 19x2. The company's year end is December 31.

Required

1. Compute the depreciation expense for 19x2 assuming the cement mixer was purchased on January 1, 19x1, using the following four methods: (a) straight-line, (b) production, (c) sum-of-the-years'-digits, (d) double-declining-balance.
2. Compute the depreciation expense for 19x2 assuming the cement mixer was purchased on July 1, 19x1, using the following methods: (a) straight-line, (b) production, (c) sum-of-the-years'-digits, (d) double-declining-balance.
3. Prepare the adjusting entry to record the depreciation calculated in **1 (a)**.
4. Show the balance sheet presentation for the cement mixer after the entry in **3** on December 31, 19x2.

Answer to Review Problem

1. Depreciation expense for 19x2 assuming purchase on January 1, 19x1:
   a. Straight-line method
      ($14,500 − $1,000) ÷ 5 = $2,700
   b. Production method
      $$\frac{(\$14{,}500 - \$1{,}000)}{7{,}500} = \$1.80 \text{ per hour} \times 2{,}675 \text{ hours} = \$4{,}725$$
   c. Sum-of-the-years'-digits method
      $$(\$14{,}500 - \$1{,}000) \times \frac{4}{15} = \$3{,}600$$

d. Double-declining-balance method
First year: $14,500 × .4 = $5,800
Second year: ($14,500 – $5,800) × .4 = $3,480

2. Depreciation expense for 19x2 assuming purchase on July 1, 19x1:
a. Straight-line method

First half: [($14,500 – $1,000) ÷ 5] × 6/12 =	$1,350
Second half: [($14,500 – $1,000) ÷ 5] × 6/12 =	1,350
19x2 Total	$2,700

(Note that depreciation is the same for each half-year under the straight-line method.)

b. Production method

$$(\$14{,}500 - \$1{,}000) \times \frac{2{,}625}{7{,}500} = \$4{,}725$$

c. Sum-of-the-years'-digits method

First half: ($14,500 – $1,000) × 5/15 × 6/12 =	$2,250
Second half: ($14,500 – $1,000) × 4/15 × 6/12 =	1,800
19x2 Total	$4,050

d. Double-declining-balance method

First half: ($14,500 × .4) × 6/12 =	$2,900
Second half: [($14,500 – $5,800*) × .4] × 6/12 =	1,740
19x2 Total	$4,640

*First full year's depreciation: $14,500 × .4 = $5,800

3. Adjusting entry for depreciation prepared:

19x2			
Dec. 31	Depreciation Expense, Cement Mixer	2,700	
	Accumulated Depreciation, Cement Mixer		2,700
	To record depreciation for 19x2 under the straight-line method		

4. Balance sheet presentation shown for December 31, 19x2:

Cement Mixer	$14,500
Less Accumulated Depreciation	5,400
	$ 9,100

Chapter Assignments

Questions

1. What are the characteristics of long-term assets?
2. Which of the following items would be classified as plant assets on the balance sheet? (a) A truck held for sale by a truck dealer, (b) an office building that was once the company headquarters but is now to be sold, (c) a typewriter used by a secretary of the company, (d) a machine that is used in the manufacturing operations but is now fully depreciated, (e) pollution-control equipment that does not reduce the cost or improve the efficiency of the factory, (f) a parking lot for company employees.
3. Why is it useful to think of a plant asset as a bundle of services?
4. Why is land different from other long-term assets?
5. What in general is included in the cost of a long-term asset?
6. Which of the following expenditures incurred in connection with the purchase of a computer system would be charged to the asset account? (a) Purchase price of the

equipment, (b) interest on debt incurred to purchase the equipment, (c) freight charges, (d) installation charges, (e) cost of special communications outlets at the computer site, (f) cost of repairing door that was damaged during installation, (g) cost of adjustments to the system during first month of operation.

7. Hale's Grocery obtained bids on the construction of a dock for receiving goods at the back of its store. The lowest bid was $22,000. The company, however, decided to build the dock itself and was able to do it for $20,000, which it borrowed. The activity was recorded as a debit to Buildings for $22,000 and credits to Notes Payable for $20,000 and Gain on Construction for $2,000. Do you agree with the entry?
8. What do accountants mean by the term *depreciation*, and what is its relationship to depletion and amortization?
9. A firm buys a piece of technical equipment that is expected to last twelve years. Why might the equipment have to be depreciated over a shorter period of time?
10. A company purchased a building five years ago. The market value of the building is now greater than it was when the building was purchased. Explain why the company should continue depreciating the building.
11. Evaluate the following statement: "A parking lot should not be depreciated because adequate repairs will make it last forever."
12. Is the purpose of depreciation to determine the value of equipment? Explain your answer.
13. Contrast the assumptions underlying the straight-line depreciation method with the assumptions underlying the production depreciation method.
14. What is the principal argument supporting accelerated depreciation methods?
15. What does the balance of the Accumulated Depreciation account represent? Does it represent funds available to purchase new plant assets?
16. If a plant asset is sold during the year, why should depreciation be computed for the partial year prior to the date of the sale?
17. What basic procedure should be followed in revising a depreciation rate?
18. Explain why and how plant assets of low unit cost can be accounted for on a basis similar to handling supplies.
19. On what basis can depreciation be taken on a group of assets rather than on individual items?
20. What is the difference between depreciation for accounting purposes and accelerated cost recovery for income tax purposes?
21. What is the distinction between capital expenditures and revenue expenditures, and why is this distinction important?
22. What will be the effect on future years' income of charging an addition to a building to repair expense?
23. In what ways do an addition, a betterment, and an extraordinary repair differ?
24. How does an ordinary repair differ from an extraordinary repair? What is the accounting treatment for each?
25. If a plant asset is discarded before the end of its useful life, how is the amount of loss measured?
26. When similar assets are exchanged, at what amount is the new asset recorded for federal income tax purposes?
27. When an exchange of similar assets occurs in which there is an unrecorded loss, is the taxpayer ever able to deduct or receive federal income tax credit for the loss?
28. Old Stake Mining Company computes the depletion rate of ore to be $2 per ton. During 19xx the company mined 400,000 tons of ore and sold 370,000 tons. What is the total depletion expense for the year?
29. Under what circumstances can a mining company depreciate its plant assets over a period of time that is less than their useful lives?
30. Because accounts receivable have no physical substance, can they be classified as intangible assets?
31. Under what circumstances can a company have intangible assets that do not appear on the balance sheet?
32. When the Accounting Principles Board indicates that accounting for intangible assets involves the same problem as accounting for tangible assets, what problem is it referring to?

33. How does the Financial Accounting Standards Board recommend that research and development costs be treated?
34. Archi Draw Company spent three years developing a new software program for designing office building structures and recently completed the detailed working program. How does accounting for the costs of software development differ before and after the completion of a successful working program?
35. How is accounting for software development costs similar to and different from accounting for research and development costs?
36. Under what conditions should goodwill be recorded? Should it remain in the records permanently once it is recorded?

Communication Skills Exercises

Communication 10-1. Ethics and Allocation of Acquisition Costs
(L.O. 2)

Signal Corporation has purchased land and a warehouse for $18,000,000. The warehouse is expected to last twenty years and to have an estimated salvage value equal to 10 percent of its cost. The chief financial officer (CFO) and controller are discussing the allocation of the purchase price. The CFO believes most of the cost should be assigned to land because this action will improve reported net income in the future. Depreciation expense will be lower because land is not depreciated. He suggests allocating one-third, or $6,000,000, of the cost to the land. This results in depreciation expense each year of $540,000 [($12,000,000 – $1,200,000)/20 years]. The controller disagrees. In his opinion, the smallest amount possible, say one-fifth of the purchase price, should be allocated to the land, thereby saving income tax since the depreciation, which is tax deductible, will be greater. Under the controller's plan, annual depreciation would be $648,000 [$14,400,000 – $1,440,000)/20 years]. The annual tax savings at a 30 percent tax rate would be $32,400 [(648,000 – $540,000) × .30]. How will this decision affect the company's cash flows? How should the purchase cost ethically be allocated? Who will be affected by the decision?

Communication 10-2. Nature of Depreciation and Amortization and Estimated Useful Lives
(L.O. 3, 10)

General Motors Corp., in its 1987 annual report, states, "In the third quarter of 1987, the Corporation revised the estimated service lives of its plants and equipment and special tools retroactive to January 1, 1987. These revisions, which were based on 1987 studies of actual useful lives and periods of use, recognized current estimates of service lives of the assets and had the effect of reducing 1987 depreciation and amortization charges by $1,236.6 million or $2.55 per share of $1-2/3 par value common stock." In 1987, General Motors's income before income taxes was $2,005.4 million. What is the purpose of depreciation and amortization? What is the estimated service life, and on what basis did General Motors change the estimates of the service lives of plants and equipment and special tools? What was the effect of this change on the corporation's income before income taxes? Is it likely that the company is in better condition economically as a result of the change? Does the company have more cash at the end of the year as a result? (Ignore income tax effects.)

Communication 10-3. Trademarks[11]
(L.O. 10)

The Quaker Oats Company's advertising campaign, "Gatorade is thirst aid for that deep down body thirst," infringed on a trademark held by Sands Taylor & Wood of Norwich, Vermont, according to a 1990 ruling by a federal judge. Sands Taylor & Wood had acquired the trademark "thirst aid" in a 1973 acquisition but was not using it when the ruling was handed down. The judge determined that Gatorade had produced $247.3 million in income over the previous six years and that the advertising campaign was responsible for 10 percent of the product's sales. He awarded Sands Taylor & Wood $24.7 million plus legal fees and interest from 1984. He also prohibited Quaker Oats from further use of the phrase "thirst aid" in any advertising campaign for Gatorade.

What is a trademark, and why is it considered an intangible asset? Why does a trademark have value? To whom does a trademark have value? How do your answers apply to the case of Quaker Oats Company's use of "thirst aid"?

11. James P. Miller, "Quaker Oats Loses Trademark Battle Over Gatorade Ad," *Wall Street Journal*, Dec. 19, 1990.

Communication 10-4. Accounting for Trademarks: U.S. and British Rules
(L.O. 10)

When the British company ***Grand Metropolitan*** (Grand Met) purchased Pillsbury in 1989, it adopted British accounting policies with regard to intangibles. Many analysts feel this gives British companies advantages over U.S. companies, especially in buyout situations.[12] There are two major differences in accounting for intangibles between U.S. accounting standards and British accounting standards. First, under the U.S. rules as discussed in this chapter, intangible assets such as trademarks are recorded at their acquisition cost, which is often nominal, and the cost is amortized over a reasonable life. Under British accounting standards, on the other hand, firms are able to record the value of trademarks for the purpose of increasing the total assets of their balance sheets. Further, they do not have to amortize the values if management can show that the values can be preserved through extensive brand support. Grand Met, therefore, elected to record such famous Pillsbury trademarks as the Pillsbury Doughboy, Green Giant vegetables, Haagen Dazs ice cream, and Van de Kamp fish at an estimated value and not to amortize them. Second, when one company purchases another company for more than the market value of the assets if purchased individually, the excess is recorded under U.S. rules as the asset goodwill, which must be amortized over a period not to exceed forty years. Although companies are required to show the expense, they cannot, under U.S. income tax laws, deduct the goodwill amortization for tax purposes. Under British accounting rules, any goodwill resulting from a purchase lowers owners' equity directly, rather than being recorded as an asset and lowering net income through amortization over a number of years. Analysts say that these two rules made Pillsbury more valuable to Grand Met than to Pillsbury stockholders and thus led to Pillsbury being bought by the British firm. Write a one- or two-page paper that addresses the following questions: What is the rationale behind the argument that the British company has an advantage because of the differences between U.S. and British accounting principles? Do you agree with the U.S. or British accounting rules with regard to intangibles and goodwill? Give reasons for your answers.

Communication 10-5. Basic Research Skills
(L.O. 7)

Public corporations are required not only to communicate with their stockholders by means of an annual report, but also to submit an annual report to the Securities and Exchange Commission (SEC). The annual report to the SEC is called a 10-K and contains information in addition to that provided to stockholders. Most college and university libraries provide access to at least a selected number of 10-Ks. These 10-Ks may be on microfiche or on file with the companies' annual reports to stockholders. In your school's library, find the 10-K for a single company. In that 10-K, Schedule 5 will contain information about the dispositions and acquisitions of property, plant, and equipment at book value. Schedule 6 will show the increases and decreases in the accumulated depreciation accounts. In the statement of cash flows under investing activities, the cash proceeds from dispositions of property, plant, and equipment will be shown. Using the information from this statement and the two related schedules, determine whether or not the company had a gain or loss from dispositions of property, plant, and equipment during the year. Be prepared to discuss your results in class.

Classroom Exercises

Exercise 10-1. Determining Cost of Long-Term Assets
(L.O. 2)

Decatur Manufacturing purchased land next to its factory to be used as a parking lot. Expenditures incurred by the company were as follows: purchase price, $150,000; broker's fees, $12,000; title search and other fees, $1,100; demolition of a shack on the property, $4,000; general grading of property, $2,100; paving parking lots, $20,000; lighting for parking lots, $16,000; and signs for parking lots, $3,200. Determine the amount that should be debited to the Land account and to the Land Improvements account.

12. Joanne Lipman, "British Value Brand Names—Literally," *Wall Street Journal*, February 9, 1989, p. B4; and "Brand Name Policy Boosts Assets," *Accountancy*, October 1988, pp. 38–39.

Exercise 10-2.
Group Purchase
(L.O. 2)

Linda Regalado went into business by purchasing a car wash for $480,000. The car wash assets included land, building, and equipment. If purchased separately, the land would have cost $120,000, the building $270,000, and the equipment $210,000. Determine the amount that should be recorded in the new business's records for land, building, and equipment.

Exercise 10-3.
Cost of Long-Term Asset and Depreciation
(L.O. 2, 3, 4)

Myron Walker purchased a used tractor for $35,000. Before the tractor could be used it required new tires, which cost $2,200, and an overhaul, which cost $2,800. Its first tank of fuel cost $150. The tractor is expected to last six years and have a residual value of $4,000. Determine the cost and depreciable cost of the tractor and calculate the first year's depreciation under the straight-line method.

Exercise 10-4.
Depreciation Methods
(L.O. 3, 4)

Findlay Oil Corporation purchased a drilling truck for $90,000. The company expected the truck to last five years or 200,000 miles, with an estimated residual value of $15,000 at the end of that time. During 19x5, the truck was driven 48,000 miles. The company's year end is December 31.

Compute the depreciation for 19x5 under each of the following methods, assuming that the truck was purchased on January 13, 19x4: (1) straight-line, (2) production, (3) sum-of-the-years'-digits, and (4) double-declining-balance. Using the amount computed in **4**, prepare the general journal entry to record depreciation expense for the second year and show how drilling trucks would appear on the balance sheet.

Exercise 10-5.
Depreciation Methods: Partial Years
(L.O. 4, 5)

Using the same data given for Findlay Oil Corporation in Exercise 10-4, compute the depreciation for calendar year 19x5 under each of the following methods, assuming that the truck was purchased on July 1, 19x4: (1) straight-line, (2) production, (3) sum-of-the-years'-digits, (4) double-declining-balance.

Exercise 10-6.
Declining-Balance Method
(L.O. 4)

Schwab Burglar Alarm Systems Company purchased a word processor for $2,240. It has an estimated useful life of four years and an estimated residual value of $240. Compute the depreciation charge for each of the four years using the double-declining-balance method.

Exercise 10-7.
Straight-Line Method: Partial Years
(L.O. 4, 5)

Idriss Manufacturing Corporation purchased three machines during the year:

February 10	Machine 1	$ 3,600
July 26	Machine 2	24,000
October 11	Machine 3	43,200

Each machine is expected to last six years and have no estimated residual value. The company's fiscal year corresponds to the calendar year. Using the straight-line method, compute the depreciation charge for each machine for the year.

Exercise 10-8.
Revision of Depreciation Rates
(L.O. 4, 5)

Broadleigh Hospital purchased a special x-ray machine for its operating room. The machine, which cost $311,560, was expected to last ten years, with an estimated residual value of $31,560. After two years of operation (and depreciation charges using the straight-line rate), it became evident that the x-ray machine would last a total of only seven years. The estimated residual value, however, would remain the same. Given this information, determine the new depreciation charge for the third year on the basis of the estimated useful life.

Exercise 10-9.
Accounting for Items of Low Unit Cost
(L.O. 5)

Kittle Air Conditioner Service Company maintains a large supply of small tools for servicing air conditioners. The company uses the inventory basis to account for the tools and assumes that annual expense is approximately equal to the cost of tools lost and discarded during the year. At the beginning of the year, the company's inventory of small tools on hand totaled $17,530. During the year, small tools were purchased at a cost of $9,560 and debited to the Small Tools account. At the end of the year (December

31), a physical inventory revealed small tools in the amount of $13,170 on hand. Prepare a general journal entry to record small tools expense for the year for Kittle Air Conditioner Service Company.

Exercise 10-10. Capital and Revenue Expenditures *(L.O. 6)*

For each of the following transactions related to an office building, tell whether each transaction is a revenue expenditure (RE) or capital expenditure (CE). In addition, indicate whether each transaction is an ordinary repair (OR), extraordinary repair (ER), addition (A), betterment (B), or none of these (N).

_____ a. The hallways and ceilings in the building are repainted at a cost of $8,300.
_____ b. The hallways, which have tile floors, are carpeted at a cost of $28,000.
_____ c. A new wing is added to the building at a cost of $175,000.
_____ d. Furniture is purchased for the entrance to the building at a cost of $16,500.
_____ e. The air conditioning system is overhauled at a cost of $28,500. The overhaul extends the useful life of the air-conditioning system by ten years.
_____ f. A cleaning firm is paid $200 per week to clean the newly installed carpets.

Exercise 10-11. Extraordinary Repairs *(L.O. 6)*

Regalado Manufacturing has an incinerator that originally cost $187,200 and now has accumulated depreciation of $132,800. The incinerator just completed its fifteenth year of service in an estimated useful life of twenty years. At the beginning of the sixteenth year, the company spent $42,800 repairing and modernizing the incinerator to comply with pollution-control standards. Therefore, instead of five years, the incinerator is now expected to last ten more years. It will not, however, have more capacity than it did in the past or a residual value at the end of its useful life.

1. Prepare the entry to record the cost of the repair.
2. Compute the book value of the incinerator after the entry.
3. Prepare the entry to record the depreciation (assuming straight-line method) for the current year.

Exercise 10-12. Disposal of Plant Assets *(L.O. 7, 8)*

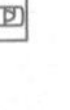

A piece of equipment that cost $32,400 and on which $18,000 of accumulated depreciation had been recorded was disposed of on January 2, the first day of business of the current year. Give general journal entries to record the disposal under each of the following assumptions:

1. It was discarded as having no value.
2. It was sold for $6,000 cash.
3. It was sold for $19,000 cash.
4. The equipment was traded in on a dissimilar machine having a list price of $48,000. A $17,600 trade-in was allowed, and the balance was paid in cash. Gains and losses are to be recognized.
5. The equipment was traded in on a dissimilar machine having a list price of $48,000. A $7,500 trade-in was allowed, and the balance was paid in cash. Gains and losses are to be recognized.
6. Same as **5** except that the items are similar and gains and losses are not to be recognized.

Exercise 10-13. Disposal of Plant Assets *(L.O. 8)*

A commercial vacuum cleaner costing $2,450, with accumulated depreciation of $1,800, was traded in on a new model that had a list price of $3,050. A trade-in allowance of $500 was given.

1. Compute the carrying value of the old vacuum cleaner.
2. Determine the amount of cash required to purchase the new vacuum cleaner.
3. Compute the amount of loss on the exchange.
4. Determine the cost basis of the new vacuum cleaner assuming (a) the loss is recognized and (b) the loss is not recognized.
5. Compute the yearly depreciation on the new vacuum cleaner for both assumptions in **4**, assuming a useful life of five years, a residual value of $800, and straight-line depreciation.

Exercise 10-14.
Disposal of Plant Assets
(L.O. 7, 8)

A microcomputer was purchased by Juniper Company on January 1, 19x1 at a cost of $5,000. It is expected to have a useful life of five years and a residual value of $500. Assuming the computer is disposed of on July 1, 19x4, record the partial year's depreciation for 19x4 using the straight-line method, and record the disposal under each of the following assumptions:

1. The microcomputer is discarded.
2. The microcomputer is sold for $800.
3. The microcomputer is sold for $2,200.
4. The microcomputer is exchanged for a new microcomputer with a list price of $9,000. A $1,200 trade-in is allowed on the cash purchase. The accounting approach to gains and losses is followed.
5. Same as **4** except a $2,400 trade-in is allowed.
6. Same as **4** except the income tax approach is followed.
7. Same as **5** except the income tax approach is followed.
8. Same as **4** except the microcomputer is exchanged for dissimilar office equipment.
9. Same as **5** except the microcomputer is exchanged for dissimilar office equipment.

Exercise 10-15.
Natural Resource Depletion and Depreciation of Related Plant Assets
(L.O. 9)

Church Mining Corporation purchased land containing an estimated 10 million tons of ore for a cost of $8,800,000. The land without the ore is estimated to be worth $1,600,000. The company expects that all the usable ore can be mined in ten years. Buildings costing $900,000 with an estimated useful life of thirty years were erected on the site. Equipment costing $960,000 with an estimated useful life of ten years was installed. Because of the remote location, neither the buildings nor the equipment has an estimated residual value. During its first year of operation, the company mined and sold 800,000 tons of ore.

1. Compute the depletion charge per ton.
2. Compute the depletion expense that Church Mining Corporation should record for the year.
3. Determine the annual depreciation expense for the buildings, making it proportional to the depletion.
4. Determine the annual depreciation expense for the equipment under two alternatives: (a) using the straight-line method and (b) making the expense proportional to the depletion.

Exercise 10-16.
Amortization of Copyrights and Trademarks
(L.O. 10)

1. Fortunato Publishing Company purchased the copyright to a basic computer textbook for $20,000. The usual life of a textbook is about four years. However, the copyright will remain in effect for another fifty years. Calculate the annual amortization of the copyright.
2. Guzman Company purchased a trademark from a well-known supermarket for $160,000. The management of the company argued that the trademark value would last forever and might even increase and so no amortization should be charged. Calculate the minimum amount of annual amortization that should be charged, according to guidelines of the appropriate Accounting Principles Board opinion.

Interpretation Case from Business

Century Steelworks Company
(L.O. 5)

Depreciation expense is a significant expense for companies in industries that have a high proportion of plant assets to other assets. The amount of depreciation expense in a given year is affected by estimates of useful life and by choice of depreciation method. In 1990, Century Steelworks Company, a major integrated steel producer, changed the estimated useful lives for its major production assets. It also changed the method of depreciation for other steel-making assets from straight-line to the production method.

The company's 1990 annual report states, "A recent study conducted by management shows that actual years-in-service figures for our major production equipment and machinery are, in most cases, higher than the estimated useful lives assigned to these assets. We have recast the depreciable lives of such assets so that equipment previously assigned a useful life of 8 to 26 years now has an extended depreciable life of 10 to 32 years." The report goes on to explain that the new production method of depreciation "recognizes that depreciation of production equipment and machinery correlates directly to both physical wear and tear and the passage of time. The production method of depreciation, which we have now initiated, more closely allocates the cost of these assets to the periods in which products are manufactured."

The report summarized the effects of both actions on the year 1990 as follows:

Incremental Increase in Net Income	In Millions	Per Share
Lengthened lives	$11.0	$ .80
Production method		
Current year	7.3	.53
Prior years	2.8	.20
Total increase	$21.1	$1.53

During 1990, Century Steelworks reported a net loss of $83,156,500 ($6.03 per share). Depreciation expense for 1990 was $87,707,200.

In explaining the changes, the controller of Century Steelworks was quoted in an article in *Business Journal* as follows: "There is no reason why Century Steelworks should continue to depreciate our assets more conservatively than our competitors do." But the article quotes an industry analyst who argues that, by slowing its method of depreciation, Century Steelworks could be viewed as reporting lower quality earnings.

Required

1. Explain the accounting treatment when there is a change in the estimated lives of depreciable assets. What circumstances must exist for the production method to produce the effect it did in relation to the straight-line method? What would have been Century Steelworks's net income or loss if the changes had not been made? What may have motivated management to make the changes?
2. What does the controller of Century Steelworks mean when he says that Century had been depreciating "more conservatively than our competitors"? Why might the changes at Century Steelworks indicate, as the analyst asserts, "lower quality earnings"? What risks might Century face as a result of its decision to use the production method of depreciation?

Problem Set A

Problem 10A-1. Determining Cost of Assets
(L.O. 2, 3, 4, 5)

Muraskas Computers, Inc. constructed a new training center in 19x2. You have been hired to manage the training center. A review of the accounting records lists the following expenditures debited to the Training Center account:

Attorney's fee, land acquisition	$ 34,900
Cost of land	598,000
Architect's fee, building design	102,000
Contractor's cost, building	1,020,000
Contractor's cost, parking lot and sidewalk	135,600
Contractor's cost, electrical (for building)	164,000
Landscaping	55,000
Costs of surveying land	9,200
Training equipment, tables, and chairs	136,400
Contractor's cost, installing training equipment	68,000
Cost of grading the land	14,000
Cost of changes in building to soundproof rooms	59,200
Total account balance	$2,396,300

During the center's construction, someone from Muraskas Computers, Inc. worked full time on the project. He spent two months on the purchase and preparation of the site, six months on the construction, one month on land improvements, and one month on equipment installation and training room furniture purchase and set-up. His salary of $64,000 during this ten-month period was charged to Administrative Expense. The training center was placed in operation on November 1.

Required

1. Prepare a schedule with the following four column (Account) headings: Land, Land Improvements, Building, and Equipment. Place each of the expenditures above in the appropriate column. Total the columns.
2. Prepare an entry on December 31 to correct the accounts associated with the training center, assuming that the company's accounts have not been closed at the end of the year.
3. Assume that the center was in operation for two months during the year. Prepare an adjusting entry to record depreciation expense, assuming that the land improvements are depreciated over twenty years with no residual value, that the building is depreciated over thirty years with no residual value, and that the equipment is depreciated over twelve years with the estimated residual value equal to 10 percent of cost. The company uses the straight-line method. Round your answers to the nearest dollar.

Problem 10A-2. Comparison of Depreciation Methods *(L.O. 3, 4)*

Larson Manufacturing Company purchased a robot for its manufacturing operations at a cost of $1,440,000 at the beginning of year 1. The robot has an estimated useful life of four years and an estimated residual value of $120,000. The robot is expected to last 20,000 hours. The robot was operated 6,000 hours in year 1; 8,000 hours in year 2; 4,000 hours in year 3; and 2,000 hours in year 4.

Required

1. Compute the annual depreciation and carrying value for the robot for each year assuming the following depreciation methods: (a) straight-line, (b) production, (c) sum-of-the-years'-digits, and (d) double-declining-balance.
2. Prepare the adjusting entry that would be made each year to record the depreciation calculated under the straight-line method.
3. Show the balance sheet presentation for the robot after the adjusting entry in year 2 using the straight-line method.
4. What conclusions can you draw from the patterns of yearly depreciation and carrying value in **1**?

Problem 10A-3. Depreciation Methods and Partial Years *(L.O. 4, 5)*

Isabel Lim purchased a laundry company that caters to young college students. In addition to the washing machines, Lim installed a tanning machine, a video game machine, and a refreshment center. Because each type of asset performs a different function, she has decided to use different depreciation methods. Data on each type of asset are summarized in the table below.

The tanning machine was operated 2,100 hours in 19x5, 3,000 hours in 19x6, and 2,400 hours in 19x7.

Asset	Date Purchased	Cost	Installation Cost	Residual Value	Estimated Life	Depreciation Method
Washing machines	3/5/x5	$30,000	$4,000	$5,200	4 years	Straight-line
Tanning machine	4/1/x5	68,000	6,000	2,000	7,500 hours	Production
Video game	6/30/x5	20,000	2,000	1,600	4 years	Sum-of-the-years'-digits
Refreshment center	10/1/x5	6,800	1,200	1,200	10 years	Double-declining-balance

Required

Assuming the fiscal year ends December 31, compute the depreciation charges for each item and in total for 19x5, 19x6, and 19x7. Round your answers to the nearest dollar and present them by filling in a table with the headings shown below.

Asset	Computations	Depreciation 19x5	19x6	19x7

Problem 10A-4. Plant Asset Transactions, Revised Depreciation, and Spare Parts *(L.O. 2, 3, 4, 5)*

Sullivan Auto Repair Company purchased auto repair equipment on January 2, 19x3 for $188,000. Delivery cost was $7,000, and installation cost was $5,000. Mr. Sullivan estimated the equipment would have a useful life of six years and a residual value of $20,000. On April 2, small tools for auto repairs were purchased for $2,950. Regular maintenance in 19x3 was $960, expended on November 1. At the end of the year, an inventory revealed $1,520 of small tools still on hand.

Regular maintenance for the equipment in 19x4 was $1,500. This expenditure was made on May 10. During 19x4, Mr. Sullivan determined that the equipment would last only four years instead of the originally estimated six years. The new estimated residual value would be only $10,000. On June 10, 19x4, $840 of small tools were purchased; the inventory of small tools at the end of the year showed $2,040 on hand.

Required

1. Prepare general journal entries for 19x3 to record the purchase of the equipment and costs associated with the purchase, maintenance costs, the transactions involving small tools, and year-end depreciation assuming the straight-line method of depreciation. Assume that all purchases are made with cash.
2. Prepare general journal entries for 19x4 for maintenance, small tools, and depreciation expense using Mr. Sullivan's revised estimates.

Problem 10A-5. Capital and Revenue Expenditure Entries *(L.O. 6, 7)*

Armand Aranyi operates several low-budget motels in the Midwest. The transactions below describe the capital and revenue expenditures for the first motel he purchased.

Dec. 21, 19x1	Purchased the motel at a cost of $1,880,000. The estimated life of the motel is twenty years, and the residual value is $280,000.
Dec. 31, 19x1	The motel was repainted and some minor roof problems were corrected at a cost of $80,000. These costs were necessary before the motel was opened to the public.
Jan. 12, 19x5	Made a small addition to the motel at a cost of $76,500. This cost did not impact on the life or residual value of the motel.
May 20, 19x5	Minor repairs were made to the doors of each room for $10,600.
Sept. 17, 19x5	Minor resurfacing was performed on the parking lot at a cost of $12,200.
Jan. 9, 19x8	Major repairs and renovation of $149,000 were completed. It was estimated that this work would extend the life of the motel by five years and increase the residual value by $20,000.

Required

1. Prepare general journal entries for each transaction. Assume that all transactions are made with cash.
2. Open ledger accounts for Motel (150) and Accumulated Depreciation, Motel (151), and post the relevant entries in **1**.
3. Compute depreciation expense for each year and partial year assuming that the straight-line method is used and the company's fiscal year ends on December 31. Enter the amounts in the account for Accumulated Depreciation, Motel.
4. Prepare general journal entries to record the partial year's depreciation and the sale of the motel on June 30, 19x9 for $1,760,000, including $160,000 cash and the remaining amount as a mortgage note. Post the relevant portions of the entries to the two accounts opened in **2**.

Problem 10A-6. Recording Disposals *(L.O. 7, 8)*

Laughlin Designs, Inc. purchased a computer that will assist it in designing factory layouts. The cost of the computer was $23,500. The expected useful life is six years. The company can probably sell the computer for $2,500 at the end of six years.

Required

Prepare journal entries to record the disposal of the computer at the end of the third year, assuming that it was depreciated using the straight-line method and making the following assumptions:

a. The computer is sold for $19,000.
b. It is sold for $10,000.
c. It is traded in on a dissimilar item (equipment) costing $36,000, a trade-in allowance of $17,500 is given, the balance is paid in cash, and gains and losses are recognized.
d. Same as **c** except the trade-in allowance is $11,000.
e. Same as **c** except it is traded for a similar computer and APB accounting rules are followed with regard to the recognition of gains or losses.

f. Same as **d** except it is traded for a similar computer and APB accounting rules are followed with regard to the recognition of gains or losses.
g. Same as **c** except it is traded for a similar computer and gains and losses are not recognized (income tax method).
h. Same as **d** except it is traded for a similar computer and gains and losses are not recognized (income tax method).

Problem 10A-7. Leasehold, Leasehold Improvements, and Amortization of Patent *(L.O. 10)*

Part 1
At the beginning of the fiscal year, Chang Company purchased an eight-year sublease on a warehouse in Peoria for $48,000. Chang will also pay rent of $1,000 a month. The warehouse needs the following improvements to meet Chang's needs:

Lighting fixtures	$18,000
Replacement of a wall	25,000
Office carpet	14,400
Heating system	30,000
Break room	12,200
Loading dock	8,400

The expected life of the loading dock and carpet is eight years. The other items are expected to last ten years. None of the improvements will have a residual value.

Required

Prepare general journal entries to record the following: (a) payment for the sublease; (b) first-year lease payment; (c) payments for the improvements; (d) amortization of leasehold for the year; (e) leasehold improvement amortization for the year.

Part 2
At the beginning of the fiscal year, Ricks Company purchased for $1,030,000 a patent that applies to the manufacture of a unique tamper-proof lid for medicine bottles. Ricks incurred legal costs of $450,000 in successfully defending the patent against use of the lid by a competitor. Ricks estimated that the patent would be valuable for at least ten years. During the first two years of operation, Ricks successfully marketed the lid. At the beginning of the third year, a study appeared in a consumers' magazine showing that the lid could, in fact, be removed by children. As a result, all orders for the lids were canceled, and the patent was rendered worthless.

Required

Prepare journal entries to record the following: (a) purchase of the patent; (b) successful defense of the patent; (c) amortization expense for the first year; and (d) write-off of the patent as worthless.

Problem Set B

Problem 10B-1. Determining Cost of Assets *(L.O. 2, 3, 4, 5)*

Flair Corporation began operation on January 1 of the current year. At the end of the year, the company's auditor discovered that all expenditures involving long-term assets were debited to an account called Fixed Assets. An analysis of the account, which has a balance at the end of the year of $2,644,972, disclosed that it contained the items presented on the following page.

The timber that was cleared from the land was sold to a firewood dealer for $5,000. This amount was credited to Miscellaneous Income. During the construction period, two supervisors devoted their full time to the construction project. These people earn annual salaries of $48,000 and $42,000, respectively. They spent two months on the purchase and preparation of the land, six months on the construction of the building (approximately one-sixth of which was devoted to improvements on the grounds), and one month on installation of machinery. The plant began operation on October 1, and the supervisors returned to their regular duties. Their salaries were debited to Factory Salary Expense.

Cost of land	$ 316,600
Surveying costs	4,100
Transfer of title and other fees required by the county	920
Broker's fees	21,144
Attorney's fees associated with land acquisition	7,048
Cost of removing unusable timber from land	50,400
Cost of grading land	4,200
Cost of digging building foundation	34,600
Architect's fee for building and land improvements (80 percent building)	64,800
Cost of building	710,000
Cost of sidewalks	11,400
Cost of parking lots	54,400
Cost of lighting for grounds	80,300
Cost of landscaping	11,800
Cost of machinery	989,000
Shipping cost on machinery	55,300
Cost of installing machinery	176,200
Cost of testing machinery	22,100
Cost of changes in building due to safety regulations required because of machinery	12,540
Cost of repairing building that was damaged in the installation of machinery	8,900
Cost of medical bill for injury received by employee while installing machinery	2,400
Cost of water damage to building during heavy rains prior to opening the plant for operation	6,820
Account balance	$2,644,972

Required

1. Prepare a schedule with the following column headings: Land, Land Improvements, Buildings, Machinery, and Losses. List the items appropriate to these accounts and sort them out into their proper accounts. Negative amounts should be shown in parentheses. Total the columns.
2. Prepare an entry to adjust the accounts based on all the information given, assuming that the company's accounts have not been closed at the end of the year.
3. Assume that the plant was in operation for three months during the year. Prepare an adjusting entry to record depreciation expense, assuming that the land improvements are depreciated over twenty years with no residual value, that the buildings are depreciated over thirty years with no estimated residual value, and that the machinery is depreciated over twelve years with the estimated residual value equal to 10 percent of cost. The company uses the straight-line method. Round your answers to the nearest dollar.

Problem 10B-2. Comparison of Depreciation Methods *(L.O. 3, 4)*

Riggio Construction Company purchased a new crane for $360,500 at the beginning of year 1. The crane has an estimated residual value of $35,000 and an estimated useful life of six years. The crane is expected to last 10,000 hours. It was used 1,800 hours in year 1; 2,000 in year 2; 2,500 in year 3; 1,500 in year 4; 1,200 in year 5; and 1,000 in year 6.

Required

1. Compute the annual depreciation and carrying value for the new crane for each of the six years (round to nearest dollar where necessary) under each of the following methods: (a) straight-line, (b) production, (c) sum-of-the-years'-digits, (d) double-declining-balance. (Use fractions instead of repeating decimals.)
2. Prepare the adjusting entry that would be made each year to record the depreciation calculated under the straight-line method.
3. Show the balance sheet presentation for the crane after the adjusting entry in year 2 using the straight-line method.

4. What conclusions can you draw from the patterns of yearly depreciation and carrying value in **1**?

Problem 10B-3. Depreciation Methods and Partial Years
(L.O. 4, 5)

Gottlieb Corporation operates four types of equipment. Because of their varied functions, company accounting policy requires the application of four different depreciation methods. Data on this equipment are summarized in the table below.

Assume that production for Equipment 4 was 2,000 hours in 19x5; 4,200 hours in 19x6; and 3,200 hours in 19x7.

Equipment	Date Purchased	Cost	Installation Cost	Estimated Residual Value	Estimated Life	Depreciation Method
1	1/12/x5	$171,000	$ 9,000	$18,000	10 years	Double-declining-balance
2	1/7/x5	230,025	8,250	22,500	6 years	Sum-of-the-years'-digits
3	7/9/x5	191,100	15,900	21,000	10 years	Straight-line
4	10/2/x5	290,700	8,100	33,600	20,000 hours	Production

Required

Assuming that the fiscal year ends December 31, compute the depreciation charges on each type of equipment and in total for 19x5, 19x6, and 19x7 by filling in a table with the headings shown below.

Equipment No.	Computations	Depreciation 19x5	19x6	19x7

Problem 10B-4. Plant Asset Transactions, Revised Depreciation, and Spare Parts
(L.O. 2, 3, 4, 5)

Rita Carrasquel entered the jewelry refinishing business in January 19x1. She was able to purchase refinishing equipment for $59,275 on January 2. It cost her $6,400 to have the equipment moved to her building and $2,340 to have it installed. It cost another $1,585 to adjust the equipment. She estimated that the equipment would have a useful life of ten years and a residual value of $6,000. Small tools were purchased on May 14 at a cost of $580, and regular maintenance of the equipment on September 16 came to $1,485. At the end of the year, an inventory revealed that $240 in small tools were still on hand. During 19x2, small tools of $725 were purchased on April 18, and the physical inventory disclosed $230 on hand at the end of the year. Regular maintenance costs for the equipment expended on October 4 were $2,070. Later in 19x2, it became apparent that the equipment would last a total of only six years instead of the originally estimated ten years, and the estimated residual value at the end of six years would be only $2,500.

Required

1. Prepare general journal entries for 19x1 to record the purchase of the equipment, the costs associated with the purchase, the transaction involving small tools, the upkeep costs, the year-end depreciation charge, and the small tools expense. Carrasquel's company uses the inventory method of recording small tools expense and the straight-line method for computing depreciation expense. Assume that all purchases are made with cash.
2. Prepare general journal entries for 19x2 for small tools, maintenance, and depreciation expense. The depreciation expense should be based on the new estimates regarding the equipment.

Problem 10B-5. Comprehensive Capital and Revenue Expenditure Entries
(L.O. 6, 7)

Beatty's, Inc. operates a chain of self-service gasoline stations in the South. The following transactions describe the capital and revenue expenditures for one station.

Construction on the station was completed on July 1, 1980, at a cost of $710,000. It was estimated that the station would have a useful life of thirty-five years and a residual value of $80,000. On September 15, 1984, scheduled painting and minor repairs affecting the appearance of the station were completed at a cost of $9,300. On July 9, 1985, a new gasoline tank was added at a cost of $160,000. The tank did not add to the useful life of the station, but it did add $22,000 to its estimated residual value. On October 22,

1989, the driveway of the station was resurfaced at a cost of $3,800. The cost of major repairs and renovation, as part of the company's planned maintenance completed on July 3, 1990, was $110,000. It was estimated that this work would extend the life of the station by five years and would not increase the residual value. A change in the routing of a major highway led to the sale of the station on January 2, 1993, for $460,000. The company received $60,000 in cash and a note for the balance.

Required

1. Prepare general journal entries for the following dates: (a) July 1, 1980; (b) September 15, 1984; (c) July 9, 1985; (d) October 22, 1989; and (e) July 3, 1990.
2. Open ledger accounts for Station (143) and for Accumulated Depreciation, Station (144), and post the relevant portions of the entries in **1**.
3. Compute depreciation expense for each year and partial year until the date of sale, assuming that the straight-line method is used and that the company's fiscal year ends on June 30. Enter the amounts in the account for Accumulated Depreciation, Station.
4. Prepare a general journal entry to record the sale of the station on January 2, 1993. Post the relevant portions of the entry to the two accounts opened in **2**.

Problem 10B-6. Recording Disposals *(L.O. 7, 8)*

Pavlic Construction Company purchased a road grader for $58,000. The road grader is expected to have a useful life of five years and a residual value of $4,000 at the end of that time.

Required

Prepare journal entries to record the disposal of the road grader at the end of the second year, assuming that the straight-line method is used and making the following additional assumptions:

a. The road grader is sold for $40,000 cash.
b. It is sold for $32,000 cash.
c. It is traded in on a dissimilar item (machinery) having a price of $66,000, a trade-in allowance of $40,000 is given, the balance is paid in cash, and gains or losses are recognized.
d. It is traded in on a dissimilar item (machinery) having a price of $66,000, a trade-in allowance of $32,000 is given, the balance is paid in cash, and gains or losses are recognized.
e. Same as **c** except it is traded for a similar road grader and Pavlic Construction Company follows APB accounting rules with regard to the recognition of gains or losses.
f. Same as **d** except it is traded for a similar road grader and Pavlic Construction Company follows APB accounting rules with regard to the recognition of gains or losses.
g. Same as **c** except it is traded for a similar road grader and gains or losses are not recognized (income tax purposes).
h. Same as **d** except it is traded for a similar road grader and gains or losses are not recognized (income tax purposes).

Problem 10B-7. Amortization of Exclusive License, Leasehold, and Leasehold Improvements *(L.O. 10)*

Part 1

On January 1, Miracle Games, Inc. purchased the exclusive license to make dolls based on the characters in a new hit television series called "Space Kids." The exclusive license cost $4,200,000, and there was no termination date on the rights. Immediately after signing the contract, the company sued a rival firm that claimed it had already received the exclusive license to the series characters. Miracle Games successfully defended its rights at a cost of $720,000. During the first year and the next, Miracle Games marketed toys based on the series. Because a successful television series lasts about five years, the company felt it could market the toys for three more years. However, before the third year of the series could get under way, a controversy arose between the two stars of the series and the producer. As a result, the stars refused to do the third year and the show was canceled, rendering exclusive rights worthless.

Required

Prepare journal entries to record the following: (a) purchase of the exclusive license; (b) successful defense of the license; (c) amortization expense, if any, for the first year; and (d) write-off of the license as worthless.

Part 2

Evelyn Miripol purchased a six-year sublease on a building from the estate of the former tenant, who had died suddenly. It was a good location for her business, and the annual rent of $7,200, which had been established ten years before, was low for such a good location. The cost of the sublease was $18,900. To use the building, Miripol had to make certain alterations. First she moved some panels at a cost of $3,400 and installed others for $12,200. Then she added carpet, lighting fixtures, and a sign at costs of $5,800, $6,200, and $2,400, respectively. All items except the carpet would last for at least twelve years. The expected life of the carpet was six years. None of the improvements would have a residual value at the end of those times.

Required

Prepare general journal entries to record the following: (a) the payment for the sublease; (b) the payments for the alterations, panels, carpet, lighting fixtures, and sign; (c) the lease payment for the first year; (d) the amortization expense, if any, associated with the sublease; and (e) the amortization expense, if any, associated with the alterations, panels, carpet, lighting fixtures, and sign.

Financial Decision Case

Kho Computer Company
(L.O. 4)

The Kho Computer Company manufactures computers that it leases to customers. On January 2, 19x5 the company completed the manufacture of a computer for a total cost of $380,000. A customer leased the computer on the same day for a five-year period at a monthly rental of $10,000. Although the computer will last longer than five years, it is likely that it will be technologically obsolete by the end of the five-year period. Kho's management estimates that if the computer is obsolete, it can be sold for $40,000 at the end of the lease, and if it is not obsolete, it can be sold for $80,000 because it would probably last for another two years. On the basis of its experience in leasing many computers, management estimates that the expenses associated with the lease of this computer will be as follows:

	Insurance and Property Taxes	Repairs and Maintenance
19x5	$14,000	$ 6,000
19x6	12,800	9,000
19x7	11,600	12,000
19x8	10,400	15,000
19x9	9,200	18,000

Required

1. What estimated useful life and estimated residual value do you recommend that Kho use for the computer? Explain.
2. Prepare two schedules that show for each year the lease revenue, expenses, and income before income taxes. The first schedule should compute depreciation by using the straight-line method, and the second schedule should use the sum-of-the-years'-digits method. Also, show on each schedule for each year the carrying value of the computer at the end of the year, and compute the ratio of income before income taxes to carrying value (return on assets). Round the ratio to one decimal place.
3. Compare the two schedules in **2**, and discuss the results. Which of the methods do you feel produces the most realistic pattern of income before taxes, and why?
4. If you were asked to determine the amount of cash generated each year from this lease (cash received minus cash disbursed), what effect, if any, would the method of depreciation have on your computations?

Answers to Self-Test

1. b	3. a	5. c	7. b	9. c
2. a	4. d	6. a	8. b	10. a

Omit Payroll Registers
Employee Earnings Record

CHAPTER 11

Current Liabilities

LEARNING OBJECTIVES

1. *Explain how the issues of recognition, valuation, and classification apply to liabilities.*
2. *Identify, compute, and record definitely determinable and estimated current liabilities.*
3. *Define* contingent *liability.*
4. *Identify and compute the liabilities associated with payroll accounting.*
5. *Record transactions associated with payroll accounting.*

Liabilities are one of the three major parts of the balance sheet. The two major kinds of liabilities are current and long-term liabilities. This chapter deals with the nature and measurement of current liabilities. The subject of long-term liabilities is covered later in the book. Because a number of current liabilities arise through the payroll process, the fundamentals of payroll accounting are also presented in this chapter. After studying this chapter, you should be able to meet the learning objectives listed on the left.

DECISION POINT

USAir Group Inc.[1]

■ **Liabilities** are the result of a company's past transactions; they are legal obligations for the future payment of assets or the future performance of services. For example, at the end of 1990, USAir Group Inc., a major U.S. airline with total assets of $6,574 million, had Accounts Payable of $474 million and Accrued Expenses of $815 million, most of which would require an outlay of cash in 1991. In addition, Traffic Balances Payable and Unused Tickets were listed at $481 million. The unused tickets represent future services that must be performed. Air travel must be provided to people who have bought tickets, or the value of the tickets must be refunded if they are not used. These are regarded as **current liabilities** because they are debts and obligations that are expected to be satisfied in one year or within the normal operating cycle, whichever is longer. USAir's management incurred these debts to provide for the smooth operation of the business. Thus, it must plan to pay or to satisfy these obligations out of current assets or with cash generated by the company's operations.

USAir also has **long-term liabilities** of $2,263 million. These liabilities are not due during the next year or normal operating cycle. Management's purpose in incurring these liabilities is very different from its purpose in incurring current liabilities. Long-term liabilities are used to finance long-term assets, such as aircraft. Management has many options for financing the business through current liabilities and long-term liabilities. This chapter and the chapter on long-term liabilities explore these options from the accounting point of view. ■

1. Information excerpted from the 1990 annual report of USAir.

Nature and Measurement of Liabilities

OBJECTIVE 1
Explain how the issues of recognition, valuation, and classification apply to liabilities

In previous chapters, the issues of recognition, valuation, and classification have been applied to transactions involving assets. These issues apply equally to liabilities.

Recognition of Liabilities

Timing is important in the recognition of liabilities. Very often failure to record a liability in an accounting period goes along with failure to record an expense. Thus, it leads to an understatement of expense and an overstatement of income. Liabilities are recorded when an obligation occurs. This rule is harder to apply than it might appear. When a transaction obligates the company to make future payments, a liability arises and is recognized, as when goods are bought on credit. However, current liabilities often are not represented by a direct transaction. One of the major reasons for adjusting entries at the end of an accounting period is to recognize unrecorded liabilities. Among these accrued liabilities are salaries payable and interest payable. Other liabilities that can only be estimated, such as taxes payable, must also be recognized by adjusting entries.

On the other hand, companies often enter into agreements for future transactions. For instance, a company may agree to pay an executive $50,000 a year for a period of three years, or a public utility may agree to buy an unspecified quantity of coal at a certain price over the next five years. These contracts, though they are definite commitments, are not considered liabilities because they are for future—not past—transactions. As there is no current obligation, no liability is recognized.

Valuation of Liabilities

Liabilities are generally valued on the balance sheet at the amount of money needed to pay the debt or at the fair market value of goods or services to be delivered. For most liabilities the amount is definitely known, but for some it must be estimated. For example, an automobile dealer who sells a car with a one-year warranty must provide parts and services during the year. The obligation is definite because the sale of the car has occurred, but the amount must be estimated. Additional disclosures of the market value of liabilities may be required in the notes to the financial statement as explained below.

Classification of Liabilities

The classification of current liabilities directly matches the classification of current assets. Two important measures of liquidity are working capital (current assets less current liabilities) and the current ratio (current assets divided by current liabilities). Long-term liabilities are usually designated in such a way that the reader of the financial statement can compute the debt to equity ratio.

Disclosure of Liabilities

Because it found past disclosure practices inadequate, the FASB required corporations to increase disclosure about all their financial instruments.[2] **Financial**

2. *Statement of Financial Accounting Standards No. 105,* "Disclosure of Information About Financial Instruments with Concentrations of Credit Risk" (Stamford, Conn.: Financial Accounting Standards Board, 1990).

instruments include cash, evidences of ownership such as common stock, and any contract that results in an asset to one entity and a liability to another entity. As such, they include financial assets. However, the FASB is more concerned with the disclosure of financial liabilities, such as loans, mortgages, bonds, leases, and other forms of debt financing, especially **off-balance-sheet liabilities**, which do not appear on the balance sheet as liabilities but that expose the company to possible loss through a credit risk. A credit risk is the possibility, however remote, that a loss might be incurred through failure of another party to perform according to the terms of a financial instrument. For example, if Maas Company guarantees the loan of Chona Corporation, no liability is recorded in the records of Maas Company, even though if Chona fails to pay the loan, Maas will have to pay it and will suffer a loss. The FASB requires that this kind of agreement be disclosed in the notes to Maas Company's financial statements.

The FASB requires that all companies disclose information about the fair value of their financial instruments, both assets and liabilities.[3] Quoted market prices generally provide the most reliable measure of fair value. Market price is defined as the amount at which a single trading unit of the instrument could be sold or bought between a willing buyer and a willing seller, excluding a forced or liquidation sale. For instance, if the fair value of a company's outstanding debt changes because of changing interest rates (see the chapter on long-term liabilities), the amount of the company's liability would not change on the balance sheet but the disclosure in the notes to the financial statements would show the current fair value. If market prices are not available, estimates based on the present value of future cash flows (discussed later in this chapter) or the market value of similar instruments could be used.

Common Categories of Current Liabilities

Current liabilities usually equal about one-fourth to one-third of total assets across all industries. They fall into two major groups: (1) definitely determinable liabilities and (2) estimated liabilities. Discussions of each follow.

Definitely Determinable Liabilities

OBJECTIVE 2
Identify, compute, and record definitely determinable and estimated current liabilities

Current liabilities that are set by contract or by statute and can be measured exactly are called **definitely determinable liabilities**. The accounting problems connected with these liabilities are to determine the existence and amount of the liability and to see that the liability is recorded properly. Definitely determinable liabilities include trade accounts payable, bank loans and commercial paper, notes payable, accrued liabilities, dividends payable, sales and excise taxes payable, current portions of long-term debt, payroll liabilities, and unearned or deferred revenues.

Accounts Payable. Accounts payable, sometimes called trade accounts payable, are short-term obligations to suppliers for goods and services. The amount in the Accounts Payable account is generally supported by an accounts payable subsidiary ledger, which contains an individual account for each person or company to whom money is owed.

3. *Statement of Financial Accounting Standards No. 107,* "Disclosures About Fair Value of Financial Instruments" (Stamford, Conn.: Financial Accounting Standards Board, 1991).

Bank Loans and Commercial Paper. Management will often establish a **line of credit** from a bank; this arrangement allows the company to borrow funds when they are needed to finance current operations. For example, Nordstrom, a chain of quality department stores, reported in its 1990 annual report that the finance division had "a $150 [million] unsecured line of credit with a group of commercial banks which is available as liquidity support for short-term debt."[4] A promissory note for the full amount of the line of credit is signed when the line of credit is granted, but the company has great flexibility in using the line of credit. The company can increase its borrowing up to the limit when it needs cash and reduce the amount borrowed when it obtains cash. Both the amount borrowed and the interest rate charged by the bank may change on a daily basis. The bank may require the company to meet certain financial goals (such as maintaining certain profit margins, current ratios, or debt to equity ratios) to retain the line of credit. Companies with excellent credit ratings may borrow short-term funds by issuing **commercial paper.** Commercial paper constitutes unsecured loans that are sold to the public, usually through professionally managed investment firms. The portion of a line of credit that has currently been borrowed and the amount of commercial paper issued are usually combined with notes payable in the current liabilities section of the balance sheet. Details are disclosed in a note to the financial statements.

Notes Payable. Short-term notes payable, which also arise out of the ordinary course of business, are obligations represented by promissory notes. These notes may be used to secure bank loans, to pay suppliers for goods and services, and to secure credit from other sources.

As with notes receivable, presented in the chapter on short-term liquid assets, the interest on notes may be stated separately on the face of the note (Case 1 in Figure 11-1), or it may be deducted in advance by discounting it from the face value of the note (Case 2). The entries to record the note in each case are as follows:

Case 1—Interest stated separately

Aug. 31	Cash	5,000	
	Notes Payable		5,000
	To record 60-day, 12% promissory note with interest stated separately		

Case 2—Interest in face amount

Aug. 31	Cash	4,900	
	Discount on Notes Payable	100	
	Notes Payable		5,000
	To record 60-day, 12% promissory note with interest included in face amount		

$$\$5{,}000 \times \frac{60}{360} \times .12 = \$100$$

Note that in Case 1 the money borrowed equaled the face value of the note, whereas in Case 2 the money borrowed ($4,900) was less than the face value ($5,000) of the note. The amount of the discount equals the amount of the interest for sixty days.[5] Discount on Notes Payable is a contra account to Notes Payable and is deducted from Notes Payable on the balance sheet.

4. Excerpted from the 1990 annual report of Nordstrom.
5. Note that although the dollar amount of interest on each of these notes is the same, the effective interest rate is slightly different in each case because the amount borrowed is slightly different ($5,000 in Case 1 versus $4,900 in Case 2).

Figure 11-1. Two Promissory Notes: One with Interest Stated Separately; One with Interest in Face Amount

Case 1 ***Interest Stated Separately***

Chicago, Illinois August 31, 19xx

Sixty days after date I promise to pay First Federal Bank the sum of $5,000 with interest at the rate of 12% per annum.

Sandra Caron
Caron Corporation

Case 2 ***Interest in Face Amount***

Chicago, Illinois August 31, 19xx

Sixty days after date I promise to pay First Federal Bank the sum of $5,000.

Sandra Caron
Caron Corporation

On October 30, when the note is paid, each alternative is recorded as follows:

Case 1—Interest stated separately

Oct.	30	Notes Payable	5,000	
		Interest Expense	100	
		Cash		5,100
		Payment of note with interest stated separately		

Case 2—Interest in face amount

Oct.	30	Notes Payable	5,000	
		Cash		5,000
		Payment of note with interest included in face amount		
	30	Interest Expense	100	
		Discount on Notes Payable		100
		Interest expense on matured note		

Accrued Liabilities. A principal reason for adjusting entries at the end of an accounting period is to recognize and record liabilities that are not already in the accounting records. This practice applies to any type of liability. For example, in previous chapters, adjustments relating to salaries payable were made. As you will see, accrued liabilities can also include estimated liabilities.

Here the focus is on interest payable, a definitely determinable liability. Interest accrues daily on interest-bearing notes. At the end of the accounting period, an adjusting entry should be made in accordance with the matching rule to record the interest obligation up to that point in time. Let us again use the example of the two notes presented above. If we assume that the accounting period ends on September 30, or thirty days after the issuance of the sixty-day notes, the adjusting entries for each case would be as shown on the next page.

Case 1—Interest stated separately

		Debit	Credit
Sept. 30	Interest Expense	50	
	Interest Payable		50
	To record interest expense for 30 days on note with interest stated separately		
	$\$5{,}000 \times \frac{30}{360} \times .12 = \$50$		

Case 2—Interest in face amount

		Debit	Credit
Sept. 30	Interest Expense	50	
	Discount on Notes Payable		50
	To record interest expense for 30 days on note with interest included in face amount		
	$\$5{,}000 \times \frac{30}{360} \times .12 = \$50$		

In Case 2, Discount on Notes Payable will now have a debit balance of $50, which will become interest expense during the next thirty days.

Dividends Payable. Cash dividends are a distribution of earnings by a corporation. The payment of dividends is solely the decision of the corporation's board of directors. A liability does not exist until the board declares the dividends. There is usually a short time between the date of declaration and the date of payment of dividends. During that short time, the dividends declared are current liabilities of the corporation. Accounting for dividends is treated extensively in the chapter on retained earnings and corporate income statements.

Sales and Excise Taxes Payable. Most states and many cities levy a sales tax on retail transactions. There are federal excise taxes on some products, such as automobile tires. The merchant who sells goods subject to these taxes must collect the taxes and remit, or pay, them periodically to the appropriate government agency. The amount of tax collected represents a current liability until it is remitted to the government. For example, assume that a merchant makes a $100 sale that is subject to a 5 percent sales tax and a 10 percent excise tax. Assuming that the sale takes place on June 1, the correct entry to record the sale is as follows:

		Debit	Credit
June 1	Cash	115	
	Sales		100
	Sales Tax Payable		5
	Excise Tax Payable		10
	Sale of merchandise and collection of sales and excise taxes		

The sale is properly recorded at $100, and tax collections are recorded as liabilities to be remitted at the proper time to the appropriate government agency.

Current Portions of Long-Term Debt. If a portion of long-term debt is due within the next year and is to be paid from current assets, then the current portion of long-term debt is properly classified as a current liability. For example, suppose that a $500,000 debt is to be paid in installments of $100,000 per year for the next five years. The $100,000 installment due in the current year should be classified as a current liability. The remaining $400,000 should be classified as a long-term liability. Note that no journal entry is necessary. The total debt of $500,000 is simply reclassified when the financial statements are prepared, as shown at the top of the next page.

Current Liabilities	
Current Portion of Long-Term Debt	$100,000
Long-Term Liabilities	
Long-Term Debt	400,000

Payroll Liabilities. A number of current liabilities are associated with payroll accounting. These liabilities are discussed in the payroll section later in this chapter.

Unearned or Deferred Revenues. **Unearned** or **deferred revenues** represent obligations for goods or services that the company must provide or deliver in a future accounting period in return for an advance payment from a customer. For example, a publisher of a monthly magazine who receives annual subscriptions totaling $240 would make the following entry:

	Debit	Credit
Cash	240	
Unearned Subscriptions		240
Receipt of annual subscriptions in advance		

The publisher now has a liability of $240 that will be reduced gradually as monthly issues of the magazine are mailed, as follows:

	Debit	Credit
Unearned Subscriptions	20	
Subscription Revenues		20
Delivery of monthly magazine issues		

Many businesses, such as repair companies, construction companies, and special-order firms, ask for a deposit or advance from a customer before they will begin work. These advances are also current liabilities until the goods or services are delivered.

Estimated Liabilities

Estimated liabilities are definite debts or obligations of a company for which the exact amount cannot be known until a later date. Since there is no doubt as to the existence of the legal obligation, the primary accounting problem is to estimate and record the amount of the liability. Examples of estimated liabilities are income taxes, property taxes, product warranties, and vacation pay.

Income Tax. The income of a corporation is taxed by the federal government, most state governments, and some cities and towns. The amount of income tax liability depends on the results of operations. Often that is not certain until after the end of the year. However, because income taxes are an expense in the year in which income is earned, an adjusting entry is necessary to record the estimated tax liability. An example of this entry follows:

		Debit	Credit
Dec. 31	Federal Income Tax Expense	53,000	
	Federal Income Tax Payable		53,000
	To record estimated federal income tax		

Remember that sole proprietorships and partnerships do *not* pay income taxes. Their owners must report their share of the firm's income on their individual tax returns.

Property Taxes Payable. Property taxes are taxes levied on real property, such as land and buildings, and on personal property, such as inventory and equipment. Property taxes are a main source of revenue for local governments. Usually they are assessed annually against the property involved. Because the fiscal years of local governments and their assessment dates rarely correspond to those of the firm, it is necessary to estimate the amount of property taxes that applies to each month of the year. Assume, for instance, that a local government has a fiscal year of July 1 to June 30, that its assessment date is November 1 for the current fiscal year that began on July 1, and that its payment date is December 15. Assume also that on July 1, Janis Corporation estimates that its property tax assessment for the coming year will be $24,000. The adjusting entry to be made on July 31, which would be repeated on August 31, September 30, and October 31, would be as follows:

July 31	Property Taxes Expense	2,000	
	Estimated Property Taxes Payable		2,000
	To record estimated property taxes expense for the month $24,000 ÷ 12 months = $2,000		

On November 1, the firm receives a property tax bill for $24,720. The estimate made in July was too low. The monthly charge should have been $2,060 per month. Because the difference between the actual assessment and the estimate is small, the company decides to absorb in November the amount undercharged in the previous four months. Therefore, the property tax expense for November is $2,300 [$2,060 + 4($60)] and is recorded as follows:

Nov. 30	Property Taxes Expense	2,300	
	Estimated Property Taxes Payable		2,300
	To record estimated property taxes		

The Estimated Property Taxes Payable account now has a balance of $10,300. The entry to record payment on December 15 would be made as follows:

Dec. 15	Estimated Property Taxes Payable	10,300	
	Prepaid Property Taxes	14,420	
	Cash		24,720
	Payment of property taxes		

Beginning December 31 and each month afterward until June 30, property tax expense is recorded by a debit to Property Taxes Expense and a credit to Prepaid Property Taxes in the amount of $2,060. The total of these seven entries will reduce the Prepaid Property Taxes account to zero on June 30.

Product Warranty Liability. When a firm places a warranty or guarantee on its product at the time of sale, a liability exists for the length of the warranty. The cost of the warranty is properly debited to an expense account in the period of sale because it is a feature of the product or service sold and thus is included in the price paid by the customer for the product. On the basis of experience, it should be possible to estimate the amount the warranty will cost in the future. Some products or services will require little warranty service; others may require much. Thus, there will be an average cost per product or service.

For example, assume that a muffler company guarantees that it will replace any muffler free of charge if it fails during the time you own your car. The company charges a small service fee for replacing the muffler. This guarantee is an important selling feature for the firm's mufflers. In the past, 6 percent of the mufflers sold have been returned for replacement under the guarantee. The average cost of a muffler is $25. Assume that during July, 350 mufflers were sold. This accrued liability would be recorded as an adjustment at the end of July as follows:

July 31	Product Warranty Expense	525	
	Estimated Product Warranty Liability		525
	To record estimated product warranty expense:		
	Number of units sold	350	
	Rate of replacements under warranty	× .06	
	Estimated units to be replaced	21	
	Estimated cost per unit	× $ 25	
	Estimated liability for product warranty	$525	

When a muffler is returned for replacement under the product warranty, the cost of the muffler is charged against the Estimated Product Warranty Liability account. For example, assume that a customer returns on December 5 with a defective muffler and pays a $10 service fee to have the muffler replaced. Assume that this particular muffler cost $20. The entry is as follows:

Dec. 5	Cash	10	
	Estimated Product Warranty Liability	20	
	Service Revenue		10
	Merchandise Inventory		20
	Replacement of muffler under warranty		

Vacation Pay Liability. In most companies, employees earn the right to paid vacation days or weeks as they work during the year. For example, an employee may earn two weeks of paid vacation for each fifty weeks of work. Therefore, she or he is paid fifty-two weeks' salary for fifty weeks' work. Theoretically, the cost of the two weeks' vacation should be allocated as an expense over the whole year so that month-to-month costs will not be distorted. The vacation pay represents 4 percent (two weeks' vacation divided by fifty weeks) of a worker's pay. Every week worked earns the employee a small fraction (4 percent) of his or her vacation pay. Vacation pay liability can amount to a substantial amount of money. For example, Delta Airlines reported at its 1989 year end a vacation pay liability of $83,083,000.[6]

Suppose that a company with this vacation policy has a payroll of $21,000, of which $1,000 was paid to employees on vacation for the week ended April 20. Since not all employees in every company will collect vacation pay because of turnover and rules regarding term of employment, it is assumed that 75 percent of employees will ultimately collect vacation pay. The computation of vacation pay expense based on the payroll of employees not on vacation ($21,000 − $1,000) is as follows: $20,000 × 4 percent × 75 percent = $600. The entry to record vacation pay expense for the week ended April 20 is as follows:

Apr. 20	Vacation Pay Expense	600	
	Estimated Liability for Vacation Pay		600
	Estimated vacation pay expense		

6. Information excerpted from the 1989 annual report of Delta Airlines.

At the time employees receive their vacation pay, an entry is made debiting Estimated Liability for Vacation Pay and crediting Cash or Wages Payable. For example, the entry to record the $1,000 paid to employees on vacation is as follows:

Aug. 31	Estimated Liability for Vacation Pay	1,000	
	Cash (or Wages Payable)		1,000
	Wages of employees on vacation		

The treatment presented in this example for vacation pay may also be applied to other payroll costs, such as bonus plans and contributions to pension plans.

Contingent Liabilities

OBJECTIVE 3
Define contingent liability

A **contingent liability** is not an existing liability. Rather, it is a potential liability because it depends on a future event arising out of a past transaction. For instance, a construction company that built a bridge may have been sued by the state for using poor materials. The past transaction is the building of the bridge under contract. The future event whose outcome is not known is the lawsuit against the company.

Two conditions have been established by the FASB for determining when a contingency should be entered in the accounting records: (1) the liability must be probable and (2) it must be reasonably estimated.[7] Estimated liabilities such as the estimated income taxes liability, warranty liability, and vacation pay liability that were described earlier in this chapter meet these conditions. Therefore, they are accrued in the accounting records. Potential liabilities that do not meet both conditions (probable and reasonably estimated) are reported in the notes to the financial statements. Losses from such potential liabilities are recorded when the conditions set by the FASB are met. The following example comes from the notes in a recent annual report of Humana Inc., one of the largest health services organizations:

The company continuously evaluates contingencies based upon the best available evidence. In addition, allowances for loss are provided currently for disputed items that have continuing significance, such as certain third-party reimbursements and tax deductions and credits that continue to be claimed in current cost reports and tax returns. Management believes that allowances for loss have been provided to the extent necessary and that its assessment of contingencies is reasonable. To the extent that resolution of contingencies results in amounts that vary from management's estimates, future earnings will be charged or credited. The principal contingencies are described below:

Third-Party Revenues. Cost reimbursements and certain other third-party payments are subject to examination by agencies administering the programs. The Company is contesting certain issues raised in audits of prior-year cost reports.

Income Taxes. The Internal Revenue Service has proposed additional taxes for prior years. The more significant issues include current deductibility of liability insurance premiums paid to an insurance subsidiary, cash-basis tax accounting, depreciable lives and investment tax credits. Settlement of these issues is not expected to have a material adverse effect on earnings. However, deferred tax credits could be reduced as a result of any such resolution.

7. *Statement of Financial Accounting Standards No. 5,* "Accounting for Contingencies" (Stamford, Conn.: Financial Accounting Standards Board, 1975).

Insurance Activities. Certain levels of professional liability risks have been underwritten by a subsidiary. Company hospitals have paid premiums, and the subsidiary has provided loss allowances, based upon actuarially-determined estimates. In addition, the Company's Group Health Division has entered into group accident and health contracts that involve actuarial estimation of medical claims reserves. Actual claim settlements and expenses incident thereto may differ from the provisions for loss.

Litigation. Various suits and claims arising in the ordinary course of business are pending against the Company.[8]

Contingent liabilities may also arise from failure to follow government regulations, from discounted notes receivable, and from guarantees of the debt of other companies.

Introduction to Payroll Accounting

OBJECTIVE 4
Identify and compute the liabilities associated with payroll accounting

A major expense of most companies is the cost of labor and related payroll taxes. In some industries, such as banking and airlines, payroll costs represent more than half the operating costs. Payroll accounting is important because of the amounts of money involved and because the employer must conform to many complex laws governing taxes on payrolls. The employer is liable for meeting reporting requirements and for the money withheld from employees' wages or salaries and for payroll taxes.

Also, the payroll accounting system is subject to complaints and to possible fraud. Every employee must be paid on time and receive a detailed explanation of the amount of his or her pay. The payroll system calls for strong internal control and efficient processing and distribution of checks, as well as accurate reporting to government agencies.

This section will focus on the liabilities, the records, and the control requirements of payroll accounting. Although the illustrations in the following sections are shown in manual format to demonstrate the concepts, most businesses (including small businesses) use a computer to process payroll. The three general kinds of liabilities associated with payroll accounting are (1) liabilities for employee compensation, (2) liabilities for employee payroll withholdings, and (3) liabilities for employer payroll taxes.

It is important to distinguish between employees and independent contractors. Payroll accounting applies only to employees of the company. Employees are paid a wage or salary by the company and are under its direct supervision and control. Independent contractors are not employees of the company, so they are not accounted for under the payroll system. They offer services to the firm for a fee, but are not under its direct control or supervision. Some examples of independent contractors are certified public accountants, advertising agencies, and lawyers.

Liabilities for Employee Compensation

The employer is liable to employees for wages and salaries. The term **wages** refers to payment for the services of employees at an hourly rate or on a piecework basis. The term **salaries** refers to the compensation for employees who are paid at a monthly or yearly rate. Generally, these employees are administrators or managers.

Besides setting minimum wage levels, the federal Fair Labor Standards Act (also called the Wages and Hours Law) regulates overtime pay. Employers who

8. Excerpts from the 1988 annual report of Humana Inc.

take part in interstate commerce must pay overtime for hours worked beyond forty hours a week or more than eight hours a day. This pay must be at least one and one-half times the regular rate. Work on Saturdays, Sundays, or holidays may also call for overtime or some sort of premium pay under separate wage agreements. Overtime pay under union or other employment contracts may exceed these minimums.

For example, suppose that the employment contract of Robert Jones calls for a regular wage of $8 an hour, one and one-half times the regular rate for work over eight hours in any weekday, and twice the regular rate for work on Saturdays, Sundays, or holidays. He works the following days and hours during the week of January 18, 19xx:

Day	Total Hours Worked	Regular Time	Overtime
Monday	10	8	2
Tuesday	8	8	0
Wednesday	8	8	0
Thursday	9	8	1
Friday	10	8	2
Saturday	2	0	2
	47	40	7

Jones's wages would be figured as follows:

Regular time	40 hours × $8	$320.00
Overtime, weekdays	5 hours × $8 × 1.5	60.00
Overtime, weekend	2 hours × $8 × 2	32.00
Total wages		$412.00

Liabilities for Employee Payroll Withholdings

The amount paid to employees is generally less than the wages they earned because the employer is required by law to withhold certain amounts from the employees' wages and send them directly to government agencies to pay taxes owed by the employees. In this group are social security and Medicare taxes, federal income taxes, and state income taxes. Also, certain withholdings are made for the employees' benefit, often at their request. These include pension payments, medical insurance premiums, life insurance premiums, union dues, and charitable contributions. No matter the reason for the withholding from employees' wages, the employer is liable for payment to the proper agency, fund, or organization.

Social Security and Medicare Taxes. With the passage of the United States social security program in the 1930s, the federal government began to take more responsibility for the well-being of its citizens. The social security program offers retirement and disability benefits, survivor's benefits, and hospitalization and other medical benefits. One of the major extensions of the program provides hospitalization and medical insurance for persons over sixty-five (Medicare).

The social security program is financed by taxes on employees, employers, and the self-employed. About 90 percent of the people working in the United States fall under the provisions of this program.

The Federal Insurance Contributions Act (FICA) set up the tax to pay for this program. The 1993 social security tax rate is 6.20 percent and the Medicare tax rate is 1.45 percent each for employers and employees. The taxes are paid by *both* employee and employer on the employee's gross wages or a portion thereof. The social security tax applies to the first $57,600 earned by an employee during the calendar year. The Medicare tax applies to the first $135,000 earned by an employee during the calendar year. This schedule is subject to change by Congress. However, we will use these figures throughout the book.

Tax rates for both the employee and the employer are the same. The employer deducts the employee's taxes from the employee's wages and sends the amount, along with other employees' withholdings of social security and Medicare taxes and the employer's matching taxes, to the government. Because of inflation and rising benefits under the social security system, these provisions are under constant study by Congress. They are subject to change and should be verified each year.

As an example of social security and Medicare taxes, suppose that Robert Jones has earned less than $57,600 this year (including his current pay). The withholding for social security and Medicare taxes on his paycheck this week is ($412.00 × .062) + ($412.00 × .0145), which equals $25.54 + $5.97 for a total of $31.51. The employer must pay equal taxes of $31.51 and remit a total of $63.02 to the government.

Federal Income Tax. The largest deduction from many employees' earnings is their estimated liability for federal income taxes. The system of tax collection for federal income taxes is to "pay as you go." The employer is required to withhold the amount of the taxes from employees' paychecks and turn it over to the Internal Revenue Service.

The amount to be withheld depends in part on the employee's earnings and on the number of the employee's exemptions. All employees are required by law to indicate exemptions by filing a Form W-4 (Employee's Withholding Exemption Certificate). Each employee is entitled to one exemption for himself or herself and one for each dependent.

The Internal Revenue Service provides employers with tables to aid them in computing the amount of withholdings. For example, Figure 11-2 is a withholding table for married employees who are paid weekly. The withholding from Robert Jones's $412.00 weekly earnings is $31.00. The amount is shown in the intersection of columns for four withholding allowances (one for Robert and one for each of his three dependents) and the $410–420 wage bracket. (This table is presented for illustrative purposes only. Actual withholding tables change periodically as changes occur in tax rates and laws.)

State Income Tax. Most states have income taxes, and in most cases the procedures for withholding are similar to those for federal income taxes.

Other Withholdings. Some of the other withholdings, such as for a retirement or pension plan, are required of each employee. Others, such as withholdings for insurance premiums or savings plans, may be requested by the employee. The payroll system must, therefore, accommodate individual employees with regard to withholdings and the records of those withholdings. The employer is liable to account for all withholdings and to make proper remittances.

Computation of an Employee's Take-Home Pay: An Illustration

OBJECTIVE 5
Record transactions associated with payroll accounting

To continue with the example of Robert Jones, let us now compute his take-home pay. We know that his total earnings for the week of January 18 are $412.00, that his social security tax is $25.54 and his Medicare tax is $5.97 (he has not earned over $57,600), and that his federal income tax withholding is $31.00. Assume also that his union dues are $2.00, his medical insurance premiums are $7.60, his life insurance premium is $6.00, he places $15.00 per week in savings bonds, and he contributes $1.00 per week to United Charities. His net (take-home) pay is computed as follows:

Gross earnings		$412.00
Deductions		
Social security tax	$25.54	
Medicare tax	5.97	
Federal income tax withheld	31.00	
Union dues	2.00	
Medical insurance	7.60	
Life insurance	6.00	
Savings bonds	15.00	
United Charities contribution	1.00	
Total deductions		94.11
Net (take-home) pay		$317.89

Payroll Register. The **payroll register** is a detailed listing of the firm's total payroll that is prepared each pay period. A payroll register is presented in Exhibit 11-1. Note that the name, hours, earnings, deductions, and net pay of each employee are listed. Compare the entry for Robert Jones in the payroll register with the January 18 entry in the employee earnings record of Robert Jones (Exhibit 11-2). Except for the first column, which lists the employee names, and the last column, which shows the wage or salary as either sales or office expense,

Figure 11-2. Wage Bracket Table

Weekly Payroll Period–Employee Married												
And the wages are–		And the number of withholding allowances claimed is–										
		0	1	2	3	4	5	6	7	8	9	10 or more
At least	*But less than*	The amount of income tax to be withheld will be–										
$300	$310	$37	$31	$26	$20	$14	$ 9	$ 3	$ 0	$ 0	$ 0	$ 0
310	320	38	33	27	22	16	10	5	0	0	0	0
320	330	40	34	29	23	17	12	6	1	0	0	0
330	340	41	36	30	25	19	13	8	2	0	0	0
340	350	43	37	32	26	20	15	9	4	0	0	0
350	360	44	39	33	28	22	16	11	5	0	0	0
360	370	46	40	35	29	23	18	12	7	1	0	0
370	380	47	42	36	31	25	19	14	8	2	0	0
380	390	49	43	38	32	26	21	15	10	4	0	0
390	400	50	45	39	34	28	22	17	11	5	0	0
400	410	52	46	41	35	29	24	18	13	7	1	0
410	420	53	48	42	37	31	25	20	14	8	3	0
420	430	55	49	44	38	32	27	21	16	10	4	0

Exhibit 11-1. Payroll Register

		Payroll Register								**Pay Period: Week Ended January 18**						
		Earnings			Deductions								Payment		Distribution	
Employee	Total Hours	Regular	Overtime	Gross	Social Security Tax	Medicare Tax	Federal Income Tax	Union Dues	Medical Insurance	Life Insurance	Savings Bonds	Other: A—United Charities	Net Earnings	Check No.	Sales Wages Expense	Office Wages Expense
Linda Duval	40	160.00		160.00	9.92	2.32	11.00		5.80				130.96	923		160.00
John Franks	44	160.00	24.00	184.00	11.41	2.67	14.00	2.00	7.60			A 10.00	136.32	924	184.00	
Samuel Goetz	40	400.00		400.00	24.80	5.80	53.00		10.40	14.00		A 3.00	289.00	925	400.00	
Robert Jones	**47**	**320.00**	**92.00**	**412.00**	**25.54**	**5.97**	**31.00**	**2.00**	**7.60**	**6.00**	**15.00**	**A 1.00**	**317.89**	**926**	**412.00**	
Billie Matthews	40	160.00		160.00	9.92	2.32	14.00		5.80				127.96	927		160.00
Rosaire O'Brian	42	200.00	20.00	220.00	13.64	3.19	22.00	2.00	5.80				173.37	928	220.00	
James Van Dyke	40	200.00		200.00	12.40	2.90	20.00		5.80				158.90	929		200.00
		1,600.00	136.00	1,736.00	107.63	25.17	165.00	6.00	48.80	20.00	15.00	14.00	1,334.40		1,216.00	520.00

the columns are the same. The columns help employers record the payroll in the accounting records and meet legal reporting requirements. The last two columns are needed to divide the expenses in the accounting records into selling and administrative categories.

Recording the Payroll. The journal entry for recording the payroll is based on the column totals from the payroll register. The journal entry to record the payroll of January 18 follows. Note that each account debited or credited is a total from the payroll register. If the payroll register is considered a special-purpose journal like those in the chapter on special-purpose journals, the column totals can be posted directly to the ledger accounts with the correct account numbers shown at the bottom of each column.

Jan.	18	Sales Wages Expense	1,216.00	
		Office Wages Expense	520.00	
		Social Security Tax Payable		107.63
		Medicare Tax Payable		25.17
		Employees' Federal Income Tax Payable		165.00
		Union Dues Payable		6.00
		Medical Insurance Premiums Payable		48.80
		Life Insurance Premiums Payable		20.00
		Savings Bonds Payable		15.00
		United Charities Payable		14.00
		Wages Payable		1,334.40
		Weekly payroll		

Employee Earnings Record. Each employer must keep a record of earnings and withholdings for each employee. Many companies today use computers to maintain these records, but small companies may still use manual records. The manual form of **employee earnings record** used for Robert Jones is shown in Exhibit 11-2. This form is designed to help the employer meet legal reporting requirements. Each deduction must be shown to have been paid to the proper agency and the employee must receive a report of the deductions made each year. Most columns are self-explanatory. Note, however, the column on the far right for cumulative earnings (earnings to date). This record helps the employer comply with the rule of applying social security and Medicare taxes only up to the maximum wage levels. At the end of the year, the employer reports to the employee on Form W-2, the Wage and Tax Statement, the totals of earnings and tax deductions for the year, which the employee uses to complete his or her individual tax return. The employer sends a copy of the W-2 to the Internal

Exhibit 11-2. Employee Earnings Record

Employee Earnings Record

Employee's Name Robert Jones
Address 777 20th Street
Marshall, Michigan 52603
Date of Birth September 20, 1962
Position Sales Assistant

Social Security Number 444-66-9999
Sex Male
Single ____ Married X
Exemptions (W-4) 4
Date of Employment July 15, 1988

Employee No. 705
Weekly Pay Rate
Hourly Rate $8
Date Employment Ended

19xx		Earnings			Deductions									Payment		
Period Ended	Total Hours	Regular	Overtime	Gross	Social Security Tax	Medicare Tax	Federal Income Tax	Union Dues	Medical Insurance	Life Insurance	Savings Bonds	Other: A—United Charities	Net Earnings	Check No.	Cumulative Gross Earnings
Jan. 4	40	320.00	0	320.00	19.84	4.64	17.00	2.00	7.60	6.00	15.00	A 1.00	246.92	717	320.00
11	44	320.00	48.00	368.00	22.82	5.34	23.00	2.00	7.60	6.00	15.00	A 1.00	285.24	822	688.00
18	47	320.00	92.00	412.00	25.54	5.97	31.00	2.00	7.60	6.00	15.00	A 1.00	317.89	926	1,100.00

Revenue Service. Thus, the IRS can check on whether the employee has reported all income earned from that employer.

Liabilities for Employer Payroll Taxes

The payroll taxes discussed so far were deducted from the employee's gross earnings, to be remitted by the employer. In addition to gross wages, there are three major taxes on salaries that the employer must pay: social security and Medicare taxes, the federal unemployment insurance tax, and the state unemployment insurance tax. These taxes are considered operating expenses.

Social Security and Medicare Taxes. The employer must pay social security and Medicare taxes equal to the amount paid by the employees. That is, from the payroll register in Exhibit 11-1, the employer would have to pay a social security tax of $107.63 and a Medicare tax of $25.17.

Federal Unemployment Insurance Tax. The Federal Unemployment Tax Act (FUTA) is another part of the U.S. social security system. It is intended to pay for operating programs to help unemployed workers. In this way, it is different from social security and Medicare taxes and state unemployment taxes. The dollars paid through FUTA (or alternatively, to state unemployment insurance, as explained below) provide for unemployment compensation. Unlike social security and Medicare taxes, which are levied on both employees and employers, the FUTA tax is assessed only against employers.

The amount of tax can vary. Recently it has been 6.2 percent of the first $7,000 earned by each employee. The employer, however, is allowed a credit against this federal tax for unemployment taxes paid to the state. The maximum credit is 5.4 percent of the first $7,000 of each employee's earnings. Most states set their rate at this maximum. Thus, the FUTA tax paid would be .8 percent (6.2 percent – 5.4 percent) of the taxable wages.

State Unemployment Insurance Tax. All state unemployment plans provide for unemployment compensation to be paid to eligible unemployed workers. This compensation is paid out of the fund provided by the 5.4 percent of the first $7,000 earned by each employee. In some states, employers with favorable employment records may be entitled to pay less than the 5.4 percent.

Recording Payroll Taxes. According to Exhibit 11-1, the gross payroll for the week ended January 18 was $1,736.00. Because it was the first month of the year, all employees had accumulated less than the $57,600 and $7,000 maximum taxable salaries. Therefore, the total social security tax was $107.63 and the total Medicare tax was $25.17 (equal to tax on employees); the total FUTA tax was $13.89 (.008 × $1,736.00); and the total state unemployment tax was $93.74 (.054 × $1,736.00). The entry to record this expense and related liability in the general journal is as follows:

Jan. 18	Payroll Tax Expense	240.43	
	Social Security Tax Payable		107.63
	Medicare Tax Payable		25.17
	Federal Unemployment Tax Payable		13.89
	State Unemployment Tax Payable		93.74
	Weekly payroll taxes expense		

Payment of Payroll and Payroll Taxes

After the weekly payroll is recorded, as illustrated earlier, a liability of $1,334.40 exists for wages payable. How this liability will be paid depends on the system used by the company. Many companies use a special payroll account against which payroll checks are drawn. Under this system, a check must first be drawn on the regular checking account for total net earnings for this payroll ($1,334.40) and deposited in the special payroll account before the payroll checks are issued to the employees. If a voucher system is combined with a special payroll account, a voucher for the total wages payable is prepared and recorded in the voucher register as a debit to Payroll Bank Account and a credit to Vouchers Payable.

The combined social security and Medicare taxes (both employees' and employer's share) and the federal income taxes must be paid at least quarterly. More frequent payments are required when the total liability exceeds $500. The federal unemployment insurance taxes are paid yearly if the amount is less than $100. If the liability for FUTA taxes exceeds $100 at the end of any quarter, a payment is necessary. Payment dates vary among the states. Other payroll deductions must be paid in accordance with the particular contracts or agreements involved.

Chapter Review

Review of Learning Objectives

1. **Explain how the issues of recognition, valuation, and classification apply to liabilities.**
   Liabilities represent present legal obligations of the firm for future payment of assets or the future performance of services. They result from past transactions and should be recognized when there is a transaction that obligates the company to make future payments. Liabilities are valued at the amount of money necessary to satisfy the obligation or the fair market value of goods or services that must be delivered. Liabilities are classified as current or long term.
2. **Identify, compute, and record definitely determinable and estimated current liabilities.**
   Two principal categories of current liabilities are definitely determinable liabilities and estimated liabilities. Although definitely determinable liabilities, such as accounts payable, notes payable, dividends payable, accrued liabilities, and the current

portion of long-term debt, can be measured exactly, the accountant must still be careful not to overlook existing liabilities in these categories. Estimated liabilities such as liabilities for income taxes, property taxes, product warranties, and others definitely exist, but the amounts must be estimated and recorded properly.

3. **Define *contingent liability.***
   A contingent liability is a potential liability arising from a past transaction and dependent on a future event. Examples are lawsuits, income tax disputes, discounted notes receivable, guarantees of debt, and the potential cost of changes in government regulations.
4. **Identify and compute the liabilities associated with payroll accounting.**
   Labor costs are a large segment of the total costs of most businesses. In addition, three important categories of liabilities are associated with the payroll. The employer is liable for the compensation to the employee, for withholdings from the employee's gross pay, and for the employer portion of payroll taxes. The most common payroll withholdings are social security and Medicare taxes, federal and state income taxes, and employee-requested withholdings. The principal employer-paid taxes are social security and Medicare (an amount equal to that of the employee) and federal and state unemployment compensation taxes.
5. **Record transactions associated with payroll accounting.**
   The salary and deductions for each employee are recorded each pay period in the payroll register. From the payroll register the details of each employee's earnings are transferred to the employee's earnings record. The column totals of the payroll register are used to prepare a general journal entry that records the payroll and accompanying liabilities. One further general journal entry is needed to record the employer's share of social security and Medicare taxes and the federal and state unemployment taxes.

Review of Concepts and Terminology

The following concepts and terms were introduced in this chapter:

(L.O. 2) **Commercial paper:** A means of borrowing funds by unsecured loans that are sold directly to the public, usually through professionally managed investment firms.

(L.O. 3) **Contingent liability:** A potential liability that depends on a future event arising out of a past transaction.

(L.O. 1) **Current liabilities:** Debts and obligations that are expected to be satisfied in one year or within the normal operating cycle, whichever is longer.

(L.O. 2) **Definitely determinable liabilities:** Current liabilities that are set by contract or by statute and can be measured exactly.

(L.O. 5) **Employee earnings record:** A record of earnings and withholdings for a single employee.

(L.O. 2) **Estimated liabilities:** Definite debts or obligations for which the exact amounts cannot be known until a later date.

(L.O. 1) **Financial instruments:** Cash, evidence of ownership, and any contract that results in an asset in one entity's records and a liability in another entity's records.

(L.O. 1) **Liabilities:** Legal obligations for the future payment of assets or the future performance of services that result from past transactions.

(L.O. 2) **Line of credit:** A preapproved arrangement with a commercial bank that allows a company to borrow funds as it needs cash.

(L.O. 1) **Long-term liabilities:** Debts or obligations that will not be due during the next year or the normal operating cycle.

(L.O. 1) **Off-balance-sheet liabilities:** Agreements that do not show up on the balance sheet as liabilities but that expose the company to possible loss through a credit risk.

(L.O. 5) **Payroll register:** A detailed listing of a firm's total payroll that is prepared each pay period.

(L.O. 4) **Salaries:** Compensation to employees who are paid at a monthly or yearly rate.

(L.O. 4) **Wages:** Payment for services of employees at an hourly rate or on a piecework basis.

(L.O. 2) **Unearned or deferred revenues:** Revenues received in advance for which the goods will not be delivered nor the services performed during the current accounting period.

Self-Test

Test your knowledge of the chapter by choosing the best answer for each of the following items.

(L.O. 1) 1. Failure to record a liability will probably
   a. have no effect on net income.
   b. result in overstated net income.
   c. result in overstated total assets.
   d. result in overstated total liabilities and owner's equity.

(L.O. 2) 2. Which of the following is most likely to be a definitely determinable liability?
   a. Property taxes payable
   b. Product warranty liability
   c. Income taxes payable
   d. Interest payable

(L.O. 2) 3. Which of the following is most likely to be an estimated liability?
   a. Deferred revenues
   b. Vacation pay liability
   c. Current portion of long-term debt
   d. Payroll liabilities

(L.O. 2) 4. The amount received by a borrower on a one-year, $3,000, 10 percent note with interest included in the face value is
   a. $3,000.
   b. $2,700.
   c. $3,300.
   d. $2,990.

(L.O. 2) 5. If product J cost $100 and had a 2 percent failure rate, the estimated warranty expense in a month in which 1,000 units were sold would be
   a. $2,000.
   b. $100.
   c. $20.
   d. $20,000.

(L.O. 2) 6. Of a company's employees, 70 percent typically qualify to receive two weeks' paid vacation per year. The amount of estimated vacation pay liability for a week in which the total payroll is $3,000 is
   a. $2,100.
   b. $42.
   c. $84.
   d. $120.

(L.O. 3) 7. A contingent liability would be recorded in the accounting records if it is
   a. not probable but can be reasonably estimated.
   b. not probable but cannot be estimated.
   c. probable and can be reasonably estimated.
   d. probable but cannot be reasonably estimated.

(L.O. 4) 8. Which of the following is a payroll tax borne by both employee and employer?
   a. Excise tax
   b. Income tax
   c. FUTA tax
   d. Social security and Medicare taxes

(L.O. 4) 9. An employee has gross earnings of $500 and withholdings of $31 for social security tax, $7 for Medicare tax, and $60 for income taxes. The employer pays $31 for social security tax, $7 for Medicare tax, and $20 for unemployment taxes. The total cost of the employee to the employer is
   a. $402.
   b. $500.
   c. $558.
   d. $596.

(L.O. 5) 10. Payroll Tax Expense includes all the following except
   a. Federal Unemployment Tax Payable.
   b. Social Security Tax Payable.
   c. Federal Income Tax Payable.
   d. State Unemployment Tax Payable.

Answers to the Self-Test are at the end of this chapter.

Review Problem
Notes Payable Transactions and End-of-Period Entries

(L.O. 2) McLaughlin, Inc., whose fiscal year ends June 30, completed the following transactions involving notes payable:

May	11	Purchased a small crane by issuing a 60-day, 12 percent note for $54,000. The face of the note does not include interest.
	16	Obtained a $40,000 loan from the bank to finance a temporary increase in receivables by signing a 90-day, 10 percent note. The face value includes interest.
June	30	Made end-of-year adjusting entry to accrue interest expense on 12 percent note.
	30	Made end-of-year adjusting entry to recognize interest expense on 10 percent note.
	30	Made end-of-year closing entry pertaining to interest expense.
July	1	Made appropriate reversing entry.
	10	Paid the note plus interest on the crane purchase.
Aug.	14	Paid off the note to the bank.

Required

1. Prepare general journal entries for the above transactions (journal Page 36).
2. Open general ledger accounts for Notes Payable (212), Discount on Notes Payable (213), Interest Payable (214), and Interest Expense (721). Post the relevant portions of the entries to these general ledger accounts.

Answer to Review Problem

1. Prepare general journal entries.

General Journal **Page 36**

Date		Description	Post. Ref.	Debit	Credit
19xx					
May	11	Equipment		54,000	
		Notes Payable	212		54,000
		Purchase of crane with 60-day, 12% note			
	16	Cash		39,000	
		Discount on Notes Payable	213	1,000	
		Notes Payable	212		40,000
		Loan from bank obtained by signing 90-day, 10% note; discount $40,000 × .10 × 90/360 = $1,000			
June	30	Interest Expense	721	900	
		Interest Payable	214		900
		To accrue interest expense $54,000 × .12 × 50/360 = $900			
	30	Interest Expense	721	500	
		Discount on Notes Payable	213		500
		To recognize interest on note $1,000 × 45/90 = $500			
	30	Income Summary		1,400	
		Interest Expense	721		1,400
		To close Interest Expense			

(continued)

Date		Description	Post. Ref.	Debit	Credit
		General Journal			**Page 36**
July	1	Interest Payable	214	900	
		Interest Expense	721		900
		To reverse interest expense accrual			
	10	Notes Payable	212	54,000	
		Interest Expense	721	1,080	
		Cash			55,080
		Payment of note on equipment			
		$54,000 × .12 × 60/360 = $1,080			
Aug.	14	Notes Payable	212	40,000	
		Cash			40,000
		Payment of bank loan			
	14	Interest Expense	721	500	
		Discount on Notes Payable	213		500
		Interest expense on matured note			
		$1,000 − $500 = $500			

2. Open general ledger accounts and post the relevant amounts.

Notes Payable — Account No. 212

Date		Item	Post. Ref.	Debit	Credit	Balance Debit	Balance Credit
May	11		J36		54,000		54,000
	16		J36		40,000		94,000
July	10		J36	54,000			40,000
Aug.	14		J36	40,000			—

Discount on Notes Payable — Account No. 213

Date		Item	Post. Ref.	Debit	Credit	Balance Debit	Balance Credit
May	16		J36	1,000		1,000	
June	30		J36		500	500	
Aug.	14		J36		500	—	

Interest Payable — Account No. 214

Date		Item	Post. Ref.	Debit	Credit	Balance Debit	Balance Credit
June	30		J36		900		900
July	1		J36	900			—

(continued)

Interest Expense **Account No. 721**

Date		Item	Post. Ref.	Debit	Credit	Balance Debit	Balance Credit
June	30		J36	900		900	
	30		J36	500		1,400	
	30		J36		1,400	—	
July	1		J36		900		900
	10		J36	1,080		180	
Aug.	14		J36	500		680	

Chapter Assignments

Questions

1. What are liabilities?
2. Why is the timing of liability recognition important in accounting?
3. At the end of the accounting period, Janson Company had a legal obligation to accept delivery and pay for a truckload of hospital supplies the following week. Is this legal obligation a liability?
4. Ned Johnson, a star college basketball player, received a contract from the Midwest Blazers to play professional basketball. The contract calls for a salary of $300,000 a year for four years, dependent on his making the team in each of those years. Should this contract be considered a liability and recorded on the books of the basketball team?
5. What is a financial instrument? Give three examples.
6. What are off-balance-sheet liabilities? Give an example.
7. What is the rule for classifying a liability as current?
8. What are a line of credit and commercial paper? Where do they appear on the balance sheet?
9. Where should the Discount on Notes Payable account appear on the balance sheet?
10. When should a portion of long-term debt be classified as a current liability?
11. Why are deferred revenues classified as liabilities?
12. What is definite about an estimated liability?
13. Why are income taxes payable considered to be estimated liabilities?
14. When does a company incur a liability for a product warranty?
15. What is a contingent liability, and how does it differ from an estimated liability?
16. What are some examples of contingent liabilities? For what reason is each a contingent liability?
17. Why is payroll accounting important?
18. How does an employee differ from an independent contractor?
19. Who pays the social security and Medicare taxes?
20. What role does the W-4 form play in determining the withholding for estimated federal income taxes?
21. What withholdings might an employee voluntarily request?
22. Why is an employee earnings record necessary, and how does it relate to the W-2 form?
23. How can the payroll register be used as a special-purpose journal?
24. What are three types of employer-related payroll liabilities?
25. A bank is offering Diane Wedge two alternatives for borrowing $2,000. The first alternative is a $2,000, 12 percent, 30-day note. The second alternative is a $2,000, 30-day note discounted at 12 percent. (a) What entries are required by Diane Wedge to record the two loans? (b) What entries are needed by Diane to record the payment of the two loans? (c) Which alternative favors Diane, and why?

Communication Skills Exercises

Communication 11-1. Identification of Current Liabilities
(L.O. 2)

Several businesses and organizations and a current liability from the balance sheet of each are listed below. Explain the nature of each current liability (whether it is a definitely determinable or an estimated liability), how each arose, and how the obligation is likely to be fulfilled.

Institute of Management Accountants: Deferred Revenues—Membership Dues
The Foxboro Company: Advances on Sales Contracts
UNC Incorporated: Current Portion of Long-Term Debt
Hurco Companies, Inc.: Accrued Warranty Expense
Affiliated Publications, Inc.: Deferred Subscription Revenues
Geo. A Hormel & Company: Accrued Advertising

Communication 11-2. Ethical Dilemma
(L.O. 4)

Tower Restaurant is a large seafood restaurant in the suburbs of Chicago. Last summer, Joe Murray, an accounting student at the local college, secured a full-time accounting job at the restaurant. Joe felt fortunate to have a good job that accommodated his class schedule because the local economy was very bad. After a few weeks on the job, Joe realized that his boss, the owner of the business, was paying the kitchen workers in cash and was not withholding federal and state income taxes or social security and Medicare taxes. Joe understands that federal and state laws require that these taxes be withheld and paid in a timely manner to the appropriate agency. Joe also realizes that if he raises this issue, he may lose his job. What alternatives are available to Joe? What action would you take if you were in Joe's position? Why did you make this choice?

Communication 11-3. Basic Research Skills
(L.O. 2, 3)

Your school library has indexes for business periodicals in which you can look up articles on topics of interest. Three of the most important of these indexes are *Business Periodicals Index,* the *Wall Street Journal Index,* and the *Accountants' Index.* Using one or more of these indexes, locate and photocopy two articles related to bank financing, commercial paper, product warranties, airline frequent flyer plans, or contingent liabilities. Keep in mind that you may have to look under related topics to find an article. For example, to find articles about contingent liabilities, you might look under litigation, debt guarantees, environmental losses, or other topics. For each of the two articles, write a short summary and tell how it relates to accounting for the topic as described in the text. Be prepared to discuss your results in class.

Classroom Exercises

Exercise 11-1. Interest Expense: Interest Not Included in Face Value of Note
(L.O. 2)

On the last day of October, Ostrand Company borrows $30,000 on a bank note for sixty days at 12 percent interest. Assume that interest is not included in the face amount. Prepare the following general journal entries: (1) October 31, recording of note; (2) November 30, accrual of interest expense; (3) November 30, closing entry; (4) December 1, reversing entry; (5) December 30, payment of note plus interest.

Exercise 11-2. Interest Expense: Interest Included in Face Value of Note
(L.O. 2)

Assume the same facts as in Exercise 11-1, except that interest is included in the face amount of the note and the note is discounted at the bank on October 31. Prepare the following general journal entries: (1) October 31, recording of note; (2) November 30, recognize interest accrued on note; (3) November 30, closing entry; (4) December 30, payment of note and recording of interest expense.

Exercise 11-3.
Sales and Excise Taxes
(L.O. 2)

Alert Dial Service billed its customers for a total of $980,400 for the month of August, including 9 percent federal excise tax and 5 percent sales tax.

1. Determine the proper amount of revenue to report for the month.
2. Prepare a general journal entry to record the revenue and related liabilities for the month.

Exercise 11-4.
Product Warranty Liability
(L.O. 2)

Keystone Company manufactures and sells electronic games. Each game costs $25 to produce and sells for $45. In addition, each game carries a warranty that provides for free replacement if it fails for any reason during the two years following the sale. In the past, 7 percent of the games sold had to be replaced under the warranty. During July, Keystone sold 26,000 games and 2,800 games were replaced under the warranty.

1. Prepare a general journal entry to record the estimated liability for product warranties during the month.
2. Prepare a general journal entry to record the games replaced under warranty during the month.

Exercise 11-5.
Vacation Pay Liability
(L.O. 2)

Crosstown Corporation currently allows each employee three weeks' paid vacation after working at the company for one year. On the basis of studies of employee turnover and previous experience, management estimates that 65 percent of the employees will qualify for vacation pay this year.

1. Assume that Crosstown's July payroll is $600,000, of which $40,000 is paid to employees on vacation. Figure the estimated employee vacation benefit for the month.
2. Prepare a general journal entry to record the employee benefit for July.
3. Prepare a general journal entry to record the pay to employees on vacation.

Exercise 11-6.
Estimated Liability
(L.O. 2)

Great Plains Airways has initiated a frequent flyer program in which enrolled passengers accumulate miles of travel that may be redeemed for rewards such as free trips or upgrades from coach to first class. Great Plains estimates that approximately 2 percent of its passengers are traveling for free as a result of this program. During 19x1, Great Plains Airways had total revenues of $16,000,000,000.

In January 19x2, passengers representing tickets of $300,000 flew free. Prepare the December 19x1 year-end adjusting entry to record the estimated liability for this program and the January 19x2 entry for the free tickets used. Can you suggest how these transactions would be recorded if the estimate of the free tickets were to be considered a deferred revenue (revenue received in advance) rather than an estimated liability? How is each treatment an application of the matching rule?

Exercise 11-7.
Social Security, Medicare, and Unemployment Taxes
(L.O. 4)

Sentinal Company is subject to a 5.4 percent state unemployment insurance tax and a .8 percent federal unemployment insurance tax after credits. Currently, both federal and state unemployment taxes apply to the first $7,000 earned by each employee. Social security and Medicare taxes in effect at this time are 6.20 and 1.45 percent, respectively, for both employee and employer on the first $57,600 (social security) and $135,000 (Medicare) earned by each employee during this year. During the current year, the cumulative earnings for each employee of the company are as follows:

Employee	Cumulative Earnings	Employee	Cumulative Earnings
Battles, W.	$28,620	Liu, K.	$ 5,120
Carlson, A.	5,260	Lopez, M.	6,420
D'Amico, T.	32,820	Maguire, T.	51,650
Essex, M.	30,130	Palermo, P.	32,100
Hyde, R.	60,000	Stein, K.	36,645
Lindstrom, D.	16,760	Zeller, C.	5,176

1. Prepare and complete a schedule with the following columns: Employee Name, Cumulative Earnings, Earnings Subject to Social Security Tax, Earnings Subject to Medicare Tax, and Earnings Subject to Unemployment Taxes. Total the columns.

2. Compute the social security and Medicare taxes and the federal and state unemployment taxes for Sentinal Company.

Exercise 11-8.
Net Pay Calculation and Payroll Entries
(L.O. 4, 5)

Marge Fender is an employee whose overtime pay is regulated by the Fair Labor Standards Act. Her hourly rate is $8, and during the week ended July 11, she worked forty-two hours. Marge claims two exemptions on her W-4 form. So far this year she has earned $8,650. Each week $12 is deducted from her paycheck for medical insurance.

1. Compute the following items related to the pay for Marge Fender for the week of July 11: (a) gross pay, (b) social security and Medicare taxes (assume rates of 6.20 percent and 1.45 percent, respectively), (c) federal income tax withholding (use Figure 11-2), and (d) net pay.
2. Prepare a general journal entry to record the wages expense and related liabilities for Marge Fender for the week ended July 11.

Exercise 11-9.
Payroll Transactions
(L.O. 4, 5)

Clarence Henry earns a salary of $60,000 per year. Social security and Medicare taxes are 6.20 percent and 1.45 percent, respectively, up to $57,600 (social security) and $135,000 (Medicare) for each employee. Federal unemployment insurance taxes are 6.2 percent of the first $7,000; however, a credit is allowed equal to the state unemployment insurance taxes of 5.4 percent on the $7,000. During the year, $15,000 was withheld for federal income taxes.

1. Prepare a general journal entry summarizing the payment of $60,000 to Henry during the year.
2. Prepare a general journal entry summarizing the employer payroll taxes on Henry's salary for the year.
3. Determine the total cost paid by Clarence Henry's employer to employ Henry for the year.

Interpretation Cases from Business

ICB 11-1.
Trans World Airlines, Inc. (TWA)[9]
(L.O. 1, 2)

Trans World Airlines, Inc. is a major airline that experienced financial difficulties in 1988 and 1989. In TWA's 1989 annual report, management refers to the company's deteriorating liquidity situation as follows:

> TWA's net working capital deficit was $55.5 million at December 31, 1989, representing a reduction of $82.6 million from net working capital of $27.1 million at December 31, 1988. Working capital deficits are not unusual in the airline industry because of the large advance ticket sales current liability account.

The company's current liabilities and current assets at December 31 for the two years are as follows (in thousands):

	1989	1988
Current liabilities:		
Current maturities of long-term debt	$ 127,301	$ 242,914
Current obligations under capital leases	93,194	60,574
Advance ticket sales	276,549	280,206
Accounts payable, principally trade	387,256	337,460
Accounts payable to affiliated companies	8,828	69,697
Securities sold, not yet purchased	82,302	240,044
Accrued expenses:		
Employee compensation and vacations earned	148,175	128,902
Contributions to retirement and pension trusts	14,711	36,766
Interest on debt and capital leases	86,761	78,795
Taxes	33,388	29,401
Other accrued expenses	122,295	140,320
Total	$1,380,760	$1,645,079

9. Information excerpted from the 1989 annual report of Trans World Airlines, Inc.

	1989	1988
Current assets:		
Cash and cash equivalents	$ 454,415	$ 632,311
Marketable securities	10,355	77,556
Receivables, less allowance for doubtful accounts, $13,432 in 1989 and $14,132 in 1988	435,061	427,092
Receivables from affiliated companies	15,506	—
Due from brokers	70,636	233,050
Spare parts, materials, and supplies, less allowance for obsolescence, $38,423 in 1989 and $32,380 in 1988	227,098	193,550
Prepaid expenses and other	112,232	108,667
Total	$1,325,303	$1,672,226

Required

1. Identify any current liabilities that do not require a current outlay of cash and identify any current estimated liabilities for 1989 and 1988. Why is management not worried about the cash flow consequences of advance ticket sales?
2. For 1989 and 1988, which current assets will not generate cash inflow, and which will most likely be available to pay for the remaining current liabilities? Compare the amount of these current assets to the amount of current liabilities other than those identified in **1** as not requiring a cash outlay.
3. In light of the calculations in **2**, comment on TWA's liquidity position for 1989 and 1988, and identify several alternative sources of additional cash.

ICB 11-2.
Texaco, Inc.[10]
(L.O. 3)

Texaco, one of the largest integrated oil companies in the world, reported its loss of the largest damage judgment in history in its 1986 annual report as follows:

Note 17. Contingent Liabilities
Pennzoil Litigation
State Court Action. On December 10, 1985, the 151st District Court of Harris County, Texas, entered judgment for Pennzoil Company of $7.5 billion actual damages, $3 billion punitive damages, and approximately $600 million prejudgment interest in *Pennzoil Company v. Texaco, Inc.*, an action in which Pennzoil claims that Texaco, Inc., tortiously interfered with Pennzoil's alleged contract to acquire a 3/7ths interest in Getty. Interest began accruing on the judgment at the simple rate of 10% per annum from the date of judgment. Texaco, Inc., believes that there is no legal basis for the judgment, which it believes is contrary to the evidence and applicable law. Texaco, Inc., is pursuing all available remedies to set aside or to reverse the judgment.

* * *

The outcome of the appeal on the preliminary injunction and the ultimate outcome of the Pennzoil litigation are not presently determinable, but could have a material adverse effect on the consolidated financial position and the results of the consolidated operations of Texaco, Inc.

At December 31, 1986, Texaco's retained earnings were $12.882 billion, and its cash and marketable securities totaled $3.0 billion. The company's net income for 1986 was $.725 billion.

After a series of court reversals and filing for bankruptcy in 1987, Texaco announced in December 1987 an out-of-court settlement with Pennzoil for $3.0 billion. Although less than the original amount, it is still the largest damage payment in history.

Required

1. The FASB has established two conditions that a contingent liability must meet before it is recorded in the accounting records. What are the two conditions? Does the situation described in "Note 17. Contingent Liabilities" meet those conditions? Explain your answer.

10. Information excerpted from the 1986 annual report of Texaco, Inc.

2. Do the events of 1987 change your answer to **1**? Explain your answer and show any journal entry that would result.
3. What will be the effect of the settlement on Texaco's retained earnings, cash and marketable securities, and net income?

Problem Set A

Problem 11A-1. Notes Payable Transactions and End-of-Period Entries *(L.O. 2)*

Landover Corporation, whose fiscal year ends June 30, completed the following transactions involving notes payable:

May	11	Signed a 90-day, 12 percent, $66,000 note payable to Village Bank for a working capital loan. The face value included interest. Proceeds received were $64,020.
	21	Obtained a sixty-day extension on an $18,000 trade account payable owed to a supplier by signing a 60-day, $18,000 note. Interest is in addition to the face value, at the rate of 14 percent.
June	30	Made end-of-year adjusting entry to accrue interest expense on 14 percent note.
	30	Made end-of-year adjusting entry to recognize interest expired on 12 percent note.
	30	Made end-of-year closing entry pertaining to interest expense.
July	1	Made appropriate reversing entry.
	20	Paid off the note plus interest due the supplier.
Aug.	9	Paid amount due bank on 90-day note.

Required

1. Prepare general journal entries for the notes payable transactions (journal Page 28).
2. Open general ledger accounts for Notes Payable (212), Discount on Notes Payable (213), Interest Payable (214), and Interest Expense (721). Post the relevant portions of the entries to these general ledger accounts.

Problem 11A-2. Property Tax and Vacation Pay Liabilities *(L.O. 2)*

Kubek Corporation prepares monthly financial statements and ends its fiscal year on June 30, the same as the local government. In July 19x1, your first month as accountant for the company, you find that the company has not previously accrued estimated liabilities. In the past, the company, which has a large property tax bill, has charged property taxes to the month in which the bill is paid. The tax bill for the year ended June 30, 19x1 was $72,000, and it is estimated that the tax will increase by 8 percent for the year ending June 30, 19x2. The tax bill is usually received on September 1, to be paid November 1.

You also discover that the company allows employees who have worked for the company for one year to take two weeks' paid vacation each year. The cost of these vacations has been charged to expense in the month of payment. Approximately 80 percent of the employees qualify for this benefit. You suggest to management that proper accounting treatment of these expenses is to spread their cost over the entire year. Management agrees and asks you to make the necessary adjustments.

Required

1. Figure the proper monthly charge to property tax expense, and prepare general journal entries for the following:

July	31	Accrual of property tax expense
Aug.	31	Accrual of property tax expense
Sept.	30	Accrual of property tax expense (assume actual bill is $81,720)
Oct.	31	Accrual of property tax expense
Nov.	1	Payment of property tax
	30	Recording of property tax expense

2. Assume that the total payroll for July is $1,136,000. This amount includes $42,600 paid to employees on paid vacations. (a) Compute the vacation pay expense for July. (b) Prepare a general journal entry on July 31 to record the accrual of vacation pay expense for July. (c) Prepare a general journal entry, dated July 31, to record the wages of employees on vacation in July (ignore payroll deductions and taxes).

Problem 11A-3. Product Warranty Liability *(L.O. 2)*

Marrero Company is engaged in the retail sale of washing machines. Each machine has a twenty-four-month warranty on parts. If a repair under warranty is required, a charge for the labor is made. Management has found that 20 percent of the machines sold require some work before the warranty expires. Furthermore, the average cost of replacement parts has been $120 per repair. At the beginning of June, the account for the estimated liability for product warranties had a credit balance of $28,600. During June, 112 machines were returned under the warranty. The cost of the parts used in repairing the machines was $17,530, and $18,884 was collected as service revenue for the labor involved. During the month, Marrero Company sold 450 new machines.

Required

1. Prepare general journal entries to record each of the following: (a) the warranty work completed during the month, including related revenue; (b) the estimated liability for product warranties for machines sold during the month.
2. Compute the balance of the Estimated Product Warranty Liability account at the end of the month.

Problem 11A-4. Payroll Entries *(L.O. 4, 5)*

The following payroll totals for the month of April were taken from the payroll register of Coover Corporation: sales salaries, $116,400; office salaries, $57,000; general salaries, $49,600; social security tax withheld, $13,826; Medicare tax withheld, $3,233.50; income taxes withheld, $31,440; medical insurance deductions, $6,580; life insurance deductions, $3,760; salaries subject to unemployment taxes, $156,600.

Required

Prepare general journal entries to record the following: (1) accrual of the monthly payroll, (2) payment of the net payroll, (3) accrual of employer's payroll taxes (assuming social security and Medicare taxes equal to the amounts for employees, a federal unemployment insurance tax of .8 percent, and a state unemployment tax of 5.4 percent), and (4) payment of all liabilities related to the payroll (assuming that all are paid at the same time).

Problem 11A-5. Payroll Register and Related Entries *(L.O. 4, 5)*

Ballini Pasta Company has seven employees. The salaried employees are paid on the last biweekly payday of each month. Employees paid hourly receive a set rate for regular hours plus one-and-one-half times their hourly rate for overtime hours. They are paid every two weeks. The employees and company are subject to social security tax of 6.20 percent and Medicare tax of 1.45 percent, up to a maximum of $57,600 (social security) and $135,000 (Medicare) for each employee. The unemployment insurance tax rates are 5.4 percent for the state and .8 percent for the federal government. The unemployment insurance tax applies to the first $7,000 earned by each employee and is levied only on the employer.

The company maintains a supplemental benefits plan that includes medical insurance, life insurance, and additional retirement funds for employees. Under the plan, each employee contributes 4 percent of her or his gross income as a payroll withholding, and the company matches the amount. Data for the November 30 payroll, the last payday of November, follow:

Employee	Hours		Pay Rate	Cumulative Gross Pay Excluding Current Pay Period	Federal Income Tax To Be Withheld
	Regular	Overtime			
Belmonte, A.	80	5	$ 8.00	$ 4,867.00	$ 71.00
Delmonico, M.	80	4	6.50	3,954.00	76.00
Lascola, R.*	Salary	—	5,000.00	55,000.00	985.00
Pastorius, T.	80	—	5.00	8,250.00	32.00
Scalera, N.*	Salary	—	2,000.00	20,000.00	294.00
Tumillo, D.	80	20	10.00	12,000.00	103.00
Wocolla, S.*	Salary	—	1,500.00	15,000.00	210.00

*Denotes administrative; the rest are sales. R. Lascola's cumulative gross pay includes a $5,000 bonus paid early in the year.

Required

1. Prepare a payroll register for the pay period ended November 30. The payroll register should have the following columns:

Employee	Deductions	Net Pay
Total Hours	Social Security Tax	Distribution
Earnings	Medicare Tax	Sales Wages Expense
Regular	Federal Income Tax	Administrative Salaries Expense
Overtime	Supplemental Benefits Plan	
Gross		
Cumulative		

2. Prepare a general journal entry to record the payroll and related liabilities for deductions for the period ended November 30.
3. Prepare general journal entries to record the employer's payroll taxes and contribution to the supplemental benefits plan.
4. Prepare the November 30 entries (a) to transfer sufficient cash from the company's regular checking account to a special Payroll Disbursement account and (b) to pay the employees.

Problem Set B

Problem 11B-1. Notes Payable Transactions and End-of-Period Entries *(L.O. 2)*

Prentiss Paper Company, whose fiscal year ends December 31, completed the following transactions involving notes payable:

19x1

Nov. 25 Purchased a new loading cart by issuing a 60-day, 10 percent note for $21,600.

Dec. 16 Borrowed $25,000 from the bank to finance inventory by signing a 90-day, 12 percent note. The face value of the note includes interest. Proceeds received were $24,250.

31 Made end-of-year adjusting entry to accrue interest expense.

31 Made end-of-year adjusting entry to recognize interest expired on note.

31 Made end-of-year closing entry pertaining to interest expense.

19x2

Jan. 2 Made appropriate reversing entry.

24 Paid off the loading cart note.

Mar. 16 Paid off the inventory note to the bank.

Required

1. Prepare general journal entries for these transactions (journal Page 41).
2. Open general ledger accounts for Notes Payable (212), Discount on Notes Payable (213), Interest Payable (214), and Interest Expense (721). Post the relevant portions of the entries to these general ledger accounts.

Problem 11B-2. Property Tax and Vacation Pay Liabilities *(L.O. 2)*

Lawrence Corporation accrues estimated liabilities for property taxes and vacation pay. The company's and the government's fiscal years end June 30, 19x1. The property tax for the year ended June 30, 19x1 was $72,000 and is expected to increase 6 percent for the year ended June 30, 19x2. Two weeks' vacation pay is given to each employee after one year of service. Lawrence management estimates that 75 percent of its employees will qualify for this benefit in the current year.

In addition, the following information is available: The property tax bill of $79,104 for the June 30, 19x2 fiscal year was received in September and paid on November 1. Total payroll for July was $196,400, which includes $18,032 paid to employees on paid vacations.

Required

1. Prepare the monthly journal entries to record the property tax for July through November and actual property tax paid.
2. a. Prepare a general journal entry to record the vacation accrual expense for July. (Round to nearest dollar.)
   b. Prepare a general journal entry to record the wages of employees on vacation in July (ignore payroll deductions and taxes).

Problem 11B-3.
Product Warranty Liability
(L.O. 2)

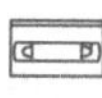

The Citation Company manufactures and sells food processors. The company guarantees the processors for five years. If a processor fails, the food processor is replaced free but the customer is charged a service fee for handling. In the past, management found only 3 percent of the processors sold required replacement under the warranty. The average food processor costs the company $120. At the beginning of September, the account for estimated liability for product warranties had a credit balance of $104,000. During September, 250 processors were returned under the warranty. The cost of replacement was $27,000. Service fees of $4,930 were collected for handling. During the month, the company sold 2,800 food processors.

Required

1. Prepare general journal entries to record the cost of food processors replaced under warranty and the estimated liability for product warranties for processors sold during the month.
2. Compute the balance of the Estimated Product Warranty Liabilities account at the end of the month.

Problem 11B-4.
Payroll Entries
(L.O. 4, 5)

At the end of October, the payroll register for Escalera Corporation contained the following totals: sales salaries, $176,220; office salaries, $80,880; administrative salaries, $113,900; social security tax withheld, $23,200; Medicare tax withheld, $5,379.50; federal income taxes withheld, $94,884; state income taxes withheld, $15,636; medical insurance deductions, $12,870; life insurance deductions, $11,712; union dues deductions, $1,368; and salaries subject to unemployment taxes, $57,240.

Required

Prepare general journal entries to record the following: (1) accrual of the monthly payroll, (2) payment of the net payroll, (3) accrual of employer's payroll taxes (assuming social security and Medicare taxes equal to the amount for employees, a federal unemployment insurance tax of .8 percent, and a state unemployment tax of 5.4 percent), and (4) payment of all liabilities related to the payroll (assuming that all are paid at the same time).

Problem 11B-5.
Payroll Register and Related Entries
(L.O. 4, 5)

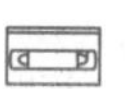

Huff Manufacturing Company employs seven people in the Drilling Division. All employees are paid an hourly wage except the foreman, who receives a monthly salary. Hourly employees are paid once a week and receive a set hourly rate for regular hours plus time-and-a-half for overtime. The employees and employer are subject to social security tax of 6.20 percent and Medicare tax of 1.45 percent on the first $57,600 (social security) and $135,000 (Medicare) earned by each employee. The unemployment insurance tax rates are 5.4 percent for the state and .8 percent for the federal government. The unemployment insurance tax applies to the first $7,000 earned by each employee and is levied only on the employer.

Each employee qualifies for the Huff Manufacturing Profit Sharing Plan. Under this plan each employee may contribute up to 10 percent of his or her gross income as a payroll withholding, and Huff Manufacturing Company matches this amount. The data for the last payday of October are presented below:

	Hours			Cumulative Gross Pay Excluding Current Pay Period	Percentage Contribution to Profit Sharing Plan	Federal Income Tax To Be Withheld
Employee	Regular	Overtime	Pay Rate			
Branch, W.	40	4	$ 9.00	$14,350.00	2	$ 40.00
Choy, T.	40	2	8.50	6,275.00	5	48.00
Duran, P.	40	5	12.70	16,510.00	7	35.00
Finnegan, M.*	Salary	—	5,500.00	53,500.00	9	760.00
Patel, B.	40	—	12.50	15,275.00	3	60.00
Sammuals, J.	40	7	9.00	11,925.00	—	23.00
Tobin, R.	40	3	7.50	10,218.00	—	20.00

*Supervisory. M. Finnegan was paid a bonus of $2,000 earlier in the year. This is included in his cumulative gross pay.

Required

1. Prepare a payroll register for the pay period ended October 31. The payroll register should have the following columns:

Employee	Deductions	Net Pay
Total Hours	Social Security Tax	Distribution
Earnings	Medicare Tax	Drilling Wages Expense
Regular	Federal Income Tax	Supervisory Salaries Expense
Overtime	Profit Sharing Plan	
Gross		
Cumulative		

2. Prepare a general journal entry to record the payroll and related liabilities for deductions for the period ended October 31.
3. Prepare general journal entries to record the expenses and related liabilities for the employer's payroll taxes (social security, Medicare, and federal and state unemployment) and contribution to the profit sharing plan.
4. Prepare the October 31 entries for the transfer of sufficient cash from the company's regular checking account to a special Payroll Disbursement account and for the subsequent payment of employees.

Financial Decision Case

Lafayette Television Repair
(L.O. 1, 2, 4)

Roosevelt Lafayette opened a small television repair shop on January 2, 19xx. He also sold a small line of television sets. Lafayette's wife was the sole salesperson for the television sets, and Lafayette was the only person doing repairs. (Lafayette had worked for another television repair store for twenty years, where he was the supervisor of six repairpersons.) The new business was such a success that he hired two assistants on March 1, 19xx. In October, Lafayette realized that he had failed to file any tax reports for his business since its inception and therefore probably owed a considerable amount of taxes. Since Lafayette has limited experience in maintaining business records, he has brought all his business records to you for help. The records include a checkbook, canceled checks, deposit slips, invoices from his suppliers, notice of annual property taxes of $9,240 due to the city November 1, 19xx, and a promissory note to his father-in-law for $10,000. He wants you to determine what his business owes to the government and other parties.

You analyze all his records and determine the following:

Unpaid supplies invoices	$ 6,320
Sales (excluding sales tax)	88,540
Workers' salaries	20,400
Repair revenues	120,600

You learn that the company has deducted $952.00 from employees' salaries for federal income tax withholding, which is owed to the government. The current social security tax is 6.20 percent on maximum earnings of $57,600 for each employee and the current Medicare tax is 1.45 percent on maximum earnings of $135,000 for each employee. The unemployment tax is 5.4 percent to the state and .8 percent to the federal government on the first $7,000 earned by each employee. Lafayette has not filed a sales tax report to the state (5 percent of sales).

Required

1. Given these limited facts, determine Lafayette Television Repair's liabilities as of October 31, 19xx.
2. What additional information would you want from Lafayette to satisfy yourself that all liabilities have been identified?

Answers to Self-Test

1. b	3. b	5. a	7. c	9. c
2. d	4. b	6. c	8. d	10. c

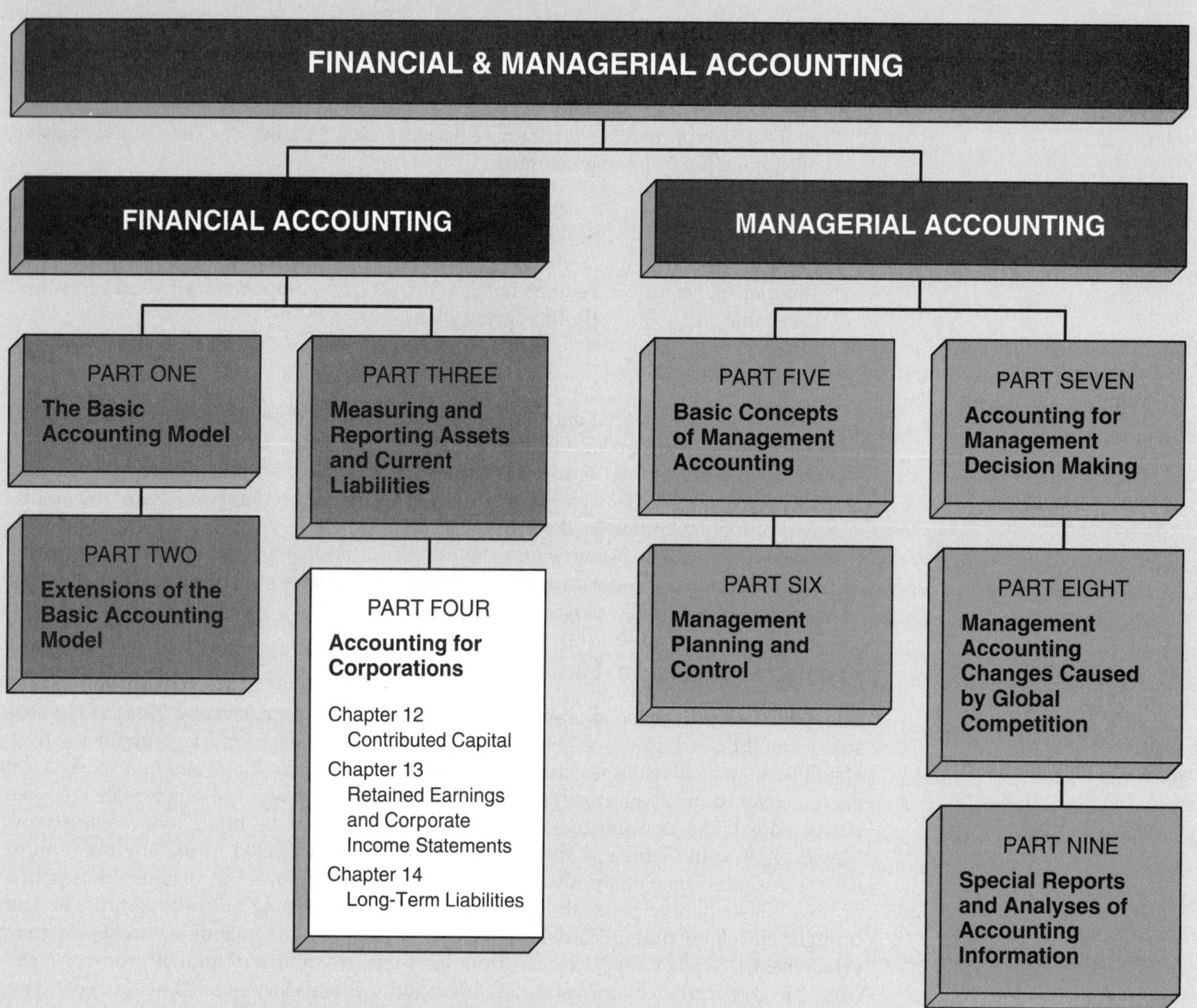

In the earlier parts of this book, the sole proprietorship has been the major form of business organization discussed. In Part Four, introductory accounting concepts and practices of corporations are presented.

PART FOUR

Accounting for Corporations

Chapter 12 introduces accounting for the corporate form of business, including the issuance of capital stock, cash dividends, and other transactions.

Chapter 13 focuses on accounting for retained earnings, a number of other transactions that affect the stockholders' equity of a corporation, and the parts that make up the corporate income statement.

Chapter 14 introduces the long-term liabilities of corporations, with special attention to accounting for bonds payable.

LEARNING OBJECTIVES

1. *Define corporation and state the advantages and disadvantages of the corporate form of business.*
2. *Account for organization costs.*
3. *Identify the components of stockholders' equity.*
4. *Account for cash dividends.*
5. *Calculate the division of dividends between common and preferred stockholders.*
6. *Account for the issuance of common and preferred stock for cash and other assets.*
7. *Account for stock subscriptions.*
8. *Account for the exercise of stock options.*

CHAPTER 12

Contributed Capital

There are fewer corporations than sole proprietorships and partnerships in the United States. However, the corporate form of business dominates the economy in total dollars of assets and output of goods and services. The corporate form of business is also well suited to today's trends toward large organizations, international trade, and professional management. After studying this chapter, you should be able to meet the learning objectives listed on the left.

DECISION POINT

Time Warner, Inc.

■ A major reason for the dominance of corporations in the U.S. economy is their ability to amass a large amount of capital. Figure 12-1 shows the amounts and sources of new funds raised by corporations during the years 1986–1990. In 1990 the amount of new corporate capital reached $314.1 billion, of which $290.3 billion, or 92.4 percent, came from new bond issues; $19.2 billion, or 6.1 percent, came from common stock issues; and $4.6 billion, or 1.5 percent, came from preferred stock issues. As you will see in the chapter on long-term liabilities, bonds are a popular way for corporations to raise new capital because of income tax advantages, flexibility, and leverage. Although much less popular than bonds, capital stock issues still are favored by many corporations. The *Wall Street Journal* recently reported that Time Warner, Inc., a major publishing and entertainment company, had raised about $2.7 billion from its common stock.[1] In light of the advantages of bond financing, what are some possible reasons for Time Warner's decision to issue common stock?

As a means of financing, common stock has disadvantages. Unlike the interest expense on bonds, dividends paid on stock are not tax-deductible. Also, by issuing more stock, the corporation dilutes its ownership. This means that the current shareholders must yield some control to the new stockholders. On the other hand, there are definite advantages to financing with common stock. First, financing with common stock issues is less risky than financing with bonds, because dividends on common stock are not paid unless management and the board of directors decide to pay them. In contrast, if the interest on bonds is not paid, a company can be forced into bankruptcy. Second, when a company does not pay a cash dividend, the cash generated by profitable operations can be invested in the company's operations. Third, and most

1. Randall Smith, "Time Warner's Offer Expires; Demand Is High," *Wall Street Journal*, August 6, 1991.

Figure 12-1. Sources of Capital Raised by Corporations in the United States

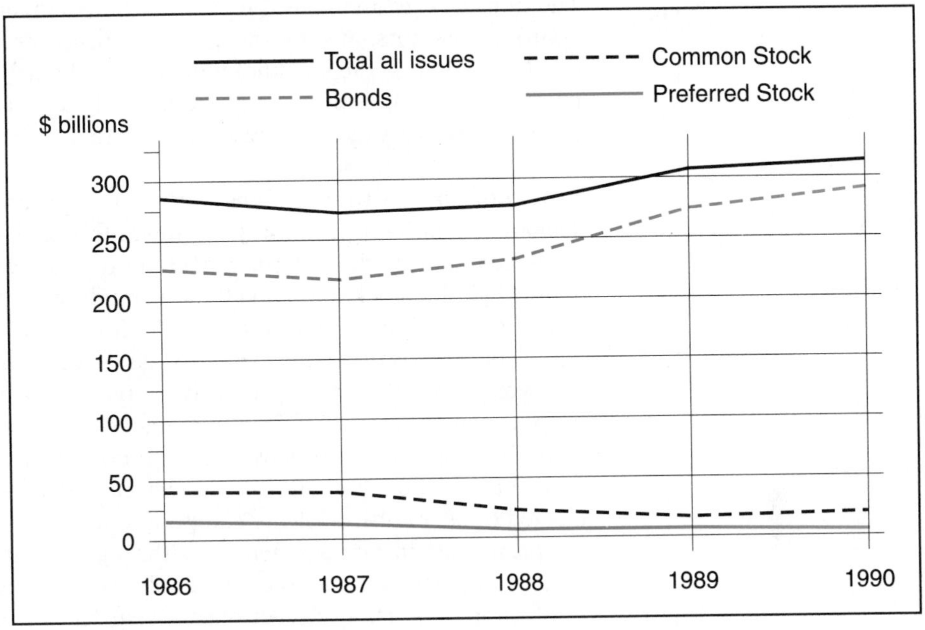

Source: Data from *Securities Industry Yearbook 1991–1992* (New York: Securities Industry Association, 1991), p. 729.

important for Time Warner, Inc., a company may need the proceeds of a common stock issue to reduce its debt and achieve a better balance between liabilities and stockholders' equity. It is important to understand the nature and characteristics of corporations as well as the process of accounting for a stock issue and other stock transactions. ■

The Corporation

OBJECTIVE 1
Define corporation *and state the advantages and disadvantages of the corporate form of business*

A **corporation** is "a body of persons granted a charter legally recognizing them as a separate entity having its own rights, privileges, and liabilities distinct from those of its members."[2] In other words, the corporation is a legal entity separate and distinct from its owners. For this reason, corporate accounting is different in some ways from accounting for proprietorships and partnerships.

Forming a Corporation

To form a corporation in most states, an application (containing the **articles of incorporation**) is filed with the proper state official. If approved by the state, the articles become, in effect, a contract between the state and the incorporators, or the *corporate charter.* After the charter is approved, the company is authorized to do business. The incorporators (usually the initial stockholders) hold a meeting to elect a board of directors and pass a set of bylaws to guide the operations of the corporation. The board of directors then holds a meeting to elect officers of the corporation. Finally, after beginning capital is raised through the issuance of shares of stock, the corporation is ready to start operating.

2. Copyright © 1991 Houghton Mifflin Company. Adapted and reprinted by permission from *The American Heritage Dictionary, Second College Edition.*

Organizing a Corporation

The authority to manage the corporation is given by the stockholders to the board of directors, and by the board of directors to the corporate officers (Figure 12-2). That is, the stockholders elect the board of directors, which sets company policies and chooses the corporate officers. The officers, in turn, carry out corporate policies by managing the business.

Stockholders. A unit of ownership in a corporation is called a **share of stock**. The articles of incorporation state the authorized stock, the maximum number of shares of a stock that the corporation is allowed to issue. The number of shares held by stockholders is the outstanding capital stock; it may be less than the number of authorized shares. To invest in a corporation, a stockholder transfers cash or other resources to the corporation. In return, the stockholder receives shares of stock representing a proportionate share of ownership in the corporation. The stockholder can transfer these shares at will.

Individual stockholders normally do not take part in the day-to-day management of a corporation. A stockholder can serve as a member of the board if elected or as an officer of the company if appointed. But, in general, stockholders participate in management only through electing the board of directors and voting on particular issues at stockholders' meetings.

Stockholders usually meet once a year to elect directors and carry on other business as provided in the company's bylaws. Business transacted at these meetings can include the election of auditors; the review of proposed mergers and acquisitions, changes in the charter, or stock option plans; and the decision to issue additional stock or finance with long-term debt. Each stockholder has one vote for each share of voting stock held. Today, ownership of large corporations is spread over the entire world. As a result, only a few stockholders may be able to attend the annual stockholders' meeting. A stockholder who cannot attend the meeting can vote by proxy. A **proxy** is a legal document, signed by a stockholder, giving another party the right to vote his or her shares. Normally, this right is given to the current management of the corporation.

Board of Directors. Again, the stockholders elect the board of directors, which in turn decides on the major business policies of the corporation and appoints managers to carry them out. Among the duties of the board are authorizing contracts, setting the level of executive salaries, and arranging major loans with banks. The declaration of dividends also is an important function of the board of directors: Only the board has the authority to declare dividends. *Dividends* are distributions of resources, generally in the form of cash, to the stockholders. They are one way of rewarding stockholders for their investment in the corporation when it has earned a profit. (The other way is a rise in the

Figure 12-2. The Corporate Form of Business

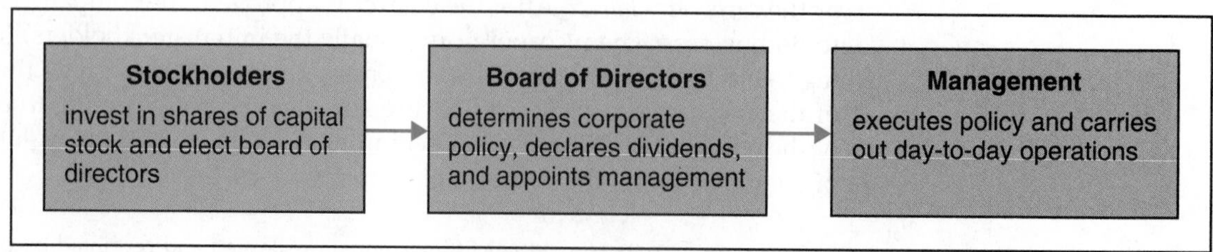

market value of the stock.) There is usually a delay of two or three weeks between the date the board declares a dividend and the date payment actually is made.

The makeup of the board of directors is different from company to company. In most cases, though, several officers of the corporation sit on the board along with several outsiders. Today, it is common to form an **audit committee** of several outside directors, to make sure that the board is objective in its evaluation of management's performance. One of the audit committee's tasks is to hire the company's independent auditors and review the scope and results of the audit.

Management. The board of directors appoints the managers of the corporation to carry out the company's policies and to run day-to-day operations. Management consists of the operating officers—generally, the president, vice presidents, controller, treasurer, and secretary. Besides being responsible for running the business, management has the duty to report the financial results of its administration to the board of directors and to the stockholders. Although management can and generally does report more often, it must report at least once a year. The annual reports of large public corporations are available to the public. We have used parts of many of them in this book.

The Advantages of a Corporation

The corporate form of business organization has several advantages over the sole proprietorship and the partnership. Among them are separate legal entity, limited liability, ease of capital generation, ease of transfer of ownership, lack of mutual agency, continuous existence, centralized authority and responsibility, and professional management.

Separate Legal Entity. A corporation is a separate legal entity that has most of the rights of a person except those of voting and marrying. As such, it can buy, sell, or own property; sue and be sued; enter into contracts; hire and fire employees; and be taxed.

Limited Liability. Because a corporation is a separate legal entity, it is responsible for its own actions and liabilities. This means that a corporation's creditors can satisfy their claims only against the assets of the corporation, not against the personal property of the owners of the company. Because the owners of a corporation are not responsible for the debts of the company, their liability is limited to the amount of their investment. The personal property of sole proprietors and partners, however, generally is available to creditors.

Ease of Capital Generation. It is fairly easy for a corporation to raise capital because shares of ownership in the business are widely available to potential investors for a small amount of money. As a result, a single corporation can be owned by many people.

Ease of Transfer of Ownership. The ownership of a corporation is represented by a transferable unit, a share of stock. An owner of shares of stock, or a stockholder, normally can buy and sell shares of stock without affecting the activities of the corporation or needing the approval of other owners.

Lack of Mutual Agency. There is no mutual agency in the corporate form of business. If a stockholder, acting as an owner, tries to enter into a contract for the corporation, the corporation is not bound by the contract. But in a partnership, because of mutual agency, all the partners can be bound by one partner's actions.

Continuous Existence. Another advantage of the corporation's being a separate legal entity is that an owner's death, incapacity, or withdrawal does not affect the life of the corporation. The life of a corporation is set by its charter and regulated by state laws.

Centralized Authority and Responsibility. The board of directors represents the stockholders and delegates the responsibility and authority for the day-to-day operation of the corporation to a single person, usually the president of the organization. This power is not divided among the many owners of the business. The president may delegate authority for certain segments of the business to others, but he or she is held accountable to the board of directors for the business. If the board is dissatisfied with the performance of the president, he or she can be replaced.

Professional Management. Large corporations are owned by many people who probably do not have the time or training to make timely decisions about the business's operations. So, in most cases, management and ownership are separate. This allows the corporation to hire the best talent available to manage the business.

The Disadvantages of a Corporation

The corporate form of business also has disadvantages. Among the more important ones are government regulation, taxation, limited liability, and separation of ownership and control.

Government Regulation. Corporations must meet the requirements of state laws. These "creatures of the state" are subject to greater control and regulation by the state than are other forms of business. Corporations must file many reports with the state in which they are chartered. Also, corporations that are held publicly must file reports with the Securities and Exchange Commission and with the stock exchanges. Meeting these requirements is very costly.

Taxation. A major disadvantage of the corporation is **double taxation**. Because the corporation is a separate legal entity, its earnings are subject to federal and state income taxes. These taxes approach 35 percent of corporate earnings. If any of the corporation's after-tax earnings then are paid out to its stockholders as dividends, the earnings are taxed again as income to the stockholders. Taxation is different for the sole proprietorship and the partnership, whose earnings are taxed only as personal income to the owners.

Limited Liability. Above, we listed limited liability as an advantage of a corporation; it also can be a disadvantage. Limited liability restricts the ability of a small corporation to borrow money. Because creditors can lay claim only to the assets of the corporation, they limit their loans to the level secured by those assets or ask stockholders to guarantee the loans personally.

Separation of Ownership and Control. Just as limited liability can be a drawback, so can the separation of ownership and control. Sometimes management makes decisions that are not good for the corporation as a whole. Poor communication also can make it hard for stockholders to exercise control over the corporation or even to recognize that management's decisions are harmful.

Organization Costs

OBJECTIVE 2
Account for organization costs

The costs of forming a corporation are called **organization costs.** These costs, which are incurred before the corporation begins operation, include state incorporation fees and attorneys' fees for drawing up the articles of incorporation. They also include the cost of printing stock certificates, accountants' fees for services rendered in registering the firm's initial stock, and other expenditures necessary for forming the corporation.

Theoretically, organization costs benefit the entire life of the corporation. For this reason, a case can be made for recording organization costs as intangible assets and amortizing them over the years of the life of the corporation. However, the life of a corporation normally is not known, so accountants amortize these costs over the early years of a corporation's life. Because federal income tax regulations allow organization costs to be amortized over five years or more, most companies amortize these costs over a five-year (sixty-month) period.[3] Organization costs normally appear as other assets or as intangible assets on the balance sheet.

To show how organization costs are accounted for, we assume that a corporation pays a lawyer $5,000 for services rendered in July 19x0, to prepare the application for a charter with the state. The entry to record this cost would be as follows:

19x0			
July 1	Organization Costs	5,000	
	Cash		5,000
	Lawyer's fee for services rendered in corporate organization		

If the corporation amortizes the organization costs over a five-year period, the entry to record the amortization at the end of the fiscal year, June 30, 19x1, would look like this:

19x1			
June 30	Organization Costs Amortization Expense	1,000	
	Organization Costs		1,000
	To amortize organization costs for one year ($5,000 ÷ 5 years = $1,000)		

The Components of Stockholders' Equity

OBJECTIVE 3
Identify the components of stockholders' equity

The assets and liabilities of a corporation are handled in the same way as they are for other forms of business. The major difference in accounting for corporations and accounting for sole proprietorships or partnerships involves the owners' equity. In a corporation's balance sheet, the owners' claims to the business are called **stockholders' equity.**

3. The FASB allows organization costs to be amortized over a period of up to forty years.

Stockholders' Equity		
Contributed Capital		
Preferred Stock—$50 par value, 1,000 shares authorized, issued, and outstanding		$ 50,000
Common Stock—$5 par value, 30,000 shares authorized, 20,000 shares issued and outstanding	$100,000	
Paid-in Capital in Excess of Par Value, Common	50,000	150,000
Total Contributed Capital		$200,000
Retained Earnings		60,000
Total Stockholders' Equity		$260,000

Notice that the equity section of the corporate balance sheet is divided into two parts: (1) contributed capital and (2) retained earnings. **Contributed capital** represents the investments made by the stockholders in the corporation. **Retained earnings** are the earnings of the corporation since its inception less any losses, dividends, or transfers to contributed capital. Retained earnings are not a pool of funds to be distributed to the stockholders; they represent instead, earnings reinvested in the corporation.

The contributed-capital part of stockholders' equity on the balance sheet, in keeping with the convention of full disclosure, gives a great deal of information about the corporation's stock: the kinds of stock; their par value; and the number of shares authorized, issued, and outstanding. The information in the contributed-capital part of stockholders' equity is the subject of the rest of this chapter. We explain retained earnings fully in the chapter on retained earnings and corporate income statements.

Capital Stock

A share of stock is a unit of ownership in a corporation. A **stock certificate** is issued to the owner. It shows the number of shares of the corporation's stock owned by the stockholder. Stockholders can transfer their ownership at will. When they do, they must sign their stock certificate and send it to the corporation's secretary. In large corporations, those listed on the organized stock exchanges, it is hard to maintain stockholders' records. These companies can have millions of shares of stock, several thousand of which change ownership every day. Therefore, they often appoint independent registrars and transfer agents (usually banks and trust companies) to help perform the secretary's duties. They are responsible for transferring the corporation's stock, maintaining stockholders' records, preparing a list of stockholders for stockholders' meetings, and paying dividends. To help with the initial issue of capital stock, corporations often use an **underwriter**—an intermediary between the corporation and the investing public. For a fee—usually less than 1 percent of the selling price—the underwriter guarantees the sale of the stock. The corporation records the amount of the net proceeds of the offering—what the public paid less the underwriter's fee, legal and printing expenses, and any other direct costs of the offering—in its capital stock and additional paid-in capital accounts.

Authorized Stock. When a corporation applies for a charter, the articles of incorporation indicate the maximum number of shares of stock the corporation is allowed to issue. This number represents **authorized stock**. Most corporations are authorized to issue more shares of stock than are necessary at the time of organization, enabling them to issue stock in the future to raise additional capital. For example, if a corporation is planning to expand later, a possible source of capital would be the unissued shares of stock that were authorized in its charter. If all authorized stock is issued immediately, before it can issue more, the corporation must change its charter by applying to the state to increase its shares of authorized stock.

The charter also shows the par value of the stock that has been authorized. **Par value** is an arbitrary amount printed on each share of stock. It must be recorded in the Capital Stock accounts and constitutes the legal capital of a corporation. **Legal capital** equals the number of shares issued times the par value; it is the minimum amount that can be reported as contributed capital. Par value usually bears little if any relationship to the market value or book value of the shares. When the corporation is formed, a memorandum entry can be made in the general journal giving the number and description of authorized shares.

Issued and Outstanding Stock. The **issued stock** of a corporation is the shares sold or otherwise transferred to stockholders. For example, a corporation can be authorized to issue 500,000 shares of stock but may choose to issue only 300,000 shares when the company is organized. The holders of those 300,000 shares own 100 percent of the corporation. The remaining 200,000 shares of stock are unissued shares. No rights or privileges are associated with them until they are issued.

Outstanding stock is stock that has been issued and is still in circulation. A share of stock is not outstanding if it has been repurchased by the issuing corporation or given back to the company that issued it by a stockholder. So, a company can have more shares issued than are currently outstanding. Issued shares that are bought back and held by the corporation are called *treasury stock*, which we talk about in the chapter on retained earnings and corporate income statements.

Common Stock

A corporation can issue two basic types of stock: common stock and preferred stock. If only one kind of stock is issued by the corporation, it is called **common stock**. Common stock is the company's **residual equity**. This means that all other creditors' and preferred stockholders' claims to the company's assets rank ahead of those of the common stockholders in case of liquidation. Because common stock is generally the only stock that carries voting rights, it represents the means of controlling the corporation.

Dividends

OBJECTIVE 4
Account for cash dividends

A **dividend** is the distribution of a corporation's assets to its stockholders. Each stockholder receives assets, usually cash, in proportion to the number of shares of stock held. The board of directors has sole authority to declare dividends.

Dividends can be paid quarterly, semiannually, annually, or at other times decided on by the board. Most states do not allow the board to declare a dividend that exceeds retained earnings. When this kind of dividend is declared, the corporation essentially is returning to the stockholders part of their contributed capital. This is called a **liquidating dividend** and normally is paid when a company is going out of business or is reducing its operations. Having sufficient retained earnings in itself does not justify the distribution of a dividend. If cash or other readily distributed assets are not available for distribution, the company might have to borrow money in order to pay a dividend—an action most boards of directors want to avoid.

There are three important dates associated with dividends. In order of occurrence, they are (1) the date of declaration, (2) the date of record, and (3) the date of payment. The *date of declaration* is the date the board of directors formally declares that a dividend is going to be paid. The *date of record* is the date on which ownership of the stock of a company, and therefore of the right to receive a dividend, is determined. Those individuals who own the stock on the date of record will receive the dividend. After that date, the stock is said to be **ex-dividend**: If one person sells the shares of stock to another, the right to the cash dividend remains with the first person; it does not transfer with the shares to the second person. The *date of payment* is the date on which the dividend is paid to the stockholders of record.

To illustrate the accounting for cash dividends, we assume that the board of directors has decided that sufficient cash is available to pay a $56,000 cash dividend to the common stockholders. The process has two steps. First, the board declares the dividend as of a certain date. Second, the dividend is paid. Assume that the dividend is declared on February 21, 19xx, for stockholders of record on March 1, 19xx, to be paid on March 11, 19xx. Here are the entries to record the declaration and payment of the cash dividend:

Date of Declaration

Feb. 21	Cash Dividends Declared	56,000	
	Cash Dividends Payable		56,000
	Declaration of a cash dividend to common stockholders		

Date of Record

Mar. 1	No entry is required. This date is used simply to determine the owners of the stock who will receive the dividends. After this date (starting March 2), the shares are ex-dividend.		

Date of Payment

Mar. 11	Cash Dividends Payable	56,000	
	Cash		56,000
	Payment of cash dividends declared February 21		

Notice that the liability for the dividend is recorded on the date of declaration because the legal obligation to pay the dividend is established on that date. No entry is required on the date of record. The liability is liquidated, or settled, on the date of payment. The Cash Dividends Declared account is a temporary stockholders' equity account that is closed at the end of the accounting period by debiting Retained Earnings and crediting Cash Dividends Declared. Retained earnings are thereby reduced by the total dividends declared during the period.

Some companies do not pay dividends very often. A company may not have any earnings. Or, a corporation may need the assets generated by the earnings kept in the company for business purposes, perhaps expansion of the plant. Investors in growth companies expect a return on their investment in the form of an increase in the market value of their stock. Stock dividends, another kind of return, are discussed in the chapter on retained earnings and corporate income statements.

Preferred Stock

The second kind of stock a company can issue is called **preferred stock**. Both common stock and preferred stock are sold to raise money. But investors in preferred stock have different investment goals from investors in common stock. Preferred stock has preference over common stock in one or more areas. There can be several different classes of preferred stock, each with distinctive characteristics to attract different investors. Most preferred stock has one or more of the following characteristics: preference as to dividends, preference as to assets of the business in liquidation, convertibility, and a callable option.

OBJECTIVE 5
Calculate the division of dividends between common and preferred stockholders

Preference as to Dividends. Preferred stocks ordinarily have a *preference* over common stock in the receipt of dividends; that is, the holders of preferred shares must receive a certain amount of dividends before the holders of common shares can receive dividends. The amount that preferred stockholders must be paid before common stockholders can be paid usually is stated in dollars per share or in a percentage of the face value of the preferred shares. For example, a corporation can issue a preferred stock and pay an annual dividend of $4 per share, or it might issue a preferred stock at $50 par value and pay a yearly dividend of 8 percent of par value, $4 annually per share.

Preferred stockholders have no guarantee of ever receiving dividends: The company must have earnings and the board of directors must declare dividends on preferred shares before any liability to pay them arises. The consequences of not declaring a dividend to preferred stockholders in the current year vary according to the exact terms under which the shares were issued. In the case of **noncumulative preferred stock**, if the board of directors fails to declare a dividend to preferred stockholders in a given year, it is under no obligation to make up the missed dividend in future years. In the case of **cumulative preferred stock**, however, the fixed dividend amount per share accumulates from year to year, and the whole amount must be paid before any common dividends can be paid. Dividends that are not paid in the year they are due are called **dividends in arrears**.

Assume that a corporation has been authorized to issue 10,000 shares of $100 par value, 5 percent cumulative preferred stock, and that the shares have been issued and are outstanding. If no dividends were paid in 19x1, at the end of the year there would be preferred dividends of $50,000 (10,000 shares × $100 × .05 = $50,000) in arrears. If dividends are paid in 19x2, the preferred stockholders' dividends in arrears plus the 19x2 preferred dividends must be paid before any dividends on common stock can be paid.

Dividends in arrears are not recognized as liabilities of a corporation because there is no liability until the board declares a dividend. A corporation cannot be sure it is going to make a profit. So, of course, it cannot promise dividends to stockholders. However, if a company has dividends in arrears, they should be reported either in the body of the financial statements or in a footnote. The following footnote appeared in a steel company's annual report a few years ago:

> On January 1, 19xx, the company was in arrears by $37,851,000 ($1.25 per share) on dividends to its preferred stockholders. The company must pay all dividends in arrears to preferred stockholders before paying any dividends to common stockholders.

Suppose that on January 1, 19x1, a corporation issued 10,000 shares of $10 par, 6 percent cumulative preferred stock and 50,000 shares of common stock. The first year's operations resulted in income of only $4,000. The corporation's board of directors declared a $3,000 cash dividend to the preferred stockholders. The dividend picture at the end of 19x1 looked like this:

19x1 dividends due preferred stockholders ($100,000 × .06)	$6,000
Less 19x1 dividends declared to preferred stockholders	3,000
19x1 preferred stock dividends in arrears	$3,000

Now, suppose that in 19x2 the company earned income of $30,000 and wanted to pay dividends to both the preferred and the common stockholders. But the preferred stock is cumulative. So the corporation must pay the $3,000 in arrears on the preferred stock, plus the current year's dividends on its preferred stock, before it can distribute a dividend to the common stockholders. For example, assume that the corporation's board of directors declared a $12,000 dividend to be distributed to preferred and common stockholders. The dividend would be distributed as follows:

19x2 declaration of dividends	$12,000	
Less 19x1 preferred stock dividends in arrears	3,000	
Available for 19x2 dividends		$9,000
Less 19x2 dividends due preferred stockholders ($100,000 × .06)		6,000
Remainder available to common stockholders		$3,000

And this is the journal entry when the dividend is declared:

Dec. 31	Cash Dividends Declared	12,000	
	Cash Dividends Payable		12,000
	Declaration of a $9,000 cash dividend to preferred stockholders and a $3,000 cash dividend to common stockholders		

Preference as to Assets. Many preferred stocks have preference in terms of the assets of the corporation in the case of liquidation. So, when the business is ended, the preferred stockholders have a right to receive the par value of their stock or a larger stated liquidation value per share before the common stockholders receive any share of the company's assets. This preference also can include any dividends in arrears owed to the preferred stockholders.

Convertible Preferred Stock. A corporation can make its preferred stock more attractive to investors by adding a convertibility feature. People who hold **convertible preferred stock** can exchange their shares of preferred stock for shares of the company's common stock at a ratio stated in the preferred stock contract. Convertibility appeals to investors for two reasons. First, like all preferred stockholders, owners of convertible stock are more likely to receive regular dividends than are common stockholders. Second, if the market value of a company's common stock rises, the conversion feature allows the preferred stockholders to share in the increase. The rise in value would come either through equal increases in the value of the preferred stock or through conversion to common stock.

For example, suppose that a company issues 1,000 shares of 8 percent, $100 par value convertible preferred stock for $100 per share. Each share of stock can be converted into five shares of the company's common stock at any time.

The market value of the common stock is now $15 per share. In the past, dividends on the common stock have been about $1 per share per year. The stockholder owning one share of preferred stock, on the other hand, now holds an investment that is worth about $100 on the market and is more likely to receive dividends than is the owner of common stock.

Assume that in the next several years, the corporation's earnings increase, and the dividends paid to common stockholders also increase, to $3 per share. In addition, the market value of a share of common stock goes up from $15 to $30. Preferred stockholders can convert each of their preferred shares into five common shares and increase their dividends from $8 on each preferred share to the equivalent of $15 ($3 on each of five common shares). Furthermore, the market value of each share of preferred stock will be close to the $150 value of the five shares of common stock because each share can be converted into five shares of common stock.

Callable Preferred Stock. Most preferred stocks are **callable preferred stocks**. That is, they can be redeemed or retired at the option of the issuing corporation at a price stated in the preferred stock contract. The stockholder must surrender a nonconvertible preferred stock to the corporation when asked to do so. If the preferred stock is convertible, the stockholder can either surrender the stock to the corporation or convert it into common stock when the corporation calls the stock. The *call price*, or redemption price, is usually higher than the par value of the stock. For example, a $100 par value preferred stock might be callable at $103 per share. When preferred stock is called and surrendered, the stockholder is entitled to (1) the par value of the stock, (2) the call premium, (3) any dividends in arrears, and (4) a prorated (by the proportion of the year to the call date) portion of the current period's dividend.

There are several reasons why a corporation would call its preferred stock. First, it may want to force conversion of the preferred stock to common stock because the cash dividend being paid on the equivalent common stock is less than the dividend being paid on the preferred shares. Second, it may be possible to replace the outstanding preferred stock on the current market with a preferred stock at a lower dividend rate or with long-term debt, which can have a lower after-tax cost. Third, the company may simply be profitable enough to retire the preferred stock.

Retained Earnings

Retained earnings, the other component of stockholders' equity, represent stockholders' claims to the assets of the company resulting from profitable operations. Again, the chapter on retained earnings and corporate income statements explains in detail the retained earnings section of the balance sheet.

Accounting for Stock Issuance

OBJECTIVE 6
Account for the issuance of common and preferred stock for cash and other assets

A share of capital stock is either a par or a no-par stock. If the capital stock is par stock, the corporation charter states the par value, and this value must be printed on each share of stock. Par value can be $.10, $1, $5, $100, or any other amount worked out by the organizers of the corporation. The par values of common stocks tend to be lower than those of preferred stocks.

Par value is the amount per share that is entered into the corporation's Capital Stock accounts and that makes up the legal capital of the corporation. A corporation cannot declare a dividend that would cause stockholders' equity to fall below the legal capital of the firm. Therefore, the par value is a minimum cushion of capital that protects creditors. Any amount in excess of par value received from the issuance of stock is recorded in the Paid-in Capital in Excess of Par Value account and represents a portion of the company's contributed capital.

No-par stock is capital stock that does not have a par value. There are several reasons for issuing stock without a par value. One is that some investors confuse par value with the market value of stock instead of recognizing it as an arbitrary figure. Another reason is that most states do not allow an original stock issue below par value and thereby limit a corporation's flexibility in obtaining capital.

No-par stock can be issued with or without a stated value. The board of directors of the corporation issuing the no-par stock can be required by state law to place a **stated value** on each share of stock or may choose to do so as a matter of convenience. The stated value can be any value set by the board, although some states do indicate a minimum stated value per share. The stated value can be set before or after the shares are issued if the state law does not specify this point.

If a company issues a no-par stock without a stated value, all proceeds of the issue are recorded in the Capital Stock account. This amount becomes the corporation's legal capital unless the amount is specified by state law. Because additional shares of the stock can be issued at different prices, the credit to the Capital Stock account per share will not be uniform. In this way, it differs from par value stock or no-par stock with a stated value.

When no-par stock with a stated value is issued, the shares are recorded in the Capital Stock account at the stated value. Any amount received in excess of the stated value is recorded in Paid-in Capital in Excess of Stated Value. The excess of the stated value is a part of the corporation's contributed capital. However, the stated value normally is considered to be the legal capital of the corporation.

Par Value Stock

When par value stock is issued, the appropriate capital stock account (usually Common Stock or Preferred Stock) is credited for the par value (legal capital) regardless of whether the proceeds are more or less than the par value. For example, assume that Bradley Corporation is authorized to issue 20,000 shares of $10 par value common stock and actually issues 10,000 shares at $10 per share on January 1, 19xx. The entry to record the stock issue at par value would be as follows:

Jan. 1	Cash	100,000	
	Common Stock		100,000
	Issued 10,000 shares of $10 par value common stock for $10 per share		

Cash is debited $100,000 (10,000 shares × $10), and Common Stock is credited an equal amount because the stock was sold for par value (legal capital).

If the stock had been issued for a price greater than par, the proceeds in excess of par would be credited to a capital account called Paid-in Capital in Excess of Par Value, Common. For example, assume that the 10,000 shares of

Bradley common stock sold for $12 per share on January 1, 19xx. The entry to record the issuance of the stock at the price in excess of par value would be as follows:

Jan. 1	Cash	120,000	
	Common Stock		100,000
	Paid-in Capital in Excess of Par Value, Common		20,000
	Issued 10,000 shares of $10 par value common stock for $12 per share		

Cash is debited for the proceeds of $120,000 (10,000 shares × $12), and Common Stock is credited at total par value of $100,000 (10,000 shares × $10). Paid-in Capital in Excess of Par Value, Common is credited for the difference of $20,000 (10,000 shares × $2). This amount is part of the corporation's contributed capital and will be included in the stockholders' equity section of the balance sheet. The stockholders' equity secton for Bradley Corporation immediately following the stock issue would appear as follows:

Contributed Capital	
Common Stock—$10 par value, 20,000 shares authorized, 10,000 shares issued and outstanding	$100,000
Paid-in Capital in Excess of Par Value, Common	20,000
Total Contributed Capital	$120,000
Retained Earnings	—
Total Stockholders' Equity	$120,000

If a corporation issues stock for less than par, an account called Discount on Capital Stock is debited for the difference. The issuance of stock at a discount rarely occurs because it is illegal in many states.

No-Par Stock

As mentioned earlier, stock can be issued without a par value. However, most states require that all or part of the proceeds from the issuance of no-par stock be designated as legal capital, which cannot be withdrawn except in liquidation. The purpose of this requirement is to protect the corporation's assets for creditors. Assume that the Bradley Corporation's capital stock is no-par common and that 10,000 shares are issued on January 1, 19xx at $15 per share. The $150,000 (10,000 shares × $15) in proceeds would be recorded as shown in the following entry:

Jan. 1	Cash	150,000	
	Common Stock		150,000
	Issued 10,000 shares of no-par common stock for $15 per share		

Because the stock does not have a stated or par value, all proceeds of the issue are credited to Common Stock and are part of the company's legal capital.

Most states allow the board of directors to put a stated value on no-par stock, and this value represents the corporation's legal capital. Assume that Bradley's board puts a $10 stated value on its no-par stock. The entry to record the issue of 10,000 shares of no-par common stock with a $10 stated value for $15 per share is shown at the top of page 480.

			Debit	Credit
Jan.	1	Cash	150,000	
		Common Stock		100,000
		Paid-in Capital in Excess of Stated Value, Common		50,000
		Issued 10,000 shares of no-par common stock of $10 stated value for $15 per share		

Notice that the legal capital credited to Common Stock is the stated value decided by the board of directors. Notice also that the account Paid-in Capital in Excess of Stated Value, Common is credited for $50,000. The $50,000 is the difference between the proceeds ($150,000) and the total stated value ($100,000). Paid-in Capital in Excess of Stated Value is presented on the balance sheet in the same way that Paid-in Capital in Excess of Par Value is presented on the balance sheet.

Issuance of Stock for Noncash Assets

Stock can be issued for assets or services other than cash. The problem here is the dollar amount that should be recorded for the exchange. The generally preferred rule is to record the transaction at the fair market value of what the corporation is giving up—in this case, the stock. If the fair market value of the stock cannot be determined, the fair market value of the assets or services received can be used to record the transaction. Transactions of this kind usually involve the use of stock to pay for land or buildings or for the services of attorneys and others who helped organize the company.

Where there is an exchange of stock for noncash assets, the board of directors has the right to determine the fair market value of the property. Suppose that when the Bradley Corporation was formed on January 1, 19xx, its attorney agreed to accept 100 shares of its $10 par value common stock for services rendered. At the time the stock was issued, its market value could not be determined. However, for similar services the attorney would have billed the company $1,500. This is the entry to record the noncash transaction:

			Debit	Credit
Jan.	1	Organization Costs	1,500	
		Common Stock		1,000
		Paid-in Capital in Excess of Par Value, Common		500
		Issued 100 shares of $10 par value common stock for attorney's services		

Now suppose that the Bradley Corporation exchanged 1,000 shares of its $10 par value common stock for a piece of land two years later. At the time of the exchange, the stock was selling on the market for $16 per share. The entry to record this exchange would be as follows:

			Debit	Credit
Jan.	1	Land	16,000	
		Common Stock		10,000
		Paid-in Capital in Excess of Par Value, Common		6,000
		Issued 1,000 shares of $10 par value common stock with a market value of $16 per share for a piece of land		

Stock Subscriptions

OBJECTIVE 7
Account for stock subscriptions

In some states, corporations can sell stock on a subscription basis. In a **stock subscription**, the investor agrees to pay for the stock on some future date or in installments at an agreed price. When a subscription is received, a contract exists and the corporation acquires an asset, Subscriptions Receivable, which represents the amount owed on the stock, and a capital item, Capital Stock Subscribed. The Capital Stock Subscribed account is used to represent the par or stated value of the stock that is not yet fully paid for and issued. (The Common Stock account is reserved for the par, or stated, value of common stock that has been issued.) The Subscriptions Receivable account should be identified as either common or preferred stock. The Capital Stock Subscribed account also should be identified as either common or preferred stock. Whether or not the subscriber is entitled to dividends on the subscribed stock depends on the laws of the state in which the company is incorporated. In certain states, the stock is considered legally issued when a subscription contract is accepted, thereby making the subscriber a legal stockholder. However, in accounting for stock subscriptions, capital stock is not issued and recorded until the subscriptions receivable pertaining to the shares are collected in full and the stock certificate is delivered to the stockholder. Likewise, dividends are not paid on common stock subscribed until it is fully paid for and the certificates issued.

To illustrate stock subscriptions, we assume that on January 1, 19xx, the Bradley Corporation received subscriptions for 15,000 shares of $10 par value common stock at $15 per share. The entry to record the subscriptions would be as follows:

Jan.	1	Subscriptions Receivable, Common	225,000	
		Common Stock Subscribed		150,000
		Paid-in Capital in Excess of Par Value, Common		75,000
		Received subscriptions for 15,000 shares of $10 par value common stock for $15 per share		

If the full subscription price for 10,000 shares was collected on January 21, 19xx (5,000 shares remain unpaid), the entry for the collection of the subscription would look like this:

Jan.	21	Cash	150,000	
		Subscriptions Receivable, Common		150,000
		Collected subscriptions in full for 10,000 shares of $10 par value common stock for $15 per share		

And because the 10,000 shares are fully paid for, the stock can be issued:

Jan.	21	Common Stock Subscribed	100,000	
		Common Stock		100,000
		Issued 10,000 shares of $10 par value common stock		

Notice that because the paid-in capital in excess of par value was recorded in the January 1 entry, there is no need to record it again.

Assume that the financial statements are prepared on January 31, 19xx, before the remaining subscriptions are collected. The balance in Subscriptions

Receivable, Common, $75,000 ($225,000 – $150,000), would be classified as a current asset unless there is some reason why it is not going to be collected in the next year. The balance of $50,000 ($150,000 – $100,000) in the Common Stock Subscribed account represents the par value of the stock yet to be issued. Common Stock Subscribed is a temporary owner's equity account. As such, it is shown as a part of stockholders' equity under contributed capital.

Contributed Capital	
Common Stock—$10 par value, 80,000 shares authorized	
Issued and outstanding, 10,000 shares	$100,000
Common Stock Subscribed, 5,000 shares	50,000
Paid-in Capital in Excess of Par Value, Common	75,000
Total Contributed Capital	$225,000

Assume that a payment of $37,500, half the remaining subscriptions receivable, is received on February 5. The entry for the collection would be as shown below:

Feb. 5	Cash	37,500	
	Subscriptions Receivable, Common		37,500
	Collected one-half payment for subscriptions to 5,000 shares of common stock		

In this case, there is no entry to issue common stock because the subscription for the stock is not paid in full (each share is one-half paid). If the subscriptions receivable are paid in full on February 20, the entry is as follows:

Feb. 20	Cash	37,500	
	Subscriptions Receivable, Common		37,500
	Collected remaining subscriptions in full for 5,000 shares of common stock		

Because the subscriptions for the stock now are paid in full, the common stock can be issued:

Feb. 20	Common Stock Subscribed	50,000	
	Common Stock		50,000
	Issued 5,000 shares of $10 par value common stock		

Exercising Stock Options

OBJECTIVE 8
Account for the exercise of stock options

Many companies encourage the ownership of the company's common stock through a **stock option plan**. A stock option plan is an agreement to issue stock to employees according to the terms of the plan. Under some plans, the option to purchase stock applies to all employees equally, and the purchase of stock is made at a price close to the market value at the time of purchase. In this situation, the stock issue is recorded in the same way any stock issue to an outsider is recorded. If, for example, we assume that on March 30 the employees of a company purchased 2,000 shares of $10 par value common stock at the current market value of $25 per share, the entry would be as follows:

Mar. 30	Cash	50,000	
	Common Stock		20,000
	Paid-in Capital in Excess of Par Value, Common		30,000
	Issued 2,000 shares of $10 par value common stock under employee stock option plan		

In other cases, the stock option plan gives the employee the right to purchase stock in the future at a fixed price. This type of plan, which usually is offered only to management personnel, both compensates and motivates the employee because the market value of a company's stock is tied to its performance. As the market value of the stock goes up, the difference between the option price and the market price increases, increasing the employee's compensation. When an option eventually is exercised and the stock is issued, the entry is similar to the one above. For example, assume that on July 1, 19x1, a company grants its key management personnel the option to purchase 50,000 shares of $10 par value common stock at the market value (as of that date) of $15 per share. Suppose that one of the firm's vice presidents exercises the option to purchase 2,000 shares on March 30, 19x2, when the market price is $25 per share. This entry would record the issue:

19x2			
Mar. 30	Cash	30,000	
	Common Stock		20,000
	Paid-in Capital in Excess of Par Value, Common		10,000
	Issued 2,000 shares of $10 par value common stock under the employee stock option plan		

Although the vice president has a gain of $20,000 (the $50,000 market value less the $30,000 option price), no compensation expense is recorded. Compensation expense would be recorded only if the option price is less than the $15 market price on July 1, 19x1, the date of grant. Methods of handling compensation in this situation are covered in more advanced courses.[4] Information pertaining to employee stock option plans should be discussed in the notes to the financial statements.

Chapter Review

Review of Learning Objectives

1. **Define *corporation* and state the advantages and disadvantages of the corporate form of business.**
   A corporation is a separate legal entity that has its own rights, privileges, and liabilities distinct from its owners. The owners are the firm's stockholders. They elect the board of directors and have the right to vote on key policies. The board determines company policy and appoints the managers, who are charged with the firm's day-to-day operations. Among the advantages of the corporate form of business are that

4. Stock options are discussed here in the context of employee compensation. They also can be important features of complex corporate capitalization arrangements.

(a) a corporation is a separate legal entity, (b) stockholders have limited liability, (c) it is easy to generate capital for a corporation, (d) stockholders can buy and sell shares of stock easily, (e) there is a lack of mutual agency, (f) the corporation has a continuous existence, (g) authority and responsibility are centralized, and (h) it is run by a professional management team. The disadvantages of corporations include (a) a large amount of government regulation, (b) double taxation, (c) difficulty of raising funds because of limited liability, and (d) separation of ownership and control.

2. **Account for organization costs.**
The costs of organizing a corporation are recorded at cost. The costs usually are amortized over five years.

3. **Identify the components of stockholders' equity.**
Stockholders' equity consists of contributed capital and retained earnings. Contributed capital includes two basic types of stock: common stock and preferred stock. When only one type of security is issued, it is common stock. Common stockholders have voting rights; they also share in the earnings of the corporation and in its assets in case of liquidation.
Preferred stock, like common stock, is sold to raise capital. But the investors have different objectives. To attract these investors, corporations usually give them a preference—in terms of receiving dividends and assets—over common stockholders. In addition, certain preferred stock is convertible. Preferred stock is often callable at the option of the corporation.
Retained earnings, the other component of stockholders' equity, represent the claim of stockholders to the assets of the company resulting from profitable operations. These are earnings that have been invested in the corporation.

4. **Account for cash dividends.**
The liability for payment of cash dividends arises on the date of declaration by the board of directors. The declaration is recorded with a debit to Cash Dividends Declared and a credit to Cash Dividends Payable. The date of record, on which no entry is required, establishes the stockholders who will receive the cash dividend on the date of payment. Payment is recorded with a debit to Cash Dividends Payable and a credit to Cash.

5. **Calculate the division of dividends between common and preferred stockholders.**
Preferred stockholders generally receive dividends before common stockholders. The dividend on preferred stock is figured first; then the remainder goes to common stock. If the preferred stock is cumulative and in arrears, the amount in arrears also has to be allocated to preferred stockholders before any allocation is made to common stockholders.

6. **Account for the issuance of common and preferred stock for cash and other assets.**
A corporation's stock normally is issued for cash and other assets or by subscription. The majority of states require that stock be issued at a minimum value called legal capital. Legal capital is represented by the par or stated value of the stock.
When stock is issued for cash at par or stated value, Cash is debited and Common Stock or Preferred Stock is credited. When stock is sold at an amount greater than par or stated value, the excess is recorded in Paid-in Capital in Excess of Par or Stated Value.
Sometimes stock is issued for noncash assets. Here, the accountant must decide how to value the stock. The general rule is to record the stock at its market value. If this value cannot be determined, then the fair market value of the asset received is used to record the transaction.

7. **Account for stock subscriptions.**
A stock subscription is an agreement to pay for stock on some future date or in installments at an agreed price. At the time the subscription is received, Subscriptions Receivable is debited and Capital Stock Subscribed is credited, as is Paid-in Capital in Excess of Par or Stated Value for any difference. Stock cannot be issued until it is fully paid. Payment is recorded by debiting Cash and crediting Subscriptions Receiv-

able; the actual issuance of stock is recorded by debiting Capital Stock Subscribed and crediting Capital Stock.

8. **Account for the exercise of stock options.**
Companywide stock option plans are used to encourage employees to own a part of the company. Other plans are offered only to management personnel, both to compensate and to motivate them. Usually, the issue of stock to employees under stock option plans is recorded in a manner similar to the issue of stock to any outsider.

Review of Concepts and Terminology

The following concepts and terms were introduced in this chapter:

(L.O. 1) **Articles of incorporation**: A contract between the state and the incorporators forming the corporation. Also called *corporate charter.*

(L.O. 1) **Audit committee**: A committee of the board of directors of a corporation, usually made up of outside directors, whose functions include hiring and monitoring the work of external auditors.

(L.O. 3) **Authorized stock**: The maximum number of shares a corporation can issue without changing its charter with the state.

(L.O. 5) **Callable preferred stock**: Preferred stock that can be redeemed and retired at the option of the corporation.

(L.O. 3) **Common stock**: Shares of stock that carry voting rights but that rank below preferred stock in terms of dividends and the distribution of assets.

(L.O. 3) **Contributed capital**: A part of stockholders' equity; the investments made by stockholders in a corporation.

(L.O. 5) **Convertible preferred stock**: Preferred stock that can be exchanged at the option of the holder for common stock.

(L.O. 1) **Corporation**: A separate legal entity having its own rights, privileges, and liabilities distinct from those of its owners.

(L.O. 5) **Cumulative preferred stock**: Preferred stock on which unpaid dividends accumulate over time and must be satisfied in any given year before a dividend can be paid to common stockholders.

(L.O. 4) **Dividend**: The distribution of a corporation's assets (usually cash) to its stockholders.

(L.O. 5) **Dividends in arrears**: Dividends on cumulative preferred stock that are not paid in the year they are due.

(L.O. 1) **Double taxation**: The act of taxing corporate earnings twice—once as the net income of the corporation and once as the dividends distributed to stockholders.

(L.O. 4) **Ex-dividend**: A description of capital stock between the date of record and the date of payment when the right to a dividend already declared on the stock remains with the person who sells the stock and does not transfer to the person who buys it.

(L.O. 3) **Issued stock**: The shares of stock sold or otherwise transferred to stockholders.

(L.O. 3) **Legal capital**: The number of shares of stock issued times the par value; the minimum amount that can be reported as contributed capital.

(L.O. 4) **Liquidating dividend**: A dividend that exceeds retained earnings; usually paid when a corporation goes out of business or reduces its operations.

(L.O. 5) **Noncumulative preferred stock**: Preferred stock that does not carry the obligation to be paid a dividend each year.

(L.O. 6) **No-par stock**: Capital stock that does not have a par value.

(L.O. 2) **Organization costs**: The costs of forming a corporation.

(L.O. 3) **Outstanding stock**: Stock that has been issued and is still in circulation.

(L.O. 3) **Par value:** The arbitrary amount printed on each share of stock; used to determine the legal capital of a corporation.

(L.O. 4) **Preferred stock:** Stock that has preference over common stock in terms of dividends and the distribution of assets.

(L.O. 1) **Proxy:** A legal document, signed by the stockholder, giving another party the right to vote his or her shares.

(L.O. 3) **Residual equity:** The common stock of a corporation.

(L.O. 3) **Retained earnings:** The accumulated earnings of a corporation from its inception less any losses, dividends, or transfers to contributed capital.

(L.O. 1) **Share of stock:** A unit of ownership in a corporation.

(L.O. 6) **Stated value:** A value assigned by the board of directors of a corporation to no-par stock.

(L.O. 3) **Stock certificate:** A document issued to a stockholder indicating the number of shares of stock the stockholder owns.

(L.O. 3) **Stockholders' equity:** The owners' claims to a corporation.

(L.O. 8) **Stock option plan:** An agreement to issue stock to employees according to the terms of a plan.

(L.O. 7) **Stock subscription:** An agreement to purchase stock on some future date or in installments at an agreed price.

(L.O. 3) **Underwriter:** An intermediary between the corporation and the public who facilitates an issue of stock or other securities for a fee.

Self-Test

Test your knowledge of the chapter by choosing the best answer for each of the following items.

(L.O. 1) 1. One disadvantage of the corporate form of business is
   a. government regulation.
   b. centralized authority and responsibility.
   c. the corporation's being a separate legal entity.
   d. continuous existence.

(L.O. 2) 2. The organization costs of a corporation should
   a. be recorded and maintained as an intangible asset for the life of the corporation.
   b. be recorded as an intangible asset and amortized over a reasonable length of time.
   c. be written off as an expense when incurred.
   d. not be incurred before the state grants the corporation its charter.

(L.O. 3) 3. All of the following normally are found in the stockholders' equity section of a corporate balance sheet *except*
   a. Paid-in Capital in Excess of Par Value.
   b. Retained Earnings.
   c. Cash Dividends Payable.
   d. Common Stock.

(L.O. 4) 4. The board of directors of the Birch Corporation declared a cash dividend on January 18, 19x8, to be paid on February 18, 19x8, to shareholders holding stock on February 2, 19x8. Given these facts, February 2, 19x8 is the
   a. date of declaration.
   b. date of record.
   c. payment date.
   d. corporate date.

(L.O. 4) 5. The journal entry to record the declaration of a cash dividend
   a. reduces assets.
   b. increases liabilities.
   c. increases total stockholders' equity.
   d. does not affect total stockholders' equity.

(L.O. 5) 6. Dividends in arrears are dividends on
   a. noncumulative preferred stock that have not been declared for some specific period of time.
   b. cumulative preferred stock that have been declared but have not been paid.
   c. cumulative preferred stock that have not been declared for some specific period of time.
   d. common stock that can never be declared.

(L.O. 6) 7. The par value of common stock represents the
   a. amount entered into the corporation's Common Stock account when shares are issued.
   b. exact amount the corporation receives when the stock is issued.
   c. liquidation value of the stock.
   d. stock's market value.

(L.O. 6) 8. The Paid-in Capital in Excess of Stated Value account is used when
   a. the par value of capital stock is greater than the stated value.
   b. capital stock is sold at an amount greater than stated value.
   c. the market value of the stock rises above its stated value.
   d. the number of shares issued exceeds the stock's stated value.

(L.O. 7) 9. Which of the following is properly classified as an asset?
   a. Subscriptions receivable
   b. Common stock subscribed
   c. Dividends in arrears
   d. Paid-in capital

(L.O. 8) 10. A plan under which employees are allowed to purchase shares of stock in a company at a specified price is called a stock
   a. option plan.
   b. subscription plan.
   c. dividend plan.
   d. compensation plan.

Answers to the Self-Test are at the end of this chapter.

Review Problem
Stock Journal Entries and Stockholders' Equity

(L.O. 2, 3, 4, 5, 6, 7) The Beta Corporation was organized in 19xx in the state of Arizona. Its charter authorized the corporation to issue 1,000,000 shares of $1 par value common stock and an additional 25,000 shares of 4 percent, $20 par value cumulative convertible preferred stock. Here are the transactions that related to the company's stock during 19xx:

Feb.	12	Issued 100,000 shares of common stock for $125,000.
	20	Issued 3,000 shares of common stock for accounting and legal services. The services were billed to the company at $3,600.
Mar.	15	Issued 120,000 shares of common stock to Edward Jackson in exchange for a building and land that had an appraised value of $100,000 and $25,000, respectively.
Apr.	2	Accepted subscriptions on 200,000 shares of common stock for $1.30 per share.
July	1	Issued 25,000 shares of preferred stock for $500,000.
Sept.	30	Collected in full subscriptions related to 60 percent of the common stock subscribed, and issued the appropriate stock to common stock subscribers. (Make two separate entries.)
Dec.	31	The company reported net income of $40,000 for 19xx, and the board declared dividends of $25,000, payable on January 15 to stockholders of record on January 8. Dividends included preferred stock cash dividends for one-half year.

Required

1. Prepare the journal entries necessary to record these transactions. Then close the Income Summary and Cash Dividends Declared accounts to Retained Earnings. Following the December 31 entry to record dividends, show dividends payable for each class of stock.
2. Prepare the stockholders' equity section of the Beta Corporation balance sheet as of December 31, 19xx.

Answer to Review Problem

1. Prepare the journal entries.

Date		Accounts and Explanation	Debit	Credit
19xx				
Feb.	12	Cash	125,000	
		Common Stock		100,000
		Paid-in Capital in Excess of Par Value, Common		25,000
		Sale of 100,000 shares of $1 par value common stock for $1.25 per share		
	20	Organization Costs	3,600	
		Common Stock		3,000
		Paid-in Capital in Excess of Par Value, Common		600
		Issue of 3,000 shares of $1 par value common stock for billed accounting and legal services of $3,600		
Mar.	15	Building	100,000	
		Land	25,000	
		Common Stock		120,000
		Paid-in Capital in Excess of Par Value, Common		5,000
		Issue of 120,000 shares of $1 par value common stock for a building and land appraised at $100,000 and $25,000		
Apr.	2	Subscriptions Receivable, Common	260,000	
		Common Stock Subscribed		200,000
		Paid-in Capital in Excess of Par Value, Common		60,000
		Subscriptions for 200,000 shares of $1 par value common stock for $1.30 per share		
July	1	Cash	500,000	
		Preferred Stock		500,000
		Sale of 25,000 shares of $20 par value preferred stock for $20 per share		
Sept.	30	Cash	156,000	
		Subscriptions Receivable, Common		156,000
		Collection in full of 60 percent of subscriptions receivable ($260,000 × .60 = $156,000)		
	30	Common Stock Subscribed	120,000	
		Common Stock		120,000
		Issue of 120,000 shares of common stock (200,000 shares × .60 = 120,000)		
Dec.	31	Income Summary	40,000	
		Retained Earnings		40,000
		To close the Income Summary account to Retained Earnings		

			Debit	Credit
Dec. 31	Cash Dividends Declared		25,000	
	Cash Dividends Payable			25,000
	Declaration of a $25,000 cash dividend to preferred and common stockholders			
	Total dividend	$25,000		
	Less preferred stock cash dividend: ($500,000 × .04 × 6/12)	10,000		
	Common stock cash dividend	$15,000		
31	Retained Earnings		25,000	
	Cash Dividends Declared			25,000
	To close the Cash Dividends Declared account to Retained Earnings			

2. Prepare the stockholders' equity section of the balance sheet.

Beta Corporation
Stockholders' Equity
December 31, 19xx

Contributed Capital		
Preferred Stock—4% cumulative convertible, $20 par value, 25,000 shares authorized, issued, and outstanding		$ 500,000
Common Stock—$1 par value, 1,000,000 shares authorized, 343,000 shares issued and outstanding	$343,000	
Common Stock Subscribed, 80,000 shares	80,000	
Paid-in Capital in Excess of Par Value, Common	90,600	513,600
Total Contributed Capital		$1,013,600
Retained Earnings		15,000
Total Stockholders' Equity		$1,028,600

Chapter Assignments

Questions

1. What is a corporation, and how is it formed?
2. What is the role of the board of directors in a corporation, and how does it differ from the role of management?
3. Who are the typical officers of a corporation, and what is an officer's role in the management of a corporation?
4. Identify and explain several advantages of the corporate form of business.
5. Identify and explain several disadvantages of the corporate form of business.
6. What are the organization costs of a corporation?
7. What is the proper accounting treatment of organization costs?
8. What is the legal capital of a corporation, and what is its significance?
9. How is the value of stock determined when stock is issued for noncash assets?

10. Describe the significance of the following dates as they relate to dividends: (a) date of declaration, (b) date of record, and (c) date of payment.
11. Explain the accounting treatment of cash dividends.
12. What is a stock subscription, and how are Subscriptions Receivable and Common Stock Subscribed classified on the balance sheet?
13. Define the terms *cumulative, convertible,* and *callable* as they apply to preferred stock.
14. What are dividends in arrears, and how should they be disclosed in the financial statements?
15. What is the proper classification of the following accounts on the balance sheet? For owners' equity accounts, indicate whether they are contributed capital or retained earnings. (a) Organization Costs; (b) Common Stock; (c) Subscriptions Receivable, Preferred; (d) Preferred Stock Subscribed; (e) Paid-in Capital in Excess of Par Value, Common; (f) Paid-in Capital in Excess of Stated Value, Common; and (g) Retained Earnings.

Communication Skills Exercises

Communication 12-1. The Corporate Form of Business and Ethical Considerations for the Accounting Profession
(L.O. 1)

Traditionally, accounting firms have organized as partnerships or as professional corporations, a form of corporation that in many ways resembles a partnership. In recent years, some accounting firms have suffered large judgments as a result of lawsuits by investors who lost money when they invested in companies that went bankrupt. In one case, a large international accounting firm went bankrupt mainly because of liabilities that were anticipated to arise from problems in the savings and loan industry. The partners dissolved the firm rather than put up the additional capital needed to keep it going. Because of the increased risk of large losses from malpractice suits, there is a movement to allow accounting firms to incorporate as long as they maintain a minimum level of partners' capital and carry malpractice insurance. Some accounting practitioners feel that incorporating would be a violation of their responsibility to the public. What features of the corporate form of business would be most advantageous to the partners of an accounting firm? Do you think it would be a violation of the public trust for an accounting firm to incorporate? (**Hint:** The characteristics of partnerships are covered in an appendix at the end of the book.)

Communication 12-2. Effect of the Omission of Preferred Dividends
(L.O. 5)

Tucson Electric Company, the *Wall Street Journal* disclosed, omitted all its preferred stock dividends indefinitely in an effort to improve liquidity. All of the company's cumulative preferred stock was affected. According to the article, "Some interpreted the drastic action as a requisite for the cash-strapped utility to secure a new credit agreement. . . . If the credit agreement falls through, the omission of preferred-stock dividends would suggest Tucson Electric is perilously close to filing for bankruptcy."[5] What are cumulative preferred shares? Why is the omission of dividends on these shares a "drastic action"? If new bank financing is not obtained, why would the company have to consider declaring bankruptcy?

Communication 12-3. Basic Research Skills
(L.O. 4, 5, 6, 8)

In your library, select the annual reports of three corporations. You can choose them from the same industry or at random, at the direction of your instructor. (**Note**: You will use these companies again in the basic research skills exercises in later chapters.) Prepare a table with a column for each corporation. Then answer the following questions for each corporation: Does the corporation have preferred stock? If so, what are the par value and the indicated dividend, and is the preferred stock cumulative or convertible? Is the common stock par value or no-par? What is the par value or stated value? What cash dividends, if any, were paid in the past year? From the notes to the financial statements, determine whether the company has an employee stock option plan. What are some of its provisions? Be prepared to discuss the characteristics of the stocks and dividends for your selected companies in class.

5. Rick Wartzman, "Tucson Electric Omits Dividends on Preferred Stock," *Wall Street Journal,* December 10, 1990.

Classroom Exercises

Exercise 12-1. Journal Entries for Organization Costs *(L.O. 2, 6)*

The Wendt Corporation was organized during 19x7. At the beginning of the fiscal year, the company incurred the following organization costs: (1) Attorney's fees, market value of services, $6,000; paid with 2,000 shares of $2 par common stock. (2) Incorporation fees paid to the state, $5,000. (3) Accountant's services that normally would be billed at $3,000; paid with 1,100 shares of $2 par value common stock.

Prepare the separate journal entries necessary to record these transactions and to amortize organization costs for the first year, assuming that the company elects to write off organization costs over five years.

Exercise 12-2. Stockholders' Equity *(L.O. 3, 7)*

The accounts and balances below were taken from the records of Jamil Corporation on December 31, 19xx.

Account	Balance Debit	Balance Credit
Preferred Stock—$100 par value, 9% cumulative, 20,000 shares authorized, 12,000 shares issued and outstanding		$1,200,000
Common Stock—$12 par value, 90,000 shares authorized, 60,000 shares issued and outstanding		720,000
Common Stock Subscribed, 4,000 shares		48,000
Paid-in Capital in Excess of Par Value, Common		340,000
Retained Earnings		46,000
Subscriptions Receivable, Common	$60,000	

Prepare a stockholders' equity section for Jamil Corporation's balance sheet.

Exercise 12-3. Characteristics of Common and Preferred Stock *(L.O. 3)*

For each of the characteristics listed below, indicate whether it is more closely associated with common stock (C) or with preferred stock (P).

_____ 1. Often receives dividends at a set rate
_____ 2. Is known as the residual equity of a company
_____ 3. Can be callable
_____ 4. Can be convertible
_____ 5. Amount of dividend more likely to vary from year to year
_____ 6. Can be entitled to receive dividends not paid in past years
_____ 7. Likely to have full voting rights
_____ 8. Receives assets first in liquidation
_____ 9. Generally receives dividends before other classes of stock

Exercise 12-4. Journal Entries and Stockholders' Equity *(L.O. 3, 6)*

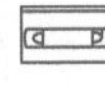

In January 19xx, the Winkler Hospital Supply Corporation was organized. The company was authorized to issue 100,000 shares of no-par common stock with a stated value of $5 per share, and 20,000 shares of $100 par value, 6 percent noncumulative preferred stock. On March 1 the company sold 60,000 shares of its common stock for $15 per share and 8,000 shares of its preferred stock for $100 per share.

1. Prepare the journal entries to record the sale of the stock.
2. Prepare the company's stockholders' equity section of the balance sheet immediately after the common and preferred stock was issued.

Exercise 12-5.
Cash Dividends
(L.O. 4)

Downey Corporation has secured authorization from the state for 200,000 shares of $10 par value common stock. There are 160,000 shares issued and 140,000 shares outstanding. On June 5, the board of directors declared a $.50 per share cash dividend to be paid on June 25 to stockholders of record on June 15. Prepare the journal entries necessary to record these events.

Exercise 12-6.
Cash Dividends
(L.O. 4)

Gayle Corporation has 500,000 authorized shares of $1 par value common stock, of which 400,000 are issued and 360,000 are outstanding. On October 15, the board of directors declared a cash dividend of $.25 per share payable on November 15 to stockholders of record on November 1. Prepare the entries, as necessary, for each of the three dates.

Exercise 12-7.
Cash Dividends with Dividends in Arrears
(L.O. 5)

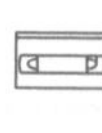

The Matsuta Corporation has 10,000 shares of its $100 par value, 7 percent cumulative preferred stock outstanding, and 50,000 shares of its $1 par value common stock outstanding. In its first four years of operation, the board of directors of Matsuta Corporation paid cash dividends as follows: 19x1, none; 19x2, $120,000; 19x3, $140,000; 19x4, $140,000.

Determine the dividends per share and total cash dividends paid to the preferred and common stockholders during each of the four years.

Exercise 12-8.
Preferred and Common Cash Dividends
(L.O. 5)

The Levinson Corporation pays dividends at the end of each year. The dividends paid for 19x1, 19x2, and 19x3 were $80,000, $60,000, and $180,000, respectively.

Calculate the total amount of dividends paid each year to the common and preferred stockholders if each of the following capital structures is assumed: (1) 20,000 shares of $100 par, 6 percent noncumulative preferred stock and 60,000 shares of $10 par common stock. (2) 10,000 shares of $100 par, 7 percent cumulative preferred stock and 60,000 shares of $10 par common stock. There were no dividends in arrears at the beginning of 19x1.

Exercise 12-9.
Issuance of Stock
(L.O. 6)

Foth Company is authorized to issue 200,000 shares of common stock. On August 1, the company sold 10,000 shares at $25 per share. Prepare journal entries to record the sale of stock for cash under each of the following independent alternatives:

1. The stock has a par value of $25.
2. The stock has a par value of $10.
3. The stock has no par value.
4. The stock has a stated value of $1 per share.

Exercise 12-10.
Journal Entries: Stated Value Stock
(L.O. 6)

The Gladstone Corporation is authorized to issue 100,000 shares of no-par stock. The company recently sold 80,000 shares for $13 per share.

1. Prepare the journal entry to record the sale of the stock assuming there is no stated value.
2. Prepare the journal entry if a $10 stated value is authorized by the company's board of directors.

Exercise 12-11.
Issuance of Stock for Noncash Assets
(L.O. 6)

On July 1, 19xx, Elk Grove, a new corporation, issued 20,000 shares of its common stock for a corporate headquarters building. The building has a fair market value of $600,000 and a book value of $400,000. Because the corporation is new, it is not possible to establish a market value for the common stock.

Record the issuance of stock for the building, assuming the following conditions: (1) The par value of the stock is $10 per share; (2) the stock is no-par stock; and (3) the stock has a stated value of $4 per share.

Exercise 12-12.
Issuance of Stock for Noncash Assets
(L.O. 6)

The Yang Corporation issued 2,000 shares of its $20 par value common stock for some land. The land had a fair market value of $60,000.

Prepare the journal entries necessary to record the stock issue for the land under each of the following conditions: (1) The stock was selling for $28 per share on the day of the transaction; and (2) management attempted to place a market value on the common stock but could not do so.

Exercise 12-13.
Stock Subscriptions
(L.O. 7)

The Spangler Corporation sold 15,000 shares of its $2 par value common stock by subscription for $8 per share on February 15, 19xx. Cash was received in installments from the purchasers: 50 percent on April 1 and 50 percent on June 1.

Prepare the journal entries necessary to record these transactions.

Exercise 12-14.
Stock Subscriptions
(L.O. 7)

The Pinto Corporation sold 50,000 shares of its no-par, $10 stated value common stock by subscription for $18 per share on March 12, 19xx. The purchasers paid for the stock in installments of 60 percent on April 1 and 40 percent on May 1.

Prepare journal entries to record these transactions.

Exercise 12-15.
Exercise of Stock Options
(L.O. 8)

Record the following equity transaction of the Evans Company in 19xx:

May 5 Walter Evans exercised his option to purchase 10,000 shares of $1 par value common stock at an option price of $12. The market price per share on the grant date was $12, and it was $24 on the exercise date.

Interpretation Case from Business

United Airlines
(L.O. 3, 6)

UAL Corporation is a holding company whose primary subsidiary is United Airlines, which provides passenger and cargo air transportation to 141 airports worldwide. On March 21, 1991, UAL announced a common stock issue in the *Wall Street Journal:*

1,500,000 Shares
UAL Corporation
Common Stock
($5 par value)
Price $146 per share

In fact, UAL sold 1,733,100 shares of stock at $146 for net proceeds of $247.2 million.

Here is a portion of the stockholders' equity section of the balance sheet from UAL's 1990 annual report:

	1990	1989
	(in thousands)	
Common Stock, $5 par value; authorized 125,000,000 shares; issued 23,467,880 shares in 1990 and 23,419,953 shares in 1989	$ 117,339	$ 117,100
Additional Paid-in Capital	52,391	47,320
Retained Earnings	1,620,885	1,526,534

Required

1. Assuming that all the shares were issued at the price indicated and that UAL received the net proceeds, prepare the entry in UAL's accounting records to record the stock issue.
2. Prepare the portion of the stockholders' equity section of the balance sheet shown above after the issue of the common stock, based on the information given. Round all answers to the nearest thousand.
3. Based on your answer in **2**, did UAL have to increase its authorized shares to undertake this stock issue?
4. What amount per share did UAL receive and how much did UAL's underwriter receive to help in issuing the stock if investors paid $146 per share? What does the underwriter do to earn his or her fee?

Problem Set A

Problem 12A-1. Organization Costs, Stock and Dividend Journal Entries, and Stockholders' Equity
(L.O. 2, 3, 4, 6)

Lasser Corporation began operations on September 1, 19xx. The corporation's charter authorized 300,000 shares of $8 par value common stock. Lasser Corporation engaged in the following transactions during its first quarter:

Sept.	1	Issued 50,000 shares of common stock, $500,000.
	1	Paid an attorney $32,000 to help organize the corporation and obtain the corporate charter from the state.
Oct.	2	Issued 80,000 shares of common stock, $960,000.
Nov.	30	The board of directors declared a cash dividend of $.40 per share to be paid on December 15 to stockholders of record on December 10.
	30	Closed the Income Summary and Cash Dividends Declared accounts for the first quarter. Revenues were $420,000 and expenses $340,000. (Assume revenues and expenses already have been closed to Income Summary.)

Required

1. Prepare general journal entries to record the first-quarter transactions and the closing entries.
2. Prepare the stockholders' equity section of Lasser Corporation's November 30, 19xx balance sheet.
3. Assuming that the payment to the attorney on September 1 was going to be amortized over five years, what adjusting entry was made on November 30?
4. How does the adjusting entry in **3** affect the balance sheet, including the resulting amount of organization costs?

Problem 12A-2. Stock Subscriptions, Stock Journal Entries, and Stockholders' Equity
(L.O. 3, 6, 7)

The corporate charter for Matlin Corporation states that the company is authorized to issue 500,000 shares of $6 par value common stock. The company was involved with several stock transactions during June 19x8, as shown in the following list. Assume no prior transactions.

June	3	Accepted subscriptions for 200,000 shares of its common stock at $11 per share.
	12	Issued 24,000 shares of stock for land and a warehouse. The land and warehouse had a fair market value of $50,000 and $200,000, respectively.
	22	Sold 50,000 shares of stock for $650,000.
	25	Collected full payment on 60,000 shares of the common stock subscribed on June 3 and issued the shares.

Required

1. Prepare the general journal entries to record the June transactions of Matlin Corporation.
2. Prepare the stockholders' equity section of Matlin Corporation's balance sheet as of June 30, 19x8. Assume that the company had net income of $16,000 during June and paid no dividends (and that all necessary entries have been made).

Problem 12A-3. Preferred and Common Stock Dividends
(L.O. 5)

The Rayner Corporation had both common stock and preferred stock outstanding from 19x4 through 19x6. Information about each stock for the three years is as follows:

Type	Par Value	Shares Outstanding	Other
Preferred	$100	40,000	7% cumulative
Common	20	600,000	

The company paid $140,000, $800,000, and $1,100,000 in dividends for 19x4 through 19x6, respectively.

Required

1. Determine the dividend per share and the total dividends paid to the common and preferred stockholders each year.
2. Repeat the computation performed in **1**, with the assumption that the preferred stock was noncumulative.

Problem 12A-4. Comprehensive Stockholders' Equity Transactions
(L.O. 2, 3, 4, 5, 6, 7)

The Loomis Plastics Corporation was chartered in the state of Wisconsin. The company was authorized to issue 20,000 shares of $100 par value, 6 percent preferred stock and 100,000 shares of no-par common stock. The common stock has a $2 stated value. The stock-related transactions for March and April 19xx were as follows:

Mar.	3	Issued 10,000 shares of common stock for $120,000 worth of services rendered in organizing and chartering the corporation.
	10	Received subscriptions for 40,000 shares of common stock at $12 per share.
	15	Issued 16,000 shares of common stock for land, which had an asking price of $200,000. The common stock had a market value of $12 per share.
	22	Issued 10,000 shares of preferred stock for $1,000,000.
	30	Closed the Income Summary account. Net income for March was $18,000.
Apr.	4	Issued 10,000 shares of common stock for $120,000.
	10	Received payment in full for 30,000 shares of the subscriptions received on March 10 and issued the appropriate stock.
	15	Declared a cash dividend for one month on the outstanding preferred stock and $.10 per share on common stock outstanding, payable on April 30 to stockholders of record on April 25.
	25	Date of record for cash dividends.
	30	Paid cash dividends.
	30	Closed the Income Summary and Cash Dividends Declared accounts. Net income for April was $28,000.

Required

1. Prepare general journal entries for March and April.
2. Prepare the stockholders' equity section of the company's balance sheet as of April 30, 19xx.

Problem 12A-5. Comprehensive Stockholders' Equity Transactions
(L.O. 2, 3, 4, 6, 7, 8)

The Omni Lighting Corporation was organized and authorized to issue 200,000 shares of 6 percent, $100 par value, noncumulative preferred stock and 3,000,000 shares of $10 par value common stock. The stock-related transactions for the first six months of 19xx operations were as follows:

Apr.	3	Issued 12,000 shares of common stock for legal and other organization fees valued at $120,000.
	29	Sold 300,000 shares of common stock for $12 per share.
May	5	Issued 40,000 shares of common stock for a building and land appraised at $300,000 and $160,000, respectively.
	17	Received subscriptions for 300,000 shares of common stock at $16 per share.
June	17	Received full payment for 200,000 shares of common stock subscribed on May 17 and issued the stock.
	30	Closed the Income Summary account for the first quarter of operations. Net income for the first quarter was $400,000. (Assume that revenues and expenses already have been closed to Income Summary.)
July	10	Issued 2,000 shares of common stock to employees under a stock option plan. The plan allows employees to purchase the stock at the current market price, $12 per share.
	17	Collected the full amount for the remaining 100,000 shares of common stock subscribed on May 17 and issued the stock.
Aug.	8	Issued 10,000 shares of common stock for $16 per share.
Sept.	11	Declared a cash dividend of $.20 per common share to be paid on September 25 to stockholders of record on September 18.
	18	Cash dividend date of record.
	25	Paid the cash dividend to stockholders of record on September 18.
	26	Issued 10,000 shares of preferred stock at par value.
	29	Accepted subscriptions for 20,000 shares of common stock at $18 per share.
	30	Closed the Income Summary and Cash Dividends Declared accounts for the second quarter of operations. Net income for the second quarter was $250,000.

Required

1. Prepare general journal entries to record the stock-related transactions of the Omni Lighting Corporation.
2. Prepare the stockholders' equity section of Omni Lighting Corporation's balance sheet as of September 30, 19xx.

Problem Set B

Problem 12B-1. Organization Costs, Stock and Dividend Journal Entries, and Stockholders' Equity
(L.O. 2, 3, 4, 6)

On March 1, 19xx, Blanco Corporation began operations with a charter from the state that authorized 100,000 shares of $4 par value common stock. Over the next quarter, the firm engaged in the following transactions:

Mar.	1	Issued 30,000 shares of common stock, $200,000.
	2	Paid fees associated with obtaining the charter and organizing the corporation, $24,000.
Apr.	10	Issued 13,000 shares of common stock, $130,000.
May	31	Closed the Income Summary account. Net income earned during the first quarter, $24,000.
	31	The board of directors declared a $.20 per share cash dividend to be paid on June 15 to shareholders of record on June 10.
	31	Closed Cash Dividends Declared to Retained Earnings.

Required

1. Prepare general journal entries to record the transactions and closing entries indicated above.
2. Prepare the stockholders' equity section of Blanco Corporation's balance sheet on May 31, 19xx.
3. Assuming that the payment for organization costs on March 2 was going to be amortized over five years, what adjusting entry was made on May 31 to record three months' amortization?
4. How does the adjusting entry in **3** affect the firm's balance sheet, including the resulting amount of organization costs?

Problem 12B-2. Stock Journal Entries and Stockholders' Equity
(L.O. 3, 6, 7)

The Ranganath Company, Inc. has been authorized by the state of Indiana to issue 1,000,000 shares of $2 par value common stock. The company began issuing its common stock in May 19xx.

During May the company had the following stock transactions:

May	10	Issued 30,000 shares of stock for a building and land with a fair market value of $64,000 and $14,000, respectively.
	15	Accepted subscriptions to 500,000 shares of its stock for $1,300,000.
	20	Collected full payment on 200,000 shares of the common stock subscribed on May 15 and issued the shares.
	23	Sold 15,000 shares of stock for $40,000 cash.
	27	Collected full payment on 100,000 shares of the common stock subscribed on May 15 and issued the shares.

Required

1. Prepare the general journal entries to record the stock transactions of Ranganath Company, Inc. for the month of May.
2. Prepare the stockholders' equity section of Ranganath's balance sheet as of May 31, 19xx. Assume that the company had net income of $36,000 for May and paid no dividends.

Problem 12B-3. Preferred and Common Stock Dividends
(L.O. 5)

The Fogel Corporation had the following stock outstanding from 19x1 through 19x4:

Preferred stock: $100 par value, 8 percent cumulative, 10,000 shares authorized, issued, and outstanding

Common stock: $10 par value, 200,000 shares authorized, issued, and outstanding

The company paid $60,000, $60,000, $188,000, and $260,000 in dividends during 19x1, 19x2, 19x3, and 19x4, respectively.

Required

1. Determine the dividend per share and the total dividends paid to common stockholders and preferred stockholders in 19x1, 19x2, 19x3, and 19x4.
2. Perform the same computations, with the assumption that the preferred stock was noncumulative.

Problem 12B-4. Comprehensive Stockholders' Equity Transactions
(L.O. 2, 3, 4, 5, 6, 7)

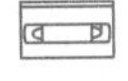

Cabrini, Inc. was organized and authorized to issue 10,000 shares of $100 par value, 9 percent preferred stock and 100,000 shares of no-par, $5 stated value common stock on July 1, 19xx. Stock-related transactions for Cabrini were as follows:

July 1 Issued 20,000 shares of common stock at $11 per share.
1 Issued 1,000 shares of common stock at $11 per share for services rendered in connection with the organization of the company.
2 Issued 2,000 shares of preferred stock at par value for cash.
10 Received subscriptions for 10,000 shares of common stock at $12 per share.
10 Issued 5,000 shares of common stock for land on which the asking price was $60,000. Market value of the stock was $12. Management wishes to record the land at full market value of the stock.
31 Closed the Income Summary account. Net income earned during July was $13,000.
Aug. 2 Received payment in full for 6,000 shares of the stock subscriptions of July 10. Issued the appropriate stocks.
10 Declared a cash dividend for one month on the outstanding preferred stock and $.02 per share on common stock outstanding, payable on August 22 to stockholders of record on August 12.
12 Date of record for cash dividends.
22 Paid cash dividends.
31 Closed the Income Summary and Cash Dividends Declared accounts. Net income during August was $12,000.

Required

1. Prepare general journal entries to record the above transactions.
2. Prepare the stockholders' equity section of the balance sheet as it would appear on August 31, 19xx.

Problem 12B-5. Comprehensive Stockholders' Equity Transactions
(L.O. 2, 3, 4, 6, 7, 8)

In January 19xx, the Rumilla Corporation was organized and authorized to issue 2,000,000 shares of no-par common stock and 50,000 shares of 5 percent, $100 par value, noncumulative preferred stock. The stock-related transactions for the first year's operations follow.

Jan. 19 Sold 30,000 shares of the common stock for $63,000. State law requires a minimum of $1 stated value per share.
21 Issued 10,000 shares of common stock to attorneys and accountants for services valued at $22,000 and provided during the organization of the corporation.
26 Accepted subscriptions for 40,000 shares of the common stock for $2.50 per share.
Feb. 7 Issued 60,000 shares of common stock for a building that had an appraised value of $156,000.
Mar. 22 Collected full payment for 24,000 shares of the common stock subscribed on January 26, 19xx and issued the stock.
June 30 Closed the Income Summary account. Reported $160,000 income for the first six months of operations, ended June 30.
July 15 Issued 10,000 shares of common stock to employees under a stock option plan that allows any employee to buy shares at the current market price, which today is $3 per share.
Aug. 1 Collected the full amount on the remaining 16,000 shares of common stock subscribed and issued the stock.
Sept. 1 Declared a cash dividend of $.15 per common share to be paid on September 25 to stockholders of record on September 15.
15 Cash dividend date of record.
25 Paid cash dividend to stockholders of record on September 15.

Oct. 30 Issued 8,000 shares of common stock for a piece of land. The stock was selling for $3 per share, and the land had a fair market value of $25,000.
Nov. 10 Accepted subscriptions for 20,000 shares of the common stock for $3.50 per share.
Dec. 15 Issued 2,200 shares of preferred stock for $100 per share.
31 Closed the Income Summary and Cash Dividends Declared accounts. Reported $40,000 income for the past six months of operations.

Required

1. Prepare the journal entries to record all of the transactions above.
2. Prepare the stockholders' equity section of Rumilla Corporation's balance sheet as of December 31, 19xx.

Financial Decision Case

Infinite Systems Corporation
(L.O. 3)

Companies offering services to the computer technology industry are growing quickly. Participating in this growth, Infinite Systems Corporation has expanded rapidly in recent years. Because of its profitability, the company has been able to grow without obtaining external financing. This fact is reflected in its current balance sheet, which contains no long-term debt. The liability and stockholders' equity sections of the balance sheet are shown below.

Infinite Systems Corporation
Partial Balance Sheet

Liabilities		
Current Liabilities		$ 1,000,000
Stockholders' Equity		
Common Stock—$20 par value, 500,000 shares authorized, 100,000 shares issued and outstanding	$2,000,000	
Paid-in Capital in Excess of Par Value, Common	3,600,000	
Total Contributed Capital	5,600,000	
Retained Earnings	3,400,000	
Total Stockholders' Equity		9,000,000
Total Liabilities and Stockholders' Equity		$10,000,000

The company is now faced with the possibility of doubling its size by purchasing the operations of a rival company for $8,000,000. If the purchase goes through, Infinite Systems will become the top company in its specialized industry in the northeastern part of the country. The problem for management is how to finance the purchase. After much study and discussion with bankers and underwriters, management has prepared three financing alternatives to present to the board of directors, which must authorize the purchase and the financing.

Alternative A: The company could issue $8,000,000 of long-term debt. Given the company's financial rating and the current market rates, management believes the company will have to pay an interest rate of 12 percent on the debt.

Alternative B: The company could issue 80,000 shares of 10 percent, $100 par value preferred stock.

Alternative C: The company could issue 100,000 additional shares of $20 par value common stock at $80 per share.

Management explains to the board that the interest on the long-term debt is tax-deductible and that the applicable income tax rate is 40 percent. The board members know that a dividend of $1.60 per share of common stock was paid last year, up from $1.20 and $.80 per share in the two years before that. The board has had a policy of regular increases in dividends of $.40 per share. The board feels that each of the three financing alternatives is feasible and now wants to study the financial effects of each alternative.

Required

1. Prepare a schedule to show how the liability and stockholders' equity side of Infinite Systems' balance sheet would look under each alternative, and figure the debt to equity ratio (total liabilities ÷ total stockholders' equity) for each.
2. Compute and compare the cash needed to pay the interest or dividends for each kind of new financing net of income taxes in the first year.
3. How might the cash needed to pay for the financing change in future years?
4. Evaluate the alternatives, giving arguments for and against each one.

Answers to Self-Test

1. a	3. c	5. b	7. a	9. a
2. b	4. b	6. c	8. b	10. a

LEARNING OBJECTIVES

1. *Define retained earnings and prepare a statement of retained earnings.*
2. *Account for stock dividends and stock splits.*
3. *Account for treasury stock transactions.*
4. *Describe the disclosure of restrictions on retained earnings.*
5. *Prepare a statement of stockholders' equity.*
6. *Calculate book value per share and distinguish it from market value.*
7. *Prepare a corporate income statement.*
8. *Show the relationships among income taxes expense, deferred income taxes, and net of taxes.*
9. *Describe the disclosure on the income statement of discontinued operations, extraordinary items, and accounting changes.*
10. *Compute earnings per share.*

CHAPTER 13

Retained Earnings and Corporate Income Statements

This chapter continues the study of the stockholders' equity section of the balance sheet. It first covers the retained earnings of a corporation, the transactions that affect them, and the statement of stockholders' equity. The rest of the chapter examines the components of the corporate income statement. After studying this chapter, you should be able to meet the learning objectives listed on the left.

DECISION POINT
International Business Machines Corporation (IBM)

■ A note to IBM's 1989 annual report outlines the company's stock repurchase plan, which already has resulted in the repurchase of a substantial number of IBM's common shares and projects the repurchase of many more shares:

> Under programs for purchasing IBM stock, 16,085,900 shares were purchased during 1989 at a cost of $1,759 million, 8,611,396 shares were repurchased during 1988 at a cost of $992 million and 11,252,000 shares during 1987 at a cost of $1,425 million. The repurchased shares were retired and restored to the status of authorized but unissued shares. In late 1989, the Board of Directors authorized the company to purchase from time to time shares of its capital stock not to exceed $5,000 million. At December 31, 1989, $4,887 million of that authorization remained.[1]

Why would management want to repurchase its company's common shares, and what are the effects of these repurchases on the company's financial statements?

There are several good reasons for a company to repurchase its common stock, as we discuss later in this chapter. The goal of IBM's management was to increase the value of the company's stock, as revealed in the following excerpt from the letter to stockholders in the annual report:

> To further enhance shareholder value, IBM has, since 1986, repurchased shares of its common stock—a total of 47 million shares through the end of 1989. Repurchase reduces shareholders' equity, distributing earnings over a smaller base and increasing returns. The benefit to IBM shareholders has been to increase return on equity by approximately 6 percent in 1988 and 1989. . . . We regard IBM stock as an attractive investment.[2]

1. Excerpted from the 1989 annual report of IBM Corporation.
2. Ibid.

Examination of IBM's statement of stockholders' equity reveals that large amounts of common stock indeed were retired in 1987, 1988, and 1989, resulting in decreases in common stock and retained earnings. The decrease in retained earnings in 1989, for example, was $1,582 million. The retirement of common stock is just one of several important transactions that affect retained earnings. The following sections explore these transactions. ■

Retained Earnings Transactions

OBJECTIVE 1
Define retained earnings and prepare a statement of retained earnings

Stockholders' equity, as presented earlier, has two parts: contributed capital and retained earnings. The **retained earnings** of a company are the part of stockholders' equity that represents claims to assets arising from the earnings of the business. Retained earnings equal the profits of a company since the date of its inception, less any losses, dividends to stockholders, or transfers to contributed capital. Exhibit 13-1 shows a statement of retained earnings for Caprock Corporation for 19x2. The beginning balance of retained earnings of $854,000 is increased by net income of $76,000 and decreased by cash dividends of $30,000. The ending balance is $900,000. The statement of retained earnings also can disclose other transactions that are explained in this chapter.

It is important to remember that retained earnings are not the assets themselves: The existence of retained earnings means that assets generated by profitable operations have been kept in the company to help it grow or to meet other business needs. A credit balance in Retained Earnings does *not* mean that cash or any designated set of assets is associated directly with retained earnings. The fact that earnings have been retained means that assets as a whole have been increased.

Retained Earnings can carry a debit balance. Generally, this happens when a company's losses and distributions to stockholders are greater than its profits from operations. In such a case, the firm is said to have a **deficit** (debit balance) in Retained Earnings. A deficit is shown in the stockholders' equity section of the balance sheet as a deduction from contributed capital.

Accountants use various terms to describe the retained earnings of a business. One is *surplus*, which implies that there are excess assets available for dividends. This usage is poor because the existence of retained earnings carries no connotation of "excess" or "surplus." Because of possible misinterpretation, the American Institute of Certified Public Accountants recommends more fitting terms, such as *retained income, retained earnings, accumulated earnings,* or *earnings retained for use in the business.*[3]

Prior period adjustments are events or transactions that relate to earlier accounting periods but that could not be determined in the earlier periods. When they occur, they are shown on the statement of retained earnings as an adjustment in the beginning balance. The Financial Accounting Standards Board identifies only two kinds of prior period adjustments. The first is to correct an error in the financial statements of a prior year. The second is needed if a company realizes an income tax gain from carrying forward a preacquisition operating loss of a purchased subsidiary.[4] Prior period adjustments are rare.

3. Committee on Accounting Terminology, *Accounting Terminology Bulletin No. 1*, "Review and Resume" (New York: American Institute of Certified Public Accountants, 1953), par. 69.
4. *Statement of Financial Accounting Standards No. 16*, "Prior Period Adjustments" (Stamford, Conn.: Financial Accounting Standards Board, 1977), par. 11.

Exhibit 13-1. A Statement of Retained Earnings

Caprock Corporation Statement of Retained Earnings For the Year Ended December 31, 19x2	
Retained Earnings, December 31, 19x1	$854,000
Net Income, 19x2	76,000
Subtotal	$930,000
Less Cash Dividends, Common	30,000
Retained Earnings, December 31, 19x2	$900,000

Stock Dividends

OBJECTIVE 2
Account for stock dividends and stock splits

A **stock dividend** is a proportional distribution of shares of the corporation's stock to its stockholders. The distribution of stock does not change the assets and liabilities of the firm because there is no distribution of assets as there is when a cash dividend is distributed.

The board of directors can declare a stock dividend for several reasons:

1. It may want to give stockholders some evidence of the success of the company without paying a cash dividend, which would affect the firm's working capital position.
2. It may seek to reduce the market price of the stock by increasing the number of shares outstanding, although this goal more often is met by stock splits.
3. It may want to make a nontaxable distribution to stockholders. Stock dividends that meet certain conditions are not considered income, so a tax is not levied on them.
4. It communicates that the permanent capital of the company has increased by transferring an amount from retained earnings to contributed capital.

The total stockholders' equity is not affected by a stock dividend. The effect of a stock dividend is to transfer a dollar amount from retained earnings to the contributed capital section on the date of declaration. The amount transferred is the fair market value (usually, the market price) of the additional shares to be issued. The laws of most states specify the minimum value of each share transferred under a stock dividend, which is normally the minimum legal capital (par or stated value). However, generally accepted accounting principles state that market value reflects the economic effect of small stock distributions (less than 20 to 25 percent of a company's outstanding common stock) better than par or stated value does. For this reason, market price should be used to account for small stock dividends.[5]

To illustrate the accounting for a stock dividend, we assume that Caprock Corporation has the following stockholders' equity structure:

Contributed Capital	
Common Stock—$5 par value, 100,000 shares authorized, 30,000 shares issued and outstanding	$ 150,000
Paid-in Capital in Excess of Par Value, Common	30,000
Total Contributed Capital	$ 180,000
Retained Earnings	900,000
Total Stockholders' Equity	$1,080,000

5. *Accounting Research Bulletin No. 43* (New York: American Institute of Certified Public Accountants, 1953), chap. 7, sec. B, par. 10.

Suppose that the corporation's board of directors declares a 10 percent stock dividend on February 24, distributable on March 31 to stockholders of record on March 15, and that the market price of the stock on February 24 is $20 per share. The entries to record the stock dividend declaration and distribution are as shown below:

Date of Declaration

Feb. 24	Stock Dividends Declared	60,000	
	Common Stock Distributable		15,000
	Paid-in Capital in Excess of Par Value, Common		45,000
	Declaration of a 10% stock dividend on common stock, distributable on March 31 to stockholders of record on March 15: 30,000 shares × .10 = 3,000 shares 3,000 shares × $20/share = $60,000 3,000 shares × $5/share = $15,000		

The Stock Dividends Declared account is used to record stock dividends; the Cash Dividends Declared account is reserved for cash dividends, as shown in the chapter on contributed capital. Retained Earnings is reduced by the amount of the stock dividend by closing the Stock Dividends Declared account to Retained Earnings at the end of the accounting period in the same way that Cash Dividends Declared is closed.

Date of Record

Mar. 15 No entry required

Date of Distribution

Mar. 31	Common Stock Distributable	15,000	
	Common Stock		15,000
	Distribution of a stock dividend of 3,000 shares		

The effect of this stock dividend is to transfer permanently the market value of the stock, $60,000, from retained earnings to contributed capital and to increase the number of shares outstanding by 3,000. Common Stock Distributable is credited for the par value of the stock to be distributed (3,000 × $5 = $15,000). In addition, when the market value is greater than the par value of the stock, Paid-in Capital in Excess of Par Value, Common must be credited for the amount by which the market value exceeds the par value. In this case, the total market value of the stock dividend ($60,000) exceeds the total par value ($15,000) by $45,000. No entry is required on the date of record. On the distribution date, the common stock is issued by debiting Common Stock Distributable and crediting Common Stock for the par value of the stock ($15,000).

Common Stock Distributable is not a liability because there is no obligation to distribute cash or other assets. The obligation is to distribute additional shares of capital stock. If financial statements are prepared between the date of declaration and the distribution of stock, Common Stock Distributable should be reported as part of contributed capital, as shown on page 504.

Contributed Capital	
Common Stock—$5 par value, 100,000 shares authorized, 30,000 shares issued and outstanding	$ 150,000
Common Stock Distributable, 3,000 shares	15,000
Paid-in Capital in Excess of Par Value, Common	75,000
Total Contributed Capital	$ 240,000
Retained Earnings	840,000
Total Stockholders' Equity	$1,080,000

Three points can be made from this example. First, the total stockholders' equity is the same before and after the stock dividend. Second, the assets of the corporation are not reduced as in the case of a cash dividend. Third, the proportionate ownership in the corporation of any individual stockholder is the same before and after the stock dividend. To illustrate these points, assume that a stockholder owns 1,000 shares before the stock dividend. After the 10 percent stock dividend is distributed, this stockholder would own 1,100 shares.

Stockholders' Equity	**Before Dividend**	**After Dividend**
Common Stock	$ 150,000	$ 165,000
Paid-in Capital in Excess of Par Value, Common	30,000	75,000
Total Contributed Capital	$ 180,000	$ 240,000
Retained Earnings	900,000	840,000
Total Stockholders' Equity	$1,080,000	$1,080,000
Shares Outstanding	30,000	33,000
Book Value per Share	$36.00	$32.73

Stockholders' Investment		
Shares owned	1,000	1,100
Shares outstanding	30,000	33,000
Percentage of ownership	3⅓%	3⅓%
Book value of investment ($1,080,000 × .03⅓)	$ 36,000	$ 36,000

Both before and after the stock dividend, the stockholders' equity totals $1,080,000 and the stockholder owns 3⅓ percent of the company. The book value (owner's equity times percentage ownership) of the investment stays at $36,000.

All stock dividends have an effect on the market price of a company's stock. But some stock dividends are so large that they have a material effect on the price per share of the stock. For example, a 50 percent stock dividend would cause the market price of the stock to drop about 33 percent. The AICPA arbitrarily has decided that large stock dividends, those greater than 20 to 25 percent, should be accounted for by transferring the par or stated value of the stock on the date of declaration from retained earnings to contributed capital.[6]

Stock Splits

A **stock split** occurs when a corporation increases the number of issued shares of stock and reduces the par or stated value proportionally. A company may

6. Ibid., par. 13.

plan a stock split when it wants to lower the market value per share of its stock and increase the liquidity of the stock. This action may be necessary when the market value per share has become so high that it hinders the trading of the company's stock. For example, suppose that the Caprock Corporation has 30,000 shares of $5.00 par value stock outstanding. The market value is $70.00 per share. The corporation plans a 2 for 1 split. This split will lower the par value to $2.50 and increase the number of shares outstanding to 60,000. A stockholder who previously owned 400 shares of the $5.00 par stock would own 800 shares of the $2.50 par stock after the split. When a stock split occurs, the market value tends to fall in proportion to the increase in outstanding shares of stock. For example, a 2 for 1 stock split would cause the price of the stock to drop by approximately 50 percent, to about $35.00. The lower price plus the increase in shares tend to promote the buying and selling of shares.

A stock split does not increase the number of shares authorized. Nor does it change the balances in the stockholders' equity section of the balance sheet. It simply changes the par value and number of shares issued, including those that are outstanding and held as treasury shares. Therefore, an entry is not necessary. However, it is appropriate to document the change by making a memorandum entry in the general journal:

July 15 The 30,000 shares of $5 par value common stock that are issued and outstanding were split 2 for 1, resulting in 60,000 shares of $2.50 par value common stock issued and outstanding.

The change for the Caprock Corporation is as follows:

Before Stock Split (from page 502)

Contributed Capital	
Common Stock—**$5 par value, 100,000 shares authorized, 30,000 shares issued and outstanding**	$ 150,000
Paid-in Capital in Excess of Par Value, Common	30,000
Total Contributed Capital	$ 180,000
Retained Earnings	900,000
Total Stockholders' Equity	$1,080,000

After Stock Split

Contributed Capital	
Common Stock—**$2.50 par value, 100,000 shares authorized, 60,000 shares issued and outstanding**	$ 150,000
Paid-in Capital in Excess of Par Value, Common	30,000
Total Contributed Capital	$ 180,000
Retained Earnings	900,000
Total Stockholders' Equity	$1,080,000

In cases where the number of split shares is going to exceed the number of authorized shares, the board of directors must secure state approval to issue additional shares at the time of the split.

Treasury Stock Transactions

OBJECTIVE 3
Account for treasury stock transactions

Treasury stock is capital stock, either common or preferred, that has been issued and reacquired by the issuing company but has not been sold or retired. The company normally gets the stock back by purchasing the shares on the market.

It is common for companies to buy and hold their own stock. In 1989, 393, or 66 percent, of 600 large companies held treasury stock.[7] There are several reasons why a company purchases its own stock:

1. It may want to have stock available to distribute to employees through stock option plans.
2. It may be trying to maintain a favorable market for the company's stock.
3. It may want to increase the company's earnings per share.
4. It may want to have additional shares of the company's stock available for such activities as purchasing other companies.
5. It may want to prevent a hostile takeover.

The effect of a treasury stock purchase is to reduce the assets and stockholders' equity of the company. It is not considered a purchase of assets, as the purchase of shares in another company would be. Treasury stock is capital stock that has been issued but is no longer outstanding. Treasury shares can be held for an indefinite period of time, reissued, or retired. Like unissued stock, treasury stock has no rights until it is reissued. Treasury stock does not have voting rights, rights to cash dividends and stock dividends, or rights to share in assets during liquidation of the company, and it is not considered to be outstanding in the calculation of book value. However, there is one major difference between unissued shares and treasury shares: A share of stock that originally was issued at par value or greater and fully paid for, and that then was reacquired as treasury stock, can be reissued at less than par value without negative consequences attaching to it.

The Purchase of Treasury Stock. When treasury stock is purchased, it normally is recorded at cost. The transaction reduces both the assets and stockholders' equity of the firm. For example, assume that on September 15 the Caprock Corporation purchases 1,000 shares of its common stock on the market at a price of $50 per share. The purchase would be recorded as follows:

Sept. 15	Treasury Stock, Common	50,000	
	Cash		50,000
	Acquired 1,000 shares of the company's common stock for $50 per share		

Notice that the treasury shares are recorded at cost. The par value, stated value, or original issue price of the stock is ignored.

The stockholders' equity section of Caprock's balance sheet shows the cost of the treasury stock as a deduction from the total of contributed capital and retained earnings:

Contributed Capital	
Common Stock—$5 par value, 100,000 shares authorized, **30,000 shares issued, 29,000 shares outstanding**	$ 150,000
Paid-in Capital in Excess of Par Value, Common	30,000
Total Contributed Capital	$ 180,000
Retained Earnings	900,000
Total Contributed Capital and Retained Earnings	$1,080,000
Less Treasury Stock, Common (1,000 shares at cost)	**50,000**
Total Stockholders' Equity	$1,030,000

7. *Accounting Trends & Techniques* (New York: American Institute of Certified Public Accountants, 1990), p. 201.

Notice that the number of shares issued, and thus the legal capital, has not changed, although the number of outstanding shares has decreased as a result of the transaction.

The Sale of Treasury Stock. Treasury shares can be sold at cost, above cost, or below cost. For example, assume that on November 15 the 1,000 treasury shares of the Caprock Corporation are sold for $50 per share. This entry records the transaction:

Nov. 15	Cash	50,000	
	Treasury Stock, Common		50,000
	Reissued 1,000 shares of treasury stock for $50 per share		

When treasury shares are sold for an amount greater than their cost, the excess of the sales price over cost should be credited to Paid-in Capital, Treasury Stock. No gain should be recorded. For example, suppose that on November 15 the 1,000 treasury shares of the Caprock Corporation are sold for $60 per share. The entry for the reissue would be as follows:

Nov. 15	Cash	60,000	
	Treasury Stock, Common		50,000
	Paid-in Capital, Treasury Stock		10,000
	Sale of 1,000 shares of treasury stock for $60 per share; cost was $50 per share		

If treasury shares are sold below their cost, the difference is deducted from Paid-in Capital, Treasury Stock. When this account does not exist or is insufficient to cover the excess of cost over the reissue price, Retained Earnings absorbs the excess. No loss is recorded. For example, suppose that on September 15, the Caprock Corporation bought 1,000 shares of its common stock on the market at a price of $50 per share. The company sold 400 shares of its stock on October 15 for $60 per share and the remaining 600 shares on December 15 for $42 per share. The entries to record these transactions are as follows:

Sept. 15	Treasury Stock, Common	50,000	
	Cash		50,000
	Purchase of 1,000 shares of treasury stock at $50 per share		
Oct. 15	Cash	24,000	
	Treasury Stock, Common		20,000
	Paid-in Capital, Treasury Stock		4,000
	Sale of 400 shares of treasury stock for $60 per share; cost was $50 per share		
Dec. 15	Cash	25,200	
	Paid-in Capital, Treasury Stock	4,000	
	Retained Earnings	800	
	Treasury Stock, Common		30,000
	Sale of 600 shares of treasury stock for $42 per share; cost was $50 per share		

In the entry for the December 15 transaction, Retained Earnings is debited $800 because the 600 shares were sold for $4,800 less than cost. That amount is $800 greater than the $4,000 of paid-in capital generated by the sale of the 400 shares on October 15.

The Retirement of Treasury Stock. If a company determines that it is not going to reissue stock it has purchased, with the approval of its stockholders it can retire the stock. When shares of stock are retired, all items related to those shares are removed from the related Capital accounts. When stock that cost less than the original contributed capital is retired, the difference is recognized in Paid-in Capital, Retirement of Stock. However, when stock that cost more than was received when the shares were first issued is retired, the difference is a reduction in stockholders' equity and is debited to Retained Earnings. For instance, suppose that instead of selling the 1,000 shares of treasury stock it purchased for $50,000, Caprock decides to retire the shares on November 15. Assuming that the $5 par value common stock originally was issued at $6 per share, this entry records the retirement:

Nov. 15	Common Stock	5,000	
	Paid-in Capital in Excess of Par Value, Common	1,000	
	Retained Earnings	44,000	
	Treasury Stock, Common		50,000
	Retirement of 1,000 shares that cost $50 per share and were issued originally at $6 per share		

Restrictions on Retained Earnings

OBJECTIVE 4
Describe the disclosure of restrictions on retained earnings

A corporation may be required or want to restrict all or a portion of retained earnings. A **restriction on retained earnings** means that dividends can be declared only to the extent of the *unrestricted* retained earnings. The following are several reasons a company might restrict retained earnings:

1. *A contractual agreement.* For example, bond indentures may place a limitation on the dividends the company can pay.
2. *State law.* Many states do not allow a corporation to distribute dividends or purchase treasury stock if doing so impairs the legal capital of the company.
3. *Voluntary action by the board of directors.* Many times a board decides to retain assets in the business for future needs. For example, the company may be planning to build a new plant and may want to show that dividends will be limited to save enough money for the building. A company also might restrict retained earnings to show the possible future loss of assets resulting from a lawsuit.

There are two ways of reporting restrictions on retained earnings to readers of financial statements: A restriction can be shown in the stockholders' equity section of the balance sheet, or it can be disclosed in a note to the financial statements.

A restriction on retained earnings does not change the total retained earnings or stockholders' equity of the company. It simply divides retained earnings into two parts, restricted and unrestricted. The restricted part indicates that assets in that amount cannot be used to pay dividends. The unrestricted amount represents earnings kept in the business that can be used for dividends and other purposes.

Assuming that Caprock's board of directors has decided to restrict retained earnings for $300,000 because of plans for plant expansion, the disclosure in Caprock's stockholders' equity section would be as follows:

Contributed Capital		
Common Stock—$5 par value, 100,000 shares authorized, 30,000 shares issued and outstanding		$ 150,000
Paid-in Capital in Excess of Par Value, Common		30,000
Total Contributed Capital		$ 180,000
Retained Earnings		
Restricted for Plant Expansion	$300,000	
Unrestricted	600,000	
Total Retained Earnings		900,000
Total Stockholders' Equity		$1,080,000

The same facts about restricted retained earnings also could be presented by reference to a note to the financial statements. For example:

Retained Earnings (Note 15)	$900,000

Note 15:
Because of plans to expand the capacity of the clothing division, the board of directors has restricted retained earnings available for dividends by $300,000.

Notice that the restriction of retained earnings does not restrict cash or other assets in any way. It simply explains to the readers of the financial statements that a certain amount of assets generated by earnings will remain in the business for the purpose stated. It is still management's job to make sure that there is enough cash or assets on hand to satisfy the restriction. Also, the removal of a restriction does not necessarily mean that the board of directors is now able to declare a dividend.

The Statement of Stockholders' Equity

OBJECTIVE 5
Prepare a statement of stockholders' equity

The **statement of stockholders' equity**, also called the *statement of changes in stockholders' equity*, summarizes the changes in the components of the stockholders' equity section of the balance sheet. Companies increasingly are using this statement in place of the statement of retained earnings because it reveals much more about the year's stockholders' equity transactions. In Exhibit 13-2, for example, the Tri-State Corporation's statement of stockholders' equity, the first line contains the beginning balances (the last period's ending balances) of each account in the stockholders' equity section. Each additional line in the statement discloses the effects of transactions that affect the accounts. It is possible to determine from this statement that during 19x2 Tri-State Corporation issued 5,000 shares of common stock for $250,000, had a conversion of $100,000 of preferred stock into common stock, declared and issued a 10 percent stock dividend on common stock, had a net purchase of treasury shares of $24,000, earned net income of $270,000, and paid cash dividends on both preferred and common stock. The ending balances of the accounts are presented at the bottom of the statement. These accounts and balances make up the stockholders' equity section of Tri-State's balance sheet on December 31, 19x2, as shown in Exhibit 13-3. Notice that the Retained Earnings column has the same components as would the statement of retained earnings, if it was prepared separately.

Exhibit 13-2. A Statement of Stockholders' Equity

Tri-State Corporation
Statement of Stockholders' Equity
For the Year Ended December 31, 19x2

	Preferred Stock $100 Par Value 8% Convertible	Common Stock $10 Par Value	Paid-in Capital in Excess of Par Value, Common	Retained Earnings	Treasury Stock	Total
Balance, December 31, 19x1	$400,000	$300,000	$300,000	$600,000	—	$1,600,000
Issuance of 5,000 Shares of Common Stock		50,000	200,000			250,000
Conversion of 1,000 Shares of Preferred Stock into 3,000 Shares of Common Stock	(100,000)	30,000	70,000			—
10 Percent Stock Dividend on Common Stock, 3,800 Shares		38,000	152,000	(190,000)		—
Purchase of 500 Shares of Treasury Stock					$(24,000)	(24,000)
Net Income				270,000		270,000
Cash Dividends						
Preferred Stock				(24,000)		(24,000)
Common Stock				(47,600)		(47,600)
Balance, December 31, 19x2	$300,000	$418,000	$722,000	$608,400	$(24,000)	$2,024,400

Exhibit 13-3. Stockholders' Equity Section of a Balance Sheet

Tri-State Corporation
Stockholders' Equity
December 31, 19x2

Contributed Capital		
Preferred Stock—$100 par value, 8% convertible, 10,000 shares authorized, 3,000 shares issued and outstanding		$ 300,000
Common Stock—$10 par value, 100,000 shares authorized, 41,800 shares issued, 41,300 shares outstanding	$418,000	
Paid-in Capital in Excess of Par Value, Common	722,000	1,140,000
Total Contributed Capital		$1,440,000
Retained Earnings		608,400
Total Contributed Capital and Retained Earnings		$2,048,400
Less Treasury Stock, Common (500 shares at cost)		24,000
Total Stockholders' Equity		$2,024,400

Stock Values

The word *value* is associated with shares of stock in several ways. The terms *par value* and *stated value* already have been explained. They are each values per share that establish the legal capital of a company. Par value or stated value is set arbitrarily when the stock is authorized. Neither has any relationship to a stock's book value or market value.

Book Value

OBJECTIVE 6
Calculate book value per share and distinguish it from market value

The **book value** of a company's stock represents the total assets of the company less its liabilities. It is simply the owners' equity of the company or, to look at it another way, the company's net assets. The book value per share, therefore, represents the equity of the owner of one share of stock in the net assets of the corporation. This value, of course, does not necessarily equal the amount the shareholder would receive if the company were sold or liquidated. It is probably different because most assets are recorded at historical cost, not at the current value at which they could be sold.

To determine the book value per share when the company has only common stock outstanding, divide the total stockholders' equity by the total common shares outstanding. In computing the shares outstanding, common stock distributable and shares subscribed but not issued are included, but treasury stock (shares previously issued and now held by the company) is not included. For example, on page 506, Caprock Corporation has total stockholders' equity of $1,030,000 and 29,000 shares outstanding after recording the purchase of treasury shares. The book value per share of Caprock's common stock is $35.52 ($1,030,000 ÷ 29,000 shares).

If a company has both preferred and common stock, the determination of book value per share is not so simple. The general rule is that the call value (or par value, if a call value is not specified) of the preferred stock plus any dividends in arrears are subtracted from total stockholders' equity to figure the equity pertaining to common stock. As an illustration, refer to the stockholders' equity section of Tri-State Corporation's balance sheet on page 510. Assuming there are no dividends in arrears and the preferred stock is callable at $105, the equity pertaining to common stock is figured as follows:

Total stockholders' equity	$2,024,400
Less equity allocated to preferred shareholders (3,000 shares × $105)	315,000
Equity pertaining to common shareholders	**$1,709,400**

There are 41,300 shares of common stock outstanding (41,800 shares issued less 500 shares of treasury stock). The book values per share would be as follows:

Preferred Stock: $315,000 ÷ 3,000 shares = $105 per share
Common Stock: $1,709,400 ÷ 41,300 shares = $41.39 per share

If we assume the same facts except that the preferred stock is 8 percent cumulative and that one year of dividends is in arrears, the stockholders' equity would be allocated as follows:

Total stockholders' equity		$2,024,400
Less: Call value of outstanding preferred shares	$315,000	
Dividends in arrears ($300,000 × .08)	24,000	
Equity allocated to preferred shareholders		**339,000**
Equity pertaining to common shareholders		**$1,685,400**

The book values per share here are as follows:

Preferred Stock: $339,000 ÷ 3,000 shares = $113 per share
Common Stock: $1,685,400 ÷ 41,300 shares = $40.81 per share

Undeclared preferred dividends fall into arrears on the last day of the fiscal year (the date when the financial statements are prepared). Also, dividends in arrears do not apply to unissued preferred stock.

Market Value

Market value is the price that investors are willing to pay for a share of stock on the open market. Whereas book value is based on historical cost, market value usually is determined by investors' expectations for the particular company and general economic conditions. That is, people's expectations about the company's future profitability and dividends per share, their perceptions of the risk attached to the company and of its current financial condition, and the state of the money market all play a part in determining the market value of a corporation's stock. Although book value per share often bears little relationship to market value per share, some investors use the relationship between the two measures as rough indicators of the relative value of the stock. For example, in early 1991 a major oil company, Texaco, had a market value per share of $65 compared with a book value per share of $34. At the same time, a large automobile company, Chrysler, had a market value per share of $14 and a book value per share of $31. Other factors being equal, investors evaluating these measures would conclude that Chrysler has more upside potential in market value than Texaco.

DECISION POINT
Eastman Kodak Company

■ Someone who does not understand the structure and use of corporate income statements may be confused by corporate earnings reports in the financial press. For example, the *Wall Street Journal* recently reported, "Eastman Kodak Co. recorded a third-quarter net loss of $206 million, or 64 cents a share, but posted a 22 percent rise in operating earnings as the company continued to benefit from restructuring moves that began in 1989."[8] How could Kodak, a well-known photographic film, chemical, and health company, have both a large net loss and an increase in operating earnings?

As will be explained in the following section, the corporate income statement has several components. Kodak's net loss reflects a $909.5 million charge for costs associated with a ruling against the company for its infringement on Polaroid Corp.'s instant photography patents. This loss is reported on the income statement below the earnings from current or continuing operations, which in one year rose by 22 percent, from $682 million to $835 million. The *Wall Street Journal* report indicates that Kodak's continuing operations are doing well, but the adverse ruling brought on a serious one-time loss—a fact that would be apparent to a reader who knows how to evaluate corporate income statements. ■

8. James S. Hirsch, "Eastman Kodak Posts Net Loss for 3rd Quarter," *Wall Street Journal*, Nov. 1, 1990, p. A3.

The Corporate Income Statement

OBJECTIVE 7
Prepare a corporate income statement

This chapter and the chapter on contributed capital show how certain transactions are reflected in the stockholders' equity section of the corporate balance sheet and in the statement of retained earnings. A separate chapter deals with the statement of cash flows. The following sections briefly describe some of the features of the corporate income statement.

Accounting organizations have not specified the format of the income statement because flexibility has been considered more important than a standard format. Either the single-step or multistep form can be used (see the chapter on accounting concepts and classified financial statements). However, the accounting profession has taken the position that income for a period should be all inclusive, **comprehensive income**.[9] This rule means that income or loss for a period should include all revenues, expenses, gains, and losses over the period, except for prior period adjustments. This approach to the measurement of income has resulted in several items being added to the income statement, among them income taxes expense, discontinued operations, extraordinary items, and accounting changes. In addition, earnings per share figures must be disclosed. Exhibit 13-4 illustrates a corporate income statement and the required disclosures. The following sections discuss the components of the corporate income statement, beginning with income taxes expense.

Income Taxes Expense

OBJECTIVE 8
Show the relationships among income taxes expense, deferred income taxes, and net of taxes

Corporations determine their taxable income (the amount on which taxes are paid) by subtracting allowable business deductions from includable gross income. The federal tax laws determine what business deductions are allowed and what must be included in taxable gross income.[10]

The tax rates that apply to a corporation's taxable income are shown in Table 13-1. A corporation with taxable income of $70,000 would have a federal income tax liability of $12,500: $7,500 (the tax on the first $50,000 of taxable income) plus $5,000 (25 percent of the $20,000 earned in excess of $50,000).

Income taxes expense is the expense recognized in the accounting records on an accrual basis to be applicable to income from continuing operations. This expense may or may not equal the amount of taxes actually paid by the corporation and recorded as income taxes payable in the current period. The amount payable is determined from taxable income, which is measured according to the rules and regulations of the income tax code. For convenience, most small businesses keep accounting records on the same basis as tax records so that the income taxes expense on the income statement equals the income taxes liability to be paid to the Internal Revenue Service (IRS). This practice is acceptable when there is no material difference between the income on an accounting basis and the income on an income tax basis. However, the purpose of accounting is to determine net income in accordance with generally accepted accounting principles; it is not to determine taxable income and tax liability.

Management has an incentive to use methods that minimize the firm's tax liability, but accountants, who are bound by accrual accounting and the materiality concept, cannot let tax procedures dictate their method of preparing

9. *Statement of Financial Accounting Concepts No. 6,* "Elements of Financial Statements" (Stamford, Conn.: Financial Accounting Standards Board, 1985), pars. 70–77.
10. Rules for calculating and reporting taxable income in specialized industries such as banking, insurance, mutual funds, and cooperatives are highly technical and may vary significantly from those shown in this chapter.

Exhibit 13-4. A Corporate Income Statement

Junction Corporation Income Statement For the Year Ended December 31, 19xx		
Revenues		$925,000
Less Costs and Expenses		500,000
Income from Continuing Operations Before Taxes		$425,000
Income Taxes Expense		119,000
Income from Continuing Operations		$306,000
Discontinued Operations		
Income from Operations of Discontinued Segment (net of taxes, $35,000)	$90,000	
Loss on Disposal of Segment (net of taxes, $42,000)	(73,000)	17,000
Income Before Extraordinary Items and Cumulative Effect of Accounting Change		$323,000
Extraordinary Gain (net of taxes, $17,000)		43,000
Subtotal		$366,000
Cumulative Effect of a Change in Accounting Principle (net of taxes, $5,000)		(6,000)
Net Income		$360,000
Earnings per Common Share:		
Income from Continuing Operations		$3.06
Discontinued Operations (net of taxes)		.17
Income Before Extraordinary Items and Cumulative Effect of Accounting Change		$3.23
Extraordinary Gain (net of taxes)		.43
Cumulative Effect of Accounting Change (net of taxes)		(.06)
Net Income		$3.60

financial statements if the result would be misleading. As a consequence, there can be a material difference between accounting and taxable incomes, especially in larger businesses. This difference in accounting and taxable incomes can result from a difference in the timing of the recognition of revenues and expenses because of different methods used in determining the respective incomes. Some possible alternatives are shown at the top of the next page.

Table 13-1. Tax Rate Schedule for Corporations, 1993*

Taxable Income		Tax Liability	
Over	But Not Over		Of the Amount Over
—	$ 50,000	0 + 15%	—
$ 50,000	75,000	$ 7,500 + 25%	$ 50,000
75,000	100,000	13,750 + 34%	75,000
100,000	335,000	22,250 + 39%	100,000
335,000	10,000,000	113,900 + 34%	335,000
10,000,000	15,000,000	3,496,650 + 35%	10,000,000
15,000,000	18,333,333	5,246,650 + 38%	15,000,000
18,333,333	—	6,513,317 + 35%	18,333,333

*Tax rates are subject to change by Congress.

	Accounting Method	Tax Method
Expense recognition	Accrual or deferral	At time of expenditure
Accounts receivable	Allowance	Direct charge-off
Inventories	Average-cost	FIFO
Depreciation	Straight-line	Accelerated cost recovery system (see the chapter on long-term assets: acquisition, depreciation, and disposal)

Deferred Income Taxes

Accounting for the difference between income taxes expense based on accounting income and the actual income taxes payable based on taxable income is accomplished by a technique called **income tax allocation**. The amount by which income taxes expense differs from income taxes payable is reconciled in an account called **Deferred Income Taxes**. For example, suppose the Junction Corporation shows income taxes expense of $119,000 on its income statement but has actual income taxes payable to the IRS of $92,000. The entry to record the income taxes expense applicable to income from continuing operations using the income tax allocation procedure would be as follows:

Dec. 31	Income Taxes Expense	119,000	
	Income Taxes Payable		92,000
	Deferred Income Taxes		27,000
	To record current and deferred income taxes		

In other years, it is possible for Income Taxes Payable to exceed Income Taxes Expense, in which case the same entry is made except that Deferred Income Taxes is debited.

The Financial Accounting Standards Board has issued new rules for recording, measuring, and classifying deferred income taxes.[11] When the Deferred Income Taxes account has a credit balance, which is its normal balance, it is classified as a liability on the balance sheet. Whether or not it is classified as a current or long-term (noncurrent) liability depends on when the timing difference is expected to reverse, to have the opposite effect. For instance, if an income tax deferral is caused by an expenditure that is deducted for income tax purposes in one year but is not an expense for accounting purposes until the next year, the deferral that is present in the first year will reverse in the second year. Here, the income tax deferral in the first year is classified as a current liability. On the other hand, if the deferral is not expected to reverse for more than one year, the deferred income taxes are classified as a long-term liability. This situation can occur when the income tax deferral is caused by a difference in depreciation methods for items of plant and equipment that have useful lives of more than one year. In other words, an income tax liability is classified as short-term or long-term based on the nature of the transactions that gave rise to the deferral and the expected date of reversal.

The Deferred Income Taxes account can have a debit balance, in which case it should be classified as an asset. In this situation, the company has prepaid its income taxes because total income taxes paid exceed income taxes expensed. Classification of the debit balance as a current asset or as a long-term asset follows the same rules as for liabilities, but the amount of the asset is subject to certain limitations, which are covered in more advanced courses.

11. *Statement of Financial Accounting Standards No. 96,* "Accounting for Income Taxes" (Stamford, Conn.: Financial Accounting Standards Board, 1987).

Each year, the balance of the Deferred Income Taxes account is evaluated to determine if it represents the expected asset or liability in light of legislated changes in income tax laws and regulations in the current year. If changes have occurred in the income tax laws, an adjusting entry is required to bring the account balance into line with the current laws. For example, a decrease in corporate income tax rates, like the one that occurred in 1987, means that a company with deferred income tax liabilities will pay less taxes in future years than indicated by the credit balance of its Deferred Income Taxes account. As a result, it would debit Deferred Income Taxes to reduce the liability and credit Gain from Reduction in Income Taxes Rates. This credit increases the reported income on the income statement. If the tax rate increases in future years, a loss would be recorded and the deferred income tax liability increased.

In any given year, the amount a company pays in income taxes is determined by subtracting (or adding, as the case may be) the deferred income taxes for that year (as reported in the notes to the financial statements) from (or to) income taxes expense, which also is reported in the notes to the financial statements. In subsequent years, the amount of deferred income taxes can vary based on changes in tax laws and rates.

Some understanding of the importance of deferred income taxes to financial reporting can be gained from studying the financial statements of six hundred large companies surveyed in a recent year. About 82 percent reported deferred income taxes with a credit balance in the long-term liability section of the income statement.[12] About 8 percent reported deferred income taxes as a current liability.[13]

Net of Taxes

The phrase **net of taxes**, as used in Exhibit 13-4 and in the discussion below, means that the effect of applicable taxes (usually income taxes) has been considered in determining the overall effect of the item on the financial statements. The phrase is used on the corporate income statement when a company has items (such as those explained below) that must be disclosed in a separate section of the income statement. Each of these items should be reported at net of the income taxes applicable to that item to avoid distorting the net operating income figure.

For example, assume that a corporation with $120,000 operating income before taxes has a high total tax liability of $66,000, which includes a tax of $30,000 on a capital gain of $100,000. Assume also that the gain is an extraordinary item (see Extraordinary Items, pages 517–518) and must be disclosed as such. This is how the tax liability would be reported on the income statement:

Operating Income Before Taxes	$120,000
Income Taxes Expense **(actual taxes are $66,000, of which $30,000 is applicable to extraordinary gain)**	36,000
Income Before Extraordinary Item	$ 84,000
Extraordinary Gain (net of taxes) **($100,000 – $30,000)**	70,000
Net Income	$154,000

12. *Accounting Trends & Techniques* (New York: American Institute of Certified Public Accountants, 1990), p. 178.
13. Ibid., p. 153.

If all the taxes payable were deducted from operating income before taxes, both the income before extraordinary items and the extraordinary gain would be distorted.

A company follows the same procedure in the case of an extraordinary loss. For example, assume the same facts as before except that total tax liability is only $6,000 because of a $100,000 extraordinary loss, which results in a $30,000 tax saving, as shown below.

Operating Income Before Taxes	$120,000
Income Taxes Expense **(actual taxes of $6,000 as a result of an extraordinary loss)**	36,000
Income Before Extraordinary Item	$ 84,000
Extraordinary Loss (net of taxes) **($100,000 – $30,000)**	(70,000)
Net Income	$ 14,000

In Exhibit 13-4, the total of the income tax items is $124,000. This amount is allocated among five statement components, as follows:

Income taxes expense on income from continuing operations	$119,000
Income tax on income from a discontinued segment	35,000
Income tax saving on the loss on disposal of the segment	(42,000)
Income tax on the extraordinary gain	17,000
Income tax saving on the cumulative effect of a change in accounting principle	(5,000)
Total income taxes expense	$124,000

Discontinued Operations

OBJECTIVE 9
Describe the disclosure on the income statement of discontinued operations, extraordinary items, and accounting changes

Large companies in the United States usually have many **segments**. A segment of a business can be a separate major line of business or serve a separate class of customer. For example, a company that makes heavy drilling equipment also may have another line of business, such as the manufacture of mobile homes. These large companies may discontinue or otherwise dispose of certain segments of their business that are not profitable. **Discontinued operations** are segments of a business that are no longer part of its ongoing operations. Generally accepted accounting principles require that gains and losses from discontinued operations be reported separately in the income statement. The reason for this requirement is that the income statement is more useful for evaluating the ongoing activities of the business if results from continuing operations are reported separately from those of discontinued operations.

In Exhibit 13-4, the disclosure of discontinued operations has two parts. One part shows that the income during the year from operations of the segment of the business that has been disposed of (or will be disposed of) after the decision date to discontinue was $90,000 (net of $35,000 taxes). The other part shows that the loss from the disposal of the segment of business was $73,000 (net of $42,000 tax savings). Computation of the gains or losses is covered in more advanced accounting courses. The disclosure has been described, however, to give a complete view of the content of the corporate income statement.

Extraordinary Items

The Accounting Principles Board, in its *Opinion No. 30,* defines **extraordinary items** as those "events or transactions that are distinguished by their unusual nature *and* by the infrequency of their occurrence."[14] As stated in the definition, the major criteria for extraordinary items are that they must be unusual and must not happen very often. Unusual and infrequent occurrences are explained in the opinion as follows:

Unusual Nature—the underlying event or transaction should possess a high degree of abnormality and be of a type clearly unrelated to, or only incidentally related to, the ordinary and typical activities of the entity, taking into account the environment in which the entity operates.

Infrequency of Occurrence—the underlying event or transaction should be of a type that would not reasonably be expected to recur in the foreseeable future, taking into account the environment in which the entity operates.[15]

If an item is both unusual and infrequent (and material in amount), it should be reported separately from continuing operations on the income statement. This disclosure allows the reader of the statement to identify gains or losses shown in the computation of income that would not be expected to happen again soon. Items that usually are treated as extraordinary include (1) an uninsured loss from flood, earthquake, fire, or theft; (2) a gain or loss resulting from the passage of a new law; (3) the expropriation (taking) of property by a foreign government; and (4) a gain or loss from early retirement of debt. Gains or losses from extraordinary items should be reported on the income statement after discontinued operations. And they should be shown net of applicable taxes. In a recent year, forty-nine (8 percent) of six hundred large companies reported extraordinary items on their income statements.[16] In Exhibit 13-4, the extraordinary gain was $43,000 after applicable taxes of $17,000.

Accounting Changes

Consistency, one of the basic conventions of accounting, means that for accounting purposes, companies must apply the same accounting principles from year to year. However, a company is allowed to make accounting changes if current procedures are incorrect or inappropriate. For example, a change from the FIFO to the LIFO inventory method can be made if there is adequate justification for the change. Adequate justification usually means that if the change occurs, the financial statements will better show the financial activities of the company. A company's wanting to lower the amount of income taxes it pays is not an adequate justification for an accounting change. If justification does exist and an accounting change is made during an accounting period, generally accepted accounting principles require the disclosure of the change in the financial statements.

The **cumulative effect of an accounting change** is the effect that the new accounting principle would have had on net income in prior periods if it, instead of the old principle, had been applied. This effect is shown on the income statement immediately after extraordinary items.[17] For example, assume that in the five years previous to 19xx, the Junction Corporation used the straight-line method to depreciate its machinery. This year, the company changes to the

14. Accounting Principles Board, *Opinion No. 30*, "Reporting the Results of Operations" (New York: American Institute of Certified Public Accountants, 1973), par. 20.
15. Ibid.
16. *Accounting Trends & Techniques* (New York: American Institute of Certified Public Accountants, 1990), p. 291.
17. Accounting Principles Board, *Opinion No. 20*, "Accounting Changes" (New York: American Institute of Certified Public Accountants, 1971), par. 20.

sum-of-the-years'-digits method of depreciation. The following depreciation charges (net of taxes) were arrived at by the controller:

Cumulative, 5-year sum-of-the-years'-digits depreciation	$16,000
Less cumulative, 5-year straight-line depreciation	10,000
Cumulative effect of accounting change	$ 6,000

Relevant information about the accounting change is shown in the notes to the financial statements. The $6,000 difference (net of $5,000 income taxes) is the cumulative effect of the change in depreciation methods. The change results in an additional $6,000 (net of taxes) depreciation expense for prior years being deducted in the current year in addition to the current year's depreciation costs included in the $500,000 costs and expenses section of the income statement. This expense must be shown in the current year's income statement as a reduction in income (see Exhibit 13-4). In a recent year, 174 (29 percent) of 600 large companies reported changes in accounting procedures.[18] Further study of accounting changes is left to more advanced accounting courses.

Earnings per Share

OBJECTIVE 10
Compute earnings per share

Readers of financial statements use earnings per share information to judge the performance of a company and to compare its performance with that of other companies. The Accounting Principles Board recognized the importance of this information in its *Opinion No. 15.* There it concludes that earnings per share of common stock should be presented on the face of the income statement.[19] As shown in Exhibit 13-4, the information generally is disclosed just below the net income figure.

An earnings per share amount always is shown for (1) income from continuing operations, (2) income before extraordinary items and the cumulative effect of accounting changes, (3) the cumulative effect of accounting changes, and (4) net income. If the statement shows a gain or loss from discontinued operations or a gain or loss on extraordinary items, earnings per share amounts also can be presented for these items.

A basic earnings per share amount is found when a company has only common stock and the same number of shares outstanding during the year. For example, Exhibit 13-4 tells us that Junction Corporation, with a net income of $360,000, had 100,000 shares of common stock outstanding for the entire year. The earnings per share of common stock were computed as follows:

$$\text{Earnings per share} = \frac{\text{net income}}{\text{shares outstanding}}$$

$$= \frac{\$360{,}000}{100{,}000 \text{ shares}}$$

$$= \$3.60 \text{ per share}$$

If the number of shares outstanding changes during the year, it is necessary to figure a weighted-average number of shares outstanding for the year. Suppose that Junction Corporation had the following amounts of common shares

18. *Accounting Trends & Techniques* (New York: American Institute of Certified Public Accountants, 1990), p. 419.
19. Accounting Principles Board, *Opinion No. 15,* "Earnings per Share" (New York: American Institute of Certified Public Accountants, 1969), par. 12.

outstanding during various periods of the year: January–March, 100,000 shares; April–September, 120,000 shares; and October–December, 130,000 shares. The weighted-average number of common shares outstanding and earnings per share would be found this way:

100,000 shares × 1/4 year	25,000
120,000 shares × 1/2 year	60,000
130,000 shares × 1/4 year	32,500
Weighted-average shares outstanding	117,500

$$\text{Earnings per share} = \frac{\$360{,}000}{117{,}500 \text{ shares}}$$

$$= \$3.06 \text{ per share}$$

If a company has nonconvertible preferred stock outstanding, the dividend for the stock must be subtracted from net income before earnings per share for common stock are computed. Suppose that Junction Corporation has preferred stock on which the annual dividend is $23,500. Earnings per share on common stock would be $2.86 [($360,000 – $23,500) ÷ 117,500 shares].

Companies with a capital structure in which there are no bonds, stocks, or stock options that could be converted into common stock are said to have a **simple capital structure**. The earnings per share for these companies are computed as shown on the previous page. Many companies, however, have a **complex capital structure**, which includes convertible stock and bonds. These convertible securities have the potential of diluting the earnings per share of common stock. *Potential dilution* means that a person's proportionate share of ownership in a company could be reduced through a conversion of stocks or bonds or the exercise of stock options, which would increase the total shares outstanding.

For example, suppose that a person owns 10,000 shares of a company, which equals 2 percent of the outstanding shares of 500,000. Now, suppose that holders of convertible bonds convert the bonds into 100,000 shares of stock. The person's 10,000 shares then would be only 1.67 percent (10,000 ÷ 600,000) of the outstanding shares. In addition, the added shares outstanding would lower earnings per share and most likely would lower market price per share.

Because stock options and convertible preferred stocks or bonds have the potential to dilute earnings per share, they are referred to as **potentially dilutive securities**. A special subset of these convertible securities is called **common stock equivalents** because these securities are considered to be similar to common stock. A convertible stock or bond is considered a common stock equivalent if the conversion feature is an important part of determining its original issue price. Special rules are applied by the accountant to determine if a convertible stock or bond is a common stock equivalent. A stock option, on the other hand, is by definition a common stock equivalent. The significance of common stock equivalents is that when they exist, they are used in the earnings per share calculations explained in the next paragraph.

When a company has a complex capital structure, it must report two earnings per share figures: primary earnings per share and fully diluted earnings per share. **Primary earnings per share** are calculated by including in the denominator the total of weighted-average common shares outstanding and common stock equivalents. **Fully diluted earnings per share** are calculated by including in the denominator the additional potentially dilutive securities that are not common stock equivalents. The latter figure shows stockholders the maximum potential effect of dilution of their ownership in the company. Here is an example of this type of disclosure:

	19x2	19x1
Net Income	$280,000	$200,000
Earnings per Share of Common Stock		
Primary	$2.25	$1.58
Fully Diluted	$2.00	$1.43

The computation of these figures is a complex process reserved for more advanced courses.

Chapter Review

Review of Learning Objectives

1. **Define *retained earnings* and prepare a statement of retained earnings.**
Retained earnings are the part of stockholders' equity that comes from retaining assets earned in business operations. They represent the claims of the stockholders against the assets of the company that arise from profitable operations. Retained earnings are different from contributed capital, which represents the claims against assets brought about by the initial and later investments by the stockholders. Both are claims against the general assets of the company, not against any specific assets that have been set aside. It is important not to confuse the assets themselves with the claims against the assets. The statement of retained earnings always shows the beginning and ending balance of retained earnings, net income or loss, and cash dividends. It also can show prior period adjustments, stock dividends, and other transactions that affect retained earnings.

2. **Account for stock dividends and stock splits.**
A stock dividend is a proportional distribution of shares of the company's stock by a corporation to its stockholders. Here is a summary of the key dates and accounting treatment of stock dividends:

Key Date	Stock Dividend
Date of declaration	Debit Stock Dividends Declared for the market value of the stock to be distributed (if it is a small stock dividend) and credit Common Stock Distributable for the stock's par value and Paid-in Capital in Excess of Par Value, Common for the excess of the market value over the stock's par value.
Date of record	No entry.
Date of distribution	Debit Common Stock Distributable and credit Common Stock for the par value of the stock that has been distributed.

A stock split usually is undertaken to reduce the market value and improve the liquidity of a company's stock. Because there is normally a decrease in the par value of the stock in proportion to the number of additional shares issued, a stock split has no effect on the dollar amounts in the stockholders' equity accounts. The split should be recorded in the general journal by a memorandum entry only.

3. **Account for treasury stock transactions.**
The treasury stock of a company is stock that has been issued and reacquired but not resold or retired. A company acquires its own stock to create stock option plans,

maintain a favorable market for the stock, increase earnings per share, and purchase other companies. Treasury stock is similar to unissued stock in that it does not have rights until it is reissued. However, treasury stock can be resold at less than par value without incurring a discount liability. The accounting treatment for treasury stock is as follows:

Treasury Stock Transaction	Accounting Treatment
Purchase of treasury stock	Debit Treasury Stock and credit Cash for the cost of the shares.
Sale of treasure stock at the cost of the shares	Debit Cash and credit Treasury Stock for the cost of the shares.
Sale of treasury stock at an amount greater than the cost of the shares	Debit Cash for the reissue price of the shares and credit Treasury Stock for the cost of the shares and Paid-in Capital, Treasury Stock for the excess.
Sale of treasury stock at an amount less than the cost of the shares	Debit Cash for the reissue price; debit Paid-in Capital, Treasury Stock for the difference between the reissue price and the cost of the shares; and credit Treasury Stock for the cost of the shares. If Paid-in Capital, Treasury Stock does not exist or is not large enough to cover the difference, Retained Earnings should absorb the difference.

4. **Describe the disclosure of restrictions on retained earnings.**
A restriction on retained earnings means that dividends can be declared only to the extent of unrestricted retained earnings. A corporation may be bound by contractual agreement or state law to restrict retained earnings, or it may do so voluntarily, to retain assets in the business for a plant expansion or a possible loss in a lawsuit. A restriction on retained earnings can be disclosed in two ways: in the stockholders' equity section of the balance sheet or, more commonly, as a note to the financial statements. Once a restriction is removed, its disclosure can be removed from the financial statements.

5. **Prepare a statement of stockholders' equity.**
A statement of stockholders' equity shows changes over the period in each component of the stockholders' equity section of the balance sheet. This statement reveals much more about the transactions that adjust stockholders' equity than does the statement of retained earnings.

6. **Calculate book value per share and distinguish it from market value.**
Book value per share is the owners' equity per share. It is calculated by dividing stockholders' equity by the number of common shares outstanding plus shares distributable and shares subscribed. When a company has both preferred and common stock, the call or par value of the preferred stock plus any dividends in arrears are deducted first from total stockholders' equity before dividing by the common shares outstanding. Market value per share is the price investors are willing to pay based on their expectations about the future earning ability of the company and general economic conditions.

7. **Prepare a corporate income statement.**
The corporate income statement shows comprehensive income—all revenues, expenses, gains, and losses for the accounting period, except for prior period adjustments. The top part of the corporate income statement includes all revenues, costs and expenses, and income taxes that pertain to continuing operations. The bottom part of the statement contains any or all of the following: discontinued operations, extraordinary items, and the cumulative effect of a change in accounting principle.

Earnings per share data should be shown at the bottom of the statement, below net income.

8. **Show the relationships among income taxes expense, deferred income taxes, and net of taxes.**
   Income taxes expense is the taxes applicable to income from operations on an accrual basis. Income tax allocation is necessary when differences between accrual-based accounting income and taxable income cause a material difference between income taxes expense as shown on the income statement and actual income tax liability. The difference between income taxes expense and income taxes payable is debited or credited to an account called Deferred Income Taxes. *Net of taxes* is a phrase used to indicate that the effect of taxes has been considered when showing an item on the income statement.
9. **Describe the disclosure on the income statement of discontinued operations, extraordinary items, and accounting changes.**
   There are several accounting items that must be disclosed separately from continuing operations and net of income taxes on the income statement because of their unusual nature. These items include a gain or loss on discontinued operations and on extraordinary items, and the cumulative effect of accounting changes.
10. **Compute earnings per share.**
   Stockholders and other readers of financial statements use earnings per share data to evaluate the performance of a company and to compare its performance with that of other companies. Therefore, earnings per share data are presented on the face of the income statement. The amounts are computed by dividing the income applicable to common stock by the common shares outstanding for the year. If the number of shares outstanding has varied during the year, then the weighted-average shares outstanding should be used in the computation. When the company has a complex capital structure, both primary and fully diluted earnings per share data must be disclosed on the face of the income statement.

Review of Concepts and Terminology

The following concepts and terms were introduced in this chapter:

(L.O. 6) **Book value:** The total assets of a company less its liabilities; owners' equity.

(L.O. 10) **Common stock equivalents:** Convertible stocks or bonds whose conversion feature is an important part of determining their original issue price.

(L.O. 10) **Complex capital structure:** A capital structure that includes securities (convertible stocks and bonds) that can be converted into common stock.

(L.O. 7) **Comprehensive income:** The concept of income or loss for a period that includes all revenues, expenses, gains, and losses, except prior period adjustments.

(L.O. 9) **Cumulative effect of an accounting change:** The effect that a new accounting principle would have had on the net income of prior periods if it had been used instead of the old principle.

(L.O. 8) **Deferred Income Taxes:** The account used to record the difference between the Income Taxes Expense and the Income Taxes Payable accounts.

(L.O. 1) **Deficit:** A debit balance in the Retained Earnings account.

(L.O. 9) **Discontinued operations:** Segments of a business that are no longer part of the ongoing operations of the company.

(L.O. 9) **Extraordinary items:** Events or transactions that are both unusual in nature and infrequent in occurrence.

(L.O. 10) **Fully diluted earnings per share:** The net income applicable to common stock divided by the sum of the weighted-average of common shares outstanding and common stock equivalents and other potentially dilutive securities.

(L.O. 8) **Income tax allocation:** An accounting method used to accrue income taxes expense on the basis of accounting income whenever there are differences between accounting and taxable income.

(L.O. 6) **Market value:** The price investors are willing to pay for a share of stock on the open market.

(L.O. 8) **Net of taxes:** Taking into account the effect of applicable taxes (usually income taxes) on an item to determine the overall effect of the item on the financial statements.

(L.O. 10) **Potentially dilutive securities:** Stock options and convertible preferred stocks or bonds, which have the potential to dilute earnings per share.

(L.O. 10) **Primary earnings per share:** The net income applicable to common stock divided by the sum of the weighted-average of common shares outstanding and common stock equivalents.

(L.O. 1) **Prior period adjustments:** Events or transactions that relate to earlier accounting periods that could not be determined in the earlier periods.

(L.O. 4) **Restriction on retained earnings:** The required or voluntary restriction of a portion of retained earnings that cannot be used to pay dividends.

(L.O. 1) **Retained earnings:** Stockholders' claims to assets arising from the earnings of the business; the accumulated earnings of a corporation from its inception, minus any losses, dividends, or transfers to contributed capital.

(L.O. 9) **Segment:** Distinct parts of business operations, such as lines of business or class of customer.

(L.O. 10) **Simple capital structure:** A capital structure with no other securities (stocks or bonds) or stock options that can be converted into common stock.

(L.O. 5) **Statement of stockholders' equity:** A financial statement that summarizes changes in the components of the stockholders' equity section of the balance sheet; also called *statement of changes in stockholders' equity.*

(L.O. 2) **Stock dividend:** A proportional distribution of shares of a corporation's stock to its stockholders.

(L.O. 2) **Stock split:** An increase in the number of outstanding shares of stock accompanied by a proportionate reduction in the par or stated value.

(L.O. 3) **Treasury stock:** Capital stock, either common or preferred, that has been issued and reacquired by the issuing company but that has not been sold or retired.

Self-Test

Test your knowledge of the chapter by choosing the best answer for each of the following items.

(L.O. 1) 1. The balance of the Retained Earnings account represents
   a. an excess of revenues over expenses for the most current operating period.
   b. the profits of a company since its inception, less any losses, dividends to stockholders, or transfers to contributed capital.
   c. cash set aside for specific future uses.
   d. cash available for daily operations.

(L.O. 2) 2. A corporation should account for the declaration of a 3 percent stock dividend by
   a. transferring from retained earnings to contributed capital an amount equal to the market value of the dividend shares.
   b. transferring from retained earnings to contributed capital an amount equal to the legal capital represented by the dividend shares.
   c. making only a memorandum entry in the general journal.
   d. transferring from retained earnings to contributed capital whatever amount the board of directors deems appropriate.

(L.O. 3) 3. Which of the following reduces total stockholders' equity?
   a. A stock split
   b. A restriction on retained earnings
   c. Treasury stock
   d. A stock dividend

(L.O. 4) 4. When retained earnings are restricted, total retained earnings
   a. increase.
   b. decrease.
   c. may increase or decrease.
   d. are unaffected.

(L.O. 5) 5. The purpose of a statement of stockholders' equity is to
   a. summarize the changes in the components of stockholders' equity over the accounting period.
   b. disclose the computation of book value per share of stock.
   c. budget for the transactions expected to occur during the forthcoming period.
   d. replace the statement of retained earnings.

(L.O. 6) 6. All of the following elements of a corporation's common stock can be determined from the accounting records *except*
   a. par value.
   b. stated value.
   c. book value.
   d. market value.

(L.O. 7) 7. Which of the following items appears on the corporate income statement before income from continuing operations?
   a. Income from operations of a discontinued segment
   b. Income taxes expense
   c. The cumulative effect of a change in accounting principle
   d. An extraordinary gain

(L.O. 8) 8. When there is a difference in the timing of revenues and expenses for accounting and for income tax purposes, it is usually necessary to
   a. prepare an adjusting entry.
   b. adjust figures on the corporate tax return.
   c. perform income tax allocation procedures.
   d. do nothing because the difference is a result of two different sets of rules.

(L.O. 9) 9. A loss due to discontinued operations should be reported in the income statement
   a. before both extraordinary items and the cumulative effect of an accounting change.
   b. before the cumulative effect of an accounting change and after extraordinary items.
   c. after both extraordinary items and the cumulative effect of an accounting change.
   d. after the cumulative effect of an accounting change and before extraordinary items.

(L.O. 10) 10. Which of the following would be involved in the computation of earnings per common share for a company with a simple capital structure?
   a. Common shares authorized
   b. Dividends declared on nonconvertible preferred stock
   c. The shares of nonconvertible preferred stock outstanding
   d. Common stock equivalents

Answers to the Self-Test are at the end of this chapter.

Review Problem
Comprehensive Stockholders' Equity Transactions

(L.O. 1, 2, 3, 4, 5, 6) The stockholders' equity on June 30, 19x5 of the Szatkowski Company is shown at the top of page 526.

Contributed Capital	
Common Stock—no par value, $6 stated value, 1,000,000 shares authorized, 250,000 shares issued and outstanding	$1,500,000
Paid-in Capital in Excess of Stated Value, Common	820,000
Total Contributed Capital	$2,320,000
Retained Earnings	970,000
Total Stockholders' Equity	$3,290,000

Stockholders' equity transactions for the next fiscal year were as follows:

a. The board of directors declared a 2 for 1 split.
b. The board of directors obtained authorization to issue 50,000 shares of $100 par value, 6 percent noncumulative preferred stock, callable at $104.
c. Issued 12,000 shares of common stock for a building appraised at $96,000.
d. Purchased 8,000 shares of the company's common stock for $64,000.
e. Issued 20,000 shares of the preferred stock for $100 per share.
f. Sold 5,000 shares of the treasury stock for $35,000.
g. Declared cash dividends of $6 per share on the preferred stock and $.20 per share on the common stock.
h. Date of record.
i. Paid the preferred and common stock cash dividends.
j. Declared a 10 percent stock dividend on the common stock. The market value was $10 per share. The stock dividend is distributable after the end of the fiscal year.
k. Net income for the year was $340,000.
l. Closed the Cash Dividends Declared and Stock Dividends Declared accounts to Retained Earnings.

Due to a loan agreement, the company is not allowed to reduce retained earnings below $100,000. The board of directors determined that this restriction should be disclosed in the notes to the financial statements.

Required

1. Make the general journal entries to record the transactions above.
2. Prepare the company's statement of retained earnings for the year ended June 30, 19x6.
3. Prepare the stockholders' equity section of the company's balance sheet on June 30, 19x6, including appropriate disclosure of the restriction on retained earnings.
4. Compute the book values per share of common stock on June 30, 19x5 and 19x6, and preferred stock on June 30, 19x6.

Answer to Review Problem

1. Prepare the journal entries.

a. Memorandum entry: 2 for 1 stock split, common, resulting in 500,000 shares issued and outstanding of no par value common stock with a stated value of $3

b. No entry required

c. Building	96,000	
Common Stock		36,000
Paid-in Capital in Excess of Stated Value, Common		60,000
Issue of 12,000 shares of common stock for a building appraised at $96,000		

	Debit	Credit
d. Treasury Stock, Common	64,000	
Cash		64,000
Purchase of 8,000 shares of common stock for the treasury for $8 per share		
e. Cash	2,000,000	
Preferred Stock		2,000,000
Sale of 20,000 shares of $100 par value preferred stock at $100 per share		
f. Cash	35,000	
Retained Earnings	5,000	
Treasury Stock, Common		40,000
Sale of 5,000 shares of treasury stock for $35,000, originally purchased for $8 per share		
g. Cash Dividends Declared	221,800	
Cash Dividends Payable		221,800
Declaration of cash dividends of $6 per share on 20,000 shares of preferred stock and $.20 per share on 509,000 shares of common stock: 20,000 × $6 = $120,000 509,000 × $.20 = 101,800 $221,800		
h. No entry required		
i. Cash Dividends Payable	221,800	
Cash		221,800
Paid cash dividend to preferred and common stockholders		
j. Stock Dividends Declared	509,000	
Common Stock Distributable		152,700
Paid-in Capital in Excess of Stated Value, Common		356,300
Declaration of a 50,900 share stock dividend (509,000 × .10) on $3 stated value common stock at a market value of $509,000 (50,900 × $10)		
k. Income Summary	340,000	
Retained Earnings		340,000
To close the Income Summary account to Retained Earnings		
l. Retained Earnings	730,800	
Cash Dividends Declared		221,800
Stock Dividends Declared		509,000
To close the Cash Dividends Declared and Stock Dividends Declared accounts to Retained Earnings		

2. Prepare a statement of retained earnings.

Szatkowski Company
Statement of Retained Earnings
For the Year Ended June 30, 19x6

Retained Earnings, June 30, 19x5		$ 970,000
Net Income, 19x6		340,000
Subtotal		$1,310,000
Less: Cash Dividends		
Preferred	$120,000	
Common	101,800	
Stock Dividends	509,000	
Treasury Stock Transaction	5,000	735,800
Retained Earnings, June 30, 19x6 (Note x)		$ 574,200

3. Prepare the stockholders' equity section of the balance sheet.

Szatkowski Company
Stockholders' Equity
June 30, 19x6

Contributed Capital		
Preferred Stock—$100 par value, 6% noncumulative, 50,000 shares authorized, 20,000 shares outstanding		$2,000,000
Common Stock—no par value, $3 stated value, 1,000,000 shares authorized, 512,000 shares issued, 509,000 shares outstanding	$1,536,000	
Common Stock Distributable, 50,900 shares	152,700	
Paid-in Capital in Excess of Stated Value, Common	1,236,300	2,925,000
Total Contributed Capital		$4,925,000
Retained Earnings (Note x)		574,200
Total Contributed Capital and Retained Earnings		$5,499,200
Less Treasury Stock, Common (3,000 shares at cost)		24,000
Total Stockholders' Equity		$5,475,200

Note x: The board of directors has restricted retained earnings available for dividends by the amount of $100,000 as required under a loan agreement.

4. Compute the book values.

June 30, 19x5
Common Stock: $3,290,000 ÷ 250,000 shares = $13.16 per share
June 30, 19x6
Preferred Stock:
Call price of $104 per share equals book value per share
Common Stock:
($5,475,200 – $2,080,000) ÷ (509,000 shares + 50,900 shares) =
$3,395,200 ÷ 559,900 shares = $6.06 per share

Chapter Assignments

Questions

1. What are retained earnings, and how do they relate to the assets of a corporation?
2. When does a company have a deficit in retained earnings?
3. What items are identified by generally accepted accounting principles as prior period adjustments?
4. Explain how the accounting treatment of stock dividends differs from that of cash dividends.
5. What is the difference between a stock dividend and a stock split? What is the effect of each on the capital structure of a corporation?
6. What is the purpose of restricting retained earnings?
7. Define treasury stock and explain why a company would purchase its own stock.
8. What is the difference between the statement of stockholders' equity and the stockholders' equity section of the balance sheet?
9. Would you expect a corporation's book value per share to equal its market value per share? Why or why not?
10. "Accounting income should be geared to the concept of taxable income because the public understands the concept of taxable income." Comment on this statement, and tell why income tax allocation is necessary.
11. Santa Fe Southern Pacific Railroad had about $1.8 billion of deferred income taxes in 1982, equal to about 31 percent of total liabilities. By 1984, deferred income taxes had reached almost $2.3 billion, or about 38 percent of total liabilities. Given management's desire to put off the payment of taxes as long as possible, the long-term growth of the economy and inflation, and the definition of a liability (probable future sacrifices of future benefits arising from present obligations), make an argument for not accounting for deferred income taxes.
12. Why should a gain or loss on discontinued operations be disclosed separately on the income statement?
13. Explain the two major criteria for extraordinary items. How should extraordinary items be disclosed in the financial statements?
14. How are earnings per share disclosed in financial statements?
15. When an accounting change occurs, what disclosures on its financial statements are necessary?
16. When does a company have a simple capital structure? A complex capital structure?
17. What is the difference between primary and fully diluted earnings per share?

Communication Skills Exercises

Communication 13-1. Ethics and Stock Dividends
(L.O. 2)

Bass Products Corporation, a public corporation, for twenty years has followed the practice of paying a cash dividend every quarter and has promoted itself to investors as a stable, reliable company. Recent competition from Asian companies in its industry has negatively affected its earnings and cash flows. As a result, Sandra Bass, president of the company, is proposing to the board of directors that the board declare a stock dividend of 5 percent this year instead of a cash dividend. She says, "This will maintain our consecutive dividend record and will not require any cash outflow." What is the difference between a cash dividend and a stock dividend? Why does a corporation usually issue them and how does each affect the financial statements? Is the action proposed by Bass ethical?

Communication 13-2. Purpose of Treasury Stock
(L.O. 3)

Atlantic Richfield Company, in its 1989 annual report, indicated that the number of common shares held in the treasury decreased from 45,546,171 in 1988 to 3,397,381 in 1989. The following also was reported:

By Board authorization, effective December 31, 1989 the Company cancelled 50 million shares of common stock held in treasury. As a result of the cancellation, common stock decreased by

$125 million, capital in excess of par value of stock decreased by $228 million, and retained earnings decreased by $3,119 million.[20]

The shares canceled or retired represent almost 25 percent of the shares of common stock issued by Atlantic Richfield. Explain the accounting for the treasury shares by Atlantic Richfield. Did the company buy any treasury shares during the year? What journal entry was made to record the cancellation or retirement of the treasury shares? At what average price were the treasury shares purchased, and at what average price were they originally issued? What do you think was management's reason for purchasing the treasury shares?

Communication 13-3. Basic Research Skills
(L.O. 2, 3, 5, 6, 7, 8, 9)

In your library, select the annual reports of three corporations. You may choose them from the same industry or at random, at the direction of your instructor. (If you completed the related basic research skills exercise in the chapter on contributed capital, use the same three companies.) Prepare a table with a column for each corporation. Then, for any year covered by the balance sheet, the statement of stockholders' equity, and the income statement, answer the following questions: Does the company own treasury stock? Was any treasury stock bought or retired? Did the company declare a stock dividend or a stock split? What other transactions appear in the statement of stockholders' equity? Has the company deferred any income taxes? Were there any discontinued operations, extraordinary items, or accounting changes? Compute the book value per common share for the company. In the *Wall Street Journal* or the financial section of another daily newspaper, find the current market price of each company's common stock and compare it to the book value you computed. Should there be any relationship between the two values? Be prepared to discuss your answers to these questions in class.

Classroom Exercises

Exercise 13-1. Statement of Retained Earnings
(L.O. 1)

The Drennan Corporation had a balance in Retained Earnings on December 31, 19x1 of $520,000. During 19x2, the company reported a profit of $224,000 after taxes. In addition, the company located an $88,000 (net of taxes) error that resulted in an overstatement of prior years' income and meets the criteria of a prior period adjustment. During 19x2, the company declared cash dividends totaling $32,000.

Prepare the company's statement of retained earnings for the year ended December 31, 19x2.

Exercise 13-2. Journal Entries: Stock Dividends
(L.O. 2)

The Geyer Company has 30,000 shares of its $1 par value common stock outstanding. Record the following transactions as they relate to the company's common stock:

July	17	Declared a 10 percent stock dividend on common stock to be distributed on August 10 to stockholders of record on July 31. Market value of the stock was $5 per share on this date.
	31	Record date.
Aug.	10	Distributed the stock dividend declared on July 17.
Sept.	1	Declared a $.50 per share cash dividend on common stock to be paid on September 16 to stockholders of record on September 10.

Exercise 13-3. Journal Entries: Stock Dividends
(L.O. 2)

On August 26, Shipley Corporation's board of directors declared a 2 percent stock dividend applicable to the outstanding shares of its $5 par value common stock, of which 150,000 shares are authorized, 130,000 are issued, and 10,000 are held in the treasury. The stock dividend was distributable on September 25 to stockholders of record on September 10. On August 26, the market value of the common stock was $12 per share. On November 26, the board of directors declared a $.20 per share cash dividend. No other stock transactions have occurred. Record the transactions on August 26, September 10, September 25, and November 26. Make the December 31 entry to close Cash Dividends Declared and Stock Dividends Declared to Retained Earnings.

20. Information excerpted from the 1989 annual report of Atlantic Richfield Company.

Exercise 13-4. Stock Split *(L.O. 2)*

The Colson Company currently has 200,000 shares of $1 par value common stock authorized outstanding. The board of directors declared a 2 for 1 split on May 15, when the market value of the common stock was $2.50 per share. The Retained Earnings balance on May 15 was $700,000. Paid-in Capital in Excess of Par Value, Common on this date was $20,000.

Prepare the stockholders' equity section of the company's balance sheet before and after the stock split. What journal entry, if any, would be necessary to record the stock split?

Exercise 13-5. Stock Split *(L.O. 2)*

On January 15, the board of directors of Fuquat International declared a 3 for 1 stock split of its $12 par value common stock, of which 800,000 shares were authorized and 200,000 were issued and outstanding. The market value on this date was $45 per share. On the same date, the balance of Paid-in Capital in Excess of Par Value, Common was $4,000,000, and the balance of Retained Earnings was $8,000,000.

Prepare the stockholders' equity section of the company's balance sheet before and after the stock split. What journal entry, if any, is needed to record the stock split?

Exercise 13-6. Treasury Stock Transactions *(L.O. 3)*

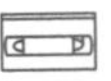

Prepare the journal entries necessary to record the following stock transactions of the Henderson Company during 19xx:

May 5 Purchased 400 shares of its own $1 par value common stock for $10 per share, the current market price.
17 Sold 150 shares of treasury stock purchased on May 5 for $11 per share.
21 Sold 100 shares of treasury stock purchased on May 5 for $10 per share.
28 Sold the remaining 150 shares of treasury stock purchased on May 5 for $9.50 per share.

Exercise 13-7. Treasury Stock Transactions Including Retirement *(L.O. 3)*

Prepare the journal entries necessary to record the following stock transactions of Nakate Corporation, which represent all treasury stock transactions entered into by the company.

June 1 Purchased 2,000 shares of its own $15 par value common stock for $35 per share, the current market price.
10 Sold 500 shares of treasury stock purchased on June 1 for $40 per share.
20 Sold 700 shares of treasury stock purchased on June 1 for $29 per share.
30 Retired the remaining shares purchased on June 1. The original issue price was $21 per share.

Exercise 13-8. Restriction of Retained Earnings *(L.O. 4)*

The board of directors of the Geroulis Company has approved plans to acquire another company during the coming year. The acquisition should cost approximately $1,100,000. The board took action to restrict retained earnings of the company in the amount of $1,100,000 on July 17, 19x1. On July 31, the company had retained earnings of $1,950,000.

1. Show two ways the restriction on retained earnings can be disclosed.
2. Assuming the purchase takes place as planned, what effect will it have on retained earnings and future disclosures?

Exercise 13-9. Statement of Stockholders' Equity *(L.O. 5)*

The stockholders' equity section of Kolb Corporation's balance sheet on December 31, 19x2 appears as follows:

Contributed Capital	
Common Stock—$2 par value, 500,000 shares authorized, 400,000 issued and outstanding	$ 800,000
Paid-in Capital in Excess of Par Value, Common	1,200,000
Total Contributed Capital	$2,000,000
Retained Earnings	4,200,000
Total Stockholders' Equity	$6,200,000

Prepare a statement of stockholders' equity for the year ended December 31, 19x3, assuming the following transactions occurred in sequence during 19x3:

a. Issued 10,000 shares of $100 par value, 9 percent cumulative preferred stock at par after obtaining authorization from the state.
b. Issued 40,000 shares of common stock in connection with the conversion of bonds having a carrying value of $600,000.
c. Declared and issued a 2 percent common stock dividend. The market value on the date of declaration was $14 per share.
d. Purchased 10,000 shares of common stock for the treasury at a cost of $16 per share.
e. Earned net income of $460,000.
f. Paid the full year's dividend on preferred stock and a dividend of $.40 per share on common stock outstanding at the end of the year.

Exercise 13-10. Book Value for Preferred and Common Stock *(L.O. 6)*

The stockholders' equity section of the Colombus Corporation's balance sheet is shown below.

Contributed Capital		
Preferred Stock—$100 per share, 6 percent cumulative, 10,000 shares authorized, 200 shares issued and outstanding*		$ 20,000
Common Stock—$5 par value, 100,000 shares authorized, 10,000 shares issued, 9,000 shares outstanding	$50,000	
Paid-in Capital in Excess of Par Value, Common	28,000	78,000
Total Contributed Capital		$ 98,000
Retained Earnings		95,000
Total Contributed Capital and Retained Earnings		$193,000
Less Treasury Stock, Common (1,000 shares at cost)		15,000
Total Stockholders' Equity		$178,000

*The preferred stock is callable at $105 per share, and one year's dividends are in arrears.

Determine the book value per share for both the preferred and the common stock.

Exercise 13-11. Corporate Income Statement *(L.O. 7)*

Assume that the Shortall Furniture Company's chief financial officer gave you the following information: Net Sales, $1,900,000; Cost of Goods Sold, $1,050,000; Extraordinary Gain (net of income taxes of $3,500), $12,500; Loss from Discontinued Operations (net of income tax benefit of $30,000), $50,000; Loss on Disposal of Discontinued Operations (net of income tax benefit of $13,000), $35,000; Selling Expenses, $50,000; Administrative Expenses, $40,000; Income Taxes Expense on Continuing Operations, $300,000.

From this information, prepare the company's income statement for the year ended June 30, 19xx. (Ignore earnings per share information.)

Exercise 13-12. Use of Corporate Income Tax Rate Schedule *(L.O. 8)*

Using the corporate tax rate schedule on page 514, compute the income tax liability for the following situations:

Situation	Taxable Income
A	$ 70,000
B	85,000
C	320,000

Exercise 13-13.
Income Tax Allocation
(L.O. 8)

The Delcampo Corporation reported the following accounting income before income taxes, income taxes expense, and net income for 19x2 and 19x3:

	19x2	19x3
Accounting income before taxes	$280,000	$280,000
Income taxes expense	88,300	88,300
Net income	$191,700	$191,700

Also, on the balance sheet, deferred income taxes liability increased by $38,400 in 19x2 and decreased by $18,800 in 19x3.

1. How much did Delcampo Corporation actually pay in income taxes for 19x2 and 19x3?
2. Prepare journal entries to record income taxes expense for 19x2 and 19x3.

Exercise 13-14.
Earnings per Share
(L.O. 10)

During 19x1, the Heath Corporation reported a net income of $1,529,500. On January 1, Heath had 700,000 shares of common stock outstanding. The company issued an additional 420,000 shares of common stock on October 1. In 19x1, the company had a simple capital structure. During 19x2, there were no transactions involving common stock, and the company reported net income of $2,016,000.

1. Determine the weighted-average number of common shares outstanding each year.
2. Compute earnings per share for each year.

Exercise 13-15.
Corporate Income Statement
(L.O. 7, 8, 9, 10)

The following items are components in the income statement of Cohen Corporation for the year ended December 31, 19x1:

Sales	$500,000
Cost of Goods Sold	(275,000)
Operating Expenses	(112,500)
Income Taxes Expense	(82,350)
Income from Operations of a Discontinued Segment	80,000
Gain on Disposal of Segment	70,000
Extraordinary Gain on Retirement of Bonds	36,000
Cumulative Effect of a Change in Accounting Principle	(24,000)
Net Income	$192,150
Earnings per Share	$.96

Recast the 19x1 income statement in proper multistep form, including allocating income taxes to appropriate items (assume a 30 percent income tax rate) and showing earnings per share figures (200,000 shares outstanding).

Exercise 13-16.
Corporate Income Statement
(L.O. 7, 8, 9, 10)

During 19x3, Shulman Corporation engaged in a number of complex transactions to restructure the business by selling off a division, retiring bonds, and changing accounting methods. The company always has issued a simple single-step income statement, and the accountant accordingly prepared the December 31 year-end income statement for 19x3 and 19x2 shown at the top of page 534.

The president of the company, Mark Shulman, is pleased to see that net income and earnings per share increased by 22 percent from 19x2 to 19x3 and intends to announce to the stockholders that the restructuring is a success.

1. Recast the 19x3 income statement in proper multistep form, including allocating income taxes to appropriate items (assume a 30 percent income tax rate) and showing earnings per share figures (200,000 shares outstanding).
2. What is your assessment of the restructuring plan?

Shulman Corporation
Income Statement
For the Years Ended December 31, 19x3 and 19x2

	19x3	19x2
Sales	$2,000,000	$2,400,000
Cost of Goods Sold	(1,100,000)	(1,200,000)
Operating Expenses	(450,000)	(300,000)
Income Taxes Expense	(329,400)	(270,000)
Income from Operations of a Discontinued Segment	320,000	
Gain on Disposal of Segment	280,000	
Extraordinary Gain on Retirement of Bonds	144,000	
Cumulative Effect of a Change in Accounting Principle	(96,000)	
Net Income	$ 768,600	$ 630,000
Earnings per Share	$3.84	$3.15

Interpretation Case from Business

Ford Motor Company[21]
(L.O. 2, 3)

In November 1987, Ford Motor Company announced a plan to buy up to $2 billion of its common stock in the open market, constituting the company's second large-scale stock repurchase since 1984. At the then current market price of $71.75, Ford estimated that it could purchase more than 27 million shares, which would effectively reduce the number of outstanding shares by more than 11 percent.

The plan represented management's belief that Ford stock was undervalued and would be an exceptional investment for both the company and its shareholders. It was an action that demonstrated management's confidence in Ford's future in the highly competitive automobile market.

Another interpretation of the action might be that Ford had generated a tremendous amount of cash for which the company had limited investment opportunities other than its own stock. By the close of 1987, it was estimated that the company would have $8 billion in cash revenues.

On October 8, eleven days before the stock market crash of October 19, Ford proposed to shareholders a 2 for 1 stock split; the new shares were expected to be issued January 12. The calculations for the buyback move were based on presplit figures. October 8 was also the day of Ford's ninth dividend increase in the past seventeen quarters; the company's quarterly dividend rose from $.75 to $1.00 a share on a presplit basis.

The condensed balance sheet for Ford on December 31, 1986 is shown on page 535.

Required

1. Assuming that the buyback was completed as planned (before December 31, 1987), prepare the journal entry to record the purchase of treasury stock (use the total dollar amount and date given above).
2. Prepare the condensed balance sheet after the buyback in **1** was recorded, assuming that the balance sheet on December 31, 1986 was the same as the balance sheet immediately before the buyback.
3. Tell whether the buyback would have increased or decreased the following ratios: current ratio, debt to equity, return on assets, return on equity, and earnings per share. Also indicate whether the increase or decrease was favorable or unfavorable.
4. Assuming that Ford decided to retire the repurchased stock, prepare the appropriate journal entry.

21. Information excerpted from the 1986 annual report of Ford Motor Company.

5. Assume that Ford did not retire the repurchased stock but went through with the proposed stock split. How would the balance sheet differ from the one you prepared in **2**, and how much would the company have paid in total quarterly dividends?

Ford Motor Company
Condensed Balance Sheet
December 31, 1986
(in billions)

Current Assets	$18.5	Current Liabilities	$15.6
Long-Term Assets	19.4	Long-Term Liabilities	7.5
	$37.9	Stockholders' Equity	
		Common Stock ($2 par value)	.5
		Paid-in Capital in Excess of Par Value, Common	.6
		Retained Earnings	13.7
		Total Liabilities and Stockholders' Equity	$37.9

Problem Set A

Problem 13A-1. Treasury Stock Transactions *(L.O. 3)*

The Spivy Corporation was involved in the following treasury stock transactions during 19x7:

a. Purchased 80,000 shares of its $1 par value common stock at $2.50 per share.
b. Purchased 16,000 shares of its common stock at $2.80 per share.
c. Sold 44,000 shares purchased in **a** for $131,000.
d. Sold the other 36,000 shares purchased in **a** for $72,000.
e. Sold 6,000 of the remaining shares of treasury stock for $1.60 per share.
f. Retired all the remaining shares of treasury stock. All shares originally were issued at $1.50 per share.

Required

Record the treasury stock transactions in general journal form.

Problem 13A-2. Stock Dividend, Stock Split, and Treasury Stock Transactions *(L.O. 2, 3)*

The stockholders' equity section of the balance sheet of Borkowski Corporation as of December 31, 19x6 was as follows:

Contributed Capital	
Common Stock—$4 par value, 500,000 shares authorized, 200,000 shares issued and outstanding	$ 800,000
Paid-in Capital in Excess of Par Value, Common	1,000,000
Total Contributed Capital	$1,800,000
Retained Earnings	1,200,000
Total Stockholders' Equity	$3,000,000

The following transactions occurred in 19x7 for Borkowski Corporation:

Jan. 21 Purchased 10,000 shares of the company's $4 par value common stock at $12 per share.
Feb. 28 The board of directors declared a 10 percent stock dividend to stockholders of record on March 25 to be distributed on April 5. The market value on this date is $16.
Mar. 25 Date of record for stock dividend.
Apr. 5 Issued stock dividend.

May 16 Sold 4,000 shares of the treasury stock purchased on January 21 for $14 per share.
June 15 Sold 5,000 shares of the treasury stock purchased on January 21 for $7 per share.
July 15 Decided to retire, effective immediately, the remaining shares held in the treasury. The shares originally were issued at $6 per share.
Aug. 3 Declared a 2 for 1 stock split.
Nov. 20 Purchased 20,000 shares of the company's common stock at $8 per share for the treasury.
Dec. 31 Declared a 5 percent stock dividend to stockholders of record on January 25 to be distributed on February 5. The market value per share was $9.
Dec. 31 Closed Stock Dividends Declared to Retained Earnings.
Dec. 31 Closed Income Summary with a credit balance of $108,000 to Retained Earnings.

Required

1. Record the transactions for Borkowski Corporation in general journal form.
2. Prepare the stockholders' equity section of the company's balance sheet as of December 31, 19x7. Assume net income for 19x7 is $108,000. (**Hint:** Use T accounts to keep track of transactions.)

Problem 13A-3. Dividend and Stock Split Transactions, Retained Earnings, and Stockholders' Equity
(L.O. 1, 2, 4)

The stockholders' equity section of the Kurland Blind and Awning Company's balance sheet as of December 31, 19x6 was as follows:

Contributed Capital	
Common Stock—$2 par value, 3,000,000 shares authorized, 500,000 shares issued and outstanding	$1,000,000
Paid-in Capital in Excess of Par Value, Common	400,000
Total Contributed Capital	$1,400,000
Retained Earnings	1,080,000
Total Stockholders' Equity	$2,480,000

The company was involved in the following stockholders' equity transactions during 19x7:

Mar. 5 Declared a $.40 per share cash dividend to be paid on April 6 to stockholders of record on March 20.
20 Date of record.
Apr. 6 Paid the cash dividend.
June 17 Declared a 10 percent stock dividend to be distributed August 17 to stockholders of record on August 5. The market value of the stock was $14 per share.
Aug. 5 Date of record.
17 Distributed the stock dividend.
Oct. 2 Split its stock 3 for 1.
Dec. 27 Declared a cash dividend of $.10 payable January 27, 19x8, to stockholders of record on January 14, 19x8.
31 Closed Income Summary with a credit balance of $400,000 to Retained Earnings.
31 Closed Cash Dividends Declared and Stock Dividends Declared to Retained Earnings.

On December 9, the board of directors restricted retained earnings for a pending lawsuit in the amount of $200,000. The restriction should be shown on the firm's financial statements.

Required

1. Record the 19x7 transactions in general journal form.
2. Prepare a statement of retained earnings, with appropriate disclosure of restriction.
3. Prepare the stockholders' equity section of the company's balance sheet as of December 31, 19x7, with an appropriate disclosure of the restriction on retained earnings. (**Hint:** Use T accounts to keep track of transactions.)

Problem 13A-4. Corporate Income Statement
(L.O. 7, 8, 9, 10)

Income statement information for the Shah Corporation during 19x1 is as follows:

a. Administrative expenses, $220,000.
b. Cost of goods sold, $880,000.
c. Cumulative effect of a change in inventory methods that decreased income (net of taxes, $56,000), $120,000.
d. Extraordinary loss from a storm (net of taxes, $20,000), $40,000.
e. Income taxes expense, continuing operations, $84,000.
f. Net sales, $1,780,000.
g. Selling expenses, $380,000.

Required

Prepare Shah Corporation's income statement for 19x1, including earnings per share information assuming a weighted average of 200,000 shares of common stock outstanding for 19x1.

Problem 13A-5. Comprehensive Stockholders' Equity Transactions
(L.O. 1, 2, 3, 4, 6)

The stockholders' equity on June 30, 19x5 of the Gagliano Company is shown below:

Contributed Capital	
Common Stock—no par value, $4 stated value, 500,000 shares authorized, 200,000 shares issued and outstanding	$ 800,000
Paid-in Capital in Excess of Stated Value, Common	1,280,000
Total Contributed Capital	$2,080,000
Retained Earnings	840,000
Total Stockholders' Equity	$2,920,000

Stockholders' equity transactions for the next fiscal year are as follows:

a. The board of directors declared a 2 for 1 split.
b. The board of directors obtained authorization to issue 200,000 shares of $100 par value, $4 noncumulative preferred stock, callable at $105.
c. Issued 10,000 shares of common stock for a building appraised at $44,000.
d. Purchased 6,000 shares of the company's common stock for $30,000.
e. Issued 30,000 shares, $100 par value, of the preferred stock for $100 per share.
f. Sold 4,000 shares of the treasury stock for $18,000.
g. Declared cash dividends of $4 per share on the preferred stock and $.20 per share on the common stock.
h. Date of record.
i. Paid the preferred and common stock cash dividends.
j. Declared a 5 percent stock dividend on the common stock. The market value was $18 per share. The stock dividend was distributable after the end of the fiscal year.
k. Net income for the year was $420,000.
l. Closed the Cash Dividends Declared and Stock Dividends Declared accounts to Retained Earnings.

Due to a loan agreement, the company is not allowed to reduce retained earnings below $200,000. The board of directors determined that this restriction should be disclosed in the notes to the financial statements.

Required

1. Make the appropriate general journal entries to record the transactions.
2. Prepare the company's statement of retained earnings for the year ended June 30, 19x6, including disclosure of restriction.
3. Prepare the stockholders' equity section of the company's balance sheet on June 30, 19x6, including an appropriate disclosure of the restriction on retained earnings. (**Hint:** Use T accounts to keep track of transactions.)
4. Compute the book values per share of preferred and common stock (including common stock distributable) on June 30, 19x5 and 19x6.

Problem Set B

Problem 13B-1. Treasury Stock Transactions
(L.O. 3)

These treasury stock transactions occurred during 19xx for the Dwyer Company:

a. Purchased 52,000 shares of its $1 par value common stock on the market for $20 per share.
b. Sold 16,000 shares of the treasury stock for $21 per share.
c. Sold 12,000 shares of the treasury stock for $19 per share.
d. Sold 20,000 shares of the treasury stock remaining for $17 per share.
e. Purchased an additional 8,000 shares for $18 per share.
f. Retired all the remaining shares of treasury stock. All shares originally were issued at $8 per share.

Required

Record these transactions in general journal form.

Problem 13B-2. Stock Dividend, Stock Split, and Treasury Stock Transactions
(L.O. 2, 3)

The stockholders' equity section of Klock Cotton Mills, Inc. as of December 31, 19x2 was as follows:

Contributed Capital	
Common Stock—$12 par value, 500,000 shares authorized, 80,000 shares issued and outstanding	$ 960,000
Paid-in Capital in Excess of Par Value, Common	300,000
Total Contributed Capital	$1,260,000
Retained Earnings	960,000
Total Stockholders' Equity	$2,220,000

A review of the stockholders' equity records of Klock Cotton Mills, Inc. disclosed the following transactions during 19x3:

Jan.	30	Purchased 20,000 shares of the company's $12 par value common stock for $21 per share. The stock originally was issued at $18 per share.
Feb.	16	Sold 6,000 shares of the company's stock purchased on January 30 for $24 per share.
Mar.	25	The board of directors declared a 5 percent stock dividend to stockholders of record on April 20 to be distributed on May 1. The market value of the common stock was $22 per share.
Apr.	20	Date of record for the stock dividend.
May	1	Issued the stock dividend.
Aug.	17	Sold 1,000 shares of the company's stock purchased on January 30 for $18 per share.
Sept.	10	Declared a 3 for 1 stock split. Assume the stock split applies to shares held in the treasury.
Oct.	5	Sold 6,000 shares of the company's stock purchased on January 30 for $4 per share. (**Hint:** Notice the effect of the stock split on the cost of the shares.)
Nov.	20	Decided to retire, effective immediately, 20,000 of the remaining shares held in the treasury.
Dec.	15	Declared a 10 percent stock dividend to stockholders of record on January 15 to be distributed on February 15. The market price on this date is $7 per share.
Dec.	31	Closed Stock Dividends Declared to Retained Earnings.
Dec.	31	Closed Income Summary with a credit balance of $94,000 to Retained Earnings.

Required

1. Record the transactions for Klock Cotton Mills, Inc. in general journal form.
2. Prepare the stockholders' equity section of the company's balance sheet as of December 31, 19x3. Assume net income for 19x3 is $94,000. (**Hint:** Use T accounts to keep track of transactions.)

Problem 13B-3.
Dividend and Stock Split Transactions, Retained Earnings, and Stockholders' Equity
(L.O. 1, 2, 4)

The balance sheet of the Yao Clothing Company disclosed the following stockholders' equity as of September 30, 19x1:

Contributed Capital	
Common Stock—$4 par value, 1,000,000 shares authorized, 300,000 shares issued and outstanding	$1,200,000
Paid-in Capital in Excess of Par Value, Common	740,000
Total Contributed Capital	$1,940,000
Retained Earnings	700,000
Total Stockholders' Equity	$2,640,000

The following stockholders' equity transactions were completed during the next fiscal year in the order presented:

19x1		
Dec.	17	Declared a 10 percent stock dividend to be distributed January 20 to stockholders of record on January 1. The market value per share on the date of declaration was $8.
19x2		
Jan.	1	Date of record.
	20	Distributed the stock dividend.
Apr.	14	Declared a $.50 per share cash dividend. The cash dividend is payable May 15 to stockholders of record on May 1.
May	1	Date of record.
	15	Paid the cash dividend.
June	17	Split its stock 2 for 1.
Sept.	15	Declared a cash dividend of $.20 per share payable October 10 to stockholders of record October 1.
	30	Closed Income Summary with a credit balance of $300,000 to Retained Earnings.
	30	Closed Cash Dividends Declared and Stock Dividends Declared to Retained Earnings.

On September 14, the board of directors restricted retained earnings for plant expansion in the amount of $300,000. The restriction should be shown in the financial statements.

Required

1. Record the above transactions in general journal form.
2. Prepare a statement of retained earnings, including disclosure of restriction.
3. Prepare the stockholders' equity section of the company's balance sheet as of September 30, 19x2, with an appropriate disclosure of the restriction of retained earnings. (**Hint:** Use T accounts to keep track of transactions.)

Problem 13B-4.
Corporate Income Statement
(L.O. 7, 8, 9, 10)

Information concerning operations of the Benedict Shoe Corporation during 19xx is as follows:

a. Administrative expenses, $180,000.
b. Cost of goods sold, $840,000.
c. Cumulative effect of an accounting change in depreciation methods that increased income (net of taxes, $40,000), $84,000.
d. Extraordinary loss from an earthquake (net of taxes, $72,000), $120,000.
e. Sales (net), $1,800,000.
f. Selling expenses, $160,000.
g. Income taxes expense applicable to continuing operations, $210,000.

Required

Prepare the corporation's income statement for the year ended December 31, 19xx, including earnings per share information. Assume a weighted average of 100,000 common shares outstanding during the year.

Problem 13B-5. Comprehensive Stockholders' Equity Transactions
(L.O. 1, 2, 3, 4, 6)

On December 31, 19x1, the stockholders' equity section of the Pucinski Company's balance sheet appeared as follows:

Contributed Capital	
Common Stock—$8 par value, 200,000 shares authorized, 60,000 shares issued and outstanding	$ 480,000
Paid-in Capital in Excess of Par Value, Common	1,280,000
Total Contributed Capital	$1,760,000
Retained Earnings	824,000
Total Stockholders' Equity	$2,584,000

Selected transactions involving stockholders' equity in 19x2 are as follows: On January 4, the board of directors obtained authorization for 20,000 shares of $40 par value noncumulative preferred stock that carried an indicated dividend rate of $4 per share and was callable at $42 per share. On January 14, the company sold 12,000 shares of the preferred stock at $40 per share and issued another 2,000 in exchange for a building valued at $80,000. On March 8, the board of directors declared a 2 for 1 stock split on the common stock. On April 20, after the stock split, the company purchased 3,000 shares of common stock for the treasury at an average price of $12 per share; 1,000 of these shares subsequently were sold on May 4 at an average price of $16 per share. On July 15, the board of directors declared a cash dividend of $4 per share on the preferred stock and $.40 per share on the common stock. The date of record was July 25. The dividends were paid on August 15. The board of directors declared a 15 percent stock dividend on November 28, when the common stock was selling for $20. The record date for the stock dividend was December 15, and the dividend was to be distributed on January 5. Net loss for 19x2 was $218,000. On December 31, Income Summary, Cash Dividends Declared, and Stock Dividends Declared were closed. The board of directors noted that footnote disclosure must be made due to a bank loan agreement that requires minimum retained earnings. No cash dividends can be declared or paid if retained earnings fall below $100,000.

Required

1. Prepare journal entries to record the transactions above.
2. Prepare the company's statement of retained earnings for the year ended December 31, 19x2, including disclosure of restriction.
3. Prepare the stockholders' equity section of the company's balance sheet as of December 31, 19x2, including an appropriate disclosure of the restriction on retained earnings. (**Hint:** Use T accounts to keep track of transactions.)
4. Compute the book value per share for preferred and common stock on December 31, 19x1 and 19x2.

Financial Decision Case

Borders Steel Corporation
(L.O. 2, 3, 6)

Borders Steel Corporation (BSC) is a small specialty steel manufacturer located in northern Alabama that has been owned by the Borders family for several generations. Myron Borders III is a major shareholder in BSC by virtue of having inherited 200,000 shares of common stock in the company. Myron has not shown much interest in the business because of his enthusiasm for archaeology, which takes him to far parts of the world. However, when he received minutes of the last board of directors meeting, he questioned a number of transactions involving the stockholders' equity of BSC. He asks you, as a person with a knowledge of accounting, to help him interpret the effect of these transactions on his interest in BSC.

You begin by examining the stockholders' equity section of BSC's January 1, 19xx balance sheet.

Borders Steel Corporation
Stockholders' Equity
January 1, 19xx

Contributed Capital	
Common Stock—$20 par value, 5,000,000 shares authorized, 1,000,000 shares issued and outstanding	$ 20,000,000
Paid-in Capital in Excess of Par Value, Common	50,000,000
Total Contributed Capital	$ 70,000,000
Retained Earnings	40,000,000
Total Stockholders' Equity	$110,000,000

Then you read the relevant parts of the minutes of the December 15, 19xx meeting of the firm's board of directors:

Item A: The president reported the following transactions involving the company's stock during the last quarter:

October 15. Sold 500,000 shares of authorized common stock through the investment banking firm of T. R. Kendall at a net price of $100 per share.

November 1. Purchased 100,000 shares for the corporate treasury from Lucy Borders at a price of $110 per share.

Item B: The board declared a 2 for 1 stock split (accomplished by halving the par value, doubling each stockholder's shares, and increasing authorized shares to 10,000,000), followed by a 10 percent stock dividend. The board then declared a cash dividend of $4 per share on the resulting shares. All these transactions are applicable to stockholders of record on December 20 and are payable on January 10. The market value of Borders stock on the board meeting date after the stock split was estimated to be $60.

Item C: The chief financial officer stated that he expected the company to report net income for the year of $8,000,000.

Required

1. Prepare a stockholders' equity section of BSC's balance sheet as of December 31, 19xx that reflects the transactions above. (**Hint:** Use T accounts to analyze the transactions. Also, use a T account to keep track of the shares of common stock outstanding.)
2. Compute the book value per share and Myron's percentage of ownership of the company at the beginning and at the end of the year. Explain the differences. Would you say that Myron's position has improved during the year? Why or why not?

Answers to Self-Test

1. b	3. c	5. a	7. b	9. a
2. a	4. d	6. d	8. c	10. b

Comprehensive Problem: Sundial Corporation

Sundial Corporation filed articles of incorporation and obtained authorization for 500,000 shares of no par common stock with a stated value of $1 per share and 20,000 shares of 9 percent cumulative preferred stock with a par value of $100 and a call price of $104. The company began operations on January 1, 19xx, as a high-tech startup in the business of making sophisticated time measuring devices. The company's first year was an exciting and profitable one, in which the company engaged in a number of transactions involving its stockholders' equity, which are listed below.

19xx

Jan. 1 Issued, for cash, 100,000 shares of common stock at a price of $6 per share.

2 Issued 12,000 shares of common stock to attorneys and others who assisted with the organization of the corporation. The value of these services was put at $72,000.

3 Issued, for cash, 12,000 shares of preferred stock at par value.

Feb. 6 Accepted subscriptions for 60,000 shares of common stock at a price of $6 per share.

Mar. 7 Issued 8,000 shares of common stock in exchange for a patent that had a value set at $50,000.

Apr. 2 Received full payment for half the stock subscription of February 6 and issued the stock.

May 5 Purchased 30,000 common shares from a stockholder for $8 per share.

19 Sold 13,000 of the common shares held in treasury from the May 5 transaction for $9 per share.

June 30 Transferred by a closing entry the net income for the first half of the year to Retained Earnings, $120,000.

July 8 Sold 7,000 more of the common shares held in treasury from the May 5 transaction for $7.

Aug. 4 Declared a 10 percent common stock dividend distributable on August 24 to stockholders of record August 14. At this time, the company's common stock was selling for $8 per share.

14 Date of record for the stock dividend.

24 Date of distribution for the stock dividend.

Sept. 9 Issued common stock for cash in connection with the exercise by management of employee stock options on 40,000 shares of common stock at $5 per share.

Oct. 10 Purchased 10,000 shares of common stock from a stockholder for $9 per share.

20 Retired the shares purchased on October 10. The shares originally were issued at $6 per share.

Nov. 1 Declared cash dividends representing the annual dividend on preferred stock and $.25 per share on common stock to stockholders of record November 11, payable on November 21.

11 Date of record for cash dividends.

21 Date of payment for cash dividends.

Dec. 16 Declared a 2 for 1 stock split on all issued and subscribed shares (including treasury stock).

31 Transferred by closing entry the net income for the second half of the year of $310,000 to Retained Earnings and closed cash and stock dividends to Retained Earnings.

Dec. 31 Due to litigation and potential loss under a lawsuit over a patent infringement, the board of directors voted to restrict retained earnings to the extent of $100,000 and to disclose this information in a note to the financial statements.

Required

1. Record the entries above in Sundial Corporation's general journal.
2. Prepare the statement of retained earnings for 19xx for Sundial Corporation.
3. Prepare the stockholders' equity section of Sundial's balance sheet on December 31, 19xx, including proper disclosure of the restriction on retained earnings.
4. Compute the book value of preferred stock and common stock at year's end.

This Comprehensive Problem covers all of the Learning Objectives in the chapter on contributed capital and Learning Objectives 1 through 6 in the chapter on retained earnings and corporate income statements.

LEARNING OBJECTIVES

1. Identify and contrast the major characteristics of bonds.
2. Record the issuance of bonds at face value and at a discount or premium.
3. Determine the value of bonds using present values.
4. Amortize (a) bond discounts and (b) bond premiums using the straight-line and effective interest methods.
5. Account for bonds issued between interest dates and make year-end adjustments.
6. Account for the retirement of bonds and the conversion of bonds into stock.
7. Explain the basic features of mortgages payable, installment notes payable, long-term leases, and pensions and other postretirement benefits as long-term liabilities.

CHAPTER 14

Long-Term Liabilities

This chapter introduces long-term liabilities. It describes the nature of bonds and the accounting treatment for bonds payable and other long-term liabilities, such as mortgages payable, installment notes payable, long-term leases, and pensions and other postretirement benefits. After studying this chapter, you should be able to meet the learning objectives listed on the left.

A corporation has many sources of funds from which to finance operations and expansion. As you learned earlier, corporations can acquire cash and other assets by earning a profit, obtaining short-term credit, and issuing stock. Another source of funds for a business is long-term debt, in the form of bonds, notes, or mortgages. When a company issues long-term debt, it promises to pay the creditor periodic interest plus the principal of the debt on a certain date in the future. Notes, bonds, and mortgages are long term if they are due more than one year from the balance sheet date. In practice, long-term notes range from two to ten years to maturity, and long-term bonds and mortgages from ten to fifty years to maturity. Although some companies carry an amount of long-term debt that exceeds 50 percent of their total assets, the average company carries much less.

DECISION POINT

RJR Nabisco

■ During the 1980s, there was an explosion in the amount of long-term debt issued by companies either to refinance their own operations or to finance takeovers of other companies. Much of this financing was accomplished through so-called **junk bonds**, unsecured, high-risk, long-term bonds that carry high rates of interest. Carrying a large amount of debt is risky for a company because interest charges on this kind of debt are very high in relation to earnings and cash flows. If a company is unable to pay the interest on its bonds, it can be forced to declare bankruptcy. Even if a company can pay the interest, its ability to improve and expand operations can be limited severely.

RJR Nabisco set a record when it issued $26 billion in junk bonds in its takeover by the securities firm of Kohlberg Kravis Roberts & Co. in February 1989. The heavy debt load proved to be a burden to RJR Nabisco. The biggest problem the company faced involved bonds whose interest rate had to be increased if the prices of the bonds on the open market declined, as they did in 1990. Some interest rates would have had to be reset at 20 percent or higher, more than double the interest rates on less risky bonds. Management now had to decide how to alleviate the situation or face the potential bankruptcy or breakup of the company.

As reported in the *Asian Wall Street Journal*, after six months of intense negotiations, RJR Nabisco's management resolved its immediate problems through a $6.9 billion refinancing plan.[1] This large refinancing package was designed to strengthen the balance sheet and ward off a potential financial crisis. Louis Gerstner, the company's chief financial officer, called the refinancing package "a comprehensive, creative program." Under the plan, RJR Nabisco would have billions of dollars at its disposal. Among the components of the plan were new long-term bonds, adjustments of interest rates on existing bonds, new issues of capital stock, new bank loans, and expansion of existing bank lines of credit. Although this financing plan is among the most complex in history, it can be understood using the concepts described in this chapter. ■

The Nature of Bonds

OBJECTIVE 1
Identify and contrast the major characteristics of bonds

A **bond** is a security, usually long term, representing money borrowed by a corporation from the investing public. (Other kinds of bonds are issued by the U.S. government, state and local governments, and foreign companies and countries to raise money.) Bonds must be repaid at a certain time and require periodic payments of interest. Interest usually is paid semiannually (twice a year). Bonds must not be confused with stocks. Because stocks are shares of ownership, stockholders are owners. Bondholders are creditors. Bonds are promises to repay the amount borrowed, called the *principal*, and interest at a certain rate on specified future dates.

The holder of a bond receives a **bond certificate** as evidence of the company's debt. In most cases, the face value (denomination) of the bond is $1,000 or some multiple of $1,000. A **bond issue** is the total number of bonds that is issued at one time. For example, a $1,000,000 bond issue could consist of a thousand $1,000 bonds. A bond issue can be bought and held by many investors. So, the corporation usually enters into a supplementary agreement, called a **bond indenture**. The bond indenture defines the rights and privileges of the bondholders and the limitations restricting them. The bond indenture generally describes such things as the maturity date of the bonds, interest payment dates, the interest rate, and characteristics of the bonds such as call features. Repayment plans and restrictions also may be covered.

The prices of bonds are stated in terms of a percentage of face value. A bond issue quoted at 103½ means that a $1,000 bond costs $1,035 ($1,000 × 1.035). When a bond sells at exactly 100, it is said to sell at face or par value. When it sells above 100, it is said to sell at a premium; below 100, at a discount. A $1,000 bond quoted at 87.62 would be selling at a discount and would cost the buyer $876.20.

A bond indenture can be written to fit the financing needs of an individual company. As a result, the bonds being issued by corporations in today's financial markets have many different features. Several of the more important ones are described here.

Secured or Unsecured Bonds

Bonds can be either secured or unsecured. If issued on the general credit of the company, they are **unsecured bonds** (also called *debenture bonds*). **Secured bonds** give the bondholders a pledge of certain assets of the company as a

1. George Anders, "RJR Nabisco Moves to Retire Most Troublesome Junk Bonds," *Asian Wall Street Journal*, July 17, 1990.

guarantee of repayment. The security identified by a secured bond can be any specific asset of the company or a general category of asset, such as property, plant, or equipment.

Term or Serial Bonds

When all the bonds of an issue mature at the same time, they are called **term bonds**. For example, a company may issue $1,000,000 worth of bonds, all due twenty years from the date of issue. If the bonds in an issue mature on several different dates, the bonds are **serial bonds**. An example of serial bonds would be a $1,000,000 issue that calls for retiring $200,000 of the principal every five years. This arrangement means that after the first $200,000 payment is made, $800,000 of the bonds would remain outstanding for the next five years. In other words, $1,000,000 is outstanding for the first five years, $800,000 for the second five years, and so on. A company may issue serial bonds to ease the task of retiring its debt.

Registered or Coupon Bonds

Most bonds that are issued today are **registered bonds**. The names and addresses of the owners of these bonds must be recorded with the issuing company. The company keeps a register of the owners and pays interest by check to the bondholders of record on the interest payment date. **Coupon bonds** generally are not registered with the corporation; instead, they bear interest coupons stating the amount of interest due and the payment date. The coupons are removed from the bonds on the interest payment dates and presented at a bank for collection.

Accounting for Bonds Payable[2]

OBJECTIVE 2
Record the issuance of bonds at face value and at a discount or premium

When the board of directors decides to issue bonds, it generally presents the proposal to the stockholders. If the stockholders agree to the issue, the company prints the certificates and draws up an appropriate legal document. The bonds then are authorized for issuance. It is not necessary to make a journal entry for the authorization, but most companies prepare a memorandum in the Bonds Payable account describing the issue. This note lists the number and value of bonds authorized, the interest rate, interest payment dates, and the life of the bonds.

Once the bonds are issued, the corporation must pay interest to the bondholders over the life of the bonds (in most cases, semiannually) and the principal of the bonds at maturity.

Balance Sheet Disclosure of Bonds

Bonds Payable and either unamortized discounts or premiums (which we explain later) generally are shown on a company's balance sheet as long-term liabilities. However, as explained in the chapter on current liabilities, if the maturity date of the bond issue is one year or less and the bonds will be retired using current assets, Bonds Payable should be listed as a current liability. If the issue is to be paid with segregated assets or replaced by another bond issue, the bonds still should be shown as a long-term liability.

2. At the time this chapter was written, the market interest rates on corporate bonds were volatile. Therefore, the examples and problems in this chapter use a variety of interest rates to demonstrate the concepts.

Important provisions of the bond indenture are reported in the notes to the financial statements. Often reported with them is a list of all bond issues, the kinds of bonds, interest rates, any securities connected with the bonds, interest payment dates, maturity dates, and effective interest rates.

Bonds Issued at Face Value

Suppose that the Vason Corporation has authorized the issuance of $100,000 of 9 percent, five-year bonds on January 1, 19x0. According to the bond indenture, interest is to be paid on January 1 and July 1 of each year. Assume that the bonds are sold on January 1, 19x0 for their face value. The entry to record the issuance is as follows:

19x0			
Jan. 1	Cash	100,000	
	Bonds Payable		100,000
	Sold $100,000 of 9%, 5-year bonds at face value		

As stated above, interest is paid on January 1 and on July 1 of each year. Therefore, the corporation would owe the bondholders $4,500 interest on July 1, 19x0:

$$\begin{aligned}\text{Interest} &= \text{principal} \times \text{rate} \times \text{time}\\ &= \$100{,}000 \times .09 \times 6/12\\ &= \$4{,}500\end{aligned}$$

The interest paid to the bondholders on each semiannual interest payment date (January 1 or July 1) would be recorded as follows:

Bond Interest Expense	4,500	
Cash (or Interest Payable)		4,500
Paid (or accrued) semiannual interest to bondholders of 9%, 5-year bonds		

Face Interest Rate and Market Interest Rate

When issuing bonds, most companies try to set the face interest rate as close as possible to the market interest rate. The **face interest rate** is the rate of interest paid to bondholders based on the face value or principal of the bonds. The rate and amount are fixed over the life of the bond. The **market interest rate** is the rate of interest paid in the market on bonds of similar risk. The market interest rate fluctuates daily. However, a company must decide well in advance of the issue date what the face interest rate will be to allow time to file with regulatory bodies, publicize the issue, and print the certificates. Because the company has no control over the market rate of interest, there is often a difference between the market or effective rate of interest and the face rate of interest on the issue date. The result is that the issue price of the bonds does not always equal the principal or face value of the bonds. If the market rate of interest is greater than the face interest rate, the issue price will be less than the face value and the bonds are said to be issued at a **discount**. The discount equals the excess of the face value over the issue price. On the other hand, if the market rate of interest is less than the face interest rate, the issue price will be more than the face value and the bonds are said to be issued at a **premium**. The premium equals the excess of the issue price over the face value.

Bonds Issued at a Discount

Suppose that the Vason Corporation issues its $100,000 of 9 percent, five-year bonds at 96.149 on January 1, 19x0, when the market rate of interest is 10 percent. In this case, the bonds are being issued at a discount because the market rate of interest exceeds the face interest rate. This entry records the issuance of the bonds at a discount:

19x0				
Jan. 1	Cash		96,149	
	Unamortized Bond Discount		3,851	
	Bonds Payable			100,000
	Sold $100,000 of 9%, 5-year bonds at 96.149			
	Face amount of bonds	$100,000		
	Less purchase price of bonds ($100,000 × .96149)	96,149		
	Unamortized bond discount	$ 3,851		

As shown, Cash is debited for the amount received ($96,149), Bonds Payable is credited for the face amount ($100,000) of the bond liability, and the difference ($3,851) is debited to Unamortized Bond Discount. If a balance sheet is prepared right after the bonds are issued at a discount, the liability for bonds payable is as follows:

Long-Term Liabilities		
9% Bonds Payable, due 1/1/x5	$100,000	
Less Unamortized Bond Discount	3,851	$96,149

Unamortized Bond Discount is a contra-liability account: Its balance is deducted from the face amount of the bonds to arrive at the carrying value or present value of the bonds. The bond discount is described as unamortized because it will be amortized (written off) over the life of the bonds.

Bonds Issued at a Premium

When bonds have a face interest rate above the market rate for similar investments, they are issued at a price above the face value, or at a premium. For example, assume that the Vason Corporation issues $100,000 of 9 percent, five-year bonds for $104,100 on January 1, 19x0, when the market rate of interest is 8 percent. This means that the bonds will be purchased by investors at 104.1 percent of their face value. The issuance would be recorded as follows:

19x0			
Jan. 1	Cash	104,100	
	Unamortized Bond Premium		4,100
	Bonds Payable		100,000
	Sold $100,000 of 9%, 5-year bonds at 104.1 ($100,000 × 1.041)		

Right after this entry is made, bonds payable would be presented on the balance sheet as follows:

Long-Term Liabilities		
9% Bonds Payable, due 1/1/x5	$100,000	
Unamortized Bond Premium	4,100	$104,100

The carrying value of the bonds payable is $104,100, which equals the face value of the bonds plus the unamortized bond premium. The cash received from the bond issue is also $104,100. This means that the purchasers were willing to pay a premium of $4,100 to buy these bonds because the face interest on them was greater than the market rate.

Bond Issue Costs

Most bonds are sold through underwriters, who receive a fee for taking care of the details of marketing the issue or for taking a chance on getting the selling price. These costs are connected with the issuance of bonds. Because bond issue costs benefit the whole life of a bond issue, it makes sense to spread the costs over that period. It is generally accepted practice to establish a separate account for bond issue costs and to amortize them over the life of the bonds. However, issue costs decrease the amount of money received by the company for the bond issue. They have the effect, then, of raising the discount or lowering the premium on the issue. As a result, bond issue costs can be spread over the life of the bonds through the amortization of a discount or premium. Because this method simplifies the recordkeeping, we assume in the text and problems of this book that all bond issue costs increase the discounts or decrease the premiums of bond issues.

Using Present Value to Value a Bond[3]

OBJECTIVE 3
Determine the value of bonds using present values

Present value is relevant here because the value of bonds is based on the present value of two components of cash flow: (1) a series of fixed interest payments and (2) a single payment at maturity. The amount of interest that a bond pays is fixed over its life. During its life, however, the market rate of interest varies from day to day. Thus, the amount that investors are willing to pay for the bond changes as well.

Assume, for example, that a particular bond has a face value of $10,000 and pays a fixed amount of interest of $450 every six months (a 9 percent annual rate). The bond is due in five years. If the market rate of interest today is 14 percent, what is the present value of the bond?

To determine the present value of the bond, we use Tables 3 and 4 in the appendix on future value and present value tables. Because the compounding period is less than a year, it is necessary to convert the annual rate to a semiannual rate of 7 percent (14 percent divided by two six-month periods per year) and to use ten periods (five years multiplied by two six-month periods per year). Using this information, we can compute the present value of the bond:

Present value of 10 periodic payments at 7% (from Table 4 in the appendix on future value and present value tables): $450 × 7.024	=	$3,160.80
Present value of a single payment at the end of 10 periods at 7% (from Table 3 in the appendix on future value and present value tables): $10,000 × 0.508	=	5,080.00
Present value of $10,000 bond	=	$8,240.80

The market rate of interest has increased so much since the bond was issued (from 9 percent to 14 percent) that the value of the bond is only $8,240.80 today. This amount is all that investors would be willing to pay at this time for income

3. A knowledge of present value concepts, as presented in the appendix on the time value of money, is necessary to an understanding of this section.

from this bond of $450 every six months and a return of the $10,000 principal in five years.

If the market rate of interest falls below the face interest rate, say to 8 percent (4 percent semiannually), the present value of the bond is greater than the face value of $10,000:

Present value of 10 periodic payments at 4% (from Table 4 in the appendix on future value and present value tables): $450 × 8.111	=	$ 3,649.95
Present value of a single payment at the end of 10 periods at 4% (from Table 3 in the appendix on future value and present value tables): $10,000 × 0.676	=	6,760.00
Present value of $10,000 bond	=	$10,409.95

Amortizing a Bond Discount

OBJECTIVE 4a
Amortize bond discounts using the straight-line and effective interest methods

In the example on page 548, Vason Corporation issued $100,000 of five-year bonds at a discount because the market interest rate of 10 percent exceeded the face interest rate of 9 percent. The bonds were sold for $96,149, resulting in an unamortized bond discount of $3,851. Because this discount, as you will see, affects interest expense in each year of the bond issue, the bond discount should be amortized (reduced gradually) over the life of the issue. This means that the unamortized bond discount will decrease gradually over time, and that the carrying value of the bond issue (face value less unamortized discount) will increase gradually. By the maturity date of the bond, the carrying value of the issue will equal its face value, and the unamortized bond discount will be zero.

Calculation of Total Interest Cost

When bonds are issued at a discount, the effective interest rate paid by the company is greater than the face interest rate on the bonds. The reason is that the interest cost to the company is the stated interest payments *plus* the amount of the bond discount. That is, although the company does not receive the full face value of the bonds on issue, it still must pay back the full face value at maturity. The difference between the issue price and the face value must be added to the total interest payments to arrive at the actual interest expense.

The full cost to the corporation of issuing the bonds at a discount is as follows:

Cash to be paid to bondholders	
Face value at maturity	$100,000
Interest payments ($100,000 × .09 × 5 years)	45,000
Total cash paid to bondholders	$145,000
Less cash received from bondholders	96,149
Total interest cost	$ 48,851

Or, alternatively:

Interest payments ($100,000 × .09 × 5 years)	$ 45,000
Bond discount	3,851
Total interest cost	$ 48,851

The total interest cost of $48,851 is made up of $45,000 in interest payments and the $3,851 bond discount. So, the bond discount increases the interest paid on the bonds from the stated to the effective interest rate. The *effective interest rate* is the real interest cost of the bond over its life.

In order for each year's interest expense to reflect the effective interest rate, the discount must be allocated over the remaining life of the bonds as an increase in the interest expense each period. The process of allocation is called *amortization of the bond discount*. Thus, interest expense for each period will exceed the actual payment of interest by the amount of the bond discount amortized over the period.

It is interesting that some companies and governmental units have begun to issue bonds that do not require periodic interest payments. These bonds, called **zero coupon bonds**, are simply a promise to pay a fixed amount at the maturity date. They are issued at a large discount, because the only interest earned by the buyer or paid by the issuer is the discount. For example, a five-year $100,000 bond issued at a time when the market rate is 14 percent, compounded semiannually, would sell for only $50,800. This amount is the present value of a single payment of $100,000 at the end of five years (from Table 3 in the appendix on future value and present value tables: 7 percent at the end of ten periods equals 0.508). The discount of $49,200 ($100,000 − $50,800) is the total interest cost; it is amortized over the life of the bond.

Methods of Amortizing a Bond Discount

There are two ways of amortizing bond discounts or premiums: the straight-line method and the effective interest method.

Straight-Line Method. The **straight-line method** is the easier of the two, with equal amortization of the discount for each interest period. Suppose that the interest payment dates for the Vason Corporation bond issue are January 1 and July 1. The amount of the bond discount amortized and the interest cost for each semiannual period are figured in four steps:

1. Total interest payments = interest payments per year × life of bonds

$$= 2 \times 5$$
$$= 10$$

2. Amortization of bond discount per interest payment

$$= \frac{\text{bond discount}}{\text{total interest payments}}$$
$$= \frac{\$3{,}851}{10}$$
$$= \$385^*$$

3. Regular cash interest payment

$$= \text{face value} \times \text{face interest rate} \times \text{time}$$
$$= \$100{,}000 \times .09 \times 6/12$$
$$= \$4{,}500$$

4. Total interest cost per interest date

$$= \text{interest payment} + \text{amortization of bond discount}$$
$$= \$4{,}500 + \$385$$
$$= \$4{,}885$$

* Rounded.

On July 1, 19x0, the first semiannual interest date, the entry would be as follows:

19x0			
July 1	Bond Interest Expense	4,885	
	Unamortized Bond Discount		385
	Cash (or Interest Payable)		4,500
	Paid (or accrued) semiannual interest to bondholders and amortized the discount on 9%, 5-year bonds		

Notice that the bond interest expense is $4,885 but that the amount paid to the bondholders is the $4,500 face interest payment. The difference of $385 is the credit to Unamortized Bond Discount. This lowers the debit balance of the Unamortized Bond Discount account and raises the carrying value of the bonds payable by $385 each interest period. Assuming that no changes occur in the bond issue, this entry will be made every six months for the life of the bonds. At the time when the bond issue matures, there will be no balance in the Unamortized Bond Discount account, and the carrying value of the bonds will be $100,000—exactly equal to the amount due the bondholders.

The straight-line method has long been used, but it has a certain weakness. Because the carrying value goes up each period and the bond interest expense stays the same, the rate of interest falls over time. Conversely, when the straight-line method is used to amortize a premium, the rate of interest rises over time. For this reason, the Accounting Principles Board has ruled that the straight-line method can be used only when it does not lead to a material difference from the effective interest method.[4] As we discuss below, the effective interest method presupposes a constant rate of interest over the life of the bonds. It is constant because the total interest expense changes only a little each interest period in response to the changing carrying value of the bonds.

Alternative Method

Effective Interest Method. To compute the interest and amortization of a bond discount for each interest period under the **effective interest method**, we have to apply a constant interest rate to the carrying value of the bonds at the beginning of the interest period. This constant rate equals the market rate at the time the bonds are issued and is called the **effective rate**. The amount to be amortized becomes the difference between the interest computed by using the effective rate and the actual interest paid to bondholders.

As an example, we use the same facts presented earlier—a $100,000 bond issue at 9 percent, with a five-year maturity, interest to be paid twice a year. The market or effective rate of interest at the time the bonds were issued was 10 percent. The bonds were sold for $96,149, at a discount of $3,851. The interest and amortization of the bond discount are shown in Table 14-1.

Here are explanations of how the amounts in the table are computed:

Column A: The carrying value of the bonds is the face value of the bonds less the unamortized bond discount ($100,000 − $3,851 = **$96,149**).

Column B: The interest expense to be recorded is the effective interest. It is found by multiplying the carrying value of the bonds by the effective interest rate for one-half year ($96,149 × .10 × 6/12 = **$4,807**).

4. Accounting Principles Board, *Opinion No. 21*, "Interest on Receivables and Payables" (New York: American Institute of Certified Public Accountants, 1971), par. 15.

Table 14-1. Interest and Amortization of Bond Discount: Effective Interest Method

	A	B	C	D	E	F
Semi-annual Interest Period	Carrying Value at Beginning of Period	Semiannual Interest Expense at 10% To Be Recorded* (5% × A)	Semiannual Interest To Be Paid to Bondholders (4½% × $100,000)	Amortization of Discount (B − C)	Unamortized Bond Discount at End of Period	Carrying Value at End of Period (A + D)
0					$3,851	$ 96,149
1	$96,149	$4,807	$4,500	$307	3,544	96,456
2	96,456	4,823	4,500	323	3,221	96,779
3	96,779	4,839	4,500	339	2,882	97,118
4	97,118	4,856	4,500	356	2,526	97,474
5	97,474	4,874	4,500	374	2,152	97,848
6	97,848	4,892	4,500	392	1,760	98,240
7	98,240	4,912	4,500	412	1,348	98,652
8	98,652	4,933	4,500	433	915	99,085
9	99,085	4,954	4,500	454	461	99,539
10	99,539	4,961**	4,500	461	—	100,000

* Rounded to nearest dollar.
** Difference due to rounding.

Column C: The interest paid in the period is the face value of the bonds multiplied by the face interest rate for the bonds multiplied by the interest time period ($100,000 × .09 × 6/12 = $4,500).

Column D: The discount amortized is the difference between the effective interest expense to be recorded and the interest to be paid on the interest payment date ($4,807 − $4,500 = $307).

Column E: The unamortized bond discount is the balance of the bond discount at the beginning of the period less the current period amortization of the discount ($3,851 − $307 = $3,544). The unamortized discount decreases each interest payment period because it is amortized as a portion of interest expense.

Column F: The carrying value of the bonds at the end of the period is the carrying value at the beginning of the period plus the amortization during the period ($96,149 + $307 = $96,456). Notice that the sum of the carrying value and unamortized discount (Column F + Column E) always equals the face value of the bonds ($96,456 + $3,544 = $100,000).

The entry to record the interest expense is exactly like the one used when the straight-line method is applied. However, the amounts debited and credited to the various accounts are different. The entry for July 1, 19x0, using the effective interest method, would be as follows:

19x0			
July 1	Bond Interest Expense	4,807	
	Unamortized Bond Discount		307
	Cash (or Interest Payable)		4,500
	Paid (or accrued) semiannual interest to bondholders and amortized the discount on 9%, 5-year bonds		

Notice that an interest and amortization table does not have to be prepared to determine the amortization of a discount for any one interest payment period. It is necessary only to multiply the carrying value by the effective interest rate and subtract the interest payment from the result. For example, the amount of discount to be amortized in the seventh interest payment period equals $412 [($98,240 × .05) – $4,500].

Visual Summary of the Effective Interest Method. The effect of the amortization of a bond discount using the effective interest method on carrying value and interest expense can be seen in Figure 14-1 (based on the data from Table 14-1). Notice that initially the carrying value (issue price) is less than the face value, but that it gradually increases toward the face value over the life of the bond issue. Notice also that interest expense exceeds interest payments by the amount of the discount amortized. Interest expense increases gradually over the life of the bond because it is based on the gradually increasing carrying value (multiplied by the market interest rate).

Figure 14-1. Carrying Value and Interest Expense—Bonds Issued at a Discount

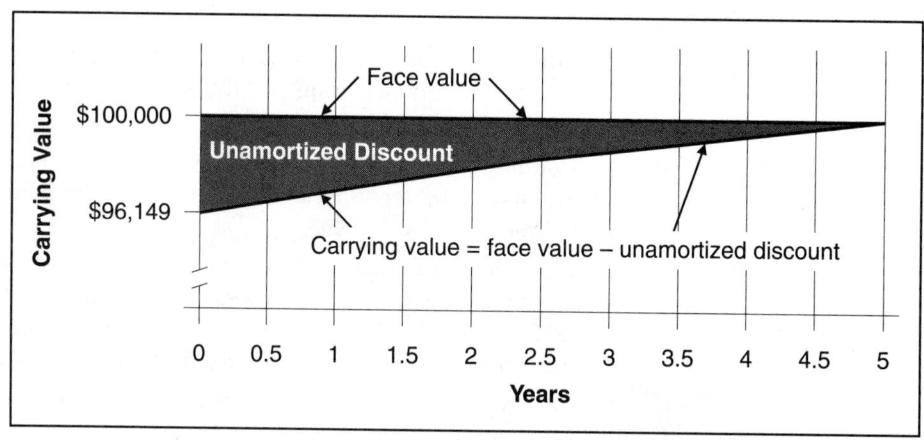

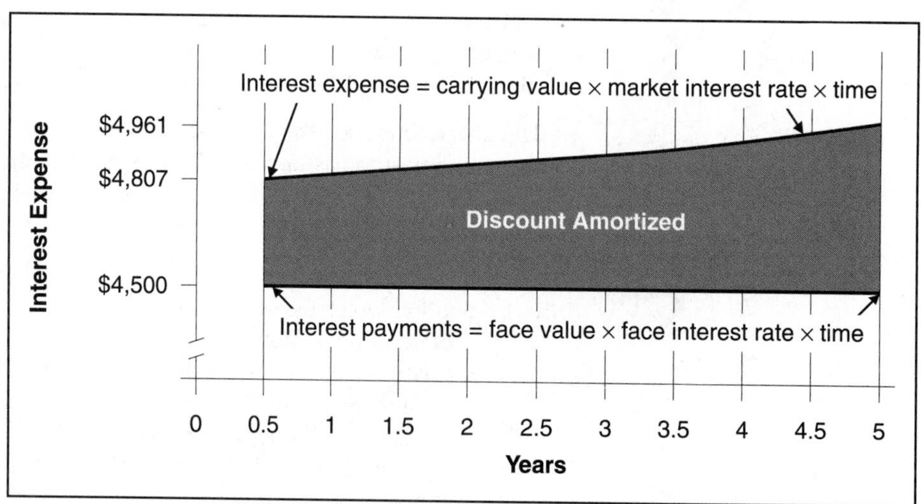

Amortizing a Bond Premium

OBJECTIVE 4b
Amortize bond premiums using the straight-line and effective interest methods

In our example on page 548, Vason Corporation issued $100,000 of five-year bonds at a premium because the market rate of interest of 8 percent was less than the face interest rate of 9 percent. The bonds were sold for $104,100, resulting in an unamortized bond premium of $4,100. Like a bond discount, a bond premium must be amortized over the life of the bonds so that it can be matched to its effects on interest expense during that period. In the following sections, the total interest cost is calculated and the bond premium is amortized using the straight-line and effective interest methods.

Calculation of Total Interest Cost

Because the bondholders paid in excess of face value for the bonds, the premium of $4,100 ($104,100 – $100,000) represents an amount that the bondholders will not receive at maturity. The premium is in effect a reduction, in advance, of the total interest paid on the bonds over the life of the bond issue.

The total interest cost over the issue's life can be computed as follows:

Cash to be paid to bondholders	
Face value at maturity	$100,000
Interest payments ($100,000 × .09 × 5 years)	45,000
Total cash paid to bondholders	$145,000
Less cash received from bondholders	104,100
Total interest cost	$ 40,900

Or, alternatively:

Interest payments ($100,000 × .09 × 5 years)	$ 45,000
Less bond premium	4,100
Total interest cost	$ 40,900

Notice that the total interest payments of $45,000 exceed the total interest costs of $40,900 by $4,100, the amount of the bond premium.

Methods of Amortizing a Bond Premium

The two methods of amortizing a bond premium are the straight-line method and the effective interest method.

Straight-Line Method. Under the straight-line method, the bond premiums are spread evenly over the life of the bond issue. As with bond discounts, the amount of the bond premium amortized and the interest cost for each semiannual period are computed in four steps:

1. Total interest payments = interest payments per year × life of bonds
   $= 2 \times 5$
   $= 10$

2. Amortization of bond premium per interest payment

$$= \frac{\text{bond premium}}{\text{total interest payments}}$$

$$= \frac{\$4{,}100}{10}$$

$$= \$410$$

3. Regular cash interest payment

= face value × face interest rate × time

= \$100,000 × .09 × 6/12

= \$4,500

4. Total interest cost per interest date

= interest payment − amortization of bond premium

= \$4,500 − \$410

= \$4,090

On July 1, 19x0, the first semiannual interest date, the entry would be:

19x0			
July 1	Bond Interest Expense	4,090	
	Unamortized Bond Premium	410	
	Cash (or Interest Payable)		4,500
	Paid (or accrued) semiannual interest to bondholders and amortized the premium on 9%, 5-year bonds		

Notice that the bond interest expense is \$4,090 but that the amount received by the bondholders is the \$4,500 face interest payment. The difference of \$410 is the debit to Unamortized Bond Premium. This lowers the credit balance of the Unamortized Bond Premium account and the carrying value of the bonds payable by \$410 each interest period. Assuming that the bond issue remains unchanged, the same entry will be made every six months over the life of the bond issue. When the bond issue matures, there will be no balance in the Unamortized Bond Premium account, and the carrying value of the bonds payable will be \$100,000, exactly equal to the amount due the bondholders.

As noted before, the straight-line method should be used only when it does not lead to a material difference from the effective interest method.

Alternative Method

Effective Interest Method. Under the straight-line method, the real or effective interest rate is changing constantly, even though the interest expense is fixed, because the effective interest rate is determined by comparing the fixed interest expense with a carrying value that is changing as a result of amortizing the discount or premium. To apply a fixed interest rate over the life of the bonds based on the actual market rate at the time of the bond issue requires the use of the effective interest method. Under this method, the interest expense decreases slightly each period (see Table 14-2, Column B) because the amount of the bond premium amortized increases slightly (Column D). This occurs because a fixed rate is applied each period to the gradually decreasing carrying value (Column A).

The first interest payment is recorded as follows:

19x0			
July 1	Bond Interest Expense	4,164	
	Unamortized Bond Premium	336	
	Cash (or Interest Payable)		4,500
	Paid (or accrued) semiannual interest to bondholders and amortized the premium on 9%, 5-year bonds		

Table 14-2. Interest and Amortization of Bond Premium: Effective Interest Method

	A	B	C	D	E	F
Semi-annual Interest Period	Carrying Value at Beginning of Period	Semiannual Interest Expense at 8% To Be Recorded* (4% × A)	Semiannual Interest To Be Paid to Bondholders (4½% × $100,000)	Amortization of Premium (C – B)	Unamortized Bond Premium at End of Period	Carrying Value at End of Period (A – D)
0					$4,100	$104,100
1	$104,100	$4,164	$4,500	$336	3,764	103,764
2	103,764	4,151	4,500	349	3,415	103,415
3	103,415	4,137	4,500	363	3,052	103,052
4	103,052	4,122	4,500	378	2,674	102,674
5	102,674	4,107	4,500	393	2,281	102,281
6	102,281	4,091	4,500	409	1,872	101,872
7	101,872	4,075	4,500	425	1,447	101,447
8	101,447	4,058	4,500	442	1,005	101,005
9	101,005	4,040	4,500	460	545	100,545
10	100,545	3,955**	4,500	545	—	100,000

* Rounded to nearest dollar.
** Difference due to rounding.

Notice that the unamortized bond premium (Column E) decreases gradually to zero as the carrying value decreases to the face value (Column F). To find the amount of premium amortized in any one interest payment period, we subtract the effective interest expense (the carrying value times the effective interest rate, Column B) from the interest payment (Column C). In semiannual interest period 5, for example, the amortization of premium equals $393 [$4,500 – ($102,674 × .04)].

Visual Summary of the Effective Interest Method. The effect of the amortization of a bond premium using the effective interest method on carrying value and interest expense can be seen in Figure 14-2 (based on data from Table 14-2). Notice that initially the carrying value (issue price) is greater than the face value, but that it gradually decreases toward the face value over the life of the bond issue. Notice also that interest payments exceed interest expense by the amount of the premium amortized, and that interest expense decreases gradually over the life of the bond because it is based on the gradually decreasing carrying value (multiplied by the market interest rate).

Other Bonds Payable Issues

OBJECTIVE 5
Account for bonds issued between interest dates and make year-end adjustments

Several other issues arise in accounting for bonds payable. Among them are the sale of bonds between interest payment dates, the year-end accrual of bond interest expense, the retirement of bonds, and the conversion of bonds into common stock.

Sale of Bonds Between Interest Dates

Bonds can be issued on an interest payment date, as in the examples above, but many times they are issued between interest payment dates. The generally

Figure 14-2. Carrying Value and Interest Expense—Bonds Issued at a Premium

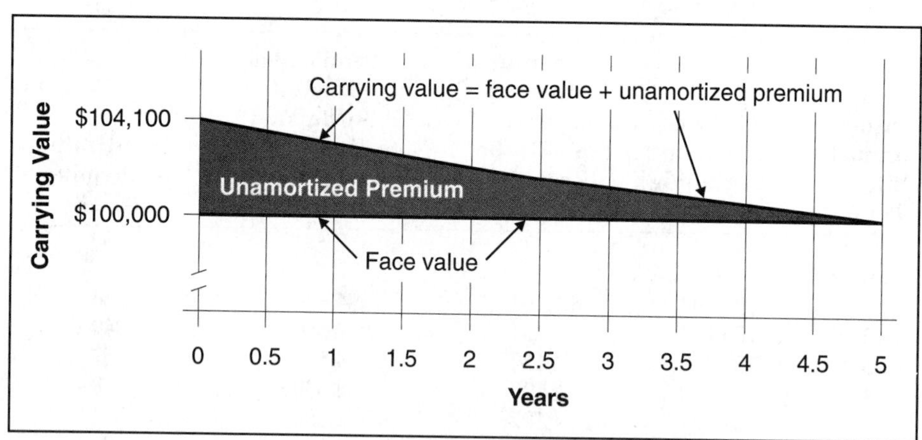

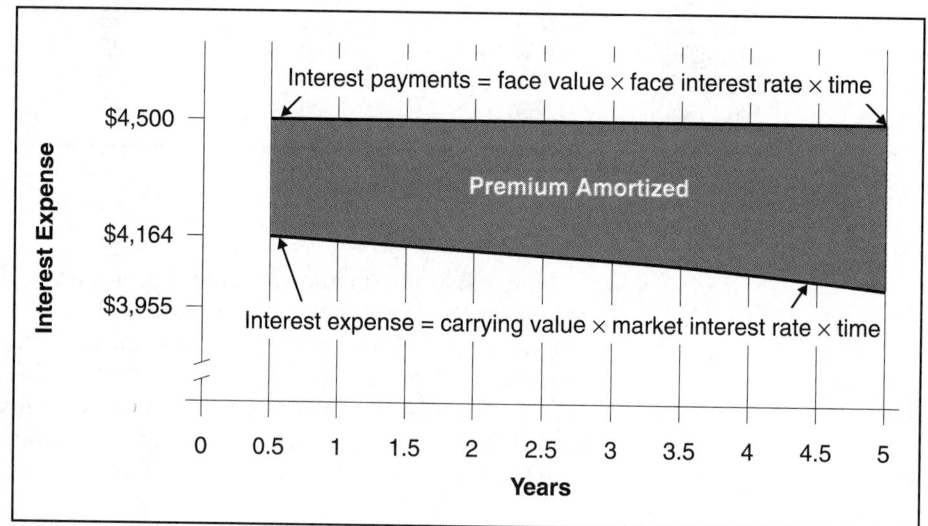

accepted method of handling bonds issued in this manner is to collect from investors the interest that has accrued since the last interest payment date. Then, when the next interest period arrives, the corporation pays investors the interest for the entire period. Thus, the interest collected when bonds are sold is returned to investors on the next interest payment date.

There are two reasons for following this procedure. The first is a practical one. If a company issued bonds on several different days and did not collect the accrued interest, records would have to be maintained for each bondholder and date of purchase. In such a case, the interest due each bondholder would have to be computed on the basis of different time periods. Clearly, large bookkeeping costs would be incurred under this kind of system. On the other hand, if accrued interest is collected when the bonds are sold, on the interest payment date the corporation can pay the interest due for the entire period, eliminating the extra computations and costs.

The second reason for collecting accrued interest in advance is that when this amount is netted against the full interest paid on the interest payment date, the resulting interest expense represents the amount for the time the money has been borrowed.

For example, assume that the Vason Corporation sold $100,000 of 9 percent, five-year bonds for face value on May 1, 19x0, rather than on January 1, 19x0, the issue date. The entry to record the sale of the bonds follows:

19x0			
May 1	Cash	103,000	
	Bond Interest Expense		3,000
	Bonds Payable		100,000
	Sold 9%, 5-year bonds at face value plus 4 months' accrued interest ($100,000 × .09 × 4/12 = $3,000)		

As shown, Cash is debited for the amount received, $103,000 (the face value of $100,000 plus four months' accrued interest of $3,000). Bond Interest Expense is credited for the $3,000 of accrued interest, and Bonds Payable is credited for the face value of $100,000.

When the first semiannual interest payment date arrives, the following entry is made:

19x0			
July 1	Bond Interest Expense	4,500	
	Cash (or Interest Payable)		4,500
	Paid (or accrued) semiannual interest ($100,000 × .09 × 6/12 = $4,500)		

Notice that here the entire half-year interest is both debited to Bond Interest Expense and credited to Cash because the corporation only pays bond interest once every six months, in full six-month amounts. This process is illustrated in Figure 14-3. The actual interest expense for the two months that the bonds were outstanding is $1,500. This amount is the net balance of the $4,500 debit to Bond Interest Expense on July 1 less the $3,000 credit to Bond Interest Expense on May 1. You can see these steps clearly in the posted entries in the ledger account for Bond Interest Expense below.

Bond Interest Expense						**Account No. 723**	
						Balance	
Date		**Item**	**Post. Ref.**	**Debit**	**Credit**	**Debit**	**Credit**
19x0							
May	1				3,000		3,000
July	1			4,500		**1,500**	

Year-End Accrual for Bond Interest Expense

It is not often that bond interest payment dates correspond to a company's fiscal year. Therefore, an adjustment must be made at the end of the accounting period to accrue the interest expense on the bonds from the last payment date to the end of the fiscal year. Further, if there is any discount or premium on the bonds, it also must be amortized for the fractional period.

Remember that in an earlier example, Vason Corporation issued $100,000 in bonds on January 1, 19x0 at 104.1 (see page 548). Suppose the company's fiscal

Figure 14-3. Effect on Bond Interest Expense When Bonds Are Issued Between Interest Dates

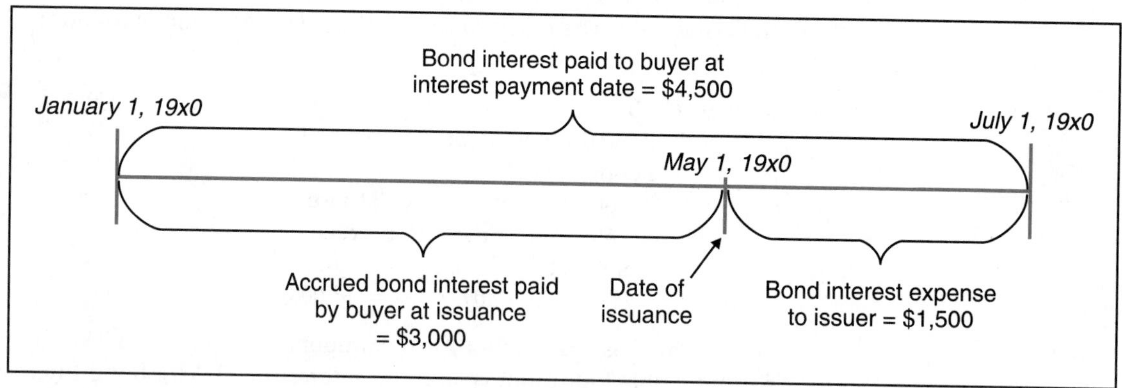

year ends on September 30, 19x0. In the period since the interest payment and amortization of the premium on July 1, three months' worth of interest has accrued, and the following adjusting entry under the effective interest method must be made:

19x0			
Sept. 30	Bond Interest Expense	2,075.50	
	Unamortized Bond Premium	174.50	
	Interest Payable		2,250.00
	To record accrual of interest on 9% bonds payable for 3 months and amortization of one-half of the premium for the second interest payment period		

This entry covers one-half of the second interest period. Unamortized Bond Premium is debited for $174.50, which is one-half of $349, the amortization of the premium for the second period from Table 14-2. Interest Payable is credited for $2,250, three months' interest on the face value of the bonds ($100,000 × .09 × 3/12). The net debit figure of $2,075.50 ($2,250 – $174.50) is the bond interest expense for the three-month period.

When the January 1, 19x1 payment date arrives, the entry to pay the bondholders and amortize the premium is as follows:

19x1			
Jan. 1	Bond Interest Expense	2,075.50	
	Interest Payable	2,250.00	
	Unamortized Bond Premium	174.50	
	Cash		4,500.00
	Paid semiannual interest including interest previously accrued, and amortized the premium for the period since the end of the fiscal year		

As shown here, one-half ($2,250) of the amount paid ($4,500) was accrued on September 30. Unamortized Bond Premium is debited for $174.50, the remaining amount to be amortized for the period ($349.00 – $174.50). The resulting bond interest expense is the amount that applies to the three-month period from October 1 to December 31.

Bond discounts are recorded at year's end in the same way as bond premiums. The difference is that the amortization of a bond discount increases interest expense instead of decreasing it, as a premium does.

Retirement of Bonds

OBJECTIVE 6
Account for the retirement of bonds and the conversion of bonds into stock

Most bond issues give the corporation a chance to buy back and retire the bonds at a specified price, usually above face value, before maturity. Such bonds are known as **callable bonds**. They give the corporation flexibility in financing its operations. For example, if bond interest rates drop, the company can call its bonds and reissue debt at a lower interest rate. Other reasons to call a company's bonds might be that the company has earned enough to pay off the debt, the reason for having the debt no longer exists, or the company wants to restructure its debt to equity ratio. The bond indenture states the time period and the prices at which the bonds can be redeemed. When a bond issue is retired before its maturity date, it is called **early extinguishment of debt**.

For example, assume that Vason Corporation can call or retire the $100,000 of bonds issued at a premium (page 548) at 105, and that it decides to do so on July 1, 19x3. (To simplify our example, we assume retirement on an interest payment date.) Because the bonds were issued on January 1, 19x0, the retirement takes place on the seventh interest payment date. Assume that the entry for the interest payment (which must be made) and for the amortization of the premium have been made. The entry to retire the bonds is as follows:

19x3			
July 1	Bonds Payable	100,000	
	Unamortized Bond Premium	1,447	
	Loss on Retirement of Bonds	3,553	
	Cash		105,000
	Retired 9% bonds at 105		

In this entry, the cash paid is the face value times the call price ($100,000 × 1.05 = $105,000). The unamortized bond premium can be found in Column E of Table 14-2. The loss on retirement of bonds occurs because the call price of the bonds is greater than the carrying value ($105,000 − $101,447 = $3,553). The loss, if material, is presented as an extraordinary item on the income statement, as explained in the chapter on retained earnings and corporate income statements.

Sometimes a rise in the market interest rate can cause the market value of bonds to fall considerably below the face value of the bonds. If it has the cash to do so, the company may find it advantageous to purchase the bonds on the open market and retire them, rather than wait and pay them off at face value. An extraordinary gain is recognized in the difference between the purchase price of the bonds and the face value of the retired bonds. For example, assume that because of a rise in interest rates, Vason Corporation is able to purchase the $100,000 bond issue on the open market at 85, making it unnecessary to call the bonds at the higher price of 105. Then, the entry would be as follows:

19x3			
July 1	Bonds Payable	100,000	
	Unamortized Bond Premium	1,447	
	Cash		85,000
	Gain on Retirement of Bonds		16,447
	Purchased and retired 9% bonds at 85		

Conversion of Bonds into Common Stock

Bonds that can be exchanged for other securities of the corporation (in most cases, common stock) are called **convertible bonds**. The conversion feature gives the investor a chance to make more money because if the market price of the common stock rises, the value of the bonds rises. However, if the price of the common stock does not rise, the investor still holds the bonds and receives the periodic interest payment as well as the principal at the maturity date.

When a bondholder wants to convert bonds into common stock, the rule is that the common stock is recorded at the carrying value of the bonds. The bond liability and associated unamortized discount or premium are written off the books. For this reason, no gain or loss is recorded on the transaction. For example, suppose that Vason Corporation's bonds are not called on July 1, 19x3. Instead, the corporation's bondholders decide to convert all the bonds to $8 par value common stock under a convertible provision of 40 shares of common stock for each $1,000 bond. The entry would be as follows:

19x3			
July 1	Bonds Payable	100,000	
	Unamortized Bond Premium	1,447	
	Common Stock		32,000
	Paid-in Capital in Excess of Par Value, Common		69,447
	Converted 9% bonds payable into $8 par value common stock at a rate of 40 shares for each $1,000 bond		

The unamortized bond premium is found in Column E of Table 14-2. At a rate of 40 shares for each $1,000 bond, 4,000 shares will be issued at a total par value of $32,000 (4,000 × $8). The Common Stock account is credited for the amount of the par value of the stock issued, and Paid-in Capital in Excess of Par Value, Common is credited for the difference between the carrying value of the bonds and the par value of the stock issued ($101,447 – $32,000 = $69,447). No gain or loss is recorded.

Other Long-Term Liabilities

OBJECTIVE 7
Explain the basic features of mortgages payable, installment notes payable, long-term leases, and pensions and other postretirement benefits as long-term liabilities

A company can have other long-term liabilities besides bonds. The most common are mortgages payable, installment notes payable, long-term leases, and pensions and other postretirement benefits.

Mortgages Payable

A **mortgage** is a long-term debt secured by real property. It usually is paid in equal monthly installments. Each monthly payment includes interest on the debt and a reduction in the debt. Table 14-3 shows the first three monthly payments on a $50,000, 12 percent mortgage. The mortgage was obtained on June 1 and the monthly payments are $800. According to the table, the entry to record the July 1 payment would be as follows:

July 1	Mortgage Payable	300	
	Mortgage Interest Expense	500	
	Cash		800
	Made monthly mortgage payment		

Table 14-3. Monthly Payment Schedule on $50,000, 12 Percent Mortgage

	A	B	C	D	E
Payment Date	Unpaid Balance at Beginning of Period	Monthly Payment	Interest for 1 Month at 1% on Unpaid Balance* (1% × A)	Reduction in Debt (B − C)	Unpaid Balance at End of Period (A − D)
June 1					$50,000
July 1	$50,000	$800	$500	$300	49,700
Aug. 1	49,700	800	497	303	49,397
Sept. 1	49,397	800	494	306	49,091

* Rounded to nearest dollar.

Notice from the entry and from Table 14-3 that the July 1 payment represents interest expense of $500 ($50,000 × .12 × 1/12) and a reduction in the debt of $300 ($800 − $500). Therefore, the unpaid balance is reduced by the July payment to $49,700. The interest expense for August is slightly less than July's because of the decrease in the debt.

Installment Notes Payable

Long-term notes can be paid at the maturity date by making a lump sum payment that includes the amount borrowed plus interest. Often, however, the terms of the note call for a series of periodic payments. When this occurs, the notes payable are called **installment notes payable** because each payment includes the interest from the previous payment to date plus a repayment of part of the amount borrowed. For example, assume that on December 31, 19x1, $100,000 is borrowed on a 15 percent installment note, to be paid annually over five years. The entry to record the note is as follows:

19x1			
Dec. 31	Cash	100,000	
	Notes Payable		100,000
	Borrowed $100,000 at 15% on a 5-year installment note		

Payments of Accrued Interest Plus Equal Amounts of Principal. Installment notes most often call for payments consisting of accrued interest plus equal amounts of principal repayment. The amount of each installment decreases because the amount of principal on which the accrued interest is owed decreases by the amount of the principal repaid. Banks use installment notes to finance equipment purchases by businesses; these notes are also common for other kinds of purchases when payment is spread over several years. They can be set up on a revolving basis, whereby the borrower can borrow additional funds as the installments are paid. Moreover, the interest rate charged on installment notes can be adjusted periodically by the bank as market rates of interest change.

Under this method of payment, the principal declines by an equal amount each year for five years, or by $20,000 per year ($100,000 ÷ 5 years). The interest is calculated on the balance of the note that remains each year. Because the balance of the note declines each year, the amount of interest also declines. For example, the entries for the first two payments of the installment note are as follows:

19x2			
Dec. 31	Notes Payable	20,000	
	Interest Expense	15,000	
	Cash		35,000
	First installment payment on note ($100,000 × .15 = $15,000)		
19x3			
Dec. 31	Notes Payable	20,000	
	Interest Expense	12,000	
	Cash		32,000
	Second installment payment on note ($80,000 × .15 = $12,000)		

Notice that the amount of the payment decreases from $35,000 to $32,000 because the amount owed on the note has decreased from $100,000 to $80,000. The difference of $3,000 is the interest on the $20,000 that was repaid in 19x2. Each subsequent payment decreases by $3,000, as the note itself decreases by $20,000 each year until it is fully paid. This example assumes that the repayment of principal and the interest rate remain the same from year to year.

Payments of Accrued Interest Plus Increasing Amounts of Principal. Less commonly, the terms of an installment note, like those used for leasing equipment, call for equal periodic (monthly or yearly) payments of accrued interest plus increasing amounts of principal. Under this method, the interest is deducted from the equal payments to determine the amount by which the principal will be reduced each year. This procedure, presented in Table 14-4, is very similar to that shown above for mortgages. Each equal payment of $29,833 is

Table 14-4. Payment Schedule on $100,000, 15 Percent Installment Note

	A	B	C	D	E
Payment Date	Unpaid Principal at Beginning of Period	Equal Annual Payment	Interest for 1 Year at 15% on Unpaid Principal* (15% × A)	Reduction in Principal (B − C)	Unpaid Principal at End of Period (A − D)
					$100,000
19x2	$100,000	$29,833	$15,000	$14,833	85,167
19x3	85,167	29,833	12,775	17,058	68,109
19x4	68,109	29,833	10,216	19,617	48,492
19x5	48,492	29,833	7,274	22,559	25,933
19x6	25,933	29,833	3,900**	25,933	—

* Rounded to the nearest dollar.

** The last year's interest equals the installment payment minus the remaining unpaid principal ($29,833 − $25,933 = $3,900); it does not exactly equal $3,890 ($25,933 × .15) because of the cumulative effect of rounding.

allocated between interest and reduction in debt (principal). Each year the interest is calculated on the remaining principal. As the principal decreases, the annual interest also decreases, and because the payment remains the same, the amount by which the principal decreases becomes larger each year. The entries for the first two years, with data taken from Table 14-4, are as follows:

19x2			
Dec. 31	Notes Payable	14,833	
	Interest Expense	15,000	
	Cash		29,833
	First installment payment on note		
19x3			
Dec. 31	Notes Payable	17,058	
	Interest Expense	12,775	
	Cash		29,833
	Second installment payment on note		

Similar entries will be made for the next three years.

How is the equal annual payment calculated? Because the $100,000 borrowed is the present value of the five equal annual payments at 15 percent interest, present value tables can be used to calculate the annual payments. Using Table 4 from the appendix on future value and present value tables, the calculation is made as follows:

Periodic payment × factor (Table 4 in the present value appendix: 15%, 5 years) = present value

Periodic payment × 3.352 = $100,000

Periodic payment = $100,000 ÷ 3.352 = $29,833

Table 14-4 shows that five equal annual payments of $29,833 at 15 percent will reduce the principal balance to zero (except for the error due to rounding).

Long-Term Leases

There are several ways in which a company can obtain new operating assets. One way is to borrow money and buy the asset. Another is to rent the equipment on a short-term lease. A third way is to obtain the equipment on a long-term lease. The first two methods do not create accounting problems. In the first case, the asset and liability are recorded at the amount paid, and the asset is subject to periodic depreciation. In the second case, the lease is short term or cancelable, and the risks of ownership lie with the lessor. This type of lease is called an **operating lease**. It is proper accounting to treat operating lease payments as an expense and to debit the amount of each monthly payment to Rent Expense.

The third case, a long-term lease, is one of the fastest-growing ways of financing operating equipment in the United States today. It has several advantages. For instance, it requires no immediate cash payment; the rental payment is deducted in full for tax purposes; and it costs less than a short-term lease. Acquiring the use of a plant asset under long-term leases does cause several accounting problems, however. Often, these leases cannot be canceled. Also, their duration may be about the same as the useful life of the asset. Finally, they may provide for the lessee to buy the asset at a nominal price at the end of the lease. The long-term lease is much like an installment purchase because the

Table 14-5. Payment Schedule on 16 Percent Capital Lease*

	A	B	C	D
Year	Lease Payment	Interest (16%) on Unpaid Obligation (D × 16%)	Reduction of Lease Obligation (A – B)	Balance of Lease Obligation
Beginning				$14,740
1	$ 4,000	$2,358	$ 1,642	13,098
2	4,000	2,096	1,904	11,194
3	4,000	1,791	2,209	8,985
4	4,000	1,438	2,562	6,423
5	4,000	1,028	2,972	3,450
6	4,000	550	3,450	—
	$24,000	$9,261	$14,739	

* Computations are rounded to the nearest dollar.

risks of ownership lie with the lessee. Both the lessee's available assets and its legal obligations (liabilities) increase because it must make a number of payments over the life of the asset.

Noting this problem, the Financial Accounting Standards Board has described this kind of long-term lease as a **capital lease**. The term reflects the provisions of the lease, which make the transaction more like a purchase or sale on installment. The FASB has ruled that in the case of a capital lease, the lessee must record an asset and a long-term liability equal to the present value of the total lease payments during the lease term. In doing so, the lessee must use the present value at the beginning of the lease.[5] In much the same way as mortgage payments are treated, each lease payment becomes partly interest expense and partly a repayment of debt. Further, depreciation expense is figured on the asset and entered on the records of the lessee.

Suppose, for example, that Isaacs Company enters into a long-term lease for a machine used in its manufacturing operations. The lease terms call for an annual payment of $4,000 for six years, which approximates the useful life of the machine (see Table 14-5.) At the end of the lease period, the title to the machine passes to Isaacs. This lease is clearly a capital lease and should be recorded according to FASB *Statement No. 13*.

A lease is a periodic payment for the right to use an asset or assets. Present value techniques, explained in the appendix on the time value of money, can be used to place a value on the asset and on the corresponding liability associated with a capital lease. If Isaacs's usual interest cost is 16 percent, the present value of the lease payments can be computed as follows:

Periodic payment	×	factor (Table 4 in the present value appendix: 16%, 6 years)	=	present value
$4,000	×	3.685	=	$14,740

5. *Statement of Financial Accounting Standards No. 13*, "Accounting for Leases" (Stamford, Conn.: Financial Accounting Standards Board, 1976), par. 10.

The entry to record the lease contract is as follows:

Equipment Under Capital Lease	14,740	
Obligations Under Capital Lease		14,740

Equipment Under Capital Lease is classified as a long-term asset; Obligations Under Capital Lease are classified as a long-term liability. Each year, Isaacs must record depreciation on the leased asset. If we assume straight-line depreciation, a six-year life, and no salvage value, this entry would record the depreciation:

Depreciation Expense	2,457	
Accumulated Depreciation, Equipment Under Capital Lease		2,457

The interest expense for each year is computed by multiplying the interest rate (16 percent) by the amount of the remaining lease obligation. Table 14-5 shows these calculations. Using the data in the table, the first lease payment would be recorded as follows:

Interest Expense (Column B)	2,358	
Obligations Under Capital Lease (Column C)	1,642	
Cash		4,000

Pensions

Most employees who work for medium-sized and large companies are covered by some sort of pension plan. A **pension plan** is a contract between the company and its employees in which the company agrees to pay benefits to the employees after they retire. Most companies contribute the full cost of the pension, but sometimes the employees also pay part of their salary or wages toward their pension. The contributions from both parties generally are paid into a **pension fund**, from which benefits are paid out to retirees. In most cases, pension benefits consist of monthly payments to employees after retirement and other payments on disability or death.

There are two kinds of pension plans. Under *defined contribution plans*, the employer is required to contribute an annual amount determined in the current year on the basis of agreements between the company and its employees or a resolution of the board of directors. Retirement payments depend on the amount of pension payments the accumulated contributions can support. Under *defined benefit plans*, the employer's required annual contribution is the amount required to fund pension liabilities that arise as a result of employment in the current year but whose amount will not be determined finally until the retirement and death of the persons currently employed. Here, the amount of the contribution required in the current year depends on a fixed amount of future benefits but uncertain current contributions; under a defined contribution plan, the uncertain future amount of pension liabilities depends on the cumulative amounts of fixed current contributions.

Accounting for annual pension expense under defined contribution plans is simple. After determining what contribution is required, Pension Expense is debited and a liability (or Cash) is credited.

Accounting for annual expense under defined benefit plans is one of the most complex topics in accounting; thus, the intricacies are reserved for advanced courses. In concept, however, the procedure is simple. First, the amount of pension expense is determined. Then, if the amount of cash contributed to the fund is less than the pension expense, a liability results, which is reported on the balance sheet. If the amount of cash paid to the pension plan exceeds the pension expense, a prepaid expense arises and appears on the asset side of the balance sheet. For example, the December 31, 1986 annual report for Goodyear Tire & Rubber Company included among other assets on the balance sheet deferred pension plan costs of $320.2 million.

In accordance with the FASB's *Statement No. 87*, all companies should use the same actuarial method to compute pension expense.[6] However, because many factors, such as the average remaining service life of active employees, the expected long-run return on pension plan assets, and expected future salary increases, must be estimated, the computation of pension expense is not simple. In addition, actuarial terminology further complicates pension accounting. In nontechnical terms, the pension expense for the year includes not only the cost of the benefits earned by people working during the year but interest costs on the total pension obligation (which are calculated on the present value of future benefits to be paid) and other adjustments. These costs are reduced by the expected return on the pension fund assets.

Since 1989, all employers whose pension plans do not have sufficient assets to cover the present value of their pension benefit obligations (on a termination basis) must record the amount of the shortfall as a liability on their balance sheets. The investor no longer has to read the notes to the financial statements to learn whether the pension plan is fully funded. However, if a pension plan does have sufficient assets to cover its obligations, then no balance sheet reporting is required or permitted.

Other Postretirement Benefits

In addition to pension benefits, many companies provide health care and other benefits for employees after retirement. In the past, these **other postretirement benefits** were accounted for on a cash basis; that is, they were expensed when the benefits were paid, after an employee had retired. The FASB has concluded, however, that these benefits are earned by the employee, and that, in accordance with the matching rule, they should be estimated and accrued while the employee is working.[7] These estimates must take into account assumptions about retirement age, mortality, and, most significantly, future trends in health care benefits. As in accounting for pension benefits, these future benefits also should be discounted to the current period. In a field test conducted by the Financial Executives Research Foundation, it was determined that this move to accrual accounting increases postretirement benefits by two to seven times the amount recognized on a cash basis. Although the new requirement was not effective for businesses until 1993, some companies elected to implement it early. For example, IBM Corporation reported its first quarterly loss ever in the first quarter of 1991, when it recorded a one-time $2.26 billion charge associated with the adoption of *Statement No. 106*.[8] This charge covered costs of postretirement benefits earned by employees in the past up to that date. Future quarters would bear only the costs associated with earnings in those quarters.

6. *Statement of Financial Accounting Standards No. 87*, "Employers' Accounting for Pensions" (Stamford, Conn.: Financial Accounting Standards Board, 1985).
7. *Statement of Financial Accounting Standards No. 106*, "Employers' Accounting for Postretirement Benefits Other Than Pensions" (Stamford, Conn.: Financial Accounting Standards Board, 1990).
8. "Earnings Drop and One-Time Charge Produce $1.7 Billion Loss at IBM," *International Herald Tribune*, April 13–14, 1991.

Chapter Review

Review of Learning Objectives

1. **Identify and contrast the major characteristics of bonds.**
A bond is a security that represents money borrowed from the investing public. When it issues bonds, the corporation enters into a contract, called a bond indenture, with the bondholders. The bond indenture identifies the major conditions of the bonds. A corporation can issue several types of bonds, each having different characteristics. For example, a bond issue may or may not require security (secured versus unsecured). It may be payable at a single time (term) or at several times (serial). And the holder may receive interest automatically (registered bond) or may have to return coupons to receive interest payable (coupon bond). The bond may be callable or convertible into other securities.

2. **Record the issuance of bonds at face value and at a discount or premium.**
When bonds are issued, the bondholders pay an amount equal to, less than, or greater than the face value of the bond. Bondholders pay face value for the bonds when the interest rate on the bonds approximates the market rate for similar investments. The issuing corporation records the bond issue as a long-term liability, in the Bonds Payable account, equal to the face value of the bonds.
Bonds are issued at a rate less than face value when the bond interest rate is below the market rate for similar investments. The difference between the face value and the issue price is called a discount and is debited to Unamortized Bond Discount.
When the interest rate on bonds is greater than the return on similar investments, investors are willing to pay more than face value for the bonds. The difference between the issue price and the face value is called a premium and is credited to Unamortized Bond Premium.

3. **Determine the value of bonds using present values.**
The value of a bond is determined by summing the present values of (a) the series of fixed interest payments of a bond issue and (b) the single payment of the face value at maturity. The third and fourth tables in the appendix on future value and present value tables should be used in making these computations.

4. **Amortize (a) bond discounts and (b) bond premiums using the straight-line and effective interest methods.**
When bonds are sold at a discount or a premium, the result is an adjustment of the interest rate on the bonds from the face rate to an effective rate that is close to the market rate when the bonds were issued. Therefore, bond discounts or premiums have the effect of increasing or decreasing the interest paid on the bonds over their life. Under these conditions, it is necessary to amortize the discount or premium over the life of the bonds by either the straight-line or effective interest method.
The straight-line method allocates a fixed portion of the bond discount or premium each interest period to adjust the interest payment to interest expense. The effective interest method, which is used when the effects of amortization are material, results in a constant rate of interest on the carrying value of the bonds. To find interest and the amortization of discounts or premiums, we apply the effective interest rate to the carrying value (face value minus the discount or plus the premium) of the bonds at the beginning of the interest period. The amount of the discount or premium to be amortized is the difference between the interest figured by using the effective rate and that obtained by using the stated or face rate. The effects of the effective interest method on bonds issued at par value, at a discount, and at a premium can be summarized as shown at the top of page 570.

	Bonds Issued at		
	Face Value	Discount	Premium
Trend in carrying value over bond term	Constant	Increasing	Decreasing
Trend in interest expense over bond term	Constant	Increasing	Decreasing
Interest expense versus interest payments	Interest expense = interest payments	Interest expense > interest payments	Interest expense < interest payments
Classification of bond discount or premium	Not applicable	Contra-liability (deducted from Bonds Payable)	Liability (added to Bonds Payable)

5. **Account for bonds issued between interest dates and make year-end adjustments.** When bonds are sold on dates between the interest payment dates, the issuing corporation collects from investors the interest that has accrued since the last interest payment date. When the next interest payment date arrives, the corporation pays the bondholders interest for the entire interest period.

   When the end of a corporation's fiscal year does not fall on an interest payment date, the corporation must accrue bond interest expense from the last interest payment date to the end of the company's fiscal year. This accrual results in the inclusion of the interest expense in the year incurred.

6. **Account for the retirement of bonds and the conversion of bonds into stock.** Callable bonds can be retired before maturity at the option of the issuing corporation. The call price is usually an amount greater than the face value of the bonds, so the corporation usually recognizes a loss on the retirement of bonds. An extraordinary gain can be recognized on the early extinguishment of debt, when a company purchases its bonds on the open market at a price below face value. This happens when a rise in the market interest rate causes the market value of the bonds to fall.

   Convertible bonds allow the bondholder to convert bonds to stock in the issuing corporation. In this case, the common stock issued is recorded at the carrying value of the bonds being converted. No gain or loss is recognized.

7. **Explain the basic features of mortgages payable, installment notes payable, long-term leases, and pensions and other postretirement benefits as long-term liabilities.** A mortgage is a long-term debt secured by real property. It usually is paid in equal monthly installments. Each payment is partly interest expense and partly debt repayment. Installment notes payable are long-term notes that are paid in a series of payments. Part of each payment is interest, and part is repayment of principal. If a long-term lease is a capital lease, the risks of ownership lie with the lessee. Like a mortgage payment, each lease payment is partly interest and partly a reduction of debt. For a capital lease, both an asset and a long-term liability should be recorded. The liability should be equal to the present value at the beginning of the lease of the total lease payments over the lease term. The recorded asset is subject to depreciation. Pension expense must be recorded in the current period. Other postretirement benefits should be estimated and accrued while the employee still is working.

Review of Concepts and Terminology

The following concepts and terms were introduced in this chapter:

(L.O. 1) **Bond:** A security, usually long term, representing money borrowed by a corporation from the investing public.

(L.O. 1) **Bond certificate:** Evidence of a company's debt to the bondholder.

(L.O. 1) **Bond indenture:** A supplementary agreement to a bond issue that defines the rights, privileges, and limitations of bondholders.

(L.O. 1) **Bond issue:** The total number of bonds issued at one time.

(L.O. 6) **Callable bonds:** Bonds that a corporation can buy back and retire at a given price, usually above face value, before maturity.

(L.O. 7) **Capital lease:** A long-term lease in which the risk of ownership lies with the lessee and whose terms resemble a purchase or sale on installment.

(L.O. 6) **Convertible bonds:** Bonds that can be exchanged for other securities of the corporation, usually its common stock.

(L.O. 1) **Coupon bonds:** Bonds that generally are not registered with the issuing corporation but instead bear interest coupons stating the amount of interest due and the payment date.

(L.O. 2) **Discount:** The amount by which the face value of a bond exceeds the issue price; for bonds issued when the market rate of interest is greater than the face interest rate.

(L.O. 6) **Early extinguishment of debt:** The purchase by a company of its own bonds on the open market in order to retire the debt at less than face value.

(L.O. 4) **Effective interest method:** A method of amortizing bond discounts or premiums that applies a constant interest rate, the effective rate (market rate) at the time the bonds were issued, to the carrying value of the bonds at the beginning of each interest period.

(L.O. 4) **Effective rate:** The market rate of interest at the time bonds are issued; the interest rate used to amortize bond discounts and premiums under the effective interest method.

(L.O. 2) **Face interest rate:** The rate of interest paid to bondholders based on the face value or principal of the bonds.

(L.O. 7) **Installment notes payable:** Long-term notes payable in a series of payments, of which part is interest and part is repayment of principal.

(L.O. 1) **Junk bonds:** Unsecured, high-risk, long-term bonds that carry high rates of interest.

(L.O. 2) **Market interest rate:** The rate of interest paid in the market on bonds of similar risk.

(L.O. 7) **Mortgage:** A long-term debt secured by real property; usually paid in equal monthly installments.

(L.O. 7) **Operating lease:** A short-term or cancelable lease for which the risks of ownership lie with the lessor, and whose payments are recorded as a rent expense.

(L.O. 7) **Other postretirement benefits:** Health care and other nonpension benefits that are paid to a worker after retirement but that are earned while the employee is working.

(L.O. 7) **Pension fund:** A fund established through contributions from an employer and sometimes employees that pays pension benefits to employees after retirement or on their disability or death.

(L.O. 7) **Pension plan:** A contract between a company and its employees under which the company agrees to pay benefits to the employees after they retire.

(L.O. 2) **Premium:** The amount by which the issue price of a bond exceeds its face value; for bonds issued when the market rate of interest is less than the face interest rate.

(L.O. 1) **Registered bonds:** Bonds for which the names and addresses of bondholders are recorded with the issuing company.

(L.O. 1) **Secured bonds:** Bonds that give the bondholders a pledge of certain assets of the company as a guarantee of repayment.

(L.O. 1) **Serial bonds:** A bond issue with several different maturity dates.

(L.O. 4) **Straight-line method:** A method of amortizing bond discounts or premiums that allocates a discount or premium equally over each interest period of the life of the bond.

(L.O. 1) **Term bonds:** Bonds of a bond issue that all mature at the same time.

(L.O. 1) **Unsecured bonds:** Bonds issued on the general credit of a company. Also called *debenture bonds.*

(L.O. 4) **Zero coupon bonds:** Bonds that do not pay periodic interest but that promise to pay a fixed amount on the maturity date.

Self-Test

Test your knowledge of the chapter by choosing the best answer for each of the following items.

(L.O. 1) 1. A bond indenture is
   a. a bond on which interest payments are past due.
   b. a bond that is secured by specific assets of the issuing corporation.
   c. an agreement between the issuing corporation and the bondholders.
   d. a bond that is unsecured.

(L.O. 2) 2. Ten $1,000 bonds issued at 98.5 on the interest date result in a debit to the Cash account for
   a. $9,850.
   b. $980.50.
   c. $985.
   d. $10,000.

(L.O. 2) 3. If the market rate of interest is lower than the face interest rate on the date of issuance, the bonds will
   a. sell at a discount.
   b. sell at a premium.
   c. sell at face value.
   d. not sell until the face interest rate is adjusted.

(L.O. 3) 4. The current value of a bond can be determined by calculating the present value of the
   a. face value of the bond.
   b. interest payments.
   c. interest payments plus any discount or minus any premium.
   d. interest payments plus the face value of the bond.

(L.O. 4) 5. When the straight-line method is used to amortize a bond discount, the interest expense for an interest period is calculated by
   a. deducting the amount of discount amortized for the period from the amount of cash paid for interest during the period.
   b. adding the amount of discount amortized for the period to the amount of cash paid for interest during the period.
   c. multiplying the face value of the bonds by the face interest rate.
   d. multiplying the carrying value of the bonds by the effective interest rate.

(L.O. 4) 6. The total interest cost on a 9 percent, ten-year, $1,000 bond that is issued at 95 is
   a. $50.
   b. $140.
   c. $900.
   d. $950.

(L.O. 4) 7. Medco Corporation issued a ten-year, 10 percent bond payable in 19x4 at a premium. During 19x5, the company's accountant failed to amortize any of the bond premium. The omission of the premium amortization
   a. does not affect the net income reported for 19x5.
   b. causes the net income for 19x5 to be overstated.
   c. causes the net income for 19x5 to be understated.
   d. causes retained earnings at the end of 19x5 to be overstated.

(L.O. 5) 8. The Kuger Corporation has authorized a bond issue with interest payment dates of January 1 and July 1. If the bonds are sold at the face amount on March 1, the cash Kuger receives is equal to the face amount of the bonds
a. plus the interest accrued from March 1 to July 1.
b. plus the interest accrued from January 1 to March 1.
c. minus the interest accrued from March 1 to July 1.
d. minus the interest accrued from January 1 to March 1.

(L.O. 6) 9. Bonds that contain a provision that allows the holders to exchange the bonds for other securities of the issuing corporation are called
a. secured bonds.
b. callable bonds.
c. debenture bonds.
d. convertible bonds.

(L.O. 7) 10. Which of the following is most likely a capital lease?
a. A five-year lease on a new building
b. A two-year lease on a truck with an option to renew for one more year
c. A five-year lease on a computer with an option to buy for a small amount at the end of the lease
d. A monthly lease on a building that can be canceled with ninety days' notice

Answers to the Self-Test are at the end of this chapter.

Review Problem
Interest and Amortization of a Bond Discount, Bond Retirement, and Bond Conversion

(L.O. 2, 4, 6) When the Merrill Manufacturing Company was expanding its metal window division, the company did not have enough capital to finance the expansion. So, management sought and received approval from the board of directors to issue bonds. The company planned to issue $5,000,000 of 8 percent, five-year bonds in 19x1. Interest would be paid on June 30 and December 31 of each year. The bonds would be callable at 104, and each $1,000 bond would be convertible into 30 shares of $10 par value common stock.

The bonds were sold at 96 on January 1, 19x1 because the market rate for similar investments was 9 percent. The company decided to amortize the bond discount by using the effective interest method. On July 1, 19x3 management called and retired half the bonds, and investors converted the other half into common stock.

Required

1. Prepare an interest and amortization schedule for the first five interest payment dates.
2. Prepare the journal entries to record the sale of the bonds, the first two interest payments, the bond retirement, and the bond conversion.

Answer to Review Problem

1. Prepare a schedule for the first five interest periods.

Interest and Amortization of Bond Discount

Semiannual Interest Payment Date	Carrying Value at Beginning of Period	Semiannual Interest Expense* (9% × 1/2)	Semiannual Interest Paid per Period (8% × 1/2)	Amortization of Discount	Unamortized Bond Discount at End of Period	Carrying Value at End of Period
Jan. 1, 19x1					$200,000	$4,800,000
June 30, 19x1	$4,800,000	$216,000	$200,000	$16,000	184,000	4,816,000
Dec. 31, 19x1	4,816,000	216,720	200,000	16,720	167,280	4,832,720
June 30, 19x2	4,832,720	217,472	200,000	17,472	149,808	4,850,192
Dec. 31, 19x2	4,850,192	218,259	200,000	18,259	131,549	4,868,451
June 30, 19x3	4,868,451	219,080	200,000	19,080	112,469	4,887,531

* Rounded to the nearest dollar.

2. Prepare the journal entries.

19x1				
Jan.	1	Cash	4,800,000	
		Unamortized Bond Discount	200,000	
		Bond Payable		5,000,000
		Sold $5,000,000 of 8%, 5-year bonds at 96		
June	30	Bond Interest Expense	216,000	
		Unamortized Bond Discount		16,000
		Cash		200,000
		Paid semiannual interest and amortized the discount on 8%, 5-year bonds		
Dec.	31	Bond Interest Expense	216,720	
		Unamortized Bond Discount		16,720
		Cash		200,000
		Paid semiannual interest and amortized the discount on 8%, 5-year bonds		
19x3				
July	1	Bonds Payable	2,500,000	
		Loss on Retirement of Bonds Payable	156,235	
		Unamortized Bond Discount		56,235
		Cash		2,600,000
		Called $2,500,000 of 8% bonds and retired them at 104 ($112,469 × 1/2 = $56,235*)		
July	1	Bonds Payable	2,500,000	
		Unamortized Bond Discount		56,234
		Common Stock		750,000
		Paid-in Capital in Excess of Par Value		1,693,766
		Converted $2,500,000 of 8% bonds into common stock: 2,500 × 30 shares = 75,000 shares 75,000 shares × $10 = $750,000 $112,469 − $56,235 = $56,234* $2,500,000 − ($56,234 + $750,000) = $1,693,766		

* Rounded.

Chapter Assignments

Questions

1. What is the difference among a bond certificate, a bond issue, and a bond indenture? What are some examples of items found in a bond indenture?
2. What are the essential differences between (a) secured and debenture bonds, (b) term and serial bonds, and (c) registered and coupon bonds?
3. Napier Corporation sold $500,000 of 5 percent $1,000 bonds on the interest payment date. What would the proceeds from the sale be if the bonds were issued at 95, at 100, and at 102?
4. If you were buying bonds on which the face interest rate was less than the market interest rate, would you expect to pay more or less than par value for the bonds? Why?

5. Why does the amortization of a bond discount increase interest expense to an amount above that of interest paid? Why does the amortization of a premium have the opposite effect?
6. When the effective interest method of amortizing a bond discount or premium is used, why does the amount of interest expense change from period to period?
7. When bonds are issued between interest dates, why is it necessary for the issuer to collect an amount equal to accrued interest from the buyer?
8. Why would a company want to exercise the callable provision of a bond when it can wait to pay off the debt?
9. What are the advantages of convertible bonds to the company issuing them and to the investor?
10. What are the two components of a uniform monthly mortgage payment?
11. What are the two methods of repayment of installment notes?
12. Under what conditions is a long-term lease called a capital lease? Why should the accountant record both an asset and a liability in connection with this type of lease? What items should appear on the income statement as the result of a capital lease?
13. What is a pension plan? What assumptions must be made to account for the expenses of such a plan?
14. What is the difference between a defined contribution plan and a defined benefit plan? In general, how is expense determined under each plan?
15. What are other postretirement benefits, and how does the matching rule apply to them?

Communication Skills Exercises

Communication 14-1. Bond Indenture and Ethics
(L.O. 1)

Xetol Corporation, a biotech company, has a bond issue outstanding of $12,000,000 that has several restrictive provisions in its bond indenture. Among these are requirements that current assets exceed current liabilities by a ratio of 2 to 1 and that income before income taxes exceed the annual interest on the bonds by a ratio of 3 to 1. If these requirements are not met, the bondholders can force the company into bankruptcy. The company is still awaiting approval from the Food and Drug Administration (FDA) of its new product XTL-14, a cancer treatment drug. Management had been counting on sales of XTL-14 in 19x4 to meet the provisions of the bond indenture. As the end of the fiscal year approaches, the company does not have sufficient current assets or income before taxes to meet the requirements. Serge Sokolov, the chief financial officer, proposes, "Since we can assume that FDA approval will occur in early 19x5, I suggest we book sales and receivables from our major customers now in anticipation of the sales we know will take place next year. This action will increase our current assets and our income before taxes. It is absolutely essential that we do this in order to save the company. Look at all the people who will be hurt if we don't do it." Is Sokolov's proposal acceptable accounting? Is it ethical? Who could be harmed by this decision? What steps might management take?

Communication 14-2. Bond Interest Rates and Market Prices
(L.O. 2)

RJR Nabisco's debt restructuring was the subject of the Decision Point that appeared at the beginning of this chapter. The following statement relates to the plan:

The refinancing plan's chief objective is to purge away most of the reset bonds of 2007 and 2009. These bonds have proved to be an immense headache for RJR. . . . That's because the bonds' interest rate must be reset so that they trade at full face value. The bonds had sunk to a deep discount earlier this year, raising the prospect that RJR might have to accept a painfully high reset rate of 20% or more to meet its reset obligations.[9]

What is a "deep discount," and what causes bonds to sell at a deep discount? Who loses when they do? What does "the bonds' interest rate must be reset so that they trade at

9. George Anders, "RJR Nabisco Moves to Retire Most Troublesome Junk Bonds," *Asian Wall Street Journal*, July 17, 1990.

full face value" mean? Why would this provision in the covenant be "an immense headache" to RJR Nabisco?

Communication 14-3. Pros and Cons of Convertible Bonds
(L.O. 6)

Sumitomo Corporation, a Japanese company that is one of the world's leading merchandisers of commodities, industrial goods, and consumer goods, has a number of issues of long-term debt. Among them are almost ¥20,000 million ($15.9 million) of 1 3/5% convertible bonds payable in Japanese yen in the year 2002.[10] (The interest rate illustrates the historically low rates in Japan.) The bonds are unsecured and are convertible into common stock at ¥1,193 per share. What reasons can you suggest for the company's issuing bonds that are convertible into common stock rather than simply issuing nonconvertible bonds or issuing common stock directly? Are there any disadvantages to this approach?

Communication 14-4. Basic Research Skills
(L.O. 2)

In your school or local library, obtain a copy of a recent issue of the *Wall Street Journal.* In the newspaper, find Section C, "Money & Investing," and turn to the page where the New York Exchange Bonds are listed. Notice, first, the Dow Jones Bond Averages of twenty bonds, ten utilities, and ten industrials. Are the averages above or below 100? Is this a premium or a discount? Is the market rate of interest above or below the face rate of the average bond? Now, identify three bonds from those listed. Choose one that sells at a discount, one that sells at a premium, and one that sells for approximately 100. For each bond, write the name of the company, the face interest rate, the year the bond is due, the current yield, and the current closing market price. (Some bonds have the letters *cv* in the Yield column. This means the bonds are convertible.) For each bond, explain the relationship among the face interest rate, the current yield, and the closing price. What other factors affect the current yield of a bond? Be prepared to discuss your findings in class.

Classroom Exercises[11]

Exercise 14-1. Journal Entries for Interest Using the Straight-Line Method
(L.O. 2, 4)

Berkshire Corporation issued $4,000,000 in 10 1/2 percent, ten-year bonds on February 1, 19x1, at 104. The semiannual interest payment dates are February 1 and August 1.

Prepare journal entries for the issue of bonds by Berkshire on February 1, 19x1, and the first two interest payments on August 1, 19x1 and February 1, 19x2, using the straight-line method. (Ignore year-end accruals).

Exercise 14-2. Journal Entries for Interest Using the Straight-Line Method
(L.O. 2, 4)

McAllister Corporation issued $8,000,000 in 8 1/2 percent, five-year bonds on March 1, 19x1, at 96. The semiannual interest payment dates are March 1 and September 1.

Prepare journal entries for the issue of the bonds by McAllister on March 1, 19x1, and the first two interest payments on September 1, 19x1 and March 1, 19x2, using the straight-line method. (Ignore year-end accruals).

Exercise 14-3. Journal Entries for Interest Using the Effective Interest Method
(L.O. 2, 4)

The Mayfair Drapery Company sold $500,000 of its 9 1/2 percent, twenty-year bonds on April 1, 19xx, at 106. The semiannual interest payment dates are April 1 and October 1. The effective interest rate is approximately 8.9 percent. The company's fiscal year ends September 30.

Prepare journal entries to record the sale of the bonds on April 1, the accrual of interest and amortization of premium on September 30, and the first interest payment on October 1. Use the effective interest method to amortize the premium.

10. Information excerpted from the 1989 annual report of Sumitomo Corporation.
11. Bond interest rates usually are quoted in eighths of a percent. Some exercises and problems in this chapter quote the rates in tenths of a percent to simplify computations.

Exercise 14-4. Journal Entries for Interest Using the Effective Interest Method *(L.O. 2, 4)*

On March 1, 19x1, the Sperlazzo Corporation issued $1,200,000 of 10 percent, five-year bonds. The semiannual interest payment dates are March 1 and September 1. Because the market rate for similar investments was 11 percent, the bonds had to be issued at a discount. The discount on the issuance of the bonds was $48,670. The company's fiscal year ends February 28.

Prepare journal entries to record the bond issue on March 1, 19x1; the payment of interest and the amortization of the discount on September 1, 19x1; the accrual of interest and the amortization of the discount on February 28, 19x2; and the payment of interest on March 1, 19x2. Use the effective interest method. (Round answers to the nearest dollar.)

Exercise 14-5. Valuing Bonds Using Present Value *(L.O. 3)*

Sessions, Inc. is considering two bond issues: (a) an $800,000 bond issue that pays semiannual interest of $64,000 and is due in twenty years; and (b) an $800,000 bond issue that pays semiannual interest of $60,000 and is due in fifteen years. Assume that the market rate of interest for each bond is 12 percent.

Calculate the amount that Sessions, Inc. will receive if both bond issues are made. (**Hint:** Calculate the present value of each bond issue and sum.)

Exercise 14-6. Valuing Bonds Using Present Value *(L.O. 3)*

Using the present value tables in the appendix on future value and present value tables, calculate the issue price of a $1,200,000 bond issue in each of the following independent cases, assuming that interest is paid semiannually:

a. A ten-year, 8 percent bond issue; the market rate of interest is 10 percent.
b. A ten-year, 8 percent bond issue; the market rate of interest is 6 percent.
c. A ten-year, 10 percent bond issue; the market rate of interest is 8 percent.
d. A twenty-year, 10 percent bond issue; the market rate of interest is 12 percent.
e. A twenty-year, 10 percent bond issue; the market rate of interest is 6 percent.

Exercise 14-7. Zero Coupon Bonds *(L.O. 1, 3)*

The Commonwealth of Kentucky needs to raise $100,000,000 for highway repairs. Officials are considering issuing zero coupon bonds, which do not require periodic interest payments. The current market rate of interest for the bonds is 10 percent. What face value of bonds must be issued to raise the needed funds, assuming the bonds will be due in thirty years and compounded annually? How would your answer change if the bonds were due in fifty years? How would both answers change if the market rate of interest were 8 percent instead of 10 percent?

Exercise 14-8. Journal Entries for Interest Payments Using the Effective Interest Method *(L.O. 4)*

The long-term debt section of the Fleming Corporation's balance sheet at the end of its fiscal year, December 31, 1991, was as follows:

Long-Term Liabilities		
Bonds Payable—8%, interest payable 1/1 and 7/1, due 12/31/03	$1,000,000	
Less Unamortized Bond Discount	80,000	$920,000

Prepare the journal entries relevant to the interest payments on July 1, 1992, December 31, 1992, and January 1, 1993. Assume an effective interest rate of 10 percent.

Exercise 14-9. Bond Issue Entries *(L.O. 2, 5)*

Graphic World, Inc. is authorized to issue $1,800,000 in bonds on June 1. The bonds carry a face interest rate of 9 percent, which is to be paid on June 1 and December 1.

Prepare journal entries for the issue of the bonds by Graphic World, Inc. under the assumptions that (a) the bonds are issued on September 1 at 100 and (b) the bonds are issued on June 1 at 105.

Exercise 14-10.
Sale of Bonds Between Interest Dates
(L.O. 5)

Reese Corporation sold $400,000 of 12 percent, ten-year bonds at face value on September 1, 19xx. The issue date of the bonds was May 1, 19xx.

1. Record the sale of the bonds on September 1 and the first semiannual interest payment on November 1, 19xx.
2. The company's fiscal year ends on December 31 and this is its only bond issue. What is the bond interest expense for the year ending December 31, 19xx?

Exercise 14-11.
Year-End Accrual of Bond Interest
(L.O. 2, 4, 5)

Swoboda Corporation issued $1,000,000 of 9 percent bonds on October 1, 19x1, at 96. The bonds are dated October 1 and pay interest semiannually. The market rate of interest is 10 percent and the company's fiscal year ends on December 31.

Prepare the entries to record the issuance of the bonds, the accrual of the interest on December 31, 19x1, and the first semiannual interest payment on April 1, 19x2. Assume the company does not use reversing entries and uses the effective interest method to amortize the bond discount.

Exercise 14-12.
Time Value of Money and Early Extinguishment of Debt
(L.O. 3, 6)

Feldman, Inc. has a $1,400,000, 8 percent bond issue that was issued a number of years ago at face value. There are now ten years left on the bond issue, and the market rate of interest is 16 percent. Interest is paid semiannually.

1. Using present value tables, figure the current market value of the bond issue.
2. Record the retirement of the bonds, assuming the company purchases the bonds on the open market at the calculated value.

Exercise 14-13.
Bond Retirement Journal Entry
(L.O. 6)

The Okado Corporation has outstanding $1,600,000 of 8 percent bonds callable at 104. On September 1, immediately after recording the payment of the semiannual interest and the amortization of the discount, the unamortized bond discount equaled $42,000. On that date, $960,000 of the bonds were called and retired.

Prepare the entry to record the retirement of the bonds on September 1.

Exercise 14-14.
Bond Conversion Journal Entry
(L.O. 6)

The Gallery Corporation has $400,000 of 6 percent bonds outstanding. There is $20,000 of unamortized discount remaining on these bonds after the July 1, 19x8 semiannual interest payment. The bonds are convertible at the rate of 40 shares of $5 par value common stock for each $1,000 bond. On July 1, 19x8, bondholders presented $300,000 of the bonds for conversion.

Prepare the journal entry to record the conversion of the bonds.

Exercise 14-15.
Mortgage Payable
(L.O. 7)

Inland Corporation purchased a building by signing a $150,000 long-term mortgage with monthly payments of $2,000. The mortgage carries an interest rate of 12 percent.

1. For the first three months, prepare a monthly payment schedule showing the monthly payment, the interest for the month, the reduction in debt, and the unpaid balance. (Round to the nearest dollar.)
2. Prepare journal entries to record the purchase and the first two monthly payments.

Exercise 14-16.
Recording Lease Obligations
(L.O. 7)

Ramos Corporation has leased a piece of equipment that has a useful life of twelve years. The terms of the lease are $43,000 per year for twelve years. Ramos currently is able to borrow money at a long-term interest rate of 15 percent. (Round answers to the nearest dollar.)

1. Calculate the present value of the lease.
2. Prepare the journal entry to record the lease agreement.
3. Prepare the entry to record depreciation of the equipment for the first year using the straight-line method.
4. Prepare the entries to record the lease payment for the first two years.

Exercise 14-17. Installment Notes Payable: Unequal Payments *(L.O. 7)*

Assume that on December 31, 19x1, $40,000 is borrowed on a 12 percent installment note, to be paid annually over four years. Prepare the entry to record the note and the first two annual payments, assuming that the principal is paid in equal annual installments and the interest on the unpaid balance accrues annually. How would your answer change if the interest rate rose to 13 percent in the second year?

Exercise 14-18. Installment Notes Payable: Equal Payments *(L.O. 7)*

Assume that on December 31, 19x1, $40,000 is borrowed on a 12 percent installment note, to be paid in equal annual payments over four years. Calculate to the nearest dollar the amount of each equal payment, using Table 4 from the appendix on future value and present value tables. Prepare a payment schedule table similar to Table 14-4, and record the first two annual payments.

Interpretation Case from Business

The Times Mirror Company[12] *(L.O. 2, 4)*

According to the long-term debt note in its annual report, the Times Mirror Company, publisher of the *Los Angeles Times, Newsday,* and other publications, engaged in the following long-term debt transactions in 1986:

a. On April 1, 1986, the company issued $100,000,000 of ten-year, 8¼ percent notes with semiannual interest payments on April 1 and October 1 at face value.
b. On October 15, 1986, the company redeemed, prior to maturity dates, all of its outstanding 10 percent notes that had been issued in connection with the acquisition of Call-Chronicle Newspapers, Inc. The redemption price was $65,000,000 plus accrued interest. The carrying value of the notes on October 15 was $65,000,000 less an unamortized discount of $7,223,000. The semiannual interest dates were June 15 and December 15.
c. On December 8, 1986, the company issued $100,000,000 of 8 percent notes due December 15, 1996, with semiannual interest payments on June 15 and December 15. The notes were issued at face value plus accrued interest.

(**Note:** Long-term notes are accounted for in a manner similar to that for bonds.)

Required

1. Prepare journal entries to record the three transactions above.
2. Prepare the entries on the interest payment dates of October 1 and December 15, 1986, and the year-end adjustment on December 31, 1986.
3. What was the total interest expense during 1986 for the three long-term notes issued, assuming that the balance in Unamortized Discount was $7,493,000 at the beginning of the year?

Problem Set A

Problem 14A-1. Bond Transactions—Straight-Line Method *(L.O. 2, 4, 5)*

Weiskopf Corporation has $8,000,000 of 9½ percent, twenty-five-year bonds dated March 1, with interest payable on March 1 and September 1. The company's fiscal year ends on November 30. It uses the straight-line method to amortize bond premiums or discounts.

Required

1. Assume the bonds are issued at 103.5 on March 1. Prepare general journal entries for March 1, September 1, and November 30.
2. Assume the bonds are issued at 96.5 on March 1. Prepare general journal entries for March 1, September 1, and November 30.
3. Assume the bonds are issued on June 1 at face value plus accrued interest. Prepare general journal entries for June 1, September 1, and November 30.

12. Information excerpted from the 1986 annual report of the Times Mirror Company.

Problem 14A-2.
Bond Transactions—Effective Interest Method
(L.O. 2, 4, 5)

Pandit Corporation has \$20,000,000 of $10\frac{1}{2}$ percent, twenty-year bonds dated June 1, with interest payment dates of May 30 and November 30. The company's fiscal year ends December 31. It uses the effective interest method to amortize bond premiums or discounts. (Round amounts to the nearest dollar.)

Required

1. Assume the bonds are issued at 103 on June 1, to yield an effective interest rate of 10.1 percent. Prepare general journal entries for June 1, November 30, and December 31.
2. Assume the bonds are issued at 97 on June 1, to yield an effective interest rate of 10.9 percent. Prepare general journal entries for June 1, November 30, and December 31.
3. Assume the bonds are issued at face value plus accrued interest on August 1. Prepare general journal entries for August 1, November 30, and December 31.

Problem 14A-3.
Bonds Issued at a Discount and a Premium
(L.O. 2, 4, 5)

Bannchi Corporation issued bonds twice during 19x1. The transactions were as follows:

19x1

- Jan. 1 Issued \$2,000,000 of $9\frac{1}{5}$ percent, ten-year bonds dated January 1, 19x1, with interest payable on June 30 and December 31. The bonds were sold at 98.1, resulting in an effective interest rate of 9.5 percent.
- Apr. 1 Issued \$4,000,000 of $9\frac{4}{5}$ percent, ten-year bonds dated April 1, 19x1, with interest payable on March 31 and September 30. The bonds were sold at 102, resulting in an effective interest rate of 9.5 percent.
- June 30 Paid semiannual interest on the January 1 issue and amortized the discount, using the effective interest method.
- Sept. 30 Paid semiannual interest on the April 1 issue and amortized the premium, using the effective interest method.
- Dec. 31 Paid semiannual interest on the January 1 issue and amortized the discount, using the effective interest method.
- 31 Made an end-of-year adjusting entry to accrue interest on the April 1 issue and to amortize half the premium applicable to the second interest period.

19x2

- Mar. 31 Paid semiannual interest on the April 1 issue and amortized the premium applicable to the second half of the second interest period.

Required

Prepare general journal entries to record the bond transactions. (Round amounts to the nearest dollar.)

Problem 14A-4.
Bond and Mortgage Transactions Contrasted
(L.O. 2, 4, 5, 7)

Christakis Manufacturing Company, whose fiscal year ends on June 30, is expanding its operations by building and equipping a new plant. It is financing the building and land with a \$20,000,000 mortgage, which carries an interest rate of 12 percent and requires monthly payments of \$236,000. The company is financing the equipment and working capital for the new plant with a \$20,000,000 twenty-year bond, which carries a face interest rate of 11 percent, payable semiannually on March 31 and September 30. To date, selected transactions related to these two issues have been as follows:

19x1

- Jan. 1 Signed mortgage in exchange for land and building. Land represents 10 percent of total price.
- Feb. 1 Made first mortgage payment.
- Mar. 1 Made second mortgage payment.
- 31 Issued bonds for cash at 96, resulting in an effective interest rate of 11.5 percent.
- Apr. 1 Made third mortgage payment.
- May 1 Made fourth mortgage payment.

19x1
June 1 Made fifth mortgage payment.
30 Made end-of-year adjusting entry to accrue interest on bonds and to amortize the discount, using the effective interest method.
July 1 Made sixth mortgage payment.
Aug. 1 Made seventh mortgage payment.
Sept. 1 Made eighth mortgage payment.
30 Made first interest payment on bonds and amortized the discount for the time period since the end of the fiscal year.

19x2
Mar. 31 Made second interest payment on bonds and amortized the discount for the time period since the last interest payment.

Required

1. Prepare a monthly payment schedule for the mortgage for ten months using these headings (round amounts to the nearest dollar): Payment Date, Unpaid Balance at Beginning of Period, Monthly Payment, Interest for One Month at 1% on Unpaid Balance, Reduction in Debt, and Unpaid Balance at End of Period.
2. Prepare the journal entries for the selected transactions. (Ignore mortgage payments made after September 1, 19x1.)

Problem 14A-5. Bond Interest and Amortization Table and Bond Retirements
(L.O. 2, 4, 6)

In 19x1, the Fender Corporation was authorized to issue $60,000,000 of six-year unsecured bonds. The bonds carried a face interest rate of 9 percent, payable semiannually on June 30 and December 31. The bonds were callable at 105 any time after June 30, 19x4. All of the bonds were issued on July 1, 19x1 at 95.568, a price yielding an effective interest rate of 10 percent. On July 1, 19x4, the company called and retired half the outstanding bonds.

Required

1. Prepare a table similar to Table 14-1, showing the interest and amortization of the bond discount for twelve interest payment periods. Use the effective interest method. (Round results to the nearest dollar).
2. Prepare general journal entries for the bond issue, interest payments and amortization of the bond discount, and bond retirement on the following dates: July 1, 19x1; December 31, 19x1; June 30, 19x4; July 1, 19x4; and December 31, 19x4.

Problem 14A-6. Comprehensive Bond Transactions
(L.O. 2, 4, 5, 6)

The Katz Corporation, a company whose fiscal year ends on June 30, engaged in the following long-term bond transactions over a three-year period:

19x5
Nov. 1 Issued $40,000,000 of 12 percent debenture bonds at face value plus accrued interest. Interest is payable on January 31 and July 31, and the bonds are callable at 104.

19x6
Jan. 31 Made the semiannual interest payment on the 12 percent bonds.
June 30 Made the year-end accrual of interest payment on the 12 percent bonds.
July 31 Issued $20,000,000 of 10 percent, fifteen-year convertible bonds at 105 plus accrued interest. Interest is payable on June 30 and December 31, and each $1,000 bond is convertible into 30 shares of $10 par value common stock. The market rate of interest is 9 percent.
31 Made the semiannual interest payment on the 12 percent bonds.
Dec. 31 Made the semiannual interest payment on the 10 percent bonds and amortized the bond premium.

19x7
Jan. 31 Made the semiannual interest payment on the 12 percent bonds.
Feb. 28 Called and retired all of the 12 percent bonds, including accrued interest.

19x7

June 30 Made the semiannual interest payment on the 10 percent bonds and amortized the bond premium.

July 1 Accepted for conversion into common stock all of the 10 percent bonds.

Required

Prepare general journal entries to record the bond transactions, making all necessary accruals and using the effective interest method. (Round all calculations to the nearest dollar.)

Problem Set B

Problem 14B-1.
Bond Transactions—Straight-Line Method
(L.O. 2, 4, 5)

Marconi Corporation has $10,000,000 of $10\frac{1}{2}$ percent, twenty-year bonds dated June 1, with interest payment dates of May 30 and November 30. The company's fiscal year ends December 31, and it uses the straight-line method to amortize bond premiums or discounts.

Required

1. Assume the bonds are issued at 103 on June 1. Prepare general journal entries for June 1, November 30, and December 31.
2. Assume the bonds are issued at 97 on June 1. Prepare general journal entries for June 1, November 30, and December 31.
3. Assume the bonds are issued at face value plus accrued interest on August 1. Prepare general journal entries for August 1, November 30, and December 31.

Problem 14B-2.
Bond Transactions—Effective Interest Method
(L.O. 2, 4, 5)

Aparicio Corporation has $8,000,000 of $9\frac{1}{2}$ percent, twenty-five-year bonds dated March 1, with interest payable on March 1 and September 1. The company's fiscal year ends on November 30. It uses the effective interest method to amortize bond premiums or discounts. (Round amounts to the nearest dollar.)

Required

1. Assume the bonds are issued at 102.5 on March 1, to yield an effective interest rate of 9.2 percent. Prepare general journal entries for March 1, September 1, and November 30.
2. Assume the bonds are issued at 97.5 on March 1, to yield an effective interest rate of 9.8 percent. Prepare general journal entries for March 1, September 1, and November 30.
3. Assume the bonds are issued on June 1 at face value plus accrued interest. Prepare general journal entries for June 1, September 1, and November 30.

Problem 14B-3.
Bonds Issued at a Discount and a Premium
(L.O. 2, 4, 5)

Maldonado Corporation sold bonds twice during 19x2. A summary of the transactions involving the bonds follows.

19x2

Jan. 1 Issued $6,000,000 of $9\frac{9}{10}$ percent, ten-year bonds dated January 1, 19x2, with interest payable on December 31 and June 30. The bonds were sold at 102.6, resulting in an effective interest rate of 9.4 percent.

Mar. 1 Issued $4,000,000 of $9\frac{1}{5}$ percent, ten-year bonds dated March 1, 19x2, with interest payable March 1 and September 1. The bonds were sold at 98.2, resulting in an effective interest rate of 9.5 percent.

June 30 Paid semiannual interest on the January 1 issue and amortized the premium, using the effective interest method.

Sept. 1 Paid semiannual interest on the March 1 issue and amortized the discount, using the effective interest method.

Dec. 31 Paid semiannual interest on the January 1 issue and amortized the premium, using the effective interest method.

31 Made an end-of-year adjusting entry to accrue the interest on the March 1 issue and to amortize two-thirds of the discount applicable to the second interest period.

19x3
Mar. 1 Paid semiannual interest on the March 1 issue and amortized the remainder of the discount applicable to the second interest period.

Required

Prepare general journal entries to record the bond transactions. (Round amounts to the nearest dollar.)

Problem 14B-4. Bond and Mortgage Transactions Contrasted
(L.O. 2, 4, 5, 7)

Idriss Grocery Stores, Inc. is expanding its operations by buying a chain of four outlets in another city. To finance the purchase of land and buildings, Idriss has obtained a $4,000,000 mortgage that carries an interest rate of 12 percent and requires monthly payments of $54,000. To finance the rest of the purchase, Idriss is issuing $4,000,000 of 12 1/2 percent unsecured bonds due in twenty years, with interest payable December 31 and June 30.

The company's fiscal year ends March 31. Selected transactions related to the two financing activities are as follows:

Jan. 1 Issued the bonds for cash at 104, to yield an effective rate of 12 percent.
Feb. 1 Issued the mortgage in exchange for land and buildings. The land represents 15 percent of the purchase price.
Mar. 1 Made first mortgage payment.
31 Made the year-end adjusting entry to accrue interest on the bonds and amortize the premium, using the effective interest method.
Apr. 1 Made second mortgage payment.
May 1 Made third mortgage payment.
June 1 Made fourth mortgage payment.
30 Made the first semiannual interest payment on the bonds and amortized the premium for the time period since the end of the fiscal year.
July 1 Made fifth mortgage payment.
Dec. 1 Made tenth mortgage payment.
31 Made the second semiannual interest payment on the bonds and amortized the premium for the time period since the last payment.

Required

1. Prepare a payment schedule for the mortgage for ten months using these headings (round amounts to the nearest dollar): Payment Date, Unpaid Balance at Beginning of Period, Monthly Payment, Interest for One Month at 1% on Unpaid Balance, Reduction in Debt, and Unpaid Balance at End of Period.
2. Prepare the journal entries for the selected transactions. (Ignore the mortgage payments for August 1 through November 1.)

Problem 14B-5. Bond Interest and Amortization Table and Bond Retirements
(L.O. 2, 4, 6)

In 19x1, Tully Corporation was authorized to issue $6,000,000 of unsecured bonds, due March 31, 19x6. The bonds carried a face interest rate of 11 3/5 percent, payable semiannually on March 31 and September 30, and were callable at 104 any time after March 31, 19x4. All the bonds were issued on April 1, 19x1 at 102.261, a price that yielded an effective interest rate of 11 percent.

On April 1, 19x4, Tully Corporation called half of the outstanding bonds and retired them.

Required

1. Prepare a table similar to Table 14-2 to show the interest and amortization of the bond premium for ten interest payment periods, using the effective interest method. (Round results to the nearest dollar).
2. Prepare general journal entries for the bond issue, interest payments and amortization of the bond premium, and the bond retirement on the following dates: April 1, 19x1; September 30, 19x1; March 31, 19x4; April 1, 19x4; and September 30, 19x4.

Problem 14B-6. Comprehensive Bond Transactions
(L.O. 2, 4, 5, 6)

Over a period of three years, DaSilva Corporation, a company whose fiscal year ends on December 31, engaged in the following transactions involving two bond issues:

19x1

July 1 Issued $20,000,000 of 12 percent convertible bonds at 96. The bonds are convertible into $20 par value common stock at the rate of 20 shares of stock for each $1,000 bond. Interest is payable on June 30 and December 31, and the market rate of interest is 13 percent.

Dec. 31 Made the semiannual interest payment and amortized the bond discount.

19x2

June 1 Issued $40,000,000 of 9 percent bonds at face value plus accrued interest. Interest is payable on February 28 and August 31. The bonds are callable at 105, and the market rate of interest is 9 percent.

30 Made the semiannual interest payment on the 12 percent bonds and amortized the bond discount.

Aug. 31 Made the semiannual interest payment on the 9 percent bonds.

Dec. 31 Made the semiannual interest payment and amortized the discount on the 12 percent bonds, and accrued interest on the 9 percent bonds.

19x3

Feb. 28 Made the semiannual interest payment on the 9 percent bonds.

June 30 Made the semiannual interest payment and amortized the bond discount on the 12 percent bonds.

July 1 Accepted for conversion into common stock all of the 12 percent bonds.

31 Called and retired all of the 9 percent bonds, including accrued interest.

Required

Prepare general journal entries to record the bond transactions, making all necessary accruals and using the effective interest method. (Round all calculations to the nearest dollar.)

Financial Decision Case

Coniglio Chemical Corporation
(L.O. 2, 7)

The Coniglio Chemical Corporation plans to build a new plant that will produce liquid fertilizer for the agricultural market. The plant is expected to cost $400,000,000 and will be located in the southwestern part of the United States. The company's chief financial officer, Terry Coniglio, has spent the last several weeks studying different means of financing the plant's construction. From his talks with bankers and other financiers, he has decided that there are two basic choices. The plant can be financed through the issuance of a long-term bond or a long-term lease. The two options follow:

a. Issuance of a $400,000,000, twenty-five-year, 16 percent bond secured by the new plant. Interest on the bonds would be payable semiannually.
b. Signing a twenty-five-year lease calling for lease payments of $32,700,000 on a semiannual basis.

Coniglio wants to know what the effect of each choice will be on the company's financial statements. He estimates that the useful life of the plant is twenty-five years, at which time it is expected to have an estimated residual value of $40,000,000.

Required

1. Prepare the entries to record the issuance of the bonds at face value in exchange for the fertilizer plant. Assume that the transaction occurs on the first day of the corporation's fiscal year, which is July 1. Also prepare the entries to pay the interest expense and interest payable and to record depreciation on the plant during the first year. Assume that the straight-line method is used. Describe the effects that these transactions will have on the balance sheet and income statement.
2. Prepare the entries required to treat the long-term lease as a capital lease. Assume that the plant is occupied on the first day of the fiscal year, July 1, and that an interest rate of 16 percent applies. Also prepare the entries to record the lease payments

and to record depreciation during the first year. Describe the effects that these transactions will have on the balance sheet and income statement. (A knowledge of present value, which is dealt with in the appendix on the time value of money and in Table 4 of the appendix on future value and present value tables, is necessary to do this part of the question.)

3. What factors would you consider important in deciding which alternative to choose? Contrast the annual cash requirement of the two alternatives.

Answers to Self-Test

1. c	3. b	5. b	7. c	9. d
2. a	4. d	6. d	8. b	10. c

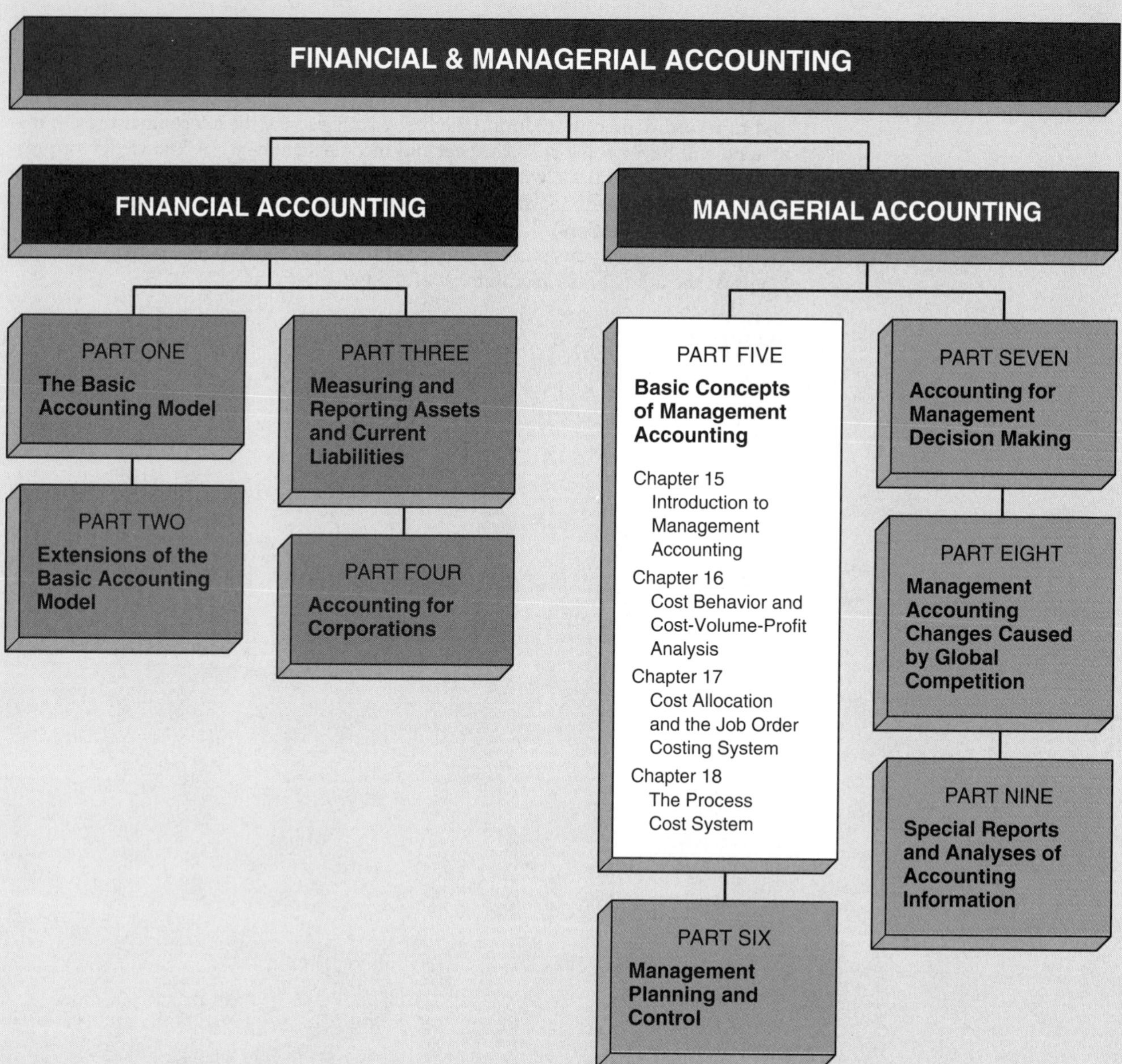

Part Five introduces you to the basic concepts, terminology, and practices underlying management accounting. Reporting of internal operations is stressed, along with methods used to establish unit costs of manufactured products.

PART FIVE

Basic Concepts of Management Accounting

Management accounting practices differ from financial accounting practices. Financial accounting concepts and procedures are designed to handle the measurement and reporting of problems pertaining to the general accounting system of an organization. The preparation of general-purpose financial statements used by people outside the business entity, such as bankers and stockholders, is also an important aspect of financial accounting. Management accounting practices and procedures are used to support the actions of internal management.

Chapter 15 describes the field of management accounting, compares management accounting with financial accounting, and focuses on the analysis of nonfinancial data, which is common in the work of the management accountant. Ethical standards of the management accountant are also introduced.

Chapter 16 analyzes the behavior of operating costs and examines the relationships among cost, volume, and profit. Specifically, this chapter focuses on variable and fixed costs, the breakeven point, contribution margin, and profit planning activities.

Chapters 17 and **18** describe and illustrate two approaches to product costing. After discussing absorption costing and predetermined overhead rates, Chapter 17 focuses on product costing within the job order cost accounting system. Chapter 18 analyzes product costing in a process cost accounting environment.

LEARNING OBJECTIVES

1. *Define* management accounting *and identify the major information needs of managers.*
2. *Distinguish between management accounting and financial accounting.*
3. *Compare the information needs of a manager of a manufacturing company, a bank, and a department store.*
4. *Prepare analyses of nonfinancial data.*
5. *Compare accounting for inventories and cost of goods sold for merchandising and manufacturing companies.*
6. *Define and give examples of the three manufacturing cost elements—direct materials costs, direct labor costs, and factory overhead costs—and compute a product's unit cost.*
7. *Describe the contents and flow of costs through the Materials Inventory, Work in Process Inventory, and Finished Goods Inventory accounts.*
8. *Prepare a statement of cost of goods manufactured and an income statement for a manufacturing company.*
9. *Identify the standards of ethical conduct for management accountants, and recognize activities that are not ethical.*

CHAPTER 15

Introduction to Management Accounting

In this chapter, we examine the relationship between management accounting and financial accounting. As we explore the information needs of managers in a manufacturing company, a service organization, and a merchandising company, you can see the role that nonfinancial as well as financial data analysis play in these three types of businesses. We compare accounting for manufacturing and merchandising companies, focusing on inventory accounts and the preparation and analysis of the statement of cost of goods manufactured and the income statement. Finally, we discuss the ethical standards that apply to the management accountant. After studying this chapter, you should be able to meet the learning objectives listed on the left.

The study of management accounting traditionally focuses on the discipline as it relates to manufacturing firms. But you should be aware that service organizations—hospitals, accounting firms, insurance agencies, banks—also must cost their "products," the services they offer. Many of the internal accounting procedures we describe in terms of manufacturing firms in this and later chapters also can be used by service organizations. For this reason, we use a service organization, a bank, as an example in this chapter. In addition, several of the Management Decision Cases in the remaining chapters focus on data that support management decisions in service-oriented companies. A work sheet analysis based on periodic and perpetual inventory systems is covered in The Windham Company Practice Case.

DECISION POINT

Caterpillar, Inc.[1]

■ Caterpillar, Inc., headquartered in Peoria, Illinois, makes large construction and earthmoving equipment. The accounting staff is responsible for the company's information needs and differentiates between financial accounting (providing information for external financial reporting purposes) and managerial accounting (providing relevant decision information to internal managers). According to Lou Jones, Caterpillar's Manager of Business Development Services and Product Cost, public reporting of business financial results is a vital activity. The function of reliable financial reporting and its related controls, records, and systems is a profound responsibility requiring technical accounting skills, a deep knowledge base, and expertise.

In the new globally competitive environment of the 1990s, these financial reporting duties have not changed at Caterpillar. But the role of the

1. Source: Lou Jones, Cost Management and Business Resources Manager, Caterpillar, Inc., Peoria, Illinois. Reprinted by permission of the author.

accountant has evolved dramatically to embrace managerial as well as financial obligations. The company must still generate reliable external financial reports, but managers depend on accountants for more than financial statements: Accountants now provide information that is used internally to manage and improve the business. Management accountants participate actively as members of the management team and make business-enhancing decisions in addition to deriving the data supporting the decisions.

Caterpillar's management accountants understand and accept their broader role. They know that the information required to run the business is not necessarily contained in the financial accounting records. These accountants provide specific, focused data that helps the organization pinpoint areas requiring change and improvement. They view the company's value chain (all activities that add value and generate revenue and profit) as one continuous customer delivery system—from product design and development, through production, marketing, and distribution, to customer service and support. They recognize that it is equally important to have a cost-effective product distribution system as it is to have a cost-effective production process. They know that all of the key business systems, processes, and activities across the customer delivery system must be well managed, controlled, and improved continuously. To ensure this, Caterpillar's management accountants identify critical success factors, establish accountability for results, set targets for improvement, and provide feedback through cost systems, performance measurements, and business analyses. This chapter discusses further the responsibilities of today's management accountants and differentiates their duties from those of financial accountants. ■

What Is Management Accounting?

OBJECTIVE 1
Define management accounting *and identify the major information needs of managers*

Today, the management accountant is expected to provide timely, accurate information—including budgets, standard costs, variance analysis, support for day-to-day operating decisions, and analyses of capital expenditures. Management accounting consists of accounting techniques and procedures for gathering and reporting financial, production, and distribution data in order to meet management's information needs. The Institute of Management Accountants defines **management accounting** as

> the process of identification, measurement, accumulation, analysis, preparation, interpretation, and communication of financial [as well as nonfinancial] information used by management to plan, evaluate, and control within the organization and to assure appropriate use and accountability for its resources.[2]

The information management accountants gather and analyze is used to support the actions of management. All business managers need accurate, timely information to support pricing, planning, operating, and many other types of decisions. Managers of production, merchandising, government, and service-oriented enterprises all depend on management accounting information. Multidivisional corporations need large amounts of information and more complex accounting and reporting systems than do small businesses. But small- and

2. Institute of Management Accountants, *Statement No. 1A* (New York, 1982). Since this definition was prepared, the importance of nonfinancial information has increased significantly. Words in brackets were added by the authors.

medium-sized businesses make use of certain types of financial and operating information as well. The types of data needed to ensure efficient operating conditions do not depend entirely on an organization's size.

Meeting Financial Information Needs

Three types of financial information are needed to manage a company effectively. First, manufacturing and service-oriented companies need product and service costing information. Cost accounting techniques are used to gather production information, assign specific costs to product batches, and calculate unit costs. Product costing techniques are discussed in the chapters on cost allocation and the job order costing system, and the process cost system.

Second, to accomplish their objectives, all companies need data to plan and control operations. In a manufacturing company, as production takes place and costs are incurred, formal control procedures are used to compare planned and actual costs. In this way, the effectiveness of operations and of management can be measured. The chapters on responsibility accounting and performance evaluation, the budgeting process, and standard costing and variance analysis focus on the planning and control functions of management accounting.

Third, managers need special reports and financial analyses to support their decisions. That is, all management decisions should be supported by analyses of alternative courses of action. The management accountant is expected to supply the information for those decisions.

Meeting Changing Needs

Management accounting is constantly evolving to meet the changing needs of management. Strong international competition has generated new operating philosophies, and these philosophies have pushed management accountants in new directions. Quality is no longer taken for granted, and the cost of scrap and rework is no longer factored into product cost. New operating methods—like the just-in-time (JIT) operating environment and total quality management—are causing companies to revamp production processes and develop new approaches to cost assignment and product costing. Totally integrated information systems are placing new pressures on the management accounting system. The role of budgeting is changing. New strategies and approaches to capital expenditure decisions are generating new forms of analysis. Many of these changes are discussed in later chapters.

The product of all of these changes is a very dynamic discipline. Small- and medium-sized companies still use many of the established practices and procedures of management accounting. But large, global companies are moving rapidly into a new operating environment that demands new management accounting techniques and analyses.

Management Accounting versus Financial Accounting

OBJECTIVE 2
Distinguish between management accounting and financial accounting

Financial accounting includes all the principles that regulate the accounting for and reporting of financial information that must be disclosed to people outside the company, to stockholders, bankers, creditors, and brokers. In contrast, management accounting exists primarily for the benefit of those inside the company, the people who are responsible for its operations.

Many of the procedures and principles that stem from financial accounting also apply to management accounting. Depreciation techniques, cash collection and disbursement procedures, inventory valuation methods, and the recognition of what is an asset or a liability are all essential to the study of management accounting. But, because their output is communicated to different audiences for different reasons, financial accountants and management accountants follow different rules. The rules of management accounting are somewhat less defined and place fewer restrictions on the accountant's day-to-day activities. In the following sections, we take a closer look at the differences between management accounting and financial accounting, differences that are summarized in Table 15-1.

The Primary Users of Information

Traditional financial statements are prepared primarily for people and organizations outside the company. In comparison, the management accountant produces internal reports and analyses that are used by all managers. These reports can be financial summaries similar to the financial statements, special financial analyses, or reports of nonfinancial data. They supply relevant information to the people who are responsible for particular activities. So the content of the reports varies depending on the level of management being served, the department or segment being analyzed, and the purpose of each report.

Table 15-1. Comparison of Financial and Management Accounting

Areas of Comparison	Financial Accounting	Management Accounting
1. Primary users of information	Persons and organizations outside the business entity	Various levels of internal management
2. Types of accounting systems	Double-entry system	Not restricted to double-entry system; any useful system
3. Restrictive guidelines	Adherence to generally accepted accounting principles	No formal guidelines or restrictions; only criterion is usefulness
4. Units of measurement	Historical dollar	Any useful monetary or physical measure, such as machine hours or labor hours; if dollars are used, can be historical or future dollars
5. Focal point for analysis	Business entity as a whole	Various segments of the business entity
6. Frequency of reporting	Periodically on a regular basis	Whenever needed; may not be on a regular basis
7. Degree of objectivity	Demands objectivity; historical in nature	Heavily subjective for planning purposes, but objective data are used when relevant; futuristic in nature

Types of Accounting Systems

Financial statements show dollar totals that reflect the balances of accounts in a company's general ledger. Before financial data are entered into the general ledger, the amounts must be in a form suitable for a double-entry accounting system. In contrast to financial accounting, management accounting uses systems that are more varied and flexible. The analyses and flow of accounting data inside a company need not depend on the double-entry format. Management accountants gather data for small segments or large divisions, and they can express those data in units of measurement other than historical dollars. The information need not be organized in general ledger accounts. Special reports can be prepared for a particular manager's use. Under these conditions, the information storage and retrieval system must be flexible and have a wide range of capabilities.

Restrictive Guidelines

Financial accounting is concerned with analyzing, classifying, recording, and reporting a company's financial activities. Accountants must adhere to generally accepted accounting principles that govern the measuring, recording, and reporting of financial information. These principles are necessary to ensure the accuracy and reliability of that information, but they confine accountants to a finite number of accounting practices.

Usually, much more information is available to managers than to people outside the company. The presentation and analysis of that information are not limited by a set of rigid rules. Management accounting has one primary guideline: The accounting practice or technique must produce *useful* information. Before tackling a problem, the management accountant must decide what information will be useful to the recipient of the report, and then must choose concepts, procedures, and techniques to generate that information. As always, the benefits of preparing each report should outweigh the costs of preparation.

Units of Measurement

The fourth area of comparison between financial and management accounting is the unit of measurement that serves as a basis for reports and analyses. Financial accounting generates financial information about events in the past. The common unit of measurement in financial accounting is the historical dollar. Management accountants, on the other hand, are not restricted to using only the historical dollar; they can employ any useful unit of measurement. Historical dollars may be used for cost control analyses and for measuring trends for routine planning. However, most management decisions require forecasts and projections that rely on estimates of future dollar flows. In addition to monetary units, the management accountant uses such nonfinancial measures as machine hours, labor hours, and product or service units.

Focal Point for Analysis

Typically, financial accounting records and reports information on the assets, liabilities, equities, and net income of a company as a whole. Financial statements summarize the transactions of an organization. Management accounting, in contrast, usually focuses on segments of a business—cost centers, profit centers, divisions, or departments—or some specific aspect of its operations. Reports can range from an analysis of revenues and expenses for an entire division to an examination of the materials used by one machine.

Frequency of Reporting

Financial statements developed for external use usually are prepared on a regular basis: monthly, quarterly, or annually. Periodic reporting at regular intervals is a basic concept of financial accounting. Management accounting reports can be prepared monthly, quarterly, or annually on a regular basis, but they also can be requested daily or on an irregular basis. What is important is that each report generated be useful and be prepared whenever it is needed.

Degree of Objectivity

The information in financial statements consists of data about transactions that have happened already. As a result, the information is determined objectively and is verifiable. In contrast, management accounting is concerned primarily with planning and controlling internal operations—activities that are often future related. Past revenue and expense transactions, although useful for establishing trends, are not used directly for planning purposes. Thus, the information prepared by management accountants typically consists of subjective estimates of future events.

The Information Needs of Management

OBJECTIVE 3
Compare the information needs of a manager of a manufacturing company, a bank, and a department store

It is customary to talk about manufacturing operations when discussing management accounting, but any manager in any business, from a conglomerate to a family grocery store, relies daily on management accounting information. Service organizations, such as banks, hotels, public accounting firms, insurance companies, and attorneys' offices, need internal accounting information to determine the costs of providing their services and the prices to charge. Retail organizations, such as Sears and Neiman-Marcus, use management accounting reports to manage operations and maximize profits. Not-for-profit and government agencies use internal accounting information to develop budgets and performance reports (see the appendix on governmental and not-for-profit accounting).

Management accounting principles and procedures are not just for accountants. Financial analysts, real estate brokers, insurance agents, bankers, market researchers, and economists are just a few of the managers who make decisions based on the information supplied by management accountants. Every person employed in a management-related job should help develop and should rely on management accounting information.

To illustrate the widespread use of management accounting information, we look at three business enterprises: a manufacturing company, a bank, and a department store.

A Manufacturing Company

A manufacturer takes raw materials, such as wood, steel, and rubber, and transforms them into finished products, such as furniture, automobiles, and tires. Product costing information is an important contribution of management accounting to a manufacturing company. Product costing information allows managers to identify weak production areas, control costs, support pricing decisions, and set inventory values.

The information used to make operating decisions also is extremely important to manufacturing managers. A manager must be knowledgeable and able to respond to pricing questions and delivery dates when special orders are received. If the company manufactures several products, constant monitoring of the different products is important. Often a manufacturer must decide whether to make a part or to purchase it. If two or more products emerge from a common raw material—for example, gasoline and motor oil from crude oil—the manufacturer must decide whether to sell the product when it first is identified or to process it further, to make a more salable and profitable product.

Information related to product costing and operating decisions accounts for only some of the information needs of managers in a manufacturing company. Budgets are used as both planning and control tools. Managers in a manufacturing company also need current information about production planning and scheduling, product-line management and development, cash management, capital expenditures, product quality levels, customer satisfaction, and selling and distribution. Information also is needed for external reporting and for computing taxes.

A Service Business—A Bank

A bank is a service business that provides financial services for a fee. Loans are available, and interest is assessed as payment for the service. To maintain checking accounts, banks usually require either a monthly fee or a minimum balance so that they can lend the money and earn interest income. A small charge is assessed for certified checks, and fees are charged for safe deposit boxes. Large banks provide other services as well.

The key to managing a bank's resources rests with its accounting information system. Balancing and monitoring cash reserves are critical. Managers are responsible for customers' savings accounts and federal deposit reserves required by the Federal Reserve Board and other government agencies.

Although normal operating decisions in banks and manufacturing companies differ in many ways, the bank manager continually must analyze the services provided and the optimal service mix, just as the manufacturing manager must analyze the products manufactured and the optimal product mix. Budgets must be prepared, and capital expenditure decisions made. Loan activities require a system for verifying credit. And monitoring loan payments and delinquent loans is very important. Recently, banks have started adopting product costing procedures. Because a bank's products are its services, it has to determine if its services are operating efficiently and are cost-effective. This means that information on the cost per loan, the cost per savings transaction, and the cost per checking account for maintenance is increasingly important to bank managers.

A Merchandising Business—A Department Store

A department store's most important asset is its merchandise. The store's manager is responsible for (1) ordering merchandise in optimal quantities, (2) safely storing merchandise once it is received, (3) displaying items so that customers are attracted to them, (4) marketing merchandise, and (5) distributing items to customers. To manage these areas of responsibility, a manager needs an accounting information system that can generate reports, requisitions, controls, and analyses. Market surveys and other research often support purchase decisions. Knowing the most economical quantity to order helps control costs. And inventory records are critical once merchandise has been received. These documents give the manager information on the quality of merchandise, deterioration, obsolescence, losses caused by theft, quantity on hand, reorder point, and current demand.

Obviously, store managers need internal accounting information to control merchandise. But store managers are involved in other areas as well, including (1) budgeting; (2) cash management; (3) product-line sales analyses; (4) capital expenditure analyses; (5) product selling cost analyses; (6) report preparation for all levels of management and tax authorities; and (7) operating decisions concerning sales mix, special orders, and personnel placement. The information reported by the management accountant helps store managers in these areas.

Analysis of Nonfinancial Data

OBJECTIVE 4
Prepare analyses of nonfinancial data

Most people associate accounting with the analysis of resources and their money equivalent. As noted earlier, however, management accountants prepare analyses expressed not only in dollars but also in nonfinancial units of measurement. Today's globally competitive operating environment has created additional demand for nonfinancial data analysis. Management has three primary concerns: (1) increasing the quality of the firm's products or services, (2) reducing the time it takes to create and deliver products or services, and (3) total customer satisfaction. What measures do managers need to monitor the company's performance in each of these areas?

To measure increased quality, management needs information and trend analysis on the number of items that require rework, the amount of scrapped materials and products, the total time devoted to inspection, and the time spent on product development, design, and testing.

The performance of the production and delivery functions can be measured by trends in throughput time (the total production time per unit per product type), total delivery time by customer and geographic location, raw materials spoilage and scrap rates, machine setup time rates, production bottlenecks (slowdowns), and completed production.

Customer satisfaction can be measured by trends in the number of product warranty claims and the number of products returned (analyzed by product line and by customer), by retention of customers, by product reorders by customers, and by time spent on product repairs and adjustments in the field.

Notice that all of these performance measures are nonfinancial and that all are critical in today's operating environment. In addition, all these measures are part of the decision-supporting data management needs, and all are expected to be supplied by the management accounting information system.

Accountants often are confronted with problems whose solutions are formulated around such measures as machine hours, labor hours, units of output, number of employees, and number of requests for a particular service. The following three cases illustrate situations in which managers require nonfinancial data to make informed decisions.

Case One: Speights Manufacturing Company. The Speights Manufacturing Company produces a product called "form-fit ski boots." Shoe moldings are cast in the molding department. This department employs seven people: three employees who run the molding machines and four support personnel. Data on the hours worked in February, 19x3 are shown in Exhibit 15-1.

Management has determined that six pairs of boots should be produced for each hour of labor worked. Here are the actual production figures for February:

Week 1: 1,590 pairs	Week 3: 1,493 pairs
Week 2: 1,544 pairs	Week 4: 1,539 pairs

Exhibit 15-1. Analysis of Nonfinancial Data—Manufacturing Company

Speights Manufacturing Company
Analysis of Labor Hours—Molding Department
For February, 19x3

Summary of Labor Hours Worked

	Hours Worked									
	Week 1		Week 2		Week 3		Week 4		Totals	
	Direct Labor	Support Labor	Direct Labor	Support Labor	Direct Labor	Support Labor	Direct Labor	Support Labor	Direct Labor	Support Labor
R. Cascio		48		48		46		48		190
R. Chen		32		48		32		48		160
L. Cox	48		36		40		44		168	
T. Greene	44		40		46		37		167	
K. Kenny		40		36		36		40		152
C. Olson	40		40		44		48		172	
P. Welsh		42		44		44		40		170
	132	162	116	176	130	158	129	176	507	672
Analysis of Production										
Units* that should have been produced: (6 × total labor hours)	1,764		1,752		1,728		1,830		7,074	
Units produced	1,590		1,544		1,493		1,539		6,166	
Units under target	174		208		235		291		908	
Percentage under target	9.86		11.87		13.60		15.90		12.84	

*Unit equals one pair of boots.

You have been asked to analyze production activity for February. Should management be concerned about productivity in the molding department? What information supports your answer?

Solution to Case One

The schedule in Exhibit 15-1 shows labor hours worked by the molding department and both the targeted and actual production output. As you can see, production consistently was under target and the percentage under target increased by almost 2 points each week. This is a bad sign, and the productivity of machine operators should be investigated. Remember, this does not mean the employees are at fault. The cause could be faulty materials, inefficient machines, or the unrealistic expectations of management. The analysis simply indicates that something is wrong, and it must be identified and corrected.

Case Two: Kings Beach National Bank. Lynda Babb supervises tellers at Kings Beach National Bank. The bank has three drive-up windows, each with a full-time teller. Historically, each teller serviced an average of thirty customers per hour. However, on November 1, 19x4, management implemented a new check-scanning procedure that has cut back the number of customers serviced per hour.

Data on the number of customers serviced for the three-month period ending December 31, 19x4 are shown in Part A of Exhibit 15-2. Each teller works an average of 170 hours per month. Window 1 is always the busiest; Windows 2

Exhibit 15-2. Analysis of Nonfinancial Data—Bank

Kings Beach National Bank
Summary of Number of Customers Serviced
For the Quarter Ended December 31, 19x4

Part A	**Number of Customers Serviced**			
Window	**October**	**November**	**December**	**Quarter Totals**
1	5,428	5,186	5,162	15,776
2	5,280	4,820	4,960	15,060
3	4,593	4,494	4,580	13,667
Totals	15,301	14,500	14,702	44,503

Part B	**Number of Customers Serviced per Hour**			
Window	**October**	**November**	**December**	**Quarter Averages**
1	31.93	30.51	30.36	30.93
2	31.06	28.35	29.18	29.53
3	27.02	26.44	26.94	26.80
Totals	90.01	85.30	86.48	87.26
Average per hour per window	30.00	28.43	28.83	29.09

and 3 receive progressively less business. The average of thirty customers per hour is an average of all three windows.

Ms. Babb is preparing a report for management on the effects of the new procedure. To help her, you have been asked to calculate a new average for customers serviced per hour for both November and December.

Solution to Case Two

Part B of Exhibit 15-2 shows an analysis of the number of customers serviced over the three months by each teller window. Using the monthly average hours worked per teller (170), you can compute the number of customers serviced per hour by dividing the number of customers serviced by 170. By averaging the customer service rates for three tellers, you get 28.43 and 28.83 for November and December, respectively. As you can see, the service rate has decreased. But December's average is higher than November's, which means the tellers, as a whole, are becoming more accustomed to the new procedure.

Case Three: Broad Street Dry Goods Store. Broad Street Dry Goods Store, a high-volume department store, offers home delivery to attract customers. Located in Bridgetown, Maine, the company uses four trucks to handle its home deliveries. Recently, demand for home delivery has increased significantly. The controller, Hank Sylvester, developed two alternatives for solving the delivery-demand problem. The first was to purchase a fifth truck and hire a fifth driver. The second was to hire someone to schedule deliveries more efficiently, thereby saving time and increasing the number of deliveries per truck. Before committing to the cost of the truck purchase alternative, Mr. Sylvester decided to try the scheduling idea.

Exhibit 15-3. Analysis of Nonfinancial Data—Department Store

Broad Street Dry Goods Store Analysis of Deliveries For the Four Weeks Ended January 28, 19x3						
Weekly Average, Previous Year		Number of Deliveries				
	Truck	Week 1	Week 2	Week 3	Week 4	Total Deliveries
400	1	360	380	440	460	1,640
450	2	480	460	500	540	1,980
400	3	390	410	420	480	1,700
500	4	520	480	560	600	2,160
1,750		1,750	1,730	1,920	2,080	7,480

Delivery data for the most recent four-week period are shown in Exhibit 15-3. The scheduler started working at the beginning of Week 3. She immediately divided the territory into four delivery regions. Actual deliveries were scheduled by location within each region to cut down mileage and backtracking. Mr. Sylvester's goal was to increase deliveries by 10 percent. Did the scheduler work out, or should Mr. Sylvester buy a fifth truck?

Solution to Case Three

Total deliveries per week were 1,750 during the first week, 1,730 during the second week, 1,920 in Week 3, and 2,080 in Week 4. To achieve Mr. Sylvester's goal, there must be at least 1,925 weekly deliveries (1,750 × 110 percent). From the information given, the new scheduler seems to be meeting that goal.

Merchandising versus Manufacturing Companies

OBJECTIVE 5
Compare accounting for inventories and cost of goods sold for merchandising and manufacturing companies

Much of what you have learned about accounting has centered on the merchandising organization. But all businesses—especially manufacturing companies—need cost information. Here, we explain how the computation of the cost of goods sold differs between merchandising and manufacturing organizations.

A merchandising company normally buys a product that is ready for resale when it is received. Nothing needs to be done to the product to make it salable except possibly to prepare a special package or display. As shown in Figure 15-1, total beginning merchandise inventory plus net purchases is the basis for computing both the cost of goods sold and ending merchandise inventory. Costs assigned to unsold items make up the ending inventory balance. The difference between the cost of goods available for sale and the ending inventory balance is the cost of goods sold during the period:

Beginning merchandise inventory	$ 2,000
Add net purchases	8,000
Cost of goods available for sale	$10,000
Less ending merchandise inventory	2,700
Cost of goods sold	$ 7,300

Figure 15-1. Cost of Goods Sold: A Merchandising Company

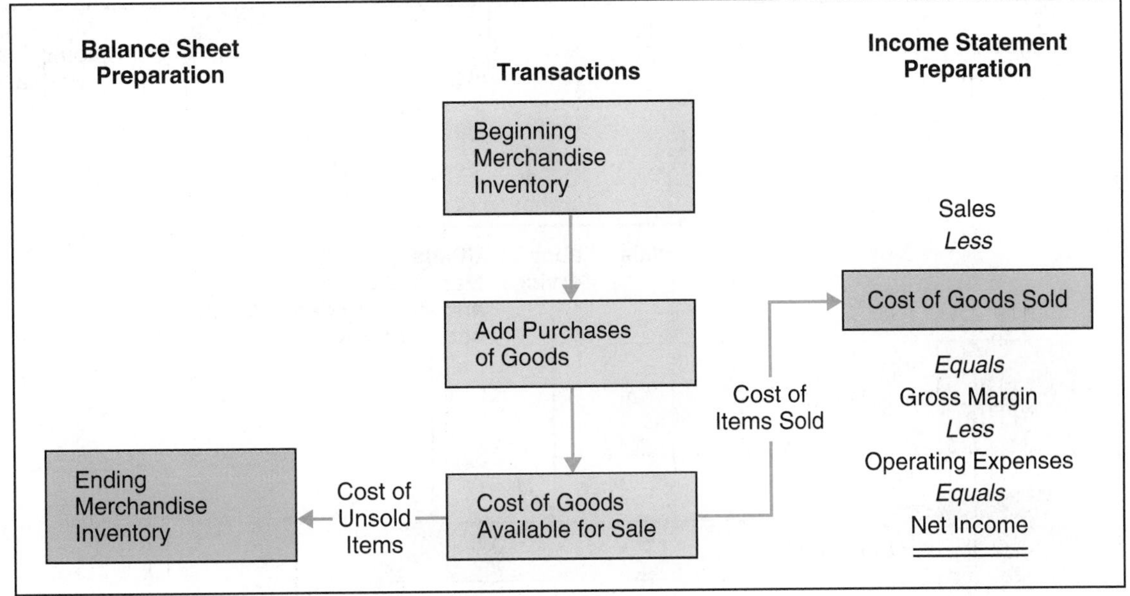

This example and Figure 15-1 show the procedure for computing the cost of goods sold for a merchandising company. Expenditures occur when goods are purchased. Any items unsold at period end make up the ending inventory balance. The cost of goods sold is computed by subtracting the ending inventory balance from the total of the beginning inventory balance and purchases made during the period.

Computing the cost of goods sold for a manufacturing company is more complex. As shown in Figure 15-2, instead of one inventory account, a manufacturer maintains three inventory accounts: Materials Inventory, Work in Process Inventory, and Finished Goods Inventory. Purchased materials unused during the production process make up the Materials Inventory balance. The cost of materials used plus the costs of labor services and factory overhead (utility costs, depreciation of factory machinery and building, supplies) are transferred to the Work in Process Inventory account once the materials, labor services, and overhead items are used in the production process.

The three types of costs discussed above often are called simply *materials, labor,* and *overhead.* These costs are accumulated in the Work in Process Inventory account during an accounting period. When a batch or order is completed, all manufacturing costs assigned to the completed units are moved to the Finished Goods Inventory account. The costs that remain in the Work in Process Inventory account belong to partly completed units. These costs make up the ending balance in the Work in Process Inventory account.

The Finished Goods Inventory account is set up in much the same way as the Ending Merchandise Inventory account in Figure 15-1. The costs of completed goods are entered into the Finished Goods Inventory account. As shown in Figure 15-2, costs attached to unsold items at year's end make up the ending balance in the Finished Goods Inventory account. All costs related to units sold are transferred to the Cost of Goods Sold account and reported on the income statement.

Figure 15-2. Cost of Goods Sold: A Manufacturing Company

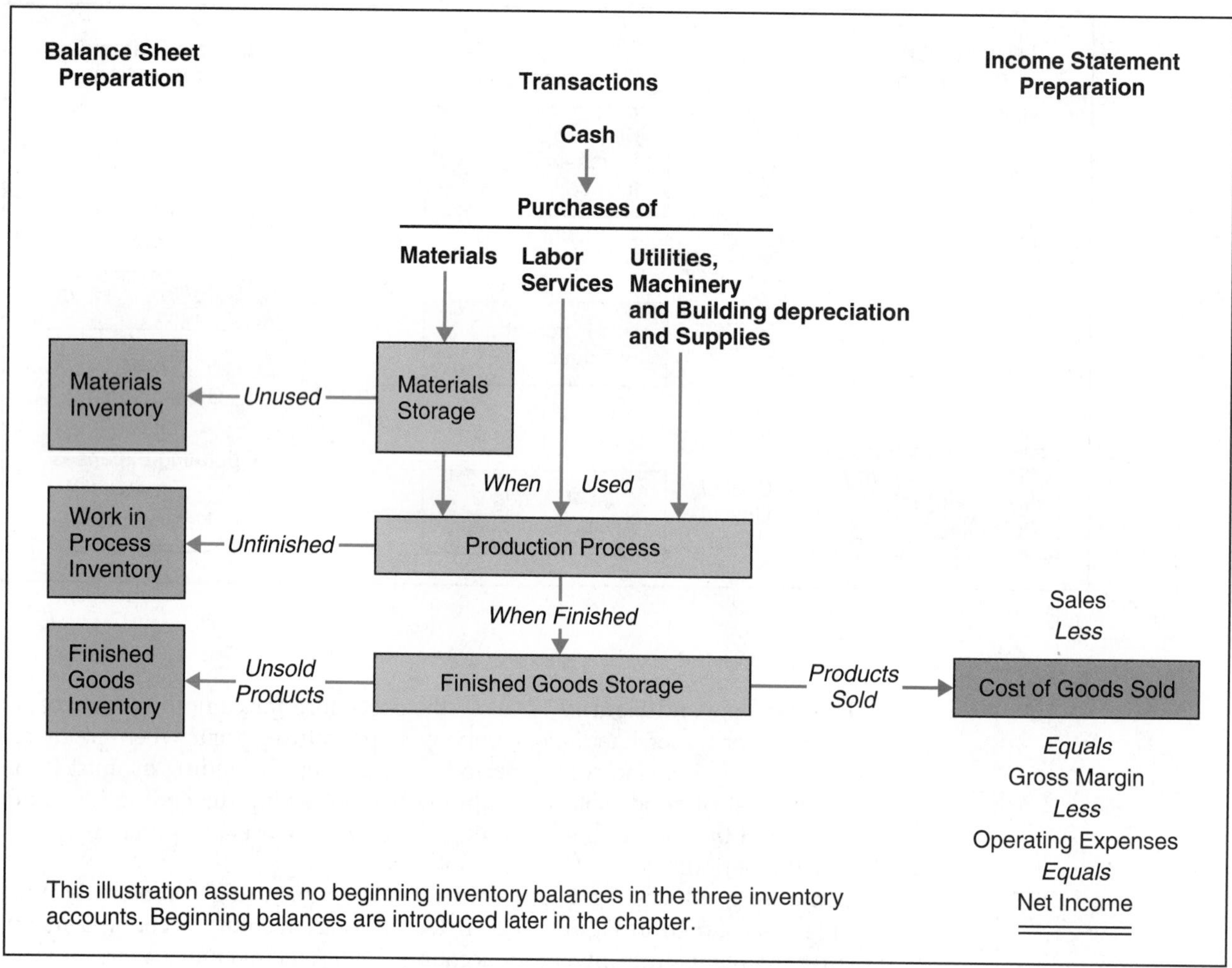

Manufacturing Cost Elements

OBJECTIVE 6
Define and give examples of the three manufacturing cost elements—direct materials costs, direct labor costs, and factory overhead costs—and compute a product's unit cost

Manufacturing costs include all costs related to the production process. They can be classified in many ways. The most common scheme groups manufacturing costs into one of three classes: (1) direct materials costs, (2) direct labor costs, or (3) indirect manufacturing costs, which often are called *factory overhead.* **Direct costs** can be traced easily to specific products. **Indirect costs** must be assigned to products by some cost assignment method.

Direct Materials Costs

All manufactured products are made from basic raw materials. The material may be iron ore for steel, sheet steel for automobiles, or flour for bread. **Direct materials** are materials that become part of a finished product and that can be conveniently and economically traced to specific product units. The costs of these materials are direct costs. Notice the words *conveniently* and *economically* in our definition of *direct materials.* In some cases, even though a material becomes part of a finished product, the time or expense involved in tracing its cost exceeds the benefits of doing so. For example, think about nails in furniture, bolts in automobiles, or rivets in airplanes. These minor materials and other production supplies that cannot be conveniently or economically traced to specific product units are accounted for as **indirect materials**. Indirect materials costs are part of factory overhead costs, which we discuss on the next page.

Direct Labor Costs

Manufacturing companies purchase labor services, both from employees working in the factory and from people and organizations outside the company. The labor costs usually associated with manufacturing include those for machine operators; setup and maintenance workers; managers and supervisors; support personnel; and employees who handle, inspect, and store materials. Because these people all are connected in some way with the production process, their wages and salaries must be accounted for as production costs and, finally, as a cost of the product.

Like direct materials costs, some labor costs are considered direct and some indirect. **Direct labor costs** include all labor costs for specific work performed on products that can be conveniently and economically traced to a product unit. The wages of machine operators are an example. Labor costs for production-related activities that cannot be conveniently or economically traced to a product unit are called **indirect labor costs**. These costs include the wages and salaries of machine helpers and other support personnel.[3] Even supervision costs can be classified as indirect labor. Like indirect materials costs, indirect labor costs are accounted for as factory overhead costs.

In addition to payroll costs, other labor-related manufacturing costs are created by agreement between management and labor and by government regulations. Management also can spend money voluntarily for the benefit of its employees. These labor-related costs fall into two main categories: employee benefits and employer payroll taxes. Employee benefits can include paid vacations, holiday and sick pay, a pension plan, life and medical insurance, performance bonuses, profit sharing, and recreational facilities. Employers also pay payroll-related taxes beyond those paid by the employee. For every dollar of social security and Medicare taxes withheld from workers' paychecks, employers usually pay an equal amount. They also must pay state and federal unemployment compensation taxes.

Most labor-related costs are incurred in direct proportion to wages and salaries earned by employees. As much as possible, labor-related costs that are dependent on direct labor costs and conveniently traceable to them should be accounted for as part of direct labor costs. All other labor-related costs should be classified as factory overhead.

Because of the size and complexity of payroll systems, most labor-related costs are not traced to individual employees. These costs normally are calculated from wages and salaries by means of a predetermined rate based on experience. For instance, a company may incur on average 12 cents of labor-related costs for every dollar of wages and salaries earned by employees. In this case, labor-related costs average 12 percent of labor costs. Therefore, if direct labor totals $6,000 for a period of time, total direct labor costs would be $6,720 ($6,000 plus 12 percent, or $720).

3. As production processes have become automated, costs such as machine setup, which initially were treated as indirect costs, have become traceable and now are classified as direct costs.

Factory Overhead

The third manufacturing cost element is a catchall for manufacturing costs that cannot be classified as direct materials or direct labor costs. **Factory overhead costs** are a varied collection of production-related costs that cannot be conveniently or economically traced directly to a product unit. This collection of costs also is called *manufacturing overhead, factory burden,* and *indirect manufacturing costs.* The following examples of the major classifications of factory overhead costs show how varied these costs are:

Indirect materials and supplies: Nails, rivets, lubricants, and small tools

Indirect labor costs: Lift-truck driver's wages, maintenance and inspection labor, engineering labor, machine helpers, and supervisors

Other factory overhead costs: Building maintenance, machinery and tool maintenance, property taxes, property insurance, pension costs, depreciation on plant and equipment, rent charges, and utility costs

A cost is classified a factory overhead cost when it cannot be traced directly to an end product. Yet a product's total cost obviously includes factory overhead costs. Somehow factory overhead costs must be identified and assigned to specific products or jobs. Methods for allocating costs are explained in the chapters on cost allocation and the job order costing system, and activity-based costing.

Determining Unit Cost

Direct materials costs, direct labor costs, and factory overhead costs constitute total manufacturing costs for a period of time or batch of products. The product unit cost for each completed job is computed by dividing the total cost of materials, labor, and factory overhead for that job by the total units produced. For example, assume that Howard Products, Inc. produced 3,000 units of output for Job 12K. Costs for Job 12K included the following: direct materials, $3,000; direct labor, $5,400; and factory overhead, $2,700. The product unit cost for Job 12K is $3.70:

Direct materials ($3,000 ÷ 3,000 units)	$1.00
Direct labor ($5,400 ÷ 3,000 units)	1.80
Factory overhead ($2,700 ÷ 3,000 units)	.90
Product unit cost ($11,100 ÷ 3,000 units)	$3.70

In this case, the unit cost was computed when the job ended, when all information was known. What if a company needs this information a month before a job starts, perhaps because it is pricing a proposed product for a customer? Here, unit cost figures have to be estimated. Assume that accounting personnel have developed the following estimates for another product: $2.50 per unit for direct materials, $4.50 per unit for direct labor, and 50 percent of direct labor costs for factory overhead. The estimated unit cost would be $9.25:

Direct materials	$2.50
Direct labor	4.50
Factory overhead ($4.50 × 50%)	2.25
Product unit cost	$9.25

The $9.25 unit cost is an estimate, but it is still useful for job costing and as a starting point for product pricing decisions.

Manufacturing Inventory Accounts

OBJECTIVE 7
Describe the contents and flow of costs through the Materials Inventory, Work in Process Inventory, and Finished Goods Inventory accounts

Most manufacturing companies use the perpetual inventory approach. In the remaining sections of this book, you should assume that a company uses the perpetual inventory system unless otherwise indicated.[4] Accounting for inventories is more complicated in manufacturing accounting than in merchandising accounting. Instead of dealing with one inventory account—Merchandise Inventory—manufacturing accounting traditionally uses three accounts: Materials Inventory, Work in Process Inventory, and Finished Goods Inventory.

Materials Inventory

The **Materials Inventory** account, also called the Stores, Raw Materials Inventory, or Materials Inventory Control account, is made up of the balances of materials, parts, and supplies on hand. This account is maintained in much the same way as the Merchandise Inventory account. The main difference is in the way that the costs of items in inventory are assigned. For a manufacturing company, materials, parts, and supplies are purchased for use in the production of a product; they are not purchased for direct resale. When an item is taken out of materials inventory and requisitioned into production, its cost is transferred to the Work in Process Inventory account. Figure 15-3 shows how it works. On January 1, 19xx, the Materials Inventory account had a beginning balance of $17,500. Over the year, purchases totaled $142,600; this amount was debited to the account. During 19xx, goods costing $139,700 were requisitioned into production. This transaction was accounted for by debiting the Work in Process Inventory account and crediting the Materials Inventory account for the amount requisitioned. At the end of the period, the balance in the Materials Inventory account was $20,400 ($17,500 + $142,600 – $139,700).

Figure 15-3. Accounting for Materials Inventory

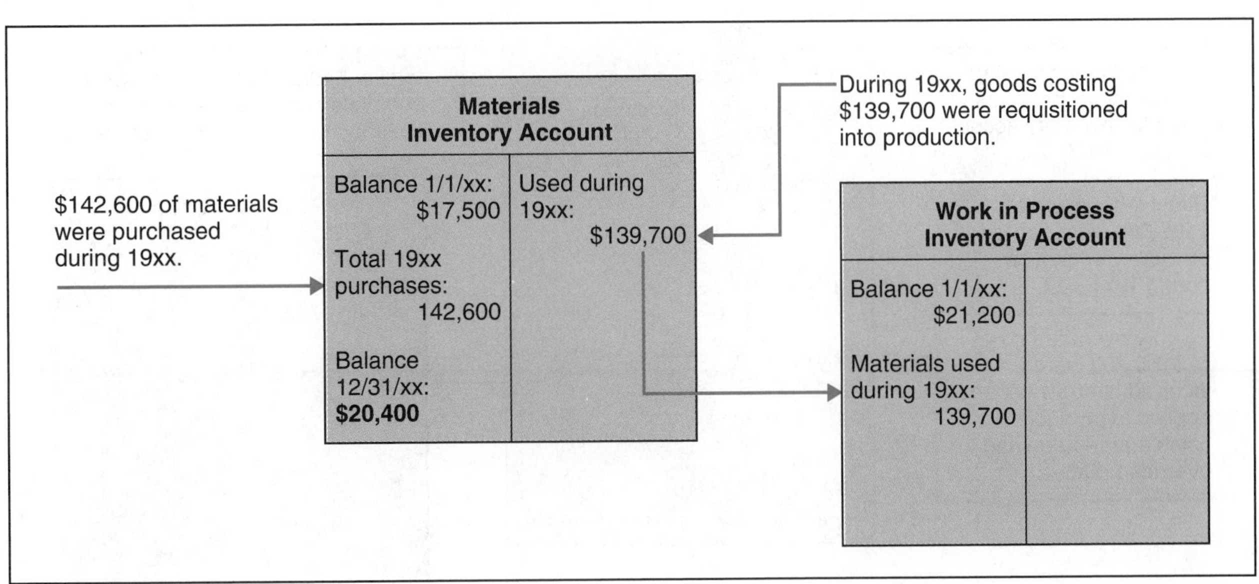

4. Both the periodic and perpetual inventory systems were discussed in the chapter on inventories. If you do not remember the distinction between the two inventory systems, review them before continuing with your study of management accounting.

Work in Process Inventory

All manufacturing costs incurred and assigned to products being produced are transferred to the **Work in Process Inventory** account. This inventory account has no counterpart in merchandise accounting. Figure 15-4 shows activity in the account over the year.

The beginning balance in the account was $21,200. The production process begins as materials are requisitioned into production. These materials must be cut, molded, assembled, or in some other way changed into a finished product. To make this change, people, machines, and other factory resources (buildings, electricity, supplies, and so on) are used. All of these costs are manufacturing cost elements, and all of them are accumulated in the Work in Process Inventory account. The materials cost flow, a total of $139,700, was debited to the account shown in Figure 15-4.

Direct labor dollars earned by factory employees are also product costs. Because these people work on specific products, their labor costs are assigned to those products by including the labor dollars earned as part of the Work in Process Inventory account. (Specific product costing techniques are the topic of the chapters on cost allocation and the job order costing system, and the process cost system. At this point, you should assume that all direct labor costs are debited to the Work in Process Inventory account.) In Figure 15-4, direct labor costs of $199,000 were earned by factory employees during 19xx and were debited to the Work in Process Inventory account.

Overhead costs also must be assigned to specific products. They, too, are included in the Work in Process Inventory account. To reduce the amount of work

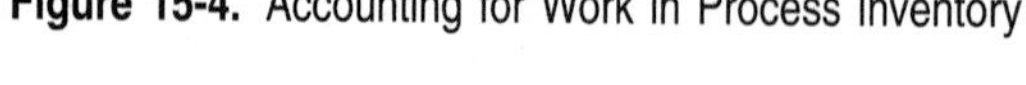

Figure 15-4. Accounting for Work in Process Inventory

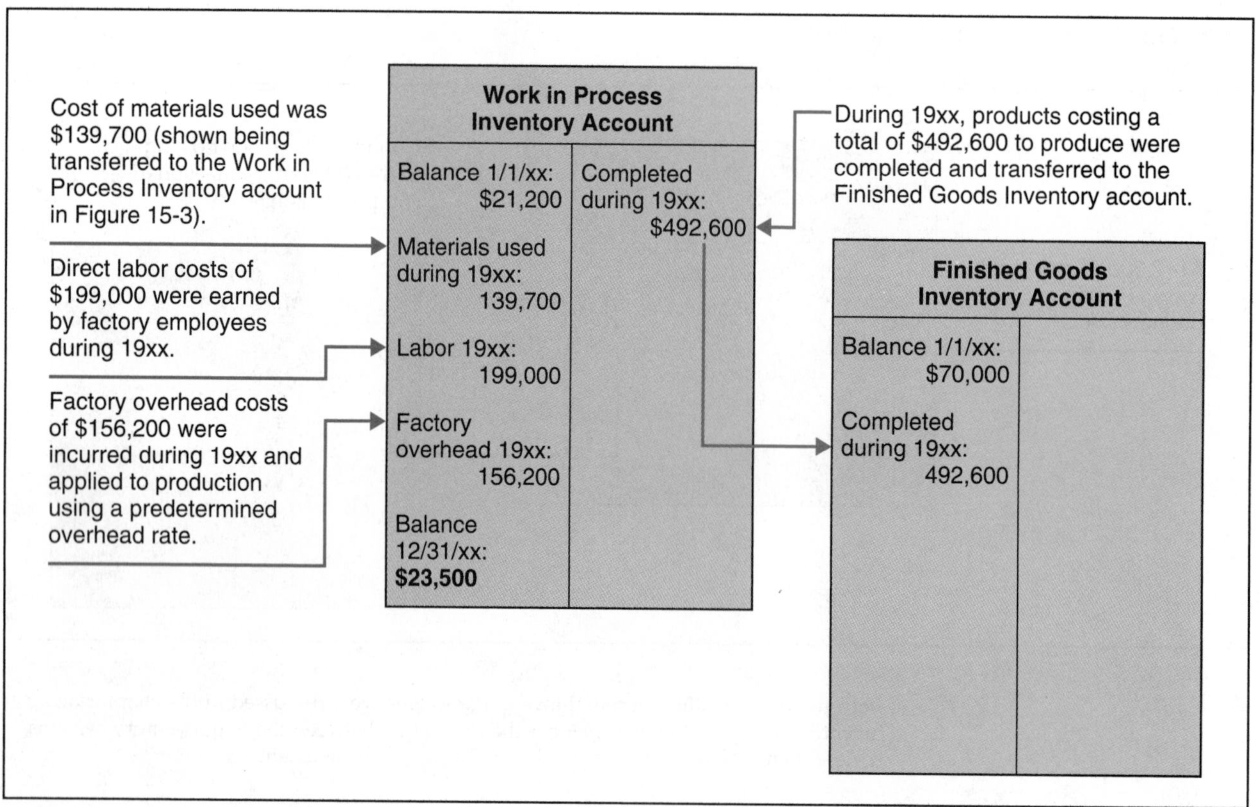

needed to assign these costs to specific products, overhead costs are accumulated in one account, Factory Overhead Control. These costs then are assigned to products using a predetermined overhead rate. (The predetermined overhead rate is discussed in the chapter on cost allocation and the job order costing system.) Using this rate, costs are transferred from the Factory Overhead Control account to the Work in Process Inventory account. In the example in Figure 15-4, factory overhead costs of $156,200 were debited to the Work in Process Inventory account.

As products are completed, they are moved into the finished goods storage area. These inventoried products now have materials, direct labor, and factory overhead costs assigned to them. Because these products are completed, their costs no longer belong to work (products) in process. So they are transferred to the Finished Goods Inventory account. As shown in Figure 15-4, completed products costing $492,600 were sent to the storage area, and their costs were transferred from the Work in Process Inventory account to the Finished Goods Inventory account. The balance remaining in the Work in Process Inventory account ($23,500) represents the costs assigned to products that were still in process at the end of the period.

Finished Goods Inventory

The **Finished Goods Inventory** account holds the costs assigned to all completed products that have not been sold. This account, like Materials Inventory, shares some characteristics with the Merchandise Inventory account. When goods or products are sold, their costs are transferred to the Cost of Goods Sold account. During 19xx, products costing $486,100 to produce were sold for $750,000. As shown in Figure 15-5, these costs were debited to Cost of Goods Sold and credited to Finished Goods Inventory. At the end of the accounting period, the balance in the Finished Goods Inventory account ($76,500) equaled the cost of products completed but unsold as of that date.

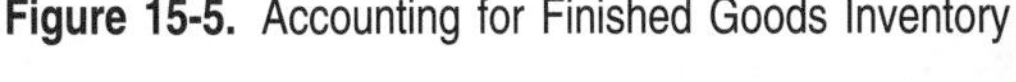

Figure 15-5. Accounting for Finished Goods Inventory

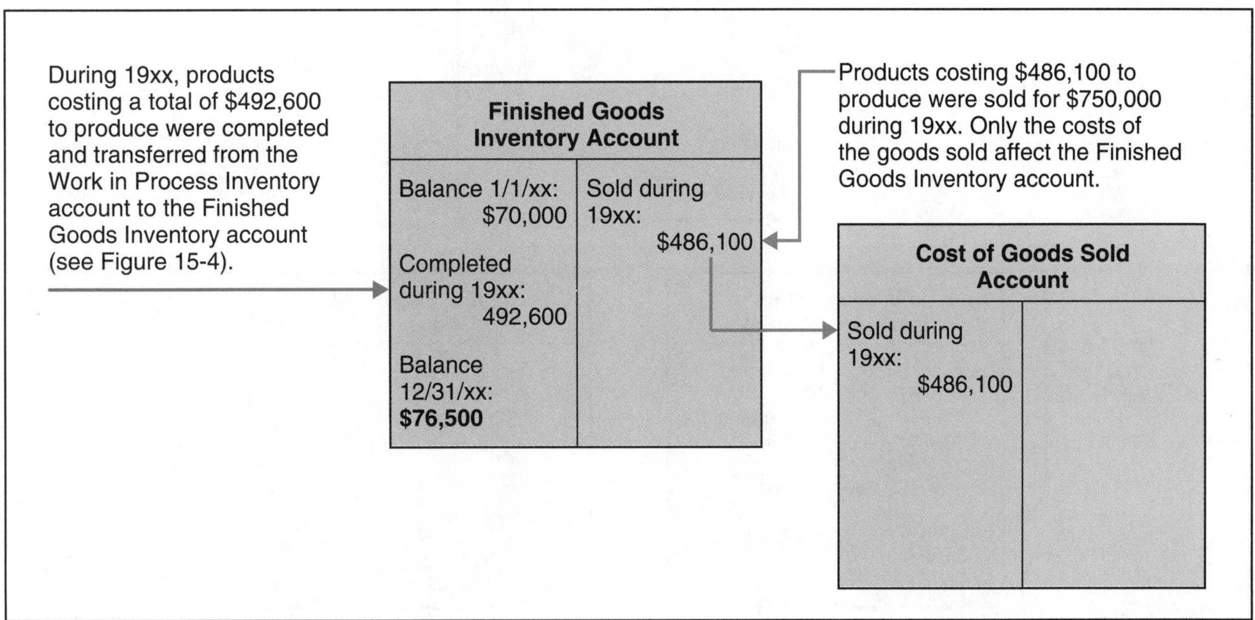

The Manufacturing Cost Flow

A defined, structured flow of manufacturing costs is the foundation for product costing, inventory valuation, and financial reporting. We outlined this manufacturing cost flow in our discussion of the three manufacturing inventory accounts. Figure 15-6 summarizes the entire cost-flow process as it relates to accounts in the general ledger.

Figure 15-6. Manufacturing Cost Flow: An Example

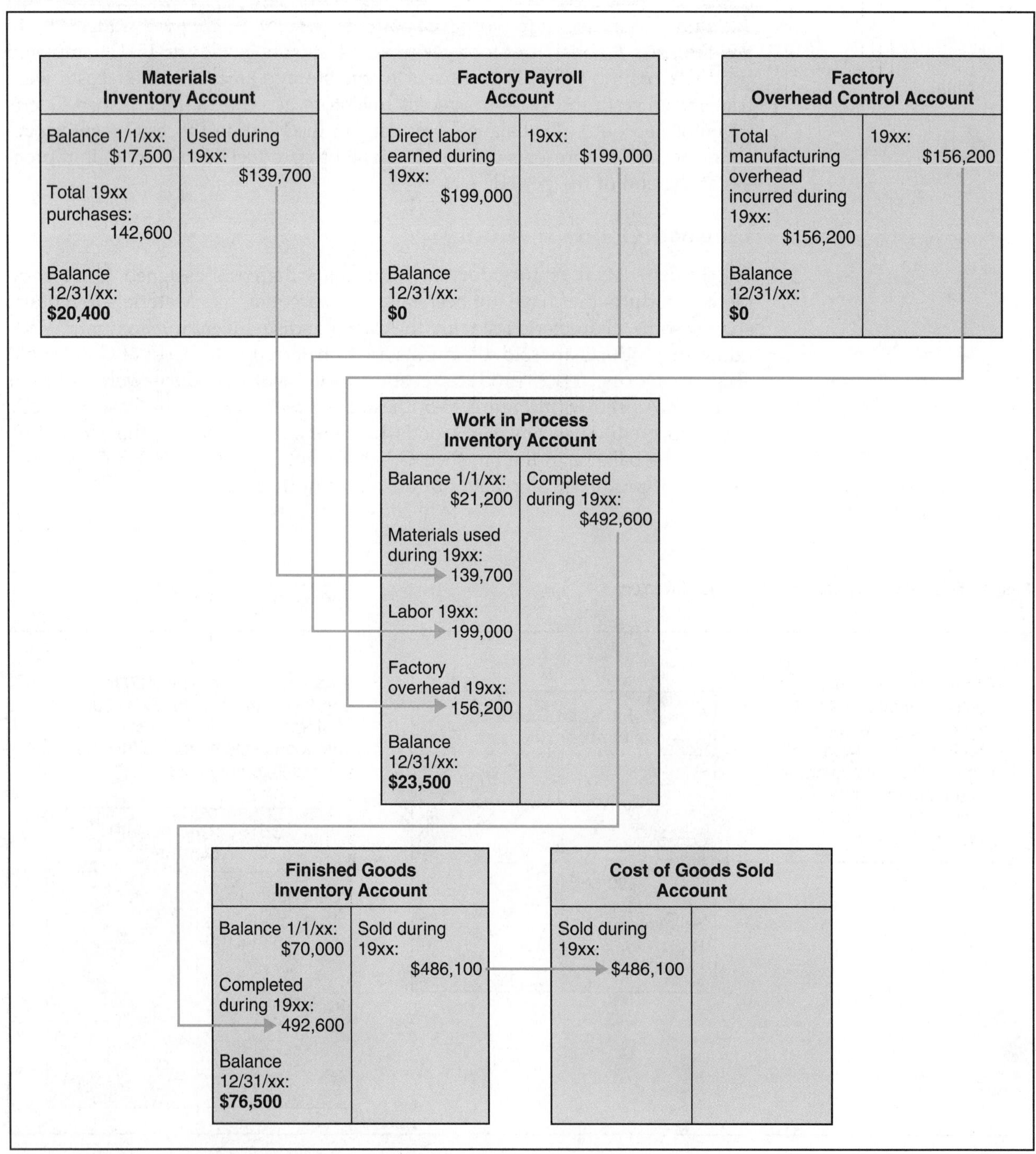

Manufacturing and Reporting

OBJECTIVE 8
Prepare a statement of cost of goods manufactured and an income statement for a manufacturing company

The financial statements of manufacturing companies differ very little from those of merchandising companies. (For a review of the financial statements used by merchandising companies, see the chapter on accounting for merchandising operations.) Account titles on the balance sheets of manufacturers are similar to those used by merchandisers. The primary difference between the balance sheets is the use of three inventory accounts by manufacturing companies versus only one by merchandising companies. Even the income statements for a merchandiser and a manufacturer are similar. However, manufacturers use the heading Cost of Goods Manufactured in place of the Purchases account. Also, the Merchandise Inventory account is replaced by the Finished Goods Inventory account. Notice these differences in the income statement shown in Exhibit 15-4.

The key to preparing an income statement for a manufacturing company is to determine the cost of goods manufactured. This dollar amount is calculated on the statement of cost of goods manufactured. This special statement is based

Exhibit 15-4. Income Statement for a Manufacturing Company

Windham Company
Income Statement
For the Year Ended December 31, 19xx

Net Sales			$750,000
Cost of Goods Sold			
Finished Goods Inventory, Jan. 1, 19xx		**$ 70,000**	
Cost of Goods Manufactured (Exhibit 15-5)		**492,600**	
Total Cost of Finished Goods Available for Sale		**$562,600**	
Less Finished Goods Inventory, Dec. 31, 19xx		**76,500**	
Cost of Goods Sold			**486,100**
Gross Margin from Sales			$263,900
Operating Expenses			
Selling Expenses			
Salaries and Commissions	$46,500		
Advertising	19,500		
Other Selling Expenses	7,400		
Total Selling Expenses		$ 73,400	
General and Administrative Expenses			
Administrative Salaries	$65,000		
Franchise and Property Taxes	72,000		
Other General and Administrative Expenses	11,300		
Total General and Administrative Expenses		148,300	
Total Operating Expenses			221,700
Income from Operations			$ 42,200
Less Interest Expense			4,600
Net Income Before Taxes			$ 37,600
Less Income Taxes Expense			11,548
Net Income			$ 26,052

on the classification of costs into categories known as product costs and period costs.

Product and Period Costs

Costs are classified as product or period costs for many reasons, among them (1) to determine unit manufacturing costs so that inventories can be valued and selling prices created and verified, (2) to report production costs on the income statement, and (3) to analyze costs for control purposes. **Product costs** consist of the three manufacturing cost elements: direct materials, direct labor, and factory overhead. They are incurred when making products and can be inventoried. That is, product costs flow through the materials, work in process, and finished goods inventories before becoming part of the cost of goods sold. They are used to compute ending inventory balances and the cost of goods sold. Product costs also can be considered unexpired costs because, as inventory balances, they are assets of the company and are expected to benefit future operations. Product costs alone make up the statement of cost of goods manufactured.

Both product and period costs are found on the income statement. **Period costs** are costs that cannot be inventoried; they are costs for services consumed during the current period. For example, selling and administrative expenses are period costs because selling and administrative resources are used up in the same period in which they originate. Period costs are not used to determine a product's unit cost or to establish ending inventory balances.

Statement of Cost of Goods Manufactured

The flow of manufacturing costs, shown in Figures 15-3 through 15-6, provides the basis for accounting for manufacturing costs. In this process, all manufacturing costs incurred are considered product costs. They are used to compute ending inventory balances and the cost of goods sold. In these figures, the costs flowing from one account to another during the year are combined into one number to show the basic idea. In fact, hundreds of transactions occur during a year, and each transaction affects part of the cost flow process. At the end of the year, the flow of all manufacturing costs incurred during the year is summarized in the **statement of cost of goods manufactured**. This statement gives the dollar amount of costs for products completed and moved to finished goods inventory during the year. The cost of goods manufactured should be the same as the amount transferred from the Work in Process Inventory account to the Finished Goods Inventory account during the year.

The statement of cost of goods manufactured is shown in Exhibit 15-5. This statement is complex, so we piece it together in three steps. The first step is to compute the cost of materials used. To do this, we add the materials purchases for the period to the beginning balance in the Materials Inventory account. This subtotal represents the cost of materials available for use during the period. Then, we subtract the ending balance of Materials Inventory from the cost of materials available for use. The difference is the cost of materials used during the accounting period.

Computation of Cost of Materials Used

Beginning Balance Materials Inventory	$ 17,500
Add Materials Purchases (net)	142,600
Cost of Materials Available for Use	$160,100
Less Ending Balance Materials Inventory	20,400
Cost of Materials Used	**$139,700**

Exhibit 15-5. Statement of Cost of Goods Manufactured

Windham Company
Statement of Cost of Goods Manufactured
For the Year Ended December 31, 19xx

Step One	Materials Used		
	Materials Inventory, Jan. 1, 19xx	$ 17,500	
	Materials Purchases (net)	142,600	
	Cost of Materials Available for Use	$160,100	
	Less Materials Inventory, December 31, 19xx	20,400	
	Cost of Materials Used		$139,700
Step Two	Direct Labor Costs		199,000
	Factory Overhead Costs		
	Indirect Labor	$ 46,400	
	Power	25,200	
	Depreciation Expense, Machinery and Equipment	14,800	
	Depreciation Expense, Factory Building	16,200	
	Small Tools Expense	2,700	
	Factory Insurance Expense	1,600	
	Supervision Expense	37,900	
	Other Factory Costs	11,400	
	Total Factory Overhead Costs		156,200
	Total Manufacturing Costs		$494,900
Step Three	Add Work in Process Inventory, January 1, 19xx		21,200
	Total Cost of Work in Process During the Year		$516,100
	Less Work in Process Inventory, December 31, 19xx		23,500
	Cost of Goods Manufactured		$492,600

Before going on to the next step, trace these numbers back to the Materials Inventory account in Figure 15-3 to see how that account is related to the statement of cost of goods manufactured.

Calculating total manufacturing costs for the year is the second step. As shown in Figure 15-4, the costs of materials used and direct labor are added to total factory overhead costs incurred during the year:

Computation of Total Manufacturing Costs

Cost of Materials Used	$139,700
Add Direct Labor Costs	199,000
Add Total Factory Overhead Costs	156,200
Total Manufacturing Costs	$494,900

The third step shown in Exhibit 15-5 changes total manufacturing costs into the total cost of goods manufactured for the period. The beginning Work in Process Inventory balance is added to total manufacturing costs for the period to arrive at the total cost of work in process during the period. From this amount, the ending Work in Process Inventory balance is subtracted to get the cost of goods manufactured:

Computation of Cost of Goods Manufactured

Total Manufacturing Costs	**$494,900**
Add Beginning Balance Work in Process Inventory	21,200
Total Cost of Work in Process During the Year	$516,100
Less Ending Balance Work in Process Inventory	23,500
Cost of Goods Manufactured	**$492,600**

The term *total manufacturing costs* should not be confused with the cost of goods manufactured. **Total manufacturing costs** are the total costs for materials used, direct labor, and factory overhead incurred and charged to production during an accounting period. The **cost of goods manufactured** consists of the total manufacturing costs attached to units of a product *completed* during an accounting period. To understand the difference between these two dollar amounts, look again at the computations above. Total manufacturing costs of $494,900 incurred during the year are added to the beginning balance in Work in Process Inventory. Costs of $21,200 in the beginning balance, by definition, are costs from an earlier period. The costs of two accounting periods are now being mixed to arrive at the total cost of work in process during the year, $516,100. The costs of products still in process ($23,500) then are subtracted from the total cost of work in process during the year. The remainder, $492,600, is the cost of goods manufactured (completed) during the year. It is assumed that the items in beginning inventory were completed first. The costs attached to the ending balance of Work in Process Inventory are part of the current period's total manufacturing costs. But they will not become part of the cost of goods manufactured until the next accounting period, when the products are completed.

Cost of Goods Sold and the Income Statement

Exhibits 15-4 and 15-5 demonstrate the relationship between the income statement and the statement of cost of goods manufactured. The total amount of the cost of goods manufactured during the period is carried over to the income statement. There, it is used to compute the cost of goods sold. The cost of goods manufactured is added to the beginning balance of Finished Goods Inventory to get the total cost of finished goods available for sale during the period. The cost of goods sold then is computed by subtracting the ending balance in Finished Goods Inventory (the cost of goods completed but not sold) from the total cost of finished goods available for sale. The cost of goods sold is considered an expense in the period in which the related products are sold.

Computation of Cost of Goods Sold

Beginning Balance Finished Goods Inventory	$ 70,000
Add Cost of Goods Manufactured	**492,600**
Total Cost of Finished Goods Available for Sale	$562,600
Less Ending Balance Finished Goods Inventory	76,500
Cost of Goods Sold	$486,100

Notice that this computation is similar to the computation of the cost of goods sold in the income statement in Exhibit 15-4. The other parts of the income statement in Exhibit 15-4 should be familiar from financial accounting.

Standards of Ethical Conduct for Management Accountants

OBJECTIVE 9
Identify the standards of ethical conduct for management accountants, and recognize activities that are not ethical

Credibility is crucial to the accounting profession. And that credibility demands that accountants adhere to high standards of ethical conduct. In your study of financial accounting, you analyzed the ethical standards that have been developed for public accountants. Ethical standards are equally important for management accountants. On June 1, 1983, the Institute of Management Accountants, formerly called the National Association of Accountants, formally adopted standards of ethical conduct for management accountants.[5] These standards specify responsibilities for competence, confidentiality, integrity, and objectivity.

Competence

In order to act ethically, management accountants first of all must be competent. In our rapidly changing world, a professional's skills can become obsolete very quickly. To keep current with management accounting issues and skills, management accountants should attend professional development and continuing education programs on an ongoing basis.

The competence required of management accountants is also far-reaching. The accountant must understand and follow all relevant laws, regulations, and technical standards that pertain to his or her duties. Professional competence must be maintained at all times when dealing with one's own company, outside entities (customers, vendors, and contractors) associated with that company, and the world marketplace in general. Furthermore, in order to develop information and reports for management, management accountants must research relevant information and approaches. Reports, financial analyses, and statements must reveal all necessary information, follow current reporting standards, and clearly state the accountant's findings.

Confidentiality

Management accountants are entrusted with information considered confidential and proprietary by management. In many cases, reports generated by the management accountant have a direct bearing on a company's profitability. Leaks of such information could give competitors an unfair advantage. Information should not be communicated to anyone, inside or outside the organization, who is not authorized to receive it, except when disclosure is required by law.

In the conduct of their responsibilities, management accountants often supervise other accountants. These subordinates should be informed whenever they are dealing with confidential or restricted information. Furthermore, the management accountant must monitor subordinates' actions to ensure that confidentiality is maintained.

Disclosure, of course, is not the only way of breaking confidentiality. It is also unethical to use confidential information, directly or through third parties,

5. Institute of Management Accountants, *Statement No. 1C*, "Standards of Ethical Conduct for Management Accountants" (Montvale, N.J., June 1, 1983).

for personal gain or to cause harm to the company, again unless the accountant is obligated legally to disclose the information.

Integrity

A management accountant must be impartial. To meet this obligation, the management accountant must avoid all actual or apparent conflicts of interest. For example, owning stock in a company that is competing with other vendors for business with his or her company is a potential conflict of interest if the accountant has direct input into the selection of vendors. The management accountant is responsible for informing all appropriate parties of the potential conflict.

The management accountant should refrain from relationships with individuals or organizations that could cause possible conflicts of interest or compromise the accountant's work. Gifts, favors, or special hospitality from an individual or organization should not be accepted.

Realistic (not blind) loyalty to one's company, industry, and country is an important aspect of integrity. Performing an act or encouraging an activity that threatens the organization's legitimate and ethical objectives is not ethical. If a management accountant gains information about disloyal, incompetent, or illegal acts that threaten the company in any way, he or she must communicate that information to management.

Management accounting reports must be accurate and truthful, regardless of whether their findings have a positive or a negative impact on the company. It is not ethical to alter a report so that targets are met or expectations exceeded.

Objectivity

The management accountant is responsible for all financial as well as many nonfinancial reports to management. Management relies on those reports to make operating decisions; and so, indirectly, do outsiders—investors, creditors, vendors, and customers. All of these people have a right to expect objective information, and the management accountant must supply it.

Internal managers in particular depend on the information generated by the management accountant. Following ethical standards is critical to carrying out these reporting responsibilities. Familiarity with ethical standards and the ability to recognize unethical actions and to avoid compromising situations should be an integral part of your knowledge and skills when you begin a career in the business world.

Chapter Review

Review of Learning Objectives

1. **Define *management accounting* and identify the major information needs of managers.**
   Management accounting is the process of identifying, measuring, accumulating, analyzing, preparing, interpreting, and communicating information used by management to plan, evaluate, and control the organization and to ensure that its resources are used and accounted for appropriately. The financial and production data generated by management accountants help managers assign costs to products or services and calculate unit costs, plan and control operations, and support their decisions.

2. **Distinguish between management accounting and financial accounting.**
There are seven areas in which the differences between management accounting and financial accounting can be compared. (1) People and organizations outside the business unit are the primary users of financial accounting information, whereas managers at all levels within the organization use management accounting information. (2) There is no restriction on the types of accounting systems that can be used in management accounting, but financial accounting centers on the double-entry system. (3) Restrictive guidelines for financial accounting are made up of generally accepted accounting principles; management accounting's only restriction is that the information be useful. (4) The historical dollar is the primary unit of measurement in financial accounting; any useful unit of measurement can be used in management accounting. (5) The business unit as a whole is the focal point of analysis in financial accounting; a management accounting analysis can focus on a division, a department, or even a machine. (6) Financial accountants prepare financial statements on a regular, periodic basis; management accountants report on an as-needed basis. (7) Financial accounting deals with data about transactions that have happened, and therefore demands objectivity; management accounting often focuses on the future and can be heavily subjective.

3. **Compare the information needs of a manager of a manufacturing company, a bank, and a department store.**
All managers need certain types of information to help them budget, make operating decisions, manage cash, and plan for capital expenditures. But the nature of a business also creates special information needs. For example, a manufacturer needs product costing information and data to help control the various types of inventory. A banker relies on special analyses to manage and control depositors' funds. And a department store manager needs merchandise control information.

4. **Prepare analyses of nonfinancial data.**
The management accountant always has been responsible for nonfinancial data analyses. Today's globally competitive operating environment has created additional demand for nonfinancial analyses centered on increasing the quality of the firm's products or services, reducing production and delivery time, and satisfying customers. Among the performance measures used in these analyses are units of output, time measures, and scrap incurrence rates.

5. **Compare accounting for inventories and cost of goods sold for merchandising and manufacturing companies.**
The merchandising firm purchases a product that is ready for resale when it is received. Only one account, Merchandise Inventory, is used to record and account for items in inventory. And the cost of goods sold is simply the difference between the cost of goods available for sale and ending merchandise inventory. The manufacturing company, because it creates a product, maintains three inventory accounts: Materials Inventory, Work in Process Inventory, and Finished Goods Inventory. Manufacturing costs flow through all three inventory accounts. At the end of the accounting period, the cost of completed products is transferred to the Finished Goods Inventory account; the cost of units that have been sold is transferred to the Cost of Goods Sold account.

6. **Define and give examples of the three manufacturing cost elements—direct materials costs, direct labor costs, and factory overhead costs—and compute a product's unit cost.**
Direct materials are materials that become part of the finished product and that can be conveniently and economically traced to specific product units. The sheet metal used to manufacture cars is an example of a direct material. Direct labor costs include all labor costs for specific work performed on products that can be conveniently and economically traced to end products. A machine operator's wages are a direct labor cost. All other production-related costs—for utilities, depreciation on equipment, and operating supplies, for example—are classified and accounted for as factory overhead costs. These costs cannot be conveniently or economically traced to end products, so they are assigned to products by some cost allocation method. The

unit cost of a product is made up of the costs of materials, labor, and factory overhead. These three cost components are accumulated for a batch of products as they are produced. Then, the number of units produced is divided into the total costs incurred to determine the product's unit cost.

7. **Describe the contents and flow of costs through the Materials Inventory, Work in Process Inventory, and Finished Goods Inventory accounts.**
The flow of costs through inventory accounts begins when costs are incurred for materials, direct labor, and factory overhead. Materials costs flow first into the Materials Inventory account, which is used to record the costs of materials when they are received and again when they are issued for use in a company's production process. All manufacturing-related costs—materials, direct labor, and factory overhead—are recorded in the Work in Process Inventory account as the production process begins. When products are completed, their costs are transferred from the Work in Process Inventory account to the Finished Goods Inventory account. Costs remain in the Finished Goods Inventory account until the products are sold, at which time they are transferred to the Cost of Goods Sold account.

8. **Prepare a statement of cost of goods manufactured and an income statement for a manufacturing company.**
The cost of goods manufactured is a key component of the income statement for a manufacturing company. Determining the cost of goods manufactured involves three steps. The first is computing the cost of materials used; the second is computing total manufacturing costs for the period; and the third is computing the cost of goods manufactured. This last figure, taken from the statement of cost of goods manufactured, is used in the income statement to compute the cost of goods sold.

9. **Identify the standards of ethical conduct for management accountants, and recognize activities that are not ethical.**
Standards of ethical conduct govern the management accountant's competence, confidentiality, integrity, and objectivity. These standards help the management accountant recognize and avoid situations and activities that compromise his or her honesty, loyalty, and ability to supply management with accurate and relevant information.

Review of Concepts and Terminology

The following concepts and terms were introduced in this chapter:

(L.O. 8) **Cost of goods manufactured:** The total manufacturing costs attached to units of a product completed during an accounting period.

(L.O. 6) **Direct costs:** Production costs that can be traced easily to specific products.

(L.O. 6) **Direct labor costs:** All labor costs for specific work performed on products that can be conveniently and economically traced to a product unit.

(L.O. 6) **Direct materials:** Materials that become part of the finished product and that can be conveniently and economically traced to specific product units.

(L.O. 6) **Factory overhead costs:** A collection of production-related costs that cannot be conveniently or economically traced directly to a product unit.

(L.O. 7) **Finished Goods Inventory:** The inventory account that holds the costs assigned to all completed products that have not been sold.

(L.O. 6) **Indirect costs:** Production costs that are not traced easily to specific products and that must be assigned by some cost assignment method.

(L.O. 6) **Indirect labor costs:** Labor costs for production-related activities that cannot be conveniently or economically traced to a product unit.

(L.O. 6) **Indirect materials:** Minor materials and other production supplies that cannot be conveniently or economically traced to specific product units.

(L.O. 1) **Management accounting:** The process of identifying, measuring, accumulating, analyzing, preparing, interpreting, and communicating financial and nonfinancial information used by management to plan, evaluate, and control the organization and to ensure that resources are used and accounted for appropriately.

(L.O. 7) **Manufacturing cost flow:** The flow of manufacturing costs (direct materials, direct labor, and factory overhead) through the Materials Inventory, Work in Process Inventory, and Finished Goods Inventory accounts to the Cost of Goods Sold account.

(L.O. 7) **Materials Inventory:** An inventory account made up of the balances of materials and supplies on hand at a given time. Also called the Stores or Materials Inventory Control account.

(L.O. 8) **Period costs:** Operating costs for services consumed during the accounting period that cannot be inventoried.

(L.O. 8) **Product costs:** The direct materials, direct labor, and factory overhead costs that are incurred in the manufacturing process and that can be inventoried.

(L.O. 8) **Statement of cost of goods manufactured:** A formal statement that summarizes the flow of all manufacturing costs incurred during an accounting period.

(L.O. 8) **Total manufacturing costs:** The total costs for materials used, direct labor, and factory overhead incurred and charged to production during an accounting period.

(L.O. 7) **Work in Process Inventory:** An inventory account that includes all manufacturing costs incurred and assigned to products that are being produced.

Self-Test

Test your knowledge of the chapter by choosing the best answer for each of the following items.

(L.O. 1) 1. When collectively applied to a company's financial, production, and distribution data, management accounting procedures
   a. guarantee the company's profitability.
   b. satisfy all of the needs of the Internal Revenue Service.
   c. satisfy management's information needs.
   d. represent the union's basic collective bargaining agreement.

(L.O. 2) 2. Which of the following statements is false?
   a. Management is responsible for a company's annual financial statements, statements that communicate information primarily to external users.
   b. Management accountants are not restricted to using the historical dollar; they can employ any unit of measurement that meets management's information needs.
   c. Financial accounting has just one real guideline: The accounting practice or technique used must produce useful information.
   d. Typically, financial accountants record and report information on the assets, liabilities, owner's equity, and net income of a company as a whole.

(L.O. 3) 3. Of the reports and analyses listed below, which would be equally important to the management of a manufacturing company, a bank, and a department store?
   a. A budget analysis
   b. A service-line management report
   c. A make-or-buy decision analysis
   d. A production planning report

(L.O. 4) 4. Nonfinancial data analysis is an important part of the management accountant's responsibilities because
   a. nonfinancial data analyses are more important to internal management than financial data reports.
   b. internal management needs information on the nonfinancial as well as the financial aspects of the business.
   c. machine hours cannot be stated in terms of dollars.
   d. external financial statements contain only nonfinancial data.

(L.O. 6) 5. Holly Company produced 5,500 outdoor chairs for Order A16. The total cost of materials was $51,700. Each chair required .6 hours of direct labor at $8.90 per hour. A total of $53,845 of factory overhead was allocated to Order A16. What is the unit cost of the order?
a. $14.74
b. $24.53
c. $19.19
d. $28.09

(L.O. 7) 6. All manufacturing costs incurred and assigned to products currently being produced are classified as
a. finished goods inventory costs.
b. materials inventory costs.
c. work in process inventory costs.
d. the cost of goods sold.

(L.O. 8) 7. If the beginning balance of the Materials Inventory account was $8,400, the ending balance was $7,880, and $43,120 of materials were used during the month, how much did the materials purchased during this time period cost?
a. $43,200
b. $43,640
c. $43,580
d. $42,600

(L.O. 8) 8. If the ending work in process inventory totaled $23,250, total manufacturing costs for the month were $99,220, and the beginning balance in the Work in Process Inventory account was $21,840, how much was the cost of goods manufactured for the period?
a. $97,810
b. $100,630
c. $97,510
d. $100,330

(L.O. 8) 9. The Storker Company had a month-end cost of goods sold of $393,910, a beginning finished goods inventory of $40,410, and an ending finished goods inventory of $42,900. What was the total cost of completed goods transferred to the Finished Goods Inventory account during the month?
a. $391,420
b. $391,120
c. $396,400
d. $393,400

(L.O. 9) 10. Ethical considerations in management accounting deal primarily with
a. the actions and interactions of people.
b. cost assignment techniques.
c. product costing approaches.
d. the financial statements of manufacturing companies.

Answers to the Self-Test are at the end of this chapter.

Review Problem
Cost of Goods Manufactured—Three Fundamental Steps

(L.O. 8) In addition to the year-end balance sheet and income statement, the management of Mison Company requires the controller to prepare a statement of cost of goods manufactured. During 19x4, $361,920 of materials were purchased. Operating cost data and inventory account balances for 19x4 follow:

Account	Balance
Direct Labor (10,430 hours at $9.50 per hour)	$ 99,085
Plant Supervision	42,500
Indirect Labor (20,280 hours at $6.25 per hour)	126,750

Account	Balance
Factory Insurance	$ 8,100
Utilities, Factory	29,220
Depreciation, Factory Building	46,200
Depreciation, Factory Equipment	62,800
Manufacturing Supplies	9,460
Repair and Maintenance	14,980
Selling and Administrative Expenses	76,480
Materials Inventory, Jan. 1, 19x4	26,490
Work in Process Inventory, Jan. 1, 19x4	101,640
Finished Goods Inventory, Jan. 1, 19x4	148,290
Materials Inventory, Dec. 31, 19x4	24,910
Work in Process Inventory, Dec. 31, 19x4	100,400
Finished Goods Inventory, Dec. 31, 19x4	141,100

Required

To review the three basic steps for computing the cost of goods manufactured, do the following:

1. Compute the cost of materials used during the year.
2. Given the cost of materials used, compute the total manufacturing costs for the year.
3. Given the total manufacturing costs for the year, compute the cost of goods manufactured during the year.

Answer to Review Problem

1. Compute the cost of materials used.

Beginning Balance Materials Inventory	$ 26,490
Add Materials Purchases (net)	361,920
Cost of Materials Available for Use	$388,410
Less Ending Balance Materials Inventory	24,910
Cost of Materials Used	$363,500

2. Compute the total manufacturing costs.

Cost of Materials Used		$363,500
Add Direct Labor Costs		99,085
Add Total Factory Overhead Costs		
Plant Supervision	$ 42,500	
Indirect Labor	126,750	
Factory Insurance	8,100	
Utilities, Factory	29,220	
Depreciation, Factory Building	46,200	
Depreciation, Factory Equipment	62,800	
Manufacturing Supplies	9,460	
Repair and Maintenance	14,980	
Total Factory Overhead Costs		340,010
Total Manufacturing Costs		$802,595

3. Compute the cost of goods manufactured.

Total Manufacturing Costs	$802,595
Add Beginning Balance Work in Process Inventory	101,640
Total Cost of Work in Process During the Year	$904,235
Less Ending Balance Work in Process Inventory	100,400
Cost of Goods Manufactured	$803,835

Chapter Assignments

Questions

1. Describe management accounting.
2. What effect does the size of a business have on the amount or type of financial information needed by management?
3. What are the three areas in which management needs information?
4. Identify the ways in which the primary users of information, types of accounting systems, and restrictive guidelines differ between financial accounting and management accounting.
5. Compare financial accounting and management accounting in terms of units of measurement, the focal point for analysis, the frequency of reporting, and the degree of objectivity.
6. Identify the types of information that are important to a manager in a manufacturing company.
7. How are the information needs of a bank manager (a) different from those of a manager in a department store and (b) similar to those of a manager in a department store?
8. Why are nonfinancial data analyses important to the management accountant?
9. Explain how the new globally competitive marketplace has increased the demand for nonfinancial data analyses. Give examples of these analyses.
10. What is the difference between a merchandising company and a manufacturing company?
11. What are the three elements of manufacturing costs?
12. How are direct costs different from indirect costs?
13. Define *direct materials.*
14. How is direct labor different from indirect labor?
15. What are the two kinds of labor-related costs? Discuss each one.
16. What characteristics are used to classify a cost as factory overhead?
17. What are the three inventory accounts used by a manufacturing company? Describe each type of inventory account.
18. Define *manufacturing cost flow.*
19. What is the difference between a product cost and a period cost?
20. How do total manufacturing costs differ from the total cost of goods manufactured?
21. How is the cost of goods manufactured used in computing the cost of goods sold?
22. Why are ethical standards of competence so important to the work of the management accountant?
23. Why is integrity so important for the management accountant to maintain?

Communication Skills Exercises

Communication 15-1. Comparing Management Accounting and Financial Accounting *(L.O. 2)*

Ann Browning, a local stockbroker, made the following comments in her speech to the Rotary Club last week: "Financial accounting relies on objective information, while management accounting deals primarily with subjective data. This means that financial accounting information is more accurate and therefore more useful to internal management's decision making." Write a response to Ms. Browning's comment for publication in the club's next newsletter to its members.

Communication 15-2. Information Needs of Managers *(L.O. 3)*

Barnett Banks, Inc. conducts banking operations in over 230 cities in Florida and Georgia. More than 560 offices comprise the network of branch banks. Some of these branches are small, employing ten to twelve people; others have over one hundred employees. Branch operating data are accumulated monthly at the corporate offices in

Jacksonville, Florida, for analysis and distribution to branch managers. Prepare a written report describing the types of information that should be included in these reports. Identify the various sources of income for the bank. What types of information, if any, do the larger branches need that are not necessary for the smaller offices? What nonfinancial information should be reported?

Communication 15-3. Scenarios on Ethics *(L.O. 9)*

For each of the two scenarios described below, identify the ethical issue or issues involved and state the appropriate solution to the problem. Be prepared to defend your answer.

1. Bob Barlev is controller for the Nashville Corporation. Bob has been with the company for seventeen years and is being considered for the job of chief financial officer (CFO). His boss, the current CFO, is going to be Nashville Corporation's new president. Bob has just discussed the year-end closing with his boss, who made the following statement during the conversation:

   Bob, why are you so inflexible? I'm only asking you to postpone the write-off of the $2,500,000 of obsolete inventory for ten days so that the write-off doesn't appear on this year's financial statements. Ten days! Do it. Your promotion is coming up, you know. Make sure you keep all of the possible outcomes in mind as you finish your year-end work. Oh, and keep this conversation confidential—just between you and me. Okay?

   Discuss the ethical implications of the CFO's instructions.

2. Frieda Maples went to work for Reno Industries five years ago. She recently was promoted to cost accounting manager and now has a new boss, Hugo King, the corporate controller. Last week, Frieda and Hugo went to a two-day professional development program on accounting changes in the new manufacturing environment. In the first hour of the first day's program, Hugo disappeared, and Frieda didn't see him again until that evening at dinner. The same thing happened on the second day. On the trip home, Frieda asked Hugo if he enjoyed the conference. He replied:

   Frieda, the golf course was excellent. You play golf. Why don't you join me during the next conference? I haven't sat in on one of those sessions in ten years. This is my R&R time. Those sessions are for the new people. My experience is enough to keep me current. Plus, I have excellent people to help me as we adjust our accounting system to the changes being implemented on the production floor.

   Does Frieda have an ethical dilemma? What, if anything, should she say to Hugo?

Communication 15-4. Basic Research Skills *(L.O. 3, 4)*

In order to be competitive in today's global marketplace, a company must be aware of its customers' level of satisfaction and continually must work to improve its relations with customers. Find an article in a recent issue of the *Wall Street Journal, Business Week, Forbes, Fortune,* or *Management Accounting* that centers on customer satisfaction awareness. Identify the industry being discussed and the financial and nonfinancial measures used to track customer satisfaction. Using actual statements from the article, describe your findings in writing and be prepared to discuss them in class.

Classroom Exercises

Exercise 15-1. Nonfinancial Data Analysis *(L.O. 4)*

Fairchild Landscapes, Inc. specializes in lawn installations using California bluegrass sod. The sod comes in 1-yard squares. The company uses the guideline of 500 square yards per person per hour to evaluate the performance of its sod layers. Each week, the most productive person is honored as "Employee of the Week."

During the first week of March, the following data were collected:

Employee	Hours Worked	Square Yards of Sod Planted
George Church	45	22,500
Ruth Crumpton	38	18,240
Ellen Marhill	42	17,640
Harris Palmetto	44	22,880
Fred Probyn	45	21,500
Jim Spry	40	19,800

Using the company's stated guideline, evaluate the performance of the six employees including the percentage over (under) target for each. Who should be selected "Employee of the Week"?

Exercise 15-2.
Merchandising Versus Manufacturing
(L.O. 5)

The following account titles were found on two sets of financial statements, one for a merchandising company and the other for a manufacturing firm. In the space provided, enter (a) if the account could only be from the merchandising company's statements, (b) if the account could only be from the manufacturing company's statements, or (c) if the account could be found on both companies' financial statements.

b 1. Work in Process Inventory
A 2. Purchases (for resale)
c 3. Accumulated Depreciation, Equipment
A 4. Merchandise Inventory
C 5. Accounts Receivable
C 6. Accounts Payable
b 7. Materials Inventory
C 8. Cash
C 9. Sales
b 10. Finished Goods Inventory

Exercise 15-3.
Direct Versus Indirect Costs, and Product Versus Period Costs
(L.O. 6, 8)

The cost accounts and amounts listed below were taken from the records of Pace Corporation's Canoe Division. In the columns, place an X to indicate (a) whether the cost is a period or a product cost and (b) for each product cost, whether it is a direct or an indirect cost.

	Period Cost	Product Cost	Direct Cost	Indirect Cost
Metal shaping labor wages, $4,320				
Production supervisor's salary, $2,500				
Lift-truck driver's wages, $890				
Interest expense on loan, $1,200				
Factory building maintenance, $1,100				
Production supplies, $570				
Factory property insurance, $320				
Raw material—sheet metal, $3,100				
Sales commissions, $1,890				
Factory electricity cost, $1,740				

Exercise 15-4.
Unit Cost Computation
(L.O. 6)

The Greer Winery is one of the finest and oldest wineries in the country. One of its most famous products is a red table wine called Olen Millot. This wine is made from Olen Millot grapes grown in Missouri's Ozark region. A fill grape called Chancellor is also used in the process. Recently, management has become concerned about the increasing cost of making Olen Millot and wants to find out if the current $10 per bottle selling price is adequate. The information is given to you for analysis at the top of page 621:

Batch size	10,500 bottles
Costs	
Materials	
Olen Millot grapes	$21,525
Chancellor grapes	8,400
Bottles	5,250
Labor	
Pickers/loaders	2,100
Crusher	630
Processors	8,820
Bottler	1,680
Storage and racking	12,600
Production overhead	
Depreciation, equipment	3,150
Depreciation, building	5,670
Utilities	1,050
Indirect labor	6,300
Supervision	7,350
Supplies	3,570
Storage fixtures	2,730
Chemicals	4,200
Repairs	2,520
Miscellaneous	420
Total production costs	$97,965

1. Compute the unit cost per bottle for materials, labor, and production overhead.
2. Is the selling price per bottle of Olen Millot wine too high, too low, or acceptable? Defend your answer.

Exercise 15-5. Cost Flow Analysis *(L.O. 7)*

Hinnen Products, Inc. makes life-sized statuettes of famous people from a rare teak wood. Highly skilled labor is required to shape the products. These were the beginning inventory balances for the period: Materials Inventory, $10,500; Work in Process Inventory, $12,400; and Finished Goods Inventory, $6,200. During April, the company purchased $6,800 of the teak wood, and $4,900 of the wood was requisitioned into production. Labor costs totaled $26,000 for the month, and factory overhead costs were $16,100. Products costing $51,300 were completed, and products costing $48,500 were sold during April.

Using T-accounts for Materials Inventory, Work in Process Inventory, Finished Goods Inventory, and Cost of Goods Sold, show the flow of costs through these accounts for April, and compute the ending balance of each account.

Exercise 15-6. Product Costs Versus Period Costs *(L.O. 8)*

The following costs were found on the monthly trial balance of the Hatfield Corporation, a manufacturer of children's toys.

Sales commissions	$14,560
President's salary	16,200
Parts for assembly	32,190
Production supplies	10,340
Indirect labor	21,380
Depreciation, sales automobiles	4,690
Advertising costs	12,170
Depreciation, machinery	7,110
Direct labor	34,120
Insurance, factory building	2,440
Small tools cost	5,660

Raw materials	$98,240
Packaging costs	9,920
Administrative support salaries	6,550

Identify those costs that would be classified as product costs and those that would be considered period costs. Explain your answers.

Exercise 15-7. Cost of Materials Used *(L.O. 8)*

On July 1, 19x4, the balance in Materials Inventory was $34,200; on July 31, 19x4, it was $61,910. During July, the company purchased $230,600 of materials on account from Lakes Company and $52,200 of materials for cash from Murphy Company. The company paid $55,000 on Lakes' account balance. Compute the cost of materials used during July 19x4.

Exercise 15-8. Computing Total Manufacturing Costs *(L.O. 8)*

The partial trial balance of Malott Millinery, Inc. appears below. Inventory accounts reflect balances at the beginning of the period. Period-end balances are $87,000, $105,800, and $56,200 for the Materials Inventory, Work in Process Inventory, and Finished Goods Inventory accounts, respectively. During the period, materials were purchased costing $431,600. From this information, prepare a schedule (in good form) showing the computation of total manufacturing costs for the period ending May 31, 19x3.

Account	Debit	Credit
Accounts Receivable	$ 87,420	
Materials Inventory	88,400	
Work in Process Inventory	64,400	
Finished Goods Inventory	41,400	
Accounts Payable		$ 79,250
Sales		893,940
Direct Labor	171,200	
Operating Supplies, Factory	22,700	
Depreciation, Machinery	64,100	
Fire Loss	92,000	
Insurance, Factory	8,700	
Indirect Labor	57,900	
Supervisory Salaries, Factory	36,700	
President's Salary	34,900	
Property Tax, Factory	10,400	
Other Indirect Manufacturing Costs	27,500	

Exercise 15-9. Statement of Cost of Goods Manufactured *(L.O. 8)*

During the month of August 19x3, the Hogan Company incurred the following manufacturing costs:

Purchases of materials: $149,000

Direct labor: 3,200 hours at $9.75 per hour

Factory overhead costs: utilities, $4,870; supervision, $15,600; indirect supplies, $7,750; depreciation, $5,200; insurance, $2,830; and miscellaneous, $2,100

Inventory accounts on August 1 were as follows: Materials Inventory, $58,600; Work in Process Inventory, $64,250; and Finished Goods Inventory, $48,500. Inventory accounts on August 31 were as follows: Materials Inventory, $60,100; Work in Process Inventory, $58,400; and Finished Goods Inventory, $47,450. From this information, prepare a statement of cost of goods manufactured.

Exercise 15-10. Computing Cost of Goods Sold *(L.O. 8)*

Maley Industries, Inc. produces a deluxe line of fruit beverages. During 19x3, the company operated at record levels, with sales totaling $995,000. The accounting department already has determined total manufacturing costs for the period, $564,500. Selling and administrative expenses for the year were $259,740. Inventory account balances were as shown at the top of page 623.

Account	Jan. 1, 19x3	Dec. 31, 19x3
Materials Inventory	$35,490	$32,810
Work in Process Inventory	67,400	66,980
Finished Goods Inventory	94,820	87,320

Assuming a 34 percent tax rate, prepare an income statement for the year ended December 31, 19x3. Round to whole dollars.

Interpretation Case from Business

Cresep Enterprises
(L.O. 2)

Cresep Enterprises is a corporation that produces and distributes household cleaning products nationally. Common and preferred stocks of the company are traded on a regional stock exchange. There are four divisions in the firm, and each is headed by a vice president. The following condensed financial statements appeared in Cresep's annual report for 19x2:

Cresep Enterprises
Income Statement
For the Year Ended December 31, 19x2

Net Sales	$200,000
Cost of Goods Sold	95,000
Gross Margin on Sales	$105,000
Selling and Administrative Expenses	80,000
Operating Income	$ 25,000
Interest Expenses	5,000
Income Before Taxes	$ 20,000
Income Taxes	5,000
Net Income ($.30 per share)	$ 15,000

Cresep Enterprises
Balance Sheet
December 31, 19x2

Assets		Liabilities and Stockholders' Equity		
Current Assets		Liabilities		
Cash	$ 20,000	Current Liabilities		
Receivables (net)	10,000	Accounts Payable	$20,000	
Inventories	30,000	Accrued Liabilities	5,000	
Prepaid Expenses	5,000	Total Current Liabilities		$ 25,000
Total Current Assets	$ 65,000	Bonds Payable		40,000
Buildings and		Total Liabilities		$ 65,000
Equipment (net)	75,000	Stockholders' Equity		
Total Assets	$140,000	Preferred Stock	$10,000	
		Common Stock	50,000	
		Retained Earnings	15,000	
		Total Stockholders' Equity		75,000
		Total Liabilities and Stockholders' Equity		$140,000

Required

Discuss the usefulness of the annual report's information in decisions and evaluations normally made by the following people:

a. Holders of Cresep common stock
b. Holders of Cresep preferred stock
c. Potential stockholders in Cresep securities
d. Company president and board of directors
e. Company bondholders
f. Vice presidents of each division
g. Plant superintendents
h. District sales managers
i. Cost center supervisors in each plant
j. Salaried employees who are nonsupervisory

Problem Set A

Problem 15A-1. Nonfinancial Data Analysis: Airport
(L.O. 4)

The Winnebago County Airport in Rockford, Illinois has experienced increased air traffic over the past year. How passenger traffic flow is handled is important to airport management. Because of the requirement that all passengers be checked for possible weapons, passenger flow has slowed significantly. Winnebago County Airport uses eight metal detector devices to screen passengers. The airport is open from 6:00 A.M. to 10:00 P.M. daily, and present machinery allows a maximum of 45,000 passengers to be checked each day.

Four of the metal detector machines have been selected for special analysis to determine if additional equipment is needed or if a passenger traffic director could solve the delay problem. The passenger traffic director would be responsible for guiding people to different machines and instructing them on the detection process. This solution is less expensive than acquiring new machines, so a suitable person is going to be assigned this function on a trial basis. Management hopes the procedure will speed passenger traffic flow by at least 10 percent. Makers of the machinery have stated that each machine can handle an average of 400 passengers per hour. Data on passenger traffic through the four machines for the past ten days is shown below.

Passengers Checked by Metal Detector Machines

Date	Machine 1	Machine 2	Machine 3	Machine 4	Totals
March 6	5,620	5,490	5,436	5,268	21,814
March 7	5,524	5,534	5,442	5,290	21,790
March 8	5,490	5,548	5,489	5,348	21,875
March 9	5,436	5,592	5,536	5,410	21,974
March 10	5,404	5,631	5,568	5,456	22,059
March 11	5,386	5,667	5,594	5,496	22,143
March 12	5,364	5,690	5,638	5,542	22,234
March 13	5,678	6,248	6,180	6,090	24,196
March 14	5,720	6,272	6,232	6,212	24,436
March 15	5,736	6,324	6,372	6,278	24,710

In the past, passenger traffic flow has favored Machine 1 because of its location. Overflow traffic goes to Machine 2, Machine 3, and Machine 4, in that order.

The passenger traffic director, Lynn Hedlund, began her duties on March 13. If this choice of alternatives results in at least a 10 percent increase in passengers handled, management plans to hire a second traffic director for the remaining four machines rather than purchase additional metal detectors.

Required

1. Calculate the average daily traffic flow for the period March 6–12 and then calculate management's traffic flow goal.
2. Calculate the average traffic flow for the period March 13–15. Did the passenger traffic director pass the minimum test set up by management, or should airport officials purchase additional metal detectors?

3. Is there anything unusual in the analysis of passenger traffic flow that management should look into? Explain your answer.

Problem 15A-2.
Unit Cost Computation
(L.O. 6)

Chen Industries, Inc. manufactures video disks for several of the leading recording studios in the United States and Europe. Department 65 is responsible for the electronic circuitry in each disk. Some parts are purchased from outside vendors, and others are produced internally. Department 62 applies the plastic-like surface to the disks and packages them for shipment. An order for 8,000 disks from the Barto Company was produced during July. For this job, Department 65 purchased miscellaneous parts costing $7,920 from Sharpe Corporation. Department 65 also incurred the following costs for the job: direct materials used, $13,600; direct labor, $6,800; and factory overhead, $7,360. Costs incurred by Department 62 included $3,920 of direct materials used, $2,560 of direct labor, and $4,800 of factory overhead. All 8,000 units ordered by the Barto Company were completed and shipped in July.

Required

1. Compute the unit cost for each of the two departments.
2. Compute the total unit cost for the Barto Company order, assuming that only Departments 62 and 65 were involved in the process.
3. The selling price for this order was $7 per unit. Was the selling price adequate? List the assumptions and/or computations upon which you based your answer. What suggestions would you make to Chen Industries' management concerning the pricing of future orders?

Problem 15A-3.
Cost of Goods Manufactured: Three Fundamental Steps
(L.O. 8)

Murat Company manufactures a line of aquatic equipment, including a new gill-like device that produces oxygen from water and replaces the large, cumbersome pressurized air tanks. Management requires that a statement of cost of goods manufactured be prepared on a quarterly basis, along with an income statement. As the company's accountant, you have determined the account balances below for the quarter ended October 31, 19x3:

Cost Account	Balance
Materials Purchases	$338,000
Small Tools	8,240
Factory Insurance	2,690
Factory Utilities	8,410
Depreciation, Factory Building	15,240
Depreciation, Factory Equipment	13,990
Selling Costs	42,600
Plant Supervisor's Salary	15,250
Direct Labor	184,700
Indirect Labor	91,400
Repairs and Maintenance, Factory	31,200
Indirect Materials and Supplies, Factory	39,400
Miscellaneous Factory Overhead	4,120
Materials Inventory, August 1, 19x3	45,600
Materials Inventory, October 31, 19x3	46,240
Work in Process Inventory, August 1, 19x3	34,020
Work in Process Inventory, October 31, 19x3	31,900
Finished Goods Inventory, August 1, 19x3	39,200
Finished Goods Inventory, October 31, 19x3	40,200

Required

1. Prepare a schedule showing the computation of the cost of materials used during the quarter.
2. Using the information calculated in **1**, determine the total manufacturing costs for the quarter.
3. Using the amount computed in **2**, prepare a final schedule to derive the cost of goods manufactured for the quarter.

Problem 15A-4. Statement of Cost of Goods Manufactured
(L.O. 8)

Holmqvist Manufacturing Company produces a line of Viking ship replicas. These models are sold at Scandinavian gift shops throughout the world. Financial records of the company show the following information:

Inventory account balances on May 1, 19x3: Materials Inventory, $180,400; Work in Process Inventory, $86,250; and Finished Goods Inventory, $42,810

Inventory account balances on April 30, 19x4: Materials Inventory, $176,250; Work in Process Inventory, $77,900; and Finished Goods Inventory, $46,620

During the fiscal year, $484,630 of materials were purchased, and payroll records indicate that direct labor costs totaled $225,970. Overhead costs for the period included indirect materials and supplies, $67,640; indirect labor, $182,710; depreciation, building, $19,900; depreciation, equipment, $14,240; heating, $19,810; electricity, $8,770; repairs and maintenance, $13,110; liability and fire insurance, $2,980; property taxes, building, $3,830; design and rework, $23,770; and supervision, $82,290. Other costs for the period included selling costs of $41,720 and administrative salaries of $102,750.

Required

Using this information, prepare a statement of cost of goods manufactured for the fiscal year ended April 30, 19x4.

Problem 15A-5. Statement Preparation: Manufacturing Company
(L.O. 8)

The Shirley River Company produces lighting fixtures. The company purchases all parts and then assembles the fixtures. Inventory account information for the quarter ended December 31, 19x3 is as follows:

Account	October 1, 19x3	December 31, 19x3
Materials Inventory		
Fixtures	$26,810	$32,020
Shades	12,660	13,940
Electrical Parts	29,890	30,470
Wire	9,250	8,840
Work in Process Inventory	82,910	85,130
Finished Goods Inventory	66,520	61,260

During the three-month period, the company purchased $82,480 of fixtures, $41,660 of shades, $62,780 of electrical parts, and $11,460 of wire. Direct labor for the period was 12,000 hours at an average wage rate of $10.50 per hour. Factory overhead costs for the period were indirect labor, $46,870; assembly supplies, $3,930; factory rent, $2,500; insurance, $1,940; repairs and maintenance, $6,880; and depreciation of equipment, $2,600. Total sales for the three months were $681,770; and general, selling, and administrative expenses totaled $286,820. Assume a federal income tax rate of 34 percent.

Required

1. Compute the cost of materials used for each of the four types of materials and the total materials cost for the quarter.
2. Prepare a statement of cost of goods manufactured for the quarter ended December 31, 19x3.
3. Prepare an income statement for the quarter ended December 31, 19x3.

Problem Set B

Problem 15B-1. Nonfinancial Data Analysis: Bank
(L.O. 4)

Colbert State Bank was formed in 1869. It has had a record of slow, steady growth since it began. Management always has kept the processing of information as current as technology allows. Leslie Oistins, manager of the Paynes Bay branch, is upgrading the check-sorting equipment in her office. There are five check-sorting machines in operation. Information on the number of checks sorted by machine for the past six weeks is summarized in the table on top of page 627.

Machine	Week 1	Week 2	Week 3	Week 4	Week 5	Week 6
AA	89,260	89,439	89,394	90,288	90,739	90,658
AC	94,830	95,020	94,972	95,922	96,401	96,315
AE	87,270	87,445	87,401	88,275	88,716	88,636
BB	91,910	92,094	92,048	92,968	93,433	93,349
BD	87,110	87,190	87,210	130,815	132,320	133,560

The Paynes Bay branch has increased its checking business significantly over the last two years. Oistins must decide whether to purchase additional check-sorting machines or attachments for the existing machines to increase productivity. Three weeks ago, the Colonnade Company convinced her to experiment with one such attachment; it was placed on Machine BD. Oistins is impressed with the attachment but has yet to decide between the two courses of action.

Required

1. Compute the average check-sorting output of the machines without the attachment and compare the average output with the output of Machine BD for each week.
2. If the Colonnade Company attachment costs about the same as a new check-sorting machine, which alternative should Oistins choose?
3. Would you change your recommendation if two attachments could be purchased for the price of one check-sorting machine?
4. If three attachments could be purchased for the price of one check-sorting machine, what action would you recommend?

Problem 15B-2.
Unit Cost Computation
(L.O. 6)

Grammer Industries has recently finished production of Job Sb-15. The corporation's cost accountant is ready to calculate the unit cost for this order. Relevant information for the month ended March 31, 19x2 is as follows.

The number of units produced was 41,480. Cost information for Department F-14 included 4,410 liters at $3.00 per liter for direct materials used, 152 hours at $8.50 per hour for direct labor incurred, and $3,514 of factory overhead. Cost data for Department G-12 included 850 liters at $5.57 per liter for direct materials used, 510 hours at $7.80 per hour for direct labor incurred, and $7,470 of factory overhead. Cost data for Department H-15 included 1,980 liters at $5.00 per liter for direct materials used, 620 hours at $8.00 per hour for direct labor incurred, and $6,810 of factory overhead. Each unit produced was processed through the three departments, F-14, G-12, and H-15, in that order. There was no ending balance in Work in Process Inventory as of March 31, 19x2.

Required

1. Compute the unit cost for each of the three separate departments, rounding to three decimal places.
2. Compute the total unit cost.
3. Order Sb-15 was specially made for the Isman Company for a selling price of $57,125. Determine whether the selling price was appropriate. List the assumptions or computations on which you base your answer. What advice, if any, would you offer to the management of Grammer Industries on the pricing of future orders?

Problem 15B-3.
Cost of Goods Manufactured: Three Fundamental Steps
(L.O. 8)

Rollins Metallurgists, Inc. is a large manufacturing firm. It prepares financial statements on a quarterly basis. Assume that you are working in the firm's accounting department. Preparing the statement of cost of goods manufactured is one of your regular duties. Account balances for the quarter ended March 31, 19x4 are as follows:

Cost Account	Balance
Materials Purchases	$1,205,330
Office Supplies	3,870
Depreciation, Plant and Equipment	35,230
President's Salary	36,000
Property Taxes, Office	1,950
Equipment Repairs, Factory	4,290
Plant Supervisors' Salaries	26,750
Insurance, Plant and Equipment	2,040
Direct Labor	228,310

Cost Account	Balance
Utilities, Plant	$ 8,420
Indirect Labor	17,000
Manufacturing Supplies	4,760
Small Tools	2,900
Materials Inventory, Jan. 1, 19x4	387,950
Materials Inventory, Mar. 31, 19x4	395,030
Work in Process Inventory, Jan. 1, 19x4	509,840
Work in Process Inventory, Mar. 31, 19x4	495,560
Finished Goods Inventory, Jan. 1, 19x4	345,010
Finished Goods Inventory, Mar. 31, 19x4	322,840

Required

1. Prepare a schedule showing the computation of the cost of materials used during the quarter.
2. Using the figure calculated in **1**, prepare a schedule to determine the total manufacturing costs for the quarter.
3. From the figure derived in **2**, prepare a final schedule to calculate the cost of goods manufactured for the quarter.

Problem 15B-4. Statement of Cost of Goods Manufactured *(L.O. 8)*

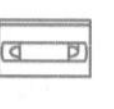

Bowman and Blunt Vineyards operates a large winery in California that produces a full line of varietal wines. The company, whose fiscal year begins on November 1, has just completed a record-breaking year ending October 31, 19x1. The vineyard's inventory and production data for this period are as follows:

Account	Nov. 1, 19x0	Oct. 31, 19x1
Materials Inventory	$2,156,200	$1,803,800
Work in Process Inventory	3,371,000	2,764,500
Finished Goods Inventory	1,596,400	1,883,200

Materials purchased during the year amounted to $6,750,000. Direct labor hours incurred totaled 142,500, at an average labor rate of $8.20 per hour. The following factory overhead costs were incurred during the year: depreciation, plant and equipment, $685,600; operating supplies, $207,300; property tax, plant and equipment, $94,200; material handlers' labor, $83,700; small tools, $42,400; utilities, $96,500; and employee benefits, $76,100.

Required

Using proper form, prepare a statement of cost of goods manufactured from the information provided.

Problem 15B-5. Statement Preparation: Manufacturing Company *(L.O. 8)*

The Polmar Pharmaceuticals Corporation manufactures a variety of drugs that are marketed internationally. Inventory information for April, 19x3 was as follows:

Account	April 1, 19x3	April 30, 19x3
Materials Inventory		
Natural Materials	$ 98,700	$ 80,600
Basic Organic Compounds	114,300	101,400
Catalysts	40,500	37,900
Suspension Agents	34,900	38,200
Work in Process Inventory	128,800	117,200
Finished Goods Inventory	101,700	104,100

The following materials were purchased in April: natural minerals, $134,610; basic organic compounds, $250,980; catalysts, $162,670; and suspension agents, $94,340. Direct labor costs were computed on the basis of 20,000 hours at $9.00 per hour. Actual factory overhead costs incurred in April were operating supplies, $9,700; janitorial and material-handling labor, $89,100; employee benefits, $70,800; heat, light, and power, $34,000; depreciation, factory, $84,400; property taxes, $9,500; and the expired portion of insurance premiums, $7,000. Net sales for April were $2,188,400. General and administrative expenses were $582,000. Income is taxed at a rate of 34 percent.

Required

1. Compute the dollar usage of each of the four types of materials during April.
2. Using good form, prepare a statement of cost of goods manufactured for the month ended April 30, 19x3.
3. Using the statement of cost of goods manufactured you prepared in **2**, prepare an income statement for the same period.

Management Decision Case

St. Peter Municipal Hospital
(L.O. 6)

Hospitals exist in a highly competitive environment, and they rely on cost data to keep their pricing structures in line with those of competitors. St. Peter Municipal Hospital is a case in point. Located in a large city, the hospital offers three broad kinds of service: general services (dietary, housekeeping, maintenance, patient care coordination, and general and administrative services), ancillary services (anesthesiology, blood bank, central and sterile supply, electrodiagnosis, laboratory, operating and recovery room, pharmacy, radiology, and respiratory therapy), and nursing care services (acute or intensive care units, intermediate care units, a neonatal nursery, and nursing administration).

The hospital's controller is Noreen Facione. She is reviewing the billing procedure for patients using the thirty intensive care units (ICUs) in the facility. Each unit contains a regular hospital bed and special equipment. One of the most important pieces of equipment at each bedside in the ICU is the cardiac monitor, which displays the patient's heartbeat. A set of central monitors at the nurses' station helps nurses watch for instances of excessively rapid or slow heartbeat, or irregular heartbeat. An alarm system attached to the monitor warns the nurses when a patient's heartbeat is over or under acceptable limits. To equip an ICU costs about $195,000 per room. Use of the equipment is billed to the patient at the rate of $280 per day. This includes a 40 percent markup to cover the hospital overhead and profit.

Other ICU patient costs include the following:

Doctors' care	2 hours per day at $260 per hour (actual)
Special nursing care	4 hours per day at $95 per hour (actual)
Regular nursing care	24 hours per day at $35 per hour (average)
Medicines	$330 per day (average)
Medical supplies	$160 per day (average)
Room rental	$300 per day (average)
Food and service	$150 per day (average)

In billing these costs, as it does with the equipment charge, the hospital adds 40 percent to cover its operating costs and profit.

Required

1. From the costs listed, identify the direct costs used in computing the cost per patient day in an ICU.
2. Compute the cost per patient per day.
3. Compute the billing per patient day using the hospital's existing markup rate to cover operating expenses and profit.
4. Many hospitals use separate markup rates for each cost when preparing billing statements. Industry averages reveal the following markup rates:

Equipment	30%	Medicines	50%
Doctors' care	50	Medical supplies	50
Special nursing care	40	Room rental	30
Regular nursing care	50	Food and service	20

   Using these rates, recompute the billing per patient day for an ICU.
5. Using the information in **3** and **4**, which billing procedure would you recommend to the hospital's director? Why?

Answers to Self-Test

1. c	3. a	5. b	7. d	9. c
2. c	4. b	6. c	8. a	10. a

LEARNING OBJECTIVES

1. Define and explain the concept of cost behavior.
2. Identify specific types of variable and fixed costs, and compute the changes in these costs caused by changes in operating activity.
3. Define semivariable cost and mixed cost, and separate their variable and fixed cost components.
4. Analyze cost behavior patterns in a service-oriented business.
5. Illustrate how changes in cost, volume, or price affect the profit formula.
6. Compute the breakeven point in units of output and in sales dollars.
7. Prepare a breakeven graph and identify its components.
8. Define contribution margin and use the concept to determine a company's breakeven point.
9. Apply contribution margin analysis to estimated levels of future sales, to compute projected profit.

CHAPTER 16

Cost Behavior and Cost-Volume-Profit Analysis

Planning and controlling selling prices, operating costs, and target profits are vital to the life of any profit-oriented business organization—a manufacturing company such as Ford Motor Company, a service company such as the Chase Manhattan Bank, or a merchandising company such as Neiman-Marcus. They also are important for not-for-profit enterprises like churches and charities. Effective cost planning produces a strong, continuous flow of operations; cost control helps the organization meet its goals, whether those goals have to do with overall profitability or the completion of a specific project. And cost planning and control activities support most of management's decisions.

To help achieve effective cost planning and control, an integrated set of techniques and procedures is employed. Collectively, these techniques are called a **budgetary control system**. This kind of system relies on a knowledge of cost behavior patterns and the relationships among cost, volume, and profit. In this chapter, we introduce these techniques and illustrate their use. After studying this chapter, you should be able to meet the learning objectives listed on the left.

DECISION POINT

Carey Construction Company[1]

■ Carey Construction Company is a medium-sized construction firm located in Lexington, Kentucky. The company specializes in road building and paving projects and uses a variety of heavy construction equipment. The costs of all of the equipment are considered fixed costs because the equipment can be used over a long period of time and on many different projects. The costs of the equipment are assigned to various projects based on usage and the duration (in weeks or months) of each project.

But equipment does not last forever. Fixed-cost equipment deteriorates, and some pieces are outdated by new, more productive models. Management must decide when equipment should be replaced as well as when to purchase additional heavy equipment so that the business can expand. What factors should management consider when it makes these decisions? Does the relationship of fixed costs to the company's volume and profit play a role in the decision process?

Carey Construction tracks the performance of all pieces of equipment. Data are recorded on (1) productive run time (the time the equipment is being used on the job), (2) travel time (being moved from one construction site to another), (3) downtime (being repaired), and (4) idle time

1. C. Douglas Poe, Gadis J. Dillion, and Kenneth Day, "Replacing Fixed Costs in the Construction Industry," *Management Accounting*, Institute of Management Accountants, August 1988, pp. 39–43.

(not being used). A computer program analyzes equipment usage to see whether the expected productivity of each piece is being maintained. If not, replacement is considered.

When making plans to expand a business, Carey Construction Company's management first must estimate the projected size and types of contracts (volume of business), the costs involved, and projected profit. With these projections in mind, management can decide how much new equipment it needs to meet the company's goals. ■

Cost Behavior Patterns

OBJECTIVE 1
Define and explain the concept of cost behavior

Before analyzing past performance, estimating a future cost, or preparing a budget, a manager must understand how costs behave. **Cost behavior** is the way costs respond to changes in volume or activity. Some costs vary with volume or operating activity; others remain fixed as volume changes. Between these two extremes are costs that exhibit characteristics of both variable and fixed costs.

Cost behavior depends on whether total costs are being analyzed or cost per unit is being computed. Variable costs vary in total: They increase in direct proportion to increases in volume or activity. But variable costs per unit remain constant as long as there are no changes in the price of materials and services consumed. Fixed costs, in contrast, react just the opposite. Total fixed costs remain constant as volume increases. But on a per unit basis, fixed costs decrease as volume increases. Because total fixed costs are constant, the more units produced, the lower the fixed cost per unit.

Consider the business of producing women's jeans. Let's say the material in the jeans costs $2 per pair. This is a constant per pair amount, but the more jeans you manufacture, the higher the total *variable* costs. That is, the total variable cost of materials for five pairs of jeans is $10; for ten pairs of jeans, it's $20. Now, think about the sewing machines used to sew the jeans together. The depreciation on those machines is a *fixed* cost. Let's say that total depreciation is $400 per month. The firm records $400 whether it manufactures one hundred pairs of jeans or one thousand. But at one hundred pairs of jeans, the fixed cost per pair is $4; at one thousand pairs, the fixed cost per pair drops to $.40.

We discuss these principles further as we examine variable and fixed costs in more detail. But it is important that you begin thinking about this pattern of cost behavior now. *Variable costs vary in total as volume or activity changes but are constant per unit; fixed costs are fixed in total but vary per unit as volume changes.*

In our discussion, we focus on cost behavior as it relates to production. But you should realize that some costs are not measured according to production volume. Sales commissions, for example, depend on the number of units sold or total sales revenue, not production measures. Another point you should keep in mind is that costs behave in much the same way in service businesses as they do in manufacturing enterprises. We look specifically at the costs of service businesses later in the chapter.

Variable-Cost Behavior

Total costs that change in direct proportion to changes in productive output (or any other measure of volume) are called **variable costs**. To explore another example of how variable costs work, consider an auto maker. Each new car has four tires, and each tire costs $48. The total cost of tires, then, is $192 for one car, $384 for two, $576 for three, $768 for four, $960 for five, $1,920 for ten, and

OBJECTIVE 2
Identify specific types of variable and fixed costs, and compute the changes in these costs caused by changes in operating activity

$19,200 for one hundred. In the production of automobiles, the total cost of tires is a variable cost. On a per unit basis, however, a variable cost remains constant. In this case, the cost of tires per automobile is $192 ($48 × 4) whether one car or one hundred cars are produced. True, the cost of tires varies depending on the number purchased, and purchases discounts are available for purchases of large quantities. But once the purchase has been made, the cost per tire is established.

Table 16-1 lists other examples of variable costs. A manufacturing company's variable costs include direct materials costs, hourly direct labor costs, hourly indirect labor costs, operating supplies, and small tools costs. Among the variable costs a bank incurs are the leasing expense for computer equipment (based on usage), hourly wages of computer operators, and the costs of operating supplies and data storage disks. A department store incurs such variable costs as the cost of merchandise, sales commissions, and hourly wages of shelf stockers. All of these costs—whether they are incurred by a manufacturer, a service-oriented business, or a merchandiser—are variable based on either productive output or total sales.

Operating Capacity. Because variable costs increase or decrease in direct proportion to volume or output, it is important to know a company's operating capacity. **Operating capacity** is the upper limit of a company's productive output capability, given its existing resources. In other words, it describes just what a company can accomplish in a given time period. Operating capacity, or volume, can be expressed in several ways, including total labor hours, total machine hours, and total units of output. Any increase in volume or activity over operating capacity requires additional expenditures for building, machinery, personnel, and operations. In our discussion of cost behavior patterns, we assume that operating capacity is constant and that all activity occurs within the limits of current operating capacity. Cost behavior patterns can change when additional operating capacity is added.

Table 16-1. Examples of Variable, Fixed, and Semivariable Costs

Costs	Manufacturing Company	Service Company—Bank	Merchandising Company—Department Store
Variable	Direct materials Direct labor (hourly) Indirect labor (hourly) Operating supplies Small tools cost	Computer equipment leasing (based on usage) Computer operators (hourly) Operating supplies Data storage disks	Cost of merchandise Sales commissions Shelf stockers (hourly)
Fixed	Depreciation, machinery and building Insurance premiums Labor (salaried) Supervisory salaries Property taxes	Depreciation, furniture and fixtures Insurance premiums Salaries: Programmers Systems designers Bank administrators Rent, buildings	Depreciation, building Insurance premiums Buyers (salaried) Supervisory salaries Property taxes (on equipment and building)
Semivariable	Electrical power Telephone Heat	Electrical power Telephone Heat	Electrical power Telephone Heat

There are three common measures, or types, of operating capacity: theoretical or ideal capacity, practical capacity, and normal capacity. **Theoretical (ideal) capacity** is the maximum productive output for a given period assuming all machinery and equipment are operating at optimum speed, without interruption. Ideal capacity is useful in estimating maximum production levels, but a company never operates at ideal capacity. In fact, the concept had little relationship to actual operations until the advent of the just-in-time operating environment. As described in the chapters on the just-in-time operating environment, and activity-based costing and measures of quality, the concept that drives the just-in-time environment is the continuous improvement of operations, with the long-term goal of approaching ideal capacity.

Practical capacity is theoretical capacity reduced by normal and expected work stoppages. Production is interrupted by machine breakdowns and downtime for retooling, repairs and maintenance, and employees' work breaks. These normal interruptions and the resulting reductions in output are considered when measuring practical capacity.

Most companies do not operate at either ideal or practical capacity. Both measures include **excess capacity**, extra machinery and equipment kept on hand on a standby basis. This extra equipment is used when regular equipment is being repaired. Also, during a slow season, a company may use only part of its equipment, or it may work just one or two shifts instead of around the clock. This is why managers often use a measure called *normal capacity*, rather than practical capacity, when planning operations. **Normal capacity** is the average annual level of operating capacity needed to meet expected sales demand. The sales demand figure is adjusted for seasonal changes and business and economic cycles. Therefore, normal capacity is a realistic measure of what a company is likely to produce, not what it can produce.

Given the concept of normal capacity, should we express capacity in terms of machine hours, direct labor hours, or units? Each variable cost should be related to an appropriate measure of capacity, but, in many cases, more than one measure of capacity applies. Operating costs can be related to machine hours used or total units produced. Sales commissions, on the other hand, usually vary in direct proportion to total sales dollars.

There are two reasons for carefully selecting the basis for measuring the activity of variable costs. First, an appropriate activity base simplifies the jobs of cost planning and control. Second, the management accountant must combine (aggregate) many variable costs with the same activity base, so that the costs can be analyzed in some reasonable way. This aggregation also provides information that allows management to predict future costs.

The general guide for selecting an activity base is to relate costs to their most logical or causal factor. For example, machinery setup costs should be considered variable in relation to the number of setup operations needed for a particular job or function. This approach allows machinery setup costs to be budgeted and controlled more effectively.

Linear Relationships and the Relevant Range. The traditional definition of a variable cost assumes that there is a linear relationship between cost and volume, that costs go up or down as volume increases or decreases. You saw this relationship in our tire example above. Figure 16-1 shows another linear relationship. Here, each unit of output requires $2.50 of labor cost. Total labor costs grow in direct proportion to the increase in units of output: For two units, total labor costs are $5.00; for six units, the company incurs $15.00 in labor costs.

Figure 16-1. A Common Variable-Cost Behavior Pattern: A Linear Relationship

Many costs, however, vary with operating activity in a nonlinear fashion. In Figure 16-2, part (a) shows the behavior of power costs as usage increases and the unit cost of power consumption falls. Part (b) shows the behavior of rental costs when each additional hour of computer usage costs more than the previous hour. And part (c) shows how labor costs vary as efficiency increases and decreases. These three nonlinear cost patterns are variable in nature, but they are different from the straight-line variable cost pattern shown in Figure 16-1.

Variable costs with linear relationships to a volume measure are easy to analyze and project for purposes of cost planning and control. Nonlinear variable costs are not easy to use. But all costs must be included in an analysis if the results are to be useful to management. To simplify cost analysis procedures and

Figure 16-2. Other Variable-Cost Behavior Patterns: Nonlinear Relationships

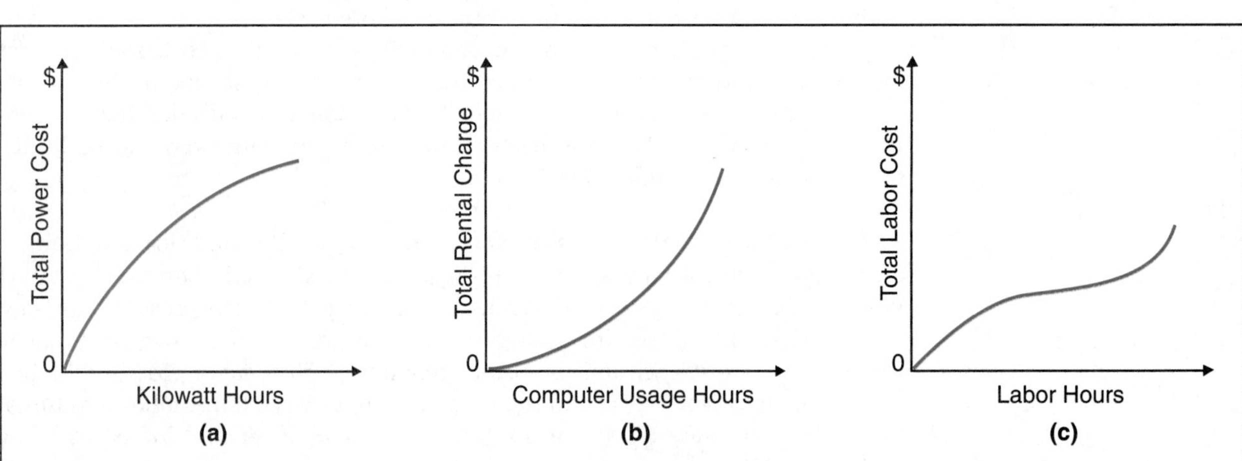

make variable costs easier to use, accountants have developed a method of converting nonlinear variable costs into linear variable costs. This method is called *linear approximation* and relies upon the concept of a relevant range of operating activity. **Relevant range** is the span of activity in which a company expects to operate. Within this range, many nonlinear costs can be estimated using the straight-line linear approximation approach that Figure 16-3 illustrates. These estimated costs then can be treated as part of the other variable costs.

A linear approximation of a nonlinear variable cost is not a precise measure, but it allows us to include nonlinear variable costs in cost behavior analysis and the loss of accuracy usually is not significant. Our objective is to help management estimate costs and prepare budgets, and linear approximation helps accomplish this goal.

Fixed-Cost Behavior

Fixed costs behave much differently from variable costs. **Fixed costs** remain constant within a relevant range of volume or activity. Remember that a relevant range of activity is the range in which actual operations are likely to occur.

Look back at Table 16-1 for examples of fixed costs. The manufacturing company, the bank, and the department store all incur depreciation costs and fixed annual insurance premiums. In addition, all salaried personnel have fixed earnings for a particular period. The manufacturing company and the department store own their buildings and must pay annual property taxes. The bank, on the other hand, pays an annual fixed rental charge for the use of its building.

As the examples in Table 16-1 suggest, reference to a particular time period is essential to the concept of fixed costs because, according to economic theory, all costs tend to be variable in the long run. Altering plant capacity, machinery, labor requirements, and other production factors causes fixed costs to increase or decrease. Thus, a cost is fixed only within a limited time period. For planning purposes, management usually considers an annual time period; fixed costs are expected to be constant within this period.

Of course, fixed costs change when activity exceeds the relevant range. An example: Let's assume that a local manufacturing company needs one supervi-

Figure 16-3. The Relevant Range and Linear Approximation

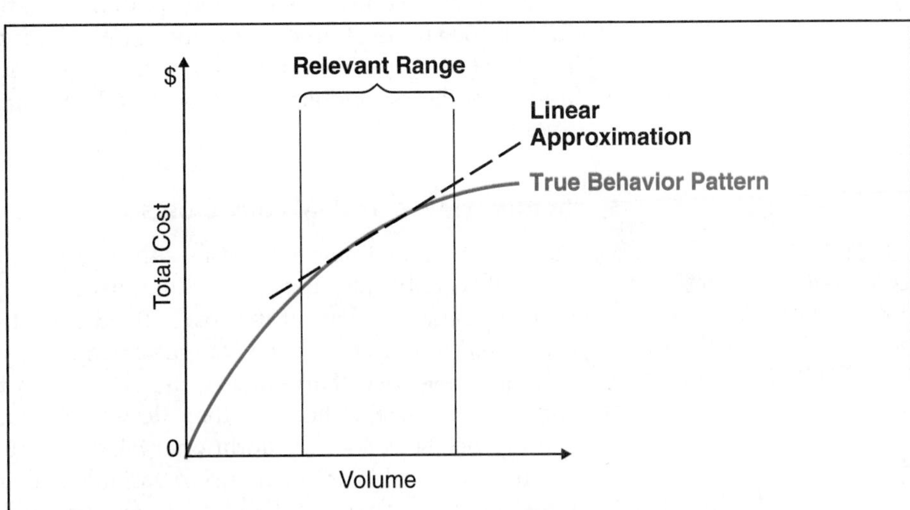

sor for an eight-hour work shift. Production can range from zero to 500,000 units per month per shift; the relevant range, then, is from zero to 500,000 units. The supervisor's salary is $4,000 per month. The cost behavior analysis is as follows:

Units of Output per Month	Total Supervisory Salaries per Month
100,000	$4,000
200,000	$4,000
300,000	$4,000
400,000	$4,000
500,000	$4,000
600,000	**$8,000**

If a maximum of 500,000 units can be produced per month per shift, any output above 500,000 units calls for another work shift and another supervisor. Like all fixed costs, this fixed cost remains constant in total within the new relevant range.

What about unit costs? Remember that the fixed costs per unit change as volume increases or decreases. *Unit fixed costs vary inversely with activity or volume.* On a per unit basis, fixed costs go down as volume goes up. This is true as long as the firm is operating within the relevant range of activity. Look at how supervisory costs per unit fall as the volume of activity increases in the relevant range:

Volume of Activity	Cost per Unit
100,000 units	$4,000 ÷ 100,000 = $.0400
200,000 units	$4,000 ÷ 200,000 = $.0200
300,000 units	$4,000 ÷ 300,000 = $.0133
400,000 units	$4,000 ÷ 400,000 = $.0100
500,000 units	$4,000 ÷ 500,000 = $.0080
600,000 units	**$8,000** ÷ 600,000 = **$.0133**

The per unit cost increases at the 600,000-unit level because this activity level is above the relevant range, which means another shift must be added and another supervisor must be hired.

Figure 16-4 shows this behavior pattern. The fixed supervisory costs for the first 500,000 units of production are $4,000. These costs hold steady at $4,000 for any level of output within the relevant range. But if output goes above 500,000 units, another supervisor must be hired, pushing fixed supervisory costs to $8,000.

Semivariable and Mixed Costs

OBJECTIVE 3
Define semivariable cost and mixed cost, and separate their variable and fixed cost components

Some costs cannot be classified as either variable or fixed. A **semivariable cost** has both variable and fixed cost components. Part of the cost changes with volume or usage, and part of the cost is fixed over the period. Telephone cost is an example. Monthly telephone charges are made up of charges for long-distance calls, and a service charge plus charges for extra telephones. The long-distance charges are variable because they depend on the amount of use; the service charge and the cost of the additional telephones are fixed costs.

Mixed costs also are made up of variable and fixed costs. **Mixed costs** result when both variable and fixed costs are charged to the same general ledger

Figure 16-4. A Common Fixed-Cost Behavior Pattern

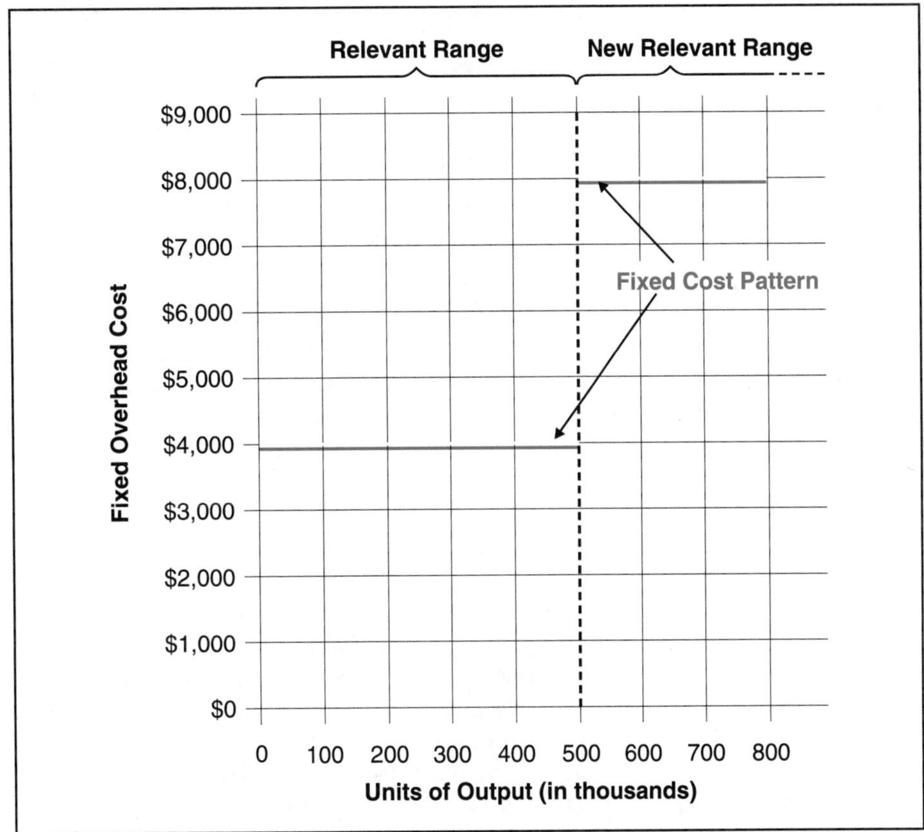

account. The Repairs and Maintenance account is a good example of an account that holds mixed costs. Labor charges to this account can vary in proportion to the amount of repairs done. However, only one repair and maintenance worker may be employed on a full-time basis (a fixed cost if he or she is salaried), with extra help hired only when needed (a variable cost). Depreciation costs for repair and maintenance machinery also are fixed costs, but costs of repair supplies depend on use.

Examples of Semivariable Costs. Many costs demonstrate both variable and fixed behavior characteristics. Utilities costs often fall in this category. Electricity, gas heat, and telephone charges normally have a fixed base amount, with additional charges based on usage. Figure 16-5 shows just three of the many types of semivariable-cost behavior patterns. Part (a) depicts the normal telephone cost for a factory. The monthly bill begins with a fixed charge for the service and increases as long-distance calls are made. Part (b) shows a special rent-labor incentive agreement found in contracts with municipalities. Factory rent has a fixed basis for the year but is reduced as labor hours are paid, down to a minimum annual guaranteed rental charge. Part (c) also depicts a special contractual arrangement: The cost of annual equipment maintenance by an outside company is variable per maintenance hour worked, up to a maximum per period. After the maximum is reached, additional maintenance is done at no cost.

Figure 16-5. Semivariable-Cost Behavior Patterns

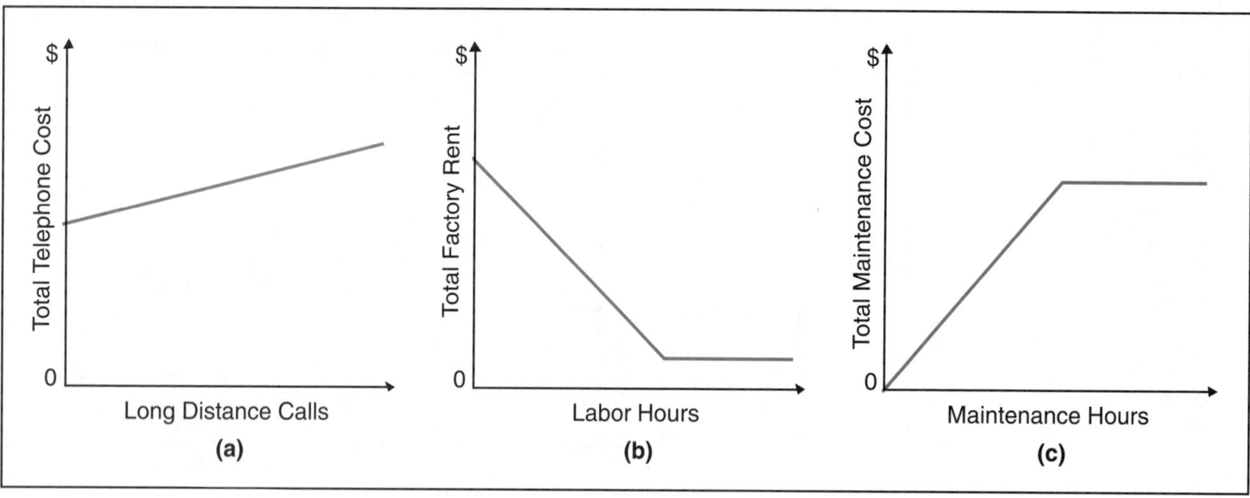

The High-Low Method of Separating Costs. For purposes of cost planning and control, semivariable and mixed costs must be divided into their respective variable and fixed cost components. This allows us to group them with other variable and fixed costs for analysis. When there is doubt about the behavior pattern of a particular cost, especially a semivariable cost, it helps to plot past costs and related measures of volume in a scatter diagram. A **scatter diagram** is a chart containing plotted points that helps determine whether there is a linear relationship between a cost item and its related activity measure. It is a form of linear approximation. If the diagram suggests that a linear relationship exists, a cost line can be imposed on the data by either visual means or statistical analysis.

Here is an example. Last year, the Evelio Corporation's Winter Park Division incurred the following machine hours and electricity costs:

Month	Machine Hours	Electricity Costs
January	6,250	$ 24,000
February	6,300	24,200
March	6,350	24,350
April	6,400	24,600
May	6,300	24,400
June	6,200	24,300
July	6,100	23,900
August	6,050	23,600
September	6,150	23,950
October	6,250	24,100
November	6,350	24,400
December	6,450	24,700
Totals	75,150	$290,500

Figure 16-6 shows a scatter diagram of these data. The diagram suggests that there is a linear relationship between machine hours and the cost of electricity.

Figure 16-6. Scatter Diagram of Machine Hours and Electricity Costs

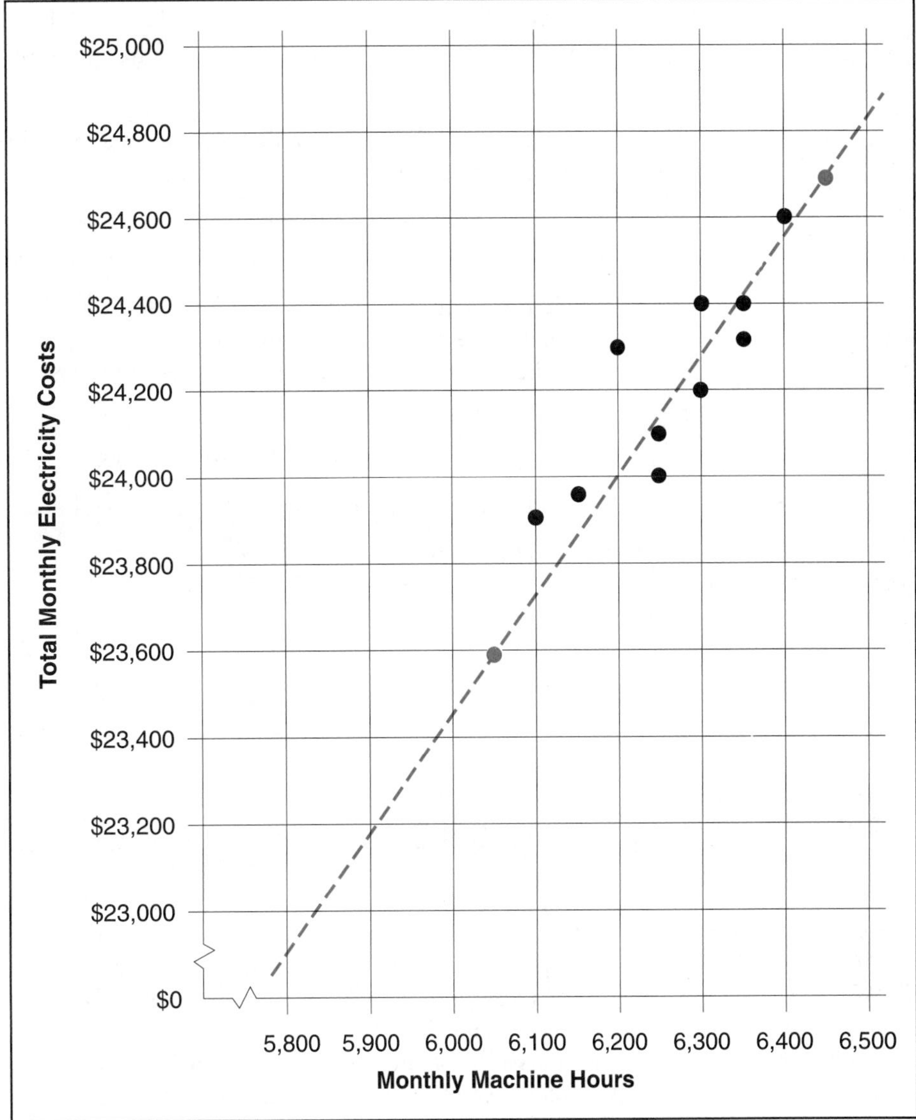

To determine the variable and fixed components of this cost, we apply the **high-low method**, a common, simple approach to separating variable and fixed costs. This method identifies a linear relationship between activity level and cost by analyzing the highest and lowest volume amounts in a period and their related costs. The change in cost between the two sets of data is divided by the change in volume to find the variable cost component of the semivariable or mixed cost. This amount, in turn, is used to compute the fixed costs at each level of activity.

Here's how it works. We begin by determining the periods of high and low activity within the accounting period. In our example, the Winter Park Division experienced high machine-hour activity in December and low machine-hour activity in August. Now, we want to find the difference between the high and low amounts for both machine hours and the related electricity costs:

Volume	Month	Activity Level	Cost
High	December	6,450 machine hours	$24,700
Low	August	6,050 machine hours	23,600
Difference		400 machine hours	$ 1,100

To determine the variable cost per machine hour, we divide the cost difference by the machine-hour difference:

Variable cost per machine hour = $1,100 ÷ 400 machine hours
= $2.75 per machine hour

Then we compute the fixed cost for any month (remember that fixed costs stay the same each month) by multiplying the machine hours times the variable rate and subtracting the amount from the total cost:

Fixed cost for December = $24,700 − (6,450 × $2.75) = $6,962.50
Fixed cost for August = $23,600 − (6,050 × $2.75) = $6,962.50

Here's the breakdown of total costs for the year:

Variable costs (75,150 × $2.75)	$206,662.50
Fixed costs [$290,500 − (75,150 × $2.75)]	83,837.50
	$290,500.00

And this is the linear relationship of the data for the Winter Park Division:

Total cost per month = $6,962.50 + $2.75 per machine hour

Cost Behavior in a Service-Oriented Business

OBJECTIVE 4
Analyze cost behavior patterns in a service-oriented business

The need to account for and control costs is fundamental to all business organizations, manufacturers, merchandisers, and service providers. But there is an important difference between the service company and the other organizations: In a service-oriented business, no physical product is produced, assembled, stored, or valued. Services are rendered; they cannot be accumulated or placed in a vault. Examples include rendering a loan service, representing someone in a court of law, selling an insurance policy, or computing a person's taxes.

How does this difference affect cost behavior patterns? Actually, only two areas of costs are affected. A service business has no materials or merchandise costs. In computing the unit cost of a service, the primary cost component is the professional labor involved. It is this direct labor cost that must be traced to the service rendered. Like other businesses, service providers also incur overhead costs. **Service overhead costs** are a varied collection of costs (excluding direct labor costs) incurred specifically to develop and provide a firm's services. Some service overhead costs vary with the number of services performed, and some are fixed in nature. Along with professional labor costs, service overhead costs are used to compute the cost per service rendered.

Assume that the home loan department of the Valencia Bank of Commerce wants to determine the total costs incurred in processing a typical loan application. For the past two years, the bank has charged $400 to process a home loan application. The chief loan officer thinks the fee is much too low; considering the way operating costs have soared in the past few years, she has proposed doubling the fee. To determine if her proposal is fair, let us compute the cost of processing a typical home loan application, including a breakdown of variable and fixed costs per loan, based on information collected for the period from January through June:

Direct professional labor: $120 per loan application

Service overhead, June:	
Chief loan officer's salary	$ 4,000
Telephone	650
Depreciation, building	2,400
Depreciation, equipment	1,400
Depreciation, automobiles	1,100
Legal advice	1,600
Legal forms and supplies	440
Credit checks	1,700
Advertising	340
Internal audits	1,900
Utilities	1,390
Clerical personnel	2,880
Miscellaneous	423
Total service overhead	$20,223

Total service overhead for the previous five months: January, $20,305; February, $20,018; March, $20,346; April, $20,182; May, $20,100.

Actual loan applications processed: January, 105; February, 98; March, 106; April, 102; May, 100; June, 103.

Appraisal and title search activities done by people contracted by the bank: $139 per loan application

Estimated average home loans processed per month next year: 100

With this information, we can compute the cost of processing a single home loan application. The first step is to determine the variable and fixed cost components of the Service Overhead account using the high-low method:

Volume	Month	Number of Loans	Cost
High	March	106	$20,346
Low	February	98	20,018
Difference		8	$ 328

Next, we determine the variable overhead costs per loan and the fixed overhead costs per month:

$$\text{Variable overhead costs per loan} = \$328 \div 8 \text{ loans} = \$41 \text{ per loan}$$

$$\text{Fixed overhead costs for March} = \$20{,}346 - (106 \text{ loans} \times \$41 \text{ per loan}) = \$16{,}000$$

$$\text{Fixed overhead costs for February} = \$20{,}018 - (98 \text{ loans} \times \$41 \text{ per loan}) = \$16{,}000$$

Now we can compute the cost per loan:

Variable costs per loan:	
Direct professional labor	$120
Contracted appraisal and title search fees	139
Variable service overhead	41
Fixed costs per loan:	
Monthly fixed service overhead ($16,000 ÷ 100 loans)	160
Estimated total cost per loan	$460

From this information, it seems that the loan officer is correct: The present fee does not cover the actual costs of processing a typical home loan application. However, raising the fee to $800 may not be appropriate. To cover costs and allow for some profit, the fee should be raised to $525 or $550.

Cost-Volume-Profit Analysis

Suppose Ford Motor Company wants to plan operations for the upcoming model year. How do managers know the correct amounts of materials and parts to purchase? Will additional workers need to be hired? Will there be enough space on existing assembly lines or must new facilities be constructed? What should the cars sell for to meet the company's target profit for the year? These questions cannot be answered until an estimate of the anticipated volume for the year is made. Once a target volume has been developed, the costs of production for the period and product pricing can be computed using cost-volume-profit analysis.

Cost-volume-profit (C-V-P) analysis is an analysis of the cost behavior patterns that underlie the relationships among cost, volume of output, and profit. C-V-P analysis is a tool for both managerial planning and control. The process involves a number of techniques and problem-solving procedures based on understanding a company's cost behavior patterns. The techniques express relationships among revenue, sales mix, cost, volume, and profits, and include breakeven analysis and profit planning activities. These relationships provide a general model of financial activity that management can use for short-range planning, evaluating performance, and analyzing decision alternatives.

Basic C-V-P Analysis

OBJECTIVE 5
Illustrate how changes in cost, volume, or price affect the profit formula

Cost-volume-profit relationships can be expressed through the use of graphs or formulas. Suppose that a company sells its product for $20, that total annual fixed costs for production and distribution are expected to be $96,000, and that variable costs for manufacturing and selling are $8 per unit.

Figure 16-7 shows the basic C-V-P relationships for this company. Total revenues and total costs are plotted by locating two points for each element and drawing a straight line through the two points. The total revenue line begins at zero dollars (no sales) and extends through $200,000 at sales of 10,000 units ($20 × 10,000 units). The total cost line begins at zero units and $96,000, the fixed costs that would be incurred if no units are sold. At the 6,000-unit mark, $144,000 of costs would be incurred ($96,000 of fixed costs plus 6,000 × $8, or $48,000 of variable costs). The point at which the two lines intersect, where total revenues equal total costs, is called the *breakeven point*. We discuss the breakeven point later in this chapter.

(The 10,000 units used to help plot the total revenue line and the 6,000 units used in identifying the total cost line in Figure 16-7 are arbitrary expressions of volume. Any amount of units could have been used.)

How Managers Use C-V-P Analysis

The graph in Figure 16-7 is a basic C-V-P model. It shows revenues, costs, volume, and profit or loss. The model is based on a set of fixed relationships. If unit prices, costs, operating efficiency, or other operating circumstances change, the model must be revised to fit the new C-V-P relationships. Similar analyses can be applied to multiproduct divisions or companies as long as a given mix of products is assumed.

Figure 16-7. Cost-Volume-Profit Relationships

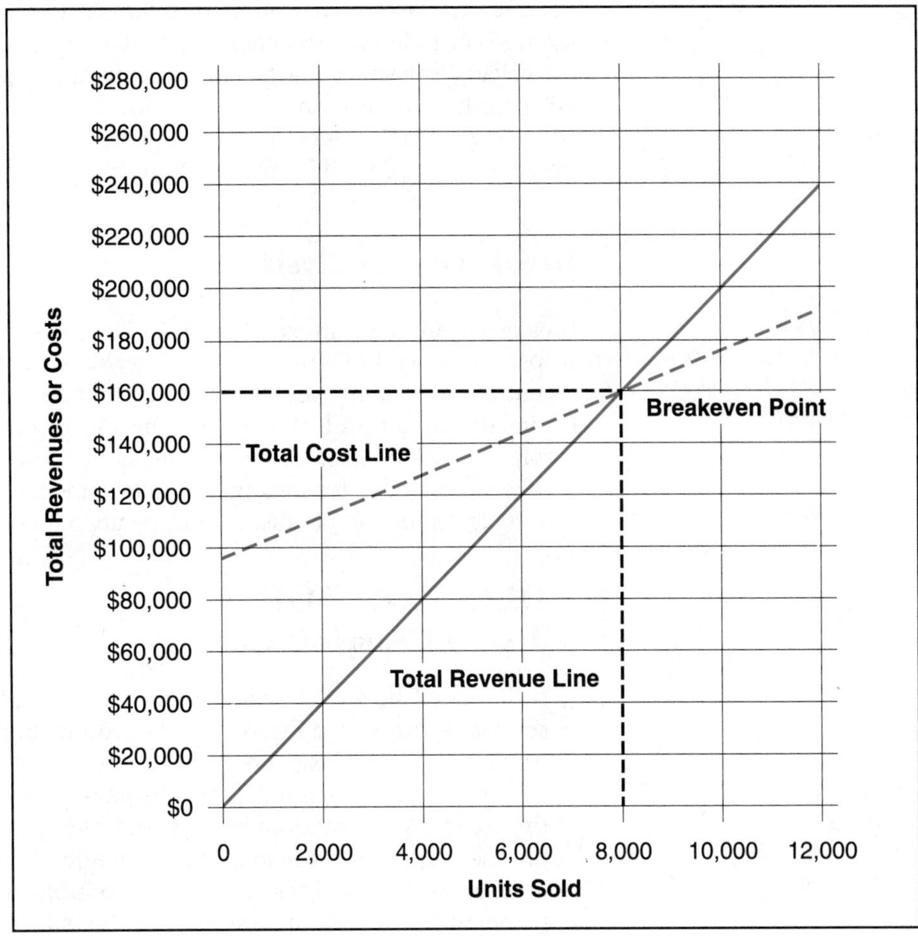

The C-V-P model is useful because it gives a general overview of a company's financial operations. For planning, managers can use C-V-P analysis to calculate profit when sales volume is known. Or, through C-V-P analysis, management can decide the level of sales needed to reach a target profit. C-V-P analysis also is used extensively in budgeting.

You can express the C-V-P relationship using this simple profit planning equation:

Sales revenue = variable costs + fixed costs + profit

Or, more simply,

$$S = VC + FC + P$$

For control, C-V-P analysis is a way of measuring how well the departments in a company are doing. At the end of a period, the company analyzes sales volume and related actual costs to find actual profit. Performance is measured by comparing actual costs with expected costs, costs that have been computed by applying C-V-P analysis to actual sales volume. The result is a performance report on which management can base the control of operations. This process is explained further in the chapter on the budgeting process and the chapter on standard costing and variance analysis.

Basic C-V-P analysis also can be applied to measure the effects of alternative choices: changes in variable and fixed costs, expansion or contraction of sales volume, increases or decreases in selling prices, or other changes in operating methods or policies. Cost-volume-profit analysis is useful for problems of product pricing, sales mix analysis (when a company produces more than one product or offers more than one service), adding or deleting a product line, and accepting special orders. In summary, there are many types of C-V-P applications, and all are used by managers to plan and control operations effectively.

Breakeven Analysis

OBJECTIVE 6
Compute the breakeven point in units of output and in sales dollars

Breakeven analysis utilizes the basic elements of cost-volume-profit relationships. As shown in Figure 16-7, the **breakeven point** is the point at which total revenues equal total costs. Breakeven, then, is the point at which a company begins to earn a profit. When new ventures or product lines are being planned, the likelihood of success can be measured quickly by finding the project's breakeven point. If, for instance, breakeven is 50,000 units and the total market is only 25,000 units, the idea should be abandoned promptly.

DECISION POINT
Mobay Chemical Corp.

■ Mobay Chemical Corp. uses breakeven analysis in a special way, consolidating breakeven figures for its product lines and divisions into one companywide analysis. From this analysis, the controller's staff develops a single graph, which the firm calls *profit geometry*, that portrays the entire company's breakeven history and plans. According to Howard Martin, the corporation's manager of strategic planning, consolidating standard breakeven analysis enables the controller, financial analyst, or planning professional to answer questions like:

How did last year's profit compare with the last time we experienced this level of capacity utilization (actual production levels relative to maximum possible production levels)?

How much have our so-called fixed costs actually increased with volume over recent years?

What level of profitability as a percent of sales and/or investment can we expect at "full" utilization of capacity?

What confidence level can we have that a recent actual or forecast future change in profitability is really significant (i.e., more than just normal variability)?[2]

How are answers to these questions useful to a manager?

Breakeven analysis can be used to examine the profitability of a new product line or an existing plant or division. A companywide analysis from a historical perspective gives management valuable direction. The analysis provides a broad view of costs that enables managers to see if costs really behave as variable or fixed. This approach also allows capacity utilization to become part of the measurement of operating performance. ■

2. Howard Martin, "Breaking Through the Breakeven Barriers," *Management Accounting*, Institute of Management Accountants, May 1985, p. 31.

The objective of breakeven analysis is to find the level of activity at which revenues from sales equal the sum of all variable and fixed costs. There is no net profit when a company just breaks even. Thus, only sales (S), variable costs (VC), and fixed costs (FC) are used to compute the breakeven point. The breakeven point can be stated in terms of sales units or sales dollars. The general equation for finding the breakeven point is:

$$S = VC + FC$$

Here is an example of how this equation can be used to find breakeven units and dollars. Keller Products, Inc. makes special wooden stands for portable compact disk players; the stands have a protective storage compartment for the disks. Variable costs are \$50 per unit, and fixed costs average \$20,000 per year. Each wooden stand sells for \$90. Given this information, we can compute the breakeven point for this product in sales units (x equals sales units):

$$S = VC + FC$$
$$\$90x = \$50x + \$20{,}000$$
$$\$40x = \$20{,}000$$
$$x = 500 \text{ units}$$

and in sales dollars:

$$\$90 \times 500 \text{ units} = \$45{,}000$$

OBJECTIVE 7
Prepare a breakeven graph and identify its components

We also can make a rough estimate of the breakeven point using a graph. This method is less exact, but it does yield meaningful data. Figure 16-8 shows a breakeven graph for Keller Products, Inc. This graph, like the standard breakeven chart, has five parts:

1. A horizontal axis in volume or units of output
2. A vertical axis in dollars
3. A line running horizontally from the vertical axis at the level of fixed costs
4. A total cost line that begins at the point where the fixed cost line crosses the vertical axis and slopes upward to the right. (The slope of the line depends on the variable cost per unit.)
5. A total revenue line that begins at the origin of the vertical and horizontal axes and slopes upward to the right. (The slope depends on the selling price per unit.)

At the point where the total revenue line crosses the total cost line, revenues equal total costs. The breakeven point, stated in either units or dollars of sales, is found by extending broken lines from this point to the axes. As Figure 16-8 shows, Keller Products, Inc. will break even when 500 wooden stands have been made and sold for \$45,000.

Contribution Margin

OBJECTIVE 8
Define contribution margin *and use the concept to determine a company's breakeven point*

A simpler method of determining the breakeven point uses the concept of a contribution margin. **Contribution margin** is the excess of revenues over all variable costs related to a particular sales volume. A product line's contribution margin represents its net contribution to paying off fixed costs and earning profits. In other words, the contribution margin (CM) is what remains after variable costs are subtracted from total sales:

$$S - VC = CM$$

Figure 16-8. Graphic Breakeven Analysis: Keller Products, Inc.

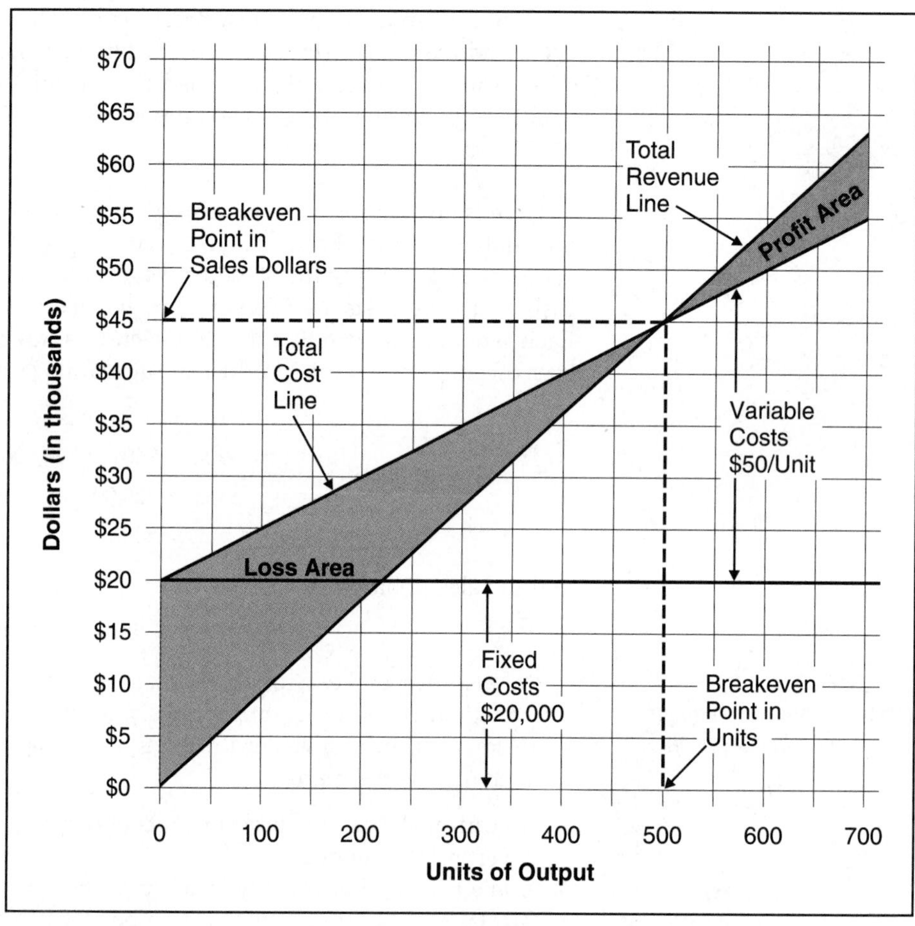

And what remains after fixed costs are paid and subtracted from the contribution margin is profit:

$$CM - FC = P$$

The following example uses the concept of the contribution margin to determine the profitability of Keller Products, Inc.:

		Units Produced and Sold		
Symbols		**250**	**500**	**750**
S	Sales revenue ($90 per unit)	$ 22,500	$45,000	$67,500
VC	Less variable costs ($50 per unit)	12,500	25,000	37,500
CM	Contribution margin	$ 10,000	$20,000	$30,000
FC	Less fixed costs	20,000	20,000	20,000
P	Profit (loss)	$(10,000)	—	$10,000

The breakeven point (BE) can be expressed as the point at which contribution margin minus total fixed costs equals zero (or the point at which contribution margin equals fixed costs). In terms of units of product, the breakeven point equation looks like this:

$$(\text{CM per unit} \times \text{BE units}) - \text{FC} = 0$$

At this point, we need to develop an equation that isolates the expression *BE units*. The equation can be rearranged as follows:

1. Move fixed costs to the right side of the equation:

$$\text{CM per unit} \times \text{BE units} = \text{FC}$$

2. Divide both sides of the equation by contribution margin per unit:

$$\frac{\text{CM per unit} \times \text{BE units}}{\text{CM per unit}} = \frac{\text{FC}}{\text{CM per unit}}$$

3. After canceling terms, the result is:

$$\text{BE units} = \frac{\text{FC}}{\text{CM per unit}}$$

To show how the equation works, we use the data for Keller Products, Inc.:

$$\text{BE units} = \frac{\text{FC}}{\text{CM per unit}} = \frac{\$20{,}000}{\$90 - \$50} = \frac{\$20{,}000}{\$40} = 500 \text{ units}$$

Profit Planning

OBJECTIVE 9
Apply contribution margin analysis to estimated levels of future sales, to compute projected profit

The primary goal of a business venture is not to break even; it is to make a profit. Breakeven analysis adjusted for a profit factor can be used as a basis for estimating the profitability of a venture. In fact, the approach is excellent for "what if" analysis, in which the accountant selects several scenarios and computes the anticipated profit for each. For instance, what if the number of units sold is increased by 17,000 items? What effect will the increase have on anticipated profits? What if the increase in units sold is only 6,000? What if fixed costs are reduced by $14,500? What if the variable unit cost increases by $1.40? All these scenarios generate different amounts of profit or loss.

To illustrate how breakeven analysis can be applied to profit planning, assume that the president of Keller Products, Inc., Don Chico, has set $10,000 in profit as the goal for the year. If all the data in our earlier example stay as they were, how many compact disk stands must Keller Products, Inc. make and sell to reach the target profit? The answer is 750 units. (Again, x equals the number of units.)

$$\begin{aligned} S &= VC + FC + P \\ \$90x &= \$50x + \$20{,}000 + \$10{,}000 \\ \$40x &= \$30{,}000 \\ x &= 750 \text{ units} \end{aligned}$$

To check the accuracy of the answer, insert all known data into the equation:

$$\begin{aligned} S - VC - FC &= P \\ (750 \text{ units} \times \$90) - (750 \times \$50) - \$20{,}000 &= \$10{,}000 \\ \$67{,}500 - \$37{,}500 - \$20{,}000 &= \$10{,}000 \end{aligned}$$

The contribution margin approach also can be used for profit planning. To do so, we simply add profit to the numerator of the contribution margin breakeven equation:

$$\text{Target sales units} = \frac{\text{FC} + \text{P}}{\text{CM per unit}}$$

Using the data from the Keller Products, Inc. example, the number of sales units needed to generate a $10,000 profit is computed this way:

$$\text{Target sales units} = \frac{\text{FC} + \text{P}}{\text{CM per unit}} = \frac{\$20{,}000 + \$10{,}000}{\$40} = \frac{\$30{,}000}{\$40} = 750 \text{ units}$$

To compute the target sales in dollars for the example above, divide the fixed costs plus profit by the contribution margin percentage. The CM percentage is computed by dividing the contribution margin per unit by the unit selling price:

$$\text{CM percent} = \frac{\$40}{\$90} = .44444 = 44.444 \text{ percent}$$

$$\text{Target sales dollars} = \frac{\text{FC} + \text{P}}{\text{CM percent}} = \frac{\$30{,}000}{.44444} = \$67{,}500$$

Cost-Volume-Profit Applications

Almost every type of business uses cost-volume-profit analysis. Manufacturing companies, service companies, and merchandisers all use C-V-P relationships for forecasting and controlling operations. As an example, let's look at the year-end planning activities of the Kalmar Corporation. Here is the information on the current year, in contribution income statement format.

Kalmar Corporation
Contribution Income Statement
For the Year Ended December 31, 19x3

Total Sales (66,000 units at $11.00 per unit)		$726,000
Less: Variable Production Costs		
(66,000 units at $4.40 per unit)	$290,400	
Variable Selling Costs		
(66,000 units at $2.80 per unit)	184,800	
Total Variable Costs		475,200
Contribution Margin		$250,800
Less: Fixed Production Costs	$130,500	
Fixed Selling and Administrative Costs	48,200	
Total Fixed Costs		178,700
Income Before Taxes		$ 72,100

Carl Nilsson, the company's controller, has asked several members of the executive committee to describe their expectations of the business environment for the coming year. Each person was asked to write up his or her personal outlook, including changes in selling prices, product demand, variable production costs, variable selling costs, fixed production costs, and fixed selling and administrative costs. In the following sections, we examine those projections and their implications.

Changes in Production Costs Only. The vice president of production believes that variable production costs will increase by 10 percent and that fixed production costs will rise by 5 percent. With no other anticipated changes, what is the projected profit for the coming year?

Solution

Total sales (66,000 units at $11.00 per unit)		$726,000
Less: **Variable production costs**		
[66,000 units at $4.84 ($4.40 × 1.10) per unit]	$319,440	
Variable selling costs		
(66,000 units at $2.80 per unit)	184,800	
Total variable costs		504,240
Contribution margin		$221,760
Less: **Fixed production costs ($130,500 × 1.05)**	$137,025	
Fixed selling and administrative costs	48,200	
Total fixed costs		185,225
Projected income before taxes		$ 36,535

As shown, if the variable and fixed production costs do change and no adjustments to selling price or volume are made, the corporation's profit will decrease by $35,565 (from $72,100 to $36,535). Because both variable and fixed production costs are projected to increase, management may want to increase the selling price to offset the rise in costs. Increasing the number of units produced and sold also would help offset the higher fixed costs. Because the vice president of production has commented on only production costs, the controller should try to augment the forecast by having other managers develop projections in their areas of expertise.

Changes in All Cost Areas. All costs will change, according to the vice president of data processing. She believes that all variable costs will go up by 10 percent, and that all fixed costs will rise by 5 percent. She does not anticipate any other changes.

Solution

Total sales (66,000 units at $11.00 per unit)		$726,000
Less: **Variable production costs**		
(66,000 units at $4.84 per unit)	$319,440	
Variable selling costs		
[66,000 units at $3.08 ($2.80 × 1.1) per unit]	203,280	
Total variable costs		522,720
Contribution margin		$203,280
Less: **Fixed production costs ($130,500 × 1.05)**	$137,025	
Fixed selling and administrative costs		
($48,200 × 1.05)	50,610	
Total fixed costs		187,635
Projected income before taxes		$ 15,645

Like the vice president of production, the vice president of data processing has concentrated only on projected costs. In this scenario, all costs are expected to increase. Profit suffers even more, pushed down to $15,645, a decrease of $56,455 ($72,100 – $15,645). Again, the controller may want to adjust this projection to include changes in volume and selling price.

Changes in Demand and in All Cost Areas. The vice president of finance anticipates volume changes as well as changes in all cost areas. He believes that unit demand in 19x4 will increase by 8 percent, all variable costs will go up by 20 percent, and all fixed costs will decrease by 10 percent.

Solution

Total sales [71,280 (66,000 × 1.08) units at $11.00 per unit]		$784,080
Less: Variable production costs [71,280 units at $5.28 ($4.40 × 1.2) per unit]	$376,358	
Variable selling costs [71,280 units at $3.36 ($2.80 × 1.2) per unit]	239,501	
Total variable costs		615,859
Contribution margin		$168,221
Less: Fixed production costs ($130,500 × .9)	$117,450	
Fixed selling and administrative costs ($48,200 × .9)	43,380	
Total fixed costs		160,830
Projected income before taxes		$ 7,391

This projection is the most pessimistic. The vice president of finance believes not only that all variable costs are going to increase but that volume also will increase. The $82,579 decrease in contribution margin far outweighs the positive aspects of lower fixed costs being spread over more units. If he is correct in his projections, something should be done to increase the selling price.

Changes in Selling Price, Product Demand, and Selling Costs. According to the vice president of sales, the corporation should increase the selling price by 10 percent, which will cause demand to fall by 8 percent. In addition, variable selling costs will go down by 5 percent, and fixed selling and administrative costs will go up by 10 percent.

Solution

Total sales [60,720 (66,000 × .92) units at $12.10 ($11 × 1.10) per unit]		$734,712
Less: Variable production costs (60,720 units at $4.40 per unit)	$267,168	
Variable selling costs [60,720 units at $2.66 ($2.80 × .95) per unit]	161,515	
Total variable costs		428,683
Contribution margin		$306,029
Less: Fixed production costs	$130,500	
Fixed selling and administrative costs ($48,200 × 1.10)	53,020	
Total fixed costs		183,520
Projected income before taxes		$122,509

The vice president of sales has the most optimistic outlook. Overall, in this scenario, profits increase by $50,409 ($122,509 – $72,100). Although the increase in selling price reduces demand, total revenue increases by $8,712. The increase in fixed selling costs is countered by an even larger decrease in variable selling costs.

Comparative Summary

Exhibit 16-1 is a comparative summary of the four executives' predictions. The controller would use a document like Exhibit 16-1 as a basis for discussing predictions for the upcoming year. From the executives' predictions and a discussion of their views, the controller can develop a portrait of the expected environment, and from that he can develop the budget for 19x4.

Exhibit 16-1. Comparative C-V-P Analysis

Kalmar Corporation
Summary of Projected Income Before Taxes
For the Year Ended December 31, 19x4

	VP Production	VP Data Processing	VP Finance	VP Sales
Total sales	$726,000	$726,000	$784,080	$734,712
Less: Variable production costs	$319,440	$319,440	$376,358	$267,168
Variable selling costs	184,800	203,280	239,501	161,515
Total variable costs	$504,240	$522,720	$615,859	$428,683
Contribution margin	$221,760	$203,280	$168,221	$306,029
Less: Fixed production costs	$137,025	$137,025	$117,450	$130,500
Fixed selling and administrative costs	48,200	50,610	43,380	53,020
Total fixed costs	$185,225	$187,635	$160,830	$183,520
Projected income before taxes	$ 36,535	$ 15,645	$ 7,391	$122,509

Assumptions Underlying C-V-P Analysis

Cost-volume-profit analysis is useful only under certain conditions and only when certain assumptions hold true. These assumptions and conditions are as follows:

1. The behavior of variable and fixed costs can be measured accurately.
2. Costs and revenues have a close linear approximation. For example, if costs rise, revenues rise proportionately.
3. Efficiency and productivity hold steady within the relevant range of activity.
4. Cost and price variables also hold steady during the period being planned.
5. The product sales mix does not change during the period being planned.
6. Production and sales volume are roughly equal.

If one or more of these conditions and assumptions are absent, the C-V-P analysis may be misleading.

Chapter Review

Review of Learning Objectives

1. **Define and explain the concept of *cost behavior*.**
   Cost behavior is the way costs respond to changes in volume or activity. Some costs vary in relation to volume or operating activity; other costs remain fixed as volume changes. Cost behavior depends on whether total costs are being analyzed or cost per unit is being computed. Variable costs vary in total as volume changes but are fixed per unit; fixed costs are fixed in total as volume changes but vary per unit.
2. **Identify specific types of variable and fixed costs, and compute the changes in these costs caused by changes in operating activity.**
   Total costs that change in direct proportion to changes in productive output (or any other volume measure) are called variable costs. Hourly wages, the cost of operating

supplies, direct materials costs, and the cost of merchandise are all variable costs. Total fixed costs remain constant within a relevant range of volume or activity. They change only when activity exceeds the anticipated relevant range, when new equipment or new buildings must be purchased, higher insurance premiums and property taxes must be paid, or additional supervisory personnel must be hired to accommodate the increased activity.

3. **Define *semivariable cost* and *mixed cost*, and separate their variable and fixed cost components.**
   A semivariable cost, such as the cost of electricity, has both variable and fixed cost components. Mixed costs result when both variable and fixed costs are charged to the same general ledger account. The balance in the Repairs and Maintenance account is an example of a mixed cost. The high-low method, which identifies a linear relationship between activity level and cost, is the easiest way to separate variable costs from fixed costs in semivariable or mixed costs.
4. **Analyze cost behavior patterns in a service-oriented business.**
   A service business's primary costs are professional labor and service overhead. Both types of costs are used to compute the cost per service rendered.
5. **Illustrate how changes in cost, volume, or price affect the profit formula.**
   Profit equals sales minus variable costs minus fixed costs. If sales, variable costs, or fixed costs change, profit changes.
6. **Compute the breakeven point in units of output and in sales dollars.**
   The breakeven point is the point at which total revenues equal total costs, the point at which sales equal variable costs plus fixed costs. Once the number of breakeven units is known, it can be multiplied by the product's selling price to get the breakeven point in sales dollars.
7. **Prepare a breakeven graph and identify its components.**
   The breakeven graph is made up of a horizontal axis (units) and a vertical axis (dollars). Three lines are plotted: The fixed cost line runs horizontally from the point on the vertical axis representing total fixed cost. The total cost line begins at the intersection of the fixed cost line and the vertical axis and runs upward to the right. The total revenue line runs from the intersection of the two axes upward to the right. The slope of the total cost line is determined by the variable cost per unit; the slope of the total revenue line is determined by the selling price per unit. The point at which the total cost and the total revenue lines cross determines the breakeven point in units and in dollars.
8. **Define *contribution margin* and use the concept to determine a company's breakeven point.**
   Contribution margin is the excess of revenues over all variable costs related to a particular sales volume. A product line's contribution margin represents its net contribution to paying off fixed costs and earning a profit. The breakeven point in units can be computed by dividing total fixed costs by the contribution margin per unit.
9. **Apply contribution margin analysis to estimated levels of future sales, to compute projected profit.**
   The addition of projected profit to the breakeven equation makes it possible to plan levels of operation that yield target profits. The formula in terms of contribution margin is

$$\text{Target sales units} = \frac{\text{FC} + \text{P}}{\text{CM per unit}}$$

Review of Concepts and Terminology

The following concepts and terms were introduced in this chapter:

(L.O. 6) **Breakeven point:** The point at which total revenues equal total costs.

(L.O. 1) **Budgetary control system:** An integrated set of techniques and procedures to help management plan and control costs.

(L.O. 8) **Contribution margin:** The excess of revenues over all variable costs related to a particular sales volume.

(L.O. 1) **Cost behavior:** The way costs respond to changes in volume or activity.

(L.O. 4) **Cost-volume-profit (C-V-P) analysis:** An analysis of the cost behavior patterns that underlie the relationships among cost, volume of output, and profit.

(L.O. 2) **Excess capacity:** Machinery and equipment kept on hand and on a standby basis.

(L.O. 2) **Fixed costs:** Cost totals that remain constant within a relevant range of volume or activity.

(L.O. 3) **High-low method:** A method that identifies the linear relationship between activity level and cost; used to separate variable from fixed costs in a semivariable or mixed cost.

(L.O. 3) **Mixed costs:** Costs that result when both variable and fixed costs (for example, repairs and maintenance costs) are charged to the same general ledger account.

(L.O. 2) **Normal capacity:** The average annual level of operating capacity needed to meet expected sales demand.

(L.O. 2) **Operating capacity:** The upper limit of a company's productive output capability, given its existing resources.

(L.O. 2) **Practical capacity:** Theoretical capacity reduced by normal and expected work stoppages.

(L.O. 2) **Relevant range:** The span of activity in which a company expects to operate.

(L.O. 3) **Scatter diagram:** A chart containing plotted points that helps determine whether there is a linear relationship between a cost item and its related activity measure.

(L.O. 3) **Semivariable costs:** Costs that have both variable and fixed cost components.

(L.O. 4) **Service overhead:** A varied collection of costs (excluding service-related direct labor costs) incurred specifically to develop and provide a firm's services.

(L.O. 2) **Theoretical capacity:** The maximum productive output for a given period assuming all machinery and equipment are operating at optimum speed without interruption. Also called *ideal capacity.*

(L.O. 1) **Variable costs:** Total costs that change in direct proportion to changes in productive output or any other measure of volume.

Self-Test

Test your knowledge of the chapter by choosing the best answer for each of the following items.

(L.O. 1) 1. "The way that costs respond to changes in volume or activity" is the definition of
   a. cost flow.
   b. cost behavior.
   c. period costs.
   d. product costs.

(L.O. 2) 2. The maximum productive output of an operating unit for a given period, assuming all machinery and equipment are operating at optimum speed without any interruptions, reduced by normal and expected work stoppages is called
   a. theoretical capacity.
   b. excess capacity.
   c. practical capacity.
   d. normal capacity.

(L.O. 2) 3. A cost that is the same for each product produced is called a(n)
   a. fixed cost.
   b. semivariable cost.
   c. variable cost.
   d. indirect cost.

(L.O. 3) 4. A cost that has both variable and fixed cost components is called a(n)
   a. direct cost.
   b. indirect cost.
   c. period cost.
   d. semivariable cost.

(L.O. 3) 5. The records of Technology Company reveal the following data about electrical costs:

Month	Activity Level	Cost
April	960 machine hours	$ 8,978
May	940 machine hours	8,842
June	1,120 machine hours	10,066

Using the high-low method, the variable cost per machine hour for the quarter was
a. $6.80. c. $7.40.
b. $8.60. d. $4.70.

(L.O. 3) 6. Assuming the same facts as in 5, the monthly fixed costs for the quarter were
a. $2,230. c. $2,540.
b. $2,450. d. $1,890.

(L.O. 6) 7. Product AB has a suggested selling price of $27 per unit and a projected variable cost per unit of $15. It is expected to increase fixed costs by $197,040 per month. The breakeven point in sales units per month is
a. 16,240. c. 11,950.
b. 11,590. d. 16,420.

(L.O. 6) 8. Assuming the same facts as in 7, the breakeven point in sales dollars per month is
a. $443,340. c. $312,930.
b. $322,650. d. $438,480.

(L.O. 9) 9. Assuming the same facts as in 7, how many units must be sold each month to earn a profit of $6,000 per month?
a. 12,450 c. 16,920
b. 16,740 d. 12,090

(L.O. 9) 10. Assuming the same facts as in 7, how many units must be sold each month to support an additional fixed monthly cost of $15,000 in advertising plus earn a profit of $9,000 per month?
a. 18,240 c. 13,590
b. 18,420 d. 13,950

Answers to the Self-Test are at the end of this chapter.

Review Problem
Breakeven/Profit Planning Analysis

(L.O. 6, 8, 9) Music City, Inc. is a major producer of pipe organs. Model D14 is a double-manual organ with a large potential market. Here is a summary of data from 19x4 operations for Model D14:

Variable costs per unit	
Direct materials	$ 2,300
Direct labor	800
Factory overhead	600
Selling expense	500
Total fixed costs	
Factory overhead	195,000
Advertising	55,000
Administrative expense	68,000
Selling price per unit	9,500

Required

1. Compute the 19x4 breakeven point in units.
2. Music City sold sixty-five D14 models in 19x4. How much profit did the firm realize?
3. Management is pondering alternative courses of action for 19x5. (Treat each alternative independently.)
   a. Calculate the number of units that must be sold to generate a $95,400 profit. Assume that costs and selling price remain constant.

b. Calculate net income if the company increases the number of units sold by 20 percent and cuts the selling price by $500 per unit.
c. Determine the number of units that must be sold to break even if advertising is increased by $47,700.
d. If variable costs are cut by 10 percent, find the number of units that must be sold to generate a profit of $125,000.

Answer to Review Problem

1. Compute the breakeven point in units for 19x4.

$$\text{Breakeven units} = \frac{\text{FC}}{\text{CM per unit}} = \frac{\$318{,}000}{\$9{,}500 - \$4{,}200} = \frac{\$318{,}000}{\$5{,}300} = 60 \text{ units}$$

2. Calculate net income from sales of sixty-five units.

Units sold	65
Units required to break even	60
Units over breakeven	5

19x4 net income = $5,300 per unit × 5 = $26,500

Contribution margin equals sales minus all variable costs. Contribution margin per unit equals the amount of sales dollars remaining, after variable costs have been subtracted, to cover fixed costs and earn a profit. If all fixed costs have been absorbed by the time breakeven is reached, the entire contribution margin of each unit sold in excess of breakeven represents profit.

3. a. Calculate the number of unit sales needed to generate a given profit.

$$\text{Target sales units} = \frac{\text{FC} + \text{P}}{\text{CM per unit}}$$

$$= \frac{\$318{,}000 + \$95{,}400}{\$5{,}300} = \frac{\$413{,}400}{\$5{,}300} = 78 \text{ units}$$

b. Calculate net income under specified conditions.

Total sales [78 (65 × 1.20) units at $9,000 per unit]	$702,000
Less variable costs (78 units × $4,200)	327,600
Contribution margin	$374,400
Less fixed costs	318,000
Projected income before taxes	$ 56,400

c. Determine the number of breakeven units under specified conditions.

$$\text{BE units} = \frac{\text{FC}}{\text{CM per unit}}$$

$$= \frac{\$318{,}000 + \$47{,}700}{\$5{,}300} = \frac{\$365{,}700}{\$5{,}300} = 69 \text{ units}$$

d. Calculate the number of sales units needed to generate a given profit under specified conditions.

CM per unit = $9,500 – ($4,200 × .9) = $9,500 – $3,780 = $5,720

$$\text{Target sales units} = \frac{\text{FC} + \text{P}}{\text{CM per unit}}$$

$$= \frac{\$318{,}000 + \$125{,}000}{\$5{,}720} = \frac{\$443{,}000}{\$5{,}720} = 77.45 \text{ or } 78 \text{ units}$$

Chapter Assignments

Questions

1. Define *cost behavior.*
2. Why is an understanding of cost behavior useful to managers?
3. What makes variable costs different from fixed costs?
4. What is the difference between theoretical capacity and practical capacity?
5. Why does a company never operate at theoretical capacity?
6. Define *excess capacity.*
7. What is normal capacity? Why is this expression of capacity considered more relevant and useful than either theoretical or practical capacity?
8. What does *relevant range of activity* mean?
9. "Fixed costs remain constant in total but decrease per unit as productive output increases." Explain this statement.
10. Why is the cost of telephone usage usually considered a semivariable cost?
11. What is a mixed cost? Give an example.
12. Describe the high-low method of separating costs.
13. "The concept of product cost is not applicable to service-oriented companies." Is this statement correct? Defend your answer.
14. Service-oriented companies do not maintain work in process and finished goods inventories. Why, then, do they need unit cost information?
15. Define *cost-volume-profit analysis.*
16. Identify two uses of C-V-P analysis and relate their significance to management.
17. Define *breakeven point.* Why is information about the breakeven point important to managers?
18. Define *contribution margin* and describe its use in breakeven analysis.
19. State the equation that determines target sales units using the elements of fixed costs, target profit, and contribution margin per unit.
20. What conditions must be met for C-V-P computations to be accurate?

Communication Skills Exercises

Communication 16-1. Concept of Cost Behavior *(L.O. 1, 2)*

Carolina Keys Shrimp Company is a very small company. It owns an ice house and shrimp preparation building, a refrigerated van, and three shrimp boats. George Conway inherited the company from his uncle two months ago. The firm employs three boat crews (there are four people in each crew) and five processing workers. Bren & Wilson, a local accounting firm, has kept the company's financial records for many years. In her last analysis of operations, Barbara Bren stated that the company's fixed-cost base is satisfactory for this type and size of business, but that the variable costs of operations are too high for the volume of business over the last two years. As a result, the company has not been operating at a profit. Conway is confused by the statement about variable and fixed costs. Prepare a response to Conway from Bren explaining the concept of cost behavior.

Communication 16-2. Costs of Providing a Service *(L.O. 2, 4)*

Orlando Medical Center (OMC) and *Infante Lawn Maintenance Company* are both service-oriented businesses that are experiencing problems with the prices of their services. OMC has increased its prices to a point where the facility is no longer competitive: It is losing business to two other private hospitals located in the same area. Tony Infante, on the other hand, apparently has priced his services too low because he now is turning away new business. Each business must analyze its service cost structure. Prepare a written analysis of the two organizations, identifying some possible reasons for their problems. As part of your analysis, identify the types of costs that would be experienced (1) in running a medical center (including the specific costs incurred to set a broken arm) and (2) in providing lawn maintenance service.

Communication 16-3. Breaking Even and Ethics
(L.O. 6)

Matt Reola is supervisor of the new product division of Farley Corp., located in Jackson, Mississippi. Reola's annual bonus is based on the success of new products and is computed on the amount of sales that are over and above each product's projected breakeven point. In reviewing the computations supporting his most recent bonus, he found that a large order for 7,500 units of product WR4, which had been refused by a customer and returned to the company, had been included in his bonus calculations. He later found out that the company's accountant had labeled the return as an overhead expense and had charged the entire cost of the returned order to the plantwide factory overhead account. The result was that product WR4 exceeded breakeven by more than 5,000 units and Matt's bonus from that product amounted to over $800. Write a memo from Matt to the accountant explaining what actions should be taken.

Communication 16-4. Basic Research Skills
(L.O. 2, 4)

Make a trip to a local fast-food restaurant. Observe all aspects of the operation, taking notes on the entire process. Describe the procedures used to take an order, process the order, fill the order, and get the food to the customer. Make a list of the costs that are being incurred by the owner based on your observations. From the costs listed, identify at least three that are fixed and three that vary based on the number of sandwiches sold. Bring your notes to class and report your findings.

Classroom Exercises

Exercise 16-1. Identification of Variable and Fixed Costs
(L.O. 2)

From the following list of costs of productive output, indicate which are usually considered variable costs and which fixed costs: (1) packaging materials for stereo components, (2) real estate taxes, (3) gasoline for a delivery truck, (4) property insurance, (5) depreciation expense of buildings (straight-line method), (6) supplies, (7) indirect materials used, (8) bottles used in the sale of liquids, (9) license fees for company cars, (10) wiring used in radios, (11) machine helper's wages, (12) wood used in bookcases, (13) city operating license, (14) machine depreciation based on machine hours of usage, (15) machine operator's hourly wage, and (16) cost of required outside inspection of each unit produced.

Exercise 16-2. Variable Cost Analysis
(L.O. 2)

Quick Oil Change has been in business for six months. Each oil-change service requires an average of four quarts of oil. The cost of oil to Quick Oil Change is $.50 per quart. The estimated number of cars that will be serviced in the next three months is 240, 288, and 360.

1. Compute the cost of oil for each of the three months as well as the total cost for all three months. Fill in the blanks in the table below.
2. Fill in the blanks in the sentences following the table with the appropriate information about cost behavior.

Month	Cars to be Serviced	Required Quarts/Car	Cost/Quart	Total Cost/Month
1	240	4	$.50	____
2	288	4	$.50	____
3	360	4	$.50	____
Three-month total	888			____

Cost Behavior:

Cost per unit ____ (increased, decreased, remained constant).
Total variable cost per month ____ (increased, decreased) as the quantity of oil used ____ (increased, decreased).

Exercise 16-3. Semivariable Costs/High-Low Method
(L.O. 3)

Herring Electronics Company manufactures major appliances. The company just had its most successful year because of increased interest in its refrigerator line. While preparing the budget for next year, Lynn Dora, the company's controller, came across the data shown at the top of page 658.

Month	Volume in Machine Hours	Electricity Costs
July	6,000	$60,000
August	5,000	53,000
September	4,500	49,500
October	4,000	46,000
November	3,500	42,500
December	3,000	39,000

Using the high-low method, determine (1) the variable electricity cost per machine hour, (2) the monthly fixed electricity cost, and (3) the total variable electricity costs and fixed electricity costs for the six-month period.

Exercise 16-4. Breakeven Analysis *(L.O. 6, 7)*

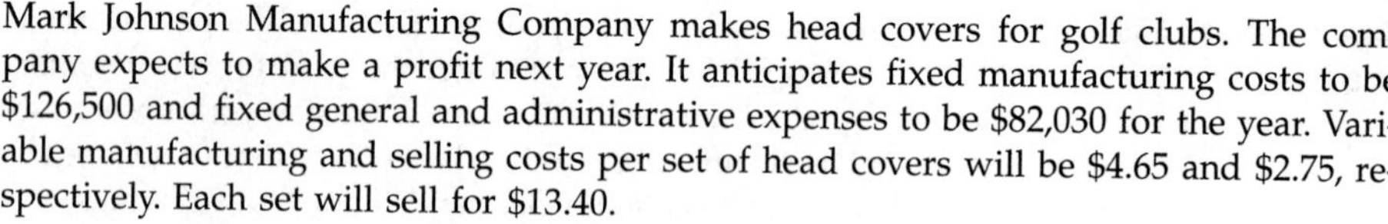

Mark Johnson Manufacturing Company makes head covers for golf clubs. The company expects to make a profit next year. It anticipates fixed manufacturing costs to be $126,500 and fixed general and administrative expenses to be $82,030 for the year. Variable manufacturing and selling costs per set of head covers will be $4.65 and $2.75, respectively. Each set will sell for $13.40.

1. Compute the breakeven point in sales units.
2. Compute the breakeven point in sales dollars.
3. If the selling price were increased to $14.00 per unit and fixed general and administrative expenses were cut by $33,465, what would the new breakeven point be in units?
4. Prepare a graph to illustrate the breakeven point found in **2**.

Exercise 16-5. Breakeven Analysis and Pricing *(L.O. 6, 8, 9)*

Harrison Company has a plant capacity of 100,000 units per year, but the 19x4 budget indicates that only 60,000 units will be produced and sold. The entire 19x4 budget is as follows:

Sales revenues (60,000 units at $4)		$240,000
Less: Cost of goods produced (based on production of 60,000 units)		
Materials (variable)	$60,000	
Labor (variable)	30,000	
Variable manufacturing costs	45,000	
Fixed manufacturing costs	75,000	
Total cost of goods produced		210,000
Gross margin		$ 30,000
Less: Selling and administrative costs		
Selling (10 percent of sales)	$24,000	
Administrative (fixed)	36,000	
Total selling and administrative costs		60,000
Net income (loss) from operations		$(30,000)

1. Given the budgeted selling price and cost data, how many units would Harrison have to produce and sell to break even?
2. Market research indicates that if Harrison were to drop its selling price to $3.80 per unit, it could sell 100,000 units in 19x4. At the new selling price, what is the company's new profit (loss) figure?
3. Would you recommend the new selling price in **2**? Explain your answer.

Exercise 16-6. Profit Planning *(L.O. 6, 8, 9)*

Short-term automobile rentals are the specialty of Sandelin Auto Rentals, Inc. Average variable operating costs have been $12.50 per day per automobile. The company owns sixty cars. Fixed operating costs for the next year are expected to be $145,500. Average daily rental revenue per automobile is expected to be $34.50. Management would like to earn $47,000 during the year.

1. Calculate the total number of daily rentals that the company must have during the year to earn the target profit.
2. On the basis of your answer to **1**, determine the number of days on the average that each automobile must be rented.
3. Find the total rental revenue for the year needed to earn the $47,000 profit.
4. What would the total rental revenue be if fixed operating costs could be lowered by $5,180 and target earnings increased to $70,000?

Exercise 16-7.
Breakeven Analysis and Profit Planning
(L.O. 6, 8, 9)

Nichole Corporation produces and distributes housing hardware, specializing in doorknobs. The present annual doorknob sales volume is 500,000 units, and the current selling price is $1.00 per unit. Variable costs amount to $.60 per unit. Fixed costs are $100,000 per year.

1. a. What is the present annual profit?
   b. What is the present breakeven point in units?
   c. What is the present breakeven point in dollars?
2. Compute the profit for each of the following changes (consider each situation independently):
   a. A per unit increase of $.02 in variable cost
   b. A 10 percent decrease in fixed costs and a 10 percent increase in sales volume
   c. A 20 percent increase in fixed costs, a 20 percent decrease in selling price, a 10 percent decrease in variable costs per unit, and a 30 percent increase in units sold
3. Compute the new breakeven point in units for each of the following changes:
   a. A 10 percent decrease in fixed costs
   b. A 10 percent increase in selling price and a $25,000 increase in fixed costs

Exercise 16-8.
Graphical Analysis
(L.O. 7, 8)

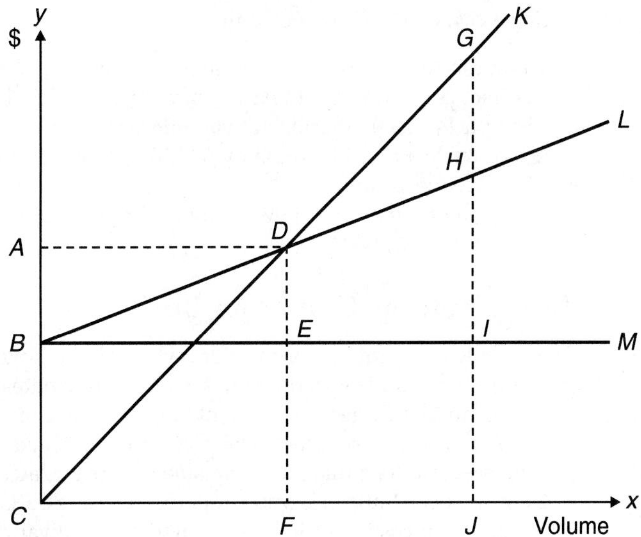

Identify the appropriate point, line segment, or area of the breakeven graph that corresponds with the following questions:

1. The maximum possible operating loss is
   a. *A*. c. *B*.
   b. *D*. d. *F*.
2. The breakeven point in sales dollars is
   a. *C*. c. *A*.
   b. *D*. d. *G*.
3. At volume *F*, total contribution margin is
   a. *C*. c. *E*.
   b. *D*. d. *G*.

4. Profits are represented by area
   a. *KDL*. c. *BDC*.
   b. *KCJ*. d. *GCJ*.
5. At volume *J*, total fixed costs are represented by
   a. *H*. c. *I*.
   b. *G*. d. *J*.
6. If volume increases from *F* to *J*, the change in total costs is
   a. *HI* minus *DE*. c. *BC* minus *DF*.
   b. *DF* minus *HJ*. d. *AB* minus *DE*.

Exercise 16-9. Cost-Volume-Profit Analysis and Pricing
(L.O. 8, 9)

The Columbia Furniture Company produces bridge tables and chairs that are sold by department and furniture stores. The current selling prices are $8 per chair and $16 per table. Based on these prices, the company is able to break even by selling 12,000 chairs and 3,000 tables. Variable manufacturing cost per chair is $4 and per table is $12. Variable selling cost per chair is $.40 and per table is $.40. In addition, manufacturing fixed costs were $37,500, and selling and administrative fixed costs were $16,500. The company's competitors recently reduced prices on similar items of equal quality to $7.50 per chair and $15 per table.

Assuming the same ratio of four chairs to one table, how many units of each would the company have to sell to meet its competitors' prices and still make a profit of $51,000?

Exercise 16-10. Contribution Margin/Profit Planning
(L.O. 8, 9)

Palmer Systems, Ltd. makes undersea missiles for nuclear submarines. Management has just been offered a government contract that may generate a profit for the company. The contract purchase price is $130,000 per unit, but the number of units to be purchased has not yet been decided. The company's fixed costs are budgeted at $3,973,500, and the variable costs are $68,500 per unit.

1. Compute the number of units that the company should agree to make at the stated contract price in order to earn a target income of $1,500,000.
2. Using a lighter material, the variable unit cost can be reduced by $1,730, but total fixed overhead will increase by $27,500. How many units must be produced to make $1,500,000 in profit?
3. Using the figures in **2**, how many additional units need to be produced to increase profit by $1,264,600?

Interpretation Case from Business

Trevor Corporation: Changes in Labor Cost
(L.O. 8, 9)

The president of Trevor Corporation, which manufactures tape decks and sells them to producers of sound-reproduction systems, anticipates that manufacturing employees (variable labor) will get a 10 percent wage increase on January 1 of next year. No other changes in costs are expected. The president has asked you to help develop the information he needs to formulate a reasonable product strategy for next year.

From a special analysis you prepared, you are satisfied that volume is the primary factor affecting costs and have separated the semivariable costs into their variable and fixed segments. You also observe that the beginning and ending inventories are never materially different. Here are current-year data for your analysis:

Current selling price per unit	$80
Variable cost per unit:	
Material	$30
Labor	12
Overhead	6
	$48
Annual sales volume	5,000 units
Fixed costs	$51,000

Required

Provide the president with the following information using cost-volume-profit analysis:

1. What increase in the selling price is necessary to cover the 10 percent wage increase and still maintain the current contribution margin ratio of 40 percent?
2. How many tape decks must be sold to maintain the current net income if the sales price remains at $80 and the 10 percent wage increase goes into affect?

(AICPA adapted)

Problem Set A

Problem 16A-1. Cost Behavior and Projection
(L.O. 2, 3, 4)

Howard Anderson Painting Company, located in Winter Haven, specializes in refurbishing exterior painted surfaces on homes and other buildings. In the humid South, exterior surfaces are hit hard with insect debris during the summer months. A special refurbishing technique, called *pressure cleaning*, is needed before the surface can be primed and repainted.

The technique involves the following steps:

1. Unskilled laborers trim trees and bushes two feet away from the structure.
2. Skilled laborers clean the building with a high-pressure cleaning machine, using about six gallons of Debris-Luse per job.
3. Unskilled laborers apply a coat of primer.
4. Skilled laborers apply oil-based exterior paint to the entire surface.

On average, specialized or skilled laborers work twelve hours per job, and unskilled, temporary laborers work eight hours.

The special pressure-cleaning and refurbishing process generated the following operating results during 19x4:

Number of structures refurbished	628
Specialized or skilled labor	$20.00 per hour
Unskilled, temporary labor	$8.00 per hour
Gallons of Debris-Luse used	3,768 gallons at $5.50 per gallon
Paint primer	7,536 gallons at $15.50 per gallon
Paint	6,280 gallons at $16.00 per gallon
Paint spraying equipment	$600.00 per month depreciation
Two leased vans	$800.00 per month total
Rent—storage building	$450.00 per month

The utilities costs for the year were as follows:

Month	Number of Jobs	Cost	Hours Worked
January	42	$ 3,950	840
February	37	3,550	740
March	44	4,090	880
April	49	4,410	980
May	54	4,720	1,080
June	62	5,240	1,240
July	71	5,820	1,420
August	73	5,890	1,460
September	63	5,370	1,260
October	48	4,340	960
November	45	4,210	900
December	40	3,830	800
Totals	628	$55,420	12,560

Required

1. Classify the cost items as variable, fixed, or semivariable costs.
2. Using the high-low method, separate semivariable costs into their variable and fixed components. Use total hours worked as a basis.
3. Compute the average cost per job for 19x4. (**Hint:** Divide 19x4's total cost for all cost items by the number of jobs completed.)

Problem 16A-2.
Breakeven Analysis
(L.O. 6, 8, 9)

Borman & Fess, a law firm in downtown San Francisco, is thinking of developing a legal clinic for middle- and low-income residents. The firm plans to hire paraprofessional help and to bill at $18 per hour. These paraprofessional employees will be law students who will work for $9 per hour. Other variable costs are anticipated to run $5.40 per hour, and annual fixed costs are expected to total $27,000.

Required

1. Compute the breakeven point in billable hours.
2. Compute the breakeven point in total billings.
3. Find the new breakeven point in total billings if fixed costs go up by $2,340.
4. Using the original figures, compute the breakeven point in total billings if the billing rate is decreased by $1 per hour, variable costs are decreased by $.40 per hour, and fixed costs are decreased by $3,600.

Problem 16A-3.
Breakeven Analysis and Profit Planning
(L.O. 6, 8, 9)

Selling citrus trees is the specialty of Orange County Nursery, Inc., which is considering adding a new line of deciduous fruit trees. Fixed costs will increase by $61,200 per year if the trees are introduced. Variable costs are expected to be $28 per tree. The average selling price is anticipated to be $45 per tree.

Required

1. From this information, compute the number of trees that must be sold per year for the company to break even on the new line of trees.
2. Determine the new breakeven point in sales units if the selling price were increased by 20 percent.
3. Assuming the original data, determine the breakeven point in sales units if fixed costs were reduced by $6,800.
4. Calculate the breakeven point in sales units if variable costs per tree were reduced to $25, assuming all other original data remain constant.
5. Compute the number of trees must be sold to earn a profit of $14,200 assuming the original data.

Problem 16A-4.
Profit Planning—Contribution Margin Approach
(L.O. 6, 8, 9)

Peck Financial Corporation is a subsidiary of Kramer Enterprises. Processing loan applications is the corporation's major task. Bob Singleton, manager of the loan department, established the policy of charging potential borrowers a fee of $250 for each application loan processed. Next year's variable costs are projected as follows: loan consultant wages, $15.50 per hour (it usually takes five hours to process a loan application); supplies, $2.40 per application; and other variable costs, $5.60 per application. Fixed costs include depreciation of equipment, $8,500; building rental, $14,000; promotional costs, $12,500; and other fixed costs, $8,099.

Required

1. Using the contribution margin approach, compute the number of loan applications the company must process (a) to break even and (b) to earn a profit of $14,476.
2. Continuing the same approach, compute the number of applications that must be processed to earn a target profit of $20,000, if promotional costs increase by $5,662.
3. Assuming the original information and the processing of 500 applications, compute the new loan application fee the company must use if the target profit is $41,651.
4. Mr. Singleton believes that 750 loan applications is the maximum his staff can handle. How much more can be spent on promotional costs if the highest fee tolerable to the customer is $280, if variable costs cannot be reduced, and if target net income for the application load is $50,000?

Problem 16A-5.
Profit Planning
(L.O. 6, 8, 9)

Baker Company, a manufacturer of quality handmade pipes, has experienced a steady growth in sales over the last five years. However, increased competition has led Alice Baker, the company president, to believe that an aggressive advertising campaign will be necessary in 19x4 to maintain the company's present growth. To prepare for the 19x4 advertising campaign, the company's accountants have presented Baker with the data in the table below, based on 19x3 operations.

Variable Cost per Pipe		Annual Fixed Costs	
Direct labor	$ 8.00	Manufacturing	$ 25,000
Direct materials	3.25	Selling	40,000
Variable overhead	2.50	Administrative	70,000
	$13.75		$135,000

Sales volume in 19x3 was 20,000 units at $25 per pipe. Target sales volume for 19x4 is $550,000, or 22,000 units. Assume a 34 percent tax rate.

Required

1. Compute the 19x3 after-tax net income.
2. Compute the breakeven volume in units for 19x3.
3. Baker believes an additional selling expense of $11,250 for advertising in 19x4, with all other costs remaining constant, will be necessary to achieve the sales target. Compute the after-tax net income for 19x4, assuming the target sales volume and expenditure for advertising occur as planned.
4. Compute the breakeven volume in sales dollars for 19x4 assuming the additional $11,250 is spent for advertising.
5. If the additional $11,250 is spent for advertising in 19x4, what is the 19x4 dollar sales volume required to earn the 19x3 after-tax net income?
6. At a 19x4 sales level of 22,000 units, what is the maximum amount that can be spent on advertising to earn an after-tax profit of $60,000?

(ICMA adapted)

Problem Set B

Problem 16B-1. Cost Behavior and Projection
(L.O. 2, 3, 4)

Having opened for business on March 1, 19x3, Alluring Auto, Inc. specializes in revitalizing automobile exteriors. *Detailing* is the term used to describe the process. The objective is to detail an automobile until it looks like it just rolled off the showroom floor. Area market research indicates that a full exterior detail should cost about $100. The company has just completed its first year of business and has asked its accountants to analyze the operating results. Management wants costs divided into variable, fixed, and semivariable components and would like them projected for the coming year. Anticipated volume for next year is 1,100 jobs.

The process used to detail a car's exterior is as follows:

1. One $20 per hour employee spends twenty minutes cleaning the car's exterior.
2. One can per car of Tars-Off, a cleaning compound, is used on the trouble spots.
3. A chemical compound called Buff Glow 7 is used to remove oxidants from the paint surface and restore the natural oils to the paint.
4. Poly Wax is applied by hand, allowed to sit for ten minutes, and then buffed off.
5. The final step is an inspection to see that all wax and debris have been removed.

On average, two hours are spent on each car, including the cleaning time and wait time for the wax. The following first-year operating information for Alluring Auto is provided to the accountant:

Number of automobiles detailed	840
Labor per auto	2 hours at $20.00 per hour
Containers of Tars-Off consumed	840 at $3.50 per can
Pounds of Buff Glow 7 consumed	105 pounds at $32.00 per pound
Pounds of Poly Wax consumed	210 pounds at $8.00 per pound
Rent	$1,400.00 per month

Here are the utilities costs for the fiscal year:

Month	Cost	Number of Jobs
March, 19x3	$ 800	40
April	850	50
May	900	65
June	1,000	85
July	1,600	105
August	1,801	110
September	1,300	90
October	850	65
November	900	75
December	925	60
January, 19x4	890	50
February	880	45
Totals	$12,696	840

Required

1. Classify the costs as variable, fixed, or semivariable.
2. Using the high-low method, separate the semivariable costs into their variable and fixed components. Use number of jobs as the basis.
3. Project these same costs for next year assuming the anticipated increase in activity and that fixed costs remain constant.
4. Compute the unit cost per job for next year.
5. Based on your answer to **4**, should the price remain at $100 per job?

Problem 16B-2.
Breakeven Analysis
(L.O. 6, 7, 8)

At the beginning of each year, the accounting department at Woolley Lighting, Ltd. must find the point at which projected sales revenue will equal total budgeted variable and fixed costs. The company manufactures custom-made, durable, low-voltage yard-lighting systems. Each system sells for an average of $435. Variable costs per unit are $210. Total fixed costs for the year are estimated to be $166,500.

Required

1. Compute the breakeven point in sales units.
2. Compute the breakeven point in sales dollars.
3. Find the new breakeven point in sales units if fixed costs go up by $10,125.
4. Using the original figures, compute the breakeven point in sales units if the selling price decreases to $425 per unit, fixed costs go up by $15,200, and variable costs decrease by $15 per unit.

Problem 16B-3.
Breakeven Analysis and Profit Planning
(L.O. 6, 7, 8, 9)

In 19x3, Altenburg Enterprises is expecting to earn a profit of $86,450. The company manufactures ornamental concrete blocks. Each lot of twenty blocks requires variable costs of $6.00 for raw materials, $3.50 for direct labor, $2.50 for manufacturing overhead, and $2.00 for selling costs. Total variable costs are $14.00 per lot. Fixed costs for 19x3 are anticipated to be $381,550. Each twenty-block lot will sell for $40.

Required

1. Determine how many lots of ornamental block the company must sell to earn its target profit, and convert this amount to sales dollars.
2. Compute breakeven sales in dollars.
3. What part of selling price represents profit beyond the breakeven point? Can this be proven by comparing the breakeven sales revenue with the sales revenue needed for the desired profit?
4. Present a graphic analysis of the projected sales and profit figures.

Problem 16B-4.
Profit Planning—Contribution Margin Approach
(L.O. 6, 8, 9)

Raoul Sanghi is president of the Baylor Plastics Division of Waco Industries. Management is considering a new product line that features a large bird posed in a running posture. Called "Chargin' Cardinal," the product is expected to have worldwide market appeal and become the mascot of many high school and university athletic teams. Expected variable unit costs are as follows: direct materials, $18.50; direct labor, $4.25; production supplies, $1.10; selling costs, $2.80; and other, $1.95. The following are annual fixed costs: depreciation, building and equipment, $36,000; advertising, $45,000; and other, $11,400. The company plans to sell the product for $55.

Required

1. Using the contribution margin approach, compute the number of products the company must sell in order (a) to break even and (b) to earn a profit of $70,224.
2. Continuing with the same approach, compute the number of products that must be sold to earn a target profit of $139,520 if advertising costs rise by $40,000.
3. Assuming the original information and sales of 10,000 units, compute the new selling price the company must use to make $131,600 profit.
4. According to the vice president of marketing, Joyce Dean, the most optimistic annual sales estimate for the product is 15,000 items. How much more can be spent on fixed advertising costs if the highest possible selling price the company can charge is $52.00, if variable costs cannot be reduced, and if target net income for 15,000 sales units is $251,000?

Problem 16B-5. Profit Planning
(L.O. 6, 8, 9)

Wheeler Company has a maximum capacity of 200,000 units per year. Variable manufacturing costs are $12 per unit. Fixed factory overhead is $600,000 per year. Variable selling and administrative costs are $5 per unit, whereas fixed selling and administrative costs are $300,000 per year. The current sales price is $23 per unit.

Required

Consider each situation independently and show all computations in good form.

1. What is the breakeven point in (a) sales units and (b) sales dollars?
2. How many units must be sold to earn a target net income of $240,000 per year?
3. A strike at a major supplier has caused a material shortage, so the current year's production and sales is limited to 160,000 units. Top management is planning to reduce fixed costs to $841,000 to partially offset the effect on profits of the reduced sales. Variable cost per unit is the same as last year. The company already has sold 30,000 units at the regular selling price of $23 per unit.
   a. How much of the fixed costs was covered by the total contribution margin of the first 30,000 units sold?
   b. What contribution margin per unit will be needed on the remaining 130,000 units to cover the remaining fixed costs and to earn a $210,000 profit this year?

Management Decision Case

Homan-Rodrigue, Ltd.
(L.O. 9)

Homan-Rodrigue, Ltd. is an international importer-exporter of fine china and other dishware. The company was formed in 1978 and is based in Portland, Oregon. Although very successful in its early years, the company's profitability has steadily declined over the last five years. Laura Homan-Rodrigue, president and chief executive officer, recently conducted a planning meeting with her officers, Jim Horzen, vice president of finance; Elyse Clayton, vice president of sales; Douglas White, vice president of purchases; and Maureen Hodgson, vice president of distribution. The purpose of the meeting was to discuss problems and to create a realistic financial plan for next year, 19x3. Before the meeting, Horzen distributed a budget for the period that had been developed by his assistant from information taken from actual and estimated data on the 19x3 budgeted income statement (shown on page 666).

Each member of the executive committee was asked to comment on the proposed plan and offer suggestions to improve its accuracy. The following comments were made at the meeting:

Horzen: "The budget developed by my assistant represents my best estimates of next year's operating results. We used the following rates for the variable costs: purchase cost of china, 35 percent of the selling price; purchase cost of other dishware, 45 percent of the selling price; distribution costs, 15 percent of the selling price; and sales commissions, 10 percent of the selling price."

Clayton: "I disagree with a few of Jim's numbers. First, the selling price of a set of china should be raised by $10; sales commissions should be raised by 2 percent of the selling price; fixed selling costs should be decreased by 10 percent; and fixed general and administrative costs should be increased by 5 percent."

White: "Jim, you did a good job as usual, but I've got a few changes to suggest, too. All purchase costs are going to go up. China will go up by 10 percent of the selling price, and other dishware will increase by 5 percent of the selling price. In addition, I think fixed purchasing costs will go down by 20 percent, and that fixed general and administrative costs will increase by 10 percent."

Hodgson: "Jim, we've already been notified that all variable distribution costs will increase by at least 3 percent of selling price over this year's amounts. I also believe that fixed distribution costs will increase by 5 percent and that fixed general and administrative costs will go down by 10 percent."

At the end of the meeting, Homan-Rodrigue instructed Horzen to have his assistant reconstruct the proposed budget based on the other officers' comments. Where more than one amount existed for the same category, an average of all amounts in that category was to be used. The revised plan would be discussed again at the next meeting.

Homan-Rodrigue, Ltd.
Budgeted Income Statement
For the Year 19x3

Sales			
China (15,000 sets at $940.00)		$14,100,000	
Other Dishware (78,000 sets at $310.00)		24,180,000	
Total Sales			$38,280,000
Less: Variable Costs			
Purchases			
China (15,000 sets at $329.00)	$ 4,935,000		
Other Dishware (78,000 sets at $139.50)	10,881,000	$15,816,000	
Distribution			
China (15,000 sets at $141.00)	$ 2,115,000		
Other Dishware (78,000 sets at $46.50)	3,627,000	5,742,000	
Sales Commissions			
China (15,000 sets at $94.00)	$ 1,410,000		
Other Dishware (78,000 sets at $31.00)	2,418,000	3,828,000	
Total Variable Costs			25,386,000
Contribution Margin			$12,894,000
Less: Fixed Costs			
Purchasing Costs		$ 2,450,000	
Distribution Costs		1,980,000	
Selling Costs		2,548,000	
General and Administrative Costs		2,236,000	
Total Fixed Costs			9,214,000
Projected Profit Before Taxes			$ 3,680,000

Required

1. Based on the information offered by each member of the executive committee, rework the proposed budget to reflect each individual forecast.
2. Develop the revised budget that will be discussed at the next meeting.
3. What do you think of the process used by the company to develop next year's budget? What changes would you make in the process?

Answers to Self-Test

1. b	3. c	5. a	7. d	9. c
2. c	4. d	6. b	8. a	10. b

LEARNING OBJECTIVES

1. *Define* cost allocation *and state the role of* cost objectives *in the cost allocation process.*
2. *Identify the uses of cost allocation in corporate accounting and reporting.*
3. *Define* supporting service function *and assign the costs of a supporting service to production departments.*
4. *Discuss the concept of absorption costing.*
5. *Compute a predetermined overhead rate and apply overhead costs to products in process using this rate.*
6. *Dispose of underapplied or overapplied overhead.*
7. *Identify the characteristics of a job order cost accounting system.*
8. *Diagram the cost flow and journalize transactions in a job order cost accounting system.*
9. *Compute the product unit cost for a specific job order.*

CHAPTER 17

Cost Allocation and the Job Order Costing System

The concept of cost allocation is introduced in this chapter together with the application and use of cost allocation techniques. In particular, we examine how to assign the costs of supporting service departments to production departments, and how to compute a predetermined overhead rate (used to apply factory overhead to products and jobs). We then explore the job order cost accounting system, record the movement of costs within the system, and compute a job order unit cost. After studying this chapter, you should be able to meet the learning objectives listed on the left.

DECISION POINT

Southwestern Bell Telephone Co.[1]

■ The telecommunications industry has had cost allocation problems since the National Bell Company was formed by Alexander Graham Bell in 1879. Even the 1984 breakup of the Bell System into many smaller local Bell companies did not solve the cost allocation problems. Allocating the costs of basic telephone equipment to the various categories of services provided by the Bell companies is the focus of the problems. These costs are indirect and are common to two or more categories of service. In most cases, they have been allocated arbitrarily. Because rates are based on cost per service, accurately allocating indirect costs to the various telephone services is very important.

Telecommunications costs are classified as either nontraffic-sensitive (NTS) costs or traffic-sensitive (TS) costs. NTS costs include the costs of the subscriber lines (running between the telephone user and the local Bell exchange company's switching equipment) that transfer calls between customers. Also included are the costs of executive compensation, business office costs, and general accounting. NTS costs have a fixed-cost behavior pattern. TS costs are incurred by providing telecommunications services that have a direct relationship to the number of messages or volume of traffic handled by a local or regional network. TS costs are either variable or semivariable in nature and can be traced directly to the three service classifications—interstate toll, intrastate toll, and local service—that generate the costs. How would you allocate NTS costs to the three services?

Because costs should be allocated fairly—not arbitrarily—on a benefits-received basis, NTS costs should be linked with the three service

1. Based on J. Patrick Cardello and Richard A. Moellenberndt, "The Cost Allocation Problem in a Telecommunications Company," *Management Accounting*, Institute of Management Accountants, September 1987, pp. 39–44.

categories by a benefits-received connection. Southwestern Bell Telephone Co., for example, uses subscriber line usage minutes. The company determines the minutes of usage of the telecommunications equipment and then divides the total into the minutes of usage for each of the three service categories. If, for instance, 10 percent of usage is traced to interstate toll calls, 10 percent of NTS costs would be allocated to that service category. ■

Cost Allocation

OBJECTIVE 1
Define cost allocation and state the role of cost objectives in the cost allocation process

Some costs (direct costs) can be traced and assigned to products or services easily; but other costs (indirect costs) must be assigned using some allocation method. The concept of cost allocation underlies every financial report the business prepares and uses—budgets, production cost forecasts, and decision support analyses. So cost allocation is important to every aspect of management, not just to the work of the management accountant.

The terms *cost allocation* and *cost assignment* often are used interchangeably, although *cost allocation* is the more popular of the two. **Cost allocation** is the process of assigning a specific cost to a specific cost objective.[2] A **cost objective** is the destination of an assigned or allocated cost.[3] If the purpose of a cost analysis is to evaluate the operating performance of a division or department, the cost objective is that department or division. But if product costing is the reason for accumulating costs, a specific product, order, or an entire contract could be the cost objective. The important point to remember is that the outcome of cost allocation depends on the cost objective being analyzed.

To understand cost allocation, you also need to understand the terms *cost center*, *direct cost*, and *indirect cost*. A **cost center** is any segment of an organization or area of activity for which there is a reason to accumulate costs. Examples of cost centers include the company as a whole, corporate divisions, specific operating plants, departments, even specific machines or work areas. No accounting report about a cost center can be prepared until all the proper cost allocation procedures have been carried out.

Finally, we need to expand the definitions of direct and indirect costs that we introduced earlier. A **direct cost** is any cost that can be conveniently and economically traced to a specific cost objective. Direct materials costs and direct labor costs normally are thought of as direct costs. However, direct costs vary with individual cost objectives. When the cost objective is a division of a company, then electricity, maintenance, and special tooling costs of the division are classified as direct costs. But when the cost objective is one of several products manufactured by the division, electricity, maintenance, and special tooling costs are indirect costs that must be allocated to that product. An **indirect cost** is any cost that cannot be conveniently or economically traced to a specific cost objective. Any production cost not classified as a direct cost is an indirect cost.

2. Cost Accounting Standard 402, promulgated by the Cost Accounting Standards Board in 1972, defined the term *allocate* as follows: "To assign an item of cost, or group of items of cost, to one or more cost objectives. This term includes both direct assignment of cost and the reassignment of a share from an indirect cost pool."
3. Cost Accounting Standard 402, promulgated by the Cost Accounting Standards Board in 1972, defined the term *cost objective* as follows: "A function, organizational subdivision, contract or other work unit for which cost data are desired and for which provision is made to accumulate and measure the cost to processes, products, jobs, capitalized projects, etc."

The Allocation of Manufacturing Costs

All manufacturing costs can be traced, or allocated, to a company's divisions, departments, or units of productive output. Direct costs, such as the cost of direct materials, can be assigned to specific jobs, products, or departments. Many manufacturing costs, however, are indirect costs that are incurred for the benefit of more than one product or department. These costs must be allocated to the products and departments that benefit from the costs. For example, a portion of the total electricity cost for a month is incurred for the benefit of all of a company's departments. The cost must be allocated to all the work done during the month. We already have discussed the fact that depreciation is actually an allocation process: A portion of the item's original depreciable cost is allocated to each period in which the item is used by the company. A similar process is used to allocate manufacturing costs.

The cost allocation process is shown in Figure 17-1. All three cost elements are included: materials, labor, and factory overhead. In this example, the cost objective is the product. The costs of lumber and the cabinetmaker's wages are direct costs of the product. The factory overhead costs include depreciation of the table saw, cleanup and janitorial services, and nails. All factory overhead costs are indirect costs of the product and must be assigned by means of an allocation method.

To summarize, the allocation of production costs calls for assigning direct and indirect manufacturing costs to specific cost objectives. The method of cost allocation depends on the specific cost objectives being analyzed. A cost can be a direct cost to a large cost objective (a division) but an indirect cost to a smaller cost objective (a product). In general, the number of costs classified as direct costs increases with the size of the cost objective.

The Role of Cost Assignment in Corporate Reporting

Accounting reports are prepared for all levels of management, from the president down to the department manager or supervisor. The president is responsible for all of the company's costs. A department manager, on the other hand, is

Figure 17-1. Cabinetmaking: Assigning Manufacturing Costs to a Product

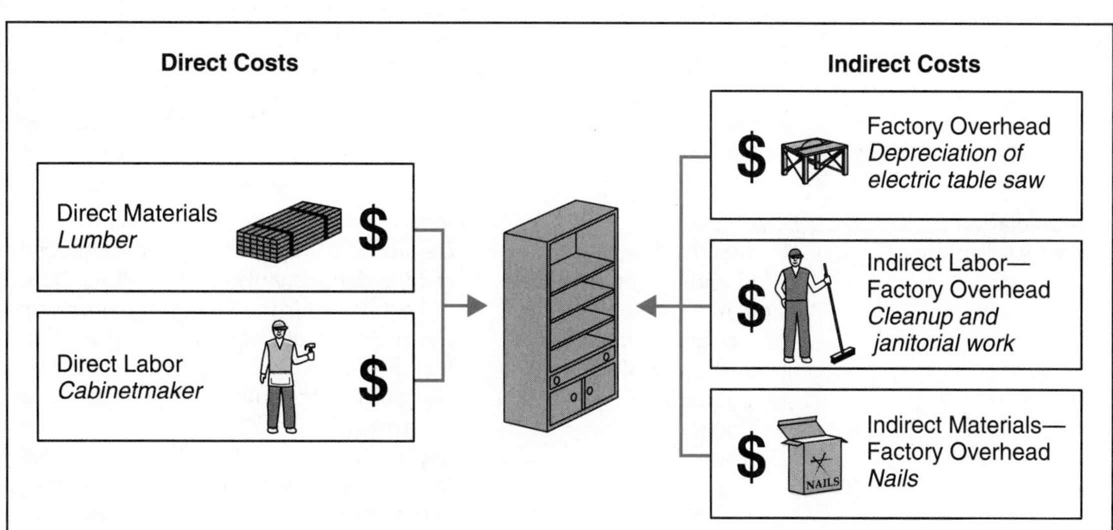

OBJECTIVE 2
Identify the uses of cost allocation in corporate accounting and reporting

responsible only for the costs connected to that one department. Reports must be prepared for all cost centers, including the company as a whole, each division, and all of the departments within each division. The same costs shown in departmental reports appear again in divisional and corporate reports but perhaps in summary form. (We expand on this subject in the chapter on responsibility accounting and the budgeting process.)

As the focus changes from one cost center or cost objective to another, so does the ease with which costs can be traced. Here is where cost allocation comes into the picture. As costs are reclassified and assigned to smaller cost centers or cost objectives, they become more difficult to trace. When the cost objective is reduced to a single product, only direct materials and direct labor costs can be traced directly. All other costs are classified as indirect and must be assigned to the product.

Table 17-1 shows how three manufacturing costs are traced as their cost objectives change. Direct materials costs can be traced directly to any level of cost objective shown. They are a direct cost at the divisional, departmental, and product levels. All 40,000 pounds of sugar were issued to Division A, so they can be traced directly to that division. Only half (20,000 pounds) was used by

Table 17-1. Manufacturing Cost Classification and Traceability

	Cost Objectives		
Costs	**Division A**	**Department XZ**	**Product AB**
Direct Materials	*Direct cost:* 40,000 pounds of sugar were issued from inventory specifically for Division A.	*Direct cost:* 20,000 of the 40,000 pounds of sugar issued from inventory were used by Department XZ (can be traced directly).	*Direct cost:* Every unit of Product AB requires one-half pound of sugar.
Depreciation of Machine 201	*Direct cost:* Machine 201 is located within Department XZ and is used exclusively by Division A. Depreciation on the machine, then, can be traced directly to Division A.	*Direct cost:* Machine 201 is used only by Department XZ. Therefore, its depreciation charges can be traced directly to Department XZ.	*Indirect cost:* The depreciation of Machine 201 cannot be traced directly to the individual products it produces. Depreciation charges are accounted for as part of factory overhead costs.
Depreciation of Factory Building G	*Direct cost:* Factory Building G is used entirely by Division A. Therefore, all depreciation expenses from the use of Factory Building G can be traced directly to Division A.	*Indirect cost:* Department XZ is one of four departments in Factory Building G. Depreciation of Factory Building G is allocated to the four departments according to the square footage used by each department.	*Indirect cost:* Depreciation of Factory Building G is an indirect product cost. It is allocated to individual products as part of factory overhead charges applied to products, using machine hours as a base.

Department XZ, so only half can be traced directly to that department. At the product level, every unit of Product AB requires one-half pound of sugar. The cost of that one-half pound is a direct cost that can be traced to the product.

Depreciation costs of Machine 201 can be traced directly to both Division A and Department XZ. When Product AB is the cost objective, however, the depreciation of the machine is considered an indirect manufacturing cost and is accounted for as a factory overhead cost. Factory overhead costs are accumulated and then allocated to the products produced in Department XZ.

Finally, the depreciation of Factory Building G, which is used entirely by Division A, can be traced directly to Division A. For smaller cost objectives, though, it becomes an indirect cost. Building depreciation must be shared by the various cost centers in the building. The costs of building depreciation must be allocated to departmental cost objectives using an allocation base such as space occupied. It is then reallocated to products.

The principles of classifying and tracing costs that we have discussed here play a part in the preparation of all internal accounting reports. In accounting for operating costs, each cost must be assigned to products, services, jobs, or departments before reports can be prepared. Without proper cost allocation techniques, management accountants cannot (1) determine product or service unit costs, (2) develop cost budgets and cost control measures for management, or (3) prepare reports and analyses to help management make and support its decisions. Each of these tasks depends on cost allocation procedures.

Assigning the Costs of Supporting Service Functions

OBJECTIVE 3
Define supporting service function *and assign the costs of a supporting service to production departments*

Every company and manufacturing process depends on the help of many supporting service functions or departments. Although not involved directly in production activities, a **supporting service function** is an operating unit or department that supports the activities of a company's production and production-related facilities. Examples include a repair and maintenance department, a production scheduling department, a central power department, an inspection department, and materials storage and handling activities.

The costs of these supporting departments are incurred for the purpose of producing a product, so they are product costs. They must be included in the overhead element of product unit costs. They should be treated as indirect manufacturing costs and assigned to products through the Factory Overhead Control account. This allocation is done in two steps. First, the costs of the supporting service function are allocated to the departments or cost centers that benefit from the services. Then, the assigned costs are included in the production department's Factory Overhead Control account and allocated to the end product.

Here, we focus on the first step: assigning the costs of supporting services to the appropriate production departments. To carry out this step, we need (1) a basis for measuring the costs of the supporting services and relating them to the production departments and (2) a method for assigning the costs.

Selecting a Basis for Allocating Costs

A service function must benefit other departments to justify its existence. The concept of benefit is the basis for assigning the costs of supporting service de-

Table 17-2. Cost Allocation Bases for Assigning the Costs of Supporting Service Functions

Possible Allocation Basis	When to Use
1. Number of service requests	Used when each service takes the same amount of time, or when a record of service requests is maintained and no other basis is available
2. Machine hours	Used when machine hours usage relates to the type of service performed
3. Kilowatt hours used	Used to distribute the costs of a central power department
4. Number of materials requisitions	Used to allocate the costs of materials storage

partments to production departments. Benefit must be measured on some basis that shows how the service relates to the department that receives the service.

Table 17-2 gives examples of bases used to allocate the costs of supporting service functions. Each basis should be used only when a close benefit relationship exists between the service and the production departments. For example, each request for service may represent an equal amount of benefit, or service, to the receiving department. In that case, the number of service requests can be the allocation basis. Or total benefit may be measured by the number of machine hours generated per service cost. Here, machine hours should be the basis of the cost allocation. Similar relationships justify the use of kilowatt hours or the number of materials requisitions as the allocation basis.

Methods Used To Allocate Service Department Costs

There are two generally recognized methods for allocating service department costs to production departments, the step method and the direct method. The **step method** is used when the services of one department are used by other service departments as well as by production departments. Here, the service department's costs are allocated to the other benefiting service departments first and then to the production departments. The **direct method** is employed when a service department's tasks benefit production departments only. In this case, the service department's costs are allocated directly to the production departments. Exhibit 17-1 shows this method of allocation: All costs are allocated directly to the production departments. Remember that a single method need not be selected for the entire process of allocating service department costs. It is possible to combine the methods: to use the step method for service departments that benefit all departments and to use the direct method for service departments that benefit only production departments.

We have to assign service department costs to production departments before these costs can be included in the calculation of factory overhead rates. Before we explain the overhead rate computation, however, we look at an example of the step and direct methods of allocating service department costs to production departments.

Exhibit 17-1. Service Department Overhead Cost Allocation Process—Direct Method

	Supporting Service Departments			Production Departments	
	Dept. 1	Dept. 2	Dept. 3	Dept. A	Dept. B
Allocation of service department costs to production departments					
Estimated overhead costs	$X,XXX	$X,XXX	$X,XXX	$ XX,XXX	$ XX,XXX
	(X,XXX) →			XXX	XXX
	$ 0				
		(X,XXX) →		XXX	XXX
		$ 0			
			(X,XXX) →	XXX	XXX
			$ 0		
Total allocated estimated overhead				$XXX,XXX	$XXX,XXX
Application of overhead costs to products					
Total allocated estimated overhead				$XXX,XXX	$XXX,XXX
÷ Estimated volume				XXX	XXX
= Predetermined overhead rate				$ XX	$ XX
				→ Product(s)	← Product(s)

Illustrative Problem
Assigning the Costs of Service Departments: Combining the Step and Direct Methods

Hazelkorn Industries, Inc. is a fastener company located in Bentley, Massachusetts. The company's factory utilizes three service departments (Repair and Maintenance, Tool and Die, and Production Scheduling) and two production departments (Heading/Slotting and Threading). The following estimates of factory overhead costs have been compiled for the year ending December 31, 19x2:

Repair and Maintenance Department	$ 51,100
Tool and Die Department	94,900
Production Scheduling Department	41,500
Heading/Slotting Department	453,800
Threading Department	211,500
Totals	$852,800

The company's controller has determined that the services of the Repair and Maintenance Department are used by all the other departments, and that the services of the Tool and Die Department and the Production Scheduling Department are used only by the production departments. In addition, the following bases for allocating costs have been selected: the number of service requests for allocating the costs of the Repair and Maintenance Department; machine

Exhibit 17-2. Allocation of Service Department Costs (Combined Method) for Hazelkorn Industries, Inc., 19x2

	Supporting Service Departments			Production Departments		
	Repair and Maintenance	Tool and Die	Production Scheduling	Heading/ Slotting	Threading	Totals
Estimated 19x2 factory overhead	$51,100	$ 94,900	$41,500	$453,800	$211,500	$852,800
Repair and Maintenance (number of service requests)	(51,100)	9,100	500	24,400	17,100	
	$ 0	$104,000	$42,000			
Tool and Die (number of machine hours)		(104,000)		62,400	41,600	
		$ 0				
Production Scheduling (number of units produced)			(42,000)	21,000	21,000	
			$ 0	$561,600	$291,200	$852,800
Detail of bases selected:						
Number of service requests		910	50	2,440	1,710	5,110
Number of machine hours				124,800 (60%)	83,200 (40%)	208,000 (100%)
Number of units produced				60,000 M* (50%)	60,000 M* (50%)	60,000 M* (same products through both departments)

*M = 1,000-unit lots.

hours for allocating the costs of the Tool and Die Department; and units produced for allocating the costs of the Production Scheduling Department. Estimates for these bases for the year are as follows:

	Service Requests	Machine Hours	Total Units Produced
Repair and Maintenance Department	0	0	0
Tool and Die Department	910	0	0
Production Scheduling Department	50	0	0
Heading/Slotting Department	2,440	124,800	60,000 M*
Threading Department	1,710	83,200	60,000 M*
Totals	5,110	208,000	120,000 M*

*M = 1,000-unit lots.

Required

Using the data given for the cost estimates and the allocation bases, prepare a schedule allocating the overhead costs of the service departments to the production departments.

Solution

The objective here is to allocate the overhead costs of the service departments to the two production departments. The allocation is illustrated in Exhibit 17-2. The estimated 19x2 factory overhead costs for the five departments are shown across the top of the exhibit.

The step method is used to allocate the costs of the Repair and Maintenance Department because it services all of the other departments. And because the allocation of costs from Repair and Maintenance affects the amounts to be allocated from the Tool and Die Department and the Production Scheduling Department, Repair and Maintenance costs are allocated first. The allocation basis is the number of service requests, which are identified at the bottom of Exhibit 17-2; the allocation rate is $10 per request ($51,100 ÷ 5,110 requests).

Notice that their share of the Repair and Maintenance costs is added to the original department overhead of the Tool and Die and Production Scheduling Departments. These total costs are allocated to production using the direct method. The Tool and Die costs, a total of $104,000, are allocated to the two production departments using machine hours as the basis. Heading/Slotting, which generated 60 percent of the machine hours during the period, is allocated 60 percent of the costs, or $62,400 ($104,000 × .60); Threading is allocated 40 percent, or $41,600 ($104,000 × .40). For Production Scheduling, the allocation basis is the number of units produced. Because an equal number of units was produced by both production departments, $21,000 ($42,000 × .50) is allocated to both the Heading/Slotting and Threading Departments.

Once we have completed the allocation process, we can check our answers by adding the columns for the Heading/Slotting and Threading Departments. In our example, $187,500 (the original costs of the service departments) has been reassigned, but the total dollar amount has not changed. The analysis still is dealing with total costs of $852,800. As long as the totals of the two production departments add up to $852,800, our computations supporting the allocation process are correct.

The Concept of Absorption Costing

OBJECTIVE 4
Discuss the concept of absorption costing

Product costing is possible only when the accounting system can define the types of manufacturing costs that must be included in the analysis. For instance, should all factory overhead costs be considered costs of making the product, or only the variable factory overhead costs? Usually, we assume that product costing is governed by the concept of absorption costing. **Absorption costing** is an approach to product costing in which a representative portion of *all* types of manufacturing costs—direct materials, direct labor, variable factory overhead, and fixed factory overhead—is assigned to individual products.

Direct materials and direct labor costs are not difficult to handle in product costing because they can be conveniently and economically traced to specific products. Factory overhead costs, on the other hand, are not as easy to trace to products. For example, how much machine depreciation should a company that manufactures lawn and garden equipment assign to a single lawnmower? How about the costs of electrical power and indirect labor? One solution would be to wait until the end of the accounting period, add all the variable and fixed factory overhead costs incurred, and divide the total by the number of units produced during the period. This procedure would work if all products were alike (and required the same manufacturing operations) and if managers could wait until the end of a period to determine product unit costs—a rare circumstance. In practice, a company usually makes many different products, and managers need product costing information to set prices before the goods are produced. The solution is to use a predetermined overhead rate to allocate factory overhead costs to products.

Predetermined Overhead Rates

OBJECTIVE 5
Compute a predetermined overhead rate and apply overhead costs to products in process using this rate

Factory overhead costs are a problem for the management accountant. Actual overhead costs fluctuate from month to month because of the timing of fixed overhead costs and the changing patterns and amounts of variable costs. The need to price out new products and to evaluate production performance prevents management from waiting until the end of the accounting period to account for these costs.

How can these costs be estimated and assigned to products or jobs before the end of an accounting period? The most common way is to use a **predetermined overhead rate** for each department or operating unit. We define this rate as a factor used to assign factory overhead costs to specific products or jobs. It is based on *estimated* overhead costs and production levels for the period.

The predetermined overhead rate is computed in three steps:

1. Estimate factory overhead costs. Using various management accounting tools and analyses, estimate all factory overhead costs. Do so for each service and production department for the coming accounting period. (Cost behavior analysis is especially useful for this procedure.) Allocate the service department costs, and then add the totals for all the production departments. For example, look back to Exhibit 17-2. The total estimated factory overhead costs assigned to the Heading/Slotting Department were $561,600.
2. Select a basis for allocating costs and estimate its amount. We have to connect overhead costs to products by using some measure of production activity—machine hours, labor hours, dollars of direct labor costs, or units of output, for example. The basis we choose should link the overhead costs to the products produced in a meaningful way. For instance, if an operation is more machine hour than labor hour intensive, then machine hours would be a good basis for overhead allocation. Suppose that this is the basis Hazelkorn Industries decides to use to allocate factory overhead costs in its Heading/Slotting Department. According to Exhibit 17-2, management estimates that the department will generate 124,800 machine hours during the year.
3. Divide the total overhead costs estimated for the period by the total estimated basis (hours, dollars, or units). The result is the predetermined overhead rate. In our Hazelkorn Industries example, the computation for the Heading/Slotting Department is as follows:

$$\begin{aligned}\text{Predetermined overhead rate per machine hour} &= \frac{\text{total estimated overhead costs}}{\text{total estimated machine hours}} \\ &= \frac{\$561{,}600}{124{,}800 \text{ machine hours}} \\ &= \$4.50 \text{ of overhead per machine hour}\end{aligned}$$

Overhead costs then are applied to each product using the predetermined overhead rate. Suppose that it takes 0.5 machine hour to produce one unit. Because the overhead rate is $4.50 per machine hour, that unit is assigned $2.25 of factory overhead costs. This amount is added to the direct materials and direct labor costs already assigned to the product, and their sum is the total unit cost.

Table 17-3 sums up the process of allocating overhead costs. In Phase I, we compute the predetermined overhead rate. To do so, we estimate total overhead costs and total production activity. In Phase II, we use the predetermined overhead rate to compute the amount of overhead costs to be applied to products or jobs during the period—a process we describe in a later section.

Table 17-3. Overhead Cost Allocation

Phase I: Computing the Predetermined Overhead Rate

Develop Overhead Cost Estimates
Estimate total overhead costs for each production department.

Develop Allocation (Activity) Basis Estimates
1. For each production department, select an allocation basis with a causal or beneficial relationship to the costs being assigned to the end product or job.
2. Carefully estimate the activity level for each department for the coming period.

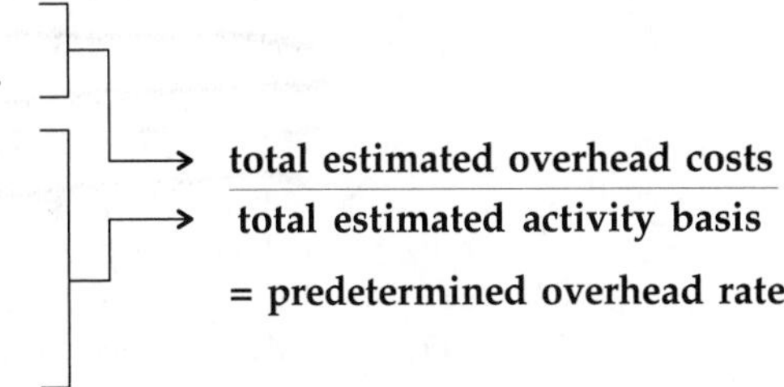

Phase II: Using the Rate to Assign Overhead Costs

Predetermined overhead rate × actual amount of activity per job order **= overhead cost assigned to that job order or batch of products**

The Importance of Good Estimates

The successful allocation of overhead costs depends on two factors. One is a careful estimate of total overhead. The other is a good forecast of the production activity that is used as the allocation basis.

Estimating total overhead costs is critical. If the estimate is wrong, the overhead rate will be wrong: Either too much or too little overhead will be assigned to the products. Therefore, in developing this estimate, the management accountant must be careful to include all factory overhead items and to forecast their costs accurately.

Overhead costs generally are estimated as part of the normal budgeting process. Expected overhead costs are gathered from all departments involved either directly or indirectly with the production process. The accounting department receives and totals each department's cost estimates. As we have seen, the costs of supporting service departments, such as the Repair and Maintenance Department, are connected only indirectly to the products, and their costs are distributed among the production departments. In this way, they are included as part of a total factory overhead when computing the predetermined overhead rate for the period.

Forecasting production activity is also critical to the success of overhead cost allocation. Once the appropriate base (machine hours, direct labor hours, direct labor cost, or units of output) has been determined, the estimated total activity base for the coming period must be computed. Assume that the activity base is machine hours. How do we estimate total machine hours for a future period? Machine hours are a function of the number of products to be produced. Each product requires a certain amount of machine time. The first step, then, is to find out how many units the manufacturing departments are planning to produce. Once this number has been determined, total estimated machine hours can be computed by multiplying total units to be produced by the number of machine hours required per unit.

Using the Predetermined Overhead Rate

A predetermined overhead rate has two primary uses. First, this rate enables the management accountant to provide cost information to sales personnel to support pricing decisions for a new product or job order. Prices are influenced by many factors, including the item's cost, and prices usually are determined before an item is produced. Factory overhead can consist of dozens, even hundreds, of types of costs, and estimating these costs every time a price must be determined would be difficult. The predetermined overhead rate significantly simplifies the price-setting process. Second, the predetermined overhead rate allows the company to attach overhead costs to items as they are worked on and completed, instead of at the end of an accounting period. Factory overhead is "applied" to the product as it moves through the production process.

Using a predetermined overhead rate changes the recordkeeping process. To this point in your study of accounting, a separate account has been maintained for each type of overhead cost incurred. When electricity or factory insurance costs were incurred, we debited the individual accounts for the amount. With the predetermined overhead rate, we introduce a new account into the recording process, the **Factory Overhead Control account**. This account is a general ledger account that contains the cumulative total of all types of factory overhead costs; it also is used to accumulate all overhead costs applied to products produced. As is the case with all control accounts, a subsidiary ledger is maintained to account for all of the individual types of costs charged to the Factory Overhead Control account. Each time an overhead cost is incurred, the Factory Overhead Control account is debited and the individual account is also debited.

Factory overhead is applied to products by debiting an amount to the Work in Process Inventory Control account. The amount is determined by multiplying the predetermined overhead rate by the amount of the basis used by the production process. (This computation is shown at the bottom of Table 17-3.) Each time the Work in Process Inventory Control account is debited for overhead costs applied, the Factory Overhead Control account is credited for the same amount. At the end of the accounting period, all overhead costs actually incurred have been debited to the Factory Overhead Control account, and all overhead costs applied to the products produced have been credited to the same account.

For example, assume that the Heading/Slotting Department of Hazelkorn Industries incurred the following overhead costs during March:

Mar. 5 Recorded usage of indirect materials and supplies, $11,890 (transferred from Materials Inventory Control account).
Mar. 10 Paid indirect labor wages, $14,220.
Mar. 15 Paid property taxes on factory building, $7,540, and utility bill, $5,200.
Mar. 31 Recorded expiration of prepaid insurance premiums, $2,820, and depreciation of machinery for the month, $4,430.

These transactions resulted in the following entries:

Mar. 5	Factory Overhead Control	11,890	
	Materials Inventory Control		11,890
	Usage of indirect materials and supplies		
10	Factory Overhead Control	14,220	
	Factory Payroll		14,220
	Distribution of indirect labor costs from the Factory Payroll account		
15	Factory Overhead Control	12,740	
	Cash		12,740
	Payment of property taxes of $7,540 and utilities of $5,200		

		Debit	Credit
Mar. 31	Factory Overhead Control	7,250	
	Prepaid Insurance		2,820
	Accumulated Depreciation, Machinery		4,430
	To record the expiration of prepaid insurance premiums and depreciation on machinery for March		

These entries record actual overhead costs of $46,100 debited to the Factory Overhead Control account. However, they neither assign the costs to products nor transfer the costs to the Work in Process Inventory Control account. This transfer must take place before factory overhead costs can be added to the costs of direct materials and direct labor so that product unit costs can be computed. This is when the predetermined overhead rate is used. Remember that the predetermined overhead rate for Hazelkorn's Heading/Slotting Department for the period is $4.50 per machine hour. The following list of jobs completed during March shows the number of machine hours required for each job and the overhead costs applied to each job:

Job	Machine Hours	×	Rate	=	Overhead Applied
16–2	3,238		$4.50		$14,571
18–6	3,038		4.50		13,671
21–5	3,884		4.50		17,478
	10,160				$45,720

The following journal entry records the application of the predetermined overhead rate to Job 16–2 (a similar entry would be made for each job worked on during March):

	Debit	Credit
Work in Process Inventory Control	14,571	
Factory Overhead Control		14,571
Application of overhead costs to Job 16–2		

This entry transfers the estimated overhead costs from the Factory Overhead Control account to the Work in Process Inventory Control account. Normally, the entry is made when production data are recorded because overhead costs can be applied only after the number of machine hours used is known.

After posting all of the overhead transactions discussed above, we compare the applied overhead costs (the amounts credited to the Factory Overhead Control account) with the actual overhead costs incurred (the amounts debited to the account). As shown below, we applied less costs than were incurred, so we have an underapplied overhead cost situation.

Factory Overhead Control

3/5	11,890	Job 16–2	14,571
3/10	14,220	Job 18–6	13,671
3/15	12,740	Job 21–5	17,478
3/31	7,250		45,720
	46,100		
Bal.	**380**		

Accounting for Underapplied or Overapplied Overhead

Although companies expend much time and effort estimating and allocating factory overhead costs, actual overhead costs and actual production activities

OBJECTIVE 6
Dispose of underapplied or overapplied overhead

seldom agree with the estimates. Because of changes in either the overhead costs or the activity-related allocation base, assigned factory overhead is either *underapplied* or *overapplied*—that is, the amount applied is less than or greater than the actual overhead costs incurred. We account for these differences by making a monthly, quarterly, or annual adjusting entry, depending on the policy of the company.

To explain this adjustment, we turn again to our Hazelkorn Industries example. The records show that at month's end, overhead costs have been underapplied by $380 ($46,100 – $45,720). More overhead was incurred than applied: The predetermined overhead rate was low; that is, the rate used did not apply all of the overhead costs incurred to the products produced. Because we have to account for all actual costs, the $380 now must be added to the production costs for the period. Assuming that most of the goods worked on during the period have been sold or that the amount is immaterial, the adjusting entry at the end of the month would charge the amount underapplied to the Cost of Goods Sold account:

Mar. 31	Cost of Goods Sold	380	
	Factory Overhead Control		380
	To record charge of underapplied overhead to the Cost of Goods Sold account		

The company should investigate any significant differences in the amount applied versus the actual overhead costs incurred; the rate may have to be recomputed if large differences persist. Here, we simply account for the $380 difference by disposing of the balance. In the chapter on standard costing and variance analysis, we investigate and identify the causes of these differences when we analyze factory overhead variances.

Product Costing Systems—Job Order Costing

Job order costing and process costing are the two basic product cost accounting systems. Actual cost accounting systems differ widely; however, all are based on one of these two systems. The choice of the general type of product costing system is influenced by the production operation itself. Industries that manufacture unique or large complicated products, such as a jet aircraft, use a type of job order system. Companies that manufacture liquid products such as paint or produce thousands of identical items in a continuous flow use some variation of the process costing system. Once the type of system has been selected, it can be adjusted to fit the particular company or operating department.

The objective of the two systems is the same: to provide product unit costs that can be used by managers to support product price development, control costs, value inventory, and prepare financial statements. End-of-period values for cost of goods sold, work in process inventory, and finished goods inventory are computed using product unit cost data. In this chapter, we concentrate on the description and operation of the job order costing system; the process costing system is discussed in the next chapter.

The Characteristics of Job Order Costing

A **job order cost accounting system** is a product costing system in which materials, labor, and factory overhead costs are assigned to specific jobs or batches

OBJECTIVE 7
Identify the characteristics of a job order cost accounting system

of product. A job order cost system is used by companies that make one-of-a-kind or special-order products, such as ships or large machines. In a job order costing system, product unit costs are computed by dividing total manufacturing costs for each job order by the number of good units produced for that order.

A job order cost system has three primary characteristics: (1) It collects all manufacturing costs and assigns them to specific jobs or batches of product; (2) it accumulates and measures costs for each job, rather than for set time periods; and (3) it uses a single Work in Process Inventory Control account, collecting on a job order cost card the costs for each job being worked on. These cards make up the subsidiary ledger of the Work in Process Inventory Control account.

The Job Order Cost Accounting System

OBJECTIVE 8
Diagram the cost flow and journalize transactions in a job order cost accounting system

Remember that a job order cost system is designed to gather manufacturing costs for a specific order or batch of products, to help determine product unit costs. A **job order** is a customer order for a specific number of specially designed, made-to-order products. Price setting, production scheduling, and other management tasks related to job orders depend on information from the cost accounting system. This is why it is necessary to maintain a system that gives timely, correct data about product costs. In the introductory chapter on management accounting, we discussed the three main cost elements—materials, labor, and factory overhead. Here, we see how these costs are accounted for in a job order cost system. Notice that all inventory balances in a job order cost system are kept on a perpetual basis, and, following the absorption costing approach, all production costs are included in the analysis.

Incurring Materials, Labor, and Factory Overhead Costs

A basic part of a job order cost system is the set of procedures, accounts, and journal entries used when the company incurs materials, labor, and factory overhead costs. To help control these costs, businesses use various documents to support each transaction. The effective use of these procedures and documents generates timely, accurate information for managers. This set of procedures also allows a smooth and continuous flow of information through the accounting records.

Materials. Careful use of materials improves a company's overall efficiency and profitability by conserving productive resources and saving their related costs. At the same time, good records ensure accountability. So, controlling the physical materials used in production and keeping good records increase the opportunity to earn a profit.

To help record and control materials costs, accountants rely on a series of documents including purchase requisitions, purchase orders, receiving reports, inventory records, and materials requisitions. Through these documents, direct materials are ordered, received, stored, and issued into production. Information from materials requisitions allows direct materials costs to be traced to specific jobs or batches of product, and identify the amount of indirect materials that should be charged to factory overhead.

Labor. Labor is one production resource that cannot be stored and used later, so it must be accounted for carefully. Labor time cards and job cards are used to record labor costs as they are incurred. Time cards keep track of the total time worked per day by an employee; labor job cards track the amount of time each employee works on a particular job or other labor classification. Labor costs that can be traced directly to a job or batch of products are debited to the Work in Process Inventory Control account; all indirect labor costs flow through the Factory Overhead Control account.

Factory Overhead. All indirect manufacturing costs are classified as factory overhead. Like direct materials and direct labor costs, factory overhead costs require documents to support the recording and payment of costs. As described above, materials requisitions support the use of indirect materials and supplies, and labor job cards track indirect labor; vendors' bills support most of the other indirect costs. Overhead costs can be accounted for in separate general ledger accounts, but this is not done in a job order cost system. Instead, they are all debited to the Factory Overhead Control account. To keep track of individual factory overhead costs, a separate subsidiary account is maintained for each type of overhead cost; these accounts make up the subsidiary ledger for the Factory Overhead Control account. Using the predetermined overhead rate, factory overhead costs are charged to individual jobs by crediting the Factory Overhead Control account and debiting the Work in Process Inventory Control account.

The Work in Process Inventory Control Account

Job order costing focuses on the flow of costs through the Work in Process Inventory Control account. All manufacturing costs incurred and charged to production are routed through this account. Figure 17-2 shows the cost flow in a job order cost system.

The costs of direct materials and indirect materials and supplies are debited to Materials Inventory Control when purchased. When used, direct materials are debited to the Work in Process Inventory Control account; indirect materials and supplies are debited to the Factory Overhead Control account. All labor costs that can be traced to specific jobs are debited to the Work in Process Inventory Control account; indirect labor costs are charged to the Factory Overhead Control account. By means of the predetermined overhead rate, we apply overhead costs to specific jobs by debiting the Work in Process Inventory Control account and crediting the Factory Overhead Control account.

Because all manufacturing costs are debited to the Work in Process Inventory Control account, we need a separate accounting procedure to link those costs to specific jobs. For this purpose, we use a subsidiary ledger made up of **job order cost cards**. One job order cost card exists for each job being worked on, and all of the costs of that job are recorded on it. As costs are debited to Work in Process Inventory Control, we also reclassify them by job and record them on the appropriate job order cost cards.

A typical job order cost card is shown in Figure 17-3. Each card has space for direct materials, direct labor, and factory overhead costs. It also includes the job order number, product specifications, the name of the customer, the date of the order, the projected completion date, and a cost summary. As each department incurs materials and labor costs, the individual job order cost cards are updated. Factory overhead, as applied, also is posted to the job order cost cards. Job order cost cards for incomplete jobs make up the subsidiary ledger for the Work in Process Inventory Control account. To be sure the ending balance in that account is correct, we compare it with the total of the costs shown on the job order cost cards. (We illustrate this process later in this section, when we examine a specific example in detail.)

Figure 17-2. Job Order Cost Flow

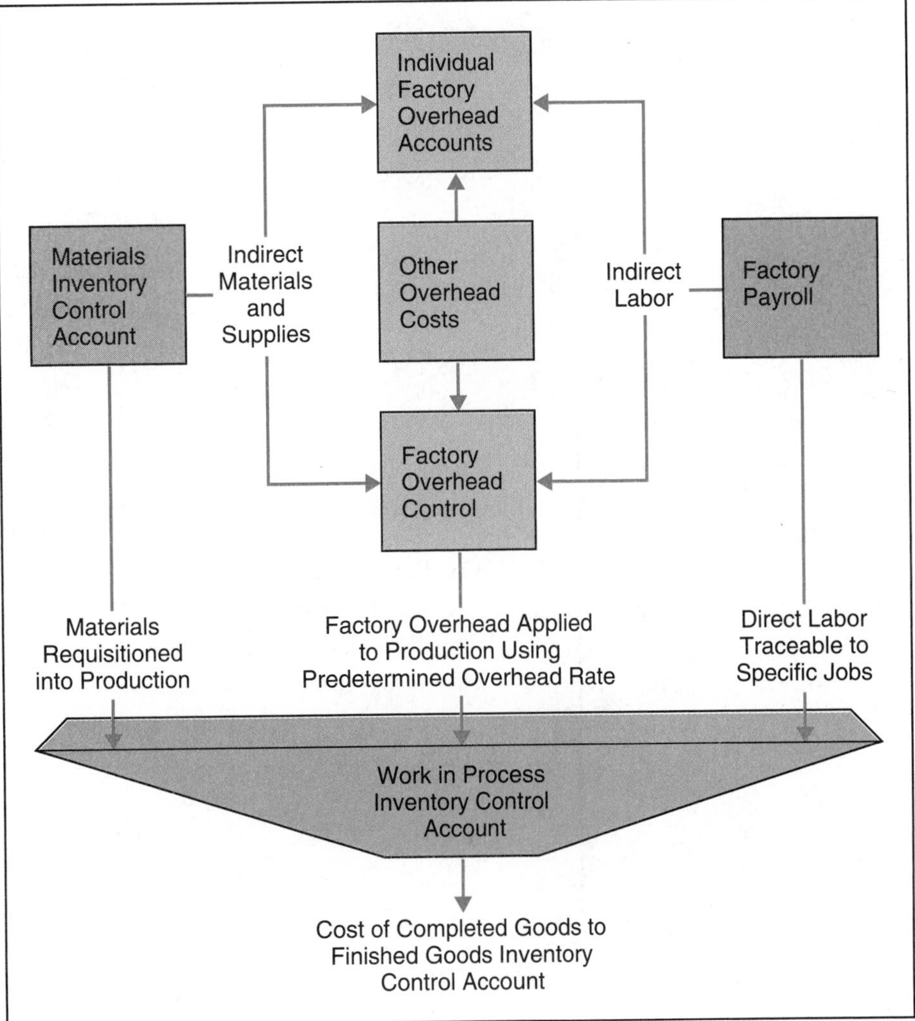

Accounting for Finished Goods

When a job has been completed, all costs assigned to that job order are transferred to the Finished Goods Inventory Control account by debiting the Finished Goods Inventory Control account and crediting the Work in Process Inventory Control account. Once this entry is made, the job order cost card is removed from the subsidiary ledger file. It then is used to help update the Finished Goods Inventory Control account.

When goods are shipped, the order for them is recorded as a sale. At this point, Accounts Receivable is debited and Sales is credited for the entire selling price. But under the perpetual inventory system, we also need to account for the cost of the goods shipped. The proper procedure is to debit Cost of Goods Sold and credit Finished Goods Inventory Control for the cost of the goods shipped.

Journal Entry Analysis

Because a job order cost system emphasizes cost flow, you should understand the journal entries that record the various costs as they are incurred. You also

Figure 17-3. Job Order Cost Card

Job Order No. 16F	Wasa Boat Company New Port Richey, Florida
Product Specs: Model GB30-Mark I: 30 foot fiberglass sailing sloop with full galley	
Customer: Hinds Yachts, Inc.	Materials: Dept. 1. $96,500 Dept. 2. 23,700 Dept. 3. -0- Total $120,200
Date of Order: February 10, 19x2	
Date of Completion: October 28, 19x2	Direct Labor: Dept. 1. $43,440 Dept. 2. 60,960 Dept. 3. 40,400 Total $144,800
Cost Summary: Materials $120,200 Direct Labor 144,800 Factory Overhead 123,080 Total $388,080 Units Completed 11 (eleven) Cost per Unit $35,280	Applied Factory Overhead: Dept. 1. $36,924 Dept. 2. 51,816 Dept. 3. 34,340 Total $123,080

388,080

should recognize the entries that are used to transfer costs from one account to another. These entries, along with job order cost cards and subsidiary ledgers for materials inventories, work in process inventories, and finished goods inventories, are a major part of the job order cost system.

To illustrate the journal entries, we go step by step through an example, using the Wasa Boat Company. As each entry is discussed, trace its number and related debits or credits to Exhibit 17-3. Also, keep in mind the cost flow shown in Figure 17-2.

Materials Purchased. The Wasa Boat Company purchased the following materials: Material 5X for $57,200 and Material 14Q for $34,000. Materials purchases are recorded at cost in the Materials Inventory Control account:

		Debit	Credit
Entry 1:	Materials Inventory Control	91,200	
	Accounts Payable (or Cash)		91,200
	Purchase of $57,200 of Material 5X and $34,000 of Material 14Q		

Notice that the debit is to an inventory account, not a purchases account. Because the inventory system is perpetual, all costs of materials flow through the inventory account. Also, the inventory account used is a control account. Some companies have hundreds of items in inventory. To keep a separate account for each item in the general ledger would crowd the ledger and make it hard to work with. When entry **1** is posted to the general ledger, the individual accounts in the materials ledger also are updated, as Exhibit 17-3 shows.

Purchase of Supplies. The company purchased \$8,200 of operating supplies for the manufacturing process.

Entry 2: Materials Inventory Control	8,200	
Accounts Payable (or Cash)		8,200
Purchase of operating supplies		

The procedures used to account for the purchase of supplies are much like those used for direct materials purchases. Operating Supplies Inventory is one of the subsidiary accounts that makes up the Materials Inventory Control account. If the supplies inventory is large, a separate general ledger account can be used. Regardless of which method is selected, the accountant should be able to justify the approach taken and then should follow it consistently.

Requisitioning Materials and Supplies. On receipt of a properly prepared materials requisition form, the following direct materials and supplies are issued from inventory to production: Material 5X, \$124,000; Material 14Q, \$64,000; and operating supplies, \$9,600.

Entry 3: Work in Process Inventory Control	188,000	
Factory Overhead Control	9,600	
Materials Inventory Control		197,600
Issuance of \$124,000 of Material 5X, \$64,000 of Material 14Q, and \$9,600 of operating supplies into production		

This entry shows that \$188,000 of direct materials and \$9,600 of indirect materials were issued. The debit to the Work in Process Inventory Control account records the cost of the direct materials issued to production. These costs can be traced directly to specific job orders. As the direct materials costs are charged to work in process, the amounts for individual jobs are entered on the job order cost cards. As shown in Exhibit 17-3, \$103,800 of materials were used on Job 16F and \$84,200 of materials were used on Job 23H. Indirect materials costs (supplies) are debited to the Factory Overhead Control account.

Labor Costs. Journal entries to record payroll for a merchandising company were illustrated and discussed in the financial accounting portion of this text. In accounting for factory labor costs, we use the same basic documents and transactions; but we need some new account titles, and we assign the costs to specific jobs or batches of product.

Recording labor costs for a manufacturing company requires three journal entries. The first records the total payroll liability of the company. Let's assume that payroll liability for the period is as follows: total direct labor wages, \$164,000; total indirect labor wages, \$76,000; total administrative salaries, \$72,000; social security and Medicare taxes withheld, \$18,720; and federal income taxes withheld, \$78,000. Although only \$215,280 of net earnings is to be paid to employees, total direct and indirect labor costs are used for product and job costing.

Exhibit 17-3. The Job Order Cost System—Wasa Boat Company

Materials Inventory Control

Beg. Bal.	123,000	Requisitions:		
(1) Purchases	91,200	Materials	188,000	(3)
(2) Purchases	8,200	Supplies	9,600	(3)
End. Bal.	**24,800**			

Work in Process Inventory Control

Beg. Bal.	40,080			
(3) Materials Used	188,000	Completed	388,080	(10)
(6) Direct Labor	164,000			
(9) Overhead	139,400			
End. Bal.	**143,400**			

Factory Payroll

(4) Wages Earned	240,000	Direct labor	164,000	(6)
		Indirect labor	76,000	(6)

Factory Overhead Control

(3) Supplies Used	9,600	Applied	139,400	(9)
(6) Indirect Labor	76,000			
(7) Other	29,500			
(8) Adjustments	24,000			
	139,100		139,400	
(13) To close	300			
	—			

Subsidiary Ledgers

Materials Ledger

Material 5X

Beg. Bal.	83,000	Used	124,000
Purchases	57,200		
End. Bal.	**16,200**		

Material 14Q

Beg. Bal.	37,000	Used	64,000
Purchases	34,000		
End. Bal.	**7,000**		

Operating Supplies

Beg. Bal.	3,000	Used	9,600
Purchases	8,200		
End. Bal.	**1,600**		

Job Order Cost Cards

Job 16F

Costs from the previous period	40,080
Materials	103,800
Direct Labor	132,000
Factory Overhead	112,200
Completed Cost	388,080

Job 23H

Materials	84,200
Direct Labor	32,000
Factory Overhead	27,200
Ending Balance	143,400

Entry 4: Factory Payroll	240,000	
Administrative Salaries Expense	72,000	
Social Security and Medicare Taxes Payable		18,720
Federal Income Tax Payable		78,000
Wages and Salaries Payable		215,280
Payroll liability for the period		

Exhibit 17-3. *(continued)*

Finished Goods Inventory Control

Beg. Bal.	—		
(10) Completed During Period	388,080	Sold	352,800 (12)
End. Bal.	**35,280**		

Cost of Goods Sold

(12) Sold During Period	352,800	Adjustment	300 (13)
End. Bal.	**352,500**		

Finished Goods Ledger

Product F

Beg. Bal.	—	Sold	352,800
Completed	388,080		
End. Bal.	**35,280**		

Product H

Beg. Bal.	—		

Entry **5** records the payment of the payroll liability established in entry **4**. This entry records the preparation of payroll checks for the period and their distribution to the employees.

Entry 5: Wages and Salaries Payable	215,280	
Cash		215,280
Payment of payroll		

A third entry is needed to account for the labor costs. The $240,000 debited to the Factory Payroll account must be moved to the production accounts. Total direct labor costs are debited to Work in Process Inventory Control, and total indirect wages (including factory supervisory salaries) are debited to Factory Overhead Control. Factory Payroll is credited to show that the total amount has been distributed to the production accounts.

Entry 6: Work in Process Inventory Control	164,000	
Factory Overhead Control	76,000	
Factory Payroll		240,000
Distribution of factory payroll to the production accounts		

In addition, the direct labor costs are recorded by job on the individual job order cost cards. This distribution of $132,000 to Job 16F and $32,000 to Job 23H is shown in Exhibit 17-3.

Other Factory Overhead Costs. As factory overhead costs other than indirect materials and indirect labor charges are incurred, the sum of these costs is charged (debited) to the Factory Overhead Control account. Each cost is identified in the journal entry explanation. In our example, factory overhead costs were paid as follows: electricity, $6,300; maintenance and repair, $16,900; insurance, $2,800; and property taxes, $3,500.

Entry 7: Factory Overhead Control	29,500	
Accounts Payable (or Cash)		29,500
Incurrence of the following overhead costs: electricity, $6,300; maintenance and repair, $16,900; insurance, $2,800; and property taxes, $3,500		

The individual subsidiary ledger accounts also are updated. Because of the amount of information in Exhibit 17-3, it does not show the subsidiary ledger for the Factory Overhead Control account. However, the subsidiary ledger would include a separate account for each type of factory overhead cost. The costs would be accounted for in much the same way that costs are accounted for in the materials ledger and job order cost cards.

The next transaction is an adjusting entry to record the depreciation of factory equipment for the period:

Entry 8: Factory Overhead Control	24,000	
Accumulated Depreciation, Equipment		24,000
To record the depreciation of factory equipment for the period		

Adjusting entries usually are prepared after all transactions for the period have been recorded. We introduce the topic at this point because depreciation of factory equipment is a part of total factory overhead cost. The actual depreciation expense account is part of the factory overhead subsidiary ledger.

Factory Overhead Applied. We apply factory overhead using a predetermined overhead rate and an allocation base (machine hours, direct labor hours, direct labor dollars, or units of output). Here, we apply factory overhead costs to production using a rate of 85 percent of direct labor dollars:

Entry 9: Work in Process Inventory Control	139,400	
Factory Overhead Control		139,400
Application of factory overhead costs to production		

The amount of overhead charged to production is found by multiplying the measurement units of the base by the predetermined overhead. In our example, we multiply the direct labor dollars ($164,000) by 85 percent, which gives us $139,400 ($164,000 × .85). This amount is debited to the Work in Process Inventory Control account. Because the application of overhead is related to direct labor dollars, we can update the job order cost cards using the same procedure. Job 16F is assigned $112,200 of overhead costs ($132,000 × .85), and Job 23H is assigned $27,200 ($32,000 × .85). These amounts have been posted to the job order cost cards in Exhibit 17-3.

Accounting for Completed Units. As various job orders are completed, their costs are moved to the Finished Goods Inventory Control account. In this case, goods costing $388,080 for Job 16F were completed and transferred to Finished Goods Inventory Control (see the job order cost card in Exhibit 17-3).

		Debit	Credit
Entry 10:	Finished Goods Inventory Control	388,080	
	Work in Process Inventory Control		388,080
	Transfer of completed goods for Job 16F from Work in Process Inventory Control to Finished Goods Inventory Control		

When a job is completed, its job order cost card is pulled from the work in process subsidiary ledger. It then is used to help update the finished goods subsidiary ledger. Specifically, costs recorded on the job order cost card are used to figure unit costs and to determine the amount of the transfer entry.

Accounting for Units Sold. The final phase of the manufacturing cost flow is the transfer of costs from the Finished Goods Inventory Control account to the Cost of Goods Sold account. At this point, ten sailing sloops from Job 16F have been shipped to the customer. The selling price for the goods shipped was $520,000. The total cost of manufacturing these products was $352,800.

		Debit	Credit
Entry 11:	Accounts Receivable	520,000	
	Sales		520,000
	Sale of a portion of Job 16F		
Entry 12:	Cost of Goods Sold	352,800	
	Finished Goods Inventory Control		352,800
	Transfer of the cost of the shipped goods for Job 16F from Finished Goods Inventory Control to Cost of Goods Sold		

Both the entry to record the sale and the entry to establish the cost of the goods sold are shown here. Entry **12** is made at the time the sale is recorded. When we transfer the costs of the products sold out of the Finished Goods Inventory Control account, we also should update the finished goods subsidiary ledger, as shown in Exhibit 17-3.

Underapplied or Overapplied Overhead Disposition. At the end of the accounting period, we total both sides of the Factory Overhead Control account to determine if we have applied the appropriate amount of factory overhead costs to the jobs and products worked on during the period. As shown on the top of page 690, we actually incurred $139,100 of factory overhead costs during the period, but we applied $139,400, a difference of $300.

Factory Overhead Control

(3)	9,600	(9)	139,400
(6)	76,000		
(7)	29,500		
(8)	24,000		
	139,100		**139,400**
		Bal.	**300**

We now make an entry to close this account and dispose of the overapplied factory overhead. During the period, we applied $300 too much to jobs worked on, so now we have to credit Cost of Goods Sold to reduce the costs of jobs completed. The debit of $300 to the Factory Overhead Control account returns the balance to zero.

Entry 13: Factory Overhead Control	300	
Cost of Goods Sold		300
To dispose of the overapplied balance and close out the Factory Overhead Control account		

Computing Product Unit Costs

OBJECTIVE 9
Compute the product unit cost for a specific job order

The process of computing product unit costs is fairly simple in a job order costing system. All costs of direct materials, direct labor, and factory overhead are recorded on the job order cost card as the job progresses toward completion. When the job is finished, the costs on the job order cost card are totaled. The unit cost is computed by dividing the total costs for the job by the number of good units produced.

Job 16F was completed in the journal entry analysis we just finished. The cost data for this job are shown on the job order cost card in Figure 17-3. Eleven sailing sloops were produced at a total cost of $388,080. This worked out to a cost of $35,280 per sloop before adjustments. Notice in Exhibit 17-3 that only ten of the sloops actually were shipped during the year. The entire $300 of overapplied overhead was credited to the ten sloops sold. One still remains in Finished Goods Inventory Control at the unadjusted cost.

Fully and Partly Completed Products

In a job order costing system, manufacturing costs are accumulated, classified, and reclassified several times. As products are produced, all manufacturing costs are linked to them. These costs then follow the products first to the Finished Goods Inventory Control account and then to the Cost of Goods Sold account. Exhibit 17-3 illustrates the accounting procedures and cost flows of units worked on during the period. The dollar amounts in Exhibit 17-3 come from posting the journal entries we've just discussed.

At the end of the period, some costs remain in the Work in Process Inventory Control account and the Finished Goods Inventory Control account. The ending balance of $143,400 in the Work in Process Inventory Control account is from costs attached to partly completed units from Job 23H. These costs are traceable to the job order cost card in the subsidiary ledger (see Exhibit 17-3). The Finished Goods Inventory Control account also has an ending balance. Of all the units completed during the accounting period, one sloop from Job 16F has not been sold or shipped. Its cost, $35,280, now appears as the ending balance in the Finished Goods Inventory Control account.

Chapter Review

Review of Learning Objectives

1. **Define *cost allocation* and state the role of cost objectives in the cost allocation process.**
Cost allocation is the process of assigning a specific cost to a specific cost objective. A cost objective is the destination of an assigned cost, and varies according to the focus of a particular report: from an entire company or division down to a particular cost center, machine, or product.

2. **Identify the uses of cost allocation in corporate accounting and reporting.**
Accounting reports are prepared for all levels of management, from the president to the department manager or supervisor. Reports must be prepared for all cost centers, including the company as a whole, each division, and all of the departments within each division. As the focus of a report changes from a larger cost center or objective to a smaller one, more and more costs become indirect and subject to cost allocation procedures.

3. **Define *supporting service function* and assign the costs of a supporting service to production departments.**
A supporting service function is an operating unit or department that supports the activities of a company's production facilities. The costs incurred by supporting service departments are accounted for as indirect operating costs. They are allocated to other operating departments and production departments on a benefit basis that reflects the relationship of the service function to the cost objective. The method used to allocate the costs often combines the step method (when the functions a service department performs benefit other service departments as well as production departments) and the direct method (when the functions a service department performs benefit only production departments).

4. **Discuss the concept of absorption costing.**
Absorption costing is an approach to product costing in which a representative portion of all manufacturing costs is assigned to individual products. Thus, direct materials, direct labor, variable factory overhead, and fixed factory overhead costs are all assigned to products.

5. **Compute a predetermined overhead rate and apply overhead costs to products in process using this rate.**
A predetermined overhead rate is a factor used to assign factory overhead costs to specific products or jobs. The rate is computed by dividing total estimated overhead costs for a period by the total expected activity basis (machine hours, labor hours, dollars of direct labor costs, units of output) for that period. Factory overhead costs are applied to a job or product by multiplying the predetermined overhead rate by the actual amount of the activity base used to produce that job or product.

6. **Dispose of underapplied or overapplied overhead.**
If at the end of a period, there is a difference between the debit and credit sides of the Factory Overhead Control account, factory overhead has been either underapplied or overapplied. When the difference is small or when most of the products worked on during the period have been sold, the underapplied or overapplied amount is eliminated with an adjusting entry that transfers the balance to the Cost of Goods Sold account.

7. **Identify the characteristics of a job order cost accounting system.**
The job order costing system is a traditional approach to product cost accounting used by companies that manufacture unique or special-order products. The system has three primary characteristics: (1) It collects all manufacturing costs and assigns them to specific jobs or batches of product; (2) it accumulates and measures costs for each job, rather than for set time periods; and (3) it uses a single Work in Process Inventory Control account (costs for each job being worked on are collected on a job order cost card).

8. **Diagram the cost flow and journalize transactions in a job order cost accounting system.**
Because a job order costing system assumes a perpetual inventory system, materials and supplies are debited to the Materials Inventory Control account, not a purchases account. Labor costs are accumulated on labor time cards and labor job cards. Direct labor costs are debited to the Work in Process Inventory Control account; indirect costs are debited to the Factory Overhead Control account. As products are manufactured, the costs of direct materials are transferred to the Work in Process Inventory Control account. Factory overhead costs are applied using a predetermined overhead rate. Applied factory overhead is debited to the Work in Process Inventory Control account and credited to the Factory Overhead Control account. When products are completed, the costs assigned to them are transferred to the Finished Goods Inventory Control account. Later, when the products are sold and shipped, the costs are transferred to the Cost of Goods Sold account.
A job order costing system requires journal entries for each of the following transactions: (a) purchase of materials; (b) purchase of operating supplies; (c) requisition of materials and supplies into production; (d) recording of payroll liability; (e) payment of payroll to employees; (f) distribution of payroll to production accounts; (g) cash payment of overhead costs; (h) recording of noncash overhead costs (depreciation of equipment, prepaid costs); (i) application of factory overhead costs to production; (j) transfer of costs of completed jobs from the Work in Process Inventory Control account to the Finished Goods Inventory Control account; (k) sale of products; (l) transfer of related costs from the Finished Goods Inventory Control account to the Cost of Goods Sold account; and (m) disposition of underapplied or overapplied factory overhead.
9. **Compute the product unit cost for a specific job order.**
Product costs are computed by first totaling all of the manufacturing costs accumulated on a particular job order cost card. This amount then is divided by the number of good units produced to find the product unit cost for the order. The unit cost information is entered on the job order cost card and used to value inventory.

Review of Concepts and Terminology

The following concepts and terms were introduced in this chapter:

(L.O. 4) **Absorption costing:** An approach to product costing in which a representative portion of all types of manufacturing costs is assigned to individual products. Also called *full costing*.

(L.O. 1) **Cost allocation:** The process of assigning a specific cost to a specific cost objective.

(L.O. 1) **Cost center:** Any organizational segment or area of activity for which there is a reason to accumulate costs.

(L.O. 1) **Cost objective:** The destination of an assigned or allocated cost.

(L.O. 1) **Direct cost:** Any cost that can be conveniently and economically traced to a specific cost objective.

(L.O. 3) **Direct method:** A method of allocating the cost of a service department that supports only production departments.

(L.O. 5) **Factory Overhead Control account:** A general ledger account that contains the cumulative total of all types of factory overhead costs incurred as well as factory overhead costs applied to the products produced.

(L.O. 1) **Indirect cost:** Any cost that cannot be conveniently and economically traced to a specific cost objective; any production cost that is not classified as a direct cost.

(L.O. 8) **Job order:** A customer order for a specific number of specially designed, made-to-order products.

(L.O. 7) **Job order cost accounting system:** A product costing system applicable to unique or special-order products, in which materials, labor, and factory overhead costs are assigned to specific jobs or batches of product.

(L.O. 8) **Job order cost card:** A document on which all of the costs incurred in the production of a particular job order are recorded; part of the subsidiary ledger for the Work in Process Inventory Control account.

(L.O. 5) **Predetermined overhead rate:** A factor used to assign factory overhead costs to specific products or jobs.

(L.O. 3) **Step method:** A method of allocating the costs of a department's services that are used to support other service departments and production departments.

(L.O. 3) **Supporting service function:** An operating unit or department that supports the activities of a company's production facilities.

Self-Test

Test your knowledge of the chapter by choosing the best answer for each of the following items.

(L.O. 1) 1. The process of assigning a specific cost to a specific cost objective is called
   a. budgeting.
   b. cost allocation.
   c. job order costing.
   d. controllable costing.

(L.O. 3) 2. The method of assigning all supporting service department costs only to production departments is known as the
   a. absorption method.
   b. step method.
   c. direct method.
   d. job costing method.

(L.O. 4) 3. An approach to product costing that assigns all types of manufacturing costs to individual products is known as
   a. absorption costing.
   b. total costing.
   c. job order costing.
   d. step costing.

(L.O. 5) 4. To compute the predetermined overhead rate, you divide the total estimated overhead costs by
   a. last year's total sales.
   b. the number of invoices expected this year.
   c. the number of products produced last year.
   d. the total estimated activity base.

(L.O. 5) 5. Based on the following estimates for the coming year and assuming the company uses machine hours as its activity base, what is the predetermined overhead rate?

   Direct labor hours: 10,400
   Machine hours: 31,200
   Estimated factory overhead costs: $65,520

   a. $2.10 per machine hour
   b. $6.30 per machine hour
   c. $2.10 per direct labor hour
   d. $6.30 per direct labor hour

(L.O. 6) 6. If actual overhead costs incurred totaled $23,780, and $23,130 of overhead was applied to jobs worked on during the period, which of the following situations is correct?
   a. Overhead is out of control.
   b. Overhead is $650 underapplied.
   c. Overhead is overspent.
   d. Overhead is $650 overapplied.

(L.O. 8) 7. When a control account is used in the accounting system, what special recordkeeping device is used to keep track of the balances in the accounts supporting the control account?
   a. General ledger
   b. Subsidiary journal
   c. Subsidiary ledger
   d. Cash payments journal

(L.O. 8) 8. The key document used to track product costs in a job order costing system is a
   a. materials requisition form.
   b. materials receiving report.
   c. job order cost card.
   d. labor time card.

(L.O. 8) 9. During April, a company using a job order costing system incurred gross pay as follows: $26,400 for direct labor and $35,600 for indirect labor. How much labor cost should have been debited directly to the Work in Process Inventory Control account during the month?

a. $62,000 c. $35,600
b. $0 d. $26,400

(L.O. 9) 10. Melnor Products, Inc. produces deluxe office desks. During January, the following costs were incurred to complete Job ACA12: direct materials, $12,210; supplies, $1,440; direct labor, $3,460; and indirect labor, $5,200. Factory overhead was applied at a rate of $35 per machine hour, and the job required 670 machine hours. If the job called for ninety-six deluxe desks, how much did each desk cost to produce?

a. $407.50 c. $232.40
b. $476.88 d. $694.06

Answers to the Self-Test are at the end of this chapter.

Review Problem
Journal Entry Analysis: Job Order Costing System

(L.O. 5, 6, 8, 9) The Madden Office Furniture Company produces "uniframe" desk and chair assemblies and study carrels. The firm uses a job order cost system and a predetermined overhead rate of 160 percent of direct labor dollars. The following transactions and events took place during September 19x3:

Sept. 4 Received direct materials costing $11,540 that were purchased on account.

7 The production department requisitioned $3,700 of direct materials (Job 259, $830; Job 260, $2,870) and $950 of operating supplies.

14 Gross factory payroll of $16,000 was paid to factory personnel. Of that amount, $12,500 represented direct labor (Job 259, $7,100; Job 260, $5,400); the remaining amount, indirect labor. (Prepare only the entry to distribute factory payroll to production accounts for this transaction and the distribution on September 28.)

14 Factory overhead costs were applied to production.

16 Received operating supplies costing $5,500 and direct materials costing $18,500. Both were ordered on 9/11/x3 and were purchased on account. Both can be inventoried.

20 Requisitioned $9,000 of direct materials (Job 260, $4,605; Job 261, $4,395) and $1,750 of operating supplies for production.

26 Paid the following overhead costs: heat, light, and power, $2,400; repairs by outside firm, $3,600; and property taxes, $1,700.

28 Gross factory payroll of $15,600 was paid to factory personnel. Of that amount, $10,200 represented direct labor (Job 259, $100; Job 260, $7,975; Job 261, $2,125); the remaining amount, indirect labor.

28 Factory overhead costs were applied to production.

29 Jobs 259 and 260, costing a total of $67,500, were transferred to finished goods inventory.

30 Depreciation of plant and equipment for September was $14,000. During the same period, $2,200 of prepaid fire insurance expired.

30 Jobs 258 and 259, costing a total of $32,750, were shipped to customers. The selling price for Job 258 was $14,760, and for Job 259, $38,950.

Required

1. Prepare the journal entries for all of these transactions.
2. Assume that the beginning balance in the Materials Inventory Control account was $4,700, the beginning balance in the Work in Process Inventory Control account was $6,200 (Job 259, $4,200; Job 260, $1,500; Job 261, $500), and the beginning balance in the Finished Goods Inventory Control account was $9,000 (Job 258). Compute the ending balances in these accounts.
3. Job 258 consisted of 36 carrels and Job 259 consisted of 95 carrels. Compute the cost and selling price per carrel.
4. Determine the amount of underapplied or overapplied overhead and prepare the journal entry to dispose of it at month end.

Answer to Review Problem

1. Prepare the journal entries.

Date	Account / Explanation	Debit	Credit
Sept. 4	Materials Inventory Control	11,540	
	Accounts Payable		11,540
	Purchase of direct materials on account		
7	Work in Process Inventory Control	3,700	
	Factory Overhead Control	950	
	Materials Inventory Control		4,650
	Issuance of direct materials and supplies into production (Job 259, $830; Job 260, $2,870)		
14	Work in Process Inventory Control	12,500	
	Factory Overhead Control	3,500	
	Factory Payroll		16,000
	Distribution of factory payroll to production accounts (Job 259, $7,100; Job 260, $5,400)		
14	Work in Process Inventory Control	20,000	
	Factory Overhead Control		20,000
	Factory overhead costs applied to production ($12,500 × 160%: Job 259, $7,100 × 160%; Job 260, $5,400 × 160%)		
16	Materials Inventory Control	24,000	
	Accounts Payable		24,000
	Purchase of $5,500 of operating supplies and $18,500 of direct materials		
20	Work in Process Inventory Control	9,000	
	Factory Overhead Control	1,750	
	Materials Inventory Control		10,750
	Issuance of direct materials and supplies into production (Job 260, $4,605; Job 261, $4,395)		
26	Factory Overhead Control	7,700	
	Cash		7,700
	Payment of overhead costs: heat, light, and power, $2,400; outside repairs, $3,600; property taxes, $1,700		
28	Work in Process Inventory Control	10,200	
	Factory Overhead Control	5,400	
	Factory Payroll		15,600
	Distribution of factory payroll to production accounts (Job 259, $100; Job 260, $7,975; Job 261, $2,125)		
28	Work in Process Inventory Control	16,320	
	Factory Overhead Control		16,320
	Factory overhead costs applied to production ($10,200 × 160%: Job 259, $100 × 160%; Job 260, $7,975 × 160%; Job 261, $2,125 × 160%)		

Date	Accounts and Explanation	Debit	Credit
Sept. 29	Finished Goods Inventory Control	67,500	
	Work in Process Inventory Control		67,500
	Transfer of costs of completed goods for Jobs 259 and 260 to finished goods inventory		
Sept. 30	Factory Overhead Control	16,200	
	Accumulated Depreciation, Plant and Equipment		14,000
	Prepaid Insurance		2,200
	To record charge to Factory Overhead Control of expired asset costs		
30	Accounts Receivable	53,710	
	Sales		53,710
	Sales for September		
30	Cost of Goods Sold	32,750	
	Finished Goods Inventory Control		32,750
	Transfer of costs from the Finished Goods Inventory account to the Cost of Goods Sold account		

2. Compute the ending balances of the inventory accounts.

Materials Inventory Control

	Debit		Credit
Beg. Bal.	4,700	9/7	4,650
9/4	11,540	9/20	10,750
9/16	24,000		
	40,240		**15,400**
End. Bal.	**24,840**		

Work in Process Inventory Control

	Debit		Credit
Beg. Bal.	6,200	9/29	67,500
9/7	3,700		
9/14	12,500		
9/14	20,000		
9/20	9,000		
9/28	10,200		
9/28	16,320		
	77,920		**67,500**
End. Bal.	**10,420**		

Finished Goods Inventory Control

	Debit		Credit
Beg. Bal.	9,000	9/30	32,750
9/29	67,500		
	76,500		**32,750**
End. Bal.	**43,750**		

Subsidiary Ledger for Finished Goods Inventory:

Job 258

	Debit		Credit
Beg. Bal.	9,000	9/30	9,000
End. Bal.	—		

Job 259

	Debit		Credit
9/29	23,750	9/30	23,750
End. Bal.	—		

Job 260

	Debit		Credit
9/29	43,750		
End. Bal.	**43,750**		

Job Order Cost Cards:

Job 259

Beg. Bal.	4,200	9/29	23,750
9/7	830		
9/14	7,100		
9/14	11,360		
9/28	100		
9/28	160		
	23,750		**23,750**
End. Bal.	—		

Job 260

Beg. Bal.	1,500	9/29	43,750
9/7	2,870		
9/14	5,400		
9/14	8,640		
9/20	4,605		
9/28	7,975		
9/28	12,760		
	43,750		**43,750**
End. Bal.	—		

Job 261

Beg. Bal.	500		
9/20	4,395		
9/28	2,125		
9/28	3,400		
End. Bal.	**10,420**		

3. Compute the cost and selling price per unit.

   Cost per unit: $32,750 ÷ 131 = $250 per unit
   Selling price per unit: $53,710 ÷ 131 = $410 per unit

4. Determine the underapplied or overapplied overhead.

Factory Overhead Control

9/7	950	9/14	20,000
9/14	3,500	9/28	16,320
9/20	1,750		
9/26	7,700		
9/28	5,400		
9/30	16,200		
	35,500		**36,320**

Factory overhead is overapplied by $820 ($36,320 – $35,500).

Prepare the entry to dispose of the overapplied overhead.

Sept. 30	Factory Overhead Control	820	
	Cost of Goods Sold		820
	To close the Factory Overhead Control account and credit the Cost of Goods Sold account with the overapplied amount		

Chapter Assignments

Questions

1. Define *cost allocation.*
2. What is a cost objective, and what is its role in management accounting?
3. "The smaller the cost center or cost objective, the more difficult it is to trace costs and revenues to it." Explain this statement.
4. What is a supporting service department? Give examples.

5. Explain the concept of absorption costing.
6. Describe the steps used to arrive at a predetermined overhead rate based on machine hours.
7. What are the keys to successfully applying overhead to products and job orders?
8. What is meant by underapplied or overapplied overhead?
9. Describe how to adjust for underapplied or overapplied overhead.
10. "At the end of the accounting period, some direct materials costs, direct labor costs, and factory overhead costs are reported in the manufacturing company's income statement, while others are reported in the company's balance sheet." Discuss the accuracy of this statement.
11. What is a job order cost accounting system? What types of companies use this kind of system?
12. What is the common objective of job order costing and process costing systems?
13. Identify the characteristics of a job order costing system.
14. How does materials usage influence the efficiency of operations?
15. "Purchased labor services cannot be stored." Discuss this statement.
16. Define *control account* and *subsidiary ledger*. How are the two related?
17. Discuss the role of the Work in Process Inventory Control account in a job order cost system.
18. What is the purpose of a job order cost card? Identify the types of information recorded on this kind of card.

Communication Skills Exercises

Communication 17-1. The Case of the $7 Aspirins[4]
(L.O. 4)

Roland County Community Hospital sent a billing statement to Anita Cooper for services performed in connection with emergency heart surgery. Included in the statement was the following item:

Pain drugs administered:	
Aspirin tablets (8 2-aspirin doses @ $7)	$56.00

Ms. Cooper questioned the amount billed, insisting that she could buy aspirin for much less at a local pharmacy. The hospital's chief administrative officer stated that in addition to the original cost of the aspirin, the charge included costs incurred to make the item available to the patient at bedside. Prepare a list of the services and related costs that you believe the hospital's CAO is referring to. Be prepared to discuss in class.

Communication 17-2. Cost Estimation and Robots[5]
(L.O. 4, 5, 7)

Sally Industries, Inc., of Jacksonville, Florida, makes robots. But these mechanical creatures are not your run-of-the-mill, everyday-variety robot. For example, the company manufactured E.T. the Extraterrestrial, a character featured at the Universal Studios theme park in Orlando. Sally Industries' products can range from an individual character, like E.T., to an entire backdrop for a ten-minute animated ride and show. Costs for these orders range from $15,000 to over $1 million. The development process includes engineering design and simulation, a machine shop for the mechanical parts, pneumatic functions (compressed air to power movements), artists, scenic creations, electronics development, computer and audio programming, and shop administration. Cost estimates and overhead application are critical to the success of this business; one significant error in projected costs could bankrupt the small company. The company develops its absorption costing–based cost estimates using a simple LOTUS 1-2-3 spreadsheet program. Should Sally Industries base its cost accumulation approach on a job order or a process costing method? Should costs be accumulated on a departmental basis, or should each job be treated individually? Would one factory overhead rate suffice, or should the company use many different rates to apply overhead to its products? Prepare a written analysis describing your perceptions of how (1) E.T. was assembled and (2) costs were accumulated and allocated to E.T.

4. Adapted from David W. McFadden, "The Legacy of the $7 Aspirin," *Management Accounting,* Institute of Management Accountants, April 1990, p. 39. Used by permission.
5. Based on Thomas L. Barton and Frederick M. Cole, "Accounting for Magic," *Management Accounting,* Institute of Management Accountants, January 1991, pp. 27–31.

Communication 17-3.
Ethical Job Order Costs
(L.O. 7)

Dean Graber, production manager for Balke Metal Products Company, has just entered the office of controller Ed Bump. "Ed, what gives here? I was charged for 330 direct labor hours on Job AD22 and my records show that we only spent 290 hours on that job. That 40 hour difference caused the total cost of labor and factory overhead for the job to increase by over $5,500. Are my records wrong or was there an error in the labor assigned to the job?" Ed responded, "Don't worry about it, Dean. This job will not be used in your quarterly performance evaluation. Job AD22 was a federal government job, a cost-plus-fixed-fee contract so the more costs we assign to it, the more profit we make. We decided to add a few hours to the job in case there is some follow-up work to do. You know how fussy the feds are with their close tolerances."

What should Dean Graber do? Discuss Ed Bump's costing procedure.

Communication 17-4.
Basic Research Skills
(L.O. 2)

Over the past fifty years, cost allocation has been one of the most discussed subjects in business and accounting literature. The main reason for interest in the subject is that every allocation method devised affects a company's net income in some way. At the library, locate the *Accountants' Index* and look under the category "Cost Allocation." Select an article published in the past three years and make a note of the name of the author(s), the title of the article, and the name and date of the publication. Identify the cost allocation issue and/or method discussed and be prepared to summarize the contents of the article for your classmates.

Classroom Exercises

Exercise 17-1.
Cost Allocation Basis
(L.O. 1, 2, 3)

A plan for cost assignment is vital to corporate reporting, product costing, and inventory valuation. Examples of costs and related cost objectives are presented below.

Cost	Cost Objective
Materials handling costs	Product
Plant depreciation costs	Division
Repair and Maintenance Department costs	One of five production departments served
Corporate president's salary	Division

1. Which costs would be direct costs of the related cost objective? Which would be indirect costs?
2. For each indirect cost, choose a cost allocation basis that provides a logical relationship between the cost and the cost objective. Defend your answers.

Exercise 17-2.
Cost Allocation—Direct Versus Indirect
(L.O. 1)

Classifying a cost as direct or indirect depends on the cost objective. Depreciation of a factory building is a direct cost when the plant is the cost objective. But when the cost objective is a product, depreciation cost is indirect.

For the following costs, indicate for each cost objective—division, department, or product—whether the cost would be indirect (I) or direct (D). Defend your answers.

	Cost Objective		
Cost	Division	Department	Product
Direct labor			
Departmental supplies			
Division head's salary			
President's salary			
Department manager's salary			
Direct materials			
Fire insurance on a specific machine			
Property taxes, division plant			
Department repairs and maintenance			

Exercise 17-3. Service Department Cost Allocation
(L.O. 3)

Demski Fundraising, Inc. has six departments that share the services of a single central computer. Management has decided that the best basis for cost allocation is minutes of computer time used by each department. Usage per department for the first week in June was as follows: 6,200 minutes for Department A; 8,400 minutes for Department B; 8,920 minutes for Department C; 4,160 minutes for Department D; 2,080 minutes for Department E; and 10,240 minutes for Department F. The total for all departments was 40,000 minutes. The total cost of operating the computer during the month was $29,056. Determine the computer expense that should be assigned to each department for the one-week period. (Carry percentages to three decimal places.)

Exercise 17-4. Concept of Absorption Costing
(L.O. 4)

Using the absorption costing concept, determine the product unit cost from the following costs incurred during March: $2,070 in liability insurance, factory; $2,900 in rent, sales office; $3,100 in depreciation, factory equipment; $14,650 in materials used; $3,480 in indirect labor, factory; $1,080 in factory supplies; $1,910 in heat, light, and power, factory; $2,600 in fire insurance, factory; $4,250 in depreciation, sales equipment; $1,850 in rent, factory; $6,420 in direct labor; $3,100 in manager's salary, factory; $5,800 in president's salary; $8,250 in sales commissions; and $2,975 in advertising expenses. The inspection department reported that 24,400 good units were produced during March.

Exercise 17-5. Computation of Predetermined Overhead Rate
(L.O. 5)

The overhead costs used by Austin Industries, Inc. to compute its predetermined overhead rate for 19x3 are listed below.

A total of 45,600 machine hours was used as the 19x3 allocation base. In 19x4, all overhead costs except depreciation, property taxes, and miscellaneous factory overhead are expected to increase by 10 percent. Depreciation should increase by 12 percent, and a 20 percent increase in property taxes and miscellaneous factory overhead is expected. Plant capacity in terms of machine hours used will increase by 4,400 hours in 19x4.

Indirect materials and supplies	$ 79,200
Repairs and maintenance	14,900
Outside service contracts	17,300
Indirect labor	79,100
Factory supervision	42,900
Depreciation, machinery	85,000
Factory insurance	8,200
Property taxes	6,500
Heat, light, and power	7,700
Miscellaneous factory overhead	5,760
	$346,560

Compute the 19x3 and 19x4 predetermined overhead rates. (Carry your answers to three decimal places.)

Exercise 17-6. Computation and Application of Overhead Rate
(L.O. 5)

Barron Compumatics specializes in the analysis and reporting of complex inventory costing projects. Materials costs are minimal, consisting entirely of operating supplies (data processing cards, inventory sheets, and other recording tools). Labor is the highest single expense item, totaling $693,000 for 75,000 hours of work in 19x3. Factory overhead costs for 19x3 were $916,000, and were applied to specific jobs on the basis of labor hours worked. In 19x4 the company anticipates a 25 percent increase in overhead costs. Labor costs will increase by $130,000, and the number of hours worked is expected to increase 20 percent.

1. Determine the total amount of factory overhead anticipated by the company in 19x4.
2. Compute the predetermined overhead rate for 19x4. (Round your answer to the nearest penny.)
3. During April 19x4, the following jobs were completed in the following times: Job 16–A4, 2,490 hours; Job 21–C2, 5,220 hours; and Job 17–H3, 4,270 hours. Prepare the journal entry required to apply overhead costs to operations for April.

Exercise 17-7.
Disposition of Overapplied Overhead (Extension of Exercise 17-6.)
(L.O. 6)

At the end of 19x4, Barron Compumatics had compiled a total of 89,920 hours worked. The actual overhead incurred was $1,143,400.

1. Using the predetermined overhead rate computed in Exercise 17-6, determine the total amount of overhead applied to operations during 19x4 to the nearest dollar.
2. Compute the amount of overapplied overhead for the year.
3. Prepare the journal entry needed to close out the overhead account and dispose of the overapplied overhead for 19x4. Assume that the amount is not significant.

Exercise 17-8.
Disposition of Underapplied Overhead
(L.O. 6)

The Cole Manufacturing Company ended the year with a total of $750 of underapplied overhead. Ending account balances were as follows: Materials Inventory Control, $214,740; Work in Process Inventory Control, $312,500; Finished Goods Inventory Control, $250,000; Cost of Goods Sold, $687,500; and Factory Overhead Control, $750. Close out the Factory Overhead Control account and dispose of the underapplied overhead. Show your work in journal entry form.

Exercise 17-9.
Cost System: Industry Linkage
(L.O. 7)

Which of the following types of manufactured products normally would be accounted for using a job order costing system? Which would be accounted for using a process costing system? (a) paint, (b) automobiles, (c) jet aircraft, (d) bricks, (e) large milling machines, (f) liquid detergent, (g) aluminum compressed-gas cylinders of standard size and capacity, (h) aluminum compressed-gas cylinders with a special fiberglass overwrap for a Mount Everest expedition, (i) standard nails produced from wire, (j) television sets, (k) printed wedding invitations, (l) a limited edition of lithographs, (m) pet flea collars, (n) high-speed lathes with special-order thread drills, (o) breakfast cereal, and (p) an original evening gown.

Exercise 17-10.
Work in Process Inventory Control Account: Journal Entry Analysis
(L.O. 8)

On July 1, Hales Specialty Company's Work in Process Inventory Control account showed a beginning balance of $29,400. Production activity for July was as follows: (a) Direct materials costing $238,820, along with $28,400 of operating supplies, were requisitioned into production. (b) Hales Specialty Company's total factory payroll for July was $140,690, of which $52,490 were payments for indirect labor. (Assume that payroll has been recorded but not distributed to production accounts.) (c) Factory overhead was applied at a rate of 150 percent of direct labor costs.

1. Prepare journal entries to record the materials, labor, and factory overhead costs for July.
2. Compute the ending balance in the Work in Process Inventory Control account. Assume a transfer of $461,400 to the Finished Goods Inventory Control account during the period.

Exercise 17-11.
Computation of Unit Cost
(L.O. 9)

Webster Corporation manufactures a full line of women's apparel. During February, Webster Corporation worked on three special orders, A–16, A–20, and B–14. Cost and production data for each order were as shown in the following table:

	Job A–16	Job A–20	Job B–14
Direct materials:			
Fabric Q	$10,840	$12,980	$17,660
Fabric Z	11,400	12,200	13,440
Fabric YB	5,260	6,920	10,900
Direct labor:			
Seamstress	8,900	10,400	16,200
Layout	6,450	7,425	9,210
Packaging	3,950	4,875	6,090
Factory overhead:			
120% of direct labor dollars	?	?	?
Number of units produced	700	775	1,482

1. Compute the total cost associated with each job. Show the subtotals for each cost category.
2. Compute the unit cost for each job. (Round your computations to the nearest penny.)

Exercise 17-12. Job Order Cost Card Preparation and Computation of Unit Cost
(L.O. 8, 9)

During the month of January, the Key Cabinet Company worked on six different orders for specialty kitchen cabinets. Job A–62, manufactured for M. J. Products, Inc. was begun and completed during the month. Partial data from Job A–62's job order cost card are summarized in the table below.

	Costs	Machine Hours Used
Direct materials:		
Cedar	$7,900	
Pine	6,320	
Hardware	2,930	
Assembly supplies	988	
Direct labor:		
Sawing Department	$2,840	120
Shaping Department	2,200	220
Finishing Department	2,250	180
Assembly Department	2,890	50

A total of thirty-four cabinets was included in Job A–62. The current predetermined factory overhead rate is $21.60 per machine hour. From the information given, prepare a job order cost card similar to Figure 17-3. The cedar and pine are placed into production in the Sawing Department. The hardware and supplies are placed into production in the Assembly Department. (Round to whole dollars where appropriate.)

Interpretation Case from Business

Jones Company and Proctor Corporation
(L.O. 5)

Both Jones Company and Proctor Corporation use predetermined overhead rates for product costing, inventory pricing, and sales quotations. The two businesses are about the same size, and they compete in the corrugated box industry. Jones Company's management believes that because the predetermined overhead rate is an estimated measure, the controller's department should spend little effort in developing it. The company computes the rate once a year based on a trend analysis of the previous year's costs. No one monitors its accuracy during the year.

Proctor Corporation takes a much more sophisticated approach. One person in the controller's office is responsible for developing predetermined overhead rates on a monthly basis. All cost estimates are checked carefully to make sure they are realistic. Accuracy checks are done routinely during each monthly closing analysis, and forecasts of changes in business activity are taken into account.

Required

1. Describe the advantages and disadvantages of each company's approach to developing predetermined overhead rates.
2. Which company has taken the more cost-effective approach to developing predetermined overhead rates? Defend your answer.
3. Is an accurate overhead rate most important for product costing, inventory valuation, or sales quotations? Why?

Problem Set A

Problem 17A-1. Service Department Cost Allocation
(L.O. 3)

Tenants at the Hicks Tower Office Complex on Palmer Avenue in Winter Park, Florida share certain supporting services. All operating costs are incurred centrally and allocated to the seven tenant businesses on the basis of usage. Word processing is one of the shared services. For August, the following costs were related to the word processing function: operator labor, ten people at $1,600 monthly salary each; supplies, $920; equipment depreciation, $1,650; space rental, $3,000; utilities, $650; and overhead charge, $2,380. Thus, total allocable costs for August amounted to $24,600. Usage of the word processing service is recorded in hours, which is the basis for allocating the cost each month. During August, tenant usage was as follows: Braun Catering Service, 128 hours; Norman Realtors, Inc., 284 hours; Drown & Cobbs, Attorneys at Law, 422 hours; Bigson Inventory Service, 170 hours; Cuthill & Teddy, CPAs, 360 hours; University Sporting Goods, 126 hours; and Pam's Hair Styling Supplies, 110 hours.

Required

1. Assign the costs of the word processing function for August to each of the seven tenant businesses on the basis of hours of usage. (Round your answers to the nearest dollar.)
2. List other bases of allocation that could have been used to assign costs in this case. Discuss the advantages and disadvantages of each.

Problem 17A-2. Application of Factory Overhead
(L.O. 5, 6)

Ray Laser Products, Inc. uses a predetermined overhead rate in its production, assembly, and testing departments. One rate is used for the entire company and is based on machine hours. The current rate was determined by analyzing data from the previous two years and projecting figures for the current year, adjusted for expected changes. Mr. Hinnen is about to compute the rate to be used in 19x3 using the data shown below.

	19x1	19x2
Machine hours	38,000	41,800
Factory overhead costs:		
Indirect materials	$ 44,500	$ 57,850
Indirect labor	21,200	25,440
Supervision	37,800	41,580
Utilities	9,400	11,280
Labor-related costs	8,200	9,020
Depreciation, factory	9,800	10,780
Depreciation, machinery	22,700	27,240
Property taxes	2,400	2,880
Insurance	1,600	1,920
Miscellaneous	4,400	4,840
Total overhead	$162,000	$192,830

Machine hours are estimated to be 45,980 for 19x3.

Required

1. Compute the predetermined overhead rate for 19x3 assuming the percentage changes are the same as those of the previous year. (Round your answer to three decimal places.)
2. During 19x3, Ray Laser Products, Inc. produced the following jobs using the machine hours shown:

Job No.	Machine Hours	Job No.	Machine Hours
H–142	7,840	H–201	10,680
H–164	5,260	H–218	12,310
H–175	8,100	H–304	2,460

Determine the amount of factory overhead that was applied to each job in 19x3. What was the total overhead applied during the year? (Round answers to the nearest dollar.)

3. Prepare the journal entry needed to close the overhead account and dispose of the under- or overapplied overhead. Actual factory overhead for 19x3 was $234,485.

Problem 17A-3. Job Order Costing: Journal Entry Analysis and T Accounts
(L.O. 5, 6, 8)

Vann Industries, Inc., the finest name in parking attendant apparel, has been in business for over thirty years. Its colorful and stylish uniforms are special ordered by exclusive hotels and country clubs all over the world. During April 19x4, Vann completed the transactions listed on page 704.

April 1 Materials costing $59,400 were purchased on account.
3 Materials costing $26,850 were requisitioned into production (all used on Job A).
4 Operating supplies were purchased for cash, $22,830.
8 The company issued checks for the following factory overhead costs: utilities, $4,310; factory insurance, $1,925; and repairs, $4,640.
10 The cutting department manager requisitioned $29,510 of materials (all used on Job A) and $6,480 of operating supplies into production.
15 Payroll was distributed to the employees. Gross wages and salaries were as follows: direct labor, $62,900 (all for Job A); indirect labor, $31,610; factory supervision, $26,900; and sales commissions, $32,980.
15 Overhead was applied to production.
22 Factory overhead costs were paid: utilities, $4,270; maintenance, $3,380; and rent, $3,250.
23 The receiving department recorded the purchase on account and receipt of $31,940 of materials and $9,260 of operating supplies.
27 Production requisitioned $28,870 of materials (Job A, $2,660; Job B, $8,400; Job C, $17,810) and $7,640 of operating supplies.
30 The following gross wages and salaries were paid to employees: direct labor, $64,220 (Job A, $44,000; Job B, $9,000; Job C, $11,220); indirect labor, $30,290; factory supervision, $28,520; and sales commissions, $36,200.
30 Factory overhead was applied to production.
30 Jobs A and B were completed and transferred to Finished Goods Inventory Control; the total cost was $322,400.
30 Job A was shipped to the customer on account. The total production cost was $294,200 and the sales price was $418,240.
30 Adjusting entries for the following were recorded: depreciation, factory equipment—$2,680; property taxes, factory, payable at month end—$1,230.

Factory overhead was applied at a rate of 120 percent of direct labor cost.

Required

1. Record the journal entries for all transactions and events in April. In the payroll entries, concern yourself only with the distribution of factory payroll to the production accounts.
2. Post the entries prepared in **1** to T accounts, and determine the partial account balances. Assume no beginning inventory balances. Assume that entries made when payroll was recorded also were posted to the Factory Payroll account. (Round your answers to the nearest whole dollar.)
3. Compute the amount of underapplied or overapplied overhead for April.

Problem 17A-4. Job Order Costing: Unknown Quantity Analysis
(L.O. 8)

Gordon Enterprises makes an assortment of computer support equipment. Joseph Dana, the new controller for the organization, can find only partial information from the past two months, which is presented below. The current year's predetermined overhead rate is 80 percent of direct labor dollars.

Account/Transaction	May	June
Materials Inventory Control, Beginning	$ 36,240	$ e
Work in Process Inventory Control, Beginning	56,480	f
Finished Goods Inventory Control, Beginning	44,260	g
Materials Purchased	a	96,120
Direct Materials Requisitioned	82,320	h
Direct Labor Costs	b	72,250
Factory Overhead Applied	53,200	i
Cost of Units Completed	c	221,400
Cost of Units Sold	209,050	j
Materials Inventory Control, Ending	38,910	41,950
Work in Process Inventory Control, Ending	d	k
Finished Goods Inventory Control, Ending	47,940	51,180

Required

Using the information given, compute the unknown values. Show your computations.

Problem 17A-5.
Job Order Cost Flow
(L.O. 5, 8, 9)

Marion Gill is chief financial officer for Johnston Industries, a company that makes special-order printers for personal computers. Her records for February, 19x4 revealed the following information:

Beginning inventory balances:	
Materials Inventory Control	$27,450
Work in Process Inventory Control	22,900
Finished Goods Inventory Control	19,200
Direct materials purchased and received:	
February 6	$ 7,200
February 12	8,110
February 24	5,890
Direct labor costs:	
February 14	$13,750
February 28	13,230
Direct materials requisitioned into production:	
February 4	$ 9,080
February 13	5,940
February 25	7,600

Job order cost cards for jobs in process on February 28 showed the following totals:

Job No.	Direct Materials	Direct Labor	Factory Overhead
AJ–10	$3,220	$1,810	$2,534
AJ–14	3,880	2,110	2,954
AJ–30	2,980	1,640	2,296
AJ–16	4,690	2,370	3,318

The predetermined overhead rate for the month was 140 percent of direct labor dollars. Sales for February totaled $152,400, which represented a 70 percent markup over the cost of production.

Required

1. Using T accounts, reconstruct the transactions for February.
2. Compute the cost of units completed during the month.
3. What was the total cost of units sold during February?
4. Determine the ending inventory balances.
5. During the first week of March, Jobs AJ–10 and AJ–14 were completed. No additional materials costs were incurred, but Job AJ–10 needed $720 more direct labor, and Job AJ–14 required additional direct labor of $1,140. Job AJ–10 was 40 units; Job AJ–14, 55 units. Compute the unit cost for both jobs.

Problem Set B

Problem 17B-1.
Service Department Cost Allocation
(L.O. 3)

Sampson Community Hospital has one respirator that is shared by the hospital's six departments. To ensure efficiency and simplify the budgeting process, each department's operating income or loss is figured separately every month. Before these calculations can be made, expenses that are considered common expenses must be allocated to each of the departments. Depreciation and maintenance expenses connected directly to the respirator are allocated to the departments according to hours of usage.

The costs for upkeep of the respirator for the month of June follow. Depreciation on the respirator was $1,400; on supplemental machinery, $340. Labor costs were $6,000 for the operators and $2,800 for maintenance. Materials costs were $5,200 for oxygen, $700 for small replacement parts, $1,050 for supplies, and $788 for other operating costs. Thus, total costs for June were $18,278. Respirator usage by department for June was as follows: 230.0 hours for the Oncology Department, 52.6 hours for the Orthopedic Department, 43.2 hours for the Nephrology Department, 113.8 hours for the Geriatric Department, 65.4 hours for the Pediatric Department, and 145.0 hours for the Maternity Department.

Required

1. Compute the cost of respirator usage per hour of use. (Round the answer to two decimal places.)
2. Assign the respirator costs for June to each of the six departments according to hourly usage. (Round the answers to the nearest dollar.)
3. Identify other bases of allocation that could be used to assign costs in this case. Be prepared to discuss the advantages and disadvantages of each allocation basis.

Problem 17B-2. Application of Factory Overhead
(L.O. 5, 6)

Crowley Cosmetics Company applies factory overhead costs on the basis of machine hours. The current predetermined overhead rate is computed by using data from the two prior years, in this case 19x0 and 19x1, adjusted to reflect expectations for the current year, 19x2. The controller prepared the overhead rate analysis for 19x2 using the information presented below.

	19x0	19x1
Machine hours	47,800	57,360
Factory overhead costs:		
Indirect labor	$ 18,100	$ 23,530
Employee benefits	22,000	28,600
Manufacturing supervision	16,800	18,480
Utilities	10,350	14,490
Factory insurance	6,500	7,800
Janitorial services	11,000	12,100
Depreciation, factory and machinery	17,750	21,300
Miscellaneous	5,750	7,475
Total overhead	$108,250	$133,775

Machine hours are expected to total 68,832.

Required

1. Compute the predetermined overhead rate for 19x2 assuming the percentage changes are the same as those of the preevious year. (Carry your answer to three decimal places.)
2. Assume that the company actually surpassed its sales and operating expectations in 19x2. Jobs completed during the year and the related machine hours used were as follows:

Job No.	Machine Hours
2214	12,300
2215	14,200
2216	9,800
2217	13,600
2218	11,300
2219	8,100

   Total machine hours were 69,300. Determine the amount of factory overhead to be applied to each job and to total production during 19x2. (Round answers to whole dollars.)
3. Prepare the journal entry needed to close the overhead accounts and dispose of the underapplied or overapplied overhead for 19x2. Assume that $165,845 of factory overhead was incurred during the year. Also assume that the difference between actual overhead costs and applied overhead costs was insignificant.

Problem 17B-3. Job Order Costing: Journal Entry Analysis and T Accounts
(L.O. 5, 6, 8)

Fordley Manufacturing, Inc. produces electric golf carts. The carts are special-order items, so the company uses a job order cost accounting system. Factory overhead is applied at the rate of 90 percent of direct labor cost. Following is a list of events and transactions for January.

Jan. 1 Direct materials costing $215,400 were purchased on account.
2 Operating supplies were purchased on account, $49,500.
4 Production personnel requisitioned direct materials costing $193,200 (all used on Job X) and operating supplies costing $38,100 into production.
10 The following overhead costs were paid: utilities, $4,400; factory rent, $3,800; and maintenance charges, $3,900.
15 Payroll was distributed to employees. Gross wages and salaries were as follows: direct labor, $120,000 (all for Job X); indirect labor, $60,620; sales commissions, $32,400; and administrative salaries, $38,000.
15 Overhead was applied to production.
19 Operating supplies costing $27,550 and direct materials listed at $190,450 were purchased on account.
21 Direct materials costing $214,750 (Job X, $178,170; Job Y, $18,170; Job Z, $18,410) and operating supplies costing $31,400 were requisitioned into production.
31 The following gross wages and salaries were paid to employees: direct labor, $132,000 (Job X, $118,500; Job Y, $7,000; Job Z, $6,500); indirect labor, $62,240; sales commissions, $31,200; and administrative salaries, $38,000.
31 Overhead was applied to production.
31 Jobs X and Y were completed and transferred to Finished Goods Inventory Control; total cost was $855,990.
31 Job X was shipped to the customer on account. The total production cost was $824,520 and the sales price was $996,800.
31 The following overhead costs (adjusting entries) were recorded: prepaid insurance expired, $3,700; property taxes (payable at year end), $3,400; and depreciation, machinery, $15,500.

Required

1. Record the journal entries for all transactions and events in January. In the payroll entries, concern yourself only with the distribution of factory payroll to the production accounts.
2. Post the entries prepared in **1** to T accounts, and determine the partial account balances. Assume no beginning inventory balances. Assume that entries made when the payroll was recorded also were posted to the Factory Payroll account.
3. Compute the amount of underapplied or overapplied overhead as of January 31.

Problem 17B-4. Job Order Costing: Unknown Quantity Analysis
(L.O. 8)

Partial operating data for the Criner Picture Company is presented below. Management has decided the predetermined overhead rate for the current year is 120 percent of direct labor dollars.

Account/Transaction	March	April
Beginning Materials Inventory Control	$ a	$ e
Beginning Work in Process Inventory Control	89,605	f
Beginning Finished Goods Inventory Control	79,764	67,660
Direct Materials Requisitioned	59,025	g
Materials Purchased	57,100	60,216
Direct Labor Costs	48,760	54,540
Factory Overhead Applied	b	h
Cost of Units Completed	c	231,861
Cost of Goods Sold	166,805	i
Ending Materials Inventory Control	32,014	27,628
Ending Work in Process Inventory Control	d	j
Ending Finished Goods Inventory Control	67,660	30,515

Required

Using the data provided, compute the unknown values. Show all your computations.

Problem 17B-5.
Job Order Cost Flow
(L.O. 5, 8, 9)

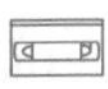

The September 1 inventory balances of Granger House, a manufacturer of high-quality children's clothing, were as follows:

Account	Balance
Materials Inventory Control	$21,360
Work in Process Inventory Control	15,112
Finished Goods Inventory Control	17,120

Job order cost cards for jobs in process as of September 30, 19x9 revealed the following totals:

Job No.	Direct Materials	Direct Labor	Factory Overhead
24–A	$1,596	$1,290	$1,677
24–B	1,492	1,380	1,794
24–C	1,984	1,760	2,288
24–D	1,608	1,540	2,002

Materials purchased and received in September:	
September 4	$33,120
September 16	28,600
September 22	31,920
Direct labor costs for September:	
September 15 payroll	$23,680
September 29 payroll	25,960
Predetermined overhead rate:	
130 percent of direct labor dollars	
Direct materials requisitioned into production during September:	
September 6	$37,240
September 23	38,960

Finished goods with a 75 percent markup over cost were sold during September for $320,000.

Required

1. Using T accounts, reconstruct the transactions for September.
2. Compute the cost of units completed during the month.
3. What was the total cost of units sold during September?
4. Determine the ending inventory balances.
5. Jobs 24–A and 24–C were completed during the first week of October. No additional materials costs were incurred, but Job 24–A required $960 more direct labor, and Job 24–C needed additional direct labor of $1,610. Job 24–A was composed of 1,200 pairs of trousers; Job 24–C, 950 shirts. Compute the unit cost for each job. (Round your answers to three places.)

Management Decision Case

Pearson Manufacturing Company
(L.O. 5, 7, 8, 9)

Pearson Manufacturing Company is a small family-owned business that makes specialty plastic products. Since it was started three years ago, the company has grown quickly and now employs ten production people. Because of its size, the company uses a job order cost accounting system that was designed around a periodic inventory system. Work sheets and special analyses are used at Pearson to account for manufacturing costs and inventory valuations.

Two months ago, in May 19x4, the company's accountant quit. You have been called in to help management. The following information has been given to you:

Beginning inventory balances (1/1/19x4):	
Materials	$50,420
Work in Process (Job K–2)	59,100
Finished Goods (Job K–1)	76,480

Direct materials requisitioned into production during 19x4:	
Job K–2	$33,850
Job K–4	53,380
Job K–6	82,400
Direct labor for the year:	
Job K–2	$25,300
Job K–4	33,480
Job K–6	45,600

The company purchased materials only once (in February), for $126,500. All jobs use the same materials. For the current year, the company has been using an overhead application rate of 150 percent of direct labor dollars. So far, two jobs, K–2 and K–4, have been completed, and Jobs K–1 and K–2 have been shipped to customers. Job K–1 contained 3,200 units; Job K–2, 5,500 units; and Job K–4, 4,600 units.

Required

1. Reconstruct the job order cost sheets for each job worked on during the period. What were the unit costs for jobs K–1, K–2, and K–4?
2. From the information given prepare a T account analysis, and compute the current balances in the three inventory accounts and the Cost of Goods Sold account.
3. The president has asked you to analyze the current job order cost accounting system. Should the system be changed? How? Why? Prepare an outline of your response to the president.

Answers to Self-Test

1. b	3. a	5. a	7. c	9. d
2. c	4. d	6. b	8. c	10. a

Comprehensive Problem: Silvoso Computer Systems, Inc.

Silvoso Computer Systems, Inc. designs unique management information systems and produces specialty computer equipment for use in the production of heavy road-construction machinery and underwater search equipment. The corporation's headquarters and operations center is located in Columbia, Missouri. The firm uses a job order costing system for internal accounting and inventory valuation purposes. The current year's predetermined overhead rate is 130 percent of direct labor dollars.

At the beginning of business on March 1, 19x3, the Materials Inventory Control account had a balance of $246,750. Materials Inventory subsidiary records revealed the following breakdown: sheet metal, $54,820; casings, $36,110; computer components, $149,880; and operating supplies, $5,940. Three jobs were in process on March 1, when the job order cost cards showed the following amounts from February:

	Job P–284	Job E–302	Job G–325
Direct Materials:			
Sheet metal	$ 28,384	$21,120	$ 5,453
Computer components	21,452	7,649	3,160
Casings	18,560	12,310	2,180
Direct Labor	20,420	8,330	1,510
Applied Factory Overhead	26,546	10,829	1,963
Totals	$115,362	$60,238	$14,266

The Work in Process Inventory Control account balance on March 1 was $189,866.

All finished goods inventory items were sold and shipped in February, so no balance existed on March 1. The Factory Payroll and Factory Overhead Control accounts are closed at the end of each month, so no balances were carried forward from February. The following transactions were completed during March:

Mar. 1 Recent purchases were received with invoices: sheet metal, $36,440; and casings, $24,980.

2 Requisitioned $3,710 of operating supplies into production.

4 Paid factory overhead costs: electricity, $3,240; water, $590; heat, $1,950; and repairs and maintenance, $2,620.

5 Received new purchases along with invoices: computer components, $52,810; casings, $22,550; and operating supplies, $4,070.

7 Requisitioned materials into production:

Job E–302: sheet metal, $7,480; and computer components, $16,270.

Job G–325: sheet metal, $18,240; casings, $5,760; and computer components, $18,960.

Job G–410: sheet metal, $15,420; casings, $6,130; and computer components, $5,230.

9 Operating supplies costing $1,840 were requisitioned into production.

14 Semimonthly payroll liability was recorded and distributed to the production accounts: total direct labor, $40,230 (Job P–284, $3,150; Job E–302, $14,720; Job G–325, $18,110; Job G–410, $4,250); indirect labor wages, $28,190; administrative salaries, $54,200; social security and Medicare taxes withheld, $9,320; and employees' federal income taxes withheld, $24,534.

Mar. 14 Factory overhead costs were applied to production.

15 Completed and transferred thirty-eight units and their costs on Job P–284 to Finished Goods Inventory Control.

16 Purchased materials were received along with invoices: sheet metal, $16,520; computer components, $29,280; casings, $15,960; and operating supplies, $4,110.

17 Job P–284 was sold and shipped to the customer. The selling price was $248,500.

18 Requisitioned materials into production:

Job E–302: casings, $8,720; and computer components, $4,890.

Job G–325: casings, $16,780; and computer components, $6,520.

Job G–410: sheet metal, $13,460; casings, $13,220; and computer components, $16,610.

Job Y–160: sheet metal, $9,810; casings, $10,730; and computer components, $6,230.

20 Operating supplies costing $5,620 were requisitioned into production.

23 Paid factory overhead costs: property taxes, $2,570; employer's share of unemployment compensation taxes, factory employees, $560; repairs, $3,680; outside-contract indirect labor, $4,170; and factory rent, $3,110.

28 Semimonthly payroll liability was recorded and distributed to the production accounts: total direct labor, $38,870 (Job E–302, $5,760; Job G–325, $5,560; Job G–410, $16,940; Job Y–160, $10,610); indirect labor wages, $40,770; administrative salaries, $56,540; social security and Medicare taxes withheld, $10,090; and employees' federal income taxes withheld, $26,510.

28 Factory overhead costs were applied to production.

29 Completed and transferred Jobs E–302 (forty-five units) and G–325 (forty-two units) to Finished Goods Inventory Control.

30 Recorded depreciation on equipment, $1,090.

31 Job E–302 was sold and shipped to the customer. The selling price was $285,000.

31 The Factory Overhead Control account was closed out, and the difference was distributed to the Cost of Goods Sold account.

Required

1. Prepare journal entries for all the transactions described above.
2. Prepare T accounts for all the general ledger and subsidiary ledger accounts relevant to the job order costing system of Silvoso Computer Systems, Inc., and enter the beginning balances where applicable.
3. Develop the job order cost cards needed for the month and enter any balances existing at the beginning of March.
4. Post the journal entries prepared in item **1** to the T accounts.
5. Enter all relevant data on the correct job order cost cards as the journal entries are posted.
6. Compute all ending balances in the T accounts.
7. Complete the job order cost cards for each job completed during March, and compute each completed job's unit cost.
8. Check the accuracy of the ending inventory control account balances by comparing them with the totals from the respective subsidiary ledger accounts.

This Comprehensive Problem covers Learning Objectives 6 through 8 in the chapter on the introduction to management accounting and Learning Objectives 5 through 9 in the chapter on cost allocation and the job order costing system.

LEARNING OBJECTIVES

1. Compare and contrast the characteristics of the job order and process cost accounting systems.
2. Explain the role of the Work in Process Inventory account(s) in a process cost accounting system.
3. Diagram the product flow and cost flow through a process cost accounting system.
4. Compute equivalent production for situations with and without units in the beginning Work in Process Inventory.
5. Compute product unit cost for a specific time period using a unit cost analysis schedule.
6. Prepare a cost summary schedule that assigns costs to units completed and transferred out during the period, and find the ending Work in Process Inventory balance.
7. Prepare the journal entry(ies) needed to transfer costs of completed units out of the Work in Process Inventory account.
8. Allocate common manufacturing costs to joint products.

CHAPTER 18

The Process Cost System

A cost accounting system is expected to provide product unit cost information, supply cost data to support management decisions, and generate ending values for the Materials, Work in Process, and Finished Goods Inventory accounts. The chapter on cost allocation and the job order costing system highlighted one approach to these objectives. A **process cost accounting system** is a product costing system used by companies that produce large amounts of similar products or have a continuous production flow. Companies adopting the just-in-time operating philosophy also employ process costing procedures. (The new global operating environments and their impact on product costing are discussed in the chapters on the just-in-time operating environment, and activity-based costing and measures of quality.)

This chapter analyzes the process cost accounting system and explains how to calculate product unit costs. It illustrates how to compute and verify the period-end balance for the Work in Process Inventory account and costs assigned to units completed. In addition, we analyze accounting for the costs of joint products. After studying this chapter, you should be able to meet the learning objectives listed on the left.

DECISION POINT
Banyon Industries

■ In the book *Crossroads: A JIT Success Story,*[1] Banyon Industries is a job-shop manufacturer that produces counters, count controls, and programmable controls. Although the company's name is fictitious, the story about implementing a new system based on work cells rather than departments is based on an actual case. Main characters Ben and Julie systematically create a new plantwide operating environment. Starting with the conversion of a single product line into a continuous flow production work cell, the story takes the reader through a complete transformation of the plant's physical layout, an improvement in employees' attitudes, a revision of the employee incentive plan, and the installation of a new accounting and performance evaluation system.

The existing job order costing system was found to be inappropriate for the new operating environment. As stated by the plant's manager,

> We identified eight major areas where changes were needed to match accounting results to plant performance. After looking at the problem, John [the controller] suggested that we change our basic cost model from job

1. Robert Stasey and Carol J. McNair, *Crossroads: A JIT Success Story,* from the Coopers & Lybrand Performance Solutions Series (Homewood, Illinois: Dow Jones–Irwin, 1990).

order to process cost. This was a major shift, resulting in a de-emphasis on labor and material reporting and an emphasis on good units produced.

What major operating system characteristic changed and required management to shift from a job order costing approach to the process costing system?

Because of the shift to a continuous product flow through production work cells, a process costing system fit management's needs perfectly. With the transition to the new operating environment, it became much easier to trace production costs to work cells than to job orders. Direct labor decreased significantly as automation was introduced. Production-related overhead costs, both fixed and variable, became traceable to the cells. Emphasis was placed on product throughput time, which meant lowering the time it took to get a product through the production process. In addition, high product quality levels, low scrap and rework levels, and an emphasis on good units produced were important elements of the new operating system. ■

The Process Cost Accounting System

A Comparison of Job Order Costing and Process Costing

OBJECTIVE 1
Compare and contrast the characteristics of the job order and process cost accounting systems

The two traditional approaches to product cost accounting systems are job order costing and process costing. Although job order costing is designed for a special order environment and process costing is used in large volume, continuous production facilities, both provide product unit cost information for pricing, cost control, inventory valuation, and the preparation of financial statements. Ending balances for the Cost of Goods Sold, Work in Process Inventory, and Finished Goods Inventory accounts are computed using product unit cost data.

The chart below summarizes the main characteristics of job order costing and process costing:

Job Order Costing	Process Costing
1. Collects manufacturing costs and assigns them to specific jobs or batches of product.	1. Collects manufacturing costs and groups them by department, work center, or work cell.
2. Measures costs for each completed job.	2. Measures costs in terms of units completed in specific time periods.
3. Utilizes one Work in Process Inventory Control account supported by a subsidiary ledger of job order cost cards.	3. Utilizes several Work in Process Inventory accounts, one for each department, work center, or work cell.

The process costing system depends on a three-schedule analysis consisting of a schedule of equivalent production, a unit cost analysis schedule, and a cost summary schedule. From the information in these three schedules, costs are traced or assigned to units that are completed and transferred out of the department or work center. Then a journal entry transfers those costs out of the department's Work in Process Inventory account. The costs remaining in the Work in Process Inventory account belong to units still in process at period end.

Cost Flow Through Work in Process Inventory Accounts

OBJECTIVE 2
Explain the role of the Work in Process Inventory account(s) in a process cost accounting system

Accounting for the costs of materials, direct labor, and factory overhead is similar for job order costing and process costing. Under both systems, costs must be recorded and eventually charged to production. Materials and supplies must be purchased and requisitioned into production. Direct labor wages must be paid to employees and charged to production accounts. Finally, factory overhead costs must be assigned to production. Journal entries like those described in the chapter on cost allocation and the job order costing system record these transactions and events. So, as you can see, the flow of costs *into* the Work in Process Inventory account is very similar in the two product costing systems.

The major difference between job order cost accounting and process cost accounting is the way in which costs are assigned to products. In a job order cost system, costs are traced to specific jobs and products. In a process cost system, an averaging technique is used. All products worked on during a specific time period (a week or a month) are used as the output base for computing unit cost. Total costs of materials, direct labor, and factory overhead accumulated in the Work in Process Inventory account (or accounts) are divided by the equivalent units for products worked on during the period. Though technical aspects make the process costing procedure more difficult than it first appears, the concept of accumulating costs by work cell or process and assigning them to good units produced supports the basic tenet of product costing.

Work in Process Inventory Accounts

The Work in Process Inventory account is the focal point of process costing. Unlike the job order system, a process cost system is not limited to one Work in Process Inventory account. In fact, process costing uses as many Work in Process Inventory accounts as there are departments or steps in the production process. The process shown in Figure 18-1 involves two departments. As shown in the figure, the three cost elements flow into the Work in Process Inventory account of Department 1. When the processed units move from Department 1 to Department 2, the total costs accumulated for those units also move from Department 1 to Department 2. In Department 2, the units from Department 1 are processed further. No more materials are needed, but as shown in the figure, more labor is added and factory overhead is assigned.

When the products are completed, they are transferred from the work in process inventory of Department 2 to the finished goods inventory. At that point each unit's cost is made up of five cost inputs, three from Department 1 and two from Department 2. A detailed breakdown, using hypothetical dollar amounts, follows.

Total Unit Cost

Department 1		
Materials	$2.55	
Direct labor	.90	
Factory overhead	.75	
Total, Department 1		$4.20
Department 2		
Direct labor	$1.20	
Factory overhead	2.05	
Total, Department 2		3.25
Total unit cost (to finished goods inventory)		$7.45

Figure 18-1. Cost Elements and Process Cost Accounts

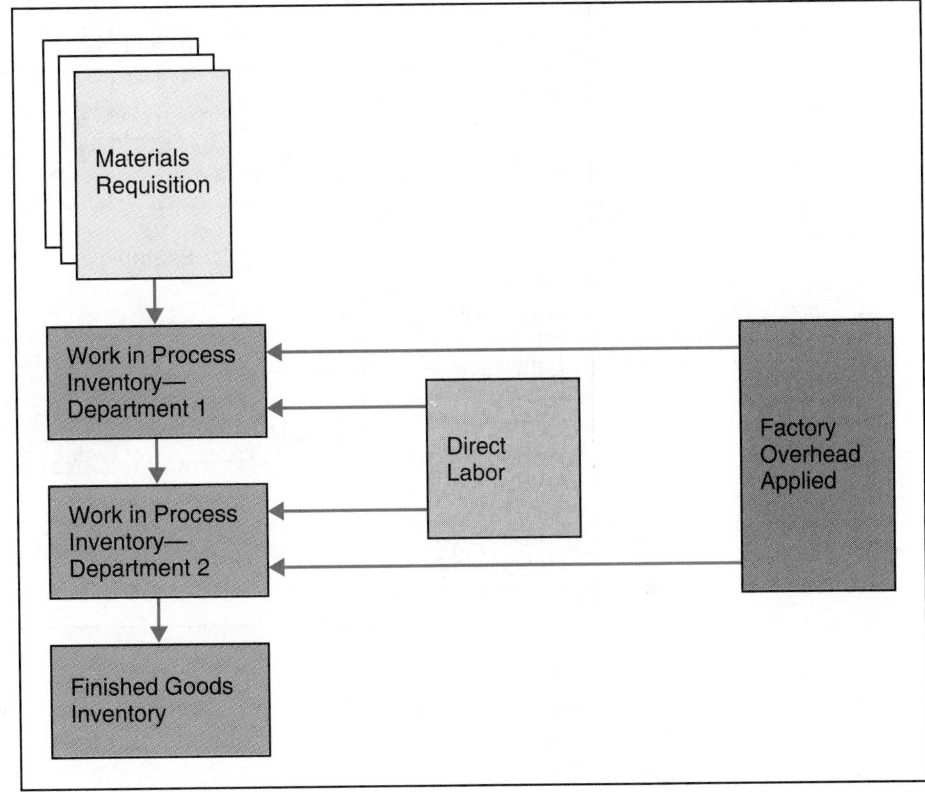

Production Flow Combinations

OBJECTIVE 3
Diagram the product flow and cost flow through a process cost accounting system

There are hundreds of ways in which product flows can combine with department production processes. Two basic structures are illustrated in Figure 18-2. Example 1 shows a series of three processes, or departments. The completed product from one department becomes the direct materials input in the next department. (Figure 18-1 also shows a series of departments.) A department series can include from two to a dozen or more departments or processes. The product unit cost is the sum of the cost elements in all departments.

Example 2 in Figure 18-2 shows a different kind of production flow. Again there are three departments, but the product does not flow through all departments in a simple 1-2-3 order. Instead, two separate products are developed, one in Department X and the other in Department Y. Both products then go to Department Z, where they are joined with a third direct material input, Material AH. The unit cost that is transferred to the Finished Goods Inventory account when the products are completed includes cost elements from Departments X, Y, and Z.

Cost Flow Assumptions

As products are developed, the costs of the necessary production activities are accumulated and assigned to those products. Because of the continuous flow nature of a process industry, products flow in a first-in, first-out (FIFO) manner. The first item entering the process must be the first one completed. If not, the

Figure 18-2. Cost Flow for Process Costing

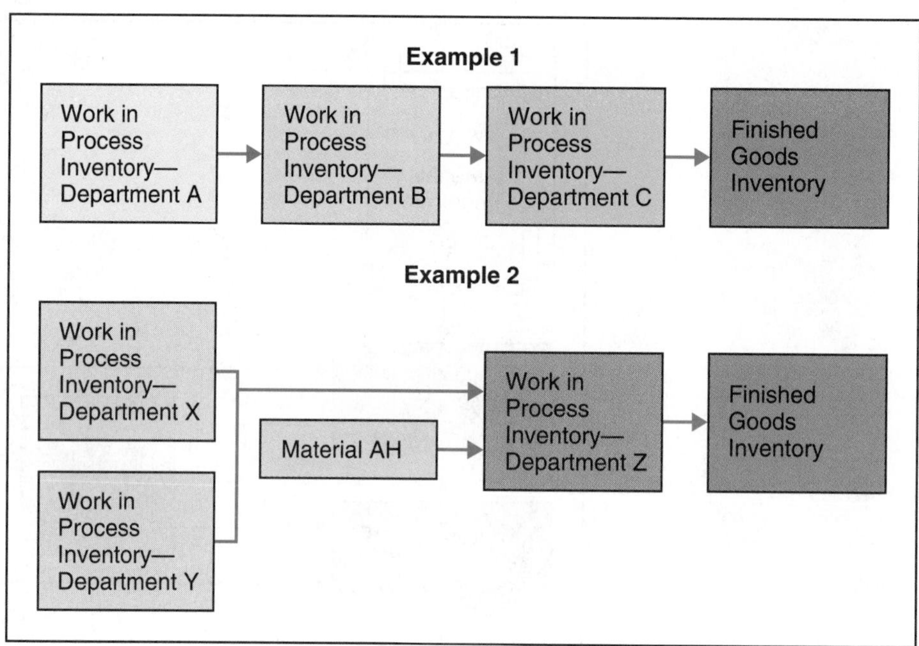

production flow has been interrupted by some unforeseen event or work stoppage. The product flows diagrammed in Figures 18-1 and 18-2 are based on a FIFO product flow.

From your study of accounting for inventories, however, you learned that cost flow does not have to be the same as product flow. Product flow may be FIFO based, but the inventory may be valued using a weighted average, FIFO, or LIFO (last-in, first-out) basis. These same alternatives are available when tracking the costs in a process costing system. In process costing, costs may be assigned to products based on either a weighted average or FIFO method.

The **FIFO costing approach**, then, is a process costing method in which cost flow follows product flow; the first products to be introduced into the production process are the first products to be completed. Costs assigned to those first products are the first costs to be transferred out of the production center or department. We have elected to use the FIFO costing method in our analysis of the process costing system for two reasons. First, since products flow through the process in a FIFO manner, it is easier to learn how to account for the costs if the same cost flow approach is used. The second reason relates to the usage of process costing in industry. A recent study determined that 52 percent of 112 companies surveyed used the process costing technique. And of those 58 companies using the process approach, 58 percent were using the FIFO cost flow assumption. Twenty-one percent used a variant of the FIFO approach. Only 21 percent of the companies surveyed used the average costing approach.[2] Since about one in five companies does use the average costing approach, we describe it as an alternative method later in this chapter.

2. Rex C. Hunter, Frank R. Urbancic, and Donald E. Edwards, "Process Costing: Is It Relevant?" *Management Accounting*, Institute of Management Accountants, December 1989, p. 53.

The Concept of Equivalent Production

OBJECTIVE 4
Compute equivalent production for situations with and without units in the beginning Work in Process Inventory

A key feature of a process cost system is the computation of equivalent units of production for each department or process for each accounting period. This computation is needed before product unit costs can be computed. Remember that in process costing, an averaging approach is used. No attempt is made to associate costs with particular job orders. Instead, all manufacturing costs incurred in a department or production process are divided by the units produced during the period. There are, however, several important questions to answer in connection with the number of units produced. Exactly how many units were produced? Do we count only those units completed during the period? What about partly completed units in the beginning work in process inventory? Do we count them even if only part of the work needed to complete them was done during the period? And what about products in the ending work in process inventory? Is it proper to focus only on those units started and completed during the period?

The answers to all these questions are linked to the concept of equivalent production. **Equivalent production** (also called **equivalent units**) is a measure of the number of equivalent whole units produced in a period of time. That is, partly completed units are restated in terms of equivalent whole units. The number of equivalent units produced is equal to the sum of (1) total units started and completed during the period and (2) an amount representing the work done on partially completed products in both the beginning and ending work in process inventories. A "percentage of completion" factor is applied to partially completed units to calculate the number of equivalent whole units.

Figure 18-3 illustrates the equivalent unit computation. One automobile was in process at the beginning of the month, three were started and completed during February, and one was still in process at period end. Actually, one-half

Figure 18-3. Equivalent Unit Computation

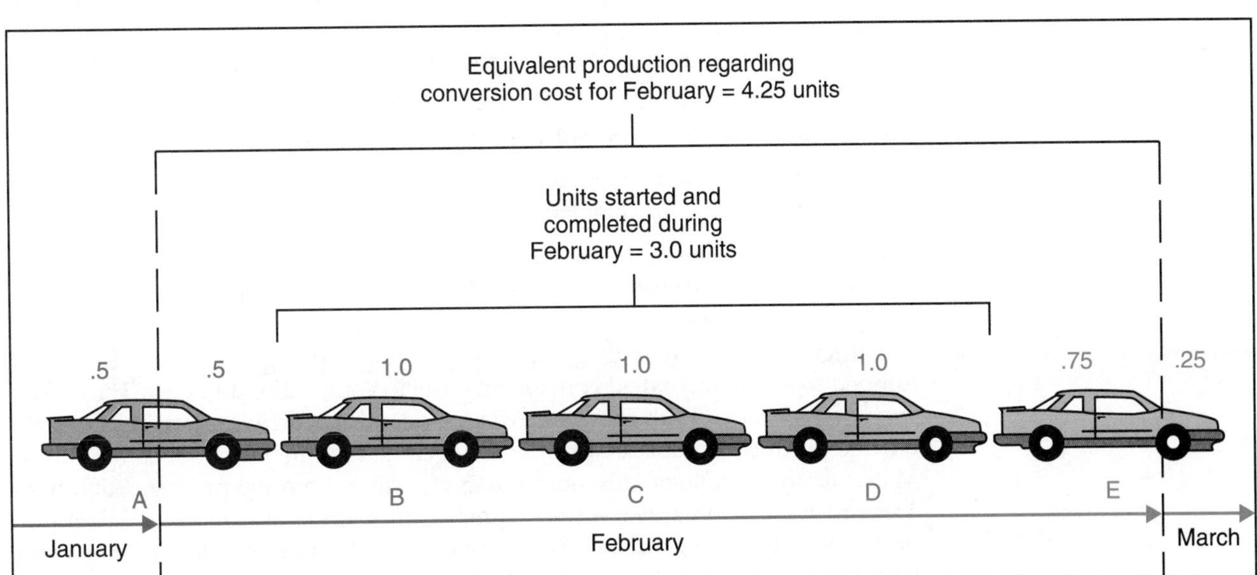

Facts: Conversion costs (those for direct labor and factory overhead) are incurred uniformly as each car moves through production. Equivalent production for February is 4.25 units as to conversion costs. But materials costs are all added to production at the beginning of the process. Since four cars entered production in February (cars B, C, D, and E), equivalent production for the month is 4.0 units as to material costs.

(.5) of Car A and three-quarters (.75) of Car E were completed during February. The total equivalent units for the month are found by adding together those units started and completed (3.0) and those units partly completed (.5 and .75). Therefore, equivalent production for February is 4.25 units.

This is the method used for determining equivalent production for direct labor and factory overhead, commonly called conversion costs. **Conversion costs** are the combined total of direct labor and factory overhead costs incurred by a production department. They are usually lumped together because they are incurred uniformly throughout the production process; combining them for unit cost determination purposes is convenient.

Raw materials are usually added at the beginning of a process, however, so equivalent units for *materials* costs are computed in a different manner. As shown in Figure 18-3, materials for Car A were added in January and therefore do not influence equivalent units for materials in February. However, materials for Car E were *all* added to production in February. So, 3.0 (units started and completed—Cars B, C, and D) is added to 1.0 (unit started but not completed—Car E) to get the equivalent units for materials for February, 4.0 units.

Once you know the number of equivalent units produced, you can compute unit costs for materials and conversion costs for each department in the production process. The equations for computing the unit cost amounts follow. (Note the role of equivalent units.)

$$\text{Unit cost for materials} = \frac{\text{total materials costs}}{\text{equivalent units—materials costs}}$$

$$\text{Unit cost for conversion costs} = \frac{\text{total labor and factory overhead costs}}{\text{equivalent units—conversion costs}}$$

No Beginning Work in Process Inventory

To begin the analysis for computing equivalent production, we will assume that there are no units in beginning work in process inventory. This assumption being true, the only remaining possibilities are (1) units started and completed during the period, and (2) units started but not completed. By definition, units started but not completed comprise the ending Work in Process Inventory unit balance. Equivalent production is computed in parts as follows:

Part 1: Units started and completed = (number of units) × 100 percent

Part 2: Equivalent units in ending work in process inventory = (number of units) × (percentage of completion)

The *sum* of these two amounts represents the equivalent whole units completed during the period. Percentage of completion factors are obtained from supervisors in the production departments.

Earlier we noted that direct labor and factory overhead costs are usually lumped together and called conversion costs in computing unit cost. The reason for doing so is that both types of costs are usually incurred uniformly throughout the production process. Combining them saves one unit cost computation. Materials costs are generally not used uniformly within the process. Such costs are usually incurred either at the beginning of the process (raw materials input) or at the end of the process (packing materials). Because of this difference, the equivalent unit amount for raw materials will not be the same as that for conversion costs. Separate computations are necessary.

We will use Karlsson Clothing, Inc. to illustrate the computation of equivalent units when there are no partially completed units in beginning work in process inventory. Assume that Karlsson's records for January 19xx contain the following information: (a) 47,500 units started during period; (b) 6,200 units partially complete at period end; (c) 60 percent completion of ending work in process inventory; (d) raw materials added at *beginning* of process, and conversion costs incurred *uniformly* throughout process; no units lost or spoiled during the month.

The **schedule of equivalent production**, in which equivalent production is computed for the period for both materials costs and conversion costs, is shown in Exhibit 18-1. Because there were no units in beginning work in process inventory, dashes are entered in the appropriate columns. All 41,300 units started and completed during the period (47,500 units started less 6,200 units not completed) have received 100 percent of the materials, labor, and overhead effort needed to complete them. Therefore, 41,300 equivalent units are recorded in both the Materials Costs and Conversion Costs columns.

Accounting for equivalent units in ending inventory is a bit more complicated. These 6,200 units have received all raw materials inputs because materials were added to each product as it entered the production process. Therefore, in the Materials Costs column, 6,200 equivalent units are entered. However, conversion costs (direct labor and factory overhead) are added uniformly as the products move through the process. The 6,200 units in ending inventory are only 60 percent complete. Equivalent whole units are determined by multiplying the number of units by the percentage completed. In Exhibit 18-1, the amount of equivalent units for conversion costs of ending inventory is computed as follows:

6,200 units × 60% completion = 3,720 equivalent units

As a result of these computations for January, there were 47,500 equivalent units for materials costs and 45,020 equivalent units for conversion costs.

Exhibit 18-1. Equivalent Units—No Beginning Inventory

Karlsson Clothing, Inc.
Schedule of Equivalent Production
For the Month Ended January 31, 19xx

		Equivalent Units	
Units—Stage of Completion	**Units To Be Accounted For**	**Materials Costs**	**Conversion Costs**
Beginning inventory—units completed in this period	—	—	—
Units started and completed in this period	41,300	41,300	41,300
Ending inventory—units started but not completed in this period	6,200		
(Materials costs—100% complete)		6,200	
(Conversion costs—60% complete)			3,720
Totals	47,500	47,500	45,020

With Beginning Work in Process Inventory

A situation where there is no beginning work in process inventory is very seldom found in industry. By definition, process costing techniques are used in industries where production flows continuously or where there are long runs of identical products. In these situations, because there is always something in process at month end, there are always units in beginning work in process inventory in the following period. Thus, we turn our analysis to this situation, expanding the example used above.

During February 19xx, unit production results for Karlsson Clothing, Inc. were as follows: (a) the 6,200 units in beginning work in process inventory (60 percent complete at the beginning of February) were finished during the month; (b) 57,500 units were started during the period, of which 5,000 units were partially complete (45 percent) at period end and comprised the ending work in process inventory.

Beginning inventories make the computation of equivalent units somewhat more difficult. February operations of Karlsson Clothing, Inc. involve both beginning and ending balances in Work in Process Inventory. To compute equivalent units for February, we must be careful to account only for the work done in February. The computation of equivalent units is illustrated in Exhibit 18-2. Units in beginning inventory were 60 percent complete as to conversion costs before the period began and 100 percent complete as to materials costs. All materials were added during the preceding period (January). Therefore, for these units, no equivalent units of materials costs were applicable to February, and only 40 percent of the conversion costs were needed during the month of Feb-

Exhibit 18-2. Equivalent Units—With Beginning Inventory

Karlsson Clothing, Inc.
Schedule of Equivalent Production
For the Month Ended February 28, 19xx

		Equivalent Units	
Units—Stage of Completion	**Units To Be Accounted For**	**Materials Costs**	**Conversion Costs**
Beginning inventory—units completed in this period	6,200		
(Materials costs—100% complete)		—	
(Conversion costs—60% complete)			2,480
Units started and completed in this period	52,500	52,500	52,500
Ending inventory—units started but not completed in this period	5,000		
(Materials costs—100% complete)		5,000	
(Conversion costs—45% complete)			2,250
Totals	63,700	57,500	57,230

ruary to complete the units. As shown in Exhibit 18-2, equivalent units of conversion costs are 2,480 (6,200 units × 40 percent, the remaining percentage of completion).

Computations involving units started and completed, as well as ending inventory computations, are similar to those for January. Units started and completed receive the full amount of raw materials and conversion costs. Therefore, the resulting equivalent units equal 52,500 (57,500 started − 5,000 not completed) for both materials and conversion costs. Ending inventory is 100 percent complete as to materials (5,000 units) and 45 percent complete as to conversion costs (5,000 × 45 percent = 2,250 units). The end result is that February produced 57,500 equivalent units that used raw materials and 57,230 equivalent units that received conversion costs.

Note that these illustrations of the computation of equivalent units cover only two of the hundreds of possible process costing situations with varying percentages of completion. These examples, however, establish the procedures necessary to solve all process costing problems utilizing the FIFO product and cost flows.

Cost Analysis Schedules

Thus far in the discussions concerning process cost accounting, we have placed primary emphasis on accounting for *units* of productive output. In the schedule of equivalent production, we have computed totals for units to be accounted for and equivalent units for materials costs and conversion costs. Once the unit information has been sorted out and equivalent unit figures have been generated, we can turn to the dollar information. Accounting for manufacturing costs, cost per equivalent unit, and inventory costing can now be brought into our analysis.

Unit Cost Analysis Schedule

OBJECTIVE 5
Compute product unit cost for a specific time period using a unit cost analysis schedule

The **unit cost analysis schedule** is a process costing statement used to (1) accumulate all costs charged to the Work in Process Inventory account of each department or production process and determine total costs to be accounted for; and (2) compute cost per equivalent unit for materials costs and conversion costs. Unit cost analysis schedules are pictured in Exhibits 18-3 and 18-5. These two schedules illustrate the calculations when there is no beginning work in process inventory (Exhibit 18-3) and when there are units in beginning work in process inventory (Exhibit 18-5). (The cost summary schedules in Exhibits 18-4 and 18-6 are discussed in the next section.)

The unit cost analysis schedule has two parts: total cost analysis and computation of equivalent unit costs. The unit cost analysis schedule functions as the accumulation point for all costs of the period, and the Total Costs To Be Accounted For column serves as a check figure for the final distribution of costs to inventories in the third schedule, the cost summary schedule. The costs making up the total costs to be accounted for may become part of ending Work in Process Inventory and remain in the account, or they may be part of the costs of completed goods transferred to the next department or to Finished Goods Inventory. The amount of total costs to be accounted for is made up of materials costs and conversion costs incurred during the current period plus those costs included in the beginning balance of Work in Process Inventory.

The second part of the unit cost analysis schedule involves the computation of costs per equivalent unit. For both materials costs and conversion costs, *cur-*

rent period costs only are divided by the respective equivalent unit amounts. Costs attached to units in beginning inventory are *not* included in computing costs per equivalent unit. Under the FIFO cost flow assumption, separate costing analyses are used for each accounting period, and costs of different periods are not averaged. Therefore, costs attached to beginning inventory are isolated and treated separately.

Cost Summary Schedule

OBJECTIVE 6
Prepare a cost summary schedule that assigns costs to units completed and transferred out during the period, and find the ending Work in Process Inventory balance

The final phase of the process costing analysis involves the distribution of total costs accumulated during the period to the units in ending Work in Process Inventory or to the units completed and transferred out of the department. This is done through the use of the **cost summary schedule**. Information used in this schedule originates in either the schedule of equivalent production or the unit cost analysis schedule. Using hypothetical amounts, the following analysis illustrates the computation of total costs transferred out of the department during the period.

Units in beginning inventory	
Costs attached to units in beginning inventory	$ 4,460
Costs necessary to complete units in beginning inventory	2,910
Total cost of units in beginning inventory	$ 7,370
Costs of units started and completed during the period	46,880
Total cost of completed units	$54,250

The computation of each of these amounts is illustrated in the next section. All costs remaining in Work in Process Inventory after costs of completed units have been transferred out represent the cost of ending units in process.

To complete the cost summary schedule, we add together the total cost of completed units transferred and the costs attached to ending Work in Process Inventory and compare their total with the total costs to be accounted for in the unit cost analysis schedule. The two totals should be equal; if they are not equal, the difference may be due to rounding or a computational error in the analysis.

Illustrative Analysis

To fully explain the form and use of the cost schedules, we will expand the Karlsson Clothing, Inc. example. In addition to the equivalent unit information analyzed earlier, the company disclosed the following cost data:

January 19xx	
Beginning Work in Process Inventory	—
Materials costs	$154,375
Conversion costs for the month	258,865
February 19xx	
Materials costs	$189,750
Conversion costs for the month	320,488

From these data, we will compute equivalent unit costs, total costs transferred to Finished Goods Inventory, and the ending balance in Work in Process Inventory for January and February 19xx.

January. Cost analysis and cost summary schedules for January are shown in Exhibits 18-3 and 18-4. Total costs to be accounted for are $413,240 for January as depicted in the unit cost analysis schedule in Exhibit 18-3. Dividing the

Exhibit 18-3. Unit Cost Determination—No Beginning Inventories

Karlsson Clothing, Inc.
Unit Cost Analysis Schedule
For the Month Ended January 31, 19xx

Total Cost Analysis	Costs from Beginning Inventory	Costs from Current Period	Total Costs To Be Accounted For
Materials costs	—	$154,375	$154,375
Conversion costs	—	258,865	258,865
Totals	—	$413,240	$413,240

Computation of Equivalent Unit Costs	Current Period Cost ÷	Equivalent Units =	Cost per Equivalent Unit
Materials costs	$154,375	47,500	$3.25
Conversion costs	258,865	45,020	5.75
Totals	$413,240		$9.00

Exhibit 18-4. Ending Inventory Computation—No Beginning Inventories

Karlsson Clothing, Inc.
Cost Summary Schedule
For the Month Ended January 31, 19xx

	Cost of Goods Transferred to Finished Goods Inventory	**Cost of Ending Work in Process Inventory**
Beginning inventory*		
Costs from preceding period	—	
Costs to complete this period	—	
Units started and completed*		
41,300 units × $9.00 per unit	$371,700	
Ending inventory*		
Materials costs: 6,200 units × $3.25		$ 20,150
Conversion costs: 3,720 units × $5.75		21,390
Totals	$371,700	$ 41,540
Computational check:		
Costs to Finished Goods Inventory		$371,700
Cost of ending Work in Process Inventory		41,540
Total costs to be accounted for (see unit cost analysis schedule)		$413,240

*Note: Unit figures come from the schedule of equivalent production for January (Exhibit 18-1).

January materials costs of $154,375 and the conversion costs of $258,865 by the equivalent unit amounts computed in Exhibit 18-1, we obtain costs per equivalent unit of $3.25 ($154,375 ÷ 47,500) for materials costs and $5.75 ($258,865 ÷ 45,020) for conversion costs. These per unit amounts are used in the cost summary schedule to compute costs transferred to Finished Goods Inventory and the cost of ending Work in Process Inventory.

The cost summary schedule for January is shown in Exhibit 18-4. No units were in process at the beginning of January, so no costs are entered for beginning inventory. (Even though there was no beginning inventory for January, the schedule headings are included because the schedule forms shown can be used for any process costing situation.) Units transferred to Finished Goods Inventory in January are made up entirely of units started and completed because there were no units in beginning inventory. These 41,300 units cost $9 each to produce (total cost per equivalent unit), so $371,700 must be transferred to Finished Goods Inventory.

Since $413,240 was debited to Work in Process Inventory during January and $371,700 of that amount was transferred to Finished Goods Inventory, the $41,540 remaining in the account is the ending inventory balance. This amount, $41,540, is verified in Exhibit 18-4. Using the ending inventory amounts from the schedule of equivalent production in Exhibit 18-1 and the costs per equivalent unit from the cost analysis schedule in Exhibit 18-3, we make the following computations:

Materials costs: 6,200 equivalent units × $3.25 per unit	$20,150
Conversion costs: 3,720 equivalent units × $5.75 per unit	21,390
Ending Work in Process Inventory balance	$41,540

The computational check at the bottom of Exhibit 18-4 verifies that all calculations are correct.

February. The cost analysis for February is more difficult because it is necessary to consider units and costs in beginning Work in Process Inventory. February operating results are analyzed in Exhibits 18-5 and 18-6. Total costs to be accounted for in February are $551,778. Included in this amount are the beginning inventory balance of $41,540 (see January computation in Exhibit 18-4) plus current period costs from February of $189,750 and $320,488 for materials costs and conversion costs, respectively.

Even though February has a beginning balance in Work in Process Inventory, the procedure to compute costs per equivalent unit is similar to the technique used in the January analysis. As shown in Exhibit 18-5, only current period costs are used. February costs of $189,750 for materials costs and $320,488 for conversion costs are divided by the equivalent unit figures computed in Exhibit 18-2. February's $8.90 cost per equivalent unit includes $3.30 per unit for raw materials ($189,750 ÷ 57,500) and $5.60 per unit for conversion costs ($320,488 ÷ 57,230).

The February cost analysis concludes with the preparation of the cost summary schedule, illustrated in Exhibit 18-6. Costs transferred to Finished Goods Inventory include costs of $41,540 attached to the 6,200 units in beginning inventory from January, the costs of completing the units in beginning inventory, and the costs of producing the 52,500 units started and completed during February. January costs of $41,540 were carried forward to February as the beginning balance in the Work in Process Inventory account (see Exhibit 18-4). In addition, as shown in Exhibit 18-2, 2,480 equivalent units of conversion costs

Exhibit 18-5. Unit Cost Determination—With Beginning Inventories

Karlsson Clothing, Inc. Unit Cost Analysis Schedule For the Month Ended February 28, 19xx				
Total Cost Analysis	Costs from Beginning Inventory	Costs from Current Period		Total Costs To Be Accounted For
Materials costs	$20,150	$189,750		$209,900
Conversion costs	21,390	320,488		341,878
Totals	$41,540	$510,238		$551,778
Computation of Equivalent Unit Costs	Current Period Cost ÷	Equivalent Units	=	Cost Per Equivalent Unit
Materials costs	$189,750	57,500		$3.30
Conversion costs	320,488	57,230		5.60
Totals	$510,238			$8.90

were required to complete the 6,200 units. Because the equivalent unit conversion cost for February is $5.60, $13,888 (2,480 units × $5.60/unit) of additional costs were required to complete units in beginning inventory. The 52,500 units started and completed in February cost $8.90 each to produce. This total of $467,250 is added to the $55,428 cost to produce the 6,200 units in beginning inventory to arrive at the $522,678 of costs transferred to Finished Goods Inventory during February.

The ending Work in Process Inventory balance of $29,100 is made up of $16,500 of materials costs (5,000 units × $3.30/unit) and $12,600 of conversion costs (5,000 units × 45 percent × $5.60/unit). The extensions of these amounts are shown in Exhibit 18-6. At the conclusion of the cost summary schedule, the computational check reveals that no calculation errors were made in the February cost analysis.

Journal Entry Analysis

OBJECTIVE 7
Prepare the journal entry(ies) needed to transfer costs of completed units out of the Work in Process Inventory account

The major emphasis in the study of process cost accounting is on the preparation of the schedules for equivalent production, unit cost analysis, and cost summary. All of the computations within these schedules involve the Work in Process Inventory account. The objective is to compute the dollar totals for goods completed and transferred to Finished Goods Inventory and for partially completed products that remain in the Work in Process Inventory account. However, the three schedules alone do not cause costs to flow through accounts in the general ledger. They only provide the information needed. Journal entries are required to effect the flow of costs from one account to another.

The culmination of a process costing analysis, then, is the preparation of a journal entry to transfer costs of completed products out of Work in Process Inventory. Remember that all of the entries analyzed in earlier chapters are also necessary in a process costing system. Only one entry is highlighted here, how-

Exhibit 18-6. Ending Inventory Computation—With Beginning Inventories

Karlsson Clothing, Inc.
Cost Summary Schedule
For the Month Ended February 28, 19xx

	Cost of Goods Transferred to Finished Goods Inventory	Cost of Ending Work in Process Inventory
Beginning inventory*		
Costs from preceding period	$ 41,540	
Costs to complete this period		
Materials costs: none	—	
Conversion costs: 2,480 units × $5.60	13,888	
Subtotal	$ 55,428	
Units started and completed*		
52,500 units × $8.90 per unit	467,250	
Ending inventory*		
Materials costs: 5,000 units × $3.30		$ 16,500
Conversion costs: 2,250 units × $5.60		12,600
Totals	$522,678	$ 29,100
Computational check:		
Costs to Finished Goods Inventory		$522,678
Costs in ending Work in Process Inventory		29,100
Total costs to be accounted for (see unit cost analysis schedule)		$551,778

*Note: Unit figures come from the schedule of equivalent production for February (Exhibit 18-2).

ever, because it is involved directly with the cost transfer of completed goods. To transfer the costs of units completed, we debit Finished Goods Inventory (or Work in Process Inventory of a subsequent department) and credit Work in Process Inventory for the amount of the cost transfer computed in the cost summary schedule.

In the example of Karlsson Clothing, Inc., the following entries would be made at the end of each time period:

Date	Account	Debit	Credit
Jan. 31	Finished Goods Inventory	371,700	
	Work in Process Inventory		371,700
	To transfer cost of units completed in January to Finished Goods Inventory		
Feb. 28	Finished Goods Inventory	522,678	
	Work in Process Inventory		522,678
	To transfer cost of units completed in February to Finished Goods Inventory		

After the entries are posted, the Work in Process Inventory account would appear as shown on the top of page 727 on February 28, 19xx.

Work in Process Inventory

Balance	—	Transferred to Finished Goods in Jan.	371,700
Jan. materials costs	154,375		
Jan. conversion costs	258,865		
Balance 1/31/xx 41,540			
Feb. materials costs	189,750	Transferred to Finished Goods in Feb.	522,678
Feb. conversion costs	320,488		
Balance 2/28/xx 29,100*			

*This amount is confirmed by the cost summary schedule in Exhibit 18-6.

In the analysis of Karlsson Clothing, Inc., the company employed only *one* production department, and the analysis centered on two consecutive monthly accounting periods. Because only one production department was used, only one Work in Process Inventory account was needed.

The following illustrative problem deals with *two* production departments in a series. The product passes from the first to the second department and then to Finished Goods Inventory and is similar to the situation depicted in Example 1 of Figure 18-2. When the production process requires two departments, the accounting system must maintain two separate Work in Process Inventory accounts, one for each department. This situation does entail more work but does not complicate the computational aspects of the process costing system. The key point to remember is to treat *each* department and its related Work in Process Inventory account as a separate analysis. The three schedules must be prepared for *each* department. Departments should be analyzed in the order in which they appear in the series.

Illustrative Problem Two Production Departments

Jens-Lena Manufacturing Company produces a liquid chemical compound used in converting salt water to fresh water. The production process involves the Mixing Department and the Cooling Department. Every unit produced must be processed by both departments, with cooling as the final operation.

In the Mixing Department, a basic chemical powder, Material BP, is blended with water, heated to 88° Celsius, and mixed actively for two hours. Assume that no evaporation takes place and that Material BP is added at the beginning of the process. Conversion costs are incurred uniformly throughout the process. Operating data for the Mixing Department for April 19xx are as follows:

Beginning Work in Process Inventory	
Units (40% complete as to conversion costs)	1,450 liters
Costs: Materials costs	$ 13,050
Conversion costs	$ 1,760
Ending Work in Process Inventory	
All units 70% complete as to conversion costs	
April operations	
Units started	55,600 liters
Costs: Materials costs	$489,280
Conversion costs	$278,975
Units completed and transferred to the Cooling Department	54,800 liters

Required

1. Using good form, prepare (a) a schedule of equivalent production, (b) a unit cost analysis schedule, and (c) a cost summary schedule.
2. Using information in the cost summary schedule, prepare the proper journal entry to transfer costs of completed units for April out of the Mixing Department to the Cooling Department.

Solution

Before doing the three schedules and preparing the journal entry, it is necessary to make a special analysis of the units (liters) worked on during April. In order to complete the schedule of equivalent production, we must first calculate the number of units started and completed and the number of units in ending work in process inventory. These amounts were not stated explicitly in the data given but can be easily computed.

Units started and completed:

	Units completed and transferred (given)	54,800 liters
Less:	Units in beginning inventory (given)	1,450 liters
Equals:	Units started and completed	53,350 liters

Units in ending inventory:

	Units started during April (given)	55,600 liters
Less:	Units started and completed (above)	53,350 liters
Equals:	Units in ending inventory	2,250 liters

With the knowledge of the number of units started and completed and the number of units in ending work in process inventory, we can now prepare the three schedules in the cost analysis.

1. The FIFO solution is shown in Exhibit 18-7. Carefully review each of the three schedules. If you have any problems following the computations, refer to Exhibits 18-1 through 18-6 for explanations.
2. The costs of completed units for April are now ready to be transferred from the Mixing Department to the Cooling Department. The required journal entry would be as follows:

Work in Process Inventory—Cooling Department	755,390	
Work in Process Inventory—Mixing Department		755,390
To transfer cost of units completed in April from Mixing Department to Cooling Department		

In the above entry, the $755,390 is being transferred from one Work in Process Inventory account to another. The $755,390 attached to the units transferred into the Cooling Department during April would be accounted for in the same way as raw materials used in the Mixing Department. All other procedures and schedules illustrated in the Mixing Department example would be used again for the Cooling Department. See the Review Problem at the end of this chapter for the accounting treatment of the Cooling Department.

Rounding of numerical answers. Unlike the problems discussed so far in this chapter, most real-world unit costs do not work out to even-numbered dollars and cents. They must be rounded. Remember these three simple rules: (a) Round off all unit cost computations to three decimal places. (b) Round off cost summary data to the nearest dollar. (c) On the cost summary schedule, any

Exhibit 18-7. FIFO Approach

Jens-Lena Manufacturing Company
Mixing Department—FIFO Process Cost Analysis
For the Month Ended April 30, 19xx

A. Schedule of Equivalent Production

Units—Stage of Completion	Units To Be Accounted For	Equivalent Units: Materials Costs	Equivalent Units: Conversion Costs
Beginning inventory—units started last period but completed this period	1,450		
(Materials costs—100% complete)		—	
(Conversion costs—40% complete)			870 (60% of 1,450)
Units started and completed in this period	53,350	53,350	53,350
Ending inventory—units started but not completed in this period	2,250		
(Materials costs—100% complete)		2,250	
(Conversion costs—70% complete)			1,575 (70% of 2,250)
Totals	57,050	55,600	55,795

B. Unit Cost Analysis Schedule

	Total Costs			Equivalent Unit Costs	
	Costs from Beginning Inventory (1)	Costs from Current Period (2)	Total Costs To Be Accounted For (3)	Equivalent Units (4)	Cost per Equivalent Unit (2÷4)
Materials costs	$13,050	$489,280	$502,330	55,600	$ 8.80
Conversion costs	1,760	278,975	280,735	55,795	5.00
Totals	$14,810	$768,255	$783,065		$13.80

C. Cost Summary Schedule

	Cost of Goods Transferred to Cooling Department	Cost of Ending Work in Process Inventory
Beginning inventory		
Beginning balance	$ 14,810	
Cost to complete: 870 units (1,450 units × 60%) × $5.00 per unit	4,350	
Total beginning inventory	$ 19,160	
Units started and completed 53,350 units × $13.80 per unit	736,230	
Ending inventory		
Materials costs: 2,250 units × $8.80 per unit		$ 19,800
Conversion costs: 1,575 units × $5.00 per unit		7,875
Totals	$755,390	$ 27,675
Check on computations:		
Costs to Cooling Department		$755,390
Costs in ending Work in Process Inventory		27,675
Total costs to be accounted for (see unit cost analysis schedule)		$783,065

difference caused by rounding should be added to or subtracted from the amount being transferred out of the department before the journal entry is prepared.

The Average Costing Approach to Process Costing

Alternative Method

Figure 18-3 illustrates how products flow through a production process in a first-in, first-out (FIFO) order. But cost flow and accountability do not have to follow the same assumptions that support the flow of products. Such is the case with the average costing approach to process cost accounting, in which costs are not accounted for in the same manner as actual product flow. The average costing method is very similar to the FIFO costing method already discussed in this chapter in that all three of the schedules used in the FIFO costing method are employed in the average costing method. The primary difference between the two methods is that the **average costing approach** assumes that the items in beginning work in process inventory were started and completed during the current period. Although less accurate than the FIFO approach, the average costing method is a bit easier to work with.

The procedures used to complete each of the three process costing schedules under the average costing approach are different from the FIFO method. The changes are described and illustrated below. The data found in the chapter's illustrative problem, the Jens-Lena Manufacturing Company, form the basis for the schedules that follow.

Schedule of Equivalent Production

No Beginning Work in Process Inventory. In a situation with no beginning work in process inventory, computing equivalent units is exactly the same in the average costing approach as it is in the FIFO method. The two approaches generate different equivalent unit amounts only when a beginning inventory is involved in the computation.

With Beginning Work in Process Inventory. The first difference between the FIFO costing and average costing methods is found in the computation of equivalent units when there is a beginning work in process inventory. Remember that when you are using the average costing approach, all units in beginning inventory are treated as if they were started and completed in the current period. However, equivalent units can still be calculated in three parts (or you can combine the first two parts since they require similar calculations):

Part 1: Units in beginning inventory = number of units × 100 percent

Part 2: Units started and completed = number of units × 100 percent

Part 3: Equivalent units in ending inventory:
Materials costs = number of units × percentage of completion
Conversion costs = number of units × percentage of completion

You should recognize that the computation of parts 2 and 3 is the same under both costing approaches.

Exhibit 18-8 (part **A**) illustrates the computation of equivalent units for Jens-Lena Manufacturing Company, using the average costing approach when beginning inventory items must be accounted for. For April 19xx, there were 1,450 units in beginning Work in Process Inventory, 100 percent complete as to materials costs and 40 percent complete as to conversion costs. In addition, 53,350 units were started and completed during the month. Ending Work in Process Inventory contained 2,250 units, 100 percent complete as to materials costs and 70 percent complete regarding conversion costs. As shown in Exhibit

Exhibit 18-8. Average Costing Approach

Jens-Lena Manufacturing Company
Mixing Department—Process Cost Analysis Using Average Costing
For the Month Ended April 30, 19xx

A. Schedule of Equivalent Production

Units—Stage of Completion	Units To Be Accounted For	Equivalent Units: Materials Costs	Equivalent Units: Conversion Costs
Beginning inventory	1,450	1,450	1,450
Units started and completed in this period	53,350	53,350	53,350
Ending inventory—units started but not completed in this period	2,250		
(Materials costs—100% complete)		2,250	
(Conversion costs—70% complete)			1,575 (70% of 2,250)
Totals	57,050	57,050	56,375

B. Unit Cost Analysis Schedule

	Total Costs: Costs from Beginning Inventory (1)	Costs from Current Period (2)	Total Costs To Be Accounted For (3)	Equivalent Unit Costs: Equivalent Units (4)	Cost per Equivalent Unit (3÷4)
Materials costs	$13,050	$489,280	$502,330	57,050	$ 8.805
Conversion costs	1,760	278,975	280,735	56,375	4.980
Totals	$14,810	$768,255	$783,065		$13.785

C. Cost Summary Schedule

	Cost of Goods Transferred to Cooling Department	Cost of Ending Work in Process Inventory
Beginning inventory		
1,450 units × $13.785 per unit	$ 19,988	
Units started and completed		
53,350 units × $13.785 per unit	735,430	
Ending inventory		
Materials costs: 2,250 units × $8.805		$ 19,811
Conversion costs: 1,575 units × $4.980		7,844
Totals	$755,418	$ 27,655
Check on computations:		
Costs to Cooling Department		$755,418
Costs in ending Work in Process Inventory		27,655
Difference due to rounding		(8)
Total costs to be accounted for (see unit cost analysis schedule)		$783,065

18-8, the 1,450 units in beginning inventory are extended at their full amount to the Materials Costs and Conversion Costs columns. This treatment is the same as that given to the 53,350 units started and completed during April. Units started and completed receive the full amount of materials costs and conversion costs. Ending inventory is 100 percent complete as to materials, so 2,250 equivalent units are extended to the Materials Costs column. Since these units are only 70 percent complete, 1,575 equivalent units (2,250 × 70 percent) are entered in the Conversion Costs column. The end result is a monthly total of 57,050 equivalent units for materials costs and 56,375 equivalent units for conversion costs for the Mixing Department at Jens-Lena Manufacturing Company.

Unit Cost Analysis Schedule

At first glance, the unit cost analysis schedule computed under the average costing method looks just like the one prepared using the FIFO method. There is, however, one significant difference between the two schedules. Following the FIFO approach, we divide the amount in the Costs from Current Period column by the respective amount in the Equivalent Units column to compute the cost per equivalent unit. Under the average costing approach, we divide the amount in the Total Costs To Be Accounted For column by the respective amount in the Equivalent Units column. Following the average costing method, costs in beginning inventory and the costs of the current period are added together and treated as current costs (averaged) just as beginning inventory units are treated as if they were started and completed this period.

As shown in part **B** of Exhibit 18-8, total unit cost computed under the average costing guidelines is $13.785 (rounded to three decimal places). Materials costs per unit are $8.805 (found by dividing the total materials costs to be accounted for, $502,330, by equivalent units of 57,050). To compute the conversion costs per unit, the total conversion costs to be accounted for—$280,735—is divided by 56,375 equivalent units to arrive at $4.980 per unit.

Cost Summary Schedule

Following the average costing method, the cost summary schedule sets out the cost of goods completed and transferred to the next department, process, or Finished Goods Inventory. Because beginning Work in Process Inventory is treated as if it were started and completed during the current period, the units in beginning inventory and the units actually started and completed this period are treated alike. Both are costed out at the total unit cost computed in the unit cost analysis schedule. Costs of units in ending Work in Process Inventory are computed exactly the same way as they were following the FIFO costing approach. The units in ending inventory are multiplied by the respective percentages of completion and cost per equivalent unit for materials costs and conversion costs to compute the ending balance of Work in Process Inventory.

Referring to the Jens-Lena Manufacturing Company example in Exhibit 18-8, part **C** shows the completed cost summary schedule. To compute the cost of goods completed and transferred to the Cooling Department during April, both the units in beginning Work in Process Inventory (1,450) and the units started and completed in April (53,350) are multiplied by the $13.785 cost per equivalent unit. The 1,450 units in beginning inventory are valued at $19,988 (1,450 × $13.785) and the 53,350 units started and completed are costed out at $735,430 (53,350 × $13.785). The total costs transferred out in April are $755,418.

The final step needed to complete the cost summary schedule is to compute the dollar amount of the units in ending Work in Process Inventory. Since all materials are added at the beginning of the process, the 2,250 units are multiplied by a 100 percent completion factor and by $8.805 to arrive at the $19,811 for total materials costs. Conversion costs of $7,844 are computed by multiplying 2,250 units times the 70 percent completion factor (equals 1,575 equivalent units) times $4.980 per unit. Total cost of the units in ending Work in Process Inventory of $27,655 is found by adding $19,811 and $7,844.

The check of computations at the bottom of Exhibit 18-8 shows that an $8 difference due to rounding was incurred in the analysis. The unit costs computed in the unit cost analysis schedule were rounded up, so too much money has been attached to the units worked on during the month. When preparing the entry to account for the costs of units completed and transferred, this small amount should be merged with the total costs transferred. In our example, the $8 overage is subtracted from the $755,418. Therefore, the adjusted total cost of the 54,800 units transferred to the Cooling Department is $755,410. The journal entry needed to record this transfer is as follows:

Work in Process Inventory—Cooling Department	$755,410	
Work in Process Inventory—Mixing Department		$755,410
To transfer costs of completed units from the Mixing Department to the Cooling Department		

Accounting for Joint Production Costs

OBJECTIVE 8
Allocate common manufacturing costs to joint products

Joint or common costs represent a special case in cost allocation. A **joint cost** (or **common cost**) is a cost that relates to two or more products produced from a common input or raw material and that can be assigned only by an arbitrary method after the products become identifiable. Joint products cannot be identified as separate products during some or all of the production process. Only at a particular point, called the **split-off point**, do separate products evolve from a common processing unit.

Petroleum refining, wood processing, and meat packing often result in joint products. In other words, more than one end product arises from a single material input. In beef processing, for example, the final cuts of meat (steaks, roasts, hamburger) do not appear until the end of the process. However, the cost of the steer and the costs of transportation, storage, hanging, and labor have been incurred in order to get the side of beef ready for final butchering. How do we assign these joint costs to specific cuts of beef? Figure 18-4 shows the accounting problem presented by joint costs. We will outline the two most commonly used methods for solving it.

Physical Volume Method

One way to allocate joint production costs to specific products is called the **physical volume method**. This approach uses a measure of physical volume (units, pounds, liters, grams) as the basis for allocating joint costs.

As an example, assume that the Fuentes Company makes two grades of paint from the same mixture of substances. During August, 75,000 liters of various ingredients were put into the production process. The final output for the month was 25,000 liters of Product AA and 50,000 liters of Product BB. Total joint production costs for August were $420,000: $210,000 for direct materials, $115,000 for direct labor, and $95,000 for factory overhead. The two products

Figure 18-4. Joint Product Cost Allocation: The Fuentes Company

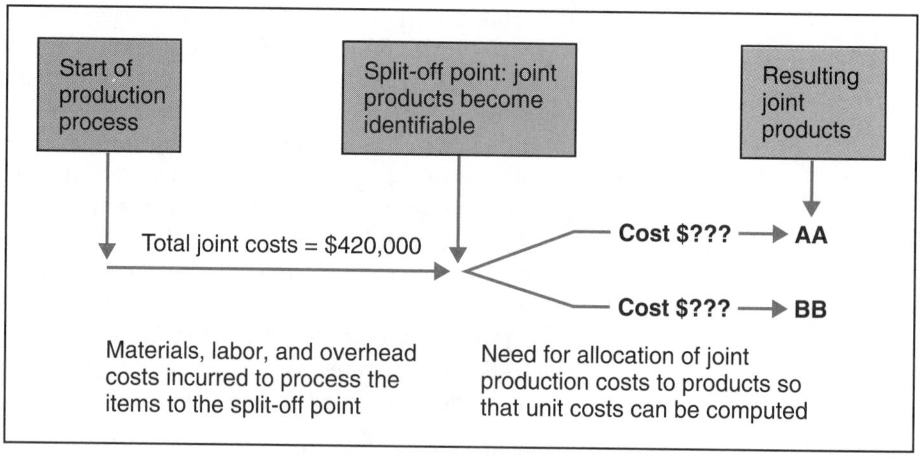

cannot be identified until the end of the production process. Product AA sells for $9 per liter and Product BB for $6 per liter. Taking total liters as the allocation basis, we apply a ratio of the physical volume of each product to total physical volume.

	Total Liters	Allocation Ratio	Joint Cost Allocation
Product AA	25,000	$\frac{25,000}{75,000}$ or ⅓	$140,000 ($420,000 × ⅓)
Product BB	50,000	$\frac{50,000}{75,000}$ or ⅔	280,000 ($420,000 × ⅔)
Totals	75,000		$420,000

Note that Product AA will generate $225,000 in revenues (25,000 liters at $9 per liter). Thus the net income for this product line will be $85,000. (We compute this by subtracting $140,000 of assigned joint costs from the total revenues of $225,000.) Product BB will sell for a total of $300,000 (50,000 liters at $6 per liter) and will show only a $20,000 profit ($300,000 minus $280,000 of assigned joint costs). Product BB's net income suffers because its high-volume content attracts two-thirds of the production costs, even though its selling price is much less than that of Product AA.

This example demonstrates the key strength and weakness of the physical volume method of allocating joint costs. It is easy to use, but it often seriously distorts net income, because the physical volume of joint products may not be proportionate to each product's ability to generate revenue.

Relative Sales Value Method

Another way to allocate joint production costs depends on the relative sales value of the products. The **relative sales value method** allocates joint production costs to products in proportion to each one's revenue-producing ability (sales value). Costs are assigned to joint products on the basis of their relative sales value when they first become identifiable as specific products—that is, at the split-off point. Extending the Fuentes Company data, we can make the analysis shown at the top of page 735.

	Liters Produced	×	Selling Price	=	Sales Value at Split-off	Allocation Ratio	Joint Cost Allocation
Product AA	25,000		$9.00		$225,000	$\frac{\$225{,}000}{\$525{,}000}$ or 3/7	$180,000 ($420,000 × 3/7)
Product BB	50,000		$6.00		300,000	$\frac{\$300{,}000}{\$525{,}000}$ or 4/7	240,000 ($420,000 × 4/7)
Totals	75,000				$525,000		$420,000

Product AA has a relative sales value of $225,000 at split-off; Product BB, $300,000. The resulting cost allocation ratios are 3/7 and 4/7, respectively. Applying these ratios to the total joint cost of $420,000, we assign $180,000 to Product AA and $240,000 to Product BB.

If we compare these results with those of the physical volume method, we see a wide difference in gross margin for the two product lines.

	Product AA		Product BB	
	Physical Volume Method	Relative Sales Value Method	Physical Volume Method	Relative Sales Value Method
Sales	$225,000	$225,000	$300,000	$300,000
Cost of goods sold	140,000	180,000	280,000	240,000
Gross margin	$ 85,000	$ 45,000	$ 20,000	$ 60,000
Gross margin as percent of sales	37.8%	20.0%	6.7%	20.0%

The major advantage of the relative sales value method is that it allocates joint costs according to a product's ability to absorb the cost. For this reason, gross margin percentages will always be equal at the split-off point, as the example shows. Under the relative sales value method, gross margin as a percentage of sales is 20% for both products.

As mentioned earlier, these approaches to assigning joint production costs are arbitrary. They are used because it is difficult to determine just how the end products (cost objectives) benefited from the incurrence of the cost. Both these approaches to allocation—the physical volume method and the relative sales value method—should be used only when it is impossible to tell how the cost benefited the cost objective.

Chapter Review

Review of Learning Objectives

1. **Compare and contrast the characteristics of the job order and process cost accounting systems.**
   Both job order costing and process costing are basic, traditional approaches to product cost accounting. However, they have different characteristics. A job order costing system is used for unique or special-order products. In such a system, materials, direct labor, and factory overhead costs are assigned to specific job orders or batches of products. In determining unit costs, the total manufacturing cost assigned to each job

order is divided by the number of good units produced for that order. A process costing system is used by companies that produce a large number of similar products or have a continuous production flow. These companies find it more economical to account for product-related costs for a period of time (a week or month) than to assign them to specific products or job orders. In a process costing system, unit costs are found by dividing total manufacturing costs for a department or work center during the week or month by the number of good units produced.

2. **Explain the role of the Work in Process Inventory account(s) in a process cost accounting system.**
The Work in Process Inventory account is the heart of the process cost accounting system. Each production department or operating unit has its own Work in Process Inventory account. All costs charged to that department flow into this inventory account. Special analysis, using three schedules, is needed at period end to determine the costs flowing out of the account. All special analyses in process cost accounting are related to costs in the Work in Process Inventory account.

3. **Diagram the product flow and cost flow through a process cost accounting system.**
Process costing is used to account for liquids or long, continuous production runs of identical products. Thus, products flow in a FIFO fashion (first in, first out). Once a product is started into production, it flows on to completion. In a process cost accounting system, manufacturing costs are handled differently than in a job order costing system. Following a FIFO costing approach, unit costs are computed using only current period cost and unit data. Costs in beginning work in process inventory are treated separately. The unit costs are assigned to completed units and to units in ending work in process inventory.

4. **Compute equivalent production for situations with and without units in the beginning Work in Process Inventory.**
Equivalent units are computed from unit information including (1) units in, and percent completion of, beginning Work in Process Inventory, (2) units started and completed during the period, and (3) units in, and percent completion of, ending Work in Process Inventory. If materials are added at the beginning of the process, no materials are added to the units in beginning inventory during the current period, so they are not included in the computation of equivalent units. All units started during the period receive the full amount of materials. Equivalent units for costs added uniformly throughout the process are computed by multiplying the percent completed in the current period by the total units in the respective categories mentioned above.

5. **Compute product unit cost for a specific time period using a unit cost analysis schedule.**
Unit costs are found by using the unit cost analysis schedule. Materials costs for units in beginning inventory and materials costs of the current period are added. The same procedure is followed for conversion costs. Total costs to be accounted for are found by adding the total materials costs and conversion costs. Following FIFO costing procedures, the unit cost for materials is found by dividing the materials costs for the *current period* by the equivalent unit amount for materials. The same procedure is followed for conversion costs. Then the unit costs for materials and conversion costs are added together to yield the total unit cost for the period.

6. **Prepare a cost summary schedule that assigns costs to units completed and transferred out during the period, and find the ending Work in Process Inventory balance.**
The first part of the cost summary schedule centers on computing the costs assigned to units completed and transferred out during the period. This part is done in two steps: (a) costs needed to complete units in beginning inventory are added to costs assigned from the previous period, and (b) units started and completed during the current period are assigned the full amount of production costs. The total of these two calculations represents costs assigned to units completed and transferred during the period. The second part of the cost summary schedule assigns costs to units still in process at period end. Unit costs for materials and conversion costs are multiplied by their respective equivalent units. The total of these two dollar amounts represents the balance in the Work in Process Inventory account at the end of the period.

7. **Prepare the journal entry(ies) needed to transfer costs of completed units out of the Work in Process Inventory account.**
   After completing the first part of the cost summary schedule (the part that assigns costs to units completed and transferred out during the period), a journal entry is prepared to transfer costs out of the Work in Process Inventory account. A credit is made to the account for the whole amount. The debit can be either to Finished Goods Inventory or to the Work in Process Inventory account of a subsequent department, depending on the network of production departments in the process.
8. **Allocate common manufacturing costs to joint products.**
   Joint products evolve from a common processing unit. They cannot be identified as specific products until the split-off point in the process. All manufacturing costs incurred prior to the split-off point are shared by all the products. After the split-off point, costs are assigned to individual products using either the physical volume method or the relative sales value method.

Review of Concepts and Terminology

The following concepts and terms were introduced in this chapter:

(L.O. 7) **Average costing approach:** A process costing method in which unit costs are computed based on the assumption that the items in beginning work in process inventory were started and completed during the current period.

(L.O. 4) **Conversion costs:** The combined total of direct labor and factory overhead costs incurred by a production department.

(L.O. 6) **Cost summary schedule:** A process costing schedule that facilitates the distribution of all production costs incurred and accumulated during the period among the units of output, either those completed and transferred out of the department or those units still in process at period end.

(L.O. 4) **Equivalent production:** A measure of the number of equivalent whole units produced in a period of time. Also called *equivalent units.*

(L.O. 3) **FIFO costing approach:** A process costing method in which cost flow follows product flow; the first products to be introduced into the production process are the first products to be completed. Costs assigned to those first products are the first costs to be transferred out of the production center or department.

(L.O. 8) **Joint cost:** A cost that relates to two or more products produced from a common input or raw material and that can be assigned only by means of arbitrary cost allocation after the products become identifiable. Also called *common cost.*

(L.O. 8) **Physical volume method:** An approach to the problem of allocating joint production costs to specific products that uses some measure of physical volume (units, pounds, liters, grams, etc.) as the basis for joint cost allocation.

(L.O. 1) **Process cost accounting system:** A product cost accounting system used by companies that make a large number of similar products or maintain a continuous production flow.

(L.O. 8) **Relative sales value method:** An approach to the problem of allocating joint production costs to specific products that uses the product's revenue-producing ability (sales value) as a basis for joint cost allocation.

(L.O. 4) **Schedule of equivalent production:** A process costing schedule in which the equivalent units are computed for the period for both materials costs and conversion costs.

(L.O. 8) **Split-off point:** A point in the manufacturing process where joint products separate and become identifiable.

(L.O. 5) **Unit cost analysis schedule:** A process costing schedule used to: (1) accumulate all costs charged to the Work in Process Inventory account of a particular department or production process and determine total costs to be accounted for; and (2) compute costs per equivalent unit for materials costs and conversion costs for the period.

Self-Test

Test your knowledge of the chapter by choosing the best answer for each of the following items.

(L.O. 1) 1. Which of the following industries is most likely to use a process costing system?
a. Bridge building company
b. Oil refining company
c. Highway construction company
d. Made-to-order boat company

(L.O. 2) 2. How many Work in Process Inventory accounts will a company using a process costing system use in its product costing process?
a. Depends on the number of products produced
b. Only one
c. One for each department or process
d. Always three

(L.O. 4) 3. If a department using a FIFO process costing system had 1,400 units in beginning Work in Process Inventory 40 percent complete, started and completed 4,900 units, and had 1,200 units in ending work in process inventory 60 percent complete, what is the number of equivalent units for materials costs, assuming materials are added at the beginning of the process?
a. 6,100
b. 7,500
c. 6,300
d. 4,900

(L.O. 4) 4. Assuming the same facts as in **3**, what is the number of equivalent units for conversion costs when these costs are incurred uniformly throughout the process?
a. 6,180
b. 7,120
c. 6,460
d. 7,500

(L.O. 4) 5. Conversion costs are
a. the total of direct labor and factory overhead costs.
b. the total of direct materials and direct labor costs.
c. all manufacturing costs.
d. all period costs.

(L.O. 5) 6. The Hood Corporation had the following information generated for May:

Beginning work in process inventory: 1,000 units, 50 percent complete; materials cost, $14,700; conversion costs, $13,550

Units started and completed: 8,000

Ending work in process inventory: 640 units, 80 percent complete

Current period costs: materials, $127,872; conversion, $243,324

Equivalent units: materials costs, 8,640 units; conversion costs, 9,012 units

Materials added at the beginning of the process and conversion costs incurred uniformly throughout the process

If the corporation uses the FIFO process costing approach, what is the unit cost for materials for May?
a. $27.10
b. $27.00
c. $14.70
d. $14.80

(L.O. 5) 7. Assuming the same facts as in **6**, what is the unit cost for conversion costs for May?
a. $27.10
b. $27.00
c. $14.70
d. $14.80

(L.O. 6) 8. Assuming the same facts as in **6**, what were the total costs transferred to Finished Goods Inventory during May?
a. $23,296
b. $41,750
c. $334,400
d. $376,150

(L.O. 6) 9. Assuming the same facts as in **6**, what was the ending balance of Work in Process Inventory?
a. $23,296
b. $41,750
c. $334,400
d. $376,150

(L.O. 8) 10. Assigning a joint cost to a product based on the product's ability to generate revenue is accomplished by using the
a. FIFO costing method.
b. physical volume method.
c. relative sales value method.
d. split-off method.

Answer to the Self-Test are at the end of this chapter.

Review Problem
Costs Transferred In

(L.O. 4, 5, 6, 7) This problem reviews the three-schedule analysis used in process costing. It also introduces a new situation common in process costing, which is how to deal with costs transferred in. Accounting for the second department's costs in a series of Work in Process Inventory accounts is very much like accounting for the first department's costs. The only difference is that instead of (or in addition to) accounting for current materials costs, we are dealing with *costs transferred in* during the period. All procedures used to account for costs transferred in are exactly the same as those used for materials costs and units. *When accounting for costs and units transferred in, treat them as you would materials added at the beginning of the process.*

This Review Problem illustrates the accounting approach for the second in a series of production departments. We will continue with the example of the Jens-Lena Manufacturing Company, concentrating this time on the Cooling Department. No new materials are added in this department; only conversion costs are added in the cooling process. Operating data for the Cooling Department for April 19xx are:

Beginning Work in Process Inventory	
Units	2,100 liters
Costs: Transferred in	$ 29,200
Conversion costs	$ 4,610
Units in beginning inventory 70% complete as to conversion costs	
Ending Work in Process Inventory	
All units 60% complete as to conversion costs	
April operations	
Units transferred in	54,800 liters
Costs: Transferred in	$755,390
Conversion costs	$169,884
Units completed and transferred to Finished Goods Inventory	54,450 liters

Required

1. Using good form and the FIFO costing method, prepare (a) a schedule of equivalent production, (b) a unit cost analysis schedule, and (c) a cost summary schedule.
2. From the cost summary schedule, prepare the journal entry to transfer costs of completed units for April to the Finished Goods Inventory account.

Answer to Review Problem

1. Before doing the three-schedule analysis on the facing page, we must first determine the following unit information.

Units started and completed:	
Units completed and transferred (given)	54,450 liters
Less units in beginning inventory (given)	2,100 liters
Units started and completed	52,350 liters
Units in ending inventory:	
Units transferred in during April (given)	54,800 liters
Less units started and completed (above)	52,350 liters
Units in ending inventory	2,450 liters

With this unit information, we can prepare the three schedules below.

Jens-Lena Manufacturing Company
Cooling Department—FIFO Process Cost Analysis
For the Month Ended April 30, 19xx

A. Schedule of Equivalent Production

Units—Stage of Completion	Units To Be Accounted For	Equivalent Units: Transferred-in Costs	Equivalent Units: Conversion Costs
Beginning inventory—units started last period but completed this period	2,100		
(Transferred-in costs—100% complete)		—	
(Conversion costs—70% complete)			630 (30% of 2,100)
Units started and completed in this period	52,350	52,350	52,350
Ending inventory—units started but not completed in this period	2,450		
(Transferred-in costs—100% complete)		2,450	
(Conversion costs—60% complete)			1,470 (60% of 2,450)
Totals	56,900	54,800	54,450

B. Unit Cost Analysis Schedule

	Total Costs: Costs from Beginning Inventory (1)	Total Costs: Costs from Current Period (2)	Total Costs: Total Costs To Be Accounted For (3)	Equivalent Unit Costs: Equivalent Units (4)	Equivalent Unit Costs: Cost per Equivalent Unit (2 ÷ 4)
Transferred-in costs	$29,200	$755,390	$784,590	54,800	$13.784
Conversion costs	4,610	169,884	174,494	54,450	3.120
Totals	$33,810	$925,274	$959,084		$16.904

C. Cost Summary Schedule

	Cost of Goods Transferred to Finished Goods Inventory	Cost of Ending Work in Process Inventory
Beginning inventory		
Beginning balance	$ 33,810	
Cost to complete: 2,100 units × 30% × $3.120 per unit	1,966	
Total beginning inventory	$ 35,776	
Units started and completed		
52,350 units × $16.904 per unit	884,924	
Ending inventory		
Transferred-in costs: 2,450 units × $13.784 per unit		$ 33,771
Conversion costs: 1,470 units × $3.120 per unit		4,586
Totals	$920,700	$ 38,357

Check on computations:	
Costs to Finished Goods Inventory	$920,700
Costs in ending Work in Process Inventory	38,357
Difference due to rounding	27
Total costs to be accounted for (see unit cost analysis schedule)	$959,084

2. The costs of completed units for April are now ready to be transferred from the Cooling Department to the Finished Goods Inventory account. The journal entry is:

Finished Goods Inventory ($920,700 + $27)	920,727	
Work in Process—Cooling Department		920,727
To transfer cost of units completed in April to Finished Goods Inventory		

Chapter Assignments

Questions

1. What types of production are best suited to a process cost accounting system?
2. "In job order costing, one Work in Process Inventory account is used for all jobs. In process costing, several Work in Process Inventory accounts are used." Explain.
3. Define the term *equivalent production (equivalent units).*
4. Why do actual unit data need to be changed to equivalent unit data for product costing purposes in a process costing system?
5. Define the term *conversion costs.* Why are conversion costs used in process costing computations?
6. What are the three schedules used in process costing analysis?
7. Why is it easier to compute equivalent units without units in beginning inventory than with them?
8. What are the purposes of the unit cost analysis schedule?
9. What are the two important dollar amounts that come from the cost summary schedule? How do they relate to the year-end financial statements?
10. Describe how to check the accuracy of the results in the cost summary schedule.
11. What is the significance of the journal entry used to transfer costs of completed products out of the Work in Process Inventory account?
12. What are costs "transferred in"? Where do they come from? Why are they handled like materials added at the beginning of the process?
13. What is a joint manufacturing cost?
14. Describe the physical volume method of allocating joint costs to products. List the advantage and disadvantage of the physical volume method.
15. Should joint costs be allocated to a product on the basis of the product's ability to generate revenue? Explain your answer.

Communication Skills Exercises

Communication 18-1. Use of Process Costing Information
(L.O. 2, 6)

Euro-Continental, Inc. produces several types of communications cable for a worldwide market. Since the manufacturing process is continuous, a process costing system is used to develop product costs. Until recently, costs were accumulated on a monthly basis and revised product costs were made available to management by the tenth of the following month. With the installation of a computer-integrated manufacturing system, cost information is now available as soon as each production run is finished. The production superintendent has asked the controller to change the accounting system so that product unit costs are available the day following production.

The controller must prepare a memorandum to the corporate vice president justifying the proposed accounting system change. Identify reasons that the controller can use to support the production superintendent's request. What benefits would be obtained from the proposed modification? Be prepared to share your ideas with your classmates.

Communication 18-2. Joint Cost Allocation[3]
(L.O. 8)

Hi-Tec Semiconductor Corp. manufactures a line of computer memory chips. In the fabrication process, identical raw materials are introduced at the beginning of the process,

3. Developed from William L. Cats-Baril, James F. Gatti, and D. Jacque Grinnell, "Joint Product Costing in the Semiconductor Industry," *Management Accounting*, Institute of Management Accountants, February 1986, pp. 28–35.

but the memory chip output contains products of varying quality and use. These products can be categorized by class, with each class having a different market. The costs of the fabrication process are joint costs of the memory chip output and can be assigned to the chip categories using the physical quantities involved (number of usable chips) or the market value of the chips at split-off. Prepare a one-page paper in which you identify the approach you believe is appropriate and the reasons for your decision.

Communication 18-3. Ethics and JIT Implementation
(L.O. 1)

Raoul Goldwasser is head of the Information Systems Department at Judd Manufacturing Company. Tom Phillips, the company's controller, is meeting with Goldwasser to discuss data gathering changes connected with the company's new automated flexible manufacturing system. Raoul opened the conversation by saying, "Tom, the old job order costing methods just will not work for the new flexible manufacturing system. The new system is based on continuous product flow, not batch processing. We need to change to a process costing approach for both data gathering and product costing purposes. Otherwise, our product costs will be way off and it will affect our pricing decisions. I found out about this needed change at a professional seminar I attended last month. You should have been there with me." Phillips responded, "Raoul, who is the accounting expert here? I know what product costing approach is best for this situation. Job order costing has provided accurate product costing information for this product line for more than fifteen years. Why should we change just because we have purchased a new machine? We've purchased several machines for this line over the years. And as for your seminar, I don't need to learn about costing methods. I was exposed to them all when I studied management accounting back in the late 1970s."

Prepare a dialogue or develop a role play with your classmates that is a follow-up to this conversation.

Communication 18-4. Basic Research Skills
(L.O. 1)

Look up a current issue of the periodical *Production and Inventory Management* at your campus library. Review the articles, paying particular attention to the type of products and production processes described. Find an example of a company that would most likely be using a process costing approach to product costing. Prepare a short report that includes the company's name, its product(s), and a description of the production process. Bring this information to class to share with your classmates. Be sure to acknowledge the title, author(s), and month of issue of the magazine.

Classroom Exercises

Exercise 18-1. Product Flow Diagram
(L.O. 3)

Layne Paint Company uses a process costing system to analyze the costs incurred in making paint. Production of Quality Brand starts in the Blending Department, where materials SM and HA are added to a water base. The solution is heated to 70° Celsius and then transferred to the Mixing Department, where it is mixed for one hour. Then the paint goes to the Settling/Canning Department, where it is cooled and put into 4-liter cans. Direct labor and factory overhead charges are incurred uniformly throughout each part of the paint-making process.

In diagram form, show the product flow for Quality Brand paint.

Exercise 18-2. Equivalent Units: No Beginning Inventories
(L.O. 4)

Jacques Stone Company produces slumpstone bricks. Though it has been in operation for only twelve months, the company already enjoys a good reputation. During its first year, materials for 580,500 bricks were put into production; 576,900 were completed and transferred to finished goods inventory. The remaining bricks were still in process at year end, 60 percent complete. In the company's process costing system, all materials are added at the beginning of the process. Conversion costs are incurred uniformly throughout the production process.

From this information, prepare a schedule of equivalent production for the year ending December 31, 19x4. Use the FIFO costing approach.

Exercise 18-3.
Equivalent Units: Beginning Inventories—FIFO Method
(L.O. 4)

Locke Enterprises makes Lola Shampoo for professional hair stylists. On January 1, 19x3, 6,200 liters of shampoo were in process, 80 percent complete as to conversion costs and 100 percent complete as to materials costs. During the month, 212,500 liters of materials were put into production. Data for work in process inventory on January 31, 19x3 were as follows: shampoo, 4,500 liters; stage of completion, 60 percent of conversion costs and 100 percent of materials content.

From this information, prepare a schedule of equivalent production for the month. Use the FIFO costing approach.

Exercise 18-4.
Equivalent Units: Beginning Inventories—FIFO Method
(L.O. 4)

The Salem Company, a major producer of liquid vitamins, uses a process cost accounting system. During February 19x3, 130,000 gallons of Material CIA and 40,000 gallons of Material CMA were put into production. Beginning work in process inventory was 15,000 gallons of product, 70 percent complete as to labor and overhead. Ending work in process inventory was made up of 12,000 gallons, 45 percent complete as to conversion costs. All materials are added at the beginning of the process.

From this information, prepare a schedule of equivalent production for February using the FIFO costing approach.

Exercise 18-5.
Work in Process Inventory Accounts: Total Unit Cost
(L.O. 5)

Scientists at Morales Laboratories, Inc. have just perfected a liquid substance called D. K. Rid, which dissolves tooth decay. The substance, which is generated from a complex process involving five departments, is very costly. Cost and equivalent unit data for the latest week are as follows (units are in ounces):

	Materials Costs		Conversion Costs	
Dept.	**Dollars**	**Equivalent Units**	**Dollars**	**Equivalent Units**
A	$12,500	1,000	$34,113	2,055
B	23,423	1,985	13,065	1,005
C	24,102	1,030	20,972	2,140
D	—	—	22,086	2,045
E	—	—	15,171	1,945

From these data, compute (a) the unit cost for each department and (b) the total unit cost of producing an ounce of D. K. Rid.

Exercise 18-6.
Unit Cost Determination
(L.O. 5)

Oertley Kitchenwares, Inc. manufactures sets of heavy-duty cookware. Production has just been completed for July 19x3. The Work in Process Inventory account showed the following costs at the beginning of July: materials costs, $31,700; conversion costs, $29,400. Cost of materials used in July was $273,728; conversion costs were $176,689. During the month, 15,190 sets were started and completed. A schedule of equivalent production for July has already been prepared. It shows a total of 16,450 equivalent sets as to materials costs and 16,210 equivalent sets as to conversion costs.

With this information, prepare a unit cost analysis schedule for July. Use the FIFO costing approach.

Exercise 18-7.
Cost Summary Schedule
(L.O. 6)

The Ammons Bakery produces Kringle coffee bread. It uses a process cost system for internal recordkeeping purposes. Production for August 19x4 was as follows: (a) Beginning inventory, 450 units, 100 percent complete as to materials costs and 10 percent as to conversion costs, had a value of $675. (b) Units started and completed during the month totaled 14,200. (c) Ending inventory was as follows: materials, 420 units, 100 percent complete as to materials costs and 70 percent as to conversion costs. (d) Unit costs per equivalent unit were computed for August: materials costs, $1.40; conversion costs, $.80.

Using the information given, compute the cost of goods transferred to the Finished Goods Inventory account, the cost remaining in the Work in Process Inventory account, and the total costs to be accounted for. Use the FIFO costing approach.

Exercise 18-8. Cost Transfer: Journal Entry Required—Average Costing Method
(L.O. 4, 7)

The following cost summary schedule based on the average costing method was prepared for the Eberle Pasta Company for the year ended July 31, 19x3.

Eberle Pasta Company
Cost Summary Schedule
For the Year Ended July 31, 19x3

	Cost of Goods Transferred to Finished Goods Inventory	Cost of Ending Work in Process Inventory
Beginning inventory		
3,140 units at $4.60	$ 14,444	
Units started and completed		
94,960 units at $4.60	436,816	
Ending inventory		
Materials costs: 4,200 units at $3.20		$13,440
Conversion costs: 2,100 units at $1.40		2,940
Totals	$451,260	$16,380

1. From the information given, prepare the journal entry for July 31, 19x3.
2. Draw up the company's schedule of equivalent production. Assume that materials are added at the beginning of the process.

Exercise 18-9. Joint Cost Allocation—Physical Volume Method
(L.O. 8)

Hawaii's Mahalo Products Company produces molasses and refined sugar, joint products that emerge from the juice extracted from sugar cane. The company uses the physical volume method to assign common or joint costs to the two products. The allocation base is liters. During February, Mahalo Products Company put 160,000 liters of sugar cane juice into production. The final products from this input were 24,000 liters of molasses and 136,000 liters of refined sugar. The following joint product costs were incurred during February: $7,280 for materials; $18,480 for direct labor; and $23,060 for factory overhead. Thus, total joint costs amounted to $48,820. Assuming no loss through evaporation, assign a portion of joint production costs to each product.

Exercise 18-10. Joint Cost Allocation—Relative Sales Value Method
(L.O. 8)

In the processing of paper, two distinct grades of wood pulp emerge from a common crushing and mixing process. Fleener Paper Products, Inc. produced 44,000 liters of pulp during January. Direct materials used during the month cost the company $172,000. Labor and overhead costs for the month were $72,000 and $112,000, respectively. Output for the month was as the following table indicates:

Product	Quantity	Market Value at Split-off
Grade A pulp	28,000 liters	$14.00 per liter
Grade B pulp	16,000 liters	$10.50 per liter

Using the relative sales value method, allocate the common production costs to Grade A pulp and Grade B pulp.

Interpretation Case from Business

Tucker Tire Corporation
(L.O. 5)

Tucker Tire Corporation makes several lines of automobile and truck tires. The company operates in a competitive marketplace, so it relies heavily on cost data from its FIFO process cost accounting system. It uses this information to set prices for its most competitive tires. The company's Blue Radial line has lost some of its market share during each of the past four years. Management believes price breaks allowed by the three competitors are the major reason for the decline in sales.

The company controller, René Smith, has been asked to review the product costing information that supports price decisions on the Blue Radial line. In preparing her report, she collected the following data related to 19x4, the last full year of operations.

		Units	Dollars
Equivalent units:	Materials costs	84,200	
	Conversion costs	82,800	
Manufacturing costs:	Materials		$1,978,700
	Direct labor		800,400
	Factory overhead applied		1,600,800
Unit cost data:	Materials costs		23.50
	Conversion costs		29.00
Work in Process Inventory:	Beginning (70% complete)	4,200	
	Ending (30% complete)	3,800	

Units started and completed during 19x4 totaled 80,400. The costs attached to the beginning Work in Process Inventory account were materials costs, $123,660, and conversion costs, $57,010. Smith found that little spoilage had occurred. The proper cost allowance for spoilage was included in the predetermined overhead rate of $2.00 per direct labor dollar. The review of direct labor cost, however, revealed that $90,500 was charged twice to the production account, the second time in error. This resulted in too much labor and applied overhead costs being charged to the above accounts.

So far in 19x5, the Blue Radial has been selling for $92 per tire. This price was based on the 19x4 unit data plus a 75 percent markup to cover operating costs and profit. During 19x5, the three competitors' prices for comparable tires have been about $87 per tire. In the company's process costing system, all materials are added at the beginning of the process, and conversion costs are incurred uniformly throughout.

Required

1. Point out how the cost-charging error is affecting the company.
2. Prepare a revised unit cost analysis schedule for 19x4.
3. What should have been the minimum selling price per tire in 19x5?
4. Suggest ways for preventing such errors in the future.

Problem Set A

Problem 18A-1. Process Costing: No Beginning Inventories
(L.O. 4, 5, 6, 7)

Druckrey Industries specializes in making Slik, a high-moisture, low-alkaline wax used to protect and preserve skis. Production of a new, improved brand of Slik began January 1, 19x4. For this new product, Materials A-14 and C-9 are introduced at the beginning of the production process, along with a wax base. During January, 640 pounds of A-14, 1,860 pounds of C-9, and 12,800 pounds of wax base were used at costs of $15,300, $29,070, and $2,295, respectively. Direct labor of $17,136 and factory overhead costs of $25,704 were incurred uniformly throughout the month. By January 31, 13,600 pounds of Slik had been completed and transferred to the finished goods inventory. Since no spoilage occurred, the leftover materials remained in production, 40 percent complete on the average.

Required

1. Using the average costing approach, prepare (a) a schedule of equivalent production, (b) a unit cost analysis schedule, and (c) a cost summary schedule for January.
2. From the cost summary schedule, prepare the journal entry to transfer costs of completed units for January to Finished Goods Inventory.

Problem 18A-2. Process Costing: With Beginning Inventories—FIFO Method
(L.O. 4, 5, 6, 7)

Callanan Liquid Extracts Company produces a line of fruit extracts for use in making homemade products such as wines, jams and jellies, pies, and meat sauces. Fruits are introduced into the production process in pounds; the product emerges in quarts (one pound of input equals one quart of output). On June 1, 19x3, 4,250 units were in process. All materials had been added and the units were 70 percent complete as to conversion costs. Materials costs of $4,607 and conversion costs of $3,535 were attached to these units in beginning work in process inventory. During June, 61,300 pounds of fruit were added: apples, 23,500 pounds costing $20,915; grapes, 22,600 pounds costing $28,153; and bananas, 15,200 pounds costing $22,040. Direct labor for the month totaled $19,760, and overhead costs applied were $31,375. On June 30, 19x3, 3,400 units remained in process. All materials had been added, and 50 percent of conversion costs had been incurred.

Required

1. Using the FIFO costing approach, prepare the following schedules for June: (a) a schedule of equivalent production, (b) a unit cost analysis schedule, and (c) a cost summary schedule.
2. From the cost summary schedule, prepare a journal entry to transfer costs of completed units to the Finished Goods Inventory account.

Problem 18A-3. Process Costing: With Beginning Inventories—Average Costing Method
(L.O. 4, 5, 6, 7)

Many of the products made by Pelliccia Plastics Company are standard replacement parts for telephones, requiring long production runs. One of the parts, a wire clip, is produced continuously. During April 19x4, materials for 25,250 units of wire clips were put into production (1 unit contains 500 clips). Total cost of materials used during April was $2,273,000. Direct labor costs totaled $1,135,000, and factory overhead was $2,043,000. The beginning work in process inventory contained 1,600 units, 100 percent complete as to materials costs and 60 percent complete as to conversion costs. Costs attached to the units in beginning inventory totaled $232,515, including $143,500 of materials costs. At month end there were 1,250 units in ending inventory; all materials had been added, and the units were 70 percent complete as to conversion costs.

Required

1. Assuming an average costing approach and no loss due to spoilage, prepare (a) a schedule of equivalent production, (b) a unit cost analysis schedule, and (c) a cost summary schedule.
2. From the cost summary schedule, prepare a journal entry to transfer costs of units completed in April to the Finished Goods Inventory account.

Problem 18A-4. Process Costing: One Process / Two Time Periods—FIFO Method
(L.O. 4, 5, 6, 7)

Paluska Laboratories produces liquid detergents that leave no soap film. All elements are biodegradable. The production process has been automated, so that the product can now be produced in one operation instead of a series of heating, mixing, and cooling operations. All materials are added at the beginning of the process, and conversion costs are incurred uniformly throughout the process. Operating data for July and August 19x3 are as follows:

	July	August
Beginning Work in Process Inventory		
Units (pounds)	2,300	?
Costs: Materials costs	$ 4,699	?
Conversion costs	$ 1,219	?
Production during the period		
Units started (pounds)	31,500	32,800
Current period costs:		
Materials costs	$65,520	$66,912
Conversion costs	$54,213	$54,774
Ending Work in Process Inventory		
Units (pounds)	3,050	3,600

Beginning Work in Process Inventory was 30 percent complete as to conversion costs. This was the point-of-completion information for ending work in process inventories: July, 60 percent; August, 50 percent. Assume that loss from spoilage and evaporation was negligible.

Required

1. Using the FIFO costing approach, prepare the following schedules for July: (a) a schedule of equivalent production, (b) a unit cost analysis schedule, and (c) a cost summary schedule.
2. From the cost summary schedule, prepare a journal entry to transfer costs of units completed in July to the Finished Goods Inventory account.
3. Repeat parts **1** and **2** for August.

Problem 18A-5.
Process Costing: With Beginning Inventories / Two Departments—FIFO Method
(L.O. 4, 5, 6, 7)

Dorr Enterprises produces dozens of products for the housing construction industry. Its most successful product is called Sta-Soft Plaster, a mixture that is used to finish off wall surfaces after dry-wall sheets have been positioned. The product's unique quality is that it will not harden until it comes into contact with the dry-wall. Sta-Soft is produced using three processes: blending, conditioning, and canning. All materials are introduced at the beginning of the blending operation except for the can, which is added in the canning process. Direct labor and factory overhead costs are applied to the products uniformly throughout each process. Production and cost information for September 19x4 follow.

Blending Department.
Beginning Work in Process Inventory contained 22,920 pounds of Sta-Soft, 60 percent complete as to conversion costs. Costs of $38,900 were assigned to these units, $28,600 of which was for materials. During September, 242,280 pounds of materials costing $302,850 were put into production. Direct labor for the month was $88,203, and an equal amount of factory overhead costs were charged to Work in Process. Ending Work in Process Inventory contained 32,480 pounds, 50 percent complete as to conversion costs.

Conditioning Department.
During September, 232,720 pounds of Sta-Soft were received from the Blending Department. Beginning Work in Process Inventory consisted of 10,500 pounds of Sta-Soft, 40 percent complete, costing $30,250 ($21,000 worth of Sta-Soft was transferred-in costs). Direct labor costs incurred during September totaled $115,625, and factory overhead costs applied were $138,751. Ending Work in Process Inventory contained 8,900 pounds, 70 percent complete as to conversion costs. Assume no measurable loss due to spoilage or waste. (**Hint:** Before completing this problem, refer to the Review Problem on pages 739–741.)

Required

1. Using the FIFO costing approach, prepare the following schedules for the Blending Department for September: (a) a schedule of equivalent production, (b) a unit cost analysis schedule, and (c) a cost summary schedule.
2. From the cost summary schedule, prepare the journal entry needed to transfer costs of completed units for September from the Blending Department to the Conditioning Department.
3. Prepare the same schedules as in **1**, but for the Conditioning Department.
4. Prepare the journal entry needed to transfer costs of completed units from the Conditioning Department to the Canning Department.

Problem 18A-6.
Joint Cost Allocation
(L.O. 8)

The processing of crude oil produces three joint products: gasoline, motor oil, and kerosene. Patterson Petroleum Products, Inc. is a Chicago-based processor. During April, the company used 1,950,000 gallons of crude oil at a cost of $.40 per gallon, paid $315,000 in direct labor wages, and applied $420,000 of factory overhead to the crude oil processing department. Production during the period yielded 950,000 gallons of gasoline, 350,000 gallons of motor oil, and 600,000 gallons of kerosene. Evaporation caused the loss of 50,000 gallons; the amount lost was normal, and its cost should be included in the cost of good units produced. Selling prices for the joint products are: $.80 per gallon of gasoline; $.95 per quart of motor oil; and $.50 per gallon of kerosene. Assume there were no beginning or ending work in process inventories, and that everything produced was sold during the period. (**Note:** Four quarts equal one gallon.)

Required

1. Using the physical volume method, allocate the joint costs to each of the three joint products.
2. Using the relative sales value method, allocate the joint costs to each of the three joint products.
3. Prepare a schedule that compares the gross profit at split-off point using the two methods of allocation. Compute gross margin both in total dollars and as a percentage of sales.

(Round answers to three decimal places where appropriate.)

Problem Set B

Problem 18B-1. Process Costing: No Beginning Inventories *(L.O. 4, 5, 6, 7)*

The Solinko Chewing Gum Company, which produces several flavors of bubble gum, began production of a new kumquat-flavored gum on June 1, 19x9. Two basic materials, gum base and kumquat-flavored sweetener, are blended at the beginning of the process. Direct labor and factory overhead costs are incurred uniformly throughout the blending process. During June, 135,000 kilograms of gum base and 270,000 kilograms of kumquat additive were used at costs of $162,000 and $81,000, respectively. Direct labor charges were $360,310, and factory overhead costs applied during June were $184,010. The ending work in process inventory was 21,600 kilograms. All materials have been added to these units, and 25 percent of the conversion costs have been assigned.

Required

1. Using the average costing approach, prepare (a) a schedule of equivalent production, (b) a unit cost analysis schedule, and (c) a cost summary schedule for the Blending Department for June.
2. Using information from the cost summary schedule, prepare the journal entry to transfer costs of completed units for June from the Blending Department to the Forming and Packing Department.

Problem 18B-2. Process Costing: With Beginning Inventories—FIFO Method *(L.O. 4, 5, 6, 7)*

Kleiner Bottling Company manufactures and sells several different kinds of soft drinks. Materials (sugar syrup and artificial flavor) are added at the beginning of production in the Mixing Department. Direct labor and factory overhead costs are applied to products throughout the process. During August 19x3, beginning inventory for the citrus flavor was 2,400 gallons, 80 percent complete. Ending inventory was 3,600 gallons, 50 percent complete. Production data showed 240,000 gallons started during August. A total of 238,800 gallons was completed and transferred to the Bottling Department. Beginning inventory costs were $600 for materials and $676 for conversion costs. Current period costs were $57,600 for materials and $83,538 for conversion costs.

Required

1. Using the FIFO costing approach, prepare the following schedules for the Mixing Department for August: (a) a schedule of equivalent production, (b) a unit cost analysis schedule, and (c) a cost summary schedule.
2. From the cost summary schedule, prepare a journal entry to transfer the cost of completed units to the Bottling Department.

Problem 18B-3. Process Costing: With Beginning Inventories—Average Costing Method *(L.O. 4, 5, 6, 7)*

O'Hara Food Products, Inc. makes high-vitamin, calorie-packed wafers used by professional sports teams to supply quick energy to players. The thin white wafers are produced in a continuous product flow. The company, which uses a process costing system based on the average costing approach, recently purchased several automated machines so that the wafers can be produced in a single department. Materials are all added at the beginning of the process. The cost for the machine operator's labor and production-related overhead are incurred uniformly throughout the process.

In February 19x2, a total of 231,200 liters of materials was put into production at a cost of $294,780. Two liters of materials were used to produce one unit of output (one unit = 144 wafers). Labor costs for February were $60,530. Factory overhead was $181,590. Beginning Work in Process Inventory on February 1 was 14,000 units, 100 percent complete as to materials and 20 percent complete as to conversion costs. The total cost of these units was $55,000, with $48,660 assigned to the cost of materials. The ending Work in Process Inventory of 12,000 units was fully complete as to materials, but only 30 percent complete as to conversion costs.

Required

1. Assuming an average costing approach and no loss due to spoilage, prepare (a) a schedule of equivalent production, (b) a unit cost analysis schedule, and (c) a cost summary schedule.
2. From the cost summary schedule you prepared in **1** above, prepare a journal entry to transfer costs of completed units in February to the Finished Goods Inventory account.

Problem 18B-4. Process Costing: One Process / Two Time Periods—FIFO Method
(L.O. 4, 5, 6, 7)

The Leclerc Products Company produces organic honey for sale to health food stores and restaurants. The company owns thousands of beehives. No materials other than the honey from the bees in the hives are used. The production operation is a simple one in which the impure honey is added at the beginning of the process. A series of filterings follows, leading to a pure finished product. Costs of labor and factory overhead are incurred uniformly throughout the filtering process. Production data for April and May 19x4 are as follows:

	April	May
Beginning Work in Process Inventory		
Units (liters)	7,100	?
Costs: Materials costs	$ 2,480	?
Conversion costs	$ 5,110	?
Production during the period		
Units started (liters)	288,000	310,000
Current period costs:		
Materials costs	$100,800	$117,800
Conversion costs	$251,550	$277,281
Ending Work in Process Inventory		
Units (liters)	12,400	16,900

April beginning inventory was 80 percent complete as to conversion costs, and ending inventory was 20 percent complete. Ending inventory for May was 30 percent complete as to conversion costs. Assume that there was no loss from spoilage or evaporation.

Required

1. Using the FIFO approach, prepare the following schedules for April: (a) a schedule of equivalent production, (b) a unit cost analysis schedule, and (c) a cost summary schedule.
2. From the cost summary schedule, prepare a journal entry to transfer costs of units completed in April to the Finished Goods Inventory account.
3. Repeat parts **1** and **2** for May.

Problem 18B-5. Process Costing: With Beginning Inventories / Two Departments—FIFO Method
(L.O. 4, 5, 6, 7)

Canned fruits and vegetables are the main products made by Storey Foods, Inc. All basic materials are added at the beginning of the Mixing Department's process. When it has been mixed, the food goes to the Cooking Department. There it is heated to 100° Celsius and simmered for twenty minutes. When cooled, the mixture goes to the Canning Department for final processing. Throughout these operations, direct labor and factory overhead costs are incurred uniformly. No materials are added in the Cooking Department stage of production.

Cost data and other information for January 19x3 were as follows:

Production Cost Data	Materials Costs	Conversion Costs
Mixing Department		
Beginning inventory	$ 28,760	$ 5,030
Current period costs	$432,000	$182,608
	Transferred-in Costs	**Conversion Costs**
Cooking Department		
Beginning inventory	$ 61,380	$ 13,320
Current period costs	?	$671,040
Work in Process Inventories		
Beginning inventories:		
Mixing Department (40% complete)	6,000 liters	
Cooking Department (20% complete)	9,000 liters	
Ending inventories:		
Mixing Department (60% complete)	8,000 liters	
Cooking Department (70% complete)	10,000 liters	

Unit Production Data	Mixing Department	Cooking Department
Units started during January	90,000 liters	88,000 liters
Units transferred out during January	88,000 liters	87,000 liters

Assume that no spoilage or evaporation loss took place during January. (**Hint:** Before completing this problem, refer to the Review Problem on pages 739–741.)

Required

1. Using the FIFO costing approach, prepare for the Mixing Department for January: (a) a schedule of equivalent production, (b) a unit cost analysis schedule, and (c) a cost summary schedule.
2. Using information from the cost summary schedule, prepare the journal entry needed to transfer costs of completed units for January from the Mixing Department to the Cooking Department.
3. Prepare the same schedules as in **1**, this time for the Cooking Department.
4. Prepare the journal entry needed to transfer costs of completed units from the Cooking Department to the Canning Department.

Problem 18B-6.
Joint Cost Allocation
(L.O. 8)

Three distinct grades of chocolate sauce are made by Mona's Toppings, Inc. The ingredients for all three grades are first blended together. Then other ingredients are added to produce the three separate grades. The Extra-Rich blend sells for $8.20 per pound. The Quality blend sells for $6.60 per pound. And the Regular blend sells for $5.00 per pound. In July, 383,000 pounds of ingredients were put into production, with output as follows: 94,218 pounds of Extra-Rich blend; 153,966 pounds of Quality blend; and 134,816 pounds of Regular blend. Joint costs for the period were $401,200 for direct materials, $146,000 for direct labor, and $196,800 for factory overhead. Assume no beginning or ending inventories and no loss of input during production.

Required

1. Using the physical volume method, allocate the joint costs to the three different blends.
2. Using the relative sales value method, allocate the joint costs to the three blends.
3. Prepare a schedule that compares the gross profit at split-off point using the two methods of allocation. Compute gross margin both in total dollars and as a percentage of sales.

(Round allocation ratios to four decimal places where appropriate.)

Management Decision Case

Murvin Cola, Inc.
(L.O. 4, 5)

For the past four years, three companies have dominated the soft drink industry, holding a combined 85 percent of market share. Murvin Cola, Inc. ranks second nationally in soft drink sales; the company attained gross revenues last year of $27,450,000. Management is thinking about introducing a new low-calorie drink called Slimit Cola.

Murvin soft drinks are processed in a single department. All materials are added at the beginning of the process. Fluids are bottled at the end of the process in bottles costing one cent each. Direct labor and factory overhead costs are applied uniformly throughout the process.

Corporate controller Samuel Ortiz believes that costs for the new cola will be very much like those for the company's Cola Plus drink. Last year, he collected the following data on Cola Plus:

	Units	Costs
Work in Process Inventory		
January 1, 19x3*	2,400	
Materials costs		$ 2,160
Conversion costs		610
December 31, 19x3†	2,800	
Materials costs		2,520
Conversion costs		840
Units started during the year	459,300	
Costs for 19x3		
Liquid materials added		413,370
Direct labor and factory overhead		229,690
Bottles		110,136

*50% complete. †60% complete. Note: Each unit is a twenty-four-bottle case.

The company's variable general administrative and selling costs are $1.10 per unit. Fixed administrative and selling costs are assigned to products at the rate of $.50 per unit. Murvin's two major competitors have already introduced a diet cola in the marketplace. Company A's product sells for $4.10 per unit, Company B's for $4.05. All costs are expected to increase by 10 percent from 19x3 to 19x4. The company tries to earn a profit of at least 15 percent on the total unit cost.

Required

1. What factors should the company consider in setting a selling price for Slimit Cola?
2. Using the FIFO costing approach, compute (a) equivalent units for materials, bottle, and conversion costs; (b) the total production cost per unit; and (c) the total cost per unit of Cola Plus for 19x3.
3. What is the expected total cost per unit of Slimit Cola for 19x4?
4. Recommend a unit selling price range for Slimit Cola for 19x4 and give the reason(s) for your choice.

Answers to Self-Test

1. b	3. a	5. a	7. b	9. a
2. c	4. c	6. d	8. d	10. c

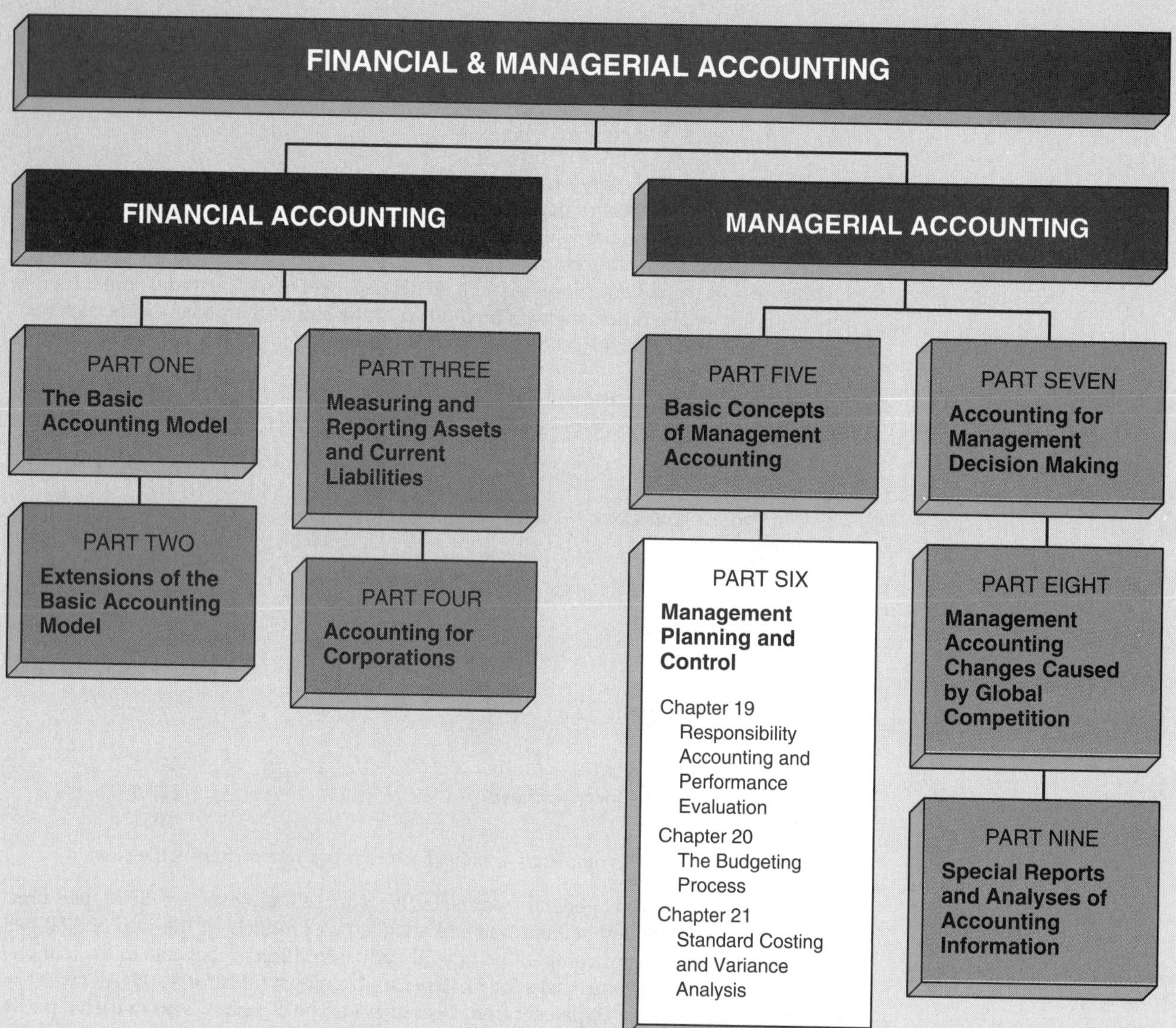

In Part Six we analyze the second aspect of the field of management accounting, which is management's need for data used for operations planning and control. Special concepts and techniques are used for cost planning and control. When integrated with an existing accounting system, these concepts and techniques are used to develop reports that facilitate managerial control activities.

PART SIX

Management Planning and Control

Chapter 19 explains the responsibility accounting system and introduces the principles of performance evaluation. The evaluations of managers of a cost/expense center, a profit center, and an investment center are illustrated.

Chapter 20 uses cost planning tools to implement the planning function of the budgetary control process. Emphasis is placed on budgeting principles and preparation, including the preparation of a cash budget.

Chapter 21 concludes your study of the budgetary control process. The standard costing system is introduced, materials and labor variances are analyzed, and your study of standard costing concludes with an analysis of the overhead variances and accounting for their disposition. Evaluating employee performance using variances is also discussed.

LEARNING OBJECTIVES

1. Define responsibility accounting and describe a responsibility accounting system.
2. Identify the cost and revenue classifications that are controllable by a particular manager.
3. Distinguish between a cost/expense center, a profit center, and an investment center.
4. Identify and describe the behavioral principles of performance evaluation.
5. State the operational principles of performance evaluation, and explain how they are interrelated.
6. Prepare a performance evaluation report for (a) a cost/expense center, (b) a profit center, and (c) an investment center.

CHAPTER 19

Responsibility Accounting and Performance Evaluation

Whenever the term *management* is used, it is safe to assume that an organization is being discussed. An organization consists of many people doing different types of jobs. Whether a company needs levels of managers depends on its size; the bigger the organization, the more managers it needs. As a company grows, its functional operations and the responsibilities associated with those functions tend to become decentralized. **Decentralization** means that control of the company's operations is spread among several people. Decentralization requires a special approach to managing an enterprise.

In this chapter we discuss how accounting helps management control the operations of a decentralized company. One approach to this task is to use a process called responsibility accounting, which is the foundation on which plans and budgets are developed in a decentralized organization. A responsibility accounting system is also important in controlling actual operations.

After defining responsibility accounting and illustrating such a system, we focus on the costs and revenues a manager can control or take responsibility for. We then emphasize the responsibilities of various centers in a decentralized company: cost/expense centers, profit centers, and investment centers. The behavioral and operational principles of performance evaluation are discussed, and the chapter concludes with a look at the performance evaluation process of a decentralized company. After studying this chapter, you should be able to meet the learning objectives listed on the left.

DECISION POINT

Martin Industries, Inc.[1]

■ Martin Industries, Inc. is a heating products manufacturer in Florence, Alabama. The company produces wood-burning stoves, gas heaters, fabricated fireplaces, dehumidifiers, and utility trailers. When James Truitt, Martin Industries' former controller and current vice president–treasurer and secretary, assumed responsibility for the accounting function, he felt that the existing management accounting system did not collect and organize information needed for decision making. The accounting system generated traditional financial statements, but it did not provide special analyses that management could use to evaluate the company's operations. How can an accounting system be expanded to improve its contribution and usefulness to management?

1. Russell F. Briner, Michael D. Akers, James W. Truitt, and James D. Wilson, "Coping with Change at Martin Industries," *Management Accounting*, Institute of Management Accountants, July 1989, pp. 45–49.

Mr. Truitt changed the company's accounting policies and procedures by implementing a variable cost accounting system. The new system produced comparative divisional income statements that measured the contribution margin of each product. When Martin Industries' managers became accustomed to following their unit's contribution margin, they could assess their performance and their impact on total company profitability. The new variable cost accounting system also generated performance analysis reports. These reports told managers how their units' productivity compared with budgeted expectations. The reports included variances for all variable costs. Managers now know the price and efficiency variances for each of their product lines. Thanks to Mr. Truitt's good decision, Martin Industries' managers now have information to guide them in their decisions. ■

Responsibility Accounting

OBJECTIVE 1
Define responsibility accounting *and describe a* responsibility accounting *system*

Responsibility accounting is an information reporting system that (1) classifies financial data according to areas of responsibility in an organization and (2) reports managers' activities by including only revenue and cost categories that a particular manager can control. Also called *profitability accounting,* a responsibility accounting system personalizes accounting reports. Such a system emphasizes responsibility centers. A **responsibility center** is an organizational unit within a responsibility accounting system for which reports are generated. Responsibility centers include (1) cost/expense centers, (2) revenue/profit centers, and (3) investment centers. By concentrating on these responsibility centers, a responsibility accounting system classifies and reports cost and revenue information according to responsibility areas assigned to managers or management positions.

REPORT VS RECORD!

Even though a company uses a responsibility accounting system, it still needs to collect normal cost and revenue data. To do so, a company must use normal recording methods and make normal debit and credit entries. A general ledger, special journals, and a defined chart of accounts are also used. **Responsibility accounting focuses on the reporting—not the recording—of operating cost and revenue data.** Once the financial data from daily operations have been recorded in the accounting system, specific costs and revenues can be reclassified and reported for specific areas of managerial responsibility.

Organizational Structure and Reporting

A responsibility accounting system is made up of several responsibility centers. There is a responsibility center for each area or level of managerial responsibility, and a report is generated for each center. The report for a responsibility center includes only those cost and revenue items the manager of that center can control. If a manager cannot control a cost or revenue item, it is either not included in the manager's report or is classified separately. This classification treatment prevents the item from influencing the manager's performance evaluation. Cost and revenue controllability is discussed in the next section.

A look at a corporate organization chart and a series of related managerial reports shows how a responsibility accounting system works. Figure 19-1 shows a typical management hierarchy, with its three vice presidents reporting to the corporate president. The sales and finance areas have been condensed, however, to emphasize the manufacturing area. The production managers of

Figure 19-1. Organization Chart Emphasizing the Manufacturing Area

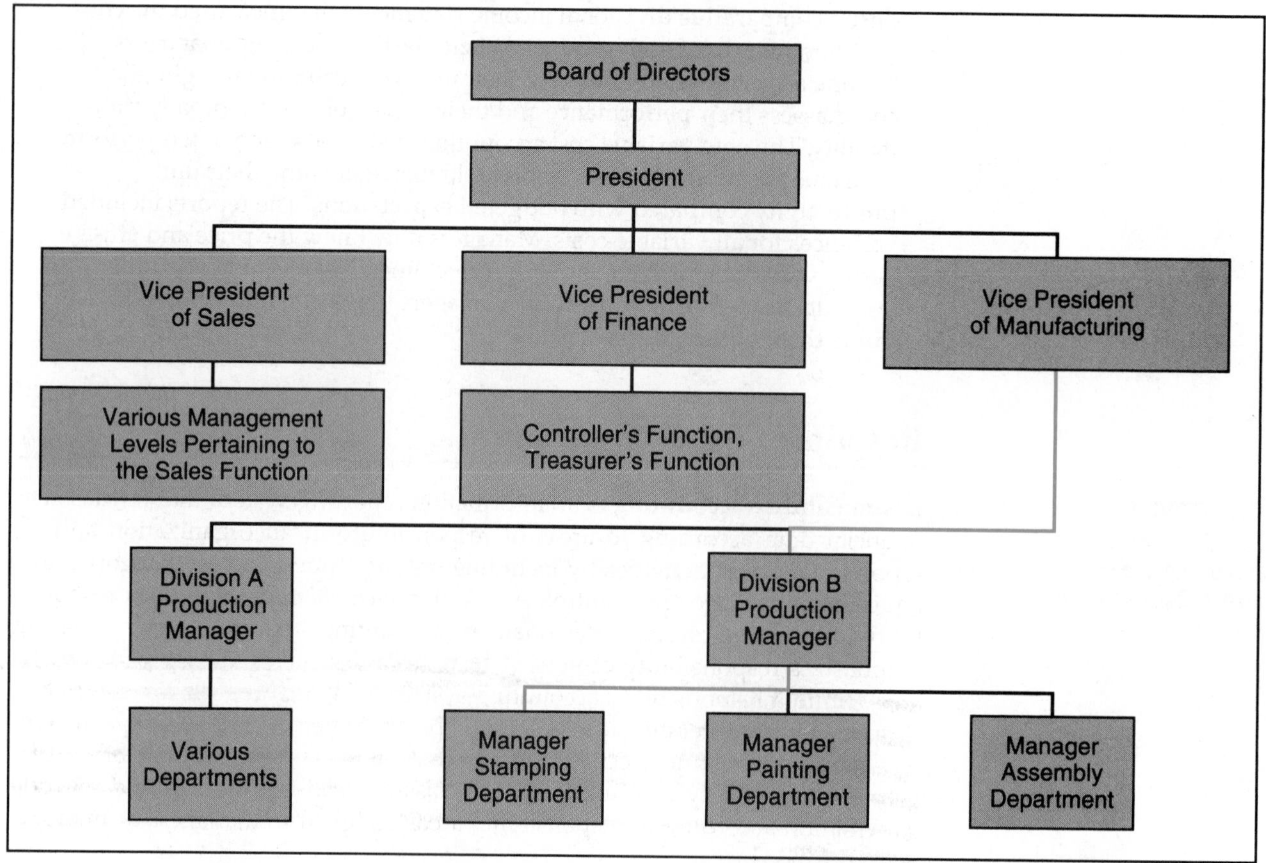

Divisions A and B report to the vice president of manufacturing. In Division B, the managers of the Stamping Department, Painting Department, and Assembly Department report to the division's production manager.

In a responsibility accounting system, operating reports for each level of management are tailored to individual needs. Because a responsibility accounting system provides a report for every manager and lower-level managers report to higher-level managers, the same costs and revenues may appear in several reports. When lower-level operating data are included in higher-level reports, the data are summarized.

Exhibit 19-1 illustrates how the responsibility reporting network is tied together. At the department level the report lists cost items under the manager's control and compares expected (or budgeted) costs with actual costs. This comparison is a measure of operating performance. The manager who receives the report on the Stamping Department should be particularly concerned with direct materials costs and maintenance salaries, for they are significantly over budget. Also, the underutilization of small tools may signal problems with that department's productivity.

The production manager of Division B is responsible for the three operating departments plus controllable divisionwide costs. The production manager's report includes a summary of results from the Stamping Department as well as from the other areas of responsibility. At the division level, the report does not present detailed data on each department; only department totals appear. As

Exhibit 19-1. Reporting Within a Responsibility Accounting System

Manufacturing: Vice President		**Monthly Report: November**	
Amount Budgeted	**Controllable Cost**	**Actual Amount**	**Over (Under) Budget**
	Central production		
$ 281,400	scheduling	$ 298,100	$16,700
179,600	Office expenses	192,800	13,200
19,800	Operating expenses	26,200	6,400
	Divisions		
339,500	A	348,900	9,400
426,200	B	399,400	(26,800)
$1,246,500	Totals	$1,265,400	$18,900

Division B: Production Manager		**Monthly Report: November**	
Amount Budgeted	**Controllable Cost**	**Actual Amount**	**Over (Under) Budget**
	Division expenses		
$101,800	Salaries	$ 96,600	$ (5,200)
39,600	Utilities	39,900	300
25,600	Insurance	21,650	(3,950)
	Departments		
46,600	Stamping	48,450	1,850
69,900	Painting	64,700	(5,200)
142,700	Assembly	128,100	(14,600)
$426,200	Totals	$399,400	$(26,800)

Stamping Department: Manager		**Monthly Report: November**	
Amount Budgeted	**Controllable Cost**	**Actual Amount**	**Over (Under) Budget**
$22,500	Direct materials	$23,900	$1,400
14,900	Factory labor	15,200	300
2,600	Small tools	1,400	(1,200)
5,100	Maintenance salaries	6,000	900
1,000	Supplies	1,200	200
500	Other costs	750	250
$46,600	Totals	$48,450	$1,850

shown in Exhibit 19-1, the data are even more condensed in the vice president's report. Only corporate and summarized divisional data on costs controllable by the vice president are included. Note that the $1,000 budgeted for supplies, shown in the Stamping Department report, is part of the vice president's report. The cost is included in the $426,200. But like all costs reported at higher levels, specific identity has been lost.

Cost and Revenue Controllability

OBJECTIVE 2
Identify the cost and revenue classifications that are controllable by a particular manager

Management wants to incur the lowest possible costs while still producing a quality product or providing a useful service. Profit-oriented businesses want to maximize their profits. Not-for-profit organizations, such as government units or charitable associations, seek to accomplish a mission while operating within their appropriations or budgets. To achieve these goals, management must know the origin of a cost or revenue item and be able to identify the person who controls it.

A manager's **controllable costs** and revenues are those that result from his or her actions, influence, and decisions. If managers can regulate or influence a cost or revenue item, the item is controllable at that level of operation. Or if managers have the authority to acquire or supervise the use of a resource or service, they control its cost.

Determining controllability is the key to a successful responsibility accounting system. In theory it means that every dollar of a company's incurred costs or earned revenue is traceable to and controllable by at least one manager. However, identifying controllable costs at lower management levels is often difficult because these managers seldom have full authority to acquire or supervise the use of resources and services. For example, if resources are shared with another department, a manager has only partial control and influence over such costs. For this reason, managers should help identify the costs for which they will be held accountable in their performance reviews. If cost and revenue items can be controlled by the person responsible for the area in which they originate, then it is possible to design an efficient, meaningful reporting system that highlights operating performance.

The activity of a responsibility center dictates the extent of the manager's responsibility. If a responsibility center only involves costs or expenditures, it is called a cost/expense center. On the other hand, if a manager is responsible for both revenues and costs, the department is called a profit center. Finally, if a manager is involved in decisions to invest in plant, equipment, and other capital resources and is also responsible for revenues and costs, the unit is called an investment center.

Cost/Expense Center

OBJECTIVE 3
Distinguish between a cost/expense center, a profit center, and an investment center

Any organizational unit, such as a department or division, whose manager is responsible only for costs incurred by that unit is known as a **cost/expense center**. The manager of a cost or expense center has no direct influence over revenue generation or decisions to invest in capital equipment. Instead, he or she is charged with the responsibility of producing a quality product or service at a reasonable cost.

The two terms *cost center* and *expense center* are both used in this discussion because both are used in business. *Cost center* is the term used more often. However, it has two distinct meanings. When discussing the accumulation of cost data, the term often refers to the smallest segment for which costs are accumulated and analyzed. Thus, if a machine were being analyzed and costs were collected for that analysis, the machine would be a cost center. When the term *cost center* is used in connection with responsibility centers and responsibility accounting, it means an organizational unit with a manager who is accountable for the unit's actions. To avoid confusion, *expense center* could be used to describe this type of responsibility center. But because that term is less widely used than *cost center,* this text refers to such organizational units as *cost/expense centers.*

What makes a cost controllable? Earlier we said a cost was controllable if the manager could influence its incurrence and amount. Operating costs incurred by the cost/expense center would fit into this category. They are variable depending on the center's activity. Fixed costs for supervising a cost/expense center should also be included in costs controllable by the manager. All other fixed costs, such as depreciation, insurance premiums, and property taxes, as well as the operating overhead allocated to the center usually cannot be controlled by the manager of a cost/expense center.

Cost/expense centers have inputs (costs) that are measurable in dollars, but their outputs (products or services) are not. Such organizational units add value to a product or service or support the business in another way. Cost/expense centers are not directly connected with the sale of a product or service. Consider the Teller Department and the Data Processing Department of a bank. Tellers are critical to good customer relations and the orderly receipt and withdrawal of funds by customers. Data Processing is responsible for accurately recording all funds received and expended by the bank. Yet neither department generates revenue. Hence both departments are considered cost/expense centers in the bank's responsibility accounting system. And respective managers are responsible only for the costs incurred to operate each department.

Profit Center

When a manager of an organizational unit is responsible for revenues, costs, and resulting profits, the responsibility center is known as a **profit center**. The term **revenue center** is sometimes used in practice. A pure revenue center, however, is one in which the department or business segment's manager is only responsible for revenue generation. The costs incurred to generate that revenue are not used to measure the manager's performance. Such a situation is quite uncommon. *Profit center* is the more common term used to describe a business unit in which the manager is responsible for generating revenues and incurring costs in such a way as to maximize profits.

Managers of profit centers are accountable for both the amount of revenues their departments generate and the costs incurred to attain that revenue level. A profit center is operated much like a business since it shows a profit or loss for its actions during a particular period. Profit centers are useful in decentralized companies. From a control standpoint, it is much easier to monitor operations if the enterprise is broken up into profit centers. Large, decentralized companies are difficult to manage because of the size and diversity of the products sold or services rendered. By operating within a responsibility accounting system, a company can place managers in charge of dozens of small profit centers. Each manager is then responsible for the expected profit from his or her operating unit.

Controllable costs for a profit center are determined much as they are for a cost/expense center. A cost is controllable only if the manager can decide if it should be incurred. Revenues of a profit center can also be controlled or influenced by the center's manager. Such revenues are used to determine a center's net income.

Large retail establishments provide a clear picture of how profit centers are used. Department stores, for example, usually have several departments, such as children's clothing, cosmetics, women's clothing, menswear, and jewelry. Each department sells directly to the public, with each manager being responsible for generating a profit from sales in his or her department.

To be a profit center, an organizational unit is not necessarily involved with selling a company's product or service. An artificial selling price can be created for the product or service even if it is not in a finished or salable condition when leaving the department. This process is known as transfer pricing and is discussed in the chapter on pricing decisions, including transfer pricing. For purposes of this discussion, however, the analysis is limited to those business units involved in direct selling activities.

Investment Center

In an investment center the concept of a responsibility center is carried one step further. The manager must be responsible for the revenues, costs, and related profits of the department or business unit for it to qualify as an investment center. In addition, the manager must be evaluated on the effective use of assets employed to generate those profits, including capital assets. In other words, an **investment center** is a profit center whose manager can make significant decisions about the assets the center uses.

On the surface there is little difference between a profit center and an investment center. However, in a profit center, top management still determines the quantity and quality of assets a department uses. If such assets are old or nonproductive, the manager can request improved equipment but cannot decide whether to replace or repair it.

Since the manager of an investment center has control over assets, he or she must be evaluated based on the effective use of those assets. Not only is the amount of profit earned important, so is the center's **return on investment**. Return on investment is computed as follows:

$$\text{Return on investment} = \frac{\text{net income}}{\begin{array}{c}\text{dollar value of the assets}\\ \text{used in generating}\\ \text{that income}\end{array}}$$

The numerator, net income, can either be before or after taxes. In the examples here, before-tax net income is used to make the analysis simpler. But remember that after-tax net income is commonly used in practice. The denominator is usually the average cost of assets used to generate a center's profit. Although much has been written and debated about the methods of assigning value to the assets used, the most common approach is to use the historical cost of the assets and not reduce their value to book value. Such an approach tends to keep the denominator constant, and the results from year to year are more comparable. If book values are used, the denominator is decreased over the life of an asset. Thus one would expect the return on investment to increase.

To evaluate the performance of an investment center's manager, one must know the quantity and value of the assets under his or her control as well as the controllable costs and revenues for the period. Controllable costs and revenues are identified in the same manner as that discussed for a profit center. Because an investment center is similar to an autonomous business enterprise, the manager usually controls more costs, such as insurance premiums, depreciation of the center's assets, and property taxes traced to the center. The value of the assets used must be computed by someone familiar with the investment center.

Later in this chapter we analyze three departments of Suchora Retail Centers, Inc. The focus is on evaluating the performance of each of the three managers. However, determining the type of responsibility center being evaluated has a direct bearing on deciding which cost and/or revenue items should be used in the evaluation process. In the Suchora case, the Maintenance Contract Department is accounted for as a cost/expense center, the Home Furnishings Department is treated as a profit center, and the Custom Draperies and Blinds Department is an investment center. But before the case can be discussed, we must study the process of performance evaluation.

Performance Evaluation

Performance evaluation is the application of financial measurement techniques in which actual operating results are compared with expectations and a manager's performance judged. An individual's performance is measured by comparing actual and budgeted results of operations. Successful performance evaluation is the result of several factors, some involving company policies, others involving human factors.

Performance evaluation is an important part of a company's budgetary control program. An effective budgetary control program includes policies and procedures for (1) preparing operational plans, (2) establishing responsibility for performance, (3) communicating operational plans to key personnel, (4) evaluating areas of responsibility, and (5) learning the causes of any variations between budgeted and actual results and making the needed corrections. Operating policies alone will not give a company an effective performance evaluation system. The human aspect is critical to its success. People do the planning and perform the actions needed to generate a profit. They are also the evaluators and the evaluated.

Behavioral Principles of Performance Evaluation

OBJECTIVE 4
Identify and describe the behavioral principles of performance evaluation

Basic guidelines regarding people must be part of any effective cost and revenue control system. Behavioral considerations should include the following:

1. Managers should have input into the standards and goals set for their areas of responsibility.
2. Top management's support of the evaluation process should be evident.
3. Only controllable cost and revenue items with significant variances should be the focus of performance reports.
4. Opportunity for manager response should be a part of the evaluation process.

All considerations assume that an effective reward system (compensation) for attaining set goals was previously established.

1. **Managers should have input into the standards and goals set for their areas of responsibility.** The manager responsible for an operating area must have direct input into the goal-setting process of his or her area. Having a desire to perform is a key factor in meeting goals and attaining targets. When a manager believes that an operating target is unrealistic, or that plans were developed without the participation of personnel from the department, the desire to reach those goals may not materialize. To prevent this negative reaction, top management should encourage participative goal setting. When departmental managers are involved in setting the targets against which they are to be evaluated, their incentive to perform is increased. They perceive such goals as attainable, not unrealistic targets set arbitrarily by top management.
2. **Top management's support of the evaluation process should be evident.** Top management must show its support by clearly communicating goals and plans, including each person's exact responsibilities. Failure to communicate plans to

managers is a common cause of inefficient operating performance. Such communication accomplishes two important aspects of the budgetary control process. First, communication spells out in detail management's expectations of each manager. Second, the development of an evaluation system and the communication of that system to managers indicates that top management is involved in the process and will support suggestions to meet the targets. Without the continued support of top management, a performance evaluation system will fail to accomplish its objectives.

3. **Only controllable cost and revenue items with significant variances should be the focus of performance reports.** Performance reports should contain only those cost and revenue categories that a manager can influence or control. Holding someone responsible for costs outside his or her control causes negative feelings and decreases the effectiveness of the system. In addition, when there are many cost and revenue categories within a manager's domain, it is more effective to limit the items reported on the performance report to those with significant variations from budget. This process focuses attention on those areas needing immediate action, so the manager will not waste time evaluating insignificant differences.
4. **Opportunity for manager response should be a part of the evaluation process.** Managers should have a chance to give top management feedback on their performance. Top management should praise good performance and not take it for granted. Silence does not imply good performance; it means bad management. If performance is poor or substandard, the responsible person should have a chance to defend his or her actions. There may be a good reason for a variance, such as the cause being beyond the person's control. The manager should be an important part of the management team, not just someone on whom blame is placed when performance is poor.

Operational Principles of Performance Evaluation

OBJECTIVE 5
State the operational principles of performance evaluation, and explain how they are interrelated

Making a performance evaluation system operable requires that a set of operational principles be followed. Note that they are linked closely with the behavioral principles already discussed. The operational principles of performance evaluation are:

1. Provide accurate and suitable measures of performance.
2. Communicate expectations to appropriate managers and segment leaders to be evaluated.
3. Identify each manager's responsibilities.
4. Compare actual performance with a suitable base.
5. Prepare performance reports that highlight areas of concern.
6. Analyze important cause-and-effect relationships.

1. **Provide accurate and suitable measures of performance.** Expectations of a manager's performance must be realistic. Accurate and suitable measures of performance should include predetermined budgets and standards, performances of other people in comparable jobs, and past performances in the same job classification. A manager will be able to do an effective job if these performance measures are provided and if they represent attainable goals. Nonfinancial measures, such as machine hours or units of output, can be used to measure performance and may be as useful as dollar measures.
2. **Communicate expectations to appropriate managers and segment leaders to be evaluated.** When developing its performance evaluation process, a company should ensure that its system of communicating expectations to managers at all

levels is well defined. The communications system should be two-way. Each level must listen to the concerns and solutions of the others. Feedback is vital to the success of a performance evaluation system.

3. **Identify each manager's responsibilities.** Before expecting a person to do something, one should inform the person of what is expected. Identifying the specific responsibilities of each manager is part of the performance evaluation process. This step is usually accomplished when the company's responsibility accounting system is devised. One way to ensure that a performance evaluation process fails is to have managers held accountable for actions they thought were another's responsibility.
4. **Compare actual performance with a suitable base.** When evaluating performance, one must compare what actually happened with a measure of what was anticipated or expected. This measure may be a budget prepared before the current period began, the average performance on a particular task during the past three or four years, a standard cost (discussed in the chapter on standard costing and variance analysis), or simply a rough estimate of expectations. Without some anticipated base, one has nothing to evaluate actual results against, and without that measurement ability, performance cannot be evaluated.
5. **Prepare performance reports that highlight areas of concern.** The preparation of performance reports is an important step in the performance evaluation process. The information in these reports should specify a manager's responsibilities. These responsibilities may be limited to cost and revenue items that depart enough from anticipated targets to warrant analysis. If a manager's area of responsibility involves only fifteen or twenty cost and revenue items, then all controllable costs and revenues may be included. But if there are more than twenty items, only those needing analysis for being far over or under target should be included. Remember, only controllable cost and revenue items belong in a manager's performance report.
6. **Analyze important cause-and-effect relationships.** Isolating a variation between a budgeted amount and an actual cost is just the beginning of the performance evaluation process. Some people believe that once this variation has been determined, someone is guilty and should be reprimanded. But a performance report is more than one set of numbers compared with another. One cost or revenue variation from budget may help cause a second reaction. A performance report should reveal cause-and-effect factors and significant relationships. If, for instance, a furniture manufacturer purchases poor-quality lumber, labor costs might soar because the wood is difficult to work with. Such qualitative information can often explain differences between budgeted and actual dollars. Much of this information must come from the manager being evaluated.

Implementing a Performance Reporting System

You have now learned about the elements needed to develop a performance reporting system:

1. A performance reporting system is based on the concept of responsibility accounting. Responsibility accounting is an information reporting system that classifies financial data according to specific areas of responsibility. If a detailed organization chart of the company is created, all managerial positions that will become part of the performance reporting system can be identified and areas of responsibility determined.
2. Adequate performance measures must be determined.

3. Specific duties and operating expectations must be identified and communicated to each manager.
4. A communications system must be established, and it must involve managers in determining their targets and goals for the period.
5. A reporting format must be devised, and it must contain only those cost and revenue items under a manager's control.
6. Once the budgeted and actual amounts have been measured and compared, the manager is expected to explain the significant differences on his or her report.
7. A manager and his or her superior must work out methods to correct problems.
8. A strong system of rewards and feedback is necessary for the performance evaluation process to succeed.

With these performance evaluation elements in mind, let us analyze the performance reporting techniques of Suchora Retail Centers, Inc.

Illustrative Case
Suchora Retail Centers, Inc.

The Suchora Retail Centers, Inc. case analysis illustrates the process of performance evaluation in a decentralized company. Emphasis is on determining the costs and revenues a manager can control and on structuring and designing performance reports. This case analysis compares performance evaluation and reporting for a cost/expense center, a profit center, and an investment center.

Suchora Retail Centers, Inc. competes directly with Sears and J. C. Penney for customers who want a store with a full line of household goods and services. Suchora's stores are in major metropolitan areas, located near Sears' and Penney's stores, and closely resemble those of competitors. Because of its large size, the company operates as a decentralized organization. In all of its 117 stores, the departments are large and supervised by experienced managers.

The following analysis concentrates on three supervisors and their performance reports. Nicole Mannarino manages a service-oriented cost/expense center, Douglas White supervises a profit center within a service business, and Karen Voorhees supervises a production and service department that is treated as an investment center.

OBJECTIVE 6a
Prepare a performance evaluation report for a cost/expense center

Maintenance Contract Department. *Organization:* Nicole Mannarino manages the Maintenance Contract Department at Suchora's Nashville, Tennessee store. The company's Appliance and Gardening departments sell maintenance contracts to customers who buy appliances and equipment. These contracts guarantee that for a set annual contract price, all labor and parts needed to keep the item in operating order will be supplied by the Maintenance Contract Department of a Suchora store. The maintenance contracts are sold by the appliance and gardening equipment salespeople, not by people working for Ms. Mannarino, so the Maintenance Contract Department and Ms. Mannarino do not have revenue responsibility.

Ms. Mannarino is responsible for thirty maintenance and repair people and a fleet of eighteen vans stocked with parts. Half the vans are involved in appliance repair activities; the others are used for lawn and garden equipment repairs. Twelve employees are support personnel involved in scheduling, purchasing, and stocking activities as well as assisting the eighteen full-time maintenance repair people who operate the vans. The department is housed in its own building, which has room for parts storage and two bays for repairing the vans.

Operating Results for March: Following are the costs identified with the Maintenance Contract Department for March, 1994. The format is the original one

Ms. Mannarino received. The report lists all costs assigned to the Contract Maintenance Department and shows both budgeted and actual data. At the bottom of the report, performance is said to be $5,630 over budget. The report, however, provides little additional information. Although the columns are totaled, there is no information on the over- or underbudget spending in individual cost categories. Also, included are several costs that Ms. Mannarino cannot control.

Suchora Retail Centers, Inc.
Maintenance Contract Department
Operating Report
For the Month Ended March 31, 19x4

Supervisor: N. Mannarino	Budgeted	Actual
Labor		
Appliance repair	$ 5,400	$ 5,940
Lawn and garden equipment repair	5,400	5,310
Support	6,000	6,240
Supervision	2,600	2,600
Labor-related benefits	3,600	3,920
Repair parts, appliances	12,500	10,800
Repair parts, lawn and garden equipment	16,400	17,250
Fuel, vans	2,250	2,520
Oil, tires, and repairs, vans	2,880	2,430
Depreciation, vans	2,400	3,000
Maintenance and upkeep, building	2,500	2,350
Property taxes, building	600	750
Depreciation, building	2,200	2,650
Insurance, building	450	510
Utilities, building	300	280
Local store overhead	2,100	4,070
Corporate general and administrative costs	6,290	8,880
Total costs	$73,870	$79,500

Performance: Operating costs were $5,630 over budget.

Suchora's national headquarters has recently installed a responsibility accounting system for all of its 117 stores. Ms. Mannarino was asked to help prepare a format for the responsibility accounting report for her department. Of the costs included in her regular monthly performance report, Ms. Mannarino determined that the following costs were not under her control:

1. Fixed/allocated costs
   a. Depreciation, vans
   b. Property taxes, building
   c. Depreciation, building
   d. Insurance, building
2. Local store overhead
3. Corporate general and administrative costs

Using this information, the controller of the Nashville store put together a new report format.

The revised performance report for the Maintenance Contract Department for March is shown in Exhibit 19-2. Costs not controllable by Ms. Mannarino are summarized at the bottom. Those costs that Ms. Mannarino can influence are reported first. She can control, and has responsibility for, labor and labor-related costs, repair parts, van costs, and building costs.

Ms. Mannarino's performance during March was much better than that stated on the old performance report. Overall, her controllable costs were $190 under budget. Areas she needs to work on are labor costs, appliance repair ($540 over budget); repair parts, lawn and garden equipment ($850 over budget); and repair parts, appliances ($1,700 under budget). There may be a connection between the low cost of parts and the high cost of labor in the appliance repair area. Repair personnel people may be using too much time trying to fix existing parts rather than replacing them. Such action could also lead to lower-quality repair service. Ms. Mannarino should take action in this area.

Exhibit 19-2. Performance Reporting: Cost/Expense Center

Suchora Retail Centers, Inc.—Nashville, Tennessee
Maintenance Contract Department
Performance Report
For the Month Ended March 31, 19x4

Supervisor: Nicole Mannarino	Budgeted	Actual	Difference Over (Under) Budget
Costs Controllable by Supervisor			
Labor costs			
Maintenance repair personnel			
Appliance repair	$ 5,400	$ 5,940	$ 540
Lawn and garden equipment repair	5,400	5,310	(90)
Support personnel	6,000	6,240	240
Supervision	2,600	2,600	—
Labor-related benefits costs	3,600	3,920	320
Repair parts			
Appliances	12,500	10,800	(1,700)
Lawn and garden equipment	16,400	17,250	850
Van costs			
Fuel	2,250	2,520	270
Oil, tires, and repairs	2,880	2,430	(450)
Building costs			
Maintenance and upkeep	2,500	2,350	(150)
Utilities	300	280	(20)
Total controllable costs	$59,830	$59,640	$ (190)
Costs Uncontrollable by Supervisor			
Fixed/allocated costs			
Depreciation, vans	$ 2,400	$ 3,000	$ 600
Property taxes, building	600	750	150
Depreciation, building	2,200	2,650	450
Insurance, building	450	510	60
Local store overhead	2,100	4,070	1,970
Corporate general and administrative costs	6,290	8,880	2,590
Total uncontrollable costs	$14,040	$19,860	$5,820
Total costs	$73,870	$79,500	$5,630

Other than those areas mentioned, she seems to be doing a good job. Although the new report format still shows the department is $5,630 over budget, Ms. Mannarino is only accountable for the controllable costs of her unit.

OBJECTIVE 6b
Prepare a performance evaluation report for a profit center

Home Furnishings Department. *Organization:* Douglas White is the supervisor of the Home Furnishings Department in Suchora's Irving, Texas store. This location is convenient for customers living in both Dallas and Fort Worth, making the Irving store one of the largest Suchora stores in the country. Home furnishings include furniture, bedding, glassware, rugs, and carpeting. This department occupies 20 percent of the store's floor space allotted to sales. Storage space for inventory takes up almost 40 percent of the warehouse space.

Since Mr. White is responsible for both the purchase and sale of all goods listed as home furnishings, his department is considered a profit center. He employs thirty salespeople, four buyers, and twelve support people who work as sales-floor stockers, warehouse personnel, and delivery people. These three areas—sales, buying, and support—are operated as minidepartments, and each has a manager who reports to Mr. White.

Operating Results for March: The original performance report received by Mr. White for the Home Furnishings Department for March is shown on page 768. The report is divided into revenue and costs sections, and department income is shown. Budgeted and actual information is reported for each category. Mr. White's performance was judged to be $6,602 under the net income budgeted for the department.

As with the Nashville store, the Irving, Texas store is shifting to the new responsibility accounting reporting system. With the cooperation of his store's controller, Mr. White identified the following items as being out of his control:

1. Depreciation, sales floor
2. Depreciation, warehouse
3. Local store overhead
4. Corporate general and administrative costs

With this input from Mr. White, the controller recast the performance report as shown in Exhibit 19-3 on page 769.

As reflected in the new report, Mr. White produced department income in March that was $12,478 over budget. With the exception of carpet costs, all cost categories were well within normal range. Selling commissions were $618 over budget, but that should be expected since sales were $15,450 over budget. Buying salaries were low, and the difference was probably caused by being one buyer short during the month.

What Exhibit 19-3 does not show, however, is the performance of the three minidepartment managers. For this purpose the sales, cost of goods sold, and gross margin from sales data are summarized in the following table:

	Budgeted	Actual	Difference Over (Under) Budget
Gross Margin from Sales			
Furniture sales	$ 75,000	$ 80,598	$ 5,598
Carpeting sales	50,500	45,360	(5,140)
Other sales	29,550	42,480	12,930
Totals	$155,050	$168,438	$13,388

Suchora Retail Centers, Inc. Home Furnishings Department Operating Report For the Month Ended March 31, 19x4		
Supervisor: D. White	**Budgeted**	**Actual**
Revenue		
Furniture sales	$187,500	$191,900
Carpeting sales	126,250	129,600
Other sales	98,500	106,200
Total revenue	$412,250	$427,700
Costs		
Cost of goods sold, furniture	$112,500	$111,302
Cost of goods sold, carpet	75,750	84,240
Cost of goods sold, other	68,950	63,720
Selling, commissions	16,490	17,108
Selling, supervision	1,200	1,250
Buying, salaries	5,600	5,000
Buying, supervision	1,200	1,200
Support, wages	8,400	8,160
Support, supervision	1,000	1,100
Department supervision	3,250	3,250
Employee benefits	7,428	7,610
Utilities, sales floor	4,200	4,450
Depreciation, sales floor	8,600	14,250
Utilities, warehouse	2,800	3,100
Depreciation, warehouse	4,700	5,900
Delivery costs	3,300	3,550
Local store overhead	13,450	15,120
Corporate general and administrative costs	26,980	37,540
Total costs	$365,798	$387,850
Department income	$ 46,452	$ 39,850

Performance: Department income was $6,602 under budget.

This analysis is revealing. Even though the department's overall gross margin was $13,388, the carpeting minidepartment had a gross margin of $5,140 under budget for March. Looking further into the data, carpet sales were $3,350 over budget, but the cost of carpet sold was $8,490 over budget. Mr. White should request information from his carpeting manager about this situation. Either someone has been buying carpet at increased prices and/or of increased quality, or sales prices are too low; these reasons may be connected. In any event, Mr. White should be concerned about these figures even though overall department income is favorable.

OBJECTIVE 6c
Prepare a performance evaluation report for an investment center

Custom Draperies and Blinds Department. *Organization:* Karen Voorhees supervises the Custom Draperies and Blinds Department at the store in Seattle, Washington. She has three full-time salespeople working for her, and they are responsible for soliciting orders for custom-made draperies and window blinds. A major portion of this department's work involves making custom draperies.

Exhibit 19-3. Performance Reporting: Profit Center

Suchora Retail Centers, Inc.—Irving, Texas
Home Furnishings Department
Performance Report
For the Month Ended March 31, 19x4

Supervisor: Douglas White	Budgeted	Actual	Difference Over (Under) Budget
Costs Controllable by Supervisor			
Revenue from sales			
Furniture	$187,500	$191,900	$ 4,400
Carpet	126,250	129,600	3,350
Other	98,500	106,200	7,700
Total revenue	$412,250	$427,700	$15,450
Cost of goods sold			
Furniture	$112,500	$111,302	$ (1,198)
Carpet	75,750	84,240	8,490
Other	68,950	63,720	(5,230)
Total cost of goods sold	$257,200	$259,262	$ 2,062
Gross margin from sales	$155,050	$168,438	$13,388
Operating costs			
Selling			
Commissions	$ 16,490	$ 17,108	$ 618
Supervision	1,200	1,250	50
Buying			
Salaries	5,600	5,000	(600)
Supervision	1,200	1,200	—
Support			
Wages	8,400	8,160	(240)
Supervision	1,000	1,100	100
Department supervision	3,250	3,250	—
Employee benefits	7,428	7,610	182
Space costs			
Utilities, sales floor	4,200	4,450	250
Utilities, warehouse	2,800	3,100	300
Delivery costs	3,300	3,550	250
Total controllable costs	$ 54,868	$ 55,778	$ 910
Controllable department income	$100,182	$112,660	$12,478
Costs Uncontrollable by Supervisor			
Depreciation, sales floor	$ 8,600	$ 14,250	$ 5,650
Depreciation, warehouse	4,700	5,900	1,200
Local store overhead	13,450	15,120	1,670
Corporate general and administrative costs	26,980	37,540	10,560
Total uncontrollable costs	$ 53,730	$ 72,810	$19,080
Net department income	$ 46,452	$ 39,850	$ (6,602)

The salespeople visit customers' homes and take all measurements for each order.

In addition to the sales staff, Ms. Voorhees employs six drapery makers, five blinds makers, and four indirect labor personnel. The department uses a job order costing system for cost accumulation purposes. Seventy percent of the department's work is custom-made goods, and 30 percent of sales are ready-made draperies and blinds. Three clerks handle sales of ready-made goods.

The company considers the Custom Draperies and Blinds Department an investment center since Ms. Voorhees is responsible for buying such capital assets as machinery and equipment to make the products. She is also responsible for three automobiles used for sales, 2,000 square feet of sales floor in the main building, and the drapery production shop located in its own building adjacent to the store.

Operating Results for March: Ms. Voorhees's performance report for March, which follows the original format, is summarized in the operating report on the next page. Because the Custom Draperies and Blinds Department is an investment center, performance is judged by both the department's income and its return on investment. As shown, Ms. Voorhees's overall performance was well below expectations. Department income was $3,881 below expectations for March. This situation meant that on the $1,559,600 investment base for the department, only a .5 percent return was realized. Target monthly return on investment was .75 percent.

As with the other stores, the Seattle, Washington store changed to a responsibility accounting reporting system in March. After reviewing the cost and revenue categories with Ms. Voorhees, the store's controller identified the following items as being out of the control of the department's supervisor:

1. Local store overhead
2. Corporate general and administrative costs

Using this information, the controller revised Ms. Voorhees's performance report; it is shown in Exhibit 19-4 on page 772.

Unlike the reports for Ms. Mannarino and Mr. White, the new reporting format for the Custom Draperies and Blinds Department does not turn an unfavorable situation into a favorable one. Ms. Voorhees has problems generating a favorable gross margin from sales. There are also two or three operating cost categories that she should be concerned about. A further look at gross margin revealed the following:

	Budgeted	Actual	Difference Over (Under) Budget
Gross Margin from Sales			
Custom draperies	$22,635	$18,810	$(3,825)
Custom blinds	11,850	13,895	2,045
Ready-mades	17,319	17,990	671
Totals	$51,804	$50,695	$(1,109)

There is a problem in the production of custom draperies. Ms. Voorhees should analyze all aspects of that area. Are cloth and other materials prices too high? Is

Suchora Retail Centers, Inc.
Custom Draperies and Blinds Department
Operating Report
For the Month Ended March 31, 19x4

Supervisor: K. Voorhees **Investment base: $1,559,600**	**Budgeted**	**Actual**
Revenue		
Custom drapery sales	$ 75,450	$ 79,410
Custom blinds sales	59,250	62,190
Ready-made sales	57,730	56,280
Total revenue	$192,430	$197,880
Costs		
Cost of goods sold		
Custom draperies, materials	$ 30,180	$ 33,480
Custom draperies, labor	15,090	19,100
Custom draperies, factory overhead	7,545	8,020
Custom blinds, materials	29,625	30,040
Custom blinds, labor	11,850	12,130
Custom blinds, factory overhead	5,925	6,125
Ready-made draperies and blinds	40,411	38,290
Selling commissions, custom-made	8,082	8,496
Selling commissions, ready-made	1,732	1,688
Automobile expenses, selling	4,620	3,750
Automobile depreciation, selling	8,160	8,430
Department supervision	2,700	2,700
Employee benefits	7,891	8,823
Utilities, sales floor	1,200	1,320
Depreciation, sales floor	1,610	1,750
Local store overhead	2,350	2,290
Corporate general and administrative costs	1,780	3,650
Total costs	$180,751	$190,082
Department income	$ 11,679	$ 7,798
Department rate of return	.75%	.50%

Performance: Department income was $3,881 under budget.
Department return on investment for March was .5% (6% annualized), which is .25% under the anticipated monthly return of .75%.

too much labor employed for the volume of business? Do the salespeople need to revise retail price figures used to develop customer quotes? There may be several possible causes for the poor performance. Other areas of concern include sales commissions for custom-made products and employee benefits. The high cost of benefits may be related to excess labor in the custom draperies area.

As shown, regardless of the result for each manager, the new reporting format has helped determine ways to improve performance. Responsibility accounting provides the tools necessary to establish a performance reporting system that highlights cost and revenue areas under the control of a manager.

Exhibit 19-4. Performance Reporting: Investment Center

Suchora Retail Centers, Inc.—Seattle, Washington
Custom Draperies and Blinds Department
Performance Report
For the Month Ended March 31, 19x4

Supervisor: Karen Voorhees Investment base: $1,559,600	Budgeted	Actual	Difference Over (Under) Budget
Costs Controllable by Supervisor			
Revenue from sales			
Custom draperies	$ 75,450	$ 79,410	$ 3,960
Custom blinds	59,250	62,190	2,940
Ready-mades	57,730	56,280	(1,450)
Total revenue from sales	$192,430	$197,880	$ 5,450
Cost of goods sold			
Custom draperies			
Materials	$ 30,180	$ 33,480	$ 3,300
Labor	15,090	19,100	4,010
Factory overhead	7,545	8,020	475
Subtotals	$ 52,815	$ 60,600	$ 7,785
Custom blinds			
Materials	$ 29,625	$ 30,040	$ 415
Labor	11,850	12,130	280
Factory overhead	5,925	6,125	200
Subtotals	$ 47,400	$ 48,295	$ 895
Ready-made draperies and blinds	$ 40,411	$ 38,290	$(2,121)
Total cost of goods sold	$140,626	$147,185	$ 6,559
Gross margin from sales	$ 51,804	$ 50,695	$(1,109)
Operating costs			
Sales commissions, custom-mades	$ 8,082	$ 8,496	$ 414
Sales commissions, ready-mades	1,732	1,688	(44)
Auto expenses	4,620	3,750	(870)
Auto depreciation	8,160	8,430	270
Department supervision	2,700	2,700	—
Employee benefits	7,891	8,823	932
Sales space costs			
Utilities, sales floor	1,200	1,320	120
Depreciation, sales floor	1,610	1,750	140
Total controllable costs	$ 35,995	$ 36,957	$ 962
Controllable department income	$ 15,809	$ 13,738	$(2,071)
Controllable department rate of return	1.01%	0.88%	−0.13%
Costs Uncontrollable by Supervisor			
Local store overhead	$ 2,350	$ 2,290	$ (60)
Corporate general and administrative costs	1,780	3,650	1,870
Total uncontrollable costs	$ 4,130	$ 5,940	$ 1,810
Net departmental income	$ 11,679	$ 7,798	$(3,881)

Chapter Review

Review of Learning Objectives

1. **Define *responsibility accounting* and describe a responsibility accounting system.**
   Responsibility accounting is an information reporting system that (1) classifies financial data according to areas of responsibility in an organization and (2) reports managers' activities by including only revenue and cost categories that a particular manager can control. A responsibility accounting system personalizes accounting reports, one for each person with responsibility for cost control in a company's organization chart.
2. **Identify the cost and revenue classifications that are controllable by a particular manager.**
   A manager's controllable costs and revenues are those that result from his or her actions, influence, and decisions. If managers can regulate or influence a cost or revenue item, it is controllable at that level of operation. If managers have the authority to acquire or supervise the use of a resource or service, they control its cost.
3. **Distinguish between a cost/expense center, a profit center, and an investment center.**
   Any organizational unit, such as a department or division, whose manager is responsible only for costs incurred by that unit is known as a cost/expense center. Cost/expense centers are not directly connected with the sale of a product or service. When a unit manager is responsible for revenues, costs, and resulting profits, the responsibility center is known as a profit center. To qualify as an investment center, the organization must evaluate its managers on how effectively assets are used to generate profits.
4. **Identify and describe the behavioral principles of performance evaluation.**
   Behavioral principles of performance evaluation state that (1) managers should have input into the standards and goals set for their areas of responsibility; (2) top management's support of the evaluation process should be evident; (3) only controllable cost and revenue items with significant variances should be the focus of performance reports; and (4) managers should be given opportunities to respond to evaluations.
5. **State the operational principles of performance evaluation, and explain how they are interrelated.**
   Operational principles of performance evaluation stipulate that management (1) provide accurate and suitable measures of performance; (2) communicate expectations to appropriate managers and segment leaders to be evaluated; (3) identify each manager's responsibilities; (4) compare actual performance with a suitable base; (5) prepare performance reports that highlight areas of concern; and (6) analyze important cause-and-effect relationships. These principles are all based on concern for the manager and his or her areas of responsibility.
6. **Prepare a performance evaluation report for (a) a cost/expense center, (b) a profit center, and (c) an investment center.**
   The key to preparing performance evaluation reports is to divide the report between those items a manager can and cannot control. A performance report for a cost/expense center contains only cost items, whereas a report for a profit and investment center contains both revenue and cost items. The report for an investment center also provides information on the center's investment base and the rate of return on invested dollars.

Review of Concepts and Terminology

The following concepts and terms were introduced in this chapter:

(L.O. 2) **Controllable costs:** Operating costs that result from a particular manager's actions, influence, and decisions.

(L.O. 3) **Cost/expense center:** A responsibility center, such as a department or division, whose manager is responsible for only the costs incurred by that center.

(L.O. 1) **Decentralization:** A system of management in which operating managers are free to make business decisions within their own department or organizational unit, as long as the decisions are consistent with the policies established for the entire company.

(L.O. 3) **Investment center:** A responsibility center whose manager is responsible for profit generation and can make significant decisions about the assets the center uses.

(L.O. 4) **Performance evaluation:** The application of financial measurement techniques in which actual operating results are compared with expectations and a manager's performance judged.

(L.O. 3) **Profit center:** A responsibility center whose manager is responsible for revenues, costs, and resulting profits.

(L.O. 1) **Responsibility accounting:** An information reporting system that (1) classifies financial data according to areas of responsibility in an organization and (2) reports managers' activities by including only revenue and cost categories that a particular manager can control. Also called *profitability accounting.*

(L.O. 1) **Responsibility centers:** Organizational units within a responsibility accounting system for which reports are generated. These include but are not limited to cost/expense centers, profit centers, revenue centers, and investment centers.

(L.O. 3) **Return on investment:** A performance measurement indicator for investment centers that relates properly measured operating income to average assets employed during the period.

(L.O. 3) **Revenue center:** A responsibility center whose manager is only responsible for revenue generation. The costs incurred to generate that revenue are not used to measure the manager's performance.

Self-Test

Test your knowledge of the chapter by choosing the best answer for each of the following items.

(L.O. 1) 1. An information reporting system that (1) classifies financial data according to areas of responsibility in an organization and (2) reports managers' activities by including only revenue and cost categories that a particular manager can control is known as
a. strategic budgeting.
b. job order costing.
c. responsibility accounting.
d. corporate planning.

(L.O. 2) 2. A controllable cost is one that
a. has a maximum limit.
b. is determined by the actions, influence, and/or decisions of a particular manager.
c. is spent within a specific time period.
d. must be authorized by the chief executive officer of a company before the expenditure can be made.

(L.O. 3) 3. A responsibility center whose manager is responsible for profit generation and can make significant decisions about the assets the center uses is known as a(n)
a. profit center.
b. revenue center.
c. cost/expense center.
d. investment center.

(L.O. 3) 4. Organizational units within a responsibility accounting system for which reports are generated are called
a. controllable units.
b. departments.
c. responsibility centers.
d. segments.

(L.O. 3) 5. A responsibility center whose manager is responsible for revenues, costs, and resulting profits is called a(n)
a. profit center.
b. revenue center.
c. cost/expense center.
d. investment center.

(L.O. 3) 6. Which of the following best describes the computation of the performance evaluation measure known as return on investment?
a. Net income divided by total assets used
b. Total assets used divided by net income
c. Gross margin divided by total sales
d. Total sales divided by cost of goods sold

(L.O. 4) 7. The application of financial measurement techniques so actual results can be compared with expectations and performance judged is the definition of
a. return on investment.
b. performance evaluation.
c. responsibility accounting.
d. management accounting.

(L.O. 4) 8. "Only controllable cost and revenue items with significant variances from target should be the focus of performance reports" is a(n)
a. operational principle of performance evaluation.
b. definition of responsibility accounting.
c. behavioral principle of performance evaluation.
d. statement without meaning in management accounting.

(L.O. 5) 9. Which of the following statements is *not* an operational principle of performance evaluation?
a. Provide accurate and suitable measures of performance.
b. Managers should have input into the standards and goals set for their areas of responsibility.
c. Prepare performance reports that highlight areas of concern.
d. Compare actual performance with a suitable base.

(L.O. 6) 10. In a typical cost/expense center, which of the following types of cost would not be controllable by the center's supervisor?
a. Labor cost
b. Cost of supplies
c. Repairs and maintenance
d. Depreciation of building

Answers to the Self-Test are at the end of this chapter.

Review Problem
Allocation of and Responsibility for Overhead

(L.O. 2, 6) Illinois Instruments Company is a high-tech firm engaged in the assembly of laser welders. The company is employee oriented and has a complete workout room and indoor track that employees can use at any time, day or night. Included in the company's health facility is a special cafeteria serving only low-cholesterol, low-sodium foods. In 19x5 the cafeteria operated at a net loss of $178,950. Company policy is to allocate this excess cost to all responsibility centers since every employee has the opportunity to eat at the cafeteria. Management is considering three allocation bases—number of employees, meals purchased by employees, and total labor hours—from which to select the allocation base. The data supporting each base under consideration are shown at the top of page 776.

Required

1. Allocate the cafeteria's net loss to the ten responsibility centers, using as a basis (a) number of employees, (b) meals purchased by employees, and (c) total labor hours.
2. For purposes of traceability, which of the three allocation bases best associates the cafeteria's cost with the cost objective (responsibility centers)? Why?
3. For performance evaluation, which of the cafeteria loss distributions computed in **1** leads to the most effective control of costs? Defend your answer.

Illinois Instruments Company
Allocation Analysis Data
For the Year Ended December 31, 19x5

Responsibility Center	Number of Employees	Meals Purchased by Employees	Total Labor Hours
Materials handling	9	655	50,400
Inventory storage	18	3,275	16,800
Electrical	63	10,480	100,800
Assembly	135	18,340	285,600
Engineering	54	9,170	134,400
Inspection	27	5,240	58,800
Accounting/Finance	9	2,620	33,600
Marketing/Sales	81	9,825	117,600
Purchasing/Shipping	18	1,965	8,400
Research/Design	36	3,930	33,600
Totals	450	65,500	840,000

Answer to Review Problem

1. Amount to be allocated: $178,950

   1a. Using number of employees basis:

Responsibility Center	Number of Employees	Percentage of Number of Employees	Amount Allocated to Each Department
Materials handling	9	2.0	$ 3,579.00
Inventory storage	18	4.0	7,158.00
Electrical	63	14.0	25,053.00
Assembly	135	30.0	53,685.00
Engineering	54	12.0	21,474.00
Inspection	27	6.0	10,737.00
Accounting/Finance	9	2.0	3,579.00
Marketing/Sales	81	18.0	32,211.00
Purchasing/Shipping	18	4.0	7,158.00
Research/Design	36	8.0	14,316.00
Totals	450	100.0	$178,950.00

1b. Using meals purchased by employees basis:

Responsibility Center	Meals Purchased by Employees	Percentage of Meals Purchased by Employees	Amount Allocated to Each Department
Materials handling	655	1.0	$ 1,789.50
Inventory storage	3,275	5.0	8,947.50
Electrical	10,480	16.0	28,632.00
Assembly	18,340	28.0	50,106.00
Engineering	9,170	14.0	25,053.00
Inspection	5,240	8.0	14,316.00
Accounting/Finance	2,620	4.0	7,158.00
Marketing/Sales	9,825	15.0	26,842.50
Purchasing/Shipping	1,965	3.0	5,368.50
Research/Design	3,930	6.0	10,737.00
Totals	65,500	100.00	$178,950.00

1c. Using total labor hours as basis:

Responsibility Center	Total Labor Hours	Percentage of Total Labor Hours	Amount Allocated to Each Department
Materials handling	50,400	6.0	$ 10,737.00
Inventory storage	16,800	2.0	3,579.00
Electrical	100,800	12.0	21,474.00
Assembly	285,600	34.0	60,843.00
Engineering	134,400	16.0	28,632.00
Inspection	58,800	7.0	12,526.50
Accounting/Finance	33,600	4.0	7,158.00
Marketing/Sales	117,600	14.0	25,053.00
Purchasing/Shipping	8,400	1.0	1,789.50
Research/Design	33,600	4.0	7,158.00
Totals	840,000	100.0	$178,950.00

2. For purposes of traceability, meals purchased by employees is the only one of the three allocation bases with a direct connection between the loss and the cost objective. The loss is directly connected with the number of meals served. Therefore, number of meals served is the best allocation base to satisfy the test of traceability.
3. For purposes of performance evaluation, none of the three bases is applicable. Only controllable costs should be included in a manager's performance evaluation. None of the managers in the departments has any control over cafeteria costs.

Chapter Assignments

Discussion Questions

1. Define *responsibility accounting*.
2. Describe a responsibility accounting system.
3. What is a responsibility center?
4. How does a company's organizational structure affect its responsibility accounting system?
5. Discuss the statement, "In a responsibility accounting system, operating reports for each level of management are tailored to individual needs."
6. What role does controllability play in a responsibility accounting system?
7. Describe a cost/expense center. Give two examples.
8. What is a profit center?
9. How does a profit center differ from a revenue center?
10. Explain the following statement: "A profit center is operated much like a separate minibusiness."
11. Describe an investment center.
12. Compare and contrast the terms *cost/expense center, profit center,* and *investment center.*
13. Describe how return on investment is computed.
14. What role does return on investment play in the evaluation of an investment center?
15. Define *performance evaluation.*
16. Identify the four behavioral principles of performance evaluation.
17. What does participative goal setting mean?
18. State the six operational principles of performance evaluation.
19. Explain the importance of a good communications system to effective performance evaluation.
20. Explain how a responsibility accounting system is linked to effective performance evaluation of managers.

Communication Skills Exercises

Communication 19-1. Individual Performance Evaluation *(L.O. 1)*

Weyerhaeuser Company[2] has adopted a new approach to individual performance evaluation that parallels the company's changing production environment. In order to remain competitive, new operating procedures and a total quality management approach have been established. The company has also adopted a policy of continuous improvement, a concept applied to the treatment of employees as well as to the operations of the company. The new individual performance appraisal system evaluates employees by looking at technical skills such as quality of work, quantity of work, job knowledge, initiative, planning, and cost control. Also evaluated are social skills such as relationships with peers, supervisor(s), the public, and clients and the ability to manage and develop subordinates. Recommendations are made regarding job performance, individual training needs, promotions, and salary adjustments. Do you think individual evaluations should contain training suggestions? Why did the company include this item when evaluating employees? What role does training play in the new manufacturing environment? Prepare a written response of your opinion of Weyerhaeuser's new evaluation approach. Include your reasoning.

Communication 19-2. Ethical Dilemma: Improving Reported Performance *(L.O. 6)*

The Northwest Division of ***Watts Insurance Agency*** handles more than $3 billion in coverage. Although the division has been very successful over its forty-five-year life, the current year has been difficult for Watts, as well as for the entire insurance industry. The Northwest Division has never shown a loss, but this year it is faced with that possibility.

2. Leslie F. Sorenson, "Appraisals at Weyerhaeuser: Improving Staff Performance," *Management Accounting,* The Institute of Management Accountants, July 1990.

The division's manager, Donna Sherman, has called the controller, Peter Gerson, to discuss the situation.

Donna Sherman: "Peter, we have a problem. I have just been promoted to Corporate Vice President, and I don't want to take a loss report from my own division to my first meeting of the Executive Committee. We have to do something about the current period's reported earnings. We're only a few thousand dollars from showing a profit. Can't we do something to postpone some costs or something? You know that you may be in line for my former job, so it's also important to you that we show a profit for the period."

Peter Gerson: "Donna, there are a number of things that we could do in the last week of the period to improve our operating results a bit. You could call Bob Terrain at Bachman Industries and offer him a discount if Bachman pays next year's premium before the end of this year. A second alternative would be to postpone Al Murphy's retirement settlement until next year. We could talk him into staying on for two more weeks. Or, we could postpone booking that $1.1 million claim from the Burnett case until next month. We only have a $1 million reserve set up for that settlement. Finally, we could simply recompute the projected future claims amount and reduce the year-end loss reserve liability needed for financial reporting purposes. After all, it is just an estimate. Which would you prefer?"

Using a group discussion approach, analyze the four alternatives offered by Peter Gerson to improve the division's operating performance. Which alternative(s) are allowable? Which are ethical? Which, if any, of the four would you recommend to Donna Sherman? Select a spokesperson for the group and create an outline of the points you feel are relevant in the evaluation of this situation. Be prepared to defend your recommended solution in class.

Communication 19-3. Professional Ethics and Performance Reporting *(L.O. 6)*

Grant Boutique is a wholesaler of women's clothing, cosmetics, and jewelry. Each product line is accounted for as a profit center, and performance reports are prepared monthly for each center's manager. During the current year, management has established an incentive system whereby a profit center's manager earns a $1,000 bonus whenever he or she exceeds the monthly profit target by at least 10 percent.

During February, a larger shipment of clothing was returned by a customer because of a significant sewing flaw in the lining of the garments. Instead of being recorded as a sales return of the Clothing Center, the company's accountant recorded the transaction as Distribution Overhead, an account that is assigned to the three centers in proportion to their monthly sales figures. The recording error resulted in lowering the month's profit amounts below the 10 percent bonus level for both the Cosmetics and Jewelry profit centers, while the Clothing Center reported a profit of 16 percent over target.

Michelle Jones is the manager of the Clothing Center. She has just received her performance report and is aware that the returned goods transaction was not recorded properly. Prepare a list of alternative actions that Ms. Jones could take and be prepared to defend your recommendations to your classmates.

Communication 19-4. Basic Research Skills *(L.O. 6)*

Measuring worker performance is an ongoing activity in most businesses. Performance can be measured by (1) comparing actual versus standard times or number of units of output, (2) generating computer printouts of output records and comparing daily or weekly figures, using industry averages as targets or goals, (3) studying the time it takes a worker to perform a particular task, and (4) observing the productive effort of various individuals and comparing their techniques and results. Observation is an important performance evaluation skill. Your assignment is to go to a large grocery store on a Saturday or Sunday when traffic is the heaviest and observe the check-out clerks in action. Determine which one is the most efficient and which is the slowest. Also identify the reasons for the one being efficient and the other having low productivity. Take notes of your observations and be prepared to report your findings to the class.

Classroom Exercises

Exercise 19-1. Responsibility Accounting/ Organization Chart
(L.O. 1)

Painted Desert Tennis and Golf Resort is in Prescott, Arizona, at the foothills of the San Francisco Peaks. Management has just hired your accounting firm to create and install a responsibility accounting system for reporting and performance evaluation purposes. Painted Desert has two eighteen-hole golf courses, twenty-four lighted tennis courts, and a 450-room lodge.

The following managerial positions are to be included in your analysis:

Manager, golf course maintenance
Manager, customer relations
Manager, collections, payables, and billings
Manager, building maintenance
Vice president, accounting and finance
Manager, resort reservations
Manager, resort grounds maintenance
Vice president, resort occupancy
President and chair of the board
Manager, tennis court maintenance
Manager, room cleaning/customer services
Manager, tennis and golf activities
Vice president, building and grounds
Manager, cash management
Manager, discount convention sales
Manager, budgeting and reporting

Use these managerial positions to prepare an organization chart for use in developing a responsibility accounting system.

Exercise 19-2. Responsibility Accounting/ Organizational Structure
(L.O. 1, 2)

The Simmons Company uses the following job titles:

Purchasing agent
Vice president, sales
Production supervisor
Controller
Cashier
President
Vice president, manufacturing
Sales manager
Vice president, administration
Treasurer
Personnel manager
Engineering research manager
Marketing manager
Warehouse manager
Supervisor, repairs and maintenance

1. Design an organization chart using these job titles.
2. For each job title, list some possible costs for which the person holding that position would be responsible.

Exercise 19-3. Controllable Versus Uncontrollable Costs
(L.O. 2, 3)

For each of the following costs, state whether it is controllable or uncontrollable for a supervisor of (1) a profit center and (2) an investment center:

Cost of goods purchased, Shoe Department
Electricity costs, allocated using an overhead application rate
Depreciation, store equipment

Insurance expense, fire insurance on equipment
Buyer's salary, Home Appliance Department
Advertising expense, Video & Sound Department
President's salary, manufacturing company
Automobile and truck repair costs, Electrical Department
Contribution to local university, Garden Tools Department
Building repair costs, Reupholstering Department

Exercise 19-4.
Identification of Controllable Costs
(L.O. 2)

Gent Corporation produces computer equipment. Production has a three-tier management structure as follows:

Vice president, production
↖ Plant superintendent
↖ Production supervisors

Various production costs are accounted for each period. Examples include:

Repair and maintenance costs
Material handling costs
Direct labor
Supervisors' salaries
Plant maintenance of grounds
Depreciation, equipment
Superintendent's salary
Materials usage costs
Storage, finished goods inventory
Property taxes, plant
Depreciation, plant

1. Identify each cost item as a variable or fixed cost.
2. Identify the manager responsible for each cost.

Exercise 19-5.
Behavioral Considerations
(L.O. 4)

An effective budget often serves as a blueprint of management's operating plans, converting management's objectives and goals into data. A budget is frequently the basis of control. Management's performance can be evaluated by comparing actual results with budgeted results.

Thus, creating the budget is essential to the success of an organization. Implementing the budget and getting to the ultimate goal require extensive use of human resources. How the people involved perceive their roles is important if the budget is to be used effectively as a management tool for planning, communicating, and controlling.

Discuss the behavioral implications of budgetary planning and control when a company's management uses

1. an imposed budgetary approach.
2. a participative budgetary approach.

(ICMA adapted)

Exercise 19-6.
Performance Report: Cost /Expense Center
(Extension of Exercise 19-1.)
(L.O. 2, 6)

The Painted Desert Tennis and Golf Resort, described in Exercise 19-1, has now been divided into responsibility centers. Mr. Thomas Gregor is manager of golf course maintenance, which has been designated as a cost/expense center. During February the following costs, shown with their respective budgeted amounts on page 782, were incurred:

Painted Desert Tennis and Golf Resort
Golf Course Maintenance
Operating Report
For the Month Ended February 28, 19x4

Supervisor: T. Gregor	Budgeted	Actual
Maintenance labor	$ 6,900	$ 7,400
Depreciation, equipment	4,200	4,500
Fuel and equipment repairs	3,650	3,400
Supervisors' salaries	2,700	2,700
Maintenance supplies	1,250	1,010
Sod and grass seed	3,900	4,140
Employee benefits	2,100	2,240
Resort overhead	6,000	6,790
Upkeep of storage sheds	1,600	1,440
Vandalism insurance	950	990
Depreciation, resort buildings	5,200	5,600
Small tools	2,400	2,260
Fertilizer and insect control powders	5,000	4,670
New trees and shrubs	2,000	2,940
Water	2,600	2,180
Sprinkler system, parts and repairs	1,800	1,260
Totals	$52,250	$53,520

Prepare a performance report for Mr. Gregor for February. Use a responsibility accounting format.

Exercise 19-7.
Performance Report: Profit Center
(L.O. 2, 6)

Surault Dry Goods, Ltd. is a worldwide merchandising concern with headquarters in Munich, Germany. Surault's store in Palm Beach, Florida is installing a responsibility accounting reporting system. Following is a summary of the Cosmetics Department's revenues and expenses for April:

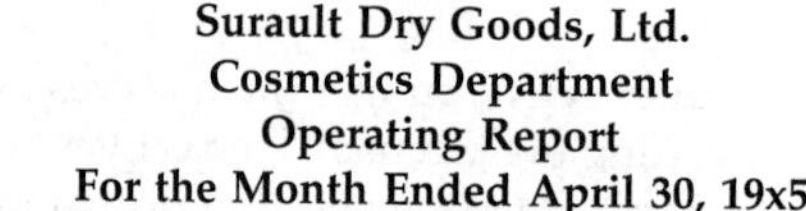

Surault Dry Goods, Ltd.
Cosmetics Department
Operating Report
For the Month Ended April 30, 19x5

Supervisor: J. Heaton	Budgeted	Actual
Sales, women's cosmetics	$67,600	$69,100
Sales, men's cosmetics	22,700	25,200
Total sales	$90,300	$94,300
Cost of goods sold, women's cosmetics	$46,000	$49,600
Cost of goods sold, men's cosmetics	14,700	16,740
Selling commissions	5,200	5,325
Buyer's salary	2,000	2,100
Supervisor's salary	2,400	2,400
Advertising	8,100	8,650
Depreciation, building	1,400	1,600
Depreciation, furniture and fixtures	800	950
Fire insurance	250	250
Travel expenses of buyer	1,640	2,110
Local store overhead charges	4,200	5,400
Total costs	$86,690	$95,125
Net income (loss) before taxes	$ 3,610	$ (825)

Assuming the Cosmetics Department is a profit center, prepare a performance report, in income statement format, for the department manager, Mr. Heaton.

Exercise 19-8. Evaluating Performance: Investment Center *(L.O. 6)*

Operating results of the Boating Accessories Department of Arohuse Industries for January 19x4 are shown below.

Arohuse Industries
Boating Accessories Department
Performance Report
For the Month Ended January 31, 19x4

Supervisor: L. Connelly Investment Base: $883,500	Budgeted	Actual	Difference Over (Under) Budget
Costs Controllable by Supervisor			
Sales			
Boat motors	$ 62,400	$ 66,340	$ 3,940
Water-sports equipment	36,500	31,890	(4,610)
Boat-repair parts	28,200	26,430	(1,770)
Total sales	$127,100	$124,660	$(2,440)
Cost of goods sold			
Boat motors	$ 46,680	$ 44,640	$(2,040)
Water-sports equipment	21,900	19,220	(2,680)
Boat-repair parts	24,560	25,690	1,130
Total cost of goods sold	$ 93,140	$ 89,550	$(3,590)
Gross margin from sales	$ 33,960	$ 35,110	$ 1,150
Less operating costs			
Heating and electricity	$ 2,460	$ 2,660	$ 200
Depreciation, building	1,980	2,240	260
Fire insurance, building	450	450	—
Employee fringe benefits	2,130	2,350	220
Supervisors' costs	3,600	3,850	250
Storewide overhead costs	2,880	3,260	380
Department overhead costs	1,920	1,430	(490)
Other operating costs	870	240	(630)
Total operating costs	$ 16,290	$ 16,480	$ 190
Controllable department income	$ 17,670	$ 18,630	$ 960
Controllable department return on investment	2.00%	2.11%	0.11%
Costs Uncontrollable by Supervisor			
Depreciation, equipment	$ 3,800	$ 3,800	—
Selling commissions	8,787	8,079	$ (708)
Repair labor	5,060	5,510	450
Total uncontrollable operating costs	$ 17,647	$ 17,389	$ (258)
Net department income before taxes	$ 23	$ 1,241	$ 1,218

Analyze this performance report. State your opinion of Ms. Connelly's performance. Was her performance report structured properly? If not, how should it have looked? As part of your analysis, prepare a gross margin report for the three sales categories.

Interpretation Case from Business

Wisconsin Produce Company
(L.O. 2, 6)

The Packing and Storage Department at Wisconsin Produce Company is run by Amy Malott. A responsibility accounting system was recently installed. A performance report is prepared monthly for each of the company's cost centers. Look at Ms. Malott's performance report for May. Top management notices that the $2,935 is 7.43 percent over budget, far above the 4 percent tolerance agreed on. Amounts allocated to the Packing and Storage Department were figured by means of appropriate allocation bases.

Wisconsin Produce Company
Packing and Storage Department
Performance Report
For the Month Ended May 31, 19x4

Supervisor: A. Malott	Budgeted	Actual	Difference Over (Under) Budget
Packing materials	$ 4,500	$ 4,600	$ 100
Packing supplies	1,800	1,700	(100)
Wages, packing	8,240	8,110	(130)
Wages, storage	6,680	6,820	140
Salaries, packing and storage	4,500	4,500	—
Salaries, vice president's staff	1,600	3,100	1,500
Depreciation, packing machinery	1,840	1,820	(20)
Depreciation, storage warehouse	3,200	3,200	—
Depreciation, companywide office building	1,250	2,500	1,250
Electric power, packing and storage	1,370	1,410	40
Electric power, main office	490	580	90
Heating, packing and storage	1,075	1,100	25
Heating, main office	380	420	40
Equipment rental, packing	780	750	(30)
Equipment rental, main office	410	450	40
Insurance, packing and storage	290	290	—
Insurance, total company	160	180	20
Equipment maintenance expense, packing and storage	460	440	(20)
Lift truck, packing and storage	220	200	(20)
Miscellaneous	250	260	10
	$39,495	$42,430	$2,935

Required

1. Using the concept of controllable costs, identify the costs that should not be in Ms. Malott's performance report.
2. Recast the performance report, using only those costs controllable by the department's supervisor.
3. How should Ms. Malott respond to top management?

Problem Set A

Problem 19A-1. Allocation and Responsibility of Overhead *(L.O. 2, 6)*

Paquette Manufacturing Company operates as a decentralized enterprise. There are seven responsibility centers in the factory area: molding, finishing, storage, receiving, shipping, scheduling, and inspection. During February, the Factory Overhead account was charged with $753,900 of indirect management-related expenses. Management wants these costs allocated to responsibility centers. It is considering three allocation bases: square footage, total costs incurred, and labor hours. The following information was provided to support the allocation analysis:

Department	Square Footage	Total Costs Incurred	Labor Hours
Molding	7,000	$ 435,060	1,024
Finishing	5,250	188,526	3,840
Storage	8,750	72,510	896
Receiving	3,150	145,020	2,304
Shipping	1,750	217,530	1,536
Scheduling	3,500	101,514	640
Inspection	5,600	290,040	2,560
Totals	35,000	$1,450,200	12,800

Required

1. Allocate the balance in the Factory Overhead account to the seven departments, using as a basis (a) square footage, (b) total costs incurred, and (c) labor hours.
2. For performance evaluation, which of the factory overhead distributions computed in 1 leads to the most effective control of costs? Defend your answer.

Problem 19A-2. Cost/Expense Centers: Performance Evaluation *(L.O. 2, 6)*

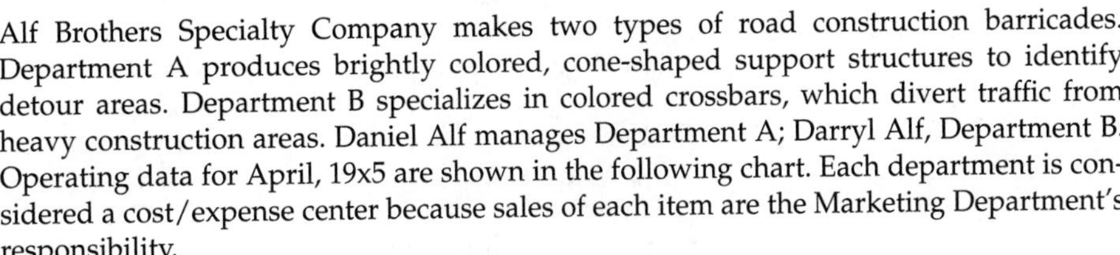

Alf Brothers Specialty Company makes two types of road construction barricades. Department A produces brightly colored, cone-shaped support structures to identify detour areas. Department B specializes in colored crossbars, which divert traffic from heavy construction areas. Daniel Alf manages Department A; Darryl Alf, Department B. Operating data for April, 19x5 are shown in the following chart. Each department is considered a cost/expense center because sales of each item are the Marketing Department's responsibility.

	Department A		Department B	
	Budgeted	Actual	Budgeted	Actual
Direct materials	$ 44,200	$ 46,100	$ 55,000	$ 54,100
Direct labor	14,100	15,400	11,000	10,200
Factory overhead				
Indirect labor	11,000	12,050	14,600	14,250
Supplies	3,400	3,520	6,400	6,650
Depreciation, building	2,100	2,350	2,700	2,800
Depreciation, equipment	3,600	3,900	3,700	4,200
Property taxes, factory	750	810	850	930
Electricity	1,340	1,360	1,480	1,400
Repairs, machinery	1,600	1,450	1,800	1,900
Insurance, building	900	1,020	950	1,100
Advertising	1,500	2,100	2,000	2,200
Packaging costs	6,400	6,600	7,100	6,940
Departmental supervision	5,900	6,100	5,900	6,240
General and administrative overhead	8,200	12,500	9,100	13,200
Interest, corporate loans	960	1,210	1,080	1,340
Total costs	$105,950	$116,470	$123,660	$127,450
Units of output	8,794	9,310	12,910	12,630

Required

1. Prepare a performance report for each of the two departments. Assume the company employs a responsibility accounting system.
2. Evaluate the performance of the two managers, using data provided in **1** above.

Problem 19A-3.
Profit Centers: Performance Evaluation
(L.O. 2, 6)

Kelliher & Roush, a national men's clothing chain, has two stores in the western United States. Charlie is the manager of the Las Vegas store; Pamela, the San Jose store. The general ledger for the western states branch revealed the data shown below for April 1–June 30, 19x5.

Kelliher & Roush
Operating Data
For the Quarter Ended June 30, 19x5

	Budgeted		Actual	
	Debit	**Credit**	**Debit**	**Credit**
Shoe sales				
Las Vegas store		$116,500		$114,100
San Jose store		112,900		116,750
Clothing sales				
Las Vegas store		296,000		286,900
San Jose store		255,000		266,200
Cost of goods sold, shoes				
Las Vegas store	$ 46,000		$ 45,940	
San Jose store	49,900		51,230	
Cost of goods sold, clothing				
Las Vegas store	272,800		269,790	
San Jose store	234,750		239,160	
Salaries and selling commissions	74,824		76,137	
Depreciation, store fixtures				
Las Vegas store	15,200		15,400	
San Jose store	12,400		12,400	
Depreciation, buildings				
Las Vegas store	8,100		8,300	
San Jose store	6,700		6,900	
Utilities	9,340		9,540	
Advertising	13,000		15,790	
Miscellaneous selling	4,660		4,679	
Insurance	2,400		2,600	
Corporate administrative salaries	12,500		14,600	
Interest, corporate loans	5,200		5,600	
Totals	$767,774	$780,400	$778,066	$783,950

Charlie and Pamela are responsible for store revenues and specific store expenditures. They do not make decisions about the buildings or fixtures. Corporate expenses are allocated to the stores by the company's home office.

Salaries of $14,500 and $13,500 were budgeted for the Las Vegas and San Jose stores, respectively. Actual costs for salaries for the three-month period were $16,200 in Las Vegas and $12,900 in San Jose.

Selling commissions were 6 percent of total sales dollars in both stores for budgeted and actual sales as shown below.

	Budgeted	Actual
Las Vegas store	$24,750	$24,060
San Jose store	$22,074	$22,977

Utilities costs were:

	Budgeted	Actual
Las Vegas store	$ 5,240	$ 5,600
San Jose store	$ 4,100	$ 3,940

Advertising costs were:

	Budgeted	Actual
Las Vegas store	$ 7,400	$ 9,640
San Jose store	$ 5,600	$6,150

Miscellaneous selling costs were:

	Budgeted	Actual
Las Vegas store	$ 2,520	$ 2,454
San Jose store	$ 2,140	$ 2,225

All insurance costs are assigned to the Las Vegas and San Jose stores on a 70 percent/30 percent basis, respectively.

All salaries and costs for corporate administration, including interest, are assigned to the Las Vegas and San Jose stores on a 60 percent/40 percent basis, respectively.

Required

1. Prepare a performance report for the quarter ended June 30, 19x5, using a responsibility accounting format for the Las Vegas store.
2. Prepare a performance report for the quarter ended June 30, 19x5, using a responsibility accounting format for the San Jose store.
3. Compare the performances of Charlie and Pamela. As part of your report, prepare a gross margin analysis for each product line.

Problem 19A-4. Performance Evaluation: Centralized Versus Decentralized Organization in an Investment Center
(L.O. 2, 4, 5, 6)

Union Leather Processors, Inc. has twelve processing plants throughout the country. Its home office is in St. Louis, Missouri. The corporation's operations are centralized, with each plant targeting operations to the goals and budgets set by the home office. The targeted rate of return on investment is 12 percent before taxes for each plant.

Two plants being investigated for low operating results are in Wisconsin, one in Oshkosh, the other just outside Milwaukee. The plant in Oshkosh specializes in leather accessories and is managed by Bill Zorr. Leather clothing is produced at the Milwaukee plant, which is managed by Carol Olson.

Leather goods are purchased centrally in raw finished form and shipped to each plant in bulk shipping cases. Each plant then cleans, shapes, and packages the goods for shipment to customers. Sales are made by salespeople connected with each plant, but advertising decisions and expenditures are made by the home office. All decisions on purchasing equipment and building space as well as truck fleet rental are made in St. Louis. Operating losses of other plants and general and administrative corporate expenses are allocated to each plant.

The performance report for the year ended May 31, 19x6 is shown on the top of page 788.

Union Leather Processors, Inc.
Performance Report
For the Year Ended May 31, 19x6

	Leather Accessories Plant		Leather Clothing Plant	
	Budgeted	**Actual**	**Budgeted**	**Actual**
Sales				
Accessories	$1,450,000	$1,510,700	—	—
Clothing	—	—	$2,650,000	$3,142,000
Miscellaneous	150,000	189,400	250,000	310,290
Total sales	$1,600,000	$1,700,100	$2,900,000	$3,452,290
Cost of materials:				
Accessories	$ 560,000	$ 649,400	—	—
Clothing	—	—	$1,237,500	$1,552,900
Miscellaneous	95,000	105,760	140,000	183,400
Cleaning and shaping labor	184,500	192,400	265,000	291,700
Outside contractual services	62,000	57,100	115,000	122,800
Corporate buyer's costs	116,600	146,250	235,000	292,100
Special packaging costs	86,200	90,700	190,000	201,040
Depreciation, equipment	32,700	35,100	52,500	52,500
Depreciation, building	26,900	27,900	44,800	51,640
Utilities	12,870	14,230	22,600	23,770
Telephone	3,200	3,470	5,400	5,880
Delivery trucks, fuel	4,250	4,510	7,500	7,390
Delivery trucks, repairs	3,900	4,110	5,800	5,410
Truck rental	10,400	10,400	24,600	28,800
Property taxes, sales equipment	7,500	9,100	4,200	3,810
Fire and liability insurance, sales	2,400	2,600	3,900	3,950
Sales commissions	66,000	74,000	124,000	146,090
Other selling costs	22,200	23,840	41,300	40,240
Advertising	49,300	67,400	84,200	102,720
Loss, Portland, Oregon plant	16,100	17,900	16,100	17,900
Plantwide overhead, factory	14,900	13,600	26,700	25,160
Corporate general and administrative costs	42,500	51,400	81,600	97,270
Total	$1,419,420	$1,601,170	$2,727,700	$3,256,470
Plant net income before taxes	$ 180,580	$ 98,930	$ 172,300	$ 195,820
Investment base	$1,588,160	$1,588,160	$2,075,830	$2,075,830
Plant return on investment	11.37%	6.23%	8.30%	9.43%

Required

1. Identify the problems inherent in the organizational structure Union Leather Processors, Inc. uses. Also identify the behavioral and operational performance evaluation principles Union is not following.
2. Recast the information given into a performance evaluation summary. Assume that Union's organizational structure is decentralized and that it uses a responsibility accounting reporting format. Also assume that everything except buyer's expenses and other corporate allocations is under the control of each manager.
3. Compute the rates of return for each plant, using the data generated in **2.**

Problem 19A-5.
Performance Evaluation
(L.O. 2, 3, 6)

Kris Kaisler was hired on July 1, 19x3 as assistant general manager of the Oviedo Division of Eubanks, Inc. Besides becoming acquainted with the division and the general manager's duties, Ms. Kaisler was given specific responsibility for developing the 19×4 and 19×5 budgets. When she was hired, it was understood that she would be elevated to general manager of the division on January 1, 19x5, when the current general manager retired. This was done. As general manager in 19×5, she was obviously responsible for the 19×6 budget.

Eubanks, Inc. is a multiproduct company that is highly decentralized. Each division is autonomous. The corporate staff approves operating budgets prepared by the divisions but seldom makes major changes in them. The corporate staff actively participates in decisions requiring capital investment for expansion or replacement and makes final decisions. Divisional management is responsible for implementing the capital investment program. The major method Eubanks, Inc. uses to measure divisional performance is contribution return on a division's net investments. The budgets below were approved by the corporation. (Revision of the 19×6 budget is considered unnecessary even though 19×5 actual data departed from the 19×5 budgeted.)

Eubanks, Inc.
Comparative Profit Report ($000 Omitted)

	Actual			Budgeted	
Oviedo Division	**19x3**	**19x4**	**19x5**	**19x5**	**19x6**
Sales	$1,000	$1,500	$1,800	$2,000	$2,400
Less:					
Divisional variable costs					
Materials and labor	$ 250	$ 375	$ 450	$ 500	$ 600
Repairs	50	75	50	100	120
Supplies	20	30	36	40	48
Less:					
Division-managed costs					
Employee training	30	35	25	40	45
Maintenance	50	55	40	60	70
Less:					
Division-committed costs					
Depreciation	120	160	160	200	200
Rent	80	100	110	140	140
Total	$ 600	$ 830	$ 871	$1,080	$1,223
Divisional net contribution	$ 400	$ 670	$ 929	$ 920	$1,177
Divisional investment					
Accounts receivable	$ 100	$ 150	$ 180	$ 200	$ 240
Inventory	200	300	270	400	480
Fixed assets	1,590	2,565	2,800	3,380	4,000
Less:					
Accounts and wages payable	(150)	(225)	(350)	(300)	(360)
Net investment	$1,740	$2,790	$2,900	$3,680	$4,360
Contribution return on net investment	23%	24%	32%	25%	27%

Required

1. Identify Ms. Kaisler's responsibilities under the management and measurement program described above.
2. Evaluate Ms. Kaisler's performance in 19x5.
3. Recommend to the president any changes in the responsibilities assigned to managers or the measurement methods used to evaluate division managers. (ICMA adapted)

Problem Set B

Problem 19B-1. Allocation and Responsibility of Overhead
(L.O. 2, 6)

A division of Rigat Enterprises makes special-order horse saddles for customers in the Southeast. Seven responsibility centers are used to manage the production operation: cutting, trimming, inspection, packing, storage/shipping, central receiving, and scheduling. Management has asked you to make a comparative analysis of the allocation methods used to assign corporate overhead costs to these centers. The following data were developed for your use:

Department	Total Costs Incurred	Labor Hours	Labor Dollars
Cutting	$ 385,308	3,360	$ 46,080
Trimming	535,150	3,120	37,440
Inspection	214,060	2,400	31,680
Packing	149,842	840	11,520
Storage/Shipping	428,120	1,080	8,640
Central Receiving	321,090	720	5,760
Scheduling	107,030	480	2,880
Totals	$2,140,600	12,000	$144,000

During July, $248,600 in corporate overhead was assigned to the Saddle Production Division for distribution to the responsibility centers.

Required

1. Allocate the balance of corporate overhead charges to the seven departments, using as a basis (a) total costs incurred, (b) labor hours, and (c) labor dollars.
2. For performance evaluation, which of the overhead distributions computed in **1** above most effectively controls costs? Defend your answer.

Problem 19B-2. Cost/Expense Center: Performance Evaluation
(L.O. 2, 6)

The city of Lyon has hired you as a consultant. Your job is to evaluate the performance of the city's Street Maintenance Department. Ms. Raphaelle Martin is the department's supervisor. To assist you in your analysis, similar costs for the Street Maintenance Department of the city of Cahors have been assembled. These data for May, 19x4 are as shown at the top of page 791.

Required

1. Prepare a performance report for each of the two departments. Assume the two cities employ responsibility accounting systems. Compute the average controllable cost per completed job as part of your analysis.
2. Evaluate Ms. Martin's performance using data provided from **1** above.

	City of Lyon Street Maintenance Department		City of Cahors Street Maintenance Department	
	Budgeted	Actual	Budgeted	Actual
Materials				
Concrete	$ 70,400	$ 68,100	$ 49,500	$ 54,600
Bedrock	42,900	38,990	32,000	34,280
Asphalt	294,800	281,420	146,100	159,200
Labor				
Heavy construction	116,740	118,410	62,400	64,100
Light construction	72,220	73,930	41,000	41,940
Overhead				
Helper labor	105,200	110,560	62,900	64,110
Equipment repairs	8,400	8,820	5,150	5,020
Vehicle repairs	4,210	4,470	2,050	2,000
Fuel cost	7,240	7,810	4,940	5,090
Depreciation, equipment	10,100	10,800	6,200	6,200
Depreciation, vehicles	16,000	18,450	10,000	12,200
Liability insurance	3,040	3,240	2,400	2,600
Operating supplies	3,210	3,620	1,800	1,890
Electricity cost	1,740	2,110	910	940
Construction-site offices	5,940	5,910	2,900	3,140
Supervision	10,280	10,280	7,100	7,310
City overhead charges	12,980	13,800	8,200	8,860
Mayor's election activities	4,200	4,400	2,600	3,600
City council charges	7,900	8,800	4,200	5,190
Total costs	$797,500	$793,920	$452,350	$482,270
Number of road repair requests honored	20	22	25	27

Problem 19B-3. Profit Centers: Performance Evaluation
(L.O. 2, 6)

Doug Schiff and Tasha Wolford manage the PM and PW branches of Sanford Appliances, Inc., respectively. All goods sold by these stores fall into two groups: white goods and brown goods. White goods include refrigerators, freezers, washing machines, and clothes dryers; brown goods include televisions, radios, and stereos. The general ledger for Sanford Appliances, Inc. for February revealed the information shown in the exhibit at the bottom of page 792.

Schiff and Wolford are responsible for store profits based on each store's sales and expenditures, which are made and approved by each manager. Neither manager makes decisions concerning fixture purchases, but both are responsible for store rent. Corporate expenses are allocated to each store from the corporation's home office.

Salaries of $8,200 and $9,600 were budgeted for the PM and PW stores, respectively. Actual salaries were $8,450 for PM and $10,410 for PW.

Selling commissions of 8 percent of sales were as follows:

	Budgeted	Actual
PM store	$17,088	$18,863
PW store	$21,984	$21,181

Utilities costs were:

	Budgeted	Actual
PM store	$ 1,640	$ 1,750
PW store	$ 1,990	$ 2,110

Advertising costs were:

	Budgeted	Actual
PM store	$6,200	$6,450
PW store	7,800	9,610

Insurance costs were assigned to the PM and PW stores on a 35 percent/65 percent basis, respectively.

Rent costs were:

	Budgeted	Actual
PM store	$3,200	$3,200
PW store	4,500	4,800

Miscellaneous selling costs were:

	Budgeted	Actual
PM store	$1,690	$1,870
PW store	2,180	2,100

Corporate administrative salaries and interest costs were assigned to the PM and PW stores on a 40 percent/60 percent basis, respectively.

Sanford Appliances, Inc.
Operating Data
For the Month Ended February 28, 19x5

	Budgeted		Actual	
	Debit	Credit	Debit	Credit
Sales, white goods				
PM store		$117,400		$128,550
PW store		144,100		138,640
Sales, brown goods				
PM store		96,200		107,240
PW store		130,700		126,120
Cost of goods sold, white goods				
PM store	$ 58,970		$ 64,560	
PW store	73,655		71,650	
Cost of goods sold, brown goods				
PM store	61,720		66,940	
PW store	82,420		80,880	
Salaries and selling commissions	56,872		58,904	
Utilities	3,630		3,860	
Advertising	14,000		16,060	
Insurance	2,400		2,600	
Depreciation, fixtures				
PM store	5,900		6,100	
PW store	8,200		9,980	
Rent	7,700		8,000	
Miscellaneous selling	3,870		3,970	
Corporate administrative salaries	8,400		8,600	
Interest, corporate loans	2,500		2,900	
Totals	$390,237	$488,400	$405,004	$500,550

Required

1. Prepare a monthly performance report, based on a responsibility accounting format, for the PM store.

2. Prepare a monthly performance report, based on a responsibility accounting format, for the PW store.
3. For your report, compare Mr. Schiff's and Ms. Wolford's performances. Include a gross margin analysis of white goods and brown goods.

Problem 19B-4. Investment Center Performance Evaluation: Centralized Versus Decentralized Organization
(L.O. 2, 4, 5, 6)

Harris Motors, Inc. is a retail automobile sales company with eight divisions in the South and Midwest. The company specializes in automobiles manufactured in Sweden and England. Organizationally, the company is operated in a centralized fashion. Each division patterns its budgets to the goals and targets set by the home office in Lake Mary, Florida. Top management has said that it expects a 14 percent rate of return on investment for the current quarter.

Two of the eight divisions have not been operating at the expected level. The troubled operations are in Atlanta, Georgia and Lexington, Kentucky. Atlanta is managed by Rob Brian; Lexington, by Doug White. The performance report for the two divisions for the quarter ended September 30, 19x6 is below.

Harris Motors, Inc.
Performance Report
For the Quarter Ended September 30, 19x6

	Atlanta, Georgia Division		Lexington, Kentucky Division	
	Budgeted	Actual	Budgeted	Actual
Sales				
Swedish-made autos	$ 936,000	$ 914,440	$ 804,000	$ 802,390
English-made autos	736,000	802,960	552,000	662,610
Parts and repairs	125,500	136,130	98,600	101,840
Total sales	$1,797,500	$1,853,530	$1,454,600	$1,566,840
Cost of goods sold				
Swedish-made autos	$ 701,600	$ 690,440	$ 572,400	$ 561,230
English-made autos	504,800	591,960	353,600	463,740
Parts	37,650	47,560	29,580	34,660
Repair labor	43,925	49,880	34,510	37,230
Sales commissions, automobiles	141,480	145,566	113,040	129,675
Corporate buyer's costs	21,250	26,900	15,460	22,310
Utilities	4,250	4,320	3,980	3,920
Demonstration automobiles cost	2,750	3,810	3,250	3,140
Depreciation, demonstration automobiles	2,100	2,260	2,800	2,990
Depreciation, equipment	3,600	3,600	3,250	3,350
Depreciation, building	2,750	2,950	2,600	2,600
Telephone charges	1,440	1,520	1,350	1,390
Advertising	11,780	14,790	21,400	23,110
Promotion costs	8,550	9,920	10,640	9,750
Other selling costs	2,340	2,440	2,280	2,280
Property taxes	920	970	880	910
Insurance, fire and liability	790	790	640	730
Divisional overhead	4,250	4,530	5,350	5,260
Loss, Lincoln, Nebraska division	2,600	3,100	2,600	3,100
Corporate general and administrative costs	7,250	7,750	6,150	6,320
Total costs	$1,506,075	$1,615,056	$1,185,760	$1,317,695
Divisional net income before taxes	$ 291,425	$ 238,474	$ 268,840	$ 249,145
Investment base	$2,081,600	$2,081,600	$1,920,280	$1,920,280
Divisional return on investment	14.00%	11.46%	14.00%	12.97%

All automobiles are purchased by the home office and shipped to the divisions. Each division then cleans and otherwise prepares the cars for sale. Sales commissions are earned by local salespeople, but advertising and promotion costs are controlled by the home office. Central management makes all decisions concerning the purchase of equipment and buildings. Operating losses of other divisions as well as corporate general and administrative expenses are allocated to the divisions.

Required

1. What problems are inherent in the organizational structure Harris Motors, Inc. uses? In your discussion, include the behavioral and operational performance evaluation principles not being followed.
2. Recast the information given into a performance evaluation summary based on a decentralized organizational structure. Use a responsibility accounting reporting format. Assume that control is shifted to each manager for everything except buyer's expenses and other corporate allocations.
3. Compute the rates of return for each division, using the data from **2.**

Problem 19B-5. Responsibility Accounting and Budgets
(L.O. 2, 3, 4, 5)

Seminole County Hospital is located in the county seat. Seminole County is a well-known summer resort area. The county's population doubles during the vacation months of May through August, and hospital activity more than doubles. Although Seminole is a relatively small hospital, its pleasant surroundings have attracted a well-trained and competent medical staff.

An administrator was hired a year ago to improve the hospital's business activities. Among the new ideas introduced was responsibility accounting. This program was announced in a memo accompanying quarterly cost reports supplied to department heads. Previously, cost data were presented to department heads infrequently. Excerpts from the announcement and the report the laundry supervisor received follow.

Seminole County Hospital
Performance Report: Laundry Department
For the Quarter Ended September 30, 19x5

	Budget	Actual	(Over) Under Budget	Percent (Over) Under Budget
Patient days	9,500	11,900	(2,400)	(25)
Pounds processed, laundry	125,000	156,000	(31,000)	(25)
Costs				
Laundry labor	$ 9,000	$12,500	$(3,500)	(39)
Supplies	1,100	1,875	(775)	(70)
Water, water heating and softening	1,700	2,500	(800)	(47)
Maintenance	1,400	2,200	(800)	(57)
Supervisor's salary	3,150	3,750	(600)	(19)
Allocated administrative costs	4,000	5,000	(1,000)	(25)
Equipment depreciation	1,200	1,250	(50)	(4)
Totals	$21,550	$29,075	$(7,525)	(35)

Administrator's comments:
Costs are significantly above budget for the quarter. Particular attention should be paid to labor, supplies, and maintenance. The hospital has adopted a responsibility accounting system. From now on you will receive quarterly reports, which will compare the costs of operating your department with budgeted costs. The reports will highlight differences (variations) so you can focus on departures from budgeted costs. (This is called management by exception.) Responsibility accounting means you are accountable for keeping the costs in your department within budget. Variations from the budget will help you identify out-of-line costs. The size of the variation will indicate which costs are most important. Your first report accompanies this announcement.

The new administrator constructed the annual budget for 19x5. Quarterly budgets were computed as one-fourth of the annual budget. The administrator compiled the budget by analyzing costs from the prior three years. The analysis showed that all costs increased each year and that the increases were more rapid between the second and third years. The administrator considered establishing a budget according to an average of the prior three years' costs, hoping that installation of the system would reduce costs to this level. However, because of rapidly increasing prices, 19x4 costs, less 3 percent, were finally chosen for the 19x5 budget. The activity level measured by patient days and pounds of laundry processed was set at 19x4 volume, which was approximately equal to the volume in each of the past three years.

Required

1. Comment on the method used to construct the budget.
2. What information should be communicated by variations from budget?
3. Does the report effectively communicate the level of efficiency of this department? Give reasons for your answer.

Management Decision Case

Kroovand Petroleum Company
(L.O. 1, 4, 5, 6)

Kroovand Petroleum Company has a large oil and natural gas project in Florida. The project has been organized into two production centers (Petroleum Production and Natural Gas Production) and one service center (Maintenance).

Ms. Tracy, Maintenance Center manager, has organized her maintenance workers into crews that serve the two production centers. The crews perform preventive maintenance and repair equipment both in the field and in the central maintenance shop.

Tracy is responsible for scheduling all maintenance work in the field and at the central shop. Preventive maintenance is performed according to a set schedule established by Tracy and approved by production center managers. Breakdowns are given immediate priority in scheduling, so downtime is minimized. Thus, preventive maintenance must occasionally be postponed, but every attempt is made to reschedule it within three weeks. Preventive maintenance is also Tracy's responsibility. However, if a significant problem is discovered during the work, a production center supervisor authorizes and supervises the repair after checking with Tracy.

When there is a breakdown in the field, the production centers contact Tracy to initiate the repairs. The work is supervised by a production center supervisor. Machinery and equipment must sometimes be replaced while they are being repaired in the central shop. This procedure is followed only when the time to make a repair would significantly interrupt operations. Equipment replacement is recommended by the maintenance work crew supervisor and approved by a production center supervisor.

Routine preventive maintenance and breakdowns of automotive and mobile equipment used in the field are completed in the central shop. All repairs and maintenance activities in the central shop are under the direction of Tracy.

Maintenance Center Accounting Activities. Tracy has records identifying the work crews assigned to each job in the field, the number of hours spent on the job, and the parts and supplies used. In addition, records for the central shop (jobs, labor hours, and parts and supplies) have been maintained. However, this detailed maintenance information is not incorporated into Kroovand's accounting system.

Tracy develops the annual budget for the maintenance center by (1) planning the preventive maintenance needed during the year, (2) estimating the number and seriousness of breakdowns, and (3) estimating shop activities. She then estimates the labor, parts, and supply costs and develops budget amounts by line item. Because the timing of the breakdowns is impossible to plan, Tracy divides the annual budget by 12 to derive monthly budgets.

All costs incurred by work crews in the field and in the central shop are accumulated monthly and are then allocated to the two production cost centers based on the field hours worked in each production center. This method of cost allocation has been used because of Tracy's recommendation that it was easy to implement and understand. Furthermore, she believed that a better allocation system was impossible to incorporate into monthly reports because of the wide range of salaries paid to maintenance workers and the fast turnover of materials and parts.

The November cost report for the Maintenance Center, provided by the Accounting Department, is shown below.

Florida Project
Maintenance Center Cost Report
For the Month Ended November 30, 1994
(in thousands of dollars)

	Budgeted	Actual	Petroleum Production	Natural Gas Production
Shop hours	2,000	1,800	—	—
Field hours	8,000	10,000	6,000	4,000
Labor, electrical	$ 25.0	$ 24.0	$ 14.4	$ 9.6
Labor, mechanical	30.0	35.0	21.0	14.0
Labor, instrumentation	18.0	22.5	13.5	9.0
Labor, automotive	3.5	2.8	1.7	1.1
Labor, heavy equipment	9.6	12.3	7.4	4.9
Labor, equipment operation	28.8	35.4	21.2	14.2
Labor, general	15.4	15.9	9.5	6.4
Parts	60.0	86.2	51.7	34.5
Supplies	15.3	12.2	7.3	4.9
Lubricants and fuels	3.4	3.0	1.8	1.2
Tools	2.5	3.2	1.9	1.3
Accounting and data processing	1.5	1.5	.9	.6
Totals	$213.0	$254.0	$152.3	$101.7

Production Center Manager's Concerns. Both production center managers have been upset with the cost allocation method. Furthermore, they believe the report is virtually useless as a cost control device. Actual costs always seem to deviate from the monthly budget, and the proportion charged to each production center varies significantly from month to month. Maintenance costs have increased substantially since 1992, and production managers believe they have no way of judging whether such an increase is reasonable.

The two production managers, Tracy, and representatives of corporate accounting met to discuss these concerns. They concluded that a responsibility accounting system should be developed to replace the current system. In their opinion a responsibility accounting system would alleviate the production managers' concerns and accurately reflect activity in the Maintenance Center.

Required

1. Explain the purposes of a responsibility accounting system. In addition, discuss how such a system could resolve the concern of the production center managers.
2. Describe behavioral advantages generally attributed to responsibility accounting systems that management should expect if the system is effectively introduced into the Maintenance Center.

3. Describe a report format for the Maintenance Center based on an effective responsibility accounting system. Explain which, if any, of the Maintenance Center's costs should be charged to the two production centers. (ICMA adapted)

Answers to Self-Test

1. c	3 d	5. a	7. b	9. b
2. b	4. c	6. a	8. c	10. d

CHAPTER 20

The Budgeting Process

LEARNING OBJECTIVES

1. Identify the objectives underlying the creation of a budget.
2. Define the concept of budgetary control.
3. Name the five groups of budgeting principles, and explain the principles in each group.
4. Identify and explain the components of a master budget.
5. Prepare a period budget.
6. State the purposes of, and prepare, a cash budget.

Budgeting is an important process for every organization, whether it is a profit-oriented business or a not-for-profit enterprise. The budgeting process pushes managers to take time to create strategies, targets, and goals before activity begins. If realistic goals have been established, comparing the actual results with the targets can help management assess how well the organization performed. This entire program of revenue and cost planning and control activities is known as budgetary control.

In this chapter the focus is on planning. We first outline and discuss the principles of budgeting, which deal with long-range and short-range organizational goals, human responsibilities, housekeeping, and follow-up. Using these principles, together with management accounting tools explained in earlier chapters, we describe the preparation of period budgets, the master budget, and the cash budget.

The budgeting process is as important in today's globally competitive operating environment as in traditional environments. In fact, budgeting becomes even more important when just-in-time (JIT) or total quality management (TQM) techniques are applied and when computers and other electronic operating and data accumulation devices are used. In these new operating settings, actual operating data are made available quickly, and budgets must be updated continuously to accommodate management's needs for performance evaluation. The basic principles of budgeting do not change in these new environments, only the speed and timing with which they are applied. After studying this chapter, you should be able to meet the learning objectives listed on the left.

DECISION POINT

Lord Corporation[1]

■ Lord Corporation is a privately held, medium-sized manufacturing and research company located in Erie, Pennsylvania. The firm sells bonded metal parts and chemical products to equipment manufacturers in aerospace and industrial companies. Recently, the company decided to computerize its budgeting process so that its 250 budget centers (located in 8 domestic manufacturing facilities and 29 office sites) are defined according to reporting and functional responsibility. The computerized budget planning system contains many features that make the budgeting process easier to implement. Five different transaction screens are available to help each segment's budget manager in his or her budget prepara-

1. Keith C. Gourley and Thomas R. Blecki, "Computerizing Budgeting at Lord Corporation," *Management Accounting*, Institute of Management Accountants, August 1986, pp. 37–40.

tion activities and make all budgets consistent within the company. The five screens include:

1. An hourly personnel screen, which determines how many labor hours and how many personnel it will take to operate a department in the upcoming year.
2. A salaries detail screen, which presents a work sheet of all employees' pay and work classification data in each budget center.
3. A salaries summary and personnel head count screen, which displays a projection of labor cost based on extensions of information on the first two screens.
4. A budget screen by account, which contains projections of all budgeted accounts in each budget center.
5. A variable overhead rate screen, which is used to create the variable overhead budgets for each budget center.

Why would a company wish to computerize its budgeting process? What benefits and costs would be analyzed in support of such a decision process?

Speed in preparation, consistency of budget format, and reduction in errors are three primary reasons (benefits) supporting the computerization of the budgeting process. Errors made at the budget center level are compounded when combined with upper-level reporting summaries. On the cost side, the initial cost of a special computer program and hardware at all 250 budget centers was offset by the reduction in managers' time devoted to the budgeting process. With the possibility of mathematical errors eliminated, Lord Corporation found that the on-line feature of the budget system, allowing budgets prepared in outlying locations to be printed at world headquarters as soon as they were finalized, improved both the accuracy and usefulness of its planning function. ■

The Budgeting Process

Establishing an effective budgeting process is the key to a successful business venture. Without a fully coordinated budgeting system, management has only a vague idea of where the company is headed financially. An effective budgeting system can supply such information as monthly cash needs, raw materials requirements, peak labor demand seasons, and timing of capital facility expenditures. At the end of an accounting period, budgets help determine areas of strength and weakness within the company through comparisons of actual operating results with budgeted amounts. These comparisons assist managers in identifying reasons why profit expectations were or were not attained.

What Is a Budget and What Does It Look Like?

OBJECTIVE 1
Identify the objectives underlying the creation of a budget

Almost everyone uses the word *budget* as if it were a cure-all for the financial problems of an enterprise. However, a budget is simply a plan, and specific management actions are needed to make it a reality. A **budget** is a planning document created before anticipated transactions occur. Often called a plan of action, a budget can be made up of financial data, nonfinancial operating data, or a combination of both. These data are projected for a series of events that have yet to occur. The primary objective of a budget is to forecast future financial and nonfinancial transactions.

Other misconceptions about budgets are obvious in innumerable reports on television and in newspapers regarding our federal budget and deficit spending by the federal government. The cure for this deficit spending, it is said, is to "balance the budget." This statement is misleading because spending processes alone cannot be used to balance the budget. To reduce or reverse the current deficit, one must ensure that revenues are greater than expenditures. There is only one way to operate within a balanced budget, and that is by first preparing a document in which planned revenues equal planned expenditures and then by operating within these constraints.

A budget can have an infinite number of shapes and forms. The structure depends on what is being budgeted, the size of the organization, the degree to which the budgeting process is integrated into the financial structure of the enterprise, and the preparer's background. Unlike the formal income statement or the balance sheet, a budget does *not* have a standard form that can be memorized. A budget can be as simple as the projected sales and costs of a corner soft drink stand or as complicated as the financial projections of Exxon Corporation or Ford Motor Company.

The actual format of the budget is developed by the budget preparer. A company may develop its own format for budgets used on a regular basis. But if a new product or service requires budget information, the document need not follow the structure or format of other budgets.

The second objective of a budget is that the information should be as accurate and as meaningful to the recipient as possible. To meet this objective, a budget should present information in an orderly manner. Too much information clouds the meaning and accuracy of the data. Too little information may result in over- or underspending because the reader did not understand the limits suggested by the document. A budget need not contain both revenues and expenses, nor does it have to be balanced. A materials purchase/usage budget, for example, contains only projected expenditures for raw materials and parts. A budget can also be made up entirely of nonfinancial data, such as hours or number of services.

Exhibit 20-1 contains two simple budgets prepared for diverse purposes. Example 1 shows the revenues and expenditures budget for a homecoming football celebration; Example 2 contains projections of hotel occupancy for a resort. Note that in Example 2, the budget contains no dollar information and is not balanced.

The examples in Exhibit 20-1 are for illustrative purposes only and should not be considered official guidelines. Common sense, however, suggests two very basic rules to follow when presenting a budget. First, make sure you begin the document with a clearly stated title or heading that includes the time period under consideration. Second, label the budget's components, and list the unit and financial data in an orderly manner.

The Need for Budgetary Control

OBJECTIVE 2
Define the concept of budgetary control

Planning and control of operations and related resources and their costs are the keys to good management. Profit planning is important to all successful profit-oriented companies as part of the budgeting program. The process of developing plans for a company's expected operations and controlling operations to help carry out those plans is known as **budgetary control**. The objectives of budgetary control are:

1. To aid in establishing procedures for preparing a company's planned revenues and costs.

Exhibit 20-1. Examples of Budgets

Example 1

State University Titans
Alumni Club
Revenue and Expenditure Budget
Homecoming Activities—19x4

Budgeted Revenues		
Football Concession Sales	$32,500	
Homecoming Dance Tickets (1,200 at $20)	24,000	
Parking Fees	1,425	
Total Budgeted Revenues		$57,925
Budgeted Expenditures		
Dance Music Group	$ 7,500	
Hall Rental	2,000	
Refreshments	2,600	
Printing Costs	1,450	
Concession Purchases	12,200	
Clean-up Costs	4,720	
Miscellaneous	800	
Total Budgeted Expenditures		31,270
Excess of Revenues Over Expenditures*		$26,655

*To be contributed to State University's Scholarship Fund.

Example 2

Albuquerque Resort
Room Occupancy Budget
For the Year Ending December 31, 19x5

	Projected Occupancy							
	Singles (50)		Doubles (80)		Mini Suites (10)		Luxury Suites (6)	
Month	Rooms	%	Rooms	%	Rooms	%	Rooms	%
January	20	40.0	30	37.5	2	20.0	1	16.7
February	24	48.0	36	45.0	3	30.0	1	16.7
March	28	56.0	42	52.5	4	40.0	2	33.3
April	32	64.0	50	62.5	5	50.0	2	33.3
May	44	88.0	60	75.0	6	60.0	2	33.3
June	46	92.0	74	92.5	7	70.0	3	50.0
July	50	100.0	78	97.5	9	90.0	4	66.7
August	50	100.0	80	100.0	10	100.0	5	83.3
September	48	96.0	78	97.5	10	100.0	6	100.0
October	34	68.0	60	75.0	8	80.0	5	83.3
November	30	60.0	46	57.5	2	20.0	3	50.0
December	34	68.0	50	62.5	4	40.0	4	66.7

2. To aid in coordinating and communicating these plans to various levels of management.
3. To formulate a basis for effective revenue and cost control.

In this chapter we deal mainly with the planning element.

A business does not benefit from budgetary control by operating haphazardly. The company must first set quantitative goals, define the roles of individuals, and establish operating targets. Short-term or one-year plans are generally formulated in a set of period budgets (also known as detailed operating budgets). A **period budget** is a forecast of operating results for a segment or function of a company for a specific period of time. It is a quantitative expression of planned activities and requires timely information and careful coordination. This process converts unit sales and production forecasts into revenue and cost estimates for each of the many operating segments of the company.

Preparing period budgets requires several management accounting tools that were discussed in earlier chapters. In particular, knowledge of responsibility accounting reporting systems, cost behavior patterns, and the use of cost-volume-profit analyses help management project revenues and costs for departments or products. Profit planning, in itself, is possible only after all cost behavior patterns have been identified. These tools, together with the concepts of cost allocation and cost accumulation, provide the foundation for preparing an organization's budget.

Basic Principles of Budgeting

OBJECTIVE 3
Name the five groups of budgeting principles, and explain the principles in each group

The preparation of an organization's budget is important to its success for three reasons. First, preparing a budget forces management to look ahead and plan both long-range and short-range goals and events. Second, the entire management team must work together in order to make and carry out the plans. Third, by comparing the budget with actual results, it is possible to review performance at all levels of management. Underlying the budgeting process is a set of principles, summarized in Table 20-1, that provides the foundation for an effective planning function. Each group of principles will be explained further to show its connection to the entire budgeting process.

Long-Range Goals Principles. Annual operating plans cannot be made unless those preparing the budget know the direction that top management expects for the organization. Long-range goals, projections covering a five- to ten-year period, must be set by top management. In doing so, management should consider economic and industry forecasts, employee-management relationships, and the structure and role of management in leading the organization. The long-range goals themselves should include statements about the expected quality of products or services, percentage-of-market targets, and growth rates.

Vague aims are not sufficient. The long-term goals should set actual targets and expected timetables and name those responsible for achieving the goals. For example, assume that O'Toole Corporation has, as one of its long-term goals, the control of 15 percent of its product's market. At present the company holds only 4 percent of the market. The company's long-term goals may state that the vice president of marketing is to develop plans and strategies so that the company controls 10 percent of the market in five years and increases its share to 15 percent by the end of ten years.

Once all of the organization's goals have been developed, they should be compiled in a total long-range plan. This plan should state a spectrum of targets

Table 20-1. Principles of Effective Budgeting

Group A: Long-Range Goals Principles

1. Develop long-range goals for the enterprise.
2. Convert the long-range goals into statements about plans for product lines or services offered and associated profit plans in broad quantitative terms.

Group B: Short-Range Goals and Strategies Principles

3. Restate the long-range plan in terms of short-range plans for product lines or services offered and a detailed profit plan.
4. Prepare a set of budget development plans and a specific timetable for the whole period.

Group C: Human Responsibilities and Interaction Principles

5. Identify the budget director and staff.
6. Identify all participants involved in the budget development process.
7. Practice participative budgeting.
8. Obtain the full support of top management and communicate this support to budget participants.
9. Practice full communications during the entire budgeting process.

Group D: Budget Housekeeping Principles

10. Practice realism in the preparation of budgets.
11. Require that all deadlines be met.
12. Use flexible application procedures.

Group E: Budget Follow-up Principles

13. Maintain a continuous budgeting process and monitor the budget at frequent points throughout the period.
14. Develop a system of periodic performance reports that are linked to assigned responsibilities.
15. Review problem areas before further planning takes place.

and goals, and it should give direction to the company's efforts to achieve those goals. The long-range plan should include future profit projections. It should spell out in general terms new product lines and services. Enlarging the scope of the company's marketplace may be a consideration. Specific statements about long-range goals, then, are the basis for preparing the annual budget.

Short-Range Goals and Strategies Principles. Using long-range goals, management prepares yearly operating plans and targets. The short-range plan or budget involves every part of the enterprise, and it is much more detailed than the long-range goals.

First, the long-range goals must be restated in terms of what should be accomplished during the next year. Decisions must be made about sales and profit targets by product or service line, personnel needs and expected changes, and plans for introducing new products or services. Budget statements must also cover needs for materials and supplies; labor needs; forecasts of overhead costs such as electric power, property taxes, and insurance; and all capital expenditures such as new buildings, machinery, and equipment. These short-range targets and goals form the basis for the organization's operating budget for the year.

Once management has set the short-range goals, the controller or budget director takes charge of preparing the budget. This person designs a complete set of budget development plans and a timetable with deadlines for all levels and parts of the year's operating plan. Specific people must be named to carry out each part of the budget's development and their responsibilities, targets, and deadlines must be described clearly.

Human Responsibilities and Interaction Principles. Budgeting success or failure is, in large part, determined by how well the human aspects of the process are handled. From top management down through the organization, all appropriate people must take part actively and honestly in the budgeting process. This kind of cooperation will occur only if each person realizes that he or she is important to the process. More specifically, the principles discussed below, related to responsibilities and interaction, underlie effective budgeting.

First, the selection of a budget director (and staff, if necessary) is very important to an effective budgeting system. This person must be able to communicate well with the people both above and below in the organization's hierarchy. Top management gives the budget targets and organizational goals to the budget director. He or she in turn assigns those targets and goals to managers at various levels. If the managers detect problem areas, they communicate this to the budget director, who analyzes and passes the information on to top management. The targets and goals are then reassessed, restructured, and passed back to the budget director, and the process begins all over again. In short, the budget director acts as an information-gathering center and clearing-house, coordinating all the different budgeting activities.

Second, we have mentioned that all participants in the budget development process should be identified and informed of their responsibilities. The identification process begins with high-level managers. These people must choose managers who will actually prepare the data under their supervision. Since the organization's main activities—whether they are forecasts for production, sales, health care, or employee training—take place at the lower levels, information must flow from the managers of these activities through the supervisory levels to top management. Each one of these people plays a part in developing the budget and implementing it. Effective budgeting, then, requires **participative budgeting**, which means that all levels of personnel take part in the budgeting process in a meaningful, active way. If every manager has significant input in setting the goals for his or her unit, then every manager will be personally motivated to ensure the success of the budgeting process.

Top management's role is also very important to the budgeting process. If targets and goals are simply dictated and sent down for implementation, participative budgeting is not being practiced. Such dictated targets are often difficult to attain and do not motivate lower-level managers to try to reach them. If top management lets the budget director handle all aspects of the process, others may feel that budgeting has a low priority and may not take it seriously. To have an effective budgeting program, top management must communicate its support and allow managers to play a meaningful role in the process.

Full communication throughout the budgeting process is our final interaction principle. In particular, the budget must be communicated clearly to the participants. After all, each participant in the budgeting process has another job in the organization. The production supervisor, for instance, is most interested in what is happening on the production floor, not in next year's activities. A key part of the budget director's job is fostering open communication, to make sure each participant knows what he or she is expected to do and when it must be done.

Budget Housekeeping Principles. Effective budgeting also requires good "housekeeping," which means that three guidelines should be followed. First, a realistic approach must be taken by the participants. Second, deadlines must be met. Third, the organization must use flexible procedures for implementing the budget.

Realism is a two-way street. Top management must first suggest attainable targets and goals. Then each manager must provide realistic information and not place departmental goals ahead of the goals of the whole organization. Inflated expenditure plans or deflated sales targets may make life easier for a manager's unit, but they can cause the entire budget to be inaccurate and difficult to use as a guide and control mechanism for the organization.

Deadlines are important because budget preparation depends on the timely cooperation of many people. If one or two people ignore a deadline for submitting information, the budget might not be ready on time. Management should communicate the importance of the timetable to all participants and should review timely submission of budget data as part of each manager's performance evaluation.

Our final principle of budget housekeeping calls for flexibility. Budgets should always be treated as guides and not as absolute truths. Budgets are important guides to the actions of management; but participants must remember that budgets are often prepared almost a year before the actual operating cycle. During that time, unexpected changes may take place. A manager cannot ignore these changes just because they were not a part of the original budget. Instead, dealing with changes in operating capacities, customer desires, and revenues and expenditures should be part of budget implementation. Each company should establish a procedure for notifying the budget director of a change and receiving approval for it. Through flexible implementation, a company can deal with change without disrupting performance.

Budget Follow-up Principles. Since the developing budget consists of projections and estimates, it is important that the budget be checked and corrected continuously. It makes more sense to correct an error than to work with an inaccurate guide. Budget follow-up and data feedback are part of the control aspect of budgeting and will be explained further in the chapter on standard costing and variance analysis.

Organizational or departmental expectations can also be unrealistic. Such problems are detected when performance reports compare actual results with budgeted results. These reports are the backbone of the responsibility accounting system. The budgeting cycle is completed after solutions to problems are identified from the performance reports and the data are restructured to become targets or goals of the next budgeting cycle.

The Master Budget

OBJECTIVE 4
Identify and explain the components of a master budget

A **master budget** is a set of period budgets that have been consolidated into forecasted financial statements for the entire company. Each period budget supplies the projected costs and revenues for a part of the company. When combined, these budgets show all anticipated transactions of the company for a future accounting period. With this information, the anticipated results of the company's operations can be put together with the beginning general ledger balances to prepare forecasted statements of the company's net income and financial position.

Three steps lead up to the completed master budget. They are: (1) The period budgets are prepared. (2) The forecasted income statement is prepared. (3) The forecasted balance sheet is prepared. After describing each of these components and illustrating the types of period budgets, we will show how the budgets are prepared.

Detailed Period Budgets

Period budgets generally are prepared for each departmental or functional segment that produces costs and revenues. Data usually are developed and transmitted to the budget director in departmental form; then they are consolidated into the following functional budgets: (1) sales budget (in units and dollars), (2) selling cost budget, (3) production budget (in units), (4) materials purchase/usage budget (in units and dollars), (5) labor budget (in hours and dollars), (6) factory overhead budget, (7) general and administrative (G&A) expense budget, and (8) capital expenditures budget.

Sales Budget. The unit sales forecast is the starting point of the budgeting process and probably the most critical component. The company's sales target is developed by top management with input from the marketing and production areas. This forecast provides the basis for the entire cost portion of the master budget.

A **sales budget** is a detailed plan, expressed in both units and dollars, that identifies expected product (or service) sales for a future period. A sales budget for the Jones Piano Company is shown in Exhibit 20-2. Sales information for all five piano models is stated in both units and dollar revenue amounts for the year under review. In addition, unit and dollar information for the current year is shown for comparison. Once the unit sales target has been agreed upon, all of the other period budgets can be prepared.

Selling Cost Budget. Information from the sales budget and the sales staff provides the basis for the **selling cost budget**. This budget details all anticipated costs related to the selling function of the business for a future period. Selling costs may be variable, such as sales commissions and automobile costs, or they may be fixed, such as advertising costs and supervisory salaries. The selling cost budget is the responsibility of the sales department and can be prepared as soon as the sales budget has been completed.

The selling cost budget for the Jones Piano Company is shown in Exhibit 20-3 on page 808. Two major cost categories are used: Selling Commissions; and Travel, Brochures, and Other Selling Support Materials. Every company will have its own approach to developing the selling cost budget, so understand that these cost categories could be unique to the Jones Piano Company.

Production Budget. Once the sales target in units has been established, the units needed from the production area (production budget) can be computed. The **production budget** is a detailed schedule that identifies the products or services that must be produced or provided to meet budgeted sales and inventory needs. Management must first determine if the finished goods inventory level should remain the same or be increased or decreased. The unit sales forecast, along with the desired changes in finished goods inventory, is then used to determine the unit production schedule.

Exhibit 20-4 (on page 809) illustrates the production budget for the Jones Piano Company. In addition to quarterly and annual production schedules, it shows a detailed view of the production schedules for the first three months of

Exhibit 20-2. Sales Budget

Jones Piano Company
Sales Budget
For the Year Ending December 31, 19x5

Unit Forecast:

	Year Ended 12/31/x4		Year Ending 12/31/x5	
	Units	**Selling Price**	**Units**	**Selling Price**
Piano Models:				
Model J-12	70	$1,800	75	$1,840
Model O-23	40	1,940	50	1,990
Model N-34	65	2,025	60	2,125
Model E-45	100	3,400	120	3,600
Model S-56	58	3,900	50	4,200

Projected Total Revenue:

	Actual Results for Year Ended 12/31/x4	Percent of Total Sales	Budget for Year Ending 12/31/x5	Percent of Total Sales
Piano Models:				
Model J-12	$126,000	13.98%	$ 138,000	13.71%
Model O-23	77,600	8.61%	99,500	9.88%
Model N-34	131,625	14.60%	127,500	12.66%
Model E-45	340,000	37.72%	432,000	42.90%
Model S-56	226,200	25.09%	210,000	20.85%
Totals	$901,425	100.00%	$1,007,000	100.00%

the budgeted year. For illustrative purposes, we have assumed that there were no anticipated changes in inventory levels of the five piano models.

Materials Purchase/Usage Budget. The production budget and anticipated changes in materials inventory levels determine materials usage. This information will generate the units of materials to be purchased. Multiplying the number of units to be purchased by the estimated purchase prices for those materials will yield the materials purchase budget. The statement of materials purchase and usage needs can be given in separate schedules or in the same document. We prefer to group these two categories in the same document. Thus, a **materials purchase/usage budget** is a detailed plan that identifies the number and timing of raw materials and parts to be purchased to meet production demands. (A merchandise purchasing budget is a similar document used by retail businesses.) The materials purchase/usage budget for the Jones Piano Company is developed in the illustrative problem at the end of this section.

Labor Budget. The **labor budget** identifies the labor needs for a future period and the labor costs associated with those needs. Like plans for materials purchase and usage, the forecasted labor hours and dollars can be structured in separate schedules or in one comprehensive schedule. Labor hours can be

Exhibit 20-3. Selling Cost Budget

Jones Piano Company
Selling Cost Budget
For the Year Ending December 31, 19x5

	Sales Regions				
	Western Region	**Southern Region**	**Midwestern Region**	**Eastern Region**	**Totals**
Selling Commissions:					
Piano Models:					
Model J-12	$ 1,350	$ 1,890	$ 1,430	$ 1,890	$ 6,560
Model O-23	1,450	1,420	1,360	1,130	5,360
Model N-34	1,730	1,810	1,720	1,830	7,090
Model E-45	4,380	4,580	5,700	4,910	19,570
Model S-56	5,040	3,120	3,210	3,540	14,910
Totals	$13,950	$12,820	$13,420	$13,300	$53,490
Travel, Brochures, and Other Selling Support Materials:					
Piano Models:					
Model J-12	$ 730	$ 690	$ 710	$ 780	$ 2,910
Model O-23	860	790	870	890	3,410
Model N-34	710	740	670	760	2,880
Model E-45	1,100	1,120	1,200	1,240	4,660
Model S-56	1,300	1,350	1,320	1,250	5,220
Totals	$ 4,700	$ 4,690	$ 4,770	$ 4,920	$19,080
Total Selling Cost Budget	$18,650	$17,510	$18,190	$18,220	$72,570

determined as soon as the unit production budget has been set. Multiplying labor hours needed per unit by the anticipated units of production gives the labor hour requirements for the budget period. These labor hours, when multiplied by the various hourly labor rates, yield the labor dollar budget.

As shown for the Jones Piano Company in Exhibit 20-5 on page 810, quarterly and annual data can be summarized in the labor budget. Some companies prefer to prepare a separate budget for direct labor only, and to account for indirect labor only in the factory overhead budget. Because Jones's production manager prefers to have all labor shown in the labor budget, indirect labor costs are included here as well as in the factory overhead budget.

Factory Overhead Budget. The **factory overhead budget** is a detailed schedule of anticipated manufacturing costs, other than direct materials and direct labor costs, that must be incurred to meet the production expectations of a future period. The budget for factory overhead has two purposes: (1) to integrate the overhead cost budgets developed by the managers of production and service departments; and (2) by accumulating this information, to compute factory overhead rates for the forthcoming accounting period.

The Jones Piano Company's factory overhead budget is illustrated in Exhibit 20-6 on page 811. Again, it shows quarterly as well as annual forecasts. Data from each of the three assembly operations (Sound System Assembly, Wood

Exhibit 20-4. Production Budget

Jones Piano Company
Production Budget
For the Year Ending December 31, 19x5

Production Schedule:

	First Quarter	Second Quarter	Third Quarter	Fourth Quarter	Totals
Piano Models:					
Model J-12	20	16	22	17	75
Model O-23	12	10	15	13	50
Model N-34	18	14	12	16	60
Model E-45	35	25	20	40	120
Model S-56	5	15	20	10	50
Totals	90	80	89	96	355

Detailed Production Schedule for First Quarter:

	January 19x5	February 19x5	March 19x5	Total Production for Quarter
Piano Models:				
Model J-12	6	9	5	20
Model O-23	4	6	2	12
Model N-34	9	5	4	18
Model E-45	15	8	12	35
Model S-56	2	2	1	5
Totals	36	30	24	90

Cabinet Assembly, and Total Piano Assembly) are grouped together within the budget shown. A more detailed breakdown of this information may be needed to help control costs and can be supplied later.

General and Administrative Expense Budget. A **general and administrative (G&A) expense budget** is a detailed plan of operating expenses, other than those of the manufacturing and selling functions, needed to support the overall operations of the business for a future period. In preparing a master budget, general and administrative expenses must be projected to provide information included in the cash budget (which is discussed later in this chapter). The G&A expense budget also serves as a means of controlling these costs. Many elements of this budget are fixed costs.

Capital Expenditures Budget. A **capital expenditures budget** is a detailed plan outlining the amount and timing of anticipated capital expenditures for a future period. Information regarding capital facility investment influences the cash budget, the interest expense on the forecasted income statement, and the plant and equipment account balances on the forecasted balance sheet. Therefore, these decisions must be anticipated and integrated into the master budget.

Exhibit 20-5. Labor Budget

Jones Piano Company
Labor Budget
For the Year Ending December 31, 19x5

Direct Labor Hours and Rate Schedule:

	Sound System Assembly		Wood Cabinet Assembly		Total Piano Assembly	
	Hours per Unit	**Rate**	**Hours per Unit**	**Rate**	**Hours per Unit**	**Rate**
Piano Models:						
Model J-12	5.6	$10.30	5.8	$11.50	12.8	$12.40
Model O-23	6.2	10.30	6.0	11.50	13.6	12.40
Model N-34	6.6	10.30	6.2	11.50	14.4	12.40
Model E-45	8.2	10.30	7.4	11.50	22.4	12.40
Model S-56	9.4	10.30	9.2	11.50	28.6	12.40

Direct Labor Budget:

	First Quarter	**Second Quarter**	**Third Quarter**	**Fourth Quarter**	**Total Direct Labor Budget**
Piano Models.*					
Model J-12	$ 5,662	$ 4,530	$ 6,228	$ 4,813	$ 21,233
Model O-23	3,618	3,015	4,522	3,919	15,074
Model N-34	5,721	4,450	3,814	5,085	19,070
Model E-45	15,656	11,183	8,946	17,893	53,678
Model S-56	2,786	8,359	11,145	5,573	27,863
Totals	$33,443	$31,537	$34,655	$37,283	$136,918
Budgeted Indirect Labor	15,240	16,220	16,180	17,260	64,900
Total Labor Budget	$48,683	$47,757	$50,835	$54,543	$201,818

*Amounts are rounded.

Determining the capital facility needs and obtaining resources for these expenditures are very complex areas of management accounting analysis. Because of their complexity, we cover them only briefly here. They are explored in more detail in an advanced management accounting course.

Relationships Among the Period Budgets. From our discussion so far, it should be apparent that the period budgets are closely related to each other. The sales unit forecast is the first step in the budgeting process. Once it is completed, the selling cost budget can be prepared. The production budget also depends on the sales forecast. The production budget in turn provides information regarding requirements for direct materials purchases and usage, as well as information for the labor and factory overhead budgets. In most cases, plans for general and administrative expenses and capital expenditures are made by top management, although much of this information may be gathered at the departmental level and included in the period budgets.

Figure 20-1 (on page 812) shows how the period budgets fit into the process of preparing a master budget. The key point to remember is that the whole

Exhibit 20-6. Factory Overhead Budget

Jones Piano Company Factory Overhead Budget For the Year Ending December 31, 19x5					
	First Quarter	Second Quarter	Third Quarter	Fourth Quarter	Totals
Factory Overhead Costs:					
Indirect Materials	$ 3,560	$ 3,850	$ 3,900	$ 4,000	$ 15,310
Indirect Labor	15,240	16,220	16,180	17,260	64,900
Assembly Supplies	1,700	1,750	1,800	1,850	7,100
Employee Benefits	9,474	9,102	10,334	11,817	40,727
Factory Supervision	15,000	15,000	15,000	15,000	60,000
Electricity Costs	1,980	2,100	2,150	2,200	8,430
Water Expense	870	900	920	950	3,640
Small Tools	1,200	1,200	1,200	1,200	4,800
Property Taxes	1,000	1,000	1,000	1,000	4,000
Insurance					
Fire	490	490	490	490	1,960
Liability	640	640	640	640	2,560
Depreciation, Machinery	3,100	3,100	3,100	3,100	12,400
Factory Rent	5,000	5,000	5,000	5,000	20,000
Repairs and Maintenance	2,800	2,900	3,000	3,000	11,700
Miscellaneous	500	500	500	500	2,000
Totals	$62,554	$63,752	$65,214	$68,007	$259,527

budgeting process begins with the sales unit forecast. In the following sections, we describe how period budgets are used to determine the effects of planned operations on the company's financial position.

Forecasted Income Statement

Once the period budgets have been prepared, the controller or the budget director can begin to compile information for the forecasted income statement. First, as Figure 20-1 shows, he or she prepares a cost of goods sold forecast from data in the materials, labor, and factory overhead budgets. Revenue information is figured from the sales budget. Then, by adding information from the selling cost and general and administrative expense budgets to the expected revenue and cost of goods sold data, the controller can prepare the forecasted income statement.

Financial Position Forecast

The last step in the master budget process is to prepare a financial position forecast or projected balance sheet for the company. As shown in Figure 20-1, all budget data are used in this process. The controller prepares a cash budget from all planned transactions requiring cash inflow or expenditure. (A more detailed explanation of cash budgeting follows later in this chapter.) When preparing the forecasted statement of financial position, the budget director must know the projected cash balance and must have determined the net income and amount of capital expenditures. All of the expected transactions shown in the period

Figure 20-1. Preparation of Master Budget

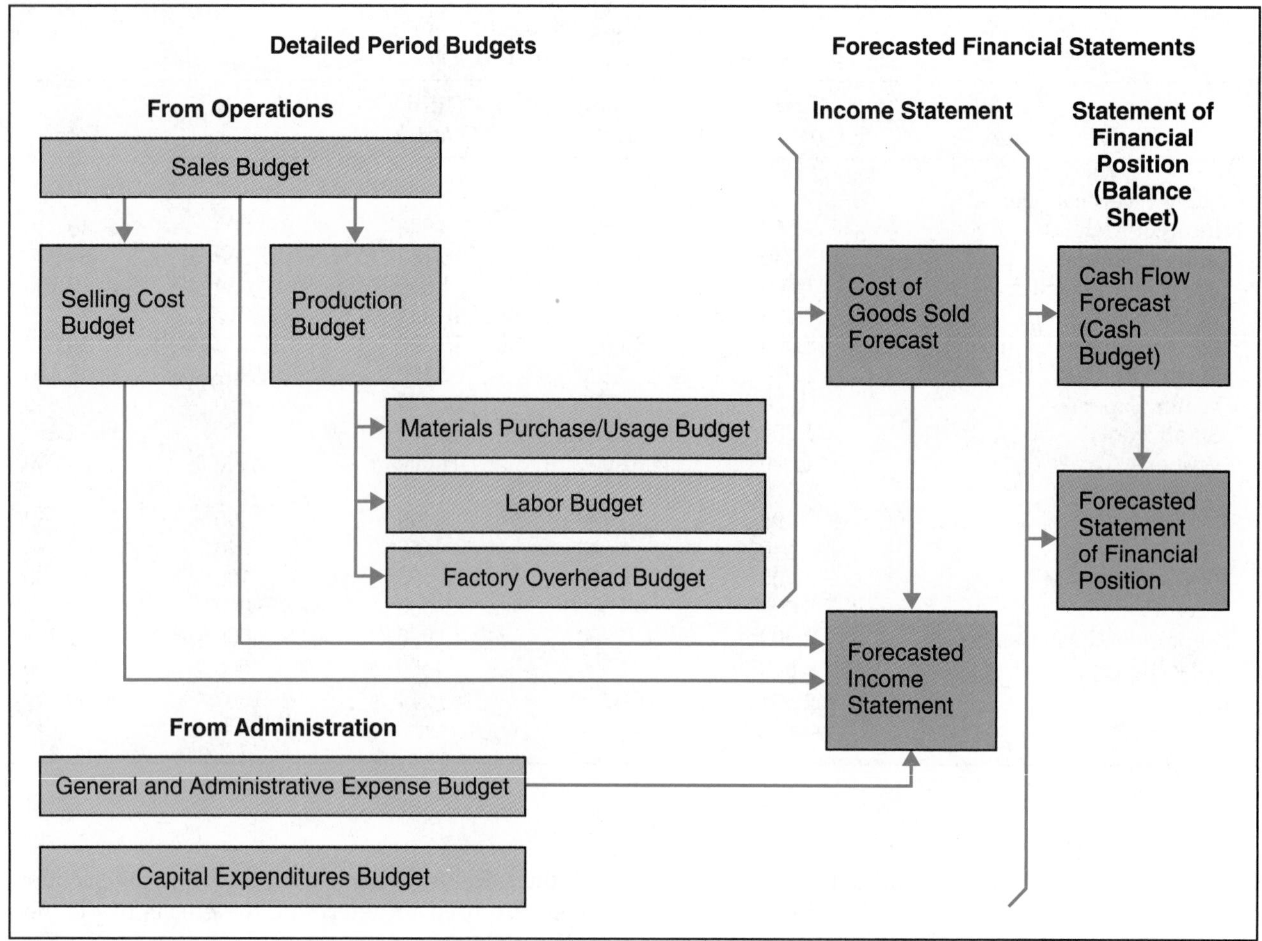

budgets must be classified and then charged to the different general ledger accounts.

The projected financial statements are the end product of the budgeting process. At this point, management must decide whether to accept the proposed master budget, as well as the planned operating results, or ask the budget director to change the plans and do parts of the budget over again.

Budget Implementation

Budget implementation is the responsibility of the budget director. Two elements discussed earlier, communication and support, determine the success of this process. Proper communication of expectations and targets to all key people in the company is essential. All employees involved in the operations of the business must know what is expected of them and they must receive directions on how to achieve their goals. Equally important, top management must support the budgeting process and encourage implementation of the budget. The process will succeed only if middle- and lower-level managers can see that top management truly is interested in the outcome and willing to reward people for meeting the budget goals.

Illustrative Problem
Period Budget Preparation

OBJECTIVE 5
Prepare a period budget

Procedures for preparing period budgets and building the master budget vary from one company to another. Since it is impossible to cover all procedures found in actual practice, the following problem illustrates one approach to preparing a period budget. Remember that by applying the tools of cost behavior and C-V-P analysis, and by working with a particular product costing method, you can prepare any kind of budget. We have already stated that there is no standard format to use for budget preparation; your only guidelines are that the budget be clear and understandable, and that it communicate the intended information to the reader.

Continuing with the Jones Piano Company example, we will develop the materials purchase/usage budget for the year ending December 31, 19x5. The company assembles and sells five piano models, each with a different quality level and market segment. The price of the purchased parts varies according to the model's quality level, and all materials and parts are purchased from outside vendors. The amounts of materials and parts to be purchased and used are derived from data found in the production budget. The company purchases such items quarterly and attempts to limit its materials inventory to the quarterly amounts. A list of parts needed for each of the three assembly operations, along with current purchase prices, follows.

Parts listing and related costs per piano:

	Model J-12	Model O-23	Model N-34	Model E-45	Model S-56
Sound System Assembly					
Wire strings	$ 14	$ 16	$ 17	$ 37	$ 40
Keyboard assembly	47	52	57	123	133
Sound chamber	94	103	113	245	265
Wire adjusters/connectors	9	10	11	25	27
Wood Cabinet Assembly					
Piano body	118	130	143	305	331
Keyboard frame	37	42	45	98	106
Top, including brace	56	62	68	147	159
Leg sets (3 per set)	42	47	51	110	119
Total Piano Assembly					
Fastener set	8	9	10	22	24
Varnishes	28	31	34	74	80
Wheel sets (3 per set)	15	17	18	39	42
	$468	$519	$567	$1,225	$1,326

Required

Prepare a materials purchase usage/budget for 19x5, and compute the amounts to be purchased for the first quarter's piano production.

Solution

The materials purchase/usage budget for the Jones Piano Company for the year ending December 31, 19x5 is shown in Exhibit 20-7. The units to be produced for the year and the first quarter were taken from the production budget in Exhibit 20-4. Each dollar amount is computed by multiplying the units by the costs per item or set described above. The company anticipates spending

Exhibit 20-7. Materials Purchase/Usage Budget

Jones Piano Company
Materials Purchase/Usage Budget
For the Year Ending December 31, 19x5

Materials Usage Projections:

	Model J-12	Model O-23	Model N-34	Model E-45	Model S-56	Total Budget
Units to be produced during year	75	50	60	120	50	355
Sound System Assembly						
Wire strings	$ 1,050	$ 800	$ 1,020	$ 4,440	$ 2,000	$ 9,310
Keyboard assembly	3,525	2,600	3,420	14,760	6,650	30,955
Sound chamber	7,050	5,150	6,780	29,400	13,250	61,630
Wire adjusters/connectors	675	500	660	3,000	1,350	6,185
Wood Cabinet Assembly						
Piano body	8,850	6,500	8,580	36,600	16,550	77,080
Keyboard frame	2,775	2,100	2,700	11,760	5,300	24,635
Top, including brace	4,200	3,100	4,080	17,640	7,950	36,970
Leg sets (3 per set)	3,150	2,350	3,060	13,200	5,950	27,710
Total Piano Assembly						
Fastener set	600	450	600	2,640	1,200	5,490
Varnishes	2,100	1,550	2,040	8,880	4,000	18,570
Wheel sets (3 per set)	1,125	850	1,080	4,680	2,100	9,835
Total Purchases	$35,100	$25,950	$34,020	$147,000	$66,300	$308,370

Detail of materials to be purchased for use during first quarter:

	Model J-12	Model O-23	Model N-34	Model E-45	Model S-56	Total Budget
Units to be produced—first quarter	20	12	18	35	5	90
Sound System Assembly						
Wire strings	$ 280	$ 192	$ 306	$ 1,295	$ 200	$ 2,273
Keyboard assembly	940	624	1,026	4,305	665	7,560
Sound chamber	1,880	1,236	2,034	8,575	1,325	15,050
Wire adjusters/connectors	180	120	198	875	135	1,508
Wood Cabinet Assembly						
Piano body	2,360	1,560	2,574	10,675	1,655	18,824
Keyboard frame	740	504	810	3,430	530	6,014
Top, including brace	1,120	744	1,224	5,145	795	9,028
Leg sets (3 per set)	840	564	918	3,850	595	6,767
Total Piano Assembly						
Fastener set	160	108	180	770	120	1,338
Varnishes	560	372	612	2,590	400	4,534
Wheel sets (3 per set)	300	204	324	1,365	210	2,403
Total Purchases—First Quarter	$9,360	$6,228	$10,206	$42,875	$6,630	**$75,299**

$308,370 on materials and parts to produce 355 pianos during 19x5, and $75,299 will be needed to pay for the first quarter's usage.

DECISION POINT
Cardinal Industries, Inc.[2]

■ Cardinal Industries, Inc. is a privately held manufacturing company and is the nation's largest manufacturer of modular shelter products. Founded in 1954, its headquarters is in Columbus, Ohio, and its manufacturing facilities are located in Atlanta, Orlando, Baltimore, Dallas, and Columbus. The company also owns and operates a motel chain, six retirement villages, apartments, single-family homes, student housing, office buildings, and rehabilitation centers located in eighteen states. Thus, although Cardinal Industries is primarily a manufacturer, it is also a construction company, mortgage financier, securities broker, real estate developer, landscape designer, and property manager.

The company grew rapidly and in many areas simultaneously. Cash budgeting was a sideline function, updated monthly at the division level. Each geographic location utilized up to four different banks and no use was made of the banks' daily balance reporting services. When an account was budgeted to be low, loans were made at the individual location. The divisions reported effective cash budgeting because low cash situations were always covered by immediate credit line transactions. But management began to be concerned about the way cash was managed. Should the company change its approach to cash management? What is wrong with the present system? What suggestions would you make to improve cash management at Cardinal Industries, Inc.?

The company decided to centralize its cash management. Instead of doing business with twenty banks at five locations, the company used only six banks. Five regional banks were selected to handle all receipts from each bank's particular region. One main bank was chosen to transact all company disbursements, and money was transferred from the location banks to the main bank daily. The need for short-term loans to cover cash shortfalls disappeared. Net annual savings from this shift in cash management was over $2 million per year. ■

Cash Budgeting

OBJECTIVE 6
State the purposes of, and prepare, a cash budget

Cash flow is one of the most important aspects of a company's operating cycle. Without cash, a business cannot function. But if cash balances are very large, funds may not earn the best possible rate of return. Low cash reserves, however, may indicate that the company cannot pay current liabilities. To prevent either of these problems, careful cash planning is necessary. The cash budget is the essential tool for this planning.

A **cash budget** (or **cash flow forecast**) is a projection of the cash receipts and cash payments for a future period. It summarizes the cash flow results of planned transactions in all phases of a master budget. Generally, a cash budget

2. Royce L. Gentzel and Mary Ann Swepston, "The Cardinal Difference in Cash Management," *Management Accounting*, Institute of Management Accountants, February 1988, pp. 43–47.

shows the company's projected ending cash balance and the cash position for each month of the year. As a result, periods of high and low cash availability can be anticipated.

The cash budget serves two purposes. First, it gives the ending cash balance, which is needed to complete the forecasted balance sheet in the master budget (see Figure 20-1). Thus, the cash budget holds a key position in the master budget preparation cycle. Second, the cash budget highlights periods of excess cash reserves or cash shortages. As a result, the budget director can advise financial executives of times when the company will need extra short-term financing because of cash shortages, and times when it will have excess cash available for short-term investments.

The cash budget has two main parts—forecasted cash receipts and forecasted cash payments. Sales budgets, cash or credit sales data, and accounts receivable collection data are used to compute the expected cash receipts. Other sources of cash, such as the sale of stock, the sale of assets, or loans, also enter into cash receipts planning. Expected cash payments are taken from the period budgets.

The Elements of a Cash Budget

The cash budget is developed after all period budgets are final and the forecasted income statement is complete. It combines information from several period budgets and brings together all elements of cash flow, both inflows (receipts) and outflows (payments). Since the master budget summarizes the expected transactions for a future period, it also includes expected cash transactions. To prepare the cash budget, then, one must analyze the master budget in terms of cash inflows and outflows.

The person preparing the cash budget must also know how the direct materials, labor, and other goods and services are going to be purchased. That is, will they be paid for immediately with cash, or will they be purchased on account, with the cash payment delayed for a time? Besides regular operating costs, cash is also used for buying equipment and paying off loans and other long-term liabilities. All of this information must be available before an accurate cash budget can be prepared.

The elements of a cash budget, examples of the receipts and disbursements (payments) of cash, and their relationships with the master budget are depicted in Table 20-2. Cash receipts information comes from several sources including the sales budget, cash collection records and trends, forecasted income statement, and the cash budgets of previous periods. Monthly sales on account must be converted to monthly cash flows before being entered in the cash budget.

Cash payment data is found by analyzing the period budgets supporting the master budget. Cash payment policies are also important. If the company holds all invoices for thirty days, the cash outflow for such items as the purchases of materials and supplies will lag the budgeted usage by a month. Cash payments information is found in the materials purchase/usage budget, factory overhead budget, labor budget, selling cost budget, general and administrative expense budget, capital expenditures budget, previous year's financial statements (income tax payments), loan records, and forecasted income statement. Each must be reviewed thoroughly to ensure that all cash payments have been included in the cash budget.

Preparing a Cash Budget

The cash budget for the Jones Piano Company for the year ending December 31, 19x5 is shown in Exhibit 20-8 on page 818. Detailed cash inflows and outflows

Table 20-2. Master Budget and Cash Budget Interrelationships

Elements of the Cash Budget	Sources of the Information
Cash Receipts	
Cash sales	Sales budget (cash sales)
Cash collections of previous sales	Sales budget (credit sales) plus collection record—percent collected in the first month, second month, etc.
Proceeds from sale of assets	Forecasted income statement and capital expenditures budget
Loan proceeds	Previous month's information on cash budget
Cash Payments	
Direct materials	Materials purchase/usage budget
Operating supplies	Factory overhead budget and materials purchase/usage budget
Direct labor	Labor budget
Factory overhead	Factory overhead budget
Selling expenses	Selling cost budget
General and administrative expenses	General and administrative expense budget
Capital expenditures	Capital expenditures budget
Income taxes	Estimated from previous year's income statement and current year's projections
Interest expense	Forecasted income statement
Loan payments	Loan record

Note: Other sources of cash receipts and cash payments exist. The above analysis covers only the most common types of cash inflows and outflows.

are presented for January, February, and March; the remaining nine months of the year are combined. It is good practice to continually update the cash budget so that as one month is completed, a new month is added to the detailed section. In our example, at the end of January, the column for January would be dropped and a new column for April added. This gives management a continuous three-month view of its cash flow projections.

To assist you in understanding how the Jones Piano Company's cash budget was developed, we will explain each line item in Exhibit 20-8. First let us analyze cash receipts. For the upcoming year, the company expects cash receipts from sales only; no other source is anticipated. Note that 60 percent of all sales generates cash in the month of sale. Forty percent are credit sales collected in the following month. Most of the necessary cash inflow information comes from the sales budget in Exhibit 20-2 and the production budget in Exhibit 20-4. There is a two-month waiting list for the company's pianos and, as a result, its pianos are shipped as soon as they are completed. So that you can determine the cash credit collections for January, you need to know that the December 19x4 sales were $90,540. December 19x5 sales are projected to be $96,520.

Information supporting cash payments comes from several sources. Every company should have an established policy about payment on account as part

Exhibit 20-8. The Cash Budget

Jones Piano Company
Cash Budget
For the Year Ending December 31, 19x5

	January	February	March	April–December	Totals
Cash Receipts					
Sales—Previous Month (40%)	$36,216	$40,210	$ 30,530	$ 27,632	$ 134,588
Sales—Current Month (60%)	60,315	45,795	41,448	722,462	870,020
Total Cash Receipts	$96,531	$86,005	$ 71,978	$750,094	$1,004,608
Cash Payments					
Direct Materials and Parts	$31,014	$22,613	$ 21,672	$233,071	$ 308,370
Direct Labor	13,590	10,640	9,213	103,475	136,918
Indirect Materials	1,490	1,075	995	11,750	15,310
Indirect Labor	6,096	5,080	4,064	49,660	64,900
Other Factory Overhead	17,910	13,795	12,049	135,563	179,317
Selling Commissions	5,340	4,055	3,670	40,425	53,490
Other Selling Costs	1,905	1,445	1,310	14,420	19,080
General and Administrative Expenses	12,063	9,159	8,290	91,328	120,840
Capital Expenditures	0	25,000	0	45,000	70,000
Income Taxes	0	0	21,430	0	21,430
Interest Expense	3,400	0	0	10,200	13,600
Total Cash Payments	$92,808	$92,862	$ 82,693	$734,892	$1,003,255
Cash Increase (Decrease)	$ 3,723	$ (6,857)	$(10,715)	$ 15,202	$ 1,353
Beginning Cash Balance	27,440	31,163	24,306	13,591	27,440
Ending Cash Balance	$31,163	$24,306	$ 13,591	$ 28,793	$ 28,793

of its cash management approach. If the policy is to pay the total within the discount period, and the terms are 2/10, net/30, cash flow would take place in ten days. If, however, the company wishes to hold its cash for the discount period, cash payments would not be made for thirty days. The Jones Piano Company's policy is to pay all invoices in the month received. Cash used to purchase materials and parts is determined from the materials purchase/usage budget in Exhibit 20-7, the individual model information in the schedule on page 813, and the detailed unit figures in the production budget.

Direct labor cash payments are derived from data in the labor budget in Exhibit 20-5 and from the detailed unit data in the production budget. Indirect materials and indirect labor are part of the factory overhead budget in Exhibit 20-6, but the company prefers to separate them out in its cash budget. They are computed using a rate based on materials and parts dollars and direct labor dollars, respectively. The remaining costs in the factory overhead budget also are assigned to time periods using a rate based on direct labor dollars. The allocation of selling commissions and other selling expenses to time periods is accomplished using data from the sales budget in Exhibit 20-2, the selling cost budget in Exhibit 20-3, and the unit data in the production budget in Exhibit 20-4.

The remaining items are not spelled out in budget exhibits in the chapter. However, general and administrative expenses would normally be a part of a separate budget. Here we need the following data to complete this section of the cash budget: cash projections for G&A expenses are January, $12,063; February, $9,159; March, $8,290; and the remaining nine months, $91,328. The company expects to spend $25,000 on capital expenditures in February, and another $45,000 in July. Federal income taxes from 19x4 of $21,430 are payable on March 15. Lastly, the company makes a $3,400 interest-only payment on a loan on the second day of the first month of each quarter.

Once the cash receipts and cash payments have been established, the cash increase or decrease for the period is computed. The resulting increase or decrease is added to the period's beginning balance to arrive at the projected cash balance at period end. In the Jones Piano Company example in Exhibit 20-8, you can see that the beginning cash balance for January was $27,440. Then each month's projected ending balance is the next month's beginning balance. In the case of the Jones Piano Company, February and March will put a heavy drain on cash reserves, but positive cash flow is expected to return during the last nine months of the year. The company seems to have a favorable cash position for the year, except at the end of March. Depending on what the company's policy is on minimum cash reserves, a small short-term loan may be anticipated. On the other hand, a $28,793 projected balance in cash at year end may be too much extra cash. At that time, management may want to make plans for investing part of this money in short-term securities.

The cash budget usually is the final segment of the master budget to be developed because to create it, all other budgets must have been completed first. When the cash budget's ending balance is determined, the forecasted balance sheet can be completed.

Chapter Review

Review of Learning Objectives

1. **Identify the objectives underlying the creation of a budget.**
   The primary objective of a budget is to forecast future financial and nonfinancial transactions of the enterprise. The second objective is to develop projected information that is as accurate and as meaningful to the recipient as possible.
2. **Define the concept of *budgetary control*.**
   The budgetary control process includes cost planning and cost control. It is the total process of developing plans for a company's expected operations, and controlling operations to help carry out those plans.
3. **Name the five groups of budgeting principles, and explain the principles in each group.**
   The five groups of budgeting principles are principles regarding: (1) long-range goals, (2) short-range goals and strategies, (3) human responsibilities and interaction, (4) budget housekeeping, and (5) follow-up. Every organization needs to set long-range goals and convert them into plans for product line or service offerings. These must be restated in terms of short-range goals and strategies, which provide plans for the annual product line or service offerings and associated profit plans. The budget development plans and timetable must also be set up. Principles regarding the human side of effective budgeting include identifying a budget director, staff, and participants. These people must be informed of their duties and responsibilities. Furthermore, it is essential to practice participative budgeting, obtain the full support of top management, and ensure full and open communication among all participants. Being realistic, requiring that all deadlines be met, and using flexible application procedures are the housekeeping principles of budgeting. Finally, budget follow-up should provide

for a continuous budgeting process, a system of periodic reports to measure performance of the operating segments, and identification of problems for analysis and inclusion in the next period's planning activities.

4. **Identify and explain the components of a master budget.**
A master budget is a set of period budgets that have been consolidated into forecasted financial statements for the whole company. First the detailed period budgets are prepared. These are the sales budget, selling cost budget, production budget, materials purchase/usage budget, labor budget, factory overhead budget, general and administrative expense budget, and capital expenditures budget. The selling cost budget and the production budget are computed from the sales budget data. Materials purchase/usage, labor, and factory overhead budgets arise from the production budget. Materials purchases can be determined only after materials needs are known. General and administrative expenses and proposed capital expenditures are determined by top management. Once these budgets have been prepared, a forecasted income statement, a forecasted cash budget, and a forecasted balance sheet can be prepared.

5. **Prepare a period budget.**
A period budget, also known as an operating budget, is a forecast of a year's operating results for a segment of a company. It is a quantitative expression of planned activities. The period budgeting process converts forecasts of unit sales and production into revenue and cost estimates for each of the many operating segments of the company.

6. **State the purposes of, and prepare, a cash budget.**
The cash budget's purposes are (1) to disclose the firm's projected ending cash balance and (2) to show the cash position for each month of the year so that periods of cash excesses or shortages can be anticipated. A cash budget or cash flow forecast is a projection of the cash receipts and cash payments for a future period. It summarizes the cash results of planned transactions in all parts of a master budget.
The preparation of a cash budget begins with the projection of all expected sources of cash (cash receipts). Next, all expected cash payments are found by analyzing all other period budgets within the master budget. The difference between these two totals is the cash increase or decrease anticipated for the period. This total, combined with the period's beginning cash balance, yields the ending cash balance.

Review of Concepts and Terminology

The following concepts and terms were introduced in this chapter:

(L.O. 1) **Budget:** A planning document created before anticipated transactions occur.

(L.O. 2) **Budgetary control:** The process of developing plans for a company's expected operations and controlling operations to help carry out those plans.

(L.O. 4) **Capital expenditures budget:** A detailed plan outlining the amount and timing of anticipated capital expenditures for a future period.

(L.O. 6) **Cash budget (or cash flow forecast):** A projection of cash receipts and cash payments for a future period.

(L.O. 4) **Factory overhead budget:** A detailed schedule of anticipated manufacturing costs, other than direct materials and direct labor costs, that must be incurred to meet the production expectations of a future period.

(L.O. 4) **General and administrative (G&A) expense budget:** A detailed plan of operating expenses, other than those of the manufacturing and selling functions, needed to support the overall operations of the business for a future period.

(L.O. 4) **Labor budget:** A detailed schedule that identifies the labor needs for a future period and the labor costs associated with those needs.

(L.O. 4) **Master budget:** A set of departmental or functional period budgets that have been consolidated into forecasted financial statements for the entire company.

(L.O. 4) **Materials purchase/usage budget:** A detailed plan developed from information on the production budget and anticipated changes in the materials inventory levels that identifies the number and timing of raw materials and parts to be purchased to meet production needs. (A merchandise purchasing budget is used by retail businesses.)

(L.O. 3) **Participative budgeting:** A managerial budget preparation process in which all levels of personnel take part creating budgets in a meaningful, active way.

(L.O. 2) **Period budget:** A forecast of operating results for a particular segment or function of a company for a specific period of time.

(L.O. 4) **Production budget:** A detailed schedule that identifies the products or services that must be produced or provided to meet budgeted sales and inventory needs.

(L.O. 4) **Sales budget:** A detailed plan, expressed in both units and dollars, that identifies the expected product (or service) sales for a future period.

(L.O. 4) **Selling cost budget:** A schedule developed from information on the sales budget and from the sales staff that details all anticipated costs related to the selling function of the business for a future period.

Self-Test

Test your knowledge of the chapter by choosing the best answer for each of the following items.

(L.O. 1) 1. A balanced federal budget exists when
   a. several expenditure categories are reduced.
   b. anticipated revenues equal anticipated expenditures.
   c. taxes are raised.
   d. taxes are raised and expenditures are reduced.

(L.O. 3) 2. Preparing a set of budget development plans and a specific timetable for the whole period is considered a
   a. short-range goals and strategies principle.
   b. long-range goals principle.
   c. human responsibilities and interaction principle.
   d. budget housekeeping principle.

(L.O. 3) 3. "Practice full communications during the entire budgeting process" is considered a
   a. short-range goals and strategies principle.
   b. long-range goals principle.
   c. human responsibilities and interaction principle.
   d. budget housekeeping principle.

(L.O. 4, 5) 4. What period budget is usually considered to be the starting point in the budgeting process?
   a. Production budget
   b. Sales budget
   c. Selling cost budget
   d. Factory overhead budget

(L.O. 4) 5. The amount of materials to be purchased can be estimated immediately after what period budget has been prepared?
   a. Selling expense budget
   b. Sales budget
   c. Production budget
   d. Materials purchase/usage budget

(L.O. 4) 6. A detailed schedule of anticipated manufacturing costs, other than direct materials and direct labor costs, that must be incurred to meet the production expectations of a future period is the definition of a
   a. master budget.
   b. capital expenditures budget.
   c. factory overhead budget.
   d. general and administrative expense budget.

(L.O. 5) 7. The sales budget of Calabria Corporation indicates that 12,500 units of product GHR and 33,100 units of product FGD are expected to be sold in October. Product GHR

sells for $22.40 whereas FGD's selling price is $32.00. Sales personnel receive a 6 percent commission on sales of GHR and 8 percent on FGD sales. How much anticipated sales commissions are budgeted for the month?
a. $105,136 c. $103,516
b. $106,276 d. $101,536

(L.O. 5) 8. Assume that Costabile Enterprises uses three gallons of material 2D, two gallons of material 4R, five gallons of material 6T, and ten gallons of material 8K to make each twenty-gallon barrel of plant food. Expected costs per gallon are: 2D, $2.40; 4R, $1.80; 6T, $10.50; and 8K, $3.30. The production budget indicates that 12,400 barrels will be produced in April, 10,800 barrels in May, and 9,800 barrels in June. Materials are purchased one month ahead of production. What is the total dollar value of budgeted materials purchases in April?
a. $1,040,040 c. $549,040
b. $1,194,120 d. $449,620

(L.O. 6) 9. The cash budget must be prepared before which of the following documents can be developed?
a. Capital expenditures budget c. Forecasted balance sheet
b. Sales budget d. Forecasted income statement

(L.O. 6) 10. Grainer Company had sales on account of $134,000 in July, $226,000 in August, and $188,000 in September. Collection experience indicates that 60 percent of credit sales are collected in the month after the sale, 36 percent in the second month after the sale, and 4 percent are uncollectible. How much cash was collected in September from sales on account?
a. $188,000 c. $226,000
b. $183,840 d. $194,160

Answers to the Self-Test are at the end of this chapter.

Review Problem
Cash Budget Preparation

(L.O. 1, 2, 4) Vertrees Information Processing Company provides word processing services for its clients. Vertrees uses state-of-the-art equipment and employs five keyboard operators, who each average 160 hours of work a month. See the table below for information developed by the budget officer.

	Actual—19x3		Forecast—19x4		
	November	December	January	February	March
Client Billings (Sales)	$25,000	$35,000	$25,000	$20,000	$40,000
Selling Costs	4,500	5,000	4,000	4,000	5,000
General and Administrative Expenses	7,500	8,000	8,000	7,000	7,500
Operating Supplies Purchased	2,500	3,500	2,500	2,500	4,000
Processing Overhead	3,200	3,500	3,000	2,500	3,500

The company has a bank loan of $12,000 at a 12 percent annual interest rate. Interest is paid monthly, and $2,000 of the principal of the loan is due on February 28, 19x4. No capital expenditures are anticipated for the first quarter of the coming year. Income taxes for calendar year 19x3 of $4,550 are due and payable on March 15, 19x4. The company's five employees earn $8.50 an hour, and all payroll-related labor benefit costs are included in processing overhead. For the items included in the table, assume the conditions outlined on the top of the next page.

Client Billings	60% are cash sales that are collected during the current period 30% are collected in the first month following the sale 10% are collected in the second month following the sale
Operating Supplies	Paid in the month purchased
Selling Costs, General and Administrative Expenses, and Processing Overhead	Paid in the month following the cost's incurrence

The beginning cash balance on January 1, 19x4 is expected to be $13,840.

Required

Prepare a monthly cash budget for Vertrees Information Processing Company for the three-month period ending March 31, 19x4.

Answer to Review Problem

Here is the three-month cash budget for Vertrees Information Processing Company:

Vertrees Information Processing Company
Monthly Cash Budget
For the Three-Month Period Ending March 31, 19x4

	January	February	March	Totals
Cash Receipts				
Client Billings	$28,000	$23,000	$32,500	$83,500
Cash Payments				
Operating Supplies	$ 2,500	$ 2,500	$ 4,000	$ 9,000
Direct Labor	6,800	6,800	6,800	20,400
Processing Overhead	3,500	3,000	2,500	9,000
Selling Costs	5,000	4,000	4,000	13,000
General and Administrative Expenses	8,000	8,000	7,000	23,000
Interest Expense	120	120	100	340
Loan Payment	—	2,000	—	2,000
Income Tax Payment	—	—	4,550	4,550
Total Disbursements	$25,920	$26,420	$28,950	$81,290
Cash Increase (Decrease)	$ 2,080	$ (3,420)	$ 3,550	$ 2,210
Beginning Cash Balance	13,840	15,920	12,500	13,840
Ending Cash Balance	$15,920	$12,500	$16,050	$16,050

Details supporting the individual computations are as follows:

	January	February	March
Cash from Client Billings			
Current month = 60%	$15,000	$12,000	$24,000
Previous month = 30%	10,500	7,500	6,000
Month before last = 10%	2,500	3,500	2,500
	$28,000	$23,000	$32,500

Operating Supplies			
All paid in the month purchased	$ 2,500	$ 2,500	$ 4,000
Direct Labor			
5 employees × 160 hours/month × $8.50/hour	6,800	6,800	6,800
Processing Overhead			
Paid in the following month	3,500	3,000	2,500
Selling Costs			
Paid in the following month	5,000	4,000	4,000
General and Administrative Expenses			
Paid in the following month	8,000	8,000	7,000
Interest Expense			
January and February = 1% of $12,000	120	120	
March = 1% of $10,000			100
Loan Payment	—	2,000	—
Income Tax Payment	—	—	4,550

The ending cash balances of $15,920, $12,500, and $16,050 for January, February, and March 19x4, respectively, appear to be comfortable but not too large for the company.

Chapter Assignments

Questions

1. Describe the concept of budgetary control. Why is it important?
2. What are the long-range goals principles of budgeting?
3. Distinguish between long-range plans and yearly operating plans.
4. What is the purpose of the following budgeting principle? "Restate the long-range plans in terms of short-range plans for product lines or services and a detailed profit plan."
5. In what ways does a well-defined organizational structure help in the preparation of budgets?
6. State the budget housekeeping principles.
7. Describe participative budgeting. Why is it necessary to identify all participants involved in budget development?
8. Why use a continuous budgeting process?
9. What is the connection between periodic performance reports and the budgeting process?
10. What is a master budget? What is its purpose?
11. Define a *period budget.*
12. Name the three main phases of the budget preparation cycle.
13. Describe the contents of a materials purchase/usage budget.
14. Identify and discuss relationships among detailed operating budgets.
15. Can a labor budget contain projections of both direct labor and indirect labor costs? What are the advantages of including both categories?
16. Why is the preparation of a cash budget so important to a company?
17. In the budget preparation process, what period budgets must precede the preparation of the cash budget?
18. How are sales and purchases on account handled when drawing up the cash budget?

Communication Skills Exercises

Communication 20-1. The Art of Budgeting Profit Targets
(L.O. 2, 3)

***University of Southern California*'s** Professor Kenneth A. Merchant conducted a field research study of twelve corporations in which he specifically looked at the levels at which profit budgets (targets) should be set. Should the budget targets be easy to reach, should their attainment be very difficult, or should the targets be set somewhere in between these extremes? Between the two extremes, literally hundreds of levels could be selected. The Merchant study showed that profit budgets influence manager behavior and that the setting of budget targets is an art as well as a science. According to Merchant, profit budget targets should be set to be "challenging but achievable." Write a statement explaining what you believe Professor Merchant meant by this statement.

Communication 20-2. Budgeting in a Small Business[3]
(L.O. 1, 3)

SubRunners is a submarine sandwich shop in Salisbury, Maryland. Opened in 1986 as a sandwich shop called Bubba's Breakaway, a franchise takeout and delivery chain, the store performed poorly and was at the brink of bankruptcy a year later. Owners Gary Gaskill and John McClellan turned the business around, in part by incorporating budgets and other planning activities in the existing accounting system. Their business has improved steadily since 1987. In 1989, they bought out their franchise agreement and are now an independent sub shop. Prepare a one-page paper identifying the uses of a budget as a tool to save a faltering business.

Communication 20-3. Ethical Considerations in the Budgeting Process
(L.O. 2)

Ernest Soto is manager of the Repairs and Maintenance (R&M) Department, a cost center at Graphics Industries. Mr. Soto is responsible for preparing the annual budget for his department. For 19x5, he turned in the following budgeted information to the company's budget director. The 19x5 figures are 20 percent above the 19x4 budget figures. Most managers in the company inflate their budget numbers by at least 10 percent because their bonuses depend upon how much below budget they operate.

Cost Category	Budget 19x4	Actual 19x4	Budget 19x5
Supplies	$ 20,000	$ 16,000	$ 24,000
Labor	80,000	82,000	96,000
Utilities	8,500	8,000	10,200
Tools	12,500	9,000	15,000
Hand-carried equipment	25,000	16,400	30,000
Cleaning materials	4,600	4,200	5,520
Miscellaneous	2,000	2,100	2,400
Totals	$152,600	$137,700	$183,120

The director has questioned some of the numbers. Mr. Soto defended them by saying that he expects a significant increase in repairs and maintenance activity in 19x5.

What are the real reasons for the increased budgeted data? What are the ethical considerations of this situation? Write a memo from the budget director to Ernest Soto that includes an analysis of the proposed budget.

Communication 20-4. Basic Research Skills
(L.O. 1, 2)

Budgets are used by every kind of enterprise, including both profit-oriented and not-for-profit concerns. Select a store, church, company, or charity that you are familiar with. Set up a meeting with the owner or manager and ask questions pertaining to the organization's use of budgets. Determine from your conversation if the person relies on budgets heavily, only once a year at preparation time, or never. Make notes on the types of budgets used. Prepare your remarks in outline form for presentation to the class.

Classroom Exercises

Exercise 20-1. Budgeting Principles
(L.O. 3)

Assume that you work in the accounting department of a small wholesale warehousing business. After attending a seminar on the values of a budgeting system at an industry association meeting, the president wants to develop a budgeting system and has asked you to direct it.

State the points that you should communicate to the president about the initial development steps of the process. Concentrate on long-range goals principles and short-range goals and strategies principles.

3. The exercise was developed from the following article: Gary T. Gaskill and J. Michael Hyland, "Starting and Managing a Small Business," *Management Accounting*, Institute of Management Accountants, December 1989, pp. 28–31.

Exercise 20-2.
Materials Quantities Budget
(L.O. 5)

Pauline Sewell, controller for Sarpu Cosmetics Corporation, is in the process of putting together the 19x5 master budget. The sales and production budgets have been assembled and Ms. Sewell is now in the process of preparing the materials purchase/usage budget for the first quarter of 19x5. The company produces three main product lines—A-1, C-3, and E-5—and each product requires different mixtures of four raw material compounds. Planned production of the three products for January–March 19x5 is as follows:

Product	Batches To Be Produced
A-1	15,000
C-3	20,000
E-5	40,000

The mixture of raw material compounds per batch of product is shown below:

	Raw Material Compounds per Batch (in gallons)			
Product	BB	DD	FF	HH
A-1	4	3	—	2
C-3	2	—	6	4
E-5	5	2	3	8

Inventory level requirements and raw material compound unit costs are:

	BB	DD	FF	HH
Inventory level (gallons):				
January 1, 19x5	2,000	1,600	900	3,000
March 31, 19x5	1,000	800	500	1,500
Projected 19x5 cost/gallon	$6	$7	$8	$10

Prepare a budget for the purchase of materials for the first quarter of 19x5 that details the total gallons to be purchased for each compound and the total cost per compound.

Exercise 20-3.
Production Budget Preparation
(L.O. 5)

The Stevens Specialty Door Company's forecast of garage door unit sales for 19x2 is as follows: January, 50,000; February, 40,000; March, 60,000; April, 70,000; May, 60,000; June, 50,000; July, 40,000; August, 50,000; September, 60,000; October, 70,000; November, 80,000; and December, 60,000.

The forecast of unit sales for January 19x3 is 50,000. Beginning finished goods inventory on January 1, 19x2 contained 15,000 doors. Company policy states that minimum finished goods inventory is 15,000 units and that the maximum is one-half of the following month's sales. Maximum productive capacity is 65,000 units per month.

Using the information given above, prepare a monthly production budget stating the number of units to be produced. Note that the company wants a fairly constant productive output so a constant work force can be maintained. How many units will be in finished goods inventory on December 31, 19x2?

Exercise 20-4.
Direct Materials Purchase Budget (Extension of Exercise 20-3)
(L.O. 5)

Refer to the data for the Stevens Specialty Door Company in Exercise 20-3. Prepare a materials purchase/usage budget for January, February, and March, 19x2, assuming the following breakdown of parts needed:

Hinges	4 sets/door	$11.00/set
Door panels	4 panels/door	$27.00/panel
Other hardware	1 lock/door	$31.00/lock
	1 handle/door	$22.50/handle
	2 roller tracks/door	$16.00/set of 2 roller tracks
	8 rollers/door	$4.00/roller

All direct materials are purchased in the month before they are used in production.

Exercise 20-5.
Factory Labor Budget
(L.O. 5)

Behme Metals Company manufactures three products in a single plant with four departments: Cutting, Grinding, Polishing, and Packing. The company has estimated costs for products T, M, and B and is currently analyzing direct labor hour requirements for the budget year 19x3. The routing sequence and departmental data follow:

Unit of Product	Estimated Hours per Unit: Cut	Grind	Polish	Pack	Total Estimated Direct Labor Hours/Unit
T	.8	1.1	.5	.3	2.7
M	1.2	—	2.9	.7	4.8
B	1.8	3.2	—	.5	5.5
Hourly labor rate	$10	$9	$7	$6	
Annual direct labor hour capacity	1,100,000	1,200,000	1,248,000	460,000	

The annual direct labor hour capacity for each department at Behme Metals is based on a normal two-shift operation. Hours of labor in excess of capacity are provided by overtime labor at 150 percent of normal hourly rates. Budgeted unit production in 19x3 for the products is 210,000 of T, 360,000 of M, and 300,000 of B.

Prepare a direct labor budget for 19x3 showing annual and monthly costs. Assume that direct labor hour capacity is the same each month. Production should be close to constant each month.

Exercise 20-6.
Sales Budget Preparation
(L.O. 5)

Sales for 19x4 for the Maruzak Manufacturing Company are shown below. The data are presented in quarterly figures because management monitors its business activity in this manner.

Maruzak Manufacturing Company
Actual Sales Revenue
For the Year Ended December 31, 19x4

Product Class	January–March	April–June	July–September	October–December	Annual Totals	Estimated 19x5 Percent Increases by Product Class
Marine Products	$ 44,500	$ 45,500	$ 48,200	$ 47,900	$ 186,100	10%
Mountain Products	36,900	32,600	34,100	37,200	140,800	5%
River Products	29,800	29,700	29,100	27,500	116,100	30%
Hiking Products	38,800	37,600	36,900	39,700	153,000	15%
Running Products	47,700	48,200	49,400	49,900	195,200	25%
Biking Products	65,400	65,900	66,600	67,300	265,200	20%
Totals	$263,100	$259,500	$264,300	$269,500	$1,056,400	

Prepare the 19x5 sales budget for the company. Show both quarterly and annual totals for each product class.

Exercise 20-7.
Factory Overhead Budget
(L.O. 5)

Robert Reid is chief financial officer for Germanna Corporation, a multinational company operating with three divisions. As part of the budgeting process, his staff is developing the factory overhead budget for 19x4. Data from the current year by division as well as projections for 19x4 have been received from each of the divisional controllers and are shown at the top of page 828.

Germanna Corporation
Factory Overhead Cost Summary Analysis
For the Year Ended December 31, 19x3

	New Orleans Division		London Division		Mexico City Division		
Cost Category	19x3 Amount	Projected 19x4 Increase	19x3 Amount	Projected 19x4 Increase	19x3 Amount	Projected 19x4 Increase	19x3 Corporate Totals
Indirect Materials	$ 77,900	10%	$ 86,900	12%	$ 97,400	10%	$ 262,200
Indirect Labor	82,100	8%	104,600	9%	112,400	6%	299,100
Factory Supervision	140,000	14%	180,000	13%	210,000	12%	530,000
Employee Benefits	64,120	20%	76,400	20%	22,600	20%	163,120
Insurance							
Casualty	3,240	5%	4,650	4%	6,940	5%	14,830
Flood	5,800	8%	6,800	5%	8,680	6%	21,280
Liability	4,120	10%	5,200	12%	6,340	15%	15,660
Taxes							
Property	16,480	4%	34,700	24%	49,700	30%	100,880
Other	2,400	10%	3,300	20%	8,640	20%	14,340
Depreciation, Machinery	78,400	2%	82,200	2%	42,100	2%	202,700
Depreciation, Buildings	62,000	4%	71,500	2%	39,600	8%	173,100
Repairs and Maintenance	24,600	4%	26,300	8%	6,800	6%	57,700
Supplies	13,200	2%	10,600	4%	3,600	8%	27,400
Special Tools	69,700	30%	45,600	25%	8,900	20%	124,200
Electricity	34,500	6%	29,800	10%	17,460	15%	81,760
Miscellaneous	2,360	5%	3,780	5%	2,200	5%	8,340
Totals	$680,920		$772,330		$643,360		$2,096,610

From the data given, prepare the 19x4 factory overhead budget for the corporation. Include divisional as well as total corporate amounts. Round to whole dollar amounts.

Exercise 20-8.
Cash Budget Preparation—Revenues
(L.O. 6)

Reihing Car Care, Inc. is an automobile maintenance and repair organization with outlets throughout the midwestern United States. Roberta Patrick, budget director for the home office, is beginning to assemble next quarter's operating cash budget. Sales are projected as follows:

	On Account	Cash
October 19x4	$452,000	$196,800
November 19x4	590,000	214,000
December 19x4	720,500	218,400

Reihing's past collection results for sales on account indicate the following pattern:

Month of sale	40%
1st month following sale	30%
2nd month following sale	28%
Uncollectible	2%

Sales on account during the months of August and September were $346,000 and $395,000, respectively.

What are the purposes of preparing a cash budget? Compute the amount of cash to be collected from sales during each month of the last quarter.

Exercise 20-9.
Cash Budget Preparation—Expenditures
(L.O. 6)

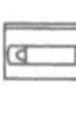

Cabernet Corporation relies on its cash budget to predict periods of high or low cash. The company considers proper cash management to be a primary short-range strategy for achieving higher profits. All materials and supplies are purchased on account, with terms of either 2/10, n/30 or 2/30, n/60. Discounts are taken whenever possible, but payment is not made until the final day of the discount period. Purchases for the next quarter of 19x2 are expected to be as follows:

Date	Terms	Gross Amount	Date	Terms	Gross Amount
July 10	2/10, n/30	$ 7,400	Aug. 31	2/10, n/30	$5,800
16	2/30, n/60	9,200	Sept. 4	2/10, n/30	8,400
24	2/30, n/60	8,400	9	2/10, n/30	7,100
Aug. 6	2/10, n/30	7,200	18	2/10, n/30	6,500
12	2/30, n/60	11,400	20	2/10, n/30	9,400
18	2/30, n/60	12,500	24	2/30, n/60	8,300
30	2/10, n/30	13,600	29	2/10, n/30	3,900

Three purchases in June affect July cash flow: June 6, 2/30, n/60, $13,200; June 21, 2/30, n/60, $11,400; and June 24, 2/10, n/30, $5,400.

From the information given, compute total cash outflow for July, August, and September resulting from the purchases identified above.

Interpretation Case from Business

Hugo Corporation
(L.O. 1, 3)

Hugo Corporation is a manufacturing company with annual sales of $25,000,000. The controller, Victor Jessie, appointed Yolanda Shirley as budget director. She created the following budget formulation policy based on a calendar-year accounting period:

May 19x3 Meeting of corporate officers and budget director to discuss corporate plans for 19x4.

June 19x3 Meeting(s) of division managers, department heads, and budget director to communicate 19x4 corporate objectives. At this time, relevant background data are distributed to all managers and a time schedule is established for development of 19x4 budget data.

July 19x3 Managers and department heads continue to develop budget data. Complete 19x4 monthly sales forecasts by product line and receive final sales estimates from sales vice president.

Aug. 19x3 Complete 19x4 monthly production activity and anticipated inventory level plans. Division managers and department heads should communicate preliminary budget figures to budget director for coordination and distribution to other operating areas.

Sept. 19x3 Development of preliminary 19x4 master budget. Revised budget data from all functional areas to be received. Budget director will coordinate staff activities, integrating labor requirements, direct materials and supplies requirements, unit cost estimates, cash requirements, and profit estimates and prepare preliminary 19x4 master budget.

Oct. 19x3 Meeting with corporate officers to discuss preliminary 19x4 master budget; any corrections, additions, or deletions to be communicated to budget director by corporate officers; all authorized changes to be incorporated into the 19x4 master budget.

Nov. 19x3 Submit final draft of 19x4 master budget to corporate officers for approval. Publish approved budget and distribute to all corporate officers, division managers, and department heads.

Required

1. Comment on the proposed budget formulation policy.
2. What changes in the policy would you recommend?

Problem Set A

Problem 20A-1.
Divisional Budget Preparation
(L.O. 5)

Jerome Spallino is budget director for Westmoreland Spectaculars, Inc., a multinational company based in Pennsylvania. Westmoreland Spectaculars, Inc. organizes and coordinates art shows and auctions throughout the world. Budgeted and actual costs and expenses for 19x3 are compared in the following schedule.

	19x3 Amounts	
Expense Item	**Budget**	**Actual**
Salary Expense, Staging	$ 240,000	$ 256,400
Salary Expense, Executive	190,000	223,600
Travel Costs	320,000	326,010
Auctioneer Services	270,000	224,910
Space Rental Costs	125,500	123,290
Printing Costs	96,000	91,250
Advertising Expense	84,500	91,640
Insurance, Merchandise	42,400	38,650
Insurance, Liability	32,000	33,550
Home Office Costs	104,600	109,940
Shipping Costs	52,500	56,280
Miscellaneous	12,500	12,914
Total Expenses	$1,570,000	$1,588,434
Net Receipts	$3,100,000	$3,184,600

For 19x4, the following fixed costs have been budgeted: executive salaries, $220,000; advertising expense, $95,000; merchandise insurance, $40,000; and liability insurance, $34,000. Additional information follows:

a. Net receipts are expected to be $3,200,000 in 19x4.
b. Staging salaries will increase 20% over 19x3 actual figures.
c. Travel costs are expected to be 11% of net receipts.
d. Auctioneer services will be billed at 9.5% of net receipts.
e. Space rental costs will go up 20% from 19x3 budgeted amounts.
f. Printing costs are expected to be $95,000 in 19x4.
g. Home office costs are budgeted for $115,000 in 19x4.
h. Shipping costs are expected to rise 20% over 19x3 budgeted amounts.
i. Miscellaneous expenses for 19x4 will be budgeted at $14,000.

Required

1. Prepare the division's forecasted income statement for 19x4. Assume that only services are being sold and that there is no cost of sales. (Net receipts equal gross margin.) Use a 34 percent federal income tax rate.
2. Should the budget director be worried about the trend in the company's operations? Be specific.

Problem 20A-2.
Factory Overhead Expense Budget
(L.O. 5)

Skinner Manufacturing Company has a home office and three operating divisions. The home office houses the top management personnel, including all accounting functions. The factory overhead costs incurred during 19x3 are summarized in the table at the top of the next page.

Expected percentage increases for 19x4 are shown for all categories except computer services. These services will increase by different amounts for each division: East Division, 25%; West Division, 30%; and Central Division, 40%. In 19x3, the home office was charged $55,000 for computer service costs. This amount is expected to rise by 25% in 19x4. During 19x4, the company will rent a new software package at an annual cost of $90,000.

Expense Categories	East Division	West Division	Central Division	Total	Expected Increase In 19x4
Indirect Labor	$ 34,500	$ 30,600	$ 39,200	$104,300	10%
Indirect Materials	12,800	13,200	14,000	40,000	20%
Supplies	11,900	12,900	12,000	36,800	10%
Utilities	14,200	15,400	11,100	40,700	10%
Computer Services	32,500	35,800	37,700	106,000	—
Insurance	11,400	12,500	13,600	37,500	10%
Repairs and Maintenance	11,600	16,000	14,400	42,000	20%
Miscellaneous	10,100	12,200	11,300	33,600	10%
Totals	$139,000	$148,600	$153,300	$440,900	

Required

1. Find the total expected cost for computer services for 19x4 for the three divisions and the home office.
2. Assume that the new software package rental charge is allocated to computer service users on the basis of their normal computer use costs as a percentage of total computer service charges. Allocate the rental charges to the three divisions and the home office. (Use the 19x4 amounts computed in **1** above, and round to one percentage decimal place.)
3. Prepare the divisional factory overhead expense budget for Skinner Manufacturing Company for 19x4.

Problem 20A-3. Master Budget
(L.O. 4, 5)

Hunt Video Company, Inc. produces and markets two popular video games, "Fifth Avenue" and "Young Adventures." The company's closing balance sheet account balances for 19x3 are as follows: Cash, $18,735; Accounts Receivable, $19,900; Materials Inventory, $18,510; Work in Process Inventory, $24,680; Finished Goods Inventory, $21,940; Prepaid Expenses, $3,420; Plant and Equipment, $262,800; Accumulated Depreciation, Plant and Equipment, $55,845; Other Assets, $9,480; Accounts Payable, $52,640; Mortgage Payable, $70,000; Common Stock, $90,000; and Retained Earnings, $110,980.

Period budgets for the first quarter of 19x4 revealed the following: materials purchases, $58,100; materials usage, $62,400; labor expense, $42,880; factory overhead expense, $51,910; selling expenses, $35,820; general and administrative expenses, $60,240; capital expenditures, $0; ending cash balances by month: January, $34,610; February, $60,190; March, $54,802; cost of goods manufactured, $163,990; and cost of goods sold, $165,440.

Sales per month are projected to be $125,200 for January, $105,100 for February, and $112,600 for March. Accounts receivable balance will double during the quarter, and accounts payable will decrease by 20 percent. Mortgage payments for the quarter will total $6,000, of which $2,000 is interest expense. Prepaid expenses are expected to go up by $20,000, and other assets are projected to increase 50 percent over the budget period. Depreciation for plant and equipment (already included in the factory overhead budget) averages 5 percent of total Plant and Equipment per year. Federal income taxes are 34 percent of profits and are payable in April. No dividends were paid.

Required

1. Prepare a forecasted income statement for the quarter ending March 31, 19x4.
2. Prepare a forecasted statement of financial position as of March 31, 19x4.

Problem 20A-4. Basic Cash Budget
(L.O. 6)

David Emerson is president of Northern Nurseries of Idaho, Inc. This corporation has four locations in the state of Idaho and has been in business for six years. Each retail outlet offers over 300 varieties of plants and trees to its customers. Sarah Stafford, the controller, has been asked to prepare a cash budget for the Southern Division for the first quarter of 19x4.

Projected data supporting the budget are summarized as follows. Collection history for the accounts receivable has shown that 30 percent of all credit sales are collected in the month of sale, 60 percent in the month following the sale, and 8 percent in the second month following the sale. Two percent of the credit sales are uncollectible. Purchases are all paid for in the month following the purchase. As of December 31, 19x3, the Southern Division had a cash balance of $4,800.

Sales (60 percent on credit)		Purchases	
November 19x3	$ 80,000	December 19x3	$43,400
December 19x3	100,000	January 19x4	62,350
January 19x4	60,000	February 19x4	49,720
February 19x4	80,000	March 19x4	52,400
March 19x4	70,000		

Salaries and wages are projected to be $12,600 in January; $16,600 in February; and $10,600 in March. Monthly costs are estimated to be: utilities, $2,110; collection fees, $850; rent, $2,650; equipment depreciation, $2,720; supplies, $1,240; small tools, $1,570; and miscellaneous, $950.

Required

1. Prepare a cash budget by month for the Southern Division for the first quarter of 19x4.
2. Should Northern Nurseries of Idaho, Inc. anticipate taking out a loan for the Southern Division during the quarter? How much should be borrowed? When? (**Note:** Management maintains a $3,000 minimum cash balance at each of its four locations.)

Problem 20A-5.
Cash Budget Preparation: Comprehensive
(L.O. 6)

Cuello's Wellness Centers, Inc. operates three fully equipped personal health facilities in Kissimmee, Florida. In addition to the health facilities, the corporation maintains a complete medical center specializing in preventive medicine. Emphasis is placed on regular workouts and medical examinations. The following projections have been made for 19x5.

Cash Receipts: First Quarter, 19x5

Membership dues:
- Memberships: December, 19x4, 870; January, 19x5, 880; February, 910; and March, 1,030
- Dues: $90 per month, payable on the 10th (80 percent collected on time, 20 percent collected one month late)

Medical examinations: January, $35,610; February, $41,840; and March, $45,610
Special aerobics classes: January, $4,020; February, $5,130; and March, $7,130
High-protein food sales: January, $4,890; February, $5,130; and March, $6,280

Cash Payments: First Quarter, 19x5

Salaries and wages:
- Corporate officers: $24,000/month
- Medical doctors: 2 @ $7,000/month
- Nurses: 3 @ $2,900/month
- Clerical staff: 2 @ $1,500/month
- Aerobics instructors: 3 @ $1,100/month
- Clinic staff: 6 @ $1,700/month
- Maintenance staff: 3 @ $900/month
- Health food servers: 3 @ $750/month

Purchases:
- Muscle-tone machines: January, $14,400; February, $13,800; and March, $0
- Pool supplies: $520 per month
- Health food: January, $3,290; February, $3,460; and March, $3,720
- Medical supplies: January, $10,400; February, $11,250; and March, $12,640
- Medical clothing: January, $7,410; February, $3,900; and March, $3,450
- Medical equipment: January, $11,200; February, $3,400; and March $5,900

Advertising: January, $2,250; February, $1,190; and March, $2,450
Utilities expense: January, $5,450; February, $5,890; and March, $6,090
Insurance:
- Fire: January, $3,470
- Liability: March, $3,980

Property taxes: $3,760 due in January
Federal income taxes: 19x4 taxes of $21,000 due in March, 19x5
Miscellaneous: January, $2,625; February, $2,800; and March, $1,150

The beginning cash balance for 19x5 is anticipated to be $9,840.

Required

Prepare a cash budget for Cuello's Wellness Centers, Inc. for the first quarter of 19x5. Use the following column headings:

Item	January	February	March	Total

Problem Set B

Problem 20B-1. Budget Preparation *(L.O. 5)*

The main product of Thomas Gregor Enterprises, Inc. is a multipurpose hammer that carries a lifetime guarantee. The steps in the manufacturing process have been combined by using modern, automated equipment. A list of cost and production information for the Gregor hammer follows:

Direct materials
- Anodized steel: 2 kilograms per hammer at $1.60 per kilogram
- Leather strapping for the handle: .5 square meter per hammer at $4.40 per square meter
- (Packing materials are returned to the manufacturer and thus are not included as part of cost of goods sold.)

Direct labor
- Forging operation: $12.50 per labor hour; 6 minutes per hammer
- Leather-wrapping operation: $12.00 per direct labor hour; 12 minutes per hammer

Factory overhead
- Forging operation: rate equals 70% of department's direct labor dollars
- Leather-wrapping operation: rate equals 50% of department's direct labor dollars

For the three months ending December 31, 19x4, Gregor's management expects to produce 54,000 hammers in October, 52,000 hammers in November, and 50,000 hammers in December.

Required

1. For the three-month period ending December 31, 19x4, prepare monthly production cost information for the manufacture of the Gregor hammer. In your budget analysis, show a detailed breakdown of all costs involved and the computation methods used.
2. Prepare a quarterly production cost budget for the hammer. Show monthly cost data and combined totals for the quarter for each cost category.

Problem 20B-2. General and Administrative Expense Budget *(L.O. 5)*

Lueck Metal Products, Inc. has four divisions and a centralized management structure. The home office is located in LaCrosse, Wisconsin. General and administrative expenses of the corporation for 19x3 and expected percentage increases for 19x4 are as follows:

Expense Categories	19x3 Expenses	Expected Increase In 19x4
Administrative Salaries	$160,000	20%
Facility Depreciation	47,000	10%
Operating Supplies	34,500	20%
Insurance and Taxes	26,000	10%
Computer Services	250,000	40%
Clerical Salaries	85,000	15%
Miscellaneous	22,500	10%
Total	$625,000	

To determine divisional profitability, all general and administrative expenses except for computer services are allocated to divisions on a total labor dollar basis. Computer service costs are charged directly to divisions on the basis of percent of total usage charges. Computer usage charges and direct labor costs in 19x3 were as follows:

	Computer Charges	Direct Labor
Division A	$ 60,000	$150,000
Division B	54,000	100,000
Division C	46,000	150,000
Division D	40,000	200,000
Home Office	50,000	—
Total	$250,000	$600,000

Required

1. Prepare the general and administrative expense budget for Lueck Metal Products, Inc. for 19x4.
2. Prepare a schedule of budgeted computer service charges to each division and the home office, assuming that percentage of usage time and cost distribution in 19x4 will be the same as in 19x3.
3. Determine the amount of general and administrative expense to be allocated to each division in 19x4, using the same direct labor cost distribution percentages as in 19x3.

Problem 20B-3.
Master Budget
(L.O. 4, 5)

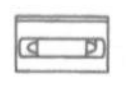

The Bank of Seminole County has asked the president of Naruse Laser Products, Inc. for a forecasted income statement and balance sheet for the quarter ending June 30, 19x1. These documents will be used to support the company's request for a loan. A quarterly master budget is prepared on a routine basis by the company, so the president indicated that the requested documents would be forwarded to the bank.

To date (April 2), the following period budgets have been developed. Sales: April, $220,400, May, $164,220, June, $165,980; materials purchases for the period, $96,840; materials usage, $102,710; labor expenses, $71,460; factory overhead, $79,940; selling expenses for the quarter, $82,840; general and administrative expenses, $60,900; capital expenditures, $125,000 (to be spent on June 29); cost of goods manufactured, $252,880; and cost of goods sold, $251,700.

Balance sheet account balances at March 31, 19x1 were: Cash, $28,770; Accounts Receivable, $26,500; Materials Inventory, $23,910; Work in Process Inventory, $31,620; Finished Goods Inventory, $36,220; Prepaid Expenses, $7,200; Plant, Furniture, and Fixtures, $498,600; Accumulated Depreciation, Plant, Furniture, and Fixtures, $141,162; Patents, $90,600; Accounts Payable, $39,600; Notes Payable, $105,500; Common Stock, $250,000; and Retained Earnings, $207,158.

Monthly cash balances for the quarter are projected to be: April 30, $20,490; May 31, $35,610; and June 30, $45,400. During the quarter, Accounts Receivable are supposed to increase by 30 percent, Patents will go up by $6,500, Prepaid Expenses will remain constant, Accounts Payable will go down by 10 percent, and the company will make a $5,000 payment on the Note Payable ($4,100 is principal reduction). The federal income tax rate is 34 percent and the second quarter's tax is paid in July. Depreciation for the quarter will be $6,420, which was already included in the factory overhead budget.

Required

1. Prepare a forecasted income statement for the quarter ending June 30, 19x1. Round answers to the nearest dollar.
2. Prepare a forecasted statement of financial position as of June 30, 19x1.

Problem 20B-4.
Basic Cash Budget
(L.O. 6)

Produce World, Inc. is the creation of Al Spallino. Spallino's dream was to develop the biggest produce store with the widest selection of fresh fruits and vegetables in the northern Illinois area. In three years, he accomplished his objective. Eighty percent of his business is conducted on credit with area retail enterprises, and 20 percent of the produce sold is to walk-in customers at his retail outlet on a cash only basis.

Collection experience has shown that 50 percent of all credit sales is collected during the month of sale, 30 percent is received in the month following the sale, and 20 percent is collected in the second month after the sale. Spallino has asked you to prepare a cash budget for the quarter ending September 30, 19x4.

Operating data for the period are as follows: Total sales in May were $132,000, and in June, $135,000. Anticipated sales include July, $139,000; August, $152,500; and September, $168,500. Purchases for the quarter are expected to be $87,400 in July; $97,850 in August; and $111,450 in September. All purchases are for cash.

Other projected costs for the quarter include salaries and wages ($36,740 in July; $38,400 in August; and $40,600 in September) and monthly costs of $2,080 for heat, light, and power; $750 for bank collection fees; $3,850 for rent; $2,240 for supplies; $3,410 for depreciation of equipment; $2,570 for equipment repairs; and $950 for miscellaneous expenses. The corporation's cash balance at June 30, 19x4 was $5,490.

Required

1. Prepare a cash budget by month for the quarter ending September 30, 19x4.
2. Should Produce World, Inc. anticipate taking out a loan during the quarter? How much should be borrowed? When? (Note: Management has a $3,000 minimum monthly cash balance policy.)

Problem 20B-5.
Cash Budget Preparation: Comprehensive
(L.O. 6)

Iowa Mountain Ski Resort, Inc. has been in business for twenty-two years. Although the skiing season is difficult to predict, the company operates under the assumption that all of its revenues will be generated during the first three months of the calendar year. Routine maintenance and repair work are done during the remaining nine-month period. The following projections for 19x5 were developed by Kristie Ann, company budget director:

Cash Receipts

Lift tickets: January, 16,800 people @ $22; February, 17,400 people @ $23; and March, 17,800 people @ $24
Food sales: January, $62,000; February, $56,000; and March, $62,000
Skiing lessons: January, $158,000; February, $134,000; and March, $158,000
Equipment sales and rental: January, $592,000; February, $496,000; and March, $592,000
Liquor sales: January, $124,000; February, $92,000; and March, $104,000

Cash Payments

Salaries:
- Ski area:
  - Lift operators: 12 people @ $2,500 per month for January, February, and March (first quarter)
  - Instruction and equipment rental: 24 people @ $2,700 per month for first quarter
- Maintenance: $35,000 per month for first quarter, and a total of $96,000 for the rest of the year
- Customer service: Shuttle bus drivers, 10 people @ $1,400 per month for first quarter
- Medical: 8 people @ $6,400 per month for first quarter
- Food service: 24 people @ $1,800 per month for first quarter

Purchases:
- Food: $30,000 per month for the first quarter
- Ski equipment: Purchases of $340,000 in both January and February plus a $700,000 purchase anticipated in December 19x5
- Liquors: $50,000 in each month of the first quarter
- Tickets and supplies: $50,000 in January, $40,000 in February, and $80,000 in December 19x5

Advertising: $40,000 in January, $30,000 in February, and a total of $90,000 from April through the end of the year
Fire and liability insurance: January and June premium payments of $8,000
Medical facility costs: $15,000 per month during first quarter

Utilities: $5,000 per month for the first quarter and $1,000 per month for the rest of the year
Lift maintenance: $25,000 per month for the first quarter and $10,000 per month for the rest of the year
Property taxes: $180,000 due in June
Federal income taxes: 19x4 taxes of $364,000 due in March

The beginning cash balance for 19x5 is anticipated to be $10,000.

Required

Prepare a cash budget for Iowa Mountain Ski Resort, Inc. for 19x5, using the following column headings:

Item	January	February	March	April–December	Total

Management Decision Case

Hayes Enterprises
(L.O. 3, 5)

During the past ten years, Hayes Enterprises has practiced participative budgeting all the way from the maintenance personnel to the president's staff. Gradually, however, the objectives of honesty and decisions made in the best interest of the company as a whole have given way to division-benefiting decisions and budgets biased in favor of divisional interests. Mr. Douglas, corporate controller, has asked Ms. Uruchurtu, budget director, to carefully analyze this year's divisional budgets before incorporating them into the company's master budget.

The Electronics Division was the first of the six divisions to submit its 19x4 budget request to the corporate office. Its summary income statement and accompanying notes are shown on page 837.

Required

1. Recast the Electronics Division's forecasted income statement into the following format (round percentages to two places):

	Budget—12/31/x3		Budget—12/31/x4	
Account	**Amount**	**Percent of Sales**	**Amount**	**Percent of Sales**

2. Actual results for 19x3 revealed the following information about revenues and cost of goods sold:

	Amount	Percent of Sales
Sales		
Radios	$ 780,000	43.94%
Appliances	640,000	36.06%
Telephones	280,000	15.77%
Miscellaneous	75,000	4.23%
Total Revenues	$1,775,000	100.00%
Less Cost of Goods Sold	763,425	43.01%
Gross Margin from Sales	$1,011,575	56.99%

On the basis of this information and your analysis in **1**, what should the budget director say to officials of the Electronics Division? Mention specific areas of the budget that need to be revised.

Answers to Self-Test

1. b	3. c	5. c	7. d	9. c
2. a	4. b	6. c	8. a	10. b

Hayes Enterprises
Electronics Division
Forecasted Income Statement
For the Years Ending December 31, 19x3 and 19x4

	Budget 12/31/x3	Budget 12/31/x4	Increase (Decrease)
Revenues			
Sales:			
Radios	$ 850,000	$ 910,000	$ 60,000
Appliances	680,000	740,000	60,000
Telephones	270,000	305,000	35,000
Miscellaneous	84,400	90,000	5,600
Total Revenues	$1,884,400	$2,045,000	$160,600
Less Cost of Goods Sold	750,960	717,500[1]	(33,460)
Gross Margin from Sales	$1,133,440	$1,327,500	$194,060
Operating Expenses			
Wages:			
Warehouse	$ 94,500	$ 102,250	$ 7,750
Purchasing	77,800	84,000	6,200
Delivery/Shipping	69,400	74,780	5,380
Maintenance	42,650	45,670	3,020
Salaries:			
Supervisory	60,000	92,250	32,250
Executive	130,000	164,000	34,000
Purchases, Supplies	17,400	20,500	3,100
Merchandise Moving Equipment:			
Maintenance	72,400	82,000	9,600
Depreciation	62,000	74,750[2]	12,750
Building Rent	96,000	102,500	6,500
Sales Commissions	188,440	204,500	16,060
Insurance:			
Fire	12,670	20,500	7,830
Liability	18,200	20,500	2,300
Utilities	14,100	15,375	1,275
Taxes:			
Property	16,600	18,450	1,850
Payroll	26,520	41,000	14,480
Miscellaneous	4,610	10,250	5,640
Total Operating Expenses	$1,003,290	$1,173,275	$169,985
Net Income Before Taxes	$ 130,150	$ 154,225	$ 24,075

1. Less expensive merchandise will be purchased in 19x4 to boost profits.
2. Depreciation is increased because of a need to buy additional equipment to handle increased sales.

LEARNING OBJECTIVES

1. *Define and state the purpose of standard costs.*
2. *Identify the six elements of, and compute, a standard unit cost.*
3. *Define and prepare a flexible budget.*
4. *Describe the concept of management by exception.*
5. *Compute and analyze (a) direct materials, (b) direct labor, and (c) factory overhead variances.*
6. *Prepare journal entries to record transactions involving variances in a standard costing system.*
7. *Evaluate managerial performance using variances.*
8. *Compute and evaluate factory overhead variances using a three-variance analysis.*

CHAPTER 21

Standard Costing and Variance Analysis

Standard cost accounting is a budgetary control technique. Standard costs are realistically predetermined costs that are developed from analyses of future prices and operating conditions. These costs usually serve as targets or goals for product costing purposes, but they can be used in the product distribution and selling cost areas as well. Once developed, standard costs are tools for planning and budgeting activities. In addition, the differences between standard costs and actual costs, called variances, provide a measure of performance that can be used to control costs. By analyzing variances, management accountants are able to separate efficient functions from inefficient functions within the departments or work cells, so managers can concentrate on areas needing improvement.

Traditionally, variances were a yardstick for measuring and evaluating operating performance in manufacturing settings. In recent years, however, a globally competitive manufacturing environment has evolved with a new approach to performance evaluation. Instead of concentrating exclusively on production efficiency and cost control, managers in the new environment are also concerned with reduced processing time, quality improvement, customer satisfaction, and on-time deliveries. This environment requires new measures of performance, which are discussed in the chapters on the just-in-time operating environment and activity-based costing and measures of quality.

In this chapter, we first look at the purpose and makeup of standard costs. After introducing flexible budgeting, we compute and analyze standard cost variances and prepare journal entries to record the variances in the accounting records. Also included is a discussion of performance evaluation, including the use of variances to measure performance. After studying this chapter, you should be able to meet the learning objectives listed on the left.

DECISION POINT

Hewlett-Packard

■ Hewlett-Packard has experimented with replacing standard costs with historical costs as a basis for recording and cost control in its new manufacturing environment.[1] Hewlett-Packard was one of the first companies to successfully update and automate its production facilities and to reduce significantly its product processing time. In a study of the Hewlett-Packard case, a group of researchers questioned the use of historical costs

1. Richard V. Calvasina, Eugene J. Calvasina, and Gerald E. Calvasina, "Beware of New Accounting Myths," *Management Accounting*, Institute of Management Accountants, December 1989, pp. 41–45.

for cost control purposes. The researchers were concerned that historical costs may have been incurred during periods of poor performance and would therefore not be a fitting measure when trying to control costs in a constantly changing environment. The researchers sought to answer the question: Should Hewlett-Packard shift from using standard costs to using historical costs as a basis for cost control analyses?

The researchers found that in the new globally competitive environment, operating conditions promote the use of standard costs. This is because an automated manufacturing environment decreases labor costs significantly, which reduces the emphasis on labor standard costs and variances. Hewlett-Packard's new system reduces the number of suppliers and advocates higher-quality goods and the use of long-term purchase contracts, all of which increases the importance of price and quality of raw materials. Updated standard costs allow materials prices and quality differences to be measured and evaluated.

Automated machinery results in a standardized, repetitive operation and a reduction of overhead costs related to scrap and rework. The use of machinery and equipment capacity must be measured through variance analysis, because in Hewlett-Packard's new manufacturing environment, inventories are kept small and facilities are idle if no orders are being processed. Factory overhead standards and variances measure these areas. The researchers concluded that these facts support an increase in the use of standard costs, rather than their elimination. ■

Standard Cost Accounting

Accountants do not build a full cost accounting system from standard costs alone. Standard costs are used with existing job order or process costing systems. When a company uses standard costs, all costs affecting the inventory accounts and the Cost of Goods Sold account are recorded using standard or predetermined costs rather than actual costs incurred. In this section, we examine the nature and purpose of standard costs—their components, their development, their use in product costing, and their related journal entries. Later in the chapter we concentrate on the way they are used, primarily as a tool for cost control.

Nature and Purpose of Standard Costs

OBJECTIVE 1
Define and state the purpose of standard costs

Standard costs are predetermined realistic costs for direct materials, direct labor, and factory overhead. They usually are expressed as cost per unit of finished product or process. Standard costs share two very important characteristics with predetermined overhead costs: both forecast the dollar amounts to be used in product costing, and both depend on projected costs for budgeted items. But that is where the similarity ends.

Unlike the predetermined overhead rate, standard costing focuses on *total* unit cost, which includes all three manufacturing cost elements. The computation of standard costs is more detailed than that of predetermined overhead costs. Whereas predetermined overhead rates usually depend on projections based on past costs, standard costs are based on engineering estimates, forecasted demand, worker input, time and motion studies, and type and quality of direct materials. One drawback to standard costing is that it is expensive to use.

Since the predetermined overhead rate does provide some of the same data as the standard overhead rate, a company that cannot afford to add standard costing to its cost system should continue to use predetermined overhead rates.

Standard costing is a total cost concept. In a fully integrated standard cost system, standard cost data replace all actual manufacturing cost data. Accounts such as Materials Inventory, Work in Process Inventory, Finished Goods Inventory, and Cost of Goods Sold are reported in terms of standard costs. All debits and credits to these accounts are in terms of standard costs, not actual costs. All inventory balances are computed using standard unit costs. The management accountant keeps separate records of actual costs to compare what should have been spent (the standard costs) with the actual costs incurred. The difference between a standard cost and an actual cost is called a **variance**. The management accountant calculates the variances at the end of the accounting period, whether weekly, monthly, or quarterly. If a variance exists, the management accountant looks for the causes of the difference between the actual and the standard costs. This process, known as variance analysis, is an effective cost control tool. We discuss it later in this chapter.

In summary, standard costs are introduced into a cost accounting system for several reasons. They are useful in preparing operating budgets. They make it easier to pinpoint production costs that must be controlled and to evaluate the performance of managers and workers. They help in setting realistic prices, and they simplify cost accounting procedures for inventories and product costing. Although expensive to set up and maintain, a standard cost accounting system can save a company money by helping to reduce waste and inefficiency.

Development of Standard Costs

OBJECTIVE 2
Identify the six elements of, and compute, a standard unit cost

A standard unit cost for a manufactured product has six parts: (1) direct materials price standard, (2) direct materials quantity standard, (3) direct labor time standard, (4) direct labor rate standard, (5) standard variable factory overhead rate, and (6) standard fixed factory overhead rate. To develop a standard unit cost, we must identify and analyze each of these elements. For service companies, only the last four apply because these companies do not use raw materials or parts in their operations.

Standard Direct Materials Cost. The **standard direct materials cost** is found by multiplying the standard price for direct materials by the standard quantity for direct materials. If the standard price for a certain item is $2.75 and a specific job calls for a standard quantity of 8 of the items, the standard direct materials cost for that job is $22.00 (8 × $2.75).

The **direct materials price standard** is a careful estimate of the cost of a certain type of direct material in the next accounting period. The purchasing agent is responsible for developing price standards for all direct materials. When estimating the direct materials price standard, the purchasing agent must take into account all possible price increases, changes in available quantities, and new sources of supply. The purchasing agent also makes the actual purchases.

The standard quantity of direct materials is one of the most difficult standards to forecast. The **direct materials quantity standard** is an estimate of the expected quantity to be used. It is influenced by product engineering specifications, the quality of direct materials, the age and productivity of machinery, and the quality and experience of the work force. Some spoilage and waste may be unavoidable and anticipated when computing the standard quantity amount. Production managers or cost accountants usually establish and police direct materials quantity standards, although engineers, purchasing agents, and machine operators may provide input into the development of these standards.

Standard Direct Labor Cost. The **standard direct labor cost** for a product, task, or job order is calculated by multiplying the standard hours of direct labor by the standard wage for direct labor. If a product takes 1.5 standard direct labor hours to produce and the standard direct labor rate is $8.40 per hour, then the product's standard direct labor cost is $12.60 ($8.40 × 1.5).

Current time and motion studies of workers and machines as well as past employee and machine performance are the basic input for a **direct labor time standard**. This standard expresses the expected time required for each department, machine, or process to complete the production of one unit or one batch. In many cases, standard time per unit is a small fraction of an hour. The direct labor time standard should be revised whenever a machine is replaced or the quality of the labor force changes. Meeting time standards is the responsibility of the department manager or supervisor.

Standard labor rates are fairly easy to develop because labor rates are either set by a labor contract or defined by the company. **Direct labor rate standards** are the hourly labor costs that are expected to prevail during the next accounting period for each function or job classification. Although rate ranges are established for each type of worker and rates vary within these ranges based on experience and length of service, an average standard rate is developed for each task. Even if the person actually making the product is paid less, the standard rate is used in calculating the standard direct labor cost.

Standard Factory Overhead Cost. The **standard factory overhead cost** is the sum of the estimates for variable and fixed factory overhead in the next accounting period. It is based on standard rates computed in much the same way as the predetermined overhead rate discussed earlier. One major difference, however, is that the standard overhead rate is made up of two parts, one for variable costs and one for fixed costs. The reason for computing the standard variable and fixed overhead rates separately is that different application bases are generally required. The **standard variable overhead rate** is total budgeted variable factory overhead costs divided by an expression of capacity, such as the expected number of standard machine hours or direct labor hours. (Other bases may be used if machine hours or direct labor hours are not good measures of variable overhead costs.) The formula using standard labor hours as the basis is:

$$\text{Standard variable overhead rate} = \frac{\text{total budgeted variable overhead costs}}{\text{expected number of standard direct labor hours}}$$

The **standard fixed overhead rate** is total budgeted fixed factory overhead costs divided by an expression of capacity, usually normal capacity in terms of standard direct labor hours. The basis is expressed in the same terms (direct labor hours, machine hours, and so forth) as that used to compute the variable overhead rate. The formula is:

$$\text{Standard fixed overhead rate} = \frac{\text{total budgeted fixed overhead costs}}{\text{normal capacity in terms of standard direct labor hours}}$$

Using normal capacity as the application basis ensures that all fixed overhead costs have been applied to units produced by the time normal capacity is reached.

Using Standards for Product Costing

Using standard costs eliminates the need to calculate unit costs from actual cost data every week or month or for each batch produced. Once standard costs are developed for direct materials, direct labor, and factory overhead, you can compute a total standard unit cost at any time.

With standard cost elements, you determine the following amounts: (1) cost of purchased direct materials entered into Materials Inventory, (2) cost of goods requisitioned out of Materials Inventory and into Work in Process Inventory, (3) cost of direct labor charged to Work in Process Inventory, (4) cost of factory overhead applied to Work in Process Inventory, (5) cost of goods completed and transferred to Finished Goods Inventory, and (6) cost of units sold and charged to Cost of Goods Sold. In other words, all transactions (and related journal entries) affecting the three inventory accounts and Cost of Goods Sold are expressed in terms of standard costs, no matter what the amount of actual costs incurred. An illustrative problem shows how standard costing works.

Illustrative Problem
Use of Standard Costs

Surrency Industries, Inc. uses a standard cost accounting system in its Swainsboro, Georgia division. Recently, the company updated the standards for its line of automatic pencils to agree with current costs for the year 19x3. New standards include the following: Direct materials price standards are $9.20 per square foot for casing materials and $2.25 for each movement mechanism. Direct materials quantity standards are .025 square foot of casing materials per pencil and one movement mechanism per pencil. Direct labor time standards are .01 hour per pencil for the Stamping Department and .05 hour per pencil for the Assembly Department. Direct labor rate standards are $8.00 per hour for the Stamping Department and $10.20 per hour for the Assembly Department. Standard factory overhead rates are $12.00 per total direct labor hours for the standard variable overhead rate and $9.00 per total direct labor hours for the standard fixed overhead rate.

Required

Compute the standard manufacturing cost of one automatic pencil.

Solution

Direct materials costs	
Casing ($9.20/sq ft × .025 sq ft)	$ .23
One movement mechanism	2.25
Direct labor costs	
Stamping Department (.01 hour/pencil × $8.00/hour)	.08
Assembly Department (.05 hour/pencil × $10.20/hour)	.51
Factory overhead	
Variable overhead (.06 hour/pencil × $12.00/hour)	.72
Fixed overhead (.06 hour/pencil × $9.00/hour)	.54
Total standard cost of one pencil	$4.33

Journal Entry Analysis

Recording standard costs is much like recording actual cost data. The major difference is that amounts for direct materials, direct labor, or factory overhead entered into the Work in Process Inventory account are recorded at standard cost. This means that any transfer of units to Finished Goods Inventory or to the Cost of Goods Sold account will automatically be stated at standard unit cost. When actual costs for direct materials, direct labor, and factory overhead differ from standard costs, the difference is recorded in a variance account. (We discuss variance accounts in the next section.) In the following journal entry analysis, it is assumed that all costs incurred are at standard cost, so no variances are shown in the entries. Again, Surrency Industries' standard costs, which were given previously, are used in the following examples.

Sample Transaction: Purchased 500 square feet of casing materials at standard cost on account.

Entry:		
Materials Inventory	4,600	
Accounts Payable		4,600
Purchase of 500 sq ft of casing material @ $9.20/sq ft		

Here it does not matter if the actual purchase price differs from the standard price. The standard cost only is entered into the Materials Inventory account.

Sample Transaction: Requisitioned 60 square feet of casing material and 240 movement mechanisms into production.

Entry:		
Work in Process Inventory	1,092	
Materials Inventory		1,092
Requisition of 60 sq ft of casing material (@ $9.20/sq ft) and 240 movement mechanisms (@ $2.25 each) into production		

Sample Transaction: During the period, 600 pencils were completed and transferred to Finished Goods Inventory.

Entry:		
Finished Goods Inventory	2,598	
Work in Process Inventory		2,598
Transfer of 600 completed units to finished goods inventory (600 pencils × $4.33/pencil)		

The preceding entries show that when a standard cost accounting system is used, standard costs, not actual costs, flow through the production and inventory accounts. Examples later in this chapter combine the recording of standard cost information with the analysis of variances.

Cost Control Through Variance Analysis

Managers of manufacturing operations, as well as those responsible for selling and service functions, constantly compare what did happen with what was expected to happen. The difference—or variance—between actual and standard costs provides information needed to evaluate managers' performance. If the variance is too great, managers can implement cost control measures. Our discussion now focuses on the differences between actual costs and budgeted or standard costs. Before budgeted data can be used to analyze performance, they must be adjusted to reflect actual productive output. The flexible budget is the management accounting tool used for this purpose.

The Flexible Budget

The type of budget used determines the accuracy of performance measurement. The budgets we discussed in the chapter on the budgeting process as part of the planning function were *static*, or fixed, budgets—budgets that describe just one level of expected sales and production activity. The master budget, including all the period budgets, usually is prepared for a single expected or normal level of output. For budgeting or planning, a set of static budgets based on a single level of output is adequate. These budgets show the desired operating results and provide a target for use in developing monthly and weekly operating plans.

Such budgets, however, often prove inadequate for judging operating results. Exhibit 21-1 presents data for NMA Industries, Inc. As you can see, actual costs exceed budgeted costs by $14,300, or 7.2 percent. Most managers would consider such an overrun to be significant. But was there really a cost overrun? The budgeted amounts are based on an expected output of 17,500 units, but actual output was 19,100 units. Thus, the static budget for 17,500 units is inadequate for judging performance. Before analyzing the performance of the Alafaya Division, we must change the budgeted data to reflect an output of 19,100 units.

OBJECTIVE 3
Define and prepare a flexible budget

Unlike a static budget, a flexible budget provides forecasted data that can be adjusted automatically for changes in the level of output. A **flexible budget** is a summary of expected costs for a *range* of activity levels, geared to changes in the level of productive output. The flexible budget (also called a variable budget) is primarily a cost control tool used in evaluating performance.

Exhibit 21-2 presents a flexible budget for NMA Industries, Inc., with budgeted data for 15,000, 17,500, and 20,000 units of output. The important part of this illustration is the flexible budget formula shown at the bottom. The **flexible budget formula** is an equation that determines the correct budgeted cost for any level of productive activity. It consists of a per unit amount for variable costs and a total amount for fixed costs. In Exhibit 21-2, the $8.60 variable cost per unit is computed in the upper right-hand column, and the $49,400 is found

Exhibit 21-1. Performance Analysis: Comparison of Actual and Budgeted Data

NMA Industries, Inc.
Performance Report—Alafaya Division
For the Year Ended December 31, 19x5

Cost Item	Budget*	Actual†	Difference Under (Over) Budget
Direct materials	$ 42,000	$ 46,000	$ (4,000)
Direct labor	68,250	75,000	(6,750)
Factory overhead			
Variable			
Indirect materials	10,500	11,500	(1,000)
Indirect labor	14,000	15,250	(1,250)
Utilities	7,000	7,600	(600)
Other	8,750	9,750	(1,000)
Fixed			
Supervisory salaries	19,000	18,500	500
Depreciation	15,000	15,000	—
Utilities	4,500	4,500	—
Other	10,900	11,100	(200)
Totals	$199,900	$214,200	$(14,300)

*Budget based on expected productive output of 17,500 units.
†Actual cost of producing 19,100 units.

Exhibit 21-2. Flexible Budget Preparation

NMA Industries, Inc.
Flexible Budget Analysis—Alafaya Division
For the Year Ended December 31, 19x5

	Unit Levels of Activity			
Cost Item	15,000	17,500	20,000	Variable Cost per Unit*
Direct materials	$ 36,000	$ 42,000	$ 48,000	$2.40
Direct labor	58,500	68,250	78,000	3.90
Variable factory overhead				
Indirect materials	9,000	10,500	12,000	.60
Indirect labor	12,000	14,000	16,000	.80
Utilities	6,000	7,000	8,000	.40
Other	7,500	8,750	10,000	.50
Total variable costs	$129,000	$150,500	$172,000	$8.60
Fixed factory overhead				
Supervisory salaries	$ 19,000	$ 19,000	$ 19,000	
Depreciation	15,000	15,000	15,000	
Utilities	4,500	4,500	4,500	
Other	10,900	10,900	10,900	
Total fixed costs	$ 49,400	$ 49,400	$ 49,400	
Total costs	$178,400	$199,900	$221,400	

Flexible budget formula:
(variable cost per unit × number of units produced) + budgeted fixed costs
= ($8.60 × units produced) + $49,400

Note: Activity expressed in units was used as the basis for this analysis. When units are used, direct material and direct labor costs are included in the analysis. Flexible budgets commonly are restricted to overhead costs. In such a situation, machine hours or direct labor hours are used in place of units produced.
*Computed by dividing the dollar amount in any column by the respective level of activity.

in the fixed cost section of the analysis. Using this formula, you can draw up a budget for the Alafaya Division at any level of output.

Exhibit 21-3 shows a performance report prepared using the flexible budget data in Exhibit 21-2. Unit variable cost amounts have been multiplied by 19,100 units to arrive at the total budgeted figures. Fixed overhead information has been carried over from the flexible budget developed in Exhibit 21-2. As the new performance report shows, costs exceeded budgeted amounts during the year by only $540, or less than three-tenths of one percent. In other words, using a flexible budget, we find that the performance of the Alafaya Division is almost on target. Performance has now been measured and analyzed accurately. In addition to being a tool for overall performance measurement, a flexible budget also is used in analyzing factory overhead cost variances, which is discussed below.

Variance Determination and Analysis

We can evaluate operating performance by comparing actual results with either budgeted data or standard cost data. Budgeted data tend to be less precise than

Exhibit 21-3. Performance Analysis Using Flexible Budget Data

NMA Industries, Inc.
Performance Report—Alafaya Division
For the Year Ended December 31, 19x5

Cost Item (Variable Unit Cost)	Budget Based on 19,100 Units Produced	Actual Costs at 19,100-Unit Level	Difference Under (Over) Budget
Direct materials ($2.40)	$ 45,840	$ 46,000	$(160)
Direct labor ($3.90)	74,490	75,000	(510)
Factory overhead			
Variable			
Indirect materials ($.60)	11,460	11,500	(40)
Indirect labor ($.80)	15,280	15,250	30
Utilities ($.40)	7,640	7,600	40
Other ($.50)	9,550	9,750	(200)
Fixed			
Supervisory salaries	19,000	18,500	500
Depreciation	15,000	15,000	—
Utilities	4,500	4,500	—
Other	10,900	11,100	(200)
Totals	$213,660	$214,200	$(540)

standard cost data, so we focus on measuring performance using standard costs.

The first step in measuring performance is to find out if a cost variance exists. Variance determination helps to locate areas of efficiency or inefficiency. But the key to effective control of operations is not just finding the amount of the variance, but finding the reason for the variance. Once the cause is known, managers can take steps to correct the problem.

OBJECTIVE 4
Describe the concept of management by exception

The process of computing the amount of and isolating the causes of differences between actual costs and standard costs is called **variance analysis.** It is employed selectively. Many companies are so big that it is impossible to review all areas of operations in detail. Only the areas of unusually good or unusually bad performance are examined, a practice called **management by exception.** Let's assume that management decides that performance within ± 4 percent of budget or target is acceptable. When reviewing performance reports, they examine only those cost areas where differences exceed these limits. In Figure 21-1, for example, only direct materials C and E are outside the 4 percent limit, so only their costs will be analyzed.

Management accountants can compute variances for whole categories, such as total direct materials cost, or for any item in a category. The more refined and detailed the analysis, the more effective it is in cost control. This chapter presents a simplified example of standard cost variance analysis. In practice, variance analyses are much more complex, taking into account all facets of production and distribution.

Management accountants compute three types of variances: direct materials variances, direct labor variances, and factory overhead variances. Although

Figure 21-1. The Management-by-Exception Technique

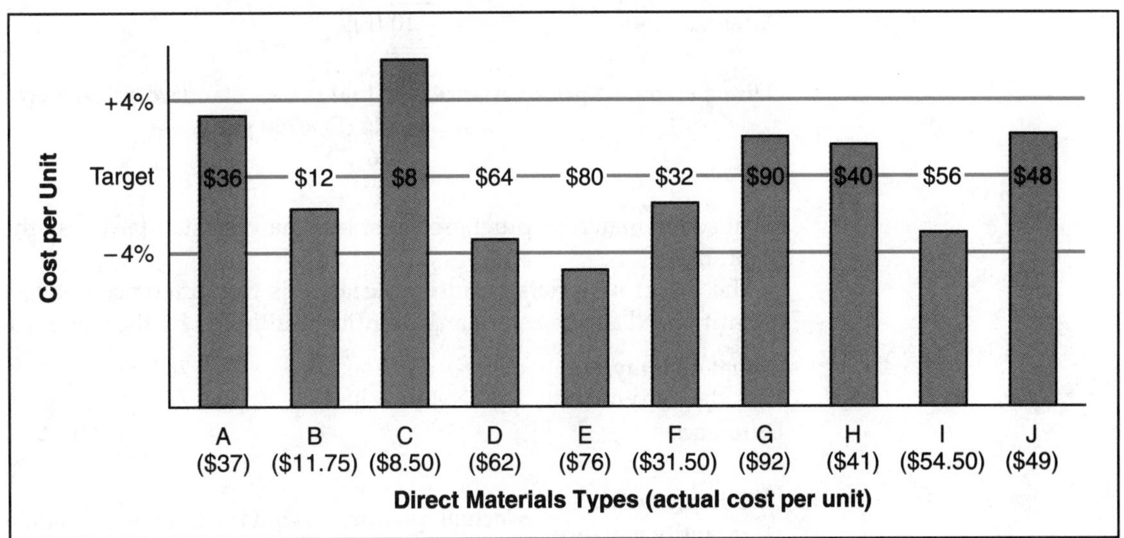

materials variances are unique to manufacturing companies, labor and overhead variances may be computed for service enterprises as well as manufacturing companies. The term *service overhead* replaces factory overhead in service companies.

OBJECTIVE 5a
Compute and analyze direct materials variances

Direct Materials Variances. The **total direct materials cost variance** is the difference between the actual materials cost incurred and the standard cost of those items. Let us assume, for example, that Boyer Company makes leather chairs. Each chair should use 4 yards of leather (standard quantity), and the standard price of leather is $6.00 per yard. During August, Boyer Company purchased 760 yards of leather costing $5.90 per yard and used the leather to produce 180 chairs. The total direct materials cost variance is as follows:

Actual cost	
Actual quantity × actual price =	
760 yd × $5.90/yd =	**$4,484**
Less standard cost	
Standard quantity × standard price =	
(180 chairs × 4 yd/chair) × $6.00/yd =	
720 yd × $6.00/yd =	**4,320**
Total direct materials cost variance	**$ 164 (U)**

Here actual cost exceeds standard cost. The situation is unfavorable, as indicated by the *U* placed in parentheses after the dollar amount. An *F* designates a favorable situation.

To find the area or people responsible for the variance, the total direct materials cost variance must be broken down into two parts: the direct materials price variance and the direct materials quantity variance. The **direct materials price variance** is the difference between the actual price and the standard price, multiplied by the actual quantity purchased. For Boyer Company, the direct materials price variance is computed as shown at the top of page 848.

Actual price	$5.90
Less standard price	6.00
Difference	$ .10 (F)

Direct materials price variance = (actual price − standard price) × actual quantity
= $.10 (F) × 760 yards
= $76 (F)

Because the materials purchased cost less than the standard cost, the variance is favorable.

The **direct materials quantity variance** is the difference between the actual quantity used and the standard quantity, multiplied by the standard price.

Actual quantity	760 yd
Less standard quantity (180 × 4 yd/chair)	720 yd
Difference	40 yd (U)

Direct materials quantity variance = (actual quantity − standard quantity) × standard price
= 40 yd (U) × $6/yd
= $240 (U)

Because more material than prescribed was used, the direct materials quantity variance is unfavorable.

If the results of these calculations are correct, the sum of the price variance and the quantity variance should equal the total direct materials cost variance, as follows:

Direct materials price variance	$ 76 (F)
Direct materials quantity variance	240 (U)
Total direct materials cost variance	$164 (U)

Normally, the purchasing agent is responsible for price variances and the production department supervisors are accountable for quantity variances. In cases like this one, however, the cheaper materials may have been of such poor quality that higher-than-expected scrap rates resulted, creating the unfavorable quantity variance. Each situation must be evaluated according to specific circumstances and not in terms of general guidelines.

Sometimes cost relationships are easier to interpret in diagram form. Figure 21-2 illustrates the analysis just described. Notice that materials are purchased at actual cost but entered into the Materials Inventory account at standard price; therefore, the materials price variance of $76 (F) is known before costs are entered into Materials Inventory. As shown in the figure, the standard quantity times the standard price is the amount entered into the Work in Process Inventory account.

OBJECTIVE 5b
Compute and analyze direct labor variances

Direct Labor Variances. The procedure for finding variances in direct labor costs parallels the procedure for finding direct materials variances. The **total direct labor cost variance** is the difference between the actual labor costs incurred and the standard labor cost for the good units produced. (Good units are the total units produced less those units scrapped or needing rework.) In the Boyer Company example, each chair requires 2.4 standard labor hours, and the standard labor rate is $8.50 per hour. During August, 450 direct labor hours

Figure 21-2. Materials Variance Analysis

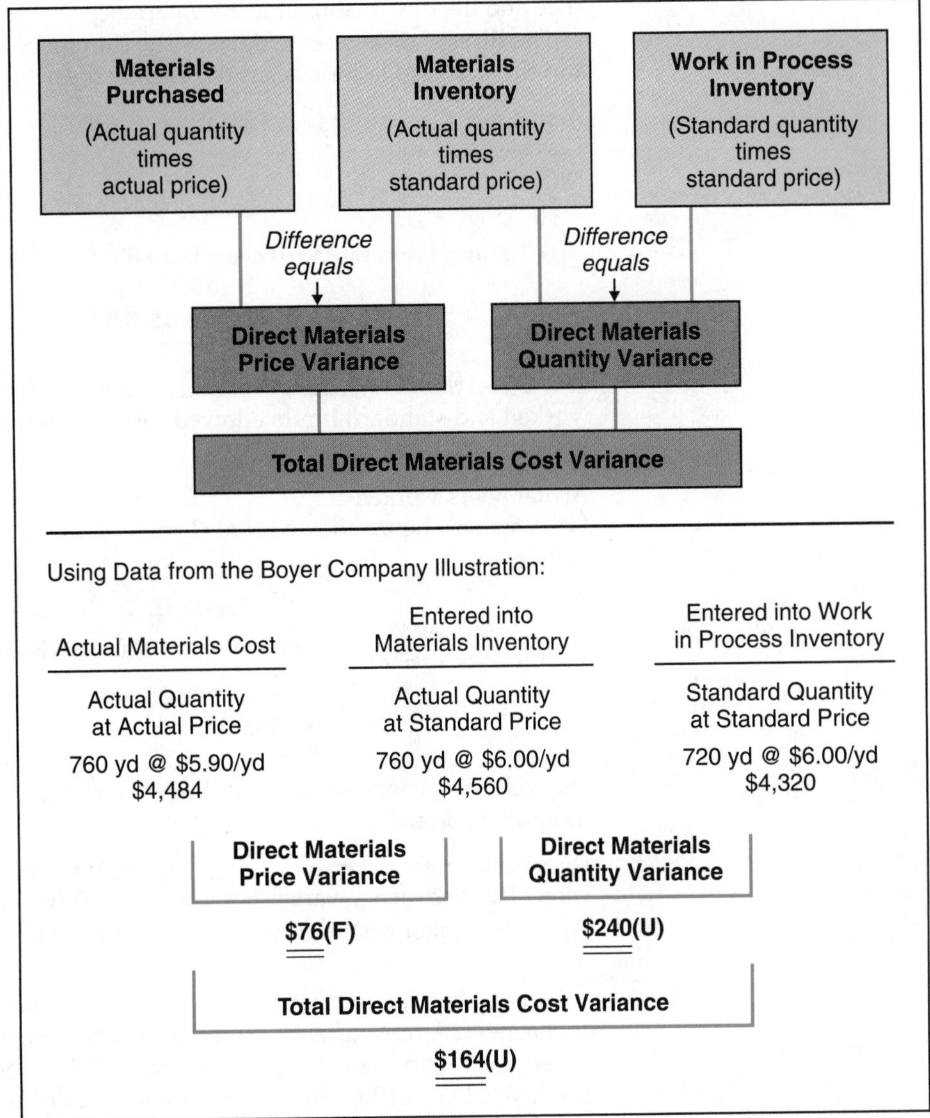

were used to make 180 chairs at an average pay rate of $9.20 per hour. The total direct labor cost variance is computed as follows.

Actual cost		
	Actual hours × actual rate = 450 hr × $9.20 =	**$4,140**
Less standard cost		
	Standard hours allowed × standard rate =	
	(180 chairs × 2.4 hr/chair) × $8.50/hr =	
	432 hr × $8.50/hr =	**3,672**
Total direct labor cost variance		**$ 468 (U)**

Both the actual hours per chair and the actual labor rate varied from the standard. For effective performance evaluation, management must know how much of the total cost arose from differing labor rates and how much from varying labor hours. This information is found by computing the direct labor rate variance and the direct labor efficiency variance.

The **direct labor rate variance** is the difference between the actual labor rate and the standard labor rate, multiplied by the actual labor hours worked.

Actual rate	$9.20
Less standard rate	8.50
Difference	$ .70 (U)

Direct labor rate variance = (actual rate − standard rate) × actual hours
= $.70 (U) × 450 hr
= $315 (U)

The **direct labor efficiency variance** is the difference between actual hours worked and standard hours allowed for the good units produced, multiplied by the standard labor rate.

Actual hours worked	450 hr
Less standard hours allowed (180 chairs × 2.4 hr/chair)	432 hr
Difference	18 hr (U)

Direct labor efficiency variance = (actual hours − standard hours allowed) × standard rate
= 18 hr (U) × $8.50/hr
= $153 (U)

The following check shows that the rate and the efficiency variances have been computed correctly.

Direct labor rate variance	$315 (U)
Direct labor efficiency variance	153 (U)
Total direct labor cost variance	$468 (U)

Direct labor rate variances are generally the responsibility of the personnel department. A rate variance can occur when a person is hired at a rate higher or lower than expected or performs the duties of a higher- or lower-paid employee. Direct labor efficiency variances can be traced to departmental supervisors. Problems in controlling labor costs arise when the wrong worker steps in to cover another's task. An example would be when a highly paid worker performs a lower-level task. For instance, a machine operator making $9.25 per hour may actually perform the work of a set-up person earning $4.50 per hour. Here, the actual cost for the work will be at variance with the standard direct labor rate. An unfavorable labor efficiency variance can also occur if an inexperienced, lower-paid person is assigned to a task requiring greater skill. Management should judge each situation according to the circumstances.

Figure 21-3 summarizes the direct labor variance analysis. Unlike materials variances, the labor rate and efficiency variances are usually computed and recorded at the same time, because labor is not stored in an inventory account before use. Data from Boyer Company in the lower portion of Figure 21-3 illustrate this approach to labor variance analysis.

Factory Overhead Variances. Controlling overhead costs is more difficult than controlling direct materials and direct labor costs because responsibility for

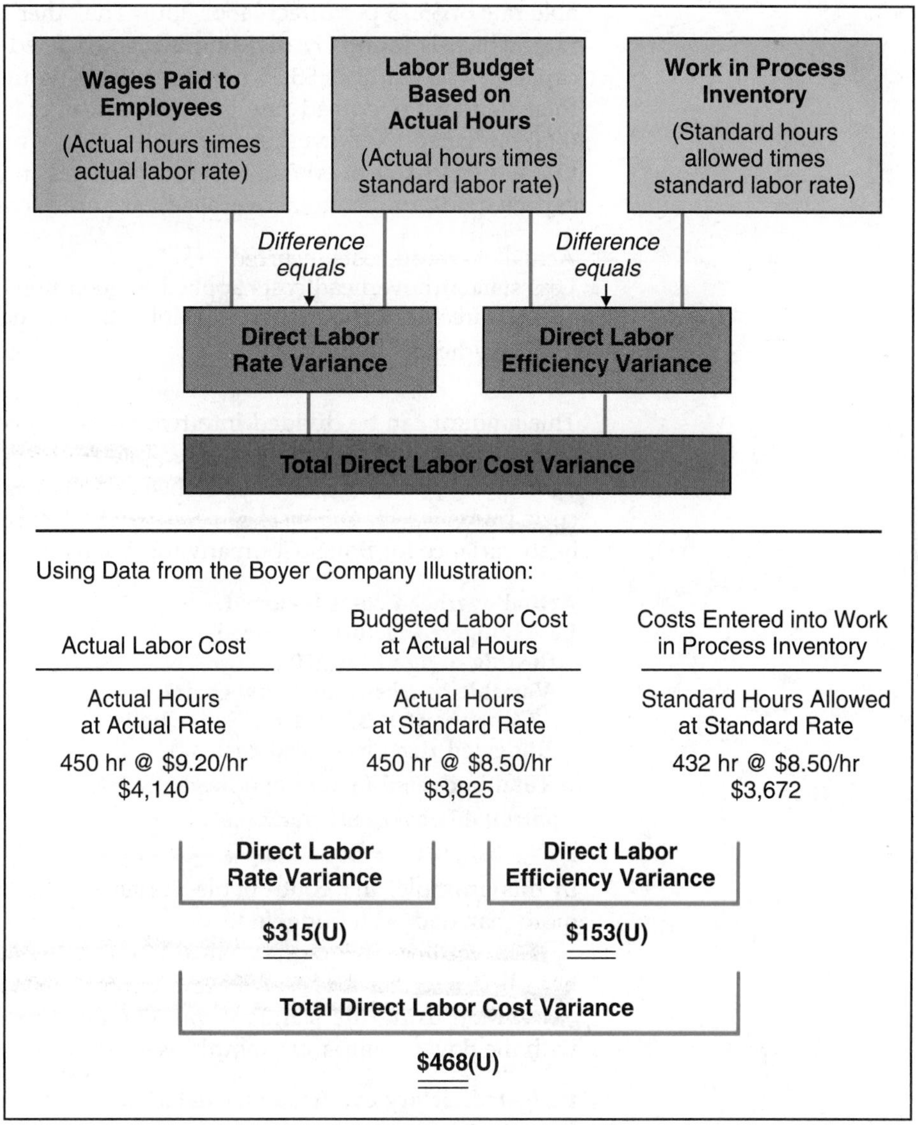

Figure 21-3. Direct Labor Variance Analysis

Using Data from the Boyer Company Illustration:

Actual Labor Cost	Budgeted Labor Cost at Actual Hours	Costs Entered into Work in Process Inventory
Actual Hours at Actual Rate	Actual Hours at Standard Rate	Standard Hours Allowed at Standard Rate
450 hr @ $9.20/hr	450 hr @ $8.50/hr	432 hr @ $8.50/hr
$4,140	$3,825	$3,672

Direct Labor Rate Variance **$315(U)**

Direct Labor Efficiency Variance **$153(U)**

Total Direct Labor Cost Variance **$468(U)**

OBJECTIVE 5c
Compute and analyze factory overhead variances

overhead costs is hard to assign. Most fixed overhead costs are not controlled by specific department managers. But if variable overhead costs can be linked to operating departments, some control is possible.

Analyses of factory overhead variances differ in sophistication. The basic approach is to first compute the **total overhead variance**, which is the difference between actual overhead costs incurred and the standard overhead costs applied to production using the standard variable and fixed overhead rates. The total overhead variance is then divided into two parts: the controllable overhead variance and the overhead volume variance.

In our example, Boyer Company budgeted standard variable overhead costs of $5.75 per direct labor hour plus $1,300 of fixed overhead costs for the month of August (flexible budget formula). Normal capacity was set at 400 direct labor hours per month. The company incurred $4,100 of actual overhead costs in August.

Before finding the overhead variances, the total standard overhead rate must be calculated. The total standard overhead rate has two parts. One is the variable rate of $5.75 per direct labor hour. The other is the standard fixed overhead rate, which is found by dividing budgeted fixed overhead ($1,300) by normal capacity. The result is $3.25 per direct labor hour ($1,300 ÷ 400 hours). So, the total standard overhead rate is $9.00 per direct labor hour ($5.75 + $3.25). The total budgeted fixed overhead costs divided by normal capacity provides a rate that assigns fixed overhead costs to products in a way that is consistent with expected output. The total overhead variance is computed as follows:

Actual overhead costs incurred	$4,100
Less standard overhead costs applied to good units produced	
$9.00/direct labor hour × (180 chairs × 2.4 hr/chair)	3,888
Total overhead variance	$ 212 (U)

This amount can be divided into two parts: the controllable overhead variance and the overhead volume variance. The **controllable overhead variance** is the difference between the actual overhead costs incurred and the factory overhead costs budgeted for the level of production reached. Thus, the controllable overhead variance for Boyer Company for August is as follows:

Actual overhead costs incurred		$4,100
Less budgeted factory overhead (flexible budget) for 180 chairs:		
Variable overhead cost (180 chairs × 2.4 hr/chair) × $5.75/direct labor hour	$2,484	
Budgeted fixed overhead cost	1,300	
Total budgeted factory overhead		3,784
Controllable overhead variance		$ 316 (U)

In this example, the controllable variance is unfavorable; the company spent more than had been budgeted.

The **overhead volume variance** is the difference between the factory overhead budgeted for the level of production achieved and the overhead applied to production using the standard variable and fixed overhead rates. Continuing with the Boyer Company example, we have the following:

Budgeted factory overhead (see detail above)	$3,784
Less factory overhead applied	
(180 chairs × 2.4 hr/chair) × $9.00/direct labor hour	3,888
Overhead volume variance	$ 104 (F)

Checking the computations, we find that the two variances do equal the total overhead variance.

Controllable overhead variance	$316 (U)
Overhead volume variance	104 (F)
Total overhead variance	$212 (U)

Because the overhead volume variance gauges the use of existing facilities and capacity, a volume variance will occur if more or less capacity than normal is used. In this example, 400 direct labor hours is considered normal use of facilities. Fixed overhead costs are applied on the basis of standard hours allowed. So in the example, overhead was applied on the basis of 432 hours, even though the fixed overhead rate was computed using 400 hours (normal capacity). Thus, more fixed costs would be applied to products than were budgeted. Because the products can absorb no more than actual costs incurred, this level of production would tend to lower unit cost. Thus, when capacity exceeds the expected amount, the result is a favorable overhead volume variance. When capacity does not meet the normal level, not all of the fixed overhead costs will be applied to units produced. It is then necessary to add the amount of underapplied fixed overhead to the cost of the good units produced, thereby increasing their unit cost. This condition is unfavorable.

Figure 21-4 summarizes the analysis of overhead variance. As explained earlier, to determine the controllable overhead variance, the management accountant subtracts the budgeted overhead amount (using a flexible budget for the

Figure 21-4. Overhead Variance Analysis

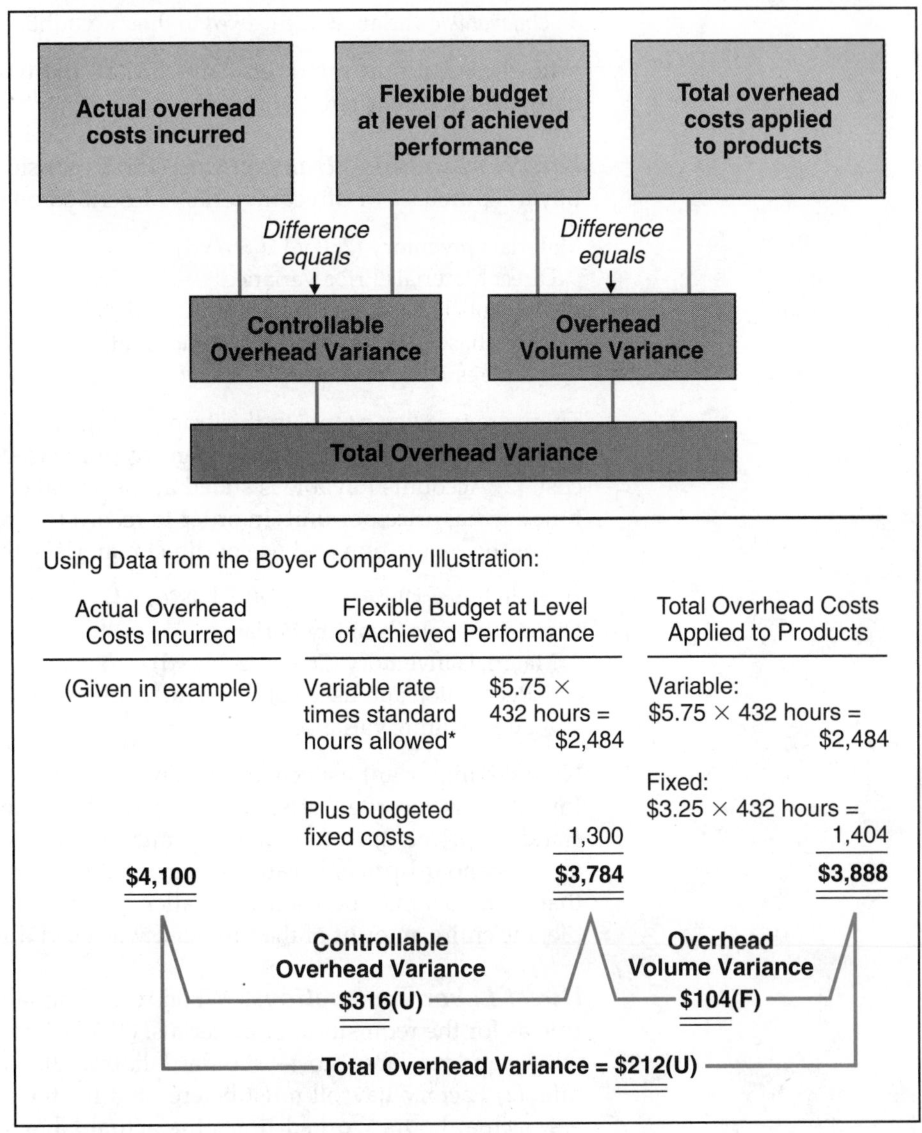

*Standard hours allowed (achieved performance level) is computed by multiplying good units produced times required standard time per unit. The computation is as follows:

180 chairs produced × 2.4 hours per chair = 432 standard hours allowed

level of output achieved) from the actual overhead costs incurred. A positive result means an unfavorable variance, because actual costs were greater than budgeted costs. The controllable overhead variance is favorable if the difference is negative. Subtracting total overhead applied from budgeted overhead at the level of output achieved yields the overhead volume variance. Again, a positive result means an unfavorable variance; a negative result, a favorable variance. The data from the Boyer Company example are shown in the lower part of Figure 21-4. Carefully check the solution in the figure with that given earlier.

Variances in the Accounting Records

OBJECTIVE 6
Prepare journal entries to record transactions involving variances in a standard costing system

Special journal entries are needed to record variances from standard costs. Three simple rules make this recording process easy to remember:

1. *All* inventory balances are recorded at standard cost.
2. Separate general ledger accounts are created for each type of variance.
3. *Unfavorable* variances are *debited* to their accounts; *favorable* variances are *credited.*

With these rules in mind, let us record all the transactions of the Boyer Company described earlier.

Direct Materials Transactions. First, consider the following entry for Boyer's purchase of direct materials (described on pages 847 and 848):

Materials Inventory (760 yd @ $6/yd)	4,560	
Direct Materials Price Variance		76
Accounts Payable (actual cost) (760 × $5.90)		4,484
Purchase of direct materials on account and resulting variance		

There are two key points to this transaction: (1) The increase in Materials Inventory is recorded at the actual quantity purchased, but priced at the standard cost. (2) Accounts Payable is stated at the actual cost (actual quantity purchased times actual price per unit) in order to record the proper liability.

For the requisition and use of direct materials, the entry would be:

Work in Process Inventory (720 yd @ $6/yd)	4,320	
Direct Materials Quantity Variance	240	
Materials Inventory (760 yd @ $6/yd)		4,560
Requisition and usage of direct materials and resulting variance		

Note the important aspects of this entry: (1) Everything in the Work in Process Inventory is recorded at standard cost, which means standard quantity times standard price. (2) Actual quantity must be removed from Materials Inventory at the standard price, because it was entered at the standard price. Remember that materials may be used in smaller quantities than purchased. In the example, the entire amount of the purchase was used during the period.

Direct Labor Transactions. When recording labor costs, the same rules hold true as for the requisition of materials. (1) Work in Process Inventory is charged with standard labor cost—standard hours allowed times the standard labor rate. (2) Factory Payroll must be credited for the actual labor cost of the workers—actual hours worked times the actual labor rate earned. The variances, if computed properly, will balance out the difference between the two amounts. The journal entry for recording labor costs for Boyer Company is shown at the top of the next page.

Work in Process Inventory (432 hr @ $8.50/hr)	3,672	
Direct Labor Rate Variance	315	
Direct Labor Efficiency Variance	153	
Factory Payroll (450 hr @ $9.20/hr)		4,140
To charge labor cost to Work in Process and to identify the resulting variances		

Application of Factory Overhead. Recording factory overhead variances differs in timing and technique from recording direct materials and direct labor variances. First, total factory overhead is charged to Work in Process Inventory at standard cost (standard labor hours allowed times the standard variable and fixed rates). The variances are identified later, when the Factory Overhead Control account is closed out at period end. The journal entries to record factory overhead for Boyer Company are:

Work in Process Inventory (432 direct labor hours @ $9/direct labor hour)	3,888	
Factory Overhead Control		3,888
To apply factory overhead costs to Work in Process at standard cost		

Since the company incurred $4,100 in overhead costs and applied only $3,888 of those costs to units produced, factory overhead has been underapplied by $212. The following entry is needed to account for the $212:

Controllable Overhead Variance	316	
Overhead Volume Variance		104
Factory Overhead Control		212
To close out Factory Overhead Control and record resulting variances		

Transfer of Completed Units to Finished Goods Inventory. There are now $11,880 of standard costs recorded in the Work in Process Inventory account (direct materials, $4,320; direct labor, $3,672; and overhead, $3,888). Assuming that the 180 chairs have been completed, the following entry would be made:

Finished Goods Inventory (180 chairs @ $66/chair)	11,880	
Work in Process Inventory		11,880
Transfer of completed units to Finished Goods Inventory		

The standard unit price of $66 is computed as follows:

Direct materials: 4 yd @ $6/yd	$24.00
Direct labor: 2.4 hr @ $8.50/hr	20.40
Factory overhead: 2.4 hr @ $9/hr	21.60
Total standard unit cost	$66.00

All costs that were entered into the Work in Process Inventory account were at standard cost, so standard cost must be used when they are transferred out of the account.

Transfer Cost of Units Sold to Cost of Goods Sold Account. The 180 chairs completed were sold on account for $169 per chair and shipped to a customer. The resulting journal entries would be as shown at the top of page 856.

Accounts Receivable (180 chairs @ $169/chair)	30,420	
Sales		30,420
Sale of 180 chairs		
Cost of Goods Sold (180 chairs @ $66 standard cost)	11,880	
Finished Goods Inventory		11,880
Transfer of standard cost of units sold to Cost of Goods Sold account		

Dispose of End-of-Period Variance Account Balances. As with over- or underapplied overhead, the balances in variance accounts at the end of the period are disposed of in one of two ways. First, if all units worked on were completed and sold, a period-end journal entry is made to close all variances to Cost of Goods Sold. Using the data from Boyer Company, the entry to close out the variance account balances is:

Cost of Goods Sold	844	
Direct Materials Price Variance	76	
Overhead Volume Variance	104	
Direct Materials Quantity Variance		240
Direct Labor Rate Variance		315
Direct Labor Efficiency Variance		153
Controllable Overhead Variance		316
To close all variance account balances to Cost of Goods Sold		

In contrast, if at period end significant balances still exist in Work in Process Inventory and Finished Goods Inventory from work performed during the period, the net amount of the variances ($844 here) should be divided among Work in Process Inventory, Finished Goods Inventory, and Cost of Goods Sold, in proportion to their balances.

Performance Evaluation

OBJECTIVE 7
Evaluate managerial performance using variances

Effective performance evaluation of managers depends on both human factors and company policies. Introducing variances from standard costs into the performance report lends a degree of accuracy to the evaluation process. The human factor is the key to meeting corporate goals. People do the planning, people perform the manufacturing operations, and people evaluate or are evaluated. Management should develop appropriate policies and get direct input from managers and employees when setting up a performance evaluation process.

More specifically, a company should establish policies or procedures for (1) preparing operational plans, (2) assigning responsibility for performance, (3) communicating operational plans to key personnel, (4) evaluating each area of responsibility, and (5) if variances exist, learning the causes and making the necessary corrections.

Variance analysis tends to pinpoint efficient and inefficient operating areas better than simple comparisons between actual and budgeted data. The key to preparing a performance report based on standard costs and related variances is to follow company policies by (1) identifying those responsible for each variance, (2) determining the causes for each variance, (3) establishing a system of management by exception, and (4) developing a reporting format suited to the

Exhibit 21-4. Performance Report Using Variance Analysis

Boyer Company
Production Department Performance Report—Cost Variance Analysis
For the Month Ended August 31, 19x5

400 hours: Normal capacity (direct labor hours)
432 hours: Capacity performance level achieved (standard hours allowed)
180 chairs: Good units produced

Cost Analysis

	Cost		Variance	
	Budgeted	**Actual**	**Amount**	**Type**
Direct materials used (leather)	$ 4,320	$ 4,560	$240 (U)	Quantity variance
Direct labor usage	3,672	3,825	153 (U)	Efficiency variance
Factory overhead	3,784	4,100	316 (U)	Controllable overhead variance
Totals	$11,776	$12,485	$709 (U)	

Reasons for Variances

Direct materials quantity variance: (1) inferior quality-control inspection; (2) cheaper grade of direct materials
Direct labor efficiency variance: (1) inferior direct materials; (2) new, inexperienced employee
Controllable overhead variance: (1) excessive indirect labor usage; (2) changes in employee overtime; (3) unexpected price changes

task. Performance reports should be tailored to a manager's responsibilities. They should be clear and accurate and should contain only those cost items that can be controlled by the manager receiving the report.

Exhibit 21-4 shows a performance report compiled using data that pertain only to the production manager at Boyer Company. This person is responsible for direct materials used (and the related direct materials quantity variance), for direct labor hours used (and the related direct labor efficiency variance), and for the costs included in the controllable overhead variance. Note that space was provided at the bottom for the manager to explain the reasons for the variances.

The report in Exhibit 21-4 is simpler than most. Normally such a report would show several items of direct materials, two or more direct labor classifications, and many overhead cost items. The report has been simplified to allow you to more easily focus on its purposes and uses.

Three-Variance Approach to Factory Overhead Variance Analysis

Alternative Method

The three-variance approach to overhead variance analysis divides the total overhead variance into three parts instead of the two parts shown earlier in the chapter. Remember, the purpose of variance analysis is to break down variations from budgeted information so that reasons for changes from planned operations can be determined. The three-variance approach to overhead variance analysis breaks the controllable overhead variance into two parts and identifies an *overhead spending variance* and an *overhead efficiency variance.* The overhead volume variance is the third overhead variance, and it is identical to its counterpart in the two-variance analysis.

OBJECTIVE 8
Compute and evaluate factory overhead variances using a three-variance analysis

The **overhead spending variance** is the difference between the actual overhead costs incurred and the amount that should have been spent, based on actual hours worked or other productive input measures. Therefore actual overhead costs incurred are compared with the costs of a flexible budget based on actual hours worked. When the Boyer Company example is expanded, the spending variance is computed as follows.

Actual overhead costs incurred		$4,100.00
Less budgeted factory overhead (flexible budget) for 450 hours worked		
Variable overhead cost 450 hours × $5.75 per direct labor hour	$2,587.50	
Budgeted fixed overhead cost	1,300.00	
Total budgeted factory overhead		3,887.50
Overhead spending variance		$ 212.50 (U)

Note that the total overhead spending variance can be broken down into its variable and fixed components. In the example, actual overhead incurred was given in total and details were not provided. If the actual variable and fixed cost components were given, however, you could easily generate a variable overhead spending variance and a fixed overhead spending variance. This further breakdown would give the supervisor additional information. If most of the spending variance involved fixed costs, much of the variance would be difficult for the manager to control. If, on the other hand, most of the spending variance were caused by noncompliance with variable cost targets, those responsible should be held accountable for the differences.

The **overhead efficiency variance** is linked directly with the labor efficiency variance. An efficiency variance occurs when actual hours worked differ from standard hours allowed for good units produced. The overhead efficiency variance is the difference between actual direct labor hours worked and standard labor hours allowed multiplied by the standard variable overhead rate. Computing the overhead efficiency variance involves comparing two flexible budgets, one based on actual hours worked and the other on standard hours allowed for good units produced. Boyer Company's overhead efficiency variance is computed as follows:

Budgeted factory overhead (flexible budget) for actual hours worked		
Variable overhead cost 450 hours × $5.75 per direct labor hour	$2,587.50	
Budgeted fixed overhead cost	1,300.00	
Total budgeted overhead for actual hours worked		$3,887.50
Budgeted factory overhead (flexible budget) for standard hours allowed		
Variable overhead cost (180 chairs × 2.4 hours per chair) × $5.75 per direct labor hour	$2,484.00	
Budgeted fixed overhead cost	1,300.00	
Total budgeted overhead for standard hours allowed		3,784.00
Overhead efficiency variance		$ 103.50 (U)

Note that by design the overhead efficiency variance is the difference between variable costs only. When two flexible budgets are compared, the fixed cost component is identical for each budget. The difference must come from the variable costs.

The overhead efficiency variance identifies the portion of the total overhead variance that occurs automatically when a labor efficiency variance develops. If the labor efficiency variance is unfavorable, the overhead efficiency variance will also be unfavorable. The person responsible for the labor efficiency variance is also responsible for the overhead efficiency variance.

As stated earlier, the overhead volume variance is computed in the same manner as in the two-variance approach. To review the computation of the two-variance approach to overhead variance analysis, refer to Figure 21-4.

In the upper part of Figure 21-5, the total overhead variance is broken down into the three variances: (1) spending, (2) efficiency, and (3) volume variances.

Figure 21-5. Three-Variance Approach to Overhead Variance Analysis

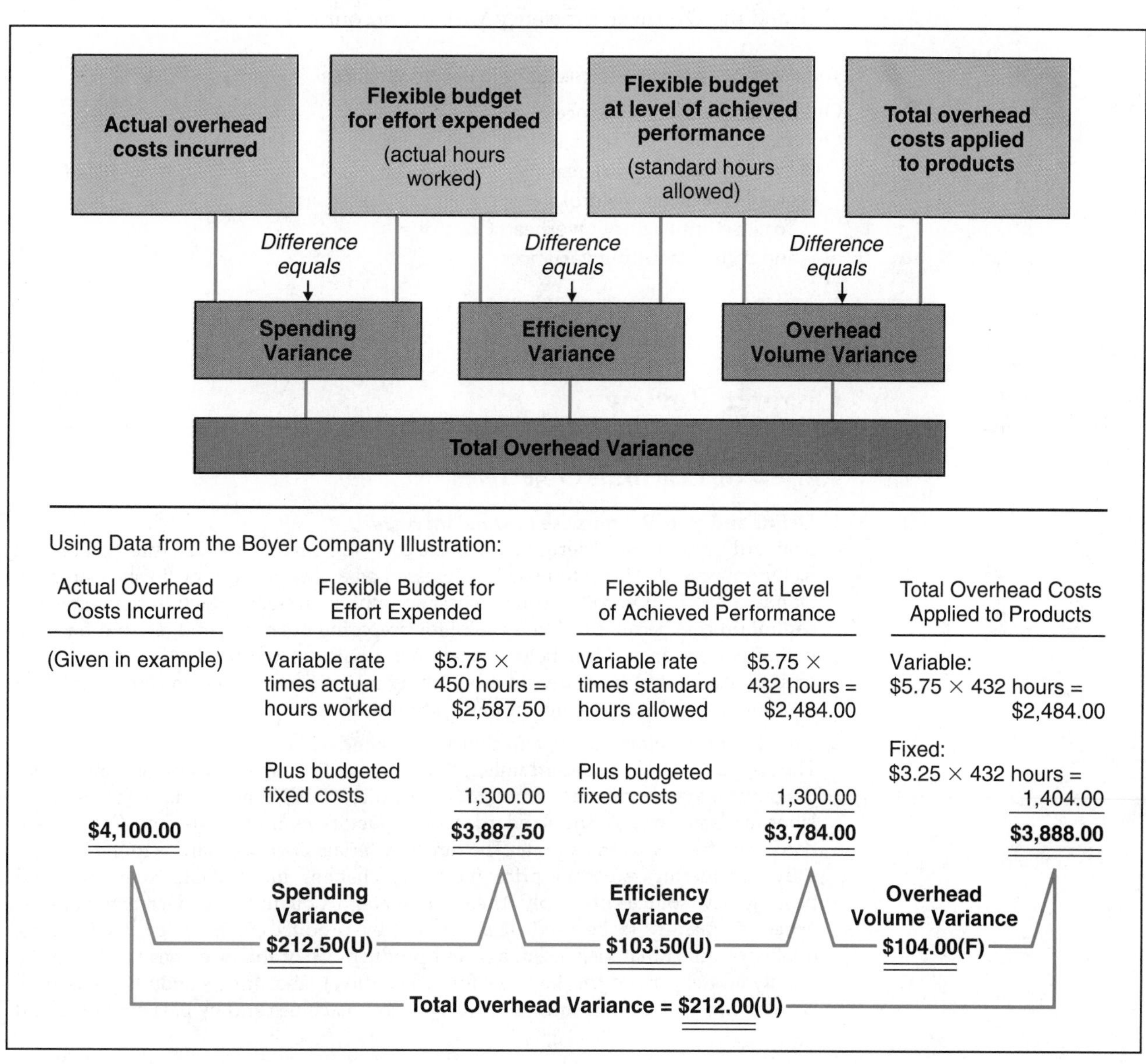

In addition, the cost totals that must be compared to arrive at each variance are identified. Note that the difference between Figures 21-4 and 21-5 is the introduction of the flexible budget for effort expended. Using this flexible budget, one can break down the controllable overhead variance into overhead spending variance and overhead efficiency variance.

In the bottom portion of Figure 21-5, the actual computation of the three variances is summarized. To check your answers to the three variances, perform the following calculation:

Overhead spending variance	$212.50 (U)
Overhead efficiency variance	103.50 (U)
Overhead volume variance	104.00 (F)
Total overhead variance	$212.00 (U)

The journal entry used to record the overhead variances in the three-variance approach is shown below. The primary difference between this entry and the one shown for the two-variance approach on page 855 is that the Controllable Overhead Variance account has been replaced by the Overhead Spending Variance and the Overhead Efficiency Variance accounts.

Three-Variance Analysis: Journal Entry to Record Variances

Overhead Spending Variance	212.50	
Overhead Efficiency Variance	103.50	
Overhead Volume Variance		104.00
Factory Overhead Control		212.00
To close out Factory Overhead Control and record resulting variances		

Chapter Review

Review of Learning Objectives

1. **Define and state the purpose of *standard costs*.**
Standard costs are predetermined realistic costs for direct materials, direct labor, and factory overhead. They are usually expressed as a cost per unit of finished product. Standard costs are introduced into a cost accounting system to help in the budgetary control process because they are useful for preparing operating budgets and for evaluating performance. They help in identifying parts of the production process that require cost control measures, in establishing realistic prices, and in simplifying cost accounting procedures for inventories and product costing.

2. **Identify the six elements of, and compute, a standard unit cost.**
The six elements of a standard unit cost are (1) the direct materials price standard, (2) the direct materials quantity standard, (3) the direct labor time standard, (4) the direct labor rate standard, (5) the standard variable factory overhead rate, and (6) the standard fixed factory overhead rate. The direct materials price standard is found by carefully considering expected price increases, changes in available quantities, and possible new sources of supply. The direct materials quantity standard expresses the expected quantity to be used. It is affected by product engineering specifications, quality of direct materials used, age and productivity of the machines used, and the quality and experience of the work force. The direct labor time standard is based on current time and motion studies of workers and machines and by past employee and

machine performance. Labor union contracts and company personnel policies influence direct labor rate standards. Standard variable and fixed factory overhead rates are found by dividing total budgeted variable and fixed factory overhead costs by an appropriate application base.

A product's total standard unit cost is computed by adding the following costs: (1) direct materials cost (equals direct materials price standard times direct materials quantity standard), (2) direct labor cost (equals direct labor time standard times direct labor rate standard), and (3) factory overhead cost (equals standard variable and standard fixed factory overhead rate times standard direct labor hours allowed per unit).

3. **Define and prepare a *flexible budget.***
A flexible budget is a summary of anticipated costs for a range of activity levels, geared to changes in productive output. Variable, fixed, and total costs are given for several levels of capacity or output. From these data the management accountant derives the flexible budget formula. This formula, which can be applied to any level of productive output, allows management to evaluate the performance of individuals, departments, or processes.

4. **Describe the concept of management by exception.**
Management by exception is the practice of analyzing only significant variances. Variances within specific limits set by management are not analyzed. This technique is especially useful in companies that control many cost centers or cost categories.

5. **Compute and analyze (a) direct materials, (b) direct labor, and (c) factory overhead variances.**
The direct materials price and quantity variances help explain differences between actual and standard direct materials costs. A direct materials price variance is computed by finding the difference between the actual price and the standard price per unit and multiplying it by the actual quantity purchased. The direct materials quantity variance is the difference between the actual quantity used and the standard quantity that should have been used, multiplied by the standard price. Actual and standard direct labor cost differences are analyzed by computing the direct labor rate variance and the direct labor efficiency variance. A direct labor rate variance is computed by determining the difference between the actual labor rate and the standard labor rate and multiplying it by the actual labor hours worked. The direct labor efficiency variance is the difference between actual hours worked and standard hours allowed for good units produced, multiplied by the standard labor rate. The controllable overhead variance and the overhead volume variance help explain differences in overhead costs. Computing the controllable overhead variance is done by finding the difference between actual overhead costs incurred and the factory overhead costs budgeted for the level of production achieved (flexible budget based on standard hours allowed). The overhead volume variance is the difference between the factory overhead budgeted for the level of production achieved and the total overhead costs applied to production using the standard variable and fixed overhead rates.

6. **Prepare journal entries to record transactions involving variances in a standard costing system.**
Journal entries are used to integrate standard cost variances into the accounting records. Unfavorable variances create debit balances, and favorable variances create credit balances. General ledger accounts are maintained for the direct materials price variance, direct materials quantity variance, direct labor rate variance, direct labor efficiency variance, controllable overhead variance, and overhead volume variance. At the close of an accounting period, balances in these accounts are disposed of by either (1) closing them to Cost of Goods Sold, if the variance balances are small or if most of the goods produced during the period were sold, or (2) dividing the net balance among Work in Process Inventory, Finished Goods Inventory, and Cost of Goods Sold, in proportion to their balances.

7. **Evaluate managerial performance using variances.**
Introducing variances from standard costs into the performance report lends accuracy to the evaluation. Variances tend to pinpoint efficient and inefficient operating areas

better than comparisons between actual and static budget data. The keys to preparing a performance report based on standard costs and related variances are to (1) identify those responsible for each variance, (2) determine the causes for each variance, (3) establish a system of management by exception, and (4) develop a reporting format suited to the task.

8. **Compute and evaluate factory overhead variances using a three-variance analysis.** If more information is desired concerning the differences in overhead costs, a more detailed analysis can be made. Using the three-variance approach, the controllable overhead variance is broken down into an overhead spending variance and an overhead efficiency variance. The overhead volume variance is the third component of the total overhead variance. Using the three-variance approach, management can determine how much of the total overhead variance was caused by unanticipated spending activities (higher or lower prices or changes in purchases) and how much was caused by changes in the level of labor or machine hour efficiency.

Review of Concepts and Terminology

The following concepts and terms were introduced in this chapter.

(L.O. 5) **Controllable overhead variance:** The difference between actual overhead costs incurred and the factory overhead costs budgeted for the level of production reached.

(L.O. 5) **Direct labor efficiency variance:** The difference between actual hours worked and standard hours allowed for the good units produced, multiplied by the standard labor rate.

(L.O. 2) **Direct labor rate standards:** The hourly labor costs that are expected to prevail during the next accounting period for each function or job classification.

(L.O. 5) **Direct labor rate variance:** The difference between the actual labor rate and the standard labor rate, multiplied by the actual labor hours worked.

(L.O. 2) **Direct labor time standard:** The expected time that it takes each department, machine, or process to complete production on one unit or one batch of output.

(L.O. 2) **Direct materials price standard:** A careful estimate of the cost of a certain type of direct material in the next accounting period.

(L.O. 5) **Direct materials price variance:** The difference between the actual price and the standard price, multiplied by the actual quantity purchased.

(L.O. 2) **Direct materials quantity standard:** An estimate of expected quantity usage that is influenced by product engineering specifications, quality of direct materials, age and productivity of machinery, and quality and experience of the work force.

(L.O. 5) **Direct materials quantity variance:** The difference between the actual quantity used and the standard quantity that should have been used, multiplied by the standard price.

(L.O. 3) **Flexible budget:** A summary of expected costs for a range of activity levels, geared to changes in the level of productive output.

(L.O. 3) **Flexible budget formula:** An equation that determines the correct budgeted cost for any level of productive output; the equation is: (the variable costs per unit of measure times the number of units) plus the total budgeted fixed costs.

(L.O. 4) **Management by exception:** The practice of locating and analyzing only the areas of unusually good or unusually bad performance.

(L.O. 8) **Overhead efficiency variance:** The difference between actual direct labor hours worked and standard labor hours allowed, multiplied by the standard variable overhead rate.

(L.O. 8) **Overhead spending variance:** The difference between the actual overhead costs incurred and the amount that should have been spent, based on actual hours worked or other productive input measures.

(L.O. 5) **Overhead volume variance:** The difference between the factory overhead budgeted for the level of production achieved and the overhead applied to production using the standard variable and fixed overhead rates.

(L.O. 1) **Standard costs:** Predetermined realistic costs for direct materials, direct labor, and factory overhead.

(L.O. 2) **Standard direct labor cost:** The standard hours of direct labor multiplied by the standard wage for direct labor.

(L.O. 2) **Standard direct materials cost:** The standard price for direct materials multiplied by the standard quantity for direct materials.

(L.O. 2) **Standard factory overhead cost:** The sum of the estimates for variable and fixed factory overhead in the next accounting period.

(L.O. 2) **Standard fixed overhead rate:** Total budgeted fixed factory overhead costs divided by an expression of capacity, usually normal capacity in terms of standard direct labor hours or standard machine hours.

(L.O. 2) **Standard variable overhead rate:** Total budgeted variable factory overhead costs divided by an expression of capacity, such as the expected number of standard direct labor hours or standard machine hours.

(L.O. 5) **Total direct labor cost variance:** The difference between actual labor costs incurred and the standard labor cost for the good units produced.

(L.O. 5) **Total direct materials cost variance:** The difference between the actual materials cost incurred and the standard cost of those same items.

(L.O. 5) **Total overhead variance:** The difference between actual overhead costs incurred and the standard overhead costs applied to production using the standard variable and fixed overhead rates.

(L.O. 1) **Variance:** The difference between a standard cost and an actual cost.

(L.O. 4) **Variance analysis:** The process of computing the amount of and isolating the causes of differences between actual costs and standard costs.

Self-Test

Test your knowledge of the chapter by choosing the best answer for each of the following items.

(L.O. 1) 1. Realistically predetermined costs for direct materials, direct labor, and factory overhead are known as
a. predetermined rates.
b. standard costs.
c. period costs.
d. variable costs.

(L.O. 2) 2. Product engineering specifications, the quality of direct materials, and the age and productivity of machinery influence the
a. direct materials quantity standard.
b. direct labor rate standard.
c. direct materials price standard.
d. direct labor time standard.

(L.O. 2) 3. To compute the standard fixed factory overhead rate, the total budgeted fixed factory overhead costs are divided by the
a. flexible budget formula.
b. actual hours worked.
c. standard hours allowed.
d. normal capacity.

(L.O. 3) 4. In the flexible budget formula for a department, the variable portion of the formula states that the variable cost per unit is multiplied by the
a. standard hours worked.
b. number of units produced.
c. standard hours allowed.
d. number of units planned.

(L.O. 4) 5. The technique of locating and analyzing the areas of unusually good or unusually bad performance is called
a. standard costing.
b. variance analysis.
c. management by exception.
d. management by objective.

(L.O. 5) 6. The Sahlen Company uses a standard cost accounting system in its glass division. The standard cost of making one glass windshield is:

Materials (60 lb @ $1/lb)	$ 60.00
Labor (3 hr @ $10/hr)	30.00
Factory overhead (3 hr @ $8/hr)	24.00
Total standard unit cost	$114.00

The current variable factory overhead rate is $3 per labor hour and the budgeted fixed factory overhead is $27,000. During January, the division produced 1,650 windshields compared to normal capacity of 1,800 windshields. The actual cost per windshield was:

Materials (58 lb @ $1.10/lb)	$ 63.80
Labor (3.1 hr @ $10/hr)	31.00
Factory overhead ($39,930/1,650 products)	24.20
Total actual unit cost	$119.00

The total materials quantity variance for January is
a. $9,570 (U).
b. $9,570 (F).
c. $3,300 (F).
d. $3,300 (U).

(L.O. 5) 7. Assuming the same facts as in **6**, the labor rate variance for January is
a. 0.
b. $1,650 (U).
c. $1,920 (F).
d. $1,650 (F).

(L.O. 5) 8. Assuming the same facts as in **6**, the controllable overhead variance for January is
a. $2,250 (U).
b. $2,250 (F).
c. $1,920 (U).
d. $1,920 (F).

(L.O. 5) 9. Assuming the same facts as in **6**, the overhead volume variance for January is
a. $2,250 (U).
b. $2,250 (F).
c. $1,920 (U).
d. $1,920 (F).

(L.O. 5) 10. Assuming the same facts as in **6**, the direct materials price variance is
a. $165 (U).
b. $9,570 (U).
c. $9,570 (F).
d. $165 (F).

Answers to the Self-Test are at the end of this chapter.

Review Problem
Variance Analysis

(L.O. 2, 5, 8) Stina Manufacturing Company has a standard cost system and keeps all cost standards up to date. The company's main product is heating pipe, which is made in a single department. The standard variable costs for one unit of finished pipe are:

Direct materials (3 sq meters @ $12.50/sq meter)	$37.50
Direct labor (1.2 hr @ $9.00/hr)	10.80
Variable overhead (1.2 hr @ $5.00/dlh)	6.00
Standard variable cost per unit	$54.30

Normal capacity is 15,000 direct labor hours, and budgeted fixed overhead costs for the year were $54,000. During the year, the company produced and sold 12,200 units. Related transactions and actual cost data for the year were as follows: Direct materials consisted of 37,500 sq meters purchased and used; unit purchase cost was $12.40 per sq meter. Direct labor consisted of 15,250 direct labor hours worked at an average labor rate of $9.20 per hour. Actual factory overhead costs incurred for the period consisted of variable overhead costs of $73,200 and fixed overhead costs of $55,000.

Using the data given, compute the following:

1. Standard hours allowed.
2. Standard fixed overhead rate.
3. Direct materials price variance.
4. Direct materials quantity variance.
5. Direct labor rate variance.
6. Direct labor efficiency variance.
7. Overhead spending variance.
8. Overhead efficiency variance.
9. Controllable overhead variance.
10. Overhead volume variance.

Answer to Review Problem

1. Standard hours allowed = good units produced × standard direct labor hours per unit

   12,200 units × 1.2 direct labor hours/unit = 14,640 hours

2. Standard fixed overhead rate = $\dfrac{\text{budgeted fixed overhead cost}}{\text{normal capacity}}$

   $= \dfrac{\$54{,}000}{15{,}000 \text{ direct labor hours}}$

   = \$3.60 per direct labor hour

3. Direct materials price variance:

Price difference:	Actual price paid	\$12.40 /sq meter
	Less standard price	12.50 /sq meter
	Difference	\$ .10 (F)

   Direct materials price variance = (actual price − standard price) × actual quantity
   = \$.10 (F) × 37,500 sq meters
   = \$3,750 (F)

4. Direct materials quantity variance:

Quantity difference:	Actual quantity used	37,500 sq meters
	Less standard quantity (12,200 units × 3 meters)	36,600 sq meters
	Difference	900 (U)

   Direct materials quantity variance = (actual quantity − standard quantity) × standard price
   = 900 (U) × \$12.50/sq meter
   = \$11,250 (U)

5. Direct labor rate variance:

Rate difference:	Actual labor rate	\$9.20 /hr
	Less standard labor rate	9.00 /hr
	Difference	\$ .20 (U)

   Direct labor rate variance = (actual rate − standard rate) × actual hours
   = \$.20 (U) × 15,250 hours
   = \$3,050 (U)

6. Direct labor efficiency variance:

Difference in hours:	Actual hours worked	15,250 hr
	Less standard hours allowed	14,640 hr*
	Difference	610 (U)

Direct labor efficiency variance = (actual hours – standard hours allowed) × standard rate
= 610 hr (U) × $9.00/hr
= $5,490 (U)

*12,200 units produced × 1.2 hr per unit = 14,640 hr

7. Overhead spending variance:

Overhead costs incurred		
Variable	$73,200	
Fixed	55,000	$128,200
Less flexible budget for effort expended		
Actual hours worked × variable overhead rate		
15,250 labor hours × $5/hour	$76,250	
Plus budgeted fixed costs	54,000	130,250
Overhead spending variance		$ 2,050 (F)

8. Overhead efficiency variance:

Flexible budget for effort expended (see computation in **7** above)		$130,250
Less flexible budget at level of achieved performance		
Standard hours allowed × variable overhead rate		
14,640 labor hours × $5/hour	$73,200	
Plus budgeted fixed costs	54,000	127,200
Overhead efficiency variance		$ 3,050 (U)

9. Controllable overhead variance

Actual overhead incurred		$128,200
Less budgeted factory overhead for 14,640 hours:		
Variable overhead cost (14,640 hr × $5.00/direct labor hour)	$73,200	
Budgeted fixed factory overhead	54,000	
Total budgeted factory overhead		127,200
Controllable overhead variance		$ 1,000 (U)

10. Overhead volume variance

Total budgeted factory overhead (see computation in **9**)		$127,200
Less factory overhead applied:		
Variable: 14,640 hr × $5.00/direct labor hour	$73,200	
Fixed: 14,640 hr × $3.60/direct labor hour	52,704	
Total factory overhead applied		125,904
Overhead volume variance		$ 1,296 (U)

Chapter Assignments

Questions

1. What is a standard cost?
2. What do predetermined overhead costing and standard costing have in common? How are they different?
3. "Standard costing is a total cost concept, in that standard unit costs are determined for direct materials, direct labor, and factory overhead." Explain this statement.
4. Name the six elements used to compute total standard unit cost.
5. What three factors could affect a direct materials price standard?
6. What general ledger accounts are affected by a standard cost system?
7. "Performance is evaluated or measured by comparing what did happen with what should have happened." What is meant by this statement? Relate your comments to the budgetary control process.
8. What is a variance?
9. How can variances help management achieve effective control of operations?
10. What is a flexible budget? What is its purpose?
11. What are the two parts of the flexible budget formula? How are they related to each other?
12. What is the formula for computing a direct materials price variance?
13. How would you interpret an unfavorable direct materials price variance?
14. Distinguish between the controllable overhead variance and the overhead volume variance.
15. If standard hours allowed exceed normal hours, will the period's overhead volume variance be favorable or unfavorable? Explain your answer.
16. Can an unfavorable direct materials quantity variance be caused, at least in part, by a favorable direct materials price variance? Explain.
17. What are the three rules that underline the recording of standard cost variances?

Communication Skills Exercises

Communication 21-1. Variances and the Factory of the Future Concept
(L.O. 1, 2)

The ***United States Air Force,*** with the assistance of Price Waterhouse, has developed a model of an advanced cost management system (ACMS) that will enable companies with newly automated factories to develop more accurate cost measures. The Electronics Systems Division of the USAF initiated the study.[2] The conceptual design features include tracking future costs, focusing on parts costs (rather than labor costs), and separating the tracking of the production process from the tracking of product costs. Variances, called planning gaps, compare the differences between predetermined estimates and actual results. Variances are classified by various causing factors and are generated for scrap, machine utilization, labor efficiency, labor utilization, set-up usage, lot size, spending, and volume. On a work sheet, separate these variance categories into two groups, those related to (1) production process control (nonfinancial data) and (2) product cost control. Be prepared to discuss in class your variance classification approach and the reasons supporting your position.

Communication 21-2. Variance Analysis
(L.O. 6, 7)

Hernden Company is a small job shop located in Sedona, Arizona. Mac Hernden, an engineer retired from a major high-tech company, started the company last year and now employs twelve factory workers and three office personnel. A local management accountant who services the accounting needs of four unrelated small businesses in the region also performs the accounting for Hernden Company. Hernden's only product line is comprised of eight different machine tools produced by machines that require

2. Daniel P. Keegan, Robert G. Eiler, and Joseph V. Anania, "An Advanced Cost Management System for the Factory of the Future," *Management Accounting,* Institute of Management Accountants, December 1988, pp. 31–37.

significant labor time. All these tools are sold to Hernden's previous employer. The management accountant has set up a standard cost system that generates traditional variances for materials, labor, and factory overhead and uses a flexible budget. Mr. Hernden has read that many companies are discarding labor variances and has questioned his accountant on this matter. Write a response to Mr. Hernden, stating your position on his question and your reasons for your position.

Communication 21-3. An Ethical Question Involving Standard Costs
(L.O. 1, 5, 7)

Chris Shoucair is manager of standard costing systems at Richard Industries, Inc. Standard costs are developed for all product-related materials, labor, and factory overhead costs and are used for pricing products, for costing all inventories, and for performance evaluation of all purchasing and production line managers. The company updates standard costs whenever costs, prices, or rates change by 3 percent or more; in addition, all standard costs are reviewed and updated annually in December. This practice provided currently attainable standards that were appropriate for use in valuing year-end inventories on Richard Industries' financial statements.

On November 30, 19x5, Chris Shoucair received a memo from the company's chief financial officer. The memo said that the company was considering a major purchase of another company and that Chris and his staff were to concentrate their full effort on analyzing the proposed transaction and ignore adjusting the standards until February or March. In late November, prices on over twenty raw materials were reduced by 10 percent or more and a new labor contract reduced several categories of labor rates. Lower standard costs would result in lower inventories, higher cost of goods sold due to inventory write-downs, and lower net income for the year. Chris believed that the company was facing an operating loss and that the assignment to evaluate the proposed major purchase was designed primarily to keep his staff from revising and lowering the standards. Chris questioned the CFO about the assignment and reiterated the need for updating the standard costs, but he was told again to ignore the update procedure and concentrate on the major purchase. The proposed major purchase never materialized and Chris and his staff were removed from the assignment in early February.

How do you assess Chris's actions regarding this situation? Did he follow all ethical paths to solve the problem? What are the consequences of not adjusting the standard costs?

Communication 21-4. Basic Research Skills
(L.O. 1, 2)

Standard costs and the materials, labor, and factory overhead variances generated by a standard costing system have been used as cost control and performance evaluation mechanisms for many years. Standard costs are also used to assist in the pricing of new products. In recent years, the standard costing approach has been criticized for being irrelevant as an operating measurement device. Locate an article written on this topic within the last five years in the periodical *Management Accounting,* published monthly by the Institute of Management Accountants (formerly the National Association of Accountants). Identify the issues addressed by the author(s). Is the article positive or negative toward standard costs? What role does the world-class competition play in the points being made by the author(s)? Prepare a formal two-page summary of the article. Also prepare an outline that you would use if called upon to report on the assignment to your classmates.

Classroom Exercises

Exercise 21-1. Development of Standard Costs
(L.O. 2)

Caspari Corp. maintains a complete standard costing system and is in the process of updating its materials and labor standards for Product 20B. The following data have been accumulated:

Materials

In the previous period, 20,500 units were produced and a total of 32,800 square yards of material was used to produce them.

(continued)

Three suppliers of material will be used in the coming period; Supplier A will provide 20 percent of the material at a cost of $3.40 per sq yd; Supplier B will be responsible for 50 percent at a cost of $3.50 per sq yd; and Supplier C will ship 30 percent at a cost of $3.60 per sq yd.

Labor

During the previous period, 57,400 direct labor hours were worked, 34,850 hours on machine H and 22,550 hours on machine K.

Machine H operators earned $8.90 per hour and machine K operators earned $9.20 per hour last period. The new labor contract calls for a 10 percent increase in labor rates for the coming period.

From the information above, compute the direct materials quantity and price standards and the direct labor time and rate standards for each machine listed for the coming accounting period.

Exercise 21-2.
Standard Unit Cost Computation
(L.O. 2)

Moustafa Aerodynamics, Inc. makes electronically equipped weather-detecting balloons for university meteorological departments. Recent nationwide inflation has caused the company management to order that standard costs be recomputed. New direct materials price standards are $620.00 per set for electronic components and $13.40 per square meter for heavy-duty canvas. Direct materials quantity standards include one set of electronic components and 95 square meters of heavy-duty canvas per balloon. Direct labor time standards are 16 hours per balloon for the Electronics Department and 19 hours per balloon for the Assembly Department. Direct labor rate standards are $11.00 per hour for the Electronics Department and $9.50 per hour for the Assembly Department. Standard factory overhead rates are $16.00 per direct labor hour for the standard variable overhead rate and $10.00 per direct labor hour for the standard fixed overhead rate.

Using the production standards provided, compute the standard manufacturing cost of one weather balloon.

Exercise 21-3.
Flexible Budget Preparation
(L.O. 3)

Fixed overhead costs for the Karolinski Kostume Company for 19x2 are expected to be as follows: depreciation, $72,000; supervisory salaries, $92,000; property taxes and insurance, $26,000; and other fixed overhead, $14,500. Total fixed overhead is thus expected to be $204,500. Variable costs per unit are expected to be as follows: direct materials, $16.50; direct labor, $8.50; operating supplies, $2.50; indirect labor, $4.00; and other variable overhead costs, $3.20.

Prepare a flexible budget for the following levels of production: 18,000 units, 20,000 units, and 22,000 units. What is the flexible budget formula for 19x2?

Exercise 21-4.
Management by Exception
(L.O. 4)

Greenawalt Instruments, Inc. produces scientific apparatus for food inspection. More than five hundred types of materials and the labor skills of more than eighty different specialists are used in the production process. During the past five years, the corporation has grown from sales of $2,800,000 to a current level of over $25,000,000. The company's rapid growth has caused numerous variances, which the controller's department has not had time to investigate. A standard cost accounting system was introduced two years ago, but it has proven impractical for analyzing all the variances. The controller has been asked by the vice president of finance to develop an improved method of controlling costs.

1. Describe the concept of management by exception.
2. Discuss how the concept could prove useful to the controller of Greenawalt Instruments, Inc.

Exercise 21-5.
Direct Materials Price and Quantity Variances
(L.O. 5)

The Marcos Elevator Company manufactures small hydroelectric elevators with a maximum capacity of ten passengers each. One of the direct materials used by the Production Department is heavy-duty carpeting for the floors of the elevators. The direct materials quantity standard used for the month ended April 30, 19x2 was 6 square yards per elevator. During April the purchasing agent purchased this carpeting at $11 per square yard;

standard price for the period was $12. Ninety elevators were completed and sold during April; the Production Department used an average of 6.6 square yards of carpet per elevator.

Calculate Marcos Elevator Company's direct materials price and quantity variances for April 19x2.

Exercise 21-6.
Direct Labor Rate and Efficiency Variances
(L.O. 5)

Loves Park Foundry, Inc. manufactures castings used by other companies in the production of machinery. For the past two years, the largest selling product has been a casting for an eight-cylinder engine block. Standard direct labor hours per engine block are 1.8 hours. The labor contract requires that $17.00 per hour be paid to all direct labor employees. During June, 16,500 engine blocks were produced. Actual direct labor hours and costs for June were 29,900 hours and $523,250, respectively.

1. Compute the direct labor rate variance for the engine block product line during June.
2. Using the same data, compute the direct labor efficiency variance for the engine block product line during June. Check your answer, assuming that the total direct labor variance is $18,350 (U).

Exercise 21-7.
Factory Overhead Variances
(L.O. 5)

The Lowry Company produces handmade clamming pots that are sold to distributors along the Atlantic coast of North Carolina. The company incurred $11,100 of actual overhead costs in May. Budgeted standard overhead costs for May were $4 of variable overhead costs per direct labor hour plus $1,250 in fixed overhead costs. Normal capacity was set at 2,000 direct labor hours per month. In May the company was able to produce 9,900 clamming pots. The time standard is .2 direct labor hours per clamming pot.

Compute the total overhead variance, the controllable overhead variance, and the overhead volume variance for May.

Exercise 21-8.
Factory Overhead Variances
(L.O. 5)

Koumans Industries uses a standard cost accounting system that includes flexible budgeting for cost planning and control. The 19x3 monthly flexible budget for factory overhead costs is $200,000 of fixed costs plus $4.80 per machine hour. Monthly normal capacity of 100,000 machine hours is used to compute the standard fixed overhead rate. During December 19x3 plant workers recorded 105,000 actual machine hours. The standard machine hours allowed for good production during December was only 98,500. Actual factory overhead costs incurred during December totaled $441,000 of variable costs and $204,500 of fixed costs.

Compute the under- or overapplied overhead during December and compute the controllable overhead variance and the overhead volume variance.

Exercise 21-9.
Standard Cost Journal Entries
(L.O. 6)

Bush-Hunt Battery Company produces batteries for automobiles, motorcycles, and mopeds. Transactions for direct materials and direct labor for March were as follows:

1. Purchased 1,000 type A battery casings for $6.50 each, on account; standard cost, $7.00 per casing.
2. Purchased 5,000 type 10C lead battery plates for $2.40 each, on account; standard cost, $2.25 per plate.
3. Requisitioned 32 type A battery casings and 248 type 10C lead plates into production. Order no. 674 called for 30 batteries, each using a standard quantity of 8 plates per casing.
4. Direct labor costs for order no. 674 were as follows:

Department H	
Actual labor	26 hr @ $10/hr
Standard labor	24 hr @ $11/hr
Department J	
Actual labor	10 hr @ $13/hr
Standard labor	12 hr @ $14/hr

Prepare journal entries for these four transactions.

Exercise 21-10.
Evaluating Performance Through Variances
(L.O. 5, 7)

Evaluating the operating performance of the Huseman Health Club is the responsibility of its controller, Joe Dean. The following information was made available for March 19x6:

	Standard	Actual
Variable costs:		
Operating labor	$12,160	$13,500
Utilities	2,880	3,360
Repairs and maintenance	5,760	7,140
Fixed costs:		
Depreciation, equipment	2,600	2,680
Rent cost	3,280	3,280
Other	1,704	1,860
Totals	$28,384	$31,820

Normal operating hours call for eight operators, working 160 hours each per month. During March nine operators worked an average of 150 hours each.

With this limited information, compute as many variances as possible for labor and overhead, and prepare a performance report for the month.

Interpretation Case from Business

Gordon Realtors, Inc.
(L.O. 3, 5, 7)

Carol Gordon, the managing partner of Gordon Realtors, Inc., received the performance report that follows. The report showed the company had experienced its biggest year in home resales since it began operating fifteen years ago. It indicates that although fees were over budget by $190,200, all cost categories were also over budget, cutting the increase in net income to only $1,847.

Gordon Realtors, Inc.
Performance Report
For the Year Ended December 31, 19x5

	Budget for the Year	Actual Fees and Costs	Variance Under (Over) Budget
Total Selling Fees	$2,052,000	$2,242,200	$(190,200)
Less Costs			
Commissions			
Salespersons	$ 513,000	$ 560,550	$ (47,550)
Listing agents	410,400	448,440	(38,040)
Listing companies	179,550	196,193	(16,643)
Other variable costs			
Automobile	36,000	39,560	(3,560)
Advertising	93,600	103,450	(9,850)
Home repairs	77,400	89,240	(11,840)
Word processing	40,500	44,310	(3,810)
General overhead costs	615,600	672,660	(57,060)
Total costs	$1,966,050	$2,154,403	$(188,353)
Net Income Before Taxes	$ 85,950	$ 87,797	$ (1,847)

During 19x5 company sales personnel marketed 202 homes averaging $185,000 per unit. Budgeted data were based on 180 homes sold at an average market value of $190,000. Selling fees for all realty work are 6 percent of the selling price. Data supporting the budget figures were as follows:

Commissions
Salespersons: 25 percent of total fees
Listing agents: 20 percent of total fees
Listing companies: 25 percent of total fees
(35 percent of homes sold by Gordon Realtors were listed by another company)

Other variable costs
Automobile, $200 per sale
Advertising, $520 per sale
Home repairs, $430 per sale
Word processing, $225 per sale

General overhead
30 percent of total fees

Required

1. Recast the performance report using a flexible budget based on the number of units sold.
2. Interpret the revised performance report for Ms. Gordon.

Problem Set A

Problem 21A-1. Development of Standards: Direct Materials
(L.O. 2)

Poole & Price, Ltd. assembles clock movements for grandfather clocks. Each movement has four components to assemble: the clock facing, the clock hands, the time movement, and the spring assembly. For the current year, 19x4, the company used the following standard costs: clock facing, $15.90; clock hands, $12.70; time movement, $66.10; and spring assembly, $52.50.

Prices and sources of materials are expected to change in 19x5. Sixty percent of the facings will be supplied by Company A at $18.50 each, and the remaining 40 percent will be purchased from Company B at $18.80 each. The hands are produced for Poole & Price, Ltd. by Sawyers Hardware, Inc., and will cost $15.50 per set in 19x5. Time movements will be purchased from three Swiss sources: Company Q, 30 percent of total need at $68.50 per movement; Company R, 20 percent at $69.50; and Company S, 50 percent at $71.90. Spring assemblies will be purchased from a French company and are expected to increase in cost by 20 percent.

Required

1. Determine the total standard direct materials cost per unit for 19x5.
2. If the company could guarantee the purchase of 2,500 sets of hands from Sawyers Hardware, Inc., the unit cost would be reduced by 20 percent. Find the resulting standard direct materials unit cost.
3. Substandard spring assemblies can be purchased at $50.00, but 20 percent of them will be unusable and cannot be returned. Compute the standard direct materials unit cost if the company follows this procedure, assuming the original facts of the case for the remaining data. The cost of the defective materials will be spread over good units produced.

Problem 21A-2. Developing and Using Standard Costs
(L.O. 2, 6)

Prefabricated houses are the specialty of Simmons Homes, Inc., of Walkertown, North Carolina. Although Simmons Homes produces many models, and customers can even special-order a home, 60 percent of the company's business comes from the sale of the El Dorado, a three-bedroom, 1,400 square foot home with an impressive front entrance. The six basic materials used to manufacture the entrance with their standard costs for 19x5 are as follows: wood framing materials, $1,820; deluxe front door, $480; door hardware, $260; exterior siding, $710; electrical materials, $580; and interior finishing materials, $1,250.

Three types of labor are used to build this section: carpenter, 20 hours at $12.00 per hour; door specialist, 4 hours at $14.00 per hour; and electrician, 8 hours at $16.00 per hour. In 19x5, the company used an overhead rate of 30 percent of total materials cost.

During 19x6, wood framing materials costs are expected to increase by 20 percent. The deluxe front door will need two suppliers: Supplier A will produce 40 percent of the company's needs at $490 per door; Supplier B, 60 percent at $500 per door. Door hardware cost will increase by 10 percent; electrical materials cost, by 20 percent. Exterior siding cost should decrease by $10 per unit. Interior finishing materials costs are expected to remain the same. Carpenter's wages will increase by $1 per hour, while door specialist's wages should remain the same. Electrician's wages will increase by $.50 per hour. Finally, the factory overhead rate will decrease to 25 percent of total materials cost.

Required

1. Compute the total standard cost per front entrance for 19x5.
2. Using your answer to **1** and other information given, compute the 19x6 standard manufacturing cost for the El Dorado's entrance.
3. From the information given, prepare journal entries for the following transactions for 19x6:

Jan. 6	Purchased 120 front doors from Supplier A for $57,120.
14	Requisitioned 60 sets of hardware into production to complete a job calling for 56 entrance units.
30	Transferred the 56 completed front entrances to finished goods inventory.

Problem 21A-3. Materials and Labor Variances
(L.O. 5)

Palm Coast Trophy Company produces a variety of athletic awards, most in the form of trophies or mounted replicas of athletes in action. Jacquelyn Landreth, president of the company, is in the process of developing a standard cost accounting system. Palm Coast produces six standard sizes. The deluxe trophy stands three feet tall above the base. Materials standards include one pound of metal and six ounces of plastic supported by an 8-ounce wooden base. Standard prices for 19x4 were $3.25 per pound of metal, $.40 per ounce of plastic, and $.25 per ounce of wood.

Direct labor is used in both the Molding and the Trimming/Finishing Departments. Deluxe trophies require labor standards of .2 hours of direct labor in the Molding Department and .4 hours in the Trimming/Finishing Department. Standard labor rates for deluxe trophies are $10.75 per hour in the Molding Department and $12.00 per hour in the Trimming/Finishing Department.

During January 19x4, 16,400 deluxe trophies were made. Actual production data were as follows:

Materials	
Metal	16,840 lb @ $3.25/lb
Plastic	99,250 oz @ $.38/oz
Wood	131,400 oz @ $.28/oz
Labor	
Molding	3,420 hr @ $10.60/hr
Trimming/Finishing	6,540 hr @ $12.10/hr

Required

1. Compute the direct materials price and quantity variances for metal, plastic, and wood.
2. Compute the direct labor rate and efficiency variances for the Molding and the Trimming/Finishing Departments.

Problem 21A-4. Direct Materials, Direct Labor, and Factory Overhead Variances
(L.O. 5)

During 19x5 Hylton Laboratories, Inc. researched and perfected a cure for the common cold. Called Cold-Gone, the product comprises a series of five tablets and sells for $28.00 per package. Standard unit costs for this product were developed in late 19x5 for use in 19x6. Per package, the standard unit costs were: chemical ingredients, 6 ounces at $1.00 per ounce; packaging, $1.20; direct labor, .8 hour at $14.00 per hour; standard variable factory overhead, $4.00 per direct labor hour; and standard fixed factory overhead, $6.00 per direct labor hour.

In the first quarter of 19x6, the peak season for colds, demand for the new product rose beyond even the wildest expectations of management. During these three months, the company produced and sold 4 million packages of Cold-Gone. During the first week in April, 50,000 packages were produced using materials for 50,200 packages costing $60,240. Chemical use was 305,000 ounces costing $289,750. Direct labor was 40,250 direct labor hours at a total cost of $571,550. Total variable factory overhead was $161,100; total fixed factory overhead, $242,000. Budgeted fixed factory overhead for the period was $240,000.

Required

Compute (1) all direct materials price variances, (2) all direct materials quantity variances, (3) the direct labor rate variance, (4) the direct labor efficiency variance, (5) the controllable overhead variance, and (6) the overhead volume variance.

Problem 21A-5. Comprehensive: Standard Cost Journal Entry Analysis
(L.O. 2, 5, 6)

DeKalb Lamp Company manufactures several lines of home and business lights and lighting systems. Mahogany table lamps are one of their most popular product lines. Since the wood is very difficult to work with, DeKalb employs skilled wood carvers. Deborah Shewman, controller, has developed the following cost, quantity, and time standards for one table lamp for the current year.

Materials: wood, 10- × 8- × 18-inch block of mahogany, $14.00; electrical fixture and cord, $5.50; and shade and mounting, $9.20.

Direct labor: wood carvers, 6 hours at $14.50 per hour; assemblers and packers, 1.2 hours at $9.00 per hour.

Factory overhead: variable rate, $1.40 per direct labor hour; fixed rate, $2.10 per direct labor hour.

Mahogany table lamps sell for $250 each.

Selected transactions for August 19x5 are as follows:

Aug. 3 Purchased 800 blocks of mahogany for $11,280, on account.
4 Requisitioned 70 blocks of wood into production for order 16, calling for 65 lamps.
5 Purchased 500 electrical fixture kits for $2,700 and 600 lamp shades and mountings for $5,580, on account.
7 Requisitioned 68 electrical fixture kits and 66 lamp shades and mountings into production for order 16.
14 Semimonthly payroll was paid, including the following wages for order 16: wood carvers, 400 hours, $5,760; assemblers and packers, 80 hours, $720. These labor efforts completed order 16.
14 Factory overhead was applied to units worked on during the payroll period. (Assume order 16 represents the only units worked on during the pay period.)
16 Requisitioned 74 blocks of wood into production for order 26, calling for 70 lamps.
19 Requisitioned 78 electrical fixture kits and 75 lamp shades and mountings into production for order 26.
30 Semimonthly payroll was paid. Labor costs associated with order 26 included: wood carvers, 434 hours, $6,293; assemblers and packers, 90 hours, $846. These labor efforts completed order 26.
30 Factory overhead was applied to the work performed during the last two weeks. (Assume order 26 represents the only units worked on during the pay period.)
30 Orders 16 and 26 were transferred to Finished Goods Inventory.
31 Orders 16 and 26 were shipped to customers at the contracted price.

During August actual factory overhead incurred for orders 16 and 26 was variable, $1,420, and fixed, $2,160. All actual overhead costs have already been recorded in the Factory Overhead Control account. Assume that budgeted fixed factory overhead was $2,697 for these two orders.

Required

1. Compute the standard cost for one mahogany table lamp.
2. Prepare the entries necessary to record the month's transactions (show calculations for each variance). For the direct labor entries, assume that everything has been recorded except the distribution of direct labor to Work in Process Inventory. Round answers to the nearest dollar.
3. Analyze the factory overhead accounts by computing the controllable overhead and overhead volume variances. Round amounts to the nearest dollar.
4. Prepare the entry to dispose of the overhead control account and record the overhead variances. (Assume that actual overhead incurred has already been debited to the control account.)
5. Close all variance account balances to the Cost of Goods Sold account. (Round answers to the nearest dollar.)

Problem 21A-6. Variance Review: Missing Information—Three-Variance Approach
(L.O. 8)

Over- or underapplied overhead is the reason for analyzing overhead variances. These variances are interrelated. Crawford Corporation and Sassani Company have standard costing systems. Each firm uses the three-variance approach to overhead variance analysis.

	Crawford Corporation	Sassani Company
Actual machine hours	8,550	?
Standard hours allowed	8,750	8,800
Normal capacity in machine hours	?	9,000
Total overhead rate per machine hour	?	?
Standard variable overhead rate	$ 2.50	$ 1.80
Actual variable and fixed overhead	?	$43,850
Total overhead costs applied	?	$44,000
Budgeted fixed overhead	$76,500	?
Total overhead variance	?	?
Overhead spending variance	$ 700 (F)	?
Overhead efficiency variance	?	$ 360 (F)
Overhead volume variance	$ 2,250 (F)	?

Required

For each company, fill in the unknown amounts by analyzing the data for each organization. Capacities are expressed in machine hours. (**Hint:** Use the structure of Figure 21-5 as a guide for your analysis.)

Problem Set B

Problem 21B-1. Development of Standards: Direct Labor
(L.O. 2)

Because of a planned change in labor structure, Shurden Salt Company must develop a new standard direct labor cost for its product. Standard direct labor costs per 1,000 pounds of salt in 19x5 were 3.5 hours in the Sodium Preparation Department at $10.00 per hour; 2.6 hours in the Chloride Mixing Department at $12.50 per hour; and 2.2 hours in the Cleaning and Packaging Department at $8.50 per hour. Labor rates are expected to increase in 19x6 by 10 percent in the Sodium Preparation Department and 20 percent in the Chloride Mixing Department, and to decrease by 10 percent in the Cleaning and Packaging Department. New machinery in the Chloride Mixing Department will lower the direct labor time standard by 20 percent per 1,000 pounds of salt. All other time standards are expected to remain the same.

Required

1. Compute the standard direct labor cost per 1,000 pounds of salt for 19x6.
2. Management has a plan to improve productive output in the Sodium Preparation Department by 20 percent. If such results are achieved in 19x6, determine (a) the

effect on the direct labor time standard and (b) the resulting total standard direct labor cost per 1,000 pounds of salt. Round to three decimal places.

3. Unskilled labor can be hired to staff all departments in 19x6, with the result that all labor rates paid in 19x5 would be cut by 30 percent in the new year. Such a change in labor skill would cause the direct labor time standards to increase by 50 percent over their 19x5 levels, based on skilled labor. Compute the standard direct labor cost per 1,000 pounds of salt if this change takes place. (Round to three decimal places.)

Problem 21B-2. Developing and Using Standard Costs *(L.O. 2, 6)*

The Singhal Supply Company manufactures swimming pool equipment and accessories. To make high-quality umbrellas for poolside tables, waterproof canvas is first sent to the Cutting Department. In the Assembly Department, the canvas is stretched over the umbrella's ribs and attached to the center pole and opening mechanism. Then the umbrella, along with a heavy mounting base, is packed for shipment.

The company uses a standard cost accounting system. Direct labor and factory overhead standards for each umbrella for 19x6 are as follows: direct labor consists of .6 hour charged to the Cutting Department at $11.00 per hour and .8 hour charged to the Assembly Department at $12.50 per hour. Variable overhead is 120 percent and fixed overhead 140 percent of total direct labor dollars.

During 19x5, the company used the following direct materials standards: waterproof canvas at $8.60 per square yard for 4 square yards per umbrella; a unit consisting of pole, ribs, and opening mechanism at $30.50 per unit; and an umbrella mounting base at $10.40 per unit.

Quantity standards are expected to remain the same during 19x6, but price changes are likely. The cost of waterproof canvas is expected to increase by 10 percent. The poles, ribs, and opening mechanism will be purchased from three vendors. Vendor A will provide 20 percent of the total supply at $31.00 per unit; Vendor B, 50 percent at $30.80; and Vendor C, 30 percent at $32.00. The cost of each umbrella mounting base is expected to increase 25 percent.

Required

1. Compute the total standard direct materials cost per umbrella for 19x6.
2. Using your answer from **1** and information from the problem, compute the standard manufacturing cost of one umbrella for 19x6.
3. Using your answers from **1** and **2,** prepare journal entries for the following transactions in 19x6:

Jan. 20	Purchased 4,500 square yards of waterproof canvas at $9.50 per square yard, on account.
Feb. 1	Requisitioned 810 pole, rib, and opening mechanism assemblies into production to complete a job calling for 800 umbrellas.
Mar. 15	Transferred 600 completed umbrellas to finished goods inventory.

Problem 21B-3. Materials and Labor Variances *(L.O. 5)*

The Winiarski Packaging Company makes plastic walnut baskets for food wholesalers. Each Type R basket is made of .8 gram of liquid plastic and .5 gram of an additive that includes color and hardening agents. The standard prices are $.12 per gram of liquid plastic and $.09 per gram of additive.

Three kinds of labor are required: molding, trimming, and packing. The labor time and rate standards per 100-basket batch are as follows: molding, .8 hour per batch at an hourly rate of $12; trimming, .6 hour per batch at an hourly rate of $10; and packing, .2 hour per batch at $9 per hour.

During 19x5, the company produced 48,000 Type R walnut baskets. Actual materials used were 38,600 grams of liquid plastic at a total cost of $4,632 and 23,950 grams of additive at a cost of $2,395. Actual direct labor included 380 hours for molding, at a total cost of $4,484; 290 hours for trimming, at $2,929; and 96 hours for packing, at $864.

Required

1. Compute the direct materials price and quantity variances for both the liquid plastic and the additive.
2. Compute the direct labor rate and efficiency variances for the molding, trimming, and packing processes.

Problem 21B-4.
Direct Materials, Direct Labor, and Factory Overhead Variances
(L.O. 5)

Stokes Shoe Company has a sandal division that produces a line of all-vinyl thongs. Each pair of thongs calls for .4 meters of vinyl material that costs $3.00 per meter. Standard direct labor hours and cost per pair of thongs are .2 hour and $1.80 (.2 hour × $9.00 per hour), respectively. The division's current standard variable overhead rate is $1.50 per direct labor hour, and the standard fixed overhead rate is $.80 per direct labor hour.

In August the sandal division manufactured and sold 60,000 pairs of thongs. During the month, 25,200 meters of vinyl material were used up, at a total cost of $73,080. The total actual overhead costs for August were $28,200, of which $18,200 were variable. The total number of direct labor hours worked was 10,800, and factory payroll for direct labor for August was $95,040. Normal monthly capacity for the year has been set at 58,000 pairs of thongs. Budgeted fixed factory overhead for the period was $9,280.

Required

Compute (1) the direct materials price variance, (2) the direct materials quantity variance, (3) the direct labor rate variance, (4) the direct labor efficiency variance, (5) the controllable overhead variance, and (6) the overhead volume variance.

Problem 21B-5.
Comprehensive: Standard Cost Journal Entry Analysis
(L.O. 2, 5, 6)

Wertheim Bottle Company makes wine bottles for many of the major wineries in California's Napa and Sonoma valleys, as well as for wineries in the grape-growing regions around Cupertino and Santa Cruz, California. Phil Cheng, controller of the company, has installed the following cost, quantity, and time standards for 19x5.

Direct materials: 4 five-gallon pails of a special silicon dioxide and phosphorus pentoxide-based compound per one gross (144) of bottles; cost, $10.00 per pail.

Direct labor: Forming Department, .2 hour per gross at $12.80 per direct labor hour; Finishing/Polishing Department, .1 hour per gross at $9.40 per direct labor hour.

Factory overhead: variable, $3.20 per direct labor hour; fixed, $2.80 per direct labor hour.

All direct materials are added at the beginning of the bottle-forming process. Much of Wertheim Bottle Company's machinery is automated, and the compound is heated, mixed, and poured into molds in a short time. Once cooled, the new bottles move via conveyor belt to the Finishing/Polishing Department. Again the process is highly automated. Machines scrape off excess material on the bottles and then polish all the outside and inside surfaces. After polishing, the bottles are fed into large cartons for shipping to customers.

During March 19x5, the following selected transactions took place:

Mar. 2 Purchased 14,000 pails of compound at $9.80 per pail, on account.

3 Requisitioned 13,240 pails of compound into production for an order calling for 3,300 gross of wine bottles.

6 Requisitioned 11,200 pails of compound into production for an order of 2,900 gross of wine bottles.

12 Transferred 5,400 gross of bottles to finished goods inventory.

15 Requisitioned 9,240 pails of compound into production for an order calling for 2,300 gross of wine bottles.

16 For the two-week period ending March 14, actual labor costs included 1,660 direct labor hours in the Forming Department at $13.00 per hour and 810 direct labor hours in the Finishing/Polishing Department at $9.50 per hour. During the pay period, 8,200 gross of good bottles were produced.

16 Factory overhead was applied to units worked on during the previous two weeks.

18 Purchased 19,000 pails of compound at $10.25 per pail, on account.

20 Requisitioned 13,960 pails of compound into production for an order of 3,500 gross of wine bottles.

28 Transferred 9,600 gross of bottles to finished goods inventory.

30 For the two-week period ending March 28, actual labor costs included 1,420 direct labor hours in the Forming Department at $12.60 per hour and 750 direct labor hours in the Finishing/Polishing Department at $9.20 per hour. During the pay period, 7,300 gross of good bottles were produced.

Mar. 30 Factory overhead was applied to units worked on during the two-week period.

31 During March, 9,800 gross of wine bottles were sold on account and shipped to customers. The selling price for these bottles was $76 per gross.

Actual factory overhead for March was $14,500 of variable and $13,300 of fixed overhead. These amounts have been recorded in the Factory Overhead Control account. Budgeted fixed factory overhead for March was $12,600. Beginning inventory information included: Materials Inventory, $42,100; Work in Process Inventory, $30,064; and Finished Goods Inventory, $146,772.

Required

1. Compute the standard cost per gross of wine bottles.
2. Prepare the entries necessary to record the above transactions (show calculations for each variance). For the direct labor entries, assume that everything except the distribution of direct labor to Work in Process Inventory has already been recorded.
3. Analyze the factory overhead accounts and compute the controllable overhead and overhead volume variances. (Assume that actual overhead incurred has already been debited to the control account.)
4. Prepare the entry to dispose of the balance in the Factory Overhead account and record the overhead variances.
5. Close all variance account balances to the Cost of Goods Sold account.

Problem 21B-6. Variance Review: Missing Information—Three-Variance Approach
(L.O. 8)

Overhead variances are interrelated. The Bruce Company and the Sparks Corporation both use standard costing systems. These systems depend on a standard overhead rate when overhead costs are applied to units produced.

	Bruce Company	Sparks Corporation
Actual machine hours	7,500	8,400
Standard hours allowed	?	8,200
Normal capacity in machine hours	?	?
Total overhead rate per machine hour	$ 3.20	?
Standard variable overhead rate	$ 1.00	$ 4.00
Actual variable and fixed overhead	$26,200	?
Total overhead costs applied	$25,600	?
Budgeted fixed overhead	?	$24,000
Total overhead variance	?	$ 600 (F)
Overhead spending variance	?	?
Overhead efficiency variance	?	$ 800 (U)
Overhead volume variance	$ 440 (F)	?
Controllable overhead variance	?	$ 8,200 (U)

Required

Fill in the unknown amounts by analyzing the data given for each company. Capacities are expressed in machine hours. (**Hint:** Use the structure of Figure 21-5 as a guide for your analysis.)

Management Decision Case

Annuity Life Insurance Company—Standard Costing In a Service Industry
(L.O. 2, 5, 7)

The Annuity Life Insurance Company (ALIC) markets several types of life insurance policies, but its permanent, twenty-year life annuity policy (P20A) is the company's most desired product. The P20A policy sells in $10,000 increments and features variable percentages of whole life insurance and single-payment annuity, depending on the potential policyholder's needs and age. There is an entire department devoted to developing and marketing the P20A policy. ALIC has determined that both the policy developer and policy salesperson contribute to creating each policy, so ALIC categorizes these people as direct labor for variance analysis, cost control, and performance evaluation purposes. For unit costing purposes, each $10,000 increment is considered 1 unit. Thus, a $90,000 policy comprises 9 units.

Standard unit cost information for the period is as follows:

Direct labor	
Policy developer	
3 hours at $12.00/hour	$ 36.00
Policy salesperson	
8.5 hours at $14.20/hour	120.70
Operating overhead	
Variable overhead	
11.5 hours at $26.00/hour	299.00
Fixed overhead	
11.5 hours at $18.00/hour	207.00
Standard unit cost	$662.70

Actual costs incurred during January for the 265 units sold were as follows:

Direct labor	
Policy developers	
848 hours at $12.50/hour	$10,600.00
Policy salespeople	
2,252.5 hours at $14.00/hour	31,535.00
Operating overhead	
Variable operating overhead	78,440.00
Fixed operating overhead	53,400.00

Normal monthly capacity was 260 units, and the budgeted fixed operating overhead for the month was $53,820.

Required

1. Compute the standard hours allowed in January for policy developers and policy salespeople.
2. What were the total actual costs incurred for January? What should the total standard costs for that period have been?
3. Compute the labor rate and efficiency variances for policy developers and policy salespeople.
4. Compute the overhead variances for January.
5. Identify possible causes for each variance, and develop possible solutions.

Answers to Self-Test

1. b	3. d	5. c	7. a	9. a
2. a	4. b	6. c	8. d	10. b

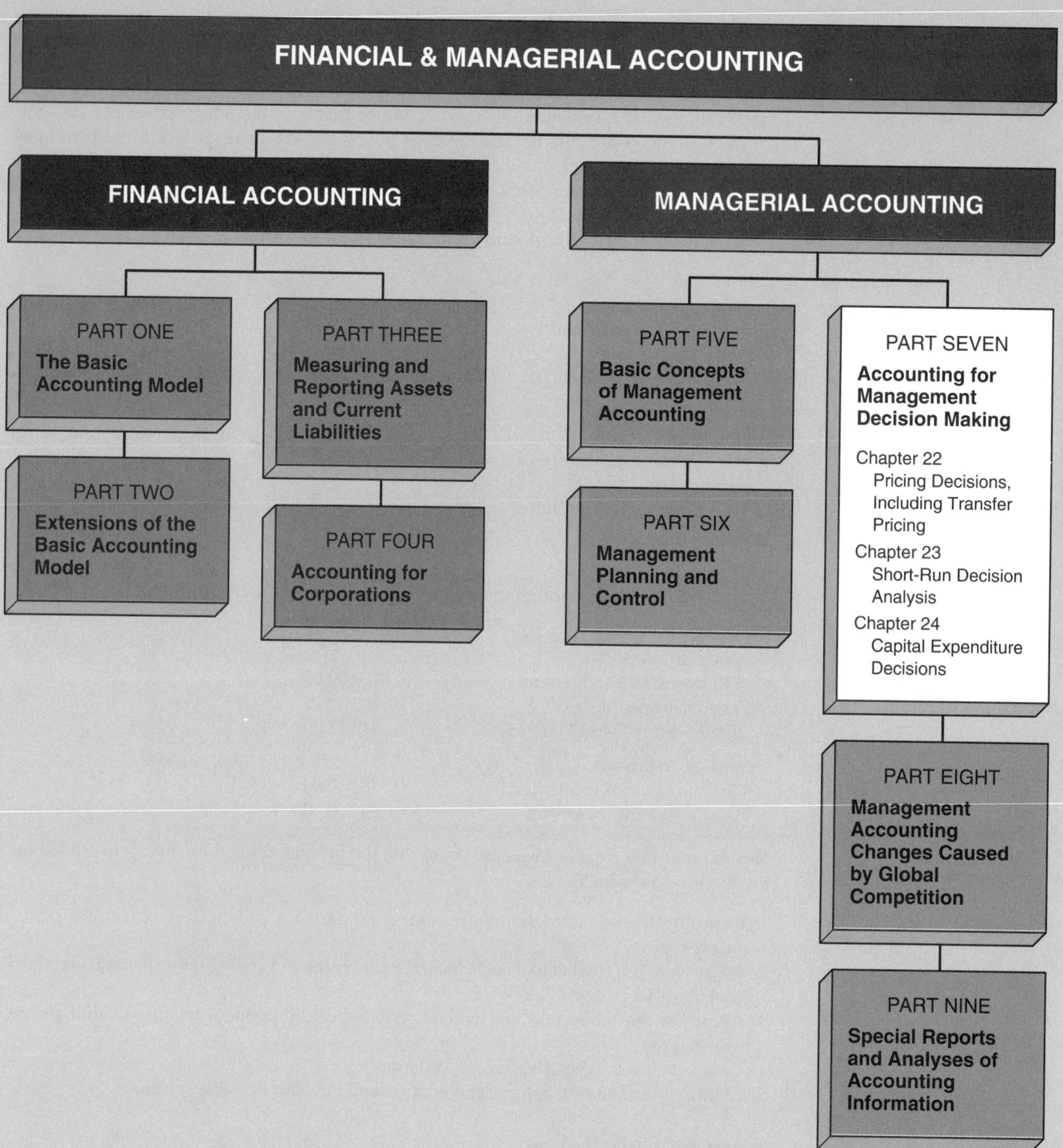

The third aspect of management accounting—providing information for management decision making—is the focal point of Part Seven. Pricing decisions, transfer pricing policies, short-run decision analyses, and capital expenditure decision analyses are fundamental applications of management accounting concepts and techniques.

PART SEVEN

Accounting for Management Decision Making

Chapter 22 exposes the difficulties of setting an accurate price for a good or a service. External as well as internal factors are used in the price setting process. Transfer pricing involves internally created prices that can be either cost- or market-based. If not applied properly, transfer prices can cause internal employee problems when used to evaluate performance.

Chapter 23 introduces the concepts of relevant decision information, variable costing, contribution margin reporting, and incremental decision analysis. Examples of short-run decisions include make or buy, special order, scarce resource/sales mix, elimination of unprofitable segments, and sell or process further considerations.

Chapter 24 first looks at the steps in the capital expenditure decision process. Then the techniques of accounting rate of return, payback period, and net present value are discussed. The concept of the time value of money and income tax influences on the capital expenditure decision analysis conclude the chapter.

LEARNING OBJECTIVES

1. Describe traditional economic pricing concepts.
2. Identify external and internal factors on which prices are based.
3. State the objectives managers use to establish prices of goods and services.
4. Create prices by applying the methods and tools of price determination.
5. Define and discuss transfer pricing.
6. Distinguish between a cost-based transfer price and a market-based transfer price.
7. Develop a transfer price.
8. Measure a manager's performance by using transfer prices.

CHAPTER 22

Pricing Decisions, Including Transfer Pricing

Deciding on an appropriate price is one of a manager's most difficult day-to-day decisions. Such decisions affect the long-term life of any profit-oriented enterprise. To stay in business, a company's selling price must (1) be equal to or lower than the competition's price; (2) be acceptable to the customer; (3) recover all costs incurred in bringing the product or service to a marketable condition; and (4) return a profit. If a manager deviates from these three pricing rules, there must be a specific short-run objective. Breaking these pricing rules for a long period will force a company into bankruptcy. Pricing using the target costing approach first looks at the competition's price, then backs into an acceptable cost.

Transfer pricing involves the setting of artificial prices on goods moving from one cost/expense center to another within a company. Because such prices are used only for internal decisions and performance evaluation, they are unknown to the outside world. A set of rules, different from those used to set external prices, governs the development of transfer prices. Transfer prices influence managers' behavior by forcing segments to compete for a company's resources. Although not as critical to a company's future as external prices, transfer prices can influence operating efficiency and profitability. After studying this chapter, you should be able to meet the learning objectives listed on the left.

DECISION POINT

American Transtech, Inc.[1]

■ American Transtech, Inc. of Jacksonville, Florida was created in the early 1980s during the divestiture of the Bell System. Formerly AT&T's Stocks and Bonds Division, the new company's primary objectives were to issue stock certificates for the seven Regional Holding Companies (RHCs) and to service the RHC shareholders. When the new company was formed, its responsibility centers were transformed from cost centers to profit centers, since management felt that by stressing profit, the company's resources would be better managed. Because the company is a service organization and each internal segment provides service to the others, pricing of service transfers within the company is a significant part of American Transtech's management control system. Therefore the company required an accounting system that would (1) track usage of all internal services so that the costs of services provided to clients could be

1. Robert J. Fox and Thomas L. Barton, "A System Is Born: Management Control at American Transtech," *Management Accounting,* Institute of Management Accountants, September 1986, pp. 37–47; and Thomas L. Barton and Robert J. Fox, "Evolution at American Transtech," *Management Accounting,* Institute of Management Accountants, April 1988, pp. 49–52.

computed and (2) create incentives for internal segments to control their usage of intracompany services.

The cost of computer operations accounts for about one-third of the company's total cost and is one of many operating units within the company. These units are called Lines of Service (LOS) and are evaluated as profit centers. In the case of Computer Operations, twenty-five computer service-related cost pools or activities have been identified and are used in charging other internal LOSs for services provided. Examples of these activities include CPU minutes, tapes mounted, disk storage space (in megabytes), and lines printed.

The Dividend Payment LOS is responsible for the issuance of dividend checks for all of AT&T's Regional Holding Companies and uses a significant amount of Computer Operations' services. From the examples of activities discussed above, how would the Dividend Payment LOS be charged for its computer service usage? How does the system of internal transfer prices safeguard the use of the company's resources?

Since the company established usage rates for each of the Computer Operations' twenty-five activities, the Dividend Payment LOS is billed at the standard rates for each service used. Because each LOS is evaluated as a profit center, managers want to minimize the charges received from Computer Operations without reducing the quality of services. Since each is a profit center too, minimizing costs helps maximize profits. Monitoring the level of internal service usage accomplishes this objective and also helps conserve the company's resources. ■

The Pricing Decision

The process of establishing a correct price is more of an art than a science. There are many mechanical approaches to price setting, and each produces a price. Six pricing methods may very well produce six different prices. The art of price setting stems from the ability to read the marketplace and anticipate customer reaction to a product and its price. Pricing methods do not provide a manager with the ability to react to the market. Market savvy is developed through experience in dealing with customers and products in an industry. Intuition also plays a major role in price setting.

The methods discussed in the following pages illustrate the process of developing a specific price under defined circumstances or objectives. Some of the methods provide the manager with the minimum price he or she can charge and still make a profit. Other prices are based on the competition and market conditions. The concept of setting prices according to "whatever the market will bear" will produce still another figure.

In making a final pricing decision, the manager must consider all these projected prices. The more data the manager has, the more he or she will be able to make a well-informed decision. But remember, pricing methods and approaches yield only decision support data. The manager must still select the appropriate price and be evaluated on that decision.

The Art of Setting a Price

Maison & Jardin is a gourmet restaurant in Altamonte Springs, Florida. The establishment is known for its excellent foods and wines. Among its selections of red wine is a 1989 Cabernet Sauvignon from Shafer Vineyards in Napa Valley, California. The restaurant's normal price for a bottle of this wine is $18.50, but, for one or more reasons, this wine is being featured as the "special selection of the month." Perhaps there is an oversupply of the wine, the wine has matured and must be sold, or the vineyard is running a special promotion.

Listed below are prices the restaurant is charging for this wine.

	Price per Bottle
Purchased by the glass, $5.25 (4 glasses per bottle)	$21.00
Purchased by the bottle with the meal	16.75
Purchased by the bottle to take home	11.95
Purchased by the case to take home ($119.50 ÷ 12)	9.96

What is the correct price for a bottle of this wine?

The listed prices are all appropriate based on differing circumstances. The $18.50 price is based on the cost of the bottle, reputation of the vineyard, prices of wines of comparable quality, vintage (1989), mixture of varietal grapes, and alcohol level.

Once a bottle of quality red wine has been opened, the wine begins to oxidize. It then spoils in two or three hours. Therefore, when wine is sold by the glass, the restaurant risks losing part of the bottle to spoilage. Thus, $5.25 per glass seems appropriate under the circumstances.

To promote a specific product, many businesses run special sales. A restaurant is no different. This month Maison & Jardin's management decided to reduce the bottle's price by $1.75 to lure customers into trying this product with their meal.

Although the take-home feature is unusual, the pricing is appropriate. Part of the cost for a bottle of wine served with a meal is for the cost of serving it. The wine steward must fetch the bottle, bring a cooling device for white wine to the table, uncork the bottle, decant a bottle of older wine, present the wine for customer approval, and continue pouring the wine during the meal. In the example, the restaurant reduced the price of a take-home bottle by $4.80. This means the cost of serving a bottle of wine and the restaurant's profit margin on this labor is somewhere around $5.00 per bottle. And that price has been included in the price shown on the wine list.

Finally, consider the price of a case. On a per bottle basis, the case price is $1.99 less than purchasing it by the bottle to take home. This reduction is known as quantity discounting, a concept widely followed in the free enterprise system. As with the take-home bottle price, reduced handling costs support the use of quantity discount pricing.

Pricing is a fascinating topic to study and learn. Any entrepreneur is a student of pricing during his or her entire career. The ability to set the one perfect price will never be mastered, for changes in circumstances will always justify a different price. Please keep this fact in mind as you begin your study of pricing decisions.

Traditional Economic Pricing Concepts

OBJECTIVE 1
Describe traditional economic pricing concepts

The traditional approach to pricing is based on microeconomic theory. Pricing has a major role in the concepts underlying the theory of the firm. At the base of this concept, the firm is in business to maximize profits. Although each product has its own set of revenues and costs, microeconomic theory states that profit will be maximized when the difference between total revenues and total costs is the greatest. Recall the discussion of breakeven analysis in the chapter on cost behavior and cost-volume-profit analysis. The figure of the graphic breakeven analysis for Keller Products, Inc. (page 646) illustrated a typical breakeven chart. To the left of the breakeven point of 500 units, the company will lose money, since total costs exceed total revenues. To the right of the breakeven point, profit will be realized, since total revenues are greater than total costs. But where is the point at which profits are maximized, and what is the role of pricing in this discussion?

Total Revenue and Total Cost Curves. By looking at the figure of the graphic breakeven analysis for Keller Products, Inc., you see that the outlook for profits is a bit misleading. The profit area seems to increase significantly as more and more products are sold. Therefore, it seems that if the company could produce an infinite number of products, maximum profit would be realized. But this situation is untrue, and microeconomic theory tells us why.

Figure 22-1A shows the economist's view of the breakeven chart. On it there are two breakeven points, between which is a large space labeled *profit area.* Notice that the total revenue line is curved rather than straight. The theory is that as one markets a product, price reductions will be necessary to sell additional units. Competition and other factors will cause such decreases. Total revenue will continue to increase, but the rate of increase will diminish as more units are sold. Therefore, the total revenue line curves toward the right.

Costs react in an opposite fashion. Over the assumed relevant range in the chapter on cost behavior and cost-volume-profit analysis, variable and fixed costs were fairly predictable, with fixed costs remaining constant and variable costs being the same per unit. The result was a straight line for total costs. Following microeconomic theory, costs per unit will increase over time, since fixed costs will change. As one moves into different relevant ranges, such fixed costs as supervision and depreciation increase. In addition, as the company pushes for more and more products from limited facilities, repair and maintenance costs increase. And as the push from management increases, total costs rise at an accelerating rate per unit. The result is that the total cost line in Figure 22-1A begins curving upward. The total revenue line and the total cost line then cross again, beyond which point the company suffers a loss on additional sales.

Profits are maximized at the point at which the difference between total revenue and total cost is the greatest. In Figure 22-1A, this point is assumed to be 7,000 units of sales. At that sales level, total revenue will be $210,000; total cost, $120,000; and profit, $90,000. In theory, if one additional unit is sold, profit per unit will drop, because total cost is rising at a faster rate than total revenues. As you can see, if the company sells 11,000 units, total profits will be almost entirely depleted by the rising costs. Therefore, in the example, 7,000 sales units is the optimum operating level, and the price charged at that level is the correct price.

Marginal Revenue and Marginal Cost Curves. Economists use the concepts of marginal revenue and marginal cost to help determine optimum price for a good or service. **Marginal revenue** is the change in total revenue caused by a one-unit change in output. **Marginal cost** is the change in total cost caused by a one-unit change in output. Graphic curves for marginal revenue and marginal cost are derived by measuring and plotting the rate of change in total revenue and total cost at various activity levels. Were you to compute marginal revenue and marginal cost for each unit sold in the example and plot them onto a graph, the lines would resemble those in Figure 22-1B. Notice that the marginal cost line crosses the marginal revenue line at 7,000 units. After that point, total profits will decrease as additional units are sold. Marginal cost will exceed marginal revenue for each unit sold over 7,000. Profit will be maximized when the marginal revenue and marginal cost lines intersect. By projecting this point

Figure 22-1. Microeconomic Pricing Theory

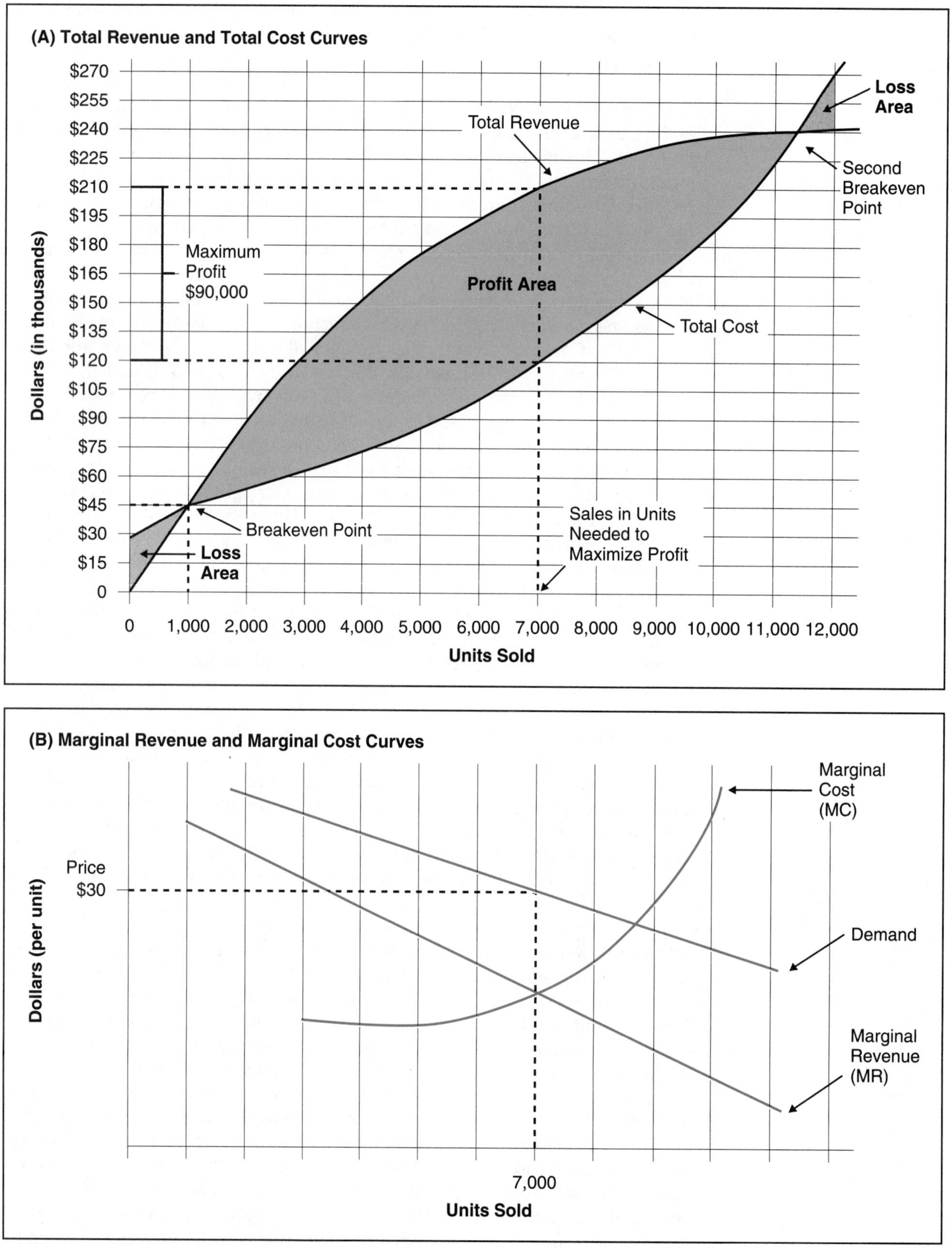

(A) Total Revenue and Total Cost Curves

Dollars (in thousands)
$270
$255
$240
$225
$210
$195
$180
$165
$150
$135
$120
$105
$90
$75
$60
$45
$30
$15
0
0 1,000 2,000 3,000 4,000 5,000 6,000 7,000 8,000 9,000 10,000 11,000 12,000
Units Sold
Total Revenue
Total Cost
Profit Area
Maximum Profit $90,000
Breakeven Point
Loss Area
Second Breakeven Point
Loss Area
Sales in Units Needed to Maximize Profit

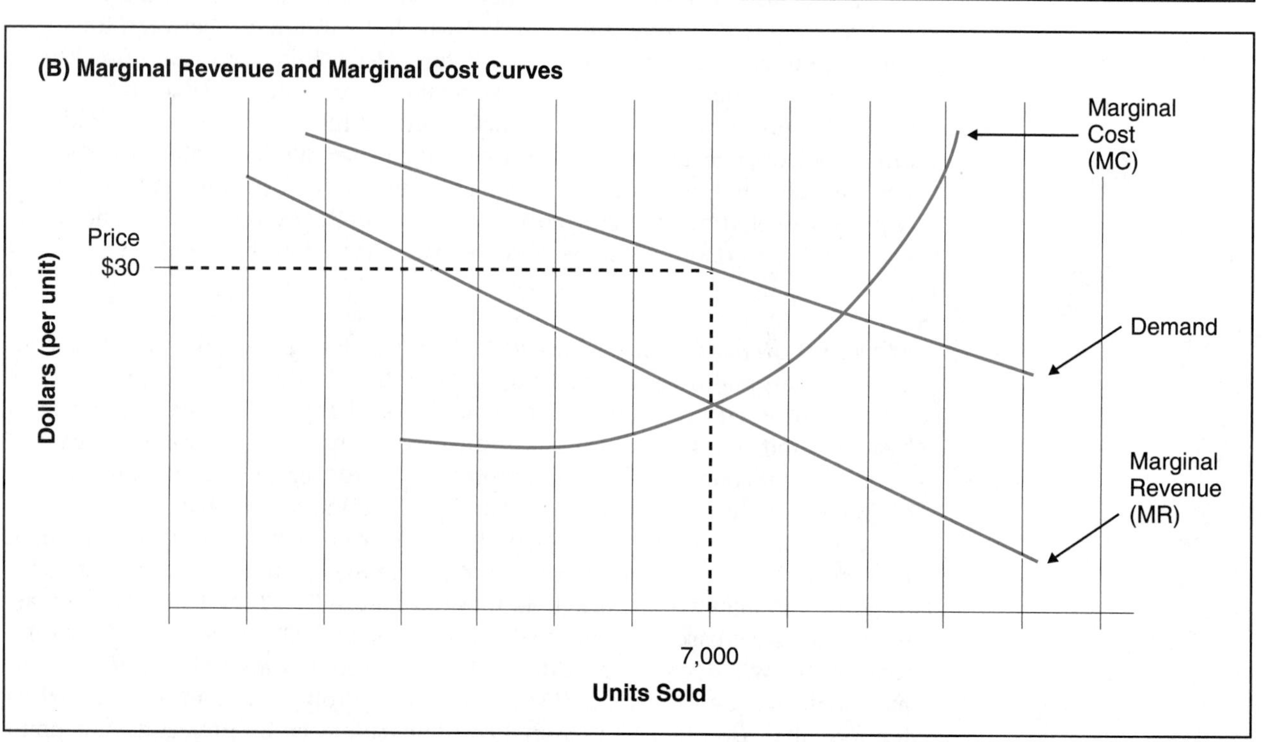

onto the product's demand curve, you can locate the optimal price, which is $30 per unit.

If all information used in microeconomic theory were certain, picking the optimal price would be fairly easy. But most information used in the previous analysis relied on projected amounts for unit sales, product costs, and revenues. Just computing total demand for a product or service from such data is difficult. And projecting repair and maintenance costs is usually done by using unsupported estimates. Nevertheless, developing such an analysis usually makes the analyst aware of cost patterns and the unanticipated influences of demand. For this reason it is important for management to consider the microeconomic approach to pricing when setting product prices. But information from this type of analysis should not be the only data relied on.

Factors Influencing the Pricing Decision

A manager must consider many factors when creating the best price for a product or service. Therefore, before exploring the methods used to compute a selling price, we will analyze those influential factors. Some of those factors are external to the company; others are internal.

OBJECTIVE 2
Identify external and internal factors on which prices are based

External Factors. Each product or service has a targeted market that determines demand. Strong consideration should be given to this market before choosing a final price. External factors to be considered in setting a price are summarized in Table 22-1. Those factors include the following considerations:

1. What is total demand for the item?
2. Are there one or several competing products in the marketplace?
3. What prices are being charged by others already selling the item?
4. Do customers want the least expensive product or are they more interested in quality than in price?
5. Is the product unique or so new that the company is the only source in the marketplace?

All these questions should be answered by the person developing the price. If competition is keen and the quality is similar, market price will set the ceiling for any new entry into the market. If, however, a product is unique, a more flexible pricing environment exists. Customers' needs and desires are important for any new product. If quality is of primary importance, as is the case for top-of-the-line automobiles, then emphasis should be placed on using quality inputs. The price will be adjusted upward accordingly.

In summary, it is important to know the marketplace, including customers' needs and the competition, before determining a final price.

Internal Factors. Several internal factors also influence the price of a good or service; these are summarized in Table 22-1 as well. Basic among these factors is an item's cost. What cost basis should be considered when determining price—variable costs, full absorption costs, or total costs? Should the price be based on a desired rate of return on assets? Is the product a loss leader, created to lure customers into considering additional, more expensive products? Where should one draw the line on the quality of materials and supplies? Is the product labor intensive or can it be produced using automated equipment? If markup percentages are used to establish prices, were they updated to reflect current operating conditions? Are the company's scarce resources being overtaxed by introducing an additional product or service, and does the price reflect this use of scarce resources?

Table 22-1. Factors To Consider When Setting a Price

External Factors:

Total demand for product or service
Number of competing products or services
Quality of competing products or services
Current prices of competing products or services
Customers' preferences for quality versus price
Sole source versus heavy competition
Seasonal demand or continual demand
Life of product or service

Internal Factors:

Cost of product or service
  Variable costs
  Full absorption costs
  Total costs
Price geared toward return on investment
Loss leader or main product
Quality of materials and labor inputs
Labor intensive or automated process
Markup percentage updated
Usage of scarce resources

As with external factors, each of these questions should be answered before a manager establishes a price for a product or service. Underlying every pricing decision is the fact that all costs incurred must be recovered in the long run or the company will no longer be in business.

Pricing Policy Objectives

OBJECTIVE 3
State the objectives managers use to establish prices of goods and services

The long-run objectives of a company should include a pricing policy. Such policies differentiate one company from another. For example, consider the pricing policies of Mercedes-Benz and Ford or Neiman-Marcus and KMart. All four companies are successful, but their pricing policies are quite different. Of primary importance in setting company objectives is identifying the market being served and meeting the needs of that market. Possible pricing policy objectives include:

1. Identifying and adhering to both short-run and long-run pricing strategies
2. Maximizing profits
3. Maintaining or gaining market share
4. Setting socially responsible prices
5. Maintaining stated rate of return on investment
6. Ensuring prices support trend of total sales increases

Pricing strategies depend on many factors and conditions. Companies producing standard items for a competitive marketplace will have different pricing strategies from firms making custom-designed items. In a competitive market, prices can be reduced to gain market share by displacing sales of competing companies. Continuous upgrading of a product or service can help in this area. The company making custom-designed items can be more conservative in its pricing strategy.

Maximizing profits has always been considered the underlying objective of any pricing policy. Maintaining or gaining market share is closely related to pricing strategies. However, market share is important only if sales are profitable. To increase market share by reducing prices below cost can be disastrous unless this move is accompanied by other compensating objectives and goals.

Although still a dominant factor in price setting, profit maximization has been tempered in recent years by other, more socially acceptable goals. Prices have a social effect, and companies are concerned about their public image. Recall the discussion about Mercedes, Ford, Neiman-Marcus, and KMart. Does not each one have an individual image in your mind? And are prices not a part of that image? Other social concerns, such as legal constraints and ethical considerations, also affect many companies' pricing policies.

Other pricing policy objectives include maintaining a minimum return on investment and concentrating on continuous sales growth. Return on investment involves markup percentages designed to provide a buffer between costs and prices and is linked closely with the profit maximization objective. Maintaining a continuous sales growth is important for several reasons. First, it provides management with a strong measure of performance for shareholders. Second, sales growth can be used to measure whether market share is increasing. Finally, such a policy provides managers with yearly incentives and targets.

Cost-Based Pricing Methods

OBJECTIVE 4
Create prices by applying the methods and tools of price determination

There are many pricing methods in business practice. Although managers may use one or two traditional approaches, at some point they also deviate from those approaches and use their experience. Several pricing methods are available that can be adopted by managers. A good starting point is for a manager to develop a price based on the cost of producing a good or service. Here, three methods based on cost will be discussed: (1) gross margin pricing; (2) profit margin pricing; and (3) return on assets pricing. Remember that in a competitive environment, market prices and conditions also influence price; however, when prices do not cover a company's costs, the company will eventually fail.

To illustrate the three methods of cost-based pricing, our example uses data on the Tom Johnson Company. The Tom Johnson Company assembles parts purchased from outside vendors into an electric car-wax buffer. Total costs and unit costs incurred in the previous accounting period to produce 14,750 wax buffers were as follows:

	Total Costs	Unit Costs
Variable production costs		
Materials and parts	$ 88,500	$ 6.00
Direct labor	66,375	4.50
Variable factory overhead	44,250	3.00
Total variable production costs	$199,125	$13.50
Fixed factory overhead	$154,875	$10.50
Selling, general, and administrative expenses		
Selling expenses	$ 73,750	$ 5.00
General expenses	36,875	2.50
Administrative expenses	22,125	1.50
Total selling, general, and administrative expenses	$132,750	$ 9.00
Total costs and expenses	$486,750	$33.00

No changes in unit costs are expected this period. Desired profit for the period is $110,625. The company uses assets totaling $921,875 in producing the wax buffers. A 12 percent return on these assets is expected.

Gross Margin Pricing

One cost-based approach to determining a selling price is known as **gross margin pricing.** Gross margin is the difference between sales and total production costs of those sales. The markup percentage under the gross margin method is designed to include everything not included in gross margin in the computation of the selling price. The gross margin markup percentage is composed of selling, general, and administrative expenses and desired profit. Because an accounting system often provides management with unit production cost data, both variable and fixed, this method of determining selling price can be easily applied. The formulas used are as follows:

$$\text{Markup percentage} = \frac{\text{desired profit} + \text{total selling, general, and administrative expenses}}{\text{total production costs}}$$

$$\text{Gross margin-based price} = \text{total production costs per unit} + (\text{markup percentage} \times \text{total production costs per unit})$$

The numerator in the markup percentage formula contains desired profit plus total selling, general, and administrative expenses. As you can see, this numerator is divided by total production costs to arrive at the markup factor.

For the Tom Johnson Company, the markup percentage and selling price are computed as follows:

$$\text{Markup percentage} = \frac{\$110{,}625 + \$132{,}750}{\$199{,}125 + \$154{,}875} = \frac{\$243{,}375}{\$354{,}000} = 68.75\%$$

$$\text{Gross margin-based price} = \$13.50 + \$10.50 + (\$24.00 \times 68.75\%) = \$40.50$$

The numerator in the markup percentage formula is the sum of the desired profit ($110,625) and the total selling, general, and administrative expenses ($132,750). The denominator contains all production costs—variable costs of $199,125 and fixed production costs of $154,875. Gross margin markup is 68.75 percent of total production costs, or $16.50 ($24 × 68.75%). Adding $16.50 to the total production cost base yields a selling price of $40.50.

Profit Margin Pricing

When using an approach known as **profit margin pricing**, the markup percentage includes only the desired profit factor. For this method to be effective, all costs and expenses must be broken down into unit cost data. Since selling, general, and administrative costs tend to be more difficult to allocate to products or services than variable and fixed production costs, only arbitrary assignments can be used. However, arbitrary allocations can be misleading and may result in poor price setting. As long as market and competition factors are accounted for before establishing a final price, profit margin pricing can be used as a starting point in any price-setting decision analysis.

In the following markup percentage computation, all costs have shifted from the numerator to the denominator.

$$\text{Markup percentage} = \frac{\text{desired profit}}{\text{total costs and expenses}}$$

Profit margin-based price = total costs and expenses per unit + (markup percentage × total costs and expenses per unit)

As shown, only desired profit remains in the numerator. The denominator contains all production and operating costs related to the product or service being priced. In the profit margin pricing formula, total costs and expenses per unit are multiplied by the markup percentage to obtain the appropriate profit margin. The selling price is computed by adding profit margin to total unit costs.

Refer again to data on the Tom Johnson Company. The markup percentage and the unit selling price using the profit margin pricing approach are computed as follows:

$$\text{Markup percentage} = \frac{\$110{,}625}{\$199{,}125 + \$154{,}875 + \$132{,}750} = \frac{\$110{,}625}{\$486{,}750} = \underline{\underline{22.73\%}}$$

$$\text{Profit margin-based price} = \$13.50 + \$10.50 + \$9.00 + (\$33.00 \times 22.73\%) = \underline{\underline{\$40.50}}$$

Only the $110,625 in desired profit margin remains in the numerator, whereas the denominator increased to $486,750. The denominator represents total costs and expenses to be incurred. Markup percentage for this situation is 22.73 percent. The selling price is again $40.50. However, in this computation the markup percentage of 22.73 percent is applied to the total cost of $33.00 to obtain the profit margin of $7.50 per unit ($33.00 + $7.50 = $40.50).

Return on Assets Pricing

Return on assets pricing changes the objective of the price determination process. Earning a profit margin on total costs is replaced by earning a profit equal to a specified rate of return on assets employed in the operation. Since a business's primary objective should be earning a minimum desired rate of return, the return on assets pricing approach has great appeal and support.

Assuming a company has a stated minimum desired rate of return, you can use the following formula to calculate return on assets-based price.

Return on assets-based price = total costs and expenses per unit + (desired rate of return × total costs of assets employed) ÷ anticipated units to be produced

The return on assets-based price is computed by first dividing the cost of assets employed by projected units to be produced. This number is then multiplied by the rate of return to obtain desired earnings per unit. Desired earnings per unit plus total costs and expenses per unit yields unit selling price.

For the Tom Johnson Company, the selling price per unit needed to earn a 12 percent return on the $921,875 asset base when estimated production is 14,750 units is calculated as follows.

$$\begin{aligned}\text{Return on assets-based price} &= \$13.50 + \$10.50 + \$9.00 \\ &\quad + [12\% \times (\$921{,}875 \div 14{,}750)] \\ &= \underline{\underline{\$40.50}}\end{aligned}$$

The desired profit amount has been replaced by an overall company rate of return on assets. By dividing cost of assets employed by projected units of output and multiplying the result by the minimum desired rate of return, one obtains a unit profit factor of $7.50 [12% × ($921,875 ÷ 14,750)]. Adding this profit factor to total unit costs and expenses determines the selling price of $40.50.

Summary of the Cost-Based Pricing Methods

The three cost-based pricing methods are summarized in Figure 22-2. All three methods—gross margin pricing, profit margin pricing, and return on assets pricing—will yield the same selling price if applied to the same data. Therefore, companies select their methods based on their degree of trust in a cost base. The cost bases from which they can choose are: (1) total product costs per unit or (2) total costs and expenses per unit. Often total product costs per unit are readily available, which makes gross margin pricing a good benchmark on which to compute selling prices. Return on assets pricing is also a good pricing method if the cost of the assets used on a product can be identified and a cost amount determined. If not, the method yields inaccurate results.

Pricing of Services

Service-oriented businesses take a different approach to pricing their products. Although a service has no physical existence, it must still be priced and billed to the customer. Most service organizations use a form of **time and materials pricing** to arrive at the price of a service. Service companies, such as appliance repair shops, home-addition specialists, pool cleaners, and automobile repair businesses, arrive at prices by using two computations, one for labor and one for materials and parts. As with the cost-based approaches, a markup percentage is used to add the cost of overhead and a profit factor to the direct costs of labor, materials, and parts. If materials and parts are not a component of the service being performed, then only direct labor costs are used as a basis for developing price. For professionals, such as attorneys, accountants, and consultants, a factor representing all overhead costs is applied to the base labor costs to establish a price for the services.

Ken's Auto Pampering just completed working on Mr. Burgess's 1983 Jaguar XJ6. Parts used to repair the vehicle cost $340. The company's 40 percent markup rate on parts covers parts-related overhead costs and profit. Labor involved nine hours of time from a Jaguar specialist whose wages are $15 per hour. The current overhead markup rate on labor is 80 percent. To see how much Mr. Burgess will be billed for these auto repairs, review the computation on the next page.

Figure 22-2. Cost-Based Pricing Methods: Tom Johnson Company

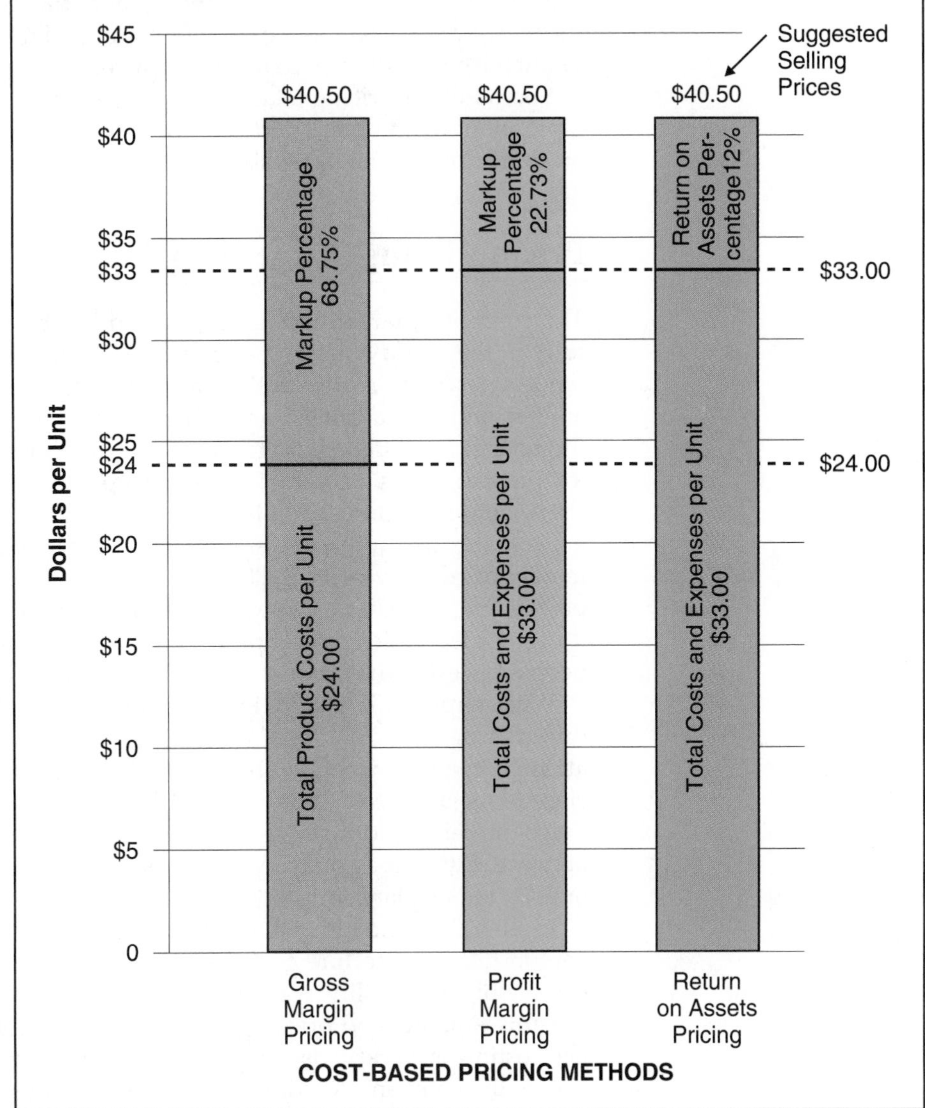

Repair parts used	$340	
Overhead charges		
$340 × 40%	136	
Total parts charges		$476
Labor charges		
9 hours @ $15/hour	$135	
Overhead charges		
$135 × 80%	108	
Total labor charges		243
Total Billing		$719

Final Notes on Cost-Based Pricing Methods

As emphasized earlier, pricing is an art, not a science. Although one can use several methods to mechanically compute the price of something, many factors external to the good or service influence price. Once the cost of a good or service is determined, the decision maker must account for such factors as competitors' prices, customers' expectations, and the cost of substitute goods and services. Pricing is a risky part of operating a business, and care must be taken to establish that all-important selling price.

Special-order pricing takes a different approach to price determination. This topic, along with other short-run operating decisions, is covered in the chapter on short-run decision analysis.

Pricing Using Target Costing

The concept of target costing, developed by the Japanese to compete successfully in the world's marketplace, is a product pricing variant of the cost-based models described earlier in this chapter. Instead of first determining the cost of an item and then adding a profit factor to identify a product's price, target costing reverses the procedure. **Target costing** is a pricing method that (1) identifies the price at which a product will be competitive in the marketplace, (2) defines the minimum desired profit to be made on that product, and (3) computes a target cost for the product by subtracting the desired profit from the competitive market price. This target cost is then given to the engineers and product design people and is used as a maximum cost for the materials, methods, and procedures needed to design and produce the product. It is the responsibility of these people to design the product at or below its target cost.

What happens if the engineers determine that the product cannot be produced at or below its target cost? First, its design should be re-evaluated and attempts made to improve the production approach. But if it still cannot come close to its target cost, the company should understand that its current productive equipment and facilities prevent it from competing in that particular marketplace. Either the company should invest in new equipment and procedures or abandon its plans for producing the product.

In a highly competitive market, product quality and price determine the winners in the quest to lure customers. Customers will purchase the product that has the highest quality at the lowest price. These two customer-decision determinants—quality and price—go together; one is not sacrificed for the other. Target costing is a very useful pricing tool in such an environment because it allows the company to critically analyze the potential for success of a product before committing resources to its production. If the company first produces a product and then finds out its cost-based price is not competitive, the company will lose money because of the resources already used to produce the product. In most cases, the potential success or failure of a product is identifiable through the use of the target costing approach.

Target costing should not be confused with the cost-based methods used for pricing decisions. In cost-based situations, if the product does not produce a desired profit, production procedures are analyzed to find areas in which costs can be cut and controlled. This approach is based on guesswork until the product hits the marketplace. A target cost is not an anticipated cost to be achieved by some midway point in a product's life cycle. The product is expected to produce a profit as soon as it is marketed. Improvements can still be made in a product's design and production methods that will reduce its cost below its target cost, but profitability is built into the selling price from the beginning.

Even though the managerial accountant is not directly involved in the process of designing a product to meet its target cost, the accountant does supply cost information to the designers during a product's development stages. In addition, the accountant is responsible for tracking the costing experience of a new product and advising the engineers of their success or failure to meet the target costs.

Transfer Pricing

OBJECTIVE 5
Define and discuss transfer pricing

In the chapter on responsibility accounting and performance evaluation, the concept of responsibility centers was introduced. As you learned, cost/expense centers and profit centers are important to a **decentralized organization** because they help alleviate some of the difficulty of controlling diverse operations. Responsibility for a company's functions is placed with managers, and their performance is measured by comparing actual results with budgeted or projected results.

Profit measurement and return on investment are important gauges of performance in decentralized divisions. But at cost/expense centers where only costs are involved, many people have difficulty measuring profitability and performance. This problem becomes more complicated when divisions within a company exchange goods or services and assume the role of customer or supplier to another division. As a result, transfer prices are used. A **transfer price** is the price at which goods are exchanged among a company's divisions. Such prices allow intracompany transactions to be measured and accounted for. These prices also affect the revenues and costs of the divisions involved. Furthermore, since a transfer price contains an estimated amount of profit, a cost/expense center manager's ability to meet a targeted profit can be measured. Although often called artificial or created prices, company transfer prices as well as related policies are closely connected with performance evaluation.

Transfer Pricing Characteristics

Transfer pricing is somewhat controversial. Some people believe in the benefits of using transfer prices. Others believe they should never be used because they are not real prices. To illustrate how transfer prices are used and to help explain their difficult operational and behavioral aspects, we will analyze two situations requiring such prices. Figure 22-3 shows how products flow at the Creative Pulp Company. This company is composed of three divisions: the Pulp Division, the Cardboard Division, and the Box Division. Example I shows the Pulp Division transferring wood pulp to the Cardboard Division for use in making cardboard. The Cardboard Division also has the option of purchasing the pulp from an outside supplier. The cost of making the pulp, including materials, labor, variable overhead, and fixed overhead, is $12.90 per pound. By adding a 10 percent factor to cover miscellaneous divisional overhead expenses as well as a small profit, the proposed transfer price amounts to $14.19 per pound. The outside supplier will sell the pulp to the company for $14.10 per pound. What should the manager of the Cardboard Division do?

Clearly, pressure is on the manager of the Pulp Division to lower the transfer price to an amount equal to or less than $14.10, the market price. If this action is taken, however, the $.09 per pound reduction will directly affect profits of the Pulp Division. In turn, that situation will affect the manager's performance. On the other hand, if the manager of the Cardboard Division agrees or is forced to pay the $14.19 price to benefit overall company operating results, that person's profit and performance will be negatively affected. Thus, the question arises: is either amount a fair price? Such a problem would not occur if costs were simply accumulated as the product travels through the production process. The Pulp

Figure 22-3. Intracompany Transfer Pricing Examples: Creative Pulp Company

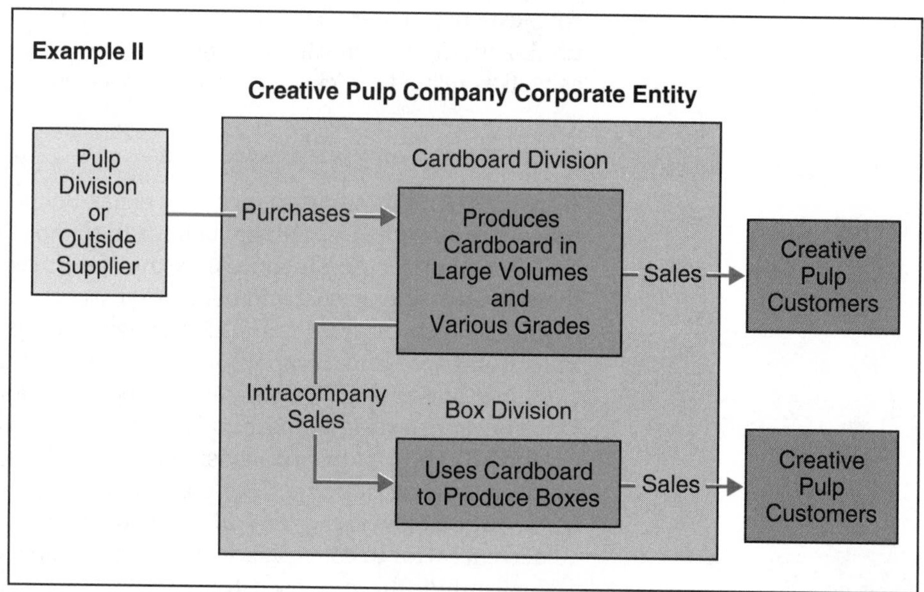

Division could be treated as a cost/expense center and the manager's performance evaluated on the basis of only budgeted and actual costs. But then the Pulp Division's return on investment could not be measured. These are the conflicting objectives of performance evaluation in a decentralized organization.

A second common situation is shown in Example II of Figure 22-3. Instead of an outside supplier's influencing an internal transfer price, the Cardboard Division has an outside customer. The manager of the Cardboard Division must decide whether to sell cardboard to the outside customer for $28.10 per pound or supply the Box Division at $27.90 per pound. (The $27.90 covers all costs plus a profit margin.)

Several possible problems must be considered here. Is the outside customer going to make boxes that compete with those of the company's Box Division? Should the Box Division pay a market value transfer price so the Cardboard Division's manager can be evaluated properly? What about the Box Division? Should that manager suffer because all profits were siphoned off by managers of the Pulp and Cardboard divisions?

These are but a few of the problems involved in using transfer prices. So, perhaps you can now better understand why there are both proponents and opponents of this concept. From the example, it is easy to understand why transfer prices often cause internal bickering between managers. But measuring a manager's performance is still a major objective of decentralized companies. And the use of transfer prices is one important approach to that objective.

Transfer Pricing Methods

OBJECTIVE 6
Distinguish between a cost-based transfer price and a market-based transfer price

There are two primary approaches to developing a transfer price.

1. The price may be based on the cost of the item until its transfer to the next department or process.
2. A market value may be used if the item has an existing external market when transferred.

Both of these pricing situations were present in the Creative Pulp Company example described earlier. There, the Pulp Division would be inclined to use the cost method, since no apparent outside market exists for the pulp product. The only user of pulp is the Cardboard Division. However, the Box Division will probably have to pay a market-related price for the cardboard, since the Cardboard Division can either sell its product outside or transfer it to the Box Division.

In a situation in which no external markets are involved, division managers in a decentralized company may agree on a *cost-plus transfer price* or a *negotiated transfer price.* A **cost-plus transfer price** is the sum of costs incurred by the producing division plus an agreed-on profit percentage. The weakness of the cost-plus pricing method is that cost recovery is guaranteed to the selling division. And guaranteed cost recovery fails to detect inefficient operating conditions as well as excessive cost incurrence.

A **negotiated transfer price,** on the other hand, is bargained for by the managers of the buying and selling divisions. From the cost-plus side, a transfer price may be based on an agreement to use a standard cost plus a profit percentage. This approach emphasizes cost control through the use of standard costs while still allowing the selling division to return a profit even though it is a cost center. A negotiated transfer price may also be based on a market price that was reduced in the bargaining process.

Market transfer prices are discussed but seldom used without being subjected to negotiations between managers. Using market prices may cause the selling division to ignore negotiation attempts from the buying division manager and sell directly to outside customers. If this causes an internal shortage of materials and forces the buying division to purchase materials from the outside, overall company profits may be lowered even when the selling division makes a profit. Such use of market prices works against a company's overall operating objectives. Therefore, when market prices are used to develop transfer prices, they are normally used only as a basis for negotiation.

Developing a Transfer Price

OBJECTIVE 7
Develop a transfer price

Many of the normal pricing considerations introduced earlier in this chapter are also present in the development of a transfer price. The first step is to compute the unit cost of the item being transferred. Next, management must determine the appropriate profit markup. If the semifinished product (1) has an existing external market for the selling division to consider or (2) can be purchased in similar condition by the buying division from an outside source, then the market price must be included in the analysis used to develop a transfer price. The final step is to have the managers negotiate a compromise between the two prices.

Now, look again at the Creative Pulp Company example. The division manager's computations supporting the $14.19 cost-plus transfer price are shown in Exhibit 22-1. This one-year budget is based on the expectation that the Cardboard Division will require 480,000 pounds of pulp. Unit costs are stated in the right column. Notice that allocated corporate overhead is not included in the computation of the transfer price. Only costs related to the Pulp Division are included. The profit markup percentage of 10 percent adds $1.29 to the final transfer price of $14.19.

At this point, management could dictate that the $14.19 price be used. On the other hand, the manager of the Cardboard Division could bring the outside purchase price of $14.10 per pound to the attention of management. Usually, such situations end up being negotiated to determine the final transfer price. Each side has a position and strong arguments to support a price. And each manager's performance will be compromised by adopting the other's price.

In the example, both managers brought their concerns to the attention of top management. A unique settlement was reached. Since internal profits must be erased before financial statements are prepared, management allowed the Pulp Division to use the $14.19 price and the Cardboard Division the $14.10 price for

Exhibit 22-1. Transfer Price Computation

Creative Pulp Company
Pulp Division—Transfer Price Computation

Cost Category	Budgeted Costs	Cost per Unit
Materials		
Wood	$1,584,000	$ 3.30
Scrap wood	336,000	0.70
Labor		
Shaving/cleaning	768,000	1.60
Pulverizing	1,152,000	2.40
Blending	912,000	1.90
Overhead		
Variable	936,000	1.95
Fixed	504,000	1.05
Subtotals	$6,192,000	$12.90
Costs allocated from corporate office	144,000	
Target profit, 10% of division's costs	619,200	1.29
Total costs and profit	$6,955,200	
Cost-plus transfer price		$14.19

purposes of performance evaluation. Obviously, the company did not want the Cardboard Division buying pulp from another company. At the same time, the Pulp Division had the right to a 10 percent profit. Such approaches are often used to maintain harmony within a corporation. In this case it allowed top management to measure the managers' performance while avoiding behavioral issues. After the period was over, all fictitious profits were canceled by using adjusting entries before preparing end-of-year financial statements. The final product, in this case the boxes, had a profit factor that took into account all operations of the business.

Measuring Performance by Using Transfer Prices

OBJECTIVE 8
Measure a manager's performance by using transfer prices

When transfer prices are used, performance reports on managers of cost/expense centers will contain revenue and income figures used in the evaluation. The Pulp Division performance report in Exhibit 22-2 is a good example.

The Pulp Division supplied 500 more pounds of pulp than anticipated for the month. Sales were priced at $14.19 per pound. The variable costs per unit shown earlier were used to extend budgeted and actual amounts for materials, labor, and variable overhead. The result was that the manager of the Pulp Division earned a March profit of $43,350, which was $1,170 over budget. The transfer price made it possible for the division to be evaluated as if it were a profit

Exhibit 22-2. Performance Report Using Transfer Prices

Creative Pulp Company
Pulp Division—Performance Report
For March 19x0

	Budget (42,000 pounds)	Actual (42,500 pounds)	Difference Over/(Under) Budget
Costs Controllable by Supervisor			
Sales to Cardboard Division	$595,980	$603,075	$7,095
Cost of goods sold			
Materials:			
Wood	$138,600	$140,250	$1,650
Scrap wood	29,400	29,750	350
Labor:			
Shaving/cleaning	67,200	68,000	800
Pulverizing	100,800	102,000	1,200
Blending	79,800	80,750	950
Overhead:			
Variable	81,900	82,875	975
Fixed	44,100	44,100	—
Total cost of goods sold	$541,800	$547,725	$5,925
Gross margin from sales	$ 54,180	$ 55,350	$1,170
Costs Uncontrollable by Supervisor			
Cost allocated from corporate office	$ 12,000	$ 12,000	—
Division's income	$ 42,180	$ 43,350	$1,170

center, even though the division does not sell to outside customers. Were the Pulp Division still accounted for as a cost/expense center, the manager would have to explain costs' being $5,925 over budget instead of divisional income's being over target.

(**Note:** Management may want the budget column restated at 42,500 pounds for evaluation purposes.)

Final Note on Transfer Prices

Problems in transfer price policy arise when buying divisions elect to purchase from outside suppliers. A selling division with adequate capacity to fulfill the buying division's demands should sell to that division at any price that recovers incremental costs. Incremental costs of intracompany sales include all variable costs of production and distribution plus any fixed costs directly traceable to intracompany sales. If a buying division can acquire products from outside suppliers at an annual cost that is less than the supplying division's incremental costs, then purchases should be made from the outside supplier. This is because overall company profits will be enhanced. A thorough analysis of the supplying division's operations should also be conducted.

Chapter Review

Review of Learning Objectives

1. **Describe traditional economic pricing concepts.**
The traditional approach to pricing is based on microeconomic theory. Microeconomic theory states that profits will be maximized at the point at which the difference between total revenue and total cost is greatest. Total revenue then tapers off, since as a product is marketed, price reductions are necessary to sell more units. Total cost increases when large quantities are produced because fixed costs change. To locate the point of maximum profit, marginal revenue and marginal cost must be computed and plotted. Profit is maximized at the point at which the marginal revenue and marginal cost curves intersect.

2. **Identify external and internal factors on which prices are based.**
Many factors influence the process of determining a selling price. Factors external to a company include: (a) total demand for the product or service; (b) number of competing products or services; (c) competitor's quality and price; (d) customer preference; (e) seasonal demand; and (f) life of the product. Internal factors are: (a) costs of producing the product or service; (b) purpose and quality of product; (c) type of process used—labor intensive versus automated; (d) markup percentage procedure; and (e) amount of scarce resources used.

3. **State the objectives managers use to establish prices of goods and services.**
The long-run objectives of a company should include statements on pricing policy. Possible pricing policy objectives include: (a) adhering to short- and long-run pricing strategies; (b) maximizing profits; (c) maintaining or gaining market share; (d) ensuring prices are socially responsible; (e) maintaining a stated rate of return on investments; and (f) ensuring prices support a trend of total sales increases.

4. **Create prices by applying the methods and tools of price determination.**
Several cost-based pricing methods can be adopted by the pricing manager. However, experience in pricing a product often leads to adjustments in the formula used. Pricing methods include: (a) gross margin pricing; (b) profit margin pricing; and (c) return on assets pricing. A pricing method often used by service-oriented businesses is time and materials pricing. Target costing is an approach to pricing developed by the

Japanese to compete successfully in the world's marketplace. Instead of being cost-based and letting total costs dictate a product's price, pricing using target costing is price-based. First, the maximum competitive price is determined. Then the company's normal profit margin is subtracted to yield the maximum allowable production and distribution costs the company can incur and still remain competitive and earn a normal profit on the product.

5. **Define and discuss transfer pricing.**
A transfer price is the price at which goods are exchanged between a company's segments. Since a transfer price contains an amount of estimated profit, a manager's ability to meet a profit target can be measured, even for a typical cost/expense center. Although often called artificial or created prices, company transfer prices and related policies are closely connected with performance evaluation.

6. **Distinguish between a cost-based transfer price and a market-based transfer price.**
There are two primary approaches to developing transfer prices: (a) the price may be based on the cost of the item up to the point at which it is transferred to the next department or process or (b) a market value may be used if an item has an existing external market when transferred. A cost-plus transfer price is the sum of costs incurred by the producing division plus an agreed-on profit percentage. A market-based transfer price is geared to external market prices. In most cases a negotiated transfer price is used, that is, one that was bargained for between the managers of the selling and buying divisions.

7. **Develop a transfer price.**
Many of the normal pricing considerations are also present in the development of a transfer price. The first step is to compute the unit cost of the item being transferred. Next, management must determine the appropriate profit markup. Then, those involved in the intracompany transfer must discuss any relevant market prices before negotiating a final transfer price.

8. **Measure a manager's performance by using transfer prices.**
When transfer prices are used, performance reports on managers of cost centers must contain revenue, cost, and income figures used in the evaluation process. Actual performance reports on cost centers will look just like those used for profit centers. Evaluation procedures will also be similar in that the manager of the cost/expense center will have to explain any differences between budgeted and actual revenues, costs, and income.

Review of Concepts and Terminology

The following concepts and terms were introduced in this chapter:

(L.O. 6) **Cost-plus transfer price:** A transfer price computed as the sum of costs incurred by the producing division plus an agreed-on percentage markup for profit.

(L.O. 5) **Decentralized organization:** An organization having several operating segments; operating control of each segment's activities is the responsibility of the segment's manager.

(L.O. 4) **Gross margin pricing:** An approach to cost-based pricing in which the price is computed using the percentage of a product's total production costs.

(L.O. 1) **Marginal cost:** The change in total cost caused by a one-unit change in output.

(L.O. 1) **Marginal revenue:** The change in total revenue caused by a one-unit change in output.

(L.O. 6) **Market transfer price:** A transfer price based on the price that a segment could demand from an external customer of the product.

(L.O. 6) **Negotiated transfer price:** A transfer price that is arrived at through bargaining between the managers of the buying and selling divisions or segments.

(L.O. 4) **Profit margin pricing:** An approach to cost-based pricing in which the price is computed using the percentage of a product's total costs and expenses.

(L.O. 4) **Return on assets pricing:** A pricing method in which the objective of price determination is to earn a profit equal to a specific rate of return on assets employed in the operation.

(L.O. 4) **Target costing:** A pricing method that (1) identifies the price at which a product will be competitive in the marketplace, (2) defines the minimum desired profit to be made on the product, and (3) computes a target cost for the product by subtracting the desired profit from the competitive market price.

(L.O. 4) **Time and materials pricing:** An approach to pricing used by service-oriented businesses in which the total billing is composed of actual materials cost and actual labor cost plus a percentage markup of each to cover overhead costs and a profit factor.

(L.O. 5) **Transfer price:** The price at which goods and services are exchanged between a company's divisions or segments.

Self-Test

Test your knowledge of the chapter by choosing the best answer for each of the following items.

(L.O. 1) 1. A company is still increasing its profit margin when
   a. marginal revenue equals marginal cost.
   b. marginal cost is greater than marginal revenue.
   c. marginal revenue is less than marginal cost.
   d. marginal revenue is greater than marginal cost.

(L.O. 2) 2. Which of the following items is *not* an external factor that should be considered when setting a price?
   a. A company's credit rating
   b. Total demand for the product or service
   c. Current prices of competing products or services
   d. Seasonal demand or continual demand

(L.O. 3) 3. Setting socially responsible prices means
   a. the customer should have the final word on price setting.
   b. the price should never be so high that society cannot afford the item or service.
   c. prices have a social effect and companies are concerned about their public image.
   d. the buyer no longer must beware.

(L.O. 4) 4. Desired profit plus total selling, general, and administrative expenses divided by total production costs computes the markup percentage for
   a. gross margin pricing.
   b. total cost pricing.
   c. profit margin pricing.
   d. return on assets pricing.

(L.O. 4) 5. Time and materials pricing is designed to be used primarily by
   a. a manufacturing company.
   b. a jewelry store.
   c. a plumbing company.
   d. a government agency.

(L.O. 4) 6. Which of the following is not true of target costing?
   a. Target costing identifies the price at which a product will be competitive in the marketplace.
   b. Target costing defines the minimum desired profit a product should make.
   c. Target costing allows a company to analyze a product's potential for success before committing resources to its production.
   d. Target costing is a cost-based method used to make pricing decisions.

(L.O. 5) 7. Transfer prices are normally used by
   a. major league ball parks.
   b. bus companies.
   c. decentralized companies whose divisions use other internally produced products.
   d. countries whose currencies are different from that of the producing country.

(L.O. 5) 8. A transfer price is
   a. an artificial price.
   b. a fee charged every time a product is transferred from department to department.
   c. a price derived from a method used primarily by service companies to establish service prices.
   d. a fee charged by bus companies to transfer from one bus line to another.

(L.O. 6) 9. A negotiated transfer price is bargained for by the
   a. purchasing agent and the stores clerk.
   b. managers of the buying and selling divisions.
   c. cost accountant and the buying department's manager.
   d. selling department's manager and the production superintendent.

(L.O. 8) 10. One of the main reasons for using transfer prices is to measure the profitability of
   a. an investment center.
   b. a profit center.
   c. a cost/expense center.
   d. the company as a whole.

Answers to the Self-Test are at the end of this chapter.

Review Problem Cost-Based Pricing

The A. H. Julia Toy Company makes a complete line of toy vehicles including three types of trucks: a pickup, a dumpster, and a flatbed. These toy trucks are produced in assembly line fashion beginning with the Stamping operation and continuing through the Welding, Painting, and Detailing Departments. Projected costs of each toy truck and allocation percentages for fixed and common costs are as follows:

Cost Categories	Total Projected Costs	Toy Pickup Truck	Toy Dumpster Truck	Toy Flatbed Truck
Materials: Metal	$137,000	$62,500	$29,000	$45,500
Axles	5,250	2,500	1,000	1,750
Wheels	9,250	3,750	2,000	3,500
Paint	70,500	30,000	16,000	24,500
Labor: Stamping	53,750	22,500	12,000	19,250
Welding	94,000	42,500	20,000	31,500
Painting	107,500	45,000	24,000	38,500
Detailing	44,250	17,500	11,000	15,750
Indirect labor	173,000	77,500	36,000	59,500
Operating supplies	30,000	12,500	7,000	10,500
Variable production costs	90,500	40,000	19,000	31,500
Fixed production costs	120,000	45%	25%	30%
Distribution costs	105,000	40%	20%	40%
Variable marketing costs	123,000	55,000	26,000	42,000
Fixed marketing costs	85,400	40%	25%	35%
General and administrative costs	47,600	40%	25%	35%

Julia's policy is to earn a minimum of 30 percent over total cost on each type of toy produced. Expected sales for 19x9 are: Pickup, 50,000 units; Dumpster, 20,000 units; and Flatbed, 35,000 units. Assume no change in inventory levels.

Required

1. Compute the selling price for each toy truck using the gross margin pricing method.
2. Check your answers in **1** by computing the selling prices using the profit margin pricing method.
3. If the competition's selling price for a similar pickup truck is around $14.00, would this influence Julia's pricing decision? Give reasons defending your answer.

Answer to Review Problem

Before the various selling prices are computed, the cost analysis must be completed and restructured in order to supply the information needed for the pricing computations.

Cost Categories	Total Projected Costs	Toy Pickup Truck	Toy Dumpster Truck	Toy Flatbed Truck
Materials: Metal	$ 137,000	$ 62,500	$ 29,000	$ 45,500
Axles	5,250	2,500	1,000	1,750
Wheels	9,250	3,750	2,000	3,500
Paint	70,500	30,000	16,000	24,500
Labor: Stamping	53,750	22,500	12,000	19,250
Welding	94,000	42,500	20,000	31,500
Painting	107,500	45,000	24,000	38,500
Detailing	44,250	17,500	11,000	15,750
Indirect labor	173,000	77,500	36,000	59,500
Operating supplies	30,000	12,500	7,000	10,500
Variable production costs	90,500	40,000	19,000	31,500
Fixed production costs	120,000	54,000	30,000	36,000
Total production costs	$ 935,000	$410,250	$207,000	$317,750
Distribution costs	$ 105,000	$ 42,000	$ 21,000	$ 42,000
Variable marketing costs	123,000	55,000	26,000	42,000
Fixed marketing costs	85,400	34,160	21,350	29,890
General and administrative costs	47,600	19,040	11,900	16,660
Total selling, general, and administrative costs	$ 361,000	$150,200	$ 80,250	$130,550
Total Costs	$1,296,000	$560,450	$287,250	$448,300
Desired Profit	$ 388,800	$168,135	$ 86,175	$134,490

1. Pricing using the gross margin approach.

Markup percentage formula:

$$\text{Markup percentage} = \frac{\text{desired profit + total selling, general, and administrative costs}}{\text{total production costs}}$$

Gross margin pricing formula:

Gross margin-based price = total production costs per unit + (markup percentage × total production costs per unit)

Pickup truck:

$$\text{Markup percentage} = \frac{\$168{,}135 + \$150{,}200}{\$410{,}250} = 77.60\%$$

$$\text{Gross margin-based price} = (\$410{,}250 \div 50{,}000) + [(\$410{,}250 \div 50{,}000) \times 77.6\%] = \$14.57$$

Dumpster truck:

$$\text{Markup percentage} = \frac{\$86{,}175 + \$80{,}250}{\$207{,}000} = \underline{\underline{80.40\%}}$$

$$\text{Gross margin-based price} = (\$207{,}000 \div 20{,}000) + [(\$207{,}000 \div 20{,}000) \times 80.4\%] = \underline{\underline{\$18.67}}$$

Flatbed truck:

$$\text{Markup percentage} = \frac{\$134{,}490 + \$130{,}550}{\$317{,}750} = \underline{\underline{83.41\%}}$$

$$\text{Gross margin-based price} = (\$317{,}750 \div 35{,}000) + [(\$317{,}750 \div 35{,}000) \times 83.41\%] = \underline{\underline{\$16.65}}$$

2. Pricing using the profit margin approach.

Markup percentage formula:

$$\text{Markup percentage} = \frac{\text{desired profit}}{\text{total costs and expenses}}$$

Profit margin pricing formula:

Profit margin-based price = total costs and expenses per unit + (markup percentage × total costs and expenses per unit)

Pickup truck:

$$\text{Markup percentage} = \frac{\$168{,}135}{\$560{,}450} = \underline{\underline{30.00\%}}$$

$$\text{Profit margin-based price} = (\$560{,}450 \div 50{,}000) + [(\$560{,}450 \div 50{,}000) \times 30\%] = \underline{\underline{\$14.57}}$$

Dumpster truck:

$$\text{Markup percentage} = \frac{\$86{,}175}{\$287{,}250} = \underline{\underline{30.00\%}}$$

$$\text{Profit margin-based price} = (\$287{,}250 \div 20{,}000) + [(\$287{,}250 \div 20{,}000) \times 30\%] = \underline{\underline{\$18.67}}$$

Flatbed truck:

$$\text{Markup percentage} = \frac{\$134{,}490}{\$448{,}300} = \underline{\underline{30.00\%}}$$

$$\text{Profit margin-based price} = (\$448{,}300 \div 35{,}000) + [(\$448{,}300 \div 35{,}000) \times 30\%] = \underline{\underline{\$16.65}}$$

3. Competition's influence on price.

If the competition's toy pickup truck was similar in quality as well as design and looks, then Julia's management would have to consider the $14.00 price range. At $14.57, they have a 30 percent profit factor built into their price. Break even is at $11.21 ($14.57 ÷ 1.3). Therefore, they have the ability to reduce the price below the competition and still make a significant profit.

Chapter Assignments

Questions

1. Identify some considerations a decision maker must allow for when setting the price of a product or service.
2. Discuss the concept of making pricing decisions based on whatever the market will bear.
3. In the traditional economic pricing concept, what role does total revenue play in maximizing profit?
4. Why is profit maximized at the point where marginal revenue equals marginal cost?
5. Identify six pricing policy objectives. Discuss each one briefly.
6. Do prices have a social effect? How or in what way?
7. List some external factors to consider when establishing an item's price.
8. List the internal factors one should use to gauge pricing decisions.
9. What is the gross profit pricing method? How is the markup percentage calculated under this method?
10. Differentiate the profit margin pricing method from the return on assets pricing method.
11. In the pricing of services, what is meant by time and materials pricing?
12. Why is the target costing approach to pricing considered more useful in a competitive marketplace than the cost-based methods?
13. What is a transfer price?
14. Why are transfer prices associated with decentralized corporations?
15. Why is a transfer price often referred to as an artificial or created price?
16. Describe the cost-plus approach to setting transfer prices.
17. How are market prices used to develop a transfer price? Under what circumstances are market prices relevant to a transfer pricing decision?
18. "Most transfer prices are negotiated prices." Explain this statement.

Communication Skills Exercises

Communication 22-1. Pricing in the Printing Business *(L.O. 3)*

The National Association of Printers and Lithographers maintains an on-going survey of pricing policies, average operating costs, and profit margins for its members in the printing business. One of its findings is that as business volume increases and a printer's capacity is more fully utilized, the profit margin increases. But when business is slow, the average printer believes that any work that keeps the shop operating is better than no business at all. Profit margins are dropped to encourage new business, with the result that the average print shop makes less than 5 percent pretax income.[2]

As a pricing solution, Wally Stettinius, head of Cadmus Communications, believes that print shop managers should first develop a profit margin large enough to cover the cost of borrowed capital and to cover unforeseen contingencies. When pricing a job, the manager must carefully project the job's total operating costs. The profit margin is then added to yield the job's target price. No hedging should be incorporated into this pricing policy to cover a change in capacity utilization. What do you think of Wally Stettinius's approach to pricing? What suggestions for improvement would you offer the print shop manager? Prepare an outline of your response and be prepared to discuss your ideas in class.

Communication 22-2. Product Differentiation and Pricing *(L.O. 1)*

Maytag Corporation can price its products higher than any other company in the home appliance industry and still maintain and even increase market share. How can the company do this? Are its costs higher, resulting in higher prices than those of its competitors? No. Will customers shop around for products with lower price tags? No. Will competitors single Maytag products out in comparative ad campaigns and try to exploit the higher prices? No. Think about the Maytag repairman television commercials that

2. Roger Ynostroza, "Pricing and Profits," *Graphic Arts Monthly*, Vol. 61, February 1989, pp. 36–42.

you have seen over the past five years. They feature a very lonely person who never gets a call to repair a Maytag product. The ads say nothing about price. They do not attack competitors' products. But the commercials do inspire customers to purchase Maytag products through what is known in the marketing area as product differentiation. Prepare a two-page paper explaining how Maytag Corporation differentiated its products from the competition. Is product cost a factor in Maytag's pricing strategy?

Communication 22-3. Ethics in Pricing *(L.O. 3)*

Norris Company has been doing business with mainland China for the last three years. The company produces leather handbags that are in great demand in the cities of China. On a recent trip to Hong Kong, Yu-Ling Chen, purchasing agent for Liu Enterprises, approached Norris salesperson Lisa Stevens to arrange for a purchase of 2,500 handbags. Norris's normal price is $75 per bag. Yu-Ling Chen wanted to purchase the handbags at $65 per bag. After an hour of haggling, the two people agreed to a final price of $68 per item. When Stevens returned to her hotel room after dinner, she found an envelope containing five new $100 bills and a note that said "Thank you for agreeing to our order of 2,500 handbags at $68 per bag. My company's president wants you to have the enclosed gift for your fine service." Stevens later learned that Yu-Ling Chen was following her company's normal business practices. What should Lisa Stevens do? Is the gift hers to keep? Write a note to Yu-Ling, either accepting or returning the gift. Be prepared to justify the note's contents.

Communication 22-4. Basic Research Skills *(L.O. 5)*

One reason that companies use transfer prices is to allow cost/expense centers to function and be evaluated as profit centers. Transfer prices are fictitious prices charged to one department by another for internally manufactured parts and products that are used by the "purchasing" department. Transfer pricing policies and methods have generated much controversy in recent years. Using *The Accountant's Index*, the *Business Periodicals Index*, and the *Wall Street Journal Index*, locate an article about transfer prices. Prepare a one-page summary of the article and use it as a basis for a classroom presentation. Include in your summary the name and date of the publication, the article's title and author(s), a list of the issues being discussed, and a brief statement about the conclusions reached by the author(s).

Classroom Exercises

Exercise 22-1. Traditional Economic Pricing Theory *(L.O. 1)*

Miller & Hood are product designers. The firm has just completed a contract to develop a portable telephone. The telephone must be recharged only once a week and can be used up to one mile from the receiver. Initial fixed costs for this product are $4,000. The designers estimate the product will break even at the $5,000/100-unit mark. Total revenues will again equal total cost at the $25,000/900-unit point. Marginal cost is expected to equal marginal revenue when 550 units are sold.

1. Sketch total revenue and total cost curves for this product. Mark the vertical axis at each $5,000 increment; the horizontal axis at each 100-unit increment.
2. From your total revenue and total cost curves in **1** above, at what unit selling price will profits be maximized?

Exercise 22-2. External and Internal Pricing Factors *(L.O. 2)*

Heber Trunnell's Tire Outlet features more than a dozen brands of tires in many sizes. Two of the brands are Yerelle and Pokohama, both imports. The tire size, 205/70—VR15, is available in both brands. The following information was obtained:

	Yerelle	Pokohama
Selling price		
Single tire, installed	$145	$124
Set of four tires, installed	520	460
Cost per tire	90	60

As shown, selling prices include installation costs. Each Yerelle tire costs $20 to mount and balance; each Pokohama tire, $15 to mount and balance.

1. Compute each brand's unit selling price for both a single tire and a set of four.
2. Was cost the major consideration in supporting these prices?
3. What other factors could have influenced these prices?

Exercise 22-3.
Pricing Policy Objectives
(L.O. 3)

Darcy Swanson, Ltd. is an international clothing company specializing in retailing medium-priced goods. Retail outlets are located throughout the United States, France, Germany, and Great Britain. Management is interested in creating an image of giving the customer the most quality for the dollar. Selling prices are developed to draw customers away from competitors' stores. First-of-the-month sales are a regular practice of all stores, and customers are accustomed to this practice. Company buyers are carefully trained to seek out quality goods at inexpensive prices. Sales are targeted to increase a minimum of 5 percent per year. All sales should yield a 15 percent return on assets. Sales personnel are expected to wear Swanson's clothing while working, and all personnel can purchase clothing at 10 percent above cost. Cleanliness and an orderly appearance are required at all stores. Competitors' prices are checked daily.

Identify the pricing policy objectives of Darcy Swanson, Ltd.

Exercise 22-4.
Price Determination
(L.O. 4)

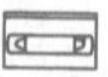

Nicoletti Industries has just patented a new product called "Toms," an automobile wax for lasting protection against the elements. Annual information developed by the company's controller for use in price determination meetings is as follows:

Variable production costs	$1,130,000
Fixed factory overhead	540,000
Selling expenses	213,000
General and administrative expenses	342,000
Desired profit	275,000

Annual demand for the product is expected to be 250,000 cans.

1. Compute the projected unit cost for one can of Toms.
2. Using the gross margin pricing method, compute the markup percentage and selling price for one can.
3. To check your answer to **2** above, compute the markup percentage and selling price of one can of Toms using the profit margin pricing method.

Exercise 22-5.
Pricing a Service
(L.O. 4)

The state of Nevada has just passed a law making it mandatory to have every head of cattle inspected at least once a year for a variety of communicable diseases. Halbert Enterprises is considering entering this inspection business. After extensive studies Mr. Halbert has developed the following annual projections:

Direct service labor	$625,000
Variable service overhead costs	150,000
Fixed service overhead costs	237,500
Marketing expenses	142,500
General and administrative expenses	157,500
Minimum desired profit	125,000
Cost of assets employed	781,250

Mr. Halbert believes his company would inspect 125,000 head of cattle per year. On average, Halbert Enterprises now earns a 16 percent return on assets.

1. Compute the projected cost of inspecting each head of cattle.
2. Determine the price to charge for inspecting each head of cattle. Use the gross margin pricing method.
3. Using the return on assets method, compute the unit price to charge for this inspection service.

Exercise 22-6.
Time and Materials Pricing
(L.O. 4)

Nicole's Home Remodeling Service specializes in refurbishing older homes. Last week Nicole was asked to bid on a remodeling job for the town's mayor. Her list of materials and labor needed to complete the job is as follows.

Materials		Labor	
Lumber	$6,380	Carpenter	$2,060
Nails/bolts	160	Floor specialist	1,300
Paint	1,420	Painter	2,000
Glass	2,890	Supervisor	1,920
Doors	730	Helpers	1,680
Hardware	610	Total	$8,960
Supplies	400		
Total	$12,590		

The company uses an overhead markup percentage for both materials (60 percent) and labor (40 percent). These markups cover all operating costs of the business. In addition, Nicole expects to make at least a 25 percent profit on all jobs.

Compute the price that Nicole should quote for the mayor's job.

Exercise 22-7.
Transfer Price Comparison
(L.O. 5, 7)

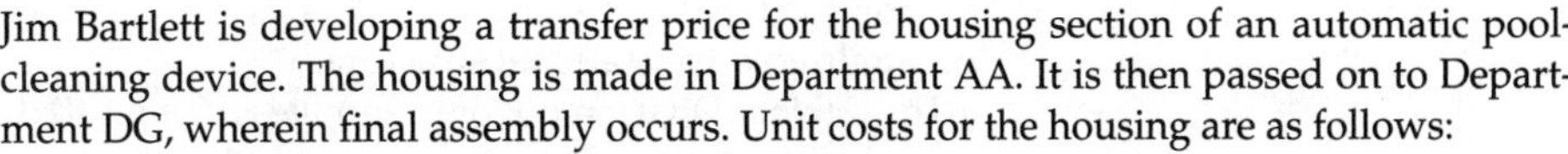

Jim Bartlett is developing a transfer price for the housing section of an automatic pool-cleaning device. The housing is made in Department AA. It is then passed on to Department DG, wherein final assembly occurs. Unit costs for the housing are as follows:

Cost Categories	Unit Costs
Materials	$4.20
Direct labor	3.30
Variable factory overhead	2.30
Fixed factory overhead	1.60
Profit markup, 20% of cost	?

An outside supplier can supply the housing for $13.60 per unit.

1. Develop a cost-plus transfer price for the housing.
2. What should the transfer price be? Support your answer.

Exercise 22-8.
Developing a Cost-Plus Transfer Price
(L.O. 7)

Management at Archer Industries has just decided to use a set of transfer prices for intra-company transfers between departments. Management's objective is to include return on assets in the performance evaluation of managers at its cost centers. Data from the Molding Department for the past six months are:

Account	Total Costs	Expected Increases/Decreases
Raw plastic	$637,300	+10%
Direct labor	507,600	− 5%
Variable factory overhead	92,300	+20%
Fixed factory overhead	125,900	—

During the six-month period, 26,250 plastic units were produced. The same number of units is expected to be completed during the next six-month period. The company uses a 15 percent profit markup percentage.

1. Compute estimated total costs for the Molding Department for the next six months.
2. Develop a cost-plus transfer price for the plastic unit. Round your answer to the nearest cent.

Exercise 22-9. Transfer Prices and Performance Evaluation
(L.O. 8)

The Ladhoff Fireplace Accessories Company uses transfer prices when evaluating division managers. Data from the Forging Department for April 19x5 are as follows:

	Budget	Actual
Direct materials	$309,960	$311,580
Direct labor	235,340	236,570
Variable factory overhead	74,620	75,010
Fixed factory overhead	34,440	34,440
Corporate selling expenses	17,410	18,700
Corporate administrative expenses	18,200	19,100

The division's transfer price is $13.11 per unit. It includes a 15% profit factor. During April the budget called for 57,400 units, and 57,700 units were actually produced and transferred.

Prepare a performance report for the Forging Division.

Interpretation Case from Business

Prescott Industries, Inc.
(L.O. 6, 7)

Two major operating divisions, the Cabinet Division and the Electronics Division, make up Prescott Industries, Inc. The company's major products are deluxe console television sets. The TV cabinets are manufactured by the Cabinet Division, while the Electronics Division produces all electronic components and assembles the sets. The company uses a decentralized organizational structure.

The Cabinet Division not only supplies cabinets to the Electronics Division, but it also sells cabinets to other TV manufacturers. Based on a normal sales order of 40 cabinets, the following unit cost breakdown for a deluxe television cabinet was developed:

Materials	$ 22.00
Direct labor	25.00
Variable factory overhead	14.00
Fixed factory overhead	16.00
Variable selling expenses	9.00
Fixed selling expenses	6.00
Fixed general and administrative expenses	8.00
Total unit cost	$100.00

The Cabinet Division's normal profit margin is 20 percent, and the regular selling price of a deluxe cabinet is $120. Divisional management recently decided that $120 will also be the transfer price used for all intracompany transactions.

Management at the Electronics Division is unhappy with that decision. They claim the Cabinet Division will show superior performance at the expense of the Electronics Division. Competition recently forced the company to lower prices. Because of a newly established transfer price for the cabinet, Electronics' portion of the profit margin on deluxe television sets was lowered to 18 percent. To counteract the new intracompany transfer price, management at the Electronics Division announced that effective immediately, all cabinets will be purchased from an outside supplier. They will be purchased in lots of 200 cabinets at a unit price of $110 per cabinet.

The corporate president, Audrey Mellor, has called a meeting of both divisions in order to negotiate a fair intracompany transfer price. The following prices were listed as possible alternatives:

Current market price	$120 per cabinet
Current outside purchase price (This price is based on a large-quantity purchase discount. It will cause increased storage costs for the Electronics Division.)	$110 per cabinet

Total unit manufacturing costs plus a normal 20 percent profit margin $77.00 + $15.40	$92.40 per cabinet
Total unit costs, excluding variable selling expenses, plus a normal 20 percent profit margin $91.00 + $18.20	$109.20 per cabinet

Required

1. What price should be established for intracompany transactions? Defend your answer by showing the shortcomings of each alternative.
2. Were there an outside market for all units produced by the Cabinet Division at the $120 price, would you change your answer to **1** above? Why?

Problem Set A

Problem 22A-1.
Pricing Decision
(L.O. 2, 4)

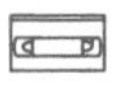

Bergin & Company is an assembly jobber specializing in home appliances. One division, Lowe Operations, focuses most efforts on assembling a standard single-slice toaster. Projected costs on this product for 19x4 are as follows:

Cost Description	Budgeted Costs
Toaster casings	$ 960,000
Electrical components	2,244,000
Direct labor	3,648,000
Variable indirect assembly costs	780,000
Fixed indirect assembly costs	1,740,000
Selling expenses	1,536,000
General operating expenses	840,000
Administrative expenses	816,000

Estimated annual demand for the single-slice toaster is 600,000 per year. The above budgeted amounts were geared to this demand. The company wants to make a $1,260,000 profit.

Competitors have just published their wholesale prices for the coming year. They range from $21.60 to $22.64 per toaster. The Bergin toaster is known for its high quality, and it competes with products at the top end of the price range. Even with its reputation, however, every $.20 increase above the top competitor's price causes a drop in demand of 60,000 units below the original estimate. Assume that all price changes are in $.20 increments.

Required

1. Compute the anticipated selling price. Use the gross margin pricing method.
2. Based on competitors' prices, what should the Bergin toaster sell for in 19x4 (assume a constant unit cost)? Defend your answer. (**Hint:** Determine the total profit at various sales levels.)
3. Would your pricing structure in **2** above change if the company had only limited competition at their quality level? If so, in what direction? Explain why.

Problem 22A-2.
Time and Materials Pricing
(L.O. 4)

Campana Construction Company specializes in additions to custom homes. Last week a potential customer called for a quote on a two-room addition to the family home. After visiting the site and taking all relevant measurements, Ned Campana returned to the office to work on drawings for the addition. As part of the process of preparing a bid, a total breakdown of cost is required.

The company follows the time and materials pricing system and uses data from the previous six months to compute markup percentages for overhead. Separate rates are used for materials and supplies and for labor. During the past six months, $35,625 of materials and supplies-related overhead was incurred and $142,500 of materials and supplies were billed. Labor cost for the six-month period was $341,600. Labor-related overhead was $170,800. Add 20 percent to each markup percentage to cover desired profit. According to Mr. Campana's design, the materials, supplies, and labor listed on the top of page 912 are needed to complete the job.

Quantity		Unit Price
Materials		
150	2″ × 4″ × 8′ cedar	$ 1.30
50	2″ × 6″ × 8′ cedar	2.20
14	2″ × 8″ × 8′ cedar	4.50
25	4′ × 8′ sheets, ½″ plywood	10.40
6	Framed windows	80.00
3	Framed doors	110.00
30	4′ × 8′ sheets, siding	14.00
Supplies		65.00

Hours		Hourly Rate
Labor		
120	Laborers/helpers	$10.50
80	Semiskilled carpenters	12.00
60	Carpenters	14.50

Required

1. Compute a markup percentage for overhead and profit for (a) materials and supplies and (b) labor.
2. Prepare a complete billing for this job. Include itemized amounts for each type of materials, supplies, and labor. Follow the time and material pricing approach and show total price for the job.

Problem 22A-3. Cost-Based Pricing *(L.O. 2, 4)*

Seltzer Coffee Company produces special types of blended coffee. Its products are used in exclusive restaurants throughout the world. Quality is the primary objective of the company. A team of consultants is employed to continuously assess the quality of the purchased coffee beans and of the blending procedures and ingredients used. The company's controller is in the process of determining prices for the coming year. Three blends are currently produced: Regular Blend, Choco Blend, and Mint Blend. Expected profit on each blend is 20 percent above costs. Expected production for 19x5 is: 360,000 pounds of Regular Blend, 150,000 pounds of Mint Blend, and 90,000 pounds of Choco Blend.

Total anticipated costs and percentages of total costs per blend are as follows for 19x5.

	Percentage of Total Costs			
Cost Categories	Regular Blend	Mint Blend	Choco Blend	Total Projected Costs
Coffee beans	60%	25%	15%	$770,000
Chocolate	0%	10%	90%	45,000
Mint leaf	10%	80%	10%	32,000
Labor				
Cleaning	60%	25%	15%	148,000
Blending	40%	30%	30%	372,000
Roasting	60%	25%	15%	298,000
Indirect labor	60%	25%	15%	110,000
Supplies	30%	40%	30%	36,500
Other variable factory overhead	60%	25%	15%	280,000
Fixed factory overhead	60%	25%	15%	166,000
Selling expenses	40%	30%	30%	138,500
General and administrative expenses	34%	33%	33%	146,000

Required

1. Compute the selling price for each blend, using the gross margin pricing method.
2. Check your answers in **1** above by computing selling prices using the profit margin pricing method.
3. If the competition's selling price for the Choco Blend averaged $7.20 per pound, should this influence the controller's pricing decision? Explain.

Problem 22A-4.
Developing Transfer Prices
(L.O. 5, 7)

Sosnow Company has two divisions, Bert Division and Pat Division. For several years Bert Division has manufactured a special glass container, which it sells to the Pat Division at the prevailing market price of $20. Bert produces the glass containers only for Pat and does not sell the product to outside customers. Annual production and sales volume is 20,000 containers. A unit cost analysis for Bert showed:

Cost Categories	Costs per Container
Direct materials	$ 3.40
Direct labor, ¼ hour	2.20
Variable factory overhead	7.60
Traceable fixed costs	
$30,000 ÷ 20,000	1.50
Corporate overhead, $18 per direct labor hour	4.50
Variable shipping costs	1.30
Unit cost	$20.50

Corporate overhead represents such allocated joint fixed costs of production as building depreciation, property taxes, fire insurance, and salaries of production executives. A normal profit allowance of 20 percent is used in determining transfer prices.

Required

1. What would be the appropriate transfer price for Bert Division to use in billing its transactions with Pat Division?
2. If Bert Division decided to sell some containers to outside customers, would your answer to **1** above change? Defend your answer.

Problem 22A-5.
Transfer Prices and Performance Evaluation
(L.O. 6, 7, 8)

Attaway Brick Company has two divisions involved in producing and selling bricks. The Mining Division produces clay, which is sold in 100-pound bags to the Production Division. All output of the Mining Division is shipped to the Production Division. These transfers are priced at the average unit cost of production and distribution. The Production Division sells each brick for $1. Each brick requires 1 pound of clay as raw material. Operating results for 19x5 for the two divisions are summarized below.

	Mining Division	Production Division
Total production costs	$ 700,000	$3,500,000*
Selling, general and administrative expenses	300,000	1,500,000
Total costs and expenses	$1,000,000	$5,000,000

*Excludes cost of clay obtained from the Mining Division.

In 19x5 the Mining Division produced and shipped 10 million pounds of clay, which were billed to the Production Division at $.10 per pound. Other mines sell comparable clay material for $.30 per pound. The Production Division manufactured and sold 10 million bricks in 19x5.

Required

1. Assume intracompany transfers are priced at average cost. Prepare an income statement for each division.
2. Assume intracompany transfers are billed at market price. Prepare an income statement for each division.
3. Which transfer price reflects a more accurate assessment of the two divisions' performance? Why?

Problem Set B

Problem 22B-1.
Pricing Decision
(L.O. 2, 4)

Craig & Dains, Ltd. designs and assembles handguns for police departments across the country. Only four other companies compete in this specialty market. The most popular police handgun is the Craig & Dains .357-caliber magnum, model 87, made of stainless steel. Craig & Dains estimates there will be 23,500 requests for this model in 19x5.

Estimated costs related to this product for 19x5 are shown in the following table. The budget is based on the demand previously stated. The company wants to earn a $846,000 profit in 19x5.

Description	Budgeted Costs
Gun casing	$ 432,400
Ammunition chamber	545,200
Trigger mechanism	1,151,500
Direct labor	1,598,000
Variable indirect assembly costs	789,600
Fixed indirect assembly costs	338,400
Selling expenses	493,500
General operating expenses	183,300
Administrative expenses	126,900

Last week the four competitors released their wholesale prices for the next year.

Gunsmith A	$256.80
Gunsmith B	245.80
Gunsmith C	239.60
Gunsmith D	253.00

Craig & Dains handguns are known for their high quality. They compete with handguns at the top of the price range. Despite the high quality, however, every $10.00 price increase above the top competitor's price causes a 5,500-unit drop in demand from what was originally estimated. (Assume all price changes are in $10.00 increments.)

Required

1. Compute the anticipated selling price. Use the gross margin pricing method.
2. Based on competitors' prices, what should the Craig & Dains handgun sell for in 19x5 (assume a constant unit cost)? Defend your answer. (**Hint:** Determine the total profit at various sales levels.)
3. Would your pricing structure in **2** above change if the company had only limited competition at this quality level? If so, in what direction? Explain why.

Problem 22B-2.
Time and Materials Pricing
(L.O. 4)

Dalton-Dale Maintenance, Inc. repairs heavy construction equipment and vehicles. Recently, the Bandy Construction Company had one of its giant earthmovers overhauled and its tires replaced. Repair work for a vehicle of this size usually takes from one week to ten days. The vehicle must be lifted enough to gain access to the engine. Parts are normally so large, a crane must be used to put them into place.

Dalton-Dale uses the time and materials pricing method for billing. A markup percentage, based on data from the previous year, is applied to the cost of parts and materials to cover materials-related overhead. A similar approach is used for labor-related overhead costs. During the previous year the company incurred $535,590 in materials-related overhead costs and paid $486,900 for materials and parts. During that same time period, direct labor employees earned $347,200, and labor-related overhead of $416,640 was incurred. A factor of 20 percent is added to markup percentages to cover desired profit.

A summary of the materials and parts used and the labor needed to repair the giant earthmover is as follows:

Quantity	Unit Price	Hours	Hourly Rate
Materials and parts		Labor	
24 Spark plugs	$ 3.40	42 Mechanic	$18.20
20 Oil, quarts	2.90	54 Assistant Mechanic	12.00
12 Hoses	11.60		
1 Water pump	764.00		
30 Coolant, quarts	6.50		
18 Clamps	5.90		
1 Distributor cap	128.40		
1 Carburetor	214.10		
4 Tires	820.00		

Required

1. Compute a markup percentage for overhead and profit for (a) materials and parts and (b) labor.
2. Prepare a complete billing for this job. Include itemized amounts for each type of material, part, and labor. Follow the time and materials pricing approach and show the total price for the job.

Problem 22B-3. Cost-Based Pricing *(L.O. 2, 4)*

Weinstein Publishing Company specializes in health awareness books. Because the field of health awareness is very competitive, Lou Weinstein, the company's president, maintains a strict policy about selecting manuscripts to publish. Weinstein wants to publish only books whose projected earnings are 20 percent above total projected costs. Three titles were accepted for publication during 19x6. The authors of these books are Laura, Scott, and Toby. Projected costs for each book and allocation percentages for fixed and common costs are shown below.

Cost Categories	Total Projected Costs	Laura Book	Scott Book	Toby Book
Labor	$487,500	$146,250	$243,750	$97,500
Royalty costs	120,000	36,000	60,000	24,000
Printing costs	248,600	74,580	124,300	49,720
Supplies	34,200	10,260	17,100	6,840
Variable production costs	142,000	42,600	71,000	28,400
Fixed production costs	168,000	35%	40%	25%
Distribution costs	194,000	30%	50%	20%
Marketing costs	194,000	61,670	90,060	42,270
General and administrative costs	52,400	35%	40%	25%

Expected sales for 19x6 are as follows: Laura, 26,000 copies; Scott, 32,000 copies; and Toby, 20,000 copies.

Required

1. Compute the selling price for each book. Use the gross margin pricing method.
2. Check your answers in **1** above by computing selling prices under the profit margin pricing method.
3. If the competition's average selling price for a book on the same subject as Toby's is $22, should this influence Weinstein's pricing decision? State your reasons.

(**Hint:** In **1** and **2**, treat royalty costs as production costs.)

Problem 22B-4. Developing Transfer Prices *(L.O. 5, 7)*

Seven years ago Teresa Vail formed the Vail Corporation and began producing sound equipment for home use. Because of the highly technical and competitive nature of the industry, Vail established the Research and Development Division. That division is responsible for continually evaluating and updating critical electronic parts used in the corporation's products. The R & D staff has been very successful, contributing to the corporation's ranking as America's leader in the industry.

Two years ago, R & D took on the added responsibility of producing all microchip circuit boards for Vail's sound equipment. One of Vail's specialties is a sound dissemination board (SDB) used in videocassette recorders (VCRs). The SDB greatly enhances the sound quality of Vail's VCRs.

Demand for the SDB has increased significantly in the past year. As a result, R & D has increased its production and assembly labor force. Three outside customers want to purchase the SDB for their sound products. To date, R & D has been producing SDBs for internal use only.

The controller of the R & D Division wants to create a transfer price for the SDBs applicable to all intracompany transfers. The following data show projections for the next six months.

Costs	
Materials:	
Boards	$ 325,350
Chips	867,600
Wire posts	397,650
Wire	289,200
Electronic glue	433,800
Labor:	
Board preparation	759,150
Assembly	1,265,250
Testing	1,012,200
Supplies	90,375
Indirect labor	524,175
Other variable overhead costs	180,750
Fixed overhead, SDBs	397,650
Other fixed overhead, corporate	506,100
Variable selling expenses, SDBs	1,337,550
Fixed selling expenses, corporate	469,950
General corporate operating expenses	795,300
Corporate administrative expenses	614,550

A profit factor of at least 25 percent must be added to total unit cost for internal transfer purposes. Outside customers are willing to pay $36 for each SDB. Estimated demand over the next six months is 235,000 SDBs for internal use and 126,500 SDBs for external customers.

Required

1. Compute the cost of producing and distributing one SDB.
2. What transfer price should R & D use? Explain the factors that influenced your decision.

Problem 22B-5. Transfer Prices and Performance Evaluation *(L.O. 6, 7, 8)*

"That Rector Division is robbing us blind!" This statement by the director of the Myers Division was heard during the board of directors meeting at June Company. The company produces umbrellas in a two-step process. The Rector Division prepares the fabric tops and transfers them to the Myers Division. The Myers Division produces the ribs and handles, secures the tops, and packs all finished umbrellas for shipment.

Because of the director's concern, the company controller gathered data on the past year as shown in the table at the top of the next page.

	Rector Division	Myers Division	Company Totals
Sales			
Regular	$700,000	$1,720,000	$2,420,000
Deluxe	900,000	3,300,000	4,200,000
Materials			
Fabric tops (from Rector Division)	—	1,600,000	1,600,000
Cloth	360,000	—	360,000
Aluminum	—	660,000	660,000
Closing mechanisms	—	1,560,000	1,560,000
Labor	480,000	540,000	1,020,000
Variable factory overhead	90,000	240,000	330,000
Fixed divisional overhead	150,000	210,000	360,000
Selling and general operating expenses	132,000	372,000	504,000
Company administrative expenses	84,000	108,000	192,000

During the year, 200,000 regular umbrellas and 150,000 deluxe umbrellas were completed and transferred or shipped by the two divisions. Transfer prices used by the Rector Division were:

Regular	$3.50
Deluxe	6.00

The regular umbrella wholesales for $8.60; the deluxe model, for $22.00. Company administrative costs are allocated to divisions by a preconceived formula.

Management has indicated the transfer price should include a 20 percent profit factor on total division costs.

Required

1. Prepare a performance report on the Rector Division.
2. Prepare a performance report on the Myers Division.
3. Compute each division's rate of return on controllable and on total division costs.
4. Do you agree with the director's statement?
5. What procedures would you recommend to the board of directors?

Management Decision Case

Heitz Company
(L.O. 4)

The Heitz Company manufactures office equipment for retail stores. Nick Rosati, vice president of Marketing, has proposed that Heitz introduce two new products, an electric stapler and an electric pencil sharpener.

Rosati has requested that the Profit Planning Department develop preliminary selling prices for the two new products for his review. Profit Planning is to follow the company's standard policy for developing potential selling prices. It is to use all data available on each product. Data accumulated by Profit Planning on the two new products are reproduced as follows.

	Electric Stapler	Electric Pencil Sharpener
Estimated annual demand in units	12,000	10,000
Estimated unit manufacturing costs	$12.00	$18.00
Estimated unit selling and administrative expenses	$5.00	Not available
Assets employed in manufacturing	$180,000	Not available

Heitz plans to use an average of $2,400,000 in assets to support operations in the current year. The condensed pro forma operating income statement presented below represents Heitz's planned costs and return on assets for the entire company for all products.

Heitz Company
Pro Forma Operating Income Statement
For the Year Ended May 31, 19x3
($000 omitted)

Revenue	$4,800
Cost of goods sold, manufacturing costs	2,880
Gross profit	$1,920
Selling and administrative expenses	1,440
Operating profit	$ 480

Required

1. Calculate a potential selling price for the:
   (a) electric stapler, using return on assets pricing.
   (b) electric pencil sharpener, using gross margin pricing.
2. Could a selling price for the electric pencil sharpener be calculated using return on assets pricing? Explain your answer.
3. Which of the two pricing methods—return on asset pricing or gross margin pricing—is more appropriate for decision analysis? Explain your answer.
4. Discuss the additional steps Nick Rosati is likely to take after he receives the potential selling prices for the two new products (as calculated in **1**) to set an actual selling price for each of the two products.

(ICMA adapted)

Answers to Self-Test

1. d	3. c	5. c	7. c	9. b
2. a	4. a	6. d	8. a	10. c

LEARNING OBJECTIVES

1. Identify the steps in the management decision cycle.
2. Define and identify relevant decision information.
3. Calculate product costs using variable costing procedures.
4. Prepare an income statement using the contribution margin reporting format.
5. Develop decision data using incremental analysis.
6. Prepare decision alternative evaluations for (a) make-or-buy decisions, (b) special order decisions, (c) sales mix analyses, (d) decisions to eliminate unprofitable segments, and (e) sell or process-further decisions.

CHAPTER 23

Short-Run Decision Analysis

Management accountants supply management with three basic types of information: (1) product costing data for pricing and inventory valuation, (2) cost analyses for operational planning and control, and (3) special analyses to support management decision making. Product costing techniques and planning and control procedures were studied in earlier chapters. Decision making is the focus of the chapters in Part Seven.

Top management often depends on the management accountant for information to support its decision-making activities. Such information reveals important data about each alternative, which helps managers make wise decisions. To evaluate alternatives, the accountant uses special decision models, analyses, and reporting techniques. Decisions concerning long-term capital expenditures are the most complex, and they are studied in depth in the next chapter. This chapter emphasizes day-to-day operating decisions and the information needed for implementation. After discussing the role of strategic planning, defining the term *relevant information*, and exploring management's decision cycle, we will examine several decision models. These models include variable costing procedures, contribution margin reporting, and the technique of incremental analysis. The remainder of the chapter focuses on five specific types of decisions: (1) make or buy, (2) special order, (3) sales mix analyses, (4) unprofitable segment elimination, and (5) sell or process further. After studying this chapter, you should be able to meet the learning objectives listed on the left.

DECISION POINT

Fireman's Fund Insurance Company[1]

■ Fireman's Fund Insurance Company is one of the top twenty property/casualty insurance companies in the United States. Fifty major field offices service the needs of the company's 6,000 independent insurance agents and brokers. Eighty percent of the company's business is commercial and the remainder is personal insurance. The company offers hundreds of different types of policies and has had trouble tracking the profitability of its numerous product lines. To set appropriate premium rates, knowledge of both policy costs and claims experience is necessary.

Fireman's Fund developed a system for tracking policy and claims costs. Based on specific activities of company personnel, operating costs are accumulated and traced to policies utilizing those services. Claims are also monitored by policy type and by geographic location. How does such

1. Michael Crane and John Meyer, "Focusing on True Costs in a Service Organization," *Management Accounting*, Institute of Management Accountants, February 1993, pp. 41–45.

a cost tracking system aid in managing the company's numerous types of insurance policies?

The new accounting system allows the company to determine the profitability of insurance policies by type as well as by geographic location. Once identified, unprofitable policy types and locations can be analyzed to determine whether or not they should be eliminated. If operating costs are too high, controls may be instituted to limit them.

Analysis of claims procedures and geographic claims experience may point to higher premiums or to policy type elimination. By improving its cost tracking ability, the company can determine the sources of its profits and can manage its resources more effectively. ■

The Decision-Making Process

The management accountant is part of an organization's decision-making team. As background to the discussion of the types of analyses an accountant prepares and the techniques used to identify potential investments, this section describes the steps in the management decision cycle and the kinds of information that are valuable in evaluating alternatives.

Management Decision Cycle

OBJECTIVE 1
Identify the steps in the management decision cycle

Although many decisions are unique and are not made according to strict rules, steps, or timetables, certain events occur frequently in the analysis of the kinds of problems facing managers. These events form a pattern called the management decision cycle (Figure 23-1).

Figure 23-1. The Management Decision Cycle

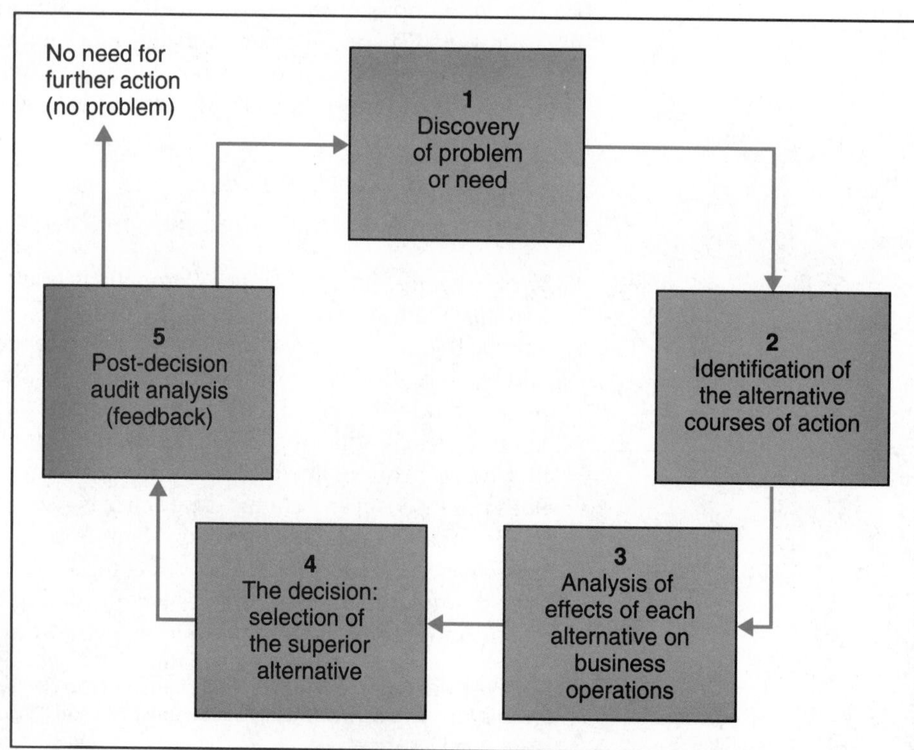

The first step in the cycle is the discovery of a problem or a need. Then in step **2,** the accountant seeks out all reasonable courses of action that will solve the problem or meet the need. In step **3,** the accountant prepares a complete analysis of each action, identifying its total cost, cost savings, or financial effects on business expectations. Each alternative may require different cost information. In step **4,** after studying the information the accountant has gathered and organized in a meaningful way, management selects the best course of action. In step **5,** after the decision has been carried out, the accountant prepares a post-decision audit to give management feedback about the results of the decision. If the solution is not completely satisfactory or if problems remain, the decision cycle begins again. If the solution solved the problem, then this decision process is complete.

Decisions and Strategic Planning

Managers are responsible for short- and long-range planning and for developing an overall strategy that determines the company's general course of action over several years. Strategic plans give direction to management's daily or monthly actions. The strategic plan specifies the company's objectives, its organizational structure, and its policies about growth and product or service lines. Identifying markets is part of the strategic plan, as are any other actions that affect the organization's structure. These strategic plans often determine the projects that managers are willing to consider.

To demonstrate how strategic planning influences the management decision cycle, consider the actions of the managers at the DataLife Corporation. DataLife markets quality computer equipment—diskettes, tape drives, and hard disk drives. In its current strategic plan, DataLife's management decided to expand operations and profitability potential by moving into new product lines. One such business venture identified in the planning process was telecommunications. After developing this strategic plan, DataLife had the option of purchasing a company specializing in telecommunications devices or upgrading an existing product line using a special, potentially high-profit telecommunications memory chip. Both projects were studied using the management decision cycle. Before the strategic plan, DataLife would have turned down both options because the company was not in the telecommunications business. With the change in its strategic plan, each option became a viable alternative, as did other telecommunications projects. Any project that management investigates for potential investment should be consistent with the organization's strategic plan.

Relevant Information for Management

OBJECTIVE 2
Define and identify relevant decision information

Once managers determine a project worthy of consideration, what information do they need to evaluate the alternatives? Managers need enough information to see how each alternative will affect the company's operations, but they should not have to wade through reams of data. The management accountant is responsible for providing relevant information for each alternative.

How does the management accountant decide what is relevant and what is not? Facts that are the same for each alternative are not relevant. If total sales are unchanged in a proposal to reduce labor costs by installing an automated machine, then that information should not appear in the evaluation of the various machines being analyzed. Similarly, although the accountant may use past data to prepare cost estimates of alternatives, historical data are not relevant to projections of future operations and do not guide managers in choosing between alternatives. The accountant should include only those cost projections or estimates that are relevant to the decision. **Relevant decision information** is data regarding future cost, revenue, and resource usage that are different for each alternative.

In the next section, the tools and reports accountants use to present financial data to management are discussed. These reports include relevant information and omit data that are common to each alternative under study.

Accounting Tools and Reports for Decision Analysis

The accountant's role in the decision-making process is to provide information that is accurate, timely, refined, and readable. To accomplish this, the accountant must gather the appropriate information and report it in a way that is meaningful to management. Two common decision tools that help accountants generate this information and the accompanying reports are variable costing and incremental analysis. Each technique helps to identify information relevant to a particular decision and each provides a special decision reporting format based on a particular decision model.

Decision Models in Management Accounting

When numerous alternatives are to be evaluated, the decision-making process becomes complex. In addition, many decisions are nonrecurring and cannot be resolved by relying on past experience. To facilitate a complex analysis, a decision model is developed. A **decision model** is a symbolic or numerical representation of the variables and parameters affecting a decision. **Decision variables** are factors controlled by management. **Decision parameters** are uncontrollable factors and operating constraints and limitations. As an example, suppose you need to develop a decision model to evaluate new product lines. Your analysis would involve such decision parameters as customer demand, market growth, competitors' actions, and production capacity limitations. Decision variables in this decision model include product selling prices, production costs, and manufacturing methods. The key to developing such a model is to identify relevant decision variables and parameters and put the information together in an informative manner.

Figure 23-2 outlines the steps in the model-building process. Decision parameters affecting the project are first defined, then possible alternatives are identified. In steps **3** and **4,** appropriate cost and revenue information is developed and analyzed. After the irrelevant information has been eliminated, the relative benefits of each alternative are summarized and presented to management. Output of the decision model is a comparative analysis, using the measurement criterion selected for the particular decision problem. This analysis is a formal report to management, and it should include a

1. Brief description of the project or problem situation
2. Comparative financial analysis of each alternative
3. Summary of the relative advantages and disadvantages of each alternative

Variable Costing

Variable costing (also called direct costing) is a method management accountants use to calculate product costs. The income statement generated by a variable costing system shows the contribution margin of the goods produced,

Figure 23-2. Steps in Developing a Decision Model

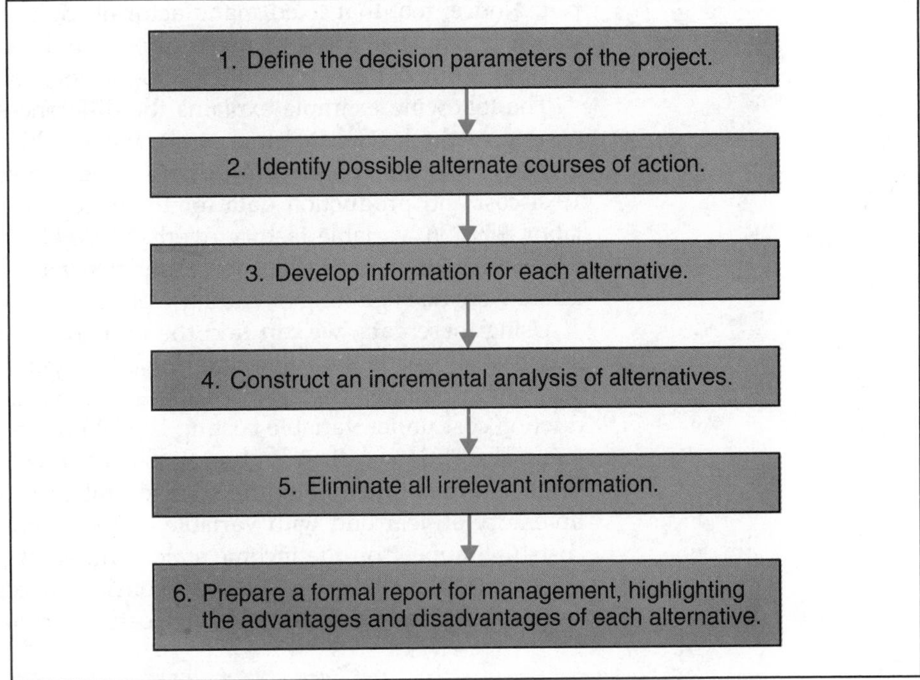

OBJECTIVE 3
Calculate product costs using variable costing procedures

information that is helpful in decision making. To understand why the contribution margin format is so useful, we first calculate and compare product costs under a variable costing system and under absorption costing (also known as full costing). We then prepare income statements under both costing procedures and observe the benefits of the contribution margin format.

Unlike absorption costing, which assigns all manufacturing costs to products, **variable costing** uses only the variable manufacturing costs for product costing and inventory valuation. Direct materials costs, direct labor costs, and variable factory overhead costs are the only cost elements used to compute product costs. Fixed factory overhead costs are considered costs of the current accounting period.

The rationale for variable costing is that a company has fixed operating costs whether it operates or not. Proponents of variable costing argue that such costs do not have a direct relationship to the product and should not be included in the product's unit cost. Fixed manufacturing costs are linked more closely with time than with productive output. Opponents of variable costing say that without fixed manufacturing costs, production would stop. They are, therefore, an integral part of a product's costs.

Whichever argument you accept, two points are certain. First, neither the Internal Revenue Service nor the public accounting profession accepts variable costing for external reporting purposes. They reject it because fixed costs are not included in inventory and cost of goods sold. Therefore variable costing cannot be used for computing federal income taxes or for reporting the results of operations and financial position to stockholders and others outside the company. Second, even with its limitations regarding financial reporting, variable costing is useful for internal management decisions and is used in many types of decision analyses, some of which are discussed later in this chapter.

Product Costing. For purposes of product costing, variable costing treats fixed manufacturing costs differently from production costs that vary with output. Notice, too, that fixed manufacturing costs are left out of all inventories, which is why the value of inventories found using variable costing is lower than the value of those computed under absorption costing.

The following example explains the differences between these two product costing methods. Gardnel Industries, Inc. produces grills for outdoor cooking. During 19x4, the company produced a new, disposable grill. A summary of 19x4 cost and production data for the grill is: direct materials, $76,384; direct labor, $59,136; variable factory overhead, $44,352; and fixed factory overhead, $36,960. There were 24,640 units completed and 22,000 units sold during 19x4. There were no beginning or ending work in process inventories.

Using these data, we can find the unit cost as well as the ending inventory and cost of goods sold amounts for 19x4 under variable costing and under absorption costing. This information is summarized in Exhibit 23-1. Unit production cost under variable costing is $7.30 per grill, whereas unit cost is $8.80 using absorption costing. Ending finished goods inventory balances are not the same because of the $1.50 difference in unit cost. Because fewer costs remain in inventory at year end with variable costing amounts, it is logical that greater costs will appear on the income statement. As shown in Exhibit 23-1, $197,560 of current manufacturing costs are considered costs of the period, to be subtracted from revenue in the variable costing income statement. Only $193,600 is

Exhibit 23-1. Variable Costing Versus Absorption Costing

Gardnel Industries, Inc.
Unit Costs and Ending Inventory Values
For the Year Ended December 31, 19x4

	Variable Costing	Absorption Costing
Unit Cost		
Direct materials ($76,384 ÷ 24,640 units)	$ 3.10	$ 3.10
Direct labor ($59,136 ÷ 24,640 units)	2.40	2.40
Variable factory overhead ($44,352 ÷ 24,640 units)	1.80	1.80
Fixed factory overhead ($36,960 ÷ 24,640 units)	—	1.50
Total unit cost	$ 7.30	$ 8.80
Total manufacturing costs to be accounted for	$216,832	$216,832
Less costs charged against income		
Cost of goods sold for 19x4		
22,000 units at $7.30	$160,600	
22,000 units at $8.80		$193,600
Fixed factory overhead	36,960	—
Costs appearing on the 19x4 income statement	$197,560	$193,600
Ending Finished Goods Inventory		
2,640 units at $7.30	$ 19,272	
2,640 units at $8.80		$ 23,232

shown as Cost of Goods Sold when absorption costing is used. The difference of $3,960 (2,640 units in inventory × $1.50 fixed costs per unit) is shown as part of inventory under absorption costing ($23,232 – $19,272).

OBJECTIVE 4
Prepare an income statement using the contribution margin reporting format

Contribution Margin Reporting Format. Variable costing produces an entirely new form of income statement because it measures the contribution margin of each product. This new form emphasizes cost variability and segment or product-line contributions to income. Costs are no longer classified as either manufacturing or nonmanufacturing costs. Instead, attention is focused on separating variable costs from fixed costs.

Referring again to the Gardnel Industries, Inc. example, assume the following additional information for 19x4: selling price per grill is $24.50; variable selling costs per grill are $4.80; fixed selling expenses are $48,210; fixed administrative expenses are $82,430. Exhibit 23-2 compares net income under variable

Exhibit 23-2. The Income Statement: Contribution Margin Versus Conventional Format

Gardnel Industries, Inc.
Disposable Grill Division
Income Statement
For the Year Ended December 31, 19x4

Contribution Margin Format

Sales (22,000 units at $24.50)		$539,000
Variable Cost of Goods Sold		
Variable Cost of Goods Available for Sale (24,640 units at $7.30)	$179,872	
Less Ending Inventory	19,272*	
Variable Cost of Goods Sold	$160,600*	
Plus Variable Selling Costs (22,000 units at $4.80)	105,600	266,200
Contribution Margin		$272,800
Less Fixed Costs		
Fixed Manufacturing Costs	$ 36,960	
Fixed Selling Expenses	48,210	
Fixed Administrative Expenses	82,430	167,600
Net Income Before Taxes		$105,200

Conventional Format

Sales		$539,000
Cost of Goods Sold		
Cost of Goods Manufactured	$216,832*	
Less Ending Inventory	23,232*	193,600*
Gross Margin from Sales		$345,400
Selling Expenses		
Variable	$105,600	
Fixed	48,210	
Administrative Expenses	82,430	236,240
Net Income (before taxes)		$109,160

*Detailed computations are in Exhibit 23-1.

costing and absorption costing. The contribution margin format is presented first. Note that the term *gross margin* is replaced by the term *contribution margin* and that only variable costs (including variable selling costs) are subtracted from sales to calculate the contribution margin. Contribution margin is the amount that each segment or product line is contributing to the company's fixed costs and profits. Net income calculated in the conventional statement appears in the lower part of Exhibit 23-2. Note that net income is different under the two methods. This difference, $3,960, is the same amount noted earlier. It is the part of fixed manufacturing overhead cost that is inventoried when absorption costing is used.

Contribution Reporting and Decisions. Variable costing and the contribution margin format of income reporting are used a great deal in decision analysis, most commonly in deciding whether to continue a segment, division, or product line. Other uses are in the evaluation of new product lines and in sales mix studies. Decisions about the contribution of sales territories also use the contribution margin approach to income reporting. These uses are explained in detail later when we look at specific kinds of decisions.

Incremental Analysis

OBJECTIVE 5
Develop decision data using incremental analysis

Incremental analysis is a technique used to compare alternative projects by focusing on the differences in their projected revenues and costs. The accountant organizes relevant information to determine which alternative contributes the most to profits or incurs the least costs. Only data that differ for each alternative appear in the report.

To illustrate how incremental analysis identifies the best alternative, consider the following situation. The management accountant is preparing a report to help the management of the Clifford Company decide which of two mill blade grinders, C or W, to buy. The accountant has collected the following annual sales and operating cost estimates for the two machines:

	Grinder C	Grinder W
Increase in revenue	$16,200	$19,800
Increase in annual operating costs		
Direct materials	4,800	4,800
Direct labor	2,200	4,100
Variable factory overhead	2,100	3,050
Fixed factory overhead (depreciation included)	5,000	5,000

An incremental analysis shows increases or decreases in revenues and costs that arise from each alternative. Since direct materials and fixed factory overhead costs are the same for each alternative, they are not included in the analysis.

If you assume that the purchase price and the useful life of the two grinders are the same, the incremental analysis in Exhibit 23-3 shows that Grinder W generates $750 more in income than Grinder C. Thus, the decision based on this report is to purchase Grinder W.

Since the incremental analysis focuses on the differences between alternatives, it isolates the benefits or drawbacks of each. A report based on incremental analysis makes the evaluation easier for the decision maker and reduces the time needed to decide on the best course of action.

Exhibit 23-3. Incremental Decision Analysis

Clifford Company
Incremental Decision Analysis

	Grinder C	Grinder W	Difference in Favor of Grinder W
Increase in revenues	$16,200	$19,800	$3,600
Increased operating costs that differ between alternatives			
Direct labor	$ 2,200	$ 4,100	$1,900
Variable factory overhead	2,100	3,050	950
Total relevant operating costs	$ 4,300	$ 7,150	$2,850
Resulting changes in income	$11,900	$12,650	$ 750

Special Decision Reports

Income statements in the contribution margin format and incremental analyses work best when comparing quantitative information. In some cases, however, managers might be considering many alternatives, each of which is best in certain circumstances. One may generate more profits, while another diversifies the company's product line. A third alternative may prevent a huge layoff, bolstering the company's goodwill. Even though several equally good alternatives may be available, management must choose only one. In such cases, qualitative information must support or replace the quantitative analyses, and the accountant must use imagination to prepare the special decision report that demonstrates which alternative is best under the circumstances.

For most special decision reports, there is no one correct, set structure. Experienced accountants prepare these reports to fit individual situations. For the purpose of this course, you can solve most of the problems by following the examples in the text. But remember that in practice, management accountants must create formats appropriate to existing circumstances. Such challenges contribute to the dynamic role of the management accountant.

Operating Decisions of Management

Many business decisions can be made using income statements generated by a variable costing system and incremental analysis. In this section, we use those tools to select the best alternative when managers face (1) make-or-buy decisions, (2) special order decisions, (3) sales mix analyses, (4) decisions to eliminate unprofitable segments, and (5) sell or process-further decisions.

Make-or-Buy Decisions

OBJECTIVE 6a
Prepare decision alternative evaluations for make-or-buy decisions

A common problem facing managers of manufacturing companies is whether to make or to buy some or all of the parts used in product assembly. The goal of **make-or-buy decision analysis** is to identify the costs of each alternative and their effect on revenue and costs and to select the more profitable choice. Listed at the top of page 928 are factors needed for this analysis.

To Make	To Buy
Need for additional machinery	Purchase price of item
Variable costs of making the item	Rent or net cash flow to be generated from vacated space in factory
Incremental fixed costs	Salvage value of unused machinery

The case of the Konert Electronics Company illustrates a make-or-buy decision. For the past five years, the firm has purchased a small transistor casing from an outside supplier at a cost of $1.25 per casing. The supplier just informed Konert Electronics that it is raising the price 20 percent, effective immediately. Konert has idle machinery that could be adjusted to produce the casings. Konert estimates the cost of direct materials at $84 per 100 casings, the amount of direct labor at three minutes of labor per casing at a rate of $8 per direct labor hour, and the cost of variable factory overhead at $4 per direct labor hour. Fixed factory overhead includes $4,000 of depreciation per year and $6,000 of other fixed costs. Annual production and usage would be 20,000 casings, the space and machinery to produce the casing would be idle if the part were purchased. Should Konert Electronics Company make or buy the casings?

Incremental analysis enables the accountant to organize the relevant data in a make-or-buy decision. From a review of decision data, management can quickly analyze all relevant costs or revenues and use that information to select the best alternative.

Exhibit 23-4 presents an incremental analysis of the two alternatives. All relevant costs are listed. Because the machinery has already been purchased and neither the machinery nor the required factory space has any other use, the depreciation costs and other fixed factory overhead costs are the same for both alternatives, so they are not relevant to the decision. The cost of making the needed casings is $28,800. The cost of buying 20,000 casings will be $30,000 at the increased purchase price. The company saves $1,200 by making the casings, and it should do so.

Special Order Decisions

OBJECTIVE 6b *Prepare decision alternative evaluations for special order decisions*

Management is often faced with **special order decisions**, that is, whether to accept or reject special product orders at prices below normal market prices. These orders usually contain large numbers of similar products to be sold in bulk (packaged in large containers). Because management did not expect the orders, they are not included in annual cost or sales estimates. And, since these orders are one-time events, they should not be included in revenue or cost estimates for subsequent years. The company should consider them only if unused capacity exists.

Before a firm accepts a special order, it must be sure that the products produced under the special order contract are sufficiently different from its regular product line to avoid violating federal price discrimination laws.

Rathman Sporting Goods, Inc. manufactures a complete line of sporting equipment. Hood Enterprises operates a large chain of discount stores. Hood has approached Rathman with a special order calling for 30,000 deluxe baseballs to be shipped in bulk packaging of 500 baseballs per box. Hood is willing to pay $2.45 per baseball.

The Rathman accounting department collected the following data: annual expected production, 400,000 baseballs; current year's production, 410,000 base-

Exhibit 23-4. Incremental Analysis: Make-or-Buy Decision

Konert Electronics Company Incremental Analysis Current Year—Annual Usage			
	Make	**Buy**	**Difference in Favor of Make**
Raw materials (20,000 ÷ 100 × $84)	$16,800	—	$(16,800)
Direct labor (20,000 ÷ 20 × $8)	8,000	—	(8,000)
Variable factory overhead (20,000 ÷ 20 × $4)	4,000	—	(4,000)
To purchase completed casings (20,000 × $1.50)	—	$30,000	30,000
Totals	$28,800	$30,000	$ 1,200

balls; and maximum production capacity, 450,000 baseballs. Additional data are:

Unit cost data	
Direct materials	$ .90
Direct labor	.60
Factory overhead	
Variable	.50
Fixed ($100,000 ÷ 400,000)	.25
Packaging per unit	.30
Advertising ($60,000 ÷ 400,000)	.15
Other fixed selling and administrative costs ($120,000 ÷ 400,000)	.30
Total	$ 3.00
Unit selling price	$ 4.00
Total estimated bulk packaging costs (30,000 baseballs: 500 per box)	$2,500

Should Rathman Sporting Goods, Inc. accept Hood's offer?

A comparative analysis in the contribution margin reporting format appears in Exhibit 23-5. The report shows net income before taxes for the Baseball Division's operations both with and without the Hood offer. The only costs affected by the order are for direct materials, direct labor, variable factory overhead, and packaging. Packaging costs will increase, but only by the amount of the added bulk packaging. All other costs will remain the same. The net result of accepting the special order is an $11,000 increase in contribution margin (and net income before taxes). This amount is verified by the following computation:

Net gain = [(unit selling price – unit variable mfg. costs) × units] – bulk packaging costs
= [($2.45 – $2.00) × 30,000] – $2,500
= $13,500 – $2,500
= $11,000

Exhibit 23-5. Contribution Margin Reporting: Special Product Order

Rathman Sporting Goods, Inc.
Comparative Decision Analysis
Special Product Order—Baseball Division

	Without Hood Order (410,000 products)	With Hood Order (440,000 products)
Sales	$1,640,000	$1,713,500
Less variable costs		
Direct materials	$ 369,000	$ 396,000
Direct labor	246,000	264,000
Variable factory overhead	205,000	220,000
Packaging costs	123,000	125,500
Total variable costs	$ 943,000	$1,005,500
Contribution margin	$ 697,000	$ 708,000
Less fixed costs		
Factory overhead	$ 100,000	$ 100,000
Advertising	60,000	60,000
Selling and administrative	120,000	120,000
Total fixed costs	$ 280,000	$ 280,000
Net income before taxes	$ 417,000	$ 428,000

Thus, the analysis reveals that Rathman should accept the special order from Hood Enterprises.

For special order analysis, both comparative contribution margin reporting and incremental analysis can be used. In this case, we used contribution margin reporting because the fixed cost data in the problem were misleading. Contribution margin reporting highlights the effect of changes in variable costs on contribution margin and net income.

Fixed costs of existing facilities would normally not change if the special orders were accepted and are, therefore, usually irrelevant to the decision. If, on the other hand, additional fixed costs are incurred to facilitate the transaction, they would be relevant to the decision. Examples of relevant fixed costs include purchase of additional machinery, increase in supervisory help, or increase in insurance premiums resulting from extra control of resources.

Sales Mix Analysis

OBJECTIVE 6c
Prepare decision alternative evaluations for sales mix analyses

Profit analysis and maximization are possible only when the profitability of all product lines is known. The question is, Which product or products contribute the most to company profitability in relation to the amount of capital assets or other scarce resources needed to produce the item(s)? To answer this question, the accountant must measure the contribution margin of each product. The next step is to determine a set of ratios of contribution margin to the required capital equipment or other resources. Once this step is completed, management should request a marketing study to set the upper limits of demand on the most profitable products. If product profitability can be computed and market demand exists for these products, management should shift production to the more profitable products.

Many kinds of decisions can be related to the approach described here. **Sales mix analysis** involves determining the most profitable combination of product sales when a company produces more than one product or offers more than one service. Closely connected with sales mix analysis is the product line profitability study designed to discover which products are losing money for the company. The same decision approach is used, but the goal is to eliminate the unprofitable product line(s). The Fireman's Fund analysis in this chapter's Decision Point involved a problem to be analyzed using the sales mix approach.

Another decision area using the sales mix approach is that of corporate segment analysis. The contribution margin analysis is again used, with the goal of isolating production costs to identify the unprofitable segment(s). If corrective action is not possible, management should eliminate the noncontributing segment(s). Even though not all of these decision areas will be discussed, it is important to remember that the same kind of analysis can be used for product line profitability studies and corporate segment analyses.

An example of this kind of analysis will aid understanding. The management of Christensen Enterprises is in the process of analyzing its sales mix. The company manufactures three products—C, S, and F—using the same production equipment for all three. The total productive capacity is being used. The product line statistics are as follows:

	Product C	Product S	Product F
Current production and sales (units)	20,000	30,000	18,000
Machine hours per product	2	1	2.5
Selling price per unit	$24.00	$18.00	$32.00
Unit variable manufacturing costs	$12.50	$10.00	$18.75
Unit variable selling costs	$6.50	$5.00	$6.25

Should the company try to sell more of one product and less of another?

Because total productive capacity is being used, the only way to expand the production of one product is to reduce the production of another. The sales mix analysis of Christensen Enterprises is shown in Exhibit 23-6. Though contribution reporting is used here, contribution margin per product is not the important figure for a decision about shifts in sales mix. In the analysis, Product F has the highest contribution margin. However, all products use the same machinery and all machine hours are being used. So machine hours become the scarce resource.

The analysis in Exhibit 23-6 goes one step beyond the computation of contribution margin per unit. A sales mix decision such as this one should use two decision variables: contribution margin per unit and machine hours required per unit. For instance, Product C requires two machine hours to generate $5 of contribution margin. But Product S would generate $6 of contribution margin using the same two machine hours. For this reason, we have calculated contribution margin per machine hour. Based on this information, management can readily see that it should produce and sell as much of Product S as possible. Next, it should push Product F. If any productive capacity remains, it should produce product C.

Product-line profitability studies are similar to sales mix analyses. They are designed to discover if any products are losing money for the company. The

Exhibit 23-6. Contribution Margin Reporting: Sales Mix Analysis

Christensen Enterprises
Sales Mix Analysis
Contribution Margin Reporting Format

	Product C	Product S	Product F
Unit sales price	$24.00	$18.00	$32.00
Variable costs			
Manufacturing	$12.50	$10.00	$18.75
Selling	6.50	5.00	6.25
Total variable costs	$19.00	$15.00	$25.00
Contribution margin per unit (A)	$ 5.00	$ 3.00	$ 7.00
Machine hours required per unit (B)	2	1	2.5
Contribution margin per machine hour (A ÷ B)	$ 2.50	$ 3.00	$ 2.80

contribution margin format is also used in this analysis, but the goal of the analysis is to eliminate unprofitable product lines or services. Identification of unprofitable corporate divisions or segments also relies on the contribution margin approach.

Decisions to Eliminate Unprofitable Segments

OBJECTIVE 6d
Prepare decision alternative evaluations for decisions to eliminate unprofitable segments

Whether to eliminate an unprofitable product, service, division, or other corporate segment is another type of operating decision management may face. The **unprofitable segment decision analysis** prepared for this type of decision is an extension of the normal performance evaluation of the segment. As an overview, the analysis of unprofitable segments compares (1) operating results of the corporation with the segment in question included against (2) operating results for the same period that do not include data from that segment. The key to this analysis is to be able to isolate the segment, product, or service in question. Variable costs associated with a product or segment are easy to identify and account for. But each product or segment also has fixed costs associated with and traceable to it that will usually be eliminated if the segment is discontinued. These fixed costs are commonly referred to as **traceable fixed costs**.

To analyze the financial consequences of eliminating a segment, one must concentrate on the incremental effect of the decision on profits. The decision analysis consists of comparing contribution margin income statements for the company. One statement includes the segment under review, and the second excludes this information. The basic decision is a problem of choosing to keep the product, service, or segment or to eliminate it.

Assume management at Hugh Corporation wants to determine if Division B should be eliminated. Exhibit 23-7 provides basic cost and revenue data and illustrates a format for evaluating alternate decisions. This analysis requires that an income statement be prepared for each alternative and that profits be compared. All traceable fixed costs of Division B are assumed to be avoidable. **Avoidable costs** are costs that will be eliminated if a particular product, service, or operating segment is discontinued. As shown in Exhibit 23-7A, the profits of Hugh Corporation will increase by $9,000 if Division B is eliminated.

Exhibit 23-7. Divisional Profit Summary and Decision Analysis

Hugh Corporation
Divisional Profit Summary and Decision Analysis
Contribution Margin Format

A. Income Statements	Divisions D and E	Division B	Total Company
Sales	$135,000	$15,000	$150,000
Less variable costs	52,500	7,500	60,000
Contribution margin	$ 82,500	$ 7,500	$ 90,000
Less traceable fixed costs	55,500	16,500	72,000
Divisional income	$ 27,000	$(9,000)	$ 18,000
Less unallocated fixed costs			12,000
Income before taxes			$ 6,000

B. Incremental Decision Analysis	Company Profitability If It Elects To: Keep Division B	Eliminate Division B	Benefit or (Cost) To Eliminate Division B	
Sales	$150,000	$135,000	$(15,000)	Sales decrease
Less variable costs	60,000	52,500	7,500	Cost reduction
Contribution margin	$ 90,000	$ 82,500	$ (7,500)	CM decrease
Less total fixed costs	84,000	67,500	16,500	Cost reduction
Income before taxes	$ 6,000	$ 15,000	$ 9,000	Profit increase

Another way of looking at this decision is to concentrate on the third column in Exhibit 23-7B. Revenue and cost factors that are different under each alternative can be analyzed to explain the profit difference of $9,000. The incremental factors are analyzed in Exhibit 23-8. If all fixed costs traceable to Division B are avoidable, then the operating loss of $9,000 is also avoidable if the division is eliminated. The primary concept is to isolate avoidable costs, which may not always correspond with traceable costs. Avoidable costs are incremental costs since these amounts are incurred only if the division exists.

In trying to understand the significance of determining an accurate amount of avoidable costs, assume you discover that executives and supervisors in Division B will be reassigned to other divisions if Division B is eliminated. Included in the $16,500 of traceable fixed costs for Division B are salaries of $12,000 for these people. This assumption now changes the profit effect of eliminating Division B, as shown below:

Advantage of eliminating Division B	
Reduction of variable expenses	$ 7,500
Reduction of fixed expenses ($16,500 − $12,000)	4,500
Total benefits	$12,000
Disadvantage of eliminating Division B	
Reduction in sales	$15,000
Decrease in profit as a result of eliminating Division B (2 − 1)	$ 3,000

Exhibit 23-8. Incremental Revenue and Cost Analysis

Hugh Corporation
Incremental Revenue and Cost Analysis

Advantage of Eliminating Division B	Amount
Increase in sales	—
Decrease in costs ($7,500 + $16,500)	$24,000
Total advantage	$24,000

Disadvantage of Eliminating Division B	Amount
Decrease in sales	$15,000
Increase in costs	—
Total disadvantage	$15,000
Incremental profit from eliminating Division B advantage less disadvantage	$ 9,000

By following these revised assumptions, you compute that avoidable fixed costs for Division B are $4,500 (traceable fixed costs of $16,500 less the $12,000 cost of people to be reassigned to other divisions). Generally, it is unprofitable to eliminate any segment for which contribution margin exceeds avoidable fixed costs. This rule is actually a condensed version of the incremental profit analysis.

If you apply this rule to the Hugh Corporation example, the analysis would be as follows:

Division B	
Contribution margin	$7,500
Less avoidable fixed costs	4,500
Profit contribution	$3,000

In such an analysis, corporate profits would actually decrease by $3,000 if Division B were eliminated. This conclusion is valid even though operating reports for Division B disclose a loss of $9,000.

As shown in Exhibit 23-7, the decision analysis used to decide about eliminating an unprofitable segment (product line, service, or division) requires two decision analysis tools: (1) contribution margin reporting and (2) incremental analysis. Contribution margin reporting helped identify traceable and avoidable fixed costs relevant to the decision, whereas incremental analysis assisted in comparing the operating results with and without the segment.

Sell or Process-Further Decisions

The **sell or process-further decision** is the choice between selling a product at the split-off point or processing it further. The decision to process a joint prod-

OBJECTIVE 6e
Prepare decision alternative evaluations for sell or process-further decisions

uct beyond the split-off point requires an analysis of incremental revenues and costs of the two alternate courses of action. Additional processing adds value to a product and increases its selling price above the amount it may have been sold for at split-off. The decision to process further depends on whether the increase in total revenue exceeds additional costs for processing beyond split-off. *Joint costs incurred before split-off do not affect the decision.* These costs are incurred regardless of the point at which the products are sold. Thus they are irrelevant to the decision. Only future costs differing between alternatives are relevant to the decision.

Maximizing company profits is the objective of sell or process-further decisions. For example, assume that Bava Gardening Supplies, Inc. produces various products to enhance plant growth. In one process, three products—Gro-Pow, Gro-Pow II, and Gro-Supreme—emerge from the joint initial phase. For each 20,000-pound batch of materials converted into products, $120,000 in joint production costs are incurred. At split-off, 50 percent of the output becomes Gro-Pow, 30 percent becomes Gro-Pow II, and 20 percent becomes Gro-Supreme. Each product must be processed beyond split-off, and the following additional variable costs are incurred:

Product	Pounds	Additional Processing Costs
Gro-Pow	10,000	$24,000
Gro-Pow II	6,000	38,000
Gro-Supreme	4,000	33,500
Totals	20,000	$95,500

Jeff & Knoll Landscapers has offered to purchase any or all joint products at split-off for the following prices per pound: Gro-Pow, $8; Gro-Pow II, $24; and Gro-Supreme, $40. To help decide whether to sell at split-off or process the products further, Bava management requested an incremental analysis. This analysis is to compare increases in revenue and increases in processing costs for each alternative.

Exhibit 23-9 reveals the selling prices of the three products at split-off and if processed further. This exhibit also contains the incremental analysis. As illustrated, products Gro-Pow and Gro-Supreme should be processed further since each will cause a significant increase in overall company profit. If Gro-Pow II can be sold to Jeff & Knoll Landscapers, the company will avoid a $2,000 loss from further processing. Note that the $120,000 in joint processing costs are irrelevant to the decision since they will be incurred with either alternative.

Measuring incremental costs for additional processing beyond split-off can create problems. Additional costs of materials, labor, and variable overhead are incremental since these costs are caused by additional processing. However, supervisors' salaries, property taxes, insurance, and other fixed costs incurred regardless of the production decision are not incremental costs. Incremental processing costs should include only production costs if a product is processed beyond split-off. Fixed overhead costs common to other production activity must be excluded from a sell or process-further incremental analysis.

Exhibit 23-9. Incremental Analysis: Sell or Process-Further Decision

Bava Gardening Supplies, Inc.
Incremental Analysis—Sell or Process-Further Decision

Unit selling price data

Product	If Sold at Split-Off	If Sold After Additional Processing
Gro-Pow	$ 8	$12
Gro-Pow II	24	30
Gro-Supreme	40	50

Incremental analysis per 20,000-pound batch

Product	(1) Pounds	(2) Total Revenue if Sold at Split-Off	(3) Total Revenue if Sold After Processing Further	(4) Incremental Revenue (3) – (2)	(5) Incremental Costs	(6) Effect on Overall Profit (4) – (5)
Gro-Pow	10,000	$ 80,000	$120,000	$40,000	$24,000	$16,000
Gro-Pow II	6,000	144,000	180,000	36,000	38,000	(2,000)
Gro-Supreme	4,000	160,000	200,000	40,000	33,500	6,500

Chapter Review

Review of Learning Objectives

1. **Identify the steps in the management decision cycle.**
The management decision cycle begins with discovery of a problem or resource need. Then alternative courses of action to solve the problem or meet the need are identified. Next, a complete analysis to determine the effects of each alternative on business operations is prepared. With these supporting data, the decision maker chooses the best alternative. After the decision has been carried out, the accountant conducts a post-audit review to see if the decision was correct or if other needs have arisen.

2. **Define and identify *relevant decision information.***
Any data that relate to future cost, revenue, or use of resources and that will be different for alternative courses of action are considered relevant decision information. Projected sales or estimated costs, such as materials or direct labor, that are different for each decision alternative are examples of relevant information.

3. **Calculate product costs using variable costing procedures.**
Variable costing uses only variable manufacturing costs for product costing and inventory valuation. Direct materials, direct labor, and variable factory overhead costs are the only cost elements used to compute product costs. Fixed factory overhead costs are considered costs of the current period and are not included in inventories.

4. **Prepare an income statement using the contribution margin reporting format.**
In an income statement in the contribution margin format, costs are categorized as variable or fixed. Variable costs of goods sold and variable selling expenses are sub-

tracted from sales to arrive at contribution margin. All fixed costs, including those from manufacturing, selling, and administrative activities, are subtracted from contribution margin to determine net income (before taxes).

5. **Develop decision data using incremental analysis.**
In incremental analysis, alternatives are compared by their information differences. After identifying the potential increases or decreases in revenues and costs that result from each alternative, the accountant highlights the relevant data. They are the values that differ among the alternatives. Only these values are included in the analysis.

6. **Prepare decision alternative evaluations for (a) make-or-buy decisions, (b) special order decisions, (c) sales mix analyses, (d) decisions to eliminate unprofitable segments, and (e) sell or process-further decisions.**
Make-or-buy decision analysis helps managers decide whether to buy a part used in product assembly or to make the part inside the company. An incremental analysis of the expected costs and revenues for each alternative identifies the best alternative. To analyze special orders, the accountant must determine if there is unused capacity and must find the lowest acceptable selling price of a product. Generally, fixed costs are irrelevant to the decision since these costs were covered by regular operations. Contribution margin reporting shows whether the special order increases net income. Sales mix analysis is used to find the most profitable combination of product sales when a company makes more than one product using a common scarce resource. (A similar approach may be used for decisions based on the profitability of sales territories, service lines, or corporate segments.) The analysis uses the contribution margin reporting format but goes beyond computation of the contribution margin to examine the contribution margin per unit of scarce resource.
The decision to eliminate unprofitable products, services, or company segments requires an incremental analysis. This analysis should compare operating results that include the questionable segment against operating results without the segment's traceable and avoidable revenues and costs. Both income statements are prepared by following the contribution margin reporting format. Sell or process-further decisions are also based on comparisons of incremental revenues and costs of the two alternatives. Joint processing costs are irrelevant to the decision since they are identical for either alternative.

Review of Concepts and Terminology

The following concepts and terms were introduced in this chapter:

(L.O. 6) **Avoidable costs:** Costs that will be eliminated if a particular product, service, or operating segment is discontinued.

(L.O. 2) **Decision model:** A symbolic or numerical representation of the variables and parameters affecting a decision.

(L.O. 2) **Decision parameters:** The uncontrollable factors and the operating constraints and limitations within a decision model.

(L.O. 2) **Decision variables:** Factors within a decision model that are controlled by management.

(L.O. 5) **Incremental analysis:** A technique used in decision analysis that compares alternatives by focusing on the differences in their projected revenues and costs.

(L.O. 6) **Make-or-buy decision analysis:** A decision analysis that helps management choose the more profitable option by identifying the costs and revenues involved in making or buying some or all parts used in product assembly operations.

(L.O. 2) **Relevant decision information:** Future cost, revenue, and resource usage data that differ for the decision alternatives being evaluated.

(L.O. 6) **Sales mix analysis:** A special analysis prepared to determine the most profitable combination of product sales when a company produces more than one product or offers more than one service.

(L.O. 6) **Sell or process-further decision:** A decision analysis designed to help management determine whether to sell a joint product at the split-off point or process it further to increase its market price and profits.

(L.O. 6) **Special order decision:** A decision analysis designed to help management determine whether to accept or reject unexpected special product orders at prices below normal market prices.

(L.O. 6) **Traceable fixed costs:** Fixed costs that are traceable to a division, department, or other operating unit or product line.

(L.O. 6) **Unprofitable segment decision analysis:** A decision analysis designed to help management decide whether to continue operating a segment or to discontinue its operations.

(L.O. 3) **Variable costing:** A costing method that uses only the variable manufacturing costs for product costing and inventory valuation purposes (as contrasted with absorption costing, which uses all product costs).

Self-Test

Test your knowledge of the chapter by choosing the best answer for each of the following items.

(L.O. 2) 1. Future cost, revenue, or resource usage data that will differ for the various decision alternatives being evaluated is the definition of
   a. incremental information.
   b. variable costing information.
   c. relevant decision information.
   d. avoidable cost information.

(L.O. 3) 2. Decision factors controlled by management are known as
   a. avoidable decision factors.
   b. decision variables.
   c. decision parameters.
   d. decision model factors.

(L.O. 2, 3) 3. When using the variable costing approach for product costing purposes, which of the following is true?
   a. Fixed manufacturing costs are inventoriable costs.
   b. Only materials and labor costs are inventoriable costs.
   c. Variable selling costs are inventoriable costs.
   d. Variable manufacturing costs are inventoriable costs.

(L.O. 3) 4. Admiral Manufacturing Company follows variable costing practices for internal purposes. Product HG has the following unit costs: materials, $4.40; labor, $1.60; variable factory overhead, $2.30; fixed factory overhead, $1.90; variable selling costs, $3.10; and fixed selling costs, $1.10. If 1,240 units of Product HG are in finished goods inventory, what would be the total inventory balance?
   a. $12,648   c. $10,292
   b. $14,136   d. $17,856

(L.O. 4) 5. Assuming the same facts for the Admiral Manufacturing Company that are included in question **4**, what would be total contribution margin if 10,200 units were sold at $25 per unit?
   a. $108,120   c. $170,340
   b. $150,960   d. $138,720

(L.O. 5) 6. An approach to decision analysis that concentrates on only those revenue and cost items that differ between decision alternatives is known as
a. contribution margin analysis.
b. incremental analysis.
c. make-or-buy decision analysis.
d. special order decision analysis.

(L.O. 6) 7. Finding unit contribution margin per scarce resource is part of the
a. sales mix decision analysis.
b. special order decision analysis.
c. make-or-buy decision analysis.
d. sell or process-further decision analysis.

(L.O. 6) 8. Four products—D, E, F, and G—are produced by the Bailey Company. Machine hours is the company's scarce resource. Data on the four products in their respective order include: contribution margins—$4.50, $6.00, $12.00, and $9.00; use of labor hours—4 hr, 6 hr, 8 hr, and 9 hr; and use of machine hours—2 hr, 4 hr, 12 hr, and 5 hr. From this limited information, which product should be pushed by the Bailey Company assuming an unlimited market for each product?
a. Product D
b. Product E
c. Product F
d. Product G

(L.O. 6) 9. A management decision to accept or reject a sizable but unusual order that generally has a reduced pricing condition is known as a
a. make-or-buy decision.
b. special order decision.
c. sell or process-further decision.
d. segment elimination decision.

(L.O. 6) 10. Products A and B can be sold at split-off point for $27.50 and $32.50, respectively. Each unit of Product A can be sold for $45.00 if the company spends an additional $15.20 per unit on the product. Product B can be sold for $50.25 per unit if an additional $17.00 is spent processing each unit. Joint costs are $12.40 per unit of Product A and $14.40 per unit of Product B. The company should
a. process only Product A further.
b. process only Product B further.
c. process both products further.
d. sell both products at the split-off point.

Answers to the Self-Test are at the end of this chapter.

Review Problem
Short-Run Operating Decision Analysis

Ten years ago, Sam Ortiz formed Home Services, Inc., a company specializing in repair and maintenance services for the home and its surroundings. To date, Home Services has six offices in major cities across the country. Fourteen services, ranging from plumbing repair to appliance repair to lawn care, are available to the home owner. During the past two years, the company's profitability has decreased, and Ortiz wants to determine which service lines are not meeting the company's profit targets. Once the unprofitable service lines are identified, he will either eliminate them or set higher prices. If higher prices are set, all variable and fixed operating, selling, and general administration costs will be covered by the price structure. The data from the most recent year-end closing shown on the top of page 940 were available for the analysis. Four service lines are under serious review.

Home Services, Inc.
Service Profit and Loss Summary
For the Year Ended December 31, 19x5

	Auto Repair Service	Boat Repair Service	Tile Floor Repair Service	Tree Trimming Service	Total Company Impact
Sales	$297,500	$114,300	$126,400	$97,600	$ 635,800
Less variable costs					
Direct labor	$119,000	$ 40,005	$ 44,240	$34,160	$ 237,405
Operating supplies	14,875	5,715	6,320	4,880	31,790
Small tools	11,900	4,572	5,056	7,808	29,336
Replacement parts	59,500	22,860	25,280	—	107,640
Truck costs	—	11,430	12,640	14,640	38,710
Selling costs	44,625	17,145	18,960	9,760	90,490
Other variable costs	5,950	2,286	2,528	1,952	12,716
Total	$255,850	$104,013	$115,024	$73,200	$ 548,087
Contribution margin	$ 41,650	$ 10,287	$ 11,376	$24,400	$ 87,713
Less traceable fixed costs	74,200	29,600	34,700	28,400	166,900
Service margin	$(32,550)	$(19,313)	$(23,324)	$(4,000)	$ (79,187)
Less nontraceable joint fixed costs					32,100
Net income before taxes					$(111,287)
Avoidable fixed costs included in traceable fixed costs above	$ 35,800	$ 16,300	$ 24,100	$ 5,200	$ 81,400

Required

1. Analyze the performance of the four services being reviewed.
2. Should Ortiz eliminate any of the service lines? Why?
3. Identify some possible causes for poor performance by the services.
4. What factors would lead you to raise the fee for a service rather than eliminate the service?

Answer to Review Problem

1. When analyzing the performance of four service lines for possible elimination, you should concentrate on the revenues and costs to be eliminated if the service is eliminated. You should start your analysis with contribution margin because all sales and variable costs will be eliminated. By subtracting the avoidable fixed costs from contribution margin, you will find the profit or loss that will be eliminated if the service is eliminated. These calculations are shown below.

	Auto Repair Service	Boat Repair Service	Tile Floor Repair Service	Tree Trimming Service	Total Company Impact
Contribution margin	$41,650	$10,287	$ 11,376	$24,400	$87,713
Less avoidable fixed costs	35,800	16,300	24,100	5,200	81,400
Profit (loss) lost if service is eliminated	$ 5,850	$(6,013)	$(12,724)	$19,200	$ 6,313

2. From the analysis in **1**, you can see that the company will improve by $18,737 ($6,013 + $12,724) if the Boat Repair Service and the Tile Floor Repair Service are eliminated.
3. There are several possible causes for poor performance by the four services, including
   a. Low service fee being charged
   b. Inadequate advertising of the service
   c. High direct labor costs
   d. Other variable costs too high
   e. Poor management of fixed cost levels
   f. Excessive management costs
4. To judge the adequacy of the service fees being charged, you should first look at the contribution margin percentages. This additional information will help support pricing decisions for the four services.

	Auto Repair Service	Boat Repair Service	Tile Floor Repair Service	Tree Trimming Service
Sales	$297,500	$114,300	$126,400	$97,600
Contribution margin	$ 41,650	$ 10,287	$ 11,376	$24,400
Contribution margin percentage	14.00%	9.00%	9.00%	25.00%

Only 9 percent of the selling price is available for fixed costs and profit from the Boat Repair and Tile Floor Repair services. This is a thin margin with which to work. An increase in fees seems appropriate. Even fees for the Auto Repair Service may need to be increased.

Also, remember that there were large amounts of unavoidable and nontraceable fixed costs reported. These costs may need to be analyzed too. Although they may or may not be avoidable, these costs must be covered by fees if the company is to remain profitable.

Chapter Assignments

Questions

1. "Strategic planning provides the basic framework for applying short-run period planning." Do you agree with this statement? If so, why?
2. Describe the five steps of the management decision cycle.
3. What is meant by relevant decision information? What are the two important characteristics of such information?
4. Describe variable costing. In what ways does variable costing differ from absorption costing?
5. Is variable costing widely used for financial reporting? Defend your answer.
6. What is the connection between variable costing and the contribution margin approach to reporting?
7. Are variable costs always relevant? Defend your response.
8. Identify and discuss the steps required to build a decision model.
9. What are the objectives of incremental analysis? What types of decision analyses depend on the incremental approach?
10. Illustrate and discuss some qualitative inputs into decision analysis.
11. How does one determine which data are relevant to a make-or-buy decision?

12. When pricing a special order, what justifies excluding fixed overhead costs from the analysis? Under what circumstances are fixed costs relevant to the pricing decision?
13. What questions must be answered in trying to make the most of product line profitability? Give examples of approaches to the solution of this question.
14. For sales mix decisions, what criteria can be used to select products that will maximize net income?
15. Why is the term *avoidable cost* used in relation to alternatives to eliminating a segment?
16. Distinguish between the terms *avoidable cost* and *traceable cost*.
17. Why are joint processing costs irrelevant to the decision to sell a product at split-off or process it further?
18. Is incremental analysis important to the sell or process-further decision? If so, why?

Communication Skills Exercises

Communication 23-1. Operating Decisions and Total Employee Involvement Groups
(L.O 2, 5)

Norfield Manufacturing Co. is a small, closely held business located in Chico, California.[2] Originally a manufacturer of pre-hung doors used in housing construction, the company's sixty employees now produce the machinery used to manufacture pre-hung doors. The company adopted the "world-class manufacturing" approach in 1987. Just-in-time manufacturing and purchasing methods are now in place. Operating decisions are made by employees, not just by managers. This team approach to decisions, known as Total Employee Involvement Groups, is used for decisions ranging from the selection of raw materials vendors to capital expenditure decisions. The implementation of this new approach took several months. Employees had to be educated, managers had to be re-educated, and the president had to communicate his support for this change. The first decision given to the employees was how to arrange the production floor to make it more productive. They responded by developing work cells and shortening the production lines. Engineers worked with production employees to create the new plant layout design. Prepare a list of benefits that Norfield Manufacturing Co. will experience from this new approach to decision making. Be prepared to share your ideas with the class.

Communication 23-2. Sophisticated, User-Driven, Decision Support Systems
(L.O. 2, 5)

Adolph Coors Brewing Company is revamping its management philosophy and its internal decision support systems.[3] Al Pipkin, vice president of finance at Coors Brewing Company, states that decision support systems are becoming paperless and invisible. Computer systems develop data, pay bills, order materials, screen deliveries for defects, and prepare budgets. Every employee in the company is considered a data source. Within this environment, routine decisions about raw materials suppliers, order quantities, and delivery schedules are made from information gathered from employees. Using a three- or four-student team, develop a decision support system that will supply the needed information for these routine decisions. Include in your system the types of information needed, where that information will come from, who is responsible for gathering it, and who will assemble the final report structure. Develop a drawing of your decision support system. Be prepared to present your group's finding to the class.

Communication 23-3. Ethics and Decision Analysis
(L.O. 6)

Michelle Pinto is assistant controller for ***Bannister Corp.,*** a leading producer of home appliances. Her friend, Eddie Mason, is supervisor of the Cookware Department. Mason has the authority to decide whether parts are purchased from outside vendors or manufactured in his department. Pinto recently conducted an internal audit of the parts being manufactured in the Cookware Department, including doing a check of the prices currently being charged by vendors for similar parts. She found over a dozen parts that could be purchased for less money than they cost the company to produce. In her discussion with Mason, she was told that if those parts were purchased from outside vendors,

2. Paul Krause and Donald E. Keller, "Bringing World-Class Manufacturing and Accounting to a Small Company," *Management Accounting,* Institute of Management Accountants, November 1988, pp. 28–33.
3. Al Pipkin, "The 21st Century Controller," *Management Accounting,* Institute of Management Accountants, February 1989, pp. 21–25.

two automated machines would be idled for several hours a week. This action would negatively influence Mason's performance evaluation and could reduce his yearly bonus. He told Pinto that he was in charge of the decision to make or purchase these parts and asked her not to pursue the matter any further.

What should Pinto do in this situation? Discuss her options.

Communication 23-4. Basic Research Skills *(L.O. 5)*

Every business organization uses machinery and/or equipment in its operations. Service organizations, such as banks, insurance companies, and law firms, and not-for-profit organizations, such as churches and local charities, rely on office equipment and computers to help them provide timely, high-quality service to their customers. Manufacturing companies transform raw materials into finished products using special machinery.

Identify a local business that you might want to work for when you graduate from college. Call the company's personnel office and ask to talk to one of its managers. Ask the manager for an interview to discuss the company's policies on the purchase of equipment. Find out what procedures the company follows when making decisions to purchase equipment. You might ask such questions as: What are the company's policies on the processing of requests for new equipment? Do policies differ for purchases of equipment under $1,000 versus equipment costing more than $10,000? Who is responsible for gathering the data to support the decision process? Who makes the final decision? Prepare a one- or two-page summary of the information gained in your interview and be prepared to present your findings to your classmates.

Classroom Exercises

Exercise 23-1. Relevant Costs and Revenues *(L.O. 2)*

Old Dominion Enterprises manufactures various household metal products, such as window frames, light fixtures, and doorknobs. In 19x1 the company produced 10,000 special oblong doorknobs but sold only 1,000 doorknobs at $20.00 each. The remaining 9,000 units cannot be sold through Old Dominion's normal channels.

For inventory purposes, costs on December 31, 19x1 included the following data on the unsold units:

Direct materials	$ 6.00
Direct labor	3.00
Variable factory overhead	1.00
Fixed factory overhead	4.00
Cost per knob	$14.00

The 9,000 oblong knobs can be sold to a scrap dealer in another state for $7.00 each. A license for doing business in this state will cost Old Dominion $400. Shipping expenses will average $0.10 per knob.

1. Identify the relevant costs and revenues for the scrap sale alternative.
2. Assume the oblong knobs can be reprocessed to produce round knobs that normally have the same $14.00 unit cost components and sell for $16.00 each. Rework costs will be $9.00 per unit. Determine the most profitable alternative: (1) doing nothing, (2) reprocessing the knobs (assuming a market exists for the reworked knobs), or (3) selling them as scrap.

Exercise 23-2. Relevant Data and Incremental Analysis *(L.O. 2, 5)*

Ruth Stuart, business manager for Stoller Industries, must select a new computer and word processing package for her secretary. Rental of Model A, which is similar to the model now being used, is $2,200 per year. Model B is a deluxe computer with Windows support for its word processing software. It rents for $2,900 per year, but will require a new desk for the secretary. The annual desk rental charge is $750. The secretary's salary of $1,200 per month will not change. If Model B is rented, $280 in annual software training costs will be incurred. Model B has greater capacity and is expected to save $1,550 per year in part-time secretarial wages. Upkeep and operating costs will not differ between the two models.

1. Identify the relevant data in this problem.
2. Prepare an incremental analysis for the business manager to aid her in making the decision.

Exercise 23-3. Variable Costing: Unit Cost Computation
(L.O. 3)

Suny Corporation produces a full line of energy-tracking devices. These devices can detect and track all forms of thermochemical energy-emitting space vehicles.

The following cost data are provided: Direct materials cost $1,185,000 for two units. Direct labor for assembly is 4,590 hours per unit at $26.50 per hour. Variable factory overhead is $48.00 per direct labor hour, and fixed factory overhead is $2,796,000 per month (based on an average production of thirty units per month). This amount includes fixed packaging overhead. Packaging materials come to $127,200 for two units, and packaging labor per unit is 420 hours per unit at $18.50 per hour. The variable factory overhead rate for packaging is $24 per packaging labor hour. Advertising and marketing cost $196,750 per month, and other fixed selling and administrative costs are $287,680 per month.

1. From these cost data, find the unit production cost, using both the variable costing and the absorption costing methods.
2. Assume that the current month's ending inventory is eight units. Compute the inventory valuation under both variable and absorption costing methods.

Exercise 23-4. Income Statement: Contribution Margin Reporting Format
(L.O. 4)

The income statement in the conventional reporting format for Brosi Products, Inc. for the year ended December 31, 19x0 appears as follows.

Brosi Products, Inc.
Income Statement
For the Year Ended December 31, 19x0

Sales		$296,400
Less Cost of Goods Sold		
Cost of Goods Available for Sale	$125,290	
Less Ending Inventory	12,540	112,750
Gross Margin from Sales		$183,650
Less Operating Expenses		
Selling Expenses		
Variable	$ 69,820	
Fixed	36,980	
Administrative Expenses	27,410	134,210
Net Income Before Taxes		$ 49,440

Fixed manufacturing costs of $17,600 and $850 are included in Cost of Goods Available for Sale and Ending Inventory, respectively. Total fixed manufacturing costs for 19x0 were $16,540. There were no beginning or ending work in process inventories. All administrative expenses are considered to be fixed.

Using this information, prepare an income statement for Brosi Products, Inc. for the year ended December 31, 19x0 using the contribution margin reporting format.

Exercise 23-5. Make-or-Buy Decision
(L.O. 6)

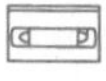

One of the parts for a radio assembly being produced by Mount Vernon Audio Systems, Inc. is presently being purchased for $225 per 100 parts. Management is studying the possibility of manufacturing these parts. Cost and production data being examined are as follows: annual production (usage) is 70,000 units; fixed costs (all of which remain unchanged whether the part is made or purchased) are $38,500; and variable costs are $.95 per unit for direct materials, $.55 per unit for direct labor, and $.60 per unit for variable manufacturing overhead.

Using incremental decision analysis, decide whether Mount Vernon Audio Systems, Inc. should manufacture the part or continue to purchase it from an outside vendor.

Exercise 23-6.
Special Order Decision
(L.O. 6)

Alvin, Cabot & Hunter, Ltd. produces antique-looking lampshades. Management has just received a request for a special design order and must decide whether or not to accept it. The special order calls for 9,000 shades to be shipped in a total of 300 bulk pack cartons. Shipping costs of $180 per carton will replace normal packing and shipping costs. Firenze Furniture Company, the purchasing company, is offering to pay $22 per shade plus packing and shipping expenses.

The following company data have been provided by the accounting department: Annual budgeted production is 350,000 shades, and the current year's production (before special order) is 360,000 shades. Maximum production capacity is 380,000 shades. Unit cost data include $9.20 for direct materials, $4.00 for direct labor, variable factory overhead of $6.80, and fixed factory overhead of $2.50 ($875,000 ÷ 350,000). Normal packaging and shipping costs per unit come to $1.50, and advertising is $.30 per unit ($105,000 ÷ 350,000). Other fixed administrative costs are $1.30 per unit ($455,000 ÷ 350,000). Total normal cost per unit is $25.60, with per unit selling price set at $38.00. Total estimated bulk packaging and shipping costs are $54,000 ($180 per carton × 300 cartons).

Determine whether this special order should be accepted.

Exercise 23-7.
Scarce Resource Usage
(L.O. 6)

Foti, Inc. manufactures two products, A and M. Although there is unlimited demand for both products, Foti could devote all its capacities to a single product. Unit prices, cost data, and processing requirements are:

	Product A	Product M
Unit selling price	$80	$220
Unit variable costs	$40	$ 90
Labor hours per unit	2	6

In 19x5 the company will be limited to 120,000 labor hours.

1. Compute the quantities of each product to be produced in 19x5.
2. Compute the contribution margin per labor hour for each product.
3. Prepare an income statement for the product volume generating the maximum contribution margin.

Exercise 23-8.
Elimination of Unprofitable Segment
(L.O. 6)

Stockholm Glass, Inc. has three divisions: Atta, Nio, and Tio. The divisional income summaries for 19x4 revealed the following:

Stockholm Glass, Inc.
Divisional Profit Summary and Decision Analysis

	Atta Division	Nio Division	Tio Division	Total Company
Sales	$290,000	$533,000	$837,000	$1,660,000
Variable costs	147,000	435,000	472,000	1,054,000
Contribution margin	$143,000	$ 98,000	$365,000	$ 606,000
Less traceable fixed costs	166,000	114,000	175,000	455,000
Divisional income	$(23,000)	$(16,000)	$190,000	$ 151,000
Less unallocated fixed costs				82,000
Net income before taxes				$ 69,000

A detailed analysis of the traceable fixed costs revealed the following information:

	Atta Division	Nio Division	Tio Division
Avoidable fixed costs	$124,000	$106,000	$139,000
Unavoidable fixed costs	42,000	8,000	36,000
Totals	$166,000	$114,000	$175,000

Based on the 19x4 income summaries, determine whether it would be profitable for the company to eliminate one or more of its segments. Identify which division(s) should be eliminated, and compute how much the resulting increase in total net income would be before taxes.

Exercise 23-9.
Sell or Process-Further Decision
(L.O. 6)

McGahey Marketeers, Inc. has developed a promotional program for a large shopping center in Tempe, Arizona. After investing $360,000 in developing the original promotion campaign, the firm is ready to present its client with an add-on contract offer that includes the original promotion areas of (1) TV advertising program, (2) series of brochures for mass mailing, and (3) special rotating BIG SALE schedule for 10 of the 28 tenants in the shopping center. Following are the revenue terms from the original contract with the shopping center and the offer for an add-on contract, which extends the original contract terms:

	Contract Terms	
	Original Contract Terms	Extended Contract Including Add-On Terms
TV advertising program	$520,000	$ 580,000
Brochure package	210,000	230,000
Rotating BIG SALE schedule	170,000	190,000
Totals	$900,000	$1,000,000

McGahey estimates that the following additional costs will be incurred by extending the contract:

	TV Program	Brochures	BIG SALE Schedule
Direct labor	$30,000	$ 9,000	$7,000
Variable overhead costs	22,000	14,000	6,000
Fixed overhead costs*	12,000	4,000	2,000

*20 percent are unavoidable fixed costs applied to this contract.

1. Compute the costs that will be incurred for each part of the add-on portion of the contract.
2. Should McGahey Marketeers, Inc. offer the add-on contract or should it ask for a final settlement check based on the original contract only? Defend your answer.
3. If management of the shopping center indicated the terms of the add-on contract were negotiable, how should McGahey respond?

Interpretation Case from Business

Hess Can Opener Company
(L.O. 6)

Hess Can Opener Company is a subsidiary of Hendricks Appliances, Inc. The can opener Hess produces is in strong demand. Sales during the present year, 19x4, are expected to hit the 1,000,000 mark. Full plant capacity is 1,150,000 units, but the 1,000,000-unit mark was considered normal capacity for the current year. The following unit price and cost breakdown is applicable in 19x4:

	Per Unit
Sales price	$22.50
Less manufacturing costs	
Materials	$ 6.00
Direct labor	2.50
Overhead: Variable	3.50
Fixed	1.50
Total manufacturing costs	$13.50
Gross margin	$ 9.00
Less selling and administrative expenses	
Selling: Variable	$ 1.50
Fixed	1.00
Administrative, fixed	1.25
Packaging, variable*	.75
Total selling and administrative expenses	$ 4.50
Net profit before taxes	$ 4.50

*Three types of packaging are available: deluxe, $.75/unit; plain, $.50/unit; and bulk pack, $.25/unit.

During November, the company received three special order requests from large chain-store companies. These orders are not part of the budgeted 1,000,000-unit sales for 19x4, but company officials think that sufficient capacity exists to accept one order. The special order will not affect normal sales to current customers. Orders received and their terms are:

Order 1: 75,000 can openers @ $20.00/unit, deluxe packaging

Order 2: 90,000 can openers @ $18.00/unit, plain packaging

Order 3: 125,000 can openers @ $15.75/unit, bulk packaging

Since these orders were made directly to company officials, no variable selling costs will be incurred.

Required

1. Analyze the profitability of each of the three special orders by computing their contribution margins.
2. Which special order should Hess accept?

Problem Set A

Problem 23A-1. Variable Costing: Contribution Approach to Income Statement
(L.O. 3, 4)

Interior designers often utilize the deluxe carpet products of Brandywine Mills, Inc. The Nassau Blend is the company's top product line. In March 19x3, Brandywine produced 187,500 square yards and sold 174,900 square yards of Nassau Blend. Factory operating data for the year included: direct materials used of $1,275,000; direct labor of .2 direct labor hour per square yard at $14.50 per hour; variable factory overhead of $431,250; and fixed factory overhead of $337,500. Other expenses included: variable selling expenses, $166,155; fixed selling expenses, $148,665; and fixed general and administrative expenses, $231,500. Total sales revenue equaled $3,935,250. All production took place in March and there was no work in process at month end. Goods are usually shipped when completed but at the end of March, 12,600 square yards still await shipment.

Required

1. Compute the unit cost, cost of goods sold for March, and ending finished goods inventory value, using (a) variable costing and (b) absorption costing procedures.
2. Prepare the month-end income statement for Brandywine Mills, Inc., using (a) the contribution margin reporting format based on variable costing data and (b) the conventional format based on absorption costing data.

Problem 23A-2.
Make-or-Buy Decision
(L.O. 6)

Lac Courte Furniture Company of Hayward, Wisconsin is famous for its dining room furniture. One full department is engaged in the production of the Cottonwood line, an elegant but affordable dining room set. To date, the company has been manufacturing all pieces of the set, including the six chairs.

Management has just received word that a company in Peoria, Illinois is willing to produce the chairs for Lac Courte Furniture Company at a total purchase price of $3,080,000 for the annual demand. Company records show that the following costs have been incurred in the production of the chairs: wood materials, $2,500 per 100 chairs; cloth materials, $900 per 100 chairs; direct labor, 1.2 hours per chair at $12.00 per hour; variable factory overhead, $8.00 per direct labor hour; fixed factory overhead, depreciation, $135,000; and fixed factory overhead, other, $105,800. Fixed factory overhead would continue whether or not the chairs are produced. Assume that idle facilities cannot be used for any other purpose and that annual usage is 56,000 chairs.

Required

Prepare an incremental decision analysis to determine whether the chairs should be made by the company or purchased from the outside supplier in Peoria.

Problem 23A-3.
Special Order Decision
(L.O. 6)

On March 26, the Harriman Boat Division of Roane Industries received a special order request for 120 ten-foot aluminum fishing boats. Operating on a fiscal year ending May 31, the division already has orders that will allow it to produce at budget levels for the period. However, extra capacity exists to produce the 120 additional boats.

Terms of the special order call for a selling price of $600 per boat and the customer will pay all shipping costs. No sales personnel were involved in soliciting this order. This special order will have no impact on current orders.

The ten-foot fishing boat has the following cost estimates: direct materials, aluminum, two 4′ × 8′ sheets at $145 per sheet; direct labor, 14 hours at $14.50 per hour; and variable factory overhead, $5.75 per direct labor hour; fixed factory overhead, $4.50 per direct labor hour; variable selling expenses, $46.50 per boat; and variable shipping expenses, $57.50 per boat.

Required

1. Prepare an analysis for management of the Harriman Boat Division to use in deciding whether to accept or reject the special order. What decision should be made?
2. To make an $8,100 profit on this order, what would be the lowest possible price that the Harriman Boat Division could charge per boat?

Problem 23A-4.
Sales Mix Analysis
(L.O. 6)

The vice president of finance for Chandler Machine Tool, Inc. is evaluating the profitability of the company's four product lines. During the current year, the company will operate at full machine-hour capacity. The following production data have been compiled:

Product	Current Year's Production (Units)	Total Machine Hours Used
24F	30,000	75,000
37N	50,000	100,000
29T	20,000	20,000
40U	90,000	45,000

Sales and operating cost data are as follows:

	Product 24F	Product 37N	Product 29T	Product 40U
Selling price per unit	$20.00	$25.00	$30.00	$35.00
Unit variable manufacturing cost	8.00	17.00	21.00	29.00
Unit fixed manufacturing cost	4.00	3.00	2.50	2.00
Unit variable selling cost	2.00	2.00	4.50	3.25
Unit fixed administrative cost	3.00	2.00	3.00	1.75

Required

1. Compute the machine hours needed to produce one unit of each product type.
2. Determine the contribution margin of each product type.
3. Which product line(s) should be pushed by the company's sales force? Why?

Problem 23A-5. Analysis to Eliminate an Unprofitable Product *(L.O. 6)*

Seven years ago, Price & Shipley Publishing Company produced its first book. Since then, the company has added four more books to its product list. Management is considering proposals for three more new books, but editorial capacity limits the company to producing only seven books. Before deciding which of the proposed books to publish, management wants you to evaluate the performance of its present book list. The revenue and cost data for the most recent year (each book is identified by the author or authors) follow:

Price & Shipley Publishing Company
Product Profit and Loss Summary
For the Year Ended December 31, 19x5

	Ray & James	Powers & Floyd	Resnik & Reed	Lyles	Hegarty	Company Totals
Sales	$813,800	$782,000	$634,200	$944,100	$707,000	$3,881,100
Less variable costs						
Materials and binding	$325,520	$312,800	$190,260	$283,230	$212,100	$1,323,910
Editorial services	71,380	88,200	73,420	57,205	80,700	370,905
Author royalties	130,208	125,120	101,472	151,056	113,120	620,976
Sales commissions	162,760	156,400	95,130	141,615	141,400	697,305
Other selling costs	50,682	44,740	21,708	18,334	60,700	196,164
Total variable costs	$740,550	$727,260	$481,990	$651,440	$608,020	$3,209,260
Contribution margin	$ 73,250	$ 54,740	$152,210	$292,660	$ 98,980	$ 671,840
Less traceable fixed costs	97,250	81,240	89,610	100,460	82,680	451,240
Product margin	$(24,000)	$(26,500)	$ 62,600	$192,200	$ 16,300	$ 220,600
Less nontraceable joint fixed costs						82,400
Net income before taxes						$ 138,200
Avoidable fixed costs included in traceable fixed costs above	$ 51,200	$ 55,100	$ 49,400	$ 69,100	$ 58,800	$ 283,600

Projected data for the proposed new books are Book A, sales, $450,000, contribution margin, $45,000; Book B, sales, $725,000, contribution margin, $25,200; and Book C, sales, $913,200, contribution margin, $115,500.

Required

1. Analyze the performance of the five books currently being published.
2. Should the company eliminate any of its present products? If so, which one(s)?
3. Identify the new books you would use to replace those eliminated. Justify your answer. (**Hint:** Consider contribution margin as a percentage of sales on all books.)

Problem Set B

Problem 23B-1. Variable Costing: Contribution Approach to Income Statement *(L.O. 3, 4)*

York Corporation is a major producer of roofing tile. The company had a particularly good year in 19x4, as is shown by the following operating data.

It produced 92,600 cases (units) of tile and sold 88,400 cases. Direct materials used cost $388,920; direct labor was $194,460; variable factory overhead was $305,580; fixed factory overhead was $166,680; variable selling expenses were $132,600; fixed selling expenses were $152,048; and fixed administrative expenses were $96,450. Selling price was $18 per case. There were no partially completed jobs in process at the beginning or the end of the year. Finished goods inventory at the beginning of the year was zero.

Required

1. Compute the unit cost, cost of goods sold for 19x4, and ending finished goods inventory value using (a) variable costing procedures and (b) absorption costing procedures.
2. Prepare the year-end income statement for York Corporation using (a) the contribution margin reporting format based on variable costing data and (b) the conventional format based on absorption costing data.

Problem 23B-2. Make-or-Buy Decision *(L.O. 6)*

The Poulson Refrigerator Company purchases and installs defrost clocks in its products. The clocks cost $138 per case, and each case contains twelve clocks. The supplier recently gave advance notice that, effective in thirty days, the price will rise by 50 percent. The company has idle equipment that could be used to produce similar defrost clocks.

The following cost estimates have been prepared under the assumption that the company could make the product itself. Direct materials would cost $100.80 per twelve clocks. Direct labor required would be ten minutes per clock at a labor rate of $18.00 per hour. Variable factory overhead would be $4.60 per clock. Fixed factory overhead, which would be incurred under either decision alternative, would be $32,420 a year for depreciation and $234,000 a year for other costs. Production and usage are estimated at 75,000 clocks a year. (Assume that any idle equipment cannot be used for any other purpose.)

Required

Prepare an incremental decision analysis to determine whether the defrost clocks should be made within the company or purchased from the outside supplier at the higher price.

Problem 23B-3. Special Order Decision *(L.O. 6)*

Randison Resorts, Ltd. has approached NAU Technical Printers, Inc. with a special order to produce 300,000 two-page brochures. Most of NAU Technical's work consists of recurring short-run orders. Randison Resorts is offering a one-time order, and NAU Technical does have the capacity to handle the order over a two-month period.

Randison's management has stated that the company is unwilling to pay more than $48 per 1,000 brochures. The following cost data were assembled by NAU Technical's controller for this decision analysis: direct materials (paper) would be $26.50 per 1,000 brochures. Direct labor costs would be $6.80 per 1,000 brochures. Direct materials (ink) would be $4.40 per 1,000 brochures. Variable production overhead would be $6.20 per 1,000 brochures. Machine maintenance (fixed cost) is $1.00 per direct labor dollar. Other fixed production overhead amounts to $2.40 per direct labor dollar. Variable packing costs would be $4.30 per 1,000 brochures. Also, the share of general and administrative expenses (fixed costs) usually allocated to printing is $5.25 per direct labor dollar.

Required

1. Prepare an analysis for NAU Technical's management to use in deciding whether to accept or reject Randison Resorts' offer. What decision should be made?
2. What is the lowest possible price NAU Technical can charge per thousand and still make a $6,000 profit on the order?

Problem 23B-4.
Sales Mix Analysis
(L.O. 6)

Management at Heckel Chemical Company is evaluating its product mix in an attempt to maximize profits. For the past two years, Heckel has produced four products, and all have a large market in which to expand market share. Cindi Henne, Heckel's controller, has gathered data from current operations and wants you to analyze it for her. Sales and operating data are as follows:

	Product AE42	Product BF53	Product CG64	Product DH75
Variable production costs	$ 71,000	$ 91,000	$ 91,920	$ 97,440
Variable selling costs	10,200	5,400	12,480	30,160
Fixed production costs	20,400	21,600	29,120	18,480
Fixed administrative costs	3,400	5,400	6,240	10,080
Total sales	122,000	136,000	156,400	161,200
Units produced and sold	85,000	45,000	26,000	14,000
Machine hours used*	17,000	18,000	20,800	16,800

*Heckel's scarce resource, machine hours, is operating at full capacity.

Required

1. Compute the machine hours needed to produce one unit of each product.
2. Determine the contribution margin per machine hour for each product.
3. Which product line(s) should be targeted for market share expansion? Why?

Problem 23B-5.
Analysis to Eliminate an Unprofitable Segment
(L.O. 6)

Tubbs Sporting Goods, Inc. is a nationwide distributor of sporting equipment. The home office is located in Las Vegas, Nevada, and four branch distributorships are in Tuba City, Alabama; Cherry Valley, Illinois; Orange, California; and Bozeman, Montana. Operating results for 19x4 (all amounts in the summary are in thousands of dollars) are as follows:

Tubbs Sporting Goods, Inc.
Segment Profit and Loss Summary
For the Year Ended December 31, 19x4

	Tuba City Branch	Cherry Valley Branch	Orange Branch	Bozeman Branch	Total Company
Sales	$6,008	$6,712	$6,473	$8,059	$27,252
Less variable costs					
Purchases	$3,471	$4,119	$3,970	$5,246	$16,806
Wages and salaries	694	702	687	841	2,924
Sales commissions	535	610	519	881	2,545
Selling expenses	96	102	79	127	404
Total variable costs	$4,796	$5,533	$5,255	$7,095	$22,679
Contribution margin	$1,212	$1,179	$1,218	$ 964	$ 4,573
Less traceable fixed costs	972	1,099	808	1,059	3,938
Branch margin	$ 240	$ 80	$ 410	$ (95)	$ 635
Less nontraceable joint costs					325
Net income before taxes					$ 310

The corporate president, Mr. Harold, is upset with overall corporate operating results, particularly those of the Bozeman branch. He has requested the controller to work up a complete profitability analysis of the four branch operations and to study the possibility of closing the Bozeman branch. The controller needed the following additional information before the analysis could be completed:

1. Shipping costs were 20 percent of the cost of goods purchased by the Bozeman branch.
2. Of the fixed costs traceable to the branch operations, the following were avoidable:

Tuba City	$782,000	Orange	$648,000
Cherry Valley	$989,000	Bozeman	$849,000

3. An analysis of sales revealed the following:

	Average Growth, Last Five Years	Growth, 19x4	Future Average Growth Rate
Tuba City	8%	7%	5%
Cherry Valley	7	5	6
Orange	10	13	8
Bozeman	22	20	10

Required

1. Analyze the performance of each branch. (**Hint:** Convert the segment profit and loss summary to a common-size statement.)
2. Should the corporation eliminate the Bozeman branch?
3. Are there other branches Harold should be concerned about? Why?
4. List possible causes for the corporation's poor performance.

Management Decision Case

Tyndall Company
(L.O. 6)

Management at Tyndall Company is considering a proposal to install a third production department within its factory building. With the company's present production setup, raw material is processed through Department I to produce materials A and B in equal proportions. Material A is then processed through Department II to yield Product C. Material B is sold as-is at $20.25 per pound. Product C has a selling price of $100.00 per pound. Current per-pound standard costs used by Tyndall Company are:

	Department I (Materials A & B)	Department II (Product C)	(Material B)
Prior department's cost	—	$53.03	$13.47
Direct materials	$20.00	—	—
Direct labor	6.00	9.00	—
Variable overhead	4.00	8.00	—
Fixed overhead			
Traceable	2.25	2.25	—
Allocated (⅔, ⅓)	1.00	1.00	—
	$33.25	$73.28	$13.47

These standard costs were developed by using an estimated production volume of 200,000 pounds of raw material as the standard volume. The company assigns Department I costs to materials A and B in proportion to their net sales values at the point of separation. These values are computed by deducting subsequent standard production costs from sales prices. The $300,000 in common fixed overhead costs are allocated to the two producing departments on the basis of the space used by the departments.

Department III is being proposed to be used to process material B into Product D. It is expected that any quantity of Product D can be sold for $30 per pound. Standard costs per pound under this proposal were developed by using 200,000 pounds of raw material as the standard volume. Those costs are as shown at the top of the next page.

	Department I (Materials A & B)	Department II (Product C)	Department III (Product D)
Prior department's cost	—	$52.80	$13.20
Direct materials	$20.00	—	—
Direct labor	6.00	9.00	3.50
Variable overhead	4.00	8.00	4.00
Fixed overhead			
Traceable	2.25	2.25	1.80
Allocated (½, ¼, ¼)	.75	.75	.75
	$33.00	$72.80	$23.25

Required

1. If (a) sales and production levels are expected to remain constant in the foreseeable future and (b) there are no foreseeable alternate uses for the factory space, should Tyndall Company install Department III and produce Product D? Show calculations to support your answer.
2. Instead of constant sales and production levels, suppose that under the present production setup, $1,000,000 in additions to the factory building must be made every ten years to accommodate growth. Also suppose that proper maintenance gives these factory additions an infinite life and that all such maintenance costs are included in the standard costs set forth in the text. How would the analysis you performed in **1** be changed if installation of Department III shortened the interval at which the $1,000,000 in factory additions are made from ten years to six years? Be as specific as possible in your answer.

(ICMA adapted)

Answers to Self-Test

1. c	3. d	5. d	7. a	9. b
2. b	4. c	6. b	8. a	10. c

CHAPTER 24

Capital Expenditure Decisions

LEARNING OBJECTIVES

1. Describe the capital expenditure decision process and identify the steps in the capital expenditure decision cycle.
2. State the purpose of the minimum desired rate of return and identify the methods used to arrive at this rate.
3. Identify and explain the measures of projected costs and revenues used to evaluate capital expenditure decision alternatives.
4. Evaluate capital expenditure proposals using (a) the accounting rate-of-return method and (b) the payback period method.
5. Apply the concept of time value of money.
6. Evaluate capital expenditure proposals using the net present value method.
7. Analyze capital expenditure decision alternatives that incorporate the effects of income taxes.
8. Rank proposals competing for limited capital expenditure funds.
9. Identify qualitative information designed to improve the capital expenditure decision process in today's globally competitive business environment.

Capital expenditure decisions involve time periods that can span several years and capital asset purchases that can represent significant dollar amounts. The success or failure of capital expenditure decisions often makes the difference between operating at a profit or a loss. These long-term decisions require projections of revenues and expenses for many years. Whenever one deals with long-range predictions, much uncertainty is incorporated into the decision process. Therefore, the management accountant must consider all likely outcomes of proposed projects and use realistic rate-of-return forecasts when preparing information for management.

This chapter first looks at the capital expenditure decision process, the steps in the decision cycle, and the meaning and computation of the minimum desired rate of return. After a review of information relevant to this decision process, the text analyzes three primary evaluation methods, including (1) accounting rate of return, (2) payback period, and (3) net present value. In relation to the net present value approach, the concept of time value of money is discussed. The capital expenditure evaluation methods are first analyzed using before-tax amounts; they are then reanalyzed, using after-tax amounts so that you can see how income taxes affect these decisions. The chapter concludes with an approach to ranking various proposals competing for limited capital expenditure funds and a look at qualitative information relevant to capital expenditure decisions in today's competitive business environment. After studying this chapter, you should be able to meet the learning objectives listed on the left.

DECISION POINT

United Architects, Inc.[1]

■ United Architects, Inc., founded in Los Angeles in 1965, is a medium-sized architectural firm with expertise in designing and developing buildings, parking garages, and other commercial structures. Like most service organizations, United Architects is labor intensive, and labor cost is a major component of each project's total cost. The company allocates service overhead to projects based on labor hours.

United Architects must make capital expenditures for its office space and furniture as well as for computer drafting equipment. The company's capital expenditure decision analyses have not changed much in the past two or three decades. United Architects uses standard practices of com-

1. John Y. Lee, "Investing in New Technology to Stay Competitive," *Management Accounting*, Institute of Management Accountants, June 1991, pp. 45–48.

puting the accounting rate of return or the payback period. In addition, it uses the net present value method to account for the time value of money. But remaining competitive in the world's marketplace means staying on the cutting edge in the use and mastery of the latest technology in the field, and standard capital budgeting decision practices do not always yield optimal results. United Architects recently experienced such a problem when it purchased a new computer-aided design system. The company opted initially to purchase an inexpensive model of computer-aided design and drafting equipment, a stand-alone personal computer system. Standard capital expenditure analyses yielded positive decision numbers because of the equipment's low cost. But competitors purchased top-of-the-line equipment, mainframe systems that had state-of-the-art programming capabilities. These companies began winning major contracts that UAI was also bidding for. Why? Because the potential customers were very impressed with the competitors' computer technology, especially their ability to render three-dimensional structural designs. What change in the capital expenditure decision analysis would support a decision to purchase the more advanced technology?

New technology is expensive and most standard capital expenditure analyses do not identify such projects as good investments because it is difficult to quantify a "competitive edge." Controller Pete Lone at United Architects, Inc. found a solution to this problem. He incorporated a factor for business gained by purchasing the equipment into his capital budgeting model. He measured this factor by the estimated increase in the contribution margin that the new piece of equipment would generate. In addition to all of the normal cash inflows and outflows, Lone added a cash inflow representing competitiveness into the net present value model. His management accepted this solution, and UAI again is in the running for major architectural contracts.

The new globally competitive business environment has changed capital expenditure decisions. When evaluating investments that enable a firm to challenge its competition, the question managers must ask is: Do we make this major investment or do we go out of business? Meeting a target rate of return means little when you cannot afford to pay your employees. Because no decision formula should be followed blindly, the health and sometimes the survival of a company depend on people, like Pete Lone, who adjust existing decision models to incorporate current business conditioning. He made a difference and probably saved his company's future. ■

The Capital Expenditure Decision Process

OBJECTIVE 1
Describe the capital expenditure decision process and identify the steps in the capital expenditure decision cycle

Among the most significant decisions facing management are those called **capital expenditure decisions**. These are decisions about when and how much to spend on capital facilities. A capital facility could include machinery, systems, or processes; building additions, renovations, or new structures; or entire new divisions or product lines. Thus, decisions about installing new equipment, replacing old equipment, expanding the production area by adding to a building, buying or building a new factory, or acquiring another company are all examples of capital expenditure decisions. Spending on capital assets is expensive. A new factory or production system may cost millions of dollars and require several years to implement. Managers must make capital expenditure decisions carefully to select the alternative that contributes the most to profits.

Capital Budgeting: A Cooperative Venture

The process of making decisions about capital expenditures is called **capital budgeting**, or **capital expenditure decision analysis**. It consists of identifying the need for a capital facility, analyzing courses of action to meet the need, preparing reports for managers, choosing the best alternative, and rationing capital expenditure funds among competing needs. People in every part of the organization participate in capital budgeting. Financial analysts supply a target cost of capital or desired rate of return and an estimate of how much money can be spent annually on capital facilities. Marketing specialists predict sales trends and new product demands. This identifies operations that need expansion or new equipment. Management personnel at all levels help identify facility needs and often prepare preliminary cost estimates of the desired capital expenditure. These same people implement the project selected and try to keep results within revenue and cost estimates.

The management accountant gathers and organizes the decision information into a workable, readable form. Generally, he or she applies one or more decision evaluation methods to the information gathered for each alternative. The most common of these methods are (1) the accounting rate-of-return method, (2) the payback period method, and (3) the net present value method. Once these methods have been applied, management can make a choice based on the criteria used for the decision. But before we can focus on the evaluation of capital expenditure proposals using each of these methods, we must explore the decision cycle, desired rate of return measures, and cost and revenue measures relevant to this decision process.

The Capital Expenditure Decision Cycle

The capital expenditure decision process involves the evaluation of alternate proposals for large capital expenditures, including considerations for financing the projects. Referred to earlier as capital budgeting, capital expenditure decision analyses affect both short-term and long-term planning activities of management. Figure 24-1 illustrates the time span of the capital expenditure planning process. Most companies have developed a long-term plan, either a five- or ten-year projection of operations. Large capital expenditures should be an integral part of a long-term plan. Anticipated additions or changes to a product line, replacements of equipment, and acquisitions of other companies are examples of items to be included in long-term capital expenditure plans. In addition, capital expenditure needs may arise from changes in current operations and may not be part of the company's long-term plan.[2]

The chapter on the budgeting process discussed the master budget. One of the period budgets in the master budget is a capital expenditure budget. The capital expenditure budget must fit into the planning process and the capital expenditure decision process. Long-term plans are not very specific; they are expressed in broad, goal-oriented terms. Each annual budget must help accomplish long-term plans. Look again at Figure 24-1. In 1995, the company plans to purchase a large, special-purpose machine. When the ten-year plan was developed, only a broad statement about a plan to purchase the machine was included. There was nothing in the ten-year plan concerning the cost of the machine or the anticipated operating details and costs. The annual master

2. The comments in this section are summarized from Henry R. Anderson and Rickard P. Schwartz, "The Capital Facility Decision." Reprinted from *Management Accounting*. Copyright by Institute of Management Accountants, Montvale, N.J. February 1971.

Figure 24-1. Time Span of Capital Expenditure Planning Process

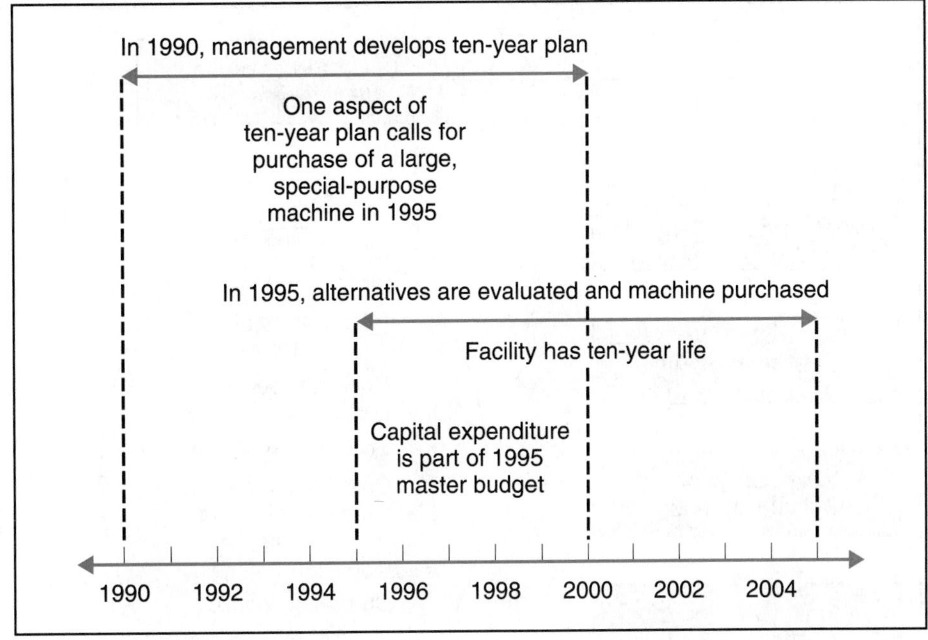

budget for 1995 contains this detailed information. And it is in 1995 that the capital expenditure decision analysis will occur. So, even though capital expenditure decisions that will affect the company for many years are discussed and estimates of future revenues and expenditures are made, the analysis is for the current period. This point is often confusing and needs to be emphasized here so the remainder of the chapter can be studied in the proper perspective. When you have finished this chapter, you will have also completed the master budget structured in the chapter on the budgeting process.

Evaluating capital expenditure proposals, deciding on proposals to be authorized, and implementing capital expenditures are long, involved procedures. Figure 24-2 depicts the capital expenditure decision cycle. The management accountant's primary responsibilities in the decision process center on three functions: (1) final evaluation of proposals, (2) methods of evaluation, and (3) postcompletion audit. The first two functions use proposal evaluation methods described later in this chapter. But the management accountant also has related responsibilities in other areas of the decision process. Figure 24-2 places the various phases of capital expenditure planning in perspective. The following paragraphs discuss each phase of that process.

Environmental Factors. The capital expenditure decision cycle occurs within a defined time period and under constraints imposed by economic policies, conditions, and objectives originating at corporate, industry, and/or national levels. Coordinating short- and long-term capital investment plans within this dynamic environment is management's responsibility, and it is vital to profitable operations.

Detection of Capital Facility Needs. Identifying the need for a new capital facility is the starting point of the decision process. Ideas for capital investment opportunities may originate from past sales experience, changes in sources and

Figure 24-2. The Capital Expenditure Decision Cycle

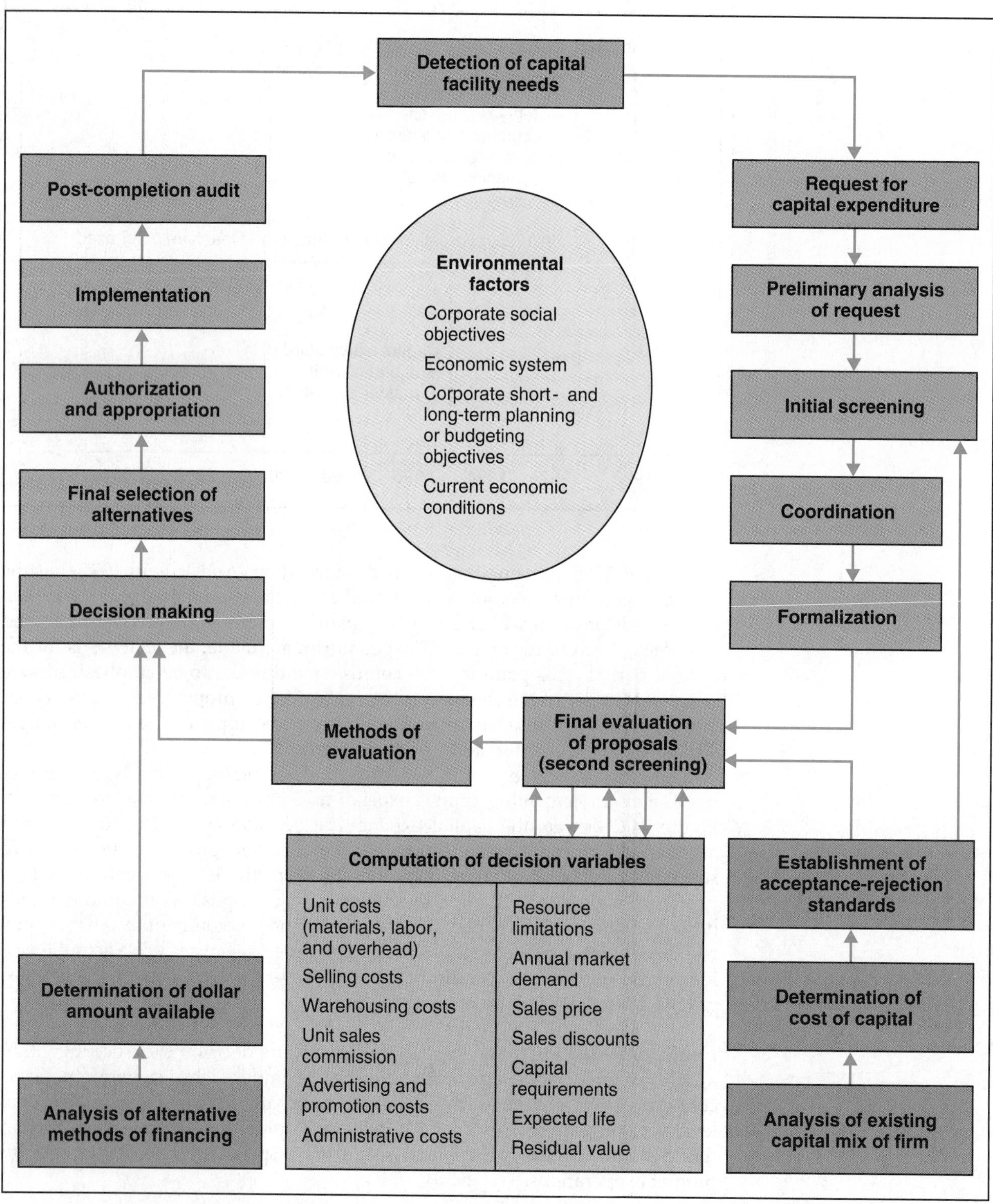

Source: Henry R. Anderson and Rickard P. Schwartz, "The Capital Facility Decision," *Management Accounting,* Institute of Management Accountants, February 1971, p. 30. Used by permission.

quality of raw materials, managerial suggestions, production bottlenecks caused by obsolete equipment, new production or distribution methods, or personnel complaints. In addition, capital facility needs are identified through proposals to

1. Add new products to the product line
2. Expand capacity in existing product lines
3. Reduce costs in production of existing products without altering operation levels
4. Automate existing production processes

Request for Capital Expenditure. To facilitate control over capital expenditures, the appropriate manager prepares a formal request for a capital expenditure. The proposed request should include a complete description of the facility under review, reasons a new facility is needed, alternate means of satisfying the need, estimated costs and related cost savings for each alternative, and engineering specifications.

Preliminary Analysis of Requests. In a large company with a highly developed capital expenditure decision process, information contained in requests for a capital expenditure is often verified before initial screening of proposals. The management accountant plays a major role in this activity by helping to identify undesirable or nonqualifying proposals, computational errors, and deficiencies in request information.

Initial Screening. Initial screening processes are used by companies with several branch plants and a highly developed program for capital expenditures. The objective of initial screening is to ensure that the only proposals going forward for further review are those meeting both company objectives and the minimum desired rate of return established by management.

Acceptance-Rejection Standards. When there are many requests for capital expenditures and limited funds for capital investment, one must establish some acceptance-rejection standard. Such a standard may be expressed as a minimum desired rate of return or as a minimum cash-flow payback period. As shown in Figure 24-2, acceptance-rejection standards are used in the screening processes to identify projects expected to yield inadequate or marginal returns. This step also identifies proposed projects with high demand and return expectations. Cost of capital information is often used to establish minimum desired rates of return on investment. Developing these rates is discussed in detail later in this chapter.

Coordination and Formalization. Before the final screening of proposed projects, alternate proposals must be coordinated and formalized for the decision maker. Coordination involves relating proposed projects to company objectives. Formalization is concerned with structuring the expenditure request to highlight its advantages and to summarize cost-benefit information for top management. Department or division managers often compete for limited capital expenditure funds. The more convincing a capital expenditure request is, the more likely it is to receive final authorization.

Final Evaluation of Proposals. Final evaluation of proposals involves verifying decision variables and applying capital expenditure proposal evaluation methods. The management accountant is the person primarily responsible for these procedures. Figure 24-2 lists several variables that may be relevant to a capital expenditure request. Generally, the variables in capital facility decisions are (1) project life, (2) estimated cash flow, and (3) investment cost. Each variable in a proposal should be checked for accuracy.

Methods of Evaluation. Techniques used for proposal evaluation include the accounting rate-of-return method, the payback period method, and the net present value method. Using management's minimum acceptance-rejection standard as a cut-off point, the management accountant evaluates all proposals, using one or more evaluation methods. The approach selected should be used consistently to facilitate project comparison.

Final Selection of Alternatives. After passing through the final screening process, acceptable capital expenditure requests are given to management for final review. Before deciding which requests to implement, management must consider the funds available for capital expenditures. Requests that have made it through screening and evaluation are ranked in order of profitability or payback potential. The final capital expenditure budget is then prepared by allocating funds to the selected proposals.

Authorization, Appropriation, and Implementation. Positive action by the board of directors on the proposed capital expenditure budget represents formal authorization. Such authorization includes the appropriation of the funds to acquire, construct, and/or install capital facilities. The implementation period begins with authorization and ends when the facility is operational.

Postcompletion Audit. The decision process does not end when the facility is operational. The accountant should perform a postcompletion audit for each project to evaluate the accuracy of forecasted results. Any weakness found in the decision process should be corrected to avoid the same problem in future decisions.

The postcompletion audit is a difficult decision step. To isolate how a decision affects a company's overall operating results requires extensive analysis. Only when an entire new plant is constructed can one isolate and identify relevant information and measure a facility's performance. The main problems in the postcompletion audit are that (1) long-term projects must be evaluated by concentrating on cash flows over the project's life, (2) a particular decision may influence the operations of existing facilities, and (3) profitability resulting from a decision may be difficult to isolate and identify.

Summary. The capital expenditure decision cycle is vital to managing a company. By making correct decisions about capital expenditures, management provides for the continued existence of the company. A series of incorrect decisions on capital expenditures could cause a company to fail. This topic by itself could fill several books. You will study various parts of the capital expenditure decision cycle in other business courses. Each exposure will help you to appreciate the importance of the decision process. In the remaining parts of this chapter, we look at aspects of a decision that are the responsibility of the management accountant, including the development of a minimum desired rate of return on investment, proposal evaluation methods, and ranking of acceptable proposals. The topic of postcompletion audit is a major responsibility of the management accountant. But as stated earlier, such a process is difficult, and its analysis will be left for a more advanced course in operational auditing.

Desired Rate of Return on Investment

OBJECTIVE 2
State the purpose of the minimum desired rate of return and identify the methods used to arrive at this rate

Choosing the best capital expenditure alternative is not always the approach taken in the decision-making process. Most companies have a set minimum rate of return, below which the expenditure request is automatically refused. If none of the capital expenditure requests is expected to meet the minimum desired rate of return, all requests will be turned down.

Why do companies use such a cutoff point? The idea is that if an expenditure request falls below the minimum rate of return, the funds can be used more profitably in another part of the company. Supporting poor-return proposals will lower the company's profitability later.

Deciding a company's minimum desired rate of return is not a simple task. Each measure that can be used to set a cutoff point has certain advantages. The most common measures used are (1) cost of capital, (2) corporate return on investment, (3) industry's average return on investment, and (4) bank interest rates. How to find the cost of capital is described in some detail, and then the use of other measures is briefly explained.

Cost of Capital Measures. Of all the measures for desired rates of return listed previously, cost of capital measures is the most widely used and discussed. The goal is to find the cost of financing the company's activities. However, to finance its activities, a company borrows funds and issues preferred and common stock. At the same time the company tries to operate at a profit. Each of these financing alternatives has a different cost rate. And each company uses a different mix of these sources to finance current and future operations.

To set a desired cutoff rate of return, management can use cost of debt, cost of preferred stock, cost of equity capital, or cost of retained earnings. In many cases a company will average these cost results to establish an **average cost of capital** measure. Sophisticated methods are used to compute these financial return measures.[3] But the purpose here is simply to identify measures used, so we present only a brief description of each type of cost of financing.

Cost of debt is the ratio of loan charges to net proceeds of the loan. The effects of income taxes and the present value of interest charges must be taken into account, but the rate is essentially the ratio of costs to loan proceeds. **Cost of preferred stock** is the stated dividend rate of the individual stock issue. Tax effects are unimportant in this case because dividends, unlike interest charges, are a nondeductible expense. **Cost of equity capital** is the rate of return to the investor and is computed by calculating net income as a percentage of invested capital. It is not just the dividend rate to the stockholder because management can raise or lower the dividend rate almost at will. This concept is very complex, but it has sound authoritative financial support.[4] **Cost of retained earnings** is the opportunity cost, or the dividends given up by the stockholder. Such a cost is linked closely with the cost of equity capital just described. The point is that a firm's cost of capital is hard to compute because it is a weighted average of the cost of various financing methods. However, this figure is the best estimate of a minimum desired rate of return.

Weighted average cost of capital is computed by first finding the cost rate for each source or class of capital-raising instrument. The second part of the computation is to figure the percentage of each source of capital to the company's

3. See David F. Scott, Jr., John D. Martin, J. William Petty, and Arthur J. Keown, "Cost of Capital," *Basic Financial Management*, 6th Edition (Englewood Cliffs, N.J.: Prentice-Hall, 1993), Chapter 8, pp. 265–281.
4. Ibid.

total debt and equity financing. Weighted average cost of capital is the sum of the products of each financing source's percentage multiplied by its cost rate. For example, assume the Uppsala Company's financing structure is as follows:

Cost Rate (Percentage)	Source of Capital	Amount	Capital Mix (Percentage of Each to Total)
10	Debt financing	$150,000	30
8	Preferred stock	50,000	10
12	Common stock	200,000	40
14	Retained earnings	100,000	20
	Totals	$500,000	100

Weighted average cost of capital of 11.4 percent would be computed the following way:

Source of Capital	Cost Rate	×	Ratio of Capital Mix	=	Portion of Weighted Average Cost of Capital
Debt financing	.10		.30		.030
Preferred stock	.08		.10		.008
Common stock	.12		.40		.048
Retained earnings	.14		.20		.028
Weighted average cost of capital					.114

Other Cutoff Measures. If cost of capital information is unavailable, management can use one of three less accurate but still useful amounts as the minimum desired rate of return. The first is average total corporate return on investment. The reasoning used to support such a measure is that any capital investment that produced a return lower than an amount earned historically by the company would negatively affect future operations. A second method is to use an industry's averages of the cost of capital. Most sizable industry associations supply such information. As a last resort, a company might use the current bank lending rate. But because most companies are both debt and equity financed, this rate seldom reflects an accurate rate of return.

Cost and Revenue Measures Used in Capital Budgeting

OBJECTIVE 3
Identify and explain the measures of projected costs and revenues used to evaluate capital expenditure decision alternatives

When evaluating a proposed capital expenditure, the management accountant must predict how the new asset will perform and how it will benefit the company. Various measures of costs and revenues are used to estimate the benefits to be derived from these projects. In this section we identify these measures and explain their relevance to the capital expenditure decision process. We also reveal measures that are not relevant to capital budgeting decision analysis but that are often incorporated into the decision process in error.

Net Income and Cash Flow. Each capital expenditure analysis must include a measure of the expected benefit from an investment project. For the accounting rate-of-return method, this measure is net income, calculated in the normal fashion. Increases in net income resulting from the capital expenditure must be determined for each alternative. All other methods of evaluating capital expenditure proposals use projected cash flows. **Net cash inflow**, the balance of increases in cash receipts over increases in cash payments resulting from the capital expenditure, is used in evaluating capital projects when either the payback period or the net present value method is employed. In some cases, equipment replacement decisions involve alternatives that do not increase current revenue. In these cases, cost savings measure the benefits resulting from the proposed capital investments. Both net cash flow and cost savings can be used as a basis for the evaluation, but you should not confuse one with the other. Each of the alternatives must be measured and evaluated consistently.

Equal Versus Unequal Cash Flows. Projected cash flows may be the same for each year of the asset's life or they may vary from year to year. Unequal cash flows are common and must be analyzed for each year of the asset's life. Proposed projects with equal annual cash flows require less detailed analysis. Evaluations for projects with both equal and unequal cash flows are illustrated and explained later in this chapter.

Book Value of Assets. **Book value** is the undepreciated portion of the original cost of a fixed asset. When evaluating a decision to replace an asset, the book value of the old asset is irrelevant since it is a past, or historical, cost and will not be altered by the decision. Net proceeds from the asset's sale or disposal are relevant, however, because the proceeds affect cash flows and may differ for each alternative. Gains or losses incurred in an exchange or sale of an old asset are also relevant, but only to the extent of their tax consequences. Gains or losses themselves (the difference between sales price and book value) do not involve cash but they do affect cash paid out in income taxes and are discussed in a later section.

Depreciation Expense. Since depreciation is a **noncash expense** requiring no cash outlay during the period, it is irrelevant to decision analyses based on cash flow. But, because depreciation expense reduces net income and income tax expense, the tax-related cash saving *is* relevant to cash-flow–based evaluations.

Disposal or Salvage Values. Proceeds from the sale of an old asset are current cash inflows and are relevant to evaluating capital expenditure decisions. Projected disposal or salvage values of replacement equipment are also relevant because these values represent future cash inflows and usually differ among alternatives. Remember, these salvage values will be received at the end of the asset's estimated life.

Capital Expenditure Evaluation Methods

Although many methods are used to evaluate capital expenditure proposals, the most common are (1) the accounting rate-of-return method, (2) the payback period method, and (3) the net present value approach, which is the most common discounted cash flow method. These three methods are discussed in the pages that follow.

Accounting Rate-of-Return Method

The **accounting rate-of-return method** is a crude but easy way to measure estimated performance of a capital investment. With this method, expected performance is measured using two variables: (1) estimated annual after-tax net

OBJECTIVE 4a
Evaluate capital expenditure proposals using the accounting rate-of-return method

income from the project and (2) average investment cost. The basic equation is as follows:

$$\text{Accounting rate of return} = \frac{\text{project's average annual after-tax net income}}{\text{average investment cost}}$$

To compute average annual after-tax net income, use the revenue and expense data prepared for evaluating the project. Average investment in the proposed capital facility is figured as follows:[5]

$$\text{Average investment} = \frac{\text{total investment} + \text{salvage value}}{2}$$

To demonstrate how this equation is used in a capital expenditure decision, assume the Boyce-Gordon Company is interested in purchasing a new bottling machine. The company's management will consider only those projects that promise to yield more than a 16 percent return. Estimates for the proposal include revenue increases of \$17,900 a year and operating cost increases of \$8,500 a year (including depreciation). The cost of the machine is \$51,000. Its salvage value is \$3,000. The company's income tax rate is 34 percent. Should the company invest in the machine? To answer the question, compute the accounting rate of return as follows:

$$\begin{aligned}\text{Accounting rate of return} &= \frac{(\$17{,}900 - \$8{,}500) \times .66}{(\$51{,}000 + \$3{,}000) \div 2} \\ &= \frac{\$6{,}204}{\$27{,}000} \\ &= \underline{\underline{22.98\,\%}}\end{aligned}$$

The projected rate of return is higher than the 16 percent minimum desired rate, so management should think seriously about making the investment.

This method is widely used because it is easy to understand and apply. It does have several disadvantages, however. First, because net income is averaged over the life of the investment, actual net income may vary and produce errors in earnings estimates. Second, the method is unreliable if estimated annual income differs from year to year. Finally, the time value of money is not considered in the computations. Thus, future and present dollars are treated as equal.

Cash Flow and the Payback Period Method

OBJECTIVE 4b
Evaluate capital expenditure proposals using the payback period method

Instead of measuring the rate of return on investments, many managers estimate the cash flow generated by a capital investment. Their goal is to determine the minimum time it will take to recover the initial investment. If two investment alternatives are being studied, management should choose the investment that pays back its initial cost in the shortest time. This period of time is known

5. The procedure of adding salvage value to the numerator may seem illogical. However, a fixed asset is never depreciated below its salvage value. Average investment is computed by determining the midpoint of the depreciable portion of the asset and adding back the salvage value. Another way of stating the above formula is

$$\text{Average investment} = \frac{\text{total investment} - \text{salvage value}}{2} + \text{salvage value}$$

Such a statement reduces to the formula used above.

as the payback period, and the method of evaluation is called the **payback period method**. You compute the payback period as follows:

$$\text{Payback period} = \frac{\text{cost of investment}}{\text{average annual net cash inflow}}$$

To apply the payback period method to the proposed capital investment of the Boyce-Gordon Company, determine the net cash flow. To do so, first find and eliminate the effects of all noncash revenue and expense items included in the analysis of net income. In this case, the only noncash expense or revenue is machine depreciation. To calculate this amount, you must know the asset's life and the depreciation method. Suppose the Boyce-Gordon Company uses the straight-line method of depreciation, and the new bottling machine will have a 10-year estimated service life. Using this information and the facts given earlier, the payback period is computed as follows:

$$\begin{aligned}\text{Annual depreciation} &= \frac{\text{cost} - \text{salvage value}}{10 \text{ (years)}}\\ &= \frac{\$51{,}000 - \$3{,}000}{10}\\ &= \$4{,}800 \text{ per year}\end{aligned}$$

$$\begin{aligned}\text{Payback period} &= \frac{\text{cost of machine}}{\text{cash revenue} - \text{cash expenses} - \text{taxes}}\\ &= \frac{\$51{,}000}{\$17{,}900 - (\$8{,}500 - \$4{,}800) - \$3{,}196^{*}}\\ &= \frac{\$51{,}000}{\$11{,}004}\\ &= \underline{\underline{4.6347}} \text{ years}\end{aligned}$$

*($17,900 – $8,500) × .34

If the company's desired payback period is five years or less, this proposal would be approved.

If a proposed capital expenditure has unequal annual net cash inflows, the payback period is determined by subtracting each annual amount (in chronological order) from the cost of the capital facility. When a zero balance is reached, you have determined the payback period. Often this will occur in the middle of a year. The portion of the final year is computed by dividing the amount needed to reach zero into the entire year's cash inflow. The Review Problem at the end of the chapter illustrates this process.

Like the accounting rate of return, the payback method is widely used because it is easy to compute and understand. However, the disadvantages of this approach far outweigh its advantages. First, the method does not measure profitability. Second, it ignores differences in the present values of cash flows from different periods; thus it does not adjust cash flows for the time value of money. Finally, the payback method emphasizes the time it takes to get out of the investment rather than the long-run return on the investment.

Time Value of Money

OBJECTIVE 5
Apply the concept of time value of money

Today there are many options for investing capital besides buying fixed assets. Consequently, management expects an asset to yield a reasonable return during its useful life. Capital expenditure decision analysis involves the evaluation of estimates of cash flows for several future time periods. It is unrealistic for cash flows from different periods to have the same values when measured in current dollars, so treating all future cash flows alike ignores the time value of money. Both the accounting rate-of-return and the payback period methods have this disadvantage.

The **time value of money** implies that cash flows of equal dollar amounts separated by an interval of time have different values. The values differ because of the effect of compound interest. For example, assume that Greg Shewman was awarded a $20,000 settlement in a lawsuit over automobile damages from an accident. The terms of the settlement dictate that the first payment of $10,000 is to be paid on December 31, 1994. The second $10,000 installment is due on December 31, 1998. What is the current (present) value of the total settlement on December 31, 1994? Assume that Shewman could earn 10 percent interest on his current funds. To compute the present value of the settlement, you must go to Table 3 in the appendix on future value and present value tables. There you will find the multiplier for four years at 10 percent, which is 0.683. The settlement's present value is computed as:

Present value of first payment on Dec. 31, 1994	$10,000
Present value of second payment to be received on Dec. 31, 1998 ($10,000 × .683)	6,830
Present value of the total settlement	$16,830

If Shewman had the choice of (1) accepting the $20,000 settlement as offered or (2) receiving $16,830 today as total compensation for the lawsuit, he would be indifferent.

As seen, the $10,000 to be received in four years is not worth $10,000 today. If funds can be invested to earn 10 percent interest, then each $1 to be received in four years is worth only $0.683 today. To prove the indifference statement above, look at the value of the total settlement to Shewman on December 31, 1998 for each choice. In this analysis, Table 1 in the appendix on future value and present value tables is used because this example deals with future values based on compounding of interest.

(1) Accepting the $20,000 settlement as offered	
December 31, 1994 payment after earning four years of interest income @ 10% annual rate ($10,000 × 1.464)	$14,640.00
December 31, 1998 payment	10,000.00
Total amount at December 31, 1998	$24,640.00
(2) Receiving $16,830 on 12/31/94 as total compensation for the lawsuit December 31, 1994 payment after earning four years of interest income @ 10% annual rate ($16,830 × 1.464)	$24,639.12*

*Difference due to rounding.

The analysis above was based on single payments received either today or on a future date. Now, assume that Debbie Trapani was just told that she won the lottery. Her winnings are $1,000,000, to be paid in $50,000 amounts at the end of each of the next twenty years. If she could choose to receive the value of the winnings today and earn 9 percent interest on her savings, how much should she settle for? Since a series of payments is being dealt with, you must use Table 4 in the appendix on future value and present value tables to locate the applicable multiplier of 9.129, which represents the discounting of twenty future payments back to the present assuming a 9 percent rate-of-return factor.

Present value of twenty annual future payments of $50,000 commencing one year from now assuming a 9% interest factor is used ($50,000 × 9.129)	$456,450

In other words, Debbie would be indifferent if given the choice of (1) receiving $1,000,000 in twenty future annual installments of $50,000 each or (2) receiving $456,450 today. To prove this point, determine the future value of the two alternatives by using data from Table 2 in the appendix on future value and present value tables. Such data are used because this example deals with a series of future payments and the compounding of interest on those payments.

(1) Receiving $1,000,000 in twenty future annual installments of $50,000 each ($50,000 × 51.16)	$2,558,000.00
(2) Receiving $456,450 today, using Table 1 because you are dealing with a single payment ($456,450 × 5.604)	$2,557,945.80*

*Difference due to rounding.

When dealing with the time value of money, use compounding to find the future value of an amount now held. To find the present value of an amount to be received, use discounting.

When determining future values, you should refer to Tables 1 and 2, in the appendix on future value and present value tables. To determine present values of future amounts of money, use Tables 3 and 4 in the appendix on future value and present value tables. Also, remember that Tables 1 and 3 deal with a single payment or amount, whereas Tables 2 and 4 are used for a series of equal annual amounts. There are additional exercises in the appendix on the time value of money if you need more practice.

Net Present Value Method

OBJECTIVE 6
Evaluate capital expenditure proposals using the net present value method

Managers expect a capital asset to yield returns for its entire useful life. Capital budgeting techniques that treat cash flows in each period as if they have the same value in current dollars do not properly value the returns from the investment. In other words, capital budgeting techniques like the accounting rate-of-return method and the payback period method ignore the time value of money.

The net present value method helps overcome the disadvantages of the accounting rate-of-return and payback period methods in evaluating capital investment alternatives. By using the present value tables in the appendix on future value and present value tables, you can discount future cash flows back to the present. This approach to capital investment analysis is called the **net present value method**. Multipliers used to find the present value of a future cash flow are in the present value tables. Which multipliers to use is determined by connecting the minimum desired rate of return and the life of the asset or length of time for which the amount is being discounted. Each cash inflow and cash outflow to be realized over the life of the asset is discounted back to the present. If the present value of all expected future net cash inflows is greater than the amount of the current investment, the expenditure meets the minimum desired rate of return, and the project should be carried out.

The net present value method is used differently depending on whether annual cash flows are equal or unequal. If all annual net cash flows (inflows less outflows) are equal, the discount factor to be used comes from Table 4 of the appendix on future value and present value tables. This table gives multipliers for the present value of $1 received each period for a given number of periods. One computation will cover the cash flows of all periods involved. If, however, expected cash inflows and outflows differ from one year to the next, each year's cash flow amount must be individually discounted back to the present. Discount factors used in this kind of analysis are found in Table 3 of the same appendix. Multipliers in this table are used to find the present value of $1 to be received (or paid out) at the end of a given number of periods.

The following example shows the difference in the present value analysis of expenditures with equal and unequal cash flows. Suppose the Keys Metal Products Company is deciding which of two stamping machines to buy. The blue machine has equal expected annual net cash inflows and the black machine has unequal annual amounts. Information on the two machines follows:

	Blue Machine	Black Machine
Purchase price: January 1, 19x4	$16,500	$16,500
Salvage value	—	—
Expected life	5 years	5 years
Estimated net cash inflows		
19x4	$5,000	$6,000
19x5	$5,000	$5,500
19x6	$5,000	$5,000
19x7	$5,000	$4,500
19x8	$5,000	$4,000

The company's minimum desired rate of return is 16 percent. Which—if either—of the two alternatives should be chosen?

The evaluation process is shown in Exhibit 24-1. The analysis of the blue machine is easier to prepare because it generates equal annual cash flows. Present value of net cash inflows for the five-year period for the blue machine is found by first locating the appropriate multiplier in Table 4 of the appendix on future value and present value tables, using the 16 percent minimum desired rate of return and a five-year life. The factor of 3.274 is then multiplied by $5,000, yielding $16,370, the present value of the total cash inflows from the blue machine. Comparing this figure with the $16,500 purchase price results in a negative net present value of $130.

Analysis of the black machine gives a different result. Multipliers for this part of the analysis are found by using the same 16 percent rate. But five multipliers must be used, one for each year of the asset's life. Table 3 in the appendix on future value and present value tables applies here since each annual amount must be discounted back to the present. For the black machine, the $16,851.50 present value of net cash inflows is more than the $16,500.00 purchase price of the machine. Thus, there is a positive net present value of $351.50.

A positive net present value means the return on the asset exceeds the 16 percent minimum desired rate of return. A negative figure means the rate of return is below the minimum cutoff point. In the Keys Metal Products case, the right decision would be to purchase the black machine.

Incorporating the time value of money into the evaluation of capital expenditure proposals is the major advantage of the net present value method. This method also measures total cash flows from the investment over its useful life, so total profitability can be brought into the analysis as well. The major disad-

Exhibit 24-1. Net Present Value Analysis: Equal Versus Unequal Cash Flows

Keys Metal Products Company Capital Expenditure Analysis 19x4	
Blue Machine	
Present value of cash inflows: ($5,000 × 3.274)	$16,370.00
Less purchase price of machine	16,500.00
Negative net present value	$ (130.00)
Black Machine	
Present value of cash inflows:	
19x4 ($6,000 × .862)	$ 5,172.00
19x5 ($5,500 × .743)	4,086.50
19x6 ($5,000 × .641)	3,205.00
19x7 ($4,500 × .552)	2,484.00
19x8 ($4,000 × .476)	1,904.00
Total	$16,851.50
Less purchase price of machine	16,500.00
Positive net present value	$ 351.50

Note: If a piece of equipment has a salvage value at the end of its useful life, the present value of that amount needs to be computed in order to determine the present value of all future net cash inflows. This technique is demonstrated in the chapter's Review Problem.

vantage of the net present value method is that the computations are more difficult than those for the payback period or the rate-of-return methods.

Income Taxes and Business Decisions

Tax Effects on Capital Expenditure Decisions

OBJECTIVE 7
Analyze capital expenditure decision alternatives that incorporate the effects of income taxes

The capital budgeting techniques discussed compare the relative benefits of proposed capital expenditures by measuring the cash receipts and payments for a project. Income taxes alter the amount and timing of cash flows of projects under consideration by for-profit companies. To assess the benefits of a capital project, you must include the effects of taxes in capital expenditure analysis.

Corporate income tax rates range from 15 percent on income under $50,000 to 35 percent on income of more than $18,333,333.

Taxable Income	Tax Rate
$0 to $50,000	15%
$50,000 to $75,000	$7,500 + 25% of amount over $50,000
$75,000 to $100,000	$13,750 + 34% of amount over $75,000
$100,000 to $335,000	$22,250 + 39% of amount over $100,000
$335,000 to $10,000,000	$113,900 + 34% of amount over $335,000
$10,000,000 to $15,000,000	$3,496,650 + 35% of amount over $10,000,000
$15,000,000 to $18,333,333	$5,246,650 + 38% of amount over $15,000,000
Over $18,333,333	$6,513,317 + 35% of amount over $18,333,333

Tax rates change yearly. To demonstrate the effect of taxes on capital expenditure decision analysis, we assume a tax rate of 34 percent on taxable income.

Suppose a project makes the following annual contribution to net income:

Cash revenues	$ 400,000
Cash expenses	(200,000)
Depreciation	(100,000)
Income before taxes	$ 100,000
Income taxes at 34%	(34,000)
Income after taxes	$ 66,000

Annual cash flow for this project can be determined by two procedures:

1. Cash flow—receipts and disbursements	
Revenues (cash inflow)	$ 400,000
Cash expenses (outflow)	(200,000)
Income taxes (outflow)	(34,000)
Net cash inflow	$ 166,000

2. Cash flow—income adjustment procedure	
Income after taxes	$ 66,000
Add noncash expenses (depreciation)	100,000
Less noncash revenues	—
Net cash inflow	$ 166,000

In both computations the net cash inflow is $166,000, and the total effect of income taxes is to lower the net cash flow by $34,000.

A closer look at income taxes reveals their two-sided effect on cash flows. First, income taxes reduce cash inflows from the receipt of revenues and proceeds from the sale of assets. Second, income taxes have the effect of reducing the amounts of potential expenses (cash outflows). Analyses of capital expenditures must include both effects.

Consider first the relationship between income taxes and cash inflows. Revenues and gains from the sale of equipment increase taxable income and tax payments. When evaluating cash inflows, you must distinguish between a gain on the sale of an asset and the proceeds received from the sale. *Gains* are the amount received over and above the book value of the asset; *proceeds* include the whole sales price and represent the cash inflow. Gains are not cash-flow items, but they do raise tax payments. If a company sells equipment with a book value of $80,000 for $180,000 in cash, it realizes a gain of $100,000. Assuming that this gain is taxable at 34 percent,[6] the cash flow is analyzed as follows:

Proceeds from sale		$180,000
Gain on sale	$100,000	
Corporate tax rate	× .34	
Cash outflow (tax increase)		(34,000)
Net cash inflow		$146,000

The relationship among income tax, expenses, and cash flow is less obvious. Cash expenses lower net income and result in cash outflows only to the extent that they exceed related tax reductions. This generalization is true for both cash operating expenses and losses on the sale of fixed assets. The examples on the top of the next page show the cash-flow effects of increases in both cash and noncash expenses and of losses on the sale of equipment.

6. Capital gains are currently taxable at the same rates as ordinary income.

Cash expenses		
Increase in cash operating expenses	$100,000	
Less tax reduction at 34%	34,000	
Net increase in cash outflow	$ 66,000	
Noncash expenses		
Annual depreciation expense	$200,000	
Corporate tax rate	× .34	
Tax reduction = cash savings	$ 68,000	
Loss on the sale of an asset		
Proceeds from sale		$150,000
Loss on sale	$100,000	
Corporate tax rate	× .34	
Reduction of taxes and cash outflow		34,000
Total cash inflow resulting from sale		$184,000

Notice that depreciation expense is not a cash-flow item, but it does provide a cash benefit equal to the amount of the reduction in taxes. Losses on the sale of fixed assets are also not cash-flow items, but they provide a cash benefit by reducing the amount of taxes to be paid in cash. For illustrations of the above ideas, see the Review Problem at the end of this chapter.

Income taxes affect the results of all capital expenditure analyses. Gains from the sale of assets increase taxes; noncash expenditures (depreciation) and losses from the sale of assets decrease taxes. Therefore, the tax impact must be analyzed for all capital investment decision variables.

Minimizing Taxes Through Planning

Businesses can minimize their tax liability in several ways. Taxation rates can be reduced in some instances by timing transactions so they fall in a given year. A corporation that is nearing a change in tax brackets for the year may elect to delay an income-producing job until after year end to avoid the higher tax rate. Or the timing of certain expenditures may be changed for the same reason. The timing of transactions involving depreciable business assets may also reduce tax liability.

A second way of minimizing tax liability is to take advantage of provisions in the tax law that give preferential treatment to certain investments and spending. The tax law often is used to encourage investment in industries important for national goals. Because these goals change over the years, the tax law has been used to promote everything from emergency war equipment to pollution-control devices. Special credits are also allowed for spending that lowers unemployment or encourages the hiring of such underemployed groups as the handicapped. Therefore, business owners or managers should keep up with current tax laws so that they can maximize their return on investment.

Ranking Capital Expenditure Proposals

OBJECTIVE 8
Rank proposals competing for limited capital expenditure funds

Generally, a company's requests for capital funds exceed the amount of dollars available for capital expenditures. Even after proposals have been evaluated and selected under minimum desired acceptance-rejection standards, there are normally too many to fund adequately. At that point the proposals must be ranked according to their rates of return or profitability. A second selection process is then imposed.

Assume that five acceptable proposals are competing for the same limited capital expenditure funds. London Enterprises has $4,500,000 to spend this year in capital improvements. It currently uses an 18 percent minimum desired rate of return. Following are the proposals under review:

Project	Rate of Return (Percentage)	Capital Expenditure
A	32	$1,460,000
B	30	1,890,000
C	28	460,000
D	24	840,000
E	22	580,000
Total		$5,230,000

How would you go about selecting the capital expenditure proposals to be implemented for the year? Projects A, B, and C are obvious contenders, and their combined dollar needs total $3,810,000. There are $690,000 in capital funds remaining. Project D should be examined to see if it can be implemented for $150,000 less. If not, then Project E should be selected. The selection of projects A, B, C, and E means there will be $110,000 in uncommitted capital expenditure funds for the year.

Capital Expenditure Decisions in a Globally Competitive Business Environment

OBJECTIVE 9
Identify qualitative information designed to improve the capital expenditure decision process in today's globally competitive business environment

In the capital expenditure evaluation methods described earlier in this chapter, the objective underlying the decision was to either meet or surpass a stated target rate of return on the investment or to meet or surpass a stated period of time needed to recoup the initial investment. The only factors used in the decision were those that could be quantified and used in the evaluation process. In the past five years, companies have begun to question the reliability of these traditional capital expenditure evaluation methods. Managers have turned down proposed investments in new technology and computer-integrated manufacturing systems because the projects could not meet the desired minimum cut-off rates of return. Yet, without this new technology, these same companies will become less competitive because other companies in their industry are able to make the investment.

The objective of a capital expenditure decision process has changed along with the technological changes in equipment. Companies now want to identify an optimal set of activities and resources that allow them to meet their strategic goals. They are striving to eliminate waste and to inject an atmosphere of continuous improvement within their organizations. In the case of United Architects, Inc. discussed in the Decision Point at the beginning of this chapter, buying a less expensive model because it meets an estimated rate of return on investment is not always the correct decision. The managers at United Architects found out the hard way that pleasing the customer is far more important than just meeting a target rate of return. Satisfying a customer means producing a quality product or service in a timely fashion and meeting projected delivery dates. To do this, a company must establish a high level of quality throughout the organization, be flexible so as to meet customer demand, and minimize throughput times (the time it takes to produce and deliver the goods to the customer). Yet when it comes to making capital expenditure decisions, how does one quantify decision elements such as quality, flexibility, and throughput time?

Capital investment decision analysis in today's globally competitive business environment should include both quantitative and qualitative factors. Each capital expenditure should be evaluated by its ability to meet the organization's total set of objectives, not just one objective such as the project's estimated rate of return on investment. Each decision should include an analysis of the proposed project's contributions to an increase in product or process quality, a decrease in the waste of resources or time, a decrease in production and delivery time, and an increase in customer satisfaction. Although more difficult, making capital expenditure decisions that include qualitative as well as quantitative factors will help ensure the company's competitive market position.

Chapter Review

Review of Learning Objectives

1. **Describe the capital expenditure decision process and identify the steps in the capital expenditure decision cycle.**
   Capital expenditure decisions are concerned with when and how much to spend on a company's capital facilities. The capital expenditure decision-making process, often referred to as capital budgeting, consists of identifying the need for a facility, analyzing courses of action to meet that need, preparing reports for management, choosing the best alternative, and rationing capital expenditure funds among competing resource needs.

   The capital expenditure decision cycle begins with detecting a facility's need. A proposal or request is then prepared and analyzed before being subjected to one or two screening processes, depending on the size of the business involved. Using various evaluation methods and a minimum desired rate of return, the proposal is determined to be either acceptable or unacceptable. If acceptable, the proposal is ranked with all other acceptable proposals. Total dollars available for capital investment are used to determine which of the ranked proposals to authorize and implement. The final step is a postcompletion audit to determine the accuracy of the forecasted data used in the decision cycle and to find out if some of the projections need corrective action.

2. **State the purpose of the minimum desired rate of return and identify the methods used to arrive at this rate.**
   The minimum desired rate of return acts as a screening mechanism by eliminating capital expenditure requests with anticipated low returns from further consideration. By using such an approach to decision making, many unprofitable requests are turned away or discouraged without a great deal of wasted executive time. The most common measures used to compute minimum desired rates of return include (1) cost of capital, (2) corporate return on investment, (3) industry's average return on investment, and (4) federal and bank interest rates. The weighted average cost of capital and average return on investment are the most widely used measures.

3. **Identify and explain the measures of projected costs and revenues used to evaluate capital expenditure decision alternatives.**
   The accounting rate-of-return method requires measures of net income. Other methods of evaluating capital expenditures evaluate net cash inflow or cash savings. The analysis process must estimate whether the cash flows are equal in each period or unequal. Book values and depreciation expense of assets awaiting replacement are irrelevant. Net proceeds from the sale of an old asset and estimated salvage value of a new facility represent future cash flows and must be part of the estimated benefit of a

project. Gains and losses on the sale of old assets and depreciation expense on replacment equipment change future cash flows because they affect cash payments for income taxes.

4. **Evaluate capital expenditure proposals using (a) the accounting rate-of-return method and (b) the payback period method.**
When using the accounting rate-of-return method to evaluate two or more capital expenditure proposals, the alternative that yields the highest ratio of net income after taxes to average cost of investment is chosen. When using the payback period method to evaluate a capital expenditure proposal, emphasis is on the shortest time period needed to recoup the original amount of the investment in cash.

5. **Apply the concept of time value of money.**
Time value of money implies that cash flows of equal dollar amounts at different times have different values because of the effect of compound interest. Of the evaluation methods discussed in this chapter, only the net present value method is based on the concept of time value of money.

6. **Evaluate capital expenditure proposals using the net present value method.**
The net present value method of evaluating capital expenditures depends on the time value of money. Present values of future cash flows are computed to see if they are greater than the current cost of the capital expenditure being evaluated.

7. **Analyze capital expenditure decision alternatives that incorporate the effects of income taxes.**
Income taxes affect the results of all capital expenditure analyses. Gains on the sale of assets increase taxes. Noncash expenditures (depreciation) and losses from the sale of assets decrease taxes. So, the impact of gains, losses, and noncash expenditures on the cash flows of the project must be examined in light of their tax consequences.

8. **Rank proposals competing for limited capital expenditure funds.**
When ranking capital expenditure proposals, acceptable projects are listed in their order of estimated rate of return. They are then authorized in their order of ranking until all capital expenditure funds appropriated for the year have been taken. If funds remain because the selection process was halted by a project too large to be funded, a smaller proposal, lower in priority, may be authorized.

9. **Identify qualitative information designed to improve the capital expenditure decision process in today's globally competitive business environment.**
Qualitative information relating a capital investment's impact on product and process quality, production flexibility, customer satisfaction, and the reduction in time needed to complete the production and distribution cycles should be analyzed and incorporated into the capital expenditure decision analysis in addition to the relevant quantitative decision variables.

Review of Concepts and Terminology

The following concepts and terms were introduced in this chapter:

(L.O. 4) **Accounting rate-of-return method:** A capital investment evaluation method designed to measure the benefit of a potential capital project. It is calculated by dividing the project's average annual after-tax net income by the average cost of the investment.

(L.O. 2) **Average cost of capital:** A minimum desired rate of return on invested capital that is computed by taking an average of the cost of debt, the cost of preferred stock, the cost of equity capital, and the cost of retained earnings.

(L.O. 3) **Book value:** The undepreciated portion of the original cost of a fixed asset.

(L.O. 1) **Capital budgeting:** The process of making decisions about capital expenditures. It includes identifying the need for a capital facility, analyzing different courses of action to meet that need, preparing the reports for management, choosing the best alternative, and rationing capital expenditure funds among the competing capital projects. Also called *capital expenditure decision analysis.*

(L.O. 1) **Capital expenditure decisions:** Management decisions about when and how much to spend on capital facilities for the company.

(L.O. 2) **Cost of debt:** A minimum desired rate of return on invested capital that is computed as the ratio of loan charges to net proceeds of the loan.

(L.O. 2) **Cost of equity capital:** A minimum desired rate of return on invested capital that is computed by calculating net income as a percentage of invested capital.

(L.O. 2) **Cost of preferred stock:** A minimum desired rate of return on invested capital that is the stated dividend rate of the individual preferred stock issues.

(L.O. 2) **Cost of retained earnings:** A minimum desired rate of return on invested capital that is the opportunity cost, or the dividends given up by the common stockholders.

(L.O. 3) **Net cash inflow:** The balance of increases in cash receipts over increases in cash payments resulting from a proposed capital expenditure.

(L.O. 6) **Net present value method:** A capital investment evaluation method based on future cash flows that are discounted back to their present value before being used to support a capital expenditure decision; the net present value of the future cash flows is compared with the amount of the proposed expenditure to determine if the investment should or should not be made.

(L.O. 3) **Noncash expense:** An expense of the period that did not require a cash outlay during the period under review.

(L.O. 4) **Payback period method:** A capital investment evaluation method that bases the decision to invest in capital equipment on the minimum length of time it will take to get back in cash the amount of the initial investment.

(L.O. 5) **Time value of money:** The concept that cash flows of equal dollar amounts that are separated by a time interval have different present values because of the effect of compound interest.

Self-Test

Test your knowledge of the chapter by choosing the best answer for each of the following items.

(L.O. 1) 1. The process of identifying the need for a facility, analyzing different courses of action to meet the need, preparing the reports for management, choosing the best alternative, and rationing capital expenditure funds among the competing capital resource projects is the definition of
   a. special order budgeting.
   b. payback period budgeting.
   c. sales mix budgeting.
   d. capital budgeting.

(L.O. 1) 2. Identify the one statement that does *not* represent a step in the capital expenditure decision cycle.
   a. Create a form for data entry.
   b. Establish the acceptance-rejection standards.
   c. Conduct a postcompletion audit.
   d. Evaluate the proposals.

(L.O. 2) 3. The ratio of loan charges to net proceeds of the loan is the definition of
   a. cost of equity capital.
   b. cost of preferred stock.
   c. average cost of capital.
   d. cost of debt.

(L.O. 3) 4. Which of the following pieces of information is not relevant when evaluating a capital investment proposal?
   a. Salvage value of the new capital asset
   b. Book value of the capital asset being replaced
   c. Net cash flow from the proposal
   d. Cost savings from the proposal

(L.O. 4) 5. A capital expenditure evaluation method based on the minimum length of time it will take to get back in cash the initial investment is known as the
a. make-or-buy method.
b. payback period method.
c. accounting rate-of-return method.
d. net present value method.

(L.O. 4) 6. Mecca Enterprises is contemplating a major investment in a new flexible manufacturing system (FMS). The company's minimum desired accounting rate of return is 16 percent. The total investment is $2,500,000 with a 10 percent salvage value at the end of its eight-year expected life. The company uses straight-line depreciation. The FMS should produce $1,400,000 of additional cash revenue annually. Annual cash operating costs are expected to be $600,000. The company is in the 34 percent tax bracket. Using the accounting rate-of-return method, what is the expected after-tax rate of return from the proposed FMS project?
a. 38.4%
b. 26.6%
c. 24.9%
d. 19.2%

(L.O. 4) 7. Assuming the same facts as in question **6,** and using the payback period method, what is the expected after-tax payback period for the proposed FMS project?
a. 3.625 years
b. 3.125 years
c. 3.954 years
d. 4.009 years

(L.O. 6) 8. Assuming the same facts as in question **6,** and using the net present value method, what is the expected after-tax net present value of the proposed FMS project?
a. Positive net present value of $1,051,450
b. Negative net present value of $12,455
c. Positive net present value of $285,277
d. Negative net present value of $62,235

(L.O. 4, 6) 9. Which of the following is not a capital expenditure evaluation method?
a. Make-or-buy method
b. Payback period method
c. Accounting rate-of-return method
d. Net present value method

(L.O. 5) 10. That cash flows of equal dollar amounts separated by an interval of time have different values is the concept of the
a. money value of time.
b. cost of debt.
c. time value of money.
d. average cost of capital.

Answers to the Self-Test are at the end of this chapter.

Review Problem
Tax Effects on a Capital Expenditure Decision

(L.O. 3, 4, 5, 6, 7) The Harold Construction Company specializes in developing large shopping centers. The company is considering the purchase of a new earth-moving machine and has gathered the following information:

Purchase price	$600,000
Salvage value	$100,000
Useful life	4 years
Effective tax rate*	34%
Depreciation method	Straight-line

*All company operations combined result in a 34 percent tax rate. Because of this, do not use specific tax rates in the tax schedule.

Desired before-tax payback period	3 years
Desired after-tax payback period	4 years
Minimum before-tax accounting rate of return	15%
Minimum after-tax accounting rate of return	9%

The before-tax cash flow estimates are as follows:

Year	Revenues	Costs	Net Cash Flow
1	$ 500,000	$260,000	$240,000
2	450,000	240,000	210,000
3	400,000	220,000	180,000
4	350,000	200,000	150,000
Totals	$1,700,000	$920,000	$780,000

Required

1. Using before-tax information, analyze the Harold Construction Company's investment in the new earth-moving machine. In your analysis use (a) the accounting rate-of-return method, (b) the payback period method, and (c) the net present value method.
2. Repeat **1** above using after-tax information.
3. Summarize your findings from **1** and **2.**

Answer to Review Problem

1. Before-tax calculations

The increase in net income is as follows:

Year	Before-Tax Net Cash Flow	Depreciation	Income Before Taxes
1	$240,000	$125,000	$115,000
2	210,000	125,000	85,000
3	180,000	125,000	55,000
4	150,000	125,000	25,000
Totals	$780,000	$500,000	$280,000

1a. (Before-tax) Accounting rate-of-return method

$$\text{Accounting rate of return} = \frac{\text{average annual net income}}{\text{average investment cost}}$$

$$= \frac{\$280{,}000 \div 4}{(\$600{,}000 + \$100{,}000) \div 2} = \frac{\$70{,}000}{\$350{,}000}$$

$$= 20\ \%$$

1b. (Before-tax) Payback period method

Total cash investment		$600,000
Less cash-flow recovery		
Year 1	$240,000	
Year 2	210,000	
Year 3 ($\frac{5}{6}$ of $180,000)	150,000	(600,000)
Unrecovered investment		0

Payback period: 2.833 ($2\frac{5}{6}$) years, or 2 years 10 months

1c. (Before-tax) Net present value method (multipliers are from Table 3 of the appendix on future value and present value tables)

Year	Net Cash Flow	Present-Value Multiplier	Present Value
1	$240,000	.870	$208,800
2	210,000	.756	158,760
3	180,000	.658	118,440
4	150,000	.572	85,800
4	100,000 (salvage)	.572	57,200
Total present value			$629,000
Less cost of original investment			600,000
Positive net present value			$ 29,000

2. After-tax calculations

The increase in net income after taxes is:

Year	Before-Tax Net Cash Flow	Depreciation	Income Before Taxes	Taxes (34%)	Income After Taxes
1	$240,000	$125,000	$115,000	$39,100	$ 75,900
2	210,000	125,000	85,000	28,900	56,100
3	180,000	125,000	55,000	18,700	36,300
4	150,000	125,000	25,000	8,500	16,500
Totals	$780,000	$500,000	$280,000	$95,200	$184,800

The after-tax cash flow is as follows:

Year	Net Cash Flow Before Taxes	Taxes	Net Cash Flow After Taxes
1	$240,000	$39,100	$200,900
2	210,000	28,900	181,100
3	180,000	18,700	161,300
4	150,000	8,500	141,500
Totals	$780,000	$95,200	$684,800

2a. (After-tax) Accounting rate-of-return method

$$\text{Accounting rate of return} = \frac{\text{average annual after-tax net income}}{\text{average investment cost}}$$

$$= \frac{\$184{,}800 \div 4}{(\$600{,}000 + \$100{,}000) \div 2} = \frac{\$46{,}200}{\$350{,}000}$$

$$= 13.2\%$$

2b. (After-tax) Payback period method

Total cash investment		$600,000
Less cash-flow recovery		
Year 1	$200,900	
Year 2	181,100	
Year 3	161,300	
Year 4 (40.1% of $141,500)	56,700	(600,000)
Unrecovered investment		0

Payback period: 3.401 years

2c. (After-tax) Net present value method (multipliers are from Table 3 of the appendix on future value and present value tables)

Year	Net Cash Inflow After Taxes	Present-Value Multiplier	Present Value
1	$200,900	.917	$184,225
2	181,100	.842	152,486
3	161,300	.772	124,524
4	141,500	.708	100,182
4	100,000 (salvage)	.708	70,800
Total present value			$632,217
Less cost of original investment			600,000
Positive net present value			$ 32,217

3. Harold Construction Company: Summary of Decision Analysis

	Before-Tax		After-Tax	
	Desired	Predicted	Desired	Predicted
Accounting rate of return	15%	20%	9%	13.2%
Payback period	3 years	2.833 years	4 years	3.401 years
Net present value	—	$29,000	—	$32,217

Based on the calculations in **1** and **2,** Harold's proposed investment in the earth-moving machine meets all company criteria for such investments. Given these results, the company should invest in the machine.

Chapter Assignments

Questions

1. What is a capital expenditure? Give examples of some types of capital expenditures.
2. Define *capital budgeting.*
3. Discuss the interrelationship of the following steps in the capital expenditure decision cycle:
   a. Determination of dollar amount available
   b. Final selection of alternatives
   c. Final evaluation of proposals
4. What are some difficulties encountered in trying to implement the postcompletion audit step in the capital expenditure decision cycle?
5. Describe some approaches used by companies in arriving at a minimum desired rate of return for their acceptance-rejection standards in capital expenditure decision making.
6. What is the importance of equal versus unequal cash flows in capital expenditure decisions? Are they relevant to the accounting rate-of-return method? The payback period method? The net present value method?
7. What is a crude but easy method for evaluating capital expenditures? List the advantages and disadvantages of this method.
8. What is the formula used for determining payback period? Is this decision-measuring technique accurate? Defend your answer.
9. Distinguish between cost savings and net cash flow.
10. Discuss the statement, "To treat all future income flows alike ignores the time value of money."
11. Explain the relationship of compound interest to determination of present value.
12. What is the objective of using discounted cash flows?

13. "In using discounted cash-flow methods, the book value of an asset is irrelevant, whereas current and future salvage values are relevant." Is this statement valid? Defend your answer.
14. Why is depreciation of the old equipment ignored when evaluating equipment replacement decisions under the net present value method?
15. What is the role of cost of capital when using the net present value method to evaluate capital expenditure proposals?
16. Why is it important to consider income taxes when evaluating a capital expenditure proposal?
17. Marquez Company replaced a machine on January 2, 19x4. During that year, it generated net cash inflow from operations of $63,000 and noncash expenditures of $12,000. The sale of the old machine netted $54,000 in proceeds and involved a $20,000 capital gain. Using the 34 percent tax rate for normal income and for capital gains, compute the company's tax liability and cash flow for the year.
18. When selecting capital expenditure proposals for implementation, final ranking of proposals may not follow the order in which they were presented. Why?
19. "Satisfying a customer means producing a quality product or service in a timely fashion and meeting a projected delivery date." What relationship does this statement have with the capital expenditure decision process?

Communication Skills Exercises

Communication 24-1. Capital Expenditures to Control Hazardous Waste *(L.O. 1, 4)*

The Upjohn Company is a leading pharmaceutical company that uses thousands of chemicals considered to be hazardous.[7] The Superfund Amendments and Reauthorization Act of 1986 (SARA) requires companies to report their operating environmental discharges, and the Upjohn Company is in compliance. Assume that Chemical XOC, a hazardous material, requires a special building for its storage. In addition, your company must regularly monitor the chemical's condition and report it to government officials. (Some chemicals must be monitored as long as thirty years.) In groups of three or four people, decide how to account for the cost of (1) the special building and (2) tracking the chemical's condition. Should these costs be capitalized or expensed in the period incurred? Can they be traced to specific products for costing purposes or should they be included in factory overhead and divided among all products? Select a spokesperson who will report the group's findings to the class and defend your position.

Communication 24-2. Capital Investments in Computer-Integrated Manufacturing *(L.O. 6)*

Hurco, Inc. is a manufacturer of computer-controlled milling machines and other automated equipment.[8] Based in Indianapolis, Indiana, the company recently revamped its production facility and invested in a flexible computer-integrated manufacturing (FCIM) system. Investing in FCIM equipment creates a unique set of problems involving capital expenditure decisions. These systems, costing millions of dollars, provide the company with high-quality, state-of-the-art production capability and are essential if the company is to remain competitive. Key elements in the FCIM capital expenditure decision process include: quality, life cycle cost, just-in-time operations and customer delivery, and the ability to change from one product to the next rapidly. These are intangible considerations that are not easily quantifiable and, as a result, are virtually ignored by traditional accounting practices. Focusing on the quality element, prepare a one-page paper describing how increased product quality will lead to increased cash flow and profitability for the company. Explain how quality can be included in the net present value approach to capital expenditure decision analysis. Be prepared to share your views with the class.

7. Gale E. Newell, Jerry G. Kreuze, and Stephen J. Newell, "Accounting for Hazardous Waste," *Management Accounting,* Institute of Management Accountants, May 1990, pp. 58–61.
8. Thornton Parker and Theodore Lettes, "Is Accounting Standing in the Way of Flexible Computer-Integrated Manufacturing?" *Management Accounting,* Institute of Management Accountants, January 1991, pp. 34–38.

Communication 24-3. Ethics, Capital Expenditure Decisions, and the New Globally Competitive Business Environment *(L.O. 6, 9)*

Marvin Ditmer is controller of ***Belstar Corporation,*** a globally competitive producer of standard and custom-designed window units for the housing industry. As part of the corporation's move to become automated, Ditmer was asked to prepare a capital expenditure decision analysis for a robot-guided aluminum extruding and stamping machine. This machine would automate the entire window-casing manufacturing line. He had just returned from a national seminar on the subject of qualitative inputs into the capital expenditure decision process and was anxious to incorporate these new ideas into the decision analysis. In addition to the normal net present value analysis (which produced a significant negative result), Ditmer factored in figures for customer satisfaction, scrap reduction, reduced inventory needs, and quality reputation. With the additional information included, the analysis produced a positive response to the decision question.

When the chief financial officer finished reviewing Ditmer's work, he threw the papers on the floor and said, "What kind of garbage is this? You know it's impossible to quantify such things as customer satisfaction and quality reputation. How do you expect me to go to the board of directors and explain your work? I want you to redo the entire analysis and follow only the traditional approach to net present value. Get it back to me in two hours!"

Write a short paper outlining Marvin's options and the possible consequences of each.

Communication 24-4. Basic Research Skills *(L.O. 1)*

Computers are important in today's business world. Every business can benefit from the capabilities of these electronic devices, which include rapid data processing, timely report generation, automated accounting systems, and the use of specialized software packages for such areas as payroll, accounts receivable, accounts payable, and tax return preparation. Make a trip to a local computer sales store. Inquire about the various personal computer (PC) models available and identify a PC that would be useful to a local nursery selling landscape plants and gardening supplies and equipment. Find out the cost of this computer. Make notes of the model name, its special features and capabilities, and its cost. After gathering this data, identify the benefits that the nursery's controller would include in the analysis to justify the purchase of the PC. For each benefit, describe its effect on cash flow and profitability. Be prepared to discuss your findings in class.

Classroom Exercises

Exercise 24-1. Capital Expenditure Decision Cycle *(L.O. 1)*

Kate Brown was just promoted to supervisor of building maintenance for the Inver Hills Theatre complex in Lake Heights, Minnesota. The complex comprises seventeen buildings. Lakes Entertainment, Inc., Brown's employer, uses an integral system for evaluating capital expenditure requests from its twenty-two supervisors. Brown has approached you, the corporate controller, for advice on preparing her first proposal. She would also like to become familiar with the entire decision cycle.

1. What advice would you give Brown before she prepares her first capital expenditure request proposal?
2. Explain the capital expenditure decision cycle to Brown.

Exercise 24-2. Minimum Desired Rate of Return *(L.O. 2)*

The controller of Faley Corporation wants to establish a minimum desired rate of return and would like to use a weighted average cost of capital. Current data about the corporation's financing structure are as follows: debt financing, 50 percent; preferred stock, 20 percent; common stock, 20 percent; and retained earnings, 10 percent. After-tax cost of debt is 9½ percent. Dividend rates on the preferred and common stock issues are 7½ and 12 percent, respectively. Cost of retained earnings is 12 percent.

Compute the weighted average cost of capital.

Exercise 24-3. Analysis of Relevant Information *(L.O. 3)*

Roland & Co., a scrap-metal company, supplies area steel companies with recycled materials. The company collects scrap metal, sorts and cleans the material, and compresses it into one-ton blocks for easy handling. Increased demand for recycled metals has caused Mr. Roland to consider purchasing an additional metal-compressing machine. He has narrowed the choice to two models. The company's management accountant has gathered the information related to each model:

	Model One	Model Two
Purchase price	$100,000	$120,000
Salvage value	12,000	20,000
Annual depreciation*	8,800	10,000
Resulting increases in annual sales	172,000	200,000
Annual operating costs		
Materials	60,000	70,000
Direct labor	40,000	40,000
Operating supplies	3,600	4,000
Indirect labor	24,000	36,000
Insurance and taxes	1,600	2,000
Plant rental	8,000	8,000
Electricity	1,000	1,120
Other overhead	5,000	5,680

*Computed using the straight-line method.

1. Identify the operating costs and revenues relevant to the decision.
2. Prepare an incremental cash-flow analysis for year 1.

Exercise 24-4. Capital Expenditure Decision: Accounting Rate-of-Return Method
(L.O. 4)

Winter Haven Corporation manufactures metal hard hats for on-site construction workers. Recently, management has tried to raise productivity to meet the growing demand from the real estate industry. The company is now thinking about a new stamping machine. Management has decided that only capital expenditures that yield a 16 percent accounting rate of return before taxes will be accepted. The following projections for the proposal are given: the new machine will cost $325,000; revenue will increase $98,400 per year; the salvage value of the new machine will be $32,500; and operating cost increases (including depreciation) will be $71,200.

Using the accounting rate-of-return method, decide whether the company should invest in the machine. (Show all computations to support your decision, and ignore income tax effects.)

Exercise 24-5. Capital Expenditure Decision: Payback Period Method
(L.O. 4)

MJK Sounds, Inc., a manufacturer of stereo speakers, is thinking about adding a new injection molding machine. This machine can produce speaker parts that the company now buys from outsiders. The machine has an estimated life of fourteen years and will cost $415,000. Gross cash revenue from the machine will be about $397,500 per year, and related cash expenses should total $265,000. Taxes on income are estimated at $45,050 a year. The payback period as set by management should be five years or less.

On the basis of the data given, use the payback period method to determine whether the company should invest in this new machine. Show your computations to support your answer.

Exercise 24-6. Using the Present Value Tables
(L.O. 5)

For each of the following situations, identify the correct multiplier to use from the tables in the appendix on future value and present value tables. Also, compute the appropriate present value.

1. Annual net cash inflow of $30,000 for five years, discounted at 16%
2. The amount of $25,000 to be received at the end of ten years, discounted at 12%
3. The amount of $21,000 to be received at the end of two years, and $15,000 to be received at the end of years four, five, and six, discounted at 10%
4. Annual net cash inflow of $22,500 for twelve years, discounted at 14%

5. The following five years of cash inflows, discounted at 10%:

Year 1	$25,000
Year 2	20,000
Year 3	30,000
Year 4	40,000
Year 5	50,000

6. The amount of $60,000 to be received at the beginning of year 7, discounted at 14%

Exercise 24-7. Present Value Computations
(L.O. 6)

Two machines (Machine A and Machine B) are being considered in a replacement decision. Both have about the same purchase price and an estimated ten-year life. The company uses a 12 percent minimum desired rate of return as its acceptance-rejection standard. Following are the estimated net cash inflows for each machine:

Year	Machine A	Machine B
1	$12,000	$17,500
2	12,000	17,500
3	14,000	17,500
4	19,000	17,500
5	20,000	17,500
6	22,000	17,500
7	23,000	17,500
8	24,000	17,500
9	25,000	17,500
10	20,000	17,500
Salvage value	20,000	10,000

1. Compute the present value of future cash flows for each machine.
2. Which machine should the company purchase assuming they both involve the same capital expenditure?

Exercise 24-8. Capital Expenditure Decision: Net Present Value Method
(L.O. 6)

Steven Altman and Associates wants to buy an automatic extruding machine. This piece of equipment would have a useful life of six years, would cost $219,500, and would increase annual after-tax net cash inflows by $57,250. Assume there is no salvage value at the end of six years. The company's minimum desired rate of return is 14 percent.

Using the net present value method, prepare an analysis to determine whether the company should purchase the machine.

Exercise 24-9. Ranking Capital Expenditure Proposals
(L.O. 8)

Managers of the Santa Ana Furniture Company have all capital expenditure proposals for the year, and they are ready to make their final selections. The following proposals and related rate-of-return amounts were all received during the period:

Project	Amount of Investment	Rate of Return (Percentage)
AB	$ 450,000	19
CD	500,000	28
EF	654,000	12
GH	800,000	32
IJ	320,000	23
KL	240,000	18
MN	180,000	16
OP	400,000	26
QR	560,000	14
ST	1,200,000	22
UV	1,600,000	20

Assume the company's minimum desired rate of return is 15 percent and $5,000,000 are available for capital expenditures during the year.

1. List the acceptable capital expenditure proposals in order of profitability.
2. Which proposals will be selected for this year?

Interpretation Case from Business

Santa Cruz Federal Bank
(L.O. 6, 7)

Automatic teller machines (ATMs) are rapidly becoming a common element of the banking industry. Several companies have developed these computerized money machines and are bombarding bank managers with salespeople and advertising brochures. Santa Cruz Federal Bank is planning to replace some old machines and has decided on the York Machine. Ms. Liu, the controller, has prepared the following decision analysis. She has recommended the purchase of the machine based on the positive net present value shown in the analysis.

Santa Cruz Federal Bank
Capital Expenditure Decision Analysis
Before-Tax Net Present Value Approach
March 2, 19x4

Year	Net Cash Inflow	Present Value Multipliers	Present Value
1	$ 55,000	.909	$ 49,995
2	80,000	.826	66,080
3	85,000	.751	63,835
4	90,000	.683	61,470
5	95,000	.621	58,995
5 (salvage)	35,000	.621	21,735
Total Present Value			$322,110
Initial Investment	$385,000		
Less Proceeds from the Sale of Existing Teller Machines	85,000		
Net Capital Investment			(300,000)
Net Present Value			$ 22,110

The York Machine has an estimated life of five years and an expected salvage value of $35,000. Its purchase price would be $385,000. Two existing ATMs, each having a book value of $25,000, would be sold for a total of $85,000 to a neighboring bank. Annual operating cash inflow is expected to increase in the following manner:

Year 1	$55,000
Year 2	80,000
Year 3	85,000
Year 4	90,000
Year 5	95,000

The bank uses straight-line depreciation. Before-tax minimum desired rate of return is 16 percent, and a 10 percent rate is used for interpreting after-tax data. Assume a 34 percent tax rate for normal operating and capital gains items.

Required

1. Analyze the work of Ms. Liu. What changes need to be made in her capital expenditure decision analysis?
2. What would be your recommendation to bank management about the York Machine purchase?

Problem Set A

Problem 24A-1.
Minimum Desired Rate of Return
(L.O. 2, 8)

Larry Carlson, controller of the Gustavus Corporation, is developing his company's minimum desired rate of return for the year. This measure will be used as an acceptance-rejection standard in capital expenditure decision analyses during the coming year. As in the past, this rate will be based on the company's weighted average cost of capital. Capital mix and respective costs (after tax) for the previous twelve months were as follows:

	Percentage of Total Financing	Cost of Capital (Percentage)
Debt financing	30	9
Preferred stock	10	11
Common stock	40	10
Retained earnings	20	12

The company will soon convert one-third of its debt financing into common stock, reducing debt financing to 20 percent of total financing and increasing common stock to 50 percent of total financing. Changes in the cost of capital are anticipated only in debt financing, where the rate is expected to increase to 12 percent.

Several capital expenditure proposals have been submitted for consideration for the current year. Those projects and their projected rates of return are as follows: Project A, 13 percent; Project B, 10 percent; Capital Equipment C, 12 percent; Project D, 9 percent; Capital Equipment E, 8 percent; and Project F, 14 percent.

Required

1. Using the anticipated adjustments to capital cost and mix, compute the weighted average cost of capital for the current year.
2. Identify the proposed capital expenditures that should be implemented on the basis of the minimum desired rate of return calculated in **1.**

Problem 24A-2.
Accounting Rate-of-Return and Payback Period Methods
(L.O. 4)

Adolphus Corporation wants to buy a new rubber-stamping machine. The machine will provide the company with a new product line, pressed rubber food trays for kitchens. Two machines are being considered; the data applicable to each machine are as follows:

	Mayer Machine	Wick Machine
Estimated annual increase in revenue	$470,000	$500,000
Purchase price	280,000	320,000
Salvage value	28,000	32,000
Traceable annual costs		
Materials	181,670	157,500
Direct labor	65,250	92,300
Factory overhead (excluding depreciation)	138,480	149,500
Estimated useful life in years	10	12

Depreciation is computed using the straight-line method net of salvage value. Assume a 34 percent income tax rate. The company's minimum desired after-tax accounting rate of return is 16 percent, and the maximum allowable payback period is 5 years.

Required

1. From the information given, compute how the company's net income after taxes will change by each alternative.
2. For each machine compute the projected accounting rate of return.
3. Compute the payback period for each machine.
4. From the information generated in **2** and **3,** decide which machine should be purchased. Why?

Problem 24A-3.
Even Versus Uneven Cash Flows
(L.O. 6, 7)

Dana Point Entertainment, Ltd. operates a tour and sightseeing business in southern California. Its trademark is the use of trolley buses. Each vehicle has its own identity and is specially made for the company. Mandy, the oldest bus, was purchased fifteen years ago and has five years of its estimated life remaining. The company paid $25,000 for Mandy, whose current market value is $15,000. Mandy is expected to generate an average annual net cash inflow of $24,000 before taxes for the remainder of its useful life.

Management wants to replace Mandy with a modern-looking vehicle called Ellery. Ellery has a purchase price of $140,000 and a useful life of twenty years. Net cash inflows before taxes are projected to be as follows for Ellery:

Years	Annual Net Cash Inflows
1–5	$40,000
6–10	45,000
11–20	50,000

Assume that (1) all cash flows occur at year end, (2) the company uses straight-line depreciation, (3) the vehicles' salvage value equals 10 percent of their purchase price, (4) the minimum desired after-tax rate of return is 16 percent, and (5) the company is in the 34 percent income tax bracket.

Required

1. Compute the net present value of the future cash flows from Mandy.
2. What would be the net present value of cash flows if Ellery were purchased?
3. Should the company keep Mandy or purchase Ellery?

Problem 24A-4. Capital Expenditure Decision: Net Present Value Method *(L.O. 6, 7)*

The Twelfth of Leo is a famous restaurant in the New Orleans French Quarter. "Bouillabaisse Kathryn" is the house specialty. Management is currently considering the purchase of a machine that would prepare all the ingredients, mix them automatically, and cook the dish to the restaurant's specifications. The machine will function for an estimated twelve years, and the purchase price including installation is $246,000. Estimated salvage value is $24,600. This labor-saving device is expected to increase cash flows by an average of $42,000 per year during its life. For purposes of capital expenditure decisions, the restaurant uses a 12 percent minimum desired before-tax rate of return.

Required

1. Using the net present value method to evaluate this capital expenditure, determine whether the company should purchase the machine. Support your answer. Ignore taxes.
2. If management had decided on a minimum desired before-tax rate of return of 14 percent, should the machine be purchased? Show all computations to support your answer.
3. Assuming straight-line depreciation, a 34 percent tax rate, and an after-tax minimum desired rate of return of 7 percent, should the company purchase the machine? Show your computations.

Problem 24A-5. Capital Expenditure Decision: Net Present Value Method *(L.O. 6, 7)*

The Haseman Hotel Syndicate owns four resort hotels in southern Iowa and Missouri. Because its Hermann, Missouri operation (Hotel 3) has been booming over the past three years, management has decided to add a new wing to increase capacity by 20 percent. A construction firm has bid on the proposed new wing. The building would have a twenty-year life, and the company uses straight-line depreciation. Deluxe accommodations are highlighted in this contractor's proposal. The new wing would cost $29,000,000 to construct, have a salvage value of $2,900,000, and is expected to generate the following cash flows:

Year	Increase in Cash Inflows from Room Rentals	Increase in Cash Operating Expenses
1–7 (each year)	$17,900,000	$12,800,000
8	20,000,000	14,600,000
9	22,100,000	15,900,000
10–20 (each year)	24,200,000	17,700,000

Capital investment projects must generate a 12 percent after-tax minimum desired rate of return to qualify for consideration. Assume a 34 percent tax rate.

Required

Evaluate the proposal from the contractor using net present value analysis, and make a recommendation to management.

Problem Set B

Problem 24B-1. Minimum Desired Rate of Return
(L.O. 2, 8)

Capital investment analysis is the main function of Lois Mahoney, special assistant to the controller of Thomas Manufacturing Company. During the previous twelve-month period, the company's capital mix and respective costs (after tax) were as follows:

	Percentage of Total Financing	Cost of Capital (Percentage)
Debt financing	25	7
Preferred stock	15	9
Common stock	50	12
Retained earnings	10	12

Plans for the current year call for a 10 percent shift in total financing, from common stock financing to debt financing. Also, the after-tax cost of debt is expected to increase to 8 percent, although the cost of the other types of financing will remain the same.

Mahoney has already analyzed several proposed capital expenditures. She expects the after-tax return on investment for each capital expenditure to be as follows: 9.5 percent on Project A; 8.5 percent on Equipment Item B; 15.0 percent on Product Line C; 6.9 percent on Project D; 10.5 percent on Product Line E; 11.9 percent on Equipment Item F; and 11.0 percent on Project G.

Required

1. Using the expected adjustments to cost and capital mix, compute the weighted average cost of capital for the current year.
2. Identify the proposed capital expenditures that should be implemented based on the minimum desired rate of return calculated in **1.**

Problem 24B-2. Accounting Rate-of-Return and Payback Period Methods
(L.O. 4)

The Burgess Company is expanding its production facilities to include a new product line, a sporty automobile tire rim. Because of a new computerized machine, tire rims can be produced with little labor cost. The controller has advised management about two machines that could do the job. Following are the details about each machine.

	Gersich Machine	Aubert Machine
Estimated annual increase in revenue	$282,010	$279,250
Purchase price	490,000	510,000
Salvage value	49,000	51,000
Traceable annual costs		
Materials	75,400	60,800
Direct labor	21,200	36,900
Factory overhead (excluding depreciation)	77,200	84,730
Estimated useful life in years	8	12

The company uses the straight-line depreciation method and is in the 34 percent tax bracket. The minimum desired after-tax accounting rate of return is 12 percent. The maximum payback period is six years. (Where necessary, round calculations to the nearest dollar.)

Required

1. From the information given, compute the change in the company's net income after taxes arising from each alternative.
2. For each machine, compute the projected accounting rate of return.
3. Compute the payback period for each machine.
4. From the information generated in **2** and **3,** which machine should be purchased? Why?

Problem 24B-3.
Net Present Value Method
(L.O. 6, 7)

Quin and Kroovand, Inc. owns and operates a group of apartment buildings. Management wants to sell one of its older four-family buildings and buy a new structure. The old building, which was purchased twenty-five years ago for $100,000, has a forty-year life. The current market value is $70,000. Annual net cash inflows before taxes on the old building are expected to average $16,000 for the remainder of its life.

The new building being considered will cost $350,000. It has a useful life of twenty-five years. Net cash inflows before taxes are expected to be $50,000 annually.

Assume that (1) all cash flows occur at year end, (2) the company uses straight-line depreciation, (3) the buildings will have a salvage value equal to 10 percent of their purchase price, (4) the minimum desired rate of return after taxes is 14 percent, and (5) the company is in the 34 percent tax bracket. Round to nearest dollar.

Required

1. Compute the net present value of future cash flows from the old building.
2. What will be the net present value of cash flows if the new building is purchased?
3. Should the company keep the old building or purchase the new one?

Problem 24B-4.
Capital Expenditure Decision: Net Present Value Method
(L.O. 6, 7)

The management of Sun Valley Plastics has recently been looking at a proposal to purchase a new plastic injection-style molding machine. With the new machine, the company would not have to buy small plastic parts to use in production. The estimated life of the machine is fifteen years, and the purchase price including all set-up charges is $395,000. Salvage value is estimated to be $39,500. The net addition to the company's cash inflow due to the savings from making the parts is estimated to be $65,000 a year. Sun Valley Plastic's management has decided on a minimum desired before-tax rate of return of 14 percent.

Required

1. Using the net present value method to evaluate this capital expenditure, determine whether the company should purchase the machine. Support your answer. Ignore taxes.
2. If management had decided on a minimum desired before-tax rate of return of 16 percent, should the machine be purchased? Show all computations to support your answer.
3. Assuming straight-line depreciation, a 34 percent tax rate, and an after-tax minimum desired rate of return of 8 percent, should the company purchase the machine? Show your computations.

Problem 24B-5.
Capital Expenditure Decision: Comprehensive
(L.O. 4, 6, 7)

The Prairie Manufacturing Company, based in Two Forks, Montana, is one of the fastest-growing companies in its industry. According to Mr. Alexander, the company's production vice president, keeping up-to-date with technological changes is what makes the company successful.

Mr. Alexander feels that a machine introduced recently would fill an important need of the company. The machine has an expected useful life of four years, a purchase price of $225,000, and a salvage value of $22,500. The company controller's estimated operating results, using the new machine, follow. The company uses straight-line depreciation for all its machinery. Mr. Alexander uses a 12 percent minimum desired rate of return and a three-year payback period for capital expenditure evaluation purposes (before-tax decision guidelines).

Cash Flow Estimates

Year	Cash Revenues	Cash Expenses	Net Cash Inflow
1	$305,000	$250,000	$55,000
2	315,000	250,000	65,000
3	325,000	250,000	75,000
4	325,000	250,000	75,000

Required

1. Ignoring income taxes, analyze the purchase of the machine and decide if the company should purchase it. Use the following evaluation approaches in your analysis: (a) the accounting rate-of-return method, (b) the payback method, and (c) the net present value method.

2. Rework **1,** assuming a 34 percent tax rate, after-tax guidelines of an 8 percent minimum desired rate of return, and a 3.5-year payback period. Does the decision change when after-tax information is used?

Management Decision Case

Mesa Grande Photo, Inc.
(L.O. 4, 6, 7)

Quality work and timely output are the benchmarks upon which Mesa Grande Photo, Inc. was organized. Now a nationally franchised company, there are over one hundred Mesa Grande Photo outlets scattered throughout the eastern and midwestern states. Part of the franchise agreement promises a centralized photo developing process with overnight delivery to the outlets.

Because of the tremendous increase in demand for its photo processing, José Jacquein, the corporation's president, is considering the purchase of a new, deluxe processing machine. At a cost of $320,000, this machine will function for an estimated five years and should have a $32,000 salvage value at the end of that period. Mr. Jacquein expects all capital expenditures to produce a 20 percent before-tax minimum rate of return and the investment should be recouped in three years or less. All fixed assets are depreciated using the straight-line method. The forecasted increases in operating results of the new machine are as follows:

Cash Flow Estimates

Year	Cash Revenues	Cash Expenses
1	$310,000	$210,000
2	325,000	220,000
3	340,000	230,000
4	300,000	210,000
5	260,000	180,000

Required

1. Ignoring income taxes, analyze the purchase of the machine and decide if the company should purchase it. Use the following evaluation approaches to your analysis: (a) the accounting rate-of-return method; (b) the payback period method; and (c) the net present value method.
2. Rework **1,** assuming a 34 percent tax rate, after-tax guidelines of a 10 percent minimum desired rate of return, and a four-year payback period. Does the decision change when after-tax information is used? (Round answers to nearest dollar where appropriate.)

Answers to Self-Test

1. d	3. d	5. b	7. d	9. a
2. a	4. b	6. c	8. c	10. c

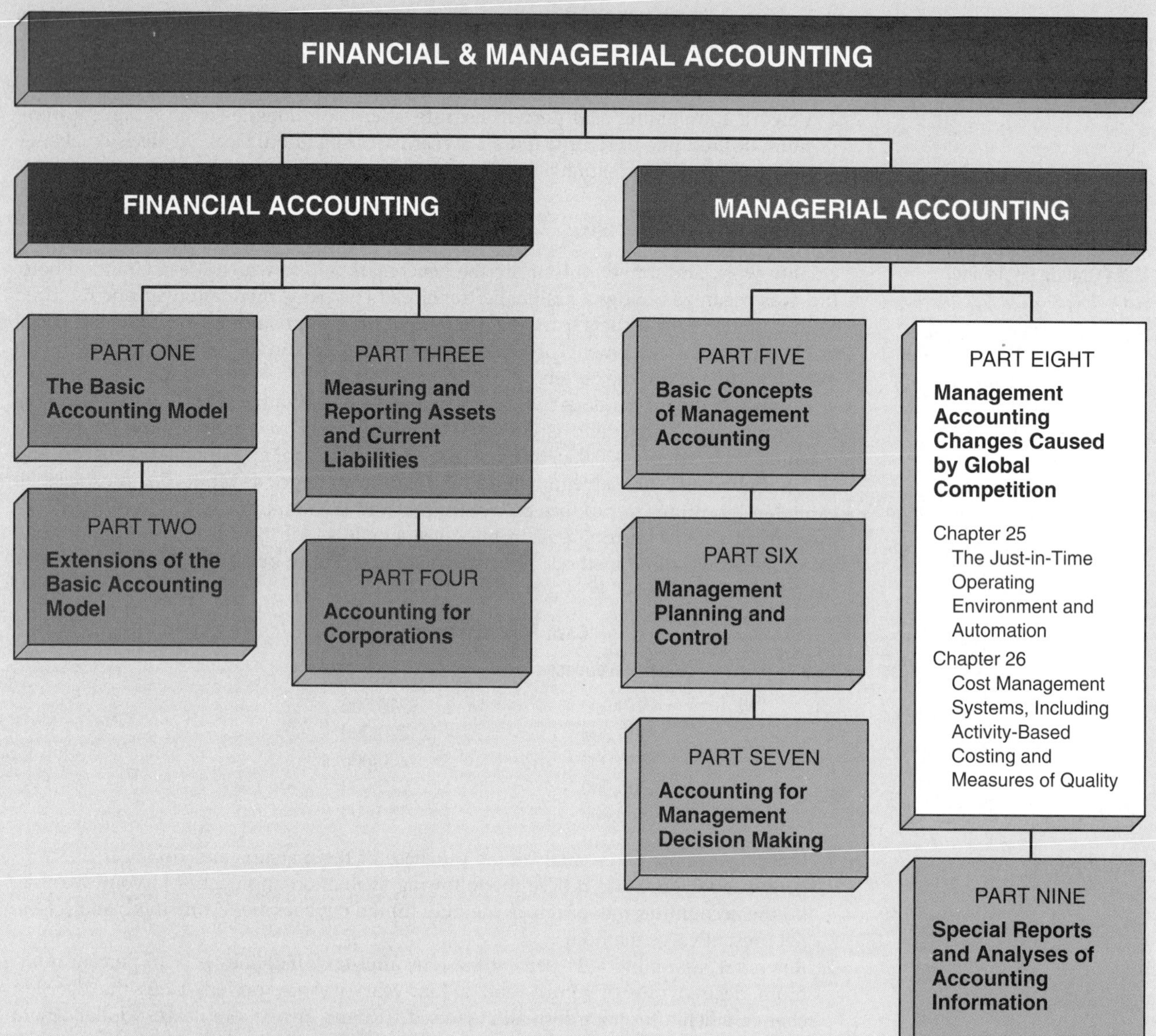

Production and service development processes have changed dramatically during the past decade. A new set of management accounting practices and policies is slowly emerging to more effectively respond to the product costing, budgeting, performance measurement, and capital investing needs of this changing operating environment. These include computer-based purchasing, manufacturing, marketing, distribution, and financial systems. These systems provide timely, accurate data that can be easily adapted to management accounting analysis.

PART EIGHT

Management Accounting Changes Caused by Global Competition

Chapter 25 focuses on the new just-in-time operating environment. The JIT approach is defined, described, and illustrated. In addition, process automation is explored. Accounting methods used in the JIT environment, including automated systems, are discussed and applied.

Chapter 26 looks at the new cost management systems area, focusing primarily on the activity-based costing approach to cost management. Then the concept of total quality management is introduced and both financial and nonfinancial measures of quality are analyzed and applied. The chapter closes with a look at performance reporting in the new operating environment.

LEARNING OBJECTIVES

1. Describe the objectives of the new operating environment and define the just-in-time management philosophy.
2. Identify the elements of a JIT operating environment.
3. Compare traditional manufacturing with just-in-time operations.
4. Identify the changes in product costing that result when firms adopt a JIT operating environment.
5. Apply process costing procedures to compute JIT product costs.
6. Record transactions involving the Raw in Process Inventory account.
7. Identify the unique aspects of product costing in an automated manufacturing process.
8. Compute a product unit cost using data from a flexible manufacturing system.

CHAPTER 25

The Just-in-Time Operating Environment and Automation

Modern businesses face more challenges today than companies did in the past. Once, U.S. firms simply had to supply goods and services to be assured of a reasonable share of the market for their products. But over the last twenty years, changes in technology and communications, the growing expertise of foreign companies, and the introduction of new restrictions in markets around the world have forced U.S. companies to reorganize in order to compete successfully with foreign firms in those markets. Foreign firms, most notably Japanese and European companies, have challenged U.S. firms by producing high-quality products at prices below those charged by many U.S. businesses for comparable goods. The result is that U.S. companies have had to revamp their production processes and rethink their basic operations. Many companies that relied on traditional production processes are changing to new manufacturing approaches, particularly the just-in-time (JIT) operating environment and total quality management (TQM). And as firms change to the new manufacturing environment, the accounting procedures and techniques they use to monitor and control operations must change too.

In this chapter, we introduce the JIT operating environment by contrasting the traditional and new manufacturing environment, focusing on the ways the new methods improve the quality and costing of products and services. Most of the management accounting techniques discussed earlier in this text are used in traditional production settings. Although some of these methods can be used to account for product costs in a JIT operating environment, others are not effective in evaluating aspects of the new manufacturing environment. An example is product costing; we analyze changes in product costing caused by the shift from traditional to JIT operations. The chapter concludes with a look at product costing in an automated production process. After studying this chapter, you should be able to meet the learning objectives listed on the left.

DECISION POINT

Grand Rapids Spring & Wire Company[1]

■ Grand Rapids Spring & Wire Company (GRS&W) opened its doors in 1960 in Grand Rapids, Michigan. The company's 125 employees manufacture compression, extension, and torsion springs; specialty wire; stampings for progressive dies; and assembly processes. In 1987, in order to compete in the world marketplace, the company changed from a traditional production process to a total quality management/just-in-time

1. Harper A. Roehm, Donald J. Klein, and Joseph F. Castellano, "Springing to World-Class Manufacturing," *Management Accounting*, Institute of Management Accountants, March 1991, p. 44.

operating environment. Changing procedures was the easy part of the transition; changing employees' attitudes and gaining their support and trust was much more difficult. Yet, without employees' involvement and trust, shifting to a new manufacturing environment is virtually impossible. What steps should management take to involve employees in a new operating environment?

GRS&W succeeded in implementing a JIT operating environment because managers broke down autocratic barriers and replaced them with full employee involvement. First, the president adamantly supported the program. Second, employee teams were formed to identify the major constraints to production in the plant. Third, employees were asked to identify and make suggestions about how to eliminate the five biggest problem areas. Fourth, management acted immediately on employees' suggestions. And, finally, employees participated in creating a group bonus plan to reward quality work. The last two steps convinced workers that management had changed and that employees' suggestions mattered. The entire culture of the organization changed over a ten-month period.

In addition to encouraging workers' participation in operating decisions, management implemented special training programs and rewarded employees for making sound suggestions. GRS&W established tuition rebates and an apprenticeship program for tool and die making. It even created family programs for weight loss, nutrition, and smoking cessation. The result was an improvement in on-time shipments from 60 percent to 97 percent, a decrease in the costs associated with achieving quality from 6 percent to just 2.7 percent of sales, and the virtual elimination of parts defects. But the real proof came at the time clock: No longer were there lines waiting to clock out; instead, workers completed their tasks before shutting down for the evening. ■

The New Manufacturing Environment: Automation and JIT Operations

OBJECTIVE 1
Describe the objectives of the new operating environment and define the just-in-time management philosophy

To gain a foothold in world markets, foreign companies looked for ways to streamline manufacturing processes and to improve productivity. The strategies they used were designed to meet the following objectives: eliminate waste in raw materials, labor, space, and production time; cut down on recordkeeping; and reduce resources that tied up working capital.

Automation and the just-in-time operating environment have emerged as effective tools in the efforts used to cut down on waste and improve productivity. By substituting automation for labor-intensive, repetitive, mechanical operations, firms found they could reduce the physical waste of scrap materials and defective units. Automated equipment—specifically computer numerically controlled (CNC) machines, flexible manufacturing systems (FMS), and computer-integrated manufacturing (CIM)—shortened production times as well.

To meet the increased efficiency necessary to compete in the new manufacturing environment, companies that adopt the just-in-time (JIT) approach to production must redesign their manufacturing facilities and the events that trigger the production process. **Just-in-time (JIT)** is an overall operating philosophy of management in which all resources, including raw materials and parts, personnel, and facilities, are used only when needed. The objectives are to improve productivity and reduce waste. JIT is based on the concept of continuous production flow and requires that each part of the production process work in concert with the others. Direct labor workers in a JIT environment are empowered with expanded responsibilities, contributing to the reduction of waste in labor cost, space, and production time. JIT production methods require virtually no materials inventory because materials and parts arrive from suppliers as needed. JIT can also reduce work in process and finished goods inventories by as much as 90 percent, significantly reducing the level of working capital devoted to inventories.

One reason for the success of Japanese industry has been the merging of these two techniques—automation and JIT operations—in a new manufacturing environment. These new methods moved Japanese industry into world prominence. Japanese manufacturers were able to improve product quality while reducing waste, and cost savings were reflected in reduced prices. Furthermore, they increased the productivity of their factories as they approached ideal capacity. Their success has prompted manufacturers in other countries to change from traditional production methods to the new manufacturing environment. And you will see a continued movement toward automation and JIT operations as more and more companies enter world markets.

Implementing a JIT Operating Environment

OBJECTIVE 2
Identify the elements of a JIT operating environment

Companies that want to adopt a JIT operating environment must reevaluate their current operations and implement new ways of manufacturing products. Underlying these new methods are several basic concepts:

Simple is better.

Product quality is critical.

The work environment must emphasize continuous improvement.

Maintaining inventories wastes resources and may hide bad work.

Any activity or function that does not add value to the product should be eliminated or reduced.

Goods should be produced only when needed.

Workers must be multiskilled and must participate in improving efficiency and product quality.

To implement a JIT operating environment—an environment based on these concepts—a company must develop an operating system that contains the following elements:

1. Maintain minimum inventory levels.
2. Develop pull-through production planning and scheduling.
3. Purchase materials and produce products as needed, in smaller lot sizes.
4. Perform quick, inexpensive machine setups.
5. Create flexible manufacturing work cells.
6. Develop a multiskilled work force.
7. Maintain high levels of product quality.
8. Enforce a system of effective preventive maintenance.
9. Encourage continuous improvement of the work environment.[2]

In this section, we discuss each element and describe its impact on costs, product quality, and productivity.

2. James B. Dilworth, *Production and Operations Management*, 3d ed. (New York: Random House, 1986), pp. 354–360.

Maintain Minimum Inventory Levels

One objective of a JIT operating environment is to maintain minimum inventory levels. In contrast to the traditional environment, in which parts, materials, and supplies are purchased far in advance and stored until the production department needs them, in a JIT environment, raw materials and parts are purchased and received only when needed. The system reduces costs by reducing (a) the space needed for inventory storage, (b) the amount of material handling, and (c) the amount of inventory obsolescence. There is less need for inventory control facilities, personnel, and recordkeeping. The amount of work in process inventory waiting to be processed, as well as the amount of working capital tied up in all inventories, is reduced significantly.

Develop Pull-Through Production Planning and Scheduling

Pull-through production is a system in which a customer order triggers the purchase of materials and the scheduling of production for the required products. In contrast, traditional manufacturing operations use the **push-through method**, whereby products are manufactured in long production runs and stored in anticipation of customers' orders. With pull-through production, the company purchases materials and parts and schedules work only as needed.

Purchase Materials and Produce Products as Needed, in Smaller Lot Sizes

With pull-through production, the size of customers' orders determines the size of production runs. Low inventory levels are maintained, but machines have to be set up more frequently, resulting in more work stoppages. Long production runs, previously thought to be more cost-effective, are no longer the rule in a JIT environment; products are not manufactured to be inventoried.

Perform Quick, Inexpensive Machine Setups

One reason that traditional production processes relied on long production runs was to reduce the number of machine setups. In the past, managers felt that it was more cost-effective to produce large inventories rather than to produce small lot sizes, which increase the number of machine setups. The success of JIT over the last ten years has disproved this belief. By placing machines in more efficient locations and scheduling similar products on common machine groupings, setup time can be minimized. In addition, workers become more experienced and more efficient with frequent setups.

Create Flexible Manufacturing Work Cells

In a traditional factory layout, all similar machines are grouped together, forming functional departments. Products are routed through each department in sequence, so that all necessary operations are completed in order. This process can take several days or weeks, depending on the size and complexity of the job.

By changing the factory layout, the JIT operating environment cuts the manufacturing time of a product from days to hours, or from weeks to days. In many cases, time can be reduced more than 80 percent by rearranging the machinery so that machines that are needed for sequential processing are placed together. This cluster of machinery forms a flexible **work cell** or **island**, an autonomous production line that can perform all required operations efficiently and continuously. The flexible work cell handles work on products of similar shape or size, what we call a "family" of products. Product families require minimum setup changes as workers move from one job to the next. The more flexible the work cell, the greater the minimization of total production time.

Develop a Multiskilled Work Force

In the flexible work cells of a JIT environment, workers may be required to operate several types of machines simultaneously. Therefore, they must learn new operating skills. Many work cells are run by only one operator, who, for example, may have to set up and retool machines, inspect the products, and even perform routine maintenance on equipment. In addition, workers are encouraged to identify inefficiencies and make recommendations for improvement. In short, a JIT operating environment requires a multiskilled work force.

Multiskilled workers have been very effective in contributing to the high levels of productivity experienced by Japanese companies. In the United States, union contracts often restrict workers to a single skill. Companies that honor these labor contracts may encounter difficulties in retraining workers to run work cells.

Maintain High Levels of Product Quality

JIT operations produce high-quality products because products are produced from high-quality raw materials and because inspections are made continuously throughout the production process. Unlike traditional manufacturing methods, in which inspection is viewed as an activity that does not add value to the product, the JIT environment incorporates inspection into the continuous production operation. JIT machine operators inspect the products as they pass through the production process. An operator who detects a flaw determines its cause. The operator even may help the engineer or quality control person find a way to correct the problem. Once an operator finds a defect, he or she shuts down the production cell and fixes the problem to prevent the production of similarly flawed products. This integrated inspection procedure, combined with quality raw materials, produces high-quality finished goods.

Enforce a System of Effective Preventive Maintenance

When a company rearranges its machinery into flexible manufacturing cells, each machine in the work cell becomes an integral part of that cell. If one machine breaks down, the entire cell stops functioning. Because the product cannot be routed easily to another machine while the malfunctioning machine is repaired, continuous JIT operations require an effective system of preventive maintenance. Preventing machine breakdowns is considered more important and more cost-effective than keeping machines running continuously. Machine operators are trained to perform minor repairs on machines as they detect problems. Machines are serviced regularly—much like an automobile—to help guarantee continued operation. The machine operator conducts routine maintenance during periods of machine downtime (caused by a lack of orders). Remember that in a JIT setting, the work cell does not operate unless there is a customer order for the product. Machine operators take advantage of downtime to perform maintenance.

Encourage Continuous Improvement of the Work Environment

The JIT environment fosters loyalty among workers, who are likely to see themselves as part of a team because they are so deeply involved in the production process. Machine operators must have the skills to run several types of machines, be able to detect defective products, suggest measures to correct problems, and maintain the machinery within their work cell. Japanese companies receive thousands of employee suggestions and implement a high percentage of them. And workers are rewarded for suggestions that improve the process. This kind of environment supports workers' initiative and benefits the company.

To sum up, a JIT operating environment does more than just lower inventory levels or cut production time. JIT operations produce high-quality products efficiently. Every action taken by machine operators, setup people, repair and maintenance personnel, and company management is dedicated to building high-quality products. Every person who participates in the production of the product is working to perform at maximum capacity.

Traditional versus Just-in-Time Production

OBJECTIVE 3
Compare traditional manufacturing with just-in-time operations

The most effective way to differentiate between traditional and JIT operating environments is to analyze and compare product flow and plant layout. We start with the traditional manufacturing process and break it down into five parts, or time frames. The total production time of a product consists of (1) actual processing time, (2) inspection time, (3) moving time, (4) queue time, and (5) storage time. Traditional manufacturing and assembly operations incorporate dozens of nonvalue-adding activities. A **nonvalue-adding activity** is a production- (or service-) related activity that adds cost to a product but does not increase its market value. JIT operations reduce or eliminate all nonvalue-adding activities from production and product distribution. Of the five time frames listed, JIT operations attempt to eliminate all but the actual processing time because inspection time, moving time, queue time, and storage time are activities that usually do not add value to a product. In this section, we compare the two manufacturing environments and examine how the JIT manufacturing environment redesigns both manufacturing facilities and the work force to eliminate nonvalue-adding activities, enabling JIT operations to produce higher-quality goods more efficiently than the traditional manufacturing process does.

The Traditional Manufacturing Environment

To study the traditional manufacturing process, we look at the production methods of a fastener company. In its factory, it produces screws, bolts, shoe nails, and specialty fasteners. Figure 25-1 shows the plant layout, and Figure 25-2 shows the operations needed to produce the fastener.

The arrows and numbers in Figure 25-1 indicate the sequence of events in the manufacturing process. Raw materials arrive at the plant as coils of wire of various thicknesses. The wire is fed into a heading machine, which cuts the wire to length and forms the head. Headed blanks then are collected in large movable

Figure 25-1. The Plant Layout of a Factory Using Traditional Manufacturing Operations

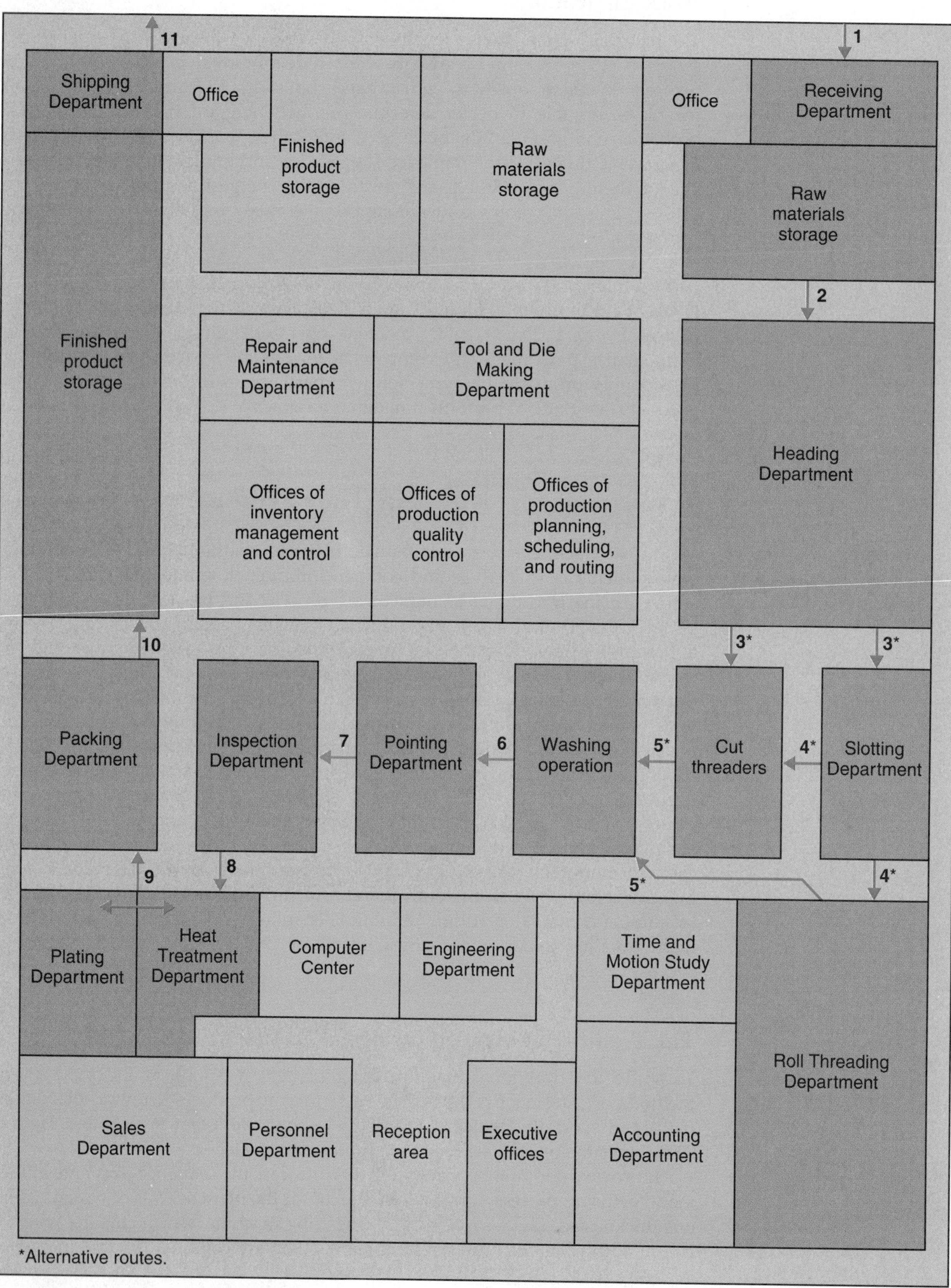

Figure 25-2. Steps in the Production of a Fastener

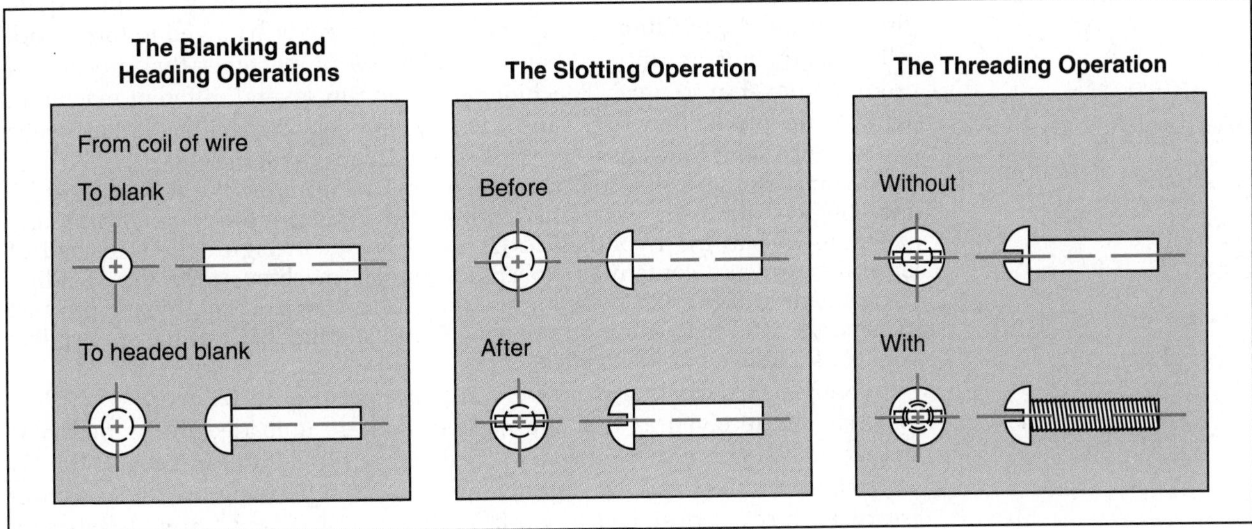

bins for temporary storage, until they are transported to the next department. If the headed blank needs a slot, it is added in the Slotting Department. Then the products again are collected in movable bins. The next operation is threading the fastener, either by cutting away the excess metal or by rolling the headed blank between two dies to form the thread (similar to rolling a pencil between your hands).

At this point, although the product looks like a screw or bolt, it needs additional operations before it becomes a finished product. These are operations **5** through **9** in Figure 25-1. The fastener may need to be pointed, and all fasteners must be washed to remove excess oils and foreign materials. Inspection is necessary to determine if the product meets specifications. Some fasteners require heat treatment and plating, and some batches need special packaging.

Throughout the process, the products are stored and moved in large bins from one operation to the next. Finally, they are transported to the finished goods storage area to await sale and shipment.

Figure 25-1 also shows the location of several support services in the traditional plant. Notice that production support services—repair and maintenance, inventory control, quality control, and scheduling and routing functions—are located in the middle of the factory. The lower part of Figure 25-1 shows other common support services. Accounting, time and motion study, engineering, computer services, sales, personnel, and executive activity functions all support the production, sale, or distribution of the company's products.

There are several nonvalue-adding activities in the layout in Figure 25-1. The most obvious are the raw materials and finished product storage areas and activities. The time taken to move the products between departments and the resulting queue time are also nonvalue-adding activities. Finally, the Inspection Department adds no value to the product, although it does contribute to the cost. Many support functions are costly to maintain and add cost to the product without increasing its market value. But, unlike the nonvalue-adding activities such as inspection and product movement, support functions are still necessary for the effective operation of the production process. Their costs can be analyzed and reduced but not eliminated.

The JIT Production Environment

The layout of a factory that operates in a JIT production environment is quite different from the traditional factory floor. Equipment is arranged to form work cells. Each manufacturing cell has a complete set of machines that produces a product from start to finish. Machine operators run several different machines, help set up production runs, and identify and repair machinery that needs maintenance. And they are encouraged to spot areas of inefficiency.

To compare the traditional manufacturing layout with the layout in a JIT operating environment, we converted the plant layout of the fastener company in Figure 25-1 to the hypothetical JIT plant layout in Figure 25-3. Instead of large departments containing dozens of similar machines (like the Heading Department in Figure 25-1), small operating cells start and complete a product in minimal time, with minimal movement and storage. Each of the six headers begins a separate operating cell.

In Subplant A, existing machinery is relocated to form JIT work cells. Raw materials are received as they are needed, and are unloaded in the materials storage area adjacent to the header scheduled to fill that order. Each of the six work cells includes heading, slotting, threading, and pointing machines, as necessary. Each cell is designed to work on different sizes and types of fasteners. Instead of work in process inventory sitting in travel bins as it moves from one department to the next, wire is fed into the header automatically. The headed blanks move on a conveyer belt to subsequent operations. If order specifications call for additional processing, such as heat treatment or plating, the computerized routing system moves the products to those locations. Packaging is the final phase; then, the goods are shipped to the customer. The fastener order is completed in a matter of hours, as compared to the days or weeks necessary when an order is moved and queued for each departmental operation.

Subplant B in Figure 25-3 shows three flexible manufacturing systems. A **flexible manufacturing system (FMS)** is a single multifunctional machine or an integrated set of computerized machines and systems designed to complete a series of operations automatically. An FMS often completes a product from beginning to end without the product being touched or moved by hand. Raw materials are fed in at one end of the FMS machine, and a finished product emerges at the other end.

Let us assume that FMS #1 in Subplant B makes a special type of fastener called a "sems screw." To manufacture a sems screw, a locking washer is placed on the screw blank before the threading operation. Once the threads have been rolled on, the washer becomes part of the finished product; it cannot be removed. This FMS cell produces all types and sizes of sems fasteners from start to finish. Each part of the cell represents a different operation—heading, slotting, lock washer fitting, threading, and pointing. All operations are computerized, and the manufacturing process is continuous. When the sems fasteners have been packaged, they are sent to the finished goods area to be shipped out to the customer.

Some aspects of the plant layout in Figure 25-3 are similar to the traditional arrangement in Figure 25-1. For example, supporting services such as the Tool and Die Center and the Repair and Maintenance Department remain close to the manufacturing operation. Heat-treating facilities are very expensive and products still are batch-processed, so both subplant layouts share the same heat-treating furnaces.

The remaining parts of the factory in Figure 25-3 have been redesigned to satisfy the needs of the JIT production process. In particular, the support functions

Figure 25-3. The Plant Layout of a Factory with a JIT Production Environment

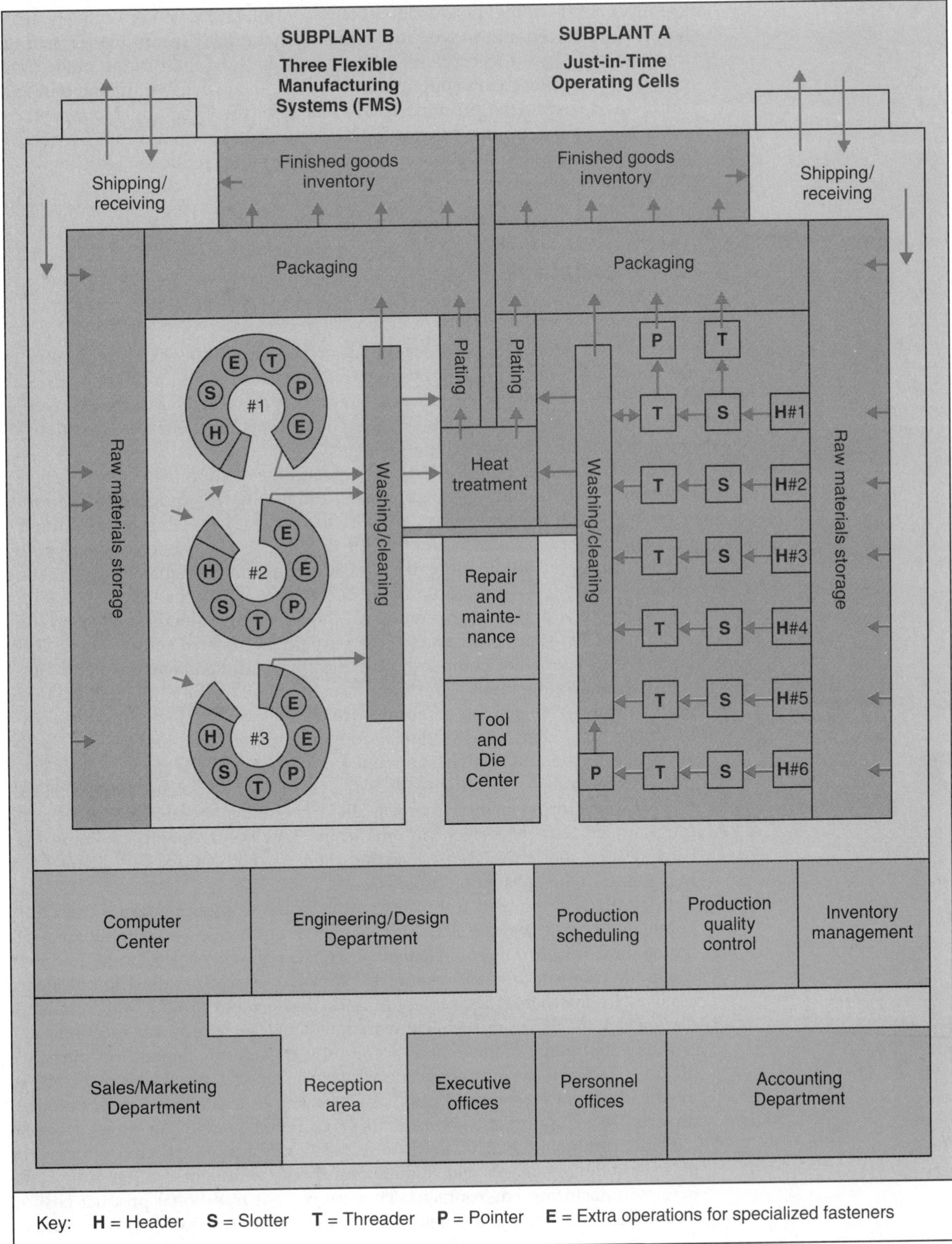

located in the lower part of the drawing are similar, but the Computer Center and the Engineering/Design Department have been enlarged in the JIT layout. Production scheduling, production quality control, and inventory management have been reduced and moved to the managerial office area; in the JIT setting, these functions need to be closer to the computer area than to the production process. In general, many support functions are too expensive to maintain and simply add cost to the product. In our example, the Time and Motion Study Department falls into this category. When a company switches to a JIT operating environment, several support functions are either reduced significantly or eliminated.

Accounting for Product Costs in the New Manufacturing Environment

OBJECTIVE 4
Identify the changes in product costing that result when firms adopt a JIT operating environment

Although the production process changes when firms shift from a traditional to the new manufacturing environment, the management accountant is still responsible for evaluating costs and controlling operations. But the changes in the manufacturing operations do affect how costs are determined and what measures are used to monitor performance.

When companies adopt a new manufacturing environment, they normally combine the JIT operating environment with automated equipment. The result is an increase in machine hours and a reduction in direct labor hours. The size of the increase in machine hours and the decrease in direct labor hours depends on the degree of automation. JIT operations are implemented by relocating existing machinery and equipment; JIT practices can be applied without automating operations. More commonly, however, firms increase their reliance on automation. Many companies use a partially automated setup, where direct labor workers operate computer numerically controlled machines and other semiautomatic equipment. **Computer numerically controlled (CNC) machines** are stand-alone pieces of computer-driven equipment, including operating machines, computer-aided design hardware and software, and robots. At the other end of the automation spectrum from a single CNC machine is a **computer-integrated manufacturing (CIM) system**, a fully computerized, plant-wide manufacturing facility, in which all parts of the manufacturing process are programmed and performed automatically. The closer operations come to a CIM system, the wider the spread between machine hours and direct labor hours used in the production process.

In addition to the shift from direct labor hours to machine hours caused by automated operations, the characteristics of labor change as a company adopts the new manufacturing environment. Direct labor workers no longer just help shape the product; they are responsible for many tasks that used to be categorized as indirect labor. Examples of tasks that are performed by direct labor workers are machine setup, machine maintenance, and product inspection.

Many traditional management accounting procedures depend on measures of direct labor. For example, accountants use direct labor to allocate factory overhead costs, find standard cost variances, and estimate the costs of potential projects. Most important, accountants have relied heavily on direct labor to compute product unit costs. Because of the significant reduction in direct labor hours and dollars, many believe that costs should be assigned differently in the new manufacturing environment. They argue that traditional product costing techniques have become obsolete, and they cite three reasons: (1) JIT operations have changed many of the relationships and cost patterns associated with traditional manufacturing; (2) automation has replaced direct labor hours with machine hours; and (3) computerized processes and systems have increased the accountant's ability to trace costs to the specific activities that generate them.[3]

In this section, we look at ways accountants can change their product costing procedures to determine accurate costs for products manufactured in the new manufacturing environment. After looking at changes in the way costs are categorized and assigned, we use the FIFO process costing method to compute product costs in an automated JIT setting.

Classifying Costs

The JIT work cell and the goal of reducing or eliminating nonvalue-adding activities change the assignment of costs in a JIT operating environment from those in a traditional manufacturing environment. To see how costs are assigned in JIT operations, we again start with the five time frames that make up the traditional production process and compare JIT operations with them.

Processing time The actual amount of time that a product is being worked on

Inspection time The time spent either looking for product flaws or reworking defective units

Moving time The time spent moving a product from one operation or department to another

Queue time The time a product spends waiting to be worked on once it arrives at the next operation or department

Storage time The time a product is in materials storage, work in process inventory, or finished goods inventory

In product costing under JIT, costs associated with actual processing time are grouped as either materials costs or conversion costs. Conversion costs include the total of direct labor and factory overhead costs incurred by a production department, JIT/FMS work cell, or other work center.

The costs associated with and traceable to the other four time classifications are not necessary to the production process and are either reduced or eliminated through process and cost control measures. Inspection costs, for instance, are reduced significantly because the cell operator performs this function. The costs associated with moving the work in process inventory from department to department are reduced because of the reconfiguration of the factory layout. Many of the costs of queue time are reduced or eliminated by using work cells. Storage costs also are reduced significantly or eliminated. When the JIT production process operates optimally, raw materials and parts arrive from vendors just in time to be used in the work cells, goods flow continuously through the work cells, and finished products are packaged and shipped immediately to customers. Thus, a large percentage of the old costs of storage are eliminated under JIT. Indirect product costs that are not eliminated still must be treated as factory overhead and charged to work cells as part of conversion costs.

Accounting for product costs under JIT is not a complicated procedure; it is summarized in Table 25-1. A product cost is classified as either a materials cost or a conversion cost. Product costs are traced to work cells. The process costing

3. Several of the ideas in this section are from Robert D. McIlhattan, "How Cost Management Systems Can Support the JIT Philosophy," *Management Accounting*, Institute of Management Accountants, September 1987, pp. 20–26.

Table 25-1. Product Costing Under JIT

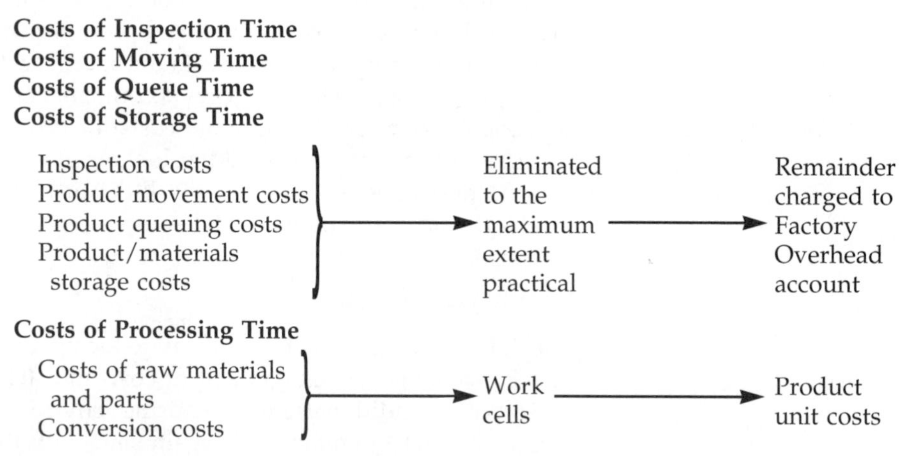

method then is used to determine product unit costs. The illustrative problem on pages 1005–1007 demonstrates this approach to product costing.

Cost Allocation

In a traditional manufacturing company, direct labor hours or dollars are a common basis for allocating factory overhead costs to products. Direct labor is usually the largest cost component of finished goods and the primary cause of factory overhead costs. Therefore, most factory overhead costs are allocated to products based on direct labor hours or dollars.

Because flexible automated work cells decrease significantly the reliance on direct labor, other measures must replace direct labor in allocating costs to finished goods in the new manufacturing environment. We describe two cost allocation changes: (1) replacing the work order with other measures of production and (2) merging direct labor and factory overhead, and accounting only for conversion costs.

The work order is a key document in a traditional manufacturing system. Labor time is accumulated as the order moves from one operation to the next. When the job is complete, the work order contains a record of all labor time required for the job. This information enables the accountant to determine the cost of direct labor and to apply factory overhead costs. Work cells and continuous production eliminate the need for work orders. Daily production schedules are maintained, and costs are assigned to the work completed during the day. Detailed reporting, such as completing documents like the work order, is not a part of the simplified JIT process.

In the JIT operating environment, indirect costs have little correlation with direct labor hours. The key measure is **throughput time**, the time it takes to get a product through the entire production process. So machine hours become more important than labor hours. Product velocity measures are used to apply conversion costs to products via process costing. In addition, theoretical capacity is used to establish conversion cost application rates. (A primary objective of the JIT environment is to produce at theoretical capacity.)

Sophisticated computer monitoring of the work cells allows many costs to be traced directly to the cells where products are being manufactured. As Table 25-2 shows, several costs that used to be treated as indirect costs and applied to products using a labor base now are treated as direct costs of a work cell. They

Table 25-2. Direct Versus Indirect Costs—Changes Caused by JIT

Traditional Environment		JIT Environment
Direct	Materials and parts	Direct
Direct	Direct labor	Direct
Indirect	Repairs and maintenance	Direct to work cell
Indirect	Materials handling	Direct to work cell
Indirect	Operating supplies	Direct to work cell
Indirect	Utility costs	Direct to work cell
Indirect	Supervision	Direct to work cell
Indirect	Depreciation	Direct to work cell
Indirect	Supporting service functions	Mostly direct
Indirect	Building occupancy	Indirect
Indirect	Insurance and taxes	Indirect

are directly traceable to the JIT production cell. If standard costs are used, products are costed using predetermined rates for materials and conversion costs. In the JIT operating environment, each cell manufactures similar products to minimize setup time. Therefore, materials and conversion costs should be nearly uniform per product per cell. The costs of materials handling, utilities, operating supplies, and supervision can be traced directly to work cells as they are incurred. Depreciation is charged on units of output, not on a time basis, so depreciation also can be charged directly to work cells based on the number of units produced. Building occupancy costs, property and casualty insurance premiums, and property taxes remain indirect costs and must be allocated to the production cells for inclusion in the conversion cost category.

JIT and Process Costing

OBJECTIVE 5
Apply process costing procedures to compute JIT product costs

The process costing method can be adapted easily to compute product unit costs in a JIT manufacturing setting. First, every manufacturing cost is classified as either materials costs (including materials-related costs) or conversion costs. After all costs have been categorized and allocated, process costing can be used to calculate product costs for the period. The following problem shows how JIT product costs are developed.

Illustrative Problem
JIT Process Costing

The Merit Company produces automobile steering wheels for all of the major car manufacturers in the United States. Three JIT operating cells are used in the process: One cell produces leather steering wheels, a second produces air-bag models, and a third makes special wood-grained wheels. The day-shift operator of each cell prepares the equipment so that the machines can run automatically during the two night shifts. Only indirect labor is used during the night shifts.

During the week ended June 15, 19x3, the JIT air-bag wheel cell produced the following data:

Units	
Beginning inventory (60 percent complete)	30
Units completed during week	4,600
Ending inventory (80 percent complete)	35

Hours worked	
Direct labor—40 hours	
Machine hours	
Nine machines in cell	
JIT air-bag wheel cell ran 110 hours during week	
Costs in beginning Work in Process Inventory	
Materials costs	$1,080
Conversion costs	378
Direct costs incurred for and traced directly to air-bag wheel cell	
Raw materials (added at beginning of process)	$138,150
Direct labor (40 hours at $14 per hour)	560
Power costs	3,056
Cell machinery depreciation	2,420
Engineering design costs	4,963
Indirect labor	11,970
Lubricants, supplies, and fasteners	7,015
Overhead rates used	
Materials handling overhead (to be added to and included as part of materials cost in process costing analysis): 20 percent of raw materials costs	
Factory overhead not traceable directly to cell: $6.50 per machine hour worked	

Required

1. Compute the total materials costs and total conversion costs for the week.
2. Using good form and the FIFO process costing approach, prepare a cost of production report, including
   a. Schedule of equivalent production
   b. Unit cost analysis schedule
   c. Cost summary schedule
3. From the cost summary schedule, prepare a journal entry to transfer the costs of completed units to the Finished Goods Inventory account.

Solution

1. Before preparing the cost of production report for the Merit Company, first compute the costs of the period. You must remember that two cost categories are used in a JIT operating environment: materials costs and conversion costs. These same categories also are used in process costing.

Raw materials costs	
In beginning work in process inventory	$ 1,080
Materials used in production during week	138,150
Materials handling overhead for week: $138,150 × 20%	27,630
Total materials costs	$166,860

Conversion costs	
In beginning inventory	$ 378
Charged to FMS cell during period	
Directly traceable costs:	
Direct labor (40 hours at $14 per hour)	560
Power costs	3,056
Cell machinery depreciation	2,420
Engineering design costs	4,963
Indirect labor	11,970
Lubricants, supplies, and fasteners	7,015
Indirect factory overhead	
110 hours × 9 machines × $6.50/machine hr	6,435
Total conversion costs	$ 36,797

2. The cost of production report is shown in Exhibit 25-1 on page 1008.
3. Prepare a journal entry to transfer the costs of completed units to Finished Goods Inventory.

Finished Goods Inventory	202,176	
Work in Process Inventory		202,176
To transfer the cost of units completed to Finished Goods Inventory		

The Raw in Process Inventory Account

OBJECTIVE 6
Record transactions involving the Raw in Process Inventory account

One of the most basic accounting changes caused by the JIT environment is the use of the **Raw in Process Inventory** account. This new inventory account replaces both the Materials Inventory and the Work in Process Inventory accounts. Because raw materials are ordered and received immediately prior to use, there is no need to debit them to a Materials Inventory account; they are debited directly to the Raw in Process Inventory account:

Raw in Process Inventory	50,000	
Accounts Payable		50,000
To record the purchase of raw materials		

In process costing situations, as goods were completed by one department and transferred to another department, the cumulative cost of the products had to be transferred from one work in process inventory account to another. This is also changed in the JIT environment. There is no need for numerous work in process inventory accounts because the products flow continuously through the flexible manufacturing cell. All conversion costs (direct labor and factory overhead costs) are debited to the single Raw in Process Inventory account. When the goods have been completed, the following entry is made:

Finished Goods Inventory	185,600	
Raw in Process Inventory		185,600
To record the transfer of completed products to Finished Goods Inventory		

If adjustments have to be made at the end of an accounting period because of over- or underapplied factory overhead, the debits or credits are made only to the Raw in Process Inventory and Finished Goods Inventory accounts. For example, assume that factory overhead was overapplied by $1,600 and that $100 should be taken back from goods in process and $500 from finished goods; the remaining $1,000 are in Cost of Goods Sold. The entry would be:

Factory Overhead Control	1,600	
Raw in Process Inventory		100
Finished Goods Inventory		500
Cost of Goods Sold		1,000
To adjust for overapplied factory overhead		

One last example helps clarify the Raw in Process Inventory account. Assume that $17,500 of raw materials were purchased and the accountant discovered that these goods were priced $1,500 over their standard cost. The entry shown at the top of page 1009 would be made to record the purchase.

Exhibit 25-1. Cost of Production Report

The Merit Company
Cost of Production Report—FIFO Method
For the Week Ended June 15, 19x3

A. Schedule of Equivalent Production

Units—Stage of Completion	Units To Be Accounted For	Equivalent Units: Materials Costs	Equivalent Units: Conversion Costs
Beginning inventory (units started last period but completed this period)	30		
(Materials costs—100% complete)		0	
(Conversion costs—60% complete)			12 (40% of 30)
Units started and completed in this period (4,600 – 30)	4,570	4,570	4,570
Ending inventory (units started but not completed in this period)	35		
(Materials costs—100% complete)		35	
(Conversion costs—80% complete)			28 (80% of 35)
Totals	4,635	4,605	4,610

B. Unit Cost Analysis Schedule

	Total Costs: Costs from Beginning Inventory (1)	Total Costs: Costs from Current Period (2)	Total Costs: Total Costs To Be Accounted For (1 + 2)	Equivalent Unit Costs: Equivalent Units (3)	Equivalent Unit Costs: Cost per Equivalent Unit (2 ÷ 3)
Materials costs	$1,080	$165,780	$166,860	4,605	$36.00
Conversion costs	378	36,419	36,797	4,610	7.90
Totals	$1,458	$202,199	$203,657		$43.90

C. Cost Summary Schedule

	Cost of Goods Transferred to Finished Goods Inventory	Cost of Ending Work in Process Inventory
Beginning inventory		
Beginning balance	$ 1,458	
Cost to complete: 30 units × 40% × $7.90 per unit	95*	
Total beginning inventory	$ 1,553	
Units started and completed: 4,570 units × $43.90 per unit	200,623	
Ending inventory		
Materials costs: 35 units × $36.00 per unit		$ 1,260
Conversion costs: 35 units × 80% × $7.90 per unit		221*
Totals	$202,176	$ 1,481
Check on computations:		
Costs to Finished Goods Inventory		$202,176
Costs in ending Work in Process Inventory		1,481
Total costs to be accounted for (see unit cost analysis schedule)		$203,657

*Rounded.

Raw in Process Inventory	16,000	
Materials Price Variance	1,500	
Accounts Payable		17,500
To record the purchase of raw materials and the related price variance		

Using the Raw in Process Inventory account is an easy adjustment to make. Remember that this new account is used in every situation in which either Materials Inventory or Work in Process Inventory was used in the past.

JIT and Automation Are Changing Management Accounting

Significant changes are underway in management accounting systems of companies that have adopted the JIT philosophy and that are employing automated manufacturing processes. These changes stem from three new areas of accounting emphasis created by the move to JIT and automated production facilities: (1) a macro versus a micro approach to control of operations, (2) the increasing importance of nonfinancial data, and (3) using theoretical capacity to evaluate actual performance.

Macro versus Micro Approach

The JIT management accountant approaches the control of operations by looking at the entire production process rather than small parts or segments of the process. Profit is maximized by supplying customers with a quality product on a timely basis at a reasonable price. With the more traditional approach, profits are thought to be increased by cutting labor time, buying large quantities of raw materials to take advantage of quantity discounts, or applying fixed overhead costs over an increased number of units of output. In a JIT setting, profitability is enhanced when the entire operation is running in a just-in-time fashion. Non-value-adding aspects such as storage time, inspection time, moving time, and queue time are the primary focus: If these wasted time periods are minimized or eliminated, profitability will increase.

Nonfinancial Data

A major part of the reporting and measurement aspects of the JIT operating environment involves nonfinancial considerations, which are linked closely with the macro approach to control of operations. Rather than being interested in labor efficiency or overhead volume variances, the management accountant must focus on time reduction, helping to determine (1) causes for excess storage time, (2) information sources that will reduce the need for separate inspection activities, (3) reporting methods that will help reduce the moving time associated with product flow through the process, and (4) causes for excessive queue time. All these analyses are nonfinancial in nature and require studies of time periods, distance factors or measures, and numbers of people involved.

The JIT environment also emphasizes product distribution and customer satisfaction. Analyses leading to control in these areas require information from such reports as number and causes of customer complaints, average delivery time, and ability to meet promised delivery dates. All these analyses involve nonfinancial data.

Emphasis on Theoretical Capacity

The chapter on cost behavior and cost-volume-profit analysis introduced the concept of normal capacity, and the chapter on standard costing and variance analysis used normal capacity as a basis for developing standard costs and computing the related variances. Normal capacity is the average anticipated level of output for a period of time. To measure performance, actual productive output is compared with expected output based on normal capacity. Variances resulting from differences between these two amounts are reported.

One major objective of the JIT philosophy is to minimize nonproductive time in the total delivery cycle, which means that the company is expected to operate at or near theoretical or ideal capacity. This goal may not be attained, but the philosophy is to work toward that ideal level. Machine operators, engineers, product designers, supervisors, salespeople, and management accountants are expected to continuously look for ways to cut nonvalue-adding time and related costs. The JIT environment exists when everyone involved in the operation of the company actively participates in a relentless effort of ongoing improvement.

Automation: Product Costing Issues

OBJECTIVE 7
Identify the unique aspects of product costing in an automated manufacturing process

Earlier, we introduced and illustrated product costing procedures related to the just-in-time philosophy. In addition to JIT, automated manufacturing facilities have also influenced the computation of a product's cost. This section takes a more detailed look at product costing in a **JIT/FMS environment**, an operating environment created by a flexible manufacturing system functioning within the just-in-time operating philosophy. Product costing methods must change as the manufacturing environment changes. And yet many companies that have automated their production facilities try to use traditional methods to cost products. In a study titled *Cost Accounting for Factory Automation* sponsored by the Institute of Management Accountants (IMA), researchers Robert E. Bennett, James A. Hendricks, David E. Keys, and Edward J. Rudnicki found that product costing problems and solutions differed with the degree of automation in the production process. These problems concern the allocation of factory overhead, the classification of costs as variable or fixed, and the changing nature of costs involving their direct versus indirect characteristics. The report was organized according to four levels of computer integration, from low to high, as follows:

1. **Computer numerically controlled (CNC) machines** — Stand-alone computer controlled machines
2. **Computer-aided design/computer-aided manufacturing (CAD/CAM)** — Using computers in product design work, planning and controlling production, and in linking CNC machines and flexible manufacturing systems to the engineering design function
3. **Flexible manufacturing systems (FMS)** — A computer-controlled production system comprised of a single, multifunctional machine or several types of machines that perform a series of operations and/or assemble a number of parts in a flexible and automatic fashion

4. **Automated material handling system (AMHS)** — A necessary component of a computer-integrated manufacturing (CIM) system in which the raw materials and partially completed product handling function is automatic, providing a continuous product flow through the entirely automated process

Computer Numerically Controlled Machines

Automating the production process begins with the introduction of computer numerically controlled (CNC) machines. Even after introducing CNC machines into the process to reduce the dependency on labor and to increase efficiency, most companies continue to allocate factory overhead based on direct labor dollars or hours for product costing purposes. This problem was a primary finding of the IMA research team's study of factory automation. They determined that there are four reasons why inaccurate factory overhead allocation exists in a CNC machine environment: (1) use of inappropriate allocation bases, (2) allocation of nonrelevant costs, (3) use of inappropriate activity levels, and (4) use of plant or companywide overhead rates rather than departmental or FMS rates.

Inappropriate Allocation Base. Direct labor is not an appropriate allocation base in an automated production setting because there is very little connection between overhead costs incurred in a CNC machine environment and direct labor hours or cost. Most of the overhead costs are associated with and caused by the operation of the machines. Machine hours differ from labor hours because of setup time, idle machine time, and the fact that one person can operate several machines simultaneously. Three machine time expressions can be used as a basis for factory overhead cost allocation: actual machine hours, **run time** (total machine hours needed less setup time), and **engineered time** (standard or predicted machine time for the product). Each expression of machine hours has advantages and disadvantages regarding cost and accuracy, but each is a better factory overhead allocation base than direct labor hours or dollars.

Relevance of Costs Being Allocated. There is still an argument that allocating fixed factory overhead costs to products tends to introduce inaccuracy into the computation of product cost. These costs tend to be unrelated to the activity levels that are often used to assign costs to work cells or products. Building occupancy costs such as building depreciation, insurance costs, and property taxes are included in this category. Even with improved cost traceability, these costs must still be considered indirect. Variable costing procedures are one answer to this concern, but to date few companies have adopted them.

Selection of Activity Levels. The selection of activity levels to be used for allocating factory overhead costs should be a primary concern for the management accountant because it is the activities within the factory that cause costs to be incurred. Therefore costs should be categorized by type of activity, and the activity itself should be used as a base for allocating those costs to the work cell or product. Approaching cost allocation from this direction will allow, for example, computer-related costs to be allocated using a computer-usage base. Activity-based costing is explained in the chapter on cost management systems, including activity-based costing and measures of quality.

Use of Work Cell or Departmental Versus Plantwide Rates. Fixed factory overhead can be more closely related to production if a company converts from a companywide or plantwide overhead rate to department or work cell overhead rates. The closer the factory overhead costs are brought to the product, the more accurate the resulting product cost. Many costs can be directly traced to a particular FMS, which further aids the product costing process.

Computer-Aided Design/ Computer-Aided Manufacturing

Most computer-aided design/computer-aided manufacturing (CAD/CAM) costs should be assigned to specific products. But the traditional methods used to accomplish this task do not usually yield accurate cost assignments. Many companies simply allocate these costs to overhead pools and then distribute them to products through the use of predetermined factory overhead rates. Yet many of these costs are traceable directly to specific orders; for instance, drafting/design costs incurred in connection with specifications for a particular order are traceable to and should be charged to that individual order. Because of sophisticated computer monitoring equipment, many CAD/CAM related costs can be easily traced to the order needing the design work. Routing these costs through plantwide overhead rates will distort product costs.

Flexible Manufacturing System

Product costing within a flexible manufacturing system (FMS) further changes the characteristics of some common variable costs, fixed costs, and direct costs. The FMS cell itself becomes the cost center. The only variable costs of an FMS are direct materials, direct labor, and some indirect materials, tooling, and power costs.

Many fixed costs can be traced directly to FMS cost centers. Costs of machine depreciation, FMS computer depreciation, computer programmers and other computer backup people working only on FMS maintenance, product line supervision, and selected off-line inspection labor can be traced to specific FMS work cells. The work and time of setup personnel and machine operators who are trouble-shooters and who move from one work cell to another can also be traced directly to specific FMS cost centers. The IMA researchers recommend that separate FMS factory overhead application rates be used because each FMS cell is usually a self-contained operating unit.

Other fixed costs are not traceable and must be allocated to the FMS cost centers. CAD/CAM costs for total system maintenance are difficult to trace to specific FMS cells and must be allocated. Common computer center costs may be allocated to cost centers based on some expression of usage. In addition, building occupancy costs such as plant depreciation, building maintenance, taxes, and insurance are usually pooled and allocated.

But what base should be used to allocate these common occupancy costs to the FMS cells? Direct labor is of little use in trying to associate overhead costs with FMS cost centers. Table 25-3 reflects the views of the IMA research team regarding overhead allocation bases relevant to the FMS environment. Four bases are identified, one focusing on units of output and three focusing on time measures. Because by definition an FMS is flexible, units of output are not identical, so units of output is not the ideal base. Each of the three time measures has advantages and disadvantages. Remember that ease of use and operating at

Table 25-3. Flexible Manufacturing Systems: Advantages and Disadvantages of Possible Overhead Allocation Bases

Overhead Allocation Base	Advantages	Disadvantages
Units of production	Simplicity; easy to use	Parts machined in the FMS often are not homogeneous and require different operations
Total time in FMS	Reflects productive capacity of entire FMS	Difficult to measure and record
Engineered machine hours	Reflects machine time that should be used; readily available	Does not represent actual machine time or total time used in FMS
Actual machine hours	Measures use of productive capacity of machine tools; can be recorded by machine computer or FMS central computer	Includes inefficiencies in operation of machine tools

Source: Robert E. Bennett, James A. Hendricks, David E. Keys, and Edward J. Rudnicki, *Cost Accounting for Factory Automation.* Reprinted from *Management Accounting.* Copyright by Institute of Management Accountants, Montvale, N.J. 1987.

theoretical capacity are goals of the JIT/FMS environment. Engineered machine hours tend to approach these requirements. Although the product costing approach for an FMS differs from the traditional approach, the objective is the same: to compute an accurate unit cost for use in pricing decisions as well as for inventory valuation and cost of goods sold information.

Automated Material Handling System

An automated material handling system (AMHS) adds the final dimension to a fully integrated computerized production process. Traditional material handling systems required manual movement of materials and parts through the manufacturing layout, and the paperwork needed to track the materials and product in process was also done manually. According to the *Cost Accounting for Factory Automation* study, companies today rely on automatic storage/retrieval systems (AS/RS) and AMHSs to move products within a computer-integrated manufacturing process.[4] Hand-pushed carts, operator-directed forklifts, and manual conveyors are being replaced by power-rolled conveyors, shuttles, and raised track, towline, or computer-guided vehicles. Computer-controlled production scheduling and material handling trace and account for all product and parts movement, replacing the old punched card and off-line tracking systems.

Traditionally, material handling costs have been included in the factory overhead cost pool and allocated to products based on direct labor. In the new manufacturing environment, there is little relationship between the amount of labor

4. Robert E. Bennett, James A. Hendricks, David E. Keys, and Edward J. Rudnicki, *Cost Accounting for Factory Automation,* Institute of Management Accountants, 1987, p. 59.

cost incurred and the amount of material handling a process or FMS work cell needs. A suggested approach for today's automated JIT environment is to account for the material handling and purchasing functions as a separate cost center. Costs associated with these functions are grouped into a cost pool and allocated as part of the materials charged to production. Materials quantity, cost, or weight may be used as the allocation basis, depending on the relationship between the costs involved and the size and complexity of the products being produced.

Illustrative Problem
Product Costing in an Automated Environment

OBJECTIVE 8
Compute a product unit cost using data from a flexible manufacturing system

As you learned in the chapter on pricing decisions, including transfer pricing, product pricing is heavily dependent on product costs. A 2 or 3 percent error in pricing a product may result in loss of customers and market share, so accurate product costs are important to a company's overall profitability. In practice, although production processes have shifted from labor intensive to capital intensive operations, direct labor hours and dollars are still the most commonly used overhead allocation bases. Even as automation begins to dominate production lines, accountants continue to use direct labor bases. Many existing allocation systems are at the point where there is little relationship between the factory overhead costs being incurred and the amount of direct labor being used. In addition, many of the indirect costs that used to be charged to overhead pools are now being traced directly to FMS operating cells.

This illustrative problem points out the significant difference in product cost that can arise when an automated company shifts from a direct labor dollar allocation basis to one based on machine hours. Accounting for a separate materials storage and handling pool is also introduced. The company also changes from using companywide overhead rates to FMS cell overhead rates.

Lesley Corporation's Foraker Division produces three products: J12, K14, and L16. Four years ago the company renovated its manufacturing facilities and installed automated flexible manufacturing systems. Each product is produced in its own FMS cell, but the allocation of factory overhead continues to be based on direct labor dollars. The following information has been made available:

	Product J12	Product K14	Product L16
Unit information:			
Raw materials cost	$3	$4	$10
Direct labor hours	.5 hours	.8 hours	.2 hours
Direct labor cost per hour	$16	$16	$16
Machine hours	3.2 hours	4 hours	5 hours
Total annual unit demand	30,000	50,000	10,000
Total factory overhead	$1,680,000	$4,480,000	$1,568,000

Foraker Division's policy is to set the selling price at 140 percent of the unit's production cost.

Required

1. Compute the division's plantwide factory overhead rate using total direct labor dollars as a basis.
2. Compute each product's total production cost and selling price using the application rate computed in **1.**

3. Compute a new factory overhead application rate assuming that
   a. Materials storage and handling overhead of 20 percent of the cost of raw materials is subtracted from the factory overhead cost totals.
   b. Machine hours is the overhead application basis.
   c. Product line overhead rates rather than a single plantwide rate are used.
4. Compute each product's total production cost and selling price using the application rates disclosed or computed in **3.**
5. Compare product selling prices. Is there a problem?

Solution

1. Factory overhead rate based on direct labor dollars computed.

	Total Factory Overhead Cost	Total Direct Labor Cost
Product J12:		
Factory overhead cost	$1,680,000	
Direct labor cost		
.5 hr × $16 × 30,000 units		$240,000
Product K14:		
Factory overhead cost	4,480,000	
Direct labor cost		
.8 hr × $16 × 50,000 units		640,000
Product L16:		
Factory overhead cost	1,568,000	
Direct labor cost		
.2 hr × $16 × 10,000 units		32,000
Totals	$7,728,000	$912,000

Factory overhead application rate
$7,728,000 ÷ $912,000 = 847.37% of direct labor cost

2. Each product's unit cost and selling price based on plantwide overhead rate computed.

	Product J12	Product K14	Product L16
Unit cost information			
Raw materials cost	$ 3.00	$ 4.00	$10.00
Direct labor cost			
.5 hr at $16/hr	8.00		
.8 hr at $16/hr		12.80	
.2 hr at $16/hr			3.20
Factory overhead cost			
$8 × 8.4737	67.79		
$12.80 × 8.4737		108.46	
$3.20 × 8.4737			27.12
Total unit cost	$ 78.79	$125.26	$40.32
Unit selling price			
J12: $78.79 × 140%	$110.31		
K14: $125.26 × 140%		$175.36	
L16: $40.32 × 140%			$56.45

3. Product line factory overhead rates based on machine hours computed.

	Net Factory Overhead Cost	Total Machine Hours Required
Product J12:		
Factory overhead cost	$1,680,000	
less materials handling cost		
$3 × 30,000 units × 20%	18,000	
Net factory overhead cost	$1,662,000	
Machine hours required		
3.2 hr × 30,000 units		96,000
Product K14:		
Factory overhead cost	$4,480,000	
less materials handling cost		
$4 × 50,000 units × 20%	40,000	
Net factory overhead cost	$4,440,000	
Machine hours required		
4 hr × 50,000 units		200,000
Product L16:		
Factory overhead cost	$1,568,000	
less materials handling cost		
$10 × 10,000 units × 20%	20,000	
Net factory overhead cost	$1,548,000	
Machine hours required		
5 hr × 10,000 units		50,000

Product line FMS factory overhead application rates:

Factory overhead rates per machine hour

J12: $1,662,000 ÷ 96,000 MH =	$17.3125 /MH
K14: $4,440,000 ÷ 200,000 MH =	$22.20 /MH
L16: $1,548,000 ÷ 50,000 MH =	$30.96 /MH

4. Each product's unit cost and selling price based on product line overhead rates computed.

	Product J12	Product K14	Product L16
Unit cost information			
Raw materials cost	$ 3.00	$ 4.00	$ 10.00
Materials handling overhead cost at 20%	0.60	0.80	2.00
Direct labor cost			
.5 hr at $16/hr	8.00		
.8 hr at $16/hr		12.80	
.2 hr at $16/hr			3.20
Factory overhead cost			
3.2 hr × $17.3125	55.40		
4 hr × $22.20		88.80	
5 hr × $30.96			154.80
Total unit cost	$67.00	$106.40	$170.00

	Product J12	Product K14	Product L16
Unit selling price			
J12: $67.00 × 140%	$93.80		
K14: $106.40 × 140%		$148.96	
L16: $170.00 × 140%			$ 238.00

5. Selling prices compared and analyzed.

Selling prices using direct labor cost allocation basis and a plantwide rate	$110.31	$175.36	$ 56.45
Selling prices using machine hours basis and product line FMS rates	93.80	148.96	238.00
Differences	$ 16.51	$ 26.40	$(181.55)

Conclusion: Products J12 and K14 are overpriced, and product L16 is extremely underpriced.

Chapter Review

Review of Learning Objectives

1. **Describe the objectives of the new operating environment and define the *just-in-time management philosophy.***
Just-in-time is an operating environment in which all resources, including raw materials and parts, personnel, and facilities, are used as they are needed. The objective of JIT operations is a continuous production flow, with all parts of the production process working in concert. JIT also enhances the role of the direct labor worker and significantly reduces waste in labor, space, and production time. JIT supporters believe that simple is better; that product quality is critical; that the company should encourage continuous quality improvement; that maintaining inventories wastes resources and often hides bad work; that any activity or function that does not add value to the product should be reduced or eliminated; that goods should be produced only when needed; and that workers should be multiskilled and should participate in improving efficiency and product quality.
2. **Identify the elements of a JIT operating environment.**
The elements that comprise a JIT operating environment are (1) maintain minimum inventory levels; (2) develop pull-through production planning and scheduling; (3) purchase materials and produce parts as needed, in smaller lot sizes; (4) perform quick, inexpensive machine setups; (5) create flexible manufacturing work cells; (6) develop a multiskilled work force; (7) maintain high levels of product quality; (8) enforce a system of effective preventive maintenance; and (9) encourage continuous improvement of the work environment.
3. **Compare traditional manufacturing with just-in-time operations.**
Traditional manufacturing plants are divided into functional departments, with similar machines grouped in each department. Products flow from department to department. Raw materials are ordered well in advance and stored until needed. Work in

process and finished goods inventories are usually large. And long production runs are scheduled to reduce setup costs and to lower fixed costs per product.

Just-in-time manufacturing operations are organized in work cells: All machines necessary for the production of a product line are grouped together to reduce the distance between operations and the time it takes to produce a product. Raw materials and parts are ordered as needed. Goods are pulled through the work cell based on actual orders received. And the size of production runs is based on the size of orders. Work in process inventories are almost nonexistent, and finished products are shipped when completed.

4. **Identify the changes in product costing that result when firms adopt a JIT operating environment.**
In the JIT operating environment, as firms increase their reliance on automation, machine hours replace direct labor hours as the dominant source of costs. This means that measures of direct labor are no longer a reliable means of determining product costs. In product costing under JIT, processing costs are grouped as either materials costs or conversion costs. The costs associated with inspection time, moving time, queue time, and storage time are reduced or eliminated. The shift to automation also affects the allocation of factory overhead costs. Other measures of production replace the work order, and direct labor and factory overhead costs are merged into conversion costs. At work here are computerized facilities that improve cost tracking, so that many costs considered indirect costs in traditional manufacturing settings, such as electricity and factory supplies, can be traced directly to work cells. Only costs associated with building occupancy, insurance, and property taxes remain indirect costs and must be allocated to work cells.

5. **Apply process costing procedures to compute JIT product costs.**
Because manufacturing costs are classified as either materials costs or conversion costs, the process costing method can be adapted easily to compute product costs in a JIT environment. Remember that there usually is very little beginning inventory in a JIT operation. So, it is easy to determine the stage of completion of goods. Unit cost analysis is used to compute product unit costs.

6. **Record transactions involving the Raw in Process Inventory account.**
The Raw in Process Inventory account has taken the place of both the Materials Inventory and the Work in Process Inventory accounts. Because raw materials are received as needed and the products flow continuously through the process, only one inventory account is needed in these areas.

7. **Identify the unique aspects of product costing in an automated manufacturing process.**
With automation, machine hours replace direct labor hours or dollars and become the primary basis for overhead allocation. The use of several overhead cost pools and appropriate cost drivers (allocation bases) is also encouraged. More costs are treated as direct costs because of their traceability to operating cells. Departmental or operating cell overhead rates are preferred over plantwide rates.

8. **Compute a product unit cost using data from a flexible manufacturing system.**
Computing a product unit cost for an FMS cell consists of determining the unit cost of materials; material handling cost overhead; and conversion costs per unit, including all traceable indirect costs and factory overhead allocations.

Review of Concepts and Terminology

The following concepts and terms were introduced in this chapter:

(L.O. 7) **Automated material handling system (AMHS):** A necessary component of a computer-integrated manufacturing system in which the raw materials and partially completed product handling function is automatic, providing a continuous product flow through the entirely automated process.

(L.O. 7) **Computer-aided design/computer-aided manufacturing (CAD/CAM):** The use of computers in product design work, planning and controlling production, and in linking CNC machines and flexible manufacturing systems to the engineering design function.

(L.O. 4) **Computer-integrated manufacturing (CIM) system:** A fully computerized, plantwide manufacturing facility, in which all parts of the manufacturing process are programmed and performed automatically.

(L.O. 4) **Computer numerically controlled (CNC) machines:** Stand-alone pieces of computer-driven equipment, including operating machines, computer-aided design hardware and software, and robots.

(L.O. 7) **Engineered time:** Standard or predicted machine time for the product.

(L.O. 3) **Flexible manufacturing system (FMS):** A single, multifunctional machine or an integrated set of computerized machines and systems designed to complete a series of operations automatically.

(L.O. 4) **Inspection time:** The time spent either looking for product flaws or reworking defective units.

(L.O. 1) **Just-in-time (JIT):** An overall operating philosophy of management in which all resources, including raw materials and parts, personnel, and facilities, are used only as needed.

(L.O. 7) **JIT/FMS environment:** An operating environment created by a flexible manufacturing system functioning within the just-in-time operating philosophy.

(L.O. 4) **Moving time:** The time spent moving a product from one operation or department to another.

(L.O. 3) **Nonvalue-adding activity:** A production- (or service-) related activity that adds cost to a product but does not increase its market value.

(L.O. 4) **Processing time:** The actual amount of time that a product is being worked on.

(L.O. 2) **Pull-through production:** A production system in which a customer order triggers the purchase of materials and the scheduling of production for the required products.

(L.O. 2) **Push-through method:** A production system in which products are manufactured in long production runs and stored in anticipation of customers' orders.

(L.O. 4) **Queue time:** The time a product spends waiting to be worked on once it arrives at the next operation or department.

(L.O. 6) **Raw in Process Inventory:** An inventory account in the just-in-time operating environment that combines the Raw Materials Inventory and the Work in Process Inventory accounts into one account.

(L.O. 7) **Run time:** Total machine hours needed less setup time.

(L.O. 4) **Storage time:** The time a product is in materials storage, work in process inventory, or finished goods inventory.

(L.O. 4) **Through-put time:** The time it takes to get a product through the entire production process.

(L.O. 2) **Work cell (island):** An autonomous production line that can perform all required operations efficiently and continuously.

Self-Test

Test your knowledge of the chapter by choosing the best answer for each of the following items.

(L.O. 2) 1. The move to a just-in-time operating environment is facilitated by
   a. creating production work cells comprised of several different types of operations.
   b. enhancing the storage functions within a factory.
   c. concentrating on areas of possible cost reduction rather than on the reduction of processing time.
   d. increasing inventories so that customers' demands can always be met.

(L.O. 2) 2. Which of the following is *not* a basic concept underlying just-in-time operations?
   a. An emphasis on quality and continuous improvement
   b. Producing goods only as they are needed
   c. Maintaining inventory levels to support probable demand
   d. The belief that simple is better

(L.O. 2) 3. Pull-through production means that
   a. the size of production runs is determined by how much can be pulled through the production process.
   b. production processes rely on long production runs to reduce the number of machine setups.
   c. it is very difficult to pull products through the production process.
   d. a customer order triggers the purchase of materials and the scheduling of production for the required products.

(L.O. 3) 4. A product- (or service-) related activity that adds costs to the product but does not increase its market value is known as a
   a. cost-adding activity.
   b. cost driver.
   c. nonvalue-adding activity.
   d. value-adding activity.

(L.O. 4) 5. A fully computerized, plantwide manufacturing facility in which all parts of the manufacturing process are programmed and performed automatically is the definition of a
   a. flexible manufacturing system.
   b. computer-integrated manufacturing system.
   c. computer numerically controlled machine.
   d. pull-through production system.

(L.O. 4) 6. The time spent either looking for product flaws or reworking defective units is called
   a. processing time.
   b. storage time.
   c. rework and spoilage time.
   d. inspection time.

(L.O. 6) 7. For a company employing the just-in-time operating philosophy, the Raw in Process Inventory account is credited when
   a. raw materials and parts are purchased and received.
   b. direct labor is charged to a particular job.
   c. indirect manufacturing costs are charged to jobs based on various overhead rates.
   d. products are completed and transferred to Finished Goods Inventory.

(L.O. 7) 8. Schooler Company's flexible manufacturing system computes the time variance for run time versus engineered time for all jobs completed. Job 22T produced an unfavorable variance of 76 minutes and had a run time of 6 hours and 16 minutes. What was the engineered time for the job?
   a. 300 minutes
   b. 452 minutes
   c. 76 minutes
   d. 376 minutes

(L.O. 8) 9. Dinger Corp. has been using direct labor hours as a basis for allocating its Drilling Department's factory overhead. This year the department used the overhead rate of \$7.40 and had anticipated direct labor hours for the period of 4,540. If the company were to switch to machine hours (MH) as the allocation basis and the anticipated machine hours for the period were 18,160, what will the new overhead rate be?
   a. \$4.00/MH
   b. \$7.40/MH
   c. \$1.85/MH
   d. \$29.60/MH

(L.O. 8) 10. Walstead Company computes total materials cost per job by including actual materials cost plus materials-handling overhead costs. If total materials cost for Job 18YT is $54,720 and the current materials-handling overhead rate is 20 percent of materials cost, what was the actual cost of materials used for the job?
   a. $10,944
   b. $45,600
   c. $65,664
   d. $43,776

Answers to the Self-Test are at the end of this chapter.

Review Problem
Unit Cost Analysis: A Comparison of Traditional and JIT/FMS Manufacturing Environments

(L.O. 4, 5) Bennett Metal Products Company has been in business for more than fifty years. At its last meeting, top management decided to implement a just-in-time philosophy and introduce a flexible manufacturing system for its DeKalb Division. DeKalb specializes in manufacturing home appliances. Its most popular item is a line of aluminum and oak barbeque grills. Various models are produced, but all are a standard shape and size. Currently, the company uses a traditional cost accounting system, and unit costs are determined by adding a manufacturing overhead factor to the unit's direct materials and direct labor amounts. Direct labor hours is the allocation base.

The controller has been asked to restructure the present manufacturing cost data so that the effect of the new system of product unit costs can be analyzed. Following are data for the past accounting period. Several changes will occur when the new system is installed. For instance, several former indirect costs will be directly traceable to the JIT/FMS work cell. Also, separate allocations will be made for materials-related costs and engineering overhead. Indirect manufacturing costs will be allocated based on machine hours; materials storage and handling overhead will be allocated based on total dollars of materials and parts incurred; and engineering overhead will be allocated based on engineering hours. Process costing procedures will be used to compute unit costs.

	Traditional Manufacturing System	JIT/Flexible Manufacturing System
Costs directly traceable to product		
Raw materials	$ 492,000	$ 492,000
Parts for assembly	1,456,000	1,456,000
Direct labor (based on 80,000 units)		
Traditional: 3.8 hr at $16/hr per unit	4,864,000	
JIT/FMS: 0.6 hr at $20/hr per unit		960,000
Total costs traceable to product	$6,812,000	$2,908,000
Costs directly traceable to FMS cell		
Electrical power		$ 60,000
Supervision		12,000
Depreciation, machinery		9,600
Setup labor		8,000
Other indirect labor		420,000
Repairs and maintenance		18,400
Operating supplies and lubricants		2,400
Total costs directly traceable to FMS cell		$ 530,400

(continued)

	Traditional Manufacturing System	JIT/Flexible Manufacturing System
Indirect manufacturing cost pool		
Electrical power	$ 240,000	
Supervision	164,500	
Depreciation, machinery	53,400	
Inspection costs	299,000	
Product rework costs	966,000	
Engineering labor	184,000	
Power costs, engineering	55,200	
Depreciation, engineering equipment	69,000	
Engineering supervision	92,000	
Other engineering overhead	35,800	
Setup labor	46,000	
Other indirect labor	1,725,000	
Repairs and maintenance	114,100	
Operating supplies and lubricants	27,600	
Depreciation, building	128,800	$ 128,800
Property taxes	18,400	18,400
Fire insurance	9,200	9,200
Liability insurance	4,600	4,600
Building maintenance	13,000	13,000
Factory utilities	32,200	32,200
Factory employee cafeteria	101,200	101,200
Purchasing costs, materials and parts	110,400	
Storage and handling, work in process inventory	736,000	
Materials/parts storage and handling	193,200	
Depreciation, materials moving trucks	41,400	
Total indirect manufacturing costs	$5,460,000	$ 307,400
Engineering overhead cost pool		
Engineering labor		$ 184,000
Power costs, engineering		55,200
Depreciation, engineering equipment		69,000
Engineering supervision		92,000
Other engineering overhead		35,800
Total engineering overhead costs		$ 436,000
Materials storage and handling overhead cost pool		
Purchasing costs, materials and parts		$ 110,400
Materials/parts storage and handling		193,200
Depreciation, materials moving trucks		41,400
Total materials storage and handling overhead costs		$ 345,000

These data have been partially restructured in anticipation of the new system. Following is a summary of the other information that will be required for the analysis:

Total actual divisional direct labor hours for the period	210,000 DLH
Total anticipated divisional machine hours for the period	1,060,000 MH
Total anticipated divisional engineering hours for the period	27,250 eng. hr

Total anticipated divisional dollar value of materials and parts for the period	$15,000,000	
Number of grills completed	80,000	grills
Anticipated machine hours for grill FMS	132,500	MH
Anticipated engineering hours for grill FMS	3,400	eng. hr
Process costing information for grill FMS		
Beginning inventory		
Materials and parts	$5,460	
Conversion costs	3,920	
Equivalent units for period		
Materials and parts	80,280	equiv. units
Conversion costs	80,200	equiv. units

Required

1. Under the traditional system,
   a. Compute the manufacturing overhead application rate.
   b. Compute the product unit cost for each grill.
2. Identify the cost categories that will likely be eliminated when the company adopts a JIT/FMS approach.
3. Compute the JIT/FMS application rates for the following:
   a. Indirect manufacturing costs
   b. Engineering overhead costs
   c. Materials storage and handling overhead costs
4. Identify the total materials costs and conversion costs for the period for the grill FMS cell.
5. Using the FIFO costing method, compute the grill unit cost under the new JIT/FMS setting.

Answer to Review Problem

1. Traditional system:

   a. Computation of manufacturing overhead application rate:

$5,460,000 ÷ 210,000 direct labor hours	$ 26.00 per DLH

   b. Computation of product unit cost:

Raw materials cost	
$492,000 ÷ 80,000 units	$ 6.15
Parts cost	
$1,456,000 ÷ 80,000 units	18.20
Direct labor cost	
$4,864,000 ÷ 80,000 units	60.80
Manufacturing overhead	
3.8 hr/unit × $26/DLH	98.80
Total unit cost	$183.95

2. The following cost categories are likely to be eliminated in a JIT/FMS setting:

Inspection costs	$ 299,000
Product rework costs	966,000
Storage and handling, work in process inventory	736,000
Total costs likely to be eliminated	$2,001,000

3. Computation of JIT/FMS overhead application rates:

   a. Indirect manufacturing costs

$307,400 ÷ 1,060,000 machine hours	$ 0.29 per MH

b. Engineering overhead costs
$436,000 ÷ 27,250 engineering hours — $16.00 per eng. hr

c. Materials storage and handling overhead costs
$345,000 ÷ $15,000,000 materials and parts purchased — 2.30% of M&P cost

4. Total costs of grill FMS cell:

Materials and materials-related costs	
Raw materials	$ 492,000
Parts for assembly	1,456,000
Materials storage and handling overhead ($492,000 + $1,456,000) × 2.3%	44,804
Total materials cost	$1,992,804
Conversion costs	
Direct labor	$ 960,000
Other directly traceable conversion costs	530,400
Indirect manufacturing costs 132,500 machine hours × $0.29 per MH	38,425
Engineering overhead costs 3,400 engineering hours × $16 per eng. hr	54,400
Total conversion costs	$1,583,225

5. Computation of grill unit cost under the new JIT/FMS approach:

Unit cost analysis schedule:

	Total Cost Analysis			Equivalent Unit Costs	
	Costs from Beginning Inventory	Costs from Current Period	Total Costs to Be Accounted For	Divided by Equivalent Units	Cost Per Equivalent Unit
Materials costs	$5,460	$1,992,804	$1,998,264	80,280	$24.823
Conversion costs	3,920	1,583,225	1,587,145	80,200	19.741
Totals	$9,380	$3,576,029	$3,585,409		$44.564

Chapter Assignments

Questions

1. Briefly describe the just-in-time operating environment.
2. What role does the elimination of waste play in the development of the just-in-time environment?
3. Describe the pull-through production concept.
4. What is a flexible manufacturing system (FMS) work cell?
5. "Preventive maintenance of machinery is critical to the operation of a flexible manufacturing system work cell." Explain this statement.
6. What are the changes in the responsibilities of the direct labor worker in the JIT operating environment?

7. How has the movement to JIT operations and automated manufacturing facilities affected the role of direct labor in management accounting practices?
8. Contrast the traditional manufacturing layout and the JIT production layout.
9. Name and describe the five time frames included in the traditional manufacturing process.
10. How has the inspection function changed in a JIT environment?
11. What is a nonvalue-adding activity?
12. Differentiate between a flexible manufacturing system and a computer-integrated manufacturing system.
13. What role does computer-integrated manufacturing play in JIT operations?
14. Identify several costs that are accounted for as direct costs in a JIT environment but that are treated as indirect costs in a traditional setting.
15. Why is the process costing method useful for computing the product unit costs of a JIT/FMS work cell?
16. Explain the meaning and use of the Raw in Process Inventory account.
17. Why is the analysis of nonfinancial data so important in a JIT environment?
18. Which level of capacity, normal or theoretical, is more important in analyzing a JIT/FMS operating cell? Why?
19. Give three examples of costs treated as indirect costs in a traditional manufacturing environment but accounted for as direct costs in a JIT setting. Explain the reasons for the three changes.
20. An automatic storage/retrieval system (AS/RS) is the key reason for the decrease in the levels of work in process inventories in a JIT/FMS environment. Why?

Communication Skills Exercises

Communication 25-1. Implementing Just-in-Time Procedures *(L.O. 2)*

J. I. Case Company is a leading manufacturer of agricultural and construction equipment and is a subsidiary of Tenneco, Inc. of Houston.[5] Case's agricultural equipment group is in the process of implementing a just-in-time operating environment. New cost management techniques utilizing nonfinancial data are required in a JIT environment to measure operating performance. These performance measures can be grouped into five general categories: quality, delivery, production process time, flexibility, and finance costs. One of the key methods used to assess product quality is to measure customer satisfaction. Working with two or three other students, develop a list of nonfinancial information and performance measures that would indicate that customers believe they have purchased a quality product. Select a spokesperson to report the group's findings to the class.

Communication 25-2. JIT, Synchronous Manufacturing Techniques, and Performance Measurement *(L.O. 1)*

General Motors Company's plant in Oshawa, Canada has changed its production process from a traditional departmental structure into nine individually focused minifactories, one for each major product line.[6] Each minifactory is a set of synchronous manufacturing work stations organized in a cell formation. Synchronous manufacturing is an offshoot of the JIT operating environment—all production is demand driven. To be synchronous, products from one station cannot be moved to the next until the receiving work station is ready to work on them. This system cuts lead times, improves quality, and reduces unit costs—all benefits of any JIT-based system.

GM's new performance measurement system has been named QUILS, which stands for quality, unit cost, inventory, lead time, and schedule. These five measures are used to monitor the plant's operating performance. Operating results are graphically displayed on large boards for easy viewing by all employees of a particular work cell. Quality is monitored using graphs of the trend of defects per million parts. Unit cost includes the cost of major components as well as the total manufacturing cost of products in a work

5. Michael R. Sellenheim, "J. I. Case Company: Performance Measurement," *Management Accounting,* Institute of Management Accountants, September 1991, pp. 50–53.
6. Anthony A. Atkinson, "GM's Innovation for Performance," *CMA Magazine,* The Society of Management Accountants of Canada, June 1990, pp. 10–14.

cell. Progress in the inventory area is measured by the trend in inventory turnover. The lead-time graphs summarize the cycle time of the products through the work cell, breaking the cycle time down into its constituent components. Schedule is depicted on a graph describing the percentage of production that was completed on time.

Prepare a short paper about GM's new performance measurement system. Respond to the following questions as part of your report: What do you think of the QUILS system? What is unique about it? Does it measure operating performance?

Communication 25-3. Ethics and JIT Implementation
(L.O. 2)

For almost a year, ***Barineau Company*** has been undergoing a change from a traditional to a JIT approach to its manufacturing process. Management has asked for employee assistance in the transition and has offered bonuses for suggestions that cut time from the production operation. Darby Lindsay and Todd Burks each identified a time-saving opportunity and, independently, turned in their suggestions to their manager, Sean McKinney.

McKinney sent the suggestions to the vice president of production and, inadvertently, they were identified as being his own. After careful analysis, the company's Production Review Committee decided that the two suggestions were worthy of reward and voted a large bonus to McKinney. When notified by the vice president, McKinney could not bring himself to identify the true authors of the suggestions.

When Lindsay and Burks heard about McKinney's ill-gained bonus, they were both very upset and confronted him with their grievance. He told them that he needed the recognition in order to be eligible for an upcoming promotion opportunity and stated that if they kept quiet about the matter, he would see to it that they both received significant raises. Prepare written responses so that you can discuss the following in class:

1. Should Lindsay and Burks keep quiet about the matter? What other avenues are open to them?
2. Having committed the fraudulent act, how should McKinney have dealt with the complaint of Lindsay and Burks?

Communication 25-4. Basic Research Skills
(L.O. 3)

Your campus library has a collection of annual reports for large, multinational companies as well as for companies in your state and local area. Many of these companies have recently installed automated just-in-time production processes in order to compete for new domestic as well as foreign business. Search through the annual reports of several manufacturers. Choose one that describes the changes made within its plant to increase product quality and to compete as a world-class manufacturer. Prepare a one-page description of those changes. Include in your report the name of the company, its geographic location, the name of the chief executive officer and/or president, and the dollar amount of total sales for the most recent year. Be prepared to present your findings to your classmates.

Classroom Exercises

Exercise 25-1. Computer-Integrated Manufacturing—Definition
(L.O. 1, 2)

Malott Plastics, Inc. has had trouble competing in world markets for the past five years. Every time the company attempts to reduce costs to maintain a price advantage, the quality of its products suffers. As the overall quality has decreased, so has the company's market share. Amy Malott, founder and president of the company, has asked the production consulting firm of Olson & Cox to develop a strategic plan that would make the company competitive again and improve the quality of its products.

Wade Cox did the fieldwork for the consulting firm before preparing the plan. Cox spent two weeks at Malott's facilities in New Jersey and obtained information from the plastics industry trade association regarding recent trends and changes in production. The latest manufacturing equipment was reviewed and compared to existing machinery. Product flow was observed. Inventory storage and management were studied. And customer complaints were analyzed.

Olson & Cox's recommendations included the following statements:

1. Adopt the just-in-time operating environment.
2. Purchase two flexible manufacturing systems to replace existing functional production lines.
3. Purchase enough computer support to enable overall production setup to be linked in a computer-integrated manufacturing system.

Explain these three statements to Amy Malott.

Exercise 25-2.
Old Versus New Manufacturing Environment
(L.O. 3)

Loomis Industries manufactures computer keyboard casings. The following machines and operations are involved in the production process:

Mixing machines — The Mixing Department has three machines that mix various chemicals to develop the raw materials used in the molding operation.

Molding machines — The Molding Department uses six molding machines. Each machine can be set up to make any keyboard casing sold by the company.

Trimming machines — In the Trimming Department, casings removed from the molds are trimmed of all excess materials. Six trimming machines are used.

Packing machines — Packing machines wrap and individually box each completed computer keyboard casing. Each of the two packing machines can keep pace with three trimming machines.

Products are moved from the mixing operation to the molding machines in 200-gallon drums. The drums usually sit one to three days before they are used. Sometimes the mixture must be remixed before it can be used by the Molding Department. From molding to trimming, the casings are stacked on wooden skids and moved by small lift trucks. The same moving procedure is used from trimming to the packing operation. Total production time can range from two weeks to three months, depending on the urgency of the order. Ed Loomis, CEO, is not happy with this rate of output. Suggest a plant layout that would change the manufacturing operation into a JIT production operation without the purchase of new equipment.

Exercise 25-3.
Direct Versus Indirect Costs
(L.O. 4)

The following cost categories are common in a manufacturing and assembly operation:

Raw materials	Operating supplies
Sheet steel	Small tools
Iron castings	Depreciation, plant
Assembly parts	Depreciation, machinery
Part 24RE6	Supervisory salaries
Part 15RF8	Electrical power
Direct labor	Insurance and taxes, plant
Engineering labor	President's salary
Indirect labor	Employee benefits

Identify each type of cost as being either direct or indirect, assuming the cost was incurred in (1) a traditional manufacturing setting and (2) a JIT/FMS environment.

State the reasons for any classification changes noted.

Exercise 25-4.
Product Costing in a Flexible Manufacturing System
(L.O. 4, 8)

Landis Enterprises, Inc. manufactures wooden serving trays using an FMS work cell. The wood is shaped and the trays assembled in one continuous operation. September's output totaled 42,300 units. Each unit requires two machine hours of effort. Materials handling cost is allocated to the product based on unit materials cost; engineering design costs are allocated based on units produced; and FMS cell overhead and building occupancy costs are allocated based on machine hours. Operating data for September are shown on page 1028.

Materials		
Wood	$97,290	
Hardware	50,760	$148,050
Materials handling		
Labor	$22,208	
Equipment depreciation	7,403	
Electrical power	4,442	
Maintenance	16,284	50,337
Direct labor		
Machinists		46,530
Engineering design		
Labor	$ 9,729	
Electrical power	5,922	
Engineering overhead	3,807	19,458
FMS cell overhead		
Indirect labor	$29,610	
Repairs and maintenance	20,304	
Supervision	16,920	
Equipment depreciation	6,768	
Operating supplies	4,230	
Electrical power	10,152	87,984
Building occupancy overhead		50,760
Total costs		$403,119

Materials handling cost allocation rate per dollar of materials:
$50,337 ÷ $148,050 = 34%

Engineering design cost allocation rate per unit:
$19,458 ÷ 42,300 = $0.46

FMS overhead allocation rate per machine hour:
$87,984 ÷ 84,600 = $1.04

Building occupancy allocation rate per machine hour:
$50,760 ÷ 84,600 = $0.60

Compute the unit cost of one wooden serving tray. Identify the six elements of the computation as part of your answer.

Exercise 25-5. Raw in Process Inventory *(L.O. 6)*

De Reyna Manufacturing Company installed a JIT/FMS environment in its Shovel Division, and the system has been operating at near capacity for about eight months. Transactions related to the JIT/FMS are recorded when incurred. The following transactions took place last week:

Sept. 5 Wooden handles for jobs 12A, 14N, and 13F were ordered and received, $3,670.
6 Sheet metal costing $5,630 received from vendor B.
7 Work begun on job 14N.
8 Job 12A completed and shipped to the customer; total cost, $13,600. (Company uses a 40 percent markup to establish selling price.)
9 Spoiled goods with a net realizable value of $1,200 were moved to the shipping dock to be sold as scrap.

Using good journal entry form, record these transactions.

Exercise 25-6.
The Changing Management Accounting Environment
(L.O. 7)

Bill Ross, president and CEO of Irving Products, Inc., has just called controller Kay Horstmann into his office. "Kay, I don't understand several parts of this request for a new management accounting system that you submitted yesterday. I thought that we already had a very modern, up-to-date system. Why this sudden request for a major change? Is your request in any way connected with our new flexible manufacturing system? If so, why does a new manufacturing system require a complete revamping of an accounting system? Can't existing accounting practices and procedures handle the new equipment?"

Prepare Kay Horstmann's reply to Bill Ross.

Exercise 25-7.
Product Costing Changes Caused by JIT and Automation
(L.O. 7)

Edberg Manufacturing Company produces high-tempered drill bits used by steel and aluminum products companies. The management accounting system uses standard costs. Cost control is accomplished by carefully computing and analyzing a series of price, rate, and efficiency variances. One factory overhead cost pool is used, and a plantwide overhead rate is the main aspect of the system. Direct labor hours is the base used to allocate factory overhead to products. Only raw materials and machinist labor are considered direct costs of the system.

Last week, the company installed its first FMS operating cell. The vice president of finance has asked the controller to identify specific changes to the management accounting system that are necessary because of the new flexible manufacturing system.

Prepare a summary of the information that should be included in the controller's response to the vice president of finance.

Exercise 25-8.
JIT's Influence on Product Unit Cost
(L.O. 4, 7)

Adamany Corporation has just installed a fully automated just-in-time production system. The entire manufacturing function comprises eight automated production cells that complete a product from beginning to end in less than two hours. Some products complete the production cycle in less than an hour. The production cycle time on the old, traditional processes took from three to five weeks. Now product orders are completed in two to three days.

What predictable effect will this production system change have on the following (give examples where appropriate)?

1. Total cost of raw materials and cost of raw materials per unit
2. Total cost of direct labor and cost of direct labor per unit
3. Total cost of factory overhead and cost of overhead per unit

Exercise 25-9.
JIT Unit Cost Computations
(L.O. 8)

DeJager Company installed an automated just-in-time production cell in its Battery Casings Division three months ago. Operating data for the first quarter of 19x4 is now available for analysis. Prior to the installation of the JIT cell, four operations were performed in functional departments to complete a casing. These departments were: Sheet Metal Cutting, Stamping, Shaping, and Finishing. Now all operations are performed in a single cell run by one machine operator. The controller is interested in a unit cost comparison and has selected casing FM20 for the analysis. Data for the last two quarters are shown on page 1030.

Compute the materials, labor, and factory overhead components of product FM20's unit cost for the last quarter of 19x3. (Round your answers to three decimal places.) Compute the materials, labor, and factory overhead components of product FM20's unit cost for the first quarter of 19x4. (Round your answers to three decimal places.) Identify the reasons for the change in total unit cost.

	Casing FM20	
	Quarter Ended 3/31/x4	Quarter Ended 12/31/x3
Units produced	39,450	21,780
Raw materials		
Sheet metal	$ 95,469	$ 56,846
Rivets	2,564	1,808
Direct labor		
Sheet metal cutting		26,136
Stamping		20,800
Shaping		16,422
Finishing		20,059
JIT cell	77,322	
Factory overhead		
Indirect labor	83,555	27,552
Operating supplies	2,998	2,047
Inspection	0	1,851
Lift truck labor	4,103	2,679
Electricity	21,106	7,405
Small tools expense	37,478	25,744
Machine depreciation	24,656	4,792
Building depreciation	3,945	2,723
Repairs and maintenance	5,089	6,207
Supervisory salaries	20,711	15,311
Lubricants	7,298	2,548
Storage space costs	2,762	11,935
Total costs incurred	$389,056	$252,865

Interpretation Case from Business

The Need for an Automated System: Hamby Woodworks, Inc.
(L.O. 2, 3)

In 1968, Ernest Hamby began tinkering with woodworking machinery in his basement in Lafayette, Indiana. His first projects were small tables, such as end tables and coffee tables for homes. After five years of part-time effort, Hamby developed his hobby into a small company: Two employees were hired, material suppliers were located, a building was leased, and new machinery was acquired. Furniture and cabinetmaking became the specialties of Hamby Woodworks, Inc.

In 1978, a famous professional golfer asked Hamby to produce a custom set of cabinets for her new home. She was so impressed with the hand-crafted features of the final product that she asked Hamby if the company could make a personalized set of persimmon wood golf clubs. Intrigued by the challenge, Hamby ordered the special wood and began making the necessary tools and dies for the wood-shaping machinery. The wood arrived, and the machines were set up for this small, precision-oriented work order. Machine shaping was used in conjunction with special hand crafting to produce the set of four golf woods. Two weeks after first being used in professional-level play, the clubs helped the pro golfer win her first professional tournament. The Hamby Club had made a very successful debut.

Since that storybook beginning, the Hamby Club has gained worldwide recognition. Demand for the product is so great that the company built a special plant that makes only custom-crafted clubs. The clubs are machine shaped but vary according to the customer's sex, height, weight, and arm length. Ten basic sets of clubs are produced, five for females and five for males. Slight variations in machine setup provide the difference in the club weights and lengths.

In the past six months, several problems have developed at the golf club plant. Even though one computer numerically controlled machine is used in the manufacturing process, the company's backlog is growing rapidly. Customers are complaining of slow delivery. Quality is declining because clubs are pushed through the production process and often shipped without proper inspection. Raw materials, work in process, and finished goods inventories are all over the plant, using up costly storage space and requiring thousands of dollars in invested working capital. Workers are complaining about the pressure to produce the backlogged orders. Machine breakdown is increasing. Production control reports are not useful because they are not timely and contain irrelevant information. Hamby's dream product has turned into a nightmare.

You have been hired by Hamby Woodworks, Inc. as a consultant to define the problem and suggest a possible solution to the current dilemma. Prepare a response to Hamby. Include in your analysis specific changes in the manufacturing process and the management reporting system. Defend each change suggested.

Problem Set A

Problem 25A-1. Production Layout Design *(L.O. 3)*

Bentley Automotive Products Company manufactures chrome automobile parts. The following manufacturing operations and functions are part of the production of all types of automobile grills:

Assembly	Connecting devices are put on the completed grill.
Stamping	The grill shape is stamped out of a piece of sheet metal.
Plating	A chrome substance is adhered to the heat-treated product.
Receiving	Sheet metal and assembly parts are received in the central receiving area.
Welding	Connector pads are attached to the heat-treated product before plating.
Washing	Products are cleaned before being inspected for the first time.
Postassembly inspection	Products are inspected just prior to being packaged.
Raw materials storage	Sheet metal and assembly parts are stored before they are used.
Drilling	Holes are drilled into the products before the connector pads are welded.
Bending	Stamped grills are bent into shape.
Heat treating	All products are heat-treated after passing the preassembly inspection point.
Sheet metal inspection	All sheet metal received is inspected.
Polishing	Plated grills are polished before being assembled.
Skid moving	All grills are moved on large wooden skids from operation to operation.
Shipping	Railroad cars are loaded for shipment to automobile manufacturers.
Packing	Grills are packed in large wooden crates.
Preassembly inspection	All grills are inspected after the washing operation.

Required

1. Arrange these operations in the order they would occur in a traditional manufacturing system.
2. Assume that a just-in-time approach is going to be taken in redesigning this production process. Identify the
   a. operations or process elements that would be eliminated.
   b. operations that would be automated.
   c. operations that could be combined into operating cells.
3. Is this company a good candidate for the JIT/FMS environment? Why or why not?

Problem 25A-2. Product Costing in a Flexible Manufacturing System
(L.O. 4, 8)

Grego Company produces a complete line of bicycle seats in its Flagstaff plant. The four versions of model J17-21 are made on flexible manufacturing system #2. The four seats have different shapes but identical processing operations and production costs. During July, the following costs were incurred and traced to FMS #2:

Materials		Engineering design	
Leather	$23,520	Labor	$ 4,116
Metal frame	38,220	Electrical power	1,176
Bolts	2,940	Engineering overhead	7,644
Materials handling		FMS overhead	
Labor	7,350	Equipment depreciation	7,056
Equipment depreciation	4,410	Indirect labor	30,870
Electrical power	2,460	Supervision	17,640
Maintenance	5,184	Operating supplies	4,410
Direct labor		Electrical power	10,584
Machinists	13,230	Repairs and maintenance	21,168
		Building occupancy overhead	52,920

July's output totaled 29,400 units. Each unit requires three machine hours of effort. Materials handling costs are allocated to the products based on unit materials cost; engineering design costs are allocated based on units produced; and FMS overhead is allocated based on machine hours.

Required

1. Compute the following:
   a. Materials handling cost allocation rate
   b. Engineering design cost allocation rate
   c. FMS overhead allocation rate
2. Compute the unit cost of one bicycle seat. Show details of your computation.

Problem 25A-3. Machine Hours Versus Labor Hours
(L.O. 4, 8)

Lou Weinstein has been in the manufacturing business for more than twenty years. Four months ago, Weinstein Products, Inc. made a major investment in automated machinery. The three new flexible manufacturing systems each have seven operating stations and produce chrome automobile bumpers in one operation. Each FMS specializes in one type of bumper; these products are identified as A-Bump, B-Bump and C-Bump, with A-Bump being the most complex and C-Bump the least difficult to make. After four months of operation, Weinstein began complaining to the controller about the ever-increasing factory overhead rate. Weinstein was under the impression that the new automated machinery was going to reduce product costs. A plantwide overhead rate is still being used, but the machinery installation consultant did suggest switching to individual FMS factory overhead rates, with materials handling costs being treated separately. These costs are currently included in the total factory overhead cost pool.

The following data are from the past month's records:

	A-Bump	B-Bump	C-Bump
Unit information			
Raw materials cost	$96	$88	$82
Direct labor hours	1.2	1.5	.8
Direct labor cost per hour	$20	$18	$16
Machine hours	4.2	3.1	3
Information totals			
Unit sales during month	50,000	70,000	100,000
Total factory overhead	$2,950,000	$1,242,500	$1,431,000

Weinstein's policy has been to set selling prices at 160 percent of a product's production cost.

Required

1. Compute the company's plantwide factory overhead rate using total direct labor dollars as a basis.
2. Compute each product's total production costs and selling price using the application rate computed in **1.**
3. Compute a new factory overhead application rate assuming:
   a. Materials storage and handling overhead equal to 5 percent of the cost of raw materials is subtracted from the factory overhead cost totals.
   b. Machine hours is the factory overhead allocation basis.
   c. Product line overhead rates are used rather than a plantwide rate.
4. Compute each product's total production cost and selling price using the allocation rates computed in **3.**
5. Compare the old and new product selling prices and comment on your findings.

Problem 25A-4. JIT and FIFO Process Costing
(L.O. 5)

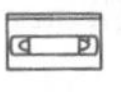

The Forest Company is located in Durango, Colorado and has been producing sink faucets for the past twelve years. The prices of the seven models of kitchen sink faucets range from $24 to $94. The Grand model is the highest-priced faucet, and its market share has declined steadily over the last four years.

Bothered by the decline in market share, management recently purchased a JIT/FMS cell for the kitchen faucet line. Two day-shift operators prepare the equipment to run automatically during the two evening shifts. Only indirect support labor is needed during the night shifts. For the week ending July 30, 19x2, the Grand model was run and the following data were generated:

Units	
Beginning work in process inventory (60 percent complete as to conversion costs, 100 percent complete as to materials costs)	45
Units completed during week	6,295
Ending work in process inventory (70 percent complete as to conversion costs, 100 percent complete as to materials costs)	50
Hours worked	
Direct labor—80 hours	
Machine hours	
Fourteen machines in cell	
Each machine in the FMS cell ran 116 hours during week	
Costs in beginning inventory	
Materials costs	$ 2,410
Conversion costs	765
Direct costs incurred by faucet JIT/FMS cell	
Raw materials	$157,458
Direct labor (80 hours at $16 per hour)	1,280
Electricity costs	6,056
JIT cell machinery depreciation	3,890
Engineering design costs	7,934
Indirect labor	12,000
Lubricants, supplies, and fasteners	8,110
Overhead rates used	
Materials handling overhead (included as part of raw materials cost in the process costing analysis): 25 percent of raw materials costs	
Factory overhead not traceable to cell: $42 per machine hour worked	

Required

1. Compute the total materials cost and total conversion cost for the week.
2. Using good form and the FIFO process costing approach, prepare (a) a schedule of equivalent production, (b) a unit cost analysis schedule, and (c) a cost summary schedule.
3. From the cost summary schedule, prepare a journal entry to transfer costs of completed units to the Finished Goods Inventory account.
4. Do you think the $94 price is too high for the Grand model? Explain your answer.

Problem 25A-5.
Traditional Versus JIT/FMS Unit Cost Analysis
(L.O. 3, 4, 5, 7, 8)

Pearson Products Company produces home products. Currently it maintains production lines for twelve different types of items, including a line of fruit juice presses. The press is adjustable to various sizes of fruits, so one press fits all needs. Diane Pearson started Pearson Products Company in her garage eleven years ago, and the company has grown to a point where it is now among the largest in the industry. The fruit juice press is assembled from parts manufactured by the company and from parts purchased from outside vendors. Pearson just installed a flexible manufacturing system for the press line. Everything is automated, including materials handling between machine ports.

The company still uses traditional methods for product costing, even though the new FMS has been operating for several weeks. You have been contacted to restructure the present accounting system to compute a more realistic product unit cost under the FMS conditions. Following are data from the current accounting period. The new system will cause several changes. Several indirect costs will be traceable directly to the FMS work cell and will not be included in the regular overhead rate computation. In addition, separate allocation rates will be needed for materials-related overhead costs and engineering costs. Costs related to inspection, rework, and work in process handling will be eliminated. The remaining indirect manufacturing costs (building occupancy costs) will be allocated using a machine hours base. Materials storage and handling overhead will be allocated based on total dollars of materials and parts incurred. Engineering hours will be used as a basis for engineering overhead allocation. Process costing procedures will be used to compute unit costs.

	Traditional Manufacturing System	JIT/Flexible Manufacturing System
Costs directly traceable to product		
Raw materials	$ 819,400	$ 819,400
Parts for assembly	482,000	482,000
Direct labor		
Traditional		
1.8 hr at $12/hr per unit	2,082,240	
JIT/FMS		
.4 hr at $15/hr per unit		578,400
Total costs traceable to product	$3,383,640	$1,879,800
Costs directly traceable to FMS cell		
Setup labor		$ 115,680
Other indirect labor		212,080
Electrical power		38,560
Repairs and maintenance		33,740
Supervision salaries		43,380
Depreciation, machinery		79,048
Operating supplies and lubricants		17,352
Total costs directly traceable to FMS cell		$ 539,840

	Traditional Manufacturing System	JIT/Flexible Manufacturing System
Companywide indirect manufacturing cost pool		
Setup labor	$ 421,780	
Electrical power, factory	163,200	
Supervision, factory	210,670	
Purchased parts, inspection costs	78,230	
Product rework costs	142,500	
Depreciation, machinery	199,600	
Other indirect labor	391,990	
Purchasing costs, materials and parts	148,200	
Materials/parts storage and handling	226,200	
Depreciation, materials moving trucks	31,200	
Engineering labor	360,000	
Electrical costs, engineering	28,800	
Depreciation, engineering equipment	32,400	
Engineering supervision	68,400	
Other engineering overhead	21,600	
Operating supplies and lubricants	38,450	
Finished goods inspection costs	89,760	
Machinery repairs and maintenance	174,560	
Storage and handling, work in process inventory	234,190	
Depreciation, building	121,400	$ 121,400
Property taxes	24,360	24,360
Fire insurance	9,860	9,860
Liability insurance	8,540	8,540
Building maintenance	34,170	34,170
Other factory utilities	19,230	19,230
Factory employee cafeteria	165,290	165,290
Total indirect manufacturing costs	$3,444,580	$ 382,850
Engineering overhead cost pool		
Engineering labor		$ 360,000
Electrical costs, engineering		28,800
Depreciation, engineering equipment		32,400
Engineering supervision		68,400
Other engineering overhead		21,600
Total engineering overhead costs		$ 511,200
Materials storage and handling overhead cost pool		
Purchasing costs, materials and parts		$ 148,200
Materials/parts storage and handling		226,200
Depreciation, materials moving trucks		31,200
Total materials storage and handling overhead costs		$ 405,600

The preceeding data have been partially restructured in anticipation of the new system. At the top of the next page is a summary of other information that will be required for the analysis.

Total companywide direct labor hours		
Actual for last period	1,216,600	DLH
Anticipated for this period	714,000	DLH
Total anticipated companywide machine hours for the period	1,850,400	MH
Total anticipated companywide engineering hours for the period	18,000	eng. hr
Total anticipated companywide dollar value of materials and parts for the period	$7,800,000	
Number of fruit juice presses produced	96,400	presses
Anticipated machine hours for press FMS	308,400	MH
Anticipated engineering hours for press FMS	7,200	eng. hr
Process costing information for press FMS		
Beginning inventory		
Materials and parts	$4,040	
Conversion costs	2,810	
Equivalent units for period		
Materials and parts	96,700	equiv. units
Conversion costs	96,600	equiv. units

Required

1. Under the traditional system,
   a. Compute the companywide manufacturing overhead application rate.
   b. Using traditional labor data, compute the product unit cost for each fruit juice press.
2. Identify the cost categories that will likely be eliminated when the company adopts a JIT/FMS approach.
3. Compute the JIT/FMS application rates for the following:
   a. Indirect manufacturing costs
   b. Engineering overhead costs
   c. Materials storage and handling overhead costs
4. Identify the total materials costs and conversion costs for the period for the press FMS cell.
5. Using the FIFO process costing method, compute the unit cost of a fruit juice press under the new JIT/FMS setting.

Problem Set B

Problem 25B-1. Production Layout Design *(L.O. 3)*

Processing and canning vegetables and fruits is a major industry in many countries. Pelican Food Products Company of Vero Beach, Florida is one of the biggest food processors in the Southeast. The following processing operations for black-eyed peas are common in this industry:

Cooking	Heating peas to a correct temperature so that consumers only have to reheat and serve
Inspecting raw peas	Weeding out inedible peas
Canning	Automatically putting cooked peas into cans
Labeling	Placing labels on processed cans
Shelling	Taking shells off raw peas
Finished goods storage	Storing canned peas while they await shipment
Cleaning	Washing peas before processing
Receiving	Central receiving area for freshly picked peas
Packing	Placing labeled cans in boxes
Lid sealing	Sealing lids on cans to prevent spoilage or leakage

Shipping	Truck loading area (cartons shipped according to customers' needs)
Bin storage	Storing raw peas before processing
Can inspection	Isolating improperly sealed cans
Cooling	Reducing temperature of cooked peas to facilitate canning operation

Required

1. Arrange these operations in the order they would occur in a traditional production system.
2. Assume that just-in-time operations are going to replace the traditional production process. Identify the
   a. operations or process elements that would be eliminated.
   b. operations that would be automated.
   c. operations that could be combined into operating cells.
3. Is this company a good candidate for the JIT/FMS environment? Be prepared to defend your answer.

Problem 25B-2. Product Costing in a Flexible Manufacturing System
(L.O. 4, 8)

Slavin Apparel, Inc. specializes in manufacturing business suits for women. The company has three basic suit lines and can produce more than a dozen variations of each basic design. Last year, because of rising backlogs and declining quality, the company installed a flexible manufacturing system for all three suit lines. Operating results to date have been very good, but management would still like to improve its delivery cycle and reduce the cost per unit.

Following are the operating data for October:

Materials		Pattern design	
Cloth material	$233,600	Labor	$ 22,806
Lining material	94,900	Electrical power	5,475
Sewing supplies	29,200	Pattern design overhead	12,775
Materials handling		FMS overhead	
Labor	4,380	Equipment depreciation	5,840
Equipment depreciation	3,285	Indirect labor	26,280
Electrical power	2,190	Supervision	49,640
Maintenance	2,920	Operating supplies	13,140
Direct labor		Electrical power	8,760
Machinists	80,300	Repairs and maintenance	7,300
		Building occupancy overhead	67,160

October's output totaled 3,650 suits. Each suit requires four machine hours of effort. Materials handling cost is allocated to the product based on unit materials cost; pattern design costs are allocated based on units produced; and FMS overhead is allocated based on machine hours.

Required

1. Compute the following:
   a. Materials handling cost allocation rate
   b. Pattern design cost allocation rate
   c. FMS overhead allocation rate
2. Compute the unit cost of one business suit. Show details of your computation.

Problem 25B-3. Machine Hours Versus Labor Hours
(L.O. 4, 8)

In 1977, Shelley Boyce and Aron Fleck formed S & A Industries, Inc. The company specializes in recreational furniture for all types of outdoor life. Portable tables are the company's best-selling product, and three models have become very popular products: the Mini, Max, and Deluxe models.

To keep up with the competition, the company purchased flexible manufacturing systems for these product lines about eight months ago. But since the purchase, factory overhead rates have been increasing, to the disappointment of Boyce and Fleck, who have asked the controller to prepare a comparative analysis of this situation.

The following data are from the past month's records:

	Mini	Max	Deluxe
Unit information			
Raw materials cost	$21	$32	$46
Direct labor hours	2.2	2.8	3.4
Direct labor cost per hour	$16	$16	$16
Machine hours	3.4	3.2	3
Information totals			
Unit sales during month	120,000	108,000	94,000
Total factory overhead	$2,904,000	$3,024,000	$2,876,400

The company's policy has been to set selling prices at 180 percent of a product's production cost.

Required

1. Compute the company's plantwide factory overhead rate using total direct labor dollars as a basis.
2. Compute each product's total production costs and selling price using the application rate computed in **1.**
3. Compute a new factory overhead application rate assuming:
   a. Materials storage and handling overhead equal to 10 percent of the cost of raw materials is subtracted from the factory overhead cost totals.
   b. Machine hours is the factory overhead allocation basis.
   c. Product line overhead rates are used rather than a plantwide rate.
4. Compute each product's total production cost and selling price using the allocation rates computed in **3.**
5. Compare the old and new product selling prices and comment on your findings.

Problem 25B-4. JIT and Process Costing—Average Method
(L.O. 5)

Enzian Corporation has manufactured ladders for both home and business use for more than twenty-five years. Ten years ago the company introduced all-aluminum models, and the Enzian Ladder became a very popular brand. But with the recent introduction of several other brands of aluminum ladders into the marketplace, the Enzian models have suffered significant sales declines. The company produces two major types of ladders: collapsible stepladders and extension ladders. Three sizes of each type of ladder are produced. Extension ladders come in 8-, 10-, and 12-foot lengths and cost $80, $100, and $125, respectively. The 12-foot model is known as the Primo Ladder.

To improve efficiency and reduce operating costs, the company purchased two JIT/flexible manufacturing systems last year, one for each type of ladder produced. Three direct labor workers run the extension ladder cell, one worker for each of the three eight-hour shifts per day. Most of the operation is run automatically, and several indirect labor support people help with setups and maintenance.

During the week ended August 12, 19x2, the extension ladder work cell produced the following data pertaining to the manufacturing of the Primo Ladder:

Units	
Beginning work in process inventory	60
Units completed during week	4,280
Ending work in process inventory (60 percent complete as to conversion costs, 100 percent complete as to materials costs)	40
Hours worked	
Direct labor—120 hours	
Machine hours	
Eleven machines in the cell	
Each machine in the FMS cell ran 112 hours during week	
Costs in beginning inventory	
Materials costs	$ 1,780
Conversion costs	1,450

Direct costs incurred by extension ladder JIT/FMS cell	
Raw materials	$96,994
Direct labor (120 hours at $19 per hour)	2,280
Electrical power costs	8,342
JIT cell machinery depreciation	2,780
Engineering design costs	8,570
Indirect labor	12,320
Lubricants, supplies, and fasteners	4,410

Overhead rates used
Materials handling overhead (included as part of raw materials cost in the process costing analysis): 30 percent of raw materials costs
Factory overhead not traceable to cell: $53 per machine hour worked

Required

1. Compute the total materials cost and the total conversion cost for the week.
2. Using good form and the average process costing approach, prepare the following schedules:
   a. schedule of equivalent production
   b. unit cost analysis schedule
   c. cost summary schedule
3. From the cost summary schedule, prepare a journal entry to transfer the costs of completed units to the Finished Goods Inventory account.
4. Do you think the $125 price is too high for the Primo Ladder? Why?

Problem 25B-5. Traditional Versus JIT/FMS Unit Cost Analysis
(L.O. 3, 4, 5, 7, 8)

Olson & Campbell Products, Inc. produces fans for home and business use. The company was created in 1974 and has grown steadily over the years. Last year management decided to install the company's first flexible manufacturing system in the Ceiling Fan Department. The deluxe ceiling fan's casing and wooden blades are manufactured by the company; the small motor and electrical parts are purchased from outside vendors and assembled by the company. Presently, the company uses a traditional cost accounting system, and unit costs are computed by adding a plantwide manufacturing overhead factor to the unit direct materials and direct labor costs. The overhead allocation basis has been direct labor hours.

You have been asked to restructure the present manufacturing cost data so that the influence of the new system on product unit costs can be analyzed. Following are data from the most recent accounting period. The new system will cause several changes. Many of the indirect costs will be directly traceable to the FMS work cell and do not have to be included in the regular overhead computation. Also, separate allocations will be made for materials-related overhead costs and engineering overhead. Remaining indirect manufacturing costs (building occupancy costs) will be allocated based on machine hours. Materials storage and handling overhead will be allocated based on total dollars of materials and parts incurred. Engineering overhead will be allocated based on engineering hours. Process costing procedures will be used to compute unit costs.

	Traditional Manufacturing System	JIT/Flexible Manufacturing System
Costs directly traceable to product		
Raw materials	$ 539,280	$ 539,280
Parts for assembly	1,823,280	1,823,280
Direct labor		
Traditional		
4.2 hr at $14/hr per unit	3,774,960	
JIT/FMS		
.8 hr at $18/hr per unit		924,480
Total costs traceable to product	$6,137,520	$3,287,040

	Traditional Manufacturing System	JIT/Flexible Manufacturing System
Costs directly traceable to FMS cell		
Electrical power		$ 65,680
Supervision		24,630
Depreciation, machinery		19,704
Setup labor		197,040
Other indirect labor		361,240
Repairs and maintenance		57,470
Operating supplies and lubricants		29,556
Total costs directly traceable to FMS cell		$755,320
Plantwide indirect manufacturing cost pool		
Product rework costs	$ 741,100	
Electrical power, factory	363,000	
Supervision, factory	246,800	
Depreciation, machinery	74,200	
Purchased motors, inspection costs	67,400	
Setup labor	231,120	
Other indirect labor	526,440	
Engineering labor	176,800	
Electrical costs, engineering	163,200	
Depreciation, engineering equipment	91,800	
Engineering supervision	104,720	
Other engineering overhead	53,040	
Operating supplies and lubricants	36,890	
Finished goods inspection costs	79,800	
Machinery repairs and maintenance	234,200	
Storage and handling, work in process inventory	432,900	
Depreciation, building	154,700	$154,700
Property taxes	28,900	28,900
Fire insurance	11,320	11,320
Liability insurance	15,540	15,540
Building maintenance	43,500	43,500
Other factory utilities	21,900	21,900
Factory employee cafeteria	134,200	134,200
Purchasing costs, materials and parts	96,700	
Materials/parts storage and handling	212,300	
Depreciation, materials moving trucks	68,700	
Total indirect manufacturing costs	$4,411,170	$410,060
Engineering overhead cost pool		
Engineering labor		$176,800
Power costs, engineering		163,200
Depreciation, engineering equipment		91,800
Engineering supervision		104,720
Other engineering overhead		53,040
Total engineering overhead costs		$589,560

	Traditional Manufacturing System	JIT/Flexible Manufacturing System
Materials storage and handling overhead cost pool		
Purchasing costs, materials and parts		$ 96,700
Materials/parts storage and handling		212,300
Depreciation, materials moving trucks		68,700
Total materials storage and handling overhead costs		$377,700

These data have been partially restructured in anticipation of the new system. Following is a summary of other information that will be required for the analysis:

Total plantwide direct labor hours	
Actual for last period	1,956,000 DLH
Anticipated for this period	782,400 DLH
Total anticipated plantwide machine hours for the period	2,475,000 MH
Total anticipated plantwide engineering hours for the period	25,340 eng. hr
Total anticipated plantwide dollar value of materials and parts for the period	$18,400,000
Number of fans produced	64,200 fans
Anticipated machine hours for fan FMS	131,360 MH
Anticipated engineering hours for fan FMS	6,800 eng. hr
Process costing information for fan FMS	
Beginning inventory	
Materials and parts	$6,420
Conversion costs	4,960
Equivalent units for period	
Materials and parts	64,320 equiv. units
Conversion costs	64,300 equiv. units

Required

1. Under the traditional system,
   a. Compute the plantwide manufacturing overhead application rate.
   b. Using traditional labor data, compute the product unit cost for each fan.
2. Identify the cost categories that will likely be eliminated when the company adopts a JIT/FMS approach.
3. Compute the JIT/FMS application rates for the following:
   a. Indirect manufacturing costs
   b. Engineering overhead costs
   c. Materials storage and handling overhead costs
4. Identify the total materials costs and conversion costs for the period for the fan FMS cell.
5. Using the FIFO process costing method, compute the fan unit cost under the new JIT/FMS setting.

Management Decision Case

Kingsley Iron Works
(L.O. 3, 4)

The management of Kingsley Iron Works has decided to convert its present traditional manufacturing system in the Castings Department to a just-in-time operation. The following tasks have been accomplished:

1. An agreement was signed with a supplier for daily deliveries of iron ingots needed for the department's iron casting products. The department supervisor is responsible for ordering the ingots.

2. Responsibility for machine repairs and maintenance and for product quality control and inspection was shifted to the machine operators in the Castings Department.
3. Three CNC machines were purchased that are capable of melting the ingots, mixing specified alloys, and molding the castings ordered to specific shapes and sizes. In addition, an automated conveyor system was purchased for work in process movement between the new machines. The entire operation is now a flexible manufacturing system and is operated in a just-in-time manner.
4. New electrical power meters were installed in all departments of the plant so that each unit's power usage can be monitored and computed. Each machine's electrical power usage in the Castings Department can be identified.
5. Insurance rates on plant machinery are broken down on a per machine hour usage basis.
6. Due to streamlining, the size of the Castings Department was reduced by 50 percent.
7. There are now eight direct labor workers in the Castings Department; there were twenty-six before the FMS was installed.

Kingsley Iron Works has a second department, the Small Tools Department, that specializes in making over twenty varieties of small iron and steel hand tools for business. The Small Tools Department still operates under the traditional methods and has only one automated machine. Thirty-six direct labor employees are needed to keep the department running. Because products are moved manually, large bins of partially completed tools are everywhere. Individual machine power usage is not metered. Repair and maintenance of machines is done on an as-needed basis. Raw materials are ordered two months in advance so that there is never a stock out.

The following facts relate to last month's operating activities:

	Castings Department	Small Tools Department	Totals
Direct labor hours	1,344	6,336	7,680
Machine hours			
Castings Department			
Machine A	484		484
Machine B	440		440
Machine C	420		420
Small Tools Department			
Semiautomatic machine		176	176
Nonprogrammed machinery*		1,920	1,920
Engineering hours used	640	320	960
Computer time usage (hours)	300	25	325
Cost of raw materials used	$96,000	$120,000	$216,000
Square footage of department (revised)	3,000	9,000	12,000

*When using nonprogrammed machine hours for distribution purposes, they should count one-tenth as much as computer-driven machine hours.

Details for the Castings Department:

	Job 101	Job 105	Job 110	Totals
Direct labor hours	168	672	504	1,344
Machine hours				
Machine A	220	132	132	484
Machine B	264	88	88	440
Machine C	84	210	126	420
Totals	568	430	346	1,344

Plantwide factory overhead costs	
Property taxes, building	$ 2,400
Wages, warehouse	8,640
Depreciation, warehouse equipment	1,296
Depreciation, factory machines	5,992
Depreciation, engineering equipment	1,440
Raw materials handling costs	25,920
Indirect support labor	15,408
Computer center costs, factory	4,030
Salaries, engineering	8,160
Operating supplies, engineering	1,728
Salaries, Accounting Department	5,136
Salaries, Personnel Department	7,104
Cafeteria expenses	4,736
Insurance, building	600
Insurance, factory machinery	3,424
Employee benefits	3,552
Repairs and Maintenance Department	2,576
Quality Control Department	3,312
Electrical power, building	10,200
Electrical power, machines	5,136
Purchasing Department expenses	3,240
Total	$124,030

Required

1. Compute the traditional plantwide factory overhead rate based on direct labor hours. Allocate the overhead costs to both departments and to the jobs in the Castings Department using this approach.
2. Recommend changes to Kingsley's management concerning the distribution of traditional indirect costs to both departments. Identify the allocation basis to be used for each cost listed.
3. Distribute the costs to both departments and to the jobs in the Castings Department using the methods you recommended in **2.** Use machine hours as the basis for the distribution of costs to Castings' jobs.
4. Highlight and explain the differences resulting from the two approaches.

Answers to Self-Test

1. a	3. d	5. b	7. d	9. c
2. c	4. c	6. d	8. a	10. b

LEARNING OBJECTIVES

1. *Define* cost management *and describe a* cost management system.
2. *Define and explain* activity-based costing, *and list examples of* cost drivers.
3. *Identify all activities that comprise a particular operating process, distinguish between value-adding and non-value-adding activities, and describe the value chain of a product or service.*
4. *Identify and compute the costs of quality for products and services.*
5. *Evaluate operating performance using nonfinancial measures of quality.*
6. *Identify the types of financial and nonfinancial analyses used in a JIT environment to evaluate the performance of (a) product delivery, (b) inventory control, (c) materials cost/scrap control, and (d) machine management and maintenance.*
7. *Define* full cost profit margin *and state the advantages of this measure of profitability.*
8. *Identify the primary areas of management reporting in a JIT/FMS environment and give examples of reports needed.*

CHAPTER 26

Cost Management Systems, Including Activity-Based Costing and Measures of Quality

In the new manufacturing environment introduced in the chapter on the just-in-time operating environment and automation, it was stressed that management accountants must assess the applicability of traditional internal accounting methods and procedures before using them with automated JIT production systems. Many of the traditional approaches to product costing, performance measurement, and operations control need to be re-evaluated in the JIT environment. In this chapter we explore newly developed cost management systems, looking first at activity-based costing methods and procedures. We then delve into total quality management (TQM), and identify and analyze the various measures of quality. The chapter concludes with an analysis of the full cost profit margin, a new measure of profitability in the JIT environment, and a closer look at JIT/FMS performance measures and management reports. After studying this chapter, you should be able to meet the learning objectives listed on the left.

DECISION POINT

Sola Optical Company[1]

■ Sola Optical Company is a manufacturer of ophthalmic spectacle lenses, located in Petaluma, California. Until 1988, the company operated in a traditional manner, experiencing continual growth in sales and profitability while holding a constant lens market share. But in 1988, Sola Optical purchased another company. The firm's management now had responsibility for new product lines and divisions that were located in three different geographic regions. Sales volume doubled, as did the number of employees. To help control the new operations and to compete globally, Sola Optical developed a TQM/JIT operating environment.

After examining the company's approach to product quality, a consultant determined that 20 percent of revenues were being spent either to create and ensure quality or to rework defective goods. Clearly, management needed a way to control the costs of quality while still ensuring high product quality. The company implemented activity-based costing. For each quality problem area, the activities involved were identified and analyzed. Costs were traced to the activities and reported to the managers and employees in each of the processes under review. The company formed

1. Richard K. Youde, "Cost of Quality Reporting: How We See It," *Management Accounting*, Institute of Management Accountants, January 1992, pp. 34–38.

quality teams that created cost-of-quality reports that were posted in each plant. Employees' suggestions were used to improve quality and to reduce quality costs. The result was a dramatic reduction in the costs of quality and an increase in the quality of all product lines.

How did management's decision to use activity-based costing increase overall product quality while significantly reducing the costs of quality?

There are "good" costs of quality and "bad" costs of quality. Good costs of quality are incurred to either prevent or uncover problems with a product or process before the product is manufactured. Bad costs of quality—the costs of poor quality—are incurred after a product is manufactured, to rework entire batches of defective products. By identifying the activities that generated costs of poor quality, Sola Optical's management was able to eliminate unnecessary activities, correct poorly implemented activities, add or modify quality-enhancing activities, and reduce the number of product defects. Although the company incurred additional costs to prevent defects, rework costs and separate inspection costs were reduced because employees began inspecting goods as production took place. The overall effect was a significant reduction in the total costs of quality, a dramatic increase in product quality, and increased profitability. ■

Cost Management Systems

OBJECTIVE 1
Define cost management *and describe a cost management system*

We have seen that many traditional management accounting techniques and practices do not produce meaningful results when applied to the new manufacturing environment. Companies have found that traditional cost allocation and product costing approaches generate erroneous unit cost information when used to measure the output of automated JIT operations. Traditional management accounting practices were not designed to identify and eliminate non-value-adding activities. Computerized facilities and computer-aided processes do enable the accountant to trace more types of costs directly to work cells or products. Traditional practices do not trace costs adequately; they do not isolate the costs of unnecessary activities; they do not penalize overproduction; and they do not quantify such nonfinancial measures as quality, throughput, and flexibility.[2] Their focus is on costs, not on the activities that generate costs.

These concerns have led to the creation of cost management systems (CMS). According to James Brimson, a partner in Coopers & Lybrand, Deloitte, United Kingdom, **cost management** is the management and control of *activities* to determine product cost accurately, to improve business processes, to eliminate waste, to identify cost drivers, to plan operations, and to set business strategies.[3] Rather than take an historical approach to cost control as most existing cost accounting systems do, a cost management system is online and interactive with current management decisions and strategies. A CMS plays a major role in planning, managing, and reducing costs. Cost cutting is not accomplished by just slashing the amount of existing resources that a department can use to produce a product, as happens in a traditional costing system. A CMS relies on the concept of continuous improvement to reduce costs while still

2. Callie Berliner and James A. Brimson, *Cost Management for Today's Advanced Manufacturing*, Computer Aided Manufacturing—International (Boston: Harvard Business School Press, 1988).
3. James A. Brimson, *Activity Accounting* (New York: John Wiley & Sons, 1991).

increasing product quality. Continuous improvement means that design engineers are continuously looking for ways to improve the product while still cutting its cost; the production process is watched constantly to find areas for improvement, thereby increasing efficiency and reducing costs; and nonvalue-adding activities are monitored continuously to find activities or resource usage that can be reduced or eliminated. In cost management systems, the primary focus is on the management of activities, not costs, for both product costing and cost control purposes. CMS advocates believe that when activities are managed effectively, a natural consequence is the effective use of money and other resources.

Another trait of a cost management system is the use of target costing, an approach to pricing that was discussed in the chapter on pricing decisions, including transfer pricing. When continuous improvement is employed, a company can increase profits by first designing the product so that its target cost is achieved. It can then make ongoing improvements to reduce costs further. Finally, cost assignment within a cost management system is far superior to traditional cost systems. By accumulating costs by activities and then tracking and tracing the usage of the activity to specific products or product types, costs can be assigned easily and accurately.

Activity-Based Costing

OBJECTIVE 2
Define and explain activity-based costing, and list examples of cost drivers

Problems arise when traditional cost allocation and product costing methods are used in automated JIT operations because of changes in direct labor. Critics insist that costs assigned to products using direct labor as a basis increasingly distort product costs as direct labor becomes a smaller and smaller factor in production. Even though many nonvalue-adding costs are reduced significantly or eliminated by adopting JIT procedures, the problem of cost traceability remains. Numerous product costing errors can result if all indirect product-related costs are charged to one Factory Overhead account and if those costs are allocated to products based on direct labor hours or dollars.[4]

Cost management systems resolve these problems with a new method of tracing and managing costs, called *activity-based costing.* **Activity-based costing (ABC)** is an approach to cost assignment that identifies all major operating activities, categorizes costs by activity, reduces or eliminates nonvalue-adding activities, and assigns costs using a basis that causes the costs to be incurred. A company that uses activity-based costing allocates product costs by identifying production and distribution activities and the events and circumstances that cause or "drive" those activities. As a result, many smaller cost pools are created, and many different cost assignments are made either directly to a product or job or to a JIT work cell. The costs traced or assigned to a work cell then are allocated to the products produced by that cell based on cost drivers.

Identifying Cost Drivers

When a company uses activity-based costing, cost drivers are the basis for cost assignment. A **cost driver** is any activity that causes a cost to be incurred.

The objective of a traditional management accounting system is cost control. Cost allocation procedures assign costs to cost objectives on a causal or beneficial basis. These assigned costs then are compared with budgeted amounts to help control costs. In the new manufacturing environment, using activity-based

4. Robin Cooper and Robert S. Kaplan, "How Cost Accounting Distorts Product Costs," *Management Accounting,* Institute of Management Accountants, April 1988, p. 21.

costing, the objective is to identify and eliminate unnecessary costs rather than just trying to reduce them through cost control procedures. But before we can eliminate a cost or account for it properly, we must know what causes the cost—what drives it. Once the cost driver has been identified, the indirect costs it generates can be either (1) treated as legitimate product costs and traced directly to a work cell or product or (2) reduced or eliminated by reducing or eliminating the activities that cause the costs to be incurred.

Table 26-1 lists ten potential cost drivers. Let's look at one—the number of engineering change orders—and develop a list of costs that it generates. Suppose an engineering change is made that leads to the reworking of products already produced as well as those in the production process. The possible costs generated by this engineering change order include the following:

1. Additional engineering time and labor costs
2. Utility and space costs associated with the extra work
3. Machine setup time and costs caused by the change order
4. Product rework time in the work cell
5. Increased conversion costs in the cell

Most engineering change orders occur because the design of the product was not refined before it was introduced into the manufacturing process. The costs associated with engineering change orders are reduced if the number of change orders is reduced. In addition, if an engineering change order is for a specific job, then all costs related to that activity are traceable and chargeable to that job. Following activity-based costing procedures, there is no need to allocate these costs through a single Factory Overhead account to all units produced, as is done by the traditional allocation method. By focusing on cost drivers and their associated costs, management can correct operating inefficiencies and reduce overall product costs. These cost reductions make price reductions possible, which can help increase sales, market share, and profitability.

Assigning Costs Using Activity-Based Costing

Cost assignment using activity-based costing principles is a two-step procedure. First, the accountant identifies activities and traces all costs attributable to and caused by those activities. Second, the accountant assigns costs to work cells,

Table 26-1. Examples of Potential Cost Drivers

Number of labor transactions
Number of material moves
Number of parts received in a month
Number of products
Number of schedule changes
Number of vendors
Number of units reworked
Number of engineering change orders
Number of direct labor employees
Number of new parts added

Source: Robert D. McIlhattan, "How Cost Management Systems Can Support the JIT Philosophy," *Management Accounting*, September 1987, p. 22. Used by permission of the Institute of Management Accountants.

jobs, or products by the amount of their use of each of the activities. Cost drivers are identified with each of the activities, and they are the mechanism for cost assignment. For example, assume that one of the activities of Forest Highlands Company is machine setup, the process of making a machine ready to run a particular product. Four specially trained indirect workers make up the machine setup team. Suppose that the costs generated and traceable to the setup activity for July totaled $17,600 and that a total of 640 setup hours were used. The cost driver is the number of setup hours. If Job AD26 involved three setups requiring a total of 18.4 hours, $506 in setup costs should be assigned to Job AD26 ($17,600 ÷ 640 = $27.50 per setup hour × 18.4 hours = $506). An actual ABC system includes cost assignments for dozens of activities. The Review Problem at the end of this chapter illustrates other aspects of activity-based costing, and it compares product costing in a traditional and a JIT/ABC system.

Process Value Analysis—Identifying the Activities

OBJECTIVE 3
Identify all activities that comprise a particular operating process, distinguish between value-adding and nonvalue-adding activities, and describe the value chain of a product or service

Identifying the activities in an operating process is an important but difficult task. How detailed should the process be? What exactly is an activity? Is every action taken throughout the company considered an activity? Obviously, the activities identified should be detailed enough so that all essential areas are included; but trying to associate costs with too many areas is not cost-effective. A balanced approach is best.

From a cost management viewpoint, a business is comprised of functions, activities, and tasks. Figure 26-1 is a schematic diagram that shows the relationships among functions, activities, and tasks. A **function** is a group of activities that have a common purpose or objective. The functions of a manufacturing company make up the product's value chain and include product design, engineering, production, distribution, marketing, and customer service follow-up. So the **value chain** of a product or service is all of the functions (and related activities) in its development path that add or contribute to its value and marketability. An **activity** is an action that is needed to accomplish the purpose or objective of a function. As shown in Figure 26-1, the activities of an engineering department might include new-product engineering, developing and maintaining bills (listings) of materials used, developing product routings, filling special orders, conducting capacity studies, implementing engineering change orders, developing ways to improve the process, laboratory testing, and designing tools. **Tasks** are the work elements or operating steps needed to perform and complete an activity. The tasks of a new-product engineering activity might include making up a list of specifications for a new product, researching similar product designs, developing an initial set of engineering drawings, and reviewing the design with production personnel. There can be hundreds of tasks for each activity, and many activities for each function.

Activity-based costing matches costs to activities. To use activity-based costing, one must (1) identify all of the activities in a product's value chain functions and (2) identify the causes of the costs of those activities. **Process value analysis (PVA)** is the process of identifying all activities and relating them to events that create or drive the need for the activities and the resources consumed. In process value analysis, management has a technique to identify those activities that add value to a product and to isolate those that simply add cost.[5] PVA forces managers to look critically at all existing phases of their operations. By reducing or eliminating nonvalue-adding activities and costs, and by

5. Michael R. Ostrenga, "Activities: The Focal Point of Total Cost Management," *Management Accounting*, Institute of Management Accountants, February 1990, p. 43.

Figure 26-1. Elements Underlying a Cost Management System

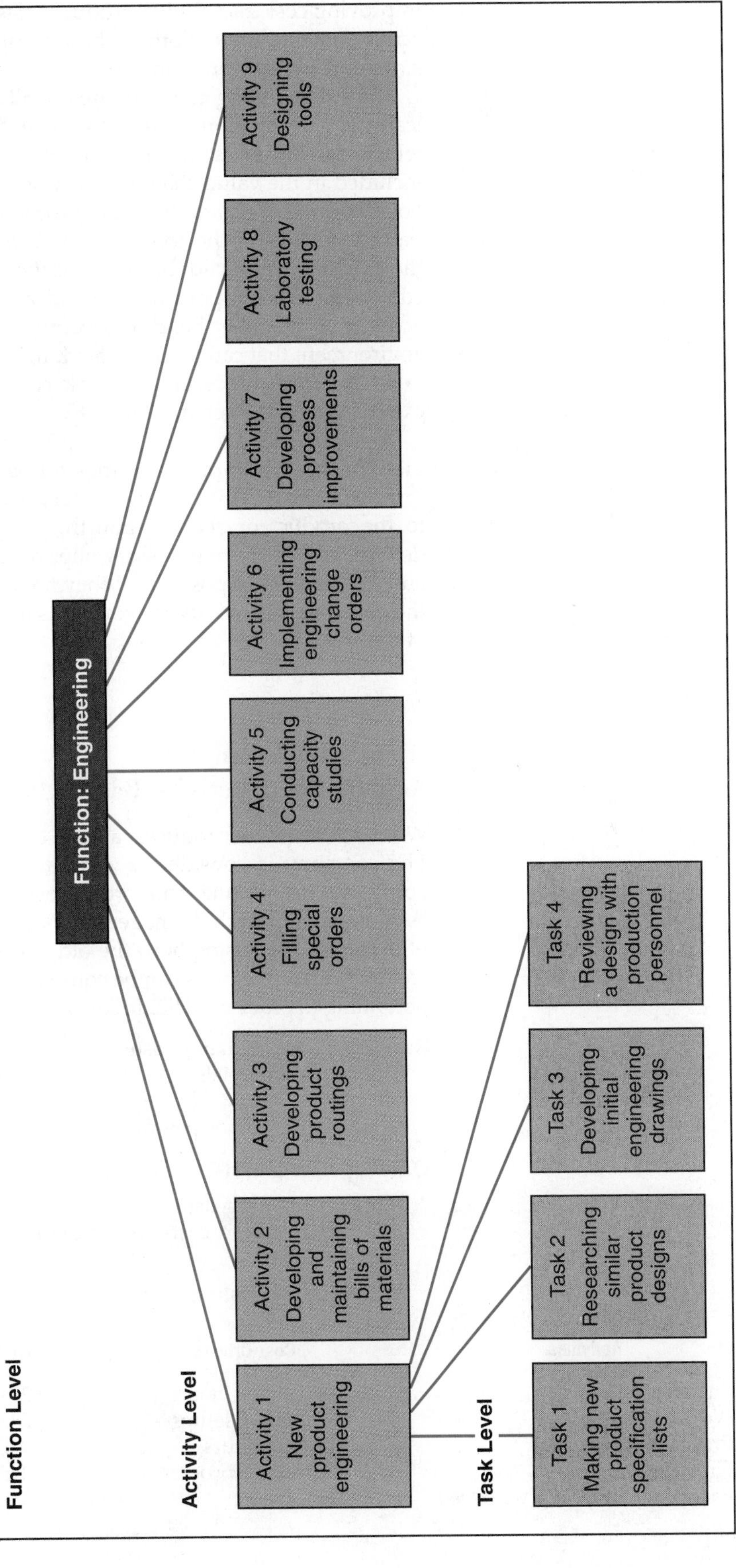

improving cost traceability, product costs normally are reduced and are significantly more accurate. Both of these results serve to improve management decisions and increase profitability.

Nonvalue-adding activities are not all wasteful and are not targeted automatically for elimination. Every company maintains support functions, without which the business would not exist. Although support activities are not included in the value chain of functions, they foster the activities of a function. For example, consider the data-processing activity in a manufacturing company, the center of the company's information system. It does not add value to the products produced, but it is a critical activity. Although its costs should be controlled, this support area should not be eliminated. A separate inspection activity, on the other hand, is a support activity of a traditional manufacturing environment that can be eliminated. In a JIT environment, inspection is incorporated into the duties of the work cell operator. The inspection support still exists, but not as a separate activity.

To summarize the steps to a successful activity-based costing system: First, identify the appropriate activities for each function. Second, accumulate costs for each activity. Third, analyze every activity to determine if it is adding value to the product or service. Fourth, analyze all nonvalue-adding activities to determine if they are necessary support areas. If they are, scrutinize their costs and reduce them if possible. If they are not, eliminate them. And, finally, assign the costs of each activity to work cells and products that consume the resources of the activities.

Illustrative Example
Activities and Activity-Based Costing

Windal Company produces a line of remote control door-opening devices. The company is considering changing from a traditional absorption costing approach for product and order costing purposes to an activity-based cost assignment approach. Management has asked the controller to compute the cost of order no. 1142 using both the old and the proposed new costing approaches so that the two methods can be compared and analyzed. A summary of the data pertaining to order no. 1142 follows.

Raw materials and labor costs

Cost of raw materials	$1,650.00
Direct labor hours	30
Average direct labor pay rate	$14.50

Other operating costs

Traditional costing data:

Factory overhead costs were assigned at a rate of 350 percent of direct labor dollars.

Activity-based costing data:

Activities	Cost Drivers	Cost Assignment Rates	Activity Usage for Order No. 1142
Engineering design	Engineering hours	$25.00 per eng. hr	12 eng. hr
Work cell setup	Number of setups	$28.00 per setup	3 setups
Production work cell	Machine hours	$17.50 per MH	24 MH
Final tuning	Number of processes	$34.00 per process	3 processes
Packaging/shipping work cell	Cell hours	$38.25 per cell hr	2 cell hr

Building occupancy-related overhead costs are allocated at a rate of $6.50 per production work cell machine hour.

Required

1. Compute the total cost of order no. 1142 following the traditional absorption costing approach.
2. Compute the total cost of order no. 1142 following the activity-based costing approach.
3. What was the difference in the amount of cost assigned to order no. 1142 resulting from the shift to the activity-based costing approach?

Solution

1 and 2. Total costs assigned to order no. 1142:

	Traditional Costing Approach	Activity-based Costing Approach
Raw materials cost	$1,650.00	$1,650.00
Direct labor cost	435.00	435.00
Factory overhead cost (traditional costing approach)	1,522.50	
Cost of activities		
Engineering design		
$25.00 per eng. hr × 12 eng. hr		300.00
Work cell setup		
$28.00 per setup × 3 setups		84.00
Production work cell		
$17.50 per MH × 24 MH		420.00
Final tuning		
$34.00 per process × 3 processes		102.00
Packaging/shipping work cell		
$38.25 per cell hr × 2 cell hr		76.50
Building occupancy-related overhead		
$6.50 × 24 MH		156.00
Total costs assigned to order no. 1142	$3,607.50	$3,223.50

3. The change to an activity-based costing approach reduced the amount of costs assigned to this order by $384.00, from $3,607.50 to $3,223.50.

Accounting for Product and Service Quality

OBJECTIVE 4
Identify and compute the costs of quality for products and services

Over the last two decades, the quality of American-made goods has slipped as manufacturers sacrificed or ignored quality in an attempt to lower prices to meet world competition. Over the same period, Japan and other countries increased the quality of their goods while lowering prices. To survive in global markets, American companies must produce a quality product at a competitive price. Quality, however, is not something that a company can apply somewhere in the production process or assume will happen automatically. Inspection points can detect bad products, but they do not ensure quality. Managers need reliable measures of quality to help them meet the goal of producing a high-quality, reasonably priced product or service. They need to create a total quality management environment. **Total quality management (TQM)** is an organizational environment in which all business functions work together to build quality into the firm's products or services. From a managerial accounting perspective, the first step toward a TQM environment is to identify and manage the costs of quality. The second step is to analyze operating performance using nonfinancial measures and require that all operating processes and products be improved continuously.

Cost-Based Measures of Quality[6]

The cost of quality is a cost classification scheme that reflects a company's commitment to quality—to produce quality output and to continuously improve both product and process. Global competition has forced manufacturing and service companies to concentrate on producing high-quality products or services. In the absence of high-quality products or services, companies lose market share to their competitors and eventually go out of business.

To the average person, quality means that one product is better than another—possibly because of design, durability, or some other attribute. In a business setting, however, **quality** is an operating environment in which a company's product or service meets or conforms to a customer's specifications the first time it is produced or delivered. The **costs of quality** are the costs specifically associated with the achievement or nonachievement of product or service quality. In other words, total costs of quality include (1) costs of good quality incurred to ensure the successful development of a product or service and (2) costs of poor quality incurred to transform a faulty product or service into one that is acceptable to the customer.

The costs of quality comprise a significant portion of a product's or service's total cost. In his book *Thriving on Chaos,* Tom Peters states that poor-quality costs consume 25 percent of all labor and assets in manufacturing firms; in service firms, the costs of poor quality can run as high as 40 percent of labor and asset costs.[7] Therefore, controlling the costs of quality has a sizable impact on profitability. Today's managers should be able to identify the activities associated with improving quality and should be aware of the cost of resources used to achieve high quality.

The costs of quality have two components: the **costs of conformance**, which are the costs incurred to produce a quality product or service, and the **costs of nonconformance**, which are the costs incurred to correct the defects or irregularities of a product or service. Costs of conformance are made up of prevention costs and appraisal costs. **Prevention costs** are the costs associated with the prevention of defects and failures in products and services. **Appraisal costs** are the costs of activities that measure, evaluate, or audit products, processes, or services to ensure conformance to quality standards and performance requirements. The costs of nonconformance include internal failure costs and external failure costs. **Internal failure costs** are the costs incurred as a consequence of the discovery of defects before the product is shipped or the service delivered to the customer. Costs incurred after the delivery of defective goods or services are called **external failure costs**. Examples of each cost category are shown in Table 26-2. You should note that there is a trade-off between the two major categories: If a company spends money on the costs of conformance, the costs of nonconformance should be reduced. If, however, little attention is paid to the costs of confor-mance, then the costs of nonconformance may escalate.

6. Many of the ideas and thoughts in this section come from John Hawley Atkinson, Jr., Gregory Hohner, Barry Mundt, Richard B. Troxel, and William Winchell, *Current Trends in Cost of Quality: Linking the Cost of Quality and Continuous Improvement,* a joint study of the Institute of Management Accountants, KPMG Peat Marwick, and William Winchell (Montvale, N.J., 1991).
7. Tom Peters, *Thriving on Chaos* (New York: Alfred A. Knopf, 1987), p. 91.

Table 26-2. Costs of Quality and Quality Measures

Costs of Conformance to Customer Standards

Prevention costs:
- Quality training of employees
- Design review
- Quality planning activities
- Quality engineering
- Preventive maintenance
- Design and development of quality equipment
- Quality improvement projects
- On-line statistical process control

Appraisal costs:
- Sample preparation
- All inspection activities
- Setup for testing
- Product simulation and development
- Vendor audits and sample testing
- Maintenance of test equipment
- Quality audits
- Maintenance of equipment used for quality enhancement

Costs of Nonconformance to Customer Standards

Internal failure costs:
- Scrap and rework
- Reinspection of rework
- Quality-related downtime
- Losses caused by vendor scrap
- Failure analysis
- Inventory control and scheduling costs
- Downgrading because of defects

External failure costs:
- Loss of goodwill and future orders
- Warranty claims and adjustments
- Customer complaint processing
- Customer service
- Returned goods
- Investigation of defects
- Product recalls
- Product liability suits

Quality Measures

Total costs of quality as a percentage of net sales
Ratio of conformance costs to total costs of quality
Ratio of nonconformance costs to total costs of quality
Nonconformance costs as a percentage of net sales

The management accountant is responsible for controlling the costs of quality. The accountant's overall objective is to avoid costs of nonconformance because internal and external failure affects customers' satisfaction as well as the company's profitability. High initial costs of conformance are justified when they minimize total costs of quality over the life cycle of the product or service. The cost-based measures of quality listed at the bottom of Table 26-2 are used and explained in the illustrative problem on pages 1055–1059.

Nonfinancial Measures of Quality

OBJECTIVE 5
Evaluate operating performance using nonfinancial measures of quality

Measuring the costs of quality tells a company how much it has spent in its efforts to improve product or service quality. But critics say that tracking historical cost data to account for quality performance does little to help production and engineering people enhance quality. What these managers need is a measurement and evaluation system that signals poor quality early enough so that they can take steps to correct problems before a product reaches the customer. Implementing a policy of continuous improvement satisfies this need and is part of the second step of total quality management.

Nonfinancial measures of operating performance, identified and reported in a timely manner to engineering and production managers, are augmenting traditional cost-based measures in JIT/TQM operations. Although cost control is still an important consideration, a commitment to ongoing product improvement encourages activities that enhance product quality, from design to delivery. As explained earlier, these activities, or cost drivers, cause costs. By controlling the nonfinancial performance measures of production activities, managers ultimately maximize the financial return from operations.

Product Design Quality Measures. Problems with quality often are the result of poor design. Most automated production operations make use of **computer-aided design (CAD)**, a computer-based engineering system with a built-in program to detect product design flaws. This computer program automatically identifies faulty design parts or manufacturing processes included in error so that engineers can correct problems before actual production begins. The management accountant is not involved directly in this process but should be aware of the existence and use of product design control measures.

High-Quality Raw Materials Input Measures. One of the most significant changes for a company that is converting to a JIT/TQM operating environment is its relationship with suppliers of raw materials and parts. Instead of dealing with dozens of suppliers, looking for the lowest cost, JIT companies analyze their materials vendors to determine which are most reliable, deal in high-quality goods, have a record of timely deliveries, and charge competitive prices. Once located, these vendors become an integral part of the production team. A JIT company works closely with its vendors to ensure a continuing supply of high-quality raw materials and parts. Vendors may even contribute to product design to ensure that the correct materials and parts are being used. The management accountant should conduct the necessary analyses to identify and monitor reliable vendors, so that high-quality, reasonably-priced materials are available when they are needed.

In-Process and Delivery Control Measures. Automated machinery linked into a flexible manufacturing system can be programmed easily with in-process product control mechanisms. Product quality problems are detected by computer-programmed control techniques, and corrective action is taken when a problem is detected. No longer is it necessary to wait for a specified inspection point to detect a product flaw. In-process controls form a continuous inspection system that highlights trouble spots, helps reduce the incidence of scrap significantly, cuts overall product rework machine time, and eliminates the nonvalue-adding product costs of traditional inspection activities. Although the management accountant is not expected to develop and program FMS in-process quality controls, the accountant should understand the control points and maintain records of the rates of defective parts produced. Product delivery is part of overall quality. The accountant also should maintain records of on-time deliveries to track the performance of the firm's delivery systems.

Customer Acceptance Measures. The sale and shipment of a product no longer marks the end of the management accountant's performance measurement duties. Customer follow-up helps evaluate total customer satisfaction. Accounting measures used to determine the degree of customer acceptance include (1) the percentage of shipments returned by customers, (2) the number and types of customer complaints, (3) the percentage of shipments accepted by customers, and (4) an analysis of the number and causes of warranty claims. Several companies have developed their own customer satisfaction indices from these measures so that they can compare different product lines over different time periods.

The nonfinancial measures of quality mentioned above are summarized in Table 26-3. This list is only a sample of the many nonfinancial measures that are used to monitor quality. These measures help a company move toward its goal of continuously seeking to produce higher-quality products and to improve production processes.

Illustrative Problem
Measuring Quality

Using many of the examples of the costs of quality identified in Table 26-2 and the nonfinancial measures of quality listed in Table 26-3, the following situations demonstrate how a company's progress toward its goal of achieving total quality management is measured and evaluated.

Part A. Evaluating the Costs of Quality. As shown in Part A of Exhibit 26-1, three companies, Able, Baker, and Cane, have taken different approaches to achieving product quality. All three companies are the same size, each generating $15 million in sales last year.

Table 26-3. Nonfinancial Measures of Quality Used by Management Accountants

High-Quality Raw Materials Input Measures	
Vendor quality analysis	An analysis of the quality of materials and parts received; prepared for each vendor used
Vendor delivery analysis	An analysis of timely vendor deliveries; prepared for each vendor used
In-Process and Delivery Control Measures	
Production quality level	Defective parts per million; usually tracked by product line
Percentage of on-time deliveries	Percentage of total shipments made by the promised date
Customer Acceptance Measures	
Returned-order percentage	Number of shipments returned by customers as a percentage of total shipments
Customer complaints	An analysis of the number and types of customer complaints
Customer acceptance percentage	Percentage of shipments accepted of total shipments, computed for each customer
Warranty claims	An analysis of the number and causes of warranty claims

Exhibit 26-1. Measures of Quality—Data Base for Case Scenarios

Part A: Costs of Quality

	Able Co.	Baker Co.	Cane Co.
Annual Sales	$15,000,000	$15,000,000	$15,000,000
Costs of Conformance to Customer Standards			
Prevention Costs:			
Quality training of employees	$ 210,000	$ 73,500	$ 136,500
Quality engineering	262,500	115,500	189,000
Design review	105,000	42,000	84,000
Preventive maintenance	157,500	84,000	115,500
Appraisal Costs:			
Setup for testing	$ 126,000	$ 63,000	$ 73,500
Product simulation and development	199,500	31,500	115,500
Quality audits	84,000	21,000	42,000
Vendor audits and sample testing	112,500	52,500	63,000
Costs of Nonconformance to Customer Standards			
Internal Failure Costs:			
Scrap and rework	$ 21,000	$ 189,000	$ 126,000
Reinspection of rework	15,750	126,000	73,500
Quality-related downtime	42,000	231,000	178,500
Losses caused by vendor scrap	26,250	84,000	52,500
External Failure Costs:			
Warranty claims	$ 47,250	$ 94,500	$ 84,000
Returned goods	15,750	68,250	36,750
Investigation of defects	26,250	78,750	57,750
Customer service	120,750	178,500	126,000

Part B: Nonfinancial Measures of Quality

	Able Co.	Baker Co.	Cane Co.
Vendor Quality Analysis:			
19x3	98.20%	94.40%	95.20%
19x4	98.40%	93.20%	95.30%
19x5	98.60%	93.10%	95.20%
Production Quality Level (product defects per million):			
19x3	1,400	4,120	2,710
19x4	1,340	4,236	2,720
19x5	1,210	4,340	2,680
Percentage of On-Time Deliveries:			
19x3	94.20%	76.20%	84.10%
19x4	94.60%	75.40%	84.00%
19x5	95.40%	73.10%	83.90%
Order-Return Percentage:			
19x3	1.30%	6.90%	4.20%
19x4	1.10%	7.20%	4.10%
19x5	0.80%	7.60%	4.00%
Number of Customer Complaints:			
19x3	22	189	52
19x4	18	194	50
19x5	12	206	46

Required

Evaluate each company's approach to quality enhancement by analyzing the costs of quality and by answering the following questions:

Which company is more likely to remain competitive in the global marketplace?

Which company is in serious trouble regarding its product's quality?

What do you feel will happen to the total costs of quality for each company over the next five years? Why?

Solution

The costs of quality have been summarized and analyzed in Exhibit 26-2. The analysis shows that each company spent between 10.22 and 10.48 percent of its sales dollars on costs of quality. The following statements are based on this analysis.

Which company is more likely to remain competitive in the global marketplace? Able Co. spent the most money on costs of quality. More importantly, however, 80 percent of the money was spent on costs of conformance. These dollars spent now will bring benefits in years to come. The company's focus on the costs of conformance means that only a small amount had to be spent on internal and external failure costs. This also would lead to customer satisfaction.

Which company is in serious trouble regarding its product's quality? Baker Co. spent the least on costs of quality but that's not the reason why the company is in serious trouble. Over 68 percent of its costs of quality ($1,050,000 of a total of $1,533,000) was spent on internal and external failure costs. Scrap costs, reinspection costs, the cost of downtime, warranty costs, and customer service costs were all high. Baker's products are very low in quality, and this will mean hard times in future years.

What do you feel will happen to the total costs of quality for each company over the next five years? Why? Money spent on costs of conformance early in a product's life cycle means that quality is integrated into the development and production processes. Once a high level of quality has been established, total costs of quality should be lower in future years. Able seems to be in this position today.

Baker's costs of conformance will have to increase significantly if the company expects to stay in business. Seven percent of its sales revenue is spent on internal and external failure costs. The products are not being accepted by the marketplace, and the company is vulnerable to its competitors. This is not a good situation to be in when a company faces global competition.

Cane is steering down the middle road. The company is spending a little more than half (53 percent) of its cost-of-quality dollars on conformance, so product quality should be increasing. But the company still is incurring high internal and external failure costs. Cane's managers must learn to prevent these costs if they expect to remain competitive.

Part B. Evaluating Nonfinancial Measures of Quality. From the information presented in Part B of Exhibit 26-1, evaluate each company's experience in its pursuit of total quality management.

Solution

The nonfinancial measures presented in Exhibit 26-1 identify trends for each company for three years, 19x3, 19x4, and 19x5. These data tend to support the findings in Part A, the analysis of the costs of quality.

Able Co. For Able Co. in 19x5, 98.6 percent of the raw materials and parts received from suppliers are high quality, and the trend is increasing. The product defect rate, measured in number of defects per million, is decreasing rapidly, proof that the costs of conformance are having a positive effect. The percentage of on-time deliveries is increasing, and both the order-return percentage and the number of customer

Exhibit 26-2. Analysis of Costs of Quality

	Able Co.	Baker Co.	Cane Co.
Annual Sales	$15,000,000	$15,000,000	$15,000,000
Costs of Conformance to Customer Standards			
Prevention Costs:			
Quality training of employees	$ 210,000	$ 73,500	$ 136,500
Quality engineering	262,500	115,500	189,000
Design review	105,000	42,000	84,000
Preventive maintenance	157,500	84,000	115,500
Subtotal	$ 735,000	$ 315,000	$ 525,000
Appraisal Costs:			
Setup for testing	$ 126,000	$ 63,000	$ 73,500
Product simulation and development	199,500	31,500	115,500
Quality audits	84,000	21,000	42,000
Vendor audits and sample testing	112,500	52,500	63,000
Subtotal	$ 522,000	$ 168,000	$ 294,000
Total conformance costs	$ 1,257,000	$ 483,000	$ 819,000
Costs of Nonconformance to Customer Standards			
Internal Failure Costs:			
Scrap and rework	$ 21,000	$ 189,000	$ 126,000
Reinspection of rework	15,750	126,000	73,500
Quality-related downtime	42,000	231,000	178,500
Losses caused by vendor scrap	26,250	84,000	52,500
Subtotal	$ 105,000	$ 630,000	$ 430,500
External Failure Costs:			
Warranty claims	$ 47,250	$ 94,500	$ 84,000
Returned goods	15,750	68,250	36,750
Investigation of defects	26,250	78,750	57,750
Customer service	120,750	178,500	126,000
Subtotal	$ 210,000	$ 420,000	$ 304,500
Total nonconformance costs	$ 315,000	$ 1,050,000	$ 735,000
Total Costs of Quality	$ 1,572,000	$ 1,533,000	$ 1,554,000
Total costs of quality as a percentage of net sales	10.48%	10.22%	10.36%
Ratio of conformance costs to total costs of quality	.80 to 1	.32 to 1	.53 to 1
Ratio of nonconformance costs to total costs of quality	.20 to 1	.68 to 1	.47 to 1
Nonconformance costs as a percentage of sales	2.10%	7.00%	4.90%

complaints are decreasing, which means that customer acceptance and satisfaction are increasing.

Baker Co. Baker Co.'s experience is not encouraging. The number of high-quality shipments of materials and parts from vendors is decreasing; the product defect rate is increasing (it seems to be out of control); on-time deliveries were bad to begin with and are getting worse; more goods are being returned each year; and customer complaints are on the rise. All of these signs reflect the company's high nonconformance costs of quality.

Cane Co. Cane Co. is making progress toward higher quality standards, but that progress is very slow. Most of the nonfinancial measures indicate a very slight positive trend. More money needs to be spent on the conformance costs of quality.

Measuring Service Quality

The quality of services rendered can be measured and analyzed. Many of the costs of product conformance and nonconformance also apply to the development and delivery of a service. Service design flaws lead to poor-quality services. Timely service delivery is as important as timely product shipments. Customer satisfaction in a service business can be measured by services accepted or rejected, the number of complaints, and the number of returning customers. Poor service development leads to internal and external failure costs. Many of the costs-of-quality categories and several of the nonfinancial measures of quality can be applied directly to services and can be adopted by any type of service company.

Performance Measures for JIT/FMS Operating Control

As with product costing, many companies have installed a flexible manufacturing system (FMS) or moved to a computer-integrated production system without changing their approaches to the monitoring and measurement of performance. One problem with the adoption of JIT production procedures is relying on an obsolete management accounting system to measure operating performance. Traditional performance evaluation measures are used, but these measures are not designed to track the objectives of automated facilities and thus are not appropriate for the new manufacturing environment. For instance, measures that center on labor efficiency or factory overhead absorption rates do not coincide with the objectives of JIT. Variance analysis based on direct labor hours will have little to measure and evaluate. JIT/FMS emphasizes minimum labor usage and a rapid, automated production process. Because building inventory levels also conflicts with the goals of JIT, measuring performance through lower overhead absorption rates is an antiquated approach.

In addition, the managerial accountant may not be familiar with the production process and thus have a difficult time identifying areas of weakness.[8] The new manufacturing environment has created a need for close cooperation between all parts of the management team. The management accountant must get closer to the actual operations and become familiar with all aspects of the manufacturing process. The accountant, the engineer, and the production manager must work closely to ensure that the production process is being monitored fairly and accurately. Without a knowledge of the production facilities, the management accountant does not know what to measure or which cost drivers are appropriate under the circumstances.

As was shown in the section on measures of quality, many nonfinancial measures have replaced traditional performance measures in a JIT/FMS setting. The primary control areas, in addition to product quality, are product delivery,

8. Robert A. Howell and Stephen R. Soucy, "Operating Controls in the New Manufacturing Environment," *Management Accounting,* Institute of Management Accountants, October 1987, p. 26.

inventory control, material costs/scrap control, and machine management and maintenance. Although cost control is still an important consideration in these areas, emphasis is on the factors that make an FMS or a product line a successful part of a profitable operation. These factors drive or cause the costs to be incurred. The belief is that control of the nonfinancial performance aspects will ultimately maximize the financial return on operations.

Product Delivery Performance

OBJECTIVE 6a
Identify the types of financial and nonfinancial analyses used in a JIT environment to evaluate product delivery performance

Besides emphasizing product quality and customer satisfaction, a JIT company is also interested in product delivery. The **delivery cycle time** is the time period between acceptance of the order and final delivery of the product. It is important for the salesperson to be able to promise accurate delivery schedules at the time the sales order is gained; the goal is for product delivery to be 100 percent on time and for the order to be filled 100 percent of the time. To meet this goal, the JIT company must establish and maintain consistency and reliability within the manufacturing process.

JIT companies place heavy importance on the delivery cycle. One company cut its delivery cycle from more than six months to less than five weeks; another company cut its four-week delivery cycle to less than five days. Such reductions in delivery time have a significant impact on income from operations. The delivery cycle is comprised of the **purchase order lead time** (the time it takes for raw materials and parts to be ordered and received so that production can begin), **production cycle time** (the time it takes for the production people to make the product available for shipment to the customer), and **delivery time** (the time period between product completion and customer receipt of the item).

The management accountant has several control measures to establish and maintain to help management minimize the delivery cycle. The accountant should maintain records and reports that are designed to monitor each product's purchase order lead time, production cycle time, delivery time, and total delivery cycle time. Trends should be highlighted, and the reports should be made available on a daily or weekly basis. Other measures designed to monitor the delivery cycle include an on-time delivery performance record and a daily or weekly report showing percentage of orders filled.

Inventory Control Performance

OBJECTIVE 6b
Identify the types of financial and nonfinancial analyses used in a JIT environment to evaluate inventory control performance

Within a JIT environment, the objective is to have no inventory. Therefore the management accountant must emphasize zero inventory balances and concentrate on measures that detect why inventory exists, not measures that lead to accurate inventory valuation. As was pointed out earlier, storage is a nonvalue-adding activity and should be reduced or eliminated. Making this shift in accounting for and controlling of inventory cost has been very difficult for accounting personnel. For decades, inventory has been one of the largest asset balances on the balance sheet, and accountants have been trained to verify inventory balances and compute the value of total inventory. JIT has made such concerns obsolete: Emphasis should be on reducing inventory.

The JIT/FMS environment utilizes only two inventory accounts, and both balances are kept at a minimum. As shown in the chapter on the just-in-time operating environment and automation, the old Materials Inventory and Work in Process Inventory accounts have been merged into the Raw in Process (RIP) Inventory account. All purchases of raw materials and parts are debited immediately to the RIP Inventory account. Because the goal is to eliminate storage as a cost, materials and parts are received only when needed. All costs of product conversion (labor and factory overhead) are also debited to the RIP Inventory account.

Inventory controls in the new manufacturing environment are designed to eliminate inventory balances and nonvalue-adding product costs. Old control measures such as the economic order quantity and reorder point computations are no longer as useful; now the concentration is on reducing the amount of space used to store raw materials, goods in process, and finished goods. Measures that detect possible product obsolescence are very important. Inventory turnover measures such as the ratio of inventory to total sales have become more important because the number of annual turnovers may double or triple with the adoption of JIT.

The inventory area remains critical to company profitability in a JIT environment. But there is heavy emphasis on nonfinancial measures to minimize the cost incurred in handling and storing inventory. The management accountant must develop measures that identify unreliable vendors because using fewer vendors who supply quality and timely raw material inputs is an objective of JIT. Another objective is to determine the amount of production time wasted because of engineering change orders and highlight the causes for management. The same approach must be applied to production schedule changes because time wasted here can be significant. Maintaining accurate records of required machine maintenance is an important JIT control measure. Cutting the downtime from machine breakdowns reduces the need for inventory. Every company's production process and inventory needs are different. When developing a set of inventory control measures, each must be tailored to a particular set of operating circumstances. Although most of these measures are nonfinancial, they are critical to gaining market share and remaining profitable.

Materials Cost/Scrap Control Performance

OBJECTIVE 6c
Identify the types of financial and nonfinancial analyses used in a JIT environment to evaluate materials cost/scrap control performance

In a traditional situation, controlling the cost of raw materials meant seeking the lowest possible price while maintaining some minimum level of quality. Responsibility for this transaction was given to the Purchasing Department. Performance was measured by analyzing the materials price variance, which is the difference between the standard price and the actual price of the goods purchased. Today, emphasis is on the quality of materials, timeliness of delivery, and reasonable price. Because materials cost is the largest single cost element in the new JIT/FMS environment, control in this area is extremely important.

Control of scrap also takes on a different focus in a JIT/FMS environment. The JIT objective is to incur no scrap in the production process, a significant difference from the traditional approach, which developed a normal scrap level or tolerance at or below which no corrective action was taken. The factory of the future sees scrap as a nonvalue-added series of costs. Each defective product has already cost the company materials costs, labor cost, as well as materials handling and factory overhead costs. In the new manufacturing environment, specific records are kept regarding scrap, rework, and defective units. Machine operators are expected to detect flaws in the production process and are also asked to suggest possible corrective action on the spot. When a flaw is detected, the FMS cell should be stopped and a solution developed immediately. Personnel should work continuously to eradicate bad or defective output.

The management accountant is responsible for developing a set of control measures for the scrap area. Although financial data on the cost of scrap are important and should be computed, nonfinancial measures should also be developed and maintained. Questions such as the following should be analyzed, answered, and reported:

1. Where was the scrap detected?
2. How often does a product flaw occur at each of these locations?
3. Was the flaw detected at the spot of machine or product failure, or were additional manufacturing costs wasted on the defective products? If so, why?
4. Who is responsible for feeding the information regarding scrap incurrence to the management accountant?
5. Who should the scrap control reports go to, and how often should the reports be prepared?

Machine Management and Maintenance Performance

OBJECTIVE 6d
Identify the types of financial and nonfinancial analyses used in a JIT environment to evaluate machine management and maintenance performance

One of the most challenging areas for the management accountant in the JIT setting is keeping records of machine maintenance and downtime. Automated equipment requires large capital expenditures. For a JIT company, the largest item on the balance sheet is often automated machinery and equipment. Each piece of equipment has a specific capability, above which continuous operation is threatened. The machine management and maintenance measures should have two objectives:

1. Evaluate performance in relation to each piece of equipment's capacity.
2. Evaluate performance of maintenance personnel to keep to a prescribed maintenance program.

Machines must operate within specified tolerances, or damage and downtime could result. Keeping track of proper machine operation is not easy, but electronic surveillance is possible because of the computer network connecting all of the machines in a JIT/FMS cell. These controls should be programmed into the system and tracked as a regular part of the operation. The accountant should help prepare the reporting format for this function and analyze and report the findings to appropriate production personnel.

Because automated equipment requires a heavy investment and unanticipated machine downtime is not tolerated in a JIT/FMS environment, machine maintenance is critical. Minor maintenance tasks are part of the machine operator's duties. When the operating cell does not have an order to process, the operator is expected to perform routine maintenance. A regular program of major maintenance should also be implemented. Timing can be flexible, based on work orders, but major maintenance cannot be ignored. Detailed records on machine maintenance should be maintained, similar to the maintenance records required for commercial aircraft. Table 26-4 is an example of a machine maintenance record.

Summary of Control Measures

Table 26-5 (page 1064) summarizes control measures in the new manufacturing environment. Quality performance is measured by tracking customer complaints, warranty claims, and vendor quality. Delivery performance is shown by on-time delivery, production backlog, lead time, cycle time, and waste time. Successful inventory performance is identified through turnover rates, space reduction, and automatic production cycle count accuracy. Materials cost/scrap control performance is measured by incoming materials inspection, materials as a percentage of total cost, actual scrap loss, and scrap as a percentage of total

Table 26-4. Machine Maintenance Record as of April 30, 19x2—Milling Machine FMS

	January	February	March	April	May	June
Small mills						
Monthly						
Wash machine	X	X	X	X		
Replace oil	X	X	X	X		
Check bearing	X	X	X	X		
Stone sand ways	X	X	X	X		
Clean moving table	X	X	X	X		
Check cutter grip	X	X	X	X		
Quarterly						
Replace bearing	X			X		
Check wiring	X			X		
Check all motors	X			X		
Replace lights	X			X		
Check scrap removal system	X			X		
Check computer system	X			X		
Materials conveyor system						
Monthly						
Clean all belts	X	X	X	X		
Oil all parts	X	X	X	X		
Check all motors	X	X	X	X		
Clean electronic contact spots	X	X	X	X		
Quarterly						
Replace small motors	X			X		
Grease gears	X			X		
Check wiring	X			X		
Check computer system	X			X		

cost. Machine management and maintenance performance is revealed through machine maintenance records, availability/downtime experience, and equipment capacity/utilization information.

Full Cost Profit Margin

OBJECTIVE 7
Define full cost profit margin *and state the advantages of this measure of profitability*

The new manufacturing environment has yet another dimension that must be analyzed when dealing with performance measures. For years, management accountants have been touting the measurement qualities of contribution margin. This number concerns itself with only revenue and those costs that are variable in relation to the products being sold. Fixed costs are excluded from the analysis so that they will not cloud the measurement of the performance of a division or a product.

As a company moves in the direction of a computer-integrated manufacturing system, more and more direct labor hours are replaced by machine hours. When a complete JIT/CIM environment is attained, very little direct labor cost is being incurred. A major part of the traditional variable product cost has been replaced by costly machinery, a fixed cost, and as a result contribution margins also get larger and, more important, less meaningful.

Today, management accountants are turning to full cost profit margin to help measure the performance of a division or a product line. Full costing has always

Table 26-5. Control Points in the New Manufacturing Environment

Quality Performance	
Customer complaints Customer surveys Warranty claims Vendor quality Quality audits	Causes of cost of quality: Scrap and rework Returns and allowances Field service Warranty claims Lost business
Delivery Performance	
On-time delivery Setup time Production backlog Lead time (order to shipment)	Order fulfillment rate Cycle time (materials receipt to product shipment) Waste time (lead time less process time)
Inventory Performance	
Turnover rates by product Cycle count accuracy Space reduction Number of inventoried items	Turnover rates by location: Raw in Process Finished goods Composite
Materials Cost/Scrap Control Performance	
Actual scrap loss Scrap by part, product, and operation Scrap percentage of total cost	Quality—incoming materials inspection Materials cost as a percentage of total cost
Machine Management and Maintenance Performance	
Availability/downtime Machine maintenance	Equipment capacity/utilization Equipment experience

Source: Robert A. Howell and Stephen R. Soucy, "Operating Controls in the New Manufacturing Environment." Reprinted from *Management Accounting*. Copyright by Institute of Management Accountants, Montvale, N.J. October 1987.

been an alternative for performance evaluation, but a stigma of inaccuracy was associated with the number because fixed costs had to be allocated to the product. Full cost profit margins are more appropriate in a capital intensive environment. A **full cost profit margin** is the difference between total revenue and total costs traceable to the work cell or product. As described in the chapter on the just-in-time operating environment and automation, the computer has enabled the accountant to more easily trace costs to FMS work cells. A CIM system can provide data that enable most costs to be treated as direct costs of the work cells. If direct traceability is not possible, new cost drivers have been established to more closely link indirect costs with cost objectives such as work cells or products. Only building occupancy costs remain as nontraceable costs to be allocated based on some causal allocation base such as machine hours or square footage occupied. Full cost profit margin, therefore, is a meaningful figure for performance evaluation as well as for new product line decision analysis.

An example points out the differences between contribution margin and full cost profit margin as measures of performance. Exhibit 26-3 shows operating data for three product lines of the Vernon Manufacturing Company. First, the

Exhibit 26-3. Contribution Margin Versus Full Cost Profit Margin

Vernon Manufacturing Company
Product Performance Evaluation

	Product 162	Product 214	Product 305
Total revenue	$2,340,000	$2,400,000	$1,560,000
Before FMS installed:			
Variable costs			
Direct materials	$ 450,000	$ 560,000	$ 270,000
Direct labor	660,000	600,000	420,000
Variable factory overhead	240,000	240,000	150,000
Variable selling expenses	90,000	80,000	60,000
Variable distribution costs	120,000	200,000	180,000
Total variable costs	$1,560,000	$1,680,000	$1,080,000
Allocated costs			
Fixed factory overhead	$ 210,000	$ 360,000	$ 240,000
Fixed selling expenses	60,000	40,000	90,000
Fixed distribution costs	150,000	128,000	135,000
Total fixed costs	$ 420,000	$ 528,000	$ 465,000
After FMS installed:			
Traceable costs			
Direct materials	$ 450,000	$ 560,000	$ 270,000
Materials-related overhead	72,000	88,000	54,000
Direct labor	90,000	128,000	84,000
Indirect labor	108,000	112,000	90,000
Setup labor	66,000	104,000	66,000
Electrical power	54,000	80,000	48,000
Supervision	96,000	120,000	96,000
Repairs and maintenance	78,000	96,000	78,000
Operating supplies/lubricants	36,000	56,000	42,000
Other traceable indirect costs	114,000	168,000	120,000
Traceable selling expenses	102,000	104,000	72,000
Traceable distribution costs	156,000	284,000	204,000
Total traceable costs	$1,422,000	$1,900,000	$1,224,000
Allocated costs			
Nontraceable factory overhead	$ 126,000	$ 244,000	$ 132,000
Nontraceable selling and distribution costs	96,000	112,000	108,000
Total nontraceable costs	$ 222,000	$ 356,000	$ 240,000

(continued)

Exhibit 26-3. *(continued)*

	Product 162	Product 214	Product 305
Product Performance Measures			
Before FMS installed:			
Contribution margin			
Total revenue	$2,340,000	$2,400,000	$1,560,000
Less variable costs	1,560,000	1,680,000	1,080,000
Contribution margin	$ 780,000	$ 720,000	$ 480,000
Less total fixed costs	420,000	528,000	465,000
Operating profit	$ 360,000	$ 192,000	$ 15,000
Contribution margin as a percent of revenue	33.33%	30.00%	30.77%
Operating profit as a percent of revenue	15.38%	8.00%	0.96%
After FMS installed:			
Full cost profit margin:			
Total revenues	$2,340,000	$2,400,000	$1,560,000
Less total traceable costs	1,422,000	1,900,000	1,224,000
Full cost profit margin	$ 918,000	$ 500,000	$ 336,000
Less total nontraceable costs	222,000	356,000	240,000
Operating profit	$ 696,000	$ 144,000	$ 96,000
Full cost profit margin as a percent of revenue	39.23%	20.83%	21.54%
Operating profit as a percent of revenue	29.74%	6.00%	6.15%

cost data are summarized as they were before the FMS was installed. Next, the data have been reclassified to reflect the increased traceability aspects of a JIT/FMS environment. The bottom portion of Exhibit 26-3 contains computations for contribution margins prior to FMS and for full cost profit margins following the installation of the new system.

The Vernon Manufacturing Company example illustrates what is likely to happen with a switch from the contribution margin to the full cost profit margin approach to performance evaluation. Better methods of cost tracing and more direct cost elements provide a more complete picture of which product lines are most profitable. In our example, the most profitable product is 162 before the FMS was installed. Product 214 is the second most profitable, with Product 305 generating the lowest profit. The order of product profitability remains the same after FMS, but look at the percent of revenue for the contribution margins and the full cost profit margins: Costs have generally shifted from Products 162 and 305 to Product 214. This shift often occurs when more direct cost relationships are uncovered and better cost tracing is made possible. Under the traditional costing methods, Product 214 had an inflated profit structure, which could have led to some bad decisions on the part of Vernon management. With full cost profit margins, management receives more accurate decision support and price determination information.

JIT/FMS Management Reporting Guidelines

OBJECTIVE 8
Identify the primary areas of management reporting in a JIT/FMS environment and give examples of reports needed

Reporting the results of operations to management is one of the management accountant's primary responsibilities. This role is amplified in the new manufacturing environment, and an entirely revised set of reports is usually required. The accountant must be careful when selecting reports prepared for the traditional manufacturing structure. Few are still relevant for automated processes. Studies have shown that well over half the reports prepared for management each month in the traditional environment have little or no relevance and are ignored by the recipients.

The management accountant faces a real challenge in the JIT/FMS management reporting area. As with performance measurement and operations control, emphasis must shift from primarily financial operating reports to a wide range of both financial and nonfinancial data reports. But the need for a responsibility accounting and reporting structure is still present in the JIT/FMS environment for the nonfinancial as well as for the financial operating results of the period. Reporting emphasis must be directed at specific areas of interest, such as customer responsiveness, product line profitability, product contribution, operating effectiveness, and asset management.

Before we discuss JIT/FMS reporting, we must mention one unique aspect of the new manufacturing environment that affects preparation of reports. For decades, the management accountant has been the production managers' only source of information for running day-to-day operations. The accountant seldom visited the manufacturing site, and reports were in traditional form, highlighting comparisons between actual and budgeted financial data. Production people were seldom asked for input concerning the content or structure of a report.

Things have changed in today's environment. Production managers have their own personal computers in the factory and know how to use them. If the management accountant will not supply needed information, these managers will develop their own reports. This factor should be an additional challenge to the accountant. Management accountants must become very familiar with the production operation and should prepare reports that are requested by those responsible for the product line or operating cell.

Customer Responsiveness Reporting

Close contact with the level of customer satisfaction is a critical issue in the new manufacturing environment. Reports prepared for management should reflect this concern. The customer is interested in receiving a quality product on a timely basis. Price is a factor, but usually the price is competitive. Other factors such as customer service and follow-up can make the difference between retaining a customer or losing a sale.

Reporting should concentrate on tracking quality through the (1) number and types of customer complaints and (2) returns and allowances. Records of promised versus actual delivery dates can be important. Continuous records of backlogged orders and delayed delivery dates are critical to maintaining customer satisfaction. A report tracking shipments from the time they leave the plant until the time they arrive at the customer's facility is also a good measure of service performance. Any report that will enhance delivery and service should be prepared. All of these reports involve nonfinancial data.

Product Line Profitability Reporting

Reporting on product line profitability should concentrate on both the manufacturing and the selling and delivery costs. Minimizing the cost of operations does not guarantee product profitability. Selling and delivery costs could easily make a product line unprofitable if they are not continuously analyzed and controlled. In the manufacturing area, reports should focus on both materials and conversion costs. Materials cost is made up of purchase price and materials handling costs once the item has been received from the vendor. Nonvalue-adding costs in the materials handling area can be eliminated in part through effective tracking and reporting procedures. Conversion costs must be analyzed continuously using a combination of traditional methods and newly created reports for scrap control, operating cell yield, and the effective use of energy.

Selling and delivery costs must be monitored very closely to ensure that waste does not occur. Reports should be tailored by sales territory, product line, and mode of transportation. This information needs to be supplied to supervisory personnel on a timely basis.

Product Contribution Reporting

A product's contribution to the absorption of a company's untraceable fixed costs is still important in a JIT/FMS environment, but as pointed out in the section on full cost profit margin, product contribution can include traceable fixed costs in a CAD/CAM or an FMS work cell situation. Contribution margin is no longer the only measure of product contribution. If contribution margin is still requested, management accounting reports should also contain information regarding full cost profit margin so that managers have additional information upon which to base their decisions.

Operating Effectiveness Reporting

Reporting to enhance operating effectiveness concentrates on the nonvalue-adding areas of a traditional system. Reports that focus on product cycle times, including the process time, lead time, and waste time, are especially good for determining operating effectiveness. Reports that track causes of downtime and defective units should be prepared. Reports on inventory turnover and space utilization can lead to significant reductions in nonvalue-adding costs. Special studies on ways to decrease throughput (processing) time of a JIT and/or FMS cell should be prepared on request. Employee suggestions for operating improvement should be encouraged and the results reported to management. Most of the reports in this category are nonfinancial and yet all help reduce operating costs.

Asset Management Reporting

The final report preparation category centers on management of the company's fixed assets. Automation caused huge increases in capital asset expenditures. Special reporting is necessary to help manage this large resource. Machine maintenance must be recorded and tracked. Records of machine time availability or the lack thereof (downtime) is important information to production managers and scheduling personnel. Space utilization must be reported periodically. Equipment capacity and experience must be logged in continuously and reports

Table 26-6. JIT Management Reporting Guidelines

Operations Reporting Areas	Nonfinancial	Financial
Customer responsiveness		
Number/types of customer complaints	X	
Returns and allowances by customers	X	X
Actual versus promised delivery	X	
Backlogged orders	X	
Product shipment tracking	X	
Product line profitability		
Materials purchasing	X	X
Materials handling costs		X
Conversion costs		X
Selling and delivery costs		X
Product contribution		
Full cost profit margins		X
Contribution margins		X
Operating effectiveness		
Product cycle times	X	
Product lead times	X	
Product waste times	X	
Scrap/defective units	X	
Machine yield rates	X	
Throughput time analyses	X	
Asset management		
Machine maintenance	X	
Machine availability/downtime	X	
Space utilization	X	
Equipment capacity/experience	X	

generated. Again, most of these reports are nonfinancial but are critical to the successful operation of the manufacturing facilities. The management accountant is expected to provide these data.

Summary

Table 26-6 depicts the reporting network described above. Some reports are primarily financial in nature, whereas others contain only nonfinancial data. A few reporting areas have both financial and nonfinancial information. The important aspect of this analysis is that the management accountant's role and responsibilities have expanded in the new manufacturing environment. The accountant must become familiar with the manufacturing facilities to be able to supply management with relevant, timely data.

Chapter Review

Review of Learning Objectives

1. **Define *cost management* and describe a cost management system.**
   Cost management is the management and control of activities to determine product costs accurately, to improve business processes, to eliminate waste, to identify cost

drivers, to plan operations, and to set business strategies. In a cost management system (CMS), the primary focus is on the management of activities, not costs, for both product costing and cost control purposes. A CMS plays a major role in planning, managing, and reducing costs. Cost cutting is not accomplished by just slashing the amount of existing resources that a department can use to produce a product, as happens in a traditional costing system. A CMS relies on the concept of continuous improvement to reduce costs while still increasing product quality. When continuous improvement is employed, a company can increase profits by first designing the product so that its target cost is achieved and then making ongoing improvements to reduce costs further. Finally, cost assignment within a cost management system is far superior to traditional cost systems.

2. **Define and explain *activity-based costing*, and list examples of cost drivers.**
   Activity-based costing is an approach to product cost assignment that identifies all major operating activities, categorizes costs by activity, reduces or eliminates nonvalue-adding activities, and assigns costs using an appropriate basis. This process allows most costs to be traced directly to a work cell or product. Building occupancy-related costs must still be allocated based on either machine hours or some other causal allocation base.

   A cost driver is any activity that causes a cost to be incurred. Before we can eliminate a cost or account for it properly, we must know what caused the cost—what drives the cost. Once the cost driver has been identified, the indirect costs it causes can either be (a) treated as legitimate product costs and traced directly to a work cell or product, or (b) reduced or eliminated by reducing or eliminating the need for the cost driver. Cost drivers include the number of machine setups, the number of schedule changes, the number of vendors, and the number of units reworked.

3. **Identify all activities that comprise a particular operating process, distinguish between value-adding and nonvalue-adding activities, and describe the value chain of a product or service.**
   A manufacturing process can be broken down into functions, activities, and tasks. Functions, such as engineering, production, or distribution, are groups of activities that have a common purpose or objective. Activities, such as new-product engineering or engineering change orders, are the actions needed to accomplish a function's purpose or objective. Tasks, such as making up a list of specifications for a new product or researching similar product designs, are the operating steps of an activity. The value chain of a product or service is all of the functions (and related activities) in its development path that add or contribute to its value and marketability. Nonvalue-adding support functions and activities that are necessary for product development are not eliminated, but their costs can be reduced. Many nonvalue-adding activities, among them separate inspection, can be eliminated.

4. **Identify and compute the costs of quality for products and services.**
   The costs of quality are measures of costs specifically related to the achievement or nonachievement of product or service quality. The costs of quality have two components. One is the cost of conforming to a customer's product or service standards, by preventing defects and failures and by appraising quality and performance. The other is the cost of nonconformance—the costs incurred when defects are discovered before a product is shipped and the costs incurred after a defective product or faulty service is delivered.

   The objective here should be to reduce or eliminate the costs of nonconformance, the internal and external failure costs that are associated with customer dissatisfaction. To this end, we can justify high initial costs of conformance if they minimize the total costs of quality over the product's or service's life cycle.

5. **Evaluate operating performance using nonfinancial measures of quality.**
   Nonfinancial measures of quality are related to product design, raw materials input, in-process and delivery control, and customer acceptance. These measures help the firm meet its goal of continuously improving product or service quality and the production process.

6. **Identify the types of financial and nonfinancial analyses used in a JIT environment to evaluate the performance of (a) product delivery, (b) inventory control, (c) materials cost/scrap control, and (d) machine management and maintenance.**
   Product delivery performance centers on tracking lead time, process time, cycle time, setup time, production backlog, and on-time deliveries. Inventory control performance looks at turnover rates by product, space reduction for storage, and number of inventoried items. Materials cost/scrap control performance looks at actual scrap loss, scrap as a percentage of total cost, materials cost as a percentage of total cost, and quality of incoming goods. Machine management and maintenance performance considers each piece of equipment's performance in relation to its capacity and how maintenance personnel follow a prescribed maintenance program.
7. **Define *full cost profit margin* and state the advantages of this measure of profitability.**
   Full cost profit margin is the difference between total revenue and total costs traceable to the work cell or product. The measure is more meaningful than contribution margin because of the additional costs brought into the analysis. Profitability is measured more accurately using the full cost profit margin.
8. **Identify the primary areas of management reporting in a JIT/FMS environment and give examples of reports needed.**
   The primary areas of management reporting in a JIT/FMS environment are (a) customer responsiveness reporting (number and types of customer complaints, backlogged orders), (b) product line profitability reporting (materials purchasing, materials handling costs), (c) product contribution reporting (full cost profit margins, contribution margins), (d) operating effectiveness reporting (product cycle times, product waste times), and (e) asset management reporting (machine maintenance, machine utilization/downtime).

Review of Concepts and Terminology

The following concepts and terms were introduced in this chapter:

(L.O. 3) **Activity:** An action that is needed to accomplish the purpose or objective of a function.

(L.O. 2) **Activity-based costing (ABC):** An approach to cost assignment that identifies all major operating activities, categorizes costs by activity, reduces or eliminates nonvalue-adding activities, and assigns costs using a basis that causes the costs to be incurred.

(L.O. 4) **Appraisal costs:** The costs of activities that measure, evaluate, or audit products, processes, or services to ensure conformance to quality standards and performance requirements; a cost of conformance.

(L.O. 5) **Computer-aided design (CAD):** A computer-based engineering system with a built-in program to detect product design flaws.

(L.O. 2) **Cost driver:** Any activity that causes a cost to be incurred.

(L.O. 1) **Cost management:** The management and control of activities to determine product cost accurately, to improve business processes, to eliminate waste, to identify cost drivers, to plan operations, and to set business strategies.

(L.O. 4) **Costs of conformance:** The costs incurred to produce a quality product or service.

(L.O. 4) **Costs of nonconformance:** The costs incurred to correct the defects or irregularities in a product or service.

(L.O. 4) **Costs of quality:** The costs specifically associated with the achievement or nonachievement of product or service quality.

(L.O. 6) **Delivery cycle time:** The time period between acceptance of an order and final delivery of the product.

(L.O. 6) **Delivery time:** The time period between product completion and customer receipt of the item.

(L.O. 4) **External failure costs:** The costs incurred as a consequence of the discovery of defects after a product or service has been delivered to a customer; a cost of nonconformance.

(L.O. 7) **Full cost profit margin:** The difference between total revenue and total costs traceable to the work cell or product.

(L.O. 3) **Function:** A group of activities that have a common purpose or objective.

(L.O. 4) **Internal failure costs:** The costs incurred as a consequence of the discovery of defects before a product is shipped or a service delivered to a customer; a cost of nonconformance.

(L.O. 4) **Prevention costs:** The costs associated with the prevention of defects and failures in products and services; a cost of conformance.

(L.O. 3) **Process value analysis (PVA):** The process of identifying all activities and relating them to events that cause or drive the need for the activities and the resources consumed.

(L.O. 6) **Production cycle time:** The time it takes for the production people to make the product available for shipment to the customer.

(L.O. 6) **Purchase order lead time:** The time it takes for raw materials and parts to be ordered and received so that production can begin.

(L.O. 4) **Quality:** An operating environment in which a company's product or service meets or conforms to a customer's specifications the first time it is produced or delivered.

(L.O. 3) **Tasks:** The work elements or operating steps needed to perform and complete an activity.

(L.O. 4) **Total quality management (TQM):** An organizational environment in which all business functions work together to build quality into the firm's products or services.

(L.O. 3) **Value chain:** All of the functions (and related activities) in the development path of a product or service that add or contribute to its value and marketability.

Self-Test

Test your knowledge of the chapter by choosing the best answer for each of the following items.

(L.O. 1) 1. The focal point of a cost management system is the management of
   a. costs.
   b. activities.
   c. functions.
   d. tasks.

(L.O. 2) 2. Activity-based costing
   a. is an operating environment in which all resources, including materials and parts, personnel, and facilities, are used as needed.
   b. is a fully integrated computer setup in which everything connected with the manufacturing system is performed automatically.
   c. identifies all operating activities and categorizes costs by activity.
   d. is the initial phase of converting to a just-in-time operating environment.

(L.O. 2) 3. Any activity that causes costs to be incurred is called a
   a. cost-adding activity.
   b. cost driver.
   c. nonvalue-adding activity.
   d. just-in-time activity.

(L.O. 3) 4. The process of identifying all activities and relating them to events that create or drive the need for the activities and the resources consumed is the definition of
   a. integrated manufacturing activities.
   b. a cost management system.
   c. process value analysis.
   d. a value chain.

(L.O. 4) 5. The commitment to product quality that underlies JIT operations would justify
a. prevention costs exceeding internal failure costs.
b. the costs of nonconformance exceeding the costs of conformance.
c. internal failure costs exceeding appraisal costs.
d. prevention costs and appraisal costs exceeding the costs of conformance.

(L.O. 5) 6. The rate of defects per million products produced is a nonfinancial measure of
a. raw materials input.
b. product design.
c. customer acceptance.
d. in-process delivery and control.

(L.O. 5) 7. Which of the following is *not* a nonfinancial measure of product quality?
a. Inventory turnover rate
b. Number of warranty claims
c. Vendor delivery data
d. Trend in number of customer complaints

(L.O. 6) 8. The time period between acceptance of the order and final delivery of the product is a description of
a. delivery time.
b. purchase order lead time.
c. production cycle time.
d. delivery cycle time.

(L.O. 7) 9. Full cost profit margin is a profitability measure represented by the difference between total revenues and a product's or work cell's
a. total costs.
b. total variable costs.
c. total traceable costs.
d. total fixed costs.

(L.O. 8) 10. Backlogged orders are a measure of
a. asset management.
b. customer responsiveness.
c. product contribution.
d. operating effectiveness.

Answers to the Self-Test are at the end of this chapter.

Review Problem
Analysis of Nonfinancial Data—Baum Products, Inc.

(L.O. 5, 6, 8) The Hadassah Motor Division of Baum Products, Inc. has been in operation for six years. Three months ago a new flexible manufacturing system was installed in the small motors department. A just-in-time approach is followed for everything from ordering materials and parts to product shipment and delivery. The division's superintendent is very interested in the initial results of the venture. The following data have been collected for your analysis:

	Weeks							
	1	2	3	4	5	6	7	8
Warranty claims	2	4	1	1	0	5	7	11
Average setup time (hours)	.3	.25	.25	.3	.25	.2	.2	.15
Average lead time (hours)	2.4	2.3	2.2	2.3	2.35	2.4	2.4	2.5
Average cycle time (hours)	2.1	2.05	1.95	2	2	2.1	2.2	2.3
Average process time (hours)	1.9	1.9	1.85	1.8	1.9	1.95	1.95	1.9
Number of inventoried items	2,450	2,390	2,380	2,410	2,430	2,460	2,610	2,720
Customer complaints	12	12	10	8	9	7	6	4
Times inventory turnover	4.5	4.4	4.4	4.35	4.3	4.25	4.25	4.35
Production backlog (units)	9,210	9,350	9,370	9,420	9,410	8,730	8,310	7,950
Machine downtime (hours)	86.5	83.1	76.5	80.1	90.4	100.6	120.2	124.9
Parts scrapped (units)	112	126	134	118	96	89	78	64
Equipment utilization rate (%)	98.2	98.6	98.9	98.5	98.1	97.3	96.6	95.7
On-time deliveries (%)	93.2	94.1	96.5	95.4	92.1	90.5	88.4	89.3
Machine maintenance time (hours)	34.6	32.2	28.5	22.1	18.5	12.6	19.7	26.4

Required

1. Analyze the performance of the Hadassah Motor Division for the eight-week period, centering your analysis on the following areas of performance:
   a. Product quality
   b. Product delivery
   c. Inventory control
   d. Materials cost/scrap control
   e. Machine management and maintenance
2. Summarize your findings in a report to the division's superintendent.

Answer to Review Problem

The data given were reorganized in the following manner, and two additional pieces of information, average waste time and estimated number of units sold, were calculated from the given information.

1. Analysis of performance

	Weeks								Weekly
	1	2	3	4	5	6	7	8	Average
Product quality performance									
Customer complaints	12	12	10	8	9	7	6	4	8.5 cmplt.
Warranty claims	2	4	1	1	0	5	7	11	3.875 claims
Product delivery performance									
On-time deliveries (%)	93.2	94.1	96.5	95.4	92.1	90.5	88.4	89.3	92.44 %
Average setup time (hours)	.3	.25	.25	.3	.25	.2	.2	.15	.238 hours
Average lead time (hours)	2.4	2.3	2.2	2.3	2.35	2.4	2.4	2.5	2.356 hours
Average cycle time (hours)	2.1	2.05	1.95	2	2	2.1	2.2	2.3	2.088 hours
Average process time (hours)	1.9	1.9	1.85	1.8	1.9	1.95	1.95	1.9	1.894 hours
Production backlog (units)	9,210	9,350	9,370	9,420	9,410	8,730	8,310	7,950	8,969 units
Waste time (hours) (lead time less process time)	.5	.4	.35	.5	.45	.45	.45	.6	.463 hours
Inventory control performance									
Number of inventoried items (units) (a)	2,450	2,390	2,380	2,410	2,430	2,460	2,610	2,720	2,481 units
Times inventory turnover (b)	4.5	4.4	4.4	4.35	4.3	4.25	4.25	4.35	4.35 times
Estimated number of units sold (a × b)	11,025	10,516	10,472	10,484	10,449	10,455	11,093	11,832	10,791 units
Materials cost/scrap control performance									
Parts scrapped (units)	112	126	134	118	96	89	78	64	102.125 units
Machine management and maintenance performance									
Machine downtime (hours)	86.5	83.1	76.5	80.1	90.4	100.6	120.2	124.9	95.288 hours
Equipment utilization rate (%)	98.2	98.6	98.9	98.5	98.1	97.3	96.6	95.7	97.74 %
Machine maintenance time (hours)	34.6	32.2	28.5	22.1	18.5	12.6	19.7	26.4	24.325 hours

2. Memorandum to division superintendent.

   My analysis of the operating data for the Hadassah Motor Division for the last eight weeks revealed the following:

   Product quality performance:
   Product quality seems to be improving, with the number of complaints decreasing rapidly. However, warranty claims rose significantly in the past three weeks, which may be a signal of quality problems ahead.

   Product delivery performance:
   Although the averages for the product delivery measures seem great when compared to our old standards, we are having trouble maintaining the averages established eight weeks ago. Waste time is increasing, which is contrary to our goals. Backlogged orders are decreasing, which is a good sign from a JIT viewpoint but could spell problems in the future. On-time deliveries percentages are slipping. On the positive side, setup time seems to be under control. Emphasis needs to be placed on reducing lead time, cycle time, and process time.

   Inventory control performance:
   This area spells trouble. Inventory size is increasing, and the number of inventory turns is decreasing. The result is increased storage costs and decreased units sold. The last two weeks do show signs of improvement.

   Materials cost/scrap control performance:
   The incidence of scrap has decreased significantly, which is very good. We had to increase cycle time to correct our manufacturing problems, which accounts for the increases in that area. With the scrap problem under control, processing and cycle time may improve in the future.

   Machine management and maintenance performance:
   Machine downtime is increasing, which is consistent with the scrap report. Also, the equipment utilization rate is down. Machine maintenance has also tailed off but has increased in the past two weeks. Department managers should be made aware of these pending problem areas.

   Overall, we can see good signs from the new equipment, but we need to stay on top of the pending problem areas mentioned above.

Chapter Assignments

Questions

1. Describe a cost management system.
2. What is activity-based costing?
3. What is a cost driver? What is its role in activity-based costing practices?
4. How is *quality* defined in business? What are the costs of quality?
5. Identify and describe the cost-of-quality categories.
6. Name five nonfinancial measures of quality and indicate what they are designed to measure in terms of product or service quality.
7. Define *total quality management.*
8. Identify four types of nonfinancial analyses that are used to measure product quality performance. Describe the kind of data used in each analysis.
9. Why is there so much emphasis on customer satisfaction in a JIT environment? How is this attention linked to the profitability of a JIT approach?
10. Inventory controls in the new manufacturing environment are designed to eliminate inventory balances and nonvalue-adding product costs. Do you agree? Why is there emphasis on inventory elimination?
11. In a JIT/FMS environment, the formal inspection departments are eliminated but product quality controls are given high priority. How is this accomplished?

12. Why are accurate records of machine maintenance so critical to an FMS operation?
13. Define *full cost profit margin* and contrast it with contribution margin.
14. What does customer responsiveness reporting mean? How does it differ from product line profitability reporting?
15. Identify and describe several of the reports needed to monitor an FMS's operating effectiveness.

Communication Skills Exercises

Communication 26-1. Optimum Performance Using Synthesis
(L.O. 8)

IBM Corporation's General Products Division uses a performance technique called optimum performance using synthesis (OPUS) to assess operating performance and identify ways to improve the process.[9] Developed by one of IBM's own senior engineers, Armin Tietze, the philosophy supports the goal of continuous ongoing improvement. Assume that the performance of a raw material used in the production process is being measured. In a perfect environment, the material would be purchased at a reasonable cost with the end product being delivered on time and possessing very high quality. Possible imperfections or causes of poor performance would include late deliveries, unexpected poor quality, and overpriced materials. Using OPUS, the imperfections are identified for each cost center or unit being analyzed. Causes for the imperfections are identified, and methods are developed to change the imperfections into a more perfect environment. This process is repeated over and over; each time the performance gets closer to being perfect. Assume that the running time performance of a particular machine is being analyzed. Running time has been averaging 6 hours per 1,000 pieces. The machine's perfection or target running time per 1,000 pieces is 4.5 hours. Write a short paper in which you identify some of the performance elements (imperfections) that would cause the machine to run below its perfection level. Explain how the OPUS philosophy would be applied to this analysis.

Communication 26-2. Using Cost Drivers as Cost Management Tools
(L.O. 2, 3)

Elgin Sweeper Company is the leading manufacturer of street sweepers in North America.[10] The company is over seventy-five years old and produces five distinct sweeper models at its Elgin, Illinois facility. In 1986 management decided to pursue a new cost management program. Its goal was the elimination of waste. A series of training sessions taught department managers to identify the major cost drivers in their areas of responsibility. Through the identification of a set of cost drivers, analyses were conducted to assess resource usage. The cost drivers also were used as a basis for preparing budgets and as a means of identifying nonvalue-adding activities. Cost variability was linked to the cost drivers. A new series of product line contribution financial statements grew from the new cost management program. The end result was that the managers were more knowledgeable about their areas and made decisions knowing what drives projected costs. Go to the library and find a recent issue of *Management Accounting*. Locate an article that has *cost driver, activity-based costing, ABC,* or *cost management* in its title. From the article, prepare a one-page paper on the topic of cost drivers. Be sure to include examples of cost drivers in your work.

Communication 26-3. Cost Management and Ethics
(L.O. 1)

Three months ago, ***Townsend Enterprises*** hired a consultant, John Swanson, to assist in the design and installation of a new cost management system for the company. Scott Craig, one of Townsend's product/systems design engineers, was assigned to work with Swanson on the project. During the three-month period, Swanson and Craig met six times and developed a tentative design and installation plan for the CMS. Before the plan was to be unveiled to top management, Craig asked his supervisor, Bethany Leftwich, to look it over and comment on the design.

9. Armin R. Tietze and Delphine R. Shaw, "OPUS: A New Concept for Mastering Cost," *Management Accounting*, Institute of Management Accountants, August 1986, pp. 27–31.
10. John P. Callan, Wesley N. Tredup, and Randy S. Wissinger, "Elgin Sweeper Company's Journey Toward Cost Management," *Management Accounting*, Institute of Management Accountants, July 1991, pp. 24–27.

Included in the plan is a consolidation of three engineering functions into one. Both of the current supervisors of the other two functions have seniority over Leftwich, so she believes that the design would lead to her losing her management position. She communicates this to Craig and ends her comments with the following statement, "If you don't redesign the system to accommodate all three of the existing engineering functions, I will see to it that you are given an unsatisfactory performance evaluation for this year!"

How should Craig respond to Leftwich's assertion? Should he handle the problem alone, keeping it inside the company or communicate the comment to Swanson? Outline Craig's options and be prepared to discuss them in class.

Communication 26-4. Basic Research Skills *(L.O. 3)*

Activity-based costing requires that all activities related to a particular function be identified and that costs be traced to those activities. Identify a set of activities required to sell an article of personal clothing. Select your favorite clothing store. Interview the manager or a salesperson, and ask what takes place between the decision to buy a particular line of clothing and the actual sale of an item to a customer. What is the normal time period between placing the purchase order and making the sale? Make a list of all of the activities involved in the process. Are any of the activities nonvalue adding? Finally, select one major activity from your list and identify the costs that could be traced to it.

Classroom Exercises

Exercise 26-1. Cost Driver Determination *(L.O. 2)*

Salesman Rick Vimmerstedt just stormed out of the office of controller Joe Umbriano. When asked what was wrong, Vimmerstedt stated that he had just been told to refuse any additional orders for goods that had to circumvent the existing three-week backlog. Umbriano had just added $2,450 in additional scheduling costs to a recent order from Blaser Corp., one of Vimmerstedt's accounts, and this charge turned a $2,200 profit into a $250 loss. (Sales personnel earn commissions on the profits their orders generate.)

Umbriano used the following analysis to back up his position regarding the Blaser Corp. order:

Costs Associated with Production Schedule Changes

Personnel overtime	$1,940
Extra computer time	1,260
Unanticipated supplies and utility costs	1,080
Communication with affected customers	620
Total costs of schedule changes	$4,900
50 percent traceable to Blaser Corp. order	$2,450

What is a cost driver? Does this case involve a cost driver? Should the cost of schedule changes be spread over all orders worked on or traced to specific orders? Do you agree with Umbriano's decision? Why or why not?

Exercise 26-2. Costs and Their Cost Drivers *(L.O. 2)*

The following items are from the trial balance of the Elmore Corporation in Huntsville, Alabama. Company accountants are in the process of establishing an overhead allocation system for factory-related costs. To help guarantee accuracy, they want to set up several cost pools based on separate activities. The company has an automated flexible manufacturing system in operation. Budgeted costs for the period were as follows:

Repairs and maintenance, plant building	$ 11,578
Engineering Department salaries	22,190
Raw materials	123,790
Depreciation, Tool and Die Department equipment	7,270
Depreciation, Engineering Department equipment	4,260
Marketing expenses	21,320
Depreciation, plant building	8,150
Tool and Die Department operating supplies	1,274

Insurance and taxes, plant building	$ 3,520
Yard maintenance, plant building	1,250
Electrical costs, Tool and Die Department	2,310
Electrical costs, plant building	3,520
Tool and Die Department wages	19,740
Electrical costs, Engineering Department	1,980

Divide these costs into separate activity cost pools. Identify the cost driver for each pool that will distribute the costs fairly. Alternative activities include direct labor hours, tool and die orders, engineering change orders, machine hours, engineering hours, tool and die labor hours, direct labor dollars, and square footage.

Exercise 26-3.
Activities and Activity-Based Costing
(L.O. 2, 3)

Ji Zeng Enterprises produces antennas for telecommunications equipment. One of the most important parts of the company's new just-in-time production process is quality control. Initially, a traditional cost accounting system was used to assign quality control costs to products. All of the costs of the Quality Control Department were included in the plant's overhead cost pool and allocated to products based on direct labor dollars. Recently, the firm implemented an activity-based costing system. The activities, cost drivers, and rates for the quality control function are summarized below, along with cost allocation information from the traditional system. Also shown is information related to one order of the Qian model antenna.

Traditional costing approach:

Quality control costs were assigned at a rate of 12 percent of direct labor dollars.
Order HQ14 was charged with $9,350 of direct labor cost.

Activity-based costing approach:

Quality Control Function

Activities	Cost Drivers	Cost Assignment Rates	Order HQ14 Activity Usage
Incoming materials inspection	Types of materials used	$17.50 per type of material	17 types of materials
In-process inspection	Number of products	$0.06 per product	2,400 products
Tool and gauge control	Number of processes per cell	$26.50 per process	11 processes
Product certification	Per order	$94.00 per order	1 order

Compute the quality control cost that would be assigned to the Qian model order HQ14 under both the traditional approach and the activity-based costing approach to cost assignment.

Exercise 26-4.
Cost of Quality
(L.O. 4)

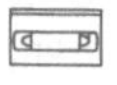

John Miller has been appointed chief accountant for Houston Industries. The business has three divisions that manufacture oil well depth gauges. The business is very competitive, and Houston Industries has lost market share in each of the last four years. Three years ago, management announced a companywide restructuring and the adoption of total quality management. Since that time, each of the divisions has been allowed to chart its own path toward TQM. Mr. Miller is new to the company and has asked to see summary figures of the costs of quality for each of the divisions. The following data were presented to him for the past six months:

Sales	Texas Division	Oklahoma Division	Arkansas Division	Company Totals
	$1,849,400	$1,773,450	$1,757,400	$5,380,250
Prevention costs	$ 32,680	$ 48,120	$ 15,880	$ 96,680
Appraisal costs	42,340	32,210	17,980	92,530
Internal failure costs	24,100	21,450	41,780	87,330
External failure costs	32,980	16,450	45,560	94,990
Total costs of quality	$ 132,100	$ 118,230	$ 121,200	$ 371,530

Evaluate the three divisions' quality control programs by first computing the costs of conformance and the costs of nonconformance of each division. Also compute quality costs as a percentage of sales for each division. Identify the division that is developing the strongest quality program. What division has been the slowest to react to the management directive of TQM? Defend your answers.

Exercise 26-5. Nonfinancial Measures of Quality and TQM *(L.O. 5)*

"A satisfied customer is the most important goal of this company!" was the opening remark of the corporate president, Peter Behr, at the monthly executive committee meeting of Stokkeland Company. The company manufactures piping products for customers in sixteen western states. Four divisions, each producing a different type of piping material, make up the company's organizational structure. Behr, a proponent of total quality management, was reacting to the latest measures of quality data from the four divisions. The data are presented below.

	Brass Division	Plastics Division	Aluminum Division	Copper Division	Company Averages
Vendor on-time delivery	96.20%	92.40%	98.10%	90.20%	94.23%
Production quality rates (defective parts per million)	1,640	2,820	1,270	4,270	2,500
On-time shipments	89.20%	78.40%	91.80%	75.60%	83.75%
Returned orders	1.10%	4.60%	0.80%	6.90%	3.35%
Number of customer complaints	24	56	10	62	38.0
Number of warranty claims	7	12	4	14	9.3*

*Rounded.

Why was Behr upset? Which division or divisions do not appear to have satisfied customers? What criteria did you use to make your decision?

Exercise 26-6. Reporting JIT Data *(L.O. 5, 8)*

Bud Archer is chief executive officer of Tubac Machinery, Inc. The company adopted a JIT operating environment about five years ago. Since then, each segment of the company has been converted, and a complete computer-integrated manufacturing system now exists in all parts of the company's five plants. Processing of Tubac's products now averages less than four days once the materials have been placed into production.

Archer is worried about customer satisfaction and has asked his controller, Sue Bailey, for some advice and help. Bailey did a quick survey of customers to determine weak areas in customer relations. Here is a summary of four customers' replies:

Customer A:
Customer for five years; waits an average of six weeks for delivery; located 1,200 miles from plant; returns an average of 3 percent of products; receives 90 percent on-time deliveries; never hears from salesperson after placing order; likes quality or would go with competitor.

Customer B:
Customer for seven years; waits an average of five weeks for delivery; orders usually sit in backlog for at least three weeks; located 50 miles from plant; returns about 5 percent of products; receives 95 percent on-time deliveries; has great rapport with salesperson; salesperson is reason why this is a loyal customer.

Customer C:
Customer for twelve years; waits an average of seven weeks for delivery; located 1,500 miles from plant; returns about 4 percent of products; receives 92 percent on-time deliveries; salesperson is available but of little help in getting faster delivery; company is thinking about dealing with another source for its product needs.

Customer D:
Customer for fifteen years; very pleased with company's product; still waits almost five weeks for delivery; located 120 miles from plant; returns only 2 percent of goods received; rapport with salesperson very good; follow-up service of salesperson excellent; would like delivery cycle time reduced to equal that of competitors; usually deals with three-week backlog.

What types of reports would you recommend be included in the management reporting system? Defend the need for each report.

Exercise 26-7.
Nonfinancial Data Analysis
(L.O. 6)

Doarn & Company makes racing bicycle products. Their Boyce model is considered top of the line within the industry. Three months ago the company purchased and installed a flexible manufacturing system for the Boyce line, with emphasis on improving quality as well as reducing production time. Management is interested in cutting time in all phases of the delivery cycle.

Following are data the controller's office gathered for the past four-week period:

	Weeks			
	1	2	3	4
Average process time (hours)	23.6	23.4	22.8	22.2
Average setup time (hours)	2.4	2.3	2.2	2.1
Customer complaints	6	5	7	8
Delivery time (hours)	34.8	35.2	36.4	38.2
On-time deliveries (%)	98.1	97.7	97.2	96.3
Production backlog (units)	8,230	8,340	8,320	8,430
Production cycle time (hours)	28.5	27.9	27.2	26.4
Purchase order lead time (hours)	38.5	36.2	35.5	34.1
Warranty claims	2	3	3	2

Analyze the performance of the Boyce model line for the four-week period, centering your analysis on the following areas of performance:

1. Product quality
2. Product delivery

Exercise 26-8.
Full Cost Profit Margin
(L.O. 7)

Mark Johnson Enterprises produces all-purpose sports vehicles. The company recently installed a flexible manufacturing system for its AJ-25 product line. The accounting system has been recast to reflect the new operating process. Following are monthly operating data for periods before and after the FMS installation:

	Product AJ-25
Average monthly revenue	$1,378,000
Total operating costs:	
For month before FMS installed	
Direct materials	$ 330,720
Direct labor	454,740
Variable factory overhead	124,020
Variable selling expenses	41,340
Variable distribution costs	55,120
Fixed factory overhead	456,200
Fixed selling expenses	132,300
Fixed distribution costs	189,700

	Product AJ-25
Total operating costs (*continued*):	
For month after FMS installed	
Direct materials	$ 330,720
Materials-related overhead	48,230
Direct labor	62,010
Indirect labor	99,216
Setup labor	66,144
Electrical power	24,804
Supervision	35,828
Repairs and maintenance	46,852
Operating supplies and lubricants	11,024
Other traceable indirect costs	30,316
Traceable selling expenses	52,364
Traceable distribution costs	57,876
Nontraceable factory overhead	245,300
Nontraceable selling and distribution costs	178,200

Using the after-FMS data, compute the full cost profit margin for product AJ-25. Also include full cost profit margin as a percent of revenue and operating profit as a percent of revenue as part of your answer.

Interpretation Case from Business

Nease Corporation
(L.O. 2, 3)

Savannah, Georgia is home of the Nease Corporation. Fifteen years ago Marsha Nease teamed up with ten financial supporters and created a roller skate manufacturing company. Company design people soon turned the roller skate idea into a riding skateboard. Twelve years and more than 4 million skateboards later, Nease Corporation finds itself an industry leader in both volume and quality.

To retain market share, Nease Corporation has decided to automate its manufacturing process. Flexible manufacturing systems have been ordered for the wheel assembly and the board shaping lines. Manual operations will be retained for the board decorating line because some hand painting is involved. All operations will be converted to a just-in-time environment.

You have been called in as a consultant to Nease, who wants some idea of the impact of the new JIT/FMS approach on the company's product costing practices.

Required

1. Summarize the elements of a JIT environment.
2. What product costing changes should be anticipated when the new automated systems are installed?
3. What are some of the cost drivers that the company should employ? In what situations?
4. Are there any other accounting practices that will be affected? Why?

Problem Set A

Problem 26A-1. Activities and Activity-Based Costing
(L.O. 2, 3)

Vanderwende Products, Inc. produces a line of FAX machines for wholesale distributors in the Pacific Northwest region. Martinek Company ordered 150 Model 14 FAX machines and Vanderwende has just completed packaging the order. Before shipping the Martinek order, the controller has asked for a unit cost analysis, comparing the amounts determined by their old traditional absorption costing system with amounts computed under their new activity-based costing system.

Raw materials, purchased parts, and production labor costs for the Martinek order are listed at the top of page 1082.

Cost of raw materials	$17,450.00
Cost of purchased parts	$14,800.00
Production direct labor hours	140
Average direct labor pay rate	$16.50

Other operating costs are as follows:

Traditional costing data:
Factory overhead costs were assigned at a rate of 240 percent of direct labor dollars.

Activity-based costing data:

Activities	Cost Drivers	Cost Assignment Rates	Activity Usage for Martinek Order
Engineering systems design	Engineering hours	$28.00 per eng. hr	18 eng. hr
Work cell setup	Number of setups	$42.00 per setup	8 setups
Parts production work cell	Machine hours	$37.50 per MH	84 MH
Product assembly cell	Cell hours	$44.00 per cell hr	36 cell hr
Packaging work cell	Cell hours	$28.50 per cell hr	28 cell hr

Building occupancy-related overhead costs are allocated at a rate of $10.40 per production work cell machine hour.

Required

1. Compute the total cost of the Martinek order following the traditional absorption costing approach.
2. Compute the total cost of the Martinek order following the activity-based costing approach.
3. What was the difference in the amount of cost assigned to the Martinek order resulting from the shift to the activity-based costing approach? Is there anything unusual about the difference?

Problem 26A-2. Costs and Nonfinancial Measures of Quality *(L.O. 4, 5)*

The Qualls Company operates as three autonomous divisions. Each division has a general manager in charge of product development, production, and distribution. Management recently adopted total quality management, and the divisions now track, record, and analyze their costs and nonfinancial measures of quality. All three divisions are competing in a worldwide, highly competitive marketplace. Sales and quality-related data for April are summarized below.

	Mills Division	Parks Division	Ross Division
Sales	$8,600,000	$9,400,000	$12,900,000
Costs of quality			
Setup for testing	$ 51,600	$ 112,800	$ 180,600
Quality audits	17,200	75,200	109,650
Failure analysis	103,200	14,100	90,300
Quality training of employees	60,200	188,000	167,700
Scrap and rework	154,800	18,800	154,800
Quality planning activities	34,400	94,000	103,200
Preventive maintenance	68,800	141,000	141,900
Warranty claims	107,500	42,300	103,200
Customer service	150,500	108,100	154,800
Quality engineering	94,600	235,000	232,200
Product simulation and development	25,800	178,600	141,900
Losses caused by vendor scrap	77,400	23,500	64,500
Returned goods	159,100	14,100	45,150
Product recalls	64,500	32,900	64,500
Total costs of quality	$1,169,600	$1,278,400	$ 1,754,400

	Mills Division	Parks Division	Ross Division
Nonfinancial measures of quality:			
Defective parts per million	3,410	1,104	1,940
Returned orders	7.40%	1.10%	3.20%
Customer complaints	62	12	30
Number of warranty claims	74	16	52

Required

1. Prepare an analysis of the costs of quality of the three divisions. Categorize the costs as follows: costs of conformance with subsets of prevention costs and appraisal costs, and costs of nonconformance with subsets of internal failure costs and external failure costs. Compute the total costs for each category for each division.
2. Compute the percent of sales of each cost-of-quality total for each division.
3. Interpret the cost-of-quality data for each division. Is each division's product of high or low quality? Explain your answers. Are the divisions headed in the right direction to be globally competitive?
4. Evaluate the nonfinancial measures of quality in terms of customer satisfaction. Are these results consistent with your analysis in 3? Explain your answers.

Problem 26A-3. Analysis of Nonfinancial Data
(L.O. 5, 6)

Henderson Electronics Company was formed in 1952. Over the years the company has become known for its high-quality electronics products and its dependability for on-time delivery. Six months ago management decided to install a flexible manufacturing system for its Electronic Components Department. With the new equipment, the entire component is produced by the FMS so the finished product is ready to be shipped when needed. Following are data the controller's staff gathered during the past eight-week period:

	Weeks							
	1	2	3	4	5	6	7	8
Average process time (hours)	11.9	12.1	11.6	11.8	12.2	12.8	13.2	14.6
Average setup time (hours)	1.5	1.6	1.6	1.8	1.7	1.4	1.2	1.2
Customer complaints	10	9	22	14	8	6	4	5
Delivery time (hours)	26.2	26.4	26.1	25.9	26.2	26.6	27.1	26.4
Equipment utilization rate (%)	97.2	97.1	97.3	98.2	98.4	97.2	97.4	96.3
Machine downtime (hours)	106.4	108.1	120.2	110.4	112.8	102.2	124.6	136.2
Machine maintenance time (hours)	66.8	68.7	74.6	76.2	78.8	68.6	82.4	90.2
Number of inventoried items	3,450	3,510	3,680	3,790	3,620	3,490	3,560	3,260
On-time deliveries (%)	97.2	97.5	97.6	98.2	98.4	96.4	94.8	92.6
Parts scrapped	243	268	279	245	256	280	290	314
Production backlog (units)	10,246	10,288	10,450	10,680	10,880	11,280	11,350	12,100
Production cycle time (hours)	16.5	16.4	16.3	16.1	16.3	17.6	19.8	21.8
Purchase order lead time (hours)	15.2	15.1	14.9	14.6	14.6	13.2	12.4	12.6
Times inventory turnover	2.1	2.3	2.2	2.4	2.2	2.1	2.1	1.9
Warranty claims	4	8	2	1	6	4	2	3

Required

1. Analyze the performance of the Electronic Components Department for the eight-week period, centering your analysis on performance in the following areas:
   a. Product quality
   b. Product delivery
   c. Inventory control
   d. Materials cost/scrap control
   e. Machine management and maintenance
2. Summarize your findings in a report to the department's superintendent.

Problem 26A-4.
Full Cost Profit Margin
(L.O. 7)

Nolan Molded Products Company produces three main products, identified as C2-24, K5-36, and R4-73. Two months ago, the company installed three fully automated flexible manufacturing systems for the product lines. The controller is anxious to see how the FMS machinery affects operating costs for the three products. Product K5-36 has been a low performer for the company and is being outpriced on the market. The line may have to be dropped.

Monthly operating data for before and after the FMS installation are as follows:

Nolan Molded Products Company
Product Performance Evaluation

	Assembly C2-24	Assembly K5-36	Assembly R4-73
Total revenue	$4,590,000	$5,180,000	$3,520,000
Total operating costs			
Before FMS installed:			
Direct materials	$1,101,600	$1,346,800	$ 774,400
Direct labor	1,514,700	1,761,200	985,600
Variable factory overhead	413,100	259,000	158,400
Variable selling expenses	137,700	155,400	123,200
Variable distribution costs	183,600	310,800	193,600
Fixed factory overhead	456,200	654,200	432,600
Fixed selling expenses	132,300	103,290	196,700
Fixed distribution costs	189,700	304,520	291,800
After FMS installed:			
Direct materials	$1,101,600	$1,346,800	$ 774,400
Materials-related overhead	160,650	150,220	112,640
Direct labor	206,550	227,920	147,840
Indirect labor	330,480	331,520	260,480
Setup labor	220,320	217,560	154,880
Electrical power	82,620	93,240	56,320
Supervision	119,340	145,040	91,520
Repairs and maintenance	156,060	160,580	130,240
Operating supplies/lubricants	36,720	46,620	28,160
Other traceable indirect costs	100,980	108,780	84,480
Traceable selling expenses	174,420	170,940	133,760
Traceable distribution costs	192,780	202,020	154,880
Nontraceable factory overhead	245,300	323,100	241,100
Nontraceable selling and distribution costs	178,200	231,400	198,760

Required

1. Recast the information given for the three products into an analysis that reveals total traceable and total nontraceable costs (a) before and (b) after the FMS was installed.
2. Describe and differentiate between full cost profit margin and contribution margin.
3. Using the before-FMS data, prepare an analysis that reveals contribution margin, operating profit, contribution margin as a percentage of revenue, and operating profit as a percentage of revenue.

4. Using the after-FMS data, prepare an analysis that reveals full cost profit margin, operating profit, full cost profit margin as a percentage of revenue, and operating profit as a percentage of revenue.
5. Should the company drop the K5-36 product line? Defend your answer.

Problem 26A-5. Traditional Versus JIT/FMS/ABC Unit Cost Analysis
(L.O. 2, 3, 6, 8)

Boyer Appliance Company produces home kitchen products. Currently, it maintains production lines for twelve different types of products, including a line of fruit juice presses. The various models of presses are adjustable to work with different sizes of fruit. Kathryn Boyer started the company in her garage fourteen years ago, and the company has grown to a point where it is now the largest in the industry. The fruit juice presses are assembled from parts manufactured by the company and from parts purchased from vendors. Two years ago, the company changed management approaches and implemented just-in-time operations. In addition, Boyer just installed a flexible manufacturing system work cell for the press line. Everything is automated, including materials handling between machine work ports. Activity-based costing is going to be applied to the engineering function to begin the process of converting all cost assignment practices to ABC.

The company still uses traditional methods for product costing, even though the new FMS has been operating for several weeks. You have been contacted to restructure the present accounting system to compute a more realistic product unit cost under the JIT/FMS conditions and one that begins to incorporate activity-based costing. Data from the current accounting period are presented below and on pages 1086 and 1087.

The new system will cause several changes. Many of the indirect costs now in the plantwide factory overhead pool will be traceable directly to the FMS work cell. Also, materials/parts storage and handling costs, which will be reduced 50 percent by the JIT/FMS system, are going to be accumulated in a separate cost pool and allocated to the work cell and other product orders based on total dollars of materials and parts incurred. The engineering function will be tracked separately by activity, and special cost drivers will be used to assign these costs to work cells and products. Any indirect costs not traceable to or handled in separate cost pools will be grouped in a plantwide overhead pool and allocated based on machine hours. Only small amounts of work in process inventory are anticipated in the new environment, and several other costs, such as setup labor, inspection, and storage costs, will be reduced significantly or eliminated by the new system. FIFO process costing procedures will be used to compute each work cell's unit costs.

	Traditional Costing Approach	JIT/FMS/ABC Costing Approach
Costs directly traceable to products in FMS cell		
Raw materials	$ 819,304	$ 819,304
Parts for assembly	482,000	482,000
Direct labor (based on 96,500 equiv. units)		
Traditional: 1.8 DLH per unit at $12 per DLH	2,084,400	
JIT/FMS: 0.4 DLH per unit at $15 per DLH		579,000
Total costs traceable to products in FMS cell	$3,385,704	$1,880,304

(continued)

	Traditional Costing Approach	JIT/FMS/ABC Costing Approach
Plantwide indirect manufacturing cost pool		
Setup labor	$ 421,780	
Electrical power, factory	163,200	
Supervision, factory	210,670	
Purchased parts, inspection costs	78,230	
Product rework costs	142,500	
Depreciation, machinery	199,600	
Other indirect labor	391,990	
Purchasing costs, materials/parts	148,200	
Materials/parts storage and handling	226,200	
Depreciation, materials/parts moving trucks	31,200	
Engineering labor	360,000	
Electrical costs, engineering	28,800	
Depreciation, engineering equipment	32,400	
Engineering supervision	68,400	
Other engineering overhead	21,600	
Operating supplies and lubricants	38,450	
Finished goods inspection costs	89,760	
Machinery repairs and maintenance	174,560	
Storage and handling, work in process inventory	234,190	
Depreciation, building	121,400	$121,400
Property taxes	24,360	24,360
Liability and fire insurance	18,400	18,400
Building maintenance	34,170	34,170
Other factory utilities	19,230	19,230
Factory employees' cafeteria	165,290	165,290
Total indirect manufacturing costs	$3,444,580	$382,850
Overhead costs directly traceable to FMS cell		
Setup labor		$115,680
Other indirect labor		212,080
Electrical power		38,560
Machinery repairs and maintenance		33,740
Supervision, factory		43,380
Depreciation, machinery		179,250
Operating supplies and lubricants		17,352
Total overhead costs directly traceable to FMS cell		$640,042
Materials/parts storage and handling overhead cost pool (original costs reduced by 50%)		
Purchasing costs, materials/parts		$ 74,100
Materials/parts storage and handling		113,100
Depreciation, materials/parts moving trucks		15,600
Total materials/parts storage and handling overhead costs		$202,800

(continued)

	JIT/FMS/ABC Costing Approach
Engineering function (all engineering costs accumulated by activity)	
Product engineering activity	$146,200
Engineering changes activity	137,600
Product testing activity	129,200
Product review activity	98,200
Total costs—engineering function	$511,200

Engineering function—Cost driver information

Activity	Cost Driver	Cost Driver Data: Total Plant	Cost Driver Data: FMS Cell
Product engineering activity	Number of different products	110	16
Engineering changes activity	Number of engineering changes	84	10
Product testing activity	Number of products	340,500	96,400
Product review activity	Number of engineering hours	18,000	7,200

These data have been partially restructured in anticipation of the new system. The following information will be required for the analysis:

Total plant direct labor hours for the period	1,216,600 DLH
Total plant machine hours for the period	1,850,400 MH
Machine hours for the fruit juice press FMS cell	308,400 MH
Total plantwide cost of materials and parts for the period	$7,800,000
Process costing information for the press FMS cell	
Beginning inventory	
Materials and parts	$1,420
Conversion costs	$1,360
Equivalent units for the period	
Materials and parts	96,400 equiv. units
Conversion costs	96,500 equiv. units

Required

1. Following the traditional costing approach,
   a. compute the plantwide factory overhead application rate.
   b. compute the product unit cost for each press produced.
2. Identify the cost categories and the total costs that are likely to be reduced significantly or eliminated when the company adopts the JIT/FMS approach.
3. Compute the new cost application rates for (a) materials/parts storage and handling overhead costs and (b) indirect manufacturing costs.
4. Compute the activity-based costing application rates per cost driver for the engineering function.

5. Identify (a) the total materials costs and (b) the total conversion costs for the period for the press FMS work cell.
6. Using the FIFO process costing method, compute the press unit cost in the new JIT/FMS setting.

Problem Set B

Problem 26B-1.
Activities and Activity-Based Costing
(L.O. 2, 3)

Goodall Computer Company, which has been in operation for ten years, produces a line of minicomputers. Cardenas Realtors, Ltd. placed an order for eighty minicomputers and the order has just been completed. Goodall recently shifted its cost assignment approach to an activity-based system. Amy Jones, the controller, is interested in finding out the impact that the ABC system had on the Cardenas order. Raw materials, purchased parts, and production labor costs for the Cardenas order are as follows:

Cost of raw materials	$36,750.00	Production direct labor hours	220
Cost of purchased parts	21,300.00	Average direct labor pay rate	$15.25

Other operating costs are as follows:

Traditional costing data:
Factory overhead costs were assigned at a rate of 270 percent of direct labor dollars.

Activity-based costing data:

Activities	Cost Drivers	Cost Assignment Rates	Activity Usage for Cardenas Order
Electrical engineering design	Engineering hours	$19.50 per eng. hr	32 eng. hr
Work cell setups	Number of setups	$29.40 per setup	11 setups
Parts production work cell	Machine hours	$26.30 per MH	134 MH
Product testing cell	Cell hours	$32.80 per cell hr	52 cell hr
Packaging work cell	Cell hours	$17.50 per cell hr	22 cell hr

Building occupancy-related overhead costs are allocated at a rate of $9.80 per production work cell machine hour.

Required

1. Compute the total cost of the Cardenas order following the traditional absorption costing approach.
2. Compute the total cost of the Cardenas order following the activity-based costing approach.
3. What was the difference in the amount of cost assigned to the Cardenas order resulting from the shift to the activity-based costing approach? Is there anything unusual about the difference?

Problem 26B-2.
Costs and Nonfinancial Measures of Quality
(L.O. 4, 5)

Maldonato Enterprises, Inc. operates as three autonomous companies. Each company has a chief executive officer who oversees its operations. At a recent corporate meeting, the company CEOs agreed to adopt total quality management for their operations and to track, record, and analyze their costs and nonfinancial measures of quality. All three companies are competing in a highly competitive worldwide market. Sales and quality-related data for September are summarized on the top of the next page.

Required

1. Prepare an analysis of the costs of quality for the three companies. Categorize the costs in the following format: costs of conformance with subsets of prevention costs and appraisal costs, and costs of nonconformance with subsets of internal failure costs and external failure costs. Compute the total costs for each category for each of the three companies.
2. Compute the percentage of sales for each cost-of-quality total for each division.
3. Interpret the cost-of-quality data for each company. Is the company's product of high or low quality? Why? Is each company headed in the right direction to be globally competitive?
4. Evaluate the nonfinancial measures of quality in terms of customer satisfaction. Are the results consistent with your analysis in **3**? Explain your answer.

	Simmons Company	Adams Company	Frye Company
Sales	$11,500,000	$13,200,000	$10,900,000
Costs of quality:			
Sample preparation	$ 69,000	$ 184,800	$ 130,800
Quality audits	57,500	112,200	141,700
Failure analysis	184,000	92,400	16,350
Design review	80,500	171,600	218,000
Scrap and rework	207,000	158,400	21,800
Quality planning activities	46,000	105,600	239,800
Preventive maintenance	92,000	158,400	163,500
Warranty adjustments	143,750	105,600	49,050
Customer service	201,250	198,000	81,750
Quality training of employees	149,500	237,600	272,500
Product simulation and development	34,500	145,200	207,100
Reinspection of rework	126,500	66,000	27,250
Returned goods	212,750	72,600	16,350
Customer complaint processing	109,250	158,400	38,150
Total costs of quality	$ 1,713,500	$ 1,966,800	$ 1,624,100
Nonfinancial measures of quality:			
Number of warranty claims	61	36	12
Customer complaints	107	52	18
Defective parts per million	4,610	2,190	1,012
Returned orders	9.20%	4.10%	0.90%

Problem 26B-3. Analysis of Nonfinancial Data
(L.O. 5, 6)

Heizenga Enterprises, Inc. manufactures several lines of small machinery. Before automated equipment was installed, the total delivery cycle for the Beki machine models averaged about three weeks. Last year management decided to purchase an FMS for the Beki line. The cost was $17,458,340 and included twelve separate work stations producing the four components needed to assemble a finished product. Each machine is linked to the next via an automated conveyor system. Assembly of the four parts, including the machine's entire electrical system, now takes only two hours. Following is a summary of operating data for the past eight weeks for the Beki line:

	Weeks							
	1	2	3	4	5	6	7	8
Average process time (hours)	8.2	8.2	8.1	8.4	8.6	8.2	7.8	7.6
Average setup time (hours)	1.2	1.2	1.1	0.9	0.9	0.8	1.0	0.9
Customer complaints	4	5	3	6	5	7	8	8
Delivery time (hours)	36.2	37.4	37.2	36.4	35.9	35.8	34.8	34.2
Equipment utilization rate (%)	99.1	99.2	99.4	99.1	98.8	98.6	98.8	98.8
Machine downtime (hours)	82.3	84.2	85.9	84.3	83.4	82.2	82.8	80.4
Machine maintenance time (hours)	52.4	54.8	51.5	48.4	49.2	47.8	46.8	44.9
Number of inventoried items	5,642	5,820	5,690	5,780	5,630	5,510	5,280	5,080
On-time deliveries (%)	92.4	92.5	93.2	94.2	94.4	94.1	95.8	94.6
Parts scrapped	98.0	96.0	102.0	104.0	100.0	98.2	98.6	100.6
Production backlog (units)	15,230	15,440	15,200	16,100	14,890	13,560	13,980	13,440
Production cycle time (hours)	12.2	12.6	11.9	11.8	12.2	11.6	11.2	10.6
Purchase order lead time (hours)	26.2	26.8	26.5	25.9	25.7	25.3	24.8	24.2
Times inventory turnover	3.2	3.4	3.4	3.6	3.8	3.8	4.2	4.4
Warranty claims	2	2	3	2	3	4	3	3

Required

1. Analyze the performance of the Beki machine line for the eight-week period, centering your analysis on performance in the following areas:
   a. Product quality
   b. Product delivery
   c. Inventory control
   d. Materials cost/scrap control
   e. Machine management and maintenance
2. Summarize your findings in a report to the company management.

Problem 26B-4.
Full Cost Profit Margin
(L.O. 7)

Denise Martinez began producing scrap-iron art works seven years ago. Her business became so profitable that she converted to an assembly line approach two years ago. Concerned about continuously rising labor costs, Martinez recently agreed to purchase flexible manufacturing systems for her three largest-selling products: the Meadow, Ridge, and Valley assemblies. Martinez is very concerned about the Valley assembly because of its recent poor profitability performance. Following are operating data from before and after the FMS installation:

Martinez Metal Products Company
Product Performance Evaluation

	Meadow Assembly	Ridge Assembly	Valley Assembly
Total revenue	$3,972,000	$6,731,000	$4,262,000
Total operating costs:			
Before FMS installed:			
Direct materials	$ 953,280	$1,750,060	$1,193,360
Direct labor	1,310,760	2,288,540	1,363,840
Variable factory overhead	357,480	336,550	230,148
Variable selling expenses	166,824	289,433	157,694
Variable distribution costs	158,880	403,860	242,934
Fixed factory overhead	461,100	647,700	515,600
Fixed selling expenses	146,100	153,400	166,700
Fixed distribution costs	191,600	299,600	249,800
After FMS installed:			
Direct materials	$ 953,280	$1,750,060	$1,193,360
Materials-related overhead	206,544	363,474	242,934
Direct labor	285,984	457,708	272,768
Indirect labor	278,040	430,784	315,388
Setup labor	190,656	282,702	187,528
Electrical power	71,496	121,158	68,192
Supervision	103,272	188,468	110,812
Repairs and maintenance	135,048	208,661	157,694
Operating supplies/lubricants	31,776	60,579	34,096
Other traceable indirect costs	87,384	141,351	102,288
Traceable selling expenses	150,936	222,123	161,956
Traceable distribution costs	166,824	262,509	183,266
Nontraceable factory overhead	276,300	341,300	253,400
Nontraceable selling and distribution costs	214,200	297,300	209,700

Required

1. Recast the information given for the three products into an analysis that reveals total traceable and total nontraceable costs (a) before and (b) after the FMS was installed.
2. Describe and differentiate between full cost profit margin and contribution margin.
3. Using the before-FMS data, prepare an analysis that reveals contribution margin, operating profit, contribution margin as a percentage of revenue, and operating profit as a percentage of revenue.
4. Using the after-FMS data, prepare an analysis that reveals full cost profit margin, operating profit, full cost profit margin as a percentage of revenue, and operating profit as a percentage of revenue.
5. Should the company drop the Valley assembly? Defend your answer.

Problem 26B-5. Traditional Versus JIT/FMS/ABC Unit Cost Analysis (Restructured version of Problem 25B-5, to include ABC)
(L.O. 2, 3, 6, 8)

Paquette Products, Inc. produces fans for homes and businesses. Last year, management decided to adopt a just-in-time operating environment and to install the company's first FMS work cell for the ceiling fan product line. Also, an activity-based costing system is going to be installed by function, beginning with the engineering function.

The deluxe ceiling fan's casing and wooden blades are manufactured by the company; the small motor and electrical parts are purchased from outside vendors and assembled by the company. Currently, the company uses a traditional cost accounting system, and unit costs are computed by adding a plantwide manufacturing overhead factor to direct materials and direct labor unit costs. The overhead allocation base has been direct labor hours.

You have been asked to restructure the present manufacturing cost data that follow so that the influence of the new system on product unit costs can be analyzed. The data are from the most recent accounting period. The new systems and operating environment will cause several changes in the unit cost analysis. Many of the indirect costs will be directly traceable to the FMS work cell and will no longer be included in the plantwide overhead computation. Also, materials/parts storage and handling costs, which will be reduced 40 percent by the JIT/FMS system, are going to be accumulated in a separate cost pool and allocated to the work cell and product orders based on total dollars of materials and parts incurred. The engineering function will be tracked separately by activity, and special cost drivers will be used to assign these costs to work cells and products. Any indirect costs not traceable to or handled in separate cost pools will be grouped in a plantwide overhead pool and allocated based on machine hours. Only small amounts of work in process inventory are anticipated in the new environment. FIFO process costing procedures will be used to compute the work cell's unit costs.

	Traditional Costing Approach	JIT/FMS/ABC Costing Approach
Costs directly traceable to products in FMS cell		
Raw materials	$ 539,072	$ 539,072
Parts for assembly	1,823,280	1,823,280
Direct labor (based on 64,300 equiv. units)		
Traditional: 4.2 hours per unit at $14/hr	3,780,840	
JIT/FMS: 0.8 hour per unit at $18/hr		925,920
Total costs traceable to products in FMS cell	$6,143,192	$3,288,272

(continued)

	Traditional Costing Approach	JIT/FMS/ABC Costing Approach
Plantwide indirect manufacturing cost pool		
Product rework costs	$ 741,100	
Electrical power, factory	363,000	
Supervision, factory	246,800	
Depreciation, machinery	74,200	
Purchased motors, inspection costs	67,400	
Setup labor	231,120	
Other indirect labor	526,440	
Engineering labor	176,800	
Electrical costs, engineering	163,200	
Depreciation, engineering equipment	91,800	
Engineering supervision	104,720	
Other engineering overhead	53,040	
Operating supplies and lubricants	36,890	
Finished goods inspection costs	79,800	
Machinery repairs and maintenance	234,200	
Storage and handling, work in process inventory	432,900	
Depreciation, building	154,700	$154,700
Property taxes	28,900	28,900
Liability and fire insurance	26,860	26,860
Building maintenance	43,500	43,500
Other factory utilities	21,900	21,900
Factory employees' cafeteria	134,200	134,200
Purchasing costs, materials/parts	96,700	
Materials/parts storage and handling	212,300	
Depreciation, materials/parts moving trucks	68,700	
Total indirect manufacturing costs	$4,411,170	$410,060
Overhead costs directly traceable to FMS cell		
Electrical power		$ 65,680
Supervision		24,630
Depreciation, machinery		119,667
Setup labor		197,040
Other indirect costs		361,240
Machinery repairs and maintenance		57,470
Operating supplies and lubricants		29,556
Total overhead costs directly traceable to FMS cell		$855,283
Materials/parts storage and handling overhead cost pool (original costs reduced by 40%)		
Purchasing costs, materials/parts		$ 58,020
Materials/parts storage and handling		127,380
Depreciation, materials/parts moving trucks		41,220
Total materials/parts storage and handling overhead costs		$226,620

(continued)

	JIT/FMS/ABC Costing Approach
Engineering function (all engineering costs accumulated by activity)	
Product engineering activity	$163,100
Engineering changes activity	152,460
Product testing activity	176,100
Product review activity	97,900
Total costs—engineering function	$589,560

Engineering function—Cost driver information

Activity	Cost Driver	Cost Driver Data: Total Plant	Cost Driver Data: FMS Cell
Product engineering activity	Number of different products	80	12
Engineering changes activity	Number of engineering changes	64	8
Product testing activity	Number of products	280,500	64,200
Product review activity	Number of engineering hours	25,340	6,800

These data have been partially restructured in anticipation of the new system. The following information will be required for the analysis:

Total plant direct labor hours for the period	956,000 DLH
Total plant machine hours for the period	2,475,000 MH
Machine hours for the fan FMS cell	332,500 MH
Total plantwide cost of materials and parts for the period	$18,400,000
Process costing information for the fan FMS cell	
Beginning inventory	
Materials and parts	$6,420
Conversion costs	$4,960
Equivalent units for the period	
Materials and parts	64,200 equiv. units
Conversion costs	64,300 equiv. units

Required

1. Following the traditional costing approach,
   a. compute the plantwide factory overhead application rate.
   b. compute the product unit cost for each fan produced.
2. Identify the cost categories, and their total costs, that are likely to be reduced significantly or eliminated when the company adopts the JIT/FMS approach.
3. Compute the new cost application rates for (a) materials/parts storage and handling overhead costs and (b) indirect manufacturing costs.
4. Compute the activity-based costing application rates per cost driver for the engineering function.
5. Identify (a) the total materials costs and (b) the total conversion costs for the period for the fan FMS work cell.

6. Using the FIFO process costing method, compute the fan unit cost in the new JIT/FMS setting.

Management Decision Case

Cooplan Saddle Company
(L.O. 3, 4)

In 1848, Bob Cooper and David Kaplan joined forces and made their first horse saddle. Cooper had been a blacksmith for twenty years, and Kaplan was famous throughout Texas for his work with leather. In two short years, the partners were known for making the finest saddle in the entire Southwest. By 1861, the two saddle makers created the Cooplan Saddle Company just outside Dallas. The company has produced saddles continuously since 1861, and today it is world famous for its three types of riding saddles.

The company's current operating process involves two plants; the Dallas plant is responsible for producing the three types of handmade saddles, and the Fort Worth plant applies a special treatment to the leather saddles that provides a long-wearing, satin finish. The Dallas plant uses some machinery for cutting and trimming leather but is highly labor intensive. Fort Worth's operation, on the other hand, is highly automated, and the steam/oil maturing process is done using programmed machinery. The model A1 saddle is made for competitive equestrian riding, model A2 is a decorative western riding saddle, and model A3 is made for long-wear, hard-use cattle ranching work.

The analysis starting at the bottom of this page shows the data you will need for this case.

Required

1. Compute projected factory overhead rates based on the following assumptions:
   a. Companywide rates based on direct labor hours and machine hours
   b. Plantwide rates at the Dallas and Fort Worth plants based on direct labor hours and on machine hours
2. Compute product unit costs for the three saddles using
   a. Companywide direct labor hour overhead rate
   b. Companywide machine hour overhead rate
   c. Plantwide rates at the Dallas plant based on direct labor hours and at the Fort Worth plant based on machine hours
   d. Plantwide rates at the Dallas plant based on machine hours and at the Fort Worth plant based on direct labor hours
3. Which set of product costs are correct? Explain your answer.
4. Would your answer to **3** change if interest expense were treated as a period cost?
5. Is research and development cost properly accounted for? How would you change the approach? Would your suggested change affect your recommendation in **3**? How? (Do not let FASB external reporting standards influence your answer—these reports are for internal use only.)

Breakdown of machine hours and labor hours for the two plants is as follows:

	Model A1	Model A2	Model A3
Dallas Plant:			
Machine hours	.2	.4	.6
Direct labor hours	3.0	2.0	1.0
Fort Worth Plant:			
Machine hours	2.0	3.0	6.0
Direct labor hours	.4	.2	.1

Other operating data for the two plants are as follows:

	Model A1	Model A2	Model A3
Dallas Plant:			
Unit raw materials cost	$92.00	$154.00	$105.00
Hourly labor rate	20.00	20.00	20.00
Fort Worth Plant:			
Unit raw materials cost	12.00	16.00	8.00
Hourly labor rate	14.00	14.00	14.00

Projected overhead costs for next year are as follows:

	Dallas Plant	Fort Worth Plant	Totals
Electricity	$ 4,100	$ 9,620	$ 13,720
Water	3,740	2,830	6,570
Heating expense	5,820	3,690	9,510
Operating supplies	8,110	14,280	22,390
Depreciation, machinery	480	13,220	13,700
Depreciation, building	9,320	8,930	18,250
Insurance expense	4,540	5,640	10,180
Property taxes	1,980	3,120	5,100
Research and development*	14,670	480	15,150
Indirect labor	26,900	18,340	45,240
Spoilage	7,740	3,160	10,900
Supervision	44,000	26,000	70,000
Interest expense†	850	5,440	6,290
Miscellaneous costs	1,870	1,310	3,180
Totals	$134,120	$116,060	$250,180

* All research and development costs were incurred in the development of saddle model A4 (designed for military and law-enforcement use).
† Interest expense was allocated to the two plants by top management based on the age and book value of the buildings and equipment.

Expected machine and labor hours per plant are as follows:

	Machine Hours	Direct Labor Hours
Dallas Plant:		
Saddle A1 (500 units):		
(500 × .2 MH)	100	
(500 × 3 DLH)		1,500
Saddle A2 (1,000 units):		
(1,000 × .4 MH)	400	
(1,000 × 2 DLH)		2,000
Saddle A3 (4,000 units):		
(4,000 × .6 MH)	2,400	
(4,000 × 1 DLH)		4,000
Subtotals	2,900	7,500
Fort Worth Plant:		
Saddle A1 (500 units):		
(500 × 2 MH)	1,000	
(500 × .4 DLH)		200
Saddle A2 (1,000 units):		
(1,000 × 3 MH)	3,000	
(1,000 × .2 DLH)		200
Saddle A3 (4,000 units):		
(4,000 × 6 MH)	24,000	
(4,000 × .1 DLH)		400
Subtotals	28,000	800
Total projected hours	30,900	8,300

Answers to Self-Test

1. b
2. c
3. b
4. c
5. a
6. d
7. a
8. d
9. c
10. b

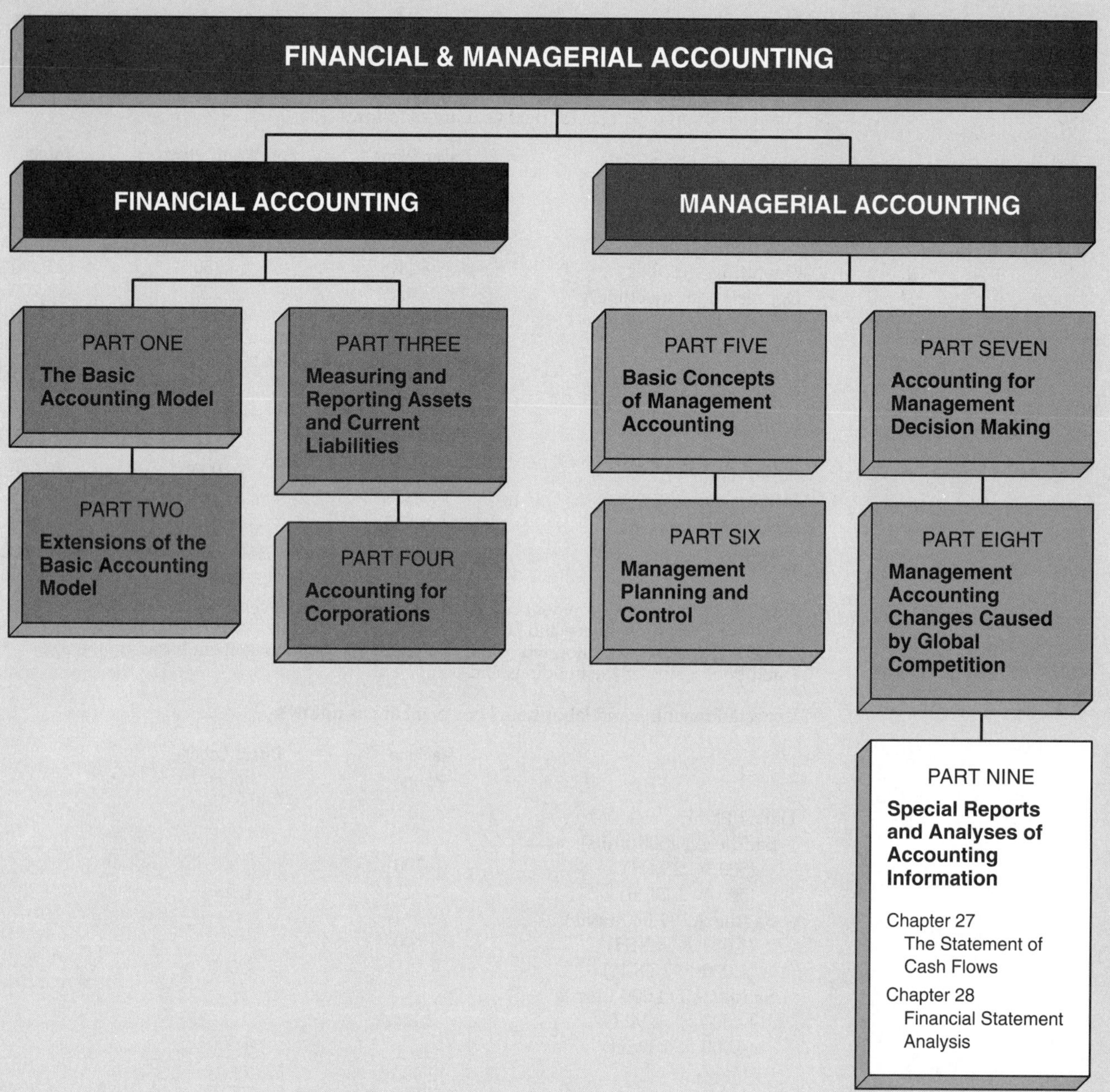

Because business organizations are so complex today, special reports are needed to present important information about their activities. To both understand and evaluate financial statements, it is necessary to learn how to analyze them. Part Nine deals with these important special reports and with the analysis of financial statements as well.

PART NINE

Special Reports and Analyses of Accounting Information

Chapter 27 presents the statement of cash flows, which explains the major operating, financing, and investing activities of a business. The chapter presents this statement using both the direct approach and the indirect approach.

Chapter 28 explains the objectives and techniques of financial statement analysis from the standpoint of the financial analyst.

LEARNING OBJECTIVES

1. *Describe the statement of cash flows, and define cash and cash equivalents.*
2. *State the principal purposes and uses of the statement of cash flows.*
3. *Identify the principal components of the classifications of cash flows, and state the significance of noncash investing and financing transactions.*
4. *Determine cash flows from operating activities using the (a) direct and (b) indirect methods.*
5. *Determine cash flows from (a) investing activities and (b) financing activities.*
6. *Prepare a statement of cash flows using the (a) direct and (b) indirect methods.*
7. *Interpret the statement of cash flows.*
8. *Prepare a work sheet for the statement of cash flows.*

CHAPTER 27

The Statement of Cash Flows

Earlier in this book you studied the balance sheet, the income statement, and the statement of stockholders' equity. In this chapter you will learn to prepare a fourth major financial statement, the statement of cash flows. After studying this chapter, you should be able to meet the learning objectives listed on the left.

DECISION POINT
Marriott Corporation

■ Marriott Corporation is a world leader in lodging and contract services. The company's annual report provides an excellent picture of management's philosophy and performance. The company's balance sheet—like that of any company—shows, at a point in time, how management has invested the company's assets and how those assets are financed by liabilities and stockholders' equity. The income statement shows how much the company earned on its assets during the year. The statement of stockholders' equity shows changes in the ownership of the business, including the cumulative income retained in the business.

While these three financial statements are essential to the evaluation of a company, several questions that they do not cover are answered by a fourth financial statement, the statement of cash flows. For example, how much cash was generated by the company's operations during the year? Marriott answers this question with the following narrative and chart (see Figure 27-1) based on the company's statement of cash flows:

> Cash provided by continuing operations increased to $423 million in 1989, reflecting higher income after adjustment for depreciation and other noncash charges.
>
> Operating cash flows, appropriately leveraged with debt, provide the company with substantial investment capacity. *Because maintaining excess investment capacity is inconsistent with the goal of maximizing shareholder value, management is continually challenged to identify investment opportunities that offer attractive returns.*[1]

This information is provided in the first part of the discussion of cash flows and indicates that Marriott is very successful in generating cash for further investment. The chart shows that cash flows from continuing operations greatly exceed net income. Other parts of the statement and discussion report where management invested the funds and the other sources of financing used by the company. In the investing and financing

1. Excerpted from the 1989 annual report of Marriott Corporation.

Figure 27-1. Cash Provided by Continuing Operations at Marriott Corporation *(in millions)*

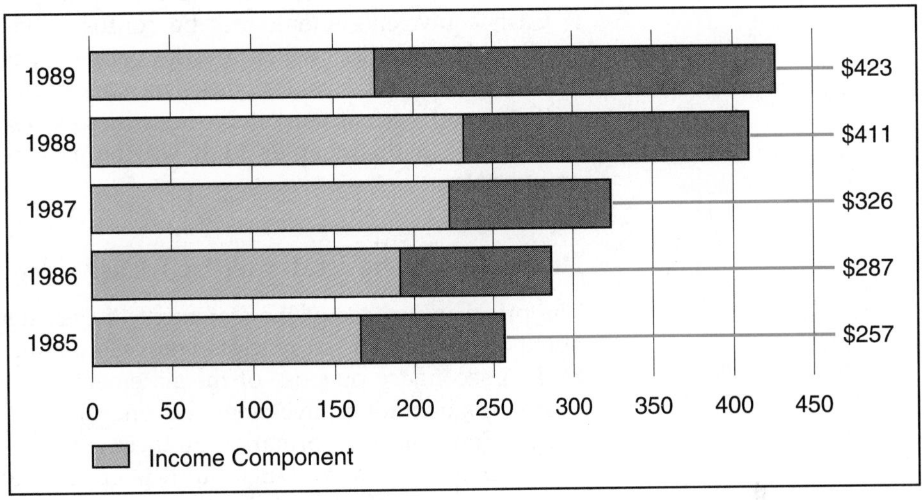

1989	$423
1988	$411
1987	$326
1986	$287
1985	$257

Source: 1989 annual report of Marriott Corporation. Used by permission of Marriott Corporation.

areas, the statement of cash flows demonstrates management's commitments for the company in ways that are not readily apparent in the other financial statements. In effect, the statement of cash flows is the most future-directed of the basic financial statements. It is required by the FASB[2] and satisfies the FASB's long-held position that a primary objective of financial statements is to provide investors and creditors with information on a company's cash flows.[3] ■

Purposes, Uses, and Components of the Statement of Cash Flows

OBJECTIVE 1
Describe the statement of cash flows, and define cash *and* cash equivalents

The **statement of cash flows** shows the effect on cash of the operating, investing, and financing activities of a company for an accounting period. It explains the net increase (or decrease) in cash during the accounting period. For purposes of preparing this statement, **cash** is defined to include both cash and cash equivalents. **Cash equivalents** are defined by the FASB as short-term, highly liquid investments, including money market accounts, commercial paper, and U.S. Treasury bills. A company maintains cash equivalents in order to earn interest on cash that otherwise would temporarily lie idle. Suppose, for example, that a company has $1,000,000 that it will not need for thirty days. To earn a return on this sum, the company may place the cash in an account that earns interest (for example, a money market account); it may loan the cash to another corporation by purchasing that corporation's short-term note (commercial paper); or it might purchase a short-term obligation of the U.S. government (a Treasury bill). In this context, short-term is defined as original maturities of ninety days or less. Since cash and cash equivalents are considered the same, transfers between the Cash account and cash equivalents are not treated as cash

2. *Statement of Financial Accounting Standards No. 95,* "Statement of Cash Flows" (Stamford, Conn.: Financial Accounting Standards Board, 1987).
3. *Statement of Financial Accounting Concepts No. 1,* "Objectives of Financial Reporting for Business Enterprises" (Stamford, Conn.: Financial Accounting Standards Board, 1978), par. 37–39.

receipts or cash payments. In effect, cash equivalents are combined with the Cash account on the statement of cash flows.

Cash equivalents should not be confused with short-term investments or marketable securities, which are not combined with the Cash account on the statement of cash flows. Purchases of marketable securities are treated as cash outflows and sales of marketable securities as cash inflows on the statement of cash flows. In this chapter, cash will be assumed to include cash and cash equivalents.

Purposes of the Statement of Cash Flows

OBJECTIVE 2
State the principal purposes and uses of the statement of cash flows

The primary purpose of the statement of cash flows is to provide information about a company's cash receipts and cash payments during an accounting period. A secondary purpose of the statement is to provide information about a company's operating, investing, and financing activities during the accounting period. Some of the information on these activities may be inferred by examining other financial statements, but it is on the statement of cash flows that all the transactions affecting cash are summarized.

Internal and External Uses of the Statement of Cash Flows

The statement of cash flows is useful internally to management and externally to investors and creditors. Management uses the statement of cash flows to assess the liquidity of the business, to determine dividend policy, and to evaluate the effects of major policy decisions involving investments and financing. In other words, management may use the statement of cash flows to determine whether or not short-term financing is needed to pay current liabilities, to decide whether to raise or lower dividends, and to plan for investing and financing needs.

Investors and creditors will find the statement useful in assessing the company's ability to manage cash flows, to generate positive future cash flows, to pay its liabilities, to pay dividends and interest, and to anticipate its need for additional financing. Also, they may use the statement to explain the differences between net income on the income statement and the net cash flows generated from operations. In addition, the statement shows both the cash and noncash effects of investing and financing activities during the accounting period.

Classification of Cash Flows

OBJECTIVE 3
Identify the principal components of the classifications of cash flows, and state the significance of noncash investing and financing transactions

The statement of cash flows classifies cash receipts and cash payments into the categories of operating, investing, and financing activities. The components of these activities are illustrated in Figure 27-2 and are summarized as follows:

1. **Operating activities** include the cash effects of transactions and other events that enter into the determination of net income. Included in this category as cash inflows are cash receipts from customers for goods and services and interest and dividends received on loans and investments. Included as cash outflows are cash payments for wages, goods and services, interest, and taxes paid to employees, suppliers, government bodies, and others. In effect, the income statement is changed from an accrual to a cash basis.
2. **Investing activities** include the acquiring and selling of long-term assets, the acquiring and selling of marketable securities other than cash equivalents, and the making and collecting of loans. Cash inflows include the cash received from

Figure 27-2. Classification of Cash Inflows and Cash Outflows

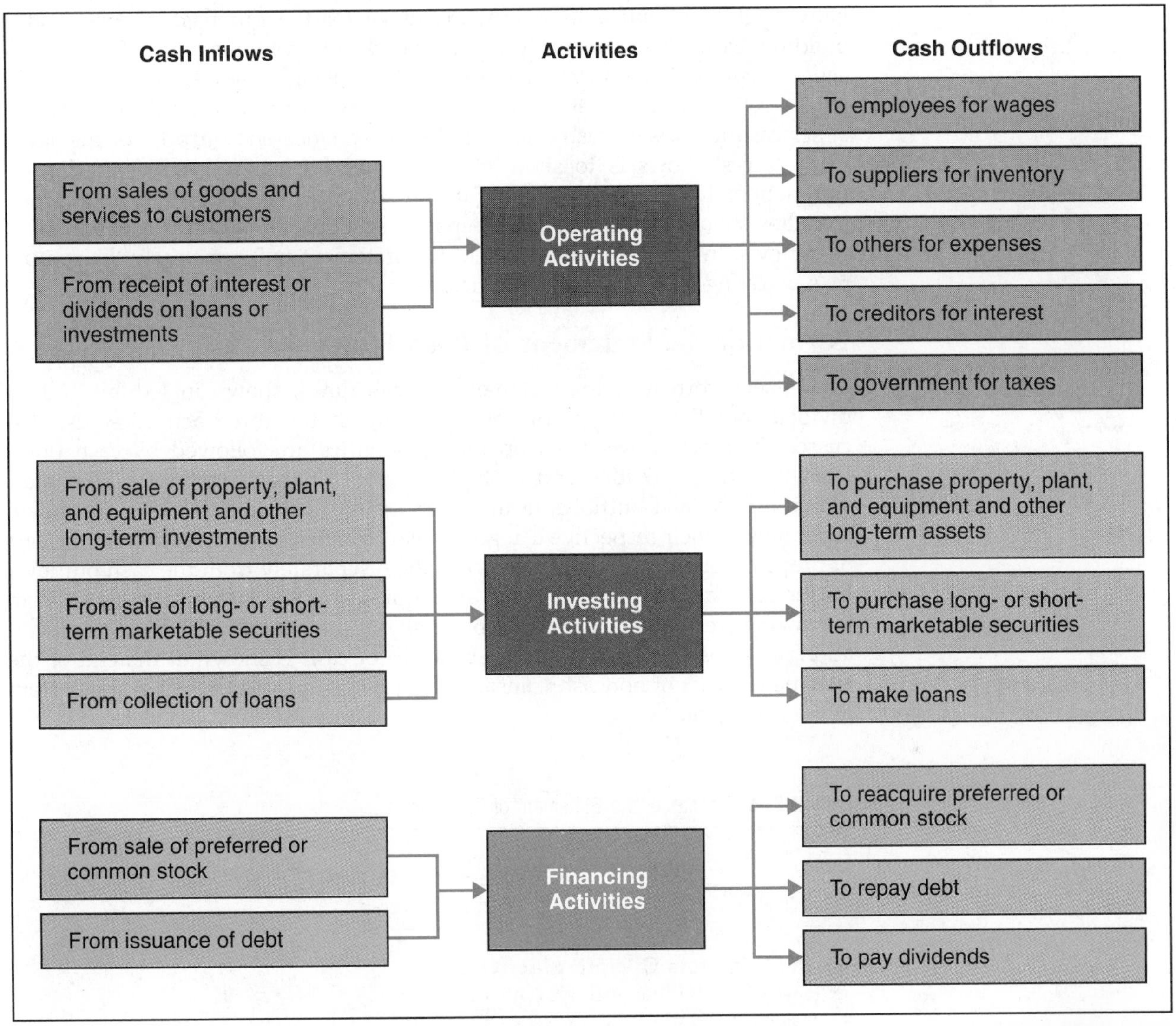

selling long-term assets and marketable securities and from collecting loans. Cash outflows include the cash expended for purchases of long-term assets and marketable securities and the cash loaned to borrowers.

3. **Financing activities** include (1) obtaining or returning resources from or to owners and providing them with a return on their investment and (2) obtaining resources from creditors and repaying the amounts borrowed or otherwise settling the obligation. Cash inflows include the proceeds from issues of stocks and from short-term and long-term borrowing. Cash outflows include the repayments of loans and payments to owners, including cash dividends. Treasury stock transactions are also considered financing activities. Repayments of accounts payable or accrued liabilities are not considered repayments of loans under financing activities, but are classified as cash outflows under operating activities.

A company will occasionally engage in significant **noncash investing and financing transactions** involving only long-term assets, long-term liabilities, or stockholders' equity, such as the exchange of a long-term asset for a long-term liability or the settlement of a debt by issuing capital stock. For instance, a company might take out a long-term mortgage for the purchase of land and a building. Or it might convert long-term bonds into common stock. These transactions represent significant investing and financing activities, but they would not be reflected on the statement of cash flows because they do not involve either cash inflows or cash outflows. However, since one purpose of the statement of cash flows is to show investing and financing activities, and since transactions like these will affect future cash flows, the FASB has determined that they should be disclosed in a separate schedule as part of the statement of cash flows. In this way, the reader of the statement will see clearly the company's investing and financing activities.

Format of the Statement of Cash Flows

The general format of the statement of cash flows, shown in Exhibit 27-1, is divided into three categories corresponding to the three activities just discussed. The cash flows from operating activities are followed by cash flows from investing activities and cash flows from financing activities. The individual inflows and outflows from investing and financing activities are shown separately in their respective categories. For instance, cash inflows from the sale of property, plant, and equipment are shown separately from the cash outflows for the purchase of property, plant, and equipment. Similarly, cash inflows from borrowing are shown separately from cash outflows to retire loans. A reconciliation of the beginning and ending balances of cash is shown at the end of the statement. A list of noncash transactions appears in the schedule at the bottom of the statement.

Exhibit 27-1. Format for the Statement of Cash Flows

Company Name Statement of Cash Flows Period Covered		
Cash Flows from Operating Activities		
(List of individual inflows and outflows)	xxx	
Net Cash Flows from Operating Activities		xxx
Cash Flows from Investing Activities		
(List of individual inflows and outflows)	xxx	
Net Cash Flows from Investing Activities		xxx
Cash Flows from Financing Activities		
(List of individual inflows and outflows)	xxx	
Net Cash Flows from Financing Activities		xxx
Net Increase (Decrease) in Cash		xx
Cash at Beginning of Year		xx
Cash at End of Year		xx
Schedule of Noncash Investing and Financing Transactions		
(List of individual transactions)		xxx

Preparing the Statement of Cash Flows

To demonstrate the preparation of the statement of cash flows, we will work an example step by step. The data for this example are presented in Exhibits 27-2 and 27-3. These two exhibits present Ryan Corporation's balance sheets for December 31, 19x1 and 19x2, and its 19x2 income statement, with additional data about transactions affecting noncurrent accounts during 19x2. Since the changes

Exhibit 27-2. Comparative Balance Sheet with Changes in Accounts Indicated for Ryan Corporation

Ryan Corporation
Comparative Balance Sheets
December 31, 19x2 and 19x1

	19x2	19x1	Change	Increase or Decrease
Assets				
Current Assets				
Cash	$ 46,000	$ 15,000	$ 31,000	Increase
Accounts Receivable (net)	47,000	55,000	(8,000)	Decrease
Inventory	144,000	110,000	34,000	Increase
Prepaid Expenses	1,000	5,000	(4,000)	Decrease
Total Current Assets	$238,000	$185,000	$ 53,000	
Investments	$115,000	$127,000	$(12,000)	Decrease
Plant Assets				
Plant Assets	$715,000	$505,000	$210,000	Increase
Accumulated Depreciation	(103,000)	(68,000)	(35,000)	Increase
Total Plant Assets	$612,000	$437,000	$175,000	
Total Assets	$965,000	$749,000	$216,000	
Liabilities				
Current Liabilities				
Accounts Payable	$ 50,000	$ 43,000	$ 7,000	Increase
Accrued Liabilities	12,000	9,000	3,000	Increase
Income Taxes Payable	3,000	5,000	(2,000)	Decrease
Total Current Liabilities	$ 65,000	$ 57,000	$ 8,000	
Long-Term Liabilities				
Bonds Payable	$295,000	$245,000	$ 50,000	Increase
Total Liabilities	$360,000	$302,000	$ 58,000	
Stockholders' Equity				
Common Stock, $5 par value	$276,000	$200,000	$ 76,000	Increase
Paid-in Capital in Excess of Par Value	189,000	115,000	74,000	Increase
Retained Earnings	140,000	132,000	8,000	Increase
Total Stockholders' Equity	$605,000	$447,000	$158,000	
Total Liabilities and Stockholders' Equity	$965,000	$749,000	$216,000	

Exhibit 27-3. Income Statement and Other Information on Noncurrent Accounts for Ryan Corporation

Ryan Corporation
Income Statement
For the Year Ended December 31, 19x2

Sales		$698,000
Cost of Goods Sold		520,000
Gross Margin from Sales		$178,000
Operating Expenses (including Depreciation Expense of $37,000)		147,000
Operating Income		$ 31,000
Other Income (Expenses)		
Interest Expense	$(23,000)	
Interest Income	6,000	
Gain on Sale of Investments	12,000	
Loss on Sale of Plant Assets	(3,000)	(8,000)
Income Before Taxes		$ 23,000
Income Taxes		7,000
Net Income		$ 16,000

Other transactions affecting noncurrent accounts during 19x2:

1. Purchased investments in the amount of $78,000.
2. Sold investments for $102,000. These investments cost $90,000.
3. Purchased plant assets in the amount of $120,000.
4. Sold plant assets that cost $10,000 with accumulated depreciation of $2,000 for $5,000.
5. Issued $100,000 of bonds at face value in a noncash exchange for plant assets.
6. Repaid $50,000 of bonds at face value at maturity.
7. Issued 15,200 shares of $5 par value common stock for $150,000.
8. Paid cash dividends in the amount of $8,000.

in the balance sheet accounts will be used in analyzing the various accounts, those changes are shown in Exhibit 27-2. For each individual account, an indication is made as to whether the change is an increase or a decrease. In addition, Exhibit 27-3 contains data about transactions that affected noncurrent accounts. These transactions would be identified by the company's accountants from the records.

There are four steps in preparing the statement of cash flows:

1. Determine cash flows from operating activities.
2. Determine cash flows from investing activities.
3. Determine cash flows from financing activities.
4. Present the information obtained in the first three steps in the form of the statement of cash flows.

Determining Cash Flows from Operating Activities

The first step in preparing the statement of cash flows is to determine cash flows from operating activities. The income statement indicates the success or failure of a business in earning an income from its operating activities, but it

Figure 27-3. Relationship of Accrual and Cash Bases of Accounting

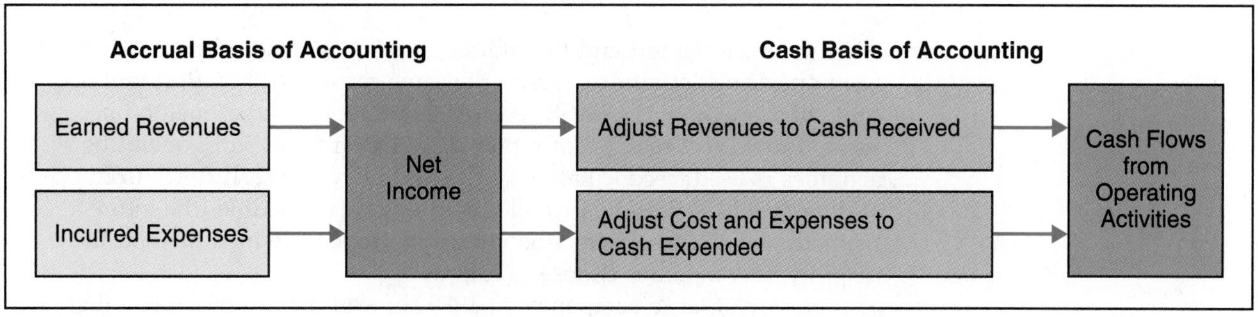

does not reflect the inflow and outflow of cash from those activities. The reason for this is that the income statement is prepared on an accrual basis. Revenues are recorded even though the cash for them may not have been received, and expenses are incurred and recorded even though cash may not yet have been expended for them. As a result, to arrive at cash flows from operations, the figures on the income statement must be converted from an accrual basis to a cash basis by adjusting earned revenues to cash received from sales and incurred costs and expenses to cash expended, as shown in Figure 27-3.

OBJECTIVE 4a
Determine cash flows from operating activities using the direct method

There are two methods of converting the income statement from an accrual basis to a cash basis: the direct method and the indirect method. The **direct method** is accomplished by adjusting each item in the income statement from the accrual basis to the cash basis. The result is a statement that begins with cash receipts from sales and then deducts cash payments for purchases, operating expenses, interest payments, and income taxes, to arrive at net cash flows from operating activities:

Cash Flows from Operating Activities		
Cash Receipts from		
Sales	xxx	
Interest and Dividends Received	xxx	xxx
Cash Payments for		
Purchases	xxx	
Operating Expenses	xxx	
Interest Payments	xxx	
Income Taxes	xxx	xxx
Net Cash Flows from Operating Activities		xxx

OBJECTIVE 4b
Determine cash flows from operating activities using the indirect method

The **indirect method**, on the other hand, does not require adjusting each item in the income statement individually, but lists only those adjustments necessary to convert net income to cash flows from operations, as follows:

Cash Flows from Operating Activities		
Net Income		xxx
Adjustments to Reconcile Net Income to Net Cash Flows from Operating Activities		
(List of individual items)	xxx	xxx
Net Cash Flows from Operating Activities		xxx

Both methods, however, analyze certain income statement items and changes in certain current assets and current liabilities.

DECISION POINT
Survey of Large Companies

■ The direct method and the indirect method of determining cash flows from operating activities produce the same results. Although it will accept either method, the FASB recommends that the direct method be used. If the direct method of reporting net cash flows from operating activities is used, reconciliation of net income to net cash flows from operating activities shall be provided in a separate schedule (the indirect method). Given these facts, it is interesting to learn which method the majority of companies choose to follow.

A survey of large companies in 1989 showed that an overwhelming majority of 97 percent chose to use the indirect method. Of 600 companies, only seventeen chose the direct approach.[4] Why did so many choose the indirect approach? The reasons for this choice may vary, but chief financial officers tend to prefer the indirect method because it is easier and less expensive to prepare. Moreover, because the FASB requires the reconciliation of net income (accrual) to cash flow (operations) as a supplemental schedule, the indirect method has to be implemented anyway.

A knowledge of the direct method helps the manager and the reader of financial statements perceive the underlying causes for the difference between reported net income and cash flows from operations. The indirect method is a practical way of presenting the differences. Since both methods have merit, the direct method will be used in the sections that follow to illustrate the conversion of the income statement to a cash basis, and the indirect method will be used to summarize the process. ■

Cash Receipts from Sales. Sales result in a positive cash flow for a company. Cash sales are direct cash inflows of the company. Credit sales are not, because they are recorded originally as accounts receivable. When they are collected, they become inflows of cash. You cannot, however, assume that credit sales are automatically inflows of cash, because the collections of accounts receivable in any one accounting period are not likely to equal credit sales. Receivables may be uncollectible, sales from a prior period may be collected in the current period, or sales from the current period may be collected next period. For example, if accounts receivable increases from one accounting period to the next, cash receipts from sales will not be as great as sales. On the other hand, if accounts receivable decreases from one accounting period to the next, cash receipts from sales will exceed sales.

The relationships among sales, changes in accounts receivable, and cash receipts from sales are reflected in the following formula:

$$\text{Cash Receipts from Sales} = \text{Sales} \begin{cases} + \text{ Decrease in Accounts Receivable} \\ \text{or} \\ - \text{ Increase in Accounts Receivable} \end{cases}$$

Refer to the balance sheets and income statement for Ryan Corporation in Exhibits 27-2 and 27-3. Note that sales were $698,000 in 19x2, and accounts receivable decreased by $8,000. Thus, cash received from sales is $706,000:

$706,000 = $698,000 + $8,000

4. *Accounting Trends & Techniques* (New York: American Institute of Certified Public Accountants, 1990), p. 350.

Ryan Corporation collected $8,000 more from sales than it sold during the year. This relationship may be illustrated as follows:

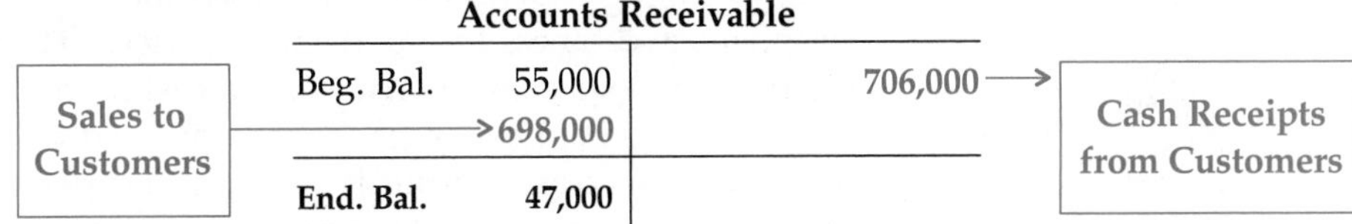

If Ryan Corporation had unearned revenues or advances from customers, an adjustment would be made for changes in those items as well.

Cash Receipts from Interest and Dividends Received. Although interest and dividends received are most closely associated with investment activity and are often called investment income, the FASB has decided to classify the cash received from these items as operating activities. To simplify the examples in this text, it is assumed that interest income equals interest received and that dividend income equals dividends received. Thus, from Exhibit 27-3, interest received by Ryan Corporation is assumed to equal $6,000, which is the amount of interest income.

Cash Payments for Purchases. Cost of goods sold (from the income statement) must be adjusted for changes in two balance sheet accounts to arrive at cash payments for purchases. First, cost of goods sold must be adjusted for changes in inventory to arrive at net purchases. Then, net purchases must be adjusted for the change in accounts payable to arrive at cash payments for purchases. If inventory has increased from one accounting period to another, net purchases will be greater than cost of goods sold; if inventory has decreased, net purchases will be less than cost of goods sold. Conversely, if accounts payable has increased, cash payments for purchases will be less than net purchases; if accounts payable has decreased, cash payments for purchases will be greater than net purchases.

These relationships may be stated in equation form as follows:

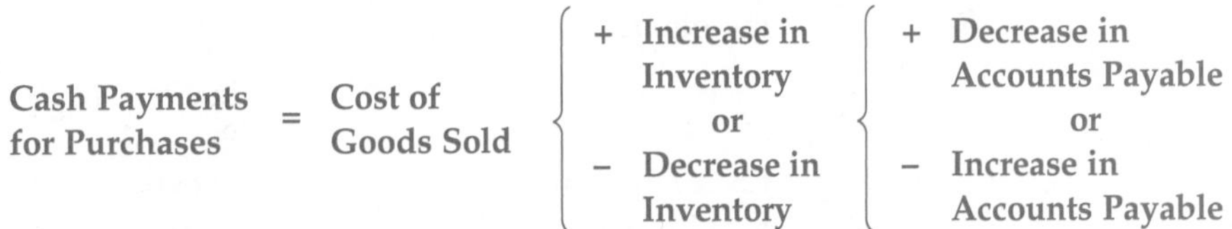

From Exhibits 27-2 and 27-3, cost of goods sold is $520,000, inventory increased by $34,000, and accounts payable increased by $7,000. Thus, cash payments for purchases is $547,000, as the following calculation shows:

$$\$547{,}000 = \$520{,}000 + \$34{,}000 - \$7{,}000$$

In this example, Ryan Corporation purchased $34,000 more inventory than it sold and paid out $7,000 less in cash than it purchased. The net result is that cash payments for purchases exceeded cost of goods sold by $27,000 ($547,000 – $520,000). These relationships can be visualized as follows:

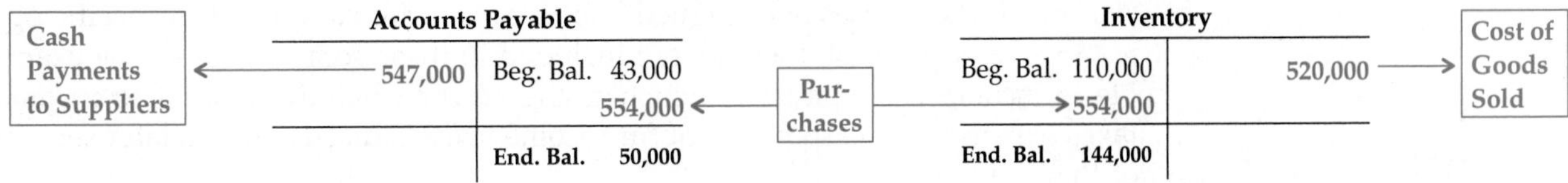

Cash Payments for Operating Expenses. Just as cost of goods sold does not represent the amount of cash paid for purchases during an accounting period, operating expenses do not match the amount of cash paid to employees, suppliers, and others for goods and services. Three adjustments must be made to operating expenses to arrive at the cash outflows. The first adjustment is for changes in prepaid expenses, such as prepaid insurance or prepaid rent. If prepaid assets increase during the accounting period, more cash will have been paid out than appears on the income statement as expenses. If prepaid assets decrease, more expenses will appear on the income statement than cash was spent.

The second adjustment is for changes in liabilities resulting from accrued expenses, such as wages payable and payroll taxes payable. If accrued liabilities increase during the accounting period, operating expenses on the income statement will exceed the cash spent. And if accrued liabilities decrease, operating expenses will fall short of cash spent.

The third adjustment is made because certain expenses do not require a current outlay of cash; these expenses must be subtracted from operating expenses to arrive at cash payments for operating expenses. The most common expenses in this category are depreciation expense, amortization expense, and depletion expense. Expenditures for plant assets, intangibles, and natural resources occur when they are purchased and are classified as an investing activity at that time. Depreciation expense, amortization expense, and depletion expense are simply allocations of the costs of those original purchases to the current accounting period; they do not affect cash flows in the current period. For example, Ryan Corporation recorded 19x2 depreciation expense as follows:

Depreciation Expense	37,000	
Accumulated Depreciation		37,000
To record depreciation on plant assets		

No cash payment is made in this transaction. Thus, to the extent that operating expenses include depreciation and similar items, an adjustment is needed to reduce operating expenses to the amount of cash expended.

The three adjustments to operating expenses are summarized in the following equation.

Cash Payments for Operating Expenses = **Operating Expenses** { **+ Increase in Prepaid Expenses** or **− Decrease in Prepaid Expenses** } { **+ Decrease in Accrued Liabilities** or **− Increase in Accrued Liabilities** } { **− Depreciation and Other Noncash Expenses** }

From Exhibits 27-2 and 27-3, Ryan's operating expenses (including depreciation of $37,000) were $147,000; prepaid expenses decreased by $4,000; and accrued liabilities increased by $3,000. As a result, Ryan Corporation's cash payments for operating expenses are $103,000, computed as follows:

$103,000 = $147,000 − $4,000 − $3,000 − $37,000

If prepaid expenses and accrued liabilities that are *not* related to specific operating expenses exist, they are not included in these computations. One example is income taxes payable, which is the accrued liability related to income taxes expense. The cash payment for income taxes is discussed in a later section of this chapter.

Cash Payments for Interest. The FASB classifies cash payments for interest as operating activities in spite of the fact that some authorities argue that they should be considered financing activities because of their association with loans incurred to finance the business. The FASB feels that interest expense is a cost of operating the business. We follow the FASB position in this text. Also, for the sake of simplicity, all examples in this text assume interest payments are equal to interest expense on the income statement. Thus, from Exhibit 27-3, Ryan Corporation's interest payments are assumed to be $23,000 in 19x2.

Cash Payments for Income Taxes. The amount of income taxes expense that appears on the income statement rarely equals the amount of income taxes actually paid during the year. One reason for this difference is that the final payments for the income taxes of one year are not due until some time in the following year. A second reason is that there may be differences between what is deducted from, or included in, income for accounting purposes and what is deducted from, or included in, income for tax purposes. The latter reason often results in a deferred income tax liability. Its effects on cash flows were discussed in the chapter on retained earnings and corporate income statements. Here, we deal only with the changes that result from increases or decreases in income taxes payable.

To determine cash payments for income taxes, income taxes expense (from the income statement) is adjusted by the change in income taxes payable. If income taxes payable increased during the accounting period, cash payments for taxes will be less than the expense shown on the income statement. If income taxes payable decreased, cash payments for taxes will exceed income taxes on the income statement. In other words, the following equation is applicable.

$$\text{Cash Payments for Income Taxes} = \text{Income Taxes} \begin{cases} + \text{ Decrease in Income Taxes Payable} \\ \text{or} \\ - \text{ Increase in Income Taxes Payable} \end{cases}$$

In 19x2, Ryan Corporation showed income taxes of $7,000 on its income statement and a decrease of $2,000 in income taxes payable on its balance sheets (see Exhibits 27-2 and 27-3). As a result, cash payments for income taxes during 19x2 were $9,000, calculated as follows:

$$\$9{,}000 = \$7{,}000 + \$2{,}000$$

Other Income and Expenses. In computing cash flows from operations, some items classified on the income statement as other income and expenses are not considered operating items because they are more closely related to financing and investing activities. Items must be analyzed individually to determine their proper classification on the statement of cash flows. For instance, we have already dealt with interest income and interest expense as operating activities. Unlike interest, however, the effects on cash flows of gains and losses are considered with the item that gave rise to the gain or loss. The effects of gains or losses on the sale of assets are considered with investing activities, and the effects of gains and losses related to liabilities are considered with financing activities. Consequently, the effects of the gain on sale of investments and of the loss on sale of plant assets reported on Ryan Corporation's income statement (Exhibit 27-3) are considered under cash flows from investing activities.

Schedule of Cash Flows from Operating Activities—Direct Method. It is now possible to prepare a schedule of cash flows from operations using the direct method and the calculations made in the preceding paragraphs. In Exhibit 27-4, Ryan Corporation had cash receipts from sales and interest received of $712,000 and cash payments for purchases, operating expenses, interest payments, and income taxes of $682,000, resulting in net cash flows from operating activities of $30,000 in 19x2.

Schedule of Cash Flows from Operating Activities—Indirect Method. It is also possible to calculate net cash flows from operations using the indirect method, as shown in Exhibit 27-5. Note that the amount for net cash flows from operating activities is the same as it was under the direct method (Exhibit 27-4).

First, under the indirect method, net income must be adjusted for expenses such as depreciation expense, amortization expense, depletion expense, and other income and expenses such as gains and losses. These are items included

Exhibit 27-4. Schedule of Cash Flows from Operating Activities—Direct Method

Ryan Corporation
Schedule of Cash Flows from Operating Activities
For the Year Ended December 31, 19x2

Cash Flows from Operating Activities		
Cash Receipts from		
Sales	$706,000	
Interest Received	6,000	$712,000
Cash Payments for		
Purchases	$547,000	
Operating Expenses	103,000	
Interest Payments	23,000	
Income Taxes	9,000	682,000
Net Cash Flows from Operating Activities		**$ 30,000**

Exhibit 27-5. Schedule of Cash Flows from Operating Activities—Indirect Method

Ryan Corporation
Schedule of Cash Flows from Operating Activities
For the Year Ended December 31, 19x2

Cash Flows from Operating Activities		
Net Income		$16,000
Adjustments to Reconcile Net Income to Net Cash Flows from Operating Activities		
Depreciation	$ 37,000	
Gain on Sale of Investments	(12,000)	
Loss on Sale of Plant Assets	3,000	
Decrease in Accounts Receivable	8,000	
Increase in Inventory	(34,000)	
Decrease in Prepaid Expenses	4,000	
Increase in Accounts Payable	7,000	
Increase in Accrued Liabilities	3,000	
Decrease in Income Taxes Payable	(2,000)	14,000
Net Cash Flows from Operating Activities		**$30,000**

on the income statement that do not affect cash flows. As a result, they are added or deducted as follows:

	Adjustments to Convert Net Income to Net Cash Flows from Operating Activities
	Add to (Deduct from) Net Income
Depreciation Expense	Add
Amortization Expense	Add
Depletion Expense	Add
Losses	Add
Gains	Deduct

Note that these adjustments to net income are made for several reasons. Depreciation expense is added because it is a noncash expense that was deducted in the income statement to arrive at net income. Adjustments are made for gains and losses because of reasons that will become clear when investing and financing activities are discussed in the next two sections.

The additions or deductions for increases and decreases in current assets and current liabilities are necessary to adjust an income statement item from an accrual basis to a cash basis.

Second, the same adjustments for the changes in current assets and current liabilities are made as under the direct method, except that they are made as additions to or subtractions from net income instead of as adjustments to the individual income statement items. For instance, under the direct method, the decrease in accounts receivable was added to sales to adjust sales from an accrual basis to a cash basis. Since sales is included in the computation of net income, the same effect is achieved by adding the decrease in accounts receivable to net income. The same logic applies to adjustments to cost of goods sold, operating expenses, and income taxes, except that the signs will be opposite for these adjustments because the adjustments are to net income, not to the individual expense items. The following table summarizes these adjustments.

	Adjustments to Convert Net Income to Net Cash Flows from Operating Activities	
	Add to Net Income	Deduct from Net Income
Current Assets		
Accounts Receivable (net)	Decrease	Increase
Inventory	Decrease	Increase
Prepaid Expenses	Decrease	Increase
Current Liabilities		
Accounts Payable	Increase	Decrease
Accrued Liabilities	Increase	Decrease
Income Taxes Payable	Increase	Decrease

Determining Cash Flows from Investing Activities

OBJECTIVE 5a
Determine cash flows from investing activities

The second step in preparing the statement of cash flows is to determine cash flows from investing activities. Each account that involves cash receipts and cash payments from investing activities is examined individually. The objective in each case is to explain the change in the account balance from one year to the next.

Investing activities center on the long-term assets shown on the balance sheet, but they also include transactions affecting short-term investments from the current asset section of the balance sheet and investment income from the income statement. From the balance sheet in Exhibit 27-2, we can see that Ryan Corporation has long-term assets of investments and plant assets, but no short-term investments. From the income statement in Exhibit 27-3, we see that Ryan has a gain on sale of investments and a loss on sale of plant assets. Also, from the schedule at the bottom of Exhibit 27-3, we find the following five items pertaining to investing activities in 19x2:

1. Purchased investments in the amount of $78,000.
2. Sold investments that cost $90,000 for $102,000, resulting in a gain of $12,000.
3. Purchased plant assets in the amount of $120,000.
4. Sold plant assets that cost $10,000 with accumulated depreciation of $2,000 for $5,000, resulting in a loss of $3,000.
5. Issued $100,000 of bonds at face value in a noncash exchange for plant assets.

The following paragraphs analyze the accounts related to investing activities to determine their effects on Ryan Corporation's cash flows.

Investments. The objective here is to explain the corporation's $12,000 decrease in investments (as shown in Exhibit 27-2) by analyzing the increases and decreases to the Investments account to determine the effects on the Cash account. Purchases increase investments and sales decrease investments. Item **1** in the list of Ryan's investing activities shows purchases of $78,000 during 19x2. This transaction is recorded as follows:

Investments	78,000	
Cash		78,000
Purchase of investments		

As we can see from the entry, the effect of this transaction is a $78,000 decrease in cash flows.

Item **2** in the list shows a sale of investments at a gain. This transaction is recorded as follows:

Cash	102,000	
Investments		90,000
Gain on Sale of Investments		12,000
Sale of investments at a gain		

The effect of this transaction is a $102,000 increase in cash flows. Note that the gain on sale of investments is included in the $102,000. This is the reason it was excluded earlier in computing cash flows from operations. If it had been included in that section, it would have been counted twice.

The $12,000 decrease in the Investments account during 19x2 has now been explained, as may be seen in the following T account:

Investments

Beg. Bal.	127,000	Sales	90,000
Purchases	78,000		
End. Bal.	**115,000**		

The cash flow effects from these transactions are shown under the cash flows from investing activities section on the statement of cash flows as follows:

Purchase of Investments	**$ (78,000)**
Sale of Investments	**102,000**

Notice that purchases and sales are disclosed separately as cash outflows and cash inflows. They are not netted against each other into a single figure. This disclosure gives the reader of the statement a more complete view of investing activity.

If Ryan Corporation had short-term investments or marketable securities, the analysis of cash flows would be the same.

Plant Assets. In the case of plant assets, it is necessary to explain the changes in both the asset account and the related accumulated depreciation account. From Exhibit 27-2, plant assets increased by $210,000 and accumulated depreciation increased by $35,000. Purchases increase plant assets and sales decrease plant assets. Accumulated depreciation is increased by the amount of depreciation expense and decreased by the removal of the accumulated depreciation associated with plant assets that are sold. Three items listed in Exhibit 27-3 affect plant assets. Item **3** in the list on page 1112 indicates that Ryan Corporation purchased plant assets totaling $120,000 during 19x2, as shown by this entry:

Plant Assets	120,000	
Cash		**120,000**
Purchase of plant assets		

This transaction results in a cash outflow of $120,000.

Item **4** states that Ryan Corporation sold plant assets for $5,000 that had cost $10,000 and had accumulated depreciation of $2,000. The entry to record this transaction is:

Cash	5,000	
Accumulated Depreciation	2,000	
Loss on Sale of Plant Assets	3,000	
Plant Assets		10,000
Sale of plant assets at a loss		

Note that in this transaction the positive cash flow is equal to the amount of cash received, or $5,000. The loss on sale of plant assets is considered here rather than in the operating activities section. The amount of a loss or gain in the sale of an asset is determined by the amount of cash received and does not represent a cash outflow or inflow.

The disclosure of these two transactions in the investing activities section of the statement of cash flows is as follows:

Purchase of Plant Assets	**$(120,000)**
Sale of Plant Assets	**5,000**

As with investments, cash outflows and cash inflows are not netted, but are presented separately to give full information to the statement reader.

Item **5** on the list of Ryan's investing activities is a noncash exchange that affects two long-term accounts, Plant Assets and Bonds Payable. It is recorded as follows:

Plant Assets	100,000	
Bonds Payable		100,000
Issued bonds at face value for plant assets		

Although this transaction is not an inflow or outflow of cash, it is a significant transaction involving both an investing activity (the purchase of plant assets) and a financing activity (the issue of bonds payable). Because one purpose of the statement of cash flows is to show important investing and financing activities, it is listed in a separate schedule, either at the bottom of the statement of cash flows or accompanying the statement, as follows:

Schedule of Noncash Investing and Financing Transactions

Issue of Bonds Payable for Plant Assets	$100,000

Through our analysis of these transactions and the depreciation expense for plant assets of $37,000, all the changes in the plant assets accounts have now been accounted for, as shown in these T accounts:

Plant Assets

Beg. Bal.	505,000	Sale	10,000
Purchase	120,000		
Noncash Purchase	100,000		
End. Bal.	**715,000**		

Accumulated Depreciation

Sale	2,000	Beg. Bal.	68,000
		Dep. Exp.	37,000
		End. Bal.	**103,000**

If the balance sheet had included specific plant asset accounts such as Buildings and Equipment and their related accumulated depreciation accounts, or other long-term asset accounts such as intangibles or natural resources, the analysis would be the same.

Determining Cash Flows from Financing Activities

OBJECTIVE 5b
Determine cash flows from financing activities

The third step in preparing the statement of cash flows is to determine cash flows from financing activities. The procedure followed in this step is the same as that applied to the analysis of investing activities, including related gains and/or losses. The only difference between the two is that the accounts to be analyzed are the short-term borrowings, long-term liability, and stockholders' equity accounts. Cash dividends from the statement of stockholders' equity must also be considered. Since Ryan Corporation does not have short-term borrowings, only long-term liability and stockholders' equity accounts are considered here. The following items from Exhibit 27-3 pertain to Ryan Corporation's financing activities in 19x2:

5. Issued $100,000 of bonds at face value in a noncash exchange for plant assets.
6. Repaid $50,000 of bonds at face value at maturity.
7. Issued 15,200 shares of $5 par value common stock for $150,000.
8. Paid cash dividends in the amount of $8,000.

Bonds Payable. Exhibit 27-2 shows that bonds payable increased by $50,000 in 19x2. This account is affected by items **5** and **6.** Item **5** was analyzed in connection with plant assets. It is reported on the schedule of noncash investing and financing transactions (see Exhibit 27-6 on page 1117), but must be remembered here in preparing the T account for Bonds Payable. Item **6** results in a cash outflow, a point that can be seen in the following transaction:

Bonds Payable	50,000	
Cash		50,000
Repayment of bonds at face value at maturity		

This cash outflow is shown in the financing activities section of the statement of cash flows as follows:

Repayment of Bonds	**$(50,000)**

From these transactions, the change in the Bonds Payable account can be explained as follows:

Bonds Payable

Repayment	50,000	Beg. Bal.	245,000
		Noncash Issue	**100,000**
		End. Bal.	**295,000**

If Ryan Corporation had notes payable, either short-term or long-term, the analysis would be the same.

Common Stock. As with plant assets, related stockholders' equity accounts should be analyzed together. For example, Paid-in Capital in Excess of Par Value should be examined together with Common Stock. In 19x2 Ryan Corporation's Common Stock account increased by $76,000 and Paid-in Capital in Excess of Par Value increased by $74,000. These increases are explained by item **7**, which states that Ryan Corporation issued 15,200 shares of stock for $150,000. The entry to record this cash inflow is as follows:

Cash	**150,000**	
Common Stock		76,000
Paid-in Capital in Excess of Par Value		74,000
Issue of 15,200 shares of $5 par value common stock		

This cash inflow is shown in the financing activities section of the statement of cash flows as follows:

Issue of Common Stock	**$150,000**

The analysis of this transaction is all that is needed to explain the changes in the two accounts during 19x2, as follows:

Common Stock

		Beg. Bal.	200,000
		Issue	**76,000**
		End. Bal.	**276,000**

Paid-in Capital in Excess of Par Value

		Beg. Bal.	115,000
		Issue	**74,000**
		End. Bal.	**189,000**

Retained Earnings. At this point in the analysis, several items that affect Retained Earnings have already been dealt with. For instance, in the case of Ryan Corporation, net income was used as part of the analysis of cash flows from operating activities. The only other item affecting the retained earnings of Ryan Corporation is the payment of $8,000 in cash dividends (item **8** on the list on page 1114), as reflected by the following transaction:

Retained Earnings	8,000	
Cash		8,000
Cash dividends for 19x2		

Ryan Corporation would have declared the dividend before paying it and debited the Dividends Declared account instead of Retained Earnings, but after paying the dividend and closing the Dividends Declared account to Retained Earnings, the effect is as shown. Cash dividends are displayed in the financing activities section of the statement of cash flows as follows:

Dividends Paid	**$(8,000)**

The change in the Retained Earnings account is explained in the T account that follows:

Retained Earnings

Dividends	8,000	Beg. Bal.	132,000
		Net Income	16,000
		End. Bal.	**140,000**

Presenting the Information in the Form of the Statement of Cash Flows

OBJECTIVE 6
Prepare a statement of cash flows using the (a) direct and (b) indirect methods

At this point in the analysis, all income statement items have been analyzed, all balance sheet changes have been explained, and all additional information has been taken into account. The resulting information may now be assembled into a statement of cash flows for Ryan Corporation. The statement in Exhibit 27-6 was prepared using the direct method and contains the operating activities section from Exhibit 27-4. The statement is just as easily prepared using the indirect approach and the data in Exhibit 27-5, as presented in Exhibit 27-7 (located on page 1118). The Schedule of Noncash Investing and Financing Transactions is presented at the bottom of each statement. When the direct method is used, a schedule explaining the difference between reported net income and cash flows from operating activities must be provided, as shown in Exhibit 27-6. This reconciliation is the same as the cash flows from operating activities section of the indirect method form of the statement (Exhibit 27-7).

Interpretation of the Statement of Cash Flows

OBJECTIVE 7
Interpret the statement of cash flows

Now that the statement is prepared, it is important to know how to interpret and use it. What can you learn about Ryan Corporation and its management by reading its statement of cash flows?

Starting with the first section of the statement in Exhibits 27-6 and 27-7, note that Ryan Corporation generated net cash flows from operating activities of $30,000, which compares very favorably with its net income of $16,000. We can see from Exhibit 27-7 that the largest positive factor is the depreciation expense of $37,000. This expense did not require a current cash outlay and is thus an important cause of the difference between net income and cash flows from operating activities.

Exhibit 27-6. The Statement of Cash Flows—Direct Method

Ryan Corporation
Statement of Cash Flows
For the Year Ended December 31, 19x2

Cash Flows from Operating Activities		
Cash Receipts from		
Sales	$706,000	
Interest Received	6,000	$712,000
Cash Payments for		
Purchases	$547,000	
Operating Expenses	103,000	
Interest Payments	23,000	
Income Taxes	9,000	682,000
Net Cash Flows from Operating Activities		$ 30,000
Cash Flows from Investing Activities		
Purchase of Investments	$ (78,000)	
Sale of Investments	102,000	
Purchase of Plant Assets	(120,000)	
Sale of Plant Assets	5,000	
Net Cash Flows from Investing Activities		(91,000)
Cash Flows from Financing Activities		
Repayment of Bonds	$ (50,000)	
Issue of Common Stock	150,000	
Dividends Paid	(8,000)	
Net Cash Flows from Financing Activities		92,000
Net Increase (Decrease) in Cash		$ 31,000
Cash at Beginning of Year		15,000
Cash at End of Year		$ 46,000

Schedule of Noncash Investing and Financing Transactions

Issue of Bonds Payable for Plant Assets	$100,000

Reconciliation of Net Income to Net Cash Flows from Operating Activities

Net Income		$ 16,000
Adjustments to Reconcile Net Income to Net Cash Flows from Operating Activities		
Depreciation	$ 37,000	
Gain on Sale of Investments	(12,000)	
Loss on Sale of Plant Assets	3,000	
Decrease in Accounts Receivable	8,000	
Increase in Inventory	(34,000)	
Decrease in Prepaid Expenses	4,000	
Increase in Accounts Payable	7,000	
Increase in Accrued Liabilities	3,000	
Decrease in Income Taxes Payable	(2,000)	14,000
Net Cash Flows from Operating Activities		$ 30,000

Exhibit 27-7. Statement of Cash Flows—Indirect Method

Ryan Corporation
Statement of Cash Flows
For the Year Ended December 31, 19x2

Cash Flows from Operating Activities		
Net Income		$ 16,000
Adjustments to Reconcile Net Income to Net Cash Flows from Operating Activities		
Depreciation	$ 37,000	
Gain on Sale of Investments	(12,000)	
Loss on Sale of Plant Assets	3,000	
Decrease in Accounts Receivable	8,000	
Increase in Inventory	(34,000)	
Decrease in Prepaid Expenses	4,000	
Increase in Accounts Payable	7,000	
Increase in Accrued Liabilities	3,000	
Decrease in Income Taxes Payable	(2,000)	14,000
Net Cash Flows from Operating Activities		$ 30,000
Cash Flows from Investing Activities		
Purchase of Investments	$ (78,000)	
Sale of Investments	102,000	
Purchase of Plant Assets	(120,000)	
Sale of Plant Assets	5,000	
Net Cash Flows from Investing Activities		(91,000)
Cash Flows from Financing Activities		
Repayment of Bonds	$ (50,000)	
Issue of Common Stock	150,000	
Dividends Paid	(8,000)	
Net Cash Flows from Financing Activities		92,000
Net Increase (Decrease) in Cash		$ 31,000
Cash at Beginning of Year		15,000
Cash at End of Year		$ 46,000

Schedule of Noncash Investing and Financing Transactions

Issue of Bonds Payable for Plant Assets	$100,000

The largest drain on cash in the operating activities section is the $34,000 increase in inventory. Management may want to explore ways of reducing inventory during the next year, unless this increase was for increased sales activities next year. Other changes in current assets and current liabilities, except for the small decrease in income taxes payable, have positive effects on cash flows in this section.

Investors and creditors may want to compare net cash flows from operating activities to dividends paid in the financing activities section to determine if the company has adequate cash flows from operations to cover its payments to investors. Ryan Corporation is in good condition in this regard. Dividends paid are $8,000, compared to $30,000 in net cash flows from operating activities. The remaining $22,000 is available for other purposes and provides a cushion for payment of dividends.

Moving to the investing activities, it is apparent that the company is expanding because there is a net cash outflow of $91,000 in this section. The company has expanded by purchasing plant assets of $120,000. Various other investing activities have reduced the cash need to $91,000. This is not the whole story on the expansion of the business, however, because the schedule of noncash investing and financing transactions reveals that the company bought another $100,000 in plant assets by issuing bonds. In other words, total purchases of plant assets were $220,000. Part of this expansion was financed by issuing bonds in exchange for plant assets and most of the rest was financed through other activities.

Net cash inflows of $92,000 were provided by financing activities to offset the $91,000 net cash outflows needed for investing activities. The company looked to its owners for financing by issuing common stock for $150,000 while repaying $50,000 in bonds payable. Taking into account the noncash transaction, bonds payable increased by $50,000.

In summary, Ryan Corporation has paid for its expansion with a combination of cash flows from operating activities, net sales of investment assets, issuance of common stock, and a net increase in bonds payable.

Preparing the Work Sheet

OBJECTIVE 8
Prepare a work sheet for the statement of cash flows

Previous sections illustrated the preparation of the statement of cash flows for Ryan Corporation, a relatively simple company. To assist in preparing the statement of cash flows in more complex companies, accountants developed a work sheet approach. The work sheet approach employs a special format that allows for the systematic analysis of all the changes in the balance sheet accounts to arrive at the statement of cash flows. In this section, the work sheet approach is demonstrated using the statement of cash flows for Ryan Corporation. The work sheet approach uses the indirect method of determining cash flows from operating activities because of its basis in changes in the balance sheet accounts.

Procedures in Preparing the Work Sheet

Alternative Method

The work sheet for Ryan Corporation is presented in Exhibit 27-8. The work sheet has four columns, labeled as follows:

Column A: Description

Column B: Account balances for the end of the prior year (19x1)

Column C: Analysis of transactions for the current year

Column D: Account balances for the end of the current year (19x2)

Five steps are followed in the preparation of the work sheet. As you read each one, refer to Exhibit 27-8.

1. Enter the account names from the balance sheet (Exhibit 27-2) in column A. Note that all accounts with debit balances are listed first, followed by all accounts with credit balances.
2. Enter the account balances for 19x1 in column B and the account balances for 19x2 in column D. In each column, total the debits and the credits. The total debits should equal the total credits in each column. (This is a check of whether all accounts were transferred from the balance sheet correctly.)
3. Below the data entered in step **2**, insert the captions: Cash Flows from Operating Activities, Cash Flows from Investing Activities, and Cash Flows from

Exhibit 27-8. Work Sheet for the Statement of Cash Flows

Ryan Corporation
Work Sheet for Statement of Cash Flows
For the Year Ended December 31, 19x2

(A) Description	(B) Account Balances 12/31/x1	(C) Analysis of Transactions Debit		(C) Analysis of Transactions Credit		(D) Account Balances 12/31/x2
Debits						
Cash	15,000	(x)	**31,000**			46,000
Accounts Receivable (net)	55,000			(b)	8,000	47,000
Inventory	110,000	(c)	34,000			144,000
Prepaid Expenses	5,000			(d)	4,000	1,000
Investments	127,000	(h)	78,000	(i)	90,000	115,000
Plant Assets	505,000	(j)	120,000	(k)	10,000	715,000
		(l)	100,000			
Total Debits	817,000					1,068,000
Credits						
Accumulated Depreciation	68,000	(k)	2,000	(m)	37,000	103,000
Accounts Payable	43,000			(e)	7,000	50,000
Accrued Liabilities	9,000			(f)	3,000	12,000
Income Taxes Payable	5,000	(g)	2,000			3,000
Bonds Payable	245,000	(n)	50,000	(l)	100,000	295,000
Common Stock	200,000			(o)	76,000	276,000
Paid-in Capital in Excess of Par Value	115,000			(o)	74,000	189,000
Retained Earnings	132,000	(p)	8,000	(a)	16,000	140,000
Total Credits	817,000		425,000		425,000	1,068,000
Cash Flows from Operating Activities						
Net Income		(a)	16,000			
Decrease in Accounts Receivable		(b)	8,000			
Increase in Inventory				(c)	34,000	
Decrease in Prepaid Expenses		(d)	4,000			
Increase in Accounts Payable		(e)	7,000			
Increase in Accrued Liabilities		(f)	3,000			
Decrease in Income Taxes Payable				(g)	2,000	
Gain on Sale of Investments				(i)	12,000	
Loss on Sale of Plant Assets		(k)	3,000			
Depreciation Expense		(m)	37,000			
Cash Flows from Investing Activities						
Purchase of Investments				(h)	78,000	
Sale of Investments		(i)	102,000			
Purchase of Plant Assets				(j)	120,000	
Sale of Plant Assets		(k)	5,000			
Cash Flows from Financing Activities						
Repayment of Bonds				(n)	50,000	
Issue of Common Stock		(o)	150,000			
Dividends Paid				(p)	8,000	
			335,000		304,000	
Net Increase in Cash				(x)	**31,000**	
			335,000		335,000	

Financing Activities, leaving several lines of space between each one. As you do the analysis in step 4, write the results in the appropriate categories.

4. Analyze the changes in each balance sheet account using information from both the income statement (see Exhibit 27-3) and from other transactions affecting noncurrent accounts during 19x2. (The procedures for this analysis are presented in the next section.) Enter the results in the debit and credit columns. Identify each item with a letter. On the first line identify the change in cash with an (x). In a complex situation, these letters will reference a list of explanations on another working paper.
5. When all the changes in the balance sheet accounts have been explained, add the debit and credit columns in both the top and bottom portions of column C. The debit and credit columns in the top portion should equal each other. They should *not* be equal in the bottom portion. If no errors have been made, the difference between columns in the bottom portion should equal the increase or decrease in the cash account identified with an (x) on the first line of the work sheet. Add this difference to the lesser of the two columns, and identify it as either an increase or decrease in cash. Label the change with an (x) and compare it with the change in cash on the first line of the work sheet, also labeled (x). The amounts should be equal, as they are in Exhibit 27-8, where the net increase in cash is $31,000.

When the work sheet is complete, the statement of cash flows may be prepared using the information in the lower half of the work sheet.

Analyzing the Changes in Balance Sheet Accounts

The most important step in the preparation of the work sheet is the analysis of the changes in the balances of the balance sheet accounts (step **4**). Although there are a number of transactions and reclassifications to analyze and record, the overall procedure is systematic and not overly complicated. It is as follows:

1. Record net income.
2. Account for changes in current assets and current liabilities.
3. Account for changes in noncurrent accounts using the information about other transactions.
4. Reclassify any other income and expense items not already dealt with. In the following explanations, the identification letters refer to the corresponding transactions and reclassifications in the work sheet.

a. ***Net Income.*** Net income results in an increase in Retained Earnings. It is also the starting point under the indirect method for determining cash flows from operating activities. Under this method, additions and deductions are made to net income to arrive at cash flows from operating activities. Work sheet entry **a** is as follows:

(a)	**Cash Flows from Operations: Net Income**	16,000	
	Retained Earnings		16,000

b–g. ***Changes in Current Assets and Current Liabilities.*** Entries **b** to **g** record the effects of the changes in current assets and current liabilities on cash flows. In each case, there is a debit or credit to the current asset or current liability to account for the change in the year and a corresponding debit or credit in the operating activities section of the work sheet. Recall that in the prior analysis, each item on the accrual-based income statement was adjusted for the change in the related current asset or current liability to arrive at the cash-based figure. The same reasoning applies in recording these changes in accounts as debits or credits in the operating activities section. For example, work sheet entry **b** records the decrease in Accounts Receivable as a credit (decrease) to Accounts Receivable and as a debit in the operating activities section because the decrease has a positive effect on cash flows, as follows:

(b) Cash Flows from Operating Activities:		
Decrease in Accounts Receivable	8,000	
Accounts Receivable		8,000

Work sheet entries **c–g** reflect the effects of the changes in the other current assets and current liabilities on cash flows from operating activities. As you study these entries, note how the effects of each entry on cash flows are automatically determined by debits or credits reflecting changes in the balance sheet accounts.

(c) Inventory	34,000	
Cash Flows from Operating Activities:		
Increase in Inventory		34,000
(d) Cash Flows from Operating Activities:		
Decrease in Prepaid Expenses	4,000	
Prepaid Expenses		4,000
(e) Cash Flows from Operating Activities:		
Increase in Accounts Payable	7,000	
Accounts Payable		7,000
(f) Cash Flows from Operating Activities:		
Increase in Accrued Liabilities	3,000	
Accrued Liabilities		3,000
(g) Income Taxes Payable	2,000	
Cash Flows from Operating Activities:		
Decrease in Income Taxes Payable		2,000

h–i. ***Investments.*** Among the other transactions affecting noncurrent accounts during 19x2 (see Exhibit 27-3), two items pertain to investments. One is the purchase for $78,000 and the other is the sale at $102,000. The purchase is recorded on the work sheet as a cash flow in the investing activities section, as follows:

(h) Investments	78,000	
Cash Flows from Investing Activities:		
Purchase of Investments		78,000

Note that instead of crediting Cash, a credit entry with the appropriate designation is made in the appropriate section in the lower half of the work sheet. The sale transaction is more complicated because it involves a gain that appears on the income statement and is included in net income. The work sheet entry accounts for this gain as follows:

(i) Cash Flows from Investing Activities:		
Sale of Investments	102,000	
Investments		90,000
Cash Flows from Operating Activities:		
Gain on Sale of Investments		12,000

This entry records the cash inflow in the investing activities section, accounts for the remaining difference in the Investments account, and removes the gain on sale of investments from its inclusion in net income.

j–m. ***Plant Assets and Accumulated Depreciation.*** Four transactions affect plant assets and the related accumulated depreciation. These are the purchase of plant assets, the sale of plant assets at a loss, the noncash exchange of plant assets for bonds, and the depreciation expense for the year. Because these transactions may appear complicated, it is important to work through them systematically when preparing the work sheet. First, the purchase of plant assets for $120,000 is entered (entry **j**) in the same way the purchase of investments was entered in entry **h**:

(j) Plant Assets	120,000	
Cash Flows from Investing Activities:		
Purchase of Plant Assets		120,000

Second, the sale of plant assets is similar to the sale of investments, except that a loss is involved, as follows:

(k) Cash Flows from Investing Activities:		
Sale of Plant Assets	5,000	
Cash Flows from Operating Activities:		
Loss on Sale of Plant Assets	3,000	
Accumulated Depreciation	2,000	
Plant Assets		10,000

The cash inflow from this transaction is $5,000. The rest of the entry is necessary to add the loss back into net income in the operating activities section of the statement of cash flows (since it was deducted to arrive at net income and no cash outflow resulted) and to record the effects on plant assets and accumulated depreciation.

The third transaction (entry **l**) is the noncash issue of bonds for the purchase of plant assets, as follows:

(l) Plant Assets	100,000	
Bonds Payable		100,000

Note that this transaction does not affect cash. Still, it needs to be recorded because the objective is to account for all the changes in the balance sheet accounts. It is listed at the end of the statement of cash flows (Exhibit 27-7) in the schedule of noncash investing and financing transactions.

At this point the increase of $210,000 ($715,000 – $505,000) in plant assets has been explained by the two purchases less the sale ($120,000 + $100,000 – $10,000 = $210,000), but the change in Accumulated Depreciation has not been completely explained. The depreciation expense for the year needs to be entered, as follows:

(m) Cash Flows from Operating Activities:		
Depreciation Expense	37,000	
Accumulated Depreciation		37,000

The debit is to the operating activities section of the work sheet because, as explained earlier in the chapter, no current cash outflow is required for depreciation expense. The effect of this debit is to add the amount for depreciation expense back into net income. The $35,000 increase in Accumulated Depreciation has now been explained by the sale transaction and the depreciation expense (–$2,000 + $37,000 = $35,000).

n. ***Bonds Payable.*** Part of the change in Bonds Payable was explained in entry **l** when a noncash transaction, a $100,000 issue of bonds in exchange for plant assets, was entered. All that remains is to enter the repayment, as follows:

(n) Bonds Payable	50,000	
Cash Flows from Financing Activities:		
Repayment of Bonds		50,000

o. ***Common Stock and Paid-in Capital in Excess of Par Value.*** One transaction affects both these accounts. It is an issue of 15,200 shares of $5 par value common stock for a total of $150,000. The work sheet entry is:

(o) Cash Flows from Financing Activities:		
Issue of Common Stock	150,000	
Common Stock		76,000
Paid-in Capital in Excess of Par Value		74,000

p. ***Retained Earnings.*** Part of the change in Retained Earnings was recognized when net income was entered (entry **a**). The only remaining effect to be recognized is the $8,000 in cash dividends paid during the year, as follows:

(p) Retained Earnings	8,000	
Cash Flows from Financing Activities:		
Dividends Paid		8,000

x. The final step is to total the debit and credit columns in the top and bottom portions of the work sheet and then to enter the net change in cash at the bottom of the work sheet. The columns in the upper half equal $425,000. In the lower half, the debit column totals $335,000 and the credit column totals $304,000. The credit difference of $31,000 (entry **x**) equals the debit change in cash on the first line of the work sheet.

Chapter Review

Review of Learning Objectives

1. **Describe the statement of cash flows, and define *cash* and *cash equivalents*.**
The statement of cash flows explains the changes in cash and cash equivalents from one accounting period to the next by showing cash inflows and cash outflows from the operating, investing, and financing activities of a company for an accounting period. For purposes of preparing the statement of cash flows, *cash* is defined to include cash and cash equivalents. *Cash equivalents* are short-term (ninety days or less), highly liquid investments, including money market accounts, commercial paper, and U.S. Treasury bills.

2. **State the principal purposes and uses of the statement of cash flows.**
The primary purpose of the statement of cash flows is to provide information about a company's cash receipts and cash payments during an accounting period. Its secondary purpose is to provide information about a company's operating, investing, and financing activities. It is useful to management as well as to investors and creditors in assessing the liquidity of a business, including the ability of the business to generate future cash flows and to pay its debts and dividends.

3. **Identify the principal components of the classifications of cash flows, and state the significance of noncash investing and financing transactions.**
Cash flows may be classified as (1) operating activities, which include the cash effects of transactions and other events that enter into the determination of net income;

(2) investing activities, which include the acquiring and selling of long- and short-term marketable securities, property, plant, and equipment, and the making and collecting of loans, excluding interest; or (3) financing activities, which include the obtaining and returning or repaying of resources, excluding interest to owners and creditors. Noncash investing and financing transactions are particularly important because they are exchanges of assets and/or liabilities that are of interest to investors and creditors when evaluating the financing and investing activities of the business.

4. **Determine cash flows from operating activities using the (a) direct and (b) indirect methods.**
The direct method of determining cash flows from operating activities is accomplished by adjusting each item in the income statement from an accrual basis to a cash basis, in the following form:

Cash Flows from Operating Activities		
Cash Receipts from		
Sales	xxx	
Interest and Dividends Received	xxx	xxx
Cash Payments for		
Purchases	xxx	
Operating Expenses	xxx	
Interest Payments	xxx	
Income Taxes	xxx	xxx
Net Cash Flows from Operating Activities		xxx

In the indirect method, net income is adjusted for all noncash effects to arrive at a cash flow basis, as follows:

Cash Flows from Operating Activities		
Net Income		xxx
Adjustments to Reconcile Net Income to Net Cash Flows from Operating Activities		
(List of individual items)	xxx	xxx
Net Cash Flows from Operating Activities		xxx

5. **Determine cash flows from (a) investing activities and (b) financing activities.**
Cash flows from investing activities are determined by identifying the cash flow effects of the transactions that affect each account relevant to investing activities. These accounts include all long-term assets and short-term marketable securities. The same procedure is followed for financing activities, except that the accounts involved are short-term notes payable, long-term liabilities, and owners' equity accounts. The effects on related accounts of gains and losses reported on the income statement must also be considered. When the change in a balance sheet account from one accounting period to the next has been explained, all the cash flow effects should have been identified.

6. **Prepare a statement of cash flows using the (a) direct and (b) indirect methods.**
The statement of cash flows lists cash flows from operating activities, investing activities, and financing activities, in that order. The section on operating activities may be prepared using either the direct or indirect method of determining cash flows from operating activities. The sections on investing and financing activities are prepared by examining individual accounts involving cash receipts and cash payments in order to explain year-to-year changes in the account balances. Significant noncash transactions are included in a schedule of noncash investing and financing transactions that accompanies the statement of cash flows. Whenever the direct method is used, a reconciliation of net income to net cash flows from operating activities is required.

7. **Interpret the statement of cash flows.**
   Interpretation of the statement of cash flows begins with an examination of the cash flows from operations, to determine if they are positive and to assess the differences between net income and net cash flows from operating activities. It is usually informative to relate cash flows from operations to dividend payments in the financing section to see if the company is comfortably covering these important cash outflows. It is also useful to examine investing activities to determine if the company is expanding, and if so, in what areas of business it is investing; or if not, in what areas it is contracting. Based on the analysis of investing, one should then look at the financing section to evaluate how the company is financing its expansion or, if it is not expanding, how it is reducing its financing obligations. Finally, it is important to evaluate the impact of the noncash investing and financing transactions listed in the lower portion of the statement of cash flows.
8. **Prepare a work sheet for the statement of cash flows.**
   A work sheet is useful in preparing the statement of cash flows for complex companies. The basic procedures in the work sheet approach are to analyze the changes in the balance sheet accounts for their effects on cash flows (in the top portion of the work sheet) and to classify those effects according to the format of the statement of cash flows (in the lower portion of the work sheet). When all the changes in the balance sheet accounts have been explained and entered on the work sheet, the change in the cash account will also be explained, and the information will be available to prepare the statement of cash flows. The work sheet approach lends itself to the indirect method of preparing the statement of cash flows.

Review of Concepts and Terminology

The following concepts and terms were introduced in this chapter:

(L.O. 1) **Cash:** Cash and cash equivalents.

(L.O. 1) **Cash equivalents:** Short-term (ninety days or less), highly liquid investments, including money market accounts, commercial paper, and U.S. Treasury bills.

(L.O. 4) **Direct method:** The procedure for converting the income statement from an accrual basis to a cash basis by adjusting each item in the income statement separately.

(L.O. 3) **Financing activities:** Business activities that involve obtaining or returning resources from or to owners and providing them with a return on their investment and obtaining resources from creditors and repaying the amounts borrowed or otherwise settling the obligation.

(L.O. 4) **Indirect method:** The procedure for converting the income statement from an accrual basis to a cash basis by adjusting net income for items that do not affect cash flows, including depreciation, amortization, depletion, gains, losses, and changes in current assets and current liabilities.

(L.O. 3) **Investing activities:** Business activities that include the acquiring and selling of long-term assets, the acquiring and selling of marketable securities other than cash equivalents, and the making and collecting of loans.

(L.O. 3) **Noncash investing and financing transactions:** Significant investing and financing transactions that do not involve an actual cash inflow or outflow but involve only long-term assets, long-term liabilities, or stockholders' equity, such as the exchange of a long-term asset for a long-term liability or the settlement of a debt by the issue of capital stock.

(L.O. 3) **Operating activities:** Business activities that include the cash effects of transactions and other events that enter into the determination of net income.

(L.O. 1) **Statement of cash flows:** A primary financial statement that shows the effect on cash of the operating, investing, and financing activities of a company for an accounting period.

Self-Test

Test your knowledge of the chapter by choosing the best answer for each of the following items.

(L.O. 1) 1. Cash equivalents include
  a. three-month Treasury bills.
  b. short-term investments.
  c. accounts receivable.
  d. long-term investments.

(L.O. 2) 2. The primary purpose of the statement of cash flows is to provide information
  a. regarding the results of operations for a period of time.
  b. regarding the financial position of a company as of the end of an accounting period.
  c. about a company's income-producing activities during an accounting period.
  d. about a company's cash receipts and cash payments during an accounting period.

(L.O. 3) 3. Which of the following is supplemental to the statement of cash flows?
  a. Operating activities
  b. Investing activities
  c. Significant noncash transactions
  d. Financing activities

(L.O. 4) 4. Which of the following would be classified as an operating activity in the statement of cash flows?
  a. Declared and paid a cash dividend
  b. Issued long-term notes for plant assets
  c. Paid interest on a long-term note
  d. Purchased a patent

(L.O. 4) 5. The direct method of preparing the operating activities section of the statement of cash flows differs from the indirect method in that it
  a. starts with the net income figure.
  b. lists the changes in current asset accounts in the operating section.
  c. begins with cash from customers, which is revenues adjusted for the change in accounts receivable.
  d. lists significant noncash transactions.

(L.O. 5) 6. Which of the following would be classified as an investing activity on the statement of cash flows?
  a. Declared and paid a cash dividend
  b. Issued long-term notes for plant assets
  c. Paid interest on a long-term note
  d. Purchased a patent

(L.O. 5) 7. Which of the following would be classified as a financing activity on the statement of cash flows?
  a. Declared and paid a cash dividend
  b. Issued long-term notes for plant assets
  c. Paid interest on a long-term note
  d. Purchased a patent

(L.O. 6) 8. On the statement of cash flows, the net amount of the major components of cash flow will equal the increase or decrease in
  a. cash and accounts receivable.
  b. working capital.
  c. cash and cash equivalents.
  d. very short-term investments.

(L.O. 7) 9. In general, to determine where the funds came from to pay for net investing activities, it is best to focus on which of the following sections of the statement of cash flows?
  a. Operating activities and financing activities
  b. Investing activities and financing activities
  c. Operating activities
  d. Financing activities

(L.O. 8) 10. A basic feature of the work sheet approach to preparing the statement of cash flows is that entries are made on the work sheet to
a. be used for reference for later entry in the general journal.
b. adjust the cash amount to an accrual basis.
c. explain the changes in income statement accounts.
d. explain the changes in balance sheet accounts.

Answers to the Self-Test are at the end of this chapter.

Review Problem
The Statement of Cash Flows

(L.O. 4, 5, 6) The comparative balance sheets for Northwest Corporation for the years 19x7 and 19x6 are presented below; the 19x7 income statement is shown on the following page.

Northwest Corporation
Comparative Balance Sheets
December 31, 19x7 and 19x6

	19x7	19x6	Change	Increase or Decrease
Assets				
Cash	$ 115,850	$ 121,850	$ (6,000)	Decrease
Accounts Receivable (net)	296,000	314,500	(18,500)	Decrease
Inventory	322,000	301,000	21,000	Increase
Prepaid Expenses	7,800	5,800	2,000	Increase
Long-Term Investments	36,000	86,000	(50,000)	Decrease
Land	150,000	125,000	25,000	Increase
Building	462,000	462,000	—	—
Accumulated Depreciation, Building	(91,000)	(79,000)	(12,000)	Increase
Equipment	159,730	167,230	(7,500)	Decrease
Accumulated Depreciation, Equipment	(43,400)	(45,600)	2,200	Decrease
Intangible Assets	19,200	24,000	(4,800)	Decrease
Total Assets	$1,434,180	$1,482,780	$ (48,600)	
Liabilities and Stockholders' Equity				
Accounts Payable	$ 133,750	$ 233,750	$(100,000)	Decrease
Notes Payable (current)	75,700	145,700	(70,000)	Decrease
Accrued Liabilities	5,000	—	5,000	Increase
Income Taxes Payable	20,000	—	20,000	Increase
Bonds Payable	210,000	310,000	(100,000)	Decrease
Mortgage Payable	330,000	350,000	(20,000)	Decrease
Common Stock—$10 par value	360,000	300,000	60,000	Increase
Paid-in Capital in Excess of Par Value	90,000	50,000	40,000	Increase
Retained Earnings	209,730	93,330	116,400	Increase
Total Liabilities and Stockholders' Equity	$1,434,180	$1,482,780	$ (48,600)	

Northwest Corporation
Income Statement
For the Year Ended December 31, 19x7

Sales		$1,650,000
Cost of Goods Sold		920,000
Gross Margin from Sales		$ 730,000
Operating Expenses (including Depreciation Expense of $12,000 on Buildings and $23,100 on Equipment and Amortization Expense of $4,800)		470,000
Operating Income		$ 260,000
Other Income (Expense)		
Interest Expense	$(55,000)	
Dividend Income	3,400	
Gain on Sale of Investments	12,500	
Loss on Disposal of Equipment	(2,300)	(41,400)
Income Before Taxes		$ 218,600
Income Taxes		52,200
Net Income		$ 166,400

The following additional information was taken from the company's records:

a. Long-term investments that cost $70,000 were sold at a gain of $12,500; additional long-term investments were made in the amount of $20,000.
b. Five acres of land were purchased for $25,000 for a parking lot.
c. Equipment that cost $37,500 with accumulated depreciation of $25,300 was sold at a loss of $2,300; new equipment costing $30,000 was purchased.
d. Notes payable in the amount of $100,000 were repaid; an additional $30,000 was borrowed by signing notes payable.
e. Bonds payable in the amount of $100,000 were converted into 6,000 shares of common stock.
f. The Mortgage Payable account was reduced by $20,000 during the year.
g. Cash dividends declared and paid were $50,000.

Required

1. Prepare a schedule of cash flows from operating activities using the (a) direct method and (b) indirect method.
2. Prepare a statement of cash flows using the indirect method.

Answer to Review Problem

1. (a) Prepare a schedule of cash flows from operating activities—direct method.

Northwest Corporation
Schedule of Cash Flows from Operating Activities
For the Year Ended December 31, 19x7

Cash Flows from Operating Activities		
Cash Receipts from		
Sales	$1,668,500 [1]	
Dividends Received	3,400	$1,671,900
Cash Payments for		
Purchases	$1,041,000 [2]	
Operating Expenses	427,100 [3]	
Interest Payments	55,000	
Income Taxes	32,200 [4]	1,555,300
Net Cash Flows from Operating Activities		$ 116,600

1. $1,650,000 + $18,500 = $1,668,500
2. $920,000 + $100,000 + $21,000 = $1,041,000
3. $470,000 + $2,000 – $5,000 – ($12,000 + $23,100 + $4,800) = $427,100
4. $52,200 – $20,000 = $32,200

1. (b) Prepare a schedule of cash flows from operating activities—indirect method.

Northwest Corporation
Schedule of Cash Flows from Operating Activities
For the Year Ended December 31, 19x7

Cash Flows from Operating Activities		
Net Income		$166,400
Adjustments to Reconcile Net Income to Net Cash Flows from Operating Activities		
Depreciation Expense, Buildings	$ 12,000	
Depreciation Expense, Equipment	23,100	
Amortization Expense, Intangible Assets	4,800	
Gain on Sale of Investments	(12,500)	
Loss on Disposal of Equipment	2,300	
Decrease in Accounts Receivable	18,500	
Increase in Inventory	(21,000)	
Increase in Prepaid Expenses	(2,000)	
Decrease in Accounts Payable	(100,000)	
Increase in Accrued Liabilities	5,000	
Increase in Income Taxes Payable	20,000	(49,800)
Net Cash Flows from Operating Activities		$116,600

2. Prepare a statement of cash flows—indirect method. (Note: This statement of cash flows is shown on the top of the next page.)

Northwest Corporation
Statement of Cash Flows
For the Year Ended December 31, 19x7

Cash Flows from Operating Activities		
Net Income		$166,400
Adjustments to Reconcile Net Income to Net Cash Flows from Operating Activities		
Depreciation Expense, Buildings	$ 12,000	
Depreciation Expense, Equipment	23,100	
Amortization Expense, Intangible Assets	4,800	
Gain on Sale of Investments	(12,500)	
Loss on Disposal of Equipment	2,300	
Decrease in Accounts Receivable	18,500	
Increase in Inventory	(21,000)	
Increase in Prepaid Expenses	(2,000)	
Decrease in Accounts Payable	(100,000)	
Increase in Accrued Liabilities	5,000	
Increase in Income Taxes Payable	20,000	(49,800)
Net Cash Flows from Operating Activities		$116,600
Cash Flows from Investing Activities		
Sale of Long-Term Investments	$ 82,500[1]	
Purchase of Long-Term Investments	(20,000)	
Purchase of Land	(25,000)	
Sale of Equipment	9,900[2]	
Purchase of Equipment	(30,000)	
Net Cash Flows from Investing Activities		17,400
Cash Flows from Financing Activities		
Repayment of Notes Payable	$(100,000)	
Issuance of Notes Payable	30,000	
Reduction in Mortgage	(20,000)	
Dividends Paid	(50,000)	
Net Cash Flows from Financing Activities		(140,000)
Net Increase (Decrease) in Cash		$ (6,000)
Cash at Beginning of Year		121,850
Cash at End of Year		$115,850

Schedule of Noncash Investing and Financing Transactions

Conversion of Bonds Payable into Common Stock	$100,000

1. $70,000 + $12,500 (gain) = $82,500
2. $37,500 − $25,300 = $12,200 (book value) − $2,300 (loss) = $9,900

Chapter Assignments

Questions

1. What is the term *cash* in the statement of cash flows understood to include?
2. In order to earn a return on cash on hand during 19x3, Sallas Corporation transferred $45,000 from its checking account to a money market account, purchased a $25,000 Treasury bill, and bought $35,000 in common stocks. How will each of these transactions affect the statement of cash flows?
3. What are the purposes of the statement of cash flows?
4. Why is the statement of cash flows needed when most of the information in it is available from a company's comparative balance sheets and the income statement?
5. What are the three classifications of cash flows? Give some examples of each.

6. Why is it important to disclose certain noncash transactions? How should they be disclosed?
7. Cell-Borne Corporation has a net loss of $12,000 in 19x1 but has positive cash flows from operations of $9,000. What conditions may have caused this situation?
8. What are the essential differences between the direct method and the indirect method of determining cash flows from operations?
9. Glen Corporation has the following other income and expense items: interest expense, $12,000; interest income, $3,000; dividend income, $5,000; and loss on retirement of bonds, $6,000. How does each of these items appear on or affect the statement of cash flows (assuming the direct method is used)?
10. What are the effects of the following items on cash flows from operations (assuming the direct method is used): (a) an increase in accounts receivable, (b) a decrease in inventory, (c) an increase in accounts payable, (d) a decrease in wages payable, (e) depreciation expense, and (f) amortization of patents?
11. What is the proper treatment on the statement of cash flows of a transaction in which a building that cost $50,000 with accumulated depreciation of $32,000 is sold for a loss of $5,000?
12. What is the proper treatment on the statement of cash flows of (a) a transaction in which buildings and land are purchased by the issuance of a mortgage for $234,000 and (b) a conversion of $50,000 in bonds payable into 2,500 shares of $6 par value common stock?
13. In interpreting the statement of cash flows, what are some comparisons that can be made with cash flows from operations? Prepare a list of reasons why a company would have a decrease in cash flows from investing activities.
14. Why is the work sheet approach considered to be more compatible with the indirect method than the direct method of determining cash flows from operations?
15. Assuming in each of the following independent cases that only one transaction occurred, what transactions would likely cause (1) a decrease in investments and (2) an increase in common stock? How would each case be treated on the work sheet for the statement of cash flows?

Communication Skills Exercises

Communication 27-1. Ethics and Cash Flow Classifications
(L.O. 3)

Chemical Waste Treatment, Inc. is a fast-growing company that disposes of chemical wastes. The company has a $800,000 line of credit at its bank. One covenant in the loan agreement stipulates that the ratio of cash flows from operations to interest expense exceed 3.0. If this ratio falls below 3.0, the company must pay down its line of credit to one-half if the funds borrowed against it currently exceed that amount. After the end of the fiscal year, the controller informs the president that "We will not meet our ratio requirements on our line of credit in 19x2 because interest expense was $1.2 million and cash flows from operations was $3.2 million. Also, we have borrowed 100 percent of our line of credit. We do not have the cash to reduce the credit line by $400,000." The president says, "This is a serious situation. To be able to pay our ongoing bills, we need our bank to increase our line of credit, not decrease it. What can we do?" "Do you recall the $500,000 two-year note payable for equipment?" replied the controller. "It is now classified as 'Proceeds from Notes Payable' in cash flows provided from financing activities in the statement of cash flows. If we move it up to cash flow from operations and call it 'Increase in Payables,' it would put us over the limit at $3.7 million." "Well, do it," ordered the president. "It surely doesn't make any difference where it is on the statement. It is an increase in both places. It would be much worse for our company in the long term if we failed to meet this ratio requirement." What is your opinion of the president's reasoning? Is the president's order ethical? Who is benefited and who is harmed if the controller follows the president's order? What are management's alternatives? What would you do?

Communication 27-2. Definitions and Interpretations of Cash Flows
(L.O. 7)

Tandy Corporation may not look the same to every analyst. Analysts tend to define and interpret cash flows in different ways. One interpretation of cash flows, presented in a *Business Week* article, is shown at the top of the next page:

Cash Flow = Net Income + Depreciation + Depletion + Amortization

Operating Cash Flow = Cash Flow + Interest + Income Tax Expense

Free Cash Flow = Cash Flow − Capital Expenditures − Dividends

According to the article, "Takeover artists and LBO operators hunt for 'operating cash flow [OCF].' That's the money generated by the company before the cost of financing and taxes comes into play. . . . While OCF is the broadest measure of a company's funds, some prefer to zero in on the narrower 'free cash flow.' That measures truly discretionary funds— company money that an owner could pocket without harming the business."[5]

The 1990 statement of cash flows for Tandy Corporation, the owner of Radio Shack and other store chains, is shown below.

Tandy Corporation and Subsidiaries
Consolidated Statements of Cash Flows[6]
Year Ended June 30, 1990
(in thousands)

Cash flows from operating activities:	
Net income	$ 290,347
Adjustments to reconcile net income to net cash provided by operating activities:	
Depreciation and amortization	92,115
Deferred income taxes and other items	(3,206)
Provision for credit losses	33,073
Changes in operating assets and liabilities, excluding the effect of businesses acquired:	
Receivables	(273,921)
Inventories	(110,336)
Other current assets	(15,110)
Accounts payable, accrued expenses and income taxes	45,445
Net cash provided by operating activities	$ 58,407
Investing activities:	
Additions to property, plant and equipment, net of retirements	$(112,515)
Acquisition of Victor Technologies	(112,856)
Payment received on InterTAN note	35,906
Other investing activities	7,853
Net cash used by investing activities	$(181,612)
Financing activities:	
Purchases of treasury stock	$(369,982)
Sales of treasury stock to employee stock purchase program	52,019
Dividends paid	(49,760)
Changes in short-term borrowings—net	479,325
Additions to long-term borrowings	133,751
Repayments of long-term borrowings	(45,349)
Net cash provided (used) by financing activities	$ 200,004
Increase (decrease) in cash and short-term investments	$ 76,799
Cash and short-term investments at the beginning of the year	$ 58,398
Cash and short-term investments at the end of the year	$ 135,197

5. Jeffrey Laderman, "Earnings, Schmernings—Look at the Cash," *Business Week*, July 24, 1989, p. 56.
6. Excerpt used with written permission from the 1990 annual report of Tandy Corporation. Copyright © 1990 by Tandy Corporation.

From the statement, compute cash flow, operating cash flow, and free cash flow as defined above. (Interest and Income Tax Expense from the income statement are $5,939,000 and $183,592,000, respectively.) How does the definition of cash flow in the formula differ from the concept followed in the statement of cash flows? (Assume that "cash and short-term investments" is equivalent to "cash and cash equivalents.") Is the definition of cash flow in the formula a substitute for net cash flows from operations? Is the concept of free cash flow, as defined, useful?

Communication 27-3.
Basic Research Skills
(L.O. 7)

In your library, select the annual reports of three corporations. You may choose them from the same industry or at random, at the direction of your instructor. (If you did a related exercise in a previous chapter, use the same three companies.) Prepare a table with a column for each corporation. Then, for any year covered by the statement of cash flows, answer the following questions: Does the company use the direct or the indirect approach? Is net income more or less than net cash flows from operating activities? What are the major causes of differences between net income and net cash flows from operating activities? Compare net cash flows from operating activities to dividends paid. Does the dividend appear secure? Did the company make significant capital expenditures during the year? How were the expenditures financed? Do you notice anything unusual about the investing and financing activities of your companies? Do the investing and financing activities provide any insights into management's plan for each company? If so, what are they? Be prepared to discuss the answers to these questions in class.

Classroom Exercises

Exercise 27-1.
Classification of Cash Flow Transactions
(L.O. 3)

Horizon Corporation engaged in the following transactions. Identify each as (1) an operating activity, (2) an investing activity, (3) a financing activity, (4) a noncash transaction, or (5) none of the above.

a. Declared and paid a cash dividend.
b. Purchased an investment.
c. Received cash from customers.
d. Paid interest.
e. Sold equipment at a loss.
f. Issued long-term bonds for plant assets.
g. Received dividends on securities held.
h. Issued common stock.
i. Declared and issued a stock dividend.
j. Repaid notes payable.
k. Paid employees for wages.
l. Purchased a 60-day Treasury bill.
m. Purchased land.

Exercise 27-2.
Cash Receipts from Sales
(L.O. 4)

During 19x2, Union Chemical Company, a distributor of farm fertilizers and herbicides, had sales of $6,500,000. The ending balance of Accounts Receivable was $850,000 in 19x1 and $1,200,000 in 19x2. Calculate cash receipts from sales in 19x2.

Exercise 27-3.
Cash Payments for Purchases
(L.O. 4)

During 19x2, Union Chemical Company had cost of goods sold of $3,800,000. The ending balance of Inventory was $510,000 in 19x1 and $420,000 in 19x2. The ending balance of Accounts Payable was $360,000 in 19x1 and $480,000 in 19x2. Calculate cash payments for purchases in 19x2.

Exercise 27-4.
Cash Payments for Operating Expenses and Income Taxes
(L.O. 4)

During 19x2, Union Chemical Company had operating expenses of $1,900,000 and income taxes expense of $200,000. Depreciation expense of $410,000 for 19x2 was included in operating expenses. The ending balance of Prepaid Expenses was $90,000 in 19x1 and $130,000 in 19x2. The ending balance of Accrued Liabilities (excluding Income Taxes Payable) was $50,000 in 19x1 and $30,000 in 19x2. The ending balance of Income Taxes Payable was $60,000 in 19x1 and $70,000 in 19x2. Calculate cash payments for operating expenses and income taxes in 19x2.

Exercise 27-5.
Cash Flows from Operating Activities—Direct Method
(L.O. 4)

Using the computations you made in Exercises 27-2, 27-3, and 27-4, prepare in good form a schedule of cash flows from operating activities for 19x2, using the direct method. The company has a December 31 year end.

Exercise 27-6.
Cash Flows from Operating Activities—Indirect Method
(L.O. 4)

The condensed single-step income statement of Union Chemical Company, a distributor of farm fertilizers and herbicides, appears as follows:

Sales		$6,500,000
Less: Cost of Goods Sold	$3,800,000	
Operating Expenses (including depreciation of $410,000)	1,900,000	
Income Taxes	200,000	5,900,000
Net Income		$ 600,000

Selected accounts from the company's balance sheets for 19x1 and 19x2 appear as shown below:

	19x2	19x1
Accounts Receivable	$1,200,000	$850,000
Inventory	420,000	510,000
Prepaid Expenses	130,000	90,000
Accounts Payable	480,000	360,000
Accrued Liabilities	30,000	50,000
Income Taxes Payable	70,000	60,000

Present in good form a schedule of cash flows from operating activities using the indirect method.

Exercise 27-7.
Computing Cash Flows from Operating Activities—Direct Method
(L.O. 4)

Europa Corporation engaged in the following transactions in 19x2. Using the direct method, compute the various cash flows from operating activities as required.

a. During 19x2, Europa Corporation had cash sales of $41,300 and sales on credit of $123,000. During the same year, accounts receivable decreased by $18,000. Determine the cash received from customers during 19x2.
b. During 19x2, Europa Corporation's cost of goods sold was $119,000. During the same year, merchandise inventory increased by $12,500 and accounts payable decreased by $4,300. Determine the cash payments for purchases during 19x2.
c. During 19x2, Europa Corporation had operating expenses of $45,000, including depreciation of $15,600. Also during 19x2, related prepaid expenses decreased by $3,100 and relevant accrued liabilities increased by $1,200. Determine the cash payments for operating expenses to suppliers of goods and services during 19x2.
d. Europa Corporation's income taxes expense for 19x2 was $4,300. Income taxes payable decreased by $230 that year. Determine the cash payments for income taxes during 19x2.

Exercise 27-8.
Computing Cash Flows from Operating Activities—Indirect Method
(L.O. 4)

During 19x1, Mayfair Corporation had a net income of $41,000. Included on the income statement was depreciation expense of $2,300 and amortization expense of $300. During the year, accounts receivable increased by $3,400, inventories decreased by $1,900, prepaid expenses decreased by $200, accounts payable increased by $5,000, and accrued liabilities decreased by $450. Prepare in good form a schedule of cash flows from operating activities using the indirect method.

Exercise 27-9.
Preparing a Schedule of Cash Flows from Operating Activities—Direct Method
(L.O. 4)

The income statement for the Karsko Corporation follows.

Karsko Corporation
Income Statement
For the Year Ended June 30, 19xx

Sales		$122,000
Cost of Goods Sold		60,000
Gross Margin from Sales		$ 62,000
Other Expenses		
Salaries Expense	$32,000	
Rent Expense	16,800	
Depreciation Expense	2,000	50,800
Income Before Income Taxes		$ 11,200
Income Taxes		2,400
Net Income		$ 8,800

Additional information: (a) All sales were on credit, and accounts receivable increased by $4,400 during the year. (b) All merchandise purchased was on credit. Inventories increased by $7,000, and accounts payable increased by $14,000 during the year. (c) Prepaid rent decreased by $1,400, while salaries payable increased by $1,000. (d) Income taxes payable decreased by $600 during the year. Prepare in good form a schedule of cash flows from operating activities using the direct method.

Exercise 27-10.
Preparing a Schedule of Cash Flows from Operating Activities—Indirect Method
(L.O. 4)

Using the data provided in Exercise 27-9, prepare in good form a schedule of cash flows from operating activities using the indirect method.

Exercise 27-11.
Computing Cash Flows from Investing Activities—Investments
(L.O. 5)

The T account for the Investments account for Krieger Company at the end of 19x3 is shown below.

Investments

Beg. Bal.	38,500	Sales	39,000
Purchases	58,000		
End. Bal.	**57,500**		

In addition, Krieger's income statement shows a loss on the sale of investments of $6,500. Compute the amounts to be shown as cash flows from investing activities and show how they are to appear on the statement of cash flows.

Exercise 27-12. Computing Cash Flows from Investing Activities—Plant Assets
(L.O. 5)

The T accounts for the Plant Assets and Accumulated Depreciation accounts for Krieger Company at the end of 19x3 are as follows:

Plant Assets

Beg. Bal.	65,000	Disposals	23,000
Purchases	33,600		
End. Bal.	**75,600**		

Accumulated Depreciation

Disposals	14,700	Beg. Bal.	34,500
		19x3 Depreciation	10,200
		End. Bal.	**30,000**

In addition, Krieger Company's income statement shows a gain on sale of plant assets of $4,400. Compute the amounts to be shown as cash flows from investing activities and show how they are to appear on the statement of cash flows.

Exercise 27-13. Determining Cash Flows from Investing and Financing Activities
(L.O. 5)

All transactions involving Notes Payable and related accounts engaged in by Krieger Company during 19x3 are as follows:

Cash	18,000	
Notes Payable		18,000
Bank loan		
Patent	30,000	
Notes Payable		30,000
Purchase of patent by issuing note payable		
Notes Payable	5,000	
Interest Expense	500	
Cash		5,500
Repayment of note payable at maturity		

Determine the amounts and how these transactions are to be shown in the statement of cash flows for 19x3.

Exercise 27-14. Preparing the Statement of Cash Flows
(L.O. 6)

Bradbury Corporation's 19x2 income statement and its comparative balance sheets for June 30, 19x2 and 19x1 follow.

Bradbury Corporation
Income Statement
For the Year Ended June 30, 19x2

Sales	$468,000
Cost of Goods Sold	312,000
Gross Margin from Sales	$156,000
Operating Expenses	90,000
Operating Income	$ 66,000
Interest Expense	5,600
Income Before Income Taxes	$ 60,400
Income Taxes	24,600
Net Income	$ 35,800

Bradbury Corporation
Comparative Balance Sheets
June 30, 19x2 and 19x1

	19x2	19x1
Assets		
Cash	$139,800	$ 25,000
Accounts Receivable (net)	42,000	52,000
Inventory	86,800	96,800
Prepaid Expenses	6,400	5,200
Furniture	110,000	120,000
Accumulated Depreciation, Furniture	(18,000)	(10,000)
Total Assets	$367,000	$289,000
Liabilities and Stockholders' Equity		
Accounts Payable	$ 26,000	$ 28,000
Income Taxes Payable	2,400	3,600
Notes Payable (long-term)	74,000	70,000
Common Stock—$10 par value	230,000	180,000
Retained Earnings	34,600	7,400
Total Liabilities and Stockholders' Equity	$367,000	$289,000

Additional information: (a) issued $44,000 in notes payable for purchase of furniture; (b) sold furniture that cost $54,000 with accumulated depreciation of $30,600 at carrying value; (c) recorded depreciation on the furniture during the year, $38,600; (d) repaid a note in the amount of $40,000; issued $50,000 of common stock at par value; and (e) declared and paid dividends of $8,600. Without using a work sheet, prepare a statement of cash flows for 19x2 using the direct method.

Exercise 27-15. Preparing a Work Sheet for the Statement of Cash Flows *(L.O. 6, 8)*

Using the information in Exercise 27-14, prepare a work sheet for the statement of cash flows for Bradbury Corporation for 19x2. From the work sheet, prepare a statement of cash flows using the indirect method.

Interpretation Case from Business

Airborne Freight Corporation *(L.O. 7)*

Airborne Freight Corporation, which is known as Airborne Express, is an air express transportation company, providing next-day, morning delivery of small packages and documents throughout the United States. Airborne Express is one of three major participants, along with Federal Express and United Parcel Service, in the air express industry. The following statement appears in "Management's discussion and analysis of results of operations and financial condition" from the company's 1990 annual report: "Capital expenditures and financing associated with those expenditures continued to be the primary factor affecting the financial condition of the company."[7] The company's consolidated statements of cash flows for 1990, 1989, and 1988 follow.

7. Excerpts from the 1990 annual report of Airborne Freight Corporation. Reprinted by permission of Airborne Freight Corporation.

Airborne Freight Corporation and Subsidiaries
Consolidated Statements of Cash Flows
Year Ended December 31

	1990	1989	1988
		(in thousands)	
Operating Activities:			
Net Earnings	$ 33,577	$ 19,083	$ 7,036
Adjustments to reconcile net earnings to net cash provided by operating activities:			
Depreciation and amortization	69,055	55,082	46,462
Provision for aircraft engine overhauls	6,224	5,703	5,823
Deferred income taxes	536	(136)	1,795
Provision for lease expense	—	4,088	—
Gain on disposition of aircraft	—	—	(1,717)
Cash Provided by Operations	109,392	83,820	59,399
Change in:			
Receivables	(19,722)	(20,152)	(16,874)
Inventories and prepaid expenses	(6,496)	(1,316)	(8,229)
Accounts payable	14,514	13,720	20,243
Accrued expenses, salaries and taxes payable	12,447	13,043	6,077
Net Cash Provided by Operating Activities	110,135	89,115	60,616
Investing Activities:			
Additions to property and equipment	(217,926)	(145,008)	(85,831)
Disposition of property and equipment	2,286	1,315	2,142
Expenditures for engine overhauls	(7,483)	(8,155)	(6,525)
Other	(1,679)	444	(1,730)
Net Cash Used in Investing Activities	(224,802)	(151,404)	(91,944)
Financing Activities:			
Proceeds from sale-leaseback of aircraft	28,464	83,904	—
Increase (decrease) in bank notes payable	(6,800)	(12,700)	37,800
Principal payments of long-term debt and capital lease obligations	(8,642)	(4,010)	(3,165)
Issuance of redeemable preferred stock	40,000	—	—
Issuance of common stock	69,461	1,410	78
Dividends paid	(7,609)	(4,168)	(4,141)
Net Cash Provided by Financing Activities	114,874	64,436	30,572
Net Increase (Decrease) in Cash	207	2,147	(756)
Cash at Beginning of Year	8,588	6,441	7,197
Cash at End of Year	$ 8,795	$ 8,588	$ 6,441

Required

1. Have operations provided significant cash flows over the past three years? What is the role of net earnings in this provision? Other than net earnings, what is the most significant factor in providing the cash flows? Have changes in working capital accounts been a significant factor?
2. Does Airborne Express generate enough net cash flows from operating activities to both pay dividends and provide additional funds for expansion?
3. Is management's statement about capital expenditures and associated financing substantiated by the figures? If your answer is yes, what were Airborne's primary means of financing the expansion in 1990?

Problem Set A

Problem 27A-1. Classification of Transactions
(L.O. 3)

Analyze the transactions in the following schedule, and place an X in the appropriate column to indicate the classification of each transaction and its effect on cash flows using the direct method.

Transaction	Cash Flow Classification				Effect on Cash		
	Operating Activity	Investing Activity	Financing Activity	Noncash Transactions	Increase	Decrease	No Effect
a. Earned a net income.							
b. Declared and paid cash dividend.							
c. Issued stock for cash.							
d. Retired long-term debt by issuing stock.							
e. Paid accounts payable.							
f. Purchased inventory.							
g. Purchased a one-year insurance policy.							
h. Purchased a long-term investment with cash.							
i. Sold marketable securities at a gain.							
j. Sold a machine at a loss.							
k. Retired fully depreciated equipment.							
l. Paid interest on debt.							
m. Purchased marketable securities.							
n. Received dividend income.							
o. Received cash on account.							
p. Converted bonds to common stock.							
q. Purchased short-term, ninety-day Treasury bill.							

Problem 27A-2. Cash Flows from Operating Activities
(L.O. 4)

The income statement for Broadwell Clothing Store is presented at the top of page 1141.

Additional information: (a) other sales and administrative expenses include depreciation expense of $104,000 and amortization expense of $36,000; (b) accrued liabilities for salaries were $24,000 less than the previous year and prepaid expenses were $40,000 more than the previous year; and (c) during the year accounts receivable (net) increased by $288,000, accounts payable increased by $228,000, and income taxes payable decreased by $14,400.

Broadwell Clothing Store Income Statement For the Year Ended June 30, 19xx		
Sales		$4,900,000
Cost of Goods Sold		
Beginning Inventory	$1,240,000	
Purchases (net)	3,040,000	
Goods Available for Sale	$4,280,000	
Ending Inventory	1,400,000	
Cost of Goods Sold		2,880,000
Gross Margin from Sales		$2,020,000
Operating Expenses		
Sales and Administrative Salaries Expense	$1,112,000	
Other Sales and Administrative Expenses	624,000	
Total Operating Expenses		1,736,000
Income Before Income Taxes		$ 284,000
Income Taxes		78,000
Net Income		$ 206,000

Required

1. Prepare a schedule of cash flows from operating activities using the direct method.
2. Prepare a schedule of cash flows from operating activities using the indirect method.

Problem 27A-3. Cash Flows from Operating Activities *(L.O. 4)*

The income statement for Springer Greeting Card Company is as follows:

Springer Greeting Card Company Income Statement For the Year Ended December 31, 19x2		
Sales		$944,000
Cost of Goods Sold		573,400
Gross Margin from Sales		$370,600
Operating Expenses (including Depreciation Expense of $42,860)		174,800
Operating Income		$195,800
Other Income (Expenses)		
Interest Expense	$(16,800)	
Interest Income	8,600	
Loss on Sale of Investments	(11,600)	(19,800)
Income Before Income Taxes		$176,000
Income Taxes		37,000
Net Income		$139,000

Relevant accounts from the comparative balance sheets for December 31, 19x2 and 19x1 are as follows:

	19x2	19x1
Accounts Receivable (net)	$37,060	$47,340
Inventory	79,280	69,980
Prepaid Expenses	4,800	17,800
Accounts Payable	69,880	45,400
Accrued Liabilities	9,380	17,660
Income Taxes Payable	9,500	35,200

Required

1. Prepare a schedule of cash flows from operating activities using the direct method.
2. Prepare a schedule of cash flows from operating activities using the indirect method.

Problem 27A-4. The Statement of Cash Flows—Direct Method *(L.O. 6, 7)*

Gutierrez Corporation's 19x7 income statement and its comparative balance sheets as of June 30, 19x7 and 19x6 appear as follows:

Gutierrez Corporation
Income Statement
For the Year Ended June 30, 19x7

Sales		$2,081,800
Cost of Goods Sold		1,312,600
Gross Margin from Sales		$ 769,200
Operating Expenses (including Depreciation Expense of $120,000)		378,400
Income from Operations		$ 390,800
Other Income (Expenses)		
Loss on Disposal of Equipment	$ (8,000)	
Interest Expense	(75,200)	(83,200)
Income Before Income Taxes		$ 307,600
Income Taxes		68,400
Net Income		$ 239,200

Gutierrez Corporation
Comparative Balance Sheets
June 30, 19x7 and 19x6

	19x7	19x6
Assets		
Cash	$ 334,000	$ 40,000
Accounts Receivable (net)	200,000	240,000
Finished Goods Inventory	360,000	440,000
Prepaid Expenses	1,200	2,000
Property, Plant, and Equipment	1,256,000	1,104,000
Accumulated Depreciation, Property, Plant, and Equipment	(366,000)	(280,000)
Total Assets	$1,785,200	$1,546,000
Liabilities and Stockholders' Equity		
Accounts Payable	$ 128,000	$ 84,000
Notes Payable (due in 90 days)	60,000	160,000
Income Taxes Payable	52,000	36,000
Mortgage Payable	720,000	560,000
Common Stock—$5 par value	400,000	400,000
Retained Earnings	425,200	306,000
Total Liabilities and Stockholders' Equity	$1,785,200	$1,546,000

Additional information about 19x7: (a) equipment that cost $48,000 with accumulated depreciation of $34,000 was sold at a loss of $8,000; (b) land and building were purchased in the amount of $200,000 through an increase of $200,000 in the mortgage payable; (c) a $40,000 payment was made on the mortgage; (d) the notes were repaid, but the company borrowed an additional $60,000 through the issuance of a new note payable; and (e) a $120,000 cash dividend was declared and paid.

Required

1. Prepare a statement of cash flows using the direct method. Include a supporting schedule of noncash investing and financing transactions.
2. What are the primary reasons for Gutierrez Corporation's large increase in cash from 19x6 to 19x7?

Problem 27A-5.
The Work Sheet and the Statement of Cash Flows—Indirect Method
(L.O. 6, 8)

Use the information for Gutierrez Corporation given in Problem 27A-4 to answer the requirements below.

Required

1. Prepare a work sheet to gather information for the preparation of the statement of cash flows.
2. From the information on the work sheet, prepare a statement of cash flows using the indirect method. Include a supporting schedule of noncash investing and financing transactions.

Problem 27A-6.
The Work Sheet and the Statement of Cash Flows—Indirect Method
(L.O. 6, 7, 8)

The comparative balance sheets for Bausch Ceramics, Inc. for December 31, 19x3 and 19x2 appear below.

Bausch Ceramics, Inc.
Comparative Balance Sheets
December 31, 19x3 and 19x2

	19x3	19x2
Assets		
Cash	$ 277,600	$ 305,600
Accounts Receivable (net)	738,800	758,800
Inventory	960,000	800,000
Prepaid Expenses	14,800	26,800
Long-Term Investments	440,000	440,000
Land	361,200	321,200
Building	1,200,000	920,000
Accumulated Depreciation, Building	(240,000)	(160,000)
Equipment	480,000	480,000
Accumulated Depreciation, Equipment	(116,000)	(56,000)
Intangible Assets	20,000	40,000
Total Assets	$4,136,400	$3,876,400
Liabilities and Stockholders' Equity		
Accounts Payable	$ 470,800	$ 660,800
Notes Payable (current)	40,000	160,000
Accrued Liabilities	10,800	20,800
Mortgage Payable	1,080,000	800,000
Bonds Payable	1,000,000	760,000
Common Stock	1,200,000	1,200,000
Paid-in Capital in Excess of Par Value	80,000	80,000
Retained Earnings	254,800	194,800
Total Liabilities and Stockholders' Equity	$4,136,400	$3,876,400

Additional information about Bausch Ceramics' operations during 19x3: (a) net income was $96,000; (b) building and equipment depreciation expense amounts were $80,000 and $60,000, respectively; (c) intangible assets were amortized in the amount of $20,000; (d) investments in the amount of $116,000 were purchased; (e) investments were sold for $150,000, on which a gain of $34,000 was made; (f) the company issued $240,000 in long-term bonds at face value; (g) a small warehouse building with the accompanying land was purchased through the issue of a $320,000 mortgage; (h) the company paid $40,000 to reduce mortgage payable during 19x3; (i) the company borrowed funds in the amount of $60,000 by issuing notes payable and repaid notes payable in the amount of $180,000; and (j) cash dividends in the amount of $36,000 were declared and paid.

Required

1. Prepare a work sheet for the statement of cash flows for Bausch Ceramics.
2. Prepare a statement of cash flows from the information in the work sheet using the indirect method. Include a supporting schedule of noncash investing and financing transactions.
3. Why did Bausch Ceramics experience a decrease in cash in a year in which it had a net income of $96,000? Discuss and interpret.

Problem Set B

Problem 27B-1. Classification of Transactions
(L.O. 3)

Analyze the transactions presented in the schedule that follows and place an X in the appropriate column to indicate the classification of each transaction and its effect on cash flows.

	Cash Flow Classification				Effect on Cash		
Transaction	Operating Activity	Investing Activity	Financing Activity	Noncash Transactions	Increase	Decrease	No Effect
a. Incurred a net loss.							
b. Declared and issued a stock dividend.							
c. Paid a cash dividend.							
d. Collected accounts receivable.							
e. Purchased inventory with cash.							
f. Retired long-term debt with cash.							
g. Sold investment for a loss.							
h. Issued stock for equipment.							
i. Purchased a one-year insurance policy for cash.							
j. Purchased treasury stock with cash.							
k. Retired a fully depreciated truck (no gain or loss).							
l. Paid interest on note.							

(continued)

Transaction	Cash Flow Classification				Effect on Cash		
	Operating Activity	Investing Activity	Financing Activity	Noncash Transactions	Increase	Decrease	No Effect
m. Received cash dividend on investment.							
n. Sold treasury stock.							
o. Paid income taxes.							
p. Transferred cash to money market account.							
q. Purchased land and building with a mortgage.							

Problem 27B-2.
Cash Flows from Operating Activities
(L.O. 4)

The income statement for Lui Food Corporation is as follows:

Lui Food Corporation
Income Statement
For the Year Ended December 31, 19xx

Sales		$980,000
Cost of Goods Sold		
Beginning Inventory	$ 440,000	
Purchases (net)	800,000	
Goods Available for Sale	$1,240,000	
Ending Inventory	500,000	
Cost of Goods Sold		740,000
Gross Margin from Sales		$240,000
Selling and Administrative Expenses		
Selling and Administrative Salaries Expense	$ 100,000	
Other Selling and Administrative Expenses	23,000	
Depreciation Expense	36,000	
Amortization Expense (Intangible Assets)	3,000	162,000
Income Before Income Taxes		$ 78,000
Income Taxes		25,000
Net Income		$ 53,000

Additional information: (a) accounts receivable (net) increased by $36,000, and accounts payable decreased by $52,000 during the year; (b) salaries payable at the end of the year were $14,000 more than last year; (c) the expired amount of prepaid insurance for the year is $1,000 and equals the decrease in the Prepaid Insurance account; and (d) income taxes payable decreased by $10,800 from last year.

Required

1. Prepare a schedule of cash flows from operating activities using the direct method.
2. Prepare a schedule of cash flows from operating activities using the indirect method.

Problem 27B-3. Cash Flows from Operating Activities *(L.O. 4)*

The income statement of Rosen Electronics, Inc. is as follows:

Rosen Electronics, Inc.
Income Statement
For the Year Ended February 28, 19x3

Sales		$1,838,000
Cost of Goods Sold		1,287,000
Gross Margin from Sales		$ 551,000
Operating Expenses (including Depreciation Expense of $42,860)		353,800
Operating Income		$ 197,200
Other Income (Expenses)		
Interest Expense	$(55,600)	
Dividend Income	28,400	
Loss on Sale of Investments	(24,200)	(51,400)
Income Before Income Taxes		$ 145,800
Income Taxes		43,000
Net Income		$ 102,800

Relevant accounts from the comparative balance sheets for February 28, 19x3 and 19x2 are as follows:

	19x3	19x2
Accounts Receivable (net)	$130,980	$ 97,840
Inventory	197,520	205,120
Prepaid Expenses	20,900	10,980
Accounts Payable	84,760	111,380
Accrued Liabilities	7,120	17,580
Income Taxes Payable	49,260	27,600

Required

1. Prepare a schedule of cash flows from operating activities using the direct method.
2. Prepare a schedule of cash flows from operating activities using the indirect method.

Problem 27B-4. The Statement of Cash Flows—Direct Method *(L.O. 6, 7)*

Meridian Corporation's 19x2 income statement and its comparative balance sheets as of December 31, 19x2 and 19x1 appear as follows:

Meridian Corporation
Income Statement
For the Year Ended December 31, 19x2

Sales		$804,500
Cost of Goods Sold		563,900
Gross Margin from Sales		$240,600
Operating Expenses (including Depreciation Expense of $23,400)		224,700
Income from Operations		$ 15,900
Other Income (Expenses)		
Gain on Disposal of Furniture and Fixtures	$ 3,500	
Interest Expense	(11,600)	(8,100)
Income Before Income Taxes		$ 7,800
Income Taxes		2,300
Net Income		$ 5,500

Meridian Corporation
Comparative Balance Sheets
December 31, 19x2 and 19x1

	19x2	19x1
Assets		
Cash	$ 82,400	$ 25,000
Accounts Receivable (net)	82,600	100,000
Merchandise Inventory	175,000	225,000
Prepaid Rent	1,000	1,500
Furniture and Fixtures	74,000	72,000
Accumulated Depreciation, Furniture and Fixtures	(21,000)	(12,000)
Total Assets	$394,000	$411,500
Liabilities and Stockholders' Equity		
Accounts Payable	$ 71,700	$100,200
Income Taxes Payable	700	2,200
Notes Payable (long-term)	20,000	10,000
Bonds Payable	50,000	100,000
Common Stock—$10 par value	120,000	100,000
Paid-in Capital in Excess of Par Value	90,720	60,720
Retained Earnings	40,880	38,380
Total Liabilities and Stockholders' Equity	$394,000	$411,500

Additional information about 19x2: (a) furniture and fixtures that cost $17,800 with accumulated depreciation of $14,400 were sold at a gain of $3,500; (b) furniture and fixtures were purchased in the amount of $19,800; (c) a $10,000 note payable was paid and $20,000 was borrowed on a new note; (d) bonds payable in the amount of $50,000 were converted into 2,000 shares of common stock; and (e) $3,000 in cash dividends were declared and paid.

Required

1. Prepare a statement of cash flows using the direct method. Include a supporting schedule of noncash investing and financing transactions. (Do not use a work sheet.)
2. What are the primary reasons for Meridian Corporation's large increase in cash from 19x1 to 19x2, despite its low net income?

Problem 27B-5. The Work Sheet and the Statement of Cash Flows—Indirect Method
(L.O. 6, 8)

Use the information for Meridian Corporation given in Problem 27B-4 to answer the following requirements.

Required

1. Prepare a work sheet to gather information for the preparation of the statement of cash flows.
2. From the information on the work sheet, prepare a statement of cash flows using the indirect approach. Include a supporting schedule of noncash investing and financing transactions.

Problem 27B-6.
The Work Sheet and the Statement of Cash Flows—Indirect Method
(L.O. 6, 7, 8)

The comparative balance sheets for Mateo Fabrics, Inc. for December 31, 19x3 and 19x2 appear below.

Mateo Fabrics, Inc.
Comparative Balance Sheets
December 31, 19x3 and 19x2

	19x3	19x2
Assets		
Cash	$ 77,120	$ 54,720
Accounts Receivable (net)	204,860	150,860
Inventory	225,780	275,780
Prepaid Expenses	—	40,000
Land	50,000	—
Building	274,000	—
Accumulated Depreciation, Building	(30,000)	—
Equipment	66,000	68,000
Accumulated Depreciation, Equipment	(29,000)	(48,000)
Patents	8,000	12,000
Total Assets	$846,760	$553,360
Liabilities and Stockholders' Equity		
Accounts Payable	$ 21,500	$ 73,500
Notes Payable (current)	20,000	—
Accrued Liabilities	—	24,600
Mortgage Payable	324,000	—
Common Stock—$20 par value	360,000	300,000
Paid-in Capital in Excess of Par Value	114,400	74,400
Retained Earnings	6,860	80,860
Total Liabilities and Stockholders' Equity	$846,760	$553,360

Additional information about Mateo Fabrics's operations during 19x3: (a) net loss, $56,000; (b) building and equipment depreciation expense amounts, $30,000 and $6,000, respectively; (c) equipment that cost $27,000 with accumulated depreciation of $25,000 sold for a gain of $10,600; (d) equipment purchases, $25,000; (e) patent amortization, $6,000; purchase of patent, $2,000; (f) borrowed funds by issuing notes payable, $50,000; notes payable repaid, $30,000; (g) land and building purchased for $324,000 by signing a mortgage for the total cost; (h) 3,000 shares of $20 par value common stock issued for a total of $100,000; and (i) cash dividend, $18,000.

Required

1. Prepare a work sheet for the statement of cash flows for Mateo Fabrics.
2. Prepare a statement of cash flows from the information in the work sheet using the indirect method.
3. Why did Mateo Fabrics have an increase in cash in a year in which it recorded a net loss of $56,000? Discuss and interpret.

Financial Decision Case

Hashimi Print Gallery
(L.O. 6, 7)

May Hashimi, president of Hashimi Print Gallery, Inc., is examining the following income statement, which has just been handed to her by her accountant, Lou Klein, CPA. After looking at the statement, Ms. Hashimi said to Mr. Klein, "Lou, the statement seems to be well done, but what I need to know is why I don't have enough cash to pay my bills this month. You show that I have earned $120,000 in 19x2, but I only have

$24,000 in the bank. I know I bought a building on a mortgage and paid a cash dividend of $48,000, but what else is going on?" Mr. Klein replied, "To answer your question, we have to look at comparative balance sheets and prepare another type of statement. Take a look at these balance sheets." The statements handed to Ms. Hashimi follow.

Hashimi Print Gallery, Inc.
Income Statement
For the Year Ended December 31, 19x2

Sales	$884,000
Cost of Goods Sold	508,000
Gross Margin from Sales	$376,000
Operating Expenses (including Depreciation Expense of $20,000)	204,000
Operating Income	$172,000
Interest Expense	24,000
Income Before Taxes	$148,000
Income Taxes	28,000
Net Income	$120,000

Hashimi Print Gallery, Inc.
Comparative Balance Sheets
December 31, 19x2 and 19x1

	19x2	19x1
Assets		
Cash	$ 24,000	$ 40,000
Accounts Receivable (net)	178,000	146,000
Inventory	240,000	180,000
Prepaid Expenses	10,000	14,000
Building	400,000	—
Accumulated Depreciation	(20,000)	—
Total Assets	$832,000	$380,000
Liabilities and Stockholders' Equity		
Accounts Payable	$ 74,000	$ 96,000
Income Taxes Payable	6,000	4,000
Mortgage Payable	400,000	—
Common Stock	200,000	200,000
Retained Earnings	152,000	80,000
Total Liabilities and Stockholders' Equity	$832,000	$380,000

Required

1. To what statement is Mr. Klein referring? From the information given, prepare the additional statement using the direct method.
2. Hashimi Print Gallery, Inc. has a cash problem despite profitable operations. Why?

Answers to Self-Test

1. a	3. c	5. c	7. a	9. a
2. d	4. c	6. d	8. c	10. d

LEARNING OBJECTIVES

1. Describe and discuss the objectives of financial statement analysis.
2. Describe and discuss the standards for financial statement analysis.
3. State the sources of information for financial statement analysis.
4. Identify the issues related to the evaluation of the quality of a company's earnings.
5. Apply horizontal analysis, trend analysis, and vertical analysis to financial statements.
6. Apply ratio analysis to financial statements in the study of an enterprise's liquidity, profitability, long-term solvency, and market tests.

CHAPTER 28

Financial Statement Analysis

This chapter presents a number of techniques intended to aid in decision making by highlighting important relationships in the financial statements. Effective decision making calls for the ability to sort out relevant information from a great many facts and to make adjustments for changing conditions. Very often, financial statements in a company's annual report run ten or more pages, including footnotes and other necessary disclosures. If these statements are to be useful in making decisions, decision makers must be able to see important relationships among figures and to make comparisons from year to year and from company to company. The many techniques that together are called **financial statement analysis** accomplish this goal. After studying this chapter, you should be able to meet the learning objectives listed on the left.

DECISION POINT

Moody's Investors Service

■ Moody's Investors Service rates the bonds and other indebtedness of companies on the basis of safety, that is, the likelihood of repayment. Investors rely on this service when making investments in bonds and other long-term company debt. The *Wall Street Journal* reported on September 19, 1990 that Moody's was reviewing $40 million of Ford Motor Company's debt for possible downgrade.[1] Moody's cited the softness in the U.S. auto market. Ford replied that the action was not warranted and questioned Moody's decision to review this debt because of what might be a short-term situation. One month later, on October 25, 1990, Moody's did in fact lower the rating on Ford's long-term debt. The rating was still in the high-grade area, but the downgrade meant that Ford would pay higher interest rates because, according to Moody's, its debt was not quite as secure as it had been. On what basis would Moody's decide to upgrade or lower the bond rating of a company?

According to the *Wall Street Journal*, "Moody's said it took the actions because Ford's returns and cash flow are vulnerable to a weaker U.S. economy, softer European sales, and volatile fuel prices. At the same time, Moody's said, Ford has committed to huge capital spending plans."[2] Ford Motor Company officials, according to the same article, said they were disappointed with the decision, as the reasons given were cyclical and transitional. This case demonstrates several features of the

1. "Ford Motor's Debt Reviewed by Moody's; Downgrade Is Possible," *Wall Street Journal*, September 19, 1990.
2. Bradley A. Stertz, "Ratings on Ford and Units' Debt Cut by Moody's," *Wall Street Journal*, October 25, 1990.

evaluation of a company's financial prospects. First, the analysis is rooted in the financial statements (for example, returns and cash flow). Second, it is directed toward the future (for example, capital spending plans). Third, the operating environment must be taken into consideration (for example, a weaker U.S. economy, softer European sales, and volatile fuel prices). Fourth, judgment is involved (for example, the disagreement between Moody's and Ford as to the seriousness of the situation). ■

Objectives of Financial Statement Analysis

OBJECTIVE 1
Describe and discuss the objectives of financial statement analysis

Users of financial statements fall into two broad categories: internal and external. Management is the main internal user. However, because those who run the company have inside information on operations, other techniques are available to them. Since these techniques are covered in managerial accounting courses, the main focus here is on the external use of financial analysis.

Creditors make loans in the form of trade accounts, notes, or bonds, on which they receive interest. They expect a loan to be repaid according to its terms. Investors buy capital stock, from which they hope to receive dividends and an increase in value. Both groups face risks. The creditor faces the risk that the debtor will fail to pay back the loan. The investor faces the risk that dividends will be reduced or not paid or that the market price of the stock will drop. For both, the goal is to achieve a return that makes up for the risk taken. In general, the greater the risk taken, the greater the return required as compensation.

Any one loan or any one investment can turn out badly. As a result, most creditors and investors put their funds into a **portfolio**, or group of loans or investments. The portfolio allows them to average both the return and the risk. Nevertheless, the portfolio is made up of a number of loans or stocks on which individual decisions must be made. It is in making these individual decisions that financial statement analysis is most useful. Creditors and investors use financial statement analysis in two general ways: (1) to judge past performance and current position and (2) to judge future potential and the risk connected with the potential.

Assessment of Past Performance and Current Position

Past performance is often a good indicator of future performance. Therefore, an investor or creditor looks at the trend of past sales, expenses, net income, cash flow, and return on investment not only as a means for judging management's past performance but also as a possible indicator of future performance. In addition, an analysis of current position will tell, for example, what assets the business owns and what liabilities must be paid. It will also tell what the cash position is, how much debt the company has in relation to equity, and how reasonable the inventories and receivables are. Knowing a company's past performance and current position is often important in achieving the second general objective of financial analysis.

Assessment of Future Potential and Related Risk

Information about the past and present is useful only to the extent that it has bearing on decisions concerning the future. An investor judges the potential earning ability of a company because that ability will affect the value of the market price of the company's stock and the amount of dividends the company will pay. A creditor judges the potential debt-paying ability of the company.

The potentials of some companies are easier to predict than those of others, and so there is less risk associated with them. The riskiness of the investment or loan depends on how easy it is to predict future profitability or liquidity. If an investor can predict with confidence that a company's earnings per share will be between $2.50 and $2.60 next year, the investment is less risky than if the earnings per share are expected to fall between $2.00 and $3.00. For example, the potential associated with an investment in an established and stable electric utility, or a loan to it, is relatively easy to predict on the basis of the company's past performance and current position. The potential associated with a small microcomputer manufacturer, on the other hand, may be much harder to predict. For this reason, the investment or loan to the electric utility carries less risk than the investment or loan to the small microcomputer company.

Often, in return for taking the greater risk, the investor in the microcomputer company will demand a higher expected return (increase in market price plus dividends) than will the investor in the utility company. Also, a creditor of the microcomputer company will need a higher interest rate and possibly more assurance of repayment (a secured loan, for instance) than a creditor to the utility company. The higher interest rate is payment to the creditor for assuming a higher risk.

Standards for Financial Statement Analysis

OBJECTIVE 2
Describe and discuss the standards for financial statement analysis

In using financial statement analysis, decision makers must judge whether the relationships they have found are favorable or unfavorable. Three standards of comparison often used are (1) rule-of-thumb measurements, (2) past performance of the company, and (3) industry norms.

Rule-of-Thumb Measures

Many financial analysts, investors, and lenders employ ideal or rule-of-thumb measures for key financial ratios. For example, it has long been thought that a current ratio (current assets divided by current liabilities) of 2:1 is acceptable. The credit rating firm of Dun & Bradstreet, in its *Key Business Ratios,* offers these guidelines:

Current debt to tangible net worth. Ordinarily, a business begins to pile up trouble when this relationship exceeds 80%.

Inventory to net working capital. Ordinarily, this relationship should not exceed 80%.

Although such measures may suggest areas that need further investigation, there is no proof they are the best for any company. A company with a higher than 2:1 current ratio may have a poor credit policy (resulting in accounts receivable being too large), too much or out-of-date inventory, or poor cash management. Another company may have a lower than 2:1 ratio resulting from excellent management in these three areas. Thus, rule-of-thumb measurements must be used with great care.

Past Performance of the Company

An improvement over the rule-of-thumb method is the comparison of financial measures or ratios of the same company over a period of time. This standard will at least give the analyst some basis for judging whether the measure or ratio is getting better or worse. It may also be helpful in showing possible future trends. However, since trends do reverse at times, such projections must be made with care. Another caution of trend analysis is that the past may not be a useful measure of adequacy. In other words, past performance may not be enough to meet present needs. For example, even if return on total investment improved from 3 percent last year to 4 percent this year, the 4 percent return may in fact not be adequate.

Industry Norms

One way of making up for the limitations of using past performance as a standard is to use industry norms. This standard will tell how the company being analyzed compares with other companies in the same industry. For example, suppose that other companies in an industry have an average rate of return on total investment of 8 percent. In such a case, 3 and 4 percent returns are probably not adequate. Industry norms can also be used to judge trends. Suppose that, because of a downward turn in the economy, a company's profit margin dropped from 12 to 10 percent. A finding that other companies in the same industry had an average drop in profit margin from 12 to 4 percent would indicate that the company being analyzed did relatively well.

There are three limitations to using industry norms as standards. First, two companies that seem to be in the same industry may not be strictly comparable. Consider two companies said to be in the oil industry. The main business of one may be marketing oil products it buys from other producers through service stations. The other, an international company, may discover, produce, refine, and market its own oil products. The operations of these two different companies cannot be compared because they are different.

Second, most large companies today operate in more than one industry. Some of these **diversified companies**, or **conglomerates**, operate in many unrelated industries. The individual segments of a diversified company generally have different rates of profitability and different degrees of risk. In analyzing the consolidated financial statements of these companies, it is often impossible to use industry norms as standards. There are simply no other companies that are closely enough related. One partial solution to this problem is a requirement by the Financial Accounting Standards Board in *Statement No. 14*. This requirement states that diversified companies must report revenues, income from operations, and identifiable assets for each of their operating segments. Depending on specific criteria, segment information may be reported for operations in different industries, in foreign markets, or to major customers.[3]

The third limitation of industry norms is that companies in the same industry with similar operations may use different acceptable accounting procedures. That is, inventories may be valued using different methods, or different depreciation methods may be used for similar assets. Even so, if little information about a company's prior performance is available, industry norms probably offer the best available standards for judging a company's current performance. They should be used with care.

DECISION POINT
Eastman Kodak Company

■ Most people think of Eastman Kodak Company as a maker of photographic film when in fact the company has diversified from its traditional business, which it calls imaging, into the information, chemical,

3. *Statement of Financial Accounting Standards No. 14*, "Financial Reporting for Segments of a Business Enterprise" (Stamford, Conn.: Financial Accounting Standards Board, 1976).

and health businesses. Since these businesses are very different, the overall success of Eastman Kodak Company as reflected in its financial statements will be affected by the relative amount of investment and earnings in each of its businesses. How is a financial analyst to assess the impact of these four businesses on the company's overall financial performance?

In accordance with FASB *Statement No. 14,* Eastman Kodak Company reports the information about these four segments, shown in Exhibit 28-1, in a note to the financial statements in its annual report. The analyst can learn much about the company from this information. For example, although the traditional imaging segment made up only about 38 percent of sales ($7,128 of $18,908) in 1990, it still produced the lion's share of earnings, about 57 percent ($1,611 of $2,844). The information segment produced sales about equal to the chemicals segment and the health segment but was much less profitable. In terms of assets, more assets were devoted to the health segment than to any other segment. Profitability ratios, such as profit margin, asset turnover, and return on assets, can be computed for each segment. The section on capital expenditures shows the analyst where the company is investing for the future. Although management is investing heavily in all segments, in the previous three years there have been increases in the information, chemical, and health segments. ■

Sources of Information

OBJECTIVE 3
State the sources of information for financial statement analysis

The external analyst is often limited to publicly available information about a company. The major sources of information about publicly held corporations are published reports, SEC reports, business periodicals, and credit and investment advisory services.

Published Reports

The annual report of a publicly held corporation is an important source of financial information. The major parts of this annual report are (1) management's analysis of the past year's operations, (2) the financial statements, (3) the notes to the statements, including the principal accounting procedures used by the company, (4) the auditors' report, and (5) a summary of operations for a five- or ten-year period. Most publicly held companies also publish **interim financial statements** each quarter. These reports present limited information in the form of condensed financial statements, which may be subject to a limited review or a full audit by the independent auditor. The interim statements are watched closely by the financial community for early signs of important changes in a company's earnings trend.[4]

SEC Reports

Publicly held corporations must file annual reports, quarterly reports, and current reports with the Securities and Exchange Commission (SEC). All such reports are available to the public at a small charge. The SEC calls for a standard

4. Accounting Principles Board, *Opinion No. 28,* "Interim Financial Reporting" (New York: American Institute of Certified Public Accountants, 1973); and *Statement of Financial Accounting Standards No. 3,* "Reporting Accounting Change in Interim Financial Statements" (Stamford, Conn.: Financial Accounting Standards Board, 1974).

Exhibit 28-1. Segment Information (in millions)

	1990	1989	1988
Sales, including intersegment sales			
Imaging	$ 7,128	$ 6,998	$ 6,642
Information	4,140	4,200	3,937
Chemicals	3,588	3,522	3,123
Health	4,349	4,009	3,597
Intersegment sales			
Imaging	(6)	(13)	(4)
Chemicals	(291)	(318)	(261)
Sales to unaffiliated customers	$18,908	$18,398	$17,034
Earnings (Losses) from operations[1]			
Imaging	$ 1,611	$ 821	$ 1,280
Information	5	(360)	311
Chemicals	602	643	630
Health	626	487	591
Earnings from operations	$ 2,844	$ 1,591	$ 2,812
Interest and other income (charges)			
Imaging	$ 10	$ 108	$ 78
Information	(8)	(35)	2
Chemicals	(6)	5	(4)
Health	(2)	3	(27)
Corporate	119	148	72
Interest expense	812	895	697
Litigation judgment	(888)	—	—
Earnings before income taxes	$ 1,257	$ 925	$ 2,236
Assets			
Imaging[2]	$ 6,623	$ 7,039	$ 7,186
Information	3,943	4,331	4,319
Chemicals	3,952	3,238	2,967
Health	8,464	7,793	7,278
Corporate[2] [3]	1,561	1,744	1,493
Intersegment receivables	(418)	(493)	(279)
Total assets at year end	$24,125	$23,652	$22,964
Depreciation expense			
Imaging	$ 371	$ 401	$ 345
Information	347	379	371
Chemicals	289	264	226
Health	161	137	115
Total depreciation expense	$ 1,168	$ 1,181	$ 1,057
Amortization expense			
Imaging	$ 18	$ 19	$ 20
Information	5	12	12
Chemicals	1	1	1
Health	117	113	93
Total amortization expense	$ 141	$ 145	$ 126
Capital expenditures			
Imaging	$ 679	$ 902	$ 854
Information	468	453	393
Chemicals	610	514	515
Health	280	249	152
Total capital expenditures	$ 2,037	$ 2,118	$ 1,914

(1) Earnings (Losses) from operations for 1989 are shown after deducting restructuring costs of $388 million for Imaging, $417 million for Information, $17 million for Chemicals and $53 million for Health.
(2) Data for 1989 and 1988 have been restated to conform to the 1990 presentation.
(3) Includes Cash, Marketable Securities and Eastman Kodak Credit Corporation assets.
Source: All information from Eastman Kodak Company reports reprinted courtesy of Eastman Kodak Company.

form for the annual report (Form 10-K) that is fuller than the published annual report. Form 10-K is, for this reason, a valuable source of information. It is available, free of charge, to stockholders of the company. The quarterly report (Form 10-Q) presents important facts about interim financial performance. The current report (Form 8-K) must be filed within a few days of the date of certain major events. It is often the first indicator of important changes that may affect the company's financial performance in the future.

Business Periodicals and Credit and Investment Advisory Services

Financial analysts must keep up with current events in the financial world. Probably the best source of financial news is the *Wall Street Journal,* which is published daily and is the most complete financial newspaper in the United States. Some helpful magazines, published every week or every two weeks, are *Forbes, Barron's, Fortune,* and the *Commercial and Financial Chronicle.*

For further details about the financial history of companies, the publications of such services as Moody's Investors Service and Standard & Poor's Industrial Surveys are useful. Data on industry norms, average ratios and relationships, and credit ratings are available from such agencies as Dun & Bradstreet Corporation. Dun & Bradstreet offers an annual analysis using 14 ratios of 125 industry groups classified as retailing, wholesaling, manufacturing, and construction in its *Key Business Ratios. Annual Statement Studies,* published by Robert Morris Associates, presents many facts and ratios for 223 different industries. Also, a number of private services are available to the analyst for a yearly fee.

An example of specialized financial reporting readily available to the public is Moody's *Handbook of Dividend Achievers,* which profiles companies that have increased their dividends consistently over the past ten years. A sample listing from this publication—of PepsiCo, Inc.—is shown in Exhibit 28-2. Within one page, a wealth of information about the company is summarized: the market action of the stock; summaries of the business operations, recent developments, and prospects; earnings and dividend data; annual financial data for the past six or seven years; and other information. From the data it is possible to do many of the trend analyses and ratios explained in this chapter.

Evaluating a Company's Quality of Earnings

OBJECTIVE 4
Identify the issues related to the evaluation of the quality of a company's earnings

It is clear from the preceding sections that current and expected earnings play an important role in the analysis of a company's prospects. In fact, a recent survey of two thousand members of the Association for Investment Management and Research indicated that the two most important economic indicators in evaluating common stocks were expected changes in earnings per share and expected return on equity.[5] Net income is an important component of both measures. Because of the importance of net income, or the "bottom line," in measures of a company's prospects, interest in evaluating the quality of the net income figure, or the *quality of earnings,* has become an important topic. The quality of a company's earnings may be affected by (1) the accounting methods and estimates the company's management chooses and/or (2) the nature of nonoperating items in the income statement.

5. Cited in *The Week in Review* (Deloitte Haskins & Sells), February 28, 1985.

Exhibit 28-2. Sample Listing from Moody's *Handbook of Dividend Achievers*

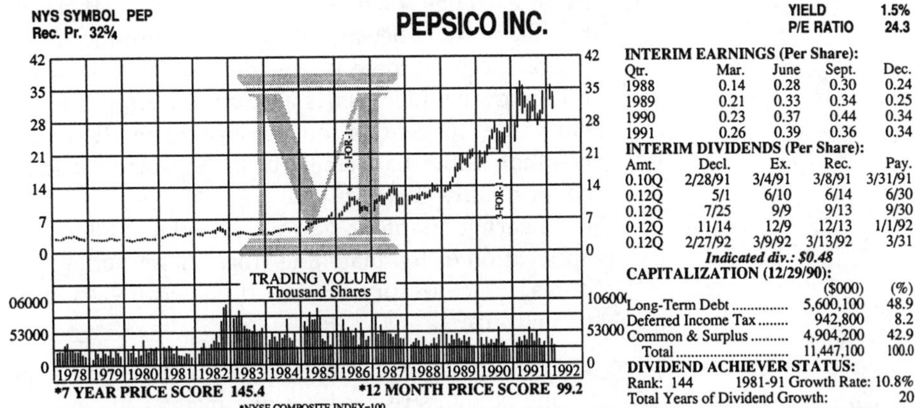

NYS SYMBOL PEP
Rec. Pr. 32¾

PEPSICO INC.

YIELD 1.5%
P/E RATIO 24.3

INTERIM EARNINGS (Per Share):

Qtr.	Mar.	June	Sept.	Dec.
1988	0.14	0.28	0.30	0.24
1989	0.21	0.33	0.34	0.25
1990	0.23	0.37	0.44	0.34
1991	0.26	0.39	0.36	0.34

INTERIM DIVIDENDS (Per Share):

Amt.	Decl.	Ex.	Rec.	Pay.
0.10Q	2/28/91	3/4/91	3/8/91	3/31/91
0.12Q	5/1	6/10	6/14	6/30
0.12Q	7/25	9/9	9/13	9/30
0.12Q	11/14	12/9	12/13	1/1/92
0.12Q	2/27/92	3/9/92	3/13/92	3/31

Indicated div.: $0.48

CAPITALIZATION (12/29/90):

	($000)	(%)
Long-Term Debt	5,600,100	48.9
Deferred Income Tax	942,800	8.2
Common & Surplus	4,904,200	42.9
Total	11,447,100	100.0

DIVIDEND ACHIEVER STATUS:
Rank: 144 1981-91 Growth Rate: 10.8%
Total Years of Dividend Growth: 20

RECENT DEVELOPMENTS: For the year ended 12/28/91, income from continuing operations was $1.08 billion, down slightly from last year. Sales increased 10% to $19.61 billion. Earnings for 1991 included a $119 million net charge for reorganization. Frito-Lay continued its price wars while Restaurants eroded from discounts offered by other eateries. International snack-foods was soft as profits declined in Britain and Spain. Profits from soft drinks rose moderately.

PROSPECTS: PEP will emerge poised from a cost basis, to compete more profitably in the near-term. Despite competition and an expected slowdown in growth of domestic per capita consumption of soft drinks, earnings should increase due to expansion overseas, increasing market share, and improving efficiencies. PEP recently formed a joint venture with Thomas J. Lipton Co. to create a new line of tea drinks to be distributed by Pepsi.

BUSINESS

PEPSICO operates on a worldwide basis within three distinct business segments; soft drinks, snack-foods and restaurants. The soft drinks segment manufactures concentrates, and markets Pepsi-Cola, Diet Pepsi, Mountain Dew, Slice and allied brands worldwide, and 7-up internationally. This segment also conducts soft drink bottling businesses principally in the United States. Snack Foods manufactures and markets snack chips through Frito-Lay Inc. Well known brands include: Doritos, Ruffles and Lays. Restaurants consists of Pizza Hut, Taco Bell and Kentucky Fried Chicken.

BUSINESS LINE ANALYSIS

(12/29/90)	Rev (%)	Inc(%)
Soft Drinks	36.6	34.5
Snack Foods	28.4	42.0
Restaurants	35.0	23.5
Total	100.0	100.0

ANNUAL EARNINGS AND DIVIDENDS PER SHARE

	12/28/91	12/29/90	12/30/89	12/31/88	12/28/87	12/27/86	12/28/85
Earnings Per Share	**1.35**	**1.37**	**1.13**	**0.97**	**[1] 0.77**	**0.58**	**[1] 0.50**
Dividends Per Share	**0.44**	**0.367**	**0.31**	**0.25**	**0.22**	**[2] 0.205**	**[3] 0.146**
Dividend Payout %	**32.6**	**26.8**	**27.1**	**26.2**	**28.7**	**35.3**	**29.0**

[1] Before disc. oper. [2] 3-for-1 stk split, 5/86 and 9/90 [3] Dec. div. paid in following year.

ANNUAL FINANCIAL DATA

	12/28/91	12/29/90	12/30/89	12/31/88	12/28/87	12/27/86	12/28/85
RECORD OF EARNINGS (IN MILLIONS):							
Total Revenues	19,607.9	17,802.7	15,242.4	13,007.0	11,485.2	9,290.8	8,056.7
Costs and Expenses	...	15,558.0	13,309.1	11,017.7	9,778.9	[1] 8,470.2	[1] 7,319.6
Depreciation & Amort	...	884.0	772.0	629.3	563.0	...	...
Operating Income	...	2,055.6	1,782.9	1,360.0	1,143.3	820.6	737.1
Inc Fr Cont Opers Bef Income Taxes	...	1,667.4	1,350.5	1,137.6	960.4	680.3	664.0
Provision for Inc Taxes	...	576.8	449.1	375.4	355.3	222.5	243.9
Net Income	[5] 1,080.2	[2] 1,090.6	901.4	762.2	[3] 605.1	457.8	[4] 420.1
Aver. Shs. Outstg. (000)	...	798,700	795,900	790,500	789,300	393,300	842,103

[1] Incl. Dep. [2] Before disc. op. dr$13,700,000. [3] Before disc. op. dr$10,300,000. [4] Before disc. op. cr$123,609,000. [5] Inc. restr. chg.

	12/28/91	12/29/90	12/30/89	12/31/88	12/28/87	12/27/86	12/28/85
BALANCE SHEET (IN MILLIONS):							
Tot Cash & Sh-tm Invests	...	1,815.7	1,533.9	1,617.8	1,352.6	920.5	912.3
Receivables, Net	...	1,414.7	1,239.7	979.3	885.6	820.2	1,024.2
Inventories	...	585.8	546.1	442.4	433.0	431.5	380.1
Gross Property	...	8,977.7	7,818.4	6,658.4	6,000.6	5,389.1	3,823.5
Accumulated Depreciation	...	3,266.8	2,688.2	2,195.9	1,883.2	1,549.0	1,251.7
Long-Term Debt	...	5,600.1	5,777.1	2,356.6	2,150.6	2,492.9	1,035.6
Capital Lease Obligations	...	...	...	...	129.3	139.7	127.1
Net Stockholders' Equity	...	4,904.2	3,891.1	3,161.0	2,508.6	2,059.1	1,837.7
Total Assets	...	17,143.4	15,126.7	11,135.3	9,022.7	8,028.6	5,861.2
Total Current Assets	...	4,081.4	3,550.8	3,264.7	2,939.6	2,503.8	2,794.5
Total Current Liabilities	...	4,770.5	3,691.8	3,873.6	2,722.8	2,223.1	1,835.7
Net Working Capital	...	d689.1	d141.0	d608.9	216.8	280.7	958.8
Year End Shs Outstg (000)	...	788,400	791,100	863,100	781,239	780,957	789,354
STATISTICAL RECORD:							
Operating Profit Margin %	...	11.5	11.7	10.5	10.0	8.8	9.1
Book Value Per Share	...	...	...	0.67	1.44	0.99	2.09
Return on Equity %	...	22.2	23.2	24.1	24.1	22.2	22.9
Return on Assets %	...	6.4	6.0	6.8	6.7	5.7	7.2
Average Yield %	1.5	1.6	1.8	2.0	1.9	2.1	2.3
P/E Ratio	26.4-17.4	20.3-13.1	19.5-11.2	14.9-10.3	18.3-11.0	20.5-12.7	16.8-9.0
Price Range	35⅝-23½	27⅞-18	22-12⅝	14½-10	14⅛-8½	11⅞-7⅜	8⅜-4½

Statistics are as originally reported.

OFFICERS:
D.W. Calloway, Chmn. & C.E.O.
R.G. Dettmer, Exec. V.P. & C.F.O.
E.V. Lahey, Jr., Sr. V.P., Gen. Coun. & Sec.
L. Schutzman, Sr. V.P. & Treas.
J.T. Cahill, V.P. & Asset. Treas.
C.E. Morf, V.P. & Asst. Treas.
INCORPORATED: NC, Dec., 1986
PRINCIPAL OFFICE: Purchase, NY 10577

TELEPHONE NUMBER: (914) 253-2000
NO. OF EMPLOYEES: 308,000
ANNUAL MEETING: In May
SHAREHOLDERS: 107,000
INSTITUTIONAL HOLDINGS:
No. of Institutions: 917
Shares Held: 428,112,151

REGISTRAR(S): Manufacturers Hanover Trust Co., New York, NY 10001

TRANSFER AGENT(S): Manufacturers Hanover Trust Co., New York, NY 10001

Source: Reprinted by permission from *Moody's Handbook of Dividend Achievers*, 1992.

Choice of Accounting Methods and Estimates

There are two aspects to the choice of accounting methods that affect the quality of earnings. First, some accounting methods are by nature more conservative than others because they tend to produce a lower net income in the current period. Second, there is considerable latitude in the choice of the estimated useful life over which assets are written off and in the amount of estimated residual value. In general, an accounting method or estimated useful life and/or residual value that results in lower current earnings is considered to produce better quality earnings.

In earlier chapters, various acceptable alternative methods were used in the application of the matching rule. These methods are based on allocation procedures, which in turn are based on certain assumptions. Here are some of these procedures:

1. For estimating uncollectible accounts expense: percentage of net sales method and accounts receivable aging method
2. For pricing the ending inventory: average-cost method; first-in, first-out (FIFO) method; and last-in, first-out (LIFO) method
3. For estimating depreciation expense: straight-line method, production method, sum-of-the-years'-digits method, and declining-balance method
4. For estimating depletion expense: production (extraction) method
5. For estimating amortization of intangibles: straight-line method

All these procedures are designed to allocate the costs of assets to the periods in which those costs contribute to the production of revenue. They are based on a determination of the benefits to the current period (expenses) versus the benefits to future periods (assets). They are estimates, and the period or periods benefited cannot be demonstrated conclusively. They are also subjective, because in practice it is hard to justify one method of estimation over another.

For this reason, it is important for the accountant as well as the financial statement user to understand the possible effects of different accounting procedures on net income and financial position. For example, suppose that two companies have similar operations, but that one uses FIFO for inventory pricing and the straight-line (SL) method for computing depreciation and the other uses LIFO for inventory pricing and the sum-of-the-years'-digits (SYD) method for computing depreciation. The income statements of the two companies might appear as follows:

	FIFO and SL	LIFO and SYD
Sales	$500,000	$500,000
Goods Available for Sale	$300,000	$300,000
Less Ending Inventory	60,000	50,000
Cost of Goods Sold	$240,000	$250,000
Gross Margin from Sales	$260,000	$250,000
Less: Depreciation Expense	$ 40,000	$ 70,000
Other Expenses	170,000	170,000
Total Operating Expenses	$210,000	$240,000
Net Income	$ 50,000	$ 10,000

This fivefold difference in income stems only from the differences in accounting methods. Differences in the estimated lives and residual values of the plant assets could cause an even greater variation. In practice, of course, differences in net income occur for many reasons, but the user must be aware of the discrepancies that can occur as a result of the methods chosen by management.

The existence of these alternatives could cause problems in the interpretation of financial statements were it not for the conventions of full disclosure and consistency described in the chapter on accounting concepts and classified financial statements. Full disclosure requires that management explain the significant accounting policies used in preparing the financial statements in a note to the statements. Consistency requires that the same accounting procedure be followed from year to year. If a change in procedure is made, the nature of the change and its monetary effect must be explained in a note.

Nature of Nonoperating Items

As seen in the chapter on retained earnings and corporate income statements, the corporate income statement consists of several components. The top of the statement presents earnings from current ongoing operations, called income from operations. The lower part of the statement can contain such nonoperating items as discontinued operations, extraordinary gains and losses, and effects of accounting changes. These items may drastically affect the bottom line, or net income, of the company. For example, Eastman Kodak Company had an unusual charge of $888 million in 1990 that related primarily to the discontinuance of its instant camera line and the loss of a patent suit with Polaroid. The loss had a detrimental effect on reported net earnings in 1990.

Such nonoperating items should be taken into consideration when interpreting a company's earnings. For example, in 1983 U.S. Steel (now USX) made an apparent turnaround by reporting first quarter earnings of $1.35 a share versus a deficit of $1.31 a year earlier. However, the "improved" earnings included a gain from sales of assets of $.45 per share and sale of tax benefits on newly acquired assets of $.40 per share, as well as other items totaling $.61 per share. These items total $1.46, an amount greater than the reported earnings for the year.[6] The opposite effect can also occur. For the first six months of 1984, Texas Instruments reported a loss of $112 million compared with a profit of $64.5 million the previous year. The loss was caused by write-offs of $58 million for nonoperating losses, $83 million for inventory, and $37 million for increased reserves for rebates, price protection for retailers, and returned inventory.[7] In reality, this large write-off was a positive step on Texas Instruments' part because getting out of the low-profit home computer business meant that TI's future cash flows would not be drained by those operations.

For practical reasons, the trends and ratios in the sections that follow are based on the assumption that net income and other components are comparable from year to year and from company to company. However, in making interpretations the astute analyst will always look beyond the ratios to the quality of the components.

Tools and Techniques of Financial Analysis

Few numbers by themselves mean very much. It is their relationship to other numbers or their change from one period to another that is important. The tools of financial analysis are intended to show relationships and changes. Among

6. Dan Dorfman, "Three Well-Known Stocks with Earnings of Dubious Quality," *Chicago Tribune*, June 28, 1984.
7. "Loss at Texas Instruments Hits $119.2 Million," *Wall Street Journal*, November 14, 1984.

the more widely used of these financial analysis techniques are horizontal analysis, trend analysis, vertical analysis, and ratio analysis.

Horizontal Analysis

OBJECTIVE 5
Apply horizontal analysis, trend analysis, and vertical analysis to financial statements

Generally accepted accounting principles call for presenting comparative financial statements that give the current year's and past year's financial information. A common starting point for studying such statements is **horizontal analysis,** which begins with the computation of dollar amount changes and percentage changes from the previous to the current year. The percentage change must be figured to show how the size of the change relates to the size of the amounts involved. A change of $1 million in sales is not so drastic as a change of $1 million in net income, because sales is a larger amount than net income.

Exhibits 28-3 and 28-4 present the comparative balance sheets and income statements, respectively, for Eastman Kodak Company, with the dollar and percentage changes shown. The percentage change is computed as follows:

$$\text{Percentage change} = 100\left(\frac{\text{amount of change}}{\text{previous year amount}}\right)$$

The **base year** in any set of data is always the first year being studied. For example, from 1989 to 1990, Kodak's total assets increased by $473 million, from $23,652 million to $24,125 million, or by 2.0 percent, computed as follows:

$$\text{Percentage increase} = 100\left(\frac{\$473\text{ million}}{\$23{,}652\text{ million}}\right) = 2.0\%$$

An examination of the comparative balance sheet in Exhibit 28-3 shows little change in the asset categories from 1989 to 1990. As shown above, there was an overall growth in total assets of 2.0 percent. Although overall total liabilities and deferred credits shows about the same increase, there was a change in the composition of liabilities. Current liabilities increased by 9.0 percent while long-term borrowings decreased by 5.2 percent.

Several interesting observations can be made about the income statement. Sales outside the United States were strong, showing an 8.6 percent increase, but sales in the United States declined by 1.8 percent. Earnings from operations showed a strong increase of 78.8 percent. This was mostly caused by the restructuring costs of $875 million, which lowered earnings in 1989. The notes to the financial statements reveal that the restructuring costs consisted primarily of write-offs of inventory and other assets as well as a provision for separation costs for employees leaving the company. Despite the increase in earnings from operations, earnings before income taxes and net earnings were up only 35.9 percent and 32.9 percent, respectively, because of a litigation judgment in 1990. The restructuring costs in 1989 and the litigation costs in 1990 are important considerations in analyzing the comparative income statements.

Care also has to be taken in the analysis of percentage changes. For example, in Exhibit 28-4, one might view the 12.8 percent increase in investment income as greater than the 9.3 percent decrease in interest expense. In dollars, though, the decrease in interest expense was more than four times the increase in investment income ($83 million versus $19 million). Dollar amounts and percentages must be considered together.

Trend Analysis

A variation of horizontal analysis is **trend analysis,** in which percentage changes are calculated for several successive years instead of two years. Trend

Exhibit 28-3. Comparative Balance Sheets with Horizontal Analysis

Eastman Kodak Company
Consolidated Balance Sheets (Statements of Financial Position)
December 31, 1990 and 1989

	(In millions)*		Increase (Decrease)	
	1990	1989	Amount	Percentage
Assets				
Current Assets				
Cash and cash equivalents	$ 735	$ 1,095	$(360)	(32.9)
Marketable securities	181	184	(3)	(1.6)
Receivables	4,333	4,245	88	2.1
Inventories	2,425	2,507	(82)	(3.3)
Deferred income tax charges	653	306	347	113.4
Prepaid charges applicable to future operations	281	254	27	10.6
Total Current Assets	$ 8,608	$ 8,591	$ 17	.2
Properties				
Land, buildings, machinery, and equipment at cost	$17,648	$16,774	$ 874	5.2
Less accumulated depreciation	8,670	8,146	524	6.4
Net Properties	$ 8,978	$ 8,628	$ 350	4.1
Other Assets				
Unamortized goodwill	$ 4,448	$ 4,579	$(131)	(2.9)
Long-term receivables and other noncurrent assets	2,091	1,854	237	12.8
Total Assets	$24,125	$23,652	$ 473	2.0
Liabilities and Shareowners' Equity				
Current Liabilities				
Payables	$ 6,413	$ 6,073	$ 340	5.6
Taxes—income and other	588	338	250	74.0
Dividends payable	162	162	0	.0
Total Current Liabilities	$ 7,163	$ 6,573	$ 590	9.0
Other Liabilities and Deferred Credits				
Long-term borrowings	$ 6,989	$ 7,376	$(387)	(5.2)
Other long-term liabilities	1,406	1,371	35	2.6
Deferred income tax credits	1,830	1,690	140	8.3
Total Liabilities and Deferred Credits	$17,388	$17,010	$ 378	2.2
Shareowners' Equity				
Common stock, par value $2.50 per share	$ 941	$ 940	$ 1	.1
Retained earnings	7,855	7,761	94	1.2
	$ 8,796	$ 8,701	$ 95	1.1
Less treasury stock at cost	2,059	2,059	0	.0
Total Shareowners' Equity	$ 6,737	$ 6,642	$ 95	1.4
Total Liabilities And Shareowners' Equity	$24,125	$23,652	$ 473	2.0

*Certain amounts have been restated as a result of the consolidation of the Eastman Kodak Credit Corporation.

analysis is important because, with its long-run view, it may point to basic changes in the nature of the business. Besides comparative financial statements, most companies give out a summary of operations and data on other key indicators for five or more years. Selected items from Kodak's summary of operations together with trend analysis are presented in Exhibit 28-5.

Exhibit 28-4. Comparative Income Statements with Horizontal Analysis

Eastman Kodak Company
Consolidated Statements of Earnings
For the Years Ended December 31, 1990 and 1989

	(In millions*)		Increase (Decrease)	
	1990	1989	Amount	Percentage
Sales to: Customers in the United States	$10,118	$10,302	$ (184)	(1.8)
Customers outside the United States	8,790	8,096	694	8.6
Total Sales	$18,908	$18,398	$ 510	2.8
Cost of goods sold	$10,966	$11,075	$ (109)	(1.0)
Sales, advertising, distribution, and administrative expenses	5,098	4,857	241	5.0
Restructuring costs	—	875	(875)	(100.0)
Total Costs and Expenses	$16,064	$16,807	$ (743)	(4.4)
Earnings from Operations	$ 2,844	$ 1,591	$1,253	78.8
Investment income	167	148	19	12.8
Interest expense	(812)	(895)	83	9.3
Litigation judgment	(888)	—	(888)	—
Other income (charges)	(54)	81	(135)	(166.7)
Earnings before income taxes	$ 1,257	$ 925	$ 332	35.9
Provision for United States, foreign, and other income taxes	554	396	158	39.9
Net Earnings	$ 703	$ 529	$ 174	32.9
Average number of common shares outstanding	324.5	324.3	.2	.1
Net earnings per share	$2.17	$1.63	$0.54	33.1

*Except per share data.

Trend analysis uses an **index number** to show changes in related items over a period of time. For index numbers, one year, the base year, is equal to 100 percent. Other years are measured in relation to that amount. For example, the 1990 index of 163.7 for sales was figured as follows:

$$\text{Index} = 100\left(\frac{\text{index year amount}}{\text{base year amount}}\right) = 100\left(\frac{\$18{,}908}{\$11{,}550}\right) = 163.7$$

An index number of 163.7 means that 1990 sales are 163.7 percent or 1.637 times 1986 sales.

A study of the trend analysis in Exhibit 28-5 shows that earnings from operations has been more volatile than sales and that net earnings per common share has been more volatile than dividends per share. Sales rose steadily over the five-year period, while dividends per share rose over the first four years and remained the same in years four and five. After a decrease in 1989, earnings from operations and net earnings per share rebounded in 1990. Over the five-year period, earnings from operations increased more rapidly than sales (392.8 versus 163.7). The contrasting volatility and steadiness are dramatically shown when graphed, as presented in Figure 28-1.

Vertical Analysis

In **vertical analysis** percentages are used to show the relationship of the different parts to the total in a single statement. The accountant sets a total figure in

Exhibit 28-5. Trend Analysis

Eastman Kodak Company
Summary of Operations
Selected Data
(Sales and Net Earnings in Millions)

	1990	1989	1988	1987	1986
Sales	$18,908	$18,398	$17,034	$13,305	$11,550
Earnings from Operations	2,844	1,591	2,812	2,078	724
Per Common Share*					
Net Earnings*	2.17	1.63	4.31	3.52	1.10
Dividends*	2.00	2.00	1.90	1.71	1.63
Trend Analysis (in percentages)					
Sales	163.7	159.3	147.5	115.2	100.0
Earnings from Operations	392.8	219.8	388.4	287.0	100.0
Per Common Share					
Net Earnings	197.3	148.2	391.8	320.0	100.0
Dividends	122.7	122.7	116.6	104.9	100.0

*Per share data restated to reflect 3-for-2 stock splits in 1985 and 1987.

the statement equal to 100 percent and computes the percentage of the total of each component of that figure. (The figure would be total assets or total liabilities and stockholders' equity on the balance sheet, and revenues or sales on the income statement.) The resulting statement of percentages is called a **common-size statement**. Common-size balance sheets and income statements for Kodak

Figure 28-1. Trend Analysis for Eastman Kodak Company

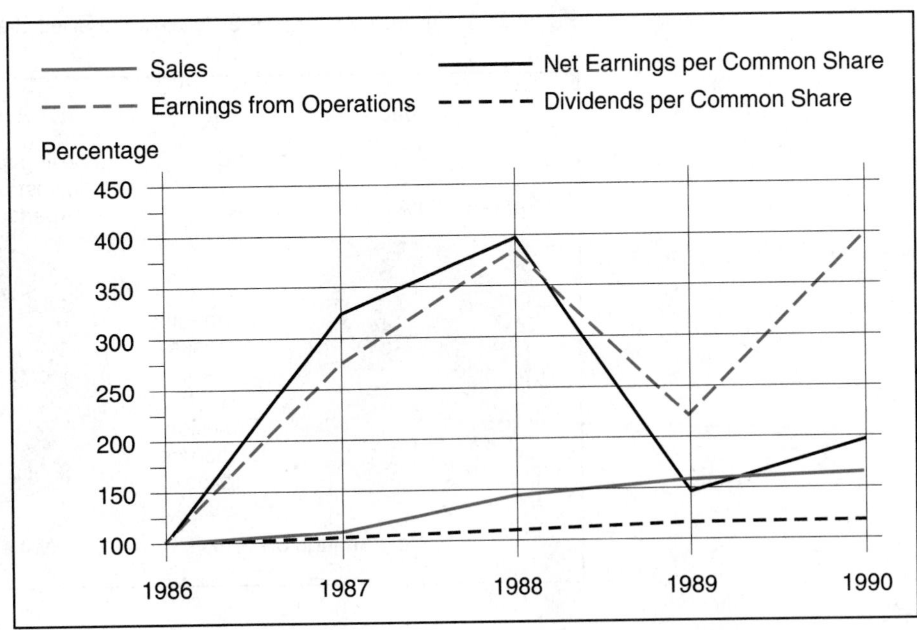

Figure 28-2. Common-Size Balance Sheets Presented Graphically

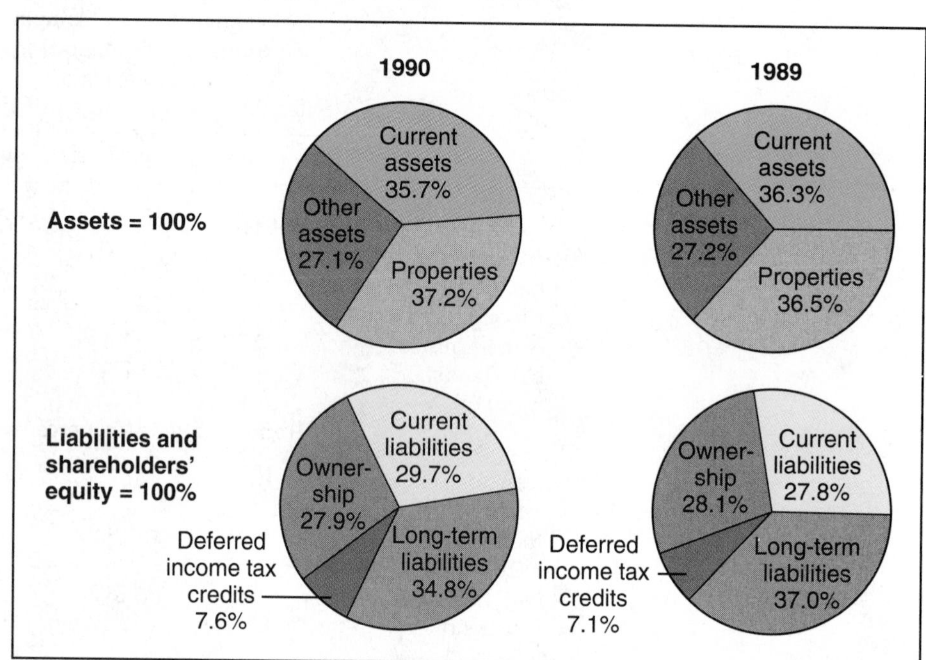

are shown in pie-chart form in Figures 28-2 and 28-3, and in financial-statement form in Exhibits 28-6 and 28-7.

Vertical analysis is useful for comparing the importance of certain components in the operation of the business. It is also useful for pointing out important changes in the components from one year to the next in comparative common-size statements. For Kodak, the composition of assets in Exhibit 28-6 did not change significantly from 1989 to 1990. About the same proportion of assets was in properties (37.2 percent versus 36.5 percent) and in current assets (35.7

Figure 28-3. Common-Size Income Statements Presented Graphically

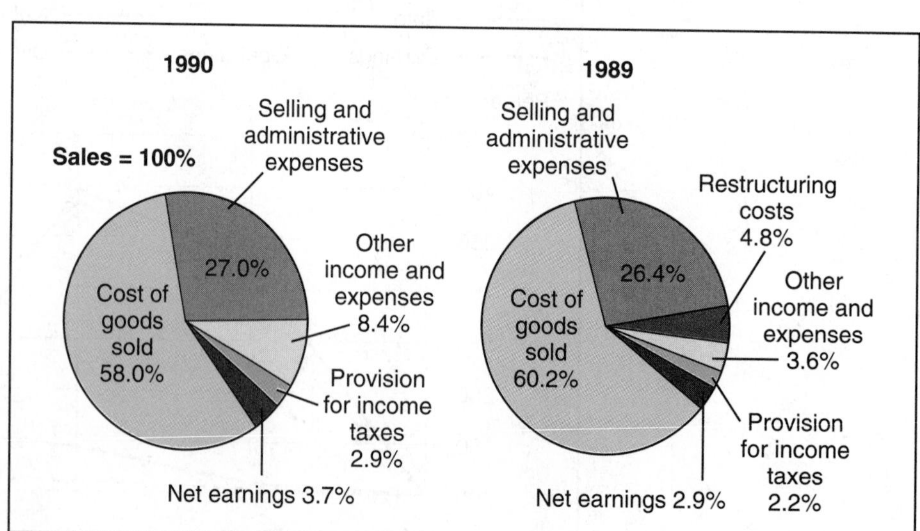

Exhibit 28-6. Common-Size Balance Sheets

Eastman Kodak Company
Common-Size Balance Sheets
December 31, 1990 and 1989

	1990*	1989*
Assets		
Current Assets	35.7%	36.3%
Properties (less Accumulated Depreciation)	37.2	36.5
Other Assets	27.1	27.2
Total Assets	100.0%	100.0%
Liabilities		
Current Liabilities	29.7%	27.8%
Long-Term Liabilities	34.8	37.0
Deferred Income Tax Credits	7.6	7.1
Total Liabilities and Deferred Credits	72.1%	71.9%
Ownership		
Common Stock	3.9%	4.0%
Retained Earnings	32.6	32.8
Treasury Stock at Cost	(8.5)	(8.7)
Total Ownership	27.9%	28.1%
Total Liabilities and Ownership	100.0%	100.0%

*Results are rounded in some cases to equal 100%.

percent versus 36.3 percent) in 1990 as in 1989. The composition of liabilities shows more change. Current liabilities increased from 27.8 percent to 29.7 percent. Correspondingly, long-term liabilities decreased from 37.0 percent to 34.8 percent.

The common-size income statements (Exhibit 28-7) show the importance of the decrease in costs and expenses from 91.4 to 85.0 percent of sales. Two factors caused this decrease. One was the one-time decrease in restructuring costs, but the other was a very favorable decrease in cost of goods sold from 60.2 percent to 58.0 percent. This decrease was a major cause of the increase in earnings from operations from 8.6 to 15.0 percent. Notice, however, the negative impact of the increase in other income and expenses from 3.6 percent to 8.4 percent and the increase in income taxes from 2.2 percent to 2.9 percent. Consequently, earnings as a percent of sales actually increased from 2.9 percent in 1989 to only 3.7 percent in 1990.

Common-size statements are often used to make comparisons between companies. They allow an analyst to compare the operating and financing characteristics of two companies of different size in the same industry. For example, the analyst may want to compare Kodak to other companies in terms of the percentage of total assets financed by debt or the percentage of general administrative and selling expenses to sales and revenues. Common-size statements would show these and other relationships.

Exhibit 28-7. Common-Size Income Statements

Eastman Kodak Company
Common-Size Income Statements (Statements of Earnings)
For Years Ended December 31, 1990 and 1989

	1990*	1989*
Sales	100.0%	100.0%
Costs and Expenses		
Cost of Goods Sold	58.0%	60.2%
Selling and Administrative Expenses	27.0	26.4
Restructuring Costs	—	4.8
Total Costs and Expenses	85.0%	91.4%
Earnings from Operations	15.0%	8.6%
Other Income and (Expenses)	(8.4)	(3.6)
Earnings Before Income Taxes	6.6%	5.0%
Provision for Income Taxes	2.9	2.2
Net Earnings	3.7%	2.9%

*Rounding causes some additions and subtractions not to total.

Ratio Analysis

Ratio analysis is an important way to state meaningful relationships between two components of a financial statement. To be most useful, a ratio must also include a study of the underlying data. Ratios are guides or short cuts that are useful in evaluating the financial position and operations of a company and in comparing them to results in previous years or to other companies. The primary purpose of ratios is to point out areas needing further investigation. They should be used in connection with a general understanding of the company and its environment. Ratios for financial analysis were introduced in the chapter on accounting concepts and classified financial statements. The following section briefly reviews the ratios covered in that chapter and expands the analysis to cover additional ratios.

Ratios may be expressed in several ways. For example, a ratio of net income of $100,000 to sales of $1,000,000 may be stated as (1) net income is 1/10 or 10 percent of sales, (2) the ratio of sales to net income is 10 to 1 (10:1) or 10 times net income, or (3) for every dollar of sales, the company has an average net income of 10 cents.

Survey of Commonly Used Ratios

In the following sections, ratio analysis is applied to four objectives: the evaluation of (1) liquidity, (2) profitability, (3) long-term solvency, and (4) market strength. The chapter on accounting concepts and classified financial statements addressed the first two objectives in an introductory way. Here we expand the evaluation to include other ratios related to those objectives and to introduce two new objectives. Data for the analyses come from the financial statements of Kodak presented in Exhibits 28-3 and 28-4. Other data are presented as needed.

Evaluating Liquidity

OBJECTIVE 6
Apply ratio analysis to financial statements in the study of an enterprise's liquidity, profitability, long-term solvency, and market tests

Liquidity is the ability to pay bills when they are due and to meet unexpected needs for cash. The ratios that relate to this goal all have to do with working capital or some part of it, because it is out of working capital that debts are paid as they mature. Some common ratios connected with evaluating liquidity are the current ratio, the quick ratio, receivable turnover, and inventory turnover.

Current Ratio. The **current ratio** expresses the relationship of current assets to current liabilities. It is widely used as a broad indicator of a company's liquidity and short-term debt-paying ability. The ratio for Kodak for 1990 and 1989 is figured as follows:

Current Ratio	1990	1989
$\frac{\text{Current assets}}{\text{Current liabilities}}$	$\frac{\$8,608}{\$7,163} = 1.20$	$\frac{\$8,591}{\$6,573} = 1.31$

The current ratio for Kodak suggests a decrease in the company's liquidity from 1989 to 1990.

Quick Ratio. One of the current ratio's faults is that it does not take into account the make-up of current assets. They may appear to be large enough, but they may not have the proper balance. Clearly, a dollar of cash or even accounts receivable is more readily available to meet obligations than is a dollar of most kinds of inventory. The **quick ratio** is designed to overcome this problem by measuring short-term liquidity. That is, it measures the relationship of the more liquid current assets (cash, marketable securities or short-term investments, and receivables) to current liabilities. This ratio for Kodak for 1990 and 1989 is figured as follows:

Quick Ratio	1990	1989
$\frac{\text{Cash + marketable securities + receivables}}{\text{Current liabilities}}$	$\frac{\$735 + \$181 + \$4,333}{\$7,163}$	$\frac{\$1,095 + \$184 + \$4,245}{\$6,573}$
	$= \frac{\$5,249}{\$7,163} = 0.73$	$= \frac{\$5,524}{\$6,573} = 0.84$

This ratio, too, suggests a decrease in liquidity from 1989 to 1990.

Receivable Turnover. The ability of a company to collect its credit sales in a timely way affects its liquidity. The **receivable turnover** ratio measures the relative size of a company's accounts receivable and the success of its credit and collection policies. It shows how many times, on average, the receivables were turned into cash during the period. However, it can also be affected by external factors, such as economic conditions and interest rates.

Turnover ratios usually consist of one balance sheet account and one income statement account. The receivable turnover is computed by dividing net sales by average accounts receivable. Theoretically, the numerator should be net credit sales, but the amount of net credit sales is rarely made available in public reports. So we will use total net sales. Further, in this ratio and others in which an average is required, we will take the beginning and ending balances and divide by 2. If we had internal financial data, it would be better to use monthly balances to find the average, because the balances of receivables, inventories, and other accounts can vary widely during the year. In fact, many companies choose a fiscal year that begins and ends at a low period of the business cycle, when inventories and receivables may be at the lowest levels of the year. When the previous year's balance is not available for computing the average, it is common practice to use the ending balance for the current year.

Using a 1988 accounts receivable ending balance of $4,071 million, Kodak's receivable turnover is computed as follows:

Receivable Turnover	1990	1989
$\dfrac{\text{Net sales}}{\text{Average accounts receivable}}$	$\dfrac{\$18{,}908}{(\$4{,}333 + \$4{,}245)/2}$	$\dfrac{\$18{,}398}{(\$4{,}245 + \$4{,}071)/2}$
	$= \dfrac{\$18{,}908}{\$4{,}289} = 4.41$ times	$= \dfrac{\$18{,}398}{\$4{,}158} = 4.42$ times

Within reasonable ranges, the higher the turnover ratio the better. With a higher turnover, the company is turning receivables into cash at a faster pace. The speed at which receivables are turned over depends on the company's credit terms. Since a company's credit terms are usually stated in days, such as 2/10, n/30, it is helpful to convert the receivable turnover to **average days' sales uncollected**. This conversion is made by dividing the length of the accounting period (usually 365 days) by the receivable turnover (as computed above), as follows:

Average Days' Sales Uncollected	1990	1989
$\dfrac{\text{Days in year}}{\text{Receivable turnover}}$	$\dfrac{365 \text{ days}}{4.41} = 82.8$ days	$\dfrac{365 \text{ days}}{4.42} = 82.6$ days

In the case of Kodak, both the receivable turnover and the average days' sales uncollected were about the same in 1989 and 1990. The average accounts receivable was turned over about 4.4 times both years. This means Kodak had to wait on average about 82 or 83 days to receive payment for credit sales.

Inventory Turnover. Inventory is two steps removed from cash (sale and collection). The **inventory turnover** ratio measures the relative size of inventory. The proportion of assets tied up in inventory, of course, affects the amount of cash available to pay maturing debts. Inventory should be maintained at the best level to support production and sales. In general, however, a smaller, faster-moving inventory means that the company has less cash tied up in inventory. There is also less chance for the inventory to become spoiled or out of date. A build-up in inventory may mean that a recession or some other factor is preventing sales from keeping pace with purchasing and production.

Using a 1988 ending inventory balance of $3,025 million, inventory turnover for 1990 and 1989 at Kodak is computed as shown at the top of the next page. There was an increase in inventory turnover from 1989 to 1990.

Inventory Turnover	1990	1989
Cost of goods sold / Average inventory	$10,966 / ($2,425 + $2,507)/2	$11,075 / ($2,507 + $3,025)/2
	= $10,966 / $2,466 = 4.45 times	= $11,075 / $2,766 = 4.00 times

Evaluating Profitability

A company's long-run survival depends on its being able to earn a satisfactory income. Investors become and remain stockholders for only one reason: They believe that the dividends and capital gains they will receive will be greater than the returns on other investments of about the same risk. An evaluation of a company's past earning power may give the investor a better basis for decision making. Also, as pointed out in the chapter on accounting concepts and classified financial statements, a company's ability to earn an income usually affects its liquidity position. For this reason, evaluating profitability is important to both investors and creditors. In judging the profitability of Kodak, five ratios will be presented: profit margin, asset turnover, return on assets, return on equity, and earnings per share. Except for earnings per share, all these ratios were introduced in the discussion of classified financial statements.

Profit Margin. The **profit margin** ratio measures the percentage of each revenue dollar that contributes to net income. It is computed for Kodak as follows:

Profit Margin[8]	1990	1989
Net income / Net sales	$703 / $18,908 = 3.7%	$529 / $18,398 = 2.9%

The ratio confirms what was clear from the common-size income statements (Exhibit 28-7): that the profit margin increased from 1989 (2.9 percent) to 1990 (3.7 percent).

Asset Turnover. **Asset turnover** is a measure of how efficiently assets are used to produce sales. It shows how many dollars in sales are produced by each dollar invested in assets. In other words, it tells how many times in the period assets were "turned over" in sales. The higher the asset turnover, the more concentrated is the use of assets. Using the data for Kodak from Exhibits 28-3 and 28-4 and 1988 total assets of $22,964 million, the asset turnover for 1990 and 1989 is computed as follows:

Asset Turnover	1990	1989
Net sales / Average total assets	$18,908 / ($24,125 + $23,652)/2	$18,398 / ($23,652 + $22,964)/2
	= $18,908 / $23,888.50	= $18,398 / $23,308
	= .79 times	= .79 times

8. In comparing companies in an industry, some analysts use net income before income taxes as the numerator to eliminate the effect of differing tax rates among firms.

Compared to companies in other industries, Kodak needs a large investment in assets for each dollar of sales. A retailer may have an asset turnover of between 4.0 and 6.0. In Kodak's case, however, asset turnover was only .79 in 1989 and in 1990. This means that Kodak makes sales of a little less than one dollar for each dollar of assets.

Return on Assets. The best overall measure of the earning power or profitability of a company is **return on assets**, which measures the amount earned on each dollar of assets invested. The return on assets for 1990 and 1989 for Kodak is computed as follows:

Return on Assets[9]	1990	1989
$\frac{\text{Net income}}{\text{Average total assets}}$	$\frac{\$703}{\$23{,}888.50} = 2.9\%$	$\frac{\$529}{\$23{,}308} = 2.3\%$

Kodak's return on assets increased from 2.3 percent in 1989 to 2.9 percent in 1990. Although it is a favorable change, the level of return would be considered low by most analysts.

One reason why return on assets is a good measure of profitability is that it combines the effects of profit margin and asset turnover. The 1990 and 1989 results for Kodak can be analyzed as follows:

	Profit Margin		Asset Turnover		Return on Assets
	$\frac{\text{Net income}}{\text{Net sales}}$	×	$\frac{\text{Net sales}}{\text{Average total assets}}$	=	$\frac{\text{Net income}}{\text{Average total assets}}$
1990	3.7%	×	.79	=	2.9%
1989	2.9%	×	.79	=	2.3%

From this analysis, it is clear that the increase in return on assets in 1990 can be attributed to the increase in profit margin.

Return on Equity. An important measure of profitability from the stockholders' standpoint is **return on equity**. This ratio measures how much was earned for each dollar invested by owners. For Kodak, this ratio for 1990 and 1989 is figured as follows (1988 owners' equity equals $6,780 million):

Return on Equity	1990	1989
$\frac{\text{Net income}}{\text{Average owners' equity}}$	$\frac{\$703}{(\$6{,}737 + \$6{,}642)/2}$	$\frac{\$529}{(\$6{,}642 + \$6{,}780)/2}$
	$= \frac{\$703}{\$6{,}689.50}$	$= \frac{\$529}{\$6{,}711}$
	= 10.5%	= 7.9%

This ratio also improved from 1989 to 1990. The increase was greater than the increase in return on assets because, although average owners' equity declined slightly from 1989 to 1990, average total assets increased.

A natural question is, Why is there a difference between return on assets and return on equity? The answer lies in the company's use of **leverage**, or debt

9. Some authorities would add interest expense to the numerator because they view interest expense as a cost of acquiring capital rather than a cost of operations.

financing. A company that has interest-bearing debt is said to be **leveraged**. If the company earns more with its borrowed funds than it must pay in interest for those funds, then the difference is available to increase the return on equity. Leverage may work against the company as well. Thus, an unfavorable situation occurs when the return on assets is less than the rate of interest paid on borrowed funds. Because of Kodak's leverage, the return on assets in 1990 of 2.9 percent created a larger return on equity of 10.5 percent for the same year. (The debt to equity ratio is presented later in this chapter.)

Earnings per Share. One of the most widely quoted measures of profitability is **earnings per share** of common stock. Exhibit 28-4 shows that the net earnings per share for Kodak improved from $1.63 to $2.17, reflecting the increase in net earnings from 1989 to 1990. These disclosures must be made in the income statement; calculations of this kind were presented in the chapter on retained earnings and corporate income statements. Earnings per share information is not comparable among companies because the number of shares varies from company to company.

Evaluating Long-Term Solvency

Long-term solvency has to do with a company's ability to survive over many years. The aim of long-term solvency analysis is to point out early if a company is on the road to bankruptcy. Studies have shown that accounting ratios can show as much as five years in advance that a company may fail.[10] Declining profitability and liquidity ratios are key signs of possible business failure. Two other ratios that analysts often consider as indicators of long-term solvency are the debt to equity ratio and the interest coverage ratio.

Debt to Equity Ratio. The existence of increasing amounts of debt in a company's capital structure is thought to be risky. The company has a legal obligation to make interest payments on time and to pay the principal at the maturity date. And this obligation holds no matter what the level of the company's earnings is. If the payments are not made, the company may be forced into bankruptcy. In contrast, dividends and other distributions to equity holders are made only when the board of directors declares them. The **debt to equity ratio** shows the amount of the company's assets provided by creditors in relation to the amount provided by stockholders. Thus, it measures the extent to which the company is leveraged. The larger the debt to equity ratio, the more fixed obligations the company has, and so the riskier the situation.

The ratio is computed as follows:

Debt to Equity Ratio	**1990**	**1989**
$\frac{\text{Total liabilities}}{\text{Owners' equity}}$	$\frac{\$17{,}388}{\$6{,}737} = 2.58$	$\frac{\$17{,}010}{\$6{,}642} = 2.56$

From 1989 to 1990, the debt to equity ratio for Kodak remained almost the same. This finding agrees with the analysis of the common-size balance sheets (Exhibit 28-6).

10. William H. Beaver, "Alternative Accounting Measures as Indicators of Failure," *Accounting Review,* January 1968; and Edward Altman, "Financial Ratios, Discriminant Analysis and the Prediction of Corporate Bankruptcy," *Journal of Finance*, September 1968.

Interest Coverage Ratio. One question that usually arises at this point is, If debt is bad, why have any? The answer is that the level of debt is a matter of balance. In spite of its riskiness, debt is a flexible means of financing certain business operations. The interest paid on debt is deductible for income taxes, whereas dividends on stock are not. Also, because it usually carries a fixed interest charge, it limits the cost of financing and creates a situation in which leverage can be used to advantage. Thus, if the company is able to earn a return on assets greater than the cost of the interest, it makes an overall profit.[11] However, the company runs the risk of not earning a return on assets equal to the cost of financing those assets, and thereby incurring a loss.

One means of measuring the degree of protection creditors have from a default on interest payments is the **interest coverage ratio**, computed as follows:

Interest Coverage Ratio	1990	1989
$\dfrac{\text{Net income before taxes + interest expense}}{\text{Interest expense}}$	$\dfrac{\$1{,}257 + \$812}{\$812}$	$\dfrac{\$925 + \$895}{\$895}$
	= 2.55 times	= 2.03 times

Although interest coverage improved in 1990, interest payments were protected by a ratio of only 2.55 times in 1990 because of the large amount of interest expense in relation to net income before taxes and interest expense.

Market Test Ratios

The market price of a company's stock is of interest to the analyst because it represents what investors as a whole think of a company at a point in time. Market price is the price at which people are willing to buy and sell the stock. It provides information about how investors view the potential return and risk connected with owning the company's stock. This information cannot be obtained simply by considering the market price of the stock by itself, however. Companies differ in number of outstanding shares and amount of underlying earnings and dividends. Thus, the market price must be related to the earnings per share, dividends per share, and price of other companies' shares. This is accomplished through the price/earnings ratio, the dividends yield, and an analysis of market risk.

Price/Earnings Ratio. The **price/earnings (P/E) ratio** measures the relationship of the current market price of a stock to the company's earnings per share. Assuming a current market price of $40 and using the 1990 earnings per share for Eastman Kodak Company of $2.17 from Exhibit 28-4, we can compute the price/earnings ratio as follows:

$$\frac{\text{Market price per share}}{\text{Earnings per share}} = \frac{\$40}{\$2.17} = 18.4 \text{ times}$$

At this time, Kodak's P/E ratio is 18.4 times its underlying earnings. The price/earnings ratio changes from day to day and from quarter to quarter as market price and earnings change. It tells how much, at any particular time, the investing public as a whole is willing to pay for $1 of a company's earnings per share.

11. In addition, there are advantages to being a debtor in periods of inflation because the debt, which is fixed in dollar amount, may be repaid with cheaper dollars.

This price/earnings ratio is very useful and widely applied because it allows companies to be compared. When a company's P/E ratio is higher than the P/E ratios for other companies, it *usually* means that investors feel that the company's earnings are going to grow at a faster rate than those of the other companies. On the other hand, a lower P/E ratio *usually* means a more negative assessment by investors. To compare two well-known companies, the market was less favorable toward IBM (11 times earnings per share) than it was toward AT&T (14 times earnings per share) in 1991.

Dividends Yield. The **dividends yield** is one measure of the current return to an investor in a stock. It is found by dividing the current annual dividend by the current market price of the stock. Assuming the same $40 per share and using the 1990 dividends of $2 per share for Kodak from Exhibit 28-5, we can compute the dividends yield thus:

$$\frac{\text{Dividends per share}}{\text{Market price per share}} = \frac{\$2}{\$40} = 5.0\%$$

Thus, an investor who owns Kodak stock at $40 had a return from dividends in 1990 of 5.0 percent.

The dividends yield is only one part of the investor's total return from investing in Eastman Kodak Company. The investor must add to or subtract from the dividends yield the percentage change (either up or down) in the market value of the stock.

Market Risk. It was pointed out earlier that besides assessing the potential return from an investment, the investor must also judge the risk associated with the investment. Many factors may be brought into assessing risk—the nature of the business, the quality of the business, the track record of the company, and so forth. One measure of risk that has gained increased attention among analysts in recent years is market risk. **Market risk** is the volatility of (or changes up and down in) the price of a stock in relation to the volatility of the prices of other stocks.

The computation of market risk is complex, involving computers and sophisticated statistical techniques such as regression analysis. The idea, however, is simple. Consider the following data on the changes in the prices of the stocks of Company A and Company B compared to the average change in price of all stocks in the market:

Average Percentage Change in Price of All Stocks	Percentage Change in Price of Company A's Stock	Percentage Change in Price of Company B's Stock
+10	+15	+5
–10	–15	–5

In this example, when the average price of all stocks went up by 10 percent, Company A's price increased 15 percent whereas Company B's increased only 5 percent. When the average price of all stocks went down by 10 percent, Company A's price decreased 15 percent but Company B's decreased only 5 percent. Thus, relative to all stocks, Company A's stock is more volatile than Company B's. If the prices of stocks go down, the risk of loss is greater in the case of Company A than in the case of Company B. If the market goes up, however, the potential for gain is greater in the case of Company A than in the case of Company B.

Market risk can be approximated by dividing the percentage change in price of a particular stock by the average percentage change in the price of all stocks, as follows:

$$\text{Company A} \quad \frac{\text{specific change}}{\text{average change}} = \frac{15}{10} = 1.5$$

$$\text{Company B} \quad \frac{\text{specific change}}{\text{average change}} = \frac{5}{10} = .5$$

This means that an investor can generally expect the value of an investment in Company A to increase or decrease 1.5 times as much as the average change in the price of all stocks. An investment in Company B can be expected to increase or decrease only .5 times as much as the price of all stocks.

Analysts call this measure of market risk **beta (β)**, after the mathematical symbol used in the formula for calculating the relationships of stock prices. The actual betas used by analysts are based on several years of data and are continually updated. Because the calculations require the use of computers, betas are usually provided by investment services.

The market risk or beta for USX in a recent year was 1.01. This means that, other things being equal, a person who invests in the stock of USX can expect its volatility or risk to be about the same as that of the stock market as a whole (which has a beta of 1.0). When one considers that USX is a mature company and the largest steel producer, with output closely related to the ups and downs in the economy as a whole, its near-neutral beta makes sense.

If the investor's objective is to assume less risk than that of the market as a whole, other companies in the steel industry might be considered. The second largest steel company in the United States, Bethlehem Steel, can be eliminated because its beta of 1.25 makes it riskier than USX. National Steel, the third largest steel processor, has been more stable over the years than its competitors, with a beta of only .75. It is a less risky stock in that there is less potential for a loss in a "down" market; but there is also less potential for gain in an "up" market. National Steel's beta is very low and compares well with that of major utilities such as American Telephone and Telegraph, which has a beta of .65.

Typically, growth stocks and speculative stocks are riskier than the stock market as a whole. Tandy Corporation (Radio Shack), a good example of a growth company, has had a beta of 1.45 in recent years. Tandy Corporation has rewarded investors' patience over the long term, but has been much more volatile and thus riskier than the average stock.

Investment decisions are not made on the basis of market risk alone, of course. First, other risk factors such as those indicated by the ratios discussed in this chapter, as well as industry, national, and world economic outlooks, must be considered. Second, the expected return must be considered. Further, most investors try to assemble a portfolio of stocks whose average beta corresponds to the degree of risk they are willing to assume in relation to their average expected return.

Chapter Review

Review of Learning Objectives

1. **Describe and discuss the objectives of financial statement analysis.**
Creditors and investors, as well as managers, use financial statement analysis to judge the past performance and current position of a company. In this way they also

judge its future potential and the risk associated with it. Creditors use the information gained from their analysis to make reliable loans that will be repaid with interest. Investors use the information to make investments that provide a return that is worth the risk.

2. **Describe and discuss the standards for financial statement analysis.**
   Three commonly used standards for financial statement analysis are rule-of-thumb measures, past performance of the company, and industry norms. Rule-of-thumb measures are weak because of the lack of evidence that they can be applied widely. The past performance of a company can offer a guideline for measuring improvement but is not helpful in judging performance relative to other companies. Although the use of industry norms overcomes this last problem, its disadvantage is that firms are not always comparable, even in the same industry.
3. **State the sources of information for financial statement analysis.**
   The major sources of information about publicly held corporations are published reports such as annual reports and interim financial statements, SEC reports, business periodicals, and credit and investment advisory services.
4. **Identify the issues related to the evaluation of the quality of a company's earnings.**
   Current and prospective net income is an important component in many ratios used to evaluate a company. The user should recognize that the quality of reported net income can be influenced by certain choices made by a company's management. First, management exercises judgment in choosing the accounting methods and estimates used in computing net income. Second, discontinued operations, extraordinary gains or losses, and changes in accounting methods may affect net income positively or negatively.
5. **Apply horizontal analysis, trend analysis, and vertical analysis to financial statements.**
   Horizontal analysis involves the computation of dollar amount changes and percentage changes from year to year. Trend analysis is an extension of horizontal analysis in that percentage changes are calculated for several years. The changes are usually computed by setting a base year equal to 100 and calculating the results for subsequent years as a percentage of that base year. Vertical analysis uses percentages to show the relationship of the component parts to the total in a single statement. The resulting financial statements, which are expressed entirely in percentages, are called common-size statements.
6. **Apply ratio analysis to financial statements in the study of an enterprise's liquidity, profitability, long-term solvency, and market tests.**
   The following table summarizes the basic information on ratio analysis.

Ratio	Components	Use or Meaning
Liquidity Ratios		
Current ratio	$\frac{\text{Current assets}}{\text{Current liabilities}}$	Measure of short-term debt-paying ability
Quick ratio	$\frac{\text{Cash + marketable securities + receivables}}{\text{Current liabilities}}$	Measure of short-term liquidity
Receivable turnover	$\frac{\text{Net sales}}{\text{Average accounts receivable}}$	Measure of relative size of accounts receivable balance and effectiveness of credit policies

(continued)

Ratio	Components	Use or Meaning
Average days' sales uncollected	Days in year / Receivable turnover	Measure of average time taken to collect receivables
Inventory turnover	Cost of goods sold / Average inventory	Measure of relative size of inventory
Profitability Ratios		
Profit margin	Net income / Net sales	Net income produced by each dollar of sales
Asset turnover	Net sales / Average total assets	Measure of how efficiently assets are used to produce sales
Return on assets	Net income / Average total assets	Overall measure of earning power or profitability of all assets employed in the business
Return on equity	Net income / Average owners' equity	Profitability of owners' investment
Earnings per share	Net income / Weighted average outstanding shares	Means of placing earnings on a common basis for comparison
Long-Term Solvency Ratios		
Debt to equity ratio	Total liabilities / Owners' equity	Measure of relationship of debt financing to equity financing
Interest coverage ratio	Net income before taxes + interest expense / Interest expense	Measure of protection of creditors from default on interest payments
Market Test Ratios		
Price/earnings (P/E) ratio	Market price per share / Earnings per share	Measure of amount the market will pay for a dollar of earnings
Dividends yield	Dividends per share / Market price per share	Measure of current return to investor
Market risk	Specific change in market price / Average change in market price	Measure of volatility of the market price of a stock in relation to that of other stocks

Review of Concepts and Terminology

The following concepts and terms were introduced in this chapter:

(L.O. 6) Asset turnover: Net sales divided by average total assets. Used to measure how efficiently assets are used to produce sales.

(L.O. 6) Average days' sales uncollected: The length of the accounting period, usually 365 days, divided by the receivable turnover. Shows the speed at which receivables are turned over—literally, the number of days, on the average, a company must wait to receive payment for credit sales.

(L.O. 5) Base year: In financial analysis, the first year to be considered in any set of data.

(L.O. 6) Beta (β): A measure of the market risk of an individual stock in relation to the average market risk of all stocks.

(L.O. 5) Common-size statement: A financial statement in which the components of a total figure are stated in terms of percentages of the total.

(L.O. 6) Current ratio: The relationship of current assets to current liabilities. Used as an indicator of a company's liquidity and short-term debt-paying ability.

(L.O. 6) Debt to equity ratio: Total liabilities divided by owners' equity. Used to measure the relationship of debt financing to equity financing, or the extent to which a company is leveraged.

(L.O. 2) Diversified companies (conglomerates): Companies that operate in more than one industry.

(L.O. 6) Dividends yield: The current annual dividend divided by the current market price of a stock. Used as a measure of the current return to an investor in a stock.

(L.O. 6) Earnings per share: Net income divided by the weighted average number of outstanding shares of common stock. Used as a measure of profitability and a means of comparison among stocks.

(L.O. 1) Financial statement analysis: A collective term for the techniques used to show important relationships among figures in financial statements.

(L.O. 5) Horizontal analysis: A technique for analyzing financial statements that involves the computation of dollar amount changes and percentage changes from the previous to the current year.

(L.O. 5) Index number: In trend analysis, a number against which changes in related items over a period of time are measured. Calculated by setting the base year equal to 100 percent.

(L.O. 6) Interest coverage ratio: Net income before taxes plus interest expense divided by interest expense. Used as a measure of the degree of protection creditors have from a default on interest payments.

(L.O. 3) Interim financial statements: Financial statements issued for a period of less than one year, usually monthly or quarterly.

(L.O. 6) Inventory turnover: The cost of goods sold divided by average inventory. Used to measure the relative size of inventory.

(L.O. 6) Leverage: Debt financing. The amount of debt financing in relation to equity financing is measured by the debt to equity ratio.

(L.O. 6) Market risk: The volatility of the price of a stock in relation to the volatility of the prices of other stocks.

(L.O. 1) Portfolio: A group of loans or investments designed to average the return and risks of a creditor or investor.

(L.O. 6) Price/earnings (P/E) ratio: Current market price per share divided by earnings per share. Used as a measure of investor confidence in a company and as a means of comparison among stocks.

(L.O. 6) **Profit margin:** Net income divided by net sales. Used to measure the percentage of each revenue dollar that contributes to net income.

(L.O. 6) **Quick ratio:** The relationship of the more liquid current assets—cash, marketable securities or short-term investments, and receivables—to current liabilities. Used as a measure of short-term liquidity.

(L.O. 5) **Ratio analysis:** A technique for analyzing financial statements in which meaningful relationships are shown between components of financial statements. (For a summary of ratios see the Review of Learning Objectives, pages 1175–1176.)

(L.O. 6) **Receivable turnover:** The relationship of net sales to average accounts receivable. Used as a measure of the relative size of a company's accounts receivable and the success of its credit and collection policies; shows how many times, on the average, receivables were turned into cash during the period.

(L.O. 6) **Return on assets:** Net income divided by average total assets. Used to measure the amount earned on each dollar of assets invested. An overall measure of earning power or profitability.

(L.O. 6) **Return on equity:** Net income divided by average owners' equity. Used to measure how much income was earned for each dollar invested by owners.

(L.O. 5) **Trend analysis:** A type of horizontal analysis in which percentage changes are calculated for several successive years instead of two years.

(L.O. 5) **Vertical analysis:** A technique for analyzing financial statements that uses percentages to show the relationship of the different parts to the total in a single statement.

Self-Test

Test your knowledge of the chapter by choosing the best answer for each of the following items.

(L.O. 1) 1. A general rule in choosing among alternative investments is the greater the risk taken, the
   a. greater the return required.
   b. lower the profits expected.
   c. lower the potential expected.
   d. greater the price of the investment.

(L.O. 2) 2. Which of the following is the most useful in evaluating whether a company has improved its position in relation to its competitors?
   a. Rule-of-thumb measures
   b. Past performance of the company
   c. Past and current performances of the company
   d. Industry averages

(L.O. 3) 3. One of the best places to look for early signals of change in a company's profitability is the
   a. interim financial statements.
   b. year-end financial statements.
   c. annual report sent to stockholders.
   d. annual report sent to the SEC.

(L.O. 4) 4. The quality of a company's earnings may be affected by
   a. the countries in which the company operates.
   b. the choice of independent auditors.
   c. the industry in which the company operates.
   d. the accounting methods used by the company.

(L.O. 5) 5. In trend analysis, each item is expressed as a percentage of the
   a. net income figure.
   b. retained earnings figure.
   c. base year figure.
   d. total assets figure.

(L.O. 5) 6. In a common-size balance sheet for a wholesale company, the 100% figure is
   a. merchandise inventory.
   b. total current assets.
   c. total property, plant, and equipment.
   d. total assets.

(L.O. 5) 7. The best way to study the changes in financial statements between two years is to prepare
   a. common-size statements.
   b. a trend analysis.
   c. a horizontal analysis.
   d. a ratio analysis.

(L.O. 6) 8. A common measure of liquidity is
   a. return on assets.
   b. profit margin.
   c. inventory turnover.
   d. interest coverage.

(L.O. 6) 9. Asset turnover is most closely related to
   a. profit margin and return on assets.
   b. profit margin and debt to equity.
   c. interest coverage and debt to equity.
   d. earnings per share and profit margin.

(L.O. 6) 10. Which of the following describes the computation of the interest coverage ratio?
   a. Net income minus interest expense divided by interest expense
   b. Net income plus interest expense divided by interest expense
   c. Net income before taxes plus interest expense divided by interest expense
   d. Net income divided by interest expense

Answers to the Self-Test are at the end of this chapter.

Review Problem
Comparative Analysis of Two Companies

(L.O. 6) Maggie Washington is considering an investment in one of two fast-food restaurant chains because she believes the trend toward eating out more often will continue. Her choices have been narrowed to Quik Burger and Big Steak, whose balance sheets and income statements follow.

Balance Sheets
(in thousands)

	Quik Burger	Big Steak
Assets		
Cash	$ 2,000	$ 4,500
Accounts Receivable (net)	2,000	6,500
Inventory	2,000	5,000
Property, Plant, and Equipment (net)	20,000	35,000
Other Assets	4,000	5,000
Total Assets	$30,000	$56,000
Liabilities and Stockholders' Equity		
Accounts Payable	$ 2,500	$ 3,000
Notes Payable	1,500	4,000
Bonds Payable	10,000	30,000
Common Stock ($1 par value)	1,000	3,000
Paid-in Capital in Excess of Par Value, Common	9,000	9,000
Retained Earnings	6,000	7,000
Total Liabilities and Stockholders' Equity	$30,000	$56,000

Income Statements
(in thousands)

	Quik Burger	Big Steak
Sales	$53,000	$86,000
Cost of Goods Sold (including restaurant operating expense)	37,000	61,000
Gross Margin from Sales	$16,000	$25,000
General Operating Expenses		
Selling Expenses	$ 7,000	$10,000
Administrative Expenses	4,000	5,000
Interest Expense	1,400	3,200
Income Taxes Expense	1,800	3,400
Total Operating Expenses	$14,200	$21,600
Net Income	$ 1,800	$ 3,400

In addition to the information on the financial statements, dividends paid were $500,000 for Quik Burger and $600,000 for Big Steak. The market prices of the stocks were $30 and $20, respectively, and their betas were 1.00 and 1.15. Financial information pertaining to prior years is not readily available to Maggie Washington. Assume that all notes payable are current liabilities and that all bonds payable are long-term liabilities.

Required

Conduct a comprehensive ratio analysis of Quik Burger and Big Steak and compare the results. The analysis should be performed using the following steps (round all ratios and percentages to one decimal place):

1. Prepare an analysis of liquidity.
2. Prepare an analysis of profitability.
3. Prepare an analysis of long-term solvency.
4. Prepare an analysis of market tests.
5. Compare the two companies by inserting the ratio calculations from the preceding four steps in a table with the following column headings: Ratio Name, Quik Burger, Big Steak, and Company with More Favorable Ratio. Indicate in the last column the company that apparently had the more favorable ratio in each case. (Consider changes of .1 or less to be indeterminate.)
6. In what ways would having access to prior years' information aid this analysis?

Answer to Review Problem

Ratio Name	Quik Burger	Big Steak
1. Liquidity analysis		
a. Current ratio	$\dfrac{\$2{,}000 + \$2{,}000 + \$2{,}000}{\$2{,}500 + \$1{,}500}$	$\dfrac{\$4{,}500 + \$6{,}500 + \$5{,}000}{\$3{,}000 + \$4{,}000}$
	$= \dfrac{\$6{,}000}{\$4{,}000} = 1.5$	$= \dfrac{\$16{,}000}{\$7{,}000} = 2.3$
b. Quick ratio	$\dfrac{\$2{,}000 + \$2{,}000}{\$2{,}500 + \$1{,}500}$	$\dfrac{\$4{,}500 + \$6{,}500}{\$3{,}000 + \$4{,}000}$
	$= \dfrac{\$4{,}000}{\$4{,}000} = 1.0$	$= \dfrac{\$11{,}000}{\$7{,}000} = 1.6$

Ratio Name	Quik Burger	Big Steak
c. Receivable turnover	$\frac{\$53{,}000}{\$2{,}000} = 26.5$ times	$\frac{\$86{,}000}{\$6{,}500} = 13.2$ times
d. Average days' sales uncollected	$\frac{365}{26.5} = 13.8$ days	$\frac{365}{13.2} = 27.7$ days
e. Inventory turnover	$\frac{\$37{,}000}{\$2{,}000} = 18.5$ times	$\frac{\$61{,}000}{\$5{,}000} = 12.2$ times
2. Profitability analysis		
a. Profit margin	$\frac{\$1{,}800}{\$53{,}000} = 3.4\%$	$\frac{\$3{,}400}{\$86{,}000} = 4.0\%$
b. Asset turnover	$\frac{\$53{,}000}{\$30{,}000} = 1.8$ times	$\frac{\$86{,}000}{\$56{,}000} = 1.5$ times
c. Return on assets	$\frac{\$1{,}800}{\$30{,}000} = 6.0\%$	$\frac{\$3{,}400}{\$56{,}000} = 6.1\%$
d. Return on equity	$\frac{\$1{,}800}{\$1{,}000 + \$9{,}000 + \$6{,}000}$ $= \frac{\$1{,}800}{\$16{,}000} = 11.3\%$	$\frac{\$3{,}400}{\$3{,}000 + \$9{,}000 + \$7{,}000}$ $= \frac{\$3{,}400}{\$19{,}000} = 17.9\%$
e. Earnings per share	$\frac{\$1{,}800}{1{,}000} = \$1.80$	$\frac{\$3{,}400}{3{,}000} = \$1.13$
3. Long-term solvency analysis		
a. Debt to equity ratio	$\frac{\$2{,}500 + \$1{,}500 + \$10{,}000}{\$1{,}000 + \$9{,}000 + \$6{,}000}$ $= \frac{\$14{,}000}{\$16{,}000} = .9$	$\frac{\$3{,}000 + \$4{,}000 + \$30{,}000}{\$3{,}000 + \$9{,}000 + \$7{,}000}$ $= \frac{\$37{,}000}{\$19{,}000} = 1.9$
b. Interest coverage ratio	$\frac{\$1{,}800 + \$1{,}800 + \$1{,}400}{\$1{,}400}$ $= \frac{\$5{,}000}{\$1{,}400} = 3.6$ times	$\frac{\$3{,}400 + \$3{,}400 + \$3{,}200}{\$3{,}200}$ $= \frac{\$10{,}000}{\$3{,}200} = 3.1$ times
4. Market test analysis		
a. Price/earnings ratio	$\frac{\$30}{\$1.80} = 16.7$ times	$\frac{\$20}{\$1.13} = 17.7$ times
b. Dividends yield	$\frac{\$500{,}000 \div 1{,}000{,}000}{\$30} = 1.7\%$	$\frac{\$600{,}000 \div 3{,}000{,}000}{\$20} = 1.0\%$
c. Market risk	1.00	1.15

5. Comparative analysis

Ratio Name	Quik Burger	Big Steak	Company with More Favorable Ratio*
1. Liquidity analysis			
a. Current ratio	1.5	2.3	Big Steak
b. Quick ratio	1.0	1.6	Big Steak
c. Receivable turnover	26.5 times	13.2 times	Quik Burger
d. Average days' sales uncollected	13.8 days	27.7 days	Quik Burger
e. Inventory turnover	18.5 times	12.2 times	Quik Burger
2. Profitability analysis			
a. Profit margin	3.4%	4.0%	Big Steak
b. Asset turnover	1.8 times	1.5 times	Quik Burger
c. Return on assets	6.0%	6.1%	Neutral
d. Return on equity	11.3%	17.9%	Big Steak
e. Earnings per share	$1.80	$1.13	Noncomparable†
3. Long-term solvency analysis			
a. Debt to equity ratio	0.9	1.9	Quik Burger
b. Interest coverage ratio	3.6 times	3.1 times	Quik Burger
4. Market test analysis			
a. Price/earnings ratio	16.7 times	17.7 times	Big Steak
b. Dividends yield	1.7%	1.0%	Quik Burger
c. Market risk	1.00	1.15	Quik Burger is less risky

*This analysis indicates the company with the apparently more favorable ratio. Class discussion may focus on conditions under which different conclusions may be drawn.

†Earnings per share are noncomparable because of the considerable difference in the number of common stockholders of the two firms. If information for prior years were available, it would be helpful in determining the earnings trend of each company.

6. Usefulness of prior years' information

Prior years' information would be helpful in two ways. First, turnover and return ratios could be based on average amounts. Second, a trend analysis could be performed for each company.

Chapter Assignments

Questions

1. What differences and similarities exist in the objectives of investors and creditors in using financial statement analysis?
2. What role does risk play in making loans and investments?
3. What standards are commonly used to evaluate financial statements, and what are their relative merits?
4. Why would a financial analyst compare the ratios of Steelco, a steel company, to the ratios of other companies in the steel industry? What factors might invalidate such a comparison?
5. Where may an investor look to find information about a company in which he or she is thinking of investing?
6. What is the basis of the statement "Accounting income is a useless measurement because it is based on so many arbitrary decisions"? Is the statement true?
7. Why would an investor want to see both horizontal and trend analyses of a company's financial statements?

8. What does the following sentence mean: "Based on 1980 equaling 100, net income increased from 240 in 1992 to 260 in 1993"?
9. What is the difference between horizontal and vertical analysis?
10. What is the purpose of ratio analysis?
11. Under what circumstances would a current ratio of 3:1 be good? Under what circumstances would it be bad?
12. In a period of high interest rates, why are receivable and inventory turnover especially important?
13. The following statements were made on page 35 of the November 6, 1978 issue of *Fortune* magazine: "Supermarket executives are beginning to look back with some nostalgia on the days when the standard profit margin was 1 percent of sales. Last year the industry overall margin came to a thin 0.72 percent." How could a supermarket earn a satisfactory return on assets with such a small profit margin?
14. Company A and Company B both have net incomes of $1,000,000. Is it possible to say that these companies are equally successful? Why or why not?
15. Circo Company has a return on assets of 12 percent and a debt to equity ratio of .5. Would you expect return on equity to be more or less than 12 percent?
16. The market price of Company J's stock is the same as the market price of Company Q's. How might you determine whether investors are equally confident about the future of these companies?
17. Why is it riskier to own a stock whose market price is more changeable than the market price of other stocks? Why might it be beneficial to own such a stock?

Communication Skills Exercises

Communication 28-1. Standards for Financial Analysis
(L.O. 2)

Helene Curtis is a well-known, publicly owned corporation. "By almost any standard, Chicago-based Helene Curtis rates as one of America's worst-managed personal care companies. In recent years its return on equity has hovered between 10% and 13%, well below the industry average of 18% to 19%. Net profit margins of 2% to 3% are half that of competitors. . . . As a result, while leading names like Revlon and Avon are trading at three and four times book value, Curtis's trades at less than two-thirds book value."[12] Considering that many companies in other industries are happy with a return on equity (owners' investment) of 10 percent to 13 percent, why is this analysis so critical of Curtis's performance? Assuming that Curtis could double its profit margin, what other information would be necessary to project the resulting return on owners' investment? Why are Revlon's and Avon's stocks trading for more than Curtis's?

Communication 28-2. Quality of Earnings[13]
(L.O. 4)

International Business Machines Corporation (IBM), the world's largest computer manufacturer, on Tuesday, January 19, 1988, reported greatly increased earnings for the fourth quarter of 1987. In spite of this reported gain in earnings, the price of IBM's stock on the New York Stock Exchange declined by $6 per share to $111.75. In sympathy with this move, most other technology stocks also declined.

Fourth-quarter net earnings rose from $1.39 billion, or $2.28 a share, to $2.08 billion, or $3.47 a share, an increase of 49.6 percent and 52.2 percent over the year-earlier period. Management declared that these results demonstrated the effectiveness of IBM's efforts to become more competitive, and that, in spite of the economic uncertainties of 1988, the company was planning for growth.

The stock price declined, however, apparently because the huge increase in income was the result of nonrecurring gains. Investment analysts pointed out that IBM's high earnings stemmed primarily from elements such as a lower tax rate. Despite most analysts' expectations of a tax rate between 40 and 42 percent, IBM's rate was down from the previous year's 45.3 percent to a low 36.4 percent.

12. *Forbes,* November 13, 1978, p. 154.
13. "Technology Firms Post Strong Earnings But Stock Prices Decline Sharply," *Wall Street Journal,* January 21, 1988; Donald R. Seace, "Industrials Plunge 57.2 Points—Technology Stocks' Woes Cited," *Wall Street Journal,* January 21, 1988.

In addition, analysts were disappointed in the revenue growth. Revenues within the United States were down, and much of the growth in revenues came through favorable currency translations, increases that may not be repeated. In fact, some estimates of the fourth-quarter earnings attributed $.50 per share to currency translations and another $.25 to tax rate changes.

Other factors contributing to the rise in earnings were one-time transactions such as the sale of Intel Corporation stock and bond redemptions, which, along with a corporate stock buyback program, reduced the amount of stock outstanding in the fourth quarter by 7.4 million shares.

The analysts are concerned about the quality of IBM's earnings. Identify four quality of earnings issues reported in the case and explain the analysts' concern about each. In percentage terms, what is the impact of the currency changes on fourth-quarter earnings? Comment on management's assessment of IBM's performance. Do you agree with management?

Communication 28-3. Basic Research Skills *(L.O. 3)*

In your school library, find either *Moody's Investors Service, Standard and Poor's Industry Guide,* or *The Value Line Investment Survey.* Locate the reports on three corporations. You may choose the corporations at random or choose them from the same industry, if directed to do so by your instructor. (If you did a related exercise in a previous chapter, use the same three companies.) Write a summary of what you learn about each company from the reference works, and be prepared to discuss your findings in class.

Classroom Exercises

Exercise 28-1. Effect of Alternative Accounting Methods *(L.O. 4)*

At the end of its first year of operations, a company could calculate its ending merchandise inventory according to three different accounting methods, as follows: FIFO, $95,000; weighted average, $90,000; LIFO, $86,000. If the weighted-average method is used by the company, net income for the year would be $34,000.

1. Determine net income if the FIFO method is used.
2. Determine net income if the LIFO method is used.
3. Which method is more conservative?
4. Will the consistency convention be violated if the company chooses to use the LIFO method?
5. Does the full-disclosure convention require disclosure of the inventory method selected by management in the financial statements?

Exercise 28-2. Effect of Alternative Accounting Methods *(L.O. 4, 6)*

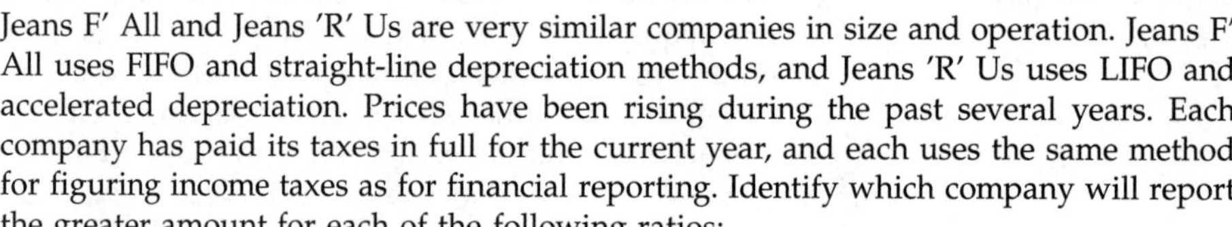

Jeans F' All and Jeans 'R' Us are very similar companies in size and operation. Jeans F' All uses FIFO and straight-line depreciation methods, and Jeans 'R' Us uses LIFO and accelerated depreciation. Prices have been rising during the past several years. Each company has paid its taxes in full for the current year, and each uses the same method for figuring income taxes as for financial reporting. Identify which company will report the greater amount for each of the following ratios:

1. Current ratio
2. Inventory turnover
3. Profit margin
4. Return on assets

If you cannot tell which company will report the greater amount, explain why.

Exercise 28-3. Horizontal Analysis *(L.O. 5)*

Compute the amount and percentage changes for the following balance sheets, and comment on the changes from 19x1 to 19x2. (Round the percentage changes to one decimal place.)

Lindquist Company
Comparative Balance Sheets
December 31, 19x2 and 19x1

	19x2	19x1
Assets		
Current Assets	$ 37,200	$ 25,600
Property, Plant, and Equipment (net)	218,928	194,400
Total Assets	$256,128	$220,000
Liabilities and Stockholders' Equity		
Current Liabilities	$ 22,400	$ 6,400
Long-Term Liabilities	70,000	80,000
Stockholders' Equity	163,728	133,600
Total Liabilities and Stockholders' Equity	$256,128	$220,000

Exercise 28-4. Trend Analysis *(L.O. 5)*

Prepare a trend analysis of the following data using 19x1 as the base year, and tell whether the situation shown by the trends is favorable or unfavorable. (Round your answers to one decimal place.)

	19x5	19x4	19x3	19x2	19x1
Sales	$25,520	$23,980	$24,200	$22,880	$22,000
Cost of Goods Sold	17,220	15,400	15,540	14,700	14,000
General and Administrative Expenses	5,280	5,184	5,088	4,896	4,800
Operating Income	3,020	3,396	3,572	3,284	3,200

Exercise 28-5. Vertical Analysis *(L.O. 5)*

Express the comparative income statements that follow as common-size statements, and comment on the changes from 19x1 to 19x2. (Round computations to one decimal place.)

Lindquist Company
Comparative Income Statements
For the Years Ended December 31, 19x2 and 19x1

	19x2	19x1
Sales	$424,000	$368,000
Cost of Goods Sold	254,400	239,200
Gross Margin from Sales	$169,600	$128,800
Selling Expenses	$106,000	$ 73,600
General Expenses	50,880	36,800
Total Operating Expenses	$156,880	$110,400
Net Operating Income	$ 12,720	$ 18,400

Exercise 28-6. Liquidity Analysis *(L.O. 6)*

Partial comparative balance sheet and income statement information for Lum Company follows.

	19x2	19x1
Cash	$ 6,800	$ 5,200
Marketable Securities	3,600	8,600
Accounts Receivable (net)	22,400	17,800
Inventory	27,200	24,800
Total Current Assets	$ 60,000	$ 56,400
Current Liabilities	$ 20,000	$ 14,100
Sales	$161,280	$110,360
Cost of Goods Sold	108,800	101,680
Gross Margin from Sales	$ 52,480	$ 8,680

The year-end balances for Accounts Receivable and Inventory were $16,200 and $25,600, respectively, in 19x0. Compute the current ratio, quick ratio, receivable turnover, average days' sales uncollected, and inventory turnover for each year. (Round computations to one decimal place.) Comment on the change in the company's liquidity position from 19x1 to 19x2.

Exercise 28-7. Turnover Analysis *(L.O. 6)*

Alberto's Men's Shop has been in business for four years. Because the company has recently had a cash flow problem, management wonders whether there is a problem with receivables or inventories. Here are selected figures from the company's financial statements (in thousands):

	19x4	19x3	19x2	19x1
Net Sales	$288	$224	$192	$160
Cost of Goods Sold	180	144	120	96
Accounts Receivable (net)	48	40	32	24
Merchandise Inventory	56	44	32	20

Compute receivable turnover and inventory turnover for each of the four years, and comment on the results relative to the cash flow problem that Alberto's Men's Shop has been experiencing. Round computations to one decimal place.

Exercise 28-8. Profitability Analysis *(L.O. 6)*

At year end, Canzoneri Company had total assets of $640,000 in 19x0, $680,000 in 19x1, and $760,000 in 19x2. Its debt to equity ratio was .67 in all three years. In 19x1, the company made a net income of $77,112 on revenues of $1,224,000. In 19x2, the company made a net income of $98,952 on revenues of $1,596,000. Compute the profit margin, asset turnover, return on assets, and return on equity for 19x1 and 19x2. Comment on the apparent cause of the increase or decrease in profitability. (Round the percentages and other ratios to one decimal place.)

Exercise 28-9. Long-Term Solvency and Market Test Ratios *(L.O. 6)*

An investor is considering investing in the long-term bonds and common stock of Companies X and Y. Both companies operate in the same industry, but Company X has a beta of 1.0 and Company Y has a beta of 1.2. In addition, both companies pay a dividend per share of $4, and a yield of 10 percent on their long-term bonds. Other data for the two companies follow:

	Company X	Company Y
Total Assets	$2,400,000	$1,080,000
Total Liabilities	1,080,000	594,000
Net Income before Taxes	288,000	129,600
Interest Expense	97,200	53,460
Earnings per Share	3.20	5.00
Market Price of Common Stock	40	47.50

Compute the debt to equity, interest coverage, price/earnings (P/E), and dividends yield ratios, and comment on the results. (Round computations to one decimal place.)

Exercise 28-10. Preparation of Statements from Ratios and Incomplete Data
(L.O. 6)

Following are the income statement and balance sheet of Pandit Corporation, with most of the amounts missing.

Pandit Corporation
Income Statement
For the Year Ended December 31, 19x1
(in thousands of dollars)

Sales		$18,000
Cost of Goods Sold		?
Gross Margin from Sales		$?
Operating Expenses		
Selling Expenses	$?	
Administrative Expenses	234	
Interest Expense	162	
Income Taxes Expense	620	
Total Operating Expenses		?
Net Income		$?

Pandit Corporation
Balance Sheet
December 31, 19x1
(in thousands of dollars)

Assets

Cash	$?	
Accounts Receivable (net)	?	
Inventories	?	
Total Current Assets		$?
Property, Plant, and Equipment (net)		5,400
Total Assets		$?

Liabilities and Stockholders' Equity

Current Liabilities	$?	
Bond Payable, 9% interest	?	
Total Liabilities		$?
Common Stock—$20 par value	$3,000	
Paid-in Capital in Excess of Par Value, Common	2,600	
Retained Earnings	4,000	
Total Stockholders' Equity		9,600
Total Liabilities and Stockholders' Equity		$?

Pandit's only interest expense is on long-term debt. Its debt to equity ratio is .5, its current ratio 3:1, its quick ratio 2:1, the receivable turnover 4.5, and its inventory turnover 4.0. The return on assets is 10 percent. All ratios are based on the current year's information. Complete the financial statements using the information presented. Show supporting computations.

Interpretation Cases from Business

ICB 28-1.
Ford Motor Company I[14]
(L.O. 6)

Standard & Poor's Corporation (S & P) offers a wide range of financial information services to investors. One of its services is rating the quality of the bond issues of U.S. corporations. Its top bond rating is AAA, followed by AA, A, BBB, BB, B, and so forth. The lowest rating, C, is reserved for companies that are in or near bankruptcy. *Business Week* reported on February 2, 1981, that S & P had downgraded the bond rating for Ford Motor Company, a leading U.S. automobile maker, from AAA to AA. The cause of the downgrading was a deterioration of Ford's financial strength as indicated by certain ratios considered important by S & P. The ratios, S & P's guidelines, and Ford's performances are summarized in the following table.

Ratio	S & P Guidelines for AAA Rating	Ford's Performance		
		1980	1979	1978
Interest Coverage	15 times	Loss	6.5 times	15.3 times
Pretax Return on Assets	15% to 20%	Loss	6.6%	13.4%
Debt to Equity	50%	63.4%	37.8%	34%
Cash Flow as a Percentage of Total Debt*	100%	91%	118.5%	152.6%
Short-Term Debt as a Percentage of Total Debt	25%	52.5%	48.3%	43.1%

*Cash flow includes net income plus noncash charges to earnings.

Required

1. Identify the objective (profitability, liquidity, long-term solvency) measured by each of the S & P ratios. Why is each ratio important to the rating of Ford's long-term bonds?
2. The *Business Week* article suggested several actions that Ford might take to regain its previous rating. Tell which of the ratios each of the following actions would improve: (a) "cutting operating costs"; (b) "scrapping at least part of its massive spending plans over the next several years"; (c) "eliminate cash dividends to stockholders"; (d) "sale of profitable nonautomobile-related operations such as its steelmaker, aerospace company, and electronic concerns."

ICB 28-2.
Ford Motor Company II[15]
(L.O. 6)

Part A:
By 1983, S & P had dropped the rating on Ford's bond issues to BBB. Selected data for the years ended December 31, 1982 and 1983, from Ford Motor Company's 1983 annual report, follow (in millions).

14. Information excerpted from the 1978, 1979, and 1980 annual reports of Ford Motor Company.
15. Information excerpted from the 1983, 1986, and 1989 annual reports of Ford Motor Company.

	1983	1982
Balance Sheet Data		
Short-Term Debt	$10,315.9	$10,424.0
Long-Term Debt	2,712.9	2,353.3
Stockholders' Equity	7,545.3	6,077.5
Total Assets	23,868.9	21,961.7
Income Statement Data		
Income (Loss) Before Income Taxes	2,166.3	(407.9)
Interest Expense	567.2	745.5
Statement of Changes in Financial Position		
Funds (Cash Basis) Provided by Operations	5,001.5	2,632.0

Required

1. Compute for 1982 and 1983 the same ratios that were used by S & P in Ford Motor Company I.
2. If you were S & P, would you raise the rating on Ford's long-term bonds in 1984? Why or why not?

Part B:

By the end of 1986, Ford's financial situation had improved enough to warrant an A rating from Standard & Poor's. Then in 1990, as discussed in the decision point at the beginning of this chapter, Ford's rating was lowered by Moody's, another bond rating company. Selected data for the years ended December 31, 1986 and 1989, from Ford Motor Company's 1986 and 1989 annual reports, follow (in millions):

	1989	1986
Balance Sheet Data		
Short-Term Debt	$20,180.6	$15,625.6
Long-Term Debt	1,137.0	2,137.1
Stockholders' Equity	22,727.8	14,859.5
Total Assets	45,819.2	37,993.0
Income Statement Data		
Income (Loss) Before Income Taxes	6,029.6	5,552.2
Interest Expense	321.1	482.9
Statement of Cash Flows		
Net Cash Flows from Operating Activities	5,623.6	7,624.4

Total assets were $31,603.6 million in 1985 and $43,127.7 million in 1988.

Required

1. Compute for 1986 and 1989 the same ratios that were used by Standard & Poor's in Ford Motor Company I.
2. Do you agree that Ford's performance had improved enough by 1986 (see Part A) to warrant an increase to an A rating?
3. Do the 1989 figures warrant a reduction in the bond rating? If not, how do you explain the downgrade described in the Decision Point at the beginning of the chapter?

ICB 28-3. PepsiCo, Inc. *(L.O. 3)*

Refer to Exhibit 28-2, which contains the listing of PepsiCo, Inc. from Moody's *Handbook of Dividend Achievers.*

Required

1. In what three business segments does PepsiCo, Inc. operate and what is the relative size of each in terms of sales and operating profit? Which business segment appears to be the most profitable?
2. What generally has been the relationship between PepsiCo's return on assets and its return on equity over the years 1985 to 1990? What does this tell you about the way the company is financed? What figures back up your conclusion?
3. What has been the trend of PepsiCo's earnings per share and dividends per share for the seven years shown? How do these trends relate to the trend of the company's stock price? What are the prospects for the trend continuing?

Problem Set A

Problem 28A-1. Effect of Alternative Accounting Methods
(L.O. 4, 6)

Albers Company began operations this year. At the beginning of the year the company purchased plant assets of $770,000, with an estimated useful life of ten years and no salvage value. During the year, the company had sales of $1,300,000, salary expense of $200,000, and other expenses of $80,000, excluding depreciation. In addition, Albers Company purchased inventory as follows:

January 15	400 units at $400	$160,000
March 20	200 units at $408	81,600
June 15	800 units at $416	332,800
September 18	600 units at $412	247,200
December 9	300 units at $420	126,000
Total	2,300 units	$947,600

At the end of the year, a physical inventory disclosed 500 units still on hand. The managers of Albers Company know they have a choice of accounting methods, but are unsure how they will affect net income. They have heard of the FIFO and LIFO inventory methods and the straight-line and sum-of-the-years'-digits depreciation methods.

Required

1. Prepare two income statements for Albers Company, one using a FIFO basis and the straight-line method, the other using a LIFO basis and the sum-of-the-years'-digits method.
2. Prepare a schedule accounting for the difference in the two net income figures obtained in **1**.
3. What effect does the choice of accounting methods have on Albers's inventory turnover? What conclusions can you draw?
4. What effect does the choice of accounting methods have on Albers's return on assets?

Use year-end balances to compute the ratios. Assume that the only other asset in addition to plant assets and inventory is $80,000 cash. Is your evaluation of Albers's profitability affected by the choice of accounting methods?

Problem 28A-2. Horizontal and Vertical Analysis
(L.O. 5)

The condensed comparative income statements and balance sheets of Mariano Corporation follow. All figures are given in thousands of dollars.

Mariano Corporation
Comparative Income Statements
For the Years Ended December 31, 19x2 and 19x1

	19x2	19x1
Sales	$3,276,800	$3,146,400
Cost of Goods Sold	2,088,800	2,008,400
Gross Margin on Sales	$1,188,000	$1,138,000
Operating Expenses		
Selling Expenses	$ 476,800	$ 518,000
Administrative Expenses	447,200	423,200
Interest Expense	65,600	39,200
Income Taxes Expense	62,400	56,800
Total Operating Expenses	$1,052,000	$1,037,200
Net Income	$ 136,000	$ 100,800

Mariano Corporation
Comparative Balance Sheets
December 31, 19x2 and 19x1

	19x2	19x1
Assets		
Cash	$ 81,200	$ 40,800
Accounts Receivable (net)	235,600	229,200
Inventory	574,800	594,800
Property, Plant, and Equipment (net)	750,000	720,000
Total Assets	$1,641,600	$1,584,800
Liabilities and Stockholders' Equity		
Accounts Payable	$ 267,600	$ 477,200
Notes Payable	200,000	400,000
Bonds Payable	400,000	—
Common Stock—$10 par value	400,000	400,000
Retained Earnings	374,000	307,600
Total Liabilities and Stockholders' Equity	$1,641,600	$1,584,800

Required

(Round percentages to one decimal place.)

1. Prepare schedules showing the amount and percentage changes from 19x1 to 19x2 for Mariano's comparative income statements and balance sheets.
2. Prepare common-size income statements and balance sheets for 19x1 and 19x2.
3. Comment on the results in **1** and **2** by identifying favorable and unfavorable changes in the components and composition of the statements.

Problem 28A-3.
Analyzing the Effects of Transactions on Ratios
(L.O. 6)

Straight Corporation engaged in the transactions listed in the first column of the following table. Opposite each transaction is a ratio and space to indicate the effect of each transaction on the ratio.

Transaction	Ratio	Effect: Increase	Effect: Decrease	Effect: None
a. Sold merchandise on account.	Current ratio			
b. Sold merchandise on account.	Inventory turnover			
c. Collected on accounts receivable.	Quick ratio			
d. Wrote off an uncollectible account.	Receivable turnover			
e. Paid on accounts payable.	Current ratio			
f. Declared cash dividend.	Return on equity			
g. Incurred advertising expense.	Profit margin			
h. Issued stock dividend.	Debt to equity ratio			
i. Issued bond payable.	Asset turnover			
j. Accrued interest expense.	Current ratio			
k. Paid previously declared cash dividend.	Dividends yield			
l. Purchased treasury stock.	Return on assets			

Required

Place an X in the appropriate column to show whether the transaction increased, decreased, or had no effect on the indicated ratio.

Problem 28A-4. Ratio Analysis *(L.O. 6)*

Additional data for Mariano Corporation in 19x2 and 19x1 follow. This information should be used together with the data in Problem 28A-2 to answer the requirements below.

	19x2	19x1
Dividends Paid	$44,000,000	$34,400,000
Number of Common Shares	40,000,000	40,000,000
Market Price per Share	$18	$30
Beta	1.40	1.25

Balances of selected accounts (in thousands) at the end of 19x0 were Accounts Receivable (net), $206,800; Inventory, $547,200; Total Assets, $1,465,600; and Stockholders' Equity, $641,200. All of Mariano's notes payable were current liabilities; all of the bonds payable were long-term liabilities.

Required

(Round percentages and ratios except earnings per share to one decimal place, and consider changes of .1 or less to be indeterminate.)

1. Conduct a liquidity analysis by calculating for each year the: (a) current ratio, (b) quick ratio, (c) receivable turnover, (d) average days' sales uncollected, and (e) inventory turnover. Indicate whether each ratio had a favorable (F) or unfavorable (U) change from 19x1 to 19x2.
2. Conduct a profitability analysis by calculating for each year the: (a) profit margin, (b) asset turnover, (c) return on assets, (d) return on equity, and (e) earnings per share. Indicate whether each ratio had a favorable (F) or unfavorable (U) change from 19x1 to 19x2.
3. Conduct a long-term solvency analysis by calculating for each year the: (a) debt to equity ratio and (b) interest coverage ratio. Indicate whether each ratio had a favorable (F) or unfavorable (U) change from 19x1 to 19x2.
4. Conduct a market test analysis by calculating for each year the: (a) price/earnings ratio, (b) dividends yield, and (c) market risk. Note the market beta measures, and indicate whether each ratio had a favorable (F) or unfavorable (U) change from 19x1 to 19x2.

Problem 28A-5. Comprehensive Ratio Analysis of Two Companies *(L.O. 6)*

Willis Rowe is considering an investment in the common stock of a chain of retail department stores. He has narrowed his choice to two retail companies, Allison Corporation and Marker Corporation, whose income statements and balance sheets follow.

	Allison Corporation	Marker Corporation
Sales	$25,120,000	$50,420,000
Cost of Goods Sold	12,284,000	29,668,000
Gross Margin from Sales	$12,836,000	$20,752,000
Operating Expenses		
Sales Expense	$ 9,645,200	$14,216,400
Administrative Expense	1,972,000	4,868,000
Interest Expense	388,000	456,000
Income Taxes Expense	400,000	600,000
Total Operating Expenses	$12,405,200	$20,140,400
Net Income	$ 430,800	$ 611,600

	Allison Corporation	Marker Corporation
Assets		
Cash	$ 160,000	$ 384,800
Marketable Securities (at cost)	406,800	169,200
Accounts Receivable (net)	1,105,600	1,970,800
Inventory	1,259,600	2,506,800
Prepaid Expenses	108,800	228,000
Property, Plant, and Equipment (net)	5,827,200	13,104,000
Intangibles and Other Assets	1,106,400	289,600
Total Assets	$9,974,400	$18,653,200
Liabilities and Stockholders' Equity		
Accounts Payable	$ 688,000	$ 1,145,200
Notes Payable	300,000	800,000
Accrued Liabilities	100,400	146,800
Bonds Payable	4,000,000	4,000,000
Common Stock—$20 par value	2,000,000	1,200,000
Paid-in Capital in Excess of Par Value, Common	1,219,600	7,137,200
Retained Earnings	1,666,400	4,224,000
Total Liabilities and Stockholders' Equity	$9,974,400	$18,653,200

During the year, Allison Corporation paid a total of $100,000 in dividends. The market price per share of its stock is currently $60. In comparison, Marker Corporation paid a total of $228,000 in dividends, and the current market price of its stock is $76 per share. An investment service has indicated that the beta associated with Allison's stock is 1.20, while that associated with Marker's stock is .95. Information for prior years is not readily available. Assume that all notes payable are current liabilities and all bonds payable are long-term liabilities.

Required

Conduct a comprehensive ratio analysis for each company using the available information and compare the results. (Round percentages and ratios except earnings per share to one decimal place, and consider changes of .1 or less to be indeterminate.) This analysis should be done in the following steps:

1. Prepare an analysis of liquidity by calculating for each company the: (a) current ratio, (b) quick ratio, (c) receivable turnover, (d) average days' sales uncollected, and (e) inventory turnover.
2. Prepare an analysis of profitability by calculating for each company the: (a) profit margin, (b) asset turnover, (c) return on assets, (d) return on equity, and (e) earnings per share.
3. Prepare an analysis of long-term solvency by calculating for each company the: (a) debt to equity ratio and (b) interest coverage ratio.
4. Prepare an analysis of market tests by calculating for each company the: (a) price/earnings ratio, (b) dividends yield, and (c) market risk.
5. Compare the two companies by inserting the ratio calculations from **1** through **4** in a table with the following column heads: Ratio Name, Allison Corporation, Marker Corporation, and Company with More Favorable Ratio. Indicate in the right-hand column which company had the more favorable ratio in each case.
6. How could the analysis be improved if prior years' information were available?

Problem Set B

Problem 28B-1. Effect of Alternative Accounting Methods *(L.O. 4, 6)*

Le Beau Company began operations by purchasing $600,000 in equipment that had an estimated useful life of nine years and an estimated residual value of $60,000.

During the year, Le Beau Company purchased inventory as presented in the following chart:

January	2,000 units at $50	$ 100,000
March	4,000 units at $48	192,000
May	1,000 units at $54	54,000
July	5,000 units at $54	270,000
September	6,000 units at $56	336,000
November	2,000 units at $58	116,000
December	3,000 units at $56	168,000
Total	23,000 units	$1,236,000

During the year the company sold 19,000 units for a total of $1,820,000 and incurred salary expenses of $340,000 and expenses other than depreciation of $240,000.

Le Beau's management is anxious to present its income statement fairly in its first year of operation. It realizes that alternative accounting methods are available for accounting for inventory and equipment. Management wants to determine the effect of various alternatives on this year's income. Two sets of alternatives are required.

Required

1. Prepare two income statements for Le Beau Company: one using a FIFO basis for inventory and the straight-line method for depreciation, the other using a LIFO basis for inventory and the sum-of-the-years'-digits method for depreciation.
2. Prepare a schedule accounting for the difference in the two net income figures obtained in **1**.
3. What effect does the choice of accounting methods have on Le Beau Company's inventory turnover? What conclusions can you draw?
4. What effect does the choice of accounting methods have on Le Beau Company's return on assets?

Use year-end balances to compute the ratios. Round all ratios and percentages to one decimal place. Assume that the only other asset in addition to plant assets and inventory is $60,000 cash. Is your evaluation of Le Beau's profitability affected by the choice of accounting methods?

Problem 28B-2. Horizontal and Vertical Analysis *(L.O. 5)*

The condensed comparative income statements and balance sheets for Kelso Corporation follow.

Kelso Corporation
Comparative Income Statements
For the Years Ended December 31, 19x2 and 19x1

	19x2	19x1
Sales	$800,400	$742,600
Cost of Goods Sold	454,100	396,200
Gross Margin from Sales	$346,300	$346,400
Operating Expenses		
Selling Expenses	$130,100	$104,600
Administrative Expenses	140,300	115,500
Interest Expense	25,000	20,000
Income Taxes Expense	14,000	35,000
Total Operating Expenses	$309,400	$275,100
Net Income	$ 36,900	$ 71,300

Kelso Corporation
Comparative Balance Sheets
December 31, 19x2 and 19x1

	19x2	19x1
Assets		
Cash	$ 31,100	$ 27,200
Accounts Receivable (net)	72,500	42,700
Inventory	122,600	107,800
Property, Plant, and Equipment (net)	577,700	507,500
Total Assets	$803,900	$685,200
Liabilities and Stockholders' Equity		
Accounts Payable	$104,700	$ 72,300
Notes Payable	50,000	50,000
Bonds Payable	200,000	110,000
Common Stock—$10 par value	300,000	300,000
Retained Earnings	149,200	152,900
Total Liabilities and Stockholders' Equity	$803,900	$685,200

Required

(Round all ratios and percentages to one decimal place.)

1. Prepare a schedule showing the amount and percentage changes from 19x1 to 19x2 for the comparative income statements and the balance sheets.
2. Prepare common-size income statements and balance sheets for 19x1 and 19x2.
3. Comment on the results in **1** and **2** by identifying favorable and unfavorable changes in the components and composition of the statements.

Problem 28B-3. Analyzing the Effects of Transactions on Ratios *(L.O. 6)*

Estevez Corporation engaged in the transactions listed in the first column of the following table. Opposite each transaction is a ratio and space to mark the effect of each transaction on the ratio.

Transaction	Ratio	Effect: Increase	Effect: Decrease	Effect: None
a. Issued common stock for cash.	Asset turnover			
b. Declared cash dividend.	Current ratio			
c. Sold treasury stock.	Return on equity			
d. Borrowed cash by issuing note payable.	Debt to equity ratio			
e. Paid salary expense.	Inventory turnover			
f. Purchased merchandise for cash.	Current ratio			
g. Sold equipment for cash.	Receivable turnover			
h. Sold merchandise on account.	Quick ratio			
i. Paid current portion of long-term debt.	Return on assets			
j. Gave sales discount.	Profit margin			
k. Purchased marketable securities for cash.	Quick ratio			
l. Declared 5% stock dividend.	Current ratio			

Required

Place an X in the appropriate column to show whether the transaction increased, decreased, or had no effect on the indicated ratio.

Problem 28B-4. Ratio Analysis
(L.O. 6)

Additional data for Kelso Corporation in 19x2 and 19x1 follow. These data should be used in conjunction with the data in Problem 28B-2.

	19x2	19x1
Dividends Paid	$31,400	$35,000
Number of Common Shares	30,000	30,000
Market Price per Share	$40	$60
Beta	1.00	.90

Balances of selected accounts at the end of 19x0 were Accounts Receivable (net), $52,700; Inventory, $99,400; Total Assets, $647,800; and Stockholders' Equity, $376,600. All of Kelso's notes payable were current liabilities; all of the bonds payable were long-term liabilities.

Required

(Round all answers except earnings per share to one decimal place, and consider changes of .1 or less to be indeterminate.)

1. Prepare a liquidity analysis by calculating for each year the: (a) current ratio, (b) quick ratio, (c) receivable turnover, (d) average days' sales uncollected, and (e) inventory turnover. Indicate whether each ratio improved or deteriorated from 19x1 to 19x2 by adding an F for favorable or a U for unfavorable.
2. Prepare a profitability analysis by calculating for each year the: (a) profit margin, (b) asset turnover, (c) return on assets, (d) return on equity, and (e) earnings per share. Indicate whether each ratio had a favorable (F) or unfavorable (U) change from 19x1 to 19x2.
3. Prepare a long-term solvency analysis by calculating for each year the: (a) debt to equity ratio and (b) interest coverage ratio. Indicate whether each ratio had a favorable (F) or unfavorable (U) change from 19x1 to 19x2.
4. Conduct a market test analysis by calculating for each year the: (a) price/earnings ratio, (b) dividends yield, and (c) market risk. Note the market risk measure, and indicate whether each ratio had a favorable (F) or unfavorable (U) change from 19x1 to 19x2.

Problem 28B-5. Comprehensive Ratio Analysis of Two Companies
(L.O. 6)

June Kim has decided to invest some of her savings in common stock. She feels that the chemical industry has good growth prospects, and she has narrowed her choice to two companies in that industry. As a final step in making the choice, she has decided to make a comprehensive ratio analysis of the two companies, Evander and Lord. Income statement and balance sheet data for the two companies follow.

	Evander	Lord
Sales	$18,972,400	$54,574,600
Cost of Goods Sold	11,624,400	36,744,800
Gross Margin from Sales	$ 7,348,000	$17,829,800
Operating Expenses		
Selling Expenses	$ 2,388,000	$ 3,911,400
Administrative Expenses	2,434,800	8,252,000
Interest Expense	540,000	2,720,000
Income Taxes Expense	900,000	1,200,000
Total Operating Expenses	$ 6,262,800	$16,083,400
Net Income	$ 1,085,200	$ 1,746,400

	Evander	Lord
Assets		
Cash	$ 252,200	$ 1,028,600
Marketable Securities (at cost)	235,000	2,400,000
Accounts Receivable (net)	913,400	5,200,000
Inventories	3,760,000	9,912,000
Prepaid Expenses	145,200	313,200
Property, Plant, and Equipment (net)	10,684,400	38,712,000
Intangibles and Other Assets	434,000	1,160,000
Total Assets	$16,424,200	$58,725,800
Liabilities and Stockholders' Equity		
Accounts Payable	$ 1,034,800	$ 4,684,000
Notes Payable	2,000,000	4,000,000
Income Taxes Payable	170,400	235,800
Bonds Payable	4,000,000	30,000,000
Common Stock—$2 par value	700,000	2,000,000
Paid-in Capital in Excess of Par Value, Common	3,494,600	10,866,600
Retained Earnings	5,024,400	6,939,400
Total Liabilities and Stockholders' Equity	$16,424,200	$58,725,800

During the year, Evander paid a total of $280,000 in dividends, and its current market price per share is $40. Lord paid a total of $1,200,000 in dividends during the year, and the current market price per share is $18. An investment service reports that the beta associated with Evander's stock is 1.05, while that associated with Lord's is .8. Information pertaining to prior years is not readily available. Assume that all notes payable are current liabilities and that all bonds payable are long-term liabilities.

Required

Conduct a comprehensive ratio analysis of Evander and of Lord using the current end-of-year data. Compare the results. (Round all ratios and percentages except earnings per share to one decimal place.) This analysis should be done in the following steps:

1. Prepare an analysis of liquidity by calculating for each company the: (a) current ratio, (b) quick ratio, (c) receivable turnover, (d) average days' sales uncollected, and (e) inventory turnover.
2. Prepare an analysis of profitability by calculating for each company the: (a) profit margin, (b) asset turnover, (c) return on assets, (d) return on equity, and (e) earnings per share.
3. Prepare an analysis of long-term solvency by calculating for each company the: (a) debt to equity ratio and (b) interest coverage ratio.
4. Prepare an analysis of market tests by calculating for each company the: (a) price/earnings ratio, (b) dividends yield, and (c) market risk.
5. Compare the two companies by inserting the ratio calculations from **1** through **4** in a table with the following column heads: Ratio Name, Evander, Lord, and Company with More Favorable Ratio. Indicate in the right-hand column of the table which company had the more favorable ratio in each case.
6. How could the analysis be improved if prior years' information were available?

Financial Decision Case

Uribe Corporation
(L.O. 4)

Victor Uribe retired at the beginning of 19x1 as president and principal stockholder in Uribe Corporation, a successful producer of word processing equipment. As an incentive to the new management, Mr. Uribe supported the board of directors' new executive compensation plan, which provides cash bonuses to key executives for the years in which the company's earnings per share equal or exceed the current dividends per share of $4.00, plus a $.40 per share increase in dividends for each future year. Thus, for management to receive the bonuses, the company must earn per-share income of $4.00 the first year, $4.40 the second, $4.80 the third, and so forth. Since Mr. Uribe owns 500,000 of the 1,000,000 common shares outstanding, the dividend income will provide for his retirement years. He is also protected against inflation by the regular increase in dividends. Earnings and dividends per share for the first three years of operation under the new management were as follows:

	19x3	19x2	19x1
Earnings per share	$5.00	$5.00	$5.00
Dividends per share	4.80	4.40	4.00

During this time, management earned bonuses totaling more than $2 million under the compensation plan. Mr. Uribe, who had taken no active part on the board of directors, began to worry about the unchanging level of earnings and decided to study the company's annual report more carefully. The notes to the annual report revealed the following information:

a. Management changed from the LIFO inventory method to the FIFO method in 19x1. The effect of the change was to decrease cost of goods sold by $400,000 in 19x1, $600,000 in 19x2, and $800,000 in 19x3.
b. Management changed from the double-declining-balance accelerated depreciation method to the straight-line method in 19x2. The effect of this change was to decrease depreciation by $800,000 in 19x2 and by $1,000,000 in 19x3.
c. In 19x3, management increased the estimated useful life of intangible assets from five to ten years. The effect of this change was to decrease amortization expense by $200,000 in 19x3.

Required

1. Compute earnings per share for each year according to the accounting methods in use at the beginning of 19x1.
2. Have the executives earned their bonuses? What serious effect has the compensation package apparently had on the net assets of Uribe Corporation? How could Mr. Uribe have protected himself from what has happened?

Answers to Self-Test

1. a	3. a	5. c	7. c	9. a
2. d	4. d	6. d	8. c	10. c

LEARNING OBJECTIVE

1. Identify the major components of a corporate annual report.

APPENDIX A

The Annotated Annual Report of Toys "R" Us, Inc.

Financial statements for major corporations can be quite complicated and have many features. The management of a corporation has a responsibility each year to report to the stockholders on the company's performance. This report, called the **annual report**, contains the annual financial statements and the notes related to them, as well as other information about the company. In addition to the financial statements and related notes, the annual report usually contains a letter to the stockholders, a multiyear summary of financial highlights, a description of the business, management's discussion of operating results and financial condition, a report of management's responsibility, the auditors' report, and a list of directors and officers of the company. This report and other data must also be filed annually with the Securities and Exchange Commission.

To illustrate the annual report of a major corporation, excerpts from the 1993 annual report of Toys "R" Us, Inc. will be used in the following sections of this appendix.[1] Toys "R" Us, Inc. is one of the most successful retailers of this generation and is famous for its stores filled with huge inventories of toys and other items for children. In recent years, the company has opened a chain of stores that sell children's clothes, called Kids "R" Us. After studying this appendix, you should be able to meet the learning objective listed on the left.

Letter to the Stockholders

OBJECTIVE 1
Identify the major components of a corporate annual report

Traditionally, the top officers of a corporation address the stockholders about the performance and prospects for the company in a letter at the beginning of the annual report. The Chief Executive Officer and the chairman of the board of Toys "R" Us wrote to the stockholders about the highlights of the past year, the outlook for the new year, corporate citizenship, and human resources. For example, they reported on the prospects for the 1993 season as follows:

> We look forward to a strong year in 1993, with profit improvements in all three Divisions. Our assessment of the February New York Toy Fair indicates another good year in basic categories such as action figures, dolls, games and juvenile as well as continued strength in video games and related categories.

Financial Highlights (Figure 1)

The financial highlights section of the annual report presents key financial statistics for a ten-year period and is often accompanied by graphical presenta-

1. Excerpts reprinted courtesy of Toys "R" Us, Inc.

Figure 1. Financial Highlights for Toys "R" Us, Inc.

TOYS"R"US, INC. AND SUBSIDIARIES

FINANCIAL HIGHLIGHTS

(Dollars in millions except per share information) — *Fiscal Year Ended*

	Jan. 30, 1993	*Feb. 1, 1992*	*Feb. 2, 1991*	*Jan. 28, 1990*	*Jan. 29, 1989*	*Jan. 31, 1988*	*Feb. 1, 1987*	*Feb. 2, 1986*	*Feb. 3, 1985*	*Jan. 29, 1984*
OPERATIONS:										
Net Sales	**$ 7,169**	$ 6,124	$ 5,510	$ 4,788	$ 4,000	$ 3,137	$ 2,445	$ 1,976	$ 1,702	$ 1,320
Net Earnings	**438**	340	326	321	268	204	152	120	111	92
Earnings Per Share	**1.47**	1.15	1.11	1.09	.91	.69	.52	.41	.39	.32
FINANCIAL POSITION AT YEAR-END:										
Working Capital	**797**	328	177	238	255	225	155	181	222	220
Real Estate-Net	**1,877**	1,751	1,433	1,142	952	762	601	423	279	185
Total Assets	**5,323**	4,583	3,582	3,075	2,555	2,027	1,523	1,226	1,099	820
Long-Term Obligations	**671**	391	195	173	174	177	85	88	88	55
Stockholders' Equity	**2,889**	2,426	2,046	1,705	1,424	1,135	901	717	579	460
NUMBER OF STORES AT YEAR-END:										
Toys"R"Us - United States	**540**	497	451	404	358	313	271	233	198	169
Toys"R"Us - International	**167**	126	97	74	52	37	24	13	5	-
Kids"R"Us	**211**	189	164	137	112	74	43	23	10	2

10 Year Growth of a 100 Share Investment in Toys"R"Us Stock

An investor would now own 761 shares as a result of the original 100 share purchase being adjusted for five stock splits.

$31,200

$35,000 · 30,000 · 25,000 · 20,000 · 15,000 · 10,000 · 5,000 · 0

As of March 15 1983 1984 1985 1986 1987 1988 1989 1990 1991 1992 1993

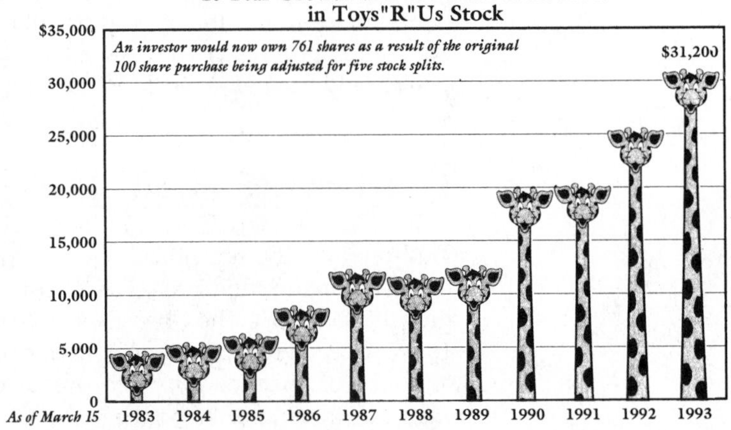

Reprinted courtesy of Toys "R" Us, Inc. The footnotes to the financial statement, which are an integral part of the report, are not included.

tions. Note, for example, that Figure 1 shows key figures for operations, financial position, and number of stores at year end for Toys "R" Us, Inc. and Subsidiaries. The growth of a one-hundred share investment in Toys "R" Us stock for the last ten years is presented graphically. Other key figures are also shown graphically at appropriate points in the report. Note that the financial highlights section often includes nonfinancial data, such as number of stores or number of employees. In addition to the financial highlights, the annual report will contain a detailed description of the products and divisions of the company. Some analysts scoff at this section of the annual report because of the glossy photographs, but many companies provide useful information about past results and future plans.

Consolidated Statements of Earnings (Figure 2)

1. Toys "R" Us calls its income statements the consolidated statements of earnings. The word **consolidated** used in the title means that Toys "R" Us consists of several companies that are combined for financial reporting purposes. Ten-year charts of consolidated net sales and consolidated net earnings are presented below the statements.
2. The consolidated statements of earnings contain data for the years ended in 1993, 1992, and 1991, shown in the columns at the right, to aid in the evaluation of the company over the years. Financial statements presented in this fashion are called **comparative financial statements**. This manner of reporting is in accordance with generally accepted accounting principles. For Toys "R" Us, the fiscal year ends on the Saturday nearest to January 31.
3. Toys "R" Us uses the single-step form of the income statement and so includes all costs and expenses as a deduction from net sales to arrive at Earnings Before Taxes on Income.
4. Taxes on Income are the expense for federal and state taxes on Toys "R" Us's corporate income. Income taxes for corporations are substantial, often exceeding 35 percent of the income before income taxes, and thus have a significant effect on company decisions. Most other taxes, such as property taxes and employment taxes, are shown among the operating expenses.
5. Earnings per share is reported by Toys "R" Us in accordance with generally accepted accounting principles. Its calculation is based on the weighted average number of common shares outstanding during the year.
6. At the bottom of each page of the financial statements, the company reminds the reader in a footnote that the notes accompanying the financial statements are an integral part of the statements and must be consulted in interpreting them.

Consolidated Balance Sheets (Figure 3)

1. Toys "R" Us also presents consolidated balance sheets in comparative form. In contrast to the statements of consolidated earnings, only two years of comparative data are used for the balance sheet.
2. Toys "R" Us has a typical set of current assets for a merchandising company.
3. Toys "R" Us has a large investment in property and equipment. More details on property and equipment, including the amounts for accumulated depreciation and amortization, are provided in the notes and shown in the discussion of explanatory notes on pages Ap-8 and Ap-9.
4. Toys "R" Us has leased property, recorded on the balance sheet as an asset.
5. In place of an investment category and an intangible asset category, Toys "R" Us has a catchall group named Other Assets.
6. The current liabilities section contains typical current liabilities.
7. Other liabilities in the Toys "R" Us balance sheet are Long-Term Debt and Obligations Under Capital Leases (excluding the current portions). Also included is Deferred Income Taxes, an account that is sometimes hard to understand. In general, deferred income taxes are income tax expenses that will not have to be paid until sometime in the future. The subject of deferred income taxes is covered in the chapter on retained earnings and corporate income statements.

Figure 2. Consolidated Statements of Earnings for Toys "R" Us, Inc.

TOYS"R"US, INC. AND SUBSIDIARIES

① **CONSOLIDATED STATEMENTS OF EARNINGS**

(In thousands except per share information)

②

			Year Ended
	January 30, 1993	*February 1, 1992*	*February 2, 1991*
③ Net sales	$ 7,169,290	$ 6,124,209	$ 5,510,001
Costs and expenses:			
Cost of sales	4,968,555	4,286,639	3,820,840
Selling, advertising, general and administrative	1,342,262	1,153,576	1,024,809
Depreciation and amortization	119,034	100,701	79,093
Interest expense	69,134	57,885	73,304
Interest and other income	(18,719)	(13,521)	(11,233)
	6,480,266	5,585,280	4,986,813
Earnings before taxes on income	689,024	538,929	523,188
④ Taxes on income	251,500	199,400	197,200
Net earnings	$ 437,524	$ 339,529	$ 325,988
⑤ Earnings per share	$ 1.47	$ 1.15	$ 1.11

⑥ See notes to consolidated financial statements.

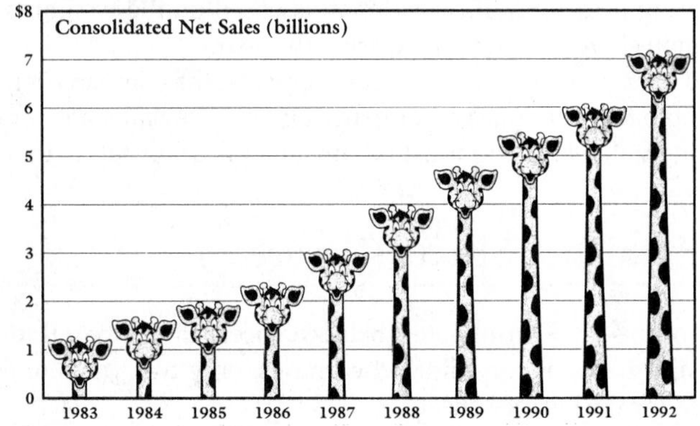

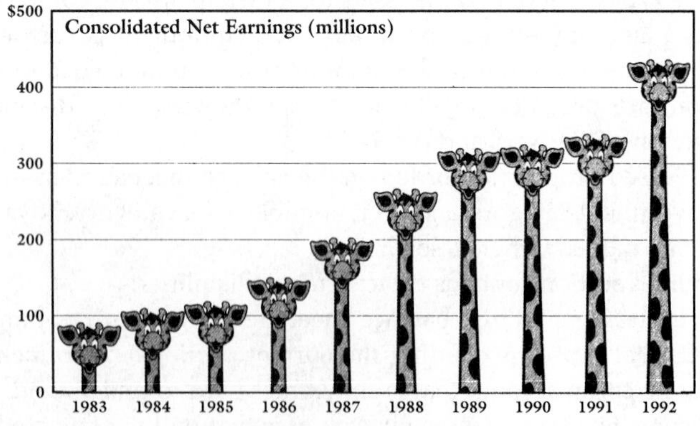

Reprinted courtesy of Toys "R" Us, Inc. The footnotes to the financial statement, which are an integral part of the report, are not included.

Figure 3. Consolidated Balance Sheets for Toys "R" Us, Inc.

TOYS"R"US, INC. AND SUBSIDIARIES

CONSOLIDATED BALANCE SHEETS

(In thousands)

	① *January 30, 1993*	*February 1, 1992*
ASSETS		
② Current Assets:		
Cash and cash equivalents	$ 763,721	$ 444,593
Accounts and other receivables	69,385	64,078
Merchandise inventories	1,498,671	1,390,605
Prepaid expenses and other	52,731	35,377
Total Current Assets	2,384,508	1,934,653
③ Property and Equipment:		
Real estate, net	1,876,835	1,751,229
Other, net	920,894	800,276
④ Leased property under capital leases, net	5,821	6,582
Total Property and Equipment	2,803,550	2,558,087
⑤ Other Assets	134,794	89,868
	$ 5,322,852	$ 4,582,608
LIABILITIES AND STOCKHOLDERS' EQUITY		
⑥ Current Liabilities:		
Short-term borrowings	$ 120,772	$ 291,659
Accounts payable	941,375	858,777
Accrued expenses and other current liabilities	361,661	332,185
Income taxes payable	163,841	123,750
Total Current Liabilities	1,587,649	1,606,371
⑦ Deferred Income Taxes	175,430	158,871
Long-Term Debt	660,488	379,880
Obligations Under Capital Leases	10,264	11,418
⑧ Stockholders' Equity:		
Common stock	29,794	29,794
Additional paid-in capital	465,494	384,803
Retained earnings	2,529,853	2,092,329
Foreign currency translation adjustments	14,317	47,967
Treasury shares, at cost	(150,437)	(127,717)
Receivable from exercise of stock options	-	(1,108)
	2,889,021	2,426,068
	$ 5,322,852	$ 4,582,608

See notes to consolidated financial statements.

Reprinted courtesy of Toys "R" Us, Inc. The footnotes to the financial statement, which are an integral part of the report, are not included.

8. There are several items in the stockholders' equity section. Common Stock represents the number of shares outstanding at par value. Additional paid-in capital represents amounts invested by stockholders in excess of the par value of the common stock. Retained earnings is the company's lifetime earnings less dividends paid to stockholders and transfers to paid-in capital. The foreign currency translation adjustment occurs because Toys "R" Us has foreign operations (see the appendices on international accounting and intercompany investments). Treasury shares is a contra stockholders' equity account that represents the cost of previously issued shares that have been bought back by the company. Finally, the receivable from exercise of stock options represents stock purchased by management and employees but not yet paid for.

The Consolidated Statements of Stockholders' Equity

Instead of a simple statement of retained earnings, Toys "R" Us presents a statement of stockholders' equity. This statement explains the changes in each of the components of stockholders' equity. The statement is covered in the chapter on retained earnings and corporate income statements.

The Consolidated Statements of Cash Flows (Figure 4)

1. The preparation of the consolidated statements of cash flows is presented in the chapter on the statement of cash flows. Whereas the income statement reflects the profitability of the company, the statement of cash flows reflects the liquidity of the company. The statement provides information about a company's cash receipts and cash payments and about its investing and financing activities during an accounting period. Three years of comparative statements are presented in Figure 4.
2. The first section of the consolidated statements of cash flows shows cash flows from operating activities. It begins with the net income (earnings) from the consolidated statements of earnings (Figure 2) and adjusts that figure, which is based on accrual accounting, to a figure that represents the net cash flows provided by operating activities. Among the adjustments are increases for depreciation and amortization, which are expenses that do not require the use of cash, and increases and decreases for the changes in the various working capital accounts. In the year ended January 30, 1993, Toys "R" Us had net earnings of $437,524,000, and its net cash inflow from these operations was $573,257,000. Added to net income are expenses that do not require a current outlay of cash, such as depreciation and amortization ($119,034,000) and deferred taxes ($13,998,000). Cash was also used to increase accounts and other receivables ($5,307,000), inventories ($108,066,000) and prepaid expenses and other operating assets ($36,249,000). An increase of $112,232,000 in accounts payable, accrued expenses, and other liabilities, and of $40,091,000 in income taxes payable had the most significant positive effect on cash flows.
3. The second major section of the consolidated statements of cash flows is cash flows from investing activities. The main item in this category is capital expenditures, net, of $421,564,000. This shows that Toys "R" Us is a growing company.
4. The third major section of the consolidated statements of cash flows is cash flows from financing activities. You can see here that the primary sources of cash from financing activities are long-term borrowings of $318,035,000 and exercise of

Figure 4. Consolidated Statements of Cash Flows for Toys "R" Us, Inc.

TOYS"R"US, INC. AND SUBSIDIARIES

CONSOLIDATED STATEMENTS OF CASH FLOWS

①

(In thousands)

			Year Ended
	January 30, 1993	*February 1, 1992*	*February 2, 1991*
CASH FLOWS FROM OPERATING ACTIVITIES			
② Net earnings	**$ 437,524**	$ 339,529	$ 325,988
Adjustments to reconcile net earnings to net cash provided by operating activities:			
Depreciation and amortization	**119,034**	100,701	79,093
Deferred income taxes	**13,998**	15,817	14,039
Changes in operating assets and liabilities:			
Accounts and other receivables	**(5,307)**	9,092	(20,072)
Merchandise inventories	**(108,066)**	(115,436)	(44,775)
Prepaid expenses and other operating assets	**(36,249)**	(16,176)	(9,043)
Accounts payable, accrued expenses and other liabilities	**112,232**	462,152	(40,130)
Income taxes payable	**40,091**	7,071	(10,424)
Total adjustments	**135,733**	463,221	(31,312)
Net cash provided by operating activities	**573,257**	802,750	294,676
CASH FLOWS FROM INVESTING ACTIVITIES			
③ Capital expenditures, net	**(421,564)**	(548,538)	(485,269)
Other assets	**(22,175)**	(17,110)	-
Net cash used in investing activities	**(443,739)**	(565,648)	(485,269)
CASH FLOWS FROM FINANCING ACTIVITIES			
④ Short-term borrowings, net	**(170,887)**	(94,811)	180,957
Long-term borrowings	**318,035**	197,802	33,152
Long-term debt repayments	**(7,926)**	(1,590)	(10,864)
Exercise of stock options	**86,323**	32,707	30,344
Share repurchase program	**(27,244)**	-	(32,692)
Net cash provided by financing activities	**198,301**	134,108	200,897
Effect of exchange rate changes on cash and cash equivalents	**(8,691)**	38,378	(16,194)
CASH AND CASH EQUIVALENTS			
⑤ Increase (decrease) during year	**319,128**	409,588	(5,890)
Beginning of year	**444,593**	35,005	40,895
End of year	**$ 763,721**	$ 444,593	$ 35,005

SUPPLEMENTAL DISCLOSURES OF CASH FLOW INFORMATION

⑥ The Company considers its highly liquid investments purchased as part of its daily cash management activities to be cash equivalents.

During the years ended January 30, 1993, February 1, 1992 and February 2, 1991, the Company made income tax payments of $151,722, $155,469 and $180,943 and interest payments (net of amounts capitalized) of $83,584, $46,763 and $77,570, respectively.

See notes to consolidated financial statements.

Reprinted courtesy of Toys "R" Us, Inc. The footnotes to the financial statement, which are an integral part of the report, are not included.

stock options of $86,323,000, which was helpful in reducing short-term borrowings by $170,887,000 and in paying for part of the capital expenditures in the investing activities section. In total, the company raised $198,301,000 from financing activities during the year.

5. At the bottom of the consolidated statements of cash flows, the net effect of the operating, investing, and financing activities on the Cash balance may be seen. Toys "R" Us had a substantial increase in cash (and cash equivalents) during the year of $319,128,000 and ended the year with $763,721,000 of cash (and cash equivalents) on hand.
6. The supplemental disclosures of cash flow information explain that Toys "R" Us intends the word *cash* to include not only cash but also highly liquid cash equivalents, which earn a return on cash that is not needed at the moment. This section also explains other significant investing and financing transactions. It is interesting to note that Cash was unfavorably affected in the amount of $8,691,000 by foreign currency fluctuations during the year.

Notes to Consolidated Financial Statements

To meet the requirements of full disclosure, the company must add **notes to the financial statements** to help the user interpret some of the more complex items in the published financial statements. The notes are considered an integral part of the financial statements. In recent years, the need for explanation and further details has become so great that the notes often take more space than the statements themselves. The notes to the financial statements can be put into three broad groups: summary of significant accounting policies, explanatory notes, and supplementary information notes.

Summary of Significant Accounting Policies

In its *Opinion No. 22,* the Accounting Principles Board requires that the financial statements include a **summary of significant accounting policies**. In most cases, this summary is presented in the first note to the financial statements or as a separate part just before the notes. In this part, the company tells which generally accepted accounting principles it has followed in preparing the statements. For example, in the Toys "R" Us report the company states the principles followed for property and equipment:

Property and equipment are recorded at cost. Depreciation and amortization are provided using the straight-line method over the estimated useful lives of the assets, or where applicable, the terms of the respective leases, whichever is shorter.

Other important accounting policies listed by Toys "R" Us deal with fiscal year, principles of consolidation, merchandise inventories, preopening costs, capitalized interest, financial instruments, and reclassification.

Explanatory Notes

Other notes explain some of the items in the financial statements. For example, Toys "R" Us showed the details of its Property and Equipment account in the second note, as shown at the top of page Ap-9.

Other notes had to do with long-term debt, leases, stockholders' equity, taxes on income, profit sharing plan, stock options, and foreign operations.

(In thousands)	Useful Life (In years)	January 30, 1993	February 1, 1992
Land		$ 642,368	$ 599,886
Buildings	45–50	1,280,850	1,164,323
Furniture and equipment	5–20	809,772	695,820
Leaseholds and leasehold improvements	12½–50	510,780	419,457
Construction in progress		72,895	83,032
Leased property under capital leases		20,193	21,172
		$3,336,858	$2,983,690
Less accumulated depreciation and amortization		533,308	425,603
		$2,803,550	$2,558,087

Supplementary Information Notes

In recent years, the FASB and SEC have ruled that certain supplemental information must be presented with financial statements. An example is the quarterly report that most companies make to their stockholders and to the Securities and Exchange Commission. These quarterly reports, which are called **interim financial statements**, are in most cases reviewed but not audited by the company's independent CPA firm. In its annual report, Toys "R" Us presented unaudited quarterly financial data from its 1993 quarterly statements, which are shown in the following table (dollars in thousands, except per share amounts). For the year ended January 30, 1993:

	First Quarter	Second Quarter	Third Quarter	Fourth Quarter
Net Sales	$1,172,476	$1,249,144	$1,345,835	$3,401,835
Cost of Sales	809,929	864,511	922,619	2,371,496
Net Earnings	28,304	32,709	36,796	339,715
Earnings per Share	$.10	$.11	$.12	$1.14

Interim data were presented for 1992 as well. Toys "R" Us also provides supplemental information on the market price of its common stock during the years. Other companies that are engaged in more than one line or type of business may present information for each business segment.

Report of Management's Responsibilities

A statement of management's responsibility for the financial statements and the system of internal control may accompany the financial statements. A part of the statement by Toys "R" Us management is printed at the top of page Ap-10.

Responsibility for the integrity and objectivity of the financial information presented in this Annual Report rests with Toys "R" Us management. The accompanying financial statements have been prepared from accounting records which management believes fairly and accurately reflect the operations and financial position of the Company. Management has established a system of internal controls to provide reasonable assurance that assets are maintained and accounted for in accordance with its policies and that transactions are recorded accurately on the Company's books and records.

The Company's comprehensive internal audit program provides for constant evaluation of the adequacy of the adherence to management's established policies and procedures. The Company has distributed to key employees its policies for conducting business affairs in a lawful and ethical manner.

The 1992 financial statements of the Company have been audited by Ernst & Young, independent auditors. Their accompanying report is based on an audit conducted in accordance with generally accepted auditing standards, including a review of internal accounting controls and financial reporting matters.

Management's Discussion and Analysis

A discussion and analysis by management of financial conditions and results of operations is also presented. In this section, management explains the difference from one year to the next. For example, the management of Toys "R" Us describes the company's sales performance in the following way:

The Company has experienced sales growth in each of its last three years; sales were up 17.1% in 1992, 11.1% in 1991 and 15.1% in 1990. Part of the growth is attributable to the opening of 136 new U.S.A. toy stores, 93 international toy stores and 75 children's clothing stores during the three year period, and a portion of the increase is due to comparable U.S.A. toy store sales increases of 6.9%, 2.4% and .3% in 1992, 1991 and 1990, respectively.

Its management of cash flows is described as follows:

The seasonal nature of the business (approximately 47% of sales take place in the fourth quarter), typically causes cash to decline from the beginning of the year through October as inventory is built up for the Christmas season and funds are used for land purchases and construction of new stores which usually open in the first ten months of the year. For these purposes, the Company has commitments and backup lines from numerous financial institutions to adequately support its short-term financing needs. Management expects that seasonal cash requirements will continue to be met primarily through operations, issuance of short-term commercial paper and bank borrowings for its foreign subsidiaries.

Report of Certified Public Accountants (Figure 5)

1. The **accountants' report** (or **auditors' report**) deals with the credibility of the financial statements. This report by independent public accountants gives the accountants' opinion about how fairly these statements have been presented. Using financial statements prepared by managers without an independent audit would be like having a judge hear a case in which he or she was personally involved or having a member of a team taking part in a soccer game act as a referee. Management, through its internal accounting system, is logically responsible for recordkeeping because it needs similar information for its own use in operating the business. The certified public accountants, acting independently,

add the necessary credibility to management's figures for interested third parties. Note that certified public accountants report to the board of directors and the stockholders rather than to management.

In form and language, most auditors' reports are like the one shown in Figure 5. Usually such a report is short, but its language is very important. The report is divided into three parts.

2. The first paragraph identifies the financial statements subject to the auditors' report. This paragraph also identifies responsibilities. Company management is responsible for financial statements, and the auditor is responsible for expressing an opinion on the financial statements based on the audit.
3. The second paragraph, or **scope section**, states that the examination was made in accordance with generally accepted auditing standards. These standards call for an acceptable level of quality in ten areas established by the American Institute of Certified Public Accountants. This paragraph also contains a brief description of the objectives and nature of the audit.
4. The third paragraph, or **opinion section**, states the results of the auditors' examination. The use of the word *opinion* is very important because the auditor does not certify or guarantee that the statements are absolutely correct. To do so would go beyond the truth since many items such as depreciation are based on estimates. Instead, the auditors simply give an opinion as to whether, overall, the financial statements "present fairly," in all material respects, the financial position, cash flows, and results of operations. This means that the statements are prepared in accordance with generally accepted accounting principles. If in the auditors' opinion they are not, the auditors must explain why and to what extent they do not meet the standards.

Figure 5. Auditors' Report for Toys "R" Us, Inc.

REPORT OF INDEPENDENT AUDITORS

① The Board of Directors and Stockholders
Toys"R"Us, Inc.

② We have audited the accompanying consolidated balance sheet of Toys"R"Us, Inc. and subsidiaries as of January 30, 1993 and the related consolidated statements of earnings, stockholders' equity and cash flows for the year then ended. These financial statements are the responsibility of the Company's management. Our responsibility is to express an opinion on these financial statements based on our audit. The financial statements of Toys"R"Us, Inc. and subsidiaries for each of the two years in the period ended February 1, 1992 were audited by other auditors whose report dated March 11, 1992, expressed an unqualified opinion on those statements.

③ We conducted our audit in accordance with generally accepted auditing standards. Those standards require that we plan and perform the audit to obtain reasonable assurance about whether the financial statements are free of material misstatement. An audit includes examining, on a test basis, evidence supporting the amounts and disclosures in the financial statements. An audit also includes assessing the accounting principles used and significant estimates made by management, as well as evaluating the overall financial statement presentation. We believe that our audit provides a reasonable basis for our opinion.

④ In our opinion, the 1992 financial statements referred to above present fairly, in all material respects, the consolidated financial position of Toys"R"Us, Inc. and subsidiaries at January 30, 1993 and the consolidated results of their operations and their cash flows for the year then ended in conformity with generally accepted accounting principles.

Ernst + Young

New York, New York
March 10, 1993

Reprinted courtesy of Toys "R" Us, Inc. The footnotes to the financial statement, which are an integral part of the report, are not included.

Questions

1. What are some of the differences between the income statement for a sole proprietorship and that for a corporation?
2. Explain earnings per share and how this figure appears on the income statement.
3. Why are notes to financial statements necessary?
4. What is the purpose of the accountants' (auditors') report?

Classroom Exercises

Exercises A-1 through A-4 pertain to the financial statements of Toys "R" Us, Inc. in Figures 1 to 5. (Note that 1993 refers to the year ended January 30, 1993, and 1992 refers to the year ended February 1, 1992.)

Exercise A-1. Consolidated Balance Sheets
(L.O. 1)

Answer the following questions pertaining to the consolidated balance sheets:

1. Did the amount of working capital increase or decrease from 1992 to 1993? By how much?
2. Did the current ratio improve from 1992 to 1993?
3. Does the company have long-term investments or intangible assets?
4. Did the capital structure of Toys "R" Us change from 1992 to 1993?
5. What is the contributed capital for 1993? How does it compare with retained earnings?

Exercise A-2. Consolidated Statements of Earnings
(L.O. 1)

Answer the following questions pertaining to the consolidated statements of earnings:

1. Did Toys "R" Us use a multistep or single-step form of income statement?
2. Is it a comparative statement?
3. What is the trend of net earnings?
4. How significant are income taxes for Toys "R" Us?
5. What is the trend of earnings per share?
6. Did the profit margin increase from 1992 to 1993?
7. Did asset turnover improve from 1992 to 1993?
8. Did the return on assets increase from 1992 to 1993?
9. Did the return on equity increase from 1992 to 1993? Total assets and total stockholders' equity for 1993 may be obtained from Figure 1.

Exercise A-3. Consolidated Statements of Cash Flows
(L.O. 1)

Answer the following questions pertaining to the consolidated statements of cash flows:

1. Compare net income in 1993 with cash provided by operating activities in 1993. Why is there a difference?
2. What are the most important investment activities in 1993?
3. What are the most important financing activities in 1993?
4. How did these investing and financing activities compare with those in prior years?
5. Where did Toys "R" Us get cash to pay for the capital expenditures?
6. How did the change in Cash and cash equivalents in 1993 compare to that in other years?

Exercise A-4. Auditors' Report
(L.O. 1)

Answer the following questions pertaining to the auditors' report:

1. What was the name of Toys "R" Us's independent auditor?
2. Who is responsible for the financial statements?
3. What is the auditor's responsibility?
4. Does the auditor examine all the company's records?
5. Did the accountants think that the financial statements presented fairly the financial situation of the company?
6. Did the company comply with generally accepted accounting principles?

Problem

Problem A-1.
Toys "R" Us, Inc.
(L.O. 1)

Toys "R" Us, Inc. has consistently been one of the best and fastest growing retailers in the country. Management is proud of its record of cost control, as witnessed by the following quotation from the company's 1987 annual report:

> Toys "R" Us expense levels are among the best controlled in retailing. . . . For example, in 1986 (year ended February 1, 1987) our expenses as a percentage of sales declined by almost 3% from 21.7% to 18.8%. As a result, we were able to operate with lower merchandise margins and still increase our earnings and return on sales.

The company's condensed single-step income statements appear in Figure 2 on page Ap-4.

Required

1. Prepare multistep income statements for Toys "R" Us for 1992 and 1993, and compute the ratios of gross margin from sales, operating expenses, income from operations, and net earnings to net sales.
2. Comment on whether the trend indicated by management in 1987 continued to be true in 1993. In 1987, gross margin was 31.2 percent, total operating expenses were 20.0 percent of net sales, and net earnings were 9.9 percent of sales.

LEARNING OBJECTIVES

1. *Distinguish between simple and compound interest.*
2. *Use compound interest tables to compute the future value of a single invested sum at compound interest and of an ordinary annuity.*
3. *Use compound interest tables to compute the present value of a single sum due in the future and of an ordinary annuity.*
4. *Apply the concept of present value to simple accounting situations.*

APPENDIX B

The Time Value of Money

Interest is an important cost to the debtor and an important revenue to the creditor. Because interest is a cost associated with time, and "time is money," it is also an important consideration in any business decision. For example, an individual who holds $100 for one year without putting that $100 in a savings account has forgone the interest that could have been earned. Thus, there is a cost associated with holding this money equal to the interest that could have been earned. Similarly, a business person who accepts a non-interest-bearing note instead of cash for the sale of merchandise is not forgoing the interest that could have been earned on that money but is including the interest implicitly in the price of the merchandise. These examples illustrate the point that the timing of the receipt and payment of cash must be considered in making business decisions. After studying this appendix, you should be able to meet the learning objectives listed on the left.

Simple Interest and Compound Interest

OBJECTIVE 1
Distinguish between simple and compound interest

Interest is the cost associated with the use of money for a specific period of time. **Simple interest** is the interest cost for one or more periods, if we assume that the amount on which the interest is computed stays the same from period to period. **Compound interest** is the interest cost for two or more periods, if we assume that after each period the interest of that period is added to the amount on which interest is computed in future periods. In other words, compound interest is interest earned on a principal sum that is increased at the end of each period by the interest of that period.

Example: Simple Interest. Joe Sanchez accepts an 8 percent, $30,000 note due in ninety days. How much will he receive in total at that time? Remember the formula for calculating simple interest, which was presented in the chapter on short-term liquid assets as part of the discussion of notes receivable:

$$\begin{aligned}\text{Interest} &= \text{principal} \times \text{rate} \times \text{time}\\ &= \$30{,}000 \times 8/100 \times 90/360\\ &= \$600\end{aligned}$$

The total that Sanchez will receive is computed as follows:

$$\begin{aligned}\text{Total} &= \text{principal} + \text{interest}\\ &= \$30{,}000 + \$600\\ &= \$30{,}600\end{aligned}$$

Example: Compound Interest. Ann Clary deposits $5,000 in a savings account that pays 6 percent interest. She expects to leave the principal and accumulated interest in the account for three years. How much will her account total at the end of three years? Assume that the interest is paid at the end of the year and is added to the principal at that time and that this total in turn earns interest. The amount at the end of three years may be computed as follows:

(1) Year	(2) Principal Amount at Beginning of Year	(3) Annual Amount of Interest (col. 2 × .06)	(4) Accumulated Amount at End of Year (col. 2 + col. 3)
1	$5,000.00	$300.00	$5,300.00
2	5,300.00	318.00	5,618.00
3	5,618.00	337.08	5,955.08

At the end of three years, Clary will have $5,955.08 in her savings account. Note that the annual amount of interest increases each year by the interest rate times the interest of the previous year. For example, between year 1 and year 2, the interest increased by $18 ($318 – $300), which exactly equals .06 times $300.

Future Value of a Single Invested Sum at Compound Interest

OBJECTIVE 2
Use compound interest tables to compute the future value of a single invested sum at compound interest and of an ordinary annuity

Another way to ask the question in the example of compound interest above is, What is the future value of a single sum ($5,000) at compound interest (6 percent) for three years? **Future value** is the amount that an investment will be worth at a future date if invested at compound interest. A business person often wants to know future value, but the method of computing the future value illustrated above is too time-consuming in practice. Imagine how tedious the calculation would be if the example were ten years instead of three. Fortunately, there are tables that make problems involving compound interest much simpler and quicker to solve. Table 1, showing the future value of $1 after a given number of time periods, is an example. It is actually part of a larger table, Table 1 in

Table 1. Future Value of $1 after a Given Number of Time Periods

Periods	1%	2%	3%	4%	5%	6%	7%	8%	9%	10%	12%	14%	15%
1	1.010	1.020	1.030	1.040	1.050	1.060	1.070	1.080	1.090	1.100	1.120	1.140	1.150
2	1.020	1.040	1.061	1.082	1.103	1.124	1.145	1.166	1.188	1.210	1.254	1.300	1.323
3	1.030	1.061	1.093	1.125	1.158	1.191	1.225	1.260	1.295	1.331	1.405	1.482	1.521
4	1.041	1.082	1.126	1.170	1.216	1.262	1.311	1.360	1.412	1.464	1.574	1.689	1.749
5	1.051	1.104	1.159	1.217	1.276	1.338	1.403	1.469	1.539	1.611	1.762	1.925	2.011
6	1.062	1.126	1.194	1.265	1.340	1.419	1.501	1.587	1.677	1.772	1.974	2.195	2.313
7	1.072	1.149	1.230	1.316	1.407	1.504	1.606	1.714	1.828	1.949	2.211	2.502	2.660
8	1.083	1.172	1.267	1.369	1.477	1.594	1.718	1.851	1.993	2.144	2.476	2.853	3.059
9	1.094	1.195	1.305	1.423	1.551	1.689	1.838	1.999	2.172	2.358	2.773	3.252	3.518
10	1.105	1.219	1.344	1.480	1.629	1.791	1.967	2.159	2.367	2.594	3.106	3.707	4.046

Source: Excerpt from Table 1 in the appendix on future value and present value tables.

the appendix on future value and present value tables. Suppose that we want to solve the problem of Clary's savings account above. We simply look down the 6 percent column in Table 1 until we reach period 3 and find the factor 1.191. This factor, when multiplied by $1, gives the future value of that $1 at compound interest of 6 percent for three periods (years in this case). Thus, we solve the problem:

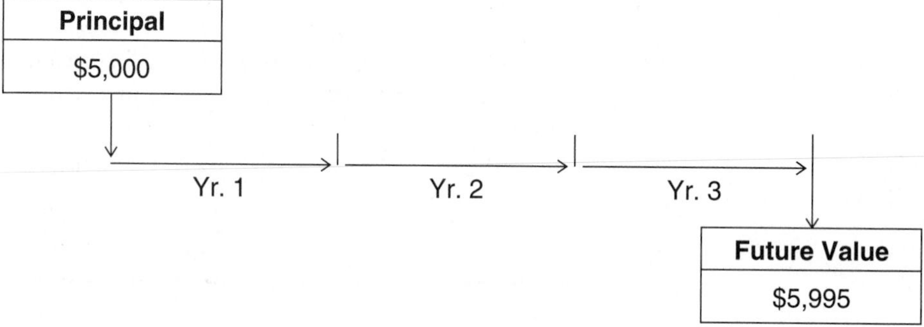

Principal × factor = future value
$5,000 × 1.191 = $5,955

Except for a rounding difference of $0.08, the answer is exactly the same as that calculated earlier.

Future Value of an Ordinary Annuity

Another common problem involves an **ordinary annuity**, which is a series of equal payments made at the end of equal intervals of time, with compound interest on these payments.

The following example shows how to find the future value of an ordinary annuity. Assume that Ben Katz makes a $200 payment at the end of each of the next three years into a savings account that pays 5 percent interest each year. How much money will he have in his account at the end of the three years? One way of computing the amount is shown in the following table:

(1) Year	(2) Beginning Balance	(3) Interest Earned (5% × col. 2)	(4) Periodic Payment	(5) Accumulated at End of Period (col. 2 + col. 3 + col. 4)
1	$ —	$ —	$200	$200.00
2	200.00	10.00	200	410.00
3	410.00	20.50	200	630.50

Katz would have $630.50 in his account at the end of three years, consisting of $600.00 in periodic payments and $30.50 in interest.

This calculation can also be simplified by using Table 2. We look down the 5 percent column until we reach period 3 and find the factor 3.153. This factor, when multiplied by $1, gives the future value of a series of three $1 payments (years in this case) at compound interest of 5 percent. Thus, we solve the problem as shown in the middle of the next page.

Table 2. Future Value of an Ordinary Annuity of $1 Paid in Each Period for a Given Number of Time Periods

Periods	1%	2%	3%	4%	5%	6%	7%	8%	9%	10%	12%	14%	15%
1	1.000	1.000	1.000	1.000	1.000	1.000	1.000	1.000	1.000	1.000	1.000	1.000	1.000
2	2.010	2.020	2.030	2.040	2.050	2.060	2.070	2.080	2.090	2.100	2.120	2.140	2.150
3	3.030	3.060	3.091	3.122	3.153	3.184	3.215	3.246	3.278	3.310	3.374	3.440	3.473
4	4.060	4.122	4.184	4.246	4.310	4.375	4.440	4.506	4.573	4.641	4.779	4.921	4.993
5	5.101	5.204	5.309	5.416	5.526	5.637	5.751	5.867	5.985	6.105	6.353	6.610	6.742
6	6.152	6.308	6.468	6.633	6.802	6.975	7.153	7.336	7.523	7.716	8.115	8.536	8.754
7	7.214	7.434	7.662	7.898	8.142	8.394	8.654	8.923	9.200	9.487	10.09	10.73	11.07
8	8.286	8.583	8.892	9.214	9.549	9.897	10.26	10.64	11.03	11.44	12.30	13.23	13.73
9	9.369	9.755	10.16	10.58	11.03	11.49	11.98	12.49	13.02	13.58	14.78	16.09	16.79
10	10.46	10.95	11.46	12.01	12.58	13.18	13.82	14.49	15.19	15.94	17.55	19.34	20.30

Source: Excerpt from Table 2 in the appendix on future value and present value tables.

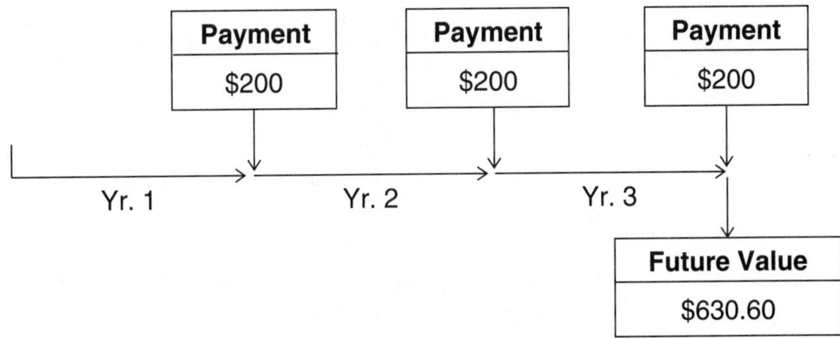

Periodic payment × factor = future value
$200.00 × 3.153 = $630.60

Except for a rounding difference of $0.10, this result is the same as the one calculated earlier.

Present Value

Suppose that you had the choice of receiving $100 today or one year from today. Intuitively, you would choose to receive the $100 today. Why? You know that if you have the $100 today, you can put it in a savings account to earn interest and will have more than $100 a year from today. Therefore, we can say that an amount to be received in the future (future value) is not worth as much today as an amount to be received today (present value) because of the cost associated with the passage of time. In fact, present value and future value are closely related. **Present value** is the amount that must be invested now at a given rate of interest to produce a given future value.

For example, assume that Sue Dapper needs $1,000 one year from now. How much should she invest today to achieve that goal if the interest rate is 5 percent per year? From earlier examples, this equation may be established:

Present value × (1.0 + interest rate) = future value
Present value × 1.05 = $1,000.00
Present value = $1,000.00 ÷ 1.05
Present value = $952.38

Thus, to achieve a future value of $1,000.00, a present value of $952.38 must be invested. Interest of 5 percent on $952.38 for one year equals $47.62, and these two amounts added together equal $1,000.00.

Present Value of a Single Sum Due in the Future

OBJECTIVE 3
Use compound interest tables to compute the present value of a single sum due in the future and of an ordinary annuity

When more than one time period is involved, the calculation of present value is more complicated. Consider the following example. Don Riley wants to be sure of having $4,000 at the end of three years. How much must he invest today in a 5 percent savings account to achieve this goal? Adapting the above equation, we compute the present value of $4,000 at compound interest of 5 percent for three years in the future.

Year	Amount at End of Year		Divide by		Present Value at Beginning of Year
3	$4,000.00	÷	1.05	=	$3,809.52
2	3,809.52	÷	1.05	=	3,628.11
1	3,628.11	÷	1.05	=	3,455.34

Riley must invest a present value of $3,455.34 to achieve a future value of $4,000.00 in three years.

This calculation is again made much easier by using the appropriate table. In Table 3, we look down the 5 percent column until we reach period 3 and find the factor .864. This factor, when multiplied by $1, gives the present value of the $1 to be received three years from now at 5 percent interest. Thus, we solve the problem:

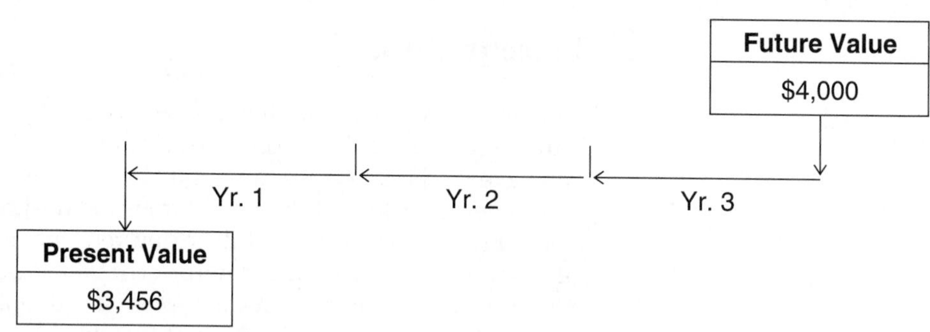

Future value × factor = present value
$4,000 × .864 = $3,456

Except for a rounding difference of $0.66, this result is the same as the one above.

Table 3. Present Value of $1 to Be Received at the End of a Given Number of Time Periods

Periods	1%	2%	3%	4%	5%	6%	7%	8%	9%	10%
1	0.990	0.980	0.971	0.962	0.952	0.943	0.935	0.926	0.917	0.909
2	0.980	0.961	0.943	0.925	0.907	0.890	0.873	0.857	0.842	0.826
3	0.971	0.942	0.915	0.889	0.864	0.840	0.816	0.794	0.772	0.751
4	0.961	0.924	0.888	0.855	0.823	0.792	0.763	0.735	0.708	0.683
5	0.951	0.906	0.883	0.822	0.784	0.747	0.713	0.681	0.650	0.621
6	0.942	0.888	0.837	0.790	0.746	0.705	0.666	0.630	0.596	0.564
7	0.933	0.871	0.813	0.760	0.711	0.665	0.623	0.583	0.547	0.513
8	0.923	0.853	0.789	0.731	0.677	0.627	0.582	0.540	0.502	0.467
9	0.914	0.837	0.766	0.703	0.645	0.592	0.544	0.500	0.460	0.424
10	0.905	0.820	0.744	0.676	0.614	0.558	0.508	0.463	0.422	0.386

Source: Excerpt from Table 3 in the appendix on future value and present value tables.

Present Value of an Ordinary Annuity

It is often necessary to compute the present value of a series of receipts or payments. When we calculate the present value of equal amounts equally spaced over a period of time, we are in fact computing the present value of an ordinary annuity.

For example, assume that Kathy Foster has sold a piece of property and is to receive $15,000 in three equal annual payments of $5,000, beginning one year from today. What is the present value of this sale, assuming a current interest rate of 5 percent? This present value may be computed by calculating a separate present value for each of the three payments (using Table 3) and summing the results, as follows:

Future Receipts (Annuity)				Present Value Factor at 5 Percent		
Year 1	Year 2	Year 3		(from Table 3)		Present Value
$5,000			×	.952	=	$ 4,760
	$5,000		×	.907	=	4,535
		$5,000	×	.864	=	4,320
Total Present Value						$13,615

The present value of this sale is $13,615. Thus, there is an implied interest cost (given the 5 percent rate) of $1,385 associated with the payment plan that allows the purchaser to pay in three installments.

We can make this calculation more easily by using Table 4. We look down the 5 percent column until we reach period 3 and find factor 2.723. This factor, when multiplied by $1, gives the present value of a series of three $1 payments (spaced one year apart) at compound interest of 5 percent. Thus, we solve the problem as shown in the middle of page Ap-20.

Table 4. Present Value of an Ordinary Annuity of $1 Received at the End of Each Period for a Given Number of Time Periods

Periods	1%	2%	3%	4%	5%	6%	7%	8%	9%	10%
1	0.990	0.980	0.971	0.962	0.952	0.943	0.935	0.926	0.917	0.909
2	1.970	1.942	1.913	1.886	1.859	1.833	1.808	1.783	1.759	1.736
3	2.941	2.884	2.829	2.775	2.723	2.673	2.624	2.577	2.531	2.487
4	3.902	3.808	3.717	3.630	3.546	3.465	3.387	3.312	3.240	3.170
5	4.853	4.713	4.580	4.452	4.329	4.212	4.100	3.993	3.890	3.791
6	5.795	5.601	5.417	5.242	5.076	4.917	4.767	4.623	4.486	4.355
7	6.728	6.472	6.230	6.002	5.786	5.582	5.389	5.206	5.033	4.868
8	7.652	7.325	7.020	6.733	6.463	6.210	5.971	5.747	5.535	5.335
9	8.566	8.162	7.786	7.435	7.108	6.802	6.515	6.247	5.995	5.759
10	9.471	8.983	8.530	8.111	7.722	7.360	7.024	6.710	6.418	6.145

Source: Excerpt from Table 4 in the appendix on future value and present value tables.

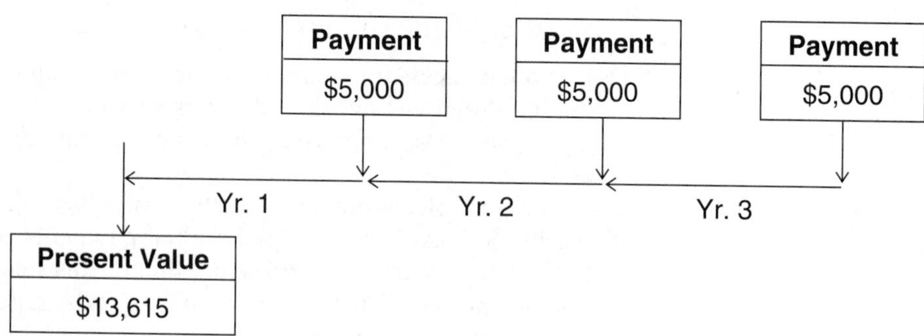

Periodic payment × factor = present value
$5,000 × 2.723 = $13,615

This result is the same as the one computed earlier.

Time Periods

In all of the previous examples, and in most other cases, the compounding period is one year, and the interest rate is stated on an annual basis. However, in each of the four tables the left-hand column refers, not to years, but to periods. This wording is intended to accommodate compounding periods of less than one year. Savings accounts that record interest quarterly and bonds that pay interest semiannually are cases where the compounding period is less than one year. To use the tables in such cases, it is necessary to (1) divide the annual interest rate by the number of periods in the year, and (2) multiply the number of periods in one year by the number of years.

For example, assume that a $6,000 note is to be paid in two years and carries an annual interest rate of 8 percent. Compute the maturity (future) value of the note, assuming that the compounding period is semiannual. Before using the table, it is necessary to compute the interest rate that applies to each compounding period and the total number of compounding periods. First, the interest rate to use is 4 percent (8% annual rate ÷ 2 periods per year). Second, the total number of compounding periods is 4 (2 periods per year × 2 years). From Table 1, therefore, the maturity value of the note may be computed as follows:

Principal × factor	= future value
$6,000 × 1.170 =	$7,020

The note will be worth $7,020 in two years.

This procedure for determining the interest rate and the number of periods when the compounding period is less than one year may be used with all four tables.

Applications of Present Value to Accounting

The concept of present value is widely applicable in the discipline of accounting. Here, the purpose is to demonstrate its usefulness in some simple applications. In-depth study of present value is deferred to more advanced courses.

Imputing Interest on Noninterest-Bearing Notes

OBJECTIVE 4
Apply the concept of present value to simple accounting situations

Clearly there is no such thing as an interest-free debt, regardless of whether the interest rate is explicitly stated. The Accounting Principles Board has declared that when a long-term note does not explicitly state an interest rate (or if the interest rate is unreasonably low), a rate based on the normal interest cost of the company in question should be assigned, or imputed.[1]

The following example applies this principle. On January 1, 19x8, Gato purchases merchandise from Haines by issuing an $8,000 noninterest-bearing note due in two years. Gato can borrow money from the bank at 9 percent interest. Gato pays the note in full after two years.

Note that the $8,000 note represents partly a payment for merchandise and partly a payment of interest for two years. In recording the purchase and sale, it is necessary to use Table 3 to determine the present value of the note. The calculation follows.

Future payment	×	present value factor (9%, 2 years)	=	present value
$8,000	×	.842	=	$6,736

The imputed interest cost is $1,264 ($8,000 – $6,736) and is recorded as a discount on notes payable in Gato's records and as a discount on notes receivable in Haines's records. The entries necessary to record the purchase in the Gato records and the sale in the Haines records are as follows:

Gato's Journal			**Haines's Journal**		
Purchases	6,736		Notes Receivable	8,000	
Discount on			Discount on		
Notes Payable	1,264		Notes Receivable		1,264
Notes Payable		8,000	Sales		6,736

On December 31, 19x8, the adjustments to recognize the interest expense and interest income will be:

Gato's Journal			**Haines's Journal**		
Interest Expense	606.24		Discount on		
Discount on			Notes Receivable	606.24	
Notes Payable		606.24	Interest Income		606.24

1. Accounting Principles Board, *Opinion No. 21*, "Interest on Receivables and Payables" (New York: American Institute of Certified Public Accountants, 1971), par. 13.

The interest is calculated by multiplying the original purchase by the interest for one year ($6,736.00 × .09 = $606.24). When payment is made on December 31, 19x9, the following entries will be made in the respective journals:

Gato's Journal

Interest Expense	657.76	
Notes Payable	8,000.00	
Discount on Notes Payable		657.76
Cash		8,000.00

Haines's Journal

Discount on Notes Receivable	657.76	
Cash	8,000.00	
Interest Income		657.76
Notes Receivable		8,000.00

The interest entries represent the remaining interest to be expensed or realized ($1,264 – $606.24 = $657.76). This amount approximates (because of rounding differences in the table) the interest for one year on the purchase plus last year's interest [($6,736 + $606.24) × .09 = $660.80].

Valuing an Asset

An asset is recorded because it will provide future benefits to the company that owns it. This future benefit is the basis for the definition of an asset. Usually, the purchase price of the asset represents the present value of these future benefits. It is possible to evaluate a proposed purchase price of an asset by comparing that price with the present value of the asset to the company.

For example, Sam Hurst wants to buy a new labor-saving machine that will reduce his annual labor cost by $700 per year and will last eight years. The interest rate that he assumes for making managerial decisions is 10 percent. What is the maximum amount (present value) that Hurst should pay?

The present value of the machine to Hurst is equal to the present value of an ordinary annuity of $700 per year for eight years at compound interest of 10 percent. (The savings in annual labor cost is assumed to occur at the end of each year.) From Table 4, we compute the value as follows:

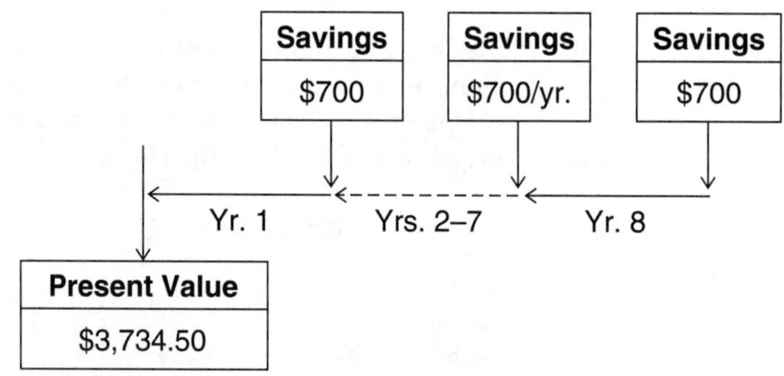

Periodic savings × factor = present value
$700 × 5.335 = $3,734.50

Hurst should not pay more than $3,734.50 for the new machine because this amount equals the present value of the benefits that will be received from owning the machine.

Deferred Payment

A seller will sometimes agree to defer payment for a sale in order to encourage the buyer to make the purchase. This practice is common, for example, in the farm implement industry, where the farmer needs the equipment in the spring but cannot pay for it until the fall crop is in. Assume that Plains Implement Corporation sells a tractor to Dana Washington for $50,000 on February 1, agreeing to take payment ten months later on December 1. When this type of agreement is made, the future payment includes not only the sales price of the tractor but also an implied (imputed) interest cost. If the prevailing annual interest rate for such transactions is 12 percent compounded monthly, the actual sale (purchase) price of the tractor would be the present value of the future payment, computed according to Table 3 (10 periods, 1 percent), as follows:

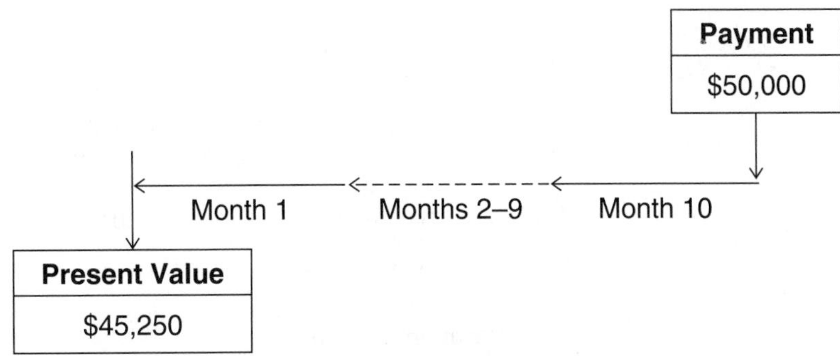

Future payment × factor = present value
$50,000 × .905 = $45,250

The purchase in Washington's records and the sale in Plains's records are recorded at the present value, $45,250. The balance consists of interest expense or interest income. The entries necessary to record the purchase in Washington's records and the sale in Plains's records are as follows:

	Washington's Journal			Plains's Journal		
Feb. 1	Tractor	45,250		Accounts Receivable	45,250	
	Accounts Payable		45,250	Sales		45,250
	Purchase of tractor			Sale of tractor		

When Washington pays for the tractor, the entries are as follows:

	Washington's Journal			Plains's Journal		
Dec. 1	Accounts Payable	45,250		Cash	50,000	
	Interest Expense	4,750		Accounts Receivable		45,250
	Cash		50,000	Interest Income		4,750
	Payment on account including imputed interest expense			Receipt on account from Washington including imputed interest income		

Investment of Idle Cash

Childware Corporation, a toy manufacturer, has just completed a successful fall selling season and has $10,000,000 in cash to invest for six months. The company places the cash in a money market account that is expected to pay 12 percent annual interest. Interest is compounded monthly and credited to the company's account each month. How much cash will the company have at the end of six months, and what entries will be made to record the investment and the monthly interest? From Table 1, the future value factor is based on six monthly periods of 1 percent (12 percent divided by 12 months), and the future value is computed as shown at the top of the next page.

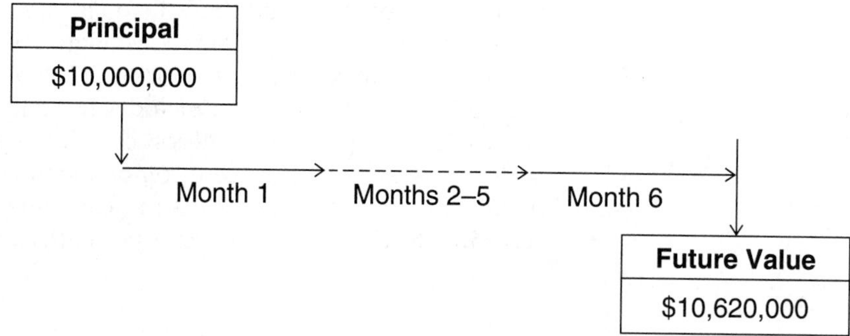

Investment × factor = future value
$10,000,000 × 1.062 = $10,620,000

When the investment is made, the journal entry is as follows:

Short-Term Investments	10,000,000	
Cash		10,000,000
Investment of cash		

After the first month, the interest is recorded by increasing the Short-Term Investments account, as follows:

Short-Term Investments	100,000	
Interest Income		100,000
One month's interest income $10,000,000 × .01 = $100,000		

After the second month, the interest is earned on the new balance of the Short-Term Investments account, as follows:

Short-Term Investments	101,000	
Interest Income		101,000
One month's interest income $10,100,000 × .01 = $101,000		

Entries would continue in a similar manner for four more months, at which time the balance of Short-Term Investments would be about $10,620,000. The actual amount accumulated may vary from this total because the interest rate paid on money market accounts can vary over time as a result of changes in market conditions.

Accumulation of a Fund

When a company owes a large fixed amount due in several years, management would be wise to accumulate a fund with which to pay off the debt at maturity. Sometimes creditors, when they agree to provide a loan, require that such a fund be established. In establishing the fund, management must determine how much cash to set aside each period in order to pay the debt. The amount will depend on the estimated rate of interest the investments will earn. Assume that Vason Corporation agrees with a creditor to set aside cash at the end of each year to accumulate enough to pay off a $100,000 note due in five years. Since the first contribution to the fund will be made in one year, five annual contributions will be made by the time the note is due. Assume also that the fund is projected to earn 8 percent, compounded annually. The amount of each annual payment is calculated from Table 2 (5 periods, 8 percent), as follows:

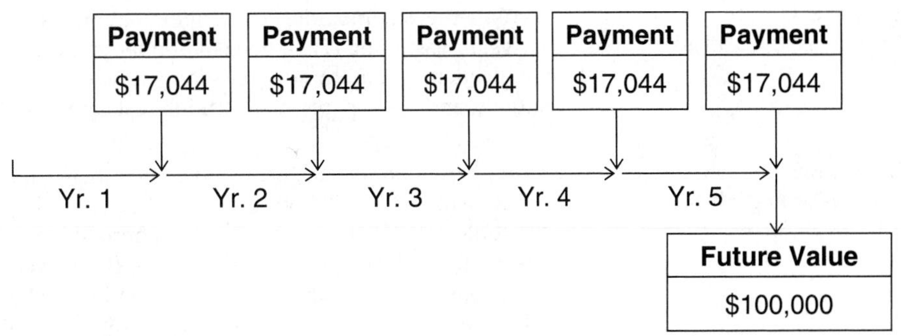

Future value of fund ÷ factor = annual investment
$100,000 ÷ 5.867 = $17,044 (rounded)

Each year's contribution to the fund is $17,044. This contribution is recorded as follows:

Loan Repayment Fund	17,044	
Cash		17,044
Annual contribution to loan repayment fund		

Other Accounting Applications

There are many other applications of present value in accounting. The uses of present value in accounting for installment notes, valuing a bond, and recording lease obligations are shown in the chapter on long-term liabilities. Present value is also applied in such areas as pension obligations; premium and discount on debt; depreciation of property, plant, and equipment; capital expenditure decisions; and generally any problem where time is a factor.

Questions

1. What is the key variable that distinguishes present value from future value?
2. What is an ordinary annuity?
3. How does the use of a compounding period of less than one year affect the computation of present value?
4. Why is present value important to accounting? (Illustrate your answer by giving concrete examples of applications in accounting.)

Classroom Exercises

Tables 1 to 4 in the appendix on future value and present value tables may be used where appropriate to solve these exercises.

Exercise B-1.
Future Value Calculations
(L.O. 1, 2)

Wieland receives a $3,000, one-year note that carries a 12 percent annual interest rate on $3,000 for the sale of a used car.

Compute the maturity value under each of the following assumptions: (1) The interest is simple interest. (2) The interest is compounded semiannually. (3) The interest is compounded quarterly. (4) The interest is compounded monthly.

Exercise B-2.
Future Value Calculations
(L.O. 2)

Find the future value of (1) a single payment of $20,000 at 7 percent for ten years, (2) ten annual payments of $2,000 at 7 percent, (3) a single payment of $6,000 at 9 percent for seven years, and (4) seven annual payments of $6,000 at 9 percent.

Exercise B-3.
Future Value Calculations
(L.O. 2)

Assume that $40,000 is invested today. Compute the amount that would accumulate at the end of seven years when the interest rate is (1) 8 percent compounded annually, (2) 8 percent compounded semiannually, and (3) 8 percent compounded quarterly.

Exercise B-4.
Future Value Calculations
(L.O. 2)

Calculate the accumulation of periodic payments of $1,000 made at the end of each of four years, assuming (1) 10 percent annual interest compounded annually, (2) 10 percent annual interest compounded semiannually, (3) 4 percent annual interest compounded annually, and (4) 16 percent annual interest compounded quarterly.

Exercise B-5.
Future Value Applications
(L.O. 2)

a. Two parents have $20,000 to invest for their child's college tuition, which they estimate will cost $40,000 when the child enters college twelve years from now.
   Calculate the approximate rate of annual interest that the investment must earn to reach the $40,000 goal in twelve years. (**Hint:** Make a calculation; then use Table 1 in the appendix on future value and present value tables.)
b. Ted Pruitt is saving to purchase a summer home that will cost about $64,000. He has $40,000 now, on which he can earn 7 percent annual interest.
   Calculate the approximate length of time he will have to wait to purchase the summer home. (**Hint:** Make a calculation; then use Table 1 in the appendix on future value and present value tables.)

Exercise B-6.
Working Backward from a Future Value
(L.O. 2)

Gloria Faraquez has a debt of $90,000 due in four years. She wants to save money to pay it off by making annual deposits in an investment account that earns 8 percent annual interest.

Calculate the amount she must deposit each year to reach her goal. (**Hint:** Use Table 2 in the appendix on future value and present value tables; then make a calculation.)

Exercise B-7.
Determining an Advance Payment
(L.O. 3)

Ellen Saber is contemplating paying five years' rent in advance. Her annual rent is $9,600. Calculate the single sum that would have to be paid now for the advance rent, if we assume compound interest of 8 percent.

Exercise B-8.
Present Value Calculations
(L.O. 3)

Find the present value of (1) a single payment of $24,000 at 6 percent for twelve years, (2) twelve annual payments of $2,000 at 6 percent, (3) a single payment of $5,000 at 9 percent for five years, and (4) five annual payments of $5,000 at 9 percent.

Exercise B-9.
Present Value of a Lump-Sum Contract
(L.O. 3)

A contract calls for a lump-sum payment of $60,000. Find the present value of the contract, assuming that (1) the payment is due in five years, and the current interest rate is 9 percent; (2) the payment is due in ten years, and the current interest rate is 9 percent; (3) the payment is due in five years, and the current interest rate is 5 percent; and (4) the payment is due in ten years, and the current interest rate is 5 percent.

Exercise B-10.
Present Value of an Annuity Contract
(L.O. 3)

A contract calls for annual payments of $1,200. Find the present value of the contract, assuming that (1) the number of payments is seven, and the current interest rate is 6 percent; (2) the number of payments is fourteen, and the current interest rate is 6 percent; (3) the number of payments is seven, and the current interest rate is 8 percent; and (4) the number of payments is fourteen, and the current interest rate is 8 percent.

Exercise B-11.
Non-Interest-Bearing Note
(L.O. 4)

On January 1, 19x8, Pendleton purchases a machine from Leyland by signing a two-year, non-interest-bearing $32,000 note. Pendleton currently pays 12 percent interest to borrow money at the bank.

Prepare entries in Pendleton's and Leyland's journals to (1) record the purchase and the note, (2) adjust the accounts after one year, and (3) record payment of the note after two years (on December 31, 19x9).

Exercise B-12.
Valuing an Asset for the Purpose of Making a Purchasing Decision
(L.O. 4)

Oscaro owns a service station and has the opportunity to purchase a car wash machine for $30,000. After carefully studying projected costs and revenues, Oscaro estimates that the car wash will produce a net cash flow of $5,200 annually and will last for eight years. Oscaro feels that an interest rate of 14 percent is adequate for his business.

Calculate the present value of the machine to Oscaro. Does the purchase appear to be a correct business decision?

Exercise B-13.
Deferred Payment
(L.O. 4)

Johnson Equipment Corporation sells a precision tool machine with computer controls to Borst Corporation for $800,000 on January 1, agreeing to take payment nine months later, on October 1. Assuming that the prevailing annual interest rate for such a transaction is 16 percent compounded quarterly, what is the actual sales (purchase) price of the machine tool, and what journal entries will be made at the time of the purchase (sale) and at the time of the payment (receipt) on the records of both Borst and Johnson?

Exercise B-14.
Investment of Idle Cash
(L.O. 4)

Scientific Publishing Company, a publisher of college books, has just completed a successful fall selling season and has $5,000,000 in cash to invest for nine months, beginning on January 1. The company places the cash in a money market account that is expected to pay 12 percent annual interest compounded monthly. Interest is credited to the company's account each month. How much cash will the company have at the end of nine months, and what entries are made to record the investment and the first two monthly (February 1 and March 1) interest amounts?

Exercise B-15.
Accumulation of a Fund
(L.O. 4)

Laferia Corporation borrows $3,000,000 from an insurance company on a five-year note. Management agrees to set aside enough cash at the end of each year to accumulate the amount needed to pay off the note at maturity. Since the first contribution to the fund will be made in one year, four annual contributions are needed. Assuming that the fund will earn 10 percent compounded annually, how much will the annual contribution to the fund be (round to nearest dollar), and what will be the journal entry for the first contribution?

Exercise B-16.
Negotiating the Sale of a Business
(L.O. 4)

Horace Raftson is attempting to sell his business to Ernando Ruiz. The company has assets of $900,000, liabilities of $800,000, and stockholders' equity of $100,000. Both parties agree that the proper rate of return to expect is 12 percent; however, they differ on other assumptions. Raftson believes that the business will generate at least $100,000 per year of cash flows for twenty years. Ruiz thinks that $80,000 in cash flows per year is more reasonable and that only ten years in the future should be considered. Using Table 4 in the appendix on future value and present value tables, determine the range for negotiation by computing the present value of Raftson's offer to sell and of Ruiz's offer to buy.

Problems

Problem B-1.
Time Value of Money Applications
(L.O. 2, 3, 4)

Neiman Corporation's management took several actions, each of which was to be effective on January 1, 19x1, and each of which involved an application of the time value of money:

a. Established a new retirement plan to take effect in three years and authorized three annual payments of $500,000 starting January 1, 19x2, to establish the retirement fund.
b. Approved plans for a new distribution center to be built for $1,000,000 and authorized five annual payments, starting January 1, 19x2, to accumulate the funds for the new center.
c. Bought out the contract of a member of top management for a payment of $50,000 per year for four years beginning January 1, 19x2.
d. Accepted a two-year non-interest-bearing note for $100,000 as payment for equipment that the company sold.
e. Set aside $300,000 for possible losses from lawsuits over a defective product. The lawsuits are not expected to be settled for three years.

Required

Assuming an annual interest rate of 10 percent and using Tables 1, 2, 3, and 4, answer the following questions:

1. In action **a,** how much will the retirement fund accumulate in three years?
2. In action **b,** how much must the annual payment be to reach the goal?
3. In action **c,** what is the cost (present value) of the buy-out?

4. In action **d,** assuming that interest is compounded semiannually, what is the selling price (present value) of the equipment?
5. In action **e,** how much will the fund accumulate to in three years?

Problem B-2. Time Value of Money Applications
(L.O. 2, 3, 4)

Effective January 1, 19x1, the board of directors of Riordan, Inc. approved the following actions, each of which is an application of the time value of money:

a. Established in a single payment of $100,000 a contingency fund for the possible settlement of a lawsuit. The suit is expected to be settled in two years.
b. Asked for another fund to be established by a single payment to accumulate to $300,000 in four years.
c. Approved purchase of a parcel of land for future plant expansion. Payments are to start January 1, 19x2, at $50,000 per year for five years.
d. Determined that a new building to be built on the property in **c** would cost $800,000 and authorized five annual payments to be made starting January 1, 19x2, into a fund for its construction.
e. Purchased Riordan common stock from a stockholder who wanted to be bought out by issuing a four-year non-interest-bearing note for $200,000.

Required

Assuming an annual interest rate of 8 percent and using Tables 1, 2, 3, and 4, answer the following questions:

1. In action **a,** how much will the fund accumulate in two years?
2. In action **b,** how much will need to be deposited initially to accumulate the desired amount?
3. In action **c,** what is the purchase price (present value) of the land?
4. In action **d,** how much would the equal annual payments need to be to accumulate enough money to construct the building?
5. In action **e,** assuming semiannual compounding of interest, what is the actual purchase price of the stock (present value of the note)?

APPENDIX C

Future Value and Present Value Tables

Table 1 provides the multipliers necessary to compute the future value of a *single* cash deposit made at the *beginning* of year 1. Three factors must be known before the future value can be computed: (1) the time period in years, (2) the stated annual rate of interest to be earned, and (3) the dollar amount invested or deposited.

Example. Determine the future value of \$5,000 deposited now that will earn 9 percent interest compounded annually for five years. From Table 1, the necessary multiplier for five years at 9 percent is 1.539, and the answer is:

$$\$5{,}000 \times 1.539 = \$7{,}695$$

Situations requiring the use of Table 2 are similar to those requiring Table 1 except that Table 2 is used to compute the future value of a *series* of *equal* annual deposits.

Example. What will be the future value at the end of thirty years if \$1,000 is deposited each year on January 1, beginning in one year, assuming 12 percent interest compounded annually? The required multiplier from Table 2 is 241.3, and the answer is:

$$\$1{,}000 \times 241.3 = \$241{,}300$$

Table 3 is used to compute the value today of a *single* amount of cash to be received sometime in the future. To use Table 3, you must first know: (1) the time period in years until funds will be received, (2) the annual rate of interest, and (3) the dollar amount to be received at the end of the time period.

Example. What is the present value of \$30,000 to be received twenty-five years from now, assuming a 14 percent interest rate? From Table 3, the required multiplier is .038, and the answer is:

$$\$30{,}000 \times .038 = \$1{,}140$$

Table 4 is used to compute the present value of a *series* of *equal* annual cash flows.

Example. Arthur Howard won a contest on January 1, 1994, in which the prize was \$30,000, payable in fifteen annual installments of \$2,000 every December 31, beginning in 1994. Assuming a 9 percent interest rate, what is the present value of Mr. Howard's prize on January 1, 1994? From Table 4, the required multiplier is 8.061, and the answer is:

$$\$2{,}000 \times 8.061 = \$16{,}122$$

Table 1. Future Value of $1 After a Given Number of Time Periods

Periods	1%	2%	3%	4%	5%	6%	7%	8%	9%	10%	12%	14%	15%
1	1.010	1.020	1.030	1.040	1.050	1.060	1.070	1.080	1.090	1.100	1.120	1.140	1.150
2	1.020	1.040	1.061	1.082	1.103	1.124	1.145	1.166	1.188	1.210	1.254	1.300	1.323
3	1.030	1.061	1.093	1.125	1.158	1.191	1.225	1.260	1.295	1.331	1.405	1.482	1.521
4	1.041	1.082	1.126	1.170	1.216	1.262	1.311	1.360	1.412	1.464	1.574	1.689	1.749
5	1.051	1.104	1.159	1.217	1.276	1.338	1.403	1.469	1.539	1.611	1.762	1.925	2.011
6	1.062	1.126	1.194	1.265	1.340	1.419	1.501	1.587	1.677	1.772	1.974	2.195	2.313
7	1.072	1.149	1.230	1.316	1.407	1.504	1.606	1.714	1.828	1.949	2.211	2.502	2.660
8	1.083	1.172	1.267	1.369	1.477	1.594	1.718	1.851	1.993	2.144	2.476	2.853	3.059
9	1.094	1.195	1.305	1.423	1.551	1.689	1.838	1.999	2.172	2.358	2.773	3.252	3.518
10	1.105	1.219	1.344	1.480	1.629	1.791	1.967	2.159	2.367	2.594	3.106	3.707	4.046
11	1.116	1.243	1.384	1.539	1.710	1.898	2.105	2.332	2.580	2.853	3.479	4.226	4.652
12	1.127	1.268	1.426	1.601	1.796	2.012	2.252	2.518	2.813	3.138	3.896	4.818	5.350
13	1.138	1.294	1.469	1.665	1.886	2.133	2.410	2.720	3.066	3.452	4.363	5.492	6.153
14	1.149	1.319	1.513	1.732	1.980	2.261	2.579	2.937	3.342	3.798	4.887	6.261	7.076
15	1.161	1.346	1.558	1.801	2.079	2.397	2.759	3.172	3.642	4.177	5.474	7.138	8.137
16	1.173	1.373	1.605	1.873	2.183	2.540	2.952	3.426	3.970	4.595	6.130	8.137	9.358
17	1.184	1.400	1.653	1.948	2.292	2.693	3.159	3.700	4.328	5.054	6.866	9.276	10.76
18	1.196	1.428	1.702	2.026	2.407	2.854	3.380	3.996	4.717	5.560	7.690	10.58	12.38
19	1.208	1.457	1.754	2.107	2.527	3.026	3.617	4.316	5.142	6.116	8.613	12.06	14.23
20	1.220	1.486	1.806	2.191	2.653	3.207	3.870	4.661	5.604	6.728	9.646	13.74	16.37
21	1.232	1.516	1.860	2.279	2.786	3.400	4.141	5.034	6.109	7.400	10.80	15.67	18.82
22	1.245	1.546	1.916	2.370	2.925	3.604	4.430	5.437	6.659	8.140	12.10	17.86	21.64
23	1.257	1.577	1.974	2.465	3.072	3.820	4.741	5.871	7.258	8.954	13.55	20.36	24.89
24	1.270	1.608	2.033	2.563	3.225	4.049	5.072	6.341	7.911	9.850	15.18	23.21	28.63
25	1.282	1.641	2.094	2.666	3.386	4.292	5.427	6.848	8.623	10.83	17.00	26.46	32.92
26	1.295	1.673	2.157	2.772	3.556	4.549	5.807	7.396	9.399	11.92	19.04	30.17	37.86
27	1.308	1.707	2.221	2.883	3.733	4.822	6.214	7.988	10.25	13.11	21.32	34.39	43.54
28	1.321	1.741	2.288	2.999	3.920	5.112	6.649	8.627	11.17	14.42	23.88	39.20	50.07
29	1.335	1.776	2.357	3.119	4.116	5.418	7.114	9.317	12.17	15.86	26.75	44.69	57.58
30	1.348	1.811	2.427	3.243	4.322	5.743	7.612	10.06	13.27	17.45	29.96	50.95	66.21
40	1.489	2.208	3.262	4.801	7.040	10.29	14.97	21.72	31.41	45.26	93.05	188.9	267.9
50	1.645	2.692	4.384	7.107	11.47	18.42	29.46	46.90	74.36	117.4	289.0	700.2	1,084

Table 4 applies to *ordinary annuities,* in which the first cash flow occurs one time period beyond the date for which the present value is to be computed. An *annuity due* is a series of equal cash flows for *N* time periods, but the first payment occurs immediately. The present value of the first payment equals the face value of the cash flow; Table 4 then is used to measure the present value of $N - 1$ remaining cash flows.

Example. Determine the present value on January 1, 1994, of twenty lease payments; each payment of $10,000 is due on January 1, beginning in 1994. Assume an interest rate of 8 percent.

$$\text{Present value} = \text{immediate payment} + \begin{cases} \text{present value of 19} \\ \text{subsequent payments at 8\%} \end{cases}$$

$$= \$10{,}000 + (\$10{,}000 \times 9.604) = \$106{,}040$$

Table 2. Future Value of $1 Paid at the End of Each Period for a Given Number of Time Periods

Periods	1%	2%	3%	4%	5%	6%	7%	8%	9%	10%	12%	14%	15%
1	1.000	1.000	1.000	1.000	1.000	1.000	1.000	1.000	1.000	1.000	1.000	1.000	1.000
2	2.010	2.020	2.030	2.040	2.050	2.060	2.070	2.080	2.090	2.100	2.120	2.140	2.150
3	3.030	3.060	3.091	3.122	3.153	3.184	3.215	3.246	3.278	3.310	3.374	3.440	3.473
4	4.060	4.122	4.184	4.246	4.310	4.375	4.440	4.506	4.573	4.641	4.779	4.921	4.993
5	5.101	5.204	5.309	5.416	5.526	5.637	5.751	5.867	5.985	6.105	6.353	6.610	6.742
6	6.152	6.308	6.468	6.633	6.802	6.975	7.153	7.336	7.523	7.716	8.115	8.536	8.754
7	7.214	7.434	7.662	7.898	8.142	8.394	8.654	8.923	9.200	9.487	10.09	10.73	11.07
8	8.286	8.583	8.892	9.214	9.549	9.897	10.26	10.64	11.03	11.44	12.30	13.23	13.73
9	9.369	9.755	10.16	10.58	11.03	11.49	11.98	12.49	13.02	13.58	14.78	16.09	16.79
10	10.46	10.95	11.46	12.01	12.58	13.18	13.82	14.49	15.19	15.94	17.55	19.34	20.30
11	11.57	12.17	12.81	13.49	14.21	14.97	15.78	16.65	17.56	18.53	20.65	23.04	24.35
12	12.68	13.41	14.19	15.03	15.92	16.87	17.89	18.98	20.14	21.38	24.13	27.27	29.00
13	13.81	14.68	15.62	16.63	17.71	18.88	20.14	21.50	22.95	24.52	28.03	32.09	34.35
14	14.95	15.97	17.09	18.29	19.60	21.02	22.55	24.21	26.02	27.98	32.39	37.58	40.50
15	16.10	17.29	18.60	20.02	21.58	23.28	25.13	27.15	29.36	31.77	37.28	43.84	47.58
16	17.26	18.64	20.16	21.82	23.66	25.67	27.89	30.32	33.00	35.95	42.75	50.98	55.72
17	18.43	20.01	21.76	23.70	25.84	28.21	30.84	33.75	36.97	40.54	48.88	59.12	65.08
18	19.61	21.41	23.41	25.65	28.13	30.91	34.00	37.45	41.30	45.60	55.75	68.39	75.84
19	20.81	22.84	25.12	27.67	30.54	33.76	37.38	41.45	46.02	51.16	63.44	78.97	88.21
20	22.02	24.30	26.87	29.78	33.07	36.79	41.00	45.76	51.16	57.28	72.05	91.02	102.4
21	23.24	25.78	28.68	31.97	35.72	39.99	44.87	50.42	56.76	64.00	81.70	104.8	118.8
22	24.47	27.30	30.54	34.25	38.51	43.39	49.01	55.46	62.87	71.40	92.50	120.4	137.6
23	25.72	28.85	32.45	36.62	41.43	47.00	53.44	60.89	69.53	79.54	104.6	138.3	159.3
24	26.97	30.42	34.43	39.08	44.50	50.82	58.18	66.76	76.79	88.50	118.2	158.7	184.2
25	28.24	32.03	36.46	41.65	47.73	54.86	63.25	73.11	84.70	98.35	133.3	181.9	212.8
26	29.53	33.67	38.55	44.31	51.11	59.16	68.68	79.95	93.32	109.2	150.3	208.3	245.7
27	30.82	35.34	40.71	47.08	54.67	63.71	74.48	87.35	102.7	121.1	169.4	238.5	283.6
28	32.13	37.05	42.93	49.97	58.40	68.53	80.70	95.34	113.0	134.2	190.7	272.9	327.1
29	33.45	38.79	45.22	52.97	62.32	73.64	87.35	104.0	124.1	148.6	214.6	312.1	377.2
30	34.78	40.57	47.58	56.08	66.44	79.06	94.46	113.3	136.3	164.5	241.3	356.8	434.7
40	48.89	60.40	75.40	95.03	120.8	154.8	199.6	259.1	337.9	442.6	767.1	1,342	1,779
50	64.46	84.58	112.8	152.7	209.3	290.3	406.5	573.8	815.1	1,164	2,400	4,995	7,218

Table 3. Present Value of $1 To Be Received at the End of a Given Number of Time Periods

Periods	1%	2%	3%	4%	5%	6%	7%	8%	9%	10%	12%
1	0.990	0.980	0.971	0.962	0.952	0.943	0.935	0.926	0.917	0.909	0.893
2	0.980	0.961	0.943	0.925	0.907	0.890	0.873	0.857	0.842	0.826	0.797
3	0.971	0.942	0.915	0.889	0.864	0.840	0.816	0.794	0.772	0.751	0.712
4	0.961	0.924	0.888	0.855	0.823	0.792	0.763	0.735	0.708	0.683	0.636
5	0.951	0.906	0.883	0.822	0.784	0.747	0.713	0.681	0.650	0.621	0.567
6	0.942	0.888	0.837	0.790	0.746	0.705	0.666	0.630	0.596	0.564	0.507
7	0.933	0.871	0.813	0.760	0.711	0.665	0.623	0.583	0.547	0.513	0.452
8	0.923	0.853	0.789	0.731	0.677	0.627	0.582	0.540	0.502	0.467	0.404
9	0.914	0.837	0.766	0.703	0.645	0.592	0.544	0.500	0.460	0.424	0.361
10	0.905	0.820	0.744	0.676	0.614	0.558	0.508	0.463	0.422	0.386	0.322
11	0.896	0.804	0.722	0.650	0.585	0.527	0.475	0.429	0.388	0.350	0.287
12	0.887	0.788	0.701	0.625	0.557	0.497	0.444	0.397	0.356	0.319	0.257
13	0.879	0.773	0.681	0.601	0.530	0.469	0.415	0.368	0.326	0.290	0.229
14	0.870	0.758	0.661	0.577	0.505	0.442	0.388	0.340	0.299	0.263	0.205
15	0.861	0.743	0.642	0.555	0.481	0.417	0.362	0.315	0.275	0.239	0.183
16	0.853	0.728	0.623	0.534	0.458	0.394	0.339	0.292	0.252	0.218	0.163
17	0.844	0.714	0.605	0.513	0.436	0.371	0.317	0.270	0.231	0.198	0.146
18	0.836	0.700	0.587	0.494	0.416	0.350	0.296	0.250	0.212	0.180	0.130
19	0.828	0.686	0.570	0.475	0.396	0.331	0.277	0.232	0.194	0.164	0.116
20	0.820	0.673	0.554	0.456	0.377	0.312	0.258	0.215	0.178	0.149	0.104
21	0.811	0.660	0.538	0.439	0.359	0.294	0.242	0.199	0.164	0.135	0.093
22	0.803	0.647	0.522	0.422	0.342	0.278	0.226	0.184	0.150	0.123	0.083
23	0.795	0.634	0.507	0.406	0.326	0.262	0.211	0.170	0.138	0.112	0.074
24	0.788	0.622	0.492	0.390	0.310	0.247	0.197	0.158	0.126	0.102	0.066
25	0.780	0.610	0.478	0.375	0.295	0.233	0.184	0.146	0.116	0.092	0.059
26	0.772	0.598	0.464	0.361	0.281	0.220	0.172	0.135	0.106	0.084	0.053
27	0.764	0.586	0.450	0.347	0.268	0.207	0.161	0.125	0.098	0.076	0.047
28	0.757	0.574	0.437	0.333	0.255	0.196	0.150	0.116	0.090	0.069	0.042
29	0.749	0.563	0.424	0.321	0.243	0.185	0.141	0.107	0.082	0.063	0.037
30	0.742	0.552	0.412	0.308	0.231	0.174	0.131	0.099	0.075	0.057	0.033
40	0.672	0.453	0.307	0.208	0.142	0.097	0.067	0.046	0.032	0.022	0.011
50	0.608	0.372	0.228	0.141	0.087	0.054	0.034	0.021	0.013	0.009	0.003

Table 3. (continued)

14%	15%	16%	18%	20%	25%	30%	35%	40%	45%	50%	Periods
0.877	0.870	0.862	0.847	0.833	0.800	0.769	0.741	0.714	0.690	0.667	1
0.769	0.756	0.743	0.718	0.694	0.640	0.592	0.549	0.510	0.476	0.444	2
0.675	0.658	0.641	0.609	0.579	0.512	0.455	0.406	0.364	0.328	0.296	3
0.592	0.572	0.552	0.516	0.482	0.410	0.350	0.301	0.260	0.226	0.198	4
0.519	0.497	0.476	0.437	0.402	0.328	0.269	0.223	0.186	0.156	0.132	5
0.456	0.432	0.410	0.370	0.335	0.262	0.207	0.165	0.133	0.108	0.088	6
0.400	0.376	0.354	0.314	0.279	0.210	0.159	0.122	0.095	0.074	0.059	7
0.351	0.327	0.305	0.266	0.233	0.168	0.123	0.091	0.068	0.051	0.039	8
0.308	0.284	0.263	0.225	0.194	0.134	0.094	0.067	0.048	0.035	0.026	9
0.270	0.247	0.227	0.191	0.162	0.107	0.073	0.050	0.035	0.024	0.017	10
0.237	0.215	0.195	0.162	0.135	0.086	0.056	0.037	0.025	0.017	0.012	11
0.208	0.187	0.168	0.137	0.112	0.069	0.043	0.027	0.018	0.012	0.008	12
0.182	0.163	0.145	0.116	0.093	0.055	0.033	0.020	0.013	0.008	0.005	13
0.160	0.141	0.125	0.099	0.078	0.044	0.025	0.015	0.009	0.006	0.003	14
0.140	0.123	0.108	0.084	0.065	0.035	0.020	0.011	0.006	0.004	0.002	15
0.123	0.107	0.093	0.071	0.054	0.028	0.015	0.008	0.005	0.003	0.002	16
0.108	0.093	0.080	0.060	0.045	0.023	0.012	0.006	0.003	0.002	0.001	17
0.095	0.081	0.069	0.051	0.038	0.018	0.009	0.005	0.002	0.001	0.001	18
0.083	0.070	0.060	0.043	0.031	0.014	0.007	0.003	0.002	0.001		19
0.073	0.061	0.051	0.037	0.026	0.012	0.005	0.002	0.001	0.001		20
0.064	0.053	0.044	0.031	0.022	0.009	0.004	0.002	0.001			21
0.056	0.046	0.038	0.026	0.018	0.007	0.003	0.001	0.001			22
0.049	0.040	0.033	0.022	0.015	0.006	0.002	0.001				23
0.043	0.035	0.028	0.019	0.013	0.005	0.002	0.001				24
0.038	0.030	0.024	0.016	0.010	0.004	0.001	0.001				25
0.033	0.026	0.021	0.014	0.009	0.003	0.001					26
0.029	0.023	0.018	0.011	0.007	0.002	0.001					27
0.026	0.020	0.016	0.010	0.006	0.002	0.001					28
0.022	0.017	0.014	0.008	0.005	0.002						29
0.020	0.015	0.012	0.007	0.004	0.001						30
0.005	0.004	0.003	0.001	0.001							40
0.001	0.001	0.001									50

Table 4. Present Value of an Ordinary Annuity of $1 Received at the End of Each Period for a Given Number of Time Periods

Periods	1%	2%	3%	4%	5%	6%	7%	8%	9%	10%	12%
1	0.990	0.980	0.971	0.962	0.952	0.943	0.935	0.926	0.917	0.909	0.893
2	1.970	1.942	1.913	1.886	1.859	1.833	1.808	1.783	1.759	1.736	1.690
3	2.941	2.884	2.829	2.775	2.723	2.673	2.624	2.577	2.531	2.487	2.402
4	3.902	3.808	3.717	3.630	3.546	3.465	3.387	3.312	3.240	3.170	3.037
5	4.853	4.713	4.580	4.452	4.329	4.212	4.100	3.993	3.890	3.791	3.605
6	5.795	5.601	5.417	5.242	5.076	4.917	4.767	4.623	4.486	4.355	4.111
7	6.728	6.472	6.230	6.002	5.786	5.582	5.389	5.206	5.033	4.868	4.564
8	7.652	7.325	7.020	6.733	6.463	6.210	5.971	5.747	5.535	5.335	4.968
9	8.566	8.162	7.786	7.435	7.108	6.802	6.515	6.247	5.995	5.759	5.328
10	9.471	8.983	8.530	8.111	7.722	7.360	7.024	6.710	6.418	6.145	5.650
11	10.368	9.787	9.253	8.760	8.306	7.887	7.499	7.139	6.805	6.495	5.938
12	11.255	10.575	9.954	9.385	8.863	8.384	7.943	7.536	7.161	6.814	6.194
13	12.134	11.348	10.635	9.986	9.394	8.853	8.358	7.904	7.487	7.103	6.424
14	13.004	12.106	11.296	10.563	9.899	9.295	8.745	8.244	7.786	7.367	6.628
15	13.865	12.849	11.938	11.118	10.380	9.712	9.108	8.559	8.061	7.606	6.811
16	14.718	13.578	12.561	11.652	10.838	10.106	9.447	8.851	8.313	7.824	6.974
17	15.562	14.292	13.166	12.166	11.274	10.477	9.763	9.122	8.544	8.022	7.120
18	16.398	14.992	13.754	12.659	11.690	10.828	10.059	9.372	8.756	8.201	7.250
19	17.226	15.678	14.324	13.134	12.085	11.158	10.336	9.604	8.950	8.365	7.366
20	18.046	16.351	14.878	13.590	12.462	11.470	10.594	9.818	9.129	8.514	7.469
21	18.857	17.011	15.415	14.029	12.821	11.764	10.836	10.017	9.292	8.649	7.562
22	19.660	17.658	15.937	14.451	13.163	12.042	11.061	10.201	9.442	8.772	7.645
23	20.456	18.292	16.444	14.857	13.489	12.303	11.272	10.371	9.580	8.883	7.718
24	21.243	18.914	16.936	15.247	13.799	12.550	11.469	10.529	9.707	8.985	7.784
25	22.023	19.523	17.413	15.622	14.094	12.783	11.654	10.675	9.823	9.077	7.843
26	22.795	20.121	17.877	15.983	14.375	13.003	11.826	10.810	9.929	9.161	7.896
27	23.560	20.707	18.327	16.330	14.643	13.211	11.987	10.935	10.027	9.237	7.943
28	24.316	21.281	18.764	16.663	14.898	13.406	12.137	11.051	10.116	9.307	7.984
29	25.066	21.844	19.189	16.984	15.141	13.591	12.278	11.158	10.198	9.370	8.022
30	25.808	22.396	19.600	17.292	15.373	13.765	12.409	11.258	10.274	9.427	8.055
40	32.835	27.355	23.115	19.793	17.159	15.046	13.332	11.925	10.757	9.779	8.244
50	39.196	31.424	25.730	21.482	18.256	15.762	13.801	12.234	10.962	9.915	8.305

Table 4. (continued)

14%	15%	16%	18%	20%	25%	30%	35%	40%	45%	50%	Periods
0.877	0.870	0.862	0.847	0.833	0.800	0.769	0.741	0.714	0.690	0.667	1
1.647	1.626	1.605	1.566	1.528	1.440	1.361	1.289	1.224	1.165	1.111	2
2.322	2.283	2.246	2.174	2.106	1.952	1.816	1.696	1.589	1.493	1.407	3
2.914	2.855	2.798	2.690	2.589	2.362	2.166	1.997	1.849	1.720	1.605	4
3.433	3.352	3.274	3.127	2.991	2.689	2.436	2.220	2.035	1.876	1.737	5
3.889	3.784	3.685	3.498	3.326	2.951	2.643	2.385	2.168	1.983	1.824	6
4.288	4.160	4.039	3.812	3.605	3.161	2.802	2.508	2.263	2.057	1.883	7
4.639	4.487	4.344	4.078	3.837	3.329	2.925	2.598	2.331	2.109	1.922	8
4.946	4.772	4.607	4.303	4.031	3.463	3.019	2.665	2.379	2.144	1.948	9
5.216	5.019	4.833	4.494	4.192	3.571	3.092	2.715	2.414	2.168	1.965	10
5.453	5.234	5.029	4.656	4.327	3.656	3.147	2.752	2.438	2.185	1.977	11
5.660	5.421	5.197	4.793	4.439	3.725	3.190	2.779	2.456	2.197	1.985	12
5.842	5.583	5.342	4.910	4.533	3.780	3.223	2.799	2.469	2.204	1.990	13
6.002	5.724	5.468	5.008	4.611	3.824	3.249	2.814	2.478	2.210	1.993	14
6.142	5.847	5.575	5.092	4.675	3.859	3.268	2.825	2.484	2.214	1.995	15
6.265	5.954	5.669	5.162	4.730	3.887	3.283	2.834	2.489	2.216	1.997	16
6.373	6.047	5.749	5.222	4.775	3.910	3.295	2.840	2.492	2.218	1.998	17
6.467	6.128	5.818	5.273	4.812	3.928	3.304	2.844	2.494	2.219	1.999	18
6.550	6.198	5.877	5.316	4.844	3.942	3.311	2.848	2.496	2.220	1.999	19
6.623	6.259	5.929	5.353	4.870	3.954	3.316	2.850	2.497	2.221	1.999	20
6.687	6.312	5.973	5.384	4.891	3.963	3.320	2.852	2.498	2.221	2.000	21
6.743	6.359	6.011	5.410	4.909	3.970	3.323	2.853	2.498	2.222	2.000	22
6.792	6.399	6.044	5.432	4.925	3.976	3.325	2.854	2.499	2.222	2.000	23
6.835	6.434	6.073	5.451	4.937	3.981	3.327	2.855	2.499	2.222	2.000	24
6.873	6.464	6.097	5.467	4.948	3.985	3.329	2.856	2.499	2.222	2.000	25
6.906	6.491	6.118	5.480	4.956	3.988	3.330	2.856	2.500	2.222	2.000	26
6.935	6.514	6.136	5.492	4.964	3.990	3.331	2.856	2.500	2.222	2.000	27
6.961	6.534	6.152	5.502	4.970	3.992	3.331	2.857	2.500	2.222	2.000	28
6.983	6.551	6.166	5.510	4.975	3.994	3.332	2.857	2.500	2.222	2.000	29
7.003	6.566	6.177	5.517	4.979	3.995	3.332	2.857	2.500	2.222	2.000	30
7.105	6.642	6.234	5.548	4.997	3.999	3.333	2.857	2.500	2.222	2.000	40
7.133	6.661	6.246	5.554	4.999	4.000	3.333	2.857	2.500	2.222	2.000	50

APPENDIX D

Accounting for Partnerships

LEARNING OBJECTIVES

1. *Identify the major characteristics, advantages, and disadvantages of the partnership form of business.*
2. *Record investments of cash and of other assets by the partners in forming a partnership.*
3. *Compute and record the income or losses that partners share, based on stated ratios, capital balance ratios, and partners' salaries and interest.*
4. *Record a person's admission to a partnership.*
5. *Record a person's withdrawal from a partnership.*
6. *Explain the distribution of assets to partners when they liquidate their partnership.*

Much of this textbook uses the sole proprietorship to illustrate the basic principles and practices of accounting. This appendix focuses on accounting for the partnership form of business organization. The Uniform Partnership Act, which has been adopted by most of the states, defines a **partnership** as "an association of two or more persons to carry on as co-owners of a business for profit." Generally, partnerships are formed when owners of small businesses want to combine capital or managerial talents for some common business purpose. After studying this appendix, you should be able to meet the learning objectives listed on the left.

Partnership Characteristics

OBJECTIVE 1
Identify the major characteristics, advantages, and disadvantages of the partnership form of business

Partnerships are treated as separate entities in accounting. They differ in many ways from the other forms of business. The next few paragraphs describe some of the important characteristics of a partnership.

Voluntary Association

A partnership is a voluntary association of individuals rather than a legal entity in itself. Therefore, a partner is responsible under the law for his or her partner's business actions within the scope of the partnership. A partner also has unlimited liability for the debts of the partnership. Because of these potential liabilities, an individual must be allowed to choose the people who join the partnership. A person should select as partners individuals who share his or her business objectives.

Partnership Agreement

A partnership is easy to form. Two or more competent people simply agree to be partners in some common business purpose. This agreement is known as a **partnership agreement**. The partnership agreement does not have to be in writing; however, it is good business practice to have a written document that clearly states the details of the partnership. The contract should describe the name, location, and purpose of the business; the partners and their respective duties; the investments of each partner; the methods for distributing income and losses; and procedures for the admission and withdrawal of partners, the withdrawal of assets allowed each partner, and the liquidation (termination) of the business.

Limited Life

Because a partnership is formed by a contract between partners, it has a **limited life**: Anything that ends the contract dissolves the partnership. A partnership is dissolved when (1) a new partner is admitted, (2) a partner withdraws, (3) a partner goes bankrupt, (4) a partner is incapacitated (to the point at which he or she cannot perform as obligated), (5) a partner retires, (6) a partner dies, or (7) the terms set out in the partnership agreement come to pass (for example, when a major project is completed). The partnership agreement can be written to cover each of these situations, allowing the partnership to continue legally. For example, the partnership agreement can state that if a partner dies, the remaining partner or partners must purchase the deceased partner's capital at book value from the heirs.

Mutual Agency

Each partner is an agent of the partnership within the scope of the business. Because of this **mutual agency**, any partner can bind the partnership to a business agreement as long as he or she acts within the scope of the company's normal operations. For example, a partner in a used-car business can bind the partnership through the purchase or sale of used cars. But this partner cannot bind the partnership to a contract for buying men's clothing or any other goods that are not related to the used-car business. Because of mutual agency, it is very important for an individual to choose business partners who have integrity and who share his or her business objectives.

Unlimited Liability

Each partner is personally liable for all the debts of the partnership. If a partnership is in poor financial condition and cannot pay its debts, the creditors first must satisfy their claims from the assets of the partnership. If the assets of the business are not enough to pay all debts, the creditors can seek payment from the personal assets of each partner. If a partner's personal assets are used up before the debts are paid, the creditors can claim additional assets from the remaining partners who are able to pay. Each partner, then, could be required by law to pay all the debts of the partnership; therefore, all the partners have **unlimited liability** for their company's debt.

Co-ownership of Partnership Property

When individuals invest property in a partnership, they give up the right to their separate use of the property. The property becomes an asset of the partnership and is owned jointly by all the partners.

Participation in Partnership Income

Each partner has the right to share in the company's income and the responsibility to share in its losses. The partnership agreement should state the method of distributing income and losses to each partner. If the agreement describes how income should be shared but does not mention losses, losses are distributed in the same way as income. If the partners fail to describe the method of income and loss distribution in the partnership agreement, the law states that income and losses must be shared equally.

Advantages and Disadvantages of Partnerships

Partnerships have both advantages and disadvantages. One advantage is that a partnership is easy to form, change, and dissolve. Also, a partnership is able to pool capital resources and individual talents; it has no corporate tax burden (because a partnership is not a legal entity, it does not have to pay a federal income tax, as do corporations, but must file an informational return); and it gives the partners a certain amount of freedom and flexibility.

On the other hand, the life of a partnership is limited; one partner can bind the partnership to a contract (mutual agency); the partners have unlimited personal liability; and it is harder in a partnership to raise large amounts of capital and to transfer ownership interest than it is for corporations.

Accounting for Partners' Equity

OBJECTIVE 2
Record investments of cash and of other assets by the partners in forming a partnership

Although accounting for a partnership is very similar to accounting for a sole proprietorship, there are differences. One is that the owners' equity of a partnership is called **partners' equity**. In accounting for partners' equity, it is necessary to maintain separate Capital and Withdrawals accounts for each partner and to divide the income and losses of the company among the partners. The differences in the Capital accounts of a sole proprietorship and a partnership are shown below.

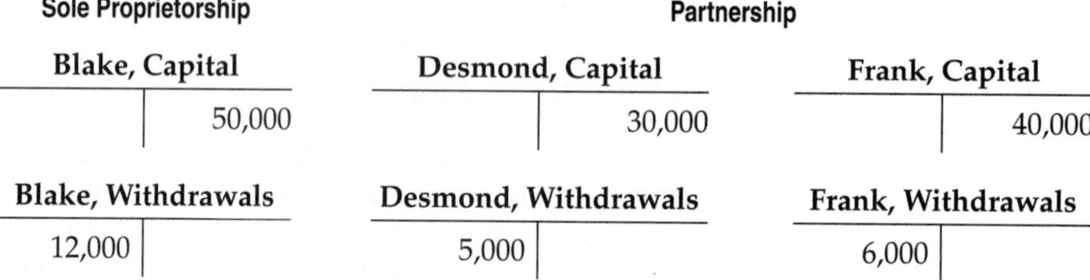

In the partners' equity section of the balance sheet, the balance of each partner's Capital account is listed separately:

Liabilities and Partners' Equity

Total Liabilities		$28,000
Partners' Equity		
Desmond, Capital	$25,000	
Frank, Capital	34,000	
Total Partners' Equity		59,000
Total Liabilities and Partners' Equity		$87,000

Each partner invests cash, other assets, or a combination in the partnership according to the partnership agreement. Noncash assets should be valued at their fair market value on the date they are transferred to the partnership. The assets invested by a partner are debited to the proper account, and the total amount is credited to the partner's Capital account.

To show how partners' investments are recorded, let's assume that Jerry Adcock and Rose Villa have agreed to combine their capital and equipment in a partnership to operate a jewelry store. According to their partnership agreement, Adcock will invest $28,000 cash and $37,000 of furniture and displays, and Villa will invest $40,000 cash and $20,000 of equipment. The general journal entries to record the partners' initial investments are as follows:

19x1				
July	1	Cash	28,000	
		Furniture and Displays	37,000	
		Jerry Adcock, Capital		65,000
		Initial investment of Jerry Adcock in Adcock and Villa		
	1	Cash	40,000	
		Equipment	20,000	
		Rose Villa, Capital		60,000
		Initial investment of Rose Villa in Adcock and Villa		

The values assigned to the assets in our example would have had to be included in the partnership agreement. These values can differ from those carried on the partners' personal books. For example, the equipment that Rose Villa contributed may have had a value of only $12,000 on her books. But suppose that after she purchased the equipment, its market value increased considerably. The book value of Villa's equipment is not important. The fair market value of the equipment at the time of transfer *is* important, however, because that value represents the amount of money that Villa has invested in the partnership. Later investments are recorded the same way.

The partnership also can assume liabilities that are related to investments. For example, suppose that after seven months, Villa invests additional equipment with a fair market value of $45,000 in the partnership. Related to the equipment is a note payable for $37,000, which the partnership assumes. This entry records the transaction:

19x2				
Feb.	1	Equipment	45,000	
		Notes Payable		37,000
		Rose Villa, Capital		8,000
		Additional investment by Rose Villa in Adcock and Villa		

Distribution of Partnership Income and Losses

OBJECTIVE 3
Compute and record the income or losses that partners share, based on stated ratios, capital balance ratios, and partners' salaries and interest

A partnership's income and losses can be distributed according to whatever method the partners specify in the partnership agreement. The agreement should be specific and clear, to avoid later disputes. If a partnership agreement does not mention the distribution of income and losses, the law requires that they be shared equally by all partners. Also, if a partnership agreement mentions only the distribution of income, the law requires that losses be distributed in the same ratio as income.

The income of a partnership normally has three components: (1) return to the partners for the use of their capital (called *interest on partners' capital*), (2) compensation for direct services the partners have rendered (partners' salaries), and (3) other income for any special characteristics or risks individual partners may bring to the partnership. The breakdown of total income into its three components helps clarify how much each partner has contributed to the firm.

If all partners are contributing equal capital, have similar talents, and are spending the same amount of time in the business, then an equal distribution of income and losses would be fair. However, if one partner works full time in the firm and another devotes only a fourth of his or her time, then the distribution of income or losses should reflect this difference. (This concept would apply to any situation in which the partners contribute unequally to the business.)

Several ways for partners to share income are (1) by stated ratios, (2) by capital balance ratios, and (3) by salaries to the partners and interest on partners' capital, with the remaining income shared according to stated ratios. *Salaries* and *interest* here are not *salaries expense* or *interest expense* in the ordinary sense of the terms. They do not affect the amount of reported net income. Instead, they refer to ways of determining each partner's share of net income or loss on the basis of time spent and money invested in the partnership.

Stated Ratios

One method of distributing income and losses is to give each partner a stated ratio of the total income or loss. If each partner is making an equal contribution to the firm, each can assume the same share of income and losses. It is important to understand that an equal contribution to the firm does not necessarily mean an equal capital investment in the firm. One partner may be devoting more time and talent to the firm, whereas the second partner may make a larger capital investment. And, if the partners contribute unequally to the firm, unequal stated ratios—60 percent and 40 percent, perhaps—can be appropriate.

Let's assume that Adcock and Villa had a net income last year of $30,000. The partnership agreement states that the percentages of income and losses distributed to Jerry Adcock and Rose Villa should be 60 percent and 40 percent, respectively. The computation of each partner's share of the income and the journal entry to show the distribution are as follows:

Adcock ($30,000 × .60)	$18,000
Villa ($30,000 × .40)	12,000
Net Income	$30,000

Date		Account	Debit	Credit
19x2				
June	30	Income Summary	30,000	
		Jerry Adcock, Capital		18,000
		Rose Villa, Capital		12,000
		Distribution of income for the year to the partners' Capital accounts		

Capital Balance Ratios

If invested capital produces the most income for the partnership, then income and losses may be distributed according to **capital balance**. One way of distributing income and losses here is to use a ratio based on each partner's capital balance at the beginning of the year. Another way is to use the average capital balance of each partner during the year. The partnership agreement must describe the method that is going to be used.

Ratios Based on Beginning Capital Balances. To show how the first method works, let's look at the beginning capital balance of the partners in Adcock and Villa. At the start of the fiscal year, July 1, 19x1, Jerry Adcock, Capital showed a $65,000 balance, and Rose Villa, Capital showed a $60,000 balance. (Actually, these balances reflect the partners' initial investment; the partnership was formed on July 1, 19x1.) The total partners' equity in the firm, then, was

$125,000 ($65,000 + $60,000). Each partner's capital balance at the beginning of the year divided by the total partners' equity at the beginning of the year is that partner's beginning capital balance ratio:

	Beginning Capital Balance	Beginning Capital Balance Ratio
Jerry Adcock	$ 65,000	65 ÷ 125 = .52 = 52%
Rose Villa	60,000	60 ÷ 125 = .48 = 48%
	$125,000	

The income that each partner should receive when distribution is based on beginning capital balance ratios is figured by multiplying the total income by each partner's capital ratio. If we assume that income for the year was $140,000, Jerry Adcock's share of that income was $72,800, and Rose Villa's share was $67,200:

Jerry Adcock	$140,000 × .52 =	$ 72,800
Rose Villa	$140,000 × .48 =	67,200
		$140,000

This journal entry shows the distribution of income to Jerry Adcock and Rose Villa:

19x2				
June	30	Income Summary	140,000	
		Jerry Adcock, Capital		72,800
		Rose Villa, Capital		67,200
		Distribution of income for the year to the partners' Capital accounts		

Ratios Based on Average Capital Balances. If Adcock and Villa use beginning capital balance ratios to determine the distribution of income, they do not consider any investments or withdrawals made during the year. But these investments and withdrawals usually change the partners' capital ratio. If the partners believe their capital balances are going to change dramatically during the year, they can choose average capital balance ratios as a fairer means of distributing income and losses.

These T accounts show the activity over the year in Adcock and Villa's partners' Capital and Withdrawals accounts:

Jerry Adcock, Capital

Debit	Credit
	7/1/x1 65,000

Jerry Adcock, Withdrawals

Debit	Credit
1/1/x2 10,000	

Rose Villa, Capital

Debit	Credit
	7/1/x1 60,000
	2/1/x2 8,000

Rose Villa, Withdrawals

Debit	Credit
11/1/x1 10,000	

Jerry Adcock withdrew $10,000 on January 1, 19x2. Rose Villa withdrew $10,000 on November 1, 19x1 and invested an additional $8,000 of equipment on February 1, 19x2. Again, the income for the year's operation (7/1/x1–6/30/x2) was $140,000. The calculations for the average capital balances and the distribution of income are as follows:

Average Capital Balances

Partner	Date	Capital Balance	×	Months Unchanged	=	Total		Average Capital Balance
Adcock	July–December	$65,000	×	6	=	$390,000		
	January–June	55,000	×	6	=	330,000		
				12		$720,000	÷ 12 =	$ 60,000
Villa	July–October	$60,000	×	4	=	$240,000		
	November–January	50,000	×	3	=	150,000		
	February–June	58,000	×	5	=	290,000		
				12		$680,000	÷ 12 =	56,667
							Total average capital	$116,667

Average Capital Balance Ratios

$$\text{Adcock} = \frac{\text{Adcock's average capital balance}}{\text{Total average capital}} = \frac{\$60{,}000}{\$116{,}667} = .514 = 51.4\%$$

$$\text{Villa} = \frac{\text{Villa's average capital balance}}{\text{Total average capital}} = \frac{\$56{,}667}{\$116{,}667} = .486 = 48.6\%$$

Distribution of Income

Partner	Income	×	Ratio	=	Share of Income
Adcock	$140,000	×	.514	=	$ 71,960
Villa	$140,000	×	.486	=	68,040
				Total income	$140,000

Notice that in order to determine the distribution of income (or loss), you have to determine (1) the average capital balances, (2) the average capital balance ratios, and (3) each partner's share of income or loss. To compute each partner's average capital balance, you have to examine the changes that have taken place during the year in each partner's capital balance, changes that are the product of further investments and withdrawals. The partner's beginning capital is multiplied by the number of months the balance remains unchanged. After the balance changes, the new balance is multiplied by the number of months it remains unchanged. The process continues until the end of the year. The totals of these computations are added together and then divided by 12 to determine the average capital balances. Once the average capital balances are determined, the method of figuring capital balance ratios for sharing income and losses is the same as that used for beginning capital balances.

The journal entry showing how the earnings for the year are distributed to the partners' Capital accounts looks like this:

19x2				
June	30	Income Summary	140,000	
		Jerry Adcock, Capital		71,960
		Rose Villa, Capital		68,040
		Distribution of income for the year to the partners' Capital accounts		

Salaries, Interest, and Stated Ratios

Partners generally do not contribute equally to a firm. To make up for unequal contributions, a partnership agreement can allow for partners' salaries, interest on partners' capital balances, or a combination of both in the distribution of income. Again, salaries and interest of this kind are not deducted as expenses before the partnership income is determined. They represent a method of arriving at an equitable distribution of income or loss.

To illustrate an allowance for partners' salaries, we assume that Adcock and Villa have agreed that they will receive salaries—$8,000 for Adcock and $7,000 for Villa—and that any remaining income will be divided equally between them. Each salary is charged to the appropriate partner's Withdrawals account when paid. If we assume the same $140,000 income for the first year, the calculations for Adcock and Villa are as follows:

	Income of Partner		Income Distributed
	Adcock	Villa	
Total Income for Distribution			$140,000
Distribution of Salaries			
Adcock	$ 8,000		
Villa		$ 7,000	(15,000)
Remaining Income After Salaries			$125,000
Equal Distribution of Remaining Income			
Adcock ($125,000 × .50)	62,500		
Villa ($125,000 × .50)		62,500	(125,000)
Remaining Income			—
Income of Partners	$70,500	$69,500	$140,000

The journal entry is as follows:

19x2			
June 30	Income Summary	140,000	
	Jerry Adcock, Capital		70,500
	Rose Villa, Capital		69,500
	Distribution of income for the year to the partners' Capital accounts		

Salaries allow for differences in the services that partners provide the business. However, they do not take into account differences in invested capital. To allow for capital differences, in addition to salary, each partner can receive a stated interest on his or her invested capital. Suppose that Jerry Adcock and Rose Villa agree to receive annual salaries of $8,000 for Adcock and $7,000 for Villa, as well as 10 percent interest on their beginning capital balances, and to share any remaining income equally. The calculations for Adcock and Villa, if we assume income of $140,000, are shown at the top of page Ap-44.

	Income of Partner		Income Distributed
	Adcock	Villa	
Total Income for Distribution			$140,000
Distribution of Salaries			
Adcock	$ 8,000		
Villa		$ 7,000	(15,000)
Remaining Income After Salaries			$125,000
Distribution of Interest			
Adcock ($65,000 × .10)	6,500		
Villa ($60,000 × .10)		6,000	(12,500)
Remaining Income After Salaries and Interest			$112,500
Equal Distribution of Remaining Income			
Adcock ($112,500 × .50)	56,250		
Villa ($112,500 × .50)		56,250	(112,500)
Remaining Income			—
Income of Partners	$70,750	$69,250	$140,000

The journal entry is as follows:

19x2			
June 30	Income Summary	140,000	
	Jerry Adcock, Capital		70,750
	Rose Villa, Capital		69,250
	Distribution of income for the year to the partners' Capital accounts		

If the partnership agreement allows for the distribution of salaries or interest or both, the amounts must be allocated to the partners even if profits are not enough to cover the salaries and interest. In fact, even if the company has a loss, these allocations still must be made. The negative balance or loss after the allocation of salaries and interest must be distributed according to the stated ratio in the partnership agreement, or equally if the agreement does not mention a ratio.

For example, let's assume that Adcock and Villa agreed to the following conditions for the distribution of income and losses:

	Salaries	Interest	Beginning Capital Balance
Adcock	$70,000	10 percent of beginning capital balances	$65,000
Villa	60,000		60,000

The income for the first year of operation was $140,000. This is the computation for the distribution of the income and loss:

	Income of Partner		Income
	Adcock	Villa	Distributed
Total Income for Distribution			$140,000
Distribution of Salaries			
Adcock	$70,000		
Villa		$60,000	(130,000)
Remaining Income After Salaries			$ 10,000
Distribution of Interest			
Adcock ($65,000 × .10)	6,500		
Villa ($60,000 × .10)		6,000	(12,500)
Negative Balance After Salaries and Interest			$ (2,500)
Equal Distribution of Negative Balance*			
Adcock ($2,500 × .50)	(1,250)		
Villa ($2,500 × .50)		(1,250)	2,500
Remaining Income			—
Income of Partners	$75,250	$64,750	$140,000

*Notice that the negative balance is distributed equally because the agreement does not indicate how income and losses should be distributed after salaries and interest are paid.

The journal entry is as follows:

19x2				
June	30	Income Summary	140,000	
		Jerry Adcock, Capital		75,250
		Rose Villa, Capital		64,750
		Distribution of income for the year to the partners' Capital accounts		

On the income statement for the partnership, the distribution of income or losses is shown below the net income figure. Exhibit 1 shows how, using the last example.

Dissolution of a Partnership

Dissolution of a partnership occurs whenever there is a change in the original association of partners. When a partnership is dissolved, the partners lose their authority to continue the business as a going concern. This does not mean that the business operation necessarily is ended or interrupted, but it does mean—from a legal and accounting standpoint—that the separate entity ceases to exist. The remaining partners can act for the partnership in finishing the affairs of the business or in forming a new partnership that will be a new accounting entity. The dissolution of a partnership takes place through the admission of a new partner, the withdrawal of a partner, or the death of a partner.

Exhibit 1. Partial Income Statement for Adcock and Villa

Adcock and Villa Partial Income Statement For the Year Ended June 30, 19x2		
Net Income		$140,000
Distribution to the Partners		
Adcock		
Salary Distribution	$70,000	
Interest on Beginning Capital Balance	6,500	
Total	$76,500	
One-Half of Remaining Negative Amount	(1,250)	
Share of Net Income		$ 75,250
Villa		
Salary Distribution	$60,000	
Interest on Beginning Capital Balance	6,000	
Total	$66,000	
One-Half of Remaining Negative Amount	(1,250)	
Share of Net Income		64,750
Net Income Distributed		$140,000

Admission of a New Partner

OBJECTIVE 4
Record a person's admission to a partnership

The admission of a new partner dissolves the old partnership because a new association has been formed. Dissolving the old partnership and creating a new one require the consent of all the old partners and the ratification of a new partnership agreement. When a new partner is admitted, a new partnership agreement should be in place.

An individual can be admitted into a firm in one of two ways: (1) by purchasing an interest in the partnership from one or more of the original partners or (2) by investing assets in the partnership.

Purchasing an Interest from a Partner. When an individual is admitted to a firm by purchasing an interest from an old partner, each partner must agree to the change. The transaction is a personal one between the old and new partners, but the interest purchased must be transferred from the Capital account of the selling partner to the Capital account of the new partner.

Suppose that Jerry Adcock decides to sell his interest, assumed to be $70,000, in Adcock and Villa to Richard Davis for $100,000 on August 31, 19x3, and that Rose Villa agrees to the sale. The entry to record the sale on the partnership books looks like this:

19x3			
Aug. 31	Jerry Adcock, Capital	70,000	
	Richard Davis, Capital		70,000
	Transfer of Jerry Adcock's equity to Richard Davis		

Notice that the entry records the book value of the equity, not the amount Davis pays. The amount Davis pays is a personal matter between him and Adcock.

Because the amount paid does not affect the assets or liabilities of the firm, it is not entered in the records.

Here's another example of a purchase: Assume that Richard Davis purchases half of Jerry Adcock's $70,000 and half of Rose Villa's interest, assumed to be $80,000, in the partnership by paying a total of $100,000 to the two partners on August 31, 19x3. The entry to record this transaction on the partnership books would be as follows:

19x3			
Aug. 31	Jerry Adcock, Capital	35,000	
	Rose Villa, Capital	40,000	
	Richard Davis, Capital		75,000
	Transfer of half of Jerry Adcock's and Rose Villa's equity to Richard Davis		

Investing Assets in a Partnership. When a new partner is admitted through an investment in the partnership, both the assets and the partners' equity in the firm increase. Why is this so? Because the assets the new partner invests become partnership assets, and as partnership assets increase, partners' equity increases as well.

For example, assume that Richard Davis wants to invest $75,000 for a one-third interest in the partnership of Adcock and Villa. The Capital accounts of Jerry Adcock and Rose Villa are assumed to be $70,000 and $80,000, respectively. The assets of the firm are valued correctly. So, the partners agree to sell Davis a one-third interest in the firm for $75,000. Davis's $75,000 investment equals a one-third interest in the firm after the investment is added to the previously existing capital of the partnership:

Jerry Adcock, Capital	$ 70,000
Rose Villa, Capital	80,000
Davis's investment	75,000
Total capital after Davis's investment	$225,000
One-third interest = $225,000 ÷ 3 =	$75,000

The journal entry to record Davis's investment is as follows:

19x3			
Aug. 31	Cash	75,000	
	Richard Davis, Capital		75,000
	Admission of Richard Davis to a one-third interest in the company		

Bonus to the Old Partners. Sometimes a partnership may be so profitable or otherwise advantageous that a new investor is willing to pay more than the actual dollar interest that he or she receives in the partnership. Suppose an individual pays $100,000 for an $80,000 interest in a partnership. The $20,000 excess of the payment over the interest purchased is a **bonus** to the original partners. The bonus must be distributed to the original partners according to the partnership agreement. When the agreement does not cover the distribution of bonuses, it should be distributed to the original partners in accordance with the method of distributing income and losses.

Assume that the Adcock and Villa Company has operated for several years and that the partners' capital balances and the stated ratios for distribution of income and loss are as follows:

Partners	Capital Balances	Stated Ratios
Adcock	$160,000	55%
Villa	140,000	45%
	$300,000	100%

Richard Davis wants to join the firm. He offers to invest $100,000 on December 1 for a one-fifth interest in the business and income. The original partners agree to the offer. This is the computation of the bonus to the original partners:

Partners' equity in the original partnership		$300,000
Cash investment by Richard Davis		100,000
Partners' equity in the new partnership		$400,000
Partners' equity assigned to Richard Davis ($400,000 × ⅕)		$ 80,000
Bonus to the original partners		
Investment by Richard Davis	$100,000	
Less equity assigned to Richard Davis	80,000	$ 20,000
Distribution of bonus to original partners		
Jerry Adcock ($20,000 × .55)	$ 11,000	
Rose Villa ($20,000 × .45)	9,000	$ 20,000

And this is the journal entry that records Davis's admission to the partnership:

19x3				
Dec.	1	Cash	100,000	
		Jerry Adcock, Capital		11,000
		Rose Villa, Capital		9,000
		Richard Davis, Capital		80,000
		Investment by Richard Davis for a one-fifth interest in the firm, and the bonus paid to the original partners		

Bonus to the New Partner. There are several reasons why a partnership might want a new partner. A firm in financial trouble might need additional cash. Or the original partners, wanting to expand the firm's markets, might need more capital than they themselves can provide. Also, the partners might know a person who would bring a unique talent to the firm. Under these conditions, a new partner could be admitted to the partnership with the understanding that part of the original partners' capital will be transferred (credited) to the new partner's Capital account as a bonus.

For example, suppose that Jerry Adcock and Rose Villa have invited Richard Davis to join the firm. Davis is going to invest $60,000 on December 1 for a one-fourth interest in the company. The stated ratios for distribution of income or loss for Adcock and Villa are 55 percent and 45 percent, respectively. If Davis is to receive a one-fourth interest in the firm, the interest of the original partners represents a three-fourths interest in the business. The computation of Davis's bonus is shown at the top of the next page.

Total equity in partnership		
Jerry Adcock, Capital		$160,000
Rose Villa, Capital		140,000
Investment by Richard Davis		60,000
Partners' equity in the new partnership		$360,000
Partners' equity assigned to Richard Davis ($360,000 × ¼)		$ 90,000
Bonus to new partner		
Equity assigned to Richard Davis	$90,000	
Less cash investment by Richard Davis	60,000	$ 30,000
Distribution of bonus from original partners		
Jerry Adcock ($30,000 × .55)	$16,500	
Rose Villa ($30,000 × .45)	13,500	$ 30,000

This is the journal entry to record the admission of Davis to the partnership:

19x3			
Dec. 1	Cash	60,000	
	Jerry Adcock, Capital	16,500	
	Rose Villa, Capital	13,500	
	Richard Davis, Capital		90,000
	To record the investment by Richard Davis of cash and a bonus from Adcock and Villa		

Withdrawal of a Partner

OBJECTIVE 5
Record a person's withdrawal from a partnership

Generally, a partner has the right to withdraw from a partnership in accord with legal requirements. However, to avoid disputes when a partner does decide to withdraw or retire from the firm, the partnership agreement should describe the procedures to be followed. The agreement should specify (1) whether or not an audit will be performed, (2) how the assets will be reappraised, (3) how a bonus will be determined, and (4) by what method the withdrawing partner will be paid.

There are several ways in which an individual can withdraw from a partnership. A partner can (1) sell his or her interest to another partner with the consent of the remaining partners, (2) sell his or her interest to an outsider with the consent of the remaining partners, (3) withdraw assets equal to his or her capital balance, (4) withdraw assets that are less than his or her capital balance (in this case, the remaining partners receive a bonus), or (5) withdraw assets that are greater than his or her capital balance (in this case, the withdrawing partner receives a bonus). These alternatives are illustrated in Figure 1.

Withdrawal by Selling Interest. When a partner sells his or her interest to another partner or to an outsider with the consent of the other partners, the transaction is personal; it does not change the partnership assets or the partners' equity. For example, let's assume that the capital balances of Adcock, Villa, and Davis are $140,000, $100,000, and $60,000, respectively, a total of $300,000.

Villa wants to withdraw from the partnership and is reviewing two offers for her interest. The offers are (1) to sell her interest to Davis for $110,000 or (2) to sell her interest to Judy Jones for $120,000. The remaining partners have agreed to either potential transaction. Because Davis and Jones would pay for Villa's interest from their personal assets, the partnership accounting records would

Figure 1. Alternative Ways for a Partner to Withdraw

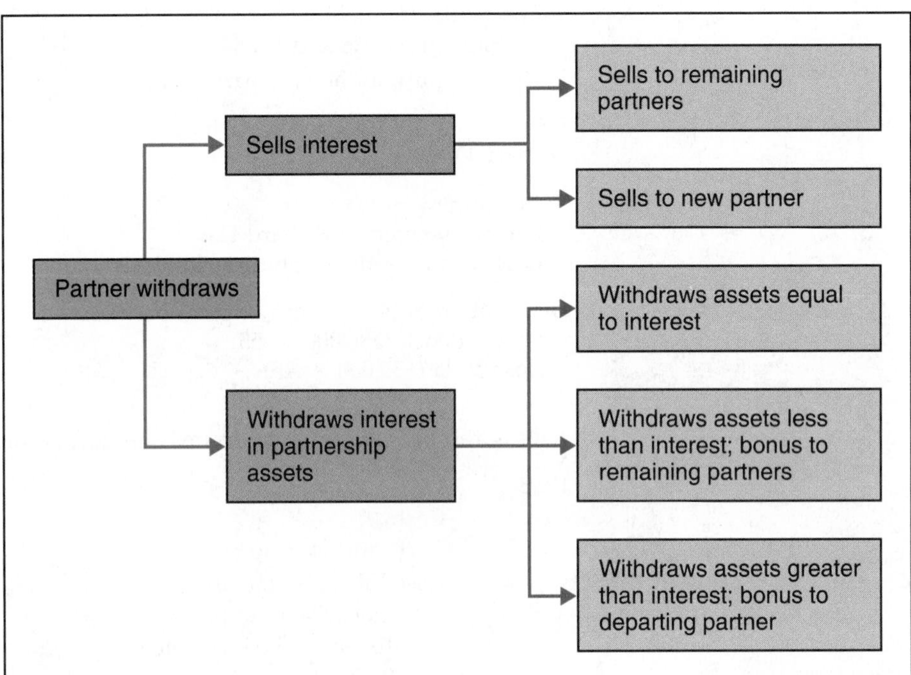

show only the transfer of Villa's interest to Davis or Jones. The entries to record these possible transfers are as follows:

1. If Villa's interest is purchased by Davis:

Rose Villa, Capital	100,000	
Richard Davis, Capital		100,000
Sale of Villa's partnership interest to Davis		

2. If Villa's interest is purchased by Jones:

Rose Villa, Capital	100,000	
Judy Jones, Capital		100,000
Sale of Villa's partnership interest to Jones		

Withdrawal by Removing Assets. A partnership agreement can allow a withdrawing partner to remove assets from the firm equal to his or her capital balance. Assume that Richard Davis decides to withdraw from Adcock, Villa, Davis & Company. Davis's capital balance is $60,000. The partnership agreement states that he can withdraw cash from the firm equal to his capital balance. If there is not enough cash, he must accept a promissory note from the new partnership for the balance. The remaining partners ask that Davis take only $50,000 in cash because of a cash shortage at the time of his withdrawal. He agrees. This is the journal entry recording Davis's withdrawal:

19x4				
Jan.	21	Richard Davis, Capital	60,000	
		Cash		50,000
		Notes Payable, Richard Davis		10,000
		Withdrawal of Richard Davis from the partnership		

When a withdrawing partner takes out assets that represent less than his or her capital balance, the equity he or she leaves in the business is divided among the remaining partners according to their stated ratios. This distribution is considered a bonus to the remaining partners. When a withdrawing partner takes out assets greater than his or her capital balance, the excess is treated as a bonus to the withdrawing partner. The remaining partners absorb the bonus according to their stated ratios. Alternative arrangements can be spelled out in the partnership agreement.

Death of a Partner

When a partner dies, the partnership is dissolved because the original association has changed. The partnership agreement should state the actions to be taken. Normally, the books are closed and financial statements prepared. These actions are necessary to determine the capital balance of each partner on the date of the death. The agreement also may indicate whether an audit should be conducted, assets appraised, and a bonus recorded, as well as the procedures for settling with the heirs. The remaining partners may purchase the deceased's equity, sell it to outsiders, or deliver certain business assets to the estate. If the firm intends to continue, a new partnership must be formed.

Liquidation of a Partnership

OBJECTIVE 6
Explain the distribution of assets to partners when they liquidate their partnership

Liquidation of a partnership is the process of ending the business, of selling enough assets to pay the partnership's liabilities and distributing any remaining assets among the partners. Liquidation is a special form of dissolution. When a partnership is liquidated, the business will not continue.

The partnership agreement should indicate the procedures to be followed in the case of liquidation. Usually, the books are adjusted and closed, with the income or loss distributed to the partners. As the assets of the business are sold, any gain or loss should be distributed to the partners according to the stated ratios. As cash becomes available, it must be applied first to outside creditors, then to partners' loans, and finally to the partners' capital balances.

Questions

1. Briefly define *partnership* and list several major characteristics of the partnership form of business.
2. What is the meaning of unlimited liability when applied to a partnership?
3. Abe and Bill are partners in a drilling operation. Abe purchased a drilling rig to be used in the partnership's operations. Is this purchase binding on Bill even though he was not involved in it? Explain your answer.
4. The partnership agreement for Karla and Jean's partnership does not disclose how they will share income and losses. How would the income and losses be shared in this partnership?
5. What are several major advantages of a partnership? What are some disadvantages?
6. Edward contributes $10,000 in cash and a building with a book value of $40,000 and fair market value of $50,000 to the Edward and Francis partnership. What is the balance of Edward's Capital account in the partnership?
7. Tom Howard and Sharon Thomas are forming a partnership. What are some of the factors they should consider in deciding how income might be divided?
8. Gayle and Henry share income and losses in their partnership in a 3:2 ratio. The firm's net income for the current year is $80,000. How would the distribution of income be recorded in the journal?

9. Opel and Paul share income in their partnership in a 2:4 ratio. Opel and Paul receive salaries of $6,000 and $10,000, respectively. How would they share a net income before salaries of $22,000?
10. Irene purchases Jane's interest in the Jane and Ken partnership for $62,000. Jane has a $57,000 capital interest in the partnership. How would this transaction be recorded in the partnership books?
11. Larry and Madison each own a $50,000 interest in a partnership. They agree to admit Nancy as a partner by selling her a one-third interest for $80,000. How large a bonus will be distributed to Larry and Madison?
12. In the liquidation of a partnership, Robert's Capital account showed a $5,000 deficit balance after all the creditors were paid. What obligation does Robert have to the partnership?
13. Describe how the dissolution of a partnership differs from the liquidation of a partnership.

Classroom Exercises

Exercise D-1.
Partnership Formation
(L.O. 2)

Martin Brill and Ruben Olivo are watch repairmen who want to form a partnership and open a jewelry store. They have an attorney prepare their partnership agreement, which indicates that assets invested in the partnership will be recorded at their fair market value and that liabilities will be assumed at book value. The assets contributed by each partner and the liabilities assumed by the partnership are as follows:

Assets (Market Value)	Martin Brill	Ruben Olivo	Total
Cash	$40,000	$30,000	$70,000
Accounts Receivable	52,000	20,000	72,000
Allowance for Uncollectible Accounts	4,000	3,000	7,000
Supplies	1,000	500	1,500
Equipment	20,000	10,000	30,000
Liabilities (Book Value)			
Accounts Payable	$32,000	$ 9,000	$41,000

Prepare the journal entries necessary to record the original investments of Brill and Olivo in the partnership.

Exercise D-2.
Distribution of Income
(L.O. 3)

Walker Parks and Lonnie Tucker agreed to form a partnership. Parks contributed $200,000 in cash, and Tucker contributed assets with a fair market value of $400,000. The partnership, in its initial year, reported net income of $120,000.

Prepare the journal entry to distribute the first year's income to the partners under each of the following conditions:

1. Parks and Tucker failed to include stated ratios in the partnership agreement.
2. Parks and Tucker agreed to share income and losses in a 3:2 ratio.
3. Parks and Tucker agreed to share income and losses in the ratio of their original investments.
4. Parks and Tucker agreed to share income and losses by allowing 10 percent interest on original investments and sharing any remainder equally.

Exercise D-3.
Distribution of Income or Losses: Salary and Interest
(L.O. 3)

Assume that the partnership agreement of Parks and Tucker in Exercise D-2 states that Parks and Tucker are to receive salaries of $20,000 and $24,000, respectively; that Parks is to receive 6 percent interest on his capital balance at the beginning of the year; and that the remainder of income and losses are to be shared equally.

Prepare the journal entries to distribute the income or losses under the conditions listed on the next page.

1. Income totaled $120,000 before deductions for salaries and interest.
2. Income totaled $48,000 before deductions for salaries and interest.
3. There was a loss of $2,000.
4. There was a loss of $40,000.

Exercise D-4. Distribution of Income: Average Capital Balance
(L.O. 3)

Fran and Laura operate a furniture rental business. Their capital balances on January 1, 19x7 were $160,000 and $240,000, respectively. Fran withdrew cash of $32,000 from the business on April 1, 19x7. Laura withdrew $60,000 cash on October 1, 19x7. Fran and Laura distribute partnership income based on their average capital balances each year. Income for 19x7 was $160,000. Compute the income to be distributed to Fran and Laura using their average capital balances in 19x7.

Exercise D-5. Admission of a New Partner: Recording a Bonus
(L.O. 4)

Jorge, Ramon, and Hubert have equity in a partnership of $40,000, $40,000, and $60,000, respectively, and they share income and losses in a ratio of 1:1:3. The partners have agreed to admit Jesse to the partnership.

Prepare journal entries to record the admission of Jesse to the partnership under the following conditions:

1. Jesse invests $60,000 for a 20 percent interest in the partnership, and a bonus is recorded for the original partners.
2. Jesse invests $60,000 for a 40 percent interest in the partnership, and a bonus is recorded for Jesse.

Exercise D-6. Withdrawal of a Partner
(L.O. 5)

Ronald, Ted, and Steve are partners. They share income and losses in the ratio of 3:2:1. Steve's Capital account has a $120,000 balance. Ronald and Ted have agreed to let Steve take $160,000 of the company's cash when he retires from the business.

What journal entry must be made on the partnership's books when Steve retires, assuming that a bonus to Steve is recognized and absorbed by the remaining partners?

Problems

Problem D-1. Partnership Formation and Distribution of Income
(L.O. 2, 3)

In January 19x1, Tom Himes and Jeff Palmer agreed to produce and sell chocolate candies. Tom contributed $240,000 in cash to the business. Jeff contributed the building and equipment, valued at $220,000 and $140,000, respectively. The partnership had an income of $84,000 during 19x1 but was less successful during 19x2, when income was only $40,000.

Required

1. Prepare the journal entry to record the investment of both partners in the partnership.
2. Determine the share of income for each partner in 19x1 and 19x2 under each of the following conditions: (a) The partners agreed to share income equally. (b) The partners failed to agree on an income-sharing arrangement. (c) The partners agreed to share income according to the ratio of their original investments. (d) The partners agreed to share income by allowing interest of 10 percent on their original investments and dividing the remainder equally. (e) The partners agreed to share income by allowing salaries of $40,000 for Himes and $28,000 for Palmer, and dividing the remainder equally. (f) The partners agreed to share income by paying salaries of $40,000 to Himes and $28,000 to Palmer, allowing interest of 9 percent on their original investments, and dividing the remainder equally.

Problem D-2. Distribution of Income: Salaries and Interest
(L.O. 3)

Ruth and Perry are partners in a tennis shop. They have agreed that Ruth will operate the store and receive a salary of $104,000 per year. Perry will receive 10 percent interest on his average capital balance during the year of $500,000. The remaining income or losses are to be shared by Ruth and Perry in a 2:3 ratio.

Required

Determine each partner's share of income and losses under each of the following conditions. In each case, the income or loss is stated before the distribution of salary and interest.

1. Income was $168,000.
2. Income was $88,000.
3. The loss was $25,600.

Problem D-3.
Admission and Withdrawal of a Partner
(L.O. 4, 5)

Pat, Connie, and Janice are partners in Manitow Woodwork Company. Their capital balances as of July 31, 19x4, are as follows:

Pat, Capital		Connie, Capital		Janice, Capital	
	45,000		15,000		30,000

Each partner has agreed to admit Felicia to the partnership.

Required

Prepare the journal entries to record Felicia's admission to or Pat's withdrawal from the partnership under each of the following independent conditions: (a) Felicia pays Pat $12,500 for 20 percent of Pat's interest in the partnership. (b) Felicia invests $20,000 cash in the partnership and receives an interest equal to her investment. (c) Felicia invests $30,000 cash in the partnership for a 20 percent interest in the business. A bonus is to be recorded for the original partners on the basis of their capital balances. (d) Felicia invests $30,000 cash in the partnership for a 40 percent interest in the business. The original partners give Felicia a bonus according to the ratio of their capital balances on July 31, 19x4. (e) Pat withdraws from the partnership, taking $52,500. The excess of assets over the partnership interest is distributed according to the balances of the Capital accounts. (f) Pat withdraws by selling her interest directly to Felicia for $60,000.

Problem D-4.
Distribution of Income: Salary and Interest
(L.O. 3)

Norman, Philip, and Daniel are partners in the South Central Company. The partnership agreement states that Norman is to receive 8 percent interest on his capital balance at the beginning of the year, Philip is to receive a salary of $100,000 a year, and Daniel will be paid interest of 6 percent on his average capital balance during the year. Norman, Philip, and Daniel will share any income or loss after salary and interest in a 5:3:2 ratio. Norman's capital balance at the beginning of the year was $600,000, and Daniel's average capital balance for the year was $720,000.

Required

Determine each partner's share of income and losses under each of the following conditions. In each case, the income or loss is stated before the distribution of salary and interest.

1. Income was $545,200.
2. Income was $155,600.
3. The loss was $56,800.

Problem D-5.
Admission and Withdrawal of a Partner
(L.O. 4, 5)

Alicia, Roberta, and Joanne are partners in the Image Gallery. The balances in the Capital accounts of Alicia, Roberta, and Joanne as of November 30, 19xx are $50,000, $60,000, and $90,000, respectively. The partners share income and losses in a ratio of 2:3:5.

Required

Prepare journal entries for each of the following independent conditions: (a) Luke pays Joanne $100,000 for four-fifths of Joanne's interest. (b) Luke is to be admitted to the partnership with a one-third interest for a $100,000 cash investment. (c) Luke is to be admitted to the partnership with a one-third interest for a $160,000 cash investment. A bonus, based on the partners' ratio for income and losses, is to be distributed to the original partners when Luke is admitted. (d) Luke is to be admitted to the partnership with a one-third interest for an $82,000 cash investment. A bonus is to be given to Luke on admission. (e) Alicia withdraws from the partnership, taking $66,000 in cash. (f) Alicia withdraws from the partnership by selling her interest directly to Luke for $70,000.

LEARNING OBJECTIVES

1. *Define* exchange rate *and record transactions that are affected by changes in foreign exchange rates.*
2. *Describe the restatement of a foreign subsidiary's financial statements in U.S. dollars.*
3. *Describe progress toward international accounting standards.*

APPENDIX E

International Accounting

Perhaps nowhere is the complexity and power of the modern corporation better demonstrated than in the expansion of its activities through international trade and through investment in the securities of other corporations. By expanding beyond national boundaries, corporations have been able to grow to sizes never thought possible. This appendix explores the fundamental accounting impact of this area of expansion. After studying this appendix, you should be able to meet the learning objectives on the left.

International Accounting[1]

OBJECTIVE 1
Define exchange rate *and record transactions that are affected by changes in foreign exchange rates*

As businesses grow, they naturally look for new sources of supply and for new markets in other countries. Today, it is common for businesses, called **multinational** or **transnational corporations**, to operate in more than one country, and many of them operate throughout the world. Table 1 shows the extent of foreign business in a few multinational corporations. IBM, for example, has operations in eighty countries and receives almost two-thirds of its sales and income from outside the United States. Unilever, the giant British/Dutch company, operates around the world and receives 75 percent of its revenues from outside its home countries. Together, the economies of such industrial countries as the United States, Japan, Great Britain, Germany, and France have given rise to numerous worldwide corporations. More than five hundred companies are listed on at least one stock exchange outside their home country.

In addition, sophisticated investors no longer restrict their investment activities to domestic securities markets. Many Americans invest in foreign securities markets, and non-Americans invest heavily in the stock market in the United States. Figure 1 shows that from 1980 to 1989, the total value of securities traded on the world's stock markets increased almost tenfold, while the U.S. share of the pie declined from 58 to 29 percent.

Foreign business transactions have two major effects on accounting. First, most sales or purchases of goods and services in other countries involve different currencies. Thus, one currency needs to be translated into another, using exchange rates. An **exchange rate** is the value of one currency in terms of another. For example, an English person purchasing goods from a U.S. company and paying in U.S. dollars must exchange British pounds for U.S. dollars before making payment. In effect, currencies are goods that can be bought and sold. Table 2 lists the exchange rates of several currencies in terms of dollars. It

1. At the time this appendix was written, exchange rates were fluctuating rapidly. Thus, the examples, exercises, and problems in this book use exchange rates in the general range for the countries involved.

Table 1. Extent of Foreign Business for Selected Companies

Company	Home Country	1989 Total Sales (Billions)	Sales Outside Home Country	Assets Outside Home Country	Shares Held Outside Home Country
Michelin	France	$ 9.4	78.0%	NA	0.0
Hoechst	Germany	27.3	77.0	NA	42.0%
Unilever	Britain/Neth.	35.3	75.0*	70.0%*	27.0
Air Liquide	France	5.0	70.0	66.0	6.0
Canon	Japan	9.4	69.0	32.0	14.0
Northern Telecom	Canada	6.1	67.1	70.5	16.0
Sony	Japan	16.3	66.0	NA	13.6
Bayer	Germany	25.8	65.4	NA	48.0
BASF	Germany	13.3	65.0	NA	NA
Gillette	U.S.	3.8	65.0	63.0	10.0*
Colgate	U.S.	5.0	64.0	47.0	10.0*
Honda	Japan	26.4	63.0	35.7	6.9
Daimler Benz	Germany	45.5	61.0	NA	25.0*
IBM	U.S.	62.7	59.0	NA	NA

**Business Week* estimates.
Source: "The Stateless Corporation: Forget Multinationals—Today's Giants Are Really Leaping Boundaries." May 14, 1990 by permission of *Business Week.* © 1990 by McGraw-Hill, Inc.

shows the exchange rate for the British pound as $1.53 per pound on a particular date. Like the price of any good or service, these prices change daily according to supply and demand for the currencies. Accounting for these price changes in recording foreign transactions and preparing financial statements for foreign subsidiaries is the subject of the next two sections.

Figure 1. Value of Securities Traded on the World's Stock Markets

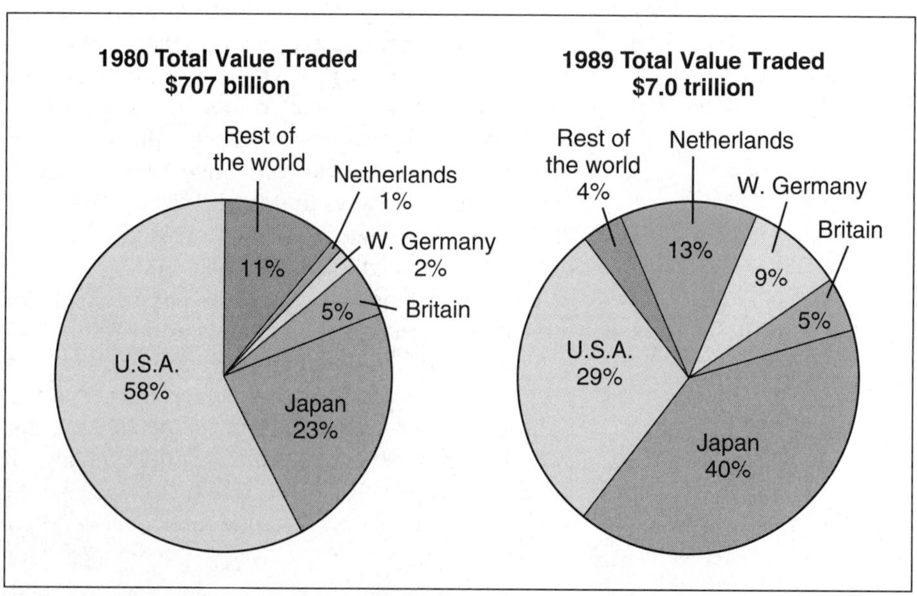

Source: From *Emerging Stock Markets Factbook* (Washington, D.C.: International Finance Corporation, 1990). Reprinted by permission.

Table 2. Partial Listing of Foreign Exchange Rates

Country	Prices in $ U.S.	Country	Prices in $ U.S.
Britain (pound)	1.53	Italy (lira)	.0007
Canada (dollar)	.78	Japan (yen)	.0094
France (franc)	.18	Mexico (peso)	.32
Germany (mark)	.61	Philippines (peso)	.037
Hong Kong (dollar)	.13	Taiwan (dollar)	.037

Source: From "World Markets/Foreign Exchange," *The Wall Street Journal,* June 11, 1993. Reprinted by permission of *Wall Street Journal,* © 1993 Dow Jones & Company, Inc. All Rights Reserved Worldwide.

The second major effect of international business on accounting is that financial standards differ from country to country, which hampers comparisons among companies from different countries. Some of the obstacles to achieving comparability and some of the progress in solving the problem are discussed later in this appendix.

Accounting for Transactions in Foreign Currencies

Among the first activities of an expanding company in the international market are the buying and selling of goods and services. For example, a U.S. maker of precision tools may expand by selling its product to foreign customers. Or it might lower its product cost by buying a less expensive part from a source in another country. Previously in this book, all transactions were recorded in dollars, and it was assumed that the dollar is a uniform measure in the same way that inches and centimeters are. But in the international marketplace, a transaction may take place in Japanese yen, British pounds, or some other currency. The values of these currencies rise and fall daily in relation to the dollar.

Foreign Sales. When a domestic company sells merchandise abroad, it may bill either in its own country's currency or in the foreign currency. If the billing and the subsequent payment are both in the domestic currency, no accounting problem arises. For example, assume that the precision toolmaker sells $170,000 worth of tools to a British company and bills the British company in dollars. The entry to record the sale and payment is familiar:

Date of sale		
Accounts Receivable, British company	170,000	
Sales		170,000
Date of payment		
Cash	170,000	
Accounts Receivable, British company		170,000

However, if the U.S. company bills the British company in British pounds and accepts payment in pounds, the U.S. company may incur an **exchange gain or loss**. A gain or loss will occur if the exchange rate of dollars to pounds changes between the date of sale and the date of payment. Since gains and losses tend to offset one another, a single account is used during the year to accumulate the activity. The net exchange gain or loss is reported on the income statement. For example, assume that the sale of $170,000 above was billed as £100,000, reflecting an exchange rate of 1.70 (that is, $1.70 per pound) on the sale date. Now assume that by the date of payment, the exchange rate has fallen to 1.65. The entries to record the transactions follow:

Date of sale		
Accounts Receivable, British company	170,000	
Sales		170,000
£100,000 × $1.70 = $170,000		
Date of payment		
Cash	165,000	
Exchange Gain or Loss	5,000	
Accounts Receivable, British company		170,000
£100,000 × $1.65 = $165,000		

The U.S. company has incurred an exchange loss of $5,000 because it agreed to accept a fixed number of British pounds in payment, and before the payment was made, the value of each pound dropped. Had the value of the pound in relation to the dollar increased, the U.S. company would have made an exchange gain.

Foreign Purchases. Purchases are the opposite of sales. So the same logic applies to them, except that the relationship of exchange gains and losses to changes in exchange rates is reversed. For example, assume that the maker of precision tools purchases $15,000 of a certain part from a Japanese supplier. If the purchase and subsequent payment are made in U.S. dollars, no accounting problem arises.

Date of purchase		
Purchases	15,000	
Accounts Payable, Japanese company		15,000
Date of payment		
Accounts Payable, Japanese company	15,000	
Cash		15,000

However, the Japanese company may bill the U.S. company in yen and be paid in yen. If so, the U.S. company will incur an exchange gain or loss if the exchange rate changes between the dates of purchase and payment. For example, assume that the transaction is for 2,500,000 yen and the exchange rates on the dates of purchase and payment are $0.0060 and $0.0055 per yen, respectively. The entries follow.

Date of purchase		
Purchases	15,000	
Accounts Payable, Japanese company		15,000
¥2,500,000 × $0.0060 = $15,000		
Date of payment		
Accounts Payable, Japanese company	15,000	
Exchange Gain or Loss		1,250
Cash		13,750
¥2,500,000 × $0.0055 = $13,750		

In this case the U.S. company received an exchange gain of $1,250 because it agreed to pay a fixed ¥2,500,000, and between the dates of purchase and payment the exchange value of the yen decreased in relation to the dollar.

Realized Versus Unrealized Exchange Gain or Loss. The preceding illustration dealt with completed transactions (in the sense that payment was completed). In each case the exchange gain or loss was recognized on the date of payment. If financial statements are prepared between the sale or purchase and the subsequent receipt or payment, and exchange rates have changed, there will be unrealized gains or losses. The Financial Accounting Standards Board, in its *Statement No. 52,* requires that exchange gains and losses "shall be included in determining net income for the period in which the exchange rate changes."[2] The requirement includes interim (quarterly) statements and applies whether or not a transaction is complete.

This ruling has caused much debate. Critics charge that it gives too much weight to fleeting changes in exchange rates, causing random changes in earnings that hide long-run trends. Others believe that the use of current exchange rates to value receivables and payables as of the balance sheet date is a major step toward economic reality (current values).

To illustrate, we will use the preceding case, in which a U.S. company buys parts from a Japanese supplier. We will assume that the transaction has not been completed by the balance sheet date, when the exchange rate is $.0051 per yen:

	Date	Exchange Rate ($ per Yen)
Date of purchase	Dec. 1	.0060
Balance sheet date	Dec. 31	.0051
Date of payment	Feb. 1	.0055

The accounting effects of the unrealized gain are as follows:

	Dec. 1	Dec. 31	Feb. 1
Purchase recorded in U.S. dollars (billed as ¥2,500,000)	$15,000	$15,000	$15,000
Dollars to be paid to equal ¥2,500,000 (¥2,500,000 × exchange rate)	15,000	12,750	13,750
Unrealized gain (or loss)	—	$ 2,250	
Realized gain (or loss)			$ 1,250

Date	Account	Debit	Credit
Dec. 1	Purchases	15,000	
	Accounts Payable, Japanese company		15,000
Dec. 31	Accounts Payable, Japanese company	2,250	
	Exchange Gain or Loss		2,250
Feb. 1	Accounts Payable, Japanese company	12,750	
	Exchange Gain or Loss	1,000	
	Cash		13,750

In this case, the original sale was billed in yen by the Japanese company. Following the rules of *Statement No. 52,* an exchange gain of $2,250 is recorded on December 31, and an exchange loss of $1,000 is recorded on February 1. Even though these large fluctuations do not affect the net exchange gain of $1,250 over the whole transaction, the effect on each year's income statements may be important.

2. *Statement of Financial Accounting Standards No. 52,* "Foreign Currency Translation" (Stamford, Conn.: Financial Accounting Standards Board, 1981), par. 15.

Restatement of Foreign Subsidiary Financial Statements[3]

OBJECTIVE 2
Describe the restatement of a foreign subsidiary's financial statements in U.S. dollars

Growing companies often expand by setting up or buying foreign subsidiaries. If a foreign subsidiary is more than 50 percent owned and if the parent company exercises control, then the foreign subsidiary should be included in the consolidated financial statements. (See discussion of parent and subsidiary companies in the appendix on intercompany investments). The consolidation procedure is the same as that for domestic subsidiaries, except that the statements of the foreign subsidiary must be restated in the reporting currency before consolidation takes place. The **reporting currency** is the currency in which the consolidated financial statements are presented. Clearly, it makes no sense to combine the assets of a Mexican subsidiary stated in pesos with the assets of the U.S. parent company stated in dollars. Most U.S. companies present their financial statements in U.S. dollars, so the following discussion assumes that the U.S. dollar is the reporting currency used.

Restatement is the stating of one currency in terms of another. The method of restatement depends on the foreign subsidiary's functional currency. The **functional currency** is the currency of the place where the subsidiary carries on most of its business. Generally, it is the currency in which a company earns and spends its cash. The functional currency to be used depends on the kind of foreign operation in which the subsidiary takes part. There are two broad types of foreign operation. Type I includes those that are fairly self-contained and integrated within a certain country or economy. Type II includes those that are mainly a direct and integral part or extension of the parent company's operations. As a general rule, Type I subsidiaries use the currency of the country in which they are located, and Type II subsidiaries use the currency of the parent company. If the parent company is a U.S. company, the functional currency of a Type I subsidiary will be the currency of the country where the subsidiary carries on its business, and the functional currency of a Type II subsidiary will be the U.S. dollar. *Statement No. 52* makes an exception when a Type I subsidiary operates in a country such as Brazil or Argentina, where there is hyperinflation (as a rule of thumb, more than 100 percent cumulative inflation over three years). In such a case, the subsidiary is treated as a Type II subsidiary, with the functional currency being the U.S. dollar.

The Search for Comparability of International Accounting Standards

OBJECTIVE 3
Describe progress toward international accounting standards

International investors need to compare the financial position and results of operations of companies from different countries. At present, however, few standards of accounting are recognized worldwide. For example, the LIFO method of valuing inventory is the most popular in the United States, but it is not acceptable in most European countries. In another example, historical cost is strictly followed in Germany, replacement cost is used by some companies in the Netherlands, and a mixed system, allowing lower of cost or market in some cases, is used in the United States and England. Even the formats of financial statements differ from country to country. In England and France, for example, the balance sheets are presented in almost reverse order to those in the United

3. This section is based on the requirements of *Statement of Financial Accounting Standards No. 52,* "Foreign Currency Translation" (Stamford, Conn.: Financial Accounting Standards Board, 1981).

States. In those countries, property, plant, and equipment is the first listing in the assets section.

A number of major problems stand in the way of setting international standards. One is that accountants and users of accounting information have not been able to agree on the goals of financial statements. Some other problems are differences in the way the accounting profession has developed in various countries, differences in the laws regulating companies, and differences in government and other requirements. Further difficulties are the failure to deal with differences among countries in the basic economic factors affecting financial reporting, inconsistencies in practices recommended by the accounting profession in different countries, and the influence of tax laws on financial reporting.[4] In the last area, for example, a survey for a major accounting firm found widely differing requirements. In nine countries, strict adherence to tax accounting was required. In eleven countries, adherence to tax accounting was required in some areas. In four countries (including the United States), adherence to tax practice was mostly forbidden.[5]

Some efforts have been made to achieve greater international understanding and uniformity of accounting practice. The Accountants International Study Group, formed in 1966 and consisting of the AICPA and similar bodies in Canada, England and Wales, Ireland, and Scotland, has issued reports that survey and compare accounting practices in the member countries. Probably the best hopes for finding areas of agreement among all the different countries are the International Accounting Standards Committee (IASC) and the International Federation of Accountants (IFAC). The IASC was formed in 1973 as a result of an agreement by accountancy bodies in Australia, Canada, France, Germany, Japan, Mexico, the Netherlands, the United Kingdom and Ireland, and the United States. More than one hundred professional accountancy bodies from over seventy countries now support the IASC.

The role of the IASC is to contribute to the development and adoption of accounting principles that are relevant, balanced, and comparable throughout the world by formulating and publicizing accounting standards and encouraging their observance in the presentation of financial statements.[6] The standards issued by the IASC are generally followed by large multinational companies that are clients of international accounting firms. The IASC has been especially helpful to companies in developing economies that do not have the financial history or resources to develop accounting standards. The IASC is currently engaged in a major project to enhance the comparability of financial statements worldwide by reducing the number of acceptable accounting methods in twelve areas, including inventory and depreciation accounting and accounting for investments and business combinations.

The IFAC, which was formed in 1977 and also consists of most of the world's accountancy organizations, fully supports the work of the IASC and recognizes the IASC as the sole body having responsibility and authority to issue pronouncements on international accounting standards. The IFAC's objective is to develop international guidelines for management accounting, auditing, ethics,

4. *Accounting Standards for Business Enterprises Throughout the World* (Chicago: Arthur Andersen, 1974), pp. 2–3.
5. *Accounting Principles and Reporting Practices: A Survey in 38 Countries* (New York: Price Waterhouse International, 1973), sec. 233.
6. "International Accounting Standards Committee Objectives and Procedures," *Professional Standards* (New York: American Institute of Certified Public Accountants, 1988), Volume B, Section 9000, par. 24–27.

and education. Every five years an International Congress is held to judge the progress toward achieving these objectives. In Europe, attempts are also being made to harmonize accounting standards. The European Community has issued a directive (4th) requiring certain minimum and uniform reporting and disclosure standards for financial statements. Other directives deal with uniform rules for preparing consolidated financial statements (7th) and qualifications of auditors (8th). At present, the European Community is paying considerable attention to the comparability of financial reporting as the organization moves toward the goal of a single European market.[7]

The road to international harmony is a difficult one. However, there is reason for optimism because an increasing number of countries are recognizing the appropriateness of international accounting standards in international trade and commerce.

Questions

1. What does it mean to say that the exchange rate for a French franc in terms of the U.S. dollar is .15? If a bottle of French perfume costs 200 francs, how much will it cost in dollars?
2. If an American firm does business with a German firm and all their transactions take place in German marks, which firm may incur an exchange gain or loss, and why?
3. What is the difference between a reporting currency and a functional currency?
4. If you as an investor were trying to evaluate the relative performance of General Motors, Volkswagen, and Toyota Motors from their published financial statements, what problems might you encounter (other than a language problem)?
5. What are some of the obstacles to uniform international accounting standards, and what efforts are being made to overcome them?

Classroom Exercises

Exercise E-1. Recording International Transactions: Fluctuating Exchange Rate *(L.O. 1)*

States Corporation purchased a special-purpose machine from Hamburg Corporation on credit for 50,000 DM (marks). At the date of purchase, the exchange rate was $0.55 per mark. On the date of the payment, which was made in marks, the value of the mark had increased to $0.60.

Prepare journal entries to record the purchase and payment in States Corporation's accounting records.

Exercise E-2. Recording International Transactions *(L.O. 1)*

U.S. Corporation made a sale on account to U.K. Company on November 15 in the amount of £300,000. Payment was to be made in British pounds on February 15. U.S. Corporation's fiscal year is the same as the calendar year. The British pound was worth $1.70 on November 15, $1.58 on December 31, and $1.78 on February 15.

Prepare journal entries to record the sale, year-end adjustment, and collection on U.S. Corporation's books.

Problems

Since foreign exchange rates can fluctuate widely, a variety of rates have been used in the following problems.

Problem E-1. Recording International Transactions *(L.O. 1)*

Mountain States Company, whose year end is June 30, engaged in the following international transactions (exchange rates in parentheses):

May 15 Purchased goods from a Japanese firm for $110,000; terms n/10 in U.S. dollars (yen = $0.0080).

7. "Comparability of Financial Statements," *Exposure Draft No. 32* (New York: International Federation of Accountants, 1989).

May 17 Sold goods to a German company for $165,000; terms n/30 in marks (mark = $0.55).
21 Purchased goods from a Mexican company for $120,000; terms n/30 in pesos (peso = $0.0004).
25 Paid for the goods purchased on May 15 (yen = $0.0085).
31 Sold goods to an Italian firm for $200,000; terms n/60 in lire (lira = $0.0005).
June 5 Sold goods to a British firm for $56,000; terms n/10 in U.S. dollars (pound = $1.30).
7 Purchased goods from a Japanese firm for $221,000; terms n/30 in yen (yen = $0.0085).
15 Received payment for the sale made on June 5 (pound = $1.80).
16 Received payment for the sale made on May 17 (mark = $0.60).
17 Purchased goods from a French firm for $66,000; terms n/30 in U.S. dollars (franc = $0.16).
20 Paid for the goods purchased on May 21 (peso = $0.0003).
22 Sold goods to a British firm for $108,000; terms n/30 in pounds (pound = $1.80).
30 Made year-end adjusting entries for incomplete foreign exchange transactions (franc = $0.17; peso = $0.0003; mark = $0.60; lira = $0.0003; pound = $1.70; yen = $0.0090).
July 7 Paid for the goods purchased on June 7 (yen = $0.0085).
19 Paid for the goods purchased on June 17 (franc = $0.15).
22 Received payment for the goods sold on June 22 (pound = $1.60).
30 Received payment for the goods sold on May 31 (lira = $0.0004).

Required

Prepare general journal entries for these transactions.

Problem E-2. Recording International Transactions *(L.O. 1)*

Tsin Import/Export Company, whose year end is December 31, engaged in the following transactions (exchange rates in parentheses):

Oct. 14 Sold goods to a Mexican firm for $20,000; terms n/30 in U.S. dollars (peso = $0.0004).
26 Purchased goods from a Japanese firm for $40,000; terms n/20 in yen (yen = $0.0040).
Nov. 4 Sold goods to a British firm for $39,000; terms n/30 in pounds (pound = $1.30).
14 Received payment in full for October 14 sale (peso = $0.0003).
15 Paid for the goods purchased on October 26 (yen = $0.0044).
23 Purchased goods from an Italian firm for $28,000; terms n/10 in U.S. dollars (lira = $0.0008).
30 Purchased goods from a Japanese firm for $35,200; terms n/60 in yen (yen = $0.0044).
Dec. 2 Paid for the goods purchased on November 23 (lira = $0.0007).
3 Received payment in full for the goods sold on November 4 (pound = $1.20).
8 Sold goods to a French firm for $66,000; terms n/30 in francs (franc = $0.11).
17 Purchased goods from a Mexican firm for $37,000; terms n/30 in U.S. dollars (peso = $0.0004).
18 Sold goods to a German firm for $90,000; terms n/30 in marks (mark = $0.30).
31 Made year-end adjusting entries for incomplete foreign exchange transactions (franc = $0.09; peso = $0.0003; pound = $1.10; mark = $0.35; lira = $0.0008; yen = $0.0050).
Jan. 7 Received payment for the goods sold on December 8 (franc = $0.10).
16 Paid for the goods purchased on December 17 (peso = $0.0002).
17 Received payment for the goods sold on December 18 (mark = $0.40).
28 Paid for the goods purchased on November 30 (yen = $0.0045).

Required

Prepare general journal entries for these transactions.

LEARNING OBJECTIVES

1. Apply the cost method and the equity method to the appropriate situations in accounting for long-term investments.
2. Explain when to prepare consolidated financial statements, and describe their uses.
3. Prepare consolidated balance sheets at acquisition date for purchase at (a) book value and (b) other than book value.
4. Prepare consolidated income statements for intercompany transactions.

APPENDIX F

Intercompany Investments

One corporation may invest in another corporation by purchasing bonds or stocks. These investments may be either short term or long term. In this section, we are concerned with long-term investments in stocks. After studying this appendix, you should be able to meet the learning objectives listed on the left.

Intercompany Investments

All long-term investments in stocks are recorded at cost, in accordance with generally accepted accounting principles. The treatment of the investment in the accounting records after the initial purchase depends on the extent to which the investing company can exercise significant influence or control over the operating and financial policies of the other company.

The Accounting Principles Board defined the important terms *significant influence* and *control* in its *Opinion No. 18*. **Significant influence** is the ability to affect the operating and financial policies of the company whose shares are owned, even though the investor holds less than 50 percent of the voting stock. Ability to influence a company may be shown by representation on the board of directors, participation in policy making, material transactions between the companies, exchange of managerial personnel, and technological dependency. For the sake of uniformity, the APB decided that unless there is proof to the contrary, an investment in 20 percent or more of the voting stock should be presumed to confer significant influence. An investment of less than 20 percent of the voting stock would not confer significant influence.[1]

Control is defined as the ability of the investing company to decide the operating and financial policies of the other company. Control is said to exist when the investing company owns more than 50 percent of the voting stock of the company in which it has invested.

Thus, in the absence of information to the contrary, a noninfluential and noncontrolling investment would be less than 20 percent ownership. An influential but noncontrolling investment would be 20 to 50 percent ownership. And a con-

1. The Financial Accounting Standards Board points out in its *Interpretation No. 35* (May 1981) that though the presumption of significant influence applies when 20 percent or more of the voting stock is held, the rule is not a rigid one. All relevant facts and circumstances should be examined in each case to find out whether or not significant influence exists. For example, the FASB notes five circumstances that may remove the element of significant influence: (1) The company files a lawsuit against the investor or complains to a government agency; (2) The investor tries and fails to become a director; (3) The investor agrees not to increase its holdings; (4) The company is operated by a small group that ignores the investor's wishes; (5) The investor tries and fails to obtain additional information from the company that is not available to other stockholders.

trolling investment would be more than 50 percent ownership. The accounting treatment differs for each kind of investment.

Noninfluential and Noncontrolling Investment

OBJECTIVE 1
Apply the cost method and the equity method to the appropriate situations in accounting for long-term investments

The **cost method** of accounting for long-term investments applies when the investor owns less than 20 percent of the voting stock. Under the cost method, the investor records the investment at cost and recognizes income as dividends are received. The Financial Accounting Standards Board states that long-term investments in marketable equity securities accounted for under the cost method should be valued at the lower of cost or market after acquisition.[2] The lower-of-cost-or-market rule is used here for the same reason it was used in the valuation of inventories. It is a conservative approach that recognizes the impairment in the value of the asset when its market value is less than cost. Conversely, a rise in the market above cost is not recognized until the investment is sold.

At the end of each accounting period, the total cost and the total market value of these long-term stock investments must be determined. If the total market value is less than the total cost, the difference must be credited to a contra-asset account called Allowance to Reduce Long-Term Investments to Market. Because of the long-term nature of the investment, the debit part of the entry, which represents a decrease in value below cost, is treated as a temporary decrease and does not appear as a loss on the income statement. It is shown in a contra-owners' equity account called Unrealized Loss on Long-Term Investments. Thus, both of these accounts are balance sheet accounts. If at some later date the market value exceeds the valuation reported in the earlier period, the Long-Term Investment account is written up to the new market value, but not to more than the acquisition cost of the investments.[3]

When long-term investments in stock are sold, the difference between the sale price and what the stock cost is recorded and reported as a realized gain or loss on the income statement. Dividend income from such investments is recorded by a debit to Cash and a credit to Dividend Income.

For example, assume the following facts about the long-term stock investments of Coleman Corporation:

June 1, 19x0	Paid cash for the following long-term investments: 10,000 shares Durbin Corporation common stock (representing 2 percent of outstanding stock) at $25 per share; 5,000 shares Kotes Corporation common stock (representing 3 percent of outstanding stock) at $15 per share.
Dec. 31, 19x0	Quoted market prices at year end: Durbin common stock, $21; Kotes common stock, $17.
Apr. 1, 19x1	Change in policy required sale of 2,000 shares of Durbin Corporation common stock at $23.
July 1, 19x1	Received cash dividend from Kotes Corporation equal to $.20 per share.
Dec. 31, 19x1	Quoted market prices at year end: Durbin common stock, $24; Kotes common stock, $13.

2. *Statement of Financial Accounting Standards No. 12,* "Accounting for Certain Marketable Securities" (Stamford, Conn.: Financial Accounting Standards Board, 1975).
3. If the decrease in value is deemed permanent, a different procedure is followed to record the decline in market value of the long-term investment. A loss account that appears on the income statement is debited instead of the Unrealized Loss account.

Entries to record these transactions follow:

Investment

		Dr.	Cr.
19x0			
June 1	Long-Term Investments	325,000	
	Cash		325,000
	Investments in Durbin common stock (10,000 shares × $25 = $250,000) and Kotes common stock (5,000 shares × $15 = $75,000)		

Year-End Adjustment

		Dr.	Cr.
19x0			
Dec. 31	Unrealized Loss on Long-Term Investments	30,000	
	Allowance to Reduce Long-Term Investments to Market		30,000
	To record reduction of long-term investment portfolio to market		

Company	Shares	Market Price	Total Market	Total Cost
Durbin	10,000	$21	$210,000	$250,000
Kotes	5,000	17	85,000	75,000
			$295,000	$325,000

Cost – market value = $325,000 – $295,000 = $30,000.

Sale

		Dr.	Cr.
19x1			
Apr. 1	Cash	46,000	
	Loss on Sale of Investment	4,000	
	Long-Term Investments		50,000
	Sale of 2,000 shares of Durbin 2,000 × $23 = $ 46,000 2,000 × $25 = (50,000) Loss $ (4,000)		

Dividend Received

		Dr.	Cr.
July 1	Cash	1,000	
	Dividend Income		1,000
	Receipt of cash dividends from Kotes stock 5,000 × $0.20 = $1,000		

Year-End Adjustment

		Dr.	Cr.
Dec. 31	Allowance to Reduce Long-Term Investments to Market	12,000	
	Unrealized Loss on Long-Term Investments		12,000
	To record the adjustment in long-term investment so it is reported at lower of cost or market		

The adjustment equals the previous balance ($30,000 from the December 31, 19x0 entry) minus the new balance ($18,000), or $12,000. The new balance of $18,000 is the difference at the present time between the total market value and the total cost of all investments. It is figured as follows:

Company	Shares	Market Price	Total Market	Total Cost
Durbin	8,000	$24	$192,000	$200,000
Kotes	5,000	13	65,000	75,000
			$257,000	$275,000

Cost − market value = $275,000 − $257,000 = $18,000.

The Allowance to Reduce Long-Term Investments to Market and the Unrealized Loss on Long-Term Investments are reciprocal contra accounts, each with the same dollar balance, as can be shown by the effects of these transactions on the T accounts:

Contra-Asset Account

Allowance to Reduce Long-Term Investments to Market

19x1	12,000	19x0	30,000
		Bal. 19x1	18,000

Contra-Owners' Equity Account

Unrealized Loss on Long-Term Investments

19x0	30,000	19x1	12,000
Bal. 19x1	18,000		

The Allowance account reduces long-term investments by the amount by which cost exceeds market of the investments; the Unrealized Loss account reduces owners' equity by a similar amount.

Influential but Noncontrolling Investment

As we have seen, ownership of 20 percent or more of a company's voting stock is considered sufficient to influence the operations of another corporation. When this is the case, the investment in the stock of the influenced company should be accounted for using the **equity method**. The equity method presumes that an investment of 20 percent or more is more than a passive investment, and that therefore the investing company should share proportionately in the success or failure of the investee company. The three main features of this method are as follows:

1. The investor records the original purchase of the stock at cost.
2. The investor records its share of the investee's periodic net income as an increase in the Investment account, with a corresponding credit to an income account. In like manner, the investor records its share of the investee's periodic loss as a decrease in the Investment account, with a corresponding debit to a loss account.
3. When the investor receives a cash dividend, the asset account Cash is increased and the Investment account decreased.

To illustrate the equity method of accounting, we will assume the following facts about an investment by the Vassor Corporation. Vassor Corporation, on January 1 of the current year, acquired 40 percent of the voting common stock of the Block Corporation for $180,000. With this share of ownership, the Vassor Corporation can exert significant influence over the operations of the Block Corporation. During the year, the Block Corporation reported net income of $80,000 and paid cash dividends of $20,000. The entries to record these transactions by the Vassor Corporation are:

Investment

Investment in Block Corporation	180,000	
Cash		180,000
Investment in Block Corporation common stock		

Recognition of Income

Investment in Block Corporation	32,000	
Income, Block Corporation Investment		32,000
Recognition of 40% of income reported by Block Corporation 40% × $80,000 = $32,000		

Receipt of Cash Dividend

Cash	8,000	
Investment in Block Corporation		8,000
Cash dividend from Block Corporation 40% × $20,000 = $8,000		

The balance of the investment in the Block Corporation account after these transactions is $204,000, as shown here:

Investment in Block Corporation

Investment	180,000	Dividends received	8,000
Share of income	32,000		
Balance	204,000		

Controlling Investment

In some cases, an investor who owns less than 50 percent of the voting stock of a company may exercise such powerful influence that for all practical purposes the investor controls the policies of the other company. Nevertheless, ownership of more than 50 percent of the voting stock is required for accounting recognition of control. When a controlling interest is owned, a parent-subsidiary relationship is said to exist. The investing company is known as the **parent company**, the other company as the **subsidiary**. Because both corporations are separate legal entities, each prepares separate financial statements. However, owing to their special relationship, they are viewed for public financial reporting purposes as a single economic entity. For this reason, they must combine their financial statements into a single set of statements called **consolidated financial statements.**

Accounting for consolidated financial statements is very complex. It is usually the subject of an advanced accounting course. However, most large public corporations have subsidiaries and must prepare consolidated financial statements. It is therefore important to have some understanding of accounting for consolidations.

The proper accounting treatments for long-term investments in stock are summarized in Table 1.

Table 1. Accounting Treatments of Long-Term Investments in Stock

Level of Ownership	Percentage of Ownership	Accounting Treatment
Noninfluential and noncontrolling	Less than 20%	Cost method; investment valued subsequent to purchase at lower of cost or market.
Influential but noncontrolling	Between 20% and 50%	Equity method; investment valued subsequently at cost plus investor's share of income (or minus investor's loss) minus dividends received.
Controlling	More than 50%	Financial statements consolidated.

Consolidated Financial Statements

OBJECTIVE 2
Explain when to prepare consolidated financial statements, and describe their uses

Most major corporations find it convenient for economic, legal, tax, or other reasons to operate in parent-subsidiary relationships. When we speak of a large company such as Ford, IBM, or Texas Instruments, we generally think of the parent company, not of its many subsidiaries. When considering investment in one of these firms, however, the investor wants a clear financial picture of the total economic entity. The main purpose of consolidated financial statements is to give such a view of the parent and subsidiary firms by treating them as if they were one company. On a consolidated balance sheet, the Inventory account includes the inventory held by the parent and all its subsidiaries. Similarly, on the consolidated income statement, the Sales account is the total revenue from sales by the parent and all its subsidiaries. This overview helps management and stockholders of the parent company judge the company's progress in meeting its goals. Long-term creditors of the parent also find consolidated statements useful because of their interest in the long-range financial health of the company.

It has been acceptable in the past not to consolidate the statements of certain subsidiaries, even though the parent owned a controlling interest, when the business of the subsidiary was not homogeneous with that of the parent. For instance, a retail company or an automobile manufacturer might have had a wholly-owned finance subsidiary that was not consolidated. However, such practices were criticized because they tended to remove certain assets (accounts and notes receivable) and certain liabilities (borrowing by the finance subsidiary) from the consolidated financial statements. For example, in 1986, General Motors's financing subsidiary, GMAC, with assets of $90 billion and liabilities of $84 billion, was carried as a long-term investment of $6 billion on GM's balance sheet. It has also been argued by those who favor consolidation that financing arrangements such as these are an integral part of the overall business. The Financial Accounting Standards Board ruled, effective in 1988, that all subsidiaries in which the parent owns a controlling interest (more than 50 percent) must be consolidated with the parent for financial reporting purposes.[4] As a result, with few exceptions, the financial statements of all majority-

4. *Statement of Financial Accounting Standards No. 94*, "Consolidation of All Majority-Owned Subsidiaries" (Stamford, Conn.: Financial Accounting Standards Board, 1987).

owned subsidiaries must now be consolidated with the parent company's financial statements for external reporting purposes.

Methods of Accounting for Business Combinations

Interests in subsidiary companies may be acquired by paying cash; issuing long-term bonds, other debt, or common or preferred stock; or working out some combination of these forms of payment, such as exchanging shares of the parent's own unissued capital stock for the outstanding shares of the subsidiary's capital stock. For parent-subsidiary relationships that arise when cash is paid or debt or preferred stock issued, it is mandatory to use the purchase method, which is explained below. For simplicity, our illustrations assume payment in cash. In the special case of establishing a parent-subsidiary relationship through an exchange of common stock, the pooling of interests method may be appropriate. This latter method is the subject of more advanced courses.

Consolidated Balance Sheet

In preparing consolidated financial statements under the **purchase method**, similar accounts from the separate statements of the parent and the subsidiaries are combined. Some accounts result from transactions between the parent and subsidiary. Examples are debt owned by one of the entities to the other and sales and purchases between the two entities. From the point of view of the consolidating group of companies as a single business, it is not appropriate to include these accounts in the group financial statements; the purchases and sales are only transfers between different parts of the business, and the payables and receivables do not represent amounts due to or receivable from outside parties. For this reason, it is important that certain **eliminations** be made. These eliminations avoid the duplication of accounts and reflect the financial position and operations from the standpoint of a single entity. Eliminations appear only on the work sheets used in preparing consolidated financial statements. They are never shown in the accounting records of either the parent or the subsidiary. There are no consolidated journals or ledgers.

Another good example of accounts that result from transactions between the two entities is the Investment in Subsidiary account in the parent's balance sheet and the stockholders' equity section of the subsidiary. When the balance sheets of the two companies are combined, these accounts must be eliminated to avoid duplicating these items in the consolidated financial statements.

To illustrate the preparation of a consolidated balance sheet under the purchase method, we will use the following balance sheets for Parent and Subsidiary companies:

Accounts	Parent Company	Subsidiary Company
Cash	$100,000	$25,000
Other Assets	760,000	60,000
Total Assets	$860,000	$85,000
Liabilities	$ 60,000	$10,000
Common Stock—$10 par value	600,000	55,000
Retained Earnings	200,000	20,000
Total Liabilities and Stockholders' Equity	$860,000	$85,000

OBJECTIVE 3a
Prepare consolidated balance sheets at acquisition date for purchase at book value

100 Percent Purchase at Book Value. Suppose that Parent Company purchases 100 percent of the stock of Subsidiary Company for an amount exactly equal to Subsidiary's book value. The book value of Subsidiary Company is $75,000 ($85,000 – $10,000). Parent Company would record the purchase as shown below:

Investment in Subsidiary Company	75,000	
Cash		75,000
Purchase of 100 percent of Subsidiary Company at book value		

It is helpful to use a work sheet like the one shown in Exhibit 1 in preparing consolidated financial statements. Note that the balance of Parent Company's Cash account is now $25,000 and that the Investment in Subsidiary Company is shown as an asset in Parent Company's balance sheet, reflecting the purchase of the subsidiary. To prepare a consolidated balance sheet, it is necessary to eliminate the investment in the subsidiary. This procedure is shown by elimination entry **1** in Exhibit 1. This elimination entry does two things. First, it eliminates the double counting that would take place when the net assets of the two companies are combined. Second, it eliminates the stockholders' equity section of Subsidiary Company.

The theory underlying consolidated financial statements is that parent and subsidiary are a single entity. The stockholders' equity section of the consolidated balance sheet is the same as that of Parent Company. So after eliminating the Investment in Subsidiary Company against the stockholders' equity of the subsidiary, we can take the information from the right-hand column in Exhibit 1 and present it in the form shown at the top of page Ap-72.

Exhibit 1. Work Sheet for Preparation of Consolidated Balance Sheet

Parent and Subsidiary Companies
Work Sheet for Consolidated Balance Sheet
As of Acquisition Date

Accounts	Balance Sheet Parent Company	Balance Sheet Subsidiary Company	Eliminations		Consolidated Balance Sheet
			Debit	Credit	
Cash	25,000	25,000			50,000
Investment in Subsidiary Company	75,000			(1) 75,000	
Other Assets	760,000	60,000			820,000
Total Assets	860,000	85,000			870,000
Liabilities	60,000	10,000			70,000
Common Stock—$10 par value	600,000	55,000	(1) 55,000		600,000
Retained Earnings	200,000	20,000	(1) 20,000		200,000
Total Liabilities and Stockholders' Equity	860,000	85,000	75,000	75,000	870,000

(1) Elimination of intercompany investment.

Parent and Subsidiary Companies
Consolidated Balance Sheet
As of Acquisition Date

Cash	$ 50,000	Liabilities	$ 70,000
Other Assets	820,000	Common Stock	600,000
		Retained Earnings	200,000
Total Assets	$870,000	Total Liabilities and Stockholders' Equity	$870,000

Less than 100 Percent Purchase at Book Value. A parent company does not have to purchase 100 percent of a subsidiary to control it. If it purchases more than 50 percent of the voting stock of the subsidiary company, it will have legal control. In the consolidated financial statements, therefore, the total assets and liabilities of the subsidiary are combined with the assets and liabilities of the parent. However, it is still necessary to account for the interests of those stockholders of the subsidiary company who own less than 50 percent of the voting stock. These are the minority stockholders, and their **minority interest** must appear on the consolidated balance sheet as an amount equal to their percentage of ownership times the net assets of the subsidiary.

Suppose that the same Parent Company buys, for $67,500, only 90 percent of Subsidiary Company's voting stock. In this case, the portion of the company purchased has a book value of $67,500 (90% × $75,000). The work sheet used for preparing the consolidated balance sheet appears in Exhibit 2. The elimination is made in the same way as in the case above, except that the minority interest must be accounted for. All of the Investment in Subsidiary Company ($67,500) is eliminated against all of Subsidiary Company's stockholders' equity ($75,000). The difference ($7,500, or 10% × $75,000) is set as minority interest.

There are two ways to classify minority interest on the consolidated balance sheet. One is to place it between long-term liabilities and stockholders' equity. The other is to consider the stockholders' equity section as consisting of (1) minority interest and (2) Parent Company's stockholders' equity, as shown here:

Minority Interest	$ 7,500
Common Stock	600,000
Retained Earnings	200,000
Total Stockholders' Equity	$807,500

OBJECTIVE 3b
Prepare consolidated balance sheets at acquisition date for purchase at other than book value

Purchase at More than or Less than Book Value. The purchase price of a business depends on many factors, such as the current market price, the relative strength of the buyer's and seller's bargaining positions, and the prospects for future earnings. Thus, it is only by chance that the purchase price of a subsidiary will equal the book value of the subsidiary's equity. Usually, it will not. For example, a parent company may pay more than the book value of a subsidiary to purchase a controlling interest if the assets of the subsidiary are understated. In that case, the recorded historical cost less depreciation of the subsidiary's assets may not reflect current market values. The parent may also pay more than book value if the subsidiary has something that the parent wants, such as an important technical process, a new and different product, or a new market. On the other hand, the parent may pay less than book value for its

Exhibit 2. Work Sheet Showing Elimination of Less than 100 Percent Ownership

Parent and Subsidiary Companies Work Sheet for Consolidated Balance Sheet As of Acquisition Date					
Accounts	Balance Sheet Parent Company	Balance Sheet Subsidiary Company	Eliminations		Consolidated Balance Sheet
			Debit	Credit	
Cash	32,500	25,000			57,500
Investment in Subsidiary Company	67,500			(1) 67,500	
Other Assets	760,000	60,000			820,000
Total Assets	860,000	85,000			877,500
Liabilities	60,000	10,000			70,000
Common Stock—$10 par value	600,000	55,000	(1) 55,000		600,000
Retained Earnings	200,000	20,000	(1) 20,000		200,000
Minority Interest				(1) 7,500	7,500
Total Liabilities and Stockholders' Equity	860,000	85,000	75,000	75,000	877,500

(1) Elimination of intercompany investment. Minority interest equals 10 percent of subsidiary's stockholders' equity.

share of the subsidiary's stock if the subsidiary's assets are not worth their depreciated cost. Or the subsidiary may have suffered heavy losses, causing its stock to sell at rather low prices.

The Accounting Principles Board has provided the following guidelines for consolidating a purchased subsidiary and its parent:

> First, all identifiable assets acquired . . . and liabilities assumed in a business combination . . . should be assigned a portion of the cost of the acquired company, normally equal to their fair values at date of acquisition.
>
> Second, the excess of the cost of the acquired company over the sum of the amounts assigned to identifiable assets acquired less liabilities assumed should be recorded as goodwill.[5]

To illustrate the application of these principles, we will assume that Parent Company purchases 100 percent of Subsidiary Company's voting stock for $92,500, or $17,500 more than book value. Parent Company considers $10,000 of the $17,500 to be due to the increased value of Subsidiary's other long-term assets and $7,500 of the $17,500 to be due to the overall strength that Subsidiary Company would add to Parent Company's organization. The work sheet used for preparing the consolidated balance sheet appears in Exhibit 3. All of the Investment in Subsidiary Company ($92,500) has been eliminated against all of the Subsidiary Company's stockholders' equity ($75,000). The excess of cost over book value ($17,500) has been debited in the amounts of $10,000 to Other

5. Accounting Principles Board, *Opinion No. 16,* "Business Combinations" (New York: Accounting Principles Board, 1970), par. 87.

Exhibit 3. Work Sheet Showing Elimination Where Purchase Cost Is Greater than Book Value

Parent and Subsidiary Companies
Work Sheet for Consolidated Balance Sheet
As of Acquisition Date

Accounts	Balance Sheet Parent Company	Balance Sheet Subsidiary Company	Eliminations		Consolidated Balance Sheet
			Debit	Credit	
Cash	7,500	25,000			32,500
Investment in Subsidiary Company	92,500			(1) 92,500	
Other Long-Term Assets	760,000	60,000	(1) 10,000		830,000
Goodwill			(1) 7,500		7,500
Total Assets	860,000	85,000			870,000
Liabilities	60,000	10,000			70,000
Common Stock—$10 par value	600,000	55,000	(1) 55,000		600,000
Retained Earnings	200,000	20,000	(1) 20,000		200,000
Total Liabilities and Stockholders' Equity	860,000	85,000	92,500	92,500	870,000

(1) Elimination of intercompany investment. Excess of cost over book value ($92,500 − $75,000 = $17,500) allocated $10,000 to Other Long-Term Assets and $7,500 to Goodwill.

Long-Term Assets and $7,500 to a new account called **Goodwill**, or **Goodwill from Consolidation**.

The amount of goodwill is determined as follows:

Cost of investment in subsidiary	$92,500
Book value of subsidiary	75,000
Excess of cost over book value	$17,500
Portion of excess attributable to undervalued long-term assets of subsidiary	10,000
Portion of excess attributable to goodwill	$ 7,500

Goodwill appears as an asset on the consolidated balance sheet representing the excess of cost of the investment over book value that cannot be allocated to any specific asset. Other Long-Term Assets appears on the consolidated balance sheet as the combined total of $830,000 ($760,000 + $60,000 + $10,000).

When the parent pays less than book value for its investment in the subsidiary, Accounting Principles Board *Opinion No. 16*, paragraph 87, requires that the excess of book value over cost of the investment be used to lower the carrying value of the subsidiary's long-term assets. The reasoning behind this is that market values of long-lived assets (other than marketable securities) are among the least reliable of estimates, since a ready market does not usually exist for such assets. In other words, the APB advises against using negative goodwill, except in very special cases.

Intercompany Receivables and Payables. If either the parent or the subsidiary company owes money to the other, there will be a receivable on the creditor company's individual balance sheet and a payable on the debtor company's individual balance sheet. When a consolidated balance sheet is prepared, both the receivable and the payable should be eliminated because, from the viewpoint of the consolidated entity, neither the asset nor the liability exists. In other words, it does not make sense for a company to owe money to itself. The eliminating entry would be made on the work sheet by debiting the payable and crediting the receivable for the amount of the intercompany loan.

Consolidated Income Statement

OBJECTIVE 4
Prepare consolidated income statements for intercompany transactions

The consolidated income statement is prepared for a consolidated entity by combining the revenues and expenses of the parent and subsidiary companies. The procedure is the same as in preparing a consolidated balance sheet. That is, intercompany transactions are eliminated to prevent double counting of revenues and expenses. Several intercompany transactions affect the consolidated income statement. They are: (1) sales and purchases of goods and services between parent and subsidiary (purchases for the buying company and sales for the selling company); (2) income and expenses on loans, receivables, or bond indebtedness between parent and subsidiary; and (3) other income and expenses from intercompany transactions.

To illustrate the eliminating entries, we will assume the following transactions between a parent and its wholly-owned subsidiary. Parent Company made sales of $120,000 in goods to Subsidiary Company, which in turn sold all the goods to others. Subsidiary Company paid Parent Company $2,000 interest on a loan from the parent.

The work sheet in Exhibit 4 shows how to prepare a consolidated income statement. The purpose of the eliminating entries is to treat the two companies

Exhibit 4. Work Sheet Showing Eliminations for Preparing a Consolidated Income Statement

Parent and Subsidiary Companies
Work Sheet for Consolidated Income Statement
For the Year Ended December 31, 19xx

Accounts	Income Statement Parent Company	Income Statement Subsidiary Company	Eliminations		Consolidated Income Statement
			Debit	Credit	
Sales	430,000	200,000	(1) 120,000		510,000
Other Revenues	60,000	10,000	(2) 2,000		68,000
Total Revenues	490,000	210,000			578,000
Cost of Goods Sold	210,000	150,000		(1) 120,000	240,000
Other Expenses	140,000	50,000		(2) 2,000	188,000
Total Deductions	350,000	200,000			428,000
Net Income	140,000	10,000	122,000	122,000	150,000

(1) Elimination of intercompany sales and purchases.
(2) Elimination of intercompany interest income and interest expense.

as a single entity. Thus, it is important to include in Sales only those sales made to outsiders and to include in Cost of Goods Sold only those purchases made from outsiders. This goal is met with the first eliminating entry, which eliminates the $120,000 of intercompany sales and purchases by a debit of that amount to Sales and a credit of that amount to Cost of Goods Sold. As a result, only sales to outsiders ($510,000) and purchases from outsiders ($240,000) are included in the Consolidated Income Statement column. The intercompany interest income and expense are eliminated by a debit to Other Revenues and a credit to Other Expenses.

Other Consolidated Financial Statements

Public corporations also prepare consolidated statements of retained earnings and consolidated statements of cash flows. For examples of these statements, see the Toys "R" Us statements in the appendix on the annotated financial statements of Toys "R" Us, Inc.

Questions

1. Why are the concepts of significant influence and control important in accounting for long-term investments?
2. For each of the following categories of long-term investments, briefly describe the applicable percentage of ownership and accounting treatment: (a) noninfluential and noncontrolling investment, (b) influential but noncontrolling investment, and (c) controlling investment.
3. What is meant by a parent-subsidiary relationship?
4. Would the stockholders of Paramount Communications, Inc. be more interested in the consolidated financial statements of Paramount Communications, Inc. than in the statements of its principal subsidiaries, such as Paramount Pictures, Madison Square Garden, or Simon & Schuster? Explain.
5. The 1987 annual report for Merchant Corporation included the following statement in its Summary of Principal Accounting Policies: "*Principles applied in consolidation.*— Majority-owned subsidiaries are consolidated, except for leasing and finance companies and those subsidiaries not considered to be material." How did this practice change in 1988, and why?
6. Also in Merchant's annual report, in the Summary of Principal Accounting Policies, was the following statement: "*Investments.*—Investments in companies, in which Merchant has significant influence in management and control, are on the equity basis." What is the equity basis of accounting for investments, and why did Merchant use it in this case?
7. Why should intercompany receivables, payables, sales, and purchases be eliminated in the preparation of consolidated financial statements?
8. The following item appears on Merchant's consolidated balance sheet: "Minority Interest—$50,000." Explain how this item arose and where you would expect to find it on the consolidated balance sheet.
9. Why may the price paid to acquire a controlling interest in a subsidiary company exceed the subsidiary's book value?
10. The following item also appears on Merchant's consolidated balance sheet: "Goodwill from Consolidation—$70,000." Explain how this item arose and where you would expect to find it on the consolidated balance sheet.
11. Subsidiary Corporation has a book value of $100,000, of which Parent Corporation purchases 100 percent for $115,000. None of the excess of cost over book value is attributed to tangible assets. What is the amount of goodwill from consolidation?
12. Subsidiary Corporation, a wholly-owned subsidiary, has total sales of $500,000, $100,000 of which were made to Parent Corporation. Parent Corporation has total sales of $1,000,000, including sales of all items purchased from Subsidiary Corporation. What is the amount of sales on the consolidated income statement?

Classroom Exercises

Exercise F-1.
Long-Term Investments: Cost Method
(L.O. 1)

Heard Corporation has the following portfolio of investments at year end:

Company	Percentage of Voting Stock Held	Cost	Year-End Market Value
N Corporation	4	$160,000	$190,000
O Corporation	12	750,000	550,000
P Corporation	5	60,000	110,000
Total		$970,000	$850,000

The Unrealized Loss on Long-Term Investments account and the Allowance to Reduce Long-Term Investments to Market account both currently have a balance of $80,000 from the last accounting period. Prepare the year-end adjustment to reflect the above information.

Exercise F-2.
Long-Term Investments: Cost and Equity Methods
(L.O. 1)

On January 1, Mueller Corporation purchased, as long-term investments, 8 percent of the voting stock of Schott Corporation for $500,000 and 45 percent of the voting stock of Choy Corporation for $2 million. During the year, Schott Corporation had earnings of $200,000 and paid dividends of $80,000. Choy Corporation had earnings of $600,000 and paid dividends of $400,000. The market value of neither investment declined during the year. Which of these investments should be accounted for using the cost method? Which with the equity method? At what amount should each investment be carried on the balance sheet at year end? Give a reason for each choice.

Exercise F-3.
Long-Term Investments: Equity Method
(L.O. 1)

On January 1, 19xx, Romano Corporation acquired 40 percent of the voting stock of Burke Corporation for $2,400,000 in cash, an amount sufficient to exercise significant influence over Burke Corporation's activities. On December 31, Romano determined that Burke paid dividends of $400,000 but incurred a net loss of $200,000 for 19xx. Prepare journal entries in Romano Corporation's records to reflect this information.

Exercise F-4.
Methods of Accounting for Long-Term Investments
(L.O. 1, 2)

Diversified Corporation has the following long-term investments:

1. 60 percent of the common stock of Calcor Corporation
2. 13 percent of the common stock of Virginia, Inc.
3. 50 percent of the nonvoting preferred stock of Camrad Corporation
4. 100 percent of the common stock of its financing subsidiary, DCF, Inc.
5. 35 percent of the common stock of the French company Maison de Boutaine
6. 70 percent of the common stock of the Canadian company Alberta Mining Company

For each of these investments, tell which of the following methods should be used for external financial reporting.

a. Cost method
b. Equity method
c. Consolidation of parent and subsidiary financial statements

Exercise F-5.
Elimination Entry for a Purchase at Book Value
(L.O. 3)

The Lardner Manufacturing Company purchased 100 percent of the common stock of the Gwynn Manufacturing Company for $300,000. Gwynn's stockholders' equity included common stock of $200,000 and retained earnings of $100,000. Prepare the eliminating entry in general journal form that would appear on the work sheet for consolidating the balance sheets of these two entities as of the acquisition date.

Exercise F-6. Elimination Entry and Minority Interest
(L.O. 3)

The stockholders' equity section of the Brandt Corporation's balance sheet appeared as follows on December 31:

Common Stock—$10 par value, 40,000 shares authorized and issued	$400,000
Retained Earnings	48,000
Total Stockholders' Equity	$448,000

Assume that Wegner Manufacturing Company owns 80 percent of the voting stock of Brandt Corporation and paid $11.20 for each share. In general journal form, prepare the entry (including minority interest) to eliminate Wegner's investment and Brandt's stockholders' equity that would appear on the work sheet used in preparing the consolidated balance sheet for the two firms.

Exercise F-7. Consolidated Balance Sheet with Goodwill
(L.O. 3)

On September 1, Y Company purchased 100 percent of the voting stock of Z Company for $960,000 in cash. The separate condensed balance sheets immediately after the purchase follow:

	Y Company	Z Company
Other Assets	$2,206,000	$1,089,000
Investment in Z Company	960,000	—
	$3,166,000	$1,089,000
Liabilities	$ 871,000	$ 189,000
Common Stock—$1 par value	1,000,000	300,000
Retained Earnings	1,295,000	600,000
	$3,166,000	$1,089,000

Prepare a work sheet for preparing the consolidated balance sheet immediately after Y Company acquired control of Z Company. Assume that any excess cost of the investment in the subsidiary over book value is attributable to goodwill from consolidation.

Exercise F-8. Preparation of Consolidated Income Statement
(L.O. 4)

Polonia Company has owned 100 percent of Cardwell Company since 19x0. The income statements of these two companies for the year ended December 31, 19x1 follow.

	Polonia Company	Cardwell Company
Sales	$3,000,000	$1,200,000
Cost of Goods Sold	1,500,000	800,000
Gross Margin from Sales	$1,500,000	$ 400,000
Less: Selling Expenses	$ 500,000	$ 100,000
General and Administrative Expenses	600,000	200,000
Total Operating Expenses	$1,100,000	$ 300,000
Net Income from Operations	$ 400,000	$ 100,000
Other Income	120,000	—
Net Income	$ 520,000	$ 100,000

Additional information: (a) Cardwell Company purchased $560,000 of inventory from Polonia Company, which had been sold to Cardwell Company customers by the end of the year. (b) Cardwell Company leased its building from Polonia Company for $120,000 per year. Prepare a consolidated income statement work sheet for the two companies for the year ended December 31, 19x1.

Problems

Problem F-1.
Long-Term Investments Transactions
(L.O. 1)

Mazurek Corporation made the following transactions in its Long-Term Investments account over a two-year period:

19x0

Apr.	1	Purchased with cash 20,000 shares of Cheevers Company stock for $152 per share.
June	1	Purchased with cash 15,000 shares of Abbado Corporation stock for $72 per share.
Sept.	1	Received a $1 per share dividend from Cheevers Company.
Nov.	1	Purchased with cash 25,000 shares of Frankel Corporation stock for $110 per share.
Dec.	31	Market values per share of shares held in the Long-Term Investments account were as follows: Cheevers Company, $140; Abbado Corporation, $32; and Frankel Corporation, $122.

19x1

Feb.	1	Because of unfavorable prospects for Abbado Corporation, sold Abbado stock for cash at $40 per share.
May	1	Purchased with cash 10,000 shares of Schulian Corporation for $224 per share.
Sept.	1	Received $2 per share dividend from Cheevers Company.
Dec.	31	Market values per share of shares held in the Long-Term Investments account were as follows: Cheevers Company, $160; Frankel Corporation, $140; and Schulian Corporation, $200.

Required

Prepare entries to record these transactions in the Mazurek Corporation records. Assume that all investments represent less than 20 percent of the voting stock of the company whose stock was acquired.

Problem F-2.
Long-Term Investment: Equity Method
(L.O. 1)

The Samir Company owns 40 percent of the voting stock of the Gorman Company. The Investment account for this company on the Samir Company's balance sheet had a balance of $600,000 on January 1, 19xx. During 19xx, the Gorman Company reported the following quarterly earnings and dividends paid:

Quarter	Earnings	Dividends Paid
1	$ 80,000	$ 40,000
2	60,000	40,000
3	160,000	40,000
4	(40,000)	40,000
	$260,000	$160,000

The Samir Company exercises a significant influence over the operations of the Gorman Company and therefore uses the equity method to account for its investment.

Required

1. Prepare the journal entries that the Samir Company must make each quarter in accounting for its investment in the Gorman Company.
2. Prepare a ledger account for the investment in common stock of the Gorman Company. Enter the beginning balance and post relevant portions of the entries made in **1**.

Problem F-3.
Consolidated Balance Sheet: Less than 100 Percent Ownership
(L.O. 3)

In a cash transaction, Kamper Company purchased 70 percent of the outstanding stock of Woolf Company for $593,600 cash on June 30, 19xx. Immediately after the acquisition, the separate balance sheets of the companies appeared as shown on the top of page Ap-80.

Additional information: (a) Woolf Company's other assets represent a long-term investment in Kamper Company's long-term debt. The debt was purchased for an amount equal to Kamper's carrying value of the debt. (b) Kamper Company owes Woolf Company $80,000 for services rendered.

Required

Prepare a work sheet for preparing a consolidated balance sheet as of the acquisition date.

	Kamper Company	Woolf Company
Assets		
Cash	$ 320,000	$ 48,000
Accounts Receivable	520,000	240,000
Inventory	800,000	520,000
Investment in Woolf Company	593,600	—
Plant and Equipment (net)	1,200,000	880,000
Other Assets	40,000	160,000
Total Assets	$3,473,600	$1,848,000
Liabilities and Stockholders' Equity		
Accounts Payable	$ 640,000	$ 400,000
Long-Term Debt	800,000	600,000
Common Stock—$10 par value	1,600,000	800,000
Retained Earnings	433,600	48,000
Total Liabilities and Stockholders' Equity	$3,473,600	$1,848,000

Problem F-4.
Consolidated Balance Sheet: Cost Exceeding Book Value
(L.O. 3)

The balance sheets of Magreb and Nicario Companies as of December 31, 19xx are as follows:

	Magreb Company	Nicario Company
Assets		
Cash	$ 120,000	$ 80,000
Accounts Receivable	200,000	60,000
Investment in Nicario Company	700,000	—
Other Assets	200,000	360,000
Total Assets	$1,220,000	$500,000
Liabilities and Stockholders' Equity		
Liabilities	$ 220,000	$ 60,000
Common Stock—$20 par value	800,000	400,000
Retained Earnings	200,000	40,000
Total Liabilities and Stockholders' Equity	$1,220,000	$500,000

Required

Prepare a consolidated balance sheet work sheet for the Magreb and Nicario Companies. Assume that the Magreb Company purchased 100 percent of Nicario's common stock for $700,000 immediately before the balance sheet date. Also assume that $160,000 of the excess of cost over book value is attributable to the increased value of Nicario Company's other assets. The rest of the excess is considered by the Magreb Company to be goodwill.

LEARNING OBJECTIVES

1. Explain and differentiate some basic concepts related to governmental and not-for-profit accounting.
2. Describe the types of funds used in governmental accounting.
3. Explain the modified accrual basis of accounting used by state and local governments.
4. Describe the financial reporting system used in governmental accounting.
5. Provide a brief introduction to other types of not-for-profit accounting.
6. Describe the unique aspects of the budgeting process in governmental and not-for-profit organizations.
7. Apply and interpret the basic techniques used by governmental and not-for-profit organizations to control costs of operations.

APPENDIX G

Overview of Governmental and Not-for-Profit Accounting

State and local governments and not-for-profit organizations account for a significant share of all spending in the American economy. This appendix provides a brief introduction to financial accounting for several categories of governmental and not-for-profit groups. They include state and local governments, colleges and universities, hospitals, and voluntary health and welfare organizations. After studying this appendix, you should be able to meet the learning objectives listed on the left.

Governmental, Not-for-Profit, and Business Accounting

Businesses in the United States are organized to produce profits for their owners or shareholders. This fact requires that the accounting system provide shareholders, creditors, and other interested parties with information that will help them evaluate the firm's success in making a profit. The rules and practices of business accounting are referred to as generally accepted accounting principles (GAAP), which are established by the Financial Accounting Standards Board (FASB). Historically, governmental GAAP have been the responsibility of the National Council on Governmental Accounting (NCGA). In 1984 the Financial Accounting Foundation founded the Governmental Accounting Standards Board (GASB). The GASB has the power to establish accounting rules and practices for governmental units. Its responsibilities parallel those of the FASB in that it defines generally accepted accounting principles for governmental units. Standards set by the GASB do not apply to nongovernmental not-for-profit organizations like private universities and hospitals. Accounting practices for these nongovernmental not-for-profit organizations fall under the pronouncements of the FASB.

Financial Reporting Objectives of Governmental Units

OBJECTIVE 1
Explain and differentiate some basic concepts related to governmental and not-for-profit accounting

State and local governments have different objectives from those of businesses, and thus they have traditionally had different GAAP. Governmental units chiefly provide services to citizens, with expenditures for these services limited to the amounts legally available. Governmental units need not be profitable in the business sense; however, they do need to limit their spending to the funds made available for specific purposes. For these reasons, the GASB has established the following financial reporting objectives for governmental units:

1. Financial reporting should assist in fulfilling government's duty to be publicly accountable and should enable users to assess that accountability.

2. Financial reporting should assist users in evaluating the operating results of the governmental entity for the year.
3. Financial reporting should assist users in assessing the level of services that can be provided by the entity and its ability to meet its obligations when due.[1]

The primary objective of governmental GAAP is, therefore, not profit measurement, but the assessment and accountability of the funds available for governmental activities. To help satisfy this objective, governmental GAAP have several unique accounting features, the most important of which are the use of funds to account for various activities and the use of modified accrual accounting. A **fund** is defined as a fiscal and accounting entity. **Modified accrual accounting** attempts to provide an accurate measure of increases and decreases in resources available (especially in cash) to fulfill governmental obligations.

The operations of state and local governments are recorded in a variety of funds, each of which is designated for a specific purpose. This means that each fund simultaneously shows (1) the financial position and results of operations during the period and (2) compliance with legal requirements of the state or local government. State and local governments rely on the following types of funds:

OBJECTIVE 2
Describe the types of funds used in governmental accounting

General fund To account for all financial resources not accounted for in any other fund. This fund accounts for most of the current operating activities of the governmental unit (administration, police, fire, health, and sanitation, for example).

Special revenue funds To account for revenues legally restricted to specific purposes.

Capital projects funds To account for the acquisition and construction of major capital projects.

Debt service fund To account for resources accumulated to pay the interest and principal of general obligation long-term debt.

Enterprise funds To account for activities that are financed and operated in a manner similar to private business activities. These funds are most appropriate for activities that charge the public for goods or services, such as municipal golf courses or utilities.

Internal service funds To account for the financing of goods or services provided by one department or agency of a governmental unit to other departments or agencies of governmental units.

Trust and agency funds To account for assets held by a governmental unit acting as a trustee or agent for individuals, private organizations, or other funds.

The first four funds are called **governmental funds**. The enterprise and internal service funds are **proprietary funds**. Trust and agency funds are **fiduciary funds**. A political unit may properly have only one general fund. There is no limit, however, on the number of other funds used. There is also no requirement that a state or local government have all of these funds; individual needs govern the type and number of funds used.

Besides these funds, state and local governments use two unique entities called **account groups** to record certain fixed assets and long-term liabilities.

General fixed assets account group To account for all long-term assets of a governmental unit except long-term assets related to specific proprietary or trust funds. This account group does not record depreciation.

1. *Concept Statement No. 1,* "Objectives of Financial Reporting" (Stamford, Conn.: Governmental Accounting Standards Board, 1987).

General long-term debt group To account for all long-term liabilities of a governmental unit except for long-term liabilities related to specific proprietary or trust funds. This account group records the principal amounts of long-term debt as well as the amounts available in the debt service fund and the amounts to be provided in the future for the retirement of the debt.

Long-term assets and long-term liabilities related to proprietary and trust funds are accounted for in essentially the same manner as in business accounting.

Modified Accrual Accounting

OBJECTIVE 3
Explain the modified accrual basis of accounting used by state and local governments

Governmental funds, as well as certain types of trust funds, use the modified accrual method of accounting. Proprietary funds, as well as certain types of trust funds, use the familiar full accrual accounting common to business organizations. This section will concentrate on the less familiar modified accrual basis of accounting.

Modified accrual accounting has several features that distinguish it from accrual accounting used in business. The measurement and recognition of revenues and expenditures, the incorporation of the budget into the formal accounting system, and the use of encumbrances to account for purchase commitments will each be described briefly.

In governmental accounting, **revenues** are defined as increases in fund resources from sources other than interfund transactions or proceeds of long-term debt. They are recognized in the accounts when "measurable and available." In most cases these conditions are met when cash is received. **Expenditures** are defined as decreases in fund resources caused by transactions other than interfund transfers. These concepts of revenues and expenditures result in some unusual situations, as the following examples illustrate.

1. Assume that a city sells a used police car for $2,500 cash. This transaction would be recorded in the general fund as follows:

Cash	2,500	
Revenues		2,500
Sale of used police car		

2. When a city purchases a new police car for $12,000 cash, the transaction would be recorded in the general fund as follows:

Expenditures	12,000	
Cash		12,000
Purchase of new police car		

The transactions are recorded in this way because they satisfy the definitions of revenues and expenditures.

To further illustrate the contrast between governmental and business-type accrual accounting, we can examine the way in which a business would record the above transactions:

1. Assume that a firm sells a used car for $2,500 cash and that the car has a carrying value of $2,000 (cost of $7,500 less accumulated depreciation of $5,500):

Cash	2,500	
Accumulated Depreciation, Car	5,500	
Car		7,500
Gain on disposal		500
Sale of used car		

Unlike governmental accounting, accrual accounting recognizes revenues only to the extent that cash received exceeds carrying value.

2. If a firm purchases a new car for $12,000 cash, the transaction would be recorded as follows:

Car	12,000	
Cash		12,000
Purchase of new car		

The car would be shown as an asset on the firm's balance sheet. No expense would be recorded until depreciation is recognized in subsequent years. As discussed throughout this book, business accounting focuses on the matching of revenues and expenses to compute net income or loss for the period. Governmental accounting, in contrast, concentrates on inflows and outflows of fund resources.

Another unique feature of governmental accounting is the formal incorporation of the budget into the accounts of the particular fund. This approach is required for the general fund and the special revenue fund and is optional for the other governmental funds. The general fund, for example, would record its budget as follows:

Estimated Revenues	1,000,000	
Appropriations		950,000
Fund Balance		50,000
To record budget for fiscal year		

This example assumes that the governmental unit expects revenues to exceed legally mandated expenditures (or appropriations). The use of budgetary accounts enables the governmental unit to have a continuous check or control on whether actual revenues and expenditures correspond to original estimates. In addition, the various funds' financial statements will show both the budgeted and actual amounts of major revenue and expenditure categories. At the end of the accounting period, the budget entry would be reversed, since its control function is no longer needed. A new budget would then be recorded in the subsequent period to control revenues and expenditures in that period. Businesses also use budgets, but they do not integrate those budgets formally into the regular accounting system.

A third unique feature of governmental accounting is the use of **encumbrance accounting**. Since governments cannot legally spend more than the amounts appropriated for specific purposes, it is necessary to keep track of anticipated, as well as actual, expenditures. Whenever a significant lapse of time is expected between a commitment to spend and the actual expenditure, governmental GAAP require the use of encumbrance accounting.

For example, a city orders $10,000 of supplies on July 1, but does not expect to receive the supplies until September 1. The bill received on September 1 amounts of $10,200. The general fund would record this transaction as follows:

July 1	Encumbrances	10,000	
	Reserve for Encumbrances		10,000
	Order of supplies		
Sept. 1	Reserve for Encumbrances	10,000	
	Encumbrances		10,000
	Reverse encumbrance upon receipt of bill for supplies		

Sept. 1	Expenditures	10,200	
	Cash (or Vouchers Payable)		10,200
	Payment for supplies		

The purpose of an encumbrance system is to ensure that the governmental unit does not exceed its spending authority. This is accomplished by recording not only actual expenditures but also anticipated expenditures under the current period's appropriations. In addition to normal expenditures, the Reserve for Encumbrances account represents that portion of the fund balance already committed to future expenditures. Regardless of the original estimated encumbrance amounts, on September 1, the encumbrance is eliminated by reversing the original entry of July 1, and Expenditures is debited for the actual amount spent.

Financial Reporting System

OBJECTIVE 4
Describe the financial reporting system used in governmental accounting

The accounting system we have described is designed to produce periodic financial statements. The financial statements recommended by the NCGA in its Government Accounting Standard No. 1 include the following:

Combined balance sheet This statement is prepared for all fund types and account groups. Each fund type and account group lists major categories of assets, liabilities, and either fund balances or owners' equity accounts.

Combined statement of revenues, expenditures, and changes in fund balances—all governmental funds This statement is prepared for all governmental fund types. Since only governmental funds are reported in this statement, all revenues and expenditures would be measured according to the principles of modified accrual accounting.

Combined statement of revenues, expenditures, and changes in fund balances—budget and actual—general and special revenue funds This statement presents budget and actual amounts for general and special revenue fund types. The statement includes the budgetary data described earlier and directly compares actual revenues and expenditures to budgeted revenues and expenditures. It indicates, for each type of revenue and expenditure, the amount by which actual amounts differ from budgeted amounts.

Combined statement of revenues, expenses, and changes in retained earnings (or equity) This statement is prepared for all proprietary fund types. It is prepared on the full accrual basis and resembles the financial statements prepared by businesses.

Combined statement of changes in financial position This statement is prepared for all proprietary fund types.

Not-for-Profit Organizations

OBJECTIVE 5
Provide a brief introduction to other types of not-for-profit accounting

This section provides a very brief view of accounting for certain types of not-for-profit organizations. Colleges and universities, hospitals, and voluntary health and welfare organizations, among others, share characteristics of both governmental and business entities. Like governments, they are not intended to make a profit; however, they lack the taxing ability of a government. Because the lack of taxing ability requires that the revenues of not-for-profit organizations at least equal expenses over the long run, these organizations rely on accrual accounting for most of their activities. These organizations also use funds to account for different types of resources and activities. The use of funds is necessary because of the legal restrictions imposed on many of the resources available to these groups.

Colleges and Universities

Colleges and universities, with a few exceptions, use full accrual accounting. Until recently, one notable exception was that depreciation on fixed assets did not have to be recorded. However, the FASB issued Statement No. 93 to eliminate this exception. Because of the controversial nature of the issue, FASB No. 93 was not implemented until 1990. Another exception is that revenues from restricted sources can be recognized only when expenditures are made for the purposes specified by the revenue source. Several types of funds are employed:

Unrestricted current fund Accounts for general operating activities.

Restricted current fund Accounts for funds available for a specific purpose, as designated by groups or individuals outside the school.

Loan funds Accounts for funds available for loans to students, faculty, and staff.

Endowment funds Accounts for gifts or bequests, the principal of which usually cannot be spent.

Annuity and life income funds Are similar to endowment funds, except that the donor receives some form of financial support from the school.

Plant funds Accounts for funds available for acquisition and replacement of plant assets, as well as retirement of debt. These funds also account for all plant assets of the school, except any that may be part of an endowment fund.

Agency funds Are similar to those used by state and local governments.

Financial statements used by colleges and universities include the following: (a) statement of current funds, revenues, expenditures, and other changes; (b) combined balance sheet; and (c) statement of changes in fund balances.

Hospitals

Accounting for not-for-profit hospitals closely resembles the accrual accounting methods used by businesses. Funds used include the following:

Unrestricted fund Accounts for the normal operating activities of the hospital. This is the only fund that records revenues and expenses. It accounts for all assets and liabilities not included in other funds, including plant assets and long-term debt.

Specific purpose fund To account for resources that are restricted by someone outside of the hospital for specific operating purposes.

Endowment and annuity and life income funds Similar to those used by colleges and universities.

Plant replacement and expansion fund Accounts for resources that are restricted by someone outside of the hospital for capital outlay purposes.

Not-for-profit hospitals prepare a statement of revenues and expenses for the unrestricted fund, as well as a statement of cash flows. They also prepare balance sheets and statements of changes in fund balances for all funds.

An important aspect of hospital accounting is the classification of revenues and expenses. Revenues must be separated by *source,* including patient service and other operating and nonoperating revenues. Expenses must be classified by *function,* including nursing services, other professional services, administrative services, and so forth. Unlike other organizations described in this appendix, hospitals recognize depreciation on plant assets.

Voluntary Health and Welfare Organizations

Voluntary health and welfare organizations encompass a broad variety of groups, such as the Sierra Club, the American Cancer Society, and the National Rifle Association. Even though accounting practices vary considerably, these organizations usually follow the full accrual basis of accounting. Their fund structure is as follows: current unrestricted fund; current restricted fund; land, building, and equipment fund; endowment funds; custodial (similar to agency) funds; and loan and annuity funds.

Three financial statements are prepared: (a) statement of support, revenue, and expenses, and changes in fund balances, (b) balance sheets, and (c) statement of functional expenses. These organizations must strictly classify revenues and expenses. Revenues must be separated into public support revenues, for which the donor expects nothing in return, and revenues from charges for goods and services. Expenses must be separated by *program* (those activities for which the organization has been established) and by *supporting services* (overhead). These classifications are useful in evaluating the relative efficiency of the groups' activities.

Summary of Funds

Governmental and not-for-profit accounting, as we have seen, shares some of the characteristics of business accounting but has its own unique features. Primary among these is the use of funds to organize transactions. Table 1 summarizes the types of funds used by various organizations and reviews some of the important details of their accounting systems.

Budgeting in Not-for-Profit Organizations

OBJECTIVE 6
Describe the unique aspects of the budgeting process in governmental and not-for-profit organizations

As pointed out earlier, the major difference between not-for-profit and profit organizations is the overall goal of each group. On the one hand, some enterprises must make a profit to exist, so making a profit must be their major objective. On the other hand, the not-for-profit organization is meant to serve some function or purpose other than making a profit. This purpose can be served, however, only if the organization carefully controls its funds and their use. For this reason, organizations that are not profit oriented depend heavily on budgeting to maintain control over their funds and to help carry out their goals.

Budgeting is a major project for large governmental organizations at the federal, state, and municipal levels. Public officials are charged with the safety and wise use of the public's money. Careful preparation of a realistic annual budget plays an important role in this process. Officials of organizations such as professional groups, civic organizations, clubs, charitable organizations, and student fraternities and sororities face the same concerns when budgeting for their organizations.

Except for the profit element, the budgeting principles illustrated in the figure on the preparation of the master budget, found in the chapter on the budgeting process (page 812) also apply to not-for-profit and government organizations. These entities must have long-term objectives as well as short-term goals and operating strategies. Human responsibilities and interaction principles are as much a part of the budgeting process in the public sector as they are in the private sector. Budget housekeeping rules apply as well as the

Table 1. Overview of Governmental and Not-for-Profit Accounting

	Type of Organization			
	Governmental Units	**Colleges and Universities**	**Hospitals**	**Voluntary Health and Welfare**
Funds and Account Groups	General	Unrestricted current	Unrestricted	Current unrestricted
	Special revenue	Restricted current	Specific purpose	Current restricted
	Capital projects	Plant	Plant replacement and expansion	Land, building, and equipment
	Debt service	Plant		
	Enterprise			
	Internal service			
	Trust and agency	Loan, Endowment, Annuity and life income, Agency	Endowment, Annuity and life income	Endowment Custodial
	General long-term assets	Plant		Land, building, and equipment
	General long-term debt			
Special Characteristics	1. Only one general fund	1. Revenues recognized in restricted funds only as specified expenditures made	1. Depreciation may be computed on a replacement cost basis	1. Revenues segregated between voluntary contributions and charges for goods or services
	2. Proprietary funds (enterprise, internal service) use full accrual accounting	2. Depreciation recorded as an expense, after implementation of FASB No. 93	2. Only unrestricted fund shows revenues and expenses	2. Expenses segregated by program services and by supporting (overhead) services
	3. Number of funds used depends on needs and complexity of governmental unit			

follow-up principles. In other words, making a profit is not the only reason for participating in the budgeting function.

However, governmental units and other not-for-profit organizations need budgeting data on anticipated changes in fund balances rather than amounts of profit or loss. Such organizations rely heavily on cash budgeting techniques since their budgets are related to expected fund changes. The budgeted amount of each cost or expense item or grouping is the maximum expenditure approved for the period. Any changes in such an amount must have official approval.

Table 1. (continued)

	Type of Organization			
	Governmental Units	**Colleges and Universities**	**Hospitals**	**Voluntary Health and Welfare**
	Basis of Accounting			
	Modified Accrual	Accrual	Accrual	Accrual
Financial Statements	Combined balance sheet—all fund types and account groups	Combined balance sheet	Balance sheet	Balance sheet
	Combined statement of revenues, expenditures, and changes in fund balances—all governmental fund types	Statement of current funds revenues, expenditures, and other changes	Statement of revenues and expenses	Statement of support, revenues, and expenses, and changes in fund balances
	Combined statement of revenues, expenditures, and changes in fund balances—budget and actual—general and special revenue fund types	Statement of changes in fund balances	Statement of changes in fund balances	Statement of functional expenses
	Combined statement of revenues, expenses, and changes in retained earnings—all proprietary fund types			
	Combined statement of changes in financial position—all proprietary fund types		Statement of cash flows	

Table 2 describes the budgeting procedure the government of the United States uses. Preparing the country's annual budget is an enormous undertaking that involves hundreds of people and agencies. The steps of the process in Table 2 take almost a whole year. Note that the process begins with the president submitting a complete budget proposal to Congress for study and approval. Thousands of hours have already been spent putting together this proposal. This early stage adds several more months to the U.S. budgeting process.

Congress and the president control the country's purse strings through budgeting. Emphasis is placed on trying to cut down overspending and waste and to prevent misuse of the taxpayers' money. Not-for-profit organizations

Table 2. Congressional Budget Process Timetable

Suggested Deadlines	Action to Be Completed
On or before:	
November 10	President submits current services budget
Fifteenth day after Congress meets [Jan. 15]	President submits budget
March 15	Committees and joint committees submit reports to Budget Committees
April 1	Congressional Budget Office submits report to Budget Committees
April 15	Budget Committees report first concurrent resolution on the budget to their houses
May 15	Committees report bills and resolutions authorizing new budget authority
May 15	Congress completes action on first concurrent resolution on the budget
7th day after Labor Day	Congress completes action on bills and resolutions providing new budget authority and new spending authority
September 15	Congress completes action on second required concurrent resolution on the budget
September 25	Congress completes action on reconciliation bill or resolution, or both, implementing second required concurrent resolution
October 1	Fiscal year begins

Source: Title III, U.S. Code Congressional and Administrative News, §300, 93rd Cong., 2d Sess., 1974, p. 336.

generally operate with a board of directors having the same sort of responsibilities as the U.S. Congress or state legislature.

To present a more detailed picture of the budgeting process of a not-for-profit organization, we turn to Beta Alpha Psi, the national accounting fraternity for honor students. Beta Alpha Psi was founded to recognize honor students in accounting and to expose them to professional issues while they are still in school. Its size makes its budgeting procedures much easier to analyze than those of the federal government.

Beta Alpha Psi's budget for the year ended April 30, 1992 and related actual expenditures are shown in Exhibit 1. The budget is prepared by the director of administration during the spring. The director first gets input from the other five directors and the national president. Past expenditure patterns and expected future events are used as the basis for projecting each revenue and expense item. An early draft of the budget is sent to board members before the organization's spring meeting. Then certain items are questioned at the meeting, and the revised budget is submitted for the board's approval about the first of June.

Actual results will, of course, be different from the budgeted figures. To control cost overruns, the board of directors should set up a policy that calls for board approval before any increases are funded. A small overrun does not call for such action. Only the significant increases must be controlled in this manner.

Exhibit 1. Typical Not-for-Profit Budget

National Council of Beta Alpha Psi
(The National Accounting Fraternity)
Statements of Revenue, Expenditures, and Changes in Fund Balance
For the Year Ended April 30, 1992

	Actual	Budget
Revenue and Support		
Initiation fees	$278,092	$245,000
Associates program contributions	150,000	132,500
Superior chapter awards contributions	67,000	74,000
Chapter fees	38,200	37,000
Annual student convention	34,791	28,000
Outstanding faculty advisor award contribution	30,000	6,000
Investment income	27,717	25,000
Charter fees	15,500	6,000
Credit card program	10,146	5,000
London summer program	8,200	0
Miscellaneous	4,172	5,000
Net decrease in unrealized loss on investment	1,153	0
Total revenue and support	$664,971	$563,500
Expenses		
General and administrative	$141,319	$138,000
National council:		
Annual student convention	84,185	60,000
Faculty advisor and student expense reimbursement	64,990	60,000
National council meetings	20,167	40,000
Chapter installations and visitations	3,195	8,000
Miscellaneous	633	500
Local chapter:		
Membership certificates	16,434	18,000
Performance awards	12,271	10,000
Banners	1,964	2,000
Special projects:		
Regional meetings	84,671	94,500
Superior chapter awards	67,000	74,000
Faculty advisor awards	30,000	6,000
Student seminar	24,294	25,000
Publications	17,508	26,000
Honorarium	1,500	1,500
Total expenses	$570,131	$563,500
Excess of Revenue and Support over Expenses	$ 94,840	$ 0
Fund Balance, Beginning of Year	407,143	407,143
Fund Balance, End of Year	$501,983	$407,143

Source: Reprinted by permission of National Council of Beta Alpha Psi.

Expenditure Control— Governmental and Not-for-Profit Organizations

OBJECTIVE 7
Apply and interpret the basic techniques used by governmental and not-for-profit organizations to control costs of operations

The way to approach effective cost control in governmental and not-for-profit organizations is through the budgeting process. These organizations rely heavily on expected revenues for the coming period, and their budgets are linked closely with this figure. For governmental organizations such as the federal government, a state university, or a municipal government unit, revenues would be the funds *appropriated* for that period of time. Sometimes dollars can be shifted from one operating fund to another during the period, but the total appropriation sets the upper limit on spending. A not-for-profit organization such as a charitable group or a professional organization (the National Association of Accountants, for example) depends on the forecast of charitable contributions or membership dues for its spending limit.

Expenditure budgets for governmental and not-for-profit enterprises are usually developed independently of the revenue projection for the period. Once both budgets are completed, the budgeted expenditures normally need to be trimmed to match the spending limit set in the revenue forecast. Budgets approved by the legislature, city council, board of trustees, or board of directors then become the standard against which all expenditures are judged.

Governmental Organizations

For governmental organizations, an *appropriation* means that expenditures have been formally approved and dollars have been set aside for specific purposes. When those dollars are gone, expenditures must cease. Therefore, administrative control over the use of these funds becomes extremely important. Each governmental unit has at least two main uses for its funds: (1) to carry out its mission and (2) to cover its day-to-day operations.

Funds to cover operating costs such as salaries, supplies, and equipment are distributed to each operating department or unit as part of the budgeting process. Each manager must then account for the specific uses of funds within her or his unit and is held responsible for any deviation from the budget. Since revenues are limited, any increase in cost over budgeted amounts must be formally requested and approved by the organization's governing body.

Expenditures used to carry out the intended mission of governmental organizations are controlled in a different manner. Let's compare cost control techniques for two types of governmental units: the Department of Defense and a municipal street department. Both these units contract with outside, profit-oriented companies for specific projects such as building a new jet fighter or paving a street. The contract itself is the cost control mechanism many government organizations use.

If at all possible, a firm fixed price contract should be obtained. With this kind of contract, the governmental unit establishes an upper expenditure limit, above which the contractor must absorb all costs and still complete the project. All costs and profits are included in the firm fixed price. Most of the projects of a municipal street department will be under firm fixed price contracts, but the Department of Defense can make only limited use of this kind of contract. Why? Because it is easy to forecast costs for paving a street, as it is for building one hundred more tanks. But what about designing and building a new jet fighter or a nuclear submarine? Imagine the amount of uncertainty involved in projecting costs for such projects. Because of this uncertainty, profit-oriented companies will not take on such a project under a firm fixed price contract. For these situations, a cost plus fixed or variable fee contract is used. Such a contract shifts the risks from the contractor to the governmental unit. These risks and uncertainties often cause cost overruns, which become targets of the news media. Without such contracts, however, no profit-oriented company would accept risky projects, and the Department of Defense would have to build its own factories for new defense projects. The government to date has been unwilling to compete with the private sector in this way. Since the Department of Defense must, as must the municipal street department, operate within set spending limits, any cost overrun that cannot be absorbed by other units within the department must come before Congress for approval. Such a procedure—submitting excess costs to a governing body for approval—is another type of cost control for governmental organizations.

Not-for-Profit Organizations

Many of the cost control procedures not-for-profit enterprises use have already been discussed in general terms. We now show how these procedures might be used in a church. The United Church has a budget committee charged with developing the church's operating budget each year. The Board of Deacons of the church then approves the budget after making adjustments for events unforeseen by the budget committee. Last year, the board approved a budget with the following items: Building Repairs, $6,500; Utility Costs, $3,450; and New Hymnals, $1,200. A hot water heater explosion, increased utility rates, and an unexpected new edition of the hymnal caused all three cost categories to be questioned during the year. Since donations and member offerings were not expected to increase much even with these unusual needs, the board had to decide how to keep costs within the set limits and still keep the church operating.

Building repairs after the explosion amounted to $10,000, $6,000 of which was covered by insurance. The $4,000 difference brought the total building repairs for the year to $7,200. Utility bills shot up 15 percent, and actual utility bills totaled $3,970. New hymnals for the church would cost $4,500. The board, after discussing these events, decided that the building repairs and payment of utility bills were necessary for the continued operation of the church. Therefore, the purchase of new hymnals was put off until the following year. The current year's appropriation of $1,200 for hymnals was diverted to Building Repairs ($700) and Utility Costs ($500) to help cover the increases. It took formal approval of the Board of Deacons to make these cost overrun payments. Cost control takes many forms in not-for-profit organizations, but all are connected with the budget and the approval/review process of the governing body.

Questions

1. How do the objectives of governmental accounting differ from the objectives of business accounting?
2. What is the purpose of a *fund,* as that term is used in governmental accounting?
3. What is a proprietary fund in governmental accounting? Why do such funds use accrual accounting?
4. Contrast the measurement of revenues and expenditures in governmental accounting with the measurement of revenues and expenses in business accounting.
5. What is the purpose of budgetary accounts in governmental accounting? Explain your answer.

6. What are the major characteristics of modified accrual accounting as used in governmental accounting?
7. What are the purposes of recording encumbrances?
8. How does accounting for colleges and universities resemble business accounting? How does it differ from business accounting?
9. Describe how revenues and expenses are classified in hospital accounting.
10. Describe and contrast the two types of revenues recognized in the accounts of voluntary health and welfare organizations.
11. Do not-for-profit organizations require budgets just as profit-oriented enterprises do? Explain your answer.
12. How do budgets help control costs for governmental and not-for-profit organizations?
13. "Contracts with outside suppliers are a common means of cost control for government organizations." Explain this statement.
14. In not-for-profit organizations, how are potential cost overruns handled? Why is this action necessary?

Classroom Exercises

Exercise G-1.
Basic Concepts and Funds
(L.O. 2, 3, 5)

Select the most appropriate answer for the following questions.

1. The fund that accounts for the day-to-day operating activities of a local government is the
   a. enterprise fund.
   b. general fund.
   c. operating fund.
   d. special revenue fund.
2. Accrual accounting is recommended for which of the following funds?
   a. Debt service fund
   b. General fund
   c. Internal service fund
   d. Capital projects fund
3. A debt service fund for a municipality is an example of what type of fund?
   a. Account fund
   b. Governmental fund
   c. Proprietary fund
   d. Fiduciary fund
4. What basis of accounting would a not-for-profit hospital use?
   a. Cash basis for all funds
   b. Modified accrual basis for all funds
   c. Accrual basis for all funds
   d. Accrual basis for some funds and modified accrual basis for other funds
5. After the implementation of FASB No. 93, which of the following types of organization does not record depreciation expense on property, plant, and equipment?
   a. State and local governments
   b. Colleges and universities
   c. Hospitals
   d. Businesses

Exercise G-2.
Recording the Budget in the General Fund
(L.O. 3)

The Village of Lancaster has adopted the following budget items for 19x4:

Estimated Revenues	$20,000,000
Appropriations	19,600,000

1. Prepare the journal entry to record the budget in the general fund for Lancaster on January 1, 19x4.
2. What entry, if any, would be required at the end of Lancaster's accounting year, December 31, 19x4?

Exercise G-3. Budgeting for Not-for-Profit Organizations *(L.O. 6)*

The Board of Directors of the Apple County Animal Shelter has been discussing budget strategy for several months. Recently, Ms. Jonathan was appointed budget director. She is now putting together the cash expenditure budget for 19x2. Following is a listing of 19x1 expenditures:

Salaries and wages	$ 80,900
Employee benefits expense	25,430
Truck expenses	6,540
Medical lab expenses	26,400
Medical supplies expense	12,600
Repairs and maintenance expense	7,260
Heating costs	2,800
Electricity expense	3,400
Water charges	200
Insect control costs	260
Building rent expense	3,500
Animal food costs	4,200
Miscellaneous expenses	620
Total	$174,110

During 19x2, salaries, wages, and related employee benefits are expected to rise by 10 percent. Medical lab and supplies expenses will go up 20 percent next year. All other expenses should be 5 percent higher in 19x2.

Prepare the cash expenditure budget for the Apple County Animal Shelter for 19x2.

Problems

Problem G-1. Journal Entries for the General Fund *(L.O. 3)*

The following transactions occurred in the city of Worthington during 19x1.

19x1

Jan. 1 The budget was adopted. Estimated revenues are $8,000,000; appropriations are $8,200,000.

Feb. 11 Supplies with an estimated cost of $44,000 were ordered.

Mar. 1 Property taxes totaling $7,000,000 were levied. Worthington expects 2 percent of this amount to be uncollectible.

Apr. 10 The supplies ordered on February 11 were received. The actual bill for these supplies amounted to $43,500.

June 1 Property tax collections totaled $6,900,000. The rest were classified as delinquent.

Aug. 10 Equipment costing $22,600 was purchased for cash.

Dec. 31 Actual revenues for 19x1 totaled $8,100,000. Actual expenditures totaled $7,950,000.

Required

Record the journal entries for these transactions in Worthington's general fund.

Problem G-2. Budget Preparation—Not-for-Profit Organization *(L.O. 6)*

Hayward College is a small liberal arts school with an enrollment of about 2,500 students. The college was founded in 1860 by a missionary and his wife and has become well known over the years. Graduates of the school have been very successful and include senators, corporate presidents, military leaders, famous academic and research personnel, and even two state governors.

The college's development program has been in operation for fifty years and is now under the direction of Dr. Jay Tontz. During the past twelve years, the college's endowment has grown from $15,500,000 to an expected $165,450,000 at the close of operation on December 31, 19x1. The breakdown of that amount is shown at the top of page Ap-96. (Information in parentheses shows how each part of the endowment is invested and its current yield.)

Unrestricted	
Corporate "silver plate" program (12% money market fund)	$ 23,400,000
Alumni open donation account (10% corporate bonds)	14,900,000
Alumni/college beneficiary insurance proceeds (14% certificate of deposit)	46,850,000
Friends of the College fund (12% money market fund)	7,280,000
Total unrestricted	$ 92,430,000
Restricted	
Endowed professorships:	
Science—6 at $1,000,000	$ 6,000,000
Business—3 at $1,000,000	3,000,000
Religion—1 at $800,000	800,000
History—1 at $600,000 (10% corporate bonds and preferred stock)	600,000
Alumni student scholarship fund (12% certificate of deposit)	4,900,000
Building maintenance program (14% second mortgage loans)	16,850,000
Capital facility expansion fund (12% government securities)	40,870,000
Total restricted	$ 73,020,000
Total college endowment	$165,450,000

After careful analysis, Dr. Tontz anticipates the following additions to the endowment next year:

Corporate "silver plate" program	$ 640,000
Alumni open donation account	110,000
Alumni/college beneficiary insurance proceeds	1,500,000
Friends of the College fund	410,000
Endowed professorships:	
One in science	1,000,000
One in social science	400,000
Alumni student scholarship fund	550,000
Building maintenance program	310,000
Capital facility expansion fund	2,500,000

Note: The endowed professorship in science and the addition to the capital facility expansion fund will be received in January. Assume that the other endowment additions earn half the normal interest for the year.

Required

1. Prepare the complete projected college endowment budget as of December 31, 19x2.
2. Compute the projected interest income for the year from each part of the endowment.
3. The interest income from the unrestricted part of the endowment must first be used to cover expenses of $2,460,000 for the development program operation. Explain what kinds of uses the college could make of the remaining funds. Give at least four examples.

APPENDIX H

LEARNING OBJECTIVES

1. Explain and differentiate some basic concepts related to income taxes and accounting.
2. Identify the major components used in determining the income tax liability of individuals.

Overview of Income Taxes for Individuals

The United States Congress first passed a permanent income tax law in 1913, after the Sixteenth Amendment to the Constitution made such a tax legal. Its original goal was to provide revenue for the U.S. government, and today the income tax is still a major source of revenue. Of course, most states and many cities also have an income tax. Because these tax laws are in many cases much like those in the federal tax system, the discussion in this appendix is limited to the federal income tax. After studying this appendix, you should be able to meet the learning objectives listed on the left.

Although an important purpose of the federal income tax laws is to produce revenue, Congress has also used its taxing power as an instrument of economic policy. Among the economic goals proposed by Congress are a fairer distribution of income, stimulation of economic growth, full employment, encouragement of exploration for oil and minerals, control of inflation, and a variety of social changes.

All three branches of the federal government have a part in the federal income tax system. The Internal Revenue Service (IRS), which is an agency of the Treasury Department, administers the system. The income tax law is based on over fifty revenue acts and other related laws that have been passed by Congress since 1913. Also, the IRS issues regulations that interpret the law. It is the federal court system, however, that must uphold these important regulations and that has final authority for interpreting the law.

The income tax has had important effects on both individuals and businesses. In 1913, an individual who earned $30,000 paid only $300 or $400 in income taxes. Under the Revenue Reconciliation Act of 1993, an individual who earns the same amount may pay as much as $5,000 or more, and corporations may pay more than one-third of their income in taxes. Clearly, the income tax is an important cost of doing business today.

Some Basic Concepts Related to Federal Income Taxes

To understand the nature of federal income taxes, it is important to distinguish between taxable income and accounting income, between tax planning and tax evasion, between cash basis and accrual basis, and among classifications of taxpayers.

Taxable Income and Accounting Income

OBJECTIVE 1
Explain and differentiate some basic concepts related to income taxes and accounting

The government assesses income taxes on **taxable income**, which usually is gross income less various exemptions and deductions specified by the law and the IRS regulations. Taxable income is generally found by referring to information in the accounting records. However, it is very unlikely that taxable income and accounting income for an entity will be the same, because they have different purposes. The government levies income taxes to obtain revenue from taxpayers and to carry out economic policies totally unrelated to the measurement of economic income, which is the purpose of accounting.

Tax Planning and Tax Evasion

The arrangement of a taxpayer's affairs in such a way as to incur the smallest legal tax is called **tax planning**. For almost every business decision, alternative courses of action are available that will affect taxable income in different ways. For example, the taxpayer may lease or buy a truck, may use LIFO, FIFO, or average cost to account for inventories, or may time an expenditure to be accounted for in one accounting period or another. Once the taxpayer chooses and acts upon an alternative, however, the IRS will usually treat this alternative as the final one for income tax determination. Therefore, in tax planning it is important to consider tax-saving alternatives before putting decisions into effect.

It is the natural goal of any taxable entity to pay as small a tax as possible; both the tax law and the IRS hold that no entity should pay more than is legally required. The best way to accomplish this goal is by careful tax planning. It is, however, illegal to evade paying taxes by concealing actual tax liabilities. This is called **tax evasion**.

Cash Basis and Accrual Basis

In general, taxpayers may use either the cash basis or the accrual basis to arrive at their taxable income. Most individuals use the **cash basis**—the reporting of items of revenue and expense when they are received or paid—because it is the simplest method. Employers usually report their employees' income on a cash basis, and companies that pay dividends and interest on a cash basis must also report them in this way.

Professional and other service enterprises, such as those of accountants, attorneys, physicians, travel agents, and insurance agents, also typically use the cash basis in determining taxable income. One advantage of this method is that fees charged to clients or customers are not considered to be earned until payment is received. Thus, it is possible to defer the taxes on these revenues until the tax year in which they are received. Similarly, expenses such as rent, utilities, and salaries are recorded when they are paid. Thus, a business can work at tax planning by carefully timing its expenditures. Still, this method does not apply to expenditures for buildings and equipment used for business purposes. Such items are treated in accordance with the accelerated cost recovery system discussed in the chapter on long-term assets: acquisition, depreciation, and disposal.

Businesses that engage in production or trading of inventories must use the **accrual basis** of accounting rather than the cash basis. In other words, they must report revenues from sales in the period in which they sold the goods, regardless of when they received the cash. And they must record purchases in the year of purchase rather than in the year of payment. They must follow the usual accounting for beginning and ending inventories in determining cost of goods sold. However, the tax laws do not require a strict accrual method in the accounting sense for manufacturing and merchandising concerns. Various modified cash and accrual bases are possible as long as they yield reasonable and consistent results from year to year.

Classifications of Taxpayers

The federal tax law recognizes four classes of taxpayers: individuals, corporations, estates, and trusts. Members of each class must file tax returns and pay taxes on taxable income. This appendix discusses only individuals. Taxation of corporations is covered in the chapter on long-term liabilities. Taxation of estates and trusts is left for a more advanced course.

Although they are business entities for accounting purposes, sole proprietorships and partnerships are not taxable entities. Instead, a proprietor must include the business income on an individual income tax return. Similarly, each partner in a business must include her or his share of the partnership income on an individual return. Each partnership, however, must file an information return showing the results of the partnership's operations and how each partner's share of the income was determined.

In contrast, corporations are taxable entities that must file tax returns and are taxed directly on their earnings. If the corporation distributes some of its after-tax earnings to its stockholders, the stockholders must report the dividend income as part of their gross income. This rule has led to the claim that corporate income is subject to **double taxation**—once when it is earned by the company and once when it is paid to the owners of the company's stock.

Income Tax for Individuals

OBJECTIVE 2
Identify the major components used in determining the income tax liability of individuals

It is important to study income tax for individuals for several reasons. First, most persons who earn taxable income must file a tax return. Second, all persons who operate proprietorships or partnerships must report the income from their businesses on their individual tax returns. Third, many of the same tax terms are used for both individuals and corporations.

The Internal Revenue Code establishes the method of calculating taxable income for individuals. The starting place for figuring taxable income is finding gross income. The next step is to find the amount of adjusted gross income by subtracting deductions from gross income. Under this heading are the expenses of running a business or profession and certain other specified expenses. Then, from adjusted gross income one subtracts a second kind of deduction, called deductions from adjusted gross income, to arrive at taxable income. Under this second heading are included (1) certain business and personal expenses or a standard minimum and (2) allowances known as exemptions. These procedures can be outlined as follows:

Gross income	$xxx	
Less deductions from gross income	xxx	
Adjusted gross income		$xxx
Less deductions from adjusted gross income:		
a. Itemized or standard deductions	$xxx	
b. Exemptions	xxx	xxx
Taxable income		$xxx

Gross Income

The Internal Revenue Code defines **gross income** as income from all sources, less allowable exclusions. Under this heading are wages, salaries, bonuses, fees, tips, interest, dividends, pensions, and annuities. Rents, royalties, alimony, prizes, profits or shares of profits from business, and gains on sale of property or stocks are also included. Income from illegal sources also must be reported as gross income.

Deductions from Gross Income

The calculation of **adjusted gross income** is important to the individual because it serves as the basis for certain personal deductions in figuring taxable income. These **deductions from gross income** are meant to give people a fairer base than gross income. For example, some people may have a high gross income but may have had many business expenditures to gain that gross income. It is fair to let them deduct the amount spent in earning the gross income.

Deductions from Adjusted Gross Income

Deductions from adjusted gross income fall under two headings: (1) the standard deduction or itemized deductions, and (2) exemptions. The **standard deduction** is an amount allowed every taxpayer for personal and business expenses. The amounts allowable to taxpayers according to their filing statuses are shown in Table 1. If the taxpayer's actual itemized allowable deductions exceed the standard deduction, the taxpayer may deduct the expenses as itemized deductions. Allowable itemized deductions for this purpose include medical and dental expenses, taxes, mortgage interest, casualty losses, contributions, employee business expenses not reimbursed by employers, and other miscellaneous expenses such as union and professional dues, all subject to certain limitations.

Besides the standard deduction and itemized deductions, the taxpayer is allowed another kind of deduction, called an **exemption**. For each exemption, the taxpayer may deduct $2,350 in 1993 from adjusted gross income. A taxpayer is allowed one exemption for herself or himself and one for each dependent. To qualify as a dependent, a person (1) must be closely related to the taxpayer or have lived in the taxpayer's house for the whole year, (2) must have received over half of her or his support during the year from the taxpayer, (3) must not file a joint return with her or his spouse, if married, (4) must have a limited amount of gross income, and (5) must be a U.S. citizen or a resident of the United States, Canada, or Mexico. If a husband and wife file a joint return, they

Table 1. Amounts Allowed as Standard Deductions

Filing Status	1993
Single individuals	$3,700*
Married filing jointly, and surviving spouses	6,200*
Married individuals filing separately	3,100*
Heads of households	5,450*

*These amounts will be adjusted by a cost of living adjustment for 1994 and years thereafter.

Exhibit 1. 1993 Tax Rate Schedules

If taxable income is:		The tax is:	
Over—	*But not over—*		*of the amount over—*
Single			
$ 0	$ 22,100	15%	$ 0
22,100	53,500	$ 3,315.00 + 28%	22,100
53,500	115,000	12,107.00 + 31%	53,500
115,000	250,000	31,172.00 + 36%	115,000
250,000	—	79,772.00 + 39.6%	250,000
Married filing jointly or qualifying widow(er)			
$ 0	$ 36,900	15%	$ 0
36,900	89,150	$ 5,535.00 + 28%	36,900
89,150	140,000	20,165.00 + 31%	89,150
140,000	250,000	35,928.50 + 36%	140,000
250,000	—	75,528.50 + 39.6%	250,000
Married filing separately			
$ 0	$ 18,450	15%	$ 0
18,450	44,575	$ 2,767.00 + 28%	18,450
44,575	70,000	10,082.50 + 31%	44,575
70,000	125,000	17,964.25 + 36%	70,000
125,000	—	37,764.25 + 39.6%	125,000
Head of household			
$ 0	$ 29,600	15%	$ 0
29,600	76,400	$ 4,440.00 + 28%	29,600
76,400	127,500	17,544.00 + 31%	76,400
127,500	250,000	33,385.00 + 36%	127,500
250,000	—	77,485.00 + 39.6%	250,000

may combine their exemptions. Elderly and blind taxpayers are no longer allowed additional exemptions for age or blindness, as they were before 1987, but they are allowed increased standard deductions.

Computing Tax Liability

In general, the income tax is a **progressive tax**, which means that the rate becomes larger as the amount of taxable income becomes larger. In other words, the higher a person's taxable income, the larger the proportion of it that goes to pay taxes.[1] Different rate schedules apply to single taxpayers, married taxpayers who file joint returns, married taxpayers who file separate returns, and single taxpayers who qualify as heads of households. Taxpayers can calculate their

1. In contrast to a progressive tax rate, a **regressive tax rate** becomes less as one's income rises. An example of a regressive tax is the social security (FICA) tax, which is levied on incomes only up to a certain amount. A **proportional tax** is one in which the rate is the same percentage regardless of income. Examples are most sales taxes and the income taxes of some states, such as Illinois.

tax liability by referring to the tax rate schedules in Exhibit 1.2 By looking at these schedules, one can easily see the progressive nature of the tax. As this book goes to press, the U.S. Congress, based on proposals by the President, is debating increases in these rates and other changes in the tax code.

Capital Gains and Losses

The income tax law accorded capital gains special treatment from 1922 through 1987. Beginning in 1988, the special treatment for net capital gains was eliminated. Nevertheless, certain limitations have been retained for taxpayers who suffer capital losses. Assets subject to these rules, called **capital assets**, usually include stocks, bonds, and other investment property. Under certain circumstances, business buildings, equipment, and land are included. Capital assets usually do not include trade receivables, inventories, and other properties created by the taxpayer, such as literary or artistic works.

One effective means of tax planning is to arrange transactions involving capital assets to reduce or defer taxes. If a taxpayer sells stock at a gain near the end of the year, the gain is taxable during that year. By waiting until just after the first day of the next year, a taxpayer can defer the tax on the gain for an entire year.

Net Capital Gain. Net capital gains are taxed at the same rate as other income of the taxpayer, subject to a maximum rate of 28 percent.

Net Capital Loss. Can a taxpayer reduce taxes by selling stock or other investments that have declined in value at a loss? In other words, can a taxpayer deduct such losses from other income, such as salary income, and thereby reduce the tax on the other income? When a taxpayer's transactions involving capital assets for a year result in a *net* capital loss, the amount of the loss that may be deducted from other income is limited. Capital losses can be offset against capital gains. Other income, however, can only be reduced by a maximum of $3,000 in any one year. Any excess *net* capital loss over the $3,000 must be carried forward to be deducted in future years.

Credit Against the Tax Liability

Tax credits are subtractions from the computed tax liability and should not be confused with deductions that are subtracted from income to determine taxable income. Since tax credits reduce tax liability dollar for dollar, they are more beneficial to taxpayers than equal dollar amounts of deductions from gross income. Tax credits are allowed to the elderly, for dependent care expenses, for income taxes paid in foreign countries, and for jobs provided to members of certain groups.

Withholding and Estimated Tax

For most individuals the tax year ends on December 31, and their return is due three and one-half months later, on April 15. If they are wage earners or salaried employees, their employer is required to withhold an estimated income tax from their pay during the year and remit it to the Internal Revenue Service. The employer reports this withholding to the employee on form W-2 on or before

2. The Internal Revenue Service provides tax tables in which the tax liabilities for specific taxable incomes for taxpayers in each filing status are calculated for taxpayers' convenience.

January 31 for the preceding year (see the chapter on current liabilities for a discussion of payroll procedures). Taxpayers who have income beyond a certain amount that is not subject to withholding must report a Declaration of Estimated Tax and pay an **estimated tax**, less any amount expected to be withheld, in four installments during the year. When taxpayers prepare their tax returns, they deduct the amount of estimated tax withheld and the amount paid in installments from the total tax liability to find the amount they must pay when they file the tax return.

Questions

1. What is the difference between tax planning and tax evasion?
2. What are the four classes of taxpayers?
3. J. Vickery's sole proprietorship had a net income of $37,500 during the taxable year. During the same year, Vickery withdrew $24,000 from the business. What income must Vickery report on his individual tax return?
4. Which of the two methods of accounting, cash or accrual, is more commonly used by individual taxpayers?
5. Why is it sometimes claimed that corporate income is subject to double taxation?
6. If a friend of yours turned down the opportunity to earn an additional $500 of taxable income because it would put him or her in a higher tax bracket, would you consider this action rational? Why?

Classroom Exercise

Exercise H-1. Computation of Tax Liability
(L.O. 2)

From Exhibit 1, figure the 1993 income tax for each of the following: (1) single individual with taxable income of $30,000, (2) single individual with taxable income of $59,000, (3) married couple filing jointly with taxable income of $11,250, (4) married couple filing jointly with taxable income of $59,000. Assume that the income tax is computed on these numbers.

Index of Company Names

Note: Boldface type denotes real companies.

Able Company, 1055, 1056(exh.), 1057, 1058(exh.)
Adcock, Villa, Davis & Company, Ap-38–Ap-39, Ap-40–Ap-45, Ap-46–Ap-51, Ap-46(exh.)
Albuquerque Resort, 801(exh.)
American Airlines, 26
American Express, 317, 318
American Greetings Corp., 92
American Transtech, Inc., 882–883
Amoco Corporation, 353–354
AMR Corporation, 26
Amre, Inc., 400–401
Arthur Andersen & Co., 27(table)
AT&T, 882

Baker Company, 1055, 1056(exh.), 1057, 1058(exh.)
Banyon Industries, 712–713
Bava Gardening Supplies, 935, 936(exh.)
Bell Atlantic Company, 306–307
Bell System, 882
Beta Alpha Psi, Ap-90, Ap-91(exh.)
Block Corporation, Ap-67–Ap-68
Boeing Company, 46
Boyce-Gordon Company, 964, 965
Boyer Company, 847–857, 849(fig.), 851(fig.), 853(fig.), 857(exh.), 858–860, 859(fig.)
Bradley Corporation, 478–482
Broad Street Dry Goods Store, 597–598, 598(exh.)

Caesars World, Inc., 92
Cane Company, 1055, 1056(exh.), 1057, 1058(exh.)
Caprock Corporation, 502–504, 505, 506–508, 509, 511
Cardinal Industries, Inc., 815
Carey Construction Company, 630–631
Carte Blanche, 318
Caterpillar, Inc., 26, 588–589
Childware Corporation, Ap-23–Ap-24
Chona Corporation, 435
Christensen Enterprises, 931, 932(exh.)
Chrysler Corporation, 512
Clifford Company, 926, 927(exh.)
Consolidated Edison, 26
Coopers & Lybrand, 27(table)
Cottage Sales Company, 310
Creative Pulp Company, 895–900, 896(fig.), 898(exh.), 899(exh.)

DataLife Corporation, 921
Dayton-Hudson Corporation, 166
Deloitte & Touche, 27(table)
Delta Airlines, 441
Department of Defense, Ap-92–Ap-93
Diners Club, 318
Dun & Bradstreet, 225, 1152, 1156

Eastman Kodak Company, 92, 512, 1153–1154, 1155(exh.), 1159, 1160, 1161(exh.), 1161–1174, 1162(exh.), 1163(fig.), 1164(fig.), 1165(exh.), 1166(exh.)
Ernst & Young, 27(table)
Evelio Corporation, 638–640, 639(fig.)

Fenwick Fashions Company, 168, 170–171, 171(exh.), 180, 181(exh.), 182–183, 183(exh.), 184(exh.), 185–188, 186(exh.), 187(exh.)
Fine Arts Gallery and Framing, 249–250
Fireman's Fund Insurance Company, 919–920
Fleetwood Credit Corporation, 317
Fleetwood Enterprises, Inc., 92, 317
Ford Motor Company, 26, 317, 888, 1150
Ford Motor Credit Company (FMCC), 317
Forest Highlands Company, 1048
Fuentes Company, 733–735

The Gap, Inc., 208
Gardnel Industries, Inc., 924(exh.), 924–926, 925(exh.)
General Electric, 26
General Foods, 26
General Motors Acceptance Corporation (GMAC), 317, Ap-69
General Motors Corporation, 15, 26, 317, Ap-69
Gerber Products Company, 2
Goodyear Tire & Rubber Company, 568
Grand Rapids Spring & Wire Company (GRS&W), 992–993
Grant Thornton, 27(table)
Hassel Company, 312
Hazelkorn Industries, Inc., 673–675, 674(exh.), 678–679, 680
Henderson Supply Company, 274
Hewlett-Packard, 838–839
H.J. Heinz Company, 386
Hood Enterprises, 928–930
Howard Products, Inc., 602
Hugh Corporation, 932–934, 933(exh.), 934(exh.)
Humana Inc., 442–443

International Business Machines Corporation (IBM), 26, 500–501, 568
International Telephone and Telegraph, 26
Isaacs Company, 566–567

Janis Corporation, 440
J.C. Penney, 318, 764
Jeff & Knoll Landscapers, 935
Jens-Lena Manufacturing Company, 727–728, 729(exh.), 730–733, 731(exh.)
Joan Miller Advertising Agency, 56–61, 62(exh.), 63(exh.), 63–64, 66, 67(exh.), 93–94, 94(exh.), 95–102, 99(exh.), 103(exh.), 104(exh.), 130–144, 133(exh.), 134(exh.), 135(exh.), 137–139(exh.), 141–143(exh.), mylar insert (Exh. 4-1–4-5)
Jones Company, 56
Jones Florist Company, 13
Jones Piano Company, 806, 808(exh.), 808–809, 810(exh.), 811(exh.), 813, 814(exh.), 815, 816–819, 818(exh.)
Junction Corporation, 514(exh.), 515, 519–520

Kalmar Corporation, 648–651, 651(exh.)
Karlsson Clothing, Inc., 718–727, 719(exh.), 720(exh.), 723(exh.), 725(exh.), 726(exh.)
Keller Products, Inc., 645, 646(fig.), 646–648, 884–885
Kennecott Copper, 26
Ken's Auto Pampering, 892
Keys Metal Products Company, 968, 969(exh.)
Kids "R" Us, Ap-1

Kings Beach National Bank, 596–597, 597(exh.)
Kmart, 354, 888
Kohlberg Kravis Roberts & Co., 544
Konert Electronics Company, 928, 929(exh.)
KPMG Peat Marwick, 27(table)

Lesley Corporation, 1014–1017
Lord Corporation, 798–799
Lorimar, 92

Maas Company, 435
Maintenance Management Company, 129–130
Maison & Jardin, 883–884
Marriott Corporation, 313–314, 1098–1099, 1099(fig.)
Marsh Tire Company, 100
Martin Industries, Inc., 754–755
Martin Maintenance Company, 274, 277, 329–330, 330(exh.)
MasterCard, 317, 318
Mattel, Inc., 92
Mercedes-Benz, 888
Merit Company, 1008(exh.)
MGC Corporation, 403
MGM/UA Communications Co., 92
Minnesota Mining and Manufacturing, 26
Mitchell's Used Car Sales, 259(exh.), 268
Mobay Chemical Corp., 644–645
Moody's Investors Service, 1150–1151
Myer Company, 313(exh.), 313–317, 314(exh.)

National Realty, 331–332
Neiman-Marcus, 593, 888
Never Flake Company, 89
NMA Industries, Inc., 844(exh.), 844–845, 845(exh.), 846(exh.)
Nordstrom, 436

O'Toole Corporation, 802

Parent Company, Ap-70–Ap-75, Ap-71(exh.), Ap-73(exh.), Ap-74(exh.), Ap-75(exh.)
Plains Implement Corporation, Ap-23
Polaroid Corp., 92, 512
Price Waterhouse, 27(table)

Rathman Sporting Goods, Inc., 928–930, 930(exh.)
RJR Nabisco, 544–545
Ryan Corporation, 1103(exh.), 1103–1104, 1104(exh.), 1106–1107, 1108, 1109–1110, 1110(exh.), 1112–1116, 1117(exh.), 1118(exh.), 1118–1119, 1120(exh.), 1121

Sears, Roebuck, 309, 317, 318, 354, 593, 764
Sears Roebuck Acceptance Corporation (SRAC), 317
Shafer Auto Parts Company, 218(exh.), 221, 222–224(exh.), 223–231
Shafer Vineyards, 883
Shannon Realty, 16–20, 22, 23(exh.), 24, 24(exh.), 52, 53, 54–55
Soda Bottling Company, 410
Sola Optical Company, 1044–1045
Southwestern Bell Telephone Co., 667–668
Speights Manufacturing Company, 595–596, 596(exh.)
State University Titans Alumni Club, 801(exh.)
ST Company, 308–309
Subsidiary Company, Ap-70–Ap-75, Ap-71(exh.), Ap-73(exh.), Ap-74(exh.), Ap-75(exh.)
Suchora Retail Centers, Inc., 760–761, 764–768, 766(exh.), 769(exh.), 770–771, 771(exh.), 772(exh.)
Surrency Industries, Inc., 842–843

Target Stores, 166
Texaco, 512
Texas Instruments, 1159
Time Warner, Inc., 466–467
Tom Johnson Company, 889–890, 891, 892, 893(fig.)
Toys "R" Us, Ap-1–Ap-11, Ap-2(fig.), Ap-4(fig.), Ap-5(fig.), Ap-7(fig.)
Tri-State Corporation, 509, 510(exh.), 511

UAL Corporation, 46
United Architects, Inc., 954–955, 972
United Church, Ap-93
Uppsala Company, 962
U.S. Steel, 1159
USAir Group Inc., 433
USX Corporation, 1159

Valencia Bank of Commerce, 640–642
Vason Corporation, 547, 548–549, 550, 551–552, 555, 559–560, 561, 562, Ap-24–Ap-25
Vassor Corporation, Ap-67–Ap-68
Vernon Manufacturing Company, 1065–1066(exh.), 1065–1067
VISA, 317, 318–319

Walt Disney Company, 92
Wasa Boat Company, 684–690, 686–687(exh.)
Windal Company, 1050–1051
Windham Company, 607(exh.), 609(exh.)

Subject Index

Note: Boldface type denotes key terms.

AAA, *see* American Accounting Association
ABC, *see* Activity-based costing
Absorption costing, 675
Accelerated Cost Recovery System (ACRS), 400
Accelerated methods, 393, 393–395, 396(fig.)
Access, to assets, limiting, 270
Account(s), 17, 48–53, 49(exh.). *See also specific accounts*
  adjusting, *see* Adjusting entries; Adjustment(s); Adjustments columns
  asset, 50–51
  balance of, *see* Balance(s)
  balance sheet, analyzing changes in, 1121–1124
  chart of, 49(exh.), 49–50
  after closing, 139–140, 141–142(exh.)
  contra, *see* Contra accounts
  contributed capital, 221
  controlling, 257, 258(exh.), 366
  expense, 53
  inventory, 603–606
  ledger account form and, 64
  liability, 51–52
  owner's equity, 52(fig.), 52–53
  permanent (real), 91
  revenue, 53
  temporary (nominal), 91
  T form of, 54–61, 62(exh.)
  titles of, 53
  uncollectible, *see* Allowance for Uncollectible Accounts account; Uncollectible accounts
  variance, *see* Variance; Variance analysis
Accountants' report, Ap-10, Ap-10–Ap-11, Ap-11(fig.)
  scope and opinion sections of, Ap-11
Account groups, Ap-82, Ap-82–Ap-83
Accounting, 3
  bookkeeping differentiated from, 4
  defined, 3(fig.), 204
Accounting cycle, 105
Accounting equation, 15
  assets and, 15
  effects of transactions on, 16–20
  financial position and, 15
  liabilities and, 15
  owner's equity and, 16, 16(fig.)
Accounting firms, 27, 27(table)
Accounting information. *See also* Financial statement(s); Report(s)
  conventions for interpretation of, 211–214
  decision making and, 4–5, 5(fig.), 6(fig.), 7–9
  disclosure of, *see* Disclosure
  objectives of, 209
  qualitative characteristics of, 210–211, 211(fig.)
  relevance of, 921–922
  types of, 590
  users of, 5, 6(fig.), 7–9, 591, 1100
Accounting period(s)
  apportioning expenses between, 95–99
  apportioning revenues between, 99–100
  disposing of end-of-period variance account balances and, 856
  merchandise inventory at end of, 178–179
  reversing entries and, 140, 143–144
Accounting period issue, 91, 91–92
Accounting practices
  changes in, 518–519
  international accounting standards and, Ap-60–Ap-62
  organizations affecting, 10–11
  quality of earnings and, 1158–1159
Accounting Principles Board (APB), 10
  on extraordinary items, 517–518
  on goodwill, 412–413
  on intangible assets, 409, 410
  on intercompany investments, Ap-64, Ap-73, Ap-74
  on interest imputation, Ap-21
  OPINIONS:
    No. 9, 399
    No. 15, 519
    No. 16, Ap-73n, Ap-74
    No. 17, 409, 412–413
    No. 18, Ap-64
    No. 20, 518n
    No. 21, 552n, Ap-21n
    No. 22, Ap-8
    No. 28, 1154n
    No. 29, 405n
    No. 30, 518n
  STATEMENTS:
    No. 4, 3n, 9n
    No. 86, 412n
Accounting rate-of-return method, 963
  capital investment performance estimation and, 963–964
Accounting standards
  international, Ap-60–Ap-62
  international comparability of, Ap-60–Ap-62
Accounting systems, 105, 105–106, 106(fig.), **250**, **269**. *See also* Job order cost accounting system; Process cost accounting system
  compatibility principle and, 251
  computerized, *see* Computer; Computerized data processing
  control principle and, 250
  cost-benefit principle and, 250
  flexibility principle and, 251
  mainframe, 253
  manual, *see* Manual data processing
  microcomputer, 253–255, 254(fig.)
  types of, 592
Account numbers, in cash receipts journal, 262
Accounts payable, 15, 435
  intercompany, Ap-75
Accounts Payable account, 17, 51
  in cash payments journal, 265, 266(exh.), 267
  in purchases journal, 259–260
Accounts payable subsidiary ledger, 257–258
Accounts receivable, 15, **309**, 309–319
  aging, 313
  credit balances in, 319
  credit card sales and, 318–319
  credit policies and, 310
  direct charge-off method for, 319
  financing, 317
  installment, 318
  intercompany, Ap-75
  uncollectible accounts and, *see* Uncollectible accounts
Accounts Receivable account, 50
  in cash receipts journal, 264
  collection of accounts and, 19
  credit balances in, 319
  in sales journal, 256–257
Accounts receivable aging method, 313, 313(exh.), 313–315, 315(exh.)
Accrual, 95
  of interest on installment notes payable, 563–565, 564(table)

Accrual *(continued)*
recognition of unrecorded expenses and, 100–102
recognition of unrecorded revenues and, 100
sale of bonds between interest dates and, 557–559, 560(fig.)
year-end, for bond interest expense, 559–561
Accrual accounting, 93, 93–94
adjusting accounts and, 94, 94(exh.)
modified accrual accounting compared with, sale of bonds between interest dates and, Ap-82, Ap-83–Ap-85
revenue and expense recognition and, 93–94
Accrual basis, Ap-98, Ap-98–Ap-99
Accrued expenses, 100, 100–102
Accrued liabilities, 437–438
Accrued revenues, 100
Accumulated depreciation, 98–99, 99(exh.)
cash flows and, 1123
Accumulated Depreciation account, 311n
ACRS, *see* Accelerated Cost Recovery System
Activity, 1048
Activity-based costing (ABC), 1046, 1046–1051
assigning costs using, 1047–1048
cost drivers and, 1046–1047, 1047(table)
illustrative example of, 1050–1051
process value analysis and, 1048, 1049(fig.), 1050
Additions, 402
Adjusted gross income, Ap-100
Adjusted gross income(s), deductions from, Ap-100(table), Ap-100–Ap-101
Adjusted trial balance, 102, 102, 103(exh.), 104(exh.)
Adjusted Trial Balance columns
adjusting entry method and, 180
closing entry method and, 185
entering and totalling balances as adjusted in, 131, mylar insert (Exh. 4-3)
extending balances to Income Statement columns or Balance Sheet columns from, 131–132, mylar insert (Exh. 4-4)
Adjusting entries, 95
adjusting entry method and, 182
closing entry method and, 185
for promissory notes, 325
recording, 133–134, 135(exh.)
Adjusting entry method, for merchandise inventory, 179, 180, 181(exh.), 182
Adjustment(s), 94–102
in accrual accounting, 94, 94(exh.)
apportioning expenses between accounting periods and, 95–99
apportioning revenues between accounting periods and, 99–100
entering and totalling in Adjustments columns, 131, mylar insert (Exh. 4-2)
preparing financial statements using adjusted trial balance and, 102, 103(exh.), 104(exh.)
prior period, 501
recognition of unrecorded expenses and, 100–102
recognition of unrecorded revenues and, 100
Adjustments columns
adjusting entry method and, 180
closing entry method and, 185
entering and totalling adjustments in, 131, mylar insert (Exh. 4-2)
Agency funds, Ap-86
Aging of accounts receivable, 313
AICPA, *see* American Institute of Certified Public Accountants
Akers, Michael D., 754n
Allowance for Bad Debts account, *see* Allowance for Uncollectible Accounts account
Allowance for depreciation, *see* Accumulated depreciation
Allowance for Uncollectible Accounts account, 310, 310–311
accounts receivable aging method and, 313(exh.), 313–315, 314(exh.)
difference between actual and estimated expense of, 316
direct charge-off method and, 319
percentage of net sales method and, 312–313, 315
recovery of written-off accounts and, 316–317
writing off uncollectible accounts and, 315–317
Allowance method, 310
uncollectible accounts and, 310–311
American Accounting Association (AAA), 11
American Institute of Certified Public Accountants (AICPA), 10, 10–11, 214
accounting defined by, 2–3
on accounting for inventories, 354
Accounting Research and Terminology Bulletin, 217n
Accounting Research Bulletin No. 43, 354n, 358n, 502n
Accounting Terminology Bulletin No. 1, 3n, 501n
Accounting Trends & Techniques, 307n, 396–397, 506n, 516n, 518n, 519n, 1106n
depreciation defined by, 390–391
OPINIONS: *No. 20*, 212n
on professional ethics, 26–27
Professional Standards, 269n, 270n, Ap-61n
on requirements for CPAs, 26
on retained earnings, 501
STATEMENTS: No. 1C, 26n
AMHS, *see* Automated material handling system
Amortization, 388
of bond discount, 550–554, 553(table), 554(fig.)
of bond premium, 555–557, 557(table), 558(fig.)
Analysis
cost analysis schedules and, 721–725, 732–733
cost-volume-profit, 642–644, 648–651
decision, 922–927
of financial statements, *see* Financial statement analysis
horizontal, 1160, 1161(exh.), 1162(exh.)
incremental, 926, 927(exh.)
of management, in annual report, Ap-10
process value, 1048, 1049(fig.), 1050
ratio, 1166
of sales mix, 930–932, 932(exh.), 933
of transactions, 55–61, 62(exh.)
trend, 1160–1162, 1163(exh.), 1163(fig.)
variance, 843–860
variance, *see* Variance analysis
vertical, 1162–1165, 1164(fig.), 1165(exh.), 1166(exh.)
Anders, George, 545n
Anderson, Henry R., 956n
Annual report, Ap-1, Ap-1–Ap-11
consolidated balance sheets in, Ap-3, Ap-5(fig.), Ap-6
consolidated statements of cash flows in, Ap-6, Ap-7(fig.), Ap-8
consolidated statements of earnings in, Ap-3, Ap-4(fig.)
consolidated statements of stockholders' equity in, Ap-6
financial highlights in, Ap-1–Ap-3, Ap-2(fig.)
as information source, 1154
letter to stockholders in, Ap-1
management's discussion and analysis in, Ap-10
notes to consolidated financial statements in, Ap-8–Ap-9
report of certified public accountants in, Ap-10–Ap-11, Ap-11(fig.)
report of management's responsibilities in, Ap-9–Ap-10
Annual Statement Studies, 1156
Annuity
future value of, Ap-16
present value of, Ap-19–Ap-20, Ap-20(table)
Annuity and life funds, Ap-86
APB, *See* Accounting Principles Board
Appraisal costs, 1052
Appropriation, Ap-92
Articles of incorporation, 467
Asset(s), 15
accounts of, 50–51
on balance sheet, 217, 219–220
book value of, *see* Book value
capital, Ap-102
corporate, distribution of, *see* Dividends
current, 217, 1121–1122

depreciable, disposal of, 403–408
exchange of, gain on, 407–408
fixed, *see* Long-term assets; Plant assets; Property, plant, and equipment
intangible, *see* Intangible assets
limiting access to, 270
liquid, *see* Short-term liquid assets
long-term, *see* Long-term assets; Plant assets; Property, plant, and equipment
of low unit cost, 399
net, 16
noncash, issuance of stock for, 480
operating, *see* Long-term assets; Plant assets; Property, plant, and equipment
other, 220
of partnership, ownership of, Ap-37
plant, *see* Plant assets; Property, plant, and equipment
preference as to, 476
purchase by incurring liabilities, 17–18
purchase with cash, 17
removing from partnership, Ap-50–Ap-51
return on, 227–229, 228(fig.), 229(fig.), 891–892, 1170
short-term liquid, *see* Short-term liquid assets
tangible, 387. *See also* Plant assets; Property, plant, and equipment
turnover of, 227–229, 228(fig.), 229(fig.)
valuation of, Ap-22
wasting, *see* Natural resources
Asset management reporting, in JIT/FMS environment, 1068–1069
Asset turnover, **227**, **1169**, 1169–1170
Atkinson, John Hawley, Jr., 1052n
At retail, defined, 368–369
Attest function, **27**. *See also* Auditing
Audit, **10**
postcompletion, capital expenditure decisions and, 960
Audit committee, **469**
Auditing, **27**
Auditors' report, **Ap-10**, Ap-10–Ap-11, Ap-11(fig.)
Authorization, internal control and, 269
Authorized stock, **472**, 472–473
Automated material handling system (AMHS), cost allocation and, 1013–1014
Automation, *see* JIT/FMS environment
Average costing approach, **730**
Average-cost method, **359**, 359–360
compared with other inventory valuation methods, 361–364
Average cost of capital, **961**
Average days' sales uncollected, **1168**
Avoidable costs, **932**

Bad debts, *see* Allowance for Uncollectible Accounts account; Uncollectible accounts
Balance, **55**
in balance defined and, 67
capital, Ap-40
Balance, compensating, 307
Balance
credit, in Accounts Receivable account, 319
deficit, 501
entering and totalling in Adjusted Trial Balance columns, 131, mylar insert (Exh. 4-3)
entering and totalling in Trial Balance columns, 131
extending from Adjusted Trial Balance columns to Income Statement columns or Balance Sheet columns, 131–132, mylar insert (Exh. 4-4)
normal, 66
trial, *see* Trial balance
Balance sheet, **22**, 22, 23(exh.)
adjusting entry method and, 180, 182
assets on, 217, 219(fig.), 219–220
classified, 216–221, 218(exh.)
combined, Ap-85
consolidated, Ap-3, Ap-5(fig.), Ap-6, Ap-70–Ap-75
disclosure of bonds on, 546–547
liabilities on, 220
owner's equity on, 220–221
relationship to other financial statements, 24
Balance sheet accounts, analyzing changes in, 1121–1124
Balance Sheet columns
closing entry method and, 185
extending account balances from Adjusted Trial Balance columns to, 131–132, mylar insert (Exh. 4-4)
totalling, 132, mylar insert (Exh. 4-5)
Bank accounts, 326–332. *See also* Bank reconciliation; Check(s)
bank statement and, 326, 328(fig.)
deposits to, 326, 327(fig.)
money market, 328
NOW, 328
Bank loans, 436
line of credit and, 436
Bank reconciliation, **326**, 326–332
illustration of, 329–330, 330(exh.)
recording transactions after, 330–331
steps in, 329
Bank statement, 275(table), **326**, 328(fig.). *See also* Bank reconciliation
Bar codes, 176, 176(fig.), 177
Barron's magazine, 1156
Barton, Thomas L., 882n
BASIC, 253
Batch processing, **253**
Beaver, William H., 1171n
Beginning inventory, **175**
equivalent production and, 718–721, 719(exh.), 720(exh.), 730, 731(exh.), 732
Bennett, Robert E., 1010, 1013n
Berliner, Callie, 1045n
Beta (β), **1174**
Betterments, **402**
Bill, 274, 275(table), 277(fig.)
Blecki, Thomas R., 798n
Blumenthal, Karen, 401n
Board of directors, 468–469
Bond(s), 544–562, **545**
amortizing discount on, 550–554, 553(table), 554(fig.)
amortizing premium on, 555–557, 557(table), 558(fig.)
balance sheet disclosure of, 546–547
callable, 561
conversion into common stock, 562
convertible, 562
coupon, 546
interest on, calculating, 550–551, 555
issue of, *see* Bond issue
junk, 544
registered, 546
retirement of, 561
sale between interest dates, 557–559, 560(fig.)
secured, 545–546
serial, 546
term, 546
unsecured, 545–546
valuing, 549–550
year-end accrual for interest expense and, 559–561
zero coupon, 551
Bond certificate, **545**
Bond indenture, **545**
Bonding, **270**
Bond issue
costs of, 549
at discount, 548
at face value, 547
interest rate and, 547
at premium, 548–549
Bonds payable, cash flows and, 1114–1115, 1123–1124
Bonds Payable account, 546–550. *See also* Bond issue
balance sheet disclosure of bonds and, 546–547
Bonus, to partners, Ap-47–Ap-49
Bookkeeping, **4**
accounting differentiated from, 4
Book of original entry, *see* Journal(s)
Book value, 388, **511**, 511–512, **963**
capital budgeting and, 963
purchase at more or less than, Ap-72–Ap-74, Ap-74(exh.)
purchase of less than 100 percent at, Ap-72, Ap-73(exh.)
purchase of 100 percent at, Ap-71(exh.), Ap-71–Ap-72
Brand names, 411(table)
Breakeven analysis, 644–645
Breakeven point, 642, **644**, 644–645
Breakeven units, 647
Brimson, James, 1045

Briner, Russell F., 754n
Brokers, as users of accounting information, 8
Budget(s), **799**, 799–800, 801(exh.)
  cash, *see* Cash budget
  flexible, 843–845, **844**, 844–845(exh.)
  master, *see* Master budget
  period, *see* Period budgets
Budgetary control system, 630
Budgeting, 798–819. *See also* Budget(s); Cash budget; Master budget; Period budgets
  basic principles of, 802–805, 803(table)
  capital, 956, 962–963
  need for budgetary control and, 800, 802
  in not-for-profit organizations, Ap-87–Ap-90, Ap-90(table), Ap-91(exh.)
Buildings. *See also* Plant assets; Property, plant, and equipment
  acquisition cost of, 390
Buildings account, 51
Business income. *See also* Income
  measurement of, 90–93
Business organizations. *See also* Corporation(s); Management; Manufacturing operations; Merchandising operations; Partnership(s); Service operations; Sole proprietorship
  forms of, 13–15, 14(table)
  as separate entities, 13
Business periodicals
  as information source, 1156
  as users of accounting information, 8
Business transactions, 12
  analysis of, 55–61, 62(exh.)
  categories of, 255
  double-entry system and, 55–61, 62(exh.)
  effect on accounting equation, 16–20
  in foreign currencies, Ap-57–Ap-59
  as object of measurement, 12–13
  recording, 62–66, 269
  recording after bank reconciliation, 330–331

CAD/CAM, *see* Computer-aided design/computer-aided manufacturing
Callable bonds, 561
Callable preferred stock, 477
Call price, 477
Calvasina, Eugene J., 838n
Calvasina, Gerald E., 838n
Calvasina, Richard V., 838n
Canceled checks, 326
Capacity
  excess, 633
  under JIT operating environment, 1010
  normal, 633
  operating, 632–633
  practical, 633
  theoretical (ideal), 633, 1010
Capital. *See also* Owner's equity; Stockholders' equity
  contributed, 221, 472. *See also* Stock
  cost of, 961
  generation of, by corporations, 469
  legal, 473
  of partners, interest on, Ap-39
  working, 225
Capital account, 52
  closing Income Summary account to, 138–139, 139(exh.)
  closing Withdrawals account to, 139, 139(exh.)
Capital assets, Ap-102
Capital balance, Ap-40
Capital balance ratios, distribution of partnership income and losses and, Ap-40–Ap-42
Capital budgeting, **956**, 962–963
  cost and revenue measures used in, 962–963
Capital expenditure(s), **401**, 401–402
Capital expenditure decision(s), 954–973, **955**
  accounting rate-of-return method and, 963–964
  capital budgeting and, 956, 962–963
  cash flow and payback period method and, 964–965
  decision cycle and, 956–960, 957(fig.), 958(fig.)
  desired rate of return and, 961–962
  in globally competitive business environment, 972–973
  net present value method and, 967–969, 969(exh.)
  ranking proposals and, 971–972
  tax effects on, 969–971
  time value of money and, 965–967
Capital expenditure decision analysis, **956**, 962–963
Capital expenditures budget, **809**, 809–810
Capital gains and losses, Ap-102
Capital lease, **566**, 566–567
Capital projects funds, Ap-82
Capital stock, *see* Stock
Capital Stock account, 478
Capital Stock Subscribed account, 481, 482
Capital structure, 520
Cardello, J. Patrick, 667n
Carrying value, **99**, 388. *See also* Book value
  remaining, 395
Cash, **307**, **1099**
  idle, investment of, Ap-23–Ap-24
  investment of, Ap-23–Ap-24
  purchase of assets with, 17
  received over the counter, control of, 272–273
  received through main, control of, 272
Cash account, 50
Cash basis, Ap-98
Cash basis of accounting, 93
Cash budget, 271, **815**, 815–819
  elements of, 816, 817(table)
  preparing, 816–819, 818(exh.)
Cash column
  in cash payments journal, 265
  in cash receipts journal, 262
Cash disbursements, control of, 273–275, 274(fig.), 275(table), 276–278(fig.), 277–278
Cash disbursements journal, *see* Cash payments journal
Cash Dividends Declared account, 474, 503
Cash equivalents, **307**, **1099**, 1099–1100
Cash flow(s). *See also* Statement of cash flows
  capital budgeting and, 962–963
  payback period method and, 964–965
Cash flow forecast, **815**. *See also* Cash budget
Cash payments journal, **265**, 265, 266(exh.), 267
  credit columns of, 265, 266(exh.)
  debit columns of, 265, 266(exh.), 267
  posting, 266(exh.), 267
Cash receipts, control of, 272–273
Cash receipts journal, **261**, 261–262, 263(exh.), 264–265
  credit columns of, 263(exh.), 264
  debit columns of, 262, 263(exh.)
  posting of, 263(exh.), 264–265
Cash Short or Over account, 273
Castellano, Joseph F., 992n
Centralization, corporations and, 470
Certified internal auditor (CIA), 28
Certified management accountant (CMA), **26**, 28
Certified public accountants (CPAs), 9–10
  employment of, 27(table), 27–28
  professional ethics and, 26–27
  report of, Ap-10–Ap-11, Ap-11(fig.)
  requirements for, 26
Chart of accounts, **49**, 49(exh.), 49–50
Check(s), **275**, 275(table), 277, 278(fig.)
  canceled, 326
  nonsufficient funds, 327–328
  outstanding, 327
Check authorization, **275**, 275(table), 277(fig.)
CIA, *see* Certified internal auditor
CIM, *see* Computer-integrated manufacturing system
Classification issue, 48
Classified financial statements, **216**, 216–221, 218(exh.)
Closing, accounts after, 139–140, 141–142(exh.)
Closing entries, 105–106, 136–140
  accounts after closing and, 139–140, 141–142(exh.)
  adjusting entry method and, 182, 183(exh.)

closing entry method and, 185–188, 186(exh.)
closing Income Statement accounts to Income Summary account and, 136–138, 137(exh.), 138(exh.)
closing Income Summary account to Capital account and, 138–139, 139(exh.)
closing Withdrawals account to Capital account and, 139, 139(exh.)
post-closing trial balance and, 140, 143(exh.)
recording, 135–136
Closing entry method, 179, 183, 184(exh.), 185–188
CMA, *see* Certified management accountant
CNC, *see* Computer numerically controlled machines
COBOL, 253
Colleges, Ap-86
Combined balance sheet, Ap-85
Combined statement of changes in financial position, Ap-85
Combined statement of revenues, expenditures, and changes in fund balances—all governmental funds, Ap-85
Combined statement of revenues, expenditures, and changes in fund balances—budget and actual—general and special revenue funds, Ap-85
Combined statement of revenues, expenditures, and changes in retained earnings (or equity), Ap-85
Commas, in financial reports, 68
Commercial paper, 436
Common costs, 733, 733–735, 734(fig.)
Common-size statement, 1163, 1163–1165, 1164(fig.), 1165(exh.), 1166(exh.)
Common stock, **473**
cash flows and, 1115, 1124
conversion of bonds into, 562
earnings per share of, 1171
Common Stock Distributable account, 503–504
Common stock equivalents, 520
Comparability convention, 211, 212
Compatibility principle, 251
Compensating balance, 307
Competence, management accounting and, 611
Complex capital structure, 520
Compound entry, 64
Compound interest, Ap-14, Ap-15. *See also* Future value; Present value
time periods and, Ap-20–Ap-21
Comprehensive income, 513
Computer, 4
Computer-aided design (CAD), 1054
Computer-aided design/computer-aided manufacturing (CAD/CAM), cost allocation and, 1012
Computer-integrated manufacturing (CIM) system, 1002
Computer integration, 1010
Computerized data processing, 251–255
batch, 253
computer system and, 251–253, 252(fig.)
mainframe accounting systems and, 253
microcomputer accounting systems and, 253–255, 254(fig.)
on-line, 253
Computer languages, 253
Computer numerically controlled (CNC) machines, 1002
cost allocation and, 1011–1012
Computer operator, 253
Condensed financial statements, 223, 223(exh.), 224(exh.)
Confidentiality, management accounting and, 611–612
Conformance, costs of, 1052
Conglomerates, 1153
Conservatism, 212, 212–213
Consignee, 357
Consignment, 357, 357–358
Consignor, 357
Consistency convention, 212
Consolidated financial statements, Ap-68
in annual report, Ap-3, Ap-4(fig.), Ap-5(fig.), Ap-6, Ap-7(fig.), Ap-8
notes to, Ap-8–Ap-9
Consulting, 28
Contingent liabilities, 324, 442, 442–443
Continuity issue, 92
Contra accounts, 98
Accumulated Depreciation account as, 98–99, 99(exh.), 311n
Allowance for Uncollectible Accounts account as, 311
Purchases Discounts account as, 172
Purchases Returns and Allowances account as, 172
Sales Discount account as, 170
Contributed capital, 221, 472. *See also* Stock
Contribution margin, 645, 645–657
reporting format and, 925(exh.), 925–926
Control, 5, 64. *See also* Internal control
budgetary, *see* Budget(s); Budgeting
of costs, *see* variance analysis
intercompany investments and, 64–68
operating, in JIT/FMS environment, 1059–1063
Control environment, 269
Controllable costs, 758
Controllable overhead variance, 852
Controller, 25
Controlling accounts, 257, 258(exh.)
Merchandise Inventory account as, 366
Control principle, 250
Control procedures, 269, 269–270
Conversion costs, 718
Convertible bonds, 562
Convertible preferred stock, 476, 476–477
Cooper, Robin, 1046n
Copyrights, 411(table)
Corporate charter, 467
Corporation(s), 14, 14(table), 14–15, 466–483. *See also* Management; Retained earnings; Stock
advantages of, 469–470
disadvantages of, 470–471
financial statements of, *see* Financial statement(s); Financial statement analysis; *specific statements*
formation of, 467
income taxes of, *see* Income taxes
multinational, Ap-55. *See also* International accounting
organization costs of, 471
organization of, 468(fig.), 468–469
owner's equity of, 221
owner's equity of, sse Stockholders' equity
transnational, Ap-55. *See also* International accounting
Cost(s), 48. *See also* Expense(s)
of acquiring plant assets, 389–390
appraisal, 1052
avoidable, 932
of bond issue, 549
breakeven analysis and, 644–645
of capital, 961–962
classifying under JIT operating environment, 1003–1004, 1004(table)
of computer software, 412
of conformance, 1052
controllable, 758
control of, *see* Variance analysis
conversion, 718
depreciable, 391
depreciation and, 391
direct, 600–601, 668
of doing business, *see* Expense(s)
expired, 91
external failure, 1052
fixed, 631, 632(table), 635–636, 637(fig.), 932
high-low method of separating, 638–640, 639(fig.)
historical, 48, 309
indirect, 600, 601, 602, 668
internal failure, 1052
of inventory, defined, 358
joint, 733–735, 734(fig.), 935
of labor, 601
manufacturing, 600–602, 610, 648–649
marginal, pricing and, 885, 886(fig.), 887
of materials, 600–601
mixed, 636–639
in new manufacturing environment, 1002–1007
of nonconformance, 1052
organization, 471
overhead, 602
period, 608

Cost(s) *(continued)*
prevention, 1052
pricing inventory at, 358–364
product, 608
of quality, 1052
of research and development, 410, 412
selling, 650
semivariable, 632(table), 636–640, 638(fig.)
standard, *see* Standard costs
total, pricing and, 885, 886(fig.)
unit, 602, 690
variable, 631–635, 632(table)
Cost Accounting Standards Board, Cost Accounting Standard 402, 668n
Cost allocation, 668, 668–690. *See also* Job order cost accounting system; Process cost accounting system
absorption costing and, 675
activity-based costing and, 1047–1048
under JIT operating environment, 1004–1005, 1005(table)
manufacturing costs and, 669, 669(fig.)
predetermined overhead rates and, 676–680, 677(table)
reports and, 669–671, 670(table)
supporting service functions and, 671–675
Cost analysis schedules, 721–725
cost summary, 722, 732–733
illustrative analysis of, 722, 723(exh.), 724–725
unit, 721–722, 732
Cost assignment, *see* Cost allocation; Job order cost accounting system; Process cost accounting system
Cost-based pricing, 889–894
gross margin, 890
profit margin, 890–891
return on assets, 891–892
of services, 892–893
Cost behavior, 631, 631–642
fixed costs and, 632(table), 635–636, 637(fig.)
semivariable and mixed costs and, 632(table), 636–640
in service organizations, 640–642
variable costs and, 631–635, 632(table)
Cost-benefit convention, 213, 213–214
Cost-benefit principle, 250
Cost center, 668
Cost drivers, 1046, 1046–1047, 1047(exh.)
Cost/expense center, 758, 758–759
Cost flow, 358
job order costing and, 682, 683(fig.), 714, 715–716
manufacturing, 606, 606(fig.)
Costing. *See also* Activity-based costing; Job order cost accounting system; Process cost accounting system
automation and, 1010–1017
product, 924(exh.), 924–925
target, 894–895
variable, 922–926
Cost management, 1044–1069, **1045**
activity-based costing and, 1046–1048, 1049(fig.), 1050–1051
cost drivers and, 1046–1047, 1047t
full cost profit margin and, 1063–1067, 1065–1066(exh.)
JIT/FMS management reporting guidelines and, 1067–1069
performance measures for JIT/FMS operating control and, 1059–1063
quality and, 1051–1059
Cost method, Ap-65
intercompany investments and, Ap-65–Ap-67
Cost objective, 668
Cost of debt, 961
Cost of equity capital, 961
Cost of goods manufactured, 610
Cost of goods sold, 167, 170–177, 171(exh.)
income statement and, 610–611
merchandise inventory and, 175–177
net purchases and, 171–174
purchases discounts and, 172–173, 174–175
Cost of Goods Sold account, 175, 689, 690
perpetual inventory system and, 364–366
transfer of cost of units sold to, 855–856
Cost of preferred stock, 961
Cost of retained earnings, 961
Cost-plus transfer price, 897
Cost principle, 48
Costs of conformance, 1052
Costs of nonconformance, 1052
Costs of quality, 1052
Cost summary schedule, 722
Cost-volume-profit (C-V-P) analysis, 642, 642–644
applications of, 648–651, 651(exh.)
assumptions underlying, 651
basic, 642, 643(fig.)
use of, 642–644
Coupon bonds, 546
Crane, Michael, 919n
Credit, 54, 55–56. *See also* Accounts payable; Accounts payable account; Accounts receivable; Accounts receivable account
line of, 436
tax, Ap-102
trade, 309
Credit and advisory services, as information source, 1156
Credit balances, in Accounts Receivable account, 319
Credit card sales, 317, 318–319
Credit columns
of cash payments journal, 265, 266(exh.)
of cash receipts journal, 263(exh.), 264
of journal, 65, 65(exh.)
of ledger, 65, 65(exh.)
Credit memorandum, 328
Creditors, as users of accounting information, 7, 1100
Credit policies, 310
Credit sales, 50
Crossfooting, 264
Cumulative effect of an accounting change, 518, 518–519
Cumulative preferred stock, 475
Currencies
functional, Ap-60
reporting, Ap-60
Current assets, 217
analyzing changes in, 1121–1122
Current liabilities, 220, 433–449. *See also* Payroll accounting
analyzing changes in, 1121–1122
contingent, 442–443
definitely determinable, 435–439
estimated, 439–442
Current ratio, 225, 225–226, 226(fig.), **1167**
Customer acceptance measures, of quality, 1054–1055
Customer responsiveness reporting, in JIT/FMS environment, 1067–1068
C-V-P, *see* Cost-volume-profit analysis

Data processing, 250
computerized, *see* Computerized data processing
manual, *see* Manual data processing
Dates
of declaration, 474
interest, sale of bonds between, 557–559, 560(fig.)
maturity, 320
of payment, 474
of record, 474
Day, Kenneth, 630n
dBASE IV, 253
Death, of partner, Ap-51
Debit, 54, 55–56
Debit columns
of cash payments journal, 265, 266(exh.), 267
of cash receipts journal, 262, 263(exh.)
of journal, 65, 65(exh.)
of ledger, 65, 65(exh.)
Debit memorandum, 328
Debt(s), 51. *See also* Bond(s); Liabilities; Loan(s); Long-term liabilities
bad, *see* Allowance for Uncollectible Accounts account; Uncollectible accounts
cost of, 961
early extinguishment of, 561
long-term, current portions of, 438–439
Debt financing, 1170–1171
Debt service fund, Ap-82
Debt to equity ratio, 229, 229–230, 230(fig.), **1171**
Decentralization, 754
Decentralized organization, 895
Decimal points, in financial reports, 68

Decision(s), 927–935. *See also* Capital expenditure decision(s); Decision making; Pricing decision
  to eliminate unprofitable segments, 932–934, 933(exh.), 934(exh.)
  make-or-buy, 927–928, 929(exh.)
  sales mix analysis and, 930–932, 932(exh.)
  sell-or-process further, 934–935, 936(exh.)
  special order, 928–930, 930(exh.)
Decision making, 920–935
  decision models in management accounting and, 922, 923(fig.)
  incremental analysis and, 926, 927(exh.)
  management decision cycle and, 920(fig.), 920–921
  relevant information for management and, 921–922
  special decision reports and, 927
  strategic planning and, 921
  variable costing and, 922–926
Decision models, **922**, 923(fig.)
Decision parameters, **922**
Decision variables, **922**
Declining-balance method, **394**, 394–395, 396(fig.)
Deduction, standard, Ap-100
Deductions from gross income, **Ap-100**
Deferral, **95**
  of expenses, 95–99
  of revenues, 99–100, 439
Deferred Income Taxes account, **515**, 515–516
Deferred revenues, **439**
Deficit, **501**
Defined benefit plans, 567
Defined contribution plans, 567
Definitely determinable liabilities, **435**, 435–439
Delivery control measures, of quality, 1054
Delivery cycle time, **1060**
Delivery time, **1060**
Demand, changes in, cost-volume-profit analysis and, 650
Depletion, **408**, 408–409
Deposit(s), in transit, 327
Deposit ticket, 275(table), **326**, 327(fig.)
Depreciable cost, **391**
Depreciation, **97**, **387**, 390–401
  accelerated methods of computing, 393–395
  accumulated, 98–99, 99(exh.), 1123
  apportioning between accounting periods, 97–98
  of assets of low unit cost, 399
  capital budgeting and, 963
  comparison of methods for computing, 395, 396(fig.)
  cost recovery for tax purposes and, 400
  declining-balance method of computing, 394–395
  defined, 390–391
  disposal of assets and, 403–408
  double-declining-balance method of computing, 394
  factors affecting computation of, 391–392
  group, 399
  income taxes and, 400
  for partial years, 397–398, 403
  production method of computing, 393
  revision of rates for, 398–399
  straight-line method of computing, 392
  sum-of-the-years'-digits method of computing, 394
Dillion, Gadis J., 630n
Dilworth, James B., 994n
Direct charge-off method, **319**
Direct cost(s), **600**, 600–601, **668**
Direct costing, *see* Variable costing
Direct labor
  rate standards for, 841
  standard cost of, 841
  time standard for, 841
Direct labor costs, **601**
Direct labor efficiency variance, **850**
Direct labor rate standards, **841**
Direct labor rate variance, **850**
Direct labor time standard, **841**
Direct labor variances, 848–850, 851(fig.), 854–855
Direct materials, **600**, 600–601
  standard cost of, 840
Direct materials price standard, **840**
Direct materials price variance, **847**, 847–848
Direct materials quantity standard, **840**, 840–841
Direct materials quantity variance, **848**
Direct materials variances, 847–848, 849(fig.), 854
Direct method, **672**
  for cost allocation, 672–675, 673(exh.), 674(exh.)
  for schedule of cash flows from operations, 1109–1110, 1110(exh.)
Disclosure
  of bonds on balance sheet, 546–547
  confidentiality and, 611
  full, 213
  of liabilities, 434–435
Discontinued operations, **517**
Discount(s), **321**, **547**
  on bonds, 547, 548
  on promissory notes, 321–323, 324–325
  purchases, 172–173
  sales, 169–170
  trade, 169
Dishonored note, **323**
Disposal value, **391**
  capital budgeting and, 963
Dissolution, **Ap-45**
  of partnership, Ap-45–Ap-51
Diversified companies, **1153**
Dividends, 221, 468–469, **473**, 473–474
  cash receipts from, 1107
  liquidating, 473
  preference as to, 475–476
  stock, 502–504
Dividends in arrears, **475**
Dividends payable, 438
Dividends yield, **1173**
Documents, 269
  source, 254
Dollar signs ($), in financial reports, 68
Double-declining-balance method, **394**
Double-entry system, 53–61, **54**
  T accounts and, 54–55
  transaction analysis and, 55–61, 62(exh.)
Double taxation, **470**, **Ap-99**
Duality, principle of, 54
Due care, **27**
Dun & Bradstreet
  Industry Norms and Ratios, 225
  Key Business Ratios, 1152, 1156
Dun & Bradstreet Corporation, 1156
Duration of note, **321**

Early extinguishment of debt, **561**
Earned Capital account, *see* Retained Earnings account
Earnings. *See also* Income; Payroll accounting; Retained earnings; Revenue(s); Salaries; Wage(s)
  quality of, 1156, 1158–1159
  ratio of price to, 1172–1173
Earnings per share, 519–521, **1171**
Economic planners, as users of accounting information, 8
Economists, as users of accounting information, 8
Education, of accountants, 26, 28
Edwards, Donald E., 716n
Effective interest method, **552**
  amortization of bond discount using, 552–554, 553(table), 554(fig.)
  amortization of bond premium using, 556–557, 557(table), 558(fig.)
Effective rate, 551, **552**
Eliminations, **Ap-70**
Embezzlement. *See also* Internal control
  vulnerability to, 268–269, 273
Employee(s). *See also* Labor
  compensation of; Payroll accounting
  embezzlement by, 268–269, 273
  pilferage by, 177, 268–269, 271–272
Employee earnings record, **447**, 447–448
Employees
  for computer system, 253
  personnel procedures and, 270
Employee's Withholding Exemption Certificate (Form W-4), 445
Ending inventory, **175**
Endowment and annuity and life income funds, **Ap-86**
Endowment funds, **Ap-86**
Engineered time, **1011**

Enterprise funds, Ap-82
Environmental factors, capital expenditure decision cycle and, 957
Environmental Protection Agency (EPA), 8
Equipment, acquisition cost of, 390
Equipment account, 51
Equity, 15, **16**. *See also* Owner's equity; Statement of owner's equity
 of partners, Ap-38–Ap-39
 ratio of debt to, 229–230, 230(fig.), 1171
 residual, 473
 return on, 1170–1171
 stockholders', 471–477. *See also* Owner's equity; Statement of stockholders' equity; Stock
Equity capital, cost of, 961
Equity method, Ap-67
 intercompany investments and, Ap-67–Ap-68
Equivalent production, **717**, 717(fig.), 717–721
 with beginning work in process inventory, 720(exh.), 720–721, 730, 731(exh.), 732
 with no beginning work in process inventory, 718–719, 719(exh.), 730
 schedule of, 730–732
Equivalent units, **717**. *See also* Equivalent production
Erasures, 103
Errors, correcting, 103–105
Estimated liabilities, **439**, 439–442
Estimated tax, Ap-102
Estimated useful life, **391**, 391–392
Estimation
 inventory valuation by, 368–370
 of overhead rates, *see* Predetermined overhead rates
 of uncollectible accounts expense, 311–315
Ethics, **25**. *See also* Professional ethics
European Community, Ap-62
Evaluation, **5**. *See also* Performance evaluation
Exception, management by, 846
Excess capacity, 633
Exchange(s), of plant assets, 405–408
Exchange gain or loss, **Ap-57**, Ap-57–Ap-59
 realized versus unrealized, Ap-59
Exchange rate, **Ap-55**
Excise taxes payable, 438
Ex-dividend, 474
Expenditure(s), **401**, **Ap-83**. *See also* Payment(s)
 capital, **401**, 401–402. *See also* Capital expenditure decision(s)
 for operating expenses, 1108
 revenue, 401–402
Expense(s), **16**, **91**. *See also* **Cost(s)**
 accrued, 100–102
 apportioning between accounting periods, 95–99
 depreciation, *see* Depreciation
 effect on accounting equation, 19–20
 general and administrative, 178
 operating, 167, 177–178
 recognition of, 93–94, 100–102
 selling, 177–178
Expense accounts, 53
Expense center, 758–759
Expired costs, 91
External failure costs, 1052
Extraordinary items, **517**, 517–518
Extraordinary repairs, 402

FAA, *see* Federal Aviation Administration
Face interest rate, 547
Face value, bonds issued at, 547
Facility needs, capital expenditure decision cycle and, 957, 959
Factor, 317
Factoring, 317
Factory burden, *see* Overhead
Factory overhead, *see* Overhead
Factory overhead budget, **808**, 808–809, 811(exh.)
Factory Overhead Control account, 671, **678**, 678–679, 682, 685, 687–688, 689–690
Factory overhead costs, 602
Factory Payroll account, 686, 687–688
Failure, costs of, 1052
FASB, *see* Financial Accounting Standards Board
Federal Aviation Administration (FAA), 8
Federal Bureau of Investigation, 28
Federal Communications Commission, 28
Federal income taxes, *see* Income taxes
Federal Insurance Contributions Act (FICA), 444–445, 448
Federal Reserve Board, 8
Federal Unemployment Tax Act (FUTA), employer's liability for taxes under, 448
FEI, *see* Financial Executives Institute
FICA, *see* Federal Insurance Contributions Act
Fiduciary funds, Ap-82
FIFO, *see* First-in, first-out method
FIFO costing approach, 716
Financial accounting, 9, 12
 concepts of, 214–216, 215(fig.)
 management accounting compared with, 590–593, 591(table)
Financial Accounting Standards Board (FASB), **10**, 11, 214
 on consolidated financial statements, Ap-69
 on contingent liabilities, 442
 on cost-benefit convention, 213, 214
 on deferred income taxes, 515
 on disclosure of liabilities, 434–435
 in full disclosure, 213
 governmental accounting and, Ap-81
 on intercompany investments, Ap-65
 INTERPRETATIONS, *No. 35*, Ap-64n
 on leases, 566
 on not-for-profit accounting, Ap-86
 on objectives of financial reporting, 209
 on organization costs, 471n
 Original Pronouncements as of July 1, 1977, 391n
 on pension expense, 568
 on postretirement benefits, 568
 on prior period adjustments, 501
 on qualitative characteristics of accounting information, 210
 on research and development costs, 412
 on short-term investments, 308
 STATEMENTS:
  No. 1, 3n, 4n, 93n, 209n, 210n, 1099n
  No. 2, 210n
  No. 5, 442n
  No. 6, 15n, 16n, 90n, 91n, 513n
  No. 12, 308, Ap-65n
  No. 13, 566
  No. 14, 1153, 1154
  No. 16, 501n
  No. 34, 389n
  No. 52, Ap-60
  No. 87, 568
  No. 94, Ap-69
  No. 95, 1099n
  No. 96, 515n
  No. 105, 434n
  No. 106, 568
  No. 107, 435n
Financial analysts and advisers, as users of accounting information, 8
Financial Executives Institute (FEI), 11
Financial information, *See* Accounting information; Financial statement(s); Report(s)
Financial instruments, 434–435
Financial position, 15
 assessment of, 1151
 forecast of, 811–812
Financial press, as user of accounting information, 8
Financial statement(s), **20**, 22–24, 23(exh.). *See also* Annual report; *specific statements*
 adjusted trial balance for preparation of, 102, 103(exh.), 104(exh.)
 common-size, 1163–1165, 1164(fig.), 1165(exh.), 1166(exh.)
 condensed, 223, 223(exh.), 224(exh.)
 consolidated, Ap-69–Ap-76
 ethics and, 216
 external, general-purpose, 209
 of foreign subsidiaries, restatement of, Ap-60
 fraudulent, 216
 frequency of, 593
 governmental, Ap-85
 interim, 129, 1154, Ap-9
 inventory valuation methods and, 358, 362, 363(fig.)

of manufacturing operations, 607(exh.), 607–611
objectivity of, 593
preparing from work sheet, 133, 133(exh.), 134(exh.)
presentation of, 68
relationships among, 24
uses of, 225–231
Financial statement analysis, 1150, 1150–1174
horizontal analysis and, 1160, 1161(exh.), 1162(exh.)
objectives of, 1151–1152
quality of earnings and, 1156, 1158–1159
ratios and, 1166–1174
sources of information for, 1154, 1156
standards for, 1152–1154
trend analysis and, 1160–1162, 1163(exh.), 1163(fig.)
vertical analysis and, 1162–1165, 1164(fig.), 1165(exh.), 1166(exh.)
Financial vice president, 25
Financing
of accounts receivable, 317
of corporations, 469
debt, 1170–1171
Financing activities, cash flows from, 1101, 1114–1116
Finished Goods Inventory account, 599, **605**, 605(fig.), 683, 689, 690
process cost accounting and, 726–727
transfer of completed units to, 855
First-in, first-out (FIFO) method, 360, 360–361
compared with other inventory valuation methods, 361–364
Fiscal year, 92
Fixed assets, 386. *See also* Long-term assets; Plant assets
Fixed costs, 631, 632(table), **635**, 635–636, 637(fig.)
traceable, 932
Flexibility, of special-purpose journals, 268
Flexibility principle, 251
Flexible budget, 843–845, **844**, 844–845(exh.)
Flexible budget formula, 844, 844–845
Flexible manufacturing system (FMS), 1000, 1001(fig.), 1002. *See also* JIT/FMS environment
cost allocation and, 1012–1013, 1013(table)
FOB destination, 173, 357
FOB shipping point, 173, 357
Folio column, *see* Posting reference column
Follow-up, budgeting and, 804
Footings, 55
Forbes magazine, 1156
Forecasting
of cash flow, *see* Cash budget
of financial position, 811–812
income statement and, 811
Form 8–K, 1156
Form 10–K, 1156
Form 10–Q, 1156
Formulas, 411(table)
Form W-2 (Wage and Tax Statement), 447–448
Form W-4 (Employee's Withholding Exemption Certificate), 445
FORTRAN, 253
Fortune magazine, 1156
Fox, Robert J., 882n
Franchises, 411(table)
Fraud, cash disbursements and, 273
Fraudulent financial reporting, 216
Freight in, 173, 173–174
Full cost profit margin, 1064
Full disclosure convention, 213
Fully diluted earnings per share, 520, 520–521
Function, 1048
Functional currency, Ap-60
Fund(s), Ap-82, Ap-87, Ap-88–Ap-89(table)
accumulation of, Ap-24–Ap-25
agency, Ap-86
annuity and life income, Ap-86
capital projects, Ap-82
debt service, Ap-82
endowment, Ap-86
endowment and annuity and life income, Ap-86
enterprise, Ap-82
fiduciary, Ap-82
general, Ap-82
governmental, Ap-82
internal service, Ap-82
loan, Ap-86
plant, Ap-86
plant replacement and expansion, Ap-86
restricted current, Ap-86
special revenue, Ap-82
specific purpose, Ap-86
trust and agency, Ap-82
unrestricted, Ap-86
unrestricted current, Ap-86
FUTA, *see* Federal Unemployment Tax Act
Future value, Ap-15
of ordinary annuity, Ap-7(table), Ap-16–Ap-17
of single invested sum at compound interest, Ap-15(table), Ap-15–Ap-16
tables of, Ap-29, Ap-30(table), Ap-31(table)

G&A, *see* General and administrative expense budget
GAAP, *see* Generally accepted accounting principles
Gains
capital, Ap-102
cash flow and, 970
exchange, Ap-57–Ap-59
on exchange of plant assets, 407–408
GASB, *see* Governmental Accounting Standards Board
General Accounting Office, 28
General and administrative expense(s), 178
General and administrative (G&A) expense budget, 809
General fixed assets account group, Ap-82
General fund, Ap-82
General journal, 63, 63(exh.), 63–64, 256, 267–268, 268(exh.)
General ledger, 49, 49(exh.), 49–50, **64**, 64–66. *See also* Ledger(s)
posting to, 64–66, 65(exh.)
General ledger software, 253, 253–254, 254(fig.)
General long-term debt group, Ap-83
Generally accepted accounting principles (GAAP), 9, 9–11
CPA's report and, 9–10
governmental accounting and, Ap-81
organizations influencing, 10–11
sources of, 214–215
General-purpose external financial statements, 209
Gentzel, Royce L., 815n
Gerstner, Louis, 545
Goethe, 54
Going concern, 92
Goods available for sale, 170
Goods flow, 358
Goodwill, 411(table), **412**, 412–413
Goodwill account, Ap-74
Gourley, Keith C., 798n
Government
regulation by, 470
as user of accounting information, 8–9
Governmental accounting, Ap-81–Ap-85
expenditure control and, Ap-92–Ap-93
financial reporting objectives and, Ap-81–Ap-83
financial reporting system and, Ap-85
modified accrual accounting and, Ap-82, Ap-83–Ap-85
Governmental Accounting Standards Board (GASB), 11, Ap-81
Concept Statement No. 1, Ap-82n
Governmental funds, Ap-82
Gross income, Ap-100
Gross margin from sales, 167
Gross margin pricing, 890
Gross method, 174
for purchases discounts, 171
Gross profit method, 369, 369–370
Gross sales, 168, 168–169
Group depreciation, 399
Group purchases, 390
Guarantees, estimated liability for, 440–441

Handbook of Dividend Achievers, 1156, 1157(fig.)
Hardware, 251, 251–252, 252(fig.)

Hendricks, James A., 1010, 1013n
High-low method, 639
  for separating costs, 638–640, 639(fig.)
Hirsch, James S., 512n
Historical costs, 48, 309
Hohner, Gregory, 1052n
Horizontal analysis, 1160, 1161(exh.), 1162(exh.)
Hospitals, Ap-86
Housekeeping, budgeting and, 804
Howell, Robert A., 1059n
Human responsibilities, budgeting and, 804
Hunter, Rex C., 716n
IASC, *see* International Accounting Standards Committee
ICC, *see* Interstate Commerce Commission

Ideal capacity, 633
IFAC, *see* International Federation of Accountants
IMA, *see* Institute of Management Accountants
Imprest system, 332
In balance, defined, 67
Income. *See also* Earnings; Payroll accounting; Revenue(s); Salaries
  adjusted gross, Ap-100
  comprehensive, 513
  gross, Ap-100
  interest, 328
  net, *see* Net income
  of partnership, distribution of, Ap-39–Ap-45
  of partnership, participation in, Ap-37
  retained, *see* Retained earnings
  taxable, Ap-98
Income from operations, 221
Income statement, 20, **22**, 23(exh.), 221, 222–224(exh.), 223, 513–521, 514(exh.)
  accounting changes and, 518–519
  consolidated, Ap-3, Ap-4(fig.), Ap-75(exh.), Ap-75–Ap-76
  cost of goods sold and, 610–611
  deferred income taxes on, 515–516
  discontinued operations and, 517
  earnings per share and, 519–521
  extraordinary items on, 517–518
  forecasted, 811
  income taxes expense on, 513–514, 515(table)
  for manufacturing operations, 610–611
  for merchandising operations, 166–168, 167(fig.), 187(exh.), 188
  multistep form of, 223, 223(exh.)
  net of taxes and, 516–517
  relationship to other financial statements, 24
  single-step form of, 223, 224(exh.)
Income Statement accounts, closing balances to Income Summary account from, 136–138, 137(exh.), 138(exh.)
Income Statement columns
  adjusting entry method and, 180, 182
  closing entry method and, 185
  extending account balances from Adjusted Trial Balance columns to, 131–132, mylar insert (Exh. 4-4)
  totalling, 132, mylar insert (Exh. 4-5)
Income Summary account, 136, 178–179
  closing balances from Income Statement accounts to, 136–138, 137(exh.), 138(exh.)
  closing to Capital account, 138–139, 139(exh.)
Income tax allocation, 515, 515–516
Income taxes
  capital expenditure decisions and, 969–971
  cash payments for, 1109
  cost recovery for, 400
  deferred, 515–516
  depreciation and, 400
  double taxation and, 470, Ap-99
  employer's liability for, 445, 446(fig.)
  estimated, 439
  income statement and, 513–517, 514(table)
  individual, *see* Individual income taxes
  inventory valuation methods and, 358, 362–364
  minimizing through planning, 971
  net of taxes and, 516–517
  tax tables and, 445, 446(fig.)
Incremental analysis, 926, 927(exh.)
Independence, 10, 27
Index number, 1162
Indirect costs, 600, 601, 602, **668**. *See also* Overhead
  allocation of, *see* Cost allocation
Indirect labor costs, 601
Indirect manufacturing costs, *see* Overhead
Indirect materials, 601
Indirect method, for schedule of cash flows from operations, 1110(exh.), 1110–1111
Individual income taxes, Ap-97–Ap-102
  capital gains and losses and, Ap-102
  cash basis and accrual basis and, Ap-98–Ap-99
  classifications of taxpayers and, Ap-99
  computing liability for, Ap-101, Ap-101(exh.)
  credits and, Ap-102
  deductions from adjusted gross income and, Ap-100(table), Ap-100–Ap-101
  deductions from gross income and, Ap-100
  employer's liability for, 445, 446(fig.)
  gross income and, Ap-100
  taxable income and accounting income and, Ap-98
  tax planning and tax evasion and, Ap-98
  tax tables and, 445, 446(fig.)
  withholding and estimated tax and, Ap-102
Industry norms, in financial statement analysis, 1153
Industry Norms and Ratios, 225
In-process measures, of quality, 1054
Installment accounts receivable, 318
Installment notes payable, 563, 563–565
Institute of Certified Management Accountants, 26
Institute of Management Accountants (IMA), 11, 26
  ethical standards of, 611
  management accounting defined by, 589
  STATEMENTS:
    No. 1A, 589n
    No. 1C, 611n
Intangible assets, 220, 388, 409–413, 411(table)
  computer software costs as, 412
  goodwill as, 412–413
  research and development costs as, 410, 412
Integrated programs, 254
Integrity, 27
  management accounting and, 612
Interactions, budgeting and, 804
Intercompany investments, Ap-64–Ap-76
  consolidated financial statements and, Ap-69–Ap-76
  controlling, Ap-68, Ap-69(table)
  influential but noncontrolling, Ap-67–Ap-68
  noninfluential and noncontrolling, Ap-65–Ap-67
Interest (expense), **321, Ap-14**. *See also* Future value; Present value
  on bonds, calculation of, 550–551, 555
  on bonds, year-end accrual for, 559–561
  cash payments for, 1109
  cash receipts from, 1107
  compound, Ap-14, Ap-15, Ap-20–Ap-21. *See also* Future value; Present value
  imputing on noninterest-bearing notes, Ap-21–Ap-22
  on installment notes, payment of, 563–565, 564(table)
  on partners' capital, Ap-39
  simple, Ap-14
  year for computation of, 321n
Interest (partner's)
  purchase of, Ap-46–Ap-47
  sale of, Ap-49–Ap-50
Interest coverage ratio, 1172
Interest income, 328
Interest rate
  on bonds, 547
  effective, 551, 552
  face, 547
  market, 547

Interim financial statements, 129, **1154**, **Ap-9**
Interim periods, 92
Internal control, 268–278, **269**
 of cash receipts, 272–273
 defined, 269–270
 limitations of, 270
 of purchases and cash disbursements, 273–275, 274(fig.), 275(table), 276–278(fig.), 277–278
Internal control structure, 269
Internal failure costs, 1052
Internal Revenue Code, 8, Ap-99
Internal Revenue Service (IRS), **11**, 28, 447–448, Ap-97. *See also* Income taxes; Individual income taxes; Internal Revenue Code
Internal service funds, Ap-82
International accounting, Ap-55–Ap-62
 international accounting standards and, Ap-60–Ap-62
 restatement of foreign subsidiary financial statements and, Ap-60
 transactions in foreign currencies and, Ap-57–Ap-59
International accounting standards, 11, Ap-60–Ap-62
International Accounting Standards Committee (IASC), 11, Ap-61
International Federation of Accountants (IFAC), 11, Ap-61
Interstate Commerce Commission (ICC), 8, 28
Inventory(ies), 353–370. *See also* Merchandise inventory; Merchandise Inventory account; Work in Process Inventory account
 accounts for, 603–606
 beginning, 175, 718–721, 719(exh.), 720(exh.), 730, 731(exh.), 732
 ending, 175
 income determination and, 354–357
 in JIT operating environment, 995
 losses from, 177
 physical, 177
Inventory control performance, in JIT/FMS environment, 1060–1061
Inventory cost, 358
Inventory measurement, 357–358
 merchandise in hand not included in inventory and, 357–358
 merchandise in transit and, 357
 perpetual inventory system and, 364–367
Inventory turnover, **1168**, 1168–1169
Inventory valuation
 average-cost method for, 359–360
 comparison of methods for, 361–364
 at cost, 358–364
 by estimation, 368–370
 first-in, first-out method for, 360–361
 last-in, first-out method for, 361
 lower-of-cost-or market rule and, 213, 367–368
 specific identification method for, 359
Investing activities, cash flows from, 1100–1101, 1111–1114
Investment(s)
 on balance sheet, 219
 cash flows and, 1122
 desired rate of return on, capital expenditure decisions and, 961–962
 of idle cash, Ap-23–Ap-24
 intercompany, *see* Intercompany investments
 owner's, 16
 in partnership, Ap-47
 short-term, 307
Investment center, **760**, 760–761
Investors, as users of accounting information, 7, 1100
Invoice, 274, 275(table), 277(fig.)
IRS, *see* Internal Revenue Service
Islands, in JIT operating environment, 995–996, 1000
Issued stock, 473
Item-by-item method, 367

JIT, *See* Just-in-time philosophy
JIT/FMS environment, 1010–1017
 automated material handling system and, 1013–1014
 computer-aided design/computer-aided manufacturing and, 1012
 computer numerically controlled machines and, 1011–1012
 flexible manufacturing system and, 1012–1013, 1013(table)
 management reporting guidelines for, 1067–1069
 performance measures for, 1059–1063
 product costing in, 1014–1017
Job order, 681
Job order cost accounting system, **680**, 680–690
 characteristics of, 680–681
 finished goods and, 683
 fully and partly completed products and, 690
 journal entries for, 683–690
 labor costs and, 681–682, 685–688
 materials costs and, 681, 684–685, 686–687(exh.)
 overhead costs and, 682, 688–690
 process cost accounting compared with, 713
 product unit costs and, 690
 Work in Process Inventory Control Account and, 383(exh.), 682, 683, 683(fig.), 684(fig.), 685, 687–689, 690
Job order cost cards, **682**, 684(fig.)
Joint costs, **733**, 733–735, 734(fig.), 935
 physical volume method and, 733–734
 relative sales value method and, 734–735
Jones, Lou, 588, 588n
Journal(s), 63
 correcting errors in, 103–105
 credit columns of, 65, 65(exh.)
 debit columns of, 65, 65(exh.)
 general, *see* General journal
 special-purpose, *see* Special-purpose journals
Journal entries, **63**, 105
 adjusting, *see* Adjusting entries
 closing, *see* Closing entries
 compound, 64
 for job order cost system, 683–690, 686–687(exh.)
 for process cost accounting, 725–727
 reversing, 140, 143–144
 for standard costs, 842–843
Journalizing, 62, **63**
Junk bonds, **544**
Just-in-time operating environment, **353**, 633, 992–1017. *See also* JIT/FMS environment
 impact on management accounting, 1009–1010
 implementing, 994–997
 macro versus micro approach and, 1009
 nonfinancial data and, 1009
 product cost in, 1002–1007
 Raw in Process Inventory account and, 1007, 1009
 theoretical capacity and, 1010
 traditional production versus, 997–1002
Just-in-time (JIT) philosophy, **993**, 993–994

Kaplan, Robert S., 1046n
Keown, Arthur J., 961n
Key Business Ratios, 1152, 1156
Keys, David E., 1010, 1013n
Klein, Donald J., 992n

Labor, 599
 direct, 601
 indirect, 601
 job order costing and, 681–682, 685–688
Labor budget, **807**, 807–808, 810(exh.)
Labor unions, as users of accounting information, 8
Land, acquisition cost of, 389
Land account, 51
Land improvements, acquisition cost of, 390
Last-in, first-out (LIFO) method, 361
 compared with other inventory valuation methods, 361–364
Lawyers, as users of accounting information, 8
LCM, *see* Lower-of-cost-or-market rule
Lease(s)
 capital, 566–567
 long-term, 565–567, 566(table)
 operating, 565

Leasehold(s), 411(table)
Leasehold improvements, 411(table)
Ledger(s), 49(exh.), 49–50
 correcting errors in, 103–105
 credit columns of, 65, 65(exh.)
 debit columns of, 65, 65(exh.)
 general, 49(exh.), 49–50, 64–66
 posting to, 65(exh.), 65–66, 256
 subsidiary, 256–258, 258(exh.)
Ledger account form, 64
Lee, John Y., 954n
Legal capital, 473
Leverage, 1170, 1170–1171
Liabilities, 15
 accounts of, 51–52
 accrued, 437–438
 on balance sheet, 220
 classification of, 434
 contingent, 324, 442–443
 current, *see* Current liabilities
 definitely determinable, 435–439
 disclosure of, 434–435
 estimated, 439–442
 long-term, *see* Bond(s); Long-term liabilities
 off-balance-sheet, 435
 payment of, 18
 payroll, 439
 product warranty, 440–441
 purchase of assets by incurring, 17–18
 recognition of, 434
 short-term, 51
 tax, Ap-101, Ap-101(exh.)
 vacation pay, 441–442
 valuation of, 434
Liability
 limited, of corporation, 469, 470
 unlimited, of partnerships, Ap-37
Licenses, 411(table)
Life
 of corporations, 470
 of long-term assets, 387
 of partnership, Ap-37
 useful, estimated, 391–392
LIFO, *see* Last-in, first-out method
LIFO liquidation, 364
Limited liability, of corporation, 469, 470
Limited life, Ap-37
Linear approximation, 635, 635(fig.)
Line of credit, 436
Liquid assets, short-term, *see* Short-term liquid assets
Liquidating dividends, 473
Liquidation, Ap-51
Liquidity, 7, 225
 evaluation of, 225–226, 1167–1169
Loan(s), 436
Loan funds, Ap-86
Lone, Pete, 955
Long-lived assets, *see* Property, plant, and equipment
Long-range goals, of budgeting, 802–803
Long-term assets, 386, 386–413
 accounting for, 388(fig.), 388–389
 acquisition cost of property, plant, and equipment and, 389–390
 depreciation of, *see* Depreciation
 life of, 387
 types of, 387–388
Long-term debt, current portions of, 438–439
Long-term leases, 565–567, 566(table)
Long-term liabilities, 52, **220**, 544–568. *See also* Bond(s)
 installment notes payable, 563–565
 leases, 565–567, 566(table)
 mortgages payable, 562–563, 563(table)
 other postretirement benefits, 568
 pensions, 567–568
Losses
 capital, Ap-102
 exchange, Ap-57–Ap-59
 on exchange of plant assets, 406–407
 from inventory, 177
 net, 16
 of partnership, distribution of, Ap-39–Ap-45
LOTUS 1-2-3, 253
Lower-of-cost-or-market (LCM) rule, 213, **367**, 367–368
 item-by-item method for, 367
 major category method for, 368
 total inventory method for, 368
LP column, *see* Posting Reference column

Machine management performance, in JIT/FMS environment, 1062
Machine setup, in JIT operating environment, 995
McIlhattan, Robert D., 1003n
McNair, Carol J., 712n
MACRS, *see* Modified Accelerated Cost Recovery System
McTague, Edward, 399n
Mainframe accounting systems, 253
Maintenance performance, in JIT/FMS environment, 1062, 1063(table)
Major category method, 368
Make-or-buy decision, 927, 927–928, 929(exh.)
Management, 7, 469, 470
 changing needs of, 590
 decision cycle of, 920(fig.), 920–921
Management, decision making by, *see* Capital expenditure decision(s); Decision(s); Decision making; Pricing decision
Management
 discussion and analysis of, in annual report, Ap-10
 information needs of, 593–595
 relevant information for, 921–922
 statement of responsibility of, Ap-9–Ap-10
 use of cost-volume-profit analysis by, 642–644
 as user of accounting information, 7, 1100
Management accounting, 9, 25, 25–26, **589**
 accounting systems for, 592
 defined, 589–590
 ethical standards for, 611–612
 financial accounting versus, 590–593, 591(table)
 focus of, 592
 frequency of reporting and, 593
 JIT and automation and, 1009–1010
 objectivity and, 593
 restrictive guidelines for, 592
 units of measurement for, 592
Management advisory services, 28
Management by exception, 846
Management information system (MIS), 4
Manual data processing, 255, 255(fig.), 255–268
Manufacturing cost(s)
 allocation of, 669, 669(fig.)
 changes in, cost-volume-profit analysis and, 648–649
 total, 610
Manufacturing cost flow, 606, 606(fig.)
Manufacturing operation
 Finished Goods Inventory account and, *see* Finished Goods inventory account
 job order costing and, *see* Job order cost accounting system
 process costing and, *see* Process cost accounting system
 statement of cost of goods manufactured and, **608**, 608–610, 609(exh.)
Manufacturing operations. *See also* JIT/FMS environment; Just-in-time operating environment; Work in Process Inventory account
 accounting information needed by, 593–594
 cost allocation and, *see* Cost allocation; Job order cost accounting system; Process cost accounting system
 cost elements and, 600–602
 cost of goods sold and, *see* Cost of goods sold; Cost of Goods Sold account
 financial statements for, 607(exh.), 607–611, 609(exh.)
 fixed, variable, and semivariable costs of, 632(table)
 inventory accounts for, 603–606
 Materials Inventory account and, 603, 603(fig.), 608, 682, 684–685, 686(exh.)
 merchandising operations compared with, 598–599, 599(fig.), 600(fig.)
 nonfinancial data needed by, 595–596, 596(exh.)
 product and period costs and, 608

Manufacturing overhead, *see* Overhead
Marginal cost, 885
pricing decision and, 885, 886(fig.), 887
Marginal revenue, 885
pricing decision and, 885, 886(fig.), 887
Market, 367
Marketable securities, 307
Market interest rate, 547
Market risk, 1172–1174, **1173**
Market test ratios, 1172–1174
Market transfer prices, 897
Market value, 367n, **512**
Martin, Howard, 644n
Martin, John D., 961n
Master budget, 805–815
detailed period budgets and, 806–811
financial position forecast and, 811–812
forecasted income statement and, 811
implementation of, 812
Matching rule, 93
uncollectible accounts and, 310–311
Material(s), 599
direct, 600–601. *See also* Direct materials variances
indirect, 601
job order costing and, 681, 684–685, 686–687(exh.)
Materiality, 212
Materials cost performance, in JIT/FMS environment, 1061–1062
Materials Inventory account, 603, 603(fig.), 608, 682, 684–685, 686(exh.)
Materials Inventory Control account, *see* Materials Inventory account
Materials purchase/usage budget, 807
Maturity date, 320
Maturity value, 321
Measurement, 12–13, 47–48
accounting period issue and, 91–92
of business income, 90–93
business transactions as object of, 12–13
classification issue and, 48
continuity issue and, 92
of inventory, *see* Inventory measurement
of liquidity, 225–226, 1167–1169
matching rule and, 93, 310–311
money measure and, 13
of net income, 1156, 1158–1159
of performance, using transfer prices, 899(exh.), 899–900
of profitability, 226–231, 1169–1171
of quality, *see* Quality
recognition issue and, 47–48
separate entity and, 13
units of, 592
valuation issue and, 48
Medicare taxes, liability for, 444–445, 448
Merchandise
on hand, not included in inventory, 357–358
in transit, 357
Merchandise inventory, 170, 354. *See also* Inventory(ies); Inventory measurement; Inventory valuation; Merchandise Inventory account
at end of accounting period, 178–179
losses from, 177
under periodic inventory system, 175–177
under perpetual inventory system, 175
Merchandise Inventory account, 175, 176
at end of accounting period, 178–179
perpetual inventory system and, 364, 365–366
Merchandising operations, 166–188. *See also* Inventory(ies); Merchandise inventory; Merchandise Inventory account
accounting information needed by, 594–595
cost of goods sold and, 170–177, 171(exh.)
fixed, variable, and semivariable costs of, 632(table)
income statement for, 166–168, 167(fig.), 187(exh.), 188
internal control and, *see* Internal control
manufacturing operations compared with, 598–599, 599(fig.), 600(fig.)
nonfinancial data needed by, 597–598, 598(exh.)
operating expenses of, 177–178
revenues from sales and, 168(exh.), 168–170
work sheet for, 180–188
Meyer, John, 919n
Microcomputer accounting systems, 253–255, 254(fig.)
MIS, *see* Management information system
Mixed costs, 636, 636–639
Modified Accelerated Cost Recovery System (MACRS), 400
Modified accrual accounting, Ap-82, Ap-83–Ap-85
Moellenberndt, Richard A., 667n
Money, time value of, 965–967, Ap-14–Ap-25. *See also* Future value; Present value
Money market accounts, 328
Money measure, 13
Moody's Investors Service, 1156
Mortgage(s), 562, 562–563, 563(table)
Multinational corporations, Ap-55. *See also* International accounting
Multiskilled work force, in JIT operating environment, 996
Multistep form, 223, 223(exh.)
Mundt, Barry, 1052n
Mutual agency, Ap-37
lack of, corporations and, 469–470

National Association of Accountants, *see* Institute of Management Accountants
National Council on Governmental Accounting (NCGA), Ap-81
National income accounting, 8
Natural resources, 387, 387–388, 408–409
depletion of, 408–409
depreciation of closely related plant assets and, 409
NCGA, *see* National Council on Governmental Accounting
Negotiated transfer price, 897
Net assets, 16
Net cash inflow, 963
Net income, 16, 16, **90**, 90–91
capital budgeting and, 962–963
evaluating, 1156, 1158–1159
Net loss, 16
Net method, 174
for purchases discounts, 174–175
Net of taxes, 516, 516–517
Net present value method, 967, 967–969, 969(exh.)
Net purchases, 171, 171–174
freight in and, 173–174
Purchases account and, 171
Purchases Discounts account and, 172–173
Purchases Returns and Allowances account and, 171–172
Net sales, 168, 312
Net worth, *see* Owner's equity
Nominal accounts, 91
Noncash assets, issuance of stock for, 480
Noncash expense, 963
Noncash investing and financing transactions, 1101, 1101–1102
Nonconformance, costs of, 1052
Noncumulative preferred stock, 475
Nonfinancial data, 595–598
under JIT operating environment, 1009
measurement of quality and, 1053–1055
Nonoperating items, quality of earnings and, 1159
Nonsufficient funds (NSF) checks, 327–328
Nonvalue-adding activity, 997
No-par stock, 478, 479–480
Normal balance, 66
Normal capacity, 633
Notes payable, 319, 436–437, 437(fig.)
Notes Payable account, 51
Notes receivable, 319, 319–325. *See also* Promissory notes
computations for, 320–323
Notes Receivable account, 50
Notes to the financial statements, Ap-8, Ap-8–Ap-9
Not-for-profit organizations, 8–9, Ap-85–Ap-87
budgeting in, Ap-87–Ap-90, Ap-90(table), Ap-91(exh.)
expenditure control in, Ap-92, Ap-93
Notice of protest, 325
NOW accounts, 328
NSF, *see* Nonsufficient funds checks

n/10, 169
n/30, 169

Objectivity, 27, 593
management accounting and, 612
Obsolescence, 391
Off-balance-sheet liabilities, 435
Office Supplies account, 51
On-line processing, 253
Operating activities, cash flows from, 1100, 1104–1111, 1105(fig.)
Operating assets, *see* Plant assets; Property, plant, and equipment
Operating capacity, 632, 632–633
Operating cycle, 217, 217(fig.)
Operating effectiveness reporting, in JIT/FMS environment, 1068
Operating expenses, 167, 177–178
cash payments for, 1108
Operating lease, 565
Operations
discontinued, 517
income from, 221
Opinion section, Ap-11
Ordinary annuity
future value of, Ap-16–Ap-17, Ap-17(table)
present value of, Ap-19–Ap-20, Ap-20(table)
Ordinary repairs, 402
Organization chart, responsibility accounting and, 755–756, 756(fig.)
Organization costs, 471
Ostrenga, Michael R., 1048n
Other Accounts column
in cash payments journal, 265, 267
in cash receipts journal, 262, 264
Other assets, 220
Other postretirement benefits, 568
Other revenues and expenses, 221, 223
Outstanding checks, 327
Outstanding stock, 473
Overapplied overhead, 679–680
Overhead, 599, 600, 602. *See also* Predetermined overhead rates
application of, 855
fixed, standard rate of, 841
job order costing and, 682, 688–690
standard cost of, 841
underapplied and overapplied, 679–680
Overhead efficiency variance, 857, **858**, 858–859
Overhead spending variance, 857, **858**
Overhead variance analysis, 857–860, 859(fig.)
Overhead variances, 850–854, 853(fig.)
Overhead volume variance, 852–853, **853**
Owner's equity, 16
accounts of, 52(fig.), 52–53
on balance sheet, 220–221
Ownership
of corporations, 469. *See also* Stock; Stockholders
of partnership property, Ap-37
separation from control, corporations and, 470–471
Owner's investments, 16
effect on accounting equation, 17
Owner's withdrawals, 16, 53, 139
effect on accounting equation, 20

Pacioli, Fra Luca, 54
Paid-in Capital, Treasury Stock account, 507–508
Paid-in Capital in Excess of Par Value account, 478–479, 503
cash flows and, 1124
Paid-in Capital in Excess of Stated Value account, 478
Parent company, Ap-68
consolidated financial statements and, Ap-69–Ap-76
Partners' equity, Ap-38, Ap-38–Ap-39
Partnership(s), 14, 14(table), Ap-36–Ap-51
accounting for partners' equity and, Ap-38–Ap-39
admission of new partner to, Ap-46–Ap-49
advantages and disadvantages of, Ap-38
characteristics of, 136–138
death of partner and, Ap-51
dissolution of, Ap-45–Ap-51
distribution of income and losses of, Ap-39–Ap-45
liquidation of, Ap-51
owner's equity of, 221
withdrawal of partner and, Ap-49–Ap-51, Ap-50(fig.)
Partnership agreement, Ap-36
Par value, 473, 477–478
Par value stock, 477–479
PASCAL, 253
Patents, 411(table)
Payback period method, 964, 964–965
Payment(s). *See also* Expenditure(s)
deferred, Ap-22–Ap-23
of income taxes, 1109
of interest, 563–565, 564(table), 1109
of liabilities, 18
of payroll and payroll taxes, 449
of principal of installment notes, 563–565, 564(table)
Payroll accounting, 443–449
computation of take-home pay and, 445–448
liabilities for employee compensation and, 443–444
liabilities for employee payroll withholdings and, 444–445
liabilities for employer payroll taxes and, 448–449
payment of payroll and payroll taxes and, 449
Payroll liabilities, 439
Payroll register, 446, 446–447, 447(exh.), 448(exh.)
Pension fund, 567
Pension plans, 567, 567–568
Percentage of net sales method, 312, 312–313, 315
Performance
measurement using transfer prices, 899(exh.), 899–900
measures of, for JIT/FMS environment, 1059–1063
past, in financial statement analysis, 1151, 1152–1153
Performance evaluation, 761, 761–771
behavioral principles of, 761–762
implementing system for, 763–771
operational principles of, 762–763
Period budgets, 802, 806–811
capital expenditures, 809–810
factory overhead, 808–809, 811(exh.)
general and administrative expense, 809
labor, 807–808, 810(exh.)
materials purchase/usage, 807
preparation of, 813, 814(exh.), 815
production, 806–807, 809(exh.)
relationships among, 810–811, 812(fig.)
sales, 806, 806(exh.)
selling cost, 806, 808(exh.)
Period costs, 608
Periodicals
as information source, 1156
as users of accounting information, 8
Periodic inventory system, 175, 176–177, **364**
Periodicity, 92
Perpetual inventory card, 366, 366(exh.)
Perpetual inventory system, 175, 364, 364–367
accounting records and, 364–366
maintaining records for, 366, 366(exh.)
physical inventories under, 366–367
Personnel, *see* Employees; Labor
Personnel procedures, internal control and, 270
P/E, *see* Price/earnings ratio
Peters, Tom, 1052
Petty, J. William, 961n
Petty cash fund, 332, 332–333
disbursements from, 332, 333(fig.)
establishing, 332
reimbursing, 332–333
Petty cash voucher, 332, 333(fig.)
Physical deterioration, 391
Physical inventory, 177
under perpetual inventory system, 366–367
Physical volume method, 733, 733–734
Pilferage, 177, 268–269, 271–272. *See also* Internal control
PL/1, 253
Planning, 5
Plant assets
acquisition cost of, 389–390
cash flows and, 1123
closely related to natural assets, depreciation of, 409
depreciation for partial year, 403

discarded, recording, 404
exchanges of, 405–408
sold for cash, 404–405
Plant funds, Ap-86
Plant replacement and expansion fund, Ap-86
Poe, C. Douglas, 630n
Portfolio, 1151
Post-closing trial balance, 141, 143(exh.)
Postcompletion audit, capital expenditure decisions and, 960
Posting, 62, **65**
of cash payments journal, 266(exh.), 267
of cash receipts journal, 263(exh.), 264–265
to general ledger, 64–66, 65(exh.), 256
Posting reference (Post. Ref.) column
in cash payments journal, 267
in cash receipts journal, 262, 264, 265
in general journal, 64
in general ledger, 64, 65, 66
in purchases journal, 260
Potential, assessment of, 1151–1152
Potentially dilutive securities, 520
Practical capacity, 633
Predetermined overhead rates, 676, 676–680, 677(table)
importance of good estimates for, 677
underapplied or overapplied overhead and, 679–680
using, 677–679
Preferred stock, 475, 475–477
cost of, 961
Premium, 547
on bonds, 547, 548–549
Prepaid expenses, 95
apportioning between accounting periods, 95–97
Prepaid Expenses account, 50–51
Prepaid Insurance account, 50–51
Present value, Ap-17, Ap-17–Ap-20
accumulation of funds and, Ap-24–Ap-25
asset valuation and, Ap-22
deferred payment and, Ap-22–Ap-23
imputing interest on noninterest-bearing notes and, Ap-21–Ap-22
investment of idle cash and, Ap-23–Ap-24
of ordinary annuity, Ap-19–Ap-20, Ap-20(table)
of single sum due in future, Ap-18, Ap-19(table)
tables of, Ap-29–Ap-30, Ap-32–Ap-35(table)
valuing bonds with, 549–550
President's Council of Economic Advisers, 8
Prevention costs, 1052
Preventive maintenance, in JIT operating environment, 996
Price
call, 477
changes in, cost-volume-profit analysis and, 650
Price/earnings (P/E) ratio, 1172, 1172–1173
Pricing, 882–900
cost-based, 889–894
target costing and, 894–895
transfer, 895–900, 899(exh.)
Pricing decision, 883–889
art of price setting and, 883–884
factors influencing, 887–888
pricing policy objectives and, 888–889
traditional economic pricing concepts and, 884–887
Primary earnings per share, 520
Principal, 545
of installment notes, payment of, 563–565, 564(table)
Principle of duality, 54
Prior period adjustments, 501
Proceeds, cash flow and, 970
Proceeds from discounting, 322, 322–323
Process(es), 411(table)
Process cost accounting system, 712, 712–735
average costing approach to, 730
cost analysis schedules and, 721–725
cost flow assumptions and, 715–716
cost summary schedule and, 732–733
equivalent production and, 717(fig.), 717–721, 730–732
under JIT operating environment, 1005–1007, 1008(exh.)
job order costing compared with, 713
joint costs and, 733–735, 734(fig.)
journal entries for, 725–727
production flow combinations and, 715, 715(fig.), 716(fig.)
unit cost analysis schedule and, 732
Work in Process Inventory accounts and, 714
Process value analysis (PVA), 1048, 1049(fig.), 1050
Product(s)
fully and partly completed, 690
quality of, *see* Quality
unit costs of, computing, 690
Product contribution reporting, in JIT/FMS environment, 1068
Product cost(s), 608
Product costing, 924(exh.), 924–925
Product delivery performance, in JIT/FMS environment, 1060
Product design, quality measures and, 1054
Production
pull-through, 995
push-through, 995
Production budget, 806, 806–807, 809(exh.)
Production cycle time, 1060
Production flow, 715, 715(fig.), 716(fig.)
Production method, 393, 395, 396(fig.)
Product line profitability reporting, in JIT/FMS environment, 1068
Product warranty liability, 440–441
Professional ethics, 25, 26–27
financial reporting and, 216
for management accounting, 611–612
Profit, 89. *See also* Cost-volume-profit analysis; Net income
gross, 167
gross profit method and, 369–370
planning, 647–648
Profitability, 7, 226
evaluation of, 226–231, 1169–1171
Profitability accounting, *see* Responsibility accounting
Profit area, 885
Profit center, 759, 759–760
Profit margin, 226, 226–227, **1169**
full cost, 1063–1067, 1065–1066(exh.)
Profit margin pricing, 890, 890–891
Program(s), 253
integrated, 254
Programmer, 253
Progressive tax, Ap-101
Promissory notes, 319, 319–325, 320(fig.)
adjusting entries for, 325
discounting, 321–323, 324–325
dishonored, 323
duration of, 321
imputing interest on, Ap-21–Ap-22
installment, 563–565
interest and interest rate on, 321
maker of, 319
maturity date of, 320
maturity value of, 321
non-interest-bearing, 321, Ap-21–Ap-22
payee of, 319
receipt of, 323
Property, plant, and equipment, 219. *See also* Plant assets
on balance sheet, 219–220
Property taxes payable, 440
Proportional tax, Ap-101n
Proprietorship, *see* Owner's equity; Sole proprietorship
Protest fee, 325
Proxy, 468
Public accounting, 26, 26–28
Pull-through production, 995
Purchase(s)
cash payments for, 1107
control of, 273–275, 274(fig.), 275(table), 276–278(fig.), 277–278
foreign, Ap-58
group, 390
of less than 100 percent at book value, Ap-72, Ap-73(exh.)
at more or less than book value, Ap-72–Ap-74, Ap-74(exh.)
net, *see* Net purchases
of 100 percent at book value, Ap-71(exh.), Ap-71–Ap-72
of partnership interest, Ap-46–Ap-47
of treasury stock, 506–507
Purchase method, Ap-70
Purchase order, 274, 275(table), 276(fig.)
Purchase order lead time, 1060

Purchase requisition, **274**, 275(table), 276(fig.)
Purchases account, 171
Purchases discounts, **172**, 172–173
 controlling using gross method, 171
 controlling using net method, 174–175
Purchases Discounts account, 172–173
Purchases Discounts column, in cash payments journal, 265
Purchases Discounts Lost account, 174–175
Purchases journal, **259**, 259–261, 261(exh.), 262(exh.)
 multicolumn, 260–261, 262(exh.)
Purchases Returns and Allowances account, 171–172
Push-through production, 995
PVA, *see* Process value analysis

Qualitative characteristics, **210**, 210–211, 211(fig.)
Quality, 1051–1059, **1052**
 cost-based measures of, 1052–1053, 1053(table)
 costs of, 1052
 illustrative problem in measuring, 1055–1059, 1056(exh.), 1058(exh.)
 in JIT operating environment, 996
 nonfinancial measures of, 1053–1055
 of services, measuring, 1059
 total quality management and, 1051–1052
Quick ratio, **1167**

Rate of return, desired, capital expenditure decisions and, 961–962
Ratio(s), 1166–1174
 asset turnover, 227, 1169–1170
 average days' sales uncollected, 1168
 capital balance, distribution of partnership income and losses and, Ap-40–Ap-42
 current, 225–226, 226(fig.), 1167
 debt to equity, 229–230, 230(fig.), 1171
 dividends yield, 1173
 earnings per share, 1171
 interest coverage, 1172
 inventory turnover, 1168–1169
 market risk, 1173–1174
 price/earnings, 1172–1173
 profit margin, 226–227, 1169
 quick, 1167
 receivable turnover, 1167–1168
 return on assets, 227–229, 228(fig.), 229(fig.), 1170
 return on equity, 230–231, 231(fig.), 1170–1171
 stated, distribution of partnership income and losses and, Ap-40, Ap-43–Ap-45, Ap-46(exh.)
Ratio analysis, **1166**
Raw in Process Inventory account, **1007**
 under JIT operating environment, 1007–1009
Raw materials, quality measures and, 1054
Raw Materials Inventory account, *see* Materials Inventory account
Real accounts, 91
Realizable value, 367n
Receivable turnover, **1167**, 1167–1168
Receiving report, **274**, 275(table)
Recognition
 of expenses, 93–94, 100–102
 of liabilities, 434
 of revenues, 93–94, 100
Recognition issue, **47**, 47–48
Records, 269
 independent verification of, 270
Registered bonds, **546**
Regressive tax, **Ap-101n**
Regulation, of corporations, 470
Regulatory agencies, as users of accounting information, 8
Relative sales value method, **734**, 734–735
Relevance, **211**
Relevant decision information, 921–922, **922**
Relevant range, **635**
Reliability, **211**, 211–212
Repairs
 extraordinary, 402
 ordinary, 402
Report(s). *See also* Annual report; Financial statement(s); *specific statements*
 cost assignment and, 669–671, 670(table)
 frequency of, 593
 governmental accounting and, Ap-81–Ap-83
 in JIT/FMS environment, 1067–1069
 of management's responsibilities, Ap-9–Ap-10
 to Securities and Exchange Commission, 1154, 1156, Ap-1
 special decisions and, 927
Reporting currency, **Ap-60**
Research and development costs, 410, 412
Reserve for Bad Debts account, *see* Allowance for Uncollectible Accounts account
Residual equity, **473**. *See also* Owner's equity
Residual value, **391**
Responsibility accounting, **755**, 755–761
 cost and revenue controllability and, 758
 cost/expense centers and, 758–759
 investment centers and, 760–761
 organizational structure and reporting and, 755–757, 756(fig.), 757(exh.)
 profit centers and, 759–760
Responsibility center, **755**
Restatement, **Ap-60**
Restricted current fund, **Ap-86**
Restriction on retained earnings, **508**, 508–509
Retail method(s), **368**, 368–369
Retained earnings, **472**, 477, **501**, 501–509, 502(exh.)
 cash flows and, 1115–1116, 1124
 cost of, 961
 restrictions on, 508–509
 stock dividends and, 502–504
 stock splits and, 504–505
 treasury stock transactions and, 505–508
Retained Earnings account, **221**
Retirement
 of bonds, 561
 of treasury stock, 508
Return on assets, **227**, 227–229, 228(fig.), 229(fig.), **1170**
Return on assets pricing, **891**, 891–892
Return on equity, **230**, 230–231, 231(fig.), **1170**, 1170–1171
Revenue(s), **16**, **90**, 90–91, **Ap-83**
 accrued, 100
 apportioning between accounting periods, 99–100
 deferred, 439
 effect on accounting equation, 18–19
 marginal, pricing and, 885, 886(fig.), 887
 recognition of, 93–94, 100
 from sales, *see* Revenues from sales
 total, pricing and, 885, 886(fig.)
 unearned, 99–100, 439
Revenue accounts, 53
Revenue center, **759**, 759–760
Revenue expenditures, **401**, 401–402
Revenue recognition, **94**
Revenues from sales, **167**, 168(exh.), 168–170
 gross sales and, 168–169
 sales discounts and, 169–170
 Sales Returns and Allowances account and, 169
 trade discounts and, 169
Reversing entries, **140**, 143–144
Risk
 assessment of, 1151–1152
 market, 1173–1174
Roehm, Harper A., 992n
Rounding off, 728, 730
Rudnicki, Edward J., 1010, 1013n
Rule-of-thumb measures, in financial statement analysis, 1152
Run time, **1011**

Salaries, **443**
 computation of take-home pay and, 445–448
 liability for, 443–444
 of partners, Ap-40
Sales. *See also* Cost of goods sold; Cost of goods sold account
 on account, 50
 on account, *see* Accounts receivable; Accounts Receivable account
 of bonds, between interest dates, 557–559, 560(fig.)
 cash receipts from, 1106–1107

credit, 50
credit card, 317, 318–319
foreign, Ap-57–Ap-58
gross, 168–169
gross margin from, 167
net, 168, 312
of partnership interest, Ap-49–Ap-50
revenues from, *see* Revenues from sales
of treasury stock, 507–508
Sales budget, 806, 807(exh.)
Sales column, in cash receipts journal, 264
Sales discount(s), 169, 169–170
Sales Discount account, 170
Sales Discount column, in cash receipts journal, 262
Sales journal, 256, 256–259, 257(exh.)
controlling accounts and subsidiary ledgers and, 256–258, 258(exh.)
sales taxes and, 259, 260(exh.)
summary of procedure for, 258–259, 259(exh.)
Sales mix analysis, 930–932, 932(exh.), **933**
Sales Returns and Allowances account, 169
Sales taxes, sales journal and, 259, 260(exh.)
Sales taxes payable, 438
Salvage value, 391
capital budgeting and, 963
Saporito, Bill, 166n
Scatter diagram, 638, 639(fig.)
Schedule of equivalent production, 719, 719(exh.)
Schwartz, Rickard P., 956n
Scope section, Ap-11
Scott, David F., Jr., 961n
Scrap control performance, in JIT/FMS environment, 1061–1062
SEC, *see* Securities and Exchange Commission
Secured bonds, 545, 545–546
Securities. *See also* Bond(s)
marketable, 307
Securities and Exchange Commission (SEC), 8, **11,** 28
on compensating balances, 307
on cost-benefit convention, 213, 214
in full disclosure, 213
reports to, 1154, 1156, Ap-1
Segments, 517
Selling cost(s), changes in, cost-volume-profit analysis and, 650
Selling cost budget, 806, 808(exh.)
Selling expenses, 177–178
Sell-or-process further decision, 934, 934–935, 936(exh.)
Semivariable costs, 632(table), **636,** 636–640, 638(fig.)
Separate entity, 13
corporation as, 469
Separation of duties, internal control and, 270, 271–272
Serial bonds, 546
Service charges, 327
Service operations
accounting information needed by, 594
cost behavior in, 640–642
fixed, variable, and semivariable costs of, 632(table)
measuring service quality and, 1059
nonfinancial data needed by, 596–597, 597(exh.)
pricing of services and, 892–893
Service overhead, 847
Share of stock, 468
Short-range goals, of budgeting, 803–804
Short-term investments, 307
Short-term liabilities, 51
Short-term liquid assets, 306, 306–333
accounting for, 307–309
accounts receivable and, 309–319
banking transactions and, 326–332
notes receivable and, 319–325, 320(fig.)
petty cash procedures and, 332–333
Signature card, 326
Significant influence, Ap-64
Simple capital structure, 520
Simple interest, Ap-14
Single-step form, 223, 224(exh.)
Small business services, 28
Smith, Randall, 466n
Social security taxes
employer's liability for, 448
liability for, 444–445
Software, 253
development costs for, 412
general ledger, 253–254, 254(fig.)
Sole proprietorship, 13, 14(table)
accounts used by, 52(fig.), 52–53
owner's equity of, 220
Solvency, evaluation of, 1171–1172
Sombart, Werner, 54
Soucy, Stephen R., 1059n
Source documents, 254
Special order decisions(s), **928,** 928–930, 930(exh.)
Special-purpose journals, 255–267
cash payments, 265, 266(exh.), 267
cash receipts, 261–262, 263(exh.), 264–265
flexibility of, 268
purchases, 259–261, 261(exh.), 262(exh.)
sales, 256–259, 257(exh.), 258(exh.), 259(exh.)
Special revenue funds, Ap-82
Specific identification method, 359
compared with other inventory valuation methods, 361–364
Specific purpose fund, Ap-86
Split-off point, 733
Staff, *see* Employees; Labor
Standard costs, 839, 839–843. *See also* Variance analysis
development of, 840–841
journal entries for, 842–843
nature and purpose of, 839–840
product costing and, 842
use of, 842
Standard deduction, Ap-100
Standard direct labor cost, 841
Standard direct materials cost, 840
Standard factory overhead cost, 841
Standard fixed overhead rate, 841
Standard & Poor's Industrial Surveys, 1156
Standard variable overhead rate, 841
Stasey, Robert, 712n
Stated ratios, distribution of partnership income and losses and, Ap-40, Ap-43–Ap-45, Ap-46(exh.)
Stated value, 478
State income taxes, employer's liability for, 445
Statement of cash flows, 22–24, **23,** 24(exh.), 224, 1098–1124, **1099**
classification of cash flows and, 1100–1102, 1101(fig.)
consolidated, Ap-6, Ap-7(fig.), Ap-8
determining cash flows from financing activities and, 1114–1116
determining cash flows from investing activities and, 1111–1114
determining cash flows from operating activities and, 1102–1111, 1105(fig.)
format of, 1102, 1102(exh.)
internal and external uses of, 1100
interpretation of, 1116, 1117(exh.), 1118(exh.), 1118–1119
presenting information in form of, 1116
purposes of, 1100
relationship to other financial statements, 24
work sheet for preparation of, 1119–1124, 1120(exh.)
Statement of changes in financial position, combined, Ap-85
Statement of changes in stockholders' equity, *see* Statement of stockholders' equity
Statement of cost of goods manufactured, 608, 608–610, 609(exh.)
Statement of financial position, *see* Balance sheet
Statement of owner's equity, 20, **22,** 23(exh.), 224, 224(exh.)
relationship to other financial statements, 24
Statement of stockholders' equity, 509, 510(exh.)
consolidated, Ap-6
State unemployment insurance tax, employer's liability for, 448
Step method, 672
for cost allocation, 673–675, 674(exh.)
Stertz, Bradley A., 1150n
Stock, 472–483
authorized, 472–473
book value of, 511–512
common, *see* Common stock
dividends on, *see* Dividends
earnings per share on, 519–521
issuance of, *see* Stock issuance
issued, 473

Stock *(continued)*
market value of, 512
no-par, 478, 479–480
outstanding, 473
par value, 477–479
preferred, 475–477, 961
share of, 468
treasury, 473, 505–508
Stock certificate, 472
Stock dividends(s), **502**, 502–504
Stock Dividends Declared account, 503
Stockholders, 468. *See also* Dividends
Stockholders' equity, 471, 471–477. *See also* Owner's equity; Statement of owner's equity; Stock
Stock issuance, 477–482
for noncash assets, 480
of no-par stock, 479–480
of par value stock, 478–479
stock subscriptions and, 481–482
Stock option plan, 482, 482–483
Stock splits, 504, 504–505
Stock subscriptions(s), **481**, 481–482
Stores account, *see* Materials Inventory account
Straight-line method, 393, 551
amortization of bond discount using, 551–552
amortization of bond premium using, 555–556
depreciation computed using, 393, 395, 396(fig.)
Strategic planning, decisions and, 921
Strategies, budgeting and, 803–804
Subscriptions Receivable account, 481–482
Subsidiary, Ap-68
consolidated financial statements and, Ap-69–Ap-76
foreign, restatement of financial statements and, Ap-60
Subsidiary ledger, 256, 256–258, 258(exh.)
Summary of significant accounting policies, Ap-8
Sundry Accounts column, in cash receipts journal, 262, 264
Supporting service function, 671, 671–675
methods used to allocate costs and, 672–675, 673(exh.), 674(exh.)
selecting basis for cost allocation and, 671–672, 672(table)
Surplus, 501
Sweptson, Mary Ann, 815n
Systems analyst, 253

T account, 54
illustration of, 54–55
transaction analysis using, 55–61, 62(exh.)
Tangible assets, 387. *See also* Plant assets; Property, plant, and equipment
Target costing, 894, 894–895
Tasks, 1048
Tax(es)
estimated, Ap-102
excise, 438
income, *see* Income taxes; Individual income taxes
Medicare, 444–445, 448
payroll, 444–445, 448–449
progressive, Ap-101
property, 440
proportional, Ap-101n
regressive, Ap-101n
sales, 259, 260(exh.), 438
social security, 444–445, 448
unemployment, 448
Taxable income, Ap-98
Tax authorities, as users of accounting information, 8
Tax credits, Ap-102
Tax evasion, Ap-98
Tax liability, 101(exh.), **Ap-101**
Tax planning, Ap-98
Tax Reform Act of 1986, 400, Ap-97
Tax services, 28
Temporary accounts, 91
Term bonds, 546
Theft, 177, 268–269, 271–272. *See also* Internal control
Theoretical capacity, 633
under JIT operating environment, 1010
Throughput time, 1004
Time
engineered, 1011
run, 1011
Time and materials pricing, 892, 892–893
Time periods, for compounding interest, Ap-20–Ap-21
Time value of money, 965–967, **966**, Ap-14–Ap-25. *See also* Future value; Present value
Total cost, pricing decision and, 885, 886
Total direct labor cost variance, 848, 848–850, 851(fig.)
Total direct materials cost variance, 847
Total inventory method, 368
Total manufacturing costs, 610
Total overhead variance, 851, 851–852
Total quality management (TQM), 1051, 1051–1052
Total revenue, pricing decision and, **885, 886**
Traceable fixed costs, 932
Trade accounts payable, *see* Accounts payable
Trade credit, 309
Trade discounts, 169
Trademarks, 411(table)
Transfer prices, 895, 895–900
characteristics of, 895–897, 896(fig.)
developing, 898(exh.), 898–899
performance measurement using, 899(exh.), 899–900
pricing methods and, 897
Transnational corporations, Ap-55. *See also* International accounting
Transportation in, 173–174
Treasurer, 25
Treasury stock, 505, 505–508
purchase of, 506–507
retirement of, 508
sale of, 507–508
Trend analysis, 1160, 1160–1162, 1163(exh.), 1163(fig.)
Trial balance, 66, 66–68, 67(exh.)
adjusted, 102, 103(exh.), 104(exh.)
post-closing, 141, 143(exh.)
Trial Balance columns
adjusting entry method and, 180
closing entry method and, 183
entering and totalling account balances in, 131
Troxel, Richard B., 1052n
Truitt, James W., 754–755, 754n
Trust and agency funds, Ap-82
2/10, 169
2/10, n/60, 169

Unamortized Bond Discount account, 552
Uncollectible accounts, 310, 310–317
credit policies and, 310
estimating expense of, 311–315
matching losses with sales and, 310–311
writing off, 315–317
Underapplied overhead, 679–680
Understandability, 211
Underwriters, 472
as users of accounting information, 8
Unearned revenues, 99, 439
apportioning between accounting periods, 99–100
recognizing, 100
Unemployment insurance taxes, employer's liability for, 448
Unexpired Insurance account, 50–51
Uniform Partnership Act, Ap-36
Unit cost(s), 602
for products, computing, 690
Unit cost analysis schedule, 721, 721–722, 732
Universal product codes (UPC), 176, 176(fig.), 177
Universities, Ap-86
Unlimited liability, Ap-37
Unprofitable segment decision analysis, 932, 932–934, 933(exh.), 934(exh.)
Unrestricted current fund, Ap-86
Unrestricted fund, Ap-86
Unsecured bonds, 545
UPC, *see* Universal product codes
Urbancic, Frank R., 716n
Usefulness, 211

Vacation pay liability, 441–442
Valuation
of assets, Ap-22
of inventory, *see* Inventory valuation
of liabilities, 434
Valuation issue, 48

Value, 48
book, *see* Book value; Carrying value
carrying, *see* Book value; Carrying value
disposal, 391, 963
face, bonds issued at, 547
future, *see* Future value
market, 367n, 512
maturity, of promissory notes, 321
par, 473, 477–478
present, *see* Present value
realizable, 367n
residual, 391
salvage, 391, 963
stated, 478
of stock, 511–512
time, of money, 965–967
Value chain, 1048
Variable cost(s), 631, 631–635, 632(table)
linear relationships and relevant range and, 633–635, 634(fig.), 635(fig.)
operating capacity and, 632–633
Variable costing, 922–926, **923**
contribution margin reporting format and, 925(exh.), 925–926
decisions and, 926
Variance, 840
Variance analysis, 843–860, **846**
cost control through, 843–856
flexible budget and, 843–845, 844–845(exh.)
of overhead, three-variance approach to, 857–860, 859(fig.)
performance evaluation and, 856–857, 857(exh.)
three-variance approach to, 857–860, 859
variance determination and, 845–854, 847(fig.)
variances in accounting records and, 854–856
Vertical analysis, 1162, 1162–1165, 1164(fig.), 1165(exh.), 1166(exh.)
Voluntary association, partnership as, Ap-36
Voluntary health and welfare organizations, Ap-87

Wage(s), 443
computation of take-home pay and, 445–448
liability for, 443–444
Wage and Tax Statement (Form W-2), 447–448
Wall Street Journal, 1156
Warranties, estimated liability for, 440–441
Wasting assets(s), 408. *See also* Natural resources
Wilson, James D., 754n
Winchell, William, 1052n
Withdrawals, *see* Owner's withdrawals
Withdrawals account, 53
closing to Capital account, 139, 139(exh.)
Withholdings, Ap-102
employer's liability for, 444–445
Without recourse, defined, 317
With recourse, defined, 317
Work cells, 995
in JIT operating environment, 995–996, 1000
Work environment, in JIT operating environment, 997
Working capital, 225
Working papers, 130
Work in Process Inventory account, 599, **604**, 604(fig.), 604–605, 609–610, 678, 679
cost flow through, 714
job order cost accounting and, 682, 683, 683(fig.), 684(fig.), 685, 686(exh.), 687–689, 690
process cost accounting and, 725–727
unit cost analysis schedule and, 721–722
Work sheet, 130, 130–136
adjusting entry method and, 180, 181(exh.), 182
closing entry method and, 183, 184(exh.), 185–188
for merchandising concern, 180–188
preparing, Exh. 4-1 to 4-5, 130–132
preparing financial statements from, 133, 133(exh.), 134(exh.)
recording adjusting entries in, 133–134, 135(exh.)
recording closing entries in, 135–136
for statement of cash flows, 1119–1124, 1120(exh.)
Writing off, of uncollectible accounts, 315–317

Year
accrual for bond interest expense at end of, 559–561
for interest computation, 321n
partial, depreciating for, 403
Youde, Richard K., 1044n

Zero coupon bonds, 551

Accounting Format Guide

Headings identify
1. Name of company
2. Name of statement
3. Date or time period

Components are indented

Totals are aligned with items to which they apply

Joan Miller Advertising Agency
Income Statement
For the Month Ended January 31, 19xx

Revenues		
Advertising Fees Earned	$4,400	
Art Fees Earned	400	
Total Revenues		$4,800
Expenses		
Office Wages Expense	$1,380	
Utility Expense	100	
Telephone Expense	70	
Rent Expense	400	
Insurance Expense	40	
Art Supplies Expense	500	
Office Supplies Expense	200	
Depreciation Expense, Art Equipment	70	
Depreciation Expense, Office Equipment	50	
Total Expenses		2,810
Net Income		**$1,990**

Joan Miller Advertising Agency
Statement of Owner's Equity
For the Month Ended January 31, 19xx

Joan Miller, Capital, January 1, 19xx		—
Add Investments by Joan Miller	$10,000	
Net Income	1,990	$11,990
Subtotal		$11,990
Less Withdrawals		1,400
Joan Miller, Capital, January 31, 19xx		$10,590

Commonly Used Formats

Accounting Records
- T Account 54–55
- General Journal 63–64
- General Ledger 64
- Combined 64–66

Work Sheets
- Service Company Mylar insert (after 130)
- (Adjusting Entry Method) Merchandising Company 183
- (Closing Entry Method) Merchandising Company 184
- Statement of Cash Flows 1120

Special Journals
- Sales Journal 257
- Purchases Journal (single-column) 261
- Purchases Journal (multi-column) 262
- Cash Receipts Journal 263
- Cash Payments Journal 266
- Voucher Register 277
- Check Register 330
- Payroll Register 447